YOUR CLEAR PATH TO SUCCESS IN THE PSYCHOLOGY COURSE

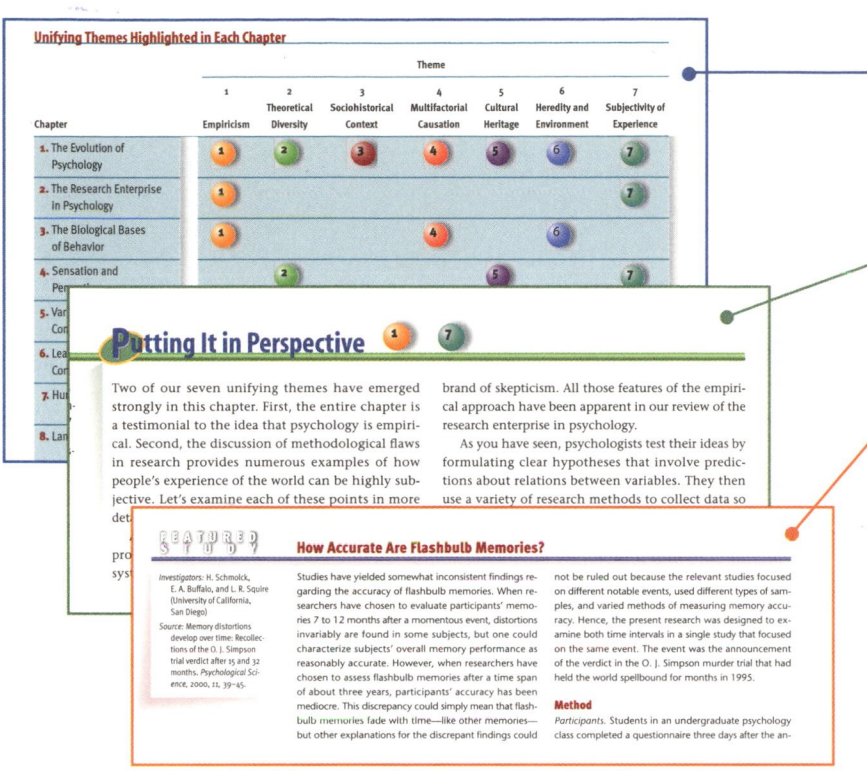

- **Unifying themes** help you make sense of it all. In Chapter 1, Wayne Weiten introduces seven themes that reappear as you move from chapter to chapter. Use these themes as a framework for organizing information as you learn.

- **Putting It in Perspective** sections at the ends of chapters put the chapters' contents into perspective by recalling the book's seven overarching themes—helping you think about important topics in new ways.

- **Featured Studies** found in every chapter (except Chapter 1) give you an over-the-shoulder look at interesting, real-life research—showing you how psychologists conduct and report their research.

- **Personal Applications** in every chapter give you practical advice that will be helpful in improving your academic performance and your daily life.

- **Critical Thinking Applications** in every chapter offer specific, concrete ways to improve your thinking skills. You'll have opportunities to practice your newly learned skills on chapter material.

- **Web links** appear throughout every chapter. This book is a rich resource for expanding your knowledge of psychology topics online. Carefully selected by Web expert Vincent Hevern (the Internet editor for the *Society for the Teaching of Psychology*), the book's Web links help you clarify your understanding of psychology and learn about current research. The URLs for these Web links appear in Appendix E at the back of the book. But because Web addresses change frequently, we recommend that you access these links through the book Web site (accessible at http://psychology.wadsworth.com/weiten_themes6e) where the URLs are periodically updated.

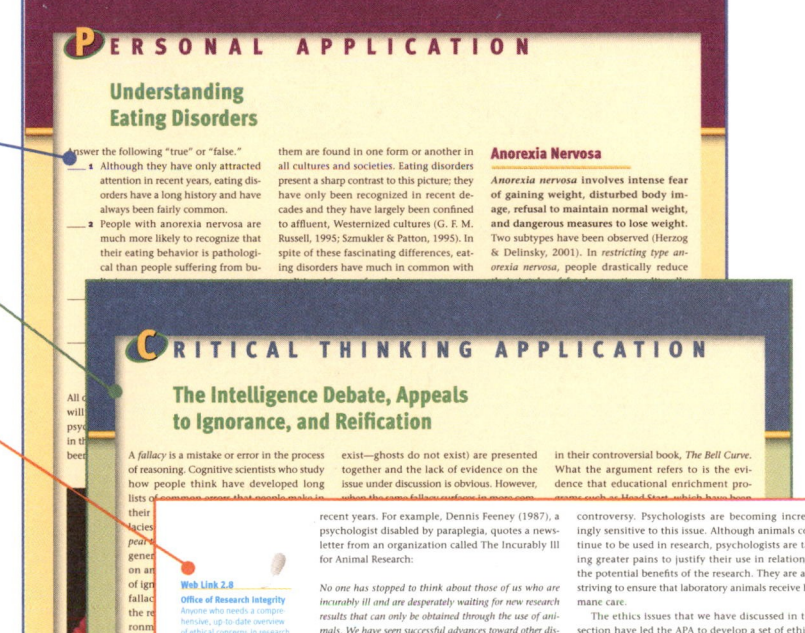

Psychology
Themes and Variations

6th EDITION

Wayne Weiten
University of Nevada, Las Vegas

With Critical Thinking Applications
By Diane F. Halpern
Claremont McKenna College

THOMSON
WADSWORTH

Australia • Canada • Mexico • Singapore • Spain
United Kingdom • United States

THOMSON

WADSWORTH

Psychology Editor: Edith Beard Brady
Developmental Editor: Sherry Symington
Assistant Editor: Jennifer Klos
Editorial Assistant: Kari Hopperstead
Technology Project Manager: Michelle Vardeman
Marketing Manager: Lori Grebe
Marketing Assistant: Laurel Anderson
Advertising Project Manager: Brian Chaffee
Project Manager, Editorial Production: Kathryn M. Stewart
Print/Media Buyer: Karen Hunt
Permissions Editor and Photo Researcher: Linda L Rill

Production Service: Thomas E. Dorsaneo
Text Designer: Gladys Rosa-Mendoza, rosa+wesley
Copy Editor: Jacqueline Estrada
Illustrator: Cyndie H. Wooley, Thompson Type, Jeff Gruenwald, Brian Wenberg
Cover Designer: Stephen Rapley
Cover Image: Illustrations courtesy of Photonica, CORBIS, and Getty. All rights reserved. Copyright © 2004.
Cover Printer: Phoenix Color Corp
Compositor: Thompson Type
Printer: Quebecor World/Versailles

Printed in the United States of America
1 2 3 4 5 6 7 07 06 05 04 03

For more information about our products, contact us at:
Thomson Learning Academic Resource Center
1-800-423-0563

For permission to use material from this text, contact us by
Phone: 1-800-730-2214   **Fax:** 1-800-730-2215
Web: http://www.thomsonrights.com

Library of Congress Control Number: 2002111203

Student Edition with InfoTrac College Edition:
  ISBN 0-534-59769-6
Student Edition without InfoTrac College Edition:
  ISBN 0-534-59770-X
Instructor's Edition: ISBN 0-534-59771-8

Wadsworth/Thomson Learning
10 Davis Drive
Belmont, CA 94002-3098
USA

Asia
Thomson Learning
5 Shenton Way, #01-01
UIC Building
Singapore 068808

Australia/New Zealand
Thomson Learning
102 Dodds Street
Southbank, Victoria 3006
Australia

Canada
Nelson
1120 Birchmount Road
Toronto, Ontario M1K 5G4
Canada

Europe/Middle East/Africa
Thomson Learning
High Holborn House
50/51 Bedford Row
London WC1R 4LR
United Kingdom

Latin America
Thomson Learning
Seneca, 53
Colonia Polanco
11560 Mexico D.F.
Mexico

Spain/Portugal
Paraninfo
Calle/Magallanes, 25
28015 Madrid, Spain

Beth,
This one is for you

To the Instructor

If I had to sum up in a single sentence what I hope will distinguish this text, that sentence would be this: I have set out to create a *paradox* instead of a *compromise*.

Let me elaborate. An introductory psychology text must satisfy two disparate audiences: professors and students. Because of the tension between the divergent needs and preferences of these audiences, textbook authors usually indicate that they have attempted to strike a compromise between being theoretical versus practical, comprehensive versus comprehensible, research oriented versus applied, rigorous versus accessible, and so forth. However, I believe that many of these dichotomies are false. As Kurt Lewin once remarked, "What could be more practical than a good theory?" Similarly, is rigorous really the opposite of accessible? Not in my dictionary. I maintain that many of the antagonistic goals that we strive for in our textbooks only *seem* incompatible and that we may not need to make compromises as often as we assume.

In my estimation, a good introductory textbook is a paradox in that it integrates characteristics and goals that appear contradictory. With this in mind, I have endeavored to write a text that is paradoxical in three ways. First, in surveying psychology's broad range of content, I have tried to show that its interests are characterized by both diversity *and* unity. Second, I have emphasized both research *and* application and how they work in harmony. Finally, I have aspired to write a book that is challenging to think about *and* easy to learn from. Let's take a closer look at these goals.

Goals

1. *To show both the unity and the diversity of psychology's subject matter.* Students entering an introductory psychology course are often unaware of the immense diversity of subjects studied by psychologists. I find this diversity to be part of psychology's charm, and throughout the book I highlight the enormous range of questions and issues addressed by psychology. Of course, psychology's diversity proves disconcerting for some students who see little continuity between such disparate areas of research as physiology, motivation, cognition, and abnormal behavior. Indeed, in this era of specialization, even some psychologists express concern about the fragmentation of the field.

However, I believe that the subfields of psychology overlap considerably and that we should emphasize their common core by accenting their connections and similarities. Consequently, I portray psychology as an integrated whole rather than as a mosaic of loosely related parts. A principal goal of this text, then, is to highlight the unity in psychology's intellectual heritage (the themes), as well as the diversity of psychology's interests and uses (the variations).

2. *To illuminate the process of research and its intimate link to application.* For me, a research-oriented book is not one that bulges with summaries of many studies but one that enhances students' appreciation of the logic and excitement of empirical inquiry. I want students to appreciate the strengths of the empirical approach and to see scientific psychology as a creative effort to solve intriguing behavioral puzzles. For this reason, the text emphasizes not only *what* psychologists know (and don't know) but *how* they attempt to find out. The book examines in some detail and encourages students to adopt the skeptical attitude of a scientist and to think critically about claims regarding behavior.

Learning the virtues of research should not mean that students cannot also satisfy their desire for concrete, personally useful information about the challenges of everyday life. Most researchers believe that psychology has a great deal to offer those outside the field and that we should share the practical implications of our work. In this text, practical insights are carefully qualified and closely tied to data, so that students can see the interdependence of research and application. I find that students come to appreciate the science of psychology more when they see that worthwhile practical applications are derived from careful research and sound theory.

3. *To make the text challenging to think about and easy to learn from.* Perhaps most of all, I have sought to create a *book of ideas* rather than a compendium of studies. I consistently emphasize concepts and theories over facts, and I focus on major issues and tough questions that cut across the subfields of psychology (for example, the extent to which behavior is governed by nature, nurture, and their interaction), as opposed to parochial debates (such as the merits of averaging versus adding in impression formation). Challenging students to think also means urging them to confront the complexity and ambiguity of psychological knowledge. Hence, the text doesn't skirt around gray areas, unresolved questions, and theo-

retical controversies. Instead, it encourages readers to contemplate open-ended questions, to examine their assumptions about behavior, and to apply psychological concepts to their own lives. My goal is not simply to describe psychology but to stimulate students' intellectual growth.

However, students can grapple with "the big issues and tough questions" only if they first master the basic concepts and principles of psychology—ideally, with as little struggle as possible. I never let myself forget that a textbook is a teaching tool. Accordingly, great care has been taken to ensure that the book's content, organization, writing, illustrations, and pedagogical aids work in harmony to facilitate instruction and learning.

Admittedly, these goals are ambitious. If you're skeptical, you have every right to be. Let me explain how I have tried to realize the objectives I have outlined.

Special Features

A variety of unusual features each contributes in its own way to the book's paradoxical nature. These special elements include unifying themes, Featured Studies, Personal Application sections, Critical Thinking Application sections, a didactic illustration program, Web Links and other Internet-related features, an integrated running glossary, Concept Checks, Preview Questions, interim Reviews of Key Points, and Practice Tests.

Unifying Themes

Chapter 1 introduces seven key ideas that serve as unifying themes throughout the text. The themes serve several purposes. First, they provide threads of continuity across chapters that help students see the connections among various areas of research in psychology. Second, as the themes evolve over the course of the book, they provide a forum for a relatively sophisticated discussion of enduring issues in psychology, thus helping to make this a "book of ideas." Third, the themes focus a spotlight on a number of basic insights about psychology and its subject matter that should leave lasting impressions on your students.

In selecting the themes, the question I asked myself (and other professors) was "What do I really want students to remember five years from now?" The resulting themes are grouped into two sets.

THEMES RELATED TO PSYCHOLOGY AS A FIELD OF STUDY
Theme 1: Psychology is empirical. This theme is used to enhance the student's appreciation of psychology's scientific nature and to demonstrate the advantages of empiricism over uncritical common sense and speculation. I also use this theme to encourage the reader to adopt a scientist's skeptical attitude and to engage in more critical thinking about information of all kinds.

Theme 2: Psychology is theoretically diverse. Students are often confused by psychology's theoretical pluralism and view it as a weakness. I don't downplay or apologize for the field's theoretical diversity, because I honestly believe that it is one of psychology's greatest strengths. Throughout the book, I provide concrete examples of how clashing theories have stimulated productive research, how converging on a question from several perspectives can yield increased understanding, and how competing theories are sometimes reconciled in the end.

Theme 3: Psychology evolves in a sociohistorical context. This theme emphasizes that psychology is embedded in the ebb and flow of everyday life. The text shows how the spirit of the times has often shaped psychology's evolution and how progress in psychology leaves its mark on our society.

THEMES RELATED TO PSYCHOLOGY'S SUBJECT MATTER
Theme 4: Behavior is determined by multiple causes. Throughout the book, I emphasize, and repeatedly illustrate, that behavioral processes are complex and that multifactorial causation is the rule. This theme is used to discourage simplistic, single-cause thinking and to encourage more critical reasoning.

Theme 5: Behavior is shaped by cultural heritage. This theme is intended to enhance students' appreciation of how cultural factors moderate psychological processes and how the viewpoint of one's own culture can distort one's interpretation of the behavior of people from other cultures. The discussions that elaborate on this theme do not simply celebrate diversity. They strike a careful balance—that accurately reflects the research in this area—highlighting both cultural variations *and* similarities in behavior.

Theme 6: Heredity and environment jointly influence behavior. Repeatedly discussing this theme permits me to air out the nature versus nurture issue in all its complexity. Over a series of chapters, students gradually learn how biology shapes behavior, how experience shapes behavior, and how scientists estimate the relative importance of each. Along the way, students

Unifying Themes Highlighted in Each Chapter

Chapter	Theme						
	1 Empiricism	2 Theoretical Diversity	3 Sociohistorical Context	4 Multifactorial Causation	5 Cultural Heritage	6 Heredity and Environment	7 Subjectivity of Experience
1. The Evolution of Psychology	1	2	3	4	5	6	7
2. The Research Enterprise in Psychology	1						7
3. The Biological Bases of Behavior	1			4		6	
4. Sensation and Perception		2			5		7
5. Variations in Consciousness		2	3		5		7
6. Learning Through Conditioning			3			6	
7. Human Memory		2		4			7
8. Language and Thought	1				5	6	7
9. Intellligence and Psychological Testing			3		5	6	
10. Motivation and Emotion		2	3	4	5	6	
11. Development Across the Life Span		2	3	4	5	6	
12. Personality: Theory, Research, and Assessment			3		5		
13. Stress, Coping, and Health				4			7
14. Psychological Disorders			3	4	5	6	
15. Treatment of Psychological Disorders		2			5	6	
16. Social Behavior	1				5		7

will gain an in-depth appreciation of what we mean when we say that heredity and environment interact.

Theme 7: People's experience of the world is highly subjective. All of us tend to forget the extent to which people view the world through their own personal lenses. This theme is used to explain the principles that underlie the subjectivity of human experience, to clarify its implications, and to repeatedly remind the readers that their view of the world is not the only legitimate view.

After introducing all seven themes in Chapter 1, I discuss different sets of themes in each chapter, as they are relevant to the subject matter. The connections between a chapter's content and the unifying themes are highlighted in a standard section near the end of the chapter, in which I reflect on the "lessons to be learned" from the chapter. The discussions of the unifying themes are largely confined to these sections, titled "Putting It in Perspective." I have not tried to make every chapter illustrate a certain number of themes. Rather, the themes were allowed to emerge naturally, and I found that two to five surfaced in any given chapter. The chart on page vii shows which themes are highlighted in each chapter. Numbered, color-coded icons at the beginning of each "Putting It in Perspective" section indicate the specific themes featured in each chapter.

Featured Studies

Each chapter except the first includes a Featured Study that provides a relatively detailed but clear summary of a particular piece of research. Each Featured Study is presented in the conventional purpose-method-results-discussion format seen in journal articles, followed by a comment in which I discuss why the study is featured (to illustrate a specific method, raise ethical issues, and so forth). By showing research methods in action, I hope to improve students' understanding of how research is done while also giving them a painless introduction to the basic format of journal articles. Additionally, the Featured Studies show how complicated research can be, so students can better appreciate why scientists may disagree about the meaning of a study. The Featured Studies are fully incorporated into the flow of discourse in the text and are *not* presented as optional boxes.

In selecting the Featured Studies, I assembled a mixture of classic and recent studies that illustrate a wide variety of methods. To make them enticing, I tilted my selections in favor of those that students find interesting. Thus, readers will encounter explorations of sleep deprivation among college students, the efficacy of subliminal audiotapes, gender differences in mating priorities, and the effects of stress on susceptibility to the common cold. This edition includes four new Featured Studies.

Personal Applications

To reinforce the pragmatic implications of theory and research stressed throughout the text, each chapter closes with a Personal Application section that highlights the practical side of psychology. Each Personal Application devotes three to six *pages* of text (rather than the usual box) to a single issue that should be of special interest to many of your students. Although most of the Personal Application sections have a "how to" character, they continue to review studies and summarize data in much the same way as the main body of each chapter. Thus, they portray

research and application not as incompatible polarities but as two sides of the same coin. Many of the Personal Applications—such as those on finding and reading journal articles, understanding art and illusion, and improving stress management—provide topical coverage unusual for an introductory text.

Critical Thinking Applications

A great deal of unusual coverage can also be found in the Critical Thinking Applications that follow the Personal Applications. Conceived by Diane Halpern (Claremont McKenna College), a leading authority on critical thinking, these applications are based on the assumption that critical thinking skills can be taught. They do not simply review research critically, as is typically the case in other introductory texts. Instead, they introduce and model a host of critical thinking *skills,* such as looking for contradictory evidence or alternative explanations; recognizing anecdotal evidence, circular reasoning, hindsight bias, reification, weak analogies, and false dichotomies; evaluating arguments systematically, and working with cumulative and conjunctive probabilities.

The specific skills discussed in the Critical Thinking Applications are listed in the accompanying table on page ix, where they are organized into five categories using a taxonomy developed by Halpern (1994). In each chapter, some of these skills are applied to topics and issues related to the chapter's content. For instance, in the chapter that covers drug abuse (Chapter 5), the concept of alcoholism is used to highlight the immense power of definitions and to illustrate how circular reasoning can seem so seductive. Skills that are particularly important may surface in more than one chapter, so students see them applied in a variety of contexts. For example, in Chapter 7 students learn how hindsight bias can contaminate memory and in Chapter 12 they see how hindsight can distort analyses of personality. Repeated practice across chapters should help students to spontaneously recognize the relevance of specific critical thinking skills when they encounter certain types of information. The skills approach taken to critical thinking and the content it has spawned are unprecedented for an introductory psychology text.

A Didactic Illustration Program

When I first outlined my plans for this text, I indicated that I wanted every aspect of the illustration program to have a genuine didactic purpose and that I wanted to be deeply involved in its development. In retrospect, I had no idea what I was getting myself into, but it has been a rewarding learning experience.

Taxonomy of Skills Covered in the Critical Thinking Applications

Verbal Reasoning Skills	
Understanding the way definitions shape how people think about issues	Chapter 5
Identifying the source of definitions	Chapter 5
Avoiding the nominal fallacy in working with definitions and labels	Chapter 5
Understanding the way language can influence thought	Chapter 8
Recognizing semantic slanting	Chapter 8
Recognizing name calling and anticipatory name calling	Chapter 8
Recognizing and avoiding reification	Chapter 9
Argument/Persuasion Analysis Skills	
Understanding the elements of an argument	Chapter 10
Recognizing and avoiding common fallacies, such as irrelevant reasons, circular reasoning, slippery slope reasoning, weak analogies, and false dichotomies	Chapters 10 and 11
Evaluating arguments systematically	Chapter 10
Recognizing and avoiding appeals to ignorance	Chapter 9
Understanding how Pavlovian conditioning can be used to manipulate emotions	Chapter 6
Developing the ability to detect conditioning procedures used in the media	Chapter 6
Recognizing social influence strategies	Chapter 16
Judging the credibility of an information source	Chapter 16
Skills in Thinking as Hypothesis Testing	
Looking for alternative explanations for findings and events	Chapters 1, 9, and 11
Looking for contradictory evidence	Chapters 1, 3, and 9
Recognizing the limitations of anecdotal evidence	Chapters 2 and 15
Understanding the need to seek disconfirming evidence	Chapter 7
Understanding the limitations of correlational evidence	Chapters 11 and 13
Understanding the limitations of statistical significance	Chapter 13
Recognizing situations in which placebo effects might occur	Chapter 15
Skills in Working with Likelihood and Uncertainty	
Utilizing base rates in making predictions and evaluating probabilities	Chapter 13
Understanding cumulative probabilities	Chapter 14
Understanding conjunctive probabilities	Chapter 14
Understanding the limitations of the representativeness heuristic	Chapter 14
Understanding the limitations of the availability heuristic	Chapter 14
Recognizing situations in which regression toward the mean may occur	Chapter 15
Understanding the limits of extrapolation	Chapter 3
Decision-Making and Problem-Solving Skills	
Using evidence-based decision making	Chapter 2
Recognizing the bias in hindsight analysis	Chapters 7 and 12
Seeking information to reduce uncertainty	Chapter 13
Making risk-benefit assessments	Chapter 13
Generating and evaluating alternative courses of action	Chapter 13
Recognizing overconfidence in human cognition	Chapter 7
Understanding the limitations and fallibility of human memory	Chapter 7
Understanding how contrast effects can influence judgments and decisions	Chapter 4
Recognizing when extreme comparitors are being used	Chapter 4

In any event, I have been intimately involved in planning every detail of the illustration program. I have endeavored to create a program of figures, diagrams, photos, and tables that work hand in hand with the prose to strengthen and clarify the main points in the text.

The most obvious results of this didactic approach to illustration are the six summary spreads that combine tabular information, photos, diagrams, and sketches to provide well-organized overviews of key ideas in the areas of history, learning, development, personality theory, psychopathology, and psychotherapy. But I hope you will also notice the subtleties of the illustration program. For instance, diagrams of important concepts (conditioning, synaptic transmission, experimental design, and so forth) are often repeated in several chapters (with variations) to highlight connections among research areas and to enhance students' mastery of key ideas. Numerous easy-to-understand graphs of research results underscore psychology's foundation in research, and photos and diagrams often bolster each other (for example, see the treatment of classical conditioning in Chapter 6). Color is used carefully as an organizational device, and visual schematics are used to simplify hard-to-visualize concepts (for example, see the figure explaining reaction range for intelligence in Chapter 9). All of these efforts were made in the service of one master: the desire to make this an inviting book that is easy to learn from.

Internet-Related Features

The Internet is rapidly altering the landscape of modern life, and students clearly need help dealing with the information explosion in cyberspace. To assist them, this text has three features. First, I recruited Web expert Vincent Hevern (Le Moyne College), the Internet editor for the Society for the Teaching of Psychology, to write a concise preface that explains the essentials of the Internet to the uninitiated. This preface, which follows the student preface, briefly explains URLs, domain names, hyperlinks, search engines, and so forth. Second, cognizant of the highly variable quality and frequently questionable validity of much of the information available on the Web, I also asked Dr. Hevern to write an essay on how to critically evaluate Web sites and online resource materials. His highly informative essay is found in the back of the book in Appendix D. Third, I also asked Professor Hevern to evaluate hundreds of psychology-related sites on the Web and come up with some recommended sites that appear to provide reasonably accurate, balanced, and empirically sound information. Short descriptions of these recommended

Web sites (called Web Links) are dispersed throughout the chapters, adjacent to related topical coverage. Because URLs change frequently, we have placed the URLs for our Web Links in an Appendix (E) in the back of the book. Insofar as students are interested in visiting these sites, we recommend that they do so through the *Psychology: Themes & Variations* home page at the Wadsworth Web site (http://psychology. wadsworth.com/weiten_themes6e). Links to all the recommended Web sites are maintained there, and the Wadsworth Webmaster periodically updates the URLs.

Integrated Running Glossary

An introductory text should place great emphasis on acquainting students with psychology's technical language—not for the sake of jargon, but because a great many of the key terms are also cornerstone concepts (for example, independent variable, reliability, and cognitive dissonance). This text handles terminology with a running glossary embedded in the prose itself. The terms are set off in boldface italics, and the definitions follow in boldface roman type. This approach retains the two advantages of a conventional running glossary: vocabulary items are made salient, and their definitions are readily accessible. However, the approach does so without interrupting the flow of discourse, while eliminating redundancy between text matter and marginal entries.

Concept Checks

To help students assess their mastery of important ideas, Concept Checks are sprinkled throughout the book (two to four per chapter). In keeping with my goal of making this a book of ideas, the Concept Checks challenge students to apply ideas instead of testing rote memory. For example, in Chapter 6 the reader is asked to analyze realistic examples of conditioning and identify conditioned stimuli and responses, reinforcers, and schedules of reinforcement. Many of the Concept Checks require the reader to put together ideas introduced in different sections of the chapter. For instance, in Chapter 2 students are asked to look for various types of deficiencies in hypothetical studies, and in Chapter 4 students are asked to identify parallels between vision and hearing. Some of the Concept Checks are quite challenging, but students find them engaging, and they report that the answers (available in Appendix A) are often illuminating.

Preview Questions and Reviews of Key Points

To help students organize and remember important ideas, each chapter includes five to eight sets of Preview Questions and companion Reviews of Key Points. Generally speaking, the Preview Questions are found at the beginning of each major section in a chapter, in the margin, adjacent to a level-one heading; the Reviews of Key Points are found at the end of each major section, just before the next level-one heading. Of course, some exceptions to this rule-of-thumb had to be made to accommodate very long or very brief sections under level-one headings. The Preview Questions are short, thought-provoking learning objectives that should help students focus on the key issues in each section. Each Review of Key Points is an interim summary that addresses the issues posed in the preceding Preview Questions. Interspersing these reviews throughout the chapters permits students to check their understanding of each section's main ideas immediately after finishing the section instead of waiting until the end of the chapter. This approach also allows students to work with more modest-sized chunks of information.

Practice Tests

Each chapter ends with a 15-item multiple-choice Practice Test that should give students a realistic assessment of their mastery of that chapter and valuable practice taking the type of test that many of them will face in the classroom (if the instructor uses the Test Bank). This feature grew out of some research that I conducted on students' use of textbook pedagogical devices (see Weiten, Guadagno, & Beck, 1996). This research indicated that students pay scant attention to some standard pedagogical devices. When I grilled my students to gain a better undertstanding of this finding, it quickly became apparent that students are very pragmatic about pedagogy. Essentially, their refrain was "We want study aids that will help us pass the next test." With this mandate in mind, I devised the Practice Tests. They should be very realistic, as I took most of the items from previous editions of the Test Bank (these items do not appear in the Test Bank for this edition).

In addition to the special features just described, the text includes a variety of more conventional, "tried and true" features. The back of the book contains a standard *alphabetical glossary*. Opening *outlines* preview each chapter, and a thorough *Recap of Key Ideas* appears at the end of each chapter, along with lists of *Key Terms* and *Key People* (important theorists and researchers). I make frequent use of *italics for emphasis*, and I depend on *frequent headings* to maximize organizational clarity. The preface for students describes these pedagogical devices in more detail.

Content

The text is divided into 16 chapters, which follow a traditional ordering. The chapters are not grouped into sections or parts, primarily because such groupings can limit your options if you want to reorganize the order of topics. The chapters are written in a way that facilitates organizational flexibility, as I always assumed that some chapters might be omitted or presented in a different order.

The topical coverage in the text is relatively conventional, but there are some subtle departures from the norm. For instance, Chapter 1 presents a relatively "meaty" discussion of the evolution of ideas in psychology. This coverage of history lays the foundation for many of the crucial ideas emphasized in subsequent chapters. The historical perspective is also my way of reaching out to the students who find that psychology just isn't what they expected it to be. If we want students to contemplate the mysteries of behavior, we must begin by clearing up the biggest mysteries of them all: "Where did these rats, statistics, synapses, and JNDs come from, what could they possibly have in common, and why doesn't this course bear any resemblance to what I anticipated?" I use history as a vehicle to explain how psychology evolved into its modern form and why misconceptions about its nature are so common.

I also devote an entire chapter (Chapter 2) to the scientific enterprise—not just the mechanics of research methods but the logic behind them. I believe that an appreciation of the nature of empirical evidence can contribute greatly to improving students' critical thinking skills. Ten years from now, many of the "facts" reported in this book will have changed, but an understanding of the methods of science will remain invaluable. An introductory psychology course, by itself, isn't going to make a student think like a scientist, but I can't think of a better place to start the process. Essential statistical concepts are introduced in Chapter 2, but no effort is made to teach actual calculations. For those who emphasize statistics, Appendix B expands on statistical concepts.

Overall, I trust you'll find the coverage up to date, although I do not believe in the common practice of piling up gratuitous references to recent studies to create an impression of currency. I think that an obsession with this year's references derogates our intellectual heritage and suggests to students that the studies we cite today will be written off tomorrow. I often chose to cite an older source over a newer one to give students an accurate feel for when an idea first surfaced or when an issue generated heated debate.

Writing Style

I strive for a down-to-earth, conversational writing style; effective communication is always the paramount goal. My intent is to talk *with* the reader rather than throw information *at* the reader. To clarify concepts and maintain students' interest, I frequently provide concrete examples that students can relate to. As much as possible, I avoid using technical jargon when ordinary language serves just as well.

Making learning easier depends, above all else, on clear, well-organized writing. For this reason, I've worked hard to ensure that chapters, sections, and paragraphs are organized in a logical manner, so that key ideas stand out in sharp relief against supportive information.

Concept Charts for Study and Review

To help your students organize and assimilate the main ideas contained in the text, I have created an entirely new supplement—a booklet of Concept Charts. This booklet contains a two-page Concept Chart for each chapter. Each Concept Chart provides a detailed visual map of the key ideas found in the main body of that chapter. These color-coded, hierarchically-organized charts create snapshots of the chapters that should allow your students to quickly see the relationships among ideas and sections.

Psyk.Trek 2.0: A Multimedia Introduction to Psychology

Psyk.Trek 2.0 is a multimedia supplement that will provide students with new opportunities for active learning and reach out to "visual learners" with greatly increased efficacy. *Psyk.Trek* is intended to give students a second pathway to learning much of the content of introductory psychology. Although it does not cover all of the content of the introductory course, I think you will see that a great many key concepts and principles can be explicated *more effectively* in an interactive audio-visual medium than in a textbook.

The revised *Psyk.Trek 2.0* consists of four components. The main component is a set of 62 *Interactive Learning Modules* that present the core content of psychology in a whole new way. These tutorials include thousands of graphics, hundred of photos, hundreds of animations, approximately four hours of narration, 35 carefully selected videos, and about 160 uniquely visual concept checks and quizzes. The *Simulations* allow students to explore complex psycho-

logical phenomena in depth. They are highly interactive, experiential demonstrations that will enhance students' appreciation of research methods. Three new simulations can be found on *Psyk.Trek 2.0*. A *Multimedia Glossary* allows students to look up over 800 psychological terms, access hundreds of pronunciations of obscure words, and pull up hundreds of related diagrams, photos, and videos. The *Video Selector* allows students to directly access the 35 video segments that are otherwise embedded in the Interactive Learning Modules.

The key strength of *Psyk.Trek* is its ability to give students new opportunities for active learning outside of the classroom. For example, students can run themselves through re-creations of classic experiments to see the complexities of data collection in action. Or they can play with visual illusions on screen in ways that will make them doubt their own eyes. Or they can stack color filters on screen to demonstrate the nature of subtractive color mixing. *Psyk.Trek* is intended to supplement and complement *Psychology: Themes & Variations*. For instance, after reading about operant conditioning in the text, a student could work through three interactive tutorials on operant principles, watch three videos, (including historic footage of B. F. Skinner shaping a rat, and then try to shape Morphy, the virtual rat), in one of the simulations.

Other Supplementary Materials

The teaching/learning package that has been developed to supplement *Psychology: Themes and Variations* also includes many other useful tools. The development of all its parts was carefully coordinated so that they are mutually supported. Moreover, the materials have been created and written by highly experienced, top-flight professors I have worked hard to recruit.

Study Guide (by Richard Stalling and Ronald Wasden)

An exceptionally thorough *Study Guide* is available to help your students master the information in the text. It was written by two of my former professors, Richard Stalling and Ronald Wasden of Bradley University. They have over 30 years of experience as a team writing study guides for introductory psychology texts, and their experience is readily apparent in the high-quality materials that they have developed.

The review of key ideas for each chapter is made up of an engaging mixture of matching exercises, fill-in-the-blank items, free-response questions, and programmed learning. Each review is organized around learning objectives written by me. The *Study Guide* is closely coordinated with the *Test Bank,* as the same learning objectives guided the construction of the questions in the *Test Bank.* The *Study Guide* also includes a review of key terms, a review of key people, and a self-test for each chapter in the text.

Instructor's Resource Manual (coordinated by Randolph Smith)

A talented roster of professors have contributed to the *Instructor's Resource Manual (IRM)* in their respective areas of expertise. The *IRM* was developed under the guidance of Randolph Smith, the editor of the journal *Teaching of Psychology.* It contains a diverse array of materials designed to facilitate efforts to teach the introductory course and includes the following sections.

- The *Instructor's Manual,* by Randolph Smith (Ouachita Baptist University), contains a wealth of detailed suggestions for lecture topics, class demonstrations, exercises, discussion questions, and suggested readings, organized around the content of each chapter in the text. It also highlights the connections between the text coverage and *Psyk.Trek* content and features an expanded collection of masters for class handouts.
- *Strategies for Effective Teaching,* by Joseph Lowman (University of North Carolina), discusses practical issues such as what to put in a course syllabus, how to handle the first class meeting, how to cope with large classes, and how to train and organize teaching assistants.
- *AV Media for Introductory Psychology,* by Russ Watson (College of DuPage), provides a comprehensive, up-to-date critical overview of educational films relevant to the introductory course.
- *The Use of Computers in Teaching Introductory Psychology,* by Susan J. Shapiro and Michael Shapiro (Indiana University–East), offers a thorough listing of computer materials germane to the introductory course and analyzes their strengths and weaknesses.
- *Integrating Writing into Introductory Psychology,* by Jane Jegerski (Elmhurst College), examines the writing-across-the-curriculum movement and provides suggestions and materials for specific writing assignments chapter by chapter.
- *Crossing Borders/Contrasting Behaviors: Using Cross-Cultural Comparisons to Enrich the Introductory Psychology Course,* by Bill Hill and Michael Reiner (Kennesaw State University), discusses the move-

ment toward "internationalizing" the curriculum and provides suggestions for lectures, exercises, and assignments that can add a cross-cultural flavor to the introductory course.

- *Teaching Introductory Psychology with the World Wide Web* by Michael R. Snyder (University of Alberta), discusses how to work Internet assignments into the introductory course and provides a guide to many psychology-related sites on the World Wide Web.
- *Using InfoTrac in Introductory Psychology* by Randolph Smith discusses how to make effective use of the *InfoTrac* subscription that is made available to students with this text. *InfoTrac College Edition* is an online database of recent full-text articles from hundreds of scholarly and popular periodicals.

Test Bank (by S. A. Hensch)

Shirley Hensch (University of Wisconsin, Marshfield/Wood County) did an excellent job revising the *Test Bank* that accompanies this text. The questions are closely tied to the chapter learning objectives and to the lists of key terms and key people found in both the text and the *Study Guide.* The items are categorized as (a) factual, (b) conceptual/applied, (c) integrative, or (d) critical thinking questions. The test bank also includes a separate section that contains about 600 multiple-choice questions based on the content of *Psyk.Trek's* Interactive Learning Modules.

Computerized Test Items

Electronic versions of the *Test Bank* are available for a variety of computer configurations. The *ExamView* software is user-friendly and allows teachers to insert their own questions and to customize those provided.

Transparencies (by Susan Shapiro)

A collection of *text-specific transparencies* has been created to enhance visual presentations in the classroom. The development of the transparencies was supervised by Susan Shapiro (Indiana University–East), who has great expertise in the use of visual media in the classroom. Suzie has done a terrific job making the transparencies clear, readable, pedagogically sound, and technically accurate. A second set of transparencies from other Wadsworth psychology texts is also available.

Challenging Your Preconceptions: Thinking Critically About Psychology (by Randolph Smith)

This brief paperback book is a wonderful introduction to critical thinking as it applies to psychological issues. Written by Randolph Smith (Ouachita Baptist University), this book helps students apply their critical thinking skills to a variety of topics, including hypnosis, advertising, misleading statistics, IQ testing, gender differences, and memory bias. Each chapter ends with critical thinking challenges that give students opportunities to practice their critical thinking skills.

Culture and Modern Life (by David Matsumoto)

If you emphasize cultural diversity in your course, this is an ideal supplementary book. Written by David Matsumoto (San Francisco State University), a lead-ing authority on cross-cultural psychology, this brief paperback will help students appreciate how cultural factors affect psychological processes. It includes chapters on self, social behavior, gender, work, and abnormal psychology.

Psychology: Themes & Variations Web Site

Both students and faculty will find a wealth of useful materials at the Psychology: Themes & Variations Web site, which is highlighted below. If you haven't done so already, I encourage you to visit the site and experience the rich diversity of resources that are available there.

 ON THE WEB

 For additional resources on the topics covered in this text, visit the *Psychology: Themes and Variations* Web site, where you will find practice quizzes, tutorials, Web links, simulations, critical thinking activities, flash cards, interactive exercises, and suggested readings available through INFOTRAC.

http://psychology.wadsworth.com/weiten_themes6e/

Acknowledgments

Creating an introductory psychology text is a complicated challenge, and a small army of people have contributed to the evolution of this book. Foremost among them are the psychology editors I have worked with at Brooks/Cole and Wadsworth—Claire Verduin, C. Deborah Laughton, Phil Curson, Eileen Murphy, and Edith Beard Brady—and the developmental editor for this book, John Bergez. They have helped me immeasurably, and each has become a treasured friend along the way. I am especially indebted to Claire, who educated me in the intricacies of textbook publishing, and to John, who has left an enduring imprint on my writing.

The challenge of meeting a difficult schedule in producing this book was undertaken by a talented team of people coordinated by Tom Dorsaneo, who did a superb job of pulling it all together. Credit for the text design goes to Gladys Rosa-Mendoza, who was very creative in building on the previous design developed by John Odam. Linda Rill handled permissions and photo research with enthusiasm and extraordinary efficiency, and Jackie Estrada did an outstanding job once again in copyediting the manuscript. Suzanne Olivier, Andrea Miles and Cyndie H. Wooley made stellar contributions to the new artwork and Alma Bell efficiently oversaw the composition process.

A host of psychologists deserve thanks for the contributions they made to this book. I am grateful to Diane Halpern for her work on the Critical Thinking Applications; to Vinny Hevern for contributing the Web Links and Internet essay; to Paul Muchinsky for writing the appendix on I/O psychology; to Rick Stalling and Ron Wasden for their work on the *Study Guide;* to Bill Addison for his work on the previous editions of the test bank; to Shirley Hensch for her work on the current edition of the test bank; to Randy Smith, Joseph Lowman, Russ Watson, Jane Jegerski, Bill Hill, Michael Reiner, Susan Shapiro, Michael Shapiro, and Michael Snyder for their contributions to the *Instructor's Resource Manual;* to Susan Shapiro for her work on the transparencies; to Randy Smith and David Matsumoto for contributing ancillary books; to Jim Calhoun for providing item analysis data for the test items; to Harry Upshaw, Larry Wrightsman, Shari Diamond, Rick Stalling, and Claire Etaugh for their help and guidance over the years; and to the chapter consultants listed on page xviii and the reviewers listed on pages xix and xx, who provided insightful and constructive critiques of various portions of the manuscript.

Many other people have also contributed to this project, and I am grateful to all of them for their efforts. Bill Roberts, Craig Barth, Nancy Sjoberg, Marjorie Sanders, Fiorella Ljunggren, Vernon Boes, Jim Brace-Thompson, Joanne Terhaar, Tanya Nigh, and Lisa Weber helped with varied aspects of previous editions. Susan Badger, Sean Wakely, Eve Howard, Stephen Rapley, Joy Westberg, Rebecca Heider, Kathryn Stewart, Lori Grebe, Jennifer Klos, and Margaret Parks made valuable contributions to the current edition. At the College of DuPage, where I taught until 1991, all of my colleagues in psychology provided support and information at one time or another, but I am especially indebted to Barb Lemme, Alan Lanning, Pat Puccio, and Don Green. I also want to thank my former colleagues at Santa Clara University (especially Tracey Kahan, Tom Plante, and Jerry Burger), who were a fertile source of new ideas, and the students at UNLV who helped complete the reference entries (Jane Karwoski, Gary Ogren, and Dionna Phillips).

I am also deeply indebted to the diverse array of people who contributed to the development of the *Psyk.Trek* CD-ROM. At Thomson Learning, Eileen Murphy, Chris Evers, Marlene Thom, May Clark, and Michelle Vardeman worked above and beyond the call of duty. At Luminair Multimedia, George Elder, Kent Johnson, Laddie Odom, John Fuller, and Jocelyn Turpin worked with maniacal intensity to deliver *Psyk.Trek* on time. Crucial contributions were also made by Alan Lanning, Roger Harnish, Linda Noble, Linda Rill, Sue Howard, and Jackie Estrada.

My greatest debt is to my wife, Beth Traylor, who has been a steady source of emotional sustenance while enduring the rigors of her medical career, and to my son T. J., for making dad laugh all the time.

Wayne Weiten

Integrated Coverage of Evolutionary Psychology

Emergence of evolutionary psychology as a major theory, pp. 14–15

Evolutionary basis of gender differences in spatial skills, pp. 15, 32–33

Overview of Darwin's original theory and key concepts, pp. 4–5, 108–109

Further refinements to evolutionary theory, including inclusive fitness, pp. 109–111

Evolutionary bases of selected animal behaviors, pp. 111–112

Parental investment theory and animal mating systems, pp. 112–114

Evolutionary significance of color vision, p. 137

Evolutionary significance of sensory adaptation, p. 128

Evolutionary basis of cortical "face detectors," p. 136

Evolution and perception of geographical slant, pp. 149–150

Evolution and gender differences in taste sensitivity, p. 161

Evolutionary roots of consciousness, pp. 178–179

Evolutionary bases of sleep, p. 187

Evolution and classical conditioning of sexual arousal, pp. 224–225

Evolution and animal foraging patterns, pp. 238–239

Evolutionary significance of conditioned taste aversion, pp. 244–245

Evolution and species-specific learning propensities, pp. 245–246

Language in evolutionary context, p. 311

Evolutionary analysis of error and bias in decision making, p. 329

Evolutionary basis of fast and frugal heuristics in decision making, pp. 329–330

Evolutionary approach to motivation, p. 383

Evolutionary explanation of increasing prevalence of obesity, pp. 388–389

Evolution and mate selection in animals, p. 393

Implications of parental investment theory for human sexual behavior, pp. 393–394

Evolution and gender differences in sexual activity, p. 394

Critique of evolutionary analyses of human sexual behavior, pp. 396–397

Evolutionary basis of mating priorities, pp. 394–396

Evolutionary significance of affiliation drive, p. 402

Evolutionary theories of emotion, pp. 413–414

Evolutionary perspective on innate cognitive abilities, p. 446

Evolutionary significance of varied attachment patterns, pp. 438–439

Adaptive implications of variations in timing of puberty, pp. 451–452

Evolutionary approach to explaining gender differences in human abilities, pp. 468–469

Evolutionary basis of Big-Five personality traits, pp. 502–503

Problem of hindsight in evolutionary analyses of personality, p. 517

Evolutionary basis of fight-or-flight response, p. 529

Evolution, preparedness, and phobias, pp. 245, 570

Evolutionary explanations of bias in person perception, p. 651

Evolutionary analyses of how aspects of physical appearance influence reproductive fitness, p. 661

Evolutionary basis of relations between infant attachment patterns and adult romantic relationships, p. 661

Evolutionary basis of mate-attraction tactics, pp. 661–662

Evolutionary basis of gender differences in the perception of sexual interest and relationship commitment, p. 662

Integrated Coverage of Cultural Factors

Increased interest in cultural diversity, pp. 13–14

Introduction of theme: Behavior is shaped by cultural heritage, pp. 24–25

Cultural variations in the pace of life, pp. 48–49

Culture and depth perception, pp. 147–148

Cultural variations in susceptibility to illusions, pp. 152–153

Cultural variations in taste preferences, p. 159

Cultural variations in pain tolerance, p. 163

Culture and patterns of sleeping, pp. 185–186

Cultural variations in the significance of dreams, pp. 194–95

Cultural similarities in the pace of language development, pp. 311–312

Effects of bilingualism, pp. 308–309

Factors influencing second language acquisition, p. 309

Linguistic relativity hypothesis, pp. 313–314

Cultural variations in cognitive style, pp. 320–322

IQ testing in non-Western cultures, p. 353

Cultural and ethnic differences in IQ scores, pp. 361–366

Cultural bias in IQ testing, pp. 365–366

Culture and food preferences, p. 387

Cross-cultural similarity of mating preferences, pp. 395–396

Cultural similarities in expressive aspects of emotions, pp. 409–410

Cultural variations in categories of emotions, display rules, p. 411

Culture and the ingredients of happiness, p. 418

Cultural variations in infant mortality, pp. 430–431

Culture and motor development, pp. 432–433

Culture and patterns of attachment, pp. 437–438

Cross-cultural validity of Piaget's theory, p. 444

Cross-cultural validity of Kohlberg's theory, p. 448

Culture and the transition to adolescence, p. 449

Culture and modal personality, p. 507

Cross-cultural validity of the Big Five trait model, pp. 507–508

Culture and independent versus interdependent views of self, pp. 508–509

Culture, self-enhancement, and self-criticism, pp. 508–509

Culture and the concept of normality, p. 562

Relativistic versus pancultural view of psychological disorders, p. 595

Culture-bound disorders, p. 596

Culture and symptom patterns, p. 596

Cultural variations in existence of eating disorders, p. 598

Contribution of Western cultural values to eating disorders, pp. 600–601

Western cultural roots of psychotherapy, p. 633

Barriers to the use of therapy by ethnic minorities, pp. 633–634

Culture, collectivism, and individualism, p. 655

Culture and attributional bias, pp. 655–656

Cultural variations in romantic relationships, pp. 660–661

Cultural variations in conformity and obedience, p. 675

Culture and social loafing, p. 678

Ethnic stereotypes and modern racism, p. 681

Contribution of attribution bias to ethnic stereotypes, pp. 682–683

Learning of ethnic stereotypes, p. 683

Outgroup homogeneity and ethnic stereotypes, p. 683

Integrated Coverage of Issues Related to Gender

Chapter Consultants

Chapter 1

Charles L. Brewer
Furman University
C. James Goodwin
Wheeling Jesuit University
David Hothersall
Ohio State University
E. R. Hilgard
Stanford University

Chapter 2

Larry Christensen
Texas A & M University
Francis Durso
University of Oklahoma
Donald H. McBurney
University of Pittsburgh
Wendy Schweigert
Bradley University

Chapter 3

Nelson Freedman
Queen's University at Kingston
Michael W. Levine
University of Illinois at Chicago
James M. Murphy
*Indiana University–Purdue University
at Indianapolis*
Paul Wellman
Texas A & M University

Chapter 4

Nelson Freedman
Queen's University at Kingston
Kevin Jordan
San Jose State University
Michael W. Levine
University of Illinois at Chicago
John Pittenger
University of Arkansas, Little Rock
Lawrence Ward
University of British Columbia

Chapter 5

Frank Etscorn
*New Mexico Institute of Mining and
Technology*
Tracey L. Kahan
Santa Clara University
Charles F. Levinthal
Hofstra University
Wilse Webb
University of Florida

Chapter 6

A. Charles Catania
University of Maryland
Michael Domjan
University of Texas, Austin
William C. Gordon
University of New Mexico
Barry Schwartz
Swarthmore College

Chapter 7

Tracey L. Kahan
Santa Clara University
Ian Neath
Purdue University
Tom Pusateri
Loras College
Stephen K. Reed
San Diego State University
Patricia Tenpenny
Loyola University, Chicago

Chapter 8

John Best
Eastern Illinois University
David Carroll
University of Wisconsin-Superior
Tom Pusateri
Loras College
Stephen K. Reed
San Diego State University

Chapter 9

Charles Davidshofer
Colorado State University
Shalynn Ford
Teikyo Marycrest University
Timothy Rogers
University of Calgary
Dennis Saccuzzo
San Diego State University

Chapter 10

Robert Franken
University of Calgary
Russell G. Geen
University of Missouri
Douglas Mook
University of Virginia
D. Louis Wood
University of Arkansas, Little Rock

Chapter 11

Ruth L. Ault
Davidson College
John C. Cavanaugh
University of Delaware
Claire Etaugh
Bradley University
Barbara Hansen Lemme
College of DuPage

Chapter 12

Susan Cloninger
Russel Sage College
Caroline Collins
University of Victoria
Christopher F. Monte
Manhattanville College

Chapter 13

Robin M. DiMatteo
University of California, Riverside
Jess Feist
McNeese State University
Chris Kleinke
University of Alaska, Anchorage

Chapter 14

David A. F. Haaga
American University
Richard Halgin
University of Massachusetts, Amherst
Chris L. Kleinke
University of Alaska, Anchorage
Elliot A. Weiner
Pacific University

Chapter 15

Gerald Corey
California State University, Fullerton
Herbert Goldenberg
California State University, Los Angeles
Jane S. Halonen
Alverno College
Thomas G. Plante
Santa Clara University

Chapter 16

Jerry M. Burger
Santa Clara University
Stephen L. Franzoi
Marquette University
Donelson R. Forsyth
Virginia Commonwealth University

Reviewers

Lyn Y. Abramson
University of Wisconsin

James R. M. Alexander
University of Tasmania

Gordon A. Allen
Miami University of Ohio

Elise L. Amel
University of St. Thomas

Ruth L. Ault
Davidson College

Jeff D. Baker
Southeastern Louisiana University

Gina J. Bates
Southern Arkansas University

Derryl K. Beale
Cerritos Community College

Ashleah Bectal
U. S. Military Academy

Robert P. Beitz
Pima County Community College

Daniel R. Bellack
Trident Technical College

Robert Bornstein
Miami University

Bette L. Bottoms
University of Illinois at Chicago

Allen Branum
South Dakota State University

Robert G. Bringle
Indiana University-Purdue University at Indianapolis

David R. Brodbeck
Sir Wilfred Grenfall College, Memorial University of Newfoundland

Dan W. Brunworth
Kishwaukee College

David M. Buss
University of Texas, Austin

James Butler
James Madison University

Mary M. Cail
University of Virginia

James F. Calhoun
University of Georgia

William Calhoun
University of Tennessee

Janet L. Chapman
U. S. Military Academy

Francis B. Colavita
University of Pittsburgh

Thomas B. Collins
Mankato State University

Stan Coren
University of British Columbia

Verne C. Cox
University of Texas at Arlington

Kenneth Cramer
University of Windsor

Dianne Crisp
Kwantlen University College

Norman Culbertson
Yakima Valley College

Betty M. Davenport
Campbell University

Stephen F. Davis
Emporia State University

Kenneth Deffenbacher
University of Nebraska

Kathy Denton
Douglas College

Marcus Dickson
Wayne State University

Deanna L. Dodson
Lebanon Valley College

Roger Dominowski
University of Illinois, Chicago

Dale V. Doty
Monroe Community College

Robert J. Douglas
University of Washington

Jim Duffy
Sir Wilfred Grenfall College, Memorial University of Newfoundland

James Eison
Southeast Missouri State University

Pamela G. Ely
St. Andrews Presbyterian College

M. Jeffrey Farrar
University of Florida

Donald Fields
University of New Brunswick

Thomas P. Fitzpatrick
Rockland Community College

Karen E. Ford
Mesa State College

Donelson R. Forsyth
Virginia Commonwealth University

William J. Froming
University of Florida

Mary Ellen Fromuth
Middle Tennessee State University

Dean E. Frost
Portland State University

Judy Gentry
Columbus State Community College

Doba Goodman
York University

Richard Griggs
University of Florida

Arthur Gutman
Florida Institute of Technology

Jane S. Halonen
Alverno College

Roger Harnish
Rochester Institute of Technology

Philip L. Hartley
Chaffey College

Brad M. Hastings
Mount Aloysius College

Glenn R. Hawkes
Virginia Commonwealth University

Myra D. Heinrich
Mesa State College

Lyllian B. Hix
Houston Community College

John P. Hostetler
Albion College

Bruce Hunsberger
Wilfrid Laurier University

Mir Rabiul Islam
Charles Sturt University

Robert A. Johnston
College of William and Mary

Robert Kaleta
University of Wisconsin, Milwaukee

Alan R. King
University of North Dakota

Melvyn B. King
State University of New York, Cortland

James Knight
Humboldt State University

Mike Knight
Central State University

Ronald Kopcho
Mercer Community College

Barry J. Krikstone
Saint Michael's College

Jerry N. Lackey
Stephen F. Austin State University

Robin L. Lashley
Kent State University, Tuscarawas

Peter Leppman
University of Guelph

Charles F. Levinthal
Hofstra University

Wolfgang Linden
University of British Columbia

John Lindsay
Georgia College & State University

Diane Martichuski
University of Colorado, Boulder

Donald McBurney
University of Pittsburgh

Siobhan McEnaney-Hayes
Chestnut Hill College

Kathleen McCormick
Ocean County College

David G. McDonald
University of Missouri

Ronald K. McLaughlin
Juniata College

Sheryll Mennicke
University of Minnesota

Mitchell Metzger
Pennsylvania State University, Shenango

Mary Morris
Northern Territory University

Darwin Muir
Queen's University at Kingston

James M. Murphy
*Indiana University-Purdue University
at Indianapolis*

Michael Murphy
Henderson State University

John Nezlek
College of William and Mary

David L. Novak
Lansing Community College

Richard Page
Wright State University

Joseph J. Palladino
University of Southern Indiana

John N. Park
Mankato State University

Bobby J. Poe
Belleville Area College

Gary Poole
Simon Fraser University

Russell Powell
Grant MacEwan College

Maureen K. Powers
Vanderbilt University

Janet Proctor
Purdue University

Robin Raygor
Anoka-Ramsey Community College

Celia Reaves
Monroe Community College

Gary T. Reker
Trent University

Daniel W. Richards
Houston Community College

Kenneth M. Rosenberg
State University of New York, Oswego

Patricia Ross
Laurentian University

Angela Sadowski
Chaffey College

Sabato D. Sagaria
Capital University

Fred Shima
*California State University
Dominguez Hills*

Susan A. Shodahl
San Bernardino Valley College

Steven M. Smith
Texas A & M University

Paul Stager
York University

Marjorie Taylor
University of Oregon

Frank R. Terrant, Jr.
Appalachian State University

Donald Tyrrell
Franklin and Marshall College

Frank J. Vattano
Colorado State University

Wayne Viney
Colorado State University

Paul Wellman
Texas A & M University

Keith D. White
University of Florida

Randall D. Wight
Ouachita Baptist University

Daniel E. Wivagg
Baylor University

D. Louis Wood
University of Arkansas, Little Rock

Cecilia Yoder
Oklahoma City Community College

Brief Contents

The Evolution of Psychology

© Kevin R. Morris/CORBIS

© Digital Vision/Getty Images

CHAPTER 3

The Biological Bases of Behavior

© Francisco Cruz/Super Stock

© Diana Ong/Super Stock

CHAPTER 4

Perception

CHAPTER 5

Variations in Consciousness

© Keren Su/CORBIS

Learning

CHAPTER 7

Human Memory

© A. Woolfitt/Robert Harding Picture Library, London

© Sally Brown/Index Stock Imagery

Intelligence and Psychological Testing

CHAPTER 9

© Adalberto Ríos Szalay/Sexto Sol/PhotoDisc-Getty Images

© Gary Buss/Taxi-Getty Images

Motivation and Emotion

CHAPTER 10

Human Development Across the Life Span

CHAPTER 11

© Adam Crowley/PhotoDisc-Getty Images

Personality: Theory, Research and Assessment

CHAPTER 12

© Bruce Stoddard/Taxi-Getty Images

Stress, Coping, and Health

© Kevin R. Morris/CORBIS

© Ed Freeman/Image Bank-Getty Images

Treatment of Psychological Disorders

CHAPTER 15

© Kit Kittle/CORBIS

Social Behavior

© Scott Barrow, Inc./SuperStock

To the Student

Welcome to your introductory psychology textbook. In most college courses, students spend more time with their textbooks than with their professors, so it helps if students *like* their textbooks. Making textbooks likable, however, is a tricky proposition. By its very nature, a textbook must introduce students to many complicated concepts, ideas, and theories. If it doesn't, it isn't much of a textbook, and instructors won't choose to use it. Nevertheless, in writing this book I've tried to make it as likable as possible without compromising the academic content that your instructor demands. I've especially tried to keep in mind your need for a clear, well-organized presentation that makes the important material stand out and yet is interesting to read. Above all else, I hope you find this book challenging to think about and easy to learn from.

Before you plunge into your first chapter, let me introduce you to the book's key features. Becoming familiar with how the book works will help you to get more out of it.

Key Features

You're about to embark on a journey into a new domain of ideas. Your text includes some important features that are intended to highlight certain aspects of psychology's landscape.

Unifying Themes

To help you make sense of a complex and diverse field of study, I introduce seven themes in Chapter 1 that reappear in a number of variations as we move from chapter to chapter. These unifying themes are meant to provoke thought about important issues and to highlight the connections between chapters. They are discussed at the end of each chapter in a section called "Putting It in Perspective."

Featured Studies

After Chapter 1, each chapter includes a Featured Study, which is an in-depth look at an interesting piece of research. The Featured Studies are presented much as if they were journal articles. I hope they will enhance your understanding of how psychologists conduct and report their research.

Personal Applications

Toward the end of each chapter you'll find a Personal Application section that shows how psychology is relevant to everyday life. Some of these sections provide concrete, practical advice that could be helpful to you in your educational endeavors, such as those on improving academic performance, improving everyday memory, and achieving self-control. So, you may want to jump ahead and read some of these Personal Applications early.

Critical Thinking Applications

Each Personal Application is followed by a two-page Critical Thinking Application that teaches and models basic critical thinking skills. I think you will find these sections refreshing and interesting. Like the Personal Applications, they are part of the text's basic content and should be read unless you are told otherwise by your instructor. Although the "facts" of psychology will gradually change after you take this course (thanks to scientific progress), the critical thinking skills modeled in these sections should prove valuable for many years to come.

Web Links and Internet Essays

To help make this book a rich resource guide, we have included dozens of Web Links, which are recommended Web sites that can provide you with additional information on many topics. The recommended sites were selected by Professor Vincent Hevern, who sought out resources that are interesting and that provide accurate, empirically sound information. The Web Links are dispersed throughout the chapters, adjacent to related topical coverage. Because Web addresses change frequently, we have placed the URLs for our Web Links in Appendix E in the back of the book. If you are interested in visiting these sites, we recommend that you do so through the *Psychology: Themes & Variations* home page at the Wadsworth Web site (http://psychology.wadsworth. com/weiten_themes6e). Links to all the recommended Web sites are maintained there and the Wadsworth Webmaster periodically updates the URLs. By the way, if you are not particularly sophisticated about the Internet, I strongly suggest that you read Professor Hevern's essay on Internet basics, which follows this preface. And even if you *are* sophisticated about the Internet, you can probably benefit from reading Appendix D, which discusses how to evaluate the quality and credibility of Web-based resources.

Learning Aids

This text contains a great deal of information. A number of learning aids have been incorporated into the book to help you digest it all.

An *outline* at the beginning of each chapter provides you with an overview of the topics covered in that chapter. Think of the outlines as road maps, and bear in mind that it's easier to reach a destination if you know where you're going.

Headings serve as road signs in your journey through each chapter. Four levels of headings are used to make it easy to see the organization of each chapter.

Preview Questions, found at the beginning of major sections, can help you focus on the key issues in the material you are about to read.

Reviews of Key Points, found at the end of major sections, are interim summaries that permit you to check your understanding of a section's main ideas immediately after finishing the section.

Italics (without boldface) are used liberally throughout the text to emphasize crucial points.

Key terms are identified with ***italicized boldface*** type to alert you that these are important vocabulary items that are part of psychology's technical language. The key terms are also listed at the end of the chapter.

An *integrated running glossary* provides an on-the-spot definition of each key term as it's introduced in the text. These formal definitions are printed in **boldface** type. Becoming familiar with psychology's terminology is an essential part of learning about the field. The integrated running glossary should make this learning process easier.

Concept Checks are sprinkled throughout the chapters to let you test your mastery of important ideas. Generally, they ask you to integrate or organize a number of key ideas, or to apply ideas to real-world situations. Although they're meant to be engaging and fun, they do check conceptual *understanding,* and some are challenging. But if you get stuck, don't worry; the answers (and explanations, where they're needed) are in the back of the book in Appendix A.

Illustrations in the text are important elements in your complete learning package. Some illustrations provide enlightening diagrams of complicated concepts; others furnish examples that help flesh out ideas or provide concise overviews of research results. Careful attention to the tables and figures in the book will help you understand the material discussed in the text.

A *Chapter Recap* at the end of each chapter provides a summary of the chapter's *Key Ideas,* a list of *Key Terms,* and a list of *Key People* (important theorists and researchers). It's wise to read over these review materials to make sure you've digested the information in the chapter.

Each chapter ends with a 15-item *Practice Test* that should give you a realistic assessment of your mastery of that chapter and valuable practice in taking multiple-choice tests.

An *alphabetical glossary* is provided in the back of the book. Most key terms are formally defined in the integrated running glossary only when they are first introduced. So if you run into a technical term a second time and can't remember its meaning, it may be easier to look it up in the alphabetical glossary than to try to find the definition where the term was originally introduced.

A Few Footnotes

Psychology textbooks customarily identify the studies, theoretical treatises, books, and articles that information comes from. These *citations* occur (1) when names are followed by a date in parentheses, as in "Smith (1993) found that . . ." or (2) when names and dates are provided together within parentheses, as in "In one study (Smith, Miller, & Jones, 2001), the researchers attempted to . . ." All of the cited publications are listed by author in the alphabetized *References* section in the back of the book. The citations and references are a necessary part of a book's scholarly and scientific foundation. Practically speaking, however, you'll probably want to glide right over them as you read. You definitely don't need to memorize the names and dates. The only names you may need to know are the handful listed under Key People in each Chapter Recap (unless your instructor mentions a personal favorite that you should know).

Concept Charts for Study and Review

Your text should be accompanied by a booklet of Concept Charts that are designed to help you organize and master the main ideas contained in each chapter. Each Concept Chart provides a detailed visual map of the key ideas found in the main body of that chapter. Seeing how it all fits together should help you to better understand each chapter. You can use these charts to preview chapters, to get a handle on how key ideas fit together, to double-check your mastery of the chapters, and to memorize the crucial principles in chapters.

Psyk.Trek: A Multimedia Introduction to Psychology

Psyk.Trek is a multimedia CD-ROM developed to accompany this textbook. It is an enormously powerful learning tool that can enhance your understanding of many complex processes and theories, provide you with an alternative way to assimilate many crucial concepts, and add a little more fun to your journey through introductory psychology. *Psyk.Trek* has been designed to supplement and complement your textbook. I strongly encourage you to use it. The CD icons that you will see in many of the headings in the upcoming chapters refer to the content of *Psyk.Trek*. An icon indicates that the textbook topic referred to in the heading is covered in the Interactive Learning Modules or Simulations found on *Psyk.Trek*. The relevant simulations (Sim1, Sim2, and so forth) and the relevant Interactive Learning Modules (1a, 1b, 1c, and so forth) are listed to the right of the icons.

A Word About the Study Guide

A *Study Guide* is available to accompany this text. It was written by two of my former professors, who introduced me to psychology years ago. They have done a great job of organizing review materials to help you master the information in the book. I suggest that you seriously consider using it to help you study.

A Final Word

I'm pleased to be a part of your first journey into the world of psychology, and I sincerely hope that you'll find the book as thought provoking and as easy to learn from as I've tried to make it. If you have any comments or advice on the book, please write to me in care of the publisher (Wadsworth Publishing Company, 10 Davis Drive, Belmont, CA 94002). You can be sure I'll pay careful attention to your feedback. Finally, let me wish you good luck. I hope you enjoy your course and learn a great deal.

Wayne Weiten

 **ON THE WEB**

For additional resources on the topics covered in this text, visit the *Psychology: Themes and Variations* Web site, where you will find practice quizzes, tutorials, Web links, simulations, critical thinking activities, flash cards, interactive exercises, and suggested readings available through INFOTRAC.

http://psychology.wadsworth.com/weiten_themes6e/

What Should Introductory Psychology Students Know About the Internet?

by Vincent W. Hevern, Le Moyne College

After dinner one night, Wayne Weiten, the author of this textbook, challenged me: Using no more than three pages, could I tell introductory psychology students the most important things they need to know about the Internet? Wait a minute, I thought, that's tough! I've been using the Net intensively for more than seven years in teaching and research with undergraduates, so I know there's an awful lot to talk about. But, after a couple of days I decided to accept his challenge. So, I'm going to share with you here what I believe to be the really important stuff about the Internet ("the Net")—information that should make your life as a student easier and, in the end, help you to learn even more about the fascinating world of psychology.

General Comments About the Internet

We now know that something of a fundamental change in the way people exchange ideas and information took place during the 1990s. For over 20 years, the Internet had been the tool of a relatively small group of lab scientists communicating mostly with each other. Suddenly, in the mid-1990s, the Net began to expand rapidly beyond the research laboratory. It first reached tens and then hundreds of millions of people as vast numbers of computers, large and small, were interconnected to form what is often called *cyberspace*. In the 21st century, learning to navigate the Internet will become as crucial as learning to read or to write—most of us will probably use the Net in some form at work or at home for the rest of our lives.

So, what are some basic notions necessary to understanding the Internet and how it works? Let me propose briefly eight crucial ideas.

1. *The goal of the Internet is communication—the rapid exchange of information—between people separated from each other.* Electronic mail (e-mail) and the World Wide Web (WWW, or just "the Web") are currently the two most important ways of communicating in cyberspace, even though the Net also uses other formats to do so.

2. *Every piece of information on the Net—every Web page, every graphic, every movie or sound, every e-mail box—has a unique, short, and structured address called a URL (or uniform resource locator).* Take, for example, the URL for materials related to psychology maintained by the publisher of this book:

http://www.wadsworth.com/psychology_d/

This example shows all three elements of a URL: (a) to the left of the double forward slashes (//) is the protocol that tells the Net how to transfer the information. Here it is *http:* which means "use hypertext transfer protocol"—the most frequent protocol on the Net; (b) to the right of the double slashes up to the first forward slash (/) is the *domain name* that indicates which computer on the Net from which to get the information. Here the name of the computer is "www.wadsworth.com"; (c) finally, everything after the first forward slash is called the *pathway* which indicates where the information is located within that particular computer. Here the pathway comprises the location "psychology_d/".

3. *The foundation of the Web rests on hypertext links ("hyperlinks"), which are contained within documents (or "Web pages") displayed online.* A hyperlink is a highlighted word, phrase, or graphic image within an onscreen document that refers to some other document or Web page elsewhere. Part of every hyperlink on a computer screen includes the URL for the document that is hidden from view but stored within the computer displaying the document. Users can easily move from one document to another on screen because of hypertext links and their URLs.

4. *Pay attention to the last element of the domain name (the "domain" itself), which indicates what type of organization sponsors the link.* Four important domains are *.com* (commercial businesses), *.edu* (colleges and universities), *.gov* (governmental agencies), and *.org* (nonprofit organizations).

5. *The Internet is too large for any one individual to know all the important resources that can be found there.* Users, even experienced ones, often need help to find what they're looking for. In the chapters ahead, you will find many recommended Web sites that I have carefully selected based on their quality and their suitability for undergraduates. In making these selections, I emphasized quality over quantity and strived to send you to excellent gateway sites that are

rich in links to related sites. I hope these suggested Web links help you begin to explore the field of psychology on the Internet.

6. *URLs are relatively unstable.* Many Web sites are moved or changed each year, as new computer systems are installed to replace older ones. Thus, links or URLs that are good one day may be useless the next. That is why we have relegated the URLs for our recommended Web sites to Appendix E found in the back of this book. If you want to check out a recommended Web site, we suggest that you do so through the *Psychology: Themes and Variations* home page at the Wadsworth Web site (http://psychology. wadsworth.com/weiten_themes6e). Links to all of the recommended Web sites will be maintained there, and the Wadsworth Webmaster will periodically update the URLs.

7. *The Web is a worldwide democracy on which anyone can post materials. Hence, the quality of information found online varies tremendously.* Some material is first-rate, up-to-date, and backed up by good research and professional judgment. But a great deal of information online is junk—based on poor or invalid research and filled with many errors. Frankly, some sites are downright wacky, and others are run by hucksters and hatemongers. Thus, users need to learn to tell the difference between reputable and disreputable Web resources (see Appendix D in the back of the book).

8. *Knowledge has a monetary value.* Although the Internet started out as a noncommerical enterprise where almost everything was free, things have changed swiftly. Owners of knowledge (the holders of commercial "copyrights") usually expect to be paid for sharing what they own over the Net. Thus, many commercial businesses, such as the publishers of academic journals or books, either do not make journal articles available on line or expect users to pay some type of fee for accessing their materials. Cognizant of this problem, the publisher of this text has entered into an agreement with a major online resource for magazine and journal articles and other types of information called *InfoTrac*. Your text may have come bundled with a subscription to *InfoTrac*, which provides easy access to full-text versions of thousands of periodicals. If you received an *InfoTrac* subscription with this book, it would be wise to take advantage of this valuable resource.

Some Suggestions for Action

In light of these ideas, how might you approach the Internet? What should you do to make the most of your time online? Let's review some general suggestions for exploring the Internet.

1. *Learn to navigate the Net before you get an assignment requiring you to do so.* If you've never used the Net before, start now to get a feel for it. Consider doing what lots of students do: Ask a friend who knows the Net to work with you directly so you can quickly get personal experience in cyberspace. What if you "hate" computers or they make you uncomfortable? Recent research has shown that students' fears of using computers tend to diminish once they get some practical experience in the course of a single semester.

2. *Learn how the software browser on your computer works.* The two most popular Web browser programs, Netscape Navigator and Microsoft Internet Explorer, are filled with many simple tricks and helpful shortcuts. Ask your friends or the computer consultants at school. Learning the tricks makes Net-based research much easier. (Hint: Find out what happens when you hold down the righthand mouse button on a PC or the whole button on a Mac once you have the cursor on top of a hyperlink.)

3. *Get to know the different types of online help to find resources on the Web.* These resources currently fall into three general categories: (a) *General guides or directories* like Yahoo! (http://www.yahoo.com) are similar to the Yellow Pages for telephones. You ask the online guide to show you what's listed in its directory under a category heading you supply. (b) *Search engines* such as Google (http://www.google.com) or AllTheWeb (http://www.alltheweb.com/), and *meta-search engines* such as ProFusion (http://www. profusion.com/) are huge databases that generally collect the names and URLs of millions of pages on the Net, along with many lines of text from these pages. They can be searched by either keywords or phrases and provide ranked listings of Web pages that contain the search target words or phrases. (c) *Expert subject guides* such as Russ Dewey's *PsychWeb* (http://www. psychwww.com/) or Jeffrey Browndyke's *Neuropsychology Central* (http://www.neuropsychologycentral. com/) provide links to online resources in more narrow or specific fields. Volunteer specialists who claim to be experts on the topic select the links.

4. *Check very carefully everything you type online because even the slightest error in spelling a URL or an e-mail address will cause a failure to retrieve the Web page or to deliver the e-mail message.* Remember that computers are stupid and will do exactly and only what you tell them to do. They don't read minds.

Using the Internet in Psychology

Here are five specific suggestions to help students of psychology when using the Net.

1. *Plan what to look for before going online.* Too many psychology students jump right to the Web when they're given a research task, before giving careful thought to what they're looking for. They easily get frustrated because the Web doesn't seem to have anything about the topic. It would be better (a) to think about the subject you are researching and what specifically you want to learn about that topic, (b) to recall what you already know that relates to the topic, especially psychological concepts and vocabulary words associated with the topic, and (c) to devise a strategy for getting the information you desire. Consult your school's reference library staff or your teachers for suggestions.

2. *Do not rely on the Internet as your principal or only source of data or references in a research project* (especially if you want a good grade). The Net may be easy to use, but your teachers will expect you to cite journal articles, books, and other printed sources more than you cite Internet materials in research. Developing your library skills is essential.

3. *As noted before, don't expect to find many full-text journal articles or other copyrighted commercial materials online for free.* Consult your school's reference librarians about online access to such materials. You are more likely to uncover government reports, specialized technical materials from nonprofit organizations, current news and opinion, and general sorts of information rather than findings of specific research studies (although, if the findings were recently in the news, you may find some news reports describing the research).

4. *Learn to recognize the characteristics of a good on-line resource site.* Good sites have Webmasters or editors personally identified by name and affiliation. Such persons may be professionals or staff members at a reputable institution such as a hospital or university. These sites tend to provide a broad set of resources, are balanced and reasonably objective in their content, and avoid sensational or one-sided viewpoints. Reputable sites tend not to promote specific products or services for money—or, if they do, they acknowledge that there are other resources that people may want to consider. The challenge of evaluating the quality of online resources is such an important skill for students to master, we have included a much more detailed discussion of this matter in Appendix D.

5. *If you contact anyone online for help, be courteous.* Introduce yourself as you would if you were standing in a faculty member's office. Give your name, your school, and a full statement of what help you are asking for and what you've tried to do that hasn't worked. Don't demand that someone help you. Be sure you've done adequate research on your own before contacting an expert on the Web. And don't be surprised if your request for help is turned down by a Webmaster or editor. Frankly, he or she has already done a lot of volunteer work by editing the site online.

I hope some of these ideas and suggestions help. The Internet offers an awesome array of learning resources related to psychology. Welcome to an exciting new world of discovery.

CHAPTER 1

© Kevin R. Morris/CORBIS

The Evolution of Psychology

What is psychology? Your initial answer to this question is likely to bear little resemblance to the picture of psychology that will emerge as you work your way through this book. I know that when I ambled into my introductory psychology course more than 30 years ago, I had no idea what psychology involved. I was a pre-law/political science major fulfilling a general education requirement with what I thought would be my one and only psychology course. I encountered two things I didn't expect. The first was to learn that psychology is about a great many things besides abnormal behavior and ways to win friends and influence people. I was surprised to discover that psychology is also about how people are able to perceive color, how hunger is regulated by the brain, whether chimpanzees can use language to communicate, and a multitude of other topics I'd never thought to wonder about. The second thing I didn't expect was that I would be so completely seduced by the subject. Before long I changed majors and embarked on a career in psychology—a decision I have never regretted.

Why has psychology continued to fascinate me? One reason is that *psychology is practical*. It offers a vast store of information about issues that concern everyone. These issues range from broad social questions, such as how to reduce the incidence of mental illness, to highly personal questions, such as how to improve your self-control. In a sense, psychology is about you and me. It's about life in our modern world. The practical side of psychology will be apparent throughout this text, especially in the end-of-chapter Personal Applications. These Applications focus on everyday problems, such as coping more effectively with stress, improving memory, enhancing performance in school, and dealing with sleep difficulties.

Another element of psychology's appeal for me is that it represents a *way of thinking*. We are all exposed to claims about psychological issues. For instance, we hear assertions that men and women have different abilities or that violence on television has a harmful effect on children. As a science, psychology de-

mands that researchers ask precise questions about such issues and that they test their ideas through systematic observation. Psychology's commitment to testing ideas encourages a healthy brand of critical thinking. In the long run, this means that psychology provides a way of building knowledge that is relatively accurate and dependable.

Of course, psychological research cannot discover an answer for every interesting question about the mind and behavior. You won't find the meaning of life or the secret of happiness in this text. But you *will* find an approach to investigating questions that has proven to be fruitful. The more you learn about psychology as a way of thinking, the better able you will be to evaluate the psychological assertions you encounter in daily life.

There is still another reason for my fascination with psychology. As you proceed through this text, you will find that psychologists study an enormous diversity of subjects, from acrophobia (fear of heights) to zoophobia (fear of animals), from problem solving in apes to the symbolic language of dreams. Psychologists look at all the seasons of human life, from development in the womb to the emotional stages that people go through in the process of dying. Psychologists study observable behaviors such as eating, fighting, and mating. But they also dig beneath the surface to investigate how hormones affect emotions and how the brain registers pain. They probe the behavior of any number of species, from humans to house cats, from monkeys to moths. This rich diversity is, for me, perhaps psychology's most appealing aspect.

Mental illness, rats running in mazes, the physiology of hunger, the mysteries of love, creativity, and prejudice—what ties all these subjects together in a single discipline? How did psychology come to be so diverse? Why is it so different from what most people expect? If psychology is a social science, why do psychologists study subjects such as brain chemistry and the physiological basis of vision? To answer these questions, we begin our introduction to psychology by retracing its development. By seeing how psychol-

© Kevin R. Morris/CORBIS

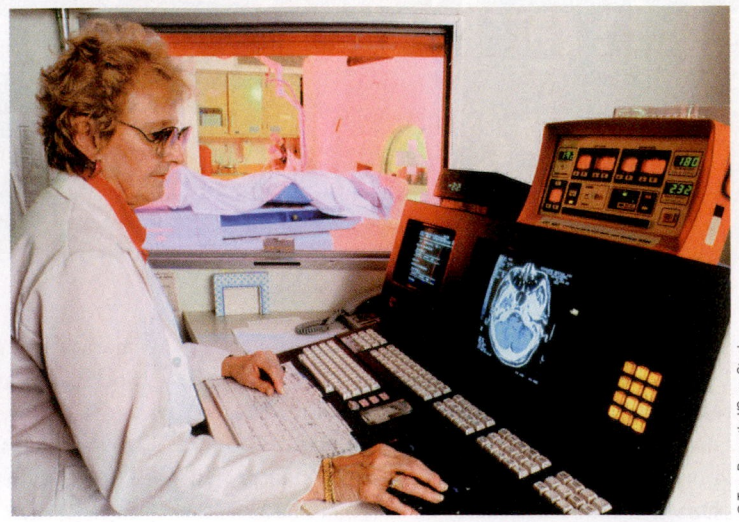

Modern psychology ranges widely in its investigations, looking at divergent topics such as work, sleep, stress, trauma, and brain function. As you progress through this book, you will see that the range and diversity of psychology's subject matter are enormous.

ogy grew and changed, you will discover why it has the shape it does today.

After our journey into psychology's past, we will examine a formal definition of psychology. We'll also look at psychology as it is today—a sprawling, multifaceted science and profession. To help keep psychology's diversity in perspective, the chapter concludes with a discussion of seven unifying themes that will serve as connecting threads in the chapters to come. Finally, in the chapter's Personal Application we'll review research that gives insights on how to be an effective student, and in the Critical Thinking Application we'll discuss how critical thinking skills can be enhanced.

From Speculation to Science: How Psychology Developed

PREVIEW QUESTIONS

- What were Wundt's and Hall's key ideas and accomplishments?
- What were the chief tenets of structuralism and functionalism?
- What was the main idea underlying behaviorism?

Psychology's story is one of people groping toward a better understanding of themselves. As psychology has evolved, its focus, methods, and explanatory models have changed. In this section we'll look at how psychology has developed from philosophical speculations about the mind into a modern science. A pictorial overview of the highlights of psychology's history can be found on pages 16–17.

The term *psychology* comes from two Greek words, *psyche,* meaning the soul, and *logos,* referring to the study of a subject. These two Greek roots were first put together to define a topic of study in the 16th century, when *psyche* was used to refer to the soul, spirit, or mind, as distinguished from the body (Boring, 1966). Not until the early 18th century did the term *psychology* gain more than rare usage among scholars. By that time it had acquired its literal meaning, "the study of the mind."

Of course, people have always wondered about the mysteries of the mind. In that sense, psychology is as old as the human race. But it was only a little over a hundred years ago that psychology emerged as a scientific discipline.

A New Science Is Born: The Contributions of Wundt and Hall

1a

Psychology's intellectual parents were the disciplines of *philosophy* and *physiology.* By the 1870s a small number of scholars in both fields were actively exploring questions about the mind. How are bodily sensations turned into a mental awareness of the outside world? Are people's perceptions of the world accurate reflections of reality? How do mind and body interact? The philosophers and physiologists who were interested in the mind viewed such questions as fascinating issues *within* their respective fields. It was a German professor, Wilhelm Wundt (1832–1920), who eventually changed this view. Wundt mounted a campaign to make psychology an independent discipline rather than a stepchild of philosophy or physiology.

The time and place were right for Wundt's appeal. German universities were in a healthy period of expansion, so resources were available for new disciplines. Furthermore, the intellectual climate favored the scientific approach that Wundt advocated. Hence, his proposals were well received by the academic community. In 1879 Wundt succeeded in establishing the first formal laboratory for research in psychology at the University of Leipzig. In deference to this landmark event, historians have christened 1879 as psychology's "date of birth." Soon afterward, in 1881, Wundt established the first journal devoted to publishing research on psychology. All in all, Wundt's campaign was so successful that today he is widely characterized as the founder of psychology.

Wundt's conception of psychology was influential for decades. Borrowing from his training in physiology, Wundt (1874) declared that the new psychology should be a *science* modeled after fields such as physics and chemistry. What was the subject matter of the new science? According to Wundt, psychology's primary focus was *consciousness*—the awareness of immediate experience. *Thus, psychology became the scientific study of conscious experience.* This orientation kept psychology focused on the mind and mental processes. But it demanded that the methods psychologists used to investigate the mind be as scientific as those of chemists or physicists.

Wundt was a tireless, dedicated scholar who generated an estimated 54,000 pages of books and articles in his career (Bringmann & Balk, 1992). Outstanding young scholars, including many Americans, came to Leipzig to study under Wundt. Many of Wundt's students then fanned out across Germany and America, establishing the research laboratories that formed the basis for the new, independent science of psychology. Indeed, it was in North America that Wundt's new science grew by leaps and bounds. Between 1883 and 1893, some 24 new psychological research laboratories sprang up in the United States and Canada, at the schools shown in Figure 1.1 (Garvey, 1929). Many of the laboratories were started by Wundt's students, or by his students' students.

G. Stanley Hall (1846–1924), who studied briefly with Wundt, was a particularly important contributor to the rapid growth of psychology in America. Toward the end of the 19th century, Hall reeled off a series of "firsts" for American psychology. To begin with, he established America's first research laboratory in psychology at Johns Hopkins University in 1883. Four years later he launched America's first psychology journal. Furthermore, in 1892 he was the driving force behind the establishment of the American Psychological Association (APA) and was elected its first president. Today the APA is the world's largest organization devoted to the advancement of psychology, with over 155,000 members and affiliates. Hall never envisioned such a vast membership when he and 26 others set up their new organization.

Exactly why Americans took to psychology so quickly is hard to say. Perhaps it was because America's relatively young universities were more open to

Web Link 1.1

HistPsyc: History of Psychology Headlines Index
More than 300 years of psychology's history and prehistory—1650 to 1959—are detailed in the form of newspaper headlines and short articles at David Likely's (University of New Brunswick) valuable site. **Note: The URLs (addresses) for the recommended web sites can be found in an appendix in the back of the book, and links to the sites can be found on the website for this text (http://wadsworth.com/psychology_d).**

"*Physiology informs us about those life phenomena that we perceive by our external senses. In psychology, the person looks upon himself as from within and tries to explain the interrelations of those processes that this internal observation discloses.*"
WILHELM WUNDT
1832–1920

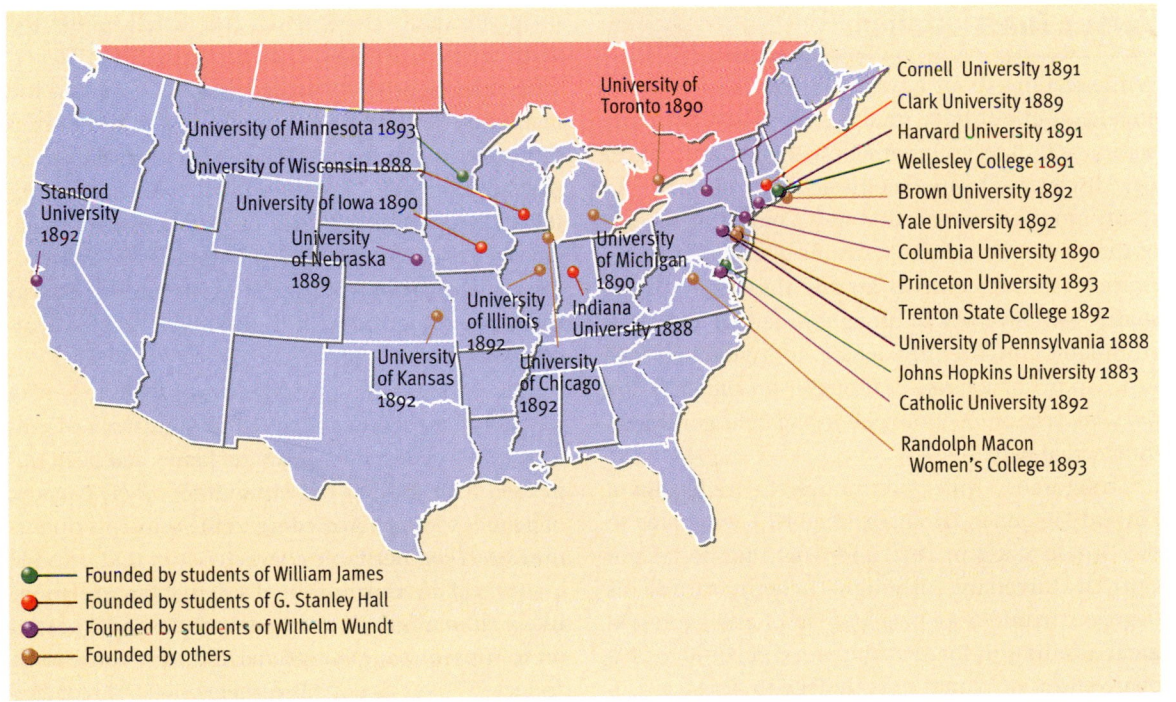

Founded by students of William James
Founded by students of G. Stanley Hall
Founded by students of Wilhelm Wundt
Founded by others

Stanford University 1892
University of Minnesota 1893
University of Wisconsin 1888
University of Iowa 1890
University of Nebraska 1889
University of Illinois 1892
University of Kansas 1892
University of Chicago 1892
Indiana University 1888
University of Michigan 1890
University of Toronto 1890
Cornell University 1891
Clark University 1889
Harvard University 1891
Wellesley College 1891
Brown University 1892
Yale University 1892
Columbia University 1890
Princeton University 1893
Trenton State College 1892
University of Pennsylvania 1888
Johns Hopkins University 1883
Catholic University 1892
Randolph Macon Women's College 1893

Figure 1.1

Early research laboratories in North America. This map highlights the location and year of founding for the first 24 psychological research labs established in North American colleges and universities. As the color coding shows, a great many of these labs were founded by the students of Wilhelm Wundt, G. Stanley Hall, and William James. (Based on Garvey, 1929; Hilgard, 1987)

The establishment of the first research laboratory in psychology by Wilhelm Wundt (far right) marked the birth of psychology as a modern science.

Archives of the History of American Psychology, University of Akron, Akron, Ohio.

new disciplines than were the older, more tradition-bound universities in Europe. In any case, although psychology was born in Germany, it blossomed into adolescence in America. Like many adolescents, however, the young science was about to enter a period of turbulence and turmoil.

The Battle of the "Schools" Begins: Structuralism Versus Functionalism

1a

While reading about how psychology became a science, you might have imagined that psychologists became a unified group of scholars who busily added new discoveries to an uncontested store of "facts." In reality, no science works that way. Competing schools of thought exist in most scientific disciplines. Sometimes the disagreements among these schools are sharp. Such diversity in thought is natural and often stimulates enlightening debate. In psychology, the first two major schools of thought, *structuralism* and *functionalism,* were entangled in the field's first great intellectual battle.

Structuralism emerged through the leadership of Edward Titchener, an Englishman who emigrated to the United States in 1892 and taught for decades at Cornell University. Although Titchener earned his degree in Wundt's Leipzig laboratory and expressed great admiration for Wundt's work, he brought his own version of Wundt's psychology to America (Hilgard, 1987; Thorne & Henley, 1997). *Structuralism*

was based on the notion that the task of psychology is to analyze consciousness into its basic elements and investigate how these elements are related. Just as physicists were studying how matter is made up of basic particles, the structuralists wanted to identify and examine the fundamental components of conscious experience, such as sensations, feelings, and images.

Although the structuralists explored many questions, most of their work concerned sensation and perception in vision, hearing, and touch. To examine the contents of consciousness, the structuralists depended on the method of *introspection,* or the careful, systematic self-observation of one's own conscious experience. As practiced by the structuralists, introspection required training to make the *subject*—the person being studied—more objective and more aware. Once trained, subjects were typically exposed to auditory tones, optical illusions, and visual stimuli under carefully controlled and systematically varied conditions and were asked to analyze what they experienced.

The functionalists took a different view of psychology's task. *Functionalism* was based on the belief that psychology should investigate the function or purpose of consciousness, rather than its structure. The chief impetus for the emergence of functionalism was the work of William James (1842–1910), a brilliant American scholar (and brother of novelist Henry James). James's formal training was in medicine. However, he did not find medicine to be intellectually challenging, and he felt he was too sickly to pursue a medical practice (Ross, 1991). Hence, when an opportunity arose in 1872, he joined the faculty of Harvard University to pursue a less arduous career in academia. Medicine's loss proved to be psychology's gain, as James quickly became an intellectual giant in the field. James's landmark book, *Principles of Psychology* (1890), became standard reading for generations of psychologists and is perhaps the most influential text in the history of psychology (Weiten & Wight, 1992).

James's thinking illustrates how psychology, like any field, is deeply embedded in a network of cultural and intellectual influences. James had been impressed with Charles Darwin's (1859, 1871) concept of *natural selection.* According to the principle of *natural selection,* heritable characteristics that provide a survival or reproductive advantage are more likely than alternative characteristics to be passed on to subsequent generations and thus come to be "selected" over time. This cornerstone notion of Darwin's evolutionary theory suggested that the typical

Web Link 1.2

Mind and Body: René Descartes to William James
Designed originally to celebrate psychology's first century as an independent discipline, this online exhibition traces three historical themes: the mind–body problem posed in the 17th century by philosopher René Descartes, the rise of experimental psychology, and the beginnings of psychology in America.

characteristics of a species must serve some purpose. Applying this idea to humans, James (1890) noted that consciousness obviously is an important characteristic of our species. Hence, he contended that psychology should investigate the *functions* rather than the *structure* of consciousness.

James also argued that the structuralists' approach missed the real nature of conscious experience. Consciousness, he argued, consists of a continuous *flow* of thoughts. In analyzing consciousness into its "elements," the structuralists were looking at static points in that flow. James wanted to understand the flow itself, which he called the "stream of consciousness."

Whereas structuralists naturally gravitated to the laboratory, functionalists were more interested in how people adapt their behavior to the demands of the real world around them. This practical slant led them to introduce new subjects into psychology. Instead of focusing on sensation and perception, functionalists such as James McKeen Cattell and John Dewey began to investigate mental testing, patterns of development in children, the effectiveness of educational practices, and behavioral differences between the sexes. These new topics may have played a role in attracting the first women into the field of psychology (see Figure 1.2).

The impassioned advocates of structuralism and functionalism saw themselves as fighting for high stakes: the definition and future direction of the new science of psychology. Their war of ideas continued energetically for many years. Who won? Most historians give the edge to functionalism. Although both schools of thought gradually faded away, functionalism fostered the development of two descendants that have dominated modern psychology: behaviorism and applied psychology.

"*It is just this free water of consciousness that psychologists resolutely overlook.*"
WILLIAM JAMES
1842–1910

Mary Whiton Calkins
(1863–1930)

Mary Calkins, who studied under William James, founded one of the first dozen psychology laboratories in America at Wellesley College in 1891, invented a widely used technique for studying memory, and became the first woman to serve as president of the American Psychological Association in 1905. Ironically, however, she never received her Ph.D. in psychology. Because she was a woman, Harvard University only reluctantly allowed her to take graduate classes as a "guest student." When she completed the requirements for her Ph.D., Harvard would only offer her a doctorate from its undergraduate sister school, Radcliffe. Calkins felt that this decision perpetuated unequal treatment of the sexes, so she refused the Radcliffe degree.

Margaret Floy Washburn
(1871–1939)

Margaret Washburn was the first woman to receive a Ph.D. in psychology. She wrote an influential book, *The Animal Mind* (1908), which served as an impetus to the subsequent emergence of behaviorism and was standard reading for several generations of psychologists. In 1921 she became the second woman to serve as president of the American Psychological Association. Washburn studied under James McKeen Cattell at Columbia University, but like Mary Calkins, she was only permitted to take graduate classes unofficially, as a "hearer." Hence, she transferred to Cornell University, which was more hospitable toward women, and completed her doctorate in 1894. Like Calkins, Washburn spent most of her career at a college for women (Vassar).

Leta Stetter Hollingworth
(1886–1939)

Leta Hollingworth did pioneering work on adolescent development, mental retardation, and gifted children. Indeed, she was the first person to use the term *gifted* to refer to youngsters who scored exceptionally high on intelligence tests. Hollingworth (1914, 1916) also played a major role in debunking popular theories of her era that purported to explain why women were "inferior" to men. For instance, she conducted a study refuting the myth that phases of the menstrual cycle are reliably associated with performance decrements in women. Her careful collection of objective data on gender differences forced other scientists to subject popular, untested beliefs about the sexes to skeptical, empirical inquiry.

Figure **1.2**

Women pioneers in the history of psychology.
Women have long made major contributions to the development of psychology (Milar, 2000; Russo & Denmark, 1987), and today nearly half of all psychologists are female. As in other fields, however, women have often been overlooked in histories of psychology (Furumoto & Scarborough, 1986). The three psychologists profiled here demonstrate that women have been making significant contributions to psychology almost from its beginning—despite formidable barriers to pursuing their academic careers.

Photos courtesy of the Archives of the History of American Psychology, University of Akron, Akron, Ohio.

Watson Alters Psychology's Course as Behaviorism Makes Its Debut

 1a, 5b

The debate between structuralism and functionalism was only the prelude to other fundamental controversies in psychology. In the early 1900s, another major school of thought appeared that dramatically altered the course of psychology. Founded by John B. Watson (1878–1958), *behaviorism is a theoretical orientation based on the premise that scientific psychology should study only observable behavior.* It is important to understand what a radical change this definition represents. Watson (1913, 1919) was proposing that psychologists *abandon the study of consciousness altogether* and focus exclusively on behaviors that they could observe directly. In essence, he was redefining what scientific psychology should be about.

Why did Watson argue for such a fundamental shift in direction? Because to him, the power of the scientific method rested on the idea of *verifiability.* In principle, scientific claims can always be verified (or disproved) by anyone who is able and willing to make the required observations. However, this power depends on studying things that can be observed objectively. Otherwise, the advantage of using the scientific approach—replacing vague speculation and personal opinion with reliable, exact knowledge—is lost. For Watson, mental processes were not a proper subject for scientific study because they are ultimately private events. After all, no one can see or touch another's thoughts. Consequently, if psychology was to be a science, it would have to give up consciousness as its subject matter and become instead the *science of behavior.*

Behavior **refers to any overt (observable) response or activity by an organism.** Watson asserted that psychologists could study anything that people do or say—shopping, playing chess, eating, complimenting a friend—but they could *not* study scientifically the thoughts, wishes, and feelings that might accompany these observable behaviors.

Watson's radical reorientation of psychology did not end with his redefinition of its subject matter. He also staked out a rather extreme position on one of psychology's oldest and most fundamental questions: the issue of *nature versus nurture.* This age-old debate is concerned with whether behavior is determined mainly by genetic inheritance ("nature") or by environment and experience ("nurture"). To oversimplify, the question is this: Is a great concert pianist or a master criminal born, or made? Watson argued that each is made, not born. In other words, he

downplayed the importance of heredity, maintaining that behavior is governed primarily by the environment. Indeed, he boldly claimed:

Give me a dozen healthy infants, well-formed, and my own special world to bring them up in and I'll guarantee to take any one at random and train him to become any type of specialist I might select—doctor, lawyer, artist, merchant-chief, and yes, even beggar-man and thief, regardless of his talents, penchants, tendencies, abilities, vocations and race of his ancestors. I am going beyond my facts and I admit it, but so have the advocates of the contrary and they have been doing it for many thousands of years. (1924, p. 82)

For obvious reasons, Watson's tongue-in-cheek challenge was never put to a test. Although this widely cited quote overstated and oversimplified Watson's views on the nature-nurture issue (Todd & Morris, 1992), his writings contributed to the strong environmental slant that became associated with behaviorism (Horowitz, 1992).

The behaviorists eventually came to view psychology's mission as an attempt to relate overt behaviors ("responses") to observable events in the environment ("stimuli"). **A *stimulus* is any detectable input from the environment.** Stimuli can range from light and sound waves to such complex inputs as the words on this page, advertisements on TV, or sarcastic remarks from a friend. Because the behaviorists investigated stimulus-response relationships, the behavioral approach is often referred to as *stimulus-response (S-R) psychology.*

Although it met resistance and skepticism in some quarters, Watson's behavioral point of view gradually took hold (Samelson, 1981, 1994). Actually, psychology had already been edging away imperceptibly from the study of consciousness toward the study of behavior for two decades before Watson made his case for behaviorism (Leahey, 1992). The gradual emergence of behaviorism was partly attributable to an important discovery made around the turn of the century by Ivan Pavlov, a Russian physiologist. As you'll learn in Chapter 6, Pavlov (1906) showed that dogs could be trained to salivate in response to an auditory stimulus such as a tone. This deceptively simple demonstration provided insight into how stimulus-response bonds are formed. Such bonds were exactly what behaviorists wanted to investigate, so Pavlov's discovery paved the way for their work.

Behaviorism's stimulus-response approach contributed to the rise of animal research in psychology. Having deleted consciousness from their scope of concern, behaviorists no longer needed to study human subjects who could report on their mental processes. Many psychologists thought that animals would make better research subjects anyway. One key reason was that experimental research is often more productive if experimenters can exert considerable *control* over their subjects. Otherwise, too many complicating factors enter into the picture and contaminate the experiment. Obviously, a researcher can exert much more control over a laboratory rat or pigeon than over a human subject, who arrives at a lab with years of uncontrolled experience and who will probably insist on going home at night. Thus, the discipline that had begun its life a few decades earlier as the study of the mind now found itself heavily involved in the study of simple responses made by laboratory animals.

Although Watson's views shaped the evolution of psychology for many decades, his ideas did not go unchallenged. In Germany opposition came from an emerging school of thought called *Gestalt psychology*. The Gestalt theorists, who were primarily concerned with perception (we'll discuss their ideas in Chapter 4), argued that psychology should continue to study conscious experience rather than overt behavior. Another alternative conception of psychology emerged from Austria, where an obscure physician named Sigmund Freud had been contemplating the mysteries of unconscious mental processes. We'll look at Freud's ideas next.

REVIEW OF KEY POINTS

- Psychology's intellectual parents were 19th-century philosophy and physiology, disciplines that shared an interest in the mysteries of the mind.
- Psychology became an independent discipline when Wilhelm Wundt established the first psychological research laboratory in 1879 at Leipzig, Germany. He defined psychology as the scientific study of consciousness.
- The new discipline grew rapidly in North America in the late 19th century, as illustrated by G. Stanley Hall's career. Hall established America's first research lab in psychology and founded the American Psychological Association.
- The structuralists, led by Edward Titchener, believed that psychology should use introspection to analyze consciousness into its basic elements.
- The functionalists, inspired by the ideas of William James, believed that psychology should focus on the purpose and adaptive functions of consciousness. Functionalism paved the way for behaviorism and applied psychology.
- Behaviorists, led by John B. Watson, argued that psychology should study only observable behavior. Thus, they campaigned to redefine psychology as the science of behavior.
- Emphasizing the importance of the environment over heredity, the behaviorists began to explore stimulus-response relationships, often using laboratory animals as subjects.

CONCEPT CHECK 1.1

Understanding the Implications of Major Theories: Wundt, James, and Watson

Check your understanding of the implications of some of the major theories reviewed in this chapter by indicating who is likely to have made each of the statements quoted below. Choose from the following theorists: (a) Wilhelm Wundt, (b) William James, and (c) John B. Watson. You'll find the answers in Appendix A in the back of the book.

_____ 1. "Our conclusion is that we have no real evidence of the inheritance of traits. I would feel perfectly confident in the ultimately favorable outcome of careful upbringing of a healthy, well-formed baby born of a long line of crooks, murderers and thieves, and prostitutes."

_____ 2. "The book which I present to the public is an attempt to mark out a new domain of science. . . . The new discipline rests upon anatomical and physiological foundations. . . . The experimental treatment of psychological problems must be pronounced from every point of view to be in its first beginnings."

_____ 3. "Consciousness, then, does not appear to itself chopped up in bits. Such words as 'chain' or 'train' do not describe it fitly. . . . It is nothing jointed; it flows. A 'river' or 'stream' are the metaphors by which it is most naturally described."

Freud Brings the Unconscious into the Picture

 1a, 10a

Sigmund Freud (1856–1939) was an Austrian physician who early in his career dreamed of achieving fame by making an important discovery. His determination was such that in medical school he dissected 400 male eels to prove for the first time that they had testes. His work with eels did not make him famous, but his subsequent work with people did. Indeed, his theories made him one of the most controversial intellectual figures of modern times.

Freud's (1900, 1933) approach to psychology grew out of his efforts to treat mental disorders. In his medical practice, Freud treated people troubled by psychological problems such as irrational fears, obsessions, and anxieties with an innovative procedure he called *psychoanalysis* (described in detail in Chapter 15). Decades of experience probing into his patients' lives provided much of the inspiration for Freud's theory. He also gathered material by looking inward and examining his own anxieties, conflicts, and desires.

His work with patients and his own self-exploration persuaded Freud of the existence of what he called the unconscious. According to Freud, the *unconscious* contains thoughts, memories, and desires that are well below the surface of conscious awareness but that nonetheless exert great influence on behavior. Freud based his concept of the unconscious on a variety of observations. For instance, he noticed that seemingly meaningless slips of the tongue (such as

PREVIEW QUESTIONS
- What did Freud have to say about the unconscious and sexuality, and why were his ideas so controversial?
- How did Freudian theory affect the mainstream of psychology?
- What basic principle of behavior did Skinner emphasize?
- What did Skinner do to stir up controversy?
- What was the impetus for the emergence of humanism?

"The unconscious is the true psychical reality; in its innermost nature it is as much unknown to us as the reality of the external world."
SIGMUND FREUD
1856–1939

"I decided to take a summer school curse") often appeared to reveal a person's true feelings. He also noted that his patients' dreams often seemed to express important feelings they were unaware of. Knitting these and other observations together, Freud eventually concluded that psychological disturbances are largely caused by personal conflicts existing at an unconscious level. More generally, his *psychoanalytic theory* attempts to explain personality, motivation, and mental disorders by focusing on unconscious determinants of behavior.

Freud's concept of the unconscious was not entirely new (Rieber, 1998). However, it was a major departure from the prevailing belief that people are fully aware of the forces affecting their behavior. In arguing that behavior is governed by unconscious forces, Freud made the disconcerting suggestion that people are not masters of their own minds. Other aspects of Freud's theory also stirred up debate. For instance, he proposed that behavior is greatly influenced by how people cope with their sexual urges. At a time when people were far less comfortable discussing sexual issues than they are today, even scientists were offended and scandalized by Freud's emphasis on sex. Small wonder, then, that Freud was soon engulfed in controversy.

In part because of its controversial nature, Freud's theory gained influence only very slowly. However, he gradually won acceptance within medicine, attracting prominent followers such as Carl Jung and Alfred Adler. Important public recognition from psychology came in 1909, when G. Stanley Hall invited Freud to give a series of lectures at Clark University in Massachusetts (see the photo below).

By 1920 psychoanalytic theory was widely known around the world, but it continued to meet with considerable resistance in psychology (Fancher, 2000). Why? The main reason was that it conflicted with the spirit of the times in psychology. Many psychologists were becoming uncomfortable with their earlier focus on conscious experience and were turning to the less murky subject of observable behavior. If they felt that *conscious* experience was inaccessible to scientific observation, you can imagine how they felt about trying to study *unconscious* experience. Most psychologists contemptuously viewed psychoanalytic theory as unscientific speculation that would eventually fade away (Hornstein, 1992).

They turned out to be wrong. Psychoanalytic ideas steadily gained credence in the culture at large, influencing thought in medicine, the arts, and literature (Rieber, 1998). According to Hornstein (1992), by the 1940s, "Psychoanalysis was becoming so popular that it threatened to eclipse psychology entirely" (p. 258). Thus, the widespread popular acceptance of psychoanalytic theory essentially forced psychologists to apply their scientific methods to the topics Freud had studied: personality, motivation, and abnormal behavior. As they turned to these topics, many of them saw merit in some of Freud's notions (Rosenzweig, 1985). Although psychoanalytic theory continued to generate heated debate, it survived to become an influential theoretical perspective. Today, many psychoanalytic concepts have filtered into the mainstream of psychology (Westen, 1998).

Skinner Questions Free Will as Behaviorism Flourishes  1a, 10b

While psychoanalytic thought was slowly gaining a foothold within psychology, the behaviorists were temporarily softening their stance on the acceptability of studying internal mental events. However, this movement toward the consideration of internal states was dramatically reversed in the 1950s by the work of B. F. Skinner (1904–1990). Skinner set out to be a writer, but he gave up his dream after a few unproductive years. "I had," he wrote later, "nothing important to say" (1967, p. 395). However, he had many important things to say about psychology, and he went on to become one of the most influential of all American psychologists.

In response to the softening that had occurred in the behaviorist position, Skinner (1953) championed a return to Watson's strict focus on observable behavior. Skinner did not deny the existence of internal mental events. However, he insisted that they could not be studied scientifically. Moreover, there was no

A portrait taken at the famous Clark University psychology conference, September 1909. Pictured are Freud, G. Stanley Hall, and four of Freud's students and associates. Seated, left to right: Freud, Hall, and Carl Jung; standing: Abraham Brill, Ernest Jones, and Sandor Ferenczi.

TIME

B. F. Skinner Says:
We Can't Afford Freedom

7x5 35

Copyright © 1971 Time Inc. Reprinted by permission.

B. F. Skinner created considerable controversy when he asserted that free will is an illusion.

need to study them. According to Skinner, if the stimulus of food is followed by the response of eating, we can fully describe what is happening without making any guesses about whether the animal is experiencing hunger. Like Watson, Skinner also emphasized how environmental factors mold behavior. Although he repeatedly acknowledged that an organism's behavior is influenced by its biological endowment, he argued that psychology could understand and predict behavior adequately without resorting to physiological explanations (Delprato & Midgley, 1992).

The fundamental principle of behavior documented by Skinner is deceptively simple: *Organisms tend to repeat responses that lead to positive outcomes, and they tend not to repeat responses that lead to neutral or negative outcomes*. Despite its simplicity, this principle turns out to be quite powerful. Working primarily with laboratory rats and pigeons, Skinner showed that he could exert remarkable control over the behavior of animals by manipulating the outcomes of their responses. He was even able to train animals to perform unnatural behaviors. For example, he once trained some pigeons to play Ping-Pong! Skinner's followers eventually showed that the principles uncovered in their animal research could be applied to complex human behaviors as well. Behavioral principles are now widely used in factories, schools, pris-

ons, mental hospitals, and a variety of other settings (see Chapter 6).

Skinner's ideas had repercussions that went far beyond the debate among psychologists about what they should study. Skinner spelled out the full implications of his findings in his book *Beyond Freedom and Dignity* (1971). There he asserted that all behavior is fully governed by external stimuli. In other words, your behavior is determined in predictable ways by lawful principles, just as the flight of an arrow is governed by the laws of physics. Thus, if you believe that your actions are the result of conscious decisions, you're wrong. According to Skinner, people are controlled by their environment, not by themselves. In short, Skinner arrived at the conclusion that *free will is an illusion.*

As you can readily imagine, such a disconcerting view of human nature was not universally acclaimed. Like Freud, Skinner was the target of harsh criticism. Much of this criticism stemmed from misinterpretations of his ideas that were disseminated in the popular press (Rutherford, 2000). For example, his analysis of free will was often misconstrued as an attack on the concept of a free society—which it was not—and he was often mistakenly condemned for advocating an undemocratic "scientific police state" (Dinsmoor, 1992). Despite all the controversy, however, behaviorism flourished as the dominant school of thought in psychology during the 1950s and 1960s (Gilgen, 1982). And when 93 psychology department chairpersons were surveyed in 1990 about the field's most important contributors (Estes, Coston, & Fournet, 1990), Skinner was ranked at the top of the list (see Figure 1.3).

Figure **1.3**

Important figures in the history of psychology. In a 1990 survey, 93 chairpersons of psychology departments ranked psychology's most important contributors (Estes, Coston, & Fournet, 1990, as cited in Korn et al., 1991). As you can see, B. F. Skinner edged out Sigmund Freud for the top ranking. Although these ratings of scholarly eminence are open to considerable debate, the data should give you some idea of the relative impact of various figures in the history of psychology.

SOURCE: Adapted from Korn, J. H., Davis, R., & Davis, S. F. (1991). Historians' and chairpersons' judgments of eminence among psychologists. *American Psychologist, 46,* 789–792. Copyright © 1991 by the American Psychological Association.

Rank	Individual	Rank Points
1	B. F. Skinner	508
2	Sigmund Freud	459
3	William James	372
4	Jean Piaget	237
5	G. Stanley Hall	216
6	Wilhelm Wundt	203
7	Carl Rogers	192
8	John B. Watson	188
9	Ivan Pavlov	152
10	E. L. Thorndike	124

Web Link 1.4

Museum of the History of Psychological Instrumentation
You can examine instruments and complex apparatus used by psychological researchers in the discipline's early decades in this "cybermuseum" maintained by Edward J. Haupt and Thomas Perera of Montclair State University.

❝*I submit that what we call the behavior of the human organism is no more free than its digestion.*❞
B. F. SKINNER
1904–1990

The Humanists Revolt

 1a, 10c

By the 1950s, behaviorism and psychoanalytic theory had become the most influential schools of thought in psychology. However, many psychologists found these theoretical orientations unappealing. The principal charge hurled at both schools was that they were "dehumanizing." Psychoanalytic theory was attacked for its belief that behavior is dominated by primitive, sexual urges. Behaviorism was criticized for its preoccupation with the study of simple animal behavior. Both theories were criticized because they suggested that people are not masters of their own destinies. Above all, many people argued, both schools of thought failed to recognize the unique qualities of *human* behavior.

Beginning in the 1950s, the diverse opposition to behaviorism and psychoanalytic theory blended into a loose alliance that eventually became a new school of thought called "humanism" (Bühler & Allen, 1972). In psychology, *humanism is a theoretical orientation that emphasizes the unique qualities of humans, especially their freedom and their potential for personal growth.* Some of the key differences between the humanistic, psychoanalytic, and behavioral viewpoints are summarized in Table 1.1, which compares six influential contemporary theoretical perspectives in psychology.

Humanists take an *optimistic* view of human nature. They maintain that people are not pawns of either their animal heritage or environmental circumstances. Furthermore, they say, because humans are fundamentally different from other animals, research on animals has little relevance to the understanding of human behavior. The most prominent architects of the humanistic movement have been Carl Rogers (1902–1987) and Abraham Maslow (1908–1970). Rogers (1951) argued that human behavior is governed primarily by each individual's sense of self, or "self-concept"—which animals presumably lack. Both he and Maslow (1954) maintained that to fully understand people's behavior, psychologists must take into account the fundamental human drive toward personal growth. They asserted that people have a basic need to continue to evolve as human beings and to fulfill their potentials. In fact, the humanists argued that many psychological disturbances are the result of thwarting these uniquely human needs.

Fragmentation and dissent have reduced the influence of humanism in recent decades, although some advocates are predicting a renaissance for the humanistic movement (Taylor, 1999). To date, the

"It seems to me that at bottom each person is asking, "Who am I, really? How can I get in touch with this real self, underlying all my surface behavior? How can I become myself?."
CARL ROGERS
1902–1987

Table 1.1 Overview of Six Contemporary Theoretical Perspectives in Psychology

Perspective and Its Influential Period	Principal Contributors	Subject Matter	Basic Premise
Behavioral (1913–present)	John B. Watson Ivan Pavlov B. F. Skinner	Effects of environment on the overt behavior of humans and animals	Only observable events (stimulus-response relations) can be studied scientifically.
Psychoanalytic (1900–present)	Sigmund Freud Carl Jung Alfred Adler	Unconscious determinants of behavior	Unconscious motives and experiences in early childhood govern personality and mental disorders.
Humanistic (1950s–present)	Carl Rogers Abraham Maslow	Unique aspects of human experience	Humans are free, rational beings with the potential for personal growth, and they are fundamentally different from animals.
Cognitive (1950s–present)	Jean Piaget Noam Chomsky Herbert Simon	Thoughts; mental processes	Human behavior cannot be fully understood without examining how people acquire, store, and process information.
Biological (1950s–present)	James Olds Roger Sperry David Hubel Torsten Wiesel	Physiological bases of behavior in humans and animals	An organism's functioning can be explained in terms of the bodily structures and biochemical processes that underlie behavior.
Evolutionary (1980s–present)	David Buss Martin Daly Margo Wilson Leda Cosmides John Tooby	Evolutionary bases of behavior in humans and animals	Behavior patterns have evolved to solve adaptive problems; natural selection favors behaviors that enhance reproductive success.

humanists' greatest contribution to psychology has probably been their innovative treatments for psychological problems and disorders. More generally, the humanists have argued eloquently for a different picture of human nature than those implied by psychoanalysis and behaviorism (Wertz, 1998).

REVIEW OF KEY POINTS

● Sigmund Freud was an Austrian physician who invented psychoanalysis. His psychoanalytic theory emphasized the unconscious determinants of behavior and the importance of sexuality.

● Freud's ideas were controversial, and they met with resistance in academic psychology. However, as more psychologists developed an interest in personality, motivation, and abnormal behavior, psychoanalytic concepts were incorporated into mainstream psychology.

● The influence of behaviorism was boosted greatly by B. F. Skinner's research. Like Watson before him, Skinner asserted that psychology should study only observable behavior.

● Working with laboratory rats and pigeons, Skinner demonstrated that organisms tend to repeat responses that lead to positive consequences and not to repeat responses that lead to neutral or negative consequences.

● Based on the belief that all behavior is fully governed by external stimuli, Skinner argued in *Beyond Freedom and Dignity* that free will is an illusion. His ideas were controversial and often misunderstood.

● Finding both behaviorism and psychoanalysis unsatisfactory, advocates of a new theoretical orientation called humanism became influential in the 1950s. Humanism, led by Abraham Maslow and Carl Rogers, emphasized the unique qualities of human behavior and humans' freedom and potential for personal growth.

Psychology Comes of Age as a Profession

The 1950s also saw psychology come of age as a profession. As you know, psychology is not all pure science. It has a highly practical side. Many psychologists provide a variety of professional services to the public. Their work falls within the domain of *applied psychology,* the branch of psychology concerned with everyday, practical problems.

This branch of psychology, so prominent today, was actually slow to develop. The first applied arm of psychology to emerge was *clinical psychology*. As practiced today, *clinical psychology* is the branch of psychology concerned with the diagnosis and treatment of psychological problems and disorders. In the early days, however, the emphasis was almost exclusively on psychological testing, and few psychologists were involved in clinical work. Although the first psychological clinic was established as early as 1896, by 1937 only about one in five members of the American Psychological Association reported an interest in clinical psychology (Goldenberg, 1983). Clinicians were a small minority in a field devoted primarily to research.

That picture was about to change with dramatic swiftness. The impetus was a world war. During World War II (1939–1945), many academic psychologists were pressed into service as clinicians. They were needed to screen military recruits and to treat soldiers suffering from trauma. Many of these psychologists (often to their surprise) found the clinical work to be challenging and rewarding, and a substantial

PREVIEW QUESTIONS

● What events stimulated the development of applied psychology and clinical psychology?

● What is the cognitive perspective, and when did it become important?

● What is the biological perspective, and when did it become important?

● Why did psychology ignore cultural variables for many years?

● What events sparked psychology's increased interest in cultural factors?

● What is the basic premise of evolutionary psychology?

CONCEPT CHECK 1.2

Understanding the Implications of Major Theories: Freud, Skinner, and Rogers

Check your understanding of the implications of some of the major theories reviewed in this chapter by indicating who is likely to have made each of the statements quoted below. Choose from the following: (a) Sigmund Freud, (b) B. F. Skinner, and (c) Carl Rogers. You'll find the answers in Appendix A at the back of the book.

_____ **1.** "In the traditional view, a person is free. . . . He can therefore be held responsible for what he does and justly punished if he offends. That view, together with its associated practices, must be reexamined when a scientific analysis reveals unsuspected controlling relations between behavior and environment."

_____ **2.** "He that has eyes to see and ears to hear may convince himself that no mortal can keep a secret. If the lips are silent, he chatters with his fingertips; betrayal oozes out of him at every pore. And thus the task of making conscious the most hidden recesses of the mind is one which it is quite possible to accomplish."

_____ **3.** "I do not have a Pollyanna view of human nature. . . . Yet one of the most refreshing and invigorating parts of my experience is to work with [my clients] and to discover the strongly positive directional tendencies which exist in them, as in all of us, at the deepest levels."

portion continued to do clinical work after the war. More significant, some 40,000 American veterans returned to seek postwar treatment in Veterans Administration (VA) hospitals for their psychological scars. With the demand for clinicians far greater than the supply, the VA stepped in to finance many new training programs in clinical psychology. These programs, emphasizing training in the treatment of psychological disorders as well as psychological testing, proved attractive. Within a few years, about half the new Ph.D.'s in psychology were specializing in clinical psychology and most went on to offer professional services to the public (Goldenberg, 1983). Thus, during the 1950s the prewar orphan of applied/professional psychology rapidly matured into a robust, powerful adult.

In the halls of academia, many traditional research psychologists were alarmed by the professionalization of the field. They argued that the energy and resources previously devoted to research would be diluted. Because of conflicting priorities, tensions between the research and professional arms of psychology have continued to grow. Although the American Psychological Association continues to work diligently to represent both the scientific and professional branches of psychology, recent decades have brought complaints from many researchers that the APA has come to be dominated by clinicians. In 1988 this rift stimulated some research psychologists to form a new organization, the American Psychological Society (APS), to serve exclusively as an advocate for the science of psychology.

Despite the conflicts, the professionalization of psychology has continued at a steady pace. In fact, the trend has spread into additional areas of psychology. Today the broad umbrella of applied psychology covers a variety of professional specialties, including school psychology, industrial and organizational psychology, and counseling psychology. Whereas psychologists were once almost exclusively academics, the vast majority of today's psychologists devote some of their time to providing professional services.

Psychology Returns to Its Roots: Renewed Interest in Cognition and Physiology

While applied psychology has blossomed in recent decades, research has continued to evolve. Ironically, two of the relatively recent trends in research hark back a century to psychology's beginning, when psychologists were principally interested in consciousness and physiology. Today psychologists are showing renewed interest in consciousness (now called "cognition") and the physiological bases of behavior. **Cognition** refers to the mental processes involved in acquiring knowledge. In other words, cognition involves thinking or conscious experience. For many decades, the dominance of behaviorism discouraged investigation of "unobservable" mental processes, and most psychologists showed little interest in cognition. During the 1950s and 1960s, however, this situation slowly began to change. The research of Swiss psychologist Jean Piaget (1954) focused increased attention on the study of children's cognitive development, while the work of Noam Chomsky (1957) elicited new interest in the psychological underpinnings of language. Around the same time, Herbert Simon and his colleagues (Newell, Shaw, & Simon, 1958) began influential, groundbreaking research on problem solving that eventually led to a Nobel prize

World War I and World War II played a major role in the growth of applied psychology, as psychologists were forced to apply their expertise to practical problems, such as ability testing and training. The top photo shows military personnel working on one of a series of tests devised to aid in the selection of air crew trainees during World War II. The bottom photo shows a booklet sold to help recruits prepare for the Army General Classification Test and other related tests. Its popularity illustrates the importance attached to the military's mental testing progam.

Archives of the History of American Psychology, University of Akron, Akron, Ohio.

for Simon (in 1978). These advances sparked a surge of interest in cognitive processes.

Since then, cognitive theorists have argued that psychology must study internal mental events to fully understand behavior (Gardner, 1985; Neisser, 1967). Advocates of the *cognitive perspective* point out that people's manipulations of mental images surely influence how they behave. Consequently, focusing exclusively on overt behavior yields an incomplete picture of why individuals behave as they do. Equally important, psychologists investigating decision making, reasoning, and problem solving have shown that methods *can* be devised to study cognitive processes scientifically. Although the methods are different from those used in psychology's early days, modern research on the inner workings of the mind has put the *psyche* back in psychology. In fact, many observers maintain that the cognitive perspective has become the dominant perspective in contemporary psychology—and some interesting data support this assertion, as can be seen in Figure 1.4 (Robins, Gosling, & Craik, 1999).

The 1950s and 1960s also saw many discoveries that highlighted the interrelations among mind, body, and behavior. For example, Canadian psychologist James Olds (1956) demonstrated that electrical stimulation of the brain could evoke emotional responses such as pleasure and rage in animals. Other work, which eventually earned a Nobel prize for Roger Sperry (in 1981), showed that the right and left halves of the brain are specialized to handle different types of mental tasks (Gazzaniga, Bogen, & Sperry, 1965). The 1960s also brought the publication of David Hubel and Torsten Wiesel's (1962, 1963) Nobel-prize–winning work on how visual signals are processed in the brain.

These and many other findings stimulated an increase in research on the biological bases of behavior. Advocates of the *biological perspective* maintain that much of human and animal behavior can be explained in terms of the bodily structures and biochemical processes that allow organisms to behave. In the 19th century the young science of psychology had a heavy physiological emphasis. Thus, the recent interest in the biological bases of behavior represents another return to psychology's heritage.

Although adherents of the cognitive and biological perspectives haven't done as much organized campaigning for their viewpoints as the proponents of the older, traditional schools of thought have, these newer perspectives have become important theoretical orientations in modern psychology. They are increasingly influential regarding what psychology

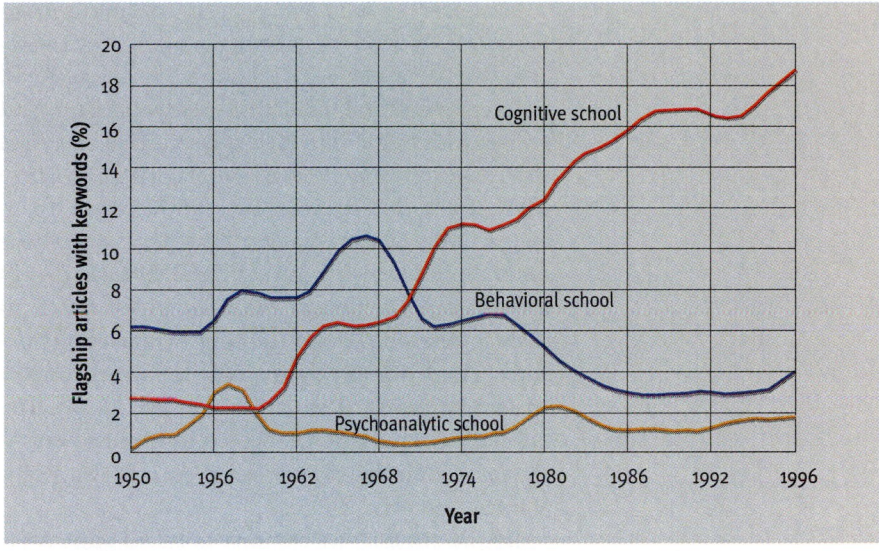

Figure 1.4

The relative prominence of three major schools of thought in psychology. To estimate the relative influence of various theoretical orientations in recent decades, Robins, Gosling, and Craik (1999) analyzed the subject matter of four prestigious general publications in psychology, measuring the percentage of articles relevant to each school of thought. Obviously, their approach is just one of many ways one might gauge the prominence of various theoretical orientations in psychology. Nonetheless, the data are thought provoking. Their findings suggest that the cognitive perspective surpassed the behavioral perspective in influence sometime around 1970. As you can see, the psychoanalytic perspective has always had a modest impact on the mainstream of psychology.

SOURCE: Adapted from Robins, R. W., Gosling, S. D., & Craik, K. H. (1999). An empirical analysis of trends in psychology. *American Psychologist, 54,* 117–128. Copyright © 1999 by the American Psychological Association. Reprinted by permission of the author.

should study and how. The cognitive and biological perspectives are compared to other contemporary theoretical perspectives in Table 1.1.

Psychology Broadens Its Horizons: Increased Interest in Cultural Diversity

Throughout psychology's history, most researchers have worked under the assumption that they were seeking to identify general principles of behavior that would be applicable to all of humanity. In reality, however, psychology has largely been a Western (North American and European) enterprise with a remarkably provincial slant (Gergen et al., 1996). The vast preponderance of psychology's research has been conducted in the United States by middle- and upper-class white psychologists who have used mostly middle- and upper-class white males as subjects (Hall, 1997; Segall et al., 1990). Traditionally, Western psychologists have paid scant attention to how well their theories and research might apply to non-Western cultures, to ethnic minorities in Western societies, or even to women as opposed to men.

Why has the focus of Western psychology been so narrow? A host of factors have probably contributed (Albert, 1988; Segall, Lonner, & Berry, 1998). First, cross-cultural research is costly, difficult, and time-consuming. It has always been cheaper, easier, and more convenient for academic psychologists to study the middle-class white students enrolled in their schools. Second, some psychologists worry that cultural comparisons may inadvertently foster stereotypes of various cultural groups, many of which already have a long history of being victimized by prejudice. Third, *ethnocentrism*—the tendency to view one's own group as superior to others and as the standard for judging the worth of foreign ways—may have contributed to Western psychologists' lack of interest in other cultures.

Despite these considerations, in recent years Western psychologists have begun to recognize that their neglect of cultural variables has diminished the value of their work, and they are devoting increased attention to culture as a determinant of behavior. What brought about this shift? Some of the impetus probably came from the sociopolitical upheavals of the 1960s and 1970s (Bronstein & Quina, 1988). The civil rights movement, the women's movement, and the gay rights movement all raised doubts about whether psychology had dealt adequately with human diversity. Above all else, however, the new interest in culture appears attributable to two recent trends: (1) advances in communication, travel, and international trade have "shrunk" the world and increased global interdependence, bringing more and more Americans and Europeans into contact with people from non-Western cultures, and (2) the ethnic makeup of the

Western world has become an increasingly diverse multicultural mosaic, as the data in Figure 1.5 show for the United States (Brislin, 1993; Hermans & Kempen, 1998; Mays et al., 1996).

These realities have prompted more and more Western psychologists to broaden their horizons and incorporate cultural factors into their theories and research (Adamopoulos & Lonner, 2001; Miller, 1999). These psychologists are striving to study previously underrepresented groups of subjects to test the generality of earlier findings and to catalog both the differences and similarities among cultural groups. They are working to increase knowledge of how culture is transmitted through socialization practices and how culture colors one's view of the world. They are seeking to learn how people cope with cultural change and to find ways to reduce misunderstandings and conflicts in intercultural interactions. In addition, they are trying to enhance understanding of how cultural groups are affected by prejudice, discrimination, and racism. In all these efforts, they are striving to understand the unique experiences of culturally diverse people *from the point of view of those people.* These efforts to ask new questions, study new groups, and apply new perspectives promise to enrich the discipline of psychology in the 21st century (Fowers & Richardson, 1996; Sue et al., 1999).

Psychology Adapts: The Emergence of Evolutionary Psychology

The most recent major development in psychology has been the emergence of evolutionary psychology, a new theoretical perspective that is likely to be in-

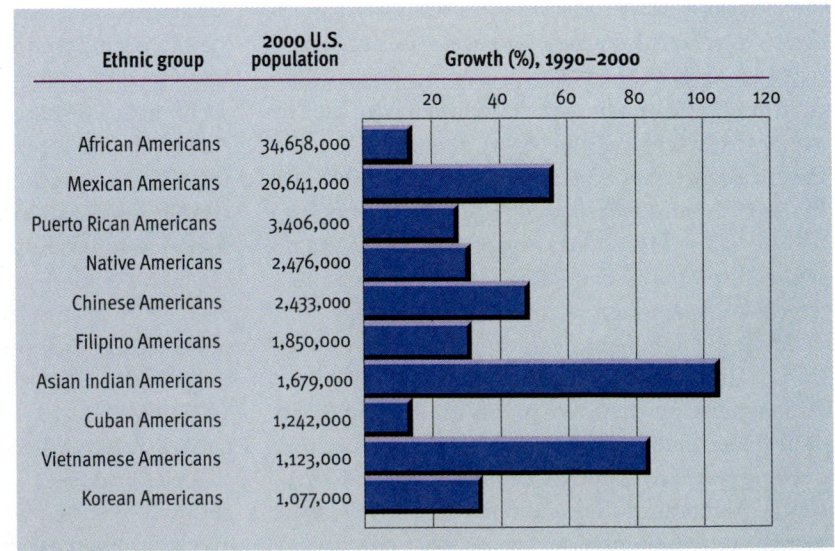

Figure 1.5

Increased cultural diversity in the United States. The 1980s and 1990s brought significant changes in the ethnic makeup of the United States. During the 1990s, the nation's Hispanic population grew by 45% and its Asian American population grew by 49%, while the white population increased by only 6%. Experts project that ethnic minorities will account for over one-third of the U.S. population within the next few decades (Hall, 1997; Sue, 1991). These realities have contributed to psychologists' increased interest in cultural factors as determinants of behavior. (Data from U.S. Bureau of the Census)

Ethnic group	2000 U.S. population	Growth (%), 1990–2000
African Americans	34,658,000	
Mexican Americans	20,641,000	
Puerto Rican Americans	3,406,000	
Native Americans	2,476,000	
Chinese Americans	2,433,000	
Filipino Americans	1,850,000	
Asian Indian Americans	1,679,000	
Cuban Americans	1,242,000	
Vietnamese Americans	1,123,000	
Korean Americans	1,077,000	

fluential in the years to come. Evolutionary psychologists assert that the patterns of behavior seen in a species are products of evolution in the same way that anatomical characteristics are. *Evolutionary psychology examines behavioral processes in terms of their adaptive value for members of a species over the course of many generations.* The basic premise of evolutionary psychology is that natural selection favors behaviors that enhance organisms' reproductive success—that is, passing on genes to the next generation. Thus, if a species is highly aggressive, evolutionary psychologists argue that it's because aggressiveness conveys a survival or reproductive advantage for members of that species, so genes that promote aggressiveness are more likely to be passed on to the next generation. Although evolutionary psychologists have a natural interest in animal behavior, they have not been bashful about analyzing the evolutionary bases of human behavior. As La Cerra and Kurzban (1995) put it, "The human mind was sculpted by natural selection, and it is this evolved organ that constitutes the subject matter of psychology" (p. 63).

Consider, for instance, evolutionary psychologists' analysis of differences between males and females in visual-spatial ability. On the average, males tend to perform slightly better than females on most visual-spatial tasks, including tasks involving mental rotation of images and navigation in space (Halpern, 2000; see Chapter 11). Irwin Silverman and his colleagues maintain that these gender differences originated in human evolution as a result of the sex-based division of labor in ancient hunting and gathering societies (Silverman & Phillips, 1998; Silverman et al., 2000). According to this analysis, males' superiority in mental rotation and navigation developed because the chore of *hunting* was largely assigned to men over the course of human history, and these skills would have facilitated success on hunting trips and thus been favored by natural selection. In contrast, women in ancient societies generally had responsibility for *gathering* food rather than hunting it. Hence, Silverman and Eals (1992) hypothesized that females ought to be superior to males on spatial skills that would have facilitated gathering, such as memory for locations, which is exactly what they found in a series of four studies. Thus, evolutionary psychologists explain gender differences in spatial ability—and many other aspects of human behavior—in terms of how such abilities evolved to meet the adaptive pressures faced by our ancestors.

Looking at behavioral patterns in terms of their evolutionary significance is not an entirely new idea (Graziano, 1995). As noted earlier, William James

and other functionalists were influenced by Darwin's concept of natural selection over a century ago. Until recently, however, applications of evolutionary concepts to *psychological* processes were piecemeal, half-hearted, and not particularly well received. The 1960s and 1970s brought major breakthroughs in the field of evolutionary *biology* (Hamilton, 1964; Trivers, 1971, 1972; Williams, 1966), but these advances had little immediate impact in psychology. The situation began to change in the 1980s. A growing cadre of evolutionary psychologists, led by David Buss (1985, 1988, 1989), Martin Daly and Margo Wilson (1985, 1988), and Leda Cosmides and John Tooby (Cosmides & Tooby, 1989; Tooby & Cosmides, 1989), published widely cited studies on a broad range of topics, including mating preferences, jealousy, aggression, sexual behavior, language, decision making, personality, and development. In 1989–1990, Buss, Daly, Wilson, Cosmides, and Tooby gathered at the Center for Advanced Study in the Behavioral Sciences in Palo Alto, California, to sketch out an ambitious research agenda for evolutionary psychology (Buss, 1999). By the mid-1990s, it became clear that psychology was witnessing the birth of its first major, new theoretical perspective since the cognitive revolution in the 1950s and 1960s.

As with all prominent theoretical perspectives in psychology, evolutionary theory has its critics (Caporael & Brewer, 1995; Gould, 1993; Rose & Rose, 2000). Among other things, they argue that many evolutionary hypotheses are untestable and that evolutionary explanations are post hoc, speculative accounts for obvious behavioral phenomena. However, evolutionary psychologists have articulated persuasive rebuttals to these and other criticisms (Bereczkei, 2000; Kenrick, 1995), and the evolutionary perspective is rapidly gaining acceptance. Advocates of the evolutionary approach have heralded it as an "immense advance over traditional perspectives" (Masters, 1995, p. 65), a "revolutionary scientific paradigm" (Buss, 1995, p. 85), and a "renaissance in the sciences of mind" (La Cerra & Kurzban, 1995, p. 62). These proclamations will probably prove to be overly enthusiastic, as is often the case when a new school of thought strives to establish its identity. Nonetheless, evolutionary psychology undeniably provides a thought-provoking, innovative perspective that is rapidly gaining influence and promises to shake things up.

Our review of psychology's past has shown the field's evolution. We have seen psychology develop from philosophical speculation into a rigorous science

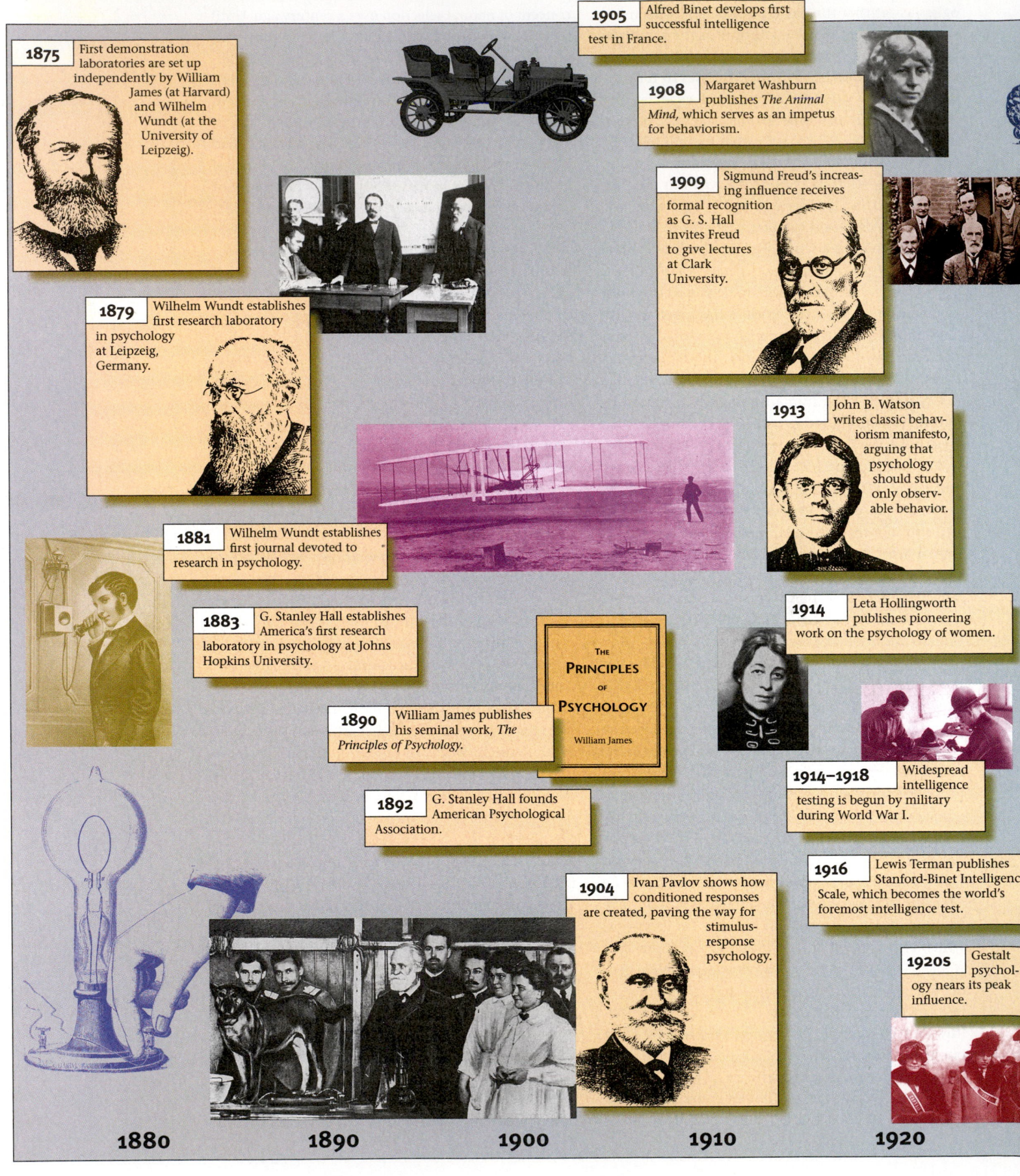

1875 First demonstration laboratories are set up independently by William James (at Harvard) and Wilhelm Wundt (at the University of Leipzeig).

1879 Wilhelm Wundt establishes first research laboratory in psychology at Leipzeig, Germany.

1881 Wilhelm Wundt establishes first journal devoted to research in psychology.

1883 G. Stanley Hall establishes America's first research laboratory in psychology at Johns Hopkins University.

1890 William James publishes his seminal work, *The Principles of Psychology.*

1892 G. Stanley Hall founds American Psychological Association.

1904 Ivan Pavlov shows how conditioned responses are created, paving the way for stimulus-response psychology.

1905 Alfred Binet develops first successful intelligence test in France.

1908 Margaret Washburn publishes *The Animal Mind,* which serves as an impetus for behaviorism.

1909 Sigmund Freud's increasing influence receives formal recognition as G. S. Hall invites Freud to give lectures at Clark University.

1913 John B. Watson writes classic behaviorism manifesto, arguing that psychology should study only observable behavior.

1914 Leta Hollingworth publishes pioneering work on the psychology of women.

1914–1918 Widespread intelligence testing is begun by military during World War I.

1916 Lewis Terman publishes Stanford-Binet Intelligence Scale, which becomes the world's foremost intelligence test.

1920s Gestalt psychology nears its peak influence.

THE PRINCIPLES OF PSYCHOLOGY

William James

1880   1890   1900   1910   1920

1933 Sigmund Freud's influence continues to build as he publishes *New Introductory Lectures on Psychoanalysis*.

1936 Hans Selye introduces concept of stress into the language of science.

1941–1945 Rapid growth in clinical psychology begins in response to huge demand for clinical services created by World War II and its aftermath.

1943 Clark Hull advocates modified behaviorism, which permits careful inferences about unobservable internal states.

1947 Kenneth and Mamie Clark publish work on prejudice that is cited in landmark 1954 Supreme Court decision outlawing segregation.

1950 Erik Erikson writes *Childhood and Society* in which he extends Freud's theory of development across the life span.

1951 Carl Rogers helps launch humanistic movement with publication of *Client-Centered Therapy*.

1953 B. F. Skinner publishes his influential *Science and Human Behavior*, advocating radical behaviorism similar to Watson's.

1954 Abraham Maslow's *Motivation and Personality* helps fuel humanistic movement.

1956 The cognitive revolution is launched at watershed conference where Herbert Simon, George Miller, and Noam Chomsky report three major advances in just one day.

1961–1964 Roger Sperry's split-brain research and work by David Hubel and Torsten Wiesel on how cortical cells respond to light help rejuvenate the biological perspective in psychology.

1963 Stanley Milgram conducts controversial study of obedience to authority, which may be the most famous single study in psychology's history.

1971 B. F. Skinner creates furor over radical behaviorism with his controversial book *Beyond Freedom and Dignity*.

1974 Eleanor Maccoby and Carol Jacklin publish their landmark review of research on gender differences, which galvanizes research in this area.

1978 Herbert Simon wins Nobel prize (in economics) for research on cognition.

1980s Increased global interdependence and cultural diversity in Western societies spark surge of interest in how cultural factors mold behavior.

1981 Roger Sperry wins Nobel prize (in physiology and medicine) for split-brain studies.

1988 Research psychologists form the American Psychological Society (APS) to serve as an advocate for the science of psychology.

1930   1940   1950   1960   1970   1980   1990

committed to research. We have seen how a highly visible professional arm involved in mental health services emerged from this science. We have seen how psychology's focus on physiology is rooted in its 19th-century origins. We have seen how and why psychologists began conducting research on lower animals. We have seen how psychology has evolved from the study of mind and body to the study of behavior. And we have seen how the investigation of mind and body has been welcomed back into the mainstream of modern psychology. We have seen how various theoretical schools have defined the scope and mission of psychology in different ways. We have seen how psychology's interests have expanded and become increasingly diverse. Above all else, we have seen that psychology is a growing, evolving intellectual enterprise.

Psychology's history is already rich, but its story has barely begun. The century or so that has elapsed since Wilhelm Wundt put psychology on a scientific footing is only an eyeblink of time in human history. What has been discovered during those years, and what remains unknown, is the subject of the rest of this book.

REVIEW OF KEY POINTS

● Stimulated by the demands of World War II, clinical psychology grew rapidly in the 1950s. Thus, psychology became a profession as well as a science. This movement toward professionalization eventually spread to other areas in psychology.

● During the 1950s and 1960s advances in the study of cognition led to renewed interest in mental processes, as psychology returned to its roots. Advocates of the cognitive perspective argue that human behavior cannot be fully understood without considering how people think.

● The 1950s and 1960s also saw advances in research on the physiological bases of behavior. Advocates of the biological perspective assert that human and animal behavior can be explained in terms of the bodily structures and biochemical processes that allow organisms to behave.

● In the 1980s, Western psychologists, who had previously been rather provincial, developed a greater interest in how cultural factors influence behavior. This trend was sparked in large part by growing global interdependence and by increased cultural diversity in Western societies.

● The 1990s witnessed the emergence of a new theoretical perspective called evolutionary psychology. The central premises of this new school of thought are that patterns of behavior are the product of evolutionary forces and that natural selection favors behaviors that enhance reproductive success.

Psychology Today: Vigorous and Diversified

PREVIEW QUESTIONS

● What evidence suggests that psychology is a vigorous, growing discipline?

● What are the main areas of research in psychology?

● What are the four professional specialties in psychology?

● How do clinical psychology and psychiatry differ?

We began this chapter with an informal description of what psychology is about. Now that you have a feel for how psychology has developed, you can better appreciate a definition that does justice to the field's modern diversity: *Psychology* **is the science that studies behavior and the physiological and cognitive processes that underlie it, and it is the profession that applies the accumulated knowledge of this science to practical problems.**

Contemporary psychology is a thriving science and profession. Its growth has been remarkable. One simple index of this growth is the dramatic rise in membership in the American Psychological Association. Figure 1.6 shows that APA membership has increased eightfold since 1950. And this membership has continued to grow despite competition from the new APS, as many research psychologists are apparently joining both organizations (Fowler, 1990). In the United States, psychology is the second most popular undergraduate major (see Figure 1.7), and the field accounts for about 9% of all doctoral degrees awarded in the sciences and humanities. The comparable figure in 1945 was only 4% (Howard et al., 1986). Of course, psychology is an international en-

Figure 1.6

Membership in the American Psychological Association, 1900–2000. The steep rise in the number of psychologists in the APA since 1950 testifies to psychology's remarkable growth as a science and a profession. If graduate student members are also counted, the APA has over 155,000 members. (Adapted from data published by the American Psychological Association, by permission.)

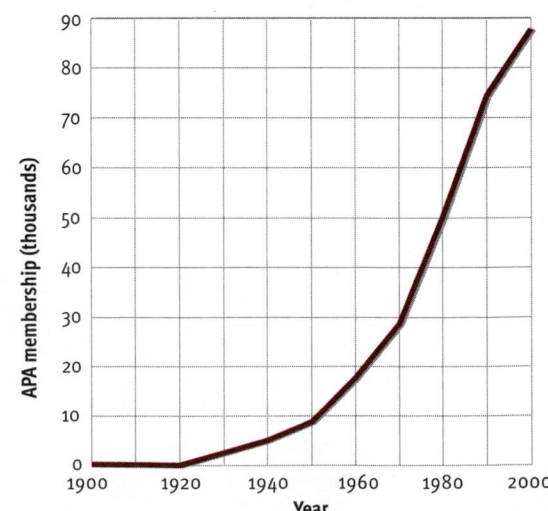

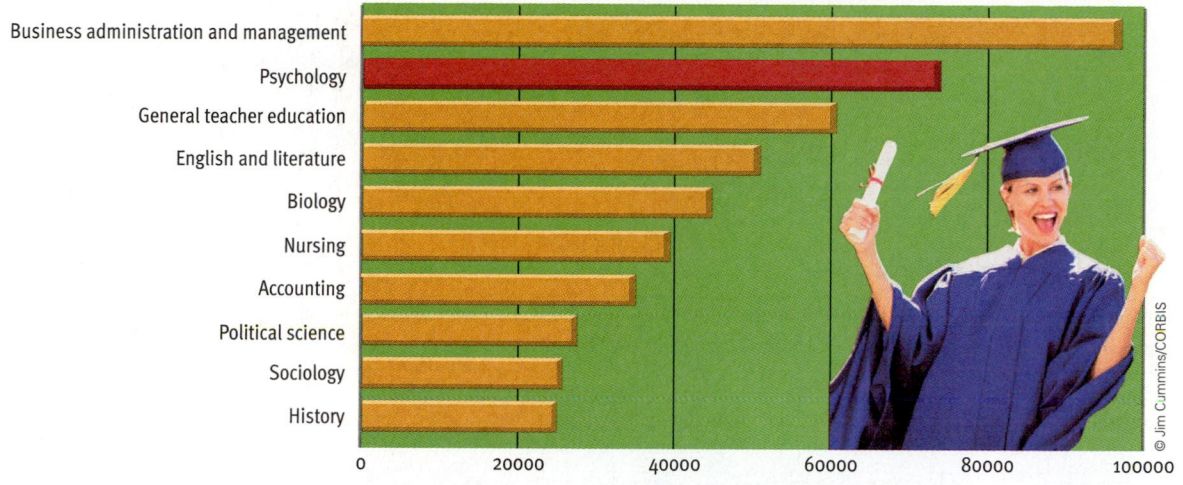

Figure 1.7

Psychology's place among leading college majors.
This list of the ten most popular undergraduate majors in the United States is based on the number of bachelor's degrees awarded in 1999–2000. As you can see, psychology ranked second only to business administration and management in the number of degrees awarded. (Data from U.S. Department of Education, National Center for Education Statistics)

© Jim Cummins/CORBIS

Business administration and management
Psychology
General teacher education
English and literature
Biology
Nursing
Accounting
Political science
Sociology
History

0   20000   40000   60000   80000   100000

Number of Bachelor's Degrees Awarded

terprise. Today, over 1800 technical journals from all over the world publish research articles on psychology. Thus, by any standard of measurement—the number of people involved, the number of degrees granted, the number of journals published—psychology is a healthy, growing field.

Psychology's vigorous presence in modern society is also demonstrated by the great variety of settings in which psychologists work. Psychologists were once found almost exclusively in the halls of academia. Today, however, colleges and universities are the primary work setting for fewer than one-third of American psychologists. The remaining two-thirds work in hospitals, clinics, police departments, research institutes, government agencies, business and industry, schools, nursing homes, counseling centers, and private practice. Figure 1.8 shows the distribution of psychologists employed in various categories of settings.

Clearly, contemporary psychology is a multifaceted field, a fact that is especially apparent when we consider the many areas of specialization within psychology today. Let's look at the current areas of specialization in both the science and the profession of psychology.

Research Areas in Psychology

Although most psychologists receive broad training that provides them with knowledge about many areas of psychology, they usually specialize when it comes to doing research. Such specialization is necessary because the subject matter of psychology has become so vast over the years. Today it is virtually impossible for anyone to stay abreast of the new research in all specialties. Specialization is also necessary because

specific skills and training are required to do research in some areas.

The seven major research areas in modern psychology are (1) developmental psychology, (2) social psychology, (3) experimental psychology, (4) physiological psychology, (5) cognitive psychology, (6) personality, and (7) psychometrics. Figure 1.9, on the next page, describes these areas briefly and shows the percentage of research psychologists in APA who identify each area as their primary interest. As you can see, social psychology and developmental psychology have become especially active areas of research.

brief descriptions of each on the next page.

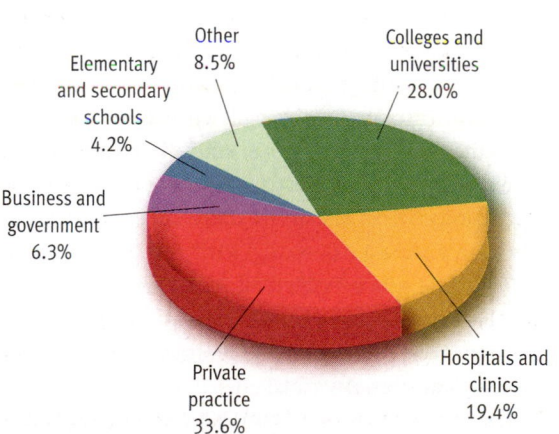

Other 8.5%
Elementary and secondary schools 4.2%
Business and government 6.3%
Private practice 33.6%
Hospitals and clinics 19.4%
Colleges and universities 28.0%

Figure 1.8

Employment of psychologists by setting. The work settings in which psychologists are employed have become very diverse. Survey data on the primary employment setting of APA members indicates that one-third are in private practice (compared to 12% in 1976) and only 28% work in colleges and universities (compared to 47% in 1976). These data may slightly underestimate the percentage of psychologists in academia, given the competition between APA and APS to represent research psychologists. (Based on *2000 APA Directory Survey*)

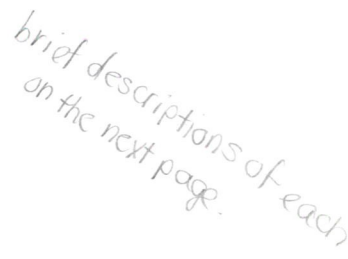

Web Link 1.5

American Psychological Association (APA)
The APA website is a treasure trove of resources on psychology in all its rich diversity. The section for the public includes electronic pamphlets on practical topics such as depression, aging, and anger. A wealth of information on career possibilities in the field is also available here.

Figure **1.9**

Major research areas in contemporary psychology.
Most research psychologists specialize in one of the seven broad areas described here. The figures in the pie chart reflect the percentage of academic and research psychologists belonging to APA who identify each area as their primary interest. (Based on *2000 APA Directory Survey*)

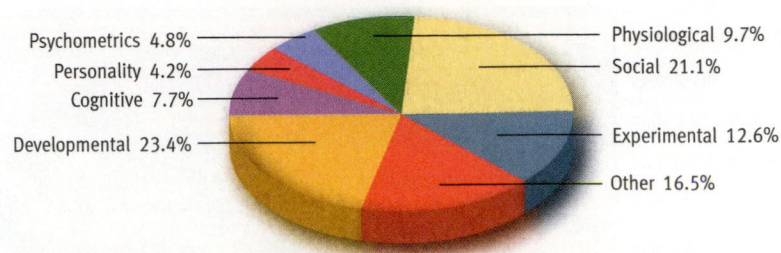

Psychometrics 4.8%
Personality 4.2%
Cognitive 7.7%
Developmental 23.4%
Physiological 9.7%
Social 21.1%
Experimental 12.6%
Other 16.5%

Area	Focus of research
Developmental psychology	Looks at human development across the life span. Developmental psychology once focused primarily on child development but today devotes a great deal of research to adolescence, adulthood, and old age.
Social psychology	Focuses on interpersonal behavior and the role of social forces in governing behavior. Typical topics include attitude formation, attitude change, prejudice, conformity, attraction, aggression, intimate relationships, and behavior in groups.
Experimental psychology	Encompasses the traditional core of topics that psychology focused on heavily in its first half-century as a science: sensation, perception, learning, conditioning, motivation, and emotion. The name experimental psychology is somewhat misleading, as this is not the only area in which experiments are done. Psychologists working in all the areas listed here conduct experiments.
Physiological psychology	Examines the influence of genetic factors on behavior and the role of the brain, nervous system, endocrine system, and bodily chemicals in the regulation of behavior.
Cognitive psychology	Focuses on "higher" mental processes, such as memory, reasoning, information processing, language, problem solving, decision making, and creativity.
Personality	Is interested in describing and understanding individuals' consistency in behavior, which represents their personality. This area of interest is also concerned with the factors that shape personality and with personality assessment.
Psychometrics	Is concerned with the measurement of behavior and capacities, usually through the development of psychological tests. Psychometrics is involved with the design of tests to assess personality, intelligence, and a wide range of abilities. It is also concerned with the development of new techniques for statistical analysis.

Web Link 1.6

Marky Lloyd's Career Page
For those who think they might want to find a job or career in psychology or a related field, Marky Lloyd of Georgia Southern University has put together a fine set of resources to help in both planning and making choices.

Web Link 1.7

A Student's Guide to Careers in the Helping Professions
Written by Melissa J. Himeline of the University of North Carolina at Asheville, this online guide provides detailed career information for 15 of the most important helping professions that psychology majors often consider entering.

Professional Specialties in Psychology

descriptions on next page

Applied psychology consists of four clearly identified areas of specialization: (1) clinical psychology, (2) counseling psychology, (3) educational and school psychology, and (4) industrial and organizational psychology. Descriptions of these specialties can be found in Figure 1.10, along with the percentage of professional psychologists in APA who are working in each area. As the graphic indicates, clinical psychology is the most prominent and widely practiced professional specialty in the field.

The data in Figures 1.9 and 1.10 are based on APA members' reports of their single, principal area of specialization. However, many psychologists work on both research and application. Some academic psychologists work as consultants, therapists, and counselors on a part-time basis. Similarly, some applied psychologists conduct basic research on issues related to their specialty. For example, many clinical psychologists are involved in research on the nature and causes of abnormal behavior.

Some people are confused about the difference between clinical psychology and psychiatry. The confusion is understandable, as both clinical psychologists and psychiatrists are involved in analyzing and treating psychological disorders. Although some overlap exists between the two professions, the training and educational requirements for the two are quite different. Clinical psychologists go to graduate school to earn one of several doctoral degrees (Ph.D., Ed.D., or Psy.D.) in order to enjoy full status in their profession. Psychiatrists go to medical school for their postgraduate education, where they receive general training in medicine and earn an M.D. degree. They then specialize by completing residency training in psychiatry at a hospital. Clinical psychologists and psychiatrists also differ in the way they tend to approach the treatment of mental disorders, as we will see in Chapter 15. To summarize, *psychiatry* **is a branch of medicine concerned with the diagnosis and treatment of psychological problems and disorders**. In contrast, clinical psychology takes a nonmedical approach to such problems.

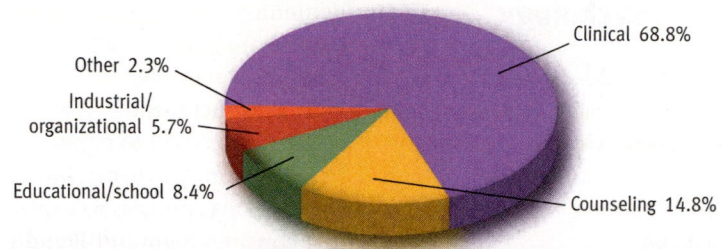

Other 2.3%

Industrial/
organizational 5.7%

Clinical 68.8%

Educational/school 8.4%

Counseling 14.8%

Figure 1.10

Principal professional specialties in contemporary psychology. Most psychologists who deliver professional services to the public specialize in one of the four areas described here. The figures in the pie chart reflect the percentage of APA members delivering professional services who identify each area as their chief specialty. (Based on *2000 APA Directory Survey*)

Specialty	Focus of professional practice
Clinical psychology	Clinical psychologists are concerned with the evaluation, diagnosis, and treatment of individuals with psychological disorders, as well as treatment of less severe behavioral and emotional problems. Principal activities include interviewing clients, psychological testing, and providing group or individual psychotherapy .
Counseling psychology	Counseling psychology overlaps with clinical psychology in that specialists in both areas engage in similar activities—interviewing, testing, and providing therapy. However, counseling psychologists usually work with a somewhat different clientele, providing assistance to people struggling with everyday problems of moderate severity. Thus, they often specialize in family, marital, or career counseling.
Educational and school psychology	Educational psychologists work to improve curriculum design, achievement testing, teacher training, and other aspects of the educational process. School psychologists usually work in elementary or secondary schools, where they test and counsel children having difficulties in school and aid parents and teachers in solving school-related problems.
Industrial and organizational psychology	Psychologists in this area perform a wide variety of tasks in the world of business and industry. These tasks include running human resources departments, working to improve staff morale and attitudes, striving to increase job satisfaction and productivity, examining organizational structures and procedures, and making recommendations for improvements.

REVIEW OF KEY POINTS

● Contemporary psychology is a diversified science and profession that has grown rapidly in recent decades. The main work settings for contemporary psychologists are (1) private practice, (2) colleges and universities, and (3) hospitals and clinics.

● Major areas of research in modern psychology include developmental psychology, social psychology, experimental psychology, physiological psychology, cognitive psychology, personality, and psychometrics.

● Applied psychology encompasses four professional specialties: clinical psychology, counseling psychology, educational and school psychology, and industrial and organizational psychology.

● Although clinical psychology and psychiatry share some of the same interests, they are different professions with different types of training. Psychiatrists are physicians who specialize in the diagnosis and treatment of mental disorders, whereas clinical psychologists take a nonmedical approach to psychological problems.

Putting It in Perspective: Seven Key Themes

The enormous breadth and diversity of psychology make it a challenging subject for the beginning student. In the pages ahead you will be introduced to many areas of research and a multitude of ideas, concepts, and principles. Fortunately, ideas are not all created equal. Some are far more important than others. In this section, I will highlight seven fundamental themes that will reappear in a number of variations as we move from one area of psychology to another in this text. You have already met some of these key ideas in our review of psychology's past and present. Now we will isolate them and highlight their significance. In the remainder of the book these

ideas serve as organizing themes to provide threads of continuity across chapters and to help you see the connections among the various areas of research in psychology.

In studying psychology, you are learning about both behavior and the scientific discipline that investigates it. Accordingly, our seven themes come in two sets. The first set consists of statements highlighting crucial aspects of psychology as a way of thinking and as a field of study. The second set consists of broad generalizations about psychology's subject matter: behavior and the cognitive and physiological processes that underlie it.

PREVIEW QUESTIONS

● What is the purpose of the text's unifying themes?

● What are the first three themes that elucidate the nature of psychology?

● What are the remaining four themes that emphasize crucial insights about behavior?

Themes Related to Psychology as a Field of Study

Looking at psychology as a field of study, we see three crucial ideas: (1) psychology is empirical, (2) psychology is theoretically diverse, and (3) psychology evolves in a sociohistorical context. Let's look at each of these ideas in more detail.

Theme 1: Psychology Is Empirical

Everyone tries to understand behavior. Most of us have our own personal answers to questions such as why some people are hard workers, why some are overweight, and why others stay in demeaning relationships. If all of us are amateur psychologists, what makes scientific psychology different? The critical difference is that psychology is *empirical*. This aspect of psychology is fundamental, and virtually every page of this book reflects it.

What do we mean by empirical? **Empiricism is the premise that knowledge should be acquired through observation.** This premise is crucial to the scientific method that psychology embraced in the late 19th century. To say that psychology is empirical means that its conclusions are based on direct observation rather than on reasoning, speculation, traditional beliefs, or common sense. Psychologists are not content with having ideas that sound plausible. They conduct research to *test* their ideas. Is intelligence higher, on average, in some social classes than in others? Are men more aggressive than women? Psychologists find a way to make direct, objective, and precise observations to answer such questions.

The empirical approach requires a certain attitude—a healthy brand of *skepticism*. Empiricism is a tough taskmaster. It demands data and documentation. Psychologists' commitment to empiricism means that they must learn to think critically about generalizations concerning behavior. If someone asserts that people tend to get depressed around Christmas, a psychologist is likely to ask, "How many people get depressed? In what population? In comparison to what baseline rate of depression? How is depression defined?" Their skeptical attitude means that psychologists are trained to ask, "Where's the evidence? How do you know?" If psychology's empirical orientation rubs off on you (and I hope it does), you will be asking similar questions by the time you finish this book.

Theme 2: Psychology Is Theoretically Diverse

Although psychology is based on observation, a string of unrelated observations would not be terribly en-

lightening. Psychologists do not set out to just collect isolated facts; they seek to explain and understand what they observe. To achieve these goals they must construct theories. **A *theory* is a system of interrelated ideas used to explain a set of observations.** In other words, a theory links apparently unrelated observations and tries to explain them. As an example, consider Sigmund Freud's observations about slips of the tongue, dreams, and psychological disturbances. On the surface, these observations appear unrelated. By devising the concept of the *unconscious*, Freud created a theory that links and explains these seemingly unrelated aspects of behavior.

Our review of psychology's past should have made one thing abundantly clear: Psychology is marked by theoretical diversity. Why do we have so many competing points of view? One reason is that no single theory can adequately explain everything that is known about behavior. Sometimes different theories focus on different aspects of behavior—that is, different collections of observations. Sometimes there is simply more than one way to look at something. Is the glass half empty or half full? Obviously, it is both. To take an example from another science, physicists wrestled for years with the nature of light. Is it a wave, or is it a particle? In the end, it proved useful to think of light sometimes as a wave and sometimes as a particle. Similarly, if a business executive lashes out at her employees with stinging criticism, is she releasing pent-up aggressive urges (a psychoanalytic view)? Is she making a habitual response to the stimulus of incompetent work (a behavioral view)? Or is she scheming to motivate her employees by using "mind games" (a cognitive view)? In some cases, all three of these explanations might have some validity. In short, it is an oversimplification to expect that one view has to be right while all others are wrong. Life is rarely that simple.

Students are often troubled by psychology's many conflicting theories, which they view as a weakness. However, contemporary psychologists increasingly recognize that theoretical diversity is a strength rather than a weakness (Hilgard, 1987). As we proceed through this text, you will see how differing theoretical perspectives often provide a more complete understanding of behavior than could be achieved by any one perspective alone.

Theme 3: Psychology Evolves in a Sociohistorical Context

Science is often seen as an "ivory tower" undertaking, isolated from the ebb and flow of everyday life. In reality, however, psychology and other sciences do not exist in a cultural vacuum. Dense intercon-

Web Link 1.8

Approaches to Psychology
Maintained at Ryerson Polytechnic University in Toronto, this site provides access to an electronic version of a book titled *Approaches to Psychology* by William E. Glassman. This e-book is organized around the various theoretical orientations that guide thinking in contemporary psychology. Visitors will find concise overviews of the biological, behavioral, cognitive, psychoanalytic, and humanistic perspectives in psychology.

Social trends and values have shaped the evolution of psychology and progress in psychology has left its mark on everyday life in our society. For example, standardized psychological tests are pervasive in our educational system where they exert great influence over students' lives.

© Bob Daemmrich/Stock Boston

nections exist between what happens in psychology and what happens in society at large (Altman, 1990; Braginsky, 1985; Danziger, 1990). Trends, issues, and values in society influence psychology's evolution. Similarly, progress in psychology affects trends, issues, and values in society. To put it briefly, psychology develops in a *sociohistorical* (social and historical) context.

Our review of psychology's past is filled with examples of how social trends have left their imprint on psychology. In the late 19th century, psychology's rapid growth as a laboratory science was due, in part, to its fascination with physics as the model discipline. Thus, the spirit of the times fostered a scientific approach rather than a philosophical approach to the investigation of the mind. Similarly, Freud's groundbreaking ideas emerged out of a specific sociohistorical context. Cultural values in Freud's era encouraged the suppression of sexuality. Hence, people tended to feel guilty about their sexual urges to a much greater extent than is common today. This situation clearly contributed to Freud's emphasis on unconscious sexual conflicts. As another example, consider the impact of World War II on the development of psychology as a profession. The rapid growth of professional psychology was largely due to the war-related surge in the demand for clinical services. Hence, World War II reshaped the landscape of psychology in a remarkably short time. Finally, in recent years we have seen how growing global interdependence and increased cultural diversity have prompted psychologists to focus new attention on cultural factors as determinants of behavior.

If we reverse our viewpoint, we can see that psychology has in turn left its mark on society. Consider, for instance, the pervasive role of mental testing in modern society. Your own career success may depend in part on how well you weave your way through a complex maze of intelligence and achievement tests made possible (to the regret of some) by research in psychology. As another example of psychology's impact on society, consider the influence that various theorists have had on parenting styles. Trends in child-rearing practices have been shaped by the ideas of John B. Watson, Sigmund Freud, B. F. Skinner, and Carl Rogers—not to mention a host of additional psychologists yet to be discussed. In short, society and psychology influence each other in complex ways. In the chapters to come, we will frequently have occasion to notice this dynamic relationship.

Themes Related to Psychology's Subject Matter

Looking at psychology's subject matter, we see four additional crucial ideas: (4) behavior is determined by multiple causes, (5) behavior is shaped by cultural heritage, (6) heredity and environment jointly influence behavior, and (7) people's experience of the world is highly subjective.

Theme 4: Behavior Is Determined by Multiple Causes

As psychology has matured, it has provided more and more information about the forces that govern behavior. This growing knowledge has led to a deeper appreciation of a simple but important fact: Behavior is exceedingly complex, and most aspects of behavior are determined by multiple causes.

Although the complexity of behavior may seem self-evident, people usually think in terms of single causes. Thus, they offer explanations such as "Andrea flunked out of school because she is lazy." Or they assert that "teenage pregnancies are increasing because of all the sex in the media." Single-cause explanations are sometimes accurate as far as they go, but they usually are incomplete. In general, psychologists find that behavior is governed by a complex network of interacting factors, an idea referred to as the *multifactorial causation of behavior.*

As a simple illustration, consider the multiple factors that might influence your performance in your introductory psychology course. Relevant personal factors might include your overall intelligence, your reading ability, your memory skills, your motivation, and your study skills. In addition, your grade could be affected by numerous situational factors, including whether you like your psychology professor, whether you like your assigned text, whether the class meets at a good time for you, whether your work schedule is light or heavy, and whether you're having any personal problems.

As you proceed through this book, you will learn that complexity of causation is the rule rather than the exception. If we expect to understand behavior, we usually have to take into account multiple determinants.

Theme 5: Behavior Is Shaped by Cultural Heritage

Among the multiple determinants of human behavior, cultural factors are particularly prominent. Just as psychology evolves in a sociohistorical context, so, too, do individuals. People's cultural backgrounds exert considerable influence over their behavior. What is *culture?* It's the human-made part of the environment. More specifically, **culture refers to the widely shared customs, beliefs, values, norms, institutions, and other products of a community that are transmitted socially across generations.** Culture is a broad construct, encompassing everything from a society's legal system to its assumptions about family roles, from its dietary habits to its political ideals, from its technology to its attitudes about time, from its modes of dress to its spiritual beliefs, and from its art and music to its unspoken rules about sexual liaisons. We tend to think of culture as belonging to entire societies or broad ethnic groups within societies—which it does—but the concept can also be applied to small

groups (a tiny Aboriginal tribe in Australia, for example) and to nonethnic groups (gay/homosexual culture, for instance).

Much of a person's cultural heritage is invisible (Brislin, 1993). Assumptions, ideals, attitudes, beliefs, and unspoken rules exist in people's minds and may not be readily apparent to outsiders. Moreover, because a cultural background is widely shared, members feel little need to discuss it with others and often take it for granted. For example, you probably don't spend much time thinking about the importance of living in rectangular rooms, trying to minimize body odor, limiting yourself to one spouse at a time, or using credit cards to obtain material goods and services. Although we generally fail to appreciate its influence, our cultural heritage has a pervasive impact on our thoughts, feelings, and behavior.

Let's look at a couple of examples of this influence. In North America, when people are invited to dinner in someone's home, they generally show their appreciation of their host's cooking efforts by eating all of the food they are served. In India, this behavior would be insulting to the host, as guests are expected to leave some food on their plates. The leftover food acknowledges the generosity of the host, implying that he or she provided so much food the guest could not eat it all (Moghaddam, Taylor, & Wright, 1993). Cultures also vary in their emphasis on punctuality. In North America, we expect people to show up for meetings on time; if someone is more than 10 to 15 minutes late we begin to get upset. We generally strive to be on time, and many of us are quite proud of our precise and dependable punctuality. However, in many Asian and Latin American countries, social obligations that arise at the last minute are given just as much priority as scheduled commitments. Hence, people often show up for important meetings an hour or two late with little remorse, and they may be quite puzzled by the consternation of their Western visitors (Brislin, 1993). These examples may seem trivial, but as you will see in upcoming chapters, culture can also influence crucial matters, such as educational success, mental health, and vulnerability to physical illnesses.

Although the influence of culture is everywhere, generalizations about cultural groups must always be tempered by the realization that great diversity also exists within any society or ethnic group. Researchers may be able to pinpoint genuinely useful insights about Ethiopian, Korean American, or Ukrainian culture, for example, but it would be foolish to assume that all Ethiopians, Korean Americans, or Ukrainians exhibit identical behavior. It is also important to re-

Web Link 1.9

Encyclopedia of Psychology
This "encyclopedia," developed by psychology faculty at Jacksonville State University, is actually a collection of over 2000 links to web pages around the world on psychological matters. The links related to the history of the field and careers in psychology are extensive, as are the links relating to theories and publications in psychology.

alize that both differences and similarities in behavior occur across cultures. As we will see repeatedly, psychological processes are characterized by both cultural variance and invariance. Caveats aside, if we hope to achieve a sound understanding of human behavior, we need to consider cultural determinants.

Theme 6: Heredity and Environment Jointly Influence Behavior

Are individuals who they are—athletic or artistic, quick-tempered or calm, shy or outgoing, energetic or laid back—because of their genetic inheritance or because of their upbringing? This question about the importance of nature versus nurture, or heredity versus environment, has been asked in one form or another since ancient times. Historically, the nature-versus-nurture question was framed as an all-or-none proposition. In other words, theorists argued that personal traits and abilities are governed either entirely by heredity or entirely by environment. John B. Watson, for instance, asserted that personality and ability depend almost exclusively on an individual's environment. In contrast, Sir Francis Galton, a pioneer in mental testing, maintained that personality and ability depend almost entirely on genetic inheritance.

Today, most psychologists agree that heredity and environment are both important. A century of research has shown that genetics and experience jointly influence an individual's intelligence, temperament, personality, and susceptibility to many psychological disorders (Plomin & Rende, 1991; Rose, 1995). If we ask whether individuals are born or made, psychology's answer is "Both." This does not mean that nature versus nurture is a dead issue. Lively debate about the *relative influence* of genetics and experience continues unabated. Furthermore, psychologists are actively seeking to understand the complex ways in which genetic inheritance and experience interact to mold behavior.

Theme 7: People's Experience of the World Is Highly Subjective

Even elementary perception—for example, of sights and sounds—is not a passive process. People actively process incoming stimulation, selectively focusing on some aspects of that stimulation while ignoring others. Moreover, they impose organization on the stimuli that they pay attention to. These tendencies combine to make perception personalized and subjective.

The subjectivity of perception was demonstrated nicely in a classic study by Hastorf and Cantril (1954). They showed students at Princeton and Dartmouth universities a film of a recent football game between the two schools. The students were told to watch for rules infractions. Both groups saw the same film, but the Princeton students "saw" the Dartmouth players engage in twice as many infractions as the Dartmouth students "saw." The investigators concluded that the game "actually was many different games and that each version of the events that transpired was just as 'real' to a particular person as other versions were to other people" (Hastorf & Cantril, 1954). In this study, the subjects' perceptions were swayed by their motives. It shows how people sometimes see what they *want* to see.

Other studies reveal that people also tend to see what they *expect* to see. For example, Harold Kelley (1950) showed how perceptions of people are influenced by their reputation. Kelley told students that their class would be taken over by a new lecturer, whom they would be asked to evaluate later. Before the class, the students were given a short description of the incoming instructor, with one important variation. Half the students were led to expect a "warm" person, while the other half were led to expect a "cold" one (see Figure 1.11). All the subjects were exposed to the same 20 minutes of lecture and interaction with the new instructor. However, the group of subjects who *expected* a warm person rated the instructor as more considerate, sociable, humorous, good natured, informal, and humane than the subjects in the group who had expected a cold person.

Figure 1.11

Manipulating person perception. Read the accompanying description of Mr. Blank carefully. If you were about to hear him give a lecture, would this description bias your perceptions of him? You probably think not, but when Kelley (1950) altered one adjective in this description (replacing the word *warm* with *cold*), the change had a dramatic impact on subjects' ratings of the guest lecturer.

SOURCE: Description from Kelley, H. H. (1950). The warm-cold variable in first impressions of persons. *Journal of Personality, 8,* 431–439. Copyright © 1950 by the Ecological Society of America. Reprinted by permission.

Mr. Blank is a graduate student in the Department of Economics and Social Science here at M.I.T. He has had three semesters of teaching experience in psychology at another college. This is his first semester teaching Ec. 70. He is 26 years old, a veteran, and married. People who know him consider him to be a very warm person, industrious, critical, practical, and determined.

Preferred Stock and Gazelle Technologies.

Thus, it is clear that motives and expectations color people's experiences. To some extent, individuals see what they want to see or what they expect to see. This subjectivity in perception turns out to explain a variety of behavioral tendencies that would otherwise be perplexing.

Human subjectivity is precisely what the scientific method is designed to counteract. In using the scientific approach, psychologists strive to make their observations as objective as possible. In some respects, overcoming subjectivity is what science is all about. Left to their own subjective experience, people might still believe that the earth is flat and that the sun revolves around it. Thus, psychologists are committed to the scientific approach because they believe it is the most reliable route to accurate knowledge.

Now that you have been introduced to the text's organizing themes, let's turn to an example of how psychological research can be applied to the challenges of everyday life. In our first Personal Application, we'll focus on a subject that should be highly relevant to you: how to be a successful student. In the Critical Thinking Application that follows it, we discuss the nature and importance of critical thinking skills.

CONCEPT CHECK 1.3

Understanding the Seven Key Themes

Check your understanding of the seven key themes introduced in the chapter by matching the vignettes with the themes they exemplify. You'll find the answers in Appendix A.

Themes

1. Psychology is empirical.
2. Psychology is theoretically diverse.
3. Psychology evolves in a sociohistorical context.
4. Behavior is determined by multiple causes.
5. Behavior is shaped by cultural heritage.
6. Heredity and environment jointly influence behavior.
7. People's experience of the world is highly subjective.

Vignettes

_____ **a.** Several or more theoretical models of emotion have contributed to our overall understanding of the dynamics of emotion.

_____ **b.** According to the stress-vulnerability model, some people are at greater risk for developing certain psychological disorders for genetic reasons. Whether these people actually develop the disorders depends on how much stress they experience in their work, families, or other areas of their lives.

_____ **c.** Physical health and illness seem to be influenced by a complex constellation of psychological, biological, and social system variables.

_____ **d.** One of the difficulties in investigating the effects of drugs on consciousness is that individuals tend to have different experiences with a given drug because of their different expectations.

REVIEW OF KEY POINTS

● As we examine psychology in all its many variations, we will emphasize seven key ideas as unifying themes. First, psychology is empirical because psychologists base their conclusions on observation through research rather than reasoning or common sense.

● Psychology is theoretically diverse, as there are many competing schools of thought in the field. This diversity has fueled progress and is a strength rather than a weakness. Psychology also evolves in a sociohistorical context, as trends, issues, and values in society influence what goes on in psychology, and vice versa.

● Behavior is determined by multiple causes, as most aspects of behavior are influenced by complex networks of interacting factors. Although cultural heritage is often taken for granted, it has a pervasive impact on people's thoughts, feelings, and behavior.

● Lively debate about the relative importance of nature versus nurture continues, but it is clear that heredity and environment jointly influence behavior. People's experience of the world is highly subjective, as they sometimes see what they want to see or what they expect to see.

PERSONAL APPLICATION

Improving Academic Performance

Answer the following "true" or "false."

_____ 1   It's a good idea to study in as many different locations (your bedroom or kitchen, the library, lounges around school, and so forth) as possible.

_____ 2   If you have a professor who delivers chaotic, hard-to-follow lectures, there is little point in attending class.

_____ 3   Cramming the night before an exam is an effective method of study.

_____ 4   In taking lecture notes, you should try to be a "human tape recorder" (that is, write down everything your professor says).

_____ 5   You should never change your answers to multiple-choice questions, because your first hunch is your best hunch.

All of the above statements are false. If you answered them all correctly, you may have already acquired the kinds of skills and habits that facilitate academic success. If so, however, you are *not* typical. Today, many students enter college with poor study skills and habits—and it's not entirely their fault. The American educational system generally provides minimal instruction on good study techniques. In this first Application, we will try to remedy this situation to some extent by reviewing some insights that psychology offers on how to improve academic performance. We will discuss how to promote better study habits, how to enhance reading efforts, how to get more out of lectures, and how to improve test-taking strategies. You may also want to jump ahead and read the Personal Application for Chapter 7, which focuses on how to improve everyday memory.

Developing Sound Study Habits

Effective study is crucial to success in college. Although you may run into a few class-mates who boast about getting good grades without studying, you can be sure that if they perform well on exams, they *do* study. Students who claim otherwise simply want to be viewed as extremely bright rather than as studious.

Learning can be immensely gratifying, but studying usually involves hard work. The first step toward effective study habits is to face up to this reality. You don't have to feel guilty if you don't look forward to studying. Most students don't. Once you accept the premise that studying doesn't come naturally, it should be apparent that you need to set up an organized program to promote adequate study. According to Siebert (1995), such a program should include the following considerations:

1. *Set up a schedule for studying.* If you wait until the urge to study strikes you, you may still be waiting when the exam rolls around. Thus, it is important to allocate definite times to studying. Review your various time obligations (work, chores, and so on) and figure out in advance when you can study. When allotting certain times to studying, keep in mind that you need to be wide awake and alert. Be realistic about how long you can study at one time before you wear down from fatigue. Allow time for study breaks—they can revive sagging concentration.

It's important to write down your study schedule. A written schedule serves as a reminder and increases your commitment to following it. You should begin by setting up a general schedule for the quarter or semester, like the one in Figure 1.12. Then, at the beginning of each week, plan the specific assignments that you intend to work on

Figure 1.12

One student's general activity schedule for a semester. Each week the student fills in the specific assignments to work on during each study period.

Weekly Activity Schedule

	Monday	Tuesday	Wednesday	Thursday	Friday	Saturday	Sunday
8 A.M.						Work	
9 A.M.	History	Study	History	Study	History	Work	
10 A.M.	Psychology	French	Psychology	French	Psychology	Work	
11 A.M.	Study	French	Study	French	Study	Work	
NOON	Math	Study	Math	Study	Math	Work	Study
1 P.M.							Study
2 P.M.	Study	English	Study	English	Study		Study
3 P.M.	Study	English	Study	English	Study		Study
4 P.M.							
5 P.M.							
6 P.M.	Work	Study	Study	Work			Study
7 P.M.	Work	Study	Study	Work			Study
8 P.M.	Work	Study	Study	Work			Study
9 P.M.	Work	Study	Study	Work			Study
10 P.M.	Work			Work			

during each study session. This approach to scheduling should help you avoid cramming for exams at the last minute. Cramming is an ineffective study strategy for most students (Underwood, 1961; Zechmeister & Nyberg, 1982). It will strain your memorization capabilities, can tax your energy level, and may stoke the fires of test anxiety.

In planning your weekly schedule, try to avoid the tendency to put off working on major tasks such as term papers and reports. Time-management experts such as Alan Lakein (1996) point out that many people tend to tackle simple, routine tasks first, saving larger tasks for later when they supposedly will have more time. This common tendency leads many individuals to repeatedly delay working on major assignments until it's too late to do a good job. A good way to avoid this trap is to break major assignments down into smaller component tasks that can be scheduled individually.

Research on the differences between successful and unsuccessful college students suggests that successful students monitor and regulate their use of time more effectively (Allgood et al., 2000). You can assess other aspects of your time-management practices by responding to the questionnaire in Figure 1.13.

2. *Find a place to study where you can concentrate.* Where you study is also important. The key is to find a place where distractions are likely to be minimal. Most people cannot study effectively while the TV or stereo is on or while other people are talking. Don't depend on willpower to carry you through such distractions. It's much easier to plan ahead and avoid the distrac-

tions altogether. In fact, you would be wise to set up one or two specific places used solely for study (Hettich, 1998).

3. *Reward your studying.* One reason that it is so difficult to be motivated to study regularly is that the payoffs often lie in the distant future. The ultimate reward, a degree, may be years away. Even short-term rewards, such as an A in the course, may be

Some locations are far more conducive to successful studying than others.

Figure 1.13

Assessing your time management. This brief questionnaire (from LeBoeuf, 1980) is designed to evaluate the quality of one's time management. It should allow you to get a rough handle on how well you manage your time.

How Well Do You Manage Your Time?

Listed below are ten statements that reflect generally accepted principles of good time management. Answer these items by circling the response most characteristic of how you perform. Please be honest. No one will know your answers except you.

1 Each day I set aside a small amount of time for planning and thinking about my responsibilities.
0. Almost never 1. Sometimes 2. Often 3. Almost always

2 I set specific, written goals and put deadlines on them.
0. Almost never 1. Sometimes 2. Often 3. Almost always

3 I make a daily "to do" list, arrange items in order of importance, and try to get the important items done as soon as possible.
0. Almost never 1. Sometimes 2. Often 3. Almost always

4 I am aware of the 80/20 rule and use it. (The 80/20 rule states that 80% of your effectiveness will generally come from achieving only 20% of your goals.)
0. Almost never 1. Sometimes 2. Often 3. Almost always

5 I keep a loose schedule to allow for crises and the unexpected.
0. Almost never 1. Sometimes 2. Often 3. Almost always

6 I delegate everything I can to others.
0. Almost never 1. Sometimes 2. Often 3. Almost always

7 I try to handle each piece of paper only once.
0. Almost never 1. Sometimes 2. Often 3. Almost always

8 I eat a light lunch so I don't get sleepy in the afternoon.
0. Almost never 1. Sometimes 2. Often 3. Almost always

9 I make an active effort to keep common interruptions (visitors, meetings, telephone calls) from continually disrupting my work day.
0. Almost never 1. Sometimes 2. Often 3. Almost always

10 I am able to say no to others' requests for my time that would prevent my completing important tasks.
0. Almost never 1. Sometimes 2. Often 3. Almost always

To get your score, give yourself	If you scored	
3 points for each "almost always"	0–15	Better give some thought to managing your time.
2 points for each "often"		
1 point for each "sometimes"	16–20	You're doing OK, but there's room for improvement.
0 points for each "almost never"	21–25	Very good.
Add up your points to get your total score.	26–30	You cheated!

Source: LeBoeuf (1980, February). Managing time means managing yourself. *Business Horizons Magazine, 23* (1), p. 45, Table 3. Copyright © 1980 by the Board of Trustees of Indiana University, Kelley School of Business. Reprinted by permission.

weeks or months away. To combat this problem, it helps to give yourself immediate, tangible rewards for studying, such as a snack, TV show, or phone call to a friend. Thus, you should set realistic study goals for yourself and then reward yourself when you meet them. The systematic manipulation of rewards involves harnessing the principles of *behavior modification* described by B. F. Skinner and other behavioral psychologists. These principles are covered in the Chapter 6 Personal Application.

Improving Your Reading

Much of your study time is spent reading and absorbing information. *These efforts must be active.* Many students deceive themselves into thinking that they are studying by running a marker through a few sentences here and there in their text. If they do so without thoughtful selectivity, they are simply turning a textbook into a coloring book. Research suggests that highlighting selected textbook material *is* a useful strategy—if students are reasonably effective in identifying the main ideas in the material and if they subsequently review the main ideas they have highlighted (Caverly, Orlando, & Mullen, 2000).

You can use a number of methods to actively attack your reading assignments. One of the more widely taught strategies is Robinson's (1970) SQ3R method. **SQ3R is a study system designed to promote effective reading, which includes five steps: survey, question, read, recite, and review.** Its name is an acronym for the five steps in the procedure:

Step 1: Survey. Before you plunge into the reading itself, glance over the topic headings in the chapter. If you know where the chapter is going, you can better appreciate and organize the information you are about to read.

Step 2: Question. Once you have an overview of your reading assignment, you should proceed through it one section at a time. Take a look at the heading of the first section and convert it into a question. Doing so is usually quite simple. If the head-

ing is "Prenatal Risk Factors," your question should be "What are sources of risk during prenatal development?" If the heading is "Stereotyping," your question should be "What is stereotyping?" Asking these questions gets you actively involved in your reading and helps you identify the main ideas.

Step 3: Read. Only now, in the third step, are you ready to sink your teeth into the reading. Read only the specific section that you have decided to tackle. Read it with an eye toward answering the question you have just formulated. If necessary, reread the section until you can answer that question. Decide whether the segment addresses any other important questions and answer them as well.

Step 4: Recite. Now that you can answer the key question for the section, recite the answer out loud to yourself in your own words. Don't move on to the next section until you understand the main ideas of the current section. You may want to write down these ideas for review later. When you have fully digested the first section, you may go on to the next. Repeat steps 2 through 4 with the next section. Once you have mastered the crucial points there, you can go on again.

Step 5: Review. When you have read the entire chapter, refresh your memory by going back over the key points. Repeat your questions and try to answer them without consulting your book or notes. This review should fortify your retention of the main ideas. It should also help you see how the main ideas are related.

The SQ3R method should probably be applied to many texts on a paragraph-by-paragraph basis. Obviously, doing so will require you to formulate some questions without the benefit of topic headings. If you don't have enough headings, you can simply reverse the order of steps 2 and 3. Read the paragraph first and then formulate a question that addresses the basic idea of the paragraph. Then work at answering the question in your own words. The point is that you can be flexible in your use of the SQ3R technique.

Using the SQ3R method does not automatically lead to improved mastery of textbook reading assignments. It won't be effective unless it is applied diligently and skillfully, and it tends to be more helpful to students with low to medium reading ability (Caverly, Orlando, & Mullen, 2000). Any strategy that facilitates active processing of text material, the identification of key ideas, and effective review of these ideas should enhance your reading.

Besides topic headings, your textbooks may contain various other learning aids you can use to improve your reading. If a book provides a chapter outline, chapter summary, learning objectives, or preview questions don't ignore them. They can help you recognize the important points in the chapter. Graphic organizers (such as the Concept Charts available for this text) can enhance understanding of text material (Nist & Holschuh, 2000). A lot of effort and thought goes into formulating these and other textbook learning aids. It is wise to take advantage of them.

Getting More Out of Lectures

Although lectures are sometimes boring and tedious, it is a simple fact that poor class attendance is associated with poor grades. For example, in one study, Lindgren (1969) found that absences from class were much more common among "unsuccessful" students (grade average C– or below) than among "successful" students (grade average B or above), as shown in Figure 1.14 on the next page. Even when you have an instructor who delivers hard-to-follow lectures, it is still important to go to class. If nothing else, you can get a feel for how the instructor thinks, which can help you anticipate the content of exams and respond in the manner expected by your professor.

Fortunately, most lectures are reasonably coherent. Studies indicate that attentive note taking *is* associated with enhanced learning and performance in college classes (Cohn, Cohn, & Bradley, 1995; O'Donnell & Dansereau, 1993). However, research also shows that many students' lecture notes are surprisingly incomplete, with the aver-

Figure **1.14**

Attendance and grades. When Lindgren (1969) compared the class attendance of successful students (B average or above) and unsuccessful students (C− average or below), he found a clear association between poor attendance and poor grades.

SOURCE: Adapted from Lindgren, H. C. (1969). *The psychology of college success: A dynamic approach.* New York: Wiley. Copyright © 1969 by Henry Clay Lindgren. Adapted by permission of H. C. Lindgren.

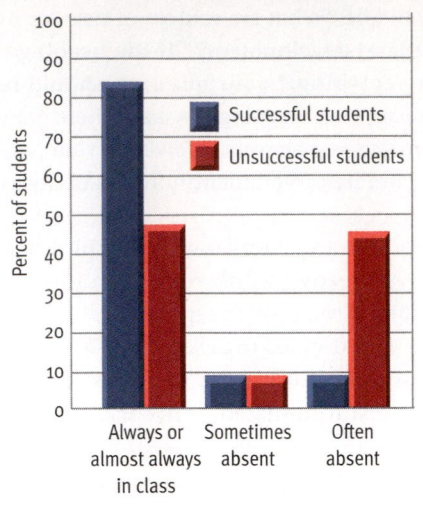

age student often recording less than 40% of the crucial ideas in a lecture (Armbruster, 2000). Thus, the key to getting more out of lectures is to stay motivated, stay attentive, and expend the effort to make your notes as complete as possible. Books on study skills (Longman & Atkinson, 2002; Sotiriou, 2002) offer a number of suggestions on how to take good-quality lecture notes, some of which are summarized here:

- Extracting information from lectures requires *active listening*. Focus full attention on the speaker. Try to anticipate what's coming and search for deeper meanings.
- When course material is especially complex, it is a good idea to prepare for the lecture by *reading ahead* on the scheduled subject in your text. Then you have less brand-new information to digest.
- You are not supposed to be a human tape recorder. Insofar as possible, try to write down the lecturer's thoughts *in your own words*. Doing so forces you to organize the ideas in a way that makes sense to you. In taking notes, pay attention to clues about what is most important. These clues may range from subtle hints, such as an instructor repeating a point, to not-so-subtle hints, such as an instructor saying "You'll run into this again."
- *Asking questions* during lectures can be helpful. Doing so keeps you actively involved in the lecture and allows you to clarify points that you may have misun-

derstood. Many students are more bashful about asking questions than they should be. They don't realize that most professors welcome questions.

Improving Test-Taking Strategies

Let's face it—some students are better than others at taking tests. *Testwiseness* is the ability to use the characteristics and format of a cognitive test to maximize one's score. Students clearly vary in testwiseness, and such variations are reflected in performance on exams (Geiger, 1997; Rogers &

Yang, 1996). Testwiseness is *not* a substitute for knowledge of the subject matter. However, skill in taking tests can help you show what you know when it is critical to do so (Flippo, Becker & Wark, 2000).

A number of myths exist about the best way to take tests. For instance, it is widely believed that students shouldn't go back and change their answers to multiple-choice questions. Benjamin, Cavell, and Shallenberger (1984) found this to be the dominant belief among college *faculty* as well as students (see Figure 1.15). However, the old adage that "your first hunch is your best hunch on tests" has been shown to be wrong. Empirical studies clearly and consistently indicate that, over the long run, changing answers pays off. Benjamin and his colleagues reviewed 20 studies on this issue; their findings are presented in Figure 1.16. As you can see, answer changes that go from a wrong answer to a right answer outnumber changes that go from a right answer to a wrong one by a sizable margin. The popular belief that answer changing is harmful is probably attributable to painful memories of right-to-wrong changes. In any case, you can see how it pays to be familiar with sound test-taking strategies.

General Tips

The principles of testwiseness were first described by Millman, Bishop, and Ebel

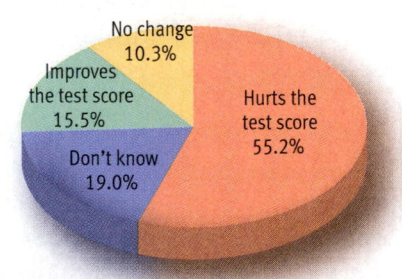

Figure 1.15

Beliefs about the effects of answer changing on tests. Ludy Benjamin and his colleagues (1984) asked 58 college faculty whether changing answers on tests is a good idea. Like most students, the majority of the faculty felt that answer changing usually hurts a student's test score, even though the research evidence contradicts this belief (see Figure 1.16).

Figure 1.16

Actual effects of changing answers on multiple-choice tests. When the data from all the relevant studies were combined by Benjamin et al. (1984), they indicated that answer changing on tests generally *increased* rather than *reduced* students' test scores. It is interesting to note the contrast between beliefs about answer changing (see Figure 1.15) and the actual results of this practice.

(1965). Let's look at some of their general ideas:

- If efficient time use appears crucial, set up a mental schedule for progressing through the test. Make a mental note to check whether you're one-third finished when a third of your time is gone.
- Don't waste time pondering difficult-to-answer questions excessively. If you have no idea at all, just guess and go on. If you need to devote a good deal of time to the question, skip it and mark it so you can return to it later if time permits.
- Adopt the appropriate level of sophistication for the test. Don't read things into questions. Sometimes students make things more complex than they were intended to be. Often, simple-looking questions are just what they appear to be.
- If you complete all of the questions and still have some time remaining, review the test. Make sure that you have recorded your answers correctly. If you were unsure of some answers, go back and reconsider them.

Tips for Multiple-Choice Exams

Sound test-taking strategies are especially important with multiple-choice (and true-false) questions. These types of questions often include clues that may help you converge on the correct answer (Mentzer, 1982; Weiten, 1984). You may be able to improve your performance on such tests by considering the following points:

- As you read the stem of each multiple-choice question, *anticipate* the answer if you can, before looking at the options. If the answer you anticipated is among the options, it is likely to be the correct one.
- Always read each question completely. Continue reading even if you find your anticipated answer among the options. A more complete option may be farther down the list.
- Learn how to quickly eliminate options that are highly implausible. Many questions have only two plausible options, accompanied by "throwaway" options for filler. You should work at spotting these implausible options so that you

can quickly discard them and narrow your task.

- Be alert to the fact that information relevant to one question is sometimes given away in another test item.
- On items that have "all of the above" as an option, if you know that just two of the options are correct, you should choose "all of the above." If you are confident that one of the options is incorrect, you should eliminate this option and "all of the above" and choose from the remaining options.
- Options that represent broad, sweeping generalizations tend to be incorrect. You should be vigilant for words such as *always, never, necessarily, only, must, completely, totally,* and so forth that create these improbable assertions.
- In contrast, options that represent carefully qualified statements tend to be correct. Words such as *often, sometimes, perhaps, may,* and *generally* tend to show up in these well-qualified statements.

Tips for Essay Exams

Little research has been done on testwiseness as it applies to essay exams. That's because there are relatively few clues to take advantage of in the essay format. Nonetheless, various books (Pauk, 1990; Walter & Siebert, 1990) offer tips based on expert advice, including the following:

- Time is usually a crucial factor on essay tests. Therefore, you should begin by looking over the questions and making time allocations on the basis of (1) your knowledge, (2) the time required to answer each question, and (3) the points awarded for answering each question. It's usually a good idea to answer the questions that you know best first.
- Many students fail to appreciate the importance of good organization in their essay responses. If your instructor can't follow where you are going with your answers, you won't get many points. Test essays are often poorly organized because students feel pressured for time and plunge into answering questions without any planning. It will pay off in the long run if you spend a minute

getting organized first. Also, many examiners appreciate it if you make your organization quite explicit by using headings or by numbering the points you're making.

- In many courses you'll learn a great deal of jargon or technical terminology. Demonstrate your learning by using this technical vocabulary in your essay answers.

In summary, sound study skills and habits are crucial to academic success. Intelligence alone won't do the job (although it certainly helps). Good academic skills do not develop overnight. They are acquired gradually, so be patient with yourself. Fortunately, tasks such as reading textbooks, writing papers, and taking tests get easier with practice. Ultimately, I think you'll find that the rewards—knowledge, a sense of accomplishment, and progress toward a degree—are worth the effort.

CRITICAL THINKING APPLICATION

Developing Critical Thinking Skills: An Introduction

If you ask any group of professors, parents, employers, or politicians, "What is the most important outcome of an education?" The most popular answer is likely to be "the development of the ability to think critically." *Critical thinking* is the use of cognitive skills and strategies that increase the probability of a desirable outcome. Such outcomes would include good career choices, effective decisions in the workplace, wise investments, and so forth. In the long run, critical thinkers should have more desirable outcomes than people who are not skilled in critical thinking (Halpern, 1996, 1998). Critical thinking is purposeful, reasoned, goal-directed thinking that involves solving problems, formulating inferences, working with probabilities, and making carefully thought-out decisions. Here are some of the skills exhibited by critical thinkers:

- They understand and use the principles of scientific investigation. (How can the effectiveness of punishment as a disciplinary procedure be determined?)
- They apply the rules of formal and informal logic. (If most people disapprove of sex sites on the World Wide Web, then why are these sites so popular?)
- They think effectively in terms of probabilities. (What is the likelihood of being able to predict who will commit a violent crime?)
- They carefully evaluate the quality of information. (Can I trust the claims made by this politician?)
- They analyze arguments for the soundness of the conclusions. (Does the rise in drug use mean that a stricter drug policy is needed?)

The topic of thinking has a long history in psychology, dating back to Wilhelm Wundt in the 19th century. Modern cognitive psychologists have found that a useful model of critical thinking has at least two components: (1) knowledge of the skills of critical thinking—the *cognitive component,* and (2) the attitude or disposition of a critical thinker—the *emotional or affective component.* Both are needed for effective critical thinking.

The Skills of Critical Thinking

Instruction in critical thinking is based on two assumptions: (1) a set of skills or strategies exists that students can learn to recognize and apply in appropriate contexts; (2) if the skills are applied appropriately, students will become more effective thinkers. Critical thinking skills that would be useful in any context might include understanding how reasons and evidence support or refute conclusions; distinguishing among facts, opinions, and reasoned judgments; using principles of likelihood and uncertainty when thinking about probabilistic events; generating multiple solutions to problems and working systematically toward a desired goal; and understanding how causation is determined. This list provides some typical examples of what is meant by the term *critical thinking skills.* Because these skills are useful in a wide variety of contexts, they are sometimes called *transcontextual skills.*

The Attitude of a Critical Thinker

It is of little use to know the skills of critical thinking if you are unwilling to exert the hard mental work to use them or if you have a sloppy or careless attitude toward thinking. A critical thinker is willing to plan, flexible in thinking, persistent, able to admit mistakes and make corrections, and mindful of the thinking process. The use of the word *critical* represents the notion of a critique or evaluation of thinking processes and outcomes. It is not meant to be negative (as in a "critical person") but rather to convey that critical thinkers are vigilant about their thinking.

The Need to Teach Critical Thinking

Decades of research on instruction in critical thinking have shown that the skills and attitudes of critical thinking need to be deliberately and consciously taught, because they often do not develop by themselves with standard instruction in a content area (Nisbett, 1993). For this reason, each chapter in this text ends with a "Critical Thinking Application." The material presented in each of these Critical Thinking Applications relates to the chapter topics, but the focus is on how to think about a particular issue, line of research, or controversy. Because the emphasis is on the thinking process, you may be asked to consider conflicting interpretations of data, judge the credibility of information sources, or generate your own testable hypotheses. The specific critical thinking skills highlighted in each Application are summarized in a table so that they are easily identified. Some of the skills will show up in multiple chapters because the goal is to help you spontaneously select the appropriate critical thinking skills when you encounter new information. Repeated practice with selected skills across chapters should help you develop this ability.

An Example

As explained in the main body of the chapter, *evolutionary psychology* is emerging as an influential school of thought. As one example of evolutionary theorizing in psychology, we looked at evolutionary analyses of gender differences in spatial abilities. To show you how critical thinking skills can be applied to psychological issues, let's reexamine the evolutionary explanation of gender differences in spatial talents, expand on it slightly, and then use some critical thinking strategies to evaluate this explanation.

Evolutionary psychologists explain gender differences in spatial abilities in terms of how they presumably evolved to meet the adaptive pressures faced by our ancient ancestors (Silverman & Eals, 1992; Silverman & Phillips, 1998). These theorists focus on how natural selection would have favored certain skills that would have been adaptive in hunting and gathering societies, as most of the human race's time on earth has been spent in such societal arrangements. Specifically, they assert that the typical division of labor between the sexes in hunting and gathering societies created different adaptive pressures for males and females. For example, it is believed that in such societies adult males often traveled long distances to hunt, while the women and children stayed closer to home to gather food. This was an efficient division of labor because women spent much of their adult lives pregnant, nursing, or caring for the young and, therefore, could not travel long distances. Building on these assumptions, evolutionary theorists assert that males tend to perform somewhat better than females on visual-spatial tasks involving mental rotation of images (see Figure 1.17), mental reconstruction of figures, map reading, and maze learning because these skills would have fostered success in the hunting tasks traditionally handled by males (by helping them to traverse long distances, aim projectiles at prey, and so forth). In contrast, the theorists argue that females exhibit a slight superiority on tasks measuring memory for locations because this talent would have fostered success in the foraging and gathering tasks traditionally handled by females.

How can you critically evaluate these claims? If your first thought was that you need more information, good for you, because you are already showing an aptitude for critical thinking. Some additional information about gender differences in cognitive abilities is presented in Chapter 11 of this text. You also need to develop the habit of asking good questions, such as, "Are there

Figure 1.17

An example of a spatial task involving mental rotation. Spatial reasoning tasks can be divided into a variety of subtypes. Studies indicate that males perform slightly better than females on most, but not all, spatial tasks. The tasks on which males are superior often involve mentally rotating objects, such as in the problem shown here. In this problem, the person has to figure out which object on the right (A through E) could be a rotation of the object at the left.

SOURCE: Stafford, R. E., & Gullikson, H. (1962). *Identical Blocks*, Form AA.

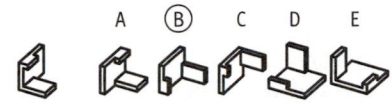

"B" is the correct answer.

alternative explanations for these results? Are there contradictory data?" Let's briefly consider each of these questions.

Are there alternative explanations for gender differences in spatial skills? Well, there certainly are other explanations for males' superiority on most spatial tasks. For example, one could attribute this finding to the gender-typed activities that males are encouraged to engage in more than females, such as playing with building blocks, Lego sets, Lincoln Logs, and various types of construction sets, as well as a host of spatially oriented video games. These gender-typed activities appear to provide boys with more practice than girls on most types of spatial tasks (Baenninger & Newcombe, 1995), and experience with spatial activities appears to enhance spatial skills (Smail, 1983; Subrahmanyam & Greenfield, 1996). If we can explain gender differences in spatial abili-

ties in terms of disparities in the everyday activities of males and females, we may have no need to appeal to natural selection.

Are there data that run counter to the evolutionary explanation for modern gender differences in spatial skills? Again, the answer is yes. Some scholars who have studied hunting and gathering societies suggest that women often traveled long distances to gather food and that women were often involved in hunting (Adler, 1993). In addition, women wove baskets and clothing and worked on other tasks that required spatial thinking (Halpern, 1997). Moreover—think about it—men on long hunting trips obviously needed to develop a good memory for locations or they might never have returned home. So, there is room for some argument about exactly what kinds of adaptive pressures males and females faced in ancient hunting and gathering societies.

Thus, you can see how considering alternative explanations and contradictory evidence weakens the evolutionary explanation of gender differences in spatial abilities. The questions we raised about alternative explanations and contradictory data are two generic critical thinking questions that can be asked in a wide variety of contexts. The answers to these questions do *not* prove that evolutionary psychologists are wrong in their explanation of gender differences in visual-spatial skills, but they do *weaken* the evolutionary explanation. In thinking critically about psychological issues, you will see that it makes more sense to talk about the *relative strength of an argument,* as opposed to whether an argument is right or wrong, because we will be dealing with complex issues that rarely lend themselves to being correct or incorrect.

Table 1.2 Critical Thinking Skills Discussed in This Application

Skill	Description
Looking for alternative explanations for findings and events	In evaluating explanations, the critical thinker explores whether there are other explanations that could also account for the findings or events under scrutiny.
Looking for contradictory evidence	In evaluating the evidence presented on an issue, the critical thinker attempts to look for contradictory evidence that may have been left out of the debate.

RECAP

Key Ideas

From Speculation to Science: How Psychology Developed

● Psychology's intellectual parents were 19th-century philosophy and physiology, which shared an interest in the mysteries of the mind. Psychology was born as an independent discipline when Wilhelm Wundt established the first psychological research laboratory in 1879 at Leipzig, Germany. He argued that psychology should be the scientific study of consciousness.

● The structuralists believed that psychology should use introspection to analyze consciousness into its basic elements. Functionalists, such as William James, believed that psychology should focus on the purpose and adaptive functions of consciousness.

● Behaviorists, led by John B. Watson, argued that psychology should study only observable behavior. Thus, they campaigned to redefine psychology as the science of behavior. Emphasizing the importance of the environment over heredity, they began to explore stimulus-response relationships, often using laboratory animals as subjects.

● Sigmund Freud's psychoanalytic theory emphasized the unconscious determinants of behavior and the importance of sexuality. Freud's ideas were controversial, and they met with resistance in academic psychology.

● Behaviorism continued as a powerful force in psychology, boosted greatly by B. F. Skinner's research. Like Watson before him, Skinner asserted that psychology should study only observable behavior, and he generated controversy by arguing that free will is an illusion.

● Finding both behaviorism and psychoanalysis unsatisfactory, advocates of a new theoretical orientation called humanism became influential in the 1950s. Humanism, led by Abraham Maslow and Carl Rogers, emphasized humans' freedom and potential for personal growth.

● Stimulated by the demands of World War II, clinical psychology grew rapidly in the 1950s. Thus, psychology became a profession as well as a science. This movement toward professionalization eventually spread to other areas in psychology.

● During the 1950s and 1960s advances in the study of cognitive processes and the physiological bases of behavior led to renewed interest in cognition and physiology, as psychology returned to its original roots.

● In the 1980s, Western psychologists, who had previously been rather provincial, developed a greater interest in how cultural factors influence thoughts, feelings, and behavior. This trend was sparked in large part by growing global interdependence and by increased cultural diversity in Western societies.

● The 1990s witnessed the emergence of a new theoretical perspective called evolutionary psychology. The central premise of this new school of thought is that patterns of behavior are the product of evolutionary forces, just as anatomical characteristics are shaped by natural selection.

Psychology Today: Vigorous and Diversified

● Contemporary psychology is a diversified science and profession that has grown rapidly in recent decades. Major areas of research in modern psychology include developmental psychology, social psychology, experimental psychology, physiological psychology, cognitive psychology, personality, and psychometrics.

● Applied psychology encompasses four professional specialties: clinical psychology, counseling psychology, educational and school psychology, and industrial and organizational psychology.

Putting It in Perspective: Seven Key Themes

● As we examine psychology in all its many variations, we will emphasize seven key ideas as unifying themes. Looking at psychology as a field of study, our three key themes are (1) psychology is empirical, (2) psychology is theoretically diverse, and (3) psychology evolves in a sociohistorical context.

● Looking at psychology's subject matter, the remaining four themes are (4) behavior is determined by multiple causes, (5) behavior is shaped by cultural heritage, (6) heredity and environment jointly influence behavior, and (7) people's experience of the world is highly subjective.

Personal Application ● Improving Academic Performance

● To foster sound study habits, you should devise a written study schedule and reward yourself for following it. You should also try to find one or two specific places for studying that are relatively free of distractions.

● You should use active reading techniques to select the most important ideas from the material you read. SQ3R, one approach to active reading, breaks a reading assigment into manageable segments and requires that you understand each segment before you move on.

● Good note taking can help you get more out of lectures. It's important to use active listening techniques and to record lecturers' ideas in your own words.

● Being an effective student also requires sound test-taking skills. In general, it's a good idea to devise a schedule for progressing through an exam, to adopt the appropriate level of sophistication, to avoid wasting time on troublesome questions, and to review your answers whenever time permits.

Critical Thinking Application ● Developing Critical Thinking Skills: An Introduction

● Critical thinking is the use of cognitive skills and strategies that increase the probability of a desirable outcome. Critical thinking is purposeful, reasoned thinking. A critical thinker is flexible, persistent, able to admit mistakes, and mindful of the thinking process.

● Evolutionary psychologists have attributed contemporary gender differences in spatial abilities to the sex-based division of labor in hunting and gathering societies. However, alternative explanations have been offered for these differences, focusing on the gender-typed activities that modern males and females engage in. There also are contradictory data regarding the adaptive pressures faced by females and males in hunting and gathering societies.

Key Terms

Applied psychology
Behavior
Behaviorism
Clinical psychology
Cognition
Critical thinking
Culture
Empiricism
Ethnocentrism
Evolutionary
  psychology
Functionalism
Humanism
Introspection
Natural selection
Psychiatry
Psychoanalytic theory
Psychology
SQ3R
Stimulus
Structuralism
Testwiseness
Theory
Unconscious

Key People

Sigmund Freud
G. Stanley Hall
William James
Carl Rogers
B. F. Skinner
John B. Watson
Wilhelm Wundt

PRACTICE TEST

1. For which of the following is Wilhelm Wundt primarily known?
   A. the establishment of the first formal laboratory for research in psychology
   B. the distinction between mind and body as two separate entities
   C. the discovery of how signals are conducted along nerves in the body
   D. the development of the first formal program for training in psychotherapy

2. G. Stanley Hall is noteworthy in the history of psychology because he:
   A. established the first American research laboratory in psychology.
   B. launched America's first psychological journal.
   C. was the driving force behind the establishment of the American Psychological Association.
   D. did all of the above.

3. Which of the following approaches might William James criticize for examining a movie frame by frame instead of seeing the motion in the motion picture?
   A. structuralism
   B. functionalism
   C. dualism
   D. humanism

4. Fred, a tennis coach, insists that he can make any reasonably healthy individual into an internationally competitive tennis player. Fred is echoing the thoughts of:
   A. Sigmund Freud.
   B. John B. Watson.
   C. Abraham Maslow.
   D. William James.

5. Which of the following approaches might suggest that forgetting to pick his mother up at the airport was Henry's unconscious way of saying that he did not welcome her visit?
   A. psychoanalytic
   B. behavioral
   C. humanistic
   D. cognitive

6. Which of the following is a statement with which Skinner's followers would agree?
   A. Most behavior is controlled by unconscious forces.
   B. The goal of behavior is self-actualization.
   C. Nature is more influential than nurture.
   D. Free will is an illusion.

7. Which of the following approaches has the most optimistic view of human nature?
   A. humanism
   B. behaviorism
   C. psychoanalysis
   D. structuralism

8. Which of the following historical events created a demand for clinicians that was far greater than the supply?
   A. World War I
   B. the Depression
   C. World War II
   D. the Korean War

9. The tendency to view one's own group as superior to others and as the standard for judging the worth of foreign ways is known as:
   A. behaviorism.
   B. ethnocentrism.
   C. humanism.
   D. functionalism.

10. The study of the endocrine system and genetic mechanisms would most likely be undertaken by a:
    A. clinical psychologist.
    B. physiological psychologist.
    C. social psychologist.
    D. educational psychologist.

11. The fact that psychologists do not all agree about the nature and development of personality demonstrates:
    A. that there are many ways of looking at the same phenomenon.
    B. the fundamental inability of psychologists to work together in developing a single theory.
    C. the failure of psychologists to communicate with one another.
    D. the possibility that personality may simply be incomprehensible.

12. A multifactorial causation approach to behavior suggests that:
    A. most behaviors can be explained best by single-cause explanations.
    B. most behavior is governed by a complex network of interrelated factors.
    C. data must be subjected to rigorous statistical analysis in order to make sense.
    D. explanations of behavior tend to build up from the simple to the complex in a hierarchical manner.

13. Psychology's answer to the question of whether we are born or made tends to be:
    A. we are born.
    B. we are made.
    C. we are both born and made.
    D. neither.

14. In regard to changing answers on multiple-choice tests, research indicates that _____ changes tend to be more common than other types of changes.
    A. wrong to right
    B. right to wrong
    C. wrong to wrong

15. Critical thinking skills:
    A. are abstract abilities that cannot be identified.
    B. usually develop spontaneously through normal content instruction.
    C. usually develop spontaneously without any instruction.
    D. need to be deliberately taught, because they often do not develop by themselves with standard content instruction.

Answers

1	A	p. 3	**6**	D	p. 9	**11**	A p. 22
2	D	p. 3	**7**	A	p. 10	**12**	B p. 24
3	A	pp. 4–5	**8**	C	pp. 11–12	**13**	C p. 25
4	B	p. 6	**9**	B	p. 14	**14**	A p. 30
5	A	pp. 7–8	**10**	B	p. 20	**15**	D p. 32

www ON THE WEB

For additional resources on the topics covered in this chapter, visit the *Psychology: Themes and Variations* Web site, where you will find practice quizzes, tutorials, Web links, simulations, critical thinking activities, flash cards, interactive exercises, and suggested readings available through INFOTRAC.

http://psychology.wadsworth.com/weiten_themes6e/

CHAPTER 2

© Digital Vision/Getty Images

The Research Enterprise in Psychology

© Digital Vision/Getty Images

- Can chronic inhibition of emotions increase people's vulnerability to physical disease?
- How does anxiety affect people's desire to be with others? Does misery love company?
- How effective are subliminal self-help audiotapes that are supposed to improve self-esteem or memory?
- Are there substantial differences among cultures when it comes to the pace of everyday life?
- What are the psychological characteristics of people who commit suicide?
- Are Internet sex sites a new source of addiction for millions of people?

Questions, questions, questions—everyone has questions about behavior. The most basic question is, how should these questions be investigated? As noted in Chapter 1, *psychology is empirical*. Psychologists rely on formal, systematic observations to address their questions about behavior. This methodology is what makes psychology a scientific endeavor.

The scientific enterprise is an exercise in creative problem solving. Scientists have to figure out how to make observations that will shed light on the puzzles they want to solve. To make these observations, psychologists use a variety of research methods because different questions call for different strategies of study. In this chapter, you will see how researchers have used such methods as experiments, case studies, surveys, and naturalistic observation to investigate the questions posed above.

Psychology's methods are worth a close look for at least two reasons. First, a better appreciation of the empirical approach will enhance your understanding of the research-based information that you will be reading about in the remainder of this book. Second, familiarity with the logic of the empirical approach should improve your ability to think critically about research. This ability is important because you are exposed to research findings nearly every day. The news media constantly report on studies that yield conclusions about how you should raise your children, improve your health, and enhance your interpersonal relationships. Learning how to evaluate these reports can help you use such information wisely.

In this chapter, we will examine the scientific approach to the study of behavior and then look at the specific research methods that psychologists use most frequently. We'll also see why psychologists use statistics in their research. After you learn how research is done, you'll also learn how *not* to do it. That is, we'll review some common flaws in doing research. Finally, we will take a look at ethical issues in behavioral research. In the Personal Application, you'll learn how to find and read journal articles that report on research. In the chapter's Critical Thinking Application, we'll examine the nature and validity of anecdotal evidence.

Looking for Laws: The Scientific Approach to Behavior

Whether the object of study is gravitational forces or people's behavior under stress, *the scientific approach assumes that events are governed by some lawful order.* As scientists, psychologists assume that behavior is governed by discernible laws or principles, just as the movement of the earth around the sun is governed by the laws of gravity. The behavior of living creatures may not seem as lawful and predictable as the "behavior" of planets. However, the scientific enterprise is based on the belief that there *are* consistencies or laws that can be uncovered. Fortunately, the plausibility of applying this fundamental assumption to psychology has been supported by the discovery of a great many such consistencies in behavior, some of which provide the subject matter for this text.

PREVIEW QUESTIONS
- What are the goals of the scientific enterprise?
- What are the key steps required by a scientific investigation?
- What are the principal advantages of the scientific approach?

Goals of the Scientific Enterprise

Psychologists and other scientists share three sets of interrelated goals: measurement and description, understanding and prediction, and application and control.

1. *Measurement and description.* Science's commitment to observation requires that an investigator figure out a way to measure the phenomenon under study. For example, a psychologist could not investigate whether men are more or less sociable than women without first developing some means of measuring sociability. Thus, the first goal of psychology is to develop measurement techniques that make it possible to describe behavior clearly and precisely.

2. *Understanding and prediction.* A higher-level goal of science is understanding. Scientists believe that they understand events when they can explain the reasons for the occurrence of the events. To evaluate their understanding, scientists make and test predictions called hypotheses. A *hypothesis* is a tentative statement about the relationship between two or more variables. *Variables* are any measurable conditions, events, characteristics, or behaviors that are controlled or observed in a study. If we hypothesized that putting people under time pressure would lower the accuracy of their time perception, the variables in our study would be time pressure and accuracy of time perception.

3. *Application and control.* Ultimately, many scientists hope that the information they gather will be of some practical value in helping to solve everyday problems. Once people understand a phenomenon, they often can exert more control over it. Today, the profession of psychology attempts to apply research findings to practical problems in schools, businesses, factories, and mental hospitals. For example, a school psychologist might use findings about the causes of math anxiety to devise a program to help students control their math phobias.

How do theories help scientists to achieve their goals? As noted in Chapter 1, psychologists do not set out just to collect isolated facts about relationships between variables. To build toward a better understanding of behavior, they construct theories. A *theory* is a system of interrelated ideas used to explain a set of observations. For example, using a handful of concepts, such as natural selection and reproductive fitness, evolutionary theory (Buss, 1995, 1996) purports to explain a diverse array of known facts about mating preferences, jealousy, aggression, sexual behavior, and so forth (see Chapter 1). Thus, by integrating apparently unrelated facts and principles into a coherent whole, theories permit psychologists to make the leap from the *description* of behavior to the *understanding* of behavior. Moreover, the enhanced understanding afforded by theories guides future research by generating new predictions and suggesting new lines of inquiry.

A scientific theory must be testable, as the cornerstone of science is its commitment to putting ideas to an empirical test. Most theories are too complex

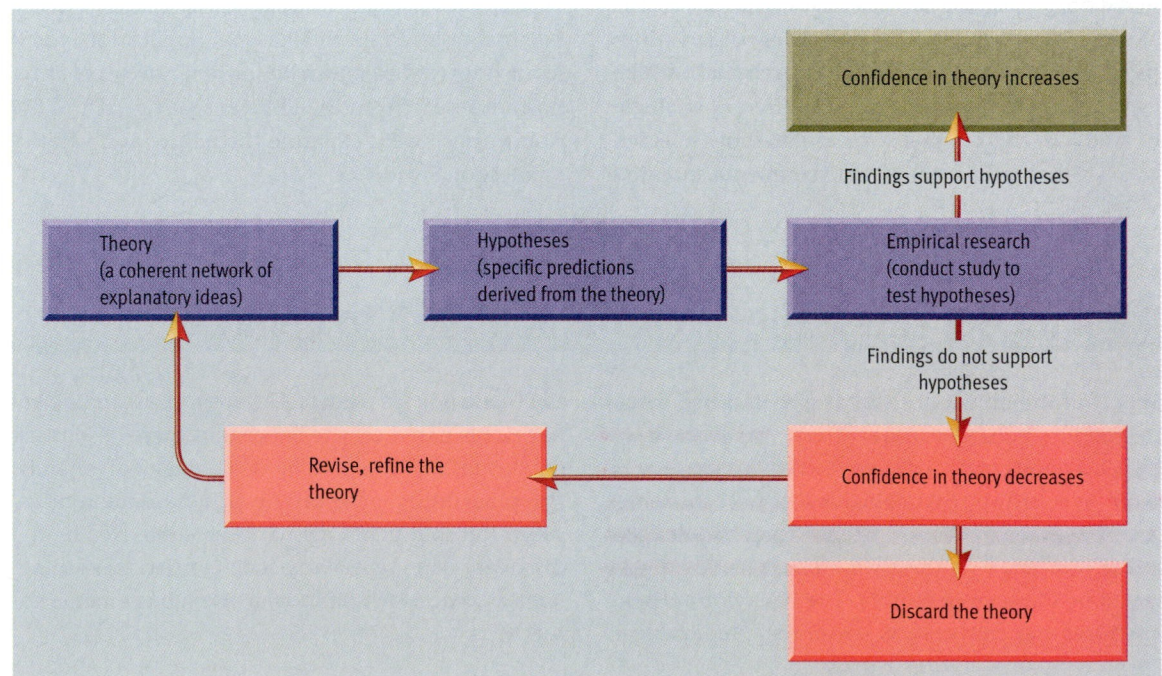

Figure 2.1

Theory construction. A good theory will generate a host of testable hypotheses. In a typical study, only one or a few of these hypotheses can be evaluated. If the evidence supports the hypotheses, our confidence in the theory they were derived from generally grows. If the hypotheses are not supported, confidence in the theory decreases and revisions to the theory may be made to accommodate the new findings. If the hypotheses generated by a theory consistently fail to garner empirical support, the theory may be discarded altogether. Thus, theory construction and testing is a gradual process.

to be tested all at once. For example, it would be impossible to devise a single study that could test all the many facets of evolutionary theory. Rather, in a typical study, investigators test one or two specific hypotheses derived from a theory. If their findings support the hypotheses, confidence in the theory that the hypotheses were derived from grows. If their findings fail to support the hypotheses, confidence in the theory diminishes, and the theory may be revised or discarded (see Figure 2.1). Thus, theory construction is a gradual, iterative process that is always subject to revision.

Steps in a Scientific Investigation

Curiosity about a question provides the point of departure for any kind of investigation, scientific or otherwise. Scientific investigations, however, are *systematic*. They follow an orderly pattern, which is outlined in Figure 2.2. Let's look at how this standard series of steps was followed in a study of psychological inhibition and physical health conducted by Steve Cole, Margaret Kemeny, Shelley Taylor, and Barbara Visscher (1996) of UCLA. Cole and his colleagues wanted to investigate whether the psychological inhibition required by gay men who conceal their homosexual identity might lead to increased vulnerability to certain kinds of physical illness.

Step 1: Formulate a Testable Hypothesis

The first step in a scientific investigation is to translate a theory or an intuitive idea into a testable hypothesis. Cole et al. (1996) noted that over the years a variety of theorists had speculated that frequent inhibition of emotions might create chronic physiological arousal that could lead to an increased incidence of physical illness. However, scientific evidence on this issue was sparse and inconsistent, in part because the concept of psychological inhibition had proven difficult to measure. Cole and his colleagues decided to approach the question in a new way. They reasoned that many gay individuals who are not "out of the closet" inhibit the public expression of their homosexuality to avoid stigmatization, discrimination, and even physical assault. They hypothesized that the vigilant inhibition of one's true feelings required by this strategy might have ramifications for gay individuals' health. Normally, hypotheses are expressed as predictions. They spell out how changes in one variable will be related to changes in another variable. Thus, Cole et al. pre-

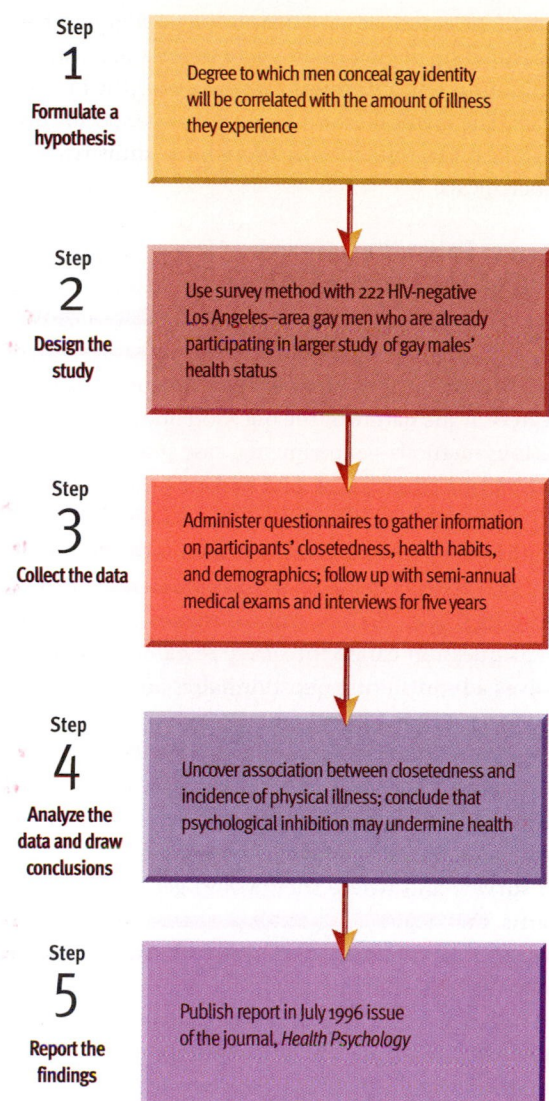

Step 1 Formulate a hypothesis
Degree to which men conceal gay identity will be correlated with the amount of illness they experience

Step 2 Design the study
Use survey method with 222 HIV-negative Los Angeles–area gay men who are already participating in larger study of gay males' health status

Step 3 Collect the data
Administer questionnaires to gather information on participants' closetedness, health habits, and demographics; follow up with semi-annual medical exams and interviews for five years

Step 4 Analyze the data and draw conclusions
Uncover association between closetedness and incidence of physical illness; conclude that psychological inhibition may undermine health

Step 5 Report the findings
Publish report in July 1996 issue of the journal, *Health Psychology*

Figure 2.2

Flowchart of steps in a scientific investigation. As illustrated in a study by Cole et al. (1996), a scientific investigation consists of a sequence of carefully planned steps, beginning with the formulation of a testable hypothesis and ending with the publication of the study, if its results are worthy of examination by other researchers.

dicted that the degree to which men concealed their gay identity would be associated with the amount of physical illness they experienced.

To be testable, scientific hypotheses must be formulated precisely, and the variables under study must be clearly defined. Researchers achieve these clear formulations by providing operational definitions of the relevant variables. **An *operational definition* describes the actions or operations that will be used to measure or control a variable.** Operational definitions—which may be quite different from concepts' dictionary definitions—establish precisely what is meant by each variable in the context of a study.

To illustrate, let's examine the operational definitions used by Cole and his colleagues. They measured concealment of homosexual identity by having gay participants rate themselves as *definitely in the closet, in the closet most of the time, half in and half out, out of the closet most of the time,* or *completely out of the closet.* The extent of participants' physical illness was measured by having them come in for a medical examination and interview every six months for five years. The medical exams focused on five specific diseases: cancer, pneumonia, bronchitis, sinusitis, and tuberculosis.

Step 2: Select the Research Method and Design the Study

The second step in a scientific investigation is to figure out how to put the hypothesis to an empirical test. The research method chosen depends to a large degree on the nature of the question under study. The various methods—experiments, case studies, surveys, naturalistic observation, and so forth—each have advantages and disadvantages. The researcher has to ponder the pros and cons and then select the strategy that appears to be the most appropriate and practical. In this case, Cole and colleagues decided that their question called for *survey* research, which involves administering questionnaires and interviews to a large number of people.

Once researchers have chosen a general method, they must make detailed plans for executing their study. Thus, Cole et al. had to decide when they would conduct their survey, how many people they needed to survey, and where they would get their participants. *Participants,* or *subjects,* **are the persons or animals whose behavior is systematically observed in a study.** For their study, Cole et al. chose to use 222 HIV-negative gay and bisexual men recruited from the Los Angeles–area gay community who had previously volunteered to participate in a larger study of gay males' health status. Although their hypothesis relating psychological inhibition to health ought to apply to both gay men and women, the researchers chose to focus on men because of the convenient availability of a local sample of gay men whose health status was already under study.

Step 3: Collect the Data

The third step in the research enterprise is to collect the data. Thus, Cole and his colleagues spent about a year collecting information on participants' concealment of their gay identity and other demographic and health-related variables (such as age, education, exercise habits, and alcohol consumption). Data on subjects' health were collected every six months for an additional five years. Researchers use a variety of *data collection techniques,* **which are procedures for making empirical observations and measurements.** Commonly used techniques include direct observation, questionnaires, interviews, psychological tests, physiological recordings, and examination of archival records (see Table 2.1). The data collection techniques used in a study depend largely on what is being investigated. For example, questionnaires are well suited for studying attitudes, psychological tests for studying personality, and physiological recordings for studying brain function.

Step 4: Analyze the Data and Draw Conclusions

The observations made in a study are usually converted into numbers, which constitute the raw data of the study. Researchers use *statistics* to analyze their data and to decide whether their hypotheses have been supported. Thus, statistics play an essential role in the scientific enterprise. Based on their statistical analyses, Cole et al. (1996) concluded that their data supported their hypothesis. As predicted, they found an association between the degree to which participants concealed their homosexual identity and the incidence of physical illness (see Figure 2.3). Al-

Table 2.1 Key Data Collection Techniques in Psychology

Technique	Description
Direct observation	Observers are trained to watch and record behavior as objectively and precisely as possible. They may use some instrumentation, such as a stopwatch or video recorder.
Questionnaire	Subjects are administered a series of written questions designed to obtain information about attitudes, opinions, and specific aspects of their behavior.
Interview	A face-to-face dialogue is conducted to obtain information about specific aspects of a subject's behavior.
Psychological test	Subjects are administered a standardized measure to obtain a sample of their behavior. Tests are usually used to assess mental abilities or personality traits.
Physiological recording	An instrument is used to monitor and record a specific physiological process in a subject. Examples include measures of blood pressure, heart rate, muscle tension, and brain activity.
Examination of archival records	The researcher analyzes existing institutional records (the archives), such as census, economic, medical, legal, educational, and business records.

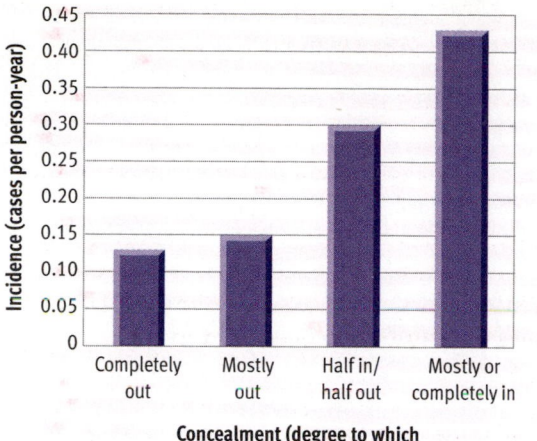

Figure 2.3

Results of the Cole et al. (1996) study. In their sample of gay and bisexual men, Cole et al. (1996) found that the more the men concealed their homosexual identity, the more likely they were to experience various diseases. The data shown here are for the combined incidence of sinusitis, bronchitis, pneumonia, and tuberculosis. A similar association was observed between closetedness and an elevated risk for skin cancer.

though the data supported the notion that psychological inhibition may be detrimental to one's health, the researchers were appropriately cautious about drawing far-reaching conclusions. Acknowledging that many variables were left uncontrolled in their correlational research, they noted that it would be premature to infer that coming out of the closet would result in improved health for gay men.

Step 5: Report the Findings

Scientific progress can be achieved only if researchers share their findings with one another and with the general public. Therefore, the final step in a scientific investigation is to write up a concise summary of the study and its findings. Typically, researchers prepare a report that is delivered at a scientific meeting and submitted to a journal for publication. A *journal* is a periodical that publishes technical and scholarly material, usually in a narrowly defined area of inquiry. The study by Cole and his colleagues (1996) was accepted for publication in a journal called *Health Psychology*.

The process of publishing scientific studies allows other experts to evaluate and critique new research findings. Sometimes this process of critical evaluation discloses flaws in a study. If the flaws are serious enough, the results may be discounted or discarded. This evaluation process is a major strength of the scientific approach because it gradually weeds out erroneous findings.

Advantages of the Scientific Approach

Science is certainly not the only method that can be used to draw conclusions about behavior. Everyone uses logic, casual observation, and good old-fashioned common sense. Because the scientific method often requires painstaking effort, it seems reasonable to ask what advantages make it worth the trouble.

Basically, the scientific approach offers two major advantages. The first is its clarity and precision. Commonsense notions about behavior tend to be vague and ambiguous. Consider the old adage "Spare the rod and spoil the child." What exactly does this generalization about child rearing amount to? How severely should children be punished if parents are not to "spare the rod"? How do we assess whether a child qualifies as "spoiled"? A fundamental problem is that such statements have different meanings, depending on the person. When people disagree about this assertion, it may be because they are talking about entirely different things. In contrast, the scientific approach requires that people specify *exactly* what they are talking about when they formulate hypotheses. This clarity and precision enhance communication about important ideas.

The second and perhaps greatest advantage offered by the scientific approach is its relative intolerance of error. Scientists are trained to be skeptical. They subject their ideas to empirical tests. They also scrutinize one another's findings with a critical eye. They demand objective data and thorough documentation before they accept ideas. When the findings of two studies conflict, the scientist tries to figure out why, usually by conducting additional research. In contrast, common sense and casual observation often tolerate contradictory generalizations, such as "Opposites attract" and "Birds of a feather flock together." Furthermore, commonsense analyses involve little effort to verify ideas or detect errors. Thus, many "truisms" about behavior that come to be widely believed are simply myths.

All this is not to say that science has an exclusive copyright on truth. However, the scientific approach does tend to yield more accurate and dependable information than casual analyses and armchair speculation do. Knowledge of scientific data can thus provide a useful benchmark against which to judge claims and information from other kinds of sources.

Now that we have had an overview of how the scientific enterprise works, we can focus on how specific research methods are used. *Research methods consist of various approaches to the observation,*

Web Link 2.1

PubMed
Few commercial databases of journal articles or abstracts in the health sciences are available online for no charge. However, the National Library of Medicine has opened the 9 million items of MEDLINE's abstracts and references to anyone wanting to research within the scientific literature of medical journals, including some important psychology publications.

Web Link 2.2

PsycINFO Direct
The definitive resource for information on the scientific literature in psychology is the PsycINFO database of abstracts maintained by the American Psychological Association (see the Personal Application for this chapter). You may be able to access this database for free through your college library. If not, you can purchase access to PsycINFO Direct via the Internet. However, it would be wise to carefully plan your research in advance, as the cost is not cheap ($9.95 for a 24-hour period).

measurement, manipulation, and control of variables in empirical studies. In other words, they are general strategies for conducting studies. No single research method is ideal for all purposes and situations. Much of the ingenuity in research involves selecting and tailoring the method to the question at hand. The next two sections of this chapter discuss the two basic types of methods used in psychology: *experimental research methods* and *descriptive/correlational research methods.*

REVIEW OF KEY POINTS

- The scientific approach assumes that there are laws of behavior that can be discovered through empirical research. The goals of the science of psychology include (1) the measurement and description of behavior, (2) the understanding and prediction of behavior, and (3) the application of this knowledge to the task of controlling behavior.

- By integrating apparently unrelated facts into a coherent whole, theories permit psychologists to make the leap from the description of behavior to the understanding of behavior. Confidence in a theory increases when hypotheses derived from it are supported by research.

- A scientific investigation follows a systematic pattern that includes five steps: (1) formulate a testable hypothesis, (2) select the research method and design the study, (3) collect the data, (4) analyze the data and draw conclusions, and (5) report the findings.

- Scientists use operational definitions to clarify what their variables mean. They depend on statistics to analyze their data. The two major advantages of the scientific approach are its clarity in communication and its relative intolerance of error.

Looking for Causes: Experimental Research

PREVIEW QUESTIONS

- What is the difference between an independent variable and a dependent variable?

- What is the purpose of experimental and control groups?

- What are extraneous variables and confounded variables?

- How can experiments vary in format?

- How did Greenwald et al. (1991) use the experimental method to evaluate the efficacy of subliminal self-help audiotapes?

- What are the strengths and weaknesses of experimental research?

Does misery love company? This question intrigued social psychologist Stanley Schachter. When people feel anxious, he wondered, do they want to be left alone, or do they prefer to have others around? Schachter's review of relevant theories suggested that in times of anxiety people would want others around to help them sort out their feelings. Thus, his hypothesis was that increases in anxiety would cause increases in the desire to be with others, which psychologists call the *need for affiliation*. To test this hypothesis, Schachter (1959) designed a clever experiment.

The *experiment* is a research method in which the investigator manipulates a variable under carefully controlled conditions and observes whether any changes occur in a second variable as a result. The experiment is a relatively powerful procedure that allows researchers to detect cause-and-effect relationships. Psychologists depend on this method more than any other.

Although its basic strategy is straightforward, in practice the experiment is a fairly complicated technique. A well-designed experiment must take into account a number of factors that could affect the clarity of the results. To see how an experiment is designed, let's use Schachter's study as an example.

Independent and Dependent Variables

 SIM1, 1b

The purpose of an experiment is to find out whether changes in one variable (let's call it X) cause changes in another variable (let's call it Y). To put it more concisely, we want to find out *how X affects Y*. In this formulation, we refer to X as the *independent variable* and to Y as the *dependent variable*.

An *independent variable* is a condition or event that an experimenter varies in order to see its impact on another variable. The independent variable is the variable that the experimenter controls or manipulates. It is hypothesized to have some effect on the dependent variable, and the experiment is conducted to verify this effect. The *dependent variable* is the variable that is thought to be affected by manipulation of the independent variable. In psychology studies, the dependent variable is usually a measurement of some aspect of the participants' behavior. The independent variable is called *independent* because it is *free* to be varied by the experimenter. The dependent variable is called *dependent* because it is thought to *depend* (at least in part) on manipulations of the independent variable.

In Schachter's experiment, *the independent variable was the subjects' anxiety level*. He manipulated anxiety level in a clever way. Participants assembled in his laboratory were told by a "Dr. Zilstein" that they would be participating in a study on the physiological effects of electric shock. They were further informed that during the experiment they would receive a series of electric shocks while their pulse and blood pressure were being monitored. Half of the subjects were warned that the shocks would be very painful. They made up the *high-anxiety* group. The other half of the participants (the *low-anxiety* group) were told that the shocks would be mild and painless. In reality, there was no plan to shock anyone at any time. These orientation procedures were simply intended to evoke different levels of anxiety. After the orientation, the experimenter indicated that there would be a delay while he prepared the shock apparatus for use. The participants were asked whether they would prefer to wait alone or in the company of others. *The participants' desire to affiliate with others was the dependent variable.*

Experimental and Control Groups

 SIM1, 1b

In an experiment the investigator typically assembles two groups of subjects who are treated differently with regard to the independent variable. These two groups are referred to as the experimental group and the control group. The *experimental group* consists of the subjects who receive some special treatment in regard to the independent variable. The *control group* consists of similar subjects who do *not* receive the special treatment given to the experimental group.

In the Schachter study, the participants in the high-anxiety condition constituted the experimental group. They received a special treatment designed to create an unusually high level of anxiety. The participants in the low-anxiety condition constituted the control group. They were not exposed to the special anxiety-arousing procedure.

It is crucial that the experimental and control groups in a study be alike, except for the different treatment that they receive in regard to the independent variable. This stipulation brings us to the logic that underlies the experimental method. If the two groups are alike in all respects *except for the variation created by the manipulation of the independent variable,* any differences between the two groups on the dependent variable *must be due to the manipulation of the independent variable.* In this way researchers isolate the effect of the independent variable on the dependent variable. Schachter, for example, isolated the impact of anxiety on the need for affiliation. As predicted, he found that increased anxiety led to increased affiliation. As Figure 2.4 indicates, the percentage of participants in the high-anxiety group who wanted to wait with others was nearly twice that of the low-anxiety group.

Extraneous Variables

 SIM1, 1b

As we have seen, the logic of the experimental method rests on the assumption that the experimental and control groups are alike except for their treatment in

regard to the independent variable. Any other differences between the two groups can cloud the situation and make it impossible to draw conclusions about how the independent variable affects the dependent variable.

In practical terms, of course, it is impossible to ensure that two groups of participants are exactly alike in *every* respect. The experimental and control groups have to be alike only on dimensions relevant to the dependent variable. Thus, Schachter did not need to worry about whether his two groups were similar in

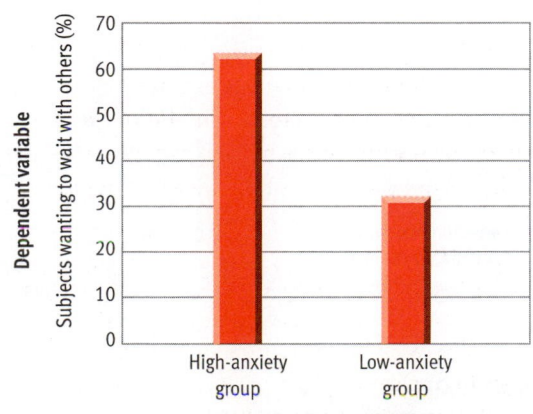

Figure 2.4

Results of Schachter's study of affiliation. The percentage of people wanting to wait with others was higher in the high-anxiety (experimental) group than in the low-anxiety (control) group, consistent with Schachter's hypothesis that anxiety would increase the desire for affiliation. The graphic portrayal of these results allows us to see at a glance the effects of the experimental manipulation on the dependent variable.

hair color, height, or interest in ballet, as these variables were unlikely to influence the dependent variable of affiliation behavior.

Instead, experimenters concentrate on ensuring that the experimental and control groups are alike on a limited number of variables that could have a bearing on the results of the study. These variables are called extraneous, secondary, or nuisance variables. *Extraneous variables* are any variables other than the independent variable that seem likely to influence the dependent variable in a specific study.

In Schachter's study, one extraneous variable would have been the subjects' tendency to be sociable. Why? Because participants' sociability could affect their desire to be with others (the dependent variable). If the participants in one group had happened to be more sociable (on the average) than those in the other group, the variables of anxiety and sociability would have been confounded. **A** *confounding of variables* **occurs when two variables are linked together in a way that makes it difficult to sort out their specific effects.** When an extraneous variable is confounded with an independent variable, a researcher cannot tell which is having what effect on the dependent variable.

Unanticipated confoundings of variables have wrecked innumerable experiments. That is why so much care, planning, and forethought must go into designing an experiment. One of the key qualities that separates a talented experimenter from a mediocre one is the ability to foresee troublesome extraneous variables and control them to avoid confoundings.

Experimenters use a variety of safeguards to control for extraneous variables. For instance, subjects are usually assigned to the experimental and control groups randomly. *Random assignment* of subjects occurs when all subjects have an equal chance of being assigned to any group or condition in the study. When experimenters distribute subjects into groups through some random procedure, they can be reasonably confident that the groups will be similar in most ways. Figure 2.5 provides an overview of the elements in an experiment, using Schachter's study as an example.

Variations in Designing Experiments  SIM1, 1b

We have discussed the experiment in only its simplest format, with just one independent variable and one dependent variable. Actually, many variations are possible in conducting experiments. Because you'll be reading about experiments with more complicated designs, these variations merit a brief mention.

First, it is sometimes advantageous to use only one group of subjects who serve as their own control group. The effects of the independent variable are evaluated by exposing this single group to two different conditions—an *experimental condition* and a *control condi-*

Figure 2.5

The basic elements of an experiment. As illustrated by the Schachter study, the logic of experimental design rests on treating the experimental and control groups exactly alike (to control for extraneous variables) except for the manipulation of the independent variable. In this way, the experimenter attempts to isolate the effects of the independent variable on the dependent variable.

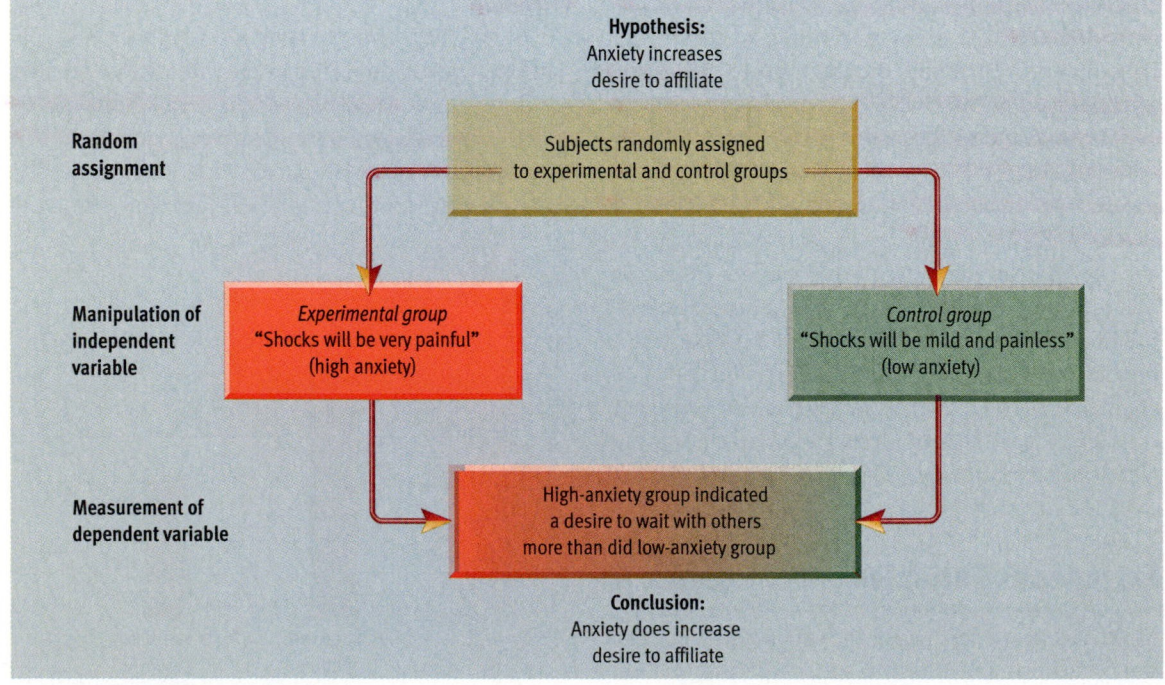

tion. For example, imagine that you wanted to study the effects of loud music on typing performance. You could have a group of participants work on a typing task while loud music was played (experimental condition) and in the absence of music (control condition). This approach would ensure that the participants in the experimental and control conditions would be alike on any extraneous variables involving their personal characteristics, such as motivation or typing skill. After all, the same people would be studied in both conditions.

Second, it is possible to manipulate more than one independent variable in a single experiment. Researchers often manipulate two or three independent variables to examine their joint effects on the dependent variable. For example, in another study of typing performance, you could vary both room temperature and the presence of distracting music (see Figure 2.6). The main advantage of this approach is that it permits the experimenter to see whether two variables interact. An *interaction* means that the effect of one variable depends on the effect of another. For instance, if we found that distracting music impaired typing performance only when room temperature was high, we would be detecting an interaction.

Third, it is also possible to use more than one dependent variable in a single study. Researchers frequently use a number of dependent variables to get a more complete picture of how experimental manipulations affect subjects' behavior. For example, in your studies of typing performance, you would probably measure two dependent variables: speed (words per minute) and accuracy (number of errors).

Now that you're familiar with the logic of the experiment, let's turn to our Featured Study for Chapter 2. You will find a Featured Study in each chapter from this point onward. These studies are provided

Figure 2.6

Manipulation of two independent variables in an experiment. As this example shows, when two independent variables are manipulated in a single experiment, the researcher has to compare four groups of subjects (or conditions) instead of the usual two. The main advantage of this procedure is that it allows an experimenter to see whether two variables interact.

to give you in-depth examples of how psychologists conduct empirical research. Each is described in a way that resembles a journal article, thereby acquainting you with the format of scientific reports (see the Personal Application at the end of the chapter for more information on this format). The Featured Study for this chapter gives you another example of an experiment in action.

Can Subliminal Audiotapes Improve Memory or Self-Esteem?

FEATURED STUDY

Subliminal perception involves the registration of sensory input without conscious awareness. As we will discuss in Chapter 4, it is a hotly debated concept. Can sensory stimuli that fall beneath the threshold of conscious awareness actually influence behavior? A great many people apparently think so, as *Time* magazine reports that subliminal self-help tapes intended to facilitate weight loss and improved sleep, self-esteem, memory, and sexual functioning have become a $50 million industry. The purpose of this study was to investigate the effectiveness of commercially sold subliminal audiotapes designed to increase self-esteem and enhance memory.

Method

Participants. Posters and newspaper advertisements in two university communities were used to recruit students and adults interested in working with subliminal tapes to improve their memory or self-esteem. Thus, the participants *were* motivated to achieve the goals

Investigators: Anthony G. Greenwald (University of Washington), Eric R. Spangenberg (Washington State University), Anthony R. Pratkanis (University of California, Santa Cruz), and Jay Eskenazi (University of California, Santa Barbara)

Source: Double-blind tests of subliminal self-help audiotapes, *Psychological Science*, 1991, *2*, 119–122.

claimed by the tapes, as is normally the case. A total of 237 participants (149 female, 88 male) completed the one-month study.

Materials. Subliminal tapes were obtained from three commercial vendors. Each tape was advertised to improve memory or self-esteem (but not both). The audible content of the tapes consisted of music or recorded nature (surf or forest) sounds.

Design. Each participant was given a subliminal tape to which a memory or self-esteem label had been *randomly* assigned. Hence, roughly half of the tapes were *mislabeled.* This manipulation was possible because the purpose of each tape (to improve self-esteem or memory) was not apparent from listening to its audible content. Thus, each participant served as both an experimental group subject and a control group subject. For instance, participants who received a self-esteem–labeled tape that was really a memory tape served as treatment subjects for the memory tape and as control subjects for the self-esteem tape. In sum, the *independent variables* were the actual purpose of the tape (memory or self-esteem) and the labeling of the tape (accurate or mislabeled).

Procedure. In the initial session, participants were given a battery of established tests that measured their self-esteem and their memory. They were then given one of the subliminal tapes and instructed to listen to it every day for one month. After the month was over, participants were given another battery of tests to assess their self-esteem and memory. They were also asked whether they felt that the tape had improved their memory or self-esteem. Thus, the *dependent variables* were improvement in memory or self-esteem as measured by the two batteries of tests and subjects' beliefs about whether they experienced an improvement.

Results

The data relevant to the efficacy of the self-esteem tapes are summarized in Figure 2.7, which shows the mean posttest self-esteem scores. If the tapes were effective, the two groups that actually listened to self-esteem messages should have higher scores. As you can see, the results are just the opposite. The data that assess the effectiveness of the memory tapes are summarized in Figure 2.8, which shows the mean posttest memory scores. Negligible differences were found between those that actually listened to memory tapes and those who did not. Curiously, though, about half the subjects reported that they *thought* the tapes had worked for them.

Figure 2.7

Effects of subliminal self-help tapes on self-esteem. This graph summarizes the data on self-esteem from the Greenwald et al. (1991) study. If the tapes with subliminal self-esteem messages had been effective, the two blue bars in the graph would be noticeably higher than the green bars. As you can see, the subjects who were given self-esteem tapes actually showed less improvement in self-esteem than those who were given memory tapes.

Source: Adapted from Greenwald, A. G., Spangenberg, E. R., Pratkanis, A. R., & Eskenazi, J. (1991). Double-blind tests of subliminal self-help audiotapes. *Psychological Science, 2,* 119–122. Copyright © 1991 by Cambridge University Press. Reprinted by permission.

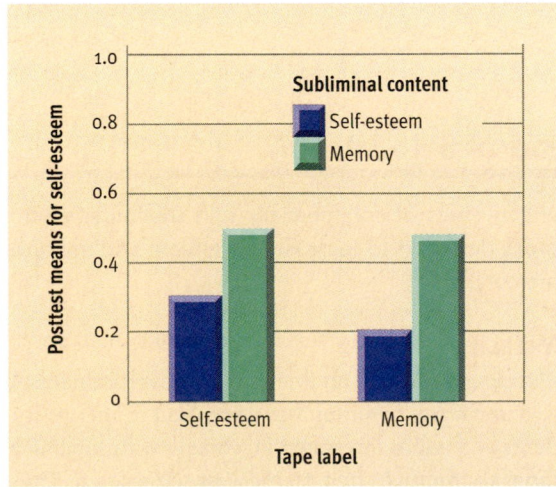

Figure 2.8

Effects of subliminal self-help tapes on memory. This graph summarizes the data on memory from the Greenwald et al. (1991) study. If the tapes with subliminal memory messages had been effective, the two green bars in the graph would be noticeably taller than the blue bars. As you can see, this was not the case.

Source: Adapted from Greenwald, A. G., Spangenberg, E. R., Pratkanis, A. R., & Eskenazi, J. (1991). Double-blind tests of subliminal self-help audiotapes. *Psychological Science, 2,* 119–122. Copyright © 1991 by Cambridge University Press. Reprinted by permission.

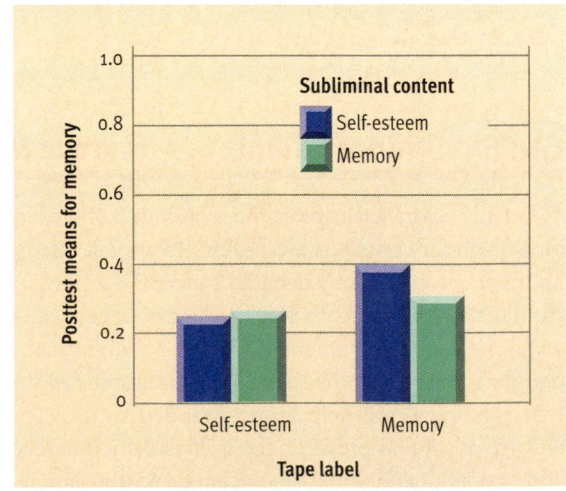

Discussion

The objective data suggest that subliminal audiotapes are not an effective means to improve either memory or self-esteem. Although the study did not examine subliminal tapes intended for other purposes (such as weight loss or better sleep), the strong results led the investigators to voice doubts about the entire spectrum of subliminal tapes, concluding "it seems most prudent to regard the general class of claims for therapeutic efficacy of subliminal audio content as lacking empirical foundation" (p. 122). The finding that about half the participants subjectively felt that the tapes had worked may explain why many people continue to tout the benefits of subliminal self-help treatments.

Comment

This study was featured because it addresses an interesting question using a reasonably straightforward experimental design. It also illustrates the importance of collecting empirical data to answer psychological questions. If asked whether subliminal audiotapes work, many people would probably answer "Yes." After all, they are sold through reputable stores and magazines. However, the findings of this carefully controlled experiment suggest that subliminal tapes are unlikely to be effective and probably represent a waste of money. Of course, a single study on an issue does not settle the matter once and for all. But without research data, we would just be guessing about the effects of subliminal tapes. ■

Advantages and Disadvantages of Experimental Research

The experiment is a powerful research method. Its principal advantage is that it permits conclusions about cause-and-effect relationships between variables. Researchers are able to draw these conclusions about causation because the precise control available in the experiment allows them to isolate the relationship between the independent variable and the dependent variable, while neutralizing the effects of extraneous variables. No other research method can duplicate this strength of the experiment. This advantage is why psychologists usually prefer to use the experimental method whenever possible.

For all its power, however, the experiment has limitations. One problem is that experiments are often artificial. Because experiments require great control over proceedings, researchers must often construct simple, contrived situations to test their hypotheses experimentally. For example, to investigate decision making in juries, psychologists have conducted many experiments in which subjects read a brief summary of a trial and then record their individual "verdicts" of innocence or guilt. This approach allows the experimenter to manipulate a variable, such as the race of the defendant, to see whether it affects the participants' verdicts. However, critics have pointed out that having a participant read a short case summary and make an individual decision cannot really compare to the complexities of real trials (Weiten & Diamond, 1979). In actual court cases, jurors may spend weeks listening to confusing testimony while making subtle judgments about the credibility of witnesses. They then retire for hours of debate to arrive at a group verdict, which is quite different from rendering an individual decision. Many researchers have failed to do justice to this complex process in their laboratory experiments. When experiments are highly artificial, doubts arise about the applicability of findings to everyday behavior outside the experimental laboratory.

Another disadvantage is that the experimental method can't be used to explore some research questions. Psychologists are frequently interested in the effects of factors that cannot be manipulated as independent variables because of ethical concerns or practical realities. For instance, you might be interested in whether a nutritionally poor diet during pregnancy increases the likelihood of birth defects. This clearly is a significant issue. However, you obviously cannot take 100 pregnant women and assign 50 of them to a condition in which they consume an inadequate diet. The potential risk to the health of the women and their unborn children would make this research strategy unethical.

In other cases, manipulations of variables are difficult or impossible. For example, you might want to know whether being brought up in an urban as opposed to a rural area affects people's values. An experiment would require you to randomly assign similar families to live in urban and rural areas, which obviously is impossible to do. To explore this question, you would have to use descriptive/correlational research methods, which we turn to next.

Web Link 2.3

Psychological Research on the Net
This site, sponsored by the American Psychological Society, is a jumping off point for people interested in participating in ongoing research projects that are collecting data over the Internet. Visitors will find a host of opportunities for taking part in genuine research.

- Experimental research involves the manipulation of an independent variable to determine its effect on a dependent variable. This research is usually done by comparing experimental and control groups, which must be alike in regard to important extraneous variables.

- Any differences between the groups in the dependent variable ought to be due to manipulation of the independent variable, as long as there are no confounds. Variables are said to be confounded when they vary together so that researchers cannot isolate the effect of the independent variable on the dependent variable.

not → necessary

- Experimental designs may vary. For example, sometimes an experimental group serves as its own control group. And many experiments have more than one independent variable or more than one dependent variable.

- Some of these variations were seen in the Featured Study, which examined the efficacy of subliminal audiotapes. The results of this experiment suggested that subliminal self-help messages are ineffective.

- An experiment is a powerful research method that permits conclusions about cause-and-effect relationships between variables. However, the experimental method is often not usable for a specific problem, and many experiments tend to be artificial.

Looking for Links: Descriptive/Correlational Research

- How did Levine and Norenzayan (1999) use naturalistic observation to estimate the pace of life in different cultures?

- How can case studies be used to look for general principles of behavior?

- Why do researchers use surveys?

- What are the strengths and weaknesses of descriptive/correlational research?

As we just saw, in some situations psychologists cannot exert experimental control over the variables they want to study. The research of Cole et al. (1996) on the relationship between psychological inhibition and vulnerability to illness provides another example of this problem. Obviously, Cole and his colleagues could not manipulate the degree to which their gay participants were in or out of the closet.

In such situations, investigators must rely on *descriptive/correlational research methods*. These methods include naturalistic observation, case studies, and surveys. What distinguishes these methods is that the researcher cannot manipulate the variables under study. This lack of control means that these methods cannot be used to demonstrate cause-and-effect relationships between variables. *Descriptive/correlational methods permit investigators to only describe patterns of behavior and discover links or associations between variables.* That is not to suggest that associations are unimportant. You'll see in this section that information on associations between variables can be extremely valuable in our efforts to understand behavior.

Naturalistic Observation

Does the pace of everyday life vary substantially from one culture to the next? Do people operate at a different speed in say, Germany, as opposed to Canada or Brazil? Are factors such as economic vitality and climate related to differences in the pace of life? These are the kinds of questions that intrigued Robert V. Levine and Ara Norenzayan (1999), who compared the pace of life in 31 countries around the world. Perhaps they could have devised an experiment to examine this question, but they wanted to focus on the pace of life in the real world rather than in the laboratory.

To study the pace of life, Levine and Norenzayan (1999) had to come up with concrete ways to measure it—their operational definition of the concept. The measure they chose depended on *naturalistic observation*. In **naturalistic observation a researcher engages in careful observation of behavior without intervening directly with the subjects.** In this instance, the researchers observed (1) the average walking speed in downtown locations, (2) the accuracy of public clocks, and (3) the speed with which postal clerks completed a simple request. Their collection of data on walking speed illustrates the careful planning required to execute naturalistic observation effectively. In the main downtown area of each city, they had to find two flat, unobstructed, uncrowded 60-foot walkways where they could unobtrusively time pedestrians during normal business hours. Only adult pedestrians walking alone and not window shopping were timed. In most cities, the observations continued until 35 men and 35 women had been timed.

Levine and Norenzayan conducted their naturalistic observations in 31 countries, typically using the largest city in each country as the locale for their research. Their findings, based on all three measures, are summarized in Table 2.2, which ranks the pace of life in the countries studied. Their data suggest that the pace of life is fastest in the countries of Western Europe and in Japan. Using archival data, they also conducted correlational analyses to see whether variations in the pace of life were associated with factors such as climate, economic vitality, or population size. Among other things, they found that the pace of life was faster in colder climates and in countries that were more economically productive.

This type of research is called *naturalistic* because behavior is allowed to unfold naturally (without in-

© Rafael Macia/Photo Researchers, Inc.

© Carl & Ann Purcell/CORBIS

Naturalistic observation can be complex and challenging, as the study by Levine and Norenzayan (1999) illustrates. One of their measures of the pace of life in 31 cultures involved estimating people's walking speed in downtown locations. To reduce the influence of confounding factors, they had to find sidewalks that were unobstructed, uncrowded, not dominated by window shoppers, and so forth. Moreover, they had to find reasonably comparable locations in 31 very different types of cities.

terference) in its natural environment—that is, the setting in which it would normally occur. The major strength of naturalistic observation is that it allows researchers to study behavior under conditions that are less artificial than in experiments. A major problem with this method is that researchers often have trouble making their observations unobtrusively so they don't affect their participants' behavior.

Case Studies

What portion of people who commit suicide suffer from psychological disorders? Which disorders are most common among victims of suicide? In health care visits during the final month of their lives, do people who commit suicide communicate their intent to do so? A research team in Finland wanted to

Table 2.2 Levine and Norenzayan's (1999) Ranking of the Pace of Life in 31 Cultures

Rank	Country	Rank	Country	Rank	Country
1	Switzerland	11	France	21	Greece
2	Ireland	12	Poland	22	Kenya
3	Germany	13	Costa Rica	23	China
4	Japan	14	Taiwan	24	Bulgaria
5	Italy	15	Singapore	25	Romania
6	England	16	United States	26	Jordan
7	Sweden	17	Canada	27	Syria
8	Austria	18	S. Korea	28	El Salvador
9	Netherlands	19	Hungary	29	Brazil
10	Hong Kong	20	Czech Republic	30	Indonesia
				31	Mexico

Source: Adapted from Levine, R. V., & Norenzayan, A. (1999). The pace of life in 31 countries. *Journal of Cross-Cultural Psychology, 30* (2), 178–205. Copyright © 1999 by Sage Publications. Reprinted by permission.

investigate the psychological characteristics of people who take their own lives (Henriksson et al., 1993; Isometsa et al., 1995). Other researchers had explored these questions, but the Finnish team planned a comprehensive, national study of unprecedented scope. Their initial sample consisted of all the known suicides in Finland for an entire year.

The research team decided that their question called for a case study approach. A *case study* is an in-depth investigation of an individual subject. When this method is applied to victims of suicide the case studies are called *psychological autopsies*. A variety of data collection techniques can be used in case studies. In normal circumstances, when the participants are not deceased, typical techniques include interviewing the subjects, interviewing people who are very close to the subjects, direct observation of the subjects, examination of records, and psychological testing. In this study, the investigators conducted thorough interviews with the families of the suicide victims and with the health care professionals who had treated them. The researchers also examined the suicide victims' medical, psychiatric, and social agency records, as well as relevant police investigations and forensic reports. Comprehensive case reports were then assembled for each person who committed suicide.

These case studies revealed that in 93% of the suicides the victim suffered from a significant psychological disorder (Henriksson et al., 1993). The most common diagnoses, by a large margin, were depression and alcohol dependence. In 571 cases, victims had a health care appointment during the last four weeks of their lives, but only 22% of these people discussed the possibility of suicide during their final visit (Isometsa et al., 1995). Even more surprising, the sample included 100 people who saw a health professional on the same day they killed themselves, yet only 21% of these individuals raised the issue of suicide. The investigators concluded that mental illness is a contributing factor in virtually all completed suicides and that the vast majority of suicidal people do not spontaneously reveal their intentions to health care professionals.

Clinical psychologists, who diagnose and treat psychological problems, routinely do case studies of their clients (see Figure 2.9). When clinicians assemble a case study for diagnostic purposes, they generally are *not* conducting empirical research. Case study *research* typically involves investigators analyzing a collection of case studies to look for patterns that permit general conclusions.

Case studies are particularly well suited for investigating certain phenomena, such as psychological

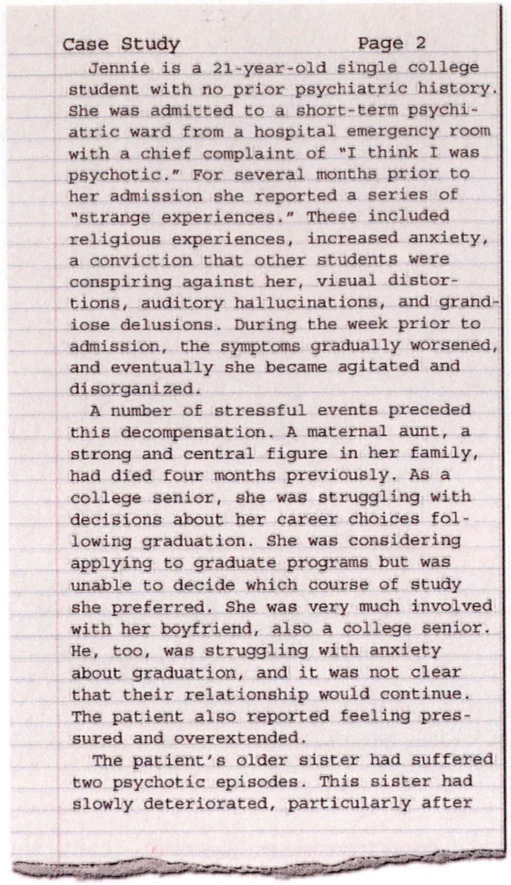

Case Study	Page 2

Jennie is a 21-year-old single college student with no prior psychiatric history. She was admitted to a short-term psychiatric ward from a hospital emergency room with a chief complaint of "I think I was psychotic." For several months prior to her admission she reported a series of "strange experiences." These included religious experiences, increased anxiety, a conviction that other students were conspiring against her, visual distortions, auditory hallucinations, and grandiose delusions. During the week prior to admission, the symptoms gradually worsened, and eventually she became agitated and disorganized.

A number of stressful events preceded this decompensation. A maternal aunt, a strong and central figure in her family, had died four months previously. As a college senior, she was struggling with decisions about her career choices following graduation. She was considering applying to graduate programs but was unable to decide which course of study she preferred. She was very much involved with her boyfriend, also a college senior. He, too, was struggling with anxiety about graduation, and it was not clear that their relationship would continue. The patient also reported feeling pressured and overextended.

The patient's older sister had suffered two psychotic episodes. This sister had slowly deteriorated, particularly after

Figure 2.9

An example of a case study report. As this example illustrates, case studies are particularly appropriate for clinical situations in which efforts are made to diagnose and treat psychological problems. Usually, one case study does not provide much basis for deriving general laws of behavior. However, if you examine a series of case studies involving similar problems, you can look for threads of consistency that may yield general conclusions.

SOURCE: Greenfield, D. (1985). *The psychotic patient: Medication and psychotherapy.* New York: The Free Press. Copyright © 1985 by David Greenfield. Reprinted by permission of the author.

disorders. They can also provide compelling, real-life illustrations that bolster a hypothesis or theory. However, the main problem with case studies is that they are highly subjective. Information from several sources must be knit together in an impressionistic way. In this process, clinicians and researchers often focus selectively on information that fits with their expectations, which usually reflect their theoretical slant. Thus, it is relatively easy for investigators to see what they expect to see in case study research.

Surveys

Millions of people visit sexually oriented websites every month. Are many of them "addicted" to cybersex, as some social critics have suggested? How much time do these people devote to online sexual pursuits? Do they feel guilty about their cybersex activities? Alvin Cooper and his colleagues (1999) set out to answer these and other questions by conducting a survey. **In a *survey* researchers use questionnaires or interviews to gather information about specific aspects of participants' behavior.** In this study, Cooper and his associates gathered data using a 59-item, online questionnaire that was posted for seven weeks at the MSNBC website. Adults who had used the Internet for sexual pursuits at least once were invited to participate in the survey. The final sample consisted of 9,177 anonymous volunteers who submitted complete surveys. The self-selected sample clearly was not representative of the general adult population in the United States, but the participants' demographic data suggested that they *were* reasonably representative of that portion of the population that visits sexually explicit websites.

What did the survey reveal? Male respondents outnumbered female respondents by about 6 to 1. Men reported mostly going to sites that featured visual erotica, whereas women were more likely to visit sexually themed chat rooms. Only 8%–9% of the respondents reported spending more than 10 hours per week in online sexual pursuits (see Figure 2.10). Although 87% of the subjects indicated that they never felt guilty about their behavior, 70% admitted keeping the extent of their online sexual activities secret from others. A majority of participants (61%) indicated that they sometimes pretended to be a different age than they really are, but a mere 5% reported pretending to be a member of the opposite sex. Only 12% of respondents reported feeling that they devoted too much time to online sexual interests. However, among

"heavy users" of Internet sex sites (more than 10 hours per week), about half admitted that their online activities were interfering with their lives. The authors conclude that "the vast majority of online users generally seem to use Internet sexual venues in casual ways that may not be problematic," but that heavy users may be at risk for psychological difficulties.

Surveys are often used to obtain information on aspects of behavior that are difficult to observe directly. Surveys also make it relatively easy to collect data on attitudes and opinions from large samples of participants. The major problem with surveys is that they depend on self-report data. As we'll discuss later, intentional deception, wishful thinking, memory lapses, and poorly worded questions can distort participants' verbal reports about their behavior (Krosnick, 1999).

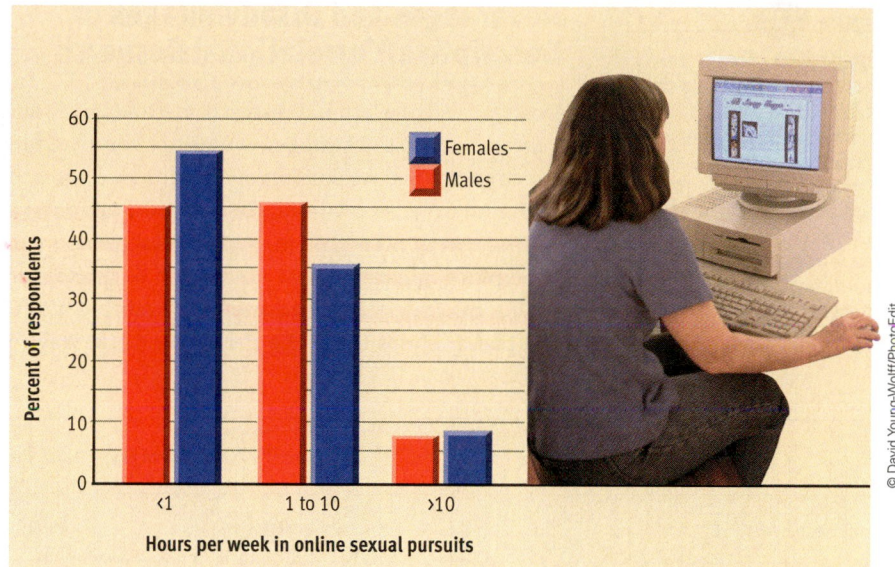

Percent of respondents vs. Hours per week in online sexual pursuits

- Females
- Males

Figure 2.10

Time devoted to Internet sexual pursuits. In the online survey conducted by Cooper and his colleagues (1999) over 9,000 respondents provided information on how much time they spend weekly visiting sexually oriented websites. As you can see, the vast majority of participants reported that they spend 10 hours or less each week in online sexual pursuits. (Based on Cooper et al., 1999)

CONCEPT CHECK 2.2

Matching Research Methods to Questions

Check your understanding of the uses and strengths of various research methods by figuring out which method would be optimal for investigating the following questions about behavioral processes. Choose from the following methods: (a) experiment, (b) naturalistic observation, (c) case study, and (d) survey. Indicate your choice (by letter) next to each question. You'll find the answers in Appendix A in the back of the book.

_____ **1.** Are people's attitudes about nuclear disarmament related to their social class or education?

_____ **2.** Do people who suffer from anxiety disorders share similar early childhood experiences?

_____ **3.** Do troops of baboons display territoriality—that is, do they mark off an area as their own and defend it from intrusion by other baboons?

_____ **4.** Can the presence of food-related cues (delicious-looking desserts in advertisements, for example) cause an increase in the amount of food that people eat?

Figure **2.11**

Comparison of major research methods. This chart pulls together a great deal of information on key research methods in psychology and gives a simple example of how each method might be applied in research on aggression. As you can see, the various research methods each have their strengths and weaknesses.

Advantages and Disadvantages of Descriptive/Correlational Research

Descriptive/correlational research methods have advantages and disadvantages, which are compared to the strengths and weaknesses of experimental research in Figure 2.11. As a whole, the foremost advantage of these methods is that they give researchers a way to explore questions that could not be examined with experimental procedures. For example, after-the-fact analyses would be the only ethical way to investigate the possible link between poor maternal nutrition and birth defects in humans. In a similar vein, if researchers hope to learn how urban and rural upbringing relate to people's values, they have to depend on descriptive methods, since they can't control where subjects grow up. Thus, *descriptive/correlational research broadens the scope of phenomena that psychologists are able to study.*

Unfortunately, descriptive methods have one significant disadvantage: Investigators cannot control events to isolate cause and effect. *Consequently, corre-*

Overview of key research methods in psychology

Research method		Description	Example	Advantages	Disadvantages
Experiment 		Manipulation of an independent variable under carefully controlled conditions to see whether any changes occur in a dependent variable	Youngsters are randomly assigned to watch a violent or nonviolent film, and their aggression is measured in a laboratory situation	Precise control over variables; ability to draw conclusions about cause-and-effect relationships	Contrived situations often artificial; ethical concerns and practical realities preclude experiments on many important questions
Naturalistic observation 		Careful, usually prolonged observation of behavior without direct intervention	Youngsters' spontaneous acts of aggression during recreational activities are observed unobtrusively and recorded	Minimizes artificiality; can be good place to start when little is known about phenomena under study	Often difficult to remain unobtrusive; can't explain why certain patterns of behavior were observed
Case studies 		In-depth investigation of a single participant using direct interview, direct observation, and other data collection techniques	Detailed case histories are worked up for youngsters referred to counseling because of excessive aggressive behavior	Well-suited for study of certain phenomena; can provide compelling illustrations to support a theory	Subjectivity makes it easy to see what one expects to see based on one's theoretical slant; clinical samples often unrepresentative
Surveys 		Use of questionnaires or interviews to gather information about specific aspects of participants' behavior	Youngsters are given questionnaire that describes hypothetical scenarios and are asked about the likelihood of aggressive behavior	Can gather data on difficult-to-observe aspects of behavior; relatively easy to collect data from large samples	Sef-report data often unreliable, due to intentional deception, social desirability bias, response sets, memory lapses, and wishful thinking

lational research cannot demonstrate conclusively that two variables are causally related. As an example, consider the cross-cultural investigation of the pace of life that we discussed earlier. Although Levine and Norenzayan (1999) found an association between colder climates and a faster pace of life, their data do not permit us to conclude that a cold climate *causes* a culture to move at a faster pace. Too many factors were left uncontrolled in the study. For example, we do not know how similar the cold and warm cities were. Climate could co-vary with some other factors, such as modernization or economic vitality, that might have led to the observed differences in the pace of life.

Looking for Conclusions: Statistics and Research

Whether researchers use experimental or correlational methods, they need some way to make sense of their data. Statistics is the use of mathematics to organize, summarize, and interpret numerical data. Statistical analyses permit researchers to draw conclusions based on their observations. Many students find statistics intimidating, but statistics are an integral part of modern life. Although you may not realize it, you are bombarded with statistics nearly every day. When you read about economists' projections for inflation, when you check a baseball player's batting average, when you see the popularity ratings of television shows, you are dealing with statistics. In this section, we will examine a few basic statistical concepts that will help you understand the research discussed throughout this book. For the most part, we won't concern ourselves with the details of statistical *computations*. These details and some additional statistical concepts are discussed in Appendix B at the back of the book. At this juncture, we will discuss only the purpose, logic, and value of the two basic types of statistics: descriptive statistics and inferential statistics.

Descriptive Statistics

Descriptive statistics are used to organize and summarize data. They provide an overview of numerical data. Key descriptive statistics include measures of central tendency, measures of variability, and the coefficient of correlation. Let's take a brief look at each of these.

Central Tendency

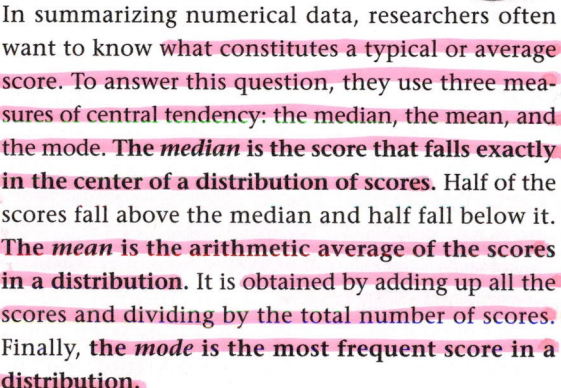

In summarizing numerical data, researchers often want to know what constitutes a typical or average score. To answer this question, they use three measures of central tendency: the median, the mean, and the mode. The *median* is the score that falls exactly in the center of a distribution of scores. Half of the scores fall above the median and half fall below it. The *mean* is the arithmetic average of the scores in a distribution. It is obtained by adding up all the scores and dividing by the total number of scores. Finally, the *mode* is the most frequent score in a distribution.

In general, the mean is the most useful measure of central tendency because additional statistical manipulations can be performed on it that are not possible with the median or mode. However, the mean is sensitive to extreme scores in a distribution, which can sometimes make the mean misleading. To illustrate, imagine that you're interviewing for a sales position at a company. Unbeknownst to you, the company's five salespeople earned the following incomes in the previous year: $20,000, $20,000, $25,000, $35,000, and $200,000. You ask how much the typical salesperson earns in a year. The sales director proudly announces that her five salespeople earned a *mean* income of $60,000 last year (the calculations are shown in Figure 2.12 on the next page). However, before you order that expensive new sports car, you had better inquire about the *median* and *modal* income for the sales staff. In this case, one extreme score ($200,000) has inflated the mean, making it un-

Web Link 2.5

HyperStat Online
For psychology researchers who find they've temporarily misplaced their statistics textbook, here's one written in hypertext by Professor David M. Lane of Rice University, and it's always available online for free. He also includes links to excellent resources involving statistics, the analysis of experimental data, and even some statistical humor.

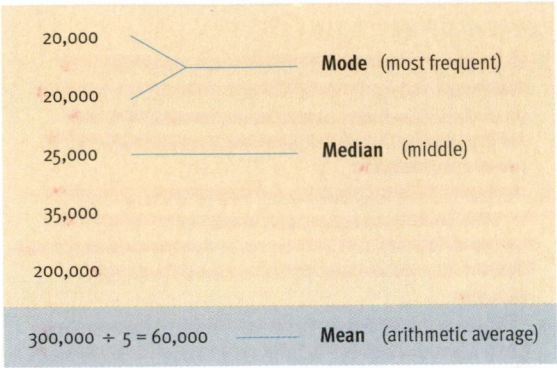

20,000		**Mode** (most frequent)
20,000		
25,000		**Median** (middle)
35,000		
200,000		
300,000 ÷ 5 = 60,000		**Mean** (arithmetic average)

Figure 2.12

Measures of central tendency. The three measures of central tendency usually converge, but that is not always the case, as these data illustrate. Which measure is most useful depends on the nature of the data. Generally, the mean is the best index of central tendency, but in this instance the median is more informative.

Speed (miles per hour)

Set A Perfection Boulevard		Set B Wild Street
35		21
34		37
33		50
37		28
38		42
40		37
36		39
33		25
34		23
30		48
35	**Mean**	35
2.87	**Standard deviation**	10.39

Figure 2.13

Variability and the standard deviation. Although these two sets of data produce the same mean, or average, an observer on Wild Street would see much more variability in the speeds of individual cars than an observer on Perfection Boulevard would. As you can see, the standard deviation for set B is higher than that for set A because of the greater variability in set B.

representative of the sales staff's earnings. In this instance, the median ($25,000) and the mode ($20,000) both provide better estimates of what you are likely to earn.

Variability

In describing a set of data it is often useful to have some estimate of the variability among the scores. *Variability* refers to how much the scores in a data set vary from each other and from the mean. The *standard deviation* is an index of the amount of variability in a set of data. When variability is great, the standard deviation will be relatively large. When variability is low, the standard deviation will be smaller. This relationship is apparent if you examine the two sets of data in Figure 2.13. The mean is the same for both sets of scores, but variability clearly is greater in set B than in set A. This greater variability yields a higher standard deviation for set B than for set A. Estimates of variability play a crucial role when researchers use statistics to decide whether the results of their studies support their hypotheses.

Correlation

A *correlation* exists when two variables are related to each other. Investigators often want to quantify the strength of an association between two variables, such as between class attendance and course grade, or between cigarette smoking and physical disease. In this effort, they depend extensively on a useful descriptive statistic: the correlation coefficient. The *correlation coefficient* is a numerical index of the degree of relationship between two variables. A correlation coefficient indicates (1) the direction (positive or negative) of the relationship and (2) how strongly the two variables are related.

Positive Versus Negative Correlation. A *positive correlation* indicates that two variables co-vary in the *same* direction. This means that high scores on variable X are associated with high scores on variable Y and that low scores on variable X are associated with low scores on variable Y. For example, there is a positive correlation between high school grade point average (GPA) and subsequent college GPA. That is, people who do well in high school tend to do well in college, and those who perform poorly in high school tend to perform poorly in college (see Figure 2.14).

In contrast, a *negative* correlation indicates that two variables co-vary in the *opposite* direction. This means that people who score high on variable X tend to score low on variable Y, whereas those who score low on X tend to score high on Y. For example, in most college courses there is a negative correlation between how frequently students are absent and how well they perform on exams. Students who have a high number of absences tend to get low exam scores, while students who have a low number of absences tend to earn higher exam scores (see Figure 2.14).

If a correlation is negative, a minus sign (−) is always placed in front of the coefficient. If a correlation is positive, a plus sign (+) may be placed in front of the coefficient, or the coefficient may be shown with no sign. Thus, if there's no sign, the correlation is positive.

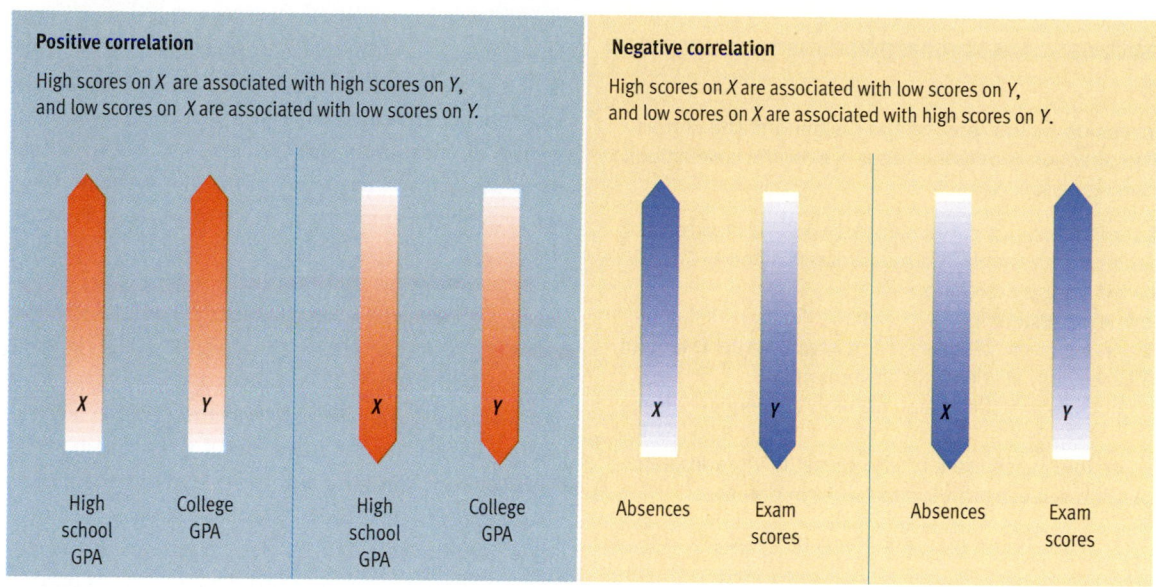

Positive correlation

High scores on *X* are associated with high scores on *Y*, and low scores on *X* are associated with low scores on *Y*.

X   Y   X   Y

High   College   High   College
school   GPA   school   GPA
GPA   GPA

Negative correlation

High scores on *X* are associated with low scores on *Y*, and low scores on *X* are associated with high scores on *Y*.

X   Y   X   Y

Absences   Exam   Absences   Exam
           scores   scores

Figure 2.14

Positive and negative correlation. Notice that the terms *positive* and *negative* refer to the direction of the relationship between two variables, not to its strength. Variables are positively correlated if they tend to increase and decrease together and are negatively correlated if one tends to increase when the other decreases.

Strength of the Correlation. Whereas the positive or negative sign indicates the direction of an association, the *size of the coefficient* indicates the *strength of an association between two variables.* The coefficient can vary between 0 and +1.00 (if positive) or between 0 and –1.00 (if negative). A coefficient near zero indicates no relationship between the variables; that is, high or low scores on variable *X* show no consistent relationship to high or low scores on variable *Y*. A coefficient of +1.00 or –1.00 indicates a perfect, one-to-one correspondence between the two variables. Most correlations fall between these extremes.

The closer the correlation to either –1.00 or +1.00, the stronger the relationship (see Figure 2.15). Thus, a correlation of .90 represents a stronger tendency for variables to be associated than a correlation of .40 does. Likewise, a correlation of –.75 represents a stronger relationship than a correlation of –.45. Keep in mind that the *strength* of a correlation depends only on the size of the coefficient. The positive or negative sign simply indicates the direction of the relationship. Therefore, a correlation of –.60 reflects a stronger relationship than a correlation of +.30.

Computation of correlation coefficients allowed Levine and Norenzayan (1999) to determine whether associations existed between various predictor variables and the pace of life in their cross-cultural study. For example, they found a robust correlation of +.74 between a measure of economic vitality (gross domestic product per capita) and overall pace, but they found a negligible correlation (–.07) between population size and the pace of life. Thus, statistical analyses permitted them to precisely quantify the associations between important cultural factors and the pace of life.

Correlation and Prediction. You may recall that one of the key goals of scientific research is accurate *prediction.* A close link exists between the magnitude of a correlation and the power it gives scientists to make predictions. *As a correlation increases in strength (gets closer to either –1.00 or +1.00), the ability to predict one variable based on knowledge of the other variable increases.*

To illustrate, consider how college admissions tests (such as the SAT or ACT) are used to predict college performance. When students' admissions test scores and first-year college GPA are correlated, re-

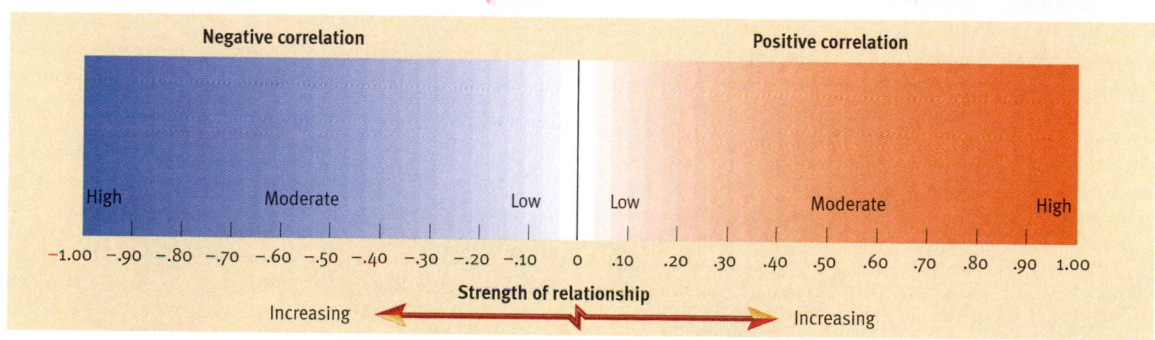

Negative correlation   **Positive correlation**

High   Moderate   Low   Low   Moderate   High

−1.00 −.90 −.80 −.70 −.60 −.50 −.40 −.30 −.20 −.10 0 .10 .20 .30 .40 .50 .60 .70 .80 .90 1.00

Strength of relationship

Increasing ←————————————→ Increasing

Figure 2.15

Interpreting correlation coefficients. The magnitude of a correlation coefficient indicates the strength of the relationship between two variables. The sign (plus or minus) indicates whether the correlation is positive or negative. The closer the coefficient comes to +1.00 or −1.00, the stronger the relationship between the variables.

Understanding Correlation

Check your understanding of correlation by interpreting the meaning of the correlation in item 1 and by guessing the direction (positive or negative) of the correlations in item 2. You'll find the answers in Appendix A.

1. Researchers have found a substantial positive correlation between youngsters' self-esteem and their academic achievement (measured by grades in school). Check any acceptable conclusions based on this correlation.

   _____ **a.** Low grades cause low self-esteem.
   _____ **b.** There is an association between self-esteem and academic achievement.
   _____ **c.** High self-esteem causes high academic achievement.
   _____ **d.** High ability causes both high self-esteem and high academic achievement.
   _____ **e.** Youngsters who score low in self-esteem tend to get low grades, and those who score high in self-esteem tend to get high grades.

2. Indicate whether you would expect the following correlations to be positive or negative.

   _____ **a.** The correlation between age and visual acuity (among adults).
   _____ **b.** The correlation between years of education and income.
   _____ **c.** The correlation between shyness and the number of friends one has.

---

searchers generally find moderate positive correlations in the .40s and .50s (Gregory, 1996). Because of this relationship, college admissions committees can predict with modest accuracy how well prospective students will do in college. Admittedly, the predictive power of these admissions tests is *far* from perfect. But it's substantial enough to justify the use of the tests as one factor in making admissions decisions. However, if this correlation were much higher, say .90, admissions tests could predict with superb accuracy how students would perform. In contrast, if this correlation were much lower, say .20, the tests' prediction of college performance would be so poor that it would be unreasonable to consider the test scores in admissions decisions.

Correlation and Causation. Although a high correlation allows us to predict one variable from another, it does not tell us whether a cause-effect relationship exists between the two variables. The problem is that variables can be highly correlated even though they are not causally related. For example, there is a sub-

stantial positive correlation between the size of young children's feet and the size of their vocabulary. That is, larger feet are associated with a larger vocabulary. Obviously, increases in foot size do not *cause* increases in vocabulary size. Nor do increases in vocabulary size cause increases in foot size. Instead, both are caused by a third variable: an increase in the children's age.

When we find that variables *X* and *Y* are correlated, we can safely conclude only that *X* and *Y* are related. We do not know *how X* and *Y* are related. We do not know whether *X* causes *Y* or *Y* causes *X* or whether both are caused by a third variable. For example, survey studies have found a positive correlation between smoking and the risk of experiencing a major depressive disorder (Breslau, Kilbey, & Andreski, 1991, 1993). Although it's clear that there is an association between smoking and depression, it's hard to tell what's causing what. The investigators acknowledge that they don't know whether smoking makes people more vulnerable to depression or whether depression increases the tendency to smoke. Moreover, they note that they can't rule out the possibility that both are caused by a third variable (*Z*). Perhaps anxiety and neuroticism increase the likelihood of both taking up smoking and becoming depressed. The plausible causal relationships in this case are diagrammed in Figure 2.16, which illustrates the "third variable problem" in interpreting correlations. This is a common problem in research, and you'll see this type of diagram again when we discuss other correlations. Thus, it is important to remember that *correlation is not equivalent to causation*.

Inferential Statistics

After researchers have summarized their data with descriptive statistics, they still need to decide whether their data support their hypotheses. *Inferential statistics* are used to interpret data and draw conclusions. Working with the laws of probability, researchers use inferential statistics to evaluate the possibility that their results might be due to the fluctuations of chance.

Figure 2.16

Three possible causal relations between correlated variables. If variables *X* and *Y* are correlated, does *X* cause *Y*, does *Y* cause *X*, or does some hidden third variable, *Z*, account for the changes in both *X* and *Y*? As the relationship between smoking and depression illustrates, a correlation alone does not provide the answer. We will encounter this problem of interpreting the meaning of correlations frequently in this text.

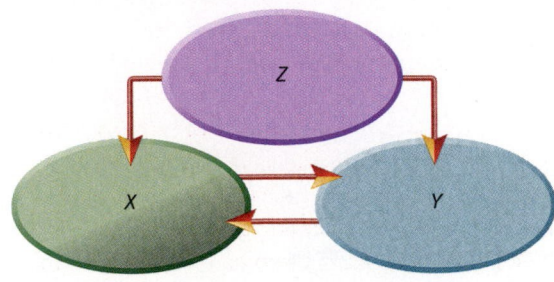
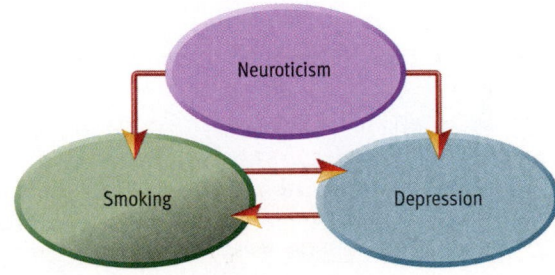

To illustrate this process, envision a hypothetical experiment. A computerized tutoring program (the independent variable) is designed to increase sixth-graders' reading achievement (the dependent variable). Our hypothesis is that program participants (the experimental group) will score higher than non-participants (the control group) on a standardized reading test given near the end of the school year. Let's assume that we compare 60 subjects in each group. We obtain the following results, reported in terms of participants' grade-level scores for reading:

Control group		Experimental group
6.3	Mean	6.8
1.4	Standard deviation	2.4

We hypothesized that the training program would produce higher reading scores in the experimental group than in the control group. Sure enough, that is indeed the case. However, we have to ask ourselves a critical question: Is this observed difference between the two groups large enough to support our hypothesis? That is, do the higher scores in the experimental group reflect the effect of the training program? Or could a difference of this size have occurred by chance? If our results could easily have occurred by chance, they don't provide meaningful support for our hypothesis.

When statistical calculations indicate that research results are not likely to be due to chance, the results are said to be *statistically significant*. You will probably hear your psychology professor use this phrase quite frequently. In discussing research, it is routine to note that "statistically significant differences were found." In statistics, the word *significant* has a precise and special meaning. **Statistical significance is said to exist when the probability that the observed findings are due to chance is very low.** "Very low" is usually defined as less than 5 chances in 100, which is referred to as the .05 level of significance.

Notice that in this special usage, *significant* does not mean "important," or even "interesting." Statistically significant findings may or may not be theoretically significant or practically significant. They simply are research results that are unlikely to be due to chance.

You don't need to be concerned here with the details of how statistical significance is calculated. However, it is worth noting that a key consideration is the amount of variability in the data. That is why the standard deviation, which measures variability, is such an important statistic. When the necessary computations are made for our hypothetical experiment, the difference between the two groups does *not* turn out to be statistically significant. Thus, our results would not be adequate to demonstrate that our tutoring program leads to improved reading achievement. Psychologists have to do this kind of statistical analysis as part of virtually every study. Thus, inferential statistics are an integral element in the research enterprise.

REVIEW OF KEY POINTS

- Psychologists use descriptive statistics to organize and summarize their numerical data. The mean, median, and mode are widely used measures of central tendency. The mean tends to be the most useful of these indexes, but it can be distorted by extreme scores. Variability is usually measured with the standard deviation, which increases as the variability in a data set grows.

- Correlations may be either positive (when two variables co-vary in the same direction) or negative (when two variables co-vary in the opposite direction). The closer a correlation is to either +1.00 or −1.00, the stronger the association is.

- As a correlation increases in strength, the ability to predict one variable based on knowledge of the other variable increases. However, a correlation is no assurance of causation. When variables are correlated, we do not know whether *X* causes *Y*, or *Y* causes *X*, or a third variable causes both.

- Hypothesis testing involves deciding whether observed findings support the researcher's hypothesis. Findings are statistically significant only when they are unlikely to be due to chance.

Looking for Flaws: Evaluating Research

Scientific research is a more reliable source of information than casual observation or popular belief. However, it would be wrong to conclude that all published research is free of errors. As we just saw, when researchers report statistically significant differences at the .05 level, there are 5 chances in 100 that the results really are a misleading by-product of chance fluctuation. This probability is pretty low, but it's not zero. Moreover, scientists' effort to minimize the prob-

ability of obtaining significant differences when none really exist increases the likelihood of the opposite mistake—failing to find significant differences when the groups really are different. Thus, even when research is conducted in a sound fashion, there's still a small chance of erroneous conclusions. Above and beyond this problem, we need to recognize that scientists are fallible human beings who do not conduct flawless research. Their personal biases in designing

PREVIEW QUESTIONS

- What is sampling bias?
- What are placebo effects and how can you guard against them?
- What is the social desirability bias?
- What are response sets?
- What is experimenter bias, and how can you guard against it?

and interpreting studies can also distort research results (MacCoun, 1998).

For these reasons, researchers are reluctant to settle scientific questions on the basis of just one empirical study. Instead, important questions usually generate a flurry of studies to see whether key findings will stand the test of replication. *Replication* **is the repetition of a study to see whether the earlier results are duplicated**. The replication process helps science identify and purge erroneous findings. Of course, the replication process sometimes leads to contradictory results. You'll see some examples in the upcoming chapters. Inconsistent findings on a research question can be frustrating and confusing for students. However, some inconsistency in results is to be expected, given science's commitment to replication.

As you will see in upcoming chapters, scientific advances often emerge out of efforts to double-check perplexing findings or to explain contradictory research results. Thus, like all sources of information, scientific studies need to be examined with a critical eye. This section describes a number of common methodological problems that often spoil studies. Being aware of these pitfalls will make you more skilled in evaluating research.

Sampling Bias

A *sample* is the collection of subjects selected for observation in an empirical study. In contrast, **the *population* is the much larger collection of animals or people (from which the sample is drawn)** that researchers want to generalize about (see Figure 2.17). For example, when political pollsters attempt to predict elections, all the voters in a jurisdiction represent the population, and the voters who are actually surveyed constitute the sample. If a researcher was interested in the ability of 6-year-old children to form concepts, those 6-year-olds actually studied would be the sample, and all similar 6-year-old children (perhaps those in modern, Western cultures) would be the population.

The strategy of observing a limited sample in order to generalize about a much larger population rests on the assumption that the sample is reasonably *representative* of the population. A sample is representative if its composition is similar to the composition of the population. *Sampling bias* **exists when a sample is not representative of the population from which it was drawn.** When a sample is not representative, generalizations about the population may be inaccurate. For instance, if a political pollster were to survey only people in posh shopping areas frequented by the wealthy, the pollster's generalizations about the voting public as a whole would be off the mark.

As we discussed in Chapter 1, historically, psychologists have tended to undersample women, ethnic minorities, and people from non-Western cultures. They have also tended to neglect older adults, while depending much too heavily on white, middle- and upper-class college students. This excessive reliance on college students may not be all that problematic for some research questions, but it certainly seems likely to distort results in many research areas (Sears,

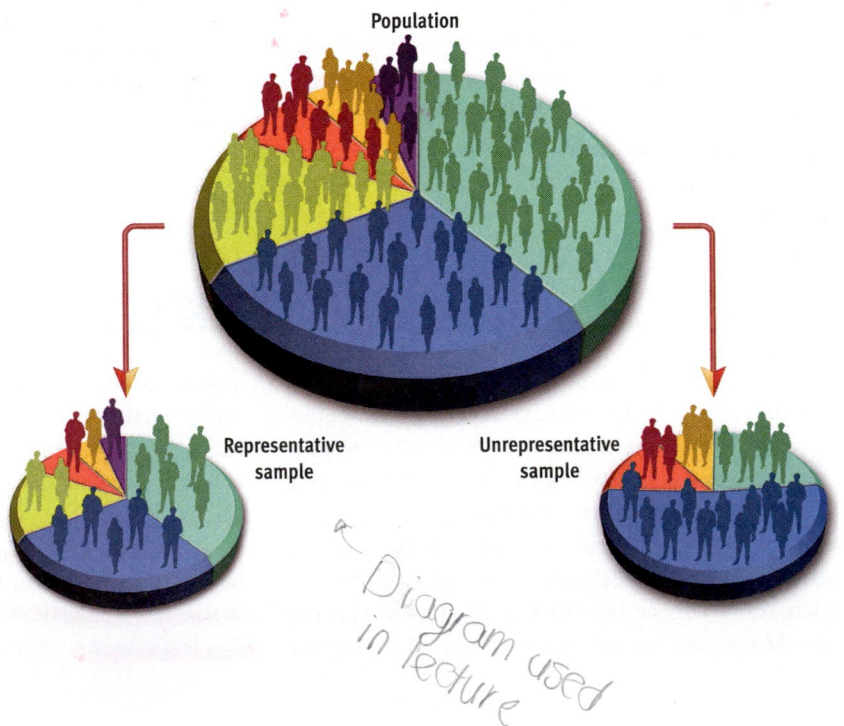

Figure 2.17

The relationship between the population and the sample. The process of drawing inferences about a population based on a sample only works if the sample is reasonably representative of the population. A sample is representative if its demographic makeup is similar to that of the population, as shown on the left. If some groups in the population are overrepresented or underrepresented in the sample, as shown on the right, inferences about the population may be skewed or inaccurate.

Population

Representative sample

Unrepresentative sample

Diagram used in lecture

Before accepting the results of a survey poll, one should know something about how the poll was conducted. A polling could, for instance, contain sampling bias. Opinions collected solely from middle-class people but generalized to the voting public as a whole would be an example of such bias.

1986). In general, then, when you have doubts about the results of a study, the first thing to examine is the composition of the sample.

Placebo Effects

In pharmacology, a *placebo* is a substance that resembles a drug but has no actual pharmacological effect. In studies that assess the effectiveness of medications, placebos are given to some subjects to control for the effects of a treacherous extraneous variable: participants' expectations. Placebos are used because researchers know that participants' expectations can influence their feelings, reactions, and behavior. Thus, *placebo effects* **occur when participants' expectations lead them to experience some change even though they receive empty, fake, or ineffectual treatment.** In medicine, placebo effects are well documented (Quitkin, 1999). Many physicians tell of patients being "cured" by prescriptions of sugar pills. Similarly, psychologists have found that participants' expectations can be powerful determinants of their perceptions and behavior when they are under the microscope in an empirical study.

For example, placebo effects have been seen in research on meditation. A number of studies have found that meditation can improve people's energy level, mental and physical health, and happiness (Alexander et al., 1990; Carrington, 1987). However, in many of the early studies of meditation, researchers assembled their experimental groups with volunteer subjects eager to learn meditation. Most of these subjects *wanted* and *expected* meditation to have beneficial effects. Their positive expectations may have colored their subsequent ratings of their energy level, happiness, and so on. Better-designed studies have shown that meditation can be beneficial (see Chapter 5). However, placebo effects have probably exaggerated these benefits in some studies (Shapiro, 1987).

Researchers should guard against placebo effects whenever subjects are likely to have expectations that a treatment will affect them in a certain way. The possible role of placebo effects can be assessed by including a fake version of the experimental treatment (a placebo condition) in a study. We saw the value of this approach in the Greenwald et al. (1991) study on the effects of subliminal self-help tapes. The mislabeled tapes served as a placebo treatment that allowed the researchers to control for the effects of participants' positive expectations about the subliminal audiotapes.

Distortions in Self-Report Data

Research psychologists often work with *self-report data*, consisting of subjects' verbal accounts of their behavior. This is the case whenever questionnaires, interviews, or personality inventories are used to measure variables. Self-report methods can be quite useful, taking advantage of the fact that people have a unique opportunity to observe themselves full-time (Baldwin, 2000). However, self-reports can be plagued by several kinds of distortion.

One of the most problematic of these distortions is the *social desirability bias,* which is a tendency to give socially approved answers to questions about oneself. Subjects who are influenced by this bias work overtime trying to create a favorable impression (DeMaio, 1984). For example, many survey respondents will report that they voted in an election or gave to a charity when in fact it is possible to determine that they did not (Granberg & Holmberg, 1991). Respondents influenced by social desirability bias also tend to report that they are healthier, happier, and less prejudiced than other types of evidence would suggest.

Other problems can also produce distortions in self-report data (Krosnick, 1999; Schuman & Kalton, 1985). Respondents misunderstand questionnaire items surprisingly often, and the way questions are worded can shape subjects' responses (Schwarz, 1999). Memory errors can undermine the accuracy of verbal reports. Response sets are yet another problem. A *response set is a tendency to respond to questions in a particular way that is unrelated to the content of the questions.* For example, some people tend to agree with nearly everything on a questionnaire (Krosnick & Fabrigar, 1998). Obviously, distortions like these can produce inaccurate results. Although researchers have devised ways to neutralize these problems—such as carefully pretesting survey instruments—we should be cautious in drawing conclusions from self-report data (Schaeffer, 2000).

Experimenter Bias

As scientists, psychologists try to conduct their studies in an objective, unbiased way so that their own views will not influence the results. However, objectivity is a *goal* that scientists strive for, not an accomplished fact that can be taken for granted (Mac-Coun, 1998). In reality, most researchers have an emotional investment in the outcome of their research. Often they are testing hypotheses that they have developed themselves and that they would like to see supported by the data. It is understandable, then, that *experimenter bias* is a possible source of error in research.

Experimenter bias occurs when a researcher's expectations or preferences about the outcome of a study influence the results obtained. Experimenter bias can slip through to influence studies in many subtle ways. One problem is that researchers, like others, sometimes *see what they want to see.* For instance, when experimenters make apparently honest mis-

CONCEPT **CHECK 2.4**

Detecting Flaws in Research

Check your understanding of how to conduct sound research by looking for methodological flaws in the following studies. You'll find the answers in Appendix A.

Study 1. A researcher announces that he will be conducting an experiment to investigate the detrimental effects of sensory deprivation on perceptual-motor coordination. The first 40 students who sign up for the study are assigned to the experimental group, and the next 40 who sign up serve in the control group. The researcher supervises all aspects of the study's execution. Experimental subjects spend two hours in a sensory deprivation chamber, where sensory stimulation is minimal. Control subjects spend two hours in a waiting room that contains magazines and a TV. All subjects then perform ten 1-minute trials on a pursuit-rotor task that requires them to try to keep a stylus on a tiny rotating target. The dependent variable is their average score on the pursuit-rotor task.

Study 2. A researcher wants to know whether there is a relationship between age and racial prejudice. She designs a survey in which respondents are asked to rate their prejudice against six different ethnic groups. She distributes the survey to over 500 people of various ages who are approached at a shopping mall in a low-income, inner-city neighborhood.

Check the flaws that are apparent in each study.

Methodological flaw	Study 1	Study 2	Methodological flaw	Study 1	Study 2
Sampling bias	_____	_____	Confounding of variables	_____	_____
Placebo effects	_____	_____	Experimenter bias	_____	_____
Distortions in self-report	_____	_____			

takes in recording subjects' responses, the mistakes tend to be heavily slanted in favor of supporting the hypothesis (O'Leary, Kent, & Kanowitz, 1975).

Research by Robert Rosenthal (1976) suggests that experimenter bias may lead researchers to unintentionally influence the behavior of their subjects. In one study, Rosenthal and Fode (1963) recruited undergraduate psychology students to serve as the "experimenters." The students were told that they would be collecting data for a study of how participants rated the success of people portrayed in photographs. In a pilot study, photos were selected that generated (on the average) neutral ratings on a scale extending from –10 (extreme failure) to +10 (extreme success). Rosenthal and Fode then manipulated the expectancies of their experimenters. Half of them were told that, based on pilot data, they would probably obtain average ratings of –5. The other half were led to expect average ratings of +5. The experimenters were forbidden from conversing with their subjects except for reading some standardized instructions. Even though the photographs were exactly the same for both groups, the experimenters who *expected* positive ratings *obtained* significantly higher ratings than those who expected negative ratings.

How could the experimenters have swayed the participants' ratings? According to Rosenthal, the experimenters may have unintentionally influenced their subjects by sending subtle nonverbal signals as the experiment progressed. Without realizing it, they may have smiled, nodded, or sent other positive cues when participants made ratings that were in line with the experimenters' expectations. Thus, experimenter bias may influence both researchers' observations and their subjects' behavior (Rosenthal, 1994).

The problems associated with experimenter bias can be neutralized by using a double-blind procedure. The *double-blind procedure* is a research strategy in which neither subjects nor experimenters know which subjects are in the experimental or control groups. It's not particularly unusual for participants to be "blind" about their treatment condition. However, the double-blind procedure keeps the experimenter in the dark as well. Of course, a member of the research team who isn't directly involved with subjects keeps track of who is in which group.

Courtesy of Robert Rosenthal

"*Quite unconsciously, a psychologist interacts in subtle ways with the people he is studying so that he may get the response he expects to get.*"
ROBERT ROSENTHAL

REVIEW OF KEY POINTS

- Scientists often try to replicate research findings to double-check their validity. Although this process leads to some contradictory findings, science works toward reconciling and explaining inconsistent results.

- Sampling bias occurs when a sample is not representative of the population of interest. Placebo effects occur when participants' expectations cause them to change their behavior in response to a fake treatment.

- Distortions in self-reports, such as response sets and the social desirability bias, are a source of concern whenever questionnaires and personality inventories are used to collect data. Experimenter bias occurs when researchers' expectations and desires distort their observations or unintentionally influence their subjects' behavior.

Looking at Ethics: Do the Ends Justify the Means?

Think back to Stanley Schachter's (1959) study on anxiety and affiliation. Imagine how you would have felt if you had been one of the subjects in Schachter's high-anxiety group. You show up at a research laboratory, expecting to participate in a harmless experiment. The room you are sent to is full of unusual electronic equipment. An official-looking man in a lab coat announces that this equipment will be used to give you a series of painful electric shocks. His statement that the shocks will leave "no permanent tissue damage" is hardly reassuring. Surely, you think, there must be a mistake. All of a sudden, your venture into research has turned into a nightmare! Your stomach knots up in anxiety. The researcher explains that there will be a delay while he prepares his apparatus. He asks you to fill out a short questionnaire

about whether you would prefer to wait alone or with others. Still reeling in dismay at the prospect of being shocked, you fill out the questionnaire. He takes it and then announces that you won't be shocked after all—it was all a hoax! Feelings of relief wash over you, but they're mixed with feelings of anger. You feel as though the experimenter has just made a fool out of you, and you're embarrassed and resentful.

Should researchers be allowed to play with your feelings in this way? Should they be permitted to deceive subjects in such a manner? Is this the cost that must be paid to advance scientific knowledge? As these questions indicate, the research enterprise sometimes presents scientists with difficult ethical dilemmas. *These dilemmas reflect concern about the possibility for inflicting harm on participants.* In psychological

PREVIEW QUESTIONS

- What are the arguments against using deception in research?
- What are the arguments in favor of allowing deception in research?
- Why are many people opposed to animal research?
- How do animal researchers defend their work?

research, the major ethical dilemmas center on the use of deception and the use of animals.

The Question of Deception

Elaborate deception, such as that seen in Schachter's study, has been fairly common in psychological research since the 1960s, especially in the area of social psychology (Epley & Huff, 1998; Korn, 1997). Over the years, psychologists have faked fights, thefts, muggings, faintings, epileptic seizures, rapes, and automobile breakdowns to explore a host of issues. They have led participants to believe that they were hurting others with electrical shocks, that they had homosexual tendencies, and that they were overhearing negative comments about themselves. Why have psychologists used so much deception in their research? Quite simply, they are trying to deal with the methodological problems discussed in the last section. Deception is used to avoid or reduce problems due to placebo effects, the unreliability of self-reports, and the like.

Critics argue against the use of deception on several grounds (Baumrind, 1985; Kelman, 1982; Ortmann & Hertwig, 1997). First, they assert that deception is only a nice word for lying, which they see as inherently immoral. Second, they argue that by deceiving unsuspecting participants, psychologists may undermine many individuals' trust in others. Third, they point out that many deceptive studies produce distress for participants who were not forewarned about that possibility. Specifically, subjects may experience great stress during a study or be made to feel foolish when the true nature of a study is explained.

Those who defend the use of deception in research maintain that many important issues could not be investigated if experimenters were not permitted to mislead participants (Bröder, 1998). They argue that most research deceptions involve "white lies" that are not likely to harm participants. Moreover, they point out that critics have *assumed* that deception studies are harmful to subjects, without collecting empirical data to document these detrimental effects. In reality, the relevant research suggests that deception studies are *not* harmful to participants (Christensen, 1988). Indeed, most subjects who participate in experiments involving deception report that they enjoyed the experience and that they didn't mind being misled. Moreover, the empirical evidence does not support the notions that deceptive research undermines subjects' trust in others, or their respect for psychology or scientific research (Kimmel, 1996; Sharpe, Adair, & Roese, 1992). Curi-

ously, the weight of the evidence suggests that researchers are more concerned about the negative effects of deception on participants than the participants themselves are (Fisher & Fyrberg, 1994; Korn, 1987). Finally, researchers who defend deception argue that the benefits—advances in knowledge that often improve human welfare—are worth the costs. They assert that it would be unethical *not* to conduct effective research on conformity, obedience, aggression, and other important social issues.

The issue of deception creates a difficult dilemma for scientists, pitting honesty against the desire to advance knowledge. Today, institutions that conduct research have committees that evaluate the ethics of research proposals before studies are allowed to proceed. These committees have often blocked studies requiring substantial deception. Many psychologists believe that this conservativism has obstructed important lines of research and slowed progress in the field. Although this belief may be true, it is not easy to write off the points made by the critics of deception. Warwick (1975) states the issue eloquently: "If it is all right to use deceit to advance knowledge, then why not for reasons of national security, for maintaining the Presidency, or to save one's own hide?" (p. 105). That's a tough question regarding a tough dilemma that will probably generate heated debate for a long time to come.

The Question of Animal Research

Psychology's other major ethics controversy concerns the use of animals in research. Psychologists use animals as research subjects for several reasons. Sometimes they simply want to know more about the behavior of a specific type of animal. In other instances, they want to see whether certain laws of behavior apply to both humans and animals. Finally, in some cases psychologists use animals because they can expose them to treatments that clearly would be unacceptable with human subjects. For example, most of the research on the relationship between deficient maternal nutrition during pregnancy and the incidence of birth defects has been done with animals.

It's this third reason for using animals that has generated most of the controversy. Some people maintain that it is wrong to subject animals to harm or pain for research purposes. Essentially, they argue that animals are entitled to the same rights as humans (Regan, 1997). They accuse researchers of violating these rights by subjecting animals to unnecessary cruelty in many "trivial" studies (Bowd & Shapiro,

1993; Hollands, 1989). They also assert that most animal studies are a waste of time because the results may not even apply to humans (Millstone, 1989). For example, Ulrich (1991) argues that "pigeons kept confined at 80% body weight in home cages that don't allow them ever to spread their wings, take a bath, or relate socially to other birds provide questionable models for humans" (pp. 200–201).

Although some animal rights activists simply advocate more humane treatment of research animals, a survey of 402 activists questioned at a Washington, D.C. rally found that 85% wanted to eliminate *all* research with animals (Plous, 1991). Some of the more militant animal rights activists have broken into laboratories, destroyed scientists' equipment and research records, and stolen experimental animals. According to David Johnson (1990), the animal rights movement has enjoyed considerable success. He notes that "the single issue citizens write about most often to their congresspersons and the President is not homelessness, not the drug problem, not crime. It is animal welfare" (p. 214).

In spite of the great furor, only 7%–8% of all psychological studies involve animals (mostly rodents and birds). Relatively few of these studies require subjecting the animals to painful or harmful manipula-

tions (American Psychological Association, 1984). Psychologists who defend animal research point to the major advances attributable to psychological research on animals, which many people are unaware of (Baldwin, 1993; Compton, Dietrich, & Smith, 1995). Among them are advances in the treatment of mental disorders, neuromuscular disorders, strokes, brain injuries, visual defects, headaches, memory defects, high blood pressure, and problems with pain (Carroll & Overmier, 2001; Domjan & Purdy, 1995). To put the problem in context, Neal Miller (1985), a prominent psychologist who has done pioneering work in several areas, noted the following:

At least 20 million dogs and cats are abandoned each year in the United States; half of them are killed in pounds and shelters, and the rest are hit by cars or die of neglect. Less than 1/10,000 as many dogs and cats were used in psychological laboratories. . . . Is it worth sacrificing the lives of our children in order to stop experiments, most of which involve no pain, on a vastly smaller number of mice, rats, dogs, and cats? (p. 427)

Far more compelling than Miller are the advocates for disabled people who have entered the fray to campaign against the animal rights movement in

Yale University

"*Who are the cruel and inhumane ones, the behavioral scientists whose research on animals led to the cures of the anorexic girl and the vomiting child, or those leaders of the radical animal activists who are making an exciting career of trying to stop all such research and are misinforming people by repeatedly asserting that it is without any value?***"**
NEAL MILLER

© James J. Broderick/International Stock

The use of rats and other animals in scientific research is now a major ethical issue. Researchers claim that experiments on animals often yield results and knowledge beneficial to humankind. Opponents maintain that humans have no right to subject animals to harm for research purposes. What is your view?

Figure 2.18

Ethics in research. Key ethical principles in psychological research, as set forth by the American Psychological Association (1992), are summarized here. These principles are meant to ensure the welfare of both human and animal subjects.

A P A   E t h i c a l   G u i d e l i n e s   f o r   R e s e a r c h

1 A subject's participation in research should be voluntary and based on informed consent. Subjects should never be coerced into participating in research. They should be informed in advance about any aspects of the study that might be expected to influence their willingness to cooperate. Furthermore, they should be permitted to withdraw from a study at any time if they so desire.

2 Participants should not be exposed to harmful or dangerous research procedures. This guideline is intended to protect subjects from psychological as well as physical harm. Thus, even stressful procedures that might cause emotional discomfort are largely prohibited. However, procedures that carry a modest risk of moderate mental discomfort may be acceptable.

3 If an investigation requires some deception of participants (about matters that do not involve risks), the researcher is required to explain and correct any misunderstandings as soon as possible. The deception must be disclosed to subjects in "debriefing" sessions as soon as it is practical to do so without compromising the goals of the study.

4 Subjects' rights to privacy should never be violated. Information about a subject that might be acquired during a study must be treated as highly confidential and should never be made available to others without the consent of the participant.

5 Harmful or painful procedures imposed upon animals must be thoroughly justified in terms of the knowledge to be gained from the study. Furthermore, laboratory animals are entitled to decent living conditions that are spelled out in detailed rules that relate to their housing, cleaning, feeding, and so forth.

6 Prior to conducting studies, approval should be obtained from host institutions and their research review committees. Research results should be reported fully and accurately, and raw data should be promptly shared with other professionals who seek to verify substantive claims. Retractions should be made if significant errors are found in a study subsequent to its publication.

Web Link 2.8

Office of Research Integrity
Anyone who needs a comprehensive, up-to-date overview of ethical concerns in research from the perspective of the U.S. government should consider visiting this site. Although the Office of Research Integrity (ORI) deals with research sponsored by the U.S. Public Health Service, it also offers links to parallel offices and resources in many other agencies.

recent years. For example, Dennis Feeney (1987), a psychologist disabled by paraplegia, quotes a newsletter from an organization called The Incurably Ill for Animal Research:

No one has stopped to think about those of us who are incurably ill and are desperately waiting for new research results that can only be obtained through the use of animals. We have seen successful advances toward other diseases, such as polio, diphtheria, mumps, measles, and hepatitis through animal research. We want the same chance for a cure, but animal rights groups would deny us this chance. (p. 595)

As you can see, the manner in which animals can ethically be used for research is a highly charged controversy. Psychologists are becoming increasingly sensitive to this issue. Although animals continue to be used in research, psychologists are taking greater pains to justify their use in relation to the potential benefits of the research. They are also striving to ensure that laboratory animals receive humane care.

The ethics issues that we have discussed in this section have led the APA to develop a set of ethical standards for researchers (American Psychological Association, 1992). Although most psychological studies are fairly benign, these ethical principles are intended to ensure that both human and animal subjects are treated with dignity. Some of the key guidelines in these ethical principles are summarized in Figure 2.18.

Putting It in Perspective

PREVIEW QUESTIONS
- How has this chapter demonstrated that psychology is empirical?
- How has this chapter illustrated the subjectivity of human experience?

Two of our seven unifying themes have emerged strongly in this chapter. First, the entire chapter is a testimonial to the idea that psychology is empirical. Second, the discussion of methodological flaws in research provides numerous examples of how people's experience of the world can be highly subjective. Let's examine each of these points in more detail.

As explained in Chapter 1, the empirical approach entails testing ideas, basing conclusions on systematic observation, and relying on a healthy brand of skepticism. All those features of the empirical approach have been apparent in our review of the research enterprise in psychology.

As you have seen, psychologists test their ideas by formulating clear hypotheses that involve predictions about relations between variables. They then use a variety of research methods to collect data so they can see whether their predictions are supported. The data collection methods are designed to make researchers' observations systematic and precise. The entire venture is saturated with skepticism. Psychologists are impressed only by research results that are highly unlikely to have occurred by chance. In planning and executing their research, they are constantly on the lookout for methodological flaws. They publish their findings so that other experts can subject their methods and conclusions to critical scrutiny. Collectively, these procedures represent the essence of the empirical approach.

The subjectivity of personal experience became apparent in the discussion of methodological problems, especially placebo effects and experimenter bias. When subjects report beneficial effects from a fake treatment (the placebo), it's because they expected to see these effects. As pointed out in Chapter 1, psychologists and other scientists are not immune to the effects of subjective experience. Although they are trained to be objective, even scientists may see what they expect to see or what they want to see. This is one reason that the empirical approach emphasizes precise measurement and a skeptical attitude. The highly subjective nature of experience is exactly what the empirical approach attempts to neutralize.

The publication of empirical studies allows us to apply a critical eye to the research enterprise. However, you cannot critically analyze studies unless you know where and how to find them. In the upcoming Personal Application, we will discuss where studies are published, how to find studies on specific topics, and how to read research reports. In the subsequent Critical Thinking Application, we'll analyze the shortcomings of anecdotal evidence, which should help you to appreciate the value of empirical evidence.

REVIEW OF KEY POINTS

- Research sometimes raises complex ethical issues. Critics argue that it is unethical to deceive subjects and to expose animals to harmful treatments. Those who defend deception in research argue that many important issues could not be investigated without misleading subjects.

- Psychologists who defend animal research argue that it has brought major advances that are worth the costs. The APA has formulated ethical principles to serve as guidelines for researchers.

- Two of the book's unifying themes are apparent in this chapter's discussion of the research enterprise in psychology: psychology is empirical, and people's experience of the world is highly subjective.

PERSONAL APPLICATION

Finding and Reading Journal Articles

Answer the following "yes" or "no."

____ **1** I have read about scientific studies in newspapers and magazines and sometimes wondered, "How did they come to those conclusions?"

____ **2** When I go to the library, I often have difficulty figuring out how to find information based on research.

____ **3** I have tried to read scientific reports and found them to be too technical and difficult to understand.

If you responded "yes" to any of the above statements, you have struggled with the information explosion in the sciences. We live in a research-oriented society. The number of studies conducted in most sciences is growing at a dizzying pace. This expansion has been particularly spectacular in psychology. Moreover, psychological research increasingly commands attention from the popular press because it is often relevant to people's personal concerns.

This Personal Application is intended to help you cope with the information explosion in psychology. It assumes that there may come a time when you need to examine original psychological research. Perhaps it will be in your role as a student (working on a term paper, for instance), in another role (parent, teacher, nurse, administrator), or merely out of curiosity. In any case, this Personal Application explains the nature of technical journals and discusses how to find and read articles in them. You can learn more about how to use library resources in psychology from an excellent little book titled *Library Use: A Handbook for Psychology* (Reed & Baxter, 1992).

The Nature of Technical Journals

As you will recall from earlier in the chapter, a *journal* is a periodical that publishes technical and scholarly material, usually in a narrowly defined area of inquiry. Scholars in most fields—whether economics, chemistry, education, or psychology—publish the bulk of their work in these journals. Journal articles represent the core of intellectual activity in any academic discipline.

In general, journal articles are written for other professionals in the field. Hence, authors assume that their readers are other interested economists or chemists or psychologists. Because journal articles are written in the special language unique to a particular discipline, they are often difficult for nonprofessionals to understand. You will be learning a great deal of psychology's special language in this course, which will improve your ability to understand articles in psychology journals.

In psychology, most journal articles are reports that describe original empirical studies. These reports permit researchers to disseminate their findings to the scientific community. Another common type of article is the review article. *Review articles* summarize and reconcile the findings of a large number of studies on a specific is-sue. Some psychology journals also publish comments or critiques of previously published research, book reviews, theoretical treatises, and descriptions of methodological innovations.

Finding Journal Articles

Reports of psychological research are commonly mentioned in newspapers and popular magazines. These summaries can be helpful to readers, but they often embrace the most sensational conclusions that might be drawn from the research. They also tend to include many oversimplifications and factual errors. Hence, if a study mentioned in the press is of interest to you, you may want to track down the original article to ensure that you get accurate information.

Most discussions of research in the popular press do not mention where you can find the original technical article. However, there is a way to find out. A computerized database called PsycINFO makes it possible to locate journal articles by specific researchers or scholarly work on specific topics. This huge, online database, which is updated constantly, contains brief summaries, or *abstracts,* of journal articles, books, and chapters in edited books, reporting, reviewing, or theorizing about psychological research. Over 1800 journals are checked regularly to select items for inclusion. The abstracts are concise—about 75 to 175 words. They briefly describe the hypotheses, methods, results, and conclusions

Craig McClain

of the studies. Each abstract should allow you to determine whether an article is relevant to your interests. If it is, you should be able to find the article in your library (or to order it) because a complete bibliographic reference is provided.

Although news accounts of research rarely mention where a study was published, they often mention the name of the researcher. If you have this information, the easiest way to find a specific article is to search PsycINFO for materials published by that researcher. For example, let's say you read a news report that summarizes an interesting study on whether alcohol hangovers affect managerial effectiveness in the business world that was published by Siegfried Streufert in the mid-1990s. To track down the original article, you would search for journal articles authored by Streufert. Given that you know the approximate year of publication, you could select the PsycINFO option to narrow your search to materials published between 1990 and 1996. If you conducted this search, you would turn up the list of 8 articles shown in Figure 2.19. The sixth item in the list appears to be the article you are interested in. Figure 2.20 on the next page shows what you would see if you clicked to obtain the Abstract and Citation for this article. As you can see, the abstract shows that the original report was published in the October 1995 issue of *Alcoholism: Clinical and Experimental Research*. Armed with this information, you could obtain the article easily.

You can also search PsycINFO for research literature on particular topics, such as achievement motivation, aggressive behavior, alcoholism, appetite disorders, or artistic ability. These computerized literature searches can be much more powerful, precise, and thorough than traditional, manual searches in a library. PsycINFO can sift through a couple million articles in a matter of seconds to identify *all* the articles on a subject, such as alcoholism. Obviously, there is no way you can match this efficiency stumbling around in the stacks at your library. Moreover, the computer allows you to pair up topics to swiftly narrow your search to exactly those issues that

interest you. For example, Figure 2.21 on the next page shows a PsycINFO search that identified all the articles on marijuana *and* memory. If you were preparing a term paper on whether marijuana affects memory, this precision would be invaluable.

The PsycINFO database can be accessed online at many libraries or via the Internet (see Web Link 2.2 on p. 41 for a description of PsycINFO Direct). The database is also available at some libraries that have the information stored on CD-ROM discs. This version of the database is updated monthly. The summaries contained in PsycINFO can also be found in a monthly print journal called *Psychological Abstracts*, but fewer and fewer libraries are subscribing to this traditional publication because it cannot match

Figure 2.19

Searching PsycINFO. If you searched PsycINFO for journal articles authored by Siegfried Streufert during the period of 1990–1996, the database would return the eight titles shown here. For each article, you can click to see its abstract or its full PsycINFO record (the abstract plus subject descriptors and other details). In some cases (depending on the version of PsycINFO that your library has ordered) you can even click to see the *full text* of some articles (those articles that appeared in journals published by APA in recent years).

SOURCE: Sample search reprinted with permission of the American Psychological Association, publisher of the PsycINFO® database. Copyright © 1887–present, American Psychological Association. All rights reserved. For more information contact psycinfo.apa.org.

found 8 documents, (8 returned).
for Your Query : *(streufert, siegfried):Author*

1. **Effects of alcohol intoxication on risk taking, strategy, and error rate in visuomotor performance.**
   By Streufert, Siegfried; Pogash, Rosanne M.; Roache, John D.; Gingrich, Dennis; et al
   Journal of Applied Psychology. 1992 Aug Vol 77(4) 515-524
   Abstract and Citation | Full PsycINFO Record | Full Text of Article

2. **Age and management team performance.**
   By Streufert, Siegfried; Pogash, Rosanne; Piasecki, Mary; Post, Gerald M.
   Psychology & Aging. 1990 Dec Vol 5(4) 551-559
   Abstract and Citation | Full PsycINFO Record | Full Text of Article

3. **Authoring of complex learning environments: Design considerations for dynamic simulations.**
   By Breuer, Klaus; Streufert, Siegfried
   Journal of Structural Learning. 1996 Nov Vol 12(4) 315-321
   Abstract and Citation | Full PsycINFO Record

4. **Effects of alprazolam on complex human functioning.**
   By Streufert, Siegfried; Satish, Usha; Pogash, Rosanne; Gingrich, Dennis; et al
   Journal of Applied Social Psychology. 1996 Nov Vol 26(21) 1912-1930
   Abstract and Citation | Full PsycINFO Record

5. **Effects of caffeine deprivation on complex human functioning.**
   By Streufert, Siegfried; Pogash, Rosanne; Miller, Jill; Gingrich, Dennis; et al
   Psychopharmacology. 1995 Apr Vol 118(4) 377-384
   Abstract and Citation | Full PsycINFO Record

6. **Alcohol hangover and managerial effectiveness.**
   By Streufert, Siegfried; Pogash, Rosanne; Braig, Daniela; Gingrich, Dennis; et al
   Alcoholism: Clinical & Experimental Research. 1995 Oct Vol 19(5) 1141-1146
   Abstract and Citation | Full PsycINFO Record

7. **Alcohol and management performance.**
   By Streufert, Siegfried; Pogash, Rosanne; Roache, John; Severs, Walter; et al
   Journal of Studies on Alcohol. 1994 Mar Vol 55(2) 230-238
   Abstract and Citation | Full PsycINFO Record

8. **Alcohol and complex functioning.**
   By Streufert, Siegfried; Pogash, Rosanne M.; Gingrich, Dennis; Kantner, Anne; et al
   Journal of Applied Social Psychology. 1993 Jun Vol 23(11) 847-866
   Abstract and Citation | Full PsycINFO Record

Figure 2.20

Example of a PsycINFO abstract. This information is what you would see if you clicked to see the abstract of item 6 in the list shown in Figure 2.19. It is a typical abstract from the online PsycINFO database. Each abstract in PsycINFO provides a summary of a specific journal article, book, or chapter in an edited book, and complete bibliographical information.

TITLE Alcohol hangover and managerial effectiveness.

ABSTRACT 21 male managers who normally drank moderate amounts of alcohol participated in a placebo-controlled, double-blind, crossover experiment to determine whether alcohol-induced hangovers would influence managerial/professional task performance characteristics. Ss consumed either placebo or alcoholic drinks to attain a breath alcohol level of 0.10 during the evening before participation in Strategic Management Simulations. By the following morning, breath alcohol levels were measured at 0.00. Questionnaire responses indicated considerable hangover discomfort. Responses to semantic differential evaluative scales suggested that Ss evaluated their own managerial performance in the simulation setting as impaired. However, multiple measures of decision-making performance obtained in the simulation task did not show any deterioration of functioning. (PsycINFO Database Record © 2000 APA, all rights reserved)

AUTHOR *Streufert, Siegfried;* Pogash, Rosanne; Braig, Daniela; Gingrich, Dennis; et al

AFFILIATION Pennsylvania State U, Coll of Medicine, Dept of Behavioral Science, Hershey, USA

SOURCE Alcoholism: Clinical & Experimental Research. 1995 Oct Vol 19(5) 1141-1146

Figure 2.21

Combining topics in a PsycINFO search. A computerized literature search can be a highly efficient way to locate the specific research that you need. For example, if you had set out in April of 2002 to find all the psychological research on marijuana and memory, using PsycINFO DIRECT (the version of PsycINFO available to the public), you would have obtained the results summarized here. At that time, the database contained 84,682 abstracts related to memory and 2076 abstracts related to marijuana (with dissertations excluded). The search depicted on the left yielded 81 abstracts that relate to both marijuana and memory. Thus, in a matter of moments, the computer can sift through nearly 2 million abstracts to find those that are most germane to a specific question, such as: Does marijuana affect memory?

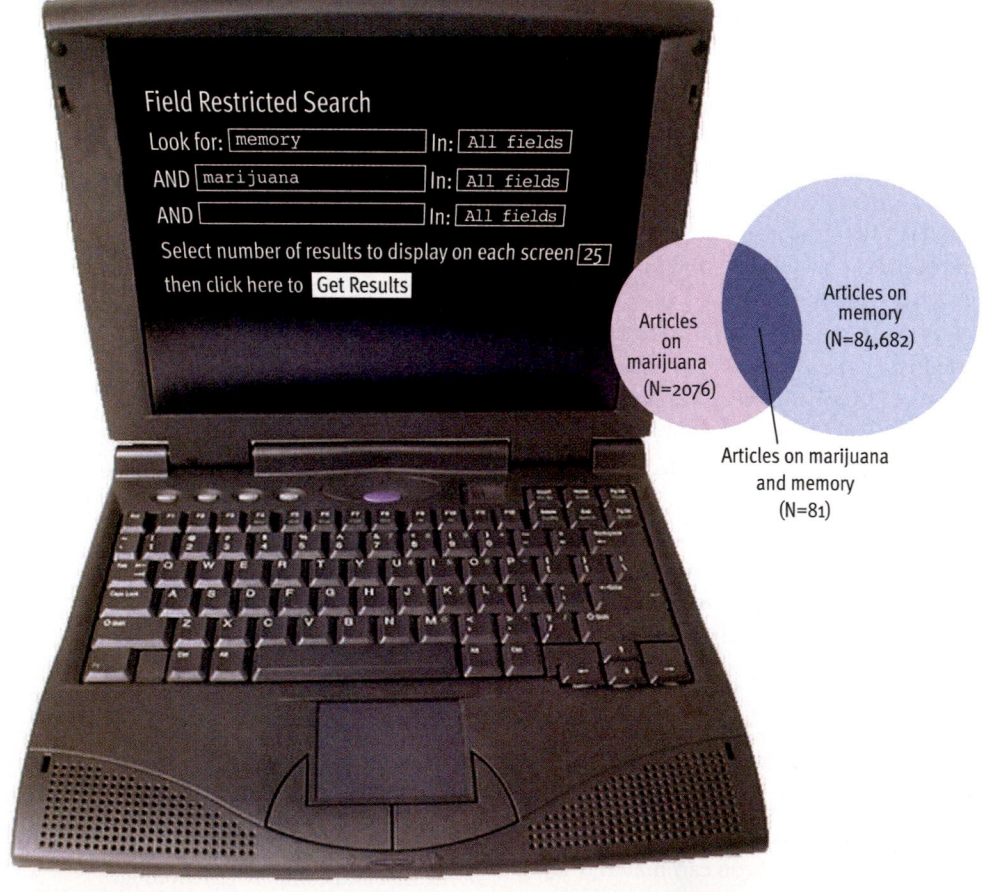

the swift and efficient search capabilities of PsycINFO.

Reading Journal Articles

Once you find the journal articles you want to examine, you need to know how to decipher them. You can process the information in such articles more efficiently if you understand how they are organized. Depending on your needs and purpose, you may want to simply skim through some of the sections. Journal articles follow a fairly standard organization, which includes the following sections and features.

Abstract

Most journals print a concise summary at the beginning of each article. This abstract allows readers scanning the journal to quickly decide whether articles are relevant to their interests.

Introduction

The introduction presents an overview of the problem studied in the research. It mentions relevant theories and quickly reviews previous research that bears on the problem, usually citing shortcomings in previous research that necessitate the present study. This review of the current state of knowledge on the topic usually progresses to a specific and precise statement regarding the hypotheses under investigation.

Method

The method section provides a thorough description of the research methods used in the study. Information is provided on the subjects used, the procedures followed, and the data collection techniques employed. This description is made detailed enough to permit another researcher to attempt to replicate the study.

Results

The data obtained in the study are reported in the results section. This section often creates problems for novice readers because it includes complex statistical analyses, figures, tables, and graphs. This section does *not* include any inferences based on the data, as such conclusions are supposed to follow in the next section. Instead, it simply contains a concise summary of the raw data and the statistical analyses.

Discussion

In the discussion section you will find the conclusions drawn by the author(s). In contrast to the results section, which is a straightforward summary of empirical observations, the discussion section allows for interpretation and evaluation of the data. Implications for theory and factual knowledge in the discipline are discussed. Conclusions are usually qualified carefully, and any limitations in the study may be ac-

knowledged. This section may also include suggestions for future research on the issue.

References

At the end of each article you will find a list of bibliographic references for any studies cited. This list permits you to examine first-hand other relevant studies mentioned in the article. The references list is often a rich source of leads about other articles that are germane to the topic that you are looking into.

The Perils of Anecdotal Evidence: "I Have a Friend Who . . ."

Here's a tough problem. Suppose you are the judge in a family law court. As you look over the cases that will come before you today, you see that one divorcing couple have managed to settle almost all of the important decisions with minimal conflict—such as who gets the house, who gets the car and the dog, and who pays which bills. However, there is one crucial issue left: Each parent wants custody of the children, and because they could not reach an agreement on their own, the case is now in your court. You will need the wisdom of the legendary King Solomon for this decision. How can you determine what is in the best interests of the children?

Child custody decisions have major consequences for all of the parties involved. As you review the case records, you see that both parents are loving and competent, so there are no obvious reasons for selecting one parent over the other as the primary caretaker. In considering various alternatives, you mull over the possibility of awarding *joint custody,* an arrangement in which the children spend half their time with each parent, instead of the more usual arrangement where one parent has primary custody and the other has visitation rights. Joint custody seems to have some obvious benefits, but you are not sure how well these arrangements actually work. Will the children feel more attached to both parents if the parents share custody equally? Or will the children feel hassled by always moving around, perhaps spending half the week at one parent's home and half at the other parent's home? Can parents who are already feuding over child custody issues make these complicated arrangements work? Or is joint custody just too disruptive to everyone's life? You really

don't know the answer to any of these vexing questions.

One of the lawyers involved in the case knows that you are thinking about the possibility of joint custody. She also understands that you want more information about how well joint custody tends to work before you render a decision. To help you make up your mind, she tells you about a divorced couple that has had a joint custody arrangement for many years and offers to have them appear in court to describe their experiences "firsthand." They and their children can answer any questions you might have about the pros and cons of joint custody. They should be in the best position to know how well joint custody works because they are living it. Sounds like a reasonable plan. What do you think?

Hopefully, you said, "No, No, No!" What's wrong with asking someone who's been there how well joint custody works? The crux of the problem is that the evidence a single family brings to the question of joint custody is **anecdotal evidence, which consists of personal stories about specific incidents and experiences.** Anecdotal evidence can be very seductive. For example, one study found that psychology majors' choices of future courses to enroll in were influenced more by a couple of students' brief anecdotes than by extensive statistics on many other students' ratings of the courses from the previous term (Borgida & Nisbett, 1977). Anecdotes readily sway people because they often are concrete, vivid, and memorable. Indeed, people tend to be influenced by anecdotal information even when they are explicitly forewarned that the information is *not* representative (Hammill, Wilson, & Nisbett, 1980). Many poli-

ticians are keenly aware of the power of anecdotes and they frequently rely on a single vivid story rather than solid data to sway voters' views. However, anecdotal evidence is fundamentally flawed.

What, exactly, is wrong with anecdotal evidence? Let's use some of the concepts introduced in the main body of the chapter to analyze the shortcomings of anecdotal evidence. First, in the language of research designs, the anecdotal experiences of one family resemble a single *case study.* The story they tell about their experiences with joint custody may be quite interesting, but their experiences—good or bad—cannot be used to generalize to other couples. Why not? Because they are only one family, and they may be unusual in some way that affects how well they manage joint custody. To draw general conclusions based on the case study approach, you need a systematic series of case studies, so you can look for threads of consistency. A single family is a sample size of one, which surely is not large enough to derive broad principles that would apply to other families.

Second, anecdotal evidence is similar to *self-report data,* which can be distorted for a variety of reasons, such as people's tendency to give socially approved information about themselves (the *social desirability bias*). When researchers use tests and surveys to gather self-report data, they can take steps to reduce or assess the impact of distortions in their data, but there are no comparable safeguards with anecdotal evidence. Thus, the family that appears in your courtroom may be eager to make a good impression and unknowingly slant their story accordingly.

Anecdotes are often inaccurate and riddled with embellishments. We will see in

People in politics understand the enormous power of a compelling anecdote. For example, former President Ronald Reagan had a marvelous ability to use anecdotes to make his points. Actress Shirley MacLaine's widely read stories of past lives also illustrate how anecdotes can spark interest. However, as the text explains, anecdotal evidence is flawed in many ways.

Chapter 7 that memories of personal experiences are far more malleable and far less reliable than widely assumed (Roediger, Wheeler, & Rajaram, 1993). And, although it would not be an issue in this case, in other situations *anecdotal evidence often consists of stories that people have heard about others' experiences.* Hearsay evidence is not accepted in courtrooms for good reason. As stories are passed on from one person to another, they often become increasingly distorted and inaccurate.

Can you think of any other reasons for being wary of anecdotal evidence? After reading the chapter, perhaps you thought about the possibility of *sampling bias.* Do you think that the lawyer will pick a couple at random from all those who have been awarded joint custody? It seems highly unlikely. If she wants you to award joint custody, she will find a couple for whom this arrangement worked very well; and if she wants you to award sole custody to her client, she will find a couple whose inability to make joint custody work had dire consequences for their children. One reason people love to work with anecdotal evidence is that it is so readily manipulated; they can usually find an anecdote or two to support their position, whether or not these anecdotes are representative of most people's experiences.

If the testimony of one family cannot be used in making this critical custody decision, what sort of evidence should you be looking for? One goal of effective critical thinking is to make decisions based on solid evidence. This process is called *evidence-based decision-making.* In this case, you would need to consider the overall experiences of a large sample of families who have tried joint custody arrangements. In general, across many different families, did the children in joint custody develop well? Was there a disproportionately high rate of emotional problems or other signs of stress for the children or the parents? Was the percentage of families who returned to court at a later date to change their joint custody arrangements higher than for other types of custody arrangements? You can probably think of additional information that you would want to collect regarding the outcomes of various custody arrangements.

In examining research reports, many people recognize the need to evaluate the evidence by looking for the types of flaws described in the main body of the chapter (sampling bias, experimenter bias, and so forth). Curiously, though, many of the same people then fail to apply the same principles of good evidence to their personal decisions in everyday life. The tendency to rely on the anecdotal experiences of a small number of people is sometimes called the *"I have a friend who" syndrome,* because no matter what the topic is, it seems that someone will provide a personal story about a friend as evidence for his or her particular point of view. In short, when you hear people support their assertions with personal stories, a little skepticism is in order.

Table 2.3 Critical Thinking Skills Discussed in This Application	
Skill	**Description**
Recognizing the limitations of anecdotal evidence	The critical thinker is wary of anecdotal evidence, which consists of personal stories used to support one's assertions. Anecdotal evidence tends to be unrepresentative, inaccurate, and unreliable.
Using evidence-based decision making	The critical thinker understands the need to seek sound evidence to guide decisions in everyday life.

RECAP

Key Ideas

Looking for Laws: The Scientific Approach to Behavior

● The scientific approach assumes that there are laws of behavior that can be discovered through empirical research. The goals of the science of psychology include (1) the measurement and description of behavior, (2) the understanding and prediction of behavior, and (3) the application of this knowledge to the task of controlling behavior.

● By integrating apparently unrelated facts into a coherent whole, theories permit psychologists to make the leap from the description of behavior to understanding behavior.

● A scientific investigation follows a systematic pattern that includes five steps: (1) formulate a testable hypothesis, (2) select the research method and design the study, (3) collect the data, (4) analyze the data and draw conclusions, and (5) report the findings. The two major advantages of the scientific approach are its clarity in communication and its relative intolerance of error.

Looking for Causes: Experimental Research

● Experimental research involves the manipulation of an independent variable to ascertain its effect on a dependent variable. This research is usually done by comparing experimental and control groups, which must be alike in regard to important extraneous variables.

● Experimental designs may vary. For example, sometimes an experimental group serves as its own control group. And many experiments have more than one independent variable or more than one dependent variable. Some of these variations were seen in the Featured Study. This experiment suggested that subliminal self-help audiotapes are unlikely to increase self-esteem or improve memory.

● An experiment is a powerful research method that permits conclusions about cause-effect relationships between variables. However, the experimental method is often not usable for a specific problem, and many experiments tend to be artificial.

Looking for Links: Descriptive/Correlational Research

● Psychologists rely on descriptive/correlational research when they are unable to manipulate the variables they want to study. Key descriptive methods include naturalistic observation, case studies, and surveys.

● Descriptive/correlational research methods allow psychologists to explore issues that might not be open to experimental investigation.

However, these research methods cannot demonstrate cause-effect relationships.

Looking for Conclusions: Statistics and Research

● Psychologists use descriptive statistics, such as measures of central tendency and variability, to organize and summarize their numerical data. The mean, median, and mode are widely used measures of central tendency. Variability is usually measured with the standard deviation.

● Correlations may be either positive (when two variables co-vary in the same direction) or negative (when two variables co-vary in the opposite direction). The closer a correlation is to either +1.00 or -1.00, the stronger the association. Higher correlations yield greater predictability. However, a correlation is no assurance of causation.

● Hypothesis testing involves deciding whether observed findings support the researcher's hypothesis. Findings are statistically significant only when they are unlikely to be due to chance.

Looking for Flaws: Evaluating Research

● Scientists often try to replicate research findings to double-check their validity. Sampling bias occurs when a sample is not representative of the population of interest. Placebo effects occur when subjects' expectations cause them to change their behavior in response to a fake treatment.

● Distortions in self-reports are a source of concern whenever questionnaires and personality inventories are used to collect data. Experimenter bias occurs when researchers' expectations and desires distort their observations or unintentionally influence their subjects' behavior.

Looking at Ethics: Do the Ends Justify the Means?

● Research sometimes raises complex ethical issues. In psychology, the key questions concern the use of deception with human subjects and the use of harmful or painful manipulations with animal subjects. The APA has formulated ethical principles to serve as guidelines for researchers.

Putting It in Perspective

● Two of the book's unifying themes are apparent in this chapter's discussion of the research enterprise in psychology: psychology is empirical, and people's experience of the world can be highly subjective.

Personal Application • Finding and Reading Journal Articles

● Journals publish technical and scholarly material. Usually they are written for other professionals in a narrow area of inquiry.

● PsycINFO is a computerized database that contains brief summaries of published journal articles, books, and chapters in edited books. Works on specific topics and publications by specific authors can be found by using the search mechanisms built into the database.

● Journal articles are easier to understand if one is familiar with the standard format. Most articles include six elements: abstract, introduction, method, results, discussion, and references.

Critical Thinking Application • The Perils of Anecdotal Evidence: "I Have a Friend Who . . ."

● Anecdotal evidence consists of personal stories about specific incidents and experiences. Anecdotes often influence people because they tend to be concrete, vivid, and memorable.

● However, anecdotal evidence is usually based on the equivalent of a single case study, which is not an adequate sample, and there are no safeguards to reduce the distortion often found in self-report data. Many anecdotes are inaccurate, second-hand reports of others' experiences. Effective critical thinking depends on evidence-based decision making.

Key Terms

Anecdotal evidence
Case study
Confounding of variables
Control group
Correlation
Correlation coefficient
Data collection techniques
Dependent variable
Descriptive statistics
Double-blind procedure
Experiment
Experimental group
Experimenter bias
Extraneous variables
Hypothesis
Independent variable
Inferential statistics
Journal
Mean
Median
Mode
Naturalistic observation
Operational definition
Participants
Placebo effects
Population
Random assignment
Replication
Research methods
Response set
Sample
Sampling bias
Social desirability bias
Standard deviation
Statistical significance
Statistics
Subjects
Survey
Theory
Variability
Variables

Key People

Neal Miller
Robert Rosenthal
Stanley Schachter

1. A tentative prediction about the relationship between two variables is:
   A. a confounding of variables.
   B. an operational definition.
   C. a theory.
   D. a hypothesis.

2. Researchers must describe the actions that will be taken to measure or control each variable in their studies. In other words, they must:
   A. provide operational definitions of their variables.
   B. decide if their studies will be experimental or correlational.
   C. use statistics to summarize their findings.
   D. decide how many subjects should participate in their studies.

3. A researcher found that clients who were randomly assigned to same-sex groups participated more in group therapy sessions than clients who were randomly assigned to coed groups. In this experiment, the independent variable was:
   A. the amount of participation in the group therapy sessions.
   B. whether or not the group was coed.
   C. the clients' attitudes toward group therapy.
   D. how much the clients' mental health improved.

4. A researcher wants to see whether a protein-enriched diet will enhance the maze-running performance of rats. One group of rats are fed the high-protein diet for the duration of the study; the other group continues to receive ordinary rat chow. In this experiment, the diet fed to the two groups of rats is the _____ variable.
   A. correlated
   B. control
   C. dependent
   D. independent

5. In a study of the effect of a new teaching technique on students' achievement test scores, an important extraneous variable would be the students':
   A. hair color.
   B. athletic skills.
   C. IQ scores.
   D. sociability.

6. Whenever you have a cold, you rest in bed, take aspirin, and drink plenty of fluids. You can't determine which remedy is most effective because of which of the following problems?
   A. sampling bias
   B. distorted self-report data
   C. confounding of variables
   D. experimenter bias

7. A psychologist monitors a group of nursery-school children, recording each instance of altruistic behavior as it occurs. The psychologist is using:
   A. the experimental method.
   B. naturalistic observation.
   C. case studies.
   D. the survey method.

8. Among the advantages of descriptive/correlational research is (are):
   A. it allows investigators to isolate cause and effect.
   B. it permits researchers to study variables that would be impossible to manipulate.
   C. it can demonstrate conclusively that two variables are causally related.
   D. a and b.

9. Which of the following correlation coefficients would indicate the strongest relationship between two variables?
   A. .58   C. −.97
   B. .19   D. −.05

10. When psychologists say that their results are statistically significant, they mean that the results:
    A. have important practical applications.
    B. have important implications for scientific theory.
    C. are unlikely to be due to the fluctuations of chance.
    D. all of the above.

11. Sampling bias exists when:
    A. the sample is representative of the population.
    B. the sample is not representative of the population.
    C. two variables are confounded.
    D. the effect of the independent variable can't be isolated.

12. The problem of experimenter bias can be avoided by:
    A. not informing subjects of the hypothesis of the experiment.
    B. telling the subjects that there are no "right" or "wrong" answers.
    C. using a research strategy in which neither subjects nor experimenter know which subjects are in the experimental and control groups.
    D. having the experimenter use only nonverbal signals when communicating with the subjects.

13. Critics of deception in research have assumed that deceptive studies are harmful to subjects. The empirical data on this issue suggest that:
    A. many deceptive studies do produce significant distress for subjects who were not forewarned about the possibility of deception.
    B. most participants in deceptive studies report that they enjoyed the experience and didn't mind being misled.
    C. deceptive research seriously undermines subjects' trust in others.
    D. a and c.

14. PsycINFO is:
    A. a new journal that recently replaced *Psychological Abstracts*.
    B. a computerized database containing abstracts of articles, chapters, and books reporting psychological research.
    C. a reference book that explains the format and techniques for writing journal articles.
    D. a computerized database containing information about studies that have not yet been published.

15. Anecdotal evidence:
    A. is often concrete, vivid, and memorable.
    B. tends to influence people.
    C. is fundamentally flawed and unreliable.
    D. is all of the above.

Answers

1	D p. 38	6	C p. 44	11	B p. 58
2	A p. 39	7	B p. 48	12	C p. 61
3	B pp. 42–43	8	B p. 52	13	B p. 62
4	D pp. 42–43	9	C p. 55	14	B pp. 66–67
5	C pp. 43–44	10	C p. 57	15	D p. 70

 ON THE WEB

For additional resources on the topics covered in this chapter, visit the *Psychology: Themes and Variations* Web site, where you will find practice quizzes, tutorials, Web links, simulations, critical thinking activities, flash cards, interactive exercises, and suggested readings available through INFOTRAC.

http://psychology.wadsworth.com/weiten_themes6e/

CHAPTER 3

© Francisco Cruz/Super Stock

The Biological Bases of Behavior

If you have ever visited an aquarium, you may have encountered one of nature's more captivating animals: the octopus. Although this jellylike mass of arms and head appears to be a relatively simple creature, it is capable of a number of interesting behaviors. The octopus has highly developed eyes that enable it to respond to stimuli in the darkness of the ocean. When threatened, it can release an inky cloud to befuddle enemies while it makes good its escape by a kind of rocket propulsion. If that doesn't work, it can camouflage itself by changing color and texture to blend into its surroundings. Furthermore, the animal is surprisingly intelligent. In captivity, an octopus can learn, for example, to twist the lid off a jar with one of its tentacles to get at a treat inside.

Despite its talents, there are many things an octopus cannot do. An octopus cannot study psychology, plan a weekend, dream about its future, or discover the Pythagorean theorem. Yet the biological processes that underlie these uniquely human behaviors are much the same as the biological processes that enable an octopus to escape from a predator or forage for food. Indeed, some of science's most important insights about how the nervous system works came from studies of a relative of the octopus, the squid.

Organisms as diverse as humans and squid share many biological processes. However, their unique behavioral capacities depend on the differences in their physiological makeup. You and I have a larger repertoire of behaviors than the octopus in large part because we come equipped with a more complex brain and nervous system. The activity of the human brain is so complex that no computer has ever come close to duplicating it. Your nervous system contains as many cells busily integrating and relaying information as there are stars in our galaxy. Whether you are scratching your nose or composing an essay, the activity of those cells underlies what you do. It is little wonder, then, that many psychologists have dedicated themselves to exploring the biological bases of behavior.

How do mood-altering drugs work? Are the two halves of the brain specialized to perform different functions? What happens inside the body when you feel a strong emotion? Are some mental illnesses the result of chemical imbalances in the brain? To what extent is intelligence determined by biological inheritance? These questions only begin to suggest the countless ways in which biology is fundamental to the study of behavior.

© Francisco Cruz/Super Stock

Communication in the Nervous System

Imagine that you are watching a scary movie. As the tension mounts, your palms sweat and your heart beats faster. You begin shoveling popcorn into your mouth, carelessly spilling some in your lap. If someone were to ask you what you are doing at this moment, you would probably say, "Nothing—just watching the movie." Yet some highly complex processes are occurring without your thinking about them. A stimulus (the light from the screen) is striking your eye. Almost instantaneously, your brain is interpreting the light stimulus, and signals are flashing to other parts of your body, leading to a flurry of activity. Your sweat glands are releasing perspiration, your heartbeat is quickening, and muscular move-

ments are enabling your hand to find the popcorn and, more or less successfully, lift it to your mouth.

Even in this simple example, you can see that behavior depends on rapid information processing. Information travels almost instantaneously from your eye to your brain, from your brain to the muscles of your arm and hand, and from your palms back to your brain. In essence, your nervous system is a complex communication network in which signals are constantly being transmitted, received, and integrated. The nervous system handles information, just as the circulatory system handles blood. In this section, we take a close look at communication in the nervous system.

PREVIEW QUESTIONS
- What are the key parts of the neuron, and what are their functions?
- What is an action potential?
- How does synaptic transmission take place?
- Which neurotransmitters regulate which aspects of behavior?

Nervous Tissue: The Basic Hardware

Your nervous system is living tissue composed of cells. The cells in the nervous system fall into two major categories: *glia* and *neurons*. *Glia* are cells found throughout the nervous system that provide structural support, nourishment, and insulation for neurons. Glia (literally "glue") help maintain the chemical environment of the neurons, which promotes more efficient signaling in the nervous system (Kandel, 2000). **Neurons are individual cells in the nervous system that receive, integrate, and transmit information.** They are the basic links that permit communication within the nervous system. The vast majority of them communicate only with other neurons. However, a small minority receive signals from outside the nervous system (from sensory organs) or carry messages from the nervous system to the muscles that move the body.

A highly simplified drawing of two "typical" neurons is shown in Figure 3.1. Actually, neurons come in such a tremendous variety of types and shapes that no single drawing can adequately represent them. Trying to draw the "typical" neuron is like trying to draw the "typical" tree. In spite of this diversity, the drawing in Figure 3.1 highlights some common features of neurons.

The *soma*, or cell body, contains the cell nucleus and much of the chemical machinery common to most cells (*soma* is Greek for "body"). The rest of the neuron is devoted exclusively to handling information. The neurons in Figure 3.1 have a number of branched, feelerlike structures called *dendritic trees* (*dendrite* is a Greek word for "tree"). Each individual branch is a *dendrite*. **Dendrites are the parts of a neuron that are specialized to receive information.**

Most neurons receive information from many other cells—sometimes thousands of others—and so have extensive dendritic trees.

From the many dendrites, information flows into the cell body and then travels away from the soma along the *axon* (from the Greek for "axle"). **The *axon* is a long, thin fiber that transmits signals away from the soma to other neurons or to muscles or glands.** Axons may be quite long (sometimes several feet), and they may branch off to communicate with a number of other cells.

In humans, many axons are wrapped in cells with a high concentration of a white, fatty substance called *myelin*. **The *myelin sheath* is insulating material, derived from glial cells, that encases some axons.** The myelin sheath speeds up the transmission of signals that move along axons. If an axon's myelin sheath deteriorates, its signals may not be transmitted effectively. The loss of muscle control seen with the disease *multiple sclerosis* is due to a degeneration of myelin sheaths (Schwartz & Westbrook, 2000).

The axon ends in a cluster of ***terminal buttons*, which are small knobs that secrete chemicals called neurotransmitters.** These chemicals serve as messengers that may activate neighboring neurons. The points at which neurons interconnect are called *synapses*. **A *synapse* is a junction where information is transmitted from one neuron to another** (*synapse* is from the Greek for "junction").

To summarize, information is received at the dendrites, is passed through the soma and along the axon, and is transmitted to the dendrites of other cells at meeting points called synapses. Unfortunately, this nice, simple picture has more exceptions than the U.S. Tax Code. For example, some neurons do not have an axon, while others have multiple axons. Also, although neurons typically synapse on the dendrites

Structure of the neuron.

Neurons are the communication links of the nervous system. This diagram highlights the key parts of a neuron, including specialized receptor areas (dendrites), the cell body (soma), the axon fiber along which impulses are transmitted, and the terminal buttons, which release chemical messengers that carry signals to other neurons. Neurons vary considerably in size and shape and are usually densely interconnected.

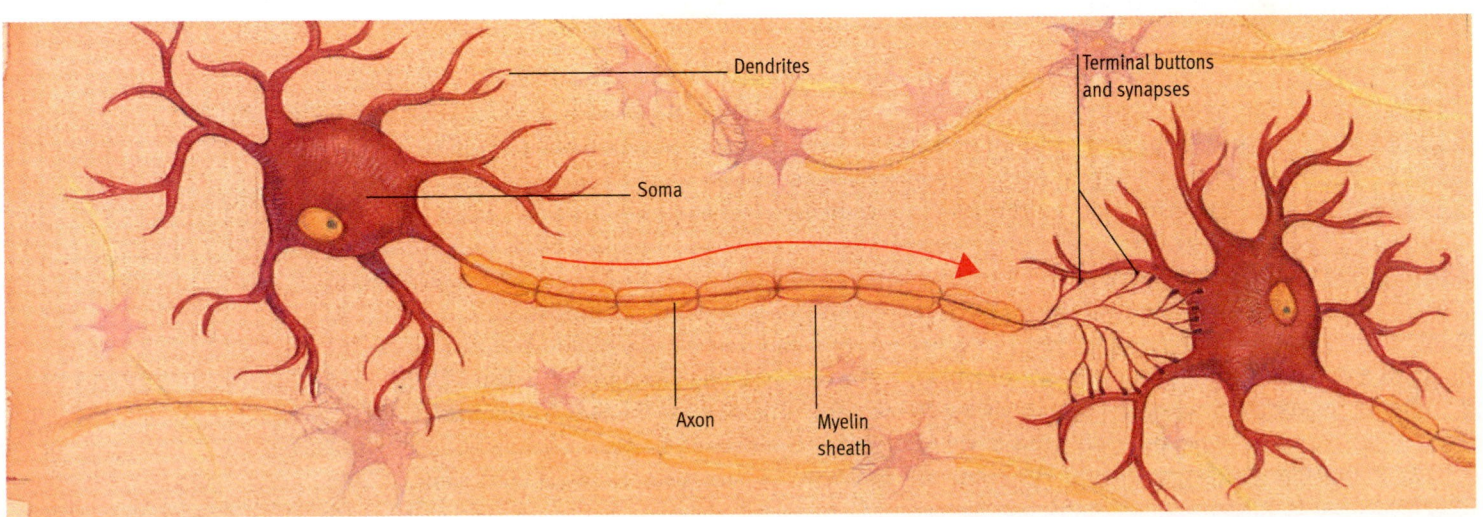

Dendrites

Terminal buttons and synapses

Soma

Axon

Myelin sheath

of other cells, they may also synapse on a soma or an axon. Despite these and other complexities, however, the fundamental function of neurons is clear: they are the nervous system's input-output devices that transmit, receive, and integrate informational signals.

The Neural Impulse: Using Energy to Send Information

What happens when a neuron is stimulated? What is the nature of the signal—the *neural impulse*—that moves through the neuron? These were the questions that Alan Hodgkin and Andrew Huxley set out to answer in their groundbreaking experiments with axons removed from squid. Why did they choose to work with squid axons? Because the squid has a pair of "giant" axons that are about a hundred times larger than those in humans (which still makes them only about as thick as a human hair). Their large size permitted Hodgkin and Huxley to insert fine wires called *microelectrodes* into them. By using the microelectrodes to record the electrical activity in individual neurons, Hodgkin and Huxley unraveled the mystery of the neural impulse.

The Neuron at Rest: A Tiny Battery

Hodgkin and Huxley (1952) learned that the neural impulse is a complex electrochemical reaction. Both inside and outside the neuron are fluids containing electrically charged atoms and molecules called *ions*. Positively charged sodium and potassium ions and negatively charged chloride ions flow back and forth across the cell membrane, but they do not cross at the same rate. The difference in flow rates leads to a slightly higher concentration of negatively charged ions inside the cell. The resulting voltage means that the neuron at rest is a tiny battery, a store of potential energy. The *resting potential* of a neuron is its stable, negative charge when the cell is inactive. As shown in Figure 3.2(a) on the next page, this charge is about –70 millivolts, roughly one-twentieth of the voltage of a flashlight battery.

The Action Potential

As long as the voltage of a neuron remains constant, the cell is quiet, and no messages are being sent. When the neuron is stimulated, channels in its cell membrane open, briefly allowing positively charged sodium ions to rush in, as shown in Figure 3.2(c). For an instant, the neuron's charge is less negative, or even positive, creating an action potential (Koester & Siegelbaum, 2000). An *action potential* is a very brief shift in a neuron's electrical charge that trav-

els along an axon. The firing of an action potential is reflected in the voltage spike shown in Figure 3.2 (b). Like a spark traveling along a trail of gunpowder, the voltage change races down the axon.

After the firing of an action potential, the channels in the cell membrane that opened to let in sodium close up, as shown in Figure 3.2(d and e). Some time is needed before they are ready to open again, and until that time the neuron cannot fire. The *absolute refractory period* is the minimum length of time after an action potential during which another action potential cannot begin. This "down time" isn't very long, only 1 or 2 milliseconds. It is followed by a brief *relative refractory period*. During the relative refractory period, the neuron can fire, but its threshold for firing is elevated, so more intense stimulation is required to initiate an action potential.

The All-or-None Law

The neural impulse is an all-or-none proposition, like firing a gun. You can't half-fire a gun. The same is true of the neuron's firing of action potentials. Either the neuron fires or it doesn't, and its action potentials are all the same size (Kandel, 2000). That is, weaker stimuli do not produce smaller action potentials.

Even though the action potential is an all-or-nothing event, neurons *can* convey information about the strength of a stimulus. They do so by varying the *rate* at which they fire action potentials. In general, a stronger stimulus will cause a cell to fire a more rapid volley of neural impulses than a weaker stimulus will.

Various neurons transmit neural impulses at different speeds. For example, thicker axons transmit neural impulses more rapidly than thinner ones do. Although neural impulses do not travel as fast as electricity along a wire, they *are* very fast, moving at up to 100 meters per second, which is equivalent to more than 200 miles per hour. The entire, complicated process of neural transmission takes only a few thousandths of a second. In the time it has taken you to read this description of the neural impulse, billions of such impulses have been transmitted in your nervous system!

The Synapse: Where Neurons Meet

In the nervous system, the neural impulse functions as a signal. For that signal to have any meaning for the system as a whole, it must be transmitted from the neuron to other cells. As noted earlier, this transmission takes place at special junctions called *synapses*, which depend on *chemical* messengers.

Web Link 3.1

Neuropsychology Central
This content-rich site, maintained by Professor Jeffrey Browndyke of Louisiana State University, is dedicated to all aspects of human neuropsychology, from the perspectives of the experimental research laboratory as well as the applied clinical setting of the hospital and professional office.

Figure 3.2

The neural impulse. The electric charge of a neuron can be measured with a pair of electrodes connected to an oscilloscope. **(a)** At rest, the neuron is like a tiny wet battery with a resting potential of about −70 millivolts. **(b)** When a neuron is stimulated, a sharp jump in its electric potential occurs, resulting in a spike on the oscilloscope recording of the neuron's electrical activity. This change in voltage, called an action potential, travels along the axon. **(c)** Biochemical changes propel the action potential along the axon. An action potential begins when sodium gates in the membrane of an axon open, permitting positively charged sodium ions to flow into the axon. **(d)** The potassium gates have opened to let potassium ions flow outward. At the next point along the axon membrane, sodium gates open and the process is repeated, thus allowing the action potential to move along the axon. **(e)** This blowup of the voltage spike associated with an action potential depicts how these biochemical changes relate to the electrical activity of the cell.

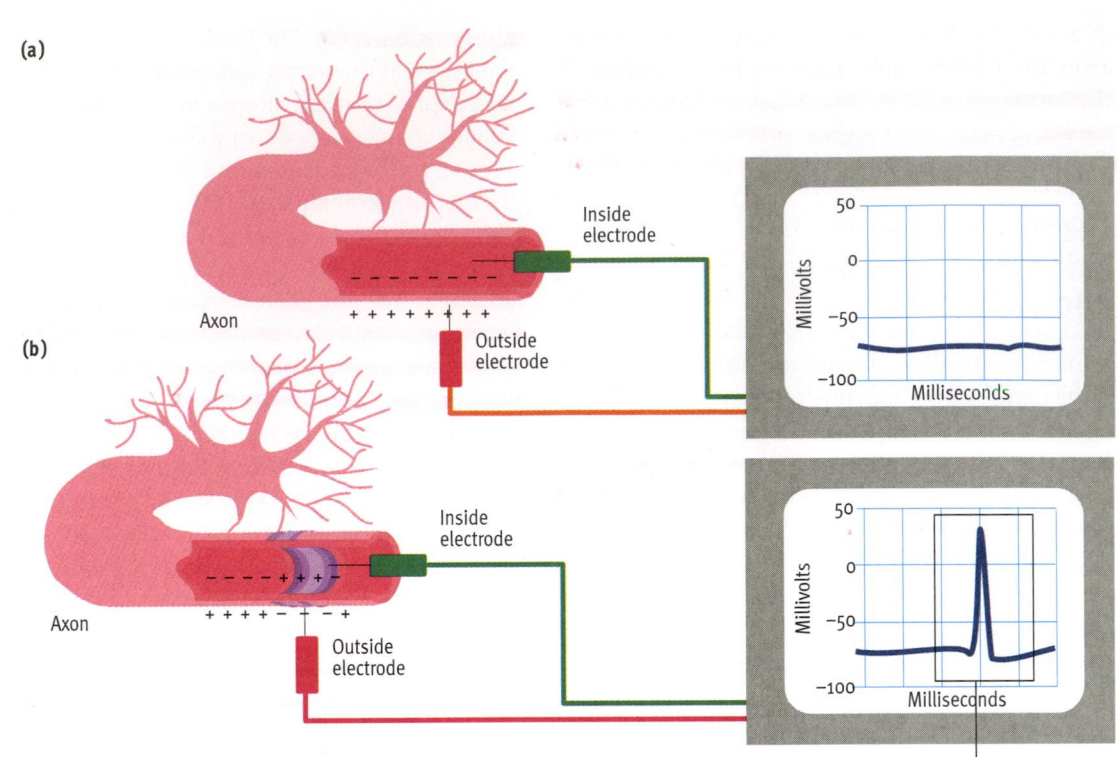

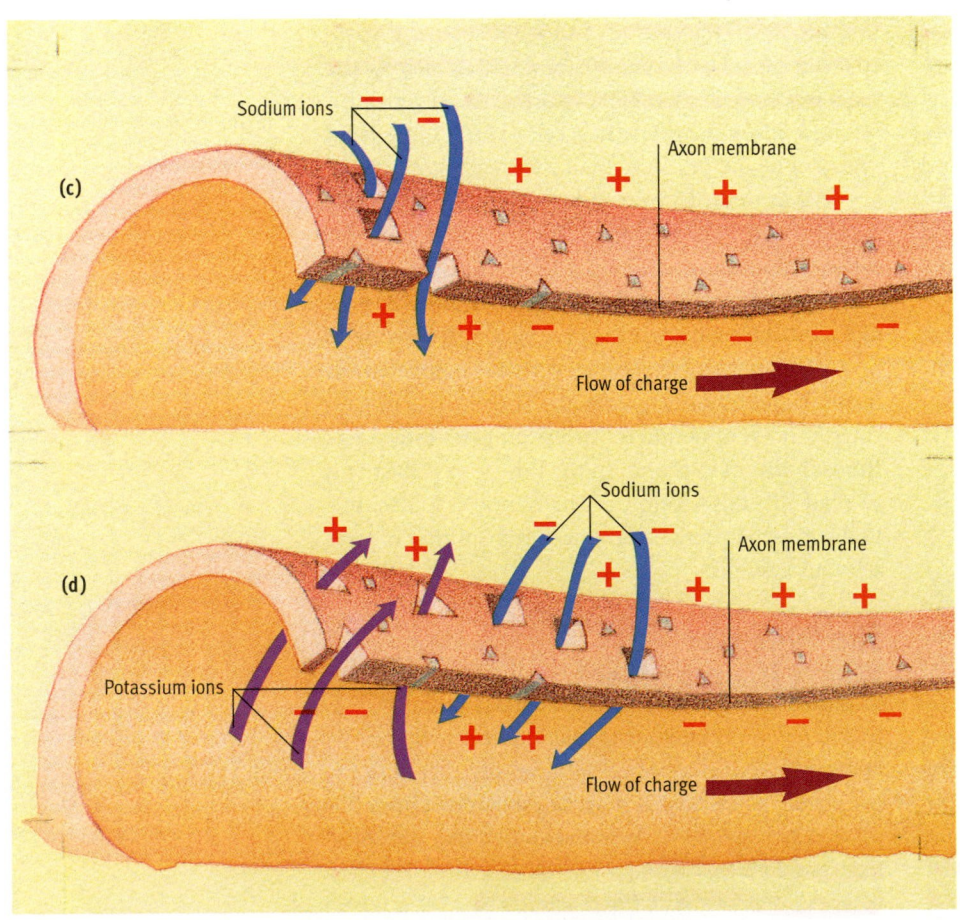

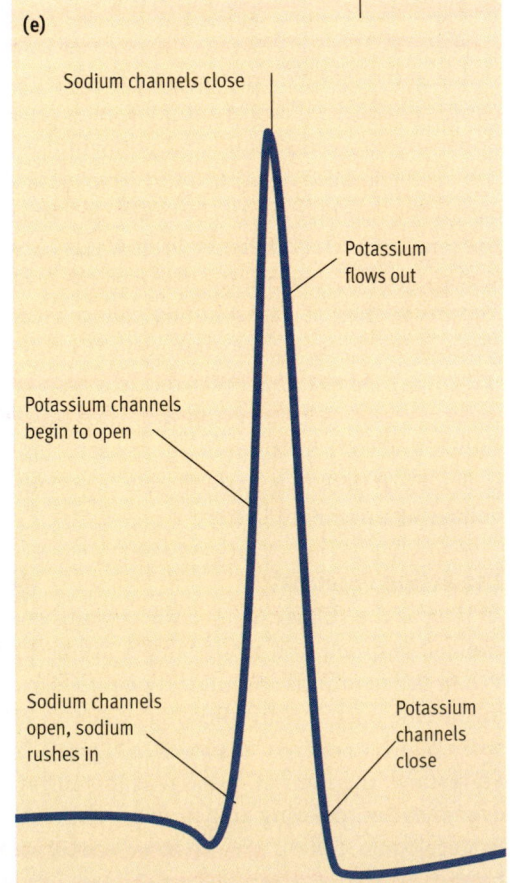

Sending Signals: Chemicals as Couriers

A "typical" synapse is shown in Figure 3.3. The first thing that you should notice is that the two neurons don't actually touch. They are separated by the *synaptic cleft,* a microscopic gap between the terminal button of one neuron and the cell membrane of another neuron. Signals have to jump this gap to permit neurons to communicate. In this situation, the neuron that sends a signal across the gap is called the *presynaptic neuron,* and the neuron that receives the signal is called the *postsynaptic neuron.*

How do messages travel across the gaps between neurons? The arrival of an action potential at an axon's terminal buttons triggers the release of *neurotransmitters—chemicals that transmit information from one neuron to another.* Within the buttons, most of these chemicals are stored in small sacs, called *synaptic vesicles.* The neurotransmitters are released when a vesicle fuses with the membrane of the presynaptic cell and its contents spill into the synaptic cleft. After their release, neurotransmitters diffuse across the synaptic cleft to the membrane of the receiving cell. There they may bind with special molecules in the postsynaptic cell membrane at various *receptor sites.* These sites are specifically "tuned" to recognize and respond to some neurotransmitters but not to others.

Receiving Signals: Postsynaptic Potentials

When a neurotransmitter and a receptor molecule combine, reactions in the cell membrane cause a *postsynaptic potential (PSP),* a voltage change at a receptor site on a postsynaptic cell membrane. Postsynaptic potentials do *not* follow the all-or-none law as action potentials do. Instead, postsynaptic potentials are *graded.* That is, they vary in size and they increase or decrease the *probability* of a neural impulse in the receiving cell in proportion to the amount of voltage change.

Two types of messages can be sent from cell to cell: excitatory and inhibitory. An *excitatory PSP* is a positive voltage shift that increases the likelihood that the postsynaptic neuron will fire action potentials. An *inhibitory PSP* is a negative voltage shift that decreases the likelihood that the postsynaptic neuron will fire action potentials. The direction of the voltage shift, and thus the nature of the PSP (excitatory or inhibitory), depends on which receptor sites are activated in the postsynaptic neuron (Kandel, 2000).

The excitatory or inhibitory effects produced at a synapse last only a fraction of a second. Then neuro-transmitters drift away from receptor sites or are inactivated by enzymes that metabolize (convert) them into inactive forms. Most are reabsorbed into the presynaptic neuron through *reuptake,* a process in which neurotransmitters are sponged up from the synaptic cleft by the presynaptic membrane. Reuptake allows synapses to recycle their materials. Reuptake and the other key processes in synaptic transmission are summarized in Figure 3.4 on the next page.

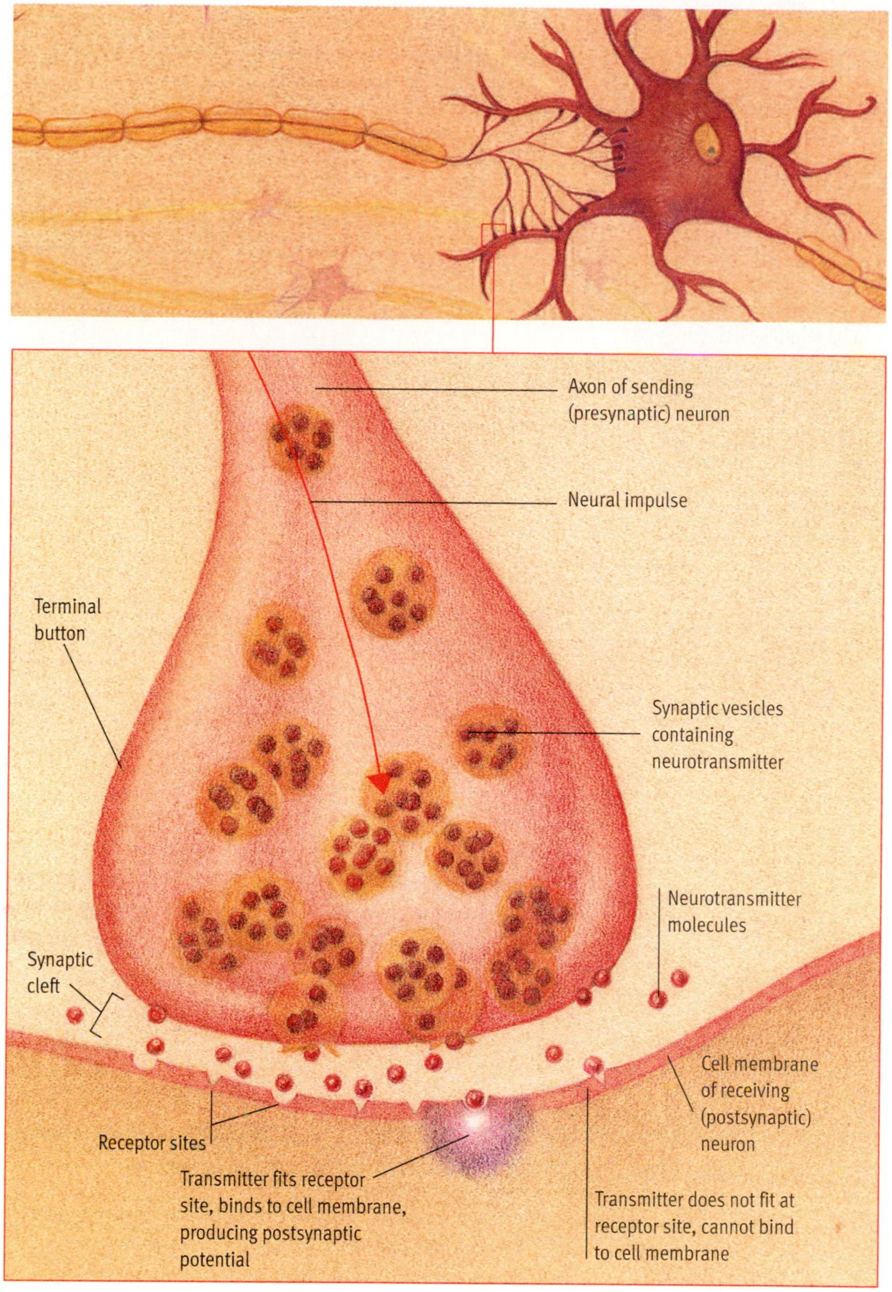

Integrating Signals: Neural Networks

A neuron may receive a symphony of signals from *thousands* of other neurons. The same neuron may

Axon of sending (presynaptic) neuron

Neural impulse

Synaptic vesicles containing neurotransmitter

Neurotransmitter molecules

Terminal button

Synaptic cleft

Cell membrane of receiving (postsynaptic) neuron

Receptor sites

Transmitter fits receptor site, binds to cell membrane, producing postsynaptic potential

Transmitter does not fit at receptor site, cannot bind to cell membrane

Figure 3.3

The synapse. When a neural impulse reaches an axon's terminal buttons, it triggers the release of chemical messengers called neurotransmitters. The neurotransmitter molecules diffuse across the synaptic cleft and bind to receptor sites on the postsynaptic neuron. A specific neurotransmitter can bind only to receptor sites that its molecular structure will fit into, much like a key must fit a lock.

Figure 3.4

Overview of synaptic transmission. The main elements in synaptic transmission are summarized here, superimposed on a blowup of the synapse seen in Figure 3.3. The five key processes involved in communication at synapses are (1) synthesis and storage, (2) release, (3) binding, (4) inactivation or removal, and (5) reuptake of neurotransmitters. As you'll see in this chapter and the remainder of the book, the effects of many phenomena—such as pain, drug use, and some diseases—can be explained in terms of how they alter one or more of these processes (usually at synapses releasing a specific neurotransmitter).

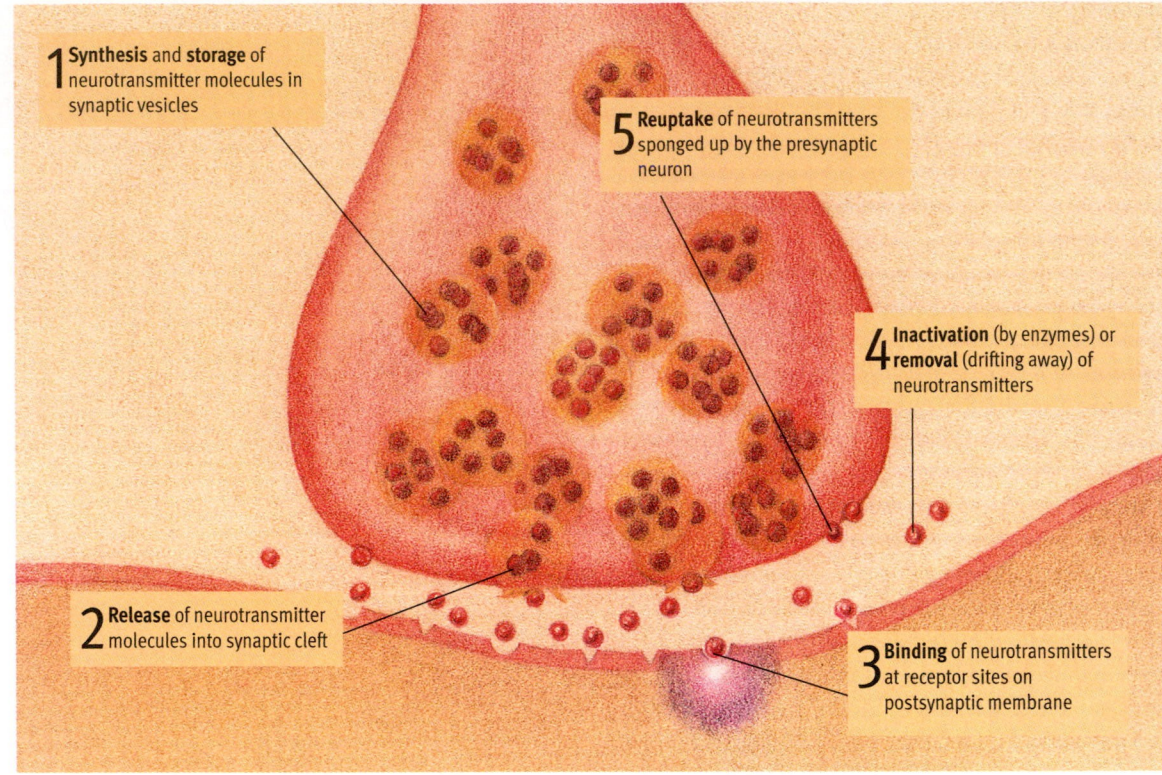

1. **Synthesis** and **storage** of neurotransmitter molecules in synaptic vesicles

5. **Reuptake** of neurotransmitters sponged up by the presynaptic neuron

4. **Inactivation** (by enzymes) or **removal** (drifting away) of neurotransmitters

2. **Release** of neurotransmitter molecules into synaptic cleft

3. **Binding** of neurotransmitters at receptor sites on postsynaptic membrane

pass its messages along to thousands of neurons as well. Thus, a neuron must do a great deal more than simply relay messages it receives. It must *integrate* signals arriving at many synapses before it "decides" whether to fire a neural impulse. If enough excitatory PSPs occur in a neuron, the electrical currents can add up, causing the cell's voltage to reach the thresh-old at which an action potential will be fired. However, if many inhibitory PSPs also occur, they will tend to cancel the effects of excitatory PSPs. Thus, the state of the neuron is a weighted balance between excitatory and inhibitory influences (Kandel & Siegelbaum, 2000).

As Rita Carter (1998, p. 19) has pointed out in *Mapping the Mind*, "The firing of a single neuron is not enough to create the twitch of an eyelid in sleep, let alone a conscious impression. . . .Millions of neurons must fire in unison to produce the most trifling thought." Most neurons are interlinked in complex chains, pathways, circuits, and networks. Our perceptions, thoughts, and actions depend on *patterns* of neural activity in elaborate neural networks. These networks consist of interconnected neurons that frequently fire together or sequentially to perform certain functions. The links in these networks are fluid, as new synaptic connections may be made while some old connections whither away. Ironically, the *elimination of old synapses* appears to play a larger role in the sculpting of neural networks than the *creation of new synapses*. The nervous system normally forms more synapses than needed and then gradually eliminates the less active synapses. For example, the number of synapses in the human visual cortex peaks at around age one and then declines, as diagrammed in Figure 3.5 (Huttenlocher, 1994). Thus, *synaptic pruning* is a key process in the formation of the neural net-

CONCEPT **CHECK 3.1**

Understanding Nervous System Hardware Using Metaphors

A useful way to learn about the structures and functions of parts of the nervous system is through metaphors. Check your understanding of the basic components of the nervous system by matching the metaphorical descriptions below with the correct terms in the following list: (a) glia, (b) neuron, (c) soma, (d) dendrite, (e) axon, (f) myelin, (g) terminal button, (h) synapse. You'll find the answers in Appendix A.

_____ **1.** Like a tree. Also, each branch is a telephone wire that carries incoming messages to you.

_____ **2.** Like the insulation that covers electrical wires.

_____ **3.** Like a silicon chip in a computer that receives and transmits information between input and output devices as well as between other chips.

_____ **4.** Like an electrical cable that carries information.

_____ **5.** Like the maintenance personnel who keep things clean and in working order so the operations of the enterprise can proceed.

_____ **6.** Like the nozzle at the end of a hose, from which water is squirted.

_____ **7.** Like a railroad junction, where two trains may meet.

works that are crucial to communication in the nervous system.

Neurotransmitters and Behavior

 **2b, 4d**

As we have seen, the nervous system relies on chemical couriers to communicate information between neurons. These *neurotransmitters* are fundamental to behavior, playing a key role in everything from muscle movements to moods and mental health.

You might guess that the nervous system would require only two neurotransmitters—one for excitatory potentials and one for inhibitory potentials. In reality, there are nine well-established, classic (small-molecule) transmitters, about 40 additional neuropeptide chemicals that function, at least part-time, as neurotransmitters, and a handful of recently recognized "novel" neurotransmitters (Schwartz, 2000). As scientists continue to discover new and increasingly diverse transmitter substances, they are being forced to reevaluate their criteria regarding what qualifies as a neurotransmitter (Snyder & Ferris, 2000).

Specific neurotransmitters work at specific kinds of synapses. You may recall that transmitters deliver their messages by binding to receptor sites on the post-

synaptic membrane. However, a transmitter cannot bind to just any site. The binding process operates much like a lock and key, as was shown in Figure 3.3. Just as a key has to fit a lock to work, a transmitter has to fit into a receptor site for binding to occur. Hence, specific transmitters can deliver signals only at certain locations on cell membranes.

Why are there many neurotransmitters, each of which works only at certain synapses? This variety and specificity reduces crosstalk between densely packed neurons, making the nervous system's communication more precise. Let's briefly review some of the most interesting findings about how neurotransmitters regulate behavior, which are summarized in Table 3.1.

Acetylcholine

 2b

The discovery that cells communicate by releasing chemicals was first made in connection with the transmitter *acetylcholine* (ACh). ACh has been found throughout the nervous system. It is the only transmitter between motor neurons and voluntary muscles. Every move you make—typing, walking, talking, breathing—depends on ACh released to your muscles by motor neurons (Kandel & Siegelbaum, 2000). ACh appears to contribute to attention, arousal, and perhaps memory.

The activity of ACh (and other neurotransmitters) may be influenced by other chemicals in the brain. Although synaptic receptor sites are sensitive to specific neurotransmitters, sometimes they can be "fooled" by other chemical substances. For example, if you

Web Link 3.2

Molecular Neurobiology: A Gallery of Animations
Site editor and physician Neil Busis brings together a set of QuickTime animations demonstrating activities at the molecular level of the synapse, such as the fusion of synaptic vesicles with the presynaptic membrane.

Figure **3.5**

Synaptic pruning. This graph summarizes data on the estimated number of synapses in the human visual cortex as a function of age (Huttenlocher, 1994). As you can see, the number of synapses in this area of the brain peaks around age 1 and then mostly declines over the course of the life span. This decline reflects the process of *synaptic pruning*, which involves the gradual elimination of less active synapses.

SOURCE: Data based on Huttenlocher, P. R. (1994). Synaptogenesis in human cerebral cortex. In G. Dawson & K. W. Fischer (Eds.), *Human behavior and the developing brain.* New York: Guilford Press. Graphic adapted from Kolb, B. & Whishaw, I. Q. (2001). *An introduction to brain and behavior.* New York: Worth Publishers.

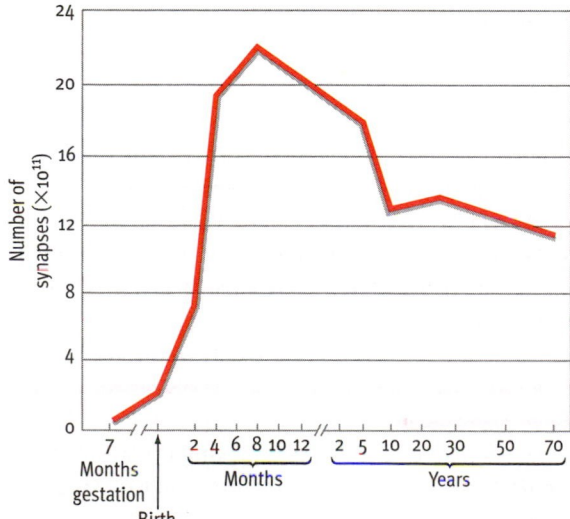

Table **3.1** Common Neurotransmitters and Some of Their Functions

Neurotransmitter	Functions and Characteristics
Acetylcholine (ACh)	Activates motor neurons controlling skeletal muscles Contributes to the regulation of attention, arousal, and memory Some ACh receptors stimulated by nicotine
Dopamine (DA)	Contributes to control of voluntary movement, pleasurable emotions Decreased levels associated with Parkinson's disease Overactivity at DA synapses associated with schizophrenia Cocaine and amphetamines elevate activity at DA synapses
Norepinephrine (NE)	Contributes to modulation of mood and arousal Cocaine and amphetamines elevate activity at NE synapses
Serotonin	Involved in regulation of sleep and wakefulness, eating, aggression Abnormal levels may contribute to depression and obsessive-compulsive disorder Prozac and similar antidepressant drugs affect serotonin circuits
GABA	Serves as widely distributed inhibitory transmitter Valium and similar antianxiety drugs work at GABA synapses
Endorphins	Resemble opiate drugs in structure and effects Contribute to pain relief and perhaps to some pleasurable emotions

© 1991 Analisa Kraft

"*When human beings engage in various activities, it seems that neurojuices are released that are associated with either pain or pleasure.*"
CANDACE PERT

© Dan McCoy/Rainbow

"*Brain research of the past decade, especially the study of neurotransmitters, has proceeded at a furious pace, achieving progress equal in scope to all the accomplishments of the preceding 50 years—and the pace of discovery continues to accelerate.*"
SOLOMON SNYDER

smoke tobacco, some of your ACh synapses will be stimulated by the nicotine that arrives in your brain. At these synapses, the nicotine acts like ACh itself. It binds to receptor sites for ACh, causing postsynaptic potentials (PSPs). In technical language, nicotine is an ACh agonist. An *agonist* is a chemical that mimics the action of a neurotransmitter.

Not all chemicals that fool synaptic receptors are agonists. Some chemicals bind to receptors but fail to produce a PSP (the key slides into the lock, but it doesn't work). In effect, they temporarily *block* the action of the natural transmitter by occupying its receptor sites, rendering them unusable. Thus, they act as antagonists. An *antagonist* is a chemical that opposes the action of a neurotransmitter. For example, the drug *curare* is an ACh antagonist. It blocks action at the same ACh synapses that are fooled by nicotine. As a result, muscles are unable to move. Some South American natives use a form of curare on arrows. If they wound an animal, the curare blocks the synapses from nerve to muscle, paralyzing the animal.

Monoamines

The *monoamines* include three neurotransmitters: dopamine, norepinephrine, and serotonin. Neurons using these transmitters regulate many aspects of everyday behavior. Dopamine (DA), for example, is used by neurons that control voluntary movements. The degeneration of such neurons apparently causes *Parkinsonism*, a disease marked by tremors, muscular rigidity, and reduced control over voluntary movements (DeLong, 2000).

Although other neurotransmitters are also involved, serotonin-releasing neurons appear to play a prominent role in the regulation of sleep and wakefulness (Vodelholzer et al., 1998) and eating behavior (Blundell & Halford, 1998). There also is considerable evidence that neural circuits using serotonin modulate aggressive behavior in animals (Bernhardt, 1997), and some preliminary evidence relating serotonin activity to aggression and impulsive behavior in humans (Dolan, Anderson, & Deakin, 2001; Nelson & Chiavegatto, 2001).

Abnormal levels of monoamines in the brain have been related to the development of certain psychological disorders. For example, people who suffer from depression appear to have lowered levels of activation at norepinephrine (NE) and serotonin synapses. Although a host of other biochemical changes may also contribute to depression, abnormalities at NE and serotonin synapses appear to play a central role, as most antidepressant drugs exert their main effects at these synapses (Garlow, Musselman, & Nemeroff, 1999).

In a similar fashion, abnormalities in activity at dopamine synapses have been implicated in the development of *schizophrenia*. This severe mental illness is marked by irrational thought, hallucinations, poor contact with reality, and deterioration of routine adaptive behavior. Afflicting roughly 1% of the population, schizophrenia requires hospitalization more often than any other psychological disorder (see Chapter 14). Studies suggest, albeit with many complications, that overactivity at DA synapses is the neurochemical basis for schizophrenia. Why? Primarily because the therapeutic drugs that tame schizophrenic symptoms are known to be DA antagonists that reduce the neurotransmitter's activity (Tamminga, 1999).

Temporary alterations at monoamine synapses also appear to account for the powerful effects of some widely abused drugs, including amphetamines and cocaine. Amphetamines and cocaine seem to exert most of their effects by creating a storm of increased activity at dopamine and norepinephrine synapses (Gold & Miller, 1997; King & Ellinwood, 1997).

GABA

Another group of transmitters consists of *amino acids*. Two of these, *gamma-aminobutyric acid* (GABA) and *glycine*, are notable in that they seem to produce only *inhibitory* postsynaptic potentials. Some transmitters, such as ACh and NE, are versatile. They can produce either excitatory or inhibitory PSPs, depending on the synaptic receptors they bind to. However, GABA and glycine appear to have inhibitory effects at virtually all synapses where either is present. GABA receptors are widely distributed in the brain and may be present at 40% of all synapses. GABA appears to be responsible for much of the inhibition in the central nervous system. Studies also suggest that GABA contributes to the regulation of anxiety in humans and that it plays a central role in the expression of seizures (Charney et al., 1996; Shank, Smith-Swintosky, & Twyman, 2000).

Endorphins

In 1970, after a horseback-riding accident, Candace Pert, a graduate student in neuroscience, lay in a hospital bed receiving frequent shots of *morphine*, a pain-killing drug derived from the opium plant. This experience left her with a driving curiosity about how morphine works. A few years later, she and Solomon Snyder rocked the scientific world by showing that *morphine exerts its effects by binding to specialized receptors in the brain* (Pert & Snyder, 1973).

This discovery raised a perplexing question: Why would the brain be equipped with receptors for morphine, a powerful, addictive opiate drug not normally found in the body? It occurred to Pert and others that the nervous system must have its own, endogenous (internally produced) morphinelike substances. Investigators dubbed these as-yet undiscovered substances *endorphins—internally produced chemicals that resemble opiates in structure and effects*. A search for the body's natural opiate ensued. In short order, a number of endogenous, opiatelike substances were identified (Hughes et al., 1975). Subsequent studies revealed that endorphins and their receptors are widely distributed in the human body and that they clearly contribute to the modulation of pain, as well as a variety of other phenomena (Basbaum & Jessell, 2000).

In this section we have highlighted just a few of the more interesting connections between neurotransmitters and behavior. These highlights barely begin to convey the rich complexity of biochemical processes in the nervous system. Most aspects of behavior are probably regulated by several types of transmitters. To further complicate matters, researchers are finding fascinating *interactions* between various neurotransmitter systems, such as serotonin and dopamine circuits (G. S. Smith et al., 1997). Although scientists have learned a great deal about neurotransmitters and behavior, much still remains to be discovered.

REVIEW OF KEY POINTS

● Behavior depends on complex information processing in the nervous system. Cells in the nervous system receive, integrate, and transmit information.

● Neurons are the basic communication links. They normally transmit a neural impulse along an axon to a synapse with another neuron. The neural impulse is a brief change in a neuron's electrical charge that moves along an axon. An

CONCEPT **CHECK 3.2**

Linking Brain Chemistry to Behavior

Check your understanding of relations between brain chemistry and behavior by indicating which neurotransmitters have been linked to the phenomena listed below. Choose your answers from the following list: (a) acetylcholine, (b) norepinephrine, (c) dopamine, (d) serotonin, (e) endorphins. Indicate your choice (by letter) in the spaces on the left. You'll find the answers in Appendix A.

_____ **1.** A transmitter involved in the regulation of sleep, eating, and aggression.

_____ **2.** The two monoamines that have been linked to depression.

_____ **3.** Chemicals that resemble opiate drugs in structure and that are involved in pain relief.

_____ **4.** A neurotransmitter for which abnormal levels have been implicated in schizophrenia.

_____ **5.** The only neurotransmitter between motor neurons and voluntary muscles.

action potential is an all-or-none event. Neurons convey information about the strength of a stimulus by variations in their rate of firing.

● Action potentials trigger the release of chemicals called neurotransmitters that diffuse across a synapse to communicate with other neurons. Transmitters bind with receptors in the postsynaptic cell membrane, causing excitatory or inhibitory PSPs.

● Whether the postsynaptic neuron fires a neural impulse depends on the balance of excitatory and inhibitory PSPs. Our thoughts and actions depend on patterns of activity in neural circuits and networks.

● The transmitter ACh plays a key role in muscular movement. Serotonin circuits may contribute to the regulation of sleep, eating, and aggression. Depression is associated with reduced activation at norepinephrine and serotonin synapses.

● Schizophrenia has been linked to overactivity at dopamine synapses. Cocaine and amphetamines appear to exert their main effects by altering activity at DA and NE synapses. GABA is an important inhibitory transmitter. Endorphins, which resemble opiates, contribute to pain relief.

Organization of the Nervous System

Clearly, communication in the nervous system is fundamental to behavior. So far we have looked at how individual cells communicate with one another. In this section, we examine the organization of the nervous system as a whole.

Experts believe that there are roughly *100 billion* neurons in the human brain (Kandel, 2000). Obviously, this is only an *estimate*. If you counted them nonstop at the rate of one per second, you'd be counting for over 3000 years! The fact that our neurons are so abundant as to be uncountable is probably why it is

widely believed that "we only use 10% of our brains." This curious tidbit of folk wisdom is utter nonsense (McBurney, 1996). There is no way to quantify the percentage of the brain that is "in use" at any specific time. And think about, if 90% of the human brain consists of unused "excess baggage," localized brain damage would not be a problem much of the time. In reality, damage in even very tiny areas of brain usually has severe, disruptive effects (Zillmer & Spiers, 2001).

In any event, the multitudes of neurons in your nervous system have to work together to keep infor-

PREVIEW QUESTIONS

● What are the subdivisions of the peripheral nervous system?

● What is the difference between afferent and efferent nerves?

● What does the autonomic nervous system regulate, and what are its subdivisions?

● What is the central nervous system made up of?

Figure **3.6**

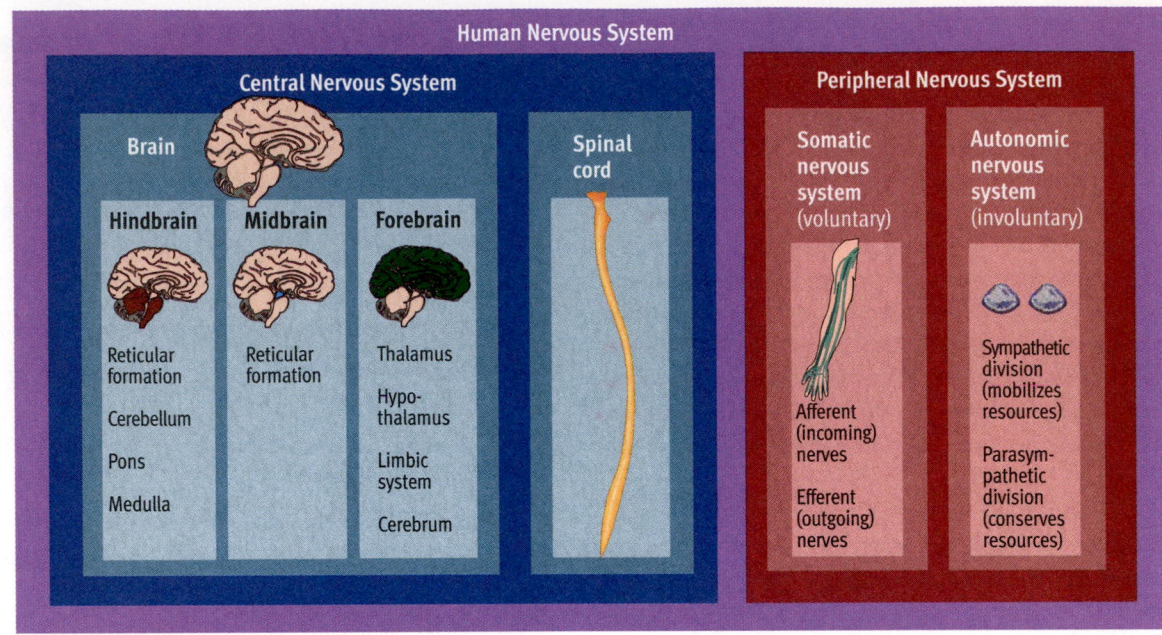

Organization of the human nervous system. This overview of the human nervous system shows the relationships of its various parts and systems. The brain is traditionally divided into three regions: the hindbrain, the midbrain, and the forebrain. The reticular formation runs through both the midbrain and the hindbrain on its way up and down the brainstem. These and other parts of the brain are discussed in detail later in the chapter. The peripheral nervous system is made up of the somatic nervous system, which controls voluntary muscles and sensory receptors, and the autonomic nervous system, which controls the involuntary activities of smooth muscles, blood vessels, and glands.

mation flowing effectively. To see how the nervous system is organized to accomplish this end, we will divide it into parts. In many instances, the parts will be divided once again. Figure 3.6 presents an organizational chart that shows the relationships of all the parts of the nervous system.

The Peripheral Nervous System

 2b, 8c

The first and most important division separates the *central nervous system* (the brain and spinal cord) from the *peripheral nervous system* (see Figure 3.7). **The *peripheral nervous system* is made up of all those nerves that lie outside the brain and spinal cord. *Nerves* are bundles of neuron fibers (axons) that are routed together in the peripheral nervous system.** This portion of the nervous system is just what it sounds like: the part that extends outside the central nervous system. The peripheral nervous system can be subdivided into the *somatic nervous system* and the *autonomic nervous system*.

The Somatic Nervous System

 2a

The *somatic nervous system* is made up of nerves that connect to voluntary skeletal muscles and to sensory receptors. These nerves are the cables that carry information from receptors in the skin, muscles, and joints to the central nervous system and that carry commands from the CNS to the muscles. These functions require two kinds of nerve fibers. *Afferent*

nerve fibers are axons that carry information inward to the central nervous system from the periphery of the body. *Efferent nerve fibers* are axons that carry information outward from the central nervous system to the periphery of the body. Each body nerve contains many axons of each type. Thus, somatic nerves are "two-way streets" with incoming

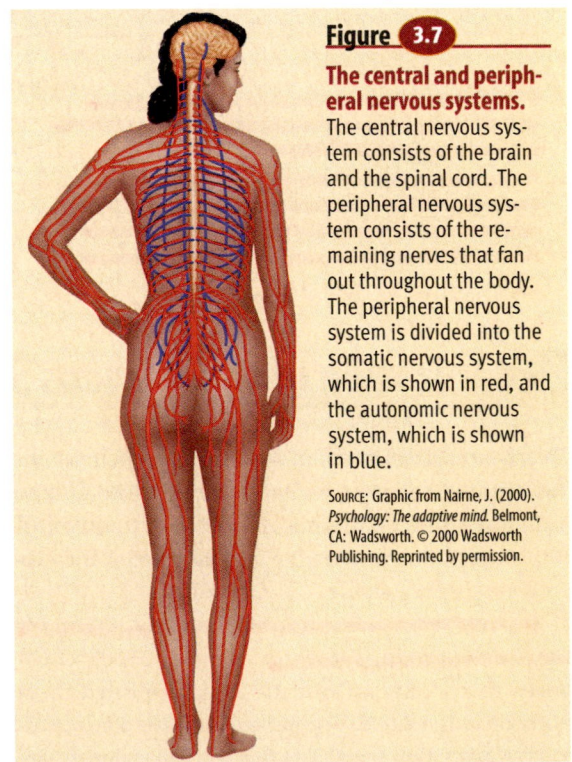

Figure **3.7**

The central and peripheral nervous systems. The central nervous system consists of the brain and the spinal cord. The peripheral nervous system consists of the remaining nerves that fan out throughout the body. The peripheral nervous system is divided into the somatic nervous system, which is shown in red, and the autonomic nervous system, which is shown in blue.

SOURCE: Graphic from Nairne, J. (2000). *Psychology: The adaptive mind.* Belmont, CA: Wadsworth. © 2000 Wadsworth Publishing. Reprinted by permission.

(afferent) and outgoing (efferent) lanes. The somatic nervous system lets you feel the world and move around in it.

The Autonomic Nervous System  2a, 8c

The *autonomic nervous system (ANS)* is made up of nerves that connect to the heart, blood vessels, smooth muscles, and glands. As its name hints, the autonomic system is a separate (autonomous) system, although it is ultimately governed by the central nervous system. The autonomic nervous system controls automatic, involuntary, visceral functions that people don't normally think about, such as heart rate, digestion, and perspiration (see Figure 3.8).

The autonomic nervous system mediates much of the physiological arousal that occurs when people experience emotions. For example, imagine that you are walking home alone one night when a seedy-looking character falls in behind you and begins to follow you. If you feel threatened, your heart rate and breathing will speed up. Your blood pressure may surge, you may get goosebumps, and your palms may begin to sweat. These difficult-to-control reactions are aspects of autonomic arousal.

Walter Cannon (1932), one of the first psychologists to study this reaction, called it the *fight-or-flight response*. Cannon carefully monitored this response in cats—after confronting them with dogs. He concluded that organisms generally respond to threat by preparing physiologically for attacking (fight) or fleeing (flight) from the enemy. Unfortunately, as you will see in Chapter 13, this fight-or-flight response can backfire if stress leaves a person in a chronic state of autonomic arousal. Prolonged autonomic arousal can eventually contribute to the development of physical diseases (Selye, 1974).

The autonomic nervous system can be subdivided into two branches: the sympathetic division and the parasympathetic division (see Figure 3.8). The *sympathetic division* is the branch of the autonomic nervous system that mobilizes the body's resources for emergencies. It creates the fight-or-flight response. Activation of the sympathetic division slows digestive processes and drains blood from the periphery, lessening bleeding in the case of an injury. Key sympathetic nerves send signals to the adrenal glands, triggering the release of hormones that ready the body for exertion. In contrast, the *parasympathetic division* is the branch of the autonomic nervous system that generally conserves bodily resources. It activates processes that allow the body to save and

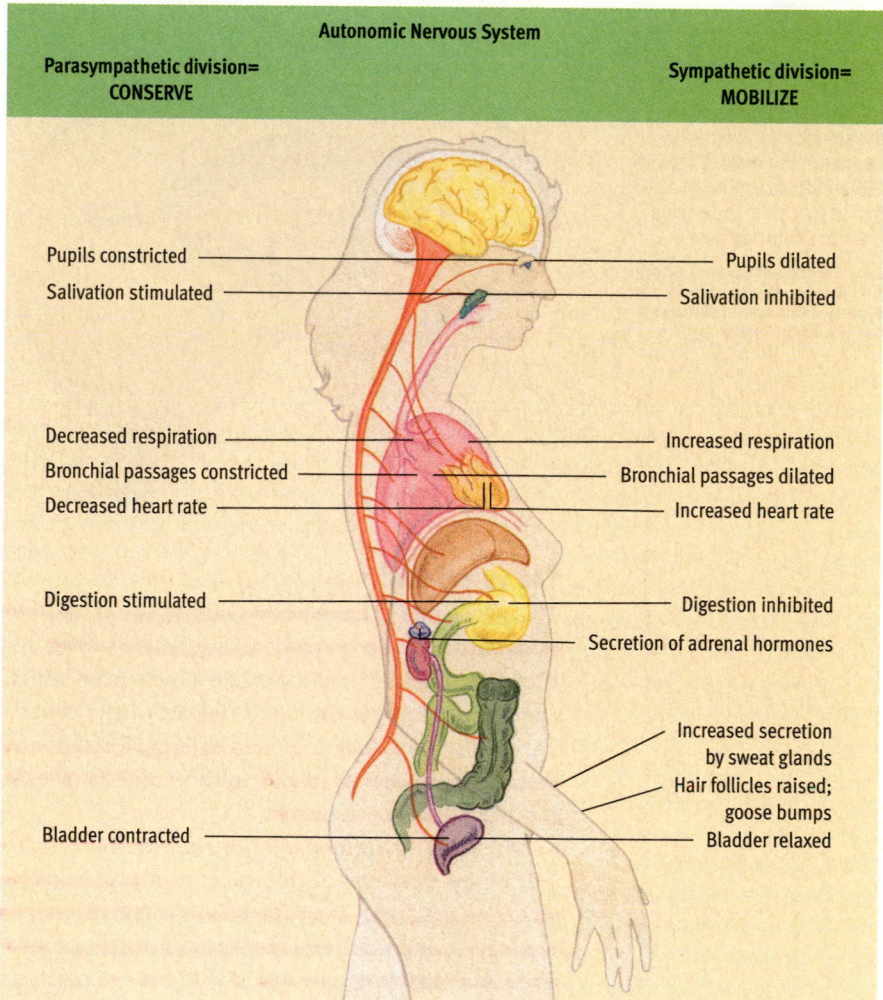

Autonomic Nervous System

Parasympathetic division= CONSERVE

Sympathetic division= MOBILIZE

Parasympathetic	Sympathetic
Pupils constricted	Pupils dilated
Salivation stimulated	Salivation inhibited
Decreased respiration	Increased respiration
Bronchial passages constricted	Bronchial passages dilated
Decreased heart rate	Increased heart rate
Digestion stimulated	Digestion inhibited
	Secretion of adrenal hormones
	Increased secretion by sweat glands
	Hair follicles raised; goose bumps
Bladder contracted	Bladder relaxed

store energy. For example, actions by parasympathetic nerves slow heart rate, reduce blood pressure, and promote digestion.

The Central Nervous System 2a

The central nervous system is the portion of the nervous system that lies within the skull and spinal column (see Figure 3.7). Thus, the *central nervous system (CNS) consists of the brain and the spinal cord.* It is protected by enclosing sheaths called the *meninges* (hence *meningitis,* the name for the disease in which the meninges become inflamed). In addition, the central nervous system is bathed in its own special nutritive "soup," the cerebrospinal fluid. The *cerebrospinal fluid (CSF) nourishes the brain and provides a protective cushion for it.* The hollow cavities in the brain that are filled with CSF are called *ventricles* (see Figure 3.9 on the next page).

Figure 3.8

The autonomic nervous system (ANS). The ANS is composed of the nerves that connect to the heart, blood vessels, smooth muscles, and glands. The ANS is divided into the sympathetic division, which mobilizes bodily resources in times of need, and the parasympathetic division, which conserves bodily resources. Some of the key functions controlled by each division of the ANS are summarized in the diagram.

Figure **3.9**

The ventricles of the brain.
Cerebrospinal fluid (CSF) circulates around the brain and the spinal cord. The hollow cavities in the brain filled with CSF are called ventricles. The four ventricles in the human brain are depicted here.

SOURCE: Graphic adapted from Starr, C. & Taggart, R. (1998). *Biology: The unity and diversity of life.* Belmont, CA: Wadsworth. © 1998 Wadsworth Publishing. Reprinted by permission.

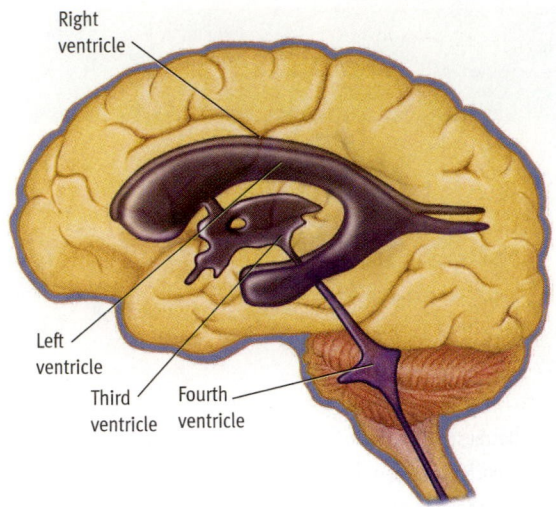

Right ventricle

Left ventricle

Third ventricle

Fourth ventricle

The Brain

The crowning glory of the central nervous system is, of course, the *brain.* Anatomically, the brain is the part of the central nervous system that fills the upper portion of the skull. Although it weighs only about three pounds and could be held in one hand, the brain contains billions of interacting cells that integrate information from inside and outside the body, coordinate the body's actions, and enable human beings to talk, think, remember, plan, create, and dream.

Because of its central importance for behavior, the brain is the subject of the next three sections of the chapter. We begin by looking at the remarkable methods that have enabled researchers to unlock some of the brain's secrets.

The Spinal Cord

The *spinal cord* connects the brain to the rest of the body through the peripheral nervous system. Although the spinal cord looks like a cable from which the somatic nerves branch, it is part of the central nervous system. Like the brain, it is enclosed by the meninges and bathed in CSF. In short, the spinal cord is an extension of the brain.

The spinal cord runs from the base of the brain to just below the level of the waist. It houses bundles of axons that carry the brain's commands to peripheral nerves and that relay sensations from the periphery of the body to the brain. Many forms of paralysis result from spinal cord damage, a fact that underscores the critical role the spinal cord plays in transmitting signals from the brain to the motor neurons that move the body's muscles.

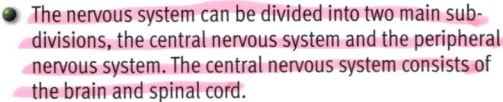

REVIEW OF KEY POINTS

- The nervous system can be divided into two main subdivisions, the central nervous system and the peripheral nervous system. The central nervous system consists of the brain and spinal cord.
- The peripheral nervous system consists of the nerves that lie outside the brain and spinal cord. It can be subdivided into the somatic nervous system, which connects to muscles and sensory receptors, and the autonomic nervous system, which connects to blood vessels, smooth muscles, and glands.
- The autonomic nervous system mediates the largely automatic arousal that accompanies emotion and the fight-or-flight response to stress. The ANS is divided into the sympathetic division, which mobilizes bodily resources, and the parasympathetic division, which conserves bodily resources.

Looking Inside the Brain: Research Methods

PREVIEW QUESTIONS
- What is an EEG and what is its output?
- How are lesioning and electrical stimulation used to study brain function?
- Which brain-imaging procedures provide information about brain structure or brain function?
- What have brain-imaging studies uncovered in schizophrenic patients?

Scientists who want to find out how parts of the brain are related to behavior are faced with a formidable task. The geography, or *structure,* of the brain can be mapped out relatively easily by examining and dissecting brains removed from animals or from deceased humans who have donated their bodies to science. Mapping of brain *function,* however, requires a working brain. Thus, special research methods are needed to discover relations between brain activity and behavior.

Investigators who conduct research on the brain or other parts of the nervous system are called *neuroscientists.* Often, brain research involves collaboration by neuroscientists from several disciplines, in-

cluding anatomy, physiology, biology, pharmacology, neurology, neurosurgery, psychiatry, and psychology. Neuroscientists use many specialized techniques to investigate connections between the brain and behavior. Among the methods they have depended on most heavily are electrical recordings, lesioning, and electrical stimulation. In addition, brain-imaging techniques have enhanced neuroscientists' ability to observe brain structure and function.

Electrical Recordings

The electrical activity of the brain can be recorded, much as Hodgkin and Huxley recorded the electrical

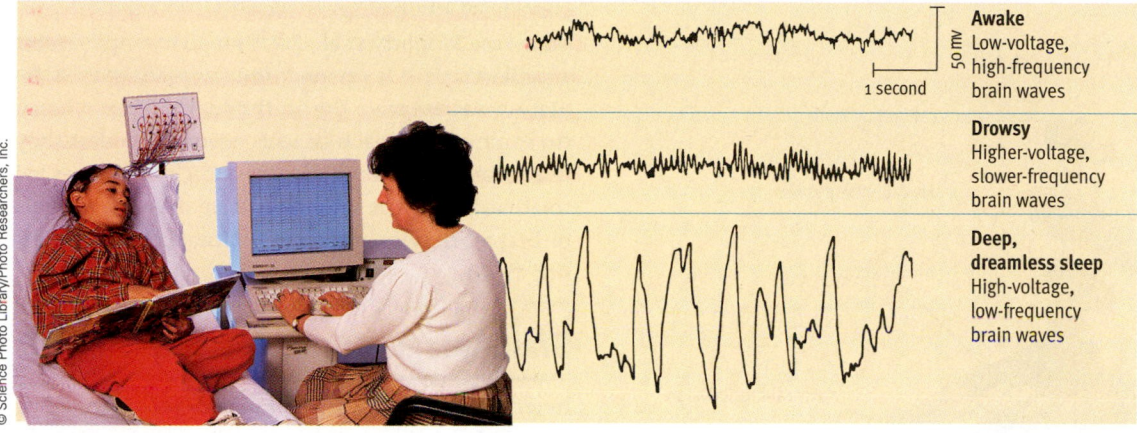

Awake
Low-voltage,
high-frequency
brain waves

50 mv
1 second

Drowsy
Higher-voltage,
slower-frequency
brain waves

Deep,
dreamless sleep
High-voltage,
low-frequency
brain waves

Figure 3.10

The electroencephalograph (EEG). Recording electrodes attached to the surface of the scalp permit the EEG to record electrical activity in the cortex over time. The EEG provides output in the form of line tracings called brain waves. Brain waves vary in frequency (cycles per second) and amplitude (measured in voltage). Various states of consciousness are associated with different brain waves. Characteristic EEG patterns for alert wakefulness, drowsiness, and deep, dreamless sleep are shown here. The use of the EEG in research is discussed in more detail in Chapter 5.

Source: Brain wave graphic adapted from Hauri, P. (1982). *Current concepts: The sleep disorders.* Kalamazoo, MI: The Upjohn Company. Reprinted by permission.

activity of individual neurons. Recordings of single cells in the brain have proven valuable, but scientists also need ways to record the simultaneous activity of many of the billions of neurons in the brain. Fortunately, in 1929 a German psychiatrist named Hans Berger invented a machine that could record broad patterns of brain electrical activity. **The *electroencephalograph (EEG)* is a device that monitors the electrical activity of the brain over time by means of recording electrodes attached to the surface of the scalp** (see Figure 3.10). An EEG electrode sums and amplifies electric potentials occurring in many thousands of brain cells.

Usually, six to ten recording electrodes are attached (with paste) at various places on the skull. The resulting EEG recordings are translated into line tracings, commonly called *brain waves*. These brain-wave recordings provide a useful overview of the electrical activity in the brain. Different brain-wave patterns are associated with different states of mental activity (Martin, 1991), as shown in Figure 3.10. The EEG is often used in the clinical diagnosis of brain damage and neurological disorders. In research applications, the EEG can be used to identify patterns of brain activity that occur when participants engage in specific behaviors or experience specific emotions. For example, in one study, researchers using EEG recordings found interesting correlations between specific types of anxiety and distinct patterns of regional brain activity (Heller et al., 1997). As you'll see in Chapter 5, the EEG has been invaluable to researchers exploring the physiology of sleep.

Lesioning

Brain tumors, strokes, head injuries, and other misfortunes often produce brain damage in people. Many major insights about brain-behavior relations have resulted from observations of behavioral changes in people who have suffered damage in specific brain areas. However, this type of research has its limitations. Subjects are not plentiful, and neuroscientists can't control the location or severity of their subjects' brain damage. Furthermore, variations in the participants' histories create a host of extraneous variables that make it difficult to isolate cause-and-effect relationships between brain damage and behavior.

To study the relations between brain and behavior more precisely, scientists sometimes observe what happens when specific brain structures in animals are purposely disabled. *Lesioning* involves destroying a piece of the brain. It is typically done by inserting an electrode into a brain structure and passing a high-frequency electric current through it to burn the tissue and disable the structure.

Lesioning requires researchers to get an electrode to a particular place buried deep inside the brain. They do so with a stereotaxic instrument, a device used to implant electrodes at precise locations in the brain. The use of this surgical device is described in Figure 3.11 on the next page. Of course, appropriate anesthetics are used to minimize pain and discomfort for the animals. The lesioning of brain structures in animals has proven invaluable in neuroscientists' research on brain functioning.

Electrical Stimulation of the Brain

Electrical stimulation of the brain (ESB) involves sending a weak electric current into a brain structure to stimulate (activate) it. The current is delivered through an electrode, but the current is different from that used in lesioning. This sort of electrical stimulation does not exactly duplicate normal signals in the brain. However, it is usually a close enough

Web Link 3.4

The Visible Human Project
This site from the National Library of Medicine provides a rich collection of online resources related to the highly detailed visual analysis of two human cadavers—a male and female—that has been carried out over the last decade. This site is a good place to explore advanced techniques in the imaging of the human body, including the central nervous system.

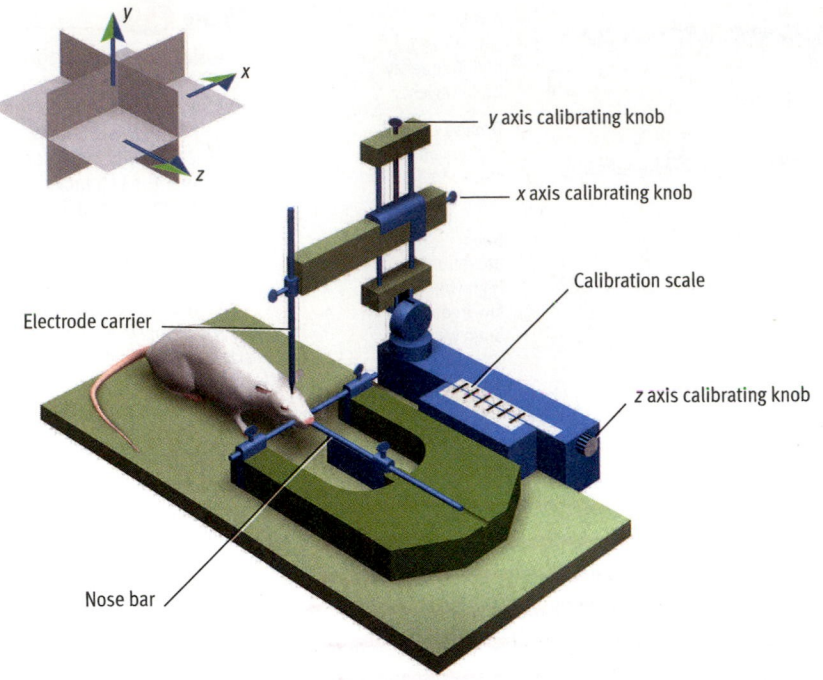

y axis calibrating knob

x axis calibrating knob

Calibration scale

Electrode carrier

z axis calibrating knob

Nose bar

Figure 3.11

An anesthetized rat in a stereotaxic instrument. This rat is undergoing brain surgery. After consulting a detailed map of the rat brain, researchers use the control knobs on the apparatus to position an electrode along the three axes (*x*, *y*, and *z*) shown in the upper left corner. This precise positioning allows researchers to implant the electrode in an exact location in the rat's brain.

Figure 3.12

CT technology. CT scans can be used in research to examine aspects of brain structure. They provide computer-enhanced X rays of horizontal slices of the brain.

approximation to activate the brain structures in which the electrodes are lodged. If areas deep within the brain are to be stimulated, the electrodes are implanted with the same stereotaxic techniques used in lesioning procedures.

Most ESB research is conducted with animals. However, ESB is occasionally used on humans in the context of brain surgery required for medical purposes (see Moriarty et al., 2001 for an example). After a patient's skull is opened, the surgeons may stimulate areas to map the individual patient's brain (to some extent, each of us is unique), so that they don't slice through critical areas. ESB research has led to advances in the understanding of many aspects of brain-behavior relations (Berman, 1991; Yudofsky, 1999).

Brain-Imaging Procedures

In recent decades, the invention of new brain-imaging devices has led to spectacular advances in science's ability to look into the brain (Bohning et al., 1998; Seibyl et al., 1999). The *CT (computerized tomography) scan* is a computer-enhanced X ray of brain structure. Multiple X rays are shot from many angles, and the computer combines the readings to create a vivid image of a horizontal slice of the brain (see Figure 3.12). The entire brain can be visualized by assembling a series of images representing successive slices of the brain. Of the new brain-imaging techniques, the CT scan is the least expensive, and it has been widely used in research. For example, many researchers have used CT scans to look for abnormalities in brain structure among people suffering from specific types of mental illness (Andreasen, 2001; G. N. Smith et al., 1997).

In research on how brain and behavior are related, *PET (positron emission tomography) scanning* is proving especially valuable (Nahas et al., 1998). Whereas CT scans can portray only brain *structure*, PET scans can examine brain *function*, mapping actual *activity* in the brain over time. In PET scans, ra-

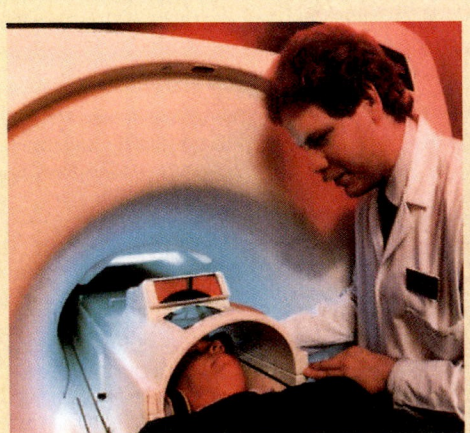

(a) The patient's head is positioned in a large cylinder, as shown here.

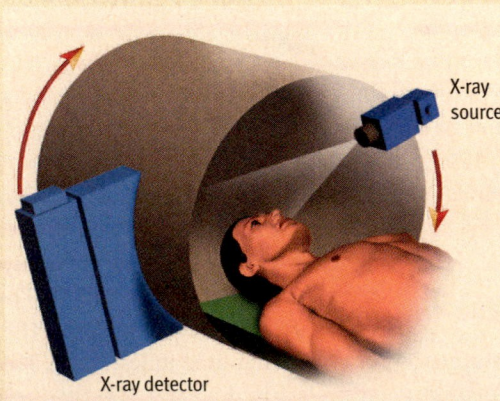

(b) An X-ray beam and X-ray detector rotate around the patient's head, taking multiple X rays of a horizontal slice of the patient's brain.

X-ray source

X-ray detector

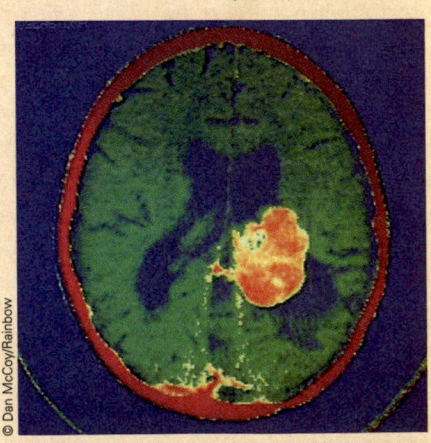

(c) A computer combines X rays to create an image of a horizontal slice of the brain. This scan shows a tumor (in red) on the right.

dioactively tagged chemicals are introduced into the brain. They serve as markers of blood flow or metabolic activity in the brain, which can be monitored with X rays. Thus, a PET scan can provide a color-coded map indicating which areas of the brain become active when subjects clench their fist, sing, or contemplate the mysteries of the universe (see Figure 3.13). In this way, neuroscientists are using PET scans to better pinpoint the brain areas that handle various types of mental activities (Craik et al., 1999; Raichle, 1994). Because PET scans monitor chemical processes, they can also be used to study the activity of specific neurotransmitters. For example, PET scans have helped researchers determine how cocaine affects activity in dopamine circuits in the human brain (Schlaepfer et al., 1997).

Research with PET scans has given neuroscientists a new appreciation of the complexity and interdependence of brain organization. The opportunity to look at ongoing brain function has revealed that even simple, routine mental operations depend on coordinated activation of several or more areas in the brain (Posner & Raichle, 1994).

The *MRI (magnetic resonance imaging) scan* uses magnetic fields, radio waves, and computerized enhancement to map out brain structure. MRI scans provide much better images of brain structure than CT scans (Bohning et al., 1998), producing three-dimensional pictures of the brain that have remarkably high resolution (see Figure 3.14a). *Functional magnetic resonance imaging (fMRI)* consists of several new variations on MRI technology that monitor blood and oxygen flow in the brain to identify areas of high activity (Lorberbaum et al., 1998). This technology is exciting because it can provide both *functional and*

structural information in the same image and monitor changes in brain activity in real time (see Figure 3.14b). For example, using fMRI scans, researchers have identified patterns of brain activity associated with cocaine craving in cocaine addicts (Wexler et al., 2001). MRI technology has proven extremely valuable in behavioral research in the last decade. Our Featured Study for this chapter is a recent MRI study that added to the growing evidence that there is an association between enlarged ventricles (the hollow, fluid-filled cavities) in the brain and schizophrenic disturbance.

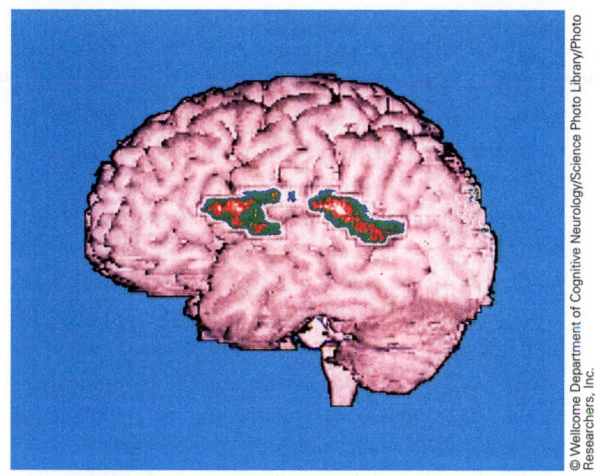

Figure 3.13

PET scans. PET scans are used to map brain activity rather than brain structure. They provide color-coded maps that show areas of high activity in the brain over time. The PET scan shown here pinpointed two areas of high activity (indicated by the red and green colors) when a research participant worked on a verbal short-term memory task.

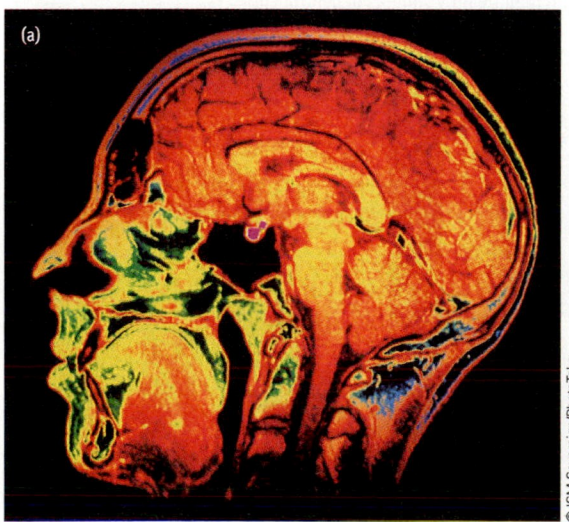

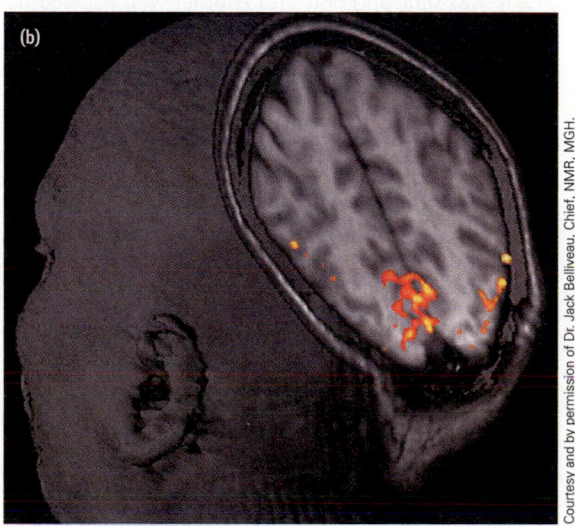

Figure 3.14

MRI scans. (a) MRI scans can be used to produce remarkably high-resolution pictures of brain structure. A vertical view of a brain from the left side is shown here. **(b)** Like PET scans, functional MRIs can monitor chemical activity in the brain. This image shows regions of the brain that were activated by the visual stimulus of a flashing light.

Probing the Anatomy of Schizophrenia

Investigators: Wouter G. Staal, Hilleke E. Hulshoff Pol, Hugo G. Schnack, Mechteld L. C. Hoogendoorn, Korne Jellema, & Rene S. Kahn (University Hospital Utrecht, the Netherlands)

Source: Structural brain abnormalities in patients with schizophrenia and their healthy siblings. *American Journal of Psychiatry*, 2000, *157*, 416–421.

Theorists have long suspected that schizophrenic disorders might be due, in part, to structural defects in the brain. Prior to the development of brain-imaging techniques, researchers had no way to test this hypothesis with live subjects. The first breakthrough in this line of research occurred when studies using CT scans reported an association between enlarged brain ventricles and schizophrenic disturbance. However, critics argued that the findings in CT studies were too weak and inconsistent to conclusively demonstrate a link between enlarged ventricles and schizophrenia.

Subsequent studies with more precise MRI scans yielded much stronger evidence of a connection between ventricular enlargement and schizophrenia. MRI studies have also found a variety of other brain structure abnormalities in schizophrenic patients, but these findings have been inconsistent from one study to the next. The Staal et al. study was conducted to gather additional data from schizophrenic participants and to see whether any brain structure abnormalities were apparent in the siblings of these subjects. Given that there is a hereditary predisposition to schizophrenia (see page 105 in this chapter), the investigators hypothesized that close relatives of schizophrenic patients might manifest similar brain abnormalities that could contribute to this genetic vulnerability.

Method

Participants. The investigators recruited 32 sets of same-sex siblings who were "discordant" for schizophrenia. Relatives are said to be discordant for a disorder when one exhibits the disorder and the other does not. Thus, each pair of siblings included one participant who clearly was schizophrenic and another who showed no signs of the disorder. The schizophrenic patients and their siblings were compared to 32 normal, control subjects who were chosen to match the age, gender, and handedness of the schizophrenic participants.

Procedure. An MRI brain scan was obtained for each participant. The same scanning techniques were used with all subjects. A computerized image analysis system was used to make numerical estimates of the volume of participants' brain ventricles and to measure other specific brain structures.

Results

The lateral ventricles were significantly larger in the schizophrenic patients than in either their siblings or the normal subjects (see Figure 3.15). The volume of the third ventricle was significantly larger in both the schizophrenic patients and their siblings than in control subjects. Significant differences were not found between the three groups in most of the other comparisons that focused on specific brain structures and regions.

Discussion

The present study adds to research that demonstrates a fairly consistent association between enlarged ventricles and schizophrenic disturbance. The authors conclude that healthy siblings share third-ventricle enlargement with their schizophrenic relatives but show no other structural brain abnormalities. They speculate that third-ventricle enlargement may be related to the genetic vulnerability to schizophrenia, whereas the increased size of the lateral ventricles may reflect the progression of schizophrenic disease.

Comment

This study was featured because it provides a simple example of how brain-imaging technologies have yielded new insights about brain-behavior relations. Science depends on observation. Improvements in our ability to observe the brain have resulted in increased knowledge of how brain structure and function are related to psy-

Figure 3.15

Enlarged brain ventricles in a schizophrenic patient. As in other studies, Staal et al. (2000) found that schizophrenic subjects tend to have enlarged brain ventricles. The data for the lateral ventricles are shown here. As you can see, the lateral ventricles of the schizophrenic subjects were about twice as large as those seen in their healthy siblings or control subjects.

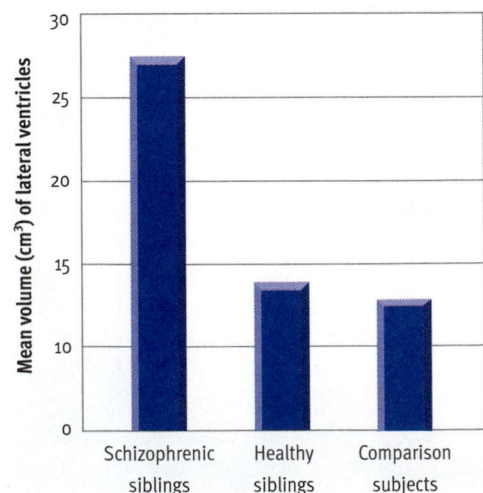

chological phenomena. Today, thanks to MRI research, we have extensive evidence of an association between ventricular enlargement and schizophrenia (McCarley et al., 1999). Most theorists believe that enlarged ventricles reflect the degeneration of nearby brain tissue or the failure of certain brain structures to develop normally (thus allowing the ventricles to grow larger). As you will see in Chapter 14, researchers are trying to figure out how abnormalities in brain structure fit in with the host of other factors implicated in the development of schizophrenic disorders. These questions can only be answered through more research. Thus, scientific inquiry is an endless process in which new knowledge stimulates new questions. ■

REVIEW OF KEY POINTS

- Neuroscientists use a variety of methods to investigate brain-behavior relations. The EEG can record broad patterns of electrical activity in the brain. Different EEG brain waves are associated with different states of consciousness.

- Lesioning involves destroying a piece of the brain. Another technique is electrical stimulation of areas in the brain in order to activate them. Both techniques depend on the use of stereotaxic instruments that permit researchers to implant electrodes at precise locations in animals' brains.

- In recent years, new brain-imaging procedures have been developed, including CT scans, PET scans, MRI scans, and fMRI scans. These techniques have enormous potential for exploring brain-behavior relations, as we saw in our Featured Study.

The Brain and Behavior

Now that we have examined selected techniques of brain research, let's look at what researchers have discovered about the functions of various parts of the brain.

The brain can be divided into three major regions: the hindbrain, the midbrain, and the forebrain. The principal structures found in each of these regions are listed in the organizational chart of the nervous system in Figure 3.6. You can see where these regions are located in the brain by looking at Figure 3.16 on the next page. They can be found easily in relation to the *brainstem*. The brainstem looks like its name—it appears to be a stem from which the rest of the brain "flowers," like a head of cauliflower. At its lower end it is contiguous with the spinal cord. At its higher end it lies deep within the brain.

We'll begin at the brain's lower end, where the spinal cord joins the brainstem. As we proceed upward, notice how the functions of brain structures go from the regulation of basic bodily processes to the control of "higher" mental processes.

The Hindbrain

The *hindbrain* includes the cerebellum and two structures found in the lower part of the brainstem: the medulla and the pons. The *medulla,* which attaches to the spinal cord, has charge of largely unconscious but vital functions, including circulating blood, breathing, maintaining muscle tone, and regulating reflexes such as sneezing, coughing, and salivating. The *pons* (literally "bridge") includes a bridge of fibers that connects the brainstem with the cerebellum. The pons also contains several clusters of cell bodies involved with sleep and arousal.

The *cerebellum* (literally "little brain") is a relatively large and deeply folded structure located adjacent to the back surface of the brainstem. The cerebellum is critical to the coordination of movement and to the sense of equilibrium, or physical balance (Ghez & Thach, 2000). Although the actual commands for muscular movements come from higher brain centers, the cerebellum plays a key role in organizing the sensory information that guides these movements. It is your cerebellum that allows you to hold your hand out to the side and then smoothly bring your finger to a stop on your nose. This is a useful roadside test for drunken driving because the cerebellum is one of the structures first depressed by alcohol. Damage to the cerebellum disrupts fine motor skills, such as those involved in writing, typing, or playing a musical instrument.

The Midbrain

The *midbrain* is the segment of the brainstem that lies between the hindbrain and the forebrain. The midbrain contains an area that is concerned with integrating sensory processes, such as vision and hearing (Stein, Wallace, & Stanford, 2000). An important system of dopamine-releasing neurons that projects into various higher brain centers originates in the midbrain. Among other things, this dopamine system is involved in the performance of voluntary

PREVIEW QUESTIONS

- What are some functions of the medulla, pons, and cerebellum?

- What are some functions of the midbrain and which structure is the brain's relay center?

- What does the hypothalamus regulate?

- What are some functions of the limbic system?

- What is each lobe in the brain known for?

- What does it mean to say that the brain is characterized by "plasticity?"

Figure 3.16

Structures and areas in the human brain. (Top left) This photo of a human brain shows many of the structures discussed in this chapter. (Top right) The brain is divided into three major areas: the hindbrain, midbrain, and forebrain. These subdivisions actually make more sense for the brains of other animals than of humans. In humans, the forebrain has become so large it makes the other two divisions look trivial. However, the hindbrain and midbrain aren't trivial; they control such vital functions as breathing, waking, and maintaining balance. (Bottom) This cross section of the brain highlights key structures and some of their principal functions. As you read about the functions of a brain structure, such as the corpus callosum, you may find it helpful to visualize it.

Wadsworth Collection.

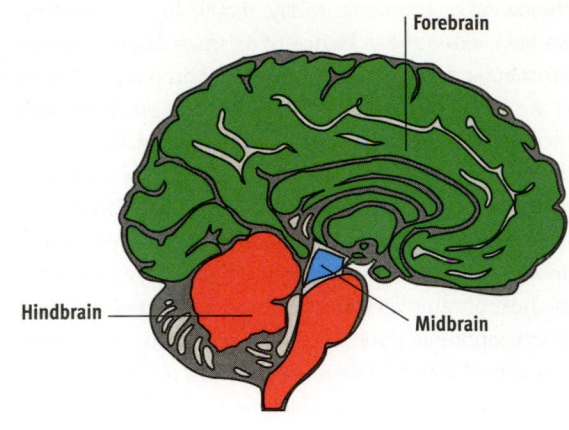

Forebrain

Hindbrain

Midbrain

Cerebrum
Responsible for sensing, thinking, learning, emotion, consciousness, and voluntary movement

Corpus callosum
Bridge of fibers passing information between the two cerebral hemispheres

Amygdala
Part of limbic system involved in emotion and aggression

Thalamus
Relay center for cortex; handles incoming and outgoing signals

Cerebellum
Structure that coordinates fine muscle movement, balance

Hypothalamus
Responsible for regulating basic biological needs: hunger, thirst, temperature control

Brainstem

Pituitary gland
"Master" gland that regulates other endocrine glands

Hippocampus
Part of limbic system involved in learning and memory

Spinal cord
Responsible for transmitting information between brain and rest of body; handles simple reflexes

Reticular formation
Group of fibers that carry stimulation related to sleep and arousal through brainstem

Medulla
Responsible for regulating largely unconscious functions such as breathing and circulation

Pons
Involved in sleep and arousal

movements. The decline in dopamine synthesis that causes Parkinsonism is due to degeneration of a structure located in the midbrain (DeLong, 2000).

Running through both the hindbrain and the midbrain is the *reticular formation* (see Figure 3.16). Lying at the central core of the brainstem, the reticular formation contributes to the modulation of muscle reflexes, breathing, and pain perception (Saper, 2000). It is best known, however, for its role in the regulation of sleep and arousal. Activity in the ascending fibers of the reticular formation contributes to arousal (Coenen, 1998).

The Forebrain  2e, 2f

The *forebrain* is the largest and most complex region of the brain, encompassing a variety of structures, including the thalamus, hypothalamus, limbic system, and cerebrum (consult Figure 3.16 once again). The thalamus, hypothalamus, and limbic system form the core of the forebrain. All three structures are located near the top of the brainstem. Above them is the *cerebrum*—the seat of complex thought. The wrinkled surface of the cerebrum is the *cerebral cortex*—the outer layer of the brain, which looks like a cauliflower.

The Thalamus: A Way Station 2e

The *thalamus* is a structure in the forebrain through which all sensory information (except smell) must pass to get to the cerebral cortex. This way station is made up of clusters of cell bodies, or somas. Each cluster is concerned with relaying sensory information to a particular part of the cortex. However, it would be a mistake to characterize the thalamus as nothing more than a passive relay station. The thalamus also appears to play an active role in integrating information from various senses.

The Hypothalamus: A Regulator of Biological Needs 2e

The *hypothalamus* is a structure found near the base of the forebrain that is involved in the regulation of basic biological needs. The hypothalamus lies beneath the thalamus (*hypo* means "under," making the hypothalamus the area under the thalamus). Although no larger than a kidney bean, the hypothalamus contains various clusters of cells that have many key functions. One such function is to control the autonomic nervous system (Iversen, Iversen, & Saper, 2000). In addition, the hypothalamus serves as a vital link between the brain and the endocrine system (a network of hormone-producing glands, discussed later in this chapter).

The hypothalamus plays a major role in the regulation of basic biological drives related to survival, including the so-called "four F's": fighting, fleeing, feeding, and mating. For example, when researchers lesion the lateral areas (the sides) of the hypothalamus, animals lose interest in eating. The animals must be fed intravenously or they starve, even in the presence of abundant food. In contrast, when electrical stimulation (ESB) is used to *activate* the lateral hypothalamus, animals eat constantly and gain weight rapidly (Grossman et al., 1978; Keesey & Powley, 1975). Does this mean that the lateral hypothalamus is the "hunger center" in the brain? Not necessarily. The regulation of hunger turns out to be complex and multifaceted, as you'll see in Chapter 10. Nonetheless, the hypothalamus clearly contributes to the control of hunger and other basic biological processes, including thirst and temperature regulation (Kupfermann, Kandel, & Iversen, 2000).

The Limbic System: The Seat of Emotion  2e

The *limbic system* is a loosely connected network of structures located roughly along the border between the cerebral cortex and deeper subcortical areas (hence the term *limbic*, which means "edge"). First described by Paul MacLean (1954), the limbic system is *not* a well-defined anatomical system with clear boundaries. Indeed, scientists disagree about which structures should be included in the limbic system (Van Hoesen, Morecraft, & Semendeferi, 1996). Broadly defined, the limbic system includes parts of the thalamus and hypothalamus, the hippocampus, the amygdala, and other structures. The limbic system is involved in the regulation of emotion, memory, and motivation.

The hippocampus and adjacent structures clearly play a role in memory processes, although the exact nature of that role is the subject of debate (Squire & Knowlton, 2000). Some theorists believe that the hippocampal region is responsible for the consolidation of memories for factual information (Gluck & Myers, 1997). In any event, many other brain structures contribute to memory processes, so the hippocampus is only one element in a complex system (see Chapter 7).

Similarly, there is ample evidence linking the limbic system to the experience of emotion, but the exact mechanisms of control are not yet well understood (Mega et al., 1997; Paradiso et al., 1997). Recent evidence suggests that the *amygdala* may play a central role in the learning of fear responses (Mori et al., 1999; Armony & LeDoux, 2000). The limbic system is also one of the areas in the brain that appears to be rich in emotion-tinged "pleasure centers." This intriguing possibility first surfaced, quite by chance, in brain stimulation research with rats. James Olds and Peter Milner (1954) accidentally discovered that a rat would press a lever repeatedly to send brief bursts of electrical stimulation to a specific spot in its brain where an electrode was implanted (see Figure 3.17). They thought that they had inserted the electrode in the rat's reticular formation. However, they learned later that the electrode had been bent during implantation and ended up elsewhere (probably in the hypothalamus). Much to their surprise, the rat kept coming back for more self-stimulation in this area. Subsequent studies showed that rats and monkeys would press a lever *thousands of times per hour,* until they sometimes collapsed from exhaustion, to stimulate certain brain sites. Although the experimenters obviously couldn't ask the animals about it, they *inferred* that the animals were experiencing some sort of pleasure.

Where are the self-stimulation centers located in the brain? Many self-stimulation sites have been found in the limbic system (Olds & Fobes, 1981). The heaviest concentration appears to be where the *medial forebrain bundle* (a bundle of axons) passes through the hypothalamus. The medial forebrain bundle is rich in dopamine-releasing neurons. The

rewarding effects of ESB at self-stimulation sites may be largely mediated by the activation of these dopamine circuits (Nakajima & Patterson, 1997). The rewarding, pleasurable effects of opiate and stimulant drugs (cocaine and amphetamines) may also depend on excitation of this dopamine system, although this conclusion is the subject of some debate (Gratton, 1996; Wise, 1999). In any event, it is clear that this dopamine system is *not* the ultimate biological basis for *all* reward (Berridge & Robinson, 1998). That is not surprising, as the brain is never that simple. Nonetheless, recent evidence suggests that the so-called "pleasure centers" in the brain may not be anatomical centers so much as neural circuits releasing dopamine.

The Cerebrum: The Seat of Complex Thought

 2f

The *cerebrum* is the largest and most complex part of the human brain. It includes the brain areas that are responsible for the most complex mental activities, including learning, remembering, thinking, and consciousness itself. **The *cerebral cortex* is the convoluted outer layer of the cerebrum.** The cortex is folded and bent, so that its large surface area—about 1.5 square feet—can be packed into the limited volume of the skull (Hubel & Wiesel, 1979).

Figure 3.17

Electrical stimulation of the brain (ESB) in the rat. Olds and Milner (1954) were using an apparatus like that depicted here when they discovered self-stimulation centers, or "pleasure centers," in the brain of a rat. In this setup, the rat's lever pressing earns brief electrical stimulation that is sent to a specific spot in the rat's brain where an electrode has been implanted.

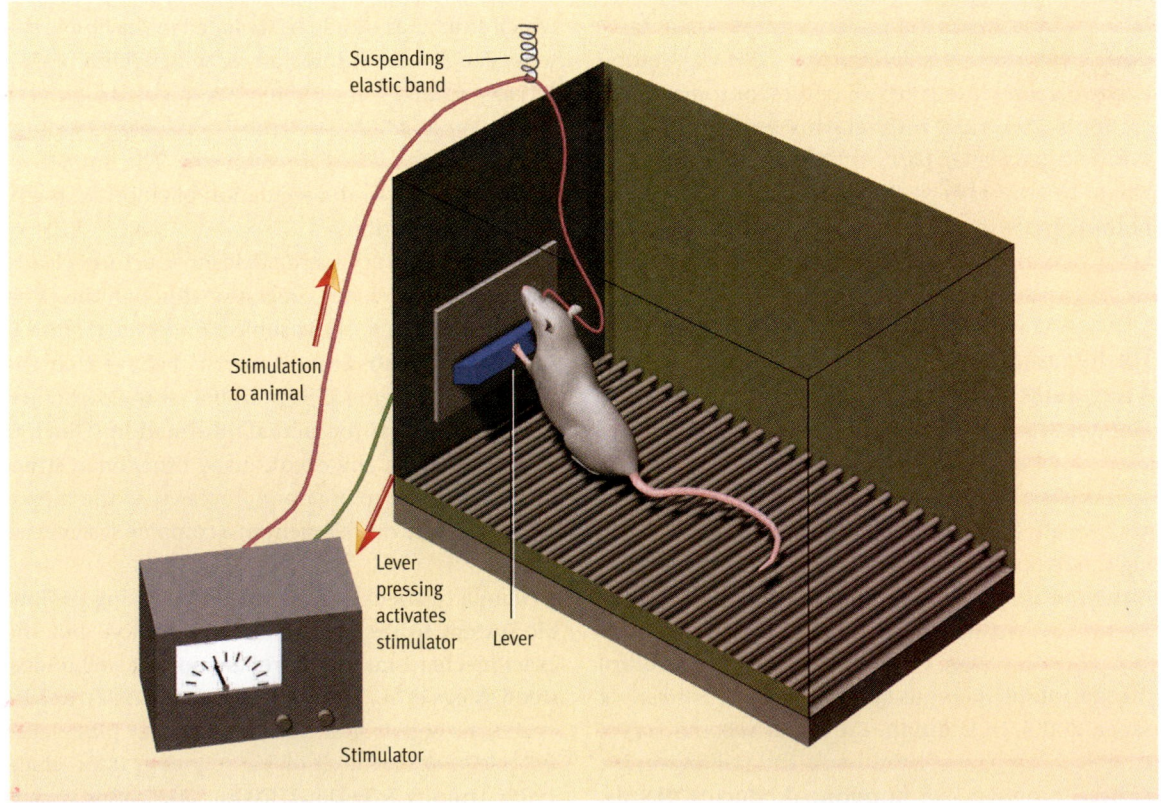

Suspending elastic band

Stimulation to animal

Lever pressing activates stimulator

Lever

Stimulator

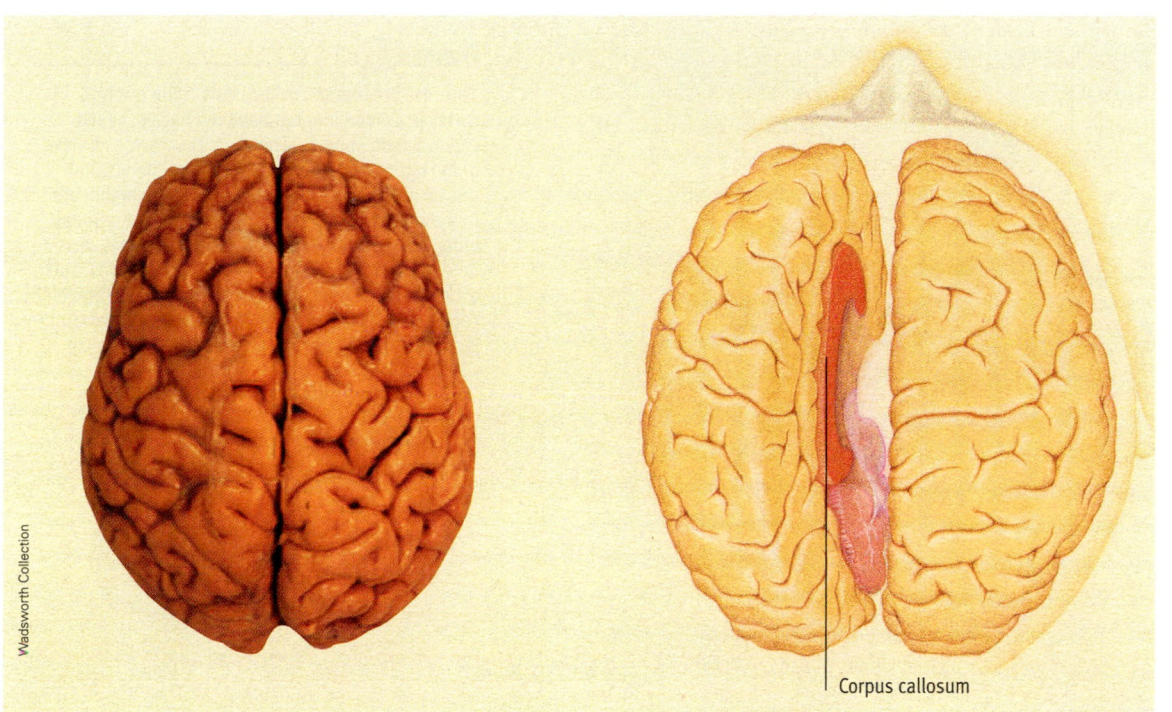

Figure 3.18

The cerebral hemispheres and the corpus callosum.
(Left) As this photo shows, the longitudinal fissure running down the middle of the brain (viewed from above) separates the left and right halves of the cerebral cortex. (Right) In this drawing the cerebral hemispheres have been "pulled apart" to reveal the corpus callosum. This band of fibers is the communication bridge between the right and left halves of the human brain.

Corpus callosum

The cerebrum is divided into two halves called hemispheres. Hence, **the *cerebral hemispheres* are the right and left halves of the cerebrum** (see Figure 3.18). The hemispheres are separated in the center of the brain by a longitudinal fissure that runs from the front to the back of the brain. This fissure descends to a thick band of fibers called the *corpus callosum* (also shown in Figure 3.18). **The *corpus callosum* is the structure that connects the two cerebral hemispheres.** We'll discuss the functional specialization of the cerebral hemispheres in the next section of this chapter. Each cerebral hemisphere is divided into four parts called *lobes.* To some extent, each of these lobes is dedicated to specific purposes. The location of these lobes can be seen in Figure 3.19 on the next page.

The *occipital lobe,* at the back of the head, includes the cortical area, where most visual signals are sent and visual processing is begun. This area is called the *primary visual cortex.* We will discuss how it is organized in Chapter 4.

The *parietal lobe* is forward of the occipital lobe. It includes the area that registers the sense of touch, called the *primary somatosensory cortex.* Various sections of this area receive signals from different regions of the body. When ESB is delivered in these parietal lobe areas, people report physical sensations—as if someone actually touched them on the arm or cheek, for example. The parietal lobe is also involved in integrating visual input and in monitoring the body's position in space.

The *temporal lobe* (meaning "near the temples") lies below the parietal lobe. Near its top, the temporal lobe contains an area devoted to auditory processing, called the *primary auditory cortex.* As we will see momentarily, damage to an area in the temporal lobe on the left side of the brain can impair the comprehension of speech and language.

Continuing forward, we find the *frontal lobe,* the largest lobe in the human brain. It contains the principal areas that control the movement of muscles, called the *primary motor cortex*. ESB applied in these areas can cause actual muscle contractions. The amount of motor cortex allocated to the control of a body part depends not on the part's size but on the diversity and precision of its movements. Thus, more of the cortex is given to parts we have fine control over, such as fingers, lips, and the tongue. Less of the cortex is devoted to larger parts that make crude movements, such as the thighs and shoulders (see Figure 3.20 on the next page).

The portion of the frontal lobe to the front of the motor cortex, which is called the *prefrontal cortex* (see the inset in Figure 3.19), is something of a mystery. This area is disproportionately large in humans, accounting for about 28% of the human cerebral cortex (Shimamura, 1996). In light of this fact, it was once assumed to house the highest, most abstract intellectual functions, but this view was eventually dismissed as an oversimplification. Still, recent studies suggest that the prefrontal cortex *does* contribute to

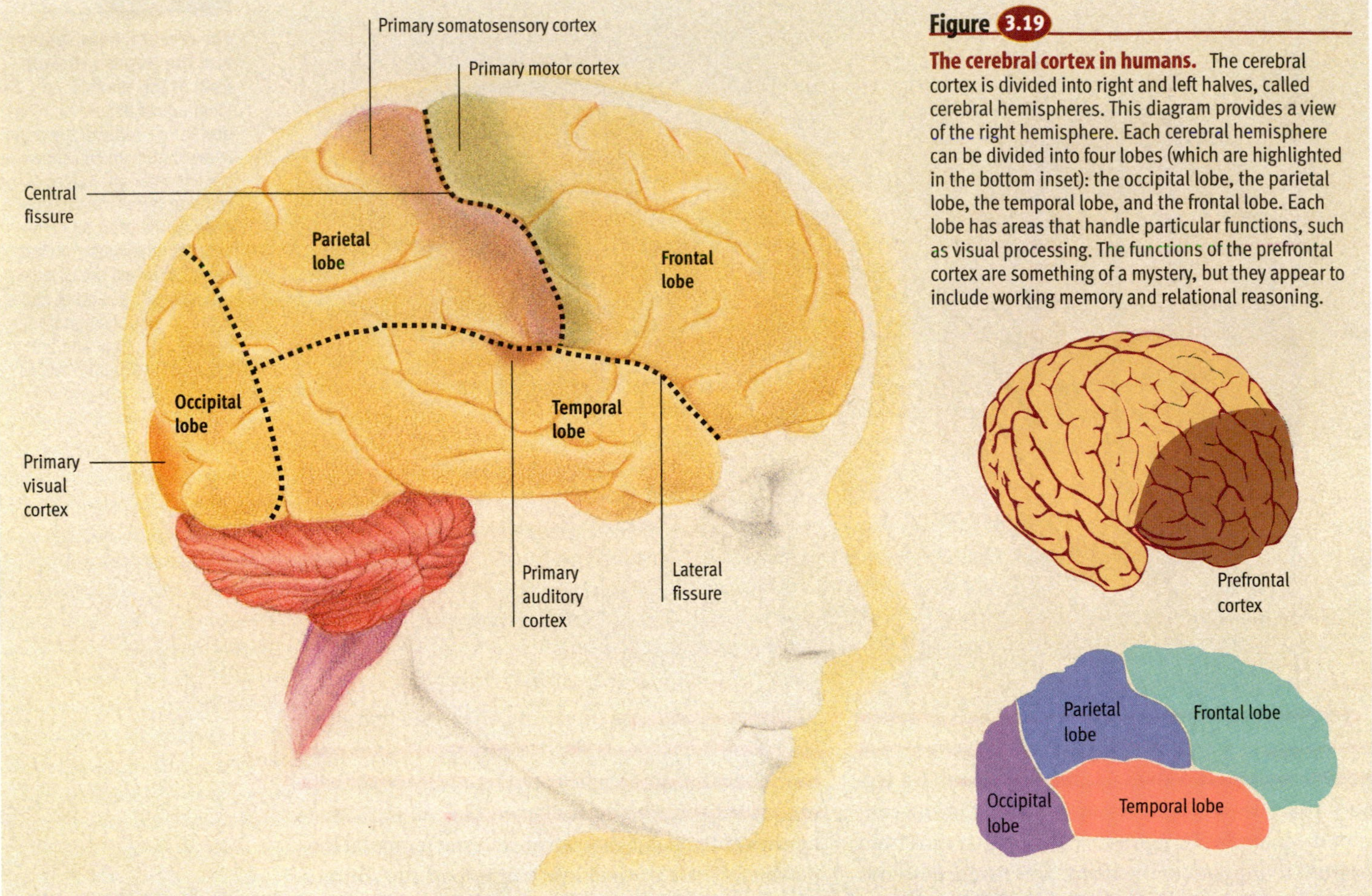

Figure 3.19

Primary somatosensory cortex

Primary motor cortex

Central fissure

Parietal lobe

Frontal lobe

Occipital lobe

Primary visual cortex

Temporal lobe

Primary auditory cortex

Lateral fissure

The cerebral cortex in humans. The cerebral cortex is divided into right and left halves, called cerebral hemispheres. This diagram provides a view of the right hemisphere. Each cerebral hemisphere can be divided into four lobes (which are highlighted in the bottom inset): the occipital lobe, the parietal lobe, the temporal lobe, and the frontal lobe. Each lobe has areas that handle particular functions, such as visual processing. The functions of the prefrontal cortex are something of a mystery, but they appear to include working memory and relational reasoning.

Prefrontal cortex

Parietal lobe

Frontal lobe

Occipital lobe

Temporal lobe

Figure 3.20

The primary motor cortex.
This diagram shows the amount of motor cortex devoted to the control of various muscles and limbs. The anatomical features in the drawing are distorted because their size is proportional to the amount of cortex devoted to their control. As you can see, more of the cortex is allocated to muscle groups that must make relatively precise movements.

SOURCE: Graphic from Sternberg, R. J. (2001). *Psychology: In search of the human mind.* Fort Worth: Harcourt. Reprinted by permission of Wadsworth Publishing.

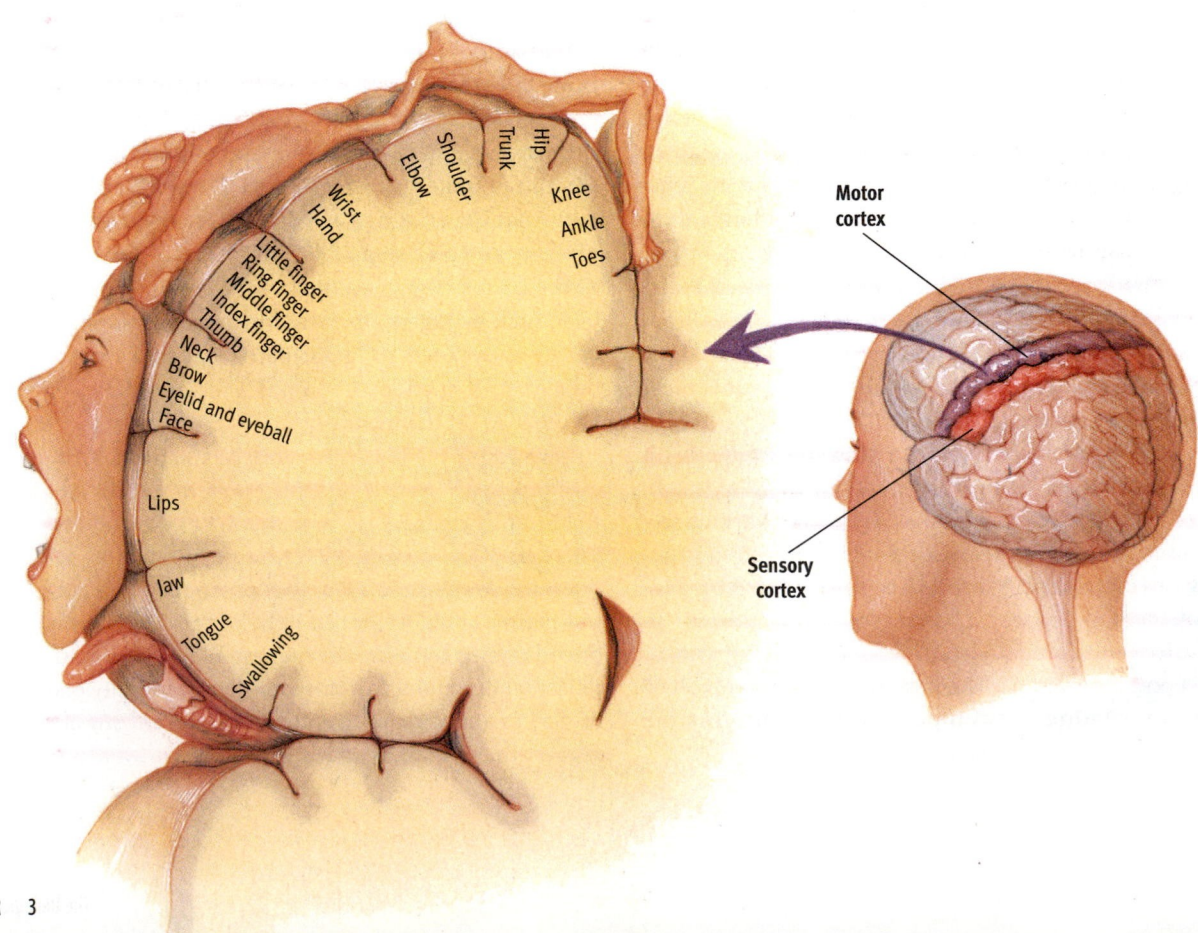

Hip
Trunk
Shoulder
Elbow
Wrist
Hand
Little finger
Ring finger
Middle finger
Index finger
Thumb
Neck
Brow
Eyelid and eyeball
Face
Lips
Jaw
Tongue
Swallowing
Knee
Ankle
Toes

Motor cortex

Sensory cortex

an impressive variety of higher-order functions, such as memory for temporal sequences (Kesner, 1998); working memory, which is a temporary buffer that processes current information (Goldman-Rakic, 1993, 1998); and reasoning about relations between objects and events (Waltz et al., 1999). Its contribution to working memory and relational reasoning have led some theorists to suggest that the prefrontal cortex houses some sort of "executive control system," which is thought to monitor, organize, and direct thought processes (Kimberg, D'Esposito, & Farah, 1997; Shimamura, 1995). Consistent with this hypothesis, people who suffer damage in the prefrontal cortex often show deficits in planning, paying attention, and getting organized (Fuster, 1996).

The Plasticity of the Brain

It was once believed that significant changes in the anatomy and organization of the brain were limited to early periods of development in both humans and animals. However, research has gradually demonstrated that the anatomical structure and functional organization of the brain is more "plastic" or malleable than widely assumed (Kolb & Whishaw, 1998; Recanzone, 2000). This conclusion is based on several lines of research.

First, studies have shown that aspects of experience can sculpt features of brain structure. For example, neuroimaging studies have shown that an area in the somatosensory cortex that receives input from the fingers of the left hand is enlarged in string musicians who constantly use the left hand to finger the strings of their instruments (Elbert et al., 1995). In a similar vein, researchers find greater dendritic branching and synaptic density in rats raised in a stimulating, enriched environment, as opposed to a dull, barren environment (Rosenzweig & Bennet, 1996; see the Critical Thinking Application).

Second, research has shown that damage to incoming sensory pathways or the destruction of brain tissue can lead to neural reorganization. For example, when scientists amputated the third finger in an owl monkey, the part of its cortex that formerly responded to the third finger gradually became responsive to the second and fourth fingers (Kaas, 2000). Neural reorganization has also been seen in response to brain damage as healthy neurons attempt to compensate for the loss of nearby neurons (Cao et al., 1994; Gilbert, 1993).

Third, recent studies indicate that the adult brain can generate new neurons. Until recently it was believed that the brain formed all its neurons by infancy at the latest. However, new evidence suggests that adult humans can form new neurons in the hippocampus (Eriksson et al., 1998). Furthermore, Elizabeth Gould and her colleagues (1999) have found that adult monkeys form *thousands* of new brain cells each day in deep subcortical areas. These new neurons then migrate to areas in the cortex where they sprout axons and form new synapses with existing neurons.

In sum, research suggests that the brain is not "hard wired" the way a computer is. It appears that the neural wiring of the brain is flexible and constantly evolving. That said, this plasticity is not unlimited. Rehabilitation efforts with people who have suffered severe brain damage clearly demonstrate that there are limits on the extent to which the brain can rewire itself (Zillmer & Spiers, 2001). And the evidence suggests that the brain's plasticity declines with age (Rains, 2002). Younger brains are more malleable than older brains. Still, the neural circuits of the brain show substantial plasticity, which certainly helps organisms adapt to their environments.

REVIEW OF KEY POINTS

- The brain has three major regions: the hindbrain, midbrain, and forebrain. Structures in the hindbrain include the medulla, pons, and cerebellum. These structures handle essential functions such as breathing, circulation, coordination of movement, and the rhythm of sleep and arousal.

- The midbrain contributes to the coordination of sensory processes. Deterioration of an area in the midbrain has been implicated as a factor in Parkinson's disease.

- The forebrain includes many structures that handle higher functions. The thalamus is primarily a relay station. The hypothalamus is involved in the regulation of basic biological drives such as hunger and sex.

- The limbic system is a network of loosely connected structures located along the border between the cortex and deeper subcortical areas. It includes the hippocampus, which appears to play a role in memory, the amygdala, which is involved in the regulation of emotion, and areas rich in self-stimulation sites.

- The cerebrum is the brain area implicated in most complex mental activities. The cortex is the cerebrum's convoluted outer layer, which is subdivided into four lobes.

- These lobes and their primary known functions are the occipital lobe (vision), the parietal lobe (touch), the temporal lobe (hearing), and the frontal lobe (movement of the body). The prefrontal cortex may contribute to working memory and relational reasoning. The structure and function of the brain appears to be more plastic than widely appreciated.

Right Brain/Left Brain: Cerebral Laterality

PREVIEW QUESTIONS

- How was the left hemisphere originally implicated in the control of language?
- How are sensory and motor information routed to the two hemispheres?
- What did split-brain research reveal about the right and left hemispheres of the brain?
- How do scientists study hemispheric specialization in normal subjects, and what have they learned?

As we noted a moment ago, the cerebrum—the seat of complex thought—is divided into two separate hemispheres (see Figure 3.18). Recent decades have seen an exciting flurry of research on the specialized abilities of the right and left cerebral hemispheres. Some theorists have gone so far as to suggest that we really have two brains in one!

Hints of this hemispheric specialization have been available for many years, from cases in which one side of a person's brain has been damaged. The left hemisphere was implicated in the control of language as early as 1861, by Paul Broca, a French surgeon. Broca was treating a patient who had been unable to speak for 30 years. After the patient died, Broca showed that the probable cause of his speech deficit was a localized lesion on the left side of the frontal lobe. Since then, many similar cases have shown that this area of the brain—known as *Broca's area*—plays an important role in the *production* of speech (see Figure 3.21). Another major language center—*Wernicke's area*—was identified in the temporal lobe of the left hemisphere in 1874. Damage in Wernicke's area (see Figure 3.21) usually leads to problems with the *comprehension* of language.

Evidence that the left hemisphere usually processes language led scientists to characterize it as the "dominant" hemisphere. Because thoughts are usually coded in terms of language, the left hemisphere was given the lion's share of credit for handling the "higher" mental processes, such as reasoning, remembering, planning, and problem solving. Meanwhile, the right hemisphere came to be viewed as the "non-dominant," or "dumb," hemisphere, lacking any special functions or abilities.

This characterization of the left and right hemispheres as major and minor partners in the brain's work began to change in the 1960s. It all started with landmark research by Roger Sperry, Michael Gazzaniga, and their colleagues who studied "split-brain" patients: individuals whose cerebral hemispheres had been surgically disconnected (Gazzaniga, 1970; Gazzaniga, Bogen, & Sperry, 1965; Levy, Trevarthen, & Sperry, 1972; Sperry, 1982). In 1981 Sperry received a Nobel prize in physiology/medicine for this work.

Bisecting the Brain: Split-Brain Research  SIM2, 2f

In *split-brain surgery* the bundle of fibers that connects the cerebral hemispheres (the corpus callosum) is cut to reduce the severity of epileptic seizures. It is a radical procedure that is chosen only in exceptional cases that have not responded to other forms of treatment. But the surgery provides scientists with an unusual opportunity to study people who have had their brain literally split in two.

To appreciate the logic of split-brain research, you need to understand how sensory and motor information is routed to and from the two hemispheres. *Each hemisphere's primary connections are to the opposite side of the body.* Thus, the left hemisphere controls, and communicates with, the right hand, right arm, right leg, right eyebrow, and so on. In contrast, the right hemisphere controls, and communicates with, the left side of the body.

Vision and hearing are more complex. Both eyes deliver information to both hemispheres, but there still is a separation of input. Stimuli in the right half of the *visual field* are registered by receptors on the left side of each eye, which send signals to the left hemisphere. Stimuli in the left half of the visual field are transmitted by both eyes to the right hemisphere (see Figure 3.22). Auditory inputs to each ear also go to both hemispheres. However, connections to the opposite hemisphere are stronger or more immediate. That is, sounds presented exclusively to the right ear (through headphones) are registered in the left hemisphere first, while sounds presented to the left ear are registered more quickly in the right hemisphere.

For the most part, people don't notice this asymmetric, "crisscrossed" organization because the two hemispheres are in close communication with each

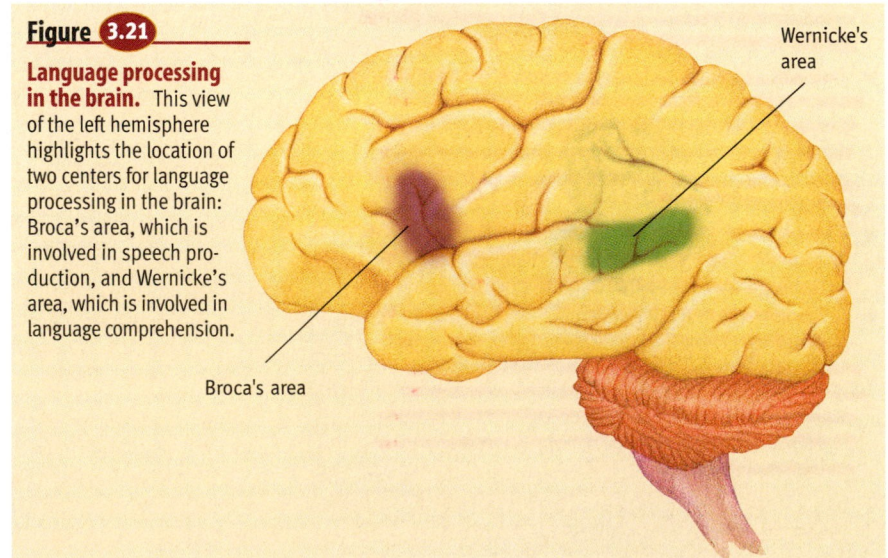

Figure 3.21

Language processing in the brain. This view of the left hemisphere highlights the location of two centers for language processing in the brain: Broca's area, which is involved in speech production, and Wernicke's area, which is involved in language comprehension.

Wernicke's area

Broca's area

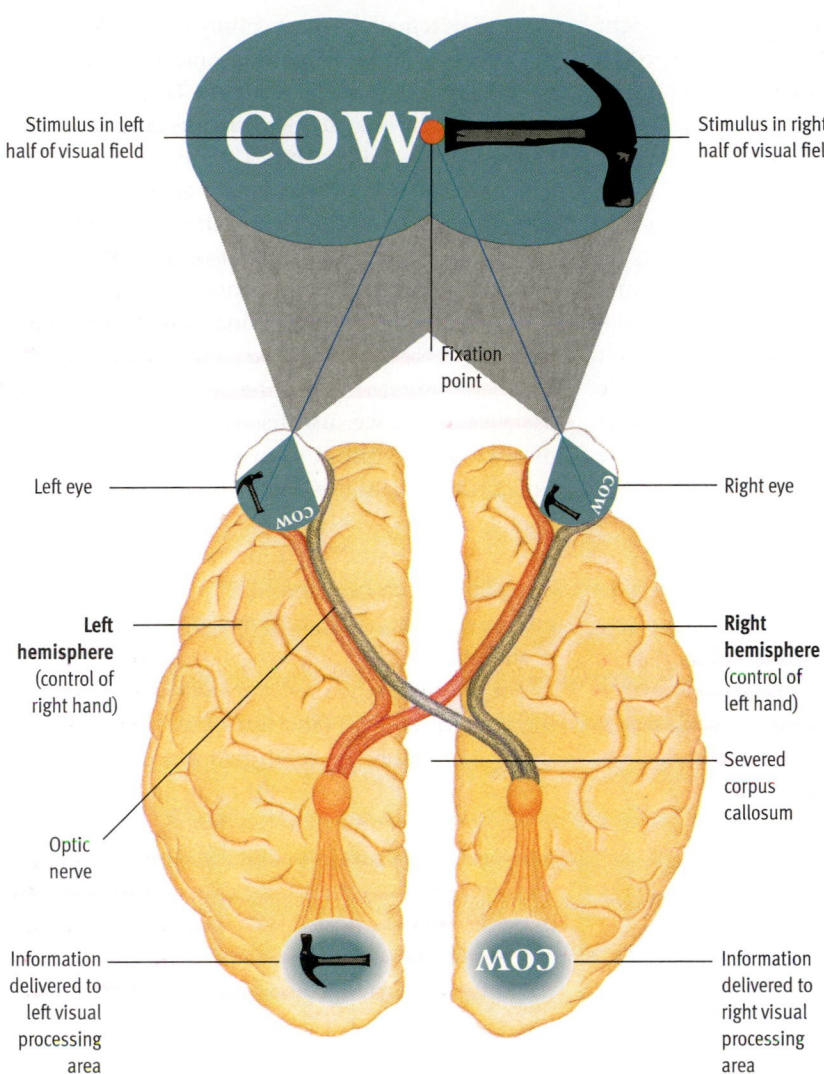

Stimulus in left half of visual field

Stimulus in right half of visual field

COW

Fixation point

Left eye

Right eye

Left hemisphere (control of right hand)

Right hemisphere (control of left hand)

Severed corpus callosum

Optic nerve

Information delivered to left visual processing area

Information delivered to right visual processing area

Courtesy of Roger Sperry

Figure 3.22

Visual input in the split brain. If a participant stares at a fixation point, the point divides the subject's visual field into right and left halves. Input from the right visual field (a picture of a hammer in this example) strikes the left side of each eye and is transmitted to the left hemisphere. Input from the left visual field strikes the right side of each eye and is transmitted to the right hemisphere. Normally, the hemispheres share the information from the two halves of the visual field, but in split-brain patients, the corpus callosum is severed, and the two hemispheres cannot communicate. Hence, the experimenter can present a visual stimulus to just one hemisphere at a time.

⟶*Both the left and right hemispheres of the brain have been found to have their own specialized forms of intellect.*⟶
ROGER SPERRY

other. Information received by one hemisphere is readily shared with the other via the corpus callosum. However, when the two hemispheres are surgically disconnected, the functional specialization of the brain becomes apparent.

In their classic study of split-brain patients, Gazzaniga, Bogen, and Sperry (1965) presented visual stimuli such as pictures, symbols, and words in a single visual field (the left or the right), so that the stimuli would be sent to only one hemisphere. The stimuli were projected onto a screen in front of the participants, who stared at a fixation point (a spot) in the center of the screen (see Figure 3.23). The images were flashed to the right or the left of the fixation point for only a split second. Thus, the subjects did not have a chance to move their eyes, and the stimuli were only glimpsed in one visual field.

When pictures were flashed in the right visual field and thus sent to the left hemisphere, the split-

brain subjects were able to name and describe the objects depicted (such as a cup or spoon). However, the subjects were *not* able to name and describe the same objects when they were flashed in the left visual field and sent to the right hemisphere. In a sim-

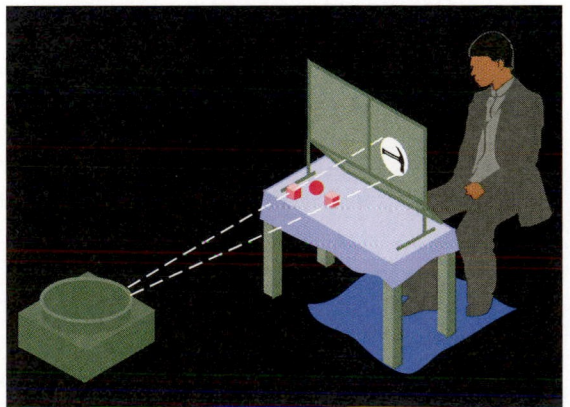

Figure 3.23

Experimental apparatus in split-brain research. On the left is a special slide projector that can present images very briefly, before the subject's eyes can move and thus change the visual field. Images are projected on one side of the screen to present stimuli to just one hemisphere. The portion of the apparatus beneath the screen is constructed to prevent participants from seeing objects that they may be asked to handle with their right or left hand, another procedure that can be used to send information to just one hemisphere.

ilar fashion, an object placed out of view in the right hand (communicating with the left hemisphere) could be named. However, the same object placed in the left hand (right hemisphere) could not be. These findings supported the notion that language is housed in the left hemisphere.

Although the split-brain subjects' right hemisphere was not able to speak up for itself, further tests revealed that it *was* processing the information presented. If subjects were given an opportunity to *point out a picture* of an object they had held in their left hand, they were able to do so. They were also able to point out pictures that had been flashed to the left visual field. Furthermore, the right hemisphere (left hand) turned out to be *superior* to the left hemisphere (right hand) in assembling little puzzles and copying drawings, even though the subjects were right-handed. These findings provided the first compelling demonstration that the right hemisphere has its own special talents. Subsequent studies of additional split-brain patients showed the right hemisphere to be better than the left on a variety of visual-spatial tasks, including discriminating colors, arranging blocks, and recognizing faces.

Hemispheric Specialization in the Intact Brain

 SIM 2, 2f

The problem with the split-brain operation, of course, is that it creates an abnormal situation. The vast ma-

jority of us remain "neurologically intact." Moreover, the surgery is done only with people who suffer from prolonged, severe cases of epilepsy. These people may have had somewhat atypical brain organization even before the operation. Thus, theorists couldn't help wondering whether it was safe to generalize broadly from the split-brain studies. For this reason, researchers developed methods that allowed them to study cerebral specialization in the intact brain.

One method involves looking at *perceptual asymmetries—left-right imbalances between the cerebral hemispheres in the speed of visual or auditory processing.* As we just discussed, it is possible to present visual stimuli to just one visual field at a time. In normal individuals, the input sent to one hemisphere is quickly shared with the other. However, subtle differences in the "abilities" of the two hemispheres can be detected by precisely measuring how long it takes subjects to recognize different types of stimuli.

For instance, when *verbal* stimuli are presented to the right visual field (and thus sent to the *left hemisphere* first), they are identified more quickly and more accurately than when they are presented to the left visual field (and sent to the right hemisphere first). The faster reactions in the left hemisphere presumably occur because it can recognize verbal stimuli on its own, while the right hemisphere has to take extra time to "consult" the left hemisphere. In contrast, the *right hemisphere* is faster than the left on *visual-*

CONCEPT CHECK 3.3

Relating Disorders to the Nervous System

Imagine that you are working as a neuropsychologist at a clinic. You are involved in the diagnosis of the cases described below. You are asked to identify the probable cause(s) of the disorders in terms of nervous system malfunctions. Based on the information in this chapter, indicate the probable location of any brain damage or the probable disturbance of neurotransmitter activity. The answers can be found in the back of the book in Appendix A.

Case 1. Miriam is exhibiting language deficits. In particular, she does not seem to comprehend the meaning of words.
_____
_____

Case 2. Camille displays tremors and muscular rigidity and is diagnosed as having Parkinsonism.
_____
_____

Case 3. Ricardo, a 28-year-old computer executive, has gradually seen his strength and motor coordination deteriorate badly. He is diagnosed as having multiple sclerosis.
_____
_____

Case 4. Wendy is highly irrational, has poor contact with reality, and reports hallucinations. She is given a diagnosis of schizophrenic disorder.
_____
_____

spatial tasks, such as locating a dot or recognizing a face (Bradshaw, 1989; Bryden, 1982).

Researchers have also used a variety of other approaches to explore hemispheric specialization in normal people. For the most part, their findings have converged nicely with the results of the split-brain studies (Reuter-Lorenz & Miller, 1998). Overall, the findings suggest that the two hemispheres are specialized, with each handling certain types of cognitive tasks better than the other (Springer & Deutsch, 1998). *The left hemisphere usually is better on tasks involving verbal processing, such as language, speech, reading, and writing. The right hemisphere exhibits superiority on many tasks involving nonverbal processing, such as most spatial, musical, and visual recognition tasks.*

Cerebral lateralization is a burgeoning area of research that has broad implications, which we will discuss further in the Personal Application. For now, however, let's leave the brain and turn our attention to the endocrine system.

REVIEW OF KEY POINTS

● The cerebrum is divided into right and left hemispheres connected by the corpus callosum. Evidence that the left cerebral hemisphere usually processes language led scientists to view it as the dominant hemisphere.

● However, studies of split-brain patients revealed that the right and left halves of the brain each have unique talents, with the right hemisphere being specialized to handle visual-spatial functions.

● Studies of perceptual asymmetries in normal subjects also showed that the left hemisphere is better equipped to handle verbal processing, whereas the right hemisphere is more adept at nonverbal processing.

The Endocrine System: Another Way to Communicate

The major way the brain communicates with the rest of the body is through the nervous system. However, the body has a second communication system that is also important to behavior. **The *endocrine system* consists of glands that secrete chemicals into the bloodstream that help control bodily functioning.** The messengers in this communication network are called hormones. ***Hormones* are the chemical substances released by the endocrine glands.** In a way, hormones are like neurotransmitters in the nervous system. They are stored for subsequent release as chemical messengers, and once released, they diffuse through the bloodstream and bind to special receptors on target cells. In fact, some chemical substances do double duty, functioning as hormones when they're released in the endocrine system and as neurotransmitters in the nervous system (norepinephrine, for example). However, there are some important differences between hormones and neurotransmitters. Neural messages generally are transmitted short distances with lightning speed (measured in milliseconds) along very specific pathways, whereas hormonal messages often travel to distant cells at a much slower speed (measured in seconds and minutes) and tend to be less specific, as they can act on many target cells throughout the body.

The major endocrine glands are shown in Figure 3.24 on the next page. Some hormones are released in response to changing conditions in the body and act to regulate those conditions. For example, hormones released by the stomach and intestines help control digestion. Kidney hormones play a part in regulating blood pressure. And pancreatic hormone (insulin) is essential for cells to use sugar from the blood. Hormone release tends to be *pulsatile*. That is, hormones tend to be released several times per day in brief bursts or pulses that last only a few minutes. The levels of many hormones increase and decrease in a rhythmic pattern throughout the day.

Much of the endocrine system is controlled by the nervous system through the *hypothalamus*. This structure at the base of the forebrain has intimate connections with the pea-sized *pituitary gland*. **The *pituitary gland* releases a great variety of hormones that fan out around the body, stimulating actions in the other endocrine glands.** In this sense, the pituitary is the "master gland" of the endocrine system, although the hypothalamus is the real power behind the throne.

The intermeshing of the nervous system and the endocrine system can be seen in the fight-or-flight response described earlier. In times of stress, the hypothalamus sends signals along two pathways—through the autonomic nervous system and through the pituitary gland—to the adrenal glands (Sapolsky, 1992). In response, the adrenal glands secrete hormones that radiate throughout the body, preparing it to cope with an emergency (see Chapter 13). The communication between the brain and the endocrine system is not a one-way street, as hormonal fluctuations can trigger responses in the brain. For example, hor-

PREVIEW QUESTIONS

● What does the endocrine system consist of?

● What are hormones, and how do they resemble and differ from neurotransmitters?

● What is the master gland of the endocrine system?

● What are some aspects of behavior regulated by hormones?

Figure 3.24

The endocrine system. This graphic depicts most of the major endocrine glands. The endocrine glands secrete hormones into the bloodstream. These chemicals regulate a variety of physical functions and affect many aspects of behavior.

SOURCE: Graphic from Starr, C. & Taggart, R. (1998). *Biology: The unity and diversity of life.* Belmont, CA: Wadsworth. © 1998 Wadsworth Publishing. Reprinted by permission.

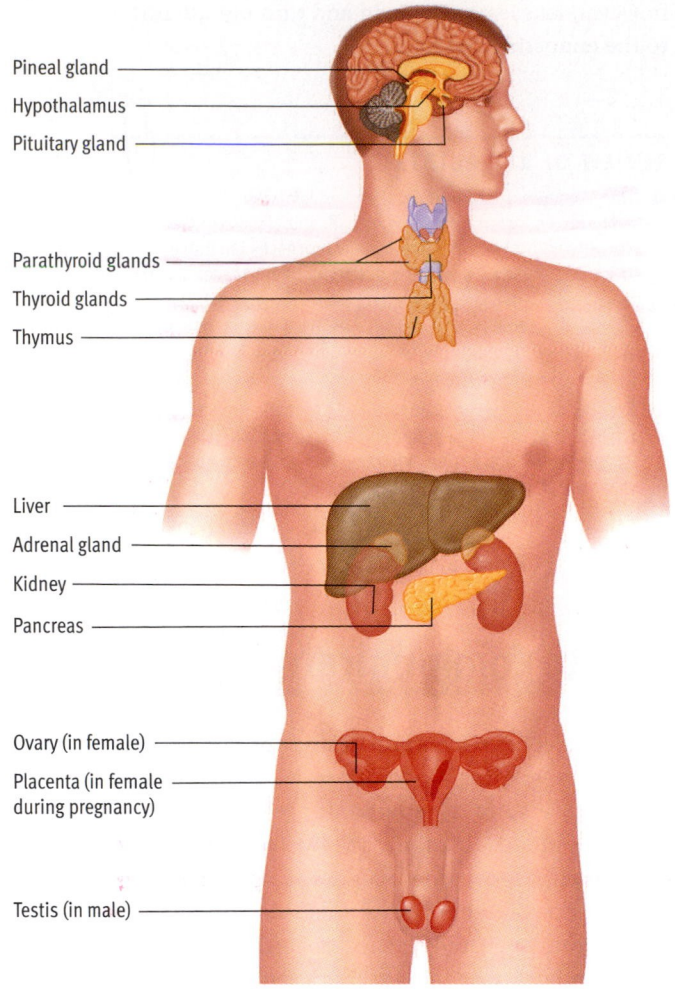

- Pineal gland
- Hypothalamus
- Pituitary gland
- Parathyroid glands
- Thyroid glands
- Thymus
- Liver
- Adrenal gland
- Kidney
- Pancreas
- Ovary (in female)
- Placenta (in female during pregnancy)
- Testis (in male)

mones secreted by the adrenal medulla in response to stress can signal the hypothalamus to inhibit further hormone output. The levels of many hormones are regulated through *negative feedback systems*. When a hormone increases to a certain level, signals are sent to the hypothalamus or the relevant endocrine gland to reduce or stop further secretion of that hormone.

Hormones play important roles in modulating human physiological development. For example, among the more interesting hormones released by the pituitary are the *gonadotropins,* which affect the *gonads,* or sexual glands. Prior to birth, these hormones direct the formation of the external sexual organs in the developing fetus (Breedlove, 1992). Thus, your sexual identity as a male or female was shaped during prenatal development by the actions of hormones. At puberty, increased levels of sexual hormones are responsible for the emergence of secondary sexual characteristics, such as male facial hair and female breasts (Litt & Vaughan, 1992). The actions of other hormones are responsible for the spurt in physical growth that occurs around puberty (see Chapter 11).

These developmental effects of hormones illustrate how genetic programming has a hand in behavior. Obviously, the hormonal actions that shaped your sex were determined by your genetic makeup. Similarly, the hormonal changes in early adolescence that launched your growth spurt and aroused your interest in sexuality were preprogrammed over a decade earlier by your genetic inheritance. Which brings us to the role of heredity in shaping behavior.

Heredity and Behavior: Is It All in the Genes?

PREVIEW QUESTIONS

- What are the basic mechanisms of hereditary transmission?
- What is the difference between one's genotype and phenotype?
- How are family studies conducted, and what can they reveal?
- How are twin studies conducted, and what have they revealed about intelligence and personality?
- How do adoption studies assess the role of genetics and environment?
- What is genetic mapping, and how will it facilitate behavioral genetics research?

As you have learned throughout this chapter, your biological makeup is intimately related to your behavior. That is why your genetic inheritance, which shapes your biological makeup, may have much to do with your behavior. Most people realize that physical characteristics such as height, hair color, blood type, and eye color are largely shaped by heredity. But what about psychological characteristics, such as intelligence, moodiness, impulsiveness, and shyness? To what extent are people's behavioral qualities molded by their genes? These questions are the central focus of *behavioral genetics*—an interdisciplinary field that studies the influence of genetic factors on behavioral traits.

As we saw in Chapter 1, questions about the relative importance of heredity versus environment are very old ones in psychology. However, research in behavioral genetics has grown by leaps and bounds

since the 1970s, and this research has shed new light on the age-old nature versus nurture debate. Ironically, although behavioral geneticists have mainly sought to demonstrate the influence of heredity on behavior, their recent work has also highlighted the importance of the environment, as we shall see in this section.

Basic Principles of Genetics

Every cell in your body contains enduring messages from your mother and father. These messages are found on the *chromosomes* that lie within the nucleus of each cell.

Chromosomes and Genes

Chromosomes are strands of DNA (deoxyribonucleic acid) molecules that carry genetic information (see Figure 3.25). Every cell in humans, except the sex cells (sperm and eggs), contains 46 chromosomes. These chromosomes operate in 23 pairs, with one chromosome of each pair being contributed by each parent. Parents make this contribution when fertilization creates a *zygote, a single cell formed by the union of a sperm and an egg.* The sex cells that form a zygote each have 23 chromosomes; together they contribute the 46 chromosomes that appear in the zygote and in all the body cells that develop from it. Each chromosome in turn contains thousands of biochemical messengers called genes. *Genes* are DNA segments that serve as the key functional units in hereditary transmission.

If all offspring are formed by a union of the parents' sex cells, why aren't family members identical clones? The reason is that a single pair of parents can produce an extraordinary variety of combinations of chromosomes. When sex cells form in each parent, it is a matter of chance as to which member of each chromosome pair ends up in the sperm or egg. Each parent's 23 chromosome pairs can be scrambled in over 8 million (2^{23}) different ways, yielding roughly 70 trillion possible configurations (2^{46}) when sperm and egg unite. Actually, this is a conservative estimate. It doesn't take into account complexities such as *mutations* (changes in the genetic code) or *crossing over* during sex-cell formation (an interchange of mate-

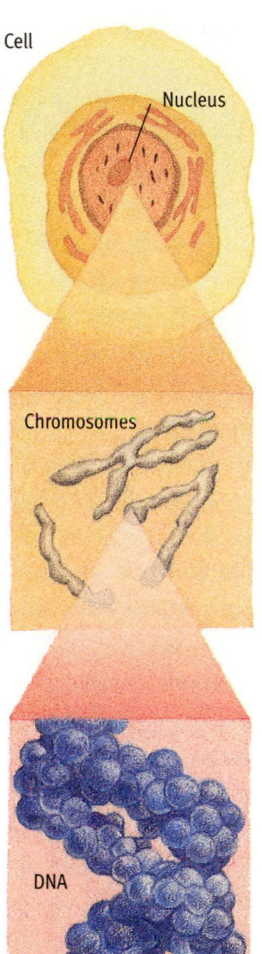

Figure 3.25

Genetic material. This series of enlargements shows the main components of genetic material. (Top) In the nucleus of every cell are chromosomes, which carry the information needed to construct new human beings. (Center) Chromosomes are thread-like strands of DNA that carry thousands of genes, the functional units of hereditary transmission. (Bottom) DNA is a spiraled double chain of molecules that can copy itself to reproduce.

Cell

Nucleus

Chromosomes

DNA

rial between chromosomes). Thus, genetic transmission is a complicated process, and everything is a matter of probability. Except for identical twins, each person ends up with a unique genetic blueprint.

Like chromosomes, genes operate in pairs, with one gene of each pair coming from each parent. In the *homozygous condition,* the two genes in a specific pair are the same. In the *heterozygous* condition, the two genes in a specific pair are different (see Figure 3.26). In the simplest scenario, a single pair of genes determines a trait. Attached versus detached earlobes provide a nice example. When both parents contribute a gene for the same type of earlobe (the *homozygous* condition), the child will have an earlobe of that type. When the parents contribute genes for different types of earlobes (the *heterozygous* condition), one gene in the pair—called the *dominant gene*—overrides or masks the other, called the *recessive gene.* Thus, **a *dominant gene* is one that is expressed when**

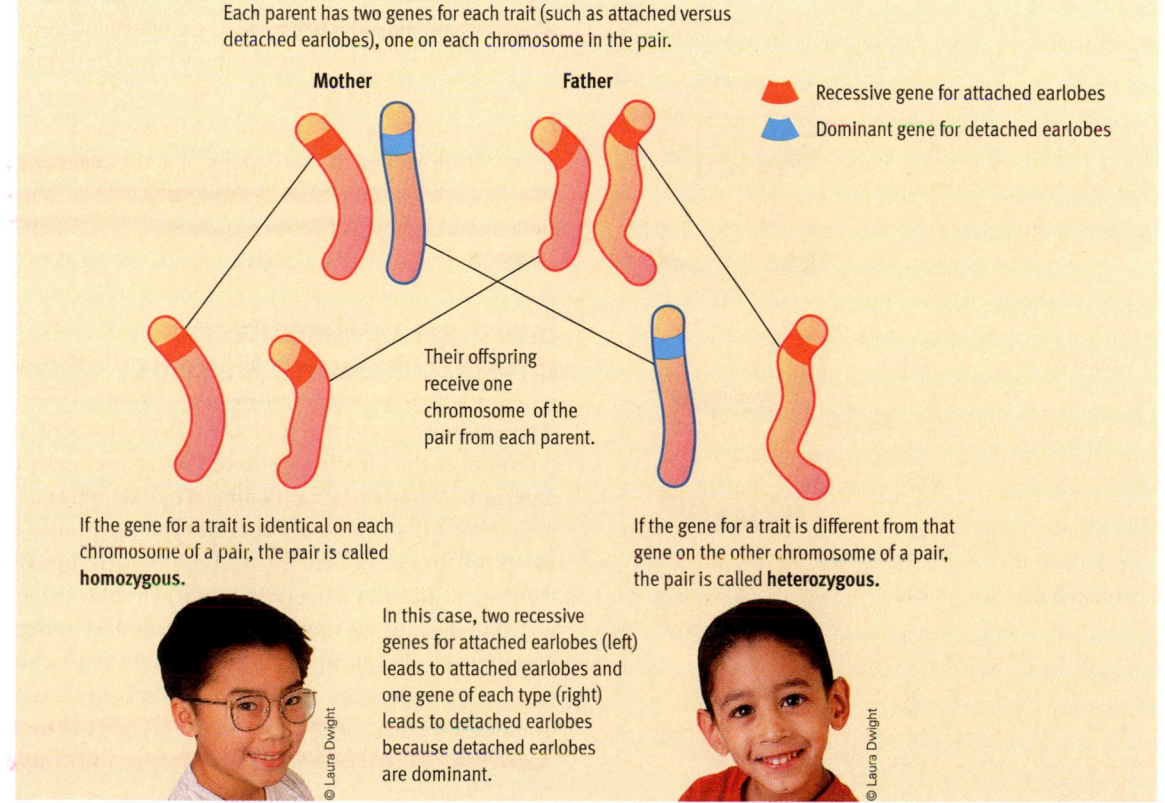

Each parent has two genes for each trait (such as attached versus detached earlobes), one on each chromosome in the pair.

Mother

Father

Recessive gene for attached earlobes

Dominant gene for detached earlobes

Their offspring receive one chromosome of the pair from each parent.

If the gene for a trait is identical on each chromosome of a pair, the pair is called **homozygous.**

If the gene for a trait is different from that gene on the other chromosome of a pair, the pair is called **heterozygous.**

In this case, two recessive genes for attached earlobes (left) leads to attached earlobes and one gene of each type (right) leads to detached earlobes because detached earlobes are dominant.

© Laura Dwight

© Laura Dwight

Figure 3.26

Homozygous and heterozygous genotypes. Like chromosomes, genes operate in pairs, with one gene in each pair coming from each parent. When paired genes are the same, they are said to be homozygous. When paired genes are different, they are said to be heterozygous. Whether people have attached or detached earlobes is determined by a single pair of genes. In the heterozygous condition, genes for detached earlobes are dominant over genes for attached earlobes.

paired genes are different. A *recessive gene* is one that is masked when paired genes are different. In the case of earlobes, genes for detached earlobes are dominant over genes for attached earlobes.

Because genes operate in pairs, a child has a 50% probability of inheriting a specific gene in a particular gene pair from each parent. Hence, the *genetic relatedness* of parents and children is said to be 50%. The genetic relatedness of other types of relatives can be calculated in the same way; the results are shown in Figure 3.27. As you can see, genetic relatedness ranges from 100% for identical twins down to 6.25% for second cousins. The numbers in Figure 3.27 are purely theoretical, and for a variety of complicated reasons they underestimate the actual genetic overlap among people. But the key to the concept of genetic relatedness is that members of a family share more of the same genes than nonmembers, and closer relatives share a larger proportion of genes than more distant relatives. These realities explain why family members tend to resemble one another and why this resemblance tends to be greater among closer relatives.

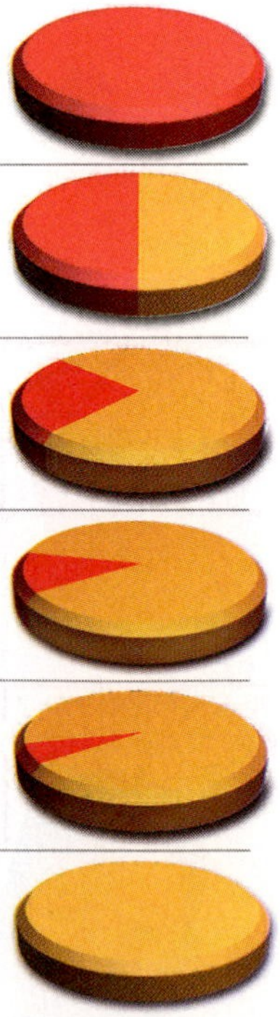

Genotype Versus Phenotype

It might seem that two parents with the same manifest trait, such as detached earlobes, should always produce offspring with that trait. However, that isn't always the case. For instance, two parents with de-

tached earlobes can produce a child with attached earlobes. This happens because there are unexpressed recessive genes in the family's gene pool—in this case, genes for attached earlobes.

This point brings us to the distinction between genotype and phenotype. *Genotype* refers to a person's genetic makeup. *Phenotype* refers to the ways in which a person's genotype is manifested in observable characteristics. Different genotypes (such as two genes for detached earlobes as opposed to one gene for detached and one for attached) can yield the same phenotype (detached earlobes). Genotype is determined at conception and is fixed forever. In contrast, phenotypic characteristics (hair color, for instance) may change over time. They may also be modified by environmental factors.

Genotypes translate into phenotypic characteristics in a variety of ways. Not all gene pairs operate according to the principles of dominance. In some instances, when paired genes are different, they produce a blend, an "averaged out" phenotype. In other cases, paired genes that are different strike another type of compromise, and both characteristics show up phenotypically. In the case of type AB blood, for example, one gene is for type A and the other is for type B.

Polygenic Inheritance

Most human characteristics appear to be *polygenic traits,* or characteristics that are influenced by more than one pair of genes. For example, three to five gene pairs are thought to interactively determine skin color. Complex physical abilities, such as motor coordination, may be influenced by tangled interactions among a great many pairs of genes. Most psychological characteristics that appear to be affected by heredity seem to involve complex polygenic inheritance (Plomin et al., 2001).

Investigating Hereditary Influence: Research Methods

How do behavioral geneticists and other scientists disentangle the effects of genetics and experience to determine whether heredity affects behavioral traits? Researchers have designed special types of studies to assess the impact of heredity. Of course, with humans they are limited to correlational rather than experimental methods, as they cannot manipulate genetic variables by assigning subjects to mate with each other (this approach, called *selective breeding,* is used in animal studies). The three most important methods in human research are family studies, twin stud-

Figure 3.27

Genetic relatedness. Research on the genetic bases of behavior takes advantage of the different degrees of genetic relatedness between various types of relatives. If heredity influences a trait, relatives who share more genes should be more similar with regard to that trait than are more distant relatives, who share fewer genes. Comparisons involving various degrees of biological relationships will come up frequently in later chapters.

Relationship	Degree of relatedness	
Identical twins		100%
Fraternal twins Brother or sister Parent or child	First degree relatives	50%
Grandparent or grandchild Uncle, aunt, nephew, or niece Half-bother or half-sister	Second degree relatives	25%
First cousin	Third degree relatives	12.5%
Second cousin	Fourth degree relatives	6.25%
Unrelated		0%

ies, and adoption studies. After examining these classic methods of research, we'll discuss the impact of new developments in genetic mapping.

Family Studies

In *family studies* researchers assess hereditary influence by examining blood relatives to see how much they resemble one another on a specific trait. If heredity affects the trait under scrutiny, researchers should find phenotypic similarity among relatives. Furthermore, they should find more similarity among relatives who share more genes. For instance, siblings should exhibit more similarity than cousins.

Illustrative of this method are the numerous family studies conducted to assess the contribution of heredity to the development of schizophrenic disorders. These disorders strike approximately 1% of the population, yet as Figure 3.28 reveals, 9% of the siblings of schizophrenic patients exhibit schizophrenia themselves (Gottesman, 1991). Thus, these first-degree relatives of schizophrenic patients show a risk for the disorder that is nine times higher than normal. This risk is greater than that observed for more distantly related, second-degree relatives, such as nieces and nephews (4%), who, in turn, are at greater risk than third-degree relatives, such as second cousins (2%). This pattern of results is consistent with the hypothesis that genetic inheritance influences the development of schizophrenic disorders (Gottesman, 1993; Gottesman & Moldin, 1998).

Family studies can indicate whether a trait runs in families. However, this correlation does not provide conclusive evidence that the trait is influenced by heredity. Why not? Because family members generally share not only genes but also similar environments. Furthermore, closer relatives are more likely to live together than more distant relatives. Thus, genetic similarity and environmental similarity *both* tend to be greater for closer relatives. Either of these confounded variables could be responsible when greater phenotypic similarity is found in closer relatives. Family studies can offer useful insights about the possible impact of heredity, but they cannot provide definitive evidence.

Twin Studies

Twin studies can yield better evidence about the possible role of genetic factors. In *twin studies* researchers assess hereditary influence by comparing the resemblance of identical twins and fraternal twins with respect to a trait. The logic of twin studies hinges on the genetic relatedness of identical and fraternal twins (see Figure 3.29 on the next page). *Identical (monozygotic) twins* emerge from one zygote that splits for unknown reasons. Thus, they have exactly the same genotype; their genetic relatedness is 100%. *Fraternal (dizygotic) twins* result when two eggs are fertilized simultaneously by different sperm cells, forming two separate zygotes. Fraternal twins are no more alike in genetic makeup than any two siblings born to a pair of parents at different times. Their genetic relatedness is only 50%.

Fraternal twins provide a useful comparison to identical twins because in both cases the twins usually grow up in the same home, at the same time, exposed to the same configuration of relatives, neighbors, peers, teachers, events, and so forth. Thus, both

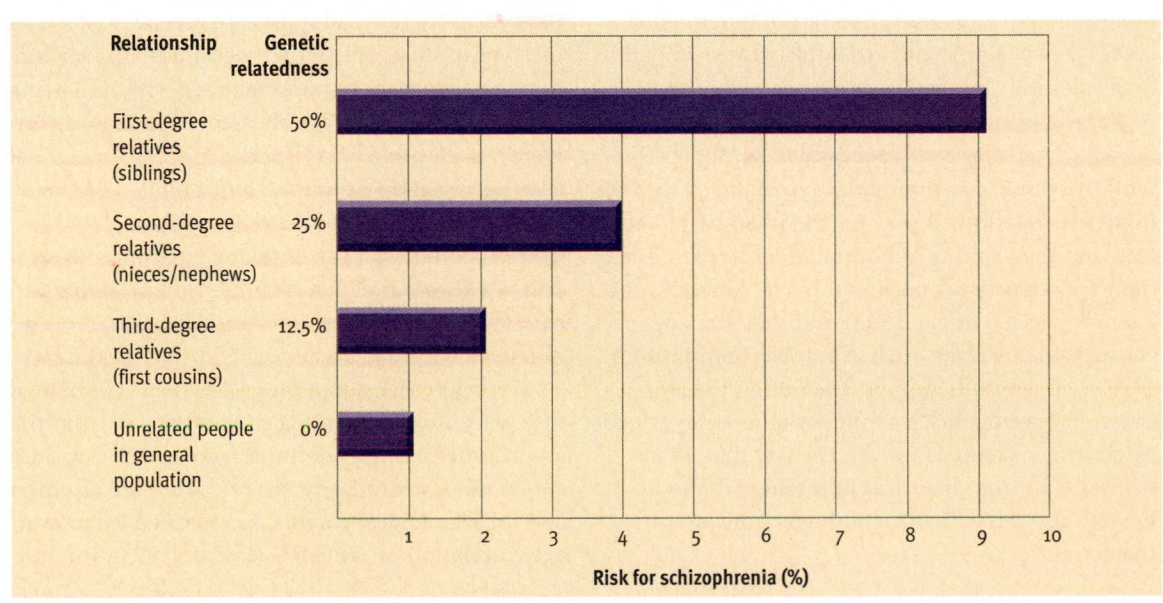

Figure 3.28

Family studies of risk for schizophrenic disorders. First-degree relatives of schizophrenic patients have an elevated risk of developing a schizophrenic disorder (Gottesman, 1991). For instance, the risk for siblings of schizophrenic patients is about 9% instead of the baseline 1% for unrelated people. Second- and third-degree relatives have progressively smaller elevations in risk for this disorder. Although these patterns of risk do not prove that schizophrenia is partly inherited, they are consistent with this hypothesis.

Relationship	Genetic relatedness
First-degree relatives (siblings)	50%
Second-degree relatives (nieces/nephews)	25%
Third-degree relatives (first cousins)	12.5%
Unrelated people in general population	0%

Risk for schizophrenia (%)

Figure 3.29

Identical versus fraternal twins. Identical (monozygotic) twins emerge from one zygote that splits, so their genetic relatedness is 100%. Fraternal (dizygotic) twins emerge from two separate zygotes, so their genetic relatedness is only 50%.

Source: Adapted from Kalat, J. (1996). *Introduction to psychology.* Belmont, CA: Wadsworth. Reprinted by permission.

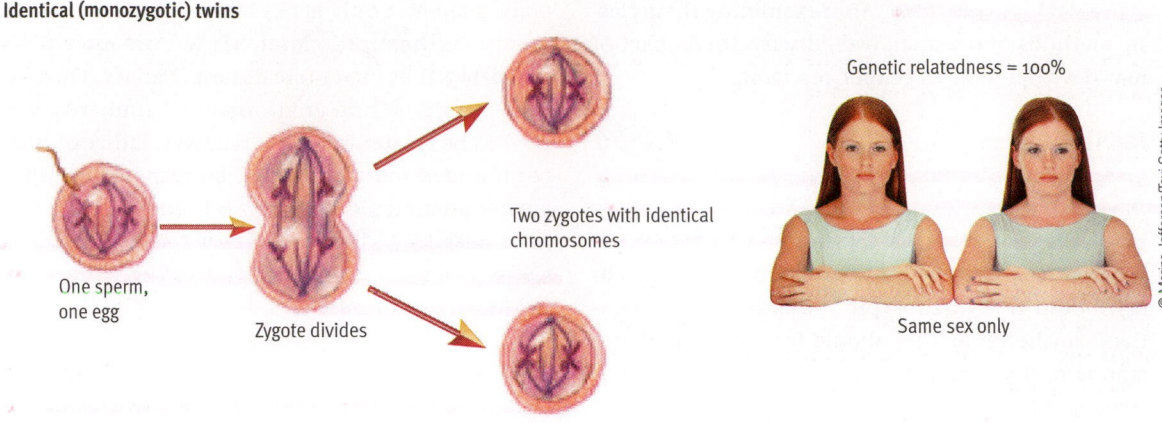

Identical (monozygotic) twins

One sperm, one egg → Zygote divides → Two zygotes with identical chromosomes

Genetic relatedness = 100%

Same sex only

© Marina Jefferson/Taxi-Getty Images

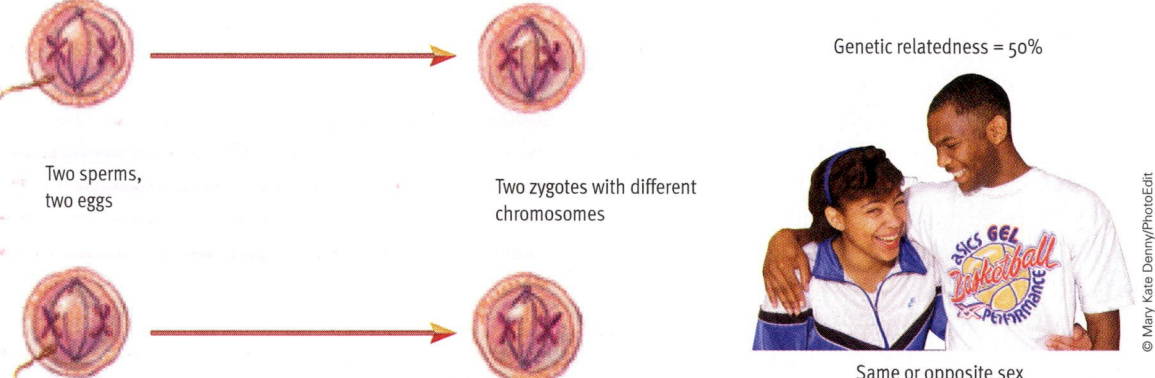

Fraternal (dizygotic) twins

Two sperms, two eggs → Two zygotes with different chromosomes

Genetic relatedness = 50%

Same or opposite sex

© Mary Kate Denny/PhotoEdit

kinds of twins normally develop under equally similar environmental conditions. However, identical twins share more genetic kinship than fraternal twins. Consequently, if sets of identical twins tend to exhibit more similarity on a trait than sets of fraternal twins do, it is reasonable to infer that this greater similarity is *probably* due to heredity rather than environment.

Twin studies have been conducted to assess the impact of heredity on a variety of traits. Some representative results are summarized in Figure 3.30. The higher correlations found for identical twins indicate that they tend to be more similar to each other than fraternal twins on measures of general intelligence (McGue et al., 1993) and measures of specific personality traits, such as extraversion (Loehlin, 1992). These results support the notion that intelligence and personality are influenced to some degree by genetic makeup. However, the fact that identical twins are far from identical in intelligence and personality also shows that environment influences these characteristics.

Adoption Studies

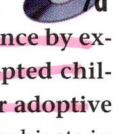

Adoption studies assess hereditary influence by examining the resemblance between adopted children and both their biological and their adoptive parents. Generally, adoptees are used as subjects in this type of study only if they were given up for adoption in early infancy and were raised without having contact with their biological parents. The logic underlying the adoption study approach is quite simple. If adopted children resemble their biological parents on a trait, even though they were not raised by them, genetic factors probably influence that trait. In contrast, if adopted children resemble their adoptive parents, even though they inherited no genes from them, environmental factors probably influence the trait.

In recent years, adoption studies have contributed to science's understanding of how genetics and the environment influence intelligence. The research shows modest similarity between adopted children and their biological parents, as indicated by an average correlation of .24 (McGue et al., 1993). Interestingly, adopted children resemble their adoptive parents just as much (also an average correlation of .24). These findings suggest that both heredity and environment have an influence on intelligence.

The Cutting Edge: Genetic Mapping

While behavioral geneticists have recently made great progress in documenting the influence of heredity on behavior, *molecular geneticists,* who study the biochemical bases of genetic inheritance, have made even more spectacular advances in their efforts to unravel the genetic code. *Genetic mapping* is the process of determining the location and chemical sequence of specific genes on specific chromosomes. New methods of manipulating DNA are now allowing scientists to create detailed physical maps of the genetic material on chromosomes in plants, animals, and humans. The Human Genome Project, a huge international enterprise intended to map out the estimated 100,000 genes found on the 23 pairs of human chromosomes, is proceeding ahead of schedule, with a working draft of the human genome having been published in 2001 (Pennisi, 2001; Roberts, 2001). Gene maps, by themselves, do not reveal which genes govern which traits. However, the compilation of a precise genetic atlas will fuel a quantum leap in the ability of scientists to pinpoint links between specific genes and specific traits and disorders. For example, medical researchers have already identified the genes responsible for cystic fibrosis, Huntington's chorea, and muscular dystrophy. Many medical researchers predict that genetic mapping will ultimately lead to revolutionary advances in the diagnosis and treatment of physical diseases (Collins & McKusick, 2001).

Will genetic mapping permit researchers to discover the genetic basis for intelligence, extraversion, musical ability, and other *behavioral* traits? Perhaps someday, but progress is likely to be painstakingly slow (Malhotra & Goldman, 1999; Turkheimer, 2000). Thus far, the major medical breakthroughs from genetic mapping have involved dichotomous traits (you either do or do not have the trait, such as muscular dystrophy) governed by a single gene pair. However, most behavioral traits do not involve a dichotomy, as everyone has varying amounts of intelligence, musical ability, and so forth. Moreover, virtually all behavioral traits appear to be *polygenic* and are shaped by many genes rather than a single gene. Because of these and a host of other complexities, scientists are not likely to find a single gene that controls intelligence, extraversion, or musical talent (Plomin

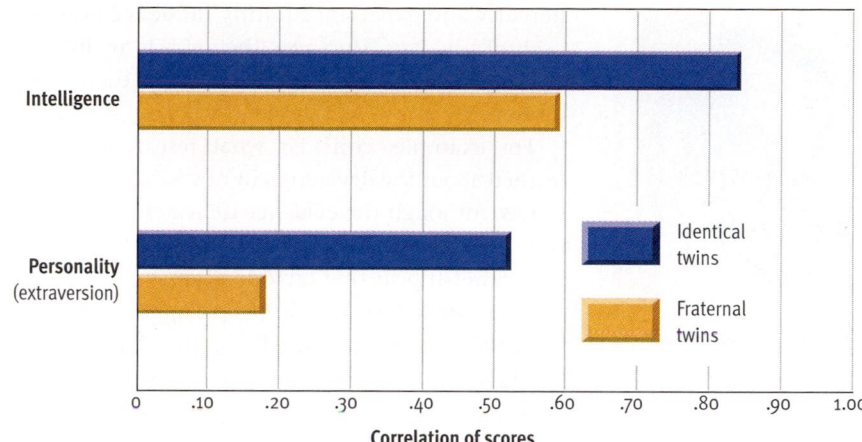

& Crabbe, 2000). The challenge will be to identify specific constellations of genes that each exert modest influence over particular aspects of behavior. What's exciting is that until recently, behavioral geneticists were largely limited to investigating *how much* heredity influences various traits. Genetic mapping will allow them to begin investigating *how* heredity influences specific aspects of behavior (Wahlsten, 1999).

The Interplay of Heredity and Environment

We began this section by asking, is it all in the genes? When it comes to behavioral traits, the answer clearly is no. According to Robert Plomin (1993), perhaps the leading behavioral genetics researcher in the last decade, what scientists find again and again is that

Figure 3.30

Twin studies of intelligence and personality. Identical twins tend to be more similar than fraternal twins (as reflected in higher correlations) with regard to intelligence and specific personality traits, such as extraversion. These findings suggest that intelligence and personality are influenced by heredity. (Intelligence data from McGue et al., 1993; extraversion data based on Loehlin, 1992)

CONCEPT CHECK 3.4

Recognizing Hereditary Influence

Check your understanding of the methods scientists use to explore hereditary influences on specific behavioral traits by filling in the blanks in the descriptive statements below. The answers can be found in the back of the book in Appendix A.

1. The findings from family studies indicate that heredity may influence a trait if _____ show more trait similarity than _____.

2. The findings from twin studies suggest that heredity influences a trait if _____ show more trait similarity than _____.

3. The findings from adoption studies suggest that heredity influences a trait if children adopted at a young age share more trait similarity with their _____ than their _____.

4. The findings from family studies, twin studies, or adoption studies suggest that heredity does not influence a trait when _____ is not related to _____.

The Pennsylvania State University Center for Development and Health Genetics

"The transformation of the social and behavioral sciences from environmentalism to biological determinism is happening so fast that I find I more often have to say, 'Yes, genetic influences are substantial, but environmental influences are important, too.'"
ROBERT PLOMIN

heredity and experience jointly influence most aspects of behavior. Moreover, their effects are interactive—genetics and experience play off each other (Rutter, 1997).

For example, consider what researchers have learned about the development of schizophrenic disorders. Although the evidence indicates that genetic factors influence the development of schizophrenia, it does *not* appear that anyone directly inherits the disorder itself. Rather, what people appear to inherit is a certain degree of *vulnerability* to the disorder (Paris, 1999). Whether this vulnerability is ever converted into an actual disorder depends on each person's experiences in life. As we will discuss in Chapter 14, certain types of stressful experience seem to evoke the disorder in people who are more vulnerable to it. Thus, as Richard Rose (1995) puts it in a major review of behavioral genetics research, "We inherit dispositions, not destinies."

The Evolutionary Bases of Behavior

To round out our look at the biological bases of behavior, we need to discuss how evolutionary forces have shaped many aspects of human and animal behavior. As you may recall from Chapter 1, *evolutionary psychology* is a major new theoretical perspective in the field that analyzes behavioral processes in terms of their adaptive significance. In this section, we will outline some basic principles of evolutionary theory and relate them to animal behavior. These ideas will create a foundation for forthcoming chapters, where we'll see how these principles can enhance our understanding of many aspects of human behavior.

Darwin's Insights

Charles Darwin, the legendary British naturalist, was *not* the first person to describe the process of evolution. Well before Darwin's time, other biologists who had studied the earth's fossil record noted that various species appeared to have undergone gradual changes over the course of a great many generations. What Darwin (1859) contributed in his landmark book, *The Origin of Species,* was a creative, new explanation for *how and why* evolutionary changes unfold over time. He identified *natural selection* as the mechanism that orchestrates the process of evolution.

The mystery that Darwin set out to solve was complicated. He wanted to explain how the characteristics of a species might change over generations and why these changes tended to be surprisingly adaptive. In other words, he wanted to shed light on why organisms tend to have characteristics that serve them well in the context of their environments. How did giraffes acquire their long necks that allow them to reach high into acacia trees to secure their main source of food? How did woodpeckers develop their sharp, chisel-shaped beaks that permit them to probe trees for insects so effectively? How did frogs develop their long and powerful hindlimbs that enable them to catapult through the air on land and move swiftly through water? Darwin's explanation for the seemingly purposive nature of evolution centered on four crucial insights.

First, he noted that organisms vary in endless ways, such as size, speed, strength, aspects of appearance, visual abilities, hearing capacities, digestive processes, cell structure, and so forth. Second, he noted that some of these characteristics are heritable—that is, they are passed down from one generation to the next. Although genes and chromosomes had not yet been discovered, the concept of heredity was well established. In Darwin's theory, variations in hereditary traits provide the crude materials for evolution. Third, borrowing from the work of Thomas Malthus, he noted that organisms tend to produce offspring at a pace that outstrips the local availability of food supplies, living space, and other crucial resources. As a population increases and resources dwindle, the competition for precious resources intensifies. Thus, it occurred to Darwin—and this was his grand insight—that variations in hereditary traits might affect organisms' ability to obtain the resources necessary for survival and reproduction. Fourth, building on this insight, Darwin argued that if a specific heritable trait contributes to an organism's survival or reproductive success, organisms with that trait should produce more offspring than those without the trait (or those with less of the trait), and the prevalence of that trait should gradually increase over generations—resulting in evolutionary change.

Although evolution is widely characterized as a matter of "survival of the fittest," Darwin recognized from the beginning that survival is only important insofar as it relates to reproductive success. Indeed, in evolutionary theory, *fitness* refers to the reproductive success (number of descendants) of an individual organism relative to the average reproductive success in the population. *Variations in reproductive success are what really fuels evolutionary change.* But survival is crucial because organisms typically need to mature and thrive before they can reproduce. So, Darwin theorized that there ought to be two ways in which traits might contribute to evolution: by providing either a survival advantage or a reproductive advantage. For example, a turtle's shell has great protective value that provides a survival advantage. In contrast, a firefly's emission of light is a courtship overture that provides a reproductive advantage.

To summarize, the principle of *natural selection* posits that heritable characteristics that provide a survival or reproductive advantage are more likely than alternative characteristics to be passed on to subsequent generations and thus come to be "selected" over time. Please note, the process of natural selection works on *populations* rather than *individual organisms.* Evolution occurs when the gene pool in a population changes gradually as a result of selection pressures. Although there are occasional exceptions (Gould & Eldredge, 1977), this process tends to be extremely gradual—it generally takes thousands to millions of generations for one trait to be selected over another.

Darwin's theory was highly controversial for at least two reasons: (a) It suggested that the awe-inspiring diversity of life is the result of an unplanned, natural process rather than divine creation, and (b) it implied that humans are not unique and that they share a common ancestry with other species. Nonetheless, Darwin's theory eventually gained considerable acceptance because it provided a compelling explanation for how the characteristics of various species gradually changed over many generations and for the functional, adaptive direction of these changes.

Subsequent Refinements to Evolutionary Theory

Although Darwin's evolutionary theory quickly acquired many articulate advocates, it also remained controversial for decades. One legitimate objection was that the theory did not provide an adequate explanation for the details of the inheritance process. This shortcoming was gradually rectified. Gregor Mendel's previously ignored work on patterns of inheritance started attracting attention around 1900. Research building on his insights led to major advances in the understanding of heredity over the next several decades. By 1937, these advances were sufficient to permit Theodore Dobzhansky to write a fairly comprehensive and convincing account of the evolutionary process in genetic terms. Dobzhansky's synthesis of Darwinian natural selection and Mendelian genetics was enormously influential, and by the 1950s the core tenets of evolutionary theory enjoyed widespread acceptance among scientists.

Contemporary models of evolution recognize that natural selection operates on the gene pool of a population. The makeup of a gene pool is also shaped by genetic drift, mutations, and gene flow. *Genetic drift* consists of random fluctuation in gene frequencies over generations, as a result of chance alone. A *mutation* is a spontaneous, heritable change in a piece of DNA that occurs in an individual organism. Mutations are unpredictable errors in DNA replication. Although infrequent, mutations increase the variability in a gene pool and give natural selection new genetic material to work with. Most mutations are not beneficial, but the minority that prove adaptive are increasingly passed on to subsequent generations. *Gene flow* occurs when gene frequencies in a population shift because some individuals leave the population (emigration) and others enter it (immigration). Gene flow operates to keep neighboring populations genetically similar. It can counterbalance gene pool differences between populations that have developed as a result of genetic drift, mutation, and natural selection. Conversely, when the gene flow between populations is minimal, the populations may evolve in divergent directions. This divergence can eventually contribute to the emergence of new species.

Bettmann/CORBIS

"Can we doubt (remembering that many more individuals are born than can possibly survive) that individuals having any advantage, however slight, over others, would have the best chance of surviving and procreating their kind? . . . This preservation of favourable variations and the rejection of injurious variations, I call Natural Selection."
CHARLES DARWIN

The fight-or-flight response discussed earlier in the chapter (see page 85), is an example of a behavior that provides a survival advantage. Although traits that convey a survival advantage can contribute to evolution, it is variations in reproductive fitness that ultimately fuel evolutionary change.

John Dominis, *Life* magazine © Time Inc.

Adaptations are the key product of the process of evolution. An *adaptation* is an inherited characteristic that increased in a population (through natural selection) because it helped solve a problem of survival or reproduction during the time it emerged. Because of the gradual, incremental nature of evolution, adaptations sometimes linger in a population even though they no longer provide a survival or reproductive advantage. For example, as noted earlier, the physiological arousal associated with the "fight or flight response" that aided humans' survival in more primitive times appears to be more detrimental than adaptive today, as it leads to a variety of stress-related diseases (see Chapter 13). Similarly, humans show a taste preference for fatty substances that was adaptive in an era of hunting and gathering, when dietary fat was a scarce source of important calories. However, in our modern world, where dietary fat is typically available in abundance, this taste preference leads many people to consume too much fat, resulting in obesity, heart disease, and other health problems. Thus, the preference for fatty foods has become a liability for human survival (although its impact on reproductive success is more difficult to gauge). Organisms' environments often undergo changes so that adaptations that were once benefical become obsolete. As you will see, evolutionary psychologists have found that many aspects of human nature reflect the adaptive demands faced by our ancient ancestors rather than contemporary demands. Of course, as natural selection continues to work, these formerly adaptive traits should gradually be eliminated, but the process is extremely slow.

In recent decades, theorists have broadened Darwin's original concept of reproductive fitness to better explain a variety of phenomena. For example, traditional evolutionary theory had difficulty explaining self-sacrifice. If organisms try to maximize their reproductive success, why does a blackbird risk death to signal the approach of a hawk to others in the flock? And why would a tribesman risk life and limb to race into a burning hut to save young children? In 1964, W. D. Hamilton proposed the theory of *inclusive fitness* to explain the paradox of self-sacrifice. According to Hamilton, an organism may contribute to passing on its genes by sacrificing itself to save others that share the same genes. Helping behavior that evolves as members of a species protect their own offspring, for example, can be extended to other, more distantly related members of the species. Thus, *inclusive fitness* is the sum of an individual's own reproductive success plus the effects the organism has on the reproductive success of related others. The concept of inclusive fitness suggests that the probability of self-sacrifice decreases as the degree of relatedness between a helper and potential recipients declines, a prediction that has been supported in studies of organisms as diverse as ground squirrels (Sherman, 1981) and humans (Burnstein, Crandall, & Kitayama, 1994).

Behaviors as Adaptive Traits

Scholarly analyses of evolution have focused primarily on the evolution of *physical characteristics* in the animal kingdom, but from the very beginning, Darwin recognized that natural selection was applicable to *behavioral traits* as well. Studying the evolution of behavior is more difficult than studying the evolution of physical traits because behavior is more transient—crucial behaviors by an organism may occur infrequently and may not last long. For example, female wood frogs are sexually receptive just one night per year. Additionally, although the fossil record *can* leave clues about past organisms' behavior (such as its prey or nesting habits), it leaves much more detailed information about organisms' physical characteristics. Nonetheless, it is clear that a species' typical patterns of behavior often reflect evolutionary solutions to adaptive problems.

Consider, for instance, the eating behavior of rats, who show remarkable caution when they encounter new foods. Rats are versatile animals that are found in an enormous range of habitats and can live off of quite a variety of foods, but this diet variety can present risks, as they need to be wary of consuming toxic

substances. When rats encounter unfamiliar foods, they consume only small amounts and won't eat two new foods together. If the consumption of a new food is followed by illness, they avoid that food in the future (Logue, 1991). These precautions allow rats to learn what makes them sick while reducing the likelihood of consuming a lethal amount of something poisonous. These patterns of eating behavior are highly adaptive solutions to the food selection problems faced by rats.

Let's look at some additional examples of how evolution has shaped organisms' behavior. Avoiding predators is a nearly universal problem for organisms. Because of natural selection, many species, such as the grasshopper, have developed physical characteristics that allow them to blend in with their environments, making detection by predators more difficult. Many organisms also engage in elaborate *behavioral maneuvers* to hide themselves. For example, the grasshopper pictured below has dug itself a small trench in which to hide and has used its midlegs to pull pebbles over its back (Alcock, 1998). This clever hiding behavior is just as much a product of evolution as the grasshopper's remarkable camouflage.

The "stotting" behavior exhibited by Thomson's gazelles when they spot a cheetah is another example of a behavioral adaptation. The cheetah is a feared predator that elicits evasive actions in Thomson's gazelles. But as the gazelles start to flee, they often slow

Web Link 3.7

Human Behavior and Evolution Society
The HBES is an interdisciplinary organization devoted to the exploration of human behavior from the perspective of evolutionary theory. This site provides a particularly rich set of links to published and online materials and organizations dealing with the evolutionary perspective on behavior.

Courtesy of John Alcock

© Mitch Reardon/National Audubon Society Collection/Photo Researchers, Inc.

The behavior that helps the grasshopper on the left hide from predators is a product of evolution, just like the physical characteristics that help it blend in with its surroundings. As explained in the text, the stotting behavior exhibited by Thomson's gazelles is adaptive in that it is intended to deter the pursuit of predators. The animal shown here is a Springbok, another species that exhibits stotting behavior.

up briefly to *stot*—that is, they jump high into the air with all four legs held straight and their white rump fully displayed. Slowing up when fleeing may not sound adaptive, but research has revealed that gazelles stot to signal to the cheetah that they have spotted the predator, they are off and running, and they will be difficult to catch. Consistent with this interpretation, stotting increases the likelihood that a cheetah will abandon its pursuit of a gazelle (Caro, 1986). Thus, stotting is a behavioral adaptation, in that it enhances the probability of survival by deterring pursuit and saves precious energy that may be needed to evade another predator.

Many behavioral adaptations are designed to improve organisms' chances of reproductive success. Consider, for instance, the wide variety of species in which females actively choose which male to mate with. In many such species, females demand material goods and services from males in return for copulation opportunities. For example, in one type of moth, males have to spend hours extracting sodium from mud puddles, which they then transfer to prospective mates, who use it to supply their larvae with an important nutritional element (Smedley & Eisner, 1996). In the black-tipped hangingfly, females insist on a nuptial gift of food before they mate. They reject suitors bringing unpalatable food, and they tie the length of subsequent copulation to the size of the nuptial gift (Thornhill, 1976).

The adaptive value of trading sex for material goods that can aid the survival of an organism and its offspring is obvious, but the evolutionary significance of other mating strategies is more perplexing. In some species characterized by female choice, the choices hinge on males' appearance and courtship

behavior. Females usually prefer males sporting larger or more brightly colored ornaments, or those capable of more extreme acoustical displays. For example, female house finches are swayed by redder feathers, whereas female wild turkeys are enticed by larger beak ornaments (see Table 3.2 for additional examples). What do females gain by selecting males with redder feathers, larger beaks, and other arbitrary characteristics? This is one of the more difficult questions in evolutionary biology, and addressing all the complexities that may be involved would take us far beyond the scope of this discussion. But, caveats aside, favored attributes generally seem to be indicators of males' relatively good genes, sound health, low parasite load, or superior ability to provide future services, such as protection or food gathering, all of which may serve to make their offspring more viable (Alcock, 1998). For example, the quality of peacocks' plumage appears to be an indicator of their parasite load (Hamilton & Zuk, 1982). So, even mating preferences for seemingly nonadaptive aspects of appearance may often have adaptive significance.

Parental Investment and Mating Systems

Given that variations in reproductive success are what really fuels evolutionary change, theorists have been particularly interested in understanding the evolutionary bases of various organisms' mating systems. In the 1970s, Robert Trivers (1972) contributed influential extensions of evolutionary theory that shed new light on patterns of mating. According to Trivers, a species' courtship and mating strategies depend primarily on sex differences in parental investment. *Parental investment* refers to what each sex has to invest—in terms of time, energy, survival risk, and forgone opportunities—to produce and nurture offspring. For example, the efforts required to guard eggs, build nests, or nourish offspring represent parental investments. In most species, there are striking disparities between males and females in their parental investment, and these discrepancies shape mating strategies. *In general, the sex that makes the smaller investment will compete for mating opportunities with the sex that makes the larger investment, and the sex with the larger investment will tend to be more discriminating in selecting its partners.*

In most mammalian species, males have to invest little beyond the act of copulation, so their reproductive potential is maximized by mating with as many females as possible. Hence, males compete with each other for mating opportunities. In contrast, fe-

Table **3.2**
Female Mate Choices Based on Differences in Males' Morphological and Behavioral Attributes

Species	Favored attribute
Scorpionfly	More symmetrical wings
Barn swallow	More symmetrical and larger tail ornaments
Wild turkey	Larger beak ornaments
House finch	Redder feathers
Satin bowerbird	Bowers with more ornaments
Cichlid fish	Taller display "bower"
Field cricket	Longer calling bouts
Woodhouse's toad	More frequent calls

Source: Adapted from Alcock, J. (1998). *Animal behavior* (p. 463). Sunderland, MA: Sinauer Associates. Copyright © 1998 John Alcock. Reprinted by permission of Sinauer Associates and the author.

Figure 3.31

Social dominance and reproductive fitness in elephant seals. These data, based on observation of a group of southern elephant seals, show that dominant males get far more copulation opportunities than less dominant males do (McCann, 1981). Thus, in male elephant seals, aggressive behavior that leads to higher dominance enhances reproductive fitness.

SOURCE: Data from McCann, T. S. (1981). Aggression and sexual activity of male Southern elephant seals, *Mirounga leonina. Journal of Zoology, 195*, 295–310. Copyright © 1981.

males typically have to invest weeks or months of effort to carry and nourish offspring, thereby limiting the number of offspring they can produce in a breeding season, regardless of how many males they mate with. Hence, females have no incentive for mating with many males. In mammalian species, females typically can optimize their reproductive potential by being discriminating in mate selection—choosing mates that can provide them with better quality genes or material resources that can be invested in offspring. Thus, *the typical result when parental investment is high for females and low for males is polygyny,* a mating system in which each male seeks to mate with multiple females, whereas each female mates with only one male. Polygyny comes in many forms and is the most common mating system in nature (Siiter, 1999).

In polygynous mating systems, natural selection favors males who compete aggressively with rivals for copulation opportunities. Thus, the males of many species engage in ferocious battles, biting, kicking, head butting, and locking horns with each other. Elephant seals, for example, hurl their huge bodies (often 1700 pounds) at each other in bitter battles to see who will control a harem of up to 50 females (see Figure 3.31). Females mate with the winners of these battles because the winners presumably have "better genes" that will provide their mutual offspring with greater strength and other adaptive traits. In this situation, natural selection obviously favors animals of larger size. Hence, in species where males fight for the right to control multiple females, the males often evolve to be much larger than the females (Alexander et al., 1979).

Although polygyny is a common mating system, other arrangements are also seen. Polyandry is the opposite of polygyny. *Polyandry* is a mating system in which each female seeks to mate with multiple males, whereas each male mates with only one female. Although polyandry is rare, as predicted by Trivers, *it tends to emerge when parental investment is high for males and low for females.* For example, female spotted sandpipers lay clutches of eggs that are then cared for by various males. With males making the greater parental investment, female spotted sandpipers compete aggressively for access to several males. The females, who have evolved to be larger and stronger than the males, compete to control territories, take the lead in courtship, and aggressively drive away intruding females (Oring, 1985). Roughly similar forms of polyandry are seen in the Galapagos hawk and northern jacana (a tropical bird), as well as some types of fish, but in general polyandry is rare because it is highly unusual for males to have a greater parental investment than females (Alcock, 1998).

Monogamy, a mating system in which one male and one female mate exclusively, or almost exclusively, with each other, is quite a bit more common than polyandry. *Monogamy tends to emerge when male and female parental investment is roughly equal, a condition typically seen when both parents need to contribute to raising their young to maximize reproductive success.* A substantial portion of bird species are predominantly monogamous, as are a small minority of mammals, such as wolves and foxes (Kleiman, 1977; Lack, 1968). As in humans, however, many monogamous relationships are more appearance than reality. For example, many supposedly monogamous birds actually mate outside their pair bond (Westneat, Sherman, & Morton, 1990).

In any event, the key point is that sex differences in parental investment appear to be a major factor shaping organisms' mating systems. Trivers's analysis can explain why males and females in many species exhibit striking differences in their mating priorities and preferences. Nature's diverse patterns of mating, which constitute especially important domains of behavior, reflect the adaptive demands that specific organisms must face to maximize their reproductive fitness.

Putting It in Perspective

PREVIEW QUESTIONS
- How did this chapter demonstrate that heredity and environment shape behavior interactively?
- How did this chapter illustrate multifactorial causation?
- How did this chapter clarify the empirical nature of psychology?

Three of our seven themes stood out in this chapter: (1) heredity and environment jointly influence behavior, (2) behavior is determined by multiple causes, and (3) psychology is empirical. Let's look at each of these points.

In Chapter 1, when it was first emphasized that heredity and environment jointly shape behavior, you may have been a little perplexed about how your genes could be responsible for your sarcastic wit or your interest in art. In fact, there are no genes for behavior per se. Experts do not expect to find genes for sarcasm or artistic interest, for example. Insofar as your hereditary endowment plays a role in your behavior, it does so *indirectly*, by molding the physiological machine that you work with. Thus, your genes influence your physiological makeup, which in turn influences your personality, temperament, intelligence, interests, and other traits. Bear in mind, however, that genetic factors do not operate in a vacuum. Genes exert their effects in an environmental context. The impact of genetic makeup depends on environment, and the impact of environment depends on genetic makeup.

It was evident throughout the chapter that behavior is determined by multiple causes, but this fact was particularly apparent in the discussions of schizophrenia. At various points in the chapter we saw that schizophrenia may be a function of (1) abnormalities in neurotransmitter activity (especially dopamine), (2) structural defects in the brain (enlarged ventricles), and (3) genetic vulnerability to the illness. These findings do not contradict one another. Rather, they demonstrate that a complex array of biological factors are involved in the development of schizophrenia. In Chapter 14, we'll see that a host of environmental factors also play a role in the multifactorial causation of schizophrenia.

The empirical nature of psychology was apparent in the numerous discussions of the specialized research methods used to study the physiological bases of behavior. As you know, the empirical approach depends on precise observation. Throughout this chapter, you've seen how investigators have come up with innovative methods to observe and measure elusive phenomena such as electrical activity in the brain, neural impulses, brain function, cerebral specialization, and the impact of heredity on behavior. The point is that empirical methods are the lifeblood of the scientific enterprise. When researchers figure out how to better observe something, their new methods usually facilitate major advances in our scientific knowledge. That is why brain-imaging techniques and genetic mapping hold such exciting promise.

The importance of empiricism will also be apparent in the upcoming Personal Application and Critical Thinking Application that follow. In both you'll see that it is important to learn to distinguish between scientific findings and conjecture based on those findings.

REVIEW OF KEY POINTS
- Darwin argued that if a heritable trait contributes to an organism's survival or reproductive success, organisms with that trait should produce more offspring than those without the trait and that the prevalence of that trait should gradually increase over generations—thanks to natural selection.
- Because of the gradual, incremental nature of evolution, adaptations sometimes linger in a population even though they no longer provide a survival or reproductive advantage. Hamilton proposed the theory of inclusive fitness to explain the paradox of self-sacrifice.
- Theorists have focused primarily on the evolution of *physical characteristics* in the animal kingdom, but from the very beginning Darwin recognized that natural selection was applicable to *behavioral traits* as well. According to Trivers, a species' courtship and mating strategies depend primarily on sex differences in parental investment.
- Three of the book's unifying themes stand out in this chapter. First, we saw how heredity interacts with experience to govern behavior. Second, the discussions of biological factors underlying schizophrenia highlighted the multifactorial causation of behavior. Third, we saw how innovations in research methods often lead to advances in knowledge, underscoring the empirical nature of psychology.

PERSONAL APPLICATION

Evaluating the Concept of "Two Minds in One"

Answer the following "true" or "false."

_____ 1 The right and left brains give people two minds in one.

_____ 2 Each half of the brain has its own special mode of thinking.

_____ 3 Some people are left-brained while others are right-brained.

_____ 4 Schools should devote more effort to teaching the overlooked right side of the brain.

Do people have two minds in one that think differently? Do some people depend on one side of the brain more than the other? Is the right side of the brain neglected? These questions are too complex to resolve with a simple true or false, but in this Application we'll take a closer look at the issues involved in these proposed applications of the findings on cerebral specialization. You'll learn that some of these ideas are plausible, but in many cases the hype has outstripped the evidence.

Earlier, we described Roger Sperry's Nobel prize–winning research with split-brain patients, whose right and left hemispheres were disconnected (to reduce epileptic seizures). The split-brain studies showed that the previously underrated right hemisphere has some special talents of its own. This discovery detonated an explosion of research on cerebral laterality.

Cerebral Specialization and Cognitive Processes

Using a variety of methods, scientists have compiled mountains of data on the specialized abilities of the right and left hemispheres. These findings have led to extensive theorizing about how the right and left brains might be related to cognitive processes. Some of the more intriguing ideas include the following:

1. *The two hemispheres are specialized to process different types of cognitive tasks* (Corballis, 1991; Ornstein, 1977). The findings of many researchers have been widely interpreted as showing that the left hemisphere handles verbal tasks, including language, speech, writing, math, and logic, while the right hemisphere handles nonverbal tasks, including spatial problems, music, art, fantasy, and creativity. These conclusions have attracted a great deal of public interest and media attention. For example, Figure 3.32 shows a *Newsweek* artist's depiction of how the brain divides its work.

2. *Each hemisphere has its own independent stream of consciousness* (Bogen, 1985; Pucetti, 1981). For instance, Joseph Bogen has asserted, "Pending further evidence, I believe that each of us has two minds in one person" (Hooper & Teresi, 1986, p. 221). Supposedly, this duality of consciousness goes largely unnoticed because of the considerable overlap between the experiences of each independent mind. Ultimately, though, the apparent unity of consciousness is but an illusion.

3. *The two hemispheres have different modes of thinking* (Banich & Heller, 1998; Joseph, 1992). According to this notion, the documented differences between the hemispheres in dealing with verbal and nonverbal materials are due to more basic differences in *how* the hemispheres process information. The standard version of this theory holds that the reason the left hemisphere handles verbal material well is that it is analytic, abstract, rational, logical, and linear. In contrast, the right hemisphere is thought to be better equipped to handle spatial and musical material because it is synthetic, concrete, nonrational, intuitive, and holistic. Robert Ornstein (1997) char-

Figure 3.32

Popular conceptions of hemispheric specialization. As this *Newsweek* diagram illustrates, depictions of hemispheric specialization in the popular press have often been oversimplified.

SOURCE: Cartoon courtesy of Roy Doty.

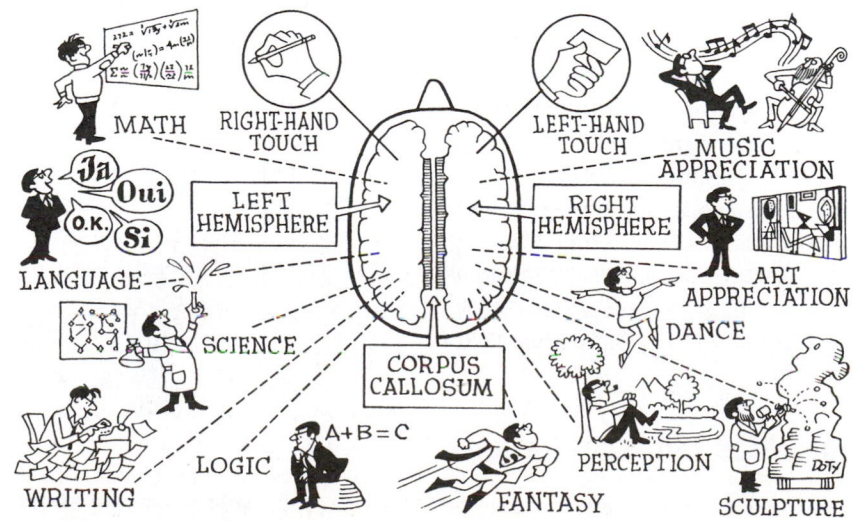

acterizes hemispheric differences in cognitive processing somewhat differently, asserting that the left hemisphere focuses on details while the right hemisphere responds to global patterns and the big picture.

4. *People vary in their reliance on one hemisphere as opposed to the other* (Bakan, 1971; Zenhausen, 1978). Allegedly, some people are "left-brained." Their greater dependence on their left hemisphere supposedly makes them analytic, rational, and logical. Other people are "right-brained." Their greater use of their right hemisphere supposedly makes them intuitive, holistic, and irrational. Being right-brained or left-brained is thought to explain many personal characteristics, such as whether an individual likes to read, is good with maps, or enjoys music. This notion of "brainedness" has even been used to explain occupational choice. Supposedly, right-brained people are more likely to become artists or musicians, while left-brained people are more likely to become writers or scientists.

5. *Schools should place more emphasis on teaching the right side of the brain* (Kitchens, 1991; Prince, 1978). "A real reform of the educational system will not occur until individual teachers learn to understand the true duality of their students' minds," says Thomas Blakeslee (1980, p. 59). Those sympathetic to his view assert that American schools overemphasize logical, analytical left-hemisphere thinking (required by English, math, and science) while short-changing intuitive, holistic right-hemisphere thinking (required by art and music). These educators have concluded that modern schools turn out an excess of left-brained graduates. They advocate curriculum reform to strengthen the right side of the brain in their students. This line of thinking has also spawned quite a collection of popular self-help books, such as *Whole-Brain Thinking* (Wonder, 1992), *Unleashing the Right Side of the Brain* (Williams & Stockmyer, 1987), and *Teaching for the Two-Sided Mind* (Williams, 1986).

Complexities and Qualifications

The ideas just outlined are the source of considerable debate among psychologists and neuroscientists. These ideas are intriguing and have clearly captured the imagination of the general public. However, the research on cerebral specialization is complex, and doubts have been raised about many of these ideas (Efron, 1990; Springer & Deutsch, 1998). Let's examine each point.

1. There *is* ample evidence that the right and left hemispheres are specialized to handle different types of cognitive tasks, *but only to a degree* (Brown & Kosslyn, 1993; Gordon, 1990). Doreen Kimura (1973) compared the abilities of the right and left hemispheres to quickly recognize letters, words, faces, and melodies in a series of perceptual asymmetry studies, like those described earlier in the chapter. She found that the superiority of one hemisphere over the other was usually quite modest, as you can see in Figure 3.33, which shows superiority ratios for four cognitive tasks.

Furthermore, in normal individuals, the hemispheres don't work alone. As Hellige (1993) notes, "In the intact brain, it is unlikely that either hemisphere is ever completely uninvolved in ongoing processing" (p. 23). Most tasks probably engage *both* hemispheres, albeit to different degrees (Beeman & Chiarello, 1998; Ornstein, 1997). For instance, imagine that you are asked the following question: "In what direction are you headed if you start north and make two right turns and a left turn?" In answering this question, you're confronted with a *spatial* task that should engage the right hemisphere. However, first you have to process the wording of the question, a *language* task that should engage the left hemisphere.

Furthermore, people differ in their patterns of cerebral specialization (Springer & Deutsch, 1998). Some people display little specialization—that is, their hemispheres seem to have equal abilities on various types of tasks. Others even reverse the usual specialization, so that verbal processing might be housed in the right hemisphere. These unusual patterns are especially common among left-handed people. For example, when Rasmussen and Milner (1977) tested subjects for the localization of speech, they found bilateral representation in 15% of the left-handers. They found a reversal of the usual specialization (speech handled by the right hemisphere) in another 15% of the left-handed subjects (see Figure 3.34). These variations in cerebral specialization are not well understood. However, they clearly indicate that the functional specialization of the cerebral hemispheres is not set in concrete.

Figure 3.33

Relative superiority of one brain hemisphere over the other in studies of perceptual asymmetry. These performance ratios from a study by Doreen Kimura (1973) show the degree to which one hemisphere was "superior" to the other on each type of task in one study of normal participants. For example, the right hemisphere was 20% better than the left hemisphere in quickly recognizing melodic patterns (ratio 1.2 to 1). Most differences in the performance of the two hemispheres are quite small. (Data from Kimura, 1973)

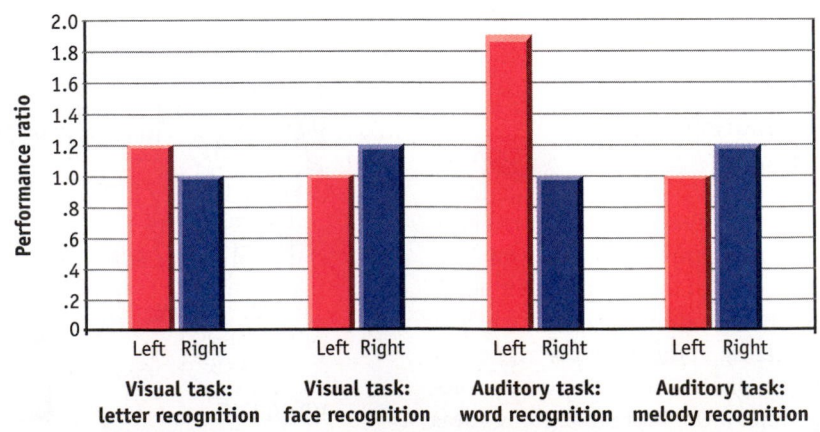

2. The evidence for the idea that people have a separate stream of consciousness in each hemisphere is weak. There *are* clear signs of such duality among *split-brain patients* (Bogen, 1990; Mark, 1996). But this duality is probably a unique by-product of the radical procedure that they have undergone—the surgical disconnection of their hemispheres (Bradshaw, 1981). In fact, many theorists have been impressed by the degree to which even split-brain patients mostly experience *unity* of consciousness. There is little empirical basis for the idea that people have two independent streams of awareness neatly housed in the right and left halves of the brain.

3. Similarly, there is little direct evidence to support the notion that each hemisphere has its own mode of thinking, or *cognitive style* (Bradshaw, 1989). This notion is plausible and there *is* some supportive evidence, but the evidence is inconsistent and more research is needed (Gordon, 1990; Reuter-Lorenz & Miller, 1998). One key problem with this idea is that aspects of cognitive style have proven difficult to define and measure (Brownell & Gardner, 1981). For instance, there is debate about the meaning of analytic versus synthetic thinking, or linear versus holistic thinking.

4. The evidence on the assertion that some people are left-brained while others are right-brained is inconclusive at best (Hellige, 1990). This notion has some plausibility—*if* it means only that some people consistently display more activation of one hemisphere than the other. However, researchers have yet to develop reliable measures of these possible "preferences" in cerebral activation. Hence, there are no convincing data linking brainedness to musical ability, occupational choice, or the like (Springer & Deutsch, 1998).

5. The idea that schools should be reformed to better exercise the right side of the brain represents intriguing but wild speculation. In neurologically intact people it is impossible to teach just one hemisphere at a time (J. Levy, 1985). Many sound arguments exist for reforming American schools to encourage more holistic, intuitive thinking, but these arguments have nothing to do with cerebral specialization.

In summary, the theories linking cerebral specialization to cognitive processes are highly speculative. There's nothing wrong with theoretical speculation. Unfortunately, the tentative, conjectural nature of these ideas about cerebral specialization has got-

ten lost in the popular book descriptions of research on the right and left hemispheres (Coren, 1992). Popular writers continue to churn out allegedly scientific books, applying brain lateralization concepts to a host of new topics on which there often is little or no real evidence. Thus, one can find books on how to have right-brain sex (Wells, 1991), develop right-brain social skills (Snyder, 1989), and lose weight with a right-brain diet (Sommer, 1987). Commenting on this popularization, Hooper and Teresi (1986) note, "A widespread cult of the right brain ensued, and the duplex house that Sperry built grew into the K mart of brain science. Today our hairdresser lectures us about the 'Two Hemispheres of the Brain,'" (p. 223). Cerebral specialization is an important and intriguing area of research. However, it is unrealistic to expect that the hemispheric divisions in the brain will provide a biological explanation for every dichotomy or polarity in modes of thinking.

REVIEW OF KEY POINTS

- Split-brain research stimulated speculation about relations between cerebral specialization and cognitive processes. Some theorists believe that each hemisphere has its own stream of consciousness and mode of thinking, which are applied to specific types of cognitive tasks.

- Some theorists also believe that people vary in their reliance on the right and left halves of the brain and that schools should work more to exercise the right half of the brain.

- The cerebral hemispheres *are* specialized for handling different cognitive tasks, but only to a degree, as most tasks engage both hemispheres. Moreover, people vary in their patterns of hemispheric specialization.

- Evidence for duality in consciousness divided along hemispheric lines is weak. Evidence on whether people vary in brainedness and whether the two hemispheres vary in cognitive style is inconclusive.

- There is no way to teach only one hemisphere of the brain, so a "right-brain curriculum" is pointless. Popular ideas about the right and left brain have gone far beyond the actual research findings.

Figure 3.34

Handedness and patterns of speech localization. Left-handed people tend to show more variety in cerebral specialization and more bilateral representation than right-handers. For example, speech processing is almost always localized in the left hemisphere of right-handed subjects. However, Rasmussen and Milner (1977) found the usual pattern of speech localization in only 70% of their left-handed subjects. (Data from Rasmussen & Milner, 1977)

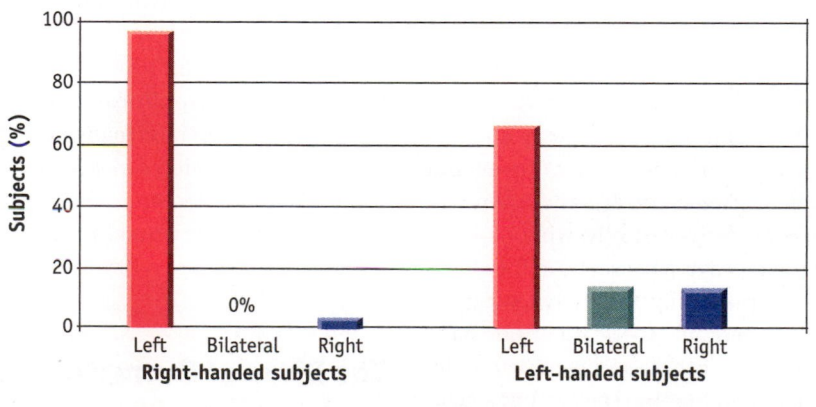

Building Better Brains: The Perils of Extrapolation

Summarizing the implications of recent research in neuroscience, science writer Ronald Kotulak (1996) concluded, "The first three years of a child's life are critically important to brain development" (pp. ix–x). Echoing this sentiment, the president of a U.S. educational commission asserted that "research in brain development suggests it is time to rethink many educational policies" (Bruer, 1999, p. 16). Based on recent findings in neuroscience, many states launched expensive programs in the 1990s intended to foster better neural development in infants. For example, Georgia Governor Zell Miller sought funding to distribute classical music tapes to the state's infants, saying, "No one doubts that listening to music, especially at a very early age, affects the spatial-temporal reasoning that underlies math, engineering, and chess" (Bruer, 1999, p. 62). Well-intended educational groups and Hollywood celebrities have argued for the creation of schools for infants on the grounds that enriched educational experiences during infancy will lead to enhanced neural development.

What are these practical, new discoveries about the brain that will permit parents and educators to optimize infants' brain development? Well, we will discuss the pertinent research momentarily, but it is not as new or as practical as suggested in many quarters. Unfortunately, as we saw in our discussion of research on hemispheric specialization, the hype in the media has greatly outstripped the realities of what scientists have learned in the laboratory (Chance, 2001).

The 1990s were recognized by the United States Congress as "The Decade of the Brain." The focus on the brain led many child-care advocates and educational reformers to use research in neuroscience as the rationale for the policies they sought to promote, as a host of books on "brain-based learning" were published (see Jensen,

2000; Sousa, 2000; Sprenger, 2001). The people advocating these ideas have good intentions, but the neuroscience rationale has been stretched to the breaking point. The result? An enlightening case study in the perils of overextrapolation.

The Key Findings on Neural Development

The education and child-care reformers who have used brain science as the basis for their campaigns have primarily cited two key findings: the discovery of critical periods in neural development and the demonstration that rats raised in "enriched environments" have more synapses than rats raised in "impoverished environments." Let's look at each of these findings.

A *critical period* is a limited time span in the development of an organism when it is optimal for certain capacities to emerge because the organism is especially responsive to certain experiences. The seminal research on critical periods in neural development was conducted by Torsten Wiesel and David Hubel (1963, 1965) in the 1960s. They showed that if an eye of a newborn kitten is sutured shut early in its development (typically the first 4 to 6 weeks), the kitten will become permanently blind in that eye, but if the eye is covered for the same amount of time at later ages (after 4 months) blindness does not result. Such studies show that certain types of visual input are necessary during a critical period of development, or neural pathways between the eye and brain will not form properly. Basically, what happens is that the inactive synapses from the closed eye are displaced by the active synapses from the open eye. Critical periods have been found for other aspects of neural development and in other species, but a great deal remains to be learned. Based on this type of research, some educational and child-care reformers have argued that the

first three years of life are a critical period for human neural development.

The pioneering work on environment and brain development was begun in the 1960s by Mark Rosenzweig and his colleagues (1961, 1962). They raised some rats in an impoverished environment, (housed individually in small, barren cages) and other rats in an enriched environment (housed in groups of 10 to 12 in larger cages, with a variety of objects available for exploration), as shown in Figure 3.35. They found that the rats raised in the enriched environment performed better on problem-solving tasks than the impoverished rats and had slightly heavier brains and a thicker cerebral cortex in some areas of the brain. Subsequent research by William Greenough demonstrated that enriched environments resulted in heavier and thicker cortical areas by virtue of producing denser dendritic branching, more synaptic contacts, and richer neural networks (Greenough, 1975; Greenough & Volkmar, 1973). Based on this type of research, some child-care reformers have argued that human infants need to be brought up in enriched environments during the critical period before age 3, to promote synapse formation and to optimize the development of their emerging neural circuits.

The findings on critical periods and the effects of enriched environments were genuine breakthroughs in neuroscience, but they certainly aren't *new* findings, as suggested by various political action groups. Moreover, one can raise many doubts about whether this research can serve as a meaningful guide for decisions about parenting practices, day-care programs, educational policies, and welfare reform (Thompson & Nelson, 2001).

The Risks of Overextrapolation

Extrapolation occurs when an effect is estimated by extending beyond some known values or conditions. Extrapolation is a nor-

Figure **3.35**

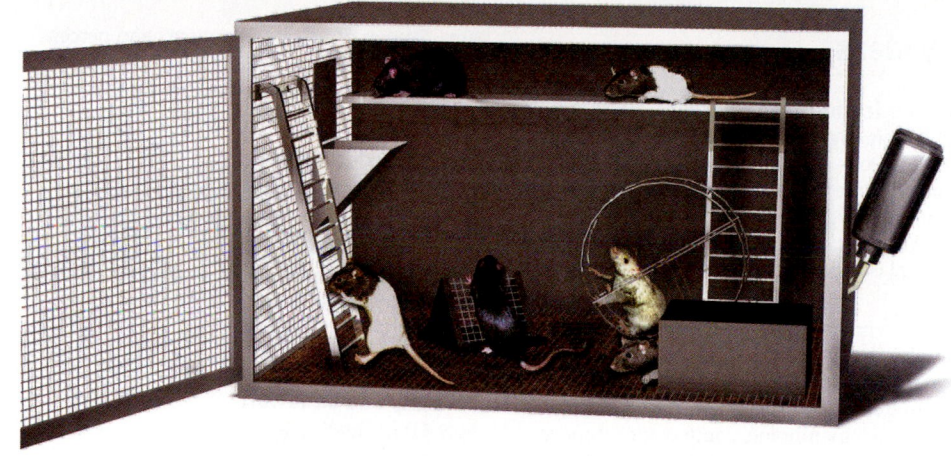

Enriched environments in the study of rats' neural development. In the studies by Rosenzweig and colleagues (1961, 1962), rats raised in an impoverished environment were housed alone in small cages, whereas rats raised in enriched environments were housed in groups and were given playthings that were changed daily. Although the enriched conditions provided more stimulating environments than what laboratory rats normally experience, they may not be any more stimulating than rats' natural habitats. Thus, the "enriched" condition may reveal more about the importance of normal stimulation than about the benefits of extra stimulation (Gopnik, Meltzoff, & Kuhl, 1999).

mal process, but some extrapolations are conservative, plausible projections drawn from directly relevant data, whereas others are wild leaps of speculation based on loosely related data. The extrapolations made regarding the educational implications of critical periods and environmental effects on synapse formation are highly conjectural *overextrapolations*. The studies that highlighted the possible importance of early experience in animals have all used extreme conditions to make their comparisons, such as depriving an animal of all visual input or raising it in stark isolation. In light of the findings, it seems plausible to speculate that children probably need normal stimulation to experience normal brain development. However, great difficulty arises when these findings are extended to conclude that adding *more* stimulation to a normal environment will be beneficial to brain development (Shatz, 1992).

The ease with which people fall into the trap of overextrapolating has been particularly apparent in recent recommendations that infants listen to classical music to enhance their brain development. These recommendations have been derived from two studies that showed that college students' performance on spatial reasoning tasks was enhanced slightly for about 10–15 minutes after listening to a brief Mozart recording (Rauscher, Shaw, & Ky, 1993, 1995). This peculiar finding, dubbed the "Mozart effect," has proven difficult to replicate (Steele, Bass, & Crook, 1999; Thompson, Schellenberg, & Husain, 2001), but the per-

tinent point here is that there was no research on how classical music affects *infants*, no research relating classical music to *brain development*, and no research on anyone showing *lasting effects*. Nonetheless, many people (including the Governor of Georgia) were quick to extrapolate the shaky findings on the Mozart effect to infants' brain development.

As discussed in Chapter 1, thinking critically about issues often involves asking questions such as: What is missing from this debate? Is there any contradictory evidence? In this case, there is some contradictory evidence that is worthy of consideration. The basis for advocating infant educational programs is the belief that the brain is malleable during the hypothesized critical period of birth to age 3 but not at later ages. However, Greenough's work on synaptic formation and other lines of research suggest that the brain remains somewhat malleable throughout life, responding to stimulation into old age (Thompson & Nelson, 2001). Thus, advocates for the aged could just as readily argue for new ed-

ucational initiatives for the elderly to help them maximize their intellectual potential. Another problem is the implicit assumption that greater synaptic density is associated with greater intelligence. As noted in the main body of the chapter, there is evidence that infant animals and humans begin life with an overabundance of synaptic connections and that learning involves selective *pruning* of inactive synapses (Huttenlocher, 1979; Rakic, Bourgeois, & Goldman-Rakic, 1994). Thus, in the realm of synapses, more may *not* be better.

In conclusion, there may be many valid reasons for increasing educational programs for infants, but research in neuroscience does not appear to provide a clear rationale for much in the way of specific infant care policies. One problem in evaluating these proposals is that few people want to argue against high-quality child care or education. But modern societies need to allocate their limited resources to the programs that appear most likely to have beneficial effects, so even intuitively appealing ideas need to be subjected to critical scrutiny.

Table 3.3 Critical Thinking Skills Discussed in This Application

Skill	Description
Understanding the limits of extrapolation	The critical thinker appreciates that extrapolations are based on certain assumptions, vary in plausibility, and ultimately involve speculation.
Looking for contradictory evidence	In evaluating the evidence presented on an issue, the critical thinker attempts to look for contradictory evidence that may have been left out of the debate.

Key Ideas

Communication in the Nervous System

● Neurons are the basic communication links in the nervous system. They normally transmit a neural impulse (an electric current) along an axon to a synapse with another neuron. The neural impulse is a brief change in a neuron's electrical charge that moves along an axon. It is an all-or-none event.

● Action potentials trigger the release of chemicals called neurotransmitters that diffuse across a synapse to communicate with other neurons. Transmitters bind with receptors in the post-synaptic cell membrane, causing excitatory or inhibitory PSPs. Most neurons are linked in neural pathways, circuits, and networks.

● ACh plays a key role in muscular movement. Disturbances in the activity of the monoamine transmitters have been related to the development of depression and schizophrenia. GABA is a widely distributed inhibitory transmitter. Endorphins contribute to the relief of pain.

Organization of the Nervous System

● The nervous system can be divided into the central nervous system and the peripheral nervous system. The central nervous system consists of the brain and spinal cord.

● The peripheral nervous system can be subdivided into the somatic nervous system, which connects to muscles and sensory receptors, and the autonomic nervous system, which connects to blood vessels, smooth muscles, and glands.

Looking Inside the Brain: Research Methods

● The EEG can record broad patterns of electrical activity in the brain. Lesioning involves destroying a piece of the brain. Another technique is electrical stimulation of areas in the brain in order to activate them. In recent years, new brain-imaging procedures have been developed, including CT scans, PET scans, MRI scans, and fMRI scans.

The Brain and Behavior

● The brain has three major regions: the hindbrain, midbrain, and forebrain. Structures in the hindbrain and midbrain handle essential functions. The thalamus is primarily a relay station. The hypothalamus is involved in the regulation of basic biological drives such as hunger and sex.

● The limbic system is involved in emotion, motivation, and memory. The cortex is the cerebrum's convoluted outer layer, which is subdivided into occipital, parietal, temporal, and frontal lobes. The brain's organization is somewhat malleable.

Right Brain/Left Brain: Cerebral Laterality

● The cerebrum is divided into right and left hemispheres connected by the corpus callo-

sum. Studies of split-brain patients and perceptual asymmetries have revealed that the right and left halves of the brain each have unique talents.

The Endocrine System: Another Way to Communicate

● The endocrine system consists of the glands that secrete hormones, which are chemicals involved in the regulation of basic bodily processes. The control centers for the endocrine system are the hypothalamus and the pituitary gland.

Heredity and Behavior: Is It All in the Genes?

● The basic units of genetic transmission are genes housed on chromosomes. Most behavioral qualities appear to involve polygenic inheritance. Researchers assess hereditary influence through a variety of methods, including family studies, twin studies, adoption studies, and genetic mapping.

The Evolutionary Bases of Behavior

● Darwin argued that if a heritable trait contributes to an organism's survival or reproductive success, organisms with that trait should produce more offspring than those without the trait and the prevalence of that trait should gradually increase over generations—thanks to natural selection.

● Darwin recognized from the beginning that natural selection was applicable to behavioral traits, as well as physical traits. According to Trivers, a species' courtship and mating strategies depend primarily on sex differences in parental investment.

Putting It in Perspective

● Three of the book's unifying themes stand out in this chapter. First, we saw how heredity interacts with experience to govern behavior. Second, the discussions of biological factors underlying schizophrenia highlighted the multifactorial causation of behavior. Third, we saw how innovations in research methods often lead to advances in knowledge, underscoring the empirical nature of psychology.

Personal Application • Evaluating the Concept of "Two Minds in One"

● The cerebral hemispheres are specialized for handling different cognitive tasks, but only to a degree, and people vary in their patterns of hemispheric specialization. Evidence on whether people vary in brainedness and whether the two hemispheres vary in cognitive style is inconclusive.

Critical Thinking Application • Building Better Brains: The Perils of Extrapolation

● Although some education and child-care reformers have used research in neuroscience

as the basis for their campaigns, research has not demonstrated that birth to three is a critical period for human neural development or that specific enrichment programs can enhance brain development. These assertions are highly conjectural overextrapolations from existing data.

Key Terms

Absolute refractory period
Action potential
Adaptation
Adoption studies
Afferent nerve fibers
Agonist
Antagonist
Autonomic nervous system (ANS)
Axon
Behavioral genetics
Central nervous system (CNS)
Cerebral cortex
Cerebral hemispheres
Cerebrospinal fluid (CSF)
Chromosomes
Corpus callosum
Critical period
Dendrites
Dominant gene
Efferent nerve fibers
Electrical stimulation of the brain (ESB)
Electroencephalograph (EEG)
Endocrine system
Endorphins
Excitatory PSP
Family studies
Fitness
Forebrain
Fraternal (dizygotic) twins
Genes
Genetic mapping
Genotype
Heterozygous condition
Hindbrain
Homozygous condition
Hormones
Hypothalamus
Identical (monozygotic) twins
Inclusive fitness
Inhibitory PSP

Lesioning
Limbic system
Midbrain
Monogamy
Mutation
Myelin sheath
Natural selection
Nerves
Neurons
Neurotransmitters
Parasympathetic division
Parental investment
Perceptual asymmetries
Peripheral nervous system
Phenotype
Pituitary gland
Polyandry
Polygenic traits
Polygyny
Postsynaptic potential (PSP)
Recessive gene
Resting potential
Reuptake
Soma
Somatic nervous system
Split-brain surgery
Sympathetic division
Synapse
Synaptic cleft
Terminal buttons
Thalamus
Twin studies
Zygote

Key People

Charles Darwin
Alan Hodgkin and Andrew Huxley
James Olds and Peter Milner
Candace Pert and Solomon Snyder
Robert Plomin
Roger Sperry and Michael Gazzaniga

PRACTICE TEST

1. A neural impulse is initiated when a neuron's charge momentarily becomes less negative, or even positive. This event is called:
   A. an action potential.
   B. a resting potential.
   C. impulse facilitation.
   D. inhibitory.

2. Neurons convey information about the strength of stimuli by varying:
   A. the size of their action potentials.
   B. the velocity of their action potentials.
   C. the rate at which they fire action potentials.
   D. all of the above.

3. Alterations in activity at dopamine synapses have been implicated in the development of:
   A. anxiety.
   B. schizophrenia.
   C. Alzheimer's disease.
   D. nicotine addiction.

4. Jim just barely avoided a head-on collision on a narrow road. With heart pounding, hands shaking, and body perspiring, Jim recognizes that these are signs of the body's fight-or-flight response, which is controlled by the:
   A. empathetic division of the peripheral nervous system.
   B. parasympathetic division of the autonomic nervous system.
   C. somatic division of the peripheral nervous system.
   D. sympathetic division of the autonomic nervous system.

5. The hindbrain consists of the:
   A. endocrine system and the limbic system.
   B. reticular formation.
   C. thalamus, hypothalamus, and cerebrum.
   D. cerebellum, medulla, and pons.

6. Juan is watching a basketball game. The neural impulses from his eyes will ultimately travel to his primary visual cortex, but first they must pass through the:
   A. amygdala.
   B. hypothalamus.
   C. thalamus.
   D. pons.

7. The _____ lobe is to hearing as the occipital lobe is to vision.
   A. frontal
   B. temporal
   C. parietal
   D. cerebellar

8. Paul has profound difficulty producing spoken language. If his problem is attributable to brain damage, the damage would probably be found in:
   A. the cerebellum.
   B. Sperry's area.
   C. Broca's area.
   D. Wernicke's area.

9. Sounds presented to the right ear are registered:
   A. only in the right hemisphere.
   B. only in the left hemisphere.
   C. more quickly in the right hemisphere.
   D. more quickly in the left hemisphere.

10. In people whose corpus callosums have not been severed, verbal stimuli are identified more quickly and more accurately:
    A. when sent to the right hemisphere first.
    B. when sent to the left hemisphere first.
    C. when presented to the left visual field.
    D. when presented auditorally rather than visually.

11. Hormones are to the endocrine system as _____ are to the nervous system.
    A. nerves
    B. synapses
    C. neurotransmitters
    D. action potentials

12. Jenny has brown hair and blue eyes and is 5'8" tall. What is being described is Jenny's:
    A. genotype.
    B. phenotype.
    C. somatotype.
    D. physiognomy.

13. Adopted children's similarity to their biological parents is generally attributed to _____; adopted children's similarity to their adoptive parents is generally attributed to _____.
    A. heredity; the environment
    B. the environment; heredity
    C. the environment; the environment
    D. heredity; heredity

14. A spontaneous, heritable change or error in DNA replication is called:
    A. genetic drift.
    B. gene flow.
    C. an adaptation.
    D. a mutation.

15. For which of the following assertions is the empirical evidence strongest?
    A. The two cerebral hemispheres are specialized to handle different types of cognitive tasks.
    B. People have a separate stream of consciousness in each hemisphere.
    C. Each hemisphere has its own cognitive style.
    D. Some people are right-brained, while others are left-brained.

Answers

1	A	p. 77	6	C	p. 93	11	C	p. 101
2	C	p. 77	7	B	pp. 95–96	12	B	p. 104
3	B	p. 82	8	C	p. 98	13	A	pp. 106–107
4	D	p. 85	9	D	p. 98	14	D	p. 109
5	D	pp. 84, 91	10	B	p. 100	15	A	pp. 116–117

WWW ON THE WEB

For additional resources on the topics covered in this chapter, visit the *Psychology: Themes and Variations* Web site, where you will find practice quizzes, tutorials, Web links, simulations, critical thinking activities, flash cards, interactive exercises, and suggested readings available through INFOTRAC.

http://psychology.wadsworth.com/weiten_themes6e/

CHAPTER 4

© Diana Ong/Super Stock

Sensation and Perception

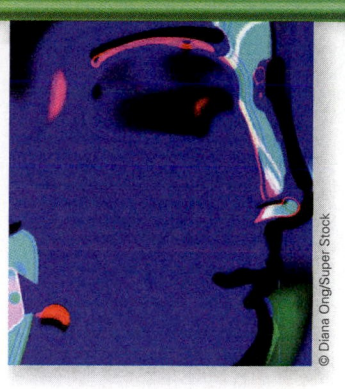

© Diana Ong/Super Stock

Take a look at the adjacent photo. What do you see? You probably answered, "a rose" or "a flower." But is that what you really see? No, this isn't a trick question. Let's examine the odd case of "Dr. P." It shows that there's more to seeing than meets the eye.

Dr. P was an intelligent and distinguished music professor who began to exhibit some worrisome behaviors that seemed to be related to his vision. Sometimes he failed to recognize familiar students by sight, though he knew them instantly by the sound of their voices. Sometimes he acted as if he saw faces in inanimate objects, cordially greeting fire hydrants and parking meters as if they were children. On one occasion, reaching for what he thought was his hat, he took hold of his wife's head and tried to put it on! Except for these kinds of visual mistakes, Dr. P was a normal, talented man.

Ultimately Dr. P was referred to Oliver Sacks, a neurologist, for an examination. During one visit, Sacks handed Dr. P a fresh red rose to see whether he would recognize it. Dr. P took the rose as if he were being given a model of a geometric solid rather than a flower. "About six inches in length," Dr. P observed, "a convoluted red form with a linear green attachment."

"Yes," Sacks persisted, "and what do you think it is, Dr. P?"

"Not easy to say," the patient replied. "It lacks the simple symmetry of the Platonic solids . . ."

"Smell it," the neurologist suggested. Dr. P looked perplexed, as if being asked to smell symmetry, but he complied and brought the flower to his nose. Suddenly, his confusion cleared up. "Beautiful. An early rose. What a heavenly smell" (Sacks, 1987, pp. 13–14).

What accounted for Dr. P's strange inability to recognize faces and familiar objects by sight? There was nothing wrong with his eyes. He could readily spot a pin on the floor. If you're thinking that he must have had something wrong with his vision, look again at the photo of the rose. What you see *is* "a convoluted red form with a linear green attachment." It doesn't occur to you to describe it that

way only because, without thinking about it, you instantly perceive that combination of form and color as a flower. This is precisely what Dr. P was unable to do. He could see perfectly well, but he was losing the ability to assemble what he saw into a meaningful picture of the world. Technically, he suffered from a condition called *visual agnosia,* an inability to recognize objects through sight. As Sacks (1987) put it, "Visually, he was lost in a world of lifeless abstractions" (p. 15).

As Dr. P's case illustrates, without effective processing of sensory input, our familiar world can become a chaos of bewildering sensations. To acknowledge the need to both take in and process sensory information, psychologists distinguish between sensation and perception. *Sensation* is the stimulation of sense organs. *Perception* is the selection, organization, and interpretation of sensory input. Sensation involves the absorption of energy, such as light or sound waves, by sensory organs, such as the eyes and ears. Perception involves organizing and translating sensory input into something meaningful (see Figure 4.1 on the next page). For example, when you look at the photo of the rose, your eyes are *sensing* the light reflected from the page, including areas of low reflectance where ink has been deposited in an irregular shape. What you *perceive,* however, is a picture of a rose.

The distinction between sensation and perception stands out in Dr. P's case of visual agnosia. His eyes were doing their job of registering sensory input and transmitting signals to the brain. However, damage in his brain interfered with his ability to put these signals together into organized wholes. Thus, Dr. P's process of visual *sensation* was intact, but his process of visual *perception* was severely impaired.

Dr. P's case is unusual, of course. Normally, the processes of sensation and perception are difficult to separate because people automatically start organizing incoming sensory stimulation the moment it arrives. The distinction between sensation and perception has been useful in organizing theory and research, but in operation the two processes merge.

Diane Padys/FPG International—Getty Images

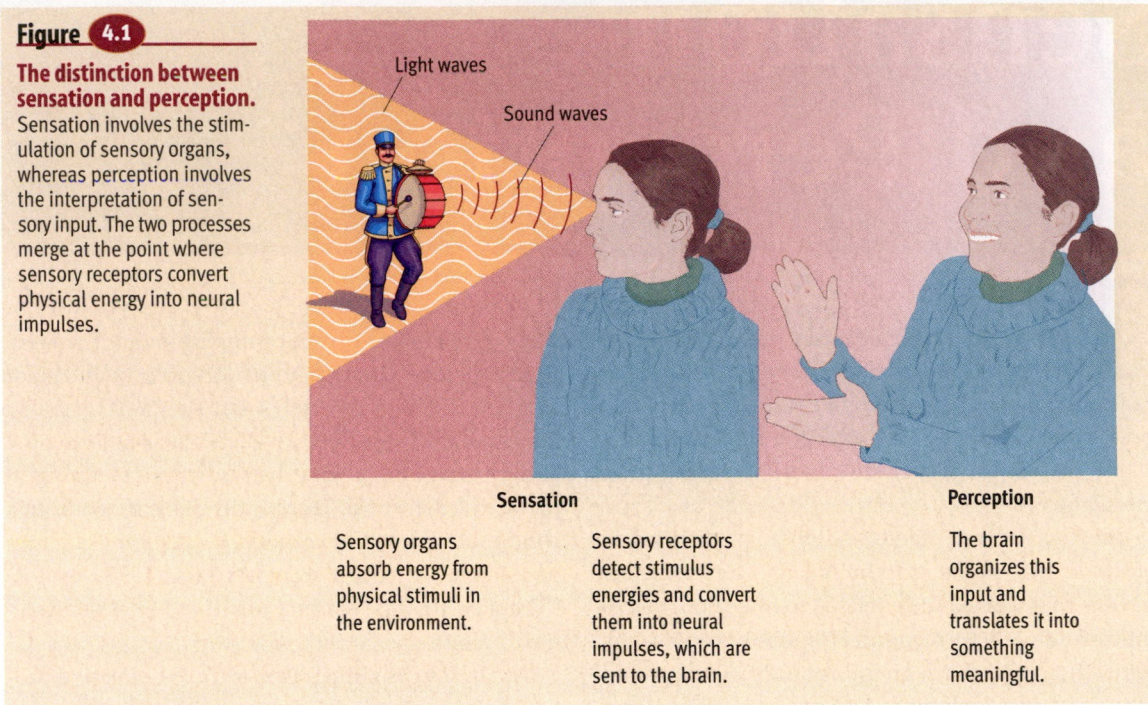

Figure 4.1

The distinction between sensation and perception. Sensation involves the stimulation of sensory organs, whereas perception involves the interpretation of sensory input. The two processes merge at the point where sensory receptors convert physical energy into neural impulses.

Light waves

Sound waves

Sensation

Sensory organs absorb energy from physical stimuli in the environment.

Sensory receptors detect stimulus energies and convert them into neural impulses, which are sent to the brain.

Perception

The brain organizes this input and translates it into something meaningful.

We'll begin our discussion of sensation and perception by examining some general concepts that are relevant to all the senses. Next, we'll examine individual senses, in each case beginning with the sensory aspects and working our way through to the perceptual aspects. The chapter's Personal Application explores how principles of visual perception come into play in art and illusion. The Critical Thinking Application discusses how perceptual contrasts can be manipulated in persuasive efforts.

Psychophysics: Basic Concepts and Issues

PREVIEW QUESTIONS

● How is stimulus intensity related to absolute thresholds?

● What is a JND, and where does it fit in with Weber's and Fechner's laws?

● What is the central idea of signal-detection theory?

● What is the practical significance of subliminal perception?

● What is sensory adaptation?

As you may recall from Chapter 1, the first experimental psychologists were interested mainly in sensation and perception. They called their area of interest *psychophysics—the study of how physical stimuli are translated into psychological experience*. A particularly important contributor to psychophysics was Gustav Fechner, who published a seminal work on the subject in 1860. Fechner was a German scientist working at the University of Leipzig, where Wilhelm Wundt later founded the first formal laboratory and journal devoted to psychological research. Unlike Wundt, Fechner was not a "campaigner" interested in establishing psychology as an independent discipline. However, his groundbreaking research laid the foundation that Wundt built upon.

Thresholds: Looking for Limits

Sensation begins with a *stimulus,* any detectable input from the environment. What counts as detectable, though, depends on who or what is doing the detecting. For instance, you might not be able to detect a weak odor that is readily apparent to your dog. Thus, Fechner wanted to know: For any given sense, what is the weakest detectable stimulus? For example, what is the minimum amount of light needed for a person to see that there is light?

Implicit in Fechner's question is a concept central to psychophysics: the threshold. *A threshold is a dividing point between energy levels that do and do not have a detectable effect.* For example, hardware stores sell a gadget with a photocell that automatically turns a lamp on when a room gets dark. The level of light intensity at which the gadget clicks on is its threshold.

An *absolute threshold* for a specific type of sensory input is the minimum amount of stimulation that an organism can detect. Absolute thresholds define the boundaries of an organism's sensory capabilities. Fechner and his contemporaries used a variety

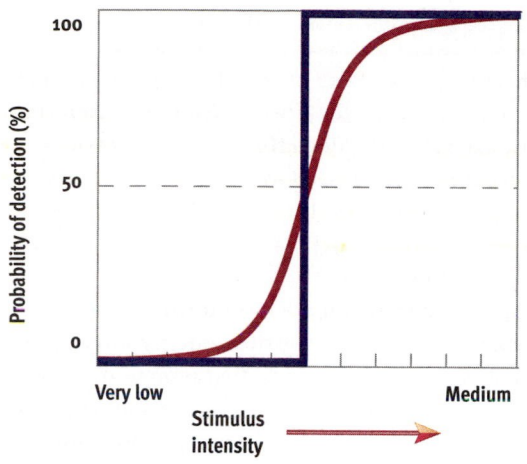

Figure 4.2

The absolute threshold. If absolute thresholds were truly absolute, then at threshold intensity the probability of detecting a stimulus would jump from 0 to 100%, as graphed here in blue. In reality, the chances of detecting a stimulus increase gradually with stimulus intensity, as shown in red. Accordingly, an "absolute" threshold is defined as the intensity level at which the probability of detection is 50%.

of methods to determine humans' absolute threshold for detecting light. They discovered that absolute thresholds are anything but absolute. When lights of varying intensity are flashed at a subject, there is no single stimulus intensity at which the subject jumps from no detection to completely accurate detection. Instead, as stimulus intensity increases, subjects' probability of responding to stimuli *gradually increases*, as shown in red in Figure 4.2. Thus, researchers had to arbitrarily define the absolute threshold as the stimulus intensity *detected 50% of the time.*

Using this definition, investigators found that under ideal conditions, human abilities to detect weak stimuli are greater than appreciated. Some concrete examples of the absolute thresholds for various senses can be seen in Table 4.1. For example, on a clear, dark night, in the absence of other distracting lights, you could see the light of a candle burning 30 miles in the distance! Of course, we're talking about ideal conditions—you would have to go out to the middle of nowhere to find the darkness required to put this assertion to a suitable test. *to do you need 20/20 vision for this to work.*

Weighing the Differences: The JND

Fechner was also interested in people's sensitivity to differences between stimuli. **A *just noticeable difference (JND)* is the smallest difference in the amount of stimulation that a specific sense can detect.** JNDs are close cousins of absolute thresholds. In fact, an

absolute threshold is simply the just noticeable difference from nothing (no stimulus input).

You might think that the JND would always have the same value for any given sense. For instance, what do you suppose is the smallest difference in weight that you can detect by lifting different objects? An ounce? Two ounces? Six ounces? As it turns out, the answer varies. The JND is greater for heavy objects than for light ones. However, the smallest detectable difference is a fairly stable *proportion* of the weight of the original object.

This principle was first demonstrated by Fechner's brother-in-law, Ernst Weber, and came to be known as Weber's law. **Weber's law states that the size of a just noticeable difference is a constant proportion of the size of the initial stimulus.** This constant proportion is called the *Weber fraction*. Weber's law applies not only to weight perception but to all the senses. However, different fractions apply to different types of sensory input. For example, the Weber fraction for lifting weights is approximately 1/30. That means that you should be just able to detect the difference between a 30-ounce weight and a 31-ounce weight (the JND for 30 ounces is 1 ounce). If you started with a 90-ounce weight, however, you would not be able to tell the difference between it and a 91-ounce weight. Why? Because the JND for 90 ounces is 3 ounces (1/30 of 90). In general, then, as stimuli increase in magnitude, the JND becomes larger.

Psychophysical Scaling

If one light has twice the energy of another, do you necessarily perceive it as twice as bright? When asked to make this kind of judgment, you are being asked to *scale* the magnitude of sensory experiences. In his work on the scaling of sensory experiences, Fechner

"*The method of just noticeable differences consists in determining how much the weights have to differ so that they can just be discriminated.*"
GUSTAV FECHNER

Table 4.1 Examples of Absolute Thresholds

Sense	Absolute Threshold
Vision	A candle flame seen at 30 miles on a dark clear night
Hearing	The tick of a watch under quiet conditions at 20 feet
Taste	One teaspoon of sugar in two gallons of water
Smell	One drop of perfume diffused into entire volume of a six-room apartment
Touch	The wing of a fly falling on your cheek from a distance of 1 centimeter

SOURCE: Galanter, E. (1962). Contemporary psychophysics. In R. Brown (Ed.), *New directions in psychology.* New York: Holt, Rinehart & Winston. © 1962 Eugene Galanter. Reprinted by permission.

used the JND as his unit of measurement. His work yielded a principle that came to be known as *Fechner's law,* which states that the magnitude of a sensory experience is proportional to the number of JNDs that the stimulus causing the experience is above absolute threshold.

An important ramification of Fechner's law is that constant increments in stimulus intensity produce smaller and smaller increases in the *perceived* magnitude of sensation. This principle is easy to illustrate. Imagine that you're in a dark room with a single lamp that has three bulbs of the same wattage. You turn a switch, and one bulb lights. After a dark room, the difference is striking. Turn again, and a second bulb comes on. The amount of light is doubled, but the room does not seem twice as bright. When you turn the third bulb on, it adds just as much light as the first or second, but you barely notice the difference. Thus, three equal increases in stimulus intensity (the amount of light) produce progressively smaller differences in the magnitude of sensation (perceived brightness).

The merit of Fechner's approach to scaling sensation was eventually questioned by S. S. Stevens (1957, 1975). His approach to scaling, called *magnitude estimation,* simply involved asking subjects to assign numbers to stimuli on the basis of how intense they appeared to be. Most modern psychophysicists believe that magnitude estimation is the best way to map the relations between stimulus intensity and sensory experience, but some of the details of this process continue to be debated (Krueger, 1989). It is clear, however, that people's inner "measurements" of sensory experiences are not a simple linear function of the physical intensity of the stimuli. What all this means is that perceptions can't be measured on absolute scales. In the domain of sensory experience virtually everything is relative.

Signal-Detection Theory

This insight applies not only to sensory scaling but to sensory thresholds as well. *Signal-detection theory* proposes that the detection of stimuli involves decision processes as well as sensory processes, which are both influenced by a variety of factors besides stimulus intensity (Egan, 1975; Swets, Tanner, & Birdsall, 1961).

Imagine that you are monitoring a radar screen, looking for signs of possible enemy aircraft. Your mission is to detect signals that represent approaching airplanes as quickly and as accurately as possible. In this situation, there are four possible outcomes, which are outlined in Figure 4.3: *hits* (detecting signals when they are present), *misses* (failing to detect signals when they are present), *false alarms* (detecting signals when they are not present), and *correct rejections* (not detecting signals when they are absent). Given these possibilities, signal-detection theory attempts to account for the influence of decision-making processes on stimulus detection. In detecting weak signals on the radar screen, you will often have to decide whether a faint signal represents an airplane or whether you're just imagining that it does. Your responses will depend in part on the *criterion* you set for how sure you must feel before you react. Setting this criterion involves higher mental processes rather than raw sensation and depends on your expectations and on the consequences of missing a signal or of reporting a false alarm.

According to signal-detection theory, your performance will also depend on the level of "noise" in the system. Noise comes from all the irrelevant stimuli in the environment and the neural activity they elicit. Noise is analogous to the background static on a radio station. The more noise in the system, the harder it will be for you to pick up a weak signal. Variations in noise provide another reason why sensory thresholds depend on more than just the intensity of stimuli.

Signal-detection theory grew out of practical efforts to understand and improve the monitoring of complex, modern equipment, such as radar. However, the theory applies equally well to a broad range of everyday experiences involving the registration of sensory inputs. Suppose, for instance, you are eagerly awaiting the delivery of a pizza at a loud, raucous party. In this situation, you want to detect a signal (the doorbell) in the midst of background noise (music, people talking), and your criteria for "hearing" the doorbell will change as the expected time of delivery approaches.

Figure 4.3

Possible outcomes in signal-detection theory. This diagram shows the four outcomes that are possible in attempting to detect the presence of weak signals. The criterion you set for how confident you want to feel before reporting a signal will affect your responding. For example, if you require high confidence before reporting a signal, you will minimize false alarms, but you'll be more likely to miss some signals.

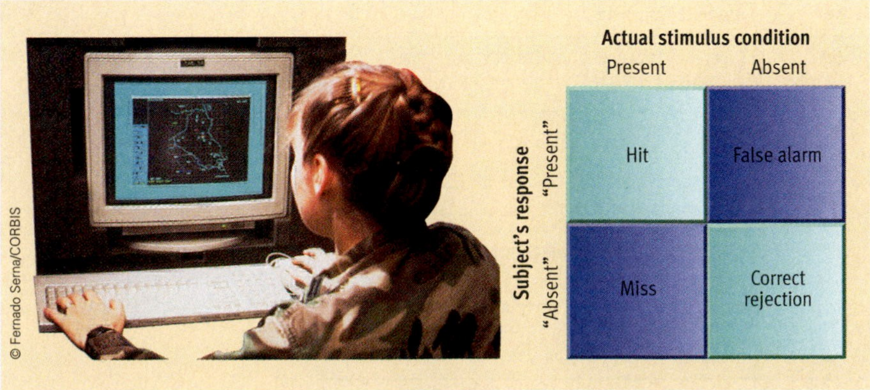

	Actual stimulus condition	
Subject's response	Present	Absent
"Present"	Hit	False alarm
"Absent"	Miss	Correct rejection

© Fernado Serna/CORBIS

The key point is that signal-detection theory replaces Fechner's sharp threshold with the concept of "detectability." Detectability is measured in terms of probability and depends on decision-making processes as well as sensory processes. In comparison to classical models of psychophysics, signal-detection theory is better equipped to explain some of the complexities of perceived experience in the real world.

Perception Without Awareness

The concepts of thresholds and detectability lie at the core of an interesting debate: Can sensory stimuli that fall beneath the threshold of awareness still influence behavior? This issue centers on the concept of *subliminal perception*—the registration of sensory input without conscious awareness (*limen* is another term for threshold, so *subliminal* means below threshold). This question might be just another technical issue in the normally staid world of psychophysics, except that subliminal perception has become tied up in highly charged controversies relating to money, sex, religion, and rock music.

The controversy began in 1957 when an executive named James Vicary placed hidden messages such as "Eat popcorn" in a film showing at a theater in New Jersey. The messages were superimposed on only a few frames of the film, so that they flashed by quickly and imperceptibly. Nonetheless, Vicary claimed in the press that popcorn sales increased by 58%, and a public outcry ensued (McConnell, Cutler, & McNeil, 1958). Since then, Wilson Brian Key, a former advertising executive, has written several books claiming that sexual words and drawings are embedded subliminally in magazine advertisements to elicit favorable unconscious reactions from consumers (Key, 1973, 1976, 1980). One such advertisement discussed by Key is shown in Figure 4.4. If you look closely, you'll find the word SEX embedded in the ice cubes. Taking the sexual manipulation theme a step further, entrepreneurs are now marketing music audiotapes containing subliminal messages that are supposed to help people seduce unsuspecting listeners. Furthermore, as noted in Chapter 2, subliminal self-help tapes intended to facilitate weight loss, sleep, memory, self-esteem, and the like have become a $50 million industry. Religious overtones were added to this controversy in the 1980s when subliminal messages encouraging devil worship were allegedly found in rock music played *backward* (Vokey & Read, 1985). Can listening to Led Zeppelin's "Stairway to Heaven" promote Satanic rituals? Can your sexual urges be manipulated by messages hidden under music? Can advertisers influence your product preferences with subliminal stimuli? Those who are concerned about subliminal messages assert that such messages are likely to be persuasive because people supposedly are defenseless against appeals operating below their threshold of awareness. How justified are these fears? Research on subliminal perception was sporadic in the 1960s and 1970s because scientists initially dismissed the entire idea as preposterous. However, empirical studies have begun to accumulate since the 1980s.

For example, Jon Krosnick and his colleagues (1992) set out to determine whether subjects' attitudes toward a target person could be shaped without their awareness. Participants were asked to attentively view a series of slides showing a target person going about her daily activities. These slides were preceded by very brief (13/1000 of a second) subliminal presentations of photos expected to arouse positive emotions (a bridal couple, a pair of kittens, and so on) or negative emotions (a skull, a werewolf, and so on). After the slide presentations, subjects rated the target person on various dimensions. The researchers found statistically significant differences in participants' attitudes toward the target person that reflected the type of subliminal photos they had seen. Thus, subliminal inputs produced measurable, although small,

Break out the frosty bottle

GILBEY'S LONDON DRY GIN

and keep your tonics dry!

Wilson Bryan Key/Mediaprobe, Inc.

Figure 4.4

Subliminal advertising: Is it all in the eye of the beholder? If you look closely at the ice cubes in this ad, you will see the word SEX spelled out. Former advertising executive Wilson Bryan Key (1973) claims advertisers routinely place subliminal stimuli in their ads. Marketing companies maintain that people are merely reading things into their ads, much like you might see familiar forms in clouds. Although subliminal perception appears to be a genuine phenomenon, Thomas Creed (1987) has pinpointed a host of fallacies in Key's analysis, which he characterizes as pseudoscience.

effects in subjects who subsequently reported that they did not consciously register the stimuli.

Since the 1980s, a host of other studies have also found support for the existence of subliminal perception (Greenwald, 1992). Using diverse methodological and conceptual approaches, researchers examining a variety of phenomena, such as unconscious semantic priming (Draine & Greenwald, 1998), subliminal affective conditioning (Bunce et al., 1999), subliminal mere exposure effects (Monahan, Murphy, & Zajonc, 2000), nonconscious learning (Lewicki, Hill, & Czyzewska, 1992), subliminal visual priming (Bar & Biederman, 1998), and subliminal psychodynamic activation (Weinberger, 1992), have found evidence that perception without awareness *can* take place. Hence, the dominant view today is that subliminal perception is a genuine phenomenon that is worthy of experimental investigation (Loftus & Klinger, 1992; Merikle & Daneman, 1998).

So, should we be worried about the threat of subliminal persuasion? The research to date suggests that there is little reason for concern. The effects of subliminal stimuli turn out to be nearly as subliminal as the stimuli themselves. Subliminal stimulation generally produces weak effects (De Houwer, Hendrickx, & Baeyens, 1997; Kihlstrom, Barnhardt, & Tataryn, 1992). These effects can be detected only by very precise measurement, under carefully controlled laboratory conditions, in which subjects are asked to focus their undivided attention on visual or auditory materials that contain the subliminal stimuli. Although these effects are theoretically interesting, they appear unlikely to have much practical importance.

In sum, there is no evidence that subliminal stimuli can lead people to buy specific products, abandon their sexual inhibitions, become Satan worshippers, or improve themselves (see the Featured Study for Chapter 2). Research has not bolstered the idea that persuasive efforts operating beneath the surface of conscious awareness are especially powerful. More research on the manipulative potential of subliminal persuasion is needed, but so far there is no cause for alarm.

Sensory Adaptation

The process of sensory adaptation is yet another factor that influences registration of sensory input. *Sensory adaptation is a gradual decline in sensitivity to prolonged stimulation.* For example, let's say you find that the garbage in your kitchen has started to smell. If you stay in the kitchen without removing the garbage, the stench will soon start to fade. In reality, the stimulus intensity of the odor is stable, but with continued exposure, your *sensitivity* to it decreases. Sensory adaptation is a pervasive aspect of everyday life. When you put on your clothes in the morning, you feel them initially, but the sensation quickly fades. Similarly, if you jump reluctantly into a pool of cold water, you'll probably find that the water temperature feels fine in a few moments after you *adapt* to it.

Sensory adaptation is an automatic, built-in process that keeps people tuned in to the *changes* rather than the *constants* in their sensory input. It allows people to ignore the obvious. After all, you don't need constant confirmation that your clothes are still on. But, like most organisms, people are interested in changes in their environment that may signal threats to safety. Thus, as its name suggests, sensory adaptation probably is a behavioral adaptation that has been sculpted by natural selection. Sensory adaptation also shows once again that there is no one-to-one correspondence between sensory input and sensory experience.

The general points we've reviewed so far begin to suggest the complexity of the relationships between the world outside and people's perceived experience of it. As we review each of the principal sensory systems in detail, we'll see repeatedly that people's experience of the world depends on both the physical stimuli they encounter and their active processing of stimulus inputs. We begin our exploration of the senses with vision—the sense that most people think of as nearly synonymous with a direct perception of reality. The case is actually quite different, as you'll see.

REVIEW OF KEY POINTS

- Psychophysicists use a variety of methods to relate sensory inputs to subjective perception. They have found that absolute thresholds are not really absolute.
- Weber's law states that the size of a just noticeable difference is a constant proportion of the size of the initial stimulus. Fechner's law asserts that larger and larger increases in stimulus intensity are required to produce just noticeable differences in the magnitude of sensation.
- According to signal-detection theory, the detection of sensory inputs is influenced by noise in the system and by decision-making strategies. Signal-detection theory replaces Fechner's sharp threshold with the concept of detectability and emphasizes that factors besides stimulus intensity influence detectability.
- In recent years, a host of researchers, using very different conceptual approaches, have demonstrated that perception can occur without awareness. However, research indicates that the effects of subliminal perception are relatively weak and of little or no practical concern.
- Prolonged stimulation may lead to sensory adaptation, which involves a reduction in sensitivity to constant stimulation.

Our Sense of Sight: The Visual System

"Seeing is believing." Good ideas are "bright," and a good explanation is "illuminating." This section is an "overview." Do you see the point? As these common expressions show, humans are visual animals. People rely heavily on their sense of sight, and they virtually equate it with what is trustworthy (seeing is believing). Although it is taken for granted, you'll see (there it is again) that the human visual system is amazingly complex. Furthermore, as in all sensory domains, what people "sense" and what they "perceive" may be quite different.

Figure 4.5

Light, the physical stimulus for vision. **(a)** Light waves vary in amplitude and wavelength. **(b)** Within the spectrum of visible light, amplitude (corresponding to physical intensity) affects mainly the experience of brightness. Wavelength affects mainly the experience of color, and purity is the key determinant of saturation. **(c)** If white light (such as sunlight) passes through a prism, the prism separates the light into its component wavelengths, creating a rainbow of colors. However, visible light is only the narrow band of wavelengths to which human eyes happen to be sensitive.

The Stimulus: Light

3a

For people to see, there must be light. *Light* is a form of electromagnetic radiation that travels as a wave, moving, naturally enough, at the speed of light. As Figure 4.5(a) shows, light waves vary in *amplitude* (height) and in *wavelength* (the distance between peaks). Amplitude affects mainly the perception of brightness, while wavelength affects mainly the perception of color. The lights humans normally see are mixtures of several wavelengths. Hence, light can also vary in its *purity* (how varied the mix is). Purity influences perception of the saturation, or richness, of colors. Saturation is difficult to describe, but if you glance at Figure 4.6,

Saturation →

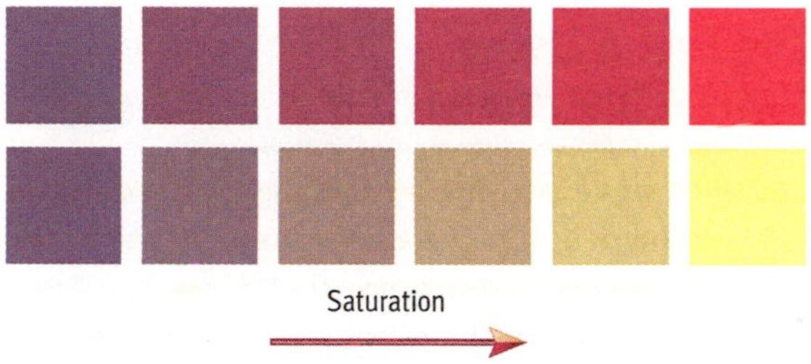

Figure 4.6

Saturation. Variations in saturation are difficult to describe, but you can see examples for two colors here.

PREVIEW QUESTIONS
- What are the three properties of light?
- What do the lens and pupil contribute to visual functioning?
- What are the functions of rods and cones?
- How do visual receptive fields typically function?
- How are visual signals routed from the eye to the primary visual cortex?
- What are feature detectors?

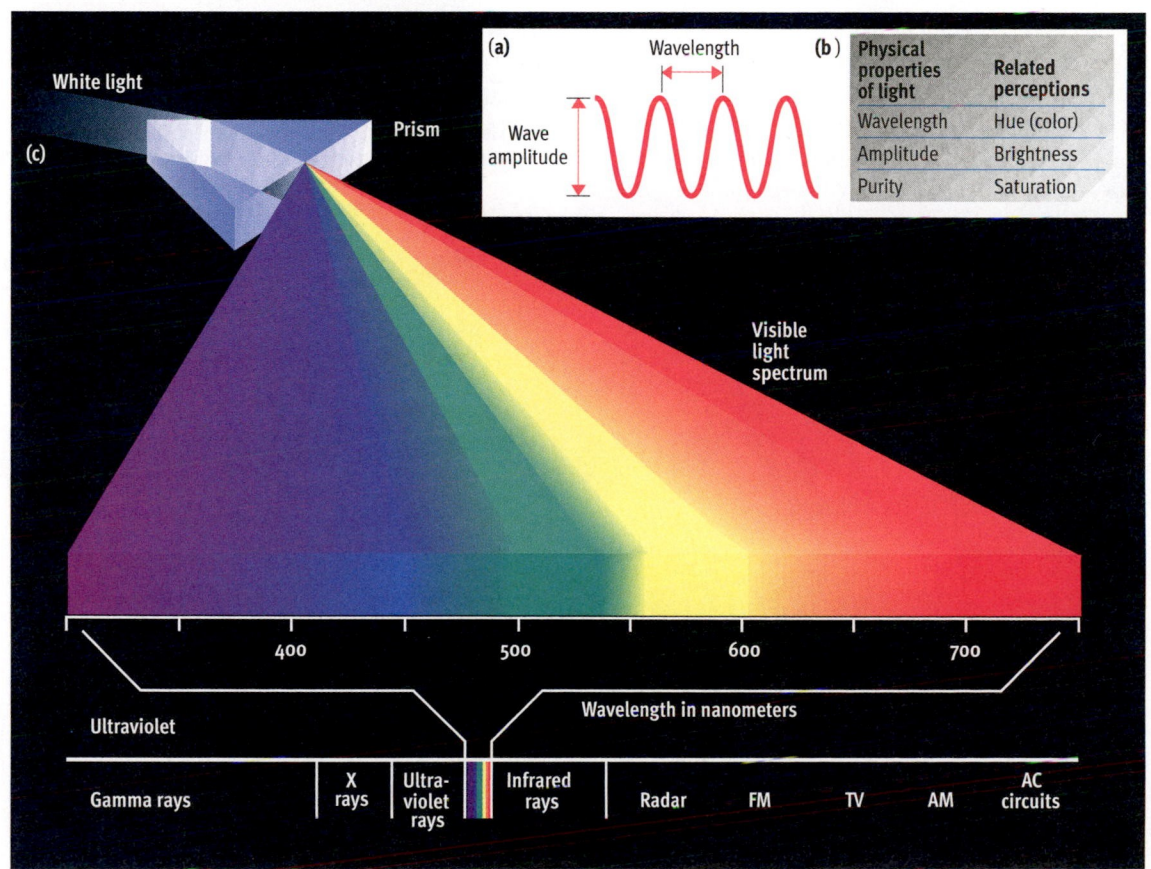

Physical properties of light	Related perceptions
Wavelength	Hue (color)
Amplitude	Brightness
Purity	Saturation

White light

Prism

(c)

(a) Wavelength

Wave amplitude

(b)

Visible light spectrum

400   500   600   700

Wavelength in nanometers

Ultraviolet

| Gamma rays | X rays | Ultra-violet rays | Infrared rays | Radar | FM | TV | AM | AC circuits |

you'll find it clearly illustrated. Of course, most objects do not emit light, they reflect it (the sun, lamps, and fireflies being some exceptions).

What most people call light includes only the wavelengths that humans can see. But as Figure 4.5(c) shows, the visible spectrum is only a slim portion of the total range of wavelengths. Vision is a filter that permits people to sense but a fraction of the real world. Other animals have different capabilities and so live in a quite different visual world. For example, many insects can see shorter wavelengths than humans can see, in the *ultraviolet* spectrum, whereas many fish and reptiles can see longer wavelengths, in the *infrared* spectrum. Although the sense of sight depends on light waves, for people to *see*, incoming visual input must be converted into neural impulses that are sent to the brain. Let's investigate how this transformation is accomplished.

The Eye: A Living Optical Instrument

The eyes serve two main purposes: They channel light to the neural tissue that receives it, called the *retina*, and they house that tissue. The structure of the eye is shown in Figure 4.7.

Each eye is a living optical instrument that creates an image of the visual world on the light-sensitive retina lining its inside back surface.

Light enters the eye through a transparent "window" at the front, the *cornea*. The cornea and the crystalline *lens*, located behind it, form an upside-down image of objects on the retina. It might seem disturbing that the image is upside down, but the brain knows the rule for relating positions on the retina to the corresponding positions in the world.

The *lens* is the transparent eye structure that focuses the light rays falling on the retina. The lens is made up of relatively soft tissue, capable of adjustments that facilitate a process called accommodation. *Accommodation* occurs when the curvature of the lens adjusts to alter visual focus. When you focus on a close object, the lens of your eye gets fatter (rounder) to give you a clear image. When you focus on distant objects, the lens flattens out to give you a better image of them.

A number of common visual deficiencies are caused by focusing problems or by defects in the lens (Guyton, 1991). For example, **in nearsightedness, close objects are seen clearly but distant objects appear blurry** because the focus of light from distant objects falls a little short of the retina (see Figure 4.8). This

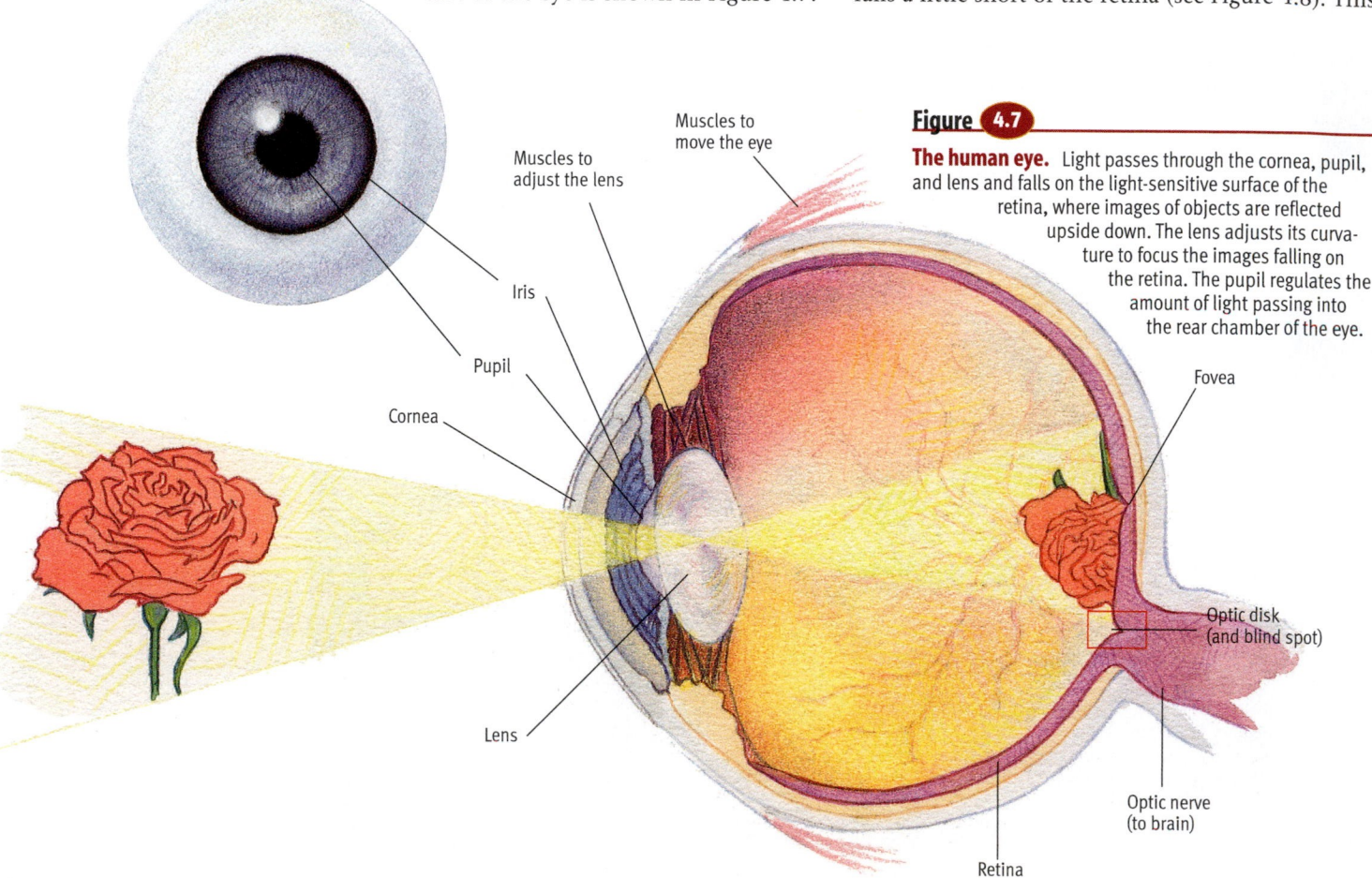

Figure 4.7

The human eye. Light passes through the cornea, pupil, and lens and falls on the light-sensitive surface of the retina, where images of objects are reflected upside down. The lens adjusts its curvature to focus the images falling on the retina. The pupil regulates the amount of light passing into the rear chamber of the eye.

Muscles to move the eye

Muscles to adjust the lens

Iris

Pupil

Cornea

Lens

Fovea

Optic disk (and blind spot)

Optic nerve (to brain)

Retina

focusing problem occurs when the cornea or lens bends light too much, or when the eyeball is too long. **In *farsightedness*, distant objects are seen clearly but close objects appear blurry** because the focus of light from close objects falls behind the retina. This focusing problem typically occurs when the eyeball is too short.

The eye can make adjustments to alter the amount of light reaching the retina. The *iris* is the colored ring of muscle surrounding the *pupil,* or black center of the eye. **The *pupil* is the opening in the center of the iris that helps regulate the amount of light passing into the rear chamber of the eye.** When the pupil constricts, it lets less light into the eye, but it sharpens the image falling on the retina. When the pupil dilates (opens), it lets more light in, but the image is less sharp. In bright light, the pupils constrict to take advantage of the sharpened image. But in dim light, the pupils dilate; image sharpness is sacrificed to allow more light to fall on the retina so that more remains visible.

The Retina: The Brain's Envoy in the Eye

3b

The *retina* is the neural tissue lining the inside back surface of the eye; it absorbs light, processes images, and sends visual information to the brain. You may be surprised to learn that the retina *processes* images. But it's a piece of the central nervous system that happens to be located in the eyeball. Much as

the spinal cord is a complicated extension of the brain, the retina is the brain's envoy in the eye. Although the retina is only a paper-thin sheet of neural tissue, it contains a complex network of specialized cells arranged in layers, as shown in Figure 4.9.

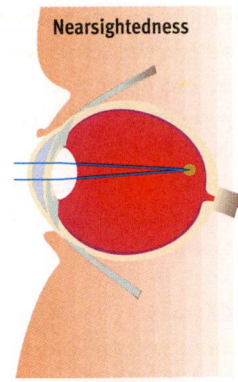

Nearsightedness

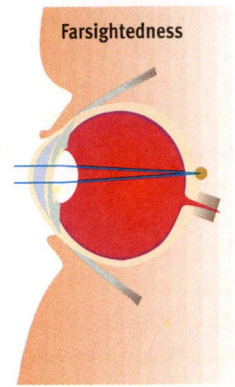

Farsightedness

Craig McClain

Figure 4.8

Nearsightedness and far-sightedness. The pictures above simulate how a scene might look to nearsighted and farsighted people. Nearsightedness occurs because light from distant objects focuses in front of the retina. Farsightedness is due to the opposite situation—light from close objects focuses behind the retina.

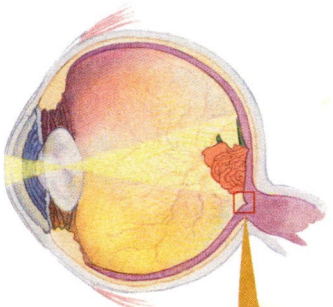

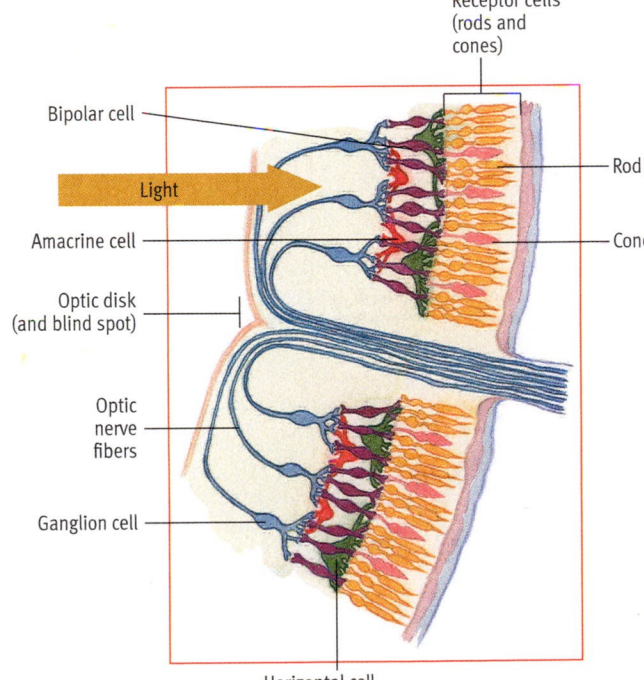

Receptor cells (rods and cones)

Bipolar cell

Light

Amacrine cell

Rod

Cone

Optic disk (and blind spot)

Optic nerve fibers

Ganglion cell

Horizontal cell

Figure 4.9

The retina. The closeup shows the several layers of cells in the retina. The cells closest to the back of the eye (the rods and cones) are the receptor cells that actually detect light. The intervening layers of cells receive signals from the rods and cones and form circuits that begin the process of analyzing incoming information before it is sent to the brain. These cells feed into many optic fibers, all of which head toward the "hole" in the retina where the optic nerve leaves the eye—the point known as the optic disk (which corresponds to the blind spot).

The axons that run from the retina to the brain converge at the *optic disk,* **a hole in the retina where the optic nerve fibers exit the eye.** Because the optic disk is a *hole* in the retina, you cannot see the part of an image that falls on it. It is therefore known as the *blind spot.* You may not be aware that you have a blind spot in each eye, as each normally compensates for the blind spot of the other.

Visual Receptors: Rods and Cones

The retina contains millions of receptor cells that are sensitive to light. Surprisingly, these receptors are located in the innermost layer of the retina. Hence, light must pass through several layers of cells before it gets to the receptors that actually detect it. Interestingly, only about 10% of the light arriving at the cornea reaches these receptors (Leibovic, 1990). The retina contains two types of receptors, *rods* and *cones.* Their names are based on their shapes, as rods are elongated and cones are stubbier. Rods outnumber cones by a huge margin, as humans have 100–125 million rods, but only 5–6.4 million cones (Frishman, 2001).

Cones **are specialized visual receptors that play a key role in daylight vision and color vision.** The cones handle most of our daytime vision, because bright lights dazzle the rods. The special sensitivities of cones also allow them to play a major role in the perception of color. However, cones do not respond well to dim light, which is why you don't see color very well in low illumination. Nonetheless, cones provide better *visual acuity*—that is, sharpness and precise detail—than rods. Cones are concentrated most heavily in the center of the retina and quickly fall off in density toward its periphery. **The fovea is a tiny spot in the center of the retina that contains only cones; visual acuity is greatest at this spot.** When you want to see something sharply, you usually move your eyes to center the object in the fovea.

Rods **are specialized visual receptors that play a key role in night vision and peripheral vision.** Rods handle night vision because they are more sensitive than cones to dim light. They handle the lion's share of peripheral vision because they greatly outnumber cones in the periphery of the retina. The density of the rods is greatest just outside the fovea and gradually decreases toward the periphery of the retina. Because of the distribution of rods, when you want to see a faintly illuminated object in the dark, it's best to look slightly above or below the place it should be. Averting your gaze this way moves the image from the cone-filled fovea, which requires more light, to the rod-dominated area just outside the fovea, which requires less light. This trick of averted vision is well known to astronomers, who use it to study dim objects viewed through the eyepiece of a telescope.

Dark and Light Adaptation

You've probably noticed that when you enter a dark theater on a bright day, you stumble around almost blindly. But within minutes you can make your way about quite well in the dim light. This adjustment is called *dark adaptation*—the process in which the eyes become more sensitive to light in low illumination. Figure 4.10 maps out the course of this process. The declining absolute thresholds over time indicate that you require less and less light to see. Dark adaptation is virtually complete in about 30 minutes, with considerable progress occurring in the first 10 minutes. The curve (in Figure 4.10) that charts this progress consists of two segments because cones adapt more rapidly than rods (Walraven et al., 1990).

When you emerge from a dark theater on a sunny day, you need to squint to ward off the overwhelming brightness, and the reverse of dark adaptation occurs. *Light adaptation* **is the process whereby the eyes become less sensitive to light in high illumination.** As with dark adaptation, light adaptation improves your visual acuity under the prevailing circumstances. Both types of adaptation are due in large part to chemical changes in the rods and cones, but neural changes in the receptors and elsewhere in the retina also contribute (Frumkes, 1990).

Information Processing in the Retina

In processing visual input, the retina transforms a pattern of light falling onto it into a very different

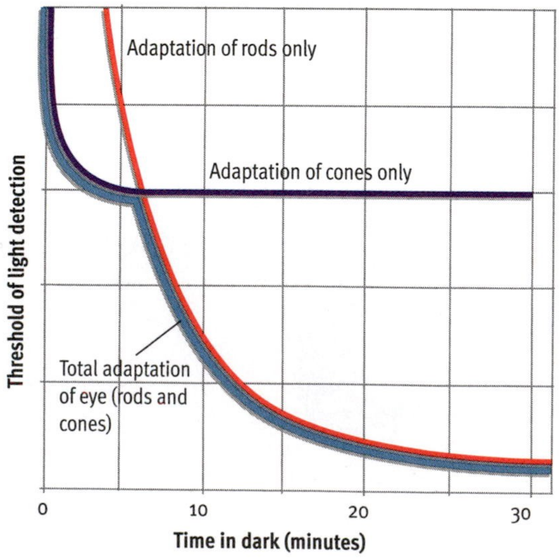

Figure 4.10

The process of dark adaptation. The declining thresholds over time indicate that your visual sensitivity is improving, as less and less light is required to see. Visual sensitivity improves markedly during the first 5 to 10 minutes after entering a dark room, as the eye's bright-light receptors (the cones) rapidly adapt to low light levels. However, the cones' adaptation, which is plotted in purple, soon reaches its limit, and further improvement comes from the rods' adaptation, which is plotted in red. The rods adapt more slowly than the cones, but they are capable of far greater visual sensitivity in low levels of light.

[Graph: Threshold of light detection (y-axis) vs. Time in dark (minutes) (x-axis, 0 to 30). Curves labeled "Adaptation of rods only," "Adaptation of cones only," and "Total adaptation of eye (rods and cones)."]

representation of the visual scene. Light striking the retina's receptors (rods and cones) triggers neural signals that pass into the intricate network of cells in the retina, which in turn send impulses along the *optic nerve*—a collection of axons that connect the eye with the brain (see Figure 4.9). These axons, which depart from the eye through the optic disk, carry visual information, encoded as a stream of neural impulses, to the brain.

A great deal of complex information processing goes on in the retina itself before visual signals are sent to the brain. Ultimately, the information from over 100 million rods and cones converges to travel along "only" 1 million axons in the optic nerve (Slaughter, 1990). The collection of rod and cone receptors that funnel signals to a particular visual cell in the retina (or ultimately in the brain) make up that cell's *receptive field*. Thus, the *receptive field of a visual cell* is the retinal area that, when stimulated, affects the firing of that cell.

Receptive fields in the retina come in a variety of shapes and sizes. Particularly common are circular fields with a center-surround arrangement (Tessier-Lavigne, 2000). In these receptive fields, light falling in the center has the opposite effect of light falling in the surrounding area (see Figure 4.11). For example, the rate of firing of a visual cell might be *increased* by light in the *center* of its receptive field and *decreased* by light in the *surrounding area,* as Figure 4.11 shows. Other visual cells may work in just the opposite way. Either way, when receptive fields are stimulated, retinal cells send signals both toward the brain and *laterally* (sideways) toward nearby visual cells. These lateral signals allow visual cells in the retina to have interactive effects on each other.

Lateral antagonism (also known as lateral inhibition) is the most basic of these interactive effects. *Lateral antagonism occurs when neural activity in a cell opposes activity in surrounding cells.* Lateral antagonism is responsible for the opposite effects that occur when light falls on the inner versus outer portions of center-surround receptive fields. Lateral antagonism allows the retina to compare the light falling in a specific area against general light-

Figure 4.11

Receptive fields in the retina. Visual cells' receptive fields—made up of rods and cones in the retina—are often circular with a center-surround arrangement, so that light striking the center of the field produces the opposite result of light striking the surround. In the receptive field depicted here, light in the center produces excitatory effects (symbolized by green at the synapse) and increased firing in the visual cell, whereas light in the surround produces inhibitory effects (symbolized by red at the synapse) and decreased firing. However, the arrangement in other receptive fields may be just the opposite. Note that no light **(a)** and light in both center and surround **(d)** produce similar baseline rates of firing. This visual cell is more sensitive to *contrast* than to absolute levels of light. In **(b)** and **(c)** there is a contrast between the light falling on the center versus the surround, producing increased or decreased activity in the visual cell.

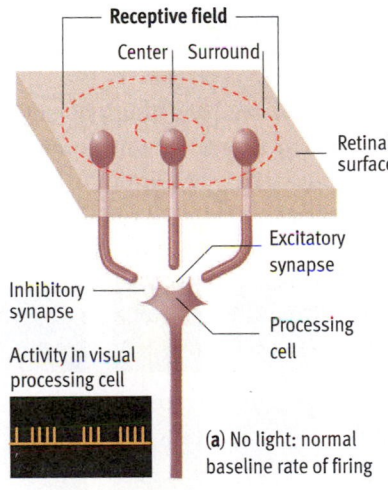

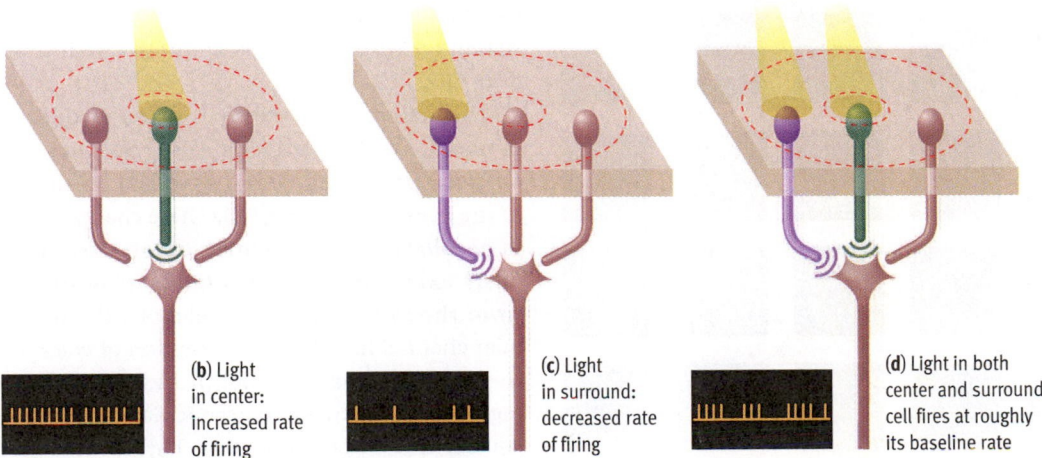

(a) No light: normal baseline rate of firing

(b) Light in center: increased rate of firing

(c) Light in surround: decreased rate of firing

(d) Light in both center and surround: cell fires at roughly its baseline rate

Understanding Sensory Processes in the Retina

Check your understanding of sensory receptors in the retina by completing the following exercises. Consult Appendix A for the answers.

1. The receptors for vision are rods and cones in the retina. These two types of receptors have many important differences, which are compared systematically in the chart below. Fill in the missing information to finish the chart.

Dimension	Rods	Cones
Physical shape	Elongated	
Number in the retina		5–6.4 million
Area of the retina in which they are dominant receptor	Periphery	
Critical to color vision		
Critical to peripheral vision		No
Sensitivity to dim light	Strong	
Speed of dark adaptation		Rapid

2. The text notes that lateral antagonism in the retina is the probable cause of the illusory dark spots seen in the intersections of the Hermann grid (consult Figure 4.12). Try to construct an explanation of how lateral antagonism might account for this phenomenon. This is no small challenge, so don't feel bad if you have to consult Appendix A for the answer. Hint: The center-surround receptive fields shown in Figure 4.11 are crucial to the explanation. It will help if you draw a center-surround receptive field at one of the intersections in the grid and another adjacent to it.

ing. This means that the visual system can compute the *relative* amount of light at a point instead of reacting to *absolute* levels of light. This attention to *contrast* is exactly what is needed because most of the

crucial information needed to recognize objects in a visual scene is contained in the pattern of contrasts (Tessier-Lavigne, 2000). If you look at Figure 4.12, you will experience a perplexing illusion attributable to lateral antagonism in the ganglion cells of the retina.

Vision and the Brain

Light falls on the eye, but you see with your brain. Although the retina does an unusual amount of information processing for a sensory organ, visual input is meaningless until it is processed in the brain.

Visual Pathways to the Brain

How does visual information get to the brain? Axons leaving the back of each eye form the optic nerves, which travel to the *optic chiasm*—**the point at which the optic nerves from the inside half of each eye cross over and then project to the opposite half of the brain.** This arrangement ensures that signals from both eyes go to both hemispheres of the brain. Thus, as Figure 4.13 shows, axons from the left half of each retina carry signals to the left side of the brain, and axons from the right half of each retina carry information to the right side of the brain.

After reaching the optic chiasm, the optic nerve fibers diverge along two pathways. The main pathway projects into the thalamus, the brain's major relay station. Here, about 90% of the axons from the retinas synapse in the *lateral geniculate nucleus* (LGN). Visual signals are processed in the LGN and then distributed to areas in the occipital lobe that make up the *primary visual cortex* (see Figure 4.13). The second visual pathway leaving the optic chiasm branches off to an area in the midbrain called the *superior colliculus* before traveling through the thalamus and on to the occipital lobe. The principal function of the second pathway appears to be the coordination of visual input with other sensory input (Stein & Meredith, 1993).

The main visual pathway is subdivided into two more specialized pathways called the *magnocellular* and *parvocellular* channels (based on the layers of the LGN they synapse in). These channels engage in *parallel processing*, **which involves simultaneously extracting different kinds of information from the same input.** For example, the parvocellular channel handles the perception of color, while the magnocellular channel processes information regarding brightness (Wurtz & Kandel, 2000). Of course, this brief description hardly does justice

Figure 4.12

The Hermann grid. If you look at this grid, you will see dark spots at the intersections of the white bars, except in the intersection you're staring at directly. This illusion is due to lateral antagonism (see Concept Check 4.1).

Figure 4.13

Visual pathways through the brain. **(a)** Input from the right half of the visual field strikes the left side of each retina and is transmitted to the left hemisphere (shown in red). Input from the left half of the visual field strikes the right side of each retina and is transmitted to the right hemisphere (shown in green). The nerve fibers from each eye meet at the optic chiasm, where fibers from the inside half of each retina cross over to the opposite side of the brain. After reaching the optic chiasm, the major visual pathway projects through the lateral geniculate nucleus in the thalamus and onto the primary visual cortex (shown with solid lines). A second pathway detours through the superior colliculus and then projects through the thalamus and onto the primary visual cortex (shown with dotted lines). **(b)** This inset shows a vertical view of how the optic pathways project through the thalamus and onto the visual cortex in the back of the brain [the two pathways mapped out in diagram **(a)** are virtually indistinguishable from this angle].

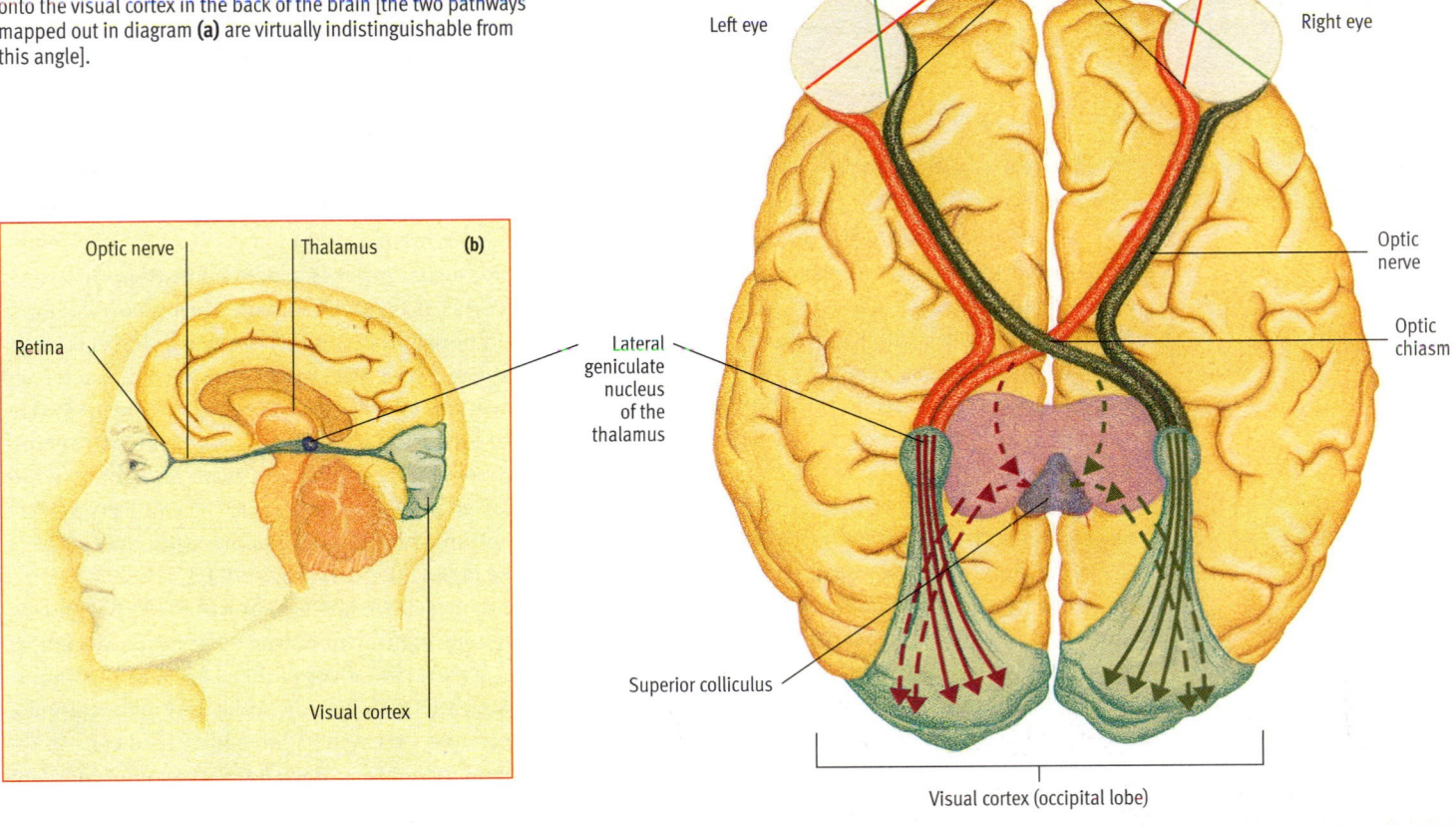

to the immense complexity of visual processing in the brain.

Information Processing in the Visual Cortex

Most visual input eventually arrives in the primary visual cortex, located in the occipital lobe. Explaining how the cortical cells in this area respond to light once posed a perplexing problem. Researchers investigating the question placed microelectrodes in the primary visual cortex of animals to record action potentials from individual cells. They would flash spots of light in the retinal receptive fields that the cells were thought to monitor, but there was rarely any response.

According to David Hubel and Torsten Wiesel (1962, 1963), they discovered the solution to this mystery quite by accident. One of the projector slides they used to present a spot to a cat had a crack in it. The spot elicited no response, but when they removed the slide, the crack moved through the cell's receptive field, and the cell fired like crazy in response to the moving dark line. It turns out that individual cells in the primary visual cortex don't really respond much to little spots—they are much more sensitive to lines, edges, and other more complicated stimuli. Armed with new slides, Hubel and Wiesel embarked on years of painstaking study of the visual cortex (see Figure 4.14 on the next page). Their work eventually earned them a Nobel prize in 1981.

One can now begin to grasp the significance of the great number of cells in the visual cortex. Each cell seems to have its own specific duties.
DAVID HUBEL

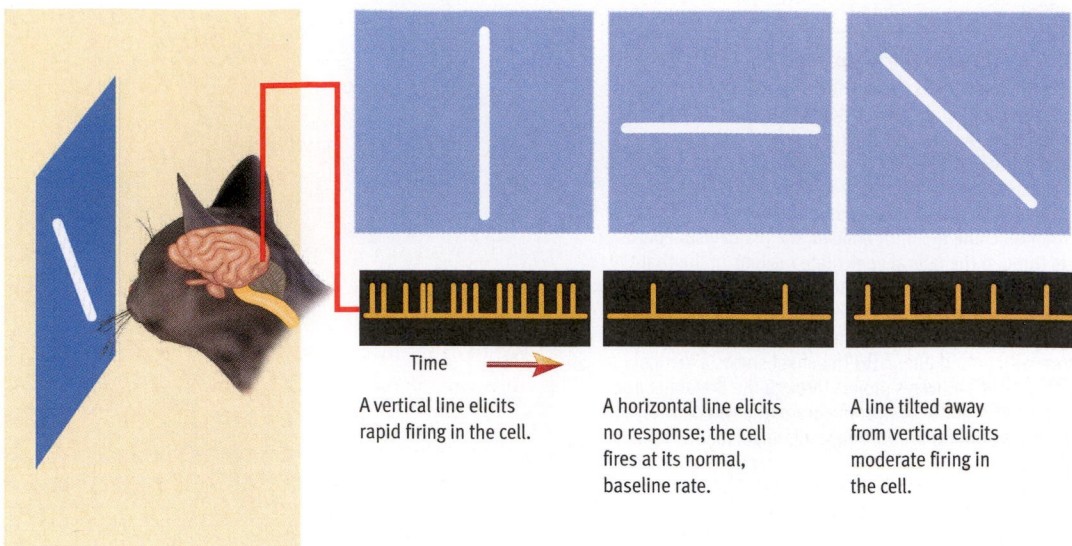

Figure 4.14

Hubel and Wiesel's procedure for studying the activity of neurons in the visual cortex. As the cat is shown various stimuli, a microelectrode records the firing of a neuron in the cat's visual cortex. The figure shows the electrical responses of a visual cell apparently "programmed" to respond to lines oriented vertically.

Time ⟶

A vertical line elicits rapid firing in the cell.

A horizontal line elicits no response; the cell fires at its normal, baseline rate.

A line tilted away from vertical elicits moderate firing in the cell.

Hubel and Wiesel (1962, 1979) identified various types of specialized cells in the primary visual cortex that respond to different stimuli. For example, *simple cells* respond best to a line of the correct width, oriented at the correct angle, and located in the correct position in its receptive field. *Complex cells* also care about width and orientation, but they respond to any position in their receptive fields. Some complex cells are most responsive if a line sweeps across their receptive field—but only if it's moving in the "right" direction. The key point of all this is that the cells in the visual cortex seem to be highly specialized. They have been characterized as *feature detectors,* **neurons that respond selectively to very specific features of more complex stimuli.** According to some theorists, most visual stimuli could ultimately be represented by combinations of lines such as those

registered by these feature detectors (Maguire, Weisstein, & Klymenko, 1990).

After visual input is processed in the primary visual cortex it is often routed to other cortical areas for additional processing. These signals travel through two streams that have sometimes been characterized as the *what and where pathways* (see Figure 4.15). The *ventral stream* processes the details of *what* objects are out there (the perception of form and color) while the *dorsal stream* processes *where* the objects are (the perception of motion and depth) (Kandel & Wurtz, 2000; Ungerleider & Haxby, 1994).

As signals move further along in the visual processing system, neurons become even more specialized or fussy about what turns them on, and the stimuli that activate them become more and more complex. For example, researchers have identified cells in the temporal lobe (along the *what* pathway) of monkeys and humans that respond best to pictures of faces (Levine, 2001; Rolls & Tovee, 1995). This incredible specificity has led researchers to joke that they may eventually find a cell that only recognizes one's grandmother (Cowey, 1994). The discovery of neurons that respond to facial stimuli raises an obvious question: Why does the cortex have face detectors? Theorists are far from sure, but one line of thinking is that the ability to quickly recognize faces—such as those of friends or foes—probably has had adaptive significance over the course of evolution (Desimone, 1991). Thus, natural selection may have wired the brains of some species to quickly respond to faces.

In any event, the discovery of the *what pathway* and the neurons inside it that respond specifically to faces has shed new light on visual disorders that have perplexed scientists for decades. For example, as noted at the beginning of the chapter (in our discussion of

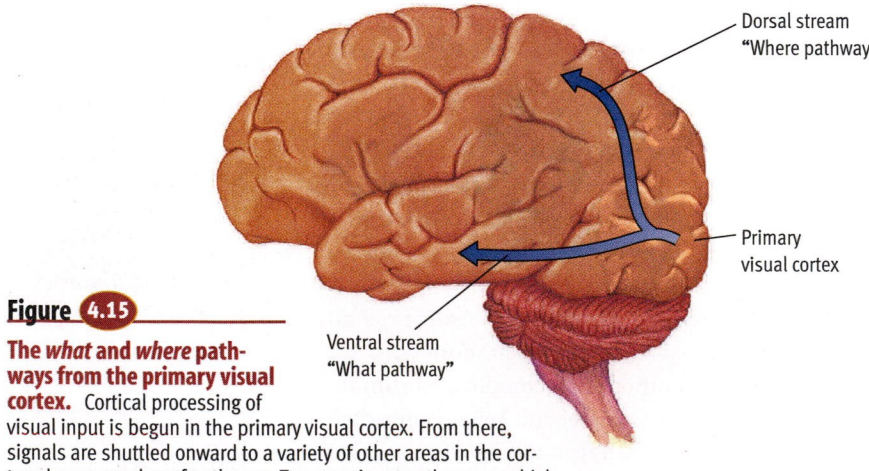

Dorsal stream "Where pathway"

Primary visual cortex

Figure 4.15

The *what* and *where* pathways from the primary visual cortex. Cortical processing of visual input is begun in the primary visual cortex. From there, signals are shuttled onward to a variety of other areas in the cortex along a number of pathways. Two prominent pathways are highlighted here. The dorsal stream, or *where* pathway, which processes information about motion and depth, moves on to areas of the parietal lobe. The ventral stream, or *what* pathway, which processes information about color and form, moves on to areas of the temporal lobe.

Ventral stream "What pathway"

Dr. P), some people exhibit **visual agnosia—an inability to recognize objects**—even though their eyes function just fine. This previously baffling condition now has a plausible explanation—it is probably the result of damage somewhere along the visual pathway that handles object recognition (Zeki, 1993).

REVIEW OF KEY POINTS

● Light varies in terms of wavelength, amplitude, and purity. Light enters the eye through the cornea and pupil and is focused upside down on the retina by the lens. Distant objects appear blurry to nearsighted people and close objects appear blurry to farsighted people.

● The retina is the neural tissue in the eye that absorbs light, processes images, and sends visual signals to the brain. Cones, which are concentrated in the fovea, play a key role in daylight vision and color perception. Rods, which have their greatest density just outside the fovea, are critical to night vision and peripheral vision. Dark adaptation and light adaptation both involve changes in the retina's sensitivity to light, allowing the eye to adapt to changes in illumination.

● The retina transforms light into neural impulses that are sent to the brain via the optic nerve. Receptive fields are areas in the retina that affect the firing of visual cells. They vary in shape and size, but center-surround arrangements are common. The optic nerves from the inside half of each eye cross at the optic chiasm and then project to the opposite half of the brain.

● Two visual pathways engage in parallel processing and send signals to different areas of the primary visual cortex. The main pathway is routed through the LGN in the thalamus. After processing in the primary visual cortex, visual information is shuttled along the *what* and *where* pathways to other cortical areas.

● Nobel prize–winning research by Hubel and Wiesel suggests that the visual cortex contains cells that function as feature detectors. The discovery of the *what pathway* and the neurons inside it that respond specifically to faces have shed new light on visual disorders that have perplexed scientists for decades.

Viewing the World in Color

So far, we've considered only how the visual system deals with light and dark. Let's journey now into the world of color. On the one hand, you can see perfectly well without seeing in color. Many animals get by with little or no color vision, and no one seemed to suffer back when all photographs, movies, or TV shows were in black and white. On the other hand, color clearly adds rich information to our perception of the world. The ability to identify objects against a complex background is enhanced by the addition of color. Quickly identifying objects probably has had adaptive value in terms of finding food and detecting predators. Indeed, some theorists have suggested that color vision evolved in humans and monkeys because it improved their ability to find fruit in the forest (Mollon, 1989). Although the purpose of color vision remains elusive, scientists have learned a great deal about the mechanisms underlying the perception of color.

The Stimulus for Color

As noted earlier, the lights people see are mixtures of various wavelengths. Perceived color is primarily a function of the dominant wavelength in these mixtures. In the visible spectrum, lights with the longest wavelengths appear red, whereas those with the shortest appear violet. Notice the word *appear*. Color is a psychological interpretation. It's not a physical property of light itself.

Although wavelength wields the greatest influence, perception of color depends on complex blends of all three properties of light. Wavelength is most closely related to hue, amplitude to brightness, and purity to saturation. These three dimensions of color are illustrated in the *color solid* shown in Figure 4.16.

PREVIEW QUESTIONS

● How are additive and subtractive color mixing different?

● How have the trichromatic and opponent process theories been reconciled to explain color vision?

● What is feature analysis, and what is the difference between top-down and bottom-up processing?

● What was the basic premise of Gestalt psychology?

● What are the Gestalt principles of form perception?

● How do perceptual hypotheses contribute to form perception?

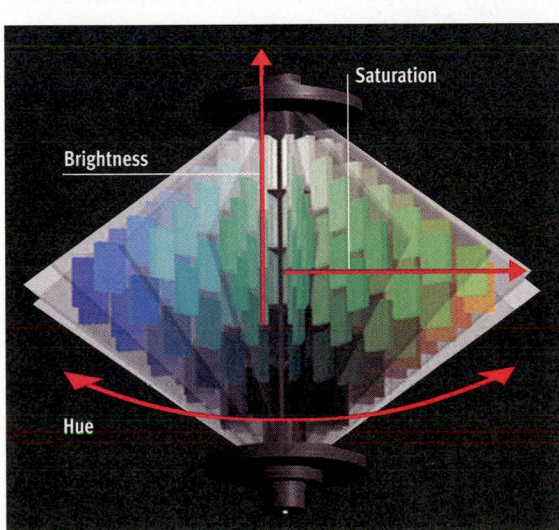

Courtesy of BASF

Figure 4.16

The color solid. The color solid shows how color varies along three perceptual dimensions: brightness (increasing from the bottom to the top of the solid), hue (changing around the solid's perimeter), and saturation (increasing toward the periphery of the solid).

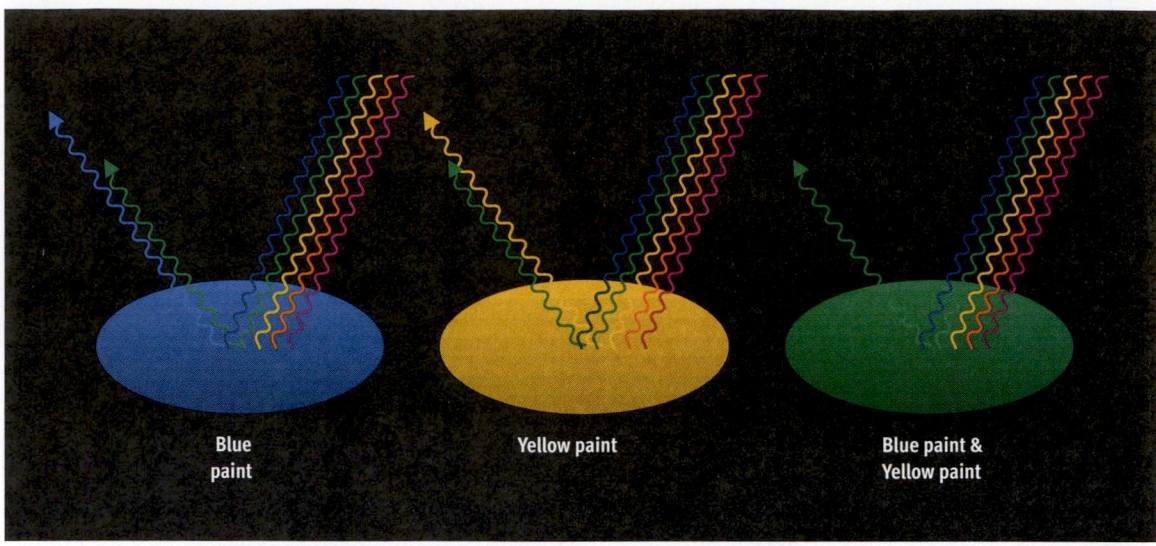

Figure 4.17

Subtractive color mixing.
Paints selectively reflect specific wavelengths that give rise to particular colors, as you can see here for blue and yellow, which both also reflect back a little green. When we mix blue and yellow paint, the mixture absorbs all the colors that blue and yellow absorbed individually. The mixture is subtractive because more wavelengths are removed than by each paint alone. The yellow paint in the mixture absorbs the wavelengths associated with blue and the blue paint in the mixture absorbs the wavelengths associated with yellow. The only wavelengths left to be reflected are some of those associated with green, so the mixture is seen as green.

SOURCE: Adapted from Goldstein, E. B. (1999). *Sensation and perception.* Belmont, CA: Wadsworth. Reprinted by permission.

As a color solid demonstrates systematically, people can perceive many different colors. Indeed, experts estimate that humans can discriminate among roughly a million colors (Boynton, 1990). Most of these diverse variations are the result of mixing a few basic colors. There are two kinds of color mixture: subtractive and additive. **Subtractive color mixing works by removing some wavelengths of light, leaving less light than was originally there.** You probably became familiar with subtractive mixing as a child when you mixed yellow and blue paints to make green. Paints yield subtractive mixing because pigments *absorb* most wavelengths, selectively reflecting specific wavelengths that give rise to particular colors (see Figure 4.17). Subtractive color mixing can also be demonstrated by stacking color filters. If you look through a sandwich of yellow and blue cellophane filters, they will block out certain wavelengths. The middle wavelengths that are left will look green.

Additive color mixing **works by superimposing lights, putting more light in the mixture than exists in any one light by itself.** If you shine red, green, and blue spotlights on a white surface, you'll have an additive mixture. As Figure 4.18 shows, additive and subtractive mixtures of the same colors produce different results. Human processes of color perception parallel additive color mixing much more closely than subtractive mixing, as you'll see in the following discussion of theories of color vision.

Trichromatic Theory of Color Vision **3d**

The *trichromatic theory* of color vision (*tri* for "three," *chroma* for "color") was first stated by Thomas Young and modified later by Hermann von Helmholtz (1852). The *trichromatic theory* **of color vision holds that the human eye has three types of receptors with differing sensitivities to different light wavelengths.** Helmholtz theorized that the eye contains specialized receptors sensitive to the specific wave-

Figure 4.18

Additive versus subtractive color mixing. Lights mix additively because all the wavelengths contained in each light reach the eye. If red, blue, and green lights are projected onto a white screen, they produce the colors shown on the left, with white at the intersection of all three lights. If paints of the same three colors were combined in the same way, the subtractive mixture would produce the colors shown on the right, with black at the intersection of all three colors.

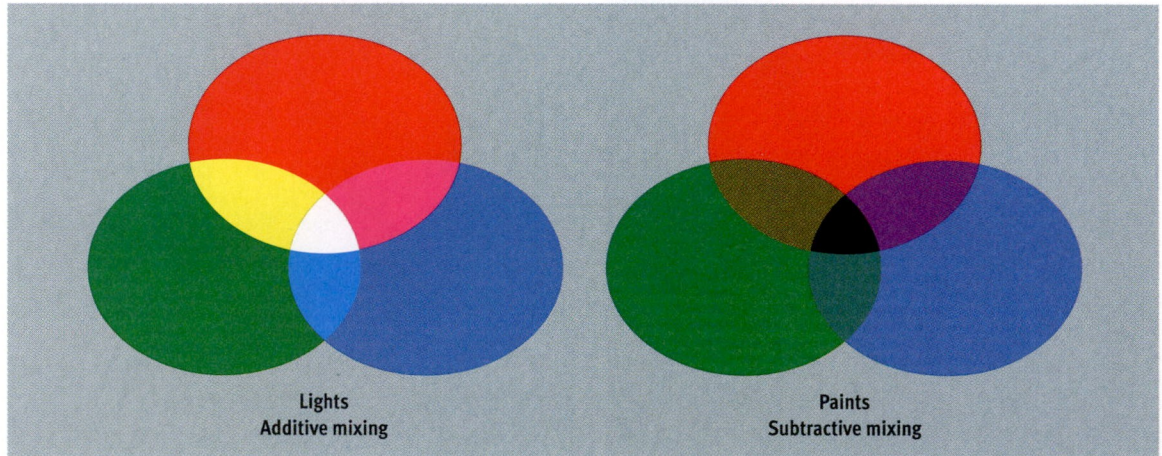

Lights
Additive mixing

Paints
Subtractive mixing

Blue paint

Yellow paint

Blue paint & Yellow paint

lengths associated with red, green, and blue. According to this model, people can see all the colors of the rainbow because the eye does its own "color mixing" by varying the ratio of neural activity among these three types of receptors.

The impetus for the trichromatic theory was the demonstration that a light of any color can be matched by the additive mixture of three *primary colors.* Any three colors that are appropriately spaced out in the visible spectrum can serve as primary colors, although red, green, and blue are usually used. Does it sound implausible that three colors should be adequate for creating all other colors? If so, consider that this is exactly what happens on your color TV screen. Additive mixtures of red, green, and blue fool you into seeing all the colors of a natural scene.

Most of the known facts about color blindness also meshed well with trichromatic theory. **Color blindness encompasses a variety of deficiencies in the ability to distinguish among colors.** Color blindness occurs much more frequently in males than in females. Actually, the term color *blindness* is somewhat misleading, since complete blindness to differences in colors is quite rare. Most people who are color blind are *dichromats;* that is, they make do with only two color channels. There are three types of dichromats, and each type is insensitive to a different color (red, green, or blue, although the latter is rare) (Gouras, 1991). The three deficiencies seen among dichromats support the notion that there are three channels for color vision, as proposed by trichromatic theory.

Opponent Process Theory of Color Vision

Although trichromatic theory explained some facets of color vision well, it ran aground in other areas. Consider complementary afterimages, for instance. *Complementary colors* **are pairs of colors that produce gray tones when mixed together.** The various pairs of complementary colors can be arranged in a *color circle,* such as the one in Figure 4.19. If you stare at a strong color and then look at a white background, you'll see an *afterimage*—**a visual image that persists after a stimulus is removed.** The color of the afterimage will be the *complement* of the color you originally stared at. Trichromatic theory cannot account for the appearance of complementary afterimages.

Here's another peculiarity to consider. If you ask people to describe colors but restrict them to using three names, they run into difficulty. For example, using only red, green, and blue, they simply don't feel comfortable describing yellow as "reddish green." However, if you let them have just one more name,

they usually choose yellow; they can then describe any color quite well (Gordon & Abramov, 2001). If colors are reduced to three channels, why are four color names required to describe the full range of possible colors?

In an effort to answer questions such as these, Ewald Hering proposed the *opponent process theory* in 1878. **The *opponent process theory* of color vision holds that color perception depends on receptors that make antagonistic responses to three pairs of colors.** The three pairs of opponent colors posited by Hering were red versus green, yellow versus blue, and black versus white. The antagonistic processes in this theory provide plausible explanations for complementary afterimages and the need for four names (red, green, blue, and yellow) to describe colors. Opponent process theory also explains some aspects of color blindness. For instance, it can explain why dichromats typically find it hard to distinguish either green from red or yellow from blue.

Reconciling Theories of Color Vision

Advocates of trichromatic theory and opponent process theory argued about the relative merits of their models for almost a century. Most researchers assumed that one theory must be wrong and the other must be right. In recent decades, however, it has become clear that *it takes both theories to explain color vision.* Eventually a physiological basis for both theories was found. Research that earned George Wald a Nobel prize demonstrated that *the eye has three types of cones,* with each type being most sensitive to a different band of wavelengths, as shown in Figure 4.20 on the next page (Lennie, 2000; Wald, 1964). The three types of cones represent the three different color receptors predicted by trichromatic theory.

Researchers also discovered a biological basis for opponent processes. They found cells in the retina,

Web Link 4.2

The Joy of Visual Perception: A Web Book
This site shows the Net at its best. Peter Kaiser of York University has crafted a comprehensive guide to human color vision, supplying plenty of graphics and demonstrations to help visitors understand what laboratory research in psychology has learned about visual perception.

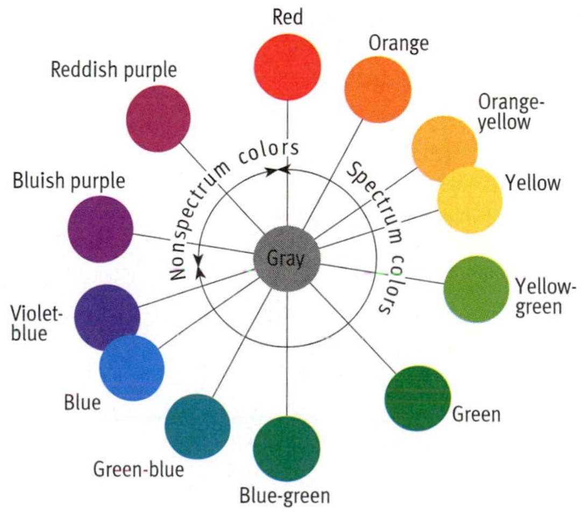

Figure 4.19

The color circle and complementary colors. Colors opposite each other on this color circle are complements, or "opposites." Additively, mixing complementary colors produces gray. Opponent process principles help explain this effect as well as the other peculiarities of complementary colors noted in the text.

Red
Orange
Reddish purple
Orange-yellow
Bluish purple
Yellow
Nonspectrum colors
Spectrum colors
Gray
Violet-blue
Yellow-green
Blue
Green
Green-blue
Blue-green

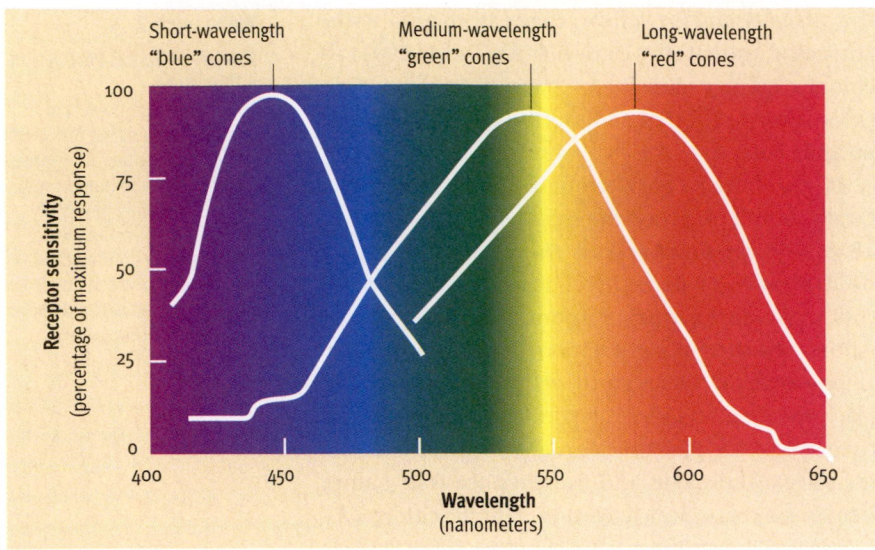

Short-wavelength "blue" cones
Medium-wavelength "green" cones
Long-wavelength "red" cones

Receptor sensitivity (percentage of maximum response)

100
75
50
25
0

400   450   500   550   600   650

Wavelength (nanometers)

Figure 4.20

Three types of cones.
Research has identified three types of cones that show varied sensitivity to different wavelengths of light. As the graph shows, these three types of cones correspond only roughly to the red, green, and blue receptors predicted by trichromatic theory, so it is more accurate to refer to them as cones sensitive to short, medium, and long wavelengths.

SOURCE: Wald, G., & Brown, P. K. (1965). Human color vision and color blindness. *Symposium Cold Spring Harbor Laboratory of Quantitative Biology, 30*, 345–359 (p. 351). Copyright © 1965. Reprinted by permission of the author.

Figure 4.21

Reconciling theories of color vision. Contemporary explanations of color vision include aspects of both the trichromatic and opponent process theories. As predicted by trichromatic theory, there are three types of receptors for color—cones sensitive to short, medium, and long wavelengths. However, these cones are organized into receptive fields that excite or inhibit the firing of higher-level visual cells in the retina, thalamus, and cortex. As predicted by opponent process theory, some of these cells respond in antagonistic ways to blue versus yellow, red versus green, and black versus white.

the LGN, and the visual cortex *that respond in opposite ways to red versus green and blue versus yellow* (DeValois & Jacobs, 1984; Zrenner et al., 1990). For example, there are ganglion cells in the retina that are excited by green and inhibited by red. Other ganglion cells in the retina work in just the opposite way, as predicted in opponent process theory.

In summary, the perception of color appears to involve sequential stages of information processing (Hurvich, 1981). The receptors that do the first stage of processing (the cones) seem to follow the principles outlined in trichromatic theory. In later stages of processing, at least some cells in the retina, the

LGN, and the visual cortex seem to follow the principles outlined in opponent process theory (see Figure 4.21). As you can see, vigorous theoretical debate about color vision produced a solution that went beyond the contributions of either theory alone.

Perceiving Forms, Patterns, and Objects

 3c, 3e

The drawing in Figure 4.22 is a poster for a circus act involving a trained seal. Take a good look at it. What do you see?

No doubt you see a seal balancing a ball on its nose and a trainer holding a fish and a whip. But suppose you had been told that the drawing is actually a poster for a costume ball. Would you have perceived it differently?

If you focus on the idea of a costume ball (stay with it a minute if you still see the seal and trainer), you will probably see a costumed man and woman in Figure 4.22. She's handing him a hat, and he has a sword in his right hand. This tricky little sketch was made ambiguous quite intentionally. It's a *reversible figure,* **a drawing that is compatible with two interpretations that can shift back and forth.** Another classic reversible figure is shown in Figure 4.23. What do you see? A rabbit or a duck? It all depends on how you look at the drawing.

The key point is simply this: *The same visual input can result in radically different perceptions.* No one-to-one correspondence exists between sensory input

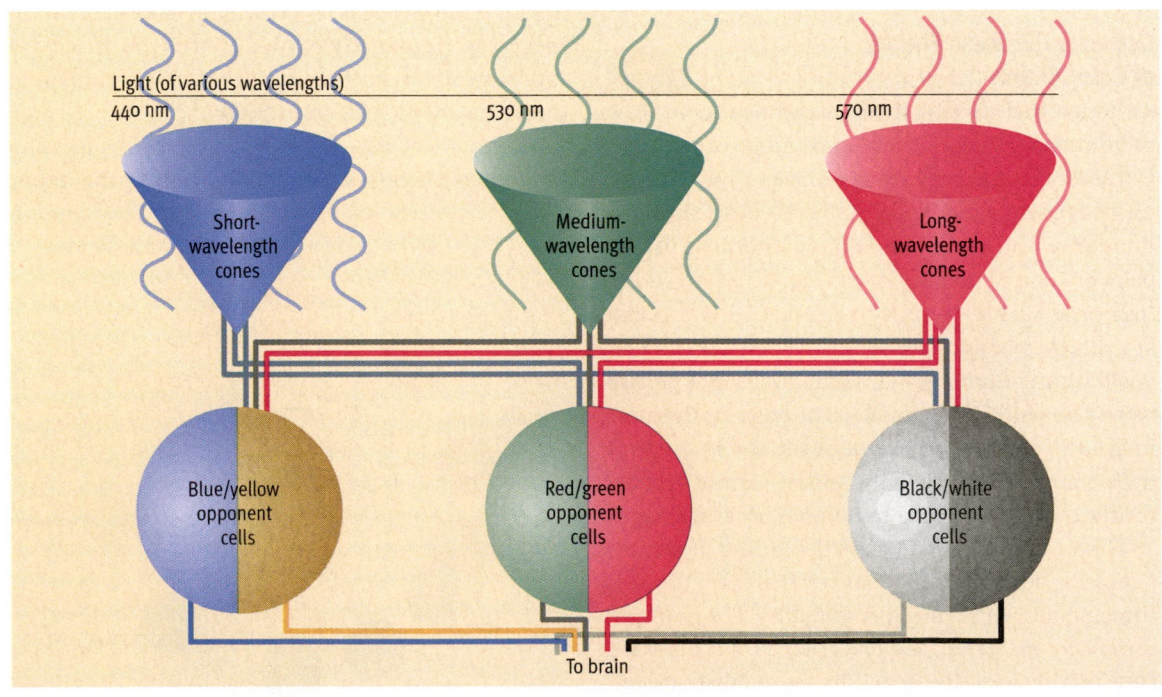

Light (of various wavelengths)
440 nm   530 nm   570 nm

Short-wavelength cones
Medium-wavelength cones
Long-wavelength cones

Blue/yellow opponent cells
Red/green opponent cells
Black/white opponent cells

To brain

Figure 4.22

A poster for a trained seal act. Or is it? The picture is an ambiguous figure, which can be interpreted as either of two scenes, as explained in the text.

and what you perceive. *This is a principal reason that people's experience of the world is subjective.* Perception involves much more than passively receiving signals from the outside world. It involves the *interpretation* of sensory input. To some extent, this interpretive process can be influenced by manipulating people's *expectations*. For example, information given to you about the drawing of the "circus act involving a trained seal" created a *perceptual set—a readiness to perceive a stimulus in a particular way.* A perceptual set creates a certain slant in how someone interprets sensory input.

Form perception also depends on the *selection* of sensory input—that is, what people focus their attention on (Chun & Wolfe, 2001). A visual scene may include many objects and forms. Some of them may capture viewers' attention while others may not. This fact has been demonstrated in dramatic fashion in studies of *inattentional blindness,* which involves the failure to see fully visible objects or events in a visual display. In one such study (Simons & Chabris, 1999), participants watched a video of a group of people in white shirts passing a basketball that was laid over another video of people in black shirts passing a basketball (the two videos were partially transparent). The observers were instructed

to focus on one of the two teams and press a key whenever that team passed the ball. Thirty seconds into the task, a woman carrying an umbrella clearly walked through the scene for four seconds. You might guess that this bizarre development would be noticed by virtually all the observers, but 44% of the participants failed to see the woman. Moreover, when someone in a gorilla suit strolled through the same scene, even more subjects (73%) missed the unexpected event! Other studies using other types of stimulus materials have demonstrated that people routinely overlook highly salient forms that are unexpected (Mack & Rock, 1998). Inattentional blindness has been attributed to subjects having a perceptual set that leads them to focus most of their attention on a specific feature in a scene (such as the basketball passes) while neglecting other facets of the scene (Most et al., 2001). The work on inattentional blindness shows that form perception is an active, selective process.

An understanding of how people perceive forms and objects also requires knowledge of how people *organize* their visual inputs. Several influential approaches to this issue emphasize *feature analysis.*

Feature Analysis: Assembling Forms  3c

The information received by your eyes would do you little good if you couldn't recognize objects and forms—ranging from words on a page to mice in your cellar and friends in the distance. According to some theories, perceptions of form and pattern entail *feature analysis* (Lindsay & Norman, 1977; Maguire et al., 1990). *Feature analysis is the process of detecting specific elements in visual input and assembling them into a more complex form.* In other words, you start with the components of a form, such as lines, edges, and corners, and build them into perceptions of squares, triangles, stop signs, bicycles, ice cream cones, and telephones. An application of this model of form perception is diagrammed in Figure 4.24 on the next page.

Feature analysis assumes that form perception involves *bottom-up processing, a progression from individual elements to the whole* (see Figure 4.25 on the next page). The plausibility of this model was bolstered greatly when Hubel and Wiesel showed that cells in the visual cortex operate as highly specialized feature detectors. Indeed, their findings strongly suggested that at least some aspects of form perception involve feature analysis.

Can feature analysis provide a complete account of how people perceive forms? Clearly not. A crucial problem for the theory is that form perception often

Figure 4.23

Another ambiguous figure. What animal do you see here? As the text explains, two very different perceptions are possible. This ambiguous figure was devised around 1900 by Joseph Jastrow, a prominent psychologist at the turn of the 20th century (Block & Yuker, 1992).

Web Link 4.3

Sensation and Perception Tutorials
John Krantz of Hanover College has assembled a collection of quality tutorials on sensation and perception. Topics covered include receptive fields, depth perception, Gestalt laws, and the use of perceptual principles in art.

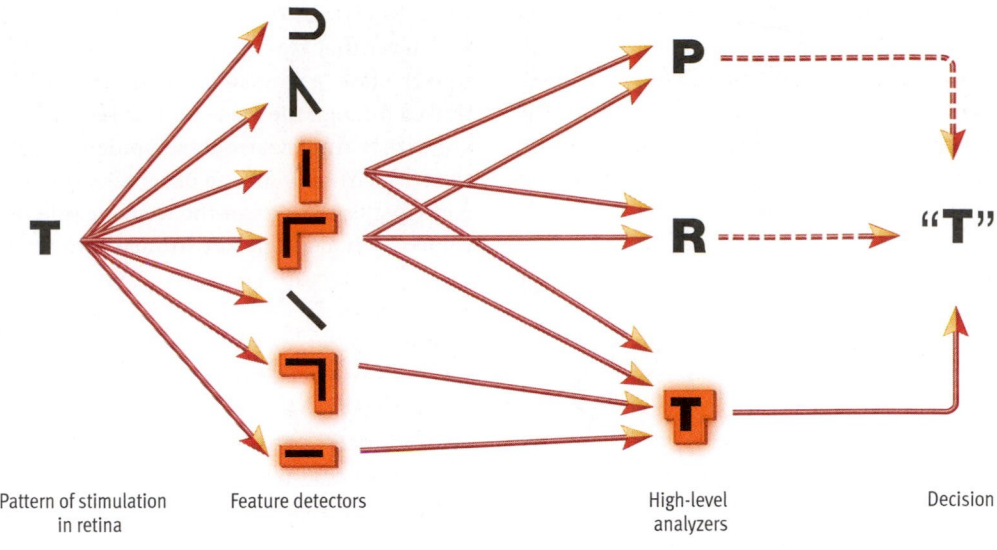

Figure 4.24

Feature analysis in form perception. One vigorously debated theory of form perception is that the brain has cells that respond to specific aspects or features of stimuli, such as lines and angles. Neurons functioning as higher-level analyzers then respond to input from these "feature detectors." The more input each analyzer receives, the more active it becomes. Finally, other neurons weigh signals from these analyzers and make a "decision" about the stimulus. In this way perception of a form is arrived at by assembling elements from the bottom up.

Pattern of stimulation in retina   Feature detectors   High-level analyzers   Decision

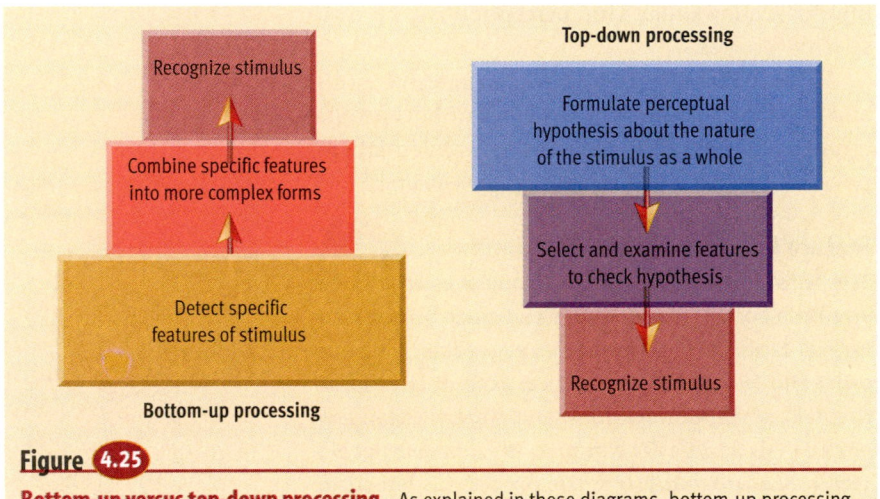

Top-down processing

Recognize stimulus

Combine specific features into more complex forms

Detect specific features of stimulus

Bottom-up processing

Formulate perceptual hypothesis about the nature of the stimulus as a whole

Select and examine features to check hypothesis

Recognize stimulus

Figure 4.25

Bottom-up versus top-down processing. As explained in these diagrams, bottom-up processing progresses from individual elements to whole elements, whereas top-down processing progresses from the whole to the individual elements.

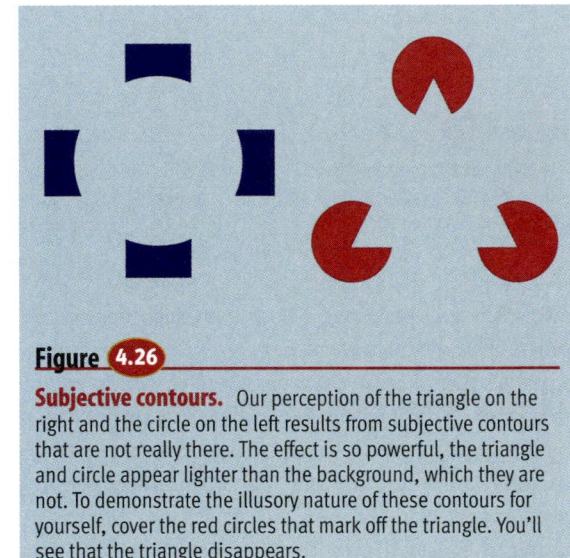

Figure 4.26

Subjective contours. Our perception of the triangle on the right and the circle on the left results from subjective contours that are not really there. The effect is so powerful, the triangle and circle appear lighter than the background, which they are not. To demonstrate the illusory nature of these contours for yourself, cover the red circles that mark off the triangle. You'll see that the triangle disappears.

does not involve bottom-up processing. In fact, there is ample evidence that perceptions of form frequently involve *top-down processing,* **a progression from the whole to the elements** (see Figure 4.25). For example, there is evidence that people can perceive a word before its individual letters, a phenomenon that has to reflect top-down processing (Johnston & McClelland, 1974). If readers depended exclusively on bottom-up processing, they would have to analyze the features of letters in words to recognize them and then assemble the letters into words. This would be a terribly time-consuming task and would slow down reading speed to a snail's pace.

Subjective contours are another phenomenon traditionally attributed to top-down processing, although

that view is changing. The phenomenon of *subjective contours* **is the perception of contours where none actually exist.** Consider, for instance, the triangle shown in Figure 4.26. We see the contours of the triangle easily, even though no physical edges or lines are present. It is hard to envision how feature detectors could detect edges that are not really there, so most theorists have argued that bottom-up models of form perception are unlikely to account for subjective contours. Until recently, the prevailing view was that subjective contours depend on viewing stimulus configurations as wholes and then filling in the blanks (Rock, 1986). However, researchers have demonstrated that feature detectors *do* respond to the edges in subjective contours (Peterhans & von der Heydt, 1991). At present, neural theories of subjective contours that emphasize bottom-up processing or both types of processing are under investigation, with promising results (Gunn et al., 2000; Lesher, 1995). In sum, it appears that both top-down and bottom-up processing have their niches in form perception.

Looking at the Whole Picture: Gestalt Principles

Top-down processing is clearly at work in the principles of form perception described by the Gestalt psychologists. As mentioned in Chapter 1, *Gestalt psychology* was an influential school of thought that emerged out of Germany during the first half of the 20th century. (*Gestalt* is a German word for "form" or "shape.") Gestalt psychologists repeatedly demonstrated that the whole can be greater than the sum of its parts.

A simple example of this principle is the *phi phenomenon*, first described by Max Wertheimer in 1912. **The *phi phenomenon* is the illusion of movement created by presenting visual stimuli in rapid succession.** You encounter examples of the phi phenomenon nearly every day. For example, movies and TV consist of separate still pictures projected rapidly one after the other. You see smooth motion, but in reality the "moving" objects merely take slightly different positions in successive frames. Viewed as a whole, a movie has a property (motion) that isn't evident in any of its parts (the individual frames). The Gestalt psychologists formulated a series of principles that describe how the visual system organizes a scene into discrete forms. Let's examine some of these principles.

Figure and Ground. Take a look at Figure 4.27. Do you see the figure as two silhouetted faces against a white background, or as a white vase against a black background? This reversible figure illustrates the Gestalt principle of *figure and ground*. Dividing visual displays into figure and ground is a fundamental way in which people organize visual perceptions (Baylis & Driver, 1995). The *figure* is the thing being looked at, and the *ground* is the background against which it stands. Figures seem to have more substance and shape, appear closer to the viewer, and seem to stand out in front of the ground. More often than not, your visual field may contain many figures sharing a background. The following Gestalt principles relate to how these elements are grouped into higher-order figures.

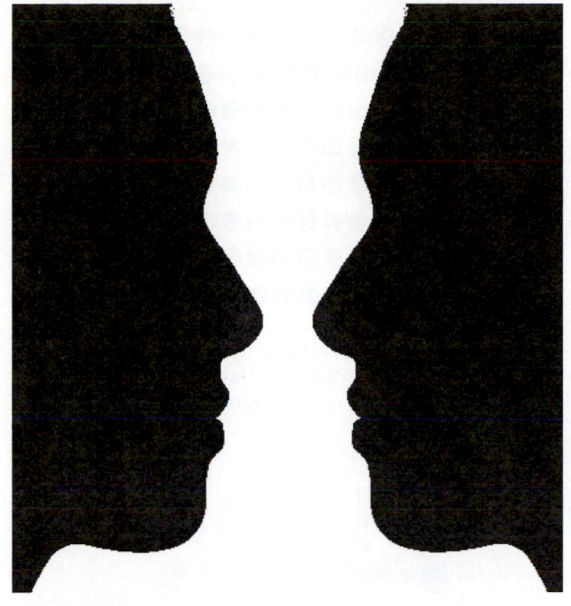

Figure 4.27

The principle of figure and ground. Whether you see two faces or a vase depends on which part of this drawing you see as figure and which as background. Although this reversible drawing allows you to switch back and forth between two ways of organizing your perception, you can't perceive the drawing both ways at once.

Proximity. Things that are near one another seem to belong together. The black dots in the upper left panel of Figure 4.28(a) on the next page could be grouped into vertical columns or horizontal rows. However, people tend to perceive rows because of the effect of proximity (the dots are closer together horizontally).

Closure. People often group elements to create a sense of *closure,* or completeness. Thus, you may "complete" figures that actually have gaps in them. This principle is demonstrated in the upper right panel of Figure 4.28(b).

Similarity. People also tend to group stimuli that are similar. This principle is apparent in Figure 4.28(c), where viewers group elements of similar lightness into the number two.

Simplicity. The Gestaltists' most general principle was the law of *Pragnanz,* which translates from German as "good form." The idea is that people tend to group elements that combine to form a good figure. This principle is somewhat vague in that it's often difficult to spell out what makes a figure "good" (Biederman, Hilton, & Hummel, 1991). Some theorists maintain that goodness is largely a matter of simplic-

"*The fundamental 'formula' of Gestalt theory might be expressed in this way: There are wholes, the behaviour of which is not determined by that of their individual elements.*"
MAX WERTHEIMER

Figure 4.28

Gestalt principles of perceptual organization.
Gestalt principles help explain some of the factors that influence form perception. **(a) Proximity:** These dots might well be organized in vertical columns rather than horizontal rows, but because of proximity (the dots are closer together horizontally), they tend to be perceived in rows. **(b) Closure:** Even though the figures are incomplete, you fill in the blanks and see a circle and a dog. **(c) Similarity:** Because of similarity of color, you see dots organized into the number 2 instead of a random array. If you did not group similar elements, you wouldn't see the number 2 here. **(d) Simplicity:** You could view this as a complicated 11-sided figure, but given the preference for simplicity, you are more likely to see it as an overlapping rectangle and triangle. **(e) Continuity:** You tend to group these dots in a way that produces a smooth path rather than an abrupt shift in direction.

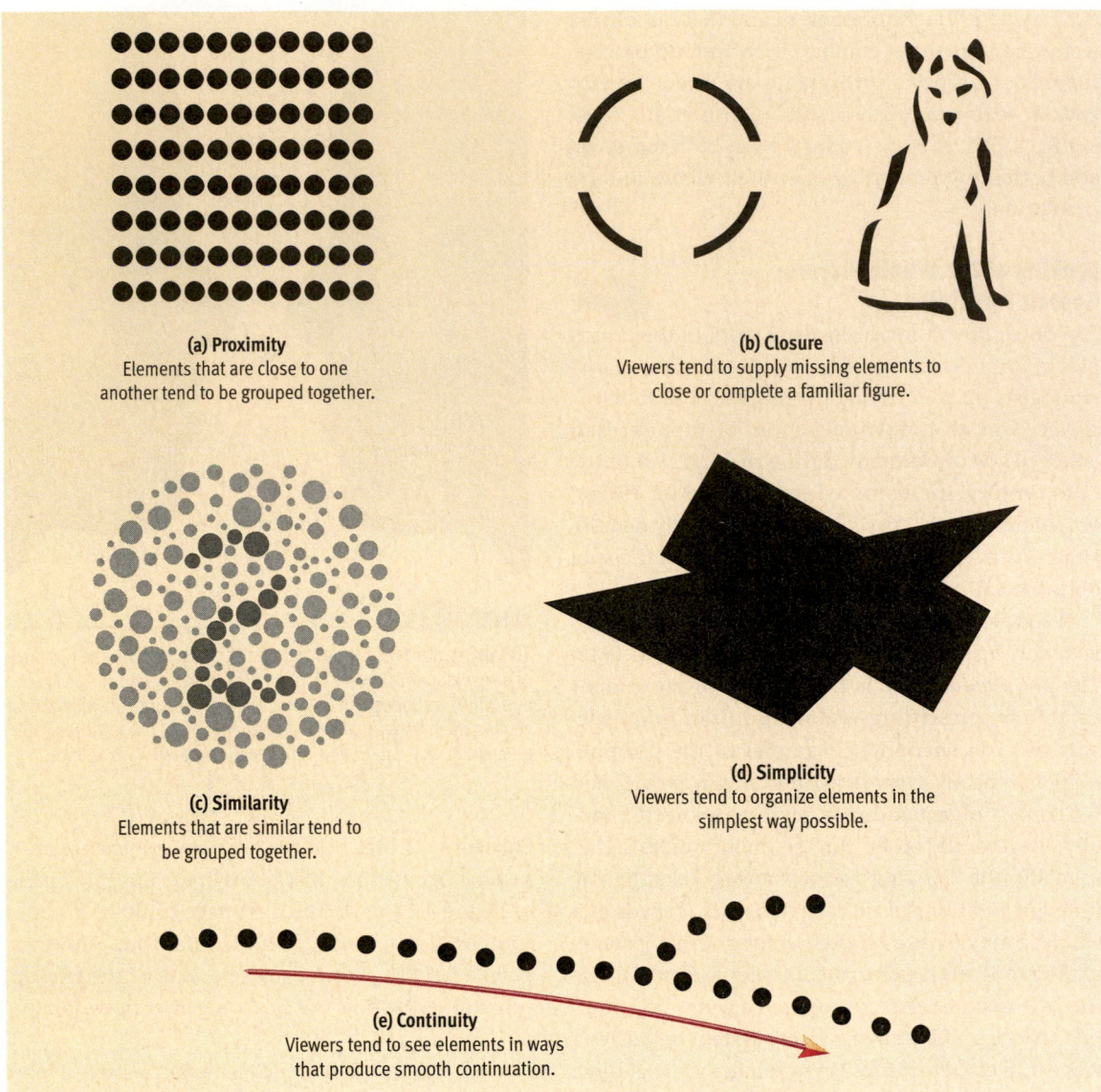

(a) Proximity
Elements that are close to one another tend to be grouped together.

(b) Closure
Viewers tend to supply missing elements to close or complete a familiar figure.

(c) Similarity
Elements that are similar tend to be grouped together.

(d) Simplicity
Viewers tend to organize elements in the simplest way possible.

(e) Continuity
Viewers tend to see elements in ways that produce smooth continuation.

ity, asserting that people tend to organize forms in the simplest way possible (see Figure 4.28d).

Continuity. The principle of continuity reflects people's tendency to follow in whatever direction they've been led. Thus, people tend to connect points that result in straight or gently curved lines that create "smooth" paths, as shown in the bottom panel of Figure 4.28(e).

Although Gestalt psychology is no longer an active theoretical orientation in modern psychology, its influence is still felt in the study of perception (Banks & Krajicek, 1991). The Gestalt psychologists raised many important questions that still occupy researchers, and they left a legacy of many useful insights about form perception that have stood the test of time (Sharps & Wertheimer, 2000).

Formulating Perceptual Hypotheses

The Gestalt principles provide some indications of how people organize visual input. However, scientists are still one step away from understanding how these organized perceptions result in a representation of the real world. Understanding the problem requires distinguishing between two kinds of stimuli: distal and proximal (Hochberg, 1988). ***Distal stimuli* are stimuli that lie in the distance (that is, in the world outside the body).** In vision, these are the objects that you're looking at. They are "distant" in that your eyes don't touch them. What your eyes do "touch" are the images formed by patterns of light falling on your retinas. These images are the ***proximal stimuli*, the stimulus energies that impinge directly on sensory receptors.** The distinction is important, because there are great differences

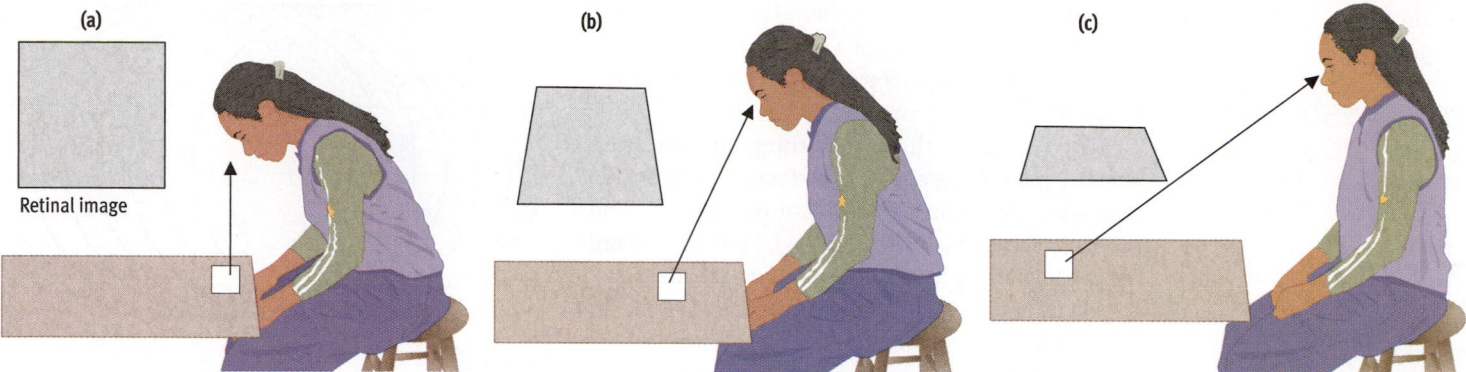

(a) Retinal image

(b)

(c)

between the objects you perceive and the stimulus energies that represent them.

In visual perception, the proximal stimuli are distorted, two-dimensional versions of their actual, three-dimensional counterparts. For example, consider the distal stimulus of a square such as the one in Figure 4.29. If the square is lying on a desk in front of you, it is actually projecting a trapezoid (the proximal stimulus) onto your retinas, because the top of the square is farther from your eyes than the bottom. Obviously, the trapezoid is a distorted representation of the square. If what people have to work with is so distorted a picture, how do they get an accurate view of the world out there?

One explanation is that people bridge the gap between distal and proximal stimuli by constantly making and testing *hypotheses* about what's out there in the real world (Gregory, 1973). Thus, **a *perceptual hypothesis* is an inference about which distal stimuli could be responsible for the proximal stimuli sensed.** In effect, people make educated guesses about what form could be responsible for a pattern of sensory stimulation. The square in Figure 4.29 may project a trapezoidal image on your retinas, but your perceptual system "guesses" correctly that it's a square—and that's what you see.

Let's look at another ambiguous drawing to further demonstrate the process of making a perceptual hypothesis. Figure 4.30 is a famous reversible figure, first published as a cartoon in a humor magazine. Perhaps you see a drawing of a young woman looking back over her right shoulder. Alternatively, you might see an old woman with her chin down on her chest. The ambiguity exists because there isn't enough information to force your perceptual system to accept only one of these hypotheses. Incidentally, studies show that people who are led to *expect* the young woman or the old woman generally see the one they expect (Leeper, 1935). This is another example of how perceptual sets influence what people see.

Psychologists have used a variety of reversible figures to study how people formulate perceptual hypotheses. Another example can be seen in Figure 4.31, which shows the *Necker cube*. The shaded surface can appear as either the front or the rear of the transparent cube. If you look at the cube for a while, your

Figure 4.30

A famous reversible figure. What do you see? Consult the text to learn what the two possible interpretations of this figure are.

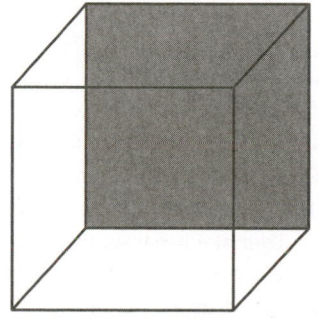

Figure 4.31

The Necker cube. The tinted surface of this reversible figure can become either the front or the back of the cube.

Figure 4.29

Distal and proximal stimuli. Proximal stimuli are often distorted, shifting representations of distal stimuli in the real world. If you look directly down at a small, square piece of paper on a desk **(a)**, the distal stimulus (the paper) and the proximal stimulus (the image projected on your retina) will both be square. But as you move the paper away on the desktop, as shown in **(b)** and **(c)**, the square distal stimulus projects an increasingly trapezoidal image on your retina, making the proximal stimulus more and more distorted. Nevertheless, you continue to perceive a square.

perception will alternate between these possibilities. People tend to experience a similar shift back and forth between two perceptions when they view the image in Figure 4.32.

The *context* in which something appears often guides people's perceptual hypotheses. To illustrate, take a look at Figure 4.33. What do you see? You probably saw the words "THE CAT." But look again; the middle characters in both words are identical. You identified an "H" in the first word and an "A" in the second because of the surrounding letters, which created an expectation—another example of top-down processing in visual perception. The power of expectations explains why typographocal errors like those in this sentence often pass unoberved (Lachman, 1996).

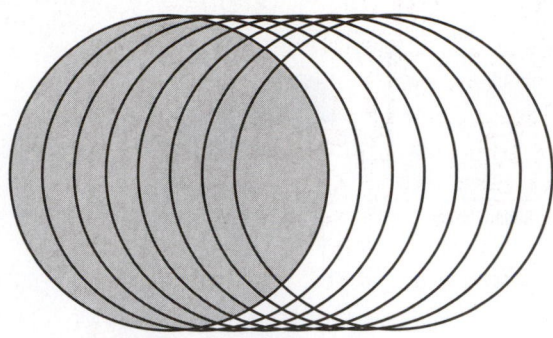

Figure 4.32

Another reversible figure. The tinted surface of this reversible figure can become either the closer or farther end of the "tube." People's perceptions of this stimulus tend to dynamically go back and forth between these interpretations.

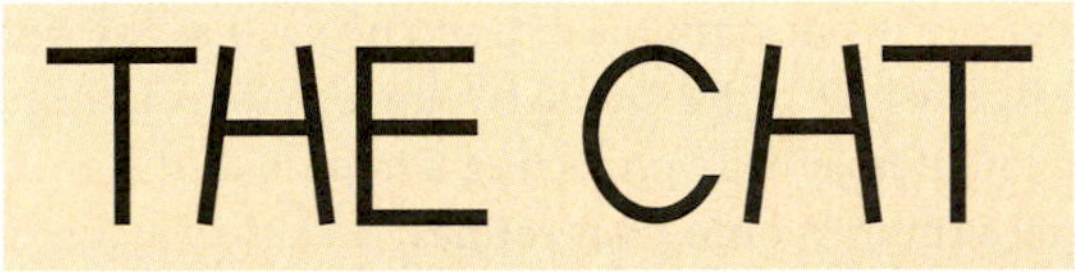

REVIEW OF KEY POINTS

- Perceptions of color (hue) are primarily a function of light wavelength, while amplitude affects brightness and purity affects saturation. There are two types of color mixing: additive and subtractive. Human color perception depends on processes that resemble additive color mixing.

- The trichromatic theory holds that people have three types of receptors that are sensitive to wavelengths associated with red, green, and blue. The opponent process theory holds that color perception depends on receptors that make antagonistic responses to red versus green, blue versus yellow, and black versus white. The evidence now suggests that both theories are necessary to account for color vision.

- Reversible figures and perceptual sets demonstrate that the same visual input can result in very different perceptions. Form perception depends on both the selection and interpretation of sensory inputs. According to feature analysis theories, people detect specific elements in stimuli and build them into recognizable forms through bottom-up processing. However, form perception also involves top-down processing, which progresses from the whole to the elements.

- Gestalt psychology emphasized that the whole may be greater than the sum of its parts (features), as illustrated by the Gestalt principles of form perception, including figure-ground, proximity, similarity, continuity, closure, and simplicity. Other approaches to form perception emphasize that people develop perceptual hypotheses about the distal stimuli that could be responsible for the proximal stimuli that are sensed.

THE CAT

Figure 4.33

Context effects. The context in which a stimulus is seen can affect your perceptual hypotheses.

Binocular Cues

Because the eyes are set apart, each eye has a slightly different view of the world. *Binocular depth cues* **are clues about distance based on the differing views of the two eyes.** "Stereo" viewers like the Viewmaster toy you may have had as a child make use of this principle by presenting slightly different flat images of the same scene to each eye. The brain then supplies the "depth," and you perceive a three-dimensional scene.

The principal binocular depth cue is *retinal disparity,* **which refers to the fact that objects within 25 feet project images to slightly different locations on the right and left retinas, so the right and left eyes see slightly different views of the object.** The closer an object gets, the greater the disparity between the images seen by each eye. Thus, retinal disparity increases as objects come closer, providing information about distance. Another binocular cue is *convergence,* **which involves sensing the eyes converging toward each other as they focus on closer objects.**

Monocular Cues

Monocular depth cues **are clues about distance based on the image in either eye alone.** There are two kinds of monocular cues to depth. One kind is

PREVIEW QUESTIONS

- What are some binocular and monocular depth cues?
- Are there cultural differences in depth perception?
- Why do hills look steeper than they are?
- What are perceptual constancies?
- What do optical illusions reveal about perceptual processes?

Perceiving Depth or Distance

More often than not, forms and figures are objects in space. Spatial considerations add a third dimension to visual perception. *Depth perception* **involves interpretation of visual cues that indicate how near or far away objects are.** To make judgments of distance, people rely on quite a variety of clues, which can be classified into two types: binocular and monocular (Hochberg, 1988).

the result of active use of the eye in viewing the world. For example, as an object comes closer, you may sense the accommodation (the change in the curvature of the lens) that must occur for the eye to adjust its focus. Furthermore, if you cover one eye and move your head from side to side, closer objects appear to move more than distant objects. In a similar vein, you may notice when driving along a highway that nearby objects (such as fenceposts along the road) appear to move by more rapidly than objects that are farther away (such as trees in the distance). Thus, you get cues about depth from **motion parallax,** which involves images of objects at different distances moving across the retina at different rates.

The other kind of monocular cues are **pictorial depth cues**—clues about distance that can be given in a flat picture. There are many pictorial cues to depth, which is why some paintings and photographs seem so realistic that you feel you can climb right into them. Six prominent pictorial depth cues are described and illustrated in Figure 4.34. *Linear perspective* is a depth cue reflecting the fact that lines converge in the distance. Because details are too small to see when they are far away, *texture gradients* can provide information about depth. If an object comes between you and another object, it must be closer to you, a cue called *interposition*. *Relative size* is a cue because closer objects appear larger. *Height in plane* reflects the fact that distant objects appear higher in a picture. Finally, the familiar effects of shadowing make *light and shadow* useful in judging distance.

There appear to be some cultural differences in the ability to take advantage of pictorial depth cues in two-dimensional drawings. These differences were first investigated by Hudson (1960, 1967), who presented pictures like that shown in Figure 4.35 on the next page to various cultural groups in South Africa. Hudson's approach was based on the assumption that subjects who indicate that the hunter is trying

Figure 4.34

Pictorial cues to depth.
Six pictorial depth cues are explained and illustrated here. Although one cue stands out in each photo, in most visual scenes several pictorial cues are present. Try looking at the light-and-shadow picture upside down. The change in shadowing reverses what you see.

Linear perspective Parallel lines that run away from the viewer seem to get closer together.

Texture gradient A texture is coarser for near areas and finer for more distant ones.

Interposition The shapes of near objects overlap or mask those of more distant ones.

Relative size If separate objects are expected to be of the same size, the larger ones are seen as closer.

Height in plane Near objects are low in the visual field; more distant ones are higher up.

Light and shadow Patterns of light and dark suggest shadows that can create an impression of three-dimensional forms.

Recognizing Pictorial Depth Cues

Painters routinely attempt to create the perception of depth on a flat canvas by using pictorial depth cues. Figure 4.34 describes and illustrates six pictorial depth cues, most of which are apparent in van Gogh's colorful piece *Corridor in the Asylum* (1889). Check your understanding of depth perception by trying to spot the depth cues in the painting.

In the list below, check off the depth cues used by van Gogh. The answers can be found in the back of the book in Appendix A. You can learn more about how artists use the principles of visual perception in the Personal Application at the end of this chapter.

van Gogh, Vincent, *Corridor in the Asylum* (1889), gouche and watercolor, 24 ⅜ × 18 ½ inches (61.5 × 47 cm). Metropolitan Museum of Art. Bequest of Abby Aldrich Rockefeller, 1948. (48.190.2) Photograph © 1998 The Metropolitan Museum of Art.

_____ **1.** Interposition   _____ **4.** Relative size

_____ **2.** Height in plane   _____ **5.** Light and shadow

_____ **3.** Texture gradient   _____ **6.** Linear perspective

---

Figure 4.35

Testing understanding of pictorial depth cues. In his cross-cultural research, Hudson (1960) asked subjects to indicate whether the hunter is trying to spear the antelope or the elephant. He found cultural disparities in subjects' ability to make effective use of the pictorial depth cues, which place the elephant in the distance and make it an unlikely target.

SOURCE: Adapted by permission from an illustration by Illi Arbel in Deregowski, J. B. (1972, November). Pictorial perception and culture. *Scientific American, 227* (5), p. 83. Copyright © 1972 by Scientific American, Inc. All rights reserved.

to spear the elephant instead of the antelope don't understand the depth cues (interposition, relative size, height in plane) in the picture, which place the elephant in the distance. Hudson found that subjects from a rural South African tribe (the Bantu), which had little exposure at that time to pictures and photos, frequently misinterpreted the depth cues in his pictures. Similar difficulties with depth cues in pictures have been documented for other cultural groups who have little experience with two-dimensional representations of three-dimensional space (Berry et al., 1992). Thus, the application of pictorial depth cues to pictures varies to some degree across cultures.

Perceiving Geographical Slant

The perception of *geographical slant* involves making judgments about how steep hills and other inclines are in relation to the norm of a flat, horizontal surface. As with depth perception, the perception of geographical slant involves juggling spatial considerations. However, unlike with depth perception, which has a rich tradition of empirical inquiry, the perception of geographical slant has largely been neglected by researchers. Nevertheless, recent work has turned up some thought-provoking findings and raised some interesting questions. We will look at this work in our Featured Study for Chapter 4.

FEATURED STUDY

Why Hills Look Steeper Than They Are

Investigators: Dennis R. Proffitt, Mukul Bhalla, Rich Gossweiler, and Jonathon Midgett (University of Virginia)

Source: Perceiving geographical slant. *Psychonomic Bulletin & Review,* 1995, 2, 409–428.

Accurate perceptions of geographical slant have obvious practical significance for people walking up hills, skiing down mountain slopes, working on pitched roofs, and so forth. Yet anecdotal accounts suggest that people tend to overestimate geographical slant. Thus, Proffitt and his colleagues set out to collect the first systematic data on everyday geographical pitch perception. They ended up conducting a series of five studies. We'll examine the first study in detail and then briefly discuss the follow-up studies.

Method

Participants. Three hundred students at the University of Virginia agreed to participate in the study when asked by an experimenter stationed near the bottom of various hills around campus. Each participant made estimates for only one hill.

Stimuli. Nine hills on the University of Virginia campus were used as stimuli. The experimenters chose hills with lots of foot traffic, unobstructed views, and wide variation in geographical slant. The inclinations of the nine hills were 2, 4, 5, 6, 10, 21, 31, 33, and 34 degrees. To put these figures in perspective, the authors note that 9 degrees is the steepest incline allowed for roads in Virginia and that a 30-degree hill is about the limit of what most people can walk up (the very steep hills on campus had stairs nearby).

Measures and apparatus. The participants were asked to estimate geographical slant in three ways. They provided a *verbal measure* by estimating the slope of the hill they were viewing in degrees. They provided a *visual measure* by adjusting the incline on the disk shown in Figure 4.36(a) to match the slope of the hill they were viewing. Finally, they provided a *haptic measure* (one based on touch) by adjusting the tilt board shown in Figure 4.36(b) to match the slope of the stimulus hill. To keep the latter measure exclusively haptic and not visual, participants were not allowed to look at their hand while they adjusted the tilt board.

Figure **4.36**

Apparatus used to measure visual and haptic estimates of geographical slant. **(a)** Visual estimates of pitch were made by adjusting the incline on a disk to match the incline of the hill. **(b)** Haptic estimates of pitch were made by adjusting a tilt board by hand without looking at it.

Source: Adapted from Proffitt, D. R., Bhalla, M., Gossweiler, R., & Midgett, J. (1995). Perceiving geographical slant. *Psychonomic Bulletin & Review, 214*, 409–428. Copyright © 1995 by Psychonomic Society Publications. Reprinted by permission.

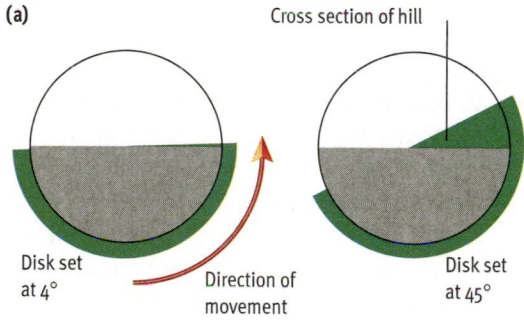

(a)

Cross section of hill

Disk set at 4°

Direction of movement

Disk set at 45°

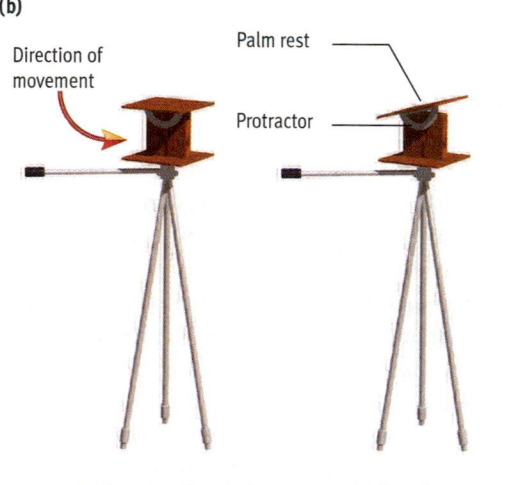

(b)

Direction of movement

Palm rest

Protractor

Tilt board resting at 0°

Tilt board set at 15°

Results

The mean slant estimates for all three measures and all nine hills are summarized graphically in Figure 4.37. As you can see, the participants' verbal and visual judgments resulted in large overestimates of all nine hills' geographic slant. For example, participants' verbal estimates for the 5-degree hill in the study averaged 20 degrees. Similarly, their visual estimates for the 10-degree hill averaged 25 degrees. In contrast, the subjects' haptic judgments were much more accurate.

Discussion

Why do hills appear substantially steeper than they are? Why are haptic judgments relatively immune to this peculiar perceptual bias? The authors argue that the data for all three measures make sense from an adaptive point of view. Subjects' verbal and visual estimates reflect their conscious awareness of how challenging hills will be to climb. Overestimates of slant are functional in that they should prevent people from undertaking climbs they are not equipped to handle, and they lead people to pace themselves and conserve energy on the steep hills they do attempt to traverse. Although overestimates of slant may be functional when people make conscious decisions about climbing hills, they would be dysfunctional if they distorted people's locomotion on hills. If people walking up a 5-degree hill raised their feet to accommodate a 20-degree slope, they would stumble. Accurate tactile perceptions are thus crucial to

Figure **4.37**

Mean slant estimates. The average pitch estimates for all three types of measures are plotted here. The red line shows where accurate estimates would fall. As you can see, verbal and visual measures yielded substantial overestimates, but haptic measures were reasonably accurate.

Source: Adapted from Proffitt, D. R., Bhalla, M., Gossweiler, R., & Midgett, J. (1995). Perceiving geographical slant. *Psychonomic Bulletin & Review, 214*, 409–428. Copyright © 1995 by Psychonomic Society Publications. Reprinted by permission.

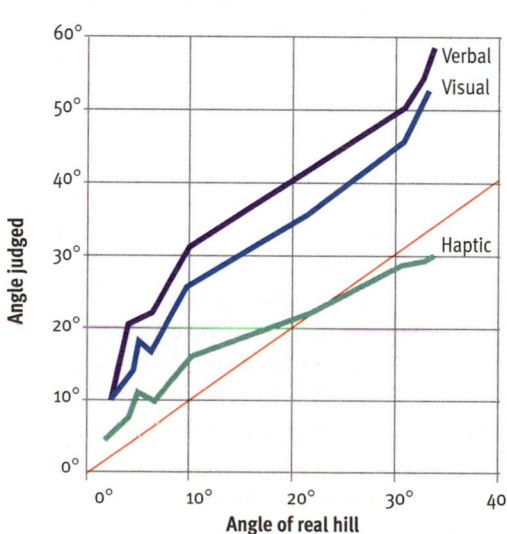

people's motor responses when they walk up a hill, so it is functional for haptic perceptions to be largely unaffected by the misperception of slant. Thus, learning, or evolution, or some combination has equipped people with perceptual responses that are adaptive.

Comment

The study of sensation and perception is one of the oldest areas of scientific research in psychology. Yet this study shows that there are still fascinating areas of inquiry that remain unexplored. It just takes some creativity and insight to recognize them. This research also illustrates the importance of using more than a single measure of the phenomenon that one is interested in.

The investigators chose to assess the dependent variable of slant perception in several ways, leading to a much richer understanding of slant perception than if only one of the three measures had been used. Finally, the highly exaggerated estimates of slant show once again that human perceptions are not simple reflections of reality, although most people tend to assume that they are. The authors note that many of their subjects were "incredulous" during their postexperimental briefings: "To look at a 10-degree hill—typically judged to be about 30 degrees by verbal reports and visual matching—and to be told that it is actually 10 degrees is an astonishing experience for anyone unfamiliar with the facts of geographical slant overestimation" (p. 425). ■

In their follow-up studies, Proffitt and his colleagues (1995) replicated and extended their original findings. In the second study, they found that verbal and visual overestimates of pitch are even more pronounced when hills are viewed from the top rather than the bottom. They argue that this bias makes functional sense because, as those who live in the San Francisco area can testify, steep hills are much harder to descend than ascend. For the third and fourth studies, they created a computer-simulated virtual reality environment in which they could confront subjects with a wider range of inclines than were readily available out-of-doors and observed the same trends in the misperception of slant. In the fifth study, subjects' fatigue was manipulated by having the participants make slant estimates before or after an exhausting run. *Consistent with their adaptive perspective, the investigators found that hills look even steeper when people are tired.* Their findings on the influence of fatigue demonstrate once again that perception is a highly subjective process.

Perceptual Constancies in Vision

When a person approaches you from a distance, his or her image on your retinas gradually changes in size. Do you perceive that the person is growing right before your eyes? Of course not. Your perceptual system constantly makes allowances for this variation in visual input. The task of the perceptual system is to provide an accurate rendition of distal stimuli based on distorted, ever-changing proximal stimuli. In doing so, it relies in part on perceptual constancies. **A *perceptual constancy* is a tendency to experience a stable perception in the face of continu-**ally changing sensory input. Among other things, people tend to view objects as having a stable size, shape, brightness, hue, and location in space.

The Power of Misleading Cues: Optical Illusions

In general, perceptual constancies, depth cues, and principles of visual organization (such as the Gestalt laws) help people perceive the world accurately. Sometimes, however, perceptions are based on inappropriate assumptions, and *optical illusions* can result. **An *optical illusion* involves an apparently inexplicable discrepancy between the appearance of a visual stimulus and its physical reality.**

One famous optical illusion is the *Müller-Lyer* illusion, shown in Figure 4.38. The two vertical lines in this figure are equally long, but they certainly don't look that way. Why not? Several mechanisms probably play a role (Day, 1965; Gregory, 1978). The figure on the left looks like the outside of a building, thrust toward the viewer, while the one on the right looks like an inside corner, thrust away (see Figure 4.39). The vertical line in the left figure therefore seems closer. If two lines cast equally long retinal images but one seems closer, the closer one is assumed to be shorter. Thus, the Müller-Lyer illusion may result from a combination of size constancy processes and misperception of depth.

The geometric illusions shown in Figure 4.40 also demonstrate that visual stimuli can be highly deceptive. The *Ponzo illusion,* which is shown at the top of Figure 4.40, appears to result from the same factors at work in the Müller-Lyer illusion (Coren & Girgus, 1978). The upper and lower horizontal lines are the

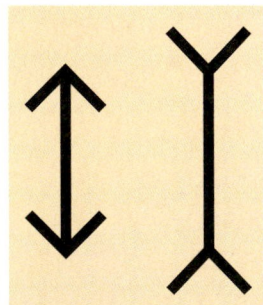

Figure 4.38

The Müller-Lyer illusion.
Go ahead, measure them: the two vertical lines are of equal length.

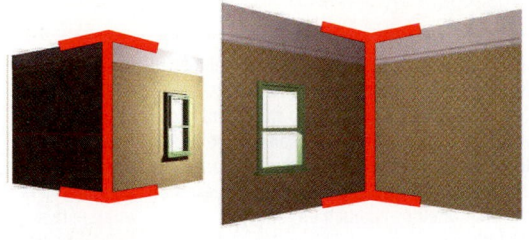

Figure 4.39

Explaining the Müller-Lyer illusion. The figure on the left seems to be closer, since it looks like an outside corner, thrust toward you, whereas the figure on the right looks like an inside corner thrust away from you. Given retinal images of the same length, you assume that the "closer" line is shorter.

same length, but the upper one appears longer. This illusion probably occurs because the converging lines convey linear perspective, a key depth cue suggesting that the upper line lies farther away. Figure 4.41 shows a drawing by Stanford University psychologist Roger Shepard (1990) that creates a similar illusion.

Figure 4.40

Four geometric illusions. **Ponzo:** The horizontal lines are the same length. **Poggendorff:** The two diagonal segments lie on the same straight line. **Upside-down T:** The vertical and horizontal lines are the same length. **Zollner:** The long diagonals are all parallel (try covering up some of the short diagonal lines if you don't believe it).

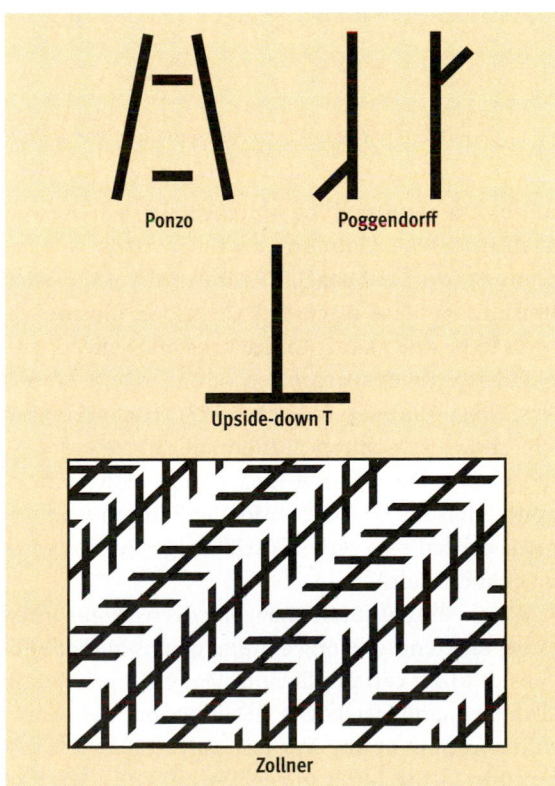

The second monster appears much larger than the first, even though they are really identical in size.

Adelbert Ames designed a striking illusion that makes use of misperception of distance. It's called, appropriately enough, the *Ames room*. It's a specially contrived room built with a trapezoidal rear wall and a sloping floor and ceiling. When viewed from the correct point, as in the picture, it looks like an ordinary rectangular room (see Figure 4.42 on the next page). But in reality, the left corner is much taller and much farther from the viewer than the right corner. Hence, bizarre illusions unfold in the Ames room. People standing in the right corner appear to be giants, while those standing in the left corner appear to be midgets. Even more disconcerting, a person who walks across the room from right to left appears to shrink before your eyes! The Ames room creates these misperceptions by toying with the perfectly reasonable assumption that the room is vertically and horizontally rectangular.

Impossible figures create another form of illusion. **Impossible figures are objects that can be represented in two-dimensional pictures but cannot**

Figure 4.41

A monster of an illusion. The principles underlying the Ponzo illusion also explain the striking illusion seen here, in which two identical monsters appear to be quite different in size.

Wayne Weiten

Figure 4.42

The Ames room. The diagram on the right shows the room as it is actually constructed. However, the viewer assumes that the room is rectangular, and the image cast on the retina is consistent with this hypothesis. Because of this reasonable perceptual hypothesis, the normal perceptual adjustments made to preserve size constancy lead to the illusions described in the text. For example, naive viewers "conclude" that one boy is much larger than the other, when in fact he is merely closer.

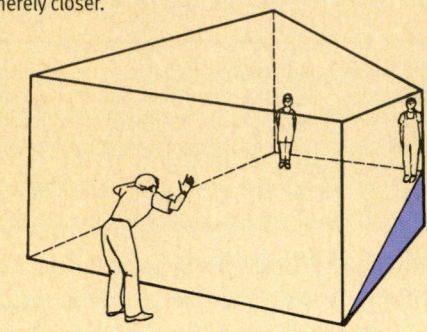

Figure 4.43

Three classic impossible figures. The figures are impossible, yet they clearly exist—on the page. What makes them impossible is that they appear to be three-dimensional representations yet are drawn in a way that frustrates mental attempts to "assemble" their features into possible objects. It's difficult to see the drawings simply as lines lying in a plane—even though this perceptual hypothesis is the only one that resolves the contradiction.

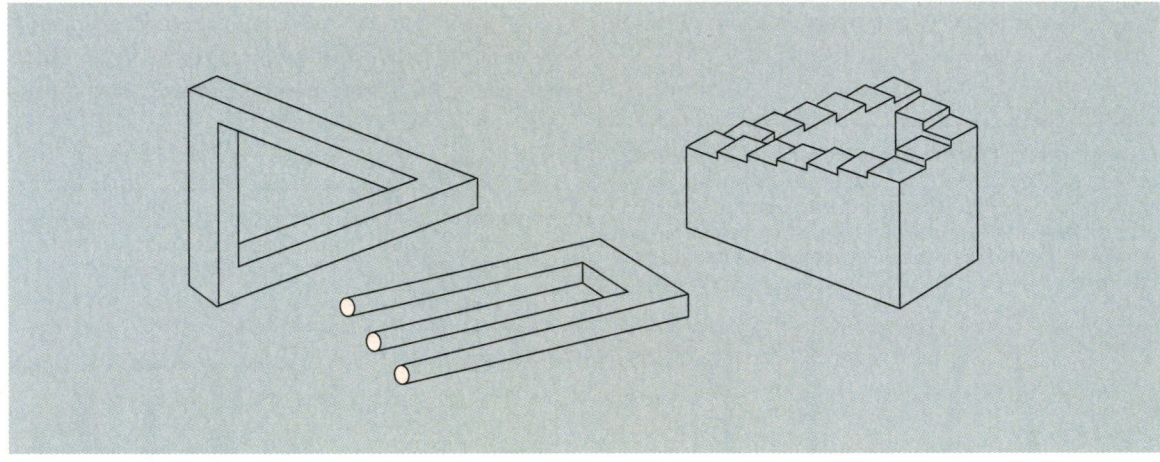

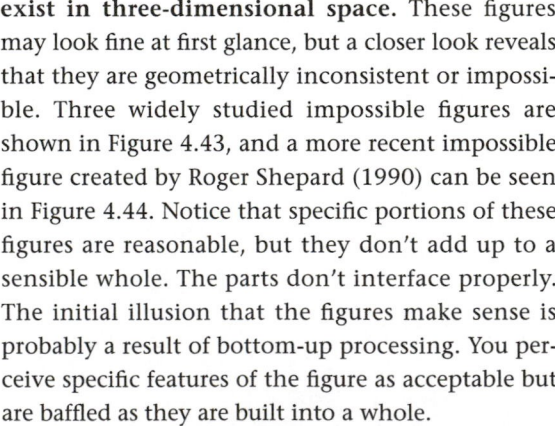

Web Link 4.4

IllusionWorks
IllusionWorks bills itself as "the most comprehensive collection of optical and sensory illusions on the World Wide Web." At both "introductory" and "advanced" levels of explanation, this is an excellent resource for experiencing some of the strangest and most thought-provoking illusions ever created.

exist in three-dimensional space. These figures may look fine at first glance, but a closer look reveals that they are geometrically inconsistent or impossible. Three widely studied impossible figures are shown in Figure 4.43, and a more recent impossible figure created by Roger Shepard (1990) can be seen in Figure 4.44. Notice that specific portions of these figures are reasonable, but they don't add up to a sensible whole. The parts don't interface properly. The initial illusion that the figures make sense is probably a result of bottom-up processing. You perceive specific features of the figure as acceptable but are baffled as they are built into a whole.

Obviously, illusions such as impossible figures and their real-life relative, the Ames room, involve a conspiracy of cues intended to deceive the viewer. Many visual illusions, however, occur quite naturally. A well-known example is the *moon illusion*. The full moon appears to be much smaller when overhead than when looming on the horizon (see the photo on the next page). As with many of the other illusions we have discussed, the moon illusion appears to be due mainly to size constancy effects coupled with the misperception of distance (Coren & Aks, 1990; Kaufman & Rock, 1962). The moon illusion shows that optical illusions are part of everyday life. Indeed, many people are virtually addicted to an optical illusion called television (an illusion of movement created by a series of still images presented in quick succession).

Cross-cultural studies have uncovered some interesting differences among cultural groups in their propensity to see certain illusions. For example, Segall, Campbell, and Herskovits (1966) found that people from a variety of non-Western cultures are less susceptible to the Müller-Lyer illusion than Western

Figure 4.44

Another impossible figure. This impossible figure, drawn by Stanford University psychologist Roger Shepard (1990), seems even more perplexing than the classic impossible figure that it is based on (the one seen in the middle of Figure 4.43).

SOURCE: Shepard, R. N. (1990). *Mind sights.* New York: W. H. Freeman. Copyright © 1990 by Roger N. Shepard. Used by permission of W. H. Freeman and Company.

Web Link 4.5

The Moon Illusion Explained
Don McCready, professor emeritus at the University of Wisconsin (Whitewater), addresses the age-old puzzle of why the moon appears much larger at the horizon than overhead. He uses a helpful collection of illustrations in a comprehensive review of alternative theories.

© N. R. Rowan/The Image Works

A puzzling perceptual illusion common in everyday life is the moon illusion: the moon looks larger when at the horizon than when overhead.

samples. What could account for this difference? The most plausible explanation is that in the West, we live in a "carpentered world" dominated by straight lines, right angles, and rectangular rooms, buildings, and furniture. Thus, our experience prepares us to readily view the Müller-Lyer figures as inside and outside corners of buildings—inferences that help foster the illusion (Segall et al., 1990). In contrast, people in many non-Western cultures, such as the Zulu (see the adjacent photo) who were tested by Segall and associates (1966), live in a less carpentered world, making them less prone to see the Müller-Lyer figures as building corners. Although there is some debate about the matter, cultural differences in illusion susceptibility suggest that people's perceptual inferences can be shaped by experience (Segall et al., 1990).

What do optical illusions reveal about visual perception? They drive home the point that people go through life formulating perceptual hypotheses about what lies out there in the real world. The fact that these are only hypotheses becomes especially striking when the hypotheses are wrong, as they are with illusions. Optical illusions also show how contextual factors such as depth cues shape perceptual hypotheses. Finally, like ambiguous figures, illusions clearly demonstrate that human perceptions are not simple reflections of objective reality. Once again, we see that

© Peter Menzel/Stock, Boston

Unlike people in Western nations, the Zulus live in a culture where straight lines and right angles are scarce, if not entirely absent. Thus, they are not affected by such phenomena as the Müller-Lyer illusion nearly as much as people raised in environments that abound with rectangular structures.

perception of the world is subjective. These insights do not apply to visual perception only. We will encounter these lessons again as we examine other sensory systems, such as hearing, which we turn to next.

REVIEW OF KEY POINTS

- Binocular cues such as retinal disparity and convergence can contribute to depth perception. Depth perception depends primarily on monocular cues, including pictorial cues such as texture gradient, linear perspective, light and shadow, interposition, relative size, and height in plane.

- People from pictureless societies have some difficulty in applying pictorial depth cues to two-dimensional pictures.

- Conscious perceptions of geographical slant, as reflected by visual and verbal estimates of pitch, tend to be greatly exaggerated, but haptic (tactile) judgments seem largely immune to this perceptual bias. Perceptual constancies in vision help viewers deal with the ever-shifting nature of proximal stimuli.

- Optical illusions demonstrate that perceptual hypotheses can be inaccurate and that perceptions are not simple reflections of objective reality. Researchers have found some interesting cultural differences in susceptibility to the Müller-Lyer and Ponzo illusions.

Our Sense of Hearing: The Auditory System

PREVIEW QUESTIONS

- What are the three key properties of sound?
- How are these properties related to auditory perceptions?
- What are the key structures in the ear involved in the processing of sound?
- What were the central ideas of place theory and frequency theory?
- How were the two theories reconciled?
- What cues do people use to locate sounds in space?

Stop reading for a moment, close your eyes, and listen carefully. What do you hear?

Chances are, you'll discover that you're immersed in sounds: street noises, a high-pitched laugh from the next room, the hum of a fluorescent lamp, perhaps some background music you put on a while ago but forgot about. As this little demonstration shows, physical stimuli producing sound are present almost constantly, but you're not necessarily aware of these sounds.

Like vision, the auditory (hearing) system provides input about the world "out there," but not until incoming information is processed by the brain. A distal stimulus—a screech of tires, someone laughing, the hum of the refrigerator—produces a proximal stimulus in the form of sound waves reaching the ears. The perceptual system must somehow transform this stimulation into the psychological experience of hearing. We'll begin our discussion of hearing by looking at the stimulus for auditory experience: sound.

The Stimulus: Sound

Sound waves are vibrations of molecules, which means that they must travel through some physical medium, such as air. They move at a fraction of the speed of light. Sound waves are usually generated by vibrating objects, such as a guitar string, a loudspeaker cone, or your vocal cords. However, sound waves can also be generated by forcing air past a chamber (as in a pipe organ), or by suddenly releasing a burst of air (as when you clap).

Like light waves, sound waves are characterized by their *amplitude,* their *wavelength,* and their *purity* (see Figure 4.45). The physical properties of amplitude, wavelength, and purity affect mainly the perceived (psychological) qualities of loudness, pitch, and timbre, respectively. However, the physical properties of sound interact in complex ways to produce perceptions of these sound qualities (Hirsh & Watson, 1996).

Human Hearing Capacities

Wavelengths of sound are described in terms of their *frequency,* which is measured in cycles per second, or *hertz (Hz).* For the most part, higher frequencies are perceived as having higher pitch. That is, if you strike the key for high C on a piano, it will produce higher-frequency sound waves than the key for low C. Although the perception of pitch depends mainly on frequency, the amplitude of the sound waves also influences it.

Just as the visible spectrum is only a portion of the total spectrum of light, so, too, what people can hear is only a portion of the available range of sounds. Humans can hear sounds ranging from a low of 20 Hz

Figure 4.45

Sound, the physical stimulus for hearing. **(a)** Like light, sound travels in waves—in this case, waves of air pressure. A smooth curve would represent a pure tone, such as that produced by a tuning fork. Most sounds, however, are complex. For example, the wave shown here is for middle C played on a piano. The sound wave for the same note played on a violin would have the same wavelength (or frequency) as this one, but the "wrinkles" in the wave would be different, corresponding to the differences in timbre between the two sounds. **(b)** The table shows the main relations between objective aspects of sound and subjective perceptions.

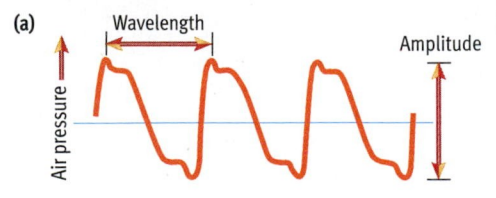

(a)

(b)

Physical properties of sound	Related perceptions
Amplitude	Loudness
Frequency	Pitch
Purity	Timbre

up to a high of about 20,000 Hz. Sounds at either end of this range are harder to hear, and sensitivity to high-frequency tones declines as adults grow older. Other organisms have different capabilities. Low-frequency sounds under 10 Hz are audible to homing pigeons, for example. At the other extreme, bats and porpoises can hear frequencies well above 20,000 Hz.

In general, the greater the amplitude of sound waves, the louder the sound perceived. Whereas frequency is measured in hertz, amplitude is measured in *decibels (dB)*. The relationship between decibels (which measure a physical property of sound) and loudness (a psychological quality) is complex. A rough rule of thumb is that perceived loudness doubles about every 10 decibels (Stevens, 1955). To make this idea less abstract, Figure 4.46 shows approximate decibel levels for a wide range of common sounds. Very loud sounds can jeopardize the quality of your hearing. Even brief exposure to sounds over 120 decibels can be painful and may cause damage to your auditory system (Henry, 1984).

As shown in Figure 4.46, the absolute thresholds for the weakest sounds people can hear differ for sounds of various frequencies. The human ear is most sensitive to sounds at frequencies near 2000 Hz. That is, these frequencies yield the lowest absolute thresholds. To summarize, amplitude is the principal determinant of loudness, but loudness ultimately depends on an interaction between amplitude and frequency.

People are also sensitive to variations in the purity of sounds. The purest sound is one that has only a single frequency of vibration, such as that produced by a tuning fork. Most everyday sounds are complex mixtures of many frequencies. The purity or complexity of a sound influences how *timbre* is perceived. To understand timbre, think of a note with precisely the same loudness and pitch played on a French horn and then on a violin. The difference you perceive in the sounds is a difference in timbre.

Sensory Processing in the Ear 3h

Like your eyes, your ears channel energy to the neural tissue that receives it. Figure 4.47 on the next page shows that the human ear can be divided into three sections: the external ear, the middle ear, and the inner ear. Sound is conducted differently in each section. The external ear depends on the *vibration of air*

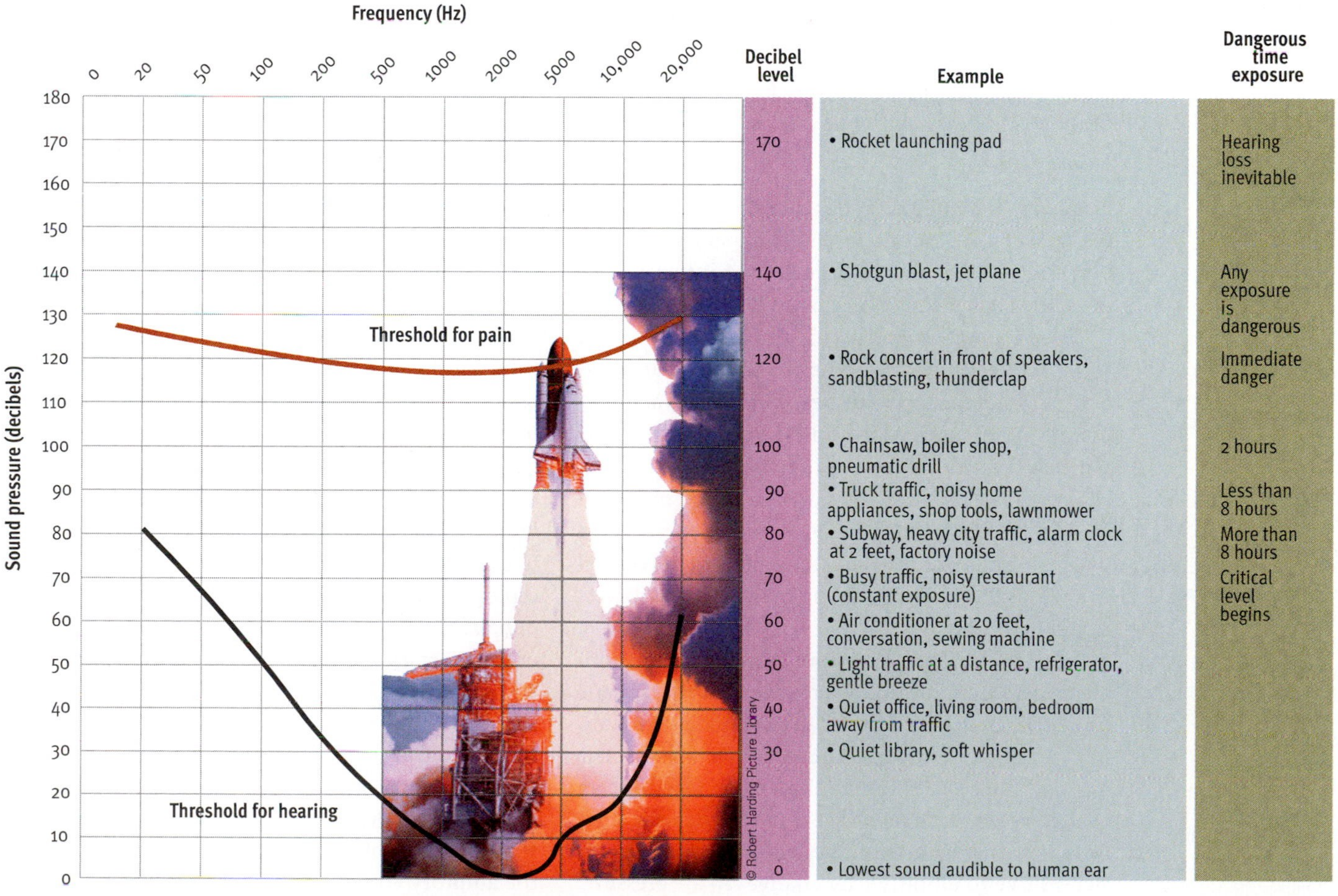

Figure 4.46

Sound pressure and auditory experience. The threshold for human hearing (graphed in green) is a function of both sound pressure (decibel level) and frequency. Human hearing is keenest for sounds at a frequency of about 2000 Hz; at other frequencies, higher decibel levels are needed to produce sounds people can detect. On the other hand, the human threshold for pain (graphed in red) is almost purely a function of decibel level. Some common sounds corresponding to various decibel levels are listed to the right, together with the amount of time at which exposure to higher levels becomes dangerous.

SOURCE: Decibel level examples from Atkinson, R. L., Atkinson, R. C., Smith, E. F., & Hilgard, E. R. (1987). *Introduction to Psychology*. San Diego: Harcourt. Reprinted by permission of Wadsworth Publishing.

Frequency (Hz)

0   20   50   100   200   500   1000   2000   5000   10,000   20,000

Sound pressure (decibels)

Threshold for pain

Threshold for hearing

© Robert Harding Picture Library

Decibel level	Example	Dangerous time exposure
170	• Rocket launching pad	Hearing loss inevitable
140	• Shotgun blast, jet plane	Any exposure is dangerous
120	• Rock concert in front of speakers, sandblasting, thunderclap	Immediate danger
100	• Chainsaw, boiler shop, pneumatic drill	2 hours
90	• Truck traffic, noisy home appliances, shop tools, lawnmower	Less than 8 hours
80	• Subway, heavy city traffic, alarm clock at 2 feet, factory noise	More than 8 hours
70	• Busy traffic, noisy restaurant (constant exposure)	Critical level begins
60	• Air conditioner at 20 feet, conversation, sewing machine	
50	• Light traffic at a distance, refrigerator, gentle breeze	
40	• Quiet office, living room, bedroom away from traffic	
30	• Quiet library, soft whisper	
0	• Lowest sound audible to human ear	

Figure 4.47

The human ear. Converting sound pressure to information processed by the nervous system involves a complex relay of stimuli. Waves of air pressure create vibrations in the eardrum, which in turn cause oscillations in the tiny bones in the inner ear (the hammer, anvil, and stirrup). As they are relayed from one bone to the next, the oscillations are magnified and then transformed into pressure waves moving through a liquid medium in the cochlea. These waves cause the basilar membrane to oscillate, stimulating the hair cells that are the actual auditory receptors (see Figure 4.48).

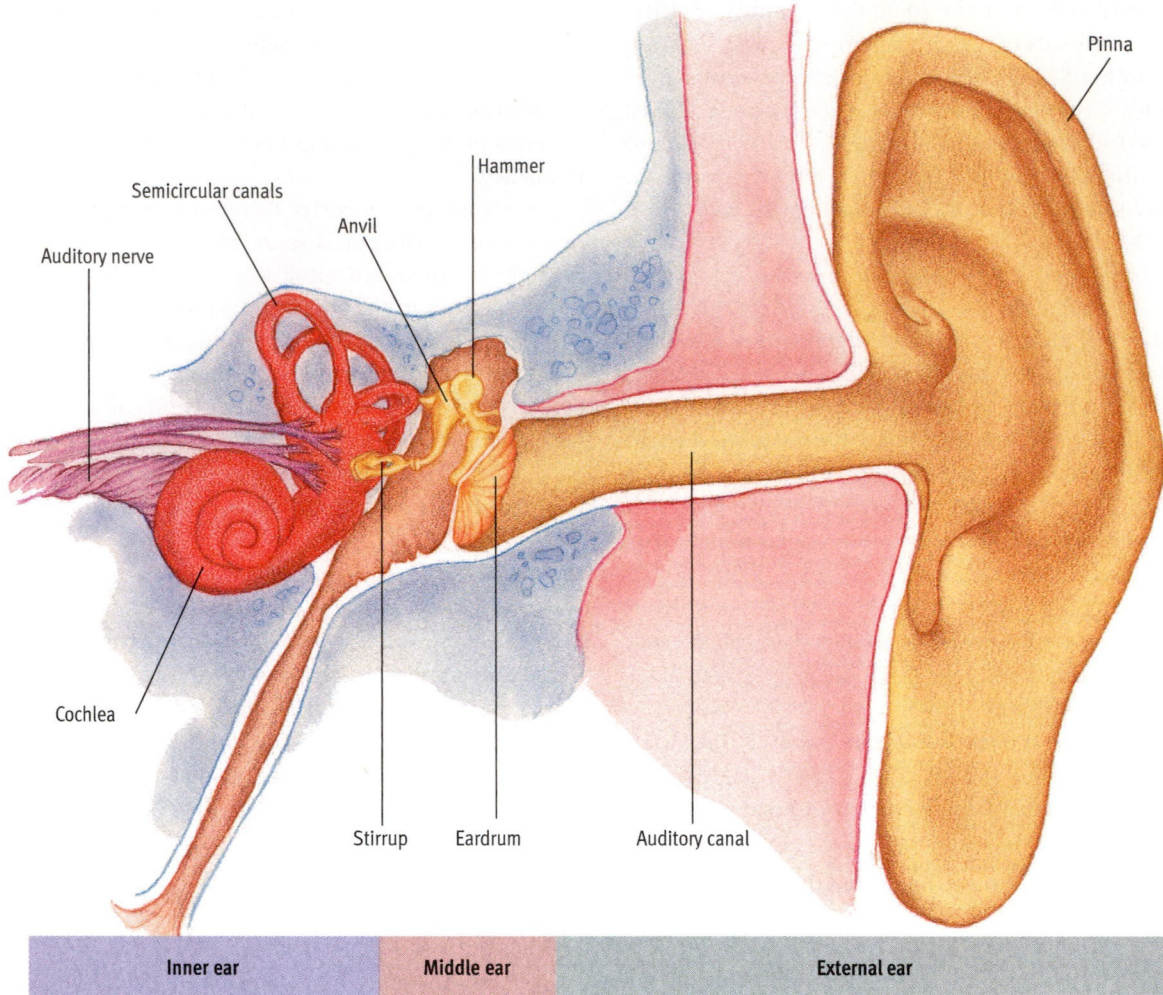

Semicircular canals / Anvil / Hammer / Pinna / Auditory nerve / Cochlea / Stirrup / Eardrum / Auditory canal

Inner ear | Middle ear | External ear

molecules. The middle ear depends on the *vibration of movable bones.* And the inner ear depends on *waves in a fluid,* which are finally converted into a stream of neural signals sent to the brain (Moore, 2001).

The *external ear* consists mainly of the *pinna,* a sound-collecting cone. When you cup your hand behind your ear to try to hear better, you are augmenting that cone. Many animals have large external ears that they can aim directly toward a sound source. However, humans can adjust their aim only crudely, by turning their heads. Sound waves collected by the pinna are funneled along the auditory canal toward the *eardrum,* a taut membrane that vibrates in response.

In the *middle ear,* the vibrations of the eardrum are transmitted inward by a mechanical chain made up of the three tiniest bones in your body (the hammer, anvil, and stirrup), known collectively as the *ossicles.* The ossicles form a three-stage lever system that converts relatively large movements with little force into smaller motions with greater force. The ossicles serve to amplify tiny changes in air pressure.

The *inner ear* consists largely of the *cochlea,* **a fluid-filled, coiled tunnel that contains the receptors for hearing.** The term *cochlea* comes from the Greek word for a spiral-shelled snail, which this chamber resembles (see Figure 4.47). Sound enters the cochlea through the *oval window,* which is vibrated by the ossicles. The ear's neural tissue, analogous to the retina in the eye, lies within the cochlea. This tissue sits on the basilar membrane that divides the cochlea into upper and lower chambers. **The *basilar membrane,* which runs the length of the spiraled cochlea, holds the auditory receptors.** The auditory receptors are called *hair cells* because of the tiny bundles of hairs that protrude from them. Waves in the fluid of the inner ear stimulate the hair cells. Like the rods and cones in the eye, the hair cells convert this physical stimulation into neural impulses that are sent to the brain (Hudspeth, 2000).

These signals are routed through the thalamus to the auditory cortex, which is located mostly in the temporal lobes of the brain. Studies demonstrate that the auditory cortex has specialized cells—similar to the feature detectors found in the visual cortex—that have special sensitivity to certain features of sound (Pickles, 1988). Evidence also suggests that the parallel processing of input seen in the visual system also occurs in the auditory pathways (Rouiller, 1997).

Auditory Perception: Theories of Hearing

Theories of hearing need to account for how sound waves are physiologically translated into the perceptions of pitch, loudness, and timbre. To date, most of the theorizing about hearing has focused on the perception of pitch, which is reasonably well understood. Researchers' understanding of loudness and timbre perception is primitive by comparison. Hence, we'll limit our coverage to theories of pitch perception.

Two theories have dominated the debate on pitch perception: *place theory* and *frequency theory.* You'll be able to follow the development of these theories more easily if you can imagine the spiraled cochlea unraveled, so that the basilar membrane becomes a long, thin sheet, lined with about 25,000 individual hair cells (see Figure 4.48).

Place Theory

Long ago, Hermann von Helmholtz (1863) proposed that specific sound frequencies vibrate specific portions of the basilar membrane, producing distinct pitches, just as plucking specific strings on a harp produces sounds of varied pitch. This model, called *place theory,* **holds that perception of pitch corresponds to the vibration of different portions, or places, along the basilar membrane.** Place theory assumes that hair cells at various locations respond independently and that different sets of hair cells are vibrated by different sound frequencies. The brain then detects the frequency of a tone according to which area along the basilar membrane is most active.

Frequency Theory

Other theorists in the 19th century proposed an alternative theory of pitch perception, called frequency theory (Rutherford, 1886). **Frequency theory holds that perception of pitch corresponds to the rate, or frequency, at which the entire basilar membrane vibrates.** This theory views the basilar membrane as more like a drumhead than a harp. According to frequency theory, the whole membrane vibrates in unison in response to sounds. However, a particular sound frequency, say 3000 Hz, causes the basilar membrane to vibrate at a corresponding rate of 3000 times per second. The brain detects the frequency of a tone by the rate at which the auditory nerve fibers fire.

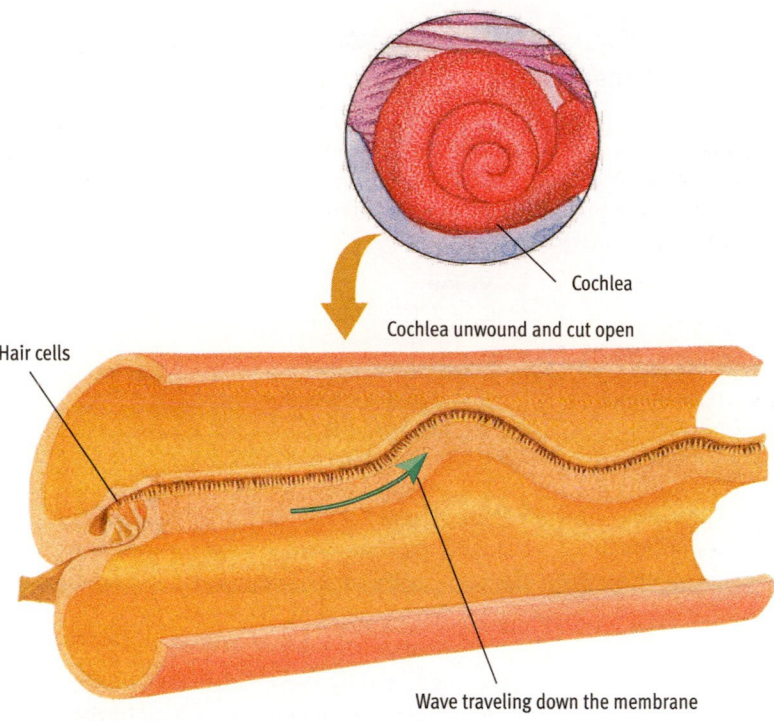

Cochlea

Cochlea unwound and cut open

Hair cells

Wave traveling down the membrane

Figure 4.48

The basilar membrane. This graphic shows how the cochlea might look if it were unwound and cut open to reveal the basilar membrane, which is covered with thousands of hair cells (the auditory receptors). Pressure waves in the fluid filling the cochlea cause oscillations to travel in waves down the basilar membrane, stimulating the hair cells to fire. Although the entire membrane vibrates, as predicted by frequency theory, the point along the membrane where the wave peaks depends on the frequency of the sound stimulus, as suggested by place theory.

Reconciling Place and Frequency Theories

The competition between these two theories is reminiscent of the dispute between the trichromatic and opponent process theories of color vision. As with that argument, the debate between place and frequency theories generated roughly a century of research. Although both theories proved to have some flaws, *both turned out to be valid in part.*

Helmholtz's place theory was basically on the mark except for one detail. The hair cells along the basilar membrane are not independent. They vibrate together, as suggested by frequency theory. The actual pattern of vibration, described in Nobel prize–winning research by Georg von Békésy (1947), is a traveling wave that moves along the basilar membrane. Place theory is correct, however, in that the wave peaks at a particular place, depending on the frequency of the sound wave.

Frequency theory was also found to be flawed when investigators learned that neurons are hard pressed to fire at a maximum rate of about 1000 impulses per second. How, then, can frequency theory account for the translation of 4000 Hz sound waves, which would require 4000 impulses per second? The

Stock Montage, Inc.

"The psychic activities, by which we arrive at the judgment that a certain object of a certain character exists before us at a certain place, are generally not conscious activities but unconscious ones. . . . It may be permissible to designate the psychic acts of ordinary perception as unconscious inferences."
HERMANN VON HELMHOLTZ

Comparing Vision and Hearing

Check your understanding of both vision and audition by comparing key aspects of sensation and perception in these senses. The dimensions of comparison are listed in the first column below. The second column lists the answers for the sense of vision. Fill in the answers for the sense of hearing in the third column. The answers can be found in Appendix A in the back of the book.

Dimension	Vision	Hearing
1. Stimulus	Light waves	
2. Elements of stimulus and related perceptions	Wavelength/hue Amplitude/brightness Purity/saturation	
3. Receptors	Rods and cones	
4. Location of receptors	Retina	
5. Main location of processing in brain	Occipital lobe, visual cortex	
6. Spatial aspect of perception	Depth perception	

generate volleys of up to 5000 impulses per second (Zwislocki, 1981).

Although the original theories had to be revised, the current thinking is that pitch perception depends on both place and frequency coding of vibrations along the basilar membrane (Goldstein, 1996). Sounds under 1000 Hz appear to be translated into pitch through frequency coding. For sounds between 1000 and 5000 Hz, pitch perception seems to depend on a combination of frequency and place coding. Sounds over 5000 Hz seem to be handled through place coding only. Again we find that theories that were pitted against each other for decades are complementary rather than contradictory.

Auditory Localization: Perceiving Sources of Sound

You're driving down a street when suddenly you hear a siren wailing in the distance. As the wail grows louder, you glance around, cocking your ear to the sound. Where is it coming from? Behind you? In front of you? From one side? This example illustrates a common perceptual task called *auditory localization*—locating the source of a sound in space. The process of recognizing where a sound is coming from is analogous to recognizing depth or distance in vision. Both processes involve spatial aspects of sensory input. The fact that human ears are set *apart* contributes to auditory localization, just as the separation of the eyes contributes to depth perception.

Many features of sounds can contribute to auditory localization, but two cues are particularly important: the intensity (loudness) and the timing of sounds arriving at each ear (Yost, 2001). For example, a sound source to one side of the head produces a greater intensity at the ear nearer to the sound. This difference is due partly to the loss of sound intensity with distance. Another factor at work is the "shadow," or partial sound barrier, cast by the head itself (see Figure 4.49). The intensity difference between the two ears is greatest when the sound source is well to one side. The human perceptual system uses this difference as a clue in localizing sounds. Because the path to the farther ear is longer, a sound takes longer to reach that ear. This fact means that sounds can be localized by comparing the timing of their arrival at each ear. Such comparison of the timing of sounds is remarkably sensitive. People can detect timing differences as small as 1/100,000 of a second (Durlach & Colburn, 1978).

answer, suggested by Wever and Bray (1937), is that groups of hair cells operate according to the volley principle. **The *volley principle* holds that groups of auditory nerve fibers fire neural impulses in rapid succession, creating volleys of impulses.** These volleys exceed the 1000-per-second limit. Studies suggest that auditory nerves can team up like this to

Figure 4.49

Cues in auditory localization. A sound coming from the left reaches the left ear sooner than the right. When the sound reaches the right ear, it is also less intense because it has traveled a greater distance and because it is in the sound shadow produced by the listener's head. These cues are used to localize the sources of sound in space.

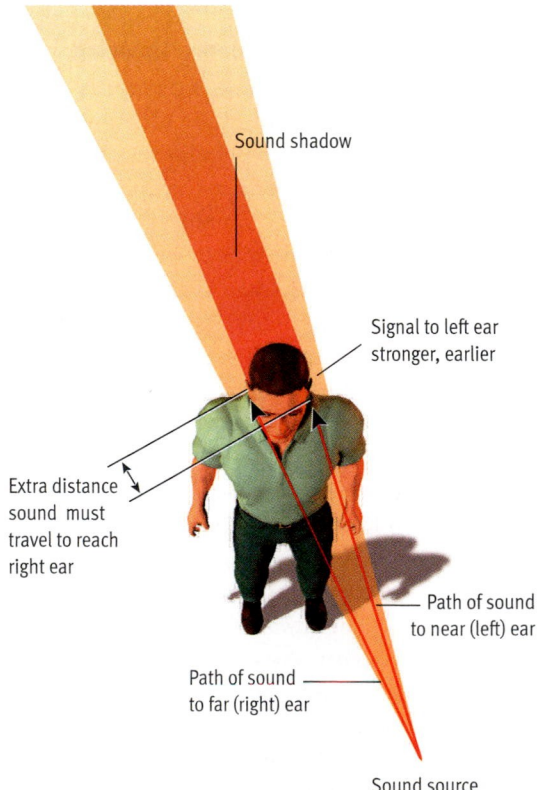

Sound shadow

Signal to left ear stronger, earlier

Extra distance sound must travel to reach right ear

Path of sound to near (left) ear

Path of sound to far (right) ear

Sound source

- Sound varies in terms of wavelength (frequency), amplitude, and purity. These properties affect mainly perceptions of pitch, loudness, and timbre, respectively. The human ear is most sensitive to sounds around 2000 Hz. Even brief exposure to sounds over 120 decibels can be painful and damaging.

- Sound is transmitted through the external ear via air conduction to the middle ear, where sound waves are translated into the vibration of tiny bones called ossicles. In the inner ear, fluid conduction vibrates hair cells along the basilar membrane in the cochlea. These hair cells are the receptors for hearing.

- Place theory proposed that pitch perception depends on where vibrations occur along the basilar membrane. Frequency theory countered with the idea that pitch perception depends on the rate at which the basilar membrane vibrates. Modern evidence suggests that these theories are complementary rather than incompatible.

- Auditory localization involves locating the source of a sound in space. People pinpoint where sounds have come from by comparing interear differences in the intensity and timing of sounds.

Our Chemical Senses: Taste and Smell

Psychologists have devoted most of their attention to the visual and auditory systems. Although less is known about the chemical senses, taste and smell also play a critical role in people's experience of the world. Let's take a brief look at what psychologists have learned about the *gustatory system*—the sensory system for taste—and its close cousin, the *olfactory system*—the sensory system for smell.

Taste: The Gustatory System

True wine lovers go through an elaborate series of steps when they are served a good bottle of wine. Typically, they begin by drinking a little water to cleanse their palate. Then they sniff the cork from the wine bottle, swirl a small amount of the wine around in a glass, and sniff the odor emerging from the glass. Finally, they take a sip of the wine, rolling it around in their mouth for a short time before swallowing it. At last they are ready to confer their approval or disapproval. Is all this activity really a meaningful way to put the wine to a sensitive test? Or is it just a harmless ritual passed on through tradition? You'll find out in this section.

The physical stimuli for the sense of taste are chemical substances that are soluble (dissolvable in water). The gustatory receptors are clusters of taste cells found in the *taste buds* that line the trenches around tiny bumps on the tongue (see Figure 4.50 on the next page). When these cells absorb chemicals dissolved in saliva, they trigger neural impulses that are routed through the thalamus to the cortex. Interestingly, taste cells have a short life, spanning only about ten days, and they are constantly being replaced. New cells are born at the edge of the taste bud and migrate inward to die at the center.

It's generally (but not universally) agreed that there are four *primary tastes:* sweet, sour, bitter, and salty (Buck, 2000). Sensitivity to these tastes is distributed somewhat unevenly across the tongue, but the variations in sensitivity are quite small and highly complicated (Bartoshuk, 1993b; see Figure 4.50). Although most taste cells respond to more than one of the primary tastes, they typically respond best to one. Perceptions of taste quality appear to depend on complex *patterns* of neural activity initiated by taste receptors (Erickson, DiLorenzo, & Woodbury, 1994).

Some basic taste preferences appear to be innate and to be automatically regulated by physiological mechanisms. In humans, for instance, newborn infants react positively to sweet tastes and negatively to strong concentrations of bitter, salty, or sour tastes (Lipsitt & Behl, 1990). To some extent, these innate taste preferences are flexible, changing to accommodate the body's nutritional needs (Scott, 1990).

Although some basic aspects of taste perception may be innate, taste preferences are largely learned and heavily influenced by social processes (Rozin, 1990). Most parents are aware of this fact and intentionally try—with varied success—to mold their children's taste preferences early in life (Casey & Rozin, 1989). This extensive social influence contributes greatly to the striking ethnic and cultural disparities found in taste preferences (Kittler & Sucher, 1998). Foods that are a source of disgust in Western cultures—such as worms, fish eyes, and blood—may be delicacies in other cultures (see Figure 4.51 on the next page). Indeed, Rozin (1990) asserts that feces may be the only universal source of taste-related disgust in humans. To a large degree, variations in taste preferences depend on what one has been exposed to (Capaldi & VandenBos, 1991; Zellner, 1991). Exposure to various foods varies along ethnic lines because different cultures have different traditions in food preparation, different agricultural resources, different climates to work with, and so forth.

PREVIEW QUESTIONS
- Where are the receptors for taste?
- How many basic tastes are there?
- How do people vary in taste sensitivity?
- Where are the receptors for smell?
- Are there primary odors?
- How well do people perform when asked to name odors?

Figure **4.50**

The tongue and taste. **(a)** Taste buds line the trenches around tiny bumps on the tongue called papillae (see the inset). **(b)** There are three types of papillae, which are distributed on the tongue as shown here. The taste buds found in each type of papillae show slightly different sensitivities to the four basic tastes, as mapped out in the graph at the top. Thus, sensitivity to the primary tastes varies across the tongue, but these variations are small, and all four primary tastes can be detected wherever there are taste receptors.

SOURCE: Adapted from Bartoshuk, L. M. (1993). Genetic and pathological taste variation: What can we learn from animal models and human disease? In D. Chadwick, J. Marsh, & J. Goode (Eds.), *The molecular basis of smell and taste transduction* (pp. 251–267). New York: Wiley.

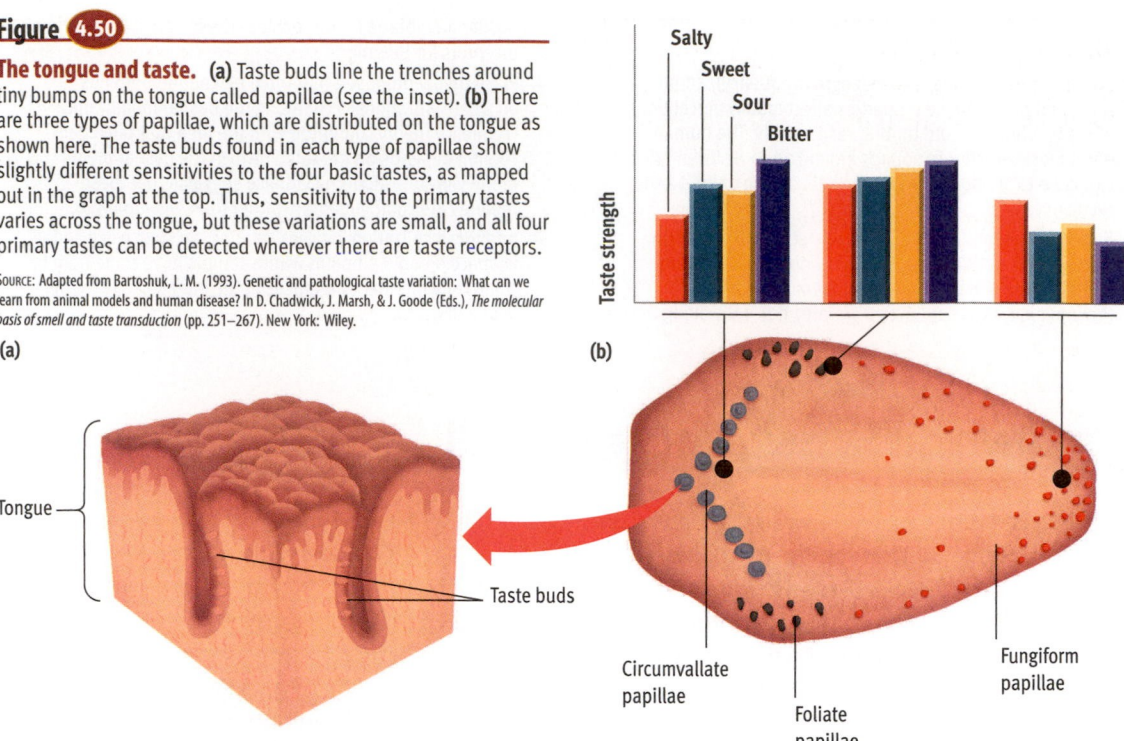

(a)

Tongue

Taste buds

(b)

Circumvallate papillae

Foliate papillae

Fungiform papillae

Research by Linda Bartoshuk and others reveals that people vary considerably in their sensitivity to certain tastes. These differences depend in part on the density of taste buds on the tongue, which appears to be a matter of genetic inheritance (Bartoshuk, 1993a). People characterized as *supertasters* tend to have about four times as many taste buds per square centimeter as people at the other end of the spectrum, who are called *nontasters* (Miller & Reedy, 1990). Women are more likely to be supertasters than men are (Bartoshuk, Duffy, & Miller, 1994). Supertasters and nontasters respond similarly to many foods, but supertasters are much more sensitive to certain sweet and bitter substances. For example, super-

Figure **4.51**

Culture and taste preferences. Taste preferences are largely learned, and they vary dramatically from one society to the next, as these examples demonstrate.

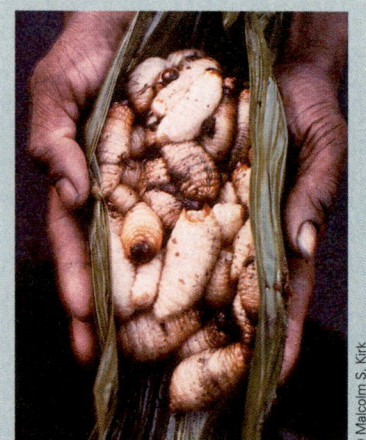

Grubs. For most North Americans, the thought of eating a worm would be totally unthinkable. For the Asmat of New Guinea, however, a favorite delicacy is the plump, white, 2-inch larva or beetle grub.

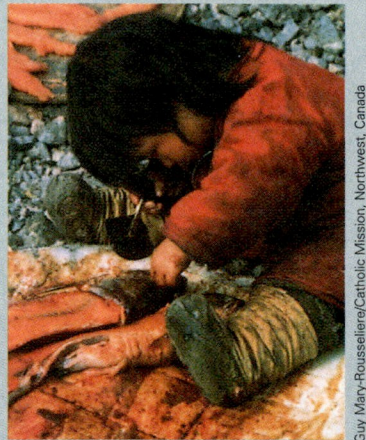

Fish eyes. For some Eskimo children, raw fish eyes are like candy. Here you see a young girl using the Eskimo's all-purpose knife to gouge out the eye of an already-filleted Arctic fish.

Blood. Several tribes in East Africa supplement their diet with fresh blood that is sometimes mixed with milk. They obtain the blood by puncturing a cow's jugular vein with a sharp arrow. The blood-milk drink provides a rich source of protein and iron.

tasters react far more strongly to the chemical (capsaicin) in hot peppers (Tepper & Nurse, 1997). Some psychologists speculate that the gender gap in this trait may have evolutionary significance. Over the course of evolution, women have generally been more involved than men in feeding children. Increased reactivity to sweet and bitter tastes would have been adaptive in that it would have made women more sensitive to the relatively scarce high-caloric foods (which often taste sweet) needed for survival and to the toxic substances (which often taste bitter) that hunters and gatherers needed to avoid.

So far, we've been discussing taste, but what we are really interested in is the *perception of flavor.* Odor contributes greatly to flavor (Lawless, 2001). Although taste and smell are distinct sensory systems, they interact extensively. The ability to identify flavors declines noticeably when odor cues are absent. You might have noticed this interaction when you ate a favorite meal while enduring a severe head cold. The food probably tasted bland, because your stuffy nose impaired your sense of smell.

Now that we've explored the dynamics of taste, we can return to our question about the value of the wine-tasting ritual. This elaborate ritual is indeed an authentic way to put wine to a sensitive test. The aftereffects associated with sensory adaptation make it wise to cleanse one's palate before tasting the wine. Sniffing the cork, and the wine in the glass, is important because odor is a major determinant of flavor. Swirling the wine in the glass helps release the wine's odor. And rolling the wine around in your mouth is especially critical, because it distributes the wine over the full diversity of taste cells. It also forces the wine's odor up into the nasal passages. Thus, each action in this age-old ritual makes a meaningful contribution to the tasting.

Smell: The Olfactory System

In many ways, the sense of smell is much like the sense of taste. The physical stimuli are chemical substances—volatile ones that can evaporate and be carried in the air. These chemical stimuli are dissolved in fluid—specifically, the mucus in the nose. The receptors for smell are *olfactory cilia,* hairlike structures located in the upper portion of the nasal passages (see Figure 4.52). They resemble taste cells in that they have a short life (30–60 days) and are constantly being replaced (Buck, 2000). Olfactory receptors have axons that synapse with cells in the olfactory bulb and then are routed directly to various areas in the cortex. This arrangement is unique. Smell is the only sensory system in which incoming information is not routed through the thalamus before it projects to the cortex.

Odors cannot be classified as neatly as tastes, since efforts to identify primary odors have proven unsatisfactory (Doty, 1991). If primary odors exist, there must be a fairly large number of them. Most olfactory receptors respond to a wide range of odors (Doty, 2001). Hence, the perception of various odors probably depends on a great many types of receptors that are uniquely responsive to specific chemical structures (Bartoshuk & Beauchamp, 1994). Like the other senses, the sense of smell shows sensory adaptation. The perceived strength of an odor usually fades to less than half its original strength within about 4 minutes (Cain, 1988).

Humans can distinguish among about 10,000 different odors (Axel, 1995). However, when people are asked to identify the sources of specific odors (such as smoke or soap), their performance is rather mediocre. For some unknown reason, people have a hard time attaching names to odors (Cowart & Rawson,

"*Good and bad are so intimately associated with taste and smell that we have special words for the experiences (e.g., repugnant, foul). The immediacy of the pleasure makes it seem absolute and thus inborn. This turns out to be true for taste but not for smell.*"
LINDA BARTOSHUK

Figure 4.52

The olfactory system. Odor molecules travel through the nasal passages and stimulate olfactory cilia. An enlargement of these hairlike olfactory receptors is shown in the inset. The olfactory nerves transmit neural impulses through the olfactory bulb to the brain.

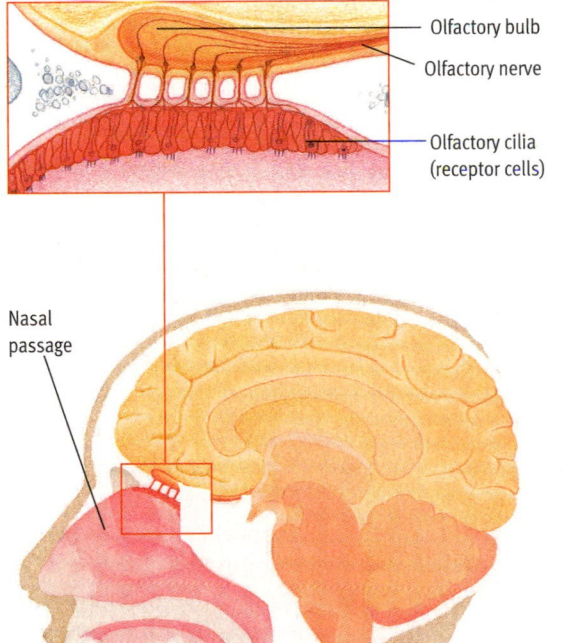

Olfactory bulb

Olfactory nerve

Olfactory cilia (receptor cells)

Nasal passage

Web Link 4.8

Seeing, Hearing, and Smelling the World
Hosted by the Howard Hughes Medical Institute, this site provides a graphically attractive review of what scientific research has discovered about human sensory systems, with suggestions about where research will be moving in the future.

2001). Gender differences have been found in the ability to identify odors, as females tend to be somewhat more accurate than males on odor recognition tasks (de Wijk, Schab, & Cain, 1995).

REVIEW OF KEY POINTS

● The taste buds are sensitive to four basic tastes: sweet, sour, bitter, and salty. Sensitivity to these tastes is distributed unevenly across the tongue, but the variations are small.

● Taste preferences are largely learned and are heavily influenced by one's cultural background. The perception of flavor is influenced greatly by the odor of food.

● Like taste, smell is a chemical sense. Chemical stimuli activate receptors, called olfactory cilia, that line the nasal passages. Most of these receptors respond to more than one odor.

Our Sense of Touch: Sensory Systems in the Skin

PREVIEW QUESTIONS

● How are tactile data routed to the brain?

● How are the two pathways for pain different?

● What does a useful theory of pain perception need to explain?

● How does the physiological evidence relate to gate-control theory?

If there is any sense that people trust almost as much as sight, it is the sense of touch. Yet, like all the senses, touch involves converting the sensation of physical stimuli into a psychological experience—and it can be fooled.

The physical stimuli for touch are mechanical, thermal, and chemical energy that impinge on the skin. These stimuli can produce perceptions of tactile stimulation (the pressure of touch against the skin), warmth, cold, and pain. The human skin is saturated with at least six types of sensory receptors. To some degree, these different types of receptors are specialized for different functions, such as the registration of pressure, heat, cold, and so forth. However, these distinctions are not as clear as researchers had originally expected (Sinclair, 1981).

Feeling Pressure

If you've been to a mosquito-infested picnic lately, you'll appreciate the need to quickly know where tactile stimulation is coming from. The sense of touch is set up to meet this need for tactile localization with admirable precision and efficiency. Cells in the nervous system that respond to touch are sensitive to specific patches of skin. These skin patches, which vary considerably in size, are the functional equivalents of *receptive fields* in vision. Like visual receptive fields, they often involve a center-surround arrangement (see Figure 4.53). Thus, stimuli falling in the center produce the opposite effect of stimuli falling in the surrounding area (Kandel & Jessell, 1991). If a stimulus is applied continuously to a specific spot on the skin, the perception of pressure gradually fades. Hence, sensory adaptation occurs in the perception of touch, as it does in other sensory systems.

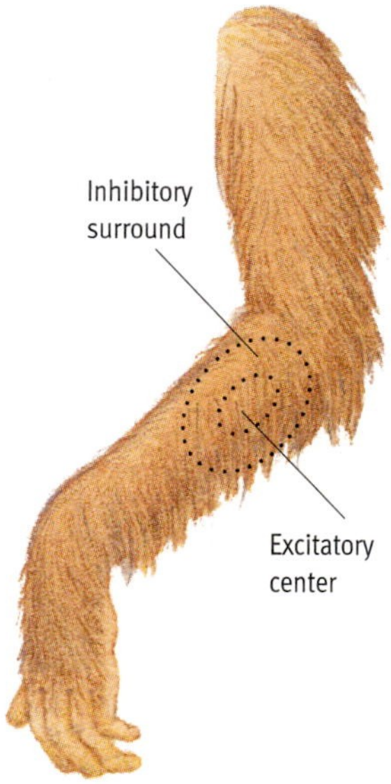

The nerve fibers that carry incoming information about tactile stimulation are routed through the spinal cord to the brainstem. There, the fibers from each side of the body cross over mostly to the opposite side of the brain. The tactile pathway then projects through the thalamus and onto the *somatosensory cortex* in the brain's parietal lobe. Some cells in the somatosensory cortex function like the *feature detectors* discovered in vision (Gardner & Kandel, 2000). They respond to specific features of touch, such as a movement across the skin in a particular direction.

Feeling Pain

As unpleasant as pain is, the sensation of pain is crucial to survival. Pain is a marvelous warning system. It tells people when they should stop shoveling snow, or it lets them know that they have a pinched nerve that requires treatment. However, chronic pain is a frustrating, demoralizing affliction that affects over 50 million people in American society, at a cost of more than $70 billion annually (Turk, 1994). Thus, there are pressing practical reasons for psychologists' keen interest in the perception of pain.

Pathways to the Brain

The receptors for pain are mostly free nerve endings in the skin. Pain messages are transmitted to the brain via two types of pathways that pass through different areas in the thalamus (Willis, 1985). One is a *fast pathway* that registers localized pain and relays it to the cortex in a fraction of a second. This is the system that hits you with sharp pain when you first cut your finger. The second system uses a *slow pathway* that lags a second or two behind the fast system. This pathway (which also carries information about temperature) conveys the less localized, longer-lasting, aching or burning pain that comes after the initial injury. The slow pathway depends on thin, unmyeli-

Figure 4.53

Receptive field for touch.
A receptive field for touch is an area on the skin surface that, when stimulated, affects the firing of a cell that responds to pressure on the skin. Shown here is a center-surround receptive field for a cell in the thalamus of a monkey.

Inhibitory surround

Excitatory center

nated neurons called *C fibers,* whereas the fast pathway is mediated by thicker, myelinated neurons called *A-delta fibers* (see Figure 4.54).

Puzzles in Pain Perception

As with other perceptions, pain is not an automatic result of certain types of stimulation. The perception of pain can be influenced greatly by expectations, personality, mood, and other factors involving higher mental processes (Rollman, 1992; Stalling, 1992). The subjective nature of pain is illustrated by placebo effects. As we saw in Chapter 2, many people suffering from pain report relief when given a placebo—an inert "sugar pill" that is presented to them as if it were a painkilling drug (Wall, 1993).

Further evidence regarding the subjective quality of pain has come from studies that have found ethnic and cultural differences in the pain associated with childbirth (Jordan, 1983) and the experience of chronic pain (Bates, Edwards, & Anderson, 1993). According to Melzack and Wall (1982), culture does not affect the process of pain perception so much as the willingness to tolerate certain types of pain, a conclusion echoed by Zatzick and Dimsdale (1990).

The psychological element in pain perception becomes clear when something distracts your attention from pain and the hurting temporarily disappears. For example, imagine that you've just hit your thumb with a hammer and it's throbbing with pain. Suddenly, your child cries out that there's a fire in the laundry room. As you race to deal with this emergency, you forget all about the pain in your thumb.

As you can see, then, tissue damage that sends pain impulses on their way to the brain doesn't necessarily result in the experience of pain. Cognitive and emotional processes that unfold in higher brain centers can somehow block pain signals coming from peripheral receptors. Thus, any useful explantion of pain perception must be able to answer a critical question: How does the central nervous system block incoming pain signals?

In an influential effort to answer this question, Ronald Melzack and Patrick Wall (1965) devised the gate-control theory of pain. *Gate-control theory* **holds that incoming pain sensations must pass through a "gate" in the spinal cord that can be closed, thus blocking ascending pain signals.** The gate in this model is not an anatomical structure but a pattern of neural activity that inhibits incoming pain signals. Melzack and Wall suggested that this imaginary gate

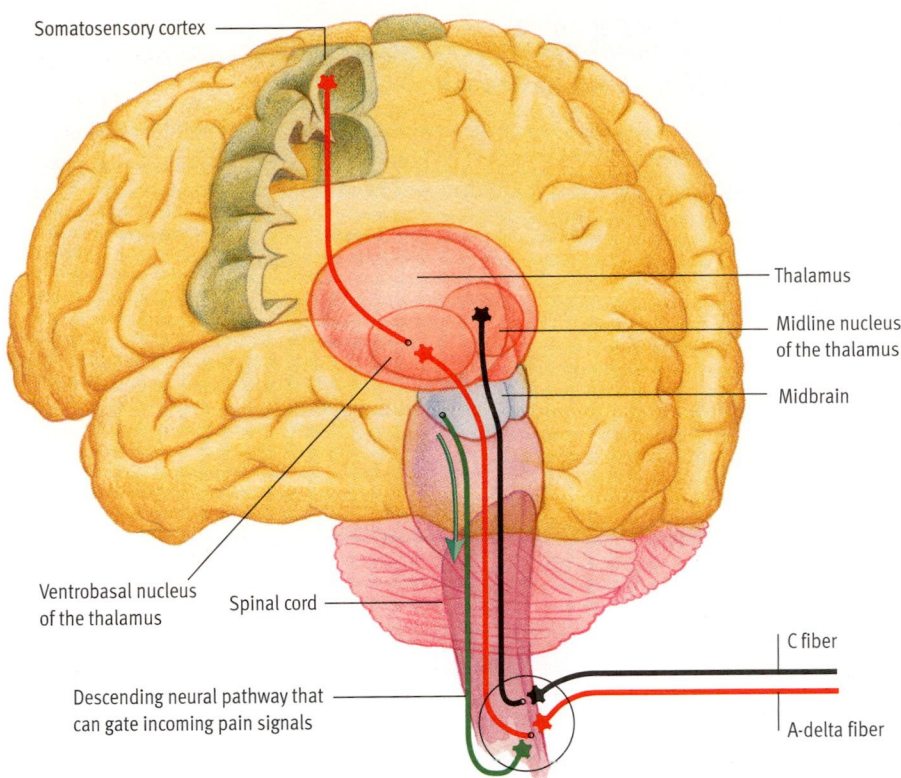

Figure 4.54

The two pathways for pain signals. Pain signals are sent from receptors to the brain along the two pathways depicted here. The fast pathway, shown in red, and the slow pathway, shown in black, depend on different types of nerve fibers and are routed through different parts of the thalamus. The gate control mechanism posited by Melzack and Wall (1965) apparently depends on descending signals originating in an area of the midbrain (the pathway shown in green).

Labels in figure: Somatosensory cortex, Thalamus, Midline nucleus of the thalamus, Midbrain, Ventrobasal nucleus of the thalamus, Spinal cord, C fiber, A-delta fiber, Descending neural pathway that can gate incoming pain signals

can be closed by signals from peripheral receptors or by signals from the brain. They theorized that the latter mechanism can help explain how factors such as attention and expectations can shut off pain signals. As a whole, research suggests that the concept of a gating mechanism for pain has merit (Craig & Rollman, 1999). However, relatively little support has been found for the neural circuitry originally hypothesized by Melzack and Wall in the 1960s. Other neural mechanisms, discovered after gate-control theory was proposed, appear to be responsible for blocking the perception of pain.

One of these discoveries was the identification of endorphins. As discussed in Chapter 3, *endorphins* are the body's own natural morphinelike painkillers. Studies suggest that the release of endorphins underlies the pain-relieving effects of placebo drugs (Fields & Levine, 1984). The analgesic effects that can be achieved through the ancient Chinese art of acupuncture may likewise involve endorphins (Murray, 1995). Endorphins are widely distributed in the central nervous system. Scientists are still working out the details of how they suppress pain.

The other discovery involved the identification of a descending neural pathway that mediates the suppression of pain (Basbaum & Jessell, 2000). This pathway appears to originate in an area of the midbrain

Comparing Taste, Smell, and Touch

Check your understanding of taste, smell, and touch by comparing these sensory systems on the dimensions listed in the first column below. A few answers are supplied; see whether you can fill in the rest. The answers can be found in Appendix A.

Dimension	Taste	Smell	Touch
1. Stimulus	_____	Volatile chemicals in the air	_____
2. Receptors	_____	_____	Many (at least 6) types
3. Location of receptors	_____	Upper areas of nasal passages	_____
4. Basic elements of perception	Sweet, sour, salty, bitter	_____	_____

called the *periaqueductal gray (PAG)*. Neural activity in this pathway is probably initiated by endorphins acting on PAG neurons, which eventually trigger impulses sent down neural circuits that mostly release serotonin. These circuits synapse in the spinal cord, where they appear to release more endorphins, thus inhibiting the activity of neurons that would normally transmit incoming pain impulses to the brain (see Figure 4.54). The painkilling effects of morphine appear to be at least partly attributable to activity in this descending pathway, as cutting the fibers in this pathway reduces the analgesic effects of morphine (Jessell & Kelly, 1991). In contrast, activation of this pathway by electrical stimulation of the brain can produce an analgesic effect. Clearly, this pathway plays a central role in gating incoming pain signals.

Our Other Senses

PREVIEW QUESTIONS
- What does the kinesthetic system monitor?
- What does the vestibular system do?
- Where is the vestibular system located?

We have discussed the dynamics of sensation and perception in five sensory domains—vision, hearing, taste, smell, and touch. Since it is widely known that humans have five senses, that should wrap up our coverage, right? Wrong! People have still other sensory systems: the kinesthetic system (which monitors positions of the body) and the vestibular system (sense of balance).

The Kinesthetic System

The *kinesthetic system* monitors the positions of the various parts of the body. To some extent, you know where your limbs are because you commanded the muscles that put them there. Nonetheless, the kinesthetic system allows you to double-check these locations. Where are the receptors for your kinesthetic sense? Some reside in the joints, indicating how much they are bending. Others reside within the muscles, registering their tautness, or extension. Most kinesthetic stimulation is transmitted to the brain along the same pathway as tactile stimulation. However, the two types of information are kept separate (Vierck, 1978).

The Vestibular System

When you're jolting along in a bus, the world outside the bus window doesn't seem to jump about as your head bounces up and down. Yet a movie taken with a camera fastened to the bus would show a bouncing world. How are you and the camera dif-

ferent? Unlike the camera, you are equipped with **a *vestibular system,* which responds to gravity and keeps you informed of your body's location in space.** The vestibular system provides the sense of balance, or equilibrium, compensating for changes in the body's position.

The vestibular system shares space in the inner ear with the auditory system. The *semicircular canals* (consult Figure 4.47 once again) make up the largest part of the vestibular system. They look like three inner tubes joined at the base. Any rotational motion of the head is uniquely represented by a combination of fluid flows in the semicircular canals (Kelly, 1991). These shifts in fluid are detected by hair cells similar to those found along the basilar membrane in the cochlea (Goldberg & Hudspeth, 2000). Your perceptual system integrates the vestibular input about your body's position with information from other senses. After all, you can see where you are and you know where you've instructed your muscles to take you.

This integration of sensory input raises a point that merits emphasis as we close our tour of the human sensory systems. Although we have discussed the various sensory domains separately, it's important to remember that all the senses send signals to the same brain, where the information is pooled. We have already encountered examples of sensory integration. For example, it's at work when the sight and smell of food influence taste. *Sensory integration is the norm in perceptual experience.* For instance, when you sit around a campfire, you *see* it blazing, you *hear* it crackling, you *smell* it burning, and you feel the *touch* of its warmth. If you cook something over it, you may even *taste* it. Thus, perception involves building a unified model of the world out of integrated input from all the senses (Stein, Wallace, & Stanford, 2001).

Putting It in Perspective

In this chapter, three of our unifying themes stand out in sharp relief. Let's discuss the value of theoretical diversity first. Contradictory theories about behavior can be disconcerting and frustrating for theorists, researchers, teachers, and students alike. Yet this chapter provides two dramatic demonstrations of how theoretical diversity can lead to progress in the long run. For decades, the trichromatic and opponent process theories of color vision and the place and frequency theories of pitch perception were viewed as fundamentally incompatible. As you know, in each case the evidence eventually revealed that both theories were needed to fully explain the sensory processes that each sought to explain individually. If it hadn't been for these theoretical debates, current understanding of color vision and pitch perception might be far more primitive, as the understanding of timbre still is.

Our coverage of sensation and perception should also have enhanced your appreciation of why human experience of the world is highly subjective. As ambiguous figures and optical illusions clearly show, there is no one-to-one correspondence between sensory input and perceived experience of the world. Perception is an active process in which people organize and interpret the information received by the senses. These interpretations are shaped by a host of factors, including the environmental context and perceptual sets. Small wonder, then, that people often perceive the same event in very different ways.

Finally, this chapter provided numerous examples of how cultural factors can shape behavior—in an area of research where one might expect to find little cultural influence. Most people are not surprised to learn that there are cultural differences in attitudes, values, social behavior, and development. But perception is widely viewed as a basic, universal process that should be invariant across cultures. In most respects it is, as the similarities among cultural groups in perception far outweigh the differences. Nonetheless, we saw cultural variations in depth perception, susceptibility to illusions, taste preferences, and pain tolerance. Thus, even a fundamental, heavily physiological process such as perception can be modified to some degree by one's cultural background.

The following Personal Application demonstrates the subjectivity of perception once again. It focuses on how painters have learned to use the principles of visual perception to achieve a variety of artistic goals.

PREVIEW QUESTIONS

- How did this chapter demonstrate the value of theoretical diversity?
- How did this chapter clarify the subjective nature of human experience?
- How did this chapter illustrate the importance of cultural influences?

REVIEW OF KEY POINTS

- Sensory receptors in the skin respond to pressure, temperature, and pain. Tactile localization depends on receptive fields similar to those seen for vision. Some cells in the somatosensory cortex appear to function like feature detectors.

- Pain signals are sent to the brain along two pathways that are characterized as fast and slow. The perception of pain is highly subjective and may be influenced by mood, attention, and culture. Gate-control theory holds that incoming pain signals can be blocked in the spinal cord. Endorphins and a descending neural pathway appear responsible for the suppression of pain by the central nervous system.

- The kinesthetic system monitors the position of various body parts. Kinesthetic receptors, located in the joints and muscles, send signals to the brain along the same pathway as tactile stimulation. The sense of balance depends primarily on activity in the semicircular canals in the vestibular system.

- This chapter underscored three of our unifying themes: the value of theoretical diversity, the subjective nature of human experience, and the influence of culture on behavior.

PERSONAL APPLICATION

Appreciating Art and Illusion

Answer the following multiple-choice question:

Artistic works such as paintings:
_____ **a** render an accurate picture of reality.
_____ **b** create an illusion of reality.
_____ **c** provide an interpretation of reality.
_____ **d** make us think about the nature of reality.
_____ **e** all of the above.

The answer to this question is (e), "all of the above." Historically, artists have pursued many and varied purposes, including each of those listed in the question (Goldstein, 2001). To realize their goals, they have had to use a number of principles of perception—sometimes quite deliberately, and sometimes not. Let's use the example of painting to explore the role of perceptual principles in art and illusion.

The goal of most early painters was to produce a believable picture of reality. This goal immediately created a problem familiar to most of us who have attempted to draw realistic pictures: The real world is three–dimensional, but a canvas or a sheet of paper is flat. Paradoxically, then, painters who set out to re-create reality have to do so by creating an *illusion* of three–dimensional reality.

Prior to the Renaissance, efforts to create a convincing illusion of reality were relatively awkward by modern standards. Why? Because artists did not understand how to use the full range of depth cues. This is apparent in Figure 4.55, a religious scene painted around 1300. The painting clearly lacks a sense of depth. The people seem paper–thin. They have no real position in space.

Although earlier artists made some use of depth cues, Renaissance artists manipulated the full range of pictorial depth cues and really harnessed the crucial cue of linear perspective (Solso, 1994). Figure 4.56

Figure 4.55

Master of the Arrest of Christ (detail, central part) by S. Francesco, Assisi, Italy (circa 1300). Notice how the paucity of depth cues makes the painting seem flat and unrealistic.

Scala/Art Resource, New York

dramatizes the resulting transition in art. It shows a scene depicted by Gentile and Giovanni Bellini, Italian Renaissance painters. It seems much more realistic and lifelike than the painting in Figure 4.55. Notice how the buildings on the sides converge to make use of linear perspective. Additionally, distant objects are smaller than nearby ones, an application of relative size. This painting also uses height in plane, light and shadow, and interposition. By taking fuller advantage of pictorial depth cues, Renaissance artists enhanced the illusion of reality in paintings.

In the centuries since the Renaissance, painters have adopted a number of viewpoints about the portrayal of reality. For instance, the Impressionists of the 19th century did not want to re-create the photographic "reality" of a scene. They set out to interpret a viewer's fleeting perception or *impression* of reality. To accomplish this end, they worked with color in unprecedented ways.

Consider for instance, Claude Monet, a French Impressionist who began to work with separate daubs of pure, bright colors that blurred together to create an alternating perceptual experience. If you view his paintings up close, you see only a shimmering mass of color. When you step back, however, the adjacent colors begin to blend, and forms begin to take shape, as you can see in Figure 4.57. Monet achieved this duality through careful use of color mixing and by working systematically with complementary colors.

Similar methods were used even more precisely and systematically by Georges Seurat, a French artist who used a technique called *pointillism*. Seurat carefully studied what scientists knew about the composi-

Figure 4.56

Brera Predica di S. Marco Pinacoteca **by Gentile and Giovanni Bellini (circa 1480).** In this painting, the Italian Renaissance artists use a number of depth cues—including linear perspective, relative size, height in plane, light and shadow, and interposition—to enhance the illusion of three-dimensional reality.

Figure 4.57

Claude Monet's *Palazzo da Mula, Venice* **(1908).** The French Impressionist Monet often used complementary colors to achieve his visual effects.

Monet, Claude, *Palazzo da Mula, Venice* (1908). Photo by Richard Carafelli, Chester Dale Collection, © Board of Trustees, National Gallery of Art.

tion of color in the 1880s, then applied this knowledge in a calculated, laboratory-like manner. Indeed, critics in his era dubbed him the "little chemist." Seurat constructed his paintings out of tiny dots of pure, intense colors. He used additive color mixing, a departure from the norm in painting, which usually depends on subtractive mixing of pigments. A famous result of Seurat's "scientific" approach to painting was his renowned *Sunday Afternoon on the Island of La Grande Jatte* (see Figure 4.58 on the next page). As the work of Seurat illustrates, modernist painters were moving away from attempts to re-create the world as it is literally seen.

If 19th-century painters liberated color, their successors at the turn of the 20th century liberated form. This was particularly true of the Cubists. Cubism was begun in 1909 by Pablo Picasso, a Spanish artist who went on to experiment with other styles in his prolific career. The Cubists didn't try to *portray* reality so much as to *reassemble* it. They attempted to reduce everything to combinations of geometric forms (lines,

Figure 4.58

Georges Seurat's *Sunday Afternoon on the Island of La Grande Jatte* (without artist's border) (1884–1886). Seurat used thousands of tiny dots of color and the principles of color mixing (see detail). The eye and brain combine the points into the colors the viewer actually sees.

circles, triangles, rectangles, and such) laid out in a flat space, lacking depth. In a sense, *they applied the theory of feature analysis to canvas,* as they built their figures out of simple features.

The resulting paintings were decidedly unrealistic, but the painters would leave realistic fragments that provided clues about the subject. Picasso liked to challenge his viewers to decipher the subject of his paintings. Take a look at the painting in Figure 4.59 and see whether you can figure out what Picasso was portraying.

The work in Figure 4.59 is titled *Violin and Grapes.* Note how Gestalt principles of perceptual organization are at work to create these forms. Proximity and similarity serve to bring the grapes together in the bottom right corner. Closure accounts for your being able to see the essence of the violin.

Other Gestalt principles are the key to the effect achieved in the painting in Figure 4.60. This painting, by Marcel Duchamp, a French artist who blended Cubism and a style called Futurism, is titled *Nude Descending a Staircase.* The effect clearly depends on the Gestalt principle of continuity.

Figure 4.59

***Violin and Grapes* by Pablo Picasso (1912).** This painting makes use of the Gestalt principles of proximity, similarity, and closure.

Figure 4.60

Marcel Duchamp's *Nude Descending a Staircase, No 2* (1912). This painting uses the Gestalt principles of continuity and common fate.

Duchamp, Marcel, 1912, *Nude Descending a Staircase, No. 2,* oil on canvas, 58" × 35" Philadelphia Museum of Art: Louise and Walter Arensburg Collection, # '50–134–69. Reproduced by permission. © 2000 Artists Rights Society (ARS), New York/ADAGP, Paris/Estate of Marcel Duchamp.

Figure 4.61

Salvador Dali's *The Hallucinogenic Toreador* (1969–1970). This surrealistic painting includes a reversible figure (the bullfighter is made up of Venus di Milo statues). Gestalt principles are crucial to the perception of the bull and the dalmatian near the bottom of the painting.

Dali, Salvador, *The Hallucinogenic Toreador* (1969–70), oil on canvas, 157 × 119 inches (398.7 × 302.3 cm). Collection of The Salvador Dali Museum, St. Petersburg, Florida, Copyright © 2000 The Salvador Dali Museum, Inc. © 2000 Foundation Gala-Salvador Dali/VEGAP/Artists Rights Society (ARP), New York.

The Surrealists toyed with reality in a different way. Influenced by Sigmund Freud's writings on the unconscious, the Surrealists explored the world of dreams and fantasy. Specific elements in their paintings are often depicted realistically, but the strange juxtaposition of elements yields a disconcerting irrationality reminiscent of dreams. A prominent example of this style is Salvador Dali's *The Hallucinogenic Tore-ador,* shown in Figure 4.61. Notice the reversible figure near the center of the painting. The bullfighter is made up of Venus de Milo sculptures. Dali often used reversible figures to enhance the ambiguity of his bizarre visions.

Perhaps no one has been more creative in manipulating perceptual ambiguity than M. C. Escher, a modern Dutch artist. Escher's chief goal was to stimulate viewers to think about the nature of reality and the process of visual perception itself. Interestingly, Escher readily acknowledged his debt to psychology as a source of inspiration (Teuber, 1974). He followed the work of the Gestalt psychologists carefully and would even cite specific journal articles that served as the point of departure for his works. For example, *Waterfall,* a 1961 lithograph by Escher, is an impossible figure

that appears to defy the law of gravity (see Figure 4.62 on the next page). The puzzling problem here is that a level channel of water terminates in a waterfall that "falls" into the *same* channel two levels "below." This drawing is made up of two impossible triangles. In case you need help seeing

them, the waterfall itself forms one side of each triangle.

The Necker cube, a reversible figure mentioned earlier, was the inspiration for Escher's 1958 lithograph *Belvedere*, shown in Figure 4.63. You have to look carefully to realize that this is another impossible figure.

Note that the top story runs at a right angle from the first story. Note also how the pillars are twisted around. The pillars that start on one side of the building end up supporting the second story on the other side! Escher's debt to the Necker cube is manifested in several places. Notice, for instance, the

Figure 4.64

Victor Vasarely's *Vega-Tek* (1969). In this painting, Vasarely manipulates a host of depth cues to create the image of a sphere inflating.

Vasarely, Victor, *Vega-Tek*. Wool Aubusson tapestry. 1969. Copyright Art Resource, NY. Private Collection. © 2000 Artists Rights Society (ARS), New York/ADAGP, Paris.

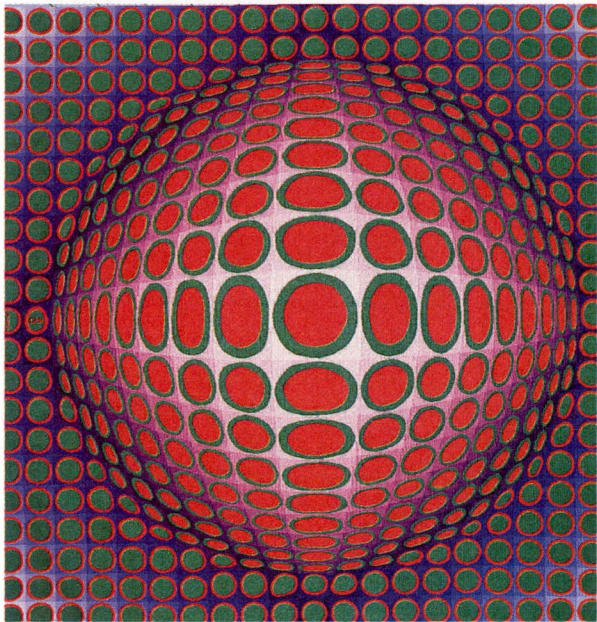

Figure 4.65

René Magritte's *Les Promenades d'Euclide* (1955). Notice how the pair of nearly identical triangles look quite different in different contexts.

Magritte, René, *Les Promenades d'Euclide*, The Minneapolis Institute of Arts, The William Hood Dunwoody Fund. Copyright © 2000 Charly Herscovic, Brussels/Artists Rights Society (ARS) New York.

drawing of a Necker cube on the floor next to the seated boy (on the lower left).

Like Escher, Victor Vasarely challenged viewers to think about the process of perception. A Hungarian artist, Vasarely pioneered an approach called Kinetic Art because of his interest in creating illusions of motion. Like Georges Seurat, he went about his work with scientific precision. His paintings are based on optical illusions, as squares seem to advance and recede, or spheres seem to inflate and deflate. For example, note how Vasarely used a variety of depth cues to convey the look of a sphere inflating in his painting *Vega-Tek*, shown in Figure 4.64.

While Escher and Vasarely challenged viewers to think about perception, Belgian artist René Magritte challenged people to think about the conventions of painting. Many of his works depict paintings on an easel, with the "real" scene continuing unbroken at the edges. The painting in Figure 4.65 is such a picture within a picture. In addition, there are two identical triangles in the painting. One represents a road and the other a nearby tower. Notice how the identical triangles are perceived differently because of the variations in *context*.

Ultimately, Magritte's painting blurs the line between the real world and the illusory world created by the artist, suggesting that there is no line—that everything is an illusion. In this way, Magritte "framed" the ageless, unanswerable question: What is reality?

REVIEW OF KEY POINTS

- The principles of visual perception are often applied to artistic endeavors. Prior to the Renaissance, efforts to create a convincing illusion of three-dimensional reality were awkward because artists did not understand how to use depth cues. After the Renaissance, painters began to routinely use pictorial depth cues to make their scenes more lifelike.

- Nineteenth-century painters, such as the Impressionists, manipulated color in creative, new ways. The Cubists were innovative in manipulating form, as they applied the theory of feature analysis to canvas. The Surrealists toyed with reality, exploring the world of fantasy and dreams.

- Modern artists such as Escher and Vasarely have tried to stimulate viewers to think about the process of perception. Among other things, Escher worked with the Necker cube and the impossible triangle.

Recognizing Contrast Effects: It's All Relative

You're sitting at home one night, when the phone rings. It's Simone, an acquaintance from school who needs help with a recreational program for youngsters that she runs for the local park district. She tries to persuade you to volunteer four hours of your time every Friday night throughout the school year to supervise the volleyball program. The thought of giving up your Friday nights and adding this sizable obligation to your already busy schedule makes you cringe with horror. You politely explain to Simone that you can't possibly afford to give up that much time and you won't be able to help her. She accepts your rebuff graciously, but the next night she calls again. This time she wants to know whether you would be willing to supervise volleyball every third Friday. You still feel like it's a big obligation that you really don't want to take on, but the new request seems much more reasonable than the original one. So, with a sigh of resignation, you agree to Simone's request.

What's wrong with this picture? Well, there's nothing wrong with volunteering your time for a good cause, but you just succumbed to a social influence strategy called the *door-in-the face technique*. **The *door-in-the-face technique* involves making a large request that is likely to be turned down as a way to increase the chances that people will agree to a smaller request later** (see Figure 4.66). The name for this strategy is derived from the expectation that the initial request will be quickly rejected (hence, the door is slammed in the salesperson's face). Although they may not be familiar with the strategy's name, many people use this manipulative tactic. For example, a husband who wants to coax his frugal wife into agreeing to buy a $25,000 sports car might begin by proposing that they purchase a $44,000 sports car. By the time the wife talks her husband out of the $44,000 car, the $25,000 price tag may look quite reasonable to her—which is what the husband wanted all along.

Research has demonstrated that the door-in-the-face technique is a highly effective persuasive strategy (Cialdini, 1993). One of the reasons it works so well is that it depends on a simple and pervasive perceptual principle. As noted in our discussion of psychophysical scaling (see p. 126), in the domain of perceptual experience, *everything is relative*. This relativity means that people are easily swayed by *contrast effects*. For example, lighting a match or a small candle in a dark room will produce a burst of light that seems quite bright, but if you light the same match or candle in a well-lit room, you may not even detect the additional illumination. The relativity of perception is apparent in the painting by Josef Albers shown in Figure 4.67. The two Xs are exactly the same color, but the X in the top half looks yellow, whereas the X in the bottom half looks brown. These varied perceptions occur because of contrast effects—the two X's are contrasted against different background colors.

The same principles of relativity and contrast that operate when we are making judgments about the intensity or color of visual stimuli also affect the way we make judgments in a wide variety of domains. For example, a 6'3" basketball player, who is really quite tall, can look downright small when surrounded by teammates who are all over 6'8". And a salary of $30,000 per year for your first full-time job may seem like a princely sum, until a close friend gets an offer of $55,000 a year. The assertion that everything is relative raises the issue of *relative to what?* **Comparitors are people, objects, events, and other stan-**

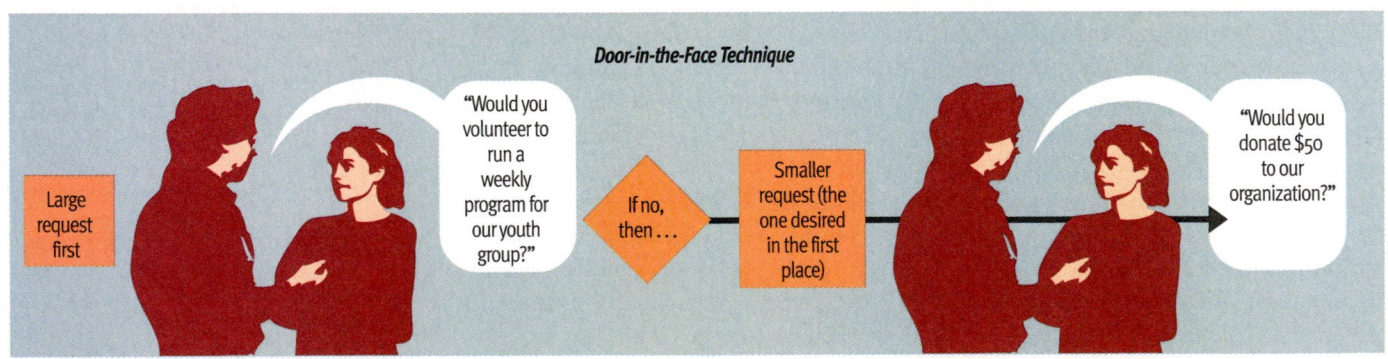

Figure 4.66

The door-in-the-face technique. The door-in-the-face technique is a frequently used compliance strategy in which you begin with a large request and work down to the smaller request you are really after. It depends in part on contrast effects.

Figure 4.67

Contrast effects in visual perception.
This composition by Joseph Albers shows how one color can be perceived differently when contrasted against different backgrounds. The top X looks yellow and the bottom X looks brown, but they're really the same color.

SOURCE: Albers, Joseph. *Interaction of Color.* Copyright © 1963 and reprinted by permission of the publisher, Yale University Press.

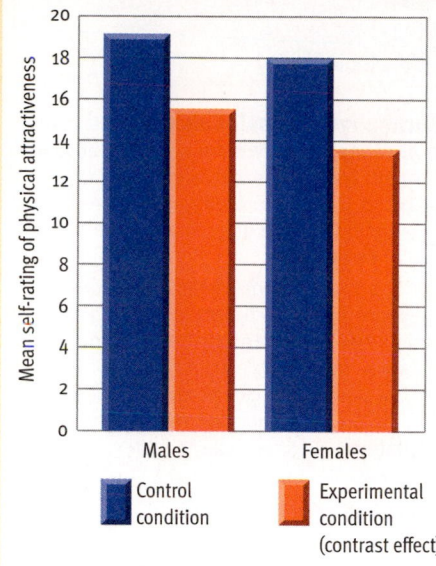

Figure 4.68

Contrast effects in judgments of physical attractiveness. Participants rated their own physical attractiveness under two conditions. In the experimental condition, the ratings occurred after subjects were exposed to a series of photos depicting very attractive models. The resulting contrast effects led to lower self-ratings in this condition. (Data based on Thornton & Moore, 1993)

dards used as a baseline for comparison in making judgments. It is fairly easy to manipulate many types of judgments by selecting *extreme* comparitors that may be unrepresentative.

The influence of extreme comparitors was demonstrated in a couple of interesting studies of judgments of physical attractiveness. In one study, undergraduate males were asked to rate the attractiveness of an average-looking female (who was described as a potential date for another male in the dorm) presented in a photo either just before or just after the participants watched a TV show dominated by strikingly beautiful women (Kenrick & Gutierres, 1980). The female was viewed as less attractive when the ratings were obtained just after the men had seen gorgeous women cavorting on TV as opposed to when they hadn't. In another investigation (Thornton and Moore, 1993), both male and female participants rated *themselves* as less attractive after being exposed to many pictures of extremely attractive models (see Figure 4.68). Thus, contrast effects can influence important social judgments that are likely to affect how people feel about themselves and others.

Anyone who understands how easily judgments can be manipulated by a care-

ful choice of comparitors could influence your thinking. For example, a politician who is caught in some illegal or immoral act could sway public opinion by bringing to mind (perhaps subtly) the fact that many other politicians have committed acts that were much worse. When considered against a backdrop of more extreme comparitors, the politician's transgression will probably seem less offensive. A defense attorney could use a similar strategy in an attempt to obtain a lighter sentence for a client by comparing the client's offense to much more serious crimes. And a realtor who wants to sell you an expensive house that will require huge mortgage payments will be quick to mention other homeowners who have taken on even larger mortgages.

In summary, critical thinking is facilitated by conscious awareness of the way comparitors can influence and perhaps distort a wide range of judgments. In particular, it pays to be vigilant about the possibility that others may manipulate contrast effects in their persuasive efforts. One way to reduce the influence of contrast effects is to consciously consider comparitors that are both worse and better than the event you are judging, as a way of balancing the effects of the two extremes.

Table 4.2 Critical Thinking Skills Discussed in This Application

Skill	Description
Understanding how contrast effects can influence judgments and decisions	The critical thinker appreciates how striking contrasts can be manipulated to influence many types of judgments.
Recognizing when extreme comparitors are being used	The critical thinker is on the lookout for extreme comparitors that distort judgments.

RECAP

Key Ideas

Psychophysics: Basic Concepts and Issues

● Absolute thresholds are not really absolute. Fechner's law asserts that larger and larger increases in stimulus intensity are required to produce just noticeable differences in the magnitude of sensation.

● According to signal-detection theory, the detection of sensory inputs is influenced by noise in the system and by decision-making strategies. In recent years, it has become apparent that perception can occur without awareness. Prolonged stimulation may lead to sensory adaptation.

Our Sense of Sight: The Visual System

● Light varies in terms of wavelength, amplitude, and purity. Light enters the eye through the cornea and pupil and is focused on the retina by the lens. Rods and cones are the visual receptors found in the retina. Cones play a key role in daylight vision and color perception, and rods are critical to night vision and peripheral vision. Dark and light adaptation both involve changes in the retina's sensitivity to light.

● The retina transforms light into neural impulses that are sent to the brain via the optic nerve. Receptive fields are areas in the retina that affect the firing of visual cells. Two visual pathways, which engage in parallel processing, send signals through the thalamus to the primary visual cortex. From there, visual signals are shuttled along pathways that have been characterized as the *what* and *where* pathways.

● Perceptions of color (hue) are primarily a function of light wavelength, while amplitude affects brightness and purity affects saturation. Perceptions of many varied colors depend on processes that resemble additive color mixing. The evidence now suggests that both the trichromatic and opponent process theories are necessary to account for color vision.

● Form perception depends on the selection and interpretation of visual inputs. According to feature analysis theories, people detect specific elements in stimuli and build them into forms through bottom-up processing. However, evidence suggests that form perception also involves top-down processing.

● Gestalt psychology emphasized that the whole may be greater than the sum of its parts (features), as illustrated by Gestalt principles of form perception. Other approaches to form perception emphasize that people develop perceptual hypotheses about the distal stimuli that could be responsible for the proximal stimuli that are sensed.

● Depth perception depends primarily on monocular cues. Binocular cues such as retinal disparity and convergence can also contribute to depth perception. Conscious perceptions of geographical slant tend to be greatly exaggerated, but haptic judgments seem largely immune to this perceptual bias.

● Perceptual constancies help viewers deal with the ever-shifting nature of proximal stimuli. Optical illusions demonstrate that perceptual hypotheses can be inaccurate and that perceptions are not simple reflections of objective reality.

Our Sense of Hearing: The Auditory System

● Sound varies in terms of wavelength (frequency), amplitude, and purity. These properties affect mainly perceptions of pitch, loudness, and timbre, respectively. Auditory signals are transmitted through the thalamus to the auditory cortex in the temporal lobe.

● Modern evidence suggests that place theory and frequency theory are complementary rather than incompatible explanations of pitch perception. People pinpoint the source of sounds by comparing interear differences in the intensity and timing of sounds.

Our Chemical Senses: Taste and Smell

● The taste buds are sensitive to four basic tastes: sweet, sour, bitter, and salty. Taste preferences are largely learned and are heavily influenced by one's cultural background. Supertasters are more sensitive to bitter and sweet tastes than others are.

● Like taste, smell is a chemical sense. Chemical stimuli activate olfactory receptors lining the nasal passages. Most of these receptors respond to more than one odor. Humans exhibit surprising difficulty attaching names to odors.

Our Sense of Touch: Sensory Systems in the Skin

● Sensory receptors in the skin respond to pressure, temperature, and pain. Pain signals are sent to the brain along two pathways characterized as fast and slow. The perception of pain is highly subjective and may be influenced by mood, attention, personality, and culture. Gate-control theory holds that incoming pain signals can be blocked in the spinal cord. Endorphins and a descending neural pathway appear responsible for the suppression of pain by the central nervous system.

Our Other Senses

● The kinesthetic system monitors the position of various body parts. The sense of balance depends on activity in the vestibular system.

Putting It in Perspective

● This chapter underscored three of our unifying themes: the value of theoretical diversity, the subjective nature of human experience, and the influence of culture on behavior.

Personal Application ●
Appreciating Art and Illusion

● The principles of visual perception are often applied to artistic endeavors. Painters routinely use pictorial depth cues to make their scenes more lifelike. Color mixing, feature analysis, Gestalt principles, reversible figures, and impossible figures have also been used in influential paintings.

Critical Thinking Application ●
Recognizing Contrast Effects: It's All Relative

● The study of perception often highlights the relativity of experience. This relativity can be manipulated by arranging for contrast effects. Critical thinking is enhanced by an awareness of how comparitors can distort many judgments.

Key Terms

Absolute threshold
Additive color mixing
Afterimage
Auditory localization
Basilar membrane
Binocular depth cues
Bottom-up processing
Cochlea
Color blindness
Comparitors
Complementary colors
Cones
Convergence
Dark adaptation
Depth perception
Distal stimuli
Door-in-the-face technique
Farsightedness
Feature analysis
Feature detectors
Fechner's law
Fovea
Frequency theory
Gate-control theory
Gustatory system
Impossible figures
Just noticeable difference (JND)
Kinesthetic system
Lateral antagonism
Lens
Light adaptation
Monocular depth cues
Motion parallax
Nearsightedness
Olfactory system
Opponent process theory
Optic chiasm
Optic disk
Optical illusion
Parallel processing
Perception
Perceptual constancy
Perceptual hypothesis
Perceptual set
Phi phenomenon
Pictorial depth cues
Place theory
Proximal stimuli
Psychophysics
Pupil
Receptive field of a visual cell
Retina
Retinal disparity
Reversible figure
Rods
Sensation
Sensory adaptation
Signal-detection theory
Subjective contours
Subliminal perception
Subtractive color mixing
Threshold
Top-down processing
Trichromatic theory
Vestibular system
Visual agnosia
Volley principle
Weber's law

Key People

Linda Bartoshuk
Gustav Fechner
Hermann von Helmholtz
David Hubel and Torsten Wiesel
Ronald Melzack and Patrick Wall
Max Wertheimer

PRACTICE TEST

1. In psychophysical research, the absolute threshold has been arbitrarily defined as:
   A. the stimulus intensity that can be detected 100% of the time.
   B. the stimulus intensity that can be detected 50% of the time.
   C. the minimum amount of difference in intensity needed to tell two stimuli apart.
   D. a constant proportion of the size of the initial stimulus.

2. A tone-deaf person would probably not be able to tell two musical notes apart unless they were very different. We could say that this person has a relatively large:
   A. just noticeable difference.
   B. relative threshold.
   C. absolute threshold.
   D. detection threshold.

3. In their study of the influence of subliminal perception on attitudes, Krosnick and his colleagues (1992) found:
   A. absolutely no evidence of such influence.
   B. overwhelming evidence that subliminal stimuli can and do influence subjects' attitudes.
   C. that subliminal stimuli do not really exist.
   D. small but measureable effects.

4. In farsightedness:
   A. close objects are seen clearly but distant objects appear blurry.
   B. the focus of light from close objects falls behind the retina.
   C. the focus of light from distant objects falls a little short of the retina.
   D. a and b.
   E. a and c.

5. The collection of rod and cone receptors that funnel signals to a particular visual cell in the retina make up that cell's:
   A. blind spot.
   B. optic disk.
   C. opponent process field.
   D. receptive field.

6. The visual pathway that has been characterized as _____ travels through the dorsal stream to the parietal lobes, whereas the pathway that has been labeled the _____ travels through the ventral stream to the temporal lobes.
   A. the *what* pathway; the *where* pathway
   B. the *where* pathway; the *what* pathway
   C. the *opponent process* pathway; the *trichromatic* pathway
   D. the *trichromatic* pathway; the *opponent process* pathway

7. Which theory would predict that the American flag would have a green, black, and yellow afterimage?
   A. subtractive color mixing
   B. opponent process theory
   C. additive color mixing
   D. trichromatic theory

8. The illusion of movement created by presenting visual stimuli in rapid succession is called:
   A. convergence.
   B. retinal disparity.
   C. motion parallax.
   D. the phi phenomenon.

9. In a painting, train tracks may look as if they go off into the distance because the artist draws the tracks as converging lines, a monocular cue to depth known as:
   A. interposition.
   B. texture gradient.
   C. convergence.
   D. linear perspective.

10. Sarah has just finished a long, exhausting 6-mile run. She and her friend Jamal are gazing at a hill they need to climb to get back to their car. Jamal asks Sarah, "Gee, how steep do you think that hill is?" Based on research by Proffitt and his colleagues, Sarah is likely to:
    A. make a reasonably accurate estimate of the hill's slant, as most people do.
    B. underestimate the hill's slant, as most people do.
    C. overestimate the hill's slant, but to a lesser degree than she would have before her exhausting run.
    D. overestimate the hill's slant to an even greater degree than she would have before her exhausting run.

11. The facts that cultural groups with little exposure to roads are less susceptible to the Ponzo illusion and that those with less exposure to buildings are less susceptible to the Müller-Lyer illusion suggest that:
    A. not all cultures test perceptual hypotheses.
    B. people in technologically advanced cultures are more gullible.
    C. optical illusions can be experienced only by cultures that have been exposed to the concept of optical illusions.
    D. perceptual inferences can be shaped by experience.

12. Perception of pitch can best be explained by:
    A. place theory.
    B. frequency theory.
    C. both place theory and frequency theory.
    D. neither theory.

13. In what way(s) is the sense of taste like the sense of smell?
    A. There are four primary stimulus groups for both senses.
    B. Both systems are routed through the thalamus on the way to the cortex.
    C. The physical stimuli for both senses are chemical substances dissolved in fluid.
    D. All of the above.
    E. None of the above.

14. Which school of painting applied the theory of feature analysis to canvas by building figures out of simple features?
    A. Kineticism   C. Surrealism
    B. Impressionism   D. Cubism

15. In the study by Kenrick and Gutierres (1980), exposing male subjects to a TV show dominated by extremely beautiful women:
    A. had no effect on their ratings of the attractiveness of a prospective date.
    B. increased their ratings of the attractiveness of a prospective date.
    C. decreased their ratings of the attractiveness of a prospective date.
    D. increased their ratings of their own attractiveness.

Answers

1	B	p. 124	**6**	B	p. 136	**11**	D	p. 153
2	A	p. 125	**7**	B	p. 139	**12**	C	pp. 157–158
3	D	pp. 127–128	**8**	D	p. 143	**13**	C	p. 161
4	B	p. 131	**9**	D	p. 147	**14**	D	p. 168
5	D	p. 133	**10**	D	pp. 149–150	**15**	C	p. 173

 ON THE WEB

For additional resources on the topics covered in this chapter, visit the *Psychology: Themes and Variations* Web site, where you will find practice quizzes, tutorials, Web links, simulations, critical thinking activities, flash cards, interactive exercises, and suggested readings available through INFOTRAC.

http://psychology.wadsworth.com/weiten_themes6e/

CHAPTER 5

© Keren Su/CORBIS

Variations in Consciousness

© Keren Su/CORBIS

Nathaniel Kleitman and Eugene Aserinsky couldn't believe their eyes—or their subjects' eyes, either. It was the spring of 1952, and Kleitman, a physiologist and prominent sleep researcher, was investigating the slow, rolling eye movements displayed by subjects at the onset of sleep. Kleitman had begun to wonder whether these slow eye movements would show up during later phases of sleep. The trouble was that watching a subject's closed eyelids all night long was a surefire way to put the *researcher* to sleep. Cleverly, Kleitman and Aserinsky, a graduate student, came up with a better way to document eye movements. They hooked subjects up to an apparatus that was connected to electrodes pasted near the eyes. The electrodes picked up the small electrical signals generated by moving eyeballs. In turn, these signals moved a pen on a chart recorder, much like an electroencephalograph (EEG) traces brain waves (see Chapter 3). The result was an objective record of subjects' eye movements during sleep that could be studied at leisure (Dement, 1992).

One night, while one of their subjects was asleep, the researchers were astonished to see a tracing in the recording that suggested a different, much more rapid eye movement. This result was so unexpected that they suspected the recording device was defective. "It was a rickety old thing, anyway," a technician in Kleitman's lab recalled (Coren, 1996, p. 21). Only when they decided to walk in and personally observe sleeping subjects were they convinced that the eye movements were real. The subjects were deeply asleep, yet the bulges in their closed eyelids showed that their eyeballs were moving laterally in sharp jerks, first in one direction and then in the other. It was almost as if the sleeping subjects were watching a chaotic movie. The researchers wondered—what in the world was going on?

In retrospect, it's amazing that no one had discovered these rapid eye movements before. It turns out that periods of rapid eye movement are a routine characteristic of sleep in humans and many animals. In fact, you can observe them for yourself in your pet dog or cat. The phenomenon had been there for everyone to see for eons, but those who noticed must not have attached any significance to it.

Kleitman and Aserinsky's discovery might have remained something of an oddity, but then they had a brainstorm. Could the rapid eye movements be related to dreaming? With the help of William Dement, a graduate student who was interested in dreams, they soon found the answer. When Dement woke up subjects during periods of rapid eye movement, about 80 percent reported that they had just been having a vivid dream. Another 10 percent reported thoughts or images that might have signified dreaming. By contrast, only a small minority of subjects awakened during other phases of sleep reported that they had been dreaming. Dement knew that he was on to something. "I was overwhelmed with excitement," he wrote later (Dement, 1992, pp. 24–25). Subsequently, EEG recordings showed that periods of rapid eye movement were also associated with marked changes in brain-wave patterns. What Kleitman and his graduate students had stumbled on was considerably more than an oddity: It was a window into the most private aspect of consciousness imaginable—the experience of dreaming.

As you will learn in this chapter, the discovery of rapid eye movement (REM) sleep blossomed into a number of other fascinating insights about what goes on in the brain during sleep. This research is just one example of how contemporary psychologists have tried to come to grips with the slippery topic of consciousness. Over time, consciousness has represented something of a paradox for psychology. On the one hand, our conscious experience—our awareness of ourselves and the world around us, our thoughts, and even our dreams—would seem to be an obvious and central concern for psychologists. On the other hand, psychology is committed to the empirical approach, which requires having objective, replicable ways of studying a given phenomenon. And consciousness is the ultimate in subjective experience. We can't directly observe another's consciousness. We have a hard enough time even describing our own conscious experience to anyone else (Schooler & Fiore, 1997). Yet in recent decades researchers have been finding inventive ways to shed some objective light on the mysteries of consciousness.

We'll begin our tour of variations in consciousness with a few general points about the nature of consciousness. After that, much of the chapter will be a "bedtime story," as we take a long look at sleep and dreaming. We'll continue our discussion of consciousness by examining hypnosis, meditation, and the effects of mind-altering drugs. The Personal Application will address a number of practical questions about sleep and dreams. Finally, the Critical Thinking Application looks at the concept of alcoholism to highlight the power of definitions.

On the Nature of Consciousness

PREVIEW QUESTIONS
- What is consciousness?
- What did Freud have to say about levels of awareness?
- Is there any awareness during sleep?
- How might consciousness be adaptive?
- How are variations in consciousness associated with EEG activity?

Consciousness is the awareness of internal and external stimuli. Your consciousness includes (1) your awareness of external events ("The professor just asked me a difficult question about medieval history"), (2) your awareness of your internal sensations ("My heart is racing and I'm beginning to sweat"), (3) your awareness of your self as the unique being having these experiences ("Why me?"), and (4) your awareness of your thoughts about these experiences ("I'm going to make a fool of myself!"). To put it more concisely, consciousness is personal awareness.

The contents of your consciousness are continually changing. Rarely does consciousness come to a standstill. It moves, it flows, it fluctuates, it wanders (Wegner, 1997). Recognizing this fact, William James (1902) christened this continuous flow the *stream of consciousness*. If you could tape-record your thoughts, you would find an endless flow of ideas that zigzag in all directions. As you will soon learn, even when you sleep your consciousness moves through a series of transitions. Constant shifting and changing seem to be part of the essential nature of consciousness.

Variations in Levels of Awareness

Whereas William James emphasized the stream of consciousness, Sigmund Freud (1900) wanted to examine what went on beneath the surface of this stream. As explained in Chapter 1, Freud argued that people's feelings and behavior are influenced by *unconscious* needs, wishes, and conflicts that lie below the surface of conscious awareness. According to Freud, the stream of consciousness has depth. Conscious and unconscious processes are different *levels of awareness*. Thus, Freud was one of the first theorists to recognize that consciousness is not an all-or-none phenomenon.

Since Freud's time, research has shown that people continue to maintain some awareness during sleep and even when they are put under anesthesia for surgery. How do we know? Because some stimuli can still penetrate awareness. For example, people under surgical anesthesia occasionally hear comments made during their surgery, which they later repeat to their surprised surgeons (Bennett, 1993; Kihlstrom et al., 1990). Other research indicates that while people are asleep they remain aware of external events to some degree (Badia, 1990; Evans, 1990). A good example is the new parent who can sleep through a loud thunderstorm or a buzzing alarm clock but who immediately hears the muffled sound of the baby crying down the hall. The parent's selective sensitivity to sounds means that some mental processing must be going on even during sleep.

The Evolutionary Roots of Consciousness

Why do humans experience consciousness? Like other aspects of human nature, consciousness must have evolved because it helped our ancient ancestors survive and reproduce (Ornstein & Dewan, 1991). That said, there is plenty of debate about exactly how consciousness proved adaptive (Guzeldere, Flanagan, & Hardcastle, 2000). One line of thinking is that consciousness allowed our ancestors to think through courses of action and their consequences—and attempt to choose the best course—without actually executing ill-advised actions (by trial and error) that may have led to disastrous consequences (Plotkin, 1998). In other words, a little forethought and planning may have proved valuable in efforts to obtain food, avoid predators, and find mates. Although this analysis seems plausible, there are a host of alternative explanations that focus on other adaptive benefits of personal awareness, and (to date) relatively little empirical evidence to judge their merits. Hence, the evolutionary bases of consciousness remain elusive.

Consciousness and Brain Activity

Consciousness does not arise from any distinct structure in the brain but rather from activity in distributed networks of neural pathways (Kinsbourne, 1997). Thus, one of the best physiological indicators of variations in consciousness is the EEG, which records activity from broad swaths of the cortex. The *electroencephalograph (EEG)* is a device that monitors the electrical activity of the brain over time by means of recording electrodes attached to the surface of the scalp. Ultimately, the EEG summarizes the rhythm of cortical activity in the brain in terms of line tracings called *brain waves*. These brain-wave tracings vary in *amplitude* (height) and *frequency* (cycles per second, abbreviated *cps*). You can see what brain waves look like if you glance ahead to Figure 5.4. Human brain-wave activity is usually divided into four principal bands based on the frequency of the brain waves. These bands, named after letters in the Greek alphabet, are *beta* (13–24 cps), *alpha* (8–12 cps), *theta* (4–7 cps), and *delta* (under 4 cps).

Different patterns of EEG activity are associated with different states of consciousness, as is summarized in Table 5.1. For instance, when you are alertly engaged in problem solving, beta waves tend to dominate. When you are relaxed and resting, alpha waves increase. When you slip into deep, dreamless sleep, delta waves become more prevalent. Although these correlations are far from perfect, changes in EEG activity are closely related to variations in consciousness (Wallace & Fisher, 1999).

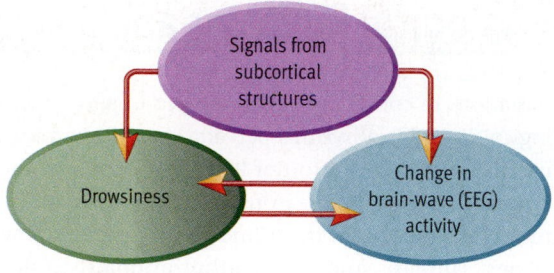

Figure 5.1

The correlation between mental states and electrical activity in the brain. As discussed in Chapter 2, correlations alone do not establish causation. For example, there are strong correlations between drowsiness and a particular pattern of cortical activity, as reflected by EEG brain waves. But does drowsiness cause a change in cortical activity, or do changes in cortical activity cause drowsiness? Or does some third variable account for the changes in both?

As is often the case with correlations, researchers are faced with a chicken-or-egg puzzle when it comes to the relationship between mental states and the brain's electrical activity. If you become drowsy while you are reading this passage, your brain-wave activity will probably change. But are these changes causing your drowsiness, or is your drowsiness causing the changes in brain-wave activity? Or are the drowsiness and the shifts in brain-wave activity both caused by a *third* factor—perhaps signals coming from a subcortical area in the brain? (See Figure 5.1.) Frankly, no one knows. All that is known for sure is that variations in consciousness are correlated with variations in brain activity.

Measures of brain-wave activity have provided investigators with a method for mapping out the mysterious state of consciousness called sleep. As we will see in the next two sections of the chapter, this state turns out to be far more complex and varied than you might expect.

Table 5.1

EEG Patterns Associated with States of Consciousness

EEG pattern	Frequency (cps)	Typical States of Consciousness
Beta (β)	13–24	Normal waking thought, alert problem solving
Alpha (α)	8–12	Deep relaxation, blank mind, meditation
Theta (θ)	4–7	Light sleep
Delta (Δ)	less than 4	Deep sleep

REVIEW OF KEY POINTS

● William James emphasized that consciousness is a continually changing stream of mental activity. Consciousness varies along a continuum of levels of awareness.

● Consciousness may have evolved because it allowed humans to think through the possible consequences of their actions and avoid some negative consequences. People maintain some degree of awareness during sleep and sometimes while under anesthesia.

● Brain waves vary in amplitude and frequency (cps) and are divided into four bands: beta, alpha, theta, and delta. Variations in consciousness are related to variations in brain activity, as measured by the EEG.

Biological Rhythms and Sleep

PREVIEW QUESTIONS
- What are biological rhythms?
- How are circadian rhythms related to falling asleep?
- Which physiological structures control our biological clocks?
- How are circadian rhythms related to jet lag?
- How do rotating work shifts tend to affect sleep?
- What are the pros and cons of using melatonin as a sleep aid?

Variations in consciousness are shaped in part by biological rhythms. Rhythms pervade the world around us. The daily alternation of light and darkness, the annual pattern of the seasons, and the phases of the moon all reflect this rhythmic quality of repeating cycles. Humans and many other animals display biological rhythms that are tied to these planetary rhythms (Schwartz, 1996). *Biological rhythms* are periodic fluctuations in physiological functioning. The existence of these rhythms means that organisms have internal "biological clocks" that somehow monitor the passage of time.

The Role of Circadian Rhythms

 4a

Circadian rhythms are the 24-hour biological cycles found in humans and many other species. In humans, circadian rhythms are particularly influential in the regulation of sleep (Lavie, 2001). However, daily cycles also produce rhythmic variations in blood pressure, urine production, hormonal secretions, and other physical functions (see Figure 5.2), as well as alertness, short-term memory, and other aspects of cognitive performance (Czeisler & Khalsa, 2000; Van Dongen & Dinges, 2000). For instance,

body temperature varies rhythmically in a daily cycle, usually peaking in the afternoon and reaching its low point in the depths of the night.

Research indicates that people generally fall asleep as their body temperature begins to drop and awaken as it begins to ascend once again (McGinty, 1993). Investigators have concluded that circadian rhythms can leave individuals physiologically primed to fall asleep most easily at a particular time of day (Richardson, 1993). This optimal time varies from person to person, depending on their schedules, but it's interesting to learn that each individual may have an "ideal" time for going to bed. This ideal bedtime may also promote better quality sleep during the night (Akerstedt et al., 1997), which is interesting in light of evidence that sleep *quality* may be more strongly correlated with health and well-being than the sheer quantity of sleep (Pilcher, Ginter, & Sadowsky, 1997).

To study biological clocks, researchers have monitored physiological processes while subjects are cut off from exposure to the cycle of day and night and all other external time cues. These studies have demonstrated that circadian rhythms generally persist even when external time cues are eliminated. However, when people are isolated in this way, their cycles run a little longer than normal, about 24.2 hours

Figure 5.2

Examples of circadian rhythms. These graphs show how alertness, core body temperature, and the secretion of growth hormone typically fluctuate in a 24-hour rhythm. Note how alertness tends to diminish with declining body temperature.

SOURCE: Adapted from Coleman, R. (1986). *Wide awake at 3:00 A.M.* New York: W. H. Freeman. Copyright © 1986 by Richard M. Coleman. Used with the permission of W. H. Freeman.

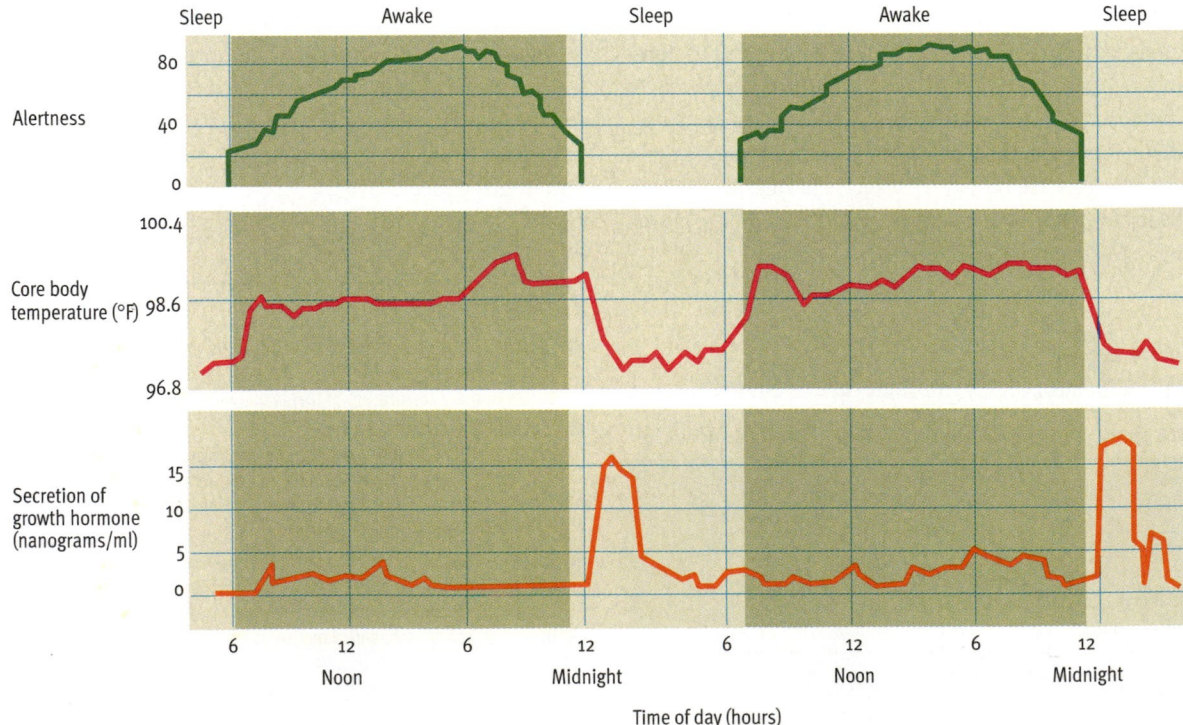

on the average (Czeisler & Khalsa, 2000). Investigators aren't sure why this drift toward a longer cycle occurs, but it is not apparent under normal circumstances because daily exposure to light *readjusts* people's biological clocks.

In fact, researchers have worked out many of the details regarding how the day-night cycle resets biological clocks. When exposed to light, some receptors in the retina send direct inputs to a small structure in the hypothalamus called the *suprachiasmatic nucleus (SCN)* (Schwartz, 1996). The SCN sends signals to the nearby *pineal gland,* whose secretion of the hormone *melatonin* plays a key role in adjusting biological clocks (Harrington & Mistlberger, 2000). Circadian rhythms in humans actually appear to be regulated by *several* internal clocks, but the central pacemaker clearly is located in the SCN.

Ignoring Circadian Rhythms 4a

What happens when you ignore your biological clock and go to sleep at an unusual time? Typically, the quality of your sleep suffers. Getting out of sync with your circadian rhythms also causes *jet lag.* When you fly across several time zones, your biological clock keeps time as usual, even though official clock time changes. You then go to sleep at the "wrong" time and are likely to experience difficulty falling asleep and poor quality sleep (Moline, 1993). This inferior sleep, which can continue to occur for several days, can make you feel fatigued, sluggish, and irritable during the daytime (Arendt, Stone, & Skene, 2000). Moreover, chronic jet lag appears to be associated

with measurable deficits in cognitive performance (Cho et al., 2000).

People differ in how quickly they can reset their biological clocks to compensate for jet lag, but a rough rule of thumb is that the readjustment process takes about a day for each time zone crossed (Moline, 1993). In addition, the speed of readjustment depends on the direction traveled. Generally, it's easier to fly westward and lengthen your day than it is to fly eastward and shorten it (Arendt et al., 2000). This east-west disparity in jet lag is sizable enough to have an impact on the performance of sports teams. Studies have found that teams flying westward perform significantly better than teams flying eastward in professional baseball (Recht, Lew, & Schwartz, 1995; see Figure 5.3) and college football (Worthen & Wade, 1999).

Of course, you don't have to hop on a jet to get out of sync with your biological clock. Just going to bed a couple hours later than usual can affect how you sleep. Rotating work shifts that force many nurses, firefighters, and other workers to keep changing their sleep schedule play havoc with biological rhythms. Shift rotation, which affects about 20% of the United States workforce, tends to be even harder to adjust to than jet lag (Monk, 2000). Studies show that workers get less total sleep and poorer quality sleep when they go on rotating shifts. Shift rotation can also have a negative impact on employees' productivity and accident–proneness at work, the quality of their social relations at home, and their physical and mental health (Costa, 1996; Cruz, della Rocco, & Hackworth, 2000; Hossain & Shapiro, 1999). For example, one

Web Link 5.1

NSF Center for Biological Timing
The role of biological rhythms in the functioning of living organisms has become an important focus of both medical and psychological research. This center's online tutorial about biological timing, or "chronobiology," is a broad and well-illustrated introduction to this field.

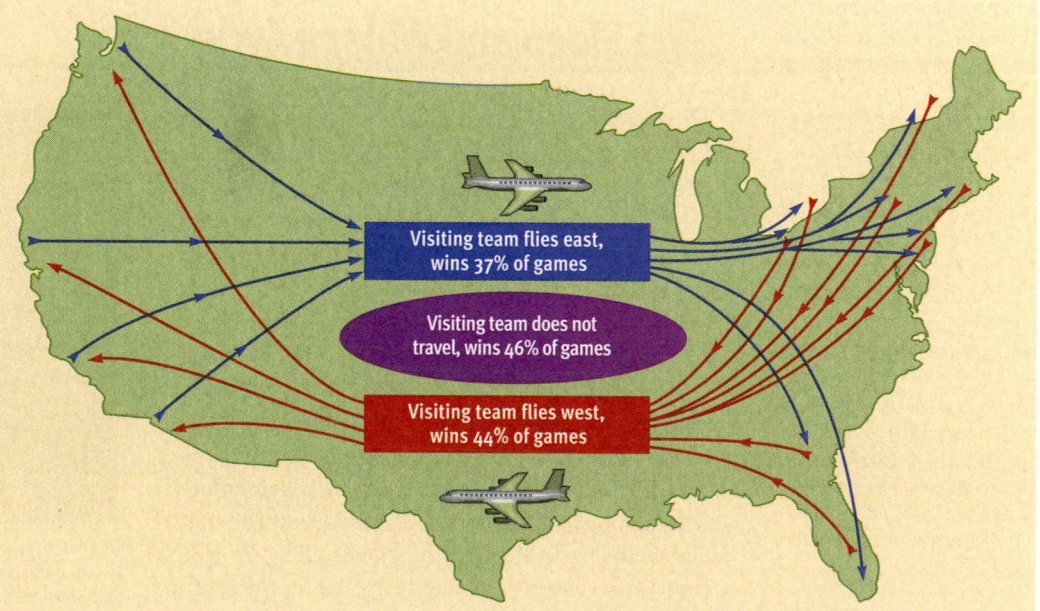

Figure 5.3

Effects of direction traveled on the performance of professional baseball teams. To gain some insight into the determinants of jet lag, Recht, Lew, and Schwartz (1995) analyzed the performance of visiting teams in major league baseball over a three-year period. In baseball, visiting teams usually play 3–4 games in each destination city, so there are plenty of games in which the visiting team has not traveled the day before. These games, which served as a baseline for comparison, were won by the visiting team 46% of the time. Consistent with the observation that flying west creates less jet lag than flying east, visiting teams that flew westward the day (or night) before performed only slightly worse, winning 44% of the time. In contrast, visiting teams that flew eastward the day before won only 37% of their games, presumably because flying east and shortening one's day creates greater jet lag.

Visiting team flies east, wins 37% of games

Visiting team does not travel, wins 46% of games

Visiting team flies west, wins 44% of games

SOURCE: Adapted from Kalat, J. W. (2001). *Biological psychology.* Belmont, CA: Wadsworth. Reprinted by permission.

study found a 40% increase in shift workers' risk for cardiovascular disease (Boggild & Knutsson, 1999).

Melatonin and Circadian Rhythms

As scientists have come to appreciate the importance of circadian rhythms, they have begun to look for new ways to help people harness their daily rhythms. A promising line of research has focused on giving people small doses of the hormone melatonin, which appears to regulate the human biological clock. The evidence from a number of studies suggests that melatonin *can* reduce the effects of jet lag by helping travelers resynchronize their biological clocks, but the research results are inconsistent (Arendt et al., 2000; Spitzer et al., 1999). One reason for the inconsistent findings is that when melatonin is used to ameliorate jet lag, the timing of the dose is crucial; because calculating the optimal timing is rather complicated, it is easy to get it wrong (Czeisler, Cajochen, & Turek, 2000). Research also suggests that melatonin may have some utility as a mild sedative (Hughes & Badia, 1997; Lavie, 1997). However, melatonin administered during the daytime, when endogenous melatonin levels are normally pretty low, is much more effective as a sedative than melatonin administered during the nighttime, when individuals' melatonin levels are already relatively high (Czeisler et al., 2000). This pattern of responsiveness suggests that melatonin can facilitate daytime naps but may have limited value in the treatment of nighttime insomnia.

Although these results are interesting, some words of caution are also in order. In Canada, Great Britain, and many other countries, melatonin is a regulated drug. In the United States, however, it is classified as a dietary supplement. It is sold in health food stores, where it is often touted as a miracle preparation that slows the aging process, enhances sex, and fights cancer and AIDS! There is little or no scientific evidence to support any of these unlikely claims (Arendt, 1996; Bonn, 1996). If people were merely wasting their money, there wouldn't be much cause for concern, but medical experts are worried that health food stores are encouraging people to take excessive doses of an untested drug that can raise melatonin levels in the blood to 1,000 times higher than normal (Czeisler et al., 2000).

REVIEW OF KEY POINTS

- The cycle of sleep and wakefulness is influenced considerably by circadian rhythms. Exposure to light resets biological clocks by affecting the activity of the suprachiasmatic nucleus and the pineal gland, which secretes the hormone melatonin.
- Ignoring your biological clock by going to sleep at an unusual time may have a negative effect on your sleep. Being out of sync with circadian rhythms is one reason for jet lag and for the unpleasant nature of rotating shift work.
- Melatonin may have value in efforts to alleviate the effects of jet lag and it may be an effective sedative in some situations, but there is little or no evidence for the other alleged benefits of this hormone.

The Sleep and Waking Cycle

PREVIEW QUESTIONS
- What happens when people fall asleep?
- How is REM sleep different from non-REM sleep?
- How do sleep stages evolve over the course of a night's sleep?
- How does age affect patterns of sleeping?
- Which aspects of sleep are influenced by culture?
- Which brain centers and neurotransmitters are involved in the modulation of sleep?

Although it is a familiar state of consciousness, sleep is widely misunderstood. Generally, people consider sleep to be a single, uniform state of physical and mental inactivity, during which the brain is "turned off." In reality, sleepers experience quite a bit of physical and mental activity throughout the night. Scientists have learned a great deal about sleep since the landmark discovery of REM sleep in the 1950s.

The advances in psychology's understanding of sleep are the result of hard work by researchers who have spent countless nighttime hours watching other people sleep. This work is done in sleep laboratories, where volunteer subjects come to spend the night. Sleep labs have one or more "bedrooms" in which the subjects retire, usually after being hooked up to a variety of physiological recording devices. In ad-

Researchers in a sleep laboratory can observe subjects while using elaborate equipment to record physiological changes during sleep. This kind of research has disclosed that sleep is a complex series of physical and mental states.

dition to an EEG, the other two crucial devices are an *electromyograph (EMG),* which records muscular activity and tension, and an *electrooculograph (EOG),* which records eye movements (Carskadon & Rechtschaffen, 2000). Typically, other instruments are also used to monitor heart rate, breathing, pulse rate, and body temperature. The researchers observe the sleeping subject through a window (or with a video camera) from an adjacent room, where they also monitor their elaborate physiological recording equipment (see the photo on page 182). For most people, it takes just one night to adapt to the strange bedroom and the recording devices and return to their normal mode of sleeping (Carskadon & Dement, 1994).

Cycling Through the Stages of Sleep

Not only does sleep occur in a context of daily rhythms, but subtler rhythms are evident within the experience of sleep itself. During sleep, people cycle through a series of five stages. Let's take a look at what researchers have learned about the changes that occur during each of these stages (Anch et al., 1988; Carskadon & Dement, 2000).

Stages 1–4

Although it may only take a few minutes, the onset of sleep is gradual and there is no obvious transition point between wakefulness and sleep (Rechtschaffen, 1994). The length of time it takes people to fall asleep varies considerably. It depends on quite an array of factors, including how long it has been since the person has slept, where the person is in his or her circadian cycle, the amount of noise or light in the sleep environment, and the person's age, desire to fall asleep, boredom level, recent caffeine or drug intake, and stress level, among other things (Broughton, 1994). In any event, stage 1 is a brief transitional stage of light sleep that usually lasts only a few (1–7) minutes. Breathing and heart rate slow as muscle tension and body temperature decline. The alpha waves that probably dominated EEG activity just before falling asleep give way to lower-frequency EEG activity in which theta waves are prominent (see Figure 5.4). *Hypnic jerks,* those brief muscular contractions that occur as people fall asleep, generally occur during stage 1 drowsiness (Broughton, 1994).

As the sleeper descends through stages 2, 3, and 4 of the cycle, respiration rate, heart rate, muscle tension, and body temperature continue to decline. During stage 2, which typically lasts about 10–25 min-

utes, brief bursts of higher-frequency brain waves, called *sleep spindles,* appear against a background of mixed EEG activity (refer to Figure 5.4 once again). Gradually, brain waves become higher in amplitude and slower in frequency, as the body moves into a deeper form of sleep, called slow-wave sleep. *Slow-wave sleep (SWS)* consists of sleep stages 3 and 4, during which high-amplitude, low-frequency delta waves become prominent in EEG recordings. Typically, individuals reach slow-wave sleep in about a half-hour and stay there for roughly 30 minutes. Then the cycle reverses itself and the sleeper gradually moves back upward through the lighter stages. That's when things start to get especially interesting.

REM Sleep

When sleepers reach what should be stage 1 once again, they usually go into the *fifth* stage of sleep, which is most widely known as *REM sleep.* As we have seen, REM is an abbreviation for the *rapid eye movements* prominent during this stage of sleep. In a sleep lab, researchers use an electrooculograph to monitor these lateral (side-to-side) movements that occur beneath the sleeping person's closed eyelids. However, they can be seen with the naked eye if you closely watch someone in the REM stage of sleep (little ripples move back and forth across his or her closed eyelids).

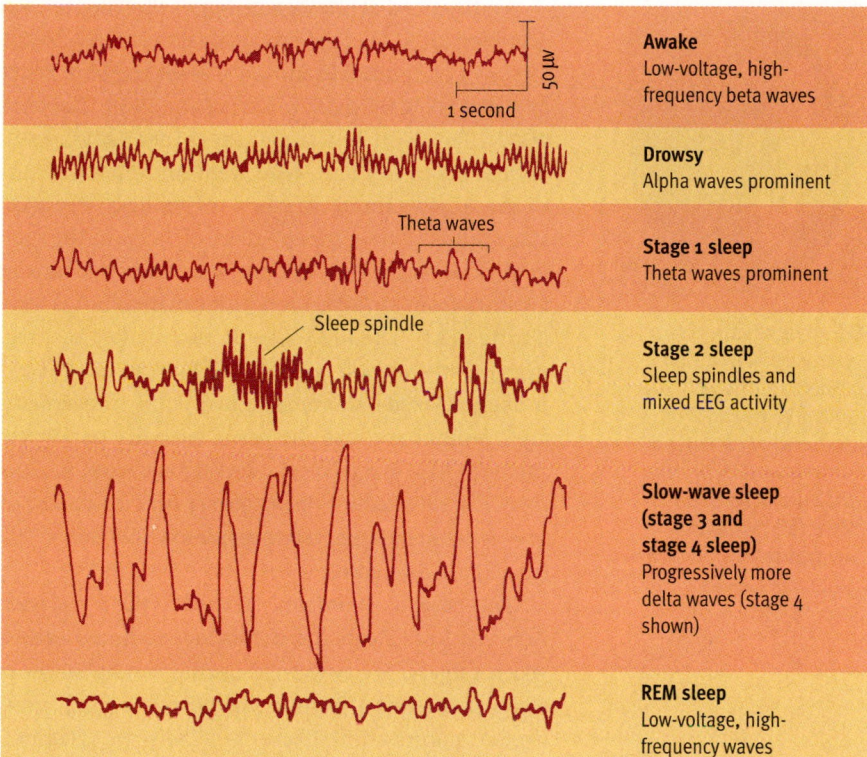

Awake
Low-voltage, high-frequency beta waves

1 second

Drowsy
Alpha waves prominent

Theta waves

Stage 1 sleep
Theta waves prominent

Sleep spindle

Stage 2 sleep
Sleep spindles and mixed EEG activity

Slow-wave sleep (stage 3 and stage 4 sleep)
Progressively more delta waves (stage 4 shown)

REM sleep
Low-voltage, high-frequency waves

Figure 5.4

EEG patterns in sleep and wakefulness. Characteristic brain waves vary depending on one's state of consciousness. Generally, as people move from an awake state through deeper stages of sleep, their brain waves decrease in frequency (cycles per second) and increase in amplitude (height). However, brain waves during REM sleep resemble "wide-awake" brain waves.

SOURCE: Adapted from Hauri, P. (1982). *Current concepts: The sleep disorders.* Kalamazoo, MI: The Upjohn Company. Reprinted by permission.

Courtesy of William Dement

"Sleep deprivation is a major epidemic in our society. . . . Americans spend so much time and energy chasing the American dream, that they don't have much time left for actual dreaming."
WILLIAM DEMENT

As discussed at the beginning of the chapter, the discovery of REM sleep was made accidentally in the 1950s in Nathaniel Kleitman's lab at the University of Chicago (Aserinsky & Kleitman, 1953; Dement, 2000). The term *REM sleep* was coined by grad student William Dement, who went on to become one of the world's foremost sleep researchers. The REM stage tends to be a "deep" stage of sleep in the conventional sense that people are relatively hard to awaken from it (although arousal thresholds vary during REM). The REM stage is also marked by irregular breathing and pulse rate. Muscle tone is extremely relaxed—so much so that bodily movements are minimal and the sleeper is virtually paralyzed. *Although REM is a relatively deep stage of sleep, EEG activity is dominated by high-frequency beta waves that resemble those observed when people are alert and awake* (see Figure 5.4 again).

This paradox is probably related to the association between REM sleep and dreaming. As noted earlier, when subjects are awakened during various stages of sleep and asked whether they are dreaming, most dream reports come from the REM stage (Dement, 1978; McCarley, 1994). Although decades of research have revealed that some dreaming occurs in the non-REM stages (Pivik, 2000), dreaming is most frequent, vivid, and memorable during REM sleep.

To summarize, *REM sleep* is a relatively deep stage of sleep marked by rapid eye movements, high-frequency, low-amplitude brain waves, and vivid dreaming. It is such a special stage of sleep that the other four stages are often characterized simply as "non-REM sleep." *Non-REM (NREM) sleep* consists of sleep stages 1 through 4, which are marked by an absence of rapid eye movements, relatively little dreaming, and varied EEG activity.

Repeating the Cycle

During the course of a night, people usually repeat the sleep cycle about four times. As the night wears on, the cycle changes gradually. The first REM period is relatively short, lasting only a few minutes. Subsequent REM periods get progressively longer, peaking at around 40–60 minutes in length. Additionally, NREM intervals tend to get shorter, and descents into NREM stages usually become more shallow. These trends can be seen in Figure 5.5, which provides an overview of a typical night's sleep cycle. These trends mean that most slow-wave sleep occurs early in the

Figure 5.5

An overview of the cycle of sleep. The white line charts how a typical, healthy, young adult moves through the various stages of sleep during the course of a night. This diagram also shows how dreams and rapid eye movements tend to coincide with REM sleep, whereas posture changes occur between REM periods (because the body is nearly paralyzed during REM sleep). Notice how the person cycles into REM four times, as descents into NREM sleep get shallower and REM periods get longer. Thus, slow-wave sleep is prominent early in the night, while REM sleep dominates the second half of a night's sleep. Although these patterns are typical, keep in mind that sleep patterns vary from one person to another and that they change with age.

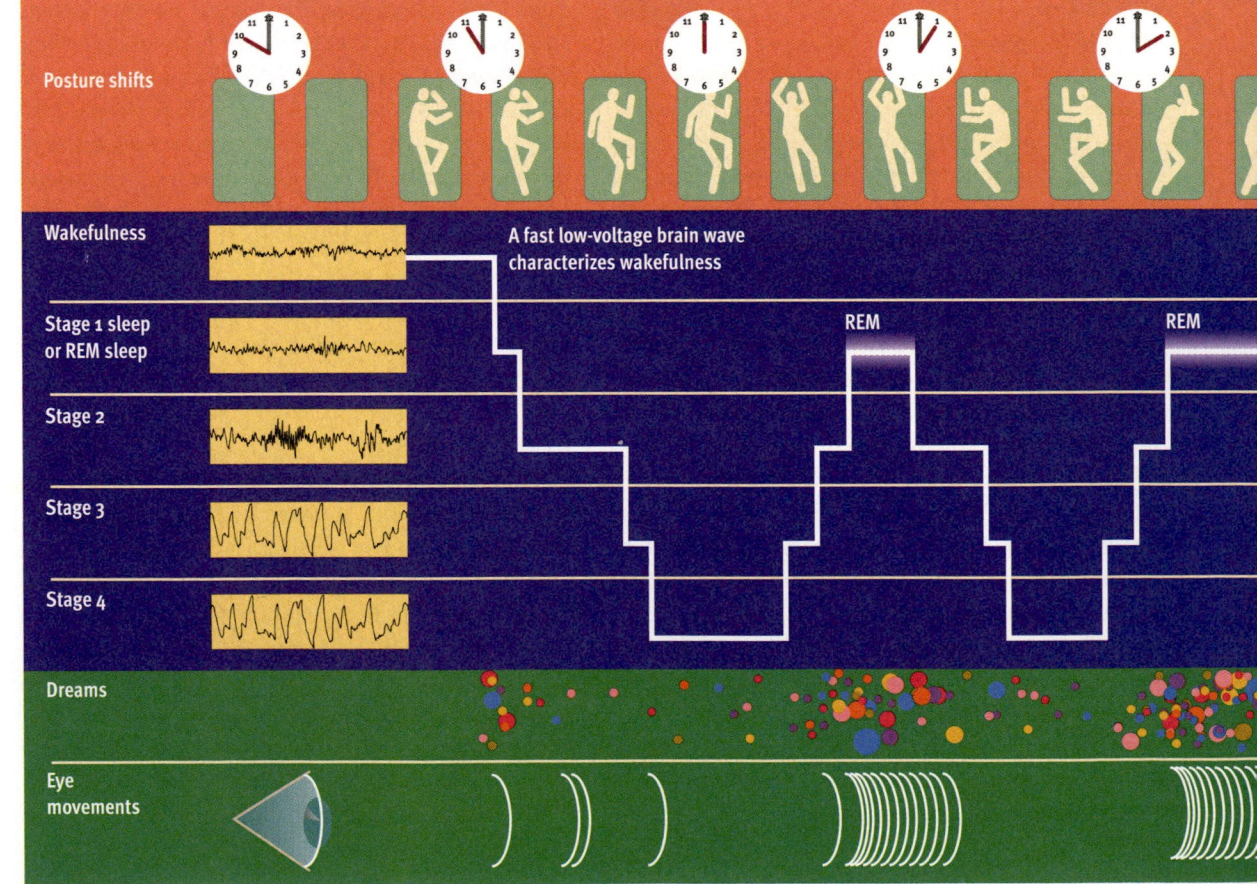

sleep cycle and that REM sleep tends to pile up in the second half of the sleep cycle. Summing across the entire cycle, young adults typically spend about 20% of their sleep time in slow-wave sleep and another 20% in REM sleep.

Age Trends in Sleep

Age alters the sleep cycle. What we have described so far is the typical pattern for young adults. Children, however, display different patterns (Bootzin et al., 2001; Roffwarg, Muzio, & Dement, 1966). Newborns will sleep six to eight times in a 24-hour period, often exceeding a total of 16 hours of sleep. Fortunately for parents, during the first several months much of this sleep begins to get consolidated into one particularly long nighttime sleep period (Webb, 1992a). Interestingly, infants spend much more of their sleep time in the REM stage than adults do. In the first few months, REM accounts for about 50% of babies' sleep, as compared to 20% of adults' sleep. During the remainder of the first year, the REM portion of infants' sleep declines to roughly 30%. The REM portion of sleep continues to decrease gradually until it levels off at about 20% (see Figure 5.6 on the next page).

During adulthood, gradual, age-related changes in sleep continue. Although the proportion of REM sleep remains fairly stable (Bliwise, 2000), the percentage of slow-wave sleep declines dramatically and the percentage of time spent in stage 1 increases slightly (Van Cauter, Leproult, & Plat, 2000). These shifts toward lighter sleep *may* contribute to the increased frequency of nighttime awakenings seen among the elderly. As Figure 5.6 shows, the average amount of total sleep time also declines with advancing age. However, these averages mask important variability, as total sleep *increases* with age in a substantial minority of older people (Webb, 1992a).

Culture and Sleep

Although age clearly affects the nature and structure of sleep itself, the psychological and physiological experience of sleep does not appear to vary systematically across cultures. Cultural disparities in sleep are limited to more peripheral matters, such as sleep-

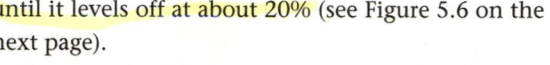

Web Link 5.2

The Sleep Well
Leading sleep researcher William Dement of Stanford University offers a major Internet resource center on sleep and sleeping disorders.

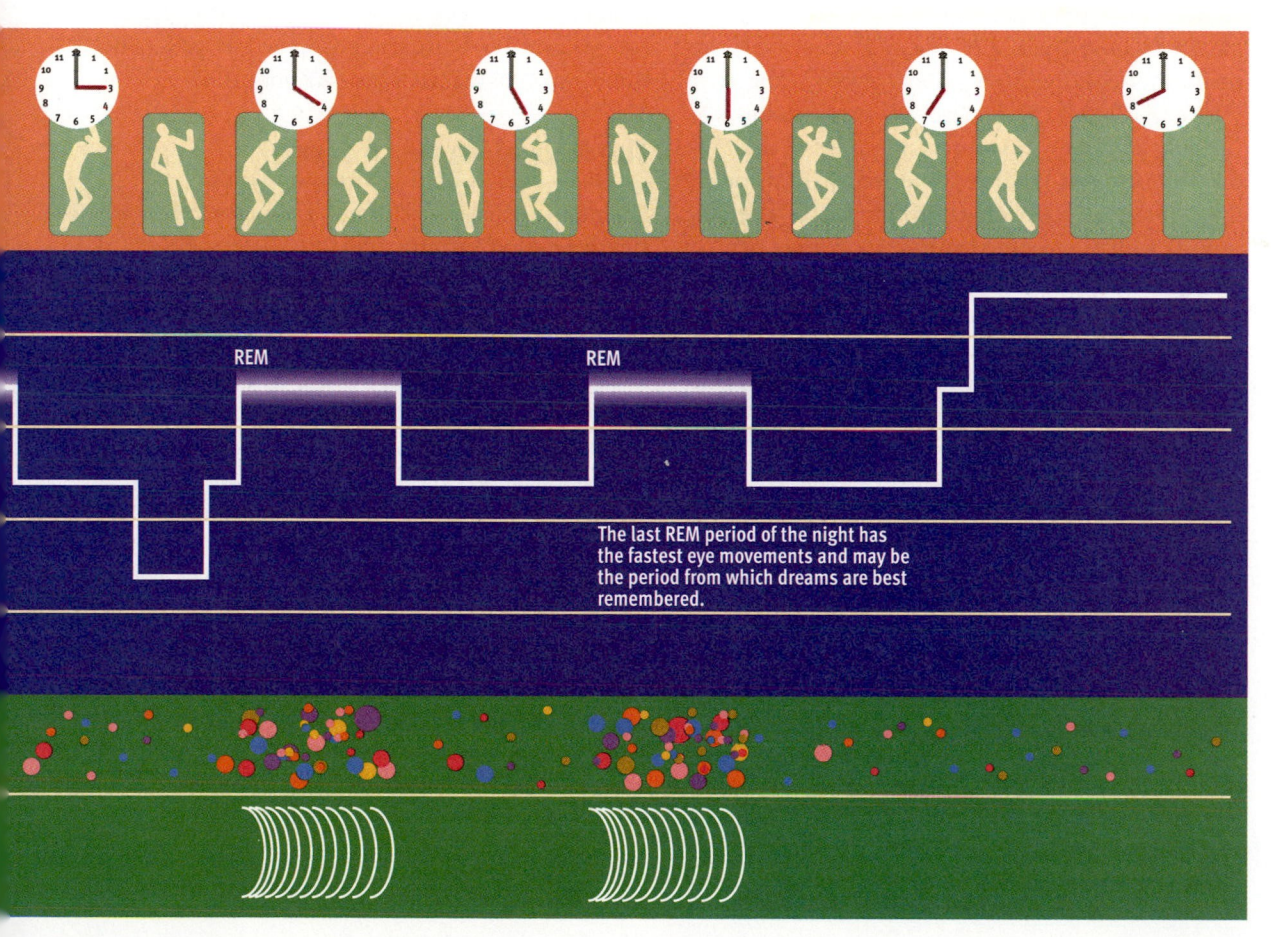

The last REM period of the night has the fastest eye movements and may be the period from which dreams are best remembered.

Figure 5.6

Changes in sleep patterns over the life span. Both the total amount of sleep per night and the portion of sleep that is REM sleep change with age. Sleep patterns change most dramatically during infancy, with total sleep time and amount of REM sleep declining sharply in the first two years of life. After a noticeable drop in the average amount of sleep in adolescence, sleep patterns remain relatively stable, although total sleep and slow-wave sleep continue to decline gradually with age.

Source: Adapted from an updated revision of a figure in Roffwarg, H. P., Muzio, J. N., & Dement, W. C. (1966). Ontogenetic development of human sleep-dream cycle. *Science, 152,* 604–609. Copyright © 1966 by the American Association for the Advancement of Science. Adapted and revised by permission of the authors.

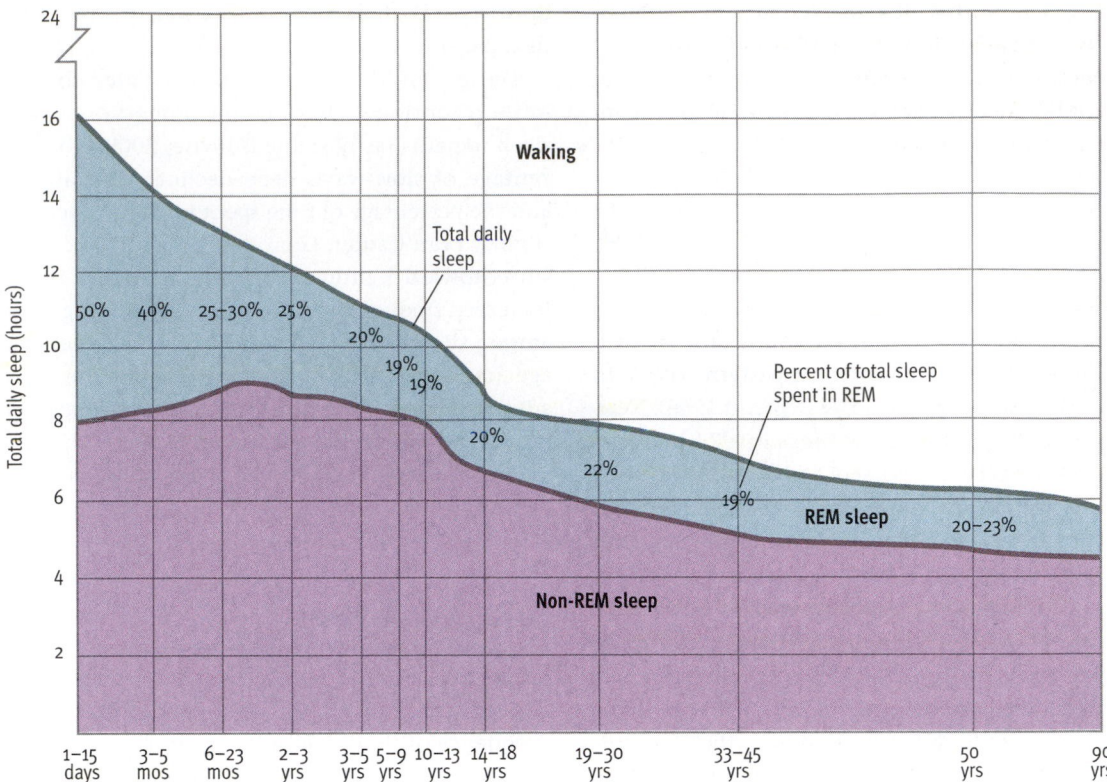

ing arrangements and napping customs. For example, there are cultural differences in *co-sleeping*, the practice of children and parents sleeping together (McKenna, 1993). In modern Western societies, co-sleeping is actively discouraged. As part of their effort to foster self-reliance, American parents teach their children to sleep alone. In contrast, co-sleeping is more widely accepted in Japanese culture, which emphasizes interdependence and group harmony (Latz et al., 1999). Around the world as a whole, co-sleeping is normative (Ball, Hooker, & Kelly, 2000). Strong pressure against co-sleeping appears to be largely an urban, Western phenomenon.

Napping practices also vary along cultural lines. In many societies, shops close and activities are curtailed in the afternoon to permit people to enjoy a 1- to 2-hour midday nap. These "siesta cultures" are found mostly in tropical regions of the world (Webb & Dinges, 1989). There, this practice is adaptive in that it allows people to avoid working during the hottest part of the day. The siesta is not a fixture in all tropical societies, however. It is infrequent among nomadic groups and those that depend on irregular food supplies. As a rule, the siesta tradition is not found in industrialized societies, where it conflicts with the emphasis on productivity and the philosophy that "time is money." Moreover, when industrialization

comes to a siesta culture, it undermines the practice. For instance, modernization in Spain has led to a decline in midday napping there (Kribbs, 1993).

The Neural Bases of Sleep

The rhythm of sleep and waking appears to be regulated by subcortical structures that lie deep within the brain. One brain structure that is important to sleep and wakefulness is the *reticular formation* in the core of the brainstem (Steriade, 2000). **The *ascending reticular activating system (ARAS)* consists of the afferent fibers running through the reticular formation that influence physiological arousal.** As you can see in Figure 5.7, the ARAS projects diffusely into many areas of the cortex. When these ascending fibers are cut in the brainstem of a cat, the result is continuous sleep (Moruzzi, 1964). Electrical stimulation along the same pathways produces arousal and alertness.

Although the ARAS contributes to the neural regulation of sleep and waking, many other brain structures are also involved (Hobson, 1995). For example, activity in the pons and adjacent areas in the midbrain seems to be critical to the generation of REM sleep (Siegel, 2000). Specific areas in the medulla, thalamus, hypothalamus, and limbic system have also been implicated in the control of sleep and waking (see Figure 5.7). Thus, the ebb and flow of sleep and waking is regulated through activity in a *constellation* of interacting brain centers.

Efforts to identify the neurotransmitters involved in the regulation of sleep and waking have uncovered similar diffusion of responsibility. Serotonin and GABA appear to play especially important roles in the regulation of sleep. However, a variety of other neurotransmitters—norepinephrine, dopamine, and acetylcholine—clearly influence the course of sleep and arousal, and several other chemicals play contributing roles (Jones, 2000; Mendelson, 2001). In summary, no single structure in the brain serves as a "sleep center," nor does any one neurotransmitter serve as a "sleep chemical." Instead, sleep depends on the interplay of many neural centers and neurotransmitters.

The Evolutionary Bases of Sleep

What is the evolutionary significance of sleep? The fact that sleep is seen in a highly diverse array of organisms and that it appears to have evolved independently in birds and mammals suggests that it has considerable adaptive value. But theorists disagree about *how* exactly sleep is adaptive. One hypothesis is that sleep evolved to conserve organisms' energy. According to this notion, sleep evolved millions of years ago in service of warmbloodedness, which requires the maintenance of a constant, high body temperature by metabolic means. An alternative hypothesis is that the immobilization associated with sleep is adaptive because it reduces exposure to predators and other sources of danger. A third hypothesis is that sleep is adaptive because it helps animals restore energy and other bodily resources depleted by waking activities. Overall, the evidence seems strongest for the energy conservation hypothesis, but there is room for extensive debate about the evolutionary bases of sleep (Zepelin, 2000).

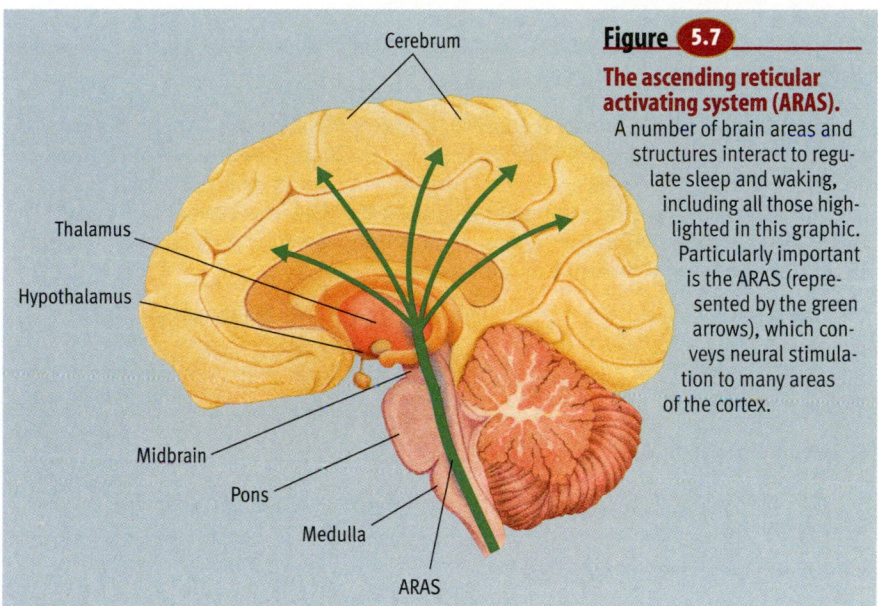

Figure 5.7

The ascending reticular activating system (ARAS). A number of brain areas and structures interact to regulate sleep and waking, including all those highlighted in this graphic. Particularly important is the ARAS (represented by the green arrows), which conveys neural stimulation to many areas of the cortex.

Cerebrum
Thalamus
Hypothalamus
Midbrain
Pons
Medulla
ARAS

REVIEW OF KEY POINTS

● Research on sleep is typically done in laboratories where volunteers come to spend the night. Participants are hooked up to an EEG, EOG, EMG, and instruments that monitor heart rate, respiration, pulse rate, and body temperature.

● When people fall asleep, they evolve through a series of stages in cycles of approximately 90 minutes. Slow-wave sleep consists of stages 3 and 4, during which delta waves are prominent. During the REM stage, sleepers experience rapid eye movements, brain waves that are characteristic of waking thought, and vivid dreaming. The sleep cycle tends to be repeated about four times a night, as REM

sleep gradually becomes more predominant and NREM sleep dwindles.

● The REM portion of sleep declines during childhood, leveling off at around 20%. During adulthood, slow-wave sleep declines. Total sleep time decreases for most elderly people, although it increases for some. Culture appears to have little impact on the physiological experience of sleep, but it does influence napping patterns and sleeping arrangements, such as co-sleeping.

● The neural bases of sleep are complex. Arousal depends on activity in the ascending reticular activating system, but a constellation of brain structures and neurotransmitters contribute to regulation of the sleep and waking cycle. Hypotheses about the evolutionary bases of sleep focus on energy conservation, reduced exposure to predators, and restoration of resources depleted by waking activity.

Doing Without: Sleep Deprivation

Scientific research on sleep deprivation presents something of a paradox. On the one hand, research suggests that sleep deprivation is not as detrimental as one might expect. On the other hand, evidence suggests that sleep deprivation may be a major social problem, undermining efficiency at work and contributing to countless accidents.

Complete Deprivation

What happens when people go completely without sleep for a period of days? As you might expect, complete deprivation of sleep has negative effects on participants' mood and on their performance on both cognitive and perceptual-motor tasks (Pilcher & Huffcutt, 1996). However, these negative effects tend to be modest, and many researchers have been impressed

PREVIEW QUESTIONS

● What are the effects of sleep deprivation?

● What is known about the causes and prevalence of insomnia?

● What is the role of sedative drugs in the treatment of insomnia?

● What are the symptoms of narcolepsy? Sleep apnea? Nightmares? Night terrors? Somnambulism?

CONCEPT CHECK 5.1

Comparing REM and NREM Sleep

A table here could have provided you with a systematic comparison of REM sleep and NREM sleep, but that would have deprived you of the opportunity to check your understanding of these sleep phases by creating your own table. Fill in each of the blanks below with a word or phrase highlighting the differences between REM and NREM sleep with regard to the various characteristics specified. You can find the answers in the back of the book in Appendix A.

Characteristic	REM sleep	NREM sleep
1. Type of EEG activity	_____	_____
2. Eye movements	_____	_____
3. Dreaming	_____	_____
4. Depth (difficulty in awakening)	_____	_____
5. Percentage of total sleep (in adults)	_____	_____
6. Increases or decreases (as percentage of sleep) during childhood	_____	_____
7. Timing in sleep cycle (dominates early or late)	_____	_____

by how *well* sleep-deprived subjects can perform if they are motivated to do so (Anch et al., 1988). The effects of complete sleep deprivation would probably be more severe except that most people have a hard time going very long without sleep. Most experience great difficulty getting beyond a third or fourth sleepless day.

Partial Deprivation

Partial sleep deprivation, or *sleep restriction*, occurs when people make do with substantially less sleep than normal over a period of time. Partial deprivation occurs far more often in everyday life than complete sleep deprivation. Indeed, many sleep experts believe that much of American society chronically suffers from partial sleep deprivation (Mitler, Dinges, & Dement, 2000). It appears that more and more people are trying to squeeze additional waking hours out of their days as they attempt to juggle work, family, household, and school responsibilities, leading William Dement to comment that "most Americans no longer know what it feels like to be fully alert" (Toufexis, 1990, p. 79).

How serious are the effects of partial sleep deprivation? Studies suggest that the effects depend on the amount of sleep lost and on the nature of the task at hand (Bonnet, 1991). Negative effects are most likely when subjects are asked to work on long-lasting, difficult, or monotonous tasks, or when subjects are asked to restrict their sleep to 5 hours or fewer for many nights (Gillberg & Akerstedt, 1998). Interestingly, people often do not appreciate the degree to which sleep deprivation has a negative impact on their functioning, a finding that was apparent in our Featured Study for this chapter.

FEATURED STUDY

Gauging the Impact of Sleep Deprivation in College Students

Investigators: June J. Pilcher and Amy S. Walters (Bradley University)

Source: How sleep deprivation affects psychological variables related to college students' cognitive performance. *Journal of American College Health,* 1997, 46, 121–126.

Whether it's because they want to fit in more time for partying or for studying, college students routinely deprive themselves of sleep. This study assessed the effects of 24 hours of sleep deprivation on students' cognitive performance and attempted to identify some factors, such as negative mood or poor attention, that might contribute to any decrements in cognitive functioning. The investigators also wanted to see whether sleep deprivation altered participants' ability to make accurate assessments of their concentration, effort, and performance.

Method

Participants. Volunteers were solicited from five psychology classes. Of the original 65 volunteers, 44 (26 women and 18 men) completed the study. Their mean age was 20.5 years.

Measures. Cognitive performance was evaluated with the Watson-Glaser Critical Thinking Appraisal, a challenging standardized test that resembles the normal tests college students encounter. Mood was assessed with the Profile of Mood States, and attention was measured with the Cognitive Interference Questionnaire. The participants also rated their effort, concentration, and performance on seven-point scales.

Procedure. After a normal day with no napping, participants reported to a sleep lab at 10 P.M. on a Friday night. At that time, the students were randomly assigned to the experimental (sleep-deprived) and control (nondeprived) groups. Members of the control group were sent home and instructed to get about eight hours of sleep. The sleep-deprived subjects remained at the lab, where they watched movies, played video and board games, and worked on personal projects, under the supervision of research assistants. The participants in both groups completed the various tests and other measures on Saturday at 10 A.M.

Results

As anticipated, the sleep-deprived group scored significantly lower on the measure of cognitive performance (see Figure 5.8). Contrary to expectation, the differences between the two groups on the Profile of Mood States and the Cognitive Interference Questionnaire were minimal and unenlightening. However, the participants' self-ratings yielded more interesting data, as the sleep-deprived subjects rated their effort, concentration, and performance significantly *higher* than the nondeprived subjects did.

Discussion

Although the sleep-deprived group performed substantially worse on the cognitive test, their subjective estimates of their effort, concentration, and performance were inconsistent with this reality. Thus, the investigators conclude that "college students are not aware of the extent to which sleep deprivation impairs their ability to complete cognitive tasks successfully" (p. 125).

Comment

This study was selected for its straightforward examination of a practical issue that is obviously relevant to students' lives. The negative impact of sleep deprivation on the participants' cognitive functioning was striking. The study also provides yet another demonstration that human experience is highly subjective. Although sleep-deprived subjects showed clear impairment on an objective measure of their cognitive performance, they *felt* that their performance was fine. ■

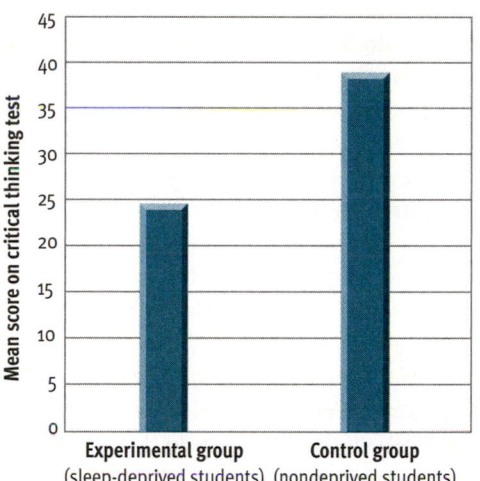

Figure 5.8

Effect of sleep deprivation on cognitive performance. Experimental subjects in the Pilcher and Walters (1997) study underwent 24 hours of sleep deprivation prior to taking the Watson-Glaser Critical Thinking Appraisal. As you can see, their performance on this cognitive test was clearly inferior to that of the control subjects, who had not experienced sleep deprivation.

Our Featured Study is representative of a great deal of recent research suggesting that the effects of sleep deprivation are not as benign as widely believed. Studies indicate that partial sleep deprivation can impair individuals' attention, reaction time, motor coordination, and decision making (Dinges, 1995; Pilcher & Huffcutt, 1996). Evidence suggests that sleep deprivation contributes to errors in medical treatment by physicians in training (medical residents), who often work 80–100 hours a week without adequate rest (Weinger & Ancoli-Israel, 2002). Sleep deprivation has also been blamed for a large proportion of transportation accidents and mishaps in the workplace (Dement, 1997; Mitler, 1993). In one survey, 23% of the respondents reported that they had fallen asleep while driving at some point in their lives (McCartt et al., 1996). Sleep deprivation seems to be particularly problematic among truck drivers, young drivers, drivers with sleep disorders, and drivers who work rotating shifts (Lyznicki et al., 1998). Studies also suggest that nighttime workers in many industries frequently fall asleep on the job (Roehrs et al., 2000). Obviously, if a person is running a punch press, driving a bus, or working as an air traffic controller, a momentary lapse in attention could be very, very costly. In recent years, a number of major disasters, such as the nuclear accidents at Three Mile Island and Chernobyl, the running aground of the Exxon *Valdez* in Alaska, and the *Challenger* space shuttle tragedy have been blamed in part on lapses in judgment and attention resulting from sleep deprivation (Doghramji, 2001). Experts have *estimated* that accidents attributed to drowsiness induced by sleep deprivation cost the U.S. economy over $56 billion annually, lead to the loss of over 52 million work days each year, and result in over 24,000 deaths per year (Coren, 1996).

Selective Deprivation

The unique quality of REM sleep led researchers to look into the effects of a special type of partial sleep deprivation—*selective deprivation.* In a number of laboratory studies, subjects were awakened over a period of nights whenever they began to go into the REM stage. These subjects usually got a decent amount of sleep in NREM stages, but they were selectively deprived of REM sleep.

What are the effects of REM deprivation? The evidence indicates that it has little impact on daytime functioning and task performance, but it *does* have some interesting effects on subjects' patterns of sleeping (Bonnet, 2000). As the nights go by in REM-deprivation studies, it becomes necessary to awaken the subjects more and more often to deprive them of their REM sleep, because they spontaneously shift into REM more and more frequently. In one study, researchers had to awaken a subject 64 times by the third night of REM deprivation, as shown in Figure 5.9 (Borbely, 1986). Furthermore, when a REM-deprivation experiment comes to an end and subjects are allowed to sleep without interruption, they experience a "rebound effect." That is, they spend extra time in REM periods for one to three nights to make up for their REM deprivation (Bonnet, 2000).

Similar results have been observed when subjects have been selectively deprived of slow-wave sleep (Klerman, 1993). As the nights go by, more awakenings are required to prevent SWS and after deprivation of SWS, people experience a rebound effect (Borbely & Achermann, 2000). In fact, by some standards, the need for slow-wave sleep appears to be even more pressing than the need for REM sleep, which may explain why, in a typical night's sleep, people get lots of SWS first, and then load up on REM sleep (Borbely, 1994). What do theorists make of these spontaneous pursuits of REM and slow-wave sleep? They conclude that people must have specific *needs* for REM and slow-wave sleep—and rather strong needs, at that (Borbely & Achermann, 2000). Some recent studies suggest that REM and perhaps slow-wave sleep contribute to firming up learning that takes place during the day—a process called *memory consolidation* (Stickgold, James, & Hobson, 2000; Stickgold et al., 2000).

Problems in the Night: Sleep Disorders

Not everyone is able to consistently enjoy the luxury of a good night's sleep. In this section we will briefly discuss what is currently known about a variety of sleep disorders.

Insomnia

Insomnia is the most common sleep disorder. *Insomnia* refers to chronic problems in getting adequate sleep. It occurs in three basic patterns: (1) difficulty in falling asleep initially, (2) difficulty in remaining asleep, and (3) persistent early-morning awakening. Difficulty falling asleep is the most common problem among young people, whereas trouble staying asleep and early-morning awakenings are the most common syndromes among middle-aged and elderly people (Hublin & Partinen, 2002). Insomnia may sound like a minor problem to those who haven't struggled with it, but it can be a very unpleasant malady. Insomniacs have to endure the agony of watching their precious sleep time tick away as they toss and turn in restless frustration. Moreover, insomnia is associated with daytime fatigue, impaired functioning, an elevated risk for accidents, reduced productivity, absenteeism at work, depression, and increased health problems (Benca, 2001; Simon & VonKorff, 1997).

Prevalence. Estimates of the prevalence of insomnia vary considerably because surveys have to depend on respondents' highly subjective judgments of whether their sleep is adequate. Another complicating consideration is that nearly everyone suffers *occasional* sleep difficulties because of stress, disruptions of biological rhythms, or other temporary circumstances. Fortunately, these problems clear up spontaneously for most people. Caveats aside, the best estimates suggest that about 34%–35% of adults report problems with insomnia and about half of these people (15%–17%) suffer from severe or frequent insomnia (Zorick & Walsh, 2000). The prevalence of insomnia increases with age and is about 50% more common in women than in men (Partinen & Hublin, 2000).

Some people may suffer from "pseudoinsomnia," or *sleep state misperception,* which means that they just *think* they are getting an inadequate amount of sleep. When actually monitored in a sleep clinic, about 5% of insomniac patients show sound patterns of sleep (Hauri, 2000). In one well-known case of exaggerated complaining, a British insomniac claimed that he hadn't slept in 10 years! When invited to stay at a sleep clinic for observation, he seemed determined to prove his chronic sleeplessness. However, on the second night he nodded out for 20 minutes. By the fourth night, he could barely keep his eyes open, and soon he was snoring blissfully for hours (Oswald & Adam, 1980). Misperceptions of sleep efficiency are

A large number of traffic accidents occur because drivers get drowsy or fall asleep at the wheel. Although the effects of sleep deprivation seem innocuous, sleep loss can be deadly.

© Joseph Sohm/ChromoSohm-CORBIS

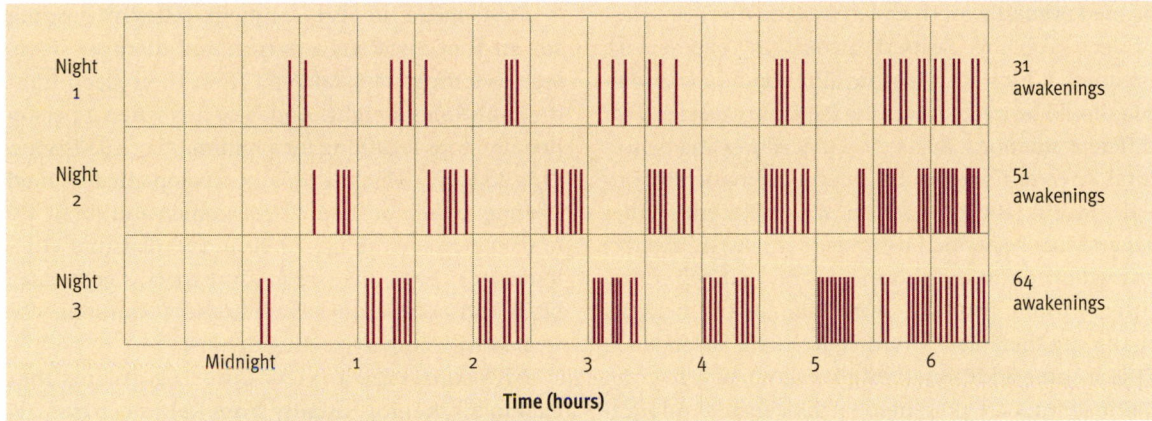

	Midnight	1	2	3	4	5	6

Night 1 — 31 awakenings

Night 2 — 51 awakenings

Night 3 — 64 awakenings

Time (hours)

Figure 5.9

The effects of REM deprivation on sleep. This graph plots how often researchers had to awaken a subject over the course of three nights of REM deprivation. Notice how the awakenings rapidly became more frequent during the course of each night and from night to night. This pattern of awakenings illustrates how a REM-deprived subject tends to compensate by repeatedly slipping back into REM sleep.

SOURCE: Adapted from Borbely, A. (1986). *Secrets of sleep* (English translation). New York: Basic Books. Copyright © 1986 by Basic Books. Reprinted by permission of Basic Books, Inc.

not unique to pseudoinsomniacs. Many people underestimate how much sleep they get (Reynolds et al., 1991). The discrepancy between individuals' feelings about how much they sleep and objective reality shows once again that states of consciousness are highly subjective.

Causes. Insomnia has many causes (Roehrs, Zorick, & Roth, 2000; Hauri, 2002). In some cases, excessive anxiety and tension prevent relaxation and keep people awake. Insomnia is frequently a side effect of emotional problems, such as depression, or of significant stress, such as pressures at work. Understandably, health problems such as back pain, ulcers, and asthma can lead to insomnia. The use of certain drugs, especially such stimulants as cocaine and amphetamines, may also lead to problems in sleeping.

Treatment. The most common approach to the treatment of insomnia is prescription of sedative drugs (sleeping pills). *Benzodiazepine medications,* which exert their effects at GABA synapses, are the most widely prescribed sedatives. These drugs are fairly effective in helping people fall asleep more quickly, and they reduce nighttime awakenings and increase total sleep (Mendelson, 2000). Nonetheless, sedative drugs may be used to combat insomnia *too* frequently. Many sleep experts argue that in the past physicians prescribed sleeping pills far too readily. As a result of this criticism, prescriptions for sleeping pills have declined significantly in recent decades (Walsh & Scweitzer, 1999). Nonetheless, about 5%–15% of adults still use sleep medication with some regularity (Hublin & Partinen, 2002).

Sedatives can be a poor long-term solution for insomnia for a number of reasons (Roehrs & Roth, 2000; Wesson et al., 1997). One problem is that sedatives have carryover effects that can make people drowsy and sluggish the next day and can lead to memory decrements. They can also cause an over-

dose in combination with alcohol or opiate drugs. Although the abuse of sleeping medications appears to be less common that widely assumed, there are legitimate concerns about people becoming physically dependent on sedatives (Ballenger, 2000). Moreover, with continued use sedatives gradually become less effective, so some people increase their dose to higher levels, creating a vicious circle of escalating dependency and daytime sluggishness (Lader, 2002; see Figure 5.10). Ironically, most sedatives also interfere with the normal cycle of sleep. Although they promote sleep, most sedatives decrease the proportion of time spent in slow-wave sleep, and some of the older drugs also reduce REM sleep (Nishino, Mignot, & Dement, 1995). Furthermore, if sleep medication is stopped abruptly, many people experience even worse insomnia than before their treatment was begun—a condition called *rebound insomnia.*

In conclusion, sedatives *do* have an important place in the treatment of insomnia, but they need to be used cautiously and conservatively. They should

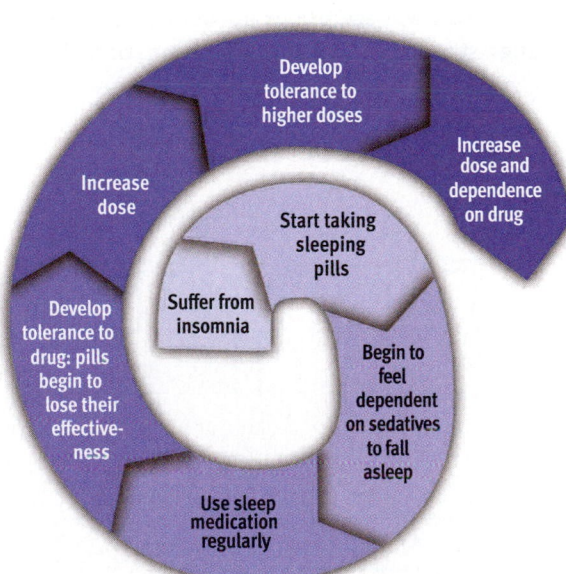

Figure 5.10

The vicious circle of dependence on sleeping pills. Because of the body's ability to develop tolerance to drugs, using sedatives routinely to "cure" insomnia can lead to a vicious circle of escalating dependency as larger and larger doses of the sedative are needed to produce the same effect.

be used primarily for short-term treatment (2-4 weeks) of sleep problems. Beyond discouraging overreliance on drugs, it is difficult to generalize about how insomnia should be treated, because its many causes call for different solutions. Relaxation procedures and behavioral interventions can be helpful for many individuals (Morin, 2002; Stepanski, 2000). Recent studies suggest that behavioral treatments are just as effective as medication in the short term and that behavioral interventions produce more long-lasting benefits than drug therapies (Morin et al., 1999; Smith et al., 2002). Some additional insights about how to combat insomnia are presented in the Personal Application at the end of this chapter.

Other Sleep Problems

Although insomnia is the most common difficulty associated with sleep, people are plagued by many other types of sleep problems as well. Let's briefly look at the symptoms, causes, and prevalence of five additional sleep problems, as described by Kryger, Roth, and Dement (2000) and Bootzin et al. (2001).

Narcolepsy **is a disease marked by sudden and irresistible onsets of sleep during normal waking periods.** A person suffering from narcolepsy goes directly from wakefulness into REM sleep, usually for a short period of time (10–20 minutes). This is a potentially dangerous condition, since some victims fall asleep instantly, even while driving a car or operating machinery. Narcolepsy is relatively infrequent, as it is seen in only about 0.05% of the population (Partinen & Hublin, 2000). Its causes are not well understood, but some people appear to be genetically predisposed to the disease (Mignot, 2000). Stimulant drugs have been used to treat this condition with modest success (Guilleminault & Anagnos, 2000). But as you will see in our upcoming discussion of drugs, stimulants carry many problems of their own.

Sleep apnea **involves frequent, reflexive gasping for air that awakens a person and disrupts sleep.** Some victims are awakened from their sleep hundreds of times a night. Apnea occurs when a person literally stops breathing for a minimum of 10 seconds. This disorder, which is usually accompanied by loud snoring, is seen in about 2% of women and about 4% of men between the ages of 30 and 60 (Bassiri & Guilleminault, 2000). As you might expect, sleep apnea often leads to insomnia as a side effect. Apnea may be treated with surgery or drug therapy.

Nightmares **are anxiety-arousing dreams that lead to awakening, usually from REM sleep** (see Figure 5.11). Typically, a person who awakens from a nightmare recalls a vivid dream and may have difficulty getting back to sleep. Significant stress in one's life is associated with increased frequency and intensity of nightmares. In adults, there is a correlation between frequent nightmares and neurotic symptoms (Berquier & Ashton, 1992). Although about 10% of adults have occasional nightmares, these frightening episodes are mainly a problem among children. Most youngsters have occasional nightmares, but *persistent* nightmares may reflect an emotional disturbance. If a child's nightmares are frequent and unpleasant, counseling may prove helpful. Otherwise, treatment is unnecessary, as most children outgrow the problem.

Night terrors **(also called sleep terrors) are abrupt awakenings from NREM sleep accompanied by intense autonomic arousal and feelings of panic.** Night terrors, which can produce remarkable accelerations of heart rate, usually occur during stage 4 sleep early in the night, as shown in Figure 5.11 (Nielsen & Zadra, 2000). Victims typically let out a piercing cry, bolt upright, and then stare into space. They do not usually recall a coherent dream, although they may remember a simple, frightening image. The panic normally fades quickly, and a return to sleep is fairly easy. Night terrors occur in adults, but they are especially common in children ages 3 to 8. Night terrors are *not* indicative of an emotional disturbance. Treatment may not be necessary, as night terrors are often a temporary problem.

Somnambulism, **or sleepwalking, occurs when a person arises and wanders about while remaining asleep.** Sleepwalking tends to occur during the first 2 hours of sleep, when individuals are in slow-wave sleep (see Figure 5.11). Episodes may last from 15 seconds to 30 minutes (Aldrich, 2000). Sleepwalkers may awaken during their journey, or they may return to bed without any recollection of their excursion. The causes of this unusual disorder are unknown, although it appears to have a genetic predisposition (Keefauver & Guilleminault, 1994). Sleepwalking does

Figure 5.11

Sleep problems and the cycle of sleep. Different sleep problems tend to occur at different points in the sleep cycle. Whereas sleepwalking and night terrors are associated with slow-wave sleep, nightmares are associated with the heightened dream activity of REM sleep.

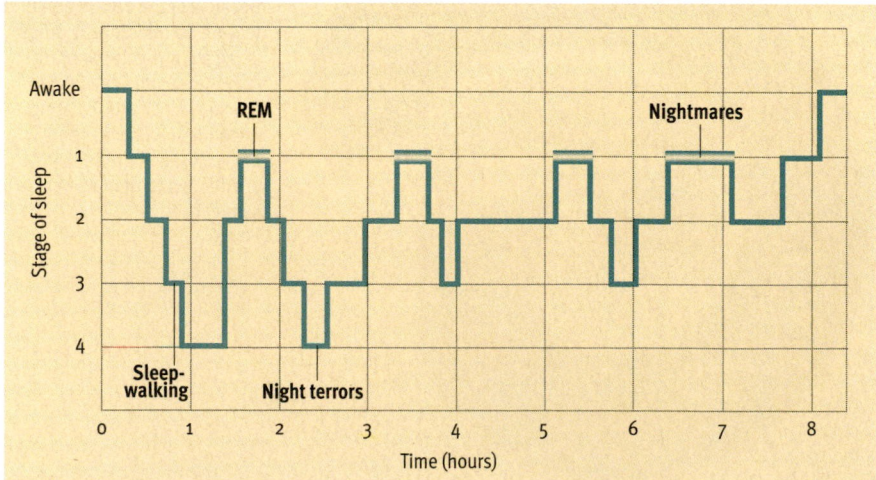

not appear to be a manifestation of underlying emotional or psychological problems (Mahowald, 1993). However, sleepwalkers *are* prone to accidents. In light of this reality, it is important to note that, contrary to popular myth, it is safe to awaken people (gently) from a sleepwalking episode—much safer than letting them wander about.

REVIEW OF KEY POINTS

- The effects of sleep deprivation depend on a variety of factors. Our Featured Study showed that college students underestimate the impact of sleep deprivation. Increased sleepiness can be a significant problem that appears to contribute to many transportation accidents and mishaps at work. Research on selective sleep deprivation suggests that people need REM sleep and slow-wave sleep.

- Many people are troubled by sleep disorders. Insomnia has a variety of causes. Sleeping pills generally are a poor solution. The optimal treatment for insomnia depends on its apparent cause.

- Narcolepsy is a disease marked by sudden, irresistible onsets of sleep during normal waking periods. Sleep apnea involves frequent gasping for air, which occurs when people stop breathing. Night terrors are abrupt awakenings from NREM sleep accompanied by panic, whereas nightmares are anxiety-arousing dreams that typically awaken one from REM sleep. Somnambulism typically occurs during slow-wave sleep.

The World of Dreams

For the most part, dreams are not taken very seriously in Western societies. Paradoxically, though, Robert Van de Castle (1994) points out that dreams have sometimes changed the world. For example, Van de Castle describes how René Descartes's philosophy of dualism, Frederick Banting's discovery of insulin, Elias Howe's refinement of the sewing machine, Mohandas Gandhi's strategy of nonviolent protest, and Lyndon Johnson's withdrawal from the 1968 presidential race were all inspired by dreams. He also explains how Mary Shelley's *Frankenstein* and Robert Louis Stevenson's *The Strange Case of Dr. Jekyll and Mr. Hyde* emerged out of their dream experiences. In his wide-ranging discussion, Van de Castle also relates how the Surrealist painter Salvador Dali characterized his works as "dream photographs," and how legendary filmmakers Ingmar Bergman, Orson Welles, and Federico Fellini all drew on their dreams in making their films. Thus, Van de Castle concludes that "dreams have had a dramatic influence on almost every important aspect of our culture and history" (p. 10).

What exactly is a dream? This question is more complex and controversial than you might guess (Pagel et al., 2001). The conventional view is that dreams are mental experiences during REM sleep that have a storylike quality, include vivid visual imagery, are often bizarre, and are regarded as perceptually real by the dreamer (Antrobus, 1993). However, theorists have begun to question virtually every aspect of this characterization. Decades of research on the contents of dreams, which we will discuss momentarily, has shown that dreams are not as bizarre as widely assumed (Cartwright, 1994). Recent years have seen renewed interest in the fact that dreams are not the exclusive property of REM sleep (Antrobus, 2000). Moreover, studies that have focused on dream reports from non-REM stages of sleep have found that these dreams appear to be less vivid, visual, and storylike than REM dreams (Verdone, 1993). And research suggests that dreamers realize they are dreaming more often than previously thought and that mental processes during sleep are more similar to waking thought processes than is widely assumed (Kahan & LaBerge, 1994, 1996). Thus, the concept of dreaming is undergoing some revision in scientific circles.

The Contents of Dreams

What do people dream about? Overall, dreams are not as exciting as advertised. Perhaps dreams are seen as exotic because people are more likely to remember their more bizarre nighttime dramas (De Koninck, 2000). After analyzing the contents of more than 10,000 dreams, Calvin Hall (1966) concluded that most dreams are relatively mundane. They tend to unfold in familiar settings with a cast of characters dominated by family, friends, and colleagues.

Certain themes tend to be more common than others in dreams. Table 5.2 on the next page lists the most common dreams reported by college students in one study (Griffith, Miyago, & Tago, 1958). If you glance through this list, you will see that people dream quite a bit about sex, aggression, and misfortune. According to Hall, dreams tend to center on classic sources of internal conflict, such as the conflict between taking chances and playing it safe. Hall was struck by how little people dream about public affairs and current events. Typically, dreams are self-centered; people dream mostly about themselves.

PREVIEW QUESTIONS

- What is a dream, and how are views on this question changing?
- What is known about the contents of people's dreams?
- Can external events affect the content of dreams?
- How does culture affect dream recall and dream content?
- How do the Freudian, cognitive, and activation-synthesis models view dreams?

Table 5.2 Common Dreams of College Students and the Percentage Having Each Type of Dream

Type of Dream	Percentage of Students	Type of Dream	Percentage of Students
Falling	83	Finding money	56
Being attacked or pursued	77	Swimming	52
Trying repeatedly to do something	71	Snakes	49
School, teachers, studying	71	Being inappropriately dressed	46
Sexual experiences	66	Being smothered	44
Arriving too late	64	Being nude in public	43
Eating	62	Fire	41
Being frozen with fright	58	Failing an examination	39
The death of a loved one	57	Seeing self as dead	33
Being locked up	56	Killing someone	26

Source: Griffith, R. M., Miyago, O, & Tago, A. (1958). The universality of typical dreams: Japanese vs. Americans. *American Anthropologist, 60*, 1173–1179. Copyright © 1958 by the American Anthropological Association. Reproduced by permission. Not for further reproduction.

Relatively little research has been done on developmental trends in dream reports, but the available data suggest that children's dreams are different from adults' dreams (Foulkes, 1982, 1999). For one thing, the rate of dream recall after REM awakenings is only 20%–30% until ages 9–11, when the recall rate begins to approach adults levels (typically around 80%). Dream reports from children under age 5 mostly consist of static, bland images with no storyline. Children ages 5 to 8 report dream narratives, but they are not well developed, and common adult themes of aggression and misfortune are notably infrequent. The contents of children's dreams don't become adult-like until around ages 11–13. These findings suggest that dreaming is a cognitive ability that develops gradually, like other cognitive abilities.

Researchers have found some modest dream-content differences between men and women that seem to reflect conventional gender roles in modern society (Van de Castle, 1993). For example, strangers show up more often in men's dreams, while women are more likely to dream of children. Men are more likely to dream about acting aggressively; women are more likely to dream about being the target of aggression. In their sexual dreams, men tend to have liaisons with attractive female strangers, whereas women are more likely to dream about sex with their boyfriends and husbands.

Links Between Dreams and Waking Life

Though dreams seem to belong in a world of their own, what people dream about is affected by what is going on in their lives (Kramer, 1994). If you're struggling with financial problems, worried about an upcoming exam, or sexually attracted to a classmate, these themes may very well show up in your dreams. As Domhoff (2001) puts it, "dream content in general is continuous with waking conceptions and emotional preoccupations" (p. 13). Freud noticed long ago that the contents of waking life tend to spill into dreams; he labeled this spillover the *day residue.*

On occasion, the content of dreams can also be affected by stimuli experienced while one is dreaming (De Koninck, 2000). For example, William Dement sprayed water on one hand of sleeping subjects while they were in the REM stage (Dement & Wolpert, 1958). Subjects who weren't awakened by the water were awakened by the experimenter a short time later and asked what they had been dreaming about. Dement found that 42% of the subjects had incorporated the water into their dreams. They said that they had dreamt that they were in rainfalls, floods, baths, swimming pools, and the like. Some people report that they occasionally experience the same sort of phenomenon at home when the sound of their alarm clock fails to awaken them. The alarm is incorporated into their dream as a loud engine or a siren, for instance. As with day residue, the incorporation of external stimuli into dreams shows that people's dream world is not entirely separate from their real world.

Culture and Dreams

Striking cross-cultural variations occur in beliefs about the nature of dreams and the importance attributed to them. In modern Western society, people typically make a distinction between the "real" world they experience while awake and the "imaginary" world they experience while dreaming. Some people realize that events in the real world can affect their dreams, but few believe that events in their dreams hold any significance for their waking life. Although a small minority of individuals take their dreams seriously, in Western cultures dreams are largely written off as insignificant, meaningless meanderings of the unconscious (Tart, 1988).

In many non-Western cultures, however, dreams are viewed as important sources of information about oneself, about the future, or about the spiritual world (Kracke, 1991). Although no culture confuses dreams with waking reality, many view events in dreams as another type of reality that may be just as important as, or perhaps even more important than, events experienced while awake. Among Australian aborigines, for example, "Dreaming is the focal point of traditional aboriginal existence and simultaneously determines their way of life, their culture, and their relationship to the physical and spiritual environment" (Dawson, 1993, p. 1). In some instances, people are even held responsible for their dream actions. Among the New Guinea Arapesh, for example, an erotic dream about someone may be viewed as the equivalent of an adulterous act. In many cultures, dreams are seen as a window into the spiritual world, permitting communication with ancestors or supernatural beings (Bourguignon, 1972). People in some cultures believe that dreams provide information about the future—good or bad omens about upcoming battles, hunts, births, and so forth (Tedlock, 1992).

In regard to dream content, both similarities and differences occur across cultures in the types of dreams that people report (Domhoff, 2000; Hunt, 1989). Some basic dream themes appear to be nearly universal (falling, being pursued, having sex). However, the contents of dreams vary some from one culture to another because people in different societies deal with different worlds while awake. For example, in a 1950 study of the Siriono, a hunting-and-gathering people of the Amazon who were almost always hungry and spent most of their time in a grim search for food, *half* of the reported dreams focused on hunting, gathering, and eating food (D'Andrade, 1961). Shared systems for interpreting the contents of dreams also vary from one society to another. Table 5.3 lists a number of common dream interpretations among the Toraja of Indonesia (Hollan, 1989). Although some of these interpretations (example: standing on mountaintop = becoming a leader) might be common in other societies, some clearly are peculiar to Toraja society (example: buffalo in the rice fields = rats will eat the rice harvest).

Theories of Dreaming

Many theories have been proposed to explain why people dream. Sigmund Freud (1900), who analyzed clients' dreams in therapy, believed that the principal purpose of dreams is *wish fulfillment*. He thought that people fulfill ungratified needs from waking hours through wishful thinking in dreams. For example, someone who is sexually frustrated might have highly erotic dreams, while an unsuccessful person might dream about great accomplishments. Although these examples involve blatant wishful thinking, Freud asserted that the wish-fulfilling quality of many dreams may not be readily apparent because the true meaning of dreams may be disguised.

"[Dreams are] the royal road to the unconscious."
SIGMUND FREUD

National Library of Medicine

Table 5.3 Examples of Common Dream Interpretations Among the Toraja of Indonesia

"Good" Dreams	Interpretation	"Bad" Dreams	Interpretation
Receive gold	Good rice harvest	Buffalo in the rice fields	Rats will eat rice harvest
Carry pig or buffalo meat	Good rice harvest	Naked	Get sick
Act "crazy"	Receive wealth	Enter a burial cave	Die
Objects are thrown at dreamer	Rain will fall	Carried off by an ancestor	Die
Stand on mountaintop	Become a leader	Objects are stolen/lost/ carried away	Lose those objects
Steal objects	Receive those objects/ become wealthy	House burns or is destroyed	Lose wealth/ become poor
Swim in ocean or river	Receive wealth		
Jump over or cross water	Become wise/clever		
Gored by a buffalo	Buy a buffalo		

SOURCE: Adapted from Hollan, D. (1989). The personal use of dream beliefs in the Toraja Highlands. *Ethos, 17*, 166–186. Copyright © 1989 by the American Anthropological Association. Reproduced by permission. Not for further reproduction.

"*One function of dreams may be to restore our sense of competence. . . . It is also probable that in times of stress, dreams have more work to do in resolving our problems and are thus more salient and memorable.*"
ROSALIND CARTWRIGHT

Freud's influential theory sounded plausible when it was proposed over 100 years ago, but research has not provided much support for Freud's conception of dreaming (Fisher & Greenberg, 1996).

Other theorists, such as Rosalind Cartwright (1977; Cartwright & Lamberg, 1992), have proposed that dreams provide an opportunity to work through everyday problems. According to her *cognitive, problem-solving view,* there is considerable continuity between waking and sleeping thought. Proponents of this view believe that dreams allow people to engage in creative thinking about problems because dreams are not restrained by logic or realism. Consistent with this view, Cartwright (1991) has found that women going through divorce frequently dream about divorce-related problems. Cartwright's analysis is thought provoking, but critics point out that just because people dream about problems from their waking life doesn't mean they are dreaming up solutions (Blagrove, 1992, 1996). At present, there is only limited support for the idea that dreams serve a problem-solving function.

J. Allan Hobson and Robert McCarley argue that dreams are simply the by-product of bursts of activity emanating from subcortical areas in the brain (Hobson & McCarley, 1977; Hobson, Pace-Schott, & Stickgold, 2000; McCarley, 1994). Their *activation-synthesis model* proposes that dreams are side effects of the neural activation that produces "wide awake" brain waves during REM sleep. According to this model, neurons firing periodically in lower brain centers send random signals to the cortex (the seat of complex thought). The cortex supposedly synthesizes (constructs) a dream to make sense out of these signals. The activation-synthesis model does *not* assume that dreams are meaningless. As Hobson (1988) puts it, "Dreams are as meaningful as they can be under the adverse working conditions of the brain in REM sleep" (p. 214). In contrast to the theories of Freud and Cartwright, this theory obviously downplays the role of emotional factors as determinants of dreams. Like other theories of dreams, the activation-synthesis model has its share of critics. They point out that the model cannot accommodate the fact that dreaming occurs outside of REM sleep and that the contents of dreams are considerably more meaningful than Hobson and McCarley would predict (Foulkes, 1996).

These approaches, summarized in Figure 5.12, are only three out of a host of theories about the functions of dreams. All these theories are based more on conjecture than solid evidence, and none of them has been tested adequately. In part, this is because the private, subjective nature of dreams makes it difficult to put the theories to an empirical test. Thus, the purpose of dreaming remains a mystery.

We'll encounter more unsolved mysteries in the next two sections of this chapter as we discuss hypnosis and meditation. Whereas sleep and dreams are familiar to everyone, most people have little familiarity with hypnosis and meditation, which both involve deliberate efforts to temporarily alter consciousness.

Figure 5.12

Three theories of dreaming. Dreams can be explained in a variety of ways. Freud stressed the wish-fulfilling function of dreams. Cartwright emphasizes the problem-solving function of dreams. Hobson and McCarley assert that dreams are merely a by-product of periodic neural activation. All three theories are speculative and have their critics.

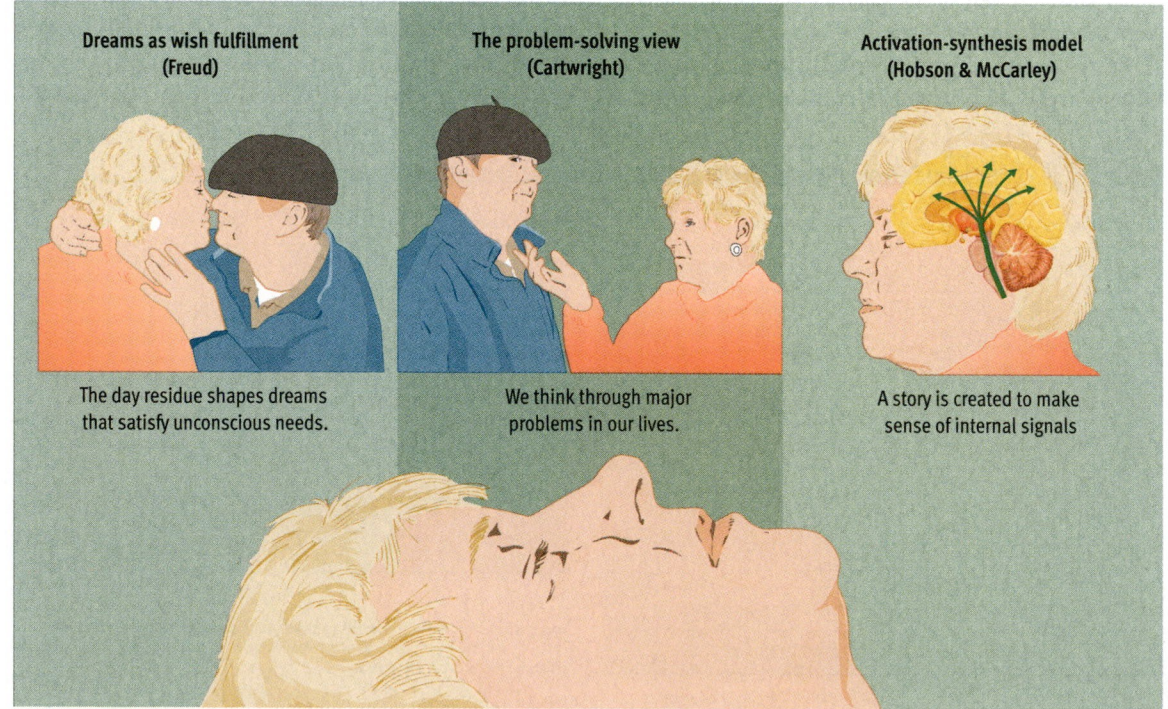

Dreams as wish fulfillment (Freud)

The day residue shapes dreams that satisfy unconscious needs.

The problem-solving view (Cartwright)

We think through major problems in our lives.

Activation-synthesis model (Hobson & McCarley)

A story is created to make sense of internal signals

REVIEW OF KEY POINTS

● The conventional view is that dreams are mental experiences during REM sleep that have a storylike quality, include vivid imagery, are often bizarre, and are regarded as real by the dreamer, but theorists have begun to question many aspects of this view.

● Researchers have found modest differences between men and women in dream content that seem to reflect conventional gender roles. The content of one's dreams may be affected by what is going on in one's life and by external stimuli that are experienced during the dream.

● In many non-Western cultures, dreams are viewed as important sources of information. Cultures vary in beliefs about the nature of dreams, dream recall, dream content, and dream interpretation.

● Freud argued that the principal purpose of dreams is wish fulfillment. Cartwright has articulated a problem-solving view, whereas Hobson and McCarley assert that dreams are side effects of the neural activation seen during REM sleep. Ultimately, theories of dreaming remain largely untested.

Hypnosis: Altered Consciousness or Role Playing?

Hypnosis has a long and checkered history. It all began with a flamboyant 18th-century Austrian physician by the name of Franz Anton Mesmer. Working in Paris, Mesmer claimed to cure people of illnesses through an elaborate routine involving a "laying on of hands." Mesmer had some complicated theories about how he had harnessed "animal magnetism." However, we know today that he had simply stumbled onto the power of suggestion. It was rumored that the French government offered him a princely amount of money to disclose how he effected his cures. He refused, probably because he didn't really know. Eventually he was dismissed as a charlatan and run out of town by the local authorities. Although officially discredited, Mesmer inspired followers—practitioners of "mesmerism"—who continued to ply their trade. To this day, our language preserves the memory of Franz Mesmer: When we are under the spell of an event or a story, we are "mesmerized."

Eventually, a Scottish physician, James Braid, became interested in the trancelike state that could be induced by the mesmerists. It was Braid who popularized the term *hypnotism* in 1843, borrowing it from the Greek word for sleep. Braid thought that hypnotism could be used to produce anesthesia for surgeries. However, just as hypnosis was catching on as a general anesthetic, more powerful and reliable chemical anesthetics were discovered, and interest in hypnotism dwindled.

Since then, hypnotism has led a curious dual existence. On the one hand, it has been the subject of numerous scientific studies. Furthermore, it has enjoyed considerable use as a clinical tool by physicians, dentists, and psychologists for over a century and has empirically supported value in the treatment of a variety of psychological and physical maladies (Lynn et al., 2000; Spiegel, Greenleaf, & Spiegel, 2000). On the other hand, however, an assortment of entertainers and quacks have continued in the less re-spectable tradition of mesmerism, using hypnotism for parlor tricks and chicanery. It is little wonder, then, that many myths about hypnosis have come to be widely accepted (see Figure 5.13 on the next page). In this section, we'll work on clearing up some of the confusion surrounding hypnosis.

Hypnotic Induction and Susceptibility

Hypnosis is a systematic procedure that typically produces a heightened state of suggestibility. It may also lead to passive relaxation, narrowed attention, and enhanced fantasy. If only in popular films, virtually everyone has seen a *hypnotic induction* enacted with a swinging pendulum. Actually many techniques can be used for inducing hypnosis (Meyer, 1992). Usually, the hypnotist will suggest to the subject that he or she is relaxing. Repetitively, softly, subjects are told that they are getting tired, drowsy, or sleepy. Often, the hypnotist vividly describes bodily sensations that should be occurring. Subjects are told that their arms are going limp, their feet are getting warm, their eyelids are getting heavy. Gradually, most subjects succumb and become hypnotized.

People differ in how well they respond to hypnotic induction. Ernest and Josephine Hilgard have done extensive research on this variability in *hypnotic susceptibility*. Not everyone can be hypnotized. About 10% of the population doesn't respond well at all. At the other end of the continuum, about 10% of people are exceptionally good hypnotic subjects (Hilgard, 1965). Responsiveness to hypnosis is a stable, measurable trait. It can be estimated pretty effectively with the Stanford Hypnotic Susceptibility Scale (SHSS) or its derivative, the Harvard Group Scale of Hypnotic Susceptibility (Perry, Nadon, & Button, 1992). The distribution of scores on the SHSS is graphed in Figure 5.14 on the next page.

PREVIEW QUESTIONS

● What is the history of hypnosis?

● What are some correlates of hypnotic susceptibility?

● What are some prominent hypnotic phenomena?

● What lines of evidence support the role-playing theory of hypnosis?

● What is Hilgard's explanation for how hypnosis works?

Hypnosis: Myth and Reality	
If you think . . .	**The reality is . . .**
Relaxation is an important feature of hypnosis.	It's not. Hypnosis has been induced during vigorous exercise.
It's mostly just compliance.	Many highly motivated subjects fail to experience hypnosis.
It's a matter of willful faking.	Physiological responses indicate that hypnotized subjects generally are not lying.
It has something to do with a sleeplike state.	It does not. Hypnotized subjects are fully awake.
Responding to hynosis is like responding to a placebo.	Placebo responsiveness and hypnotizability are not correlated.
People who are hypnotized lose control of themselves.	Subjects are perfectly capable of saying no or terminating hypnosis.
Hypnosis can enable people to "relive" the past.	Age-regressed adults behave like adults play-acting as children.
When hypnotized, people can remember more accurately.	Hypnosis may actually muddle the distinction between memory and fantasy and may artificially inflate confidence.
Hypnotized people do not remember what happened during the session.	Posthypnotic amnesia does not occur spontaneously.
Hypnosis can enable people to perform otherwise impossible feats of strength, endurance, learning, and sensory acuity.	Performance following hypnotic suggestions for increased muscle strength, learning and sensory acuity does not exceed what can be accomplished by motivated subjects outside hypnosis.

Figure 5.13

Misconceptions regarding hypnosis. Mistaken ideas about the nature of hypnosis are common. Some widely believed myths about hypnosis are summarized here along with more accurate information on each point, based on an article by Michael Nash (2001), a prominent hypnosis researcher. Many of these myths and realities are discussed in more detail in the text.

SOURCE: Adapted from Nash, M. R. (2001, July). The truth and the hype of hypnosis. *Scientific American, 285,* 36–43. Copyright © 2001 by Scientific American, Inc.

What makes some people highly susceptible to hypnosis? Variations in hypnotic susceptibility have traditionally been attributed to basic differences between people in personality traits, but decades of research on personality and hypnotizability have actually turned up relatively little (Dixon & Laurence, 1992). The only personality factors found to be related to hypnotic susceptibility are the overlapping traits of *absorption* and *imaginativeness*. People who can become deeply absorbed in an intense experience and people with a vivid imagination tend to be more susceptible to hypnosis, but the correlations are rather weak (Kirsch & Council, 1992).

Research has recently demonstrated that people who are responsive to suggestion under hypnosis are just as responsive to suggestion without being hypnotized (Braffman & Kirsch, 1999). In other words, their "hypnotic susceptibility" is not unique to hypnosis and is part of a broader trait that Kirsch and Braffman (2001) characterize as *imaginative suggestibility*. Kirsch and Braffman argue that future research should focus on measuring the determinants and repercussions of this broader trait. It remains to be seen whether this proposal will enhance our understanding of why some people are more responsive to hypnosis than others.

Hypnotic Phenomena

Many interesting effects can be produced through hypnosis. Some of the more prominent include:

1. *Anesthesia*. Under the influence of hypnosis, some participants can withstand treatments that would normally cause considerable pain (Finer, 1980).

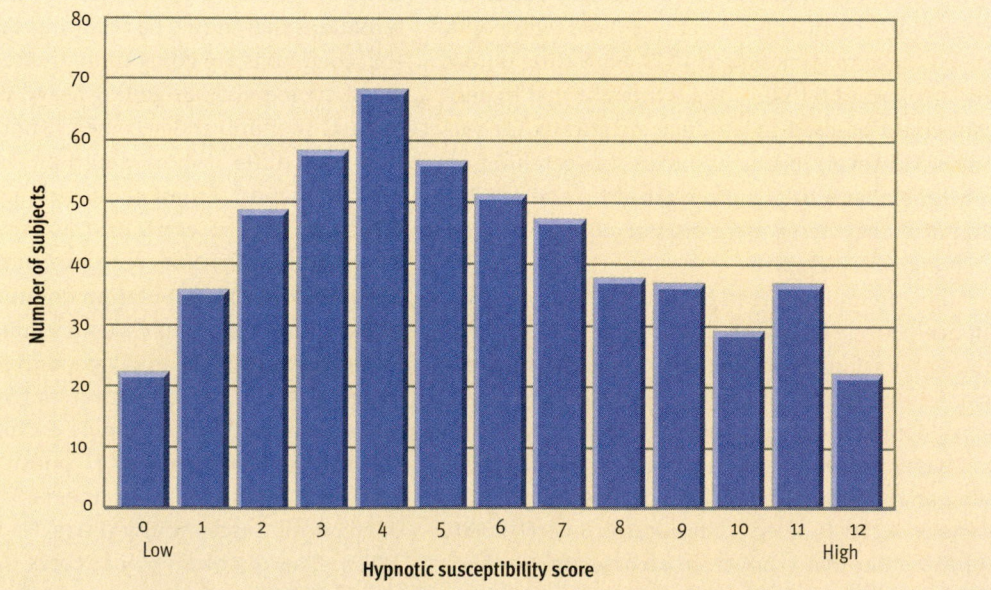

Figure 5.14

Variation in hypnotic susceptibility. This graph shows the distribution of scores of more than 500 subjects on the Stanford Hypnotic Susceptibility Scale. As you can see, responsiveness to hypnotism varies widely, and many people are not very susceptible to hypnotic induction.

SOURCE: Adapted from Hilgard, E. (1965). *Hypnotic susceptibility.* San Diego: Harcourt Brace Jovanovich. Copyright © 1965 by Ernest R. Hilgard. Reprinted by permission of Ernest R. Hilgard.

As a result, some physicians and dentists have used hypnosis as a substitute for anesthetic drugs. Admittedly, drugs are far more reliable pain relievers, making hypnosis something of a scientific curiosity as a solo treatment for acute pain (Gibson & Heap, 1991). Nonetheless, hypnosis can be a surprisingly effective anesthetic for some people (Montgomery, DuHamel, & Redd, 2000).

2. *Sensory distortions and hallucinations.* Hypnotized participants may be led to experience auditory or visual hallucinations. They may hear sounds or see things that are not there, or fail to hear or see stimuli that are present. In one study, for instance, hypnotized participants were induced to "see" a cardboard box that blocked their view of a television (Spiegel et al., 1985). Subjects may also have their sensations distorted so that something sweet tastes sour or an unpleasant odor smells fragrant.

3. *Disinhibition.* Generally, it is difficult to get hypnotized participants to do things that they would normally consider unacceptable. Nonetheless, hypnosis *can* sometimes reduce inhibitions that would normally prevent subjects from acting in ways that they would see as socially undesirable. In experiments, hypnotized participants have been induced to throw what they believed to be nitric acid into the face of a research assistant. Similarly, stage hypnotists are sometimes successful in getting people to disrobe in public. One lay hypnotist even coaxed a man into robbing a bank (Deyoub, 1984). This disinhibition effect may occur simply because hypnotized people feel that they cannot be held responsible for their actions while they are hypnotized.

4. *Posthypnotic suggestions and amnesia.* Suggestions made during hypnosis may influence a subject's later behavior (Barnier & McConkey, 1998; Kihlstrom, 1985). The most common posthypnotic suggestion is the creation of posthypnotic amnesia. That is, participants are told that they will remember nothing that happened while they were hypnotized. Such subjects usually claim to remember nothing, as ordered. However, when pressed, many of these subjects acknowledge that they have not really forgotten the information (Kirsch & Lynn, 1998).

Theories of Hypnosis

Although a number of theories have been developed to explain hypnosis, it is still not well understood. One popular view is that hypnotic effects occur because participants are put into a special, altered state of consciousness, called a *hypnotic trance*. Although hypnotized subjects may feel as though they are in an altered state, their patterns of EEG activity can-

not be distinguished from their EEG patterns in normal waking states (Dixon & Laurence, 1992; Orne & Dinges, 1989). The failure to find any special physiological changes associated with hypnosis has led some theorists to conclude that hypnosis is a normal state of consciousness that is simply characterized by dramatic role playing.

Hypnosis as Role Playing

Theodore Barber (1979) and Nicholas Spanos (1986; Spanos & Coe, 1992) have been the leading advocates of the view that hypnosis produces a normal mental state in which suggestible people act out the role of a hypnotic subject and behave as they think hypnotized people are supposed to. According to this notion, it is subjects' role expectations that produce hypnotic effects, rather than a special trancelike state of consciousness.

Two lines of evidence support the role-playing view. First, many of the seemingly amazing effects of hypnosis have been duplicated by nonhypnotized participants or have been shown to be exaggerated (Kirsch, 1997). For example, much has been made of the fact that hypnotized subjects can be used as "human planks," but it turns out that nonhypnotized subjects can easily match this feat (Barber, 1986). In a similar vein, anecdotal reports that hypnosis can enhance memory have not stood up well to empirical testing. Although hypnosis may occasionally facilitate recall in some people, experimental studies have tended to find that hypnotized participants make more memory errors than nonhypnotized participants, even though they often feel more confident about their recollections (McConkey, 1992; Whitehouse et al., 1988). These findings suggest that no special state of consciousness is required to explain hypnotic feats.

Web Link 5.5

States of Consciousness
PsychWeb, Russ Dewey's (Georgia Southern University) superb resource page, hosts this fine collection of scientifically grounded guides to three topics that too often provoke nonsensical claims: hypnosis, out-of-body experiences, and dreaming.

Biomedical Research Foundation

"Thousands of books, movies, and professional articles have woven the concept of 'hypnotic trance' into the common knowledge. And yet there is almost no scientific support for it."
THEODORE BARBER

APWide World Photos

Some feats performed under hypnosis can be performed equally well by nonhypnotized subjects. Here "the Amazing Kreskin" demonstrates that proper positioning is the only requirement for the famous human plank feat.

Courtesy of Ernest R. Hilgard

"*Many psychologists argue that the hypnotic trance is a mirage. It would be unfortunate if this skeptical view were to gain such popularity that the benefits of hypnosis are denied to the numbers of those who could be helped.*"
ERNEST HILGARD

The second line of evidence involves demonstrations that hypnotized participants are often acting out a role. For example, Martin Orne (1951) regressed hypnotized subjects back to their sixth birthday and asked them to describe it. They responded with detailed descriptions that appeared to represent great feats of hypnosis-enhanced memory. However, instead of accepting this information at face value, Orne compared it with information that he had obtained from the subjects' parents. It turned out that many of the participants' memories were inaccurate and invented! Many other studies have also found that age-regressed subjects' recall of the distant past tends to be more fanciful than factual (Green, 1999; Perry, Kusel, & Perry, 1988). Thus, the role-playing explanation of hypnosis suggests that situational factors lead some subjects to act out a certain role in a highly cooperative manner.

Hypnosis as an Altered State of Consciousness

Despite the doubts raised by role-playing explanations, many prominent theorists still maintain that hypnotic effects are attributable to a special, altered state of consciousness (Beahrs, 1983; Fromm, 1979, 1992; Hilgard, 1986). These theorists argue that it is doubtful that role playing can explain all hypnotic phenomena. For instance, they assert that even the most cooperative subjects are unlikely to endure surgery without a drug anesthetic just to please their physician and live up to their expected role. They also cite studies in which hypnotized participants have continued to display hypnotic responses when they thought they were alone and not being observed (Perugini et al., 1997). If hypnotized participants were merely acting, they would drop the act when alone. The most impressive research undermining the role-playing view has come from recent brain-imaging studies, which suggest that hypnotized participants experience changes in brain activity that appear consistent with their reports of hypnosis-induced hallucinations (Szechtman et al., 1998) or pain suppression (Rainville et al., 1997).

The most influential explanation of hypnosis as an altered state of awareness has been offered by Ernest Hilgard (1986, 1992). According to Hilgard, hypnosis creates a *dissociation* in consciousness. *Dissociation* is a splitting off of mental processes into two separate, simultaneous streams of awareness. In other words, Hilgard theorizes that hypnosis splits consciousness into two streams. One stream is in communication with the hypnotist and the external world, while the other is a difficult-to-detect "hidden observer." Hilgard believes that many hypnotic effects are a product of this divided consciousness. For instance, he suggests that a hypnotized subject might appear unresponsive to pain because the pain isn't registered in the portion of consciousness that communicates with other people.

One appealing aspect of Hilgard's theory is that *divided consciousness* is a common, normal experience. For example, people will often drive a car a great distance, responding to traffic signals and other cars, with no recollection of having consciously done so. In such cases, consciousness is clearly divided between driving and the person's thoughts about other matters. Interestingly, this common experience has long been known as *highway hypnosis*. In this condition, there is even an "amnesia" for the component of consciousness that drove the car, similar to posthypnotic amnesia. In summary, Hilgard presents hypnosis as a plausible variation in consciousness that has continuity with everyday experience.

The debate about whether hypnosis involves an altered or normal state of consciousness appears likely to continue for the foreseeable future (Kihlstrom, 1998a; Kirsch & Lynn, 1998). As you will see momentarily, a similar debate has dominated the scientific discussion of meditation.

Meditation: Pure Consciousness or Relaxation?

PREVIEW QUESTIONS
- What is meditation and how is it practiced?
- How does meditation affect physiological responding?
- What's the evidence on the long-term benefits of meditation?

Recent years have seen growing interest in the ancient discipline of meditation. *Meditation* refers to a family of practices that train attention to heighten awareness and bring mental processes under greater voluntary control. There are many approaches to meditation. In North America, the most widely practiced approaches are those associated with yoga, Zen, and transcendental meditation (TM). All three of these approaches are rooted in Eastern religions (Hinduism, Buddhism, and Taoism). However, meditation has been practiced throughout history as an element of all religious and spiritual traditions, including Judaism and Christianity. Moreover, the practice of meditation can be largely divorced from religious beliefs. In fact, most Americans who meditate have only vague ideas regarding its religious significance. Of interest to psychology is the fact that meditation involves a deliberate effort to alter consciousness.

Most meditative techniques are deceptively simple. For example, in TM a person is supposed to sit in a comfortable position with eyes closed and silently focus attention on a *mantra*. A mantra is a specially assigned Sanskrit word that is personalized to each meditator. This exercise in mental self-discipline is to be practiced twice daily for about 20 minutes. The technique has been described as "diving from the active surface of the mind to its quiet depths" (Bloomfield & Kory, 1976, p. 49). Most proponents of TM believe it involves an altered state of "pure consciousness" that has many unique benefits. Many skeptics counter that meditation is only an effective relaxation technique. Let's look at the evidence.

Physiological Correlates

What happens when an experienced meditator goes into the meditative state? One intriguing finding is that alpha waves and theta waves become more prominent in EEG recordings. Many studies also find that subjects' heart rate, skin conductance, respiration rate, oxygen consumption, and carbon dioxide elimination decline (see Figure 5.15; Dillbeck & Orme-Johnson, 1987; Fenwick, 1987; Travis, 2001). Taken together, these changes suggest that meditation leads to a potentially beneficial physiological state characterized by suppression of bodily arousal. However, some researchers have argued that a variety of systematic relaxation training procedures can produce similar results (Holmes, 1987; Shapiro, 1984). Mere relaxation hardly seems like an adequate explanation for the transcendant experiences reported by many meditators. Hence, debate continues about whether there are physiological changes associated with meditation that are unique to a special state of consciousness (Shear & Jevning, 1999; Travis & Pearson, 2000).

To shed new light on this lingering question, some researchers have begun to use new brain-imaging technologies in an effort to identify the neural circuits that are affected by meditation. For example, using a special type of CT scan to track blood flow in the brain, Andrew Newberg and his colleagues (2001) examined patterns of brain activity during meditation in a sample of eight experienced Tibetan Buddhist meditators. Among other things, they observed high activity in the prefrontal cortex, which is consistent with the focused attention that is central to meditation. They also found unusually low activity in an area in the parietal lobe that is known to process information on the body's location in space. This finding is interesting in that skilled meditators often report that their sense of individuality and separateness from others diminishes as they experience a sense of oneness with the world. This melting away

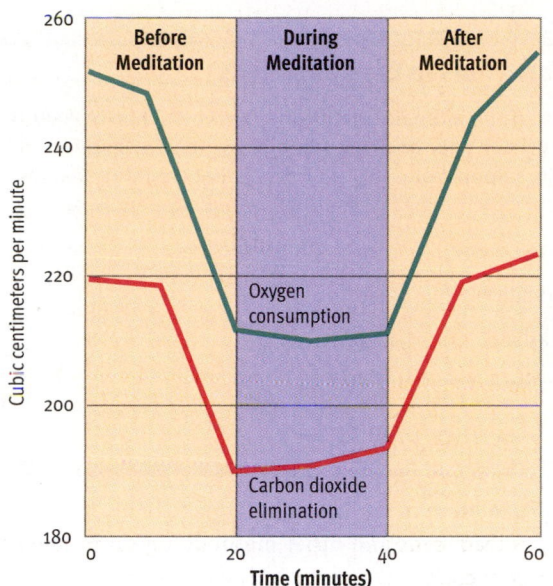

Figure 5.15

The suppression of physiological arousal during transcendental meditation.
The physiological changes shown in the graph are evidence of physical relaxation during the meditative state. However, critics argue that similar changes may also be produced by systematic relaxation procedures.

SOURCE: Adapted from Wallace, R. K., & Benson, H. (1972, February). The physiology of meditation. *Scientific American, 226,* 85–90. Graphic redrawn from illustration on p. 86 by Lorelle A. Raboni. Copyright © 1972 by Scientific American, Inc.

of personal boundaries may be associated with the low activity observed in the area of the brain that registers the sensation of a physically delimited body. The intriguing findings of Newberg et al. (2001) are preliminary and need to be replicated in additional samples, but they suggest that it may be possible to pinpoint the neural bases of meditative experiences that previously seemed inexplicable.

Long-Term Benefits

What about the long-term benefits that have been claimed for meditation? Research suggests that meditation may have some value in reducing the effects of stress (Anderson et al., 1999; Winzelberg & Luskin, 1999). In particular, regular meditation is associated with lower levels of some "stress hormones" (Infante et al., 2001). Research also suggests that meditation can improve mental health while reducing anxiety and drug abuse (Alexander et al., 1994). Other studies report that meditation may have beneficial effects on blood pressure (Barnes, Treiber, & Davis, 2001), self-esteem (Emavardhana & Tori, 1997), mood and one's sense of control (Easterlin & Cardena, 1999), happiness (Smith, Compton, & West, 1995), and overall physical health and well-being (Reibel et al., 2001). One recent study even reported that regular meditation led to increased creativity and intelligence in a sample of high school students (So & Orme-Johnson, 2001). At first glance these results are profoundly impressive, but they need to be viewed with some caution. At least some of these effects may be just as attainable through systematic relaxation or other mental focusing procedures (Shapiro, 1984; Smith, 1975). Critics also wonder whether placebo effects,

Relating EEG Activity to Variations in Consciousness

Early in the chapter we emphasized the intimate relationship between brain activity and variations in consciousness. Check your understanding of this relationship by indicating the kind of EEG activity (alpha, beta, theta, or delta) that would probably be dominant in each of the following situations. The answers are in Appendix A.

_____ **1.** You are playing a video game.

_____ **2.** You are deep in meditation.

_____ **3.** You have just fallen asleep.

_____ **4.** You are sleepwalking across the lawn.

_____ **5.** You are in the midst of a terrible nightmare.

much more than mere relaxation, as meditation advocates insist. Certainly, it is hard to envision mere relaxation providing such a diverse constellation of benefits. At present, however, there is great debate about the notion that meditation produces a unique state of "pure consciousness" and healthy skepticism about some of its alleged long-term benefits.

REVIEW OF KEY POINTS

- Hypnosis has had a long and curious history since the era of Mesmerism in the 18th century. Hypnotic susceptibility is a stable trait. It is only weakly correlated with personality, but highly hypnotizable people tend to score somewhat higher than others in absorption and imaginativeness. Hypnosis can produce anesthesia, sensory distortions, disinhibition, and posthypnotic amnesia.

- One approach to hypnosis is to view it as a normal state of consciousness in which subjects assume a hypnotic role. Another approach asserts that hypnosis leads to an altered state in which consciousness is split into two streams of awareness.

- Meditation refers to a family of practices that train attention to heighten awareness and bring mental processes under greater voluntary control. Evidence suggests that meditation leads to a potentially beneficial physiological state characterized by suppression of bodily arousal. However, some experts suggest that the benefits of meditation are not unique to meditation and are a product of any effective relaxation procedure.

sampling bias, and other methodological problems may contribute to some of the reported benefits of meditation (Bishop, 2002; Shapiro, 1987). In a recent and relatively enthusiastic review of meditation research, the authors acknowledge that many meditation studies "do not use rigorous research design (including lack of randomization, lack of followup, and imprecise measurement of constructs) and sometimes are based on small samples (Shapiro, Schwartz, & Santerre, 2002).

In summary, it seems safe to conclude that meditation is a potentially worthwhile relaxation strategy. And it's entirely possible that meditation involves

Altering Consciousness with Drugs

PREVIEW QUESTIONS

- What are the principal categories of abused drugs, and what are their main effects?

- What kinds of factors influence drug experiences?

- Where do drugs exert their effects in the brain?

- What is the difference between physical and psychological dependence?

- What are the three ways in which abused drugs can harm health?

- What are the health risks associated with the use of marijuana and MDMA?

Like hypnosis and meditation, drugs are commonly used in deliberate efforts to alter consciousness. In this section, we focus on the use of drugs for nonmedical purposes, commonly referred to as "drug abuse" or "recreational drug use." Drug abuse reaches into every corner of modern society. Although some modest declines occurred in the overall abuse of drugs during the 1980s and early 1990s, survey data indicate that illicit drug use has mostly been increasing since 1992 (Johnston, O'Malley, & Bachman, 2001). In spite of extraordinary efforts to reduce drug abuse, it seems reasonable to conclude that widespread recreational drug use is here to stay for the foreseeable future.

As with other controversial social problems, recreational drug use often inspires more rhetoric than reason. For instance, a former president of the American Medical Association made headlines when he declared that marijuana "makes a man of 35 sexually like a man of 70." In reality, the research findings do not support this assertion. This influential physician later retracted

his statement, admitting that he had made it simply to campaign against marijuana use (Leavitt, 1995). Unfortunately, such scare tactics can backfire by undermining the credibility of drug education efforts.

Recreational drug use involves personal, moral, political, and legal issues that are not matters for science to resolve. However, the more knowledgeable you are about drugs, the more informed your decisions and opinions about them will be. Accordingly, this section describes the types of drugs that are most commonly used for recreational purposes and summarizes their effects on consciousness, behavior, and health.

Principal Abused Drugs and Their Effects

 4c

The drugs that people use recreationally are *psychoactive*. **Psychoactive drugs are chemical substances that modify mental, emotional, or behavioral functioning.** Not all psychoactive drugs produce effects that lead to recreational use. Generally, people prefer drugs that elevate their mood or produce other pleasurable alterations in consciousness.

The principal types of recreational drugs are described in Table 5.4. The table lists representative drugs in each of six categories. It also summarizes how the drugs are taken, their medical uses, their effects on consciousness, and their common side effects (based on Julien, 2001; Levinthal, 1999; Lowinson et al., 1997). The six categories of psychoactive drugs that we will focus on are narcotics, sedatives, stimulants, hallucinogens, cannabis, and alcohol. We will also discuss one specific drug that is not listed in the table (because it does not fit into traditional drug categories) but that cannot be ignored in light of its escalating popularity: MDMA, better known as "ecstasy."

Narcotics, or *opiates,* are drugs derived from opium that are capable of relieving pain. The main drugs in this category are heroin and morphine, although less potent opiates such as codeine, Demerol, and methadone are also abused. In sufficient dosages these drugs can produce an overwhelming sense of euphoria or well-being. This euphoric effect has a re-

laxing, "Who cares?" quality that makes the high an attractive escape from reality. Frequent side effects include lethargy, nausea, and impaired mental and motor functioning.

Sedatives are sleep-inducing drugs that tend to decrease central nervous system (CNS) activation and behavioral activity. People abusing sedatives, or "downers," generally consume larger doses than are prescribed for medical purposes. The desired effect is a euphoria similar to that produced by drinking large amounts of alcohol. Feelings of tension or dejection are replaced by a relaxed, pleasant state of intoxication, accompanied by loosened inhibitions. Prominent side effects include drowsiness, unpredictable emotional swings, and severe impairments in motor coordination and mental functioning.

Stimulants are drugs that tend to increase central nervous system activation and behavioral activity. Stimulants range from mild, widely available drugs, such as caffeine and nicotine, to stronger, carefully regulated ones, such as cocaine. We will focus on cocaine and amphetamines. Cocaine is a natural substance that comes from the coca shrub. In con-

Web Link 5.6

Web of Addictions
From the earliest days of the World Wide Web, this page at The Well has been regularly recognized as a primary source for accurate and responsible information about alcohol and other drugs.

Table 5.4 Psychoactive Drugs: Methods of Ingestion, Medical Uses, and Effects

Drugs	Methods of Ingestion	Principal Medical Uses	Desired Effects	Potential Short-Term Side Effects
Narcotics (opiates) Morphine Heroin	Injected, smoked, oral	Pain relief	Euphoria, relaxation, anxiety reduction, pain relief	Lethargy, drowsiness, nausea, impaired coordination, impaired mental functioning, constipation
Sedatives Barbiturates (e.g., Seconal) Nonbarbiturates (e.g., Quaalude)	Oral, injected	Sleeping pill, anticonvulsant	Euphoria, relaxation, anxiety reduction, reduced inhibitions	Lethargy, drowsiness, severely impaired coordination, impaired mental functioning, emotional swings, dejection
Stimulants Amphetamines Cocaine	Oral, sniffed, injected, freebased, smoked	Treatment of hyperactivity and narcolepsy, local anesthetic (cocaine only)	Elation, excitement, increased alertness, increased energy, reduced fatigue	Increased blood pressure and heart rate, increased talkativeness, restlessness, irritability, insomnia, reduced appetite, increased sweating and urination, anxiety, paranoia, increased aggressiveness, panic
Hallucinogens LSD Mescaline Psilocybin	Oral	None	Increased sensory awareness, euphoria, altered perceptions, hallucinations, insightful experiences	Dilated pupils, nausea, emotional swings, paranoia, jumbled thought processes, impaired judgment, anxiety, panic reaction
Cannabis Marijuana Hashish THC	Smoked, oral	Treatment of glaucoma and chemotherapy—induced nausea and vomiting; other uses under study	Mild euphoria, relaxation, altered perceptions, enhanced awareness	Bloodshot eyes, dry mouth, reduced short-term memory, sluggish motor coordination, sluggish mental functioning, anxiety
Alcohol	Drinking	None	Mild euphoria, relaxation, anxiety reduction, reduced inhibitions	Severely impaired coordination, impaired mental functioning, increased urination, emotional swings, depression, quarrelsomeness, hangover

Overindulging in alcohol is particularly widespread among college students.

trast, amphetamines are synthesized in a pharmaceutical laboratory. Cocaine and amphetamines have fairly similar effects, except that cocaine produces a briefer high. Stimulants produce a euphoria very different from that created by narcotics or sedatives. They produce a buoyant, elated, energetic "I can conquer the world!" feeling accompanied by increased alertness. In recent years, cocaine and amphetamines have become available in much more potent (and dangerous) forms than before. "Freebasing" is a chemical treatment used to extract nearly pure cocaine from ordinary street cocaine. "Crack" is the most widely distributed by-product of this process, consisting of chips of pure cocaine that are usually smoked. Amphetamines are increasingly sold as a crystalline powder, called "crank," that may be snorted or injected intravenously. Drug dealers are also beginning to market a smokable form of methamphetamine called "ice." Side effects of stimulants vary with dosage and potency but may include restlessness, anxiety, paranoia, and insomnia.

Hallucinogens are a diverse group of drugs that have powerful effects on mental and emotional functioning, marked most prominently by distortions in sensory and perceptual experience. The principal hallucinogens are LSD, mescaline, and psilocybin. These drugs have similar effects, although they vary in potency. Hallucinogens produce euphoria, increased sensory awareness, and a distorted sense of time. In some users, they lead to profound, dreamlike, "mystical" feelings that are difficult to describe. The latter effect is why they have been used in religious ceremonies for centuries in some cultures. Unfortunately, at the other end of the emotional spectrum hallucinogens can also produce nightmarish feelings of anxiety and paranoia, commonly called a "bad trip." Other side effects include impaired judgment and jumbled thought processes.

Cannabis is the hemp plant from which marijuana, hashish, and THC are derived. Marijuana is a mixture of dried leaves, flowers, stems, and seeds taken from the plant. Hashish comes from the plant's resin. Smoking is the usual route of ingestion for both marijuana and hashish. THC, the active chemical ingredient in cannabis, can be synthesized for research purposes (for example, to give to animals, who can't very well smoke marijuana). When smoked, cannabis has an immediate impact that may last several hours. The desired effects of the drug are a mild, relaxed euphoria and enhanced sensory awareness. Unintended effects may include anxiety, sluggish mental functioning, and impaired memory.

Alcohol encompasses a variety of beverages containing ethyl alcohol, such as beers, wines, and distilled spirits. The concentration of ethyl alcohol varies from about 4% in most beers to 40% in 80-proof liquor—and occasionally more in higher-proof liquors. When people drink heavily, the central effect is a relaxed euphoria that temporarily boosts self-esteem, as problems seem to melt away and inhibitions diminish. Common side effects include severe impairments in mental and motor functioning, mood swings, and quarrelsomeness. Alcohol is the most widely used recreational drug in our society. Because alcohol is legal, many people use it casually without even thinking of it as a drug.

MDMA is a compound drug related to both amphetamines and hallucinogens, especially mescaline. MDMA was originally formulated in 1912 but was not widely used in the United States until the 1990s, when as *ecstasy* it became popular in the context of raves and dance clubs. MDMA produces a short-lived high that typically lasts a few hours or more. Users report that they feel warm, friendly, euphoric, sensual, insightful, and empathetic, but alert and energetic. Problematic side effects include increased blood pressure, muscle tension, sweating, blurred vision, insomnia, and transient anxiety.

Factors Influencing Drug Effects

The drug effects summarized in Table 5.4 are the *typical* ones. Drug effects can vary from person to person and even for the same person in different situations. The impact of any drug depends in part on the user's age, mood, motivation, personality, previous experience with the drug, body weight, and physiology. The dose and potency of a drug, the method of administration, and the setting in which a drug is taken also influence its effects (Leavitt, 1995). Our theme of *multifactorial causation* clearly applies to the effects of drugs.

So, too, does our theme emphasizing the *subjectivity of experience*. Expectations are potentially powerful factors that can influence the user's perceptions of a drug's effects. You may recall from our discussion of placebo effects in Chapter 2 that some people who are misled to *think* that they are drinking alcohol show signs of intoxication (Wilson, 1982). If people *expect* a drug to make them feel giddy, serene, or profound, their expectation may contribute to the feelings they experience.

A drug's effects can also change as the person's body develops a tolerance for the chemical as a result of continued use. **Tolerance** *refers to a progressive decrease in a person's responsiveness to a drug.* Tolerance usually leads people to consume larger and larger doses of a drug to attain the effects they desire. Most drugs produce tolerance effects, but some do so more rapidly than others. For example, tolerance to alcohol usually builds slowly, while tolerance to heroin increases much more quickly. Table 5.5 indicates whether various categories of drugs tend to produce tolerance rapidly or gradually.

Mechanisms of Drug Action

Most drugs have effects that reverberate throughout the body. However, psychoactive drugs work primarily by altering neurotransmitter activity in the brain. As we discussed in Chapter 3, neurotransmitters are chemicals that transmit information between neurons at junctions called *synapses*.

The actions of amphetamines and cocaine illustrate how drugs have selective, multiple effects on neurotransmitter activity (see Figure 5.16). Amphetamines exert their main effects on two of the monoamine neurotransmitters: norepinephrine (NE) and dopamine (DA). Indeed, the name *amphetamines* reflects the kinship between these drugs and the *mono-*

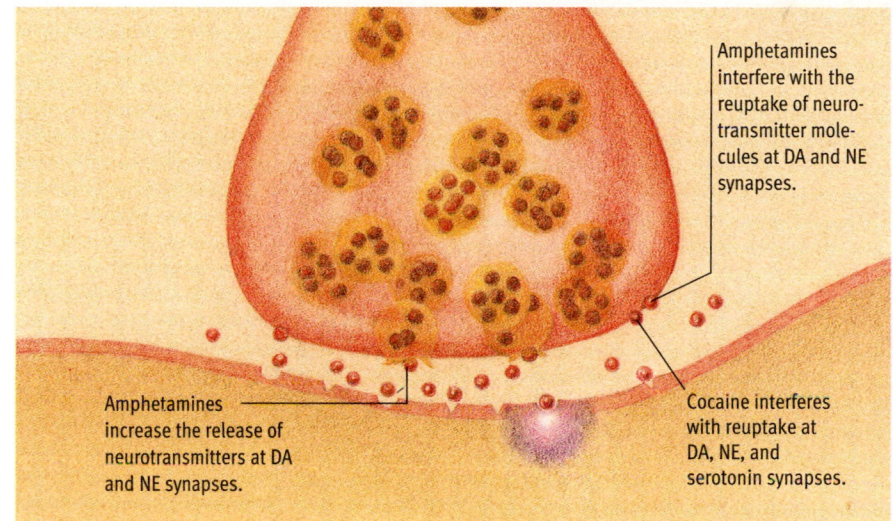

Amphetamines interfere with the reuptake of neurotransmitter molecules at DA and NE synapses.

Amphetamines increase the release of neurotransmitters at DA and NE synapses.

Cocaine interferes with reuptake at DA, NE, and serotonin synapses.

amines. Amphetamines mainly increase the release of DA and NE by presynaptic neurons. They also interfere with the reuptake of DA and NE from synaptic clefts (Cooper, Bloom, & Roth, 1996; Snyder, 1996). These actions serve to increase the levels of dopamine and norepinephrine at the affected synapses. Cocaine shares some of these actions, which is why cocaine and amphetamines produce similar stimulant effects. Cocaine mainly blocks reuptake at DA, NE, and serotonin synapses. For both amphetamines and cocaine, elevated activity in certain *dopamine circuits* is believed to be crucial to the drugs' pleasurable, rewarding effects.

The cellular mechanisms underlying stimulant drugs' effects also explain why cocaine and amphetamine highs are often followed by an emotional crash, marked by depression and exhaustion (see Figure 5.17 on the next page). The slowing of reuptake leaves more neurotransmitter in the affected synapses

Figure 5.16

Stimulant drugs and neurotransmitter activity. Like other psychoactive drugs, amphetamines and cocaine alter neurotransmitter activity at specific synapses. Amphetamines primarily increase the release of dopamine (DA) and norepinephrine (NE) and secondarily inhibit the reuptake of these neurotransmitters. Cocaine slows the reuptake process at DA, NE, and serotonin synapses. The psychological and behavioral effects of the drugs have largely been attributed to their impact on dopamine circuits, but recent evidence suggests that altered activity in serotonin circuits may play a larger role in the cocaine high than previously suspected (Julien, 2001).

Table 5.5 Psychoactive Drugs: Tolerance, Dependence, Potential for Fatal Overdose, and Health Risks

Drugs	Tolerance	Risk of Physical Dependence	Risk of Psychological Dependence	Fatal Overdose Potential	Health Risks
Narcotics (opiates)	Rapid	High	High	High	Infectious diseases, accidents, immune suppression
Sedatives	Rapid	High	High	High	Accidents
Stimulants	Rapid	Moderate	High	Moderate to high	Sleep problems, malnutrition, nasal damage, hypertension, respiratory disease, stroke, liver disease, heart attack
Hallucinogens	Gradual	None	Very low	Very low	Accidents
Cannabis	Gradual	None	Low to moderate	Very low	Accidents, lung cancer, respiratory disease, pulmonary disease
Alcohol	Gradual	Moderate	Moderate	Low to high	Accidents, liver disease, malnutrition, brain damage, neurological disorders, heart disease, stroke, hypertension, ulcers, cancer, birth defects

Figure 5.17

The "crash" after use of cocaine or amphetamines. Stimulant drugs induce an emotional high that is often followed by an emotional letdown called a "crash." Larger doses of the drugs tend to precipitate bigger crashes. As the text explains, the crash is attributable to the depletion of certain neurotransmitters.

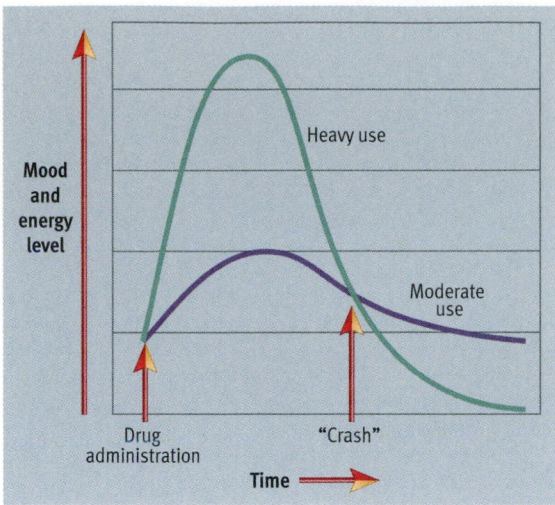

to stimulate increased activity, but it also gives enzymes that metabolize the neurotransmitter more opportunity to swoop in and inactivate more of the neurotransmitter, and there is more opportunity for the neurotransmitter to drift away from affected synapses. Hence, the use of cocaine or amphetamines can eventually lead to a depletion of dopamine and

Figure 5.18

The "reward pathway" in the brain. The neural circuits shown here in purple make up the *mesolimbic dopamine pathway*. Axons in this pathway run from an area in the midbrain through the medial forebrain bundle to the *nucleus accumbens* and on to the prefrontal cortex. Recreational drugs affect a variety of neurotransmitter systems, but theorists believe that heightened dopamine activity in this pathway—especially the portion running from the midbrain to the nucleus accumbens—is responsible for the reinforcing effects of most abused drugs.

SOURCE: Adapted from Kalat, J. W. (2001). *Biological psychology.* Belmont, CA: Wadsworth. Reprinted by permission.

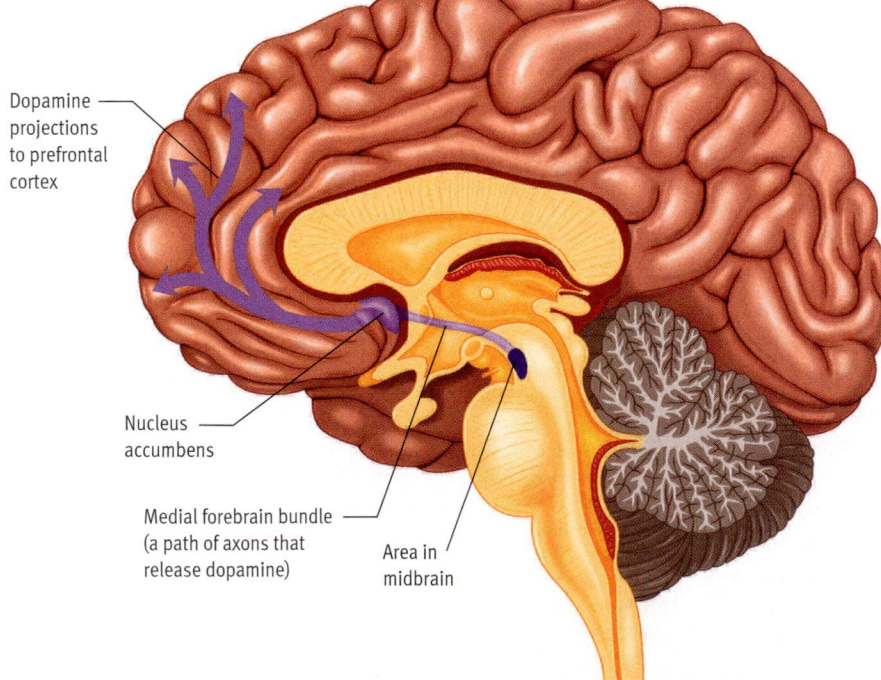

norepinephrine. This depletion appears to be the cause of the emotional crash experienced by many users.

The effects of other drugs can also be explained in terms of their impact on specific types of neurotransmitter activity. Sedatives are thought to exert their key effects by increasing activity at GABA synapses (Brady, Myrick, & Malcolm, 1999). Changes in GABA activity are also thought to be the main culprit underlying alcohol intoxication, although alcohol has additional effects on dopamine, serotonin, and other neurotransmitter systems (Moak & Anton, 1999). The finding that alcohol and sedatives converge on many of the same (GABA) synapses probably explains why these drugs are *synergistic.* Drugs are said to be synergistic when their combined effect is greater than the sum of their individual effects. Synergistic effects explain why the combination of alcohol and sedatives has caused many fatal overdoses by depressing CNS activity excessively.

The discovery of special receptor sites in the brain for opiate drugs and endogenous opiates (endorphins) has led to new insights about the actions of narcotic drugs (see Chapter 3). These drugs apparently bind to specific subtypes of opiate receptors, and their actions at these receptor sites indirectly elevate dopamine activity (Koob & Bloom, 1988; Stine & Kosten, 1999). Scientists have recently found receptors in the brain for THC, the active chemical ingredient in marijuana (Stephens, 1999). They have also found an internally produced chemical, christened *anandamide* (from a Sanskrit word for internal bliss), that activates these receptors (Wiley, 1999). It appears that anandamide shares many of the pharmacological properties of THC (Stahl, 1998). The discovery of this endogenous cannabinoid promises to gradually shed new light on how marijuana produces its effects.

Although specific drugs exert their initial effects in the brain on a wide variety of neurotransmitter systems, many theorists believe that virtually all abused drugs eventually increase activity in a particular neural pathway, called the *mesolimbic dopamine pathway.* This neural circuit, which runs from the midbrain, through the *nucleus accumbens,* and on to the prefrontal cortex (see Figure 5.18), has been characterized as a "reward pathway." Increased dopamine release along this pathway is thought to be the principal source of the reinforcing effects of most abused drugs (Gardner, 1997; Koob, 1997).

Drug Dependence

People can become either physically or psychologically dependent on a drug. Physical dependence is a common problem with narcotics, sedatives, alcohol, and stimulants. *Physical dependence* **exists when a person must continue to take a drug to avoid withdrawal illness.** The symptoms of withdrawal illness depend on the specific drug. Withdrawal from heroin, barbiturates, and alcohol can produce fever, chills, tremors, convulsions, vomiting, cramps, diarrhea, and severe aches and pains. Withdrawal from stimulants can lead to a more subtle syndrome, marked by fatigue, apathy, irritability, depression, and feelings of disorientation.

Psychological dependence **exists when a person must continue to take a drug to satisfy intense mental and emotional craving for the drug.** Psychological dependence is more subtle than physical dependence, but the need it creates can be powerful. Cocaine, for instance, can produce an overwhelming psychological need for continued use. Psychological dependence is possible with all recreational drugs, although it seems rare for hallucinogens.

Both types of dependence are established gradually with repeated use of a drug. It was originally assumed that only physical dependence has a physiological basis, but theorists now believe that both types of dependence reflect alterations in synaptic transmission (Di Chara, 1999; Self, 1997). Drugs vary in their potential for creating either physical or psychological dependence. Table 5.5 provides estimates of the risk of each kind of dependence for the six categories of recreational drugs covered in our discussion.

Drugs and Health

The use of recreational drugs can be damaging to health. The harmful effects of drugs were illustrated dramatically in a widely cited study of rats that were given unlimited access to heroin or cocaine (Bozarth & Wise, 1985). In this study, the rats "earned" drug injections delivered through tubes implanted in their bodies by pressing a lever in an experimental chamber. Even though unlimited food and water were available, rats on cocaine lost an average of 29% of their body weight. Their health deteriorated rapidly, and by the end of the 30-day study 90% of them had died. The health of the rats on heroin deteriorated less rapidly, but 36% of them also died during the course of the study. As is true for many human drug users, serious aversive effects did not deter the rats from continuing their "drug abuse." Many of the rats on cocaine experienced severe and highly unpleasant seizures. However, they would resume their lever pressing as soon as they stopped writhing from convulsions!

In humans, recreational drug use can affect health in a variety of ways. The three principal ways are by triggering an overdose, by producing various types of physiological damage (direct effects), and by causing health-impairing behavior (indirect effects).

Overdose

Any drug can be fatal if a person takes enough of it, but some drugs are much more dangerous than others. Table 5.5 shows estimates of the risk of accidentally consuming a lethal overdose of each listed drug. Drugs that are CNS depressants—sedatives, narcotics, and alcohol—carry the greatest risk of overdose. It's important to remember that these drugs are synergistic with each other, so many overdoses involve lethal *combinations* of CNS depressants. What happens when a person overdoses on these drugs? The respiratory system usually grinds to a halt, producing coma, brain damage, and death within a brief period.

Fatal overdoses with CNS stimulants usually involve a heart attack, stroke, or cortical seizure. Deaths due to overdoses of stimulant drugs used to be relatively infrequent, but cocaine overdoses have increased sharply as more people have experimented with freebasing, smoking crack, and other more dangerous modes of ingestion (Gold, 1997). Similar increases in amphetamine overdoses seem likely if more potent forms of speed (crank and ice) become more widely available.

Direct Effects

In some cases, drugs cause tissue damage directly. For example, snorting cocaine can damage nasal membranes. Cocaine can also alter cardiovascular functioning in ways that increase the risk of heart attack and stroke, and crack smoking is associated with a host of respiratory problems (Kerfoot, Sakoulas, & Hyman, 1996; Weaver & Schnoll, 1999). Long-term, excessive alcohol consumption is associated with an elevated risk for a wide range of serious health problems, including liver damage, ulcers, hypertension, stroke, heart disease, neurological disorders, and some types of cancer (Goodwin & Gabrielli, 1997; Moak & Anton, 1999).

Indirect Effects

The negative effects of drugs on physical health are often indirect results of the drugs' impact on behavior. For instance, people using stimulants tend not to eat or sleep properly. Sedatives increase the risk of accidental injuries because they severely impair motor coordination. People who abuse downers often trip down stairs, fall off stools, and suffer other mishaps. Many drugs impair driving ability, increasing the risk of automobile accidents. Alcohol, for instance, may contribute to roughly 40% of all automobile fatalities (Liu et al., 1997). Intravenous drug users risk

Web Link 5.7

National Institute on Alcohol Abuse and Alcoholism
Just two of the many research sources here include the entire collection of the bulletin *Alcohol Alert*, issued since 1988 on specific topics related to alcoholism, and the ETOH Database, a searchable repository of more than 100,000 records on alcoholism and alcohol abuse.

contracting infectious diseases that can be spread by unsterilized needles. In recent years, acquired immune deficiency syndrome (AIDS) has been transmitted at an alarming rate through the population of intravenous drug users (Des Jarlais, Hagan, & Friedman, 1997).

The major health risks (other than overdose) of various recreational drugs are listed in the sixth column of Table 5.5. As you can see, alcohol appears to have the most diverse negative effects on physical health. The irony, of course, is that alcohol is the only recreational drug listed that is legal.

Controversies Concerning Marijuana

The possible health risks associated with marijuana use have generated considerable debate in recent years. The preponderance of evidence suggests that heavy use of marijuana *probably* increases the chances for respiratory and pulmonary disease, including lung cancer (Stephens, 1999). Reasonably convincing evidence also indicates that marijuana increases the risk of automobile accidents (Ramaekers, Robbe, & O'Hanlon, 2000). These dangers are listed in Table 5.5, but many other widely publicized dangers are omitted because the findings on these other risks have been exaggerated or remain debatable. Here is a brief overview of the evidence on some of these controversies.

- *Does marijuana reduce one's immune response?* Research with animals suggests that cannabis may suppress the body's natural immune response slightly. However, infectious diseases do *not* appear to be more common among marijuana smokers than among nonsmokers. Hence, marijuana's effect on immune functioning apparently is too small to have any practical importance (Hall, Solowij, & Lemon, 1994; Hollister, 1988).

- *Does marijuana lead to impotence and sterility in men?* Cannabis appears to produce a small, reversible decline in sperm count among male smokers and may have temporary effects on hormone levels (Bloodworth, 1987). Citing these findings, the popular media have frequently implied that marijuana therefore makes men sterile and impotent. However, the evidence suggests that marijuana has little lasting impact on male smokers' fertility or sexual functioning (Grinspoon & Bakalar, 1997).

- *Does marijuana have long-term negative effects on cognitive functioning?* It has long been known that marijuana has a negative impact on attention and memory while users are high, but until recently studies had failed to find any permanent cognitive deficits attributable to cannabis use. However, a spate of recent studies using more elaborate and precise assessments of cognitive functioning *have* found an association between chronic, heavy marijuana use and measurable impairments in attention and memory (see Figure 5.19) that show up when users are not high (Ehrenreich et al., 1999; Solowij et al., 2002). That said, the cognitive deficits that have been observed are very modest and certainly not disabling, and one study found that the deficits vanished after a month of marijuana abstinence (Pope, Gruber, & Yurgelun-Todd, 2001; Pope et al., 2001). More research is needed, but the recent studies in this area provide some cause for concern.

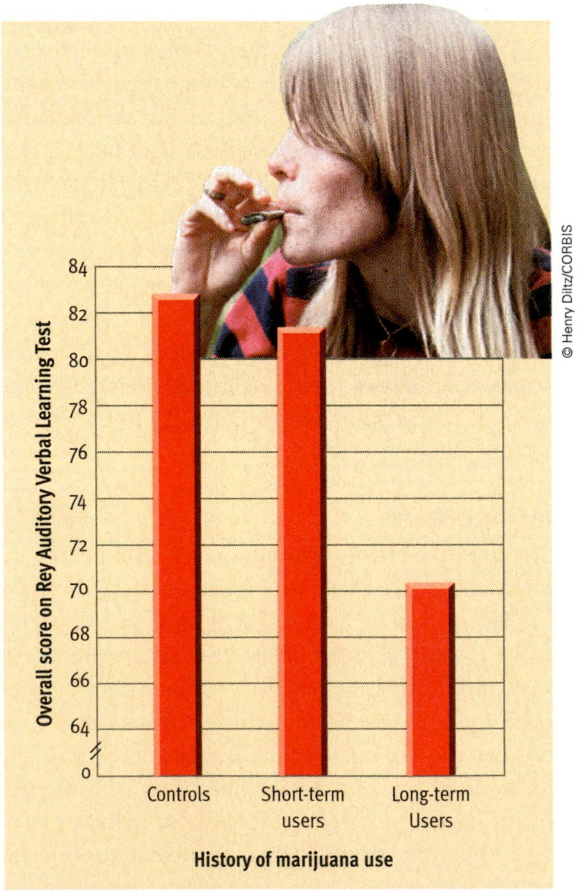

New Findings Regarding Ecstasy

Like marijuana, ecstasy is viewed as a harmless drug in some quarters, but accumulating empirical evidence is beginning to alter that perception. Research on MDMA is in its infancy, so conclusions about its risks must be tentative. MDMA does not appear to be especially addictive, but psychological dependence clearly can become a problem for some people. MDMA has been implicated in cases of stroke and heart attack, seizures, heat stroke, and liver damage, but its exact contribution is hard to gauge, given

Figure 5.19

Chronic cannabis use and cognitive performance.
Solowij and associates (2002) administered a battery of neuropsychological tests to 51 long-term cannabis users who had smoked marijuana regularly for an average of 24 years, 51 short-term cannabis users who had smoked marijuana regularly for an average of 10 years, and 33 control subjects who had little or no history of cannabis use. The cannabis users were required to abstain from smoking marijuana for a minimum of 12 hours prior to their testing. The study found evidence suggestive of subtle cognitive impairments among the long-term cannabis users on many of the tests. The graph shown here depicts the results observed for overall performance on the Rey Auditory Verbal Learning Test, which measures several aspects of memory functioning.

© Henry Diltz/CORBIS

all the other drugs that MDMA users typically consume (Burgess, O'Donohoe, & Gill, 2000; Grob & Poland, 1997). Chronic, heavy use of ecstasy appears to be associated with sleep disorders, depression, and elevated anxiety and hostility (Morgan, 2000). Moreover, studies of former MDMA users suggest that ecstasy may have subtle, long-term effects on cognitive functioning (Parrott, 2000). Quite a few studies have found memory deficits in former users (Bhattachary & Powell, 2001; Zakzanis & Young, 2001). Other studies have found decreased performance on laboratory tasks requiring attention and learning (Gouzoulis-Mayfrank et al., 2000). Thus, although a great deal of additional research is needed, the preliminary evidence suggests that MDMA may be more harmful than widely assumed.

Putting It in Perspective

This chapter highlights four of our unifying themes. First, we can see how psychology evolves in a sociohistorical context. Psychology began as the science of consciousness in the 19th century, but consciousness proved difficult to study empirically. Research on consciousness dwindled after John B. Watson and others redefined psychology as the science of behavior. However, in the 1960s people began to turn inward, showing a new interest in altering consciousness through drug use, meditation, hypnosis, and biofeedback. Psychologists responded to these social trends by beginning to study variations in consciousness in earnest. This renewed interest in consciousness shows how social forces can have an impact on psychology's evolution.

A second theme that predominates in this chapter is the idea that people's experience of the world is highly subjective. We encountered this theme at the start of the chapter when we mentioned the difficulty that people have describing their states of consciousness. The subjective nature of consciousness was apparent elsewhere in the chapter, as well. For instance, we found that the alterations of consciousness produced by drugs depend significantly on personal expectations.

Third, we saw once again how culture molds some aspects of behavior. Although the basic physiological process of sleep appears largely invariant from one society to another, culture influences certain aspects of sleep habits and has a dramatic impact on whether people remember their dreams and how they interpret and feel about their dreams. If not for space constraints, we might also have discussed cross-cultural differences in patterns of recreational drug use, which vary considerably from one society to the next.

Finally, the chapter illustrates psychology's theoretical diversity. We discussed conflicting theories about dreams, hypnosis, and meditation. For the most part, we did not see these opposing theories converging toward reconciliation, as we did in the areas of sensation and perception. However, it's important to emphasize that rival theories do not always merge neatly into tidy models of behavior. Many theoretical controversies go on indefinitely. This fact does not negate the value of theoretical diversity. While it's always nice to resolve a theoretical debate, the debate itself can advance knowledge by stimulating and guiding empirical research.

Indeed, our upcoming Personal Application demonstrates that theoretical debates need not be resolved in order to advance knowledge. Many theoretical controversies and enduring mysteries remain in the study of sleep and dreams. Nonetheless, researchers have accumulated a great deal of practical information on these topics, which we'll discuss in the next few pages.

PREVIEW QUESTIONS

- How did this chapter show that psychology evolves in a sociohistorical context?
- How did this chapter illustrate the subjective nature of human experience?
- How did this chapter illustrate the importance of cultural influences?
- How did this chapter highlight psychology's theoretical diversity?

REVIEW OF KEY POINTS

- The principal categories of abused drugs are narcotics, sedatives, stimulants, hallucinogens, cannabis, and alcohol. Although it's possible to describe the typical effects of various drugs, the actual effect on any individual depends on a host of factors, including subjective expectations and tolerance to the drug.

- Psychoactive drugs exert their main effects in the brain, where they alter neurotransmitter activity at synaptic sites in a variety of ways. For example, amphetamines increase the release of DA and NE, and like cocaine, they slow reuptake at DA and NE synapses. The mesolimbic dopamine pathway may mediate the reinforcing effects of most abused drugs.

- Recreational drug use can prove harmful to health by producing an overdose, by causing tissue damage, or by increasing health-impairing behavior. The chances of accidentally consuming a lethal overdose are greatest for the CNS depressants and cocaine. Direct tissue damage occurs most frequently with alcohol and cocaine.

- The health risks of marijuana have generated debate. Preliminary evidence suggests that MDMA may be more dangerous than widely assumed.

- Four of our unifying themes were highlighted in this chapter. We saw that psychology evolves in a sociohistorical context, that experience is highly subjective, that culture influences many aspects of behavior, and that psychology is characterized by extensive theoretical diversity.

PERSONAL APPLICATION

Addressing Practical Questions About Sleep and Dreams

Indicate whether the following statements are "true" or "false."

_____ **1** Naps rarely have a refreshing effect.

_____ **2** Some people never dream.

_____ **3** When people cannot recall their dreams, it's because they are trying to repress them.

_____ **4** Only an expert in symbolism, such as a psychoanalytic therapist, can interpret the real meaning of dreams.

These assertions were all drawn from the Sleep and Dreams Information Questionnaire (Palladino & Carducci, 1984), which measures practical knowledge about sleep and dreams. Are they true or false? You'll see in this Application.

Common Questions About Sleep

How much sleep do people need? The average amount of daily sleep for young adults is 7.5 hours. However, there is considerable variability in how long people sleep. Based on a synthesis of data from many studies, Webb (1992b) estimates that sleep time is normally distributed as shown in Figure 5.20. Thus, sleep needs vary from person to person. That said, many sleep experts believe that most people would function more effectively if they increased their amount of sleep (Maas, 1998).

Can short naps be refreshing? Some naps are beneficial and some are not. The effectiveness of napping varies from person to person. Also, the benefits of any specific nap depend on the time of day and the amount of sleep one has had recently (Dinges, 1993). On the negative side, naps are not very *efficient* ways to sleep because you're often just getting into the deeper stages of sleep when your nap time is up. Another potential problem is that overly long naps or naps that occur too close to bedtime can disrupt nighttime sleep (Dinges, 1989).

Nonetheless, many highly productive people (including Thomas Edison, Winston Churchill, and John F. Kennedy) have made effective use of naps. On the positive side, most naps enhance subsequent alertness and task performance and reduce sleepiness (Gillberg et al., 1996; Hayashi, Watanabe, & Hori, 1999). In conclusion, naps can be refreshing for most people (so the first statement opening this Application is false), and they can pay off in the long run if they don't interfere with nighttime sleep.

How do alcohol and drugs affect sleep? Obviously, stimulants such as cocaine and amphetamines make it difficult to sleep. More surprising is the finding that most of the CNS depressants that facilitate sleep (such as alcohol, analgesics, sedatives, and tranquilizers) actually disrupt the normal sleep cycle. The principal problem is that they reduce the time spent in REM sleep

and slow-wave sleep (Carskadon & Dement, 2000). Unfortunately, these are the sleep stages that appear to be most important to a refreshing night's sleep.

Is there such a thing as sleep learning? Yes, but it won't get you through college. Studies show that cognitive responding to external stimuli can occur during the lighter stages (1 and 2) of sleep (Ogilvie, Wilkinson, & Allison, 1989). This and other lines of evidence suggest that sleep learning is a legitimate possibility (Eich, 1990). However, studies indicate that people have minimal ability to assimilate information of any complexity into memory while asleep (Badia, 1990). It would be nice if people could learn Spanish by listening to an audiotape while they slept, but the evidence indicates that trying to do so is pointless.

Can people learn to awaken without an alarm clock? Some people who have consis-

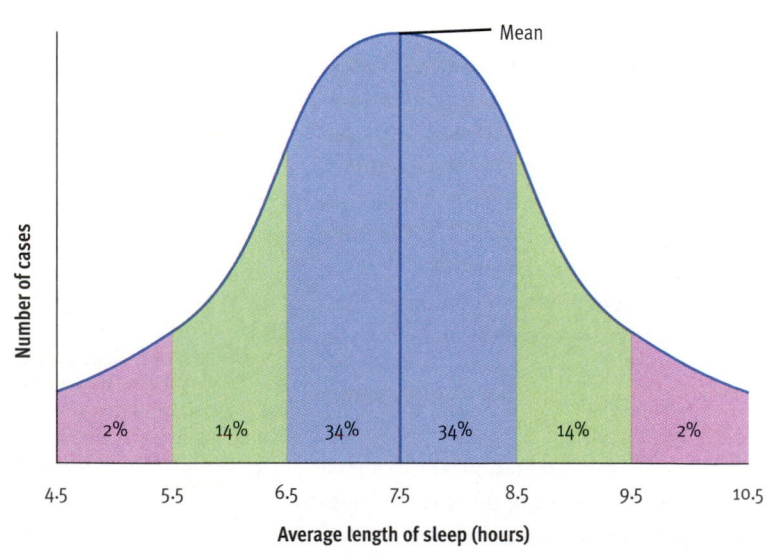

Figure 5.20

Variation in sleep needs. Based on data from a variety of sources, Webb (1992b) estimates that average sleep length among young adults is distributed normally, as shown here. Although most young adults sleep an average of 6.5 to 8.5 hours per night, some people need less and some people need more sleep.

SOURCE: Adapted from Webb, W. B. (1992). *Sleep, the gentle tyrant* (2nd Ed.). Bolton, MA: Anker Publishing Co. Copyright © 1992 by Anker Publishing Co. Adapted by permission.

tent sleep habits find themselves awakening on their own just before their alarm clock goes off. This phenomenon is fairly common and presumably reflects the influence of circadian rhythms. A smaller number of people claim that they can reliably awaken themselves at predetermined, nonhabitual times. However, when some of these people have been tested carefully in sleep laboratories, their performance has been inconsistent (Zepelin, 1993). Thus, people who claim that they have an adjustable internal alarm clock are probably exaggerating its reliability.

What do yawning and snoring have to do with sleep? Yawning is a universal phenomenon seen in all cultural groups—not to mention other mammals, birds, fish, and reptiles (Baenninger, 1997). Contrary to popular belief, yawning is not a response to a buildup of carbon dioxide or a shortage of oxygen. However, as reputed, yawning *is* correlated with sleepiness and boredom, although the association with sleepiness may not be as strong as widely assumed. Whether yawning facilitates or impedes sleep, or has no effect, is not yet known (Provine, 1993). According to one theory, the principal function of yawning is to modify cortical arousal in situations where there is little external stimulation (Baenninger, 1997). The most fascinating and perplexing facet of yawning is that it is contagious—seeing others yawn creates a powerful urge to follow suit. Contagious yawning is not well understood, although Provine (1989) argues that it is a neurologically programmed, reflexive response.

Snoring is a common phenomenon seen in about 20% of adults (Lugaresi et al., 1994). Snoring increases after age 35, occurs in men more than women, and is more frequent among people who are overweight (Kryger, 1993; Stoohs et al., 1998). Many factors, including colds, allergies, smoking, and some drugs, can contribute to snoring, mainly by forcing people to breathe through their mouths while sleeping. Some people who snore loudly disrupt their own sleep as well as that of their bed partners. It can be difficult to prevent snoring in some people, whereas others are able to reduce their snoring by simply losing weight or by sleep-

People typically get very upset when they have difficulty falling asleep. Unfortunately, the emotional distress tends to make it even harder for people to get to sleep.

ing on their side instead of their back (Lugaresi et al., 1994). Snoring may seem like a trivial problem, but it is associated with sleep apnea and cardiovascular disease, and it may have considerably more medical significance than most people realize (Dement & Vaughn, 1999).

What can be done to avoid sleep problems? There are many ways to improve your chances of getting satisfactory sleep (see Figure 5.21). Most of them involve developing sensible daytime habits that won't interfere with sleep (Catalano, 1990; Dement & Vaughn, 1999; Maas, 1998; Zarcone, 2000). For example, if you've been having trouble sleeping at night, it's wise to avoid daytime naps, so you will be *tired* when bedtime arrives. Some people find that daytime exercise helps them fall asleep more readily at bedtime (King et al., 1997). Of course, the exercise should be part of a regular regimen that doesn't leave one sore or aching.

It's also a good idea to minimize consumption of stimulants such as caffeine or nicotine. Because coffee and cigarettes aren't prescription drugs, people don't appreciate how much the stimulants they contain can heighten physical arousal. Many foods (such as chocolate) and beverages (such as cola drinks) contain more caffeine than people

Figure 5.21

Suggestions for better sleep. In his book, *Power Sleep*, James Maas (1998) offers the following advice for people concerned about enhancing their sleep. Maas argues convincingly that good daytime habits can make all the difference in the world to the quality of one's sleep.

SOURCE: Adapted from Maas, J. B. (1998). *Power sleep.* New York: Random House. Copyright © 1998 by James B. Mass, Ph. D. Reprinted by permission of Villard Books, a division of Random House, Inc.

1. Reduce stress as much as possible.
2. Exercise to stay fit.
3. Keep mentally stimulated during the day.
4. Eat a proper diet.
5. Stop smoking.
6. Reduce caffeine intake.
7. Avoid alcohol near bedtime.
8. Take a warm bath before bed.
9. Maintain a relaxing atmosphere in the bedroom.
10. Establish a bedtime ritual.
11. Have pleasurable sexual activity.
12. Clear your mind at bedtime.
13. Try some bedtime relaxation techniques.
14. Avoid trying too hard to get to sleep.
15. Learn to value sleep.

realize. Also, bear in mind that ill-advised eating habits can interfere with sleep. Try to avoid going to bed hungry, uncomfortably stuffed, or soon after eating foods that disagree with you.

In addition to these prudent habits, two other preventive measures are worth mentioning. First, try to establish a reasonably regular bedtime. This habit will allow you to take advantage of your circadian rhythm, so you'll be trying to fall asleep when your body is primed to cooperate. Second, create a favorable environment for sleep. This advice belabors what should be obvious, but many people fail to heed it. Make sure you have a good bed that is comfortable for you. Take steps to ensure that your bedroom is quiet enough and that the humidity and temperature are to your liking.

What can be done about insomnia? First, don't panic if you run into a little trouble sleeping. An overreaction to sleep problems can begin a vicious circle of escalating problems, like that depicted in Figure 5.22. If you jump to the conclusion that you are becoming an insomniac, you may approach sleep with anxiety that will aggravate the problem. The harder you work at falling asleep, the less success you're likely to have. As noted earlier, temporary sleep problems are common and generally clear up on their own.

One sleep expert, Dianne Hales (1987), lists 101 suggestions for combating insomnia in her book *How to Sleep Like a Baby*. Many involve "boring yourself to sleep" by playing alphabet games, reciting poems, or listening to your clock. Another recommended strategy is to engage in some not-so-engaging activity. For instance, you might try reading your dullest textbook. It could turn out to be a superb sedative. Whatever you think about, try to avoid ruminating about the current stresses and problems in your life. Research has shown that the tendency to ruminate is one of the key factors contributing to insomnia (Kales et al., 1984), as the data in Figure 5.23 show.

Anything that relaxes you—whether it's music, meditation, prayer, or a warm bath—can aid you in falling asleep. Experts have also devised systematic relaxation procedures that can make relaxation efforts more effective. You may want to learn about techniques such as *progressive relaxation* (Jacobson, 1938), *autogenic training* (Schultz & Luthe, 1959), or the *relaxation response* (Benson & Klipper, 1988).

Common Questions About Dreams

Does everyone dream? Yes. Some people just don't *remember* their dreams. However,

when these people are brought into a sleep lab and awakened from REM sleep, they report having been dreaming—much to their surprise (Hall & Nordby, 1972). Thus, statement 2 at the start of this Application is false.

Why don't some people remember their dreams? The evaporation of dreams appears to be quite normal. Given the lowered level of awareness during sleep, it's understandable that memory of dreams is mediocre. Dream recall is best when people are awakened during or very soon after a dream (Goodenough, 1991). Most of the time, people who *do* recall dreams upon waking are remembering either their *last* dream from their final REM period or a dream that awakened them earlier in the night. Hobson's (1989) educated guess is that people probably forget 95%–99% of their dreams. This forgetting is natural and is not due to repression, so statement 3 is also false. People who never remember their dreams probably have a sleep pattern that puts too much time between their last REM/dream period and awakening, so even their last dream is forgotten.

Can people improve their recall of dreams? Yes. Most people don't have any significant reason to work at recalling their dreams, so they just let them float away. However, many people have found that they can re-

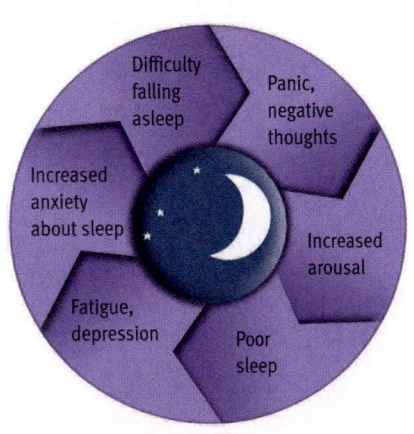

Figure 5.22

The vicious circle of anxiety and sleep difficulty. Anxiety about sleep difficulties leads to poorer sleep, which increases anxiety further, which in turn leads to even greater difficulties in sleeping.

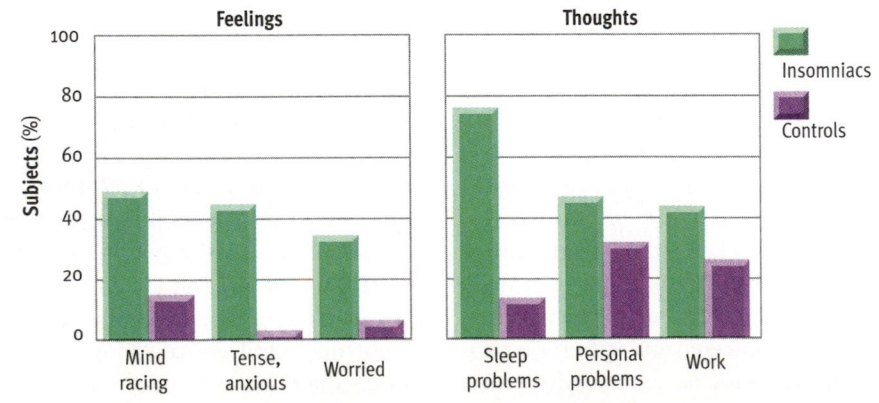

Figure 5.23

Thoughts and emotions associated with insomnia. This graph depicts the percentage of insomniacs and control subjects reporting various presleep feelings and thoughts. Insomniacs' tendency to ruminate about their problems contributes to their sleep difficulties.

SOURCE: Data from Kales, A., & Kales, J. D. (1984). *Evaluation and treatment of insomnia.* New York: Oxford University Press. Copyright © 1984 by Oxford University Press. Reprinted by permission.

member more dreams if they merely place that goal uppermost in their minds as they go to sleep (Goodenough, 1991). Dream recall is also aided by making a point of trying to remember dreams upon first awakening, before opening one's eyes or getting out of bed.

Are dreams instantaneous? No. It has long been speculated that dreams flash through consciousness almost instantaneously. According to this notion, complicated plots that would require 20 minutes to think through in waking life could bolt through the dreaming mind in a second or two. However, modern research shows that this isn't the case (Weinstein, Schwartz, & Arkin, 1991).

Do dreams require interpretation? Most theorists would say yes, but interpretation may not be as difficult as generally assumed. People have long believed that dreams are symbolic and that it is necessary to interpret the symbols to understand the meaning of dreams. Freud, for instance, made a distinction between the *manifest content* and the *latent content* of a dream. **The manifest content consists of the plot of a dream at a surface level. The latent content refers to the hidden or disguised meaning of the events in the plot.** Thus, a Freudian therapist might equate such dream events as walking into a tunnel or riding a horse with sexual intercourse.

Freudian theorists assert that dream interpretation is a complicated task requiring considerable knowledge of symbolism. However, many dream theorists argue that symbolism in dreams is less deceptive and mysterious than Freud thought (Faraday, 1974; Foulkes, 1985; Hall, 1979). Calvin Hall makes the point that dreams require some interpretation simply because they are more visual than verbal. That is, pictures need to be translated into ideas. According to Hall, dream symbolism is highly personal and the dreamer may be the person best equipped to decipher a dream (statement 4 is also false). Thus, it is not unreasonable for you to try to interpret your own dreams. Unfortunately, you'll never know whether you're "correct," because there is no definitive way to judge the validity of different dream interpretations.

Can people learn to influence their dreams? Quite possibly, but it is not easy. Researchers in a number of studies have instructed subjects to try to dream about a particular topic. Subjects have been successful often enough to suggest that some dream control is possible (Nikles et al., 1998). However, there have been many failures as well, suggesting that dream control may be fairly difficult (Tart, 1990).

What is lucid dreaming? Generally, when people dream, they are not aware that they are dreaming. Occasionally, however, some people experience "lucid" dreams in which they recognize that they are dreaming. Typically, normal dreams become lucid when people puzzle over something bizarre in a dream and recognize that they must be dreaming. **In *lucid dreams* people can think clearly about the circumstances of waking life and the fact that they are dreaming, yet they remain asleep in the midst of a vivid dream.** Perhaps the most intriguing aspect of this dual consciousness is that people can often exert some control over the events unfolding in their lucid dreams (LaBerge, 1990; Tart, 1988).

Reports of lucid dreams have a long history, but the inability of one person to experience another person's dream has always made it difficult to verify the existence of these exotic, paradoxical dreams (LaBerge, 1988). However, Stephen LaBerge reasoned that if lucid dreamers can act deliberately in their dreams, they should be able to make prearranged special eye movements to signal the occurrence of lucid dreams while being carefully monitored with physiological recording devices in a sleep lab. The ability to send such signals while dreaming would provide evidence of some degree of lucidity. This clever utilization of modern sleep monitoring techniques has allowed LaBerge and his colleagues to gather objective evidence that lucid dreaming is a genuine phenomenon that usually occurs during the REM stage (LaBerge et al., 1981). The ability of lucid dreamers to communicate with sleep researchers while dreaming may provide new opportunities for investigators to explore the world of dreams (Kahan & LaBerge, 1994).

Could a shocking dream be fatal? According to folklore, if you fall from a height in a dream, you'd better wake up on the plunge downward, for if you hit the bottom the shock to your system will be so great that you will actually die in your sleep. Think about this one for a moment. *If* it were a genuine problem, who would have reported it? You can be sure that no one has ever testified to experiencing a fatal dream. This myth presumably exists because many people do awaken during the downward plunge, thinking that they've averted a close call. A study by Barrett (1988–1989) suggests that dreams of one's own death are relatively infrequent. However, people do have such dreams—and live to tell about them.

REVIEW OF KEY POINTS

- People's sleep needs vary in a normal distribution. The value of short naps depends on many factors, including one's biological rhythm. Alcohol and many other widely used drugs have a negative effect on sleep.

- Sleep learning is possible, but only in primitive ways. People's internal alarm clocks are not as reliable as often claimed. Yawning appears to be associated with boredom and sleepiness but is not well understood. Snoring occurs exclusively during sleep, increases after age 35, and may have more medical significance than most people realize.

- People can do many things to avoid or reduce sleep problems. Mostly, it's a matter of developing good daytime habits that do not interfere with sleep. Individuals troubled by transient insomnia should avoid panic, pursue effective relaxation, and try distracting themselves so they don't work too hard at falling asleep.

- Everyone dreams, but some people don't remember their dreams, probably because of the nature of their sleep cycle. Dream recall can be improved, and some people have even been taught to influence the course of their dreams.

- Freud distinguished between the manifest and latent content of dreams and asserted that dreams require interpretation. Most theorists agree that dreams require some interpretation, but doing so may not be as complicated as Freud assumed.

- In lucid dreams, people consciously recognize that they are dreaming and exert some control over the events in their dreams. Dreams are not instantaneous, and there's no evidence that they can be fatal.

Is Alcoholism a Disease? The Power of Definitions

Alcoholism is a major problem in most, perhaps all, societies. As we saw in the main body of the chapter, alcohol is a dangerous drug. Alcoholism destroys countless lives, tears families apart, and is associated with an elevated risk for a host of physical maladies (Goodwin & Gabrielli, 1997). With roughly 19 million problem drinkers in the United States (Winick, 1992), it seems likely that alcoholism has touched the lives of a majority of Americans.

In almost every discussion about alcoholism someone will ask, "Is alcoholism a disease?" If alcoholism is a disease, it is a strange one, because the alcoholic is the most direct cause of his or her own sickness. If alcoholism is *not* a disease, then what else might it be? Over the course of history, alcoholism has been categorized under many labels, from a personal weakness to a crime, a sin, a mental disorder, and a physical illness (Meyer, 1996). Each of these definitions carries important personal, social, political, and economic implications.

Consider, for instance, the consequences of characterizing alcoholism as a disease. If that is the case, then alcoholics should be treated like diabetics, heart patients, or victims of other physical illnesses. That is, they should be viewed with sympathy and should be given appropriate medical and therapeutic interventions to foster recovery from their illness. These treatments should be covered by medical insurance and delivered by health care professionals. Just as important, if alcoholism is defined as a disease, it should lose much of its stigma. After all, we don't blame people with diabetes or heart disease for their illnesses. Yes, alcoholics admittedly contribute to their own disease (by drinking too much), but so do many victims of diabetes and heart disease, who eat the wrong foods, fail to control their weight, and so forth (McLellan et al., 2000). And, as is the case with many physical illnesses, one can inherit a genetic vulnerability to alcoholism (Anthenelli & Schuckit, 1997), so it is difficult to argue that alcoholism is caused solely by one's behavior.

However, if alcoholism is defined as a personal failure or a moral weakness, alcoholics are less likely to be viewed with sympathy and compassion. They might be admonished to quit drinking, be put in prison, or be punished in some other way. These responses to their alcoholism would be administered primarily by the legal system rather than the health care system, as medical interventions are not designed to remedy moral failings. Obviously, the interventions that would be available would not be covered by health insurance, which would have enormous financial repercussions (for both health care providers and alcoholics).

The key point here is that definitions lie at the center of many complex debates, and they can have profound and far-reaching implications. People tend to think of definitions as insignificant, arbitrary, abstruse sets of words found buried in the obscurity of thick dictionaries compiled by ivory tower intellectuals. Well, much of this characterization may be accurate, but definitions are *not* insignificant. They are vested with enormous power to shape how people think about important issues. And an endless array of issues boil down to matters of definition. For example, the next time you hear people arguing over whether a particular movie is pornographic, whether the death penalty is cruel and unusual punishment, or whether spanking is child abuse, you'll find it helps to focus the debate on clarifying the definitions of the crucial concepts.

The Power to Make Definitions

So, how can we resolve the debate about whether alcoholism is a disease? Scientists generally try to resolve their debates by conducting research to achieve a better understanding of the phenomena under scrutiny. You may have noticed already that the assertion "We need more research on this issue . . ." is a frequent refrain in this text. Is more research the answer in this case? For once, the answer is "no." There is no conclusive way to determine whether alcoholism is a disease. It is not as though there is a "right" answer to this question that we can discover through more and better research.

The question of whether alcoholism is a disease is a *matter of definition:* Does alcoholism fit the currently accepted definition of what constitutes a disease? If you consult medical texts or dictionaries, you will find that *disease is typically defined as an impairment in the normal functioning of an organism that alters its vital functions.* Given that alcoholism clearly impairs people's normal functioning and disrupts a variety of vital functions (see Figure 5.24), it seems reasonable to characterize it as a disease, and this has been the dominant view in the United States since the middle of the 20th century (Maltzman, 1994; Meyer, 1996). Still, many critics express vigorous doubts about the wisdom of defining alcoholism as a disease (Peele, 1989). They often raise a question that comes up frequently in arguments about definitions: Who should have the power to make the definition? In this case, the power lies in the hands of the medical community, which seems sensible, given that disease is a medical concept. But some critics argue that the medical community has a strong bias in favor of defining conditions as diseases because this creates new markets and fuels economic growth for the health industry (Nikelly, 1994). Thus, debate about whether alcoholism is a disease seems likely to continue for the indefinite future.

To summarize, definitions generally do not emerge out of research. They are typically crafted by experts or authorities in a specific field who try to reach a consensus about how to best define a particular concept. Thus, in analyzing the validity of a definition, you need to look not only at the definition itself but at where it came from. Who decided what the definition should be? Does the source of the definition seem legitimate and appropriate? Did the authorities who formulated the definition have any biases that should be considered?

Definitions, Labels, and Circular Reasoning

There is one additional point about definitions that is worth discussing. Perhaps because definitions are imbued with so much power, people have an interesting tendency to incorrectly use them as *explanations* for the phenomena they describe. This logical error, which equates *naming* something with *explaining* it, is sometime called the *nominal fallacy*. Names and labels that are used as explanations may sound reasonable at first glance, but definitions do not really have any explanatory value; they simply specify what certain terms mean. Consider an example. Let's say your friend, Frank, has a severe drinking problem. You are sitting around with some other friends discussing why Frank drinks so much. Rest assured, at least one of these friends will assert that "Frank drinks too much because he is an alcoholic." This is circular reasoning, which is just as useless as explaining that Frank is an alcoholic because he drinks too much. It tells us nothing about *why* Frank has a drinking problem. The diagnostic labels that are used in the classification of mental disorders—labels such as schizophrenia, depression, autism, and obsessive-compulsive disorder—seem to invite this type of circular reasoning. For example, people often say things like "That person is delusional because she is schizophrenic," or "He is afraid of small, enclosed places because he is claustrophobic." These statements are just as logical as saying "She is a redhead because she has red hair." The logical fallacy of mistaking a label for an explanation will get us as far in our understanding as a dog gets in chasing its own tail.

Figure 5.24

Physiological malfunctions associated with alcoholism. This chart amply demonstrates that alcoholism is associated with a diverse array of physiological maladies. In and of itself, however, this information does not settle the argument about whether alcoholism should be regarded as a disease. It all depends on one's definition of what constitutes a disease.

SOURCE: Edlin, G., & Golanty, E. (1992). *Health and wellness: A holistic approach.* Boston: Jones & Bartlett. Copyright © 1992 by Jones & Bartlett Publishers, Inc. www.jbpub.com. Reprinted by permission.

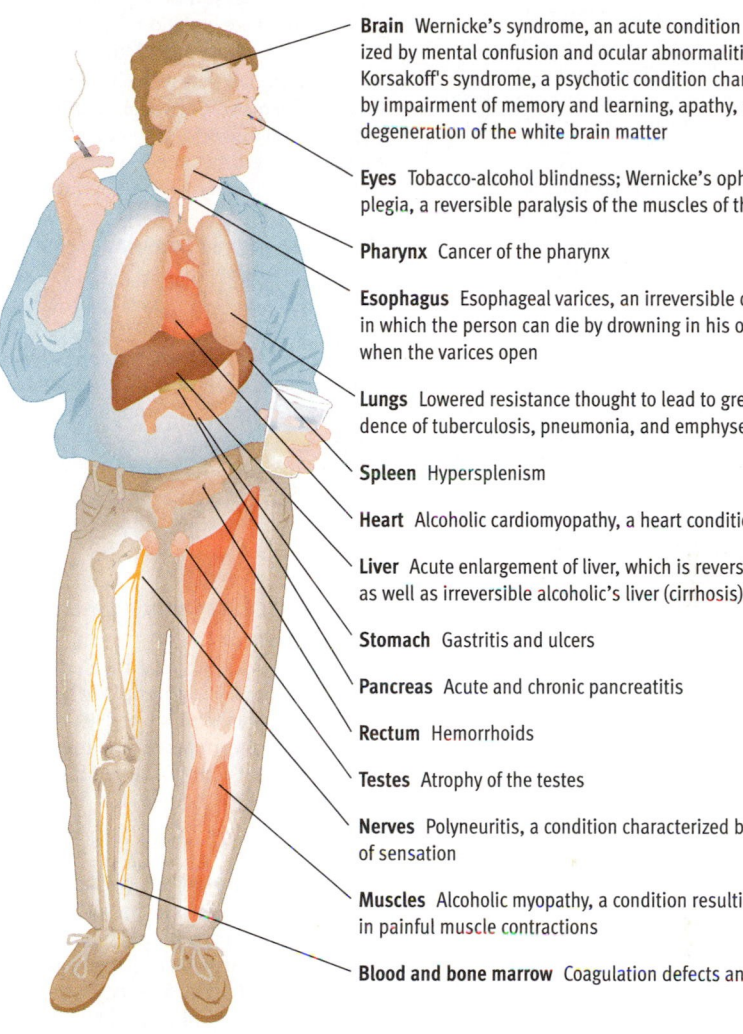

Brain Wernicke's syndrome, an acute condition characterized by mental confusion and ocular abnormalities; Korsakoff's syndrome, a psychotic condition characterized by impairment of memory and learning, apathy, and degeneration of the white brain matter

Eyes Tobacco-alcohol blindness; Wernicke's ophthalmoplegia, a reversible paralysis of the muscles of the eye

Pharynx Cancer of the pharynx

Esophagus Esophageal varices, an irreversible condition in which the person can die by drowning in his own blood when the varices open

Lungs Lowered resistance thought to lead to greater incidence of tuberculosis, pneumonia, and emphysema

Spleen Hypersplenism

Heart Alcoholic cardiomyopathy, a heart condition

Liver Acute enlargement of liver, which is reversible, as well as irreversible alcoholic's liver (cirrhosis)

Stomach Gastritis and ulcers

Pancreas Acute and chronic pancreatitis

Rectum Hemorrhoids

Testes Atrophy of the testes

Nerves Polyneuritis, a condition characterized by loss of sensation

Muscles Alcoholic myopathy, a condition resulting in painful muscle contractions

Blood and bone marrow Coagulation defects and anemia

Table 5.6 Critical Thinking Skills Discussed in This Application

Skill	Description
Understanding the way definitions shape how people think about issues	The critical thinker appreciates the enormous power of definitions and the need to clarify definitions in efforts to resolve disagreements.
Identifying the source of definitions	The critical thinker recognizes the need to determine who has the power to make specific definitions and to evaluate their credibility.
Avoiding the nominal fallacy in working with definitions and labels	The critical thinker understands that labels do not have explanatory value.

Key Ideas

On the Nature of Consciousness

● Consciousness is the continually changing stream of mental activity. There is some degree of awareness during sleep and sometimes even when patients are under anesthesia.

● Consciousness clearly is adaptive, but the question of exactly why it evolved is open to debate. Variations in consciousness are related to brain activity, as measured by the EEG.

Biological Rhythms and Sleep

● The cycle of sleep and wakefulness is influenced by circadian rhythms. Exposure to light resets biological clocks by affecting the activity of the suprachiasmatic nucleus and the pineal gland, which secretes melatonin.

● Being out of sync with circadian rhythms is one reason for jet lag and for the unpleasant nature of rotating shift work. Melatonin may have some value in treating jet lag and other sleep problems, but more research is needed.

The Sleep and Waking Cycle

● During a night's sleep, you evolve through a series of stages in cycles of approximately 90 minutes. During the REM stage you experience rapid eye movements, brain waves characteristic of waking thought, and vivid dreaming. The sleep cycle tends to be repeated four times in a night, as REM sleep gradually becomes more predominant and NREM sleep dwindles.

● The REM portion of sleep declines during childhood, leveling off at around 20%. During adulthood, slow-wave sleep declines. Culture appears to have little impact on the physiological experience of sleep, but it does influence sleeping arrangements and napping patterns.

● The modulation of sleep and arousal depends on a constellation of brain structures and a variety of neurotransmitters. Hypotheses about the evolutionary bases of sleep focus on energy conservation, reduced exposure to predators, and restoration of depleted resources.

● People often underestimate the impact of sleep deprivation. Going without sleep appears to contribute to many transportation accidents and mishaps at work. Research on selective sleep deprivation suggests that people need REM sleep and slow-wave sleep.

● Many people are troubled by sleep disorders. Foremost among these disorders is insomnia, which has a variety of causes. Other common sleep problems include narcolepsy, sleep apnea, night terrors, nightmares, and somnambulism.

The World of Dreams

● The conventional view is that dreams are mental experiences during REM sleep that have a storylike quality, include vivid imagery, are often bizarre, and are regarded as real by the dreamer, but theorists have begun to question many aspects of this view.

● The content of one's dreams may be affected by one's age and gender, events in one's life, and external stimuli experienced during the dream. There are variations across cultures in dream recall, content, and interpretation.

● Freud argued that the purpose of dreams is wish fulfillment. Cartwright has articulated a problem-solving view, whereas Hobson and McCarley assert that dreams are side effects of the neural activation seen during REM sleep.

Hypnosis: Altered Consciousness or Role Playing?

● Hypnosis has a long and curious history. People vary greatly in their susceptibility to hypnosis. Among other things, hypnosis can produce anesthesia, sensory distortions, disinhibition, and posthypnotic amnesia.

● There are two major theoretical approaches to hypnosis that view it either as an altered state of consciousness or as a normal state of consciousness in which subjects assume a hypnotic role.

Meditation: Pure Consciousness or Relaxation?

● Evidence suggests that meditation leads to a potentially beneficial physiological state characterized by suppression of bodily arousal. However, the long-term benefits of meditation may not be unique to meditation and critics are worried about methodological flaws in meditation research.

Altering Consciousness with Drugs

● Recreational drug use involves an effort to alter consciousness with psychoactive drugs. Psychoactive drugs exert their main effects in the brain, where they alter neurotransmitter activity in a variety of ways. The mesolimbic dopamine pathway may mediate the reinforcing effects of most abused drugs.

● Drugs vary in their potential for psychological and physical dependence. Likewise, the dangers to health vary depending on the drug. Recreational drug use can prove harmful to health by producing an overdose, by causing tissue damage, or by increasing health-impairing behavior.

Putting It in Perspective

● Four of our unifying themes were highlighted in this chapter. We saw that psychology evolves in a sociohistorical context, that experience is highly subjective, that culture influences many aspects of behavior, and that psychology is characterized by theoretical diversity.

Personal Application ● Addressing Practical Questions About Sleep and Dreams

● People's sleep needs vary, and the value of short naps depends on many factors. Sleep learning is possible, but only in primitive ways. People's internal alarm clocks are not as reliable as often claimed.

● People can do many things to avoid or reduce sleep problems. Mostly, it's a matter of developing good daytime habits that do not interfere with sleep. Individuals troubled by transient insomnia should avoid panic, pursue relaxation, and try distracting themselves.

● Everyone dreams, but some people cannot remember their dreams, probably because of the nature of their sleep cycle. In lucid dreams, people consciously recognize that they are dreaming and exert some control over the events in their dreams. Most theorists believe that dreams require some interpretation, but this may not be as complicated as once assumed.

Critical Thinking Application ● Is Alcoholism a Disease? The Power of Definitions

● Like many questions, the issue of whether alcoholism should be regarded as a disease is a matter of definition. In evaluating the validity of a definition, one should look not only at the definition but also at where it came from. People have a tendency to use definitions as explanations for the phenomena they describe, but doing so involves circular reasoning.

Key Terms

Alcohol
Ascending reticular activating system (ARAS)
Biological rhythms
Cannabis
Circadian rhythms
Dissociation
Electroencephalograph (EEG)
Electromyograph (EMG)
Electrooculograph (EOG)
Hallucinogens
Hypnosis
Insomnia
Latent content
Lucid dreams
Manifest content
MDMA
Meditation
Narcolepsy
Narcotics
Night terrors
Nightmares
Non-REM (NREM) sleep
Opiates
Physical dependence
Psychoactive drugs
Psychological dependence
REM sleep
Sedatives
Sleep apnea
Slow-wave sleep (SWS)
Somnambulism
Stimulants
Tolerance

Key People

Theodore Barber
Rosalind Cartwright
William Dement
Sigmund Freud
Calvin Hall
Ernest Hilgard
J. Alan Hobson
William James

8/15

1. An EEG would indicate primarily _____ activity while you take this test.
- A. alpha
- B. beta
- C. delta
- D. theta

2. Other things being equal, which of the following flights would lead to the greatest difficulty with jet lag?
- A. northward
- B. southward
- C. eastward
- D. westward

3. Slow-wave sleep consists of stages _____ of sleep and is dominated by _____ waves.
- A. 1 and 2; beta
- B. 2 and 3; alpha
- C. 3 and 4; delta
- D. 1 and 2; delta

4. As the sleep cycle evolves through the night, people tend to:
- A. spend more time in REM sleep and less time in NREM sleep.
- B. spend more time in NREM sleep and less time in REM sleep.
- C. spend a more or less equal amount of time in REM sleep and NREM sleep.
- D. spend more time in stage 4 sleep and less time in REM sleep.

5. Newborn infants spend about _____% of their sleep time in REM, while adults spend about _____% of their sleep time in REM.
- A. 20; 50
- B. 50; 20
- C. 20; 20
- D. 50; 50

6. Tamara has taken part in a 3-day study in which she was awakened every time she went in to REM sleep. Now that she is home sleeping without interference, it is likely that she will:
- A. exhibit psychotic symptoms for a few nights.
- B. experience severe insomnia for about a week.
- C. spend extra time in REM sleep for a few nights.
- D. spend less time in REM sleep for a few nights.

7. Which of the following generally occurs during REM sleep?
- A. sleep apnea
- B. somnambulism
- C. night terrors
- D. nightmares

8. Which of the following is *not* true of cultural influences on dream experiences?
- A. The ability to recall dreams is fairly consistent across cultures.
- B. In some cultures, people are held responsible for their dream actions.
- C. In many cultures, dreams are seen as a window into the spiritual world.
- D. People in some cultures believe that dreams provide information about the future.

9. The activation-synthesis theory of dreaming contends that:
- A. dreams are simply the by-product of bursts of activity in the brain.
- B. dreams provide an outlet for energy invested in socially undesirable impulses.
- C. dreams represent the brain's attempt to process information taken in during waking hours.
- D. dreams are an attempt to restore a neurotransmitter balance within the brain.

10. A common driving experience is "highway hypnosis," in which one's consciousness seems to be divided between the driving itself and one's conscious train of thought. This phenomenon is consistent with the idea that hypnosis is:
- A. an exercise in role playing.
- B. a dissociated state of consciousness.
- C. a goal-directed fantasy.
- D. not an altered state of consciousness.

11. Stimulant is to depressant as:
- A. cocaine is to alcohol.
- B. mescaline is to barbiturates.
- C. caffeine is to amphetamines.
- D. alcohol is to barbiturates.

12. Amphetamines work by increasing the levels of _____ in a variety of ways.
- A. GABA and glycine
- B. melatonin
- C. acetylcholine
- D. norepinephrine and dopamine

13. Which of the following drugs would be most likely to result in a fatal overdose?
- A. LSD
- B. mescaline
- C. marijuana
- D. sedatives

14. Which of the following is a true statement about naps?
- A. Daytime naps invariably lead to insomnia.
- B. Daytime naps are invariably refreshing and an efficient way to rest.
- C. Daytime naps are not very efficient ways to sleep, but their effects are sometimes beneficial.
- D. Taking many naps during the day can substitute for a full night's sleep.

15. Definitions:
- A. generally emerge out of research.
- B. often have great explanatory value.
- C. generally exert little influence over how people think.
- D. are usually constructed by experts or authorities in a specific field.

Answers

1	B	p. 179	**6**	C	pp. 190–191	**11**	A	pp. 203–204
2	C	p. 181	**7**	D	p. 192	**12**	D	p. 205
3	C	p. 183	**8**	A	p. 195	**13**	D	pp. 205, 207
4	A	pp. 184–185	**9**	A	p. 196	**14**	C	p. 210
5	B	pp. 185–186	**10**	B	p. 200	**15**	D	pp. 214–215

ON THE WEB

For additional resources on the topics covered in this chapter, visit the *Psychology: Themes and Variations* Web site, where you will find practice quizzes, tutorials, Web links, simulations, critical thinking activities, flash cards, interactive exercises, and suggested readings available through INFOTRAC.

http://psychology.wadsworth.com/weiten_themes6e/

CHAPTER 6

© Katy Knootz/Mira. All rights reserved.

Learning

- You're sitting in the waiting room of your dentist's office. You cringe when you hear the whirring of a dental drill coming from the next room.
- A four-year-old boy pinches his hand in one of his toys and curses loudly. His mother looks up in dismay and says to his father, "Where did he pick up that kind of language?"
- A young girl goes to the front closet, takes out a chain leash for her dog, and jingles the chain loudly. The dog leaps off the couch and comes running, wagging its tail with excitement.
- A seal waddles across the stage, bows ceremoniously, and "doffs his cap" by flipping it into the air and catching it in his mouth. The spectators at the aquatic show clap appreciatively as the trainer tosses the seal a fish as a reward.
- The crowd hushes as an Olympic diver prepares to execute her dive. In a burst of motion she propels herself into the air and glides smoothly through a dazzling corkscrew somersault.

What do all of these scenarios have in common? At first glance, very little. They are a diverse collection of events, some trivial, some impressive. However, they do share one common thread: *They all involve learning*. This may surprise you. When most people think of learning, they envision students reading textbooks or novices working to acquire a specific skill, such as riding a bicycle or skiing. Although such activities do involve learning, they represent only the tip of the iceberg in psychologists' eyes.

Learning **refers to a relatively durable change in behavior or knowledge that is due to experience.** This broad definition means that learning is one of the most fundamental concepts in all of psychology. Learning includes the acquisition of knowledge and skills, but it also shapes personal habits, such as nailbiting; personality traits, such as shyness; emotional responses, such as a fear of storms; and personal preferences, such as a taste for tacos or a distaste for formal clothes. Much of your behavior is the result of learning. If it were possible to strip away your learned responses, little behavior would be left. You would not be able to read this book, find your way home, or cook yourself a hamburger. You would be about as complex and exciting as a turnip.

Although you and I depend on learning, it is *not* an exclusively human process. Most organisms are capable of learning. Even the lowly flatworm can acquire a learned response. As this chapter unfolds, you may be surprised to see that much of the research on learning has been conducted using animals as subjects. Why? Mainly because researchers can exert much better experimental control over animal subjects than human subjects. As we saw in Chapter 1, that was one of the reasons that the noted behaviorist John B. Watson advocated the study of animal behavior. For the most part, Watson's plan has worked out well. Decades of research have shown that many principles of learning discovered in animal research apply quite well to humans.

In this chapter, we will focus most of our attention on a specific kind of learning: conditioning. *Conditioning* involves learning associations between events that occur in an organism's environment. In investigating conditioning, psychologists study learning at a very fundamental level. This strategy has paid off with fruitful insights that have laid the foundation for the study of more complex forms of learning, including learning by means of observation. In the Personal Application, you'll see how you can harness the principles of conditioning to improve your self-control. The Critical Thinking Application shows how conditioning procedures can be used to manipulate emotions.

Classical Conditioning

PREVIEW QUESTIONS

- What happens in classical conditioning?
- What are the key elements in this type of learning?
- What types of emotional responses are modulated by classical conditioning?
- What are some physiological processes governed by classical conditioning?
- How are conditioned responses acquired and weakened?
- What is higher-order conditioning?

Do you go weak in the knees at the thought of standing on the roof of a tall building? Does your heart race when you imagine encountering a harmless garter snake? If so, you can understand, at least to some degree, what it's like to have a phobia. *Phobias are irrational fears of specific objects or situations*. Mild phobias are commonplace (Eaton, Dryman, & Weissman, 1991). Over the years, students in my classes have described their phobic responses to a diverse array of stimuli, including bridges, elevators, tunnels, heights, dogs, cats, bugs, snakes, professors, doctors, strangers, thunderstorms, and germs. If you have a phobia, you may have wondered how you managed to acquire such a perplexing fear. Chances are, it was through classical conditioning (Ayres, 1998).

Classical conditioning is a type of learning in which a stimulus acquires the capacity to evoke a response that was originally evoked by another stimulus. The process was first described around 1900 by Ivan Pavlov, and it is sometimes called *Pavlovian conditioning* in tribute to him. The term *conditioning* comes from Pavlov's determination to discover the "conditions" that produce this kind of learning.

Pavlov's Demonstration: "Psychic Reflexes"

Ivan Pavlov was a prominent Russian physiologist who did Nobel prize–winning research on digestion. Something of a "classic" himself, he was an absent-minded but brilliant professor obsessed with his research. Legend has it that Pavlov once reprimanded an assistant who arrived late for an experiment because of trying to avoid street fighting in the midst of the Russian Revolution. The assistant defended his

tardiness, saying, "But Professor, there's a revolution going on with shooting in the streets!" Pavlov supposedly replied, "What the hell difference does a revolution make when you've work to do in the laboratory? Next time there's a revolution, get up earlier!" Apparently, dodging bullets wasn't an adequate excuse for delaying the march of scientific progress (Fancher, 1979; Gantt, 1975).

Pavlov was studying the role of saliva in the digestive processes of dogs when he stumbled onto what he called "psychic reflexes" (Pavlov, 1906). Like many great discoveries, Pavlov's was partly accidental, although he had the insight to recognize its significance. His subjects were dogs restrained in harnesses in an experimental chamber (see Figure 6.1). Their saliva was collected by means of a surgically implanted tube in the salivary gland. Pavlov would present meat powder to a dog and then collect the resulting saliva. As his research progressed, he noticed that dogs accustomed to the procedure would start salivating *before* the meat powder was presented. For instance, they would salivate in response to a clicking sound made by the device that was used to present the meat powder.

Intrigued by this unexpected finding, Pavlov decided to investigate further. To clarify what was happening, he paired the presentation of the meat powder with various stimuli that would stand out in the laboratory situation. For instance, in some experiments he used a simple auditory stimulus—the presentation of a tone. After the tone and the meat powder had been presented together a number of times, the tone was presented alone. What happened? The dogs responded by salivating to the sound of the tone alone.

What was so significant about a dog salivating when a tone was presented? The key is that the tone started out as a *neutral* stimulus. That is, it did not originally produce the response of salivation. However, Pavlov managed to change that by pairing the tone with a stimulus (meat powder) that did produce the salivation response. Through this process, the tone acquired the capacity to trigger the response of salivation. What Pavlov had demonstrated was how learned associations—which were viewed as the basic building blocks of the entire learning process—were formed by events in an organism's environment. Based on this insight, he built a broad theory of learning that attempted to explain aspects of emo-

Surrounded by his research staff, the great Russian physiologist Ivan Pavlov (center, white beard) demonstrates his famous classical conditioning experiment with dogs.

© CORBIS-Bettmann

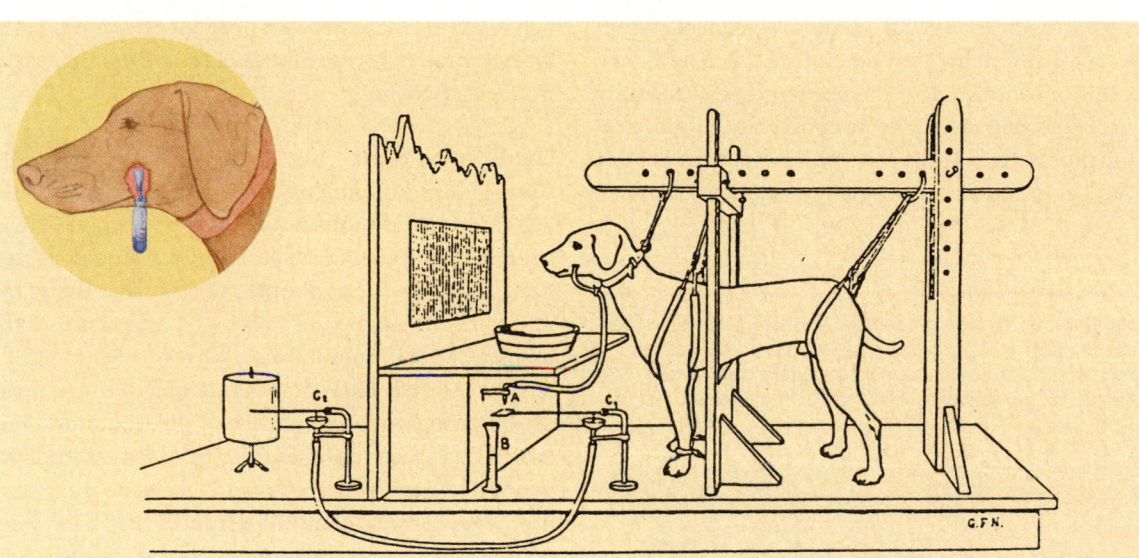

Figure 6.1

Classical conditioning apparatus. An experimental arrangement similar to the one depicted here (taken from Yerkes & Morgulis, 1909) has typically been used in demonstrations of classical conditioning, although Pavlov's original setup (see inset) was quite a bit simpler. The dog is restrained in a harness. A tone is used as the conditioned stimulus (CS), and the presentation of meat powder is used as the unconditioned stimulus (UCS). The tube inserted into the dog's salivary gland allows precise measurement of its salivation response. The pen and rotating drum of paper on the left are used to maintain a continuous record of salivary flow. (Inset) The less elaborate setup that Pavlov originally used to collect saliva on each trial is shown here (Goodwin, 1991).

tion, temperament, neuroses, and language (Windholz, 1997).

Terminology and Procedures 5a

There is a special vocabulary associated with classical conditioning. It often looks intimidating to the uninitiated, but it's really not all that mysterious. The bond Pavlov noted between the meat powder and salivation was a natural, unlearned association. It did not have to be created through conditioning. It is therefore called an *unconditioned* association. Thus, **the *unconditioned stimulus (UCS)* is a stimulus that evokes an unconditioned response without previous conditioning. The *unconditioned response (UCR)* is an unlearned reaction to an unconditioned stimulus that occurs without previous conditioning.**

In contrast, the link between the tone and salivation was established through conditioning. It is therefore called a *conditioned* association. Thus, **the *conditioned stimulus (CS)* is a previously neutral stimulus that has, through conditioning, acquired the capacity to evoke a conditioned response. The *conditioned response (CR)* is a learned reaction to a conditioned stimulus that occurs because of previous conditioning.** Ironically, the names for the four key elements in classical conditioning (the UCS, UCR, CS, and CR) are the by-product of a poor translation of Pavlov's writing into English. Pavlov actually used the words condition*al* and uncondition*al* to refer to these concepts (Todes, 1997).

To avoid possible confusion, it is worth noting that the unconditioned response and conditioned response often consist of the same behavior, although there may be subtle differences between them. In Pavlov's initial demonstration, the UCR and CR were both salivation. When evoked by the UCS (meat powder), salivation was an unconditioned response. When evoked by the CS (the tone), salivation was a conditioned response. The procedures involved in classical conditioning are outlined in Figure 6.2 on the next page.

Pavlov's "psychic reflex" came to be called the *conditioned reflex.* Classically conditioned responses have traditionally been characterized as reflexes and are said to be *elicited* (drawn forth) because most of them are relatively automatic or involuntary. However, research in recent decades has demonstrated that classical conditioning is involved in a wider range of human and animal behavior than previously appreciated, including some types of nonreflexive responding (Allan, 1998). Finally, **a *trial* in classical conditioning consists of any presentation of a stimulus or pair of stimuli.** Psychologists are interested in how many trials are required to establish a particular conditioned bond. The number needed to form an association varies considerably. Although classical conditioning generally proceeds gradually, it *can* occur quite rapidly, sometimes in just one pairing of the CS and UCS.

Classical Conditioning in Everyday Life 5a

In laboratory experiments on classical conditioning, researchers have generally worked with extremely

"Next time there's a revolution, get up earlier!"
Ivan Pavlov

simple responses. Besides salivation, frequently studied favorites include eyelid closure, knee jerks, the flexing of various limbs, and fear responses. The study of such simple responses has proven both practical and productive. However, these responses do not even begin to convey the rich diversity of everyday behaviors regulated by classical conditioning. Let's look at some examples of classical conditioning taken from everyday life.

Conditioned Fears 5a

Classical conditioning often plays a key role in shaping emotional responses such as fears. Phobias are a good example of such responses. Case studies of patients suffering from phobias suggest that many irrational fears can be traced back to experiences that involve classical conditioning (Ayres, 1998; McAllister & McAllister, 1995). It is easy to imagine how such conditioning can occur outside of the laboratory. For example, a student of mine was troubled by a bridge phobia so severe that she couldn't drive on interstate highways because of all the viaducts that had to be crossed. She was able to pinpoint as the source of her phobia something that had happened during her childhood (see Figure 6.3). Whenever her family drove to visit her grandmother, they had to cross a little-used, rickety, dilapidated bridge out in the country-side. Her father, in a misguided attempt at humor, made a major production out of these crossings. He would stop short of the bridge and carry on about the enormous danger. Obviously, he thought the bridge was safe or he wouldn't have driven across it. However, the naive young girl was terrified by her father's scare tactics. Hence, the bridge became a conditioned stimulus eliciting great fear. Unfortunately, the fear spilled over to *all* bridges. Forty years later she was still carrying the burden of this phobia.

Everyday fear responses that are less severe than phobias may also be products of classical conditioning. For instance, if you cringe when you hear the sound of a dentist's drill, this response is due to classical conditioning. In this case, the pain you have experienced from dental drilling is the UCS. This pain has been paired with the sound of the drill, which became a CS eliciting your cringe.

Figure 6.2

The sequence of events in classical conditioning. **(a)** Moving downward, this series of three panels outlines the sequence of events in classical conditioning, using Pavlov's original demonstration as an example. **(b)** As we encounter other examples of classical conditioning throughout the book, we will see many diagrams like the one in this panel, which will provide snapshots of specific instances of classical conditioning.

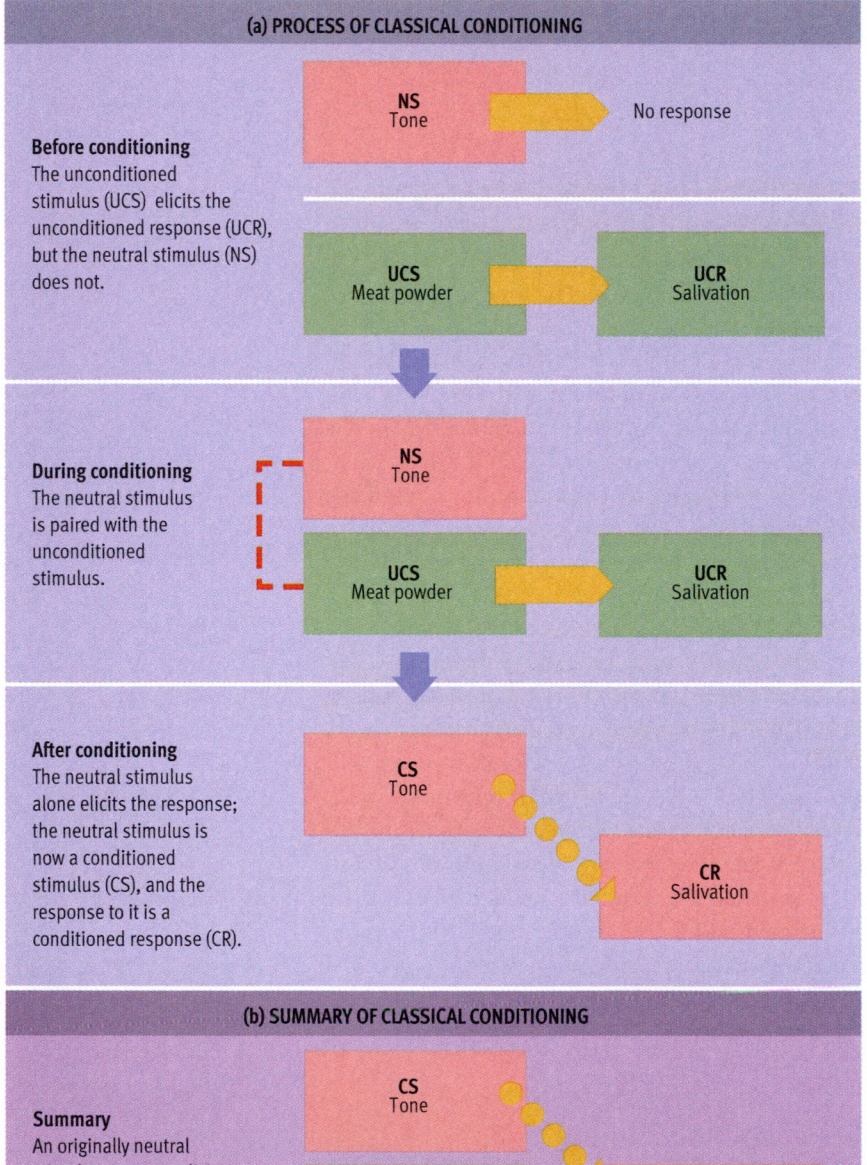

Figure 6.3

Classical conditioning of a fear response. Many emotional responses that would otherwise be puzzling can be explained by classical conditioning. In the case of one woman's bridge phobia, the fear originally elicited by her father's scare tactics became a conditioned response to the stimulus of bridges.

Other Conditioned Emotional Responses 5a

Classical conditioning is not limited to producing unpleasant emotions such as fear. Many pleasant emotional responses are also acquired through classical conditioning. Consider the following example, described by a woman who wrote a letter to newspaper columnist Bob Greene about the news that a company was bringing back a discontinued product—Beemans gum. She wrote:

That was the year I met Charlie. I guess first love is always the same. . . . Charlie and I went out a lot. He chewed Beemans gum and he smoked. . . . We would go to all the passion pits—the drive-in movies and the places to park. We did a lot of necking, but we always stopped at a certain point. Charlie wanted to get married when we got out of high school . . . [but] Charlie and I drifted apart. We both ended up getting married to different people.

And the funny thing is . . . for years the combined smell of cigarette smoke and Beemans gum made my knees weak. Those two smells were Charlie to me. When I would smell the Beemans and the cigarette smoke, I could feel the butterflies dancing all over my stomach.

The writer clearly had a unique and long-lasting emotional response to the smell of Beemans gum and cigarettes. The credit for this *pleasant* response goes to classical conditioning (see Figure 6.4).

Advertising campaigns often try to take advantage of classical conditioning. Advertisers frequently pair their products with UCSs that elicit pleasant emotions (Allen & Shimp, 1990). The most common strategy is to present a product in association with an attractive person or enjoyable surroundings (see Figure 6.5). Advertisers hope that these pairings will

Figure 6.4

Classical conditioning and romance. Pleasant emotional responses can be acquired through classical conditioning, as illustrated by one woman's unusual conditioned response to the aroma of Beemans gum and cigarette smoke.

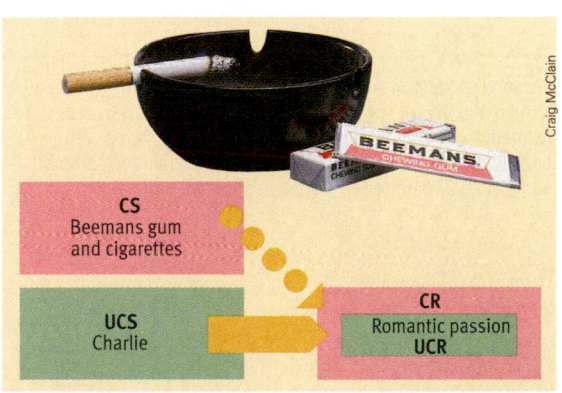

make their products conditioned stimuli that evoke good feelings. For example, Kodak used a child playing with puppies in one of its TV commercials to help associate warm feelings with its film products.

Conditioning and Physiological Responses 5a

Classical conditioning affects not only overt behaviors but physiological processes as well. Consider, for example, your body's immune functioning. When an infectious agent invades your body, your immune system attempts to repel the invasion by producing specialized proteins called *antibodies*. The critical importance of the immune response becomes evident when the immune system is disabled, as occurs with the disease AIDS (acquired immune deficiency syndrome).

Recent advances have revealed that the functioning of the immune system can be influenced by psychological factors, including conditioning (Ader, 2001). Robert Ader and Nicholas Cohen (1984, 1993) have shown that classical conditioning procedures can lead to *immunosuppression*—a decrease in the production of antibodies. In a typical study, animals are injected with a drug (the UCS) that *chemically* causes immunosuppression while they are simultaneously given an unusual-tasting liquid to drink (the CS). Days later, after the chemical immunosuppression has ended, some of the animals are reexposed to the CS by giving them the unusual-tasting solution. Mea-

Figure 6.5

Classical conditioning in advertising. Many advertisers attempt to make their products conditioned stimuli that elicit pleasant emotional responses by pairing their products with attractive or popular people or sexual imagery.

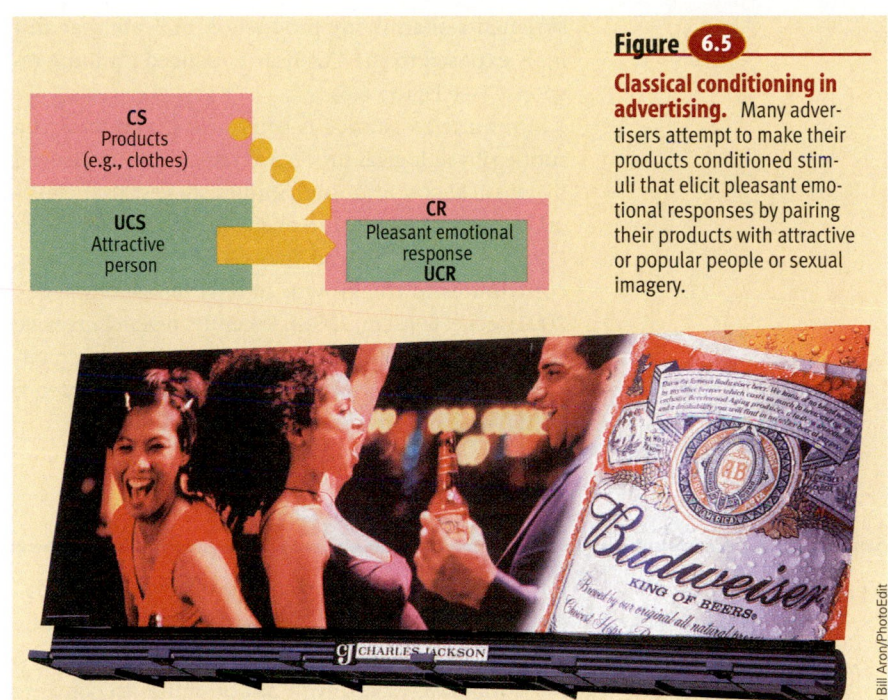

surements of antibody production indicate that animals exposed to the CS show a reduced immune response (see Figure 6.6).

Immune resistance is only one example of the subtle physiological processes that can be influenced by classical conditioning. Studies suggest that classical conditioning can also elicit *allergic reactions* (MacQueen et al., 1989) and that classical conditioning contributes to the growth of *drug tolerance* (Siegel, 2001; Siegel & Allan, 1998). Recently, researchers have shown an interest in how classical conditioning modulates sexual responding (Pfaus, Kippin, & Centeno, 2001), which brings us to our Featured Study.

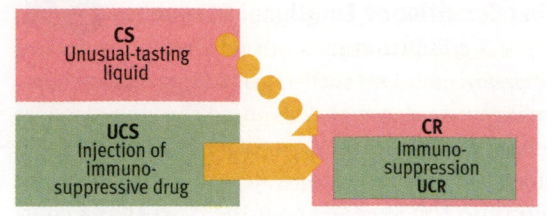

Figure 6.6

Classical conditioning of immunosuppression. When a neutral stimulus is paired with a drug that chemically causes immunosuppression, it can become a CS that elicits immunosuppression on its own. Thus, even the immune response can be influenced by classical conditioning.

FEATURED STUDY

Sex and the Single Quail

Investigators: Michael Domjan (University of Texas, Austin), Elisabeth Blesbois, and John Williams (Institut National de Recherche Agronomique, Centre de Tours, France)

Source: The adaptive significance of sexual conditioning: Pavlovian control of sperm release. *Psychological Science*, 1998, *9*, 411–415.

Previous research had shown that male Japanese quail could be conditioned to become sexually aroused by an originally neutral stimulus. The neutral stimulus—a red light—was paired with opportunities to copulate with a female. These pairings eventually made the red light a CS that elicited excitement in the male subjects—and led them to copulate more quickly if females were made available in the presence of the red light (Domjan, 1992, 1994). The present study examined the evolutionary significance of this type of sexual conditioning. The investigators hypothesized that this type of conditioning might have a favorable impact on organisms' reproductive fitness by increasing the quantity or quality of sperm released.

Method

Subjects. Twenty-nine adult male Japanese quail were used in the experiment. Fifteen came from a line of experimental animals previously bred for high sociality and fourteen from a line bred for low emotionality.

Apparatus. The conditioned stimulus was a distinctive chamber (painted white with a wire mesh floor) in which the males were given copulation opportunities. On test trials, the subjects' semen was collected by allowing them to mount a taxidermically prepared artificial female made of terrycloth and polyester fiber.

Procedure. The subjects in the experimental group went through six conditioning trials, each of which involved giving them access to a receptive female in the distinctive chamber (see Figure 6.7). The subjects in the control group were given similar opportunities for copulation, but in their home cages. Thus, both groups received equivalent handling and sexual opportunities, but only the experimental group learned to associate the distinctive chamber with sexual reinforcement. Test trials, with the artificial female in the distinctive chamber, were conducted after the fourth and sixth condi-

tioning trials. The researchers measured semen volume, estimated the number of spermatozoa per ejaculate, and evaluated sperm quality (the percentage of viable sperm).

Results

No significant differences were found between the groups in sperm quality. However, the experimental subjects ejaculated a greater volume of semen, which resulted in the release of a greater number of spermatozoa. As you can see in Figure 6.8, the experimental subjects released roughly twice as many sperm as the control subjects.

Discussion

The physiological mechanisms underlying the enhanced sperm release will require further investigation. Domjan and his colleagues speculate that the conditioned stimulus *may* have elicited greater muscular contractions during ejaculation. Obviously, a conditioned response that results in the ejaculation of a greater number of spermatozoa should facilitate the fertilization of eggs and result in increased offspring. Thus, the investigators conclude that their study "demonstrates an important way

Figure 6.7

Classical conditioning of sexual arousal. Working with quail, Domjan and his colleagues (1998) paired the neutral stimulus of a distinctive chamber with a receptive female and the opportunity to copulate. Hence, the chamber became a conditioned stimulus that elicited a conditioned response of sexual arousal.

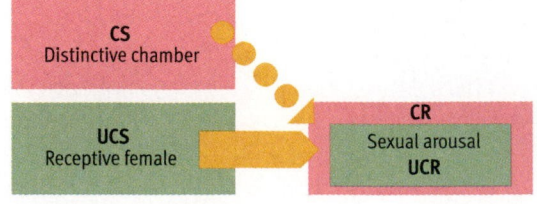

in which Pavlovian conditioning can alter reproductive fitness" (pp. 412–413).

Comment

This study was featured because it highlights the growing influence of the evolutionary perspective in psychology. Researchers are increasingly investigating Pavlovian conditioning by trying to discern its adaptive significance (Hollis, 1997). This research is also extremely interesting for what it implies about human sexual functioning. Psychologists have long suspected that stimuli routinely paired with sex, such as seductive nightgowns, mood music, lit candles, and the like, probably become conditioned stimuli that elicit arousal, but this hypothesis is not readily investigated in the laboratory with human subjects. Elucidating the role of classical conditioning in sexual functioning may also shed new light on how humans' sexual tastes can go awry in the form of *fetishes* for inanimate objects. If quail can be conditioned to find a

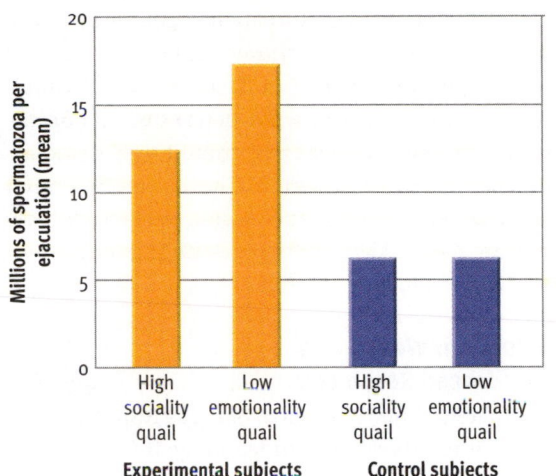

Figure 6.8

Effect of classical conditioning on sperm release. The conditioning of sexual arousal in the two experimental groups clearly enhanced sperm release in these groups, as compared to the two control groups.

SOURCE: Adapted from Domjan, M., Blesbois, E., & Williams, J. (1998). The adaptive significance of sexual conditioning: Pavlovian control of sperm release. *Psychological Science, 9,* 411–415. Blackwell Publishers. Adapted by permission.

red light or a distinctive chamber arousing, it seems likely that humans may be conditioned to be aroused by objects such as shoes, boots, leather, and undergarments. ■

Basic Processes in Classical Conditioning

Classical conditioning is often portrayed as a mechanical process that inevitably leads to a certain result. This view reflects the fact that most conditioned responses are reflexive and difficult to control—Pavlov's dogs would have been hard pressed to withhold their salivation. Similarly, most people with phobias have great difficulty suppressing their fear. However, this vision of classical conditioning as an "irresistible force" is misleading because it fails to consider the many factors involved in classical conditioning (Kehoe & Macrae, 1998). In this section, we'll look at basic processes in classical conditioning to expand on the rich complexity of this form of learning.

Acquisition: Forming New Responses

We have already discussed *acquisition* without attaching a formal name to the process. **Acquisition refers to the initial stage of learning something.** Pavlov theorized that the acquisition of a conditioned response depends on *stimulus contiguity*. Stimuli are contiguous if they occur together in time and space.

Stimulus contiguity is important, but learning theorists now realize that contiguity alone doesn't automatically produce conditioning. People are bombarded daily by countless stimuli that could be perceived as being paired, yet only some of these pairings produce classical conditioning. Consider the woman who developed a conditioned emotional reaction to

the smell of Beemans gum and cigarettes. There were no doubt other stimuli that shared contiguity with her boyfriend, Charlie. He smoked, so ashtrays were

CONCEPT **CHECK 6.1**

Identifying Elements in Classical Conditioning

Check your understanding of classical conditioning by trying to identify the unconditioned stimulus (UCS), unconditioned response (UCR), conditioned stimulus (CS), and conditioned response (CR) in each of the examples below. Fill in the diagram next to each example. You'll find the answers in Appendix A in the back of the book.

1. Sam is 3 years old. One night his parents build a roaring fire in the family room fireplace. The fire spits out a large ember that hits Sam in the arm, giving him a nasty burn that hurts a great deal for several hours. A week later, when Sam's parents light another fire in the fireplace, Sam becomes upset and fearful, crying and running from the room.

2. Melanie is driving to work on a rainy highway when she notices that the brake lights of all the cars just ahead of her have come on. She hits her brakes but watches in horror as her car glides into a four-car pileup. She's badly shaken up in the accident. A month later she's driving in the rain again and notices that she tenses up every time she sees brake lights come on ahead of her.

3. At the age of 24, Tyrone has recently developed an allergy to cats. When he's in the same room with a cat for more than 30 minutes, he starts wheezing. After a few such allergic reactions, he starts wheezing as soon as he sees a cat in a room.

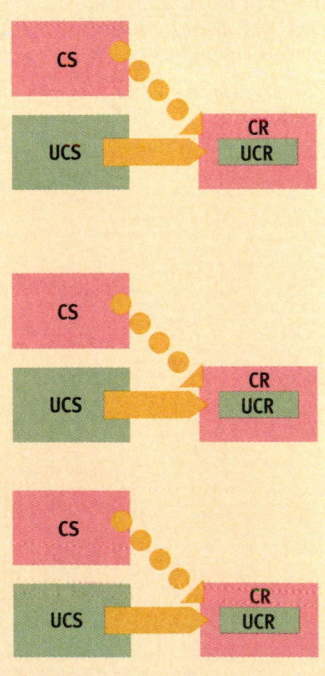

Web Link 6.1

Behaviour Analysis and Learning
A multitude of annotated links, all focusing on learning through conditioning, can be found at the excellent Psychology Centre site at Athabasca University (Alberta, Canada).

probably present, but she doesn't get weak in the knees at the sight of an ashtray.

If conditioning does not occur to all the stimuli present in a situation, what determines its occurrence? Evidence suggests that stimuli that are novel, unusual, or especially intense have more potential to become CSs than routine stimuli, probably because they are more likely to stand out among other stimuli (Hearst, 1988).

Extinction: Weakening Conditioned Responses

Fortunately, a newly formed stimulus-response bond does not necessarily last indefinitely. If it did, learning would be inflexible, and organisms would have difficulty adapting to new situations. Instead, the right circumstances produce **extinction, the gradual weakening and disappearance of a conditioned response tendency.**

What leads to extinction in classical conditioning? The consistent presentation of the conditioned stimulus *alone,* without the unconditioned stimulus. For example, when Pavlov consistently presented *only* the tone to a previously conditioned dog, the tone gradually lost its capacity to elicit the response of salivation. Such a sequence of events is depicted in the tan portion of Figure 6.9, which graphs the amount of salivation by a dog over a series of conditioning trials. Note how the salivation response declines during extinction.

For an example of extinction from outside the laboratory, let's assume that you cringe at the sound of a dentist's drill, which has been paired with pain in the past. You take a job as a dental assistant and you start hearing the drill (the CS) day in and day out

without experiencing any pain (the UCS). Your cringing response will gradually diminish and extinguish altogether.

How long does it take to extinguish a conditioned response? That depends on many factors, but particularly the strength of the conditioned bond when extinction begins. Some conditioned responses extinguish quickly, while others are difficult to weaken.

Spontaneous Recovery: Resurrecting Responses

Some conditioned responses display the ultimate in tenacity by "reappearing from the dead" after having been extinguished. Learning theorists use the term *spontaneous recovery* to describe such a resurrection from the graveyard of conditioned associations. **Spontaneous recovery is the reappearance of an extinguished response after a period of nonexposure to the conditioned stimulus.**

Pavlov (1927) observed this phenomenon in some of his pioneering studies. He fully extinguished a dog's CR of salivation to a tone and then returned the dog to its home cage for a "rest interval" (a period of nonexposure to the CS). On a subsequent day, when the dog was brought back to the experimental chamber for retesting, the tone was sounded and the salivation response reappeared. Although it had returned, the rejuvenated response was weak. The salivation was less than when the response was at its peak strength. If Pavlov consistently presented the CS by itself again, the response reextinguished quickly. However, in some of the dogs the response made still another spontaneous recovery (typically even weaker than the first) after they had spent another period in their cages (consult Figure 6.9 once again).

Recent studies have also demonstrated that if a response is extinguished in a different environment than it was acquired, the extinguished response will reappear if the animal is returned to the original environment where acquisition took place (Bouton, 1994). This phenomenon, called the *renewal effect,* along with the evidence on spontaneous recovery, suggests that extinction somehow suppresses a conditioned response rather than erasing a learned association. In other words, *extinction does not appear to lead to unlearning* (Bouton & Nelson, 1998). The theoretical meaning of spontaneous recovery and the renewal effect is complex and the subject of some debate. However, their practical meaning is quite simple: Even if you manage to rid yourself of an unwanted conditioned response (such as cringing when you hear a dental drill), there is an excellent chance that it may make a surprise reappearance later.

Figure 6.9

Acquisition, extinction, and spontaneous recovery.
During acquisition, the strength of the dog's conditioned response (measured by the amount of salivation) increases rapidly and then levels off near its maximum. During extinction, the CR declines erratically until it's extinguished. After a "rest" period in which the dog is not exposed to the CS, a spontaneous recovery occurs, and the CS once again elicits a (weakened) CR. Repeated presentations of the CS alone re-extinguish the CR, but after another "rest" interval, a weaker spontaneous recovery occurs.

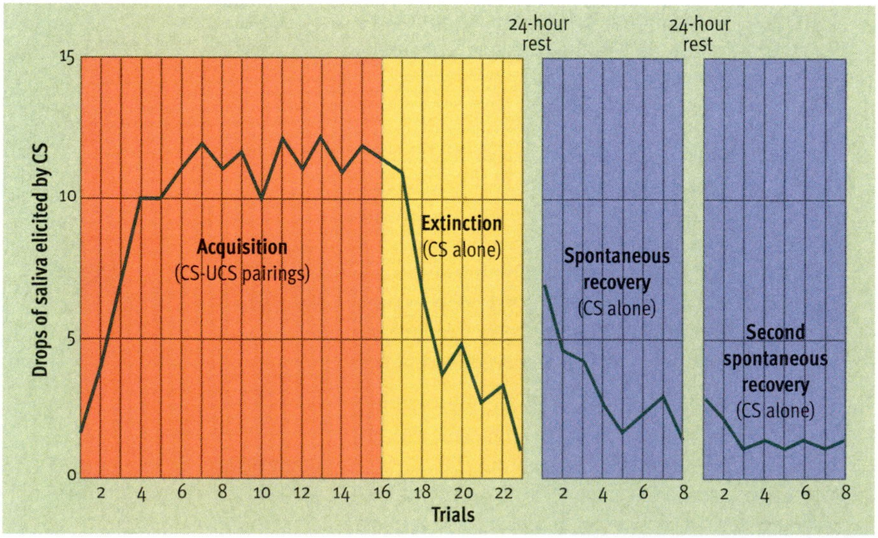

Stimulus Generalization and the Case of Little Albert

After conditioning has occurred, organisms often show a tendency to respond not only to the exact CS used but also to other, similar stimuli. For example, Pavlov's dogs might have salivated in response to a different-sounding tone, or you might cringe at the sound of a jeweler's as well as a dentist's drill. These are examples of stimulus generalization. ***Stimulus generalization occurs when an organism that has learned a response to a specific stimulus responds in the same way to new stimuli that are similar to the original stimulus.*** Generalization is adaptive given that organisms rarely encounter the exact same stimulus more than once (Thomas, 1992). Stimulus generalization is also commonplace. We have already discussed a real-life example: the woman who acquired a bridge phobia during her childhood because her father scared her whenever they went over a particular old bridge. The original CS for her fear was that specific bridge, but her fear was ultimately *generalized* to all bridges.

John B. Watson, the founder of behaviorism (see Chapter 1), conducted an influential early study of generalization. Watson and a colleague, Rosalie Rayner, examined the generalization of conditioned fear in an 11-month-old boy, known in the annals of psychology as "Little Albert." Like many babies, Albert was initially unafraid of a live white rat. Then Watson and Rayner (1920) paired the presentation of the rat with a loud, startling sound (made by striking a steel gong with a hammer). Albert *did* show fear in response to the loud noise. After seven pairings of the rat and the gong, the rat was established as a CS eliciting a fear response (see Figure 6.10). Five days later, Watson and Rayner exposed the youngster to other stimuli that resembled the rat in being white and furry. They found that Albert's fear response generalized to a variety of stimuli, including a rabbit, a dog, a fur coat, a Santa Claus mask, and Watson's hair.

What happened to Little Albert? Did he grow up with a phobia of Santa Claus? Unfortunately, we have no idea. He was taken from the hospital where Watson and Rayner conducted their study before they got around to extinguishing the conditioned fears that they had created, and he was never heard of again. Watson and Rayner were roundly criticized in later years for failing to ensure that Albert experienced no lasting ill effects. Their failure to do so was fairly typical for their era but clearly remiss by today's much stricter code of research ethics.

The likelihood and amount of generalization to a new stimulus depend on the similarity between the

Figure 6.10

The conditioning of Little Albert. The diagram shows how Little Albert's fear response to a white rat was established. Albert's fear response to other white, furry objects illustrates generalization. In the photo, made from a 1919 film, John B. Watson's collaborator, Rosalie Rayner, is shown with Little Albert before he was conditioned to fear the rat.

new stimulus and the original CS (Balsam, 1988). The basic law governing generalization is this: *The more similar new stimuli are to the original CS, the greater the generalization.* This principle can be quantified in graphs called *generalization gradients,* such as those shown in Figure 6.11 on the next page. These generalization gradients map out how a dog conditioned to salivate to a tone of 1200 hertz might respond to other tones. As you can see, the strength of the generalization response declines as the similarity between the new stimuli and the original CS decreases.

Stimulus Discrimination

Stimulus discrimination is just the opposite of stimulus generalization. ***Stimulus discrimination occurs when an organism that has learned a response to a specific stimulus does *not* respond in the same way to new stimuli that are similar to the original stimulus.*** Like generalization, discrimination is adaptive in that an animal's survival may hinge on its being able to distinguish friend from foe, or edible from poisonous food (Thomas, 1992). Organisms can gradually learn to discriminate between an original CS and similar stimuli if they have adequate experience with both. For instance, let's say your pet dog runs around, excitedly wagging its tail, whenever it hears your car pull up in the driveway. Initially it will probably respond to *all* cars that pull into the driveway (stimulus generalization). However, if there is anything distinctive about the sound of your car, your dog may gradually respond with excitement to only your car and not to other cars (stimulus discrimination).

The development of stimulus discrimination usually requires that the original CS (your car) continue to be paired with the UCS (your arrival) while similar stimuli (the other cars) not be paired with the UCS. As with generalization, a basic law governs discrimination: *The less similar new stimuli are to the original*

"Surely this proof of the conditioned origin of a fear response puts us on natural science grounds in our study of emotional behavior."
JOHN B. WATSON

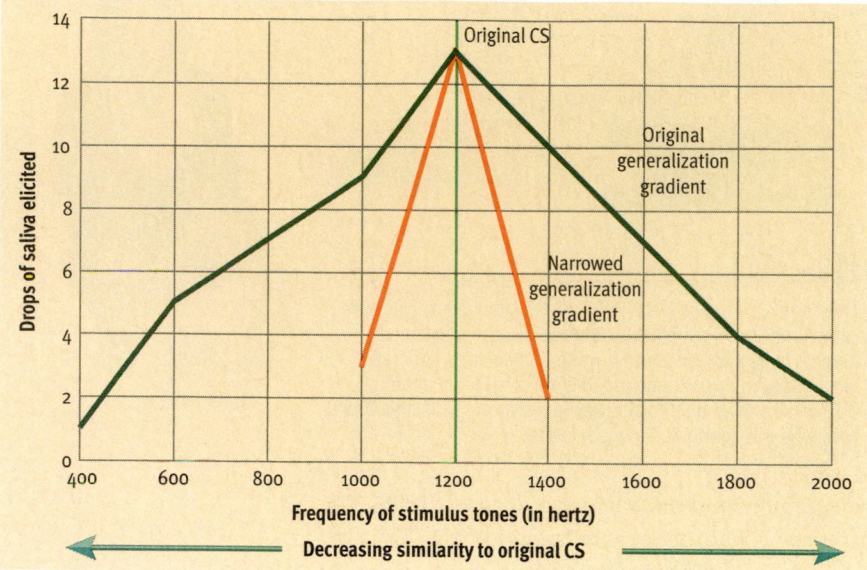

Figure 6.11

Generalization gradients. In a study of stimulus generalization, an organism is typically conditioned to respond to a specific CS, such as a 1200 hertz tone, and then is tested with similar stimuli, such as other tones between 400 and 2000 hertz. Graphs of the organism's responding are called *generalization gradients*. The graphs normally show, as depicted here, that generalization declines as the similarity between the original CS and the new stimuli decreases. When an organism gradually learns to *discriminate* between a CS and similar stimuli, the generalization gradient tends to narrow around the original CS.

CS, the greater the likelihood (and ease) of discrimination. Conversely, if a new stimulus is quite similar to the original CS, discrimination will be relatively difficult to learn. What happens to a generalization gradient when an organism learns a discrimination? The generalization gradient gradually narrows around the original CS, which means that the organism is generalizing to a smaller and smaller range of similar stimuli (consult Figure 6.11 again).

Higher-Order Conditioning  5b

Imagine that you were to conduct the following experiment. First, you condition a dog to salivate in response to the sound of a tone by pairing the tone with meat powder. Once the tone is firmly established as

a CS, you pair the tone with a new stimulus, let's say a red light, for 15 trials. You then present the red light alone, without the tone. Will the dog salivate in response to the red light?

The answer is "yes." Even though the red light has never been paired with the meat powder, it will acquire the capacity to elicit salivation by virtue of being paired with the tone (see Figure 6.12). This is a demonstration of **higher-order conditioning, in which a conditioned stimulus functions as if it were an unconditioned stimulus.** Higher-order conditioning shows that classical conditioning does not depend on the presence of a genuine, natural UCS. An already established CS will do just fine. In higher-order conditioning, new conditioned responses are built on the foundation of already established conditioned responses. Many human conditioned responses are the product of higher-order conditioning (Rescorla, 1980). The phenomenon of higher-order conditioning greatly extends the reach of classical conditioning.

REVIEW OF KEY POINTS

● Learning is defined as a relatively durable change in behavior or knowledge due to experience. Classical conditioning explains how a neutral stimulus can acquire the capacity to elicit a response originally elicited by another stimulus. This kind of conditioning was originally described by Ivan Pavlov, who conditioned dogs to salivate in response to the sound of a tone.

● In classical conditioning, the unconditioned stimulus (UCS) is a stimulus that elicits an unconditioned response without previous conditioning. The unconditioned response (UCR) is an unlearned reaction to an unconditioned stimulus that occurs without previous conditioning. The conditioned stimulus (CS) is a previously neutral stimulus that has acquired the capacity to elicit a conditioned response. The conditioned response (CR) is a learned reaction to a conditioned stimulus.

● Classically conditioned responses are said to be elicited. Many kinds of everyday responses are regulated through classical conditioning, including phobias, mild fears, and pleasant emotional responses. Even subtle physiological responses such as immune system functioning respond to

Figure 6.12

Higher-order conditioning. Higher-order conditioning involves a two-phase process. In the first phase, a neutral stimulus (such as a tone) is paired with an unconditioned stimulus (such as meat powder) until it becomes a conditioned stimulus that elicits the response originally evoked by the UCS (such as salivation). In the second phase, another neutral stimulus (such as a red light) is paired with the previously established CS, so that it also acquires the capacity to elicit the response originally evoked by the UCS.

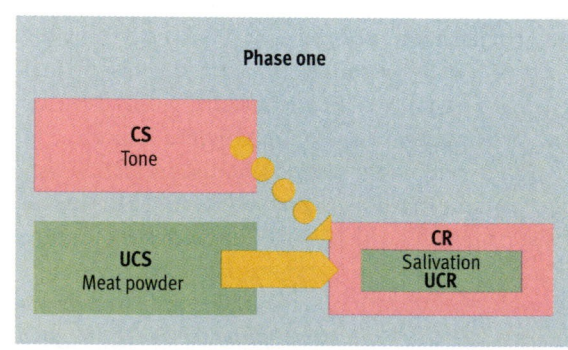

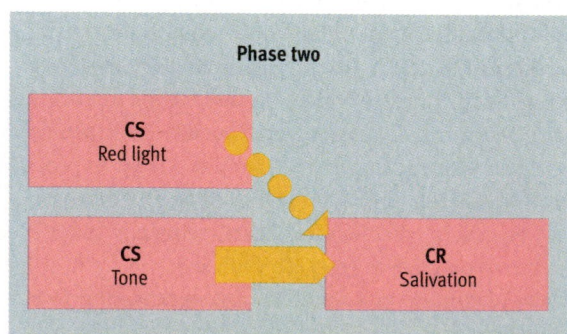

classical conditioning. Our Featured Study showed that sexual arousal can be influenced by Pavlovian conditioning and that this process may have adaptive significance.

- Stimulus contiguity plays a key role in the acquisition of new conditioned responses. A conditioned response may be weakened and extinguished entirely when the CS is no longer paired with the UCS. In some cases, spontaneous recovery occurs, and an extinguished response reappears after a period of nonexposure to the CS.

- Conditioning may generalize to additional stimuli that are similar to the original CS. Watson and Rayner conducted an influential early study of generalization with a subject known as Little Albert, whose fear response to a rat generalized to a variety of other white, furry objects.

- The opposite of generalization is discrimination, which involves not responding to stimuli that resemble the original CS. When an organism learns a discrimination, the generalization gradient narrows around the original CS. Higher-order conditioning occurs when a CS functions as if it were a UCS.

Operant Conditioning

Even Pavlov recognized that classical conditioning is not the only form of conditioning. Classical conditioning best explains reflexive responding that is largely controlled by stimuli that *precede* the response. However, humans and other animals make a great many responses that don't fit this description. Consider the response that you are engaging in right now: studying. It is definitely not a reflex (life might be easier if it were). The stimuli that govern it (exams and grades) do not precede it. Instead, your studying is mainly influenced by stimulus events that *follow* the response—specifically, its *consequences*.

In the 1930s, this kind of learning was christened *operant conditioning* by B. F. Skinner. The term was derived from his belief that in this type of responding, an organism "operates" on the environment instead of simply reacting to stimuli. Learning occurs because responses come to be influenced by the outcomes that follow them. Thus, **operant conditioning is a form of learning in which responses come to be controlled by their consequences.** Learning theorists originally distinguished between classical and operant conditioning on the grounds that the former regulated reflexive, involuntary responses, whereas the latter governed voluntary responses. This distinction holds up much of the time, but it is not absolute. Research in recent decades has shown that classical conditioning sometimes contributes to the regulation of voluntary behavior, that operant conditioning can influence involuntary, visceral responses, and that the two types of conditioning jointly and interactively govern some aspects of behavior (Allan, 1998; Turkkan, 1989).

Thorndike's Law of Effect

Another name for operant conditioning is *instrumental learning,* a term introduced earlier by Edward L. Thorndike (1913). Thorndike wanted to empha-size that this kind of responding is often *instrumental* in obtaining some desired outcome. His pioneering work provided the foundation for many of the ideas proposed later by Skinner. Thorndike began studying animal learning around the turn of the century. Setting out to determine whether animals could think, he conducted some classic studies of problem solving in cats. In these studies, a hungry cat was placed in a small cage or "puzzle box" with food available just outside. The cat could escape to obtain the food by performing a specific response, such as pulling a wire or depressing a lever (see Figure 6.13). After each escape, the cat was rewarded with a small amount of food and then returned to the cage for another trial. Thorndike monitored how long it took the cat to get out of the box over a series of trials. If the cat could think, Thorndike reasoned, there would be a

PREVIEW QUESTIONS

- How did Thorndike's law of effect anticipate Skinner's findings?
- What are the key elements in operant conditioning?
- How do organisms acquire new responses through operant conditioning?
- What is resistance to extinction, and why does it matter?
- How does stimulus control fit into operant responding?
- How do primary and secondary reinforcers differ?

Figure 6.13

The learning curve of one of Thorndike's cats. The inset shows one of Thorndike's puzzle boxes. The cat had to perform three separate acts to escape the box, including depressing the pedal on the right. The learning curve shows how the cat's escape time declined gradually over a number of trials.

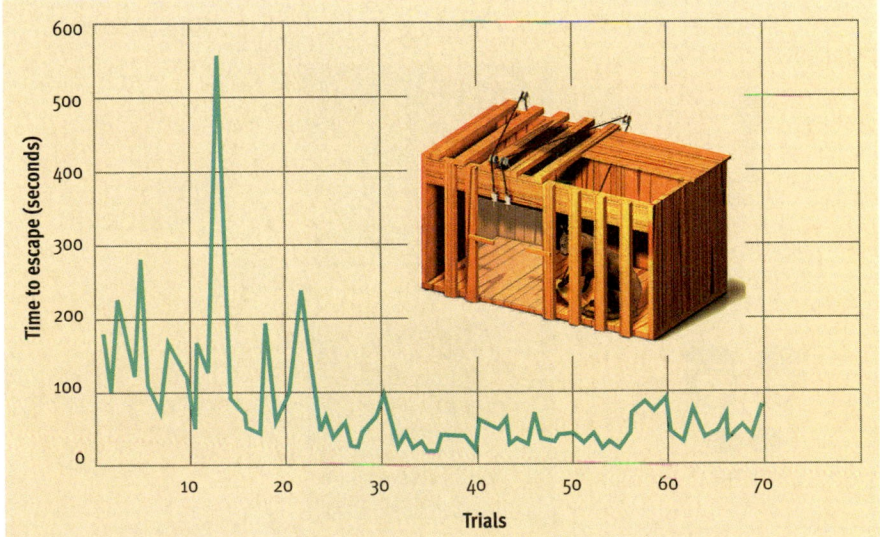

sudden drop in the time required to escape when the cat recognized the solution to the problem.

Instead of a sudden drop, Thorndike observed a gradual, uneven decline in the time it took cats to escape from his puzzle boxes (see the graph in Figure 6.13). The decline in solution time showed that the cats *were learning*. But the gradual nature of this decline suggested that this learning did *not* depend on thinking and understanding. Instead, Thorndike attributed this learning to a principle he called the *law of effect*. According to the *law of effect,* if a response in the presence of a stimulus leads to satisfying effects, the association between the stimulus and the response is strengthened. Thorndike viewed instrumental learning as a mechanical process in which successful responses are gradually "stamped in" by their favorable effects. His law of effect became the cornerstone of Skinner's theory of operant conditioning, although Skinner used different terminology.

Skinner's Demonstration: It's All a Matter of Consequences

Like Pavlov, Skinner (1953, 1969, 1984) conducted some deceptively simple research that became enormously influential (Lattal, 1992). Ironically, he got off to an inauspicious start. His first book, *The Behavior of Organisms* (1938), sold only 80 copies in its first four years in print. Nonetheless, he went on to become, in the words of historian Albert Gilgen (1982), "without question the most famous American psychologist in the world" (p. 97).

The fundamental principle of operant conditioning is uncommonly simple and was anticipated by

Thorndike's law of effect. *Skinner demonstrated that organisms tend to repeat those responses that are followed by favorable consequences.* This fundamental principle is embodied in Skinner's concept of reinforcement. **Reinforcement occurs when an event following a response increases an organism's tendency to make that response.** In other words, a response is strengthened because it leads to rewarding consequences (see Figure 6.14).

The principle of reinforcement may be simple, but it is immensely powerful. Skinner and his followers have shown that much of everyday behavior is regulated by reinforcement. For example, you put money in a soda vending machine and you get a soft drink back as a result. You go to work because this behavior leads to your receiving paychecks. Perhaps you work extra hard because promotions and raises tend to follow such behavior. You tell jokes, and your friends laugh—so you tell some more. The principle of reinforcement clearly governs complex aspects of human behavior. Paradoxically, though, this principle emerged out of Skinner's research on the behavior of rats and pigeons in exceptionally simple situations. Let's look at that research.

Terminology and Procedures

Like Pavlov, Skinner created a prototype experimental procedure that has been repeated (with variations) thousands of times. In this procedure, an animal, typically a rat or a pigeon, is placed in an *operant chamber* that has come to be better known as a "Skinner box." **An *operant chamber*, or *Skinner box,* is a small enclosure in which an animal can make a specific response that is recorded while the consequences of the response are systematically controlled.** In the boxes designed for rats, the main response made available is pressing a small lever mounted on one side wall (see Figure 6.15). In the boxes made for pigeons, the designated response is pecking a small disk mounted on a side wall. Because operant responses *tend* to be voluntary, they are said to be *emitted* rather than *elicited*. **To *emit* means to send forth.**

The Skinner box permits the experimenter to control the reinforcement contingencies that are in effect for the animal. **Reinforcement contingencies are the circumstances or rules that determine whether responses lead to the presentation of reinforcers.** Typically, the experimenter manipulates whether positive consequences occur when the animal makes the designated response. The main positive consequence is usually delivery of a small bit of food into a food cup mounted in the chamber. Because the an-

Figure 6.14

Reinforcement in operant conditioning. According to Skinner, reinforcement occurs when a response is followed by rewarding consequences and the organism's tendency to make the response increases. The two examples diagrammed here illustrate the basic premise of operant conditioning—that voluntary behavior is controlled by its consequences. These examples involve positive reinforcement (for a comparison of positive and negative reinforcement, see Figure 6.21).

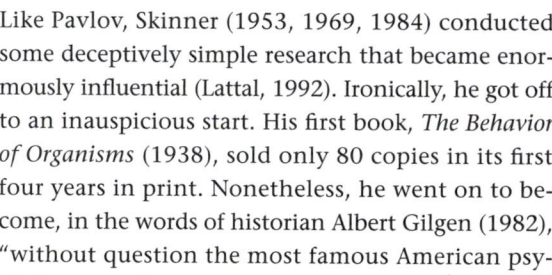

Behavior	Consequence	Effect on behavior
Response Go to Elmo's Bistro for dinner	**Rewarding stimulus presented** Great meal	Tendency to patronize Elmo's Bistro increases
Response Tell jokes	**Rewarding stimulus presented** Friends laugh	Tendency to tell jokes increases

imals are deprived of food for a while prior to the experimental session, their hunger virtually ensures that the food serves as a reinforcer.

The key dependent variable in most research on operant conditioning is the subjects' *response rate* over time. An animal's rate of lever pressing or disk pecking in the Skinner box is monitored continuously by a device known as a cumulative recorder (see Figure 6.15). **The *cumulative recorder* creates a graphic record of responding and reinforcement in a Skinner box as a function of time.** The recorder works by means of a roll of paper that moves at a steady rate underneath a movable pen. When there is no responding, the pen stays still and draws a straight horizontal line, reflecting the passage of time. Whenever the designated response occurs, however, the pen moves upward a notch. The pen's movements produce a graphic summary of the animal's responding over time. The pen also makes slash marks to record the delivery of each reinforcer.

The results of operant-conditioning studies are usually portrayed in graphs. In these graphs, the horizontal axis is used to mark the passage of time, while the vertical axis is used to plot the accumulation of responses, as shown in Figure 6.16 on the next page. In interpreting these graphs, the key consideration is the *slope* of the line that represents the record of responding. *A rapid response rate produces a steep slope,* *whereas a slow response rate produces a shallow slope.* Because the response record is cumulative, the line never goes down. It can only go up as more responses are made or flatten out if the response rate slows to zero. The magnifications shown in Figure 6.16 show how slope and response rate are related.

Basic Processes in Operant Conditioning

 SIM4, 5c

Although the principle of reinforcement is strikingly simple, many other processes involved in operant

Figure 6.15

Skinner box and cumulative recorder. **(a)** This diagram highlights some of the key features of an operant chamber, or Skinner box. In this apparatus designed for rats, the response under study is lever pressing. Food pellets, which may serve as reinforcers, are delivered into the food cup on the right. The speaker and light permit manipulations of visual and auditory stimuli, and the electric grid gives the experimenter control over aversive consequences (shock) in the box. **(b)** A cumulative recorder connected to the box keeps a continuous record of responses and reinforcements. A small segment of a cumulative record is shown here. The entire process is automatic as the paper moves with the passage of time; each lever press moves the pen up a step, and each reinforcement is marked with a slash. **(c)** This photo shows the real thing—a rat being conditioned in a Skinner box. Note the food dispenser on the left, which was omitted from the diagram.

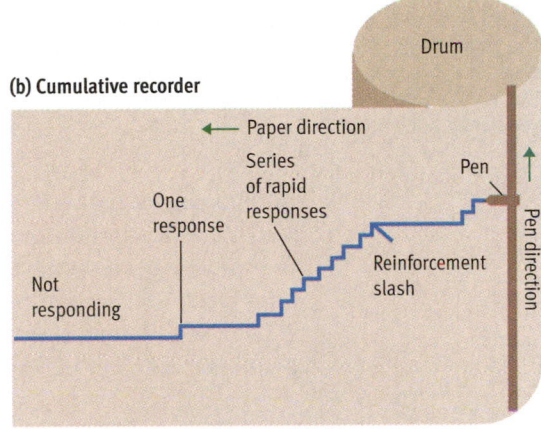

(b) Cumulative recorder

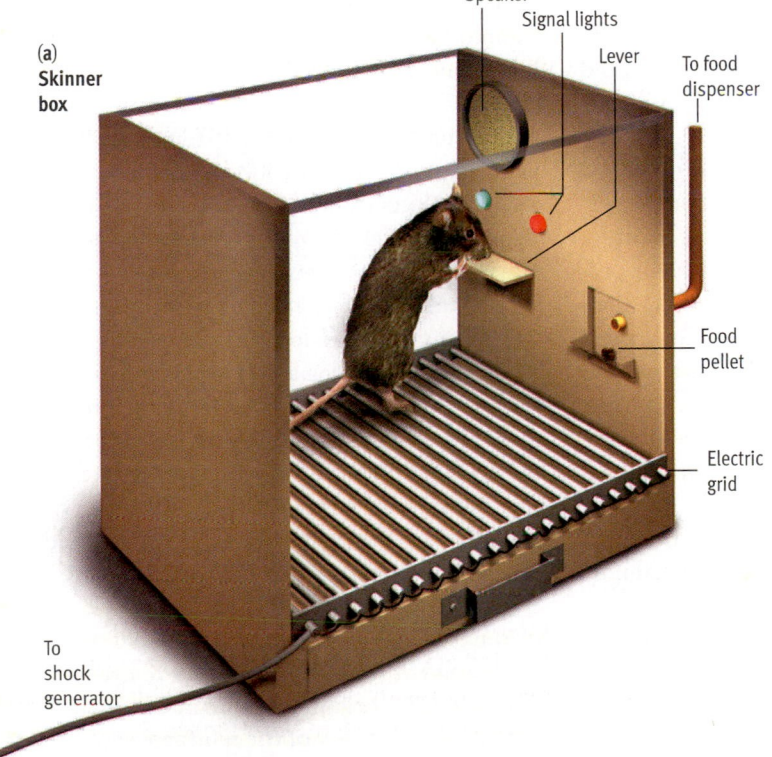

(a)
Skinner box

(c)

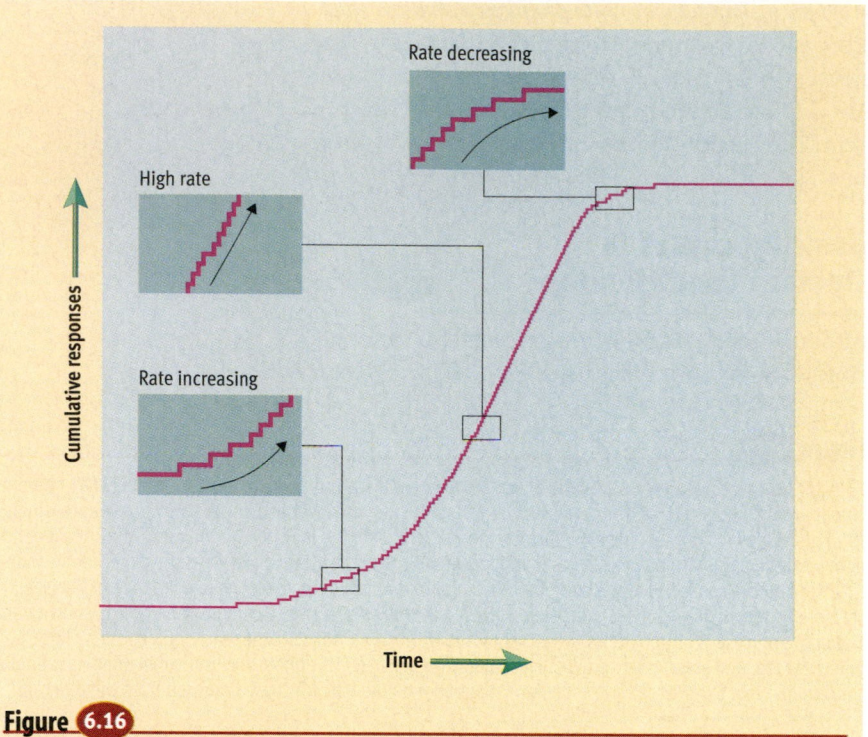

Rate decreasing

High rate

Rate increasing

Cumulative responses

Time

Figure 6.16

A graphic portrayal of operant responding. The results of operant conditioning are often summarized in a graph of cumulative responses over time. The insets magnify small segments of the curve to show how an increasing response rate yields a progressively steeper slope (bottom); a high, steady response rate yields a steep, stable slope (middle); and a decreasing response rate yields a progressively flatter slope (top).

"Operant conditioning shapes behavior as a sculptor shapes a lump of clay."
B. F. SKINNER

conditioning make this form of learning just as complex as classical conditioning. In fact, some of the *same* processes are involved in both types of conditioning. In this section, we'll discuss how the processes of acquisition, extinction, generalization, and discrimination occur in operant conditioning.

Acquisition and Shaping

As in classical conditioning, *acquisition* in operant conditioning refers to the initial stage of learning some new pattern of responding. However, the procedures used to establish a tendency to emit an operant response are different from those used to create the typical conditioned response. Operant responses are usually established through a gradual process called *shaping,* which consists of the reinforcement of closer and closer approximations of a desired response.

Shaping is necessary when an organism does not, on its own, emit the desired response. For example, when a rat is first placed in a Skinner box, it may not press the lever at all. In this case an experimenter begins shaping by releasing food pellets whenever the rat moves toward the lever. As this response becomes more frequent, the experimenter starts requiring a closer approximation of the desired response, possi-

bly releasing food only when the rat actually touches the lever. As reinforcement increases the rat's tendency to touch the lever, the rat will spontaneously press the lever on occasion, finally providing the experimenter with an opportunity to reinforce the designated response. These reinforcements will gradually increase the rate of lever pressing.

The mechanism of shaping is the key to training animals to perform impressive tricks. When you go to a zoo, circus, or marine park and see bears riding bicycles, monkeys playing the piano, and whales leaping through hoops, you are witnessing the results of shaping. To demonstrate the power of shaping techniques, Skinner once trained some pigeons so that they appeared to play Ping-Pong. They would run about on opposite ends of a Ping-Pong table and peck the ball back and forth. Keller and Marian Breland, a couple of psychologists influenced by Skinner, went into the business of training animals for advertising and entertainment purposes. One of their better known feats was shaping "Priscilla, the Fastidious Pig" to turn on a radio, eat at a kitchen table, put dirty clothes in a hamper, run a vacuum, and then "go shopping" with a shopping cart. Of course, Priscilla picked the sponsor's product off the shelf in her shopping expedition (Breland & Breland, 1961).

Extinction

In operant conditioning, *extinction* refers to the gradual weakening and disappearance of a response tendency because the response is no longer followed by a reinforcer. Extinction begins in operant conditioning whenever previously available reinforcement is stopped. In laboratory studies with rats, this usually means that the experimenter stops delivering food when the rat presses the lever. When the extinction process is begun, a brief surge often occurs in the rat's responding, followed by a gradual decline in response rate until it approaches zero.

The same effects are generally seen in the extinction of human behaviors. Let's say that a child routinely cries at bedtime and that this response is reinforced by attention from mom and dad. If the parents decided to cut off further reinforcement by ignoring the crying, they would be attempting to extinguish this undesirable response. Typically, the child increases its crying behavior for a few days, and then the crying tapers off fairly quickly (Williams, 1959).

A key issue in operant conditioning is how much *resistance to extinction* an organism will display when reinforcement is halted. *Resistance to extinction occurs when an organism continues to make a response after delivery of the reinforcer has been terminated*. The greater the resistance to extinction,

Courtesy of Animal Behavior Enterprises, Inc.

© Gerald Davis by permission of Karen Davis

Shaping—an operant technique in which an organism is rewarded for closer and closer approximations of the desired response—is used in teaching both animals and humans. It is the main means of training animals to perform unnatural tricks. Breland and Breland's (1961) famous subject, "Priscilla, the Fastidious Pig," is shown on the left.

the longer the responding will continue. Thus, if a researcher stops giving reinforcement for lever pressing and the response tapers off slowly, the response shows high resistance to extinction. However, if the response tapers off quickly, it shows relatively little resistance to extinction.

Resistance to extinction may sound like a matter of purely theoretical interest, but it's actually quite practical. People often want to strengthen a response in such a way that it will be relatively resistant to extinction. For instance, most parents want to see their child's studying response survive even if the child hits a rocky stretch when studying doesn't lead to reinforcement (good grades). In a similar fashion, a casino wants to see patrons continue to gamble, even if they encounter a lengthy losing streak. Thus, a high degree of resistance to extinction can be desirable in many situations. Resistance to extinction depends on a variety of factors. Chief among them is the *schedule of reinforcement* used during acquisition, a matter that we will discuss a little later in this chapter.

Stimulus Control: Generalization and Discrimination

Operant responding is ultimately controlled by its consequences, as organisms learn response-outcome (R-O) associations (Colwill, 1993). However, stimuli that *precede* a response can also exert considerable influence over operant behavior. When a response is consistently followed by a reinforcer in the presence of a particular stimulus, that stimulus comes to serve as a "signal" indicating that the response is likely to

lead to a reinforcer. Once an organism learns the signal, it tends to respond accordingly (Honig & Alsop, 1992). For example, a pigeon's disk pecking may be reinforced only when a small light behind the disk is lit. When the light is out, pecking does not lead to the reward. Pigeons quickly learn to peck the disk only when it is lit. The light that signals the availability of reinforcement is called a discriminative stimulus. *Discriminative stimuli* are cues that influence operant behavior by indicating the probable consequences (reinforcement or nonreinforcement) of a response.

Discriminative stimuli play a key role in the regulation of operant behavior. For example, birds learn that hunting for worms is likely to be reinforced after a rain. Children learn to ask for sweets when their parents are in a good mood. Drivers learn to slow down when the highway is wet. Human social behavior is also regulated extensively by discriminative stimuli. Consider the behavior of asking someone out for a date. Many people emit this response only cautiously, after receiving many signals (such as eye contact, smiles, encouraging conversational exchanges) that reinforcement (a favorable answer) is fairly likely. The potential power of discriminative stimuli to govern behavior has recently been demonstrated in dramatic fashion by research (Talwar et al., 2002) showing that it is possible to use operant procedures to train what *Time* magazine called "roborats," radio-controlled rodents that can be precisely directed through complex environments (see Figure 6.17 on the next page).

Web Link 6.2

The B. F. Skinner Foundation
This site is a fine place to become better acquainted with the psychologist who pioneered the study of operant conditioning. The site features Skinner's short autobiography, a complete bibliography of his publications, and annotated introductions to all of his books.

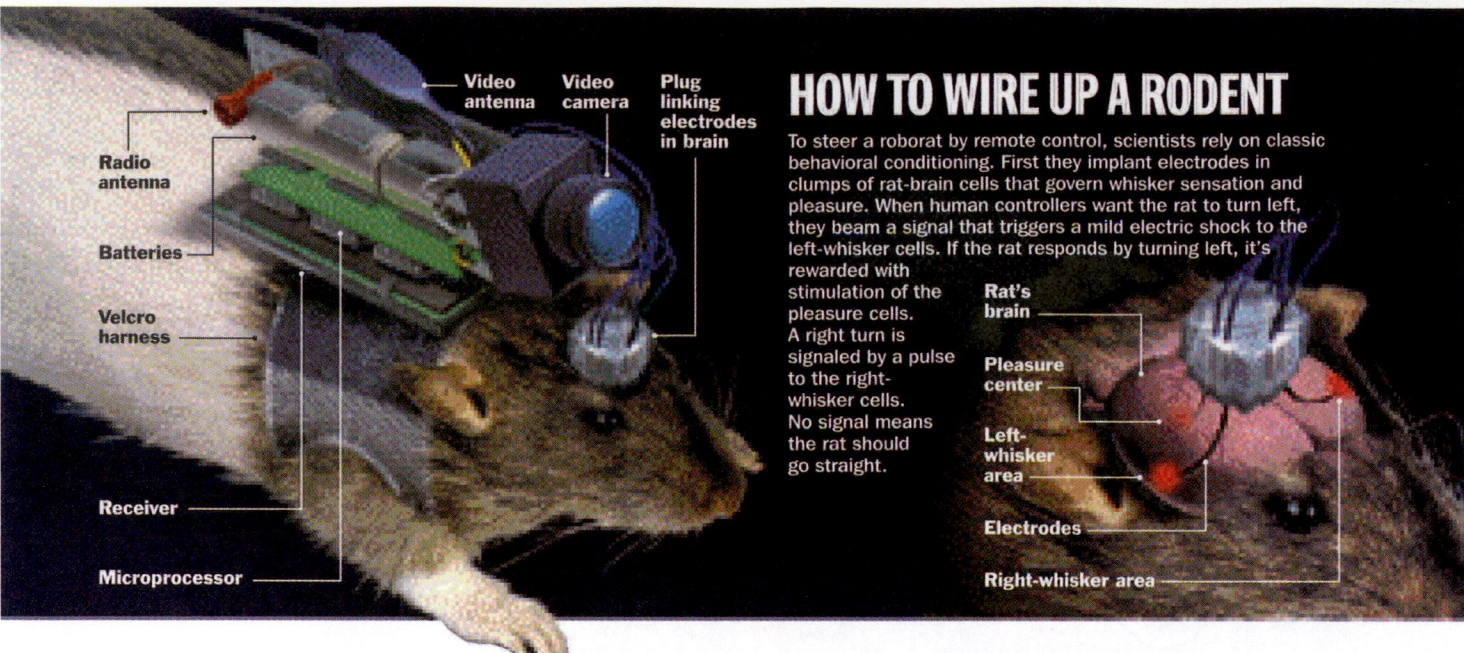

HOW TO WIRE UP A RODENT

To steer a roborat by remote control, scientists rely on classic behavioral conditioning. First they implant electrodes in clumps of rat-brain cells that govern whisker sensation and pleasure. When human controllers want the rat to turn left, they beam a signal that triggers a mild electric shock to the left-whisker cells. If the rat responds by turning left, it's rewarded with stimulation of the pleasure cells. A right turn is signaled by a pulse to the right-whisker cells. No signal means the rat should go straight.

Labels: Radio antenna; Batteries; Velcro harness; Receiver; Microprocessor; Video antenna; Video camera; Plug linking electrodes in brain; Rat's brain; Pleasure center; Left-whisker area; Electrodes; Right-whisker area

Figure 6.17

Remote-controlled rodents: An example of operant conditioning in action. In a study that almost reads like science fiction, Sanjiv Talwar and colleagues (2002) used operant conditioning procedures to train radio-controlled "roborats" that could have a variety of valuable applications, such as searching for survivors in a collapsed building. As this *Time* magazine graphic explains, radio signals can be used to direct the rat to go forward or turn right or left, while a video feed is sent back to a control center. The *reinforcer* in this setup is brief electrical stimulation of a pleasure center in the rat's brain (see Chapter 3), which can be delivered by remote control. The brief shocks sent to the right or left whiskers are *discriminative stimuli* that indicate which types of responses will be reinforced. The entire procedure depended on extensive *shaping*.

SOURCE: Graphic from Lemonick, M. D. (2002, May 13). Send in the roborats. *Time, 159* (19), p. 61. © 2002 Time, Inc. Reprinted by permission.

Reactions to a discriminative stimulus are governed by the processes of *stimulus generalization* and *stimulus discrimination*, just like reactions to a CS in classical conditioning. For instance, envision a cat that comes running into the kitchen whenever it hears the sound of a can opener because that sound has become a discriminative stimulus signaling a good chance of its getting fed. If the cat also responded to the sound of a new kitchen appliance (say a blender), this response would represent *generalization*—responding to a new stimulus as if it were the original. *Discrimination* would occur if the cat learned to respond only to the can opener and not to the blender.

As you have learned in this section, the processes of acquisition, extinction, generalization, and discrimination in operant conditioning parallel these same processes in classical conditioning. Table 6.1 compares these processes in the two kinds of conditioning.

Reinforcement: Consequences That Strengthen Responses

 5e

Although it is convenient to equate reinforcement with reward and the experience of pleasure, strict behaviorists object to this practice. Why? Because the experience of pleasure is an unobservable event that takes place within an organism. As explained in Chapter 1, most behaviorists believe that scientific assertions must be limited to what can be observed.

In keeping with this orientation, Skinner said that reinforcement occurs whenever an outcome strength-

Table 6.1 Comparison of Basic Processes in Classical and Operant Conditioning

Process and Definition	Description in Classical Conditioning	Description in Operant Conditioning
Acquisition: The initial stage of learning	CS and UCS are paired, gradually resulting in CR.	Responding gradually increases because of reinforcement, possibly through shaping.
Extinction: The gradual weakening and disappearance of a conditioned response tendency	CS is presented alone until it no longer elicits CR.	Responding gradually slows and stops after reinforcement is terminated.
Stimulus generalization: An organism's responding to stimuli other than the original stimulus used in conditioning	CR is elicited by new stimulus that resembles original CS.	Responding increases in the presence of new stimulus that resembles original discriminative stimulus.
Stimulus discrimination: An organism's lack of response to stimuli that are similar to the original stimulus used in conditioning	CR is not elicited by new stimulus that resembles original CS.	Responding does not increase in the presence of new stimulus that resembles original discriminative stimulus.

ens a response, as measured by an increase in the rate of responding. This definition avoids the issue of what the organism is feeling and focuses on observable events. Thus, the central process in reinforcement is the *strengthening of a response tendency*. To know whether an event is reinforcing, researchers must make it contingent on a response and observe whether the rate of this response increases after the supposed reinforcer has been presented.

Thus, reinforcement is defined *after the fact*, in terms of its *effect* on behavior. Something that is clearly reinforcing for an organism at one time may not function as a reinforcer later (Catania, 1992). Food will reinforce lever pressing by a rat only if the rat is hungry. Similarly, something that serves as a reinforcer for one person may not function as a reinforcer for another person. For example, parental approval is a potent reinforcer for most children, but not all.

Delayed Reinforcement

In operant conditioning, a favorable outcome is much more likely to strengthen a response if the outcome follows *immediately*. If a delay occurs between a response and the positive outcome, the response may not be strengthened. Furthermore, studies show that the longer the delay between the designated response and the delivery of the reinforcer, the more slowly conditioning proceeds (Church, 1989; Mazur, 1993).

Conditioned Reinforcement

Operant theorists make a distinction between unlearned, or primary, reinforcers as opposed to conditioned, or secondary, reinforcers. **Primary reinforcers are events that are inherently reinforcing because they satisfy biological needs.** A given species has a limited number of primary reinforcers because they are closely tied to physiological needs. In humans, primary reinforcers include food, water, warmth, sex, and perhaps affection expressed through hugging and close bodily contact.

Secondary, or conditioned, reinforcers **are events that acquire reinforcing qualities by being associated with primary reinforcers.** The events that function as secondary reinforcers vary among members of a species because they depend on learning. Examples of common secondary reinforcers in humans include money, good grades, attention, flattery, praise, and applause. Most of the material things that people work hard to earn are secondary reinforcers. For example, people learn to find stylish clothes, sports cars, fine jewelry, elegant china, and state-of-the-art stereos reinforcing.

Intermittent Reinforcement: Effects of Basic Schedules  5d

Organisms make innumerable responses that do not lead to favorable consequences. It would be nice if people were reinforced every time they took an exam, watched a movie, hit a golf shot, asked for a date, or made a sales call. However, in the real world most responses are reinforced only some of the time. How does this fact affect the potency of reinforcers? To find out, operant psychologists have devoted an enormous amount of attention to how *intermittent schedules of reinforcement* influence operant behavior (Ferster & Skinner, 1957; Skinner, 1938, 1953).

A *schedule of reinforcement* **determines which occurrences of a specific response result in the presentation of a reinforcer.** The simplest pattern is continuous reinforcement. *Continuous reinforcement* **occurs when every instance of a designated response is reinforced.** In the laboratory, experimenters often use continuous reinforcement to shape and establish a new response before moving on to more realistic schedules involving intermittent reinforcement. *Intermittent, or partial, reinforcement*

PREVIEW QUESTIONS

● What are the typical effects of various schedules of reinforcement?

● How do researchers study choice in operant behavior, and what have they discovered?

● How do positive and negative reinforcement differ?

● How does two-process theory explain the persistence of avoidance behavior?

● What is the difference between negative reinforcement and punishment?

● What are some side effects of punishment and some factors that influence its efficacy?

occurs when a designated response is reinforced only some of the time.

Which do you suppose leads to longer-lasting effects—being reinforced every time you emit a response, or being reinforced only some of the time? Studies show that, given an equal number of reinforcements, *intermittent* reinforcement makes a response more resistant to extinction than continuous reinforcement does (Falls, 1998; Schwartz & Robbins, 1995). In other words, organisms continue responding longer after removal of reinforcers when a response has been reinforced only *some* of the time. In fact, schedules of reinforcement that provide only sporadic delivery of reinforcers can yield great resistance to extinction. This finding explains why behaviors that are reinforced only occasionally—such as youngsters' temper tantrums—can be very durable and difficult to eliminate.

Reinforcement schedules come in many varieties, but four particular types of intermittent schedules have attracted the most interest. These schedules are described here along with examples drawn from the laboratory and everyday life (see Figure 6.18 for additional examples).

Ratio schedules require the organism to make the designated response a certain number of times to gain each reinforcer. **With a *fixed-ratio (FR) schedule*, the reinforcer is given after a fixed number of nonreinforced responses.** *Examples:* (1) A rat is reinforced for every tenth lever press. (2) A salesperson receives a bonus for every fourth set of encyclopedias sold. **With a *variable-ratio (VR) schedule*, the** reinforcer is given after a variable number of nonreinforced responses. The number of nonreinforced responses varies around a predetermined average. *Examples:* (1) A rat is reinforced for every tenth lever press on the average. The exact number of responses required for reinforcement varies from one time to the next. (2) A slot machine in a casino pays off once every six tries on the average. The number of nonwinning responses between payoffs varies greatly from one time to the next.

Interval schedules require a time period to pass between the presentation of reinforcers. **With a *fixed-interval (FI) schedule,* the reinforcer is given for the first response that occurs after a fixed time interval has elapsed.** *Examples:* (1) A rat is reinforced for the first lever press after a 2-minute interval has elapsed and then must wait 2 minutes before being able to earn the next reinforcement. (2) A man washing his clothes periodically checks to see whether each load is finished. The reward (clean clothes) is available only after a fixed time interval (corresponding to how long the washer takes to complete a cycle) has elapsed, and checking responses during the interval are not reinforced. **With a *variable-interval (VI) schedule,* the reinforcer is given for the first response after a variable time interval has elapsed.** The interval length varies around a predetermined average. *Examples:* (1) A rat is reinforced for the first lever press after a 1-minute interval has elapsed, but the following intervals are 3 minutes, 2 minutes, 4 minutes, and so on—with an average length of 2 minutes. (2) A person repeatedly dials a busy phone number (getting through is the reinforcer).

More than 50 years of research has yielded an enormous volume of data on how these schedules of reinforcement are related to patterns of responding (Williams, 1988; Zeiler, 1977). Some of the more prominent findings are summarized in Figure 6.19, which depicts typical response patterns generated by each schedule. For example, with fixed-interval schedules, a pause in responding usually occurs after each reinforcer is delivered, and then responding gradually increases to a rapid rate at the end of the interval. This pattern of behavior yields a "scalloped" response curve. In general, ratio schedules tend to produce more rapid responding than interval schedules. Why? Because faster responding leads to reinforcement sooner when a ratio schedule is in effect. Variable schedules tend to generate steadier response rates and greater resistance to extinction than their fixed counterparts.

Most of the research on reinforcement schedules was conducted on rats and pigeons in Skinner boxes. However, the available evidence suggests that humans

Figure 6.18

Reinforcement schedules in everyday life. Complex human behaviors are regulated by schedules of reinforcement. Piecework in factories is reinforced on a fixed-ratio schedule. Playing slot machines is based on variable-ratio reinforcement. Watching the clock at work is rewarded on a fixed-interval basis (the arrival of quitting time is the reinforcer). Surfers waiting for a big wave are rewarded on a variable-interval basis.

Fixed   Variable

Ratio

© Julian Cotton/International Stock

Interval

© David Woods/CORBIS/The Stock Market

© Rick Doyle/Uniphoto-PICTOR

Figure 6.19

Schedules of reinforcement and patterns of response. Each type of reinforcement schedule tends to generate a characteristic pattern of responding. In general, ratio schedules tend to produce more rapid responding than interval schedules (note the steep slopes of the FR and VR curves). In comparison to fixed schedules, variable schedules tend to yield steadier responding (note the smoother lines for the VR and VI schedules on the right) and greater resistance to extinction.

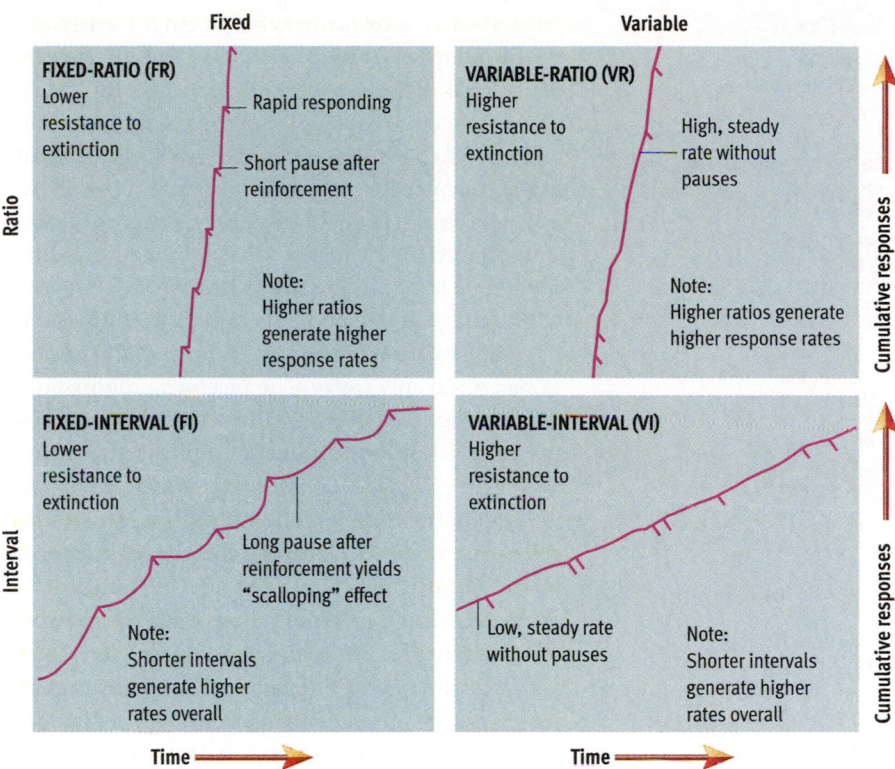

react to schedules of reinforcement in much the same way as animals (De Villiers, 1977; Perone, Galizio, & Baron, 1988). For example, when animals are placed on ratio schedules, shifting to a higher ratio (that is, requiring more responses per reinforcement) tends to generate faster responding. Managers of factories that pay on a piecework basis (a fixed-ratio schedule) have seen the same reaction in humans. Shifting to a higher ratio (more pieces for the same pay) usually stimulates harder work and greater productivity (although workers often complain).

There are many other parallels between animals' and humans' reactions to different schedules of reinforcement. For instance, with rats and pigeons, variable-ratio schedules yield steady responding and great resistance to extinction. Similar effects are routinely observed among people who gamble. Most gambling is reinforced according to variable-ratio schedules, which tend to produce rapid, steady responding and great resistance to extinction—exactly what casino operators want. The scalloped response curve seen when animals are placed on a fixed-interval schedule is also seen when humans work under this schedule. For example, consider what happens when the exams in a course occur every three weeks (a fixed-interval schedule). There's usually a pause in responding (studying) after each reinforcer (exam), and responding becomes very rapid (cramming) as each interval comes to an end.

Concurrent Schedules of Reinforcement and the Study of Choice

The schedules of reinforcement discussed thus far clearly are powerful determinants of responding, but they only begin to suggest the complexity of the reinforcement contingencies that regulate behavior. Humans and other organisms constantly have to make choices between two or more responses that are governed by independent schedules of reinforcement. For example, on a given night, you might have to choose between going to a movie or attending a party. Each response has the potential to yield a different type of reinforcement and each has its own

history of intermittent reinforcement. Similarly, animals foraging for their next meal must choose between different behaviors that have been reinforced according to different schedules.

To gain insight into how organisms make choices among operant responses, researchers have studied *concurrent schedules of reinforcement,* which

CONCEPT CHECK 6.2

Recognizing Schedules of Reinforcement

Check your understanding of schedules of reinforcement in operant conditioning by indicating the type of schedule that would be in effect in each of the examples below. In the spaces on the left, fill in CR for continuous reinforcement, FR for fixed-ratio, VR for variable-ratio, FI for fixed-interval, and VI for variable-interval. The answers can be found in Appendix A in the back of the book.

_____ **1.** Sarah is paid on a commission basis for selling computer systems. She gets a bonus for every third sale.

_____ **2.** Juan's parents let him earn some pocket money by doing yard work approximately once a week.

_____ **3.** Martha is fly-fishing. Think of each time that she casts her line as the response that may be rewarded.

_____ **4.** Jamal, who is in the fourth grade, gets a gold star from his teacher for every book he reads.

_____ **5.** Skip, a professional baseball player, signs an agreement that his salary increases will be renegotiated every third year.

consist of two or more reinforcement schedules that operate simultaneously and independently, each for a different response. In the simplest experiments, animals are placed in Skinner boxes that allow for two responses that are reinforced according to independent schedules. For example, a pigeon might be able to peck either of two disks, one of which is reinforced on a variable interval schedule and the other on a fixed ratio schedule (see Figure 6.20). How will the pigeon distribute its responses in this complicated situation? Even simple organisms turn out to be remarkably savvy. The pigeon's proportion of responding to each disk will correspond closely to the relative amount of overall reinforcement each disk can yield (Nevin, 1998; Shettleworth, 1998). This phenomenon is called the *matching law,* which states that under concurrent schedules of reinforcement, organisms' relative rate of responding to each alternative tends to match each alternative's relative rate of reinforcement. Moreover, if the *magnitude* or *quality* of reinforcement earned by each alternative is manipulated, organisms will adjust their responding to match up well with these factors as well (Gibbon & Fairhurst, 1994). Of course, animals don't match their responding to the realities of reinforcement perfectly, but they come surprisingly close (B. A. Williams, 1994).

Although there is healthy debate about the details, most explanations of matching assume that organisms are working to maximize their overall reinforcement (Nevin, 1998). This conclusion may seem far-fetched, but the maximizing found in the laboratory may simply reflect behavioral adaptations seen in the real world. Scientists studying the foraging behavior of many species in their natural environments have been impressed by how optimized their patterns of food seeking are (Krebs & McCleery, 1984;

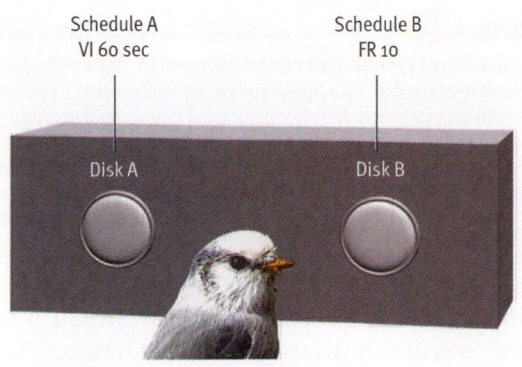

Schedule A
VI 60 sec

Schedule B
FR 10

Disk A

Disk B

Figure 6.20

An example of concurrent schedules of reinforcement. In this example of a study of pigeons responding to concurrent schedules of reinforcement, pecking disk A is reinforced according to a VI-60 seconds schedule, whereas responding to disk B is reinforced according to a FR-10 schedule. Experimental arrangements such as these allow operant psychologists to study complex choice behavior under controlled laboratory conditions.

SOURCE: Adapted from Domjan, M. (1998). *Principles of learning and behavior.* Belmont, CA: Wadsworth. Reprinted by permission.

Parker & Smith, 1990). According to *optimal foraging theory,* the food-seeking behaviors of many animals maximize the nutrition gained in relation to the energy expended to locate, secure, and consume various foods. For example, in choosing whether to pursue several small prey that are easy to catch or one large prey that will take more effort to subdue, or in choosing whether to continue foraging in a depleting patch of food or move on to another patch, animals tend to make sound choices that approximate optimal responding. Exactly *how* animals achieve these impressive results is not well understood. Obviously, they are not capable of making complex calculations about future costs, benefits, and probabilities. Rather, it appears that they follow some simple rules of thumb that yield surprisingly good results.

Research on the foraging strategies of animals has revealed that they tend to make surprisingly good choices. This discovery led to the formulation of optimal foraging theory.

These response tendencies appear to be learned the same way other operant responses are learned—through the principles of reinforcement (Shettleworth, 1998). However, theorists suspect that evolution also contributes to optimal foraging. Animals are probably preprogrammed by evolution to attend to, remember, and be guided by crucial features of the environment that allow them to readily learn effective foraging behaviors based on their reinforcement history.

Positive Reinforcement Versus Negative Reinforcement 5e, 5f

According to Skinner, reinforcement can take two forms, which he called *positive reinforcement* and *negative reinforcement*. **Positive reinforcement occurs when a response is strengthened because it is followed by the presentation of a rewarding stimulus.** Thus far, for purposes of simplicity, our examples of reinforcement have involved positive reinforcement. Good grades, tasty meals, paychecks, scholarships, promotions, nice clothes, nifty cars, attention, and flattery are all positive reinforcers.

In contrast, *negative reinforcement* occurs when a response is strengthened because it is followed by the removal of an aversive (unpleasant) stimulus. Don't let the word *negative* confuse you. Negative reinforcement *is* reinforcement. As with all reinforcement, it involves a favorable outcome that *strengthens* a response tendency. However, this strengthening takes place because a response leads to the *removal of an aversive stimulus* rather than the arrival of a pleasant stimulus (see Figure 6.21).

In laboratory studies, negative reinforcement is usually accomplished as follows. While a rat is in a Skinner box, a moderate electric shock is delivered to the animal through the floor of the box. When the rat presses the lever, the shock is turned off for a period of time. Thus, lever pressing leads to removal of an aversive stimulus (shock). Although this sequence of events is different from those for positive reinforcement, it reliably strengthens the rat's lever-pressing response.

Everyday human behavior is regulated extensively by negative reinforcement. Consider a handful of examples. You rush home in the winter to get out of the cold. You clean house to get rid of a disgusting mess. You give in to your child's begging to halt the whining. You take medication to get rid of pain or discomfort. You give in to a roommate or spouse to bring an unpleasant argument to an end.

Negative Reinforcement and Avoidance Behavior 5f

You have probably noticed that many people tend to avoid facing awkward situations, difficult challenges, and sticky personal problems. Consistent reliance on avoidance is not a very effective coping strategy. How do people learn to rely on such a strategy? In large part, it may be through negative reinforcement.

Escape Learning 5f

The roots of avoidance lie in escape learning. In *escape learning* an organism acquires a response that decreases or ends some aversive stimulation. Psychologists often study escape learning in the labora-

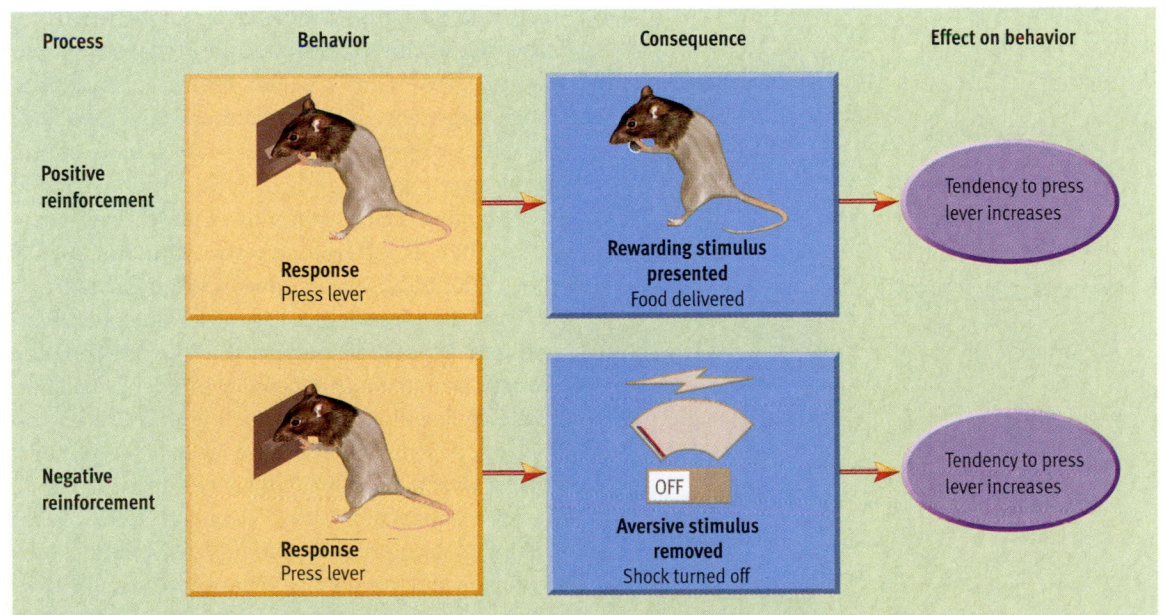

Process	Behavior	Consequence	Effect on behavior
Positive reinforcement	Response Press lever	Rewarding stimulus presented Food delivered	Tendency to press lever increases
Negative reinforcement	Response Press lever	Aversive stimulus removed Shock turned off	Tendency to press lever increases

Figure 6.21

Positive reinforcement versus negative reinforcement. In positive reinforcement, a response leads to the presentation of a rewarding stimulus. In negative reinforcement, a response leads to the removal of an aversive stimulus. Both types of reinforcement involve favorable consequences and both have the same effect on behavior: The organism's tendency to emit the reinforced response is strengthened.

tory with rats that are conditioned in a *shuttle box*. The shuttle box has two compartments connected by a doorway, which can be opened and closed by the experimenter, as depicted in Figure 6.22(a). In a typical study, an animal is placed in one compartment and an electric current in the floor of that chamber is turned on, with the doorway open. The animal learns to escape the shock by running to the other compartment. This escape response leads to the removal of an aversive stimulus (shock), so it is strengthened through negative reinforcement. If you were to leave a party where you were getting picked on by peers, you would be engaging in an escape response. Escape learning doesn't necessarily entail leaving the scene of the aversive stimulation. Any behavior that decreases or ends aversive stimulation (for example, turning on the air conditioner to get rid of stifling heat) represents escape learning.

Avoidance Learning 5f

Escape learning often leads to avoidance learning. In *avoidance learning* an organism acquires a re-

sponse that prevents some aversive stimulation from occurring. In laboratory studies of avoidance learning, the experimenter simply gives the animal a signal that shock is forthcoming. The typical signal is a light that goes on a few seconds prior to the shock. At first the rat runs only when shocked (escape learning). Gradually, however, the animal learns to run to the safe compartment as soon as the light comes on, demonstrating avoidance learning. Similarly, if you were to quit going to parties because of your concern about being picked on, this would represent avoidance learning. Turning on air conditioning *before* a room gets hot would also represent avoidance learning.

Avoidance learning presents an interesting puzzle for learning theorists. Avoidance responses tend to be long-lasting even though the mechanism of continuing reinforcement is obscure. For example, when an animal in a shuttle box learns to avoid shock entirely, it seems to have no opportunity for continued negative reinforcement. After all, the animal can't remove shock that never occurs. In theory, the avoidance response should gradually extinguish, because it is no longer followed by the removal of an aversive stimulus. However, avoidance responses usually remain strong. The best explanation of this paradox appears to be the two-process theory of avoidance, which integrates the processes of classical and operant conditioning (Miller, 1951; Mowrer, 1947; Rescorla & Solomon, 1967).

Two-Process Theory of Avoidance 5f

According to the two-process theory, the warning light that goes on in the shuttle box becomes a CS (through classical conditioning) eliciting conditioned fear in the animal. The behavior of fleeing to the other side of the box is an operant response that produces negative reinforcement, even after shock is no longer experienced, *because it reduces conditioned fear.* In short, two-process theory appears to solve our riddle by asserting that the avoidance response removes an *internal* aversive stimulus—conditioned fear—rather than an external aversive stimulus, such as shock. This idea is diagrammed in Figure 6.22(b).

There are some "holes" in the two-process theory and some alternative theories that provide better explanations for certain aspects of avoidance behavior (Bolles & Fanselow, 1980; Hineline, 1981). Nonetheless, the two-process theory remains "the standard against which all other explanations of avoidance behavior are always measured" (Domjan, 1998, p. 255). One of its strengths is that it provides a simple, compelling account for why avoidance behaviors—such as phobias—are so resistant to extinction (Levis, 1989).

Figure 6.22

Escape and avoidance learning. (a) Escape and avoidance learning are often studied with a shuttle box like that shown here. Warning signals, shock, and the animal's ability to flee from one compartment to another can be controlled by the experimenter. (b) According to Mowrer's two-process theory, avoidance begins because classical conditioning creates a conditioned fear that is elicited by the warning signal (panel 1). Avoidance continues because it is maintained by operant conditioning (panel 2). Specifically, the avoidance response is strengthened through negative reinforcement, since it leads to removal of the conditioned fear.

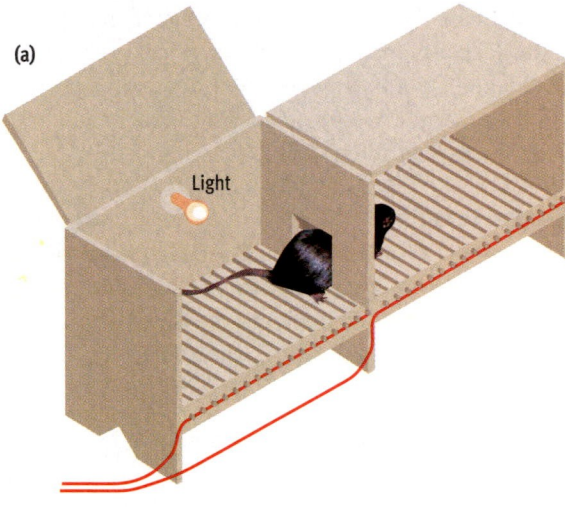

(a)

Light

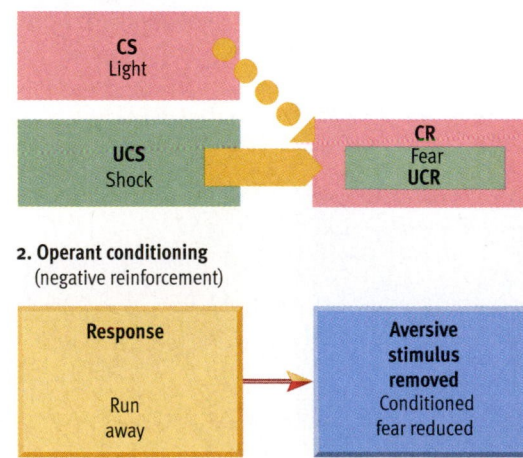

(b) 1. Classical conditioning

CS
Light

UCS
Shock

CR
Fear
UCR

2. Operant conditioning
(negative reinforcement)

Response

Run away

Aversive stimulus removed
Conditioned fear reduced

According to two-process theory, phobias are highly resistant to extinction for two reasons. First, a phobia usually leads to an avoidance response that earns negative reinforcement each time it is made. Second, avoidance behavior prevents opportunities to extinguish the phobic conditioned response because the person doesn't get much exposure to the conditioned (phobic) stimulus.

Punishment: Consequences That Weaken Responses

 5e

Reinforcement is defined in terms of its consequences. It *increases* an organism's tendency to make a certain response. Are there also consequences that *decrease* an organism's tendency to make a particular response? Yes. In Skinner's model of operant behavior, such consequences are called *punishment*.

Punishment occurs when an event following a response weakens the tendency to make that response. In a Skinner box, the administration of punishment is very simple. When a rat presses the lever or a pigeon pecks the disk, it receives a brief shock. This procedure usually leads to a rapid decline in the animal's response rate (Dinsmoor, 1998). Punishment typically involves presentation of an aversive stimulus (for instance, spanking a child). However, punishment may also involve the removal of a rewarding stimulus (for instance, taking away a child's TV-watching privileges).

The concept of punishment in operant conditioning is confusing to many students on two counts.

First, they often confuse it with negative reinforcement, which is entirely different. Negative reinforcement involves the *removal* of an aversive stimulus, thereby *strengthening* a response. Punishment, on the other hand, involves the *presentation* of an aversive stimulus, thereby *weakening* a response. Thus, punishment and negative reinforcement are opposite procedures that yield opposite effects on behavior (see Figure 6.23).

The second source of confusion involves the tendency to equate punishment with *disciplinary procedures* used by parents, teachers, and other authority figures. In the operant model, punishment occurs any time undesirable consequences weaken a response tendency. Defined in this way, the concept of punishment goes far beyond things like parents spanking children and teachers handing out detentions. For example, if you wear a new outfit and your schoolmates make fun of it, your behavior will have been punished and your tendency to emit this response (wear the same clothing) will probably decline. Similarly, if you go to a restaurant and have a horrible meal, your response will have been punished, and your tendency to go to that restaurant will probably decline.

Although punishment in operant conditioning encompasses far more than disciplinary acts, it *is* used frequently for disciplinary purposes. In light of this reality, it is worth looking at the implications of operant research for the use of punishment as a disciplinary measure. One key problem with punishment is that even when it is effective in weakening a

Web Link 6.5

Journal of the Experimental Analysis of Behavior & Journal of Applied Behavioral Analysis
Two important journals devoted to behavioral analysis share a site at the University of Rochester's Environmental Health Sciences Center. Among the site's many resources are a searchable abstract database for both journals and an archive of audio and video clips demonstrating selected learning principles.

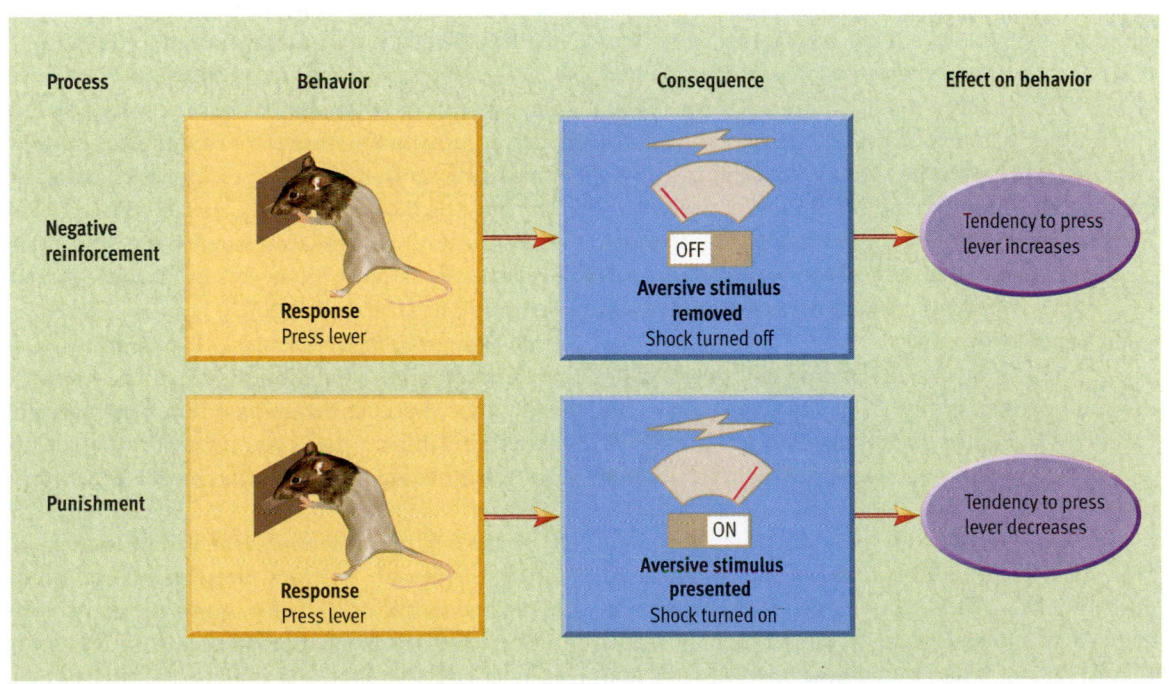

Figure 6.23

Comparison of negative reinforcement and punishment. Although punishment can occur when a response leads to the removal of a rewarding stimulus, it more typically involves the presentation of an aversive stimulus. Students often confuse punishment with negative reinforcement because they associate both with aversive stimuli. However, as this diagram shows, punishment and negative reinforcement represent opposite procedures that have opposite effects on behavior.

Although physical punishment is frequently administered to suppress aggressive behavior, in the long run it actually is associated with an increase in aggressive behavior.

response, it can have unintended side effects (Newsom, Favell, & Rincover, 1983; Van Houten, 1983). For example, punishment can trigger *strong emotional responses,* including anxiety, anger, and resentment, and it can generate hostility toward the source of the punishment, such as a parent. Another very serious problem is that *physical* punishment often leads to an increase in *aggressive behavior.* Children who are subjected to a lot of physical punishment tend to become more aggressive than average, an effect that typically continues through adolescence and adulthood (Parke & Slaby, 1983; Straus & Kantor, 1994). You'll see why shortly, when we discuss observational learning. The potential side effects of punishment make it less than ideal as a disciplinary procedure. Research on operant conditioning suggests that disciplinary goals can often be accomplished more effectively by *reinforcing desirable behavior* than by *punishing undesirable behavior.*

Although punishment is probably overused in disciplinary efforts, it does have a role to play. The following guidelines summarize evidence on how to make punishment effective while reducing its side effects.

1. *Apply punishment swiftly.* A delay in delivering punishment—like a delay in delivering reinforcement—tends to undermine its impact (Abramowitz & O'Leary, 1990). When a mother says, "Wait until your father gets home . . ." she is making a fundamental mistake in the use of punishment. This problem with delayed punishment also explains the ineffectiveness of punishing a pet hours after it has misbehaved, when the owner finally returns home. For instance, it won't do any good to hit your dog with a newspaper while shoving its face in the feces it previously left on your carpet. This common punishment doesn't teach your dog to stop defecating on your carpet—it teaches the dog to keep its face out of its feces.

2. *Use punishment just severe enough to be effective.* The intensity of punishment is a two-edged sword. Severe punishments usually are more effective in weakening unwanted responses. However, they also increase the likelihood of undesirable side effects. Thus, it's best to use the least severe punishment that seems likely to have the necessary impact (Powell, Symbaluk, & MacDonald, 2002).

3. *Make punishment consistent.* If you want to eliminate a response, you should punish the response every time it occurs. When parents are inconsistent about punishing a particular behavior, they create more confusion than learning (Acker & O'Leary, 1996).

4. *Explain the punishment.* When children are punished, the reason for their punishment should be explained as fully as possible, given the constraints of their age. Punishment combined with reasoning is more effective than either alone (Larzelere et al.,

1996). The more that children understand why they were punished, the more effective the punishment tends to be.

5. *Minimize dependence on physical punishment.* Modest physical punishment may be necessary when children are too young to understand a verbal reprimand or the withdrawal of privileges. Otherwise, physical punishment should be avoided, because it tends to increase aggressive behavior in children (Stormshak et al., 2000). Also, physical punishment often isn't as effective as most parents assume. Even a vigorous spanking isn't felt by a child an hour later. In contrast, withdrawing valued privileges can give children hours to contemplate the wisdom of changing their ways.

REVIEW OF KEY POINTS

● Schedules of reinforcement influence patterns of operant responding. Continuous reinforcement occurs when every designated response is reinforced. Intermittent schedules of reinforcement include fixed-ratio, variable-ratio, fixed-interval, and variable-interval schedules.

● Intermittent schedules produce greater resistance to extinction than similar continuous schedules. Ratio schedules tend to yield higher rates of response than interval schedules. Shorter intervals and higher ratios are associated with faster responding.

● Concurrent schedules of reinforcement permit researchers to study how organisms make choices among operant responses. The matching law suggests that organisms strive to maximize their reinforcement. Optimal foraging theory asserts that animals' food-seeking behaviors optimize the nutrition gained in relation to the effort expended.

● Responses can be strengthened either through the presentation of positive reinforcers or through the removal of negative reinforcers. Negative reinforcement regulates escape and avoidance learning. The two-process theory provides the best explanation of avoidance behavior and may shed light on why phobias are so difficult to eliminate.

● Punishment involves unfavorable consequences that lead to a decline in response strength. Problems associated with the application of punishment as a disciplinary procedure include emotional side effects and increased aggressive behavior. To be effective, punishment of children should be swift, consistent, explained, non-physical, and just severe enough to have an impact.

CONCEPT CHECK 6.3

Recognizing Outcomes in Operant Conditioning

Check your understanding of the various types of consequences that can occur in operant conditioning by indicating whether the examples below involve positive reinforcement (PR), negative reinforcement (NR), punishment (P), or extinction (E). The answers can be found in Appendix A.

_____ **1.** Antonio gets a speeding ticket.

_____ **2.** Diane's supervisor compliments her on her hard work.

_____ **3.** Leon goes to the health club for a rare workout and pushes himself so hard that his entire body aches and he throws up.

_____ **4.** Audrey lets her dog out so she won't have to listen to its whimpering.

_____ **5.** Richard shoots up heroin to ward off tremors and chills associated with heroin withdrawal.

_____ **6.** Sharma constantly complains about minor aches and pains to obtain sympathy from colleagues at work. Three co-workers who share an office with her decide to ignore her complaints instead of responding with sympathy.

Changing Directions in the Study of Conditioning

As you learned in Chapter 1, science is constantly evolving and changing in response to new research and new thinking. Such change has certainly occurred in the study of conditioning. In this section, we will examine two major changes in thinking about conditioning. First, we'll consider the recent recognition that an organism's biological heritage can limit or channel conditioning. Second, we'll discuss the increased appreciation of the role of cognitive processes in conditioning.

Recognizing Biological Constraints on Conditioning

Learning theorists have traditionally assumed that the fundamental laws of conditioning have great generality—that they apply to a wide range of species. Although no one ever suggested that hamsters could learn physics, until the 1960s most psychologists assumed that associations could be conditioned between any stimulus an organism could register and any response it could make. However, findings in recent decades have demonstrated that there are limits to the generality of conditioning principles—limits imposed by an organism's biological heritage.

Instinctive Drift: The Case of the Miserly Raccoons

One biological constraint on learning is instinctive drift. *Instinctive drift* occurs when an animal's innate response tendencies interfere with conditioning processes. Instinctive drift was first described by

PREVIEW QUESTIONS
● What is instinctive drift?
● Why are conditioned taste aversions so easy to acquire?
● Why are some phobias much more common than others?
● To what degree are the laws of learning universal across species?
● How does the predictive value of a CS affect conditioning?
● Are responses that are followed by favorable consequences always strengthened?

❝Taste aversions do not fit comfortably within the present framework of classical or instrumental conditioning: These aversions selectively seek flavors to the exclusion of other stimuli. Inter-stimulus intervals are a thousandfold too long.❞
JOHN GARCIA

the Brelands, the operant psychologists who went into the business of training animals for commercial purposes (Breland & Breland, 1966). They have described many amusing examples of their "failures" to control behavior through conditioning. For instance, they once were training some raccoons to deposit coins in a piggy bank. They were successful in shaping the raccoons to pick up a coin and put it into a small box, using food as the reinforcer. However, when they gave the raccoons a couple of coins, an unexpected problem arose: The raccoons wouldn't give the coins up! In spite of the reinforcers available for depositing the coins, they would sit and rub the coins together like so many little misers.

What had happened to disrupt the conditioning program? Apparently, associating the coins with food had brought out the raccoons' innate food-washing behavior. Raccoons often rub things together to clean them. The Brelands report that they have run into this sort of instinct-related interference on many occasions with a wide variety of species.

Conditioned Taste Aversion: The "Sauce Béarnaise Syndrome"

A number of years ago, a prominent psychologist, Martin Seligman, dined out with his wife and enjoyed a steak with sauce béarnaise. About 6 hours afterward, he developed a wicked case of stomach flu and endured severe nausea. Subsequently, when he ordered sauce béarnaise, he was chagrined to discover that its aroma alone nearly made him throw up.

Seligman's experience was not unique. Many people develop aversions to food that has been followed by nausea from illness, alcohol intoxication, or food poisoning. However, Seligman was puzzled by what he called his "sauce béarnaise syndrome" (Seligman & Hager, 1972). On the one hand, it appeared to be the straightforward result of classical conditioning. A neutral stimulus (the sauce) had been paired with an unconditioned stimulus (the flu), which caused an unconditioned response (the nausea). Hence, the sauce béarnaise became a conditioned stimulus eliciting nausea (see Figure 6.24).

On the other hand, Seligman recognized that his aversion to béarnaise sauce seemed to violate certain

basic principles of conditioning. First, the lengthy delay of 6 hours between the CS (the sauce) and the UCS (the flu) should have prevented conditioning from occurring. In laboratory studies, a delay of more than *30 seconds* between the CS and UCS makes it difficult to establish a conditioned response, yet this conditioning occurred in just one pairing. Second, why was it that *only* the béarnaise sauce became a CS eliciting nausea? Why not other stimuli that were present in the restaurant? Shouldn't plates, knives, tablecloths, or his wife, for example, also trigger Seligman's nausea?

The riddle of Seligman's sauce béarnaise syndrome was solved by John Garcia (1989) and his colleagues. They conducted a series of studies on *conditioned taste aversion* (Garcia, Clarke, & Hankins, 1973; Garcia & Koelling, 1966; Garcia & Rusiniak, 1980). In these studies, they manipulated the kinds of stimuli preceding the onset of nausea and other noxious experiences in rats, using radiation to artificially induce the nausea (see Figure 6.25). They found that when taste cues were followed by nausea, rats quickly acquired conditioned taste aversions. However, when taste cues were followed by other types of noxious stimuli (such as shock), rats did *not* develop conditioned taste aversions. Furthermore, visual and auditory stimuli followed by nausea also failed to produce conditioned aversions. In short, Garcia and his co-workers found that it was almost impossible to create certain associations, whereas taste-nausea associ-

Figure 6.25

Garcia and Koelling's research on conditioned taste aversion. In a landmark series of studies, Garcia and Koelling (1966) demonstrated that some stimulus-response associations are much easier to condition than others. Their apparatus is depicted here. Rats drink saccharin-flavored water out of the tube on the right. When they make contact with the tube, they may trigger a bright light and buzzer, or a brief electric shock, or radiation exposure that will make them nauseated. This setup allowed Garcia and Koelling to pair various types of stimuli, as discussed in your text.

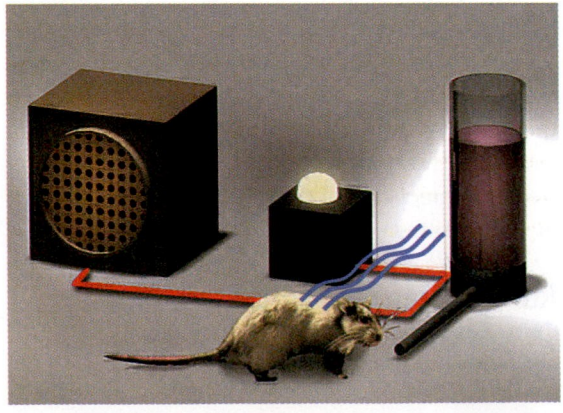

Figure 6.24

Conditioned taste aversion. Taste aversions can be established through classical conditioning, as in the "sauce béarnaise syndrome." However, as the text explains, taste aversions can be acquired in ways that seem to violate basic principles of classical conditioning.

CS Sauce béarnaise → **CR** Nausea **UCR**

UCS Flu

People tend to develop phobias to snakes very easily but to electrical outlets rarely, even though the latter are just as dangerous. Preparedness theory can explain this paradox.

ations (and odor-nausea associations) were almost impossible to prevent.

What is the theoretical significance of this unique readiness to make connections between taste and nausea? Garcia argues that it is a by-product of the evolutionary history of mammals. Animals that consume poisonous foods and survive must learn not to repeat their mistakes. Natural selection will favor organisms that quickly learn what *not* to eat. Thus, evolution may have biologically programmed some organisms to learn certain types of associations more easily than others.

Preparedness and Phobias

According to Martin Seligman, evolution has also programmed organisms to acquire certain fears more readily than others, because of a phenomenon he calls *preparedness*. **Preparedness involves a species-specific predisposition to be conditioned in certain ways and not others.** Seligman (1971) believes that preparedness can explain why certain phobias are vastly more common than others. People tend to develop phobias to snakes, spiders, heights, and darkness relatively easily. However, even after painful experiences with hammers, knives, hot stoves, and electrical outlets, phobic fears of these objects are infrequent. What characteristics do common phobic objects share? Most were once genuine threats to our ancestors. Consequently, a fear response to such objects has survival value for our species. According to Seligman, evolutionary forces gradually programmed humans to acquire conditioned fears of these objects

easily and rapidly. Laboratory simulations of phobic conditioning have provided some support for the concept of preparedness (LoLordo & Droungas, 1989; Mineka & Hamida, 1998).

Evolutionary Perspectives on Learning

Clearly, several lines of research suggest that there are species-specific biological constraints on conditioning. So, what is the current thinking on the idea that the laws of learning are *universal* across various species? The predominant view among learning theorists seems to be that the basic mechanisms of learning are *similar* across species but that these mechanisms have sometimes been modified in the course of evolution as species have adapted to the specialized demands of their environments (Shettleworth, 1998). According to this view, learning is a very general process because the neural substrates of learning and the basic problems confronted by various organisms are much the same across species. For example, developing the ability to recognize stimuli that signal important events is probably adaptive for virtually any organism. However, given that different organisms confront different adaptive problems to survive and reproduce, it makes sense that learning has evolved along somewhat different paths in different species (Hollis, 1997; Sherry, 1992).

Some evolutionary psychologists take this line of reasoning one step further. The consensus view just described assumes that an organism's biological heritage—which has been shaped by natural selection—places certain constraints on the learning process.

The more radical view espoused by some theorists is that there is no such thing as *the* learning process. Rather, there are many learning processes, sculpted by evolution, as specialized mechanisms designed to solve particular types of adaptive problems for particular species. For example, C. R. Gallistel (2000) asserts, "Most theorizing assumes that there is a general-purpose learning process in the brain. . . . this assumption is equivalent to assuming that there is a general-purpose sensory organ" (p. 1179). According to this more radical view, the adaptive problems faced by different types of organisms are extraordinarily diverse and often have little in common. For example, the problems faced by a migratory bird that needs to navigate its way over thousands of miles, a star-nosed mole that needs to detect worms underground, and a male squirrel monkey that needs to remember the locations of females about to enter into estrus are entirely different. Hence, the solutions to these problems depend on highly specialized learning mechanisms that were crafted by evolution to meet the unique needs of various species. Thus, some evolutionary psychologists completely reject the idea that there are universal laws of learning.

CONCEPT CHECK 6.4

Distinguishing Between Classical Conditioning and Operant Conditioning

Check your understanding of the usual differences between classical conditioning and operant conditioning by indicating the type of conditioning process involved in each of the following examples. In the space on the left, place a C if the example involves classical conditioning, an O if it involves operant conditioning, or a B if it involves both. The answers can be found in Appendix A.

_____ **1.** Whenever Midori takes her dog out for a walk, she wears the same old blue windbreaker. Eventually, she notices that her dog becomes excited whenever she puts on this windbreaker.

_____ **2.** The Creatures are a successful rock band with three hit albums to their credit. They begin their U.S. tour featuring many new, unreleased songs, all of which draw silence from their concert fans. The same fans cheer wildly when the Creatures play any of their old hits. Gradually, the band reduces the number of new songs it plays and starts playing more of the old standbys.

_____ **3.** When Cindy and Mel first fell in love, they listened constantly to the Creatures' hit song "Transatlantic Obsession." Although several years have passed, whenever they hear this song they experience a warm, romantic feeling.

_____ **4.** For nearly 20 years Ralph has worked as a machinist in the same factory. His new foreman is never satisfied with his work and criticizes him constantly. After a few weeks of heavy criticism, he experiences anxiety whenever he arrives at work. He starts calling in sick more and more frequently to evade this anxiety.

Recognizing Cognitive Processes in Conditioning

Pavlov, Skinner, and their followers traditionally viewed conditioning as a mechanical process in which stimulus-response associations are stamped in by experience. Learning theorists asserted that if creatures such as flatworms can be conditioned, conditioning can't depend on higher mental processes. Although this viewpoint did not go entirely unchallenged (for example, Tolman, 1922, 1932), mainstream theories of conditioning did not allocate a major role to cognitive processes. In recent decades, however, research findings have led theorists to shift toward more cognitive explanations of conditioning. Let's review some of these findings and the theories that have resulted.

Signal Relations

The cognitive element in conditioning is especially prominent in research conducted by Robert Rescorla (1978, 1980; Rescorla & Wagner, 1972). Rescorla asserts that environmental stimuli serve as signals and that some stimuli are better, or more dependable, signals than others. Hence, he has manipulated *signal relations* in classical conditioning—that is, CS-UCS relations that influence whether a CS is a good signal. A "good" signal is one that allows accurate prediction of the UCS.

In essence, Rescorla manipulates the *predictive value* of a conditioned stimulus. How does he do so? He varies the proportion of trials in which the CS and UCS are paired. Consider the following example. A tone and shock are paired 20 times for one group of rats. Otherwise, these rats are never shocked. For these rats the CS (tone) and UCS (shock) are paired in 100% of the experimental trials. Another group of rats also receive 20 pairings of the tone and shock. However, the rats in this group are also exposed to the shock on 20 other trials when the tone does *not* precede it. For this group, the CS and UCS are paired in only 50% of the trials. Thus, the two groups of rats have had an equal number of CS-UCS pairings, but the CS is a better signal or predictor of shock for the 100% CS-UCS group than for the 50% CS-UCS group.

What did Rescorla find when he tested the two groups of rats for conditioned fear? He found that the CS elicits a much stronger response in the 100% CS-UCS group than in the 50% CS-UCS group. Given that the two groups have received an equal number of CS-UCS pairings, this difference must be due to the greater predictive power of the CS for the 100% group. Numerous studies of signal relations have shown that the predictive value of a CS is an influential factor governing classical conditioning (Rescorla, 1978).

Response-Outcome Relations and Reinforcement

Studies of response-outcome relations and reinforcement also highlight the role of cognitive processes in conditioning. Imagine that on the night before an important exam you study hard while repeatedly playing a Smash Mouth song. The next morning you earn an A on your exam. Does this result strengthen your tendency to play Smash Mouth's music before exams? Probably not. Chances are, you will recognize the logical relation between the response of studying hard and the reinforcement of a good grade, and only the response of studying will be strengthened (Killeen, 1981).

Thus, reinforcement is *not* automatic when favorable consequences follow a response. People actively reason out the relations between responses and the outcomes that follow. When a response is followed by a desirable outcome, the response is more likely to be strengthened if the person thinks that the response *caused* the outcome. You might guess that only humans would engage in this causal reasoning. However, evidence suggests that under the right circumstances even pigeons can learn to recognize causal relations between responses and outcomes (Killeen, 1981).

In sum, modern, reformulated models of conditioning view it as a matter of detecting the *contingencies* among environmental events (Matute & Miller, 1998). According to these theories, organisms actively try to figure out what leads to what (the contingencies) in the world around them. Stimuli are viewed as signals that help organisms minimize their aversive experiences and maximize their pleasant experiences. The new, cognitively oriented theories of conditioning are quite a departure from older theories that depicted conditioning as a mindless, mechanical process. We can also see this new emphasis on cognitive processes in our next subject, observational learning.

REVIEW OF KEY POINTS

- Recent decades have brought profound changes in our understanding of conditioning. Instinctive drift occurs when an animal's innate response tendencies interfere with conditioning. Conditioned taste aversions can be readily acquired even when there is a lengthy delay between the CS and UCS. Seligman's concept of preparedness may explain why certain phobias are far more common than others.
- The findings on instinctive drift, conditioned taste aversion, and preparedness have led to the recognition that there are species-specific biological constraints on conditioning. Some evolutionary psychologists argue that learning processes vary immensely across species because different species have to grapple with very different adaptive problems.
- Rescorla's work on signal relations showed that the predictive value of a CS is an influential factor governing classical conditioning. When a response is followed by a desirable outcome, the response is more likely to be strengthened if it appears that the response caused the outcome. Studies of signal relations in classical conditioning and response-outcome relations in operant conditioning suggest that cognitive processes play a larger role in conditioning than originally believed.

University of Pennsylvania

"Pavlovian conditioning is a sophisticated and sensible mechanism by which organisms represent the world. . . . I encourage students to think of animals as behaving like little statisticians. . . . They really are very finely attuned to small changes in the likelihood of events."
ROBERT RESCORLA

Observational Learning

Can classical and operant conditioning account for all learning? Absolutely not. Consider how people learn a fairly basic skill such as driving a car. They do not hop naively into an automobile and start emitting random responses until one leads to favorable consequences. On the contrary, most people learning to drive know exactly where to place the key and how to get started. How are these responses acquired? Through *observation*. Most new drivers have years of experience observing others drive, and they put those observations to work. Learning through observation accounts for a great deal of learning in both animals and humans.

Observational learning occurs when an organism's responding is influenced by the observation of others, who are called models. This process has been investigated extensively by Albert Bandura (1977, 1986). Bandura does not see observational learning as entirely separate from classical and operant conditioning. Instead, he asserts that it greatly extends the reach of these conditioning processes. Whereas previous conditioning theorists emphasized the organism's direct experience, Bandura has demonstrated that both classical and operant conditioning can take place vicariously through observational learning.

Essentially, observational learning involves being conditioned indirectly by virtue of observing another's conditioning (see Figure 6.26 on the next page). To illustrate, suppose you observe a friend be-

PREVIEW QUESTIONS
- How can conditioning occur indirectly?
- What are the key processes in observational learning?
- What does Bandura have to say about acquisition versus performance?
- What are some practical implications of observational learning?

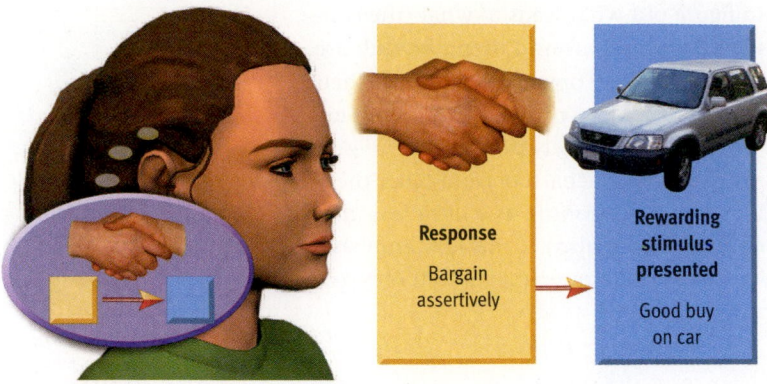

Figure 6.26

Observational learning.
In observational learning, an observer attends to and stores a mental representation of a model's behavior (example: assertive bargaining) and its consequences (example: a good buy on a car). If the observer sees the modeled response lead to a favorable outcome, the observer's tendency to emit the modeled response will be strengthened.

"Most human behavior is learned by observation through modeling."
ALBERT BANDURA

having assertively with a car salesperson. You see your friend's assertive behavior reinforced by the exceptionally good buy she gets on the car. Your own tendency to behave assertively with salespeople might well be strengthened as a result. Notice that the reinforcement is experienced by your friend, not you. The good buy should strengthen your friend's tendency to bargain assertively, but your tendency to do so may also be strengthened indirectly.

Basic Processes

Bandura has identified four key processes that are crucial in observational learning. The first two—attention and retention—highlight the importance of cognition in this type of learning.

- *Attention*. To learn through observation, you must pay attention to another person's behavior and its consequences.
- *Retention*. You may not have occasion to use an observed response for weeks, months, or even years. Hence, you must store a mental representation of what you have witnessed in your memory.
- *Reproduction*. Enacting a modeled response depends on your ability to reproduce the response by converting your stored mental images into overt behavior. This may not be easy for some responses. For example, most people cannot execute a breathtaking windmill dunk after watching Kobe Bryant do it in a basketball game.
- *Motivation*. Finally, you are unlikely to reproduce an observed response unless you are motivated to do so. Your motivation depends on whether you encounter a situation in which you believe that the response is likely to pay off for you.

Observational learning has proven especially valuable in explaining complex human behaviors, but animals can also learn through observation. A simple

example is the thieving behavior of the English titmouse, a small bird renowned for its early-morning raids on its human neighbors. The titmouse has learned how to open cardboard caps on bottles of milk delivered to the porches of many homes in England. Having opened the bottle, the titmouse skims the cream from the top of the milk. This clever learned behavior has been passed down from one generation of titmouse to the next through observational learning.

Acquisition Versus Performance

Bandura points out that people have many learned responses that they may or may not perform, depending on the situation. Thus, he distinguishes between the *acquisition* of a learned response and the *performance* of that response. He maintains that reinforcement affects which responses are actually performed more than which responses are acquired. People emit those responses that they think are likely to be reinforced. For instance, you may study hard for a course in which the professor gives fair exams, because you expect studying to lead to reinforcement in the form of a good grade. In contrast, you may hardly open the text for a course in which the professor gives arbitrary, unpredictable exams, because you do not expect studying to be reinforced. Your performance is different in the two situations because you think the reinforcement contingencies are different. Thus, like Skinner, Bandura asserts that reinforcement is a critical determinant of behavior. However, Bandura maintains that reinforcement influences performance rather than learning per se.

Applications

It is the power of observational learning that makes television such an influential determinant of behavior. Young children are especially impressionable, and extensive evidence indicates that they pick up many responses—including aggressive behaviors—from viewing models on TV (Huston & Wright, 1982; Liebert & Sprafkin, 1988). Bandura's theory of observational learning also explains why physical punishment tends to increase aggressive behavior in children, even when it is intended to do just the opposite. Parents who depend on physical punishment often punish a child for hitting other children—by hitting the child. The parents may sincerely intend to reduce the child's aggressive behavior, but they are unwittingly serving as *models* of such behavior. Although they may tell the child that "hitting people won't accomplish anything," they are in the midst of hitting the child in order to accomplish something. Because parents usually accomplish their immediate goal of stopping the child's hitting, the child witnesses the reinforcement of aggressive behavior. In this situation, actions speak louder than words—because of observational learning.

Clearly, observational learning plays an important role in regulating behavior. It represents a third major type of learning that builds on the first two types—classical conditioning and operant conditioning. These three basic types of learning are summarized and compared in a pictorial table on pages 250–251.

Observational learning occurs in both humans and animals. For example, the English titmouse has learned how to break into containers to swipe cream from its human neighbors and this behavior has been passed across generations through observational learning. In a similar vein, children acquire a diverse array of responses from role models.

Putting It in Perspective

Two of our seven unifying themes stand out in this chapter. First, you can see how nature and nurture interactively govern behavior. Second, looking at psychology in its sociohistorical context, you can see how progress in psychology spills over to affect trends and values in society at large. Let's examine each of these points in more detail.

In regard to nature versus nurture, research on learning clearly demonstrates the enormous power of the environment in shaping behavior. Pavlov's model of classical conditioning shows how experiences can account for everyday fears and other emotional responses. Skinner's model of operant conditioning shows how reinforcement and punishment can mold everything from a child's bedtime whimpering to an adult's restaurant preferences. Indeed, many learning theorists once believed that *all* aspects of behavior could be explained in terms of environmental determinants. In recent decades, however, evidence on instinctive drift, conditioned taste aversion, and preparedness has shown that there are biological constraints on conditioning. Thus, even in explanations of learning—an area once dominated by nurture theories—we see once again that heredity and environment jointly influence behavior.

The history of research on conditioning also shows how progress in psychology can seep into every corner of society. For example, the behaviorists' ideas about reinforcement and punishment have influenced patterns of discipline in our society. Research on operant conditioning has also affected management styles in the business world, leading to an increased emphasis on positive reinforcement. In the educational arena, the concept of individualized, programmed learning is a spinoff from behavioral research. The fact that the principles of conditioning are routinely applied in homes, businesses, schools, and factories clearly shows that psychology is not an ivory tower endeavor.

In the upcoming Personal Application, you will see how you can apply the principles of conditioning to improve your self-control, as we discuss the technology of behavior modification.

PREVIEW QUESTIONS

● How did this chapter demonstrate that nature and nurture jointly influence behavior?

● How did this chapter show that psychology evolves in a sociohistorical context?

REVIEW OF KEY POINTS

● In observational learning, an organism is conditioned vicariously by watching a model's conditioning. Both classical and operant conditioning can occur through observational learning, which depends on the processes of attention, retention, reproduction, and motivation.

● According to Bandura, reinforcement influences which of several already acquired responses one will perform more than it influences the acquisition of new responses. Observational learning can account for the influence of mass media (such as television) on behavior. The principles of observational learning have also been used to explain why physical punishment increases aggressive behavior.

● Two of our key themes were especially apparent in our coverage of learning and conditioning. One theme involves the interaction of heredity and environment in learning. The other involves the way progress in psychology affects society at large.

Type of learning	Procedure	Diagram	Result
Classical conditioning Ivan Pavlov 	A neutral stimulus (for example, a tone) is paired with an unconditioned stimulus (such as food) that elicits an unconditioned response (salivation).		The neutral stimulus becomes a conditioned stimulus that elicits the conditioned response (for example, a tone triggers salivation).
Operant conditioning B. F. Skinner 	In a stimulus situation, a response is followed by favorable consequences (reinforcement) or unfavorable consequences (punishment).	**Response** Press lever → **Rewarding or aversive stimulus presented or removed** Food delivery or shock	If reinforced, the response is strengthened (emitted more frequently); if punished, the response is weakened (emitted less frequently).
Observational learning Albert Bandura 	An observer attends to a model's behavior (for example, aggressive bargaining) and its consequences (for example, a good buy on a car).	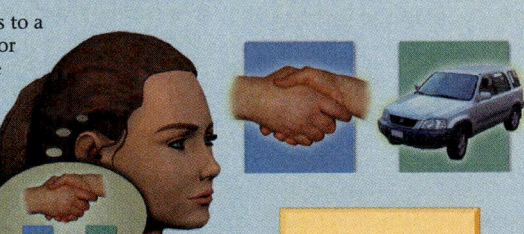 **Response** Bargain assertively → **Rewarding stimulus presented** Good buy on car	The observer stores a mental representation of the modeled response; the observer's tendency to emit the response may be strengthened or weakened, depending on the consequences observed.

Typical kinds of responses	Examples in animals	Examples in humans

Mostly (but not always) involuntary reflexes and visceral responses

Dogs learn to salivate to the sound of a tone that has been paired with meat powder.

CORBIS-Bettmann

Little Albert learns to fear a white rat and other white, furry objects through classical conditioning

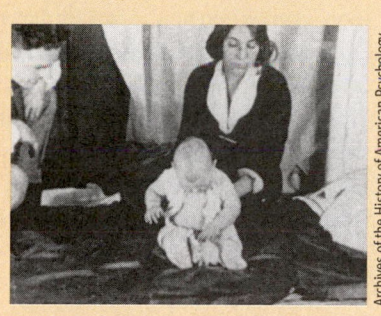

Archives of the History of American Psychology, University of Akron, Akron, Ohio

Mostly (but not always) voluntary, spontaneous responses

Trained animals perform remarkable feats because they have been reinforced for gradually learning closer and closer approximations of responses they do not normally emit.

© Gerald Davis by permission of Karen Davis

Casino patrons tend to exhibit high, steady rates of gambling, as most games of chance involve complex variable-ratio schedules of reinforcement.

© David Falconer/Folio, Inc.

A young boy performs a response that he has acquired through observational learning.

© Laura Dwight/CORBIS

Mostly voluntary responses, often consisting of novel and complex sequences

An English titmouse learns to break into milk bottles by observing the thievery of other titmice.

© J. Markham/Bruce Coleman, Inc.

PERSONAL APPLICATION

Achieving Self-Control Through Behavior Modification

Answer the following "yes" or "no."

____ **1** Do you have a hard time passing up food, even when you're not hungry?
____ **2** Do you wish you studied more often?
____ **3** Would you like to cut down on your smoking or drinking?
____ **4** Do you experience difficulty in getting yourself to exercise regularly?
____ **5** Do you wish you had more willpower?

If you answered "yes" to any of these questions, you have struggled with the challenge of self-control. This Personal Application discusses how you can use the techniques of behavior modification to improve your self-control. If you stop to think about it, self-control—or rather a lack of it—underlies many of the personal problems that people struggle with in everyday life.

Behavior modification is a systematic approach to changing behavior through the application of the principles of conditioning. Advocates of behavior modification assume that behavior is a product of learning, conditioning, and environmental control. They further assume that *what is learned can be unlearned.* Thus, they set out to "recondition" people to produce more desirable patterns of behavior.

The technology of behavior modification has been applied with great success in schools, businesses, hospitals, factories, child-care facilities, prisons, and mental health centers (Kazdin, 1982; O'Donohue, 1998; Rachman, 1992). Moreover, behavior modification techniques have proven particularly valuable in efforts to improve self-control. Our discussion will borrow liberally from an excellent book on self-modification by David Watson and Roland Tharp (2002). We will discuss five steps in the process of self-modification, which are outlined in Figure 6.27.

Specifying Your Target Behavior

The first step in a self-modification program is to specify the target behavior(s) that you want to change. Behavior modification can only be applied to a clearly defined, overt response, yet many people have difficulty pinpointing the behavior they hope to alter. They tend to describe their problems in terms of unobservable personality *traits* rather than overt *behaviors*. For example, asked what behavior he would like to change, a man might say, "I'm too irritable." That may be true, but it is of little help in designing a self-modification program. To use a behavioral approach, vague statements about traits need to be translated into precise descriptions of specific target behaviors.

To identify target responses, you need to ponder past behavior or closely observe future behavior and list specific *examples* of responses that lead to the trait description. For instance, the man who regards himself as "too irritable" might identify two overly frequent responses, such as arguing with his wife and snapping at his children. These are specific behaviors for which he could design a self-modification program.

Gathering Baseline Data

The second step in behavior modification is to gather baseline data. You need to systematically observe your target behavior for a period of time (usually a week or two) before you work out the details of your program. In gathering your baseline data, you need to monitor three things.

First, you need to determine the initial response level of your target behavior. After all, you can't tell whether your program is working effectively unless you have a baseline for comparison. In most cases, you would simply keep track of how often the target response occurs in a certain time

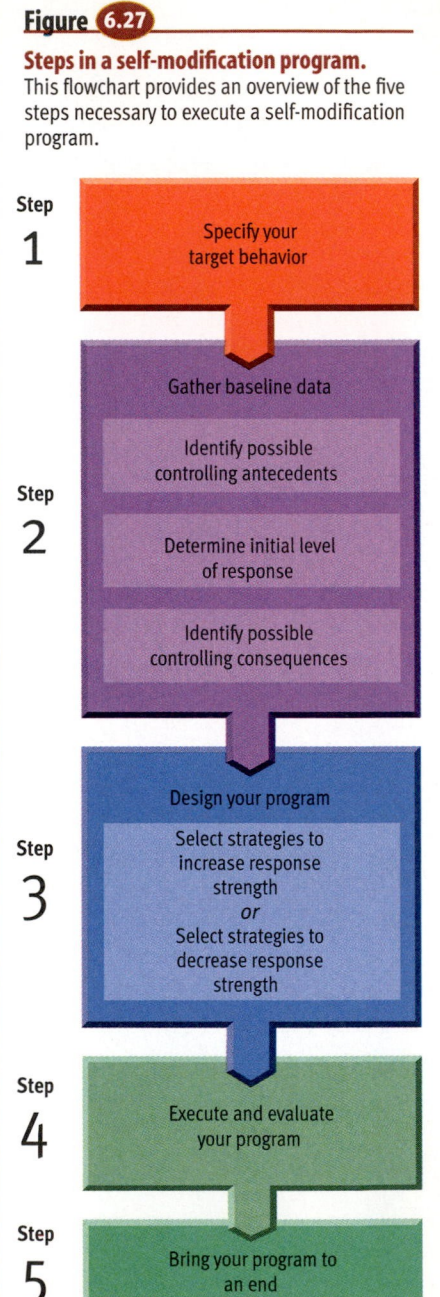

Figure 6.27

Steps in a self-modification program. This flowchart provides an overview of the five steps necessary to execute a self-modification program.

Step 1 Specify your target behavior

Step 2 Gather baseline data
- Identify possible controlling antecedents
- Determine initial level of response
- Identify possible controlling consequences

Step 3 Design your program
- Select strategies to increase response strength *or* Select strategies to decrease response strength

Step 4 Execute and evaluate your program

Step 5 Bring your program to an end

interval. Thus, you might count the daily frequency of snapping at your children, smoking cigarettes, or biting your fingernails. If studying is your target behavior, you will probably monitor hours of study. If you want to modify your eating, you will probably keep track of how many calories you consume. Whatever the unit of measurement, *it is crucial to gather accurate data*. You should keep permanent written records, and it is usually best to portray these records graphically (see Figure 6.28).

Second, you need to monitor the antecedents of your target behavior. ***Antecedents* are events that typically precede the target response.** Often these events play a major role in evoking your target behavior. For example, if your target is overeating, you might discover that the bulk of your overeating occurs late in the evening while you watch TV. If you can pinpoint this kind of antecedent-response connection, you may be able to design your program to circumvent or break the link.

Third, you need to monitor the typical consequences of your target behavior. Try to identify the reinforcers that are maintaining an undesirable target behavior or the unfavorable outcomes that are suppressing a desirable target behavior. In trying to identify reinforcers, remember that avoidance behavior is usually maintained by negative reinforcement. That is, the payoff for avoidance is usually the removal of something aversive, such as anxiety or a threat to self-esteem. You should also take into account the fact that a response may not be reinforced every time, as most behavior is maintained by intermittent reinforcement.

Designing Your Program

Once you have selected a target behavior and gathered adequate baseline data, it is time to plan your intervention program. Generally speaking, your program will be designed either to increase or to decrease the frequency of a target response.

Increasing Response Strength

Efforts to increase the frequency of a target response depend largely on the use of pos-

Figure 6.28

Example of record keeping in a self-modification program. Graphic records are ideal for tracking progress in behavior modification efforts. The records shown here illustrate what people would be likely to track in a behavior modification program for weight loss.

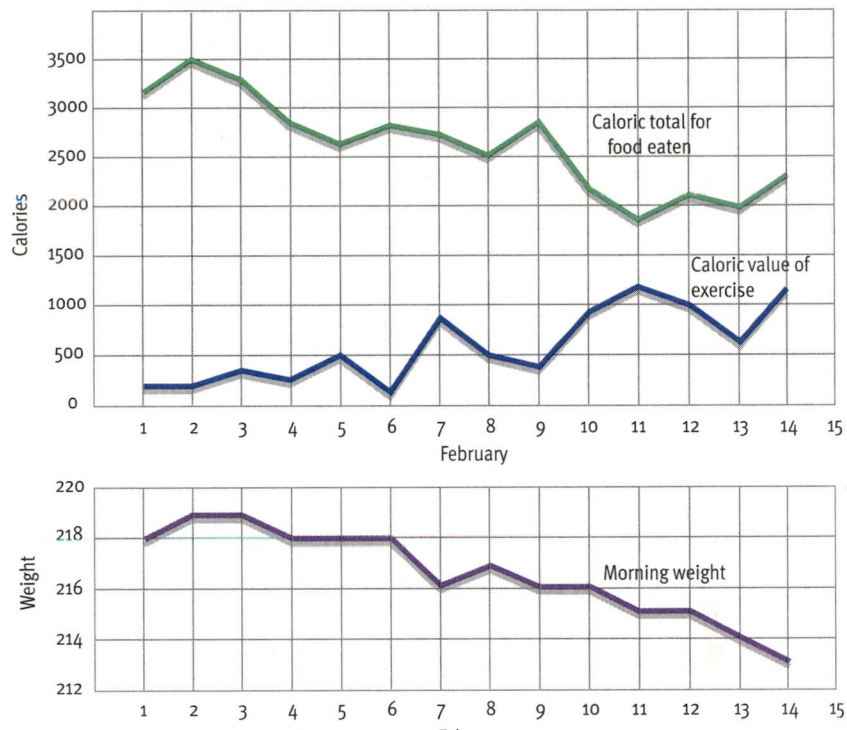

Overeating is just one of the many types of maladaptive behavior that can be changed with a self-modification program.

itive reinforcement. In other words, you reward yourself for behaving properly. Although the basic strategy is quite simple, doing it skillfully involves a number of considerations.

Selecting a Reinforcer. To use positive reinforcement, you need to find a reward that will be effective for you. Reinforcement is subjective—what is reinforcing for one person may not be reinforcing for another. Figure 6.29 lists questions you can ask your-self to help you determine your personal reinforcers. Be sure to be realistic and choose a reinforcer that is really available to you.

You don't have to come up with spectacular new reinforcers that you've never experienced before. *You can use reinforcers that you are already getting.* However, you have to restructure the contingencies so that you get them only if you behave appropriately. For example, if you normally buy two compact discs per week, you might make these purchases contingent on studying a certain number of hours during the week. Making yourself earn rewards that you used to take for granted is often a useful strategy in a self-modification program.

Arranging the Contingencies. Once you have chosen your reinforcer, you have to set up reinforcement contingencies. These contingencies will describe the exact behavioral goals that must be met and the reinforcement that may then be awarded. For example, in a program to increase exercise, you might make spending $40 on clothes (the reinforcer) contingent on having jogged 15 miles during the week (the target behavior).

Try to set behavioral goals that are both challenging and realistic. You want your goals to be challenging so that they lead to improvement in your behavior. However, setting unrealistically high goals—a common mistake in self-modification—often leads to unnecessary discouragement.

You also need to be concerned about doling out too much reinforcement. If reinforcement is too easy to get, you may become *satiated,* and the reinforcer may lose its motivational power. For example, if you were to reward yourself with virtually all the compact discs you wanted, this reinforcer would lose its incentive value.

One way to avoid the satiation problem is to put yourself on a token economy. A **token economy is a system for doling out symbolic reinforcers that are exchanged later for a variety of genuine reinforcers.** Thus, you might develop a point system for exercise behavior, accumulating points that can be spent on compact discs,

Figure 6.29

Selecting a reinforcer. Finding a good reinforcer to use in a behavior modification program can require a lot of thought. The questions listed here can help people identify their personal reinforcers.

Source: Adapted from Watson, D. L., & Tharp, R. G. (1997). *Self-directed behavior: Self-modification for personal adjustment.* Belmont, CA: Wadsworth. Reprinted by permission.

1. What will be the rewards of achieving your goal?
2. What kind of praise do you like to receive, from yourself and others?
3. What kinds of things do you like to have?
4. What are your major interests?
5. What are your hobbies?
6. What people do you like to be with?
7. What do you like to do with those people?
8. What do you do for fun?
9. What do you do to relax?
10. What do you do to get away from it all?
11. What makes you feel good?
12. What would be a nice present to receive?
13. What kinds of things are important to you?
14. What would you buy if you had an extra $20? $50? $100?
15. On what do you spend your money each week?
16. What behaviors do you perform every day? (Don't overlook the obvious or commonplace.)
17. Are there any behaviors you usually perform instead of the target behavior?
18. What would you hate to lose?
19. Of the things you do every day, which would you hate to give up?
20. What are your favorite daydreams and fantasies?
21. What are the most relaxing scenes you can imagine?

Figure 6.30

Example of a token economy. This token economy was set up to strengthen three types of exercise behavior (jogging, tennis, and situps). The person can exchange the tokens earned for four types of reinforcers that require different numbers of tokens. A token economy allows for immediate reinforcement (you can award yourself tokens each time you exercise) and it can allow you to employ a variety of reinforcers.

Response earning tokens

Response	Amount	Number of tokens
Jogging	1/2 mile	4
Jogging	1 mile	8
Jogging	2 miles	16
Tennis	1 hour	4
Tennis	2 hours	8
Sit-ups	25	1
Sit-ups	50	2

Redemption value of tokens

Reinforcer	Tokens required
Purchase one compact disc of your choice	30
Go to movie	50
Go to nice restaurant	100
Take special weekend trip	500

movies, restaurant meals, and so forth (see Figure 6.30).

Decreasing Response Strength

Let's turn now to the challenge of reducing the frequency of an undesirable response. You can go about this task in a number of ways. Your principal options include reinforcement, control of antecedents, and punishment.

Reinforcement. Reinforcers can be used in an indirect way to decrease the frequency of a response. This may sound paradoxical, since you have learned that reinforcement strengthens a response. The trick lies in how you define the target behavior. For example, in the case of overeating you might define your target behavior as eating more than 1600 calories a day (an excess response that you want to decrease) or eating less than 1600 calories a day (a deficit response

that you want to increase). You can choose the latter definition and reinforce yourself whenever you eat less than 1600 calories in a day. Thus, you can reinforce yourself for not emitting a response, or for emitting it less, and thereby decrease a response through reinforcement.

Control of Antecedents. A worthwhile strategy for decreasing the occurrence of an undesirable response may be to identify its antecedents and avoid exposure to them. This strategy is especially useful when you are trying to decrease the frequency of a consummatory response, such as smoking or eating. In the case of overeating, for instance, the easiest way to resist temptation is to avoid having to face it. Thus, you might stay away from enticing restaurants, minimize time spent in your kitchen, shop for groceries just after eating (when willpower is higher), and avoid purchasing favorite foods. Control of antecedents can also be helpful in a program to increase studying. The key often lies in *where* you study. You can reduce excessive socializing by studying somewhere devoid of people. Similarly, you can reduce loafing by studying someplace where there is no TV, stereo, or phone to distract you.

Punishment. The strategy of decreasing unwanted behavior by punishing yourself for that behavior is an obvious option that people tend to overuse. The biggest problem with punishment in a self-modification effort is that it is difficult to follow through and punish yourself. Nonetheless, there may be situations in which your manipulations of reinforcers need to be bolstered by the threat of punishment.

If you're going to use punishment, keep two guidelines in mind. First, do not use punishment alone. Use it in conjunction with positive reinforcement. If you set up a program in which you can earn only negative consequences, you probably won't stick to it. Second, use a relatively mild punishment so that you will actually be able to administer it to yourself. Nurnberger and Zimmerman (1970) developed a creative method of self-punishment. They had subjects write out a check to an organization they hated (for instance, the campaign of a political candidate whom they despised). The check was held by a third party who mailed it if subjects failed to meet their behavioral goals. Such a punishment is relatively harmless, but it can serve as a strong source of motivation.

Executing and Evaluating Your Program

Once you have designed your program, the next step is to put it to work by enforcing the contingencies that you have carefully planned. During this period, you need to continue to accurately record the frequency of your target behavior so you can evaluate your progress. The success of your program depends on your not "cheating." The most common form of cheating is to reward yourself when you have not actually earned it.

You can do two things to increase the likelihood that you will comply with your program. One is to make up a *behavioral contract*—a written agreement outlining a promise to adhere to the contingencies of a behavior modification program. The formality of signing such a contract in front of friends or family seems to make many people take their program more seriously. You can further reduce the likelihood of cheating by having someone other than you dole out the reinforcers and punishments.

Behavior modification programs often require some fine-tuning, so don't be surprised if you need to make a few adjustments. Several flaws are especially common in designing self-modification programs. Among those that you should look out for are (1) depending on a weak reinforcer, (2) permitting lengthy delays between appropriate behavior and delivery of reinforcers, and (3) trying to do too much too quickly by setting unrealistic goals. Often, a small revision or two can turn a failing program around and make it a success.

Ending Your Program

Generally, when you design your program you should spell out the conditions under which you will bring it to an end. Doing so involves setting terminal goals such as reaching a certain weight, studying with a certain regularity, or going without cigarettes for a certain length of time. Often, it is a good idea to phase out your program by planning a gradual reduction in the frequency or potency of your reinforcement for appropriate behavior.

If your program is successful, it may fade away without a conscious decision on your part. Often, new, improved patterns of behavior become self-maintaining. Responses such as eating right, exercising regularly, and studying diligently may become habitual. Whether or not you end your program intentionally, you should always be prepared to reinstitute the program if you find yourself slipping back to your old patterns of behavior.

REVIEW OF KEY POINTS

● In behavior modification, the principles of learning are used to change behavior directly. Behavior modification techniques can be used to increase one's self-control. The first step in self-modification involves specifying the overt target behavior to be increased or decreased.

● The second step involves gathering baseline data about the initial rate of the target response and identifying any typical antecedents and consequences associated with the behavior.

● The third step is to design a program. If you are trying to increase the strength of a response, you'll depend on positive reinforcement. The reinforcement contingencies should spell out exactly what you have to do to earn your reinforcer. A number of strategies can be used to decrease the strength of a response, including reinforcement, control of antecedents, and punishment.

● The fourth step involves executing and evaluating your program. Self-modification programs often require some fine-tuning. The final step is to determine how and when you will phase out your program.

Manipulating Emotions: Pavlov and Persuasion

With all due respect to the great Ivan Pavlov, when we focus on his demonstration that dogs can be trained to slobber in response to a tone, it is easy to lose sight of the importance of classical conditioning. At first glance, most people do not see a relationship between Pavlov's slobbering dogs and anything that they are even remotely interested in. However, in the main body of the chapter, we saw that classical conditioning actually contributes to the regulation of many important aspects of behavior, including fears, phobias, and other emotional reactions; immune function and other physiological processes; food preferences; and even sexual arousal. In this Application you will learn that classical conditioning is routinely used to manipulate emotions in persuasive efforts. If you watch TV, you have been subjected to Pavlovian techniques. An understanding of these techniques can help you recognize when your emotions are being manipulated by advertisers, politicians, and the media.

Perhaps the most interesting aspect of classically conditioned emotional responses is that people often are unaware of the origin of these responses, or even that they feel the way they do. Consistent with this observation, research has shown that attitudes can be shaped through classical conditioning without participants' conscious awareness (Olson & Fazio, 2001). The key to the process is simply to manipulate the automatic, subconscious associations that people make in response to various stimuli. Let's look at how this manipulation is done in advertising, business negotiations, and the world of politics.

Classical Conditioning in Advertising

The art of manipulating people's associations has been perfected by the advertising industry. Advertisers consistently endeavor to pair the products they are peddling with stimuli that seem likely to elicit positive emotional responses. An extensive variety of stimuli are used for this purpose. Products are paired with well-liked celebrity spokespersons; depictions of warm, loving families; beautiful pastoral scenery; cute, cuddly pets; enchanting, rosy-cheeked children; upbeat, pleasant music; opulent surroundings that reek of wealth; and, above all else, extremely attractive models—especially, glamorous, alluring women. Advertisers also like to pair their products with exciting events, such as the NBA Finals, and cherished symbols, such as flags and the Olympic rings insignia.

Advertisers mostly seek to associate their products with stimuli that evoke pleasurable feelings of a general sort, but in some cases they try to create more specific associations. For example, cigarette brands sold mainly to men are frequently paired with tough-looking men in rugged settings to create an association between the cigarettes and masculinity. In contrast, cigarette brands that are mainly marketed to women are paired with images that evoke feelings of femininity. In a similar vein, manufacturers of designer jeans typically seek to forge associations between their products and things that are young, urban, and hip. Advertisers marketing expensive automobiles or platinum credit cards pair their products with symbols of affluence, luxury, and privilege, such as mansions, butlers, and dazzling jewelry.

Classical Conditioning in Business Negotiations

In the world of business interactions, two standard practices are designed to get customers to make an association between one's business and pleasurable feelings. The first is to take customers out to dinner at fine restaurants. The provision of delicious food and fine wine in a luxurious environment is a powerful unconditioned stimulus that reliably elicits pleasant feelings that are likely to be associated with one's host. The second practice is the strategy of entertaining customers at major events, such as concerts and football games. Over the last decade, America's sports arenas have largely

The practice of taking customers out to dinner at expensive, luxurious restaurants takes advantage of the process of classical conditioning.

been rebuilt with vastly more "luxury sky-boxes" to accommodate this business tactic. It reaches its zenith every year at the Super Bowl, where most of the seats go to the guests of Fortune 500 corporations. This practice pairs the host with both pleasant feelings and the excitement of a big event.

It is worth noting that these strategies take advantage of other processes besides classical conditioning. They also make use of the *reciprocity norm*—the social rule that one should pay back in kind what one receives from others (Cialdini, 1993). Thus, wining and dining clients creates a sense of obligation that they should reciprocate their hosts' generosity—presumably in their business dealings.

Classical Conditioning in the World of Politics

Like advertisers, candidates running for election need to influence the attitudes of many people quickly, subtly, and effectively—and they depend on classical conditioning to help them do so. For example, have you noticed how politicians show up at an endless variety of pleasant public events (such as the opening of a new mall) that often have nothing to do with their public service? When a sports team wins some sort of championship, local politicians are drawn like flies to the subsequent celebrations. They want to pair themselves with these positive events, so that they are associated with pleasant emotions.

Election campaign ads use the same techniques as commercial ads. Candidates are paired with popular celebrities, wholesome families, pleasant music, and symbols of patriotism. Cognizant of the power of classical conditioning, politicians also exercise great care to ensure that they are not paired with people or events that might trigger negative feelings. For example, in 1999, when the U.S. government finally turned control of the Panama Canal over to Panama, President Clinton and Vice-President Gore chose to not attend the ceremonies because this event was viewed negatively in some quarters.

The ultimate political perversion of the principles of classical conditioning proba-

bly occurred in Nazi Germany. The Nazis used many propaganda techniques to create prejudice toward Jews and members of other targeted groups (such as Gypsies). One such strategy was the repeated pairing of disgusting, repulsive images with stereotypical pictures of Jews. For example, the Nazis would show alternating pictures of rats or roaches crawling over filthy garbage and stereotypical Jewish faces, so that the two images would become associated in the minds of the viewers. Thus, the German population was conditioned to have negative emotional reactions to Jews and to associate them with vermin subject to extermination. The Nazis reasoned that if people would not hesitate to exterminate rats and roaches, then why not human beings associated with these vermin?

Becoming More Aware of Classical Conditioning Processes

How effective are the efforts to manipulate people's emotions through Pavlovian conditioning? It's hard to say. In the real world, these strategies are always used in combination with other persuasive tactics, which creates multiple confounds that make it difficult to assess the impact of the Pavlovian techniques. Laboratory research can eliminate these confounds, but surprisingly little research on these strategies has been published, and virtually all of it has dealt with advertising. The advertising studies suggest that classical conditioning can be effective and leave enduring imprints on consumers' attitudes (Grossman & Till, 1998; Stuart, Shimp, & Engle, 1987), but a great deal of additional research is

Political candidates are very savvy about the potential power of classical conditioning. For example, they like to be seen in public with popular celebrities who elicit positive feelings among many voters.

needed. Given the monumental sums that advertisers spend using these techniques, it seems reasonable to speculate that individual companies have data on their specific practices to demonstrate their efficacy, but these data are not made available to the public.

What can you do to reduce the extent to which your emotions are manipulated through Pavlovian procedures? Well, you could turn off your radio and TV, close up your magazines, stop your newspaper, disconnect your modem, and withdraw into a media-shielded shell, but that hardly seems realistic for most people. Realistically, the best defense is to make a conscious effort to become more aware of the pervasive attempts to condition your emotions and attitudes. Some research on persuasion suggests that *to be forewarned is to be forearmed* (Pfau et al., 1990). In other words, if you know how media sources try to manipulate you, you should be more resistant to their strategies.

Table 6.2 Critical Thinking Skills Discussed in This Application

Skill	Description
Understanding how Pavlovian conditioning can be used to manipulate emotions	The critical thinker understands how stimuli can be paired together to create automatic associations that people may not be aware of.
Developing the ability to detect conditioning procedures used in the media	The critical thinker can recognize Pavlovian conditioning tactics in commercial and political advertisements.

RECAP

Key Ideas

Classical Conditioning

● Classical conditioning explains how a neutral stimulus can acquire the capacity to elicit a response originally evoked by another stimulus. This kind of conditioning was originally described by Ivan Pavlov.

● Many kinds of everyday responses are regulated through classical conditioning, including phobias, fears, and pleasant emotional responses. Even physiological responses such as immune and sexual functioning respond to classical conditioning.

● A conditioned response may be weakened and extinguished entirely when the CS is no longer paired with the UCS. In some cases, spontaneous recovery occurs, and an extinguished response reappears after a period of nonexposure to the CS.

● Conditioning may generalize to additional stimuli that are similar to the original CS. The opposite of generalization is discrimination, which involves not responding to stimuli that resemble the original CS. Higher-order conditioning occurs when a CS functions as if it were a UCS, to establish new conditioning.

Operant Conditioning

● Operant conditioning involves largely voluntary responses that are governed by their consequences. Following the lead of E. L. Thorndike, B. F. Skinner investigated this form of conditioning, working mainly with rats and pigeons in Skinner boxes.

● The key dependent variable in operant conditioning is the rate of response over time. When this responding is shown graphically, steep slopes indicate rapid responding. New operant responses can be shaped by gradually reinforcing closer and closer approximations of the desired response. In operant conditioning, extinction occurs when reinforcement for a response is terminated and the rate of that response declines.

● Operant responses are regulated by discriminative stimuli that are cues for the likelihood of obtaining reinforcers. These stimuli are subject to the same processes of generalization and discrimination that occur in classical conditioning.

● Delayed reinforcement slows the process of conditioning. Primary reinforcers are unlearned; secondary reinforcers acquire their reinforcing quality through conditioning.

● Intermittent schedules of reinforcement produce greater resistance to extinction than similar continuous schedules. Ratio schedules tend to yield higher rates of response than interval schedules. Shorter intervals and higher ratios are associated with faster responding.

● Concurrent schedules of reinforcement permit researchers to study how organisms make choices among operant responses. The matching law suggests that organisms strive to maximize their reinforcement. Optimal foraging theory asserts that animals' food-seeking behaviors optimize the nutrition gained in relation to the effort expended.

● Responses can be strengthened through either the presentation of positive reinforcers or the removal of negative reinforcers. Negative reinforcement regulates escape and avoidance learning. The two-process theory provides the best explanation of avoidance behavior and may shed light on why phobias are so difficult to eliminate.

● Punishment involves unfavorable consequences that lead to a decline in response strength. Some of the problems associated with punishment as a disciplinary procedure are emotional side effects and increased aggressive behavior.

Changing Directions in the Study of Conditioning

● The findings on instinctive drift, conditioned taste aversion, and preparedness have led to the recognition that there are species-specific biological constraints on conditioning. Some evolutionary psychologists argue that learning processes vary considerably across species.

● Studies of signal relations in classical conditioning and response-outcome relations in operant conditioning suggest that cognitive processes play a larger role in conditioning than originally believed.

Observational Learning

● In observational learning, an organism is conditioned by watching a model's conditioning. Both classical and operant conditioning can occur through observational learning, which depends on the processes of attention, retention, reproduction, and motivation.

● Observational learning can account for the influence of mass media (such as television) on behavior. The principles of observational learning have also been used to explain why physical punishment increases aggressive behavior.

Putting It in Perspective

● Two of our key themes were especially apparent in our coverage of learning and conditioning. One theme involves the interaction of heredity and environment in learning. The other involves the way progress in psychology affects society at large.

Personal Application ● Achieving Self-Control Through Behavior Modification

● The first step in self-modification is specifying the target behavior to be increased or decreased. The second step is gathering baseline data.

● The third step is to design a program, using procedures such as reinforcement, control of antecedents, and punishment. The fourth step involves executing and evaluating your program. The final step is to determine how and when you will phase out your program.

Critical Thinking Application ● Manipulating Emotions: Pavlov and Persuasion

● Advertisers routinely pair their products with stimuli that seem likely to elicit positive emotions or other specific feelings. The practice of taking customers out to dinner or to major events also takes advantage of Pavlovian conditioning. Politicians also work to pair themselves with positive events. The best defense against these tactics is to become more aware of efforts to manipulate your emotions.

Key Terms

Acquisition
Antecedents
Avoidance learning
Behavior modification
Behavioral contract
Classical conditioning
Concurrent schedules
  of reinforcement
Conditioned reinforcers
Conditioned response
  (CR)
Conditioned stimulus
  (CS)
Continuous
  reinforcement
Cumulative recorder
Discriminative stimuli
Elicit
Emit
Escape learning
Extinction
Fixed-interval (FI)
  schedule
Fixed-ratio (FR)
  schedule
Higher-order
  conditioning
Instinctive drift
Instrumental learning
Intermittent
  reinforcement
Law of effect
Learning
Matching law
Negative reinforcement
Observational learning
Operant chamber
Operant conditioning
Optimal foraging
  theory

Partial reinforcement
Pavlovian conditioning
Phobias
Positive reinforcement
Preparedness
Primary reinforcers
Punishment
Reinforcement
Reinforcement
  contingencies
Resistance to extinction
Schedule of
  reinforcement
Secondary reinforcers
Shaping
Skinner box
Spontaneous recovery
Stimulus discrimination
Stimulus generalization
Token economy
Trial
Unconditioned
  response (UCR)
Unconditioned
  stimulus (UCS)
Variable-interval (VI)
  schedule
Variable-ratio (VR)
  schedule

Key People

Albert Bandura
John Garcia
Ivan Pavlov
Robert Rescorla
Martin Seligman
B. F. Skinner
E. L. Thorndike
John B. Watson

PRACTICE TEST

1. After repeated pairings of a tone with meat powder, Pavlov found that a dog will salivate when the tone is presented. Salivation to the tone is a(n):
   A. unconditioned stimulus.
   B. unconditioned response.
   C. conditioned stimulus.
   D. conditioned response.

2. Sam's wife always wears the same black nightgown whenever she is "in the mood" for sexual relations. Sam becomes sexually aroused as soon as he sees his wife in the nightgown. For Sam, the nightgown is a(n):
   A. unconditioned stimulus.
   B. unconditioned response.
   C. conditioned stimulus.
   D. conditioned response.

3. Watson and Rayner (1920) conditioned "Little Albert" to fear white rats by banging a hammer on a steel bar as the child played with a white rat. Later, it was discovered that Albert feared not only white rats but white stuffed toys and Santa's beard as well. Albert's fear of these other objects can be attributed to:
   A. the law of effect.
   B. stimulus generalization.
   C. stimulus discrimination.
   D. an overactive imagination.

4. The phenomenon of higher-order conditioning shows that:
   A. only a genuine, natural UCS can be used to establish a CR.
   B. auditory stimuli are easier to condition than visual stimuli.
   C. visual stimuli are easier to condition than auditory stimuli.
   D. an already established CS can be used in the place of a natural UCS.

5. Which of the following statements is (are) true?
   A. Classical conditioning regulates reflexive, involuntary responses exclusively.
   B. Operant conditioning regulates voluntary responses exclusively.
   C. The distinction between the two types of conditioning is not absolute, with both types jointly and interactively governing some aspects of behavior.
   D. a and b.

6. A pigeon in a Skinner box is pecking the disk at a high, steady rate. The graph portraying this pigeon's responding will have:
   A. a steep, unchanging slope.
   B. a shallow, unchanging slope.
   C. a progressively steeper slope
   D. a progressively shallower slope.

7. A primary reinforcer has _____ reinforcing properties; a secondary reinforcer has _____ reinforcing properties.
   A. biological; acquired
   B. conditioned; unconditioned
   C. potent; weak
   D. immediate; delayed

8. The steady, rapid responding of a person playing a slot machine is an example of the pattern of responding typically generated on a _____ schedule.
   A. fixed-ratio
   B. variable-ratio
   C. fixed-interval
   D. variable-interval

9. Positive reinforcement _____ the rate of responding; negative reinforcement _____ the rate of responding.
   A. increases; decreases
   B. decreases; increases
   C. increases; increases
   D. decreases; decreases

10. According to the two-process theory, a fear response is acquired due to _____ conditioning; it is maintained due to _____ conditioning.
    A. classical; operant
    B. operant; classical
    C. classical; classical
    D. operant; operant

11. Nolan used to love tequila. However, a few weeks ago he drank way too much tequila and became very, very sick. His tendency to drink tequila has since declined dramatically. In operant terms, this sequence of events represents:
    A. avoidance learning.
    B. negative reinforcement.
    C. escape learning.
    D. punishment.

12. According to Rescorla, the strength of a conditioned response depends on:
    A. the number of trials in which the CS and UCS are paired.
    B. the number of trials in which the CS is presented alone.
    C. the percentage of trials in which the CS and UCS are paired.
    D. resistance to extinction.

13. Skinner maintained that reinforcement determines the acquisition of a response; Bandura maintains that reinforcement determines the _____ of a response.
    A. acquisition
    B. development
    C. performance
    D. generalization

14. The link between physical punishment and subsequent aggressive behavior is probably best explained by:
    A. observational learning.
    B. noncontingent reinforcement.
    C. resistance to extinction.
    D. the matching law.

15. The *second* step in a self-modification program is to:
    A. specify the target behavior.
    B. design your program.
    C. gather baseline data.
    D. set up a behavioral contact.

Answers

1	D p. 221	**6**	A pp. 231–232	**11**	D p. 241
2	C pp. 221–223	**7**	A p. 235	**12**	C pp. 246–247
3	B p. 227	**8**	B pp. 236–237	**13**	C p. 248
4	D p. 228	**9**	C p. 239	**14**	A pp. 248–249
5	C p. 229	**10**	A pp. 240–241	**15**	C p. 252

ON THE WEB

For additional resources on the topics covered in this chapter, visit the *Psychology: Themes and Variations* Web site, where you will find practice quizzes, tutorials, Web links, simulations, critical thinking activities, flash cards, interactive exercises, and suggested readings available through INFOTRAC.

http://psychology.wadsworth.com/weiten_themes6e/

CHAPTER 7

© A. Woolfitt/Robert Harding Picture Library, London

Human Memory

If you live in the United States, you've undoubtedly handled thousands upon thousands of American pennies. Surely, then, you remember what a penny looks like—or do you? Take a look at Figure 7.1. Which drawing corresponds to a real penny? Did you have a hard time selecting the real one? If so, you're not alone. Nickerson and Adams (1979) found that most people can't recognize the real penny in this collection of drawings. And their surprising finding was not a fluke. Undergraduates in England showed even worse memory for British coins (Jones, 1990). How can that be? Why do most of us have so poor a memory for an object we see every day?

Let's try another exercise. A definition of a word follows. It's not a particularly common word, but there's a good chance that you're familiar with it. Try to think of the word.

Definition: Favoritism shown or patronage granted by persons in high office to relatives or close friends.

If you can't think of the word, perhaps you can remember the letter of the alphabet it begins with, or what it sounds like. If so, you're experiencing the *tip-of-the-tongue phenomenon,* in which forgotten information feels like it's just out of reach. In this case, the word you may be reaching for is *nepotism.*

You've probably endured the tip-of-the-tongue phenomenon while taking exams. You blank out on a term that you're sure you know. You may feel as if you're on the verge of remembering the term, but you can't quite come up with it. Later, perhaps while you're driving home, the term suddenly comes to you. "Of course," you may say to yourself, "how could I forget that?" That's an interesting question. Clearly, the term was stored in your memory.

As these examples suggest, memory involves more than taking information in and storing it in some mental compartment. In fact, psychologists probing the workings of memory have had to grapple with three enduring questions: (1) How does information get *into* memory? (2) How is information *maintained* in memory? and (3) How is information pulled *back out* of memory? These three questions correspond to the three key processes involved in memory (see Figure 7.2 on the next page): *encoding* (getting information in), *storage* (maintaining it), and *retrieval* (getting it out).

Encoding **involves forming a memory code.** For example, when you form a memory code for a word, you might emphasize how it looks, how it sounds, or what it means. Encoding usually requires attention, which is why you may not be able to recall exactly what a penny looks like—most people don't pay much attention to the appearance of a penny. *Storage* **involves maintaining encoded information in memory over time.** Psychologists have focused much of their memory research on trying to identify just what factors help or hinder memory storage. But, as the tip-of-the-tongue phenomenon shows, information storage isn't enough to guarantee that you'll remember something. You need to be able to get information out of storage. *Retrieval* **involves recovering information from memory stores.** Research issues concerned with retrieval include the study of how people search memory and why some retrieval strategies are more effective than others.

Most of this chapter is devoted to an examination of memory encoding, storage, and retrieval. As you'll

© A. Woolfitt/Robert Harding Picture Library, London

Figure 7.1

A simple memory test.
Nickerson and Adams (1979) presented these 15 versions of an object most people have seen hundreds or thousands of times and asked, "Which one is correct?" Can you identify the real penny shown here?

SOURCE: Nickerson, R. S., & Adams, M. J. (1979). Long-term memory for a common object. *Cognitive Psychology, 11,* 287–307. Copyright © 1979 Elsevier Science USA, reproduced with permission from the publisher.

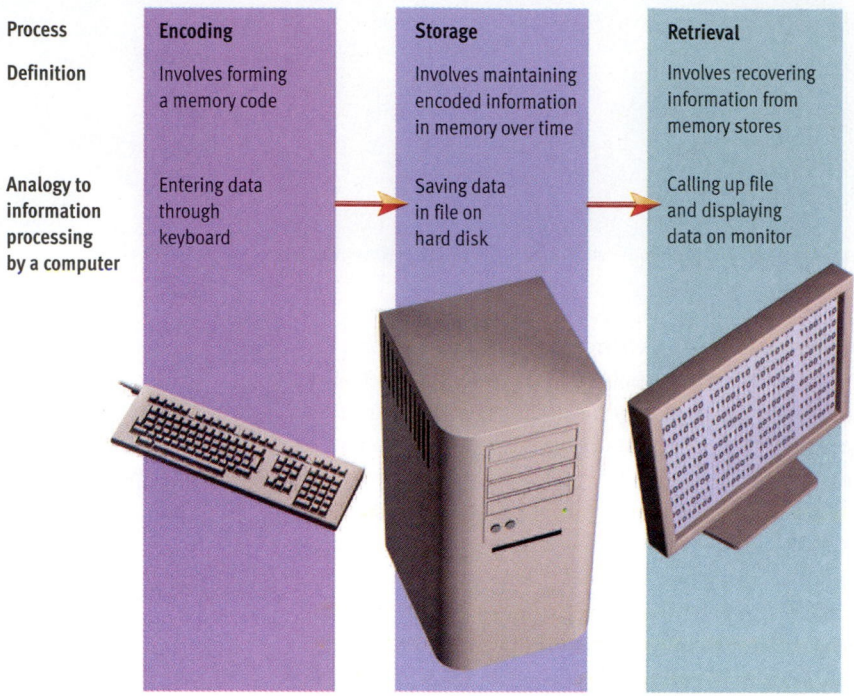

Process	Encoding	Storage	Retrieval
Definition	Involves forming a memory code	Involves maintaining encoded information in memory over time	Involves recovering information from memory stores
Analogy to information processing by a computer	Entering data through keyboard	Saving data in file on hard disk	Calling up file and displaying data on monitor

Figure 7.2

Three key processes in memory. Memory depends on three sequential processes: encoding, storage, and retrieval. Some theorists have drawn an analogy between these processes and elements of information processing by computers, as depicted here. The analogies for encoding and retrieval work pretty well, but the storage analogy is somewhat misleading. When information is stored on a hard drive, it remains unchanged indefinitely and you can retrieve an exact copy. As you will learn in this chapter, memory storage is a much more dynamic process. Our memories change over time and are rough reconstructions rather than exact copies of past events.

see, these basic processes help explain the ultimate puzzle in the study of memory: why people forget. Just as memory involves more than storage, forgetting involves more than "losing" something from the memory store. Forgetting may be due to deficiencies in any of the three key processes in memory—encoding, storage, or retrieval. After our discussion of forgetting, we will take a brief look at the physiological bases of memory. Finally, we will discuss the theoretical controversy about whether there are separate memory systems for different types of information. The chapter's Personal Application provides some practical advice on how to improve your memory. The Critical Thinking Application discusses some reasons that memory is less reliable than people assume it to be.

Encoding: Getting Information into Memory

PREVIEW QUESTIONS
- What does attention have to do with memory?
- What types of encoding produce deeper processing?
- How do levels of processing relate to retention?
- How does elaboration enhance encoding?
- How does the use of visual imagery improve memory?
- What is self-referent encoding?

Have you ever been introduced to someone and then realized only 30 seconds into your interaction that you had already "forgotten" his or her name? More often than not, this familiar kind of forgetting results from a failure to form a memory code for the name. When you're introduced to people, you're often busy sizing them up and thinking about what you're going to say. With your attention diverted in this way, names go in one ear and out the other. You don't remember them because they aren't encoded for storage into memory. Psychologists have observed a similar phenomenon in the laboratory, which they have dubbed the *next-in-line effect*. If participants in a small group take turns speaking to the group, subsequent memory tests reveal that the subjects tend to not recall much of what was said just before they took their turn (Bond, Pitre, & Van Leeuwen, 1991). Why? Because when participants are next in line to speak, they are too preoccupied rehearsing to pay attention to what is being said.

Like the problem of forgetting people's names just after you've met them, the next-in-line effect illustrates that active encoding is a crucial process in memory. In this section, we discuss the role of attention in encoding, various types of encoding, and ways to enrich the encoding process.

The Role of Attention

Although there are some fascinating exceptions, you generally need to pay attention to information if you intend to remember it (Craik et al., 1996; Mulligan, 1998). For example, if you sit through a class lecture but pay little attention to it, you're unlikely to remember much of what the professor had to say.

Attention involves focusing awareness on a narrowed range of stimuli or events. If you pause to devote a little attention to the matter, you'll realize that selective attention is critical to everyday functioning. If your attention were distributed equally among all stimulus inputs, life would be utter chaos. If you weren't able to filter out most of the potential stimulation around you, you wouldn't be able to read a book, converse with a friend, or even carry on a coherent train of thought.

Attention is often likened to a *filter* that screens out most potential stimuli while allowing a select few to pass through into conscious awareness. However, a great deal of debate has been devoted to *where* the filter is located in the information-processing system. The key issue in this debate is whether stimuli are screened out *early,* during sensory input, or *late,* after the brain has processed the meaning or significance of the input (see Figure 7.3).

Evidence on the "cocktail party phenomenon" suggests the latter. For example, imagine a young woman named Claudia at a crowded party where many conversations are taking place. Claudia is paying attention to her conversation with a friend and filtering out the other conversations. However, if someone in another conversation mentions her name, Claudia may notice it, even though she has been ignoring that conversation. In experimental simulations of this situation about 35% of participants report hearing their own name (Wood & Cowan, 1995). If selection is early, how can these people register input they've been blocking out? This cocktail party phenomenon suggests that attention involves *late* selection, based on the *meaning* of input.

Which view is supported by the weight of scientific evidence—early selection or late selection? Studies have found ample evidence for *both* as well as for intermediate selection (Cowan, 1988; Posner & DiGirolamo, 2000). These findings have led some theorists to conclude that the location of the attention filter may be flexible rather than fixed (Shiffrin, 1988).

Wherever filtering occurs, it is clear that people have difficulty if they attempt to focus their attention on two or more inputs simultaneously. For example, if Claudia tried to continue her original conversation while also monitoring the other conversation in which she was mentioned, she would struggle in her efforts to attend to both conversations and would remember less of her original conversation. Studies indicate that when participants are forced to divide their attention between memory encoding and some other task, large reductions in memory performance

are seen (Craik, 2001; Craik & Kester, 2000). Actually, the negative effects of divided attention are not limited to memory. Divided attention can have a negative impact on the performance of quite a variety of tasks, especially when the tasks are complex or unfamiliar (Pashler, Johnston, & Ruthruff, 2001). This principle appears to apply to the controversy about the advisability of driving while conversing on a cellular telephone. One recent study of a simulated driving task suggests that cellular conversations double the chances of missing traffic signals and slow reactions to signals that are detected (Strayer & Johnston, 2001).

Levels of Processing  SIM5, 6a

Attention is critical to the encoding of memories, but not all attention is created equal. You can attend to things in different ways, focusing on different aspects of the stimulus input. According to some theorists, these qualitative differences in *how* people attend to information are the main factors influencing how much they remember. For example, Fergus Craik and Robert Lockhart (1972) argue that different rates of forgetting occur because some methods of encoding create more durable memory codes than others.

Craik and Lockhart propose that incoming information can be processed at different levels. For instance, they maintain that in dealing with verbal information, people engage in three progressively deeper levels of processing: structural, phonemic, and semantic encoding (see Figure 7.4 on the next page). *Structural encoding* is relatively shallow processing that emphasizes the physical structure of the stimulus. For example, if words are flashed on a screen, structural encoding registers such things as how they were printed (capital, lowercase, and so on) or the length of the words (how many letters). Further analysis may result in *phonemic encoding,* which emphasizes what a word sounds like. Phonemic encoding involves

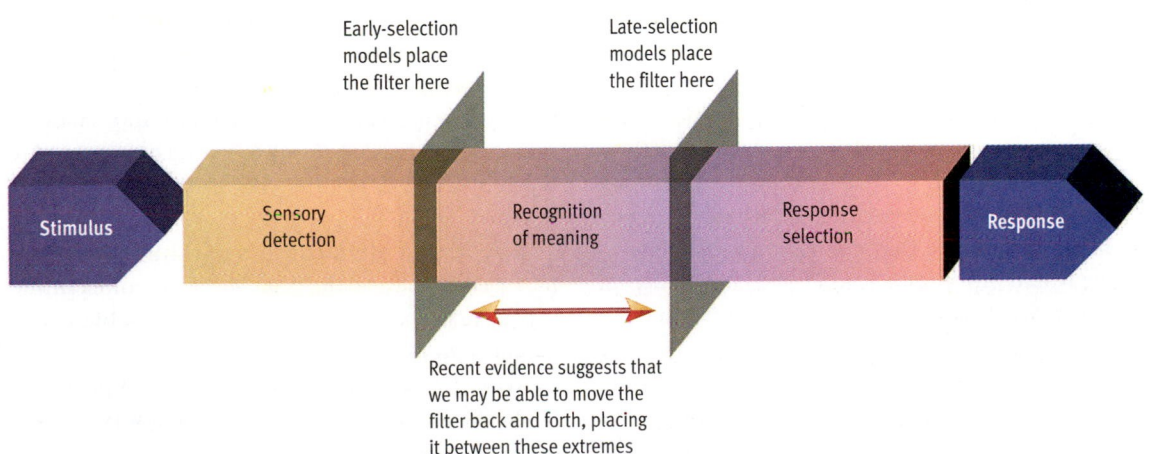

Early-selection models place the filter here

Late-selection models place the filter here

Stimulus

Sensory detection

Recognition of meaning

Response selection

Response

Recent evidence suggests that we may be able to move the filter back and forth, placing it between these extremes

Figure 7.3

Models of selective attention. Early-selection models propose that input is filtered before meaning is processed. Late-selection models hold that filtering occurs after the processing of meaning. There is evidence to support early, late, and intermediate selection, suggesting that the location of the attentional filter may not be fixed.

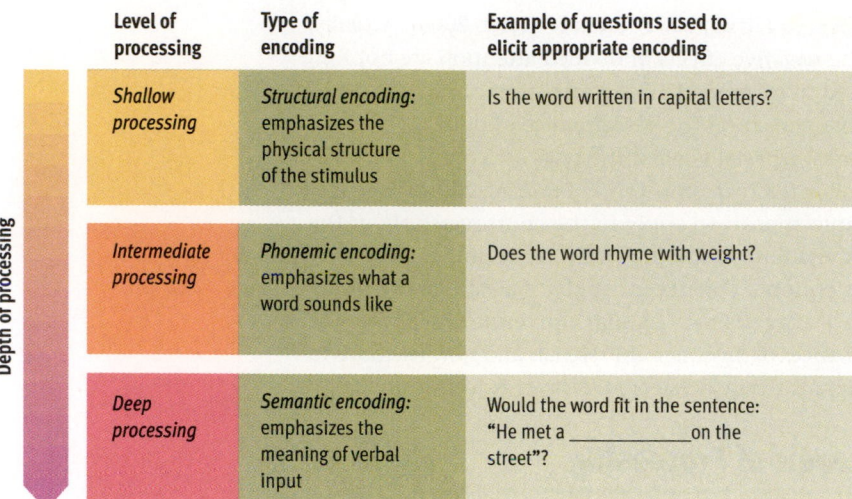

Level of processing	Type of encoding	Example of questions used to elicit appropriate encoding
Shallow processing	Structural encoding: emphasizes the physical structure of the stimulus	Is the word written in capital letters?
Intermediate processing	Phonemic encoding: emphasizes what a word sounds like	Does the word rhyme with weight?
Deep processing	Semantic encoding: emphasizes the meaning of verbal input	Would the word fit in the sentence: "He met a _____ on the street"?

Depth of processing

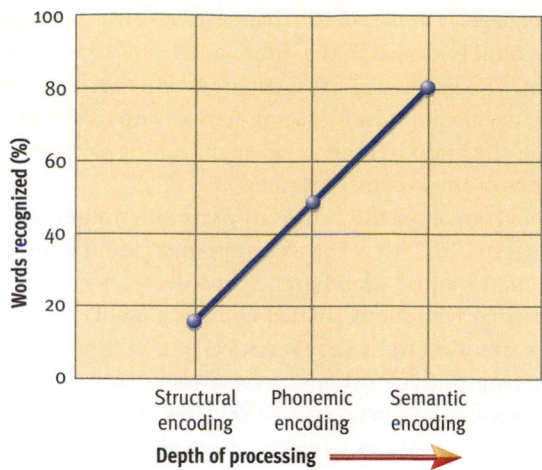

Depth of processing ⟶

Figure 7.5

Retention at three levels of processing. In accordance with levels-of-processing theory, Craik and Tulving (1975) found that structural, phonemic, and semantic encoding, which involve progressively deeper levels of processing, led to progressively better retention. (Data from Craik & Tulving, 1975)

Figure 7.4

Levels-of-processing theory. According to Craik and Lockhart (1972), structural, phonemic, and semantic encoding—which can be elicited by questions such as those shown on the right—involve progressively deeper levels of processing, which should result in more durable memories.

naming or saying (perhaps silently) the words. Finally, *semantic encoding* emphasizes the meaning of verbal input; it involves thinking about the objects and actions the words represent. **Levels-of-processing theory proposes that deeper levels of processing result in longer-lasting memory codes.**

In one experimental test of levels-of-processing theory, Craik and Tulving (1975) compared the durability of structural, phonemic, and semantic encoding. They directed subjects' attention to particular aspects of briefly presented stimulus words by asking them questions about various characteristics of the words (see Figure 7.4). The questions were designed to engage the subjects in different levels of processing. The key hypothesis was that retention of the stimulus words would increase as subjects moved from structural to phonemic to semantic encoding. After responding to 60 words, the subjects received an unexpected test of their memory for the words. As predicted, the subjects' recall was low after structural encoding, notably better after phonemic encoding, and highest after semantic encoding (see Figure 7.5).

The hypothesis that deeper processing leads to enhanced memory has been replicated in many studies (Koriat & Melkman, 1987; Lockhart & Craik, 1990). Nonetheless, the levels-of-processing model is not without its weaknesses. Critics ask, what exactly is a "level" of processing? And how do we determine whether one level is deeper than another? Craik and Lockhart had hoped that the *time required for processing* would prove to be a good indicator of depth. However, Craik and Tulving (1975) found that it's possible to design a task in which structural encoding takes longer than semantic encoding. This finding indicates that processing time is not a reliable index

of depth of processing. Thus, the levels in levels-of-processing theory remain vaguely defined.

Enriching Encoding

Structural, phonemic, and semantic encoding do not exhaust the options when it comes to forming memory codes. There are other dimensions to encoding, dimensions that can enrich the encoding process and thereby improve memory.

Elaboration

Semantic encoding can often be enhanced through a process called elaboration. **Elaboration is linking a stimulus to other information at the time of encoding.** For example, let's say you read that phobias are often caused by classical conditioning, and you apply this idea to your own fear of spiders. In doing so, you are engaging in elaboration. The additional associations created by elaboration usually help people remember information. Differences in elaboration can help explain why different approaches to semantic processing result in varied amounts of retention (Craik & Tulving, 1975; Willoughby, Motz, & Wood, 1997).

Elaboration often consists of thinking of examples that illustrate an idea. The value of examples was demonstrated in a study in which subjects read 32 paragraphs of information about a fictitious African country (Palmere et al., 1983). Each paragraph communicated one main idea, which was followed

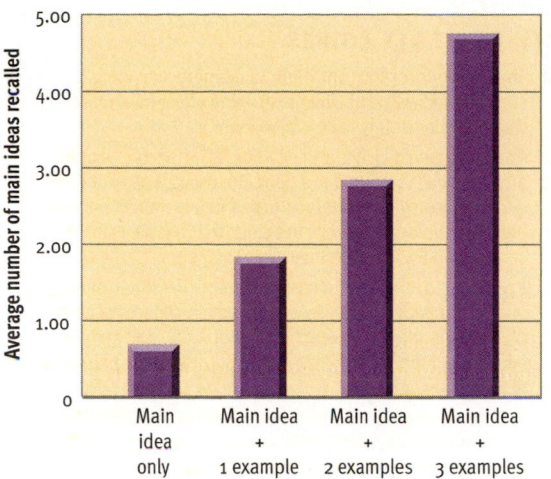

Figure 7.6

Effects of examples on retention of ideas. Palmere et al. (1983) manipulated the number of examples provided to illustrate the main idea of various paragraphs. As the number of examples increased from none to three, so did participants' retention of the main ideas. These results are consistent with the notion that elaboration enhances retention. (Data from Palmere et al., 1983)

by no example, one example, two examples, or three examples. The effect of examples on memory was dramatic. As you can see in Figure 7.6, additional examples led to better memory. In this study, the examples were provided to the students, but self-generated examples created through elaboration would probably be even more valuable in enhancing memory.

Visual Imagery

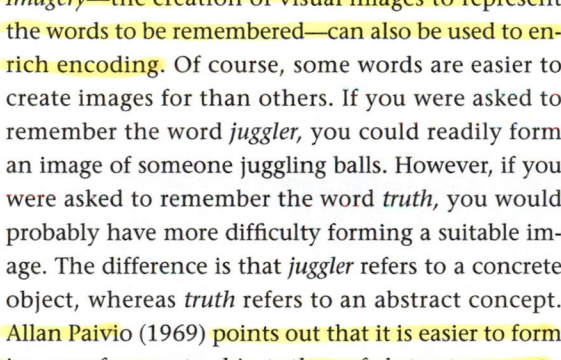 6a

Imagery—the creation of visual images to represent the words to be remembered—can also be used to enrich encoding. Of course, some words are easier to create images for than others. If you were asked to remember the word *juggler,* you could readily form an image of someone juggling balls. However, if you were asked to remember the word *truth,* you would probably have more difficulty forming a suitable image. The difference is that *juggler* refers to a concrete object, whereas *truth* refers to an abstract concept. Allan Paivio (1969) points out that it is easier to form images of concrete objects than of abstract concepts. He believes that this ease of image formation affects memory.

The beneficial effect of imagery on memory was demonstrated in a study by Paivio, Smythe, and Yuille (1968). They asked subjects to learn a list of 16 pairs of words. They manipulated whether the words were concrete, high-imagery words or abstract, low-imagery words. In terms of imagery potential, the list contained four types of pairings: high-high (*juggler-dress*),

high-low (*letter-effort*), low-high (*duty-hotel*), and low-low (*quality-necessity*). Figure 7.7 shows the recall for each type of pairing. The impact of imagery is quite evident. The best recall was of high-high pairings, and the worst recall was of low-low pairings, showing that high-imagery words are easier to remember than low-imagery words. Similar results were observed in a more recent study that controlled for additional confounding factors (Paivio, Khan, & Begg, 2000).

According to Paivio (1986), imagery facilitates memory because it provides a second kind of memory code, and two codes are better than one. His *dual-coding theory* holds that memory is enhanced by forming semantic and visual codes, since either can lead to recall. Although some aspects of dual-coding theory have been questioned, it's clear that the use of mental imagery can enhance memory in many situations (Marschark, 1992; McCauley, Eskes, & Moscovitch, 1996).

Self-Referent Encoding

Making material *personally* meaningful can also enrich encoding. For example, if you ride a bus regularly, you've probably heard the driver call out the names of the stops day in and day out for months. Do you remember all of the stops? If you haven't made an effort to memorize them, probably not. But you could probably list those that you've used, or even the ones where your friends get on or off. People's recall of information tends to be slanted in favor of material that is personally relevant (Kahan & Johnson, 1992).

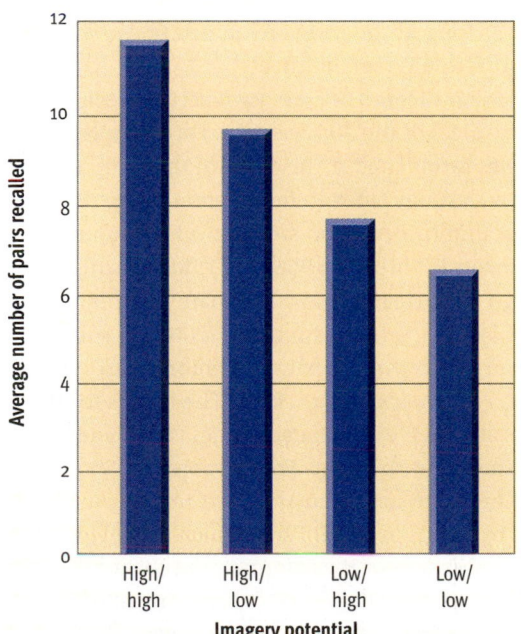

Figure 7.7

The effect of visual imagery on retention. Participants given pairs of words to remember showed better recall for high-imagery pairings than for low-imagery pairings, demonstrating that visual imagery can enrich encoding. (Data from Paivio, Smythe, & Yuille, 1968)

Self-referent encoding involves deciding how or whether information is personally relevant. This approach to encoding was compared to structural, phonemic, and semantic encoding in a study by Rogers, Kuiper, and Kirker (1977). Like Craik and Tulving (1975), these researchers manipulated encoding by asking their subjects certain kinds of questions. To induce self-referent encoding, subjects were asked to decide whether adjectives flashed on a screen applied to them personally. The results showed that self-referent encoding led to improved recall of the adjectives. Self-referent encoding appears to enhance recall by promoting additional elaboration and better organization of information (Symons & Johnson, 1997).

The value of self-referent encoding demonstrates once again that encoding plays a critical role in memory. But encoding is only one of the three key processes in memory. We turn next to the process of storage, which for many people is virtually synonymous with memory.

REVIEW OF KEY POINTS

● Three key processes contribute to memory: encoding, storage, and retrieval. The next-in-line effect illustrates that active encoding is crucial to memory.

● Attention, which facilitates encoding, is inherently selective and has been compared to a filter. The cocktail party phenomenon suggests that input is screened late in mental processing. The empirical evidence indicates that people may have some flexibility in where they place their attention filter.

● According to levels-of-processing theory, the kinds of memory codes people create depend on which aspects of a stimulus are emphasized. Structural, phonemic, and semantic encoding emphasize the structure, sound, and meaning of words, respectively.

● Deeper processing results in better recall of information. Structural, phonemic, and semantic encoding represent progressively deeper levels of processing.

● Elaboration enriches encoding by linking a stimulus to other information, such as examples of an idea. The creation of visual images to represent words can enrich encoding. Visual imagery may help by creating two memory codes rather than just one. Encoding that emphasizes personal self-reference may be especially useful in facilitating retention.

Storage: Maintaining Information in Memory

PREVIEW QUESTIONS

● What is sensory memory?

● What is the duration and capacity of the short-term store?

● What are the components of working memory?

● Is long-term storage permanent?

● Why have some theorists questioned the distinction between short-term and long-term memory?

● How is information organized and represented in memory?

In their efforts to understand memory storage, theorists have historically related it to the technologies of their age (Roediger, 1980). One of the earliest models used to explain memory storage was the wax tablet. Both Aristotle and Plato compared memory to a block of wax that differed in size and hardness for various individuals. Remembering, according to this analogy, was like stamping an impression into the wax. As long as the image remained in the wax, the memory would remain intact.

Modern theories of memory reflect the technological advances of the 20th century. For example, many theories formulated at the dawn of the computer age drew an analogy between information storage by computers and information storage in human memory (Atkinson & Shiffrin, 1968, 1971; Broadbent, 1958; Waugh & Norman, 1965). The main contribution of these *information-processing theories* was to subdivide memory into three separate memory stores (Estes, 1999; Pashler & Carrier, 1996). The names for these stores and their exact characteristics varied some from one theory to the next. For purposes of simplicity, we'll organize our discussion around the model devised by Atkinson and Shiffrin, which proved to be the most influential of the information-processing theories. According to their model, incoming information passes through two temporary storage buffers—the sensory store and short-term store—before it is transferred into a long-term store (see Figure 7.8). Like the wax tablet before it, the information-processing model of memory is a metaphor; the three memory stores are not viewed as anatomical structures in the brain, but rather as functionally distinct types of memory.

Sensory Memory 6b

The *sensory memory* preserves information in its original sensory form for a brief time, usually only

Because the image of the sparkler persists briefly in sensory memory, when the sparkler is moved fast enough, the blending of afterimages causes people to see a continuous stream of light instead of a succession of individual points.

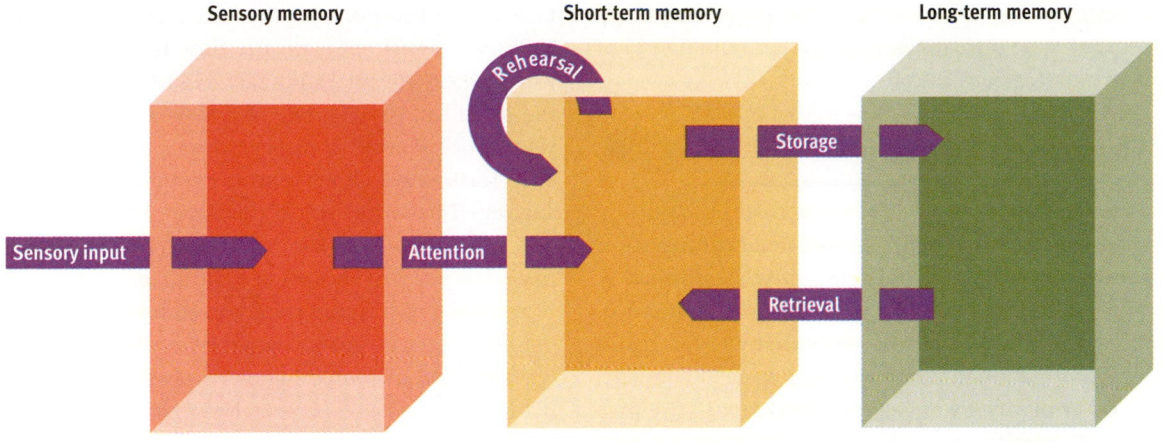

Sensory memory   Short-term memory   Long-term memory

Rehearsal

Sensory input

Attention

Storage

Retrieval

Figure 7.8

The Atkinson and Shiffrin model of memory storage. Atkinson and Shiffrin (1971) proposed that memory is made up of three information stores. *Sensory memory* can hold a large amount of information just long enough (a fraction of a second) for a small portion of it to be selected for longer storage. *Short-term memory* has a limited capacity, and unless aided by rehearsal, its storage duration is brief. *Long-term memory* can store an apparently unlimited amount of information for indeterminate periods.

a fraction of a second. Sensory memory allows the sensation of a visual pattern, sound, or touch to linger for a brief moment after the sensory stimulation is over. In the case of vision, people really perceive an *afterimage* rather than the actual stimulus. You can demonstrate the existence of afterimages for yourself by rapidly moving a lighted sparkler or flashlight in circles in the dark. If you move a sparkler fast enough, you should see a complete circle even though the light source is only a single point (see the photo on the previous page). The sensory memory preserves the sensory image long enough for you to perceive a continuous circle rather than separate points of light.

The brief preservation of sensations in sensory memory gives you additional time to try to recognize stimuli. However, you'd better take advantage of sensory storage immediately, because it doesn't last long. This fact was demonstrated in a classic experiment by George Sperling (1960). His subjects saw three rows of letters flashed on a screen for just 1/20 of a second. A tone following the exposure signaled which row of letters the subject should report to the experimenter (see Figure 7.9). Subjects were fairly accurate when the signal occurred immediately. However, their accuracy steadily declined as the delay of the tone increased to 1 second. Why? Because the memory trace in the visual sensory store decays in

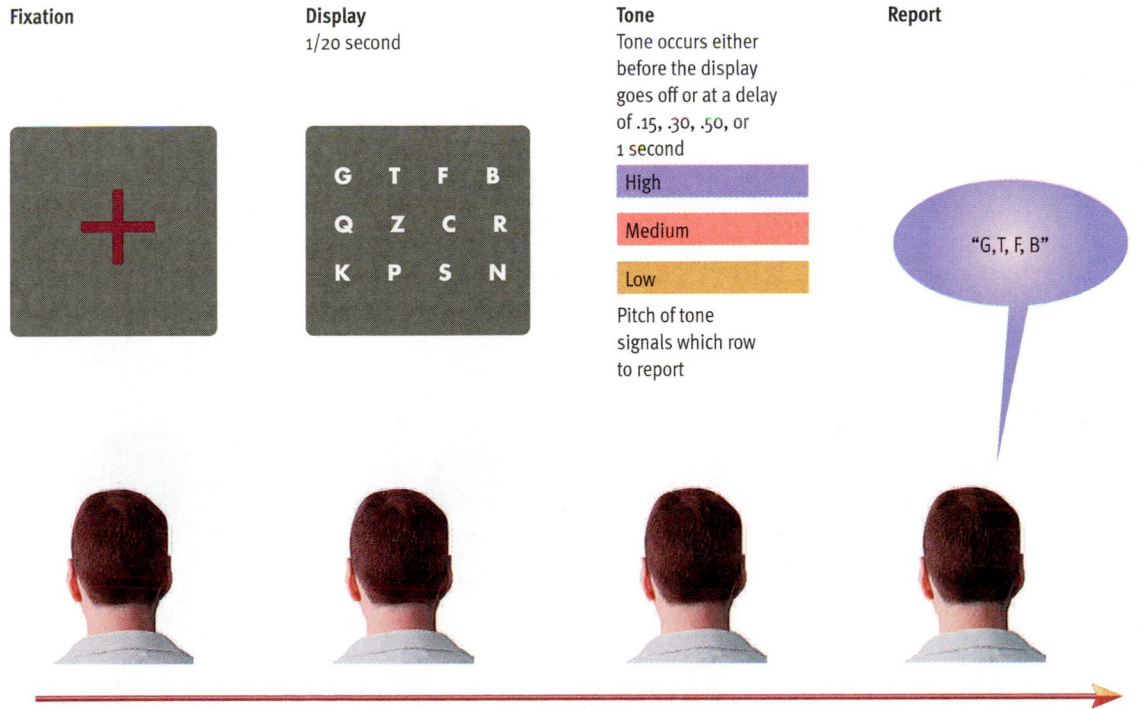

Fixation

Display
1/20 second

G T F B
Q Z C R
K P S N

Tone
Tone occurs either before the display goes off or at a delay of .15, .30, .50, or 1 second

High

Medium

Low

Pitch of tone signals which row to report

Report

"G, T, F, B"

Time (fractions of seconds)

Figure 7.9

Sperling's (1960) study of sensory memory. After the participants had fixated on the cross, the letters were flashed on the screen just long enough to create a visual afterimage. High, medium, and low tones signaled which row of letters to report. Because subjects had to rely on the afterimage to report the letters, Sperling (1960) was able to measure how rapidly the afterimage disappeared by varying the delay between the display and the signal to report.

Web Link 7.1

The Magic Number Seven Plus or Minus Two

In 1956, Princeton psychology professor George A. Miller published one of the most famous papers in the history of psychology: "The Magic Number Seven Plus or Minus Two: Some Limits on Our Capacity for Processing Information." At this site, you'll find a copy of the original text with tables so you can see why this is such an important research milestone in psychology.

about ¼ of a second. Memory traces in the auditory sensory store also appear to last approximately ¼ of a second (Massaro & Loftus, 1996).

Short-Term Memory 6b

Short-term memory (STM) is a limited-capacity store that can maintain unrehearsed information for up to about 20 seconds. In contrast, information stored in long-term memory may last weeks, months, or years. However, there is a way that you can maintain information in your short-term store indefinitely. How? Primarily, by engaging in *rehearsal—the process of repetitively verbalizing or thinking about the information.* You surely have used the rehearsal process on many occasions. For instance, when you look up a phone number, you probably recite it over and over until you can dial it. Rehearsal keeps recycling the information through your short-term memory. In theory, this recycling could go on forever, but in reality something eventually distracts you and breaks the rehearsal loop.

Durability of Storage 6b

Without rehearsal, information in short-term memory is lost in less than 20 seconds (Wickens, 1999). This rapid loss was demonstrated in a study by Peterson and Peterson (1959). They measured how long undergraduates could remember three consonants if they couldn't rehearse them. To prevent re-

hearsal, the Petersons required the students to count backward by threes from the time the consonants were presented until they saw a light that signaled the recall test (see Figure 7.10). Their results showed that subjects' recall accuracy was pretty dismal after only 15 seconds. Other approaches to the issue have suggested that the typical duration of STM storage may even be shorter (Baddely, 1986). Theorists originally believed that the loss of information from short-term memory was due purely to time-related *decay* of memory traces, but follow-up research showed that *interference* from competing material also contributes (Cowan et al., 1997; Nairne, Neath, & Serra, 1997).

Capacity of Storage 6b

Short-term memory is also limited in the number of items it can hold. The small capacity of STM was pointed out by George Miller (1956) in a famous paper called "The Magical Number Seven, Plus or Minus Two: Some Limits on Our Capacity for Processing Information." Miller noticed that people could recall only about seven items in tasks that required them to remember unfamiliar material. The common thread in these tasks, Miller argued, was that they required the use of STM. The limited capacity of STM constrains people's ability to perform tasks in which they need to mentally juggle various pieces of information (Baddeley & Hitch, 1974).

You can increase the capacity of your short-term memory by combining stimuli into larger, possibly

Figure 7.10

Peterson and Peterson's (1959) study of short-term memory. After a warning light was flashed, the participants were given three consonants to remember. The researchers prevented rehearsal by giving the subjects a three-digit number at the same time and telling them to count backward by three from that number until given the signal to recall the letters. By varying the amount of time between stimulus presentation and recall, Peterson and Peterson (1959) were able to measure how quickly information is lost from short-term memory.

Warning
Green signal light: trial about to begin

Stimulus presentation
3 letters and a 3-digit number

Retention interval
Subject counts backward by threes for intervals of 3 to 18 seconds

Recall signal and report
Red signal light: recall letters

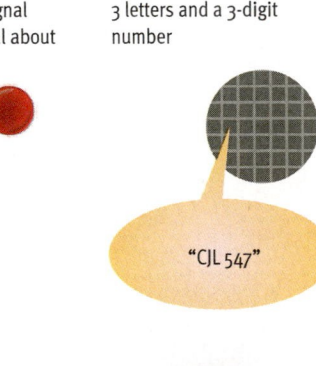

"CJL 547"

547...
544...
541...
538...
535...

"CJL ?"

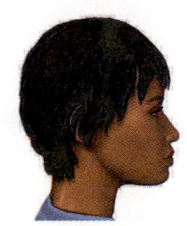

Time (seconds)

higher-order units, called *chunks* (Simon, 1974). **A chunk is a group of familiar stimuli stored as a single unit.** You can demonstrate the effect of chunking by asking someone to recall a sequence of 12 letters grouped in the following way:

FB - ITW - AC - IAIB - M

As you read the letters aloud, pause at the hyphens. Your subject will probably attempt to remember each letter separately because there are no obvious groups or chunks. But a string of 12 letters is too long for STM, so errors are likely. Now present the same string of letters to another person, but place the pauses in the following locations:

FBI - TWA - CIA - IBM

The letters now form four familiar chunks that should occupy only four slots in STM, resulting in successful recall (Bower & Springston, 1970).

To successfully chunk the letters I B M, a subject must first recognize these letters as a familiar unit. This familiarity has to be stored somewhere in long-term memory. Hence, in this case information was transferred from long-term into short-term memory. This is not unusual. People routinely draw information out of their long-term memory banks to evaluate and understand information that they are working with in short-term memory.

Short-Term Memory as "Working Memory" 6b

Research eventually uncovered a number of problems with the original model of short-term memory (Bower, 2000). Among other things, studies showed that short-term memory is *not* limited to phonemic encoding as originally thought and that decay is *not* the only process responsible for the loss of information from STM. These and other findings suggested that short-term memory involves more than a simple rehearsal buffer, as originally envisioned. To make sense of such findings, Alan Baddeley (1986, 1989, 1992) proposed a more complex, modularized model of short-term memory that characterizes it as "working memory."

The original conception of working memory consisted of three components, but Baddely (2001) has recently added a fourth element (see Figure 7.11). The first is the *phonological rehearsal loop* that represented all of STM in earlier models. This component is at work when you use recitation to temporarily hold on to a phone number. The second component in working memory is a *visuospatial sketchpad* that

permits people to temporarily hold and manipulate visual images. This component is at work when you try to mentally rearrange the furniture in your bedroom. The third component is an *executive control system*. It controls the deployment of attention, switching the focus of attention and dividing attention as needed. The fourth component is the *episodic buffer*, a temporary, limited capacity store that allows the various components of working memory to integrate information and that serves as an interface between working memory and long-term memory.

The two key characteristics that originally defined short-term memory—small capacity and short storage duration—are still present in the concept of working memory. However, Baddeley's model accounts for evidence that STM handles a greater variety of functions and depends on more complicated processes than previously thought.

Long-Term Memory 6b

Long-term memory (LTM) is an unlimited capacity store that can hold information over lengthy periods of time. Unlike sensory and short-term memory, which have very brief storage durations, LTM can store information indefinitely. In fact, one point of view is that all information stored in long-term memory is stored there *permanently*. According to this view, forgetting occurs only because people sometimes cannot *retrieve* needed information from LTM.

The notion that LTM storage may be permanent is certainly intriguing. A couple of interesting lines of research have seemed to provide compelling evidence of permanent storage. However, each line of research turns out to be less compelling than it appears at first glance. The first line of research consisted of some landmark studies conducted by Cana-

"The Magical Number Seven, Plus or Minus Two."
GEORGE MILLER

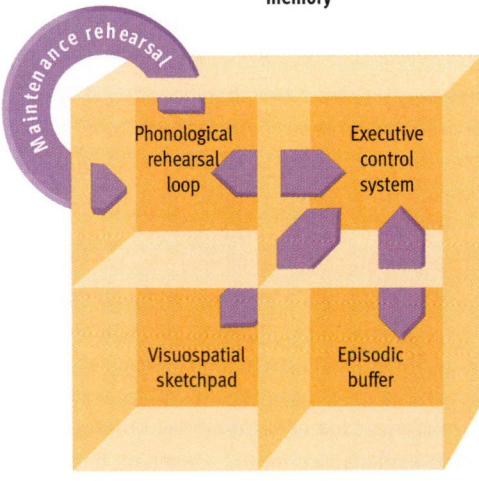

Working (short-term) memory

Maintenance rehearsal

Phonological rehearsal loop

Executive control system

Visuospatial sketchpad

Episodic buffer

Figure 7.11

Short-term memory as working memory. This diagram depicts the revised model of the short-term store proposed by Alan Baddeley. According to Baddeley (2001), working memory includes four components: a phonological rehearsal loop, a visuospatial sketchpad, an executive control system, and an episodic buffer.

Flashbulb memories are vivid and detailed recollections of momentous events. For example, many people will long remember exactly where they were and how they felt when they learned about the terrorist attacks on the World Trade Center.

The second line of research centers on the phenomenon of *flashbulb memories,* which are unusually vivid and detailed recollections of momentous events. For instance, many older adults in the United States can remember exactly where they were, what they were doing, and how they felt when they learned that President John F. Kennedy had been shot. You may have a similar recollection related to the death of Princess Diana or the terrorist attacks that took place in New York and Washington, DC, on September 11, 2001. The vivid detail of people's memories of President Kennedy's assassination 40 years ago would seem to provide a striking example of permanent storage.

So, why don't these lines of evidence demonstrate that LTM storage is permanent? Let's look at each. Closer scrutiny eventually showed that the remarkable "memories" activated by ESB in Penfield's studies often included major distortions or factual impossibilities. For instance, the person who recalled being in a lumberyard had never actually been to one. The ESB-induced recollections of Penfield's subjects apparently were hallucinations, dreams, or loose reconstructions of events rather than exact replays of the past (Squire, 1987). In a similar vein, subsequent research has undermined the notion that flashbulb memories represent an instance of permanent storage. Although flashbulb memories tend to be strong, vivid, and detailed, studies suggest that they are neither as accurate nor as special as once believed (Neisser & Harsch, 1992). Like other memories, they become less detailed and complete with time and are often inaccurate (McCloskey, 1992; Weaver, 1993). This observation brings us to our Featured Study for this chapter, which examined the accuracy of students' flashbulb memories of the announcement of the verdict in the 1995 O. J. Simpson murder trial.

dian neuroscientist Wilder Penfield in the 1960s. He reported triggering long-lost memories through electrical stimulation of the brain (ESB) during brain surgeries (Penfield & Perot, 1963). When Penfield used ESB (see Chapter 3) to map brain function in patients undergoing surgery for epilepsy, he found that stimulation of the temporal lobe sometimes elicited vivid descriptions of events long past. Patients would describe events that apparently came from their childhood—such as "being in a lumberyard" or "watching Mom make a phone call"—as if they were there once again. Penfield and others inferred that these descriptions were exact playbacks of long-lost memories unearthed by electrical stimulation of the brain.

FEATURED STUDY

How Accurate Are Flashbulb Memories?

Investigators: H. Schmolck, E. A. Buffalo, and L. R. Squire (University of California, San Diego)

Source: Memory distortions develop over time: Recollections of the O. J. Simpson trial verdict after 15 and 32 months. *Psychological Science,* 2000, *11*, 39–45.

Studies have yielded somewhat inconsistent findings regarding the accuracy of flashbulb memories. When researchers have chosen to evaluate participants' memories 7 to 12 months after a momentous event, distortions invariably are found in some subjects, but one could characterize subjects' overall memory performance as reasonably accurate. However, when researchers have chosen to assess flashbulb memories after a time span of about three years, participants' accuracy has been mediocre. This discrepancy could simply mean that flashbulb memories fade with time—like other memories—but other explanations for the discrepant findings could

not be ruled out because the relevant studies focused on different notable events, used different types of samples, and varied methods of measuring memory accuracy. Hence, the present research was designed to examine both time intervals in a single study that focused on the same event. The event was the announcement of the verdict in the O. J. Simpson murder trial that had held the world spellbound for months in 1995.

Method

Participants. Students in an undergraduate psychology class completed a questionnaire three days after the announcement of the Simpson verdict. The subjects were then divided into two groups that were matched for the intensity of their reported emotional reactions and for whether they agreed with the verdict. One group was contacted 15 months after the verdict and the other group was contacted 32 months after the verdict. The follow-up questionnaires were completed by 28 members of the first group (evaluated at 15 months) and 35 members of the second group (evaluated at 32 months). At follow-up, roughly 80% of the subjects in both groups met the usual criteria (based on Brown & Kulik, 1977) for having a flashbulb memory of the Simpson verdict announcement.

Materials. The questionnaire administered three days after the verdict and many months later asked subjects nine specific questions about their experiences, such as: What time was it when you first heard the news of the verdict? Where were you? What were you doing? Who told you? Participants were also asked to write a paragraph describing how they heard about the verdict and to rate their emotional reaction to it and their agreement with it. The follow-up questionnaire also asked participants to rate how confident they were about the accuracy of their recollections.

Results

The principal finding was that recollections containing no distortions predominated at 15 months, whereas recollections containing major distortions predominated at 32 months. After a 32-month time interval, over 40% of subjects' recollections contained major distortions and more than 30% contained minor distortions (see Figure 7.12). Interestingly, 61% of the subjects who exhibited major memory distortions indicated that they had high confidence in their recollections.

Discussion

The authors conclude that flashbulb memories fade gradually over time, just like other memories, and that flashbulb memories are not all that accurate just three years after a momentous event. They also interpret their findings as undermining the notion that flashbulb memo-

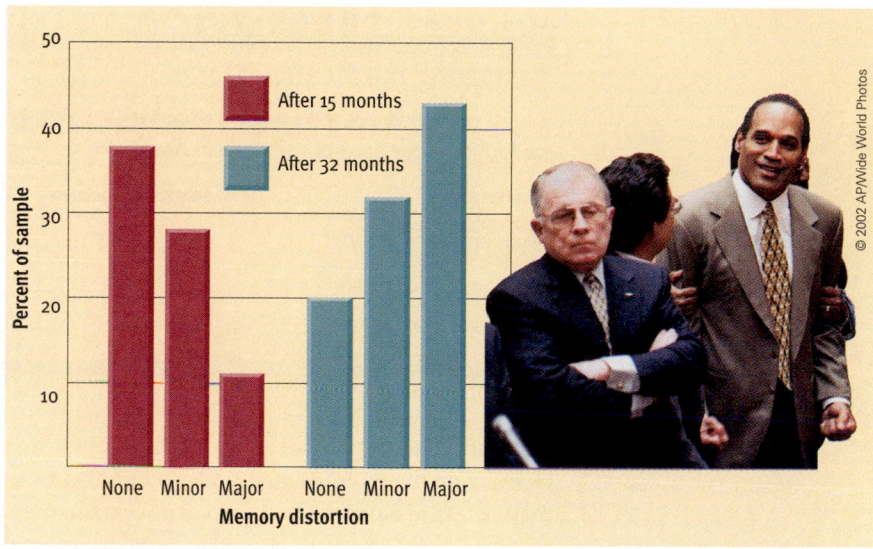

Figure 7.12

Accuracy of flashbulb memories. Schmolck, Buffalo, and Squire (2000) assessed the accuracy of participants' flashbulb memories of the announcement of the O. J. Simpson murder trial verdict after 15 and 32 months. As you can see, there was a substantial deterioration in subjects' recollections between 15 and 32 months, and distorted memories were quite common after 32 months. (Note: The two sets of numbers do not add up to 100% because the graph does not include subjects who were scored as "don't remember.")

SOURCE: Schmolck, H., Buffalo, E. A., & Squire, L. R. (2000). Memory distortions develop over time: Recollections of the O. J. Simpson trial verdict after 15 and 32 months. *Psychological Science, 11,* 39–45. Blackwell Publishers. Reprinted by permission.

ries have special characteristics that make them less vulnerable to forgetting than ordinary memories.

Comment

This research was featured because it examined a very timely question in light of the September 2001 terrorist attacks in the United States. If ever there was a momentous event that ought to create indelible memories, it ought to be the 9/11 attacks. Many flashbulb memory investigations were launched in the aftermath of the traumatic assaults on the World Trade Center and the Pentagon, and it will be interesting to see what these studies discover in the years ahead. This study was also featured because it demonstrates that human memory is not as reliable as we assume it to be, a conclusion that will be echoed throughout this chapter. ■

Returning to the question at hand, the results of our Featured Study clearly conflict with the hypothesis that memory storage is permanent. Although the possibility cannot be ruled out completely, there is no convincing evidence that memories are stored away permanently and that forgetting is all a matter of retrieval failure (Payne & Blackwell, 1998; Schacter, 1996).

Are Short-Term Memory and Long-Term Memory Really Separate?

The partitioning of memory into the sensory, short-term, and long-term stores has dominated thinking about memory for many decades, but over the years some theorists have expressed doubts about whether there really are separate memory stores. A handful

Comparing the Memory Stores

Check your understanding of the three memory stores by filling in the blanks in the table below. The answers can be found in the back of the book in Appendix A.

Feature	Sensory memory	Short-term memory	Long-term memory
Main encoding format	*copy of input*	_____	*largely semantic*
Storage capacity	*limited*	_____	_____
Storage duration	_____	*up to 20 seconds*	_____

of theorists have questioned the concept of sensory memory on the grounds that it may be nothing more than perceptual processes at work, rather than memory. A larger number of theorists have questioned the concept of short-term memory on the grounds that it really isn't all that different from long-term memory (Crowder, 1993; Healy & McNamara, 1996; Nairne, 1996). The view of short-term memory and long-term memory as independent systems was originally based, in part, on the belief that they depended on different types of encoding and were subject to different mechanisms of forgetting. STM was thought to depend on *phonemic* encoding (based on sound), whereas LTM encoding was thought to be largely *semantic* (based on meaning). Information loss from STM was believed to be mostly due to time-related *decay,* whereas *interference* was viewed as the principal mechanism of LTM forgetting. However, decades of research have undermined both of these distinctions, as both semantic encoding and interference effects have been found in research on short-term memory (Meiser & Klauer, 1999; Walker & Hulme, 1999).

How do theorists who doubt the existence of separate memory stores view the structure of memory?

Their views vary considerably (Nairne, 2002). One perspective is to view short-term memory as a tiny and constantly changing portion of long-term memory that happens to be in a heightened state of activation (Cowan, 1995). Other, more radical views assert that there is a single, unitary, "generic" memory store that is governed by one set of rules and processes (Nairne, 2001). The outcome of the debate about whether there are separate memory stores is difficult to predict. At present, the multiple stores viewpoint remains dominant, but alternative approaches are becoming increasingly influential.

How Is Knowledge Represented and Organized in Memory?

Over the years memory researchers have wrestled endlessly with another major question relating to memory storage: How is knowledge represented and organized in memory? In other words, what forms do our mental representations of information take? Most theorists seem to agree that our mental representations probably take a variety of forms, depending on the nature of the material that needs to be tucked away in memory. For example, memories of visual scenes, of how to perform actions (such as typing or hitting a backhand stroke in tennis), and of factual information (such as definitions or dates in history) are probably represented and organized in very different ways. Most of the theorizing to date has focused on how factual knowledge may be represented in memory. In this section, we'll look at a small sample of the organizational structures that have been proposed for semantic information.

Clustering and Conceptual Hierarchies

If you were to memorize the list of 60 words in Figure 7.13, your recall of the list at a later time would demonstrate how the mind spontaneously organizes information stored in memory. Each of the words

Figure 7.13

Clustering. The words in this list fall into four categories: animals, men's names, vegetables, and professions. Even when the words are presented in mixed order, people tend to recall them in these groupings. This phenomenon is called clustering.

SOURCE: Adapted from Bousfield, W. A. (1953). The occurrence of clustering in the recall of randomly arranged associates. *Journal of General Psychology, 49,* 229–240. Published by Heldref Publications. Reprinted with permission of the Helen Dwight Reid Education Foundation.

Giraffe	Plumber	Owen	Lettuce
Parsnip	Otto	Parsley	Donkey
Zebra	Noah	Otter	Blacksmith
Radish	Chipmunk	Grocer	Eggplant
Diver	Adam	Badger	Garlic
Broker	Chemist	Camel	Wildcat
Spinach	Turnip	Baboon	Jason
Baker	Simon	Florist	Leopard
Woodchuck	Howard	Rhubarb	Printer
Dancer	Milkman	Melon	Bernard
Weasel	Gerard	Mustard	Carrot
Pumpkin	Panther	Wallace	Sherman
Amos	Oswald	Dentist	Waiter
Typist	Druggist	Muskrat	Moses
Byron	Reindeer	Mushroom	Cabbage

in this list fits into one of four categories: animals, men's names, vegetables, or professions. Bousfield (1953) showed that subjects recalling this list engage in clustering. *Clustering* **is the tendency to remember similar or related items in groups.** Even though the words are not presented in organized groups, you would tend to remember them in bunches that belong in the same category.

Factual information is routinely represented in categories, and when possible, this information is organized into conceptual hierarchies. **A** *conceptual hierarchy* **is a multilevel classification system based on common properties among items.** A conceptual hierarchy that a person might construct for minerals can be found in Figure 7.14. According to Gordon Bower (1970), organizing information into a conceptual hierarchy can improve recall dramatically.

Schemas 6b

Imagine that you've just visited Professor Smith's office, which is shown in the adjacent photo. Take a brief look at the photo and then cover it up. Now pretend that you want to describe Professor Smith's office to a friend. Write down what you saw in the office (the picture).

After you finish, compare your description with the picture. Chances are, your description will include elements—books or filing cabinets, for instance—that were *not* in the office. This common phenomenon demonstrates how *schemas* can influence memory. **A** *schema* **is an organized cluster of knowledge about a particular object or event abstracted from previous experience with the object or event.** For example, college students have schemas for what professors' offices are like. When Brewer and Treyens (1981) tested the recall of 30 subjects who had briefly visited the office shown in the photo, most subjects recalled the desks and chairs, but few recalled the

Courtesy of W. F. Brewer

wine bottle or the picnic basket, which aren't part of a typical office schema. Moreover, nine subjects in the Brewer and Treyens study falsely recalled that the office contained books. Perhaps you made the same mistake.

These results suggest that *people are more likely to remember things that are consistent with their schemas than things that are not*. Although this principle seems applicable much of the time, the inverse is also true: *people sometimes exhibit better recall of things that violate their schema-based expectations* (Rojahn & Pettigrew, 1992). If information really clashes with a schema, it may attract extra attention and deeper processing and become very memorable. Thus, the impact of schemas on memory can be difficult to predict, but either way

Professor Smith's office is shown in this photo. Follow the instructions in the text to learn how Brewer and Treyens (1981) used it in a study of memory.

Level					
1			Minerals		
2		Metals		Stones	
3	Rare	Common	Alloys	Precious	Masonry
4	Platinum Silver Gold	Aluminum Copper Lead Iron	Bronze Steel Brass	Sapphire Emerald Diamond Ruby	Limestone Granite Marble Slate

Figure 7.14

Conceptual hierarchies and long-term memory. Some types of information can be organized into a multilevel hierarchy of concepts, like the one shown here, which was studied by Bower and others (1969). They found that subjects remember more information when they organize it into a conceptual hierarchy.

SOURCE: Adapted from Bower, G. (1970). Organizational factors in memory. *Cognitive Psychology, 1* (1), 18–46. Copyright © 1970 Elsevier Science USA, reproduced with permission from the publisher.

Web Link 7.2

Memory Principles
This brief overview of practical guidelines for improving recall of academic material is maintained by Carolyn Hopper at Middle Tennessee State University. Ten basic principles are outlined succinctly. Elsewhere at this site you will find other worthwhile materials intended to help students improve their study techniques.

it is apparent that information stored in memory is often organized around schemas.

Semantic Networks

Of course, not all information fits neatly into conceptual hierarchies or schemas. Much knowledge seems to be organized into less systematic frameworks, called semantic networks (Collins & Loftus, 1975). A *semantic network* consists of nodes representing concepts, joined together by pathways that link related concepts. A small semantic network is shown in Figure 7.15. The ovals are the nodes, and the words inside the ovals are the interlinked concepts. The lines connecting the nodes are the pathways. A more detailed figure would label the pathways to show how the concepts are related to one another. However, in this instance, the relations should be fairly clear. The length of each pathway represents the degree of association between two concepts. Shorter pathways imply stronger associations.

Semantic networks have proven useful in explaining why thinking about one word (such as *butter*) can make a closely related word (such as *bread*) easier to remember (Meyer & Schvaneveldt, 1976). According to Collins and Loftus (1975), when people think about a word, their thoughts naturally go to related words. These theorists call this process *spreading activation* within a semantic network. They assume that activation spreads out along the pathways of the semantic network surrounding the word. They also theorize that the strength of this activation decreases as it

travels outward, much as ripples decrease in size as they radiate outward from a rock tossed into a pond. Consider again the semantic network shown in Figure 7.15. If subjects see the word *red*, words that are closely linked to it (such as *orange*) should be easier to recall than words that have longer links (such as *sunrises*).

Connectionist Networks and Parallel Distributed Processing (PDP) Models

Instead of taking their cue from how computers process information, *connectionist models* of memory take their inspiration from how neural networks appear to handle information. As we noted in our discussion of visual perception in Chapter 4, the human brain appears to depend extensively on *parallel distributed processing*—that is, simultaneous processing of the same information that is spread across networks of neurons. Based on this insight and basic findings about how neurons operate, *connectionist*, or *parallel distributed processing (PDP), models* assume that cognitive processes depend on patterns of activation in highly interconnected computational networks that resemble neural networks (McClelland, 2000; McClelland & Rumelhart, 1985; Smolensky, 1995). A PDP system consists of a large network of interconnected computing units, or *nodes,* that operate much like neurons. These nodes may be inactive or they may send either excitatory or inhibitory signals to other units. Like an individual neuron, a specific node's level of activation reflects the weighted

Figure 7.15

A semantic network. Much of the organization of long-term memory depends on networks of associations among concepts. In this highly simplified depiction of a fragment of a semantic network, the shorter the line linking any two concepts, the stronger the association between them. The coloration of the concept boxes represents activation of the concepts. This is how the network might look just after a person hears the words *fire engine.*

Source: Adapted from Collins, A. M., & Loftus, E. F. (1975). A spreading activation theory of semantic processing. *Psychological Review, 82,* 407–428. Copyright © 1975 by the American Psychological Association. Adapted by permission of the authors.

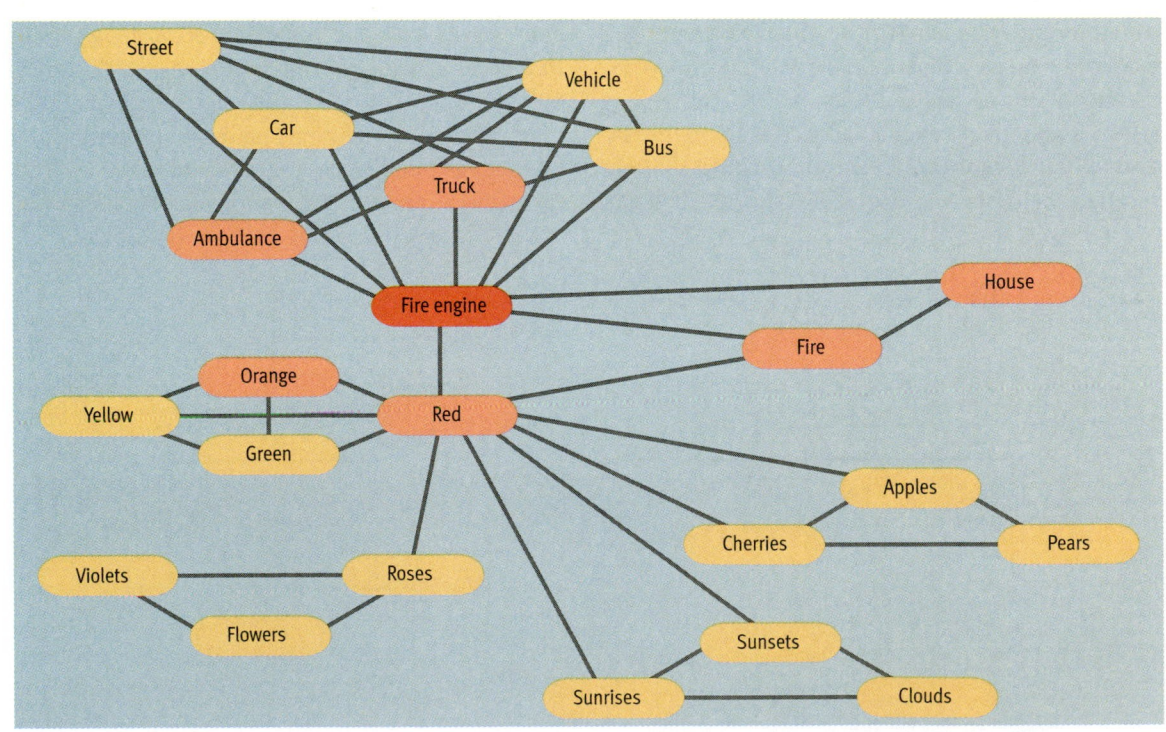

balance of excitatory and inhibitory inputs from many other units. Given this framework, *PDP models assert that specific memories correspond to particular patterns of activation in these networks* (McClelland, 1992). Connectionist networks bear some superficial resemblance to semantic networks, but there is a crucial difference. In semantic networks, specific nodes represent specific concepts or pieces of knowledge. In connectionist networks, a piece of knowledge is represented by a particular *pattern* of activation across an entire network. Thus, the information lies in the strengths of the *connections,* which is why the PDP approach is called "connectionism."

I hasten to note that PDP models are much more general in scope than the other organizational structures that we have discussed in this section. Conceptual hierarchies, schemas, and semantic networks are largely limited to explaining how factual information might be represented in memory. In contrast, other forms of knowledge, such as memory for visual images or motor skills, could be explained with connectionist networks. In fact, PDP models have been applied to a broad range of phenomena, including perception, learning, problem solving, and decision making. Indeed, PDP models have provided a fresh, new way of thinking about cognitive processes in general (Clark, 1997).

What are the strengths of the PDP approach? For one thing, connectionist models provide a highly plausible account for how mental structures may be derived from neural structures. In other words, they make sense in light of what research has revealed about neurophysiology. Another strength is that the emphasis on parallel processing seems to explain the blazing speed of humans' cognitive functioning more persuasively than alternative models do. You may not always *feel* like your mental processes are blaz-

ingly fast, but the reality is that a routine act like recognizing a complex visual stimulus typically takes a scant 300 milliseconds. Most other models implicitly assume that thinking involves *serial processing,* which requires executing operations in a single sequence. However, serial processing appears much too slow to account for how the brain fires millions of neural impulses to accomplish simple actions.

REVIEW OF KEY POINTS

- Information-processing theories of memory assert that people have three kinds of memory stores: a sensory memory, a short-term memory, and a long-term memory. The sensory store preserves information in its original form, probably for only a fraction of a second.

- Short-term memory has a limited capacity of about seven chunks of information. STM can maintain unrehearsed information for up to about 20 seconds. Short-term memory is working memory, and it appears to involve more than a simple rehearsal loop. According to Baddeley, working memory also includes a visuospatial sketchpad, an executive control system, and an episodic buffer.

- Long-term memory is an unlimited capacity store that may hold information indefinitely. Penfield's ESB research and the existence of flashbulb memories suggest that LTM storage may be permanent, but the evidence is not convincing. Our Featured Study showed that flashbulb memories are not as accurate as claimed. Some theorists have questioned the distinction between short-term and long-term memory.

- Information in long-term memory can be organized in simple clusters or multilevel classification systems called conceptual hierarchies. A schema is an organized cluster of knowledge about a particular object or sequence of events.

- Semantic networks consist of concepts joined by pathways. Research suggests that activation spreads along the paths of semantic networks to activate closely associated words. Parallel distributed processing models of memory assert that specific memories correspond to particular patterns of activation in connectionist networks.

Web Link 7.3

Mind Tools—Tools for Improving Your Memory
The Mind Tools site details practical techniques to help people improve their cognitive efficiency in many areas. The subpage dedicated to memory functioning offers an excellent collection of suggestions for ways to enhance memory.

Retrieval: Getting Information Out of Memory

Entering information into long-term memory is a worthy goal, but an insufficient one if you can't get the information back out again when you need it. Some theorists maintain that understanding retrieval is the key to understanding human memory (Roediger, 2000).

Using Cues to Aid Retrieval

At the beginning of this chapter we discussed the *tip-of-the-tongue phenomenon—the temporary in-*

ability to remember something you know, accompanied by a feeling that it's just out of reach. The tip-of-the-tongue phenomenon is a common experience that is typically triggered by a name that one can't quite recall. Most people experience this temporary frustration about once a week, although its occurrence increases with age (A. Brown, 1991). The tip-of-the-tongue phenomenon clearly constitutes a failure in retrieval. However, the exact mechanisms underlying this failure are the subject of debate, as a host of explanations have been

PREVIEW QUESTIONS

- What does the tip-of-the-tongue phenomenon reveal about memory?
- Why does reinstating the context of an event aid in its recall?
- What is the misinformation effect?
- How can source-monitoring errors shed light on eyewitness suggestibility and inadvertent plagiarism?
- What is reality monitoring?

proposed for the tip-of-the-tongue phenomenon (Schwartz, 1999).

Fortunately, memories can often be jogged with *retrieval cues*—stimuli that help gain access to memories. This was apparent when Roger Brown and David McNeill (1966) studied the tip-of-the-tongue phenomenon. They gave subjects definitions of obscure words and asked them to come up with the words. Our example at the beginning of the chapter (the definition for *nepotism*) was taken from their study. Brown and McNeill found that subjects groping for obscure words were correct in guessing the first letter of the missing word 57% of the time. This figure far exceeds chance and shows that partial recollections are often headed in the right direction.

Reinstating the Context of an Event

Let's test your memory: What did you have for breakfast two days ago? If you can't immediately answer, you might begin by imagining yourself sitting at the breakfast table. Trying to recall an event by putting yourself back in the context in which it occurred involves working with *context cues* to aid retrieval.

Context cues often facilitate the retrieval of information (Smith, 1988). Most people have experienced the effects of context cues on many occasions. For instance, when people return after a number of years to a place where they used to live, they typically are flooded with long-forgotten memories. Or consider how often you have gone from one room to another to get something (scissors, perhaps), only to discover that you can't remember what you were after. However, when you return to the first room (the original context), you suddenly recall what it was ("Of course, the scissors!"). These examples illustrate the potentially powerful effects of context cues on memory.

The technique of reinstating the context of an event has been used effectively in legal investigations to enhance eyewitness recall (Chandler & Fisher, 1996). The eyewitness may be encouraged to retrieve information about a crime by replaying the sequence of events. The value of reinstating the context of an event may account for how hypnosis occasionally stimulates eyewitness recall (Meyer, 1992). The hypnotist usually attempts to reinstate the context of the event by telling the witness to imagine being at the scene of the crime once again. Unfortunately, research suggests that hypnosis often increases subjects' tendencies to report *incorrect* information (Lynn et al., 1997; McConkey, Barnier, & Sheehan, 1998). Concerns about the accuracy of hypnosis-aided recall have led courts to be cautious about allowing hypnosis-aided recollections as admissible testimony.

Reconstructing Memories and the Misinformation Effect

When you retrieve information from long-term memory, you're not able to pull up a "mental videotape" that provides an exact replay of the past. To some extent, your memories are sketchy *reconstructions* of the past that may be distorted and may include details that did not actually occur (Roediger, Wheeler, & Rajaram, 1993). The reconstructive nature of memory was first highlighted many years ago by Sir Frederic Bartlett, a prominent English psychologist. Bartlett (1932) had his subjects read the tale "War of the Ghosts," reproduced in Figure 7.16. Subjects read the story twice and waited 15 minutes. Then they were asked to write down the tale as best they could recall it.

What did Bartlett find? As you might expect, subjects condensed the story, leaving out boring details. Of greater interest was Bartlett's discovery that subjects frequently *changed* the tale to some extent. The canoe became a boat or the two young men were

Figure 7.16

A story used in a study of reconstructive memory by Bartlett (1932). Subjects recalling the story tended to change details and to "remember" elements not in the original at all.

SOURCE: Excerpt from Bartlett, F. C. (1932). *Remembering: A study in experimental and social psychology.* New York: Cambridge University Press, p. 65. Copyright © 1932. Reprinted with the permission of Cambridge University Press.

WAR OF THE GHOSTS

One night two young men from Egulac went down to the river to hunt seals, and while they were there it became foggy and calm. Then they heard war cries, and they thought: "Maybe this is a war party." They escaped to the shore, and hid behind a log. Now canoes came up, and they heard the noise of paddles, and saw one canoe coming up to them. There were five men in the canoe, and they said:

"What do you think? We wish to take you along. We are going up the river to make war on the people."

One of the young men said: "I have no arrows."

"Arrows are in the canoe," they said.

"I will not go along. I might be killed. My relatives do not know where I have gone. But you," he said, turning to the other, "may go with them."

So one of the young men went, but the other returned home.

And the warriors went up to the river to a town on the other side of Kalama. The people came down to the water, and they began to fight, and many were killed. But presently the young man heard one of the warriors say: "Quick, let us go home: that Indian has been hit." Now he thought: "Oh, they are ghosts." He did not feel sick, but they said he had been shot.

So the canoes went back to Egulac and the young man went ashore to his house, and made a fire. And he told everybody and said: "Behold I accompanied the ghosts, and we went to fight. Many of our fellows were killed, and many of those who attacked us were killed. They said I was hit, and I did not feel sick."

He told it all, and then he became quiet. When the sun rose he fell down. Something black came out of his mouth. His face became contorted. The people jumped up and cried.

He was dead.

hunting beavers instead of seals. Subjects often introduced entirely *new elements* and twists. For instance, in one case, the death at the end was attributed to fever and the character was described as "foaming at the mouth" (instead of "something black came out of his mouth"). Bartlett concluded that the distortions in recall occurred because subjects reconstructed the tale to fit with their established schemas. Modern schema theories also emphasize the reconstructive nature of memory (Hirt, McDonald, & Markman, 1998). These theories propose that part of what people recall about an event is the details of that particular event and part is a reconstruction of the event based on their schemas.

Research by Elizabeth Loftus (1979, 1992) and others on the *misinformation effect* has shown that reconstructive distortions show up frequently in eyewitness testimony. Studies of the misinformation effect include three stages. In the first stage, subjects view an event. In the second stage, they are exposed to information about this event, some of which is misleading. In the third stage, their recall of the original event is tested to see if the postevent misinformation altered their memory of the original event. For example, in one study Loftus and Palmer (1974) showed subjects a videotape of an automobile accident. Subjects were then "grilled" as if they were providing eyewitness testimony, and biasing information was introduced. Some subjects were asked, "How fast were the cars going when they *hit* each other?" Other subjects were asked, "How fast were the cars going when they *smashed into* each other?" A week later, subjects' recall of the accident was tested and they were asked whether they remembered seeing any broken glass in the accident (there was none). Subjects who had earlier been asked about the cars *smashing into* each other were more likely to "recall" broken glass. Why would they add this detail to their reconstructions of the accident? Probably because broken glass is consistent with their schema for cars *smashing* together (see Figure 7.17).

The misinformation effect has been replicated in numerous studies by Loftus and other researchers (Ayers & Reder, 1998; Lindsay, 1993). Indeed, the effect is difficult to escape, as even subjects who have been forewarned can be swayed by postevent misinformation (Koriat, Goldsmith, & Pansky, 2000). However, there is considerable debate about the mechanisms underlying the effect (Ceci & Bruck, 1993). Loftus (1979) has argued for an "overwriting" explanation in which the new misinformation destroys and replaces the original memory of the event (much

like saving a new version of a file on a computer). An alternative explanation is that the new misinformation interferes with the retrieval of the original memory (Chandler, 1991). Other theorists argue that subjects can access both the original memory and the altered memory but have difficulty distinguishing which one was the original (Lindsay & Johnson, 1989). This explanation attributes the misinformation effect to difficulties in *source monitoring*, an interesting memory process that we'll discuss next. A review of the extensive evidence on the misinformation effect concluded that all three proposed mechanisms probably contribute to this phenomenon (Ayers & Reder, 1998).

Source Monitoring and Reality Monitoring

The misinformation effect appears to be due, in part, to the unreliability of source monitoring (Mitchell & Johnson, 2000). *Source monitoring is the process of making attributions about the origins of memories.* Marcia Johnson and her colleagues maintain that source monitoring is a crucial facet of memory retrieval that contributes to many of the mistakes that people make in reconstructing their experiences (Johnson, 1996; Johnson, Hashtroudi, & Lindsay, 1993). According to Johnson, memories are not tagged with labels that specify their sources. Hence, when people pull up specific memory records, they have to make decisions *at the time of retrieval* about where the memories came from (example: "Did I read that in the *New York Times* or *Rolling Stone*?"). Much of the time, these decisions are so easy and automatic, people make them without being consciously aware of the source-monitoring process. In other instances,

University of Washington News and Information Office

❝One reason most of us, as jurors, place so much faith in *eyewitness testimony* is that we *are* unaware of how many factors influence its accuracy.❞
ELIZABETH LOFTUS

Figure 7.17

The misinformation effect.
In an experiment by Loftus and Palmer (1974), participants who were asked leading questions in which cars were described as *hitting* or *smashing* each other were prone to recall the same accident differently one week later, demonstrating the reconstructive nature of memory.

Leading question asked during witness testimony	Possible schemas activated	Response of subjects asked one week later, "Did you see any broken glass?" (There was none.)
"About how fast were the cars going when they hit each other?"		"Yes"—14%
"About how fast were the cars going when they smashed into each other?"		"Yes"—32%

Denise Applewhite/Communications Department, Princeton University

"Our long-term goal is to develop ways of determining which aspects of mental experience create one's sense of a personal past and one's conviction (accurate or not) that memories, knowledge, beliefs, attitudes, and feelings are tied to reality in a veridical fashion."
MARCIA K. JOHNSON

however, they may consciously struggle to pinpoint the source of a memory. **A *source-monitoring error* occurs when a memory derived from one source is misattributed to another source.** For example, you might attribute something that your roommate said to your psychology professor, or something you heard on *Oprah* to your psychology textbook. Inaccurate memories that reflect source-monitoring errors may seem quite compelling, and people often feel quite confident about their authenticity even though the recollections really are inaccurate (Lampinen, Neuschatz, & Payne, 1999).

Source-monitoring errors appear to be commonplace and may shed light on many interesting memory phenomena. For instance, in studies of eyewitness suggestibility, some subjects have gone so far as to insist that they "remember" seeing something that was only verbally suggested to them. Most theories have a hard time explaining how people can have memories of events that they never actually saw or experienced, but this paradox doesn't seem all that perplexing when it is explained as a source-monitoring error. The source-monitoring approach can also make sense of *cryptomnesia*—inadvertent plagiarism that occurs when people come up with an idea that they think is original, when they were actually exposed to it earlier (Landau & Marsh, 1997). Source-monitoring errors also appear to underlie the common tendency for people to mix up fictional information from novels and movies with factual information from news reports and personal experiences. For example, a veteran of the Vietnam war might unwittingly describe a scene from the movie *Apocalypse Now* as a personal experience from his war days.

Marcia Johnson's source-monitoring theory has built and expanded on an earlier concept that she called *reality monitoring*, which she now views as a subtype of source monitoring. **Reality monitoring refers to the process of deciding whether memories are based on external sources (one's perceptions of actual events) or internal sources (one's thoughts and imaginations).** People engage in reality monitoring when they reflect on whether something actually happened or they only thought about it happening. This dilemma may sound like an odd problem that would arise only infrequently, but it isn't. People routinely ponder questions like "Did I pack the umbrella or only think about packing it?" "Did I take my morning pill or only intend to do so?" "Did I turn off the stove, or did I imagine doing it?" Studies indicate that people focus on several types of clues in making their reality-monitoring decisions (Johnson & Raye, 1981; Johnson, Kahan, & Raye, 1984; Kahan et al., 1999). When memories are rich in sensory information (you can recall the feel of shoving the umbrella into your suitcase) or contextual information (you can clearly see yourself in the hallway packing your umbrella), or when memories can be retrieved with little effort, one is more likely to infer that the event really happened. In contrast, one is more likely to infer that an event did *not* actually occur when memories of it lack sensory or contextual details or are difficult to retrieve.

REVIEW OF KEY POINTS

- The tip-of-the-tongue phenomenon shows that recall is often guided by partial information about a word. Reinstating the context of an event can facilitate recall. This factor may account for cases in which hypnosis appears to aid recall of previously forgotten information. However, hypnosis seems to increase people's tendency to report incorrect information.

- Memories are not exact replicas of past experiences. As Bartlett showed many years ago, memory is partially reconstructive. Research on the misinformation effect shows that information learned after an event can alter one's memory of it.

- Source monitoring is the process of making attributions about the origins of memories. Source-monitoring errors appear to be common and may explain why people sometimes "recall" something that was only suggested to them or something they only imagined. Reality monitoring involves deciding whether memories are based on perceptions of actual events or on just thinking about the events.

In recent years, Doris Kearns Goodwin (shown above) and several other prominent historians have been accused of plagiarizing the work of others. We can only speculate, but perhaps these incidents involved cryptomnesia—inadvertent plagiarism that occurs when people come up with an idea that they think is original, when they really were exposed to it earlier. Cryptomnesia may occur beccause of source-monitoring errors in retrieval.

© Seth Resnick/CORBIS

Forgetting: When Memory Lapses

Why do people forget information—even information they would like to remember? Many theorists believe that there isn't one simple answer to this question. They point to the complex, multifaceted nature of memory and assert that forgetting can be caused by deficiencies in encoding, storage, retrieval, or some combination of these processes.

How Quickly We Forget: Ebbinghaus's Forgetting Curve

The first person to conduct scientific studies of forgetting was Hermann Ebbinghaus. He published a series of insightful memory studies way back in 1885. Ebbinghaus studied only one subject—himself. To give himself lots of new material to memorize, he invented *nonsense syllables*—consonant-vowel-consonant arrangements that do not correspond to words (such as BAF, XOF, VIR, and MEQ). He wanted to work with meaningless materials that would be uncontaminated by his previous learning.

Ebbinghaus was a remarkably dedicated researcher. For instance, in one study he went through over 14,000 practice repetitions, as he tirelessly memorized 420 lists of nonsense syllables (Slamecka, 1985). He tested his memory of these lists after various time intervals. Figure 7.18 shows what he found. This diagram, called a *forgetting curve,* graphs retention and forgetting over time. Ebbinghaus's forgetting curve shows a precipitous drop in retention during the first few hours after the nonsense syllables were memorized. Thus, he concluded that most forgetting occurs very rapidly after learning something.

That's a depressing conclusion. What is the point of memorizing information if you're going to forget it all right away? Fortunately, subsequent research showed that Ebbinghaus's forgetting curve was unusually steep (Postman, 1985). Forgetting isn't usually quite as swift or as extensive as Ebbinghaus thought. One problem was that he was working with such meaningless material. When subjects memorize more meaningful material, such as prose or poetry, forgetting curves aren't nearly as steep. Studies of how well people recall their high school classmates suggest that forgetting curves for autobiographical information are much shallower (Bahrick, 2000). Also, different methods of measuring forgetting yield varied estimates of how quickly people forget. This variation underscores the importance of the methods used to measure forgetting, the matter we turn to next.

Measures of Forgetting

SIM5, SIM6

To study forgetting empirically, psychologists need to be able to measure it precisely. Measures of forgetting inevitably measure retention as well. **Retention refers to the proportion of material retained (remembered).** In studies of forgetting, the results may be reported in terms of the amount forgotten or the amount retained. In these studies, the *retention interval* is the length of time between the presentation of materials to be remembered and the measurement of forgetting. The three principal methods used to measure forgetting are recall, recognition, and relearning (Lockhart, 1992).

Who is the current U.S. secretary of state? What movie won the Academy Award for best picture last year? These questions involve recall measures of retention. **A *recall* measure of retention requires subjects to reproduce information on their own without any cues.** If you were to take a recall test on a list of 25 words you had memorized, you would simply be told to write down on a blank sheet of paper as many of the words as you could remember.

In contrast, in a recognition test you might be shown a list of 100 words and asked to choose the 25 words that you had memorized. **A *recognition* measure of retention requires subjects to select pre-**

PREVIEW QUESTIONS

● What did Ebbinghaus discover about how quickly people forget?

● What are the three methods for measuring retention?

● What is the difference between the decay and interference explanations of forgetting?

● When are retrieval failures likely to occur?

● Why do some experts believe that recovered memories of childhood sexual abuse are mostly genuine, while other experts are skeptical?

Figure 7.18

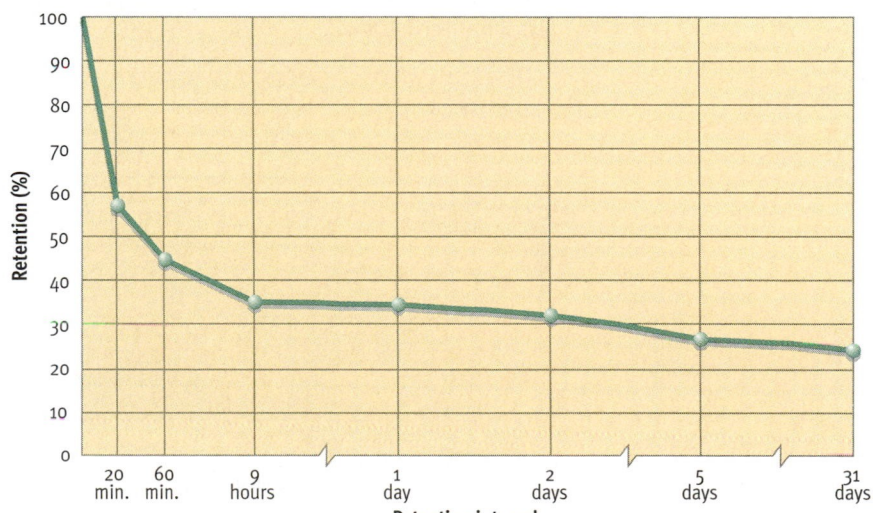

Ebbinghaus's forgetting curve for nonsense syllables. From his experiments on himself, Ebbinghaus concluded that forgetting is extremely rapid immediately after the original learning and then levels off. Although this generalization remains true, subsequent research has shown that forgetting curves for nonsense syllables are unusually steep. (Data from Ebbinghaus, 1885)

Welcome Institute for the History of Medicine, London

"*Left to itself every mental content gradually loses its capacity for being revived. . . . Facts crammed at examination time soon vanish.*"
HERMANN EBBINGHAUS

viously learned information from an array of options. Subjects not only have cues to work with, they have the answers right in front of them. In educational testing, essay questions and fill-in-the-blanks questions are recall measures of retention. Multiple-choice, true-false, and matching questions are recognition measures.

If you're like most students, you probably prefer multiple-choice tests over essay tests. This preference is understandable, because evidence shows that recognition measures tend to yield higher scores than recall measures of memory for the same information (Lockhart, 2000). This reality was demonstrated many decades ago by Luh (1922), who measured subjects' retention of nonsense syllables with both a recognition test and a recall test. As Figure 7.19 shows, subjects' performance on the recognition measure was far superior to their performance on the recall measure. There are two ways of looking at this disparity between recall and recognition tests. One view is that recognition tests are especially *sensitive* measures of retention. The other view is that recognition tests are excessively *easy* measures of retention.

Actually, there is no guarantee that a recognition test will be easier than a recall test. This tends to be the case, but the difficulty of a recognition test can vary greatly, depending on the number, similarity, and plausibility of the options provided as possible answers. To illustrate, see whether you know the answer to the following multiple-choice question:

Figure 7.19

Recognition versus recall in the measurement of retention. Luh (1922) had participants memorize lists of nonsense syllables and then measured their retention with either a recognition test or a recall test at various intervals up to two days. As you can see, the forgetting curve for the recall test was quite steep, whereas the recognition test yielded much higher estimates of subjects' retention. (Data from Luh, 1922)

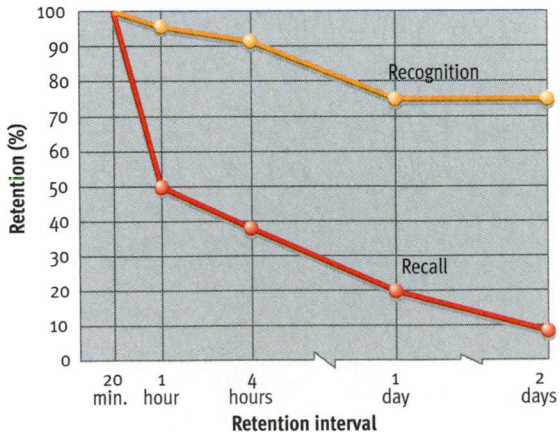

The capital of Washington is:
a. Seattle
b. Spokane
c. Tacoma
d. Olympia

Most students who aren't from Washington find this a fairly difficult question. The answer is Olympia. Now take a look at the next question:

The capital of Washington is:
a. London
b. New York
c. Tokyo
d. Olympia

Virtually anyone can answer this question because the incorrect options are readily dismissed. Although this illustration is a bit extreme, it shows that two recognition measures of the same information can be dramatically different in difficulty.

The third method of measuring forgetting is relearning. A *relearning* measure of retention requires a subject to memorize information a second time to determine how much time or how many practice trials are saved by having learned it before. Subjects' *savings scores* provide an estimate of their retention. Relearning measures can detect retention that is overlooked by recognition tests (Crowder & Greene, 2000).

Why We Forget

Measuring forgetting is only the first step in the long journey toward explaining why forgetting occurs. In this section, we explore the possible causes of forgetting, looking at factors that may affect encoding, storage, and retrieval processes.

Ineffective Encoding

A great deal of forgetting may only *appear* to be forgetting. The information in question may never have been inserted into memory in the first place. Since you can't really forget something you never learned, this phenomenon is sometimes called *pseudoforgetting*. We opened the chapter with an example of pseudoforgetting. People usually assume that they know what a penny looks like, but most have actually failed to encode this information. Pseudoforgetting is usually due to *lack of attention*.

Even when memory codes *are* formed for new information, subsequent forgetting may be the result of ineffective or inappropriate encoding (Brown & Craik, 2000). The research on levels of processing shows that some approaches to encoding lead to more forgetting than others (Craik & Tulving, 1975). For example, if you're distracted while you read your textbooks, you may be doing little more than saying the words to yourself. This is *phonemic encoding,* which is inferior to *semantic encoding* for retention of verbal material. When you can't remember the information that you've read, your forgetting may be due to ineffective encoding.

Decay

Instead of focusing on encoding, decay theory attributes forgetting to the impermanence of memory *storage.* **Decay theory** **proposes that forgetting occurs because memory traces fade with time.** The implicit assumption is that decay occurs in the physiological mechanisms responsible for memories. According to decay theory, the mere passage of time produces forgetting. This notion meshes nicely with commonsense views of forgetting.

As we noted earlier, evidence suggests that decay does contribute to the loss of information from the sensory and short-term memory stores. However, the critical task for theories of forgetting is to explain the loss of information from long-term memory. Researchers have *not* been able to demonstrate that decay causes LTM forgetting (Slamecka, 1992).

If decay theory is correct, the principal cause of forgetting should be the passage of time. In studies of long-term memory, however, researchers have repeatedly found that time passage is not as influential as what happens during the time interval. Research has shown that forgetting depends not on the amount of time that has passed since learning but on the amount, complexity, and type of information that subjects have had to assimilate *during* the retention interval. The negative impact of competing information on retention is called *interference.*

Interference

Interference theory **proposes that people forget information because of competition from other material.** Although demonstrations of decay in long-term memory have remained elusive, hundreds of studies have shown that interference influences forgetting (Anderson & Neely, 1996; Bjork, 1992). In many of these studies, researchers have controlled interference by varying the *similarity* between the original material given to subjects (the test material) and the material studied in the intervening period.

Interference is assumed to be greatest when intervening material is most similar to the test material. Decreasing the similarity should reduce interference and cause less forgetting. This is exactly what McGeoch and McDonald (1931) found in an influential study. They had subjects memorize test material that consisted of a list of two-syllable adjectives. They varied the similarity of intervening learning by having subjects then memorize one of five lists. In order of decreasing similarity to the test material, they were synonyms of the test words, antonyms of the test words, unrelated adjectives, nonsense syllables, and numbers. Later, subjects' recall of the test material was measured. Figure 7.20 shows that as the similarity of the intervening material decreased, the amount of forgetting also decreased—because of reduced interference.

There are two kinds of interference: *retroactive* interference and *proactive* interference (Jacoby, Hessels, & Bopp, 2001). **Retroactive interference** **occurs when new information impairs the retention of previously learned information.** Retroactive interference occurs between the original learning and the retest on that learning, during the retention interval (see Figure 7.21 on the next page). For example, the in-

Figure 7.20

Effects of interference. According to interference theory, more interference from competing information should produce more forgetting. McGeoch and McDonald (1931) controlled the amount of interference with a learning task by varying the similarity of an intervening task. The results were consistent with interference theory. The amount of interference is greatest at the left of the graph, as is the amount of forgetting. As interference decreases (moving to the right on the graph), retention improves. (Data from McGeoch & McDonald, 1931)

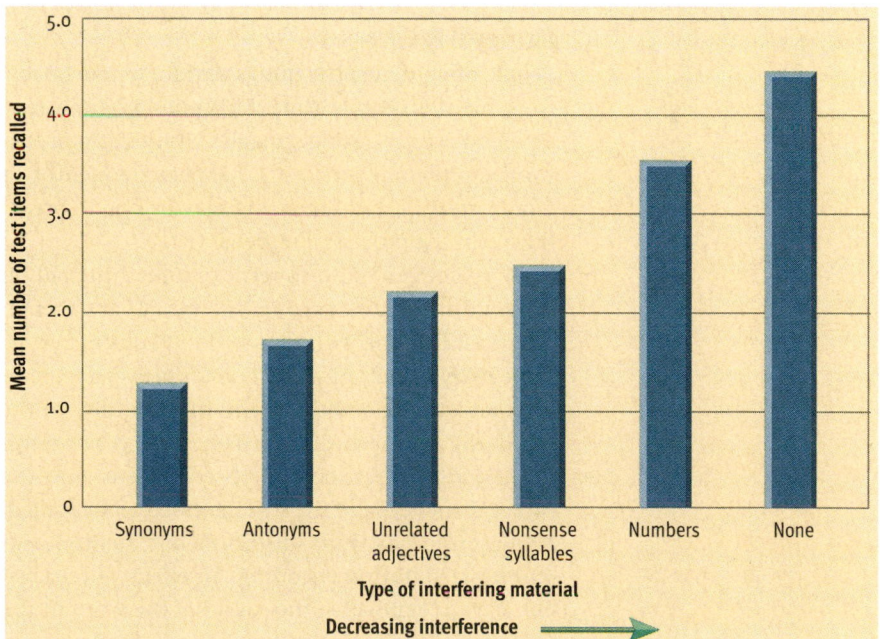

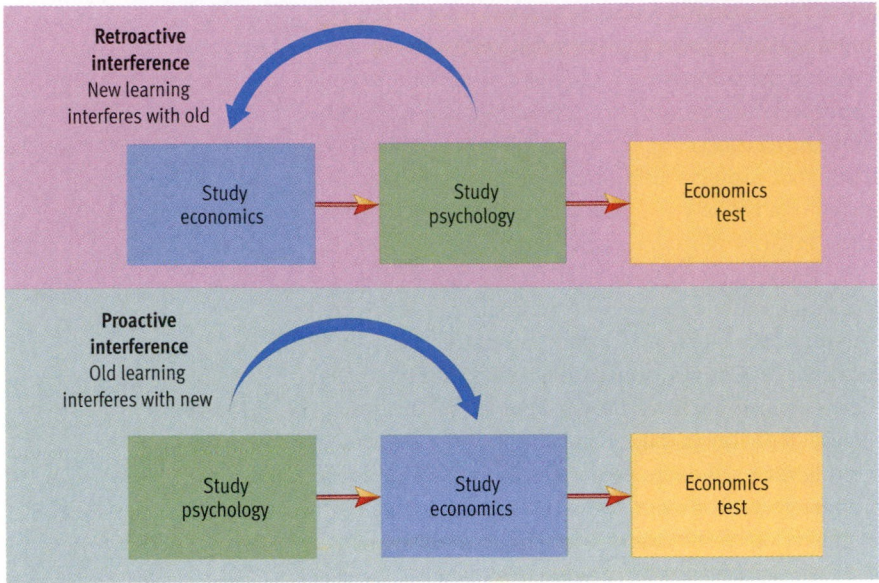

Retroactive interference
New learning interferes with old

Study economics → Study psychology → Economics test

Proactive interference
Old learning interferes with new

Study psychology → Study economics → Economics test

Figure 7.21

Retroactive and proactive interference. Retroactive interference occurs when learning produces a "backward" effect, reducing recall of previously learned material. Proactive interference occurs when learning produces a "forward" effect, reducing recall of subsequently learned material. For example, if you were to prepare for an economics test and then study psychology, the interference from the psychology study would be retroactive interference. However, if you studied psychology first and then economics, the interference from the psychology study would be proactive interference.

terference manipulated by McGeoch and McDonald (1931) was retroactive interference. In contrast, *proactive interference* occurs when previously learned information interferes with the retention of new information. Proactive interference is rooted in learning that comes *before* exposure to the test material.

Retrieval Failure

People often remember things that they were unable to recall at an earlier time. This phenomenon may be obvious only during struggles with the tip-of-the-tongue phenomenon, but it happens frequently. In fact, a great deal of forgetting may be due to breakdowns in the process of retrieval.

Why does an effort to retrieve something fail on one occasion and succeed on another? That's a tough question. One theory is that retrieval failures may be more likely when a mismatch occurs between retrieval cues and the encoding of the information you're searching for. According to Tulving and Thomson (1973), a good retrieval cue is consistent with the original encoding of the information to be recalled. If the sound of a word—its phonemic quality—was emphasized during encoding, an effective retrieval cue should emphasize the sound of the word. If the meaning of the word was emphasized during encoding, semantic cues should be best.

A general statement of the principle at work here was formulated by Tulving and Thomson (1973). **The encoding specificity principle states that the value of a retrieval cue depends on how well it corresponds to the memory code.** This principle provides one explanation for the inconsistent success of retrieval efforts.

Another line of research also indicates that memory is influenced by the "fit" between the processing during encoding and retrieval. *Transfer-appropriate processing* occurs when the initial processing of information is similar to the type of processing required by the subsequent measure of retention. For example, Morris, Bransford, and Franks (1977) gave subjects a list of words and a task that required either semantic or phonemic processing. Retention was measured with recognition tests that emphasized either the meaning or the sound of the words. Semantic processing yielded higher retention when the testing emphasized semantic factors, while phonemic processing yielded higher retention when the testing emphasized phonemic factors. Thus, retrieval failures are more likely when there is a poor fit between the processing done during encoding and the processing invoked by the measure of retention (Roediger & Guynn, 1996).

Motivated Forgetting

Many years ago, Sigmund Freud (1901) came up with an entirely different explanation for retrieval failures. As we noted in Chapter 1, Freud asserted that people often keep embarrassing, unpleasant, or painful memories buried in their unconscious. For example, a person who was deeply wounded by perceived slights at a childhood birthday party might suppress all recollection of that party. In his therapeutic work with patients, Freud recovered many such buried memories. He theorized that the memories were there all along, but their retrieval was blocked by unconscious avoidance tendencies.

The tendency to forget things one doesn't want to think about is called *motivated forgetting,* or to use Freud's terminology, *repression.* In Freudian theory, *repression refers to keeping distressing thoughts and feelings buried in the unconscious* (see Chapter 12). Although it is difficult to demonstrate the operation of repression in laboratory studies (Holmes, 1990), a number of experiments suggest that people don't remember anxiety-laden material as readily as emotionally neutral material, just as Freud proposed (Guenther, 1988; Reisner, 1998). Thus, when you forget unpleasant things such as a dental appointment, a promise to help a friend move, or a term paper deadline, motivated forgetting *may* be at work.

The Repressed Memories Controversy

Although the concept of repression has been around for a century, interest in this phenomenon has surged in recent years, thanks to a spate of prominent reports involving the return of individuals' long-lost memories of sexual abuse and other traumas during childhood. The media have been flooded with reports of adults accusing their parents, teachers, and neighbors of horrific child abuse decades earlier, based on previously repressed memories of these travesties. For the most part, these parents, teachers, and neighbors have denied the allegations. Many of them have seemed genuinely baffled by the accusations, which have torn some previously happy families apart (Loftus & Ketcham, 1994; Wylie, 1998). In an effort to make sense of the charges, some accused parents have argued that their children's recollections are false memories created inadvertently by well-intentioned therapists through the power of suggestion.

The controversy surrounding repressed memories is complex and difficult to sort out. The crux of the problem is that child abuse usually takes place behind closed doors. In the absence of corroborative evidence, there is no way to reliably distinguish genuine recovered memories from false ones. A handful of recovered memory incidents have been substantiated by independent witnesses or belated admissions of guilt from the accused (Bull, 1999; Duggal & Sroufe, 1998; Reisner, 1998; Schooler, 1999). But in the vast majority of cases, the allegations of abuse have been vehemently denied, and independent corroboration has not been available. What do psychologists and psychiatrists have to say about the authenticity of repressed memories? They are sharply divided on the issue.

Many psychologists and psychiatrists, especially clinicians involved in the treatment of psychological disorders, largely accept recovered memories of abuse at face value (Banyard & Williams, 1999; Briere & Conte, 1993; Herman, 1992, 1994; Terr, 1994; Whitfield, 1995). They assert that sexual abuse in childhood is far more widespread than most people realize. For example, a recent, large-scale survey (MacMillan et al., 1997), using a random sample of 9953 residents of Ontario, found that 12.8% of the females and 4.3% of the males reported that they had been victims of sexual abuse during childhood (see Figure 7.22). They further assert that there is ample evidence that it is common for people to bury traumatic incidents in their unconscious (Del Monte, 2000; Karon & Widener, 1997). For instance, in one widely cited study, L. M. Williams (1994) followed up on 129 female

CONCEPT CHECK 7.2

Figuring Out Forgetting

Check your understanding of why people forget by identifying the probable causes of forgetting in each of the following scenarios. Choose from (a) motivated forgetting (repression), (b) decay, (c) ineffective encoding, (d) proactive interference, (e) retroactive interference, or (f) retrieval failure. You will find the answers in Appendix A.

_____ **1.** Ellen can't recall the reasons for the Webster-Ashburton Treaty because she was daydreaming when it was discussed in history class.

_____ **2.** Rufus hates his job at Taco Heaven and is always forgetting when he is scheduled to work.

_____ **3.** Ray's new assistant in the shipping department is named John Cocker. Ray keeps calling him Joe, mixing him up with the rock singer Joe Cocker.

_____ **4.** Tania studied history on Sunday morning and sociology on Sunday evening. It's Monday, and she's struggling with her history test because she keeps mixing up prominent historians with influential sociologists.

children who had been brought to a hospital emergency room for treatment of sexual abuse. When interviewed approximately 17 years later about a variety of things, including their history of sexual abuse, 38% of the women failed to report the original incident, which Wiliams largely attributed to amnesia for the incident. In a recent study of psychiatric patients hospitalized for posttraumatic or dissociative disorders (see Chapter 14), one-third of those who

Figure 7.22

Estimates of the prevalence of childhood physical and sexual abuse. In one of the better efforts to estimate the prevalence of child abuse, MacMillan and her colleagues (1997) questioned a random sample of almost 10,000 adults living in the province of Ontario, Canada, about whether they were abused during childhood. As you can see, males were more likely to have experienced physical abuse and females were more likely to have suffered from sexual abuse. The data support the assertion that millions of people have been victimized by childhood sexual abuse, which is far from rare. (Based on data from MacMillan et al., 1997)

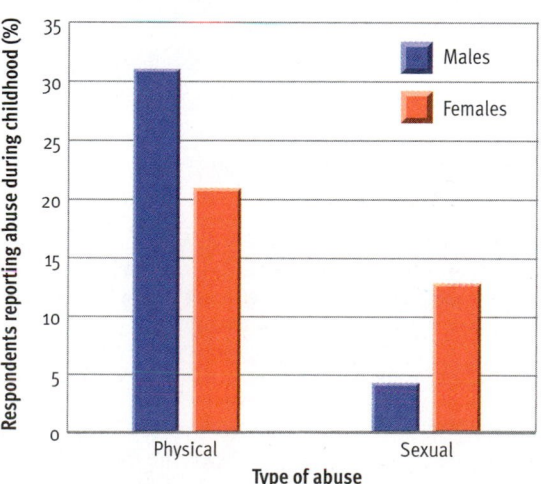

reported childhood sexual abuse said that they experienced complete amnesia for the abuse at some point in their lives (Chu et al., 1999). According to Freyd (1996), sexual abuse by a parent evokes coping efforts that attempt to block awareness of the abuse because that awareness would interfere with normal attachment processes. The clinicians who accept the authenticity of recovered memories of abuse attribute the recent upsurge in recovered memories to therapists' and clients' increased sensitivity to an issue that people used to be reluctant to discuss.

In contrast, many other psychologists, especially memory researchers, have expressed skepticism about the recent upsurge of recovered memories of abuse (Kihlstrom, 1998b; Lindsay & Poole, 1995; Loftus, 1993b, 1998; Lynn & Nash, 1994). They point out that the women in the Williams (1994) study may have failed to report their earlier sexual abuse for a variety of reasons besides amnesia, including embarrassment, poor rapport with the interviewer, normal forgetfulness, or a conscious preference not to revisit painful experiences from the past (Loftus, Garry & Feldman, 1998; Pope & Hudson, 1998). Many memory researchers are also skeptical about retrospective self-reports of amnesia—such as those seen in the Chu et al. (1999) study—because self-assessments of personal memory are often distorted and because it is difficult to distinguish between a period when a memory was not *accessed* versus a period when a memory

AP/Wide World Photos

Tom Rutherford (shown here with his wife, Joyce) received a $1 million settlement in a suit against a church therapist and a Springfield, Missouri, church in a false memory case. Under the church counselor's guidance, the Rutherfords' daughter, Beth, had "recalled" childhood memories of having been raped repeatedly by her minister father, gotten pregnant, and undergone a painful coat-hanger abortion. Her father lost his job and was ostracized. After he later revealed he'd had a vasectomy when Beth was age 4, and a physical exam revealed that at age 23 she was still a virgin, the memories were shown to be false.

was not *available* due to repression (Belli et al., 1998; Schooler, 1999).

The skeptics do *not* say that people are lying about their previously repressed memories. Rather, they maintain that some suggestible people wrestling with emotional problems have been convinced by persuasive therapists that their emotional problems must be the result of abuse that occurred years before. Critics blame a minority of therapists who presumably have good intentions but who operate under the dubious assumption that virtually all psychological problems are attributable to childhood sexual abuse (Lindsay & Read, 1994; Spanos, 1994). Using hypnosis, dream interpretation, and leading questions, they supposedly prod and probe patients until they inadvertently create the memories of abuse that they are searching for. Consistent with this view, Yapko (1994) reviews evidence that some therapists are (1) overly prone to see signs of abuse where none has occurred, (2) unsophisticated about the extent to which memories can be distorted, and (3) naive about how much their expectations and beliefs can influence their patients' efforts to achieve self-understanding.

Psychologists who doubt the authenticity of repressed memories support their analysis by pointing to discredited cases of recovered memories (Brown, Goldstein, & Bjorklund, 2000). For example, with the help of a church counselor, one woman recovered memories of how her minister father had repeatedly raped her, got her pregnant, and then aborted the

Figure  7.23

A case of recovered memories recanted. Revelations of repressed memories of sexual abuse are viewed with skepticism in some quarters. One reason is that some people who have recovered previously repressed recollections of child abuse have subsequently realized that their "memories" were the product of suggestion. A number of case histories, such as the one summarized here (from Jaroff, 1993), have demonstrated that therapists who relentlessly search for memories of child abuse in their patients sometimes instill the memories they are seeking.

SOURCE: Jaroff, L. (1993, November 29). Lies of the mind. *Time*, pp. 52–59. Copyright © 1993 Time Inc. Reprinted by permission.

A Case History of Recovered Memories Recanted

Suffering from a prolonged bout of depression and desperate for help, Melody Gavigan, 39, a computer specialist from Long Beach, California, checked herself into a local psychiatric hospital. As Gavigan recalls the experience, her problems were just beginning. During five weeks of treatment there, a family and marriage counselor repeatedly suggested that her depression stemmed from incest during her childhood. While at first Gavigan had no recollection of any abuse, the therapist kept prodding. "I was so distressed and needed help so desperately, I latched on to what he was offering me," she says. "I accepted his answers."

When asked for details, she wrote page after page of what she believed were emerging repressed memories. She told about running into the yard after being raped in the bathroom. She incorporated into another lurid rape scene an actual girlhood incident, in which she had dislocated a shoulder. She went on to recall being molested by her father when she was only a year old—as her diapers were being changed—and sodomized by him at five. Following what she says was the therapist's advice, Gavigan confronted her father with her accusations, severed her relationship with him, moved away, and formed an incest survivors' group.

But she remained uneasy. Signing up for a college psychology course, she examined her newfound memories more carefully and concluded that they were false. Now Gavigan has begged her father's forgiveness and filed a lawsuit against the psychiatric hospital for the pain that she and her family suffered.

pregnancy with a coat-hanger; however, subsequent evidence revealed that the woman was still a virgin and that her father had had a vasectomy years before (Loftus, 1997; Testa, 1996). The skeptics also point to published case histories that clearly involved suggestive questioning and to cases in which patients have recanted recovered memories of sexual abuse (see Figure 7.23) after realizing that these memories were implanted by their therapists (Goldstein & Farmer, 1993; Loftus, 1994).

Those who question the accuracy of repressed memories also point to findings on the misinformation effect, research on source-monitoring errors, and other studies that demonstrate the relative ease of creating "memories" of events that never happened. For example, working with college students, Ira Hyman and his colleagues have managed to implant recollections of fairly substantial events (such as spilling a punch bowl at a wedding, being in a grocery store when the fire sprinkler system went off, being hospitalized for an earache) in about 25% of their subjects, just by asking them to elaborate on events supposedly reported by their parents (Hyman, Husband, & Billings, 1995; Hyman & Kleinknecht, 1999).

In a similar vein, Roediger and McDermott (1995, 2000) have devised a simple laboratory paradigm involving the learning of word lists that is remarkably reliable in producing memory illusions. In this paradigm, a series of lists of 15 words are presented to participants, who are asked to recall the words immediately after each list is presented and are given a recognition measure of their retention at the end of the session. The trick is that each list consists of a set of words (such as *bed, rest, awake, tired*) that are strongly associated with another target word that is not on the list (in this case, *sleep*). When subjects *recall* the words on each list, they remember the non-presented target word over 50% of the time, and when they are given the final *recognition* test, they typically indicate that about 80% of the nonstudied target words were presented in the lists (see Figure 7.24).

The trivial memory illusions created in this experiment may seem a far cry from the vivid, detailed recollections of previously forgotten sexual abuse that have generated the repressed memories controversy. But these false memories can be reliably created in normal, healthy participants in a matter of minutes, with little effort and no pressure or misleading information. Thus, the Roediger and McDermott paradigm provides a dramatic demonstration of how easy it is to get people to remember that they saw something they really didn't see. The simplicity and reliability of the paradigm are also permitting investigators to

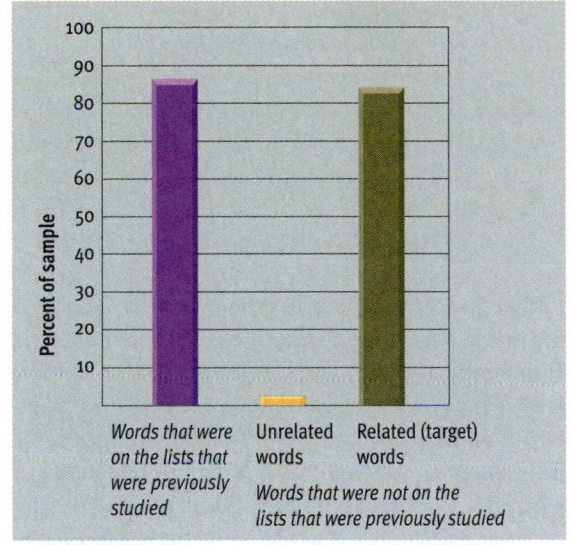

Figure 7.24

The prevalence of false memories observed by Roediger and McDermott (1995). The graph shown here summarizes the recognition test results in Study 1 conducted by Roediger and McDermott (1995). Participants correctly identified words that had been on the lists that they had studied 86% of the time and only misidentified unrelated words that had not been on the lists 2% of the time, indicating that they were paying careful attention to the task. Nonetheless, they mistakenly reported that they "remembered" related target words that were *not* on the lists 84% of the time—a remarkably high prevalence of false memories. (Data from Roediger & McDermott, 1995)

explore personal correlates of the tendency to falsely remember target words. For example, researchers who have used this paradigm have found an elevated rate of false recollections among women who have reported recovering memories of abuse (Clancy et al., 2000) and among victims of emotional trauma (Zoellner et al., 2000).

Skepticism about the validity of recovered memories of abuse has also been fueled by the following observations and research findings.

- Many repressed memories of abuse have been recovered under the influence of hypnosis. However, an extensive body of research indicates that hypnosis tends to increase memory distortions while paradoxically making people feel more confident about their recollections (Lynn et al., 1997; Whitehouse et al., 1988).
- Many repressed memories of abuse have been recovered through therapists' dream interpretations. But as you learned in Chapter 5, dream interpretation depends on highly subjective guesswork that cannot be verified. Moreover, research shows that bogus dream interpretations can lead normal subjects to believe that they actually experienced

Web Link 7.4

False Memory Syndrome Foundation (FMSF) Online
This site marshals evidence that recovered memories of childhood abuse are often false, therapist induced, and grounded in shoddy and non-objective scientific claims. Dealing with perhaps the most bitterly contested topic in current psychology, the FMSF has elicited fierce opposition, as the material presented at the site described in the next Web Link demonstrates.

Web Link 7.5

"False Memory Syndrome" Facts
Social worker and psychotherapist Linda Chapman, editor of the online *Wounded Healer Journal*, has brought together scientific and clinical evidence that "false memory syndrome" is a misleading label and that adults may indeed recover repressed memories of childhood abuse.

the events suggested in the dream analyses (Loftus, 2000; Loftus & Mazzoni, 1998).

- Some recovered memories have described incidents of abuse that occurred before the victim reached age 3. However, when adults are asked to recall their earliest memories, their oldest recollections typically don't go back that far (Bruce, Dolan, & Phillips-Grant, 2000; Eacott & Crawley, 1998).

Of course, psychologists who believe in recovered memories have mounted rebuttals to the numerous arguments raised by the skeptics. For example, Kluft (1999) argues that a recantation of a recovered memory of abuse does not prove that the memory was false. Gleaves (1994) points out that individuals with a history of sexual abuse often vacillate between denying and accepting that the abuse occurred. Harvey (1999) argues that laboratory demonstrations that it is easy to create false memories have involved insignificant memory distortions that do not resemble the emotionally wrenching recollections of sexual abuse that have been recovered in therapy. Olio (1994) concludes that "The possibility of implanting entire multiple scenarios of horror that differ markedly from the individual's experience, such as memories of childhood abuse in an individual who does not have a trauma history, remains an unsubstantiated hypothesis" (p. 442). Moreover, even if one accepts the assertion that therapists *can* create false memories of abuse in their patients, some critics have noted that there is virtually no direct evidence on how often this occurs and no empirical basis for the claim that there has been an *epidemic* of such cases (Berliner & Briere, 1999; Calof, 1998; Pope & Brown, 1996).

Although both sides seem genuinely concerned about the welfare of the people involved, the debate about recovered memories of sexual abuse has grown increasingly bitter and emotionally charged (Lindsay, 1998; Pope, 1996). So, what can we conclude about the recovered memories controversy? It seems pretty clear that therapists can unknowingly create false memories in their patients and that a significant portion of recovered memories of abuse are the product of suggestion. But it also seems likely that some cases of recovered memories are authentic (Brown, Scheflin, & Whitfield, 1999). At this point, we don't have adequate data to estimate what proportion of recovered memories of abuse fall in each category (Brown, Scheflin, & Hammond, 1998; Gow, 1999). Thus, the matter needs to be addressed with great caution. On the one hand, people should be extremely careful about accepting recovered memories of abuse in the absence of convincing corroboration. On the other hand, recovered memories of abuse cannot be sum-

marily dismissed, and it would be tragic if the repressed memories controversy made people overly skeptical about the all-too-real problem of childhood sexual abuse.

The repressed memories controversy deserves one last comment regarding its impact on memory research and scientific conceptions of memory. The controversy has helped inspire a great deal of research that has increased our understanding of just how fragile, fallible, malleable, and subjective human memory is. It is presumptuous to trust memory—whether recovered or not—to provide accurate recollections of the past. Moreover, the implicit dichotomy underlying the repressed memories debate—that some memories are true, whereas others are false—is misleading and oversimplified. Research demonstrates that all our memories are imperfect reconstructions of the past that are subject to many types of distortion. Although Schacter (1999) has argued convincingly that the imperfections of memory may be adaptive in the long run, the fact remains that memory is surprisingly unreliable.

REVIEW OF KEY POINTS

- Ebbinghaus's early studies of nonsense syllables suggested that people forget very rapidly. Subsequent research showed that Ebbinghaus's forgetting curve was exceptionally steep.

- Forgetting can be measured by asking people to recall, recognize, or relearn information. Different methods of measuring retention often produce different estimates of forgetting. Recognition measures tend to yield higher estimates of retention than recall measures.

- Some forgetting, including pseudoforgetting, is due to ineffective encoding of information. Decay theory proposes that forgetting occurs spontaneously with the passage of time. It has proven difficult to show that decay occurs in long-term memory.

- Interference theory proposes that people forget information because of competition from other material. Proactive interference occurs when old learning interferes with new information. Retroactive interference occurs when new learning interferes with old information.

- Forgetting may also be a matter of retrieval failure. According to the encoding specificity principle, the effectiveness of a retrieval cue depends on how well it corresponds to the memory code that represents the stored item.

- Repression involves the motivated forgetting of painful or unpleasant memories. Recent years have seen a surge of reports of recovered memories of sexual abuse in childhood. The authenticity of these repressed memories is the subject of controversy because empirical studies have demonstrated that it is not all that difficult to create false memories.

- The evidence suggests that therapists can unknowingly create false memories in their patients and that a significant portion of recovered memories of abuse are the product of suggestion. But it also seems likely that some cases of recovered memories are authentic.

In Search of the Memory Trace: The Physiology of Memory

For decades, neuroscientists have ventured forth in search of the physiological basis for memory, often referred to as the "memory trace." On several occasions scientists have been excited by new leads, only to be led down blind alleys. For example, as we noted earlier, Wilder Penfield's work with electrical stimulation of the brain during surgery suggested that the cortex houses exact tape recordings of past experiences (Penfield & Perot, 1963). At the time, scientists believed that this was a major advance. Ultimately, it was not.

Similarly, James McConnell rocked the world of science when he reported that he had chemically transferred a specific memory from one flatworm to another. McConnell (1962) created a conditioned reflex (contraction in response to light) in flatworms and then transferred RNA (a basic molecular constituent of all living cells) from trained worms to untrained worms. The untrained worms showed evidence of "remembering" the conditioned reflex. McConnell boldly speculated that in the future, chemists might be able to formulate pills containing the information for Physics 201 or History 101! Unfortunately, the RNA transfer studies proved difficult to replicate (Rilling, 1996). Today, 30 years after McConnell's "breakthrough," we are still a long way from breaking the chemical code for memory.

Investigators continue to explore a variety of leads about the physiological bases for memory. In light of past failures, these lines of research should probably be viewed with guarded optimism, but we'll look at some of the more promising approaches. You may want to consult Chapter 3 if you need to refresh your memory about the physiological processes and structures discussed in this section.

The Biochemistry of Memory 6c

One line of research suggests that memory formation results in *alterations in synaptic transmission* at specific sites. According to this view, specific memories depend on biochemical changes that occur at specific synapses. Like McConnell, Eric Kandel and his colleagues have studied conditioned reflexes in a simple organism—a sea slug. In research that earned a Nobel Prize for Kandel, they showed that specific forms of learning in the sea slug result in an increase or decrease in the release of neurotransmitters by presynaptic neurons (Kandel & Schwartz, 1982; Kennedy, Hawkins, & Kandel, 1992). Kandel believes that durable changes in synaptic transmission may be the

neural building blocks of more complex memories as well. Of course, critics point out that it's risky to generalize from marine mollusks to humans.

Manipulations that alter hormone levels shortly after an organism has learned a new response can affect memory storage in a variety of animals. These hormonal changes can either facilitate or impair memory, depending on the specific hormone and the amount of change (McGaugh, Roozendaal, & Cahill, 2000). James McGaugh (1995, 2000) theorizes that hormones influence memory storage by modulating activity in the amygdala and a variety of neurotransmitter systems in the brain. Other animal studies suggest that adequate protein synthesis is necessary for the formation of memories (Rose, 1992; Rosenzweig, 1996). For example, the administration of drugs that interfere with protein synthesis impairs long-term memory storage in chicks and rats.

The Neural Circuitry of Memory 6c

Richard F. Thompson (1989, 1992) and his colleagues have shown that specific memories may depend on *localized neural circuits* in the brain. In other words, memories may create unique, reusable pathways in the brain along which signals flow. Thompson has traced the pathway that accounts for a rabbit's memory of a conditioned eyeblink response. The key link in this circuit is a microscopic spot in the *cerebellum*, a structure in the hindbrain (see Figure 7.25). When

PREVIEW QUESTIONS
- What do synaptic transmission and hormonal fluctuations have to do with memory?
- What type of memory has been explained in terms of a localized neural circuit?
- Which brain structures appear to be involved in memory?

Figure 7.25

The anatomy of memory. All the brain structures identified here have been implicated in efforts to discover the anatomical structures involved in memory. Although its exact contribution to memory remains the subject of debate, the hippocampus is thought to play an especially central role in memory.

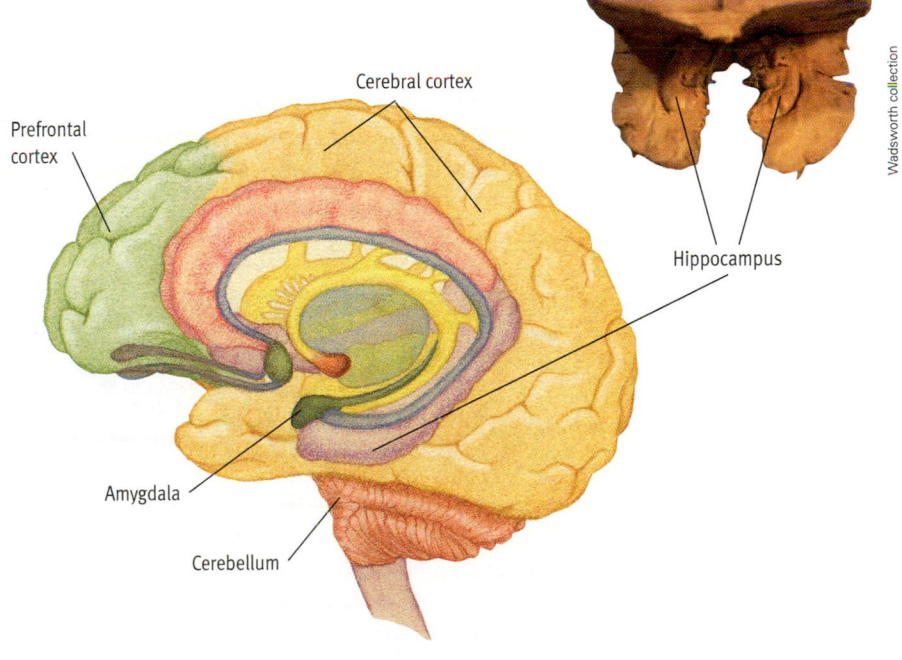

Cerebral cortex

Prefrontal cortex

Hippocampus

Amygdala

Cerebellum

Wadsworth collection

Web Link 7.6

Alzheimer Page
The Alzheimer Disease Research Center at Washington University has fashioned a companion site to ALZHEIMER, a Usenet discussion group for clinicians, researchers, and the various publics affected by this memory-destroying disease. A broad, annotated set of links as well as a search facility for the massive archives of the discussion group itself invite further exploration of all facets of this illness.

this spot is destroyed, the conditioned stimulus no longer elicits the eyeblink response, even though the unconditioned stimulus still does (Steinmetz, 1998). This finding does *not* mean that the cerebellum is the key to all memory. Other memories presumably create entirely different pathways in other areas of the brain. The key implication of this work is that it may be possible to map out specific neural circuits that correspond to at least some types of specific memories.

Evidence on *long-term potentiation* also supports the idea that memory traces consist of specific neural circuits. **Long-term potentiation (LTP) is a long-lasting increase in neural excitability at synapses along a specific neural pathway.** Thus far, researchers have produced LTP artificially by sending a burst of high-frequency electrical stimulation along a neural pathway (Racine & deJonge, 1988). Many theorists suspect that natural events produce the same sort of potentiated neural circuit when a memory is formed (Martinez, Barea-Rodriguez, & Derrick, 1998).

In some cases, memory formation may stimulate neural growth and the emergence of new neural circuits (Rosenzweig, 1996). For instance, new branches in the dendritic trees of certain neurons are found in rats that learn to run a series of mazes (Greenough, 1985). As you may recall from Chapter 3, dendritic trees are specialized to receive signals from other neurons. Hence, increased dendritic branching probably leads to the formation of additional synapses and the creation of new neural pathways. These new neural circuits may reflect the storage of learned information.

The Anatomy of Memory 6c

Cases of *organic amnesia*—extensive memory loss due to head injury—are another source of clues about the physiological bases of memory (Mayes, 1992). There are two basic types of amnesia: retrograde and anterograde (see Figure 7.26). **Retrograde amnesia involves the loss of memories for events that occurred prior to the onset of amnesia.** For example, a 25-year-old gymnast who sustains a head trauma might find the prior three years, or seven years, or her entire lifetime erased. **Anterograde amnesia involves the loss of memories for events that occur after the onset of amnesia.** For instance, after her accident, the injured gymnast might suffer impaired ability to remember people she meets, where she has parked her car, and so on.

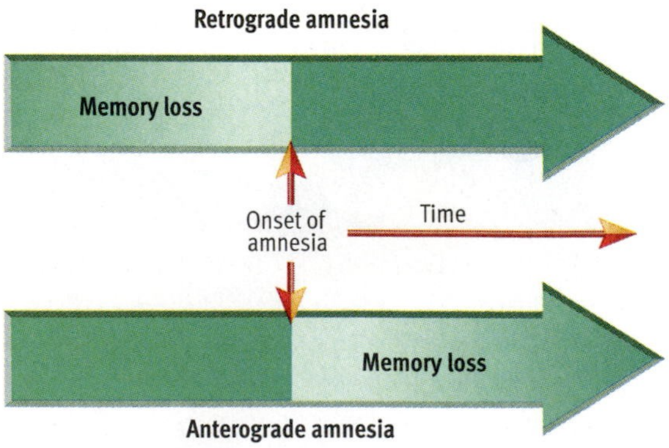

The study of anterograde amnesia has proven to be an especially rich source of information about the brain and memory. One well-known case, that of a man referred to as H. M., has been followed by Brenda Milner and her colleagues since 1953 (Corkin, 1984; Milner, Corkin, & Teuber, 1968; Scoville & Milner, 1957). H. M. had surgery to relieve debilitating epileptic seizures. Unfortunately, the surgery inadvertently wiped out most of his ability to form long-term memories. H. M.'s short-term memory is fine, but he has no recollection of anything that has happened since 1953 (other than about the most recent 20–30 seconds of his life). He doesn't recognize the doctors treating him and he can't remember routes to and from places. He can read a magazine story over and over, thinking he is reading it for the first time each time. He can't remember what he did yesterday, let alone what he has done for the last 50 years. He doesn't even recognize a current photo of himself, as aging has changed his appearance considerably.

H. M.'s memory losses were originally attributed to the removal of his *hippocampus* (see Figure 7.25), although theorists now understand that other nearby structures that were removed also contributed to H. M.'s dramatic memory deficits (Delis & Lucas, 1996). Based on decades of additional research, scientists now believe that the entire *hippocampal region* (including the hippocampus, dentate gyrus, subiculum, and entorhinal cortex) and the adjacent *parahippocampal region* are critical for many types of long-term memory (Zola & Squire, 2000). Consistent with this conclusion, it is interesting to note that the hippocampal region is one of the first areas of the brain to sustain significant damage in the course of Alzheimer's disease, which produces severe memory impairment in many people, typically after age 65 (Ashford, Mattson, & Kumar, 1998).

Do these findings mean that memories are stored in the hippocampal region and adjacent areas? Probably not. Many theorists believe that the hippocampal region plays a key role in the *consolidation* of memories (Alvarez & Squire, 1994; Gluck & Myers, 1997). *Consolidation* is a hypothetical process involving

Figure 7.26

Retrograde versus anterograde amnesia. In retrograde amnesia, memory for events that occurred prior to the onset of amnesia is lost. In anterograde amnesia, memory for events that occur subsequent to the onset of amnesia suffers.

Retrograde amnesia

Memory loss

Onset of amnesia   Time

Memory loss

Anterograde amnesia

the gradual conversion of information into durable memory codes stored in long-term memory. According to this view, memories are consolidated in the hippocampal region and then stored in diverse and widely distributed areas of the cortex (Markowitsch, 2000).

Theorists who have been influenced by parallel distributed processing (PDP) models of memory have come up with a slightly different take on the hippocampal region's contribution to memory. They suggest that the hippocampal area functions to *bind together* the individual elements of a specific memory, which are stored in widely distributed areas of the cortex (Cohen et al., 1999; Nadel & Jacobs, 1998). For example, your memory of attending a baseball game might include a variety of elements—such as when and where it occurred, the final score, certain key plays, the location of your seat, who went with you, and the weather—that are stored in dispersed brain modules. The hippocampal complex may provide a mechanism for bringing these disaggregated elements of a memory together by activating certain ensembles of neurons. In other words, the hippocampal area may play a key role in organizing neural networks that represent specific memories. This analysis is not entirely incompatible with the notion that the hippocampal region handles the consolidation of long-term memories.

Neuroscientists continue to forge ahead in their efforts to identify the anatomical bases of memory. One recent advance has been the demonstration that the *amygdala seems to be critical to the formation of memories for learned fears* (Armony & LeDoux, 2000).

This subcortical structure, which is a close neighbor of the hippocampus (see Figure 7.25), may also contribute to other emotional memories (Cahill & McGaugh, 1998). Investigators are also intrigued by recent evidence regarding the role of the prefrontal cortex in memory (see Figure 7.25). *The prefrontal cortex appears to contribute to memory for temporal sequences and to short-term, working memory* (Gershberg & Shimamura, 1998; Smith, 2000).

As you can see, a host of biochemical processes, neural circuits, and anatomical structures have been implicated as playing a role in memory. Looking for the physiological basis for memory is only slightly less daunting than looking for the physiological basis for thought itself.

Montreal Neurological Institute

"Some effects of temporal lobe lesions in man are hard to reconcile with any unitary-process theory of memory."
BRENDA MILNER

REVIEW OF KEY POINTS

● Memory traces may reflect alterations in neurotransmitter release at specific locations. Manipulations of hormone levels and protein synthesis can affect memory.

● Thompson's research suggests that memory traces may consist of localized neural circuits. Memories may also depend on long-term potentiation, which is a durable increase in neural excitability at synapses along a specific neural pathway. Memory formation may also stimulate neural growth.

● In retrograde amnesia, a person loses memory for events prior to the amnesia. In anterograde amnesia, a person shows memory deficits for events subsequent to the onset of the amnesia. Studies of amnesia and other research suggests that the hippocampal complex is involved in the consolidation of memories.

Are There Multiple Memory Systems?

Some theorists believe that evidence on the physiology of memory is confusing because investigators are unwittingly probing into several distinct memory systems that have different physiological bases. A number of research findings inspired this view, foremost among them being the discovery of *implicit memory*. Let's look at this perplexing phenomenon.

Implicit Versus Explicit Memory

As noted earlier, patients with anterograde amnesia often appear to have no ability to form long-term memories. If they're shown a list of words and subsequently given a test of retention, their performance is miserable. However, different findings emerge when

"sneaky" techniques are used to measure their memory indirectly. For instance, they might be asked to work on a word recognition task that is not presented as a measure of retention. In this task, they are shown fragments of words (example: _ss_ss__ for assassin) and are asked to complete the fragments with the first appropriate word that comes to mind. The series of word fragments includes ones that correspond to words on a list they saw earlier. In this situation, the amnesiac subjects respond with words that were on the list just as frequently as normal subjects who also saw the initial list (Schacter, Chiu, & Ochsner, 1993). Thus, the amnesiacs *do* remember words from the list. However, when asked, they don't even remember having been shown the list.

PREVIEW QUESTIONS

● What is the difference between implicit and explicit memory?

● How does this distinction relate to declarative versus procedural memory?

● Which type of memory is like an encyclopedia and which is like an autobiography?

● What is prospective memory?

"Memory systems constitute the major subdivisions of the overall organization of the memory complex. . . . An operating component of a system consists of a neural substrate and its behavioral or cognitive correlates."
ENDEL TULVING

The demonstration of long-term retention in amnesiacs who previously appeared to have no long-term memory shocked memory experts when it was first reported by Warrington and Weiskrantz (1970). However, this surprising finding has been replicated in many subsequent studies. This phenomenon has come to be known as implicit memory. *Implicit memory is apparent when retention is exhibited on a task that does not require intentional remembering.* Implicit memory is contrasted with *explicit memory, which involves intentional recollection of previous experiences.*

Is implicit memory peculiar to people suffering from amnesia? No. When normal subjects are exposed to material and their retention of it is measured indirectly, they, too, show implicit memory (Schacter, 1987, 1989). To draw a parallel with everyday life, implicit memory is simply incidental, unintentional remembering (Mandler, 1989). People frequently remember things that they didn't deliberately store in memory. For example, you might recall the color of a jacket that your professor wore yesterday. Likewise, people remember things without deliberate retrieval efforts. For instance, you might be telling someone about a restaurant, which somehow reminds you of an unrelated story about a mutual friend.

Research has uncovered many interesting differences between implicit and explicit memory (Roediger, 1990; Tulving & Schacter, 1990). Explicit memory is conscious, is accessed directly, and can be best assessed with recall or recognition measures of retention. Implicit memory is unconscious, must be accessed indirectly, and can be best assessed with variations on relearning (savings) measures of retention. Implicit memory is largely unaffected by amnesia, age, the administration of certain drugs (such as alcohol), the length of the retention interval, and manipulations of interference. In contrast, explicit memory is affected very much by all these factors.

Some theorists think these differences are found because implicit and explicit memory rely on *different cognitive processes* in encoding and retrieval (Graf & Gallie, 1992; Jacoby, 1988; Roediger, 1990). However, many other theorists argue that the differences exist because implicit and explicit memory are handled by *independent memory systems* (Schacter, 1992, 1994; Squire, 1994). These independent systems are referred to as declarative and procedural memory.

Declarative Versus Procedural Memory

6c

Many theorists have suggested that people have separate memory systems for different kinds of information (see Figure 7.27). The most basic division of memory into distinct systems contrasts *declarative memory* with *nondeclarative* or *procedural memory* (Squire & Zola, 1996; Winograd, 1975). The *declarative memory system* handles factual information. It contains recollections of words, definitions, names, dates, faces, events, concepts, and ideas. The *nondeclarative* or *procedural memory system* houses memory for actions, skills, operations, and conditioned responses. It contains memories of how to execute such actions as riding a bike, typing, and tying one's shoes. To illustrate the distinction, if you know the rules of tennis (the number of games in a set, scoring, and such), this factual information is stored in declarative memory. If you remember how to hit a serve and swing through a backhand, these perceptual-motor skills are stored in procedural memory.

Some theorists believe that an association exists between implicit memory and the procedural memory system (Squire, Knowlton, & Musen, 1993). Why? Because memory for skills is largely unconscious. People execute perceptual-motor tasks such as playing

Figure 7.27

Theories of independent memory systems. There is some evidence that different types of information are stored in separate memory systems, which may have distinct physiological bases. The diagram shown here, which blends the ideas of several theorists, is an adaptation of Larry Squire's (1987) scheme. Note that implicit and explicit memory are not memory systems. They are observed behavioral phenomena that appear to be handled by different hypothetical memory systems (the procedural and declarative memory systems), which cannot be observed directly.

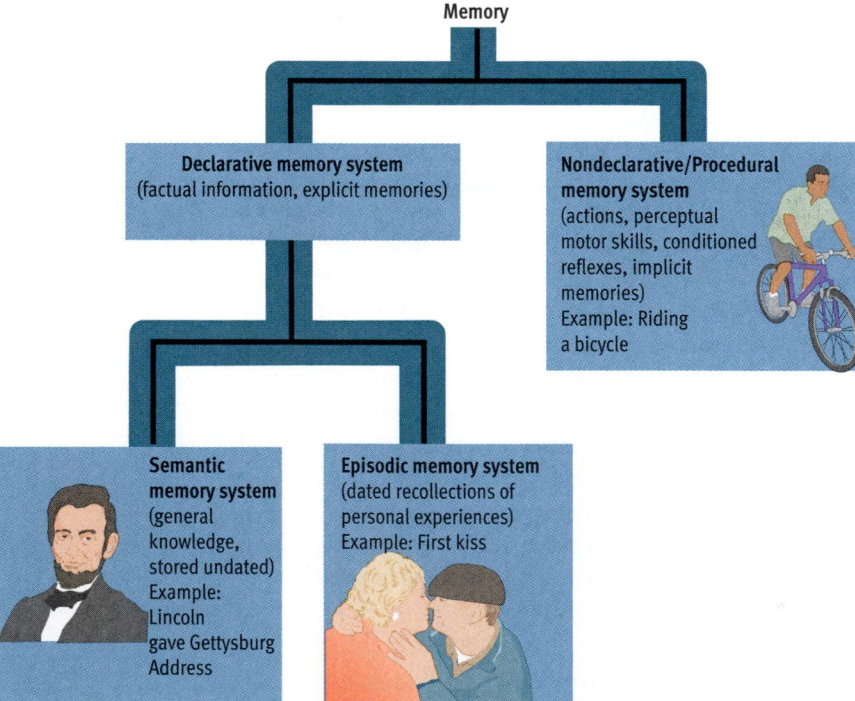

Memory

Declarative memory system (factual information, explicit memories)

Nondeclarative/Procedural memory system (actions, perceptual motor skills, conditioned reflexes, implicit memories) Example: Riding a bicycle

Semantic memory system (general knowledge, stored undated) Example: Lincoln gave Gettysburg Address

Episodic memory system (dated recollections of personal experiences) Example: First kiss

the piano or typing with little conscious awareness of what they're doing. In fact, performance on such tasks often deteriorates if people think too much about what they're doing. Another parallel with implicit memory is that the memory for skills (such as typing and bike riding) doesn't decline much over long retention intervals. Thus, the procedural memory system may handle implicit remembering, while the declarative memory system handles explicit remembering.

Although much remains to be learned, researchers have made some progress toward identifying the neural bases of declarative versus nondeclarative memory. Declarative memory appears to be handled by the hippocampal complex and the far-flung areas of the cortex with which it communicates (Eichenbaum 1997). It has proven more difficult to pinpoint the neural bases of nondeclarative memory because it consists of more of a hodgepodge of memory functions; however, structures such as the cerebellum and amygdala appear to contribute (Delis & Lucas, 1996; Squire & Knowlton, 2000).

Semantic Versus Episodic Memory

Endel Tulving (1986, 1993) has further subdivided declarative memory into episodic and semantic memory (see Figure 7.27). Both contain factual information, but episodic memory contains *personal facts* and semantic memory contains *general facts*. The *episodic memory system* is made up of chronological, or temporally dated, recollections of personal experiences. Episodic memory is a record of things you've done, seen, and heard. It includes information about *when* you did these things, saw them, or heard them. It contains recollections about being in a ninth-grade play, visiting the Grand Canyon, attending a Depeche Mode concert, or going to a movie last weekend. Tulving (2001) emphasizes that the function of episodic memory is "time travel"— that is, to allow one to reexperience the past. He also speculates that episodic memory may be unique to humans.

The *semantic memory system* contains general knowledge that is not tied to the time when the information was learned. Semantic memory contains information such as Christmas is December 25, dogs have four legs, and Phoenix is located in Arizona. You probably don't remember when you learned these facts. Information like this is usually stored undated. The distinction between episodic and semantic memory can be better appreciated by drawing an analogy to books: Episodic memory is like an autobiography, while semantic memory is like an encyclopedia.

Research suggests that memory for perceptual-motor skills, such as the skilled strokes that make Jennifer Capriati a tennis star, are stored in the procedural (nondeclarative) memory system. In contrast, memory for factual information, such as the rules of tennis or game strategies that have worked in the past, are thought to be stored in the declarative memory system.

© 2002 AP/Wide World Photos

Figure 7.28

Retrospective versus prospective memory. Most memory research has explored the dynamics of *retrospective memory*, which focuses on recollections from the past. However, *prospective memory*, which requires people to remember to perform actions in the future, also plays an important role in everyday life.

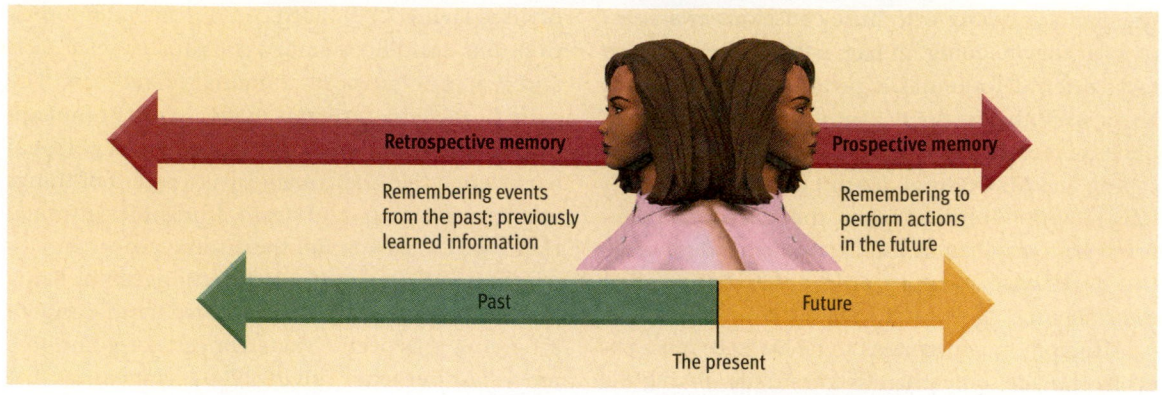

Retrospective memory — Remembering events from the past; previously learned information

Prospective memory — Remembering to perform actions in the future

Past — The present — Future

The memory deficits seen in some cases of amnesia suggest that episodic and semantic memory are separate systems. For instance, some amnesiacs forget most personal facts, while their recall of general facts is largely unaffected (Wood, Ebert, & Kinsbourne, 1982). However, debate continues about whether episodic and semantic memory have distinct neural bases (Barba et al., 1998; Wiggs, Weisberg, & Martin, 1999).

CONCEPT CHECK 7.3

Recognizing Various Types of Memory

Check your understanding of the various types of memory discussed in this chapter by matching the definitions below with the following: (a) declarative memory, (b) episodic memory, (c) explicit memory, (d) implicit memory, (e) long-term memory, (f) procedural memory, (g) prospective memory, (h) retrospective memory, (i) semantic memory, (j) sensory memory, and (k) short-term memory. The answers can be found in Appendix A.

_____ **1.** Memory for factual information.

_____ **2.** An unlimited capacity store that can hold information over lengthy periods of time.

_____ **3.** The preservation of information in its original sensory form for a brief time, usually only a fraction of a second.

_____ **4.** Type of memory apparent when retention is exhibited on a task that does not require intentional remembering.

_____ **5.** Chronological, or temporally dated, recollections of personal experiences.

_____ **6.** The repository of memories for actions, skills, operations, and conditioned responses.

_____ **7.** General knowledge that is not tied to the time when the information was learned.

_____ **8.** Remembering to perform future actions.

_____ **9.** A limited-capacity store that can maintain unrehearsed information for about 20 seconds.

Prospective Versus Retrospective Memory

A 1984 paper with a clever title, "Remembering to Do Things: A Forgotten Topic" (Harris, 1984), introduced yet another distinction between types of memory: *prospective memory* versus *retrospective memory* (see Figure 7.28). **Prospective memory involves remembering to perform actions in the future.** Examples of prospective memory tasks include remembering to walk the dog, to call someone, to grab the tickets for the big game, and to turn off your lawn sprinkler. In contrast, *retrospective memory* **involves remembering events from the past or previously learned information.** Retrospective memory is at work when you try to recall who won the Super Bowl last year, when you reminisce about your high school days, or when you try to recall what your professor said in a lecture last week. Prospective memory has been a "forgotten" topic in that it has been the subject of relatively little study. But that has begun to change, as research on prospective memory has increased in recent years (Einstein & McDaniel, 1996).

Researchers interested in prospective memory argue that the topic merits far more study because it plays such a pervasive role in everyday life (Graf & Uttl, 2001). Think about it—a brief trip to attend class at school can be saturated with prospective memory tasks. You may need to remember to pack your notebook, take your umbrella, turn off your coffeemaker, and grab your car keys before you even get out the door. People seem to vary tremendously in their ability to successfully carry out prospective memory tasks (Searleman, 1996). Individuals who appear deficient in prospective memory are often characterized as "absent-minded."

Much remains to be learned about the factors that influence prospective memory. *Habitual tasks,* such as remembering to pick up your mail, appear to be easier to remember than *infrequent tasks,* such as remembering to stop your mail delivery for an upcoming vacation (Searleman, 1996). Another key factor appears to be whether a prospective memory task is tied to some sort of cue. *Event-based tasks* involve future actions that should be triggered by a specific cue. For example, remembering to give a message to a friend is cued by seeing the friend, or remembering to take medication with one's meal is cued by the meal. *Time-based tasks* require that an action be performed at a certain time or after a certain length of time has elapsed. For example, you might want to start your video recorder at a specific time to tape an interesting show, or you might need to remember to turn off the oven after an hour of baking. Evidence suggests that the cues available in event-based prospective memory tasks make these tasks easier to remember than time-based tasks (Einstein & McDaniel, 1996). Age appears to be another factor that influences the functioning of prospective memory. Older adults seem to be somewhat more vulnerable to problems with prospective memory than younger people are (Einstein et al., 1998).

Putting It in Perspective

One of our integrative themes—the idea that people's experience of the world is subjective—stood head and shoulders above the rest in this chapter. Let's briefly review how the study of memory has illuminated this idea.

First, our discussion of attention as inherently selective should have shed light on why people's experience of the world is subjective. To a great degree, what you see in the world around you depends on where you focus your attention. This is one of the main reasons that two people can be exposed to the "same" events and walk away with entirely different perceptions. Second, the reconstructive nature of memory should further explain people's tendency to view the world with a subjective slant. When you observe an event, you don't store an exact copy of the event in your memory. Instead, you store a rough, "bare bones" approximation of the event that may be reshaped as time goes by.

A second theme that was apparent in our discussion of memory is psychology's theoretical diversity. We saw illuminating theoretical debates about the nature of memory storage, the causes of forgetting, and the existence of multiple memory systems. Finally, the multifaceted nature of memory demonstrated once again that behavior is governed by multiple causes. For instance, your memory of a specific event may be influenced by your attention to it, your level of processing, your elaboration, your exposure to interference, how you search your memory store, how you reconstruct the event, and so forth. Given the multifaceted nature of memory, it should come as no surprise that there are many ways to improve memory. We discuss a variety of strategies in the Personal Application section.

PREVIEW QUESTIONS
- How did this chapter demonstrate the subjectivity of experience?
- How did this chapter highlight psychology's theoretical diversity and multifactorial causation?

REVIEW OF KEY POINTS

- Implicit memory involves unintentional remembering, whereas explicit memory involves intentional recall. Implicit memory is unconscious, must be accessed indirectly, and is largely unaffected by amnesia, age, drugs, and the length of the retention interval.

- Declarative memory is memory for facts, while procedural memory is memory for actions and skills. Theorists suspect that the declarative memory system handles explicit memory, whereas the procedural memory system handles implicit memory.

- Declarative memory can be subdivided into episodic memory, for personal facts, and semantic memory, for general facts. Theorists have also distinguished between retrospective memory (remembering past events) and prospective memory (remembering to do things in the future).

- Our discussion of memory enhances our understanding of why people's experience of the world is highly subjective. Work in this area also shows that behavior is governed by multiple causes and that psychology is characterized by theoretical diversity.

Improving Everyday Memory

Answer the following "true" or "false."

____ **1** Memory strategies were recently invented by psychologists.

____ **2** Imagery can be used to help remember concrete words only.

____ **3** Overlearning of information leads to poor retention.

____ **4** Outlining what you read is not likely to affect retention.

____ **5** Massing practice in one long study session is better than distributing practice across several shorter sessions.

Mnemonic devices **are methods used to increase the recall of information.** They have a long history, so the first statement is false. In fact, one of the mnemonic devices covered in this Application—the method of loci—was described in Greece as early as 86–82 B.C. (Yates, 1966). Actually, mnemonic devices were much more important in ancient times than they are today. In ancient Greece and Rome, for instance, paper and pencils were not readily available for people to write down things they needed to remember, so they had to depend heavily on mnemonic devices.

Are mnemonic devices the key to improving one's everyday memory? No. Mnemonic devices can clearly be helpful in some situations (Wilding & Valentine, 1996), but they are not a panacea. They can be difficult to use and difficult to apply to many everyday situations. Most books and training programs designed to improve memory probably overemphasize mnemonic techniques (Searleman & Herrmann, 1994). Although less exotic strategies such as increasing rehearsal, engaging in deeper processing, and organizing material are more crucial to everyday memory, we will discuss some popular mnemonics as we proceed through this Application. Along the way, you'll learn that all of our opening true-false statements are false.

Engage in Adequate Rehearsal

Practice makes perfect, or so you've heard. In reality, practice is not likely to guarantee perfection, but it usually leads to improved retention. Studies show that retention improves with increased rehearsal. This improvement presumably occurs because rehearsal helps to transfer information into long-term memory. Continued rehearsal may also improve your *understanding* of assigned material, as your increased familiarity with the material may permit you to focus selectively on the most important points (Bromage & Mayer, 1986).

It even pays to overlearn material (Driskell, Willis, & Copper, 1992). **Overlearning refers to continued rehearsal of material after you first appear to have mastered it.** In one study, after subjects had mastered a list of nouns (they recited the list without error), Krueger (1929) required them to continue rehearsing for 50% or 100% more trials. Measuring retention at intervals up to 28 days, Krueger found that greater overlearning was related to better recall of the list. The practical implication of this finding is simple: You should not quit rehearsing material as soon as you appear to have mastered it. One other precaution is also worth mentioning. If you are memorizing some type of list, be aware of the serial position effect, which is often observed when subjects are tested on their memory of lists (Murdock, 2001). **The *serial-position effect* occurs when subjects show better recall for items at the beginning and end of a list than for items in the middle** (see Figure 7.29). The reasons for the serial-position effect are complex and need not concern us, but its pragmatic implications are clear: If you need to learn a list, allocate extra practice trials to items in the middle of the list and check your memorization of those items very carefully.

Schedule Distributed Practice and Minimize Interference

Let's assume that you need to study 9 hours for an exam. Should you "cram" all your studying into one 9-hour period (massed practice)? Or is it better to distribute your study among, say, three 3-hour periods on successive days (distributed practice)? The evidence indicates that retention tends to be greater after distributed practice than after massed practice (Glenberg, 1992; Payne & Wenger, 1996). For instance, Underwood (1970) studied children (ages 9 to 14) who practiced a list of words four times, either in one long session or in four separate sessions. He found that distributed practice led to better recall than a similar amount of massed practice (see Figure 7.30). The superiority of distributed practice suggests that cramming is an ill-advised approach to studying for exams (Dempster, 1996).

Because interference is a major cause of forgetting, you'll probably want to think about how you can minimize it. This issue is especially important for students, because memorizing information for one course can interfere with the retention of information for another course. It may help to allocate study for specific courses to separate days. Thorndyke and Hayes-Roth (1979) found that similar material produced less interference when it was learned on different days. Thus, the day before an exam in a course, you should study for that course only—if possible. If demands in other courses make that plan impossible, you should study the test material last.

Emphasize Deep Processing and Organize Information

Research on levels of processing suggests that how *often* you go over material is less critical than the *depth* of processing that you engage in (Craik & Tulving, 1975).

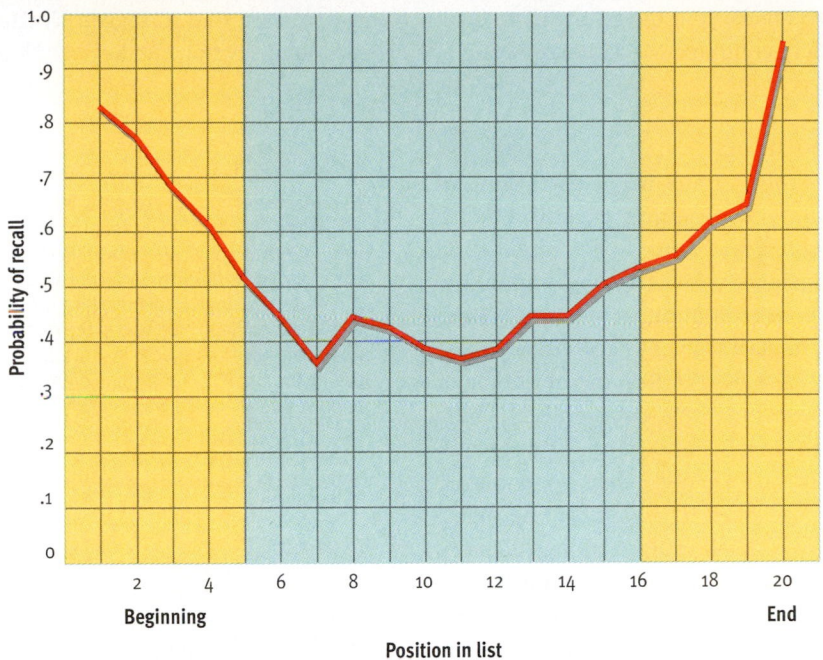

Figure 7.29

The serial-position effect. After learning a list of items to remember, people tend to recall more of the items from the beginning and the end of the list than from the middle, producing the characteristic U-shaped curve shown here. This phenomenon is called the serial-position effect.

SOURCE: Adapted from Rundus, D. (1971). Analysis of rehearsal processes in free recall. *Journal of Experimental Psychology, 89*, 63–77. Copyright © 1971 by the American Psychological Association. Adapted by permission of the author.

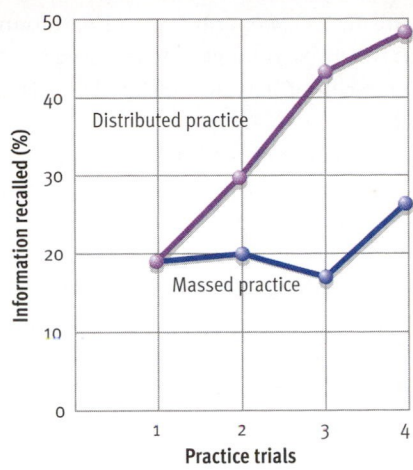

Figure 7.30

Effects of massed versus distributed practice on retention. Children in the Underwood (1970) study showed better recall of information when practice sessions were distributed over time as opposed to being massed together in one session.

SOURCE: Adapted from Underwood, B. J. (1970). A breakdown of the total-time law in free-recall learning. *Journal of Verbal Learning and Verbal Behavior, 9*, 573–580. Copyright © 1970 Elsevier Science USA, reproduced with permission from the publisher.

Thus, if you expect to remember what you read, you have to wrestle fully with its meaning. Many students could probably benefit if they spent less time on rote repetition and devoted more effort to actually paying attention to and analyzing the meaning of their reading assignments. In particular, it is useful to make material *personally* meaningful. When you read your textbooks, try to relate information to your own life and experience. For example, when you read about classical conditioning, try to think of responses that you display that are attributable to classical conditioning.

Retention tends to be greater when information is well organized. The value of organization has been apparent in studies of people who exhibit remarkable memory capability. For example, Ericsson and Polson (1988) have studied a waiter, known as J. C., who can remember up to 20 complicated dinner orders without taking notes. They found that control subjects tried to memorize dinner requests in the order in which the requests were presented, whereas J. C. reorganized information by dinner element (salad dressings, vegetables, and so on).

Gordon Bower (1970) has shown that hierarchical organization is particularly helpful when it is applicable. Thus, it may be a good idea to *outline* reading assignments for school. Consistent with this reasoning, there is some empirical evidence that outlining material from textbooks can enhance retention of the material (McDaniel, Waddill, & Shakesby, 1996).

Enrich Encoding with Verbal Mnemonics

When you memorize abstract information, it helps to make the information personally meaningful, but it's not always easy to do so. For instance, when you study chemistry you may have a hard time relating to polymers at a personal level. Thus, many mnemonic devices—such as acrostics, acronyms, and narrative methods—are designed to make abstract material more meaningful.

Acrostics and Acronyms

Acrostics are phrases (or poems) in which the first letter of each word (or line) functions as a cue to help you recall information to be remembered. For instance, you may remember the order of musical notes with the saying "Every good boy does fine" (or "deserves favor"). A slight variation on acrostics is the *acronym*—a word formed out of the first letters of a series of words. Students memorizing the order of colors in the light spectrum often store the name "Roy G. Biv" to remember red, orange, yellow, green, blue, indigo, and violet. Notice that this acronym takes advantage of the principle of chunking.

Narrative Methods

Another useful way to remember a list of words is to create a story that includes the words in the appropriate order. The narrative both increases the meaningfulness of the words and links them in a specific order.

Examples of this technique can be seen in Figure 7.31. Bower and Clark (1969) found that this procedure greatly enhanced subjects' recall of lists of unrelated words (as shown in Figure 7.31).

Why—and how—would you use the narrative method? Let's assume that you always manage to forget to put one item in your gym bag on your way to the pool. Short of pasting a list on the inside of the bag, how can you remember everything you need? You could make up a story like the following that includes the items you need:

The wind and rain in COMBINATION nearly LOCKed out the rescue efforts. CAP, the flying ace, TOWELed the soap from his eyes, pulled his GOGGLES from his SUIT pocket, and COMBed the BRUSH for survivors.

Rhymes

Another verbal mnemonic that people often rely on is rhyming. You've probably repeated, "I before E except after C . . ." thousands of times. Perhaps you also remember the number of days in each month with the old standby, "Thirty days hath September . . ." Rhyming something to remember it is an old and useful trick.

Enrich Encoding with Visual Mnemonics

Memory can be enhanced by the use of visual imagery. As you may recall, Allan Paivio (1986) believes that visual images create a second memory code and that two codes are better than one for enhancing recall. Many popular mnemonic devices depend on visual imagery, including the link method, method of loci, and keyword method.

Link Method

The *link method* involves forming a mental image of items to be remembered in a way that links them together. For instance, suppose you need to remember some items to pick up at the drugstore: a news magazine, shaving cream, film, and pens. To remember these items, you might visualize a public figure on the magazine cover shaving with a pen while being photographed.

There is some evidence that the more bizarre you make your image, the more helpful it is likely to be (McDaniel & Einstein, 1986).

Method of Loci

The *method of loci* involves taking an imaginary walk along a familiar path where images of items to be remembered are associated with certain locations. The first step is to commit to memory a series of loci, or places along a path. Usually these loci are specific locations in your home or neighborhood. Then envision each thing you want to remember in one of these locations. Try to form distinctive, vivid images. When you need to remember the items, imagine yourself walking along the path. The various loci on your path should serve as cues for the retrieval of the images that you formed (see Figure 7.32). Evidence suggests that the method of loci can be effective in increasing retention (Cornoldi & De Beni, 1996). Moreover, this method ensures that items are remembered in their *correct order* because the order is determined by the sequence of locations along the pathway.

Keyword Method

Visual images are also useful when you need to form an association between a pair of items, such as a person's name and face or a foreign word and its English translation. However, there is a potential problem that you may recall from our earlier discussion of visual imagery. It's difficult to generate images to represent abstract words (Paivio, 1969). A way to avoid this problem is to use the *keyword method,* in which you associate a concrete word with an abstract word and generate an image to represent the concrete word.

A practical use of this method is to help you remember the names of people you meet (Morris, Jones, & Hampson, 1978). Just associate a concrete word with the name and then form an image of the associated word. The associated word, which is the *keyword,* should sound like the name that's being learned. For example, you might use Garden as a keyword for *Gordon.* And *debtor man* might be a good keyword for

Detterman, if you form an image of Mr. Detterman dressed in ragged clothes. Research suggests that the keyword method

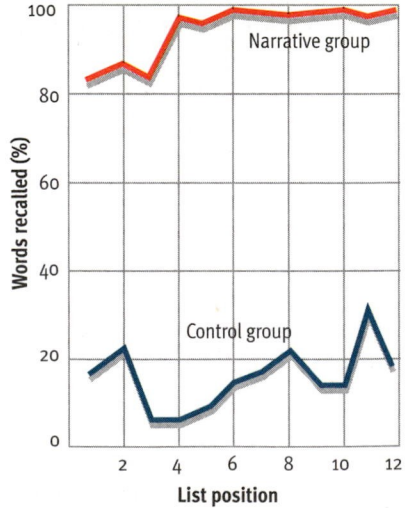

Figure 7.31

Narrative methods of remembering.
Bower and Clark (1969) presented participants with 12 lists of words. Subjects in the "narrative group" were asked to recall the words by constructing a story out of them (like the two stories shown here). Subjects in the control group were given no special instructions. Recoding the material in story form dramatically improved recall, as the graph clearly shows.

SOURCE: Adapted from Bower, G. H., & Clark, M. C. (1969). Narrative stories as mediators of serial learning. *Psychonomic Science, 14*, 181–182. Copyright © 1969 by the Psychonomic Society. Adapted by permission of the Psychonomic Society.

Word lists	Stories
Bird	A man dressed in a *Bird Costume*
Costume	and wearing a *Mailbox* on his
Mailbox	*Head* was seen leaping into
Head	the *River*. A *Nurse* ran out of a
River	nearby *Theater* and applied *Wax*
Nurse	to his *Eyelids*, but her efforts
Theater	were in vain. He died and was
Wax	tossed into the *Furnace*.
Eyelid	
Furnace	

Word lists	Stories
Rustler	A *Rustler* lived in a *Penthouse* on
Penthouse	top of a *Mountain*. His specialty
Mountain	was the three-toed *Sloth*. He
Sloth	would take his captive animals
Tavern	to a *Tavern* where he would
Fuzz	remove *Fuzz* from their *Glands*.
Gland	Unfortunately, all this exposure
Antler	to sloth fuzz caused him to grow
Pencil	*Antlers*. So he gave up his pro-
Vitamin	fession and went to work in a
	Pencil factory. As a precaution
	he also took a lot of *Vitamin* E.

Figure 7.32

The method of loci. In this example from Bower (1970), a person about to go shopping pairs items to remember with familiar places (loci) arranged in a natural sequence: (1) hot dogs/driveway; (2) cat food/garage interior; (3) tomatoes/front door; (4) bananas/coat closet shelf; (5) whiskey/kitchen sink. The shopper then uses imagery to associate the items on the shopping list with the loci, as shown in the drawing: (1) giant hot dog rolls down a driveway; (2) a cat noisily devours cat food in the garage; (3) ripe tomatoes are splattered on the front door; (4) bunches of bananas are hung from the closet shelf; (5) the contents of a bottle of whiskey gurgle down the kitchen sink. As the last panel shows, the shopper recalls the items by mentally touring the loci associated with them.

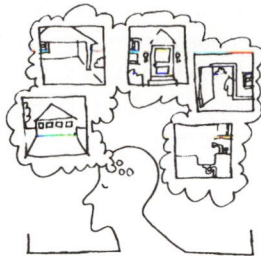

SOURCE: From Bower, G. H. (1970). Analysis of a mnemonic device. *American Scientist, 58,* 496–499. Copyright © 1970 by Scientific Research Society. Reprinted by permission.

can enhance the retention of foreign language and other types of educational material (Bellezza, 1996; Gruneberg, Sykes, & Gillett, 1994).

Levin and Levin (1990) trained students to apply the keyword method to unfamiliar terms in a plant classification system. They coupled this approach with the link method, which was used to group terms that belonged together in categories. The researchers found that these methods enhanced students' memory of the classification system (see Figure 7.33).

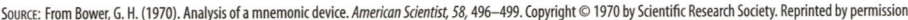

REVIEW OF KEY POINTS

- Mnemonic devices are methods used to increase the recall of information. Rehearsal, even when it involves overlearning, facilitates retention, although one should be wary of the serial-position effect. Distributed practice tends to be more efficient than massed practice.

- It is wise to plan study sessions so as to minimize interference and maximize deep processing. Evidence also suggests that organization enhances retention, so outlining texts may be valuable.

- Meaningfulness can be enhanced through the use of verbal mnemonics such as acrostics, acronyms, and narrative methods. The link method, the method of loci, and the keyword method are mnemonic devices that depend on the value of visual imagery.

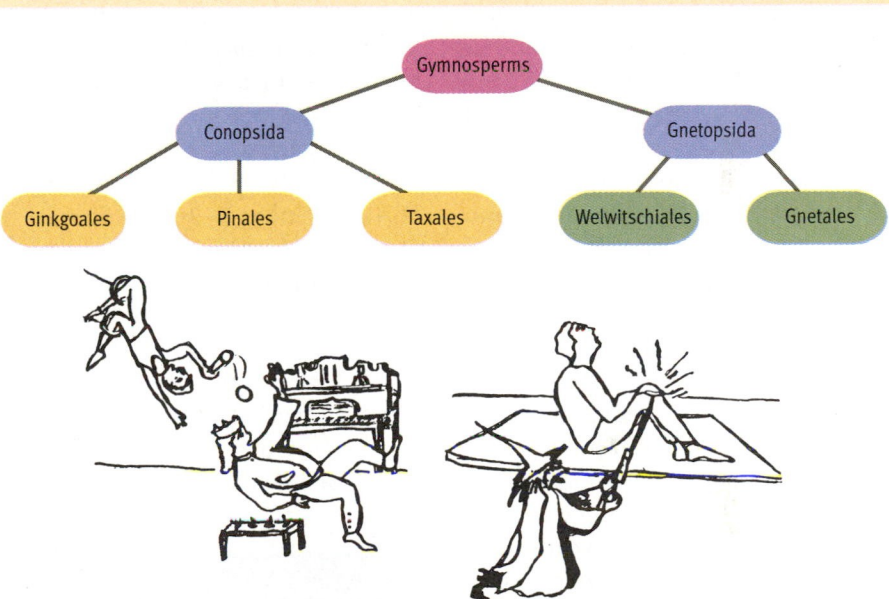

To remember that the subdivision *gymnosperms* includes the class *conopsida*, which in turn includes the three orders *ginkgoales*, *pinales*, and *taxales*, study the picture of the swinging gymnast with the ice cream cone in his hand. The ice cream is about to splat in the face of the king who is leaping from the bench of his royal piano after sitting on some tacks.

To remember that the subdivision *gymnosperms* includes the class *gnetopsida*, which in turn includes the two orders *welwitschiales* and *gnetales*, study the picture of the fallen gymnast holding his sore knee tops. He is being treated (or tricked!) by a witch doctor who is sticking a very long needle into his injured knee.

Figure 7.33

Combining the keyword and link methods to aid recall. Levin and Levin (1990) set out to help students memorize a difficult plant classification system (a portion of the system is shown in the top part of the figure). They taught students to use a technique that essentially combines the keyword and link methods. Students were trained to generate keywords for the abstract terms in the hierarchy and to form images that linked the keywords that corresponded to portions of the classification system (two examples are shown in the bottom part of the figure). This creative use of visual imagery enhanced students' recall of the plant classification system.

SOURCE: Adapted from Levin, M. E., & Levin, J. R. (1990). Scientific mnemonomies: Methods for maximizing more than memory. *American Educational Research Journal, 27* (2), 301–321. Copyright © 1990 by American Educational Research Association. Adapted by permission.

Understanding the Fallibility of Eyewitness Accounts

A number of years ago, the Wilmington, Delaware, area was plagued by a series of armed robberies committed by a perpetrator who was dubbed the "gentleman bandit" by the press because he was an unusually polite and well-groomed thief. The local media published a sketch of the gentleman bandit and eventually an alert resident turned in a suspect who resembled the sketch. Much to everyone's surprise, the accused thief was a Catholic priest named Father Bernard Pagano—who vigorously denied the charges. Unfortunately for Father Pagano, his denials and alibis were unconvincing and he was charged with the crimes. At the trial, *seven* eyewitnesses confidently identified Father Pagano as the gentleman bandit. The prosecution was well on its way to a conviction when there was a stunning turn of events—another man, Ronald Clouser, confessed to the police that he was the gentleman bandit. The authorities dropped the charges against Father Pagano and the relieved priest was able to return to his normal existence (Rodgers, 1982).

This bizarre tale of mistaken identity—which sounds like it was lifted from a movie script—raises some interesting questions about memory. How could seven people "remember" seeing Father Pagnano commit armed robberies that he had nothing to do with? How could they mistake him for Ronald Clouser, when the two really didn't look very similar (see photos)? How could they be so confident when they were so wrong? Perhaps you're thinking that this is just one case and it must be unrepresentative (which would be sound critical thinking). Well, yes, it *is* a rather extreme example of eyewitness fallibility, but researchers have compiled mountains of evidence that eyewitness testimony is not nearly as reliable or as accurate as widely assumed (Cutler & Penrod, 1995; Kassin et al., 2001). This finding is ironic in that people are most

confident about their assertions when they can say, "I saw it with my own eyes." Television news shows like to use the title "Eyewitness News" to create the impression that they chronicle events with great clarity and accuracy. And our legal system accords special status to eyewitness testimony because it is considered much more dependable than hearsay or circumstantial evidence.

So, why are eyewitness accounts surprisingly inaccurate? Well, a host of factors and processes contribute to this inaccuracy. Let's briefly review some of the relevant processes that were introduced in the main body of the chapter; then we'll focus on two common errors in thinking that also contribute.

Can you think of any memory phenomena described in the chapter that seem likely to undermine eyewitness accuracy? You could point to the fact that *memory is a reconstructive process,* and eyewitness recall is likely to be distorted by the schemas that people have for various events. A second consideration is that *witnesses sometimes make source-monitoring errors* and get confused about where they saw a face. For example, one rape victim mixed up her as-

sailant with a guest on a TV show that she was watching when she was attacked. Fortunately, the falsely accused suspect had an airtight alibi, as he could demonstrate that he was on live television when the rape occurred (Schacter, 1996). Perhaps the most pervasive factor is the misinformation effect (Loftus, 1993). *Witnesses' recall of events is routinely distorted by information introduced after the event* by police officers, attorneys, news reports, and so forth. In addition to these factors, eyewitness inaccuracy is fueled by the *hindsight bias* and *overconfidence effects.*

The Contribution of Hindsight Bias

The *hindsight bias* is the tendency to **mold our interpretation of the past to fit how events actually turned out.** When you know the outcome of an event, this knowledge slants your recall of how the event unfolded and what your thinking was at the time. With the luxury of hindsight, there is a curious tendency to say, "I knew it all along" when explaining events that objectively would have been difficult

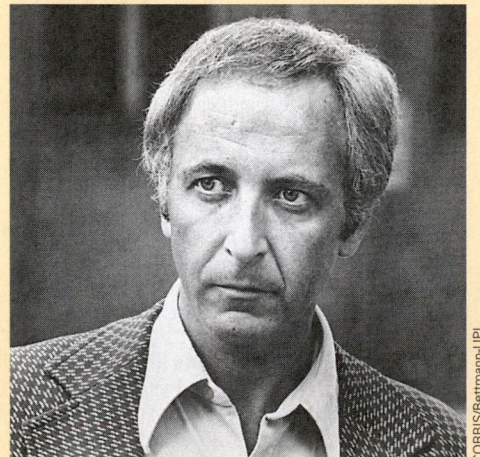

Although he doesn't look that much like the real "gentleman bandit," who is shown on the left, seven eyewitnesses identified Father Pagnano (right) as the gentleman bandit, showing just how unreliable eyewitness accounts can be.

Although courts give special credence to eyewitness testimony, scientific evidence indicates that eyewitness accounts are less reliable than widely assumed.

to foresee. With regard to eyewitnesses, their recollections may often be distorted by knowing that a particular person has been arrested and accused of the crime in question. For example, Wells and Bradfield (1998) had simulated eyewitnesses select a perpetrator from a photo lineup. The eyewitnesses' confidence in their identifications tended to be quite modest, which made sense given that the actual perpetrator was not even in the lineup. But when some subjects were told, "Good, you identified the actual suspect," they became highly confident about their identifications, which obviously were incorrect. In another study, participants read identical scenarios about a couple's first date that either had no ending or ended in a rape (described in one additional sentence). The subjects who received the rape ending reconstructed the story to be more consistent with their stereotypes of how rapes occur (Carli, 1999).

The Contribution of Overconfidence

Another flaw in thinking that contributes to inaccuracy in eyewitness accounts is people's tendency to be overconfident about the reliability of their memory. When tested for their memory of general information, people tend to overestimate their accuracy (Lichtenstein, Fischhoff, & Phillips, 1982). In studies of eyewitness recall, participants also tend to be overconfident about their recollections. Although jurors tend to be more convinced by eyewitnesses who appear confident, the evidence indicates that

there is only a modest correlation between eyewitness confidence and eyewitness accuracy (Bornstein & Zickafoose, 1999).

Strategies to Reduce Overconfidence

Can you learn to make better judgments of the accuracy of your recall of everyday events? Yes, with effort you can get better at making accurate estimates of how likely you are to be correct in the recall of some fact or event. One reason that people tend to be overconfident is that if they can't think of any reasons that they might be wrong, they assume they must be right. Thus, overconfidence is fueled by yet another common error in thinking—*the failure to seek disconfirming evidence.* Even veteran scientists fall prey to this weakness, as most people don't seriously consider reasons that they might be wrong about something (Mynatt, Doherty, & Tweney, 1978).

Thus, to make more accurate assessments of what you know and don't know, it helps to engage in a deliberate process of considering why you might be wrong. Here is an example. Based on your reading of Chapter 1, write down the schools of thought associated with the following major theorists: William James, John B. Watson, and Carl Rogers. After you provide your answers, rate your confidence that the information you just provided is correct. Now, write three reasons that your answers might be wrong and three reasons they might be

correct. Most people will balk at this exercise, arguing that they cannot think of any reasons that they might be wrong, but after some resistance, they can come up with several. Such reasons might include "I was half asleep when I read that part of the chapter" or "I might be confusing Watson and James." Reasons that you think you're right could include "I distinctly recall discussing this with my friend" or "I really worked on those names in Chapter 1." After listing reasons that you might be right and reasons that you might be wrong, rate your confidence in your accuracy once again. Guess what? Most people are less confident after going through such an exercise than they were before (depending, of course, on the nature of the topic).

The new confidence ratings tend to be more realistic than the original ratings (Koriat, Lichtenstein, & Fischhoff, 1980). Why? Because this exercise forces you to think more deeply about your answers and to search your memory for related information. Most people stop searching their memory as soon as they generate an answer they believe to be correct. Thus, the process of considering reasons that you might be wrong about something—a process that people rarely engage in—is a useful critical thinking skill that can reduce overconfidence effects. Better assessment of what you know and don't know can be an important determinant of the quality of the decisions you make and the way you solve problems and reason from evidence.

Table 7.1 Critical Thinking Skills Discussed in This Application	
Skill	**Description**
Understanding the limitations and fallibility of human memory	The critical thinker appreciates that memory is reconstructive and that even eyewitness accounts may be distorted or inaccurate.
Recognizing the bias in hindsight analysis	The critical thinker understands that knowing the outcome of events biases our recall and interpretation of the events.
Recognizing overconfidence in human cognition	The critical thinker understands that people are frequently overconfident about the accuracy of their projections for the future and their recollections of the past.
Understanding the need to seek disconfirming evidence	The critical thinker understands the value of thinking about how or why one might be wrong about something.

Key Ideas

Encoding: Getting Information into Memory

● The multifaceted process of memory begins with encoding. Attention, which facilitates encoding, is inherently selective and has been compared to a filter.

● According to levels-of-processing theory, the kinds of memory codes people create depend on which aspects of a stimulus are emphasized; deeper processing results in better recall of information. Structural, phonemic, and semantic encoding represent progressively deeper and more effective levels of processing.

● Elaboration enriches encoding by linking a stimulus to other information. Visual imagery may work in much the same way, creating two memory codes rather than just one. Encoding that emphasizes personal self-reference may be especially useful in facilitating retention.

Storage: Maintaining Information in Memory

● Sensory memory preserves information in its original form, for only a fraction of a second. Short-term memory has a limited capacity (capable of holding about seven chunks of information) and can maintain unrehearsed information for up to about 20 seconds. Short-term memory is working memory and appears to involve more than a simple rehearsal loop.

● Long-term memory is an unlimited capacity store that may hold information indefinitely. Certain lines of evidence suggest that LTM storage may be permanent, but the evidence is not convincing. Some theorists have raised doubts about whether short-term and long-term memory are really separate.

● Information in LTM can be organized in simple clusters, conceptual hierarchies, or semantic networks. A schema is an organized cluster of knowledge about a particular object or sequence of events. PDP models of memory assert that specific memories correspond to particular patterns of activation in connectionist networks.

Retrieval: Getting Information Out of Memory

● Reinstating the context of an event can facilitate recall. This factor may account for cases in which hypnosis appears to aid recall. Memories are not exact replicas of past experiences. Memory is partially reconstructive.

● Research on the misinformation effect shows that information learned after an event can alter one's memory of it. Source-monitoring and reality-monitoring errors may explain why people sometimes "recall" something that was only suggested to them or something they only imagined.

Forgetting: When Memory Lapses

● Ebbinghaus's early studies of nonsense syllables suggested that people forget very rapidly. Subsequent research showed that Ebbinghaus's forgetting curve was exceptionally steep. Forgetting can be measured by asking people to recall, recognize, or relearn information.

● Decay theory proposes that forgetting occurs spontaneously with the passage of time. It has proven difficult to show that decay occurs in long-term memory. Interference theory proposes that people forget information because of competition from other material.

● Repression involves the motivated forgetting of painful or unpleasant memories. Recent years have seen a surge of reports of repressed memories of sexual abuse in childhood. The authenticity of these recovered memories is the subject of controversy.

In Search of the Memory Trace: The Physiology of Memory

● Memory traces may reflect alterations in neurotransmitter release at specific locations. Memory traces may also consist of localized neural circuits that undergo long-term potentiation. The study of amnesia and other research has implicated the hippocampal region as a key player in memory processes. The hippocampal region may be responsible for the consolidation of memories, but its exact role remains the subject of debate.

Are There Multiple Memory Systems?

● Differences between implicit and explicit memory suggest that people may have several separate memory systems. Declarative memory is memory for facts, whereas nondeclarative or procedural memory is memory for actions and skills. Declarative memory can be subdivided into episodic memory, for personal facts, and semantic memory, for general facts. Theorists have also distinguished between retrospective and prospective memory.

Putting It in Perspective

● Our discussion of attention and memory enhances understanding of why people's experience of the world is highly subjective. Work in this area also highlights the field's theoretical diversity and shows that behavior is governed by multiple causes.

Personal Application ● Improving Everyday Memory

● Rehearsal, even when it involves overlearning, facilitates retention, although one should be wary of the serial-position effect. Distributed practice tends to be more efficient than massed practice. It is wise to plan study sessions so as to minimize interference. Processing during rehearsal should be deep.

● Meaningfulness can be enhanced with verbal mnemonics such as acrostics, acronyms, and narrative methods. The link method, the method of loci, and the keyword method are mnemonic devices that depend on visual imagery.

Critical Thinking Application ● Understanding the Fallibility of Eyewitness Accounts

● Research indicates that eyewitness memory is not nearly as reliable or as accurate as widely believed. Two common errors in thinking that contribute to this situation are the hindsight bias and overconfidence effects. The hindsight bias is the tendency to reshape one's interpretation of the past to fit with known outcomes.

Key Terms

Anterograde amnesia
Attention
Chunk
Clustering
Conceptual hierarchy
Connectionist models
Consolidation
Decay theory
Declarative memory system
Dual-coding theory
Elaboration
Encoding
Encoding specificity principle
Episodic memory system
Explicit memory
Flashbulb memories
Forgetting curve
Hindsight bias
Implicit memory
Interference theory
Keyword method
Levels-of-processing theory
Link method
Long-term memory (LTM)
Long-term potentiation (LTP)
Method of loci
Mnemonic devices
Nondeclarative memory system
Overlearning
Parallel distributed processing (PDP) models
Proactive interference
Procedural memory system
Prospective memory
Reality monitoring
Recall
Recognition
Rehearsal
Relearning
Repression
Retention
Retrieval
Retroactive interference
Retrograde amnesia
Retrospective memory
Schema
Self-referent encoding
Semantic memory system
Semantic network
Sensory memory
Serial-position effect
Short-term memory (STM)
Source monitoring
Source-monitoring error
Storage
Tip-of-the-tongue phenomenon
Transfer-appropriate processing

Key People

Richard Atkinson and Richard Shiffrin
Fergus Craik and Robert Lockhart
Hermann Ebbinghaus
Marcia Johnson
Elizabeth Loftus
George Miller
Brenda Milner
Endel Tulving

PRACTICE TEST

1. Getting information into memory is called _____; getting information out of memory is called _____.
   - A. storage; retrieval
   - B. encoding; storage
   - C. encoding; retrieval
   - D. storage; encoding

2. The word *big* is flashed on a screen. A mental picture of the word big represents a _____ code; the definition "large in size" represents a _____ code; "sounds like pig" represents a _____ code.
   - A. structural; phonemic; semantic
   - B. phonemic; semantic; structural
   - C. structural; semantic; phonemic
   - D. phonemic; structural; semantic

3. Miles is listening as his mother rattles through a list of fifteen or so things that he needs to remember to pack for an upcoming trip. According to George Miller, if Miles doesn't write the items down as he hears them, he will probably remember:
   - A. fewer than 5 items from the list.
   - B. about 10 to 12 items from the list.
   - C. all the items from the list.
   - D. 5 to 9 items from the list.

4. Which statement best represents current evidence on the durability of long-term storage?
   - A. All forgetting involves breakdowns in retrieval.
   - B. LTM is like a barrel of marbles in which none of the marbles ever leak out.
   - C. There is no convincing evidence that all one's memories are stored away permanently.
   - D. All long-term memories gradually decay at a constant rate.

5. An organized cluster of knowledge about a particular object or event is called a:
   - A. semantic network.
   - B. conceptual hierarchy.
   - C. schema.
   - D. retrieval cue.

6. The tip-of-the-tongue phenomenon:
   - A. is a temporary inability to remember something you know, accompanied by a feeling that it's just out of reach.
   - B. is clearly due to a failure in retrieval.
   - C. reflects a permanent loss of information from LTM.
   - D. is both a and b.

7. Roberto is telling Rachel about some juicy gossip when she stops him and informs him that she is the one who passed this gossip on to him about a week ago. In this example, Roberto has:
   - A. been fooled by the misinformation effect.
   - B. made a reality-monitoring error.
   - C. made a source-monitoring error.
   - D. made a prospective memory error.

8. If decay theory is correct:
   - A. information can never be permanently lost from long-term memory.
   - B. forgetting is simply a case of retrieval failure.
   - C. the principal cause of forgetting should be the passage of time.
   - D. all of the above.

9. Bulldog McRae was recently traded to a new football team. He is struggling to remember the plays for his new team because he keeps mixing them up with the plays from his previous team. Bulldog's problem illustrates the operation of:
   - A. retroactive interference.
   - B. proactive interference.
   - C. transfer-inappropriate processing.
   - D. parallel distributed processing.

10. Many amnesiacs demonstrate _____ memory, even though their _____ memory is extremely impaired.
    - A. declarative; procedural
    - B. conscious; unconscious
    - C. implicit; explicit
    - D. semantic; episodic

11. Your memory of how to brush your teeth is contained in your _____ memory.
    - A. declarative
    - B. procedural
    - C. structural
    - D. episodic

12. Your knowledge that birds fly, that the sun rises in the east, and that 2 + 2 = 4 is contained in your _____ memory.
    - A. structural
    - B. procedural
    - C. implicit
    - D. semantic

13. Dorothy memorized her shopping list. When she got to the store, however, she found she had forgotten many of the items from the middle of the list. This is an example of:
    - A. inappropriate encoding.
    - B. retrograde amnesia.
    - C. proactive interference.
    - D. the serial-position effect.

14. Overlearning:
    - A. refers to continued rehearsal of material after the point of apparent mastery.
    - B. promotes improved recall.
    - C. should not be done, since it leads to increased interference.
    - D. both a and b.

15. The tendency to mold one's interpretation of the past to fit how events actually turned out is called:
    - A. the overconfidence effect.
    - B. selective amnesia.
    - C. retroactive interference.
    - D. the hindsight bias.

Answers

1	C pp. 261–262	6	D p. 275	11	B p. 290
2	C pp. 263–264	7	C pp. 277–278	12	D pp. 290–291
3	D pp. 268–269	8	C p. 281	13	D pp. 294–295
4	C pp. 270–271	9	B pp. 281–282	14	D p. 294
5	C p. 273	10	C pp. 289–290	15	D p. 298

ON THE WEB

For additional resources on the topics covered in this chapter, visit the *Psychology: Themes and Variations* Web site, where you will find practice quizzes, tutorials, Web links, simulations, critical thinking activities, flash cards, interactive exercises, and suggested readings available through INFOTRAC.

http://psychology.wadsworth.com/weiten_themes6e/

CHAPTER 8

© Sally Brown/Index Stock Imagery

Language and Thought

"*Mr. Watson—Mr. Sherlock Holmes,*" said Stamford, *introducing us.*

"*How are you?*" *he said, cordially, gripping my hand with a strength for which I should hardly have given him credit.* "*You have been in Afghanistan, I perceive.*"

"*How on earth did you know that?*" *I asked, in astonishment.*

(From A Study in Scarlet *by Arthur Conan Doyle)*

If you've ever read any Sherlock Holmes stories, you know that the great detective continually astonished his stalwart companion, Dr. Watson, with his extraordinary deductions. Obviously, Holmes could not arrive at his conclusions without a chain of reasoning. Yet to him even an elaborate reasoning process was a simple, everyday act. Consider his feat of knowing at once, on first meeting Watson, that the doctor had been in Afghanistan. When asked, Holmes explained his reasoning as follows:

"*I knew you came from Afghanistan. From long habit the train of thought ran so swiftly through my mind that I arrived at the conclusion without being conscious of the intermediate steps. There were such steps, however. The train of reasoning ran: 'Here is a gentleman of a medical type, but with the air of a military man. Clearly an army doctor, then. He has just come from the tropics, for his face is dark, and that is not the natural tint of his skin, for his wrists are fair. He has undergone hardship and sickness, as his haggard face says clearly. His left arm has been injured. He holds it in a stiff and unnatural manner. Where in the tropics could an English army doctor have seen much hardship and got his arm wounded? Clearly in Afghanistan.' The whole train of thought did not occupy a second.*"

Admittedly, Sherlock Holmes's deductive feats are fictional. But even to read about them appreciatively—let alone imagine them, as Sir Arthur Conan Doyle did—is a remarkably complex mental act. Our everyday thought processes seem ordinary to us only because we take them for granted, just as Holmes saw

nothing extraordinary in what to him was a simple deduction.

In reality, everyone is a Sherlock Holmes, continually performing magical feats of thought. Even elementary perception—for instance, watching a football game or a ballet—involves elaborate cognitive processes. People must sort through distorted, constantly shifting perceptual inputs and deduce what they see out there in the real world. Imagine, then, the complexity of thought required to read a book, fix an automobile, or balance a checkbook. Of course, all this is not to say that human thought processes are flawless or unequaled. You probably own a $10 calculator that can run circles around you when it comes to computing square roots. As we'll see, some of the most interesting research in this chapter focuses on ways in which people's thinking can be limited, simplistic, or illogical.

In any event, as we have noted before, **cognition refers to the mental processes involved in acquiring knowledge.** In other words, cognition involves thinking. When psychology first emerged as an independent science in the 19th century, it focused on the mind. Mental processes were explored through *introspection*—analysis of one's own conscious experience (see Chapter 1). Unfortunately, early psychologists' study of mental processes ran aground, as the method of introspection yielded unreliable results. Psychology's empirical approach depends on observation, and private mental events proved difficult to observe. Furthermore, during the first half of the 20th century, the study of cognition was actively discouraged by the theoretical dominance of behaviorism. Herbert Simon, a pioneer of cognitive psychology, recalls that "you couldn't use a word like *mind* in a psychology journal—you'd get your mouth washed out with soap" (Holden, 1986).

Although it wasn't fully recognized until much later, the 1950s brought a "cognitive revolution" in psychology (Baars, 1986). Renegade theorists, such as Herbert Simon, began to argue that behaviorists' exclusive focus on overt responses was doomed to

"*You couldn't use a word like* mind *in a psychology journal—you'd get your mouth washed out with soap.*"
HERBERT SIMON

yield an incomplete understanding of human functioning. More important, creative new approaches to research on cognitive processes led to exciting progress. For example, in his book on the cognitive revolution, Howard Gardner (1985) notes that three major advances were reported at a watershed 1956 conference—in just one day! First, Herbert Simon and Allen Newell described the first computer program to successfully simulate human problem solving. Second, Noam Chomsky outlined a new model that changed the way psychologists studied language. Third, George Miller delivered the legendary paper that we discussed in Chapter 7, arguing that the capacity of short-term memory is seven (plus or minus two) items. Since then, cognitive science has grown into a robust, interdisciplinary enterprise (Simon, 1992). Besides memory (which we covered in Chapter 7), cognitive psychologists investigate the complexities of language, problem solving, decision making, and reasoning. We'll look at all these topics in this chapter, beginning with language.

Language: Turning Thoughts into Words

PREVIEW QUESTIONS
- What are the four key properties of language?
- How is language structured?
- How do children progress in their use of words and sentences?
- What types of mistakes do they tend to make?
- Does learning two languages at the same time affect language or cognitive development?
- What age is best for learning a second language?

Language obviously plays a fundamental role in human behavior. Indeed, if you were to ask people, "What characteristic most distinguishes humans from other living creatures?" a great many would reply, "Language." In this section, we'll discuss the nature, structure, and development of language and related topics, such as bilingualism and whether animals can learn language.

What Is Language?

A *language* consists of symbols that convey meaning, plus rules for combining those symbols, that can be used to generate an infinite variety of messages. Language systems include a number of critical properties.

First, language is *symbolic*. People use spoken sounds and written words to represent objects, actions, events, and ideas. The word *lamp,* for instance, refers to a class of objects that have certain properties. The symbolic nature of language greatly expands what people can communicate about. Symbols allow one to refer to objects that may be in another place and to events that happened at another time (for example, a lamp broken at work yesterday). Language symbols are flexible in that a variety of somewhat different objects may be called by the same name (consider the diversity of lamps, for example).

Second, language is *semantic,* or meaningful. The symbols used in a language are arbitrary in that no built-in relationship exists between the look or sound of words and the objects they stand for. Take, for instance, the writing object that you may have in your hand right now. It's represented by the word *pen* in English, *stylo* in French, and *pluma* in Spanish. Although these words are arbitrary (others could have been chosen), they have *shared meanings* for people who speak English, French, and Spanish.

Third, language is *generative*. A limited number of symbols can be combined in an infinite variety of ways to *generate* an endless array of novel messages. Everyone has some "stock sayings," but every day you create sentences that you have never spoken before. You also comprehend many sentences that you have never encountered before (like this one).

Fourth, language is *structured*. Although people can generate an infinite variety of sentences, these sentences must be structured in a limited number of ways. Rules govern the arrangement of words into phrases and sentences; some arrangements are acceptable and some are not. For example, you might say, "The swimmer jumped into the pool," but you would never recombine the same words to say, "Pool the into the jumped swimmer." The structure of language allows people to be inventive with words and still understand each other. Let's take a closer look at the structural properties of language.

The Structure of Language

Human languages have a hierarchical structure (Ratner, Gleason, & Narasimhan, 1998). As Figure 8.1 shows, basic sounds are combined into units with meaning, which are combined into words. Words are combined into phrases, which are combined into sentences.

Phonemes

At the base of the language hierarchy are *phonemes*, the smallest speech units in a language that can be distinguished perceptually. Considering that an unabridged English dictionary contains more than

450,000 words, you might imagine that there must be a huge number of phonemes. In fact, linguists estimate that humans are capable of recognizing only about 100 such basic sounds. Moreover, no one language uses all of these phonemes. Different languages use different groups of about 20 to 80 phonemes.

For all its rich vocabulary, the English language is composed of about 40 phonemes, corresponding roughly to the 26 letters of the alphabet plus several variations (see Table 8.1). A letter in the alphabet can represent more than one phoneme if it has more than one pronunciation. For example, the letter *a* is pronounced differently in the words *father, had, call,* and *take*. Each of these pronunciations corresponds to a different phoneme. In addition, some phonemes are represented by combinations of letters, such as *ch* and *th*. Working with this handful of basic sounds, people can understand and generate all the words in the English language—and invent new ones besides.

Morphemes and Semantics

Morphemes are the smallest units of meaning in a language. There are approximately 50,000 English morphemes, which include root words as well as prefixes and suffixes. Many words, such as *fire, guard,* and *friend,* consist of a single morpheme. Many others represent combinations of morphemes. For example, the word *unfriendly* consists of three morphemes: the root word *friend,* the prefix *un,* and the suffix *ly.* Each of the morphemes contributes to the meaning of the entire word. *Semantics* is the area of language concerned with understanding the meaning of words and word combinations. Learning about semantics entails learning about the infinite variety of objects and actions that words refer to. A word's meaning may consist of both its *denotation*, which is its dictionary definition, and its *connotation*, which includes its emotional overtones and secondary implications.

Syntax

Of course, most utterances consist of more than a single word. As we've already noted, people don't combine words randomly. *Syntax is a system of rules that specify how words can be arranged into sentences.* A simple rule of syntax is that a sentence must have both a *noun phrase* and a *verb phrase*. Thus, "The

Table 8.1 Phonemic Symbols for the Sounds of American English

Consonants								Vowels			
/p/	pill	/t/	toe	/g/	gill			/i/	beet	/ɪ/	bit
/b/	bill	/d/	doe	/ŋ/	ring			/e/	bait	/ɛ/	bet
/m/	mill	/n/	no	/h/	hot			/u/	boot	/ʊ/	foot
/f/	fine	/s/	sink	/ʔ/	uh-oh			/o/	boat	/ɔ/	caught
/v/	vine	/z/	zinc	/l/	low			/æ/	bat	/a/	pot
/θ/	thigh	/č/	choke	/r/	row			/ʌ/	but	/ə/	sofa
/ð/	thy	/ǰ/	joke	/y/	you			/aɪ/	bite	/au/	out
/š/	shoe	/k/	kill	/w/	win			/ɔɪ/	boy		
/ž/	treasure										

SOURCE: Hoff, E. (2001). *Language development.* Belmont, CA: Wadsworth. Reprinted by permission.

Figure 8.1

An analysis of a simple English sentence. As this example shows, verbal language has a hierarchical structure. At the base of the hierarchy are the *phonemes*, which are units of vocal sound that do not, in themselves, have meaning. The smallest units of meaning in a language are *morphemes*, which include not only root words but such meaning-carrying units as the past-tense suffix *ed* and the plural *s*. Complex rules of syntax govern how the words constructed from morphemes may be combined into phrases, and phrases into meaningful statements, or sentences.

SOURCE: Clarke-Stewart, A., Friedman, S., & Koch, J. (1985). *Child development: A topical approach* (p. 417). New York: Wiley. Reprinted by permission of John Wiley & Sons, Inc.

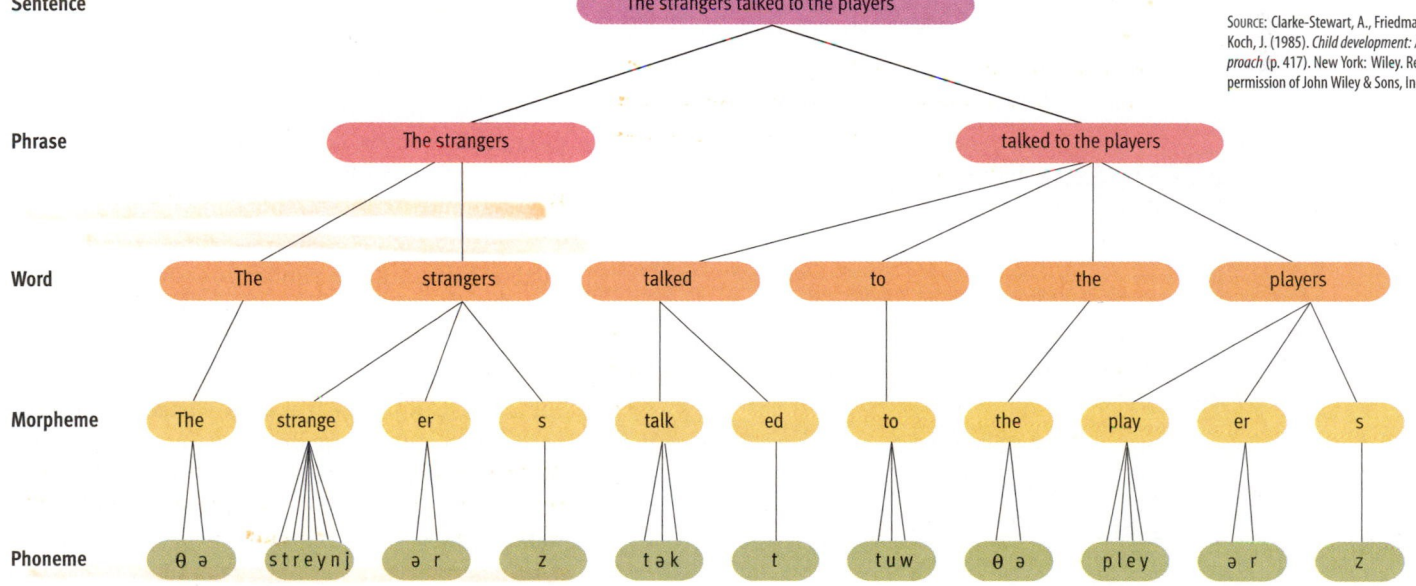

sound of cars is annoying" is a sentence. However, "The sound of cars" is not a sentence, because it lacks a verb phrase.

Rules of syntax underlie all language use, even though you may not be aware of them. Thus, although they may not be able to verbalize the rule, virtually all English speakers know that an *article* (such as *the*) comes before the word it modifies. For example, you would never say *swimmer the* instead of *the swimmer*. How children learn the complicated rules of syntax is one of the major puzzles investigated by psychologists interested in language. Like other aspects of language development, children's acquisition of syntax seems to progress at an amazingly rapid pace. Let's look at how this remarkable development unfolds.

Milestones in Language Development

Learning to use language requires learning a number of skills that become important at various points in a child's development (Siegler, 1998). We'll examine this developmental sequence by looking first at how

children learn to pronounce words, then at their use of single words, and finally at their ability to combine words to form sentences (see Table 8.2).

Moving Toward Producing Words

Three-month-old infants display a surprising language-related talent: They can distinguish phonemes from all the world's languages, including phonemes that they do not hear in their environment. In contrast, adults cannot readily discriminate phonemes that are not used in their native language. Actually, neither can 1-year-old children, as this curious ability gradually disappears between 4 months and 12 months of age (Werker & Desjardins, 1995). The exact mechanisms responsible for this transition are not understood, but it is clear that long before infants utter their first words, they are making remarkable progress in learning the sound structure of their native language. Progress toward understanding words also occurs during the first year. By 7.5 months, infants begin to recognize common word forms (Jusczyk & Hohne, 1997), and by 8 months many infants show the first signs of understanding the meanings of familiar words (Fenson et al., 1994).

During the first six months of life, a baby's vocalizations are dominated by crying, cooing, and laughter, which have limited value as a means of communication. Soon, infants are *babbling*, producing a wide variety of sounds that correspond to phonemes and, eventually, many repetitive consonant-vowel combinations, such as "lalalalalala." Babbling gradually becomes more complex and increasingly resembles the language spoken by parents and others in the child's environment (De Boysson-Bardies & Vihman, 1991). These trends probably reflect ongoing neural development and the maturation of the infant's vocal apparatus (Sachs, 1985), as well as the impact of experience (Kuhl & Meltzoff, 1997). Babbling lasts until around 18 months, continuing even after children utter their first words.

At around 10 to 13 months of age, most children begin to utter sounds that correspond to words. Most infants' first words are similar in phonetic form and meaning—even in different languages (Gleason & Ratner, 1998). The initial words resemble the syllables that infants most often babble spontaneously. For example, words such as *dada, mama,* and *papa* are names for parents in many languages because they consist of sounds that are easy to produce.

Using Words

After children utter their first words, their vocabulary grows slowly for the next few months (Barrett,

Table 8.2 Overview of Typical Language Development

Age	General Characteristics
Months	
1–5	*Reflexive communication:* Vocalizes randomly, coos, laughs, cries, engages in vocal play, discriminates language from nonlanguage sounds
6–18	*Babbling:* Verbalizes in response to speech of others; responses increasingly approximate human speech patterns
10–13	*First words:* Uses words; typically to refer to objects
12–18	*One-word sentence stage:* Vocabulary grows slowly; uses nouns primarily; overextensions begin
18–24	*Vocabulary spurt:* Fast-mapping facilitates rapid acquisition of new words
Years	
2	*Two-word sentence stage:* Uses telegraphic speech; uses more pronouns and verbs
2.5	*Three-word sentence stage:* Modifies speech to take listener into account; overregularizations begin
3	Uses complete simple active sentence structure; uses sentences to tell stories that are understood by others; uses plurals
3.5	*Expanded grammatical forms:* Expresses concepts with words; uses four-word sentences
4	Uses imaginary speech; uses five-word sentences
5	*Well-developed and complex syntax:* Uses more complex syntax; uses more complex forms to tell stories
6	Displays metalinguistic awareness

NOTE: Children often show individual differences in the exact ages at which they display the various developmental achievements outlined here.

1995). Toddlers typically can say between 3 and 50 words by 18 months. However, their *receptive vocabulary* is larger than their *productive vocabulary*. That is, they can comprehend more words spoken by others than they can actually produce to express themselves (Dan & Gleason, 2001). Thus, toddlers can *understand* 50 words months before they can *say* 50 words. Toddlers' early words tend to refer most often to *objects* and secondarily to familiar *actions* (Menyuk, Liebergott, & Schultz, 1995). Children generally acquire nouns before verbs because the meanings of nouns, which often refer to distinct, concrete objects, tend to be easier to encode than the meanings of verbs, which often refer to more abstract relationships (Gentner & Rattermann, 1991). However, this generalization may not apply to all languages (Bates, Devescovi, & Wulfeck, 2001).

Youngsters' vocabularies soon begin to grow at a dizzying pace, as a *vocabulary spurt* often begins at around 18–24 months (Bates & Carnevale, 1993; see Figure 8.2). By the first grade, the average child has a vocabulary of approximately 10,000 words, which builds to an astonishing 40,000 words by the fifth grade (Anglin, 1993; see Figure 8.3). In building these impressive vocabularies, some 2-year-olds learn as many as 20 new words every week. *Fast mapping* appears to be one factor underlying this rapid growth of vocabulary (Mervis & Bertrand, 1994). *Fast mapping* is the process by which children map a word onto an underlying concept after only one exposure. Thus, children often add words like *tank, board,* and *tape* to their vocabularies after their first encounter with objects that illustrate these concepts. The vocabulary spurt may be attributable to children's improved articulation skills, improved understanding of syntax, underlying cognitive development, or some combination of these factors (MacWhinney, 1998).

Of course, these efforts to learn new words are not flawless. Toddlers often make errors, such as overextensions and underextensions (Dan & Gleason, 2001). An *overextension* occurs when a child incorrectly uses a word to describe a wider set of objects or actions than it is meant to. For example, a child might use the word *ball* for anything round—oranges, apples, even the moon. Overextensions usually appear in children's speech between ages 1 and 2½. Specific overextensions typically last up to several months. Toddlers also tend to be guilty of *underextensions*, which occur when a child incorrectly uses a word to describe a narrower set of objects or actions than it is meant to. For example, a child might use the word *doll* to refer only to a single, favorite doll. Overextensions and underextensions show

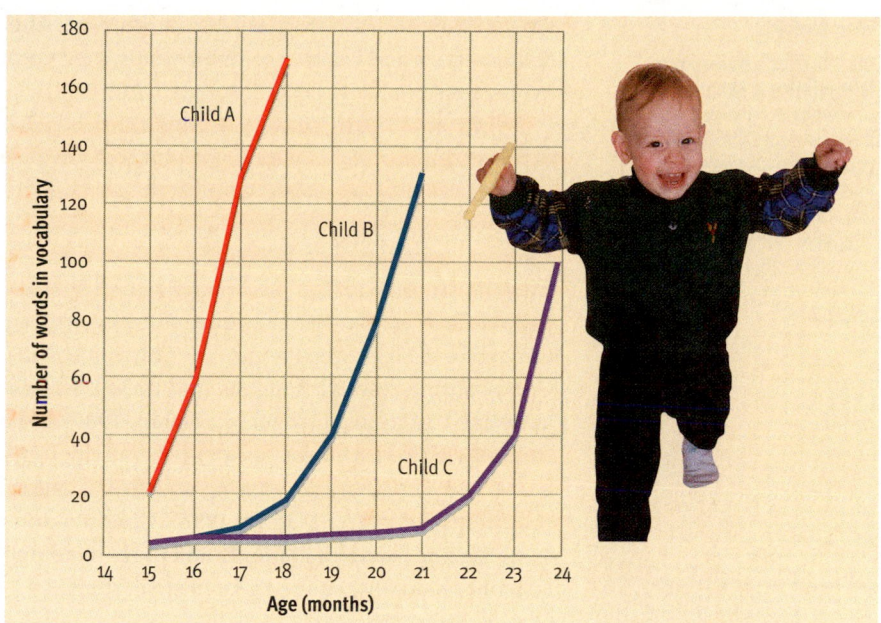

that toddlers are actively trying to learn the rules of language—albeit with mixed success.

Combining Words

Children typically begin to combine words into sentences near the end of their second year. Early sentences are characterized as "telegraphic" because they resemble telegrams. *Telegraphic speech* consists mainly of content words; articles, prepositions, and other less critical words are omitted. Thus, a child might say, "Give doll" rather than "Please give me the doll." Although not unique to the English language, telegraphic speech is not cross-culturally universal, as once thought (de Villiers & de Villiers, 1992).

Researchers sometimes track language development by keeping tabs on subjects' *mean length of utterance (MLU)*—the average length of youngsters'

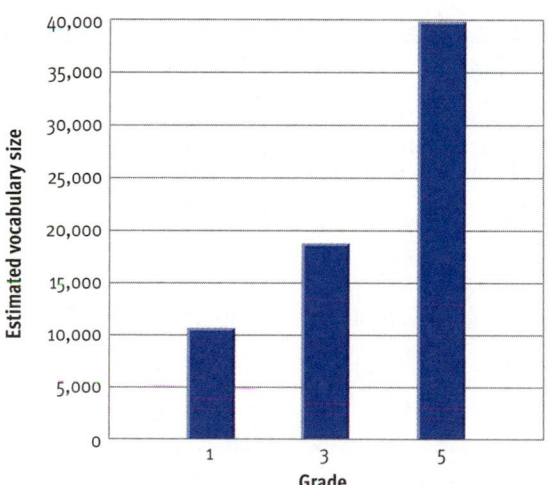

Figure 8.2

The vocabulary spurt.
Children typically acquire their first 10–15 words very slowly, but they soon go through a vocabulary spurt—a period during which they rapidly acquire many new words. The vocabulary spurt usually begins at around 18–24 months, but children vary, as these graphs of three toddlers' vocabulary growth show.

SOURCE: Adapted from Goldfield, B. A., & Resnick, J. S. (1990). Early lexical acquisition: Rate, content, and the vocabulary spurt. *Journal of Child Language, 17,* 171–183. Copyright © 1990 by Cambridge University Press. Adapted by permission. Photo: Courtesy of Wayne Weiten

Figure 8.3

The growth of school children's vocabulary.
Vocabulary growth is rapid during the early years of grade school. Youngsters' estimated vocabulary doubles about every two years between first grade and fifth grade.

SOURCE: Anglin, J. M. (1993). Vocabulary development: A morphological analysis. *Child Development, 58,* Serial 238. Copyright © 1993 The Society for Research in Child Development. Reprinted by permission.

Web Link 8.1

John Lawler's Homepage (Linguistics & Language)
University of Michigan linguistics professor John Lawler has constructed a seemingly endless guide to Net resources for the study of linguistics and language, a field allied with psychology. His homepage is a goldmine of references and guides.

spoken statements (measured in morphemes). After children grow and begin to combine words, their vocal expressions gradually become longer (Hoff, 2001).

By the end of their third year, most children can express complex ideas such as the plural or the past tense. However, their efforts to learn the rules of language continue to generate revealing mistakes. *Overregularizations* occur when grammatical rules are incorrectly generalized to irregular cases where they do not apply. For example, children will say things like "The girl goed home" or "I hitted the ball." Cross-cultural research suggests that these overregularizations occur in all languages (Slobin, 1985). Most theorists believe that overregularizations demonstrate that children are working actively to master the *rules* of language (Marcus, 1996). Children don't learn the fine points of grammar and usage in a single leap but gradually acquire them in small steps.

Refining Language Skills

Youngsters make their largest strides in language development in their first 4 to 5 years. However, they continue to refine their language skills during their school-age years. They generate longer and more complicated sentences as they receive formal training in written language.

As their language skills develop, school-age children begin to appreciate ambiguities in language. They can, for instance, recognize two possible meanings in sentences such as "Visiting relatives can be bothersome." This interest in ambiguities indicates that they're developing *metalinguistic awareness*—the ability to reflect on the use of language. As metalinguistic awareness grows, children begin to "play" with language, coming up with puns and jokes. They begin to make more frequent and sophisticated use of metaphors, such as "We were packed in the room

like sardines" (Gentner, 1988). They also learn to recognize hidden meanings often found in everyday discourse, such as sarcastic comments (Capelli, Nakagawa, & Madden, 1990).

Learning More Than One Language: Bilingualism

Given the complexities involved in acquiring one language, you may be wondering about the ramifications of being asked to learn *two* languages. *Bilingualism* is the acquisition of two languages that use different speech sounds, vocabulary, and grammatical rules. Although not the norm in the United States, bilingualism is quite common in Europe and many other regions, and nearly half of the world's population grows up bilingual (Hakuta, 1986; Snow, 1998). Moreover, bilingualism is far from rare even in the English-dominated United States, where roughly 6 million children speak a language other than English at home. Bilingualism has sparked considerable controversy in the United States, as a host of new laws and court rulings have reduced the availability of bilingual educational programs in many school systems (Hakuta, 1999). These laws are based on the implicit assumption that bilingualism hampers language development and has a negative impact on youngsters' educational progress. But does the empirical evidence support this assumption? Let's take a look at the research on bilingualism.

Does Learning Two Languages in Childhood Slow Down Language Development?

If youngsters are learning two languages simultaneously, does one language interfere with the other so that the acquisition of both is impeded? Given the far-reaching sociopolitical implications of this question, you might guess that many relevant studies have been conducted, but in reality there is only a modest body of research. Some studies *have* found that bilingual children have smaller vocabularies in each of their languages than monolingual children have in their one language (Umbel et al., 1992). But when their two overlapping vocabularies are added, their total vocabulary is similar to that of children learning a single language (Pearson, Fernandez, & Oller, 1993). Taken as a whole, the available evidence suggests that bilingual and monolingual children are largely similar in the course and rate of their language development (de Houwer, 1995; Nicoladis & Genesee, 1997) Thus, although more research is needed, so far, there is little empirical support for the assumption that bilingualism has a negative effect on language development.

CONCEPT CHECK 8.1

Tracking Language Development

Check your understanding of how language skills progress in youngsters. Number the utterances below to indicate the developmental sequence in which they would probably occur. The answers can be found in Appendix A in the back of the book.

_____ **1.** "Doggie," while pointing to a cow.

_____ **2.** "The dogs runned away."

_____ **3.** "Doggie run."

_____ **4.** "The dogs ran away."

_____ **5.** "Doggie," while pointing to a dog.

_____ **6.** "Tommy thinks like his head is full of mashed potatoes."

Does Bilingualism Affect Cognitive Processes and Skills?

Does knowing two languages make thinking more difficult, or could bilingualism enhance thought processes? Once again the evidence is mixed, depending on the variables measured and the exact nature of the subject populations that are compared. When middle-class bilingual subjects who are fluent in both languages are studied, they tend to score somewhat *higher* than monolingual subjects on measures of cognitive flexibility, analytical reasoning, selective attention, and metalinguistic awareness (Bialystok, 1999; Campbell & Sais, 1995; Lambert, 1990). However, on some types of tasks, bilinguals may have a slight disadvantage in terms of raw language-processing *speed* (Taylor & Taylor, 1990). Nonetheless, when researchers control for the effects of social class, they do not find significant cognitive deficits in bilingual youngsters.

What Factors Influence the Acquisition of a Second Language?

A great many bilingual individuals do not learn their two languages simultaneously. Rather, they learn their native language first and then learn a second language later. Do any key considerations influence the learning of a second language? Yes, the evidence clearly indicates that *age* is a significant correlate of how effectively people can acquire a second language—and younger is better. For example, Figure 8.4, from a study by Johnson and Newport (1989), maps out the relationship between immigrants' age of arrival in the U.S. and their subsequent mastery of English grammar. As you can see, people who started learning English at an early age achieved greater mastery than those who began later. For reasons that are not well understood, language learning unfolds more effectively when initiated prior to age 7, and younger continues to be better up through age 15. Older children and adults can certainly become proficient in a second language, but only a small minority become as proficient as native speakers are (Birdsong, 1999). The other factor that influences the acquisition of a second language is *acculturation*—the degree to which a person is socially and psychologically integrated into a new culture. As you might guess, greater acculturation facilitates more rapid acquisition of the new culture's language (Schumann, 1978, 1993). This finding highlights the fact that language learning is more than a purely cognitive process. Language is a communication tool that is used in varied social contexts. Moreover, language lies at the very core of a nation's culture, which is probably why the debate about bilingualism has been so vigorous. In any event,

The utility of bilingual education programs has been a hotly debated local issue across the United States and Canada. Critics argue that bilingualism has a negative effect on children's language and cognitive development, but there is relatively little empirical support for this assertion.

we turn next to another vigorous debate about language acquisition—the debate over whether animals can learn language.

REVIEW OF KEY POINTS

- During the first half of the 20th century, the study of cognition was largely suppressed by the theoretical dominance of behaviorism. However, the 1950s brought a cognitive revolution in psychology, as Simon, Chomsky, Miller, and many others reported major advances in the study of mental processes.

- Languages are symbolic, semantic, generative, and structured. Human languages are structured hierarchically. At the bottom of the hierarchy are the basic sound units, called phonemes. At the next level are morphemes, the smallest units of meaning.

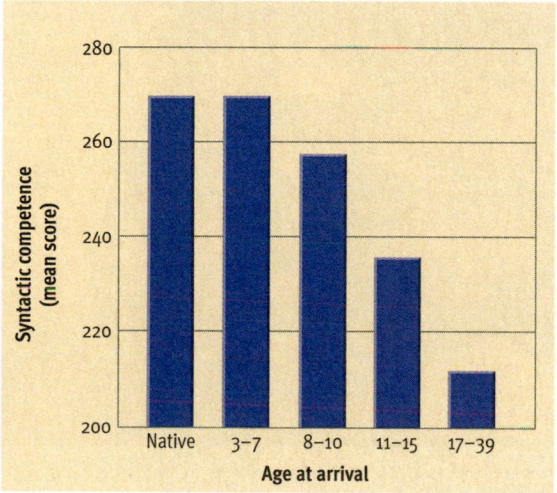

Figure 8.4

Age and second language learning. In a study of how well immigrants to the United States master English as a second language, Johnson and Newport (1989) examined the relationship between the subjects' age of arrival and their mastery of syntax. As you can see, it was advantageous to start learning English at an earlier age, up through about age 15. After that, age of arrival did not make a difference. For example, those who started at 20 were no better off than those who started at 30. (Data from Johnson & Newport, 1989)

- The initial vocalizations by infants are similar across languages, but their babbling gradually begins to resemble the sounds from their surrounding language. Children typically utter their first words around their first birthday. Vocabulary growth is slow at first, but a vocabulary spurt often begins at around 18–24 months.

- Most children begin to combine words by the end of their second year. Their early sentences are telegraphic, in that they omit many nonessential words. Over the next several years, children gradually learn the complexities of syntax.

- Research does not support the assumption that bilingualism has a negative effect on language development or on cognitive development. The learning of a second language is facilitated by starting at a younger age and by acculturation.

Can Animals Develop Language?

PREVIEW QUESTIONS
- What kind of progress has been made in teaching animals language?
- What is the evolutionary significance of language?
- Do humans have an innate facility for learning language?
- Does language shape thought?

Can other species besides humans develop language? Although this issue does not have the practical, socio-political repercussions of the debate about bilingualism, it has intrigued researchers for many decades and led to some fascinating research. Scientists have taught some language-like skills to a number of species, including dolphins (Herman, Kuczaj, & Holder, 1993), sea lions (Schusterman & Gisiner, 1988), and an African gray parrot (Pepperberg, 1990, 1993), but their greatest success has come with the chimpanzee, an intelligent primate widely regarded as humans' closest cousin.

In early studies, researchers tried to teach chimps to *speak* (Hayes & Hayes, 1951). However, investigators quickly concluded that chimps simply didn't have the appropriate vocal apparatus to acquire human speech. But is speech the only way to use language? Of course not. At this moment you're reading a written expression of language.

Like speech, writing may not be a realistic form of communication for chimps, but researchers have tried training chimps to use a nonoral human language: American Sign Language (ASL). ASL is a complex language of hand gestures and facial expressions used by thousands of deaf people in the United States. The first effort of this sort was begun by Allen and Beatrice Gardner (1969), who worked with a chimp named Washoe. The Gardners approached the task as if Washoe were a deaf child. They signed to her regularly, rewarded her imitations, and taught her complex signs by physically moving her hands through the required motions. In four years, Washoe acquired a sign vocabulary of roughly 160 words. She learned to combine these words into simple sentences, such as "Washoe sorry," "Gimme flower," and "More fruit."

Although these accomplishments were impressive, critics expressed doubts about whether Washoe and the other chimps that learned ASL had really acquired language skills. For example, Herbert Terrace (1986) argued that these chimps showed little evidence of mastering *rules* of language. According to Terrace, the chimps' sentences were the products of imitation and operant conditioning, rather than spontaneous generations based on linguistic rules.

In more recent years, Sue Savage-Rumbaugh and her colleagues have reported some striking advances with *bonobo pygmy chimpanzees* that have fueled additional debate (Savage-Rumbaugh, 1991; Savage-Rumbaugh et al., 1986; Savage-Rumbaugh, Shanker, & Taylor, 1998). In this line of research, the bonobos have been trained to communicate with their caretakers by touching geometric symbols that represent words on a computer-monitored keyboard. Savage-Rumbaugh's star pupil has been a chimp named Kanzi, although many of his feats have been duplicated by his younger sister, Panbanisha. Kanzi has acquired hundreds of words and has used them in thousands of combinations. Many of these combinations were spontaneous and seemed to follow rules of language. For example, to specify whether he wanted to chase or be chased, Kanzi had to differentiate between symbol combinations in a way that appeared to involve the use of grammatical rules.

As the years went by, Kanzi's trainers noticed that he often seemed to understand the normal utterances that they exchanged with each other. Hence, they began to systematically evaluate his comprehension of spoken English. At age nine, they tested his understanding of 660 sentences that directed Kanzi to execute simple actions, such as "Put the collar in

Kanzi, a pygmy chimpanzee, has learned to communicate with his caretakers in surprisingly sophisticated ways via computer-controlled symbol boards, thus raising some doubt about whether language is unique to humans.

© Michael Nichols/Magnum Photos

the water." To make sure that he really *understood* the sentences, they included many novel constructions in which the actions were not obvious given the objects involved, such as "Put the raisins in the shoe," or "Go get the balloon that's in the microwave." Kanzi correctly carried out 72% of the 660 requests. Moreover, he demonstrated remarkable understanding of sentence structure, as he could reliably distinguish the actions requested by "Pour the Coke in the lemonade," as opposed to "Pour the lemonade in the Coke."

How have the linguistics experts reacted to Kanzi's surprising progress in language development? Many remain skeptical about whether Kanzi's communications demonstrate all the basic properties of a language (Kako, 1999; Seidenberg & Petitto, 1987; Wallman, 1992). Yet, even *critics* such as Kako (1999) acknowledge that "Kanzi clearly comprehends more than just the words in these sentences: He comprehends both the words *and* their relations to one another, as specified by the structure" (p. 10). Overall, it seems reasonable to conclude that the ability to use language may *not* be unique to humans, as has been widely assumed.

However, even if language is *not* unique to humans, they do appear to be exceptionally well suited for learning language. There's no comparison between human linguistic abilities and those of apes or other animals. As remarkable as the language studies with apes are, they should make us marvel even more at the fluency, flexibility, and complexity of human language. A normal human toddler quickly surpasses even the most successfully trained chimps. In mastering language, children outstrip chimps the way jet airplanes outrace horse-drawn buggies. Why are humans so well suited for learning language? According to some theorists, this talent for language is a product of evolution. Let's look at their thinking.

Language in Evolutionary Context

All human societies depend on complex language systems. Even primitive cultures employ languages that are just as complicated as those used in modern societies. The universal nature of language suggests that it is an innate human characteristic. Consistent with this view, Steven Pinker (1994) argues that humans' special talent for language is a species-specific trait that is the product of natural selection. According to Pinker, language is a valuable means of communication that has enormous adaptive value. As Pinker and Bloom (1992) point out, "There is an obvious advantage in being able to acquire information about the world secondhand . . . one can avoid having to duplicate the possibly time-consuming and dangerous trial-and-error process that won that knowledge"

(p. 460). Dunbar (1996) argues that language evolved as a device to build and maintain social coalitions in increasingly larger groups. Although the impetus for the evolution of language remains a matter of speculation, it does not take much imagination to envision how more-effective communication among our ancient ancestors could have aided hunting, gathering, fighting, mating, and the avoidance of poisons, predators, and other dangers.

Although the adaptive value of language seems obvious, some scholars take issue with the assertion that human language is the product of evolution. For example, David Premack (1985) has expressed skepticism that small differences in language skill would influence reproductive fitness in primitive societies where all one had to communicate about was the location of the closest mastadon herd. In an effort to refute this argument, Pinker and Bloom (1992) point out that very small adaptive disparities are sufficient to fuel evolutionary change. For example, they cite an estimate that a 1% difference in mortality rates among overlapping Neanderthal and human populations could have led to the extinction of Neanderthals in just 30 generations. They also note that a trait variation that produces on average just 1% more offspring than its alternative genetic expression would increase in prevalence from 0.1% to 99.9% of the population in 4000 generations. Four thousand generations may seem like an eternity, but in the context of evolution, it is a modest amount of time.

Whether or not evolution gets the credit, language acquisition in humans seems remarkably rapid. As you will see in the next section, this reality looms large in theories of language acquisition.

Theories of Language Acquisition

Since the 1950s, a great debate has raged about the key processes involved in language acquisition. As with arguments we have seen in other areas of psychology, this one centers on the *nature versus nurture* issue. The debate was stimulated by the influential behaviorist B. F. Skinner (1957), who argued that environmental factors govern language development. His provocative analysis brought a rejoinder from Noam Chomsky (1959), who emphasized biological determinism. Let's examine their views and subsequent theories that stake out a middle ground.

Behaviorist Theories

The behaviorist approach to language was first outlined by Skinner in his book *Verbal Behavior* (1957). He argued that children learn language the same way they learn everything else: through imitation, rein-

"What Kanzi tells us is that humans are not the only species that can acquire language if exposed to it at an early age."
SUE SAVAGE-RUMBAUGH

"If human language is unique in the modern animal kingdom, as it appears to be, the implications for a Darwinian account of its evolution would be as follows: none. A language instinct unique to modern humans poses no more of a paradox than a trunk unique to modern elephants."
STEVEN PINKER

forcement, and other established principles of conditioning. According to Skinner, vocalizations that are not reinforced gradually decline in frequency. The remaining vocalizations are shaped with reinforcers until they are correct. Behaviorists assert that by controlling reinforcement, parents encourage their children to learn the correct meaning and pronunciation of words (Staats & Staats, 1963). For example, as children grow older, parents may insist on closer and closer approximations of the word *water* before supplying the requested drink.

Behavioral theorists also use the principles of imitation and reinforcement to explain how children learn syntax. According to the behaviorists' view, children learn how to construct sentences by imitating the sentences of adults and older children. If children's imitative statements are understood, parents are able to answer their questions or respond to their requests, thus reinforcing their verbal behavior.

Nativist Theories

Skinner's explanation of language acquisition soon inspired a critique and rival explanation from Noam Chomsky (1959, 1965). Chomsky pointed out that there are an infinite number of sentences in a language. It's therefore unreasonable to expect that children learn language by imitation. For example, in English, we add *ed* to the end of a verb to construct past tense. Children routinely overregularize this rule, producing incorrect verbs such as *goed, eated,* and *thinked*. Mistakes such as these are inconsistent with Skinner's emphasis on imitation, because most adult speakers don't use ungrammatical words like *goed*. Children can't imitate things they don't hear. According to Chomsky, children learn *the rules of language*, not specific verbal responses, as Skinner proposed.

Critics have also challenged the behaviorist position that children learn to construct correct sentences through reinforcement. An influential study by Brown and Hanlon (1970) indicated that parents typically respond to meaning and factual accuracy in their youngsters' speech rather than to grammar. Thus, a mother curling her daughter's hair probably won't correct the ungrammatical statement "Her curl my hair," because it is factually accurate. In other words, parents may not engage in much of the language shaping that is critical to the behavioral explanation of language development (Maratsos, 1983; Pinker, 1990).

An alternative theory favored by Chomsky and others is that humans have an inborn or "native" propensity to develop language (Chomsky, 1975, 1986; Crain, 1991; McNeill, 1970). In this sense, *native* is a variation on the word *nature* as it's used in the na-

"Even at low levels of intelligence, at pathological levels, we find a command of language that is totally unattainable by an ape."
NOAM CHOMSKY

MIT photo by Donna Coveney/MIT News Office

ture versus nurture debate. *Nativist theory* proposes that humans are equipped with a **language acquisition device (LAD)—an innate mechanism or process that facilitates the learning of language**. According to this view, humans learn language for the same reason that birds learn to fly—because they're biologically equipped for it. The exact nature of the LAD has not been spelled out in nativist theories. It presumably consists of brain structures and neural wiring that leave humans well prepared to discriminate among phonemes, to fast-map morphemes, to acquire rules of syntax, and so on.

Why does Chomsky believe that children have an innate capacity for learning language? One reason is that children seem to acquire language quickly and effortlessly. How could they develop so complex a skill in such a short time unless they have a built-in capacity for it? Another reason is that language development tends to unfold at roughly the same pace for most children, even though children obviously are reared in diverse home environments. This finding suggests that language development is determined by biological maturation more than personal experience. The nativists also cite evidence that the early course of language development is similar across very different cultures (Gleitman & Newport, 1996; Slobin, 1992). They interpret this to mean that children all over the world are guided by the same innate capabilities.

Interactionist Theories

Like Skinner, Chomsky has his critics (Bohannon & Bonvillian, 2001). They ask: What exactly is a language acquisition device? How does the LAD work? What are the neural mechanisms involved? They argue that the LAD concept is terribly vague. Other critics question whether the rapidity of early language development is as exceptional as nativists assume. They assert that it isn't fair to compare the rapid progress of toddlers, who are immersed in their native language, against the struggles of older students, who may devote only 10–15 hours per week to their foreign language course. Nativist theories have also been undermined by evidence that parents *do* provide their children with subtle corrective feedback about grammar (Bohannon, MacWhinney, & Snow, 1990; Saxton et al., 1998).

The problems apparent in Skinner's and Chomsky's explanations of language development have led some psychologists to outline *interactionist theories* of language acquisition. These theories assert that biology and experience *both* make important contributions to the development of language. Interactionist theories come in at least three flavors. *Cognitive theories* assert that language development is simply an important aspect of more general cognitive development—which depends on both maturation and experience (Meltzoff & Gopnik, 1989; Piaget, 1983). *Social communication theories* emphasize the functional value of interpersonal communication and the social context in which language evolves (Bohannon & Warren-Leubecker, 1989; Farrar, 1990). *Emergentist theories* argue that the neural circuits supporting language are not prewired but *emerge* gradually in response to language learning experiences (Bates, 1999; MacWhinney, 1999). These theories tend to assume that incremental changes in connectionist networks (see Chapter 7) underlie children's gradual acquisition of various language skills (Elman, 1999). Practically speaking, emergentist models emphasize the importance of children's learning experiences and their information processing. In recent years, these models have guided some interesting research that has shown infants to have a surprising capacity to draw sophisticated inferences about the workings of language from their linguistic environments (Aslin, Saffran, & Newport, 1999).

Like the nativists, interactionists believe that the human organism is biologically well equipped for learning language. They also agree that much of this learning involves the acquisition of rules. However, like the behaviorists, they believe that social exchanges with parents and others play a critical role in molding language skills. Thus, interactionist theories maintain that a biological predisposition *and* a supportive environment both contribute to language development (see Figure 8.5).

Culture, Language, and Thought

Another long-running controversy in the study of language concerns the relations between culture, language, and thought. Obviously, people from different cultures generally speak different languages. But does your training in English lead you to think about certain things differently than someone who was raised to speak Chinese or French? In other words, does a cultural group's language determine their thought? Or does thought determine language?

Benjamin Lee Whorf (1956) has been the most prominent advocate of *linguistic relativity,* the hypothesis that one's language determines the nature of one's thought. Whorf speculated that different languages lead people to view the world differently. His classic example compared English and Eskimo views of snow. He asserted that the English language

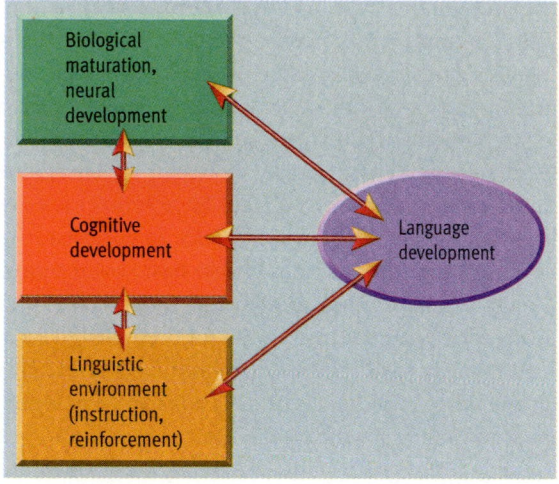

Figure 8.5

Interactionist theories of language acquisition. The interactionist view is that nature and nurture are both important to language acquisition. Maturation is thought to drive language development directly and to influence it indirectly by fostering cognitive development. Meanwhile, verbal exchanges with parents and others are also thought to play a critical role in molding language skills. The complex bidirectional relations depicted here shed some light on why there is room for extensive debate about the crucial factors in language acquisition.

has just one word for snow, whereas the Eskimo language has many words that distinguish among falling snow, wet snow, and so on. Because of this language gap, Whorf argued that Eskimos perceive snow differently than English-speaking people do. However, Whorf's conclusion about these perceptual differences was based on casual observation rather than systematic cross-cultural comparisons of perceptual processes. Moreover, critics subsequently noted that advocates of the linguistic relativity hypothesis had carelessly overestimated the number of Eskimo words for snow, while conveniently ignoring the variety of English words that refer to snow, such as slush and blizzard (Martin, 1986; Pullum, 1991).

Nonetheless, Whorf's hypothesis has been the subject of spirited debate. In one of the better-designed

Does the language you speak determine how you think? Yes, said Benjamin Lee Whorf, who argued that the Eskimo language, which has numerous words for snow, leads Eskimos to perceive snow differently than English speakers. However, the overall evidence provides little support for the strong version of Whorf's hypothesis.

© Wayne R. Bilenduke/Stone-Getty Images

experimental tests of this hypothesis, Eleanor Rosch (1973) compared the color perceptions of English-speaking people with those of the Dani, an agricultural people who live in New Guinea. The Dani were chosen because their language includes relatively few *basic color terms* (widely used words for widely agreed upon colors). In fact, the Dani have terms for only two basic colors (bright and dark). In contrast, the English language includes eleven basic color terms. Previous research had shown that English speakers learn arbitrary, nonsense names for these eleven basic colors more easily than for nonbasic colors. If language determines thought, this advantage in learning new names for the eleven basic colors should not be seen among the Dani, since they don't think in terms of these colors. However, the Dani also found it easier to learn nonsense names for the eleven basic colors. Thus, Rosch concluded that the Dani think about color much as English speakers do, even though their language treats color differently. Rosch's findings clearly contradict Whorf's hypothesis.

So, what is the status of the linguistic relativity hypothesis? The preponderance of evidence provides little support for the original, strong version of the hypothesis—that a given language makes certain ways of thinking obligatory or impossible (Berry et al., 1992; Eysenck, 1984). However, a weaker version of the linguistic relativity hypothesis—that a given language makes certain ways of thinking easier or more difficult—may still be tenable.

REVIEW OF KEY POINTS

- Efforts to teach chimpanzees American Sign Language were impressive, but doubts were raised about whether the chimps learned rules of language. Sue Savage-Rumbaugh's work with Kanzi suggests that some animals are capable of some genuine language acquisition. Many theorists believe that humans' special talent for language is the product of natural selection.

- According to Skinner and other behaviorists, children acquire a language through imitation and reinforcement. Nativist theories assert that humans have an innate capacity to learn language rules. Today, theorists are moving toward interactionist perspectives, which emphasize the role of both biology and experience.

- The theory of linguistic relativity asserts that language determines thought, thus suggesting that people from different cultures may think about the world somewhat differently. The evidence supports only a weak version of the linguistic relativity hypothesis.

Problem Solving: In Search of Solutions

PREVIEW QUESTIONS

- What types of problems have psychologists studied?
- What are some common mistakes that thwart problem-solving efforts?
- What are algorithms and heuristics in problem solving?
- What are some useful problem-solving strategies?
- What is field dependence-independence?
- How is culture related to cognitive style?

Look at the two problems below. Can you solve them?

In the Thompson family there are five brothers, and each brother has one sister. If you count Mrs. Thompson, how many females are there in the Thompson family?

Fifteen percent of the people in Topeka have unlisted telephone numbers. You select 200 names at random from the Topeka phone book. How many of these people can be expected to have unlisted phone numbers?

These problems, borrowed from Sternberg (1986, p. 214), are exceptionally simple, but many people fail to solve them. The answer to the first problem is *two:* The only females in the family are Mrs. Thompson and her one daughter, who is a sister to each of her brothers. The answer to the second problem is *none*—you won't find any people with *unlisted* phone numbers in the phone book.

Why do many people fail to solve these simple problems? You'll learn why in a moment, when we discuss barriers to effective problem solving. But first, let's examine a scheme for classifying problems into a few basic types.

Types of Problems

Problem solving refers to active efforts to discover what must be done to achieve a goal that is not readily attainable. Obviously, if a goal is readily attainable, there isn't a problem. But in problem-solving situations, one must go beyond the information given to overcome obstacles and reach a goal. Jim Greeno (1978) has proposed that problems can be categorized into three basic classes:

1. *Problems of inducing structure* require people to discover the relations among numbers, words, symbols, or ideas. The *series completion problems* and the *analogy problems* in Figure 8.6 are examples of problems of inducing structure.

2. *Problems of arrangement* require people to arrange the parts of a problem in a way that satisfies some criterion. The parts can usually be arranged in many

A. Analogy

What word completes the analogy?

Merchant : Sell : : Customer : _____

Lawyer : Client : : Doctor : _____

B. String problem

Two strings hang from the ceiling but are too far apart to allow a person to hold one and walk to the other. On the table are a book of matches, a screwdriver, and a few pieces of cotton. How could the strings be tied together?

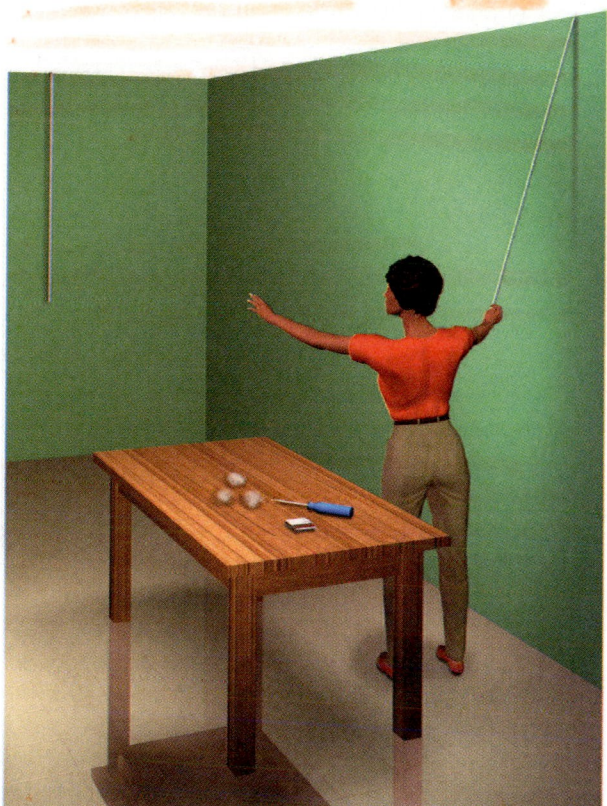

C. Hobbits and orcs problem

Three hobbits and three orcs arrive at a river bank, and they all wish to cross onto the other side. Fortunately, there is a boat, but unfortunately, the boat can hold only two creatures at one time. Also, there is another problem. Orcs are vicious creatures, and whenever there are more orcs than hobbits on one side of the river, the orcs will immediately attack the hobbits and eat them up. Consequently, you should be certain that you never leave more orcs than hobbits on either river bank. How should the problem be solved? It must be added that the orcs, though vicious, can be trusted to bring the boat back! (From Matlin, 1989, p. 319)

D. Water jar problem

Suppose that you have a 21-cup jar, a 127-cup jar, and a 3-cup jar. Drawing and discarding as much water as you like, you need to measure out exactly 100 cups of water. How can this be done?

E. Anagram

Rearrange the letters in each row to make an English word.

RWAET

KEROJ

F. Series completion

What number or letter completes each series?

1 2 8 3 4 6 5 6 _____

A B M C D M _____

Figure 8.6

Six standard problems used in studies of problem solving. Try solving the problems and identifying which class each belongs to before reading further. The problems can be classified as follows. The *analogy problems* and *series completion problems* are problems of inducing structure. The solutions for the analogy problems are *Buy* and *Patient*. The solutions for the series completion problems are *4* and *E*. The *string problem* and the *anagram problems* are problems of arrangement. To solve the string problem, attach the screwdriver to one string and set it swinging as a pendulum. Hold the other string and catch the swinging screwdriver. Then you need only untie the screwdriver and tie the strings together. The solutions for the anagram problems are *WATER* and *JOKER*. The *hobbits and orcs problem* and the *water jar problem* are problems of transformation. The solutions for these problems are outlined in Figures 8.7 and 8.8.

ways, but only one or a few of the arrangements form a solution. The *string problem* and the *anagrams* in Figure 8.6 fit in this category. Arrangement problems are often solved with a burst of insight. **Insight is the sudden discovery of the correct solution following incorrect attempts based primarily on trial and error** (Mayer, 1995).

3. *Problems of transformation* require people to carry out a sequence of transformations in order to reach a specific goal. The *hobbits and orcs problem* and the *water jar problem* in Figure 8.6 are examples of transformation problems. Transformation problems can be challenging. Even though you know exactly what the goal is, it's often not obvious how the goal can be achieved.

Greeno's list is not an exhaustive scheme for classifying problems, but it provides a useful system for understanding some of the variety seen in everyday problems.

Figure 8.7

Solution to the hobbits and orcs problem. This problem is difficult because it is necessary to temporarily work "away" from the goal.

Figure 8.8

The method for solving the water jar problem. As explained in the text, the correct formula is B – A – 2C.

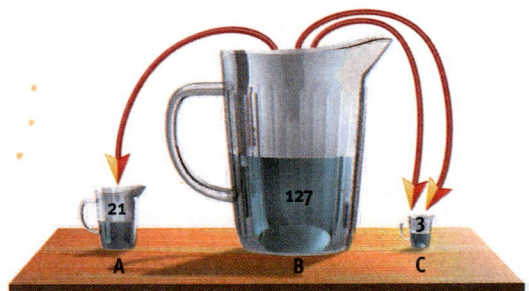

Barriers to Effective Problem Solving

On the basis of their studies of problem solving, psychologists have identified a number of barriers that frequently impede subjects' efforts to arrive at solutions. Common obstacles to effective problem solving include a focus on irrelevant information, functional fixedness, mental set, and the imposition of unnecessary constraints.

Irrelevant Information

We began our discussion of problem solving with two simple problems that people routinely fail to solve (see page 314). The catch is that these problems contain *irrelevant information* that leads people astray. In the first problem, the number of brothers is irrelevant in determining the number of females in the Thompson family. In the second problem, subjects tend to focus on the figures of 15% and 200 names. But this numerical information is irrelevant, since all the names came out of the phone book.

Sternberg (1986) points out that people often incorrectly assume that all the numerical information in a problem is necessary to solve it. They therefore try to figure out how to use quantitative information before they even consider whether it's relevant. Focusing on irrelevant information can have adverse effects on reasoning and problem solving (Gaeth & Shanteau, 2000). Hence, effective problem solving requires that you attempt to figure out what information is relevant and what is irrelevant before proceeding.

Functional Fixedness

Another common barrier to successful problem solving, identified by Gestalt psychologists, is *functional fixedness*—the tendency to perceive an item only in terms of its most common use. Functional fixedness has been seen in the difficulties that people have with the string problem (Maier, 1931). Solving this problem requires finding a novel use for one of the objects: the screwdriver. Subjects tend to think of the screwdriver in terms of its usual functions—turning screws and perhaps prying things open. They have a hard time viewing the screwdriver as a weight. Their rigid way of thinking about the screwdriver illustrates functional fixedness (Dominowski & Bourne, 1994). Ironically, young children appear to be less vulnerable to functional fixedness than older children or adults because they have less knowledge about the conventional uses of various objects (German & Defeyter, 2000).

Mental Set

Rigid thinking is also at work when a mental set interferes with effective problem solving. A *mental set* exists when people persist in using problem-solving strategies that have worked in the past. The effects of mental set were seen in a classic study by Gestalt psychologist Abraham Luchins (1942). He asked subjects to work a series of water jar problems, like the one introduced earlier. Six such problems are outlined in Figure 8.9, which shows the capacities of the

	Capacity of empty jars			Desired amount of water
Problem	A	B	C	
1	14	163	25	99
2	18	43	10	5
3	9	42	6	21
4	20	59	4	31
5	23	49	3	20
6	28	76	3	25

Figure 8.9

Additional water jar problems. Using jars A, B, and C, with the capacities indicated in each row, figure out how to measure out the desired amount of water specified on the far right. The solutions are shown in Figure 8.13. (Based on Luchins, 1942)

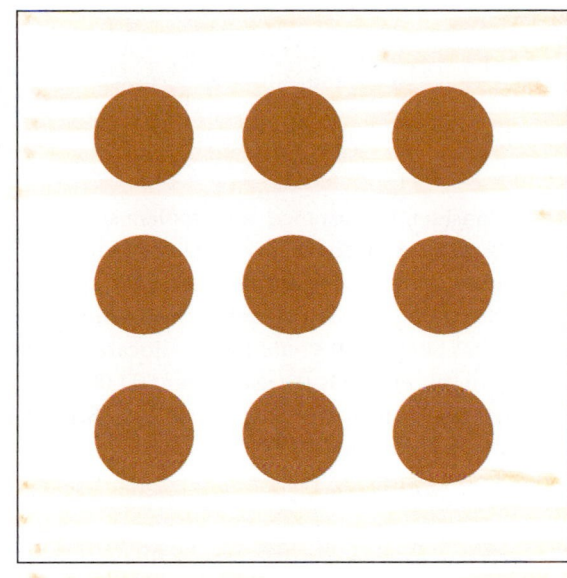

Figure 8.10

The nine-dot problem. Without lifting your pencil from the paper, draw no more than four lines that will cross through all nine dots. For possible solutions, see Figure 8.14.

SOURCE: Adams, J. L. (1980). *Conceptual block-busting: A guide to better ideas.* New York: W. H. Freeman. Copyright © 1980 by James L. Adams. Reprinted by permission of W. H. Freeman & Co.

three jars and the amounts of water to be measured out. Try solving these problems.

Were you able to develop a formula for solving these problems? The first four all require the same strategy, which was described in Figure 8.8. You have to fill jar B, draw off the amount that jar A holds once, and draw off the amount that jar C holds twice. Thus, the formula for your solution is B – A – 2C. Although there is an obvious and much simpler solution (A – C) for the fifth problem (see Figure 8.13 on page 319), Luchins found that most subjects stuck with the more cumbersome strategy that they had used in problems 1–4. Moreover, most subjects couldn't solve the sixth problem in the allotted time, because they kept trying to use their proven strategy, which does *not* work for this problem. The subjects' reliance on their "tried and true" strategy is an illustration of mental set in problem solving. This tendency to let one's thinking get into a rut is a common barrier to successful problem solving (Smith, 1995).

Unnecessary Constraints

Effective problem solving requires specifying all the constraints governing a problem *without assuming any constraints that don't exist*. An example of a problem in which people place an unnecessary constraint on the solution is shown in Figure 8.10 (Adams, 1980). Without lifting your pencil from the paper, try to draw four straight lines that will cross through all nine dots. Most people will not draw lines outside the imaginary boundary that surrounds the dots. Notice that this constraint is not part of the problem statement. It's imposed only by the problem solver. Correct solutions, two of which are shown in Figure 8.14

on page 319, extend outside the imaginary boundary. People often make assumptions that impose unnecessary constraints on problem-solving efforts.

Approaches to Problem Solving

In their classic treatise on problem solving, Allen Newell and Herbert Simon (1972) use a spatial metaphor to describe the process of problem solving. They use the term *problem space* to refer to the set of possible pathways to a solution considered by the problem solver. Thus, they see problem solving as a search in space. The problem solver's task is to find a solution path among the potential pathways that could lead from the problem's initial state to its goal state. The problem space metaphor highlights the fact that people must choose from among a variety of conceivable pathways or strategies in attempting to solve problems (Hunt, 1994). In this section, we'll examine some general strategies.

Using Algorithms and Heuristics

Trial and error is a common approach to solving problems. *Trial and error* involves trying possible solutions and discarding those that are in error until one works. Trial and error is often applied haphazardly, but people sometimes try to be systematic. An *algorithm* is a methodical, step-by-step procedure for trying all possible alternatives in searching for a solution to a problem. For instance, to solve the anagram IHCRA, you could write out all the possible arrangements of these letters until you eventually reached an answer (CHAIR). If an algorithm is avail-

Figure 8.11

The matchstick problem. Move two matches to form four equal squares. A solution can be found in Figure 8.15.

Source: Kendler, H. H. (1974). *Basic psychology.* Menlo Park, CA: Benjamin-Cummings. Copyright © 1974 The Benjamin-Cummings Publishing Co. Adapted by permission of Howard H. Kendler.

Figure 8.12

The tower of Hanoi problem. Your mission is to move the rings from peg A to peg C. You can move only the top ring on a peg and can't place a larger ring above a smaller one. The solution is explained in the text.

able for a problem, it guarantees that one can eventually find a solution.

Algorithms can be effective when there are relatively few possible solutions to be tried out. However, algorithms do not exist for many problems, and they can become impractical when the problem space is large. Consider, for instance, the problem shown in Figure 8.11. The challenge is to move just two matches to create a pattern containing four equal squares. Sure, you could follow an algorithm in moving pairs of matches about. But you'd better allocate plenty of time to this effort, as there are over 60,000 possible rearrangements to check out (see Figure 8.15 on page 319 for the solution).

Because algorithms are inefficient, people often use shortcuts called *heuristics* in problem solving. A *heuristic* is a guiding principle or "rule of thumb" used in solving problems or making decisions. In solving problems, a heuristic allows you to discard some alternatives while pursuing selected alternatives that appear more likely to lead to a solution (Holyoak, 1995). Heuristics can be useful because they selectively narrow the problem space, but they don't guarantee success. Helpful heuristics in problem solving include forming subgoals, working backward, searching for analogies, and changing the representation of a problem.

Forming Subgoals

A useful strategy for many problems is to formulate *subgoals*, intermediate steps toward a solution. When you reach a subgoal, you've solved part of the problem. Some problems have fairly obvious subgoals, and research has shown that people take advantage of them. For instance, in analogy problems, the first subgoal usually is to figure out the possible relations between the first two parts of the analogy. In a study by Simon and Reed (1976), subjects working on complex problems were given subgoals that weren't obvious. Providing subgoals helped the subjects solve the problems much more quickly.

The wisdom of formulating subgoals can be seen in the *tower of Hanoi problem,* depicted in Figure 8.12. The terminal goal for this problem is to move all three rings on peg A to peg C, while abiding by two restrictions: only the top ring on a peg can be moved, and a ring must never be placed above a smaller ring. See whether you can solve the problem before continuing.

Dividing this problem into subgoals facilitates a solution (Kotovsky, Hayes, & Simon, 1985). If you think in terms of subgoals, your first task is to get ring 3 to the bottom of peg C. Breaking this task into sub-subgoals, subjects can figure out that they should move ring 1 to peg C, ring 2 to peg B, and ring 1 from peg C to peg B. These maneuvers allow you to place ring 3 at the bottom of peg C, thus meeting your first subgoal. Your next subgoal—getting ring 2 over to peg C—can be accomplished in just two steps: move ring 1 to peg A and ring 2 to peg C. It should then be obvious how to achieve your final subgoal—getting ring 1 over to peg C.

Working Backward

Try to work the *lily pond problem* described below:

The water lilies on the surface of a small pond double in area every 24 hours. From the time the first water lily appears until the pond is completely covered takes 60 days. On what day is half of the pond covered with lilies?

If you're working on a problem that has a well-specified end point, you may find the solution more readily if you begin at the end and work backward. This strategy is the key to solving the lily pond problem. If the entire pond is covered on the 60th day, and the area covered doubles every day, how much is covered on the 59th day? One-half of the pond will be covered, and that happens to be the exact point you were trying to reach. The lily pond problem is remarkably simple when you work backward. In contrast, if you move forward from the starting point, you wrestle with questions about the area of the pond and the size of the lilies, and you find the problem riddled with ambiguities.

Searching for Analogies

Searching for analogies is another of the major heuristics for solving problems (Holyoak & Thagard, 1997). If you can spot an analogy between problems, you may be able to use the solution to a previous problem to solve a current one. Of course, using this strategy depends on recognizing the similarity between two problems, which may itself be a challenging problem. People often are unable to recognize that two problems are similar (Gilhooly, 1996). One prominent

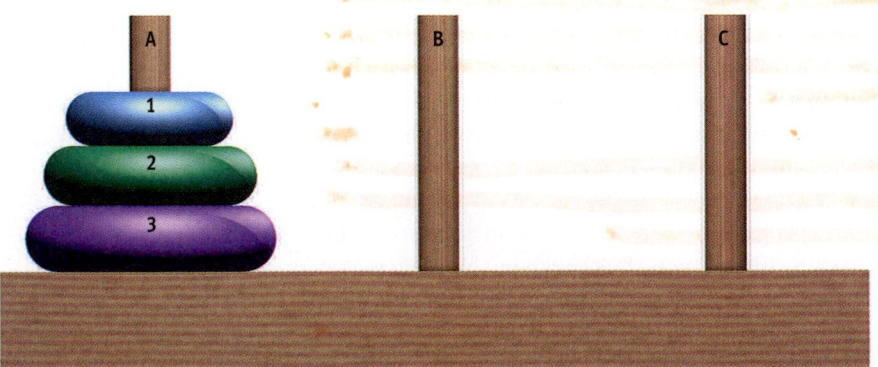

Figure 8.13

Solutions to the additional water jar problems. The solution for problems 1–4 is the same (B – A – 2C) as the solution shown in Figure 8.8. This method will work for problem 5, but there also is a simpler solution (A – C), which is the only solution for problem 6. Many subjects exhibit a mental set on these problems, as they fail to notice the simpler solution for problem 5.

Figure 8.14

Two solutions to the nine-dot problem. The key to solving the problem is to recognize that nothing in the problem statement forbids going outside the imaginary boundary surrounding the dots.

SOURCE: Adams, J. L. (1980). *Conceptual blockbusting: A guide to better ideas.* New York: W. H. Freeman. Copyright © 1980 by James L. Adams. Reprinted by permission of W. H. Freeman & Co.

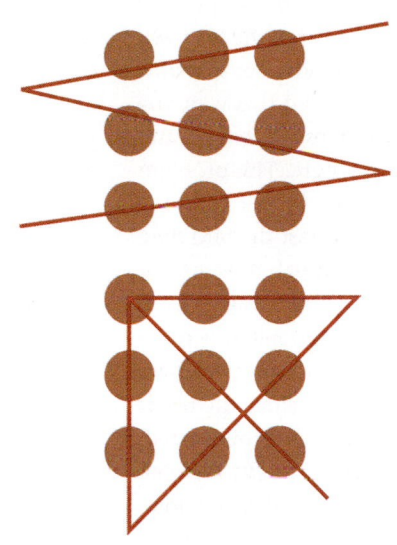

Figure 8.15

Solution to the matchstick problem. The key to solving this problem is to "open up" the figure, something many subjects are reluctant to do because they impose unnecessary constraints on the problem.

SOURCE: Kendler, H. H. (1974). *Basic psychology.* Menlo Park, CA: Benjamin-Cummings. Copyright © 1974 The Benjamin-Cummings Publishing Co. Adapted by permission of Howard H. Kendler.

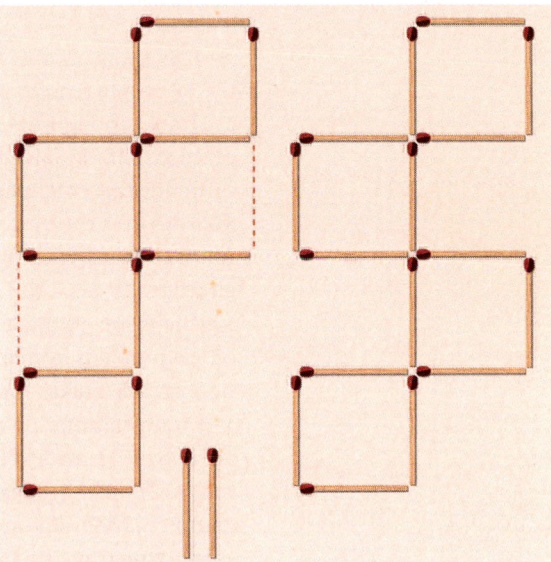

reason that people have difficulty recognizing analogies between problems is that they tend to focus on superficial, surface features of problems rather than their underlying structure (VanderStoep & Seifert, 1994). Nonetheless, analogies can be a powerful tool in efforts to solve problems. Try to make use of analogies to solve the following two problems:

A teacher had 23 pupils in his class. All but 7 of them went on a museum trip and thus were away for the day. How many students remained in class that day?

Susan gets in her car in Boston and drives toward New York City, averaging 50 miles per hour. Twenty minutes later, Ellen gets in her car in New York City and starts driving toward Boston, averaging 60 miles per hour. Both women take the same route, which extends a total of 220 miles between the two cities. Which car is nearer to Boston when they meet?

These problems, taken from Sternberg (1986, pp. 213 and 215), resemble the ones that opened our discussion of problem solving. Each has an obvious solution that's hidden in irrelevant quantitative information. If you recognized this similarity, you probably solved the problems easily. If not, take another look now that you know what the analogy is. Neither problem requires any calculation whatsoever. The answer to the first problem is *7.* As for the sec-

ond problem, when the two cars meet they're in the same place. Obviously, they have to be the same distance from Boston.

Changing the Representation of the Problem

Whether you solve a problem often hinges on how you envision it—your *representation of the problem.* Many problems can be represented in a variety of ways, such as verbally, mathematically, or spatially. You might represent a problem with a list, a table, an equation, a graph, a matrix of facts or numbers, a hierarchical tree diagram, or a sequential flowchart (Halpern, 1996). Some studies have shown that diagrams can facilitate reasoning on some types of problems by making it easier to find crucial information and by making alternative possibilities more salient (Bauer & Johnson-Laird, 1993). There isn't one ideal way to represent problems. The best representation will depend on the nature of the problem. But when you fail to make progress with your initial representation, changing your representation is often a good strategy. As an illustration, see whether you can solve the *bird and train problem* (from Bransford & Stein, 1993, p. 11):

Two train stations are 50 miles apart. At 1 P.M. on Sunday a train pulls out from each of the stations and the trains start toward each other. Just as the trains pull out from the stations, a hawk flies into the air in front of the

Web Link 8.2

Critical Thinking Consortium
The many resources at the Critical Thinking Consortium are directed primarily toward teachers at every level to help them develop their students' critical thinking skills. Visitors will find many online pamphlets on critical thinking and active learning.

first train and flies ahead to the front of the second train. When the hawk reaches the second train, it turns around and flies toward the first train. The hawk continues in this way until the trains meet. Assume that both trains travel at the speed of 25 miles per hour and the hawk flies at a constant speed of 100 miles per hour. How many miles will the hawk have flown when the trains meet?

This problem asks about the *distance* the bird will fly, so people tend to represent the problem spatially, as shown in Figure 8.16. Represented this way, the problem can be solved, but the steps are tedious and difficult. But consider another angle. The problem asks how far the bird will fly in the time it takes the trains to meet. Since we know how fast the bird flies, all we really need to know is how much *time* it takes for the trains to meet. Changing the representation of the problem from a question of *distance* to a question of *time* makes for an easier solution, as follows: The train stations are 50 miles apart. Since the trains are traveling toward each other at the same speed, they will meet midway and each will have traveled 25 miles. The trains are moving at 25 miles per hour. Hence, the time it takes them to meet 25 miles from each station is 1 hour. Since the bird flies at 100 miles per hour, it will fly 100 miles in the hour it takes the trains to meet.

Let's consider one more problem in which representation plays a crucial role. See whether you can solve the *Buddhist monk problem:*

At sunrise, a Buddhist monk sets out to climb a tall mountain. He follows a narrow path that winds around the mountain and up to a temple. He stops frequently to rest and climbs at varying speeds, arriving around sunset. After staying a few days, he begins his return journey. As before, he starts at sunrise, rests often, walks at varying speeds, and arrives around sunset. Prove that there must be a spot along the path that the monk will pass on both trips at precisely the same time of day.

Why should there be such a spot? The monk's walking speed varies. Shouldn't it all be a matter of coincidence if he reaches a spot at the same time each day? Moreover, if there is such a spot, how would you prove it? Subjects who represent this problem in terms of verbal, mathematical, or spatial information struggle. Subjects who work with a graphic representation fare much better. The best way to represent the problem is to envision the monk (or two different monks) ascending and descending the mountain at the same time. The two monks must meet at some point. If you construct a graph (see Figure 8.17) you can vary the speed of the monk's descent in endless ways, but you can see that there's always a place where they meet. The location of this place and the time of day can vary, but there will always be a crossing point where the monk(s) is (are) in the same place at the same time.

Culture, Cognitive Style, and Problem Solving

Do the varied experiences of people from different cultures lead to cross-cultural variations in problem solving? Yes, at least to some degree, as researchers have found cultural differences in the cognitive style that people exhibit in solving problems.

Figure 8.16

Representing the bird and train problem. The typical inclination is to envision this problem spatially, as shown here. However, as the text explains, this representation makes the problem much more difficult than it really is.

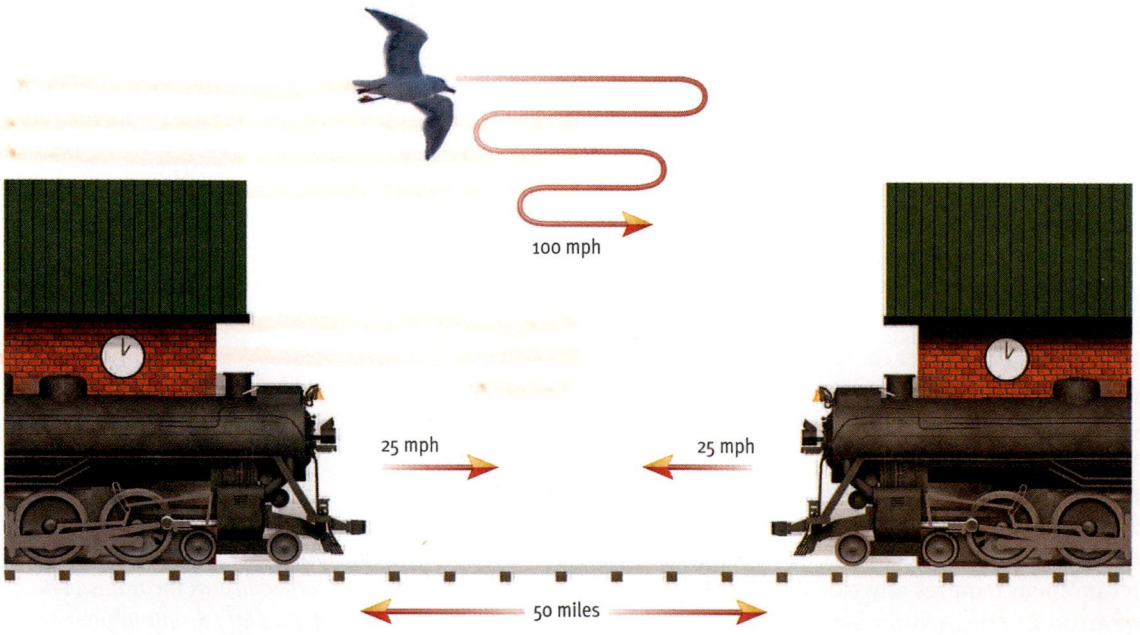

100 mph

25 mph   25 mph

50 miles

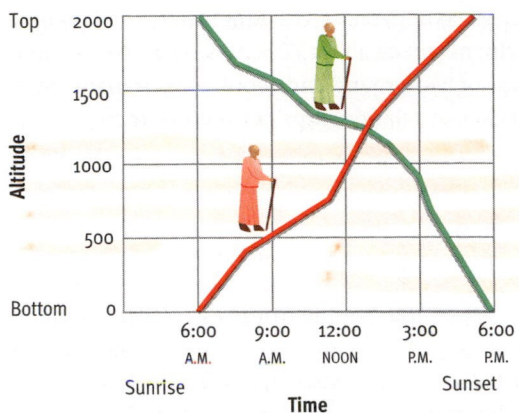

Figure 8.17

Solution to the Buddhist monk problem. If you represent this problem graphically and think in terms of two monks, it is readily apparent that the monk does pass a single spot at the same time each day.

Back in the 1940s, Herman Witkin was intrigued by the observation that some airplane pilots would fly into a cloud bank upright but exit it upside down without realizing that they had turned over. Witkin's efforts to explain this aviation problem led to the discovery of an interesting dimension of cognitive style (Witkin, 1950; Witkin et al., 1962). *Field dependence-independence* refers to individuals' tendency to rely primarily on external versus internal frames of reference when orienting themselves in space. People who are *field dependent* rely on external frames of reference and tend to accept the physical environment as a given instead of trying to analyze or restructure it. People who are *field independent* rely on internal frames of reference and tend to analyze and try to restructure the physical environment rather than accepting it as is. In solving problems, field-dependent people tend to focus on the total context of a problem instead of zeroing in on specific aspects or breaking it into component parts. In contrast, field-independent people are more likely to focus on specific features of a problem and to reorganize the component parts.

Research has shown that field dependence-independence is related to diverse aspects of cognitive, emotional, and social functioning (Witkin & Goodenough, 1981). Each style has its strengths and weaknesses, but studies have shown that field-independent subjects outperform field-dependent subjects on a variety of classic laboratory problems, including the string problem, matchstick problem, candle problem, and water jar problem (Witkin et al., 1962). Field-independent subjects' superiority on these types of problems has been attributed to their pro-

CONCEPT **CHECK 8.2**

Thinking About Problem Solving

Check your understanding of problem solving by answering some questions about the following problem. Begin by trying to solve the problem.

The candle problem. Using the objects shown—candles, a box of matches, string, and some tacks—figure out how you could mount a candle on a wall so that it could be used as a light.

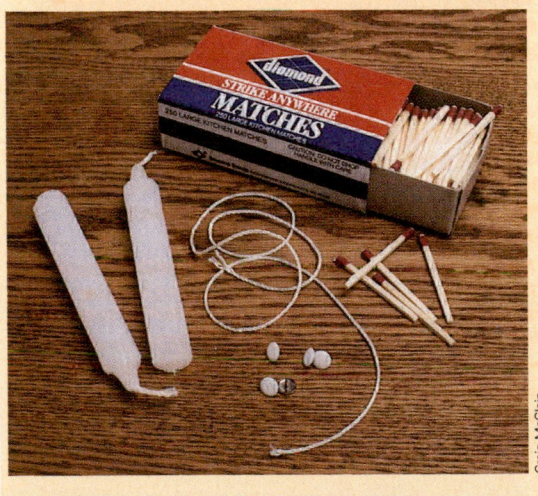

Work on the problem for a while, then turn to page 322 to see the solution. After you've seen the solution, respond to the following questions. The answers are in Appendix A.

1. If it didn't occur to you that the matchbox could be converted from a container to a platform, this illustrates _____ _____.

2. While working on the problem, if you thought to yourself, "How can I create a platform attached to the wall?" you used the heuristic of _____ _____.

3. If it occurred to you suddenly that the matchbox could be used as a platform, this realization would be an example of _____.

4. If you had a hunch that there might be some similarity between this problem and the string problem in Figure 8.6 (the similarity is the novel use of an object), your hunch would illustrate the heuristic of _____ _____ _____.

5. In terms of Greeno's three types of problems, the candle problem is a(n) _____ problem.

The solution to the candle problem in Concept Check 8.2.

Figure 8.18

Cultural disparities in cognitive style. In one of the studies conducted by Masuda and Nisbett (2001), the participants were asked to describe computer-animated visual scenes. As you can see, the initial comments made by American subjects referred more to focal objects in the scenes, whereas the initial comments made by Japanese subjects referred more to background elements in the scenes. These findings are consistent with the hypothesis that Easterners see wholes (a holistic cognitive style) where Westerners see parts (an analytic cognitive style). (Data from Masuda & Nisbett, 2001)

pensity to analyze and rearrange the elements of a problem and their ability to overcome the context in which problems are presented.

An extensive body of research suggests that some cultures encourage a field-dependent cognitive style, whereas others foster a field-independent style (Berry, 1990; Mishra, 2001). The educational practices in modern Western societies seem to nourish field independence. A field-independent style is also more likely to be predominant in nomadic societies that depend on hunting and gathering for subsistence and in societies that encourage personal autonomy. In contrast, a field-dependent style is found more in sedentary agricultural societies and in societies that stress conformity.

In a related line of research, Richard Nisbett and his colleagues (2001) have argued that people from East Asian cultures (such as China, Japan, and Korea) display a *holistic cognitive style* that focuses on context and relationships among elements in a field, whereas people from Western cultures (America and Europe) exhibit an *analytic cognitive style* that focuses on objects and their properties rather than context. To put it simply, Easterners see wholes where Westerners see parts. Nisbett et al. (2001) trace Eastern societies' holistic style of thinking back to ancient Chinese philosophies, while they trace Western societies' analytic style of thinking back to ancient Greek philosophies. Although these contrasting cognitive styles are rooted in ancient traditions, Nisbett et al. argue that these styles continue to influence reasoning and problem solving in our contemporary world.

To demonstrate this influence, Masuda and Nisbett (2001) presented computer-animated scenes of fish and other underwater objects to Japanese and American participants and asked them to report what they had seen. The initial comments of American subjects typically referred to the focal fish, whereas the initial comments of Japanese subjects usually referred to background elements (see Figure 8.18). Fur-

thermore, compared to the Americans, the Japanese participants made about 70% more statements about context or background and about twice as many statements about relationships between elements in the scenes. Other studies have shown that cultural variations in analytic versus holistic thinking influence subjects' patterns of logical reasoning, their vulnerability to hindsight bias (see Chapter 7), and their tolerance of contradictions (Nisbett et al., 2001). Research also suggests that people from Eastern cultures tend to be more field-dependent than their Western counterparts (Ji, Peng, & Nisbett, 2000), but Nisbett and his colleagues view field dependence-independence as just one facet of a broader preference for holistic versus analytic thinking. Based on these and many other findings, Nisbett et al. (2001) conclude that cultural disparities in cognitive style are substantial and that "literally different cognitive processes are often invoked by East Asians and Westerners dealing with the same problem" (p. 305).

Problems are not the only kind of cognitive challenge that people grapple with on a regular basis. Life also seems to constantly demand decisions. As you might expect, cognitive psychologists have shown great interest in the process of decision making, which is our next subject.

REVIEW OF KEY POINTS

- In studying problem solving, psychologists have differentiated among several types of problems. In problems that require inducing structure, the problem solver must discover the relations among the parts of a problem. Transformation problems require that the problem solver carry out a sequence of transformations (moves) in order to reach a specific goal. Arrangement problems require the problem solver to arrange the parts in a way that satisfies a general goal.

- Common barriers to problem solving include functional fixedness, mental set, getting bogged down in irrelevant information, and placing unnecessary constraints on one's solutions. An algorithm is a procedure for trying all possible alternatives in searching for a solution to a problem.

- A variety of strategies, or heuristics, are used for solving problems. When people form subgoals, they try breaking the problem into several parts. Sometimes it is useful to start at the goal state and work backward toward the initial state. Other general strategies include searching for analogies between new problems and old problems, and changing the representation of problems.

- Some cultures encourage a field-dependent cognitive style, whereas others foster more field independence. People who are field independent tend to analyze and restructure problems more than those who are field dependent. Research suggests that Eastern cultures exhibit a more holistic cognitive style, whereas Western cultures display a more analytic cognitive style.

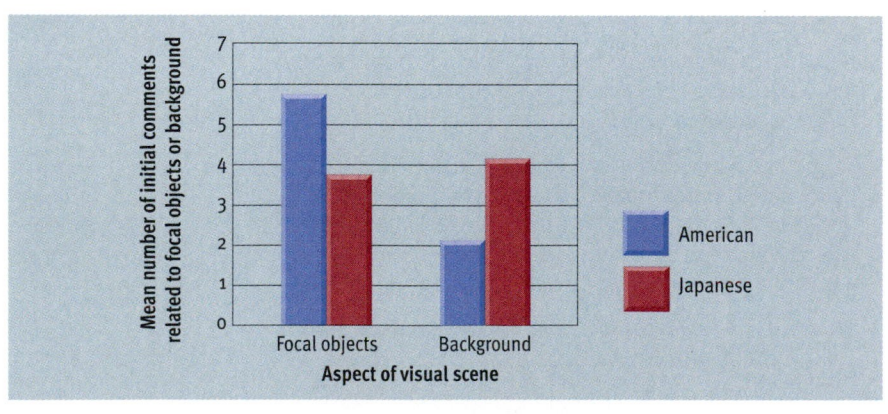

Decision Making: Choices and Chances

Decisions, decisions. Life is full of them. You decided to read this book today. Earlier today you decided when to get up, whether to eat breakfast, and if so, what to eat. Usually you make routine decisions like these with little effort. But on occasion you need to make important decisions that require more thought. Big decisions—such as selecting a car, a home, or a job—tend to be difficult. The alternatives usually have a number of attributes that need to be weighed. For instance, in choosing among several cars, you may want to compare their costs, roominess, fuel economy, handling, acceleration, stylishness, reliability, safety features, and warranties.

Decision making involves evaluating alternatives and making choices among them. Most people try to be systematic and rational in their decision making. However, the work that earned Herbert Simon the 1978 Nobel prize in economics showed that people don't always live up to these goals. Before Simon's work, most traditional theories in economics assumed that people make rational choices to maximize their economic gains. Simon (1957) demonstrated that people have a limited ability to process and evaluate information on numerous facets of possible alternatives. Thus, Simon's *theory of bounded rationality* asserts that people tend to use simple strategies in decision making that focus on only a few facets of available options and often result in "irrational" decisions that are less than optimal.

Spurred by Simon's analysis, psychologists have devoted several decades to the study of how cognitive biases distort people's decision making. The results of this research have sometimes been disturbing, leading some theorists to conclude that "normal adult human subjects do a singularly bad job at the business of reasoning, even when they are calm, clearheaded, and under no pressure to perform quickly" (Stich, 1990, pp. 173–174). Researchers' focus on *biases and mistakes* in making decisions may seem a little peculiar, but as Kahneman (1991) has pointed out, the study of people's misguided decisions has illuminated the process of decision making, just as the study of illusions and forgetting has enhanced our understanding of visual perception and memory, respectively.

Making Choices: Selecting an Alternative

Many decisions involve choices about *preferences*, which can be made using a variety of strategies (Ho-

garth, 1987). For instance, imagine that Boris has found two reasonably attractive apartments and is trying to decide between them. How should he go about selecting between his alternatives? Let's look at some strategies Boris might use in trying to make his decision.

If Boris wanted to use an *additive strategy*, he would list the attributes that influence his decision. Then he would rate the desirability of each apartment on each attribute. For example, let's say that Boris wants to consider four attributes: rent, noise level, distance to campus, and cleanliness. He might make ratings from –3 to +3, like those shown in Table 8.3, add up the ratings for each alternative, and select the one with the largest total. Given the ratings in Table 8.3, Boris should select apartment B.

To make an additive strategy more useful, you can *weight* attributes differently, based on their importance (Goldstein, 1990). For example, if Boris considers distance to campus to be twice as important as the other considerations, he could multiply his ratings of this attribute by 2. The distance rating would then be +6 for apartment A and –2 for apartment B, and apartment A would become the preferred choice.

People also make choices by gradually eliminating less attractive alternatives (Slovic, 1990; Tversky, 1972). This strategy is called *elimination by aspects* because it assumes that alternatives are eliminated by evaluating them on each attribute or aspect in turn. Whenever any alternative fails to satisfy some minimum criterion for an attribute, it is eliminated from further consideration.

To illustrate, suppose Juanita is looking for a new car. She may begin by eliminating all cars that cost over $18,000. Then she may eliminate cars that don't average at least 20 miles per gallon of gas. By continuing to reject choices that don't satisfy some minimum

Table 8.3 Application of the Additive Model to Choosing an Apartment

Attribute	Apartment	
	A	B
Rent	+1	+2
Noise level	–2	+3
Distance to campus	+3	–1
Cleanliness	+2	+2
Total	**+4**	**+6**

PREVIEW QUESTIONS
- How do people make choices about preferences?
- What factors are important in risky decision making?
- What shortcuts do people use in judging probabilities?
- What is the alternative outcomes effect?
- What do evolutionary psychologists have to say about error and bias in human decision making?

criterion on selected attributes, she can gradually eliminate alternatives until only a single car remains.

The final choice in elimination by aspects depends on the order in which attributes are evaluated. For example, if cost was the last attribute Juanita evaluated, she could have previously eliminated all cars that cost under $18,000. If she has only $18,000 to spend, her decision-making strategy would not have brought her very far. Thus, when using elimination by aspects, it's best to evaluate attributes in the order of their importance.

Both the additive and the elimination-by-aspects strategies have advantages, but which strategy do people actually tend to use? Research by John Payne (1976) suggests that when decisions involve relatively few options that need to be evaluated on only a few attributes, people tend to use additive strategies. However, as more options and factors are added to a decision task, people tend to shift to elimination by aspects. Thus, people adapt their approach to the demands of the task. When their choices become very complex, they shift toward simpler decision strategies (Payne, Bettman, & Johnson, 1992).

Difficulties in choosing between alternatives can also lead people to delay their decisions. Tversky and Shafir (1992) note that "the experience of conflict is the price one pays for the freedom to choose" (p. 358). They argue that when alternatives are not dramatically different in attractiveness, people struggle with conflict and often defer decisions, taking additional time to look for a new car, apartment, or whatever.

The research of Tversky and Shafir (1992) suggests that these delayed decisions are common even when the available alternatives are quite satisfactory. As an everyday illustration of this phenomenon, they describe a friend who had decided to buy an expensive encyclopedia for his children. Much to his chagrin, when he visited a bookstore to make his purchase he discovered that there were two appealing encyclopedias available. Although both encyclopedias were acceptable, he found it difficult to choose between the two, and as a result he bought neither.

Delaying a decision allows one to seek additional information. However, people have a perplexing tendency to pursue information that ought not alter their decision (Bastardi & Shafir, 2000). For example, in one study by Bastardi and Shafir (1998), participants were asked to make a hypothetical decision about whether they would buy a new CD player that was on sale for half-price, even though they just learned that their amplifier would require repairs costing $90. In the *simple condition,* subjects were told that their amplifier warranty had expired and they would have to pay the $90 for repairs. The vast majority (91%) of these subjects indicated that they would purchase the attractively priced CD player anyway. This result suggests that most people would buy the CD player whether or not they had to pay for the repairs. However, in the *uncertain condition,* when participants were told that they would have to wait a day to find out if their amplifier warranty would cover the $90 repair, 69% of the subjects chose to wait to find out about the repair before making a decision. Thus the introduction of uncertainty led over two-thirds of the participants to seek information that was really useless, since it would not alter most people's decisions.

Even more perplexing, this seemingly useless information actually influenced their decisions. The subjects who chose to wait were told that they would have to pay for the repairs after all. Over half (58%) of these subjects decided *not* to buy the CD player—even though the vast majority would have bought it in the simple condition. Thus, it appears that the decision to pursue additional information made that information seem more important than it otherwise would have been. Obviously, in many situations seeking more information can facilitate effective decision making. However, the research by Bastardi and Shafir (1998, 2000) shows that additional information is not always beneficial and that people need to think about whether specific information is really worth pursuing.

People often have to decide between alternative products, such as computers, cars, refrigerators, and so forth, that are not all that different. They often struggle with the abundant choices and delay making a decision. However, as the text explains, extra deliberation does not necessarily lead to better decisions.

© Arthur Tilley/Taxi-Getty Images

Taking Chances: Factors Weighed in Risky Decisions

Suppose you have the chance to play a dice game in which you might win some money. You must decide whether it would be to your advantage to play. You're going to roll a fair die. If the number 6 appears, you win $5. If one of the other five numbers appears, you win nothing. It costs you $1 every time you play. Should you participate?

This problem calls for a type of decision making that is somewhat different from making choices about preferences. In selecting alternatives that reflect preferences, people generally weigh known outcomes (apartment A will require a long commute to campus, car B will get 30 miles per gallon, and so forth). In contrast, *risky decision making* involves making choices under conditions of uncertainty. Uncertainty exists when people don't know what will happen. At best, they know the probability that a particular event will occur.

One way to decide whether to play the dice game would be to figure out the *expected value* of participation in the game. To do so, you would need to calculate the average amount of money you could expect to win or lose each time you play. The value of a win is $4 ($5 minus the $1 entry fee). The value of a loss is –$1. To calculate expected value, you also need to know the probability of a win or loss. Since a die has six faces, the probability of a win is 1 out of 6, and the probability of a loss is 5 out of 6. Thus, on five out of every six trials, you lose $1. On one out of six, you win $4. The game is beginning to sound unattractive, isn't it? We can figure out the precise expected value as follows:

Expected value = ($\frac{1}{6}$ × 4) + ($\frac{5}{6}$ × –1)
= $\frac{4}{6}$ + (–$\frac{5}{6}$) = –$\frac{1}{6}$

The expected value of this game is –$\frac{1}{6}$ of a dollar, which means that you lose an average of about 17 cents per turn. Now that you know the expected value, surely you won't agree to play. Or will you?

If we want to understand why people make the decisions they do, the concept of expected value is not enough. People frequently behave in ways that are inconsistent with expected value (Slovic, Lichtenstein, & Fischhoff, 1988). Anytime the expected value is negative, a gambler should expect to lose money. Yet a great many people gamble at racetracks and casinos and buy lottery tickets. Although they realize that the odds are against them, they continue to gamble. Even people who don't gamble buy home-

owner's insurance, which has a negative expected value. After all, when you buy insurance, your expectation (and hope!) is that you will lose money on the deal.

To explain decisions that violate expected value, some theories replace the objective value of an outcome with its *subjective utility* (Fischhoff, 1988). Subjective utility represents what an outcome is personally worth to an individual. For example, buying a few lottery tickets may allow you to dream about becoming wealthy. Buying insurance may give you a sense of security. Subjective utilities like these vary from one person to another. If we know an individual's subjective utilities, we can better understand that person's risky decision making.

Another way to improve our understanding of risky decision making is to consider individuals' estimates of the *subjective probability* of events (Shafer & Tversky, 1988). If people don't know actual probabilities, they must rely on their personal estimates of probabilities. These estimates can have interesting effects on the perceived utility of various outcomes.

Heuristics in Judging Probabilities

- What are your chances of passing your next psychology test if you study only 3 hours?
- How likely is a major downturn in the stock market during the upcoming year?
- What are the odds of your getting into graduate school in the field of your choice?

These questions ask you to make probability estimates. Amos Tversky and Daniel Kahneman (1974, 1982; Kahneman & Tversky, 2000) have conducted extensive research on the *heuristics,* or mental shortcuts, that people use in grappling with probabilities. This research on heuristics earned Kahneman the Nobel Prize in Economics in 2002 (unfortunately, his collaborator, Amos Tversky, died in 1996). *Availability* is one such heuristic. The *availability heuristic* involves basing the estimated probability of an event on the ease with which relevant instances come to mind. For example, you may estimate the divorce rate by recalling the number of divorces among your friends' parents. Recalling specific instances of an event is a reasonable strategy to use in estimating the event's probability. However, if instances occur frequently but you have difficulty retrieving them from memory, your estimate will be biased. For instance, it's easier to think of words that

Courtesy of Daniel Kahneman

"The human mind suppresses uncertainty. We're not only convinced that we know more about our politics, our businesses, and our spouses than we really do, but also that what we don't know must be unimportant."
DANIEL KAHNEMAN

"*People treat their own cases as if they were unique, rather than part of a huge lottery. You hear this silly argument that 'The odds don't apply to me.' Why should God, or whoever runs this lottery, give you special treatment?*"
AMOS TVERSKY

begin with a certain letter than words that contain that letter at some other position. Hence, people should tend to respond that there are more words starting with the letter *K* than words having a *K* in the third position. To test this hypothesis, Tversky and Kahneman (1973) selected five consonants (*K, L, N, R, V*) that occur more frequently in the third position of a word than in the first. Subjects were asked whether each of the letters appears more often in the first or third position. Most of the subjects erroneously believed that all five letters were much more frequent in the first than in the third position, confirming the hypothesis.

Representativeness is another guide in estimating probabilities identified by Kahneman and Tversky (1982). **The *representativeness heuristic* involves basing the estimated probability of an event on how similar it is to the typical prototype of that event.** To illustrate, imagine that you flip a coin six times and keep track of how often the result is heads (H) or tails (T). Which of the following sequences is more likely?

1. T T T T T T
2. H T T H T H

People generally believe that the second sequence is more likely. After all, coin tossing is a random affair, and the second sequence looks much more representative of a random process than the first. In reality, the probability of each exact *sequence* is pre-

cisely the same ($\frac{1}{2} \times \frac{1}{2} \times \frac{1}{2} \times \frac{1}{2} \times \frac{1}{2} \times \frac{1}{2} = \frac{1}{64}$). Let's look at another phenomenon in which the representativeness heuristic plays a key role.

The Tendency to Ignore Base Rates

Steve is very shy and withdrawn, invariably helpful, but with little interest in people or in the world of reality. A meek and tidy soul, he has a need for order and structure and a passion for detail. Do you think Steve is a salesperson or a librarian? (Adapted from Tversky & Kahneman, 1974, p. 1124)

Using the *representativeness heuristic*, subjects tend to guess that Steve is a librarian because he resembles their prototype of a librarian (Tversky & Kahneman, 1982). In reality, this is not a very wise guess, because it *ignores the base rates* of librarians and salespeople in the population. Virtually everyone knows that salespeople outnumber librarians by a wide margin (roughly 75 to 1 in the United States). This fact makes it much more likely that Steve is in sales. But in estimating probabilities, people often ignore information on base rates.

Although people do not *always* neglect base rate information, it is a persistent phenomenon (Case, Fantino, & Goodie, 1999; Koehler, 1996). Moreover, people are particularly bad about applying base rates to themselves. For instance, Weinstein (1984;

CONCEPT CHECK 8.3

Recognizing Heuristics in Decision Making

Check your understanding of heuristics in decision making by trying to identify the heuristics used in the following example. Each numbered element in the anecdote below illustrates a problem-solving heuristic. Write the relevant heuristic in the space on the left. You can find the answers in Appendix A.

_____ **1.** Marsha can't decide on a college major. She evaluates all the majors available at her college on the attributes of how much she would enjoy them (likability), how challenging they are (difficulty), and how good the job opportunities are in the field (employability). She drops from consideration any major that she regards as "poor" on any of these three attributes.

_____ **2.** When she considers history as a major, she thinks to herself, "Gee, I know four history graduates who are still looking for work," and concludes that the probability of getting a job using a history degree is very low.

_____ **3.** She finds that every major gets a "poor" rating on at least one attribute, so she eliminates everything. Because this is unacceptable, she decides she has to switch to another strategy. Marsha finally focuses her consideration on five majors that received just one "poor" rating. She uses a 4-point scale to rate each of these majors on each of the three attributes she values. She adds up the ratings and selects the major with the highest total as her leading candidate.

Weinstein & Klein, 1995) has found that people underestimate the risks of their own health-impairing habits while viewing others' risks much more accurately. Thus, smokers are realistic in estimating the degree to which smoking increases someone else's risk of heart attack but underestimate the risk for themselves. Similarly, people starting new companies ignore the high failure rate for new businesses, and burglars underestimate the likelihood that they will end up in jail. Thus, in risky decision making, people often think that they can beat the odds. As Amos Tversky puts it, "People treat their own cases as if they were unique, rather than part of a huge lottery. You hear this silly argument that 'The odds don't apply to me.' Why should God, or whoever runs this lottery, give you special treatment?" (McKean, 1985, p. 27).

The Conjunction Fallacy 6e

Imagine that you're going to meet a man who is an articulate, ambitious, power-hungry wheeler-dealer. Do you think it's more likely that he's a college teacher or a college teacher who's also a politician?

People tend to guess that the man is a "college teacher who's a politician" because the description fits with the typical prototype of politicians. But stop and think for a moment. The broader category of college teachers completely includes the smaller subcategory of college teachers who are politicians (see Figure 8.19). The probability of being in the subcategory cannot be higher than the probability of being in the broader category. It's a logical impossibility!

Tversky and Kahneman (1983) call this error the *conjunction fallacy*. The *conjunction fallacy* occurs when people estimate that the odds of two uncertain events happening together are greater than the odds of either event happening alone. The conjunction fallacy has been observed in a number of studies and has generally been attributed to the pow-

College professors

College professors who are also politicians

Figure 8.19

The conjunction fallacy. People routinely fall victim to the conjunction fallacy, but as this diagram makes obvious, the probability of being in a subcategory (college teachers who are politicians) cannot be higher than the probability of being in the broader category (college teachers). As this case illustrates, it often helps to represent a problem in a diagram.

erful influence of the representativeness heuristic (Epstein, Donovan, & Denes-Raj, 1999).

The Alternative Outcomes Effect

Like the conjunction fallacy, the alternative outcomes effect seems irrational. In this case, two different scenarios that represent the same probability situation lead to surprisingly discrepant estimates of the likelihood of an event. According to Paul Windschitl and Gary Wells (1998) the *alternative outcomes effect* occurs when people's belief about whether an outcome will occur changes depending on how alternative outcomes are distributed, even though the summed probability of the alternative outcomes is held constant. Let's look at the research that documented this peculiar effect in decision making.

Even Objective Probabilities Are Subjective

The authors begin by citing evidence that people's feelings about the likelihood of an event can be influenced by a variety of factors—even when the objective probability of the event is known. For example, research has shown that people like their chances of winning better when they draw a bean from a bowl that contains 10 winning beans and 90 losing beans as opposed to a bowl containing 1 winning bean and 9 losing beans, in spite of the obvious fact that the two situations involve the same probability of winning. To explore this type of perplexing subjectivity in risky decision making, Windschitl and Wells conducted a series of six studies in which they typically held the probability of a "focal outcome" constant while tinkering with the distribution of probabilities for alternative outcomes. Their first two studies are summarized here.

FEATURED STUDY

Investigators: Paul D. Windschitl (University of Iowa) and Gary L. Wells (Iowa State University)

Source: The alternative outcomes effect. *Journal of Personality and Social Psychology*, 1998, 75, 1411–1423.

Study 1

Method. Half of the participants considered the following scenario: *Imagine you are at a casino-style charity party where a raffle is held for a $200 prize. Of the 88 raffle tickets, you hold 21 tickets, Mary has 14, Simon has 13, Amman has 15, Tara has 12, and George has 13.* The other half of the participants read about the same situation, but were given a different ticket distribution. *Of the 88 raffle tickets, you hold 21 tickets, Mary has 52, Simon has 6, Amman has 2, Tara has 2, and George has 5.* Ninety-six undergraduates rated the likelihood that they would win the raffle prize on an 11-point scale ranging from 0 (*impossible*) to 10 (*certain*).

Results. Although the objective probability of winning the raffle was the same in both conditions ($^{21}/_{88}$), subjects who worked with the 21–14–13–15–12–13 distribution of tickets rated their chances of winning significantly higher than did the subjects exposed to the 21–52–6–2–2–5 distribution.

Study 2

Method. Half of the participants considered the following scenario: *After dinner, young Katie is told that she can have one cookie, which she must pull out of a cookie jar without looking. She is hoping to snag a chocolate chip cookie from the jar, which contains 2 chocolate chip cookies, 1 oatmeal, 1 raisin, 1 butterscotch, 1 rum, 1 peanut butter, 1 pecan, and 1 sugar cookie.* The other half of the participants read about the same situation, but they were informed that *the jar contains 2 chocolate chip cookies and 7 oatmeal cookies.* Ninety-six undergraduates rated the likelihood that Katie would get her chocolate chip cookie on the same 11-point scale used in Study 1.

Results. Although the objective probability of Katie getting a chocolate chip cookie was the same in both conditions and very easy to calculate ($^{2}/_{9}$), subjects who worked with the 2–1–1–1–1–1–1–1 distribution of cookies liked Katie's chances significantly better than the subjects exposed to the 2-7 distribution.

Discussion

The results seen in these two studies demonstrate that the perceived likelihood of a focal outcome is influenced by the distribution of alternative outcomes. It appears that participants focus heavily on comparisons between the focal outcome and the most likely alternative. When these simple comparisons do not favor the focal outcome, subjective estimates of its likelihood decrease. The authors speculate that these subjective distortions in the evaluation of probabilities could influence many real-world decisions.

Comment

This research was featured because it provided an interesting and convincing demonstration that even objective probabilities are ultimately very subjective—a result that once again highlights the text's theme about the subjectivity of human experience. This research also fleshes out Simon's (1957) concept of *bounded rationality,* which was introduced at the beginning of the section on decision making. Consistent with Simon's theory, research has repeatedly shown that in evaluating their alternatives, people tend to use simple strategies that focus on only a few facets of the situation, which can lead to peculiarities that are often characterized as irrational. ■

Figure 8.20

The alternative outcomes effect in a study of hurricane projections. In one of their six studies, Windschitl and Wells (1998) showed participants these two maps, which depict the estimated probability of a hurricane coming ashore in the fictitious town of Sunbury, Georgia. As in their other studies, the distribution of alternative outcomes influenced subjects' perceptions about the likelihood of the focal event. The people who saw Map A were more worried about the hurricane hitting Sunbury than those who saw Map B.

Source: Windschitl, P. D., & Wells, G. L. (1998). The alternative outcomes effect. *Journal of Personality and Social Psychology, 75* (6), 1411–1423. Copyright © 1998 by the American Psychological Association. Reprinted by permission of the author.

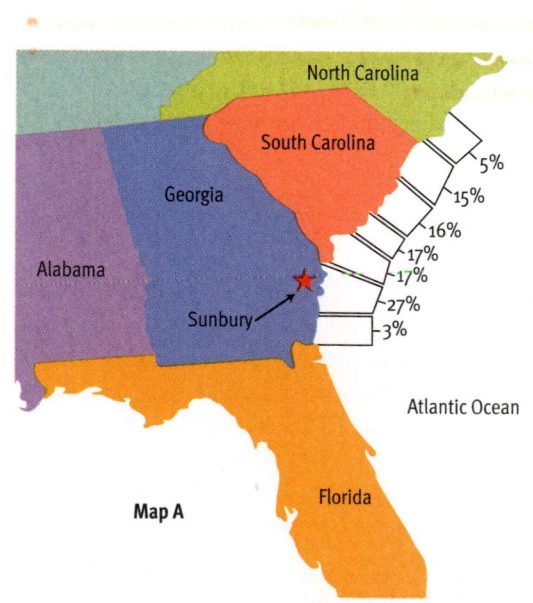

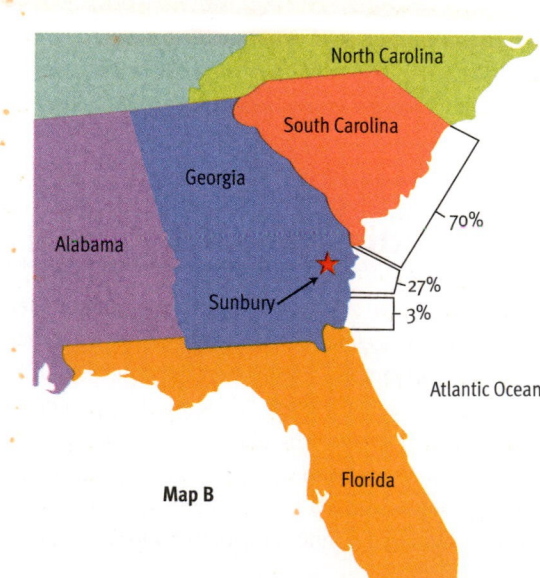

The alternative outcomes effect discovered by Windschitl and Wells appears to be reliable, as it showed up in one form or another in all six of their studies, which involved quite a variety of situations. These situations included some more realistic scenarios where the given probabilities were only *estimates* rather than *known realities*. For example, in one study subjects were told that they lived in the coastal town of Sunbury, Georgia, and that a hurricane was headed their way. The estimated probabilities of the hurricane coming ashore at various places along the coast were given to subjects in the two maps shown in Figure 8.20. As predicted, subjects who saw Map A were more worried about the hurricane coming ashore in Sunbury than those who saw Map B, even though the crucial estimated probability was 27% on both maps.

Evolutionary Analyses of Flaws in Human Decision Making

Consistent with our Featured Study, a central conclusion of the last 25 years of research on decision making has been that human decision-making strategies are riddled with errors and biases that yield surprisingly irrational results (Goldstein & Hogarth, 1997; Shafir & LeBoeuf, 2002). Theorists have discovered that people have "mental limitations" and have concluded that people are not as bright and rational as they think they are. Conversely, over the same period of time, researchers studying the behavior of animals in their natural environments have been increasingly impressed by how the animals tend to make sound choices that approximate optimal decision making (see Chapter 6) consistent with elaborate mathematical models of optimality (Real, 1991; Shettleworth, 1998). So, we have quite a paradox: How can humans appear so dumb, when animals appear so bright? This paradox has led some evolutionary psychologists to reconsider the work on human decision making, and their take on the matter is quite interesting. First, they argue that traditional decision research has imposed an invalid and unrealistic standard of rationality, which assumes that people should be impeccable in applying the laws of deductive logic and statistical probability while objectively and precisely weighing multiple factors in arriving at decisions (Gigerenzer, 2000). Second, they argue that humans only *seem* irrational because cognitive psychologists have been asking the wrong questions and formulating problems in the wrong ways—ways that have nothing to do with the adaptive problems that the human mind has evolved to solve (Cosmides & Tooby, 1996).

According to Leda Cosmides and John Tooby (1994, 1996), the human mind consists of a large number of specialized cognitive mechanisms that have emerged over the course of evolution to solve specific adaptive problems, such as finding food, shelter, and mates and dealing with allies and enemies. Thus, human decision and problem-solving strategies have been tailored to handle real-world adaptive problems. Participants perform poorly in cognitive research, say Cosmides and Tooby, because it confronts them with contrived, artificial problems that do not involve natural categories and have no adaptive significance.

For example, evolutionary psychologists argue that the human mind is wired to think in terms of *raw frequencies* rather than *base rates and probabilities* (Gigerenzer, 1997, 2000). Asking about the probability of a single event is routine in today's world, where we are inundated with statistical data ranging from batting averages to weather predictions. But our ancient ancestors had access to little data other than their own observations, which were accumulating counts of natural frequencies, such as "we had a good hunt three out of the last five times we went to the north plains." Thus, evolutionary theorists assert that many errors in human reasoning, such as neglect of base rates and the conjunction fallacy, should vanish if classic laboratory problems are reformulated in terms of raw frequencies rather than probabilities and base rates.

Consistent with this analysis, evolutionary psychologists have shown that some errors in reasoning that are seen in laboratory studies disappear or are decreased when problems are presented in ways that resemble the type of input humans would have processed in ancestral times (Brase, Cosmides & Tooby, 1998; Gigerenzer & Hoffrage, 1999; Hertwig & Gigerenzer, 1999). Although there is plenty of room for debate (Mellers, Hertwig & Kahneman, 2001; Shafir & LeBoeuf, 2002), this evidence and a couple of other lines of research are gradually reducing cognitive psychologists' tendency to characterize human reasoning as "irrational."

Fast and Frugal Heuristics

Working from an evolutionary point of view, Gerd Gigerenzer has argued that humans' reasoning largely depends on "fast and frugal heuristics" that are quite a bit simpler than the complicated inferential processes studied in traditional cognitive research (Gigerenzer, 2000; Goldstein & Gigerenzer, 1999; Todd & Gigerenzer, 2000). According to Gigenrenzer, organisms from toads to stockbrokers have to make fast decisions under demanding circumstances with limited information. In most instances organisms (in-

Web Link 8.4

Has Natural Selection Shaped How Humans Reason?
This link will take you to a recorded talk by Leda Cosmides and John Tooby (University of California, Santa Barbara) in which they discuss their evolutionary perspective on human decision making.

Courtesy of John Tooby

Courtesy of Leda Cosmides

"*The problems our cognitive devices are designed to solve do not reflect the problems our modern life experiences lead us to see as normal . . . Instead, they are the ancient and seemingly esoteric problems that our hunter-gatherer ancestors encountered generation after generation over hominid evolution.*"
JOHN TOOBY AND
LEDA COSMIDES

Courtesy of Gerd Gigerenzer

"These 'fast and frugal' heuristics operate with simple psychological principles that satisfy the constraints of limited time, knowledge, and computational might, rather than those of classical rationality.**"**
GERD GIGERENZER

Web Link 8.5

**Simple Minds—
Smart Choices**
This link leads to an article from *Science News* on Gerd Gigerenzer's research, which suggests that decisions can be made quickly and accurately with remarkably simple strategies.

cluding humans) do not have the time, resources, or cognitive capacities to gather all the relevant information, consider all the possible options, calculate all the probabilities and risks, and then make the statistically optimal decision. Instead, they use quick and dirty heuristics that are less than perfect but that work well enough most of the time to be adaptive in the real world.

To explore these fast and frugal heuristics, Gigerenzer and his colleagues have typically studied inferences from *memory*, which challenge participants to search some portion of their general knowledge, rather than inferences from *givens*, which challenge participants to draw logical conclusions from information provided by the experimenter (example: you hold 21 of the 88 raffle tickets, Mary has 14, and so forth). Gigerenzer (2000) maintains that the traditional approach of studying inferences from givens is contrived because in the real world people are rarely given all the information relevant to their decisions; they normally have to search for useful information and base their decisions on limited knowledge. To model this process, Gigerenzer and his colleagues have often asked subjects to draw inferences based on their knowledge of geography, which tends to be limited and imperfect. In a typical study, participants are asked to make a series of choices between pairs of alternatives based on some quantitative dimension, such as deciding which of two cities is larger.

What has this research revealed? It has demonstrated that fast and frugal heuristics can be surprisingly effective. One heuristic that is often used in selecting between alternatives based on some quantitative dimension is the *recognition heuristic,* which works as follows: If one of two alternatives is recog-

nized and the other is not, infer that the recognized alternative has the higher value. Consider the following questions—Which city has more inhabitants: San Diego or San Antonio? Hamburg or Munich? In choosing between U.S. cities, American college students weighed a lifetime of facts useful for inferring population and made the correct choice 71% of the time; in choosing between German cities about which they knew very little, the same students depended on the recognition heuristic and chose correctly 73% of the time (Goldstein & Gigerenzer, 2002). Thus, the recognition heuristic allowed students to perform just as well with very limited knowledge as they did with extensive knowledge. In another test of the efficacy of the recognition heuristic, researchers compiled imaginary stock portfolios made up of the 10 German stocks that were most highly recognized by American subjects and the 10 American stocks that were most highly recognized by German subjects (Borges et al., 1999). Over the six-month period of the study, these portfolios, which were assembled on the basis of minimal knowledge and a simple selection strategy, outperformed their respective market indexes by substantial margins.

Gigerenzer and his colleagues have studied a variety of other quick, one-reason decision-making strategies and demonstrated that they can yield inferences that are just as accurate as much more elaborate and time-consuming strategies that carefully weigh a multiplicity of relevant factors. And they have demonstrated that people actually use these fast and frugal heuristics in a diverse array of situations (Gigerenzer & Todd, 1999; Rieskamp & Hoffrage, 1999). Thus, the study of fast and frugal heuristics promises to be an intriguing new line of research in the study of human decision making.

Putting It in Perspective

PREVIEW QUESTIONS
- Where did the nature versus nurture debate surface in this chapter?
- How did this chapter highlight the importance of research methods?
- How did this chapter illustrate both cultural variance and invariance?
- How did this chapter demonstrate the subjectivity of experience?

Four of our unifying themes have been especially prominent in this chapter. The first is the continuing question about the relative influences of heredity and environment. The controversy about how children acquire language skills replays the nature versus nurture debate. The behaviorist theory, that children learn language through imitation and reinforcement, emphasizes the importance of the environment. The nativist theory, that children come equipped with an innate language acquisition device, argues for the importance of biology. The debate is far from settled,

but the accumulating evidence suggests that language development depends on both nature and nurture, as more recent interactionist theories have proposed.

The second pertinent theme is the empirical nature of psychology. For many decades, psychologists paid little attention to cognitive processes, because most of them assumed that thinking is too private to be studied scientifically. During the 1950s and 1960s, however, psychologists began to devise creative new ways to measure mental processes. These innovations fueled the cognitive revolution that put the *psyche* (the mind) back in psychology. Thus, once again, we see how empirical methods are the lifeblood of the scientific enterprise.

Third, the study of cognitive processes shows how there are both similarities and differences across cultures in behavior. On the one hand, we saw that language development unfolds in much the same way in widely disparate cultures and that thought processes are largely invariant in spite of sharp differences in cultures' linguistic heritage. On the other hand, we learned that there are interesting cultural variations in cognitive style.

The fourth theme is the subjective nature of human experience. We have seen that decision making is a highly subjective process. For example, probabilities weighed in decisions that are objectively identical can subjectively seem very different. The subjectivity of decision processes will continue to be prominent in the upcoming Personal Application, which discusses some more common pitfalls in reasoning about decisions.

REVIEW OF KEY POINTS

- Simon's theory of bounded rationality suggests that human decision strategies are simplistic and often yield irrational results. An additive decision model is used when people make decisions by rating the attributes of each alternative and selecting the alternative that has the highest sum of ratings.

- When elimination by aspects is used, people gradually eliminate alternatives whose attributes fail to satisfy some minimum criterion. To some extent, people adapt their decision-making strategy to the situation, moving toward simpler strategies when choices become complex. In making decisions, people have a curious tendency to pursue information that is not likely to alter their decisions.

- Models of how people make risky decisions focus on the expected value or subjective utility of various outcomes and the objective or subjective probability that these outcomes will occur.

- People use the representativeness and availability heuristics in estimating probabilities. These heuristics can lead people to ignore base rates and to fall prey to the conjunction fallacy. In the alternative outcomes effect, two scenarios that represent the same probability situation lead to surprisingly discrepant estimates of the likelihood of an event.

- Evolutionary psychologists maintain that many errors and biases in human reasoning are greatly reduced when problems are presented in ways that resemble the type of input humans would have processed in ancestral times. Gigerenzer argues that people largely depend on fast and frugal decision heuristics that are adaptive in the real world.

- Four of our unifying themes surfaced in the chapter. Our discussion of language acquisition revealed once again that all aspects of behavior are shaped by both nature and nurture. The recent progress in the study of cognitive processes showed how science depends on empirical methods. Research on decision making illustrated the importance of subjective perceptions, and we saw that cognitive processes are moderated—to a limited degree—by cultural factors.

Understanding Pitfalls in Reasoning About Decisions

Consider the following scenario:

Laura is in a casino watching people play roulette. The 38 slots in the roulette wheel include 18 black numbers, 18 red numbers, and 2 green numbers. Hence, on any one spin, the probability of red or black is slightly less than 50-50 (.474 to be exact). Although Laura hasn't been betting, she has been following the pattern of results in the game very carefully. The ball has landed in red seven times in a row. Laura concludes that black is long overdue and she jumps into the game, betting heavily on black.

Has Laura made a good bet? Do you agree with Laura's reasoning? Or do you think that Laura misunderstands the laws of probability? You'll find out momentarily, as we discuss how people reason their way to decisions—and how their reasoning can go awry.

The pioneering work of Amos Tversky and Daniel Kahneman (1974, 1982) led to an explosion of research on risky decision making. In their efforts to identify the heuristics that people use in decision making, investigators stumbled onto quite a few misconceptions, oversights, and biases. It turns out that people deviate in predictable ways from optimal decision strategies—with surprising regularity (Goldstein & Hogarth, 1997). As explained in the chapter, recent evolutionary research on decision making has offered a new explanation for *why* our decision making appears to be muddled. And evolutionary theorists argue that our decision strategies actually are rational—when viewed as evolved mechanisms designed to solve the adaptive problems faced in ancestral times (Cosmides & Tooby, 1996).

But, while the evolutionary explanations for our foibles in reasoning *may* be on target, the fact remains that *we do not live in ancestral times*. We live in the information age and we have to deal with base rates, probabilities, and percentages on a routine basis. In our modern world, reproductive fitness surely depends more on SAT scores than on counting berries. So, mainstream cognitive research on flaws in human reasoning about decisions remains relevant. Fortunately, there is evidence that increased awareness of common shortcomings in reasoning about decisions can lead to improved decision making (Agnoli & Krantz, 1989; Fischhoff, 1982; Keren, 1990). With this goal in mind, let's look at some common pitfalls in decision making.

The Gambler's Fallacy

As you may have guessed by now, Laura's reasoning in our opening scenario is flawed. A great many people tend to believe that Laura has made a good bet (Rogers, 1998; Tversky & Kahneman, 1982). However, they're wrong. Laura's behavior illustrates the *gambler's fallacy*—the belief that the odds of a chance event increase if the event hasn't occurred recently. People believe that the laws of probability should yield fair results and that a random process must be self-correcting. These aren't bad assumptions in the long run. However, they don't apply to individual, independent events.

The roulette wheel does not remember its recent results and make adjustments for them. Each spin of the wheel is an independent event. The probability of black on each spin remains at .474, even if red comes up 100 times in a row! The gambler's fallacy reflects the pervasive influence of the *representativeness heuristic*. In betting on black, Laura is predicting that future results will be more representative of a random process. This logic can be used to estimate the probability of black across a *string of spins*. But it doesn't apply to a *specific spin* of the roulette wheel.

The Law of Small Numbers

Envision a small urn filled with a mixture of red and green beads. You know that two-thirds of the beads are one color and one-third are the other color. However, you don't know whether red or green predominates. A blindfolded person reaches into the urn and comes up with 3 red beads and 1 green bead. These beads are put back in the urn and a second person scoops up 14 red beads and 10 green beads. Both samplings suggest that red beads outnumber green beads in the urn. But which sample provides better evidence? (Adapted from McKean, 1985, p. 25)

Many subjects report that the first sampling is more convincing, because of the greater preponderance of red over green. What are the actual odds that each sampling accurately reflects the dominant color in the urn? The odds for the first sampling are 4 to 1. These aren't bad odds, but the odds that the second sampling is accurate are much higher—16 to 1. Why? Because the second sample is substantially larger than the first. The likelihood of misleading results is much greater in a small sample than a large one. For example, in flipping a fair coin, the odds of getting all heads in a sample of 5 coin flips dwarfs the odds of getting all heads in a sample of 100 coin flips.

Most people appreciate the value of a large sample as an abstract principle, but they don't fully understand that results based on small samples are more variable and more likely to be a fluke (Well, Pollatsek, & Boyce, 1990). Hence, they frequently assume that results based on small samples are representative of the population (Poulton, 1994). Tversky and Kahneman (1971) call this the *belief in the law of small numbers*. This misplaced faith in small numbers explains why people are often willing to draw general conclusions based on a few individual cases.

Overestimating the Improbable

Various causes of death are paired up below. In each pairing, which is the more likely cause of death?

Asthma or tornadoes?

Syphilis or botulism (food poisoning)?

Tuberculosis or floods?

Suicide or murder?

Table 8.4 shows the actual mortality rates for each of the causes of death just listed. As you can see, the first choice in each pair is the more common cause of death. If you guessed wrong for several pairings, don't feel bad. Like many other people, you may be a victim of the tendency to *overestimate the improbable.* People tend to greatly overestimate the likelihood of dramatic, vivid—but infrequent—events that receive heavy media coverage. Thus, the number of fatalities due to tornadoes, floods, food poisonings, and murders is usually overestimated (Slovic, Fischhoff, & Lichtenstein, 1982). Fatalities due to asthma and other common diseases, which receive less media coverage, tend to be underestimated. For instance, a majority of subjects estimate that tornadoes kill more people than asthma, even though asthma fatalities outnumber tornado fatalities by a ratio of 80 to 1. This tendency to exaggerate the improbable reflects the operation of the *availability heuristic.* Instances of floods, tornadoes, and such are readily available in memory because people are exposed to a great deal of publicity about such events.

The availability heuristic can be dramatized by juxtaposing the unrelated phenomena of floods and tuberculosis (TB). Many people are killed by floods, but far more die from tuberculosis (see Table 8.4). However, since the news media report flood fatalities frequently and prominently, but rarely focus on deaths from tuberculosis, people tend to assume that flood-related deaths are more common.

Confirmation Bias and Belief Perseverance

Imagine a young physician examining a sick patient. The patient is complaining of a high fever and a sore throat. The physician must decide on a diagnosis from among a myriad possible diseases. The physician thinks that it may be the flu. She asks the patient if he feels "achey all over." The answer is "yes." The physician asks if the symptoms began a few days ago. Again, the response is "yes." The physician concludes that the patient has the flu. (Adapted from Halpern, 1984, pp. 215–216)

Do you see any flaws in the physician's reasoning? Has she probed into the causes of the patient's malady effectively? No, she has asked about symptoms that would be consistent with her preliminary diagnosis, but she has not inquired about symptoms that could rule it out. Her questioning of the patient illustrates *confirmation bias*—the **tendency to seek information that supports one's decisions and beliefs while ignoring disconfirming information** (see Figure 8.21 on the next page). This bias is common in medical diagnosis and other forms of decision making (Nickerson, 1998). There's nothing wrong with searching for confirming evidence to support one's decisions. However, people should also seek disconfirming evidence—which they often neglect to do.

Confirmation bias contributes to another, related problem called *belief perseverance*—the **tendency to hang onto beliefs in the face of contradictory evidence** (Gorman, 1989). It is difficult to dislodge an idea after having embraced it. To investigate this phenomenon, researchers have given subjects evidence to establish a belief (example: high risk takers make better firefighters) and later exposed the subjects to information discrediting the idea. These studies have shown that the disconfirming

Table 8.4 Actual Mortality Rates for Selected Causes of Death			
Cause of Death	Rate	Cause of Death	Rate
Asthma	2,000	Tornadoes	25
Accidental falls	6,021	Firearms accidents	320
Tuberculosis	400	Floods	44
Suicide	11,300	Homicide	6,800

NOTE: Mortality rates are per 100 million people and are based on the *Statistical Abstract of the United States, 2001.*

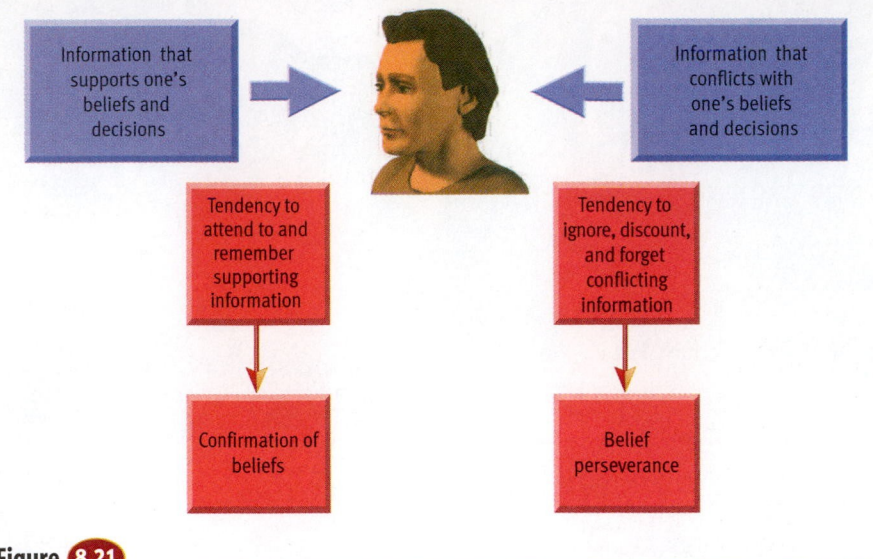

Figure **8.21**

Confirmation bias and belief perseverance. Confirmation bias exists when people seek out and react favorably to information that supports their beliefs. Belief perseverance is the tendency to cling to beliefs despite exposure to contradictory evidence.

evidence tends to fall on deaf ears (Ross & Anderson, 1982). Thus, once people arrive at a decision, they are prone to accept supportive evidence at face value while subjecting contradictory evidence to tough, skeptical scrutiny.

The Overconfidence Effect  6e

Make high and low estimates of the total U.S. Defense Department budget in the year 2000. Choose estimates far enough apart to be 98% confident that the actual figure lies between them. In other words, you should feel that there is only a 2% chance that the correct figure is lower than your low estimate or higher than your high estimate. Write your estimates in the spaces provided, before reading further.

   High estimate: _____
   Low estimate: _____

When working on problems like this one, people reason their way to their best estimate and then create a confidence interval around it. For instance, let's say that you arrived at $200 billion as your best estimate of the defense budget. You would then expand a range around that estimate— say $150 billion to $250 billion—that you're sure will contain the correct figure. The answer in this case is $281 billion. If the answer falls outside your estimated range, you are not unusual. In making this type of estimate, people consistently tend to make their confidence intervals too narrow (Lichtenstein, Fischhoff, & Phillips, 1982). For example, subjects' 98% confidence intervals should include the correct answer 98% of the time, but they actually do so only about 60% of the time.

The crux of the problem is that people tend to put too much faith in their estimates, beliefs, and decisions, even when they should know better, a principle called the *overconfidence effect*. People vary considerably in their tendency to be overconfident (Stanovich, 1999), but overconfidence effects have been seen in perceptual judgments, predictions of sports results, and economic forecasts, among many other things (West & Stanovich, 1997). The overconfidence effect is seen even when people make probability predictions about themselves. For instance, in one study (Vallone et al., 1990), college students were asked to make predictions about personal matters for the upcoming fall quarter and the entire academic year. Their predictions concerned such things as whether they would drop any courses, whether they would vote in an upcoming election, or whether they would break up with their boyfriend or girlfriend. The subjects were also asked to rate their confidence in each of their predictions, from 50% confidence to 100% confidence (the predictions were either-or propositions, making 50% a chance level of accuracy and the lowest possible level of confidence). The accuracy of the subjects' predictions was assessed at the end of the year. The analyses of thousands of predictions revealed that the students were more confident than accurate. Moreover, the more confident subjects were about their predictions, the more likely it was that they were overconfident (see Figure 8.22).

The overconfidence effect is also seen among experts in many walks of life (Fischhoff, 1988). Studies have shown that physicians, weather forecasters, military leaders, gamblers, investors, and scientists tend to be overconfident about their predictions. As Daniel Kahneman puts it, "The human mind suppresses uncertainty. We're not only convinced that we know more about our politics, our businesses, and our spouses than we really do, but also that what we don't know must be unimportant" (McKean, 1985, p. 27).

The Effects of Framing 6e

Another consideration in making decisions involving risks is the framing of questions (Tversky & Kahneman, 1988, 1991). *Framing* **refers to how decision issues are posed or how choices are structured.** People often allow a decision to be shaped by the language or context in which it's presented, rather than explore it from different perspectives. Consider the following scenario, which is adapted from Kahneman and Tversky (1984, p. 343):

Imagine that the U.S. is preparing for the outbreak of a dangerous disease, which is expected to kill 600 people. Two alternative programs to combat the disease have been proposed. Assume that the exact scientific estimates of the consequences of the programs are as follows.

• *If Program A is adopted, 200 people will be saved.*

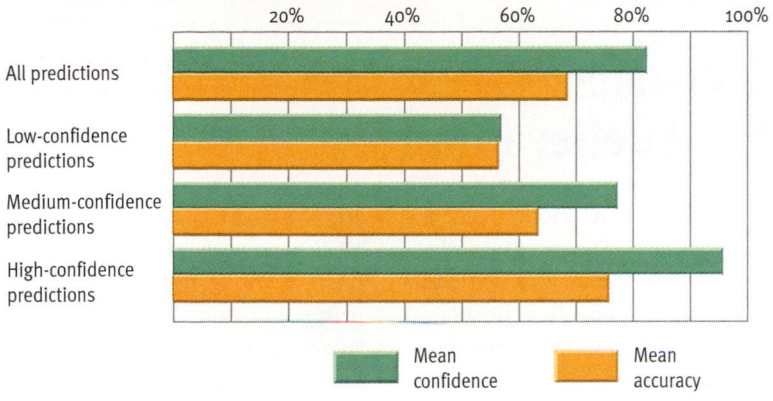

Figure 8.22

Results of the Vallone et al. (1990) study. The subjects in this study (sample 1) made 3776 predictions about personal matters. Their mean confidence level for all these predictions was 82.3%, but their mean accuracy was only 68.2%. When the predictions were divided into low-, medium-, and high-confidence predictions, an interesting pattern emerged. As subjects' confidence level went up, the gap between their confidence and their accuracy increased. This finding suggests that the more confident you are about a personal prediction, the more likely it is that you are overconfident. (Data from Vallone at al., 1990)

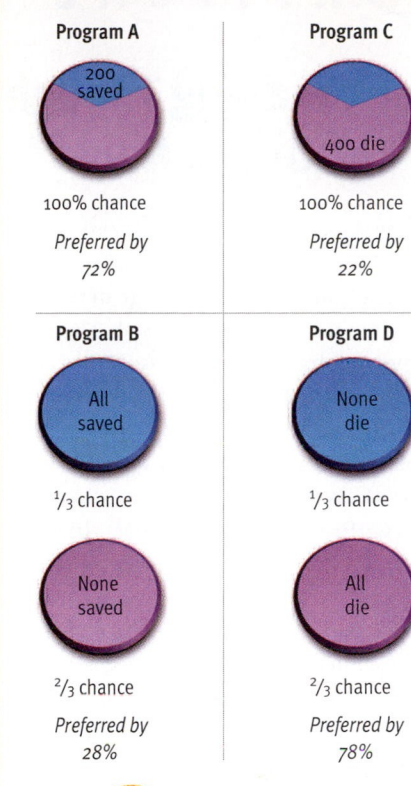

Figure 8.23

The framing of questions. This chart shows that Programs A and C involve an identical probability situation, as do Programs B and D. When choices are framed in terms of possible gains, people prefer the safer plan. However, when choices are framed in terms of losses, people are more willing to take a gamble.

- *If Program B is adopted, there is a one-third probability that all 600 people will be saved and a two-thirds probability that no people will be saved.*

Kahneman and Tversky found that 72% of their subjects chose the "sure thing" (Program A) over the "risky gamble" (Program B). However, they obtained different results when the alternatives were reframed as follows:

- *If Program C is adopted, 400 people will die.*
- *If Program D is adopted, there is a one-third probability that nobody will die and a two-thirds probability that all 600 people will die.*

Although framed differently, Programs A and B represent exactly the same probability situation as Programs C and D (see Figure 8.23). In spite of this equivalence, 78% of the subjects chose Program D. Thus, subjects chose the sure thing when the decision was framed in terms of lives saved, but they went with the risky gamble when the decision was framed in terms of lives lost. Additional experiments have shown that these results reflect a general trend in thinking about decisions. *When seeking to obtain gains, people tend to avoid risky options. However, when seeking to cut their losses, people are much more likely to take risks.*

Obviously, sound decision making should yield consistent decisions that are not altered dramatically by superficial changes in how options are presented, so framing effects once again highlight the foibles of human decision making. Fortunately, however, there are some limiting conditions that reduce the likelihood of framing effects (Mellers, Schwartz, & Cooke, 1998).

Nonetheless, research shows that framing is a factor in many of the choices people face in everyday life, including medical decisions (Gurm & Litaker, 2000) and consumer choices (Park, Jun, & Macinnis, 2000). For instance, some oil companies charge gas station patrons an extra nickel or so per gallon when they pay with a credit card. This fee clearly is a credit surcharge that results in a small financial loss. However, the oil companies never explicitly label it as a surcharge. Instead, they assert that they offer a discount for cash. Thus, they frame the decision as a choice between the normal price or an opportunity for a gain. They understand that it's easier for customers to foresake a gain than it is to absorb a loss.

Shaping Thought with Language: "Only a Naive Moron Would Believe That"

As explained in the chapter, the strong version of the *linguistic relativity hypothesis*— the idea that people's language determines how they think about things—has *not* been supported by research (Hunt & Agnoli, 1991). But research does show that carefully chosen words can exert subtle influence on people's feelings about various issues (Calvert, 1997; Johnson & Dowling-Guyer, 1996; Weatherall, 1992). In everyday life, many people clearly recognize that language can tilt thought along certain lines. This possibility is the basis for some of the concerns that have been expressed about sexist language. Women who object to being called "girls," "chicks," and "babes" believe that these terms influence the way people think about and interact with women. In a similar vein, used car dealers that sell "preowned cars" and airlines that outline precautions for "water landings" are manipulating language to influence thought. Indeed, bureaucrats, politicians, advertisers, and big business have refined the art of shaping thought by tinkering with language, and to a lesser degree the same techniques are used by many people in everyday interactions. Let's look at two of these techniques: semantic slanting and name calling.

Semantic Slanting

Semantic slanting refers to deliberately choosing words to create specific emotional responses. For example, consider the crafty word choices made in the incendiary debate about abortion (Halpern, 1996). The anti-abortion movement recognized that it is better to be *for* something than to be *against* something and then decided to characterize its stance as "pro-life" rather than "anti-choice." Likewise, the faction that favored abortion did not like the connotation of an "anti-life" or "pro-abortion"

campaign, so they characterized their position as "pro-choice." The position advocated is exactly the same either way, but the label clearly influences how people respond. Thinking along similar lines, some "pro-life" advocates have asserted that the best way to win the debate about abortion is to frequently use the words *kill* and *baby* in the same sentence (Kahane, 1992). Obviously, these are words that push people's buttons and trigger powerful emotional responses.

In his fascinating book *Doublespeak*, William Lutz (1989) describes an endless series of examples of how government, business, and advertisers manipulate language to bias people's thoughts and feelings. For example, in the language of the military, an invasion is a "preemptive counterattack," bombing the enemy is providing "air support," a retreat is a "backloading of augmentation personnel," civilians accidentally killed or wounded by military strikes

are "collateral damage," and troops killed by their own troops are "friendly casualties." In the world of business, layoffs and firings become "headcount reductions," "workforce adjustments," or "career alternative enhancement programs," whereas bad debts become "nonperforming assets." And in the language of bureaucrats, hospital deaths become "negative patient care outcomes" and tax increases become "revenue enhancement initiatives," leading Lutz to quip that "Nothing in life is certain except negative patient care outcome and revenue enhancement." You can't really appreciate how absurd this process can become until you go shopping for "genuine imitation leather" or "real counterfeit diamonds."

Of course, you don't have to be a bureaucrat or military spokesperson to use semantic slanting. For example, if a friend of yours is annoyed at her 60-year-old professor for giving a tough exam and describes

Semantic slanting, which consists of carefully choosing words to create specific emotional reactions, has been used extensively by both sides in the debate about abortion.

Briefings on the status of miliary actions are renowned for their creative but unintelligible manipulation of language, which is often necessary to obscure the unpleasant realities of war.

him as an "old geezer," she would be using semantic slanting. She would have communicated that the professor's age is a negative factor—one that is associated with a host of unflattering stereotypes about older people. And she would have implied that he gave an inappropriate exam because of his antiquated expectations or senile incompetence—all with a couple of well-chosen words. We are all the recipients of many such messages containing emotionally laden words and content. An important skill of critical thinking is to recognize when semantic slanting is being used to influence how you think so you can resist this subtle technique.

In becoming sensitive to semantic slanting, notice how the people around you and those whom you see on television and read about in the newspapers refer to people from other racial and ethnic groups. You can probably determine a politician's attitudes toward immigration, for example, by considering the words he or she uses when speaking about people from other countries. Are the students on your campus who come from other countries referred to as "international students" or "foreign students"? The term "international" seems to convey a more positive image, with associations of being cosmopolitan and worldly. On the other hand, the term "foreign" suggests someone who is strange. Clearly, it pays to be careful when selecting the words you use in your own communication.

Name Calling

Another way that word choice influences thinking is in the way people tend to label and categorize others through the strategy of *name calling.* People often attempt to neutralize or combat views they don't like by attributing such views to "radical feminists," "knee-jerk liberals," "right-wingers," "religious zealots," or "extremists." In everyday interactions, someone who inspires our wrath may be labeled as a "bitch," a "moron," or a "cheapskate." In these examples, the name calling is not subtle and is easy to recognize. But name calling can also be used with more cunning and finesse. Sometimes, there is an *implied threat* that if you make an unpopular decision or arrive at a conclusion that is not favored, a negative label will be applied to you. For example, someone might say, "Only a naive moron would believe that" to influence your attitude on an issue. This strategy of *anticipatory name calling* makes it difficult for you to declare that you favor the negatively valued belief because it means that you make yourself look like a "naive moron." Anticipatory name calling can also invoke positive group memberships, such as asserting that "all good Americans will agree . . ." or "people in the know think that . . ." Anticipatory name calling is a shrewd tactic that can be effective in shaping people's thinking.

Regardless of your position on these issues, how would you respond to someone who says, "Only a knee-jerk liberal would support racial quotas or affirmative action programs that give unfair advantages to minorities." Or "Only a stupid bigot would oppose affirmative action programs that rectify the unfair discrimination that minorities face." Can you identify the anticipatory name calling and the attempts at semantic slanting in each of these examples? More important, can you resist attempts like these to influence how you think about a host of complicated social issues?

Table 8.5 Critical Thinking Skills Discussed in This Application

Skill	Description
Understanding the way language can influence thought	The critical thinker appreciates that when you want to influence how people think, you should choose your words carefully.
Recognizing semantic slanting	The critical thinker is vigilant about how people deliberately choose certain words to elicit specific emotional responses.
Recognizing name calling and anticipatory name calling	The critical thinker is on the lookout for name calling and the implied threats used in anticipatory name calling.

Key Ideas

The Cognitive Revolution in Psychology

● During the first half of the 20th century, the study of cognition was largely suppressed by the theoretical dominance of behaviorism. However, the 1950s brought a cognitive revolution in psychology, as Simon, Chomsky, Miller, and many others reported major advances in the study of mental processes.

Language: Turning Thoughts into Words

● Languages are symbolic, semantic, generative, and structured. Human languages are structured hierarchically. At the bottom of the hierarchy are the basic sound units, called phonemes. At the next level are morphemes, the smallest units of meaning.

● Children typically utter their first words around their first birthday. Vocabulary growth is slow at first, but a vocabulary spurt often begins at around 18–24 months. Children begin to combine words by the end of their second year. Their early sentences are telegraphic, in that they omit many nonessential words. Over the next several years, children gradually learn the complexities of syntax.

● Research does not support the assumption that bilingualism has a negative effect on language development or on cognitive development. The learning of a second language is facilitated by starting at a younger age and by acculturation.

● Sue Savage-Rumbaugh's work with Kanzi suggests that some animals are capable of some genuine language acquisition. Many theorists believe that humans' special talent for language is the product of natural selection.

● According to Skinner and other behaviorists, children acquire a language through imitation and reinforcement. Nativist theories assert that humans have an innate capacity to learn language rules. Today, theorists are moving toward interactionist perspectives, which emphasize the role of both biology and experience. The evidence supports only a weak version of the linguistic relativity hypothesis.

Problem Solving: In Search of Solutions

● Psychologists have differentiated among several types of problems, including problems of inducing structure, problems of transformation, and problems of arrangement. Common barriers to problem solving include functional fixedness, mental set, getting bogged down in irrelevant information, and placing unnecessary constraints on one's solutions.

● A variety of strategies, or heuristics, are used for solving problems, including trial and error, forming subgoals, working backward, searching for analogies, and changing the representation of a problem.

● Some cultures encourage a field-dependent cognitive style, whereas others foster more field independence. People who are field independent tend to analyze and restructure problems more than those who are field dependent. Research suggests that Eastern cultures exhibit a more holistic cognitive style, whereas Western cultures display a more analytic cognitive style.

Decision Making: Choices and Chances

● Simon's theory of bounded rationality suggests that human decision strategies are simplistic and often yield irrational results. An additive decision model is used when people make decisions by rating the attributes of each alternative and selecting the alternative that has the highest sum of ratings.

● When elimination by aspects is used, people gradually eliminate alternatives if their attributes fail to satisfy some minimum criterion. To some extent, people adapt their decision-making strategy to the situation, moving toward simpler strategies when choices become complex.

● Models of how people make risky decisions focus on the expected value or subjective utility of various outcomes and the objective or subjective probability that these outcomes will occur.

● People use the representativeness and availability heuristics in estimating probabilities. These heuristics can lead people to ignore base rates and to fall for the conjunction fallacy. In the alternative outcomes effect, two scenarios that represent the same probability situation lead to surprisingly discrepant estimates of the likelihood of an event.

● Evolutionary psychologists maintain that many errors and biases in human reasoning are greatly reduced when problems are presented in ways that resemble the type of input humans would have processed in ancestral times. Gigerenzer argues that people largely depend on fast and frugal decision heuristics that are adaptive in the real world.

Putting It in Perspective

● Four of our unifying themes surfaced in the chapter. Our discussion of language acquisition revealed once again that all aspects of behavior are shaped by both nature and nurture. The recent progress in the study of cognitive processes showed how science depends on empirical methods. Research on decision making illustrated the importance of subjective perceptions. We also saw that cognitive processes are moderated—to a limited degree—by cultural factors.

Personal Application ● Understanding Pitfalls in Reasoning About Decisions

● The heuristics that people use in decision making lead to various flaws in reasoning. For instance, the use of the representativeness heuristic contributes to the gambler's fallacy and faith in small numbers. The availability heuristic underlies the tendency to overestimate the improbable.

● People tend to cling to their beliefs in spite of contradictory evidence, in part because they exhibit confirmation bias. People generally fail to appreciate these shortcomings, which leads to the overconfidence effect. In evaluating choices, it is wise to understand that decisions can be influenced by the language in which they are framed.

Critical Thinking Application ● Shaping Thought with Language: "Only a Naive Moron Would Believe That"

● Language can exert subtle influence over how people feel about various issues. Semantic slanting refers to the deliberate choice of words to create specific emotional responses, as has been apparent in the debate about abortion. In anticipatory name calling, there is an implied threat that a negative label will apply to you if you express certain views.

Key Terms

Acculturation
Algorithm
Alternative outcomes effect
Availability heuristic
Belief perseverance
Bilingualism
Cognition
Confirmation bias
Conjunction fallacy
Decision making
Fast mapping
Field dependence-independence
Framing
Functional fixedness
Gambler's fallacy
Heuristic
Insight
Language
Language acquisition device (LAD)
Linguistic relativity
Mean length of utterance (MLU)
Mental set
Metalinguistic awareness

Morphemes
Overextension
Overregularization
Phonemes
Problem solving
Problem space
Representativeness heuristic
Risky decision making
Semantics
Syntax
Telegraphic speech
Theory of bounded rationality
Trial and error
Underextensions

Key People

Noam Chomsky
Leda Cosmides & John Tooby
Gerd Gigerenzer
Daniel Kahneman
Steven Pinker
Sue Savage-Rumbaugh
Herbert Simon
B. F. Skinner
Amos Tversky

PRACTICE TEST

1. The 2-year-old child who refers to every four-legged animal as "dog-gie" is making which of the following errors?
   A. underextension
   B. overextension
   C. overregularization
   D. underregularization

2. Research suggests that bilingualism has a negative effect on:
   A. language development.
   B. cognitive development.
   C. metalinguistic awareness.
   D. none of the above.

3. Based on the work with Kanzi, which statement best summarizes the current status of the research on whether chimps can learn language?
   A. Chimps can acquire the use of symbols but cannot combine them into sentences or learn rules of language.
   B. Chimps are as well suited for learning and using language as humans.
   C. Chimps are incapable even of learning the symbols of a language.
   D. Chimps can learn some genuine language skills, including the use of rules, but the linguistic capacities of humans are far superior.

4. Chomsky proposed that children learn a language:
   A. because they possess an innate language acquisition device.
   B. through imitation, reinforcement, and shaping.
   C. as the quality of their thought improves with age.
   D. because they need to in order to get their increasingly complex needs met.

5. The linguistic relativity hypothesis is the notion that:
   A. one's language determines the nature of one's thought.
   B. one's thought determines the nature of one's language.
   C. language and thought are separate and independent processes.
   D. language and thought interact, with each influencing the other.

6. Arrangement problems are often solved:
   A. suddenly in a burst of insight.
   B. gradually in small, incremental steps.
   C. through fast mapping.
   D. by maximizing mental set.

7. Problems that require a common object to be used in an unusual way may be difficult to solve because of:
   A. mental set.
   B. irrelevant information.
   C. unnecessary constraints.
   D. functional fixedness.

8. A heuristic is:
   A. a flash of insight.
   B. a guiding principle or "rule of thumb" used in problem solving.
   C. a methodical procedure for trying all possible solutions to a problem.
   D. a way of making a compensatory decision.

9. In solving problems, people who are field dependent:
   A. rely on external frames of reference.
   B. tend to accept the physical environment as a given.
   C. tend to focus on specific features of a problem.
   D. all of the above.
   E. a and b.

10. According to Nisbett, Eastern cultures tend to favor a(n) _____ cognitive style, whereas Western cultures tend to display a(n) _____ cognitive style.
    A. analytic; holistic
    B. holistic; analytic
    C. holistic; field dependent
    D. field independent; field dependent

11. When Bastardi and Shafir (1998) asked subjects to make a decision about buying a CD player for a bargain price, they found:
    A. that participants' decision making was not affected by uncertainty about whether they would have to pay for a $90 repair to their amplifier.
    B. that participants showed a curious tendency to seek "useless" information that was unlikely to affect their decisions.
    C. that participants' decisions were influenced by seemingly "useless" information.
    D. a and b
    E. b and c

12. When you estimate the probability of an event by judging the ease with which relevant instances come to mind, you are relying on:
    A. an additive decision-making model.
    B. the representativeness heuristic.
    C. the availability heuristic.
    D. a noncompensatory model.

13. The belief that the probability of heads is higher after a long string of tails:
    A. is rational and accurate.
    B. is an example of the "gambler's fallacy."
    C. reflects the influence of the representativeness heuristic.
    D. b and c.

14. The more confident you are about your predictions of upcoming events in your life:
    A. the less likely it is that your predictions are accurate.
    B. the less likely it is that your predictions are overconfident.
    C. the more likely it is that your predictions are overconfident.
    D. a and b.

15. If someone says, "Only a congenital pinhead would make that choice," this use of language would represent:
    A. confirmation bias.
    B. syntactic slanting.
    C. anticipatory name calling.
    D. telegraphic speech.

Answers

1	B	p. 307	6	A	p. 315	11	E	p. 324
2	D	pp. 308–309	7	D	p. 316	12	C	p. 325
3	D	pp. 310–311	8	B	p. 318	13	D	p. 332
4	A	p. 312	9	E	p. 321	14	C	pp. 334–335
5	A	p. 313	10	B	p. 322	15	C	p. 337

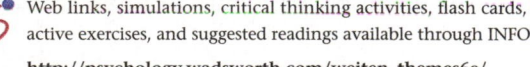

www ON THE WEB

For additional resources on the topics covered in this chapter, visit the *Psychology: Themes and Variations* Web site, where you will find practice quizzes, tutorials, Web links, simulations, critical thinking activities, flash cards, interactive exercises, and suggested readings available through INFOTRAC.

http://psychology.wadsworth.com/weiten_themes6e/

CHAPTER 9

© Adalberto Rios Szalay/Sexto Sol/PhotoDisc-Getty Images

Intelligence and Psychological Testing

Have you ever thought about the role that psychological testing has played in your life? In all likelihood, your years in grade school and high school were punctuated with a variety of intelligence tests, achievement tests, creativity tests, aptitude tests, and occupational interest tests. In the lower grades, you were probably given standardized achievement tests once or twice a year. For instance, you may have taken the Iowa Tests of Basic Skills, which measured your progress in reading, language, vocabulary, mathematics, and study skills. Perhaps you still have vivid memories of the serious atmosphere in the classroom, the very formal instructions ("Do not break the seal on this test until your examiner tells you to do so"), and the heavy pressure to work fast (I can still see Sister Dominic marching back and forth with her intense gaze riveted on her stopwatch).

Where you're sitting at this very moment may have been influenced by your performance on standardized tests. That is, the college you chose to attend may have hinged on your SAT or ACT scores. Moreover, your interactions with standardized tests may be far from finished. Even at this point in your life, you may be selecting your courses to gear up for the Graduate Record Exam (GRE), the Law School Admission Test (LSAT), the Medical College Admission Test (MCAT), or certification tests in fields such as accounting or nursing. After graduation, when you go job hunting, you may find that prospective employers expect you to take still more batteries of psychological tests as they attempt to assess your personality, your motivation, and your talents.

The vast enterprise of modern testing evolved from psychologists' pioneering efforts to measure *general intelligence*. The first useful intelligence tests, which were created soon after the turn of the twentieth century, left a great many "descendants." Today, there are over 2600 published psychological tests that measure a diverse array of mental abilities and other behavioral traits. Indeed, psychological testing has become a big business that annually generates millions of dollars of revenues.

Clearly, American society has embraced psychological testing (Hanson, 1993). Each year in the United States alone, people take *hundreds of millions* of intelligence and achievement tests. Scholarships, degrees, jobs, and self-concepts are on the line as Americans attempt to hurdle a seemingly endless succession of tests. Because your life is so strongly affected by how you perform on psychological tests, it pays to be aware of their strengths and limitations. In this chapter we'll explore many questions about testing, including the following:

- How did psychological testing become so prevalent in modern society?
- How do psychologists judge the validity of their tests?
- What exactly do intelligence tests measure?

Most children become familiar with standardized psychological tests—intelligence, achievement, and aptitude tests—in school settings.

- Is intelligence inherited? If so, to what extent?
- How do psychological tests measure creativity?

We'll begin by introducing some basic concepts in psychological testing. Then we'll explore the history of intelligence tests because they provided the model for subsequent psychological tests. Next we'll address practical questions about how intelligence tests work. After examining the nature versus nurture debate as it relates to intelligence, we'll explore some new directions in the study of intelligence. In the Personal Application, we'll discuss efforts to measure and understand another type of mental ability: creativity. In the Critical Thinking Application, we will critique some of the reasoning used in the vigorous debate about the roots of intelligence.

Key Concepts in Psychological Testing

PREVIEW QUESTIONS

- Why is it wise to be cautious when interpreting test results?
- What are the two main categories of psychological tests?
- What makes a test standardized?
- What are test norms and percentile scores?
- What is reliability, and how can it be measured?
- What are the three types of test validity?

A *psychological test* is a standardized measure of a sample of a person's behavior. Psychological tests are measurement instruments. They're used to measure the *individual differences* that exist among people in abilities, aptitudes, interests, and aspects of personality.

Your responses to a psychological test represent a *sample* of your behavior. The word *sample* should alert you to one of the key limitations of psychological tests: A particular behavior sample may not be representative of your characteristic behavior. Everyone has bad days. A stomachache, a fight with a friend, a problem with your car—all might affect your responses to a particular test on a particular day.

This sampling problem is not unique to psychological testing. It's an unavoidable problem for any measurement technique that relies on sampling. For example, a physician taking your blood pressure might get an unrepresentative reading. Likewise, a football scout clocking a prospect's 40-yard sprint time might get a misleading figure. Because of the limitations of the sampling process, test scores should always be interpreted *cautiously*.

Principal Types of Tests

Psychological tests are used extensively in research, but most of them were developed to serve a practical purpose outside of the laboratory. Most tests can be placed in one of two broad categories: mental ability tests and personality tests.

Mental Ability Tests

Psychological testing originated with efforts to measure general mental ability. Today, tests of mental abilities remain the most common kind of psychological test. This broad class of tests includes three principal subcategories: intelligence tests, aptitude tests, and achievement tests.

Intelligence tests measure general mental ability. They're intended to assess intellectual potential rather than previous learning or accumulated knowledge. *Aptitude tests* are also designed to measure potential more than knowledge, but they break mental ability into separate components. Thus, *aptitude tests assess specific types of mental abilities*. For example, the Differential Aptitude Tests assess verbal reasoning, numerical ability, abstract reasoning, perceptual speed and accuracy, mechanical reasoning, space relations, spelling, and language usage (see Figure 9.1). Like aptitude tests, *achievement tests* have a specific focus, but they're supposed to measure previous learning instead of potential. Thus, *achievement tests gauge a person's mastery and knowledge of various subjects* (such as reading, English, or history).

Personality Tests

If you had to describe yourself in a few words, what words would you use? Are you introverted? Independent? Ambitious? Enterprising? Conventional? Assertive? Domineering? Words such as these refer to personality traits. These *traits* can be assessed systematically with personality tests, of which there are more than 500. *Personality tests measure various aspects of personality, including motives, interests, values, and attitudes*. Many psychologists prefer to call these tests personality *scales* because, unlike tests of mental abilities, the questions do not have right and wrong answers. We'll look at the various types of personality scales in our upcoming chapter on personality (Chapter 12).

Standardization and Norms

Both personality scales and tests of mental abilities are *standardized* measures of behavior. *Standardization refers to the uniform procedures used in the administration and scoring of a test*. All subjects get the same instructions, the same questions, and the same time limits so that their scores can be compared meaningfully. This means, for instance, that a

Web Link 9.1

ERIC/AE Test Locator
Educational Testing Service (ETS) has made available online the ETS Test Collection database listing more than 10,000 tests and research instruments. Users can search the database to discover basic information about each test and its availability.

Figure 9.1

Examples of aptitude tests.

Aptitude tests measure specific mental abilities instead of general mental ability. The questions shown here illustrate the specific types of abilities assessed by the Differential Aptitude Tests.

SOURCE: Sample items from the *Differential Aptitude Tests*, 5th edition. Copyright © 1990 by The Psychological Corporation, a Harcourt Assessment Company. Reproduced by permission. All rights reserved.

Verbal reasoning

Choose the correct pair of words to fill the blanks. The first word of the pair goes in the blank space at the beginning of the sentence; the second word of the pair goes in the blank at the end of the sentence.

_____ is to fin as bird is to _____

A water–feather   C fish–wing
B shark–nest   D flipper–fly
            E fish–sky

The correct answer is **C.**

Numerical reasoning

Choose the correct answer for the problem.

        18
        10
       +17   A 13
       ─────   B 11
                    C 7
                    D 6
                    E none of these

The correct answer is **E.**

Abstract reasoning

The four "problem figures" make a series. Find the one among the "answer figures" that would be next in the series.

Problem figures   Answer figures

                        A   B   C   D   E

The correct answer is **C.**

Perceptual speed and accuracy

In each test item, one of the five combinations is underlined. Find the same combination on the answer sheet and mark it.

Test items

1.	XY	Xy	XX	<u>YX</u>	Yy
2.	6g	<u>6G</u>	G6	Gg	g6
3.	<u>nm</u>	mn	mm	nn	nv

Sample of answer sheet

	Xy	Yy	YX	XX	XY
1	○	○	●	○	○
	g6	Gg	6g	G6	6G
2	○	○	○	○	●
	nn	mn	nv	nm	mm
3	○	○	○	●	○

Mechanical reasoning

A   B   C

Which load will be easier to pull through soft sand?

The correct answer is **C.**

Space relations

Which one of the following figures could be made by folding the pattern at the left? The pattern always shows the outside of the figure.

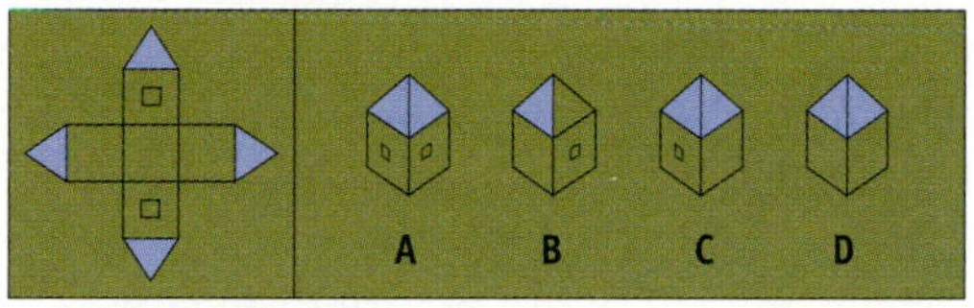

                A   B   C   D

The correct answer is **C.**

Spelling

Decide which word is not spelled correctly.

A numeral
B interest
C desloyal
D salary

The correct answer is **C.**

Language usage

Decide which of the lettered parts of the sentence contains an error and mark the corresponding letter on the answer sheet. If there is no error, mark *No Error*.

Jane and Tom / is going / to the office / this morning.
      A   B   C   D

The correct answer is **B.**

---

person taking the Differential Aptitude Tests (DAT) in 1984 in San Diego, another taking the DAT in 1994 in Baltimore, and another taking it in 2004 in Peoria all confront exactly the same test-taking task.

The standardization of a test's scoring system includes the development of test norms. *Test norms provide information about where a score on a psychological test ranks in relation to other scores on that test.* Why are test norms needed? Because in psychological testing, everything is relative. Psychological tests tell you how you score *relative to other people*. They tell you, for instance, that you are average in creativity or slightly above average in clerical ability. These interpretations are derived from the test norms that help you understand what your test score means.

Usually, test norms allow you to convert your "raw score" on a test into a *percentile*. A *percentile score* indicates the percentage of people who score at or below the score one has obtained. For example, imagine that you take a 40-item assertiveness scale and obtain a raw score of 26. In other words, you indicate a preference for the assertive option on 26 of the questions. Your score of 26 has little meaning until you consult the test norms and find out that it places you at the 82nd percentile. This normative information would indicate that you appear to be as assertive as or more assertive than 82% of the sample of people who provided the basis for the test norms.

The sample of people that the norms are based on is called a test's *standardization group*. Ideally, test norms are based on a large sample of people who

Web Link 9.2

ERIC Clearinghouse on Assessment and Evaluation
This site assembles the most comprehensive set of links regarding psychological testing and assessment on the web. A recent addition is the full-text library of more than 250 scholarly and professional books and articles regarding assessment.

were carefully selected to be representative of the broader population. For example, the norms for most intelligence tests are based on samples of 2000–6000 people whose demographic characteristics closely match the overall demographics of the United States (Woodcock, 1994). Although intelligence tests have been standardized pretty carefully, the representativeness of standardization groups for other types of tests varies considerably from one test to another.

Reliability

Any kind of measuring device, whether it's a tire gauge, a stopwatch, or a psychological test, should be reasonably consistent. That is, repeated measurements should yield reasonably similar results. Psychologists call this quality *reliability*. To better appreciate the importance of reliability, think about how you would react if a tire pressure gauge were to give you several very different readings for the same tire. You would probably conclude that the gauge is broken and toss it into the trash. Consistency in measurement is essential to accuracy in measurement. *Reliability* refers to the measurement consistency of a test (or of other kinds of measurement techniques). Like most other types of measuring devices, psychological tests are not perfectly reliable. A test's reliability can be estimated in several ways. One widely used approach is to check *test-retest reliability*, which is estimated by comparing subjects' scores on two administrations of a test. If we wanted to check the test-retest reliability of a newly developed test of assertiveness, we would ask a group of subjects to take the test on two occasions, probably a few weeks apart (see Figure 9.2). The underlying assumption is that assertiveness is a fairly stable aspect of personality that won't change in a matter of a few weeks. Thus,

changes in participants' scores across the two administrations of the test would presumably reflect inconsistency in measurement.

Reliability estimates require the computation of correlation coefficients, which we introduced in Chapter 2 (see Figure 9.3 for a brief recapitulation). A *correlation coefficient* is a numerical index of the degree of relationship between two variables. In estimating test-retest reliability, the two variables that must be correlated are the two sets of scores from the two administrations of the test. If people get fairly similar scores on the two administrations of our hypothetical assertiveness test, this consistency yields a substantial positive correlation. The magnitude of the correlation gives us a precise indication of the test's consistency. The closer the correlation comes to +1.00, the more reliable the test is.

There are no absolute guidelines about acceptable levels of reliability. What's acceptable depends to some extent on the nature and purpose of the test (Reynolds, 1994). The reliability estimates for most psychological tests are above .70. Many exceed .90. The higher the reliability coefficient, the more consistent the test is. As reliability goes down, concern about measurement error increases.

Validity

Even if a test is quite reliable, we still need to be concerned about its validity. *Validity* refers to the ability of a test to measure what it was designed to measure. If we develop a new test of assertiveness, we have to provide some evidence that it really measures assertiveness. Increasingly, the term *validity* is also used to refer to the accuracy or usefulness of the inferences or decisions based on a test (Moss, 1994). This broader conception of validity highlights the

Figure 9.2

Test-retest reliability. In each panel, subjects' scores on the first administration of an assertiveness test are represented on the left, and their scores on a second administration of the same test a few weeks later are shown on the right. If participants obtain similar scores on both administrations, as in the left panel, the test measures assertiveness consistently and has high test-retest reliability. If they get very different scores on the second administration, as in the right panel, the test has low reliability.

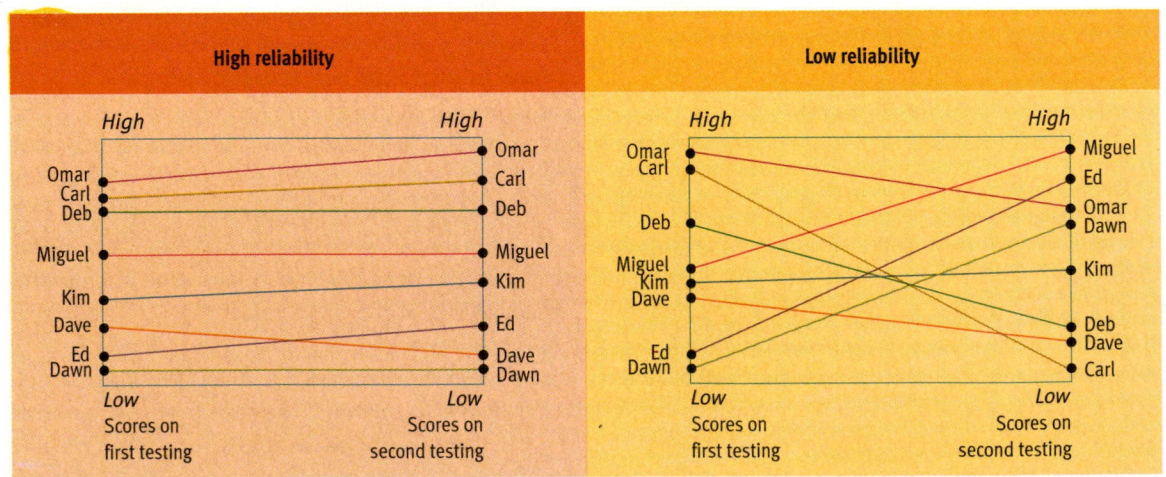

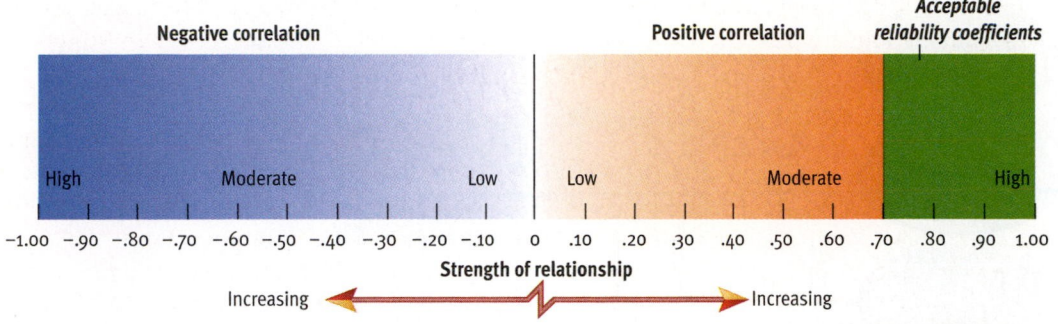

Negative correlation   Positive correlation   **Acceptable reliability coefficients**

High   Moderate   Low   Low   Moderate   High

−1.00 −.90 −.80 −.70 −.60 −.50 −.40 −.30 −.20 −.10   0   .10 .20 .30 .40 .50 .60 .70 .80 .90 1.00

Strength of relationship

Increasing ← → Increasing

Figure 9.3

Correlation and reliability.
As explained in Chapter 2, a positive correlation means that two variables co-vary in the *same* direction; a negative correlation means that two variables co-vary in the *opposite* direction. The closer the correlation coefficient gets to either −1.00 or +1.00, the stronger the relationship. At a minimum, reliability estimates for psychological tests must be moderately high positive correlations. Most reliability coefficients fall between .70 and .95.

fact that a specific test might be valid for one purpose, such as placing students in school, and invalid for another purpose, such as making employment decisions for a particular occupation. Validity can be estimated in several ways, depending on the nature and purpose of a test (Golden, Sawicki, & Franzen, 1990).

Content Validity

 7b

Achievement tests and educational tests such as classroom exams should have adequate content validity. *Content validity* refers to the degree to which the content of a test is representative of the domain it's supposed to cover. Imagine a poorly prepared physics exam that includes questions on material that was not covered in class or in assigned reading. The professor has compromised the content validity of the exam. Content validity is evaluated with logic more than with statistics.

Criterion-Related Validity

 7b

Psychological tests are often used to make predictions about specific aspects of individuals' behavior. They are used to predict performance in college, job capability, and suitability for training programs, as just a few examples. Criterion-related validity is a central concern in such cases. *Criterion-related validity* is estimated by correlating subjects' scores on a test with their scores on an independent criterion (another measure) of the trait assessed by the test. For example, let's say you developed a test to measure aptitude for becoming an airplane pilot. You could check its validity by correlating subjects' scores on your aptitude test with subsequent ratings of their performance in their pilot training (see Figure 9.4). The performance ratings would be the independent criterion of pilot aptitude. If your test has reasonable validity, there ought to be a reasonably strong positive correlation between the test and the criterion measure. Such a correlation would help validate your test's predictive ability.

Construct Validity

 SIM8, 7b

Many psychological tests attempt to measure abstract personal qualities, such as creativity, intelligence, extraversion, or independence. No obvious criterion measures exist for these abstract qualities, which are called *hypothetical constructs*. In measuring abstract qualities, psychologists are concerned about *construct validity*—the extent to which there is evidence that a test measures a particular hypothetical construct.

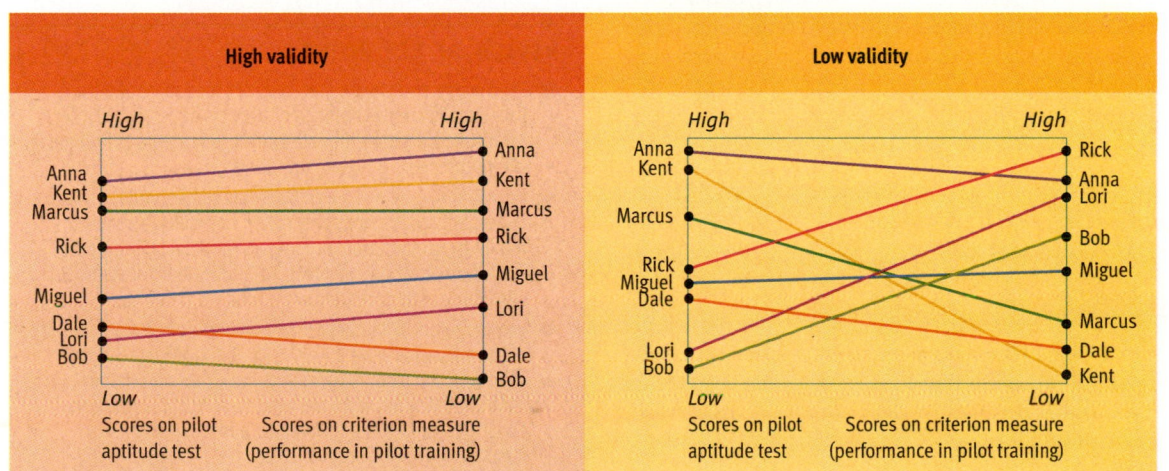

Figure 9.4

Criterion-related validity.
To evaluate the criterion-related validity of a pilot aptitude test, a psychologist would correlate subjects' test scores with a criterion measure of their aptitude, such as ratings of their performance in a pilot training program. The validity of the test is supported if the people who score high on the test also score high on the criterion measure (as shown in the left panel), yielding a substantial correlation between the two measures. If little or no relationship exists between the two sets of scores (as shown in the right panel), the data do not provide support for the validity of the test.

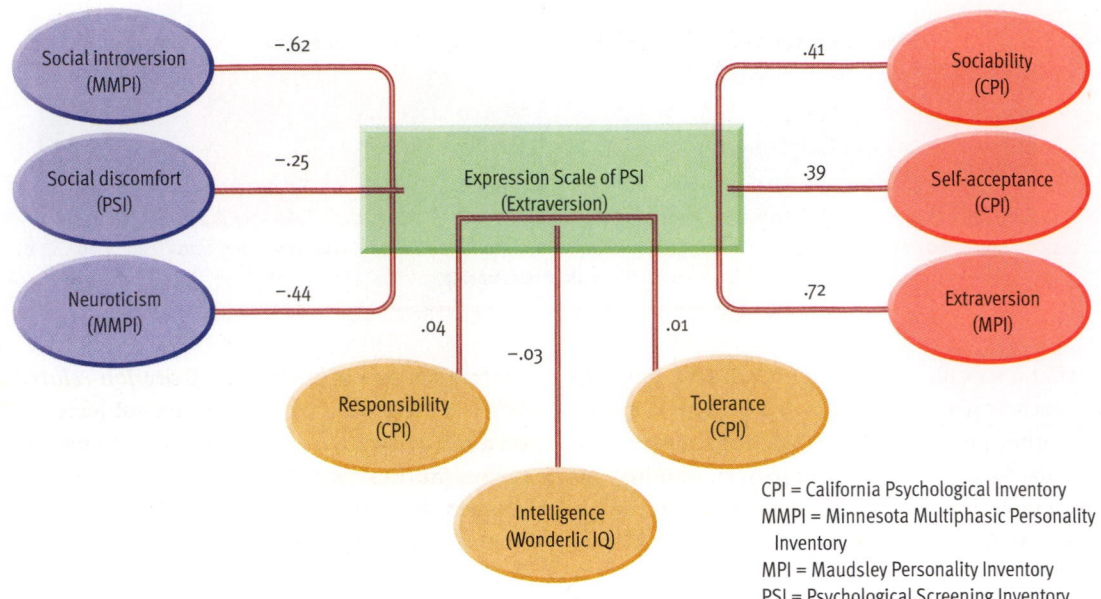

Figure 9.5

Construct validity. Some of the evidence on the construct validity of the Expression Scale from the Psychological Screening Inventory is summarized here. This scale is supposed to measure the personality trait of *extraversion*. As you can see on the left side of this network of correlations, the scale correlates negatively with measures of social introversion, social discomfort, and neuroticism, just as one would expect if the scale is really tapping extraversion. On the right, you can see that the scale is correlated positively with measures of sociability and self-acceptance and another index of extraversion, as one would anticipate. At the bottom, you can see that the scale does not correlate with several traits that should be unrelated to extraversion. Thus, the network of correlations depicted here supports the idea that the Expression Scale measures the construct of extraversion.

The process of demonstrating construct validity can be complicated. It usually requires a series of studies that examine the correlations between the test and various measures *related* to the trait in question. A thorough demonstration of construct validity requires looking at the relations between a test and many other measures. For example, some of the evidence on the construct validity of a measure of extraversion (the Expression scale from the Psychological Screening Inventory) is summarized in Figure 9.5. This network of correlation coefficients shows that the Expression scale correlates negatively, positively, or not at all with various measures, much as one would expect if the scale is really assessing extraversion. Ultimately, it's the overall pattern of correlations that provides convincing (or unconvincing) evidence of a test's construct validity.

The complexities involved in demonstrating construct validity will be apparent in our upcoming discussion of intelligence testing. The ongoing debate about the construct validity of intelligence tests is one of the oldest debates in psychology. We'll look first at the origins of intelligence tests; this historical review will help you appreciate the current controversies about intelligence testing.

CONCEPT CHECK 9.1

Recognizing Basic Concepts in Testing

Check your understanding of basic concepts in psychological testing by answering the questions below. Select your responses from the following concepts. The answers are in Appendix A.

Test norms   Criterion-related validity
Test-retest reliability   Construct validity
Split-half reliability   Content validity

1. At the request of the HiTechnoLand computer store chain, Professor Charlz develops a test to measure aptitude for selling computers. Two hundred applicants for sales jobs at HiTechnoLand stores are asked to take the test on two occasions, a few weeks apart. A correlation of +.82 is found between applicants' scores on the two administrations of the test. Thus, the test appears to possess reasonable _test-retest reliability_

2. All 200 of these applicants are hired and put to work selling computers. After six months Professor Charlz correlates the new workers' aptitude test scores with the dollar value of the computers that each sold during the first six months on the job. This correlation turns out to be –.21. This finding suggests that the test may lack _criterion related_

3. Back at the university, Professor Charlz is teaching a course in theories of personality. He decides to use the same midterm exam that he gave last year, even though the exam includes questions about theorists that he did not cover or assign reading on this year. There are reasons to doubt the _content validity_ of Professor Charlz's midterm exam.

The Evolution of Intelligence Testing

Psychological tests may play a prominent role in contemporary society, but this wasn't always so. The first psychological tests were invented only a little over a hundred years ago. Since then, the reliance on psychological tests has grown gradually. In this section, we discuss the pioneers who launched psychological testing with their efforts to measure general intelligence.

Galton's Studies of Hereditary Genius

It all began with the work of a British scholar, Sir Francis Galton, in the later part of the 19th century. Galton studied family trees and found that success and eminence appeared consistently in some families over generations. For the most part, these families were much like Galton's: well-bred, upper-class families with access to superior schooling and social connections that pave the way to success. Yet Galton discounted the advantages of such an upbringing. In his book *Hereditary Genius*, Galton (1869) concluded that success runs in families because great intelligence is passed from generation to generation through genetic inheritance.

To better demonstrate that intelligence is governed by heredity, Galton needed an objective measure of intelligence. His approach to this problem was guided by the theoretical views of his day. Thus, he assumed that the contents of the mind are built out of elementary *sensations*, and he hypothesized that exceptionally bright people should exhibit exceptional sensory acuity. Working from this premise, he tried to assess innate mental ability by measuring simple sensory processes. Among other things, he measured sensitivity to high-pitched sounds, color perception, and reaction time (the speed of one's response to a stimulus). His efforts met with little success. Research eventually showed that the sensory processes that he measured were largely unrelated to other criteria of mental ability that he was trying to predict, such as success in school or in professional life (Kaufman, 2000).

In pursuing this line of investigation, Galton coined the phrase *nature versus nurture* to refer to the heredity-environment issue (Hilgard, 1989). Along the way, he also invented the concepts of *correlation* and *percentile test scores*. Although Galton's mental tests were a failure, his work created an interest in the measurement of mental ability, setting the stage for a subsequent breakthrough by Alfred Binet, a prominent French psychologist.

Binet's Breakthrough 7c

In 1904 a commission on education in France asked Alfred Binet to devise a test to identify mentally subnormal children. The commission was motivated by admirable goals: It wanted to single out youngsters in need of special training. It also wanted to avoid complete reliance on teachers' evaluations, which might often be subjective and biased.

In response to this need, Binet and a colleague, Theodore Simon, published the first useful test of general mental ability in 1905. They had the insight to load it with items that required abstract reasoning skills, rather than the sensory skills Galton had measured (Brody, 2000). Their scale was a success because it was inexpensive, easy to administer, objective, and capable of predicting children's performance in school fairly well (Siegler, 1992). Thanks to these qualities, its use spread across Europe and America.

The Binet-Simon scale expressed a child's score in terms of "mental level" or "mental age." A child's **mental age indicated that he or she displayed the mental ability typical of a child of that chronological (actual) age.** Thus, a child with a mental age of 6 performed like the average 6-year-old on the test. Binet realized that his scale was a somewhat crude initial effort at measuring mental ability. He revised it in 1908 and again in 1911. Unfortunately, his revising came to an abrupt end with his death in 1911. However, other psychologists continued to build on Binet's work.

Terman and the Stanford-Binet 7c

In America, Lewis Terman and his colleagues at Stanford University soon went to work on a major expansion and revision of Binet's test. Their work led to the 1916 publication of the Stanford-Binet Intelligence Scale (Terman, 1916). Although this revision was quite loyal to Binet's original conceptions, it incorporated a new scoring scheme based on the "intelligence quotient" suggested by William Stern (1914). **An *intelligence quotient (IQ)* is a child's mental age divided by chronological age, multiplied by 100.** As you can see, IQ scores originally involved actual quotients:

$$IQ = \frac{\text{Mental age}}{\text{Chronological age}} \times 100$$

The ratio of mental age to chronological age made it possible to compare children of different ages. In

PREVIEW QUESTIONS
- When and how did intelligence testing begin?
- What were Binet's contributions to the progress of intelligence testing?
- What is an IQ score, and with what test did it originate?
- How did Wechsler improve intelligence testing?

Wellcome Institute for the History of Medicine, London

"There is no escape from the conclusion that nature prevails enormously over nurture when the differences in nurture do not exceed what is commonly to be found among persons of the same rank of society and in the same country."
SIR FRANCIS GALTON

CORBIS-Bettmann

"The intelligence of anyone is susceptible of development. With practice, enthusiasm, and especially with method one can succeed in increasing one's attention, memory, judgment, and in becoming literally more intelligent than one was before."
ALFRED BINET

Web Link 9.4

History of the Influences in the Development of Intelligence Theory & Testing
A graphic approach to the history of intelligence testing is taken at this site, which uses colored arrows to show academic lineage and connections among various theorists. Maintained by Jonathan Plucker of Indiana University, this site covers all the major intelligence theorists and there are excellent discussions of contemporary topics.

Table 9.1 Calculating the Intelligence Quotient

Measure	Child 1	Child 2	Child 3	Child 4
Mental age (MA)	6 years	6 years	9 years	12 years
Chronological age (CA)	6 years	9 years	12 years	9 years
$IQ = \dfrac{MA}{CA} \times 100$	$\dfrac{6}{6} \times 100 = 100$	$\dfrac{6}{9} \times 100 = 67$	$\dfrac{9}{12} \times 100 = 75$	$\dfrac{12}{9} \times 100 = 133$

It is the method of tests that has brought psychology down from the clouds and made it useful to men; that has transformed the 'science of trivialities' into the 'science of human engineering.'
LEWIS TERMAN

The subtests [of the WAIS] are different measures of intelligence, not measures of different kinds of intelligence.
DAVID WECHSLER

Binet's system, such comparisons were awkward. The IQ ratio placed all children (regardless of age) on the same scale, which was centered at 100 if their mental age corresponded to their chronological age (see Table 9.1 for examples of IQ calculations).

Terman's technical and theoretical contributions to psychological testing were modest, but he made an articulate case for the potential educational benefits of testing and became the key force behind American schools' widespread adoption of IQ tests (Chapman, 1988). As a result of his efforts, the Stanford-Binet quickly became the world's foremost intelligence test and the standard of comparison for virtually all intelligence tests that followed (White, 2000). Since its publication in 1916, the Stanford-Binet has been updated periodically—in 1937, 1960, 1973, and 1986. Although the most recent (1986) revision introduced some major changes in the organizational structure of the test (see pages 367–368), the modern Stanford-Binet remains loyal to the conception of intelligence originally formulated by Binet and Terman.

Wechsler's Innovations

 7c

As chief psychologist at New York's massive Bellevue Hospital, David Wechsler was charged with overseeing the psychological assessment of thousands of adult patients. He found the Stanford-Binet somewhat unsatisfactory for this purpose. Thus, Wechsler set out to improve on the measurement of intelligence *in adults.* In 1939 he published the first high-quality IQ test designed specifically for adults, which came to be known as the Wechsler Adult Intelligence Scale (WAIS) (Wechsler, 1955, 1981). Ironically, Wechsler (1949, 1967, 1991) eventually devised downward extensions of his scale for children.

The Wechsler scales were characterized by at least two major innovations (Prifitera, 1994). First, Wechsler made his scales less dependent on subjects' verbal ability than the Stanford-Binet. He included many items that required nonverbal reasoning. To highlight the distinction between verbal and nonverbal ability, he formalized the computation of separate scores for verbal IQ, performance (nonverbal) IQ, and full-scale (total) IQ.

Second, Wechsler discarded the intelligence quotient in favor of a new scoring scheme based on the *normal distribution.* This scoring system has since been adopted by most other IQ tests, including the Stanford-Binet. Although the term *intelligence quotient* lingers on in our vocabulary, scores on intelligence tests are no longer based on an actual quotient. We'll take a close look at the modern scoring system for IQ tests a little later.

Intelligence Testing Today

Today, psychologists and educators have many IQ tests available for their use. Basically, these tests fall into two categories: *individual tests* and *group tests.* Individual IQ tests are administered only by psychologists who have special training for this purpose. A psychologist works face to face with a single examinee at a time. The Stanford-Binet and the Wechsler scales are both individual IQ tests.

The problem with individual IQ tests is that they're expensive and time-consuming to administer. Therefore, researchers have developed a number

The Wechsler Intelligence Scale for Children includes subtests that measure verbal and performance abilities. This block design task is one of the performance subtests.

of IQ tests that can be administered to large groups of people at once (Kaufman, 2000). Because of their cost-effectiveness, group tests such as the Otis-Lennon School Ability Test and the Cognitive Abilities Test enjoy wide usage at all educational levels. Indeed, if you've taken an IQ test, chances are that it was a group test. As you'll see in the next section, many school districts routinely administer group IQ tests.

REVIEW OF KEY POINTS

- The first crude efforts to devise intelligence tests were made by Sir Francis Galton, who wanted to show that intelligence is inherited. Galton is also known for inventing correlation and percentile test scores.

- Modern intelligence testing began with the work of Alfred Binet, a French psychologist who published the first useful intelligence test in 1905. Binet's scale measured a child's mental age.

- Lewis Terman revised the original Binet scale to produce the Stanford-Binet in 1916. It introduced the intelligence quotient and became the standard of comparison for subsequent intelligence tests.

- David Wechsler devised an improved measure of intelligence for adults and a series of IQ tests that reduced the emphasis on verbal ability. He also introduced a new scoring system based on the normal distribution.

- Today, there are many individual and group intelligence tests. An individual IQ test is administered to a single examinee by a psychologist who has special training for this purpose. Group IQ tests can be administered to many people simultaneously.

Basic Questions About Intelligence Testing

Misconceptions abound when it comes to intelligence tests. In this section we'll use a question-and-answer format to explain the basic principles underlying intelligence testing.

What Kinds of Questions Are on Intelligence Tests?

The nature of the questions found on IQ tests varies somewhat from test to test. These variations depend on whether the test is intended for children or adults (or both) and whether the test is designed for individuals or groups. Overall, the questions are fairly diverse in format. The Wechsler scales, with their numerous subtests, provide a representative example of the kinds of items that appear on most IQ tests. As you can see in Figure 9.6 on the next page, the items in the Wechsler subtests require subjects to furnish information, recognize vocabulary, and demonstrate basic memory. Generally speaking, examinees are required to manipulate words, numbers, and images through abstract reasoning.

What Do Modern IQ Scores Mean?

As we've discussed, scores on intelligence tests once represented a ratio of mental age to chronological age. However, this system has given way to one based on the normal distribution and the standard deviation (see Chapter 2). The *normal distribution* is a symmetric, bell-shaped curve that represents the pattern in which many characteristics are dispersed in the population. When a trait is normally distributed, most cases fall near the center of the distribution (an average score) and the number of cases gradually declines as one moves away from the center in either direction (see Figure 9.7 on page 351).

The normal distribution was first discovered by 18th-century astronomers. They found that their measurement errors were distributed in a predictable way that resembled a bell-shaped curve. Since then, research has shown that many human traits, ranging from height to running speed to spatial ability, also follow a normal distribution. Psychologists eventually recognized that intelligence scores also fall into a normal distribution. This insight permitted David Wechsler to devise a more sophisticated scoring system for his tests that has been adopted by virtually all subsequent IQ tests. In this system, raw scores are translated into *deviation IQ scores* that locate subjects precisely within the normal distribution, using the standard deviation as the unit of measurement.

For most IQ tests, the mean of the distribution is set at 100 and the standard deviation (SD) is set at 15. These choices were made to provide continuity with the original IQ ratio (mental age to chronological age) that was centered at 100. In this system, which is depicted in Figure 9.7, a score of 115 means that a person scored exactly one SD (15 points) above the mean. A score of 85 means that a person scored one SD below the mean. A score of 100 means that a person showed average performance. You don't really need to know how to work with standard deviations to understand this system (but if

PREVIEW QUESTIONS

- What types of items are found on IQ tests?
- What role does the normal distribution play in the scoring system for modern IQ tests?
- Do IQ tests assess innate intellectual potential?
- Are IQ tests reliable?
- What type of evidence is used to support the validity of IQ tests?
- How well do IQ tests predict occupational attainment and job success?
- Do non-Western cultures make much use of IQ tests?

Wechsler Adult Intelligence Scale (WAIS)		
Test	**Description**	**Example**
Verbal scale		
Information	Taps general range of information	On what continent is France?
Comprehension	Tests understanding of social conventions and ability to evaluate past experience	Why are children required to go to school?
Arithmetic	Tests arithmetic reasoning through verbal problems	How many hours will it take to drive 150 miles at 50 miles per hour?
Similarities	Asks in what way certain objects or concepts are similar; measures abstract thinking	How are a calculator and a typewriter alike?
Digit span	Tests attention and rote memory by orally presenting series of digits to be repeated forward or backward	Repeat the following numbers backward: 2 4 3 5 1 8 6
Vocabulary	Tests ability to define increasingly difficult words	What does audacity mean?
Performance scale		
Digit symbol	Tests speed of learning through timed coding tasks in which numbers must be associated with marks of various shapes	Shown: 1 2 3 4 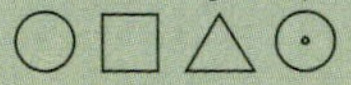 Fill in: 1 4 3 2
Picture completion	Tests visual alertness and visual memory through presentation of an incompletely drawn figure; the missing part must be discovered and named	Tell me what is missing: 
Block design	Tests ability to perceive and analyze patterns by presenting designs that must be copied with blocks	Assemble blocks to match this design: 
Picture arrangement	Tests understanding of social situations through a series of comic-strip-type pictures that must be arranged in the right sequence to tell a story	Put the pictures in the right order: 
Object assembly	Tests ability to deal with part/whole relationships by presenting puzzle pieces that must be assembled to form a complete object	Assemble the pieces into a complete object: 

Figure 9.6

Subtests on the Wechsler Adult Intelligence Scale (WAIS). The WAIS is divided into scales that yield separate verbal and performance (nonverbal) IQ scores. The verbal scale consists of six subtests and the performance scale is made up of five subtests. Examples of low-level (easy) test items that closely resemble those on the WAIS are shown on the right.

you're interested, consult Appendix B). *The key point is that modern IQ scores indicate exactly where you fall in the normal distribution of intelligence*. Thus, a score of 120 does not indicate that you answered 120 questions correctly. Nor does it mean that you have 120 "units" of intelligence. A deviation IQ score places you at a specific point in the normal distribution of intelligence.

Deviation IQ scores can be converted into percentile scores (see Figure 9.7). In fact, a major advantage of this scoring system is that a specific score on a specific test always translates into exactly the

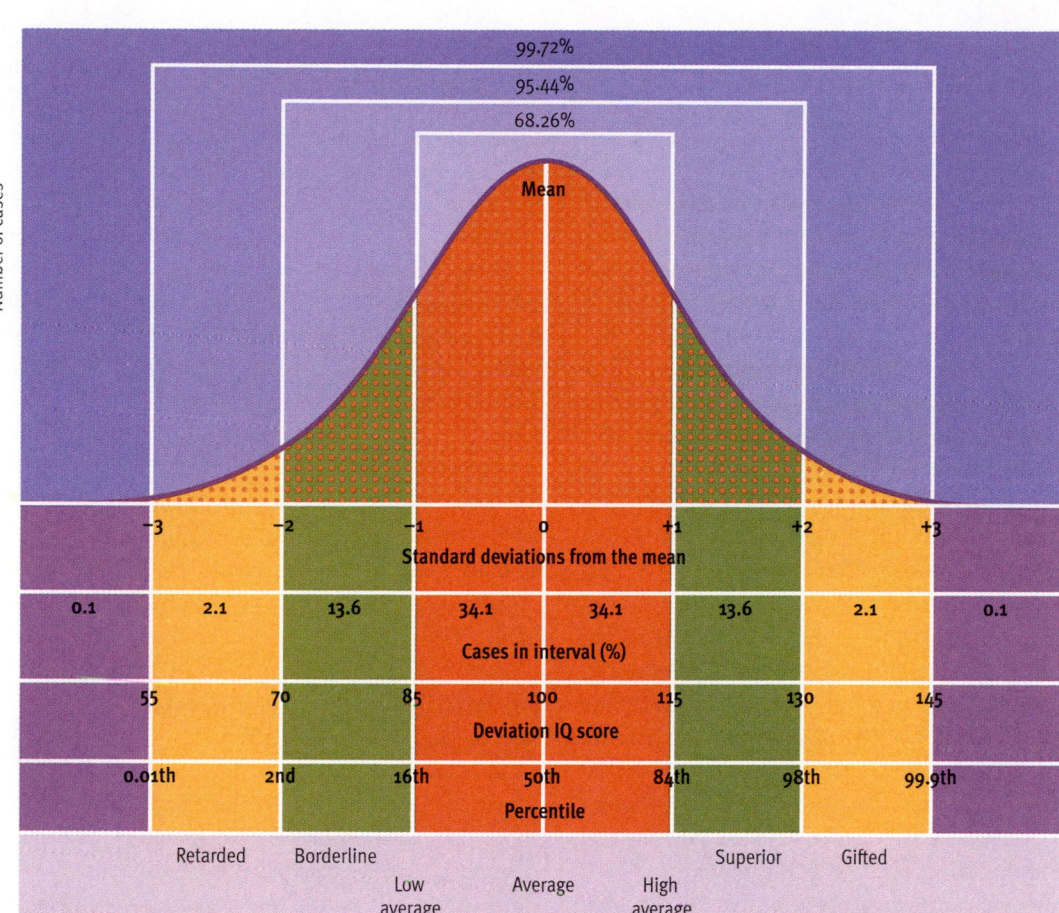

Figure 9.7

The normal distribution.
Many characteristics are distributed in a pattern represented by this bell-shaped curve. The horizontal axis shows how far above or below the mean a score is (measured in plus or minus standard deviations). The vertical axis is used to graph the number of cases obtaining each score. In a normal distribution, the cases are distributed in a fixed pattern. For instance, 68.26% of the cases fall between +1 and −1 standard deviation. Modern IQ scores indicate where a person's measured intelligence falls in the normal distribution. On most IQ tests, the mean is set at an IQ of 100 and the standard deviation at 15. Any deviation IQ score can be converted into a percentile score. The mental classifications at the bottom of the figure are descriptive labels that roughly correspond to ranges of IQ scores.

same percentile score, regardless of the person's age group. The old system of IQ ratio scores lacked this consistency.

Do Intelligence Tests Measure Potential or Knowledge?

Intelligence tests are intended to measure intellectual potential. They do so by presenting novel questions that require test takers to think on their feet, rather than questions that simply tap factual knowledge. However, because people's backgrounds differ, it's not easy to devise items that are completely unaffected by differences in knowledge. Test developers try to circumvent this problem by requiring subjects to *apply* relatively *common* knowledge. Nevertheless, IQ tests unavoidably contain items that are influenced by the test taker's previous learning. *Hence, IQ tests measure a blend of potential and knowledge.* Test developers try to tilt the balance toward the assessment of potential as much as possible, but factual knowledge clearly has an impact on intelligence test scores (Glaser, 1991; Zigler & Seitz, 1982).

Do Intelligence Tests Have Adequate Reliability?

Do IQ tests produce consistent results when people are retested? Yes. Most IQ tests report commendable reliability estimates. The correlations generally range into the .90s (Kaufman, 2000). In comparison to most other types of psychological tests, IQ tests are exceptionally reliable. However, like other tests, they *sample* behavior, and a specific testing may yield an unrepresentative score.

Variations in examinees' motivation to take an IQ test or in their anxiety about the test can sometimes produce misleading scores (Spielberger & Sydeman, 1994; Zimmerman & Woo-Sam, 1984). The most common problem is that low motivation or high anxiety may drag a person's score down on a particular occasion. For instance, a fourth-grader who is made to feel that the test is terribly important may get jittery and be unable to concentrate. The same child might score much higher on a subsequent testing by another examiner who creates a more comfortable atmosphere. Although the reliability of IQ tests is excellent, caution is always in order in interpreting test scores.

Do Intelligence Tests Have Adequate Validity?

Do intelligence tests measure what they're supposed to measure? Yes, but this answer has to be qualified very carefully. IQ tests are valid measures of the kind of intelligence that's necessary to do well in academic work. But if the purpose is to assess intelligence in a broader sense, the validity of IQ tests is questionable.

As you may recall, intelligence tests were originally designed with a relatively limited purpose in mind: to predict school performance. This has continued to be the principal purpose of IQ testing. Efforts to document the validity of IQ tests have usually concentrated on their relationship to grades in school. Typically, positive correlations in the .40s and .50s are found between IQ scores and school grades (Kline, 1991). Even higher correlations (between .60 and .80) are found between IQ scores and the number of years of school that people complete (Ceci, 1991). However, the meaning of this finding is complicated by the fact that the causal links between IQ and schooling are bidirectional. Although high IQ clearly fosters success in school, schooling also has a positive effect on IQ (Ceci & Williams, 1997).

In any event, these correlations are about as high as one could expect, given that many factors besides a person's intelligence are likely to affect grades and school progress. For example, school grades may be influenced by a student's motivation, diligence, or personality, not to mention teachers' subjective biases. Thus, IQ tests are reasonably valid indexes of school-related intellectual ability, or academic intelligence.

However, over the years people have mistakenly come to believe that IQ tests measure mental ability in a truly general sense. In reality, IQ tests have always focused on the abstract reasoning and verbal fluency that are essential to academic success. The tests do not tap social competence, practical problem solving, creativity, mechanical ingenuity, or artistic talent.

When Robert Sternberg and his colleagues (1981) asked people to list examples of intelligent behavior, they found that the examples fell into three categories: (1) *verbal intelligence,* (2) *practical intelligence,* and (3) *social intelligence* (see Figure 9.8). Thus, people generally recognize three basic components of intelligence. For the most part, IQ tests assess only the first of these three components. Although IQ tests are billed as measures of *general* mental ability, they actually focus somewhat narrowly on a specific type of intelligence: academic/verbal intelligence (Sternberg, 1998).

Do Intelligence Tests Predict Vocational Success?

Vocational success is a vague, value-laden concept that's difficult to quantify. Nonetheless, researchers have attacked this question by examining correlations between IQ scores and specific indicators of vocational success, such as the prestige of subjects' occupations or ratings of subjects' job performance. On the positive side of the ledger, it's clear that IQ is related to occupational attainment. *People who score high on IQ tests are more likely than those who score low to end up in high-status jobs* (Austin & Hanisch, 1990; Herrnstein & Murray, 1994; Ree & Earles, 1992). Be-

Figure 9.8

Laypersons' conceptions of intelligence. Robert Sternberg and his colleagues (1981) asked participants to list examples of behaviors characteristic of intelligence. The examples tended to sort into three groups that represent the three types of intelligence recognized by the average person: verbal intelligence, practical intelligence, and social intelligence. The three well-known individuals shown here are prototype examples of verbal intelligence (Ted Koppel), practical intelligence (Bill Gates), and social intelligence (Oprah Winfrey).

SOURCE: Adapted from Sternberg, R. J., Conway, B. E., Keton, J. L., & Bernstein, M. (1981). People's conceptions of intelligence. *Journal of Personality and Social Psychology, 41* (1), 37–55. Copyright © 1981 by the American Psychological Association. Adapted by permission of the author.

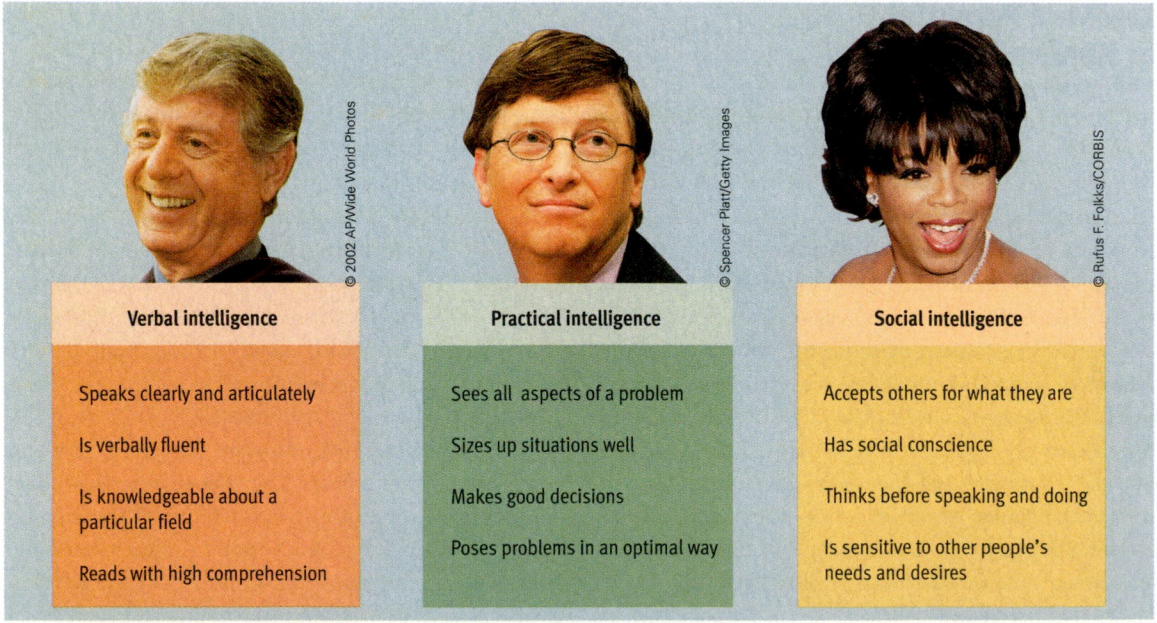

Verbal intelligence	Practical intelligence	Social intelligence
Speaks clearly and articulately	Sees all aspects of a problem	Accepts others for what they are
Is verbally fluent	Sizes up situations well	Has social conscience
Is knowledgeable about a particular field	Makes good decisions	Thinks before speaking and doing
Reads with high comprehension	Poses problems in an optimal way	Is sensitive to other people's needs and desires

cause IQ tests measure school ability fairly well and school performance is important in reaching certain occupations, this link between IQ scores and job status makes sense. Of course, the correlations between IQ and occupational attainment are moderate, and there are plenty of exceptions to the general trend. Some people plow through the educational system with bulldog determination and hard work, in spite of limited ability as measured by IQ tests. Such people may go on to prestigious jobs, while people who are brighter (according to their test results), but less motivated, settle for lower-status jobs.

On the negative side of the ledger, there is considerable debate about whether IQ scores are effective predictors of performance *within* a particular occupation (Hunter & Schmidt, 1996; McClelland, 1993; Sternberg & Wagner, 1993; Wagner, 1997). For example, in summarizing data for 446 occupations, Jensen (1993a) reported an unimpressive median correlation of .27 between general intelligence and job performance. On the other hand, in another summary of research involving 515 jobs, Schmidt and Hunter (1998) calculated a much more respectable mean correlation of .51 between measures of general mental ability and job performance. Doubts about the ability of IQ tests to predict job performance and concerns about possible cultural bias in the tests have led to controversy over the use of IQ tests in employee selection. In fact, the use of intelligence testing in making employment decisions has been challenged on legal grounds. Because of these challenges, the practice has declined (Gatewood & Perloff, 1990).

Essentially, court rulings and laws now require that tests used in employment selection measure specific abilities that are clearly related to job performance (Schmidt, Ones, & Hunter, 1992). Companies are increasingly turning to personality tests to select employees who are conscientious, calm under pressure, persistent, reliable, and so forth (Hogan, Hogan, & Roberts, 1996). Psychologists are also trying to develop tests of practical intelligence to aid employers in their hiring decisions (Sternberg et al., 1995). Thus, psychological tests that measure abilities relevant to specific jobs continue to be valuable tools in selecting employees (Landy, Shankster, & Kohler, 1994).

Are IQ Tests Widely Used in Other Cultures?

In other Western cultures with European roots, the answer to this questions is yes. In most non-Western cultures, the answer is only very little. IQ testing has a long history and continues to be a major enterprise in many Western countries, such as Britain, France, Norway, Canada, and Australia (Irvine & Berry, 1988). However, efforts to export IQ tests to non-Western societies have met with mixed results. The tests have been well received in some non-Western cultures, such as Japan, where the Binet-Simon scales were introduced as early as 1908 (Iwawaki & Vernon, 1988), but they have been met with indifference or resistance in other cultures, such as China and India (Chan & Vernon, 1988; Sinha, 1983).

The bottom line is that Western IQ tests do not translate well into the language and cognitive frameworks of many non-Western cultures (Berry, 1994). Using an intelligence test with a cultural group other than the one for which it was originally designed can be problematic. The entire process of test administration, with its emphasis on rapid information processing, decisive responding, and the notion that ability can be quantified, is foreign to some cultures. Moreover, different cultures have different conceptions of what intelligence is and value different mental skills (Das, 1994; Sternberg & Kaufman, 1998). In a landmark treatise on culture and cognition, Cole and his colleagues (1971) concluded that "people will be good at doing things that are important to them and that they have occasion to do often" (p. xi). *In other words, the ingredients of intelligence are culture-specific.* Even when a non-Western culture is largely in agreement with Western views about the ingredients of intelligent behavior, it can be difficult to construct equivalent tests that measure these ingredients with equal reliability and validity in both cultural contexts (Greenfield, 1997).

REVIEW OF KEY POINTS

- Intelligence tests contain a diverse mixture of questions. In the modern scoring system, deviation IQ scores indicate where people fall in the normal distribution of intelligence for their age group. On most tests, the mean is set at 100 and the standard deviation is set at 15.

- Although they are intended to measure potential for learning, IQ tests inevitably assess a blend of potential and knowledge. IQ tests are exceptionally reliable, with reliability coefficients typically ranging into the .90s.

- IQ tests are reasonably valid measures of academic intelligence in that they predict school grades and the number of years of school that people complete. However, they do not tap social or practical intelligence, and they do not measure intelligence in a truly general sense.

- IQ scores are correlated with occupational attainment. However, there is active debate about whether they predict performance within an occupation very well.

- Intelligence testing is largely a Western enterprise and IQ tests are not widely used in most non-Western cultures. One reason is that different cultures have different conceptions of intelligence.

Web Link 9.5

Educational Psychology Interactive: Intelligence
This site, maintained by Bill Huitt of Valdosta State University, leads to a helpful review of psychological approaches to intelligence and is an excellent resource for other topics in educational psychology.

Extremes of Intelligence

PREVIEW QUESTIONS

- What are the different levels of retardation and how common are they?
- How often is retardation due to a known biological cause?
- How are children typically selected for gifted programs?
- Are most gifted children lonely and maladjusted?
- Do most gifted children achieve eminence as adults?
- Which contributes more to extraordinary achievement: innate talent or hard work?

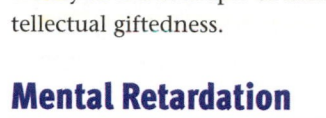

Web Link 9.6

The ARC
The ARC is a "national organization of and for people with mental retardation and related developmental disabilities and their families." Materials available here include overviews of the causes of mental retardation, education and employment of the mentally retarded, and the rights of mentally retarded individuals, among many other things.

What are the cutoff scores for extremes in intelligence that lead children to be designated as retarded or gifted? On the low end, IQ scores roughly two standard deviations or more below the mean are regarded as subnormal. On the high end, children who score more than two or three standard deviations above the mean are regarded as gifted. However, designations of mental retardation and giftedness should not be based exclusively on IQ test results. Let's look more closely at the concepts of mental retardation and intellectual giftedness.

Mental Retardation

According to the American Association on Mental Retardation (AAMR), *mental retardation* refers to subaverage general mental ability accompanied by deficiencies in adaptive skills, originating before age 18. Adaptive skills consist of everyday living skills in ten domains, including communication (example: writing a letter), self-care (dressing oneself), home living (preparing meals), social interaction (coping with others' demands), community use (shopping), and health/safety (recognizing illness).

There are two noteworthy aspects to this definition. First, the IQ criterion of subnormality is arbitrary. In the most recent release of its manual on mental retardation, the AAMR (1992) set a flexible cutoff line, which is an IQ score of 70 to 75 or below. This cutoff line could be drawn elsewhere. Indeed, the AAMR has changed the cutoff four times in the last four decades (Ramey & Ramey, 2000). Second, the requirement of deficits in everyday living skills is included because experts feel that retardation should not be determined solely on the basis of individuals'

test ability (Bunch, 1994). This requirement acknowledges that "school learning" is not the only important kind of learning. Unfortunately, there are no objective methods of measuring everyday living skills, so this assessment is necessarily subjective (Detterman, Gabriel, & Ruthsatz, 2000).

Levels of Retardation

Approximately 2%–3% of the school-age population is diagnosed as mentally retarded (Frazier, 1999). Mental retardation has traditionally been classified into four levels characterized as mild, moderate, severe, or profound. Table 9.2 lists the IQ range for each level and the typical behavioral and educational characteristics of individuals at each level.

As Figure 9.9 shows, the vast majority of retarded people fall in the *mildly retarded* category. Only about 15% of retarded people exhibit the obvious mental deficiencies that most people envision when they think of retardation. Many mildly retarded individuals are not all that easily distinguished from the rest of the population. The mental deficiency of children in the mildly retarded category often is not noticed until they have been in school a few years. Outside of school, many are considered normal. Furthermore, many of these children manage to shed the label of retardation when they reach adulthood and leave the educational system (Jacobson & Mulick, 1992; Landesman & Ramey, 1989). A significant portion of them become self-supporting and are integrated into the community.

Origins of Retardation

Many organic conditions can cause mental retardation. For example, *Down syndrome* is a condition

Table 9.2 Categories of Mental Retardation

Category of Retardation	IQ Range	Education Possible	Life Adaptation Possible
Mild	51–70	Sixth grade (maximum) by late teens; special education helpful	Can be self-supporting in nearly normal fashion if environment is stable and supportive; may need help with stress
Moderate	36–50	Second to fourth grade by late teens; special education necessary	Can be semi-independent in sheltered environment; needs help with even mild stress
Severe	20–35	Limited speech, toilet habits, and so forth with systematic training	Can help contribute to self-support under total supervision
Profound	below 20	Little or no speech; not toilet-trained; relatively unresponsive to training	Requires total care

NOTE: As explained in the text, diagnoses of retardation should not be made on the basis of IQ scores alone.

marked by distinctive physical characteristics (such as slanted eyes, stubby limbs, and thin hair) that is associated with mild to severe retardation. Most children exhibiting this syndrome carry an extra chromosome. *Phenylketonuria* is a metabolic disorder (due to an inherited enzyme deficiency) that can lead to retardation if it is not caught and treated in infancy. In *hydrocephaly,* an excessive accumulation of cerebrospinal fluid in the skull destroys brain tissue and causes retardation. Although over 350 such organic syndromes are known to cause retardation (King, Hodapp, & Dykens, 2000), diagnosticians are able to pin down an organic cause for retardation in fewer than 25% of cases (Popper & West, 1999). However, this percentage appears to be increasing as scientists unravel more of the genetic bases for various kinds of disorders (Simonoff, Bolton, & Rutter, 1998).

The cases of unknown origin tend to involve milder forms of retardation. A number of theories attempt to identify the factors that underlie retardation in the absence of a known organic pathology (Hodapp, 1994). Some theorists believe that subtle, difficult-to-detect physiological defects contribute to many of these cases. However, the predominant view is that the cases not involving obvious organic pathology are mainly caused by a variety of unfavorable environmental factors. Consistent with this hypothesis, the vast majority of mildly retarded children come from the lower socioeconomic classes (see Figure 9.10), where a host of factors—such as greater marital instability and parental neglect, inadequate nutrition and medical care, and lower-quality schooling—may contribute to children's poor intellectual development.

Giftedness

Like mental retardation, giftedness is widely misunderstood. This misunderstanding is a result, in part, of television and movies inaccurately portraying gifted children as social misfits and "nerds."

Identifying Gifted Children

Some curious discrepancies exist between ideals and practice in how gifted children are identified. The experts who shape government policy consistently assert that giftedness should not be equated with high intelligence and they recommend that schools not rely too heavily on IQ tests to select gifted children (Gallagher & Courtright, 1986; Robinson & Clinkenbeard, 1998). In practice, however, efforts to identify gifted children focus almost exclusively on IQ scores and rarely consider qualities such as creativity, leader-

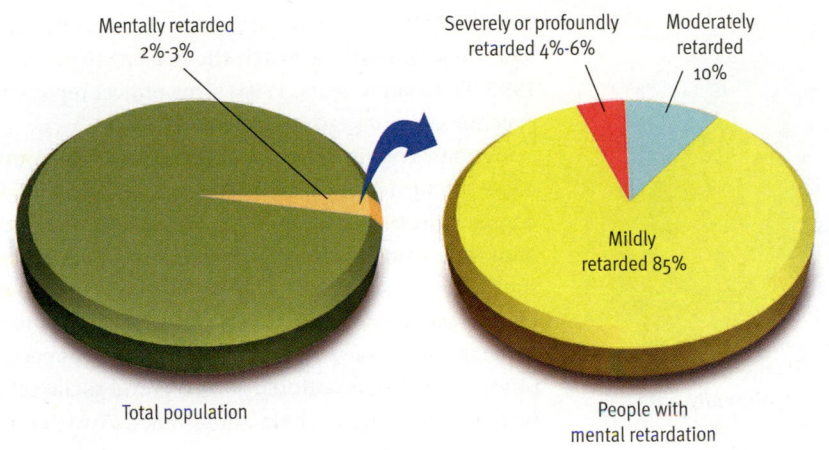

Total population

People with mental retardation

Figure 9.9

The prevalence and severity of mental retardation. The overall prevalence of mental retardation is 2%–3% of the general population. The vast majority (85%) of the retarded population falls in the mildly retarded category (IQ: 51–70). Only about 15% of the retarded population falls into the subcategories of moderate, severe, or profound retardation.

ship, or special talent (Callahan, 2000). Most school districts consider children who fall in the upper 2%–3% of the IQ distribution to be gifted. Thus, the minimum IQ score for gifted programs usually falls somewhere around 130.

Personal Qualities of the Gifted

Gifted children have long been stereotyped as weak, sickly, socially inept "bookworms" who are often emotionally troubled. The empirical evidence *largely* contradicts this view. The best evidence comes from a major longitudinal study of gifted children begun by Lewis Terman in 1921 (Terman, 1925; Terman &

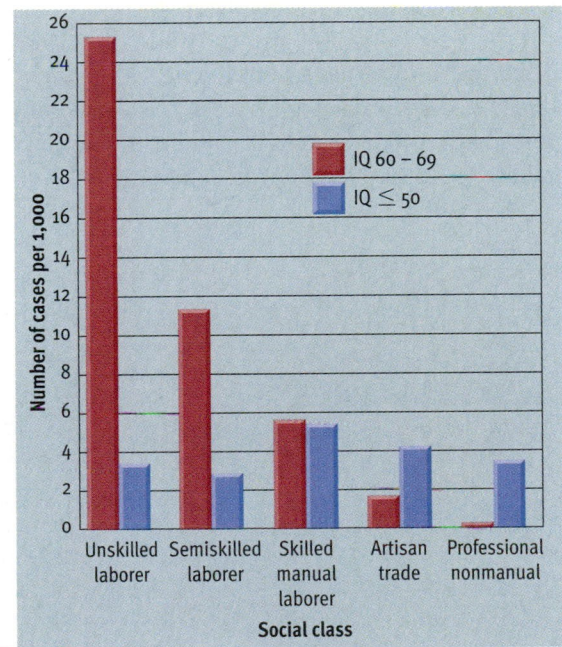

Figure 9.10

Social class and mental retardation. This graph charts the prevalence of mild retardation (IQ 60 to 69) and more severe forms of retardation (IQ below 50) in relation to social class. Severe forms of retardation are distributed pretty evenly across the social classes, a finding that is consistent with the notion that they are the product of biological aberrations that are equally likely to strike anyone. In contrast, the prevalence of mild retardation is greatly elevated in the lower social classes, a finding that meshes with the notion that mild retardation is largely a product of unfavorable environmental factors. (Data from Popper and Steingard, 1994)

"*Moderately gifted children are very different from profoundly gifted children. . . . Most gifted children do not grow into eminent adults.*"
ELLEN WINNER

Oden, 1959). Other investigators have continued to study this group through the present (Cronbach, 1992; Holahan & Sears, 1995). This project represents psychology's longest-running study.

Terman's original subject pool consisted of around 1500 youngsters who had an average IQ of 150. In comparison to normal subjects, Terman's gifted children were found to be above average in height, weight, strength, physical health, emotional adjustment, mental health, and social maturity. As a group, Terman's subjects continued to exhibit better-than-average physical health, emotional stability, and social satisfaction throughout their adult years. A variety of other studies have also found that samples of high-IQ children are either average or above average in social and emotional development (Garland & Zigler, 1999; Robinson & Clinkenbeard, 1998).

However, some other lines of research raise some questions about this conclusion. For instance, Ellen Winner (1997, 1998) asserts that moderately gifted children (those with an IQ of 130–150) are very different from profoundly gifted children (those with an IQ above 180). She asserts that profoundly gifted children are often introverted and socially isolated. She also estimates that the incidence of interpersonal and emotional problems in this group is about twice as high as in other children. Another line of research, which is discussed in more detail in the Personal Application, has focused on samples of people who have displayed truly exceptional creative achievement. Contrary to the findings of the Terman study, investigators have found elevated rates of mental illness in these samples (Ludwig, 1995). Thus, the psychosocial adjustment of gifted individuals may depend in part on their level of giftedness.

Giftedness and Achievement in Life

Terman's gifted children grew up to be very successful by conventional standards. By midlife they had produced 92 books, 235 patents, and nearly 2200 sci-

Young Nirav Gathani made exam history in England when he became the youngest student to pass the General Certificate of Secondary Education at age 7. As amazing as this feat was, it is hard to say whether Nirav will go on to achieve eminence, which typically requires a combination of exceptional intelligence, motivation, and creativity.

entific articles. Although Terman's gifted children accomplished a great deal, no one in the group achieved recognition for genius-level contributions. In retrospect, this finding may not be surprising. The concept of giftedness is applied to two very different groups. One consists of high-IQ children who are the cream of the crop in school. The other consists of eminent adults who make enduring contributions in their fields. According to Siegler and Kotovsky (1986), a sizable gap exists between these two groups. The accomplishments of the latter group involve a much higher level of giftedness. Joseph Renzulli (1986, 1999, 2002) theorizes that this rarer form of giftedness depends on the intersection of three factors: high intelligence, high creativity, and high motivation (see Figure 9.11). He emphasizes that high intelligence alone does not usually foster genuine greatness. Thus, the vast majority of children selected for gifted school programs do not achieve eminence as adults or make genius-like contributions to society (Callahan, 2000; Richert, 1997).

Another hot issue in the study of giftedness concerns the degree to which extraordinary achievement depends on innate talent as opposed to intensive training and hard work. In recent years, the emphasis

Figure 9.11

A three-ring conception of eminent giftedness. According to Renzulli (1986), high intelligence is only one of three requirements for achieving eminence. He proposes that a combination of exceptional ability, creativity, and motivation leads some people to make enduring contributions in their fields.

SOURCE: Adapted from Renzulli, J. S. (1986). The three-ring conception of giftedness: A developmental model for creative productivity. In R. J. Sternberg & J. E. Davidson (Eds.), *Conceptions of Giftedness* (pp. 53–92). New York: Cambridge University Press. Copyright © 1986 Cambridge University Press. Adapted by permission.

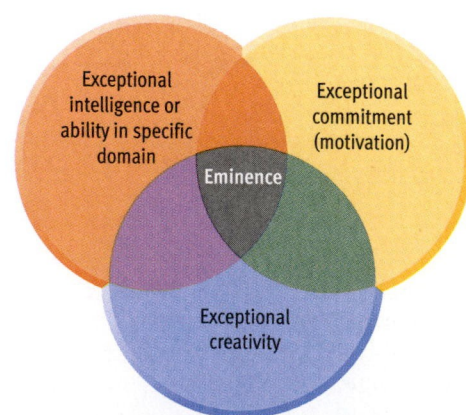

has been on what Simonton (2001) calls the "drudge theory" of exceptional achievement. According to this view, eminence primarily or entirely depends on dogged determination; endless, tedious practice; and outstanding mentoring and training (Bloom, 1985; Ericsson & Lehman, 1996; Howe, 1999). This conclusion is based on studies of eminent scientists, artists, writers, musicians, and athletes, which show that they push themselves much harder and engage in far more deliberate practice than their less successful counterparts. The essence of the drudge theory is captured by the reaction of one violin virtuoso after a critic hailed him as a genius: "A genius! For 37 years I've practiced fourteen hours a day, and now they call me a genius!" (quoted in Simonton, 1999). Although the evidence linking strenuous training and prodigious effort to world-class achievement is convincing, Winner (2000) points out that obsessive hard work and inborn ability may be confounded in retrospective analyses of eminent individuals. The youngsters who work the hardest may be those with the greatest innate talent, who are likely to find their efforts more rewarding than others. In other words, innate ability may be the key factor fostering the single-minded commitment that seems to be crucial to greatness. Simonton (1999) has devised an elaborate theory of talent development that allocates a significant role to both innate ability and a host of supportive environmental factors. In sum, recent research

has clearly demonstrated that quality training, monumental effort, and perseverance are crucial factors in greatness, but many experts on giftedness maintain that extraordinary achievement also requires rare, innate talent.

REVIEW OF KEY POINTS

- IQ scores below 70–75 are usually diagnostic of mental retardation, but these diagnoses should not be based solely on test results, as adaptive behavior should also be evaluated carefully. Four levels of retardation have been distinguished. The vast majority of retarded people are mildly retarded.

- Although over 350 biological conditions can cause retardation, biological causes can be pinpointed in only a minority of cases. Research suggests that cases of unknown origin are mostly caused by unfavorable environmental factors, such as poverty, neglect, and poor nutrition.

- Children who obtain IQ scores above 130 may be viewed as gifted, but cutoffs for accelerated programs vary, and schools rely too much on IQ scores. Research by Terman showed that gifted children tend to be socially mature and well adjusted. However, Winner has expressed some concerns about the adjustment of profoundly gifted individuals.

- Gifted youngsters typically go on to be very successful in life. However, most do not make genius-level contributions because these depend on a combination of high intelligence, creativity, and motivation. Research suggests that intensive training and hard work are crucial to achieving eminence, but many theorists are reluctant to dismiss the importance of innate talent.

Heredity and Environment as Determinants of Intelligence

Most early pioneers of intelligence testing maintained that intelligence is inherited (Cravens, 1992). Small wonder, then, that this view lingers on among many people. Gradually, however, it has become clear that both heredity and environment influence intelligence (Locurto, 1991; Plomin & Petrill, 1997, Scarr, 1997). Does this mean that the nature versus nurture debate has been settled with respect to intelligence? Absolutely not. Theorists and researchers continue to argue vigorously about which of the two is more important, in part because the issue has such far-reaching sociopolitical implications.

Theorists who believe that intelligence is largely inherited downplay the value of special educational programs for underprivileged groups (Herrnstein & Murray, 1994; Jensen, 1980, 2000). They assert that a child's intelligence cannot be increased noticeably, because a child's genetic destiny cannot be altered. Other theorists take issue with this point, asserting that inherited characteristics are not necessarily un-

changeable (Angoff, 1988; Wahlsten, 1997). The people in this camp tend to maintain that even more funds should be allocated for remedial education programs, improved schooling in lower-class neighborhoods, and college financial aid for the underprivileged. Because the debate over the role of heredity in intelligence has direct relevance to important social issues and political decisions, we'll take a detailed look at this complex controversy.

Evidence for Hereditary Influence

Galton's observation that intelligence runs in families was quite accurate. However, *family studies* can determine only whether genetic influence on a trait is *plausible,* not whether it is certain (see Chapter 3). Family members share not just genes, but similar environments. If high intelligence (or low intelligence) appears in a family over several generations, this con-

PREVIEW QUESTIONS

- What types of evidence suggest that intelligence is inherited?
- What is heritability, and what are some limitations of heritability estimates?
- How has research demonstrated that environment influences IQ?
- How is the concept of reaction range used to explain the interaction of heredity and environment?
- How have Jensen and Herrnstein and Murray explained cultural disparities in average IQ scores?
- What are some alternative explanations for ethnic differences in average IQ scores?

sistency could reflect the influence of either shared genes or shared environment. Because of this problem, researchers must turn to *twin studies* and *adoption studies* to obtain more definitive evidence on whether heredity affects intelligence.

Twin Studies

The best evidence regarding the role of genetic factors in intelligence comes from studies that compare identical and fraternal twins. The rationale for twin studies is that both identical and fraternal twins normally develop under similar environmental conditions. However, identical twins share more genetic kinship than fraternal twins. Hence, if pairs of identical twins are more similar in intelligence than pairs of fraternal twins, it's presumably because of their greater genetic similarity. (See Chapter 3 for a more detailed explanation of the logic underlying twin studies.)

What are the findings of twin studies regarding intelligence? The data from over 100 studies of intellectual similarity for various kinds of kinship relations and child-rearing arrangements are summarized in Figure 9.12. This figure plots the average correlation observed for various types of relationships. As you can see, the average correlation reported for identical twins (.86) is very high, indicating that identical twins tend to be quite similar in intelligence. The average correlation for fraternal twins (.60) is significantly lower. This correlation indicates that fraternal twins also tend to be similar in intelligence, but noticeably less so than identical twins. These results support the notion that IQ is inherited to a considerable degree (Bouchard, 1998).

Of course, critics have tried to poke holes in this line of reasoning. They argue that identical twins are more alike in IQ because parents and others treat them more similarly than they treat fraternal twins. This environmental explanation of the findings has some merit. After all, identical twins are always the same sex, and gender influences how a child is raised. However, this explanation seems unlikely in light of the evidence on identical twins reared apart because of family breakups or adoption (Bouchard, 1997; Bouchard et al., 1990). *Although reared in different environments, these identical twins still display greater similarity in IQ (average correlation: .72) than fraternal twins reared together (average correlation: .60).* Moreover, the gap in IQ similarity between identical twins reared apart and fraternal twins reared together appears to widen in middle and late adulthood, suggesting paradoxically that the influence of heredity increases with age (Pedersen et al., 1992).

Adoption Studies

Research on adopted children also provides evidence about the effects of heredity (and of environment, as

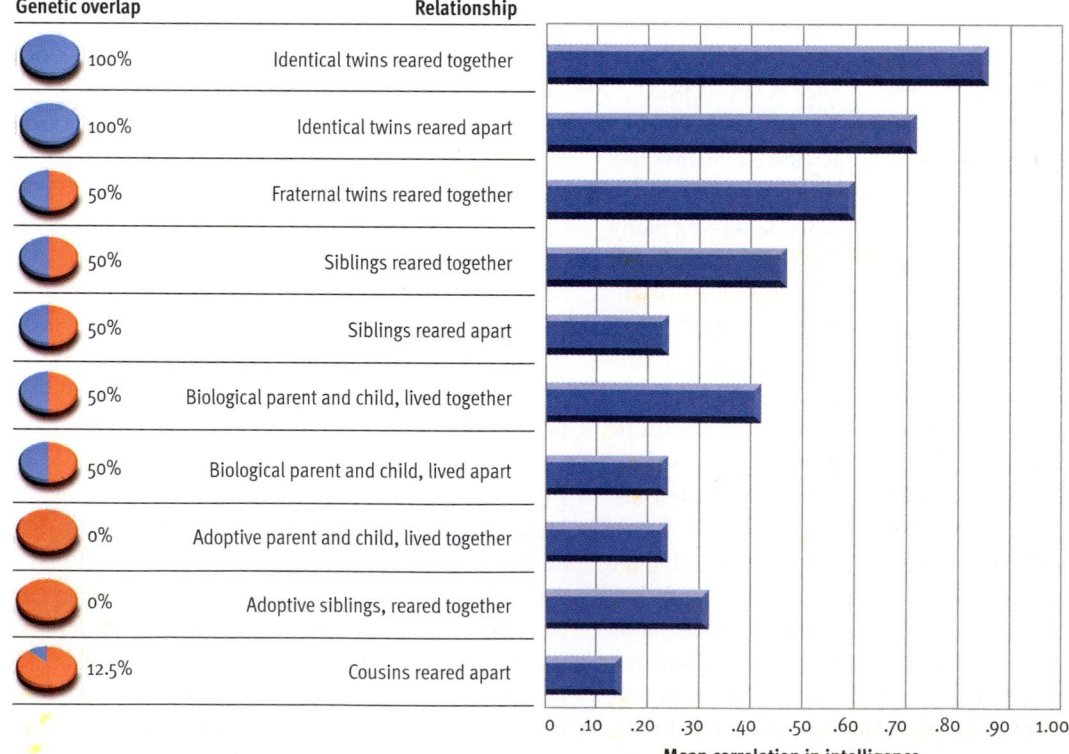

Figure 9.12

Studies of IQ similarity. The graph shows the mean correlations of IQ scores for people of various types of relationships, as obtained in studies of IQ similarity. Higher correlations indicate greater similarity. The results show that greater genetic similarity is associated with greater similarity in IQ, suggesting that intelligence is partly inherited (compare, for example, the correlations for identical and fraternal twins). However, the results also show that living together is associated with greater IQ similarity, suggesting that intelligence is partly governed by environment (compare, for example, the scores of siblings reared together and reared apart). (Data from McGue et al., 1993)

we shall see). If adopted children resemble their biological parents in intelligence even though they were not reared by these parents, this finding supports the genetic hypothesis. The relevant studies indicate that there is indeed more than chance similarity between adopted children and their biological parents (Turkheimer, 1991; refer again to Figure 9.12).

Heritability Estimates

Various experts have sifted through mountains of correlational evidence to estimate the *heritability* of intelligence. A *heritability ratio* is an estimate of the proportion of trait variability in a population that is determined by variations in genetic inheritance. Heritability can be estimated for any trait. For example, the heritability of height is estimated to be around 90% (Plomin, 1994). Heritability can be estimated in a variety of ways that appear logically and mathematically defensible (Loehlin, 1994; Schonemann, 1994). Given the variety of methods available and the strong views that experts bring to the IQ debate, it should come as no surprise that heritability estimates for intelligence vary considerably (see Figure 9.13).

At the high end, a few theorists, such as Arthur Jensen (1980, 1998), maintain that the heritability of IQ ranges as high as 80%. That is, they believe that only about 20% of the variation in intelligence is attributable to environmental factors. Most studies suggest that the heritability of IQ is between 50% and 70% (Bouchard et al., 1990; Loehlin, 1989). The consensus estimate of experts hovers around 60% (Snyderman & Rothman, 1987). Even the estimates at the low end, such as the 48% figure reported by Devlin, Daniels, and Roeder (1997), suggest that heredity has a substantial impact on intelligence.

However, it's important to understand that heritability estimates have certain limitations (Ceci et al., 1997; Grigorenko, 2000; Waldman, 1997). First, a heritability estimate is a *group statistic* based on studies of trait variability within a specific group. A heritability estimate cannot be applied meaningfully to *individuals*. In other words, even if the heritability of intelligence is 60%, this does not mean that each individual's intelligence is 60% inherited. Second, the heritability of a specific trait may vary from one group to another depending on a variety of factors. For instance, in a group with a given gene pool, heritability will increase if there's a shift toward rearing group members in more similar circumstances. Why? Because the extent of environmental differences will be reduced. To date, heritability estimates for intelligence have been based largely on research with white,

middle-class subjects. Hence, they should be applied only to such groups.

Evidence for Environmental Influence

Heredity unquestionably influences intelligence, but a great deal of evidence indicates that upbringing also affects mental ability. In this section, we'll examine various approaches to research that show how life experiences shape intelligence.

Adoption Studies

Research with adopted children provides useful evidence about the impact of experience as well as heredity (Locurto, 1990; Loehlin, Horn, & Willerman, 1997). Many of the correlations in Figure 9.12 reflect the influence of the environment. For example, adopted children show some resemblance to their foster parents in IQ. This similarity is usually attributed to the fact that their foster parents shape their environment. Adoption studies also indicate that siblings reared together are more similar in IQ than siblings reared apart. This is true even for identical twins who have the same genetic endowment. Moreover, entirely unrelated children who are raised in the same home also show a significant resemblance in IQ. All of these findings indicate that environment influences intelligence.

Environmental Deprivation and Enrichment

If environment affects intelligence, children who are raised in substandard circumstances should experience a gradual decline in IQ as they grow older (since other children will be progressing more rapidly). This *cumulative deprivation hypothesis* was tested decades ago. Researchers studied children consigned to understaffed orphanages and children raised in the

Heritability estimates for intelligence

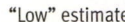

"High" estimate

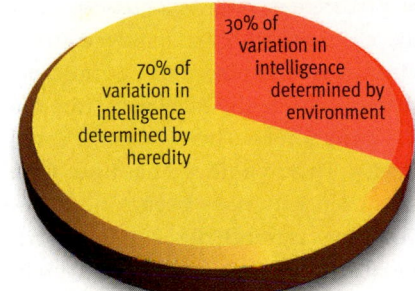

70% of variation in intelligence determined by heredity

30% of variation in intelligence determined by environment

"Low" estimate

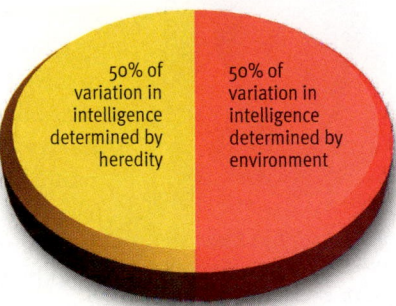

50% of variation in intelligence determined by heredity

50% of variation in intelligence determined by environment

Figure 9.13

The concept of heritability.
A heritability ratio is an estimate of the portion of variation in a trait determined by heredity—with the remainder presumably determined by environment—as these pie charts illustrate. Typical heritability estimates for intelligence range between a high of 70% and a low of 50%, although some estimates have fallen outside this range. Bear in mind that heritability ratios are *estimates* and have certain limitations that are discussed in the text.

"My research has been aimed at asking in what kind of environments genetic differences shine through and when do they remain hidden."
SANDRA SCARR

poverty and isolation of the back hills of Appalachia (Sherman & Key, 1932; Stoddard, 1943). Generally, investigators *did* find that environmental deprivation led to the predicted erosion in IQ scores.

Conversely, children who are removed from a deprived environment and placed in circumstances more conducive to learning should benefit from their environmental enrichment. Their IQ scores should gradually increase. This hypothesis has been tested by studying children who have been moved from disadvantaged homes into middle- and upper-class adoptive homes (Scarr & Weinberg, 1977, 1983; Schiff & Lewontin, 1986; Skodak & Skeels, 1947). Although there are limits on the improvements seen, the IQs of these children tend to increase noticeably (typically 10–12 points). These findings also show that environment influences IQ.

Home Environment and Schooling Effects

Researchers have detected the influence of environment on intelligence in still other ways. One approach involves going into intact homes (mother and father living together with their children) to make an elaborate, systematic assessment of the quality of the intellectual environment there. If environment shapes intelligence, these assessments of home environments should correlate with youngsters' IQ scores, which they do (Okagaki, 1994). Schooling effects also demonstrate the impact of environment. Ceci and Williams (1997) have reviewed seven lines of evidence that show that school attendance has a positive impact on measured IQ.

Generational Changes: The Flynn Effect

The most interesting, albeit perplexing, evidence showcasing the importance of the environment is the finding that performance on IQ tests has steadily increased over generations. This trend was not widely appreciated until recently because the tests are renormed periodically with new standardization groups, so that the mean IQ always remains at 100. However, in a study of the IQ tests used by the U.S. military, James Flynn noticed that the level of performance required to earn a score of 100 jumped upward every time the tests were renormed. Curious about this unexpected finding, he eventually gathered extensive data from 20 nations and demonstrated that IQ performance has been rising steadily all over the industrialized world since the 1930s (Flynn, 1987, 1994, 1998, 1999). Thus, the performance that today would earn you an average score of 100 would have earned you an IQ score of about 120 back in the 1930s (see Figure 9.14). Researchers who study intelligence are now scrambling to explain this trend, which has been dubbed the "Flynn effect." About the only thing they mostly agree on is that the Flynn effect has to be attributed to environmental factors, as the modern world's gene pool could not have changed overnight (in evolutionary terms, 70 years is more like a fraction of a second) (Dickens & Flynn, 2001; Neisser, 1998).

At this point, the proposed explanations for the Flynn effect are conjectural, but it is worth reviewing some of them, as they highlight the diversity of environmental factors that may shape IQ performance. Some theorists attribute generational gains in IQ test performance to reductions in the prevalence of severe malnutrition among children (Lynn, 1998; Sigman & Whaley, 1998). Patricia Greenfield (1998) argues that advances in technology, including much maligned media such as television and video games, have enhanced visuospatial skills and other specific cognitive skills that contribute to performance on IQ tests. Wendy Williams (1998) discusses the importance of a constellation of factors, including improved schools, smaller families, better-educated parents, and higher-quality parenting. All of these speculations have some plausibility but are open to rebuttals as well. Thus, the causes of the Flynn effect remain obscure.

The Interaction of Heredity and Environment

Clearly, heredity and environment both influence intelligence to a significant degree. Indeed, many theorists now assert that the question of which is

Figure 9.14

Generational increases in measured IQ. IQ tests are renormed periodically so that the mean score remains at 100. However, research by James Flynn has demonstrated that performance on IQ tests around the world has been increasing throughout most of the century. This graph traces the estimated increases in IQ in the United States from 1918 to 1995. In relation to the axis on the right, the graph shows how average IQ would have increased if IQ tests continued to use 1918 norms. In relation to the axis on the left, the graph shows how much lower the average IQ score would have been in earlier years if 1995 norms were used. The causes of the "Flynn effect" are unknown, but they have to involve environmental factors.

SOURCE: Adapted from Flynn, J. R. (1998). IQ gains over time: Toward finding the causes. In U. Neisser (Ed.), *The rising curve: Long-term gains in IQ and related measures* (p. 37). Washington, DC: American Psychological Association. Copyright © by the American Psychological Association. Reprinted by permission of the author.

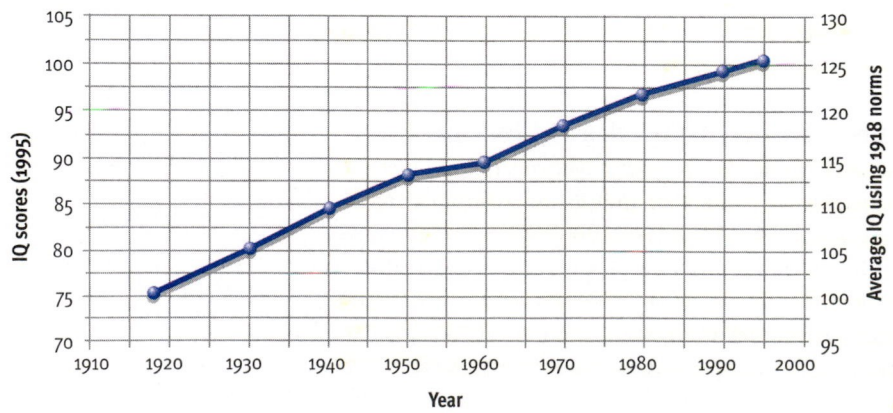

more important ought to take a back seat to the question of *how they interact* to govern IQ.

The current thinking, perhaps championed most prominently by Sandra Scarr (1991), is that heredity may set certain limits on intelligence and that environmental factors determine where individuals fall within these limits (Bouchard, 1997; Weinberg, 1989). According to this idea, genetic makeup places an upper limit on a person's IQ that can't be exceeded even when environment is ideal. Heredity is also thought to place a lower limit on an individual's IQ, although extreme circumstances (for example, being locked in an attic until age 10) could drag a person's IQ beneath this boundary. Theorists use the term *reaction range* to refer to these genetically determined limits on IQ (or other traits).

According to the reaction-range model, children reared in high-quality environments that promote the development of intelligence should score near the top of their potential IQ range (see Figure 9.15). Children reared under less ideal circumstances should score lower in their reaction range. The reaction range for most people is *estimated* to be around 20–25 points on the IQ scale (Weinberg, 1989).

The concept of a reaction range can explain why high-IQ children sometimes come from poor environments. It can also explain why low-IQ children sometimes come from very good environments. Moreover, it can explain these apparent paradoxes without discounting the role that environment undeniably plays. But how can the genetic boundaries on a person's intelligence be measured? That's the problem with the reaction-range concept. There is no readily apparent way to measure the range, which makes it difficult to test the reaction-range model empirically. The impossibility of measuring individuals'

CONCEPT **CHECK 9.2**

Understanding Correlational Evidence on the Heredity-Environment Question

Check your understanding of how correlational findings relate to the nature versus nurture issue by indicating how you would interpret the meaning of each "piece" of evidence described below. The numbers inside the parentheses are the mean IQ correlations observed for the relationships described (based on McGue et al., 1993), which are shown in Figure 9.12. In the spaces on the left, enter the letter H if the findings suggest that intelligence is shaped by heredity, enter the letter E if the findings suggest that intelligence is shaped by the environment, and enter the letter B if the findings suggest that intelligence is shaped by both (or either) heredity and environment. The answers can be found in Appendix A.

_____ **1.** Identical twins reared apart are more similar (.72) than fraternal twins reared together (.60).

_____ **2.** Identical twins reared together are more similar (.86) than identical twins reared apart (.72).

_____ **3.** Siblings reared together are more similar (.47) than siblings reared apart (.24).

_____ **4.** Biological parents and the children they rear are more similar (.42) than unrelated persons who are reared apart (no correlation if sampled randomly).

_____ **5.** Adopted children show similarity to their biological parents (.24) and to their adoptive parents (.24).

genetically determined intellectual potential also makes it difficult to resolve the debate about the causes of ethnic differences in IQ scores. We'll try to sort through this complex issue in the next section.

Cultural Differences in IQ Scores

The age-old nature versus nurture debate lies at the core of the current controversy about ethnic differences in average IQ. Although the full range of IQ

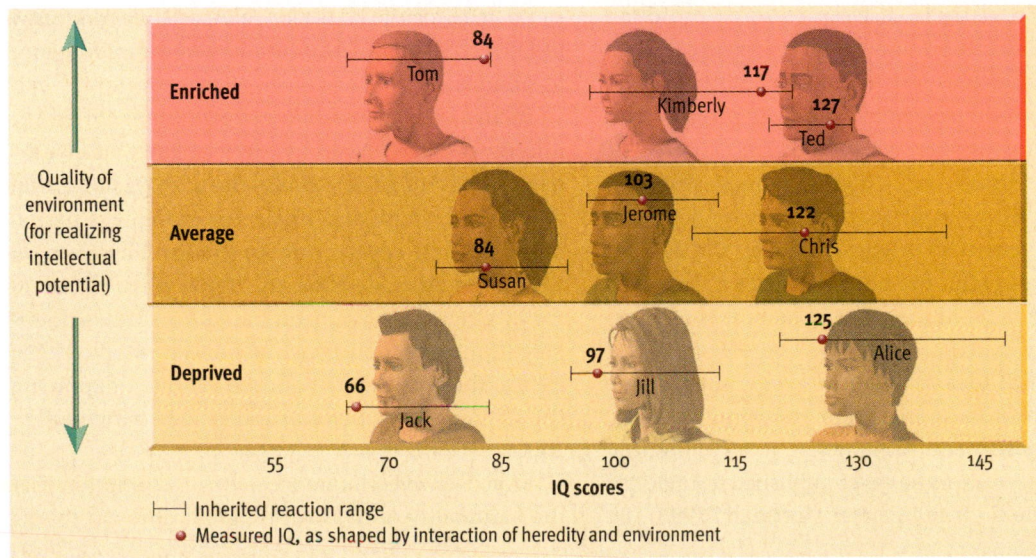

Quality of environment (for realizing intellectual potential)

IQ scores

├─┤ Inherited reaction range

● Measured IQ, as shaped by interaction of heredity and environment

Figure 9.15

Reaction range. The concept of reaction range posits that heredity sets limits on one's intellectual potential (represented by the horizontal bars), while the quality of one's environment influences where one scores within this range (represented by the dots on the bars). People raised in enriched environments should score near the top of their reaction range, whereas people raised in poor-quality environments should score near the bottom of their range. Genetic limits on IQ can be inferred only indirectly, so theorists aren't sure whether reaction ranges are narrow (like Ted's) or wide (like Chris's). The concept of reaction range can explain how two people with similar genetic potential can be quite different in intelligence (compare Tom and Jack) and how two people reared in environments of similar quality can score quite differently (compare Alice and Jack).

Courtesy of Arthur R. Jensen

❝Despite more than half a century of repeated efforts by psychologists to improve the intelligence of children, particularly those in the lower quarter of the IQ distribution relative to those in the upper half of the distribution, strong evidence is still lacking as to whether or not it can be done.❞

ARTHUR JENSEN

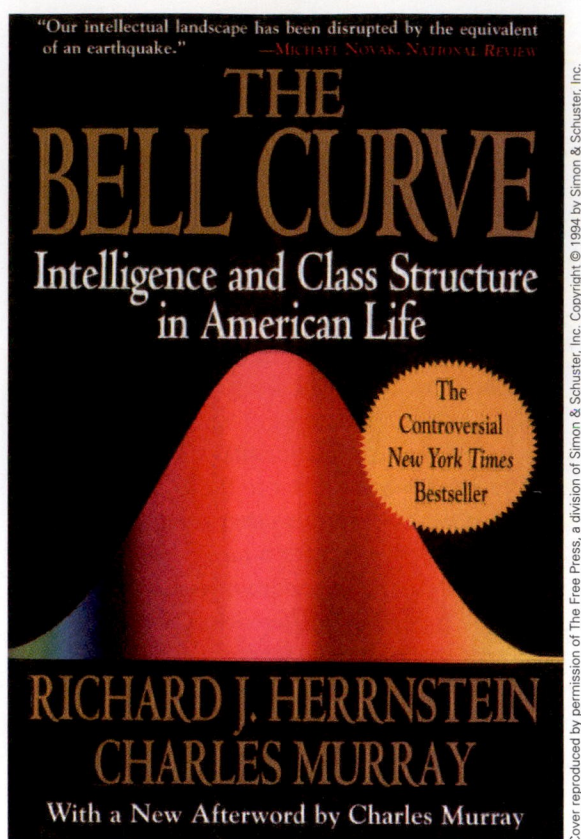

Cover reproduced by permission of The Free Press, a division of Simon & Schuster, Inc. Copyright © 1994 by Simon & Schuster, Inc.

In their 1994 best-seller, Herrnstein and Murray added fuel to the fire of the race-intelligence controversy.

Web Link 9.7

Upstream-Issues:
The Bell Curve
The editors of Upstream, champions of "politically incorrect" conversation, have assembled perhaps the broadest collection of commentaries on the Net regarding Herrnstein and Murray's *The Bell Curve*. Despite the marked political conservatism of this site, it contains a full range of opinion and analyses of the book.

scores is seen in all ethnic groups, the average IQ for many of the larger minority groups in the United States (such as African Americans, Native Americans, and Hispanics) is somewhat lower than the average for whites. The disparity ranges from 3 to 15 points, depending on the group tested and the IQ scale used (Loehlin, 2000; Perlman & Kaufman, 1990; Suzuki & Vraniak, 1994). There is little argument about the existence of these group differences, variously referred to as racial, ethnic, or cultural differences in intelligence. The controversy concerns *why* the differences are found. A vigorous debate continues as to whether cultural differences in intelligence are mainly due to the influence of heredity or of environment.

Heritability as an Explanation

In 1969 Arthur Jensen sparked a heated war of words by arguing that cultural differences in IQ are largely due to heredity. The cornerstone for Jensen's argument was his analysis suggesting that the heritability of intelligence is about 80%. Essentially, he asserted that (1) intelligence is largely genetic in origin, and (2) therefore, genetic factors are "strongly implicated" as the cause of ethnic differences in intelligence. Jensen's article triggered outrage, bitter criticism, and even death threats, as well as a flurry of research that shed additional light on the determinants of intelligence.

Twenty-five years later, Richard Herrnstein and Charles Murray (1994) reignited the same controversy with the publication of their widely discussed book *The Bell Curve*. Their main thesis is that in recent decades intellectual ability, which they believe is largely inherited, has become the primary determinant of individuals' success in life. They go on to argue that ethnic and cultural differences in average intelligence are substantial and not easily reduced and that these differences have profound and disturbing implications. Perhaps having learned from Jensen's nightmarish experiences, they try to tiptoe around the incendiary issue of whether ethnic differences in average IQ are due to heredity. But their discussions of "dysgenic pressures" in ethnic groups clearly imply that these disparities are at least partly genetic in origin. Moreover, the implicit message throughout the book is that disadvantaged groups cannot avoid their fate because it is their genetic destiny.

The central idea of *The Bell Curve*, that we are evolving toward a meritocracy based on intellect, may have some merit. Nonetheless, it is curious that neither of the authors has ever published a single scientific article on intelligence (Dorfman, 1995). By choosing to present their data exclusively in a popular book intended for the general reader, Herrnstein and Murray avoided having their data analyses subjected to the critical scrutiny that scientific data must withstand. It is not unusual for scientists to describe their work in a popular book, but doing so normally occurs *after* the scientists have published many technical articles on a topic, which they then attempt to summarize for the layperson. Herrnstein and Murray did not have any work of their own on intelligence to summarize.

In any event, heritability explanations for ethnic differences in IQ have a variety of flaws and weaknesses (Devlin et al., 2002; Horn, 2002; Myerson et al., 1998; Sternberg, 1995). For example, a heritability estimate applies only to the specific group on which the estimate is based. Heritability estimates for intelligence have been based on studies dominated almost entirely by white subjects (Brody, 1992). Hence, there is doubt about the validity of applying this estimate to other cultural groups (Grigerenko, 2000).

Moreover, even if one accepts the assumption that the heritability of IQ is very high, it does not follow logically that differences in *group averages* must be due largely to heredity. Leon Kamin has presented a compelling analogy that highlights the logical fallacy in this reasoning (see Figure 9.16):

We fill a white sack and a black sack with a mixture of different genetic varieties of corn seed. We make certain that the proportions of each variety of seed are identical in each sack. We then plant the seed from the white sack in fertile Field A, while that from the black sack is planted in barren Field B. We will observe that within Field A, as within Field B, there is considerable variation in the height of individual corn plants. This variation will be due largely to genetic factors (seed differences). We will also observe, however, that the average height of plants in Field A is greater than that in Field B. That difference will be entirely due to environmental factors (the soil). The same is true of IQs: differences in the average IQ of various human populations could be entirely due to environmental differences, even if within each population all variation were due to genetic differences! (Eysenck & Kamin, 1981, p. 97)

Kamin's analogy shows that even if the heritability of intelligence is high, group differences in average IQ *could* still be caused entirely (or in part) by environmental factors, a reality acknowledged by Arthur Jensen (1994b) and the authors of *The Bell Curve*.

The available evidence certainly does not allow us to rule out the possibility that ethnic and cultural disparities in average intelligence are partly genetic. And the hypothesis should not be dismissed without study simply because many people find it offensive or distasteful. However, there are several alternative explanations for the culture gap in intelligence that seem more plausible. Let's look at them.

Socioeconomic Disadvantage as an Explanation

Some theorists have approached the issue by trying to show that socioeconomic disadvantages are the main cause of ethnic differences in average IQ. Many social scientists argue that minority students' IQ scores are depressed because these children tend to grow up in deprived environments that create a disadvantage—both in school and on IQ tests. Obviously, living circumstances vary greatly within ethnic groups, but there is no question that, on the average, whites and minorities tend to be raised in very different circumstances. Most minority groups have endured a long history of economic discrimination and are greatly overrepresented in the lower social classes. A lower-class upbringing tends to carry a number of disadvantages that work against the development of

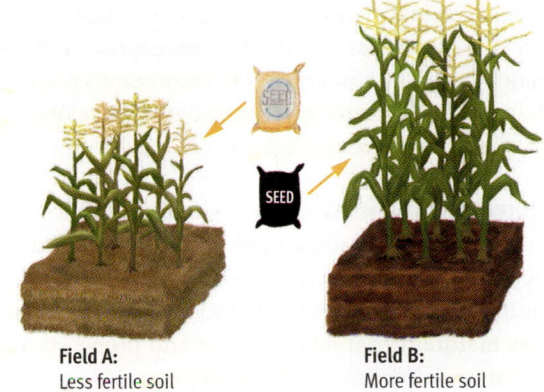

Individual variation in corn plant heights within each group (cause: genetic variation in the seeds)

Field A: Less fertile soil

Field B: More fertile soil

Differences in average corn plant height between groups (cause: the soils in which the plants were grown)

Figure 9.16

Genetics and between-group differences on a trait. Leon Kamin's analogy (see text) shows how between-group differences on a trait (the average height of corn plants) could be due to environment, even if the trait is largely inherited. The same reasoning presumably applies to ethnic group differences in average intelligence.

a youngster's full intellectual potential (Blau, 1981; Lott, 2002; McLoyd, 1998; Seifer, 2001). In comparison to the middle and upper classes, lower-class children are more likely to come from large families and from single-parent homes, factors that may often limit the parental attention they receive. Lower-class children also tend to be exposed to fewer books, to have fewer learning supplies, to have less privacy for concentrated study, and to get less parental assistance in learning. Typically, they also have poorer role models for language development, experience less pressure to work hard on intellectual pursuits, and attend poorer-quality schools that are underfunded and understaffed. Many of these children grow up in crime-, drug-, and gang-infested neighborhoods where it is far more important to develop street intelligence than school intelligence. Some theorists also argue that children in the lower classes are more likely to suffer from malnutrition or to be exposed to environmental toxins (Brody, 1992). Either of these circumstances could interfere with youngsters' intellectual development (Bellinger & Adams, 2001; Grantham-McGregor, Ani, & Fernald, 2001).

In light of these disadvantages, it's not surprising that average IQ scores among children from lower social classes tend to run about 15 points below the average scores obtained by children from middle and upper class homes (Seifer, 2001; Williams & Ceci, 1997). This is the case even if race is factored out of the picture by studying whites exclusively. Admittedly, there is room for argument about the direction of the causal relationships underlying this association between social class and intelligence (Turkheimer, 1994). Nonetheless, given the overrepresentation of minorities in the lower classes, many researchers argue that ethnic differences in intelligence are really social class differences in disguise.

Stereotype Vulnerability as an Explanation

Socioeconomic disadvantages probably are a major factor in various minority groups' poor performance on IQ and other standardized tests, but some theorists maintain that other factors and processes are also at work. For example, Claude Steele (1992, 1997), a social psychologist at Stanford University, has argued that derogatory stereotypes of stigmatized groups' intellectual capabilities create unique feelings of vulnerability in the educational arena. These feelings of *stereotype vulnerability* can undermine group members' performance on tests, as well as other measures of academic achievement.

Steele points out that demeaning stereotypes of stigmatized groups are widely disseminated, creating a subtle climate of prejudice, even in the absence of overt discrimination. He further notes that members of minority groups are keenly aware of any negative stereotypes that exist regarding their intellect. Hence, when an African American or Hispanic American does poorly on a test, he or she must confront a disturbing possibility: *that others will attribute the failure to racial inferiority.* Steele maintains that females face the same problem when they venture into academic

domains where stereotypes suggest that they are inferior to males, such as mathematics, engineering, and the physical sciences. That is, *they worry about people blaming their failures on their sex.* According to Steele, minorities and women in male-dominated fields are in a no-win situation. When they do well and contradict stereotypes, people tend to view their success with suspicion, but when they do poorly, people readily view their failure as vindication of the stereotypes.

Steele maintains that stigmatized groups' apprehension about "confirming" people's negative stereotypes can contribute to academic underachievement in at least two ways. First, it can undermine their emotional investment in academic work. As Steele notes, "Doing well in school requires a belief that school achievement can be a promising basis of self-esteem, and that belief needs constant reaffirmation even for advantaged students" (1992, p. 72). When this belief is relentlessly undercut instead of frequently reaffirmed, students tend to "disidentify" with school and write off academic pursuits as a source of self-worth. Their academic motivation declines and their performance suffers as a result. Second, standardized tests such as IQ tests may be especially anxiety arousing for members of stigmatized groups because the importance attributed to the tests makes one's stereotype vulnerability particularly salient. This anxiety may impair students' test performance by temporarily disrupting their cognitive functioning. We'll look at how Steele tested his theory in our Featured Study.

"I believe that in significant part the crisis in black Americans' education stems from the power of this vulnerability to undercut identification with schooling."
CLAUDE STEELE

Investigators: Claude M. Steele (Stanford University) and Joshua Aronson (University of Texas, Austin)

Source: Stereotype threat and the intellectual performance of African Americans. *Journal of Personality and Social Psychology,* 1995, 69, 797–811.

FEATURED STUDY

Racial Stereotypes and Test Performance

In this article, Steele and Aronson report on a series of four studies that tested various aspects of Steele's theory about the ramifications of stereotype vulnerability. We will examine their first study in some detail and then discuss the remaining studies more briefly. The purpose of the first study was to test the hypothesis that raising the threat of stereotype vulnerability would have a negative impact on African American students' performance on a mental ability test.

Method

Participants. The participants were 114 black and white undergraduates attending Stanford University who were recruited through campus advertisements. As expected, given Stanford's highly selective admissions, both groups

of students were well above average in academic ability, as evidenced by their mean scores on the verbal subtest of the SAT. The study compared black and white students with high and roughly equal ability and preparation (based on their SAT scores) to rule out cultural disadvantage as a factor.

Procedure. The participants were asked to take a challenging, 30-minute test of verbal ability composed of items from the verbal subtest of the Graduate Record Exam (GRE). In one condition, the issue of stereotype vulnerability was not made salient, as the test was presented to subjects as a device to permit the researchers to analyze participants' problem-solving strategies. In another condition, the specter of stereotype vulnerability was raised, as the test was presented as an excellent index of one's general verbal ability. The principal dependent variable was subjects' performance on the verbal test.

Results

When the African American students' stereotype vulnerability was not made salient, the performance of the black and white students did not differ, as you can see in Figure 9.17. However, when the same test was presented in a way that increased blacks' stereotype vulnerability, the African American students scored significantly lower than their white counterparts (see Figure 9.17).

Discussion

Based on their initial study, the authors inferred that stereotype vulnerability does appear to impair minority group members' test performance. They went on to replicate their finding in a second study of 40 black and white female students. In a third study, they demonstrated that their manipulations of stereotype vulnerability were indeed activating thoughts about negative stereotypes, ability-related self-doubts, and performance apprehension in their African American participants. Their fourth study showed that stereotype vulnerability can be activated even when a test is not explicitly presented as an index of one's ability.

Comment

More evidence is clearly needed on the effects of stereotype vulnerability, but Steele's theory has been supported in a number of additional studies (Aronson et al., 1999; Croizet & Claire, 1998; Spencer, Steele, & Quinn,

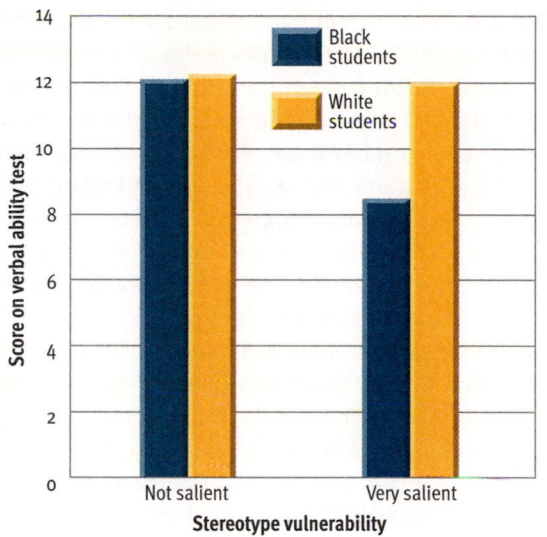

Figure 9.17

Stereotype vulnerability and test performance.
Steele and Aronson (1995) compared the performance of African American and white students of equal ability on a 30-item verbal ability test constructed from difficult GRE questions. When the black students' stereotype vulnerability was not salient, their performance did not differ from that of the white students; but when the specter of stereotype vulnerability was raised, the African American students performed significantly worse than the white students.

SOURCE: Adapted from Steele, C. M., & Aronson, J. (1995). Stereotype threat and the intellectual test performance of African Americans. *Journal of Personality and Social Psychology, 69,* 797–811. Copyright © 1995 by the American Psychological Association. Reprinted by permission of the author.

1999). The concept of stereotype vulnerability has the potential to clear up some of the confusion surrounding the controversial issue of racial disparities in IQ scores. It seems likely that socioeconomic disadvantage makes a substantial contribution to cultural differences in average IQ, but various lines of evidence suggest that this factor cannot account for the culture gap by itself (Neisser et al., 1996). For years, many theorists have argued that test bias accounts for the rest of the culture gap, but as we will discuss momentarily, recent research suggests otherwise. Thus, Steele's groundbreaking research gives scientists an entirely new explanatory tool for understanding the vexing cultural disparities in average IQ. ∎

Cultural Bias on IQ Tests as an Explanation

Some critics of IQ tests have argued that cultural differences in IQ scores are partly due to a cultural bias built into IQ tests. They argue that because IQ tests are constructed by white, middle-class psychologists, they naturally draw on experience and knowledge typical of white, middle-class lifestyles and use language and vocabulary that reflect the white, middle-class origins of their developers (Cohen, 2002; Helms, 1992; Hilliard, 1984; Williams et al., 1980). Given these concerns, many testing experts assert that minority students' IQ scores should be interpreted with extra caution (Puente, 1990). However, the balance of evidence suggests that the cultural slant on IQ tests is modest to negligible. The charges of bias stimulated a great deal of research on the issue in the

1970s and 1980s. *As a whole, the accumulated evidence suggests that cultural bias produces only weak and inconsistent effects on the IQ scores of minority examinees* (Hunter & Schmidt, 2000; Kaplan, 1985; Reynolds, 2000). However, Suzuki and Valencia (1997) express some caution about this conclusion, noting that the studies of test bias may use culturally biased criteria of academic success to evaluate the tests. They also assert that little research has been done on some widely used tests and with some minority populations.

Taken as a whole, the various alternative explanations for cultural and ethnic disparities in average IQ provide serious challenges to genetic explanations, which appear weak at best—and suspiciously racist at worst. Unfortunately, since the earliest days of IQ testing some people have used IQ tests to further elitist goals. The current controversy about ethnic differences in IQ is just another replay of a record that has been heard before. For instance, beginning in 1913, Henry Goddard tested a great many immigrants to the United States at Ellis Island in New York. Goddard reported that the vast majority of Italian, Hungarian, and Jewish immigrants tested out as *feebleminded* (Kamin, 1974). As you can see, claims about ethnic deficits in intelligence are nothing new—only the victims have changed.

The debate about ethnic differences in intelligence illustrates how IQ tests have often become entangled in thorny social conflicts. This is unfortunate, because it brings politics to the testing enterprise. Intelligence testing has many legitimate and valuable uses. However, the controversy associated with intelligence tests has undermined their value, leading to some of the new trends that we discuss in the next section.

REVIEW OF KEY POINTS

- The debate about the influence of heredity and environment on intelligence has important sociopolitical implications. Twin studies show that identical twins, even when raised apart, are more similar in IQ than fraternal twins, suggesting that intelligence is inherited. Adoption studies reveal that people resemble their parents in intelligence even when not raised by them. Estimates of the heritability of intelligence mostly range from 50% to 70%, but heritability ratios have certain limitations.

- Many lines of evidence, including adoption studies, studies of environmental deprivation and enrichment, home-environment studies, and research on the Flynn effect indicate that environment is also an important determinant of intelligence. The concept of reaction range posits that heredity places limits on one's intellectual potential while the environment determines where one falls within these limits.

- Arthur Jensen sparked great controversy by arguing that cultural differences in average IQ are largely due to heredity. Although the authors of *The Bell Curve* tried to sidestep the issue, their book ignited the same controversy.

- Genetic explanations for cultural differences in IQ have been challenged on a variety of grounds. Even if the heritability of IQ is great, group differences in average intelligence may not be due to heredity. Moreover, ethnicity varies with social class, so socioeconomic disadvantage may account for low IQ scores among minority students.

- Claude Steele has collected some thought-provoking data suggesting that stereotype vulnerability contributes to the culture gap in average IQ. Cultural bias on IQ tests may also contribute a little to ethnic differences in IQ, but it does not appear to be a crucial factor.

New Directions in the Assessment and Study of Intelligence

PREVIEW QUESTIONS

- Do modern IQ tests emphasize general ability or specific talents?
- Do measures of mental speed correlate with intelligence?
- What are the key features of Sternberg's theory of successful intelligence?
- What is Gardner's thesis about the nature of intelligence?
- What is emotional intelligence and can it be measured?

Intelligence testing has been through a period of turmoil, and changes are on the horizon. In fact, many changes have occurred already. Let's discuss some of the major new trends and projections for the future.

Increasing Emphasis on Specific Abilities

Although the pendulum may be starting to swing back the other way, recent years have brought an increased emphasis on the measurement of *specific mental abilities* as opposed to *general mental ability* (Daniel, 1997; Das, 1992; Gardner, 1993). Intelligence testing grew out of a particular theoretical climate in the first few decades of this century. At that time, Charles Spearman's (1904, 1923) ideas about the structure of intellect were dominant. Spearman developed an advanced statistical procedure called factor analysis. In *factor analysis*, correlations among many variables are analyzed to identify closely related clusters of variables. If a number of variables correlate highly with one another, the assumption is that a single factor is influencing all of them. Factor analysis attempts to identify these hidden factors.

Spearman used factor analysis to examine the correlations among tests of many specific mental abilities. He concluded that all cognitive abilities share an important core factor, which he labeled *g* for general mental ability. Spearman recognized that people also have "special" abilities (such as numerical reasoning or memory). However, he thought that individuals' ability in these specific areas is largely determined by their general mental ability (see Figure 9.18). Thus, test developers came to see *g* as the Holy Grail in their quest to measure mental ability. Since then, intelligence tests have usually been designed to tap as much of *g* as possible.

A very different view of the structure of intellect began to emerge in the 1940s. Using a somewhat different approach to factor analysis, L. L. Thurstone (1938, 1955) concluded that intelligence involves multiple abilities. Thurstone argued that Spearman and his followers placed far too much emphasis on *g*. In contrast, Thurstone found that he could carve intelligence into seven distinct factors called *primary*

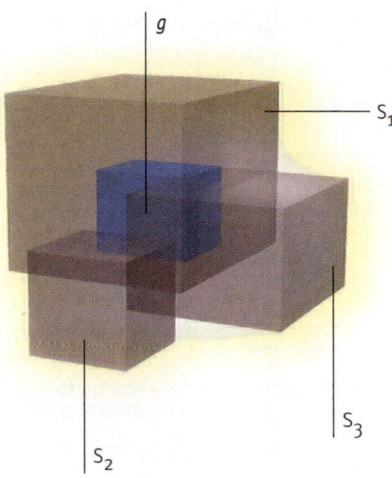

Figure 9.18

Spearman's *g*. In his analysis of the structure of intellect, Charles Spearman found that *specific* mental talents (S1, S2, S3, and so on) were highly intercorrelated. Thus, he concluded that all cognitive abilities share a common core, which he labeled *g* for general mental ability.

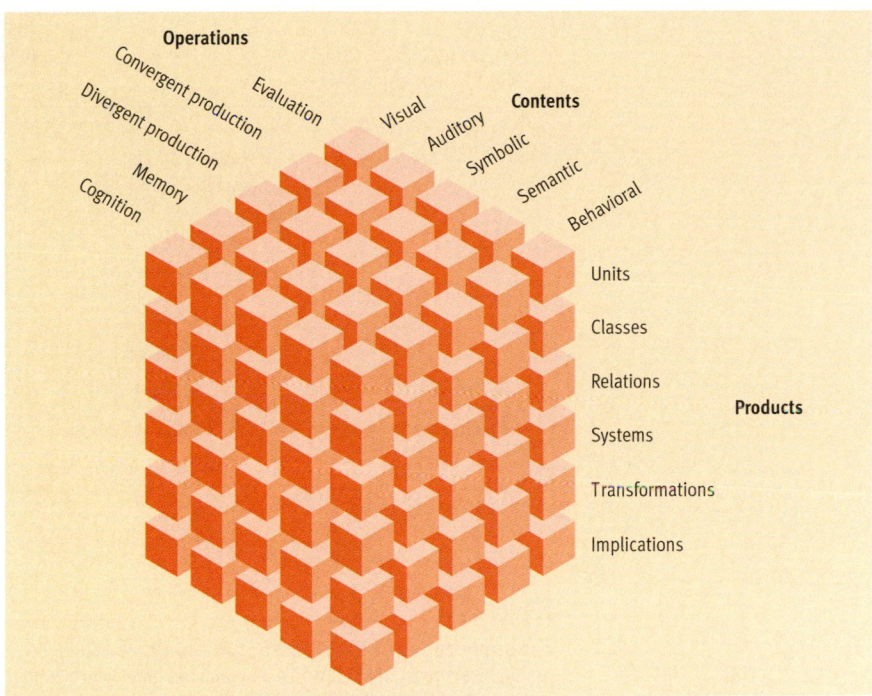

Figure 9.19

Guilford's model of mental abilities. In contrast to Spearman (see Figure 9.18), J. P. Guilford concluded that intelligence is made up of many separate abilities. According to his analysis, we may have as many as 150 distinct mental abilities that can be characterized in terms of the operations, contents, and products of intellectual activity.

mental abilities: word fluency, verbal comprehension, spatial ability, perceptual speed, numerical ability, inductive reasoning, and memory. Following in this tradition, J. P. Guilford (1959, 1985) upped the ante. His theory divided intelligence into *150* separate abilities—and did away with *g* entirely (see Figure 9.19). Thurstone's and Guilford's theories attracted favorable attention, but their ideas had relatively little effect on the day-to-day enterprise of intelligence testing (Horn, 1979).

However, another approach to carving up intelligence *has* had some impact. This approach was originally proposed by Raymond Cattell (1963) and was further developed by John Horn (1985). They suggest that *g* should be divided into *fluid intelligence* and *crystallized intelligence.* **Fluid intelligence** involves reasoning ability, memory capacity, and speed of information processing. *Crystallized intelligence* involves ability to apply acquired knowledge and skills in problem solving. Cattell originally assumed that fluid intelligence is largely determined by biological factors, and crystallized intelligence by education and experience. However, not all theorists who use the fluid-crystallized distinction assume that fluid intelligence has a stronger biological basis (Lohman, 1989).

The distinction between fluid and crystallized intelligence is central to the hierarchical model of intelligence that guided the most recent revision of the Stanford-Binet IQ test (Thorndike, Hagen, & Sattler, 1986). For the first 70 years of its existence, the Stanford-Binet yielded just one score, which was widely viewed as the ultimate index of general intelligence. However, the Stanford-Binet was broken into subtests for the first time in its long history in the 1986 revision. As Figure 9.20 on the next page shows, the modern Stanford-Binet includes 15 subtests. This major change in the structure of the Stanford-Binet seems to reflect a general trend toward devising tests of mental ability that assess specific abilities.

Exploring Biological Indexes of Intelligence

Although specific abilities are increasingly emphasized in the world of education, in the world of research some investigators continue to stalk *g* with single-minded determination. In particular, biologically oriented theorists, such as Arthur Jensen (1987, 1993b, 1998) and Hans Eysenck (1988, 1989), have attempted to find raw physiological indicators of general intelligence. Their search for a "culture-free" measure of intelligence has led them to focus on sensory processes, much as Sir Francis Galton did over a hundred years ago. Armed with much more sophisticated equipment, they hope to succeed where Galton failed.

Jensen's (1982, 1987, 1992) studies of mental speed are representative of this line of inquiry. In his studies, Jensen measures *reaction time* (RT), using a panel of paired buttons and lights. On each trial, the subject rests a hand on a "home button." When one of the lights is activated, the subject is supposed to push

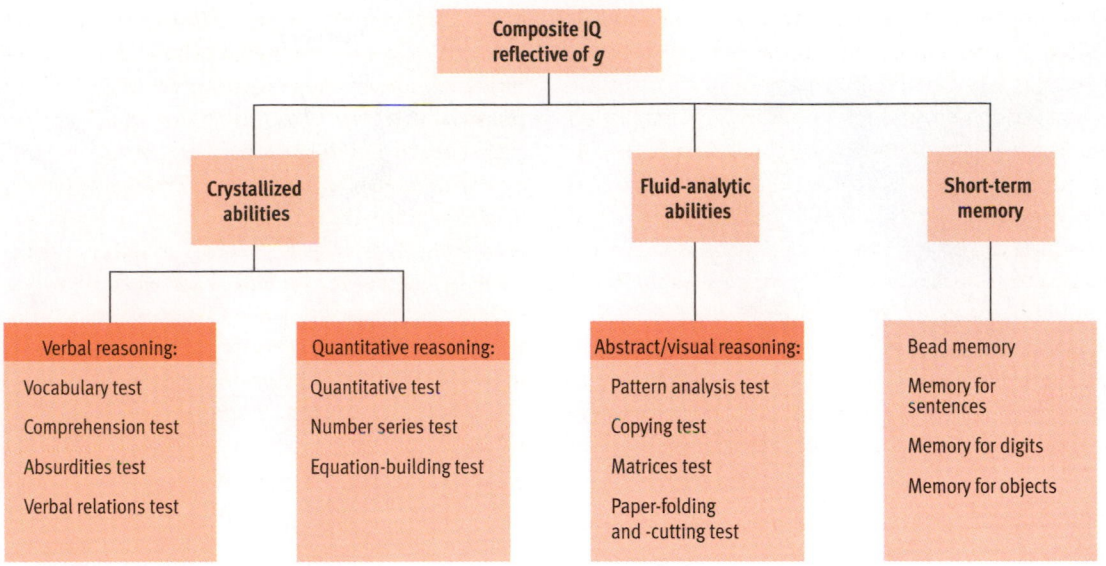

Figure 9.20

The organization of the modern Stanford-Binet. The 1986 edition of the classic Stanford-Binet Intelligence Test is based on the hierarchical model of intelligence diagrammed here, which is built around the distinction between fluid and crystallized intelligence. The modern Stanford-Binet yields a composite score that presumably reflects *g*, four second-order scores for broad types of mental ability (verbal reasoning, quantitative reasoning, abstract/visual reasoning, and short-term memory), and scores on 15 subtests that measure specific mental abilities.

SOURCE: Adapted from Thorndike, R. L., Hagen, E. P., & Sattler, J. M. (1986). *Stanford-Binet Intelligence Scale: Guide for administering and scoring* (4th Ed.). Chicago: Riverside Publishing Company. Reprinted with permission of The Riverside Publishing Company, Copyright © 1986.

the button for that light as quickly as possible. RT is typically averaged over a number of trials involving varied numbers of lights. Modest correlations (.20s to .30s) have been found between faster RTs and higher scores on conventional IQ tests.

Jensen's findings suggest an association between raw mental speed and intelligence, as Galton originally suggested. This correlation is theoretically interesting and, in retrospect, not all that surprising. Many conventional IQ tests have imposed demand-

ing time limits on examinees, working under the assumption that "fast is smart." However, the correlation between RT and IQ appears to be too weak to give RT any practical value as an index of intelligence.

However, another approach to measuring mental speed may have more practical potential. Measures of *inspection time* assess how long it takes participants to make simple perceptual discriminations that meet a certain criterion of accuracy (Deary & Stough, 1996). For example, in a series of trials, participants may be

Figure 9.21

Research on inspection time as a biological index of intelligence.
(Left) In studies of inspection time, participants are shown stimuli for very brief durations and are asked to make accurate judgments about them (such as whether the longer line is on the right or the left). (Right) Each participant's accuracy in making these perceptual discriminations is graphed as a function of exposure duration. A subject's inspection time for a particular task is the exposure duration required to achieve a certain level of accuracy. In this case, 85% accuracy is the criterion and the participant's inspection time for the task is 14 milliseconds.

SOURCE: Graph adapted from Deary, I. J., Caryl, P. G., & Gibson, G. J. (1993). Non-stationarity and the measurement of psychophysical response in a visual inspection time task. *Perception, 22,* 1245–1256. Copyright © 1993 by Pion Ltd. Adapted by permission.

asked repeatedly to indicate which of two lines is shorter. The pairs of lines are presented for very brief exposures and participants are told to concentrate on making *accurate* judgments. A person's inspection time is the exposure duration required for that person to achieve a specific level of accuracy, such as 85% correct judgments (see Figure 9.21). Correlations in the .40s been found between participants' inspection time scores and their scores on measures of fluid intelligence (Deary, 2000). These correlations are high enough to have some practical potential, although a great deal of work remains to be done to standardize inspection time measures and to figure out why they are associated with intelligence.

Investigating Cognitive Processes in Intelligent Behavior

As noted in Chapters 1 and 8, psychologists are increasingly taking a cognitive perspective in their efforts to study many topics. For over a century, the investigation of intelligence has been approached primarily from a *testing perspective*. This perspective emphasizes measuring the *amount* of intelligence people have and figuring out why some have more than others. In contrast, the *cognitive perspective* focuses on how people *use* their intelligence. The interest is in process rather than amount. In particular, cognitive psychologists focus on the information-processing strategies that underlie intelligence.

The application of the cognitive perspective to intelligence has been spearheaded by Robert Sternberg (1985, 1988b, 1991). His *triarchic theory of human intelligence* consists of three parts: the contextual, experiential, and componential subtheories. In his *contextual subtheory,* Sternberg argues that intelligence is

a culturally defined concept. He asserts that different manifestations of intelligent behavior are valued in different contexts. For example, the verbal skills emphasized in North American culture may take a back seat to hunting skills in another culture.

In his *experiential subtheory,* Sternberg explores the relationships between experience and intelligence. He emphasizes two factors as the hallmarks of intelligent behavior. The first is the ability to deal effectively with novelty—new tasks, demands, and situations. The second factor is the ability to learn how to handle familiar tasks automatically and effortlessly. Sternberg's *componential subtheory* describes three types of mental processes that intelligent thought depends on: metacomponents, performance components, and knowledge-acquisition components (see Figure 9.22). This part of the theory has guided extensive research on the specific thinking strategies that contribute to intelligent problem solving. Investigations of cognitive processes in intelligent behavior have some interesting implications for intelligence testing. Cognitive research has shown that more-intelligent subjects spend more time figuring out how to best represent problems and planning how to solve them than less-intelligent subjects do. Because planning takes time, Sternberg (1985) argues that traditional IQ tests place too much emphasis on speed.

Michael Marsland/Yale University

"*To understand intelligent behavior, we need to move beyond the fairly restrictive tasks that have been used both in experimental laboratories and in psychometric tests of intelligence.*"
ROBERT STERNBERG

Figure 9.22

Sternberg's triarchic theory of intelligence. Sternberg's model of intelligence consists of three parts: the contextual subtheory, the experiential subtheory, and the componential subtheory. Much of Sternberg's research has been devoted to the componential subtheory, as he has attempted to identify the cognitive processes that contribute to intelligence. He believes that these processes fall into three groups: metacomponents, performance components, and knowledge-acquisition components. All three component processes contribute to each of three aspects or types of intelligence: analytical intelligence, practical intelligence, and creative intelligence.

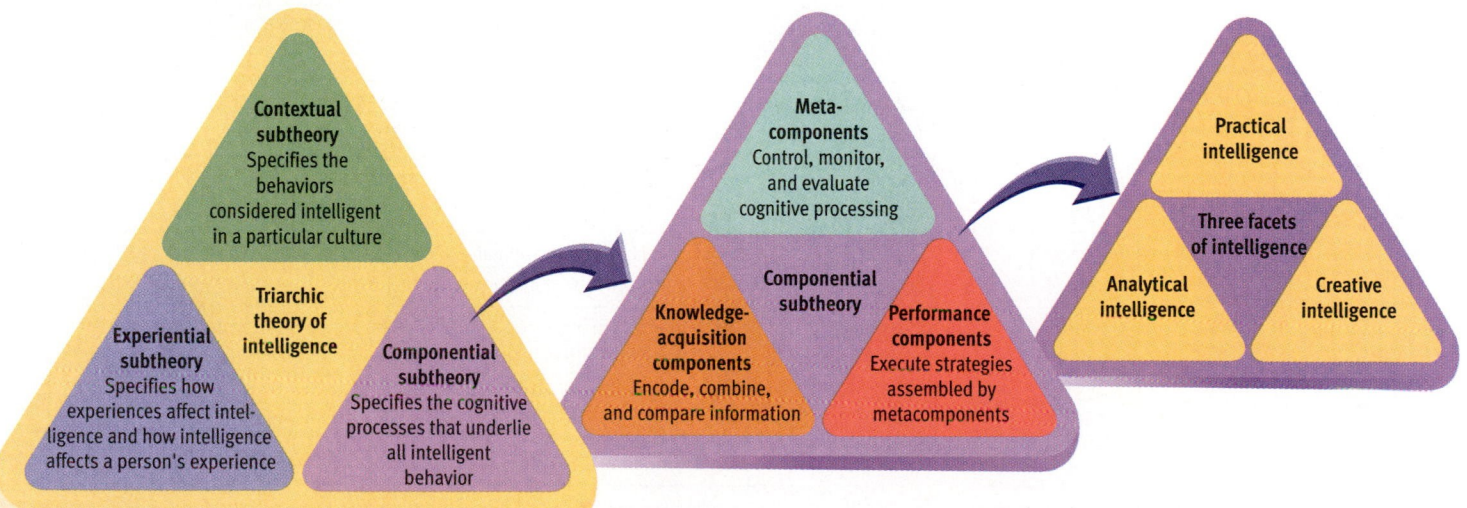

In more recent extensions of his theory, Sternberg (1999, 2000) has asserted that there are three aspects or facets of what he calls "successful intelligence": analytical intelligence, creative intelligence, and practical intelligence. *Analytical intelligence* involves abstract reasoning, evaluation, and judgment. It is the type of intelligence that is crucial to most schoolwork and that is assessed by conventional IQ tests. *Creative intelligence* involves the ability to generate new ideas and to be inventive in dealing with novel problems. *Practical intelligence* involves the ability to deal effectively with the kinds of problems that people encounter in everyday life, such as on the job or at home. A big part of practical intelligence involves learning what one needs to know to work efficiently in an environment that is not explicitly taught and that often is not even verbalized.

According to Sternberg, all three of the component processes underlying intelligence (metacomponents, performance components, and knowledge-acquisition components) contribute to each of the three facets of intelligence (analytical, creative, and practical intelligence). In a series of studies, Sternberg and his colleagues have gathered data suggesting that (1) all three facets of intelligence can be measured reliably, (2) the three facets of intelligence are relatively independent (uncorrelated), and (3) the assessment of all three aspects of intelligence can improve the prediction of intelligent behavior in the real world (Grigorenko & Sternberg, 2001; Sternberg et al., 1999, 2001). A great deal of additional research will be needed to explore the predictive validity and value of Sternberg's new measures of analytical, creative, and practical intelligence. Nonetheless, he certainly has been an articulate voice arguing for a broader, expanded concept of intelligence, which is a theme that has been echoed by others.

Expanding the Concept of Intelligence

In recent years, a number of theorists besides Sternberg have concluded that the focus of traditional IQ tests is too narrow (Ceci, 1990; Greenspan & Driscoll, 1997). These theorists argue that to assess intelligence in a truly general sense, tests should sample from a wider range of tasks. The most prominent proponent of this view has been Howard Gardner (1983, 1993, 1998).

According to Gardner, IQ tests have generally emphasized verbal and mathematical skills, to the exclusion of other important skills. He suggests the existence of a number of relatively autonomous *human intelligences*, which are listed in Table 9.3. To build his list of separate intelligences, Gardner reviewed the evidence on cognitive capacities in normal individuals, people suffering from brain damage, and special populations, such as prodigies and idiot sa-

Courtesy of Howard Gardner, photo © Jay Gardner

"It is high time that the view of intelligence be widened to incorporate a range of human computational capacities. . . . But where is it written that intelligence needs to be determined on the basis of tests?"
HOWARD GARDNER

Table 9.3 Gardner's Eight Intelligences

Intelligence	End-States	Core Components
Logical-mathematical	Scientist Mathematician	Sensitivity to, and capacity to discern, logical or numerical patterns; ability to handle long chains of reasoning
Linguistic	Poet Journalist	Sensitivity to the sounds, rhythms, and meanings of words; sensitivity to the different functions of language
Musical	Composer Violinist	Abilities to produce and appreciate rhythm, pitch, and timbre; appreciation of the forms of musical expressiveness
Spatial	Navigator Sculptor	Capacities to perceive the visual-spatial world accurately and to perform transformations on one's initial perceptions
Bodily-kinesthetic	Dancer Athlete	Abilities to control one's body movements and to handle objects skillfully
Interpersonal	Therapist Salesperson	Capacities to discern and respond appropriately to the moods, temperaments, motivations, and desires of other people
Intrapersonal	Person with detailed, accurate self-knowledge	Access to one's own feelings and the ability to discriminate among them and draw upon them to guide behavior; knowledge of one's own strengths, weaknesses, desires, and intelligences
Naturalist	Biologist Naturalist	Abilities to recognize and categorize objects and processes in nature

SOURCE: Adapted from Gardner, H., & Hatch, T. (1989). Multiple intelligences go to school: Educational implications of the theory of multiple intelligences. *Educational Researcher, 18* (8), 4–10. American Educational Research Association. Additional information from Gardner, 1998.

vants. He concluded that humans exhibit eight intelligences: logical-mathematical, linguistic, musical, spatial, bodily-kinesthetic, interpersonal, intrapersonal, and naturalist. These intelligences obviously include quite a variety of talents that are not assessed by conventional IQ tests. Gardner is investigating the extent to which these intelligences are largely independent, as his theory asserts. For the most part, he has found that people tend to display a mixture of strong, intermediate, and weak abilities, which is consistent with idea that the various types of intelligence are independent.

Gardner's books have been very popular and his theory clearly resonates with many people. His ideas have had an impact on educators around the world. He has done a superb job of synthesizing research from neuropsychology, developmental psychology, cognitive psychology, and other areas to arrive at fascinating speculations about the structure of human abilities. He has raised thought-provoking questions about what abilities should be included under the rubric of intelligence. However, he has his critics (Hunt, 2001; Klein, 1997; Morgan, 1996). Some argue that his use of the term *intelligence* is so broad, encompassing virtually any valued human ability, it makes the term almost meaningless. These critics wonder whether there is any advantage to relabeling talents such as musical ability and motor coordination as forms of intelligence. Critics also note that Gardner's theory has not generated much research on the predictive value of measuring individual differences in the eight intelligences he has described. This research would require the development of tests to measure the eight intelligences, but Gardner is not particularly interested in the matter of assessment and he loathes conventional testing. This reality makes it difficult to predict where Gardner's theory will lead, as research is crucial to the evolution of a theory.

Measuring Emotional Intelligence

In yet another highly publicized effort to expand the concept of intelligence, a variety of theorists have argued that the measurement of *emotional intelligence* can enhance the prediction of success at school, at work, and in interpersonal relationships. The concept of emotional intelligence was originally developed by Peter Salovey and John Mayer (1990). Their concept languished in relative obscurity until Daniel Goleman (1995) wrote a compelling book titled *Emotional Intelligence,* which made the best-seller lists. Since then, empirical research on the measurement of emotional intelligence has increased dramatically.

Emotional intelligence consists of the ability to perceive and express emotion, assimilate emotion in thought, understand and reason with emotion, and regulate emotion. Emotional intelligence includes four essential components (Mayer & Salovey, 1997). First, people need to be able to accurately perceive emotions in themselves and others and have the ability to express their own emotions effectively. Second, people need to be aware of how their emotions shape their thinking, decisionmaking, and coping with stress. Third, people need to be able to understand and analyze their emotions, which may often be complex and contradictory. Fourth, people need to be able to regulate their emotions so that they can dampen negative emotions and make effective use of positive emotions.

Several tests of emotional intelligence have already been developed. The test that has the strongest empirical foundation is the Multifactor Emotional Intelligence Scale (MEIS) devised by Mayer, Caruso, and Salovey (1999). They have strived to make this test a performance-based measure of the cognitive ability to deal effectively with emotions rather than a measure of personality or temperament. Preliminary results suggest that they have made considerable progress toward this goal, as evidenced by data on the test's reliability, validity, and factor structure (Mayer, Salovey, & Caruso, 2000) and the scale's ability to predict intelligent management of emotions in real-world situations (Ciarrochi, Dean & Anderson, 2002; Lam & Kirby, 2002; Mayer et al., 2001).

CONCEPT CHECK 9.3

Recognizing Theories of Intelligence

Check your understanding of various theories on the nature of intelligence by matching the names of their originators with the brief descriptions of the theories' main themes that appear below. Choose from the following theorists: (a) Sir Francis Galton, (b) Howard Gardner, (c) Arthur Jensen, (d) Sandra Scarr, (e) Robert Sternberg, (f) Alfred Binet, and (g) David Wechsler. The answers are in Appendix A.

_____ 1. This theorist posited eight human intelligences: logical-mathematical, linguistic, musical, spatial, bodily-kinesthetic, interpersonal, intrapersonal, and naturalist.

_____ 2. On the basis of a study of eminence and success in families, this theorist concluded that intelligence is inherited.

_____ 3. This theorist stated that the heritability of intelligence is about 80% and that IQ differences between ethnic groups are mainly due to genetics.

_____ 4. This theorist stated that heredity sets certain limits on intelligence and that environmental factors determine where one falls within those limits.

_____ 5. This person's theory of intelligence is divided into contextual, experiential, and componential subtheories and posits three facets of intelligence: analytical, practical, and creative intelligence.

Skeptics have questioned whether sophistication about emotion should be viewed as a form of intelligence, and they have correctly pointed out that a great deal of additional research will be needed to fully validate the MEIS and to fully document the adaptive significance of emotional intelligence (Izard, 2001; Roberts, Zeidner, & Matthews, 2001). However, advocates for the concept of emotional intelligence—unlike advocates for the concept of multiple intelligences—seem to relish that challenge, and serious research on emotional intelligence is flourishing. It will be interesting to see where this research leads over the next decade.

Putting It in Perspective

PREVIEW QUESTIONS

- What did this chapter reveal about the importance of cultural factors and the nature versus nurture debate?
- How did this chapter illustrate the connections between psychology and the world at large?

As you probably noticed, three of our integrative themes surfaced in this chapter. Our discussions illustrated that cultural factors shape behavior, that psychology evolves in a sociohistorical context, and that heredity and environment jointly influence behavior.

Pervasive psychological testing is largely a Western phenomenon. The concept of general intelligence also has a special, Western flavor to it. Many non-Western cultures have very different ideas about the nature of intelligence. Within Western societies, the observed ethnic differences in average intelligence also illustrate the importance of cultural factors, as these disparities appear to be due in large part to cultural disadvantage and other culture-related considerations. Thus, we see once again that if we hope to achieve a sound understanding of behavior, we need to appreciate the cultural contexts in which behavior unfolds.

Human intelligence is shaped by a complex interaction of hereditary and environmental factors. We've drawn similar conclusions before in other chapters where we examined other aspects of behavior. However, this chapter should have enhanced your appreciation of this idea in at least two ways. First, we examined more of the details of how scientists arrive at the conclusion that heredity and environment jointly shape behavior. Second, we encountered dramatic illustrations of the immense importance attached to the nature versus nurture debate. For example, Arthur Jensen has been the target of savage criticism. After his controversial 1969 article, he was widely characterized as a racist. When he gave speeches, he was often greeted by protestors carrying signs, such as "Kill Jensen" and "Jensen Must Perish." As you can see, the debate about the inheritance of intelligence inspires passionate feelings in many people. In part, this is because the debate has far-reaching social and political implications, which brings us to another prominent theme in the chapter.

There may be no other area in psychology where the connections between psychology and society at large are so obvious. Prevailing social attitudes have always exerted some influence on testing practices and the interpretation of test results. In the first half of the 20th century, a strong current of racial and class prejudice was apparent in the United States and Britain. This prejudice supported the idea that IQ tests measured innate ability and that "undesirable" groups scored poorly because of their genetic inferiority. Although these beliefs did not go unchallenged within psychology, their widespread acceptance in the field reflected the social values of the time. It's ironic that IQ tests have sometimes been associated with social prejudice. When used properly, intelligence tests provide relatively objective measures of mental ability that are less prone to bias than the subjective judgments of teachers or employers.

Today, psychological tests serve many diverse purposes. In the upcoming Personal Application, we focus on creativity tests and on the nature of creative thinking and creative people.

REVIEW OF KEY POINTS

- Modern intelligence tests place a greater emphasis on the measurement of specific mental abilities and less emphasis on tapping Spearman's *g* than their predecessors. The distinction between fluid and crystallized intelligence is the basis for the most recent revision of the Stanford-Binet IQ test.

- Although reaction time indexes of intelligence are being explored, they seem to have little practical utility. Measures of inspection time may prove more useful, although additional research is needed.

- Research on intelligence increasingly uses a cognitive perspective, which emphasizes the need to understand how people use their intelligence. Many modern theorists, such as Robert Sternberg and Howard Gardner, argue that the concept of intelligence should be expanded to encompass a greater variety of skills. Researchers have made some progress in their efforts to measure emotional intelligence.

- Three of our integrative themes stood out in the chapter. Our discussions of intelligence showed how heredity and environment interact to shape behavior, how psychology evolves in a sociohistorical context, and how one has to consider cultural contexts to fully understand behavior.

Understanding Creativity

Answer the following "true" or "false."

____ **1.** Creative ideas often come out of nowhere.

____ **2.** Creativity usually occurs in a burst of insight.

____ **3.** Creativity depends on inspiration far more than on perspiration.

Intelligence is not the only type of mental ability that psychologists have studied. They have devised tests to explore a variety of mental abilities. Among these, creativity is certainly one of the most interesting. People tend to view creativity as an essential trait for artists, musicians, and writers, but it is important in *many* walks of life. In this Application, we'll discuss psychologists' efforts to measure and understand creativity. As we progress, you'll learn that all the statements above are false.

The Nature of Creativity

What makes thought creative? *Creativity involves the generation of ideas that are original, novel, and useful.* Creative thinking is fresh, innovative, and inventive. But novelty by itself is not enough. In addition to being unusual, creative thinking must be adaptive. It must be appropriate to the situation and problem.

Does Creativity Occur in a Burst of Insight?

It is widely believed that creativity usually involves sudden flashes of insight and great leaps of imagination. Robert Weisberg (1986) calls this belief the "aha! myth." Undeniably, creative bursts of insight do occur (Feldman, 1988). However, the evidence suggests that major creative achievements generally are logical extensions of existing ideas, involving long, hard work and many small, faltering steps forward (Weisberg, 1993). Creative ideas do not come out of nowhere. Creative ideas come from a deep well

of experience and training in a specific area, whether it's music, painting, business, or science (Weisberg, 1999). As Snow (1986) puts it, "Creativity is not a light bulb in the mind, as most cartoons depict it. It is an accomplishment born of intensive study, long reflection, persistence, and interest" (p. 1033).

Does Creativity Depend on Unconscious Thought Processes?

Some fascinating reports have attributed creative breakthroughs to unconscious thought processes (Ghiselin, 1952). For example, creative giants such as Mozart, Dostoyevsky, and Coleridge reported that dazzling insights came to them while sleeping or daydreaming. These stories have led some theorists to conclude that creativity depends on the unconscious, which is not constrained by normal logic and rationality (Kris, 1952).

As a whole, however, reports of unconscious breakthroughs are few and of dubious accuracy. In at least some cases, it appears that artists have fabricated stories of unconscious breakthroughs to attract publicity, to confound rivals, or to enhance the legend of their genius (Weisberg, 1993). Most cognitive psychologists have concluded that creativity emerges out of normal problem-solving efforts that depend on conscious thought processes (Hayes, 1989; Klahr & Simon, 1999) and that creativity can be learned or enhanced, at least to some degree (Nickerson, 1999).

Does Creativity Depend on Divergent Thinking?

According to many theorists, the key to creativity lies in *divergent thinking*—thinking "that goes off in different directions," as J. P. Guilford (1959) put it. In his model of mental abilities (see Figure 9.19 on page 367), Guilford distinguished between convergent thinking and divergent thinking. In *convergent thinking* one tries to narrow down a list of alternatives to converge on

a single correct answer. For example, when you take a multiple-choice exam, you try to eliminate incorrect options until you hit on the correct response. Most training in school encourages convergent thinking. In *divergent thinking* one tries to expand the range of alternatives by generating many possible solutions. Imagine that you work for an advertising agency. To come up with as many slogans as possible for a client's product, you must use divergent thinking. Some of your slogans may be clear losers, and eventually you will have to engage in convergent thinking to pick the best, but coming up with the range of new possibilities depends on divergent thinking.

Thirty years of research on divergent thinking has yielded mixed results. As a whole, the evidence suggests that divergent thinking contributes to creativity, but it clearly does not represent the essence of creativity, as originally proposed (Brown, 1989; Plucker & Renzulli, 1999). In retrospect, it was probably unrealistic to expect creativity to depend on a single cognitive skill. According to Sternberg (1988a), the cognitive processes that underlie creativity are multifaceted.

Measuring Creativity

Although its nature may be elusive, creativity clearly is important in today's world. Creative masterpieces in the arts and literature enrich human existence. Creative insights in the sciences illuminate people's understanding of the world. Creative inventions fuel technological progress. Thus, it is understandable that psychologists have been interested in measuring creativity with psychological tests.

How Do Psychological Tests Measure Creativity?

A diverse array of psychological tests have been devised to measure individuals' creativity (Cooper, 1991). Usually, the items on creativity tests assess divergent thinking by giving respondents a specific starting point and then requiring them to generate as many possibilities as they can in a short period of time. Typical items on a creativity test might include the following: (1) List as many uses as you can for a newspaper. (2) Think of as many fluids that burn as you can. (3) Imagine that people no longer need sleep and think of as many consequences as you can. Subjects' scores on these tests depend on the *number* of alternatives they generate and on the *originality* and *usefulness* of the alternatives.

One seminal test of creativity is the Remote Associates Test (RAT) developed by Sarnoff and Martha Mednick (1967). This test is based on the assumption that creative people see unusual relationships and make nonobvious connections between ideas. Items on the test require subjects to figure out the obscure links (the remote associations) among three words by coming up with a fourth word that is related to the three stimulus words. Examples of items similar to those found on the RAT are shown in Figure 9.23.

How Well Do Tests Predict Creative Productivity?

In general, studies indicate that creativity tests are mediocre predictors of creative achievement in the real world (Hocevar & Bachelor, 1989; Plucker & Renzulli, 1999). Why? One reason is that these tests measure creativity in the abstract, as a *general trait*. However, the accumulation of evidence suggests that *creativity is specific to particular domains* (Amabile, 1990, 1996; Baer, 1994). Despite some rare exceptions, creative people usually excel in a single field, in which they typically have considerable training and expertise (Policastro & Gardner, 1999). A remarkably innovative physicist might have no potential to be a creative poet or an inventive advertising executive. Measuring this person's creativity outside of physics may be meaningless. Thus, creativity tests may have limited value because they measure creativity out of context.

Why Is Creative Achievement So Difficult to Predict?

Even if better tests of creativity were devised, predicting creative achievement would probably still prove difficult. Why? Because creative achievement depends on many factors besides creativity (Cropley, 2000). Creative productivity over the course of an individual's career will depend on his or her motivation, personality, and intelligence, as well as situational factors, including training, mentoring, and good fortune (Amabile, 1983; Feldman, 1999).

Motivational factors may be particularly important. People who make creative breakthroughs tend to have a single-minded, "workaholic," commitment to their endeavors and show great perseverance in the face of obstacles and setbacks (Simonton, 1999). Although their ideas are often attacked or dismissed, they do not give up easily. To underscore this point, Sternberg (2000, 2001) asserts that creativity appears to be in large part a *decision*. By this he means that highly creative people often have to make a choice to defy conventional thinking.

Correlates of Creativity

What are creative people like? Are they brighter, or more open minded, or less well adjusted than average? A great deal of research has been conducted on the correlates of creativity.

Is There a Creative Personality?

Creative people exhibit the full range of personality traits, but investigators have found modest correlations between certain personality characteristics and creativity (Ochse, 1990). Based on a meta-analysis of over 80 studies, Feist (1998) concludes that highly creative people "are more autonomous, introverted, open to new experiences, norm-doubting, self-confident, self-accepting, driven, ambitious, dominant, hostile, and impulsive" (p. 299). At the core of this set of personality characteristics are the related traits of independence and nonconformity. Creative people tend to think for themselves and are less easily influenced by the opinions of others than the average person is. Sternberg and Lubart (1992) also suggest that creative people are willing to grow and change and willing to take risks.

Are Creativity and Intelligence Related?

Are creative people exceptionally smart? Conceptually, creativity and intelligence represent different types of mental ability. Thus, it's not surprising that correlations between measures of creativity and measures of intelligence are generally weak (Stern-

Figure 9.23

Remote associates as an index of creativity. One groundbreaking creativity test is the Remote Associates Test (RAT) developed by Sarnoff and Martha Mednick (1967). The items shown here are similar to those on the RAT. See whether you can identify the remote associations between the three stimulus words by coming up with a fourth word that is related to all three. The answers can be found in Figure 9.24.

SOURCE: Matlin, M. W. (1994). *Cognition* (3rd Ed.). Fort Worth, TX: Harcourt Brace. Reprinted by permission of the author.

Instructions: For each set of three words, try to think of a fourth word that is related to all three words. For example, the words ROUGH, RESISTANCE, and BEER suggest the word DRAFT because of the phrases ROUGH DRAFT, DRAFT RESISTANCE, and DRAFT BEER.

1.	CHARMING	STUDENT	VALIANT
2.	FOOD	CATCHER	HOT
3.	HEARTED	FEET	BITTER
4.	DARK	SHOT	SUN
5.	CANADIAN	GOLF	SANDWICH
6.	TUG	GRAVY	SHOW
7.	ATTORNEY	SELF	SPENDING
8.	MAGIC	PITCH	POWER
9.	ARM	COAL	PEACH
10.	TYPE	GHOST	STORY

berg & O'Hara, 1999). Creativity and intelligence are not entirely unrelated, however, as creative achievements in most fields require a minimum level of intelligence. Hence, most highly creative people are probably well above average in intelligence (Simonton, 1999).

Is There a Connection Between Creativity and Mental Illness?

There may be a connection between truly exceptional creativity and mental illness. The list of creative geniuses who suffered from psychological disorders is endless (Prentky, 1989). Kafka, Hemingway, Rembrandt, Van Gogh, Chopin, Tchaikovsky, Descartes, and Newton are but a few examples (see Figure 9.25). Of course, a statistical association cannot be demonstrated by citing a handful of examples.

In this case, however, some statistical data are available. And these data *do* suggest a correlation between creative genius and maladjustment—in particular, mood disorders such as depression. When Andreasen (1987) studied 30 accomplished writers who had been invited as visiting faculty to the prestigious Iowa Writers Workshop, she found that 80% of her sample had suffered a mood disorder at some point in their lives. In a similar study of 59 female writers from another writers' conference, Ludwig (1994) found that 56% had experienced depression. These figures are far above the base rate (roughly 15%) for mood disorders in the general population. Other studies have also found an association between creativity and mood disorders, as well as other kinds of psychological disorders (Frantom & Sherman, 1999; Jamison, 1988; Ludwig, 1998; Post, 1996;

Schildkraut, Hirshfeld, & Murphy, 1994). Perhaps the most ambitious examination of the issue has been Arnold Ludwig's (1995) analyses of the biographies of 1004 people who achieved eminence in 18 fields. He found greatly elevated rates of depression and other disorders among eminent writers, artists, and composers.

Thus, accumulating empirical data tentatively suggest that there may be a correlation between major creative achievement and vulnerability to mood disorders. According to Andreasen (1996), creativity and maladjustment probably are *not* causally related. Instead, she speculates that certain cognitive styles may both foster creativity and predispose people to psychological disorders. Another, more mundane possibility is that creative individuals' elevated pathology may simply reflect all the difficulty and frustration they experience as they struggle to get their ideas or works accepted in artistic fields that enjoy relatively little public support (Csikszentmihalyi, 1994, 1999).

REVIEW OF KEY POINTS

- Creativity involves the generation of original, novel, and useful ideas. Creativity does not usually involve sudden insight and it does not depend on unconscious thought processes. Divergent thinking contributes to creativity but does not represent its essence.

- Creativity tests are mediocre predictors of creative productivity in the real world. One problem is that creativity is specific to particular domains of expertise. Another problem is that creative achievement depends on a host of factors besides one's creativity.

- Creative people are more likely than others to exhibit certain personality traits, but the correlations between creativity and personality are weak. The association between creativity and intelligence is also modest, although creativity probably requires above-average intelligence. Recent evidence suggests that creative geniuses may exhibit heightened vulnerability to mood disorders.

Figure 9.24

Answers to the remote associates items.

Source: Matlin, M. W. (1994). *Cognition* (3rd Ed.). Fort Worth, TX: Harcourt Brace. Reprinted by permission of the author.

10. WRITER	5. CLUB
9. PIT	4. GLASSES
8. BLACK	3. COLD
7. DEFENSE	2. DOG
6. BOAT	1. PRINCE

Figure 9.25

Examples of people who achieved creative eminence and suffered from psychological disorders.

As these brief lists show, it is easy to compile rosters of great artists, scientists, composers, and writers who struggled with mental illness. However, while interesting, anecdotal evidence such as this cannot demonstrate that there is an association between creative eminence and mental disorder. [Based on information from Prentky (1980) and Rothenberg (1990)]

Artists	Scientists	Composers	Writers
Bosch	Copernicus	Beethoven	Blake
Durer	Descartes	Berlioz	Coleridge
Goya	Kepler	Chopin	Dostoyevsky
Kandinsky	Linnaeus	Handel	Hemingway
Raphael	Mendel	Saint-Saens	Kafka
Rembrandt	Newton	Schubert	Poe
Van Gogh	Pascal	Tchaikovsky	Plath

Rembrandt
Rembrandt, Harmensz, van Rijn, *Self-Portrait with Beard*. Museu de Arte, Sao Paulo, Brazil. Giraudon/Art Resource, NY.

Chopin
Delacroix, Eugene, *Portrait of Chopin*, Louvre, Paris: Giraudon/Art Resource, NY.

Copernicus
Pomerian, 16th cent. *Portrait of Nicolas Copernicus*. Museum, Torun, Poland. Erich Lessing/Art Resource, NY.

The Intelligence Debate, Appeals to Ignorance, and Reification

A *fallacy* is a mistake or error in the process of reasoning. Cognitive scientists who study how people think have developed long lists of common errors that people make in their reasoning processes. One of these fallacies has a curious name, which is the *appeal to ignorance*. It involves misusing the general lack of knowledge or information on an issue (a lack of knowledge is a kind of ignorance) to support an argument. This fallacy often surfaces in the debate about the relative influence of heredity and environment on intelligence. Before we tackle the more difficult issue of how this fallacy shows up in the debate about intelligence, let's start with a simpler example.

Appeal to Ignorance

Do ghosts exist? This is probably not the kind of question you expected to find in your psychology textbook, but it can clarify the appeal to ignorance. Those who assert that ghosts *do* exist will often support their conclusion by arguing that no one can prove that ghosts do *not* exist; therefore ghosts must exist. The lack of evidence or inability to show that ghosts do not exist is used to conclude the opposite. Conversely, those who assert that ghosts *do not* exist often rely on the same logic. They argue that no one can prove that ghosts exist; therefore, they must not exist. Can you see what is wrong with these appeals to ignorance? The lack of information on an issue cannot be used to support any conclusion—other than the conclusion that we are too ignorant to draw a conclusion.

One interesting aspect of the appeal to ignorance is that the same appeal can be used to support two conclusions that are diametrically opposed to each other. This paradox is a telltale clue that appeals to ignorance involve flawed reasoning. It is easy to see what is wrong with appeals to ignorance when the opposite arguments (ghosts exist—ghosts do not exist) are presented together and the lack of evidence on the issue under discussion is obvious. However, when the same fallacy surfaces in more complex debates and the appeal to ignorance is not as blatant, the strategy can be more difficult to recognize. Let's look at how the appeal to ignorance has been used in the debate about intelligence.

As you saw in the main body of the chapter, the debate about the relative contributions of nature and nurture to intelligence is one of psychology's longest-running controversies. This complex and multifaceted debate is exceptionally bitter and acrimonious because it has far-reaching sociopolitical repercussions. In this debate, one argument that has frequently been made is that we have little or no evidence that intelligence can be increased by environmental (educational) interventions; therefore, intelligence must be mostly inherited. In other words, the argument runs: No one has demonstrated that intelligence is largely shaped by environment, so it must be largely inherited. This argument was part of Jensen's (1969) landmark treatise that greatly intensified the debate about intelligence, and it was one of the arguments made by Herrnstein and Murray (1994)

in their controversial book, *The Bell Curve*. What the argument refers to is the evidence that educational enrichment programs such as Head Start, which have been designed to enhance the intellectual development of underprivileged children, generally have not produced substantial, long-term gains in IQ (Bentler & Woodward, 1978; Neisser et al., 1996). These findings may have some important implications for government policy in the educational arena, but the way in which they have been applied to the nature-nurture debate regarding intelligence has resulted in an appeal to ignorance. In its simplest form, the absence of evidence showing that environmental changes can increase intelligence is used to support the conclusion that intelligence is mostly determined by genetic inheritance. But the absence of evidence (ignorance) cannot be used to argue for or against a position.

By the way, if you have assimilated some of the critical thinking skills discussed in earlier chapters, you may be thinking, "Wait a minute. Aren't there alternative explanations for the failure of educational enrichment programs to increase IQ scores?" Yes, one could argue that the programs failed to yield the expected increments in IQ scores

For the most part, educational enrichment programs for underprivileged children, such as Head Start, have not produced durable increases in participants' IQ scores. However, as the text explains, this finding does not provide logically sound support for the notion that intelligence is largely inherited.

because they were poorly planned, poorly executed, too brief, or underfunded (Ramey, 1999; Zigler & Styfco, 1994). The inability of the enrichment programs to produce enduring increases in IQ does not necessarily imply that intelligence is unchangeable because it is largely a product of heredity.

You may also be wondering, "Aren't there contradictory data?" Once again, the answer is yes. Some lesser-known educational enrichment programs attempted with smaller groups of children *have* yielded durable gains in IQ scores or other measures of academic achievement (Barnett, 1995; Ramey, Ramey, & Lanzi, 2001; Reynolds et al., 2001). Moreover, completely different approaches to gauging the impact of environmental enrichment—such as studies of children adopted from underprivileged homes into middle-class homes—have demonstrated that an improved environment can lead to meaningful increases in IQ (Scarr & Weinberg, 1983).

But we're supposed to be discussing appeals to ignorance, and there was another notable example of this fallacy in the chapter. Can you identify where this slippery logic was used? It surfaced in the discussion of the causes of mental retardation. As you may recall, roughly 25% of the time diagnosticians can pinpoint a biological cause for retardation. The remaining 75% of the cases are of unknown origin, but they are typically assumed to be due to environmental factors. In other words, the reasoning goes, *we don't have any evidence that these cases are due to biological anomalies, so they must be environmental in origin.* This is an appeal to ignorance, and the assertion that most cases of retardation must be due to environmental factors is open to some questioning.

Reification

The dialogue on intelligence has also been marred by the tendency to engage in reification. **Reification occurs when a hypothetical, abstract concept is given a name and then treated as though it were a concrete, tangible object.** Some hypothetical constructs just become so familiar and so taken for granted that we begin to think

about them as if they were real. People often fall into this trap with the Freudian personality concepts of id, ego, and superego (see Chapter 12). They begin to think of the *ego,* for instance, as a genuine entity that can be strengthened or controlled, when the ego is really nothing more than a hypothetical abstraction. The concept of intelligence has also been reified in many quarters. Like the ego, intelligence is nothing more than a useful abstraction—a hypothetical construct that is estimated, rather arbitrarily, by a collection of paper-and-pencil measures called IQ tests. Yet people routinely act as if intelligence is a tangible commodity, fighting vitriolic battles over whether it can be measured precisely, whether it can be changed, and whether it can ensure job success. This reification clearly contributes to the tendency for people to attribute excessive importance to the concept of intelligence. It would be wise to remember that intelligence is no more real than the concept of "environment," or "cyberspace," or "the American dream."

Reification has also occurred in the debate about the *degree* to which intelligence is inherited. Arguments about the heritability coefficient for intelligence often imply that there is a single, true number lurking somewhere "out there" waiting to be discovered. In reality, heritability is a hypothetical construct that can be legitimately estimated in several ways that can lead to somewhat different results. Moreover, heritability ratios will vary from one popula-

Reification occurs when we think of hypothetical constructs as if they were real. Like intelligence, the concept of cyberspace has been subject to reification. The fact that cyberspace is merely an abstraction becomes readily apparent when artists are asked to "draw" cyberspace for conference posters or book covers.

tion to the next, depending on the amount of genetic variability and the extent of environmental variability in the populations. No exactly accurate number that corresponds to "true heritability" awaits discovery. Thus, it is important to understand that hypothetical constructs have great heuristic value in the study of complex phenomena such as human thought and behavior, but they do not actually exist in the world—at least not in the same way that a table or a person exists.

Table 9.4 Critical Thinking Skills Discussed in This Application	
Skill	**Description**
Recognizing and avoiding appeals to ignorance	The critical thinker understands that the lack of information on an issue cannot be used to support an argument.
Recognizing and avoiding reification	The critical thinker is vigilant about the tendency to treat hypothetical constructs as if they were concrete things.
Looking for alternative explanations for findings and events	In evaluating explanations, the critical thinker explores whether there are other explanations that could also account for the findings or events under scrutiny.
Looking for contradictory evidence	In evaluating the evidence presented on an issue, the critical thinker attempts to look for contradictory evidence that may have been left out of the debate.

RECAP

Key Ideas

Key Concepts in Psychological Testing

● Psychological tests are standardized measures of behavior—usually mental abilities or aspects of personality. Test scores are interpreted by consulting test norms to find out what represents a high or low score. Psychological tests should produce consistent results, a quality called reliability.

● Validity refers to the degree to which there is evidence that a test measures what it was designed to measure. Content validity is crucial on classroom tests. Criterion-related validity is critical when tests are used to predict performance. Construct validity is critical when a test is designed to measure a hypothetical construct.

The Evolution of Intelligence Testing

● The first crude efforts to devise intelligence tests were made by Sir Francis Galton, who wanted to show that intelligence is inherited. Modern intelligence testing began with the work of Alfred Binet, who devised a scale to measure a child's mental age.

● Lewis Terman revised the original Binet scale to produce the Stanford-Binet in 1916. It introduced the intelligence quotient and became the standard of comparison for subsequent tests. David Wechsler devised an improved measure of intelligence for adults and a new scoring system based on the normal distribution.

Basic Questions About Intelligence Testing

● In the modern scoring system, deviation IQ scores indicate where people fall in the normal distribution of intelligence for their age group. Although they are intended to measure potential for learning, IQ tests inevitably assess a blend of potential and knowledge.

● IQ tests are exceptionally reliable. They are reasonably valid measures of academic intelligence, but they do not tap social or practical intelligence.

● IQ scores are correlated with occupational attainment, but their ability to predict performance within occupations is the subject of debate. Intelligence testing is largely a Western enterprise; IQ tests are not widely used in most non-Western cultures.

Extremes of Intelligence

● IQ scores below 70–75 are usually diagnostic of mental retardation, but these diagnoses should not be based solely on test results. Four levels of retardation have been distinguished. Most of the retarded population falls in the mildly retarded category. Although many biological conditions can cause retardation, biological causes can be pinpointed in only about 25% of cases.

● Children who obtain IQ scores above 130 may be viewed as gifted, but cutoffs for accelerated programs vary. Research by Terman showed that gifted children tend to be socially mature and well adjusted, although Winner has raised concerns about the adjustment of profoundly gifted individuals. Extraordinary achievement seems to depend on intensive training and hard work, but innate talent may also contribute.

Heredity and Environment as Determinants of Intelligence

● Twin studies show that identical twins are more similar in IQ than fraternal twins, suggesting that intelligence is inherited, at least in part. Estimates of the heritability of intelligence mostly range from 50% to 70%, but heritability ratios have certain limitations.

● Many lines of evidence indicate that environment is also an important determinant of intelligence. Of particular interest is the recent discovery of generational increases in measured IQ. The concept of reaction range posits that heredity places limits on one's intellectual potential while the environment determines where one falls within these limits.

● Genetic explanations for cultural differences in IQ have been challenged on a variety of grounds. Even if the heritability of IQ is great, group differences in average intelligence may not be due to heredity. Moreover, ethnicity varies with social class, so socioeconomic disadvantage may account for low IQ scores among minority students. Stereotype vulnerability and cultural bias on IQ tests may also contribute to ethnic differences in average IQ.

New Directions in the Assessment and Study of Intelligence

● In contemporary testing, there is a greater emphasis on the measurement of specific mental abilities and less emphasis on tapping Spearman's *g*. The distinction between fluid and crystallized intelligence is the basis for the most recent revision of the Stanford-Binet IQ test.

● Biological indexes of intelligence are being explored; however, they seem to have little practical utility, although the inspection time measure appears to have potential. Research on intelligence increasingly takes a cognitive perspective, which emphasizes the need to understand how people use their intelligence. Many modern theorists, such as Robert Sternberg and Howard Gardner, argue that the concept of intelligence should be expanded to encompass a greater variety of skills.

Putting It in Perspective

● Three of our integrative themes stood out in the chapter. Our discussions of intelligence showed how heredity and environment interact to shape behavior, how psychology evolves in a sociohistorical context, and how one has to consider cultural contexts to fully understand behavior.

Personal Application ●
Understanding Creativity

● Creativity involves the generation of original, novel, and useful ideas. Creativity does not usually involve sudden insight, and it consists of more than divergent thinking. Creativity tests are mediocre predictors of creative productivity in the real world.

● Creativity is only weakly related to intelligence. The correlations are modest, but some personality traits are associated with creativity. Recent evidence suggests that creative geniuses may exhibit heightened vulnerability to psychological disorders, especially mood disorders.

Critical Thinking Application ●
The Intelligence Debate, Appeals to Ignorance, and Reification

● The appeal to ignorance involves misusing the general lack of knowledge or information on an issue to support an argument. This fallacy has surfaced in the debate about intelligence, wherein it has been argued that because we have little or no evidence that intelligence can be increased by environmental interventions, intelligence must be mostly inherited.

● Reification occurs when a hypothetical construct is treated as though it were a tangible object. The concepts of intelligence and heritability have both been subject to reification.

Key Terms

Achievement tests
Aptitude tests
Construct validity
Content validity
Convergent thinking
Correlation coefficient
Creativity
Criterion-related
  validity
Crystallized
  intelligence
Deviation IQ scores
Divergent thinking
Emotional intelligence
Factor analysis
Fluid intelligence
Heritability ratio
Intelligence quotient
  (IQ)
Intelligence tests
Mental age
Mental retardation
Normal distribution
Percentile score
Personality tests
Psychological test
Reaction range
Reification
Reliability
Standardization
Test norms
Validity

Key People

Alfred Binet
Sir Francis Galton
Howard Gardner
Arthur Jensen
Sandra Scarr
Claude Steele
Robert Sternberg
Lewis Terman
David Wechsler

1. Which of the following does not belong with the others?
   - A. aptitude tests
   - B. personality tests
   - C. intelligence tests
   - D. achievement tests

2. If you score at the 75th percentile on a standardized test, this means that:
   - A. 75% of those who took the test scored better than you did.
   - B. 25% of those who took the test scored less than you did.
   - C. 75% of those who took the test scored the same or less than you did.
   - D. you answered 75% of the questions correctly.

3. If a test has good test-retest reliability:
   - A. there is a strong correlation between items on the test.
   - B. it accurately measures what it says it measures.
   - C. it can be used to predict future performance.
   - D. the test yields similar scores if taken at two different times.

4. Which of the following is a true statement regarding Francis Galton?
   - A. He took the position that intelligence is largely determined by heredity.
   - B. He advocated the development of special programs to tap the intellectual potential of the culturally disadvantaged.
   - C. He developed tests that identified those children who were unable to profit from a normal education.
   - D. He took the position that intelligence is more a matter of environment than heredity.

5. On most modern IQ tests, a score of 115 would be:
   - A. about normal.
   - B. about 15% higher than the average of one's agemates.
   - C. an indication of genius.
   - D. one standard deviation above the mean.

6. IQ tests have proven to be good predictors of:
   - A. social intelligence.
   - B. practical problem-solving intelligence.
   - C. school performance.
   - D. all of the above.

7. Mr. and Mrs. Proudparent are beaming because their son, little Newton, has been selected for a gifted children program at school. They think Newton is a genius. What sort of advice do they need to hear?
   - A. Youngsters with a 130–140 IQ tend to be very maladjusted.
   - B. Most gifted children do not go on to make genius-level, major contributions to society that earn them eminence.
   - C. They should prepare to be famous, based on their parentage of Newton.
   - D. They should be warned that gifted children often have deficits in fluid intelligence.

8. Which of the following is a true statement about mental retardation?
   - A. Most retarded people are unable to live normal lives because of their mental deficiencies.
   - B. With special tutoring, a mentally retarded person can attain average intelligence.
   - C. The majority of mentally retarded people fall in the mildly retarded category.
   - D. Diagnoses of mental retardation should be based exclusively on IQ scores.

9. Most school districts consider children who _____ to be gifted.
   - A. have IQ scores above 115
   - B. score in the upper 2%-3% of the IQ distribution
   - C. have parents in professional careers
   - D. demonstrate high levels of leadership and creativity

10. In which of the following cases would you expect to find the greatest similarity in IQ?
    - A. between fraternal twins
    - B. between identical twins
    - C. between nontwin siblings
    - D. between parent and child

11. Evidence indicating that upbringing affects one's mental ability is provided by which of the following findings?
    - A. that identical twins are more similar in IQ than fraternal twins
    - B. that there is more than a chance similarity between adopted children and their biological parents
    - C. that siblings reared together are more similar in IQ than siblings reared apart
    - D. that identical twins reared apart are more similar in IQ than siblings reared together

12. Which of the following is a likely consequence of stereotype vulnerability for members of minority groups?
    - A. Academic motivation declines.
    - B. Academic performance often suffers.
    - C. Standardized tests may be especially anxiety arousing.
    - D. All of the above are likely consequences.

13. Which of the following is a current trend in the assessment of intelligence?
    - A. using biological indexes of intelligence in the schools
    - B. narrowing the concept of intelligence
    - C. greater emphasis on measuring g rather than specific abilities
    - D. greater emphasis on measuring specific abilities rather than g

14. When you try to narrow down a list of alternatives to arrive at a single correct answer, you engage in:
    - A. convergent thinking.
    - B. divergent thinking.
    - C. creativity.
    - D. insight.

15. Nora has a blind date with Nick who, she's been told, is considered a true genius by the faculty in the art department. Now she's having second thoughts, because she's always heard that geniuses are a little off their rocker. Does she have reason to be concerned?
    - A. Yes. It's been well documented that the stress of creative achievement often leads to schizophrenic symptoms.
    - B. No. Extensive research on creativity and psychological disorders shows no evidence for any connection.
    - C. Perhaps. There is evidence of a correlation between major creative achievement and vulnerability to mood disorders.
    - D. Of course not. The stereotype of the genius who's mentally ill is purely a product of the jealousy of untalented people.

Answers

1	B p. 342	6	C p. 352	11	C pp. 358–359
2	C p. 343	7	B p. 356	12	D pp. 364–365
3	D p. 344	8	C pp. 354–355	13	D pp. 366–367
4	A p. 347	9	B p. 355	14	A p. 373
5	D pp. 349–351	10	B p. 358	15	C p. 375

 ON THE WEB

For additional resources on the topics covered in this chapter, visit the *Psychology: Themes and Variations* Web site, where you will find practice quizzes, tutorials, Web links, simulations, critical thinking activities, flash cards, interactive exercises, and suggested readings available through INFOTRAC.

 http://psychology.wadsworth.com/weiten_themes6e/

CHAPTER 10

© Gary Buss/Taxi-Getty Images

Motivation and Emotion

I t was a bright afternoon in May 1996, and 41-year-old Jon Krakauer was on top of the world—literally. Krakauer had just fulfilled a boyhood dream by climbing Mount Everest, the tallest peak on Earth. Clearing the ice from his oxygen mask, he looked down on a sweeping vista of ice, snow, and majestic mountains. His triumph should have brought him intense joy, but he felt strangely detached. "I'd been fantasizing about this moment, and the release of emotion that would accompany it, for many years," he wrote later. "But now that I was finally here, standing on the summit of Mount Everest, I just couldn't summon the energy to care" (Krakauer, 1998, p. 6).

Why were Krakauer's emotions so subdued? A major reason was that he was physically spent. Climbing Mount Everest is an incredibly grueling experience. At just over 29,000 feet, the mountain's peak is at the altitude flown by jumbo jets. Because such high altitudes wreak havoc on the human body, Krakauer and his fellow climbers couldn't even approach the summit until they had spent six weeks acclimating at Base Camp, 17,600 feet above sea level. Even getting that far would test the limits of most people's endurance. At Base Camp, Krakauer found that ordinary bodily functions became painfully difficult. On most nights, he awoke three or four times, gasping for breath and feeling like he was suffocating. His appetite vanished, and his oxygen-starved digestive system failed to metabolize food normally. "My body began consuming itself for sustenance. My arms and legs gradually began to wither to sticklike proportions" (Krakauer, 1998, p. 87).

At this point you may be wondering why anyone would willingly undergo such extreme discomfort, but Base Camp was just the beginning. From Base Camp it is another two vertical miles through the aptly named Death Zone to the summit. Even for a fully acclimated climber, the final leg of the ascent is excruciating. By the time Krakauer reached the summit, every step was labored, every gasping breath hurt. He hadn't slept in 57 hours, and he had two separated ribs from weeks of violent coughing. He was

bitterly cold and utterly exhausted. Instead of elation, he felt only apprehension. Even though his oxygen-starved brain was barely functioning, he understood that getting down from the summit would be fully as dangerous as getting up.

Tragically, events proved just how dangerous an assault on Everest can be. During Krakauer's descent, a sudden, howling storm hit the mountain. Winds exceeding 100 miles per hour whipped the snow into a blinding white blur and sent the temperature plummeting. While Krakauer barely escaped with his life, twelve men and women died on the mountain, including several in Krakauer's own party. Some of them perished needlessly because they had fallen victim to "summit fever." Once they got close to the top, they refused to turn back despite extreme exhaustion and the obvious threat posed by the storm.

The saga of Jon Krakauer and the other climbers is packed with motivation riddles. Why would people push on toward a goal even at the risk of their lives? Why would they choose to endure such a punishing and hazardous ordeal in the first place? In the case of Mount Everest, perhaps the most obvious motive is simply the satisfaction of conquering the world's tallest peak. When British climber George Leigh Mallory was asked why he wanted to climb Everest in the 1920s, his famous reply was, "Because it is there." Some people seem to have an intense desire to take on the toughest challenges imaginable, to achieve something incredibly difficult. Yet—as is usually the case with human behavior—things are not quite so simple. Krakauer observed that a wide variety of motives drove the climbers and professional expedition leaders he met on Everest, including desires for "minor celebrity, career advancement, ego massage, ordinary bragging rights, filthy lucre," and even a quest for "a state of grace" (Krakauer, 1998, p. 177).

Krakauer's story is also filled with strong emotions. He anticipated that he would experience a transcendent emotional high when he reached the summit of Mount Everest. As it turned out, his triumph was accompanied more by anxiety than by ecstasy. And

Jon Krakauer (the third person) and other climbers are seen here during their ascent of Mount Everest at an elevation of about 28,200 feet.

though the harrowing events that followed left him emotionally numb at first, he was soon flooded with intense feelings of despair, grief, and guilt over the deaths of his companions. His tale illustrates the intimate connection between motivation and emotion—the topics we'll examine in this chapter.

Motivational Theories and Concepts

PREVIEW QUESTIONS
- What is the distinction between drive and incentive theories of motivation?
- How do evolutionary theories explain various motives?
- What are the two major categories of human motives?

Motives are the needs, wants, interests, and desires that propel people in certain directions. In short, *motivation* involves goal-directed behavior. There are a number of theoretical approaches to motivation. Let's look at some of these theories and the concepts they employ.

Drive Theories

Many theories view motivational forces in terms of *drives*. The drive concept appears in a diverse array of theories that otherwise have little in common, such as psychoanalytic (Freud, 1915) and behaviorist formulations (Hull, 1943). This approach to understanding motivation was explored most fully by Clark Hull in the 1940s and 1950s.

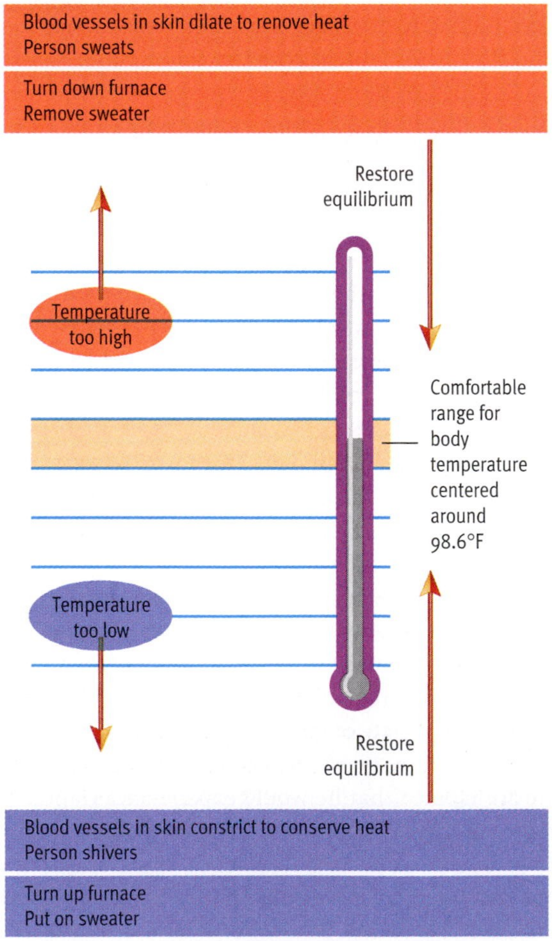

Hull's concept of drive was derived from Walter Cannon's (1932) observation that organisms seek to maintain *homeostasis*, a state of physiological equilibrium or stability. The body maintains homeostasis in various ways. For example, human body temperature normally fluctuates around 98.6 degrees Fahrenheit (see Figure 10.1). If your body temperature rises or drops noticeably, automatic responses occur: If your temperature goes up, you'll perspire; if your temperature goes down, you'll shiver. These reactions are designed to move your temperature back toward 98.6 degrees. Thus, your body reacts to many disturbances in physiological stability by trying to restore equilibrium.

Drive theories apply the concept of homeostasis to behavior. A *drive* is an internal state of tension that motivates an organism to engage in activities that should reduce this tension. These unpleasant states of tension are viewed as disruptions of the preferred equilibrium. According to drive theories, when individuals experience a drive, they're motivated to pursue actions that will lead to *drive reduction*. For example, the hunger motive has usually been conceptualized as a drive system. If you go without food for a while, you begin to experience some discomfort. This internal tension (the drive) motivates you to obtain food. Eating reduces the drive and restores physiological equilibrium.

Drive theories have been very influential, and the drive concept continues to be widely used in modern psychology. *However, drive theories cannot explain all motivation.* Homeostasis appears irrelevant to some human motives, such as a "thirst for knowledge." Also, motivation may exist without drive arousal. This point is easy to illustrate. Think of all the times that you've eaten when you weren't the least bit hungry. You're driving or walking home from class, amply filled by a solid lunch, when an ice cream parlor beckons seductively. You stop in and have a couple of scoops of your favorite flavor. Not only are you motivated to eat in the absence of internal tension, you may cause yourself some internal tension—from overeating. Because drive theories assume that people always try to reduce internal tension, they can't explain this behavior very well. Incentive theories,

Figure 10.1

Temperature regulation as an example of homeostasis.
The regulation of body temperature provides a simple example of how organisms often seek to maintain homeostasis, or a state of physiological equilibrium. When your temperature moves out of an acceptable range, automatic bodily reactions (such as sweating or shivering) occur that help restore equilibrium. Of course, these automatic reactions may not be sufficient by themselves, so you may have to take other actions (such as turning a furnace up or down) to bring your body temperature back into its comfort zone.

Blood vessels in skin dilate to remove heat
Person sweats

Turn down furnace
Remove sweater

Restore equilibrium

Temperature too high

Comfortable range for body temperature centered around 98.6°F

Temperature too low

Restore equilibrium

Blood vessels in skin constrict to conserve heat
Person shivers

Turn up furnace
Put on sweater

which represent a different approach to motivation, can account for this behavior more readily.

Incentive Theories

Incentive theories propose that external stimuli regulate motivational states (Bolles, 1975; McClelland, 1975; Skinner, 1953). **An *incentive* is an external goal that has the capacity to motivate behavior.** Ice cream, a juicy steak, a monetary prize, approval from friends, an A on an exam, and a promotion at work are all incentives. Some of these incentives may reduce drives, but others may not.

Drive and incentive models of motivation are often contrasted as *push versus pull* theories. Drive theories emphasize how *internal* states of tension *push* people in certain directions. Incentive theories emphasize how *external* stimuli *pull* people in certain directions. According to drive theories, the source of motivation lies *within* the organism. According to incentive theories, the source of motivation lies *outside* the organism, in the environment. This means that incentive models don't operate according to the principle of homeostasis, which hinges on internal changes in the organism. Thus, in comparison to drive theories, incentive theories emphasize environmental factors and downplay the biological bases of human motivation.

As you're painfully aware, people can't always obtain the goals they desire, such as good grades or choice promotions. *Expectancy-value models* of motivation are incentive theories that take this reality into account (Atkinson & Birch, 1978). According to expectancy-value models, one's motivation to pursue a particular course of action will depend on two factors: (1) *expectancy* about one's chances of attaining the incentive and (2) the *value* of the desired incentive. Thus, your motivation to pursue a promotion at work will depend on your estimate of the likelihood that you can snare the promotion (expectancy) and on how appealing the promotion is to you (value).

Evolutionary Theories

Psychologists who take an evolutionary perspective assert that human motives and those of other species are the products of evolution, just as anatomical characteristics are. They argue that natural selection favors behaviors that maximize reproductive success—that is, passing on genes to the next generation. Thus, they explain motives such as affiliation, achievement, dominance, aggression, and sex drive in terms of their adaptive value. If dominance is a crucial motive for a species, they say, it's because dominance provides a reproductive or survival advantage.

Evolutionary analyses of motivation are based on the premise that motives can best be understood in terms of the adaptive problems they have solved over the course of human history. For example, the need for dominance is thought to be greater in men than women because it could facilitate males' reproductive success in a variety of ways including (1) females may prefer mating with dominant males, (2) dominant males may poach females from subordinate males, (3) dominant males may intimidate male rivals in competition for sexual access, and (4) dominant males may acquire more material resources, which may increase mating opportunities (Buss, 1999). Consider, also, the *affiliation motive,* or need for belongingness. As we will discuss later, the adaptive benefits of affiliation for our ancestors probably included help with offspring, collaboration in hunting or defense, opportunities for sexual interaction, and so forth (Baumeister & Leary, 1995). David Buss (1995) points out that it is not by accident that achievement, power (dominance), and intimacy are among the most heavily studied social motives, as the satisfaction of each of these motives is likely to affect one's reproductive success.

The Range and Diversity of Human Motives

Motivational theorists of all persuasions agree on one point: Humans display an enormous diversity of motives. Most theories (evolutionary theories being a notable exception) distinguish between *biological motives* that originate in bodily needs, such as hunger, and *social motives* that originate in social experiences, such as the need for achievement.

People have a limited number of biological needs. According to K. B. Madsen (1968, 1973), most theories identify 10 to 15 such needs, some of which are listed on the left side of Figure 10.2 on the next page. As you can see, most biological motives reflect needs that are essential to survival, such as the needs for food, water, and maintenance of body temperature within an acceptable range.

People all share the same biological motives, but their social motives vary depending on their experiences. For example, we all need to eat, but not everyone acquires a need for orderliness. Although people have a limited number of biological motives, they can acquire an unlimited number of social motives through learning and socialization. Some examples of social motives—from an influential list compiled

Examples of Biological Motives in Humans	Examples of Social Motives in Humans
Hunger motive Thirst motive Sex motive Temperature motive (need for appropriate body temperature) Excretory motive (need to eliminate bodily wastes) Sleep and rest motive Activity motive (need for optimal level of stimulation and arousal) Aggression motive	Achievement motive (need to excel) Affiliation motive (need for social bonds) Autonomy motive (need for independence) Nurturance motive (need to nourish and protect others) Dominance motive (need to influence or control others) Exhibition motive (need to make an impression on others) Order motive (need for orderliness, tidiness, organization) Play motive (need for fun, relaxation, amusement)

Figure 10.2

The diversity of human motives. People are motivated by a wide range of needs, which can be divided into two broad classes: biological motives and social motives. The list on the left (adapted from Madsen, 1973) shows some important biological motives in humans. The list on the right (adapted from Murray, 1938) provides examples of prominent social motives in humans. The distinction between biological and social motives is not absolute.

by Henry Murray (1938)—are shown on the right side of Figure 10.2. He theorized that most people have needs for achievement, autonomy, affiliation, dominance, exhibition, and order, among other things. Of course, the strength of these motives varies from person to person, depending on personal history.

Although the distinction between biological and social needs is not absolute, this dichotomy allows us to impose some organization on the diverse motives seen in human behavior. Given the range and diversity of human motives, we can examine only a handful in depth. To a large degree, our choices reflect the motives psychologists have studied the most. Specifically, we'll draw two examples each from the two broad classes of human needs, biological and social. We'll focus on hunger and sexual motivation to show how researchers have dissected biological needs. Then we'll examine affiliation and achievement to illustrate how psychologists have analyzed social motives.

The Motivation of Hunger and Eating

PREVIEW QUESTIONS
- Which brain centers appear to control the experience of hunger?
- How do fluctuations in blood glucose and hormones contribute to hunger?
- How is eating influenced by the availability of food, learned habits, and stress?
- How common and how dangerous is obesity?
- What have scientists learned about the causes of obesity?

Why do people eat? Because they're hungry. What makes them hungry? A lack of food. Any grade-school child can explain these basic facts. So hunger is a simple motivational system, right? Wrong! Hunger is deceptive. It only looks simple. Actually, it's a puzzling and complex motivational system. Despite extensive studies of hunger, scientists are still struggling to understand the factors that regulate eating behavior. Let's examine a few of these factors.

Biological Factors in the Regulation of Hunger  2e, 8a

You have probably had embarrassing occasions when your stomach growled loudly at an inopportune moment. Someone may have commented, "You must be starving!" Most people equate a rumbling stomach with hunger, and, in fact, the first scientific theories of hunger were based on this simple equation. In an elaborate 1912 study, Walter Cannon and A. L. Washburn verified what most people have noticed based on casual observation: There is an association between stomach contractions and the experience of hunger.

Based on this correlation, Cannon theorized that stomach contractions *cause* hunger. However, as we've seen before, correlation is no assurance of causation, and his theory was eventually discredited. Stomach contractions often accompany hunger, but they don't

cause it. How do we know? Because later research showed that people continue to experience hunger even after their stomachs have been removed out of medical necessity (Wangensteen & Carlson, 1931). If hunger can occur without a stomach, then stomach contractions can't be the cause of hunger. This realization led to more elaborate theories of hunger that focus on (1) the role of the brain, (2) blood sugar level, and (3) hormones.

Brain Regulation  2e, 8a

Research with laboratory animals eventually suggested that the experience of hunger is controlled in

The rat in front has had its ventromedial hypothalamus lesioned, resulting in a dramatic increase in weight.

the brain—specifically, in two centers located in the hypothalamus. As we have noted before, the *hypothalamus* is a tiny structure involved in the regulation of a variety of biological needs related to survival (see Figure 10.3). Investigators found that when they lesioned animals' *lateral hypothalamus (LH),* the animals showed little or no interest in eating, as if their hunger center had been destroyed (Anand & Brobeck, 1951). In contrast, when researchers lesioned animals' *ventromedial nucleus of the hypothalamus (VMH),* the animals ate excessively and gained weight rapidly, as if their ability to recognize satiety (fullness) had been destroyed (Brobeck, Tepperman, & Long, 1943). Given these results, investigators concluded that the LH and VMH were the brain's on-off switches for the control of hunger (Stellar, 1954). However, over the course of several decades, a host of empirical findings complicated this simple picture and undermined the dual-centers model of hunger (Valenstein, 1973; Winn, 1995). The current thinking is that the lateral and ventromedial areas of the hypothalamus are elements in the neural circuitry that regulates hunger but are not the key elements and not simple on-off centers. Today, scientists believe that another area of the hypothalamus—the *paraventricular nucleus (PVN)*—plays a larger role in the modulation of hunger (Woods et al., 2000) (see Figure 10.3).

Contemporary theories of hunger focus more on *neural circuits* that pass through the hypothalamus, rather than on *anatomical centers* in the brain. These circuits depend on a variety of neurotransmitters, with neuropeptide Y and serotonin playing particularly prominent roles (Halford & Blundell, 2000; Seeley & Schwartz, 1997). Accumulating evidence suggests that the hypothalamus contains a confluence of interacting systems that regulate eating by monitoring a diverse array of physiological processes. Let's look at some other physiological processes that appear to provide input to these systems.

Glucose and Digestive Regulation

Much of the food taken into the body is converted into *glucose,* which circulates in the blood. *Glucose is a simple sugar that is an important source of energy.* Manipulations that decrease blood glucose level can increase hunger. Manipulations that increase glucose level can make people feel satiated. Based on these findings, Jean Mayer (1955, 1968) proposed that hunger is regulated by the rise and fall of blood glucose levels. *Glucostatic theory* proposed that fluctuations in blood glucose level are monitored in the brain by *glucostats*—neurons sensitive to glucose in the surrounding fluid. Like the dual-centers theory, the glucostatic theory of hunger grad-

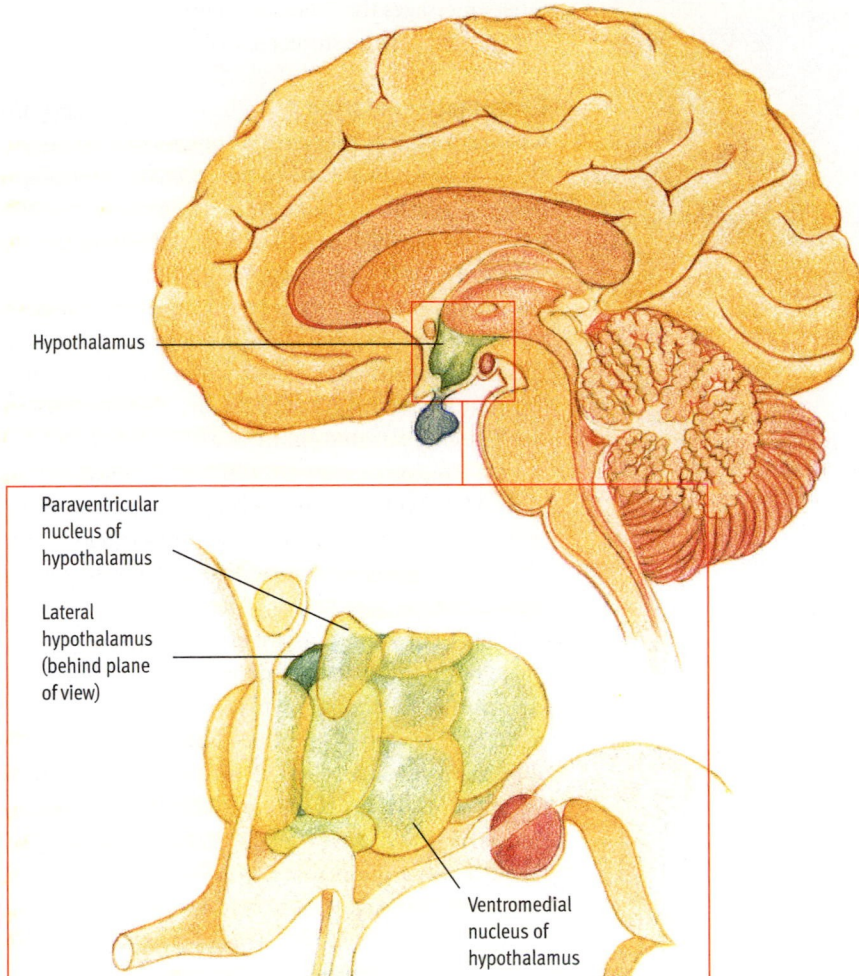

Hypothalamus

Paraventricular nucleus of hypothalamus

Lateral hypothalamus (behind plane of view)

Ventromedial nucleus of hypothalamus

Figure 10.3

The hypothalamus. This small structure at the base of the forebrain plays a role in regulating a variety of human biological needs, including hunger. The detailed blowup shows that the hypothalamus is made up of a variety of discrete areas. Scientists used to believe that the lateral and ventromedial areas were the brain's on-off centers for eating. However, more recent research suggests that the paraventricular nucleus may be more crucial to the regulation of hunger, and that it makes more sense to think in terms of neural circuits than anatomical centers.

ually ran into a host of complications, not the least of which was that glucose levels in the blood really don't fluctuate all that much or all that fast (LeMagnen, 1981). Nonetheless, some researchers continue to believe that glucostatic mechanisms *contribute* to the modulation of eating (Smith & Campfield, 1993).

The digestive system also includes other mechanisms that influence hunger. It turns out that Walter Cannon was not entirely wrong in hypothesizing that the stomach regulates hunger. After you have consumed food, cells in the stomach can send signals to the brain that inhibit further eating (Deutsch, 1990). For example, the vagus nerve carries information about the stretching of the stomach walls that indicates when the stomach is full. Other nerves carry

"People's metabolic machinery is constituted in such a way that the fatter they are, the fatter they are primed to become."

JUDITH RODIN

satiety messages that depend on how rich in nutrients the contents of the stomach are.

Hormonal Regulation

 8a

A variety of hormones circulating in the bloodstream also appear to contribute to the regulation of hunger. *Insulin* is a hormone secreted by the pancreas. It must be present for cells to extract glucose from the blood. Indeed, an inadequate supply of insulin is what causes diabetes. The secretion of insulin is associated with increased hunger. And, in landmark research that blurred the distinction between biological and environmental determinants of hunger, Judith Rodin (1985) demonstrated that the mere sight and smell of enticing food can stimulate the secretion of insulin. Moreover, insulin levels appear to be sensitive to fluctuations in the body's fat stores (Seeley et al., 1996). These findings suggest that insulin secretions play a role in the fluctuation of hunger.

Finally, the recent discovery of a previously undetected hormone, since christened *leptin,* has shed new light on the hormonal regulation of hunger (Halaas et al., 1995). Leptin is produced by fat cells throughout the body and released into the bloodstream. Higher levels of fat generate higher levels of leptin (Schwartz et al., 1996). Leptin circulates through the bloodstream and ultimately provides the hypothalamus with information about the body's fat stores (Campfield, 2002). When leptin levels are high, the propensity to feel hungry diminishes. Leptin apparently activates receptors in the brain that inhibit the release of neuropeptide Y, which leads to activity in the paraventricular nucleus of the hypothalamus, which inhibits eating (Stephens et al., 1995). Researchers are currently exploring whether leptin itself, or drugs that affect leptin levels might be helpful to people trying to lose weight (Heshka & Heymsfield, 2002).

If all this sounds confusing, it is, and I haven't even mentioned *all* the physiological processes involved in the regulation of hunger and eating. Frankly, researchers are still struggling to figure out exactly how all these processes work together, as hunger depends on complex interactions between neural circuits, neurotransmitter systems, digestive processes, and hormonal fluctuations.

Environmental Factors in the Regulation of Hunger

 8a

Hunger clearly is a biological need, but eating is not regulated by biological factors alone. Studies show that social and environmental factors govern eating to a considerable extent. Three key environmental factors are (1) the availability of food, (2) learned preferences and habits, and (3) stress.

Food Availability and Related Cues

 8a

Most of the research on the physiological regulation of hunger has been based on the assumption that hunger operates as a drive system in which homeostatic mechanisms are at work. However, some theorists emphasize the incentive value of food and argue that humans and other animals are often motivated to eat not by the need to compensate for energy deficits but by the anticipated pleasure of eating (Hetherington & Rolls, 1996; Ramsay et al., 1996). According to this perspective, the availability and palatability of food are the key factors regulating hunger. This view is bolstered by the observation made earlier that the presence of tasty food often leads people to eat even though they are already quite full from recently consumed food. Consistent with the incentive view, research shows that hunger is influenced by food availability and palatability (Pinel, Assanand, & Lehman, 2000; Schachter & Rodin, 1974).

Hunger can also be triggered by exposure to environmental cues that have been associated with eating. You have no doubt had your hunger aroused by television commercials for delicious-looking food or by seductive odors coming from the kitchen. Consistent with this observation, studies have shown that hunger can be increased by exposure to pictures, written descriptions, and video depictions of attractive foods (Herman, Ostovich, & Polivy, 1999; Marcelino et al., 2001; Oakes & Slotterback, 2000). Thus, it's clear that hunger and eating are governed in part by the availability of food and the presence of a variety of food-related cues.

According to incentive models of hunger, the availability and palatability of food are key factors regulating hunger. An abundance of diverse foods tends to lead to increased eating.

Learned Preferences and Habits **8a**

Are you fond of eating calves' brains? How about eels or snakes? Could I interest you in a grasshopper or some dog meat? Probably not, but these are delicacies in some regions of the world. Arctic Eskimos like to eat maggots! You probably prefer chicken, apples, eggs, lettuce, potato chips, pizza, cornflakes, or ice cream. These preferences are acquired through learning. People from different cultures display very different patterns of food consumption (Kittler & Sucher, 1998). If you doubt this fact, just visit a grocery store in an ethnic neighborhood (not your own, of course). As Paul Rozin (1996) points out, immigrant groups "seem to retain their ethnic identity through food long after they have become assimilated in most other ways" (p. 20).

Humans do have some innate taste preferences of a general sort. For example, a preference for sweet tastes is present at birth (Menella & Beauchamp, 1996), and humans' preference for high-fat foods appears to be at least partly genetic in origin (Schiffman et al., 1998). Evidence also suggests that an unlearned preference for salt emerges at around four months of age in humans (Birch & Fisher, 1996). Nonetheless, learning wields a great deal of influence over what people prefer to eat (Booth, 1994). Taste preferences are partly a function of learned associations formed through classical conditioning (Capaldi, 1996). For example, youngsters can be conditioned to prefer flavors paired with high caloric intake or other pleasant events. Of course, as we learned in Chapter 6, taste aversions can also be acquired through conditioning when foods are followed by nausea (Schafe & Bernstein, 1996).

Eating habits are also shaped by observational learning (see Chapter 6). To a large degree, food preferences are a matter of exposure (Rozin, 1990). People generally prefer familiar foods. But geographical, cultural, religious, and ethnic factors limit people's exposure to various foods. Young children are more likely to taste an unfamiliar food if an adult tries it first. Repeated exposures to a new food usually lead to increased liking. However, as many parents have learned the hard way, forcing a child to eat a specific food can backfire—coercion tends to have a negative effect on a youngster's preference for the mandated food (Birch & Fisher, 1996). Learned habits and social considerations also influence *when* and *how much* people eat. For example, a key determinant of when we eat is our memory of how much time has passed since we ate our last meal and what we consumed (Rozin et al., 1998). These expectations about how

The fact that culture influences food preferences is evident in these photos, in which you can see delicacies such as grilled bat (left) and crocodile soup (right).

© Michael Freeman/Aurora Photos

© Michael Freeman/Aurora Photos

often and how much we should eat are the product of years of learning.

Stress and Eating

When I have an exceptionally stressful day, I often head for the refrigerator, a grocery store, or a restaurant—usually in pursuit of something chocolate. My response is not particularly unusual. Studies have shown that stress leads to increased eating in a substantial portion of people (Greeno & Wing, 1994; Laitinen, Ek, & Sovio, 2002). Some studies suggest that stress-induced eating may be especially common among chronic dieters (Heatherton, Striepe, & Wittenberg, 1998). Some theorists believe that it is stress-induced *physiological arousal* rather than stress itself that stimulates eating (Striegel-Moore & Rodin, 1986). Other researchers suspect that it is the *negative emotions* often evoked by stress that promote additional eating (Macht & Simons, 2000). Some people respond to emotional distress by eating tasty foods because they expect the enjoyable treats to make them feel better (Tice, Bratslavsky, & Baumeister, 2001). Unfortunately, this strategy of emotional regulation does not appear to be very effective, as eating does not usually lead to lasting mood changes (Thayer, 1996). In any event, stress is another environmental factor that can influence hunger, although it's not clear whether the effects are direct or indirect.

Eating and Weight: The Roots of Obesity

We just saw that hunger is regulated by a complex interaction of biological and psychological factors. The same kinds of complexities emerge when investigators explore the roots of *obesity*, the condition of being overweight. The criteria of obesity vary considerably. One simple, intermediate criterion is to classify people as obese if their weight exceeds their ideal body weight by 20%. If this criterion is used, 31% of men and 35% of women in the United States qualify as obese (Brownell & Wadden, 2000). Many experts prefer to assess obesity in terms of *body mass index (BMI)*—weight (in kilograms) divided by height (in meters) squared (kg/m^2). This increasingly used index of weight controls for variations in height. A BMI of 25–29.9 is typically regarded as overweight and a BMI of over 30 as obese (Bjorntorp, 2002). Although American culture seems to be obsessed with slimness, recent surveys show surprisingly sharp increases in the incidence of obesity (Jeffery, 2001; Mokdad et al., 1999). If a BMI over 25 is used as the cutoff, over 50% of American adults are struggling with weight problems!

If obesity merely frustrated people's vanity, there would be little cause for concern. Unfortunately, obesity is a significant health problem that elevates one's mortality risk (Allison et al., 1999; Bender et al., 1999). Overweight people are more vulnerable than others to cardiovascular diseases, diabetes, hypertension, respiratory problems, gallbladder disease, stroke, arthritis, muscle and skeletal pain, and some types of cancer (Manson, Skerrett, & Willet, 2002; Pi-Sunyer, 2002). For example, Figure 10.4 shows how the prevalence of diabetes, hypertension, coronary disease, and musculoskeletal pain are elevated as BMI increases.

Evolutionary-oriented researchers have a plausible explanation for the dramatic increase in the prevalence of obesity (Pinel et al., 2000). They point out that over the course of history, most animals and humans have lived in environments in which there was fierce competition for limited, unreliable food resources and where starvation was a very real threat. Hence, warm-blooded, foraging animals evolved a

Figure 10.4

Weight and the prevalence of various diseases. This graph shows how obesity, as indexed by BMI, is related to the prevalence of four common types of illness. The prevalence of diabetes, heart disease, muscle pain, and hypertension all increase as BMI goes up. Clearly, obesity is a significant health risk. (Based on data in Brownell & Wadden, 2000)

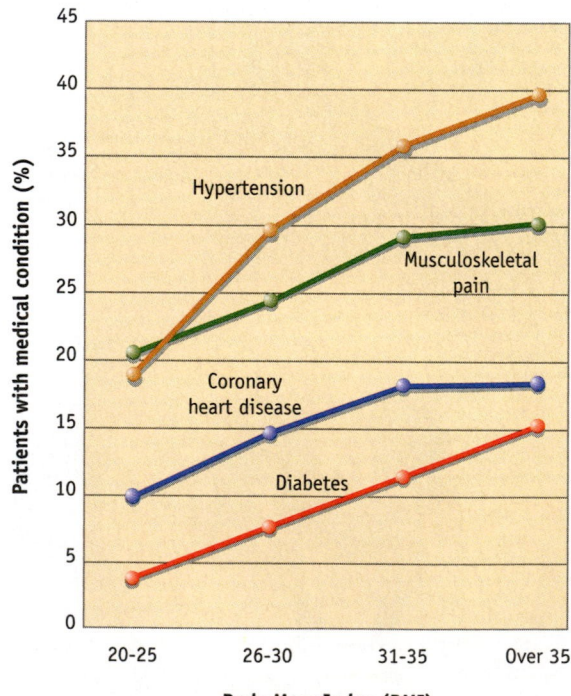

propensity to consume more food than immediately necessary when the opportunity presented itself because food might not be available later. Excess calories were stored in the body (as fat) to prepare for future food shortages. This approach to eating remains adaptive for most species of animals which continue to struggle with the ebb and flow of unpredictable food supplies. However, in today's modern, industrialized societies, the vast majority of humans live in environments which provide an abundant, reliable supply of tasty, high-calorie food. In these environments, humans' evolved tendency to overeat when food is plentiful leads most people down a pathway of chronic, excessive food consumption. According to this line of thinking, most people in food-replete environments tend to overeat in relation to their physiological needs, but because of variations in genetics, metabolism, and other factors only some become overweight.

Cognizant of the health problems associated with obesity, many people attempt to lose weight. At any given time, about 21% of men and 39% of women are dieting (Hill, 2002). Although concerns have been raised that dieting carries its own risks, the evidence clearly indicates that weight loss efforts involving moderate changes in eating and exercise are more beneficial than harmful to people's health (Devlin, Yanovski, & Wilson, 2000). Given the health concerns associated with weight problems, scientists have devoted a great deal of attention to the causes of obesity. Let's look at some of the factors they have identified.

Genetic Predisposition

You may know some people who can eat constantly without gaining weight. You may also know less fortunate people who get chubby eating far less. Differences in physiological makeup must be the cause of this paradox. Research suggests that these differences have a genetic basis (Bouchard, 2002).

In one influential study, adults raised by foster parents were compared with their biological and foster parents in regard to body mass index (Stunkard et al., 1986). The investigators found that the adoptees resembled their biological parents much more than their adoptive parents. In a subsequent *twin study,* Stunkard and colleagues (1990) found that identical twins reared apart were far more similar in BMI than fraternal twins reared together (see Figure 10.5). In another study of over 4000 twins, Allison and colleagues (1994) estimated that genetic factors account for 61% of the variation in weight among men, and

73% among women. Thus, it appears that some people inherit a genetic *vulnerability* to obesity (Schwartz & Seeley, 1997).

Excessive Eating and Inadequate Exercise

The bottom line for overweight people is that their energy intake from food consumption chronically exceeds their energy expenditure from physical activities and resting metabolic processes. In other words, they eat too much in relation to their level of exercise. In modern America, the tendency to overeat is easy to understand. Tasty, caloric, high-fat foods in ever-increasing portions are readily available nearly everywhere, not just in restaurants and grocery stores but in shopping malls, airports, gas stations, schools, and factories (Brownell, 2002). Unfortunately, the increased availability of highly caloric food in America has been paralleled by declining physical activity (Hill & Peters, 1998). Modern conveniences, such as cars and elevators, and changes in the world of work, such as the shift to more desk jobs, have conspired to make American lifestyles more sedentary than ever before.

The Concept of Set Point

People who lose weight on a diet have a rather strong (and depressing) tendency to gain back all the weight they lose. The reverse is also true. People who have to work to put weight on often have trouble keeping it on. According to Richard Keesey (1995), these observations suggest that your body may have a *set point,* or a natural point of stability in body weight. *Set-point theory* proposes that the body monitors fat-cell levels to keep them (and weight) fairly stable. When fat stores slip below a crucial set point, the body supposedly begins to compensate for this change (Keesey, 1993). This compensation apparently leads to increased hunger and decreased metabolism.

Web Link 10.1

American Obesity Association
This nonprofit organization's mission is to change public policy and make obesity a public health priority. It has an incredibly rich and well-organized website. In-depth information is available on the causes, consequences, and treatments of obesity.

Figure **10.5**

The heritability of weight. These data from a twin study by Stunkard et al. (1990) reveal that identical twins are much more similar in body mass index than fraternal twins, suggesting that genetic factors account for much of the variation among people in the propensity to become overweight. (Data from Stunkard et al., 1990)

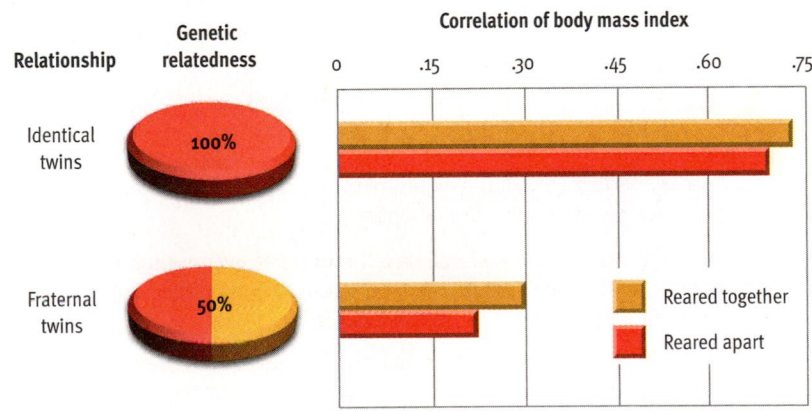

Studies have raised some doubts about various details of set-point theory, leading some researchers to propose an alternative called *settling-point theory* (Pinel et al., 2000). **Settling-point theory proposes that weight tends to drift around the level at which the constellation of factors that determine food consumption and energy expenditure achieve an equilibrium.** According to this view, weight tends to remain stable as long as there are no durable changes in any of the factors that influence it. Settling-point theory casts a much wider net than set-point theory, which attributes weight stability to very specific physiological processes. Another difference is that set-point theory asserts that an obese person's body will initiate processes that actively defend an excessive weight, whereas settling-point theory suggests that if an obese person makes long-term changes in eating or exercise that person's settling point will drift downward without active resistance. Thus, settling-point theory is a little more encouraging to those who hope to lose weight.

Dietary Restraint

Some investigators have proposed that vacillations in *dietary restraint* contribute to obesity (Polivy & Herman, 1995; Wardle et al., 2000). According to this theory, chronic dieters are *restrained eaters*—people who consciously work overtime to control their eating impulses and who feel guilty when they fail. To lose weight, restrained eaters go hungry much of the time, but they are constantly thinking about food. However, when their cognitive control is disrupted, they become *disinhibited* and eat to excess (Lowe, 2002). The crux of the problem is that restrained eaters assume, "Either I am on a diet, or I am out of control." A variety of events, such as drinking alcohol or experiencing emotional distress, can disrupt restrained eaters' control. But for many, the most common source of disinhibition is simply the perception that they have cheated on their diet. "I've already blown it," they think to themselves after perhaps just one high-calorie appetizer, "so I might as well enjoy as much as I want." They then proceed to consume a large meal or to go on an eating binge for the remainder of the day. Paradoxically, then, dietary restraint is thought to lead to frequent overeating and thus contribute to obesity.

CONCEPT CHECK 10.1

Understanding Factors in the Regulation of Hunger

Check your understanding of the effects of the various factors that influence hunger by indicating whether hunger would tend to increase or decrease in each of the situations described below. Indicate your choice by marking an I (increase), a D (decrease), or a ? (can't be determined without more information) next to each situation. You'll find the answers in Appendix A at the back of the book.

_____ 1. The ventromedial nucleus of a rat's brain is destroyed by lesioning.

_____ 2. The glucose level in Marlene's bloodstream decreases.

_____ 3. Norman just ate, but his roomate just brought home his favorite food—a pizza that smells great.

_____ 4. You're offered an exotic, strange-looking food from another culture and told that everyone in that culture loves it.

_____ 5. You are participating in an experiment on the effects of leptin and have just been given an injection of leptin.

_____ 6. Elton has been going crazy all day. It seems like everything's happening at once, and he feels totally stressed out. Finally he's been able to break away for a few minutes so he can catch a bite to eat.

_____ 7. You have been on a successful diet, but you just broke down and ate some appetizers at a party.

REVIEW OF KEY POINTS

- Drive theories apply a homeostatic model to motivation. They assume that organisms seek to reduce unpleasant states of tension called drives. In contrast, incentive theories emphasize how external goals energize behavior.

- Evolutionary theorists explain motives in terms of their adaptive value. Madsen's list of biological needs and Murray's list of social needs illustrate that a diverse array of motives govern human behavior.

- Eating is regulated by a complex interaction of biological and environmental factors. In the brain, the lateral and ventromedial areas of the hypothalamus were once viewed as on-off centers for the control of hunger, but their exact role is now unclear. Recent research suggests that hunger is regulated by neural circuits rather than anatomical centers in the brain.

- Fluctuations in blood glucose also seem to play a role in hunger, but the exact location of the "glucostats" and their mode of functioning are yet to be determined. Hormonal regulation of hunger depends primarily on insulin and leptin.

- Incentive-oriented models assert that eating is regulated by the availability and palatability of food. Learning processes, such as classical conditioning and observational learning, exert a great deal of influence over both what people eat and how much they eat. Cultural traditions also shape food preferences. Stress can stimulate eating.

- Surveys suggest that perhaps as many as 50% of people in the United States are struggling with weight problems. Obesity is a serious health problem that elevates the risk of many diseases. Evidence indicates that there is a genetic predisposition to obesity.

- Weight problems occur when people eat too much in relation to their exercise level. According to set-point theory, the body monitors fat stores to keep them fairly stable. Settling-point theory suggests that a multitude of factors contribute to weight stability. Vacillations in dietary restraint resulting in disinhibition may contribute to obesity in some people.

Sexual Motivation and Behavior

How does sex resemble food? Sometimes it seems that people are obsessed with both. People joke and gossip about sex constantly. Magazines, novels, movies, and television shows are saturated with sexual activity and innuendo. The advertising industry uses sex to sell everything from mouthwash to designer jeans to automobiles. This intense interest in sex reflects the importance of sexual motivation. In this portion of the chapter, we'll examine the factors that influence sexual desire and sexual orientation, and we'll describe the physiology of the human sexual response.

Determinants of Sexual Desire

Sex is essential for the survival of a species, but it's not essential to an *individual's* survival. Sexual motivation is not driven by deprivation to the extent that hunger is—you can live out a long life without sex, but without food your life will be very short. Like hunger, sexual desire is influenced by a complicated network of biological and social factors.

Hormonal Regulation

Hormones secreted by the *gonads*—the ovaries in females and the testes in males—can influence sexual motivation (consult Chapter 3, Figure 3.24). *Estrogens* are the principal class of gonadal hormones in females. *Androgens* are the principal class of gonadal hormones in males. Actually, both classes of hormones are produced in both sexes, but the relative balance is much different. The hypothalamus and the pituitary gland regulate these hormonal secretions.

The influence of hormones on sexual desire can be seen quite vividly in the animal kingdom (Feder, 1984). In many species, females are sexually receptive only just prior to ovulation, coinciding with an elevation in circulating levels of gonadal hormones. Hormones also influence sexual desire in males. For instance, if a male rat's testes are removed, the lack of a key androgen (testosterone) results in a lack of sexual interest. Testosterone injections can revive sexual desire in such castrated animals. Thus, it's clear that gonadal hormones regulate the sex drive in many animals.

Moving up the phylogenetic scale from rats to primates, hormones exert less and less influence over sexual behavior (Chambers & Phoenix, 1987). However, several lines of evidence suggest that they do *contribute* to the modulation of sexual desire in humans. For example, males who develop an endocrine disorder called *hypogonadism* during adulthood exhibit abnormally low levels of androgens and reduced sexual motivation, which can be revived by hormone replacement therapy (Rabkin, Wagner, & Rabkin, 2000). Experiments with male sex offenders suggest that drugs that drastically lower testosterone levels can be used to reduce sexual interest, although they certainly do not preclude further sexual assaults (Prentky, 1997). Curiously, *androgen* levels seem related to sexual motivation in *both* sexes. Higher levels of testosterone correlate with higher rates of sexual activity in both males (Schiavi et al., 1997) and females (Davis, 2000). And rising testosterone levels predict the onset of sexual activity in adolescent females (Halpern, Udry, & Suchindran, 1997).

The links between hormone levels and sexual activity in humans are interesting, but the correlations are modest, and much of the evidence comes from abnormal syndromes that may tell us little about normal sexual functioning. Furthermore, it is difficult to sort out the causal relations, as sexual activity can increase testosterone levels (Stoleru et al., 1993). At present, we can only conclude that hormonal fluctuations probably have a small impact on sexual desire in humans.

Erotic Materials

Erotic reading material, photographs, and films can stimulate sexual desire in many people. Of course, people don't all respond favorably to sexually explicit media (Fisher et al., 1988). Men are more likely than women to report that they find erotic materials enjoyable and arousing (Gardos & Mosher, 1999; Koukounas & McCabe, 1997). However, this finding may simply reflect the fact that the vast majority of erotic materials are scripted to appeal to males and often portray women in degrading roles that elicit negative reactions from female viewers (Mosher & MacIan, 1994; Pearson & Pollack, 1997).

How much impact does erotic material have on actual sexual behavior? The empirical data on this hotly debated question are inconsistent and are open to varied interpretations (Seto, Maric, & Barbaree, 2001). The balance of evidence suggests that exposure to erotic material elevates the likelihood of overt sexual activity for a few hours immediately after the exposure (Donnerstein, Linz, & Penrod, 1987). This relatively modest effect may explain why attempts to find a link between the availability of erotica and sex crime rates have largely yielded negative results.

PREVIEW QUESTIONS
- How much do hormones influence sexual desire in humans?
- How do erotic materials affect sexual behavior?
- How does attraction to a potential partner influence sexual behavior?
- What has evolutionary-oriented research revealed about gender differences in sexual activity and mating preferences?

For the most part, researchers have not found correlations between greater availability of pornography and elevated rates of sex crimes (Kimmel & Linders, 1996; Kutchinsky, 1991; Nemes, 1992; Winick & Evans, 1996). Although most sex offenders admit to an extensive history of using pornographic materials, a review of the relevant research indicated that sex offenders typically do not have earlier or more extensive exposure to pornography in childhood or adolescence than other people (Bauserman, 1996).

Although erotic materials don't appear to incite overpowering sexual urges, they may alter *attitudes* in ways that eventually influence sexual behavior. Zillmann and Bryant (1984) found that male and female undergraduates exposed to a large dose of pornography (three or six films per week for six weeks) developed more liberal attitudes about sexual practices. For example, they came to view premarital and extramarital sex as more acceptable. Another study by Zillmann and Bryant (1988) suggests that viewing sexually explicit films may make some people dissatisfied with their own sexual interactions. In comparison to control subjects, the subjects exposed to a steady diet of pornography reported less satisfaction with their partners' physical appearance, sexual curiosity, and sexual performance. Thus, pornography may create unrealistic expectations about sexual relations.

Moreover, research on *aggressive pornography* has raised some serious concerns about its effects. Aggressive pornography typically depicts violence against women. Many films show women who gradually give in to and enjoy rape and other sexually degrading acts after some initial resistance. Some studies indicate that this type of material increases male subjects' aggressive behavior toward women, at least in the context of the research laboratory (Donnerstein & Malamuth, 1997; Zillmann & Weaver, 1989). In the typical study, male subjects work on a laboratory task and are led to believe (falsely) that they are delivering electric shocks to other subjects. In this situation, their aggression toward females tends to be elevated after exposure to aggressive pornography. Exposure to aggressive pornography may also make sexual coercion seem less offensive and may desensitize males to the horror of sexual violence (Mullin & Linz, 1995). In particular, it helps perpetuate the myth that women enjoy being raped and ravaged (Allen et al., 1995). This effect is not limited to sexually explicit media. Mainstream (R-rated) movies suggesting that women enjoy rape can also influence males' attitudes about sexual coercion (Milburn, Mather, & Conrad, 2000).

The effects of aggressive pornography are especially worrisome in light of evidence about rape. Although it is difficult to obtain accurate information about the prevalence of rape (some experts believe that 90% of all rapes are never reported), the incidence of rape appears to be growing (Kilpatrick, Edmunds, & Seymour, 1992). Estimates suggest that as many as one-quarter of young women in the United States may be victims of rape or attempted rape (Koss, 1993; Parrot & Bechhofer, 1991). Only a minority of reported rapes are committed by strangers (see Figure 10.6). Particularly common is *date rape,* which occurs when a woman is forced to have sex in the context of dating. Research suggests that date rape is a serious problem on college campuses. In one survey of students at 32 colleges, 1 in 7 women reported that they had been victimized by date rape or an attempted date rape (Koss, Gidycz, & Wisniewski, 1987). Moreover, 1 in 12 men admitted either to having forced a date into sex or to having tried to do so. However, *none* of these men identified himself as a rapist. Although other factors are surely at work, many theorists believe that aggressive pornography has contributed to this failure to see sexual coercion for what it is (Malamuth, Addison, & Koss, 2000).

Attraction to a Partner

Obviously, another key consideration governing sexual desire is the availability of a potential partner and attraction to that partner. Humans are not unique in this regard. Many organisms respond to the external stimulus of an available partner. In fact, a *new* part-

Figure 10.6

Rape victim–offender relationships. Based on a national survey of 3187 college women, Mary Koss and her colleagues (1988) identified a sample of 468 women who indicated that they had been a victim of rape and who provided information on their relationship to the offender. Contrary to the prevailing stereotype, only a small minority (11%) of these women were raped by a stranger. As you can see, many of the women were raped by men they were dating. (Based on data from Koss et al., 1988)

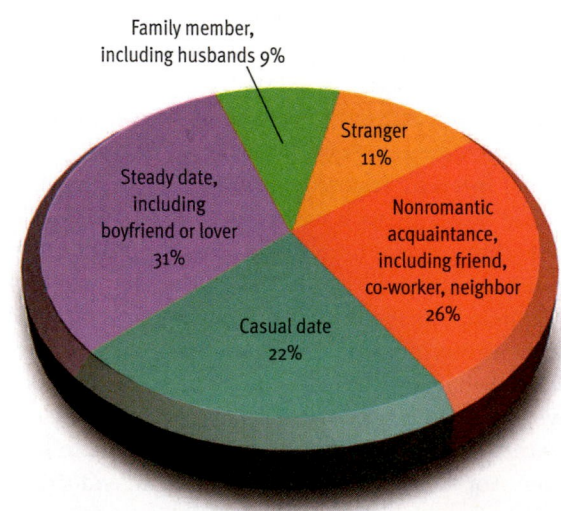

ner can revive dwindling sexual interest in many animals. This phenomenon has a curious name, *the Coolidge effect*, which derives from the following story. President Calvin Coolidge and his wife were touring a farm. Mrs. Coolidge was informed that a rooster on the farm often copulated 20 or more times in a day. "Tell *that* to Mr. Coolidge," she supposedly said. When informed of the rooster's feat, the president asked if it was always with the same hen. He was told that the rooster enjoyed a different hen each time. "Tell that to Mrs. Coolidge," was his reply. Today, no one is sure whether the story is true, but the Coolidge effect refers to the preference for variety in sexual partners that is seen in males of many species, including rats, bulls, and monkeys (Dewsbury, 1981; Fiorino, Coury, & Phillips, 1997).

Most species of animals are *selective* in their attraction to sexual partners. As we discussed in Chapter 3, in many species females choose who they will mate with based on the males' appearance, courtship behavior, or material assets (Alcock, 1998). Females typically prefer males who have larger or brighter ornaments. For example, female house finches are enticed by redder feathers. In other species, mating opportunities are awarded to males who can provide certain types of material goods. The female African village weaverbird, for instance, sizes up a male's mating potential by carefully inspecting the quality of the nest he has built. If she decides that the nest isn't solid enough to protect her offspring, she moves on to look for a male with a better nest (Buss, 1998). The strategies that organisms follow in mate selection appear to be a product of natural selection, which brings us to evolutionary analyses of human sexual behavior.

Evolutionary Analyses of Human Sexual Behavior

As you have already seen in previous chapters, the relatively new evolutionary perspective in psychology has generated intriguing hypotheses related to a host of topics, including perception, learning, language, and problem solving. However, evolutionary theorists' analyses of sexual behavior have drawn the most attention. Obviously, the task of explaining sexual behavior is crucial to the evolutionary perspective, given its fundamental thesis that natural selection is fueled by variations in reproductive success. The thinking in this area has been guided by Robert Trivers's (1972) *parental investment theory,* which we introduced in Chapter 3. To quickly recapitulate, Trivers maintains that a species' mating patterns depend on what each sex has to invest—in terms of time, energy, and survival risk—to produce and nurture offspring. According to Trivers, *the sex that makes the smaller investment will compete for mating opportunities with the sex that makes the larger investment, and the sex with the larger investment will tend to be more discriminating in selecting its partners.* In Chapter 3, we saw how this rule of thumb predicted mating patterns in many types of animals. Let's look at how this analysis applies to humans.

Like many mammalian species, human males are *required* to invest little in the production of offspring beyond the act of copulation, so their reproductive potential is maximized by mating with as many females as possible. The situation for females is quite different. Females have to invest nine months in pregnancy, and our female ancestors typically had to devote at least several additional years to nourishing offspring through breastfeeding. These realities place a ceiling on the number of offspring women can produce, regardless of how many males they mate with. Hence, females have little or no incentive for mating with many males. Instead, females can optimize their reproductive potential by being selective in mating. Thus, in humans, males are thought to compete with other males for the relatively scarce and valuable "commodity" of reproductive opportunities. Parental investment theory predicts that in comparison to women, men will show more interest in sexual activity, more desire for variety in sexual partners, and more willingness to engage in uncommitted sex (see Figure 10.7). In contrast, females are thought to be the conservative, discriminating sex that is highly

Web Link 10.2

The Evolutionary Psychology FAQ
Maintained by Edward Hagen (Institute for Theoretical Biology, Humboldt University, Berlin), this site provides answers to a host of controversial questions on the subject of evolutionary psychology. Covered questions include: What is an adaptation? How can we identify psychological adaptations? Is evolutionary psychology sexist? If my genes made me do it, am I still responsible? Why do some people hate evolutionary psychology?

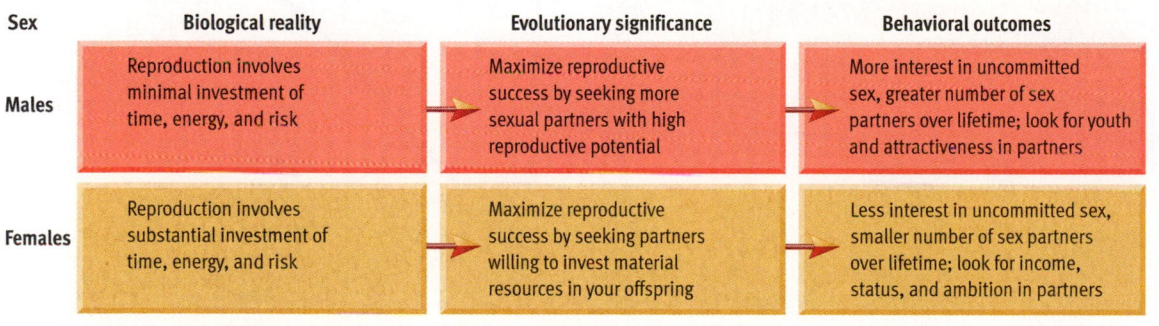

Sex	Biological reality	Evolutionary significance	Behavioral outcomes
Males	Reproduction involves minimal investment of time, energy, and risk	Maximize reproductive success by seeking more sexual partners with high reproductive potential	More interest in uncommitted sex, greater number of sex partners over lifetime; look for youth and attractiveness in partners
Females	Reproduction involves substantial investment of time, energy, and risk	Maximize reproductive success by seeking partners willing to invest material resources in your offspring	Less interest in uncommitted sex, smaller number of sex partners over lifetime; look for income, status, and ambition in partners

Figure 10.7

Parental investment theory and mating preferences. Parental investment theory suggests that basic differences between males and females in parental investment have great adaptive significance and lead to gender differences in mating propensities and preferences, as outlined here.

selective in choosing partners. This selectivity supposedly entails seeking partners who have the greatest ability to contribute toward feeding and caring for offspring. Why? Because in the world of our ancient ancestors, males' greater strength and agility would have been crucial assets in the never-ending struggle to find food and shelter and defend one's territory. A female who chose a mate who was lazy or unreliable or who had no hunting, fighting, building, farming, or other useful economic skills would have suffered a substantial disadvantage in her efforts to raise her children and pass on her genes.

Gender Differences in Patterns of Sexual Activity

Consistent with evolutionary theory, males generally show a greater interest in sex than females do. Men think about sex more often than women (see Figure 10.8), they initiate sex more frequently (Morokoff et al., 1997), and they are more interested in sex for its own sake (Whitley, 1988). Some theorists also argue that men's greater liking of pornography reflects the influence of evolutionary forces that have made males more interested in sex (Malamuth, 1996).

Men also are more motivated than women to pursue sex with a variety of partners. Buss and Schmitt (1993) found that college men indicate that they would ideally like to have 18 sex partners across their lives, whereas college women report that they would prefer only 5 partners (see Figure 10.9). Surveys inquiring about adults' actual sexual histories also indicate that men engage in sex with a larger number of partners than women do, on the average (Janus & Janus, 1993; Laumann et al., 1994).

Clear gender disparities are also seen in regard to people's willingness to engage in casual or uncommitted sex. For example, Buss and Schmitt (1993)

asked undergraduates about the likelihood that they would consent to sex with someone they found desirable whom they had known for one hour, one day, one week, one month, or longer periods. Men were much more likely than women to have sex with someone they had known for only a brief period.

In a definitive review of the empirical evidence, Roy Baumeister and colleagues (2001) conclude, "Across many different studies and measures, men have been shown to have more frequent and more intense sexual desires than women, as reflected in spontaneous thoughts about sex, frequency and variety of sexual fantasies, desired frequency of intercourse, desired number of partners, masturbation, liking for various sexual practices, willingness to forego sex, and other measures. No contrary findings (indicating stronger sexual motivation among women) were found" (p. 242).

Gender Differences in Mate Preferences

According to evolutionary theorists, if males were left to their own devices over the course of history, they probably would have shown little interest in long-term mating commitments, but females have generally demanded long-term commitments from males before consenting to sex (Buss, 1994a). Hence,

---

Figure 10.8

The gender gap in how much people think about sex. This graph summarizes data on how often males and females think about sex, based on a large-scale survey by Laumann, Gagnon, and Michaels (1994). As evolutionary theorists would predict, based on parental investment theory, males seem to manifest more interest in sexual activity than their female counterparts do. (Data from Laumann et al., 1994)

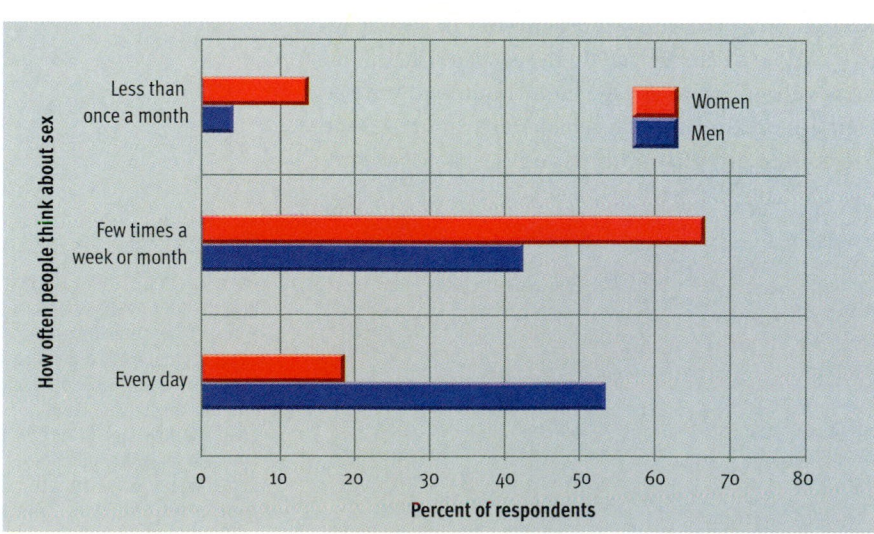

Figure 10.9

The gender gap in desire for a variety of sexual partners. Buss and Schmitt (1993) asked college students about how many sexual partners they ideally would like to have for various time intervals ranging up to one's entire lifetime. As evolutionary theorists would predict, males are interested in having considerably more partners than females are.

Source: Buss, D. M., & Schmitt, D. P. (1993). Sexual strategies theory: An evolutionary perspective on human mating. *Psychological Review, 100,* 204–232. Copyright © 1993 by the American Psychological Association. Reprinted by permission of the authors.

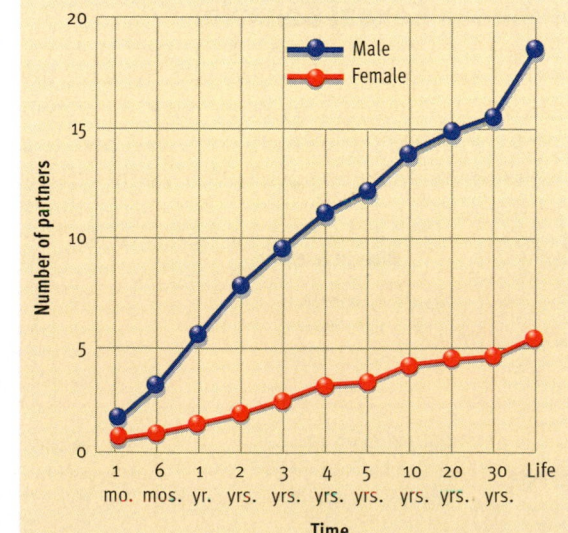

long-term mating commitments are a normal part of the social landscape in human societies. However, parental investment theory suggests that there should be some glaring disparities between men and women in what they look for in a long-term mate (consult Figure 10.7 again).

The adaptive problem for our male ancestors was to find a female with good reproductive potential who would be sexually faithful and effective in nurturing children. Given these needs, evolutionary theory predicts that men should place more emphasis than women on partner characteristics such as youthfulness (which allows for more reproductive years) and attractiveness (which is assumed to be correlated with health and fertility). In contrast, the adaptive problem for our female ancestors was to find a male who could provide material resources and protect his family and who was dependable and willing to invest his resources in his family. Given these needs, evolutionary theory predicts that women should place more emphasis than men on partner characteristics such as intelligence, ambition, income, and social status (which are associated with the ability to provide more material resources). Evolutionary theorists are quick to point out that these differing priorities *do not reflect conscious strategies*. For the most part, people do not think about sex in terms of maximizing their reproductive potential. Instead, these different priorities are viewed as subconscious preferences that have been hardwired into the human brain by evolutionary forces. In any event, gender differences in mating preferences have been the subject of much research, including our Featured Study for this chapter.

Web Link 10.3

Go Ask Alice!
One of the longest-standing and most popular sources of frank information on the Net has been *Alice!* from Columbia University's Health Education Program. Geared especially to the needs of undergraduate students, the site offers direct answers to questions about relationships, sexuality and sexual health, alcohol and drug consumption, emotional health, and general health.

Evolution, Culture, and Mating Priorities

FEATURED STUDY

According to evolutionary theories, human females enhance their chances of passing on their genes by seeking male partners who possess or are likely to acquire more material resources that can be invested in children. Thus, women should emphasize education, income, status, ambition, and industriousness in potential partners. Men, on the other hand, are assumed to maximize their reproductive outlook by seeking female partners with good breeding potential. Thus, men are thought to look for youth, attractiveness, good health, and other characteristics presumed to be associated with higher fertility. If these evolutionary analyses of sexual motivation are on the mark, gender differences in mating preferences should be virtually universal and thus transcend culture.

Method

To test this hypothesis, David Buss coordinated the efforts of 50 scientists from around the world, who collected data on what people want in a mate. They surveyed more than 10,000 people from 37 cultures distributed across six continents and five islands. Subjects responded to two questionnaires, which asked them to rate the importance of 32 characteristics in potential mates.

Results

The findings revealed that males and females exhibit both similarities and differences in mating preferences. Many characteristics, such as kindness, emotional stability, dependability, and a pleasant disposition, were rated very highly by both sexes. However, a few crucial differences between males' and females' priorities were found, and these differences were universal across cultures. As a group, women placed a higher value than men on potential partners' status, ambition, and financial prospects (see Figure 10.10 on the next page). These priorities were not limited to industrialized or capitalist countries; they were apparent in third-world

Investigator: David M. Buss (University of Michigan)

Source: Sex differences in human mate preferences: Evolutionary hypotheses tested in 37 cultures. *Behavioral and Brain Sciences*, 1989, *12*, 1–49.

Evolutionary theory posits that men can maximize their reproductive fitness by seeking youthful partners, whereas women can maximize their reproductive success by searching for mates that are rich in material resources that can be invested in children. Obviously, this theory can explain why attractive young women often become romantically involved with much older men who happen to be wealthy.

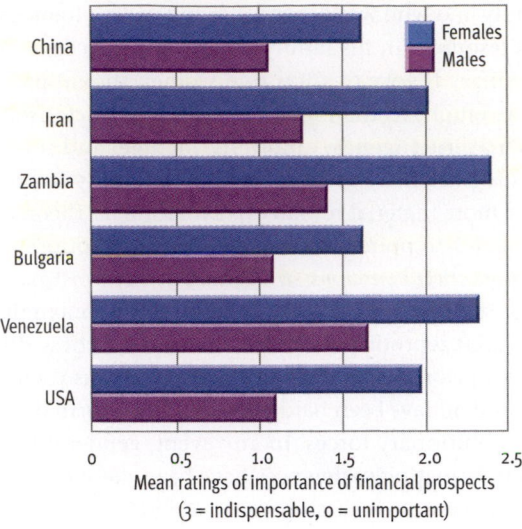

Figure 10.10

Gender and potential mates' financial prospects. Consistent with evolutionary theory, Buss (1989) found that females place more emphasis on potential partners' financial prospects than males do. Moreover, he found that this trend transcended culture. The specific results for 6 of the 37 cultures studied by Buss are shown here. (Based on data from Buss, 1989)

Figure 10.11

Gender and potential mates' physical attractiveness. Consistent with evolutionary theory, Buss (1989) found that all over the world, males place more emphasis on potential partners' good looks than females do. The specific results for 6 of the 37 cultures studied by Buss are shown here. (Based on data from Buss, 1989)

Courtesy of David M. Buss

"*Evolutionary psychologists develop hypotheses about the psychological mechanisms that have evolved in humans to solve particular adaptive problems that humans have faced under ancestral conditions.*"
DAVID BUSS

cultures, socialist countries, and all varieties of economic systems. In contrast, men consistently showed more interest than women in potential partners' youthfulness and physical attractiveness (see Figure 10.11). Cross-cultural variations in mate preferences were relatively modest. The most prominent variation was in the emphasis placed on female chastity—a woman's lack of previous sexual intercourse. Chastity was highly valued in some societies but viewed with indifference in others.

Discussion

According to Buss, social scientists have traditionally assumed that mating preferences are shaped by learning and that they vary considerably from culture to culture. His findings suggest that culture matters, but only in a limited way. He also concludes that his data provide striking support for evolutionary theories of sexual mo-

tivation. As predicted, women emphasized males' prospects for acquisition of material resources, whereas men emphasized females' reproductive capacity.

Comment

Besides supporting evolutionary theories of sexual motivation, this study exemplifies the rich potential of psychology's new commitment to cross-cultural research (see Chapter 1). Interestingly, though, Buss (1994b) notes that his data "were extraordinarily difficult to obtain." Authorities in some countries tried to sabotage the study, while others banned it completely. These nightmares and the logistical difficulties inherent in gathering data from 37 disparate cultures illustrate the extra-challenging nature of cross-cultural research. Of course, sexual behavior is a particularly sensitive topic of study, as we'll see throughout this section. ■

Subsequent studies have provided additional support for the existence of gender disparities in mating preferences. For example, Sprecher, Sullivan, and Hatfield (1994) examined a large, representative sample of adults in the United States and replicated the findings that men look for youth and attractiveness in partners, whereas women are more concerned about potential partners' education and income potential. In a study of personal ads placed in newspapers and

magazines, Wiederman (1993) found that female advertisers explicitly sought financial resources in potential partners eleven times as often as male advertisers did.

Criticism and Alternative Explanations

So, the findings on gender differences in sexual behavior mesh very nicely with predictions derived from evolutionary theory. But, in the world of science, everyone is a critic—so you may be wondering: What types of criticism has this line of research generated? One set of concerns centers on the fact that the findings do not paint a very flattering picture of human nature. Men end up looking like sordid sexual predators; women come across as cynical, greedy materialists; and evolutionary theory appears to endorse these ideas as the inevitable outcome of natural selection. As Buss (1998) acknowledges, "Much of what I discovered about human mating is not nice" (p. 408). This controversy demonstrates once again that psychological theories can have far-reaching social and political ramifications, but the sociopolitical fallout has no bearing on evolutionary theory's scientific validity or utility.

However, some critics *have* expressed doubts about the validity of evolutionary explanations of gender differences in sexual behavior. They note that one can posit alternative explanations for the findings. For example, women's emphasis on males' material resources could be a by-product of cultural and economic forces rather than the result of biological imperatives (Wallen, 1989). Women may have learned to value males' economic clout because their own economic potential has been severely limited in virtually all cultures by a long history of discrimination (Hrdy, 1997; Kasser & Sharma, 1999). In a similar vein, Roy Baumeister, who has convincingly documented that men have stronger sexual motivation than women (Baumeister et al., 2001), has argued that this disparity may be largely due to extensive cultural processes that serve to suppress female sexuality (Baumeister & Twenge, 2002). Evolutionary theorists counter these arguments by pointing out that the cultural and economic processes at work may themselves be products of evolution. At present, evolutionary theory appears to provide a more complete account for gender disparities in sexual behavior than the alternative explanations (Archer, 1996). But more research is needed—and given the controversial nature of the findings, you can rest assured more research will be conducted.

REVIEW OF KEY POINTS

- Hormones exert considerable influence over sexual motivation in many animals. Some interesting correlations between testosterone fluctuations and sexual activity in humans suggest that hormonal swings may have a small impact on human sexual desire.
- People respond to a variety of erotic materials, which may elevate sexual desire for only a few hours but may have an enduring impact on attitudes about sex. Aggressive pornography may make sexual coercion seem less offensive and may contribute to date rape. Attraction to a potential part-

ner is a critical determinant of sexual interest in both animals and humans.

- According to parental investment theory, males are thought to compete with other males for reproductive opportunities and females are assumed to be the discriminating sex that is selective in choosing partners. Consistent with evolutionary theory, males tend to think about and initiate sex more than females do and to have more sexual partners and more interest in casual sex than females.
- The Featured Study by Buss demonstrated that there are gender differences in mating preferences that largely transcend cultural boundaries. Males emphasize potential partners' youthfulness and attractiveness, whereas females emphasize potential partners' status and financial prospects.

The Mystery of Sexual Orientation

Sex must be a contentious topic, as the controversy swirling around evolutionary explanations of gender differences in sexuality is easily equaled by the controversy surrounding the determinants of *sexual orientation*. *Sexual orientation* refers to a person's preference for emotional and sexual relationships with individuals of the same sex, the other sex, or either sex. *Heterosexuals* seek emotional-sexual relationships with members of the other sex, *bisexuals* with members of either sex, and *homosexuals* with members of the same sex. In recent years, the terms *gay* and *straight* have become widely used to refer to homosexuals and heterosexuals, respectively. Although *gay* can refer to homosexuals of either sex, most homosexual women prefer to call themselves *lesbians*.

People tend to view heterosexuality and homosexuality as an all-or-none distinction. However, in a large-scale survey of sexual behavior, Alfred Kinsey and his colleagues (1948, 1953) discovered that many people who define themselves as heterosexuals have had homosexual experiences—and vice versa. Thus, Kinsey and others have concluded that it is more accurate to view heterosexuality and homosexuality as end points on a continuum (Haslam, 1997). Indeed, Kinsey devised a seven-point scale, shown in Figure 10.12 on the next page, that can be used to characterize individuals' sexual orientation.

How common is homosexuality? No one knows for sure. Part of the problem is that this question is vastly more complex than it appears at first glance (LeVay, 1996). Given that sexual orientation is best represented as a continuum, where do you draw the lines between heterosexuality, bisexuality, and homosexuality? And how do you handle the distinction between overt behavior and desire? Where, for instance, do you put a person who is married and has never engaged in homosexual behavior but who re-

PREVIEW QUESTIONS

- Is sexual orientation an either-or distinction?
- How common is homosexuality?
- How have theorists explained the development of homosexuality?
- What are the four phases of the human sexual response?

Figure 10.12

Homosexuality and hetero-sexuality as endpoints on a continuum. Sex research-ers view heterosexuality and homosexuality as falling on a continuum rather than make an all-or-none distinction. Kin-sey and his associates (1948, 1953) created this seven-point scale (from 0 to 6) to describe people's sexual orientation. They used the term *ambisex-ual* to describe those who fall in the middle of the scale, but such people are commonly called *bisexual* today.

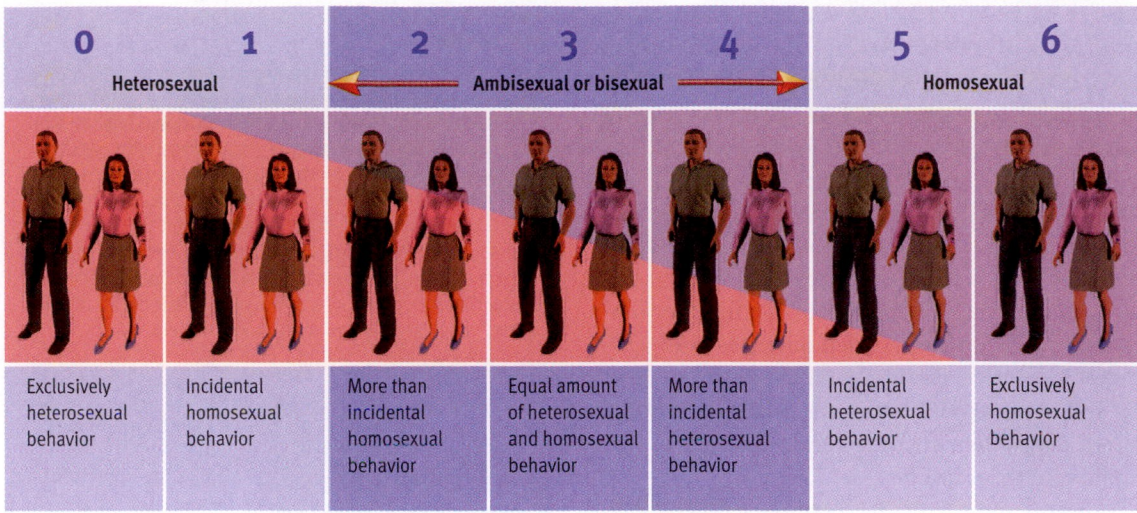

0	1	2	3	4	5	6
Heterosexual		Ambisexual or bisexual			Homosexual	
Exclusively heterosexual behavior	Incidental homosexual behavior	More than incidental homosexual behavior	Equal amount of heterosexual and homosexual behavior	More than incidental heterosexual behavior	Incidental heterosexual behavior	Exclusively homosexual behavior

ports homosexual fantasies and acknowledges be-ing strongly drawn to members of the same sex? The other part of the problem is that many people have extremely prejudicial attitudes about homosexuality, which makes gays cautious and reluctant to give can-did information about their sexuality (Herek, 1996, 2000). Small wonder then that estimates of the por-tion of the population that is homosexual vary pretty widely. A frequently cited estimate of the number of people who are gay is 10%, but recent surveys sug-

Figure 10.13

How common is homosexuality? The answer to this question is both complex and controversial. Michaels (1996) brought together data from two large-scale surveys to arrive at the estimates shown here. If you look at how many people have actually had a same-sex partner in the last five years, the figures are relatively low, but if you count those who have had a same-sex partner since puberty the figures more than double. Still another way to look at it is to ask people whether they are attracted to people of the same sex (regardless of their actual behavior). This approach suggests that about 8% of the population could be characterized as homosexual. (Data from Michaels, 1996)

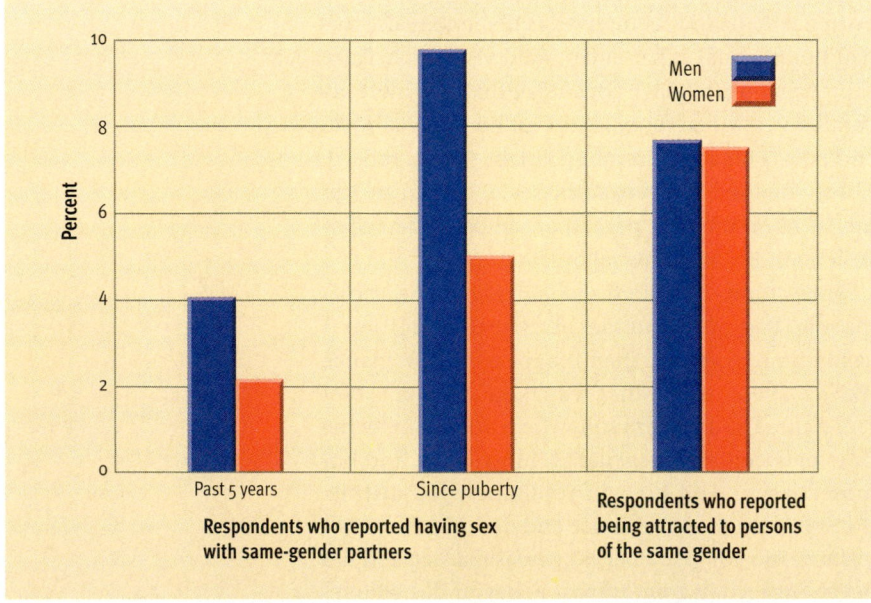

gest that this percentage may be an overestimate. Mi-chaels (1996) has combined data from two of the better large-scale surveys in recent years to arrive at the estimates seen in Figure 10.13. As you can see, the numbers are open to varying interpretations, but as a whole they suggest that about 5%–8% of the popula-tion could reasonably be characterized as homosexual.

Environmental Theories

Over the years many environmental theories have been floated to explain the origins of homosexuality, but when tested empirically, these theories have gar-nered remarkably little support. For example, psycho-analytic and behavioral theorists, who usually agree on very little, both proposed environmental expla-nations for the development of homosexuality. The Freudian theorists argued that a male is likely to be-come gay when raised by a weak, detached, ineffec-tual father who is a poor heterosexual role model and by an overprotective, close-binding mother, with whom the boy identifies. Behavioral theorists argued that homosexuality is a learned preference acquired when same-sex stimuli have been paired with sexual arousal, perhaps through chance seductions by adult homosexuals. Extensive research on homosexuals' upbringing and childhood experiences have failed to support either of these theories (Bell, Weinberg, & Hammersmith, 1981).

However, efforts to research homosexuals' per-sonal histories have yielded a number of interesting insights. Extremely feminine behavior in young boys or masculine behavior in young girls does predict the subsequent development of homosexuality (Bailey & Zucker, 1995). For example, 75%–90% of highly feminine young boys eventually turn out to be gay (Blanchard et al., 1995). Consistent with this find-ing, most gay men and women report that they can

Both biological and environmental factors appear to contribute to homosexuality, although its precise developmental roots remain obscure.

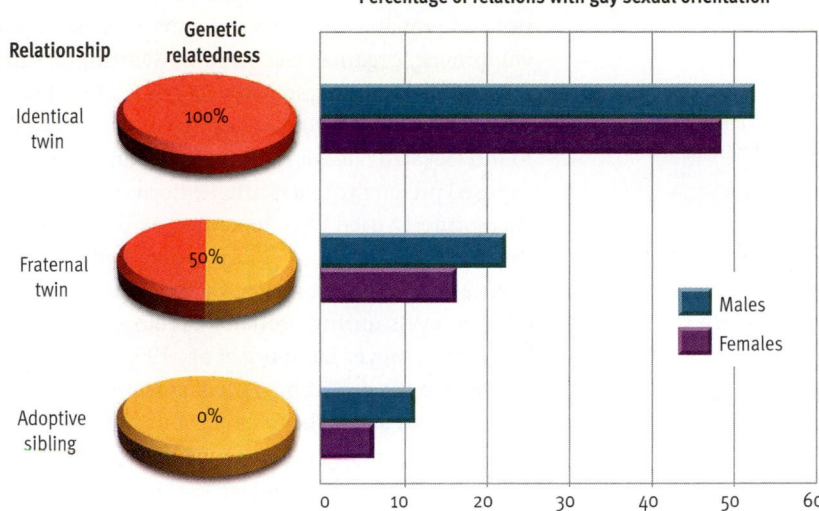

Percentage of relations with gay sexual orientation

Relationship	Genetic relatedness
Identical twin	100%
Fraternal twin	50%
Adoptive sibling	0%

Males
Females

0 10 20 30 40 50 60

trace their homosexual leanings back to their early childhood, even before they understood what sex was really about (Garnets & Kimmel, 1991). Most also report that because of negative parental and societal attitudes about homosexuality, they initially struggled to deny their sexual orientation. Hence, they felt that their homosexuality was not a matter of choice and not something that they could readily change (Breedlove, 1994). These findings obviously suggest that the roots of homosexuality are more biological than environmental.

Biological Theories

Nonetheless, initial efforts to find a biological basis for homosexuality met with little success. Most theorists originally assumed that hormonal differences between heterosexuals and homosexuals must underlie a person's sexual orientation (Doerr et al., 1976; Dorner, 1988). However, studies comparing circulating hormone levels in gays and straights found only small, inconsistent differences that could not be linked to sexual orientation in any convincing way (Garnets & Kimmel, 1991; Gladue, 1988).

Thus, like environmental theorists, biological theorists were stymied for quite a while in their efforts to explain the roots of homosexuality. However, that picture changed in the 1990s when a pair of behavioral genetics studies reported findings suggesting that homosexuality has a hereditary basis. In the first study, conducted by Bailey and Pillard (1991), the subjects were gay men who had either a twin brother or an adopted brother. They found that 52% of the subjects' identical twins were gay, that 22% of their fraternal twins were gay, and that 11% of their adoptive brothers were gay. A companion study (Bailey et al., 1993) of lesbians yielded a similar pattern of results (see Figure 10.14). Given that identical twins share more genetic overlap than fraternal twins, who

share more genes than unrelated adoptive siblings, these results suggest that there is a genetic predisposition to homosexuality (see Chapter 3 for an explanation of the logic underlying twin and adoption studies). More recent twin studies, with larger and more representative samples, have provided further support for the conclusion that heredity influences sexual orientation (Bailey, Dunne, & Martin, 2000; Kendler et al., 2000). However, these newer studies have yielded smaller estimates of genetic influence, which have been attributed to improved sampling. The sampling method used in the earlier studies—although appropriate for exploratory investigations—probably led to somewhat inflated estimates of genetic influence.

In another line of research, LeVay (1991, 1993) has reported anatomical differences between gay and straight men in a region of the brain thought to influence sexual behavior. He focused on a tiny cluster of neurons in the anterior hypothalamus that is known to be larger in men than women. Because the structure is too small to be measured effectively in the living brain, it is studied posthumously. LeVay compared the autopsied brains of 19 homosexual and 16 heterosexual men and found that the targeted structure tended to be about half as large in the gay men. LeVay (1996) stresses that his findings on brain structure should be interpreted with caution, as most of his subjects had died of AIDS, which clearly can wreak havoc in the brain. Although the data on disparities in brain structure are preliminary, they point to a biological basis for sexual orientation.

Many theorists suspect that disparities between heterosexuals and homosexuals in brain structure may reflect the organizing effects of prenatal hormones on neurological development. Several lines of research

Figure 10.14

Genetics and sexual orientation. If relatives who share more genetic relatedness show greater similarity on a trait than relatives who share less genetic overlap, this evidence suggests a genetic predisposition to the characteristic. Studies of both gay men and lesbian women have found a higher prevalence of homosexuality among their identical twins than their fraternal twins, who, in turn, are more likely to be homosexual than their adoptive siblings. These findings suggest that genetic factors influence sexual orientation. (Data from Bailey & Pillard, 1991; Bailey et. al., 1993)

Web Link 10.4

Queer Resources Directory (QRD)
In its 1994 mission statement, the *Queer Resources Directory* described itself as "an electronic research library specifically dedicated to sexual minorities—groups that have traditionally been labeled as 'queer' and systematically discriminated against." Composed of more than 22,000 files and still growing, QRD offers a rich array of resources.

suggest that hormonal secretions during critical periods of prenatal development may shape sexual development, organize the brain in a lasting manner, and influence subsequent sexual orientation (Berenbaum & Snyder, 1995). For example, researchers have found elevated rates of homosexuality among women exposed prenatally to a synthetic hormone (DES) that was formerly used to reduce the risk of miscarriage (by their mothers) and among women who have an adrenal disorder that results in abnormally high androgen levels during prenatal development (Breedlove, 1994; Meyer-Bahlburg et al., 1995).

Despite the recent breakthroughs, much remains to be learned about the determinants of sexual orientation. The pathways to homosexuality appear to be somewhat different for males as opposed to females (Gladue, 1994). The behavioral genetics data suggest that the hereditary predisposition to homosexuality is not overpowering. Environmental influences of some kind probably contribute to the development of homosexuality, but the nature of these environmental factors remains a mystery.

Once again, though, we can see that the nature versus nurture debate can have far-reaching social and political implications. Homosexuals have long been victims of extensive—and in many instances *legal*—discrimination. Gays generally cannot legally formalize their unions in marriage, they are not allowed to openly join the U.S. military, and they are barred from some jobs (for example, many school districts will not hire gay teachers). However, if research were to show that being gay is largely a matter of biological destiny, much like being Hispanic or female or short, many of the arguments against equal rights for gays would disintegrate. Why ban gays from teaching, for instance, if their sexual preference cannot "rub off" on their students? Although I would argue that discrimination against gays should be brought to an end either way, many individuals' opinions about gay rights may be swayed by the outcome of the nature-nurture debate on the roots of homosexuality.

The Human Sexual Response

Assuming people are motivated to engage in sexual activity, exactly what happens to them physically? This may sound like a simple question. But scientists really knew very little about the physiology of the human sexual response before William Masters and Virginia Johnson did groundbreaking research in the 1960s. Although our society seems obsessed with sex, until relatively recently (the 1980s) it did not encourage scientists to study sex. At first Masters and Johnson even had difficulty finding journals that were willing to publish their studies.

Masters and Johnson used physiological recording devices to monitor the bodily changes of volunteers engaging in sexual activities. They even equipped an artificial penile device with a camera to study physiological reactions inside the vagina! Their observations of and interviews with subjects yielded a detailed description of the human sexual response and won them widespread acclaim.

Masters and Johnson (1966, 1970) divide the sexual response cycle into four stages: excitement, plateau, orgasm, and resolution. Figure 10.15 shows how the intensity of sexual arousal changes as women and men progress through these stages. Let's take a closer look at these phases in the human sexual response.

Excitement Phase

During the initial phase of excitement, the level of physical arousal usually escalates rapidly. In both sexes, muscle tension, respiration rate, heart rate, and blood pressure increase quickly. *Vasocongestion*—engorgement of blood vessels—produces penile erection and swollen testes in males. In females, vaso-

Figure 10.15

The human sexual response cycle. There are similarities and differences between men and women in patterns of sexual arousal. Pattern A, which culminates in orgasm and resolution, is the ideal sequence for both sexes but not something one can count on. Pattern B, which involves sexual arousal without orgasm followed by a slow resolution, is seen in both sexes but is more common among women (see Figure 10.16). Pattern C, which involves multiple orgasms, is seen almost exclusively in women, as men go through a refractory period before they are capable of another orgasm.

SOURCE: Based on Masters, W. H., & Johnson, V. E. (1966). *Human sexual response.* Boston: Little, Brown. Copyright ©1966 Little, Brown and Company.

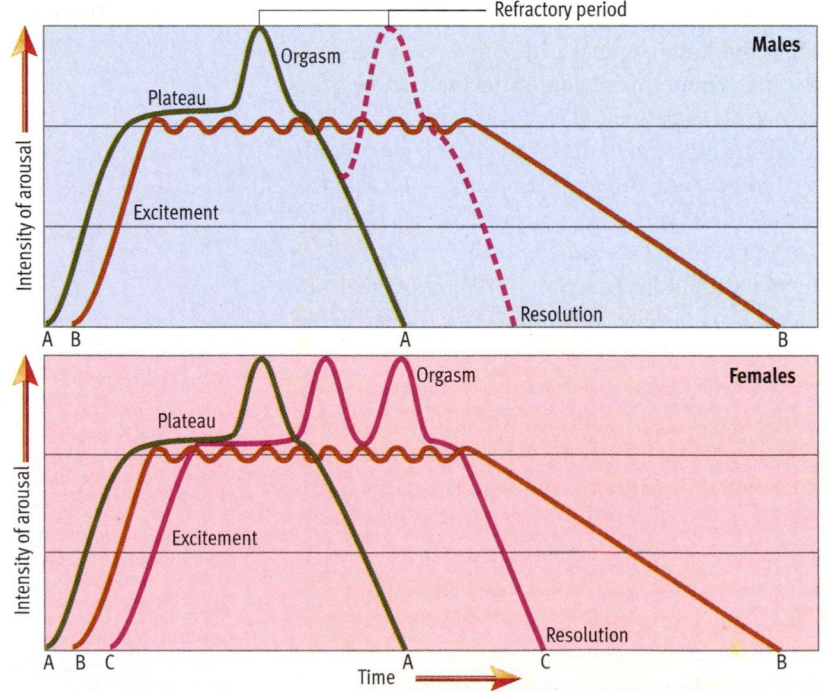

congestion leads to a swelling and hardening of the clitoris, expansion of the vaginal lips, and vaginal lubrication.

Plateau Phase

During the plateau phase, physiological arousal usually continues to build, but at a much slower pace. In women, further vasocongestion produces a tightening of the vaginal entrance, as the clitoris withdraws under the clitoral hood. Many men secrete a bit of fluid at the tip of the penis. This is not ejaculate, but it may contain sperm. When foreplay is lengthy, fluctuation in arousal is normal for both sexes. This fluctuation is more apparent in men; erections may increase and decrease noticeably. In women, this fluctuation may be reflected in changes in vaginal lubrication.

Orgasm Phase

Orgasm occurs when sexual arousal reaches its peak intensity and is discharged in a series of muscular contractions that pulsate through the pelvic area. Heart rate, respiration rate, and blood pressure increase sharply during this exceedingly pleasant spasmodic response. In males, orgasm is accompanied by ejaculation of the seminal fluid. The subjective experience of orgasm appears to be very similar for men and women.

However, there *are* some interesting gender differences in the orgasm phase of the sexual response cycle. On the one hand, women are more likely than men to be *multiorgasmic*. A woman is said to be multiorgasmic if she experiences more than one climax in a very brief time period (pattern C in Figure 10.15). On the other hand, women are more likely than men to engage in intercourse without experiencing an orgasm (see Figure 10.16; Laumann et al., 1994). Whether these differences reflect attitudes and sexual practices versus physiological processes is open to debate. On the one hand, it is easy to argue that males' greater orgasmic consistency must be a product of evolution, as it would have obvious adaptive significance for men's reproductive fitness. On the other hand, over the years theorists have come up with a variety of plausible environmental explanations for this disparity, such as gender differences in the socialization of guilt feelings about sex, and sexual scripts and practices that are less than optimal for women (Lott, 1987).

Resolution Phase

During the resolution phase, the physiological changes produced by sexual arousal subside. If orgasm has not occurred, the reduction in sexual ten-

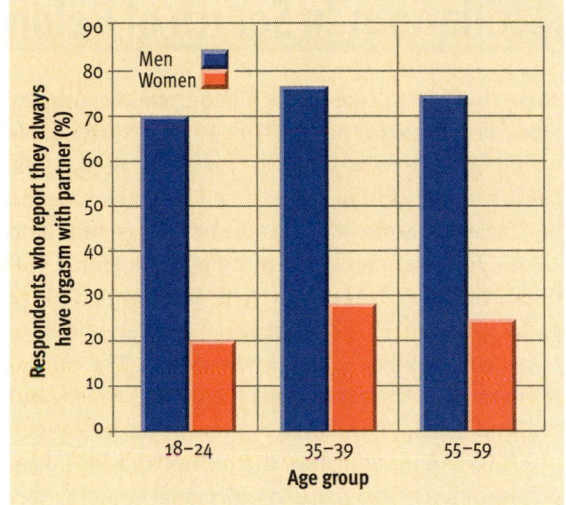

Figure 10.16

The gender gap in orgasm consistency. In their sexual interactions, men seem to reach orgasm more reliably than women. The data shown here suggest that the gender gap in orgasmic consistency is pretty sizable. Both biological and sociocultural factors may contribute to this gender gap. (Data from Laumann et al., 1994)

sion may be relatively slow and sometimes unpleasant. After orgasm, men experience a *refractory period, a time following orgasm during which males are largely unresponsive to further stimulation.* The length of the refractory period varies from a few minutes to a few hours and increases with age.

Masters and Johnson's exploration of the human sexual response led to major insights into the nature and causes of sexual problems. Ironically, although Masters and Johnson broke new ground in studying the *physiology* of sexual arousal, their research demonstrated that sexual problems are typically caused by *psychological* factors. Their conclusion shows once again that human sexuality involves a fascinating blend of biological and social processes. We turn next to the related motive of affiliation, which is more social in origin.

"*The conviction has grown that the most effective treatment of sexual incompatibility involves the technique of working with both members of the family unit.*"
WILLIAM MASTERS AND VIRGINIA JOHNSON

REVIEW OF KEY POINTS

- Modern theorists view heterosexuality and homosexuality not as an all-or-none distinction but as endpoints on a continuum. Recent data on the prevalence of homosexuality suggest that 5%–8% of the population may be gay. Although most gays can trace their homosexual leanings back to early childhood, research has not supported Freudian or behavioral theories of sexual orientation.

- Recent studies suggest that there is a genetic predisposition to homosexuality and that some subtle disparities in brain structure may be associated with homosexuality. Idiosyncrasies in prenatal hormonal secretions may also contribute to the development of homosexuality.

- The human sexual response cycle can be divided into four stages: excitement, plateau, orgasm, and resolution. The subjective experience of orgasm is fairly similar for both sexes. Intercourse leads to orgasm in women less consistently than in men, but women are much more likely to be multiorgasmic.

Affiliation: In Search of Belongingness

PREVIEW QUESTIONS
- What is the evolutionary significance of affiliation?
- What is the affiliation motive? How is it measured?
- How do those who score high in the need for affiliation differ from those who score low?

How would you like to spend the rest of your life alone on a pleasant but deserted island? Most people would find this to be a terrible fate. Why? Because the fundamental human need to be with others would be thwarted. Some animals (bears, tigers, and bald eagles, for example) don't mind going it alone. Humans, however, react badly to prolonged periods of social isolation. Humans are social animals and have to have meaningful contact with others. The *affiliation motive* is the need to associate with others and maintain social bonds. Affiliation encompasses one's needs for companionship, friendship, and love. People need more than mere interpersonal contact, they need enduring social bonds marked by mutual concern for one another.

In an overview of research on affiliation, Roy Baumeister and Mark Leary (1995) argued that it has a strong evolutionary basis, as social bonds offer a host of survival and reproductive benefits. They noted that by joining together, our ancestors could share food, provide better care for their offspring, engage in more effective hunting or gathering, enhance their defense against predators, diffuse risks, and provide more opportunities for mating. Small wonder, then, that humans seem to form bonds readily and go to great lengths to preserve their interpersonal attachments. In discussing the significance of affiliation, Baumeister and Leary described evidence that the quality of people's personal relationships is a major determinant of their happiness. They also discussed the strong link between affiliation issues and negative emotions—how the threat of rejection triggers anxiety, how concern about losing a partner evokes jealousy, and how loneliness is associated with depression. In sum, Baumeister and Leary made an eloquent case for the pervasive importance of affiliation, asserting that "much of what human beings do is done in the service of belongingness" (p. 498).

Although virtually everyone exhibits the need for belongingness, some people have stronger affiliation needs than others. Much of the research on affiliation has looked into these individual differences. In this research, investigators usually measure subjects' need for affiliation with some variant of Henry Murray's Thematic Apperception Test (Morgan & Murray, 1935; Murray, 1943). The Thematic Apperception Test (TAT) is a *projective test,* a test that requires subjects to respond to vague, ambiguous stimuli in ways that may reveal personal motives and traits (see Chapter 12). The stimulus materials for the TAT are pictures of people in ambiguous scenes open to interpretation. Examples include a man working at a desk and a woman seated in a chair staring off into space. Subjects are asked to write or tell stories about what's happening in the scenes and what the characters are feeling. The themes of these stories are then scored to measure the strength of various needs. Figure 10.17 shows examples of stories dominated by affiliation and achievement themes.

How do people who score high in the need for affiliation differ from those who score low? First, *they devote more time to interpersonal activities.* For example, they join more social groups such as clubs and church organizations (Smart, 1965). They make more phone calls and visits to friends (McClelland

---

Figure 10.17

Measuring motives with the Thematic Apperception Test (TAT). Subjects taking the TAT tell or write stories about what is happening in a scene, such as this one showing a man at work. The two stories shown here illustrate strong affiliation motivation and strong achievement motivation. The italicized parts of the stories are thematic ideas that would be identified by a TAT scorer.

Source: Stories reprinted by permission of Dr. David McClelland.

Affiliation arousal
George is an engineer who is working late. He is *worried that his wife will be annoyed* with him for neglecting her. She has been *objecting* that he cares more about his work than his wife and family. He seems *unable to satisfy* both his boss and his wife, but he *loves her* very much and will do his best to *finish up* fast and get home to her.

Achievement arousal
George is an engineer who *wants to win* a competition in which the man with the *most practicable drawing* will be awarded the contract to build a bridge. He is taking a moment to think *how happy he will be* if he wins. He has been *baffled by how to make such a long span strong,* but he remembers to *specify a new steel alloy* of great strength, submits his entry, but does not win, and is *very unhappy.*

& Winter, 1969), and they tend to devote more time to conversations and letter writing than others do (McAdams & Constantian, 1983). Second, *people with strong affiliation needs worry more about acceptance than those with a low affiliation drive do* (Koest-

ner & McClelland, 1992). For example, they experience greater anxiety when they're being evaluated socially by peers. They also go out of their way to avoid being argumentative in groups, because they fear rejection.

Achievement: In Search of Excellence

At the beginning of this chapter, we discussed Jon Krakauer's laborious, grueling effort to reach the summit of Mount Everest. He and the other climbers confronted incredible perils and endured extraordinary hardships to achieve their goal. What motivates people to push themselves so hard? In all likelihood, it's a strong need for achievement. The *achievement motive* is the need to master difficult challenges, to outperform others, and to meet high standards of excellence. Above all else, the need for achievement involves the desire to excel, especially in competition with others.

David McClelland and his colleagues (McClelland et al., 1953; McClelland, 1985) have been studying the achievement motive for about 40 years. McClelland believes that achievement motivation is of the utmost importance. He has estimated the average achievement motivation for *entire societies* by using TAT-like scoring procedures to assess the themes in representative examples of literature from those societies (rather than individuals' stories). These estimates of entire societies' need for achievement at specific times correlate with progress and productivity in those societies (Winter, 1992). For example, estimates of changes in achievement motivation in ancient Greece relate closely to the rise and fall of Greek civilization (McClelland, 1961). Also, estimates of achievement need in the United States have fluctuated in tandem with inventive activity as measured by the U.S. Patent Index (deCharms & Moeller, 1962).

McClelland sees the need for achievement as the spark that ignites economic growth, scientific progress, inspirational leadership, and masterpieces in the creative arts. It's difficult to argue with his assertion about the immense importance of achievement motivation. Consider how much poorer our culture would be if people such as Charles Darwin, Thomas Edison, Ernest Hemingway, Pablo Picasso, Marie Curie, Abraham Lincoln, Susan B. Anthony, Winston Churchill, and Martin Luther King hadn't had a fire burning in their hearts.

Individual Differences in the Need for Achievement

 8b

You've no doubt heard the stories of Lincoln as a young boy, reading through the night by firelight. Find a biography of any high achiever, and you'll probably find a similar drive—throughout the person's life. The need for achievement is a fairly stable aspect of personality. Hence, research in this area has focused mostly on individual differences in achievement motivation. Subjects' need for achievement can be measured effectively with the Thematic Apperception Test (C. Smith, 1992; Spangler, 1992).

The research on individual differences in achievement motivation has yielded interesting findings on the characteristics of people who score high in the need for achievement. They tend to work harder and more persistently on tasks than people low in the need for achievement (Brown, 1974). And they handle negative feedback about task performance more effectively than others (Fodor & Carver, 2000). They also are more future oriented than others and more likely to delay gratification in order to pursue long-term goals (Mischel, 1961; Raynor & Entin, 1982). In terms of careers, they typically go into competitive, entrepreneurial occupations that provide them with an opportunity to excel (McClelland, 1987). Apparently, their persistence and hard work often pay off. High achievement motivation correlates positively with measures of career success and with upward social mobility among lower-class men (Crockett, 1962; McClelland & Boyatzis, 1982).

Do people high in achievement need always tackle the biggest challenges available? Not necessarily. A curious finding has emerged in laboratory studies in which subjects have been asked to choose how difficult a task they want to work on. Subjects high in the need for achievement tend to select tasks of intermediate difficulty (McClelland & Koestner, 1992). For instance, in one study, where subjects playing a ring-tossing game were allowed to stand as close to or far away from the target peg as they wanted, high achiev-

Courtesy of David C. McClelland

"People with a high need for achievement are not gamblers; they are challenged to win by personal effort, not by luck."
DAVID MCCLELLAND

Most people attribute Michael Jordan's success in basketball to his remarkable ability, which was undeniably important. But the contribution of his extremely high need for achievement should not be underestimated. Jordan's competitive zeal was legendary, and he was widely regarded as one of the hardest working athletes in professional sports.

© Getty Images

ers tended to prefer a moderate degree of challenge (Atkinson & Litwin, 1960).

Situational Determinants of Achievement Behavior 8b

Your achievement drive is not the only determinant of how hard you work. Situational factors can also influence achievement strivings. John Atkinson (1974, 1981, 1992) has elaborated extensively on McClelland's original theory of achievement motivation and has identified some important situational deter-

minants of achievement behavior. Atkinson theorizes that the tendency to pursue achievement in a particular situation depends on the following factors:

- The strength of one's *motivation* to *achieve success*. This is viewed as a stable aspect of personality.
- One's estimate of the *probability of success* for the task at hand. This varies from task to task.
- The *incentive value of success*. This depends on the tangible and intangible rewards for success on the specific task.

The last two variables are situational determinants of achievement behavior (see Figure 10.18). That is, they vary from one situation to another. According to Atkinson, the pursuit of achievement increases as the probability and incentive value of success go up.

Let's apply Atkinson's model to a simple example. According to his theory, your tendency to pursue a good grade in calculus should depend on your general motivation to achieve success, your estimate of the probability of getting a good grade in the class, and the value you place on getting a good grade in calculus. Thus, given a certain motivation to achieve success, you will pursue a good grade in calculus less vigorously if your professor gives impossible exams (thus lowering your expectancy of success) or if a good grade in calculus is not required for your major (lowering the incentive value of success).

The joint influence of these situational factors may explain why high achievers prefer tasks of intermediate difficulty. Atkinson notes that the probability of success and the incentive value of success on tasks are interdependent to some degree. As tasks get easier, success becomes less satisfying. As tasks get harder, success becomes more satisfying, but its likelihood obviously declines. When the probability

Figure 10.18

Determinants of achievement behavior. According to John Atkinson, a person's pursuit of achievement in a particular situation depends on several factors. Some of these factors, such as need for achievement or fear of failure, are relatively stable motives that are part of the person's personality. Many other factors, such as the likelihood and value of success or failure, vary from one situation to another, depending on the circumstances.

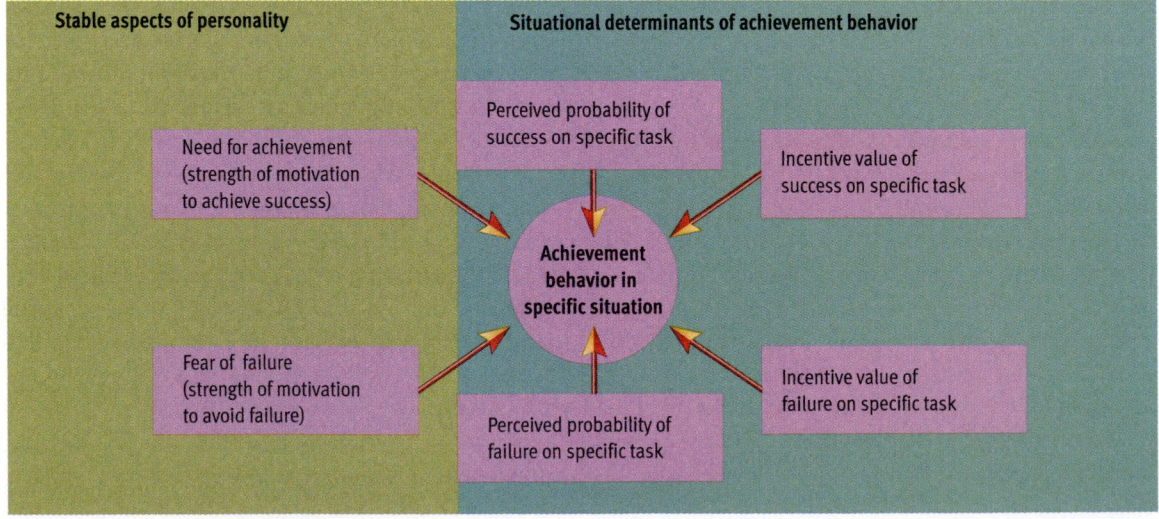

Stable aspects of personality | Situational determinants of achievement behavior

Need for achievement (strength of motivation to achieve success)

Perceived probability of success on specific task

Incentive value of success on specific task

Achievement behavior in specific situation

Fear of failure (strength of motivation to avoid failure)

Perceived probability of failure on specific task

Incentive value of failure on specific task

and incentive value of success are weighed together, moderately challenging tasks seem to offer the best overall value in terms of maximizing one's sense of accomplishment.

According to Atkinson, a person's fear of failure must also be considered to understand achievement behavior (Atkinson & Birch, 1978). He maintains that people vary in their *motivation to avoid failure*. This motive is considered a stable aspect of personality. Together with situational factors such as the probability of failure and the negative value placed on failure, it influences achievement strivings. Figure 10.18 diagrams all the factors in Atkinson's model that are thought to govern achievement behavior.

Fear is one of the most fundamental emotions. Thus, the relationship between achievement behavior and *fear* of failure illustrates how motivation and emotion are often intertwined. On the one hand, *emotion can cause motivation*. For example, *anger* about your work schedule may motivate you to look for a new job. *Jealousy* of an ex-girlfriend may motivate you to ask out her roommate. On the other hand, *motivation can cause emotion*. For example, your motivation to win a photography contest may lead to great *anxiety* during the judging and either great *joy* if you win or great *gloom* if you don't. Although motivation and emotion are closely related, they're *not* the same thing. We'll analyze the nature of emotion in the next section.

REVIEW OF KEY POINTS

● Affiliation encompasses various needs for social bonds. Affiliation probably had many adaptive benefits for our ancestors. Individual differences in the need for affiliation are usually measured with the TAT. People who are rela-tively high in the need for affiliation tend to devote more time to interpersonal activities and to worry more about acceptance than others do.

● Achievement involves the need to excel, especially in competition with others. The need for achievement is usually measured with the TAT. People who are relatively high in the need for achievement work harder and more persistently than others. They delay gratification well and pursue competitive careers.

● Situational factors also influence achievement behavior. The pursuit of achievement tends to increase when the probability of success and the incentive value of success are high.

CONCEPT CHECK 10.2

Understanding the Determinants of Achievement Behavior

According to John Atkinson, one's pursuit of achievement in a particular situation depends on several factors. Check your understanding of these factors by identifying each of the following vignettes as an example of one of the following four determinants of achievement behavior: (a) need for achievement, (b) perceived probability of success, (c) incentive value of success, (d) fear of failure. The answers can be found in Appendix A.

_____ 1. Donna has just received a B in biology. Her reaction is typical of the way she responds to many situations involving achievement: "I didn't get an A, it's true, but at least I didn't flunk; that's what I was really worried about."

_____ 2. Belinda is nervously awaiting the start of the finals of the 200-meter dash in the last meet of her high school career. "I've gotta win this race! This is the most important race of my life!"

_____ 3. Corey grins as he considers the easy time he's going to have this semester. "This class is supposed to be a snap. I hear the professor gives an A to nearly everyone."

_____ 4. Diana's just as hard-charging as ever. She's gotten the highest grade on every test throughout the semester, yet she's still up all night studying for the final. "I know I've got an A in the bag, but I want to be the best student Dr. McClelland's ever had!"

The Elements of Emotional Experience

The most profound and important experiences in life are saturated with emotion. Think of the *joy* that people feel at weddings, the *grief* they feel at funerals, the *ecstasy* they feel when they fall in love. Emotions also color everyday experiences. For instance, you might experience *anger* when a professor treats you rudely, *dismay* when you learn that your car needs expensive repairs, and *happiness* when you see that you aced your economics exam. In some respects, emotions lie at the core of mental health. The two most common complaints that lead people to seek psychotherapy are *depression* and *anxiety*. Clearly, emotions play a pervasive role in people's lives. Reflecting this reality, modern psychologists have in-creased their research on emotion in recent decades (Cacioppo & Gardner, 1999).

But exactly what is an emotion? Everyone has plenty of personal experience with emotion, but it's an elusive concept to define (LeDoux, 1995). Emotion includes cognitive, physiological, and behavioral components, which are summarized in the following definition: **Emotion** involves (1) **a subjective conscious experience (the cognitive component)** accompanied by (2) **bodily arousal (the physiological component) and by (3) characteristic overt expressions (the behavioral component)**. That's a pretty complex definition. Let's take a closer look at each of these three components of emotion.

PREVIEW QUESTIONS

● How do emotions affect autonomic activity?

● How does a lie detector work?

● Which brain centers contribute to the experience of emotions?

● What is the connection between emotion and body language?

● Are there cultural differences in how people recognize, describe, or express their emotions?

The Cognitive Component: Subjective Feelings

Over 550 words in the English language refer to emotions (Averill, 1980). Ironically, however, people often have difficulty describing their emotions to others (Zajonc, 1980). Emotion is a highly personal, subjective experience. In studying the cognitive component of emotions, psychologists generally rely on subjects' verbal reports of what they're experiencing. Their reports indicate that emotions are potentially intense internal feelings that sometimes seem to have a life of their own. People can't click their emotions on and off like a bedroom light. If it was as simple as that, you could choose to be happy whenever you wanted. As Joseph LeDoux puts it, "Emotions are things that happen to us rather than things we will to occur" (1996, p. 19). Actually, some degree of emotional control is possible (Thayer, 1996), but emotions tend to involve automatic reactions that are difficult to regulate (see Chapter 13).

People's cognitive appraisals of events in their lives are key determinants of the emotions they experience (R. Lazarus, 1991, 1995; Parkinson, 1997). A specific event, such as giving a speech, may be highly threatening and thus anxiety arousing for one person but a "ho-hum," routine matter for another. The conscious experience of emotion includes an *evaluative* aspect. People characterize their emotions as pleasant or unpleasant (Lang, 1995; Schlosberg, 1954). Of course, individuals often experience "mixed emotions" that include both pleasant and unpleasant qualities (Cacioppo & Berntson, 1999). For example, an executive just given a promotion with challenging new responsibilities may experience both happiness and anxiety. A young man who has just lost his virginity may experience a mixture of apprehension, guilt, and delight.

Emotions involve automatic reactions that can be difficult to control.

For the most part, researchers have paid more attention to negative emotions than positive ones (Fredrickson, 1998). Why have positive emotions been neglected? Fredrickson and Branigan (2001) note that there appear to be fewer positive emotions than negative ones and that positive emotions are less clearly differentiated from each other than negative emotions. Another consideration is that negative emotions appear to have more powerful effects than positive emotions (Baumeister et al., 2001). Although these factors probably have contributed, the neglect of positive emotions is symptomatic of a broad and deeply rooted bias in the field of psychology, which has historically focused on pathology, weaknesses, and suffering (and how to heal these conditions) rather than health, strengths, and resilience (Fredrickson, 2002). In recent years, the architects of the "positive psychology movement" have set out to shift the field's focus away from negative experiences (Seligman, 2002; Seligman & Csikszentmihalyi, 2000). The advocates of *positive psychology* argue for increased research on contentment, well-being, human strengths, and positive emotions. One outgrowth of this movement has been increased interest in the dynamics of happiness. We will discuss this research in the upcoming Personal Application.

The Physiological Component: Diffuse and Multifaceted

Emotional processes are closely tied to physiological processes, but the interconnections are enormously complex. The biological bases of emotions are diffuse, involving many areas in the brain and many neurotransmitter systems, as well as the autonomic nervous system and the endocrine system.

Autonomic Arousal

Imagine your reaction as your car spins out of control on an icy highway. Your fear is accompanied by a variety of physiological changes. Your heart rate and breathing accelerate. Your blood pressure surges, and your pupils dilate. The hairs on your skin stand erect, giving you "goose bumps," and you start to perspire. Although the physical reactions may not always be as obvious as in this scenario, *emotions are accompanied by visceral arousal* (Cacioppo et al., 1993). Surely you've experienced a "knot in your stomach" or a "lump in your throat"—thanks to anxiety.

Much of the discernible physiological arousal associated with emotion occurs through the actions of the *autonomic nervous system,* which regulates the activity of glands, smooth muscles, and blood vessels

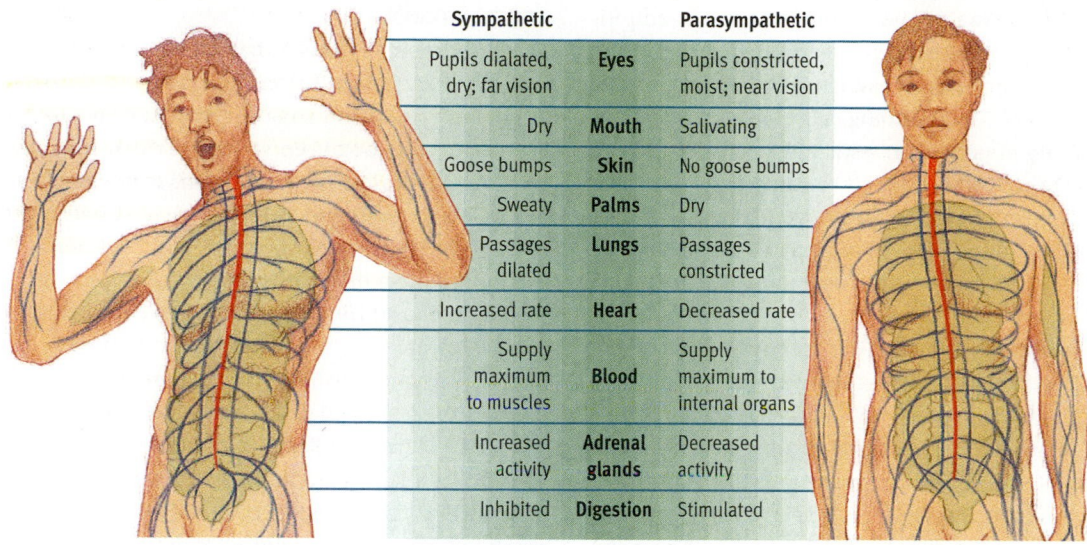

	Sympathetic		Parasympathetic
Pupils dilated, dry; far vision	**Eyes**		Pupils constricted, moist; near vision
Dry	**Mouth**		Salivating
Goose bumps	**Skin**		No goose bumps
Sweaty	**Palms**		Dry
Passages dilated	**Lungs**		Passages constricted
Increased rate	**Heart**		Decreased rate
Supply maximum to muscles	**Blood**		Supply maximum to internal organs
Increased activity	**Adrenal glands**		Decreased activity
Inhibited	**Digestion**		Stimulated

Figure 10.19

Emotion and autonomic arousal. The autonomic nervous system (ANS) is composed of the nerves that connect to the heart, blood vessels, smooth muscles, and glands (consult Figure 3.8 for a more detailed view). The ANS is divided into the *sympathetic system,* which mobilizes bodily resources in response to stress, and the *parasympathetic system,* which conserves bodily resources. Emotions are frequently accompanied by sympathetic ANS activation, which leads to goose bumps, sweaty palms, and the other physical responses listed on the left side of the diagram.

(see Figure 10.19). As you may recall from Chapter 3, the autonomic nervous system is responsible for the highly emotional *fight-or-flight response,* which is largely modulated by the release of adrenal *hormones* that radiate throughout the body. Hormonal changes clearly play a crucial role in emotional responses to stress and may contribute to many other emotions as well (Baum, Grunberg, & Singer, 1992).

One prominent part of emotional arousal is **the galvanic skin response (GSR), an increase in the electrical conductivity of the skin that occurs when sweat glands increase their activity.** GSR is a convenient and sensitive index of autonomic arousal that has been used as a measure of emotion in many laboratory studies.

The connection between emotion and autonomic arousal provides the basis for the ***polygraph,* or lie detector, a device that records autonomic fluctuations while a subject is questioned.** A polygraph can't actually detect lies. It's really an emotion detector. It monitors key indicators of autonomic arousal, typically heart rate, blood pressure, respiration rate, and GSR. The assumption is that when subjects lie, they experience emotion (presumably anxiety) that produces noticeable changes in these physiological indicators (see Figure 10.20). The polygraph examiner asks a subject a number of nonthreatening questions to establish the subject's baseline on these autonomic indicators. Then the examiner asks the critical questions (for example, "Where were you on the night of the burglary?") and observes whether the subject's autonomic arousal changes.

Polygraph advocates claim that lie detector tests are about 85%–90% accurate and that the validity of

Figure 10.20

Emotion and the polygraph. A lie detector measures the autonomic arousal that most people experience when they tell a lie. After using nonthreatening questions to establish a baseline, a polygraph examiner looks for signs of arousal (such as the sharp change in GSR shown here) on incriminating questions. Unfortunately, the polygraph is not a very dependable index of whether people are lying.

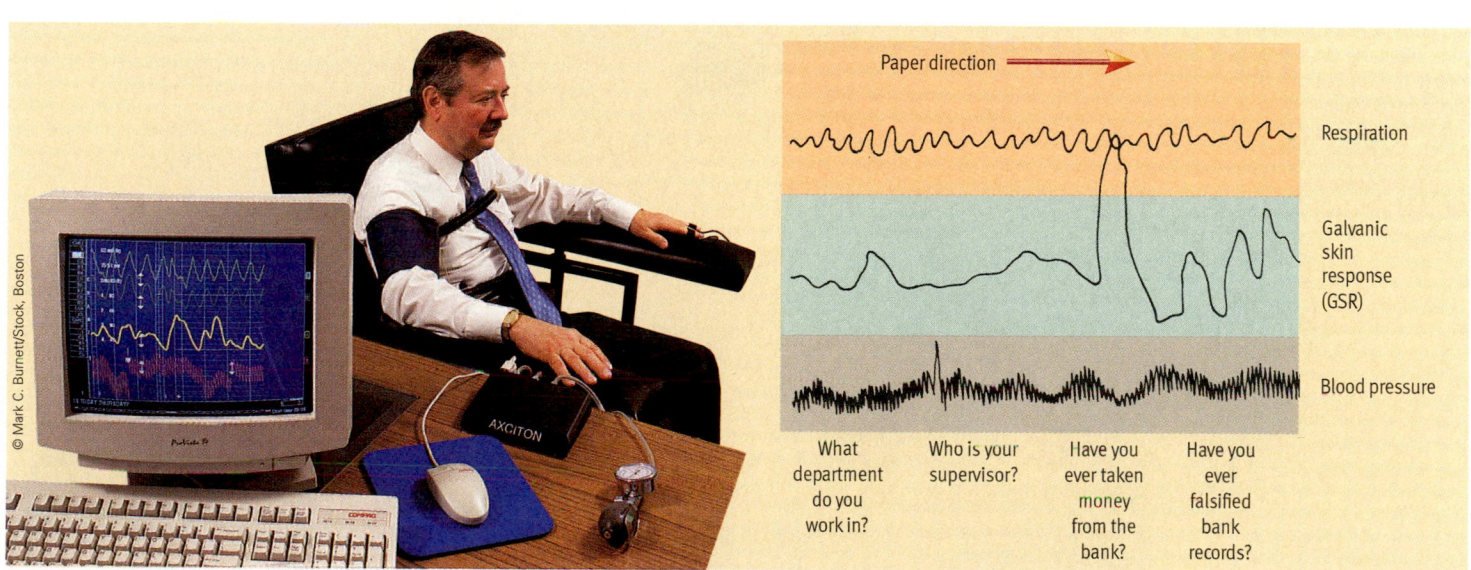

❝*In situations of danger, it is very useful to be able to respond quickly. The time saved by the amygdala in acting on the thalamic information, rather than waiting for the cortical input, may be the difference between life and death.*❞
JOSEPH LEDOUX

polygraph testing has been demonstrated in empirical studies, but these claims clearly are not supported by the evidence (Iacono & Patrick, 1999; Iacono & Lykken, 1997). Methodologically sound research on the validity of polygraph testing is surprisingly sparse (largely because it is difficult research to do), and the limited evidence available is not very impressive (Lykken, 1998; Saxe & Ben-Shakhar, 1999). Part of the problem is that people who are telling the truth may experience emotional arousal when they respond to incriminating questions. Thus, polygraph tests sometimes lead to accusations of lying against people who are innocent. Another problem is that some people can lie without experiencing anxiety or autonomic arousal. The crux of the problem, as Leonard Saxe (1994) notes, is that "there is no evidence of a unique physiological reaction to deceit" (p. 71). The polygraph *is* a potentially useful tool that can help police check out leads and alibis. However, polygraph results are not reliable enough to be submitted as evidence in most types of courtrooms.

Neural Circuits

 8c

The autonomic responses that accompany emotions are ultimately controlled in the brain. The hypothalamus, amygdala, and adjacent structures in the *limbic system* have long been viewed as the seat of emotions in the brain (Izard & Saxton, 1988; MacLean, 1993). Recent evidence suggests that the *amygdala* (see Figure 10.21) plays a particularly central role in the modulation of emotion. Joseph LeDoux (1986, 1993, 1996) and his colleagues have conducted extensive research on the classical conditioning of fear responses in animals. They have demonstrated that if an animal's amygdala is destroyed, the animal is unable to learn conditioned fear responses. Moreover, brain-imaging studies with human participants indicate that the amygdala is activated when subjects are shown emotion-arousing stimuli, such as pictures of mutilated bodies (Irwin et al., 1996) and when subjects are shown pictures depicting facial expressions of fear (Morris et al., 1996). That's *not* to say that the amygdala processes emotion by itself, as it appears

Figure 10.21

The amygdala and fear.
Emotions are controlled by a constellation of interacting brain systems, but the amygdala appears to play a particularly crucial role. According to LeDoux (1996), sensory inputs that can trigger fear (such as seeing a snake while out walking) arrive in the thalamus and then are routed along a fast pathway (shown in red) directly to the amygdala, and along a slow pathway (shown in blue) that allows the cortex time to think about the situation. Activity in the fast pathway also elicits the autonomic arousal and hormonal responses that are part of the physiological component of emotion. (Adapted from LeDoux, 1994)
Photo: © C. H. Wooley.

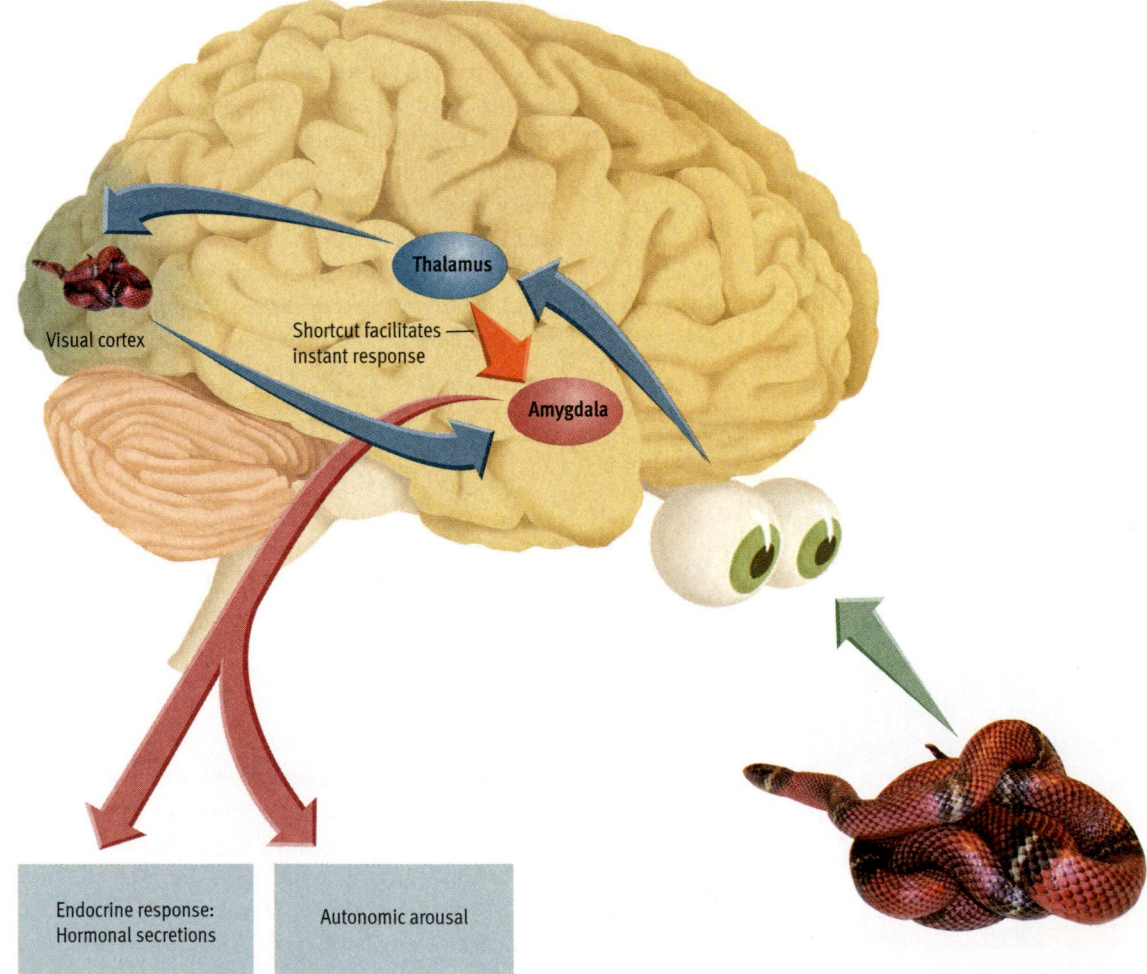

Thalamus

Visual cortex

Shortcut facilitates instant response

Amygdala

Endocrine response: Hormonal secretions

Autonomic arousal

to modulate activity in the cortex (Kapp, Supple, & Whalen, 1994). Recent studies suggest that areas in the *prefrontal cortex* make important contributions to the processing of emotional events (Davidson, Jackson, & Kalin, 2000; Teasdale et al., 1999).

According to LeDoux (1996), the amygdala lies at the core of a complex set of neural circuits that process emotion. He believes that sensory inputs capable of eliciting emotions arrive in the thalamus, which simultaneously routes the information along two separate pathways: a fast pathway to the nearby amygdala and a slower pathway to areas in the cortex (see Figure 10.21). The amygdala processes the information quickly, and if it detects a threat it almost instantly triggers neural activity that leads to the autonomic arousal and endocrine (hormonal) responses associated with emotion. The processing in this pathway is extremely fast, so that emotions may be triggered even before the brain has had a chance to really "think" about the input. Meanwhile, the information shuttled along the other pathway is subjected to a more "leisurely" cognitive appraisal in the cortex. This slower system, which can encode more details about a potential threat and evaluate the threat more thoroughly, then sends additional information to the amygdala, which is the "hub" of the system. LeDoux believes that the rapid-response pathway evolved because it is a highly adaptive warning system that can "be the difference between life and death." Although the amygdala has been widely characterized as a brain center for emotion in general, the research has mainly focused on the single emotion of fear. Hence, Whalen (1998) suggests that it might be more accurate to characterize the amygdala as the hub of a "vigilance" system.

The Behavioral Component: Nonverbal Expressiveness

At the behavioral level, people reveal their emotions through characteristic overt expressions such as smiles, frowns, furrowed brows, clenched fists, and slumped shoulders. In other words, *emotions are expressed in "body language," or nonverbal behavior.*

Facial expressions reveal a variety of basic emotions. In an extensive research project, Paul Ekman and Wallace Friesen have asked subjects to identify what emotion a person was experiencing on the basis of facial cues in photographs. They have found that subjects are generally successful in identifying six fundamental emotions: happiness, sadness, anger, fear, surprise, and disgust (Ekman & Friesen, 1975, 1984). These studies have been criticized on the grounds that they have used a rather small set of artificial,

highly posed photographs that don't do justice to the variety of facial expressions that can accompany specific emotions (Carroll & Russell, 1997). Still, the overall evidence indicates that people are reasonably skilled at deciphering emotions from others' facial expressions (Galati, Scherer, & Ricci-Bitti, 1997).

Some theorists believe that muscular feedback from one's own facial expressions contributes to one's conscious experience of emotions (Izard, 1990; Tomkins, 1991). Proponents of the *facial-feedback hypothesis* assert that facial muscles send signals to the brain and that these signals help the brain recognize the emotion that one is experiencing (see Figure 10.22 on the next page). According to this view, smiles, frowns, and furrowed brows help create the subjective experience of various emotions. Consistent with this idea, studies show that if subjects are instructed to contract their facial muscles to mimic facial expressions associated with certain emotions, they tend to report that they actually experience these emotions to some degree (Kleinke, Peterson, & Rutledge, 1998; Levenson, 1992).

The facial expressions that go with various emotions may be largely innate (Eibl-Ebesfeldt, 1975). For the most part, people who have been blind since birth smile and frown much like everyone else, even though they've never seen a smile or frown (Galati et al., 1997). The idea that facial expressions of emotion might be biologically built in has led to extensive cross-cultural research on the dynamics of emotion. Let's look at what investigators have learned about culture and the elements of emotional experience.

Culture and the Elements of Emotion

Are emotions innate reactions that are universal across cultures? Or are they socially learned reactions that are culturally variable? The voluminous research on this lingering question has not yielded a simple answer. Investigators have found both remarkable similarities and dramatic differences between cultures in the experience of emotion.

Cross-Cultural Similarities in Emotional Experience

After demonstrating that Western subjects could discern specific emotions from facial expressions, Ekman and Friesen (1975) took their facial-cue photographs on the road to other societies to see whether nonverbal expressions of emotion transcend cultural boundaries. Testing subjects in Argentina, Spain, Japan, and other countries, they found considerable cross-cultural agreement in the identification of happi-

Web Link 10.5

UCSC Perceptual Science Laboratory
Perceptions of other people, especially speech perception and facial expression, serve as a primary focus for research at this laboratory at the University of California, Santa Cruz. The site offers a broad set of resources, including a comprehensive guide to nonverbal facial analysis research being conducted in laboratories worldwide.

Figure 10.22

The facial feedback hypothesis. According to the facial feedback hypothesis, inputs to subcortical centers automatically evoke facial expressions associated with certain emotions, and the facial muscles then feed signals to the cortex that help it to recognize the emotion that one is experiencing. According to this view, facial expressions help create the subjective experience of various emotions.

Source: Smith, R. E. (1993). *Psychology*. St. Paul, MN: West Publishing. Copyright © 1993 by West Publishing. Reprinted by permission of Wadsworth Publishing.

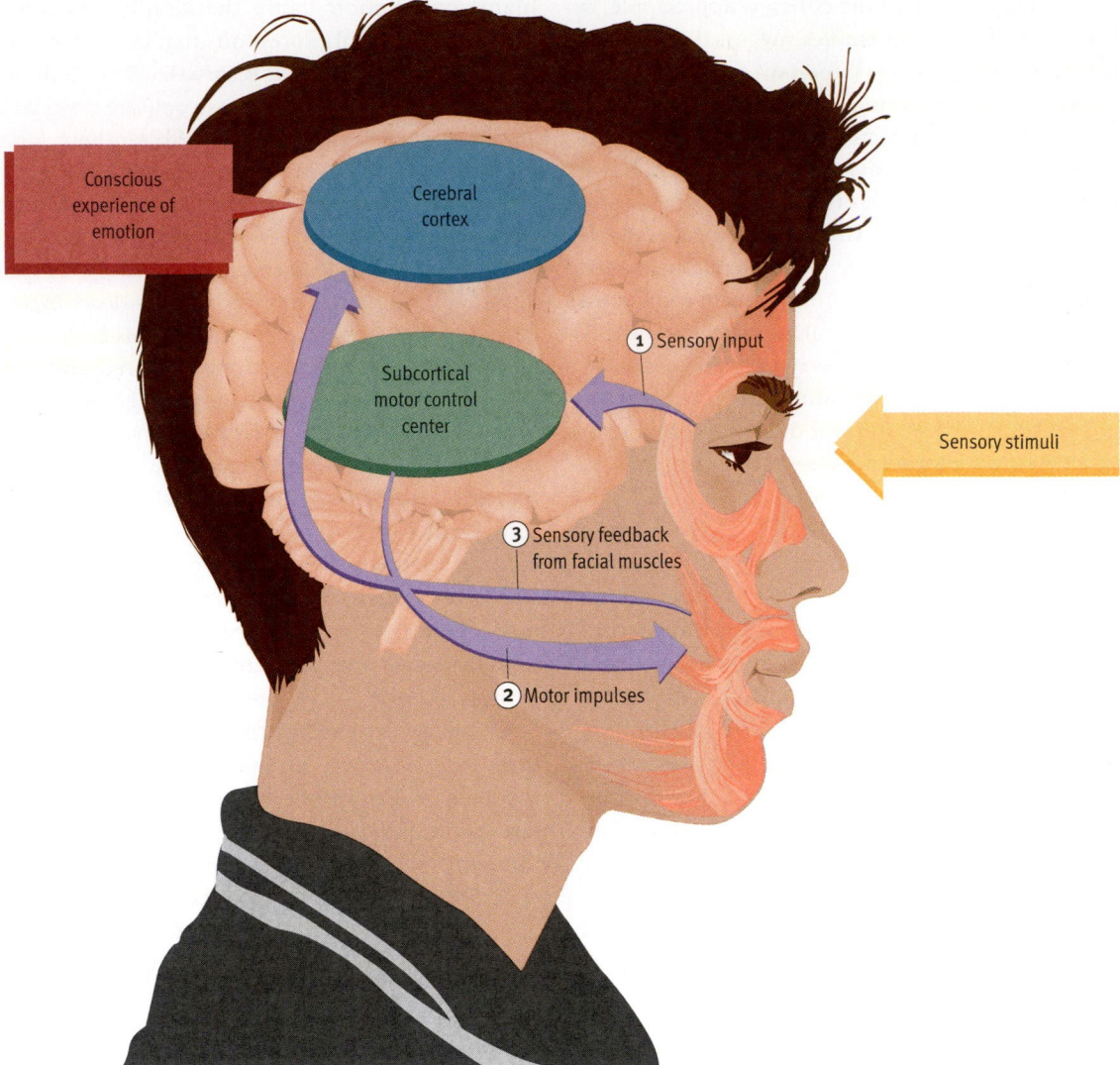

ness, sadness, anger, fear, surprise, and disgust based on facial expressions (see Figure 10.23). Still, Ekman and Friesen wondered whether this agreement might be the result of learning rather than biology, given that people in different cultures often share considerable exposure to Western mass media (magazines, newspapers, television, and so forth), which provide many visual depictions of people's emotional reactions. To rule out this possibility, they took their photos to a remote area in New Guinea and showed them to a group of natives (the Fore) who had had virtually no contact with Western culture. Even the people from this preliterate culture did a fair job of identifying the emotions portrayed in the pictures (see the data in the bottom row of Figure 10.23). Subsequent comparisons of many other societies have also shown considerable cross-cultural congruence in the judgment of facial expressions (Biehl et al., 1997; Ekman, 1992, 1993). Although some theorists

disagree (Russell, 1994, 1995), there is reasonably convincing evidence that people in widely disparate cultures express their emotions and interpret those expressions in much the same way (Izard, 1994; Matsumoto, 2001).

Cross-cultural similarities have also been found in the cognitive and physiological elements of emotional experience (Scherer & Wallbott, 1994). For example, in making cognitive appraisals of events that might elicit emotional reactions, people from different cultures generally think along the same lines (Mauro, Sato, & Tucker, 1992; Mesquita & Frijda, 1992). That is, they evaluate situations along the same dimensions (pleasant versus unpleasant, expected versus unexpected, fair versus unfair, and so on). Understandably, then, the types of events that trigger specific emotions are fairly similar across cultures (Frijda, 1999; Scherer, 1997). Around the globe, achievements lead to joy, injustices lead to anger,

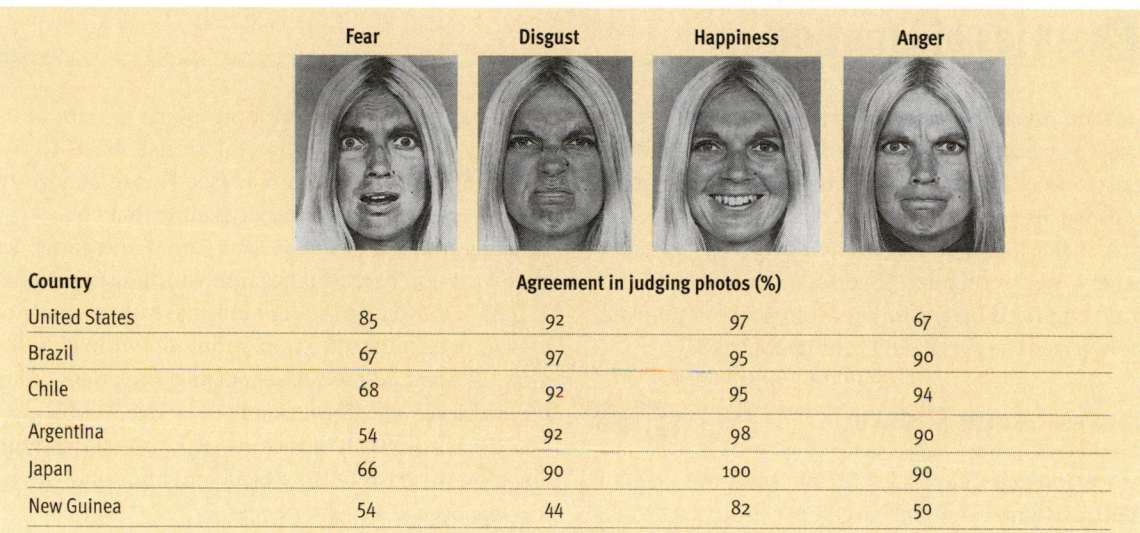

Country	Agreement in judging photos (%)			
	Fear	Disgust	Happiness	Anger
United States	85	92	97	67
Brazil	67	97	95	90
Chile	68	92	95	94
Argentina	54	92	98	90
Japan	66	90	100	90
New Guinea	54	44	82	50

Figure 10.23

Cross-cultural comparisons of people's ability to recognize emotions from facial expressions. Ekman and Friesen (1975) found that people in highly disparate cultures showed fair agreement on the emotions portrayed in these photos. This consensus across cultures suggests that facial expressions of emotions may be universal and that they have a strong biological basis.

SOURCE: Data from Ekman, P., & Friesen, W. V. (1975). *Unmasking the face.* Englewood Cliffs, NJ: Prentice-Hall. © 1975 by Paul Ekman, photographs courtesy of Paul Ekman.

and risky situations lead to fear. Finally, as one might expect, the physiological arousal that accompanies emotion also appears to be largely invariant across cultures (Wallbott & Scherer, 1988). Thus, researchers have found a great deal of cross-cultural continuity and uniformity in the cognitive, physiological, and behavioral (expressive) elements of emotional experience.

Cross-Cultural Differences in Emotional Experience

The cross-cultural similarities in emotional experience are impressive, but researchers have also found many cultural disparities in how people think about and express their emotions (Mesquita, 2001). Foremost among these disparities are the fascinating variations in how cultures categorize emotions. Some basic categories of emotion that are universally understood in Western cultures appear to go unrecognized—or at least unnamed—in some non-Western cultures. James Russell (1991) has compiled numerous examples of English words for emotions that have no equivalent in other languages. For example, Tahitians have no word that corresponds to *sadness*. Many non-Western groups, including the Yoruba of Nigeria, the Kaluli of New Guinea, and the Chinese, lack a word for *depression*. The concept of *anxiety* seems to go unrecognized among Eskimos, and the Quichua of Ecuador lack a word for *remorse*.

Cultural disparities have also been found in regard to nonverbal expressions of emotion. Although the natural facial expressions associated with basic emotions appear to be pancultural, people can and do learn to control and modify these expressions. *Display rules* are norms that regulate the appropri-ate expression of emotions. They prescribe when, how, and to whom people can show various emotions. These norms vary from one culture to another (Ekman, 1992), as do attitudes about specific emotions (Eid & Diener, 2001). For instance, the Ifaluk (a Pacific island culture) severely restrict expressions of happiness because they believe that this emotion often leads people to neglect their duties (Lutz, 1987). Japanese culture emphasizes the suppression of negative emotions in public. More so than in other cultures, the Japanese are socialized to mask emotions such as anger, sadness, and disgust with stoic facial expressions or polite smiling. Thus, nonverbal expressions of emotions vary somewhat across cultures because of culture-specific attitudes and display rules.

REVIEW OF KEY POINTS

- Emotion is made up of cognitive, physiological, and behavioral components. The cognitive component involves subjective feelings that have an evaluative aspect.

- The most readily apparent aspect of the physiological component of emotion is autonomic arousal. This arousal is the basis for the lie detector, which is really an emotion detector. Polygraphs are not all that accurate in assessing individuals' veracity. The amygdala appears to be the hub of an emotion-processing system in the brain.

- At the behavioral level, emotions are expressed through body language, with facial expressions being particularly prominent. Ekman and Friesen have found considerable cross-cultural agreement in the identification of emotions based on facial expressions.

- Cross-cultural similarities have also been found in the cognitive and physiological components of emotion. However, there are some striking cultural variations in how people categorize and display their emotions.

Theories of Emotion

PREVIEW QUESTIONS
- What are the differences between the James-Lange and Cannon-Bard theories of emotion?
- How did the two-factor theory of emotion try to reconcile these differences?
- How do evolutionary theorists explain emotions?

How do psychologists explain the experience of emotion? A variety of theories and conflicting models exist. Some have been vigorously debated for over a century. As we describe these theories, you'll recognize a familiar bone of contention. Like so many other types of theories, theories of emotion differ in their emphasis on the innate biological basis of emotion versus the social, environmental basis.

James-Lange Theory

As we noted in Chapter 1, William James was a prominent early theorist who urged psychologists to explore the functions of consciousness. James (1884) developed a theory of emotion over 100 years ago that remains influential today. At about the same time, he and Carl Lange (1885) independently proposed that *the conscious experience of emotion results from one's perception of autonomic arousal.* Their theory stood common sense on its head. Everyday logic suggests that when you stumble onto a rattlesnake in the woods, the conscious experience of fear leads to visceral arousal (the fight-or-flight response). The

James-Lange theory of emotion asserts the opposite: that the perception of visceral arousal leads to the conscious experience of fear (see Figure 10.24). In other words, while you might assume that your pulse is racing because you're fearful, James and Lange argued that you're fearful because your pulse is racing.

The James-Lange theory emphasizes the physiological determinants of emotion. According to this view, *different patterns of autonomic activation lead to the experience of different emotions.* Hence, people supposedly distinguish emotions such as fear, joy, and anger on the basis of the exact configuration of physical reactions they experience.

Cannon-Bard Theory

Walter Cannon (1927) found the James-Lange theory unconvincing. Cannon pointed out that physiological arousal may occur without the experience of emotion (if one exercises vigorously, for instance). He also argued that visceral changes are too slow to precede the conscious experience of emotion. Finally, he argued that people experiencing very different

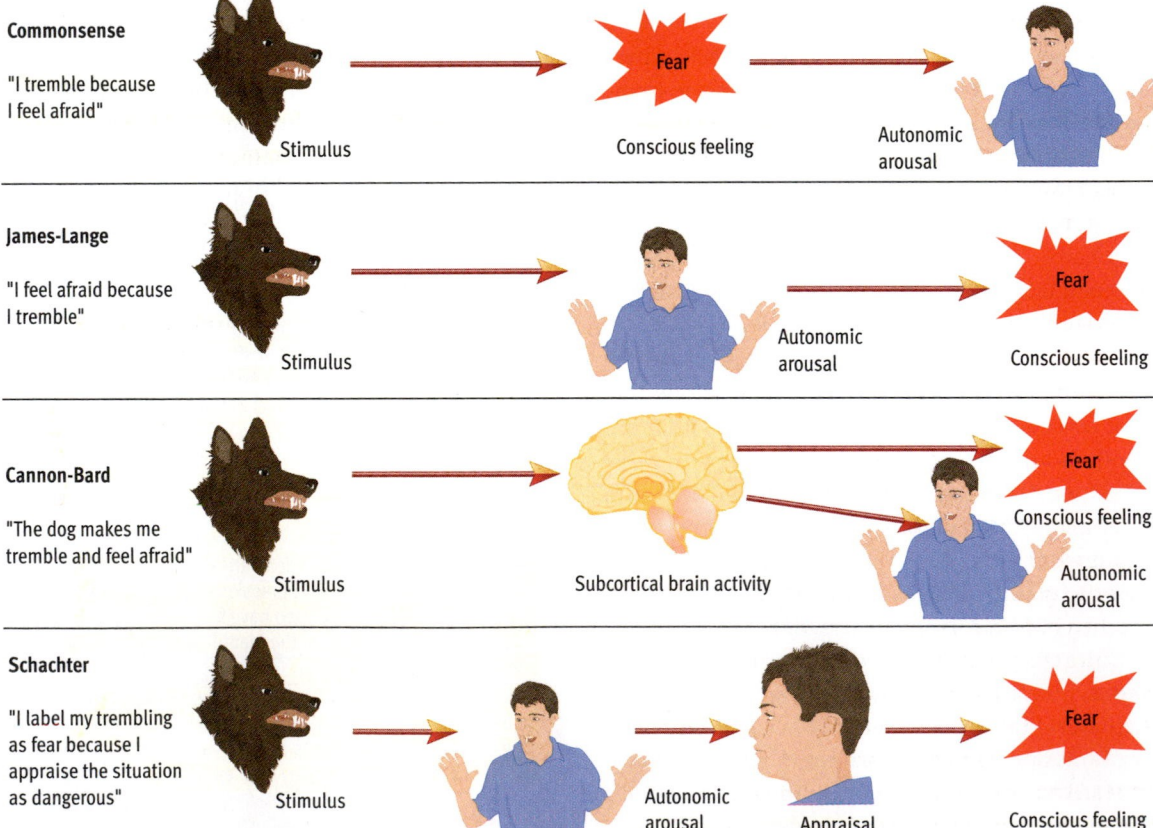

Figure 10.24

Theories of emotion. Three influential theories of emotion are contrasted with one another and with the common-sense view. The James-Lange theory was the first to suggest that feelings of arousal cause emotion, rather than vice versa. Schachter built on this idea by adding a second factor—interpretation (appraisal and labeling) of arousal.

Commonsense

"I tremble because I feel afraid"

Stimulus → Fear (Conscious feeling) → Autonomic arousal

James-Lange

"I feel afraid because I tremble"

Stimulus → Autonomic arousal → Fear (Conscious feeling)

Cannon-Bard

"The dog makes me tremble and feel afraid"

Stimulus → Subcortical brain activity → Fear (Conscious feeling) / Autonomic arousal

Schachter

"I label my trembling as fear because I appraise the situation as dangerous"

Stimulus → Autonomic arousal → Appraisal → Fear (Conscious feeling)

emotions, such as fear, joy, and anger, exhibit almost identical patterns of autonomic arousal.

Thus, Cannon espoused a different explanation of emotion. Later, Philip Bard (1934) elaborated on it. The resulting Cannon-Bard theory argues that emotion occurs when the thalamus sends signals *simultaneously* to the cortex (creating the conscious experience of emotion) and to the autonomic nervous system (creating visceral arousal). The Cannon-Bard model is compared to the James-Lange model in Figure 10.24. Cannon and Bard were off the mark a bit in pinpointing the thalamus as the neural center for emotion. However, many modern theorists agree with the Cannon-Bard view that emotions originate in subcortical brain structures (LeDoux, 1996; Panksepp, 1991; Rolls, 1990) and with the assertion that people do not discern their emotions from different patterns of autonomic activation (Frijda, 1999; Wagner, 1989).

Schachter's Two-Factor Theory

In another influential analysis, Stanley Schachter asserted that people look at situational cues to differentiate between alternative emotions. According to Schachter (1964; Schachter & Singer, 1962, 1979), the experience of emotion depends on two factors: (1) autonomic arousal and (2) cognitive interpretation of that arousal. Schachter proposed that when you experience visceral arousal, you search your environment for an explanation (see Figure 10.24 again). If you're stuck in a traffic jam, you'll probably label your arousal as anger. If you're taking an important exam, you'll probably label it as anxiety. If you're celebrating your birthday, you'll probably label it as happiness.

Schachter agreed with the James-Lange view that emotion is inferred from arousal. However, he also agreed with the Cannon-Bard position that different emotions yield indistinguishable patterns of arousal. He reconciled these views by arguing that people look to external rather than internal cues to differentiate and label their specific emotions. In essence, Schachter suggested that people think along the following lines: "If I'm aroused and you're obnoxious, I must be angry."

Although the two-factor theory has received support, studies have revealed some limitations as well (Leventhal & Tomarken, 1986). Situations can't mold emotions in just any way at any time. And in searching to explain arousal, subjects don't limit themselves to the immediate situation (Sinclair et al., 1994). Thus, emotions are not as pliable as the two-factor theory initially suggested.

Evolutionary Theories of Emotion

As the limitations of the two-factor theory were exposed, theorists began returning to ideas espoused by Charles Darwin over a century ago. Darwin (1872) believed that emotions developed because of their adaptive value. Fear, for instance, would help an organism avoid danger and thus would aid in survival. Hence, Darwin viewed human emotions as a product of evolution. This premise serves as the foundation for several prominent theories of emotion developed independently by S. S. Tomkins (1980, 1991), Carroll Izard (1984, 1991), and Robert Plutchik (1984, 1993).

These *evolutionary theories* consider emotions to be largely innate reactions to certain stimuli. As such, emotions should be immediately recognizable under most conditions without much thought. After all, primitive animals that are incapable of complex thought seem to have little difficulty in recognizing their emotions. Evolutionary theorists believe that emotion evolved before thought. They assert that thought plays a relatively small role in emotion, although they admit that learning and cognition may have some influence on human emotions. Evolutionary theories generally assume that emotions originate in subcortical brain structures that evolved before the higher brain areas in the cortex associated with complex thought.

Evolutionary theories also assume that evolution has equipped humans with a small number of innate emotions with proven adaptive value. Hence, the principal question that evolutionary theories of emotion wrestle with is, *What are the fundamental emotions?* Figure 10.25 summarizes the conclusions of the leading theorists in this area. As you can see, Tomkins, Izard, and Plutchik have not come up with identical

"*Cognitive factors play a major role in determining how a subject interprets his bodily feelings.*"
STANLEY SCHACHTER

Figure 10.25

Primary emotions. Evolutionary theories of emotion attempt to identify primary emotions. Three leading theorists—Silvan Tomkins, Carroll Izard, and Robert Plutchik—have compiled different lists of primary emotions, but this chart shows great overlap among the basic emotions identified by these theorists. (Based on Mandler, 1984)

Silvan Tomkins	Carroll Izard	Robert Plutchik
Fear	Fear	Fear
Anger	Anger	Anger
Enjoyment	Joy	Joy
Disgust	Disgust	Disgust
Interest	Interest	Anticipation
Surprise	Surprise	Surprise
Contempt	Contempt	
Shame	Shame	
	Sadness	Sadness
Distress		
	Guilt	
		Acceptance

Understanding Theories of Emotion

Check your understanding of theories of emotion by matching the theories we discussed with the statements below. Let's borrow William James's classic example: Assume that you just stumbled onto a bear in the woods. The first statement expresses the commonsense explanation of your fear. Each of the remaining statements expresses the essence of a different theory; indicate which theory in the spaces provided. The answers are provided in Appendix A.

1. You tremble because you're afraid.

Common Sense
_____

2. You're afraid because you're trembling.

_____

3. You're afraid because situational cues (the bear) suggest that's why you're trembling.

_____

4. You're afraid because the bear has elicited an innate primary emotion.

_____

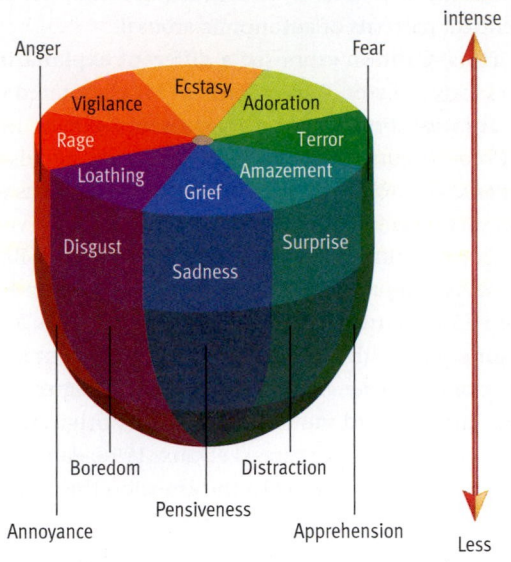

Figure 10.26

Emotional intensity in Plutchik's model. According to Plutchik, diversity in human emotion is a product of variations in emotional intensity, as well as blendings of primary emotions. Each vertical slice in the diagram is a primary emotion that can be subdivided into emotional expressions of varied intensity, ranging from most intense (top) to least intense (bottom).

SOURCE: Based on art in Plutchik, R. (1980). A language for emotions. *Psychology Today, 13* (9), 68–78. Reprinted with permission from Psychology Today Magazine. Copyright © 1980 by Sussex Publishers.

lists, but there is considerable agreement. All three conclude that people exhibit eight to ten primary emotions. Moreover, six of these emotions appear on all three lists: fear, anger, joy, disgust, interest, and surprise.

Of course, people experience more than just eight to ten emotions. How do evolutionary theories account for this variety? They propose that the many emotions that people experience are produced by (1) blends of primary emotions and (2) variations in intensity. For example, Robert Plutchik (1980, 1993)

has devised an elegant model of how primary emotions such as fear and surprise may blend into secondary emotions such as awe. Plutchik's model also posits that various emotions, such as apprehension, fear, and terror, involve one primary emotion experienced at different levels of intensity (see Figure 10.26).

Putting It in Perspective

Five of our organizing themes were particularly prominent in this chapter: the influence of cultural contexts, the dense connections between psychology and society at large, psychology's theoretical diversity, the interplay of heredity and environment, and the multiple causes of behavior.

Our discussion of motivation and emotion demonstrated once again that there are both similarities and differences across cultures in behavior. The neural, biochemical, genetic, and hormonal processes underlying hunger and eating, for instance, are universal. But cultural factors influence what people prefer

to eat, how much they eat, and whether they worry about dieting. In a similar vein, researchers have found a great deal of cross-cultural congruence in the cognitive, physiological, and expressive elements of emotional experience, but they have also found cultural variations in how people think about and express their emotions. Thus, as we have seen in previous chapters, psychological processes are characterized by both cultural variance and invariance.

Our discussion of the controversies surrounding evolutionary theory, aggressive pornography, and the determinants of sexual orientation show once again that psychology is not an ivory tower enterprise. It evolves in a sociohistorical context that helps to shape the debates in the field, and these debates often have far-reaching social and political ramifications for society at large. We ended the chapter with a discussion of various theories of emotion, which showed once again that psychology is characterized by great theoretical diversity.

Finally, we repeatedly saw that biological and environmental factors jointly govern behavior. For example, we learned that eating behavior, sexual desire, and the experience of emotion all depend on complicated interactions between biological and environmental determinants. Indeed, complicated interactions permeated the entire chapter, demonstrating that if we want to fully understand behavior, we have to take multiple causes into account. In the upcoming Personal Application, we will continue our discussion of emotion, looking at recent research on the correlates of happiness. In the Critical Thinking

Application that follows, we discuss how to carefully analyze the types of arguments that permeated this chapter.

REVIEW OF KEY POINTS

- The James-Lange theory asserts that emotion results from one's perception of autonomic arousal. The Cannon-Bard theory counters with the proposal that emotions originate in subcortical areas of the brain.

- According to Schachter's two-factor theory, people infer emotion from arousal and then label the emotion in accordance with their cognitive explanation for the arousal. Evolutionary theories of emotion maintain that emotions are innate reactions that require little cognitive interpretation.

- Our look at motivation and emotion showed once again that psychology is characterized by theoretical diversity, that biology and environment shape behavior interactively, that behavior is governed by multiple causes, that psychological processes are characterized by both cultural variance and invariance, and that psychology evolves in a sociohistorical context.

ERSONAL APPLICATION

Exploring the Ingredients of Happiness

Answer the following "true" or "false."

____ **1** The empirical evidence indicates that most people are relatively unhappy.

____ **2** Although wealth doesn't *guarantee* happiness, wealthy people are much more likely to be happy than the rest of the population.

____ **3** People who have children are happier than people without children.

____ **4** Good health is an essential requirement for happiness.

____ **5** Good-looking people are happier than those who are unattractive.

The answer to all these questions is "false." These assertions are all reasonable and widely believed hypotheses about the correlates of happiness, but they have *not* been supported by empirical research. Recent years have brought a surge of interest in the correlates of *subjective well-being*— **individuals' personal perceptions of their overall happiness and life satisfaction.** The findings of these studies are quite in-

teresting. As you have already seen from our true-false questions, many common-sense notions about happiness appear to be inaccurate.

How Happy Are People?

One of these inaccuracies is the apparently widespread assumption that most people are relatively unhappy. Writers, social scientists, and the general public seem to believe that people around the world are predominantly dissatisfied and unhappy, yet empirical surveys consistently find that the vast majority of respondents—even those who are poor or disabled—characterize themselves as fairly happy (Diener & Diener, 1996; Myers & Diener, 1995). When people are asked to rate their happiness, only a small minority place themselves below the neutral point on the various scales used (see Figure 10.27). When the average subjective well-being of entire nations is computed, based on almost 1000 surveys, the means cluster toward the positive end of the scale, as shown in Fig-

ure 10.28 (Veenhoven, 1993). That's not to say that everyone is equally happy. Researchers find substantial and thought-provoking disparities among people in subjective well-being, which we will analyze momentarily, but the overall picture seems rosier than anticipated.

Factors That Do Not Predict Happiness

Let us begin our discussion of individual differences in happiness by highlighting those things that turn out to be relatively unimportant determinants of subjective well-being. Quite a number of factors that you might expect to be influential appear to bear little or no relationship to general happiness.

Money. There *is* a positive correlation between income and subjective feelings of happiness, but in modern, affluent cultures the association is surprisingly weak (Myers & Diener, 1995). For example, one study found a correlation of just .12 between income and happiness in the United States (Diener et al., 1993). Admittedly, being very poor can make people unhappy, but once people ascend above the poverty level, little relation is seen between income and happiness. On the average, even wealthy people are only marginally happier than those in the middle classes. The problem with money is that in this era of voracious consumption, most of us find a way to spend all our money and come out short no matter how much we make. Complaints about not having enough money are routine even among people who earn six-figure incomes. Interestingly, there is some evidence that people who place an especially strong emphasis on the pursuit of wealth and materialistic goals tend to be somewhat less happy than others (Ryan & Deci, 2001).

Figure 10.27

Measuring happiness with a nonverbal scale. Researchers have used a variety of methods to estimate the distribution of happiness. For example, in one study in the United States, respondents were asked to examine the seven facial expressions shown and select the one that "comes closest to expressing how you feel about your life as a whole." As you can see, the vast majority of participants chose happy faces. (Data adapted from Myers, 1992)

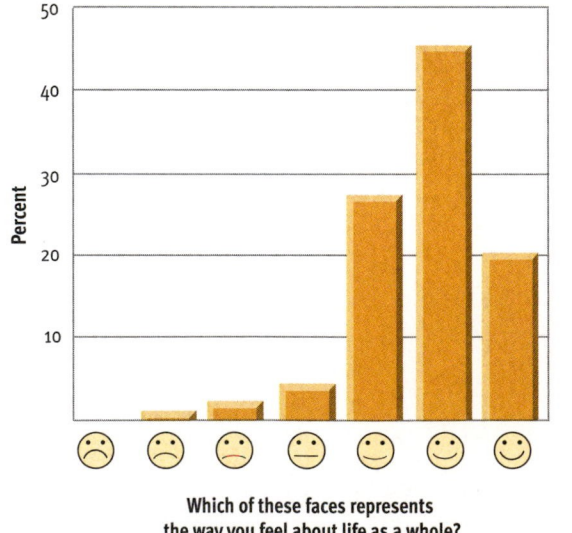

Which of these faces represents the way you feel about life as a whole?

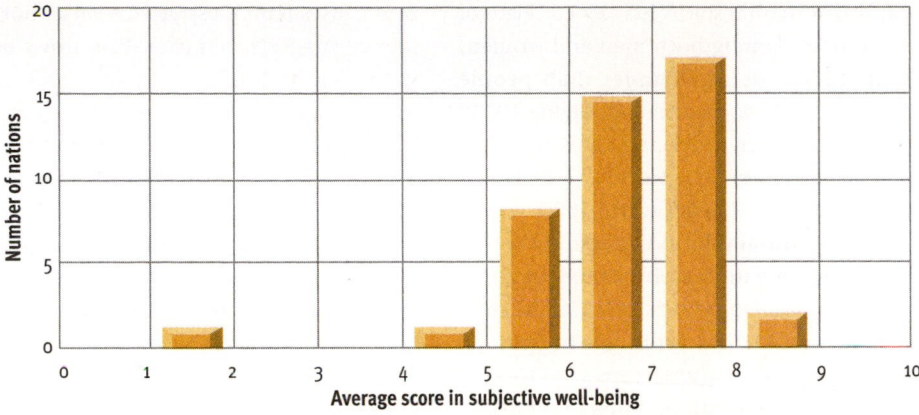

Figure 10.28

The subjective well-being of nations.
Veenhoven (1993) combined the results of almost 1000 surveys to calculate the average subjective well-being reported by representative samples from 43 nations. The mean happiness scores clearly pile up at the positive end of the distribution, with only two scores falling below the neutral point of 5. (Data adapted from Diener and Diener, 1996)

Age. Age and happiness are consistently found to be unrelated. Age accounts for less than 1 percent of the variation in people's happiness (Inglehart, 1990; Myers & Diener, 1997). The key factors influencing subjective well-being may shift some as people grow older—work becomes less important, health more so—but people's average level of happiness tends to remain remarkably stable over the life span.

Parenthood. Children can be a tremendous source of joy and fulfillment, but they can also be a tremendous source of headaches and hassles. Compared to childless couples, parents worry more and experience more marital problems (Argyle, 1987). Apparently, the good and bad aspects of parenthood balance each other out, because the evidence indicates that people who have children are neither more nor less happy than people without children.

Intelligence. Intelligence is a highly valued trait in modern society, but researchers have not found an association between IQ scores and happiness (Diener, 1984). Educational attainment also appears to be unrelated to life satisfaction (Ross & Van Willigen, 1997).

Physical Attractiveness. Good-looking people enjoy a variety of advantages in comparison to unattractive people (see Chapter 16). Given that physical attractiveness is an important resource, we might expect that attractive people would be happier than others, but the available data indicate that the correlation between attractiveness and happiness is negligible (Diener, Wolsic, & Fujita, 1995).

Moderately Good Predictors of Happiness

Research has identified four facets of life that appear to have a *moderate* association with subjective well-being: health, social activity, religious belief, and culture.

Health. Good physical health would seem to be an essential requirement for happiness, but people adapt to health problems. Research reveals that individuals who develop serious, disabling health conditions aren't as unhappy as one might guess (Myers, 1992). Furthermore, Freedman (1978) argues that good health does not, by itself, produce happiness, because people tend to take good health for granted. Considerations such as these may help to explain why researchers find only a moderate positive correlation (average = .32) between health status and subjective well-being (Argyle, 1999).

Social Activity. Humans are social animals, and interpersonal relations *do* appear to contribute to people's happiness. Those who are satisfied with their social support and friendship networks and those who are socially active report above-average levels of happiness (Cooper, Okamura, & Gurka, 1992; Myers, 1999). And people who are exceptionally happy tend to report greater satisfaction with their social relations than those who are average or low in subjective well-being (Diener & Seligman, 2002).

Religion. The link between religiosity and subjective well-being is modest, but a number of large-scale surveys suggest that people with heartfelt religious convictions are more likely to be happy than people who

If beauty, wealth, fame, and success bring happiness, then actress Halle Berry should be as happy as they come, but her past struggles with depression demonstrate that the ingredients of happiness are more subjective and complex than one might guess.

characterize themselves as nonreligious (Argyle, 1999; Poloma & Pendleton, 1990). Researchers aren't sure how religious faith fosters happiness, but Myers (1992) offers some interesting conjectures. Among other things, he discusses how religion can give people a sense of purpose and meaning in their lives, help them accept their setbacks gracefully, connect them to a caring, supportive community, and comfort them by putting their ultimate mortality in perspective.

Culture. Researchers have found some modest cultural variations in average subjective well-being and in the key sources of happiness (Diener, Diener, & Diener, 1995; Suh et al., 1998). These variations have mostly been related to cultural differences in *individualism versus collectivism*. **Individualism involves putting personal goals ahead of group goals and defining one's identity in terms of personal attributes rather than group memberships.** In contrast, *collectivism* **involves putting group goals ahead of personal goals and defining one's identity in terms of the groups one belongs to** (such as one's family, tribe, work group, social class, caste, and so on). In comparison to individualistic cultures, collectivist cultures place a higher priority on shared values and resources, cooperation, mutual interdependence, and concern for how one's actions will affect other group members. Consistent with these realities, *relationship harmony* appears to be a more important determinant of happiness in collectivist cultures than in individualistic cultures (Kwan, Bond, & Singelis, 1997).

Strong Predictors of Happiness

The list of factors that turn out to have fairly strong associations with happiness is surprisingly short. The key ingredients of happiness appear to involve love, work, and personality.

Love and Marriage. Romantic relationships can be stressful, but people consistently rate being in love as one of the most critical ingredients of happiness (Myers, 1999). Furthermore, although people complain a lot about their marriages, the evidence indicates that marital status is a key correlate of happiness. Among both men and women, married people are happier than people who are single or divorced (see Figure 10.29; Myers & Diener, 1995), and this relationship holds around the world in widely different cultures (Diener et al., 2000). However, the causal relations underlying this correlation are unclear. It may be that happiness causes marital satisfaction more than marital satisfaction promotes happiness. Perhaps people who are happy tend to have better intimate relationships and more stable marriages, while people who are unhappy have more difficulty finding and keeping mates.

Work. Given the way people often complain about their jobs, one might not expect work to be a key source of happiness, but it is. Although less critical than love and marriage, job satisfaction has a substantial association with general happiness (Warr, 1999). Studies also show that unemployment has strong negative effects on subjective well-being (Argyle, 1999). It is difficult to sort out whether job satisfaction causes happiness or vice versa, but evidence suggests that causation flows both ways (Argyle, 1987).

Personality. The best predictor of individuals' future happiness is their past happiness (Diener & Lucas, 1999). Some people seem destined to be happy and others unhappy, regardless of their triumphs or setbacks. The limited influence of life events was apparent in a stunning study that found only marginal differences in overall happiness between recent lottery winners and recent accident victims who became quadriplegics (Brickman, Coates, & Janoff-Bulman, 1978). Investigators were amazed that extremely fortuitous and horrible events like these didn't have a dramatic impact on happiness. Actually, *several* lines of evidence suggest that happiness does not depend on external circumstances—buying a nice house, getting promoted—so much as internal factors, such as one's outlook on life (Lykken & Tellegen, 1996). With this fact in mind, researchers have begun to look for links between personality and subjec-

Figure 10.29

Happiness and marital status. This graph shows the percentage of adults characterizing themselves as "very happy" as a function of marital status (Myers, 1999). Among both women and men, happiness shows up more in those who are married as opposed to those who are separated, are divorced, or have never married. These data and many others suggest that marital satisfaction is a key ingredient of happiness.

Source: Myers, D. G. (1999). Close relationships and quality of life. In D. Kahneman, E. Diener, & N. Schwarz (Eds.), *Well-being: The foundations of hedonic psychology.* New York: Russell Sage Foundation. Copyright © 1999. Reprinted by permission of the Russell Sage Foundation.

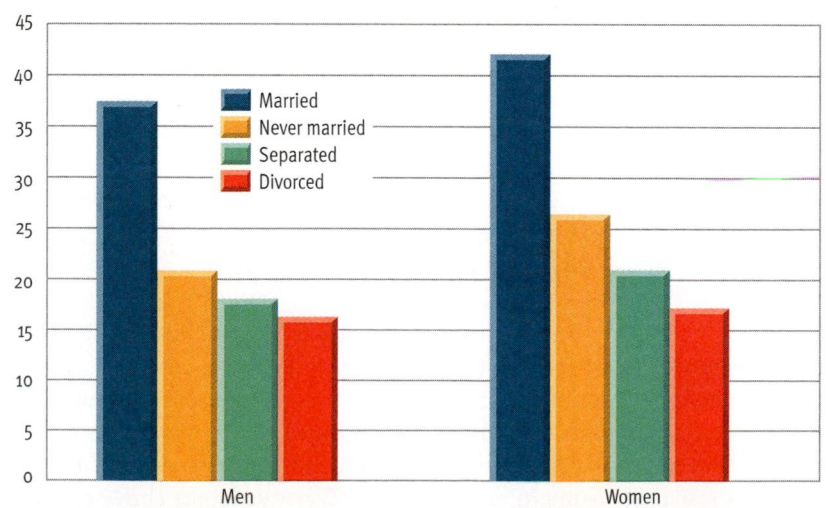

tive well-being, and they have found some intriguing correlations. For example, *extraversion* is one of the better predictors of happiness. People who are outgoing, upbeat, and sociable tend to be happier than others. Additional positive correlates of happiness include self-esteem and optimism (Lucas, Diener, & Suh, 1996).

Conclusions About Subjective Well-Being

We must be cautious in drawing inferences about the causes of happiness because the available data are correlational (see Figure 10.30). Nonetheless, the empirical evidence suggests that many popular beliefs about the sources of happiness are unfounded. The data also demonstrate that happiness is shaped by a complex constellation of variables. In spite of this complexity, however, a number of worthwhile insights about the ingredients of happiness can be gleaned from the recent flurry of research.

First, research on happiness demonstrates that the determinants of subjective well-being are precisely that: subjective. *Objective realities are not as important as subjective feelings.* In other words, your health, your wealth, and your job are not as influential as how you *feel* about your health, wealth, and job (Schwarz & Strack, 1999). These feelings are likely to be influenced by what your *expectations* were. Research suggests that bad outcomes feel worse when unexpected than when expected and good outcomes feel better when unexpected than when expected (Shepperd & McNulty, 2002). Thus, the same objective event, such as a pay raise of $2000 annually, may generate positive feelings in someone who wasn't expecting a raise and negative feelings in someone expecting a much larger increase in salary.

Second, *when it comes to happiness everything is relative* (Argyle, 1999; Hagerty, 2000). In other words, you evaluate what you have relative to what the people around you have. Generally, we compare ourselves with others who are similar to us. Thus, people who are wealthy assess what they have by comparing themselves with their wealthy friends and neighbors. This is one reason that there is little correlation between wealth and happiness. You might have a lovely home, but if it sits next door to a neighbor's palatial mansion, it might be a source of more dissatisfaction than happiness.

Third, *research on subjective well-being indicates that people often adapt to their circumstances.* This adaptation effect is one reason why increases in income don't necessarily bring increases in happiness. Thus **hedonic adaptation occurs when the mental scale that people use to judge the pleasantness-unpleasantness of their experiences shifts so that their neutral point, or baseline for comparison, changes.** Unfortunately, when people's experiences improve, hedonic adaptation may *sometimes* put them on a *hedonic treadmill*—their neutral point moves upward, so that the improvements yield no real benefits (Kahneman, 1999). However, when people have to grapple with major setbacks, hedonic adaptation probably helps protect their mental and physical health. For example, people who are sent to prison and people who develop debilitating diseases are not as unhappy as one might assume, because they adapt to their changed situations and evaluate events from a new perspective (Frederick & Loewenstein, 1999).

This effect is probably related to the fourth conclusion we can draw about subjective well-being: *Research shows that the quest for happiness is never hopeless* (Freedman, 1978; Myers, 1992). Although there are no simple recipes for happiness, the evidence indicates that some people find happiness in spite of seemingly insurmountable problems. There is nothing, short of terminal illness—no setback, shortcoming, difficulty, or inadequacy—that makes happiness impossible.

REVIEW OF KEY POINTS

- Research on happiness reveals that many commonsense notions about the roots of happiness appear to be incorrect, including the notion that most people are unhappy. Factors such as income, age, parenthood, intelligence, and attractiveness are largely uncorrelated with subjective well-being.

- Physical health, good social relationships, religious faith, and culture appear to have a modest impact on feelings of happiness. The only factors that are good predictors of happiness are love and marriage, work satisfaction, and personality.

- Research on happiness indicates that objective realities are not as important as subjective feelings and that subjective well-being is a relative concept. The evidence also indicates that people adapt to their circumstances and that the quest for happiness is almost never hopeless.

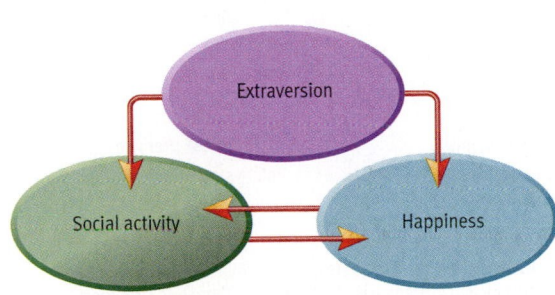

Figure 10.30

Possible causal relations among the correlates of happiness. Although we have considerable data on the correlates of happiness, it is difficult to untangle the possible causal relationships. For example, we know that a moderate positive correlation exists between social activity and happiness, but we can't say for sure whether high social activity causes happiness or whether happiness causes people to be more socially active. Moreover, in light of the research showing that a third variable—extraversion—correlates with both variables, we have to consider the possibility that extraversion causes both greater social activity and greater happiness.

Analyzing Arguments: Making Sense out of Controversy

Consider the following argument. "Dieting is harmful to your health because the tendency to be obese is largely inherited." What is your reaction to this reasoning? Do you find it convincing? We hope not, as this argument is seriously flawed. Can you see what's wrong? There is no relationship between the conclusion that "dieting is harmful to your health" and the reason given that "the tendency to be obese is largely inherited." The argument is initially seductive because you know from reading this chapter that obesity *is* largely inherited, so the reason provided represents a true statement. But the reason is unrelated to the conclusion advocated. This scenario may strike you as odd, but if you start listening carefully to discussions about controversial issues, you will probably notice that people often cite irrelevant considerations in support of their favored conclusions.

This chapter was loaded with controversial issues that sincere, well-meaning people could argue about for weeks. Does the availability of pornography increase the prevalence of sex crimes? Are gender differences in mating preferences a product of evolution or of modern economic realities? Is there a biological basis for homosexuality? Unfortunately, arguments about issues such as these typically are unproductive in terms of moving toward resolution or agreement because most people know little about the rules of argumentation. In this application, we will explore what makes arguments sound or unsound in the hope of improving your ability to analyze and think critically about arguments.

The Anatomy of an Argument

In everyday usage, the word *argument* is used to refer to a dispute or disagreement between two or more people, but in the technical language of rhetoric, **an *argument* consists of one or more premises that are used to provide support for a conclusion.** *Premises* **are the reasons that are presented to persuade someone that a conclusion is true or probably true.** *Assumptions* **are premises for which no proof or evidence is offered.** Assumptions are often left unstated. For example, suppose that your doctor tells you that you should exercise regularly because regular exercise is good for your heart. In this simple argument, the conclusion is "You should exercise regularly." The premise that leads to this conclusion is the idea that "exercise

is good for your heart." An unstated assumption is that everyone wants a healthy heart.

In the language of argument analysis, premises are said to support (or not support) conclusions. A conclusion may be supported by one reason or by many reasons. One way to visualize these possibilities is to draw an analogy between the reasons that support a conclusion and the legs that support a table (Halpern, 1996). As shown in Figure 10.31, a table top (conclusion) could be supported by one strong leg (a single strong reason) or many thin legs (lots of weaker reasons). Of course, the reasons provided for a conclusion may fail to support the conclusion. Returning to our table analogy, the table top might not be supported because the legs are too thin (very weak reasons) or because the legs are not attached (irrelevant reasons).

Arguments can get pretty complicated, as they usually have more parts than just reasons and conclusions. In addition, there often are *counterarguments,* which are reasons that take support away from a conclusion. And sometimes the most important part of an argument is a part that is not there—reasons that have been omitted, either deliberately or not, that would lead to

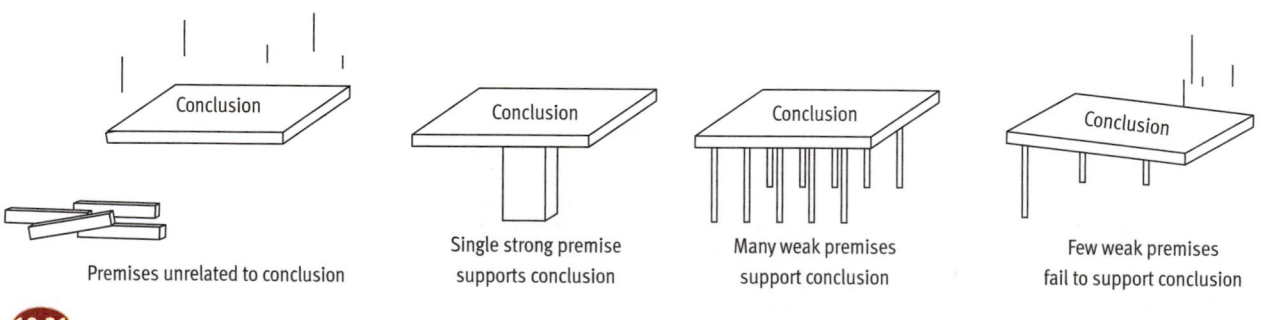

| Premises unrelated to conclusion | Single strong premise supports conclusion | Many weak premises support conclusion | Few weak premises fail to support conclusion |

Figure 10.31

An analogy for understanding the strength of arguments. Halpern (1996) draws an analogy between the reasons that support a conclusion and the legs that support a table. She points out that a conclusion may be supported effectively by one strong premise or many weak premises. Of course, the reasons provided for a conclusion may also *fail* to provide adequate support.

SOURCE: Halpern, D. F. (1996). *Thought & knowledge: An introduction to critical thinking.* Mahwah, NJ: Erlbaum. Copyright © 1996 Lawrence Erlbaum Associates. Reprinted by permission.

a different conclusion if they were supplied. Given all the complex variations that are possible in arguments, it is impossible to give you simple rules for judging arguments, but we can highlight some common fallacies and then provide some criteria that you can apply in thinking critically about arguments.

Common Fallacies

As noted in previous chapters, cognitive scientists have compiled lengthy lists of fallacies that people frequently display in their reasoning. These fallacies often show up in arguments. In this section we will describe five common fallacies. To illustrate each one, we will assume the role of someone arguing that pornographic material on the Internet (cyberporn) should be banned or heavily regulated.

Irrelevant Reasons. Reasons cannot provide support for an argument unless they are relevant to the conclusion. Arguments that depend on irrelevant reasons—either intentionally or inadvertently—are quite common. You already saw one example at the beginning of this application. The Latin term for this fallacy is *non sequitur,* which literally translates to "it doesn't follow." In other words, the conclusion does not follow from the premise. For example, in the debate about Internet pornography, you might hear the following *non sequitur:* "We need to regulate cyberporn because research has shown that most date rapes go unreported."

Circular Reasoning. In *circular reasoning* the premise and conclusion are simply restatements of each other. People vary their wording a little so it isn't obvious, but when you look closely, the conclusion *is* the premise. For example, in arguments about Internet pornography you might hear someone assert, "We need to control cyberporn because it currently is unregulated."

Slippery Slope. The concept of *slippery slope* argumentation takes its name from the notion that if you are on a slippery slope and you don't dig your heels in, you will slide and slide until you reach bottom. A slippery slope argument typically asserts that

if you allow X to happen, things will spin out of control and far worse events will follow. The trick is that there is no inherent connection between X and the events that are predicted to follow. For example, in the debate about medical marijuana, opponents have argued, "If you legalize medical marijuana, the next thing you know cocaine and heroin will be legal." In the debate about cyberporn, a slippery slope argument might go, "If we don't ban cyberporn, the next thing you know, grade-school children will be watching smut all day long in their school libraries."

Weak Analogies. An *analogy* asserts that two concepts or events are similar in some way. Hence, you can draw conclusions about event B because of its similarity to event A. Analogies are useful in thinking about complex issues, but some analogies are weak or inappropriate because the similarity between A and B is superficial, minimal, or irrelevant to the issue at hand. For example, in the debate about Internet erotica, someone might argue, "Cyberporn is morally offensive, just like child molestation. We wouldn't tolerate child molestation, so we shouldn't permit cyberporn."

False Dichotomy. A *false dichotomy* creates an either-or choice between two outcomes: the outcome advocated and some obviously horrible outcome that any sensible person would want to avoid. These outcomes are presented as the only two possibilities, when

in reality there could be other outcomes, including ones that lie somewhere between the extremes depicted in the false dichotomy. In the debate about Internet pornography, someone might argue, "We can ban cyberporn, or we can hasten the moral decay of modern society."

Evaluating the Strength of Arguments

In everyday life, you may frequently need to assess the strength of arguments made by friends, family, co-workers, politicians, media pundits, and so forth. You may also want to evaluate your own arguments when you write papers or speeches for school or prepare presentations for your work. The following questions can help you make systematic evaluations of arguments (adapted from Halpern, 1996):

- What is the conclusion?
- What are the premises provided to support the conclusion? Are the premises valid?
- Does the conclusion follow from the premises? Are there any fallacies in the chain of reasoning?
- What assumptions have been made? Are they valid assumptions? Should they be stated explicitly?
- What are the counterarguments? Do they weaken the argument?
- Is there anything that has been omitted from the argument?

Table 10.1 Critical Thinking Skills Discussed in This Application

Skill	Description
Understanding the elements of an argument	The critical thinker understands that an argument consists of premises and assumptions that are used to support a conclusion.
Recognizing and avoiding common fallacies, such as irrelevant reasons, circular reasoning, slippery slope reasoning, weak analogies, and false dichotomies	The critical thinker is vigilant about conclusions based on unrelated premises, conclusions that are rewordings of premises, unwarranted predictions that things will spin out of control, superficial analogies, and contrived dichotomies.
Evaluating arguments systematically	The critical thinker carefully assesses the validity of the premises, assumptions, and conclusions in an argument, and considers counterarguments and missing elements.

RECAP

Key Ideas

Motivational Theories and Concepts

● Drive theories apply a homeostatic model to motivation. They assume that organisms seek to reduce unpleasant states of tension called drives. In contrast, incentive theories emphasize how external goals energize behavior.

● Evolutionary theorists explain motives in terms of their adaptive value. Madsen's list of biological needs and Murray's list of social needs illustrate that a diverse array of motives govern human behavior.

The Motivation of Hunger and Eating

● Eating is regulated by a complex interaction of biological and environmental factors. In the brain, the lateral, ventromedial, and paraventricular areas of the hypothalamus appear to be involved in the control of hunger, but their exact role is unclear.

● Fluctuations in blood glucose also seem to play a role in hunger. The stomach can send two types of satiety signals to the brain. Hormonal regulation of hunger depends primarily on insulin and leptin secretions.

● Incentive-oriented models assert that eating is regulated by the availability and palatability of food. Learning processes, such as classical conditioning and observational learning, exert a great deal of influence over both what people eat and how much they eat. Cultural traditions also shape food preferences. Stress can stimulate eating.

● Evidence indicates that there is a genetic predisposition to obesity. According to set-point theory, the body monitors fat stores to keep them fairly stable. Settling-point theory suggests that a multitude of factors contribute to weight stability. Vacillations in dietary restraint resulting in disinhibition may contribute to obesity in some people.

Sexual Motivation and Behavior

● Scientists are not sure, but hormonal swings appear to have a modest impact on human sexual desire. People respond to a variety of erotic materials, which may elevate sexual desire for only a few hours but may have an enduring impact on attitudes about sex. Aggressive pornography may make sexual coercion seem less offensive and may contribute to date rape.

● Consistent with evolutionary theory, males tend to think about and initiate sex more than females and to have more sexual partners and more interest in casual sex than females. The Featured Study by Buss demonstrated that there are gender differences in mating preferences that largely transcend cultural boundaries. Males emphasize potential partners' youthfulness and attractiveness, whereas females emphasize potential partners' financial prospects.

● The determinants of sexual orientation are not well understood. Recent studies suggest that there may be a genetic predisposition to homosexuality and that idiosyncrasies in prenatal hormonal secretions may contribute, but much remains to be learned. The human sexual response cycle can be divided into four stages: excitement, plateau, orgasm, and resolution.

Affiliation: In Search of Belongingness

● Affiliation probably had many adaptive benefits for our ancestors. Individual differences in the need for affiliation are usually measured with the TAT. People who are relatively high in the need for affiliation tend to devote more time to interpersonal activities and to worry more about acceptance than others do.

Achievement: In Search of Excellence

● McClelland pioneered the use of the TAT to measure achievement motivation. People who are high in the need for achievement work harder and more persistently than others, although they often choose to tackle challenges of intermediate difficulty. The pursuit of achievement tends to increase when the probability of success and the incentive value of success are high.

The Elements of Emotional Experience

● Emotion is made up of cognitive, physiological, and behavioral components. The cognitive component involves subjective feelings that have an evaluative aspect. In the peripheral nervous system, the physiological component is dominated by autonomic arousal. In the brain, the amygdala seems to be the hub of the neural circuits that process emotion. At the behavioral level, emotions are expressed through body language, with facial expressions being particularly prominent.

● Ekman and Friesen have found considerable cross-cultural agreement in the identification of emotions based on facial expressions. Cross-cultural similarities have also been found in the cognitive and physiological components of emotion. However, there are cultural variations in how people categorize and display their emotions.

Theories of Emotion

● The James-Lange theory asserts that emotion results from one's perception of autonomic arousal. The Cannon-Bard theory counters with the proposal that emotions originate in subcortical areas of the brain. According to Schachter's two-factor theory, people infer emotion from arousal and then label the emotion in accordance with their cognitive explanation for the arousal. Evolutionary theories of emotion maintain that emotions are innate reactions that require little cognitive interpretation.

Putting It in Perspective

● Our look at motivation and emotion showed once again that psychology is characterized by theoretical diversity, that biology and environment shape behavior interactively, that behavior is governed by multiple causes, that psychological processes are characterized by both cultural variance and invariance, and that psychology evolves in a sociohistorical context.

Personal Application ● Exploring the Ingredients of Happiness

● Factors such as income, age, parenthood, intelligence, and attractiveness are largely uncorrelated with subjective well-being. Physical health, good social relationships, religious faith, and culture appear to have a modest impact on feelings of happiness. Strong predictors of happiness include love and marriage, work satisfaction, and personality.

● Research on happiness indicates that objective realities are not that important, that happiness is relative, that people adapt to their circumstances, and that the quest for happiness is almost never hopeless.

Critical Thinking Application ● Analyzing Arguments: Making Sense out of Controversy

● An argument consists of one or more premises used to provide support for a conclusion. Arguments are often marred by fallacies in reasoning, such as irrelevant reasons, circular reasoning, slippery slope scenarios, weak analogies, and false dichotomies. Arguments can be evaluated more effectively by applying systematic criteria.

Key Terms

Achievement motive
Affiliation motive
Androgens
Argument
Assumptions
Bisexuals
Body mass index (BMI)
Collectivism
Display rules
Drive
Emotion
Estrogens
Galvanic skin response (GSR)
Glucose
Glucostats
Hedonic adaptation
Heterosexuals
Homeostasis
Homosexuals
Incentive
Individualism
Lie detector
Motivation
Obesity
Orgasm
Polygraph
Premises
Refractory period
Set-point theory
Settling-point theory
Sexual orientation
Subjective well-being
Vasocongestion

Key People

John Atkinson
David Buss
Walter Cannon
Paul Ekman and Wallace Friesen
William James
Joseph LeDoux
William Masters and Virginia Johnson
David McClelland
Henry Murray
Stanley Schachter

1. Jackson had a huge breakfast this morning and is still feeling stuffed when he arrives at work. However, one of his colleagues has brought some delicious-looking donuts to the morning staff meeting and Jackson just can't resist. Although he feels full, he eats three donuts. His behavior is inconsistent with:
   A. incentive theories of motivation.
   B. drive theories of motivation.
   C. evolutionary theories of motivation.
   D. the Cannon-Bard theory of motivation.

2. The heritability of weight appears to be:
   A. virtually impossible to demonstrate.
   B. very low.
   C. in the range of 60%–70%
   D. irrelevant to the understanding of obesity.

3. Which of the following is the most common source of disinhibition for restrained eaters?
   A. emotional distress
   B. the fear of becoming too thin
   C. drinking alcohol in small quantities
   D. the perception that they have cheated on their diet

4. Some recent studies suggest that exposure to aggressive pornography:
   A. may increase males' aggressive behavior toward women.
   B. may perpetuate the myth that women enjoy being raped.
   C. both a and b.
   D. neither a nor b.

5. Which of the following has *not* been found in research on gender differences in sexual interest?
   A. Men think about sex more than women.
   B. Men initiate sex more frequently than women.
   C. Women are more interested in having many partners than men are.
   D. Women are less interested in uncommitted sex.

6. Kinsey maintained that sexual orientation:
   A. depends on early classical conditioning experiences.
   B. should be viewed as a continuum.
   C. depends on normalities and abnormalities in the amygdala.
   D. should be viewed as an either-or distinction.

7. In research on affiliation, individual differences in affiliation are usually measured:
   A. by observing subjects' actual social behavior.
   B. by asking subjects about their affiliation needs.
   C. with the Thematic Apperception Test.
   D. with the Minnesota Multiphasic Personality Inventory.

8. The determinant of achievement behavior that increases when a college student enrolls in a class that is *required* for graduation is:
   A. the probability of success.
   B. the need to avoid failure.
   C. the incentive value of success.
   D. the fear of success.

9. A polygraph (lie detector) works by:
   A. monitoring physiological indices of autonomic arousal.
   B. directly assessing the truthfulness of a person's statements.
   C. monitoring the person's facial expressions.
   D. all of the above.

10. Which of the following statements about cross-cultural comparisons of emotional experience is *not* true?
    A. The types of events that trigger specific emotions are fairly similar across cultures.
    B. The physiological reactions that accompany emotions tend to be similar across cultures.

C. People of different cultures tend to categorize emotions somewhat differently.
D. All of the above statements are true.

11. According to the James-Lange theory of emotion:
    A. the experience of emotion depends on autonomic arousal and on one's cognitive interpretation of that arousal.
    B. different patterns of autonomic activation lead to the experience of different emotions.
    C. emotion occurs when the thalamus sends signals simultaneously to the cortex and to the autonomic nervous system.
    D. emotions develop because of their adaptive value.

12. Which theory of emotion implies that people can change their emotions simply by changing the way they label their arousal?
    A. the James-Lange theory
    B. the Cannon-Bard theory
    C. Schachter's two-factor theory
    D. opponent-process theory

13. The fact that eating behavior, sexual desire, and the experience of emotion all depend on interactions between biological and environmental determinants lends evidence to which of your text's organizing themes?
    A. psychology's theoretical diversity
    B. psychology's empiricism
    C. people's experience of the world is subjective
    D. the joint influence of biology and environment

14. Which of the following statements is (are) true?
    A. For the most part, people are pretty happy.
    B. Age is unrelated to happiness.
    C. Income is largely unrelated to happiness.
    D. All of the above.

15. The sales pitch "We're the best dealership in town because the other dealerships just don't stack up against us" is an example of:
    A. a false dichotomy.
    B. semantic slanting.
    C. circular reasoning.
    D. slippery slope.

Answers

1	B	p. 383	6	B	pp. 397–398	11	B p. 412
2	C	p. 389	7	C	p. 402	12	C p. 413
3	D	p. 390	8	C	p. 404	13	D p. 415
4	C	p. 392	9	A	p. 407	14	D pp. 416–417
5	C	p. 394	10	D	pp. 410–411	15	C p. 421

www ON THE WEB

For additional resources on the topics covered in this chapter, visit the *Psychology: Themes and Variations* Web site, where you will find practice quizzes, tutorials,

Web links, simulations, critical thinking activities, flash cards, interactive exercises, and suggested readings available through INFOTRAC.

http://psychology.wadsworth.com/weiten_themes6e/

CHAPTER **11**

© Adam Crowley/PhotoDisc-Getty Images

Human Development Across the Life Span

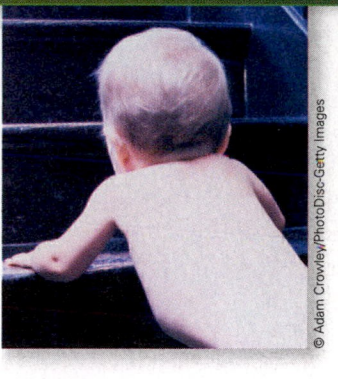

On July 29, 1981, 20-year-old Diana Spencer stood before more than 2,000 guests at St. Paul's Cathedral in London and fumbled through an exchange of wedding vows, nervously transposing two of her husband's middle names. Diana could hardly believe what was happening. Just a few months before, she had been a giggly teenager with a playful sign on her bedroom door that read "Chief Chick." Dubbed "Shy Di" by the hordes of photographers who followed her every move, she had never even had a boyfriend (Morton, 1998). Now she was getting married to Charles, Prince of Wales, the heir to the British throne, in an ostentatious wedding ceremony that was televised around the world.

Marriage—let alone to a future king—is a major transition for most people, but for Diana it was only the beginning of an extraordinary series of changes. When Diana became engaged, she was a pretty if slightly pudgy 19-year-old who was just on the threshold of adulthood. A high school dropout, she had few serious interests or ambitions. Her most obvious talent was her rapport with young children, who adored her. Far from a fashion plate, she owned "one long dress, one silk skirt, one smart pair of shoes, and that was it" (Morton, 1998, p. 66).

Yet, like Cinderella, the "fairy tale princess" soon blossomed. "It happened before our very eyes," said one photographer, "the transformation from this shy teenager who hid beneath big hats, and hung her head, into the self-assured woman and mother, confident in her beauty" (Clayton & Craig, 2001, p. 113). The Shy Di who sometimes burst into tears at the sight of crowds became Disco Di, a svelte beauty celebrated for her stylish clothes and hairstyles. Then came Dynasty Di, the doting mother of Princes William and Harry. Finally, as her marriage to Charles crumbled and she sought a new and more fulfilling role for herself, still another Diana emerged. Now she was Dedicated Di, a poised and effective spokesperson for important causes, such as AIDS and the removal of land mines from war-torn areas. No longer a frightened young princess or her husband's beautiful accessory, by her 30s Diana was a seemingly confident and independent woman who could publicly rebuke the royal family for their treatment of her and declare that she would rather be the "Queen of people's hearts" than the Queen of England (Edwards, 1999, p. 342).

Diana's transformations were startling, yet there was also a strong element of continuity in her life. As an adult, Diana continued to display qualities she had shown as a child, including her mischievous sense of humor, her love of swimming and dancing, and even her attachment to stuffed animals (S. B. Smith, 2000). Her childhood feeling of destiny ultimately blossomed into a deep sense of mission that took her to homeless shelters, clinics for lepers, and the bedsides of AIDS patients. Although cynics doubted the genuineness of her empathy for society's "outcasts,"

The story of Princess Diana's metamorphosis from an awkward teenager into an elegant, self-assured public figure provides a dramatic demonstration of how human development is marked by both continuity and transition.

she had displayed a similar caring and naturalness as a young teenager dancing with patients in wheelchairs at a hospital for the mentally and physically handicapped (Clayton & Craig, 2001).

Other, more troubling, continuities also marked Diana's turbulent passage through life. Despite her growing mastery of her public roles, privately she remained vulnerable, moody, and insecure. Diana's parents had divorced when she was 6, and fears of abandonment never left her. As a young girl being taken to boarding school, she had begged her father, "If you love me, don't leave me here"—a plea she later echoed in tearful arguments with Prince Charles (Smith, 2000, p. 53). Her childhood feelings of intellectual inferiority continued to plague her as an adult. "A brain the size of a pea I've got," she would say (Clayton & Craig, 2001, p. 22). Throughout her marriage, she suffered bouts of bulimia (an eating disorder) and depression. While she projected a new confidence and maturity after her separation from Prince Charles, some observers felt that she was as needy and insecure as ever. A succession of relationships with men, before and after her divorce, seemed to bring her no closer to the love and security she craved. One biographer argues that in fundamental ways she had changed little, if at all (Smith, 2001). Others, however, believed that a new chapter in her life was just beginning and that many more changes were undoubtedly in store when Diana was tragically killed in an auto accident at the age of 36.

What does Princess Diana have to do with developmental psychology? Although her story is obviously unique in many ways, it provides an interesting illustration of the two themes that permeate the study of human development: *transition* and *continuity*. In investigating human development, psychologists study how people evolve through transitions over time. In looking at these transitions, developmental psychologists inevitably find continuity with the past. This continuity may be the most fascinating element in Diana's story. The metamorphosis of the shy, awkward teenager into an elegant, self-assured public figure was a more radical transformation than most people go through. Nonetheless, the threads of continuity connecting Diana's childhood to the development of her adult personality were quite obvious.

Development is the sequence of age-related changes that occur as a person progresses from conception to death. It is a reasonably orderly, cumulative process that includes both the biological and behavioral changes that take place as people grow older. An infant's newfound ability to grasp objects, a child's gradual mastery of grammar, an adolescent's spurt in physical growth, a young adult's increasing commitment to a vocation, and an older adult's transition into the role of grandparent all represent development. These transitions are predictable changes that are related to age.

Traditionally, psychologists have been most interested in development during childhood. Our coverage reflects this emphasis. However, decades of research have clearly demonstrated that development is a lifelong process. We'll divide the life span into four broad periods: (1) the prenatal period, between conception and birth, (2) childhood, (3) adolescence, and (4) adulthood. We'll examine aspects of development that are especially dynamic during each period. Let's begin by looking at events that occur before birth, during prenatal development.

Progress Before Birth: Prenatal Development

PREVIEW QUESTIONS
- What are the three stages of prenatal development and what happens in each stage?
- Can maternal nutrition affect the fetus?
- How about maternal drug use?
- Which maternal illnesses can be dangerous to the fetus?
- How important is prenatal health care?

Development begins with conception. Conception occurs when fertilization creates a *zygote,* a one-celled organism formed by the union of a sperm and an egg. All the other cells in your body developed from this single cell. Each of your cells contains enduring messages from your parents carried on the *chromosomes* that lie within its nucleus. Each chromosome houses many *genes,* the functional units in hereditary transmission. Genes carry the details of your hereditary blueprints, which are revealed gradually throughout life (see Chapter 3 for more information on genetic transmission).

The *prenatal period* extends from conception to birth, usually encompassing nine months of pregnancy. A great deal of important development occurs before birth. In fact, development during the prenatal period is remarkably rapid. If you were an average-sized newborn and your physical growth had continued during the first year of your life at a prenatal pace, by your first birthday you would have weighed 200 pounds! Fortunately, you didn't grow at that rate—and no human does—because in the final weeks before birth the frenzied pace of prenatal development tapers off dramatically. In this section, we'll examine the usual course of prenatal development and discuss how environmental events can leave their mark on development even before birth exposes the newborn to the outside world.

The Course of Prenatal Development

The prenatal period is divided into three phases: (1) the germinal stage (the first two weeks), (2) the embryonic stage (two weeks to two months), and (3) the fetal stage (two months to birth). Some key developments in these phases are outlined here.

Germinal Stage

The *germinal stage* is the first phase of prenatal development, encompassing the first two weeks after conception. This brief stage begins when a zygote is created through fertilization. Within 36 hours, rapid cell division begins, and the zygote becomes a microscopic mass of multiplying cells. This mass of cells slowly migrates along the mother's fallopian tube to the uterine cavity. On about the seventh day, the cell mass begins to implant itself in the uterine wall. This process takes about a week and is far from automatic. Many zygotes are rejected at this point. As many as one in five pregnancies end with the woman never being aware that conception has occurred (Wilcox et al., 1988).

During the implantation process, the placenta begins to form. The *placenta* is a structure that allows oxygen and nutrients to pass into the fetus from the mother's bloodstream and bodily wastes to pass out to the mother. This critical exchange takes place across thin membranes that block the passage of blood cells, keeping the fetal and maternal bloodstreams separate.

Embryonic Stage

The *embryonic stage* is the second stage of prenatal development, lasting from two weeks until the end of the second month. During this stage, most of the vital organs and bodily systems begin to form in the developing organism, which is now called an *embryo*. Structures such as the heart, spine, and brain emerge gradually as cell division becomes more specialized. Although the embryo is typically only about an inch long at the end of this stage, it's already beginning to look human. Arms, legs, hands, feet, fingers, toes, eyes, and ears are already discernible.

The embryonic stage is a period of great vulnerability because virtually all the basic physiological structures are being formed. If anything interferes with normal development during the embryonic phase, the effects can be devastating. Most miscarriages occur during this period (Simpson, 1991). Most major structural birth defects are also due to problems that occur during the embryonic stage (Mortensen, Sever, & Oakley, 1991).

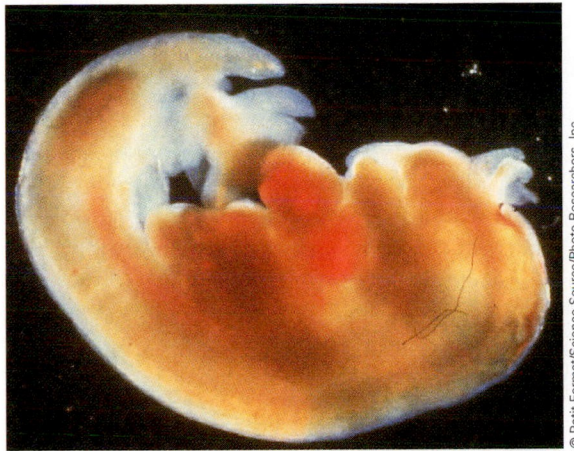
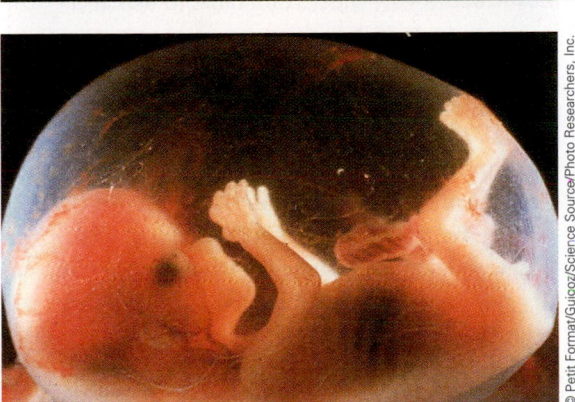
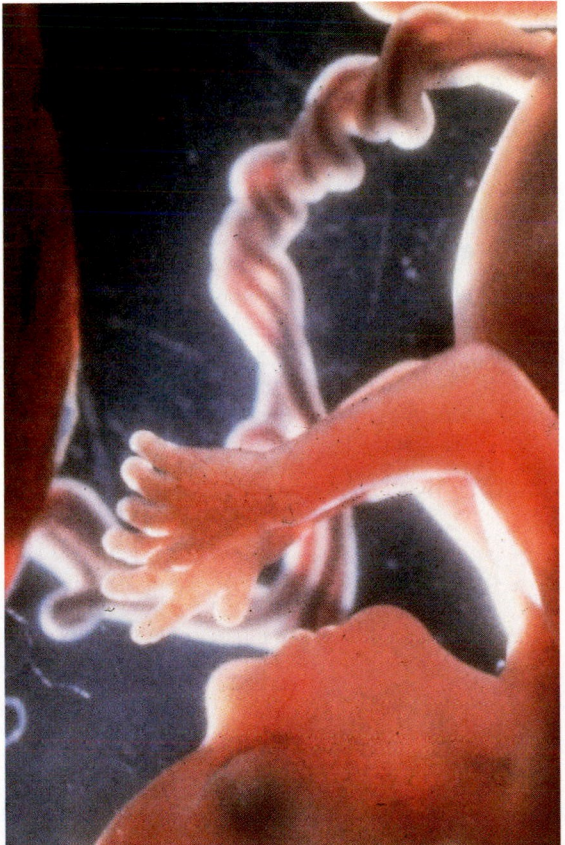

Prenatal development is remarkably rapid. (top left) This 30-day-old embryo is just 6 millimeters in length. (bottom left) At 14 weeks, the fetus is approximately 2 inches long. Note the well-developed fingers. The fetus can already move its legs, feet, hands, and head and displays a variety of basic reflexes. (right) After 4 months of prenatal development, facial features are beginning to emerge.

Figure 11.1

Overview of fetal development. This chart outlines some of the highlights of development during the fetal stage.

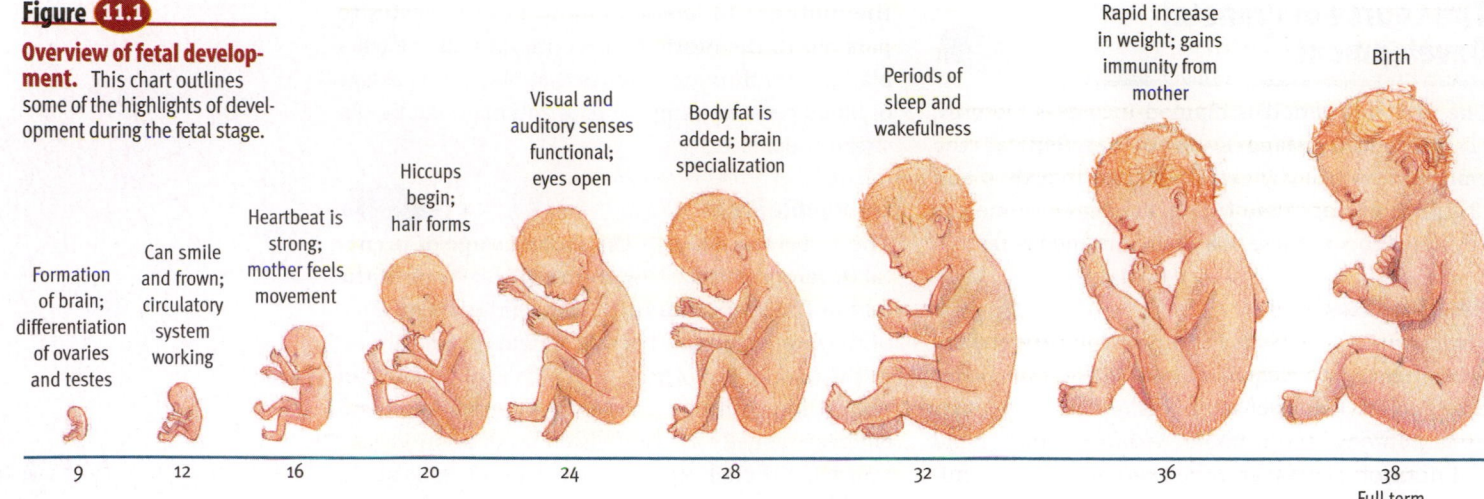

Formation of brain; differentiation of ovaries and testes

Can smile and frown; circulatory system working

Heartbeat is strong; mother feels movement

Hiccups begin; hair forms

Visual and auditory senses functional; eyes open

Body fat is added; brain specialization

Periods of sleep and wakefulness

Rapid increase in weight; gains immunity from mother

Birth

| 9 | 12 | 16 | 20 | 24 | 28 | 32 | 36 | 38 |

Weeks since conception

Full term

Fetal Stage

9a

The *fetal stage* is the third stage of prenatal development, lasting from two months through birth. Some highlights of fetal development are summarized in Figure 11.1. The first two months of the fetal stage bring rapid bodily growth, as muscles and bones begin to form (Moore & Persaud, 1998). The developing organism, now called a *fetus,* becomes capable of physical movements as skeletal structures harden. Organs formed in the embryonic stage continue to grow and gradually begin to function. Sex organs start to develop during the third month.

During the final three months of the prenatal period, brain cells multiply at a brisk pace. A layer of fat is deposited under the skin to provide insulation, and the respiratory and digestive systems mature. All of these changes ready the fetus for life outside the cozy, supportive environment of its mother's womb. Sometime between 22 weeks and 26 weeks the fetus reaches the *age of viability*—the age at which a baby can survive in the event of a premature birth. The probability of survival is still pretty slim at 22 or 23 weeks, but it climbs steadily over the next month to an 85% survival rate at 26 to 28 weeks (Hack & Fanaroff, 1999; Main & Main, 1991).

Environmental Factors and Prenatal Development

Although the fetus develops in the protective buffer of the womb, events in the external environment can affect it indirectly through the mother. Because the developing organism and its mother are linked through the placenta, a mother's eating habits, drug use, and physical health, among other things, can affect prenatal development. Figure 11.2 shows the periods of prenatal development during which various structures are most vulnerable to damage.

Maternal Nutrition

The developing fetus needs a variety of essential nutrients. Thus, it's not surprising that severe maternal malnutrition increases the risk of birth complications and neurological defects for the newborn (Coutts, 2000; Fifer, Monk, & Grose-Fifer, 2001). The effects of severe malnutrition are a major problem in underdeveloped nations where food shortages are common. The impact of moderate malnutrition, which is more common in modern societies, is more diffi-

CONCEPT CHECK 11.1

Understanding the Stages of Prenatal Development

Check your understanding of the stages of prenatal development by filling in the blanks in the chart below. The first column contains descriptions of a main event from each of the three stages. In the second column, write the name of the stage; in the third column, write the term used to refer to the developing organism during that stage; and in the fourth column, write the time span (in terms of weeks or months) covered by the stage. The answers are in Appendix A at the back of the book.

Event	Stage	Term for organism	Time span
1. Uterine implantation	_____	_____	_____
2. Muscle and bone begin to form	_____	_____	_____
3. Vital organs and body systems begin to form	_____	_____	_____

cult to gauge, in part because maternal malnutrition is often confounded with other risk factors associated with poverty, such as drug abuse and limited access to health care (Worthington-Roberts & Klerman, 1990). Recent research suggests that prenatal malnutrition may have negative effects decades after a child's birth. For example, prenatal malnutrition has been linked to vulnerability to schizophrenia and other psychiatric disorders in adolescence and early adulthood (Susser, Brown, & Matte, 1999). And low birth weight is associated with an increased risk of heart disease and diabetes in middle adulthood (Forsen et al., 2000; Rich-Edwards et al., 1997). Although birth weight is influenced by factors besides maternal nutrition (Osrin & de L Costello, 2000), these findings are alarming.

Maternal Drug Use

A major source of concern about fetal and infant well-being is the mother's consumption of drugs, including such widely used substances as tobacco and alcohol, as well as prescription and recreational drugs. Unfortunately, most drugs consumed by a pregnant woman can pass through the membranes of the placenta.

Virtually all "recreational" drugs (see Chapter 5) can be harmful, with sedatives, narcotics, and cocaine being particularly dangerous. Babies of heroin users are born addicted to narcotics and have an increased risk of early death due to prematurity, birth defects, respiratory difficulties, and problems associated with their addiction (Finnegan & Kandall, 1997). Prenatal exposure to cocaine is associated with increased risk of birth complications (Bendersky & Lewis, 1999) and a variety of cognitive deficits that are apparent in childhood (Singer et al., 2002). Problems can also be caused by a great variety of drugs prescribed for legitimate medical reasons, and even some over-the-counter drugs (Niebyl, 1991). The impact of drugs on the embryo or fetus varies greatly depending on the drug, the dose, and the phase of prenatal development.

Alcohol consumption during pregnancy also carries risks. It has long been clear that *heavy* drinking by a mother can be hazardous to a fetus. **Fetal alcohol syndrome is a collection of congenital (inborn) problems associated with excessive alcohol use during pregnancy.** Typical problems include microcephaly (a small head), heart defects, irritability, hyperactivity, and delayed mental and motor development (Hannigan & Armant, 2000). Fetal alcohol syndrome is one of the leading causes of mental retardation (Kaemingk & Paquette, 1999), and it is related to an increased incidence of depression, suicide, and criminal behavior in adulthood (Kelly, Day, & Streissguth, 2000). Furthermore, there are many children who fall short of the criteria for fetal alcohol syndrome but still show serious impairments attributable to their mothers' drinking during pregnancy (Abel, 1998). Even normal social drinking during pregnancy can have enduring negative effects on children, including deficits in IQ, reaction time, motor skills, attention span, and math skills, and increased impulsive, antisocial, and delinquent behavior (Hunt et al., 1995; Streissguth et al., 1989; Streissguth et al., 1999). There appears to be a correlation between the amount of alcohol that pregnant women consume and the severity of the damage inflicted on their offspring (Ott, Tarter, & Ammerman, 1999).

Tobacco use during pregnancy is also hazardous to prenatal development. Smoking produces a number of subtle physiological changes in the mother that appear to reduce the flow of oxygen and nutrients to the fetus. Pregnant women who smoke have an increased risk for miscarriage, stillbirth, prematurity, and other birth complications (Andres & Day, 2000). Maternal smoking may also increase a child's risk for sudden infant death syndrome (Fullilove & Dieudonne, 1997), slower than average cognitive development (Trasti et al., 1999), and attention deficit disorder (Milberger et al., 1998). Even maternal exposure to second-hand smoke may be dangerous to a fetus (Windham, Eaton, & Hopkins, 1999).

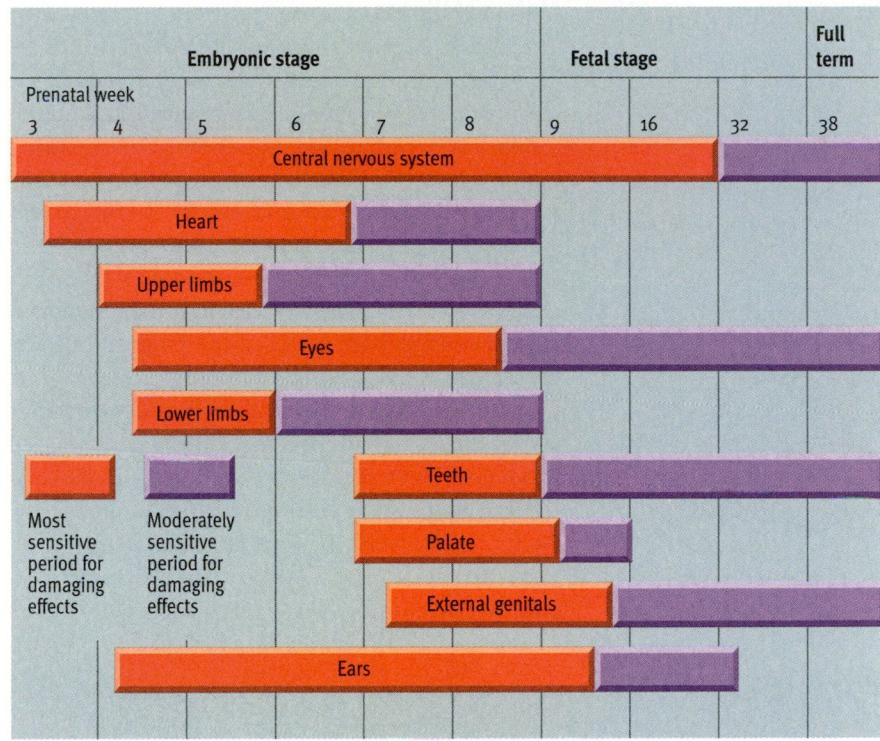

Figure 11.2

Periods of vulnerability in prenatal development.
Generally, structures are most susceptible to damage when they are undergoing rapid development. The red regions of the bars indicate the most sensitive periods for various organs and structures, while the purple regions indicate periods of continued, but lessened, vulnerability. As a whole, sensitivity is greatest in the embryonic stage, but some structures remain vulnerable throughout prenatal development.

Source: Adapted from Moore, K. L., & Persaud, T. V. N. (1998). *Before we are born: Essentials of embryology and birth defects.* Philadelphia: W. B. Saunders. Copyright © 1998 Elsevier Science (USA). All rights reserved. Reprinted by permission.

Maternal Illness

The fetus is largely defenseless against infections because its immune system matures relatively late in the prenatal period. The placenta screens out quite a number of infectious agents, but not all. Thus, many maternal illnesses can interfere with prenatal development. Diseases such as rubella (German measles), syphilis, cholera, smallpox, mumps, and even severe cases of the flu can be hazardous to the fetus (Isada & Grossman, 1991). The nature of any damage depends, in part, on when the mother contracts the illness.

Genital herpes and acquired immune deficiency syndrome (AIDS) are two very deadly diseases that pregnant women can also transmit to their offspring. Genital herpes is typically transmitted during the birth process itself when newborns come into contact with their mothers' genital lesions (Gosden, Nicolaides, & Whitting, 1994). Herpes can cause microcephaly, paralysis, deafness, blindness, and brain damage in infants and is fatal for many newborns (Ismail, 1993). The transmission of AIDS may occur prenatally through the placenta, during birth, or through breast feeding (Eldred & Chaisson, 1996). About 20%–30% of pregnant women who carry the virus for AIDS pass the disease on to their babies (Nourse & Butler, 1998), although improved antiviral drugs can reduce this percentage considerably (Culnane et al., 1999).

Prenatal Health Care 9a

Many of the prenatal dangers that we have discussed are preventable if pregnant women receive adequate care and guidance from health professionals. Good quality medical care that begins early in pregnancy is associated with reduced prematurity and higher survival rates for infants (Malloy, Kao, & Lee, 1992). Because of poverty and a related constellation of problems, however, many pregnant women in the United States receive little or no prenatal medical care (Cook et al., 1999). This problem is particularly acute among racial minorities, especially African Americans (McAllister & Boyle, 1998). Other factors surely contribute, but the lack of readily available health care for low-income groups is thought to be the main cause of the surprisingly high infant mortality rate in the United States. In spite of its relative affluence and its leadership in medical technology, the United States ranks an embarrassing 21st in the world in the prevention of infant mortality (see Figure 11.3). Ex-

Figure 11.3

Cross-cultural comparisons of infant mortality. Infant mortality is the death rate per 1000 births during the first year of life. Although the United States takes pride in its modern, sophisticated medical system, it ranks only 21st in the prevention of infant mortality. One of the main factors underlying this poor showing appears to be low-income mothers' limited access to medical care during pregnancy.

SOURCE: Adapted from Berk, L. E. (2002). *Infants, children, and adolescents.* Boston: Allyn & Bacon. Reprinted by permission.

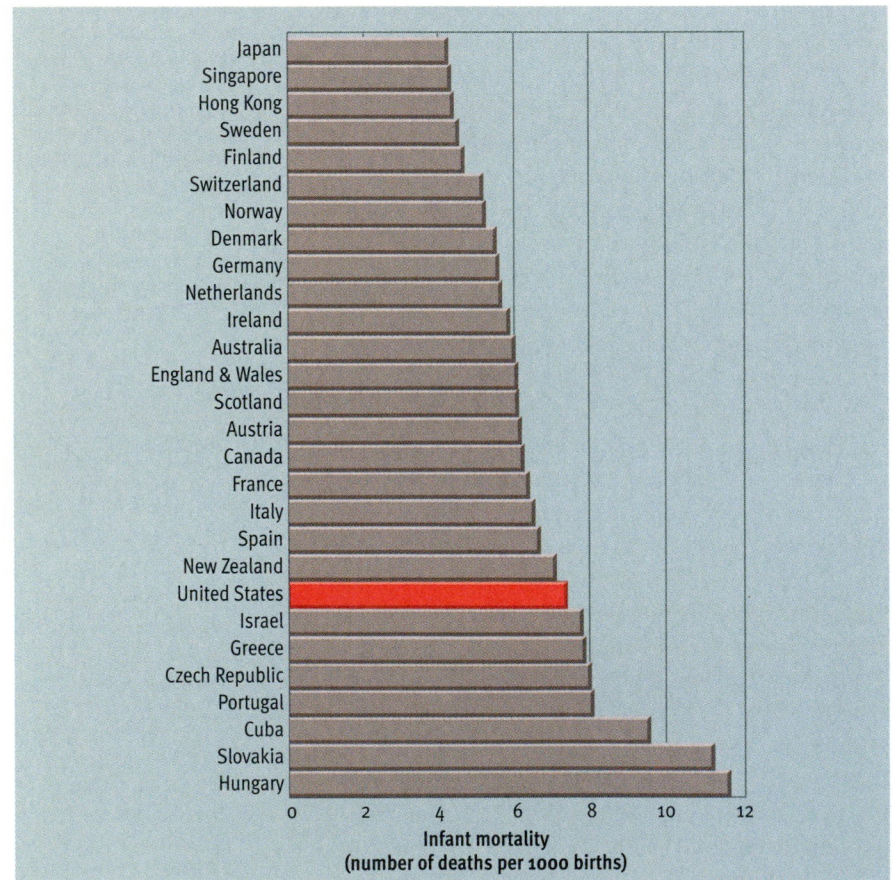

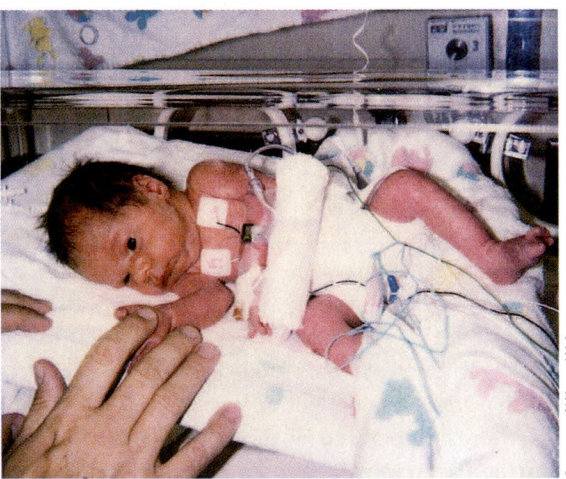

Premature births and infant deaths are much more common in the United States than most people realize. Shown here is the author's son, born prematurely in September 1992, receiving postnatal treatment in a hospital intensive care unit. Although prematurity is associated with a variety of developmental problems, T. J., like a great many premature infants, has matured into a robust, healthy child (see page 307 for a picture of him at age 15 months).

perts on child development from psychology, medicine, and many other fields have argued that the U.S. government sorely needs to increase its funding of prenatal health care for low-income groups. Given the high cost of intensive care for prematurely born infants, this investment would almost surely save money in the long run (see Figure 11.4). Unfortunately, in recent years, federal spending on children's programs has *declined* rather than increased.

Science has a long way to go before it uncovers all the factors that shape development before birth. For example, the prenatal effects of fluctuations in maternal emotions are not well understood. Nonetheless, it's clear that critical developments unfold quickly during the prenatal period. In the next section, you'll learn that development continues at a fast pace during the early years of childhood.

REVIEW OF KEY POINTS

- Prenatal development proceeds through the germinal, embryonic, and fetal stages as the zygote is differentiated into a human organism. The embryonic stage is a period of great vulnerability, as most physiological structures are being formed.

- Maternal malnutrition during the prenatal period has been linked to birth complications and other subsequent problems. Maternal drug use can be very dangerous, although the risks depend on the drug used, the dose, and phase of prenatal development.

- Fetal alcohol syndrome is a collection of congenital problems caused by a mother's excessive alcohol use during pregnancy. A variety of maternal illnesses can interfere with prenatal development.

- Genital herpes and AIDS can be transmitted to offspring during the birth process. Many problems can be avoided if expectant mothers have access to good health care.

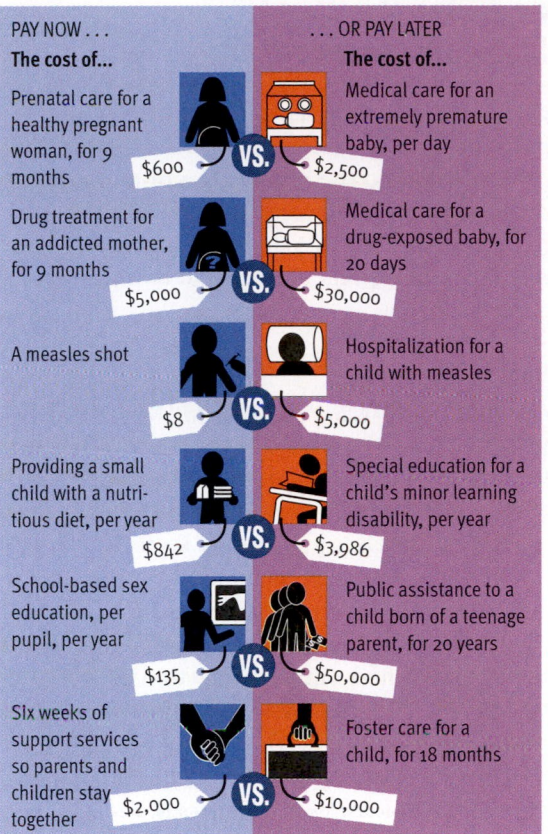

Figure 11.4

The high cost of not investing in preventive care for children.
This *Time* magazine graphic shows why it would be financially prudent to spend more public funds on preventive health care measures for young children. As you can see, the cost of providing medical care to pregnant women who cannot afford it is a pittance in comparison to the cost that government agencies often absorb later when a child is born prematurely. Infants born six to eight weeks early often spend a month or more in an intensive care unit, at a cost of $75,000 to $100,000.

SOURCE: From a chart by Steve Hart in *Time*, October 8, 1990, p. 45. Copyright © 1990 by Time Inc. Reproduced by permission.

The Wondrous Years of Childhood

A certain magic is associated with childhood. Young children have an extraordinary ability to captivate adults' attention, especially their parents'. Legions of parents apologize repeatedly to friends and strangers alike as they talk on and on about the cute things their kids do. Most wondrous of all are the rapid and momentous developmental changes of the childhood years. Helpless infants become curious toddlers almost overnight. Before parents can catch their breath, these toddlers are schoolchildren engaged in spirited play with young friends. Then, suddenly, they're insecure adolescents, worrying about dates, part-time jobs, cars, and college. The whirlwind transitions of childhood often seem miraculous.

Of course, the transformations that occur in childhood only *seem* magical. In reality, they reflect an orderly, predictable, gradual progression. In this section you'll see what psychologists have learned about this progression. We'll examine various aspects of development that are especially dynamic during childhood. Language development is omitted from this section because we covered it in the chapter on language and thought (see Chapter 8). Let's begin by looking at motor development.

PREVIEW QUESTIONS

- How uneven is physical growth during infancy?
- How important is maturation to motor development?
- How much does culture influence motor development?
- What is the difference between cross-sectional and longitudinal research?
- What kinds of temperaments have been observed in infancy?

Exploring the World: Motor Development

One of the earliest topics studied by developmental psychologists was motor development. *Motor development* refers to the progression of muscular coordination required for physical activities. Basic motor skills include grasping and reaching for objects, manipulating objects, sitting up, crawling, walking, and running.

Basic Principles

A number of principles are apparent in motor development. One is the *cephalocaudal trend*—the head-to-foot direction of motor development. Children tend to gain control over the upper part of their bodies before the lower part. You've seen this trend in action if you've seen an infant learn to crawl. Infants gradually shift from using their arms for propelling themselves to using their legs. The *proximodistal trend* is the center-outward direction of motor development. Children gain control over their torso before their extremities. Thus, infants initially reach for things by twisting their entire body, but gradually they learn to extend just their arms.

Early motor development depends in part on physical growth, which is not only rapid during infancy but apparently more uneven than previously appreciated. Infants typically grow to quadruple their birth weight during the first year, while height increases by 75%. Until recently, it was assumed that this physical growth involved a gradual, steady process that yielded smooth, continuous growth curves. But improved research methods have demonstrated that early growth is actually very irregular. In a study of infants from birth to 21 months, Lampl, Veldhuis, and Johnson (1992) found that lengthy periods of no growth were punctuated by sudden bursts of growth. These growth spurts tended to be accompanied by restlessness and irritability. More research is needed to determine whether this pattern of episodic growth continues beyond infancy, but parents who sometimes feel that their children are changing overnight may not be imagining it!

Early progress in motor skills has traditionally been attributed almost entirely to the process of maturation. *Maturation is development that reflects the gradual unfolding of one's genetic blueprint.* It is a product of genetically programmed physical changes that come with age—as opposed to experience and learning. However, recent research that has taken a closer look at the *process* of motor development suggests that infants are active agents rather than passive organisms waiting for their brain and limbs to mature (Thelen, 1995). According to the new view, the driving force behind motor development is infants' ongoing exploration of their world and their need to master specific tasks (such as grasping a larger toy or looking out a window). Progress in motor development is attributed to infants' experimentation and their learning and remembering of the consequences of their activities. Although modern researchers acknowledge that maturation facilitates motor development, they argue that its contribution has been oversimplified and overestimated (Bertenthal & Clifton, 1998).

Understanding Developmental Norms

Parents often pay close attention to early motor development, comparing their child's progress with developmental norms. *Developmental norms* indicate the median age at which individuals display various behaviors and abilities (see Chapter 2 for a discussion of the median). For example, the generalizations that "average children" say their first word at about 12 months and start combining words into sentences at around 24 months are developmental norms. Developmental norms are useful benchmarks as long as parents don't expect their children to progress exactly at the pace specified in the norms.

Some parents get unnecessarily alarmed when their children fall behind developmental norms, but variations from the typical age of accomplishment are entirely normal. This normal variation stands out in Figure 11.5, which shows norms for many basic motor skills. The left side, interior mark, and right side of the bars in the diagram indicate the ages at which 25%, 50%, and 90% of youngsters can demonstrate each motor skill. Typically, information on developmental norms includes only the median age of attainment indicated by the interior (50%) mark in each bar. This exclusive focus on the central tendency or typical progress fails to convey the immense variability seen in youngsters' development. As Figure 11.5 shows, a substantial portion of normal, healthy children often don't achieve a particular milestone until long after the median time cited in norms.

Cultural Variations and Their Significance

Cross-cultural research has highlighted the dynamic interplay between experience and maturation in motor development. Relatively rapid motor development has been observed in some cultures that provide special practice in basic motor skills. For example, the Kipsigis people of Kenya begin active efforts to train their infants to sit up, stand, and walk soon after birth. Thanks to this training, Kipsigis children achieve these developmental milestones (but not

Web Link 11.1

PBS: The Whole Child
Coordinated with the videotape series of the same name, this Public Broadcasting System site assembles a broad collection of information for parents, caregivers, and others about the developing child from birth through age 5. Presented in English and Spanish, the resources here include an interactive timeline of developmental milestones, reading lists, and a guide to other online sites dealing with child development.

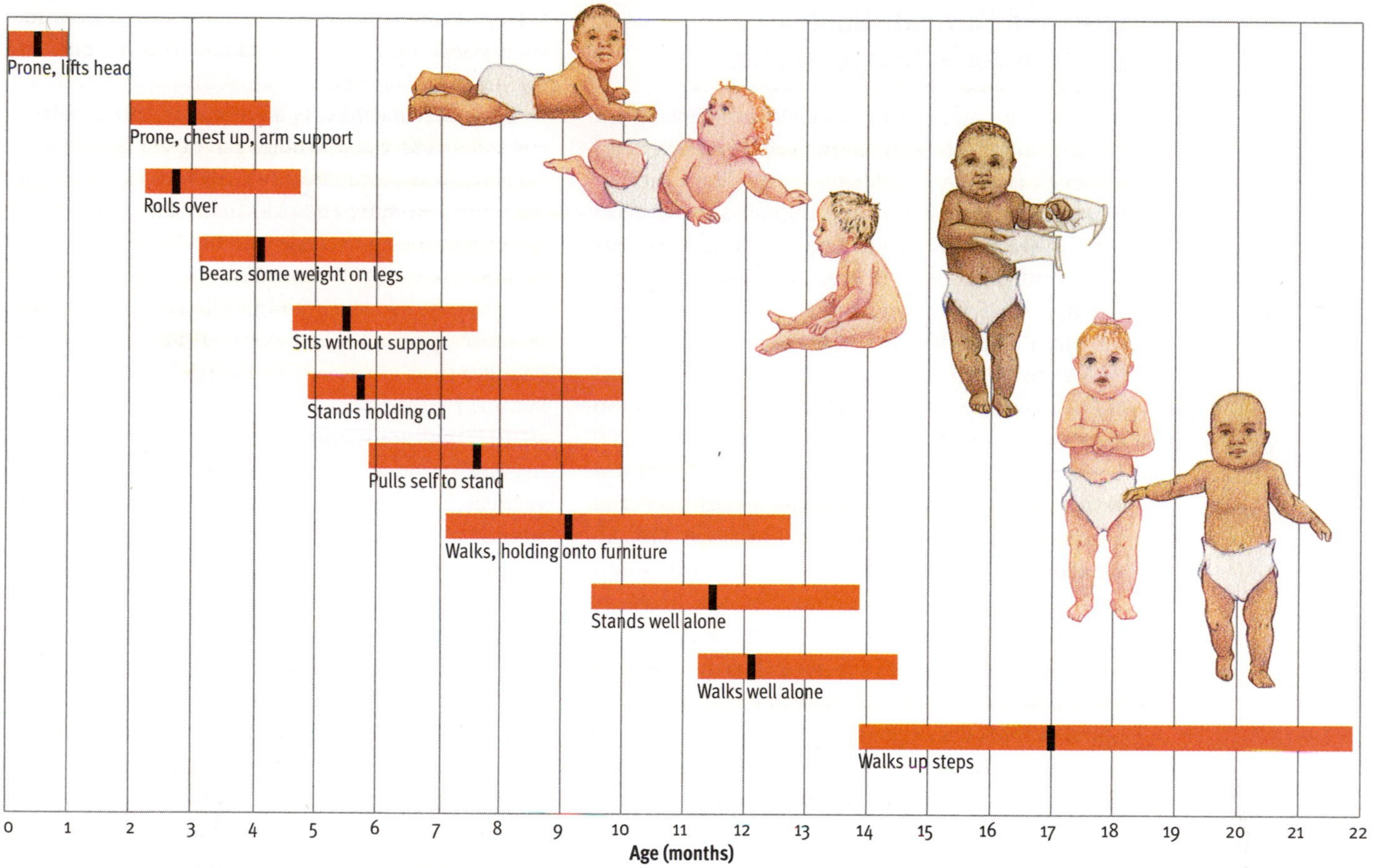

Prone, lifts head

Prone, chest up, arm support

Rolls over

Bears some weight on legs

Sits without support

Stands holding on

Pulls self to stand

Walks, holding onto furniture

Stands well alone

Walks well alone

Walks up steps

| 0 | 1 | 2 | 3 | 4 | 5 | 6 | 7 | 8 | 9 | 10 | 11 | 12 | 13 | 14 | 15 | 16 | 17 | 18 | 19 | 20 | 21 | 22 |

Age (months)

others) about a month earlier than babies in the United States (Super, 1976). West Indian children in Jamaica also exhibit advanced motor development that has been linked to a special regimen of motor exercises practiced in early infancy (Hopkins & Westra, 1988, 1990). In contrast, relatively slow motor development has been found in some cultures that discourage motor exploration. For example, among the Ache, a nomadic people living in the rain forests of Paraguay, safety concerns dictate that children under 3 rarely venture more than three feet from their mothers, who carry them virtually everywhere. As a result of these constraints, Ache children are delayed in acquiring a variety of motor skills and typically begin walking about a year later than other children (Kaplan & Dove, 1987).

Cultural variations in the emergence of basic motor skills demonstrate that environmental factors can accelerate or slow early motor development. Nonetheless, the similarities across cultures in the sequence and timing of early motor development outweigh the differences. This fact suggests that *early* motor development depends to a considerable extent on maturation. *Later* motor development is another matter, however. As children in any culture grow older, they acquire more specialized motor skills, some of which may be unique to their culture. Maturation becomes less influential and experience becomes more critical. Obviously, maturation by itself will never lead to the development of ballet or football skills, for example, without exposure to appropriate training.

Tribes across the world use a variety of methods to foster rapid development of motor abilities in their children. The Kung San of the Kalahari, Botswana, teach their young to dance quite early, using poles to develop the kinesthetic sense of balance.

© Konner/AnthroPhoto

Figure 11.5

Landmarks in motor development. The left edge, interior mark, and right edge of each bar indicate the age at which 25%, 50%, and 90% of infants have mastered each motor skill shown. Developmental norms typically report only the median age of mastery (the interior mark), which can be misleading in light of the variability in age of mastery apparent in this chart.

Easy and Difficult Babies: Differences in Temperament

Infants show considerable variability in temperament. *Temperament* **refers to characteristic mood, activity level, and emotional reactivity.** From the very beginning, some babies seem animated and cheerful while others seem sluggish and ornery. Infants show consistent differences in emotional tone, tempo of activity, and sensitivity to environmental stimuli very early in life (Rothbart & Bates, 1998).

Alexander Thomas and Stella Chess have conducted a major *longitudinal* study of the development of temperament (Thomas & Chess, 1977, 1989; Thomas, Chess, & Birch, 1970). **In a *longitudinal* design investigators observe one group of participants repeatedly over a period of time.** This approach to the study of development is often contrasted with the cross-sectional approach (the logic of both approaches is diagrammed in Figure 11.6). **In a *cross-sectional design* investigators compare groups of participants of differing age at a single point in time.** For example, in a cross-sectional study an investigator tracing the growth of children's vocabulary might compare 50 six-year-olds, 50 eight-year-olds, and 50 ten-year-olds. In contrast, an investigator using the longitudinal method would assemble one group of 50 six-year-olds and measure their vocabulary at age six, again at age eight, and once more at age ten.

Each method has its advantages and disadvantages. Cross-sectional studies can be completed more quickly, easily, and cheaply than longitudinal studies, which often extend over many years. And when a longitudinal study takes years to complete, participants often drop out because they move away or lose interest. However, longitudinal designs tend to be more sensitive to developmental influences and changes than cross-sectional designs (Magnusson & Stattin, 1998).

To some extent, the choice of a research design to investigate development depends on what the investigators want to learn about. Thomas and Chess wanted to learn about the long-term stability of children's temperaments. Given this goal, they needed to follow the same children in a longitudinal study to assess their temperamental stability over time. They began their study in 1956 with a group of 141 middle-class children. In 1961 they added a second group of 95 children of working-class parents. They have tracked the development of most of these subjects into adolescence and adulthood.

Thomas and Chess found that "temperamental individuality is well established by the time the in-

Figure 11.6

Longitudinal versus cross-sectional research. In a longitudinal study of development between ages 6 and 10, the same children would be observed at 6, again at 8, and again at 10. In a cross-sectional study of the same age span, a group of 6-year-olds, a group of 8-year-olds, and a group of 10-year-olds would be compared simultaneously. Note that data collection could be completed immediately in the cross-sectional study, whereas the longitudinal study would require 4 years to complete.

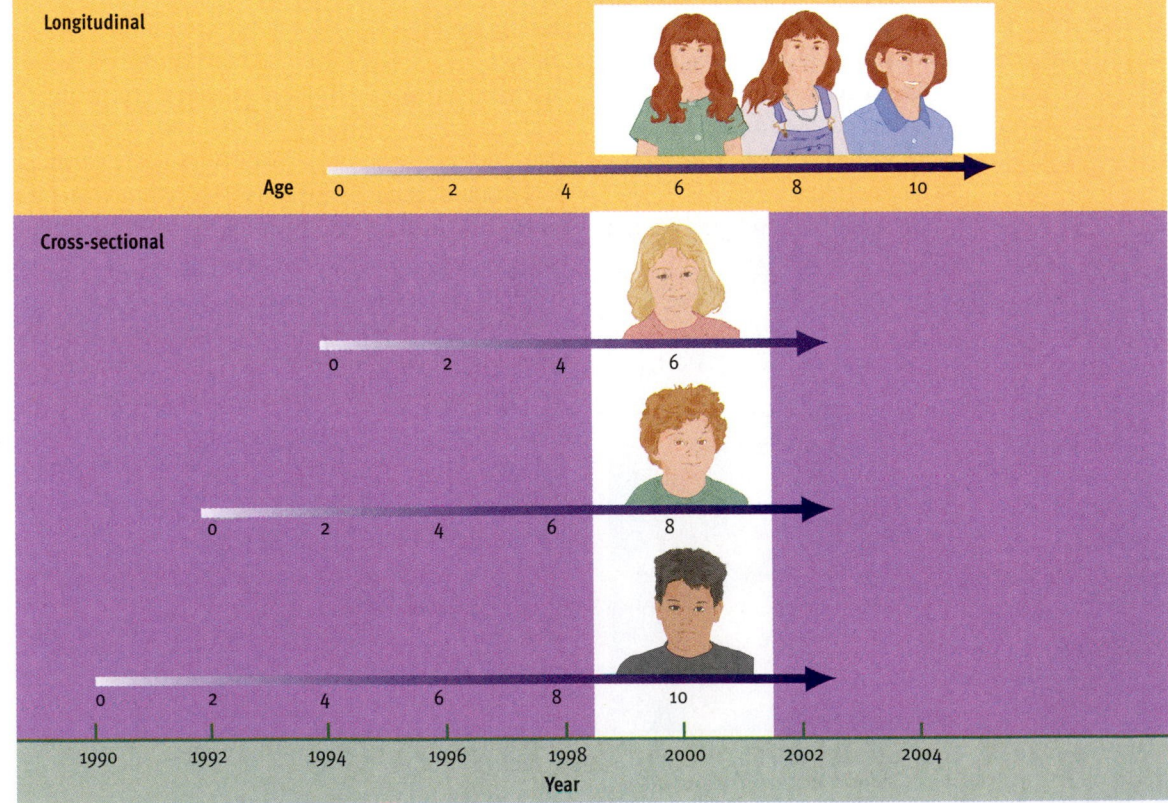

fant is two to three months old" (Thomas & Chess, 1977, p. 153). They identified three basic styles of temperament that were apparent in most of the children. About 40% of the youngsters were *easy children* who tended to be happy, regular in sleep and eating, adaptable, and not readily upset. Another 15% were *slow-to-warm-up children* who tended to be less cheery, less regular in their sleep and eating, and slower in adapting to change. These children were wary of new experiences, and their emotional reactivity was moderate. *Difficult children* constituted 10% of the group. They tended to be glum, erratic in sleep and eating, resistant to change, and relatively irritable. The remaining 35% of the children showed mixtures of these three temperaments.

A child's temperament at three months was a fair predictor of the child's temperament at age ten. Infants categorized as "difficult" developed more emotional problems requiring counseling than other children did. Although basic changes in temperament were seen in some children, temperament was generally stable over time (Chess & Thomas, 1996).

Some critics have expressed concern because Thomas and Chess's data were based on parents' highly subjective ratings of their children's temperament (Mebert, 1991). But other investigators, who have used a variety of methods to assess infant temperament, have also found it to be fairly stable (Calkins, Fox, & Marshall, 1996; Gest, 1997; Rothbart, Ahadi, & Evans, 2000), although the evidence indicates that temperament tends to stabilize a little later (around age 1 or 2) than Thomas and Chess suggested (Lemery et al., 1999).

One prominent example of contemporary research on temperament is the work of Jerome Kagan and his colleagues, who have relied on direct observations of children in their studies of temperament (Kagan & Snidman, 1991; Kagan, Snidman, & Arcus, 1992). They have found that about 15%–20% of infants display an *inhibited temperament* characterized by shyness, timidity, and wariness of unfamiliar people, objects, and events. In contrast, about 25%–30% of infants exhibit an *uninhibited temperament*. These children are less restrained, approaching unfamiliar people, objects, and events with little trepidation. Evidence suggests that these temperamental styles have a genetic basis and that they are reasonably stable into middle childhood (Kagan, Reznick, & Snidman, 1999). Research also indicates that about one-third of those who exhibit an inhibited temperament in their second year of life develop problems with anxiety during their adolescent years (Kagan & Snidman, 1999).

REVIEW OF KEY POINTS

- Motor development follows cephalocaudal (head-to-foot) and proximodistal (center-outward) trends and depends in part on physical growth, which appears to be more uneven than previously appreciated.

- Early motor development depends on both maturation and learning. Developmental norms for motor skills and other types of development are only group averages, and parents should not be alarmed if their children's progress does not match these norms exactly. Cultural variations in the pacing of motor development demonstrate the importance of learning.

- Cross-sectional and longitudinal studies are both well suited to developmental research. Cross-sectional studies are quicker, easier, and less expensive to conduct. Longitudinal studies are more sensitive to developmental changes.

- Temperamental differences among children are apparent during the first few months of life. Thomas and Chess found that most infants could be classified as easy, slow-to-warm-up, or difficult children. These differences in temperament are fairly stable and probably have a genetic basis.

Early Emotional Development: Attachment

Do mothers and infants forge lasting emotional bonds in the first few hours after birth? Do early emotional bonds affect later development? These are just some of the questions investigated by psychologists interested in attachment. **Attachment refers to the close, emotional bonds of affection that develop between infants and their caregivers.** Researchers have shown a keen interest in how infant-mother attachments are formed early in life. Children eventually may form attachments to many people, including their fathers, grandparents, and others (Cassidy, 1999). However, a child's first important attachment usually occurs with his or her mother because in most cultures she is the principal caregiver, especially in the early years of life (Lamb et al., 1999).

Contrary to popular belief, infants' attachment to their mothers is *not* instantaneous. Initially, babies show little in the way of a special preference for their mothers. They can be handed over to strangers such as babysitters with relatively little difficulty. This situation typically changes at around 6 to 8 months of age, when infants begin to show a preference for their mother's company and often protest when separated from her (Lamb, Ketterlinus, & Fracasso, 1992). This is the first manifestation of *separation anxiety*—**emotional distress seen in many infants when they are separated from people with whom they have formed an attachment.** Separation anxiety, which may occur with fathers and other familiar caregivers

PREVIEW QUESTIONS

- What are the three patterns of attachment seen in infants?
- Does day care disrupt attachment processes?
- What kinds of cultural variations have been observed in attachment patterns?
- What is the evolutionary significance of attachment patterns?
- What do stage theories have in common?
- How did Erikson explain personality development?
- What are the strengths and weaknesses of Erikson's theory?

"*Where familial security is lacking, the individual is handicapped by the lack of what might be called a secure base from which to work.*"
MARY SALTER AINSWORTH

as well as with mothers, typically peaks at around 14 to 18 months and then begins to decline.

Patterns of Attachment

Research by Mary Ainsworth and her colleagues (Ainsworth, 1979; Ainsworth et al., 1978) suggests that attachment emerges out of a complex interplay between infant and mother. Studies reveal that mothers who are sensitive and responsive to their children's needs tend to evoke more secure attachments than mothers who are relatively insensitive or inconsistent in their responding (Isabella, 1995; van den Boom, 1994). However, the correlation between maternal sensitivity and attachment security is modest, so other factors must also be involved (de Wolff & van IJzendoorn, 1997). One obvious factor is that infants are not passive bystanders as this process unfolds. They are active participants who influence the process with their crying, smiling, fussing, and babbling. Difficult infants who are prone to distress, spit up most of their food, make bathing a major battle, refuse to go to sleep, and rarely smile may sometimes undermine a mother's responsiveness (Mangelsdorf et al., 1990).

Infant-mother attachments vary in quality. Ainsworth and her colleagues (1978) found that these attachments follow three patterns (see Figure 11.7). Fortunately, most infants develop a *secure attachment*. They play and explore comfortably with their mother present, become visibly upset when she leaves, and are quickly calmed by her return. However, some children display a pattern called *anxious-ambivalent attachment*. They appear anxious even when their mother is near and protest excessively when she leaves, but they are not particularly comforted when she returns. Children in the third category seek little contact with their mothers and often are not distressed when she leaves, a condition labeled *avoidant attachment*. The type of attachment that emerges between an infant and mother may depend in part on the infant's temperament (Seifer et al., 1996). Although the correlations between infant temperament and attachment security are modest, the evidence suggests that insecure (ambivalent or avoidant) attachments occur more often with temperamentally difficult infants who are fussy, fretful, and irritable (Vaughn & Bost, 1999). Some interesting (albeit modest) correlations have also been noted between parents' marital quality and infants' attachment security. Secure attachments are somewhat more likely in homes where parents are happy with each other, probably because marital satisfaction fosters maternal sensitivity (Belsky, 1990, 1999a).

Effects of Secure Attachment

Clearly, some children have stronger attachments to their mothers than other children do. Evidence suggests that the quality of these attachment relationships can have important consequences for children. Infants with a relatively secure attachment tend to become resilient, competent toddlers with high self-esteem (Goldsmith & Harman, 1994). In their preschool years, they exhibit more persistence, curiosity, self-reliance, and leadership and have better peer relations (Weinfeld et al., 1999), while experiencing fewer negative emotions and more positive emotions (Kochanska, 2001). In middle childhood they display better social skills and have richer friendship networks than youngsters who lacked a secure attachment during infancy (Elicker, Englund, & Sroufe,

Figure 11.7

Overview of the attachment process. The unfolding of attachment depends on the interaction between a mother (or other caregiver) and an infant. Research by Mary Ainsworth and others suggests that attachment relations fall into three categories—secure, avoidant, and anxious-ambivalent—which depend on how sensitive and responsive caregivers are to their children's needs. The feedback loops shown in the diagram reflect the fact that babies are not passive bystanders in the attachment drama; their reactions to caregivers can affect the caregivers' behavior.

SOURCE: Adapted from Shaver, P. R., & Hazan, C. (1994). Attachment. In A. Weber & J. H. Harvey (Eds.), *Perspectives on close relationships.* Boston: Allyn & Bacon. Copyright © 1994 by Allyn and Bacon. Reprinted by permission.

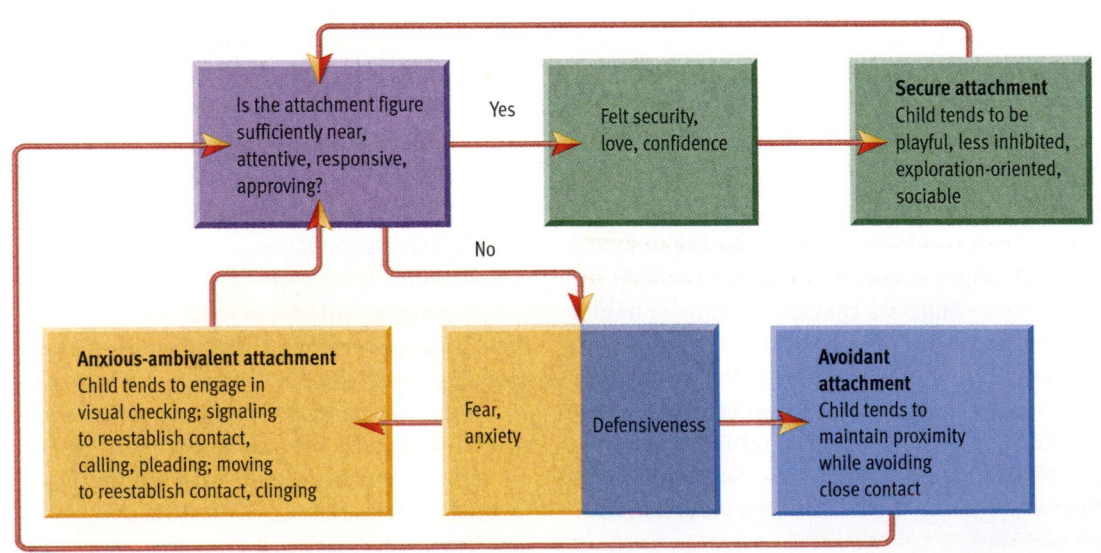

Infant-mother attachments vary in strength and quality and these variations in attachment relations may have long-lasting repercussions.

1992; Schneider, Atkinson, & Tardif, 2001). Furthermore, research suggests that children who have a secure attachment to *both* their parents are better off than those who have a secure attachment to only one parent (Cabrera et al., 2000). However, it is worth noting that all the relevant data on attachment effects are correlational (experimenters cannot manipulate caregiver-infant attachments), so we cannot assume that secure attachment *causes* all these favorable outcomes. Secure attachment could co-vary with other important factors that contribute to high self-esteem, self-reliance, and so forth.

The repercussions of attachment patterns in infancy appear to even reach into adulthood. In Chapter 16 we'll discuss thought-provoking evidence that infant attachment patterns set the tone for people's romantic relationships in adulthood, not to mention their gender roles, religious beliefs, and patterns of self-disclosure (Feeney, 1999; Kirkpatrick, 1999; Shaver & Hazan, 1993, 1994).

Day Care and Attachment

The impact of day care on attachment is the subject of heated debate. The crucial question is whether frequent infant-mother separations might disrupt the attachment process. The issue is an important one, given that about two-thirds of the children under age 5 in the United States receive some nonmaternal care (Scarr, 1998; see Figure 11.8). Research by Jay Belsky (1988, 1992) suggests that babies who receive nonmaternal care for more than 20 hours per week have an increased risk of developing insecure attachments to their mothers. Belsky's findings have raised many eyebrows, but they need to be put in perspective. First, even the most "alarming" data suggest that the proportion of day-care infants who exhibit insecure attachments is only slightly higher than the

norm in American society and even lower than the norm in some other societies (Lamb, Sternberg, & Prodromidis, 1992). Second, the preponderance of evidence suggests that day care is *not* harmful to children's attachment relationships (Booth et al., 2002; Lamb, 1998), including the evidence from a recent ten-site study in the United States funded by the National Institute of Child Health and Human Development (NICHD) that has been characterized as the "most rigorous, and most systematic evaluation of day care ever undertaken" (Rutter & O'Connor, 1999, p. 828). Third, given the deprived child-rearing conditions found in many homes, there is evidence that day care can have *beneficial effects* on some youngsters' social development (Andersson, 1992; Egeland & Hiester, 1995).

Culture and Attachment

Separation anxiety emerges in children at about 6–8 months and peaks at about 14–18 months in cultures around the world (Grossmann & Grossmann, 1990). These findings, which have been replicated in quite a variety of non-Western cultures, suggest that attachment is a universal feature of human development (van IJzendoorn & Sagi, 1999). However, studies have found some interesting cultural variations in the proportion of infants who fall into the three attachment categories described by Ainsworth. Working with white, middle-class subjects in the United States, Ainsworth and colleagues (1978) found that 67% of infants displayed a secure attachment, 21% an anxious-ambivalent attachment, and 12% an avoidant attachment. As Table 11.1 on the next page shows, studies in Germany and Japan have yielded

Web Link 11.3

Child Development Abstracts & Bibliography (CDAB) Online Edition
The CDAB database is sponsored by the Society for Research in Child Development. Now student researchers can access this database online to find abstracts for resources about growth and development published in CDAB since 1990.

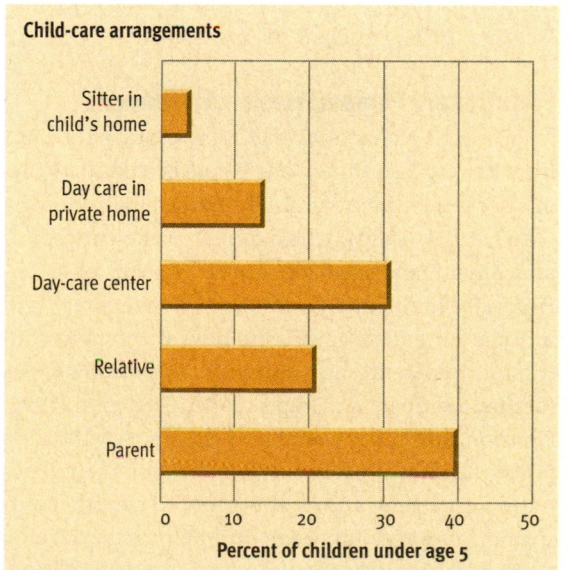

Child-care arrangements

Percent of children under age 5

Figure 11.8

Day care in the United States. This graph shows the distribution of child-care arrangements in 1995 for children under age 5 who were not enrolled in school. The percentages add up to more than 100% because some children experienced more than one type of care. As you can see, about two-thirds of children receive some type of day care. (Data from Scarr, 1998)

Table 11.1 Patterns of Attachment (%) From Three Different Cultures

Country (Study)	Avoidant	Secure	Anxious-Ambivalent
USA (Ainsworth et al., 1978)	21	67	12
Germany (Grossmann et al., 1981)	52	35	13
Japan (Takahashi, 1986)	0	68	32

Source: Cole, M. (1999). Culture in development. In M. H. Bornstein & M. E. Lamb (Eds.), *Developmental psychology: An advanced textbook.* Mahwah, NJ: Erlbaum. Copyright © 1999 Lawrence Erlbaum Associates. Reprinted by permission.

very different figures (Cole, 1999). Avoidant attachments were far more common in the German sample but were nonexistent in the Japanese sample, which yielded more anxious-ambivalent attachments than the U.S. sample.

Researchers have attributed these disparities in attachment patterns to cultural variations in child-rearing practices (Greenfield & Suzuki, 1998). More so than American parents, German parents intentionally try to encourage independence rather than clinging dependence at an early age, thus producing more avoidant attachments (Grossmann et al., 1985). In contrast, Japanese parents do not attempt to foster a similar kind of early independence, and infants are rarely away from their mothers during the first year, so avoidant attachments are rare (Takahashi, 1990). Although these explanations seem plausible, some critics have argued that cultural disparities in attachment processes have been underestimated by Western researchers who have exhibited an ethnocentric slant in their cross-cultural investigations (Rothbaum et al., 2000). These critics assert that there are significant cultural variations in what represents a secure parent-child attachment and in the effects of secure attachment. The validity of this criticism is currently the subject of vigorous debate (Chao, 2001; Kondo-Ikemura, 2001; Posada & Jacobs, 2001).

Evolutionary Perspectives on Attachment

Attachment theory has had an evolutionary slant from its very beginning, long before evolutionary theory became influential in psychology. John Bowlby (1969, 1973, 1980), who originated the concept of attachment, analyzed attachment in terms of its *survival value* for infants. In contrast, contemporary evolutionary theorists emphasize how attachment contributes to parents' and children's *reproductive fitness* (Belsky, Steinberg, & Draper, 1991; Chisholm, 1996; Simpson, 1999). For example, contemporary theorists point out that if parents expect to pass their genes on to future generations, they need to raise their offspring to reproductive age and help them develop the social maturity required for successful mating. Parent-child attachments make crucial contributions

to these outcomes by fostering social and emotional development in children (Kobak, 1999).

Contemporary theorists also have some interesting hypotheses about the evolutionary significance of the specific patterns of attachment seen in children. Jay Belsky (1999b) asserts that *the nature of children's early attachment experiences depends on the character of their environments and that these experiences chart the course of children's social development in ways that are adaptive for their environmental circumstances.* Belsky has outlined hypotheses for all three types of attachment, but we will limit our discussion to the simpler and more fully described comparison between secure and insecure attachments. According to Belsky, over the course of evolutionary history, if parents had the time and energy to be sensitive and responsive to infants' needs, the local environment was probably relatively safe and rich in resources. Sensitive care presumably promoted secure attachments and conveyed to infants that the world is safe, others can be trusted, and relationships are enduring. When securely attached children reached adulthood, this mindset supposedly fostered a reproductive strategy that emphasized *quality* in mating relationships, resulting in relatively few sexual partners, more stable, durable romantic bonds, and more parental investment in offspring. In contrast, Belsky theorizes that, historically, when parents were insensitive and unresponsive to infants' needs, the local environment was probably relatively unsafe and resources depleted. Unresponsive care presumably promoted insecure attachments and conveyed to infants that the world is harsh, others cannot be trusted, and relationships are fleeting. When children with insecure attachments reached adulthood, this mindset supposedly fostered an opportunistic reproductive strategy that emphasized *quantity* in mating relationships, resulting in relatively more sexual partners, less-stable romantic bonds, and less parental investment in offspring (consult Figure 11.18 on page 451).

Belsky's (1999b) key point is that each reproductive strategy was adaptive for the environment in which it tended to occur. In other words, individuals' reproductive potential was probably maximized by being sexually opportunistic in harsh, depleted environments, where long-term survival was precarious, and by emphasizing enduring relationships and high parental investment in benign, abundant environments, where long-term survival appeared more promising.

Is there any empirical evidence to support Belsky's theory? Yes, in Chapter 16 you will see that childhood attachments correlate with adult patterns of romantic relations in ways that mesh reasonably well with Belsky's hypotheses. And in our discussion of adolescence in this chapter, you will see that Belsky's theory has generated some novel predictions about sexual maturation that have received some support. However, most aspects of the theory remain largely untested and some aspects of the theory need to be more fully elucidated.

Becoming Unique: Personality Development

How do individuals develop their unique constellations of personality traits over time? Many theories have addressed this question. The first major theory of personality development was put together by Sigmund Freud back around 1900. As we'll discuss in Chapter 12, he claimed that the basic foundation of an individual's personality is firmly laid down by age 5. Half a century later, Erik Erikson (1963) proposed a sweeping revision of Freud's theory that has proven influential. Like Freud, Erikson concluded that events in early childhood leave a permanent stamp on adult personality. However, unlike Freud, Erikson theorized that personality continues to evolve over the entire life span.

Building on Freud's earlier work, Erikson devised a stage theory of personality development. As you'll see in reading this chapter, many theories describe development in terms of stages. A *stage* is a developmental period during which characteristic patterns of behavior are exhibited and certain capacities become established. Stage theories assume that (1) individuals must progress through specified stages in a particular order because each stage builds on the previous stage, (2) progress through these stages is strongly related to age, and (3) development is marked by major discontinuities that usher in dramatic transitions in behavior (see Figure 11.9).

Erikson's Stage Theory

Erikson partitioned the life span into eight stages, each of which brings a *psychosocial crisis* involving transitions in important social relationships. According to Erikson, personality is shaped by how individuals deal with these psychosocial crises. Each crisis involves a struggle between two opposing tendencies, such as trust versus mistrust or initiative versus guilt, both of which are experienced by the person. Erikson described the stages in terms of these antagonistic tendencies, which represent personality traits that people display in varying degrees over the remainder of their lives. Although the names for Erikson's stages suggest either-or outcomes, he viewed each stage as a tug of war that determined the subsequent *balance* between opposing polarities in personality. All eight stages in Erikson's theory are charted in Figure 11.10. We describe the first four childhood

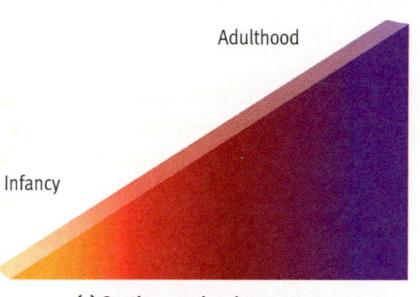

(a) Continuous development   (b) Discontinuous development (stages)

Figure 11.9

Stage theories of development. Some theories view development as a relatively continuous process, albeit not as smooth and perfectly linear as depicted on the left. In contrast, stage theories assume that development is marked by major discontinuities (as shown on the right) that bring fundamental, qualitative changes in capabilities or characteristic behavior.

Figure 11.10

Erikson's stage theory. Erikson's theory of personality development posits that people evolve through eight stages over the life span. Each stage is marked by a *psychosocial crisis* that involves confronting a fundamental question, such as "Who am I and where am I going?" The stages are described in terms of alternative traits that are potential outcomes from the crises. Development is enhanced when a crisis is resolved in favor of the healthier alternative (which is listed first for each stage).

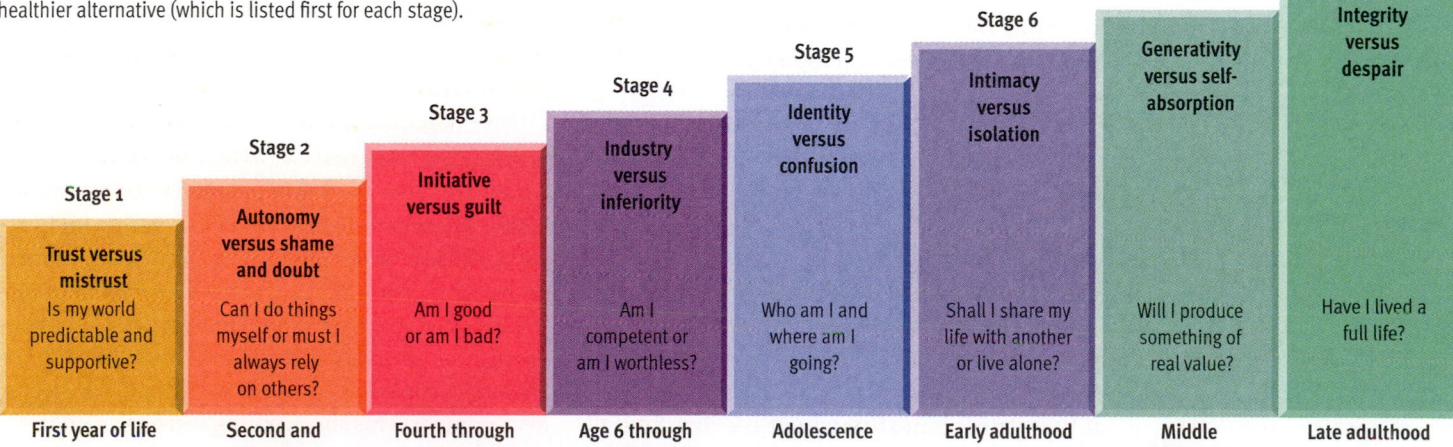

Stage 1	Stage 2	Stage 3	Stage 4	Stage 5	Stage 6	Stage 7	Stage 8
Trust versus mistrust	Autonomy versus shame and doubt	Initiative versus guilt	Industry versus inferiority	Identity versus confusion	Intimacy versus isolation	Generativity versus self-absorption	Integrity versus despair
Is my world predictable and supportive?	Can I do things myself or must I always rely on others?	Am I good or am I bad?	Am I competent or am I worthless?	Who am I and where am I going?	Shall I share my life with another or live alone?	Will I produce something of real value?	Have I lived a full life?
First year of life	Second and third years	Fourth through sixth years	Age 6 through puberty	Adolescence	Early adulthood	Middle adulthood	Late adulthood

"Human personality in principle develops according to steps predetermined in the growing person's readiness to be driven toward, to be aware of, and to interact with a widening social radius."

ERIK ERIKSON

AP/Wide World Photos

Web Link 11.4

Erik Erikson Tutorial Homepage
Margaret Anderson, who teaches at Cortland College in New York, has developed a set of tutorials on major figures of importance to educational psychology. Her Erik Erikson tutorial includes a summary of his eight stages of development, biographical details, some controversies regarding his theories, and links to other online sources.

stages here and discuss the remaining stages in the upcoming sections on adolescence and adulthood.

Trust Versus Mistrust. Erikson's first stage encompasses the first year of life, when an infant has to depend completely on adults to take care of its basic needs for such necessities as food, a warm blanket, and changed diapers. If an infant's basic biological needs are adequately met by his or her caregivers and sound attachments are formed, the child should develop an optimistic, trusting attitude toward the world. However, if the infant's basic needs are taken care of poorly, a more distrusting, pessimistic personality may result.

Autonomy Versus Shame and Doubt. Erikson's second stage unfolds during the second and third years of life, when parents begin toilet training and other efforts to regulate the child's behavior. The child must begin to take some personal responsibility for feeding, dressing, and bathing. If all goes well, he or she acquires a sense of self-sufficiency. But, if parents are never satisfied with the child's efforts and there are constant parent-child conflicts, the child may develop a sense of personal shame and self-doubt.

Initiative Versus Guilt. In Erikson's third stage, lasting roughly from ages 3 to 6, children experiment and take initiatives that may sometimes conflict with their parents' rules. Overcontrolling parents may begin to instill feelings of guilt, and self-esteem may suffer. Parents need to support their children's emerging independence while maintaining appropriate controls. In the ideal situation, children will retain their sense of initiative while learning to respect the rights and privileges of other family members.

Industry Versus Inferiority. In the fourth stage (age 6 through puberty), the challenge of learning to function socially is extended beyond the family to the broader social realm of the neighborhood and school. Children who are able to function effectively in this less nurturant social sphere where productivity is highly valued should learn to value achievement and to take pride in accomplishment, resulting in a sense of competence.

Evaluating Erikson's Theory

The strength of Erikson's theory is that it accounts for both continuity and transition in personality development. It accounts for transition by showing how new challenges in social relations stimulate personality development throughout life. It accounts

© Bill Bachman/PhotoEdit

According to Erik Erikson, school-age children face the challenge of learning how to function in social situations outside of their family, especially with peers and at school. If they succeed, they will develop a sense of competence; if they fail, they may feel inferior.

for continuity by drawing connections between early childhood experiences and aspects of adult personality. One measure of a theory's value is how much research it generates, and Erikson's theory continues to guide a fair amount of research (Thomas, 2000).

On the negative side of the ledger, Erikson's theory has depended heavily on illustrative case studies, which are open to varied interpretations (Thomas, 2000). Another weakness is that the theory provides an "idealized" description of "typical" developmental patterns. Thus, it's not well suited for explaining the enormous personality differences that exist among people. Inadequate explanation of individual differences is a common problem with stage theories of development. This shortcoming surfaces again in the next section, where we'll examine Jean Piaget's stage theory of cognitive development.

Figure 11.11

Piaget's stage theory. Piaget's theory of cognitive development identifies four stages marked by fundamentally different modes of thinking through which youngsters evolve. The approximate age norms and some key characteristics of thought at each stage are summarized here.

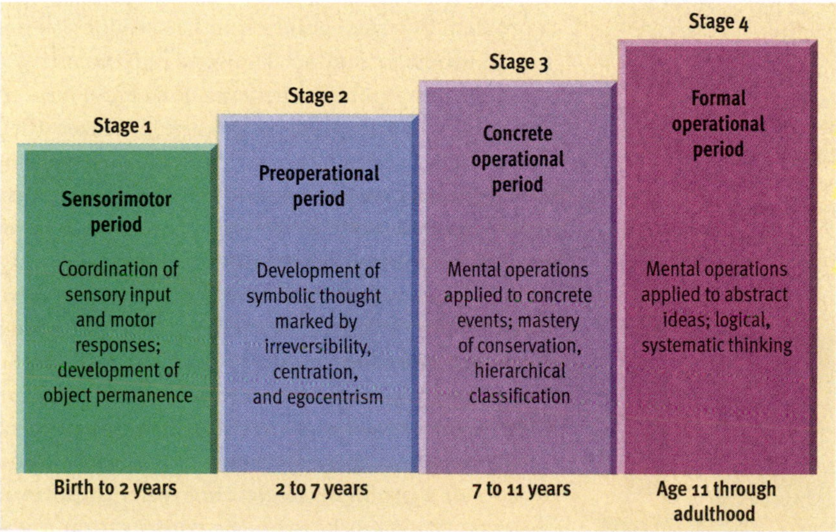

Stage 1	Stage 2	Stage 3	Stage 4
Sensorimotor period	**Preoperational period**	**Concrete operational period**	**Formal operational period**
Coordination of sensory input and motor responses; development of object permanence	Development of symbolic thought marked by irreversibility, centration, and egocentrism	Mental operations applied to concrete events; mastery of conservation, hierarchical classification	Mental operations applied to abstract ideas; logical, systematic thinking
Birth to 2 years	2 to 7 years	7 to 11 years	Age 11 through adulthood

The Growth of Thought: Cognitive Development

 9c

Cognitive development refers to transitions in youngsters' patterns of thinking, including reasoning, remembering, and problem solving. The investigation of cognitive development was dominated in most of the second half of the 20th century by the theory of Jean Piaget (Kessen, 1996). Much of our discussion of cognitive development is devoted to Piaget's theory and the research it generated, although we'll also delve into other approaches to cognitive development.

Overview of Piaget's Stage Theory

 9c

Jean Piaget (1929, 1952, 1983) was an interdisciplinary scholar whose own cognitive development was exceptionally rapid. In his early 20s, after he had earned a doctorate in natural science and published a novel, Piaget's interest turned to psychology. He met Theodore Simon, who had collaborated with Alfred Binet in devising the first useful intelligence tests (see Chapter 9). Working in Simon's Paris laboratory, Piaget administered intelligence tests to many children to develop better test norms. In doing this testing, Piaget became intrigued by the reasoning underlying the children's *wrong* answers. He decided that measuring children's intelligence was less interesting than studying how children *use* their intelligence. In 1921 he moved to Geneva, where he spent the rest of his life studying cognitive development. Many of his ideas were based on insights gleaned from careful observations of his own three children during their infancy.

Like Erikson's theory, Piaget's model is a *stage theory* of development. Piaget proposed that youngsters progress through four major stages of cognitive development, which are characterized by fundamentally different thought processes: (1) the *sensorimotor period* (birth to age 2), (2) the *preoperational period* (ages 2 to 7), (3) the *concrete operational period* (ages 7 to 11), and (4) the *formal operational period* (age 11 onward). Figure 11.11 provides an overview of each of these periods. Piaget regarded his age norms as approximations and acknowledged that transitional ages may vary, but he was con-

"It is virtually impossible to draw a clear line between innate and acquired behavior patterns."
JEAN PIAGET

Figure 11.12

Piaget's conservation task.
After watching the transformation shown, a preoperational child will usually answer that the taller beaker contains more water. In contrast, the child in the concrete operational period tends to respond correctly, recognizing that the amount of water in beaker C remains the same as the amount in beaker A.

vinced that all children progress through the stages of cognitive development in the same order.

Noting that children actively explore the world around them, Piaget asserted that interaction with the environment and maturation gradually alter the way children think. According to Piaget, children progress in their thinking through the complementary processes of assimilation and accommodation. *Assimilation* involves interpreting new experiences in terms of existing mental structures without changing them. In contrast, *accommodation* involves changing existing mental structures to explain new experiences. Accommodation and assimilation often occur interactively. For instance, a child who has learned to call four-legged pets "puppies" may apply this scheme the first time she encounters a cat (assimilation), but she will eventually discover that puppies and cats are different types of animals and make adjustments to her mental schemes (accommodation). With the companion processes of assimilation and accommodation in mind, let's turn now to the four stages in Piaget's theory.

Sensorimotor Period. One of Piaget's foremost contributions was to greatly enhance our understanding of mental development in the earliest months of life. The first stage in his theory is the *sensorimotor period,* which lasts from birth to about age 2. Piaget called this stage *sensorimotor* because infants are developing the ability to coordinate their sensory input with their motor actions.

The major development during the sensorimotor stage is the gradual appearance of symbolic thought. At the beginning of this stage, a child's behavior is dominated by innate reflexes. But by the end of the stage, the child can use mental symbols to represent objects (for example, a mental image of a favorite toy). The key to this transition is the acquisition of the concept of object permanence.

Object permanence develops when a child recognizes that objects continue to exist even when they are no longer visible. Although you surely take the permanence of objects for granted, infants aren't aware of this permanence at first. If you show a 4-month-old an eye-catching toy and then cover the toy with a pillow, the child will not attempt to search for the toy. Piaget inferred from this observation that the child does not understand that the toy continues to exist under the pillow. The notion of object permanence does not dawn on children overnight. The first signs of this insight usually appear between 4 and 8 months of age, when children will often pursue an object that is *partially* covered in their presence. Progress is gradual, and Piaget believed that children typically don't master the concept of object permanence until they're about 18 months old.

Preoperational Period. During the *preoperational period,* which extends roughly from age 2 to age 7, children gradually improve in their use of mental images. Although progress in symbolic thought continues, Piaget emphasized the *shortcomings* in preoperational thought.

Consider a simple problem that Piaget presented to youngsters. He would take two identical beakers and fill each with the same amount of water. After a child had agreed that the two beakers contained the same amount of water, he would pour the water from one of the beakers into a much taller and thinner beaker (see Figure 11.12). He would then ask the child whether the two differently shaped beakers still contained the same amount of water. Confronted with a problem like this, children in the preoperational period generally said no. They typically focused on the higher water line in the taller beaker and insisted that there was more water in the slender beaker. They had not yet mastered the principle of conservation. *Conservation* is Piaget's term for the awareness that physical quantities remain constant in spite of changes in their shape or appearance.

Why are preoperational children unable to solve conservation problems? According to Piaget, their inability to understand conservation is due to some basic flaws in preoperational thinking. These flaws include centration, irreversibility, and egocentrism. *Centration* is the tendency to focus on just one feature of a problem, neglecting other important aspects. When working on the conservation problem with water, preoperational children tend to con-

Step 1
The child agrees that beakers A and B contain the same amount of water.

Step 2
The child observes as the water from beaker B is poured into beaker C, which is shaped differently.

Step 3
The child is asked: "Do beakers A and C contain the same amount of water?"

centrate on the height of the water while ignoring the width. They have difficulty focusing on several aspects of a problem at once.

Irreversibility **is the inability to envision reversing an action.** Preoperational children can't mentally "undo" something. For instance, in grappling with the conservation of water, they don't think about what would happen if the water were poured back from the tall beaker into the original beaker.

Egocentrism **in thinking is characterized by a limited ability to share another person's viewpoint.** Indeed, Piaget felt that preoperational children fail to appreciate that there are points of view other than their own. For instance, if you ask a preoperational girl whether her sister has a sister, she'll probably say no if they are the only two girls in the family. She's unable to view sisterhood from her sister's perspective (this also shows irreversibility).

A notable feature of egocentrism is *animism*—**the belief that all things are living,** just like oneself. Thus, youngsters attribute lifelike, human qualities to inanimate objects, asking questions such as, "When does the ocean stop to rest?" or "Why does the wind get so mad?"

As you can see, Piaget emphasized the weaknesses apparent in preoperational thought. Indeed, that is why he called this stage *pre*operational. The ability to perform *operations*—internal transformations, manipulations, and reorganizations of mental structures—emerges in the next stage.

Concrete Operational Period. The development of mental operations marks the beginning of the *concrete operational period,* which usually lasts from about age 7 to age 11. Piaget called this stage *concrete* operations because children can perform operations only on images of tangible objects and actual events.

Among the operations that children master during this stage are reversibility and decentration. *Reversibility* permits a child to mentally undo an action. *Decentration* allows the child to focus on more than one feature of a problem simultaneously. The newfound ability to coordinate several aspects of a problem helps the child appreciate that there are several ways to look at things. This ability in turn leads to a *decline in egocentrism* and *gradual mastery of conservation* as it applies to liquid, mass, number, volume, area, and length (see Figure 11.13 on the next page).

As children master concrete operations, they develop a variety of new problem-solving capacities. Let's examine another problem studied by Piaget. Give a preoperational child seven carnations and three daisies. Tell the child the names for the two types of flowers and ask the child to sort them into carnations and daisies. That should be no problem. Now ask the child whether there are more carnations or more daisies. Most children will correctly respond that there are more carnations. Now ask the child whether there are more carnations or more flowers. At this point, most preoperational children will stumble and respond incorrectly that there are more carnations than flowers. Generally, preoperational children can't handle *hierarchical classification* problems that require them to focus simultaneously on two levels of classification. However, the child who has advanced to the concrete operational stage is not as limited by centration and can work successfully with hierarchical classification problems.

Formal Operational Period. The final stage in Piaget's theory is the *formal operational period,* which typically begins around 11 years of age. In this stage, children begin to apply their operations to *abstract* concepts in addition to concrete objects. Indeed, during this stage, youngsters come to *enjoy* the heady contemplation of abstract concepts. Many adolescents spend hours mulling over hypothetical possibilities related to abstractions such as justice, love, and free will.

According to Piaget, youngsters graduate to relatively adult modes of thinking in the formal operations stage. He did *not* mean to suggest that no further cognitive development occurs once children reach this stage. However, he believed that after children achieve formal operations, further developments in thinking are changes in *degree* rather than fundamental changes in the *nature* of thinking.

Adolescents in the formal operational period become more *systematic* in their problem-solving efforts. Children in earlier developmental stages tend to attack problems quickly, with a trial-and-error approach. In contrast, children who have achieved formal operations are more likely to think things through. They envision possible courses of action and try to use logic to reason out the likely consequences of each possible solution before they act. Thus, thought processes in the formal operational period can be characterized as abstract, systematic, logical, and reflective.

Evaluating Piaget's Theory

Jean Piaget made a landmark contribution to psychology's understanding of children in general and their cognitive development in particular (Beilin, 1992). He founded the field of cognitive development and fostered a new view of children that saw them as active agents constructing their own worlds (Fischer & Hencke, 1996). Above all else, he sought answers to new questions. As he acknowledged in a 1970 inter-

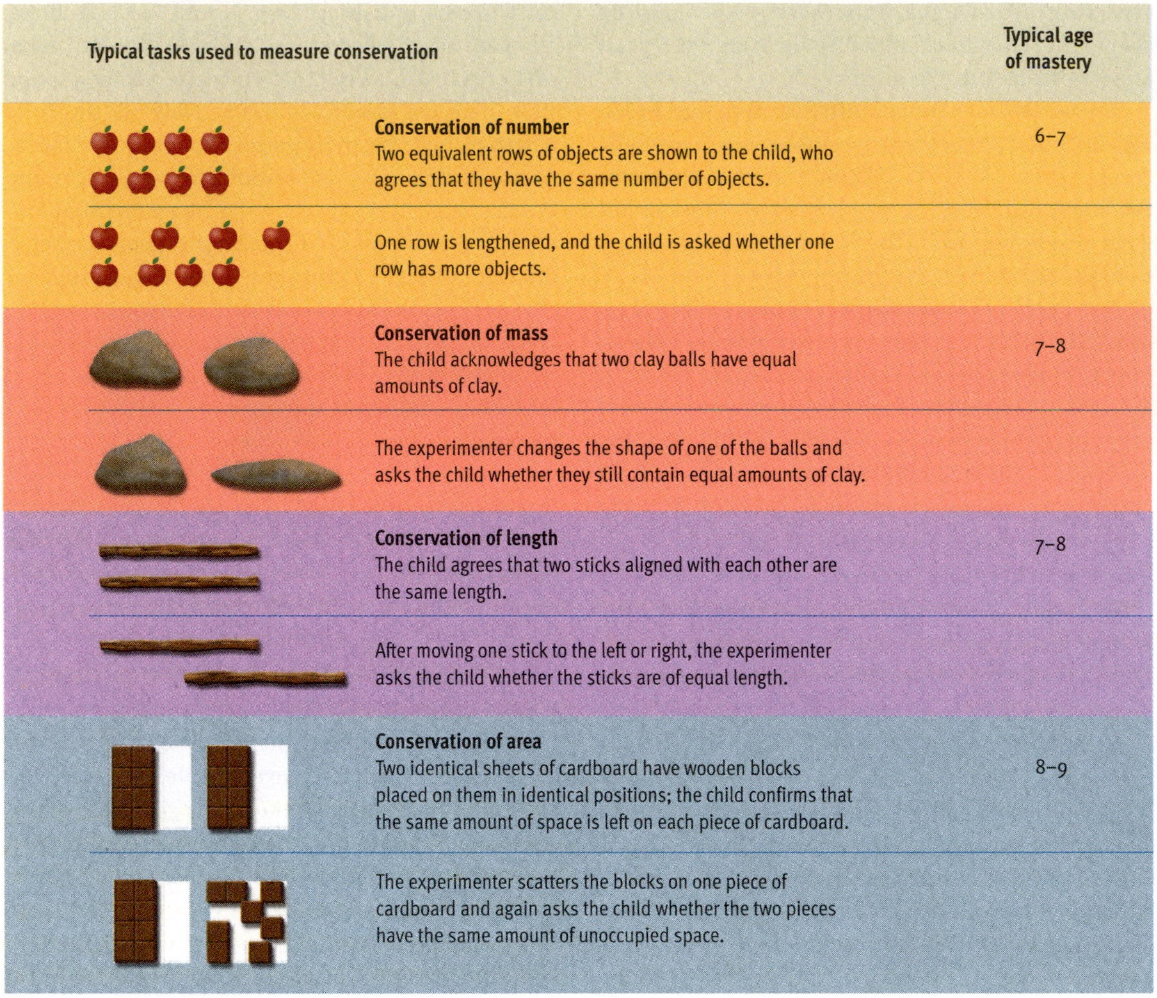

Figure 11.13

The gradual mastery of conservation. Children master conservation during the concrete operational period, but their mastery is gradual. As outlined here, children usually master the conservation of number at age 6 or 7, but they may not understand the conservation of area until age 8 or 9.

Typical tasks used to measure conservation	Typical age of mastery
Conservation of number Two equivalent rows of objects are shown to the child, who agrees that they have the same number of objects.	6–7
One row is lengthened, and the child is asked whether one row has more objects.	
Conservation of mass The child acknowledges that two clay balls have equal amounts of clay.	7–8
The experimenter changes the shape of one of the balls and asks the child whether they still contain equal amounts of clay.	
Conservation of length The child agrees that two sticks aligned with each other are the same length.	7–8
After moving one stick to the left or right, the experimenter asks the child whether the sticks are of equal length.	
Conservation of area Two identical sheets of cardboard have wooden blocks placed on them in identical positions; the child confirms that the same amount of space is left on each piece of cardboard.	8–9
The experimenter scatters the blocks on one piece of cardboard and again asks the child whether the two pieces have the same amount of unoccupied space.	

view, "It's just that no adult ever had the idea of asking children about conservation. It was so obvious that if you change the shape of an object, the quantity will be conserved. Why ask a child? The novelty lay in asking the question" (Hall, 1987, p. 56). Piaget's theory guided an enormous volume of productive research that continues through today (Brainerd, 1996). This research has supported many of Piaget's central propositions (Flavell, 1996). In such a far-reaching theory, however, there are bound to be some weak spots. Let's briefly examine some criticisms of Piaget's theory:

1. In many areas, Piaget appears to have underestimated young children's cognitive development (Lutz & Sternberg, 1999). For example, researchers have found evidence that children begin to develop object permanence much earlier than Piaget thought, perhaps as early as 3 to 4 months of age (Baillargeon, 1987, 1994). Others have marshaled evidence that preoperational children exhibit less egocentrism and animism than Piaget believed (Newcombe & Huttenlocher, 1992).

2. Piaget's model suffers from problems that plague most stage theories. Like Erikson, Piaget had little to say about individual differences in development (Siegler, 1994). Also, people often simultaneously display patterns of thinking that are characteristic of several stages. This "mixing" of stages calls into question the value of organizing development in terms of stages (Bjorklund, 2000; Siegler & Ellis, 1996).

3. Piaget believed that his theory described universal processes that should lead children everywhere to progress through uniform stages of thinking at roughly the same ages. Subsequent research has shown that the *sequence* of stages is largely invariant, but the *timetable* that children follow in passing through these stages varies considerably across cultures (Dasen, 1994; Rogoff, 1990). Thus, Piaget underestimated the influence of cultural factors on cognitive development.

As with any theory, Piaget's is not flawless. However, without Piaget's theory to guide research, many crucial questions about children's development might not have been confronted until decades later (if at all). By some measures, the influence of Piaget is declining (Bjorklund, 1997), but ironically, even many of the new directions in the study of cognitive development grew out of efforts to test, revise, or discredit Piaget's theory (Flavell, 1996). Let's look at some of these new directions.

Are Some Cognitive Abilities Innate?

The frequent finding that Piaget underestimated infants' cognitive abilities has led to a rash of research suggesting that infants have a surprising grasp of many complex concepts. The new findings have been made possible by some innovative research methods that permit investigators to draw inferences about the abilities of very young children. Many studies have made use of the *habituation-dishabituation paradigm*. *Habituation* is a gradual reduction in the strength of a response when a stimulus event is presented repeatedly. If you show infants the same event over and over (such as an object dropping onto a platform), they habituate to it—their heart and respiration rates decline and they spend less time looking at the stimulus. *Dishabituation* occurs if a new stimulus elicits an increase in the strength of an habituated response. Patterns of dishabituation can give researchers insights into what types of events infants can tell apart, which events surprise or interest them, and which events violate their expectations.

Working mostly with the habituation-dishabituation paradigm, researchers have discovered that infants understand basic properties of objects and some of the rules that govern them. At 3 to 4 months of age, infants understand that objects are distinct entities with boundaries, that objects move in continuous paths, that one solid object cannot pass through another, that an object cannot pass through an opening that is smaller than the object, and that objects on slopes roll down rather than up (Kim & Spelke, 1992; Spelke & Newport, 1998). Other research has shown that infants' ability to categorize objects is much more advanced than previously appreciated. At 9 to 12 months of age, infants can recognize whether common objects belong to sensible categories, such as foods, animals, and vehicles (Quinn & Eimas, 1996, 1998).

In this line of research, perhaps the most stunning discovery has been the finding that *infants seem to be able to add and subtract small numbers* (Bremner, 2001). If 5-month-old infants are shown a sequence of events in which one object is added to another behind a screen, they expect to see two objects when the screen is removed, and they exhibit surprise when their expectation is violated (see Figure 11.14). This expectation suggests that they understand that 1 + 1

CONCEPT CHECK 11.2

Recognizing Piaget's Stages

Check your understanding of Piaget's theory by indicating the stage of cognitive development illustrated by each of the examples below. For each scenario, fill in the letter for the appropriate stage in the space on the left. The answers are in Appendix A.

a. Sensorimotor period   **c.** Concrete operational period
b. Preoperational period   **d.** Formal operational period

_____ **1.** Upon seeing a glass lying on its side, Sammy says, "Look, the glass is tired. It's taking a nap."

_____ **2.** Maria is told that a farmer has nine cows and six horses. The teacher asks, "Does the farmer have more cows or more animals?" Maria answers, "More animals."

_____ **3.** Alice is playing in the living room with a small red ball. The ball rolls under the sofa. She stares for a moment at the place where the ball vanished and then turns her attention to a toy truck sitting in front of her.

= 2 (Wynn, 1992, 1996). Similar manipulations suggest that infants also understand that 2 – 1 = 1, that 2 + 1 = 3, and that 3 – 1 = 2 (Hauser & Carey, 1998; Wynn, 1998).

Again and again in recent years, research has shown that infants appear to understand surprisingly complex concepts that they have had virtually no opportunity to learn about. These findings have led some theorists to conclude that certain basic cognitive abilities are biologically built into humans' neural architecture. The theorists who have reached

Figure 11.14

The procedure used to test infants' understanding of number. To see if 5-month-old infants have some appreciation of addition and subtraction, Wynn (1992, 1996) showed them sequences of events like those depicted here. If children express surprise (primarily assessed by time spent looking) when the screen drops and they see only one object, this result suggests that they understand that 1 + 1 = 2. Wynn and others have found that infants seem to have some primitive grasp of simple addition and subtraction.

SOURCE: Adapted from Wynn, K. (1992). Addition and subtraction by human infants. *Nature, 358,* 749–750. Copyright © 1992 Macmillan Magazines, Ltd. Reprinted with permission.

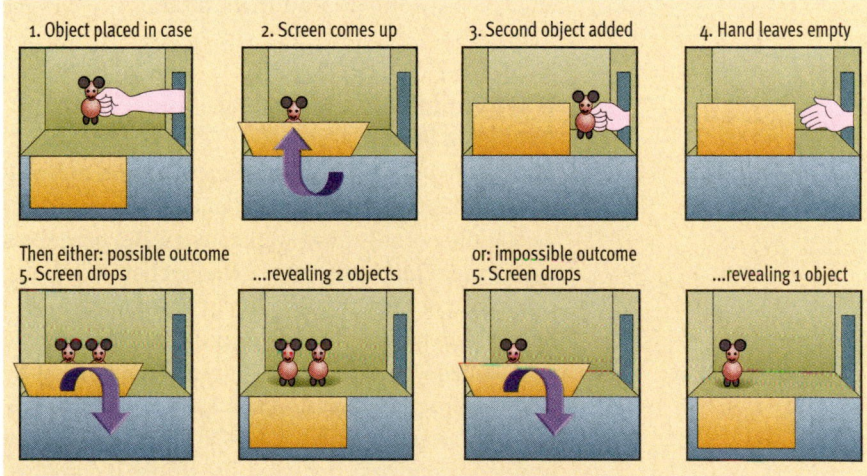

1. Object placed in case   2. Screen comes up   3. Second object added   4. Hand leaves empty

Then either: possible outcome 5. Screen drops   ...revealing 2 objects   or: impossible outcome 5. Screen drops   ...revealing 1 object

this conclusion tend to fall into two camps: nativists and evolutionary theorists. The *nativists* simply assert that humans are prewired to readily understand certain concepts without making any assumptions about *why* humans are prewired in these ways (Spelke, 1994; Spelke & Newport, 1998). Their principal interest is to sort out the complex matter of what is prewired and what isn't.

Evolutionary theorists agree with the nativists that humans are prewired for certain cognitive abilities, but they are keenly interested in *why.* As you might expect, they maintain that this wiring is a product of natural selection, and they strive to understand its adaptive significance (Hauser & Carey, 1998; Wynn, 1998). For example, evolutionary theorists are interested in how basic addition-subtraction abilities may have enhanced our hominid ancestors' success in hunting, foraging, and social bargaining. The evolutionary theorists also argue that the findings on infants' surprising abilities *demonstrate that the human mind is modular*—that it is made up of domain-specific modules that have been crafted by natural selection to solve specific adaptive problems, such as recognizing faces, discriminating simple speech sounds, and understanding basic properties of objects (Gelman & Williams, 1998; Leslie, 1994).

I hasten to add that the question about whether some cognitive abilities are hardwired is much more complicated than it may appear at first glance. Critics assert that infants' dishabituation responses to various events can be interpreted and explained in a variety of ways without assuming that infants possess innate knowledge of objects, categories, and number (Fischer & Bidell, 1991; Haith & Benson, 1998). For example, infants may spend more time looking at novel events simply because these events require more time for perceptual processing and memory encoding (Bogartz & Shinskey, 1998). Thus, the newly emerging debate about whether infants have some innate knowledge of the world around them promises to be very interesting.

What Do Children Understand About the Mind?

Another red-hot topic in the area of cognitive development has been the question of how children's understanding of the mind and mental states progresses over time (Bjorklund, 2000). Researchers exploring this aspect of cognitive development study when and how children come to understand that other people have knowledge, beliefs, and desires that may be quite different from their own. Consider the following scenario. An experimenter shows a 5-year-old child a candy box and asks her what she thinks it contains.

She answers, "candy." The child is then allowed to look inside the box and discovers that it really contains crayons. Then the experimenter asks the girl what another child who has *not* seen the contents of the box will think it contains. "Candy," she replies, showing her understanding of the planned deception. Now imagine the same experiment with a 3-year-old boy. Events unfold in the same way until the experimenter asks what another child will think the candy box contains. The 3-year-old typically will say "crayons," thinking that the other child will know what he knows about the hidden contents of the box. More perplexing yet, if questioned further, the 3-year-old will probably insist that he originally thought and said that there were crayons in the candy box (Flavell, 1999). Why does the 3-year-old respond in this way? Because most children under age 4 do not yet appreciate that people can hold *false beliefs* that do not accurately reflect reality.

Researchers have mapped out some milestones in the development of children's understanding of mental states (Bartsch & Wellman, 1995; Flavell & Miller, 1998). Around age 2 children begin to distinguish between mental states and overt behavior. The first mental states they understand are *desires* and *emotions*. By age 3, children are talking about others' *beliefs* and *thoughts,* as well as their desires. It is not until about age 4, however, that children consistently make the connection between mental states and behavior. That is, they begin to understand how people's beliefs, thoughts, and desires motivate and direct their behavior. Thus, they can appreciate that Darius *wants* to get some Pokemon cards, which would make him very *happy,* that he *believes* they will be available at the mall, and that these mental states will *motivate* Darius to ask his dad to take him to the mall.

Children's understanding of the mind seems to turn a corner between ages 3 and 4, so that 4-year-olds typically begin to grasp the fact that people may hold false beliefs (Wellman & Gelman, 1998). After age 4, youngsters' reasoning about mental states continues to improve. For example, 4-year-olds are relatively poor at introspection, as they struggle when asked to reconstruct their recent thoughts about something, but their capacity for introspection gradually increases over the next several years (Flavell, 1999).

The Development of Moral Reasoning

In Europe, a woman was near death from cancer. One drug might save her, a form of radium that a druggist in the same town had recently discovered. The druggist was charging $2,000, ten times what the drug cost him to

make. The sick woman's husband, Heinz, went to everyone he knew to borrow the money, but he could only get together about half of what it cost. He told the druggist that his wife was dying and asked him to sell it cheaper or let him pay later. But the druggist said, "No." The husband got desperate and broke into the man's store to steal the drug for his wife. Should the husband have done that? Why? (Kohlberg, 1969, p. 379)

What's your answer to Heinz's dilemma? Would you have answered the same way three years ago? In the fifth grade? Can you guess what you might have said at age 6?

By presenting similar dilemmas to subjects and studying their responses, Lawrence Kohlberg (1976, 1984; Colby & Kohlberg, 1987) devised a model of how moral reasoning develops. What is morality? That's a complicated question that philosophers have debated for centuries. For our purposes, it will suffice to say that *morality* involves the ability to discern right from wrong and to behave accordingly.

Kohlberg's Stage Theory

9d

Kohlberg's model is the most influential of a number of competing theories that attempt to explain how youngsters develop a sense of right and wrong. His work was derived from much earlier work by Jean Piaget (1932), who theorized that moral development is determined by cognitive development. By this he meant that the way individuals think out moral issues depends on their level of cognitive development. This assumption provided the springboard for Kohlberg's research.

Kohlberg's theory focuses on moral *reasoning* rather than overt *behavior*. This point is best illustrated by describing Kohlberg's method of investigation. He presented his subjects with thorny moral questions such as Heinz's dilemma. He then asked them what the actor in the dilemma should do, and more im-

portant, why. It was the *why* that interested Kohlberg. He examined the nature and progression of subjects' moral reasoning.

The result of this work is the stage theory of moral reasoning outlined in Figure 11.15. Kohlberg found that individuals progress through a series of three levels of moral development, each of which can be broken into two sublevels, yielding a total of six stages. Each stage represents a different approach to thinking about right and wrong.

Younger children at the *preconventional level* think in terms of external authority. Acts are wrong because they are punished or right because they lead to positive consequences. Older children who have reached the *conventional level* of moral reasoning see rules as necessary for maintaining social order. They therefore accept these rules as their own. They "internalize" these rules not to avoid punishment but to be virtuous and win approval from others. Moral thinking at this stage is relatively inflexible. Rules are viewed as absolute guidelines that should be enforced rigidly.

During adolescence, some youngsters move on to the *postconventional level,* which involves working out a personal code of ethics. Acceptance of rules is less rigid, and moral thinking shows some flexibility. Subjects at the postconventional level allow for the possibility that someone might not comply with some of society's rules if they conflict with personal ethics. For example, subjects at this level might applaud a newspaper reporter who goes to jail rather than reveal a source of information who was promised anonymity.

Evaluating Kohlberg's Theory

How has Kohlberg's theory fared in research? The central ideas have received reasonable support. Progress in moral reasoning is indeed closely tied to cognitive development (Walker, 1988). Studies also show that

"Children are almost as likely to reject moral reasoning beneath their level as to fail to assimilate reasoning too far above their level."
LAWRENCE KOHLBERG

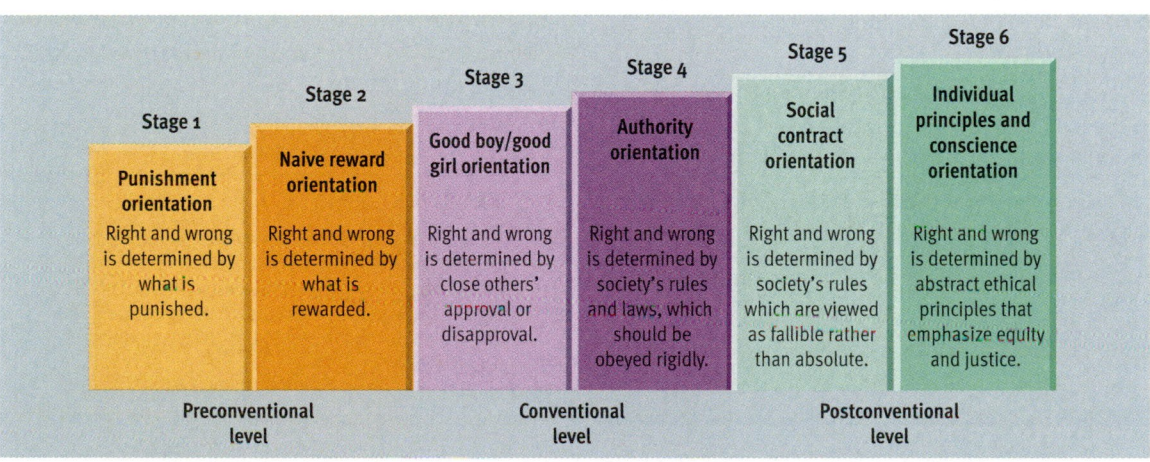

Stage 1	Stage 2	Stage 3	Stage 4	Stage 5	Stage 6
Punishment orientation	**Naive reward orientation**	**Good boy/good girl orientation**	**Authority orientation**	**Social contract orientation**	**Individual principles and conscience orientation**
Right and wrong is determined by what is punished.	Right and wrong is determined by what is rewarded.	Right and wrong is determined by close others' approval or disapproval.	Right and wrong is determined by society's rules and laws, which should be obeyed rigidly.	Right and wrong is determined by society's rules which are viewed as fallible rather than absolute.	Right and wrong is determined by abstract ethical principles that emphasize equity and justice.
Preconventional level		**Conventional level**		**Postconventional level**	

Figure 11.15

Kohlberg's stage theory.
Kohlberg's model posits three levels of moral reasoning, each of which can be divided into two stages. This chart summarizes some of the key facets in how individuals think about right and wrong at each stage.

Figure 11.16

Age and moral reasoning.
The percentages of different types of moral judgments made by subjects at various ages are graphed here (based on Kohlberg, 1963, 1969). As predicted, preconventional reasoning declines as children mature, conventional reasoning increases during middle childhood, and postconventional reasoning begins to emerge during adolescence. But at each age, children display a mixture of various levels of moral reasoning.

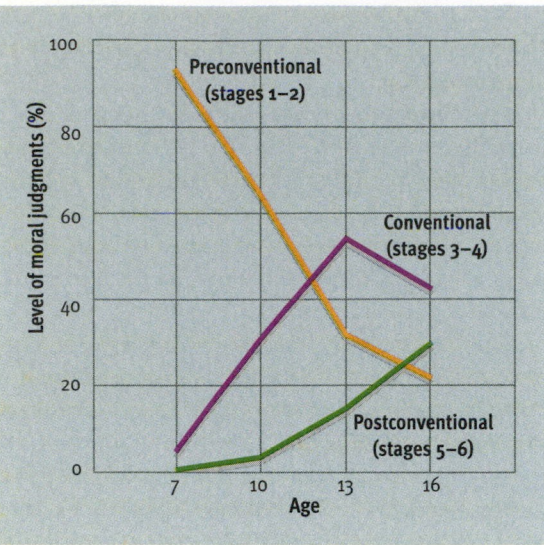

youngsters generally do progress through Kohlberg's stages of moral reasoning in the order that he proposed (Walker & Taylor, 1991). Furthermore, relations between age and level of moral reasoning are in the predicted directions (Rest, 1986; Walker, 1989). Representative age trends are shown in Figure 11.16. As children get older, stage 1 and stage 2 reasoning declines, while stage 3 and stage 4 reasoning increases.

CONCEPT CHECK 11.3

Analyzing Moral Reasoning

Check your understanding of Kohlberg's theory of moral development by analyzing hypothetical responses to the following moral dilemma.

A midwest biologist has conducted numerous studies demonstrating that simple organisms such as worms and paramecia can learn through conditioning. It occurs to her that perhaps she could condition fertilized human ova, to provide a dramatic demonstration that abortions destroy adaptable, living human organisms. This possibility appeals to her, as she is ardently opposed to abortion. However, there is no way to conduct the necessary research on human ova without sacrificing the lives of potential human beings. She desperately wants to conduct the research, but obviously, the sacrifice of human ova is fundamentally incompatible with her belief in the sanctity of human life. What should she do? Why? [Submitted by a student (age 13) to Professor Barbara Banas at Monroe Community College]

In the spaces on the left of each numbered response, indicate the level of moral reasoning shown, choosing from the following: (a) preconventional level, (b) conventional level, or (c) postconventional level. The answers are in Appendix A.

_____ **1.** She should do the research. Although it's wrong to kill, there's a greater good that can be realized through the research.

_____ **2.** She shouldn't do the research because people will think that she's a hypocrite and condemn her.

_____ **3.** She should do the research because she may become rich and famous as a result.

However, there is great variation in the age at which people reach specific stages. Finally, evidence suggests that moral *reasoning* is predictive of moral *behavior,* although the association is modest (Bruggerman & Hart, 1996). That is, youngsters who are at higher stages of moral development are somewhat more likely to be altruistic, conscientious, and honest than youngsters at lower stages (Fabes et al., 1999; Taylor & Walker, 1997). Although these findings support the utility of Kohlberg's model, like all influential theorists, he has his critics. They have raised the following issues:

1. It's not unusual to find that a person shows signs of several adjacent levels of moral reasoning at a particular point in development (Walker & Taylor, 1991). As we noted in the critique of Piaget, this mixing of stages is a problem for virtually all stage theories.

2. Researchers have focused too heavily on how people reason about the specific dilemmas devised by Kohlberg. As Wark and Krebs (1996) put it, "It is somewhat disconcerting to consider how much we have learned about people's judgments about Heinz and his dilemma, and how little we have learned about real-life moral judgment" (pp. 220–221).

3. Sizable cultural disparities have been found in people's progress through Kohlberg's stages (Miller, 2001). When subjects from small, technologically unsophisticated village societies are tested, they rarely show reasoning beyond stage 3 in Kohlberg's scheme (Snarey, 1995). The concerns about social justice that are paramount in Kohlberg's analysis of morality are not necessarily emphasized in other societies (Walker & Moran, 1991). Evidence is mounting that Kohlberg's dilemmas may not be valid indicators of moral development in some cultures (Eckensberger & Zimba, 1997). Some critics believe that the value judgments built into Kohlberg's theory reflect a liberal, individualistic ideology characteristic of modern Western nations that is much more culture-specific than Kohlberg appreciated (Shweder, Mahapatra, & Miller, 1990).

REVIEW OF KEY POINTS

● According to Piaget's theory of cognitive development, the key advance during the sensorimotor period is the child's gradual recognition of the permanence of objects. The preoperational period is marked by certain deficiencies in thinking—notably, centration, irreversibility, and egocentrism.

● During the concrete operations period, children develop the ability to perform operations on mental representations, making them capable of conservation and hierarchical classification. The stage of formal operations ushers in more abstract, systematic, and logical thought.

- Piaget may have underestimated some aspects of children's cognitive development and his theory, like other stage theories, does not explain individual differences very well. Nonetheless, his work has greatly improved psychology's understanding of cognitive development.

- Recent research has shown that infants appear to understand surprisingly complex concepts that they have had virtually no opportunity to learn about, leading some theorists to conclude that basic cognitive abilities are biologically built into humans' neural architecture. Children's understanding of the mind seems to turn a corner between ages 3 and 4.

- According to Kohlberg, moral reasoning progresses through six stages that are related to age and determined by cognitive development. Age-related progress in moral reasoning has been found in research, although a great deal of overlap occurs between adjacent stages.

The Transition of Adolescence

Adolescence is a transitional period between childhood and adulthood. Its age boundaries are not exact, but in our society adolescence begins at around age 13 and ends at about age 22. Although most societies have at least a brief period of adolescence, it is *not* universal across cultures (Schlegel & Barry, 1991; Whiting, Burbank, & Ratner, 1986). In some cultures, young people move directly from childhood to adulthood. A protracted period of adolescence is seen primarily in industrialized nations. In these societies, rapid technological progress has made lengthy education, and therefore prolonged economic dependence, the norm. Thus, in our own culture junior high school, high school, and college students often have a "marginal" status. They are capable of reproduction and so are physiologically mature. Yet they have not achieved the emotional and economic independence from their parents that are the hallmarks of adulthood. Let's begin our discussion of adolescent development with its most visible aspect: the physical changes that transform the body of a child into that of an adult.

Puberty and the Growth Spurt

Recall for a moment your junior high school days. Didn't it seem that your body grew so fast about this time that your clothes just couldn't "keep up"? This phase of rapid growth in height and weight is called the *adolescent growth spurt*. Brought on by hormonal changes, it typically starts at about 11 years of age in girls and about two years later in boys (Malina, 1990). Scientists are not sure about what triggers the hormonal changes that underlie the adolescent growth spurt, but recent evidence suggests that rising levels of *leptin*, the recently discovered hormone that reflects the body's fat cell storage (see Chapter 10), may provide the crucial signals (Spear, 2000).

The term *pubescence* is used to describe the two-year span preceding puberty during which the changes leading to physical and sexual maturity take place. In addition to growing taller and heavier during pubescence, children begin to develop the physical features that characterize adults of their respective sexes. These features are termed *secondary sex characteristics—physical features that distinguish one sex from the other but that are not essential for reproduction.* For example, males go through a voice change, develop facial hair, and experience greater skeletal and muscle growth in the

The timing of sexual maturation can have important implications for adolescents. Youngsters who mature unusually early or unusually late often feel uneasy about this transition.

PREVIEW QUESTIONS

- When do children reach pubescence and puberty?
- What changes do these landmarks bring?
- How do early attachment relations appear to be related to the timing of sexual maturation?
- Does the empirical evidence support the notion that adolescence is a time of great turmoil?
- What is the chief challenge of adolescence, according to Erikson?
- What are Marcia's four identity statuses?

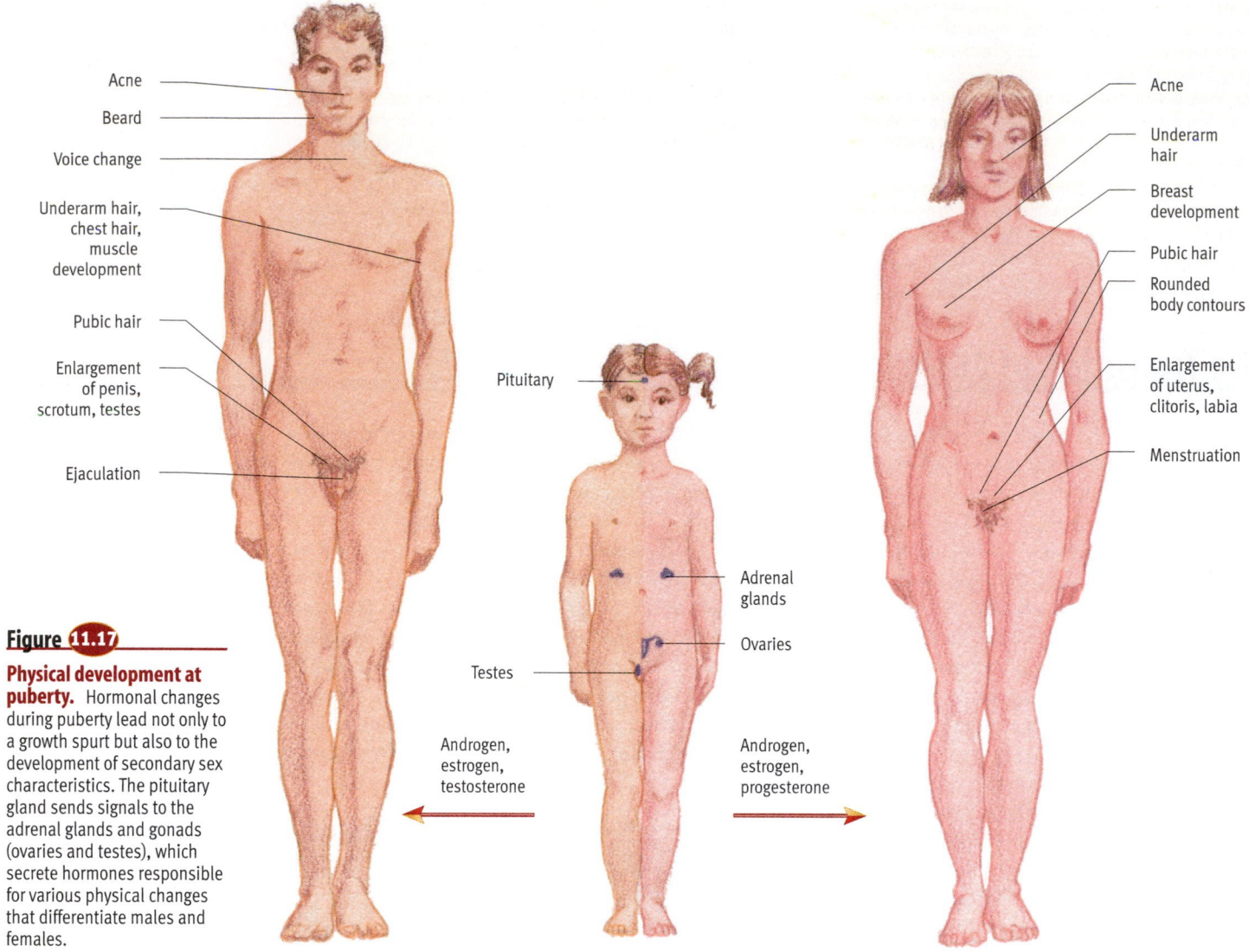

Acne
Beard
Voice change
Underarm hair, chest hair, muscle development
Pubic hair
Enlargement of penis, scrotum, testes
Ejaculation

Pituitary

Adrenal glands
Ovaries
Testes

Androgen, estrogen, testosterone

Androgen, estrogen, progesterone

Acne
Underarm hair
Breast development
Pubic hair
Rounded body contours
Enlargement of uterus, clitoris, labia
Menstruation

Figure 11.17

Physical development at puberty. Hormonal changes during puberty lead not only to a growth spurt but also to the development of secondary sex characteristics. The pituitary gland sends signals to the adrenal glands and gonads (ovaries and testes), which secrete hormones responsible for various physical changes that differentiate males and females.

Web Link 11.5

Adolescence Directory OnLine
Browsers visiting this site hosted by the University of Indiana will find guides to resources about adolescence that cover many of the health, mental health, safety, personal, and parenting issues important to this phase of development.

upper torso, leading to broader shoulders (see Figure 11.17). Females experience breast growth and a widening of the pelvic bones plus increased fat deposits in this area, resulting in wider hips (Litt & Vaughan, 1992).

Note, however, that the capacity to reproduce is not attained in pubescence. This comes later. *Puberty is the stage during which sexual functions reach maturity, which marks the beginning of adolescence.* It is during puberty that the *primary sex characteristics—the structures necessary for reproduction*—develop fully. In the male these include the testes, penis, and related internal structures. In the female they include the ovaries, vagina, uterus, and other internal structures.

In females, the onset of puberty is typically signaled by *menarche—the first occurrence of menstruation*, which reflects the culmination of a series of hormonal changes (Dorn et al., 1999). American

girls typically reach menarche at about age 12½, with further sexual maturation continuing until approximately 16. Most American boys begin to produce sperm by age 14, with complete sexual maturation occurring around 18 (Brooks-Gunn & Reiter, 1990). Interestingly, there have been *generational* changes in the timing of puberty. Today's adolescents begin puberty at a younger age, and complete it more rapidly, than did their counterparts in earlier generations. This trend apparently reflects improvements in nutrition and medical care (Brooks-Gunn, 1991). The timing of puberty varies from one adolescent to the next over a range of about 5 years (10–15 for girls, 11–16 for boys). Much of this variability is governed by hereditary differences (Kaprio et al., 1995), but other factors also are influential. One interesting factor may be the quality of a person's family relationships during early childhood, the subject of our Featured Study for this chapter.

Evolution and the Timing of Sexual Maturation

Interest in the possible link between family relations and the timing of puberty emerged out of Jay Belsky's evolutionary analyses of attachment patterns, discussed earlier in this chapter (see pp. 438–439). According to Belsky, children have been programmed by evolution to respond to insensitive parenting (which historically would have been associated with harsh ancestral environments) with attachment patterns that eventually cultivate opportunistic reproductive strategies that would have been adaptive in precarious environments with scarce resources (Belsky, 1999b; Belsky, Steinberg, and Draper, 1991). Belsky's theory generated the novel hypothesis that stress in early family relations (rejection, inconsistent parenting, family discord) might accelerate the process of sexual maturation, thus leading to a relatively early onset of puberty (see Figure 11.18). Over the course of evolutionary history, early sexual maturation would have enhanced reproductive fitness by giving individuals extra years of reproductive capacity and by giving them a sexual headstart on their age mates (remember, reproductive fitness is relative). The purpose of this study was to test Belsky's hypothesis as applied to females, using a longitudinal design.

Method

Participants. The data were collected as part of an ongoing study of socialization processes conducted in three cities in the United States (Nashville and Knoxville, Tennessee, and Bloomington, Indiana) with a total of 585 families. The participants in this study were 281 mothers from this demographically diverse sample and their daughters, who were 4 to 5 years old when the study began in 1987.

Procedure. The data on the quality of family relationships were collected at the beginning of the study, while the girls were in preschool. Their mothers provided information on discipline, family conflict, parental support-

iveness, time devoted to child care, and so forth in 90-minute recorded interviews conducted in their homes. A subset of the families also agreed to let researchers observe their interactions in two home visits, which yielded additional ratings of parent-child relations. The data on pubertal development were collected in year 8 of the study from the daughters, who were interviewed either at home or at school. As is normal in longitudinal studies, some of the participants dropped out, so that only 217 of the original 281 girls were available for the second part of the study.

Results

Modest but statistically significant associations were found between measures of family relations and pubertal timing. Earlier sexual maturation was correlated with family stress as indexed by lower scores on measures of parental supportiveness (.25), time spent by the father in child care (.23), mother-daughter affection (.29), and father-daughter affection (.43). However, the correlations between pubertal timing and the measures of parental conflict and harshness of discipline were not significant.

Discussion

The investigators conclude that Belsky's central hypothesis relating the quality of early family relations to sexual maturation "received reasonable support." They also infer from their data that daughters' relations with their fathers have greater impact on their maturation than their relations with their mothers. They speculate that father-daughter relations may be more influential because males' parental investment tends to be more variable than that of females.

Comment

This study was featured because it illustrates how events early in life can have long-term consequences for de-

Investigators: Bruce J. Ellis, Steven McFadyen-Ketchum (Vanderbilt University) Kenneth A. Dodge (Duke University), Gregory S. Petit (Auburn University), and John E. Bates (Indiana University)

Source: Quality of early family relationships and individual differences in the timing of pubertal maturation in girls: A longitudinal test of an evolutionary model. *Journal of Personality and Social Psychology,* 1999, *77,* 387–401.

Figure 11.18

Belsky's analysis relating family relations to sexual maturation. Based on his evolutionary analysis of the possible significance of infants' attachment patterns, Belsky hypothesized that stress in early family relations (unresponsive, inconsistent parenting) might accelerate sexual maturation, as outlined here (Belsky, 1999; Belsky, Steinberg, & Draper, 1991). Our Featured Study attempted to evaluate this hypothesis as applied to girls in an 8-year longitudinal study.

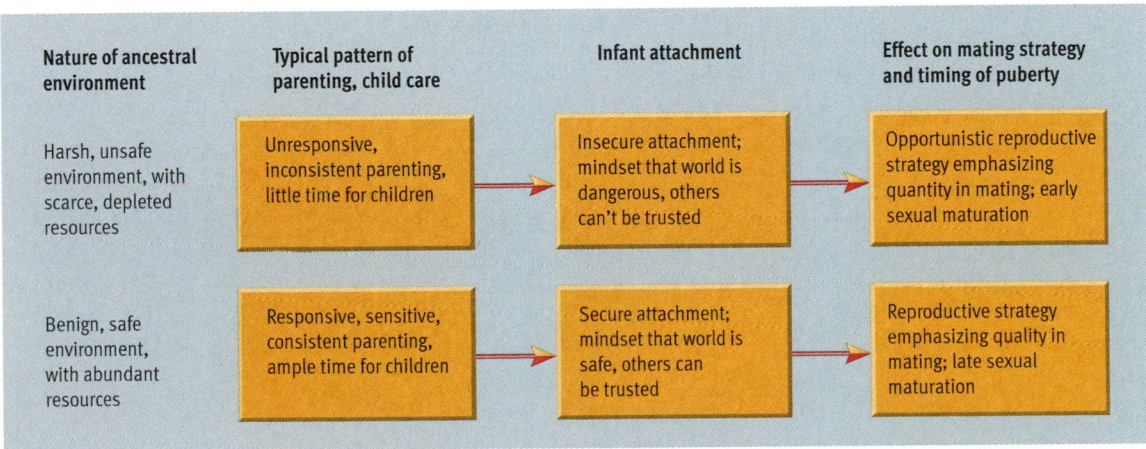

Nature of ancestral environment	Typical pattern of parenting, child care	Infant attachment	Effect on mating strategy and timing of puberty
Harsh, unsafe environment, with scarce, depleted resources	Unresponsive, inconsistent parenting, little time for children	Insecure attachment; mindset that world is dangerous, others can't be trusted	Opportunistic reproductive strategy emphasizing quantity in mating; early sexual maturation
Benign, safe environment, with abundant resources	Responsive, sensitive, consistent parenting, ample time for children	Secure attachment; mindset that world is safe, others can be trusted	Reproductive strategy emphasizing quality in mating; late sexual maturation

velopment in complex ways that are often difficult to anticipate. The study also illustrates how the recently emerging evolutionary perspective in psychology is generating fresh, new thinking on many topics. However, the study also demonstrates how evolutionary hypotheses tend to be difficult to test directly. The findings provided decent support for the idea that family stress predicts early sexual maturation, but they don't demonstrate that this association exists for the evolutionary reasons spelled out by Belsky. Still, it is an inter-

esting study that blunts one of the frequent criticisms of evolutionary theory—that it merely generates after-the-fact explanations for known realities, such as the long-recognized differences between males and females in mating priorities (Cornell, 1997). The predicted link between family stress and early maturation is *not* an obvious phenomenon like gender differences in mating priorities, and the association is not readily explained by any competing theories. ■

Although the determinants of the timing of puberty remain open to debate, more is known about the *consequences* of variation in the onset of puberty. Generally, *girls who mature early and boys who mature late seem to have more emotional difficulties with the transition to adolescence* (Ge, Conger, & Elder, 1996; Graber et al., 1997). However, in both males and females, early maturation is associated with greater use of alcohol and drugs, more high-risk behavior, and more trouble with the law (Steinberg & Morris, 2001). Among females, early maturation is also correlated with poorer school performance, earlier experience of intercourse, more unwanted pregnancies, and greater risk for eating problems and disorders (Graber et al., 1994; Stattin & Magnusson, 1990). Thus, we might speculate that early maturation often thrusts both sexes (but especially females) toward the adult world too soon.

Time of Turmoil?

Back around the turn of the century, G. Stanley Hall (1904), one of psychology's great pioneers (see Chapter 1), proposed that the adolescent years are characterized by convulsive instability and disturbing inner

turmoil. Hall attributed this turmoil to adolescents' erratic physical changes and resultant confusion about self-image. Over the decades, a host of theorists have agreed with Hall's characterization of adolescence as a stormy period.

Statistics on *adolescent suicide* would seem to support the idea that adolescence is a time marked by turmoil, but the figures can be interpreted in various ways. On the one hand, suicide rates among adolescents have risen alarmingly in recent decades (see Figure 11.19a). On the other hand, even with this steep increase, suicide rates for adolescents are lower than those for older age groups (see Figure 11.19b). Actually, the suicide crisis among teenagers involves *attempted* suicide more than *completed* suicide. It is difficult to compile accurate data on suicide attempts (which are often covered up), but experts estimate that when all age groups are lumped together, suicide attempts outnumber actual suicidal deaths by a ratio of at least 8 to 1 and perhaps as high as 25 to 1. However, this ratio of attempted to completed suicides is much higher for adolescents. It is estimated to range anywhere from 100:1 to 200:1 (Maris, Berman, & Silverman, 2000). Thus, attempted suicide is a major problem during adolescence. About 2% of

Figure 11.19

Adolescent suicide. (a) The suicide rate for adolescents and young adults (15–24 years old) has increased 198% since 1960. (b) Nonetheless, suicide rates for this youthful age group remain lower than suicide rates for older age groups. (Source: Centers for Disease Control and Prevention)

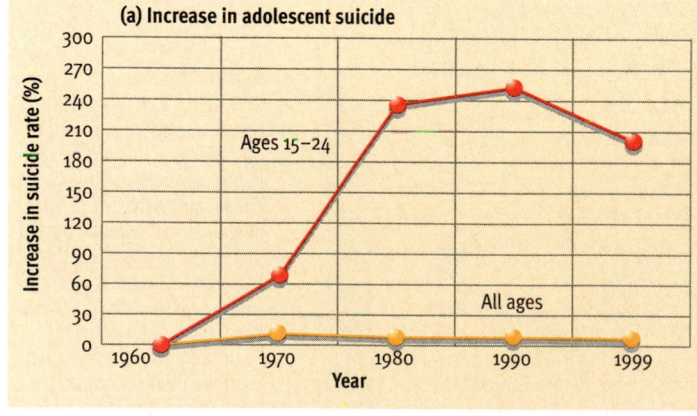

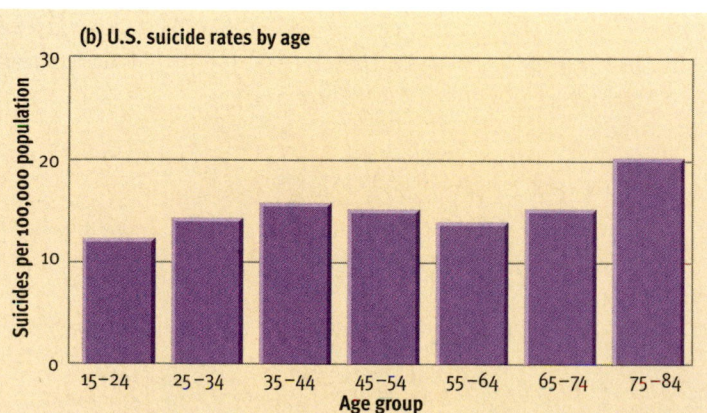

adolescent males and about 5% of adolescent females attempt suicide each year in the United States (Blum & Rinehart, 2000).

In recent years, the highly publicized problem of *adolescent violence* has led many people to conclude that adolescence is indeed a time of turmoil. The tragic shootings at Columbine High School and similar incidents at other schools have created the impression that disaffected teenagers are running amuck and that schools are extremely perilous combat zones. As we saw with adolescent suicide, the data on adolescent violence can be viewed in different ways. Arrest rates for violent crimes (assault, rape, robbery, and murder) *do* climb through the adolescent years until age 18 and then gradually decline (see Figure 11.20). And youngsters under the age of 18 accounted for 27% of the arrests for serious crimes in the United States in 1999 (Federal Bureau of Investigation, 1999). So, there *is* a distressing association between adolescence and the prevalence of violent crime.

That said, the vast majority of this violence occurs in settings outside of school. The perception that school shootings are common and rapidly increasing is not accurate. The incidence of school violence has been stable since the late 1980s and violent deaths at school remain infrequent (Mulvey & Cauffman, 2001). Less than 1% of homicides and suicides among school-aged children occur at school, and most youngsters are much safer in their schools than they are on the way to or from their schools. Parents and school authorities grossly overestimate the likelihood of shootings at school because of all the media coverage these tragic events have (understandably) garnered. Although there has been a public outcry for efforts to identify adolescents who are likely to lash out with violence at school, the offenders do not have any unique characteristics that would permit reliable prediction of these rare outbursts of violence (Steinberg, 2000). That's not to say that nothing can be done in the way of psychological interventions. Programs that strive to reduce student alienation and foster healthy, supportive school environments appear to have some value in reducing school violence (Franke, 2000; Howard, Flora, & Griffin, 1999). But programs designed to single out perpetrators in advance who have not made any overt threats are doomed to failure (Mulvey & Cauffman, 2001).

Returning to our original question, does the weight of evidence support the idea that adolescence is usually a period of turmoil and turbulence? Overall, the recent consensus of the experts has been that adolescence is *not* an exceptionally difficult period (Petersen et al., 1993; Steinberg & Levine, 1997). How-

ever, in a recent reanalysis of the evidence, Jeffrey Arnett (1999) has argued convincingly that "not all adolescents experience storm and stress, but storm and stress is more likely during adolescence than at other ages" (p. 317). Arnett supports his intermediate position by summarizing research on adolescents' moods, risky behaviors, and conflicts with their parents. Research shows that adolescents do experience more volatile and more negative emotions than their parents or younger children do (Larson & Richards, 1994). Studies also show that various types of risky behavior, such as substance abuse, careless sexual practices, and dangerous driving peak during late adolescence (Arnett, 1992, 1995). Finally, adolescence *does* bring an increase in parent-child conflicts (Laursen, Coy, & Collins, 1998). Arnett is quick to emphasize that turmoil in adolescence is far from universal, but he maintains that, on the average, adolescence is somewhat more stressful than other developmental periods. However, he notes that this conclusion *may* only apply to modern, Western cultures characterized by shifting values and an emphasis on individualism. Adolescence appears to be less stressful in traditional, preindustrial cultures.

Although turbulence and turmoil are not *universal* features of adolescence, challenging adaptations *do* have to be made during this period. In particular, most adolescents struggle to some extent in their effort to achieve a sound sense of identity.

The Search for Identity 9b

Erik Erikson was especially interested in personality development during adolescence, which is the fifth

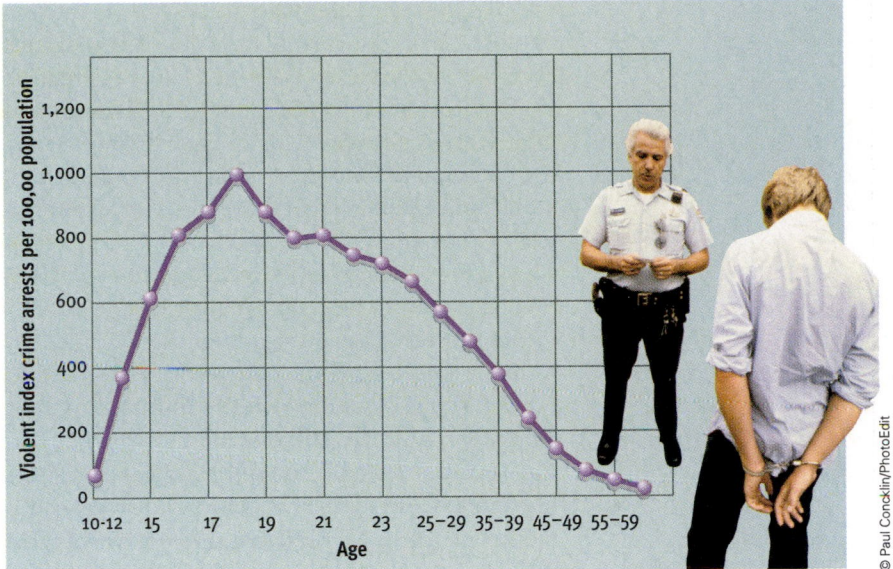

© Paul Conklin/PhotoEdit

Figure 11.20

Age and violent crime. FBI statistics for the United States show that there is a substantial relationship between age and the likelihood of being arrested for a violent crime. As you can see, the prevalence of violent criminal activity definitely peaks in adolescence and then declines throughout adulthood. (Data based on FBI *Uniform Crime Reports for the United States*, 1999)

Web Link 11.6

Adolescent Health and Mental Health
This site on issues related to adolescence is edited by Michael Fenichel, a prominent psychologist interested in using the Internet to distribute quality professional information to the public.

of the eight major life stages he described. The psychosocial crisis during this stage pits *identity* against *confusion*. According to Erikson (1968), the premiere challenge of adolescence is the struggle to form a clear sense of identity. This struggle involves working out a stable concept of oneself as a unique individual and embracing an ideology or system of values that provides a sense of direction. In Erikson's view, adolescents grapple with questions such as "Who am I, and where am I going in life?"

Erikson recognized that the process of identity formation begins before adolescence and often extends beyond it, as his own life illustrates (Coles, 1970; Roazen, 1976). Erikson's mother, who was Jewish, was abandoned by his Danish father before Erik's birth in 1902 in Germany. Within a few years, his mother married a Jewish doctor and the two of them raised Erik in the Jewish faith as Erik Homburger. Erik was viewed as a Jew by his schoolmates, but he was viewed as a gentile at his temple because of his decidedly Scandinavian appearance. Thus, Erikson struggled with identity confusion early in life.

During adolescence Erikson began to resist family pressures to study medicine. Instead, he wandered about Europe until he was 25, trying to "find himself" as an artist. His interest in psychoanalysis was sparked by an introduction to Sigmund Freud's youngest daughter, Anna, a pioneer of child psychoanalysis. After his psychoanalytic training, he moved to the United States. When he became a naturalized citizen in 1939, he changed his surname from Homburger to Erikson. Clearly, Erikson was struggling with the question of "Who am I?" well into adulthood. Small wonder, then, that he focused a great deal of attention on identity formation.

Although the struggle for a sense of identity is a lifelong process (Waterman & Archer, 1990), it does tend to be especially intense during adolescence. Adolescents deal with identity formation in a variety of ways. According to James Marcia (1966, 1980, 1994), the presence or absence of a sense of commitment (to life goals and values) and a sense of crisis (active questioning and exploration) can combine to produce four different *identity statuses* (see Figure 11.21). These are not stages that people pass through, but orientations that may occur at a particular time. In order of increasing maturity, Marcia's four identity statuses are as follows (Meeus, 1996).

- *Identity diffusion* is a state of rudderless apathy. Some people simply refuse to confront the challenge of charting a life course and committing to an ideology. Although this stance allows them to evade the crisis of identity, the lack of direction can become problematic, as people in this status exhibit more social and psychological problems than others (Adams, Gullotta, & Montemayor, 1992).
- *Identity foreclosure* is a premature commitment to visions, values, and roles—typically those prescribed by one's parents. This path allows a person to circumvent much of the struggle for an identity. However, it may backfire and cause problems later (Kroger, 1995).
- An *identity moratorium* involves delaying commitment for a while to experiment with alternative ideologies and careers. Such experimentation can be valuable. Unfortunately, some people remain indefinitely in what should be a temporary phase. Identity moratorium is associated with self-doubt and confusion (Flum, 1994).
- *Identity achievement* involves arriving at a sense of self and direction after some consideration of alternative possibilities. Commitments have the strength of some conviction, although they're not absolutely irrevocable. Identity achievement is associated with higher self-esteem, greater security, and a variety of other healthy traits (Marcia et al., 1993).

Age trends in identity status are depicted in Figure 11.22. Consistent with Marcia's theory, identity moratorium and achievement increase with age while identity diffusion and foreclosure decline (Meuus et al., 1999). Although the age trends seen in Figure 11.22 make sense, they mask the extent to which a sizable majority of adolescents shift back and forth among the four identity statuses (Berzonsky & Adams, 1999). Moreover, people tend to reach identity achievement at later ages than originally envisioned by Marcia. By late adolescence, only a small minority of individuals have reached identity achievement, so the struggle for a sense of identity routinely extends into young adulthood. Actually, even after people reach identity achievement, the process of identity formation continues (Kroger, 1996).

Figure 11.21

Marcia's four identity statuses. According to Marcia (1980), the occurrence of identity crisis and exploration and the development of personal commitments can combine into four possible identity statuses, as shown in this diagram. The progressively darker shades of blue signify progressively more mature identity statuses.

Source: Adapted from Marcia, J. E. (1980). Identity in adolescence. In J. Adelson (Ed.), *Handbook of adolescent psychology* (pp. 159–210). New York: John Wiley. Copyright © 1980 by John Wiley. Adapted by permission.

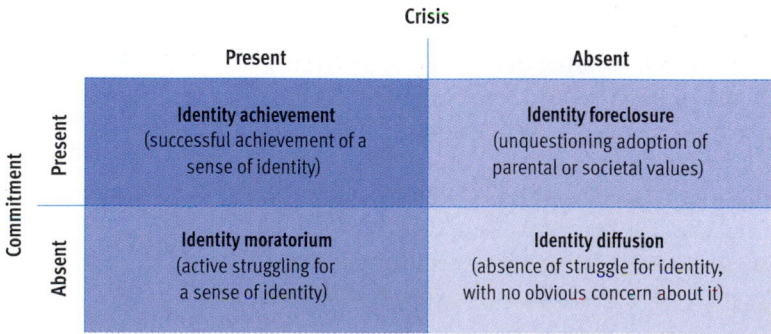

		Crisis	
		Present	**Absent**
Commitment	**Present**	**Identity achievement** (successful achievement of a sense of identity)	**Identity foreclosure** (unquestioning adoption of parental or societal values)
	Absent	**Identity moratorium** (active struggling for a sense of identity)	**Identity diffusion** (absence of struggle for identity, with no obvious concern about it)

Erikson, Marcia, and many other theorists believe that adequate identity formation is a cornerstone of sound psychological health. Identity confusion can interfere with important developmental transitions that should unfold during the adult years, as you'll see in the next section, which takes a look at developmental trends during adulthood.

REVIEW OF KEY POINTS

- The growth spurt at puberty is a prominent event involving the development of reproductive maturity and secondary sex characteristics. Belsky's theory that stress in early family relations might accelerate the process of sexual maturation has received some support, at least for girls. Early sexual maturation is associated with a variety of problems, especially among females.

- Adolescent suicide rates have climbed dramatically in recent decades, and attempted suicides have increased even more. Although school shootings remain rare, there is an association between adolescence and the prevalence of violent crime. Most theorists do not view adolescence as a time of turmoil, but Arnett argues that adolescence is slightly more stressful than other periods of life.

- According to Erikson, the key challenge of adolescence is to make some progress toward a sense of identity. Marcia identified four patterns of identity formation: foreclosure, moratorium, identity diffusion, and identity achievement.

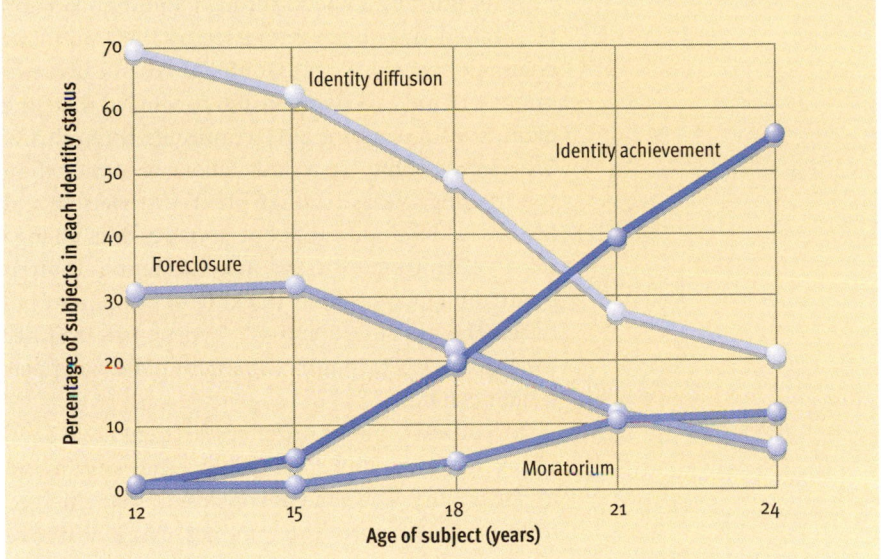

Figure 11.22

Age and identity status. These data from Meilman (1979) summarize the relationship between age and Marcia's (1980) identity statuses. The less mature statuses (diffusion and foreclosure) become less common as people move into young adulthood and the more mature statuses (moratorium and identity achievement) become more common. As you can see, at age 18, relatively few people have reached identity achievement.

SOURCE: Adapted from Meilman, P. W. (1979). Cross-sectional age changes in ego identity status during adolescence. *Developmental Psychology, 15,* 230–231. Copyright © 1979 by the American Psychological Association. Reprinted by permission of the author.

The Expanse of Adulthood

The concept of development was once associated almost exclusively with childhood and adolescence, but today it is widely appreciated that development is a life-long journey. The life-span approach to development assumes that important changes occur throughout the life cycle. Recent years have also brought increasing recognition that the historical context people live in can have profound impact on their developmental trajectories. As Stewart and Ostrove (1998) put it, "It makes sense that generations raised with different expectations and in different historical circumstances may age differently" (p. 1185). Events such as the Great Depression, the Vietnam war, the women's movement, the AIDS epidemic, the emergence of television, and the rise of the Internet can leave a lasting mark on the people exposed to them. Complicating the picture further, developmental patterns are becoming increasingly diverse. The boundaries between young, middle, and late adulthood are becoming blurred as more and more people have children later than one is "supposed" to, retire earlier than one is "supposed" to and so forth. In the upcoming pages we will look at some of the major developmental transitions in adult life, but you should bear in mind that in adulthood (even more so than childhood or adolescence) there are many divergent pathways and timetables.

Personality Development 9b

In recent years, research on adult personality development has been dominated by one key question: How stable is personality over the life span? We'll look at this issue, the question of the midlife crisis, and Erikson's view of adulthood in our discussion of personality development in the adult years.

The Question of Stability

At midlife, Jerry Rubin went from being an outraged, radical political activist to being a subdued, conventional Wall Street businessman. His transformation illustrates that major personality changes sometimes occur during adulthood. But how common are such changes? Is a grouchy 20-year-old going to be a grouchy 40-year-old and a grouchy 65-year-old? Or can the grouchy young adult become a mellow senior citizen?

PREVIEW QUESTIONS

- How stable is personality over the life span?
- How did Erikson describe adult development?
- How does marital satisfaction tend to evolve over the life span?
- How difficult are the transitions to parenthood and the empty nest?
- What kinds of physical changes occur in middle and late adulthood?
- What is dementia, and what is its chief cause in old age?
- How well do intelligence and memory hold up in middle and late adulthood?

After tracking subjects through adulthood, many researchers have been impressed by the amount of change observed. Roger Gould (1975) studied two samples of men and women and concluded that "the evolution of a personality continues through the fifth decade of life." In a study following women from their college years through their 40s, Helson and Moane (1987) found that "personality does change from youth to middle age in consistent and often predictable ways." After tracking development between the ages of 20 and 42, Whitbourne and her colleagues (1992) found "consistent patterns of personality change."

In contrast, many other researchers have been struck by the stability and durability they have found in personality. The general conclusion that emerged from several longitudinal studies using objective assessments of personality traits was that personality tends to be quite stable over periods of 20 to 40 years (Block, 1981; Caspi & Herbener, 1990; Costa & McCrae, 1994, 1997). Moreover, a recent review of 150 relevant studies, involving almost 50,000 participants, concluded that personality in early adulthood was a good predictor of personality in late adulthood and that the stability of personality increases with age up to about age 50 (Roberts & DelVecchio, 2000).

In sum, researchers assessing the stability of personality in adulthood have reached very different conclusions (Kogan, 1990). How can these contradictory conclusions be reconciled? This appears to be one of those debates in which researchers are eyeing the same findings but from different perspectives. Hence, some conclude that the glass is half full, whereas others conclude that it's half empty. In his discussion of this controversy, Lawrence Pervin (1994) concludes that personality is characterized by *both* stability and change. It appears that some personality traits tend to remain stable, while others tend to change systematically as people grow older. For example, in a recent study of personality functioning between the ages of 18 and 26, the investigators found a great deal of stability, but they also found some interesting changes in the direction of greater maturity (Roberts, Caspi, & Moffitt, 2001). Specifically, the young adults in this study became more controlled and confident and less angry and alienated.

The Question of the Midlife Crisis

There has also been a spirited debate about whether most people go through a *midlife crisis*—a difficult, turbulent period of doubts and reappraisal of one's life. The two most influential studies of adult development in the 1970s (Gould, 1978; Levinson et al., 1978) both concluded that a midlife crisis is a normal transition experienced by a majority of people. However, since these landmark studies, a host of subsequent studies have failed to detect an increase in emotional turbulence at midlife (Eisler & Ragsdale, 1992; Roberts & Newton, 1987; Rosenberg, Rosenberg, & Farrell, 1999).

How can we explain this discrepancy? Levinson and Gould both studied samples that were less than ideal. Levinson's was unusually small, and Gould's was not very representative. Moreover, both researchers depended primarily on interview and case study methods to gather their data. As we noted in Chapter 2, when knitting together impressionistic case studies, it is easy for investigators to see what they expect to see. Given that the midlife crisis has long been part of developmental folklore, Levinson and Gould may have been prone to interpret their case study data in this light (McCrae & Costa, 1984). In any case, investigators relying on more objective measures of emotional stability have found signs of midlife crises in only a tiny minority (2%–5%) of subjects (Chiriboga, 1989; McCrae & Costa, 1990). Midlife may bring a period of increased reflection as people contemplate the remainder of their lives, but it's clear that the fabled midlife *crisis* is not typical (Lemme, 1999).

Erikson's View of Adulthood

Insofar as personality changes during the adult years, Erik Erikson's (1963) theory offers some clues about the nature of changes people can expect. In his eight-stage model of development over the life span, Erikson divided adulthood into three stages (see again Figure 11.11).

Intimacy Versus Isolation. In early adulthood, the key concern is whether one can develop the capacity to share intimacy with others. Successful resolution of the challenges in this stage should promote empathy and openness, rather than shrewdness and manipulativeness.

Generativity Versus Self-Absorption. In middle adulthood, the key challenge is to acquire a genuine concern for the welfare of future generations, which results in providing unselfish guidance to younger people and concern with one's legacy. Self-absorption is characterized by self-indulgent concerns with meeting one's own needs and desires.

Integrity Versus Despair. During the retirement years, the challenge is to avoid the tendency to dwell on the mistakes of the past and on one's imminent death. People need to find meaning and satisfaction in their lives, rather than wallow in bitterness and resentment.

Empirical research on the adult stages in Erikson's theory has been sparse, but generally supportive of the theory. For example, research by Susan Whitbourne and her colleagues (1992) suggests that personality development proceeds in an orderly sequence of stages and that favorable resolutions of psychosocial crises in earlier stages lead to more favorable outcomes in later stages. And *generativity* has proven to be a measurable trait that increases between young adulthood and middle-age as originally envisioned by Erikson (McAdams, de St. Aubin, & Logan, 1993).

Transitions in Family Life

Many of the important transitions in adulthood involve changes in family responsibilities and relationships. Predictable patterns of development can be seen in families, just as they can in individuals (Carter & McGoldrick, 1988, 1999). The *family life cycle* is a sequence of stages that families tend to progress through. However, in contemporary American society, shifting social trends are altering the traditional family life cycle. In the eyes of most people, the typical American family consists of a husband and wife who have never been married to anyone else, rearing two or more children, with the man serving as the principal breadwinner and the woman filling the homemaker role (Coontz, 2000). This configuration was never as dominant as widely assumed, and today it is estimated that only a small minority of American families match this idealized image. The increasing prevalence of people remaining single, cohabitating, getting divorced, being single parents, having stepfamilies, voluntarily remaining childless, or having children out of wedlock, and of wives and mothers working has made the traditional nuclear family a deceptive mirage that does not reflect the diversity of family life in America.

Diversity aside, everyone emerges from families, and most people go on to form their own families. However, the transitional period during which young adults are "between families" until they form a new family is being prolonged by more and more individuals. The percentage of young adults who are postponing marriage until their late twenties or early thirties has risen dramatically (Teachman, Polonko, & Scanzoni, 1999; see Figure 11.23). This trend is probably the result of a number of factors. Chief among them are the availability of new career options for women, increased educational requirements in the

world of work, and increased emphasis on personal autonomy. Remaining single is a much more acceptable option today than it was a few decades ago (De-Frain & Olson, 1999). Nonetheless, over 90% of adults eventually marry.

Adjusting to Marriage

The newly married couple usually settle into their roles as husband and wife gradually. Difficulties with this transition are more likely when spouses come into a marriage with different expectations about marital roles (Lye & Biblarz, 1993). Unfortunately, substantial differences in role expectations seem particularly likely in this era of transition in gender roles (Brewster & Padavic, 2000).

Women may be especially vulnerable to ambivalence about shifting marital roles. More and more women are aspiring to demanding careers. Yet, research shows that husbands' careers continue to take priority over their wives' vocational ambitions (Haas, 1999). Moreover, many husbands maintain traditional role expectations about housework, child care, and decision making (Blair, 1993). Men's contribution to housework has increased slightly in recent decades, but studies indicate that wives are still doing the bulk of the household chores in America, even when they work outside the home (Coltrane, 2001; Robinson & Godbey, 1997). Although married women perform about two-thirds of all housework, only about one-third of wives characterize their division of labor as unfair, because most women don't expect a 50-50 split (Coltrane, 2001). Research shows that women who have nontraditional attitudes about gender roles are more likely to perceive their share of housework as

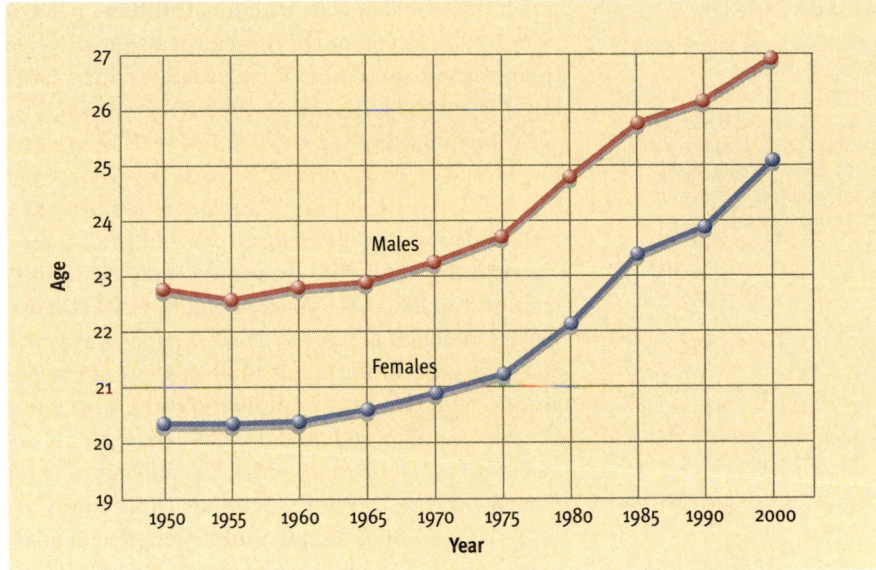

Figure 11.23

Median age at first marriage. The median age at which people in the United States marry for the first time has been creeping up for both males and females since the mid-1960s. This trend indicates that more people are postponing marriage. (Data from the U.S. Bureau of the Census)

Web Link 11.7

National Parent Information Network (NPIN)
Parents are faced with all sorts of questions about development; the NPIN site describes many guides to online and other resources for answering those questions.

unfair than women with traditional attitudes (Greenstein, 1996). As you might expect, wives who perceive their housework burden to be unfair tend to report lower levels of marital satisfaction (Haas, 1999).

In general, however, the first few years of married life tend to be characterized by great happiness—the proverbial "marital bliss." Numerous studies have measured spouses' overall satisfaction in different stages of the family life cycle and found a U-shaped relationship like that shown in Figure 11.24 (Glenn, 1990; Orbuch et al., 1996). This U shape reflects the fact that satisfaction tends to be greatest at the beginning and end of the family life cycle, with a noticeable decline in the middle. The conventional explanation for this pattern is that the burdens of child rearing, and resulting reduction in time spent together, undermine couples' satisfaction, which gradually climbs back up again as children grow up and these burdens ease. However, marital satisfaction tends to decline in the early years of marriage even when there are no children, so other factors and processes may also contribute to this U-shaped pattern (Bradbury, 1998; Glenn, 1998).

The prechildren phase of the family life cycle used to be rather short for most newly married couples. Traditionally, couples just *assumed* that they would proceed to have children. In recent decades, however, ambivalence about the prospect of having children clearly has increased (T. W. Smith, 1999), and the percentage of childless couples has doubled since 1960 (Groat et al., 1997). Hence, more and more couples are finding themselves struggling to decide *whether* to have children. Interestingly, intentions about having children are not as stable over time as one might expect. In one study that followed adult participants

over a span of six years, about one-quarter of the respondents changed their plans (Heaton et al., 1999). These subjects were almost evenly split between those who planned to remain childless but subsequently decided they wanted to have children and those who intended to have children but subsequently expressed a preference for remaining child-free.

Adjusting to Parenthood

Although an increasing number of people are choosing to remain childless, the vast majority of married couples continue to have children, and they rate parenthood as a highly positive experience (Demo, 1992). Nonetheless, the arrival of the first child represents a *major* transition, and the disruption of old routines can be extremely stressful (Carter, 1999). The new mother, already physically exhausted by the birth process, is particularly prone to postpartum stress (Hock et al., 1995). Wives are especially vulnerable when they have to shoulder the major burden of infant care (Kalmuss, Davidson, & Cushman, 1992).

Crisis during the transition to first parenthood is far from universal, however (Cox et al., 1999). Couples who have high levels of affection and commitment prior to the first child's birth are likely to maintain a stable level of satisfaction after the birth (Shapiro, Gottman, & Carrere, 2000). The key to making this transition less stressful may be to have *realistic expectations* about parental responsibilities (Belsky & Kelly, 1994). Studies find that stress is greatest in new parents who have overestimated the benefits and underestimated the costs of their new role.

As children grow up, parental influence over them tends to decline, and the early years of parenting—that once seemed so difficult—are often recalled with

Figure 11.24

Marital satisfaction across the family life cycle. This graph depicts the percentage of husbands and wives who said their marriage was going well "all the time" at various stages of the family life cycle. Rollins and Feldman (1970) broke the family life cycle into eight stages. The U-shaped relationship shown here has been found in other studies as well, although its relevance is limited to families that have children in the traditional childbearing years.

SOURCE: Adapted from Rollins, B. C., & Feldman, H. (1970). Marital satisfaction over the family cycle. *Journal of Marriage and Family, 32,* 20–28. Copyright © 1975 by the National Council on Family Relations. Reprinted by permission.

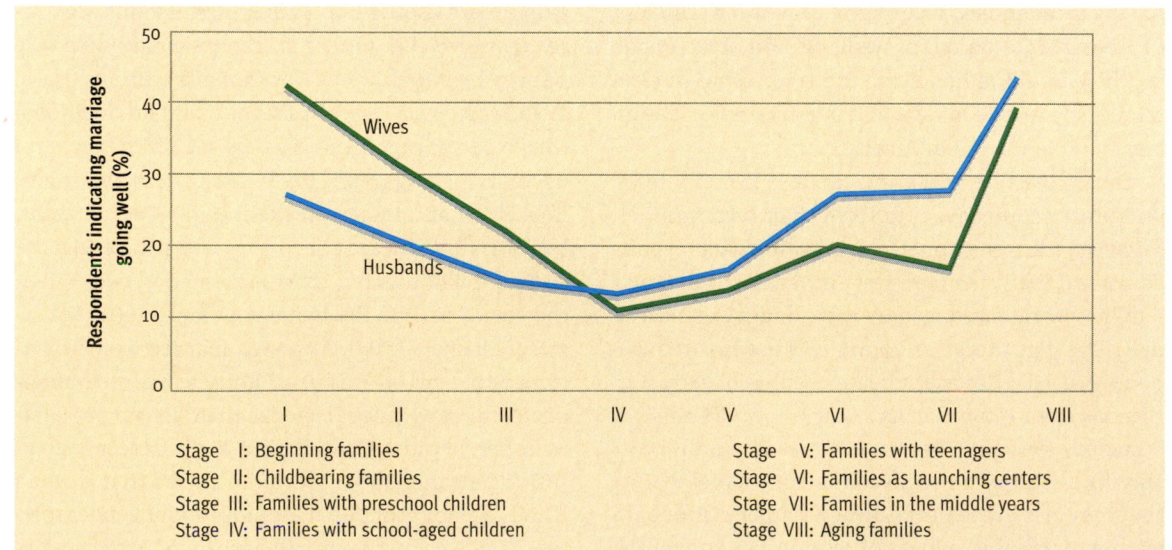

Stage I: Beginning families
Stage II: Childbearing families
Stage III: Families with preschool children
Stage IV: Families with school-aged children
Stage V: Families with teenagers
Stage VI: Families as launching centers
Stage VII: Families in the middle years
Stage VIII: Aging families

Although children can be unparalleled sources of joy and satisfaction, the transition to parenthood can be extremely stressful, especially for mothers.

fondness. When youngsters reach adolescence and seek to establish their own identities, gradual realignments occur in parent-child relationships. On the one hand, parent-adolescent relations generally are not as bitter or contentious as widely assumed (Laursen, Coy, & Collins, 1998). On the other hand, adolescents do spend less time in family activities (Larson et al., 1996) and their closeness to their parents declines while conflicts become more frequent (Grotevant, 1997). The conflicts tend to involve everyday matters (chores and appearance) more than substantive issues (sex and drugs) (Barber, 1994). When conflicts occur, they seem to have more adverse effects on the parents than the children (Steinberg & Steinberg, 1994). Ironically, although research has shown that adolescence is not as turbulent or difficult for youngsters as once believed, their parents *are* stressed out (Steinberg, 2001).

Adjusting to the Empty Nest

When parents do manage to get all their children launched into the adult world, they find themselves faced with an "empty nest." This period was formerly thought to be a difficult transition for many parents, especially mothers who were familiar only with the maternal role. In recent decades, however, more women have experience with other roles outside the home. Hence, recent evidence suggests that most parents adjust effectively to the empty nest transition and are more likely to have problems if their children *return* to the once-empty nest (Blacker, 1999).

The postparental period often provides couples with new freedom to devote attention to each other. Many couples take advantage of this opportunity by traveling or developing new leisure interests. However, spouses do have to adapt to spending more time with each other and often need to renegotiate

role expectations (Walsh, 1999). Of course, age-related considerations that are independent of the relationship, such as the increased likelihood of physical illness, can make the later years stressful. In general, however, the trend is for couples to report fairly high satisfaction until one of the spouses (usually the husband) dies.

Aging and Physical Changes

People obviously experience many physical changes as they progress through adulthood. In both sexes, hair tends to thin out and become gray, and many males confront receding hairlines and baldness. To the dismay of many, the proportion of body fat tends to increase with age, while the amount of muscle tissue decreases. Overall, weight tends to increase in most adults through the mid-50s, when a gradual decline may begin. These changes have little functional significance, but in our youth-oriented society, they often have an impact on self-concept, leading many people to view themselves as unattractive (Whitbourne, 1999).

In the sensory domain, the key developmental changes occur in vision and hearing. The proportion of people with 20/20 visual acuity declines with age. Farsightedness, difficulty adapting to darkness, and poor recovery from glare are common among older people (Fozard, 1990). Sensitivity to color and contrast also decline (Fozard & Gordon-Salant, 2001). Hearing sensitivity begins declining gradually in early adulthood but usually isn't noticeable until after age 50. Hearing loss tends to be greater in men than in women and for high-frequency sounds more than low-frequency sounds (Yost, 2000). These sensory losses could be problematic, but in modern society they can usually be compensated for with eyeglasses, contacts, and hearing aids.

Age-related changes also occur in hormonal functioning during adulthood. Among women, these changes lead to *menopause*. This ending of menstrual periods, accompanied by a loss of fertility, typically occurs at around age 50 (Avis, 1999). Most women experience at least some unpleasant symptoms (such as hot flashes, headaches, night sweats, mood changes), but the amount of discomfort varies considerably. Not long ago, menopause was thought to be almost universally accompanied by severe emotional strain. However, it is now clear that most women experience relatively modest psychological distress (Dennerstein, 1996). Although people sometimes talk about "male menopause," men don't really

Web Link 11.8

Adult Development and Aging (APA Division 20)
Psychological researchers interested in adulthood and aging form a distinct division with the American Psychological Association, Division 20. The division's homepage contains a wide range of educational, instructional, and clinical resources and references for this area of concern.

go through an equivalent experience. Starting in middle-age, testosterone levels *do* decline substantially (Morley, 2001), but these decreases are gradual and are not associated with a constellation of symptoms comparable to what women experience (Jacobs, 2001).

The amount of brain tissue and brain weight decline gradually after age 60 (Vinters, 2001). These trends appear to reflect both a decrease in the number of active neurons in some areas of the brain and shrinkage of still-active neurons, with neuron loss perhaps being less important than once believed (Albert & Killiany, 2001). Although this gradual loss of brain tissue sounds alarming, it is a normal part of the aging process. Its functional significance is the subject of some debate, but it doesn't appear to be a key factor in any of the age-related dementias. **A dementia is an abnormal condition marked by multiple cognitive deficits that include memory impairment.** Dementia can be caused by quite a variety of diseases, such as Alzheimer's disease, Parkinson's disease, Huntington's disease, and AIDS, to name just a few (Caine & Lyness, 2000). Because many of these diseases are more prevalent in older adults, dementia is seen in about 15%–20% of people over age 75 (Wise, Gray, & Seltzer, 1999). However, it is important to emphasize that dementia and "senility" are not part of the normal aging process. As Cavanaugh (1993) notes, "The term *senility* has no valid medical or psychological meaning, and its continued use simply perpetuates the myth that drastic mental decline is a product of normal aging" (p. 85).

Alzheimer's disease accounts for roughly 70% of all cases of dementia (Fromholt & Bruhn, 1999). Alzheimer's disease is accompanied by major structural deterioration in the brain. Alzheimer's patients exhibit profound and widespread loss of neurons and brain tissue and the accumulation of characteristic neural abnormalities known as neuritic plaques and neurofibrillary tangles (Vinters, 2001). In the early stages of the disease, this damage is largely centered in the hippocampal region, which is known to play a crucial role in many facets of memory, but as the disease advances it spreads throughout much of the brain (Rabins, Lyketsos, & Steele, 1999). The causes that launch this debilitating neural meltdown are not well understood.

Alzheimer's disease is a vicious affliction that can strike during middle-age but usually emerges after age 65. The beginnings of Alzheimer's disease are so subtle they are often recognized only after the disease has progressed for a year or two. The hallmark early symptom is the forgetting of newly learned information after surprisingly brief periods of time (Albert & Killiany, 2001). The course of the disease is one of progressive deterioration, typically over a period of eight to ten years, ending in death (Rabins et al., 1999). In the beginning, victims simply lose the thread of conversations or forget to follow through on tasks they have started. Gradually, much more obvious problems begin to emerge, including difficulties in speaking, comprehending, and performing complicated tasks, as well as depression and sleep disturbance. Job performance deteriorates noticeably as victims forget important appointments and suffer indignities such as getting lost while driving and paying the same bill several times. From this point, profound memory loss develops. For example, patients may fail to recognize familiar people, something particularly devastating to family and friends. Many patients become very restless and experience hallucinations, delusions, and paranoid thoughts. Eventually, victims become completely disoriented and are unable to care for themselves. There are some encouraging leads for treatments that might slow the progression of this horrific disease, but a cure does not appear to be on the horizon.

Aging and Cognitive Changes

The evidence indicates that general intelligence is fairly stable throughout most of adulthood, with a small decline in *average* test scores often seen after age 60 (Schaie, 1990, 1994, 1996). However, this seemingly simple assertion masks many complexities and needs to be qualified carefully. First, group averages can be deceptive in that mean scores can be dragged down by a small minority of people who show a decline. For example, when Schaie (1990) calculated the percentage of people who maintain stable performance on various abilities (see Figure 11.25), he found that about 80% showed no decline by age 60 and that about two-thirds were still stable through age 81. Second, even when age-related decreases in intellectual performance are found, they tend to be small in all but a few individuals (Salthouse, 1991). Third, some forms of intelligence are more vulnerable to aging than others. As we noted in Chapter 9, many theorists distinguish between *fluid intelligence*, which refers to basic information-processing skills, and *crystallized intelligence*, which refers to the application of accumulated knowledge. Research suggests that fluid intelligence is much more likely to decline with age, whereas crystallized intelligence tends to remain stable (Baltes, Staudinger, & Lindenberger, 1999; Horn & Hofer, 1992).

Web Link 11.9

USDHHS: Administration on Aging
The U.S. Department of Health and Human Services provides a content-rich site devoted to all aspect of aging; it includes one of the best available guides to online information about older Americans.

Contrary to widespread stereotypes, many people remain active and productive in their 70s, 80s, and even beyond. Pictured here is the author's Auntie Mildred, at age 99, having a little fun at a child's birthday party held at a rock-climbing facility. Now 102, Mildred still composes poetry and you can't pull her away from her personal computer.

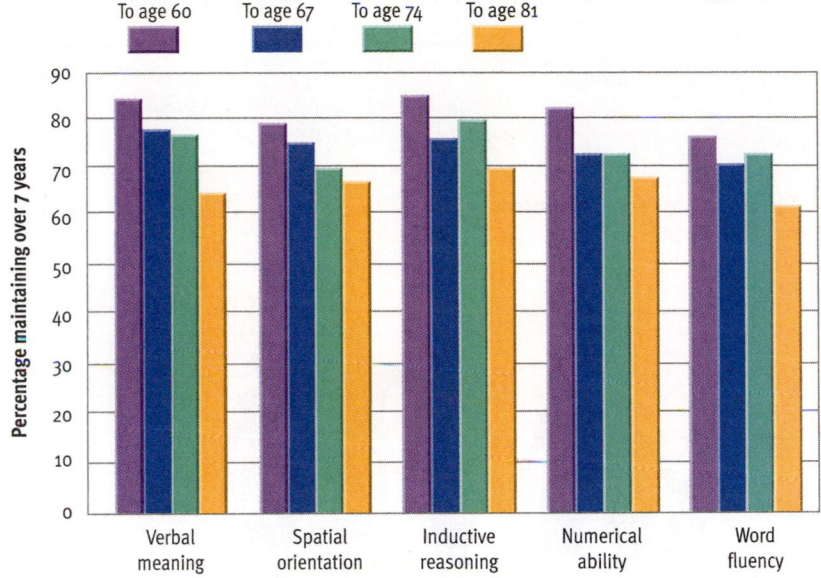

Figure 11.25

Age and the stability of primary mental abilities. In his longitudinal study of cognitive performance begun in 1956, Schaie (1983, 1993) has repeatedly assessed the five basic mental abilities listed along the bottom of this chart. The data graphed here show the percentage of subjects who maintained stable levels of performance on each ability through various ages up to age 81. As you can see, even through the age of 81, the majority of subjects show no significant decline on most abilities. (From Schaie, 1990)

SOURCE: Adapted from Schaie, K. W. (1990). Intellectual development in adulthood. In J. E. Birren and K. W. Schaie (Eds.), *Handbook of the psychology of aging* (pp. 291–309). San Diego: Academic Press. Copyright © 1990 Elsevier Science (USA), reproduced with permission from the publisher.

What about memory? Numerous studies report decreases in older adults' memory capabilities (Backman et al., 1999). But the memory losses associated with normal aging tend to be moderate and are *not* universal (Shimamura et al., 1995). A major consideration is the type of memory that is assessed (see Chapter 7 for a review of the various types of memory). The most reliable decrements are usually seen in *episodic memory* and *working memory*, with less consistent losses observed on tasks involving *procedural memory* and *semantic memory* (Backman, Small, & Wahlin, 2001). According to Salthouse (1994), it is the age-related decline in the capacity of working memory that underlies older adults' poorer performance on a wide range of cognitive tasks. He attributes most of the decline in working memory to age-related decreases in the raw speed of mental processing.

In the cognitive domain, aging does seem to take its toll on *speed* first. Many studies indicate that speed in learning, solving problems, and processing information tends to decline with age (Salthouse, 1996). The evidence suggests that the erosion of processing speed may be a gradual, lengthy trend beginning in middle adulthood (Verhaeghen & Salthouse, 1997). The general nature of this trend (across differing tasks) suggests that it may be the result of age-related changes in neurological functioning (Salthouse, 2000), although doubts have been raised about this conclusion (Bashore, Ridderinkhof, & van der Molen, 1997). Although mental speed declines with age, problem-solving ability remains largely unimpaired if older people are given adequate time to compensate for their reduced speed.

It should be emphasized that many people remain capable of great intellectual accomplishments well into their later years (Simonton, 1990, 1997). This fact was verified in a study of scholarly, scientific, and artistic productivity that examined lifelong patterns of work among 738 men who lived at least through the age of 79. Dennis (1966) found that the 40s decade was the most productive in most professions. However, productivity was remarkably stable through the 60s and even the 70s in many areas.

An Overview of Human Development

Stage of development	Infancy (birth–2)

Physical and sensorimotor development

Rapid brain growth; 75% of adult brain weight is attained by age 2.

Ability to localize sounds is apparent at birth; ability to recognize parent's voice occurs within first week.

Rapid improvement occurs in visual acuity; depth perception is clearly present by 6 months, perhaps earlier.

Landmarks in motor development: Infants sit without support around 6 months, walk around 12–14 months, run freely around 2 years.

Major stage theories		
Piaget	Sensorimotor	
Kohlberg	Premoral	
Erikson	Trust vs. mistrust	Autonomy vs. shame
Freud (see Chapter 12)	Oral	Anal

Cognitive development

Object permanence gradually develops.

Infant shows orienting response (pupils dilate, head turns) and attention to new stimulus, habituation (reduced orienting response) to repeated stimulus.

Babbling increasingly resembles spoken language.

First word is used around age 1; vocabulary spurt begins around 18 months; frequent overextensions (words applied too broadly) occur.

Social and personality development

Temperamental individuality is established by 2–3 months; infants tend to be easy, difficult, or slow to warm up.

Attachment to caregiver(s) is usually evident around 6–8 months; secure attachment facilitates exploration.

"Stranger anxiety" often appears around 6–8 months; separation anxiety peaks around 14–18 months.

© George Silver/The Stock Market-CORBIS

Information compiled by Barbara Hansen Lemme, College of DuPage

Early childhood
(2–6)

Connections among neurons continue to increase in density.

Visual acuity reaches 20/20.

Bladder and bowel control is established.

Hand preference is usually solidified by 3–4 years; coordination improves; children learn to dress themselves.

Middle childhood
(6–12)

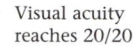

In girls, growth spurt begins around age 11, bringing dramatic increases in height and weight.

Level of pituitary activity and sex hormones increases.

In girls, puberty begins around age 12; menstruation starts.

Girls' secondary sex characteristics (such as breast development and widening hips) begin to emerge.

Preoperational	Concrete operational
Preconventional	Conventional
Initiative vs. guilt	Industry vs. inferiority
Phallic	Latency

Thought is marked by egocentrism (limited ability to view world from another's perspective).

Thought is marked by centration (inability to focus on more than one aspect of a problem at a time) and irreversibility (inability to mentally undo an action).

Telegraphic speech (omitting nonessential words) appears at 2–3 years; syntax is well developed by age 5; vocabulary increases dramatically.

Short-term memory capacity increases from two items at age 2 to five items around age 6–7; attention span improves.

Conservation (understanding that physical qualities can remain constant in spite of transformations in shape) is gradually mastered.

Child develops decentration (ability to focus on more than one feature of a problem at a time) and reversibility (ability to mentally undo an action).

Metalinguistic awareness (ability to reflect on use of language) leads to play with language, use of puns, riddles, metaphors.

Long-term memory improves with increasing use of encoding strategies of rehearsal and organization.

© David Young-Wolff/PhotoEdit

Child realizes that gender does not change and begins to learn gender roles and form gender identity; social behavior is influenced by observational learning, resulting in imitation.

Child progresses from parallel (side-by-side, noninteractive) play to cooperative play.

Social world is extended beyond family; first friendships are formed.

© Jon Feingersh/The Stock Market-CORBIS

Child experiences great increase in social skills, improved understanding of others' feelings; social world is dominated by same-sex peer relationships.

Role-taking skills emerge; fantasy is basis for thoughts about vocations and jobs.

Altruism tends to increase, aggression tends to decrease; aggression tends to become verbal rather than physical, hostile more than instrumental.

Adolescence
(12–20)

In boys, growth spurt begins around age 13, bringing dramatic increases in height and weight.

Level of pituitary activity and hormones increases.

Boys' secondary sex characteristics (such as voice change and growth of facial hair) begin to emerge.

In boys, puberty begins around age 14; boys become capable of ejaculation.

Young adulthood
(20–40)

Reaction time and muscular strength peak in early to mid-20s.

External signs of aging begin to show in 30s; skin loses elasticity; hair is thinner, more likely to be gray.

Maximum functioning of all body systems, including senses, attained; slow decline begins in 20s.

Lowered metabolic rate contributes to increased body fat relative to muscle; gain in weight is common.

Formal operational

Postconventional (if attained)

Identity vs. confusion

Intimacy vs. isolation

Genital

Deductive reasoning improves; problem solving becomes more systematic, with alternative possibilities considered before solution is selected.

Thought becomes more abstract and reflective; individual develops ability to mentally manipulate abstract concepts as well as concrete objects.

Individual engages in idealistic contemplation of hypotheticals, "what could be."

Long-term memory continues to improve as elaboration is added to encoding strategies.

Intellectual abilities and speed of information processing are stable.

Greater emphasis is on application, rather than acquisition, of knowledge.

There is some evidence of a trend toward dialectical thought (ideas stimulate opposing ideas), leading to more contemplation of contradictions, pros and cons.

Person experiences increased interactions with opposite-sex peers; dating begins.

Attention is devoted to identify formation, questions such as "Who am I?" and "What do I want out of life?"

Realistic considerations about abilities and training requirements become more influential in thoughts about vocations and jobs.

Energies are focused on intimate relationships, learning to live with marriage partner, starting a family, managing a home.

Trial period is given for occupational choices, followed by stabilization of vocational commitment; emphasis is on self-reliance, becoming one's own person.

For many, close relationship develops with mentor (older person who serves as role model, adviser, and teacher).

© David Young-Wolff/PhotoEdit

© Jeffry W. Myers/Stock, Boston

Middle adulthood
(40–65)

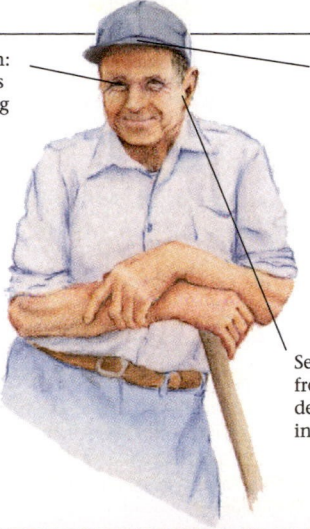

Changes occur in vision: increased farsightedness and difficulty recovering from glare; slower dark adaptation.

The amount of brain tissue declines, but significance of this neural loss is unclear.

In women, menopause occurs around age 50; in both sexes, sexual activity declines, although capacity for arousal changes only slightly.

Sensitivity to high-frequency sounds decreases especially in males after age 55.

Late adulthood
(65 and older)

Height decreases slightly because of changes in vertebral column; decline in weight also common.

Sensitivity of vision, hearing, and taste noticeably decreases.

Chronic diseases, especially heart disease, cancer, and stroke, increase.

Rate of aging is highly individualized.

Generativity vs. self-absorption

Integrity vs. despair

There is some evidence for a trend toward improved judgment or "wisdom" based on accumulation of life experiences.

Effectiveness of retrieval from long-term memory begins slow decline, usually not noticeable until after age 55.

Individual experiences gradual decline in speed of learning, problem solving, and information processing.

In spite of decreased speed in cognitive processes, intellectual productivity and problem-solving skills usually remain stable.

Individual experiences gradual decline in cognitive speed and effectiveness of working memory.

Intellectual productivity depends on factors such as health and lifestyle; many people in 60s and 70s remain quite productive.

Decision making tends to become more cautious.

Fluid intelligence often declines, but crystallized intelligence remains stable or increases.

Midlife transition around age 40 leads to reflection, increased awareness of mortality and passage of time, but usually is not a personal crisis.

"Sandwich generation" is caught between needs of aging parents and children reaching adulthood.

Career development peaks; there is some tendency to shift energy from career concerns to family concerns.

© Tony Freeman/PhotoEdit

© John Henley/The Stock Market-CORBIS

Physical changes associated with aging require adjustments that affect life satisfaction.

Marital satisfaction often increases, but eventually death of spouse presents coping challenge.

Living arrangements are a significant determinant of satisfaction, as 60%–90% of time is spent at home.

PREVIEW QUESTIONS
- How did this chapter illustrate the interplay of heredity and environment?
- What other unifying themes surfaced in this chapter?

Many of our seven integrative themes surfaced to some degree in our coverage of human development. We saw theoretical diversity in the discussions of attachment, cognitive development, and personality development. We saw that psychology evolves in a sociohistorical context, investigating complex, real-world issues such as the controversy over the effects of day care. We encountered multifactorial causation of behavior in the development of temperament and attachment, among other things. We saw cultural invariance and cultural diversity in our examination of attachment, motor development, cognitive development, and moral development.

But above all else, we saw how heredity and environment jointly mold behavior. We've encountered the dual influence of heredity and environment before, but this theme is rich in complexity, and each chapter draws out different aspects and implications. Our discussion of development amplified the point that genetics and experience work *interactively* to shape behavior. In the language of science, an interaction means that the effects of one variable depend on the effects of another. In other words, heredity and environment do not operate independently. Children with "difficult" temperaments will elicit different reactions from different parents, depending on the parents' personalities and expectations. Likewise, a particular pair of parents will affect children in different ways, depending on the inborn characteristics of the children. An interplay, or feedback loop, exists between biological and environmental factors. For instance, a temperamentally difficult child may elicit negative reactions from parents, which serve to make the child more difficult, which evokes more negative reactions. If this child develops into an ornery 11-year-old, which do we blame—genetics or experience? Clearly, this outcome is due to the reciprocal effects of both.

All aspects of development are shaped jointly by heredity and experience. We often estimate their relative weight or influence, as if we could cleanly divide behavior into genetic and environmental components. Although we can't really carve up behavior that neatly, such comparisons can be of great theoretical interest, as you'll see in our upcoming Personal Application, which discusses the nature and origins of gender differences in behavior.

REVIEW OF KEY POINTS
- During adulthood, personality is marked by both stability and change. Doubts have surfaced about whether a midlife crisis is a normal developmental transition. Adults who move successfully through the three stages of adulthood posited by Erikson should develop intimacy, generativity, and integrity.
- Many landmarks in adult development involve transitions in family relationships. Difficulty adjusting to marriage is more likely when spouses have different role expectations. Marital satisfaction tends to be highest at the beginning and end of the family life cycle.
- Unrealistic expectations make the adjustment to parenthood more stressful. Parent-adolescent relations are not as contentious as widely assumed. For most parents, the empty nest transition no longer appears to be as stressful as it once was.
- During adulthood, age-related physical transitions include changes in appearance, sensory losses (especially in vision and hearing), and hormonal changes. Menopause is not as problematic as widely suggested. Drastic mental decline is not a part of the normal aging process. However, 15%–20% of adults over age 75 suffer from some form of dementia.
- In the cognitive domain, general intelligence is fairly stable, with a small decline in average test scores seen after the age of 60. Many studies have found decreases in older adults' memory capabilities, but the losses are moderate and variable. Mental speed declines in late adulthood. Nonetheless, many people remain productive well into old age.
- Many of our seven integrative themes stood out in this chapter. But above all else, our discussion of development showed how heredity and environment interactively shape behavior.

Understanding Gender Differences

Answer the following "true" or "false."

_____ **1** Females are more socially oriented than males.

_____ **2** Males outperform females on most spatial tasks.

_____ **3** Females are more irrational than males.

_____ **4** Males are less sensitive to nonverbal cues than females.

_____ **5** Females are more emotional than males.

Are there genuine behavioral differences between the sexes similar to those mentioned above? If so, why do these differences exist? How do they develop? These are the complex and controversial questions that we'll explore in this Application.

Before proceeding further, we need to clarify how some key terms are used, as terminology in this area of research has been evolving and remains a source of confusion (Deaux, 1993; Unger & Crawford, 1993). Although not everyone agrees, we will distinguish between *sex,* **which refers to the biologically based categories of female and male,** and *gender,* **which refers to culturally constructed distinctions between femininity and masculinity.** According to this distinction, individuals are *born* female or male, but they *become* feminine or masculine through complex developmental processes that take years to unfold.

In any event, the statements at the beginning of this Application reflect popular gender stereotypes in our society. *Gender stereotypes* **are widely held beliefs about females' and males' abilities, personality traits, and social behavior.** Table 11.2 lists some characteristics that are part of the masculine and feminine stereotypes in North American society. The table shows something you may have already noticed on your own. The male stereotype is much more flattering, suggesting that men have virtually cornered the market on compe-

tence and rationality. After all, everyone knows that females are more dependent, emotional, irrational, submissive, and talkative than males. Right? Or is that not the case? Let's look at the research.

How Do the Sexes Differ in Behavior?

Gender differences **are actual disparities between the sexes in typical behavior or average ability.** Mountains of research, literally thousands of studies, exist on gender differences. It's difficult to sort through this huge body of research, but fortunately, many review articles on gender differences have been published in recent years. As noted in Chapter 2, review articles summarize and reconcile the findings of a large number of studies on a specific issue. Reviews that use meta-analysis have been particularly valuable. *Meta-analysis* **combines**

the statistical results of many studies of the same question, yielding an estimate of the size and consistency of a variable's effects.

What does this research show? Are the stereotypes of males and females accurate? Well, the findings are a mixed bag. The research indicates that genuine behavioral differences *do* exist between the sexes and that people's stereotypes are not entirely inaccurate (Eagly, 1995; Swim, 1994). But the differences are fewer in number, smaller in size, and far more complex than stereotypes suggest. As you'll see, only two of the differences mentioned in our opening true-false questions (the even-numbered items) have been largely supported by the research.

Cognitive Abilities

In the cognitive domain, it appears that there are three genuine gender differences. First, on the average, females tend to ex-

---

Table 11.2 Elements of Traditional Gender Sterotypes

Masculine	Feminine
Active	Aware of other's feelings
Adventurous	Considerate
Aggressive	Creative
Ambitious	Cries easily
Competitive	Devotes self to others
Dominant	Emotional
Independent	Enjoys art and music
Leadership qualities	Excitable in a crisis
Likes math and science	Expresses tender feelings
Makes decisions easily	Feelings hurt
Mechanical aptitude	Gentle
Not easily influenced	Home oriented
Outspoken	Kind
Persistent	Likes children
Self-confident	Neat
Skilled in business	Needs approval
Stands up under pressure	Tactful
Takes a stand	Understanding

SOURCE: Adapted from Ruble, T. L. (1983). Sex stereotypes: Issues of change in the 70s. *Sex Roles, 9,* 397–402. Copyright © 1983 Plenum Publishing Group. Adapted by permission

hibit slightly better *verbal skills* than males. Females tend to start speaking a little earlier, and they have larger vocabularies and better reading scores during the grade-school years (Halpern, 2000). In particular, females seem stronger on tasks that require rapid access to semantic and other information in long-term memory (Halpern, 1997). Second, starting during high school, males show a slight advantage on tests of *mathematical ability*. When all students are compared, males' advantage is fairly small (Feingold, 1988a; Hyde, Fennema, & Lamon, 1990). However, at the high end of the ability distribution, the gender gap is larger, as far more males than females are found to be mathematically precocious (Stumpf & Stanley, 1996). Third, starting in the grade-school years, males tend to score higher than females on various measures of *visual-spatial ability* (Voyer, Voyer, & Bryden, 1995). The size of these gender differences varies from moderate to small depending on the exact nature of the spatial task. Males appear to be strongest on tasks that require visual transformations in working memory (Halpern, 1997). Some researchers believe that gender disparities in mathematical ability and visual-spatial ability are intimately related, as most advanced topics in math (geometry, trigonometry, calculus) draw on spatial skills.

Social Behavior and Personality

In regard to social behavior and personality, research findings support some additional gender differences that are reasonably well documented. First, studies indicate that males tend to be more *aggressive* than females, both verbally and physically (Coie & Dodge, 1997; Knight, Fabes, & Higgins, 1996). This disparity shows up early in childhood. Its continuation into adulthood is supported by the fact that men account for a grossly disproportionate number of the violent crimes in our society (Halpern, 2000). However, it is worth noting that females engage in more covert and relational aggression, such as snubbing, ignoring, and undermining others (Crick, Casas, & Mosher, 1997; Crick & Rose, 2000). Second, there are gender differences in *nonverbal communication*. The evidence indicates

that females are more sensitive than males to subtle nonverbal cues (Hall, 1990, 1998; McClure, 2000). Third, males score somewhat higher than females on various assessments of risk taking (Byrnes, Miller, & Schafer, 1999). Fourth, males are more sexually active than females in a variety of ways, and they have more permissive attitudes about casual, premarital, and extramarital sex (Baumeister et al, 2001; Oliver & Hyde, 1993). In regard to personality, the disparities are small but males score a little higher on measures of assertiveness and global self-esteem, whereas females score somewhat higher on measures of anxiety and agreeableness (Costa, Terracciano, & McCrae, 2001; Feingold, 1994; Kling et al., 1999).

Some Qualifications

Although there are some genuine gender differences in behavior, bear in mind that these are *group* differences that indicate nothing about individuals. Essentially, research results compare the "average man" with the "average woman." However, you are—and every individual is—unique. The average female and male are ultimately figments of our imagination. Furthermore, most of the genuine group differences noted are relatively modest in magnitude. Figure 11.26 shows how scores on a trait, perhaps verbal ability, might be distributed for men and women. Although the group averages are detectably different, you can see the great variability within each group (sex) and the huge overlap between the two group distributions.

To summarize, the actual behavioral differences between males and females are fewer and smaller than popular stereotypes suggest. Many supposed gender differences have turned out to be more mythical than real (Tavris, 1992). Nonetheless, the few genuine gender differences require explanation, which is the matter we'll attend to next.

Biological Origins of Gender Differences

What accounts for the development of the gender differences that do exist? To what degree are they the product of learning or of biology? This question is yet another manifestation of the nature versus nurture issue. Investigations of the biological origins of gender differences have centered on the evolutionary bases of behavior, on hormones, and on brain organization.

Evolutionary Explanations

Evolutionary psychologists argue that gender differences in behavior reflect different natural selection pressures operating on the sexes over the course of human history (Archer, 1996). Evolutionary analyses usually begin by arguing that gender differences in behavior transcend culture because cultural invariance suggests that biological factors are at work (Kenrick & Trost, 1993). Although research has turned up some fascinating exceptions, the better-documented gender differences in cognitive abilities, aggression, and sexual behavior do appear to be pancultural (Beller & Gafni, 1996; Halpern, 1997).

Figure  11.26

The nature of gender differences. Gender differences are group differences that indicate little about individuals because of the great overlap between the groups. For a given trait, one sex may score higher on the average, but far more variation occurs within each sex than between the sexes.

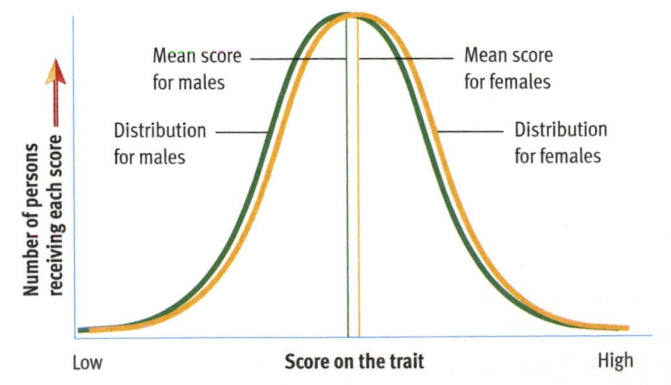

According to evolutionary psychologists, these differences are found around the world because males and females have confronted different adaptive demands (Buss & Kenrick, 1998). For example, as we discussed in Chapter 10, males supposedly are more sexually active and permissive because they invest less than females in the process of procreation and can maximize their reproductive success by seeking many sexual partners (Buss, 1996). The gender gap in aggression is also explained in terms of reproductive fitness. Because females are more selective about mating than males, males have to engage in more competition for sexual partners than females do. Greater aggressiveness is thought to be adaptive for males in this competition for sexual access because it should foster social dominance over other males and facilitate the acquisition of the material resources emphasized by females when they evaluate potential partners (Kenrick & Trost, 1993). Evolutionary theorists assert that gender differences in spatial ability reflect the division of labor in ancestral hunting and gathering societies in which males typically handled the hunting and females the gathering. Males' superiority on most (but not all) spatial tasks has been attributed to the adaptive demands of hunting versus gathering (Kimura, 1999; Silverman & Phillips, 1998; see Chapter 1).

Evolutionary analyses of gender differences are interesting, but critics are plentiful. On the one hand, it seems eminently likely that evolutionary forces could have led to some divergence between males and females in typical behavior. On the other hand, evolutionary hypotheses are highly speculative and difficult to test empirically (Eagly & Wood, 1999; Halpern, 1997). For example, it is quite a leap to infer that modern paper-and-pencil tests of spatial ability assess a talent that would have made high scorers superior hunters millions of years ago. But the crux of the problem for some critics is that evolutionary analyses are so "flexible" they can be used to explain almost anything. For example, if the situation regarding spatial ability were reversed—if females scored higher than males—evolutionary theorists might attribute females'

superiority to the adaptive demands of gathering food, weaving baskets, and making clothes—and it would be difficult to prove otherwise (Cornell, 1997).

The Role of Hormones

Hormones play a key role in sexual differentiation during prenatal development. The high level of androgens (the principal class of male hormones) in males and the low level of androgens in females appears to be the main factor leading to the differentiation of male and female genital organs. The critical role of prenatal hormones becomes apparent when something interferes with normal prenatal hormonal secretions. About a half-dozen endocrine disorders can cause overproduction or underproduction of specific gonadal hormones during prenatal development. Scientists have also studied children born to mothers who were given an androgenlike drug to prevent miscarriage. The general trend in this research is that females exposed prenatally to abnormally high levels of androgens exhibit more male-typical behavior than other females do and that males exposed prenatally to abnormally low levels of androgens exhibit more female-typical behavior than other males (Collaer & Hines, 1995). For example, girls with *congenital adrenal hyperplasia* tend to show "tomboyish" interests in vigorous outdoor activities and in "male" toys and have elevated scores on measures of aggressiveness and spatial ability.

These findings suggest that prenatal hormones contribute to the shaping of gender differences in humans. But there are a few problems with this evidence (Basow, 1992; Fausto-Sterling, 1992). First, the evidence is much stronger for females than for males. Second, it's always dangerous to draw conclusions about the general population based on small samples of people who have abnormal conditions. Third, most of the endocrine disorders studied have multiple effects (besides altering hormone levels) that create a variety of sometimes worrisome confounds in the research.

A handful of more recent studies have reported associations between circulating levels of male and female hormones and measures of specific traits, such as aggres-

siveness (Inoff-Germain et al., 1988) and spatial ability (Kimura & Hampson, 1993). For example, testosterone given to normal aging men to enhance their sexual functioning also increases their performance on visual-spatial tests (Janowsky, Oviatt, & Orwoll, 1994). Looking at the evidence as a whole, it does seems likely that hormones contribute to gender differences in behavior. However, the findings in this line of research have been equivocal and inconsistent, and a great deal remains to be learned.

Disparities in Brain Organization

Interpretive problems have also cropped up in efforts to link gender differences to specialization of the cerebral hemispheres in the brain (see Figure 11.27). As you may recall from Chapter 3, in most people the left hemisphere is more actively involved in verbal processing, whereas the right hemisphere is more active in visual-spatial processing (Sperry, 1982; Springer & Deutsch,

Figure 11.27

The cerebral hemispheres and the corpus callosum. In this drawing the cerebral hemispheres have been "pulled apart" to reveal the corpus callosum, the band of fibers that connects the right and left halves of the brain. Research has shown that the right and left hemispheres are specialized to handle different types of cognitive tasks (see Chapter 3), leading some theorists to speculate that patterns of hemispheric specialization might contribute to gender differences in verbal and spatial abilities.

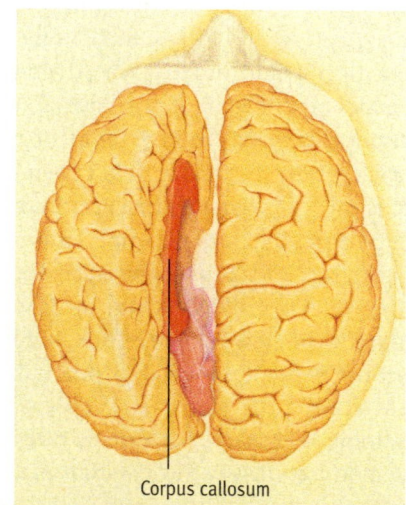

Corpus callosum

1998). After these findings surfaced, theorists began to wonder whether this division of labor in the brain might be related to gender differences in verbal and spatial skills. Consequently, they began looking for sex-related disparities in brain organization.

Some thought-provoking findings *have* been reported. For instance, some studies have found that *males tend to exhibit more cerebral specialization than females* (Hellige, 1993; Voyer, 1996). In other words, there's a trend for males to depend more heavily than females do on the left hemisphere in verbal processing and more heavily on the right in spatial processing. Some studies also suggest that *females tend to have a larger corpus callosum* (Bigler et al., 1997), which might allow for better transfer of information between hemispheres, which in turn might underlie the more bilateral organization of females' brains (Innocenti, 1994; Steinmetz et al., 1995). Thus, some theorists have concluded that differences between the sexes in brain organization are responsible for gender differences in verbal and spatial ability (Geschwind & Galaburda, 1987; Kimura & Hampson, 1993).

This idea is intriguing, but psychologists have a long way to go before they can explain gender differences in terms of right brain/left brain specialization. Studies have not been consistent in finding that males have stronger cerebral lateralization than females (Halpern, 1992; Kinsbourne, 1980), and the finding of a larger corpus callosum in females has proven controversial (Bishop & Wahlsten, 1997; Byne & Parsons, 1993). Moreover, it seems peculiar that strong lateralization would produce an advantage for males on one kind of task (spatial) and a disadvantage on another kind of task (verbal). Thus, the theory linking cerebral specialization to gender differences in mental abilities has received some empirical support, but it remains highly speculative.

In summary, researchers have made some intriguing progress in their efforts to document the biological roots of gender differences in behavior. However, the idea that "anatomy is destiny" has proven difficult to demonstrate. Many theorists remain convinced that gender differences are largely shaped by experience. Let's examine their evidence.

Environmental Origins of Gender Differences

Socialization **is the acquisition of the norms and behaviors expected of people in a particular society.** It includes all the efforts made by a society to ensure that its members learn to behave in a manner that's considered appropriate. The socialization process has traditionally included efforts to train children about gender roles. *Gender roles* **are expectations about what is appropriate behavior for each sex.** Investigators have identified three key processes involved in the socialization of gender roles: operant conditioning, observational learning, and self-socialization. First we'll examine these processes. Then we'll look at the principal sources of gender-role socialization: families, schools, and the media.

Operant Conditioning

In part, gender roles are shaped by the power of reward and punishment—the key processes in *operant conditioning* (see Chapter 6). Parents, teachers, peers, and others often reinforce (usually with tacit approval) "gender-appropriate" behavior and respond negatively to "gender-inappropriate" behavior (Bussey & Bandura, 1999; Fagot, Leinbach, & O'Boyle, 1992). If you're a man, you might recall getting hurt as a young boy and being told that "men don't cry." If you succeeded in inhibiting your crying, you may have earned an approving smile or even something tangible like an ice cream cone. The reinforcement probably strengthened your tendency to "act like a man" and suppress emotional displays. If you're a woman, chances are your crying wasn't discouraged as gender-inappropriate. Studies suggest that fathers may encourage and reward gender-appropriate behavior in their youngsters more than mothers do and that boys experience more pressure to behave in gender-appropriate ways than girls do (Levy, Taylor, & Gelman, 1995). Thus, a 10-year-old boy who enjoys playing with dollhouses is particularly likely to elicit disapproval from his parents, especially his father.

Observational Learning

As a young girl, did you imitate the behavior of your mother, your aunts, and your older sisters? As a young boy, did you imitate your father and other male role models? Such behaviors reflect *observational learning,* in which behavior is shaped by the observation of others' behavior and its consequences (see Chapter 6). In everyday language, observational learning results in *imitation.*

Children imitate both males and females, but most children tend to imitate same-sex role models more than opposite-sex role models (Bussey & Bandura, 1984; Frey & Ruble, 1992). Thus, imitation often leads young girls to play with dolls, dollhouses, and toy stoves. Young boys are more likely to tinker with toy trucks, miniature gas stations, or toolkits. Parents and other adults are not the only role models who contribute to the process of observational learning; same-sex peers may be even more influential than adults (Maccoby, 1998). In fact, one recent study found that the more time children spend playing with same-sex peers, the more gender-typed their behavior becomes (Martin & Fabes, 2001).

Self-Socialization

Children themselves are active agents in their own gender-role socialization. Several *cognitive theories* of gender-role development emphasize self-socialization (Bem, 1985, 1993; Cross & Markus, 1993; Serbin et al., 1993). Self-socialization entails three steps. First, children learn to classify themselves as male or female and to recognize their sex as a permanent quality (around ages 5 or 6). Second, this self-categorization motivates them to value those characteristics and behaviors associated with their sex. Third, they strive to bring their behavior in line with what is considered gender-appropriate in their culture. In other words, children get involved in their own socialization, working diligently to discover the rules that are supposed to govern their behavior. After gender stereotypes are internalized, they probably continue to influence behavior throughout life (Geis, 1993).

Sources of Gender-Role Socialization

Three *main* sources influence gender-role socialization: families, schools, and the media. Of course, we are now in an era of transition in gender roles, so the generalizations that follow may say more about how you were socialized than about how children will be socialized in the future.

Families. A great deal of gender-role socialization takes place in the home. One review of research (Lytton & Romney, 1991) suggests that parents don't treat girls and boys as differently as one might expect, but there are disparities (Lott & Maluso, 1993; Turner & Gervai, 1995). For example, fathers engage in more "rough-housing" play with their sons than with their daughters, even in infancy (McBride-Chang & Jacklin, 1993). And parents are more likely to explain science concepts to boys than to girls (Crowley et al., 2001). As children grow, boys and girls are encouraged to play with different types of toys (Etaugh & Liss, 1992). Generally, boys have less leeway to play with "feminine" toys than girls do with "masculine" toys.

When children are old enough to help with household chores, the assignments tend to depend on sex (McHale et al., 1990). For example, girls wash dishes and boys mow the lawn. Likewise, the leisure activities that children are encouraged to engage in vary by sex. Johnny plays in Little League and Mary practices the piano. Given these patterns, it's not surprising that parents' traditional or nontraditional attitudes about gender roles have been shown to influence the gender roles acquired by their children (Weisner & Wilson-Mitchell, 1990). Older siblings may also influence youngsters' gender-role socialization (Wagner, Schubert, & Schubert, 1993).

Schools. Schools and teachers clearly contribute to the socialization of gender roles. The books that children use in learning to read can influence their ideas about what

is suitable behavior for males and females (Oskamp, Kaufman, & Wolterbeek, 1996). Traditionally, males have been more likely to be portrayed as clever, heroic, and adventurous in these books, while females have been more likely to be shown doing domestic chores. The depiction of stereotypical gender roles in textbooks has declined considerably since the 1970s, but researchers still find subtle differences in how males and females tend to be portrayed (Kortenhaus & Demarest, 1993; Noddings, 1992; Turner-Bowker, 1996).

Preschool and grade-school teachers frequently reward gender-appropriate behavior in their pupils (Fagot et al., 1985; Ruble & Martin, 1998). Interestingly, teachers tend to pay greater attention to males, helping them, praising them, and scolding them more than females (Sadker & Sadker, 1994). As youngsters progress through the school system, they are often channeled in career directions considered appropriate for their gender (Read, 1991). For example, males have been more likely to be encouraged to study mathematics and to work toward becoming engineers or doctors. Females have often been encouraged to take classes in home economics and to work toward becoming nurses or homemakers.

Media. Television is another source of gender-role socialization (Luecke-Aleksa et al., 1995). There has been some improvement in recent years, but television shows have traditionally depicted men and women in highly stereotypic ways (Signorielli & Bacue, 1999; Zillman, Bryant, & Huston, 1994). Women are often portrayed as submissive, passive, and emotional. Men are more likely to be portrayed as independent, assertive, and competent. Another form of gender bias in television is its inordinate emphasis on physical attractiveness in women. Men on television may or may not be good-looking, but the vast majority of women are young, attractive, and sexy (Davis, 1990). TV commercials are especially likely to portray men and women in stereotypical ways (Bretl & Cantor, 1988; Signorielli, McLeod, & Healy, 1994); women are routinely shown worrying about trivial matters such as the

whiteness of their laundry or the shine of their dishes.

Conclusion

As you can see, the findings on gender and behavior are complex and confusing. Nonetheless, the evidence does permit one very general conclusion—a conclusion that you have seen before and will see again. Taken as a whole, the research in this area suggests that biological factors and environmental factors both contribute to gender differences in behavior—as they do to all other aspects of development.

REVIEW OF KEY POINTS

- Sex refers to the biological reality of being male or female, whereas gender refers to distinctions between being masculine or feminine. Gender differences in behavior are fewer in number and smaller in magnitude than gender stereotypes suggest.

- In the cognitive domain, research reviews suggest that there are genuine gender differences in verbal ability, mathematical ability, and spatial ability. In regard to social behavior and personality, differences have been found in aggression, nonverbal communication, risk taking, sexual behavior, and a handful of personality traits.

- Evolutionary theorists maintain that gender differences transcend culture because males and females have confronted different adaptive demands over the course of human history. Extensive evidence suggests that prenatal hormones contribute to human gender differences, but the research is marred by interpretive problems. Research linking gender differences to cerebral specialization is intriguing, but much remains to be learned.

- A vast research literature shows that gender differences are shaped by socialization processes. Operant conditioning, observational learning, and self-socialization contribute to the development of gender differences. Families, schools, and the media are among the main sources of gender-role socialization.

Are Fathers Essential to Children's Well-Being?

Are fathers essential for children to experience normal, healthy development? This question is currently the subject of heated debate. In recent years, a number of social scientists have mounted a thought-provoking argument that father absence is the chief factor underlying a host of modern social ills. For example, David Blankenhorn (1995) argues that "fatherlessness is the most harmful demographic trend of this generation. It is the leading cause of declining child well-being in our society" (p. 1). Expressing a similar view, David Popenoe (1996) maintains that "today's fatherlessness has led to social turmoil-damaged children, unhappy children, aimless children, children who strike back with pathological behavior and violence" (p.192).

The Basic Argument

What is the evidence for the proposition that fathers are essential to healthy development? Over the last 40 years, the proportion of children growing up without a father in the home has more than doubled (see Figure 11.28). During the same time, we have seen dramatic increases in teenage pregnancy, juvenile delinquency, violent crime, drug abuse, eating disorders, teen suicide, and family dysfunction. Moreover, mountains of studies have demonstrated an association between father absence and an elevated risk for these problems. Summarizing this evidence, Popenoe (1996) asserts that "fatherless children have a risk factor two to three times that of fathered children for a wide range of negative outcomes, including dropping out of high school, giving birth as a teenager, and becoming a juvenile delinquent" (p. 192), which leads him to infer that "fathers have a unique and irreplaceable role to play in child development" (p. 197). Working from this premise, Popenoe concludes, "If present trends continue, our society could

be on the verge of committing social suicide" (p. 192). Echoing this dire conclusion, Blankenhorn (1995) comments that "to tolerate the trend of fatherlessness is to accept the inevitability of continued societal recession" (p. 222).

You might be thinking "What's all the fuss about?" Surely, proclaiming the importance of fatherhood ought to be no more controversial than advocacy for motherhood or apple pie. But the assertion that a father is essential to a child's well-being has some interesting sociopolitical implications. It suggests that heterosexual marriage is the only appropriate context in which to raise children and that other family configurations are fundamentally deficient. Based on this line of reasoning, some people have argued for new laws that would make it more difficult to obtain a divorce and other policies and programs that would favor traditional families over families headed by single mothers, cohabiting parents, and

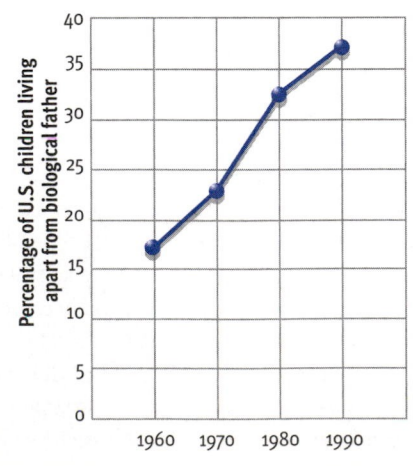

Figure 11.28

Increasing father absence in the United States. Since 1960 the percentage of U.S. children who live in a home without their biological father has risen steadily and probably exceeds 40% today. (Data from Hernandez, 1993)

gay and lesbian parents (Silverstein & Auerbach, 1999). Thus, the question about the importance of fathers is creating a great deal of controversy, because it is really a question about alternatives to traditional family structure.

Evaluating the Argument

In light of the far-reaching implications of the view that fathers are essential to normal development, it makes sense to subject this view to critical scrutiny. How could you use critical thinking skills to evaluate this argument? At least three previously discussed ideas seem germane.

First, it is important to recognize that the position that fathers are essential for healthy development rests on a foundation of correlational evidence, and as we have seen repeatedly, *correlation is no assurance of causation.* Yes, there has been an increase in fatherlessness that has been paralleled by increases in teenage pregnancy, drug abuse, eating disorders, and other disturbing social problems. But think of all the other changes that have occurred in American culture over the last 40 years, such as the decline of organized religion, the growth of mass media, dramatic shifts in sexual mores, and so forth. Increased fatherlessness has co-varied with a host of other cultural trends. Hence, it is highly speculative to infer that father absence is the chief cause of most modern social maladies.

Second, it always pays to think about whether there are specific, *alternative explanations* for findings that you might have doubts about. What other factors might account for the association between father absence and children's maladjustment? Think for a moment: What is the most frequent cause of father absence? Obviously, it is divorce. Divorces tend to be highly stressful events that disrupt children's entire lives. Although the evidence suggests that a ma-

Are fathers crucial to children's well-being? This seemingly simple question has sparked heated debate.

jority of children seem to survive divorce without lasting, detrimental effects, it is clear that divorce elevates youngsters' risk for a wide range of negative developmental outcomes (Amato & Keith, 1991; Hetherington, Bridges, & Insabella, 1998). Given that father absence and divorce are inextricably intertwined, it is possible that the negative effects of divorce account for much of the association between father absence and social problems.

Are there any other alternative explanations for the correlation between fatherlessness and social maladies? Yes, critics point out that the prevalence of father absence co-varies with socioeconomic status. Father absence is much more common in low-income families. Thus, the effects of father absence are entangled to some extent with the many powerful, malignant effects of poverty, which might account for much of the correlation between fatherlessness and negative outcomes (McLoyd, 1998).

A third possible strategy in thinking critically about the effects of father absence would be to look for some of the *fallacies in reasoning* introduced in Chapter 10 (irrelevant reasons, circular reasoning, slippery slope, weak analogies, and false dichotomy). A couple of the quotes from Popenoe and Blankenhorn were chosen to give you an opportunity to detect two of these fallacies in a new context. Take a look at the quotes once again and see whether you can spot the fallacies.

Popenoe's assertion that "if present trends continue, our society could be on the verge of social suicide" is an example of *slippery slope argumentation,* which involves predictions that if one allows X to happen, things will spin out of control and catastrophic events will follow. "Social suicide" is a little vague, but it sounds as if Popenoe is predicting that father absence will lead to the destruction of modern American culture. The other fallacy that you might have spotted was the *false dichotomy* apparent in Blankenhorn's assertion that "to tolerate the trend of fatherlessness is to accept the inevitability of continued societal recession." A false dichotomy creates an either-or choice between the position one wants to advocate (in this case, new social policies to reduce father absence) and some obviously horrible outcome that any sensible person would want to avoid (social decay), while ignoring other possible outcomes that might lie between these extremes.

In summary, we can find a number of flaws and weaknesses in the argument that fathers are *essential* to normal development. However, our critical evaluation of this argument *does not mean that fathers are unimportant.* Many types of evidence suggest that fathers generally make significant contributions to their children's development (Phares, 1996; Rohner & Veneziano, 2001). We could argue with merit that fathers typically provide a substantial advantage for children that fatherless children do not have. But there is a crucial distinction between arguing that fathers *promote* normal, healthy development and arguing that fathers are *necessary* for normal, healthy development. If fathers are *necessary,* children who grow up without them could not achieve the same level of well-being as those who have fathers, yet it is clear that a great many children from single-parent homes turn out just fine.

Fathers surely are important, and it seems likely that father absence *contributes* to a variety of social maladies. So, why do Blankenhorn (1995) and Popenoe (1996) argue for the much stronger conclusion—that fathers are *essential?* They appear to prefer the stronger conclusion because it raises much more serious questions about the viability of nontraditional family forms. Thus, they seem to want to advance a *political agenda* that champions traditional family values. They are certainly entitled to do so, but when research findings are used to advance a political agenda—whether conservative or liberal—a special caution alert should go off in your head. When a political agenda is at stake, it pays to scrutinize arguments with extra care, because research findings are more likely to be presented in a slanted fashion. The field of psychology deals with a host of complex questions that have profound implications for a wide range of social issues. The skills and habits of critical thinking can help you find your way through the maze of reasons and evidence that hold up the many sides of these complicated issues.

Table 11.3 Critical Thinking Skills Discussed in This Application	
Skill	**Description**
Understanding the limitations of correlational evidence	The critical thinker understands that a correlation between two variables does not demonstrate that there is a causal link between the variables.
Looking for alternative explanations for findings and events	In evaluating explanations, the critical thinker explores whether there are other explanations that could also account for the findings or events under scrutiny.
Recognizing and avoiding common fallacies, such as irrelevant reasons, circular reasoning, slippery slope reasoning, weak analogies, and false dichotomies	The critical thinker is vigilant about conclusions based on unrelated premises, conclusions that are rewordings of premises, unwarranted predictions that things will spin out of control, superficial analogies, and contrived dichotomies.

Key Ideas

Progress Before Birth: Prenatal Development

● Prenatal development proceeds through the germinal, embryonic, and fetal stages as the zygote is differentiated into a human organism. During this period, development may be affected by maternal malnutrition, maternal drug use, and some maternal illnesses.

The Wondrous Years of Childhood

● Motor development follows cephalocaudal and proximodistal trends. Early motor development depends on both maturation and learning. Developmental norms for motor skills and other types of development only reflect typical performance.

● Temperamental differences among children are apparent during the first few months of life. These differences are fairly stable and may have far-reaching effects. Research shows that attachment emerges out of an interplay between infant and mother.

● Infant-mother attachments fall into three categories: secure, anxious-ambivalent, and avoidant. The effects of day care on attachment are a source of concern, but the evidence is hotly debated. Cultural variations in child rearing can affect the patterns of attachment seen in a society.

● Belsky theorizes that children have been programmed by evolution to respond to sensitive or insensitive care with different attachment patterns, which eventually cultivate reproductive strategies that would have been adaptive in the environments that have historically fostered sensitive or insensitive care.

● Erik Erikson's theory of personality development proposes that individuals evolve through eight stages over the life span. In each stage the person wrestles with changes (crises) in social relationships.

● According to Piaget's theory of cognitive development, the key advance during the sensorimotor period is the child's gradual recognition of the permanence of objects. The preoperational period is marked by certain deficiencies in thinking—notably, centration, irreversibility, and egocentrism.

● During the concrete operations period, children develop the ability to perform operations on mental representations, making them capable of conservation and hierarchical classification. The stage of formal operations ushers in more abstract, systematic, and logical thought.

● Recent research has shown that infants appear to understand surprisingly complex concepts that they have had virtually no opportunity to learn about, leading some theorists to conclude that basic cognitive abilities are innate. Children's understanding of the mind seems to turn a corner between ages 3 and 4.

● According to Kohlberg, moral reasoning progresses through three levels that are related to age and determined by cognitive development. Age-related progress in moral reasoning has been found in research, although a great deal of overlap occurs between adjacent stages.

The Transition of Adolescence

● The growth spurt at puberty is a prominent event involving the development of reproductive maturity and secondary sex characteristics. Belsky's theory that stress in early family relations might accelerate the process of sexual maturation has received some support, at least for girls.

● Recent decades have brought a surge in attempted suicide by adolescents and there is an association between adolescence and the prevalence of violent crime. Evidence suggests that adolescence may be slightly more stressful than other periods of life. According to Erikson, the key challenge of adolescence is to make some progress toward a sense of identity. Marcia identified four patterns of identity formation.

The Expanse of Adulthood

● During adulthood, personality is marked by both stability and change. Doubts have surfaced about whether a midlife crisis is a normal developmental transition. Many landmarks in adult development involve transitions in family relationships, including adjusting to marriage, parenthood, and the empty nest.

● During adulthood, age-related physical transitions include changes in appearance, sensory losses, and hormonal changes. Drastic mental decline is not a part of the normal aging process. However, 15%–20% of adults over age 75 suffer from some form of dementia. In late adulthood, mental speed declines and working memory suffers, but many people remain productive well into old age.

Putting It in Perspective

● Many of our seven integrative themes stood out in this chapter. But above all else, our discussion of development showed how heredity and environment interactively shape behavior.

Personal Application • Understanding Gender Differences

● Gender differences in behavior are fewer in number and smaller in magnitude than gender stereotypes suggest. Research reviews suggest that there are genuine (albeit small) gender differences in verbal ability, mathematical ability, spatial ability, aggression, nonverbal communication, risk taking, sexual behavior, and several personality traits.

● Evolutionary theorists believe that gender differences reflect the influence of natural selection. Some research does link gender differences in humans to hormones and brain organization, but the research is marred by interpretive problems. Operant conditioning, observational learning, and self-socialization contribute to the development of gender differences.

Critical Thinking Application • Are Fathers Essential to Children's Well-Being?

● Some social scientists have argued that father absence is the chief cause of a host of social problems and that fathers are essential for normal, healthy development. Critics have argued that there are alternative explanations for the association between father absence and negative developmental outcomes.

Key Terms

Accommodation
Age of viability
Animism
Assimilation
Attachment
Centration
Cephalocaudal trend
Cognitive development
Conservation
Cross-sectional design
Dementia
Development
Developmental norms
Dishabituation
Egocentrism
Embryonic stage
Family life cycle
Fetal alcohol syndrome
Fetal stage
Gender
Gender differences
Gender roles
Gender stereotypes
Germinal stage
Habituation
Irreversibility
Longitudinal design
Maturation
Menarche

Meta-analysis
Midlife crisis
Motor development
Object permanence
Placenta
Prenatal period
Primary sex characteristics
Proximodistal trend
Puberty
Pubescence
Secondary sex characteristics
Separation anxiety
Sex
Socialization
Stage
Temperament
Zygote

Key People

Mary Ainsworth
Jay Belsky
John Bowlby
Erik Erikson
Lawrence Kohlberg
Jean Piaget
Alexander Thomas and Stella Chess

PRACTICE TEST

1. The stage of prenatal development during which the developing organism is most vulnerable to injury is the:
   A. zygotic stage.
   C. fetal stage.
   B. germinal stage.
   D. embryonic stage.

2. The cephalocaudal trend in the motor development of children can be described simply as a:
   A. head-to-foot direction.
   B. center-outward direction.
   C. foot-to-head direction.
   D. body-appendages direction.

3. Developmental norms:
   A. can be used to make extremely precise predictions about the age at which an individual child will reach various developmental milestones.
   B. indicate the maximum age at which a child can reach a particular developmental milestone and still be considered "normal."
   C. indicate the average age at which individuals reach various developmental milestones.
   D. involve both a and b.

4. When the development of the same subjects is studied over a period of time, the study is called a:
   A. cross-sectional study.
   C. longitudinal study.
   B. life history study.
   D. sequential study.

5. The quality of infant-caregiver attachment depends:
   A. on the quality of bonding in the first few hours of life.
   B. exclusively on the infant's temperament.
   C. on the interaction between the infant's temperament and the caregiver's responsiveness.
   D. on how stranger anxiety is handled.

6. During the second year of life, toddlers begin to take some personal responsibility for feeding, dressing, and bathing themselves in an attempt to establish what Erikson calls a sense of:
   A. superiority.
   C. generativity.
   B. industry.
   D. autonomy.

7. Five-year-old David watches as you pour water from a short, wide glass into a tall, narrow one. He says there is now more water than before. This response demonstrates that:
   A. David understands the concept of conservation.
   B. David does not understand the concept of conservation.
   C. David's cognitive development is "behind" for his age.
   D. both b and c.

8. Which of the following is *not* one of the criticisms of Piaget's theory of cognitive development?
   A. Piaget may have underestimated the cognitive skills of children in some areas.
   B. Piaget may have underestimated the influence of cultural factors on cognitive development.
   C. The theory does not clearly address the issue of individual differences in development.
   D. Evidence for the theory is based on children's answers to questions.

9. If a child's primary reason for not drawing pictures on the living room wall with crayons is to avoid the punishment that would inevitably follow this behavior, she would be said to be at which level of moral development?
   A. conventional
   C. preconventional
   B. postconventional
   D. unconventional

10. The Featured Study on the effects of early family relations on sexual maturation found:
    A. no association between early family stress and the timing of puberty.
    B. that early family stress was strongly associated with later sexual maturation in females.
    C. that early family stress was moderately associated with earlier sexual maturation in females.
    D. no support for the evolutionary hypothesis posited by Belsky.

11. Girls who mature _____ and boys who mature _____ seem to have more emotional difficulties with the transition to adolescence.
    A. early; early
    C. late; early
    B. early; late
    D. late; late

12. Sixteen-year-old Foster wants to spend a few years experimenting with different lifestyles and careers before he settles on who and what he wants to be. Foster's behavior illustrates the identity status of:
    A. identity moratorium.
    C. identity achievement.
    B. identity foreclosure.
    D. identity diffusion.

13. Although women perform about _____ of all housework, about _____ of wives characterize their household division of labor as unfair.
    A. one-half; one-half
    B. two-thirds; three-quarters
    C. two-thirds; one-third
    D. three-quarters; one-tenth

14. Males have been found to differ slightly from females in three well-documented areas of mental abilities. Which of the following is *not* one of these?
    A. verbal ability
    C. intelligence
    B. mathematical ability
    D. visual-spatial abilities

15. Research suggests that males exhibit _____ than females and that females have a _____ than males.
    A. less cerebral specialization; smaller corpus callosum
    B. less cerebral specialization; larger corpus callosum
    C. more cerebral specialization; smaller corpus callosum
    D. more cerebral specialization; larger corpus callosum

Answers

1	D	pp. 427, 429	**6**	D	pp. 439–440	**11**	B	p. 452
2	A	p. 432	**7**	B	p. 442	**12**	A	p. 454
3	C	p. 432	**8**	D	p. 444	**13**	C	p. 457
4	C	p. 434	**9**	C	p. 447	**14**	C	pp. 467–468
5	C	p. 436	**10**	C	p. 451	**15**	D	p. 470

 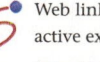 **ON THE WEB**

For additional resources on the topics covered in this chapter, visit the *Psychology: Themes and Variations* Web site, where you will find practice quizzes, tutorials, Web links, simulations, critical thinking activities, flash cards, interactive exercises, and suggested readings available through INFOTRAC.

http://psychology.wadsworth.com/weiten_themes6e/

CHAPTER 12

© Bruce Stoddard/Taxi-Getty Images

Personality: Theory, Research, and Assessment

atching Steve Irwin on television, you feel like he's about to jump right out of the set and into your living room. Known to millions of viewers around the world as the Crocodile Hunter, the Australian Irwin is famous—some would say notorious—for his frenetic energy, seeming love of danger, and exuberant affection for some of the world's most terrifying creatures. As one writer described it, "Like some crazed cross between Tarzan and a frat pledge, Steve Irwin flings himself on top of a thrashing crocodile. Slick with mud and blood (his), Irwin wrestles the beast into restraints, then declares to the TV camera, "She's a beauty!" (Lee, 2000).

You don't need to have seen Steve Irwin in action to appreciate that he has what most people would describe as an unusual *personality*. He routinely seeks out situations that would give many of us nightmares—getting covered with biting green ants, swimming with killer sharks, grabbing venomous snakes by the tail, hurling himself out of a boat at night onto the back of a 12-foot crocodile whose powerful jaws could easily crush his legs. And he does it all with wide-eyed, boisterous enthusiasm. "One bite and I'm a goner," he'll say as he dodges a spitting cobra or a snapping crocodile. "But isn't he a beaut! Crikey!"

Apparently, it isn't all showmanship. By all accounts, Irwin is just as wildly energetic and thrill seeking off camera as he is on television. One less than friendly interviewer described him as "like a boy with attention deficit disorder after a very serious Hershey's binge" (White, 1997). And if Irwin seems unusually demonstrative in his affection for deadly creatures, that, too, seems to be genuine. When he is not filming, he devotes his time to directing Australia's largest private zoo, and he has declared that educating people about conservation is his life's work. Saving a crocodile that is threatened by poachers can bring him to tears (Irwin & Irwin, 2001).

The example of Steve Irwin points to the mystery of personality. While Irwin may be unusual in many respects, all individuals can be described in terms of characteristics that make up their personalities. But what exactly is personality? How does it develop over

time? Are we born with a certain personality, or is experience critical in shaping the qualities that make us who we are? Consider that many of Steve Irwin's qualities were evident from a very early age. Irwin himself has said, "I get called an adrenaline junkie every other minute, and I'm just fine with that. You know what though, mate? I'm doing exactly what I've done from when I was a small boy" (Simpson, 2001). His late mother agreed. She once recalled, "He's always been very, very active—on the verge of hyperactive, really, very much so. If he went missing, you could always look up a tree; there he'd be" (Stainton, 1999). On the other hand, Irwin's life story points to the role of environment in shaping personality. Irwin clearly had an unusual upbringing. His parents were both lovers of wildlife who opened their own zoo, where Steve grew up. When he was 6 years old, his birthday present from his parents was a 12-foot python. If Irwin is genuinely fond of snakes, is it because that trait is "in his blood," or

Steve Irwin, better known as the Crocodile Hunter, clearly manifests a very powerful and unusual personality. But everyone has their own unique personality, which makes the study of personality a fascinating area of inquiry in psychology.

is it because he was exposed to them from very early in life?

Psychologists have approached questions like these from a variety of perspectives. Traditionally, the study of personality has been dominated by "grand theories" that attempt to explain a great many facets of behavior. Our discussion will reflect this emphasis, as we'll devote most of our time to the sweeping theories of Freud, Jung, Skinner, Rogers, and several others. In recent decades, however, the study of personality has shifted toward narrower research programs that examine specific aspects of personality. The last several sections of the chapter will reflect this trend, as we review biological, cultural, and other contemporary empirical approaches to personality. In the Personal Application, we'll discuss how psychological tests are used to measure various aspects of personality. In the Critical Thinking Application, you'll see how hindsight bias can taint people's analyses of personality.

The Nature of Personality

PREVIEW QUESTIONS
- What are the essential features of the concept of personality?
- What are personality traits?
- How many personality traits are necessary to describe personality adequately?

Personality is a complex hypothetical construct that has been defined in a variety of ways. Let's take a closer look at the concepts of personality and personality traits.

Defining Personality: Consistency and Distinctiveness

What does it mean to say that someone has an optimistic personality? This assertion indicates that the person has a fairly *consistent tendency* to behave in a cheerful, hopeful, enthusiastic way, looking at the bright side of things, across a wide variety of situations. Although no one is entirely consistent in behavior, this quality of *consistency across situations* lies at the core of the concept of personality.

Distinctiveness is also central to the concept of personality. Personality is used to explain why not everyone acts the same way in similar situations. If you were stuck in an elevator with three people, each might react differently. One might crack jokes to relieve the tension. Another might make ominous predictions that "we'll never get out of here." The third might calmly think about how to escape. These varied reactions to the same situation occur because each person has a different personality. Each person has traits that are seen in other people, but each individual has his or her own distinctive *set* of personality traits.

In summary, the concept of personality is used to explain (1) the stability in a person's behavior over time and across situations (consistency) and (2) the behavioral differences among people reacting to the same situation (distinctiveness). We can combine these ideas into the following definition: *Personality refers to an individual's unique constellation of consistent behavioral traits.* Let's look more closely at the concept of *traits*.

Personality Traits: Dispositions and Dimensions

Everyone makes remarks like "Jan is very *conscientious.*" Or you might assert that "Bill is too *timid* to succeed in that job." These descriptive statements refer to personality traits. A *personality trait* is a durable disposition to behave in a particular way in a variety of situations. Adjectives such as *honest, dependable, moody, impulsive, suspicious, anxious, excitable, domineering,* and *friendly* describe dispositions that represent personality traits.

Most approaches to personality assume that some traits are more basic than others. According to this notion, a small number of fundamental traits determine other, more superficial traits. For example, a person's tendency to be impulsive, restless, irritable, boisterous, and impatient might all be derived from a more basic tendency to be excitable.

A number of psychologists have taken on the challenge of identifying the basic traits that form the core of personality. For example, Raymond Cattell (1950, 1966, 1990) used the statistical procedure of *factor analysis* to reduce a huge list of personality traits compiled by Gordon Allport (1937) to just 16 basic dimensions of personality. As you may recall from Chapter 9, in *factor analysis,* correlations among many variables are analyzed to identify closely related clusters of variables. If the measurements of a number of variables (in this case, personality traits) correlate highly with one another, the assumption is that a single factor is influencing all of them. Factor analysis is used to identify these hidden factors. In factor analyses of personality traits, these hidden factors are viewed as very basic, higher-order traits that determine less basic, more specific traits. Based on his factor analytic work, Cattell concluded that an individual's personality can be described completely by measuring just 16 traits. The 16 crucial traits are listed in Figure 12.20, which can be found in the Personal Application, where we discuss a personality test that Cattell designed to assess these traits.

The Five-Factor Model of Personality Traits

In recent years, Robert McCrae and Paul Costa (1987, 1997, 1999) have used factor analysis to arrive at an even simpler, *five-factor model of personality* (see Figure 12.1). McCrae and Costa maintain that most personality traits are derived from just five higher-order traits that have come to be known as the "Big Five": extraversion, neuroticism, openness to experience, agreeableness, and conscientiousness. Let's take a closer look at these traits:

1. *Extraversion.* People who score high in extraversion are characterized as outgoing, sociable, upbeat, friendly, assertive, and gregarious. Referred to as *positive emotionality* in some trait models, extraversion has been studied extensively in research for many decades (Watson & Clark, 1997).

2. *Neuroticism.* People who score high in neuroticism tend to be anxious, hostile, self-conscious, insecure, and vulnerable. Like extraversion, this trait has been the subject of thousands of studies. In some trait models it is called *negative emotionality* (Church, 1994).

3. *Openness to experience.* Openness is associated with curiosity, flexibility, vivid fantasy, imaginativeness, artistic sensitivity, and unconventional attitudes. McCrae (1996) maintains that its importance has been underestimated. Citing evidence that openness fosters liberalism, he argues that this trait is the key determinant of people's political attitudes and ideology.

4. *Agreeableness.* Those who score high in agreeableness tend to be sympathetic, trusting, cooperative, modest, and straightforward. People who score at the opposite end of this personality dimension are characterized as suspicious, antagonistic, and aggressive. Agreeableness may have its roots in childhood temperament and appears to promote altruistic (helping) behavior in social interactions (Graziano & Eisenberg, 1997).

5. *Conscientiousness.* Conscientious people tend to be diligent, disciplined, well-organized, punctual, and dependable. Referred to as *constraint* in some trait models, conscientiousness is associated with higher productivity in a variety of occupational areas (Hogan & Ones, 1997).

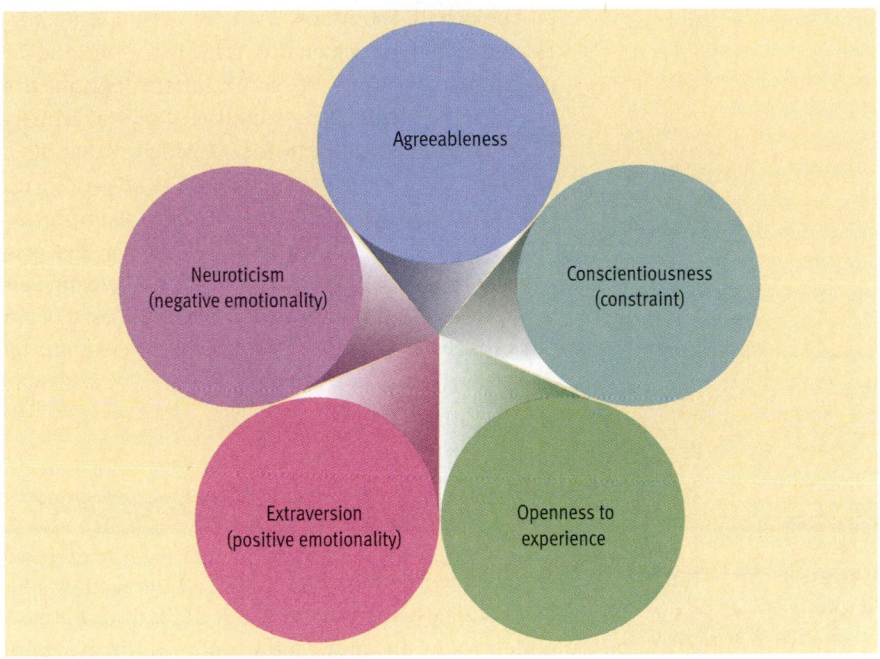

Like Cattell, McCrae and Costa maintain that personality can be described adequately by measuring the basic traits that they've identified. Their bold claim has been supported in many studies by other researchers, and the five-factor model has become the dominant conception of personality structure in contemporary psychology (John & Srivastava, 1999; Wiggins & Trapnell, 1997). These traits have been characterized as the "latitude and longitude" along which personality should be mapped (Ozer & Reise, 1994, p. 361). Thousands of studies have been conducted, exploring correlations between the Big Five traits and other characteristics such as self-esteem (Watson, Suls, & Haig, 2002), transformational leadership (Judge & Bono, 2000), social status (Anderson et al., 2001), and well-being at midlife (Siegler & Brummett, 2000).

However, some theorists have been critical of the model. For example, Dan McAdams (1992) points out that the model is purely descriptive and provides no insight into the causes or development of personality. Jack Block (1995) has questioned the generality of the model. He points out that the higher-order traits that emerge in factor analyses depend to some extent on the exact mix of the much larger set of specific traits that are measured in the first place. Thus, he asserts that the five-factor model is more arbitrary than widely appreciated. Other critics of the five-factor model maintain that more than five traits are necessary to account for most of the variation seen in human personality (Benet & Waller, 1995; Paunonen, 1998; Wiggins, 1992).

Figure 12.1

The five-factor model of personality. Trait models attempt to analyze personality into its basic dimensions. McCrae and Costa (1985, 1987, 1997) maintain that personality can be described adequately with the five higher-order traits identified here, which are widely referred to as the Big Five.

The debate about how many dimensions are necessary to describe personality is likely to continue for many years to come. As you'll see throughout the chapter, the study of personality is an area in psychology that has a long history of "dueling theories." We'll divide these diverse personality theories into four broad groups that share certain assumptions, emphases, and interests: (1) psychodynamic perspectives, (2) behavioral perspectives, (3) humanistic perspectives, and (4) biological perspectives. We'll begin our discussion of personality theories by examining the life and work of Sigmund Freud.

Psychodynamic Perspectives

Psychodynamic theories **include all the diverse theories descended from the work of Sigmund Freud, which focus on unconscious mental forces.** Freud inspired many brilliant scholars who followed in his intellectual footsteps. Some of these followers simply refined and updated Freud's theory. Others veered off in new directions and established independent, albeit related, schools of thought. Today, the psychodynamic umbrella covers a large collection of loosely related theories that we can only sample from in this text. In this chapter, we'll examine the ideas of Sigmund Freud in some detail. Then we'll take a briefer look at the psychodynamic theories of Carl Jung and Alfred Adler.

Freud's Psychoanalytic Theory

Born in 1856, Sigmund Freud grew up in a middle-class Jewish home in Vienna, Austria. He showed an early interest in intellectual pursuits and became an intense, hardworking young man, driven to achieve fame. He experienced his share of inner turmoil and engaged in regular self-analysis for over 40 years. Freud lived in the Victorian era, which was marked by sexual repression. His life was also affected by the first great World War, which devastated Europe, and by the growing anti-Semitism of the times. We'll see that the sexual repression and aggressive hostilities that Freud witnessed left their mark on his view of human nature.

Freud was a physician specializing in neurology when he began his medical practice in Vienna toward the end of the 19th century. Like other neurologists in his era, he often treated people troubled by nervous problems such as irrational fears, obsessions, and anxieties. Eventually he devoted himself to the treatment of mental disorders using an innovative procedure he had developed, called *psychoanalysis,* that required lengthy verbal interactions with patients during which Freud probed deeply into their lives.

Freud's (1901, 1924, 1940) *psychoanalytic theory* grew out of his decades of interactions with his clients in psychoanalysis. Psychoanalytic theory attempts to explain personality, motivation, and psychological disorders by focusing on the influence of early childhood experiences, on unconscious motives and conflicts, and on the methods people use to cope with their sexual and aggressive urges.

Most of Freud's contemporaries were uncomfortable with his theory for at least three reasons. First, in arguing that people's behavior is governed by unconscious factors of which they are unaware, Freud made the disconcerting suggestion that individuals are not masters of their own minds. Second, in claiming that adult personalities are shaped by childhood experiences and other factors beyond one's control, he suggested that people are not masters of their own destinies. Third, by emphasizing the great importance of how people cope with their sexual urges, he offended those who held the conservative, Victorian values of his time.

Thus, Freud endured a great deal of criticism, condemnation, and outright ridicule, even after his work began to attract more favorable attention. Consider the following recollection from one of Freud's friends: "In those days when one mentioned Freud's name everyone would begin to laugh, as if someone had told a joke. Freud was the queer fellow who wrote a book about dreams . . . He was the man who saw sex in everything. It was considered bad taste to bring up Freud's name in the presence of ladies" (Donn, 1988, p. 57). Let's examine the ideas that generated so much controversy.

"*No one who, like me, conjures up the most evil of those half-tamed demons that inhabit the human beast, and seeks to wrestle with them, can expect to come through the struggle unscathed.*"
SIGMUND FREUD

Structure of Personality

Freud divided personality structure into three components: the id, the ego, and the superego (see Figure 12.2). He saw a person's behavior as the outcome of interactions among these three components.

The *id* is the primitive, instinctive component of personality that operates according to the pleasure principle. Freud referred to the id as the reservoir of psychic energy. By this he meant that the id houses the raw biological urges (to eat, sleep, defecate, copulate, and so on) that energize human behavior. The id operates according to the *pleasure principle,* **which demands immediate gratification of its urges.** The id engages in *primary-process thinking,* which is primitive, illogical, irrational, and fantasy oriented.

The *ego* is the decision-making component of personality that operates according to the reality principle. The ego mediates between the id, with its forceful desires for immediate satisfaction, and the external social world, with its expectations and norms regarding suitable behavior. The ego considers social realities—society's norms, etiquette, rules, and customs—in deciding how to behave. The ego is guided by the *reality principle,* **which seeks to delay gratification of the id's urges until appropriate outlets and situations can be found.** In short, to stay out of trouble, the ego often works to tame the unbridled desires of the id.

In the long run, the ego wants to maximize gratification, just as the id does. However, the ego engages in *secondary-process thinking,* which is relatively rational, realistic, and oriented toward problem solving. Thus, the ego strives to avoid negative consequences from society and its representatives (for example, punishment by parents or teachers) by behaving "properly." It also attempts to achieve long-range goals that sometimes require putting off gratification.

While the ego concerns itself with practical realities, the *superego* **is the moral component of personality that incorporates social standards about what represents right and wrong.** Throughout their lives, but especially during childhood, people receive training about what constitutes good and bad behavior. Many social norms regarding morality are eventually internalized. The superego emerges out of the ego at around 3 to 5 years of age. In some people, the superego can become irrationally demanding in its striving for moral perfection. Such people are plagued by excessive feelings of guilt. According to Freud, the id, ego, and superego are distributed differently across three levels of awareness, which we'll describe next.

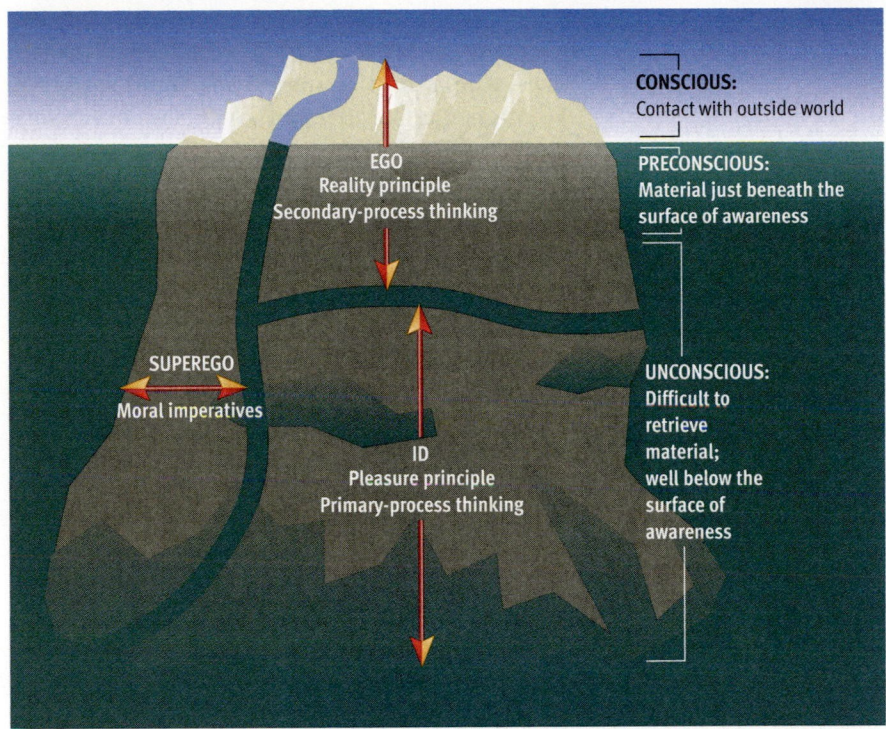

Figure 12.2

Freud's model of personality structure. Freud theorized that people have three levels of awareness: the conscious, the preconscious, and the unconscious. The enormous size of the unconscious is often dramatized by comparing it to the portion of an iceberg that lies beneath the water's surface. Freud also divided personality structure into three components—id, ego, and superego—which operate according to different principles and exhibit different modes of thinking. In Freud's model, the id is entirely unconscious, but the ego and superego operate at all three levels of awareness.

Levels of Awareness

Perhaps Freud's most enduring insight was his recognition of how unconscious forces can influence behavior. He inferred the existence of the unconscious from a variety of observations that he made with his patients. For example, he noticed that "slips of the tongue" often revealed a person's true feelings. He also realized that his patients' dreams often expressed hidden desires. Most important, through psychoanalysis he often helped patients to discover feelings and conflicts of which they had previously been unaware.

Freud contrasted the unconscious with the conscious and preconscious, creating three levels of awareness. **The *conscious* consists of whatever one is aware of at a particular point in time.** For example, at this moment your conscious may include the train of thought in this text and a dim awareness in the back of your mind that your eyes are getting tired and you're beginning to get hungry. **The *preconscious* contains material just beneath the surface of awareness that can easily be retrieved.** Examples might include your middle name, what you had for supper last night, or an argument you had with a

Web Link 12.1

The Victorian Web
Psychoanalysis initially developed within a late-19th-century context that is comprehensively portrayed in English Professor George Landow's (Brown University) important hypertext archive.

friend yesterday. **The *unconscious* contains thoughts, memories, and desires that are well below the surface of conscious awareness but that nonetheless exert great influence on behavior.** Examples of material that might be found in your unconscious include a forgotten trauma from childhood, hidden feelings of hostility toward a parent, and repressed sexual desires.

Freud's conception of the mind is often compared to an iceberg that has most of its mass hidden beneath the water's surface (see Figure 12.2). He believed that the unconscious (the mass below the surface) is much larger than the conscious or preconscious. As you can see in Figure 12.2, he proposed that the ego and superego operate at all three levels of awareness. In contrast, the id is entirely unconscious, expressing its urges at a conscious level through the ego. Of course, the id's desires for immediate satisfaction often trigger internal conflicts with the ego and superego. These conflicts play a key role in Freud's theory.

Conflict and the Tyranny of Sex and Aggression

Freud assumed that behavior is the outcome of an ongoing series of internal conflicts. He saw internal battles between the id, ego, and superego as routine. Why? Because the id wants to gratify its urges immediately, but the norms of civilized society frequently dictate otherwise. For example, your id might feel an urge to clobber a co-worker who constantly irritates you. However, society frowns on such behavior, so your ego would try to hold this urge in check. Hence, you would find yourself in conflict. You may be experiencing conflict at this very moment. In

Freudian terms, your id may be secretly urging you to abandon reading this chapter so that you can fix a snack and watch some television. Your ego may be weighing this appealing option against your society-induced need to excel in school.

Freud believed that people's lives are dominated by conflict. He asserted that individuals career from one conflict to another. The following scenario provides a concrete illustration of how the three components of personality interact to create constant conflicts:

Imagine lurching across your bed to shut off your alarm clock as it rings obnoxiously. It's 7 A.M. and time to get up for your history class. However, your id (operating according to the pleasure principle) urges you to return to the immediate gratification of additional sleep. Your ego (operating according to the reality principle) points out that you really must go to class since you haven't been able to decipher the textbook on your own. Your id (in its typical unrealistic fashion) smugly assures you that you will get the A grade that you need and suggests lying back to dream about how impressed your roommates will be. Just as you're relaxing, your superego jumps into the fray. It tries to make you feel guilty about all the money your parents paid in tuition for the class that you're about to skip. You haven't even gotten out of bed yet, but there's already a pitched battle in your psyche.

Let's say your ego wins the battle. You pull yourself out of bed and head for class. On the way, you pass a donut shop and your id clamors for cinnamon rolls. Your ego reminds you that you're supposed to be on a diet. Your id wins this time. After you've attended your history lecture, your ego reminds you that you need to do some library research for a paper in philosophy. However, your id insists on returning to your apartment to watch some sitcom reruns. As you reenter your apartment, you're overwhelmed by how messy it is. It's your roommates' mess, and your id suggests that you tell them off. As you're about to lash out, however, your ego convinces you that diplomacy will be more effective. Three sitcoms later you find that you're in a debate with yourself about whether to go to the gym to work out or to the student union to play pool. It's only midafternoon—and already you've been through a series of internal conflicts.

Freud believed that conflicts centering on sexual and aggressive impulses are especially likely to have far-reaching consequences. Why did he emphasize sex and aggression? Two reasons were prominent in his thinking. First, he thought that sex and aggression are subject to more complex and ambiguous social controls than other basic motives. The norms governing sexual and aggressive behavior are subtle,

Freud's psychoanalytic theory was based on decades of clinical work. He treated a great many patients in the consulting room pictured here. The room contains numerous artifacts from other cultures—and the original psychoanalytic couch.

© Peter Aprahamian/CORBIS

and people often get inconsistent messages about what's appropriate. Thus, Freud believed that these two drives are the source of much confusion. Second, he noted that the sexual and aggressive drives are thwarted more regularly than other basic biological urges. Think about it: If you get hungry or thirsty, you can simply head for a nearby vending machine or a drinking fountain. But if a department store clerk infuriates you, you aren't likely to reach across the counter and slug him or her. Likewise, when you see a person who inspires lustful urges, you don't normally walk up and propose a tryst in a nearby broom closet. There's nothing comparable to vending machines or drinking fountains for the satisfaction of sexual and aggressive urges. Freud ascribed great importance to these needs because social norms dictate that they be routinely frustrated.

Anxiety and Defense Mechanisms

Most internal conflicts are trivial and are quickly resolved one way or the other. Occasionally, however, a conflict will linger for days, months, or even years, creating internal tension. More often than not, such prolonged and troublesome conflicts involve sexual and aggressive impulses that society wants to tame. These conflicts are often played out entirely in the unconscious. Although you may not be aware of these unconscious battles, they can produce *anxiety* that slips to the surface of conscious awareness. The anxiety can be attributed to your ego worrying about (1) the id getting out of control and doing something terrible that leads to severe negative consequences or (2) the superego getting out of control and making you feel guilty about a real or imagined transgression.

The arousal of anxiety is a crucial event in Freud's theory of personality functioning (see Figure 12.3). Anxiety is distressing, so people try to rid themselves of this unpleasant emotion any way they can. This effort to ward off anxiety often involves the use of defense mechanisms. *Defense mechanisms* **are largely unconscious reactions that protect a person from unpleasant emotions such as anxiety and guilt** (see Table 12.1). Typically, they're mental maneuvers that work through self-deception. Consider *rationalization,* **which is creating false but plausible excuses to justify unacceptable behavior.** For example, after cheating someone in a business transaction, you might reduce your guilt by rationalizing that "everyone does it."

Characterized as "the flagship in the psychoanalytic fleet of defense mechanisms" (Paulhus, Fridhandler, & Hayes, 1997), repression is the most basic and widely used defense mechanism. *Repression* **is keep-**ing distressing thoughts and feelings buried in the unconscious. People tend to repress desires that make them feel guilty, conflicts that make them anxious, and memories that are painful. Repression has been called "motivated forgetting." If you forget a dental appointment or the name of someone you don't like, repression may be at work.

Self-deception can also be seen in projection and displacement. *Projection* **is attributing one's own thoughts, feelings, or motives to another.** Usually, the thoughts one projects onto others are thoughts that would make one feel guilty. For example, if lusting for a co-worker makes you feel guilty, you might attribute any latent sexual tension between the two of you to the *other person's* desire to seduce you. *Displacement* **is diverting emotional feelings (usually anger) from their original source to a substitute target.** If your boss gives you a hard time at work and you come home and slam the door, kick the dog, and scream at your spouse, you're displacing your anger onto irrelevant targets. Unfortunately, social constraints often

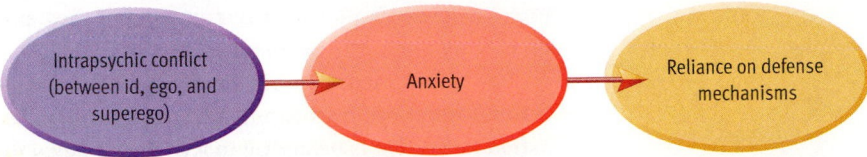

Figure 12.3

Freud's model of personality dynamics. According to Freud, unconscious conflicts between the id, ego, and superego sometimes lead to anxiety. This discomfort may lead to the use of defense mechanisms, which may temporarily relieve anxiety.

Table 12.1 Defense Mechanisms, with Examples

Defense Mechanism	Definition	Example
Repression	Keeping distressing thoughts and feelings buried in the unconscious	A traumatized soldier has no recollection of the details of a close brush with death.
Projection	Attributing one's own thoughts, feelings, or motives to another	A woman who dislikes her boss thinks she likes her boss but feels that the boss doesn't like her.
Displacement	Diverting emotional feelings (usually anger) from their original source to a substitute target	After parental scolding, a young girl takes her anger out on her little brother.
Reaction formation	Behaving in a way that is exactly the opposite of one's true feelings	A parent who unconsciously resents a child spoils the child with outlandish gifts.
Regression	A reversion to immature patterns of behavior	An adult has a temper tantrum when he doesn't get his way.
Rationalization	Creating false but plausible excuses to justify unacceptable behavior	A student watches TV instead of studying, saying that "additional study wouldn't do any good anyway."
Identification	Bolstering self-esteem by forming an imaginary or real alliance with some person or group	An insecure young man joins a fraternity to boost his self-esteem.

NOTE: See Table 13.2 for additional examples of defense mechanisms.

force people to hold back their anger, and they end up lashing out at the people they love most.

Other prominent defense mechanisms include reaction formation, regression, and identification. *Reaction formation* is behaving in a way that's exactly the opposite of one's true feelings. Guilt about sexual desires often leads to reaction formation. For example, Freud theorized that many males who ridicule homosexuals are defending against their own latent homosexual impulses. The telltale sign of reaction formation is the exaggerated quality of the opposite behavior. *Regression* is a reversion to immature patterns of behavior. When anxious about their self-worth, some adults respond with childish boasting and bragging (as opposed to subtle efforts to impress others). For example, a fired executive having difficulty finding a new job might start making ridiculous statements about his incomparable talents and achievements. Such bragging is regressive when it's marked by massive exaggerations that virtually anyone can see through. *Identification* is bolstering self-esteem by forming an imaginary or real alliance with some person or group. Youngsters often shore up precarious feelings of self-worth by identifying with rock stars, movie stars, or famous athletes. Adults may join exclusive country clubs or civic organizations as a means of identification.

Recent years have brought a revival of interest in research on defense mechanisms. For example, a series of studies have identified a *repressive coping style* and shown that "repressors" have an impoverished memory for emotional events and negative feedback and that they habitually avoid unpleasant emotions by distracting themselves with pleasant thoughts

and memories (Boden & Baumeister, 1997; Weinberger & Davidson, 1994). In another line of research, Newman, Duff, and Baumeister (1997) have shed new light on the cognitive dynamics of *projection*. Newman et al. showed that people actively work to suppress thoughts about the possibility that they might have an undesirable trait (say, dishonesty), but this ongoing effort makes thoughts about the unwanted trait highly accessible, so they chronically use this trait concept to explain others' behavior and end up routinely attributing the trait to others. Another very interesting study provided support for the Freudian hypothesis that reaction formation underlies homophobia in males. Adams, Wright, and Lohr (1996) found that when homophobic men are shown an erotic videotape depicting homosexual activity, they exhibit sexual arousal not seen in nonhomophobic subjects.

A great variety of theorists have made extensive additions to Freud's original list of defenses (Vaillant, 1992). We'll examine some of these additional defense mechanisms in the next chapter, when we discuss the role of defenses in coping with stress. For now, however, let's turn our attention to Freud's ideas about the development of personality.

Development: Psychosexual Stages

Freud believed that "the child is father to the man." In fact, he made the rather startling assertion that the basic foundation of an individual's personality has been laid down by the tender age of 5. To shed light on these crucial early years, Freud formulated a stage theory of development. He emphasized how young children deal with their immature but power-

---

CONCEPT **CHECK 12.1**

Identifying Defense Mechanisms

Check your understanding of defense mechanisms by identifying specific defenses in the story below. Each example of a defense mechanism is underlined, with a number beneath it. Write in the defense at work in each case in the numbered spaces after the story. The answers are in Appendix A.

My girlfriend recently broke up with me after we had dated seriously for several years. At first, I cried a great deal and <u>locked myself in my room, where I pouted endlessly.</u>[1] I was sure that my former girlfriend felt as miserable as I did. <u>I told several friends that she was probably lonely and depressed.</u>[2] Later, I decided that I hated her. <u>I was happy about the breakup and talked about how much I was going to enjoy my newfound freedom.</u>[3] I went to parties and socialized a great deal and just forgot about her. <u>It's funny—at one point I couldn't even remember her phone number!</u>[4] Then I started pining for her again. But eventually I began to look at the situation more objectively. I realized that she had many faults and that <u>we were bound to break up sooner or later, so I was better off without her.</u>[5]

1. _____   4. _____

2. _____   5. _____

3. _____

ful sexual urges (he used the term *sexual* in a general way to refer to many urges for physical pleasure). According to Freud, these sexual urges shift in focus as children progress from one stage of development to another. Indeed, the names for the stages (oral, anal, genital, and so on) are based on where children are focusing their erotic energy during that period. Thus, *psychosexual stages* are developmental periods with a characteristic sexual focus that leave their mark on adult personality.

Freud theorized that each psychosexual stage has its own, unique developmental challenges or tasks (see Table 12.2). The way these challenges are handled supposedly shapes personality. The process of *fixation* plays an important role in this process. *Fixation is a failure to move forward from one stage to another as expected.* Essentially, the child's development stalls for a while. Fixation can be caused by *excessive gratification* of needs at a particular stage or by *excessive frustration* of those needs. Either way, fixations left over from childhood affect adult personality. Generally, fixation leads to an overemphasis on the psychosexual needs prominent during the fixated stage. Freud described a series of five psychosexual stages. Let's examine some of the highlights in this sequence.

Oral Stage. This stage encompasses the first year of life. During this period, the main source of erotic stimulation is the mouth (in biting, sucking, chewing, and so on). In Freud's view, the handling of the child's feeding experiences is crucial to subsequent development. He attributed considerable importance to the manner in which the child is weaned from the breast or the bottle. According to Freud, fixation at the oral stage could form the basis for obsessive eating or smoking later in life (among many other things).

Anal Stage. In their second year, children get their erotic pleasure from their bowel movements, through either the expulsion or retention of feces. The cru-

© Michael Newman/PhotoEdit

According to Freud, early childhood experiences such as toilet training (a parental attempt to regulate a child's biological urges) can influence an individual's personality, with consequences lasting throughout adulthood.

Web Link 12.2

Sigmund Freud Museum, Vienna, Austria
This online museum, in both English and German versions, offers a detailed chronology of Freud's life and an explanation of the most important concepts of psychoanalysis. The highlights here, though, are the rich audiovisual resources, including photos, amateur movie clips, and voice recordings of Freud.

cial event at this time is toilet training, which represents society's first systematic effort to regulate the child's biological urges. Severely punitive toilet training leads to a variety of possible outcomes. For example, excessive punishment might produce a latent feeling of hostility toward the "trainer," usually the mother. This hostility might generalize to women as a class. Another possibility is that heavy reliance on punitive measures could lead to an association between genital concerns and the anxiety that the punishment arouses. This genital anxiety derived from severe toilet training could evolve into anxiety about sexual activities later in life.

Table 12-2 Freud's Stages of Psychosexual Development

Stage	Approximate Ages	Erotic Focus	Key Tasks and Experiences
Oral	0–1	Mouth (sucking, biting)	Weaning (from breast or bottle)
Anal	2–3	Anus (expelling or retaining feces)	Toilet training
Phallic	4–5	Genitals (masturbating)	Identifying with adult role models; coping with Oedipal crisis
Latency	6–12	None (sexually repressed)	Expanding social contacts
Genital	Puberty onward	Genitals (being sexually intimate)	Establishing intimate relationships; contributing to society through working

Phallic Stage. Around age 4, the genitals become the focus for the child's erotic energy, largely through self-stimulation. During this pivotal stage, the *Oedipal complex* emerges. That is, little boys develop an erotically tinged preference for their mother. They also feel hostility toward their father, whom they view as a competitor for mom's affection. Similarly, little girls develop a special attachment to their father. Around the same time, they learn that little boys have very different genitals, and supposedly they develop *penis envy*. According to Freud, young girls feel hostile toward their mother because they blame her for their anatomical "deficiency."

To summarize, **in the *Oedipal complex* children manifest erotically tinged desires for their opposite-sex parent, accompanied by feelings of hostility toward their same-sex parent.** The name for this syndrome was taken from a tragic myth from ancient Greece. In this story, Oedipus was separated from his parents at birth. Not knowing the identity of his real parents, when he grew up he inadvertently killed his father and married his mother.

According to Freud, the way parents and children deal with the sexual and aggressive conflicts inherent in the Oedipal complex is of paramount importance. The child has to resolve the Oedipal dilemma by purging the sexual longings for the opposite-sex parent and by crushing the hostility felt toward the same-sex parent. In Freud's view, healthy psychosexual development hinges on the resolution of the Oedipal conflict. Why? Because continued hostility toward the same-sex parent may prevent the child from identifying adequately with that parent. Freudian theory predicts that without such identification, sex typing, conscience, and many other aspects of the child's development won't progress as they should.

Latency and Genital Stages. From around age 6 through puberty, the child's sexuality is largely suppressed—it becomes *latent*. Important events during this *latency stage* center on expanding social contacts beyond the immediate family. With puberty, the child progresses into the *genital stage*. Sexual urges reappear and focus on the genitals once again. At this point, sexual energy is normally channeled toward peers of the other sex, rather than toward oneself as in the phallic stage.

In arguing that the early years shape personality, Freud did not mean that personality development comes to an abrupt halt in middle childhood. However, he did believe that the foundation for adult personality has been solidly entrenched by this time. He maintained that future developments are rooted in early, formative experiences and that significant conflicts in later years are replays of crises from childhood.

In fact, Freud believed that unconscious sexual conflicts rooted in childhood experiences cause most personality disturbances. His steadfast belief in the psychosexual origins of psychological disorders eventually led to bitter theoretical disputes with two of his most brilliant colleagues: Carl Jung and Alfred Adler. Jung and Adler both argued that Freud overemphasized sexuality. Freud rejected their ideas, and the other two theorists felt compelled to go their own way, developing their own theories of personality.

Jung's Analytical Psychology

Carl Jung was born to middle-class Swiss parents in 1875. The son of a Protestant pastor, he was a deeply introverted, lonely child, but an excellent student. Jung had earned his medical degree and was an established young psychiatrist in Zurich when he began to write to Freud in 1906. When the two men had their first meeting, they were so taken by each other's insights, they talked nonstop for 13 hours! They exchanged 359 letters before their friendship and theoretical alliance were torn apart. Their relationship was ruptured irreparably in 1913 by a variety of theoretical disagreements.

Jung called his new approach *analytical psychology* to differentiate it from Freud's psychoanalytic theory. Jung's analytical psychology eventually attracted many followers. Perhaps because of his conflicts with Freud, Jung claimed to deplore the way schools of thought often become dogmatic, discouraging new ideas. Although many theorists came to characterize themselves as "Jungians," Jung himself often remarked, "I am not a Jungian" and said, "I do not want anybody to be a Jungian. I want people above all to be themselves" (van der Post, 1975).

Like Freud, Jung (1921, 1933) emphasized the unconscious determinants of personality. However, he proposed that the unconscious consists of two layers. The first layer, called the *personal unconscious*, is essentially the same as Freud's version of the unconscious. **The *personal unconscious* houses material that is not within one's conscious awareness because it has been repressed or forgotten.** In addition, Jung theorized the existence of a deeper layer he called the collective unconscious. **The *collective unconscious* is a storehouse of latent memory traces inherited from people's ancestral past.** According to Jung, each person shares the collective unconscious with the entire human race (see Figure 12.4). It contains the "whole spiritual heritage of mankind's evolution, born anew in the brain structure of every individual" (Jung, quoted in Campbell, 1971, p. 45).

Culver Pictures, Inc.

"I am not a Jungian . . . I do not want anybody to be a Jungian. I want people above all to be themselves."
CARL JUNG

Web Link 12.3

C. G. Jung, Analytical Psychology, & Culture
Synchronicity, archetypes, collective unconscious, introversion, extraversion—these and many other important concepts arising from analytical psychology and Jung's tremendously influential theorizing are examined at this comprehensive site.

Jung called these ancestral memories *archetypes*. They are not memories of actual, personal experiences. Instead, *archetypes* **are emotionally charged images and thought forms that have universal meaning.** These archetypal images and ideas show up frequently in dreams and are often manifested in a culture's use of symbols in art, literature, and religion. According to Jung, symbols from very different cultures often show striking similarities because they emerge from archetypes that are shared by the whole human race. For instance, Jung found numerous cultures in which the *mandala*, or "magic circle," has served as a symbol of the unified wholeness of the self (see Figure 12.4). Jung felt that an understanding of archetypal symbols helped him make sense of his patients' dreams. This was of great concern to him, as he thought that dreams contain important messages from the unconscious. Like Freud, he depended extensively on dream analysis in his treatment of patients.

Jung's unusual ideas about the collective unconscious had little impact on the mainstream of thinking in psychology. Their influence was felt more in other fields, such as anthropology, philosophy, art, and religious studies. However, many of Jung's other ideas *have* been incorporated into the mainstream of psychology. For instance, Jung was the first to describe the introverted (inner-directed) and extraverted (outer-directed) personality types. **Introverts tend to be preoccupied with the internal world of their own thoughts, feelings, and experiences.** Like Jung himself, they generally are contemplative and aloof. In contrast, *extraverts* **tend to be interested in the external world of people and things.** They're more likely to be outgoing, talkative, and friendly, instead of reclusive.

Adler's Individual Psychology

Like Freud, Alfred Adler grew up in Vienna in a middle-class Jewish home. He was a sickly child who struggled to overcome rickets and an almost fatal case of pneumonia. At home, he was overshadowed by an exceptionally bright and successful older brother. Nonetheless, he went on to earn his medical degree, and he practiced ophthalmology and general medicine before his interest turned to psychiatry. He was a charter member of Freud's inner circle—the Vienna Psychoanalytic Society. However, he soon began to develop his own theory of personality, perhaps because he didn't want to be dominated once again by an "older brother" (Freud). His theorizing was denounced by Freud in 1911, and Adler was forced to

Culver Pictures, Inc.

❝*The goal of the human soul is conquest, perfection, security, superiority.*❞
ALFRED ADLER

Figure 12.4

Jung's vision of the collective unconscious. Much like Freud, Jung theorized that each person has conscious and unconscious levels of awareness. However, he also proposed that the entire human race shares a collective unconscious, which exists in the deepest reaches of everyone's awareness. He saw the collective unconscious as a storehouse of hidden ancestral memories, called archetypes. Jung believed that important cultural symbols emerge from these universal archetypes. Thus, he argued that remarkable resemblances among symbols from disparate cultures (such as the mandalas shown here) are evidence of the existence of the collective unconscious.

SOURCE: Images from C. G. Jung Bild Und Wort, © Walter-Verlag AG, Olten, Switzerland, 1977

Mandalas from various cultures

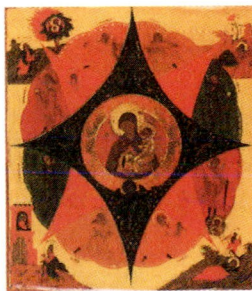
Russia

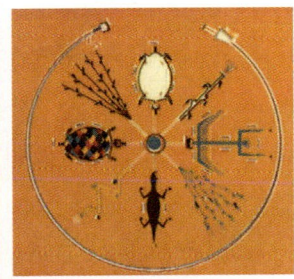
Navajo Indians

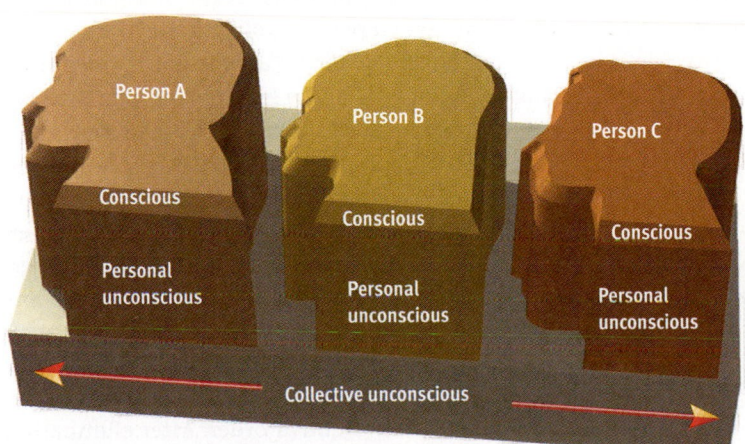

Tibet

resign from the Psychoanalytic Society. He took 9 of its 23 members with him to form his own organization. Adler's new approach to personality was christened *individual psychology*.

Like Jung, Adler (1917, 1927) argued that Freud had gone overboard in centering his theory on sexual conflicts. According to Adler, the foremost source of human motivation is a striving for superiority. In his view, this striving does not necessarily translate into the pursuit of dominance or high status. Adler saw *striving for superiority* **as a universal drive to adapt, improve oneself, and master life's challenges.** He noted that young children understandably feel weak and helpless in comparison with more competent older children and adults. These early inferiority feelings supposedly motivate them to acquire new skills and develop new talents. Thus, Adler maintained that striving for superiority is the prime goal of life, rather than physical gratification (as suggested by Freud).

Adler asserted that everyone has to work to overcome some feelings of inferiority—a process he called compensation. *Compensation* **involves efforts to overcome imagined or real inferiorities by developing one's abilities.** Adler believed that compensation is entirely normal. However, in some people inferiority feelings can become excessive, resulting in what is widely known today as an *inferiority complex*—

exaggerated feelings of weakness and inadequacy. Adler thought that either parental pampering or parental neglect could cause an inferiority complex. Thus, he agreed with Freud on the importance of early childhood experiences, although he focused on different aspects of parent-child relations.

Adler explained personality disturbances by noting that excessive inferiority feelings can pervert the normal process of striving for superiority. He asserted that some people engage in *overcompensation* to conceal, even from themselves, their feelings of inferiority. Instead of working to master life's challenges, people with an inferiority complex work to achieve status, gain power over others, and acquire the trappings of success (fancy clothes, impressive cars, or whatever looks important to them). They tend to flaunt their success in an effort to cover up their underlying inferiority complex. However, the problem is that such people engage in unconscious self-deception, worrying more about *appearances* than *reality*.

Adler's theory stressed the social context of personality development (Hoffman, 1994). For instance, it was Adler who first focused attention on the possible importance of *birth order* as a factor governing personality. He noted that first-borns, second children, and later-born children enter varied home environments and are treated differently by parents and that these experiences are likely to affect their personality. For example, he hypothesized that only children are often spoiled by excessive attention from parents and that first-borns are often problem children because they become upset when they're "dethroned" by a second child. Adler's theory stimulated hundreds of studies on the effects of birth order, but these studies generally failed to support his hypotheses and did not uncover any reliable correlations between birth order and personality (Ernst & Angst, 1983; Harris, 2000).

In recent years, however, Frank Sulloway (1995, 1996) has argued persuasively that birth order *does* have an impact on personality. Sulloway's reformulated hypotheses focus on how the Big Five traits are shaped by competition among siblings as they struggle to find a "niche" in their family environments. For example, he hypothesizes that first-borns should be more conscientious but less agreeable and open to experience than later-borns. In light of these personality patterns, he further speculates that first-borns tend to be conventional and achievement oriented, whereas later-borns tend to be liberal and rebellious. To evaluate his hypotheses, Sulloway reexamined decades of research on birth order. After eliminating

Adler's theory has been used to analyze the tragic life of the legendary actress Marilyn Monroe (Ansbacher, 1970). During her childhood, Monroe suffered from parental neglect that left her with acute feelings of inferiority. Her inferiority feelings led her to overcompensate by flaunting her beauty, marrying celebrities (Joe DiMaggio and Arthur Miller), keeping film crews waiting for hours, and seeking the adoration of her fans.

Bettmann/CORBIS

many studies that failed to control for important confounding variables, such as social class and family size, he concluded that the results of the remaining, well-controlled studies provided impressive evidence in favor of his hypotheses. Some subsequent studies have provided additional support for Sulloway's analyses (Paulhus, Trapnell, & Chen, 1999), but others have not (Freese, Powell, & Steelman, 1999; Harris, 2000). More studies will be needed, as research on birth order is enjoying a bit of a renaissance.

Evaluating Psychodynamic Perspectives

The psychodynamic approach has provided a number of far-reaching, truly "grand" theories of personality. These theories yielded some bold new insights when they were first presented. Although one might argue about exact details of interpretation, research has demonstrated that (1) unconscious forces can influence behavior, (2) internal conflict often plays a key role in generating psychological distress, (3) early childhood experiences can have powerful influences on adult personality, and (4) people do use defense mechanisms to reduce their experience of unpleasant emotions (Westen, 1998; Westen & Gabbard, 1999).

In addition to being praised, psychodynamic formulations have also been criticized on several grounds, including the following (Eysenck, 1990b; Fine, 1990; Macmillan, 1991; Torrey, 1992):

1. *Poor testability.* Scientific investigations require testable hypotheses. Psychodynamic ideas have often been too vague and conjectural to permit a clear scientific test. For instance, how would you prove or disprove the assertion that the id is entirely unconscious?

2. *Inadequate evidence.* The empirical evidence on psychodynamic theories has often been characterized as "inadequate." Psychodynamic theories depend too heavily on clinical case studies in which it's much too easy for clinicians to see what they expect to see. Reexaminations of Freud's own clinical work suggest that he frequently distorted his patients' case histories to make them mesh with his theory (Esterson, 1993; Powell & Boer, 1995). Insofar as researchers have accumulated evidence on psychodynamic theories, the evidence has provided only modest support for many of the central hypotheses (Fisher & Greenberg, 1985, 1996; Westen & Gabbard, 1999).

3. *Sexism.* Many critics have argued that psychodynamic theories are characterized by a sexist bias against women. Freud believed that females' penis envy made them feel inferior to males. He also thought that females tended to develop weaker superegos and to be more prone to neurosis than males. The sex bias in modern psychodynamic theories has been reduced considerably. Nonetheless, the psychodynamic approach has generally provided a rather male-centered point of view (Lerman, 1986; Person, 1990).

It's easy to ridicule Freud for concepts such as penis envy, and it's easy to point to Freudian ideas that have turned out to be wrong. However, you have to remember that Freud, Jung, and Adler began to fashion their theories over a century ago. It's not entirely fair to compare these theories to other models that are only a decade or two old. That's like asking the Wright brothers to race the Concorde. Freud and his colleagues deserve great credit for breaking new ground with their speculations about psychodynamics. In psychology as a whole, no other school of thought has been as influential, with the exception of behaviorism, which we turn to next.

REVIEW OF KEY POINTS

- Psychodynamic approaches include all the theories derived from Freud's insights. Freud described personality structure in terms of three components—the id, ego, and superego—which are routinely involved in an ongoing series of internal conflicts.

- Freud described three levels of awareness: the conscious, the preconscious, and the unconscious. His theory emphasized the importance of unconscious processes. Freud theorized that conflicts centering on sex and aggression are especially likely to lead to significant anxiety. According to Freud, anxiety and other unpleasant emotions such as guilt are often warded off with defense mechanisms.

- Freud believed that the first five years of life are extremely influential in shaping adult personality. He described a series of five psychosexual stages of development: oral, anal, phallic, latency, and genital. Certain experiences during these stages can have lasting effects on adult personality. Resolution of the Oedipal complex is thought to be particularly critical to healthy development.

- Jung's most innovative concept was the collective unconscious, a storehouse of latent memory traces inherited from people's ancestral past. Archetypes are emotionally charged images that have universal meaning. Jung also provided the first description of introversion and extraversion.

- Adler's individual psychology emphasizes how people strive for superiority to compensate for their feelings of inferiority. He explained personality disturbances in terms of overcompensation and inferiority complexes.

- Overall, psychodynamic theories have produced many groundbreaking insights about the unconscious, the role of internal conflict, and the importance of early childhood experiences in personality development. However, psychodynamic theories have been criticized for their poor testability, their inadequate base of empirical evidence, and their male-centered views.

Behavioral Perspectives

PREVIEW QUESTIONS

- How can Skinner's theory explain personality and its development?
- How did Bandura revise the behavioral approach to personality?
- What is self-efficacy, and how does it affect behavior?
- How did Mischel question the concept of personality?
- What are the strengths and weaknesses of the behavioral approach?

Behaviorism is a theoretical orientation based on the premise that scientific psychology should study only observable behavior. As we saw in Chapter 1, behaviorism has been a major school of thought in psychology since 1913, when John B. Watson began campaigning for the behavioral point of view. Research in the behavioral tradition has focused largely on learning. For many decades behaviorists devoted relatively little attention to the study of personality. However, their interest in personality began to pick up after John Dollard and Neal Miller (1950) attempted to translate selected Freudian ideas into behavioral terminology. Dollard and Miller showed that behavioral concepts could provide enlightening insights about the complicated subject of personality.

In this section, we'll examine three behavioral views of personality, as we discuss the ideas of B. F. Skinner, Albert Bandura, and Walter Mischel. For the most part, you'll see that behaviorists explain personality the same way they explain everything else—in terms of learning.

Skinner's Ideas Applied to Personality

As we noted in Chapters 1 and 6, modern behaviorism's most prominent theorist has been B. F. Skinner, an American psychologist who lived from 1904 to 1990. After earning his doctorate in 1931, Skinner spent most of his career at Harvard University. There he achieved renown for his research on the principles of learning, which were mostly discovered through the study of rats and pigeons. Skinner's (1953, 1957) concepts of *operant conditioning* were never meant to be a theory of personality. However, his ideas have affected thinking in all areas of psychology and have been applied to the explanation of personality. Here we'll examine Skinner's views as they relate to personality structure and development.

Personality Structure: A View from the Outside

Skinner made no provision for internal personality structures similar to Freud's id, ego, and superego because such structures can't be observed. Following in the tradition of Watson's radical behaviorism, Skinner showed little interest in what goes on "inside" people. He argued that it's useless to speculate about private, unobservable cognitive processes. Instead, he focused on how the external environment molds overt behavior. Indeed, he argued for a strong brand of *determinism*, asserting that behavior is fully determined by environmental stimuli. He claimed that free will is but an illusion, saying, "There is no place in the scientific position for a self as a true originator or initiator of action" (Skinner, 1974, p. 225).

How can Skinner's theory explain the consistency that can be seen in individuals' behavior? According to his view, people show some consistent patterns of behavior because they have some stable *response tendencies* that they have acquired through experience. These response tendencies may change in the future, as a result of new experience, but they're enduring enough to create a certain degree of consistency in a person's behavior. Implicitly, then, Skinner viewed an individual's personality as a *collection of response tendencies that are tied to various stimulus situations*. A specific situation may be associated with a number of response tendencies that vary in strength, depending on past conditioning (see Figure 12.5).

Personality Development as a Product of Conditioning

Skinner's theory accounts for personality development by explaining how various response tendencies are acquired through learning. He believed that most human responses are shaped by the type of conditioning that he described: operant conditioning. As we discussed in Chapter 6, Skinner maintained that environmental consequences—reinforcement, punishment, and extinction—determine people's pat-

---

Figure 12.5

A behavioral view of personality. Staunch behaviorists devote little attention to the structure of personality because it is unobservable, but they implicitly view personality as an individual's collection of response tendencies. A possible hierarchy of response tendencies for a particular person in a specific stimulus situation (a large party) is shown here.

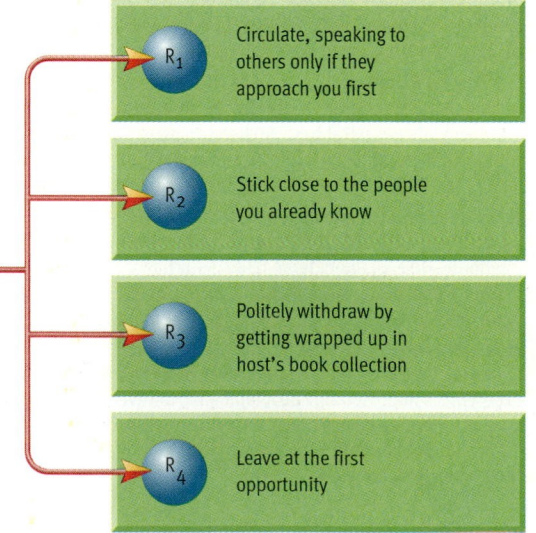

Stimulus situation

Large party where you know relatively few people

Operant response tendencies

R₁ Circulate, speaking to others only if they approach you first

R₂ Stick close to the people you already know

R₃ Politely withdraw by getting wrapped up in host's book collection

R₄ Leave at the first opportunity

terns of responding. On the one hand, when responses are followed by favorable consequences (reinforcement), they are strengthened. For example, if your joking at a party pays off with favorable attention, your tendency to joke at parties will increase (see Figure 12.6). On the other hand, when responses lead to negative consequences (punishment), they are weakened. Thus, if your impulsive decisions always backfire, your tendency to be impulsive will decline.

Because response tendencies are constantly being strengthened or weakened by new experiences, Skinner's theory views personality development as a continuous, lifelong journey. Unlike Freud and many other theorists, Skinner saw no reason to break the developmental process into stages. Nor did he attribute special importance to early childhood experiences.

Skinner believed that conditioning in humans operates much the same as in the rats and pigeons that he studied in his laboratory. Hence, he assumed that conditioning strengthens and weakens response tendencies "mechanically"—that is, without the person's conscious participation. Thus, Skinner was able to explain consistencies in behavior (personality) without being concerned about individuals' cognitive processes.

Skinner's ideas continue to be highly influential, but his mechanical, deterministic, noncognitive view of personality has not gone unchallenged by other behaviorists. In recent decades, several theorists have developed somewhat different behavioral models with a more cognitive emphasis.

Bandura's Social Cognitive Theory

Albert Bandura is a modern theorist who has helped reshape the theoretical landscape of behaviorism. Bandura grew up in Canada and earned his doctorate in psychology at the University of Iowa. He has spent his entire academic career at Stanford University, where he has conducted influential research on behavior therapy and the determinants of aggression.

Cognitive Processes and Reciprocal Determinism

Bandura is one of several theorists who have added a cognitive flavor to behaviorism since the 1960s. Bandura (1977), Walter Mischel (1973), and Julian Rotter (1982) take issue with Skinner's "pure" behaviorism. They point out that humans obviously are conscious, thinking, feeling beings. Moreover, these theorists argue that in neglecting cognitive processes, Skinner ignored the most distinctive and important feature of human behavior. Bandura and like-minded theorists originally called their modified brand of behaviorism *social learning theory*. Today, Bandura refers to his model as *social cognitive theory*.

Bandura (1982, 1986) agrees with the fundamental thrust of behaviorism in that he believes that personality is largely shaped through learning. However, he contends that conditioning is not a mechanical process in which people are passive participants. Instead, he maintains that "people are self-organizing, proactive, self-reflecting, and self-regulating, not just reactive organisms shaped and shepherded by external events" (Bandura, 1999, p. 154). Bandura (2001, p. 7) also emphasizes the important role of forward-directed planning, noting that "people set goals for themselves, anticipate the likely consequences of prospective actions, and select and create courses of action likely to produce desired outcomes and avoid detrimental ones."

Comparing his theory to Skinner's highly deterministic view, Bandura advocates a position called *reciprocal determinism*. According to this notion, the

Figure 12.6

Personality development and operant conditioning. According to Skinner, people's characteristic response tendencies are shaped by reinforcers and other consequences that follow behavior. Thus, if your joking at a party leads to attention and compliments, your tendency to be witty and humorous will be strengthened.

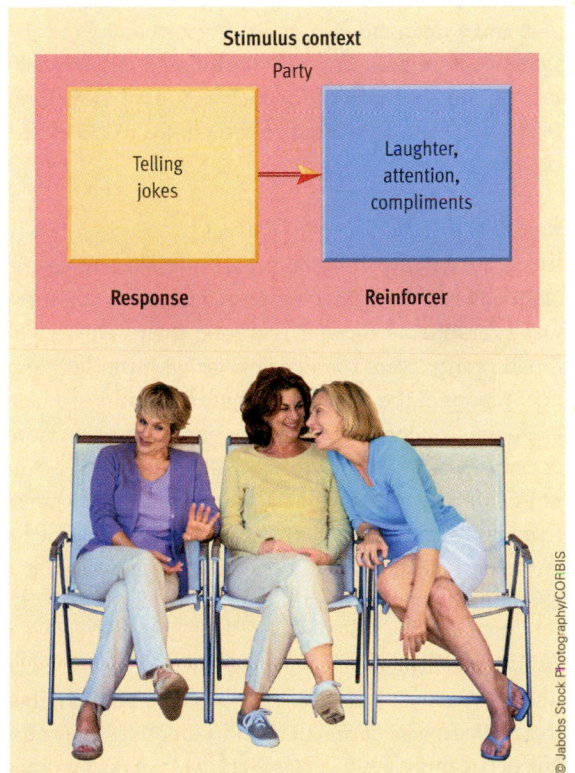

"The practice of looking inside the organism for an explanation of behavior has tended to obscure the variables which are immediately available for a scientific analysis. These variables lie outside the organism, in its immediate environment and in its environmental history. . . . The objection to inner states is not that they do not exist, but that they are not relevant."
B. F. SKINNER

"Most human behavior is learned by observation through modeling."
ALBERT BANDURA

environment does determine behavior (as Skinner would argue). However, behavior also determines the environment (in other words, people can act to alter their environment). Moreover, personal factors (cognitive structures such as beliefs and expectancies) determine and are determined by both behavior and the environment (see Figure 12.7). Thus, *reciprocal determinism* is the idea that internal mental events, external environmental events, and overt behavior all influence one another. According to Bandura, humans are neither masters of their own destiny nor hapless victims buffeted about by the environment. To some extent, people shape their environments, an observation that brings us to our Featured Study, which looked at how individuals mold their physical environments—and the clues that these environments can provide about personality.

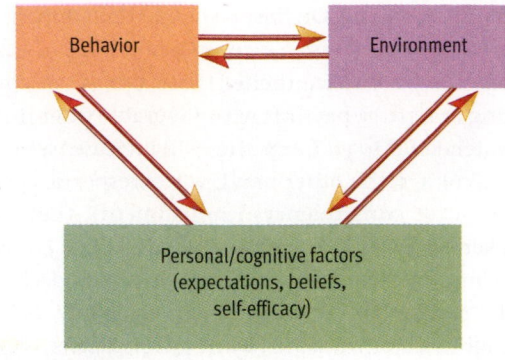

Figure 12.7

Bandura's reciprocal determinism. Bandura rejects Skinner's highly deterministic view that behavior is governed by environment and that freedom is an illusion. Bandura argues that internal mental events, external environmental contingencies, and overt behavior all influence one another.

Investigators: Samuel D. Gosling and Sei Jin Ko (University of Texas at Austin), Thomas Mannarelli (INSEAD, Singapore), and Margaret E. Morris (Sapient, San Francisco)

Source: A room with a cue: Personality judgments based on offices and bedrooms. *Journal of Personality and Social Psychology,* 2002, *82,* 379–398.

FEATURED STUDY

Can Rooms *Really* Have Personality?

You may have heard someone comment that a particular house or specific room "has personality." This metaphor is usually intended to convey that the house or room is unusual or distinctive. But Bandura's point that people proactively choose and shape their environments raises the possibility that rooms could *literally* have personality—the personality of their occupants.

A variety of theories assert that individuals select and create their social and physical environments to match their dispositions and self-views. For example, people who choose formal or informal furniture or conventional versus unconventional decorating convey something about who they are, as do people who display a Kurt Cobain poster or photos of their travels. In places where they dwell, people also leave a *behavioral residue*—remnants of their activities, such as books, magazines, computer printouts, drawings, musical instruments, snacks, and discarded beer cans. Cognizant of these realities, Samuel Gosling and his colleagues set out to determine just how much observers can infer about an individual's personality based on visiting the person's office or bedroom. We will examine the study of offices in more detail and then summarize the results of the study of bedrooms.

Method

Occupants and observations. Ninety-four office occupants in five urban office buildings agreed to participate. Eight independent observers examined each participant's office and rated the occupant (who was not present) on a 44-item scale that assessed the Big Five personality traits. All photos of the occupants and refer-

ences to their names were covered before the observers visited the offices. The intent was to see how ordinary people arrive at everyday impressions, so the observers had no special training or expertise.

Assessments of accuracy. To gauge the accuracy of the observers' personality inferences, the office occupants were asked to submit personality ratings of themselves and to suggest two peers who knew them well and who could also rate their personality (on the same 44-item scale used by the observers). The self-ratings and peer-ratings for each occupant were combined and then compared to the ratings made by the observers.

Results

Moderate positive correlations were found among the eight observers' personality ratings, indicating that there was a reasonable consensus among them. Their combined ratings were then correlated with the self- and peer-ratings of the occupants. These correlations, which averaged .22, indicated that the observers were more accurate at judging some traits than others (see Figure 12.8). The assessments of the occupants' openness to experience were very impressive and the judgments of the occupants' extraversion, conscientiousness, and emotional stability were substantial.

Follow-Up Study

A second study, focusing on individuals' bedrooms rather than offices, was conducted using identical methods. The occupants were 83 college students or recent graduates living near a university in apartments, houses, and dormitories. Once again, there was reasonable consensus among the observers' personality ratings. However, the accuracy of the ratings based on people's bedrooms was noticeably higher (average correlation of .37) than it was for offices. As in the first study, the inferences about some traits were more accurate than others (see Figure 12.8), with ratings of openness to experience yielding the greatest accuracy.

Discussion

The authors conclude that "much can be learned about persons from the spaces in which they dwell" (p. 397) and that personal dwellings yield more valid cues for certain traits than for others. To put their findings in context, they note that on some personality traits, the room-based ratings were more accurate than similar ratings from other studies that were based on long-term acquaintance! They speculate that bedrooms may be richer sources of information about their occupants than offices because people have more freedom to decorate bedrooms as they please and less need to project a professional image.

Comment

This study was featured because it took a creative approach to exploring an interesting phenomenon that has never before been subjected to scientific analysis. In retrospect, it seems readily apparent that people try to convey something about themselves in their dwellings and that visitors do form impressions based on these cues—but no one had previously thought to study these processes empirically. The creativity required to launch an entirely new line of research is apparent in one of its quirks: Who were the subjects? The occupants of the rooms? The observers who made the personality

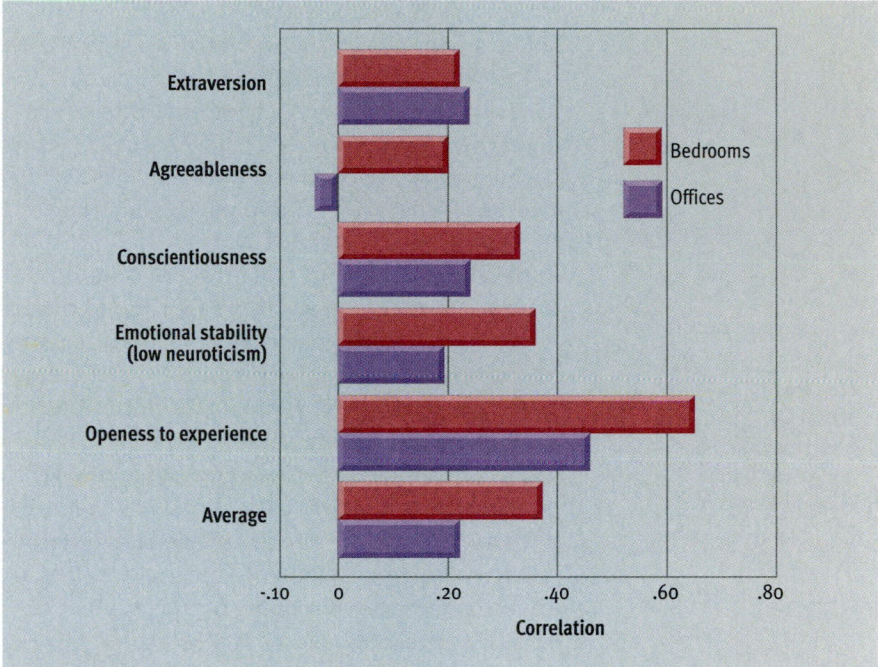

Figure 12.8

Accuracy of personality ratings based on people's rooms. To assess the accuracy of observers' personality ratings based on visiting people's offices or bedrooms, Gosling et al. (2002) correlated the observers' aggregated ratings with the combined self- and peer-ratings of the occupants of the rooms. Higher correlations are indicative of greater accuracy. If observers were not able to infer anything meaningful about occupants' personalities based on visiting their offices or bedrooms, these correlations would hover near zero, which was true in only one case (the ratings of agreeableness based on office visits). (Based on data from Gosling et al., 2002)

ratings? The participants in research are normally obvious—but in this case it is rather ambiguous. In any event, this study demonstrated that the relationship between personality and environment is a reciprocal one, as envisioned by Bandura. ■

Observational Learning

Bandura's foremost theoretical contribution has been his description of observational learning, which we introduced in Chapter 6. **Observational learning occurs when an organism's responding is influenced by the observation of others, who are called models.** According to Bandura, both classical and operant conditioning can occur vicariously when one person observes another's conditioning. For example, watching your sister get cheated by someone giving her a bad check for her old stereo could strengthen your tendency to be suspicious of others. Although your sister would be the one actually experiencing the negative consequences, they might also influence you—through observational learning.

Bandura maintains that people's characteristic patterns of behavior are shaped by the *models* that they're exposed to. He isn't referring to the fashion models who dominate the mass media—although they do qualify. In observational learning, a *model* is a person whose behavior is observed by another. At one time or another, everyone serves as a model for others. Bandura's key point is that many response tendencies are the product of imitation.

As research has accumulated, it has become apparent that some models are more influential than others (Bandura, 1986). Both children and adults tend to imitate people they like or respect more than people they don't. People are also especially prone to imitate the behavior of people whom they con-

Web Link 12.4

Television & Violence—Media and Communications Studies Site
Albert Bandura's early studies on the effect of television watching on the development of aggression spawned a wide spectrum of research about media influences on personality and behavior. This subpage at Daniel Chandler's well-known site gathers important research and reflections on the issue.

"It seems remarkable how each of us generally manages to reconcile his seemingly diverse behavior into one self-consistent whole."
WALTER MISCHEL

sider attractive or powerful (such as rock stars). In addition, imitation is more likely when people see similarity between models and themselves. Thus, children tend to imitate same-sex role models somewhat more than opposite-sex models. Finally, people are more likely to copy a model if they observe that the model's behavior leads to positive outcomes.

Self-Efficacy

Bandura discusses how a variety of personal factors (aspects of personality) govern behavior. In recent years, the factor he has emphasized most is self-efficacy (Bandura, 1990, 1993, 1995). *Self-efficacy* refers to one's belief about one's ability to perform behaviors that should lead to expected outcomes. When self-efficacy is high, individuals feel confident that they can execute the responses necessary to earn reinforcers. When self-efficacy is low, individuals worry that the necessary responses may be beyond their abilities. Perceptions of self-efficacy are subjective and specific to certain kinds of tasks. For instance, you might feel extremely confident about your ability to handle difficult social situations but doubtful about your ability to handle academic challenges.

Perceptions of self-efficacy can influence which challenges people tackle and how well they perform. Studies have found that feelings of greater self-efficacy are associated with greater success in giving up smoking (Boudreaux et al., 1998), greater adherence to an exercise regimen (Rimal, 2001), better outcomes in substance abuse treatment (Bandura, 1999), more success in coping with medical rehabilitation (Waldrop et al., 2001), better self-care among diabetics (Williams & Bond, 2002), greater persistence and effort in academic pursuits (Zimmerman, 1995), higher levels of academic performance (Chemers, Hu, & Garcia, 2001), reduced vulnerability to anxiety and depression in childhood (Muris, 2002), enhanced performance in athletic competition (Kane et al., 1996), greater receptiveness to technological training (Christoph, Schoenfeld, & Tansky, 1998), higher work-related performance (Stajkovic & Luthans, 1998), and greater resistance to stress (Jex et al., 2001), among many other things.

What are the developmental antecedents of high self-efficacy? Schneewind (1995) asserts that parents can foster self-efficacy by providing a stimulating environment and by being responsive to their children's behavior. An emphasis on warm support for children, early independence training, and nonpunitive disciplinary techniques is also helpful. In contrast, parents who are authoritarian, intrusive, overprotective, or neglectful are likely to undermine self-efficacy in their offspring.

Mischel and the Person-Situation Controversy

Walter Mischel was born in Vienna, not far from Freud's home. His family immigrated to the United States in 1939, when he was 9. After earning his doctorate in psychology, he spent many years on the faculty at Stanford, as a colleague of Bandura's. He has since moved to Columbia University.

Like Bandura, Mischel (1973, 1984) is an advocate of social learning theory. Mischel's chief contribution to personality theory has been to focus attention on the extent to which situational factors govern behavior. According to social learning theory, people try to gauge the reinforcement contingencies and adjust their behavior to the circumstances. For example, if you believe that hard work in your job will pay off by leading to raises and promotions, you'll probably be diligent and industrious. But if you think that hard work in your job is unlikely to be rewarded, you may act lazy and irresponsible. Thus, social learning theory predicts that people will often behave differently in different situations.

Mischel (1968, 1973) reviewed decades of research and concluded that, indeed, people exhibit far less consistency across situations than had been widely assumed. For example, studies show that a person who is honest in one situation may be dishonest in another. Someone who wouldn't dream of being dishonest in a business deal might engage in wholesale cheating in filling out tax returns. Similarly, some people are quite shy in one situation and outgoing in another. In light of these realities, Mischel maintains that behavior is characterized by more *situational specificity* than consistency.

Mischel's position has generated great controversy because it strikes at the heart of the concept of personality itself. As we discussed at the beginning of the chapter, the concept of personality is used to explain consistency in people's behavior over time and situations. If there isn't much consistency, there isn't much need for the concept of personality.

Mischel's views have attracted many critics who have sought to defend the value of the personality concept. For instance, Epstein (1980, 1986) argued that the methods used in much of the research reviewed by Mischel led to an underestimate of cross-situational consistency. Critics also noted that it is unreasonable to expect complete cross-situational consistency, because specific traits are more easily expressed in some situations than others (Kenrick & Funder, 1991). For example, a person's fun-loving, humorous qualities aren't likely to be apparent at a funeral where everyone is expected to be somber.

University photographer Joe Pineiro: Columbia University

Thus, Mischel's provocative theories have sparked a robust debate about the relative importance of the *person* as opposed to the *situation* in determining behavior. This debate has led to a growing recognition that *both* the person and the situation are important determinants of behavior (Funder, 2001; Mischel & Shoda, 1999).

Evaluating Behavioral Perspectives

Behavioral theories are firmly rooted in extensive empirical research rather than clinical intuition. Skinner's ideas have shed light on how environmental consequences and conditioning mold people's characteristic behavior. Bandura's social cognitive theory has expanded the horizons of behaviorism and increased its relevance to the study of personality. Mischel deserves credit for increasing psychology's awareness of how situational factors shape behavior.

Of course, each theoretical approach has its weaknesses and shortcomings, and the behavioral approach is no exception. Major lines of criticism include the following (Liebert & Liebert, 1998; Maddi, 1989):

1. *Overdependence on animal research.* Many principles in behavioral theories have been discovered through research on rats and other animals. Some critics argue that behaviorists have depended too much on animal research and that they have indiscriminately generalized from animal behavior to human behavior.

2. *Dehumanizing nature of radical behaviorism.* Skinner and other radical behaviorists have been criticized heavily for denying the existence of free will and the importance of cognitive processes. The critics argue that the radical behaviorist viewpoint strips

human behavior of its most uniquely human elements and that it therefore cannot provide an accurate model of human functioning.

3. *Fragmentation of personality.* Behaviorists have also been criticized for providing a fragmented view of personality. The behavioral approach carves personality up into stimulus-response associations. There are no unifying structural concepts (such as Freud's ego) that tie these pieces together. Humanistic theorists, whom we shall cover next, have been particularly vocal in criticizing this piecemeal analysis of personality.

REVIEW OF KEY POINTS

● Behavioral theories explain how personality is shaped through learning. Skinner had little interest in unobservable cognitive processes and embraced a strong determinism.

● Skinner's followers view personality as a collection of response tendencies tied to specific stimulus situations. They assume that personality development is a lifelong process in which response tendencies are shaped and reshaped by learning, especially operant conditioning.

● Social learning theory focuses on how cognitive factors such as expectancies regulate learned behavior. Bandura's concept of observational learning accounts for the acquisition of responses from models. High self-efficacy has been related to successful health regimens, academic success, and athletic performance, among other things.

● Mischel has questioned the degree to which people display cross-situational consistency in behavior. Mischel's arguments have increased psychologists' awareness of the situational determinants of behavior.

● Behavioral approaches to personality are based on rigorous research. They have provided ample insights into how environmental factors and learning mold personalities. The behaviorists have been criticized for their overdependence on animal research, their fragmented analysis of personality, and radical behaviorism's dehumanizing view of human nature.

Humanistic Perspectives

Humanistic theory emerged in the 1950s as something of a backlash against the behavioral and psychodynamic theories that we have just discussed (Cassel, 2000; DeCarvalho, 1991). The principal charge hurled at these two models was that they are dehumanizing. Freudian theory was criticized for its belief that behavior is dominated by primitive, animalistic drives. Behaviorism was criticized for its preoccupation with animal research and for its mechanistic, fragmented view of personality. Critics argued that both schools of thought are too deterministic and that both fail to recognize the unique qualities of human behavior.

Many of these critics blended into a loose alliance that came to be known as humanism, because of its exclusive focus on human behavior. **Humanism is a theoretical orientation that emphasizes the unique qualities of humans, especially their freedom and their potential for personal growth.** Humanistic psychologists don't believe that animal research can reveal anything of any significance about the human condition. In contrast to most psychodynamic and behavioral theorists, humanistic theorists take an optimistic view of human nature. They assume that (1) people can rise above their primitive animal her-

PREVIEW QUESTIONS

● What led to the emergence of humanism, and what are its central assumptions?

● How did Rogers explain the development of the self and defensive behavior?

● How did Maslow organize motives?

● What was Maslow's view of the healthy personality?

● What are the strengths and weaknesses of the humanistic approach?

itage and control their biological urges, and (2) people are largely conscious and rational beings who are not dominated by unconscious, irrational needs and conflicts.

Humanistic theorists also maintain that a person's subjective view of the world is more important than objective reality. According to this notion, if you think that you're homely or bright or sociable, this belief will influence your behavior more than the realities of how homely, bright, or sociable you actually are. Therefore, the humanists embrace the *phenomenological approach*, which assumes that one has to appreciate individuals' personal, subjective experiences to truly understand their behavior. As Carl Rogers (1951) put it, "The best vantage point for understanding behavior is from the internal frame of reference of the individual himself" (p. 494). Let's look at Rogers's ideas.

Rogers's Person-Centered Theory

Carl Rogers (1951, 1961, 1980) was one of the founders of the human potential movement. This movement emphasizes self-realization through sensitivity training, encounter groups, and other exercises intended to foster personal growth. Rogers grew up in a religious, upper-middle-class home in the suburbs of Chicago. He was a bright student, but he had to rebel against his parents' wishes in order to pursue his graduate study in psychology. While he was working at the University of Chicago in the 1940s, Rogers devised a major new approach to psychotherapy. Like Freud, Rogers based his personality theory on his extensive therapeutic interactions with many clients. Because of its emphasis on a person's subjective point of view, Rogers's approach is called a *person-centered theory*.

The Self

Rogers viewed personality structure in terms of just one construct. He called this construct the *self*, although it's more widely known today as the *self-concept. A self-concept is a collection of beliefs about one's own nature, unique qualities, and typical behavior*. Your self-concept is your own mental picture of yourself. It's a collection of self-perceptions. For example, a self-concept might include beliefs such as "I'm easygoing" or "I'm sly and crafty" or "I'm pretty" or "I'm hardworking." According to Rogers, individuals are aware of their self-concept. It's not buried in their unconscious.

Rogers stressed the subjective nature of the self-concept. Your self-concept may not be entirely consistent with your experiences. Most people tend to

Courtesy of the Center for Studies of the Person

"*I have little sympathy with the rather prevalent concept that man is basically irrational, and that his impulses, if not controlled, will lead to destruction of others and self. Man's behavior is exquisitely rational, moving with subtle and ordered complexity toward the goals his organism is endeavoring to achieve.*"
CARL ROGERS

distort their experiences to some extent to promote a relatively favorable self-concept. For example, you may believe that you're quite bright, but your grade transcript might suggest otherwise. Rogers called the gap between self-concept and reality incongruence. *Incongruence is the degree of disparity between one's self-concept and one's actual experience.* In contrast, if a person's self-concept is reasonably accurate, it's said to be *congruent* with reality (see Figure 12.9). Everyone experiences *some* incongruence. The crucial issue is how much. As we'll see, Rogers maintained that too much incongruence undermines one's psychological well-being.

Development of the Self

In terms of personality development, Rogers was concerned with how childhood experiences promote congruence or incongruence between one's self-concept and one's experience. According to Rogers, people have a strong need for affection, love, and acceptance from others. Early in life, parents provide most of this affection. Rogers maintained that some parents make their affection *conditional*. That is, it depends on the child's behaving well and living up to expectations. When parental love seems conditional, children often block out of their self-concept those experiences that make them feel unworthy of love. They do so because they're worried about parental acceptance, which appears precarious. At the other end of the spectrum, some parents make their affection *unconditional*. Their children have less need to block out unworthy experiences because they've been

Figure 12.9

Rogers's view of personality structure. In Rogers's model, the self-concept is the only important structural construct. However, Rogers acknowledged that one's self-concept may not be consistent with the realities of one's actual experience—a condition called incongruence.

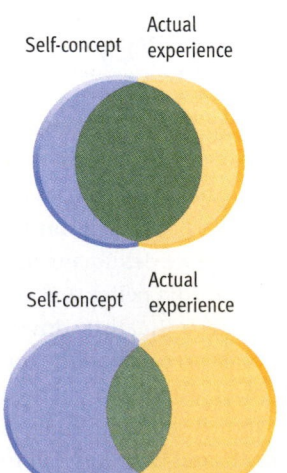

Self-concept / Actual experience

Congruence
Self-concept meshes well with actual experience (some incongruence is probably unavoidable)

Self-concept / Actual experience

Incongruence
Self-concept does not mesh well with actual experience

assured that they're worthy of affection, no matter what they do.

Hence, Rogers believed that unconditional love from parents fosters congruence and that conditional love fosters incongruence. He further theorized that if individuals grow up believing that affection from others is highly conditional, they will go on to distort more and more of their experiences in order to feel worthy of acceptance from a wider and wider array of people (see Figure 12.10).

Anxiety and Defense

According to Rogers, experiences that threaten people's personal views of themselves are the principal cause of troublesome anxiety. The more inaccurate your self-concept, the more likely you are to have experiences that clash with your self-perceptions. Thus, people with highly incongruent self-concepts are especially likely to be plagued by recurrent anxiety (see Figure 12.10).

To ward off this anxiety, individuals often behave defensively in an effort to reinterpret their experience so that it appears consistent with their self-concept. Thus, they ignore, deny, and twist reality to protect and perpetuate their self-concept. Consider a young woman who, like most people, considers herself a "nice person." Let's suppose that in reality she is rather conceited and selfish. She gets feedback from both boyfriends and girlfriends that she is a "self-centered, snotty brat." How might she react in order to protect her self-concept? She might ignore or block out those occasions when she behaves selfishly. She might attribute her girlfriends' negative comments to their jealousy of her good looks. Perhaps she would blame her boyfriends' negative remarks on their disappointment because she won't get more serious with them. As you can see, people will sometimes go to great lengths to defend their self-concept.

Maslow's Theory of Self-Actualization

Abraham Maslow, who grew up in Brooklyn, described his childhood as "unhappy, lonely, [and] isolated." To follow through on his interest in psychology, he had to resist parental pressures to go into law. Maslow spent much of his career at Brandeis University, where he created an influential theory of motivation and provided crucial leadership for the fledgling humanistic movement. Like Rogers, Maslow (1968, 1970) argued that psychology should take an optimistic view of human nature instead of dwelling on the causes of disorders. "To oversimplify the matter somewhat," he said, "it's as if Freud supplied to us the sick half of psychology and we must now fill it out with the healthy half" (1968, p. 5). Maslow's key contributions were his analysis of how motives are organized hierarchically and his description of the healthy personality.

Hierarchy of Needs

Maslow proposed that human motives are organized into a *hierarchy of needs*—**a systematic arrangement of needs, according to priority, in which basic needs must be met before less basic needs are aroused.** This hierarchical arrangement is usually portrayed as a pyramid (see Figure 12.11 on the next page). The needs toward the bottom of the pyramid, such as physiological or security needs, are the most basic. Higher levels in the pyramid consist of progressively less basic needs. When a person manages to satisfy a level of needs reasonably well (complete satisfaction is not necessary), *this satisfaction activates needs at the next level.*

Like Rogers, Maslow argued that humans have an innate drive toward personal growth—that is, evolution toward a higher state of being. Thus, he described the needs in the uppermost reaches of his hierarchy as *growth needs*. These include the needs for knowledge, understanding, order, and aesthetic beauty. Foremost among them is the *need for self-actualization*, which is the need to fulfill one's potential; it is the highest need in Maslow's motivational hierarchy. Maslow summarized this concept with a simple statement: "What a man *can* be, he *must* be." According to Maslow, people will be frustrated if they are unable to fully utilize their talents or pursue their true interests. For example, if you have great musical tal-

"*It is as if Freud supplied to us the sick half of psychology and we must now fill it out with the healthy half.*"
ABRAHAM MASLOW

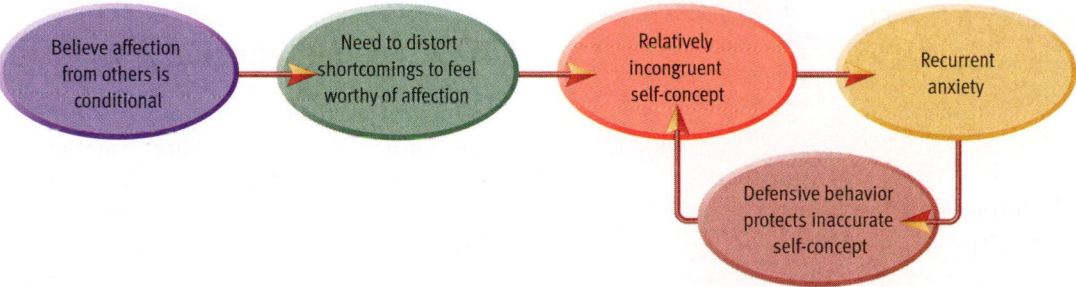

Figure 12.10

Rogers's view of personality development and dynamics. Rogers's theory of development posits that conditional love leads to a need to distort experiences, which fosters an incongruent self-concept. Incongruence makes one prone to recurrent anxiety, which triggers defensive behavior, which fuels more incongruence.

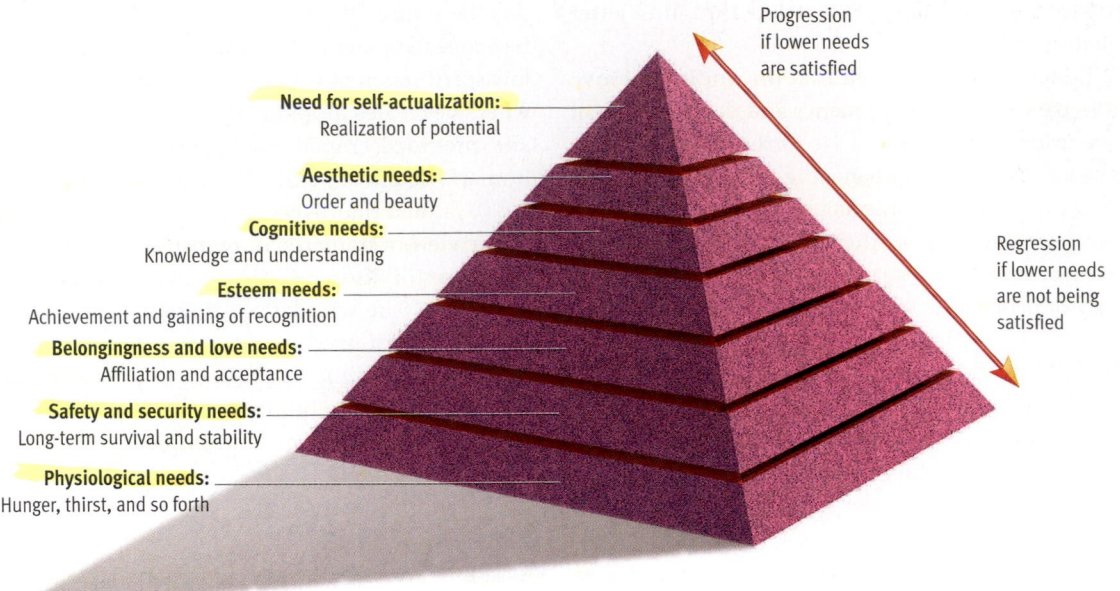

Figure 12.11

Maslow's hierarchy of needs. According to Maslow, human needs are arranged in a hierarchy, and people must satisfy their basic needs before they can satisfy higher needs. In the diagram, higher levels in the pyramid represent progressively less basic needs. Individuals progress upward in the hierarchy when lower needs are satisfied reasonably well, but they may regress back to lower levels if basic needs are no longer satisfied.

Figure 12.12

Maslow's view of the healthy personality. Humanistic theorists emphasize psychological health instead of maladjustment. Maslow's description of characteristics of self-actualizing people evokes a picture of the healthy personality.

SOURCE: Adapted from Potkay, C. R., & Allen, B. P. (1986). *Personality: Theory, research and application*. Pacific Grove, CA: Brooks/Cole. Copyright © 1986 by C. R. Potkay & B. P. Allen. Adapted by permission of the author.

ent but must work as an accountant, or if you have scholarly interests but must work as a sales clerk, your need for self-actualization will be thwarted.

The Healthy Personality 10c

Because of his interest in self-actualization, Maslow set out to discover the nature of the healthy personality. He tried to identify people of exceptional mental health so that he could investigate their characteristics. In one case, he used psychological tests and interviews to sort out the healthiest 1% of a sizable population of college students. He also studied admired historical figures (such as Thomas Jefferson and William James) and personal acquaintances characterized by superior adjustment. Over a period of years, he accumulated his case histories and gradually sketched, in broad strokes, a picture of ideal psychological health.

According to Maslow, *self-actualizing persons are people with exceptionally healthy personalities, marked by continued personal growth.* Maslow identified various traits characteristic of self-actualizing people. Many of these traits are listed in Figure 12.12. In brief, Maslow found that self-actualizers are accurately tuned in to reality and that they're at peace with themselves. He found that they're open and spontaneous and that they retain a fresh appreciation of the world around them. Socially, they're sensitive to others' needs and enjoy rewarding interpersonal relations. However, they're not dependent on others for approval or uncomfortable with solitude. They thrive on their work, and they enjoy their sense of humor. Maslow also noted that they have "peak experiences" (profound emotional highs) more often than others. Finally, he found that they strike a nice balance between many polarities in personality. For instance, they can be both childlike and mature, both rational and intuitive, both conforming and rebellious.

Characteristics of self-actualizing people

- Clear, efficient perception of reality and comfortable relations with it
- Spontaneity, simplicity, and naturalness
- Problem centering (having something outside themselves they "must" do as a mission)
- Detachment and need for privacy
- Autonomy, independence of culture and environment
- Continued freshness of appreciation
- Mystical and peak experiences
- Feelings of kinship and identification with the human race
- Strong friendships, but limited in number
- Democratic character structure
- Ethical discrimination between good and evil
- Philosophical, unhostile sense of humor
- Balance between polarities in personality

Evaluating Humanistic Perspectives

The humanists added a refreshing new perspective to the study of personality. Their argument that a person's subjective views may be more important than objective reality has proven compelling. As we noted earlier, even behavioral theorists have begun to take into account subjective personal factors such

Recognizing Key Concepts in Personality Theories

Check your understanding of psychodynamic, behavioral, and humanistic personality theories by identifying key concepts from these theories in the scenarios below. The answers can be found in Appendix A.

1. Thirteen-year-old Sarah watches a TV show in which the leading female character manipulates her boyfriend by acting helpless and purposely losing a tennis match against him. The female lead repeatedly expresses her slogan, "Never let them [men] know you can take care of yourself." Sarah becomes more passive and less competitive around boys her own age.

Concept: _____

2. Yolanda has a secure, enjoyable, reasonably well-paid job as a tenured English professor at a state university. Her friends are dumbfounded when she announces that she's going to resign and give it all up to try writing a novel. She tries to explain, "I need a new challenge, a new mountain to climb. I've had this lid on my writing talents for years, and I've got to break free. It's something I have to try. I won't be happy until I do."

Concept: _____

3. Vladimir, who is 4, seems to be emotionally distant from and inattentive to his father. He complains whenever he's left with his dad. In contrast, he often cuddles up in bed with his mother and tries very hard to please her by behaving properly.

Concept: _____

as beliefs and expectancies. The humanistic approach also deserves some of the credit for making the self-concept an important construct in psychology. Today, theorists of many persuasions use the self-concept in their analyses of personality. Finally, one could argue that the humanists' optimistic, growth- and health-oriented approach laid the foundation for the emergence of the positive psychology movement that is increasingly influential in contemporary psychology (Sheldon & Kasser, 2001; Taylor, 2001).

Of course, there's a negative side to the balance sheet as well. Critics have identified some weaknesses in the humanistic approach to personality, including the following (Burger, 1997; Geller, 1982):

1. *Poor testability.* Like psychodynamic theorists, the humanists have been criticized for generating hypotheses that are difficult to put to a scientific test. Humanistic concepts such as personal growth and self-actualization are difficult to define and measure.

2. *Unrealistic view of human nature.* Critics also charge that the humanists have been unrealistic in their assumptions about human nature and their descriptions of the healthy personality. For instance, Maslow's self-actualizing people sound nearly *perfect*. In reality, Maslow had a hard time finding such people. When he searched among the living, the results were so disappointing that he turned to the study of historical figures. Thus, humanistic portraits of psychological health are perhaps a bit too optimistic.

3. *Inadequate evidence.* For the most part, humanistic psychologists haven't been particularly research

oriented. Although Rogers and Maslow both conducted and encouraged empirical research, many of their followers have been scornful of efforts to quantify human experience to test hypotheses. Much more research is needed to catch up with the theorizing in the humanistic camp. This is precisely the opposite of the situation that we'll encounter in the next section, which examines biological approaches to personality.

Web Link 12.5

The Personality Project
William Revelle, director of the graduate program in personality at Northwestern University's Psychology Department, has assembled a directory to many Internet-based resources in the study of personality.

REVIEW OF KEY POINTS

- Humanistic theories are phenomenological and take an optimistic view of people's conscious, rational ability to chart their own courses of action. Rogers focused on the self-concept as the critical aspect of personality. Incongruence is the degree of disparity between one's self-concept and actual experience.

- Rogers maintained that unconditional love fosters congruence, whereas conditional love fosters incongruence. Incongruence makes one vulnerable to recurrent anxiety, which tends to trigger defensive behavior that protects one's inaccurate self-concept.

- Maslow theorized that needs are organized hierarchically and that psychological health depends on fulfilling one's need for self-actualization, which is the need to realize one's human potential. His work led to the description of self-actualizing persons as idealized examples of psychological health.

- Humanistic theories deserve credit for highlighting the importance of subjective views of oneself and for confronting the question of what makes for a healthy personality. Humanistic theories lack a firm base of research, are difficult to put to an empirical test, and may be overly optimistic about human nature.

Biological Perspectives

PREVIEW QUESTIONS
- How did Eysenck explain variations in extraversion-introversion?
- To what degree is personality heritable?
- Do family environments have much impact on personality?
- What do evolutionary theorists have to say about personality?
- What are the strengths and weaknesses of the biological approach?

Like many identical twins reared apart, Jim Lewis and Jim Springer found they had been leading eerily similar lives. Separated four weeks after birth in 1940, the Jim twins grew up 45 miles apart in Ohio and were reunited in 1979. Eventually, they discovered that both drove the same model blue Chevrolet, chain-smoked Salems, chewed their fingernails, and owned dogs named Toy. Each had spent a good deal of time vacationing at the same three-block strip of beach in Florida. More important, when tested for such personality traits as flexibility, self-control, and sociability, the twins responded almost exactly alike. (Leo, 1987, p. 63)

So began a *Time* magazine summary of a major twin study conducted at the University of Minnesota Center for Twin and Adoption Research. Since 1979 the investigators at this center have been studying the personality resemblance of identical twins reared apart. Not all the twin pairs have been as similar as Jim Lewis and Jim Springer, but many of the parallels have been uncanny (Lykken et al., 1992). Identical twins Oskar Stohr and Jack Yufe were separated soon after birth. Oskar was sent to a Nazi-run school in Czechoslovakia while Jack was raised in a Jewish home on a Caribbean island. When they were reunited for the first time during middle age, they showed up wearing similar mustaches, haircuts, shirts, and wire-rimmed glasses! A pair of previously separated female twins both arrived at the Minneapolis airport wearing seven rings on their fingers. One had a son named Richard Andrew and the other had a son named Andrew Richard!

Could personality be largely inherited? These anecdotal reports of striking resemblances between identical twins reared apart certainly raise this possibility. In this section we'll discuss Hans Eysenck's theory, which emphasizes the influence of heredity, look at recent behavioral genetics research on the heritability of personality, and outline the evolutionary perspective on personality.

Eysenck's Theory

Hans Eysenck was born in Germany but fled to London during the era of Nazi rule. He went on to become one of Britain's most prominent psychologists. Eysenck (1967, 1982, 1990a) views personality structure as a hierarchy of traits, in which many superficial traits are derived from a smaller number of more basic traits, which are derived from a handful of fundamental higher-order traits, as shown in Figure 12.13. His studies suggest that all aspects of personality emerge from just three higher-order traits: extraversion, neuroticism, and psychoticism. *Extraversion* involves being sociable, assertive, active, and lively. *Neuroticism* involves being anxious, tense, moody, and low in self-esteem. *Psychoticism* involves being egocentric, impulsive, cold, and antisocial.

According to Eysenck, "Personality is determined to a large extent by a person's genes" (1967, p. 20). How is heredity linked to personality in Eysenck's model? In part, through conditioning concepts borrowed from behavioral theory. Eysenck theorizes that some people can be conditioned more readily than others because of differences in their physiological functioning. These variations in "conditionability" are assumed to influence the personality traits that people acquire through conditioning processes.

Eysenck has shown a special interest in explaining variations in *extraversion-introversion*, the trait dimension first described years earlier by Carl Jung. He has proposed that introverts tend to have higher levels of physiological arousal, or perhaps higher "arousability," which make them more easily conditioned than extraverts. According to Eysenck, people who condition easily acquire more conditioned inhibi-

"*Personality is determined to a large extent by a person's genes.*"
HANS EYSENCK

Figure 12.13

Eysenck's model of personality structure. Eysenck described personality structure as a hierarchy of traits. In this scheme, a few higher-order traits, such as extraversion, determine a host of lower-order traits, which determine a person's habitual responses.

SOURCE: Eysenck, H. J. (1976). *The biological basis of personality.* Springfield, IL: Charles C. Thomas. Reprinted by permission of the publisher.

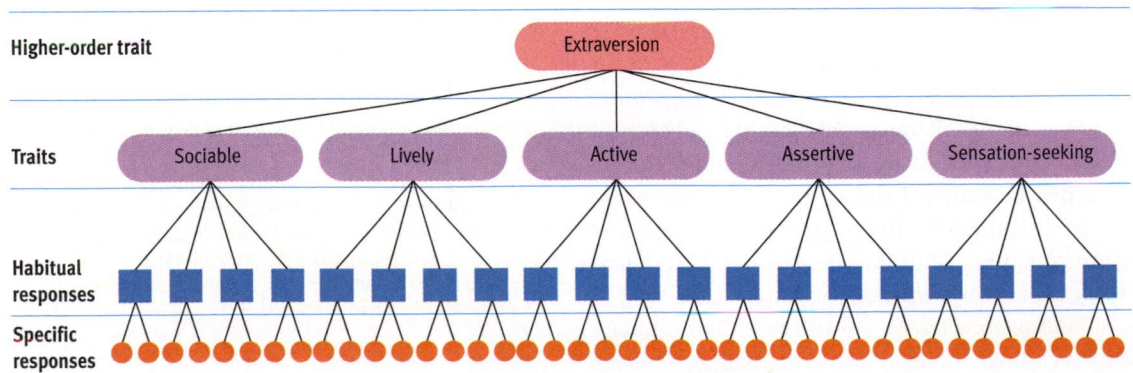

Higher-order trait			Extraversion		
Traits	Sociable	Lively	Active	Assertive	Sensation-seeking
Habitual responses					
Specific responses					

tions than others. These inhibitions make them more bashful, tentative, and uneasy in social situations. This social discomfort leads them to turn inward. Hence, they become introverted.

Behavioral Genetics and Personality

Recent research in behavioral genetics has provided impressive support for the idea that many personality traits are largely inherited (Plomin & Caspi, 1999; Rowe, 1997). For instance, Figure 12.14 shows the mean correlations observed for identical and fraternal twins in studies of the Big Five personality traits summarized by Loehlin (1992). Higher correlations are indicative of greater similarity on a trait. On all five traits, identical twins have been found to be much more similar than fraternal twins. Based on these and many other data, Loehlin (1992) concludes that genetic factors exert considerable influence over personality (see Chapter 3 for an explanation of the logic of twin studies).

Some skeptics wonder whether identical twins might exhibit more trait similarity than fraternal twins because they're treated more alike. In other words, they wonder whether environmental factors (rather than heredity) could be responsible for identical twins' greater personality resemblance. This nagging question can be answered only by studying identical twins reared apart, which is why the twin study at the University of Minnesota has been so impor-

tant. The Minnesota study (Tellegen et al., 1988) was the first to administer the same personality test to identical and fraternal twins reared apart, as well as together. Most of the twins reared apart were separated quite early in life (median age of 2.5 months) and remained separated for a long time (median period of almost 34 years).

The results revealed that identical twins reared apart were substantially more similar in personality than fraternal twins reared together. The *heritability estimates* (see Chapter 9) for the traits examined ranged from 40% to 58%. The investigators concluded that their results support the hypothesis that genetic blueprints shape the contours of personality.

Another large-scale twin study of the Big Five traits conducted in Germany and Poland yielded similar conclusions (Riemann, Angleitner, & Strelau, 1997). The heritability estimates based on the data from this study are in the same range as the estimates from the Minnesota study (see Figure 12.15 on the next page). Moreover, a unique feature of this study was that it obtained peer ratings of subjects' personality traits, as well as the usual measures based on participants' responses to personality tests, and these independent ratings yielded roughly similar estimates of heritability. Thus, recent behavioral genetics research suggests that personality is shaped to a considerable degree by hereditary factors.

Research on the heritability of personality has inadvertently turned up an interesting finding that was apparent in the Riemann et al. (1997) study. As you

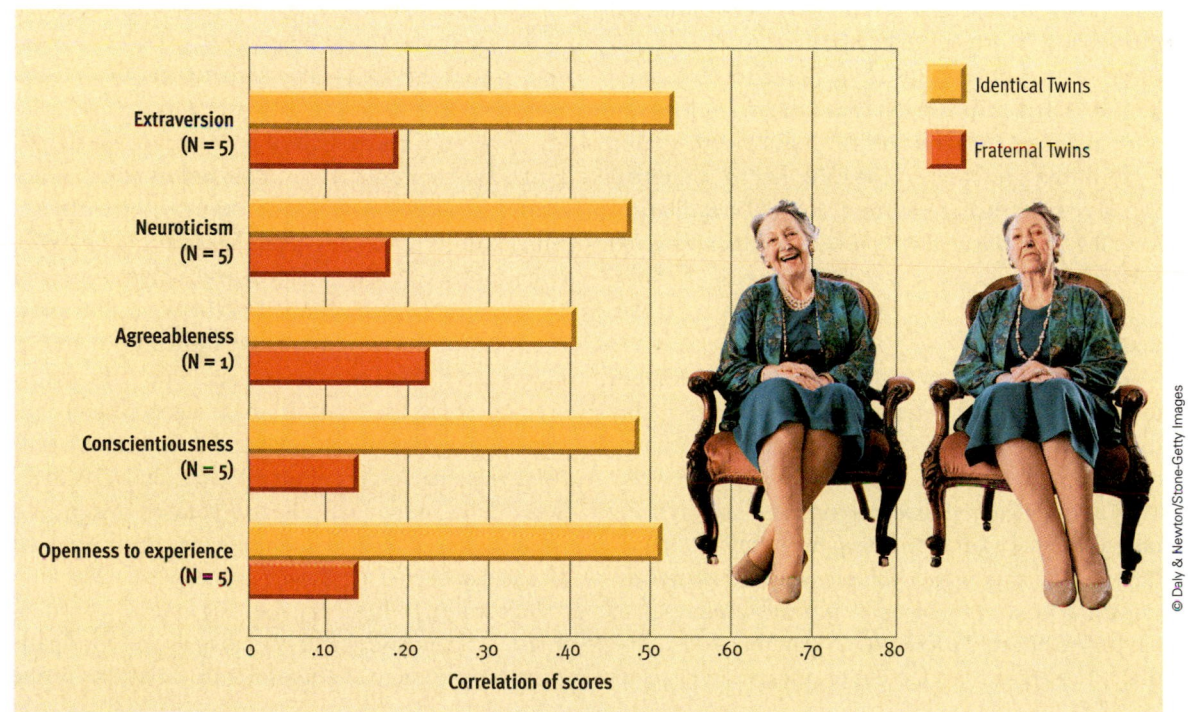

Figure 12.14

Twin studies of personality. Loehlin (1992) has summarized the results of twin studies that have examined the Big Five personality traits. The N under each trait indicates the number of twin studies that have examined that trait. The chart plots the average correlations obtained for identical and fraternal twins in these studies. As you can see, identical twins have shown greater resemblance in personality than fraternal twins have, suggesting that personality is partly inherited. (Based on data from Loehlin, 1992)

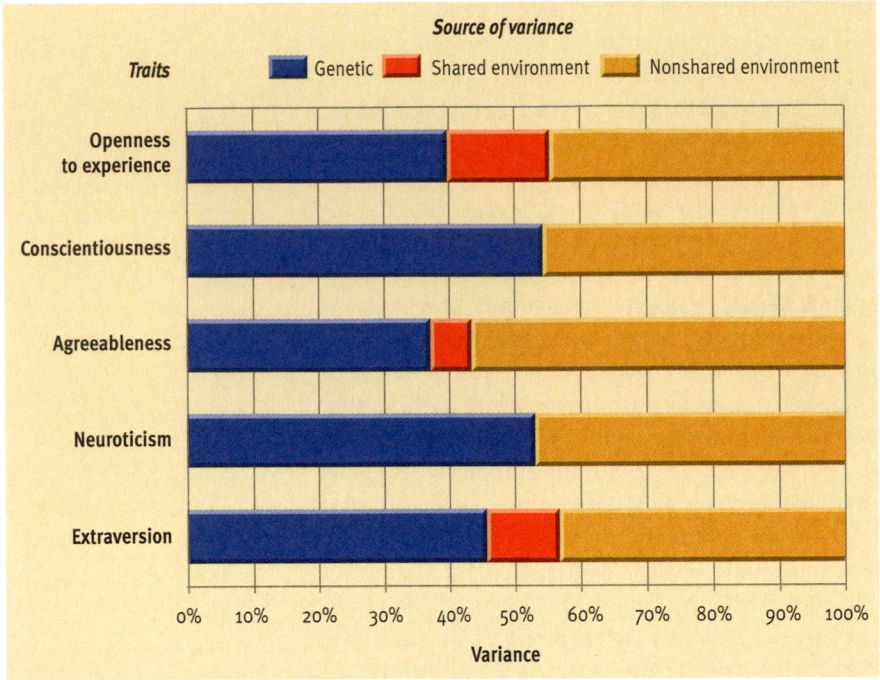

Source of variance

| Traits | ■ Genetic | ■ Shared environment | ■ Nonshared environment |

Openness to experience
Conscientiousness
Agreeableness
Neuroticism
Extraversion

0% 10% 20% 30% 40% 50% 60% 70% 80% 90% 100%

Variance

Figure 12.15

Heritability and environmental variance for the Big Five traits. Based on the twin study data of Riemann et al. (1997), Plomin and Caspi (1999) estimated the heritability of each of the Big Five traits. The data also allowed them to estimate the amount of variance on each trait attributable to shared environment and nonshared environment. As you can see, the heritability estimates hovered in the vicinity of 40%, with two exceeding 50%. As in other studies, the influence of shared family environment was very modest.

Source: Adapted from Plomin R., & Caspi, A. (1999). Behavioral genetics and personality. In L. A. Pervin & O. P. John (Eds.), *Handbook of personality: Theory and research.* New York: Guilford Press.

Web Link 12.6

Great Ideas in Personality
Northwestern University personality psychologist G. Scott Acton demonstrates that scientific research programs in personality generate broad and compelling ideas about what it is to be a human being. He charts the contours of 12 research perspectives, including behaviorism, behavioral genetics, and sociobiology, and backs them up with extensive links to published and online resources associated with each perspective.

can see in Figure 12.15, *shared family environment* appears to have remarkably little impact on personality. This unexpected finding has been observed quite consistently in behavioral genetics research (Beer, Arnold, & Loehlin, 1998; Halverson & Wampler, 1997). It is surprising in that social scientists have long assumed that the family environment shared by children growing up together led to some personality resemblance among them. *These findings have led some theorists to conclude that parents don't matter—that they wield very little influence over how their children develop* (Cohen, 1999; Harris, 1998; Rowe, 1994).

Critics have argued with merit that the methods used in behavioral genetics studies have probably underestimated the impact of shared environment on personality (Collins et al., 2000; Stoolmiller, 1999). They also note that shared experiences—such as being raised with authoritarian discipline—may often have different effects on two siblings, which obscures the impact of environment but is not the same result as having no effect (Turkheimer & Waldron, 2000). And the critics argue that decades of research in develop-

mental psychology have clearly demonstrated that parents have significant influence on their children (Maccoby, 2000).

Although the assertion that "parents don't matter" seems premature and overstated, the perplexing findings in behavioral genetics studies of personality have led researchers to investigate why children from the same family are often so different. Thus far, the evidence suggests that children in the same family experience home environments that are not nearly as homogeneous as previously assumed (Hetherington, Reiss, & Plomin, 1994; Pike et al., 2000). Children in the same home may be treated quite differently, because gender and birth order can influence parents' approaches to child rearing. Temperamental differences between children may also evoke differences in parenting. Focusing on how environmental factors vary *within* families represents a promising new way to explore the determinants of personality.

The Evolutionary Approach to Personality

In the realm of biological perspectives on personality, another recent development has been the emergence of evolutionary theory. Evolutionary theorists assert that personality has a biological basis because natural selection has favored certain traits over the course of human history. Thus, evolutionary analyses focus on how various personality traits—and the ability to recognize these traits in others—may have contributed to reproductive fitness in ancestral human populations.

For example, David Buss (1991, 1995, 1997) has argued that the Big Five personality traits stand out as important dimensions of personality across a variety of cultures because those traits have had significant adaptive implications. Buss points out that humans historically have depended heavily on groups, which afford protection from predators or enemies, opportunities for sharing food, and a diverse array of other benefits. In the context of these group interactions, people have had to make difficult but crucial judgments about the characteristics of others, asking such questions as: Who will make a good member of my coalition? Who can I depend on when in need? Who will share their resources? Thus, Buss (1995) argues, "those individuals able to accurately discern and act upon these individual differences likely enjoyed a considerable reproductive advantage" (p. 22).

According to Buss, the Big Five emerge as fundamental dimensions of personality because humans have evolved special sensitivity to variations in the ability to bond with others (extraversion), the willingness to cooperate and collaborate (agreeableness), the tendency to be reliable and ethical (conscientiousness), the capacity to be an innovative problem solver (openness to experience), and the ability to handle stress (low neuroticism). In a nutshell, Buss argues that the Big Five reflect the most salient features of others' adaptive behavior over the course of evolutionary history. MacDonald (1998) takes this line of thinking one step further, asserting that the traits themselves (as opposed to the ability to recognize them) are products of evolution that were adaptive in ancestral environments.

Evaluating Biological Perspectives

Researchers have compiled convincing evidence that biological factors exert considerable influence over personality. Nonetheless, we must take note of some weaknesses in biological approaches to personality:

1. David Funder (2001, p. 207) makes the observation that behavioral genetics researchers exhibit something of an "obsession with establishing the exact magnitude of heritability coefficients." As we discussed in Chapter 9, heritability ratios are ballpark estimates that will vary depending on sampling procedures and other considerations. There is no one magic number awaiting discovery, so the inordinate focus on heritability does seem ill-advised.

2. The results of efforts to carve behavior into genetic and environmental components are ultimately artificial. The effects of nature and nurture are twisted together in complicated interactions that can't be separated cleanly (Brody & Crowley, 1995).

3. At present there's no comprehensive biological theory of personality. Eysenck's model doesn't provide a systematic overview of how biological factors govern personality structure and development (and was never intended to). In regard to personality, evolutionary theory currently is even more limited in scope than Eysenck's theory. Additional theoretical work is needed to catch up with recent empirical findings on the biological basis for personality.

Courtesy of David M. Buss

In sum, the five factors of personality, in this account, represent important dimensions of the social terrain that humans were selected to attend to and act upon.
DAVID BUSS

REVIEW OF KEY POINTS

- Contemporary biological theories stress the genetic origins of personality. Eysenck views personality structure as a hierarchy of traits. He believes that heredity influences individual differences in physiological functioning that affect how easily people acquire conditioned inhibitions.

- Twin studies of the Big Five personality traits find that identical twins are more similar in personality than fraternal twins, thus suggesting that personality is partly inherited. Estimates for the heritability of personality hover in the vicinity of 40%. Recent research in behavioral genetics has suggested that shared family environment has surprisingly little impact on personality, although a variety of theorists have been critical of this conclusion.

- Evolutionary analyses of personality suggest that certain traits and the ability to recognize them may have contributed to reproductive fitness. The biological approach has been criticized because of methodological problems with heritability ratios and because it offers no systematic model of how physiology shapes personality.

CONCEPT CHECK 12.3

Understanding the Implications of Major Theories: Who Said This?

Check your understanding of the implications of the personality theories we've discussed by indicating which theorist is likely to have made the statements below. The answers are in Appendix A.

Choose from the following theorists:

Alfred Adler

Albert Bandura

Hans Eysenck

Sigmund Freud

Abraham Maslow

Walter Mischel

Quotes

1. _____ "If you deliberately plan to be less than you are capable of being, then I warn you that you'll be deeply unhappy for the rest of your life."

2. _____ "I feel that the major, most fundamental dimensions of personality are likely to be those on which [there is] strong genetic determination of individual differences."

3. _____ "People are in general not candid over sexual matters . . . they wear a heavy overcoat woven of a tissue of lies, as though the weather were bad in the world of sexuality."

Four Views of Personality

Theorist and orientation	Source of data and observations	Key motivational forces
A psychodynamic view Sigmund Freud 	Case studies from clinical practice of psychoanalysis  © Peter Aprahamian/CORBIS	Sex and aggression; need to reduce tension resulting from internal conflicts
A behavioral view B. F. Skinner 	Laboratory experiments, primarily with animals  © Richard Wood/Index Stock	Pursuit of primary (unlearned) and secondary (learned) reinforcers; priorities depend on personal history
A humanistic view Carl Rogers 	Case studies from clinical practice of client-centered therapy  © Tom Stewart/CORBIS	Actualizing tendency (motive to develop capacities, and experience personal growth) and self-actualizing tendency (motive to maintain self-concept and behave in ways that are consistent with self-concept)
A biological view Hans Eysenck 	Twin, family, and adoption studies of heritability; factor analysis studies of personality structure  © Daly & Newton/Stone-Getty Images	No specific motivational forces singled out

Model of personality structure

Three interacting components (id, ego, superego) operating at three levels of consciousness

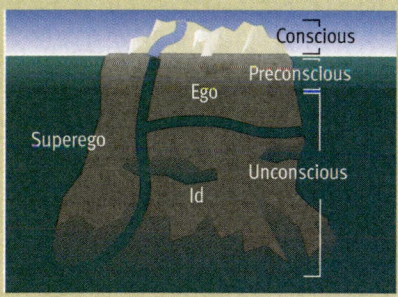

Collections of response tendencies tied to specific stimulus situations

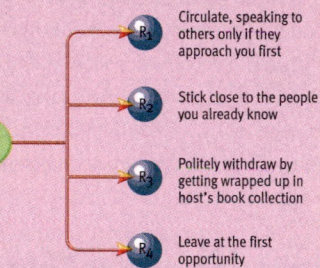

Self-concept, which may or may not mesh well with actual experience

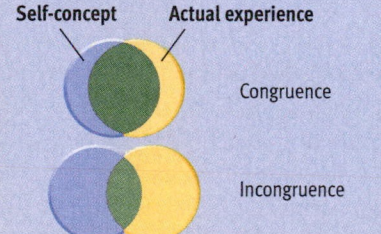

Hierarchy of traits, with specific traits derived from more fundamental, general traits

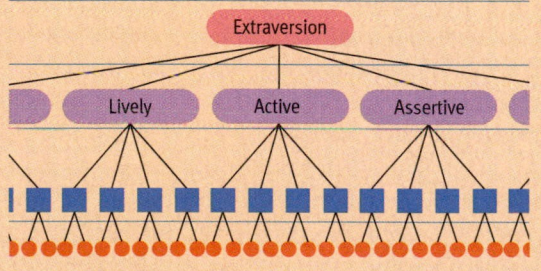

View of personality development

Emphasis on fixation or progress through psychosexual stages; experiences in early childhood (such as toilet training) can leave lasting mark on adult personality

© Peter Aprahamian/CORBIS

Personality evolves gradually over the life span (not in stages); responses (such as extraverted joking) followed by reinforcement (such as appreciative laughter) become more frequent

© Richard Wood/Index Stock

Children who receive unconditional love have less need to be defensive; they develop more accurate, congruent self-concept; conditional love fosters incongruence

© Tom Stewart/CORBIS

Emphasis on unfolding of genetic blueprint with maturation; inherited predispositions interact with learning experiences

Roots of disorders

Unconscious fixations and unresolved conflicts from childhood, usually centering on sex and aggression

Maladaptive behavior due to faulty learning; the "symptom" is the problem, not a sign of underlying disease

Incongruence between self and actual experience (inaccurate self-concept); overdependence on others for approval and sense of worth

Genetic vulnerability activated in part by environmental factors

Contemporary Empirical Approaches to Personality

PREVIEW QUESTIONS
- What is sensation seeking?
- How does it influence adjustment and mental health?
- What is self-monitoring?
- What effects does it have on interpersonal behavior?

So far, our coverage has been devoted to grand, panoramic theories of personality. In this section we'll examine some contemporary empirical approaches that are narrower in scope, tending to focus on specific traits. In modern personality research programs, investigators attempt to describe and measure an important personality trait, shed light on its development, and ascertain its relationship to other traits and behaviors. To get a sense of this kind of research, we'll take a look at two such traits in this section: sensation seeking and self-monitoring.

Sensation Seeking: Life in the Fast Lane

The "adrenaline junkie," Steve Irwin, profiled at the beginning of this chapter provides a prototype example of high sensation seeking. *Sensation seeking* **is a generalized preference for high or low levels of sensory stimulation.** People who are high in sensation seeking prefer a high level of stimulation, or "life in the fast lane." They're always looking for new and exhilarating experiences. People who are low in sensation seeking prefer more modest levels of stimulation. They tend to choose tranquillity over excitement. Sensation seeking was first described by Marvin Zuckerman (1971, 1979), a biologically oriented theorist influenced by Hans Eysenck's views. Zuckerman (1990, 1991, 1996) believes that there is a strong genetic predisposition to high or low sensation seeking.

Sensation-seeking tendencies are measured by Zuckerman's (1984) Sensation Seeking Scale (see Figure 12.16). Sensation seeking is distributed along a continuum, and many people fall in the middle. Factor analyses indicate that the personality trait of sensation seeking consists of four related components. When compared to low sensation seekers, those high in sensation seeking display the following four sets of characteristics (Zuckerman, 1979, 1994):

- *Thrill and adventure seeking.* They're more willing to engage in activities that may involve a physical risk. Thus, they're more likely to go mountain climbing, skydiving, surfing, and scuba diving.
- *Experience seeking.* They're more willing to volunteer for unusual experiments or activities that they may know little about. They tend to relish extensive travel, provocative art, wild parties, and unusual friends.
- *Disinhibition.* High sensation seekers are relatively uninhibited. Hence, they are prone to engage in

heavy drinking, recreational drug use, gambling, and sexual experimentation.
- *Susceptibility to boredom.* High sensation seekers' chief foe is monotony. They have a low tolerance for routine and repetition, and they quickly and easily become bored.

How do high sensation seekers stack up in terms of adjustment and mental health? On the positive side of the ledger, high sensation seekers are relatively tolerant of stress. They find many types of potentially stressful events to be less threatening and anxiety arousing than others (Franken, Gibson, & Rowland, 1992). On the negative side of the ledger, high sensation seekers are more likely than others to exhibit impulsive, last-minute decision making (Franken, 1993), poor health habits (Watanabe, 1998), reckless driving (Jonah, 1997) and high-risk sexual behavior (McCoul & Haslam, 2001). High sensation seeking is also associated with problem drinking (Parent & Newman, 1999), recreational drug use and gambling (Zuckerman & Kuhlman, 2000), delinquency (Luengo et al., 1994), and criminal behavior (Arnett, 1996). Thus, high sensation seeking may be more maladaptive than adaptive.

Self-Monitoring: Life as Theater

The trait of self-monitoring, originally unearthed by Mark Snyder, has been the subject of hundreds of studies since the mid-1970s (Gangestad & Snyder, 2000). *Self-monitoring* **refers to the degree to which people attend to and control the impression they make on others in social interactions.** According to Snyder (1979, 1987), people vary in their awareness of how they're being perceived by others. People who are high in self-monitoring are very sensitive to how their self-presentation is going over. They seek information about how they're expected to behave in a situation, and, when necessary, they shrewdly adjust their behavior to create the right impression. For high self-monitors, "All the world's a stage."

Being tuned in to how others view you is one thing, but high self-monitors also show a gift for creating the right impression. They tend to be skilled at adjusting their self-presentations to produce desired audience responses (Larkin, 1988). In other words, they are good actors. They control their emotions well and can feign emotions when necessary. They deliberately regulate nonverbal signals (for instance, facial expressions and gestures) that are fairly spon-

Answer "true" or "false" to each of the items listed below by circling "T" or "F." A "true" means that the item expresses your preference most of the time. A "false" means that you do not agree that the item is generally true for you. After completing the test, score your responses according to the instructions that follow the test items.

T F   1. I would really enjoy skydiving.
T F   2. I can imagine myself driving a sports car in a race and loving it.
T F   3. My life is very secure and comfortable—the way I like it.
T F   4. I usually like emotionally expressive or artistic people, even if they are sort of wild.
T F   5. I like the idea of seeing many of the same warm, supportive faces in my everyday life.
T F   6. I like doing adventurous things and would have enjoyed being a pioneer in the early days of this country.
T F   7. A good photograph should express peacefulness creatively.
T F   8. The most important thing in living is fully experiencing all emotions.
T F   9. I like creature comforts when I go on a trip or vacation.
T F   10. Doing the same things each day really gets to me.
T F   11. I love snuggling in front of a fire on a wintry day.
T F   12. I would like to try several types of drugs as long as they didn't harm me permanently.
T F   13. Drinking and being rowdy really appeals to me on the weekend.
T F   14. Rational people try to avoid dangerous situations.
T F   15. I prefer Figure A to Figure B.

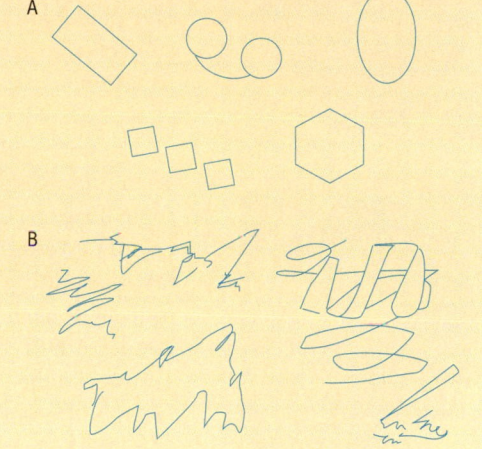

A

B

Give yourself 1 point for answering "true" to the following items: 1, 2, 4, 6, 8, 10, 12, and 13. Also give yourself 1 point for answering "false" to the following items: 3, 5, 7, 9, 11, 14, and 15. Add up your points, and compare your total to the following norms: 11–15, high sensation seeker; 6–10, moderate sensation seeker; 1–5, low sensation seeker. Bear in mind that this is a shortened version of the Sensation Seeking Scale and that it provides only a rough approximation of your status on this personality trait.

Figure 12.16

A brief scale to assess sensation seeking. Follow the instructions for this scale to obtain a rough estimate of your own sensation-seeking tendencies.

Source: Grasha, A. F., & Kirschenbaum, D. S. (1986). *Adjustment and competence: Concepts and applications.* St. Paul, MN: West Publishing. Reprinted by permission of Anthony F. Grasha.

taneous in most people. One recent study found that high self-monitors indicated that they would be better than others at feigning romantic interest in someone and that they would enjoy it more than others (Leck & Simpson, 1999). People who are high in self-monitoring tend to invest a lot of effort in "reading" and remembering others' self-presentations (Beers, Lassiter, & Flannery, 1997). Ironically, they are good at spotting deceptive impression management *in other people.* For instance, they can tell when others are trying to butter them up. They are also better than low self-monitors at accurately judging others' personalities (Sanz, Sanchez-Bernardos, & Avia, 1996). Like sensation seeking, self-monitoring appears to be determined in part by people's genetic makeup (Gangestad & Simpson, 1993).

Culture and Personality

Are there connections between culture and personality? The investigation of this question dates back to the 1940s and 1950s, when researchers set out to describe various cultures' *modal personality* (Kardiner & Linton, 1945) or *national character* (Kluckhohn & Murray, 1948). These investigations, which were largely guided by Freud's psychoanalytic theory, met with relatively little success (Bruner, 1974). Part of the problem may have been the rather culture-bound, Eurocentric nature of Freudian theory, but the crux of the problem was that it was unrealistic to expect to find a single, dominant personality type in each culture (Draguns, 1979). As we have seen repeatedly, given the realities of multifactorial causation, behavior is never that simple. In retrospect, the research on modal personality overestimated the impact of cultural contexts and the uniformity of people within societies.

Studies of the links between culture and personality dwindled after the disappointments of the 1940s and 1950s. However, in recent years psychology's new interest in cultural factors has led to a renaissance of culture-personality research. This research has sought to determine whether Western personality constructs are relevant to other cultures and whether cultural differences can be seen in the prevalence of specific personality traits. As with cross-cultural research in other areas of psychology, these studies have found evidence of both continuity and variability across cultures.

For the most part, continuity has been apparent in cross-cultural comparisons of the *trait structure* of

PREVIEW QUESTIONS
- Does the five-factor model have any relevance in non-Western cultures?
- How do conceptions of self vary across cultures?
- How does an interdependent view of self relate to self-enhancement?

Photo and Campus Services, University of Michigan

Courtesy of Shinobu Kitayama

"*Most of what psychologists currently know about human nature is based on one particular view—the so-called Western view of the individual as an independent, self-contained, autonomous entity.*"
HAZEL MARKUS AND
SHINOBU KITAYAMA

personality. When English language personality scales have been translated and administered in other cultures, the predicted dimensions of personality have emerged from the factor analyses (Paunonen & Ashton, 1998). For example, when scales that tap the Big Five personality traits have been administered and subjected to factor analysis in other cultures, the usual five traits have typically emerged (Katigbak et al., 2002; McCrae, 2001).

The cross-cultural similarities observed thus far seem impressive, but skepticism has been voiced in some quarters. Critics argue that the strategy of "exporting" Western tests to other cultures is slanted in favor of finding cross-cultural compatibility and is unlikely to uncover culture-specific traits (Church & Lonner, 1998). They also note that the non-Western samples studied thus far have not been all that culturally different from Western samples (Triandis & Suh, 2002). Furthermore, even though the Big Five traits are replicated in many cultures, this finding does not demonstrate that the traits have the same predictive meaning in those cultures (Markus & Kitayama, 1998). In other words, the correlates of a high neuroticism score in China may be different from the correlates that have been observed in Western cultures. In sum, preliminary research tentatively suggests that the basic dimensions of personality trait structure may be pancultural, but additional research is needed.

Perhaps the most interesting recent work on culture and personality has been that of Hazel Markus and Shinobu Kitayama (1991, 1994), comparing

American and Asian conceptions of the self. According to Markus and Kitayama, American parents teach their children to be self-reliant, to feel good about themselves, and to view themselves as special individuals. Children are encouraged to excel in competitive endeavors and to strive to stand out from the crowd. They are told that "the squeaky wheel gets the grease" and that "you have to stand up for yourself." Thus, Markus and Kitayama argue that *American culture fosters an independent view of the self.* American youngsters learn to define themselves in terms of their personal attributes, abilities, accomplishments, and possessions. Their unique strengths and achievements become the basis for their sense of self-worth. Hence, they are prone to emphasize their uniqueness.

Most of us take this individualistic mentality for granted. Indeed, Markus and Kitayama maintain that "most of what psychologists currently know about human nature is based on one particular view—the so-called Western view of the individual as an independent, self-contained, autonomous entity" (1991, p. 224). However, they marshal convincing evidence that this view is *not* universal. They argue that in Asian cultures such as Japan and China, socialization practices foster a more *interdependent view of the self,* which emphasizes the fundamental connectedness of people to each other (see Figure 12.17). In these cultures, parents teach their children that they can rely on family and friends, that they should be modest about their personal accomplishments so they don't diminish others' achievements, and that they should view themselves as part of a larger social matrix. Children are encouraged to fit in with others and to avoid standing out from the crowd. A popular adage in Japan reminds children that "the nail that stands out gets pounded down." Hence, Markus and Kitayama assert that Asian youngsters typically learn to define themselves in terms of the groups they belong to. Their harmonious relations with others and their pride in group achievements become the basis for their sense of self-worth. Because their self-esteem does not hinge so much on personal strengths, they are less likely to emphasize their uniqueness. Consistent with this analysis, Markus and Kitayama report that Asian subjects tend to view themselves as more similar to their peers than American subjects do.

The ramifications of these discrepant views of self are many. For example, these differing self-views lead to cultural disparities in self-enhancement. *Self-enhancement* involves focusing on positive feedback from others, exaggerating one's strengths, and seeing oneself as above average. These tenden-

© Keren Su/Stone-Getty Images

Culture can shape personality. Children in Asian cultures, for example, grow up with a value system that allows them to view themselves as interconnected parts of larger social units. Hence, they tend to avoid positioning themselves so that they stand out from others.

508 CHAPTER 12

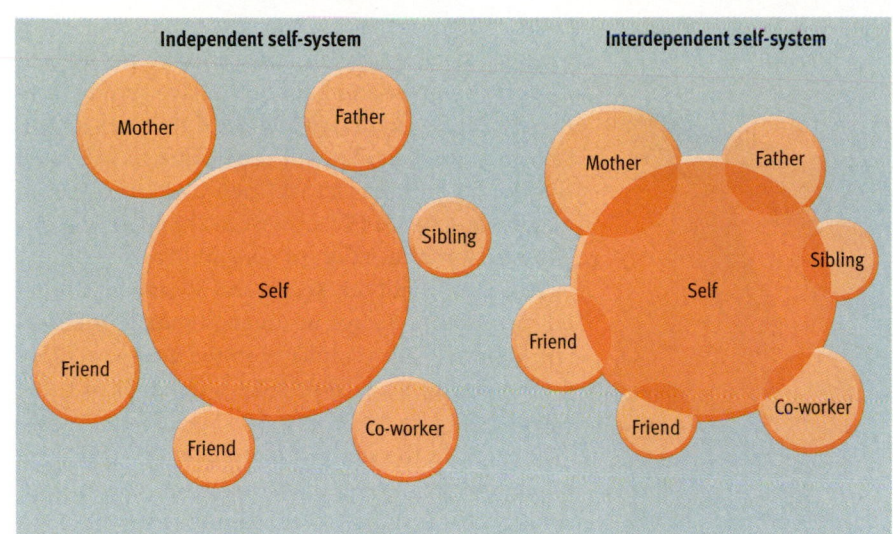

Figure 12.17

Culture and conceptions of self. According to Markus and Kitayama (1991), Western cultures foster an independent view of the self as a unique individual who is separate from others, as diagrammed on the left. In contrast, Asian cultures encourage an interdependent view of the self as part of an interconnected social matrix, as diagrammed on the right. The interdependent view leads people to define themselves in terms of their social relationships (for instance, as someone's daughter, employee, colleague, or neighbor).

Source: Adapted from Markus, H. R., & Kitayama, S. (1991). Culture and the self: Implications for cognition, emotion, and motivation. *Psychological Review, 98,* 224–253. Copyright © 1991 by the American Psychological Association. Adapted by permission of the author.

cies are pervasive in Western cultures but are quite rare in Asian cultures, where the norm is to be more sensitive to negative feedback, to reflect on one's shortcomings, and to look for avenues of improvement (Cross & Markus, 1999). In the hopes of fitting in better and contributing more to the group, people with interdependent self-views seem to be more interested in *self-criticism* than self-enhancement. Does all this self-criticism lead to lower self-esteem, on the average, in some cultures? Preliminary research suggests that the answer may be yes (Heine et al., 1999; Kitayama et al., 1997). But, ironically, low self-esteem may not have the same significance in cultures that encourage interdependent self-views. In Japan, for instance, self-esteem does not correlate with subjective well-being the way it does in Western cultures (Diener & Diener, 1995). This finding demonstrates once again that we cannot assume that Western models of psychological processes will apply equally well in other cultures.

Putting It in Perspective

The preceding discussion of culture and personality obviously highlighted the text's theme that people's behavior is influenced by their cultural heritage. This chapter has also been ideally suited for embellishing two other unifying themes: psychology's theoretical diversity and the idea that psychology evolves in a sociohistorical context.

No other area of psychology is characterized by as much theoretical diversity as the study of personality, where there are literally dozens of insightful theories. Some of this diversity exists because different theories attempt to explain different facets of behavior. However, much of this theoretical diversity reflects genuine disagreements on basic questions about personality. These disagreements are apparent on pages 504–505, which present an illustrated comparative overview of the ideas of Freud, Skinner, Rogers, and Eysenck, as representatives of the psychodynamic, behavioral, humanistic, and biological approaches to personality.

The study of personality also highlights the sociohistorical context in which psychology evolves. Personality theories have left many marks on modern culture; we can mention only a handful as illustrations. The theories of Freud, Adler, and Skinner have had an enormous impact on child-rearing practices. The ideas of Freud and Jung have found their way into literature (influencing the portrayal of fictional characters) and the visual arts. For example, Freud's theory helped inspire surrealism's interest in the world of dreams (see Figure 12.18 on the next page). Social learning theory has become embroiled in the public policy debate about whether media violence should be controlled, because of its effects on viewers' aggressive behavior. Maslow's hierarchy of needs and Skinner's affirmation of the value of positive reinforcement have influenced approaches to management in the world of business and industry.

Sociohistorical forces also leave their imprint on psychology. This chapter provided many examples

PREVIEW QUESTIONS
- How did the chapter illustrate psychology's theoretical diversity?
- How did the chapter show that psychology evolves in a sociohistorical context?

Figure 12.18

Freud and surrealism. The theories of Freud and Jung had considerable influence on the arts. For instance, their ideas about the unconscious guided the surrealists' explorations of the irrational world of dreams. Salvador Dali's 1936 painting *Soft Construction with Boiled Beans: Premonition of Civil War* is a bizarre image that symbolizes how a society can tear itself apart. Freud once commented, "I was tempted to consider the surrealists, which apparently have chosen me for their patron saint, as a bunch of complete nuts . . . [but] the young Spaniard [Dali], with the magnificent eyes of a fanatic and his undeniable technical mastery, has caused me to reconsider" (quoted in Gerard, 1968).

SOURCE: Salvador Dali, *Soft Construction with Boiled Beans: Premonitions of Civil War (1936)*. Photo by Graydon Wood, 1995, Philadelphia Museum of Art: The Louise and Walter Arensberg Collection. © 2000 Foundation Gala-Salvador Dali/VEGAP/Artists Rights Society (ARS), New York.

of how personal experiences, prevailing attitudes, and historical events have contributed to the evolution of ideas in psychology. For example, Freud's pessimistic view of human nature and his emphasis on the dark forces of aggression were shaped to some extent by his exposure to the hostilities of World War I and prevailing anti-Semitic sentiments. Freud's emphasis on sexuality was surely influenced by the Victorian climate of sexual repression that existed in his

youth. Adler's views also reflected the social context in which he grew up. His interest in inferiority feelings and compensation appear to have sprung from his own sickly childhood and the difficulties he had to overcome. Likewise, it's reasonable to speculate that Jung's childhood loneliness and introversion may have sparked his interest in the introversion-extraversion dimension of personality. In a similar vein, we saw that both Rogers and Maslow had to resist parental pressures in order to pursue their career interests. Their emphasis on the need to achieve personal fulfillment may have originated in these experiences.

Progress in the study of personality has also been influenced by developments in other areas of psychology. For instance, the enterprise of psychological testing originally emerged out of efforts to measure general intelligence. Eventually, however, the principles of psychological testing were applied to the challenge of measuring personality. In the upcoming Personal Application we discuss the logic and limitations of personality tests.

REVIEW OF KEY POINTS

- Modern personality research programs have tended to focus on specific personality traits. Sensation seeking is a trait describing the degree to which people seek high or low levels of sensory stimulation. High sensation seekers are willing to take risks, are open to new experiences, and are susceptible to boredom.

- Self-monitoring is the degree to which people attend to and control the impressions they make on others. High self-monitors are skilled at impression management and sensitive to others' self-presentations.

- Some studies suggest that the basic trait structure of personality may be much the same across cultures. However, some critics have voiced doubts about this conclusion.

- Markus and Kitayama assert that American culture fosters an independent conception of self, whereas Asian cultures foster an interdependent view of the self. These different views of the self lead to cultural disparities in the tendency to engage in self-enhancement.

- The study of personality illustrates how psychology is characterized by great theoretical diversity. The study of personality also demonstrates how ideas in psychology are shaped by sociohistorical forces and how cultural factors influence psychological processes.

Understanding Personality Assessment

Answer the following "true" or "false."

____ **1** Responses to personality tests are subject to unconscious distortion.

____ **2** The results of personality tests are often misunderstood.

____ **3** Personality test scores should be interpreted with caution.

____ **4** Personality tests serve many important functions.

If you answered "true" to all four questions, you earned a perfect score. Yes, personality tests are subject to distortion. Admittedly, test results are often misunderstood, and they should be interpreted cautiously. In spite of these problems, however, psychological tests can be quite useful.

Everyone engages in efforts to size up his or her own personality as well as that of others. When you think to yourself that "Mary Ann is shrewd and poised," or when you remark to a friend that "Howard is timid and submissive," you're making personality assessments. In a sense, then, personality assessment is an ongoing part of daily life. Given the popular interest in personality assessment, it's not surprising that psychologists have devised formal measures of personality.

The Uses of Personality Scales

Why are psychological tests used to measure personality? They have a variety of purposes. Benjamin Kleinmuntz (1985) lists four principal uses of personality tests:

1. Personality tests are used extensively by mental health professionals in the *clinical diagnosis* of psychological disorders. Although diagnoses are not made on the basis of test results alone, personality scales can be helpful in arriving at diagnostic decisions.

2. Personality measurement may be done for the purpose of *counseling* individuals about a variety of normal, everyday problems. Counselors often use personality scales to help people chart career plans and make vocational decisions.

3. Formal personality assessment often plays a key role in *personnel selection* in business, industry, government, and the military services. This use of personality testing has become controversial in recent years. Nonetheless, many organizations continue to use personality scales to assess applicants' suitability for various jobs.

4. Personality scales are frequently used in *psychological research*. Empirical studies on a great variety of issues require precise measurement of some aspect of personality. For instance, let's say you want to investigate whether introversion is related to a certain style of child rearing. Your task is simplified greatly if you have a personality test that measures introversion.

Personality tests can be divided into two broad categories: *self-report inventories* and *projective tests*. In this Application, we'll discuss some representative tests from both categories and discuss their strengths and weaknesses.

Self-Report Inventories

Self-report inventories **are personality tests that ask individuals to answer a series of questions about their characteristic behavior.** The logic underlying this approach is simple: Who knows you better? Who has known you longer? Who has more access to your private feelings? Some self-report inventories, such as the Sensation Seeking Scale and the Self-Monitoring Scale, are designed to measure one specific personality trait. Others can be used to measure many dimensions of personality simultaneously.

Single-trait scales are used primarily in research. In clinical, counseling, and personnel work, psychologists rely more on multitrait inventories. We'll discuss three examples of multitrait scales: the MMPI, the 16PF, and the NEO Personality Inventory.

The MMPI

The most widely used multitrait scale is the Minnesota Multiphasic Personality Inventory (MMPI). This test was developed in the 1940s (Hathaway & McKinley, 1943) but underwent a major revision and modernization in the 1980s. The authors of MMPI-2 set out to maintain the original character of the scale while replacing obsolete items, eliminating sexist language, and updating the test norms (Graham, 1990).

The MMPI was originally designed to aid clinicians in the diagnosis of psychological disorders. Consequently, it measures mostly aspects of personality that, when manifested to an extreme degree, are thought to be symptoms of disorders. Examples include traits such as paranoia, depression, and hysteria.

The MMPI is a rather lengthy test. The revised version consists of 567 statements to which the subject answers "true," "false," or "cannot say." The MMPI yields scores on the 14 subscales described in Table 12.3 on the next page. Four of the subscales are *validity scales* that provide indications about whether a subject has been careless or deceptive in taking the test. The remaining 10 are *clinical scales* that measure various aspects of personality.

Are the MMPI clinical scales valid? That is, do they measure what they were designed to measure? The validity of the MMPI has been investigated in hundreds of studies (Butcher & Keller, 1984). Originally, it was assumed that the 10 clinical subscales would provide direct indexes of specific types of disorders. In other words, a high score on the depression scale would be in-

Table 12.3 Personality Characteristics Associated with High MMPI Scores

Scale	Characteristics Associated with Higher Scores
Validity scale	
Cannot say (?)	May increase evasiveness.
Lie scale (L)	Indicates a tendency to present oneself in an overly favorable or highly virtuous light.
Infrequency scale (F)	Items on this scale are endorsed very infrequently by most people. Suggests carelessness, confusion, or "faking illness."
Subtle defensiveness (K)	Measures defensiveness of a subtle nature.
Clinical scale	
Hypochondriasis (Hs)	Indicates person is preoccupied with self, complaining, hostile, and presenting numerous physical problems that tend to be chronic.
Depression (D)	Indicates person is moody, shy, despondent, pessimistic, and distressed; one of the most frequently elevated scales in clinical patients.
Hysteria (Hy)	Indicates person tends to rely on neurotic defenses such as denial and repression to deal with stress and tends to be dependent, naive, outgoing, infantile, and narcissistic.
Psychopathic deviation (Pd)	May indicate rebelliousness, impulsiveness, hedonism, antisocial behavior, difficulty in marital or family relationships, and trouble with the law or authority in general.
Masculinity/femininity (MF)	Indicates departure from traditional gender roles. High-scoring men are described as sensitive, aesthetic, passive, or feminine. They may show conflicts over sexual identity and low heterosexual drive. Because the direction of scoring is reversed, high-scoring women are seen as masculine, rough, aggressive, self-confident, unemotional, and insensitive.
Paranoia (Pa)	Often indicates person is suspicious, aloof, shrewd, guarded, worrisome, and overly sensitive and likely to project or externalize blame.
Psychasthenia (Pt)	Indicates person is tense, anxious, ruminative, preoccupied, obsessional, phobic, rigid, and frequently self-condemning and feeling inferior and inadequate.
Schizophrenia (Sc)	Often indicates person is withdrawn, shy, unusual, or strange and has peculiar thoughts or ideas, poor reality contact, and perhaps delusions and hallucinations.
Hypomania (Ma)	Indicates person is social, outgoing, impulsive, overly energetic, optimistic, and in some cases amoral, flighty, grandiose, and impulsive.
Social introversion (Sie)	Indicates person is introverted, shy, withdrawn, socially reserved, submissive, overcontrolled, lethargic, conventional, tense, inflexible, and guilt-prone.

SOURCE: Keller, L. S., Butcher, J. N. & Slutske, W. S. (1990). Objective personality assessment. In G. Goldstein & M. Hersen (Eds.). *Handbook of psychological assessment* (pp. 345–386). New York: Pergamon Press. Copyright © 1990 Pergamon Press, Ltd. Adapted by permission.

dicative of depression, a high score on the paranoia scale would be indicative of a paranoid disorder, and so forth. However, research revealed that the relations between MMPI scores and various types of pathology are much more complex than anticipated. People with most types of disorders show elevated scores on *several* MMPI subscales. This means that certain score *profiles* are indicative of specific disorders (see Figure 12.19). Thus, the interpretation of the MMPI is quite complicated. Nonetheless, the MMPI can be a helpful diagnostic tool for the clinician. The fact that the inventory has been translated into more than 115 languages is a testimonial to its usefulness (Butcher, 1990).

The 16PF and NEO Personality Inventory

Raymond Cattell (1957, 1965) set out to identify and measure the *basic dimensions* of the *normal* personality. He started with a previously compiled list of 4504 personality traits. This massive list was reduced to 171 traits by weeding out terms that were virtually synonymous. Cattell then used factor analysis to identify clusters of closely related traits and the factors underlying them. Eventually, he reduced the list of 171 traits

to 16 *source traits*. The Sixteen Personality Factor (16PF) Questionnaire is a 187-item scale that assesses these 16 basic dimensions of personality (Cattell, Eber, & Tatsuoka, 1970), which are listed in Figure 12.20.

As we noted in the main body of the chapter, some theorists believe that only five trait dimensions are required to provide a full description of personality. This view has led to the creation of a relatively new test—the NEO Personality Inventory. Developed by Paul Costa and Robert McCrae (1985, 1992), the NEO Inventory is designed to measure the Big Five traits: neuroticism, extraversion, openness to experience, agree-

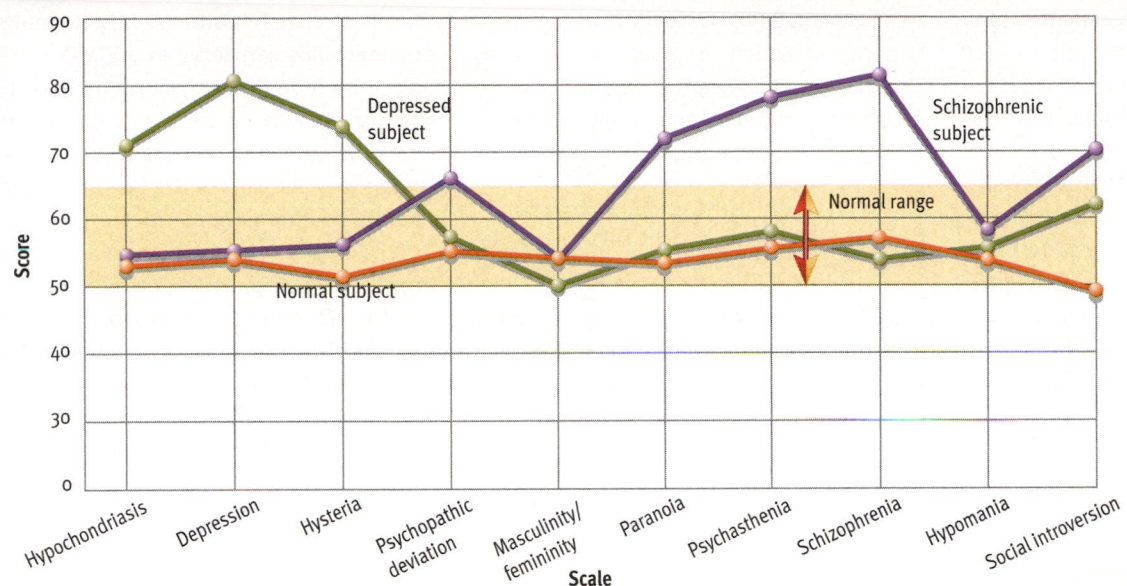

Figure 12.19

MMPI profiles. Scores on the 10 clinical scales of the MMPI are often plotted as shown here to create a profile for a client. The normal range for scores on each subscale is 50 to 65. People with disorders frequently exhibit elevated scores on several clinical scales rather than just one.

ableness, and conscientiousness. In spite of its short life span, the NEO is already widely used in research and clinical work.

Strengths and Weaknesses of Self-Report Inventories

To appreciate the strengths of self-report inventories, consider how else you might inquire about an individual's personality. For instance, if you want to know how assertive someone is, why not just ask the person? Why administer an elaborate 50-item personality inventory that measures assertiveness? The advantage of the personality inventory is that it can provide a more objective and more precise estimate, one that is better grounded in extensive comparative data. Take a moment to consider: How assertive are you? You probably have some vague idea, but to accurately gauge your assertiveness you would need a great deal of comparative information about others' assertiveness, data which you lack. In contrast, a self-report

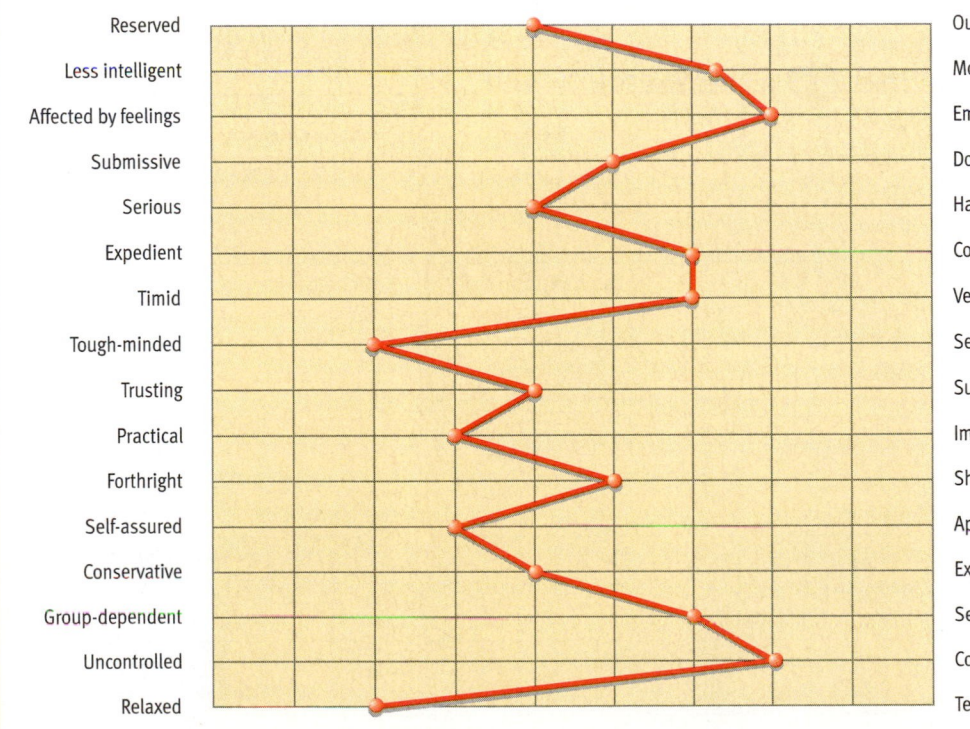

Figure 12.20

The Sixteen Personality Factor Questionnaire (16PF). Unlike the MMPI, Cattell's 16PF is designed to assess normal aspects of personality. The pairs of traits listed across from each other in the figure define the 16 factors measured by this self-report inventory. The profile shown is the average profile seen among a group of airline pilots who took the test.

Source: Cattell, R. B. (1973, July). Personality pinned down. *Psychology Today*, 40–46. Reprinted by permission of Psychology Today Magazine. Copyright © 1973 Sussex Publishers, Inc.

inventory inquires about your typical behavior in a variety of circumstances requiring assertiveness and generates an exact comparison with the typical behavior reported by many other respondents for the same circumstances.

Although self-report inventories are much more thorough and precise than casual observations, they are only as accurate as the information that respondents provide. They are susceptible to several sources of error (Kline, 1995; Paulhus, 1991; Rosse et al., 1998; Shedler, Mayman, & Manis, 1993), including the following:

1. *Deliberate deception.* Some self-report inventories include many questions whose purpose is easy to figure out. This problem makes it possible for some respondents to intentionally fake particular personality traits.

2. *Social desirability bias.* Without realizing it, some people consistently respond to questions in ways that make them look good. The social desirability bias isn't a matter of deception so much as wishful thinking.

3. *Response sets.* A response set is a systematic tendency to respond to test items in a particular way that is unrelated to the content of the items. For instance, some people, called "yea-sayers," tend to agree with virtually every statement on a test. Other people, called "nay-sayers," tend to disagree with nearly every statement.

Test developers have devised a number of strategies to reduce the impact of deliberate deception, social desirability bias, and response sets (Berry, Wetter, & Baer, 1995; Lanyon & Goodstein, 1997). For instance, it's possible to insert a "lie scale" into a test to assess the likelihood that a respondent is engaging in deception. The MMPI has a lie scale made up of 15 items that ask the subject to acknowledge minor faults that virtually everyone has. Subjects who report themselves to be nearly faultless on these questions are probably being deceptive.

The best way to reduce the impact of social desirability bias is to identify items that are sensitive to this bias and drop them

from the test. Problems with response sets can be reduced by systematically varying the way in which test items are worded. The key is to balance the items so that responses of agreement and disagreement are equally likely to be indicative of the trait being measured.

Projective Tests

Projective tests, which all take a rather indirect approach to the assessment of personality, are used extensively in clinical work. ***Projective tests* ask subjects to respond to vague, ambiguous stimuli in ways that may reveal the subjects' needs, feelings, and personality traits** (see Table 12.4 for examples). The Rorschach test, for instance, consists of a series of ten inkblots. Respondents are asked to describe what they see in the blots (see the photo on page 515). In the Thematic Apperception Test (TAT), a series of pictures of simple scenes are presented to subjects, who are asked to tell stories about what is happening in the scenes and what the characters are feeling. For instance, one TAT card shows a young boy contemplating a violin resting on a table in front of him (see Figure 12.21 for another example).

The Projective Hypothesis

The "projective hypothesis" is that ambiguous materials can serve as a blank screen onto which people project their characteristic concerns, conflicts, and desires (Frank, 1939). Thus, a competitive person who is shown the TAT card of the boy at the table with the violin might concoct a story about how the boy is contemplating an upcoming musical competition at which he hopes to excel. The same card shown to a person high in impulsiveness might elicit a story about how the boy is planning to sneak out the door to go dirt-bike riding with friends.

The scoring and interpretation of projective tests is very complicated. Rorschach responses may be analyzed in terms of content, originality, the feature of the inkblot that determined the response, and the amount of the inkblot used, among other criteria. In fact, five different systems exist for scoring the Rorschach (Edberg, 1990). TAT stories are examined in terms of heroes, needs, themes, and outcomes.

Strengths and Weaknesses of Projective Tests

Proponents of projective tests assert that the tests have two unique strengths. First, they are not transparent to subjects. That is, the

Table 12.4 Representative Projective Tests

Test	Stimuli Presented	Response Request
Rorschach test (Rorschach, 1942)	10 cards, each with a bilaterally symmetric inkblot	"Tell me what this might be."
Thematic Apperception Test (TAT) (Murray, 1943)	10 to 12 (out of 30 available) cards depicting simple scenes	"Tell me a story about each picture. Tell me what is happening, what the characters are thinking and feeling . . ."
Menninger Word Association Test (Rapaport, Gill, & Schafer, 1968)	60 nouns	"Tell me the first word that comes to mind."
Rotter Incomplete Sentence Blank (Rotter & Rafferty, 1950)	40 sentence stems such as "My greatest fear is . . ."	"Finish the sentence in writing as rapidly as possible."
Draw-a-Person Test (Machover, 1949)	Blank sheet of paper	"Draw a whole person." (When finished: "Draw a person of the other sex.")

Figure 12.21

The Thematic Apperception Test (TAT). In taking the TAT, a respondent is asked to tell stories about scenes such as this one. The themes apparent in each story can be scored to provide insight about the respondent's personality.

SOURCE: Murray. H. A. (1971). *Thematic Apperception Test.* Cambridge, MA: Harvard University Press. Copyright © 1943 by The President and Fellows of Harvard College, Copyright © 1971 by Henry A. Murray. Reprinted by permission of the publisher.

subject doesn't know how the test provides information to the tester. Hence, it's difficult for people to engage in intentional deception (Groth-Marnat, 1997). Second, the indirect approach used in these tests may make them especially sensitive to unconscious, latent features of personality.

Unfortunately, there is inadequate evidence for the reliability (consistency) and validity of projective measures (Lanyon & Goodstein, 1997; Lilienfeld, Wood & Garb, 2000). In particular, doubts have been raised about the research evidence on the Rorschach test (Garb, Florio, & Grove, 1998; Wood, Nezworski, & Stejskal, 1996). In spite of these problems, projective tests continue to be widely used by clinicians (Watkins et al., 1995). About 40 years ago, a reviewer characterized the critics of projective tests as "doubting statisticians" and the users of projective tests as "enthusiastic clinicians" (Adcock, 1965). Decades of research not withstanding, little has changed since then.

The continued popularity of the Rorschach and other projective techniques suggests that they are effective in eliciting information that is valuable to many clinicians (Groth-Marnat, 1997). Although the subjectivity of the projective tests raises serious concerns about their use in clinical diagnosis, some projective measures have shown adequate reliability and validity when used for limited, specific purposes, such as the assessment of achievement motivation (Spangler, 1992).

Although the problems associated with self-report inventories and projective tests can't be eliminated entirely, these measurement strategies have proven useful in personality assessment. In light of the potential for distortion, however, the results of personality tests should be interpreted with caution. Of course, as we saw in Chapter 9, prudence is always in order when interpreting psychological test results of any kind.

REVIEW OF KEY POINTS

- Personality assessment is useful in clinical diagnosis, counseling, personnel selection, and research. Personality scales can be divided into self-report inventories and projective tests.

- Self-report measures ask subjects to describe themselves. The MMPI is a widely used inventory that measures pathological aspects of personality. The 16PF assesses 16 dimensions of the normal personality. The NEO personality inventory measures the Big Five personality traits.

- Self-report inventories are vulnerable to certain sources of error, including deception, the social desirability bias, and response sets.

- Projective tests, such as the Rorschach and TAT, assume that subjects' responses to ambiguous stimuli reveal something about their personality. While the projective hypothesis seems plausible, projective tests' reliability and validity are disturbingly low.

When individuals are given the Rorschach test, they are shown a series of 10 inkblots and they are asked to describe the forms that they see in these ambiguous stimuli. Evidence on the reliability and validity of the Rorschach is not particularly impressive, but the test is still used by many clinicians.

© Laura Dwight/PhotoEdit

Hindsight in Everyday Analyses of Personality

Consider the case of two close sisters who grew up together: Lorena and Christina. Lorena grew into a frugal adult who is careful about spending her money, only shops when there are sales, and saves every penny she can. In contrast, Christina became an extravagant spender who lives to shop and never saves any money. How do the sisters explain their striking personality differences? Lorena attributes her thrifty habits to the fact that her family was so poor when she was a child that she learned the value of being careful with money. Christina attributes her extravagant spending to the fact that her family was so poor that she learned to really enjoy any money that she might have. Now, it *is* possible that two sisters could react to essentially the same circumstances quite differently, but the more likely explanation is that both sisters have been influenced by the **hindsight bias—the tendency to mold one's interpretation of the past to fit how events actually turned out.** We saw how hindsight can distort memory in Chapter 7. Here, we will see how hindsight tends to make everyone feel as if they are personality experts and how it creates interpretive problems even for scientific theories of personality.

The Prevalence of Hindsight Bias

Hindsight bias is *ubiquitous,* which means that it occurs in many different settings, with all sorts of people. Most of the time, people are not aware of the way their explanations are skewed by the fact that the outcome is already known. The experimental literature on hindsight bias offers a rich array of findings on how the knowledge of an outcome biases the way people think about its causes (Hawkins & Hastie, 1990). For example, when college students were told the results of hypothetical experiments, each group of students could "ex-plain" why the studies turned out the way they did, even though different groups were given opposite results to explain (Slovic & Fischhoff, 1977). The students believed that the results of the studies were obvious when they were told what the experimenter found, but when they were given only the information that was available before the outcome was known, it was not obvious at all. This bias is also called the "I knew it all along" effect because that is the typical re-frain of people when they have the luxury of hindsight. Indeed, after the fact, people often act as if events that would have been difficult to predict had in fact been virtually *inevitable.* Looking back at the disintegration of the Soviet Union and the end of the Cold War, for instance, many people today act as though these events were bound to happen, but in reality these landmark events were predicted by almost no one.

Hindsight bias shows up in many contexts. For example, when a couple announces that they are splitting up, many people in their social circle will typically claim they "saw it coming." When a football team loses in a huge upset, you will hear many fans claim, "I knew they were overrated and vulnerable." When public officials make a difficult decision that leads to a disastrous outcome—such as the FBI's 1993 attack on the Branch Davidian compound in Waco, Texas—many of the pundits in the press are quick to criticize, often asserting that only incompetent fools could have failed to foresee the catastrophe. Interestingly, people are not much kinder to themselves when they make ill-fated decisions. When individuals make tough calls that lead to negative results—such as buying a car that turns out to be a lemon, or investing in a stock that plummets—they often say things like, "Why did I ignore the obvious warning signs?" or "How could I be such an idiot?"

Hindsight and Personality

Hindsight bias appears to be pervasive in everyday analyses of personality. Think about it: If you attempt to explain why you are so suspicious, why your mother is so domineering, or why your best friend is so

Governor Tom Ridge

When public officials make tough decisions that backfire, critics are often quick to argue that the officials should have shown greater foresight (which may have been much more difficult than the critics suggest). This type of hindsight bias has been apparent in discussions of whether the 9/11 terrorist attacks could have been prevented. Here, U.S. Homeland Security Director Tom Ridge testifies before a congressional committee.

© 2002 AP/Wide World Photos

insecure, the starting point in each case will be the personality outcome. It would probably be impossible to reconstruct the past without being swayed by your knowledge of these outcomes. Thus, hindsight makes everybody an expert on personality, as we can all come up with plausible explanations for the personality traits of people we know well. Perhaps this is why Judith Harris (1998) ignited a firestorm of protest when she wrote a widely read book arguing that parents have relatively little effect on their children's personalities beyond the genetic material that they supply.

In her book *The Nurture Assumption,* Harris summarizes behavioral genetics research and other evidence suggesting that family environment has surprisingly little impact on children's personality (see pp. 501–502). As we discussed in the main body of the chapter, there is room for plenty of debate on this complex issue (Kagan, 1998; Tavris, 1998), but our chief interest here is that Harris made a cogent, compelling argument in her book that attracted extensive coverage in the press, which generated an avalanche of commentary from angry parents who argued that *parents do matter.* For example, *Newsweek* magazine received 350 letters, mostly from parents who provided examples of how they thought they influenced their children's personalities. However, parents' retrospective analyses of their children's personality development have to be treated with great skepticism, as they are likely to be distorted by hindsight bias (not to mention the selective recall frequently seen in anecdotal reports).

Unfortunately, hindsight bias is so prevalent it also presents a problem for scientific theories of personality. For example, the spectre of hindsight bias has been raised in many critiques of psychoanalytic theory (Torrey, 1992). Freudian theory was originally built mainly on a foundation of case studies of patients in therapy. Obviously, Freudian therapists who knew what their patients' adult personalities were like probably went looking for the types of childhood experiences hypothesized by Freud (oral fixations, punitive toilet training, Oedipal conflicts, and so forth) in their efforts to explain their patients' personalities.

Another problem with hindsight bias is that once researchers know an outcome, more often than not they can fashion some plausible explanation for it. For instance, Torrey (1992) describes a study inspired by Freudian theory that examined breast-size preferences among men. The original hypothesis was that men who scored higher in dependence—thought to be a sign of oral fixation—would manifest a stronger preference for women with large breasts. When the actual results of the study showed just the opposite—that dependence was associated with a preference for smaller breasts—the finding was attributed to reaction formation on the part of the men. Instead of failing to support Freudian theory, the unexpected findings were simply reinterpreted in a way that was consistent with Freudian theory.

Hindsight bias also presents thorny problems for evolutionary theorists, who generally work backward from known outcomes to reason out how adaptive pressures in humans' ancestral past may have led to those outcomes (Cornell, 1997). Consider, for instance, evolutionary theorists' assertion that the Big Five traits are found to be fundamental dimensions of personality around the world because those specific traits have had major adaptive implications over the course of human history (Buss, 1995; MacDonald, 1998). Their explanation makes sense, but what would have happened if some *other traits* had shown up in the Big Five? Would the evolutionary view have been weakened if dominance, or paranoia, or high sensation seeking had turned up in the Big Five? Probably not. With the luxury of hindsight, evolutionary theorists surely could have constructed plausible explanations for how these traits promoted reproductive success in the distant past. Thus, hindsight bias is a fundamental feature of human cognition,

and the scientific enterprise is not immune to this problem.

Other Implications of "20/20 Hindsight"

Our discussion of hindsight has focused on its implications for thinking about personality, but there is ample evidence that hindsight can bias thinking in all sorts of domains. For example, consider the practice of obtaining second opinions on medical diagnoses. The doctor providing the second opinion usually is aware of the first physician's diagnosis, which creates a hindsight bias (Arkes et al., 1981). Second opinions would probably be more valuable if the doctors rendering them were not aware of previous diagnoses. Hindsight also has the potential to distort legal decisions in cases involving allegations of negligence. Jurors' natural tendency to think "how could they have failed to foresee this problem," may exaggerate the appearance of negligence (LaBine & LaBine, 1996).

Hindsight bias is very powerful. The next time you hear of an unfortunate outcome to a decision made by a public official, carefully examine the way news reporters describe the decision. You will probably find that they believe that the disastrous outcome should have been obvious, because they can clearly see what went wrong after the fact. Similarly, if you find yourself thinking "Only a fool would have failed to anticipate this disaster" or "I would have foreseen this problem," take a deep breath and try to review the decision *using only information that was known at the time the decision was being made.* Sometimes good decisions, based on the best available information, can have terrible outcomes. Unfortunately, the clarity of "20/20 hindsight" makes it difficult for people to learn from their own and others' mistakes.

Table 12.5 Critical Thinking Skill Discussed in This Application

Skill	Description
Recognizing the bias in hindsight analysis	The critical thinker understands that knowing the outcome of events biases our recall and interpretation of the events.

RECAP

Key Ideas

The Nature of Personality

● The concept of personality explains the consistency in people's behavior over time and situations while also explaining their distinctiveness. There is considerable debate as to how many trait dimensions are necessary to account for the variation in personality, but the Big Five model has become the dominant conception of personality structure.

Psychodynamic Perspectives

● Freud's psychoanalytic theory emphasizes the importance of the unconscious. Freud described personality structure in terms of three components—the id, ego, and superego—which are routinely involved in an ongoing series of internal conflicts.

● Freud theorized that conflicts centering on sex and aggression are especially likely to lead to anxiety. According to Freud, anxiety and other unpleasant emotions such as guilt are often warded off with defense mechanisms.

● Freud described a series of five stages of development: oral, anal, phallic, latency, and genital. Certain experiences during these stages can have lasting effects on adult personality.

● Jung's most innovative and controversial concept was the collective unconscious. Adler's individual psychology emphasizes how people strive for superiority to compensate for their feelings of inferiority.

● Overall, psychodynamic theories have produced many groundbreaking insights about the unconscious, the role of internal conflict, and the importance of early childhood experiences in personality development. However, psychodynamic theories have been criticized for their poor testability, their inadequate base of empirical evidence, and their male-centered views.

Behavioral Perspectives

● Behavioral theories view personality as a collection of response tendencies tied to specific stimulus situations. They assume that personality development is a lifelong process in which response tendencies are shaped and reshaped by learning, especially operant conditioning.

● Social learning theory focuses on how cognitive factors such as expectancies and self-efficacy regulate learned behavior. Bandura's concept of observational learning accounts for the acquisition of responses from models. Mischel has questioned the degree to which people display cross-situational consistency in behavior.

● Behavioral approaches to personality are based on rigorous research. They have provided ample insights into how environmental factors

and learning mold personalities. The behaviorists have been criticized for their overdependence on animal research, their fragmented analysis of personality, and radical behaviorism's dehumanizing view of human nature.

Humanistic Perspectives

● Humanistic theories are phenomenological and take an optimistic view of human potential. Rogers focused on the self-concept as the critical aspect of personality. Maslow theorized that psychological health depends on fulfilling one's need for self-actualization.

● Humanistic theories deserve credit for highlighting the importance of subjective views of oneself and for helping to lay the foundation for positive psychology. Humanistic theories lack a firm base of research, are difficult to put to an empirical test, and may be overly optimistic about human nature.

Biological Perspectives

● Contemporary biological theories stress the genetic origins of personality. Eysenck suggests that heredity influences individual differences in physiological functioning that affect how easily people acquire conditioned responses. Research on the personality resemblance of twins provides impressive evidence that genetic factors shape personality.

● Evolutionary theorists argue that the major dimensions of personality reflect humans' adaptive landscape. The biological approach has demonstrated that personality is partly heritable, but it has been criticized for its narrow focus on heritability and because it offers no systematic model of how physiology shapes personality.

Contemporary Empirical Approaches to Personality

● Sensation seeking is a trait describing the degree to which people seek high or low levels of sensory stimulation. Self-monitoring is the degree to which people attend to and control the impressions they make on others.

Culture and Personality

● Some studies suggest that the basic trait structure of personality may be much the same across cultures. However, notable differences have been found when researchers have compared cultural groups' conceptions of self.

Putting It in Perspective

● The study of personality illustrates how psychology is characterized by great theoretical diversity. It also demonstrates how ideas in psychology are shaped by sociohistorical forces and how cultural factors influence psychological processes.

Personal Application ●
Understanding Personality Assessment

● Personality assessment is useful in clinical diagnosis, counseling, personnel selection, and research. Self-report measures ask subjects to describe themselves. Self-report inventories are vulnerable to certain sources of error, including deception, the social desirability bias, and response sets.

● Projective tests assume that subjects' responses to ambiguous stimuli reveal something about their personality. While the projective hypothesis seems plausible, projective tests' reliability and validity are disturbingly low.

Critical Thinking Application ●
Hindsight in Everyday Analyses of Personality

● Hindsight bias often leads people to assert that "I knew it all along" in discussing outcomes that they did not actually predict. Thanks to hindsight, people can almost always come up with plausible-sounding explanations for known personality traits.

Key Terms

Archetypes
Behaviorism
Collective unconscious
Compensation
Conscious
Defense mechanisms
Displacement
Ego
Extraverts
Factor analysis
Fixation
Hierarchy of needs
Hindsight bias
Humanism
Id
Identification
Incongruence
Introverts
Model
Need for self-
  actualization
Observational learning
Oedipal complex
Personal unconscious
Personality
Personality trait
Phenomenological
  approach
Pleasure principle
Preconscious
Projection
Projective tests

Psychodynamic
  theories
Psychosexual stages
Rationalization
Reaction formation
Reality principle
Reciprocal
  determinism
Regression
Repression
Self-actualizing
  persons
Self-concept
Self-efficacy
Self-enhancement
Self-monitoring
Self-report inventories
Sensation seeking
Striving for superiority
Superego
Unconscious

Key People

Alfred Adler
Albert Bandura
Hans Eysenck
Sigmund Freud
Carl Jung
Abraham Maslow
Walter Mischel
Carl Rogers
B. F. Skinner

PRACTICE TEST

1. Harvey Hedonist has devoted his life to the search for physical pleasure and immediate need gratification. Freud would say that Harvey is dominated by:
   A. his ego.
   B. his superego.
   C. his id.
   D. Bacchus.

2. Furious at her boss for what she considers to be unjust criticism, Tyra turns around and takes out her anger on her subordinates. Tyra may be using the defense mechanism of:
   A. displacement.
   B. reaction formation.
   C. identification.
   D. replacement.

3. Freud believed that most personality disturbances are due to:
   A. the failure of parents to reinforce healthy behavior.
   B. a poor self-concept resulting from excessive parental demands.
   C. unconscious and unresolved sexual conflicts rooted in childhood experiences.
   D. the exposure of children to unhealthy role models.

4. According to Alfred Adler, the prime motivating force in a person's life is:
   A. physical gratification.
   B. existential anxiety.
   C. striving for superiority.
   D. the need for power.

5. Which of the following learning mechanisms does B. F. Skinner see as being the major means by which behavior is learned?
   A. classical conditioning
   B. operant conditioning
   C. observational learning
   D. insight learning

6. Always having been a good student, Irving is confident that he will do well in his psychology course. According to Bandura's social cognitive theory, Irving would be said to have:
   A. strong feelings of self-efficacy.
   B. a sense of superiority.
   C. strong feelings of self-esteem.
   D. strong defense mechanisms.

7. Which of the following approaches to personality is least deterministic?
   A. the humanistic approach
   B. the psychoanalytic approach
   C. Skinner's approach
   D. the behavioral approach

8. Which of the following did Carl Rogers believe fosters a congruent self-concept?
   A. conditional love
   B. appropriate role models
   C. immediate-need gratification
   D. unconditional love

9. The strongest support for the theory that personality is heavily influenced by genetics is provided by strong personality similarity between:
   A. identical twins reared together.
   B. identical twins reared apart.
   C. fraternal twins reared together.
   D. nontwins reared together.

10. Which of the following is the best way to regard heritability estimates?
    A. as reliable but not necessarily valid estimates
    B. as ballpark estimates of the influence of genetics
    C. as accurate estimates of the influence of genetics
    D. as relatively useless estimates of the influence of genetics

11. People who are high in self-monitoring:
    A. are sensitive to how their self-presentations go over.
    B. are good judges of others' personality.
    C. readily adjust their self-presentations to create certain impressions.
    D. all of the above.

12. If given a choice between staying home to read a good book and spending the day at an amusement park, Eldridge is likely to stay home. Marvin Zuckerman would say that Edridge is probably:
    A. a low self-monitor.
    B. an introvert.
    C. relatively low in sensation seeking.
    D. psychologically repressed.

13. In which of the following cultures is an independent view of the self most likely to be the norm?
    A. China
    B. Japan
    C. Africa
    D. United States

14. Which of the following is *not* a shortcoming of self-report personality inventories?
    A. The accuracy of the results is a function of the honesty of the respondent.
    B. Respondents may attempt to answer in a way that makes them look good.
    C. There is sometimes a problem with "yea-sayers" or "nay-sayers."
    D. They are objective measures that are easy to administer and score.

15. In *The Nurture Assumption*, Judith Harris argues that the evidence indicates that family environment has _____ on children's personalities.
    A. largely positive effects
    B. largely negative effects
    C. surprisingly little effect
    D. a powerful effect

Answers

1	C	p. 481	**6**	A	p. 494	**11**	D	pp. 506–507
2	A	p. 483	**7**	A	pp. 495–496	**12**	C	p. 506
3	C	p. 486	**8**	D	pp. 496–497	**13**	D	pp. 508–509
4	C	p. 488	**9**	B	p. 501	**14**	D	p. 514
5	B	pp. 490–491	**10**	B	p. 503	**15**	C	p. 517

ON THE WEB

For additional resources on the topics covered in this chapter, visit the *Psychology: Themes and Variations* Web site, where you will find practice quizzes, tutorials, Web links, simulations, critical thinking activities, flash cards, interactive exercises, and suggested readings available through INFOTRAC.

http://psychology.wadsworth.com/weiten_themes6e/

CHAPTER 13

© Kevin R. Morris/CORBIS

Stress, Coping, and Health

You're in your car headed home from school with a classmate. Traffic is barely moving. A radio report indicates that the traffic jam is only going to get worse. You groan audibly as you fiddle impatiently with the radio dial. Another motorist nearly takes your fender off trying to cut into your lane. Your pulse quickens as you shout insults at the unknown driver, who can't even hear you. You think about the term paper that you have to work on tonight. Your stomach knots up as you recall all the crumpled drafts you tossed into the wastebasket last night. If you don't finish that paper soon, you won't be able to find any time to study for your math test, not to mention your biology quiz. Suddenly, you remember that you promised the person you're dating that the two of you would get together tonight. There's no way. Another fight looms on the horizon. Your classmate asks how you feel about the tuition increase that the college announced yesterday. You've been trying not to think about it. You're already in debt up to your ears. Your parents are bugging you about changing schools, but you don't want to leave your friends. Your heartbeat quickens as you contemplate the debate you're sure to have with your parents. You feel wired with tension as you realize that the stress in your life never seems to let up.

Many circumstances can create stress. It comes in all sorts of packages: big and small, pretty and ugly, simple and complex. All too often, the package comes as a surprise. In this chapter we'll try to sort out these packages. We'll discuss the nature of stress, how people cope with stress, and the potential effects of stress.

Our examination of the relationship between stress and physical illness will lead us into a broader discussion of the psychology of health. The way people in health professions think about physical illness has changed considerably in the past 20 years. The tradi-tional view of physical illness as a purely biological phenomenon has given way to a biopsychosocial model of illness (Smilkstein, 1990). **The *biopsychoso-cial model* holds that physical illness is caused by a complex interaction of biological, psychologi-cal, and sociocultural factors.** This model does not suggest that biological factors are unimportant. It simply asserts that these factors operate in a psycho-social context that is also influential.

What has led to this shift in thinking? In part, it's a result of changing patterns of illness. Prior to the 20th century, the principal threats to health were *contagious diseases* caused by infectious agents—dis-eases such as smallpox, typhoid fever, diphtheria, yel-low fever, malaria, cholera, tuberculosis, and polio. Today, none of these diseases is among the leading killers in the United States. They were tamed by im-provements in nutrition, public hygiene, sanitation, and medical treatment (Grob, 1983). Unfortunately, the void left by contagious diseases has been filled all too quickly by *chronic diseases* that develop grad-ually, such as heart disease, cancer, and stroke (see Figure 13.1 on the next page). Psychosocial factors, such as stress and lifestyle, play a large role in the de-velopment of these chronic diseases. The growing recognition that psychological factors influence phys-ical health has led to the emergence of a new spe-cialty in psychology. *Health psychology* is concerned with how psychosocial factors relate to the pro-motion and maintenance of health and with the causation, prevention, and treatment of illness. In the second half of this chapter, we'll explore this new domain of psychology. In the Personal Applica-tion, we'll focus on strategies for enhancing stress management, and in the Critical Thinking Applica-tion we'll discuss strategies for improving health-related decision making.

Figure 13.1

Changing patterns of illness. Trends in the death rates for various diseases during the 20th century reveal that contagious diseases (shown in blue) have declined as a threat to health. However, the death rates for stress-related chronic diseases (shown in red) have remained quite high. The pie chart (inset) shows the results of these trends: three chronic diseases (heart disease, cancer, and stroke) account for 60.3% of all deaths. (Based on data from the U.S. National Center for Health Statistics)

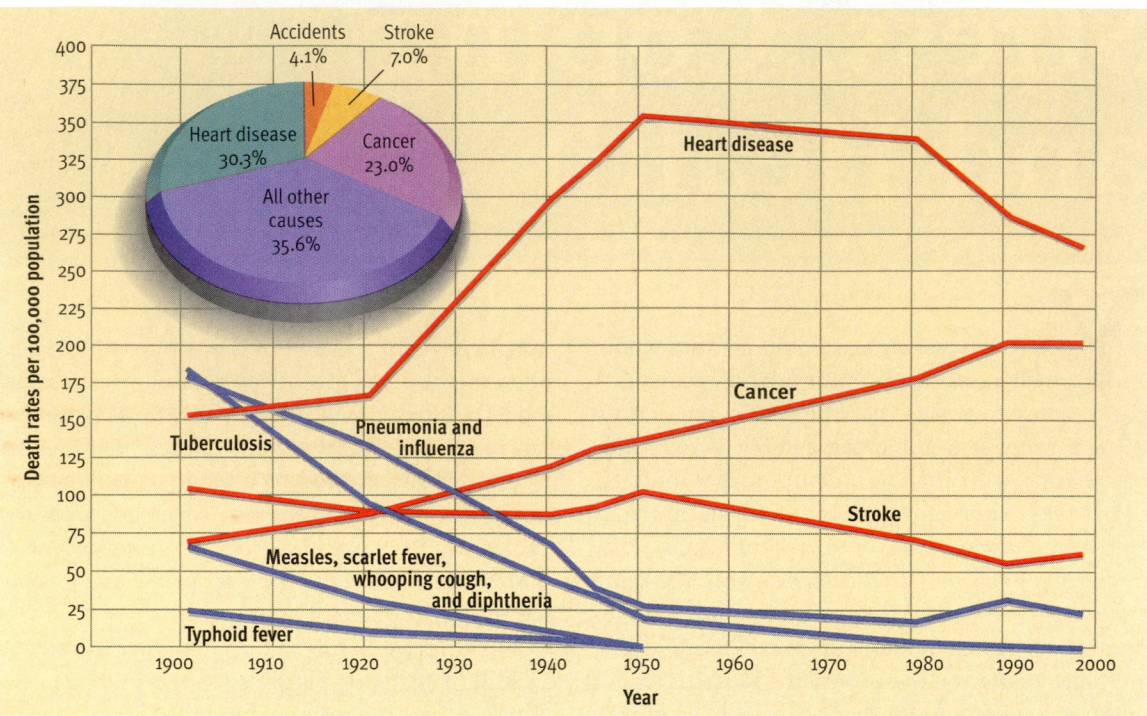

The Nature of Stress

PREVIEW QUESTIONS
- What is stress?
- How significant are minor, everyday stressors?
- How objective are our appraisals of stress?

"We developed the Hassle Scale because we think scales that measure major events miss the point. The constant, minor irritants may be much more important than the large, landmark changes."
RICHARD LAZARUS

The word *stress* has been used in different ways by different theorists. We'll define **stress as any circumstances that threaten or are perceived to threaten one's well-being and that thereby tax one's coping abilities.** The threat may be to immediate physical safety, long-range security, self-esteem, reputation, peace of mind, or many other things that one values. Stress is a complex concept, so let's explore a little further.

Stress as an Everyday Event

The word *stress* tends to spark images of overwhelming, traumatic crises. People may think of tornadoes, hurricanes, floods, and earthquakes. Undeniably, major disasters of this sort are extremely stressful events. Studies conducted in the aftermath of natural disasters typically find elevated rates of psychological problems and physical illness in the communities affected by these disasters (Brende, 2000; Raphael & Dobson, 2000). However, these unusual events are only a small part of what constitutes stress. Many everyday events, such as waiting in line, having car trouble, shopping for Christmas presents, misplacing your checkbook, and staring at bills you can't pay are also stressful. Researchers have found that everyday problems and the minor nuisances of life

are also important forms of stress (Kohn, Lafreniere, & Gurevich, 1991). Of course, major and minor stressors are not entirely independent. A major stressful event, such as going through a divorce, can trigger a cascade of minor stressors, such as looking for an attorney, changing bank accounts, taking on new household responsibilities, and so forth (Pillow, Zautra, & Sandler, 1996).

You might guess that minor stresses would produce minor effects, but that isn't necessarily true. Richard Lazarus and his colleagues, who developed a scale to measure everyday hassles, have shown that routine hassles may have significant harmful effects on mental and physical health (Delongis, Folkman, & Lazarus, 1988). Why would minor hassles be related to mental health? The answer isn't entirely clear yet, but it may be because of the *cumulative* nature of stress (Seta, Seta, & Wang, 1991). Stress adds up. Routine stresses at home, at school, and at work might be fairly benign individually, but collectively they could create great strain.

Appraisal: Stress Lies in the Eye of the Beholder

The experience of feeling stressed depends on what events one notices and how one chooses to appraise or interpret them (Lazarus, 1999). Events that are stressful for one person may be routine for another. For example, many people find flying in an airplane somewhat stressful, but frequent fliers may not be bothered at all. Some people enjoy the excitement of going out on a date with someone new; others find the uncertainty terrifying.

Often, people aren't very objective in their appraisals of potentially stressful events. A study of hospitalized patients awaiting surgery showed only a slight correlation between the objective seriousness of a person's upcoming surgery and the amount of fear experienced by the patients (Janis, 1958). Clearly, some people are more prone than others to feel threatened by life's difficulties. A number of studies have shown that anxious, neurotic people report more stress than others (Watson, David, & Suls, 1999), as do people who are relatively unhappy (Seidlitz & Diener, 1993). Thus, stress lies in the eye (actually, the mind) of the beholder. People's appraisals of stressful events are highly subjective.

Major Types of Stress

An enormous variety of events can be stressful for one person or another. Although they're not entirely independent, the four principal types of stress are (1) frustration, (2) conflict, (3) change, and (4) pressure. As you read about each, you'll surely recognize four very familiar adversaries.

Frustration

I had a wonderful relationship with a nice man for three months. One day when we planned to spend the entire day together, he called and said he wouldn't be meeting me and that he had decided to stop seeing me. I cried all morning. The grief was like losing someone through death. I still hurt, and I wonder if I'll ever get over him.

This scenario illustrates frustration. As psychologists use the term, *frustration* occurs in any situation in which the pursuit of some goal is thwarted. In essence, you experience frustration when you want something and you can't have it. Everyone has to deal with frustration virtually every day. Traffic jams, difficult daily commutes, and annoying drivers, for instance, are a routine source of frustration that can elicit anger and aggression (Hennessy & Wiesenthal, 1999; Rasmussen, Knapp, & Garner, 2000). Fortunately, most frustrations are brief and insignificant. You may be quite upset when you go to a repair shop to pick up your ailing VCR and find that it hasn't been fixed as promised. However, a week later you'll probably have your VCR back, and the frustration will be forgotten.

Of course, some frustrations can be sources of significant stress. Failures and losses are two common kinds of frustration that are often highly stressful. Everyone fails in at least some of his or her endeavors. Some people make failure almost inevitable by setting unrealistically high goals for themselves. For example, many business executives tend to forget that for every newly appointed vice president in the business world, there are dozens of middle-level executives who don't get promoted. Losses can be especially frustrating because people are deprived of something that they're accustomed to having. For example, few things are more frustrating than losing a dearly loved boyfriend, girlfriend, spouse, or parent.

Conflict

Should I or shouldn't I? I became engaged at Christmas. My fiance surprised me with a ring. I knew if I refused the ring he would be terribly hurt and our relationship would suffer. However, I don't really know whether or not I want to marry him. On the other hand, I don't want to lose him either.

Like frustration, conflict is an unavoidable feature of everyday life. The perplexing question "Should I or shouldn't I?" comes up countless times in everyone's life. *Conflict* occurs when two or more incompatible motivations or behavioral impulses compete for expression. As we discussed in Chapter 12, Sigmund Freud proposed over a century ago that internal conflicts generate considerable psychological distress. This link between conflict and distress was measured with new precision in studies by Laura King and Robert Emmons (1990, 1991). They used an elaborate questionnaire to assess the overall amount of internal conflict experienced by subjects. They found that higher levels of conflict were associated with higher levels of anxiety, depression, and physical symptoms.

Conflicts come in three types, which were originally described by Kurt Lewin (1935) and investigated extensively by Neal Miller (1944, 1959). These three basic types of conflict—approach-approach, avoidance-avoidance, and approach-avoidance—are diagrammed in Figure 13.2 on the next page.

PREVIEW QUESTIONS
- What is frustration?
- What are the three types of conflict?
- Which types of conflict are especially stressful?
- What evidence led to the conclusion that life changes are stressful?
- What is pressure?

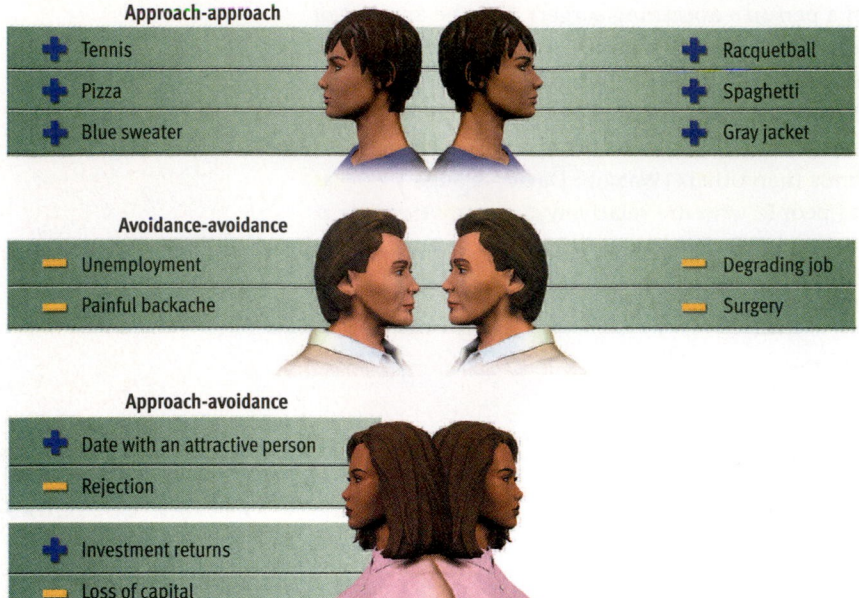

Figure 13.2

Types of conflict. Psychologists have identified three basic types of conflict. In approach-approach and avoidance-avoidance conflicts, a person is torn between two goals. In an approach-avoidance conflict, there is only one goal under consideration, but it has both positive and negative aspects.

Approach-approach
- + Tennis
- + Pizza
- + Blue sweater
- + Racquetball
- + Spaghetti
- + Gray jacket

Avoidance-avoidance
- − Unemployment
- − Painful backache
- − Degrading job
- − Surgery

Approach-avoidance
- + Date with an attractive person
- − Rejection
- + Investment returns
- − Loss of capital

In an *approach-approach conflict* a choice must be made between two attractive goals. The problem, of course, is that you can choose just one of the two goals. For example: You have a free afternoon; should you play tennis or racquetball? You're out for a meal; do you want the pizza or the spaghetti? You can't afford both—should you buy the blue sweater or the gray jacket?

Among the three kinds of conflict, the approach-approach type tends to be the least stressful. People don't usually stagger out of restaurants exhausted by the stress of choosing which of several appealing entrees to eat. Approach-approach conflicts typically have a reasonably happy ending, whichever way you decide to go. Nonetheless, approach-approach con-

flicts over important issues may sometimes be troublesome. If you're torn between two appealing college majors or two attractive boyfriends, you may find the decision-making process quite stressful, since whichever alternative is not chosen represents a loss of sorts.

In an *avoidance-avoidance conflict* a choice must be made between two unattractive goals. Forced to choose between two repelling alternatives, you are, as they say, "caught between a rock and a hard place." For example, should you continue to collect unemployment checks, or should you take that degrading job at the car wash? Or suppose you have painful backaches. Should you submit to surgery that you dread, or should you continue to live with the back pain? Obviously, avoidance-avoidance conflicts are most unpleasant and highly stressful.

In an *approach-avoidance conflict* a choice must be made about whether to pursue a single goal that has both attractive and unattractive aspects. For instance, imagine that you're offered a career promotion that will mean a large increase in pay, but you'll have to move to a city where you don't want to live. Approach-avoidance conflicts are common and can be quite stressful. Any time you have to take a risk to pursue some desirable outcome, you're likely to find yourself in an approach-avoidance conflict. Should you risk rejection by asking out a person that you are attracted to? Should you risk your savings by investing in a new business that could fail?

Approach-avoidance conflicts often produce *vacillation*. That is, you go back and forth, beset by indecision. You decide to go ahead, then you decide not to, and then you decide to go ahead again. Humans are not unique in this respect. Many years ago, Neal Miller (1944) observed the same vacillation in his groundbreaking research with rats. He created approach-avoidance conflicts in hungry rats by alternately feeding and shocking them at one end of a runway apparatus. Eventually, these rats tended to hover near the center of the runway, alternately approaching and retreating from the goal box at the end of the alley.

Change

After my divorce, I lived alone for four years. Six months ago I married a wonderful woman who has two children from her previous marriage. My biggest stress is suddenly having to adapt to living with three people instead of by myself. I was pretty set in my ways. I had certain routines. Now everything is chaos. I love my wife and I'm fond of the kids. They're not really doing anything wrong. But my house and my life just aren't the same, and I'm having trouble dealing with it all.

CONCEPT CHECK 13.1

Identifying Types of Conflict

Check your understanding of the three basic types of conflict by identifying the type experienced in each of the following examples. The answers are in Appendix A.

Examples

_____ **1.** John can't decide whether to take a demeaning job in a car wash or to go on welfare.

_____ **2.** Desiree wants to apply to a highly selective law school, but she hates to risk the possibility of rejection.

_____ **3.** Vanessa has been shopping for a new car and is torn between a nifty little sports car and a classy sedan, both of which she really likes.

Types of conflict

a. approach-approach
b. avoidance-avoidance
c. approach-avoidance

It has been proposed that life changes, such as a change in marital status, represent a key type of stress. *Life changes* are any noticeable alterations in one's living circumstances that require readjustment. The importance of life changes was first demonstrated by Thomas Holmes, Richard Rahe, and their colleagues in the 1960s (Holmes & Rahe, 1967; Rahe & Arthur, 1978). Theorizing that stress might make people more vulnerable to illness, they interviewed thousands of tuberculosis patients to find out what kinds of events had preceded the onset of their disease. Surprisingly, the most frequently cited events were not uniformly negative. There were plenty of aversive events, as expected. But there were also many seemingly positive events, such as getting married, having a baby, or getting promoted.

Why would positive events, such as moving to a nicer home, produce stress? According to Holmes and Rahe, it's because they produce *change.* In their view, changes in personal relationships, changes at work, changes in finances, and so forth can be stressful even when the changes are welcomed.

Based on this analysis, Holmes and Rahe (1967) developed the Social Readjustment Rating Scale (SRRS) to measure life change as a form of stress. The scale assigns numerical values to 43 major life events. These values are supposed to reflect the magnitude of the readjustment required by each change (see Table 13.1). In using the scale, respondents are asked to indicate how often they experienced any of these 43 events during a certain time period (typically, the past year). The numbers associated with each event checked are then added. This total is an index of the amount of change-related stress the person has recently experienced.

The SRRS and similar scales based on it have been used in thousands of studies by researchers all over the world. Overall, these studies have shown that people with higher scores on the SRRS tend to be more vulnerable to many kinds of physical illness and to many types of psychological problems as well (Derogatis & Coons, 1993; Gruen, 1993; Scully, Tosi, & Banning, 2000). These results have attracted a great deal of attention, and the SRRS has been reprinted in many popular newspapers and magazines. The attendant publicity has led to the widespread conclusion that life change is inherently stressful.

More recently, however, experts have criticized this research, citing problems with the methods used and raising questions about the meaning of the findings (Critelli & Ee, 1996; Monroe & McQuaid, 1994; Wethington, 2000). At this point, it's a key interpretive issue that concerns us. Many critics have argued that the SRRS does not measure *change* exclusively.

The main problem is that the list of life changes on the SRRS is dominated by events that are clearly negative or undesirable (death of a spouse, being fired from a job, and so on). These negative events probably generate great frustration. Although there are some positive events on the scale, it turns out that negative life events cause most of the stress tapped by the SRRS (McLean & Link, 1994; Turner & Wheaton,

Table 13.1 Social Readjustment Rating Scale

Life Event	Mean Value
Death of a spouse	100
Divorce	73
Marital separation	65
Jail term	63
Death of a close family member	63
Personal injury or illness	53
Marriage	50
Fired at work	47
Marital reconciliation	45
Retirement	45
Change in health of family member	44
Pregnancy	40
Sex difficulties	39
Gain of a new family member	39
Business readjustment	39
Change in financial state	38
Death of a close friend	37
Change to a different line of work	36
Change in number of arguments with spouse	35
Mortgage or loan for major purchase (home, etc.)	31
Foreclosure of mortgage or loan	30
Change in responsibilities at work	29
Son or daughter leaving home	29
Trouble with in-laws	29
Outstanding personal achievement	28
Spouse begins or stops work	26
Begin or end school	26
Change in living conditions	25
Revision of personal habits	24
Trouble with boss	23
Change in work hours or conditions	20
Change in residence	20
Change in school	20
Change in recreation	19
Change in church activities	19
Change in social activities	18
Mortgage or loan for lesser purchase (car, TV, etc.)	17
Change in sleeping habits	16
Change in number of family get-togethers	15
Change in eating habits	15
Vacation	13
Christmas	12
Minor violations of the law	11

SOURCE: Adapted from Holmes, T. H., & Rahe, R. (1967). The Social Readjustment Rating Scale. *Journal of Psychosomatic Research, 11,* 213–218. Copyright © 1967 by Elsevier Science Publishing Co. Reprinted by permission.

Web Link 13.1

The Web's Stress Management & Emotional Wellness Page
Ernesto Randolfi (Montana State University) has gathered a comprehensive set of resources dealing with stress management. Topics covered include cognitive restructuring, relaxation techniques, and stress in the workplace and in college life.

1995). Thus, it has become apparent that the SRRS assesses a wide range of stressful experiences, not just life change. At present, there's little reason to believe that change is inherently or inevitably stressful. Undoubtedly, some life changes may be quite challenging, but others may be quite benign.

Pressure

My father questioned me at dinner about some things I didn't want to talk about. I know he doesn't want to hear my answers, at least not the truth. My father told me when I was little that I was his favorite because I was "pretty near perfect." I've spent my life trying to keep up that image, even though it's obviously not true. Recently, he has begun to realize this, and it's made our relationship very strained and painful.

At one time or another, most people have remarked that they're "under pressure." What does this mean? *Pressure* involves expectations or demands that one behave in a certain way. You are under pressure to *perform* when you're expected to execute tasks and responsibilities quickly, efficiently, and successfully. For example, salespeople are usually under pressure to move merchandise. Professors at research institutions are often under pressure to publish in prestigious journals. Stand-up comedians are under intense pressure to make people laugh. Pressures to *conform* to others' expectations are also common in our lives. People in the business world are expected to dress in certain ways. Suburban homeowners are expected to keep their lawns well manicured. Teenagers are expected to adhere to their parents' values and rules.

Although widely discussed by the general public, the concept of pressure has received scant attention from researchers. However, Weiten (1988b, 1998) has devised a scale to measure pressure as a form of life stress. It assesses self-imposed pressure, pressure from work and school, and pressure from family relations, peer relations, and intimate relations. In research with this scale, a strong relationship has been found between pressure and a variety of psychological symptoms and problems. In fact, pressure has turned out to be more strongly related to measures of mental health than the SRRS and other established measures of stress are (see Figure 13.3).

Figure 13.3

Pressure and psychological symptoms. A comparison of pressure and life change as sources of stress suggests that pressure may be more strongly related to mental health than change is. In one study, Weiten (1988b) found a correlation of .59 between scores on the Pressure Inventory (PI) and symptoms of psychological distress. In the same sample, the correlation between SRRS scores and psychological symptoms was only .28.

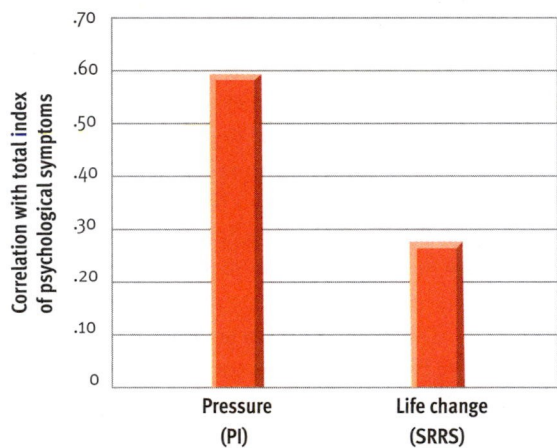

CONCEPT CHECK 13.2

Recognizing Sources of Stress

Check your understanding of the major sources of stress by indicating which type or types of stress are at work in each of the examples below. Bear in mind that the four basic types of stress are not mutually exclusive. There's some potential for overlap, so a specific experience might include both change and pressure, for instance. The answers are in Appendix A.

Examples

_____ **1.** Marie is late for an appointment but is stuck in line at the bank.

_____ **2.** Tamika decides that she won't be satisfied unless she gets straight A's this year.

_____ **3.** Jose has just graduated from business school and has taken an exciting new job.

_____ **4.** Morris has just been fired from his job and needs to find another.

Types of stress

a. frustration
b. conflict
c. change
d. pressure

Responding to Stress

People's response to stress is complex and multidimensional. Stress affects the individual at several levels. Consider again the chapter's opening scenario, in which you're driving home in heavy traffic and thinking about overdue papers, tuition increases, and parental pressures. Let's look at some of the reactions that were mentioned. When you groan in reaction to the traffic report, you're experiencing an *emotional response* to stress, in this case annoyance and anger. When your pulse quickens and your stomach knots up, you're exhibiting *physiological responses* to stress. When you shout insults at another driver, your verbal aggression is a *behavioral response* to the stress at hand. Thus, we can analyze a person's reactions to stress at three levels: (1) emotional responses, (2) physiological responses, and (3) behavioral responses. Figure 13.4, which diagrams these three levels of response, provides an overview of the stress process.

Emotional Responses

When people are under stress, they often react emotionally. Studies that have tracked stress and mood on a daily basis have found intimate relationships between the two (Affleck et al., 1994; van Eck, Nicolson, & Berkhof, 1998).

Emotions Commonly Elicited

No simple one-to-one connections have been found between certain types of stressful events and particular emotions. However, researchers *have* begun to uncover some strong links between *specific cognitive reactions to stress* (appraisals) and specific emotions (Smith & Lazarus, 1993). For example, self-blame tends to lead to guilt, helplessness to sadness, and so forth. Although many emotions can be evoked by stressful events, some are certainly more likely than others. Common emotional responses to stress include (a) annoyance, anger, and rage, (b) apprehension, anxiety, and fear, and (c) dejection, sadness and grief (Lazarus, 1993; Woolfolk & Richardson, 1978).

Although investigators have tended to focus heavily on the connection between stress and negative emotions, research shows that positive emotions also occur during periods of stress (Folkman, 1997). Although this finding seems counterintuitive, research-

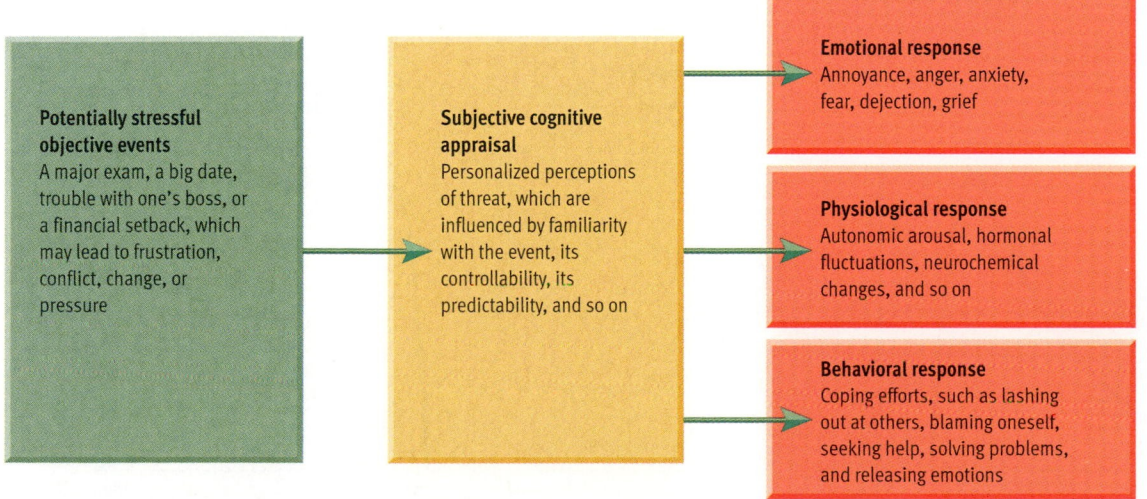

Figure 13.4

Overview of the stress process. A potentially stressful event, such as a major exam, elicits a subjective appraisal of how threatening the event is. If the event is viewed with alarm, the stress may trigger emotional, physiological, and behavioral reactions, as people's response to stress is multidimensional.

Potentially stressful objective events
A major exam, a big date, trouble with one's boss, or a financial setback, which may lead to frustration, conflict, change, or pressure

Subjective cognitive appraisal
Personalized perceptions of threat, which are influenced by familiarity with the event, its controllability, its predictability, and so on

Emotional response
Annoyance, anger, anxiety, fear, dejection, grief

Physiological response
Autonomic arousal, hormonal fluctuations, neurochemical changes, and so on

Behavioral response
Coping efforts, such as lashing out at others, blaming oneself, seeking help, solving problems, and releasing emotions

ers have found that people experience a diverse array of pleasant emotions even while enduring the most dire of circumstances. Consider, for example, the results of a five-year study of coping patterns in 253 caregiving partners of men with AIDS (Folkman et al., 1997). Surprisingly, over the course of the study, the caregivers reported experiencing positive emotions about as often as they experienced negative emotions—except during the time immediately surrounding the death of their partners. Moreover, Susan Folkman and Judith Moskowitz (2000) argue that positive emotions experienced while under duress have important adaptive significance. They review evidence suggesting that positive emotions can promote creativity and flexibility in problem solving, facilitate the processing of important information about oneself, and reduce the adverse physiological effects of stress. Consistent with their analysis, recent research suggests that positive emotions may reduce vulnerability to heart disease in older adults (Ostir et al., 2001).

Effects of Emotional Arousal

Emotional responses are a natural and normal part of life. Even unpleasant emotions serve important purposes. Like physical pain, painful emotions can serve as warnings that one needs to take action. However, strong emotional arousal can also interfere with efforts to cope with stress. For example, there is evidence that high emotional arousal can interfere with attention and memory retrieval and can impair judgment and decision making (Janis, 1993; Mandler, 1993).

Although emotional arousal may hurt coping efforts, that isn't *necessarily* the case. The *inverted-U hypothesis* predicts that task performance should improve with increased emotional arousal—up to a point, after which further increases in arousal become disruptive and performance deteriorates (An-

derson, 1990; Mandler, 1993). This idea is referred to as the inverted-U hypothesis because when performance is plotted as a function of arousal, the resulting graphs approximate an upside-down U (see Figure 13.5). In these graphs, the level of arousal at which performance peaks is characterized as the *optimal level of arousal* for a task.

This optimal level of arousal appears to depend in part on the complexity of the task at hand. The conventional wisdom is that *as a task becomes more complex, the optimal level of arousal (for peak performance) tends to decrease.* This relationship is depicted in Figure 13.5. As you can see, a fairly high level of arousal should be optimal on simple tasks (such as driving 8 hours to help a friend in a crisis). However, performance should peak at a lower level of arousal on complex tasks (such as making a major decision in which you have to weigh many factors).

The research evidence on the inverted-U hypothesis is inconsistent and subject to varied interpretations (Neiss, 1988, 1990). Hence, it may be risky to generalize this principle to the complexities of everyday coping efforts. Nonetheless, the inverted-U hypothesis provides a plausible model of how emotional arousal could have either beneficial or disruptive effects on coping, depending on the nature of the stressful demands.

Physiological Responses

As we just discussed, stress frequently elicits strong emotional responses. Now we'll look at the important physiological changes that often accompany these responses.

The Fight-or-Flight Response

Walter Cannon (1932) was one of the first theorists to describe the fight-or-flight response. The *fight-or-*

Figure 13.5

Arousal and performance.
Graphs of the relationship between emotional arousal and task performance tend to resemble an inverted U, as increased arousal is associated with improved performance up to a point, after which higher arousal leads to poorer performance. The optimal level of arousal for a task depends on the complexity of the task. On complex tasks, a relatively low level of arousal tends to be optimal. On simple tasks, however, performance may peak at a much higher level of arousal.

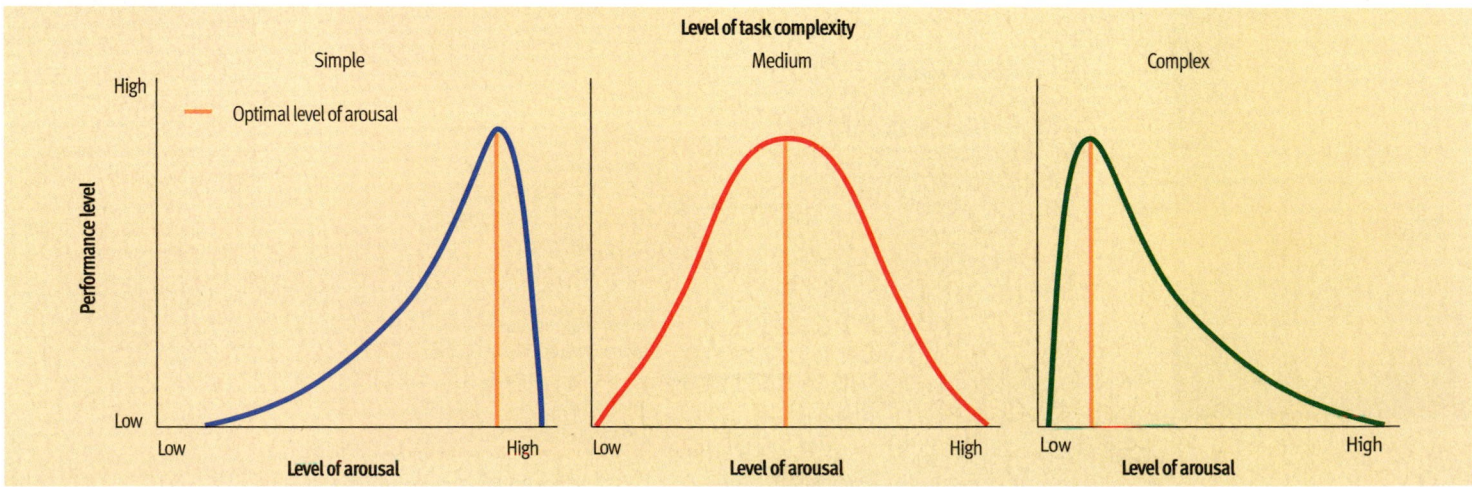

flight response **is a physiological reaction to threat in which the autonomic nervous system mobilizes the organism for attacking (fight) or fleeing (flight) an enemy.** As you may recall from Chapter 3, the *autonomic nervous system (ANS)* controls blood vessels, smooth muscles, and glands. The fight-or-flight response is mediated by the *sympathetic division* of the ANS. In one experiment, Cannon studied the fight-or-flight response in cats by confronting them with dogs. Among other things, he noticed an immediate acceleration in their breathing and heart rate and a reduction in their digestive processes.

The physiological arousal associated with the fight-or-flight response is also seen in humans. In a sense, this automatic reaction is a "leftover" from humanity's evolutionary past. It's clearly an adaptive response in the animal kingdom, where the threat of predators often requires a swift response of fighting or fleeing. But in our modern world, the fight-or-flight response may be less adaptive for human functioning than it was thousands of generations ago (Neese & Young, 2000). Most human stresses can't be handled simply through fight or flight. Work pressures, marital problems, and financial difficulties require far more complex responses. Moreover, people's stresses often continue for lengthy periods of time, so that their fight-or-flight response leaves them in a state of enduring physiological arousal. Concern about the effects of prolonged physical arousal was first voiced by a Canadian scientist who conducted extensive research on stress. Let's look at his ideas.

The General Adaptation Syndrome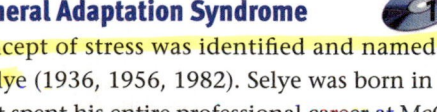

The concept of stress was identified and named by Hans Selye (1936, 1956, 1982). Selye was born in Vienna but spent his entire professional career at McGill University in Montreal. Beginning in the 1930s, Selye exposed laboratory animals to a diverse array of both physical and psychological stressors (heat, cold, pain, mild shock, restraint, and so on). The patterns of physiological arousal seen in the animals were largely the same, regardless of the type of stress. Thus, Selye concluded that stress reactions are *nonspecific*. In other words, he maintained that the reactions do not vary according to the specific type of stress encountered. Initially, Selye wasn't sure what to call this nonspecific response to a variety of noxious agents. In the 1940s he decided to call it *stress,* and the word has been part of our vocabulary ever since.

Selye (1956, 1974) formulated an influential theory of stress reactions called the general adaptation syndrome. **The *general adaptation syndrome* is a model of the body's stress response, consisting of three stages: alarm, resistance, and exhaustion.** In the first stage of the general adaptation syndrome, an *alarm reaction* occurs when an organism first recognizes the existence of a threat. Physiological arousal occurs as the body musters its resources to combat the challenge. Selye's alarm reaction is essentially the fight-or-flight response originally described by Cannon.

However, Selye took his investigation of stress a few steps further by exposing laboratory animals to *prolonged* stress, similar to the chronic stress often endured by humans. As stress continues, the organism may progress to the second phase of the general adaptation syndrome, the *stage of resistance*. During this phase, physiological changes stabilize as coping efforts get under way. Typically, physiological arousal continues to be higher than normal, although it may level off somewhat as the organism becomes accustomed to the threat.

If the stress continues over a substantial period of time, the organism may enter the third stage, the *stage of exhaustion*. According to Selye, the body's resources for fighting stress are limited. If the stress can't be overcome, the body's resources may be depleted, and physiological arousal will decrease. Eventually, the organism may collapse from exhaustion. During this phase, the organism's resistance declines. This reduced resistance may lead to what Selye called "diseases of adaptation."

Brain-Body Pathways

Even in cases of moderate stress, you may notice that your heart has started beating faster, you've begun to breathe harder, and you're perspiring more than usual. How does all this (and much more) happen? It appears that there are two major pathways along which the brain sends signals to the endocrine system in response to stress (Dallman, Bhatnagar, & Viau, 2000; Felker & Hubbard, 1998). As we noted in Chapter 3, the *endocrine system* consists of glands located at various sites in the body that secrete chemicals called hormones. The *hypothalamus* is the brain structure that appears to initiate action along these two pathways.

The first pathway (see Figure 13.6 on the next page) is routed through the autonomic nervous system. In response to stress, your hypothalamus activates the sympathetic division of the ANS. A key part of this activation involves stimulating the central part of the adrenal glands (the adrenal medulla) to release large amounts of *catecholamines* into the bloodstream. These hormones radiate throughout your body, producing the physiological changes seen in the fight-or-flight response. The net result of catecholamine elevation is that your body is mobilized

>*There are two main types of human beings: 'racehorses,' who thrive on stress and are only happy with a vigorous, fast-paced lifestyle; and 'turtles,' who in order to be happy require peace, quiet, and a generally tranquil environment.*
>HANS SELYE

Figure **13.6**

Brain-body pathways in stress. In times of stress, the brain sends signals along two pathways. The pathway through the autonomic nervous system controls the release of catecholamine hormones that help mobilize the body for action. The pathway through the pituitary gland and the endocrine system controls the release of corticosteroid hormones that increase energy and ward off tissue inflammation.

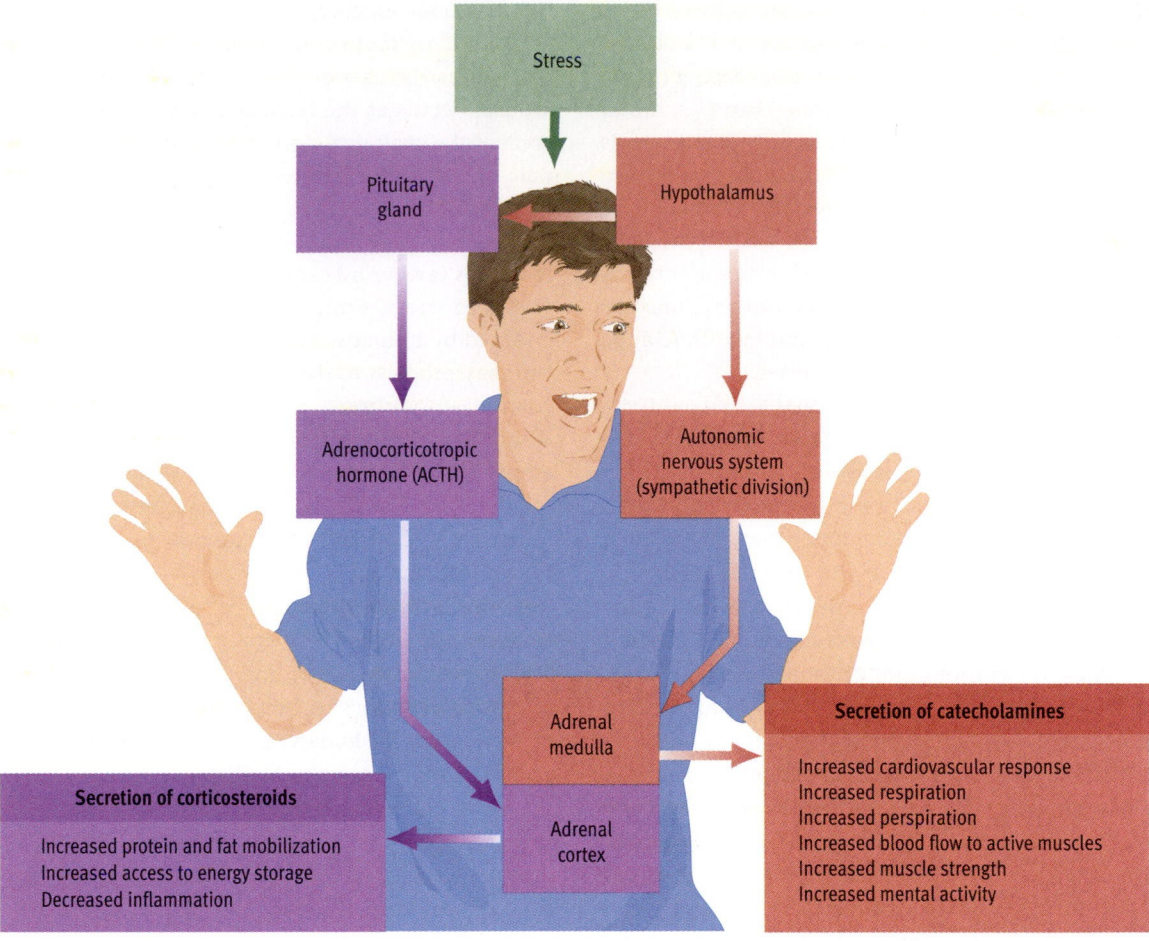

for action (Lundberg, 2000). Heart rate and blood flow increase, and more blood is pumped to your brain and muscles. Respiration and oxygen consumption speed up, which facilitates alertness. Digestive processes are inhibited to conserve your energy. The pupils of your eyes dilate, increasing visual sensitivity.

The second pathway involves more direct communication between the brain and the endocrine system (see Figure 13.6). The hypothalamus sends signals to the so-called master gland of the endocrine system, the pituitary. In turn, the pituitary secretes a hormone (ACTH) that stimulates the outer part of the adrenal glands (the adrenal cortex) to release another important set of hormones—*corticosteroids*. These hormones stimulate the release of chemicals that help increase your energy and help inhibit tissue inflammation in case of injury (Munck, 2000).

Behavioral Responses 11g

Although people respond to stress at several levels, it's clear that *behavior* is the crucial dimension of their reactions. Most behavioral responses to stress involve coping. *Coping* **refers to active efforts to master, reduce, or tolerate the demands created by stress.** Notice that this definition is neutral as to whether coping efforts are healthful or maladaptive. The popular use of the term often implies that coping is inherently healthful. When people say that someone "coped with her problems," the implication is that she handled them effectively.

In reality, however, coping responses may be adaptive or maladaptive (Moos & Schaefer, 1993; Vaillant, 2000). For example, if you were flunking a history course at midterm, you might cope with this stress by (1) increasing your study efforts, (2) seeking help from a tutor, (3) blaming your professor, or (4) giving up on the class without really trying. Clearly, the first two of these coping responses would be more adaptive than the last two.

People cope with stress in many ways, but most individuals exhibit certain styles of coping that are fairly consistent across situations (Carver & Scheier, 1994; Heszen-Niejodek, 1997). Given the immense variety in coping strategies, we can only highlight a few of the more common patterns. In this section we'll focus most of our attention on styles of coping that tend to be less than ideal. We'll discuss a variety

Giving Up and Blaming Oneself

When confronted with stress, people sometimes simply give up and withdraw from the battle. Some people routinely respond to stress with fatalism and resignation, passively accepting setbacks that might be dealt with effectively. This syndrome is referred to as *learned helplessness* (Seligman, 1974, 1992). *Learned helplessness is passive behavior produced by exposure to unavoidable aversive events.* Learned helplessness seems to occur when individuals come to believe that events are beyond their control. As you might guess, giving up is not a highly regarded method of coping. Carver and his colleagues (1989, 1993) have studied this coping strategy, which they refer to as *behavioral disengagement,* and found that it is associated with increased rather than decreased distress. Furthermore, many studies suggest that learned helplessness can contribute to depression (Seligman & Isaacowitz, 2000).

Blaming oneself is another common response when people are confronted by stressful difficulties. The tendency to become highly self-critical in response to stress has been noted by a number of influential theorists. Albert Ellis (1973, 1987) calls this phenomenon "catastrophic thinking." According to Ellis, catastrophic thinking causes, aggravates, and perpetuates emotional reactions to stress that are often problematic (see the Personal Application for this chapter). In a similar vein, Aaron Beck (1976, 1987) argues that negative self-talk can contribute to the development of depressive disorders (see Chapter 15). Although there is something to be said for recognizing one's weaknesses and taking responsibility for one's failures, Ellis and Beck agree that excessive self-blame can be very unhealthy.

Striking Out at Others

People often respond to stressful events by striking out at others with aggressive behavior. *Aggression is any behavior that is intended to hurt someone, either physically or verbally.* Many years ago, a team of psychologists (Dollard et al., 1939) proposed the *frustration-aggression hypothesis,* which held that aggression is always caused by frustration. Decades of research have supported this idea of a causal link between frustration and aggression (Berkowitz, 1989). However, this research has also shown that there isn't an inevitable, one-to-one correspondence between frustration and aggression.

Frequently people lash out aggressively at others who had nothing to do with their frustration, appar-

ently because they can't vent their anger at the real source. For example, you'll probably suppress your anger rather than lash out verbally at your boss or at a police officer who's giving you a speeding ticket. Twenty minutes later, however, you might be verbally brutal to a colleague at work. As we discussed in Chapter 12, this diversion of anger to a substitute target was noticed long ago by Sigmund Freud, who called it *displacement.* Unfortunately, research suggests that when people are provoked, displaced aggression is a common response (Marcus-Newhall et al., 2000).

Freud theorized that behaving aggressively could get pent-up emotion out of one's system and thus be adaptive. He coined the term *catharsis* to refer to this release of emotional tension. There is some experimental evidence to support Freud's theory of catharsis (Hokanson & Burgess, 1962). However, the balance of evidence indicates that aggressive behavior does *not* reliably lead to catharsis (Tavris, 1989). As Carol Tavris notes, "Aggressive catharses are almost impossible to find in continuing relationships because parents, children, spouses, and bosses usually feel obliged to aggress back at you" (1982, p. 131). Thus, the interpersonal conflicts that often emerge from aggressive behavior may increase rather than relieve stress. For example, if you pick a fight with your spouse after a terrible day at work, you may create new stress for yourself.

Indulging Oneself

Stress sometimes leads to reduced impulse control, or *self-indulgence* (Tice, Bratslavsky, & Baumeister, 2001). When troubled by stress, many people engage in excessive consumption—unwise patterns of eating, drinking, smoking, using drugs, spending money, and so forth. For example, I have a friend who copes with stress by making a beeline for the nearest shopping mall to indulge in a spending spree. It appears that my friend is not unusual. It makes sense that when things are going poorly in one area of their lives, people may try to compensate by pursuing substitute forms of satisfaction. When this happens, self-indulgent responses tend to be relatively easy to execute and highly pleasurable. Thus, it's not surprising that studies have linked stress to increases in eating (Grunberg & Straub, 1992), smoking (Cohen & Lichtenstein, 1990), and consumption of alcohol and drugs (Colder, 2001; Pihl, 1999).

A new manifestation of this coping strategy that has attracted much attention recently is the tendency to immerse oneself in the online world of the Internet. Kimberly Young (1996, 1998) has described a syndrome called *Internet addiction,* which consists of spending an inordinate amount of time on

"People largely disturb themselves by thinking in a self-defeating, illogical, and unrealistic manner."
ALBERT ELLIS

Experts disagree about whether excessive Internet use should be characterized as an addiction, but the inability to control online activity appears to be an increasingly common syndrome that illustrates the coping strategy of indulging oneself.

Defensive Coping  10a, 11g

Many people exhibit consistent styles of defensive coping in response to stress (Vaillant, 1994). We noted in the previous chapter that Sigmund Freud originally developed the concept of the *defense mechanism*. Though rooted in the psychoanalytic tradition, this concept has gained widespread acceptance from psychologists of most persuasions (Cramer, 2000). Building on Freud's initial insights, modern psychologists have broadened the scope of the concept and added to Freud's list of defense mechanisms.

Defense mechanisms are largely unconscious reactions that protect a person from unpleasant emotions such as anxiety and guilt. Many specific defense mechanisms have been identified. For example, Laughlin (1979) lists 49 different defenses. We described seven common defense mechanisms in our discussion of Freud's theory in the previous chapter. Table 13.2 introduces another five defenses that people use with some regularity. Although widely discussed in the popular press, defense mechanisms are often misunderstood. To clear up some of the misconceptions, we'll use a question/answer format to elaborate on the nature of defense mechanisms.

What exactly do defense mechanisms defend against? Above all else, defense mechanisms shield the individual from the emotional discomfort that's so often elicited by stress. Their main purpose is to ward off unwelcome emotions or to reduce their intensity. Foremost among the emotions guarded against is *anxiety*. Defenses are also used to suppress dangerous feelings of *anger* so that they don't explode into acts of aggression. *Guilt* and *dejection* are two other emotions that people often try to evade through defensive maneuvers.

the Internet and inability to control online use. People who exhibit this syndrome tend to feel anxious, depressed, or empty when they are not online (Kandell, 1998). Their Internet use is so excessive, it begins to interfere with their functioning at work, at school, or at home, which leads victims to start concealing the extent of their dependence on the Internet. It is difficult to estimate the prevalence of Internet addiction, but the syndrome does *not* appear to be rare (Greenfield, 1999; Morahan-Martin & Schumacher, 2000). Research suggests that Internet addiction is not limited to shy, male computer nerds, as one might expect (Young, 1998). Although there is active debate about the wisdom of characterizing excessive Internet surfing as an *addiction* (Griffiths, 1999), it is clear that this new coping strategy is likely to become increasingly common.

Table 13.2 Additional Defense Mechanisms

Mechanism	Description	Example
Denial of reality	Protecting oneself from unpleasant reality by refusing to perceive or face it	A smoker concludes that the evidence linking cigarette use to health problems is scientifically worthless
Fantasy	Gratifying frustrated desires by imaginary achievements	A socially inept and inhibited young man imagines himself chosen by a group of women to provide them with sexual satisfaction
Intellectualization (isolation)	Cutting off emotion from hurtful situations or separating incompatible attitudes so that they appear unrelated	A prisoner on death row awaiting execution resists appeal on his behalf and coldly insists that the letter of the law be followed
Undoing	Atoning for or trying to magically dispel unacceptable desires or acts	A teenager who feels guilty about masturbation ritually touches door knobs a prescribed number of times following each occurrence of the act
Overcompensation	Covering up felt weakness by emphasizing some desirable characteristics, or making up for frustration in one area by overgratification in another	A dangerously overweight woman goes on eating binges when she feels neglected by her husband

SOURCE: Adapted from Carson, R. C., Butcher, J. N., & Coleman, J. C. (1988). *Abnormal psychology and modern life*. Glenview, IL: Scott, Foresman. Copyright © 1988 by Scott, Foresman and Company. Adapted by permission of the publisher.
NOTE: See Table 12.1 for another list of defense mechanisms.

How do they work? Through *self-deception*. Defense mechanisms accomplish their goals by distorting reality so that it doesn't appear so threatening. For example, suppose you're not doing well in school and you're in danger of flunking out. Initially you might use *denial* to block awareness of the possibility that you could flunk. This defense might temporarily fend off feelings of anxiety. If it becomes difficult to deny the obvious, you could resort to *fantasy*. You might daydream about how you'll salvage adequate grades by getting spectacular scores on the upcoming final exams, when the objective fact is that you're hopelessly behind in your studies. Thus, defense mechanisms work their magic by bending reality in self-serving ways.

Are they conscious or unconscious? Both. Freudian theory originally assumed that defenses operate entirely at an unconscious level. However, the concept of the defense mechanism has been broadened by other theorists to include maneuvers that people may be aware of. Thus, defense mechanisms may operate at varying levels of awareness, although they're largely unconscious (Cramer, 2001; Erdelyi, 2001).

Are they normal? Definitely. Everyone uses defense mechanisms on a fairly regular basis. They're entirely normal patterns of coping. The notion that only neurotic people use defense mechanisms is inaccurate.

Are they healthy? This is a much more complicated question. More often than not, the answer is "no." Generally, defensive coping is less than optimal for a number of reasons. First, defensive coping is an avoidance strategy, and avoidance rarely provides a genuine solution to problems (Holahan & Moos, 1985, 1990). Second, a repressive coping style has been related to poor health, in part because repression often leads people to delay facing up to their problems (Weinberger, 1990). For example, if you were to block out obvious warning signs of cancer or diabetes and fail to obtain needed medical care, your defensive behavior could be fatal. Third, defenses such as denial and fantasy represent wishful thinking, which is likely to accomplish little (Bolger, 1990).

Although defensive behavior tends to be relatively unhealthful, Shelley Taylor and Jonathon Brown (1988, 1994) have reviewed several lines of evidence suggesting that "positive illusions" may be adaptive for mental health and well-being. First, they note that "normal" people tend to have overly favorable self-images. In contrast, depressed subjects exhibit less favorable—but more realistic—self-concepts. Second, normal subjects overestimate the degree to which they control chance events. In comparison, depressed subjects are less prone to this illusion of control. Third, normal individuals are more likely than depressed subjects to display unrealistic optimism in making projections about the future.

The findings on whether positive illusions are healthy are contradictory and controversial (Asendorpf & Ostendorf, 1998; Colvin, Block, & Funder, 1995), so it is hard to make sweeping generalizations

Courtesy of Shelley Taylor

"Rather than perceiving themselves, the world, and the future accurately, most people regard themselves, their circumstances, and the future as considerably more positive than is objectively likely. . . . These illusions are not merely characteristic of human thought; they appear actually to be adaptive, promoting rather than undermining good mental health."
SHELLEY TAYLOR

CONCEPT CHECK 13.3

Identifying More Defense Mechanisms

In the last chapter you checked your understanding of several defense mechanisms by identifying instances of them in a story. In this chapter, you've learned about five additional defense mechanisms that are sometimes used as ways of coping with stress. Check your understanding of these defense mechanisms by identifying them in the story below. Each example of a defense mechanism is underlined, with a number beneath it. Write the name of the defense mechanism exemplified in each case in the numbered spaces after the story. The answers are in Appendix A.

The guys at work have been trying to break it to me gently that they think my job's on the line because I've missed work too many days this year. I don't know how they came up with that idea; I've got nothing to worry about. Besides, every day I missed, I always did a lot of cleaning up and other chores around the house here. One of these days the boss will finally recognize how really valuable I am to the company, and I'll be getting a big promotion. Anyway, since the guys have been dropping these hints about my not missing any more days, I've been trying really hard to make a good impression by saying "Hi" to everyone I see, especially the boss, and telling jokes. You know, it's really pretty interesting to observe how all these relationships unfold between guys who work together and the people who manage them.

1. _____   4. _____

2. _____   5. _____

3. _____

about the adaptive value of self-deception. Roy Baumeister (1989) theorizes that it's all a matter of degree and that there is an "optimal margin of illusion." According to Baumeister, extreme distortions of reality are maladaptive, but small illusions are often beneficial.

Constructive Coping

Our discussion thus far has focused on coping strategies that usually are less than ideal. Of course, people also exhibit many healthful strategies for dealing with stress. We'll use the term *constructive coping to refer to relatively healthful efforts that people make to deal with stressful events*. No strategy of coping can *guarantee* a successful outcome. Even the healthiest coping responses may turn out to be ineffective in some circumstances. Thus, the concept of constructive coping is simply meant to connote a healthful, positive approach, without promising success.

What makes certain coping strategies constructive? Frankly, it's a gray area in which psychologists' opinions vary to some extent. Nonetheless, a consensus about the nature of constructive coping has emerged from the sizable literature on stress management. Key themes in this literature include the following:

1. Constructive coping involves confronting problems directly. It is task relevant and action oriented. It entails a conscious effort to rationally evaluate your options so that you can try to solve your problems.

2. Constructive coping is based on reasonably realistic appraisals of your stress and coping resources. A little self-deception may sometimes be adaptive, but excessive self-deception and highly unrealistic negative thinking are not.

3. Constructive coping involves learning to recognize, and in some cases inhibit, potentially disruptive emotional reactions to stress.

4. Constructive coping includes making efforts to ensure that your body is not especially vulnerable to the possibly damaging effects of stress.

These principles provide a rather general and abstract picture of constructive coping. We'll look at patterns of constructive coping in more detail in the Personal Application, which discusses various stress management strategies that people can use.

REVIEW OF KEY POINTS

- Stress often triggers emotional reactions. These reactions typically include anger, fear, and sadness. In times of stress, emotions are not uniformly negative and positive emotions may foster resilience. Emotional arousal may interfere with coping. According to the inverted-U hypothesis, task performance improves with increased arousal up to a point and then declines. The optimal level of arousal on a task depends on the complexity of the task.

- Physiological arousal in response to stress was originally called the fight-or-flight response by Cannon. This automatic response has limited adaptive value in our modern world. Selye's general adaptation syndrome describes three stages in physiological reactions to stress: alarm, resistance, and exhaustion. Diseases of adaptation may appear during the stage of exhaustion.

- There are two major pathways along which the brain sends signals to the endocrine system in response to stress. The first pathway releases a class of hormones called catecholamines. The second pathway releases a class of hormones called corticosteroids.

- The behavioral response to stress takes the form of coping. Some relatively unhealthy coping responses include giving up, blaming oneself, and striking out at others with acts of aggression. Self-indulgence is another coping pattern that tends to be of limited value.

- Defensive coping is quite common. Defense mechanisms protect against emotional distress through self-deception. Several lines of evidence suggest that positive illusions may be healthful, but there is some debate about the matter. It is probably a matter of degree. Relatively healthful coping tactics are called constructive coping.

The Effects of Stress on Psychological Functioning

PREVIEW QUESTIONS

- Can stress interfere with task performance?
- What is burnout, and what are its causes?
- What is posttraumatic stress disorder, and how common is it?
- What kinds of experiences cause PTSD?
- What other psychological problems and mental disorders are stress related?

People struggle with many stresses every day. Most stresses come and go without leaving any enduring imprint. However, when stress is severe or when many stressful demands pile up, one's psychological functioning may be affected.

Research on the effects of stress has focused mainly on negative outcomes, so our coverage is slanted in that direction. However, it's important to emphasize that stress is not inherently bad. You would probably suffocate from boredom if you lived a stress-free existence. Stress makes life challenging and interesting. Along the way, though, stress can be harrowing, sometimes leading to impairments in performance, to burnout, and to other problems.

Impaired Task Performance

Frequently, stress takes its toll on the ability to perform effectively on a task at hand. For instance, Roy Baumeister's work shows how pressure can interfere with performance. Baumeister's (1984) theory assumes that pressure to perform often makes people self-conscious and that this elevated self-consciousness disrupts their attention. He found support for his theory in a series of laboratory experiments in which he manipulated the pressure to perform well on a simple perceptual-motor task and found that many people tend to "choke" under pressure (Butler & Baumeister, 1998; Baumeister, 1984). His theory has also received some support in studies of the past performance of professional sports teams (Baumeister, 1995; Baumeister & Steinhilber, 1984).

Other research suggests that Baumeister is on the right track in looking to *attention* to explain how stress impairs task performance. In a study of stress and decision making, Keinan (1987) found that stress disrupted two out of the three aspects of attention measured in the study. Stress increased subjects' tendency (1) to jump to a conclusion too quickly without considering all their options and (2) to do an unsystematic, poorly organized review of their available options. In a more recent study, Keinan and colleagues (1999) found that stress impaired performance on cognitive tasks. The results suggested that stress makes it harder for people to suppress competing thoughts. Research also suggests that stress can have detrimental effects on certain memory functions (Kellog, Hopko, & Ashcraft, 1999; Klein & Boals, 2001).

Burnout

Burnout is an overused buzzword that means different things to different people. Nonetheless, a few researchers have described burnout in a systematic way that has facilitated scientific study of the syndrome (Maslach & Leiter, 1997; Pines, 1993). **Burnout involves physical and emotional exhaustion, cynicism, and a lowered sense of self-efficacy that can be brought on gradually by chronic work-related stress.** Exhaustion, which is central to burnout, includes chronic fatigue, weakness, and low energy. Cynicism is manifested in highly negative attitudes toward oneself, one's work, and life in general. Reduced self-efficacy involves declining feelings of competence at work which give way to feelings of hopelessness and helplessness.

What causes burnout? Factors in the workplace that appear to promote burnout include work overload, struggling with interpersonal conflicts at work, lack of control over work responsibilities and outcomes, and inadequate recognition for one's work (Leiter & Maslach, 2001; see Figure 13.7). As you might expect, burnout is associated with increased

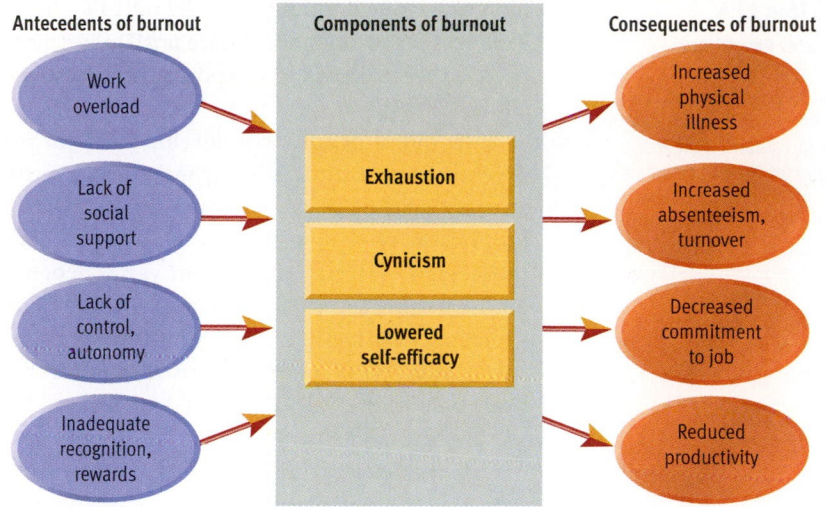

Antecedents of burnout — Work overload; Lack of social support; Lack of control, autonomy; Inadequate recognition, rewards

Components of burnout — Exhaustion; Cynicism; Lowered self-efficacy

Consequences of burnout — Increased physical illness; Increased absenteeism, turnover; Decreased commitment to job; Reduced productivity

Figure 13.7

The antecedents, components, and consequences of burnout. Christina Maslach and Michael Leiter have developed a systematic model of burnout that specifies the antecedents, components, and consequences of burnout. The antecedents on the left in the diagram are the stressful features of the work environment that cause burnout. The burnout syndrome itself consists of the three components shown in the center of the diagram. Some of the unfortunate results of burnout are listed on the right. (Based on Leiter & Maslach, 2001)

absenteeism and reduced productivity at work, as well as increased vulnerability to a variety of health problems (Maslach & Leiter, 2000). Burnout is a potential problem in a wide variety of occupations (Lee & Ashforth, 1996).

Posttraumatic Stress Disorders

Extremely stressful, traumatic incidents can leave a lasting imprint on victims' psychological functioning. **The *posttraumatic stress disorder (PTSD)* involves enduring psychological disturbance attributed to the experience of a major traumatic event.** Researchers began to appreciate the frequency and severity of posttraumatic stress disorders after the Vietnam war ended in 1975 and a great many psychologically scarred veterans returned home. These veterans displayed a diverse array of psychological problems and symptoms that in many cases lingered much longer than expected (Schlenger et al., 1992).

Although posttraumatic stress disorders are widely associated with the experiences of Vietnam veterans, they are seen in the aftermath of other traumatic events as well. For example, PTSD is often seen after a rape or assault, a severe automobile accident, a natural disaster, or the witnessing of someone's death (Koren, Arnon, & Klein, 1999; Stein et al., 1997; Vernberg et al., 1996). Unfortunately, traumatic experiences such as these appear to be much more com-

Web Link 13.3

National Center for PTSD
This site offers numerous resources devoted to posttraumatic stress disorder (PTSD). Visitors also have access to the PILOTS database, a free searchable guide to the worldwide literature on traumatic stress.

Web Link 13.4

Disaster Psychiatry
In light of the traumatic terror-ist attacks on 9/11 and their aftermath, the importance of first-rate information about how to respond to disasters is obvious. This site, maintained by the American Psychiatric Association, provides many valuable insights and links related to professional as-sistance at times of major emergencies.

Web Link 13.5

David Baldwin's Trauma Information Pages
This site has long been recog-nized as the premier reposi-tory for web-based and other resources relating to emotional trauma, traumatic stress, and posttraumatic stress disorder. David Baldwin has assembled more than 1,000 links to infor-mation about these issues.

mon than widely assumed (see Figure 13.8). In some instances, PTSD does not surface until many months or years after a person's exposure to severe stress (Holen, 2000).

How many people will develop PTSD or other psychological disorders in the wake of the terrorist attacks that took place on September 11, 2001? The proportion of people who develop psychological problems after a traumatic event varies depending on the nature, severity, and duration of the trauma. Averaging over many types of trauma, it is estimated that about 9% of people exposed to a traumatic stressor develop PTSD (Everly, 2000). However, stud-ies suggest that deliberate violence, such as that seen in terrorist attacks, tends to produce more severe neg-ative effects on mental health than accidents or nat-ural disasters. The closest precedent for making pre-dictions is the 1995 bombing of the Murrah Federal Building in Oklahoma City. In a study of survivors who were directly exposed to this terrorist act, re-searchers found that 45% eventually developed a psychological disorder (North et al., 1999). The most common disorders were PTSD, which was seen in 34% of the sample, and major depression. Generally speaking, watching, reading, or listening to media coverage of major disasters does *not* lead to PTSD or other serious psychological problems (Korn, 2001). That said, research on the Oklahoma City tragedy

demonstrated that indirect exposure to a traumatic event through graphic television coverage *can* lead to PTSD, at least in children (Pfefferbaum et al., 2000). Given the graphic video footage of the destruction of the World Trade Center and the pervasive media coverage of the terrorist assaults, it seems likely that the 9/11 terrorist attacks will lead to the emergence of posttraumatic stress disorder in some people who were not at the scene of the attacks.

Research suggests a variety of factors are predic-tors of individuals' risk for PTSD (McNally, 1999; Norris et al., 2001; Ursano, Fullerton, & Norwood, 2001). As you might expect, increased vulnerability is associated with greater personal injuries and losses, greater intensity of exposure to the traumatic event, and more exposure to the grotesque aftermath of the event. The likelihood of PTSD is higher among women than men and among people who were al-ready struggling with psychological problems before they were exposed to a traumatic event (Halligan & Yehuda, 2001). Vulnerability to PTSD is not limited to victims, survivors, and witnesses of traumatic events. Rescue workers and cleanup crews who have to grap-ple with the gruesome carnage of major disasters, dangerous working conditions, and tremendous fa-tigue also have a highly elevated risk for PTSD (Ur-sano et al., 1999).

What are the symptoms of posttraumatic stress disorders? Common symptoms include reexperienc-ing the traumatic event in the form of nightmares and flashbacks, emotional numbing, alienation, prob-lems in social relations, an increased sense of vul-nerability, and elevated arousal, anxiety, anger, and guilt (Flannery, 1999; Shalev, 2001). PTSD is also as-sociated with an elevated risk for substance abuse, depression, and suicide attempts (Warshaw et al., 1993), as well as a great variety of physical health problems (Beckham et al., 1998). The frequency and severity of posttraumatic symptoms usually decline gradually over time, but recovery tends to be grad-ual, and in many cases the symptoms never com-pletely disappear.

Psychological Problems and Disorders

Posttraumatic stress disorders are caused by a single episode of extreme stress. Of greater relevance to most of us are the effects of chronic, prolonged, everyday stress. On the basis of clinical impressions, psychol-ogists have long suspected that chronic stress might contribute to many types of psychological problems

Figure 13.8

The prevalence of traumatic events. We tend to think that traumatic events are relatively unusual and infrequent, but research by Stein et al. (1997) suggests otherwise. They interviewed over 1000 people in Winnipeg, and found that 74.2% of the women and 81.3% of the men reported experiencing at least one highly traumatic event. The percentage of respondents reporting specific types of traumatic events are summarized in this graph. (Based on data from Stein et al., 1997)

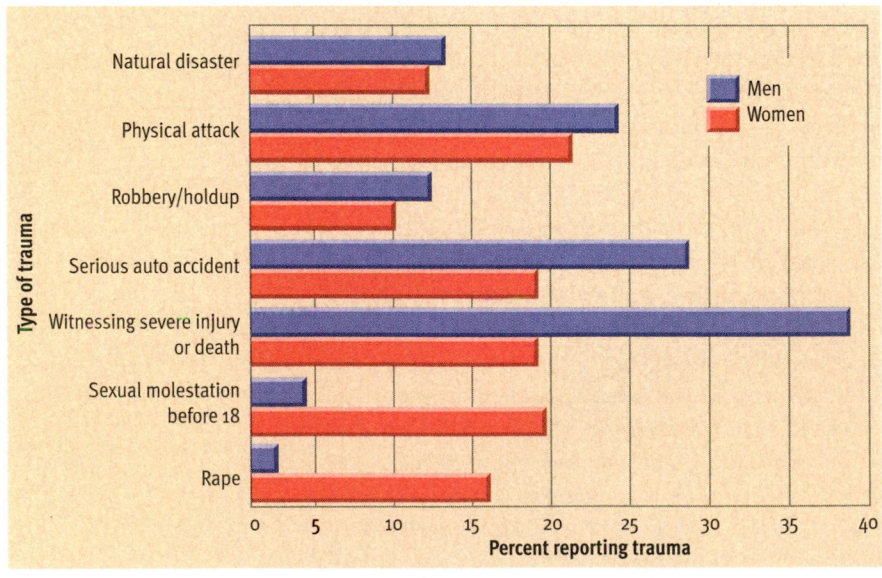

and mental disorders. Since the late 1960s, advances in the measurement of stress have allowed researchers to verify these suspicions in empirical studies. In the domain of common psychological problems, studies indicate that stress may contribute to poor academic performance (Dawod, 1995), insomnia and other sleep disturbances (Vgontzas, Bixler, & Kales, 2000), sexual difficulties (Lemack, Uzzo, & Poppas, 1998), alcohol abuse (Colder, 2001), and drug abuse (Franco, Hubbard, & Martin, 1998).

Above and beyond these everyday problems, research reveals that stress often contributes to the onset of full-fledged psychological disorders, including depression (Kessler, 1997), schizophrenia (Fowles, 1992), anxiety disorders (Falsetti & Ballenger, 1998), and eating disorders (Cooper, 1995). We'll discuss these relations between stress and mental disorders in detail in Chapter 14. Of course, stress is only one of many factors that may contribute to psychological disorders. Nonetheless, it's sobering to realize that stress can have a dramatic impact on one's mental health.

Positive Effects

The effects of stress are not entirely negative. Recent years have brought increased interest in the positive aspects of the stress process, including favorable outcomes that follow in the wake of stress (Folkman & Moskowitz, 2000). To some extent, the new focus on the possible benefits of stress reflects a new emphasis on "positive psychology." As we noted in Chapter 10, some theorists have argued that the field of psychology has historically devoted too much attention to pathology and suffering (Seligman & Csikszentmihalyi, 2000). The advocates of positive psychology argue for increased research on well-being, hope, courage, perseverance, tolerance, and other human strengths and virtues. One of these strengths is resilience in the face of stress.

Recent research on resilience suggests that stress can promote personal growth or self-improvement (Tedeschi, Park, & Calhoun, 1998). For example, studies of people grappling with major health problems show that the majority of respondents report that they derived benefits from their adversity (Tennen & Affleck, 1999). Stressful events sometimes force people to develop new skills, reevaluate priorities, learn new insights, and acquire new strengths. In other words, the adaptation process initiated by stress may lead to personal changes that are changes for the better. Confronting and conquering a stressful

Major disasters are just one of about a half-dozen types of calamitous events that can lead to post-traumatic stress disorder.

© Chin Allan/CORBIS Sygma

challenge may lead to improvements in specific coping abilities and to an enhanced self-concept. Moreover, even if people do not conquer stressors, they may be able to learn from their mistakes. Thus, researchers have begun to explore the growth potential of stressful events (Calhoun & Tedeschi, 2001; Park, 1998).

REVIEW OF KEY POINTS

- Several lines of research, including Baumeister's work on choking under pressure, suggest that stress can interfere with task performance. Burnout involves exhaustion, cynicism, and lowered self-efficacy as a result of chronic work-related stress.

- Posttraumatic stress disorders are disturbances that surface in the aftermath of a major stressful event. PTSD appears to be fairly common and can be caused by a diverse array of traumatic experiences, ranging from auto accidents to natural disasters.

- Stress can contribute to a host of common problems, such as poor academic performance, insomnia, and sexual difficulties. Stress has also been related to the development of various psychological disorders, including depression, schizophrenia, anxiety disorders, and eating disorders. Research on the effects of stress has concentrated on negative outcomes, but positive effects may also occur.

The Effects of Stress on Physical Health

PREVIEW QUESTIONS

- What is the Type A personality, and how is hostility related to heart disease?
- Can stress trigger emotional reactions that cause heart attacks?
- How is depression related to heart disease?
- How does stress affect immune function and vulnerability to the common cold?
- How strong is the association between stress and illness?

The effects of stress are not limited to mental health. Stress can also have an impact on one's physical health. The idea that stress can contribute to physical ailments is not entirely new. Evidence that stress can cause physical illness began to accumulate back in the 1930s. By the 1950s, the concept of *psychosomatic disease* was widely accepted. **Psychosomatic diseases were genuine physical ailments that were thought to be caused in part by stress and other psychological factors.** The classic psychosomatic illnesses were high blood pressure, peptic ulcers, asthma, skin disorders such as eczema and hives, and migraine and tension headaches (Kaplan, 1989; Rogers, Fricchione, & Reich, 1999). Please note, these diseases were not regarded as *imagined* physical ailments. The term *psychosomatic* has often been misused to refer to physical ailments that are "all in one's head," but that is an entirely different syndrome (see Chapter 14). Rather, psychosomatic diseases were viewed as *authentic* organic maladies that were heavily stress-related.

Since the 1970s, the concept of psychosomatic disease has gradually fallen into disuse because research has shown that stress can contribute to the development of a diverse array of other diseases previously believed to be purely physiological in origin (Dougall & Baum, 2001; Hubbard & Workman, 1998). Thus, it has become apparent that there is nothing unique about the psychosomatic diseases that requires a special category. Modern evidence continues to demonstrate that the classic psychosomatic diseases are influenced by stress, but as you will see, so are a host of other diseases (Levenson et al., 1999). In this section we'll look at the evidence on the apparent link between stress and physical illness, beginning with heart disease, which is far and away the leading cause of death in North America.

Type A Personality, Hostility, and Heart Disease

Heart disease accounts for nearly 40% of the deaths in the United States every year. *Coronary heart disease* involves a reduction in blood flow in the coronary arteries, which supply the heart with blood. This type of heart disease accounts for about 90% of heart-related deaths.

Atherosclerosis is the principal cause of coronary heart disease. This condition is characterized by a gradual narrowing of the coronary arteries. A buildup of fatty deposits and other debris on the inner walls of the arteries is the usual cause of this narrowing. Atherosclerosis progresses slowly over a period of years. However, when a narrowed coronary artery is blocked completely (by a blood clot, for instance), the abrupt interruption of blood flow can produce a heart attack. Atherosclerosis is more prevalent in men than women and tends to increase with age. Other established risk factors for atherosclerosis include smoking, lack of exercise, high cholesterol levels, and high blood pressure (Ketterer & Randall, 2000).

Recently, attention has shifted to the possibility that inflammation may contribute to atherosclerosis and elevated coronary risk (Roivainen et al., 2000). Evidence is mounting that inflammation plays a key role in the initiation and progression of atherosclerosis, as well as the acute complications that trigger heart attacks (Albert et al., 2002; Libby, Ridker, & Maseri, 2002). Fortunately, researchers have found a marker—levels of C-reactive protein (CRP) in the blood—that may help physicians estimate individuals' coronary risk more accurately than was possible previously (Ridker, 2001). Figure 13.9 shows how combined levels of CRP and cholesterol appear to be related to coronary risk.

Research on the relationship between *psychological* factors and heart attacks began in the 1960s and 1970s, when a pair of cardiologists, Meyer Friedman and Ray Rosenman (1974), discovered an apparent connection between coronary risk and a syndrome they called the *Type A personality*, which involves self-imposed stress and intense reactions to stress. **The Type A personality includes three elements: (1) a strong competitive orientation, (2) impatience and time urgency, and (3) anger and hostility.** Type A's are ambitious, hard-driving perfectionists who are exceedingly time-conscious. They routinely try to do several things at once. They fidget frantically over the briefest delays. Often they are highly competitive, achievement-oriented workaholics who drive themselves with many deadlines. They are easily irritated and are quick to anger. In contrast, **the Type B personality is marked by relatively relaxed, patient, easygoing, amicable behavior.** Type B's are less hurried, less competitive, and less easily angered than Type A's.

Decades of research uncovered a tantalizingly modest correlation between Type A behavior and increased coronary risk. More often than not, studies

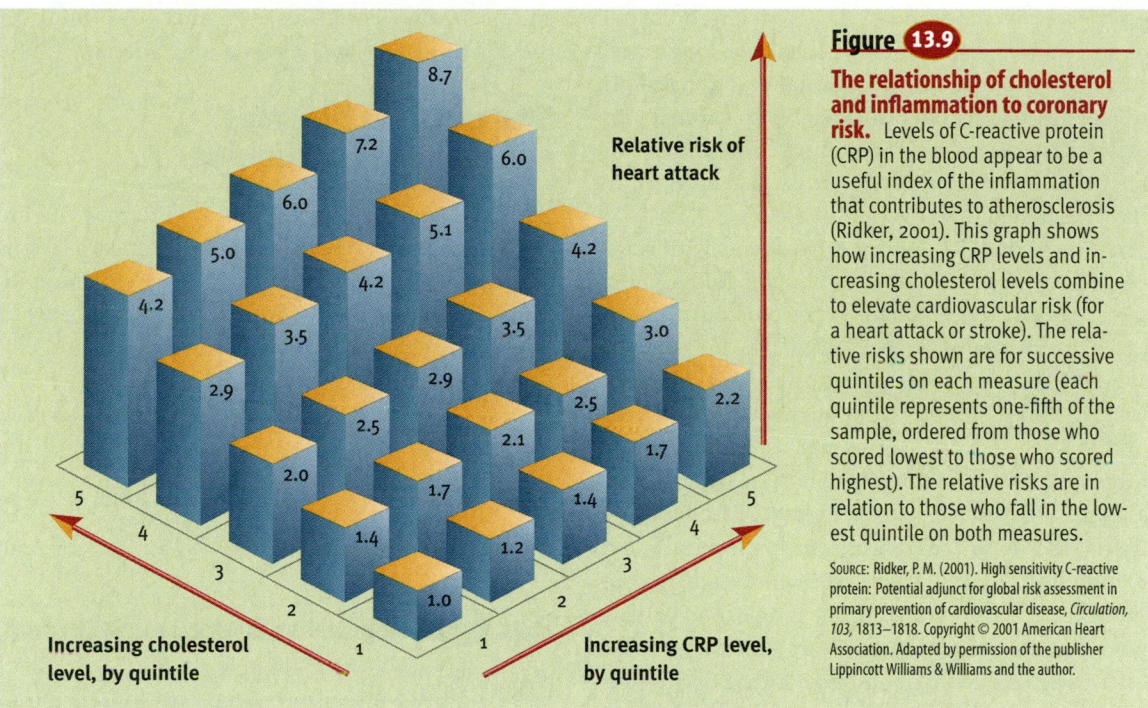

Figure 13.9

The relationship of cholesterol and inflammation to coronary risk. Levels of C-reactive protein (CRP) in the blood appear to be a useful index of the inflammation that contributes to atherosclerosis (Ridker, 2001). This graph shows how increasing CRP levels and increasing cholesterol levels combine to elevate cardiovascular risk (for a heart attack or stroke). The relative risks shown are for successive quintiles on each measure (each quintile represents one-fifth of the sample, ordered from those who scored lowest to those who scored highest). The relative risks are in relation to those who fall in the lowest quintile on both measures.

SOURCE: Ridker, P. M. (2001). High sensitivity C-reactive protein: Potential adjunct for global risk assessment in primary prevention of cardiovascular disease, *Circulation, 103,* 1813–1818. Copyright © 2001 American Heart Association. Adapted by permission of the publisher Lippincott Williams & Williams and the author.

found an association between Type A personality and an elevated incidence of heart disease, but the findings were not as strong or as consistent as expected (Ragland & Brand, 1988; Smith & Gallo, 2001). However, in recent years, researchers have found a stronger link between personality and coronary risk by focusing on a specific component of the Type A personality—*anger and hostility* (Rozanski, Blumenthal, & Kaplan, 1999). For example, in one study of almost 13,000 men and women who had no prior history of heart disease (Williams et al., 2000), investigators found an elevated incidence of heart attacks among participants who exhibited an angry temperament. The participants, who were followed for a median period of 4.5 years, were classified as being low (37.1%), moderate (55.2%), or high (7.7%) in anger. Among participants with normal blood pressure, the high-anger subjects experienced almost three times as many coronary events as the low-anger subjects (see Figure 13.10). In another study, CT scans were used to look for signs of atherosclerosis in a sample of 374 young men and women whose hostility had been assessed a decade earlier when they were 18 to 30 years old (Irabarren et al., 2000). Participants with above-average hostility scores were twice as likely to exhibit atherosclerosis as participants with below-average hostility scores. Thus, recent research suggests that hostility may be the crucial toxic element in the Type A syndrome.

Emotional Reactions, Depression, and Heart Disease

Although work on personality risk factors has dominated research on how psychological functioning contributes to heart disease, recent studies suggest that emotional reactions may also be critical. *One line of research has supported the hypothesis that transient mental stress and the resulting emotions that people*

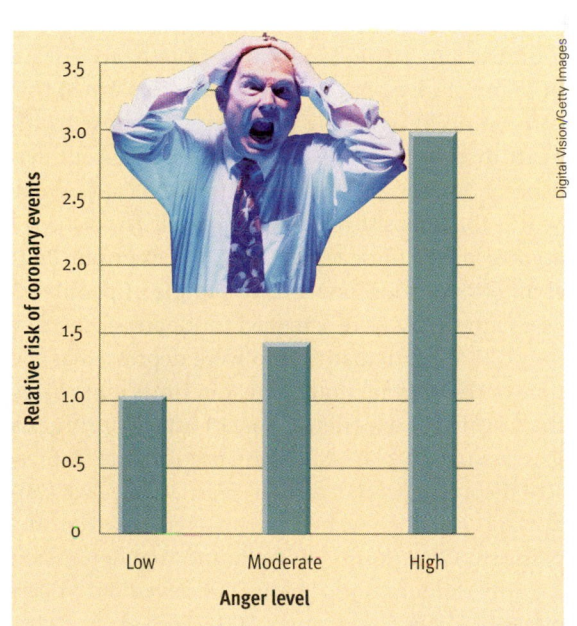

Digital Vision/Getty Images

Figure 13.10

Anger and coronary risk. Working with a large sample of healthy men and women who were followed for a median of 4.5 years, Williams et al. (2000) found an association between anger and the likelihood of a coronary event. Among subjects who manifested normal blood pressure at the beginning of the study, a moderate anger level was associated with a 36% increase in coronary attacks and a high level of anger nearly tripled participants' risk for coronary disease. (Based on data in Williams et al., 2000)

experience can tax the heart. Based on anecdotal evidence, cardiologists and laypersons have long voiced suspicions that strong emotional reactions might trigger heart attacks in individuals with coronary disease, but it has been difficult to document this connection. However, advances in cardiac monitoring have facilitated investigation of the issue.

As suspected, laboratory experiments with cardiology patients have shown that brief periods of mental stress can trigger acute symptoms of heart disease (Gottdiener et al., 1994). Overall, the evidence suggests that mental stress can elicit cardiac symptoms in about 30%–70% of patients with stable coronary disease (Kop, Gottdiener, & Krantz, 2001). Moreover, research indicates that these patients have a higher risk for heart attack than the cardiology patients who do not manifest ischemia in response to mental stress (Krantz et al., 2000). In a study that approached the issue from another angle, 660 patients who experienced a nonfatal heart attack were subsequently interviewed about events that occurred in the 6 hours prior to the onset of their heart attack (Moller et al., 1999). The interviews suggested that episodes of anger were a frequent trigger for the participants' heart attacks. Taken together, these studies suggest that emotional reactions to stressful events may precipitate heart attacks in people with coronary disease.

Another line of research has recently implicated depression as a risk factor for heart disease (Krantz & McCeney, 2002). *Depressive disorders,* which are characterized by persistent feelings of sadness and despair, are a fairly common form of mental illness (see Chapter 14). Elevated rates of depression have been found among patients suffering from heart disease in many studies, but most theorists explained this correlation by asserting that being diagnosed with heart disease makes people depressed. Recent evidence, however, suggests that the causal relations may be just the opposite—*that the emotional dysfunction of depression may cause heart disease.* For example, Pratt et al. (1996) examined a large sample of people 13 years after they were screened for depression. They found that participants who were depressed at the time of the original study were four times more likely than others to experience a heart attack during the intervening 13 years. Since the participants' depressive disorders preceded their heart attacks, we cannot argue that their heart disease caused their depression. Other studies have found that depression roughly doubles one's chances of developing heart disease (Cohen & Alderman, 2001; Ford et al., 1998). Moreover, the predictive link between depression

and heart disease remains even after controlling for the effects of smoking (Glassman & Shapiro, 1998).

Stress, Other Diseases, and Immune Functioning

The development of questionnaires to measure life stress has allowed researchers to look for correlations between stress and a variety of diseases. These researchers have uncovered many connections between stress and illness. For example, Thomason and colleagues (1992) found an association between life stress and the course of rheumatoid arthritis. Another study found an association between stressful life events and the emergence of lower back pain (Lampe et al., 1998). Other studies have connected stress to the development of genital herpes (VanderPlate, Aral,

Table 13.3 Health Problems That May Be Linked to Stress

Health Problem	Representative Evidence
AIDS	Ironson et al. (1994)
Appendicitis	Creed (1989)
Asthma	Sriram & Silverman (1998)
Cancer	Holland & Lewis (1993)
Chronic back pain	Lampe et al. (1998)
Common cold	Stone et al. (1992)
Complications of pregnancy	Dunkel-Schetter et al. (2001)
Coronary heart disease	Orth-Gomer et al. (2000)
Diabetes	Riazi & Bradley (2000)
Epileptic seizures	Kelly & Schramke (2000)
Hemophilia	Buxton et al. (1981)
Herpes virus	Padgett & Sheridan (2000)
Hypertension	Pickering et al. (1996)
Hyperthyroidism	Yang, Liu, & Zang (2000)
Inflammatory bowel disease	Searle & Bennett (2001)
Migraine headaches	Ramadan (2000)
Multiple sclerosis	Grant et al. (1989)
Periodontal disease	Marcenes & Sheiham (1992)
Premenstrual distress	Wu-Holt & Boutte (1994)
Rheumatoid arthritis	Huyser & Parker (1998)
Skin disorders	Arnold (2000)
Stroke	Harmsen et al. (1990)
Ulcers	Murison (2001)
Vaginal infections	Williams & Deffenbacher (1983)

Web Link 13.6

Healthfinder
Through the Department of Health and Human Services, the U.S. government has opened an ambitious online gateway to consumer-oriented information about health in all its aspects. Annotated descriptions are available for all resources identified in no-cost searches of this database.

& Magder, 1988), periodontal disease (Green et al., 1986), and flare-ups of inflammatory bowel disease (Olden, 1998).

These are just a handful of representative examples of studies relating stress to physical diseases. Table 13.3 provides a longer list of health problems that have been linked to stress. Many of these stress-illness connections are based on tentative or inconsistent findings, but the sheer length and diversity of the list is remarkable. Why should stress increase the risk for so many kinds of illness? A partial answer may lie in immune functioning.

The apparent link between stress and many types of illness raises the possibility that stress may undermine immune functioning. The *immune response* is the body's defensive reaction to invasion by bacteria, viral agents, or other foreign substances. The immune response works to protect the body from many forms of disease. Immune reactions are multifaceted, but they depend heavily on actions initiated by specialized white blood cells, called *lymphocytes*.

A wealth of studies indicate that experimentally induced stress can impair immune functioning *in animals* (Moynihan & Ader, 1996). That is, stressors such as crowding, shock, food restriction, and restraint reduce various aspects of immune reactivity in laboratory animals (Chiappelli & Hodgson, 2000).

Studies by Janice Kiecolt-Glaser and her colleagues have also related stress to suppressed immune activity *in humans* (Kiecolt-Glaser & Glaser, 1995). In one study, medical students provided researchers with blood samples so that their immune response could be assessed (Kiecolt-Glaser et al., 1984). The students provided the baseline sample a month before final exams and contributed the "high-stress" sample on the first day of their finals. The subjects also responded to the SRRS as a measure of recent stress. Reduced levels of immune activity were found during the extremely stressful finals week. Reduced immune activity was also correlated with higher scores on the SRRS.

Other studies have found evidence of reduced immune activity among people who scored relatively high on a stress scale measuring daily hassles (Levy et al., 1989), among recently divorced or separated men (Kiecolt-Glaser et al., 1988), and among people recently traumatized by a hurricane (Ironson et al., 1997). Thus, scientists are beginning to assemble some impressive evidence that stress can temporarily suppress human immune functioning, which may make people more vulnerable to infections, inflammation, and a diverse array of diseases (Kiecolt-Glaser et al., 2002). This possibility brings us to our Featured Study, which broke new ground exploring the possible link between stress and the common cold.

Connecting Stress to the Common Cold

Researchers have consistently found an association between stress and suppressed immune functioning, but as Sheldon Cohen and his colleagues note, "It is unclear whether the immune changes related to stress in these studies are of the type or magnitude that would influence susceptibility to infection" (p. 131). The handful of studies that have linked stress to actual infections have been plagued by a number of methodological shortcomings (Cohen & Williamson, 1991). For instance, these studies have usually failed to control for variations in subjects' personality, health habits, exposure to infected friends and family, and preexisting antibodies to the virus used. Hence, Cohen, Tyrrell, and Smith set out to conduct a more carefully controlled study of whether stress elevates vulnerability to infectious disease.

Method

Participants and procedure. The subjects were 154 men and 266 women who volunteered to participate in trials at the Medical Research Council's Common Cold Unit in Salisbury, England, where they were given free accommodations and quarantined for nine days. The volunteers' ages ranged from 18 to 54 (mean = 34). During their first two days on the unit, the participants were given medical exams to verify that they were in good health and were administered a series of questionnaires to assess their recent stress, aspects of their personality, and various health habits. They were then given—with their informed consent—nasal drops that contained either a respiratory virus or a harmless saline solution. A double-blind procedure was used so that neither the subjects nor the investigators knew who received the virus. The subjects were subsequently followed for six days to see whether they developed a viral infection (based on cultures of their nasal secretions) or cold symptoms (based on daily temperature readings for fever and clinical examinations for sore throat, nasal stuffiness, and so on).

Measurement instruments. Participants provided information about their recent stress by filling out a major life events scale similar to the SRRS, a measure of their subjective, perceived stress, and an assessment of their emotional tone during the previous week. These scales were examined individually and combined into an over-

Investigators: Sheldon Cohen (Carnegie-Mellon University), David A. J. Tyrrell (Medical Research Council, Salisbury, England), and Andrew P. Smith (University of Wales College of Cardiff)

Source: Negative life events, perceived stress, negative affect, and susceptibility to the common cold. *Journal of Personality and Social Psychology,* 1993, *64,* 131–140.

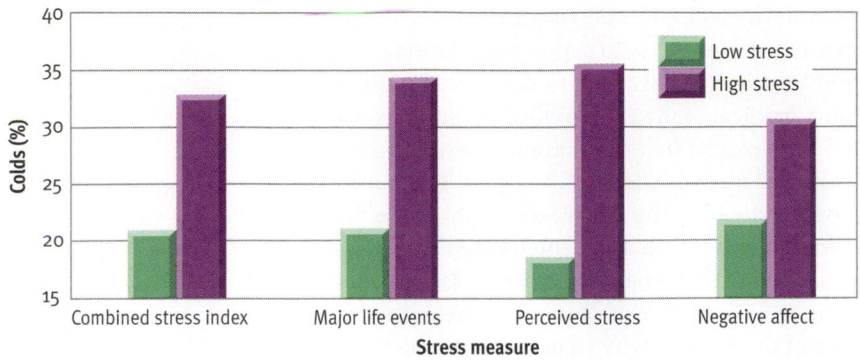

CHAPTER 13

Figure 13.11

Stress and vulnerability to the common cold. After exposing subjects to a respiratory virus, Cohen, Tyrrell, and Smith (1993) compared low-stress and high-stress subjects to see if the latter were more susceptible to colds. The data shown here are for subjects who did *not* have an infected roommate. As you can see, all four measures of stress were predictive of the incidence of colds, with high-stress subjects consistently developing more colds.

SOURCE: Adapted from Cohen, S., Tyrrell, D. A. J., & Smith, A. P. (1993). Negative life events, perceived stress, negative affect, and susceptibility to the common cold. *Journal of Personality and Social Psychology, 64,* 131–140. Copyright © 1993 by the American Psychological Association. Reprinted by permission of the author.

all stress index. The subjects also responded to personality scales that measured their self-esteem, self-efficacy, and extraversion. Their health practices were assessed with questionnaires that inquired about their exercise, dietary, sleep, and alcohol consumption habits.

Results

Participants were divided into high-stress and low-stress subjects based on whether they scored above or below the median on each of the stress scales. When the entire sample was analyzed, high-stress subjects were somewhat more likely than low-stress subjects to develop a viral infection and to manifest cold symptoms. However, the results revealed that being housed with a person who became infected (and thus infectious) partly obscured the effects of stress on colds, because these subjects were re-exposed to the virus (from their roommate's sneezing, coughing, and so on). Hence, the most telling comparisons were the analyses of cold rates in the subsample of subjects who did not have an infectious roommate, which are shown in Figure 13.11. In these comparisons, on all the stress measures high-stress subjects were more likely to develop colds than low-stress subjects. The associations between high stress and an increased incidence of colds were still significant even after the investigators controlled statistically for variations in subjects' personality and health practices.

Discussion

The authors assert that their control procedures eliminated a variety of possible alternative explanations for the apparent link between stress and vulnerability to infection. Hence they conclude that their study demonstrates "what up to now has been somewhat speculative, that psychological stress is associated with increased susceptibility to biologically verified infectious disease processes" (p. 139).

Comment

As you can see in Figure 13.11, the differences between the high-stress and low-stress subjects in the incidence of colds were not particularly large, but as we will discuss momentarily, these results are consistent with other research suggesting that the association between stress and illness is modest in strength. What makes this study outstanding is the enormous effort that the researchers went through to control for possible confounding variables. The quarantine conditions, which were highly unusual, obviously reduced the likelihood that participants would develop colds from other sources besides the virus tested. The monitoring of infections and colds with reliable biological measures (daily temperature readings, nasal cultures, and so on) circumvented the possibility that high-stress subjects might simply report more subjective symptoms of illness than low-stress subjects. By statistically controlling for subjects' health practices, the investigators eliminated the possibility that the stress-illness association might be due to unhealthy habits (smoking, drinking, and so on) that could undermine immune resistance. The investigators neutralized other possible confounds by using a double-blind procedure and by controlling for various demographic variables, preexisting antibodies, and personality differences. Given the enormous multiplicity of factors that influence behavior, one can never control for every possible confound and conduct "the perfect study." However, this study illustrates the great lengths that researchers go to in the hopes of coming close. ■

Sizing Up the Link Between Stress and Illness

A wealth of evidence shows that stress is related to physical health, and converging lines of evidence suggest that stress contributes to the *causation* of illness. But we have to put this intriguing finding in perspective. Virtually all of the relevant research is correlational, so it can't demonstrate *conclusively* that stress causes illness (Smith & Gallo, 2001). Subjects'

elevated levels of stress and illness could both be due to a third variable, perhaps some aspect of personality (see Figure 13.12). For instance, some evidence suggests that neuroticism may make people overly prone to interpret events as stressful and overly prone to interpret unpleasant sensations as symptoms of illness, thus inflating the correlation between stress and illness (Watson & Pennebaker, 1989).

In spite of methodological problems favoring inflated correlations, the research in this area consistently indicates that the *strength* of the relationship between stress and health is *modest*. The correlations typically fall in the .20s and .30s (Cohen, Kessler, & Gordon, 1995). Clearly, stress is not an irresistible force that produces inevitable effects on health. Actually, this fact should come as no surprise, as stress is but one factor operating in a complex network of biopsychosocial determinants of health. Other key factors include one's genetic endowment, exposure to infectious agents and environmental toxins, nutrition, exercise, alcohol and drug use, smoking, use of medical care, and cooperation with medical advice. Furthermore, some people handle stress better than others, which is the matter we turn to next.

REVIEW OF KEY POINTS

- Stress appears to play a role in many types of illnesses, not just psychosomatic diseases. The Type A personality has been implicated as a contributing cause of coronary heart disease, but hostility may be the most toxic element of the Type A syndrome. Transient, stress-induced emo-

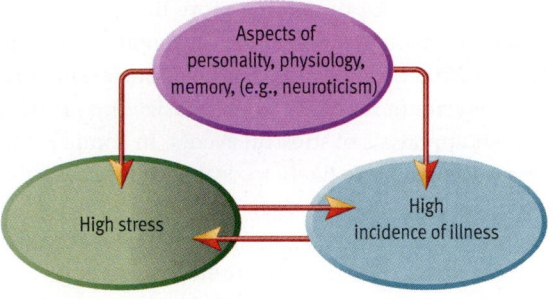

Figure 13.12

The stress-illness correlation. One or more aspects of personality, physiology, or memory could play the role of a postulated third variable in the relationship between high stress and high incidence of illness. For example, neuroticism may lead some subjects to view more events as stressful and to remember more illness, thus inflating the apparent correlation between stress and illness.

tional reactions and depression have also been identified as cardiovascular risk factors.

- Researchers have found associations between stress and the onset of a great variety of specific diseases, although the evidence on many is highly tentative. Stress may play a role in a host of diseases because it can temporarily suppress the effectiveness of the immune system. The Featured Study provided a well-controlled demonstration of how stress may increase susceptibility to the common cold.

- Although there's little doubt that stress can contribute to the development of physical illness, the link between stress and illness is modest. Stress is only one factor in a complex network of biopsychosocial variables that shape health.

Factors Moderating the Impact of Stress

Some people seem to be able to withstand the ravages of stress better than others (Holohan & Moos, 1994). Why? Because a number of *moderator variables* can lessen the impact of stress on physical and mental health. We'll look at three key moderator variables—social support, optimism, and conscientiousness—to shed light on individual differences in how well people tolerate stress.

Social Support

Friends may be good for your health! This startling conclusion emerges from studies on social support as a moderator of stress. **Social support refers to various types of aid and succor provided by members of one's social networks.** In one study, Jemmott and Magloire (1988) examined the effect of social support on immune functioning in a group of students going through the stress of final exams. They found that students who reported stronger social support had higher levels of an antibody that plays a key role in warding off respiratory infections. Positive correlations between high social support and greater immune functioning have also been found in other studies (Uchino, Uno, & Holt-Lunstad, 1999).

Over the last two decades, a vast body of studies have found evidence that social support is favorably related to physical health (Wills & Fegan, 2001). Social support seems to be good medicine for the mind as well as the body, as most studies also find an association between social support and mental health (Davis, Morris, & Kraus, 1998). It appears that social support serves as a protective buffer during times of high stress, reducing the negative impact of stressful events—and that social support has its own positive effects on health, which may be apparent even when people aren't under great stress (Peirce et al., 1996; Wills & Fegan, 2001). The stress-buffering effects of social support were apparent in a study which found that strong social support was a key factor reducing the likelihood of posttraumatic stress disorders among Vietnam veterans (King et al., 1998).

Optimism and Conscientiousness

Defining *optimism* as a **general tendency to expect good outcomes**, Michael Scheier and Charles Carver (1985) found a correlation between optimism and relatively good physical health in a sample of college students. Another study found optimism to be associated with more effective immune functioning (Segerstrom et al., 1998). Research suggests that optimists cope with stress in more adaptive ways than pessimists (Aspinwall, Richter, & Hoffman, 2001; Carver &

PREVIEW QUESTIONS

- How does social support influence people's health?
- How is optimism related to health?
- How is conscientiousness related to health?

Scheier, 1999). Optimists are more likely to engage in action-oriented, problem-focused coping. They are more willing than pessimists to seek social support, and they are more likely to emphasize the positive in their appraisals of stressful events. In comparison, pessimists are more likely to deal with stress by giving up or engaging in denial.

In a related line of research, Christopher Peterson and Martin Seligman have studied how people explain bad events (personal setbacks, mishaps, disappointments, and such). They identified a *pessimistic explanatory style* in which people tend to blame setbacks on their own personal shortcomings versus an *optimistic explanatory style* which leads people to attribute setbacks to temporary situational factors. In two retrospective studies of people born many decades ago, they found an association between this optimistic explanatory style and relatively good health (Peterson, Seligman, & Vaillant, 1988) and increased longevity (Peterson et al., 1998). Many other studies have linked this optimistic explanatory style to superior physical health (Peterson & Bossio, 2001), as well as higher academic achievement, increased job productivity, enhanced athletic performance, and higher marital satisfaction (Gillham et al., 2001).

Optimism versus pessimism is not the only dimension of personality that has been examined as a possible moderator of physical health. Howard Friedman and his colleagues have found evidence that *conscientiousness*, one of the Big Five personality traits discussed in Chapter 12, may have an impact on physical health. Friedman et al. (1993) related personality measures to longevity in the gifted individuals first studied by Lewis Terman (see Chapter 9), who have been followed closely by researchers since 1921. Data were available on six personality traits, which were measured when the subjects were children. The one trait that predicted greater longevity was conscientiousness. Friedman et al. (1993) reasoned, logically enough, that conscientiousness may simply have fostered better health habits, but a follow-up study (Friedman et al., 1995) found little evidence that this was the case. Hence, the investigators have now turned their attention to how conscientiousness may have affected subjects' coping or stress tolerance.

Individual differences among people in social support, optimism, and conscientiousness explain why stress doesn't have the same impact on everyone. Differences in lifestyle may play an even larger role in determining health. We'll examine some critical aspects of lifestyle in the next section.

Courtesy of Martin E. P. Seligman

"*The concept of explanatory style brings hope into the laboratory, where scientists can dissect it in order to understand how it works.*"
MARTIN SELIGMAN

REVIEW OF KEY POINTS

- There are individual differences in how much stress people can tolerate without experiencing ill effects. Social support is a key moderator of the relationship between stress and both physical and mental health.

- Optimism may lead to more effective coping with stress, whereas pessimism has been related to passive coping and poor health practices. A recent study of Terman's sample of gifted children suggests that conscientiousness is associated with greater longevity.

Health-Impairing Behavior

PREVIEW QUESTIONS

- Why does smoking increase mortality?
- What are some examples of links between nutrition and health?
- What are the health benefits of exercise?
- What are some misconceptions about HIV transmission?
- How do health-impairing habits get started?

Some people seem determined to dig an early grave for themselves. They do precisely those things that are bad for their health. For example, some people drink heavily even though they know that they're damaging their liver. Others eat all the wrong foods even though they know that they're increasing their risk of a second heart attack. Behavior that's downright *self-destructive* is surprisingly common. In this section we'll discuss how health is affected by smoking, nutrition, exercise, and drug use, and we'll look at behavioral factors in AIDS. We'll also discuss *why* people develop health-impairing lifestyles.

Smoking

The smoking of tobacco is widespread in our culture, with current consumption running around 2400 cigarettes a year per adult in the United States. The percentage of people who smoke has declined noticeably since the mid-1960s (see Figure 13.13). Nonetheless, about 26% of adult men and 22% of adult women in the United States continue to smoke regularly.

The evidence clearly shows that smokers face a much greater risk of premature death than nonsmokers (Schmitz, Jarvik & Schneider, 1997). For example, a 25-year-old male who smokes two packs a day has an estimated life expectancy *8.3 years shorter* than that of a similar nonsmoker (Schlaadt & Shannon, 1994). The overall risk is positively related to the number of cigarettes smoked and their tar and nicotine content. Cigar smoking, which has increased dramatically in recent years, elevates health risks almost as much as cigarette smoking (Baker et al., 2000). Jarvik and Schneider (1992) put the health costs of smoking in perspective by noting that smoking accounts for roughly 60 times as many deaths per year as cocaine and heroin use combined.

Why are mortality rates higher for smokers? Smoking increases the likelihood of developing a surprisingly large range of diseases (Thun, Apicella, & Henley, 2000). Lung cancer and heart disease kill the largest number of smokers. However, smokers also have an elevated risk for oral, bladder, and kidney cancer, as well as cancers of the larynx, esophagus, and pancreas; for arteriosclerosis, hypertension, stroke, and other cardiovascular diseases; and for bronchitis, emphysema, and other pulmonary diseases. Most smokers know about the risks associated with tobacco use, but they tend to underestimate the actual risks as applied to themselves (Ayanian & Cleary, 1999).

The dangers of smoking are not limited to smokers themselves. Family members and co-workers who spend a lot of time around smokers are exposed to *second-hand smoke* or *environmental tobacco smoke*, which can increase their risk for a variety of illnesses, including lung cancer (Wells, 1998), heart disease (Howard et al., 1998), and breast cancer in women (Lash & Aschengrau, 1999). Young children with asthma are particularly vulnerable to the effects of second-hand smoke (Stoddard & Miller, 1995).

Studies show that if people can give up smoking, their health risks decline reasonably quickly (Samet, 1992; see Figure 13.14). Evidence suggests that most smokers would like to quit but are reluctant to give up a major source of pleasure, and they worry about craving cigarettes, gaining weight, becoming anxious and irritable, and feeling less able to cope with stress (Grunberg, Faraday, & Rahman, 2001).

Unfortunately, it's difficult to give up cigarettes. People who enroll in formal smoking cessation programs aren't any more successful than people who try to quit on their own (Cohen et al., 1989). Long-term success rates are in the vicinity of only 25%, and some studies report even lower figures. For example, in one study of self-quitters, after six months only 3% had maintained complete abstinence from smoking (Hughes et al., 1992). Relapse rates for quitting smoking are often as bad as those seen in efforts to give up heroin or alcohol (Hunt & Matarazzo, 1982). Nonetheless, the fact that there are nearly 40 million ex-smokers in the United States indicates that it is possible to quit smoking successfully. Interestingly, many people fail several or more times before they eventually succeed. Evidence suggests that the readiness to give up smoking builds gradually as people cycle through periods of abstinence and relapse (Herzog et al., 1999; Prochaska, 1994).

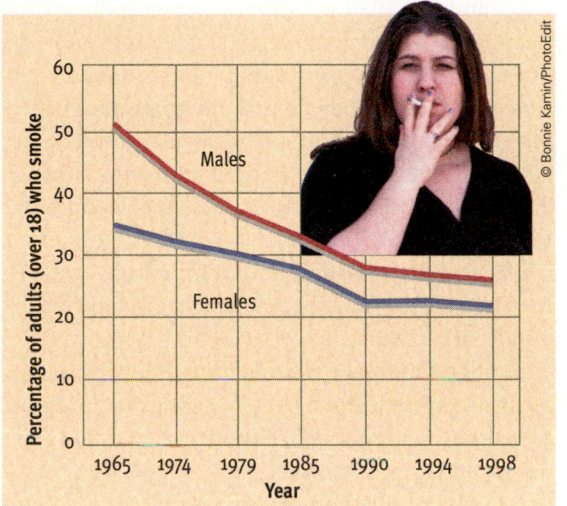

Figure 13.13

The prevalence of smoking in the United States. This graph shows how the percentage of U.S. adults who smoke has declined steadily since the mid-1960s. Although considerable progress has been made, smoking still accounts for about 400,000 premature deaths each year. (Based on data from the Centers for Disease Control and Prevention)

Poor Nutritional Habits

Evidence is accumulating that patterns of nutrition influence susceptibility to a variety of diseases and health problems. In addition to the problems associated with obesity, which we discussed in Chapter 10, other possible connections between eating patterns and health include the following:

1. Heavy consumption of foods that elevate serum cholesterol level (eggs, cheeses, butter, shellfish, sau-

Figure 13.14

Quitting smoking and health risk. Research suggests that various types of health risks associated with smoking decline gradually after people give up tobacco. The data shown here, from the U.S. Surgeon General's (1990) report on smoking, illustrate the overall effects on mortality rates. (Based on data from U.S. Department of Health and Human Services, 1990)

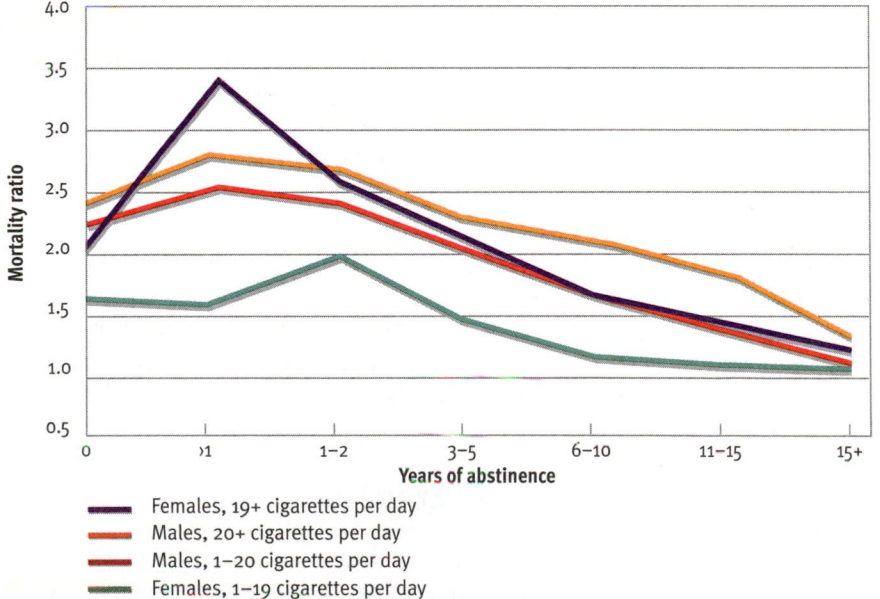

sage, and the like) appears to increase the risk of heart disease (Stamler et al., 2000). Eating habits are only one of several factors that influence serum cholesterol level, but they do make an important contribution. Vulnerability to cardiovascular diseases may also be influenced by other dietary factors. For example, low-fiber diets may increase the likelihood of coronary disease (Ludwig et al., 1999; Wolk et al., 1999), and low consumption of fruit and vegetables may be associated with vulnerability to stroke (Joshipura et al., 1999).

2. High salt intake is thought to be a contributing factor to the development of hypertension (Messerli, Schmieder, & Weir, 1997), although there is still some debate about its exact role.

3. Some studies have suggested that high caffeine consumption may elevate one's risk for hypertension (Lovallo et al., 1996) and for coronary disease (Grossarth-Maticek & Eysenck, 1991). However, the findings are inconsistent, and one large-scale study of over 45,000 subjects found no association between caffeine consumption and cardiovascular risk (Grobbee et al., 1990).

4. High-fat diets have been implicated as possible contributors to some forms of cancer, especially prostate cancer (Rose, 1997), colon and rectal cancer (Shike, 1999), and breast cancer (Wynder et al., 1997). Some studies also suggest that high-fiber diets may reduce one's risk for colon and rectal cancer (Reddy, 1999), but the evidence is not conclusive.

5. Vulnerability to osteoporosis, an abnormal loss of bone mass observed most commonly in postmenopausal women, appears to be elevated by a lifelong pattern of inadequate calcium intake (Fahey & Gallagher-Allred, 1990).

6. Nutritional patterns play a role in the course and management of a host of diseases, among them gallstones, kidney stones, gout, peptic ulcers, and rheumatoid arthritis (Werbach, 1988). Eating habits may also contribute to the causation of some of these diseases, although the evidence is less compelling on this point.

Of course, nutritional habits interact with other factors—genetics, exercise, environment, and so on—to determine whether one develops a particular disease. Nonetheless, the examples just described indicate that eating habits can influence one's physical health.

Lack of Exercise

There is considerable evidence linking lack of exercise to poor health. Research indicates that regular

Web Link 13.7

Exercise and Sport Psychology
For anyone wondering about how psychological science deals with sports and athletics, this site, maintained by Division 47 of the American Psychological Association, is an excellent starting point, especially for those looking for career information.

exercise is associated with increased longevity (Lee, Hsieh, & Paffenbarger, 1995). Why would exercise help people live longer? For one thing, an appropriate exercise program can enhance cardiovascular fitness and thereby reduce susceptibility to deadly cardiovascular problems (Lee et al., 2001; Phillips, Kiernan, & King, 2001). Second, fitness may indirectly reduce one's risk for a variety of obesity-related health problems, such as diabetes and respiratory difficulties (Epstein et al., 1995). Third, recent studies suggest that physical fitness is also associated with a decreased risk for colon cancer in men and for breast and reproductive cancer in women (Marcus, Bock, & Pinto, 1997; Thune et al., 1997). The apparent link between exercise and reduced cancer risk has been a pleasant surprise for scientists, who are now scrambling to figure out the physiological mechanisms underlying this association. Fourth, exercise can serve as a buffer that reduces the potentially damaging physical effects of stress (Plante, 1999; Plante, Caputo, & Chizmar, 2000). This buffering effect may occur because people high in fitness show less physiological reactivity to stress than those who are less fit.

Alcohol and Drug Use 4c

Recreational drug use is another common health-impairing habit. The risks associated with the use of various drugs were discussed in detail in Chapter 5. Unlike smoking, poor eating habits, and inactivity, drugs can kill directly and immediately when they are taken in an overdose or when they impair the user enough to cause an accident. In the long run, various recreational drugs may also elevate one's risk for infectious diseases; respiratory, pulmonary, and cardiovascular diseases; liver disease; gastrointestinal problems; cancer; neurological disorders; and pregnancy complications (see Chapter 5). Ironically, the greatest physical damage in the population as a whole is caused by alcohol, the one recreational drug that's legal.

Behavior and AIDS

At present, some of the most problematic links between behavior and health may be those related to AIDS. AIDS stands for *acquired immune deficiency syndrome,* a disorder in which the immune system is gradually weakened and eventually disabled by the human immunodeficiency virus (HIV). Being infected with the HIV virus is *not* equivalent to having AIDS. AIDS is the final stage of the HIV infection process, typically manifested about ten years after the original infection (Treisman, 1999). With the onset of AIDS, one is left virtually defenseless against a host of opportunistic infectious agents. AIDS inflicts its harm indirectly by opening the door to other diseases. The symptoms of AIDS vary widely depending on the specific constellation of diseases that one develops. Unfortunately, the worldwide prevalence of this deadly disease continues to increase at an alarming rate.

Prior to 1996–1997, the average length of survival for people after the onset of the AIDS syndrome was about 18 to 24 months. Encouraging advances in the treatment of AIDS with drug regimens referred to as *highly active antiretroviral therapy* hold out promise for *substantially* longer survival (Kirchner, 2001). But these drugs have been rushed into service and their long-term efficacy is yet to be determined (Lee et al., 2001; Tang & Glatt, 2001). Medical experts are concerned that the general public has gotten the impression that these treatments have transformed AIDS from a fatal disease to a manageable one, which is a premature conclusion (Mitka, 1999). HIV strains are evolving, and many have developed resistance to the currently available antiretroviral drugs (Tang & Glatt, 2001). Moreover, many patients do not respond well to the new drugs, and many patients who are responsive have difficulty sticking to the complicated drug administration regimens that often require people to take 20–30 pills daily and that often have adverse side effects (Catz & Kelly, 2001).

Transmission

The HIV virus is transmitted through person-to-person contact involving the exchange of bodily fluids, primarily semen and blood. The two principal modes of transmission in the United States have been sexual contact and the sharing of needles by intravenous (IV) drug users. In the United States, sexual transmission has occurred primarily among gay and bisexual men, but heterosexual transmission has increased in recent years (Rosenberg & Biggar, 1998). In the world as a whole, infection through heterosexual relations has been much more common from the beginning (see Figure 13.15). In heterosexual relations, male-to-female transmission is estimated to be about eight times more likely than female-to-male transmission (Ickovics, Thayaparan, & Ethier, 2001). The HIV virus can be found in the tears and saliva of infected individuals, but the concentrations are low and there is no evidence that the infection can be spread through casual contact. Even most forms of noncasual contact, including kissing, hugging, and sharing food with infected individuals, appear safe (Kalichman, 1995).

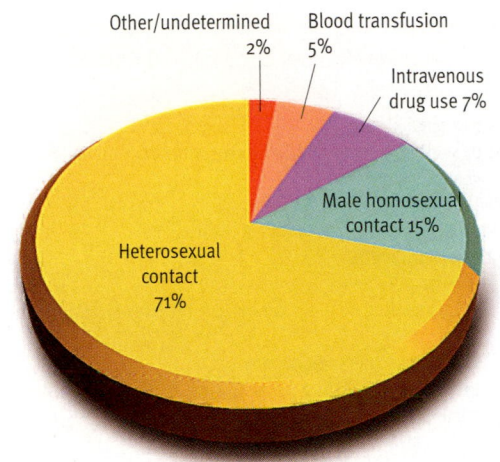

Figure 13.15

HIV transmission worldwide. In the United States, about 80% of HIV transmission thus far has occurred among gay men or intravenous drug users, perhaps leading to misconceptions about the ease of transmission via heterosexual relations. In the world as a whole, heterosexual relations are the predominant mode of transmission, as these data show.

SOURCE: Mann, J., Tarantola, D. J. M., & Netter, T. W. (1992). *A global report: AIDS in the world.* New York: Oxford University Press.

Misconceptions

Misconceptions about AIDS are widespread. Ironically, the people who hold these misconceptions fall into two polarized camps. On the one hand, a great many people have unrealistic fears that AIDS can be readily transmitted through casual contact with infected individuals. These people worry unnecessarily about contracting AIDS from a handshake, a sneeze, or an eating utensil. They tend to be paranoid about interacting with homosexuals, thus fueling discrimination against gays in regard to housing, employment, and so forth. Some people also believe that it is dangerous to donate blood, when in fact blood donors are at no risk whatsoever.

On the other hand, many young heterosexuals who are sexually active with a variety of partners foolishly downplay their risk for HIV, naively assuming that they are safe as long as they avoid IV drug use and sexual relations with gay or bisexual men. They greatly underestimate the probability that their sexual partners previously may have used IV drugs or had unprotected sex with an infected individual. They don't understand, for instance, that most bisexual men do not disclose their bisexuality to their female partners (Kalichman et al., 1998). Also, because AIDS is usually accompanied by discernible symptoms, many young people believe that prospective sexual partners who carry the HIV virus will exhibit telltale signs of illness. However, as we have al-

AIDS Risk Knowledge Test

Answer the following "true" or "false."

T	F	**1.**	The AIDS virus cannot be spread through kissing.
T	F	**2.**	A person can get the AIDS virus by sharing kitchens and bathrooms with someone who has AIDS.
T	F	**3.**	Men can give the AIDS virus to women.
T	F	**4.**	The AIDS virus attacks the body's ability to fight off diseases.
T	F	**5.**	You can get the AIDS virus by someone sneezing, like a cold or the flu.
T	F	**6.**	You can get AIDS by touching a person with AIDS.
T	F	**7.**	Women can give the AIDS virus to men.
T	F	**8.**	A person who got the AIDS virus from shooting up drugs cannot give the virus to someone by having sex.
T	F	**9.**	A pregnant woman can give the AIDS virus to her unborn baby.
T	F	**10.**	Most types of birth control also protect against getting the AIDS virus.
T	F	**11.**	Condoms make intercourse completely safe.
T	F	**12.**	Oral sex is safe if partners "do not swallow."
T	F	**13.**	A person must have many different sexual partners to be at risk for AIDS.
T	F	**14.**	It is more important to take precautions against AIDS in large cities than in small cities.
T	F	**15.**	A positive result on the AIDS virus antibody test often occurs for people who do not even have the virus.
T	F	**16.**	Only receptive (passive) anal intercourse transmits the AIDS virus.
T	F	**17.**	Donating blood carries no AIDS risk for the donor.
T	F	**18.**	Most people who have the AIDS virus look quite ill.

Answers: 1.T 2.F 3.T 4.T 5.F 6.F 7.T 8.F 9.T 10.F 11.F 12.F 13.F 14.F 15.F 16.F 17.T 18.F

Figure 13.16

A quiz on knowledge of AIDS. Because misconceptions about AIDS abound, it may be wise to take this brief quiz to test your knowledge of AIDS. The answers are shown at the bottom of the figure.

Adapted from Kalichman, S. C. (1995). *Understanding AIDS: A guide for mental health professionals.* Washington, DC: American Psychological Association. Reprinted by permission of the author.

ready noted, having AIDS and being infected with HIV are not the same thing, and HIV carriers often remain healthy and symptom-free for many years after they are infected. In sum, many myths about AIDS persist, in spite of extensive efforts to educate the public about this complex and controversial disease. Figure 13.16 contains a short quiz to test your knowledge of the facts about AIDS.

Prevention

The behavioral changes that minimize the risk of developing AIDS are fairly straightforward, although making the changes is often much easier said than done (Coates & Collins, 1998). In all groups, the more sexual partners a person has, the higher the risk that one will be exposed to the HIV virus. Thus, people can reduce their risk by having sexual contacts with fewer partners and by using condoms to control the exchange of semen. It is also important to curtail certain sexual practices (in particular, anal sex) that increase the probability of semen/blood mixing. The 1980s and early 1990s saw considerable progress towards wider use of safe sex practices, but new cohorts of young people appear to be much less concerned about the risk of HIV infection than the generation that witnessed the original emergence of AIDS (Catania et al., 2001). For example, a recent study of 15- to 22-year-old gay men found alarmingly high rates of risky sexual practices, such as unprotected anal sex (Valleroy et al., 2000). These findings do not bode well for efforts to slow the spread of AIDS.

How Does Health-Impairing Behavior Develop?

It may seem puzzling that people behave in self-destructive ways. How does this happen? Several factors are involved. First, many health-impairing habits creep up on people slowly. For instance, drug use may grow imperceptibly over years, or exercise habits may decline ever so gradually. Second, many health-impairing habits involve activities that are quite pleasant at the time. Actions such as eating favorite foods, smoking cigarettes, or getting "high" are potent reinforcing events. Third, the risks associated with most health-impairing habits are chronic diseases such as cancer that usually lie 10, 20, or 30 years down the road. It's relatively easy to ignore risks that lie in the distant future.

Finally, people have a curious tendency to underestimate the risks that accompany their own health-impairing behaviors while viewing the risks associated with others' self-destructive behaviors much more accurately (Weinstein & Klein, 1995, 1996). Many people are well aware of the dangers associated with certain habits, but when it's time to apply this information to themselves, they often discount it. They figure, for instance, that smoking will lead to cancer or a heart attack in *someone else*.

So far, we've seen that physical health may be affected by stress and by aspects of lifestyle. Next, we'll look at the importance of how people react to physical symptoms, health problems, and health care efforts.

REVIEW OF KEY POINTS

- People frequently display health-impairing lifestyles. Smokers have much higher mortality rates than nonsmokers because they are more vulnerable to a host of diseases. Health risks decline reasonably quickly for people who give up smoking, but quitting is difficult and relapse rates are high.

- Poor nutritional habits have been linked to heart disease, hypertension, and cancer, among other things. Lack of exercise elevates one's risk for cardiovascular diseases. Alcohol and drug use carry the immediate risk of overdose and elevate the long-term risk of many diseases.

- Aspects of behavior influence one's risk of AIDS, which is transmitted through person-to-person contact involving the exchange of bodily fluids, primarily semen and blood. Misconceptions about AIDS are common, and the people who hold these misconceptions tend to fall into polarized camps, either overestimating or underestimating their risk of infection.

- Health-impairing habits tend to develop gradually and often involve pleasant activities. The risks may be easy to ignore because they lie in the distant future and because people tend to underestimate risks that apply to them personally.

Reactions to Illness

Some people respond to physical symptoms and illnesses by ignoring warning signs of developing diseases, while others engage in active coping efforts to conquer their diseases. Let's examine the decision to seek medical treatment, communication with health providers, and compliance with medical advice.

Deciding to Seek Treatment

Have you ever experienced nausea, diarrhea, stiffness, headaches, cramps, chest pains, or sinus problems? Of course you have; we all experience some of these problems periodically. However, whether we view these sensations as *symptoms* is a matter of individual interpretation. When two persons experience the same unpleasant sensations, one may shrug them off as a nuisance while the other may rush to a physician. Studies suggest that people who are relatively high in anxiety and neuroticism tend to report more symptoms of illness than others do (Feldman et al., 1999; Leventhal et al., 1996). Those who are extremely attentive to bodily sensations and health concerns also report more symptoms than the average person (Barsky, 1988).

Variations in the perceived seriousness and disruptiveness of symptoms help explain the differences among people in their readiness to seek medical treatment (Cameron, Leventhal, & Leventhal, 1993). The biggest problem in regard to treatment seeking is the tendency of many people to delay the pursuit of needed professional consultation. Delays can be critical because early diagnosis and quick intervention may facilitate more effective treatment of many health problems. Unfortunately, procrastination is the norm even when people are faced with a medical emergency, such as a heart attack. Why do people dawdle in the midst of a crisis? Robin DiMatteo (1991), a leading expert on patient behavior, mentions a number of reasons, noting that people delay because they often (a) misinterpret and downplay the significance of their symptoms, (b) fret about looking silly if the problem turns out to be nothing, (c) worry about "bothering" their physician, (d) are reluctant to disrupt their plans (to go out to dinner, see a movie, and so forth), and (e) waste time on trivial matters (such as taking a shower, gathering personal items, or packing clothes) before going to a hospital emergency room.

Communicating with Health Providers

About half of medical patients depart their doctors' offices not understanding what they have been told and what they are supposed to do (DiMatteo, 1991). This reality is most unfortunate because good communication is a crucial requirement for sound medical decisions, informed choices about treatment, and appropriate follow-through by patients (Gambone, Reiter, & DiMatteo, 1994).

There are many barriers to effective provider-patient communication (Beisecker, 1990; DiMatteo, 1997). Economic realities dictate that medical visits are generally quite brief, allowing little time for discussion. Many providers use too much medical jargon and overestimate their patients' understanding of technical terms. Patients who are upset and worried about their illness may simply forget to report some symptoms or to ask questions they meant to ask. Other patients are evasive about their real

PREVIEW QUESTIONS
- What is the biggest problem related to people's decisions to seek medical treatment?
- What are some barriers to effective communication between patients and their health providers?
- What can patients do to improve communication?
- How much of a problem is nonadherence to medical advice?
- What are the causes of nonadherence?

Communication between health care providers and patients tends to be far from optimal, for a variety of reasons.

"*A person will not carry out a health behavior if significant barriers stand in the way, or if the steps interfere with favorite or necessary activities.*"
ROBIN DiMATTEO

concerns because they fear a serious diagnosis. Many patients are reluctant to challenge doctors' authority and are too passive in their interactions with providers.

What can you do to improve your communication with health care providers? The key is to not be a passive consumer of medical services (Ferguson, 1993; Kane, 1991). Arrive at a medical visit on time, with your questions and concerns prepared in advance. Try to be accurate and candid in replying to your doctor's questions. If you don't understand something the doctor says, don't be embarrassed about asking for clarification. If you have doubts about the suitability or feasibility of your doctor's recommendations, don't be afraid to voice them.

Adhering to Medical Advice

Many patients fail to adhere to the instructions they receive from physicians and other health care professionals. The evidence suggests that nonadherence to medical advice may occur 30% to 60% of the time (DiMatteo, 1994). Nonadherence takes many forms. Patients may fail to begin a treatment regimen, stop the regimen early, reduce or increase the levels of treatment that were prescribed, or be inconsistent and unreliable in following treatment procedures (Dunbar-Jacob & Schlenk, 2001).

This point is not intended to suggest that you should passively accept all professional advice from medical personnel. However, when you have doubts about a prescribed treatment, you should speak up and ask questions. Passive resistance can backfire. For instance, if a physician sees no improvement in a patient who falsely insists that he has been taking his medicine, the physician may abandon an accurate diagnosis in favor of an inaccurate one. The inaccurate diagnosis could then lead to inappropriate treatments that might be harmful to the patient.

Why don't people comply with the advice that they've sought out from highly regarded health care professionals? Physicians tend to attribute noncompliance to patients' personality traits, but research indicates that other factors are more important. In many cases, patients simply forget about the requirements of their treatment regimen (Dunbar-Jacob & Schlenk, 2001). Three other considerations are also especially prominent (DiMatteo & Friedman, 1982; Evans & Haynes, 1990; Ley, 1997):

1. Frequently, noncompliance is a result of the patient's failure to understand the instructions as given. Highly trained professionals often forget that what seems obvious and simple to them may be obscure and complicated to many of their patients.

2. Another key factor is how aversive or difficult the instructions are. If the prescribed regimen is unpleasant, compliance will tend to decrease. And the more that following instructions interferes with routine behavior, the less probable it is that the patient will cooperate successfully.

3. If a patient has a negative attitude toward a physician, the probability of noncompliance will increase. When patients are unhappy with their interactions with the doctor, they're more likely to ignore the medical advice provided.

In response to the noncompliance problem, some health psychologists are exploring ways to increase patients' adherence to medical advice. They've found that the communication process between the practitioner and the patient is of critical importance. Courtesy, encouragement, reassurance, taking time to answer questions, and decreased reliance on medical jargon can improve compliance (DiNicola & DiMatteo, 1984; Hall, Roter, & Katz, 1988). Thus, there's a new emphasis in medicine on enhancing health care professionals' communication skills.

Putting It in Perspective

PREVIEW QUESTIONS
● How did this chapter illustrate multifactorial causation?
● How did this chapter highlight the subjectivity of human experience?

Which of our themes were prominent in this chapter? As you probably noticed, our discussion of stress and health illustrated multifactorial causation and the subjectivity of experience. As we noted in Chapter 1, people tend to think simplistically, in terms of single causes. In recent years, the highly publicized research linking stress to health has led many people to point automatically to stress as an explanation for illness. In reality, stress has only a modest impact on physical health. Stress can increase the risk for illness, but health is governed by a dense network of factors. Important factors include inherited vulnerabilities, physiological reactivity, exposure to infectious agents, health-impairing habits, reactions to symptoms, treatment-seeking behavior, compliance with medical advice, personality, and social support. In other words, stress is but one actor on a crowded stage. This should be apparent in

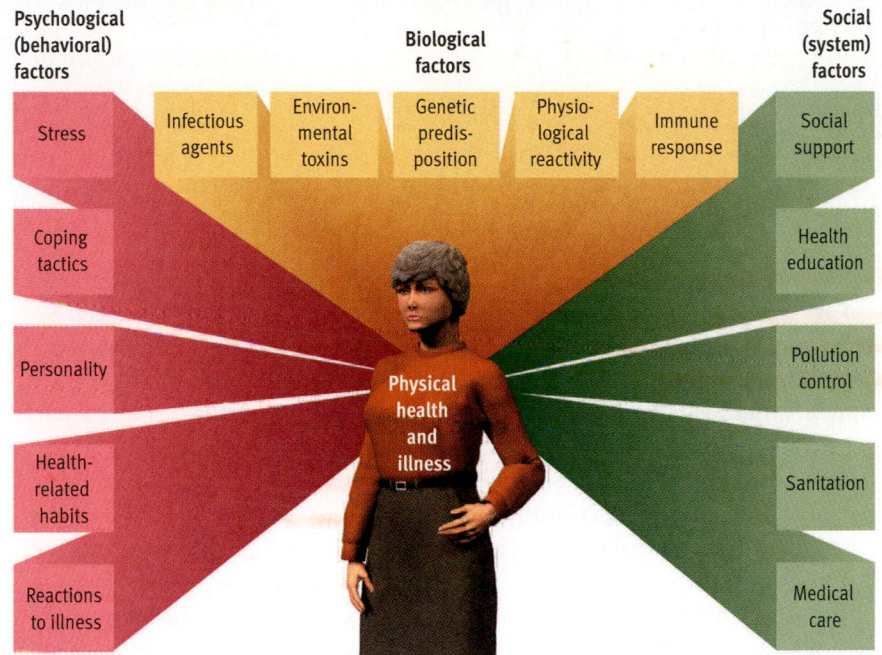

Psychological (behavioral) factors

Stress

Coping tactics

Personality

Health-related habits

Reactions to illness

Biological factors

Infectious agents

Environmental toxins

Genetic predisposition

Physiological reactivity

Immune response

Physical health and illness

Social (system) factors

Social support

Health education

Pollution control

Sanitation

Medical care

Figure 13.17, which shows the multitude of biopsychosocial factors that jointly influence physical health. It illustrates multifactorial causation in all its complexity.

The subjectivity of experience was demonstrated by the frequently repeated point that stress lies in the eye of the beholder. The same job promotion may be stressful for one person and invigorating for another. One person's pressure is another's challenge. When it comes to stress, objective reality is not nearly as important as subjective perceptions. More than anything else, the impact of stressful events seems to depend on how people view them. The critical importance of individual stress appraisals will continue to be apparent in the Personal Application on coping and stress management. Many stress management strategies depend on altering one's appraisals of events.

REVIEW OF KEY POINTS

- Ignoring physical symptoms may result in the delay of medical treatment. There are many barriers to effective communication between patients and health care providers.

- Noncompliance with medical advice is a major problem. The likelihood of nonadherence is greater when instructions are difficult to understand, when recommendations are difficult to follow, and when patients are unhappy with their doctor.

- Two of our integrative themes were prominent in this chapter. First, we saw that behavior and health are influenced by multiple causes. Second, we saw that experience is highly subjective, as stress lies in the eye of the beholder.

Improving Coping and Stress Management

Answer the following "true" or "false."

_____ **1** The key to managing stress is to avoid or circumvent it.

_____ **2** It's best to suppress emotional reactions to stress.

_____ **3** Laughing at one's problems is immature.

Courses and books on stress management have multiplied at a furious pace in the last couple decades. They summarize experts' advice on how to cope with stress more effectively. How do these experts feel about the three statements above? As you'll see in this Application, most would agree that all three are false.

The key to managing stress does *not* lie in avoiding it. Stress is an inevitable element in the fabric of modern life. As Hans Selye (1973) noted, "Contrary to public opinion, we must not—and indeed can't—avoid stress" (p. 693). Thus, most stress management programs encourage people to confront stress rather than sidestep it. This requires training people to engage in action-oriented, rational, reality-based *constructive coping*.

As we noted earlier, some coping tactics are more healthful than others. In this Application, we'll examine a variety of constructive coping tactics, beginning with Albert Ellis's ideas about changing one's appraisals of stressful events.

Reappraisal: Ellis's Rational Thinking

Albert Ellis (1977, 1985, 1996) is a prominent theorist who believes that people can short-circuit their emotional reactions to stress by altering their appraisals of stressful events. Ellis's insights about stress appraisal are the foundation for a widely used system of therapy that he devised.

Rational-emotive therapy **is an approach that focuses on altering clients' patterns of irrational thinking to reduce maladaptive emotions and behavior.**

Ellis maintains that *you feel the way you think*. He argues that problematic emotional reactions are caused by negative self-talk, which he calls catastrophic thinking. *Catastrophic thinking* **involves unrealistically negative appraisals of stress that exaggerate the magnitude of one's problems.** Ellis uses a simple A-B-C sequence to explain his ideas (see Figure 13.18):

A: Activating event. The A in Ellis's system stands for the activating event that pro-duces the stress. The activating event may be any potentially stressful transaction. Examples might include an automobile accident, the cancellation of a date, a delay while waiting in line at the bank, or a failure to get a promotion you were expecting.

B: Belief system. B stands for your belief about the event, or your appraisal of the stress. According to Ellis, people often view minor setbacks as disasters. Thus, they engage in catastrophic thinking: "How awful this is. I can't stand it! Things never turn out fair for me. I'll never get promoted."

C: Consequence. C stands for the consequences of your negative thinking. When your appraisals of stressful events are overly

---

Figure 13.18

Albert Ellis's A-B-C model of emotional reactions. Although most people attribute their negative emotional reactions directly to negative events that they experience, Ellis argues that events themselves do *not* cause emotional distress, rather distress is caused by the way people *think* about negative events. According to Ellis, the key to managing stress is to change one's appraisal of stressful events.

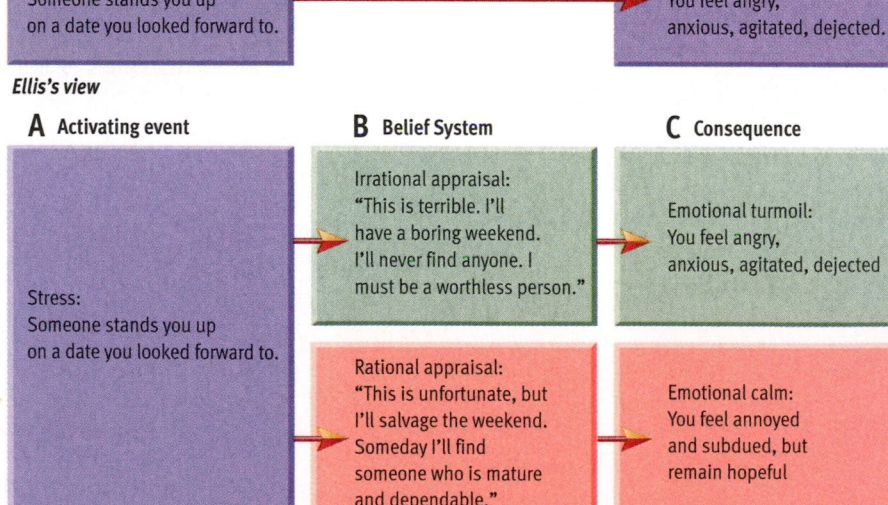

---

negative, the consequence tends to be emotional distress. Thus, people feel angry, anxious, panic stricken, or dejected.

Ellis asserts that most people don't understand the importance of phase B in this three-stage sequence. They unwittingly believe that the activating event (A) causes the consequent emotional turmoil (C). However, Ellis maintains that A does *not* cause C. It only appears to do so. Instead, Ellis asserts, B causes C. One's emotional distress is actually caused by one's catastrophic thinking.

According to Ellis, it's commonplace for people to turn inconvenience into disaster and to make mountains out of molehills. Ellis theorizes that unrealistic appraisals of stress are derived from irrational assumptions that people hold. He maintains that if you scrutinize your catastrophic thinking, you'll find that your reasoning is based on a logically indefensible premise, such as "I must have approval from everyone" or "I must perform well in all endeavors." These faulty assumptions, which people often hold unconsciously, generate catastrophic thinking and emotional turmoil.

How can you reduce your unrealistic appraisals of stress? Ellis asserts that you must learn (1) how to detect catastrophic thinking and (2) how to dispute the irrational assumptions that cause it. Detection involves acquiring the ability to spot unrealistic pessimism and wild exaggeration in your thinking. Disputing your irrational assumptions requires subjecting your reasoning process to scrutiny. Try to root out the assumptions from which you derive your conclusions. Once the underlying premises are unearthed, their irrationality may be obvious.

Using Humor as a Stress Reducer

A number of years ago, the Chicago area experienced its worst flooding in about a century. Thousands of people saw their homes wrecked when two rivers spilled over their banks. As the waters receded, the flood victims returning to their homes were subjected to the inevitable TV interviews. A remarkable number of victims, surrounded by the ruins of their homes, *joked* about their misfortune. When the going gets tough, it may pay to laugh about it. In a study of coping styles, McCrae (1984) found that 40% of his subjects used humor to deal with stress.

Empirical evidence showing that humor moderates the impact of stress has been accumulating over the last 25 years (Abel, 1998; Lefcourt, 2001). Lefcourt and colleagues (1995) argue that high-humor people may benefit from not taking themselves as seriously as low-humor people. As they put it, "If persons do not regard themselves too seriously and do not have an inflated sense of self-importance, then defeats, embarrassments, and even tragedies should have less pervasive emotional consequences for them" (p. 375).

Releasing Pent-Up Emotions

As we discussed in the main body of the chapter, stress often leads to emotional arousal. When this happens, there's merit in the commonsense notion that you should try to release the emotions welling up inside. Why? Because the physiological arousal that accompanies emotions can become problematic. For example, research suggests that people who inhibit the expression of anger and other emotions are somewhat more likely than other people to have elevated blood pressure (Jorgensen et al., 1996). Moreover, research suggests that efforts to actively suppress emotions result in increased autonomic arousal (Gross, 1998, 2001) and decreased immune function (Petrie, Booth, & Pennebaker, 1998).

Although there's no guarantee of it, you can sometimes reduce your physiological arousal by *expressing* your emotions. Evidence is accumulating that writing or talking about life's difficulties can be valuable in dealing with stress (Clark, 1993; Smyth & Pennebaker, 1999). For example, in one study of college students, half the subjects were asked to write three essays about their difficulties in adjusting to college. The other half wrote three essays about superficial topics. The subjects who wrote about their personal problems enjoyed better health in the following months than the other subjects did (Pennebaker, Colder, & Sharp, 1990). Subsequent, similar studies have replicated this finding (Francis & Pennebaker, 1992; Greenberg, Wortman, & Stone, 1996) and shown that emotional disclosure is associated with better immune functioning (Smyth & Pennebaker, 2001). So, if you can find a good listener, you may be able to discharge problematic emotions by letting your secret fears, misgivings, and suspicions spill out in a candid conversation.

Managing Hostility and Forgiving Others

Scientists have compiled quite a bit of evidence that hostility is related to increased risk for heart attacks and other types of illness (Williams, 2001). In light of this reality, many experts assert that people should strive to learn how to manage their feelings of hostility more effectively (Williams & Williams, 2001). The goal of hostility management is not merely to suppress the overt expression of hostility that may continue to seethe beneath the surface, but to actually reduce the frequency and intensity of one's hostile feelings.

We tend to experience hostility and other negative emotions when we feel "wronged"—that is when we believe that the actions of another person were harmful, immoral, or unjust. When we feel wronged, our natural inclination is either to seek revenge or to avoid further contact with the offender (McCullough, 2001). *Forgiving* someone involves counteracting these natural tendencies and releasing the person from further liability for his or her transgression. Research suggests that forgiving is associated with better adjustment and well-being (Thoresen, Harris, & Luskin, 1999). For example, in one study of divorced or permanently separated women reported by McCollough (2001), the extent to which the women had forgiven their former husbands was positively related to several measures of well-being and inversely related to measures of anxiety and depression. Research also shows that vengefulness is correlated with more rumination and negative emotion and with lower life satisfaction (McCullough et al., 2001). Taken together, these findings suggest that it may be healthful for people to learn to forgive others more readily.

Learning to Relax

Relaxation is a valuable stress management technique that can soothe emotional turmoil and reduce problematic physiological arousal (Lehrer & Woolfolk, 1984, 1993; Smyth et al., 2001). The value of relaxation became apparent to Herbert Benson (1975; Benson & Klipper, 1988) as a result of his research on meditation. Benson, a Harvard Medical School cardiologist, believes that relaxation is the key to the beneficial effects of meditation. According to Benson, the elaborate religious rituals and beliefs associated with meditation are irrelevant to its effects. After "demystifying" meditation, Benson set out to devise a simple, nonreligious procedure that could provide similar benefits. He calls his procedure the *relaxation response*. Although there are several other worthwhile approaches to relaxation training, we'll examine Benson's procedure, as its simplicity makes it especially useful. From his study of a variety of relaxation techniques, Benson concluded that four factors promote effective relaxation:

1. *A quiet environment.* It's easiest to induce the relaxation response in a distraction-free environment. After you become experienced with the relaxation response, you may be able to practice it in a crowded subway. Initially, however, you should practice it in a quiet, calm place.

2. *A mental device.* To shift attention inward and keep it there, you need to focus your attention on a constant stimulus, such as a sound or word recited repetitively.

3. *A passive attitude.* It's important not to get upset when your attention strays to distracting thoughts. You must realize that such distractions are inevitable. Whenever your mind wanders from your attentional focus, calmly redirect attention to your mental device.

4. *A comfortable position.* Reasonable body comfort is essential to avoid a major source of potential distraction. Simply sitting up straight generally works well. Lying down is too conducive to sleep.

Benson's simple relaxation procedure is described in Figure 13.19. For full benefit, it should be practiced daily.

Minimizing Physiological Vulnerability

Your body is intimately involved in your response to stress, and the wear and tear of stress can be injurious to your health. To combat this potential problem, it helps to keep your body in relatively sound shape. It's a good idea to consume a nutritionally balanced diet, get adequate sleep, and engage in at least a moderate amount of exercise. It's also a good idea to learn how to control overeating and the use of tobacco, alcohol, and other drugs. Doing these things will not make you immune to the ravages of stress. However, failure to do them may increase your vulnerability to stress-related diseases. We've discussed sleep patterns, drug use, and eating habits in other chapters, so the coverage here will focus exclusively on exercise.

The potential benefits of regular exercise are substantial. Fortunately, evidence indicates that you don't have to be a dedicated athlete to benefit from exercise (Blair

Figure 13.19

Benson's relaxation procedure. Herbert Benson's relaxation procedure is described here. According to Benson, his simple relaxation response can yield benefits similar to meditation. To experience these benefits, you should practice the procedure daily.

Source: Benson, H., & Klipper, M. Z. (1975, 1988). *The relaxation response.* New York: Morrow. Copyright © 1975 by William Morrow & Co. Reprinted by permission of HarperCollins Publishers.

1 Sit quietly in a comfortable position.

2 Close your eyes.

3 Deeply relax all your muscles, beginning at your feet and progressing up to your face. Keep them relaxed.

4 Breathe through your nose. Become aware of your breathing. As you breathe out, say the word "one" silently to yourself. For example, breath in . . . out, "one"; in . . . out, "one"; and so forth. Breathe easily and naturally.

5 Continue for 10 to 20 minutes. You may open your eyes to check the time, but do not use an alarm. When you finish, sit quietly for several minutes, at first with your eyes closed and later with your eyes opened. Do not stand up for a few minutes.

6 Do not worry about whether you are successful in achieving a deep level of relaxation. Maintain a passive attitude and permit relaxation to occur at its own pace. When distracting thoughts occur, try to ignore them by not dwelling on them, and return to repeating "one." With practice, the response should come with little effort. Practice the technique once or twice daily but not within two hours after any meal, since digestive processes seem to interfere with the elicitation of the relaxation response.

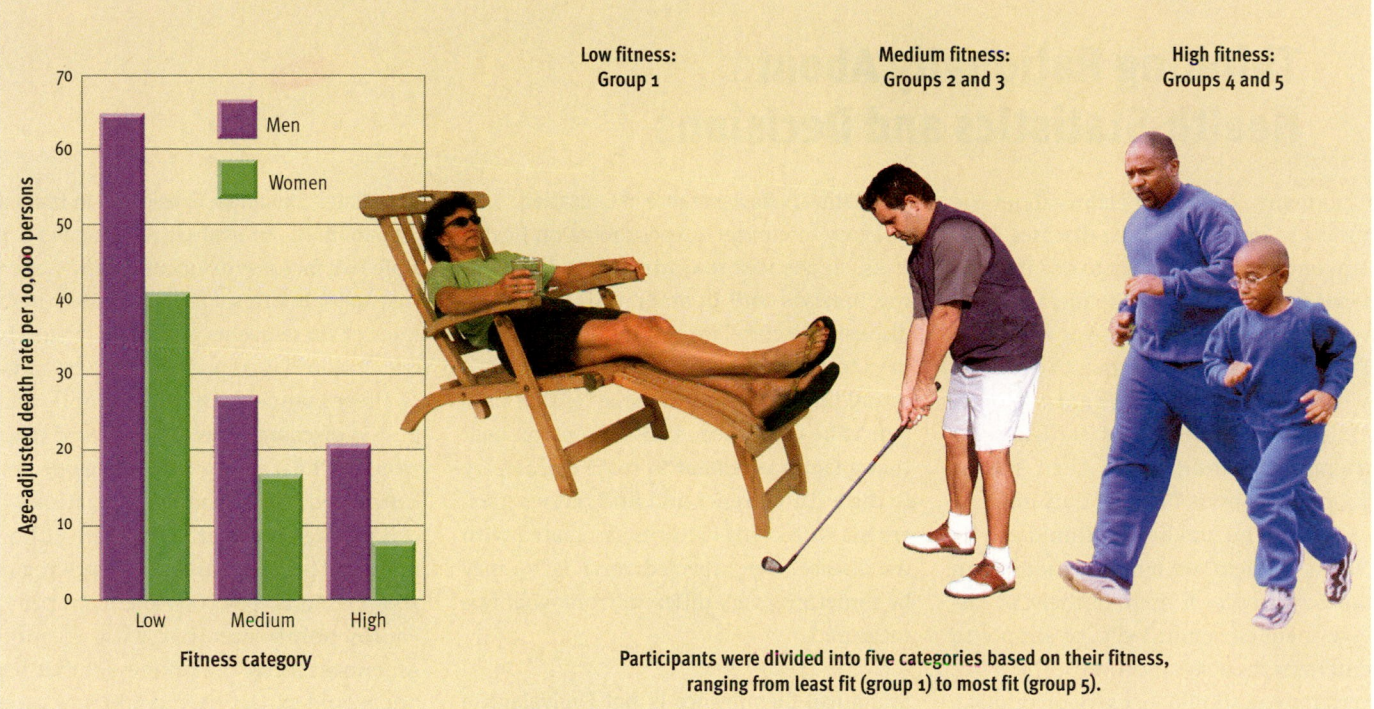

Low fitness:
Group 1

Medium fitness:
Groups 2 and 3

High fitness:
Groups 4 and 5

Participants were divided into five categories based on their fitness,
ranging from least fit (group 1) to most fit (group 5).

Figure 13.20

Physical fitness and mortality. Blair and colleagues (1989) studied death rates among men and women who exhibited low, medium, or high fitness. As you can see, fitness was associated with lower mortality rates in both sexes.

SOURCE: Adapted from Blair, S. N., Kohl, W. H., Paffenbarger, R. S., Clark, D. G., Cooper, K. H., & Gibbons, L. W. (1989). Physical fitness and all-cause mortality. *Journal of the American Medical Association, 262*, 2395–2401. Copyright © 1989 American Medical Association. Reprinted by permission. (Photos: left, © C. H. Wooley; middle, © Paul Francis Photo; right, © Michael Newman/PhotoEdit)

et al., 1989). Even a moderate amount of exercise—such as taking a brisk, half-hour walk each day—can reduce your risk of disease (see Figure 13.20). Successful participation in an exercise program can also lead to improvements in your mood and ability to deal with stress (Hays, 1999; Plante, 1999). For example, King, Taylor, and Haskell (1993) found that an exercise regimen led to a decline in depression and anxiety in a study of older adults who also benefited from reductions in perceived stress.

Embarking on an exercise program is difficult for many people. Exercise is time-consuming, and if you're out of shape, your initial attempts may be discouraging. To avoid these problems, it's wise to do the following (Greenberg, 1993):

1. Select an activity that you find enjoyable.
2. Increase your participation gradually.
3. Exercise regularly without overdoing it.
4. Reinforce yourself for your efforts.

If you choose a competitive sport (such as tennis), try to avoid falling into the competition trap. If you become obsessed with winning, you'll put yourself under pressure and *add* to the stress in your life.

REVIEW OF KEY POINTS

- Action-oriented, realistic, constructive coping can be helpful in managing the stress of daily life. Ellis emphasizes the importance of reappraising stressful events to detect and dispute catastrophic thinking. According to Ellis, emotional distress is often due to irrational assumptions that underlie one's thinking.

- Humor may be useful in efforts to redefine stressful situations. In some cases, it may pay to release pent-up emotions. Talking it out may help drain off negative emotions and foster better health. Stress can also be reduced by learning to manage one's hostile feelings more effectively and by learning to be more forgiving toward others.

- Relaxation techniques, such as Benson's relaxation response, can reduce the wear and tear of stress. Physical vulnerability may also be reduced by following a regular exercise regimen.

CRITICAL THINKING APPLICATION

Thinking Rationally About Health Statistics and Decisions

With so many conflicting claims about the best ways to prevent or treat diseases, how can anyone ever decide what to do? It seems that every day a report in the media claims that yesterday's health news was wrong.

The inconsistency of health news is only part of the problem. We are also overwhelmed by health-related statistics. As mathematics pundit John Allen Paulos (1995, p. 133) puts it, "Health statistics may be bad for our mental health. Inundated by too many of them, we tend to ignore them completely, to accept them blithely, to disbelieve them closemindedly, or simply to misinterpret their significance."

Perhaps you should just give up or make health decisions based on your own intuitions or the flip of a coin. Is that the right answer? Of course not. Personal decisions about health-related issues can be extremely important, even a matter of life and death. It may not be easy, but it is particularly important to try to think rationally and systematically about health issues. In this Application, we will discuss a few insights that can help you to think critically about statistics on health risks, then we'll briefly outline a systematic approach to thinking through health decisions.

Evaluating Statistics on Health Risks

News reports seem to suggest that there are links between virtually everything people do, touch, and consume and some type of physical illness. For example, media have reported that coffee consumption is related to hypertension, that sleep loss is related to mortality, and that a high-fat diet is related to heart disease. It's enough to send even the most subdued person into a panic. Fortunately, your evaluation of data on health risks can become more sophisticated by considering the following.

Correlation Is No Assurance of Causation. It is not easy to conduct experiments on health risks, so the vast majority of studies linking lifestyle and demographic factors to diseases are correlational studies. Hence, it pays to remember that there may not be a causal link between two variables that happen to be correlated. Thus, when you hear that a factor is related to some disease, try to dig a little deeper and find out why scientists think this factor is associated with the disease. The suspected causal factor may be something very different from what was measured.

Statistical Significance Is Not Equivalent to Practical Significance. Reports on health statistics often emphasize that the investigators uncovered "statistically significant" findings. As explained in Chapter 2, statistically significant findings are findings that are not likely to be due to chance fluctuations. Statistical significance is a useful concept, but it can sometimes be misleading (Matthey, 1998). Medical studies are often based on rather large samples, because they tend to yield more reliable conclusions than small samples. However, when a large sample is used, weak relationships and small differences between groups can turn out to be statistically significant, and these small differences may not have much practical importance. For example, in one study of sodium (salt) intake and cardiovascular disease, which used a sample of over 14,000 participants, He et al. (1999) found a statistically significant association between high sodium intake and the prevalence of hypertension among normal-weight subjects. However, this statistically significant difference was not particularly large. The prevalence of hypertension among subjects with the lowest sodium intake was 19.1% compared to 21.8% for subjects with the highest sodium intake—not exactly a difference worthy of panic.

Base Rates Should Be Considered in Evaluating Probabilities. In evaluating whether a possible risk factor is associated with some disease, people often fail to consider the base rates of these events and draw far-reaching conclusions based on what may be a matter of sheer coincidence. For example, Paulos (1995) discusses how a handful of cases in which cellular phone users developed brain cancer led to unfounded allegations that cell phones cause brain cancer. Although brain cancer is a rare disease, striking only about 6 out of 100,000 Americans per year, Paulos points out that with 10 million Americans using cell phones (at that time), one would expect to find 600 new cases of brain cancer annually among cell phone users. Given the paucity of reported cases, he playfully concludes that cellular phones must prevent brain cancer.

It is also useful to consider base rates in evaluating percentage increases in diseases. If the base rate of a disease is relatively low, a small increase can sound quite large if it is reported as a percentage. For example, in the He et al. (1999) study, the prevalence of diabetes among subjects with the lowest sodium intake was 2.1% compared to 3.8% for subjects with the highest sodium intake. Based on this small but statistically significant difference, one could say (the investigators did not) that high sodium intake was associated with a 81% increase (3.8 – 2.1/2.1) in the prevalence of diabetes, an assertion that would exaggerate the role of sodium intake in the development of diabetes.

Thinking Systematically About Health Decisions

Health decisions are oriented toward the future, which means that there are always uncertainties. And they usually involve weighing potential risks and benefits. None of these variables is unique to health decisions—uncertainty, risks, and benefits play prominent roles in economic and political decisions as well as in personal decisions. Let's apply some basic principles of quantitative reasoning to a treatment decision involving whether to prescribe Ritalin for a boy who has been diagnosed with attention deficit disorder (ADD). Keep in mind that the general principles applied in this example can be used for a wide variety of decisions.

Seek Information to Reduce Uncertainty. Gather information and check it carefully for accuracy, completeness, and the presence or absence of conflicting information. For example, is the diagnosis of ADD correct? *Look for conflicting information* that does not fit with this diagnosis. For example, if the child can sit and read for a long period of time, maybe the problem is an undetected hearing loss that makes him appear to be hyperactive in some situations, or perhaps he is just a very active child who prefers physical activity to the sedentary. This is an important first step that is often omitted.

As you consider the additional information, begin *quantifying the degree of uncertainty* or its "flip side," your degree of confidence that the diagnosis is correct. A specific value is usually not possible, but a general approximation along a dimension ranging from "highly confident" to "not at all confident" is useful in helping you think about the next step. If you decide that you are not confident about the diagnosis, you may be trying to solve the wrong problem.

Make Risk-Benefit Assessments. What are the risks and benefits of Ritalin? How likely is this child to benefit from Ritalin, and just how much improvement can be expected? If the child is 8 years old and unable to read and is miserable in school and at home, any treatment that could reduce his problems deserves serious consideration. As in the first step, the quantification is at an approximate level. A child who is two years behind at school and has no friends is, in a roughly quantifiable sense, worse off than one who is only 6 months behind in school and has at least one or two friends. How likely and how severe are the risks associated with Ritalin? If there is evidence that children do not grow as well when

they are on Ritalin, for example, can they be taken off Ritalin over the summer months so that they can catch up?

List Alternative Courses of Action. What are the alternatives to Ritalin? How well do they work? What are the risks associated with the alternatives, including the risk of falling further behind in school? *Consider the pros and cons of each alternative.* A special diet that sometimes works might be a good first step along with the decision to start drug therapy if the child does not show improvement over some time period. What are the relative success rates for different types of treatment for children like the one being considered? To answer these questions, you will need to use probability estimates in your decision making.

As you can see from this example, many parts of the problem are quantified (confidence in the diagnosis, likelihood of improvement, probability of negative outcomes, and so forth). Precise probability values were not used because often the actual numbers are not known. Some of the values that are quantified reflect value judgments, others reflect likelihoods, and others assess the degree of uncertainty. The decision will have a different outcome de-

pending on the particular child in question, the expected degree of success for alternative modes of treatment, and the associated risks for each. It is important to avoid the (understandable) tendency to give up and do nothing or to just do what the experts say to do, because every course of action has associated risks. It is also important to remember that doing nothing is also a decision, and it may not be the best one.

The decision-making process is not complete even after a decision is made. New decisions are needed as the future unfolds. When new information and new alternatives become available, the decision needs to be reviewed. Decision makers need to adopt deliberate strategies that require them to look for and seriously consider information that conflicts with any decision that was previously made, to avoid the tendency to notice and act only on information that confirms what you already believe to be true.

If you are thinking that the quantification of many unknowns in decision making is a lot of work, you are right. But, it is work worth doing. Whenever there are important decisions to be made about health, the ability to think with numbers will help you reach a better decision. And yes, that assertion is a virtual certainty.

Table 13.4 Critical Thinking Skills Discussed in This Application

Skill	Description
Understanding the limitations of correlational evidence	The critical thinker understands that a correlation between two variables does not demonstrate that there is a causal link between the variables.
Understanding the limitations of statistical significance	The critical thinker understands that weak relationships can be statistically significant when large samples are used in research.
Utilizing base rates in making predictions and evaluating probabilities	The critical thinker appreciates that the initial proportion of some group or event needs to be considered in weighing probabilities.
Seeking information to reduce uncertainty	The critical thinker understands that gathering more information can often decrease uncertainty, and reduced uncertainty can facilitate better decisions.
Making risk-benefit assessments	The critical thinker is aware that most decisions have risks and benefits that need to be weighed carefully.
Generating and evaluating alternative courses of action	In problem solving and decision making, the critical thinker knows the value of generating as many alternatives as possible and assessing their advantages and disadvantages.

RECAP

Key Ideas

The Nature of Stress

● Stress is a common, everyday event, and even seemingly minor stressors or hassles can be problematic. To a large degree, stress lies in the eye of the beholder, as appraisals of stress are highly subjective.

● Major types of stress include frustration, conflict, change, and pressure. Frustration occurs when an obstacle prevents one from attaining some goal. There are three principal types of conflict: approach-approach, avoidance-avoidance, and approach-avoidance.

● A large number of studies with the SRRS suggest that change is stressful. Although this may be true, it is now clear that the SRRS is a measure of general stress rather than just change-related stress. Two kinds of pressure (to perform and conform) also appear to be stressful.

Responding to Stress

● Emotional reactions to stress typically include anger, fear, and sadness, although positive emotions may also occur. Emotional arousal may interfere with coping. The optimal level of arousal on a task depends on the complexity of the task.

● Physiological arousal in response to stress was originally called the fight-or-flight response by Cannon. Selye's general adaptation syndrome describes three stages in physiological reactions to stress: alarm, resistance, and exhaustion.

● There are two major pathways along which the brain sends signals to the endocrine system in response to stress. Actions along these paths release two sets of hormones, catecholamines and corticosteroids, into the bloodstream.

● Some coping responses are less than optimal. Among these are giving up, blaming oneself, and striking out at others with acts of aggression. Indulging oneself is another coping pattern that tends to be of limited value. Defense mechanisms protect against emotional distress through self-deception. Small positive illusions about oneself may sometimes be adaptive.

The Effects of Stress on Psychological Functioning

● Common negative effects of stress in terms of psychological functioning include impaired task performance, burnout, posttraumatic stress disorders, and a variety of other psychological problems and disorders. Stress may also have positive effects, stimulating personal growth and the acquisition of new strengths.

The Effects of Stress on Physical Health

● The Type A personality has been implicated as a contributing cause of coronary heart dis-

ease, but hostility may be the toxic element of the Type A syndrome. Transient emotional reactions to stressful events and depression have also been identified as cardiovascular risk factors.

● Stress may play a role in a host of diseases because it can temporarily suppress the effectiveness of the immune system. The Featured Study provided a well-controlled demonstration of how stress may increase susceptibility to the common cold. Although there's little doubt that stress can contribute to the development of physical illness, the link between stress and illness is modest.

Factors Moderating the Impact of Stress

● Social support is a key moderator of the relationship between stress and illness and it is associated with better mental and physical health. Optimism and conscientiousness may lead to more effective coping with stress.

Health-Impairing Behavior

● People display many forms of health-impairing behavior. Smokers have much higher mortality rates than nonsmokers because they are more vulnerable to a host of diseases.

● Poor nutritional habits have been linked to heart disease, hypertension, and cancer, among other things. Lack of exercise elevates one's risk for cardiovascular diseases. Alcohol and drug use carry the immediate risk of overdose and elevate the long-term risk of many diseases.

● Aspects of behavior also influence one's risk of AIDS. Misconceptions about AIDS are common, and the people who hold these misconceptions tend to fall into polarized camps, either overestimating or underestimating their risk of infection. Health-impairing habits tend to develop gradually and often involve pleasant activities.

Reactions to Illness

● Ignoring physical symptoms may result in the delay of needed medical treatment. There are many barriers to effective communication between patients and health care providers. Noncompliance with medical advice is a major problem.

Putting It in Perspective

● Two of our integrative themes were prominent in this chapter. First, we saw that behavior and health are influenced by multiple causes. Second, we saw that experience is highly subjective, as stress lies in the eye of the beholder.

Personal Application • Improving Coping and Stress Management

● Action-oriented, realistic, constructive coping can be helpful in managing the stress of daily life. Ellis emphasizes the importance of reappraising stressful events to detect and dis-

pute catastrophic thinking. Humor may be useful in efforts to redefine stressful situations.

● In some cases, it may pay to release pent-up emotions by expressing them. Managing hostility and forgiving others' transgressions can also reduce stress. Relaxation techniques, such as Benson's relaxation response, can be helpful in stress management. Regular exercise can help to make one less vulnerable to the ravages of stress.

Critical Thinking Application • Thinking Rationally About Health Statistics and Decisions

● Evaluations of statistics on health risks can be enhanced by remembering that correlation is no assurance of causation, statistical significance is not equivalent to practical significance, and base rates need to be considered in assessing probabilities. In trying to think systematically about health decisions, one should seek information to reduce uncertainty, make risk-benefit assessments, and consider alternative courses of action.

Key Terms

Acquired immune deficiency syndrome (AIDS)
Aggression
Approach-approach conflict
Approach-avoidance conflict
Avoidance-avoidance conflict
Biopsychosocial model
Burnout
Catastrophic thinking
Catharsis
Conflict
Constructive coping
Coping
Defense mechanisms
Fight-or-flight response
Frustration
General adaptation syndrome
Health psychology
Immune response
Internet addiction
Learned helplessness
Life changes
Optimism
Posttraumatic stress disorder (PTSD)
Pressure
Psychosomatic diseases
Rational-emotive therapy
Social support
Stress
Type A personality
Type B personality

Key People

Walter Cannon
Robin DiMatteo
Albert Ellis
Meyer Friedman and Ray Rosenman
Thomas Holmes and Richard Rahe
Janice Kiecolt-Glaser
Richard Lazarus
Neal Miller
Hans Selye
Shelley Taylor

PRACTICE TEST

1. It is the weekend before a major psychology exam on Monday, and Janine is experiencing total panic even though she is thoroughly prepared and aced the previous two psychology exams. Janine's panic illustrates that:
   A. high arousal is optimal on complex tasks.
   B. the appraisal of stress is quite objective.
   C. the appraisal of stress is highly subjective.
   D. her adrenal cortex is malfunctioning.

2. The four principal sources of stress are:
   A. frustration, conflict, pressure, and anxiety.
   B. frustration, anger, pressure, and change.
   C. anger, anxiety, depression, and annoyance.
   D. frustration, conflict, pressure, and change.

3. When your boss tells you that a complicated report that you have not yet begun to write must be on her desk by this afternoon, you may experience:
   A. burnout.   C. a double bind.
   B. pressure.   D. catharsis.

4. You want very badly to ask someone for a date, but you are afraid to risk rejection. You are experiencing:
   A. an approach-avoidance conflict.
   B. an avoidance-avoidance conflict.
   C. frustration.
   D. self-imposed pressure.

5. Research suggests that a high level of arousal may be most optimal for the performance of a task when:
   A. the task is complex.
   B. the task is simple.
   C. the rewards are high.
   D. an audience is present.

6. The alarm stage of Hans Selye's general adaptation syndrome is essentially the same as:
   A. the fight-or-flight response.
   B. constructive coping.
   C. catharsis.
   D. secondary appraisal.

7. The brain structure responsible for initiating action along the two major pathways through which the brain sends signals to the endocrine system is the:
   A. hypothalamus.   C. corpus callosum.
   B. thalamus.   D. medulla.

8. You have been doing poorly in your psychology class and you are in danger of flunking. Which of the following qualifies as a defense mechanism in response to this situation?
   A. You seek the aid of a tutor.
   B. You decide to withdraw from the class and take it another time.
   C. You deny the reality that you are hopelessly behind in the class, convinced that you will somehow ace the final without seeking help.
   D. You consult with the instructor to see what you can do to pass the class.

9. Physical and emotional exhaustion, cynicism, and lowered self-efficacy attributable to chronic work-related stress is referred to as:
   A. learned helplessness.
   B. burnout.
   C. fallout.
   D. posttraumatic stress disorder.

10. Which personality trait seems to be most strongly related to increased coronary risk?
    A. Type B personality
    B. perfectionism
    C. competitiveness
    D. hostility

11. Many students often develop colds and other minor ailments during final exams. This probably happens because:
    A. stress is associated with the release of corticosteroid hormones.
    B. stress is associated with the release of catecholamine hormones.
    C. burnout causes colds.
    D. stress can suppress immune functioning.

12. Research has found that optimists are more likely than pessimists to:
    A. take their time in confronting problems.
    B. identify the negatives before they identify the positives.
    C. engage in action-oriented, problem-focused coping.
    D. blame others for their personal problems.

13. Which of the following has *not* been found to be a mode of transmission for the HIV virus?
    A. sexual contact among homosexual men
    B. the sharing of needles by intravenous drug users
    C. sexual contact among heterosexuals
    D. sharing food

14. The three phases in Albert Ellis's explanation of emotional reactions are:
    A. alarm, resistance, exhaustion.
    B. id, ego, superego.
    C. activating event, belief system, consequence.
    D. antecedent conditions, behavior, consequence.

15. In evaluating health statistics, it is useful to:
    A. remember that statistical significance is equivalent to practical significance.
    B. remember that correlation is a reliable indicator of causation.
    C. consider base rates in thinking about probabilities.
    D. all of the above.

Answers

1	C pp. 522–523	**6**	A p. 529	**11**	D pp. 541–542
2	D pp. 523–526	**7**	A pp. 529–530	**12**	C pp. 543–544
3	B p. 526	**8**	C pp. 530–533	**13**	D p. 547
4	A p. 524	**9**	B p. 535	**14**	C pp. 552–553
5	B p. 528	**10**	D p. 538–539	**15**	C pp. 556–557

 ## ON THE WEB

For additional resources on the topics covered in this chapter, visit the *Psychology: Themes and Variations* Web site, where you will find practice quizzes, tutorials, Web links, simulations, critical thinking activities, flash cards, interactive exercises, and suggested readings available through INFOTRAC.

http://psychology.wadsworth.com/weiten_themes6e/

CHAPTER 14

© Ed Freeman/Image Bank-Getty Images

Psychological Disorders

© Ed Freeman/Image Bank-Getty Images

"*The government of the United States was overthrown more than a year ago! I'm the president of the United States of America and Bob Dylan is vice president!*" So said Ed, the author of a prominent book on journalism, who was speaking to a college journalism class, as a guest lecturer. Ed also informed the class that he had killed both John and Robert Kennedy, as well as Charles de Gaulle, the former president of France. He went on to tell the class that all rock music songs were written about him, that he was the greatest karate expert in the universe, and that he had been fighting "space wars" for 2000 years. The students in the class were mystified by Ed's bizarre, disjointed "lecture," but they assumed that he was putting on a show that would eventually lead to a sensible conclusion. However, their perplexed but expectant calm was shattered when Ed pulled a hatchet from the props he had brought with him and hurled the hatchet at the class! Fortunately, he didn't hit anyone, as the hatchet sailed over the students' heads. At that point, the professor for the class realized that Ed's irrational behavior was not a pretense. The professor evacuated the class quickly while Ed continued to rant and rave about his presidential administration, space wars, vampires, his romances with female rock stars, and his personal harem of 38 "chicks." (Adapted from Pearce, 1974)

Clearly Ed's behavior was abnormal. Even *he* recognized that when he agreed later to be admitted to a mental hospital, signing himself in as the "President of the United States of America." What causes such abnormal behavior? Does Ed have a mental illness, or does he just behave strangely? What is the basis for judging behavior as normal versus abnormal? Are people who have psychological disorders dangerous? How common are such disorders? Can they be cured? These are just a few of the questions that we will address in this chapter as we discuss psychological disorders and their complex causes.

Abnormal Behavior: Myths, Realities, and Controversies

Misconceptions about abnormal behavior are common. Hence, we need to clear up some preliminary issues before we describe the various types of disorders. In this section, we will discuss (1) the medical model of abnormal behavior, (2) the criteria of abnormal behavior, (3) stereotypes regarding psychological disorders, (4) the classification of psychological disorders, and (5) how common such disorders are.

The Medical Model Applied to Abnormal Behavior

In Ed's case, there's no question that his behavior was abnormal. But does it make sense to view his unusual and irrational behavior as an illness? This is a controversial question. The *medical model* proposes that it is useful to think of abnormal behavior as a disease. This point of view is the basis for many of the terms used to refer to abnormal behavior, including mental *illness*, psychological *disorder*, and psychopathology (*pathology* refers to manifestations of disease). The medical model gradually became the dominant way of thinking about abnormal behavior during the 18th and 19th centuries, and its influence remains strong today.

The medical model clearly represented progress over earlier models of abnormal behavior. Prior to the 18th century, most conceptions of abnormal behavior were based on superstition. People who behaved strangely were thought to be possessed by demons, to be witches in league with the devil, or to be victims of God's punishment. Their disorders were "treated" with chants, rituals, exorcisms, and such. If the people's behavior was seen as threatening, they were candidates for chains, dungeons, torture, and death (see Figure 14.1 on the next page).

The rise of the medical model brought improvements in the treatment of those who exhibited abnormal behavior. As victims of an illness, they were viewed with more sympathy and less hatred and fear.

PREVIEW QUESTIONS
- What is the medical model?
- What criteria are used to judge abnormality?
- How easy is it to distinguish normality from abnormality?
- What classification system is used to diagnose psychological disorders?
- How common are mental disorders?

Figure 14.1

Historical conceptions of mental illness. In the Middle Ages people who behaved strangely were sometimes thought to be in league with the devil. The top drawing depicts some of the cruel methods used to extract confessions from suspected witches and warlocks. Some psychological disorders were also thought to be caused by demonic possession. The bottom illustration depicts an exorcism.

SOURCE: (Right) Culver Pictures, Inc. (Below) *St. Catherine of Siena Exorcising a Possessed Woman*, c. 1500–1510. Girolamo Di Benvenuto. Denver Art Museum Collection, Gift of Samuel H. Kress Foundation Collection, 1967.171 © 2001 Denver Art Museum.

❝*Minds can be 'sick' only in the sense that jokes are 'sick' or economies are 'sick.'*❞
THOMAS SZASZ

Although living conditions in early asylums were typically deplorable, gradual progress was made toward more humane care of the mentally ill. It took time, but ineffectual approaches to treatment eventually gave way to scientific investigation of the causes and cures of psychological disorders.

However, in recent decades, some critics have suggested that the medical model may have outlived its usefulness (Kiesler, 1999). A particularly vocal critic has been Thomas Szasz (1974, 1990). He asserts that "strictly speaking, disease or illness can affect only the body; hence there can be no mental illness. . . . Minds can be 'sick' only in the sense that jokes are 'sick' or economies are 'sick'" (1974, p. 267). He further argues that abnormal behavior usually involves a deviation from social norms rather than an illness. He contends that such deviations are "problems in living" rather than medical problems. According to Szasz, the medical model's disease analogy converts

moral and social questions about what is acceptable behavior into medical questions.

Although Szasz's criticism of the medical model has some merit, we'll take the position that the disease analogy continues to be useful, although one should remember that it is *only* an analogy. Medical concepts such as *diagnosis, etiology,* and *prognosis* have proven valuable in the treatment and study of abnormality. *Diagnosis* involves distinguishing one illness from another. *Etiology* refers to the apparent causation and developmental history of an illness. A *prognosis* is a forecast about the probable course of an illness. These medically based concepts have widely shared meanings that permit clinicians, researchers, and the public to communicate more effectively in their discussions of abnormal behavior.

Criteria of Abnormal Behavior

If your next-door neighbor scrubs his front porch twice every day and spends virtually all his time cleaning and recleaning his house, is he normal? If your sister-in-law goes to one physician after another seeking treatment for ailments that appear imaginary, is she psychologically healthy? How are we to judge what's normal and what's abnormal? More important, who's to do the judging?

These are complex questions. In a sense, *all* people make judgments about normality in that they all express opinions about others' (and perhaps their own) mental health. Of course, formal diagnoses of psychological disorders are made by mental health professionals. In making these diagnoses, clinicians rely on a variety of criteria, the foremost of which are the following:

1. *Deviance.* As Szasz has pointed out, people are often said to have a disorder because their behavior deviates from what their society considers acceptable. What constitutes normality varies somewhat from one culture to another, but all cultures have such norms. When people violate these standards and expectations, they may be labeled mentally ill. For example, *transvestic fetishism* is a sexual disorder in which a man achieves sexual arousal by dressing in women's clothing. This behavior is regarded as disordered because a man who wears a dress, brassiere, and nylons is deviating from our culture's norms. This example illustrates the arbitrary nature of cultural standards regarding normality, as the same overt behavior (cross-sex dressing) is acceptable for women but deviant for men.

2. *Maladaptive behavior.* In many cases, people are judged to have a psychological disorder because their

everyday adaptive behavior is impaired. This is the key criterion in the diagnosis of substance use (drug) disorders. In and of itself, alcohol and drug use is not terribly unusual or deviant. However, when the use of cocaine, for instance, begins to interfere with a person's social or occupational functioning, a substance use disorder exists. In such cases, it is the maladaptive quality of the behavior that makes it disordered.

3. *Personal distress*. Frequently, the diagnosis of a psychological disorder is based on an individual's report of great personal distress. This is usually the criterion met by people who are troubled by depression or anxiety disorders. Depressed people, for instance, may or may not exhibit deviant or maladaptive behavior. Such people are usually labeled as having a disorder when they describe their subjective pain and suffering to friends, relatives, and mental health professionals.

Although two or three criteria may apply in a particular case, people are often viewed as disordered when only one criterion is met. As you may have already noticed, diagnoses of psychological disorders involve *value judgments* about what represents normal or abnormal behavior (Widiger & Sankis, 2000). The criteria of mental illness are not nearly as value-free as the criteria of physical illness. In evaluating physical diseases, people can usually agree that a malfunctioning heart or kidney is pathological, regardless of their personal values. However, judgments about mental illness reflect prevailing cultural values, social trends, and political forces, as well as scientific knowledge (Kutchins & Kirk, 1997; Mechanic, 1999).

This man clearly exhibits a certain type of deviance, but does that mean that he has a psychological disorder? The critieria of mental illness are more subjective and complicated than most people realize, and to some extent, judgments of mental health represent value judgments.

© 2001 AP/Wide World Photos

Web Link 14.1

Mental Health Net
This is arguably the premier site on the Net to explore all aspects of mental health, including psychological disorders and treatment, professional issues, and information for consumers. It is a great starting point, with links to more than 8000 resources.

CONCEPT CHECK 14.1

Applying the Criteria of Abnormal Behavior

Check your understanding of the criteria of abnormal behavior by identifying the criteria met by each of the examples below and checking them off in the table provided. Remember, a specific behavior may meet more than one criterion. The answers are in Appendix A.

Behavioral examples

1. Alan's performance at work has suffered because he has been drinking alcohol to excess. Several co-workers have suggested that he seek help for his problem, but he thinks that they're getting alarmed over nothing. "I just enjoy a good time once in a while," he says.
2. Monica has gone away to college and feels lonely, sad, and dejected. Her grades are fine, and she gets along okay with the other students in the dormitory, but inside she's choked with gloom, hopelessness, and despair.
3. Boris believes that he's Napoleon reborn. He believes that he is destined to lead the U.S. military forces into a great battle to recover California from space aliens.
4. Natasha panics with anxiety whenever she leaves her home. Her problem escalated gradually until she was absent from work so often that she was fired. She hasn't been out of her house in nine months and is deeply troubled by her problem.

Criteria met by each example

	Maladaptive behavior	Deviance	Personal distress
1. Alan	_____	_____	_____
2. Monica	_____	_____	_____
3. Boris	_____	_____	_____
4. Natasha	_____	_____	_____

Stanford University News Service

"How many people, one wonders, are sane but not recognized as such in our psychiatric institutions?"

DAVID ROSENHAN

Antonyms such as *normal* versus *abnormal* and *mental health* versus *mental illness* imply that people can be divided neatly into two distinct groups: those who are normal and those who are not. In reality, it is often difficult to draw a line that clearly separates normality from abnormality. On occasion, everybody acts in deviant ways, everyone displays some maladaptive behavior, and everyone experiences personal distress. People are judged to have psychological disorders only when their behavior becomes *extremely* deviant, maladaptive, or distressing. Thus, normality and abnormality exist on a continuum. It's a matter of degree, not an either-or proposition (see Figure 14.2).

Stereotypes of Psychological Disorders

We've seen that mental illnesses are not diseases in a strict sense and that judgments of mental health are not value-free. However, still other myths about abnormal behavior need to be exposed as such. Let's examine three stereotypes about psychological disorders that are largely inaccurate:

1. *Psychological disorders are incurable.* Admittedly, there are mentally ill people for whom treatment is largely a failure. However, they are greatly outnumbered by people who do get better, either spontaneously or through formal treatment (Lambert & Bergin, 1992). The vast majority of people who are diagnosed as mentally ill eventually improve and lead normal, productive lives. Even the most severe psychological disorders can be treated successfully.

2. *People with psychological disorders are often violent and dangerous.* Only a modest association has been found between mental illness and violence-prone tendencies (Monahan, 1997; Tardiff, 1999). This stereotype exists because incidents of violence involving the mentally ill tend to command media attention. For example, our opening case history,

which described Ed's breakdown and the incident with the hatchet, was written up in a national news magazine. People such as John Hinckley, Jr., whose mental illness led him to attempt an assassination of President Ronald Reagan (and wounding of press secretary James Brady), receive extensive publicity. However, these individuals are not representative of the large number of people who have struggled with psychological disorders.

3. *People with psychological disorders behave in bizarre ways and are very different from normal people.* This is true only in a small minority of cases, usually involving relatively severe disorders. As noted earlier, the line between normal and abnormal behavior can be difficult to draw. At first glance, people with psychological disorders usually are indistinguishable from those without disorders. A classic study by David Rosenhan (1973) showed that even mental health professionals may have difficulty distinguishing normality from abnormality. To study diagnostic accuracy, Rosenhan arranged for a number of normal people to seek admission to mental hospitals. These "pseudopatients" arrived at the hospitals complaining of one false symptom—hearing voices. Except for this single symptom, they acted as they normally would and gave accurate information when interviewed about their personal histories. *All* the pseudopatients were admitted, and the average length of their hospitalization was 19 days!

Why is it so hard to distinguish normality from abnormality? The pseudopatients' observations about life on the psychiatric wards offer a clue. They noted that the real patients acted normal most of the time and only infrequently acted in a deviant manner. As you might imagine, Rosenhan's study evoked quite a controversy about our diagnostic system for mental illness. Let's take a look at how this diagnostic system has evolved.

Psychodiagnosis: The Classification of Disorders

Obviously, we cannot lump all psychological disorders together without giving up all hope of understanding them better. A sound taxonomy of mental disorders can facilitate empirical research and enhance communication among scientists and clinicians (Williams, 1999). Hence, a great deal of effort has been invested in devising an elaborate system for classifying psychological disorders (see Figure 14.3).

Guidelines for psychodiagnosis were extremely vague and informal prior to 1952 when the Ameri-

Figure 14.2

Normality and abnormality as a continuum. There isn't a sharp boundary between normal and abnormal behavior. Behavior is normal or abnormal in degree, depending on the extent to which one's behavior is deviant, personally distressing, or maladaptive.

Normal | Deviance | Personal distress | Maladaptive behavior | Abnormal

can Psychiatric Association unveiled its *Diagnostic and Statistical Manual of Mental Disorders* (Grob, 1991). This classification scheme described about 100 disorders. Revisions intended to improve the system were incorporated into the second edition (DSM-II) pub- lished in 1968, but the diagnostic guidelines were still pretty sketchy. However, the third edition (DSM-III), published in 1980, represented a major advance, as the diagnostic criteria were made much more explicit, concrete, and detailed to facilitate more con-

Figure 14.3

Overview of the DSM diagnostic system. Published by the American Psychiatric Association, the *Diagnostic and Statistical Manual of Mental Disorders* is the formal classification system used in the diagnosis of psychological disorders. It is a *multiaxial* system, which means that information is recorded on the five axes described here. (Based on American Psychiatric Association, 1994, 2000)

SOURCE: Adapted with permission from the *Diagnostic and Statistical Manual of Mental Disorders, 4th ed. (DSM–TR)*. Copyright © 2000 American Psychiatric Association.

Axis I
Clinical Syndromes

1. **Disorders usually first diagnosed in infancy, childhood, or adolescence**
   This category includes disorders that arise before adolescence, such as attention deficit disorders, autism, enuresis, and stuttering.

2. **Organic mental disorders**
   These disorders are temporary or permanent dysfunctions of brain tissue caused by diseases or chemicals. Examples are delirium, dementia, and amnesia.

3. **Substance-related disorders**
   This category refers to the maladaptive use of drugs and alcohol. This category requires an abnormal pattern of use, as with alcohol abuse and cocaine dependence.

4. **Schizophrenia and other psychotic disorders**
   The schizophrenias are characterized by psychotic symptoms (for example, grossly disorganized behavior, delusions, and hallucinations) and by over six months of behavioral deterioration. This category also includes delusional disorder and schizoaffective disorder.

5. **Mood disorders**
   The cardinal feature is emotional disturbance. These disorders include major depression, bipolar disorder, dysthymic disorder, and cyclothymic disorder.

6. **Anxiety disorders**
   These disorders are characterized by physiological signs of anxiety (for example, palpitations) and subjective feelings of tension, apprehension, or fear. Anxiety may be acute and focused (panic disorder) or continual and diffuse (generalized anxiety disorder).

7. **Somatoform disorders**
   These disorders are dominated by somatic symptoms that resemble physical illnesses. These symptoms cannot be fully accounted for by organic damage. This category includes somatization and conversion disorders and hypochondriasis.

8. **Dissociative disorders**
   These disorders all feature a sudden, temporary alteration or dysfunction of memory, consciousness, and identity, as in dissociative amnesia and dissociative identity disorder.

9. **Sexual and gender-identity disorders**
   There are three basic types of disorders in this category: gender identity disorders (discomfort with identity as male or female), paraphilias (preference for unusual acts to achieve sexual arousal), and sexual dysfunctions (impairments in sexual functioning).

10. **Eating Disorders**
    Eating disorders are severe disturbances in eating behavior characterized by preoccupation with weight concerns and unhealthy efforts to control weight. Examples include anorexia nervosa and bulimia nervosa.

Axis II
Personality Disorders or Mental Retardation

Personality disorders are longstanding patterns of extreme, inflexible personality traits that are deviant or maladaptive and lead to impaired functioning or subjective distress. *Mental retardation* refers to subnormal general mental ability accompanied by deficiencies in adaptive skills, originating before age 18.

Axis III
General Medical Conditions

Physical disorders or conditions are recorded on this axis. Examples include diabetes, arthritis, and hemophilia.

Axis IV
Psychosocial and Environmental Problems

Axis IV is for reporting psychosocial and environmental problems that may affect the diagnosis, treatment, and prognosis of mental disorders (Axes I and II). A psychosocial or environmental problem may be a negative life event, an environmental difficulty or deficiency, a familial or other interpersonal stress, an inadequacy of social support or personal resources, or another problem that describes the context in which a person's difficulties have developed.

Axis V
Global Assessment of Functioning (GAF) Scale

Code	Symptoms
100	Superior functioning in a wide range of activities
90	Absent or minimal symptoms, good functioning in all areas
80	Symptoms transient and expectable reactions to psychosocial stressors
70	Some mild symptoms or some difficulty in social, occupational, or school functioning, but generally functioning pretty well
60	Moderate symptoms or difficulty in social, occupational, or school functioning
50	Serious symptoms or impairment in social, occupational, or school functioning
40	Some impairment in reality testing or communication or major impairment in family relations, judgment, thinking, or mood
30	Behavior considerably influenced by delusions or hallucinations, serious impairment in communication or judgment, or inability to function in almost all areas
20	Some danger of hurting self or others, occasional failure to maintain minimal personal hygiene, or gross impairment in communication
10	Persistent danger of severely hurting self or others
1	

Web Link 14.2

National Alliance for the Mentally Ill (NAMI)
NAMI describes itself as "a grassroots, self-help support and advocacy organization of families and friends of people with serious mental illness, and those persons themselves." Its online site responds to their needs with extensive and current information about schizophrenia, bipolar disorder, and other severe disorders.

sistent diagnoses across clinicians (Blacker & Tsuang, 1999). The current, fourth edition (DSM-IV), which was released in 1994, made use of intervening research to refine the criteria introduced in DSM-III. Each revision of the DSM system has expanded the list of disorders covered. The current version describes about three times as many types of psychological disorders as DSM-I (Houts, 2002).

The publication of DSM-III in 1980 introduced a new multiaxial system of classification, which asks for judgments about individuals on five separate dimensions, or "axes." Figure 14.3 provides an overview of the five axes. The diagnoses of disorders are made on Axes I and II. Clinicians record most types of disorders on Axis I. They use Axis II to list long-running personality disorders or mental retardation. People may receive diagnoses on both Axes I and II.

The remaining axes are used to record supplemental information. A patient's physical disorders are listed on Axis III (General Medical Conditions). On Axis IV (Psychosocial and Environmental Problems), the clinician makes notations regarding the types of stress experienced by the individual in the past year. On Axis V (Global Assessment of Functioning), estimates are made of the individual's current level of adaptive functioning (in social and occupational behavior, viewed as a whole) and of the individual's highest level of functioning in the past year. Figure 14.4 shows an example of a multiaxial evaluation. Most theorists agree that the multiaxial system is a step in the right direction because it recognizes the importance of information besides a traditional diagnostic label.

A great deal of progress had been made in the last two decades in the effort to make psychodiagnosis more reliable, more valid, and more scientific (Blashfield & Livesley, 1999). That said, a host of conceptual headaches and controversial issues remain (Adams, Luscher, & Bernat, 2001; Garfield, 2001). The quest for a scientific system of psychodiagnosis is an ongoing challenge, and there is a great deal of room for further progress (Widiger & Clark, 2000).

Web Link 14.3

Mental Health: A Report of the Surgeon General
In late 1999, the Surgeon General issued the first comprehensive survey of the state of mental health in the United States. This report will provide a crucial foundation of statistics and other information for understanding the needs for mental health care in the first decade of the 21st century.

The Prevalence of Psychological Disorders

How common are psychological disorders? What percentage of the population is afflicted with mental illness? Is it 10%? Perhaps 25%? Could the figure range as high as 40% or 50%?

Such estimates fall in the domain of ***epidemiology*—the study of the distribution of mental or physical disorders in a population**. The 1980s and 1990s brought major advances in psychiatric epidemiology, as a host of large-scale investigations provided a huge, new database on the distribution of mental disorders (Murphy, Tohen, & Tsuang, 1999). In epidemiology, ***prevalence* refers to the percentage of a population that exhibits a disorder during a specified time period.** In the case of mental disorders, the most interesting data are the estimates of *lifetime prevalence,* the percentage of people who endure a specific disorder at any time in their lives.

Estimates of lifetime prevalence suggest that psychological disorders are more common than most people realize. Prior to the advent of DSM-III, studies suggested that about *one-fifth* of the population exhibited clear signs of mental illness at some point in their lives (Neugebauer, Dohrenwend, & Dohrenwend, 1980). However, the older studies did not assess alcohol and drug-related disorders very effectively, because these disorders were vaguely described in DSM-I and DSM-II. Studies published in the 1980s and early 1990s, using the explicit criteria for substance use disorders in DSM-III, found psychological disorders in roughly *one-third* of the population (Regier & Kaelber, 1995; Robins, Locke, & Regier, 1991). Subsequent research, which has focused on a somewhat younger sample (ages 18–54 instead of over age 18), suggests that about 44% of the adult population will struggle with some sort of psychological disorder at some point in their lives (Kessler & Zhao, 1999; Regier & Burke, 2000). Obviously, all these figures are *estimates* that depend to some extent on the sampling and assessment techniques used (Wakefield, 1999). Some of the increase in the prevalence of mental illness is more apparent than real, as it is partly attributable to more effective tabulation of certain disorders. However, research also suggests that there has been a genuine increase in the prevalence of mental

Figure 14.4

Example of a multiaxial evaluation. A multiaxial evaluation for a depressed man with a cocaine problem might look like this.

A DSM multiaxial evaluation (patient 49-year-old male)	
Axis I	Major depressive disorder Cocaine abuse
Axis II	Borderline personality disorder (provisional, rule out dependent personality disorder)
Axis III	Hypertension
Axis IV	Psychosocial stressors: recent divorce, permitted to see his children only infrequently, job is in jeopardy
Axis V	Current global assessment of functioning (GAF): 46

disorders among more recent age cohorts (Smith & Weissman, 1992). In any event, as Figure 14.5 shows, the most common classes of disorders are (1) substance (alcohol and drugs) use disorders, (2) anxiety disorders, and (3) mood disorders.

We are now ready to start examining the specific types of psychological disorders. Obviously, we cannot cover all of the disorders listed in DSM-IV. However, we will introduce most of the major categories of disorders to give you an overview of the many forms abnormal behavior takes (see Chapter 5 for a discussion of substance abuse). In discussing each set of disorders, we will begin with brief descriptions of the specific syndromes or subtypes that fall in the category. Then we'll focus on the *etiology* of the disorders in that category. Although many paths can lead to specific disorders, some are more common than others. We'll highlight some of the common paths to enhance your understanding of the roots of abnormal behavior.

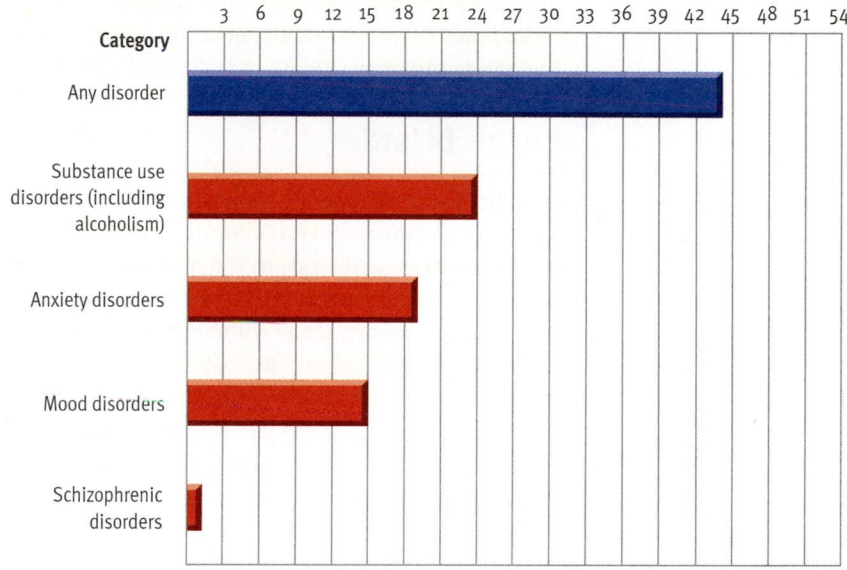

Figure 14.5

Lifetime prevalence of psychological disorders. The estimated percentage of people who have, at any time in their life, suffered from one of four types of psychological disorders or from a disorder of any kind (top bar) is shown here. Prevalence estimates vary somewhat from one study to the next, depending on the exact methods used in sampling and assessment. The estimates shown here are based on pooling data from Wave 1 and 2 of the Epidemiological Catchment Area studies and the National Comorbidity Study, as summarized by Regier and Burke (2000) and Dew, Bromet, and Switzer (2000). These studies, which collectively evaluated over 28,000 subjects, provide the best data to date on the prevalence of mental illness in the United States.

REVIEW OF KEY POINTS

- The medical model assumes that it is useful to view abnormal behavior as a disease. This view has been criticized on the grounds that it turns questions about deviance into medical questions. Nonetheless, the medical model has proven useful, although one should remember that it is only an analogy.

- Three criteria are used in deciding whether people suffer from psychological disorders: deviance, personal distress, and maladaptive behavior. Often it is difficult to clearly draw a line between normality and abnormality. Contrary to popular stereotypes, people with psychological disorders are not particularly bizarre or dangerous, and even the most severe disorders are treatable.

- Research by David Rosenhan showed that pseudopatients were routinely admitted to mental hospitals, which were unable to detect the patients' normalcy. His study showed

that the distinction between normality and abnormality is not clear-cut.

- DSM-IV is the official psychodiagnostic classification system in the United States. This system asks for information about patients on five axes, or dimensions. It is difficult to obtain good data on the prevalence of psychological disorders. Nonetheless, it is clear that they are more common than widely believed.

Anxiety Disorders

Everyone experiences anxiety from time to time. It is a natural and common reaction to many of life's difficulties. For some people, however, anxiety becomes a chronic problem. These people experience high levels of anxiety with disturbing regularity. *Anxiety disorders are a class of disorders marked by feelings of excessive apprehension and anxiety.* There are four principal types of anxiety disorders: generalized anxiety disorder, phobic disorder, obsessive-compulsive disorder, and panic disorder. These disorders are not mutually exclusive, as many people who develop one anxiety syndrome often suffer from another at some point in their lives (Hunt & Andrews, 1995).

Generalized Anxiety Disorder

The generalized anxiety disorder is marked by a chronic, high level of anxiety that is not tied to any specific threat. This anxiety is sometimes called "free-floating anxiety" because it is nonspecific. People with this disorder worry constantly about yesterday's mistakes and tomorrow's problems. In particular, they worry about minor matters related to family, finances, work, and personal illness (Sanderson & Barlow, 1990). They often dread decisions and brood over them endlessly. Their anxiety is commonly accompanied by physical symptoms, such as trembling,

PREVIEW QUESTIONS

- What are the four major anxiety disorders and what are their chief symptoms?

- Which biological factors have been implicated in anxiety disorders?

- How do conditioning and learning contribute to anxiety disorders?

- How do cognition and stress contribute to anxiety disorders?

muscle tension, diarrhea, dizziness, faintness, sweating, and heart palpitations. Generalized anxiety disorder tends to have a gradual onset and is seen more frequently in females than males (Brown, 1999).

Phobic Disorder

In a phobic disorder, an individual's troublesome anxiety has a specific focus. **A *phobic disorder* is marked by a persistent and irrational fear of an object or situation that presents no realistic danger.** Although mild phobias are extremely common, people are said to have a phobic disorder only when their fears seriously interfere with their everyday behavior. Phobic reactions tend to be accompanied by physical symptoms of anxiety, such as trembling and palpitations (Rapee & Barlow, 2001). The following case provides an example of a phobic disorder:

Hilda is 32 years of age and has a rather unusual fear. She is terrified of snow. She cannot go outside in the snow. She cannot even stand to see snow or hear about it on the weather report. Her phobia severely constricts her day-to-day behavior. Probing in therapy revealed that her phobia was caused by a traumatic experience at age 11. Playing at a ski lodge, she was buried briefly by a small avalanche of snow. She had no recollection of this experience until it was recovered in therapy. (Adapted from Laughlin, 1967, p. 227)

As Hilda's unusual snow phobia illustrates, people can develop phobic responses to virtually anything. Nonetheless, certain types of phobias are more common than others. Particularly common are acrophobia (fear of heights), claustrophobia (fear of small, enclosed places), brontophobia (fear of storms), hydrophobia (fear of water), and various animal and insect phobias (Eaton, Dryman, & Weissman, 1991). People troubled by phobias typically realize that their fears are irrational, but they still are unable to calm themselves when confronted by a phobic object. Among many of them, even *imagining* a phobic object or situation can trigger great anxiety (Thorpe & Salkovskis, 1995).

Panic Disorder and Agoraphobia

A *panic disorder* is characterized by recurrent attacks of overwhelming anxiety that usually occur suddenly and unexpectedly. These paralyzing panic attacks are accompanied by physical symptoms of anxiety. After a number of panic attacks, victims often become apprehensive, wondering when their next panic will occur. Their concern about exhibiting panic in public may escalate to the point where they are afraid to leave home. This creates a condition called *agoraphobia*, which is a common complication of panic disorders.

Agoraphobia **is a fear of going out to public places** (its literal meaning is "fear of the marketplace or open places"). Because of this fear, some people become prisoners confined to their homes, although many will venture out if accompanied by a trusted companion (Hollander, Simeon, & Gorman, 1999). As its name suggests, agoraphobia has traditionally been viewed as a phobic disorder. However, more recent evidence suggests that agoraphobia is mainly a complication of panic disorder. About two-thirds of people who suffer from panic disorder are female (Horwath & Weissman, 2000). The onset of panic disorder typically occurs during late adolescence or early adulthood (Pine, 2000).

Obsessive-Compulsive Disorder

Obsessions are *thoughts* that repeatedly intrude on one's consciousness in a distressing way. Compulsions are *actions* that one feels forced to carry out. Thus, **an *obsessive-compulsive disorder* (OCD) is marked by persistent, uncontrollable intrusions of unwanted thoughts (obsessions) and urges to engage in senseless rituals (compulsions).** To illustrate, let's examine the bizarre behavior of a man once reputed to be the wealthiest person in the world:

The famous industrialist Howard Hughes was obsessed with the possibility of being contaminated by germs. This led him to devise extraordinary rituals to minimize the possibility of such contamination. He would spend hours methodically cleaning a single telephone. He once wrote a three-page memo instructing assistants on exactly how to open cans of fruit for him. The following is just a small portion of the instructions that Hughes provided for a driver who delivered films to his bungalow. "Get out of the car on the traffic side. Do not at any time be on the side of the car between the car and the curb. . . . Carry only one can of film at a time. Step over the gutter opposite the place where the sidewalk deadends into the curb from a point as far out into the center of the road as possible. Do not ever walk on the grass at all, also do not step into the gutter at all. Walk to the bungalow keeping as near to the center of the sidewalk as possible." (Adapted from Barlett & Steele, 1979, pp. 227–237)

Obsessions often center on inflicting harm on others, personal failures, suicide, or sexual acts. People troubled by obsessions may feel that they have lost control of their mind. Compulsions usually involve stereotyped rituals that temporarily relieve anxiety. Common examples include constant handwashing, repetitive cleaning of things that are already clean, and endless rechecking of locks, faucets, and such (Foa & Kozak, 1995). Specific types of obsessions tend to be associated with specific types of compulsions. For example, obsessions about contamination tend to be paired with cleaning compulsions and obsessions about symmetry tend to be paired with ordering and arranging compulsions (Leckman et al., 1997).

Although many of us can be compulsive at times, full-fledged obsessive-compulsive disorders occur in roughly 2.5% of the population (Turner et al., 2001). The prevalence of obsessive-compulsive disorder seems to be increasing, but this trend may simply reflect changes in clinicians' diagnostic tendencies (Stein et al., 1997). Most cases of OCD emerge before the age of 35 (Otto et al., 1999).

Etiology of Anxiety Disorders

Like most psychological disorders, anxiety disorders develop out of complicated interactions among a variety of biological and psychological factors.

Biological Factors

In studies that assess the impact of heredity on psychological disorders, investigators look at *concordance rates*. A *concordance rate* indicates the percentage of twin pairs or other pairs of relatives who exhibit the same disorder. If relatives who share more genetic similarity show higher concordance rates than relatives who share less genetic overlap, this finding supports the genetic hypothesis. The results of both *twin studies* (see Figure 14.6) and *family studies* (see Chapter 3 for discussions of both methods) suggest that there is a moderate genetic predisposition to anxiety disorders (Fyer, 2000; Hettema, Neale, & Kendler, 2001).

Another line of research suggests that *anxiety sensitivity* may make people vulnerable to anxiety disorders (Reiss, 1991; Weems et al., 2002). According to this notion, some people are highly sensitive to the internal physiological symptoms of anxiety and are prone to overreact with fear when they experience these symptoms. Anxiety sensitivity may fuel an inflationary spiral in which anxiety breeds more anxiety, which eventually spins out of control in the form of an anxiety disorder.

Recent evidence suggests that a link may exist between anxiety disorders and neurochemical activity

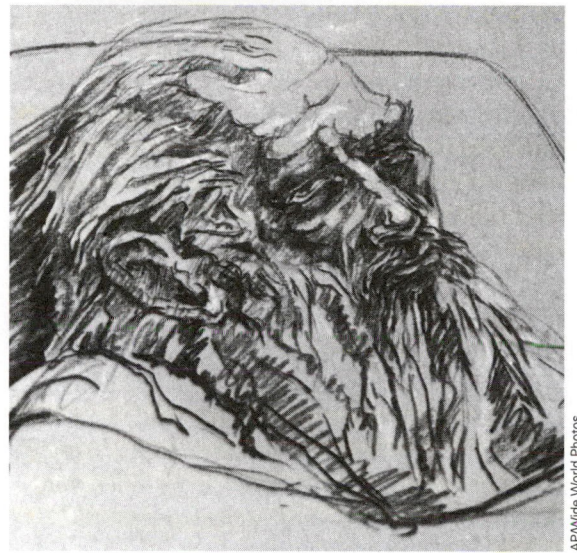

As a young man (shown in the photo), Howard Hughes was a handsome, dashing daredevil pilot and movie producer who appeared to be reasonably well adjusted. However, as the years went by, his behavior gradually became more and more maladaptive, as obsessions and compulsions came to dominate his life. In his later years (shown in the drawing), he spent most of his time in darkened rooms, naked, unkempt, and dirty, following bizarre rituals to alleviate his anxieties. (The drawing was done by an NBC artist and was based on descriptions from men who had seen Hughes.)

in the brain. As you learned in Chapter 3, *neurotransmitters* are chemicals that carry signals from one neuron to another. Therapeutic drugs (such as Valium) that reduce excessive anxiety appear to alter neurotransmitter activity at GABA synapses. This finding and other lines of evidence suggest that disturbances in the neural circuits using GABA may play a role in some types of anxiety disorders (Longo, 1998). Abnormalities in neural circuits using serotonin have recently been implicated in panic and obsessive-compulsive disorders (Sullivan & Coplan, 2000). Thus, scientists are beginning to unravel the neurochemical bases for anxiety disorders.

Figure 14.6

Twin studies of anxiety disorders. The concordance rate for anxiety disorders in identical twins is higher than that for fraternal twins, who share less genetic overlap. These results suggest that there is a genetic predisposition to anxiety disorders. (Data based on Noyes et al., 1987; Slater & Shields, 1969; Torgersen, 1979, 1983)

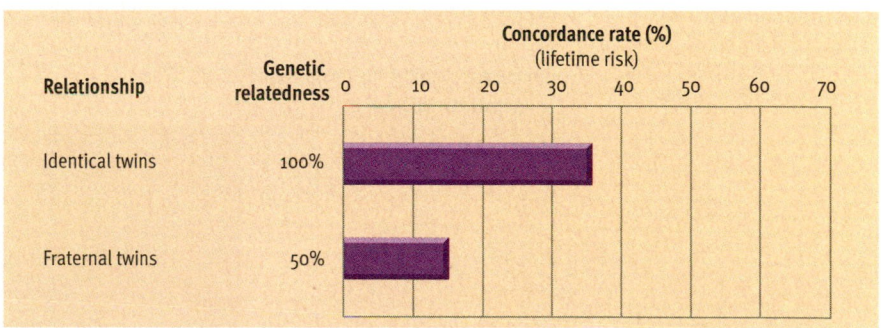

Conditioning and Learning

Many anxiety responses may be *acquired through classical conditioning and maintained through operant conditioning* (see Chapter 6). According to Mowrer (1947), an originally neutral stimulus (the snow in Hilda's case, for instance) may be paired with a frightening event (the avalanche) so that it becomes a conditioned stimulus eliciting anxiety (see Figure 14.7a). Once a fear is acquired through classical conditioning, the person may start avoiding the anxiety-producing stimulus. The avoidance response is negatively reinforced because it is followed by a reduction in anxiety. This process involves operant conditioning (see Figure 14.7b). Thus, separate conditioning processes may create and then sustain specific anxiety responses (Levis, 1989). Consistent with this view, studies find that a substantial portion of people suffering from phobias can identify a traumatic conditioning experience that probably contributed to their anxiety disorder (King, Eleonora, & Ollendick, 1998; Stemberger et al., 1995).

The tendency to develop phobias of certain types of objects and situations may be explained by Martin Seligman's (1971) concept of *preparedness*. Like many theorists, Seligman believes that classical conditioning creates most phobic responses. *However, he suggests that people are biologically prepared by their evolutionary history to acquire some fears much more easily than others.* His theory would explain why people develop phobias of ancient sources of threat (such as snakes and spiders) much more readily than modern sources of threat (such as electrical outlets or hot irons). Some laboratory studies of conditioned fears have yielded evidence that supports Seligman's theory, but the evidence is inconsistent (Rapee & Barlow, 2001).

Critics note a number of problems with conditioning models of phobias (Rachman, 1990). For instance, many people with phobias cannot recall or identify a traumatic conditioning experience that led to their phobia. Conversely, many people endure extremely traumatic experiences that should create a phobia but do not. To provide better explanations for these complexities, conditioning models of anxiety disorders are currently being revised to include a larger role for cognitive factors (de Jong & Merckelbach, 2000), much like conditioning theories in general, as we saw in Chapter 6.

One of these revisions is an increased emphasis on how observational learning can lead to the development of conditioned fears. *Observational learning* occurs when a new response is acquired through watching the behavior of another (consult Chapter 6). Studies suggest that conditioned fears can be created through observational learning (Fredrikson, Annas, & Wik, 1997; Rachman, 1990). In particular, parents frequently pass on their anxieties to their children. Thus, if a father hides in a closet every time there's a thunderstorm, his children may acquire their father's fear of storms.

Cognitive Factors

Cognitive theorists maintain that certain styles of thinking make some people particularly vulnerable to anxiety disorders. According to these theorists, some people are more likely to suffer from problems with anxiety because they tend to (a) misinterpret harmless situations as threatening, (b) focus excessive attention on perceived threats, and (c) selectively recall information that seems threatening (Beck, 1997; McNally, 1994, 1996). In one intriguing test of the cognitive view, anxious and nonanxious subjects were asked to read 32 sentences that could be interpreted in either a threatening or a nonthreatening manner (Eysenck et al., 1991). For instance, one such sentence was "The doctor examined little Emma's growth," which could mean that the doctor checked her height or the growth of a tumor. As Figure 14.8 shows, the anxious participants interpreted the sentences in a threatening way more often than the nonanxious participants did. Thus, consistent with our theme that human experience is highly subjective, the cognitive view holds that some people are prone to anxiety disorders because they see threat in every corner of their lives (Williams et al., 1997).

Stress

Finally, studies have supported the long-held suspicion that anxiety disorders are stress related. For instance, Faravelli and Pallanti (1989) found that pa-

Figure 14.7

Conditioning as an explanation for phobias. **(a)** Many phobias appear to be acquired through classical conditioning when a neutral stimulus is paired with an anxiety-arousing stimulus. **(b)** Once acquired, a phobia may be maintained through operant conditioning. Avoidance of the phobic stimulus reduces anxiety, resulting in negative reinforcement.

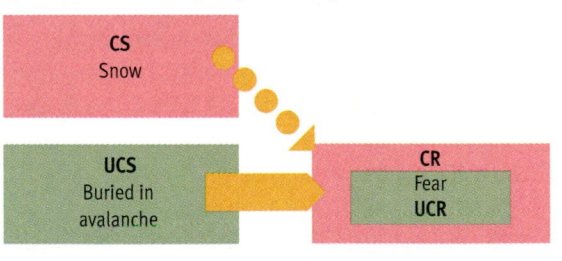

(a) Classical conditioning: Acquisition of phobic fear

CS
Snow

UCS
Buried in avalanche

CR
Fear
UCR

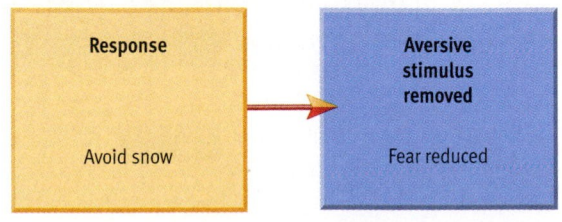

(b) Operant conditioning: Maintenance of phobic fear (negative reinforcement)

Response

Aversive stimulus removed

Avoid snow

Fear reduced

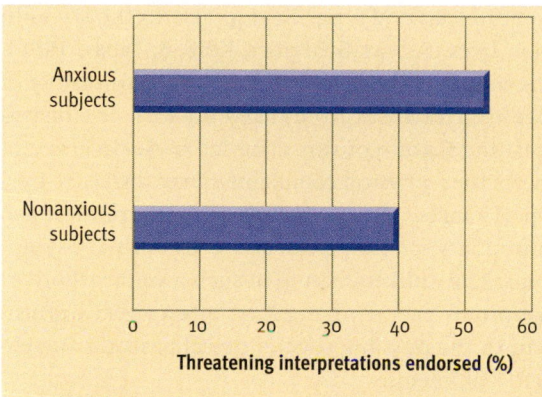

Figure 14.8

Cognitive factors in anxiety disorders. Eysenck and his colleagues (1991) compared how subjects with anxiety problems and nonanxious subjects tended to interpret sentences that could be viewed as threatening or nonthreatening. Consistent with cognitive models of anxiety disorders, anxious subjects were more likely to interpret the sentences in a threatening light.

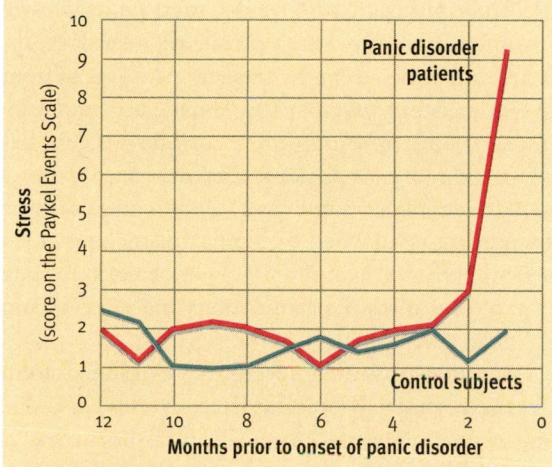

Figure 14.9

Stress and panic disorder. Faravelli and Pallanti (1989) assessed the amount of stress experienced during the 12 months before the onset of panic disorder in a group of 64 patients with this disorder and in a control group drawn from hospital employees and their friends. As you can see, there was a dramatic increase in stress in the month prior to the onset of the patients' panic disorders. These data suggest that stress may contribute to the development of panic disorders.

SOURCE: Adapted from Faravelli, C., & Pallanti, S. (1989). Recent life events and panic disorders. *American Journal of Psychiatry, 146*, 622–626. Copyright © 1989 by the American Psychiatric Association.

tients with panic disorder had experienced a dramatic increase in stress in the month prior to the onset of their disorder (see Figure 14.9). In another study, Brown et al. (1998) found an association between stress and the development of social phobia. Thus, there is reason to believe that high stress often helps to precipitate the onset of anxiety disorders.

REVIEW OF KEY POINTS

- The anxiety disorders include generalized anxiety disorder, phobic disorder, panic disorder, and obsessive-compulsive disorder. Many people who develop one anxiety disorder also suffer from another.

- Twin studies suggest that there is a weak genetic predisposition to anxiety disorders. These disorders may be more likely in people who are especially sensitive to the physiological symptoms of anxiety. Abnormalities in neurotrans-

mitter activity at GABA synapses or serotonin synapses may also play a role in anxiety disorders.

- Many anxiety responses, especially phobias, may be caused by classical conditioning and maintained by operant conditioning. Parents who model anxiety may promote these disorders through observational learning.

- Cognitive theorists maintain that certain styles of thinking—especially a tendency to overinterpret harmless situations as threatening—make some people more vulnerable to anxiety disorders. Stress may also predispose people to anxiety disorders.

Somatoform Disorders

Chances are, you have met people who always seem to be complaining about aches, pains, and physical maladies of doubtful authenticity. You may have thought to yourself, "It's all in his head" and concluded that the person exhibited a "psychosomatic" condition. However, as we discussed in Chapter 13, the term *psychosomatic* has been widely misused. *Psychosomatic diseases* involve *genuine* physical ailments caused in part by psychological factors, especially reactions to stress. These diseases, which include maladies such as ulcers, asthma, and high blood pressure, are not imagined ailments.

They are recorded on the DSM axis for physical problems (Axis III). When physical illness appears *largely* psychological in origin, we are dealing with somatoform disorders, which are recorded on Axis I. *Somatoform disorders* are physical ailments that cannot be fully explained by organic conditions and are largely due to psychological factors. Although their symptoms are more imaginary than real, victims of somatoform disorders are *not* simply faking illness. Deliberate feigning of illness for personal gain is another matter altogether, called *malingering*.

PREVIEW QUESTIONS

- How do psychosomatic diseases and somatoform disorders differ?

- What are the three major somatoform disorders, and what are their chief symptoms?

- What factors have been implicated in the etiology of somatoform disorders?

People with somatoform disorders typically seek treatment from physicians practicing neurology, internal medicine, or family medicine, instead of from psychologists or psychiatrists. Making accurate diagnoses of somatoform disorders can be difficult, because the causes of physical ailments are sometimes hard to identify. In some cases, somatoform disorders are misdiagnosed when a genuine organic cause for a person's physical symptoms goes undetected in spite of extensive medical examinations and tests (Martin & Yutzy, 1999).

We will discuss three specific types of somatoform disorders: somatization disorder, conversion disorder, and hypochondriasis. Diagnostic difficulties make it hard to obtain sound data on the prevalence of somatoform disorders (Bouman, Eifert, & Lejuez, 1999).

Somatization Disorder

Individuals with somatization disorder are often said to "cling to ill health." A *somatization disorder* is marked by a history of diverse physical complaints that appear to be psychological in origin. Somatization disorder occurs mostly in women (Guggenheim, 2000) and often coexists with depression and anxiety disorders (Gureje et al., 1997). Victims report an endless succession of minor physical ailments that seem to wax and wane in response to the stress in their lives (Servan-Schreiber, Kolb, & Tabas, 1999). They usually have a long and complicated history of medical treatment from many doctors. The distinguishing feature of this disorder is the diversity of the victims' physical complaints. Over the years, they report a mixed bag of cardiovascular, gastrointestinal, pulmonary, neurological, and genitourinary symptoms. The unlikely nature of such a smorgasbord of symptoms occurring together often alerts a physician to the possible psychological basis for the patient's problems.

Conversion Disorder

Conversion disorder is characterized by a significant loss of physical function (with no apparent organic basis), usually in a single organ system. Common symptoms include partial or complete loss of vision, partial or complete loss of hearing, partial paralysis, severe laryngitis or mutism, and loss of feeling or function in limbs, such as that seen in the following case:

Mildred was a rancher's daughter who lost the use of both of her legs during adolescence. Mildred was at home alone one afternoon when a male relative attempted to assault her. She screamed for help, and her legs gave way as she slipped to the floor. She was found on the floor a few minutes later when her mother returned home. She could not get up, so she was carried to her bed. Her legs buckled when she made subsequent attempts to walk on her own. Due to her illness, she was waited on hand and foot by her family and friends. Neighbors brought her homemade things to eat or to wear. She became the center of attention in the household. (Adapted from Cameron, 1963, pp. 312–313)

People with conversion disorder are usually troubled by more severe ailments than people with somatization disorder. In some cases of conversion disorder, telltale clues reveal the psychological origins of the illness because the patient's symptoms are not consistent with medical knowledge about their apparent disease. For instance, the loss of feeling in one hand that is seen in "glove anesthesia" is inconsistent with the known facts of neurological organization (see Figure 14.10).

Hypochondriasis

Hypochondriacs constantly monitor their physical condition, looking for signs of illness. Any tiny alteration from their physical norm leads them to con-

Figure 14.10

Glove anesthesia. In conversion disorders, the physical complaints are sometimes inconsistent with the known facts of physiology. For instance, given the patterns of nerve distribution in the arm shown in **(a),** it is impossible that a loss of feeling in the hand exclusively, as shown in **(b),** has a physical cause, indicating that the patient's problem is psychological in origin.

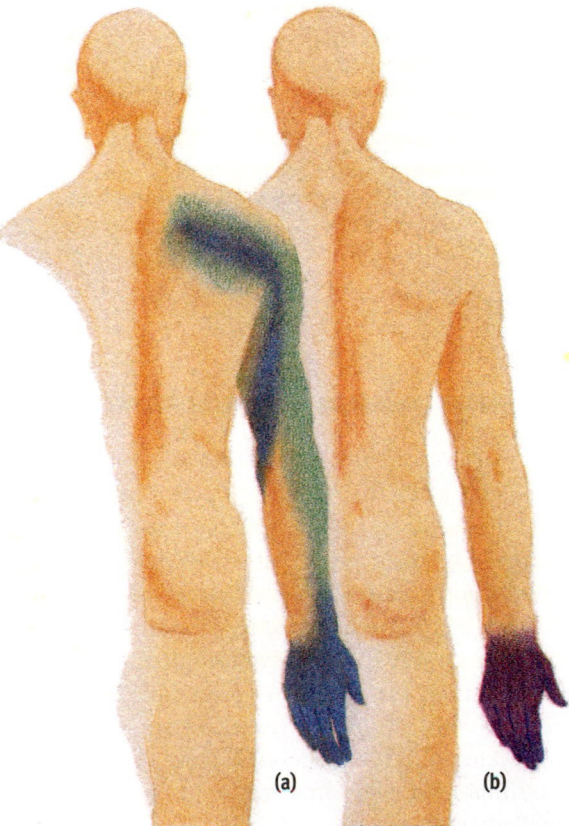

(a)   (b)

clude that they have contracted a disease. *Hypochondriasis* (more widely known as hypochondria) is characterized by excessive preoccupation with health concerns and incessant worry about developing physical illnesses. The following case illustrates the nature of hypochondria:

Jeff is a middle-aged man who works as a clerk in a drug store. He spends long hours describing his health problems to anyone who will listen. Jeff is an avid reader of popular magazine articles on medicine. He can tell you all about the latest medical discoveries. He takes all sorts of pills and vitamins to ward off possible illnesses. He's the first to try every new product on the market. Jeff is constantly afflicted by new symptoms of illness. His most recent problems were poor digestion and a heartbeat that he thought was irregular. He frequently goes to physicians who can find nothing wrong with him physically. They tell him that he is healthy. He thinks they use "backward techniques." He suspects that his illness is too rare to be diagnosed successfully. (Adapted from Suinn, 1984, p. 236)

When hypochondriacs are assured by their physician that they do not have any real illness, they often are skeptical and disbelieving (Starcevic, 2001). As in Jeff's case, they frequently assume that the physician must be incompetent, and they go shopping for another doctor. Hypochondriacs don't subjectively suffer from physical distress as much as they *overinterpret* every conceivable sign of illness. Hypochondria frequently appears alongside other psychological disorders, especially anxiety disorders and depression (Iezzi, Duckworth, & Adams, 2001). For example, Howard Hughes's obsessive-compulsive disorder was coupled with profound hypochondria.

Etiology of Somatoform Disorders

Inherited aspects of physiological functioning, such as a highly reactive autonomic nervous system, may predispose some people to somatoform disorders (Weiner, 1992). However, available evidence suggests that these disorders are largely a function of personality and cognitive factors. Let's look at personality factors first.

Personality Factors

People with certain types of personality traits seem to develop somatoform disorders more readily than others. The prime candidates appear to be people with *histrionic* personality characteristics (Nemiah, 1985; Slavney, 1990). The histrionic personality tends to be self-centered, suggestible, excitable, highly emo-

tional, and overly dramatic. Such people thrive on the attention that they get when they become ill. The personality trait of *neuroticism* also seems to elevate individuals' susceptibility to somatoform disorders (Kirmayer, Robbins, & Paris, 1994).

Cognitive Factors

In recent years, theorists have devoted increased attention to how cognitive peculiarities might contribute to somatoform disorders. For example, Barsky (2001) asserts that some people focus excessive attention on their internal physiological processes and amplify normal bodily sensations into symptoms of distress, which lead them to pursue unnecessary medical treatment. Recent evidence suggests that people with somatoform disorders tend to draw catastrophic conclusions about minor bodily complaints (Salkovskis & Warwick, 2001). They also seem to apply a faulty standard of good health, equating health with a complete absence of symptoms and discomfort, which is unrealistic (Barsky et al., 1993).

The Sick Role

Another consideration is that some people grow fond of the role associated with being sick (Pilow-

CONCEPT CHECK 14.2

Distinguishing Anxiety and Somatoform Disorders

Check your understanding of the nature of anxiety and somatoform disorders by making preliminary diagnoses for the cases described below. Read each case summary and write your tentative diagnosis in the space provided. The answers are in Appendix A.

1. Malcolm religiously follows an exact schedule every day. His showering and grooming ritual takes two hours. He follows the same path in walking to his classes every day, and he always sits in the same seat in each class. He can't study until his apartment is arranged perfectly. Although he tries not to, he thinks constantly about flunking out of school. Both his grades and his social life are suffering from his rigid routines.

   Preliminary diagnosis: _____

2. Jane has been unemployed for the last eight years because of poor health. She has suffered through a bizarre series of illnesses of mysterious origin. Troubles with devastating headaches were followed by months of chronic back pain. Then she developed respiratory problems, frequently gasping for breath. Her current problem is stomach pain. Physicians have been unable to find any physical basis for her maladies.

   Preliminary diagnosis: _____

3. Nathan owns a small restaurant that's in deep financial trouble. He dreads facing the possibility that his restaurant will fail. One day, he suddenly loses all feeling in his right arm and the ability to control the arm. He's hospitalized for his condition, but physicians can't find any organic cause for his arm trouble.

   Preliminary diagnosis: _____

sky, 1993). Their complaints of physical symptoms may be reinforced by indirect benefits derived from their illness (Schwartz, Slater, & Birchler, 1994). What are the benefits commonly associated with physical illness? One payoff is that becoming ill is a superb way to avoid having to confront life's challenges. Many people with somatoform disorders are avoiding facing up to marital problems, career frustrations, family responsibilities, and the like. After all, when you're sick, others cannot place great demands on you. Another benefit is that physical problems can provide a convenient excuse when people fail, or worry about failing, in endeavors that are critical to their self-esteem (Organista & Miranda, 1991).

Attention from others is another payoff that may reinforce complaints of physical illness. When people become ill, they command the attention of family, friends, co-workers, neighbors, and doctors. The sympathy that illness often brings may strengthen the person's tendency to feel ill. This clearly occurred in Mildred's case of conversion disorder. Her illness paid handsome dividends in terms of attention, consolation, and kindhearted assistance from others.

Dissociative Disorders

PREVIEW QUESTIONS
- What are the principal types of dissociative disorders, and what are their chief symptoms?
- Why is the dissociative identity disorder controversial?

Dissociative disorders are among the more unusual syndromes that we will discuss. *Dissociative disorders are a class of disorders in which people lose contact with portions of their consciousness or memory, resulting in disruptions in their sense of identity.* We'll describe three dissociative syndromes—dissociative amnesia, dissociative fugue, and dissociative identity disorder—all of which are relatively uncommon.

Dissociative Amnesia and Fugue

Dissociative amnesia and fugue are overlapping disorders characterized by serious memory deficits. *Dissociative amnesia is a sudden loss of memory for important personal information that is too extensive to be due to normal forgetting.* Memory losses may occur for a single traumatic event (such as an automobile accident or home fire) or for an extended period of time surrounding the event. Cases of amnesia have been observed after people have experienced disasters, accidents, combat stress, physical abuse, and rape, or after they have witnessed the violent death of a parent, among other things (Arrigo & Pezdek, 1997; Loewenstein, 1996). In *dissociative fugue, people lose their memory for their entire lives along with their sense of personal identity.* These people forget their name, their family, where they live, and where they work! In spite of this wholesale forgetting, they remember matters unrelated to their identity, such as how to drive a car and how to do math.

Dissociative Identity Disorder

Dissociative identity disorder (DID) involves the coexistence in one person of two or more largely complete, and usually very different, personalities. The name for this disorder used to be *multiple personality disorder,* which still enjoys informal use. In dissociative identity disorder, the divergences in behavior go far beyond those that people normally display in adapting to different roles in life. People with "multiple personalities" feel that they have more than one identity. Each personality has his or her own name, memories, traits, and physical mannerisms. Although rare, this "Dr. Jekyll and Mr. Hyde" syndrome is frequently portrayed in novels, television shows, and movies, such as the *Three Faces of Eve,* a 1957 film starring Joanne Woodward. In popular media portrayals, the syndrome is often mistakenly called *schizophrenia.* As you will see later, schizophrenic disorders are entirely different.

In dissociative identity disorder, the various personalities are often unaware of each other (Eich et al., 1997). In other words, the experiences of a specific personality are only recalled by that personality and not the others. The alternate personalities commonly display traits that are quite foreign to the original personality. For instance, a shy, inhibited person might develop a flamboyant, extraverted alternate personality. Transitions between identities often occur suddenly. The disparities between identities can be bizarre, as different personalities may assert that they are different in age, race, gender, and sexual orientation (Kluft, 1996). Dissociative identity disorder rarely occurs in isolation. Most DID patients also have a history of anxiety, mood, or personality disorders (Ross, 1999).

Starting in the 1970s, there was a dramatic increase in the diagnosis of multiple-personality disorder (Kihlstrom, 2001). There were only about 100 published cases accumulated up through 1970, but by the mid-1990s about 6,000 new cases were being reported *each year* (Milstone, 1997). Some theorists believe that these disorders used to be underdiagnosed—that is, they often went undetected (Saxe et al., 1993; Spiegel & Maldonado, 1999). However, other theorists argue that a handful of clinicians have begun overdiagnosing the condition and that some clinicians even *encourage and contribute* to the emergence of DID (McHugh, 1995; Powell & Gee, 1999). Consistent with this view, a survey of all the psychiatrists in Switzerland found that 90% of them had never seen a case of dissociative identity disorder, whereas three of the psychiatrists had each seen more than 20 DID patients (Modestin, 1992). The data from this study suggest that 6 psychiatrists (out of 655 surveyed) accounted for two-thirds of the dissociative identity disorder diagnoses in Switzerland.

Etiology of Dissociative Disorders

Psychogenic amnesia and fugue are usually attributed to excessive stress. However, relatively little is known about why this extreme reaction to stress occurs in a tiny minority of people but not in the vast majority who are subjected to similar stress. Some theorists speculate that certain personality traits—fantasy proneness and a tendency to become intensely absorbed in personal experiences—may make some people more susceptible to dissociative disorders, but adequate evidence is lacking on this line of thought (Kihlstrom, Glisky, & Angiulo, 1994).

The causes of dissociative identity disorders are particularly obscure. Some skeptical theorists, such as Nicholas Spanos (1994, 1996) and others (Lilienfeld et al., 1999) believe that people with multiple personalities are engaging in intentional role playing to use mental illness as a face-saving excuse for their personal failings. Spanos also argues that a small minority of therapists help create multiple personalities in their patients by subtly encouraging the emergence of alternate personalities. According to Spanos, dissociative identity disorder is a creation of modern North American culture, much as demonic possession was a creation of early Christianity. To bolster his argument, he discusses how multiple-personality patients' symptom presentations seem to have been influenced by popular media. For example, the typical patient with dissociative identity disorder used to report having two or three personalities, but since the publication of *Sybil* (Schreiber, 1973) and other books describing patients with many personalities, the average number of alternate personalities has climbed to about 15. In a similar vein, there has been a dramatic upsurge in the number of dissociative patients reporting that they were victims of ritual satanic abuse during childhood that dates back to the publication of *Michelle Remembers* (Smith & Pazder, 1980), a book about a multiple-personality patient who purportedly was tortured by a satanic cult.

In spite of these concerns, many clinicians are convinced that dissociative identity disorder is an authentic disorder (Gleaves, May, & Cardena, 2001; Kihlstrom, Tataryn, & Hoyt, 1993). They argue that there is no incentive for either patients or therapists to manufacture cases of multiple personalities, which are often greeted with skepticism and outright hostility. They maintain that most cases of dissociative identity disorder are rooted in severe emotional trauma that occurred during childhood (Draijer & Langeland, 1999). A substantial majority of people with dissociative identity disorder report a childhood history of rejection from parents and physical and sexual abuse (Lewis et al., 1997; Scroppo et al., 1998). However, this link is not unique to DID, as a history of child abuse elevates the likelihood of *many* disorders, especially among females (MacMillan et al., 2001). In the final analysis, very little is known about the causes of dissociative identity disorder, which remains a controversial diagnosis. In one recent survey of American psychiatrists, only one-quarter of the respondents indicated that they felt there was solid evidence for the scientific validity of the DID diagnosis (Pope et al., 1999).

REVIEW OF KEY POINTS

● Somatoform disorders are physical ailments that cannot be fully explained by organic conditions. They are different from psychosomatic diseases, which are genuine physical ailments caused in part by psychological factors.

● Somatoform disorders include somatization disorder, conversion disorder, and hypochondriasis. These disorders often emerge in people with highly suggestible, histrionic personalities and in people who focus excess attention on their internal physiological processes. Somatoform disorders may be a learned avoidance strategy reinforced by attention and sympathy.

● Dissociative disorders include dissociative amnesia, fugue, and dissociative identity disorder (multiple-personality disorder). These disorders are uncommon and their causes are not well understood.

● Some theorists believe that people with dissociative identity disorder are engaging in intentional role playing to use an exotic mental illness as a face-saving excuse for their personal failings. These disorders may be rooted in emotional trauma that occurred during childhood.

Mood Disorders

PREVIEW QUESTIONS

- What are the principal mood disorders, and what are their chief symptoms?
- Which biological factors have been implicated in mood disorders?
- How do cognitive processes contribute to depressive disorders?
- How do social skills and stress contribute to depressive disorders?

What did Abraham Lincoln, Marilyn Monroe, Kurt Cobain, Vincent Van Gogh, Ernest Hemingway, Winston Churchill, Janis Joplin, and Leo Tolstoy have in common? Yes, they all achieved great prominence, albeit in different ways at different times. But, more pertinent to our interest, they all suffered from severe mood disorders. Although mood disorders can be terribly debilitating, people with mood disorders may still achieve greatness, because such disorders tend to be *episodic*. In other words, mood disturbances often come and go, interspersed among periods of normality. These episodes of disturbance can vary greatly in length, but they typically last 3–12 months (Akiskal, 2000).

Of course, everybody has ups and downs in terms of mood. Life would be dull indeed if people's emotional tone were constant. Everyone experiences depression occasionally. Likewise, everyone has days that he or she sails through on an emotional high. Such emotional fluctuations are natural, but some people are subject to extreme and sustained distortions of mood. *Mood disorders* are a class of disorders marked by emotional disturbances of varied kinds that may spill over to disrupt physical, perceptual, social, and thought processes.

There are two basic types of mood disorders: unipolar and bipolar (see Figure 14.11). People with *unipolar disorder* experience emotional extremes at just one end of the mood continuum, as they are troubled only by *depression*. People with *bipolar disorder* are vulnerable to emotional extremes at both ends of the mood continuum, going through periods of both *depression* and *mania* (excitement and elation).

Major Depressive Disorder

The line between normal dejection and unhappiness and abnormal depression can be difficult to draw (Kendler & Gardner, 1998). Ultimately, it requires a subjective judgment. Crucial considerations in this judgment include the duration of the depression and its disruptive effects. When a depression significantly impairs everyday adaptive behavior for more than a few weeks, there is reason for concern.

In *major depressive disorder* people show persistent feelings of sadness and despair and a loss of interest in previous sources of pleasure. Negative emotions form the heart of the depressive syndrome, but many other symptoms may also appear. The most common symptoms of major depression are summarized and compared with the symptoms of mania in Table 14.1. Depressed people often give up activities that they used to find enjoyable. For example, a depressed person might quit going bowling or might give up a favorite hobby such as photogra-

Figure 14.11

Episodic patterns in mood disorders. Time-limited episodes of emotional disturbance come and go unpredictably in mood disorders. People with unipolar disorders suffer from bouts of depression only, whereas people with bipolar disorders experience both manic and depressive episodes. The time between episodes of disturbance varies greatly with the individual and the type of disorder.

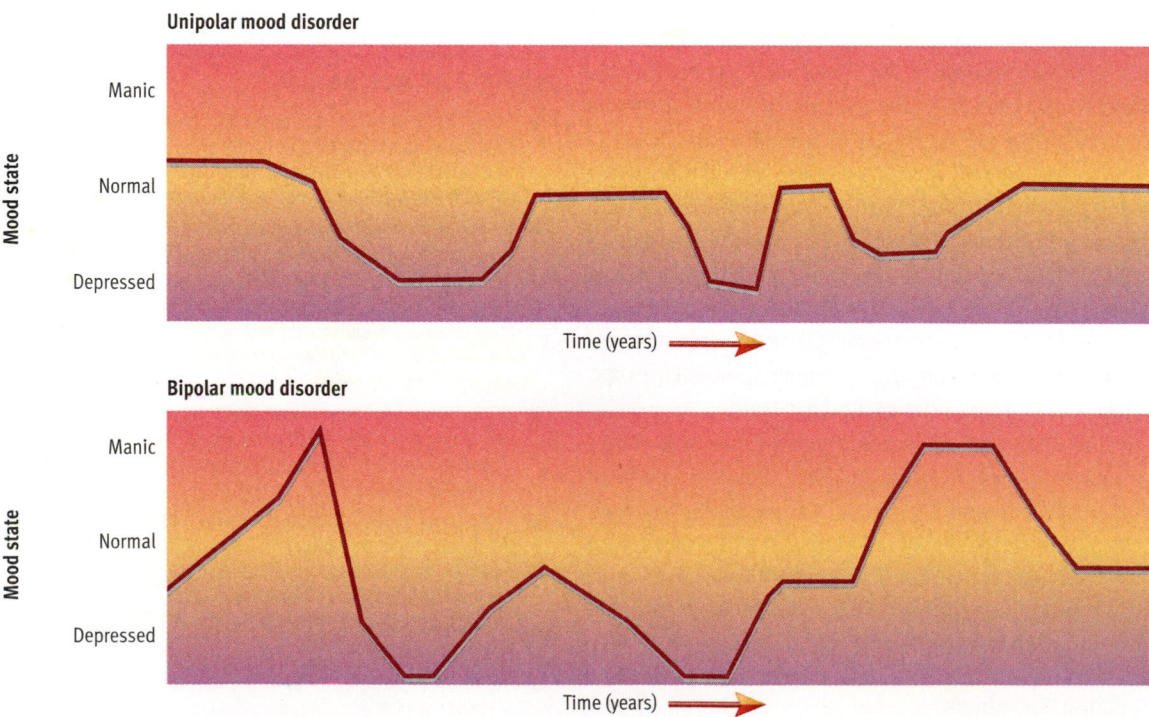

phy. Alterations in appetite and sleep patterns are common. People with depression often lack energy. They tend to move sluggishly and talk slowly. Anxiety, irritability, and brooding are commonly observed. Self-esteem tends to sink as the depressed person begins to feel worthless. Depression plunges people into feelings of hopelessness, dejection, and boundless guilt. To make matters worse, people who suffer from depression often exhibit other disorders as well (Boland & Keller, 2002). Coexisting anxiety disorders and substance use disorders are particularly frequent.

The onset of depression can occur at any point in the life span. The median duration of depressive episodes is 5 months (Solomon et al., 1997). The vast majority (75%–95%) of people who suffer from depression experience more than one episode over the course of their lifetime (Dubovsky & Buzan, 1999). In one longitudinal study, after recovery from one's first episode of depression, the cumulative probability of recurrence was 25% after 1 year, 42% after two years, and 60% after 5 years (Solomon et al., 2000). The severity of depressive disorders varies considerably. When people display relatively mild symptoms of depression, they're given a diagnosis of *dysthymic disorder,* which consists of chronic depression that is insufficient in severity to justify diagnosis of a major depressive episode.

How common are depressive disorders? Very common. Research suggests that about 7% to 18% of Americans endure a depressive disorder at some time in their lives (Blazer, 2000; Regier & Burke, 2000). Estimates of the prevalence of depression vary quite a bit because of the previously mentioned difficulty in drawing a line between normal dejection and abnormal depression. Hence, different researchers using different procedures and cutoff points obtain varied estimates. Moreover, evidence suggests that the prevalence of depression is increasing, as it is higher in more recent age cohorts (Rehm, Wagner, & Ivens-Tyndal, 2001). In particular, age cohorts born since World War II appear to have an elevated risk for depression (Kessler, 2002). The factors underlying this rise in depression are not readily apparent, and researchers are scrambling to collect data that might shed light on this unanticipated trend.

Researchers also find that the prevalence of depression is about twice as high in women as it is in men (Nolen-Hoeksema, 2002). This gender gap in depression opens up during mid to late adolescence (Hankin et al., 1998). The many possible explanations for this gender gap are the subject of considerable debate. Susan Nolen-Hoeksema (2001) argues that women experience more depression than men because they are far more likely to be victims of sex-

ual abuse and somewhat more likely to endure poverty, harassment, and role constraints. In other words, she attributes the higher prevalence of depression among women to their experience of greater stress and adversity. Nolen-Hoeksema also believes that women have a greater tendency than men to *ruminate* about setbacks and problems. Evidence suggests that this tendency to dwell on one's difficulties elevates vulnerability to depression, as we will discuss momentarily.

Drew Barrymore and Art Buchwald are two well-known figures who have struggled with mood disorders.

Bipolar Disorder 11b

***Bipolar disorder* (formerly known as manic-depressive disorder) is characterized by the experience of one or more manic episodes as well as periods of depression.** One manic episode is sufficient to qualify for this diagnosis. The symptoms seen in

Table 14.1 Comparisons of Common Symptoms in Manic and Depressive Episodes

Characteristics	Manic Episode	Depressive Episode
Emotional	Elated, euphoric, very sociable, impatient at any hindrance	Gloomy, hopeless, socially withdrawn, irritable
Cognitive	Characterized by racing thoughts, flight of ideas, desire for action, and impulsive behavior; talkative, self-confident; experiencing delusions of grandeur	Characterized by slowness of thought processes, obsessive worrying, inability to make decisions, negative self-image, self-blame and delusions of guilt and disease
Motor	Hyperactive, tireless, requiring less sleep than usual, showing increased sex drive and fluctuating appetite	Less active, tired, experiencing difficulty in sleeping, showing decreased sex drive and decreased appetite

Source: Sarason, I. G., & Sarason, B. G. (1987). *Abnormal psychology: The problem of maladaptive behavior.* Upper Saddle River, NJ: Prentice-Hall. © 1987 Prentice-Hall, Inc. Reprinted by permission.

manic periods generally are the opposite of those seen in depression (see Table 14.1 for a comparison). In a manic episode, a person's mood becomes elevated to the point of euphoria. Self-esteem skyrockets as the person bubbles over with optimism, energy, and extravagant plans. He or she becomes hyperactive and may go for days without sleep. The individual talks rapidly and shifts topics wildly, as his or her mind races at breakneck speed. Judgment is often impaired. Some people in manic periods gamble impulsively, spend money frantically, or become sexually reckless. Like depressive disorders, bipolar disorders vary considerably in severity. People are given a diagnosis of *cyclothymic disorder* when they exhibit chronic but relatively mild symptoms of bipolar disturbance.

You may be thinking that the euphoria in manic episodes sounds appealing. If so, you are not entirely wrong. In their milder forms, manic states can seem attractive. The increases in energy, self-esteem, and optimism can be deceptively seductive. Because of the increase in energy, many bipolar patients report temporary surges of productivity and creativity (Goodwin & Jamison, 1990).

Although manic episodes may have some positive aspects, these periods often have a paradoxical negative undercurrent of irritability and depression (Dilsaver et al., 1999). Moreover, mild manic episodes usually escalate to higher levels that become scary and disturbing. Impaired judgment leads many victims to do things that they greatly regret later, as you'll see in the following case history:

Robert, a dentist, awoke one morning with the idea that he was the most gifted dental surgeon in his tristate area. He decided that he should try to provide services to as many people as possible, so that more people could bene-fit from his talents. Thus, he decided to remodel his two-chair dental office, installing 20 booths so that he could simultaneously attend to 20 patients. That same day he drew up plans for this arrangement, telephoned a number of remodelers, and invited bids for the work. Later that day, impatient to get rolling on his remodeling, he rolled up his sleeves, got himself a sledgehammer, and began to knock down the walls in his office. Annoyed when that didn't go so well, he smashed his dental tools, washbasins, and X-ray equipment. Later, Robert's wife became concerned about his behavior and summoned two of her adult daughters for assistance. The daughters responded quickly, arriving at the family home with their husbands. In the ensuing discussion, Robert—after bragging about his sexual prowess—made advances toward his daughters. He had to be subdued by their husbands. (Adapted from Kleinmuntz, 1980, p. 309)

Although not rare, bipolar disorders are much less common than unipolar disorders. Bipolar disorder affects about 1% to 2% of the population (Dubovsky & Buzan, 1999). Unlike depressive disorder, bipolar disorder is seen equally often in males and females (Tohen & Goodwin, 1995). As Figure 14.12 shows, the onset of bipolar disorder is age related, with the peak of vulnerability occurring between the ages of 20 and 29 (Goodwin & Jamison, 1990). The mood swings in bipolar disorder can be patterned in many ways. About 20% of bipolar patients exhibit a *rapid-cycling pattern*, which means they go through four or more manic or depressive episodes within a year.

Etiology of Mood Disorders 11b

Quite a bit is known about the etiology of mood disorders, although the puzzle certainly hasn't been assembled completely. There appear to be a number of routes into these disorders, involving intricate interactions between psychological and biological factors.

Genetic Vulnerability 11b

The evidence strongly suggests that genetic factors influence the likelihood of developing major depression or bipolar disorder (Kalidindi & McGuffin, 2003; Sullivan, Neale, & Kendler, 2000). *Twin studies* have found a sizable disparity between identical and fraternal twins in concordance rates for mood disorders (see Figure 14.13). This evidence suggests that heredity can create a *predisposition* to mood disorders. Environmental factors probably determine whether this predisposition is converted into an actual disorder. Research suggests that genetic vulnerability may play a larger role in women's depression than in men's

Figure 14.12

Age of onset for bipolar mood disorder. The onset of bipolar disorder typically occurs in adolescence or early adulthood. The data graphed here, which were combined from 10 studies, show the distribution of age of onset for 1304 bipolar patients. As you can see, bipolar disorder emerges most frequently during the 20s decade.

Source: Goodwin, F. K., & Jamison, K. R. (1990). *Manic-depressive illness* (p. 132). New York: Oxford University Press. Copyright © 1990 Oxford University Press., Inc. Reprinted by permission.

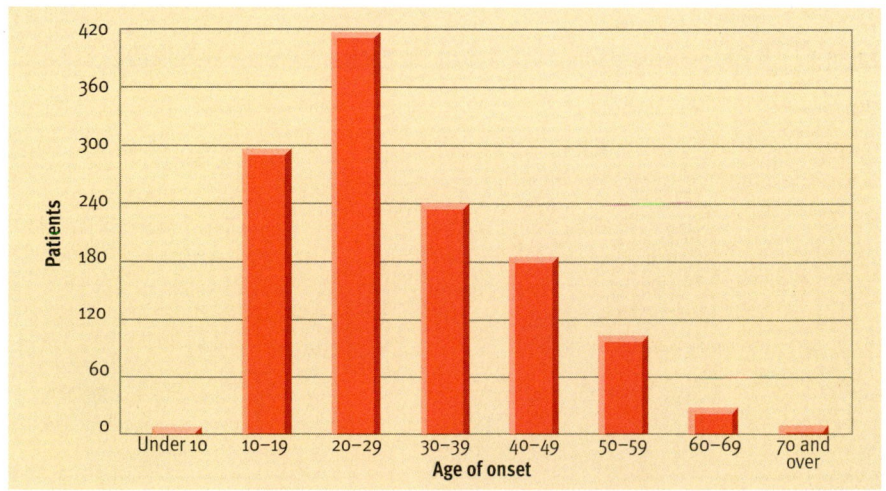

(Bierut et al., 1999). The influence of genetic factors also appears to be stronger for bipolar disorders than for unipolar disorders (Knowles, Kaufmann, & Rieder, 1999). Although genetic mapping technology (see Chapter 3) holds great promise for pinpointing the specific genes that shape vulnerability to mood disorders, scientists do *not* appear to be on the verge of unraveling the genetic code for mood disorders, which probably depend on constellations of many genes (Ambrosio et al., 2001; Knowles et al., 1999).

Neurochemical Factors

Heredity may influence susceptibility to mood disorders by creating a predisposition toward certain types of neurochemical abnormalities in the brain. Correlations have been found between mood disorders and abnormal levels of two neurotransmitters in the brain: norepinephrine and serotonin (Nemeroff, 1998; Rothschild, 1999), although other neurotransmitter disturbances may also contribute (Thase, Jindal, & Howland, 2002). The details remain elusive, but it seems clear that a neurochemical basis exists for at least some mood disorders. A variety of drug therapies are fairly effective in the treatment of severe mood disorders. Most of these drugs are known to affect the availability (in the brain) of the neurotransmitters that have been related to mood disorders (Garlow, Musselman, & Nemeroff, 1999). Since this effect is unlikely to be a coincidence, it bolsters the plausibility of the idea that neurochemical changes produce mood disturbances.

If alterations in neurotransmitter activity are the basis for many mood disorders, what causes the alterations in neurotransmitter activity? These changes probably depend on people's reactions to environmental events. Thus, a number of psychological factors have been implicated in the etiology of mood disorders. We'll examine evidence on the role of cognitive factors next.

Cognitive Factors

A variety of theories emphasize how cognitive factors contribute to depressive disorders (Abramson et al., 2002). We will discuss Aaron Beck's (1976, 1987) influential cognitive theory of depression in Chapter 15, where his approach to therapy is described. In this section, we'll examine Martin Seligman's *learned helplessness model* of depression and its most recent descendant, *hopelessness theory*. Based largely on animal research, Seligman (1974) proposed that depression is caused by *learned helplessness*—passive "giving up" behavior produced by exposure to unavoidable aversive events (such as uncontrollable shock in the lab-

oratory). He originally considered learned helplessness to be a product of conditioning but eventually revised his theory, giving it a cognitive slant. The reformulated theory of learned helplessness postulates that the roots of depression lie in how people explain the setbacks and other negative events that they experience (Abramson, Seligman, & Teasdale, 1978). According to Seligman (1990), people who exhibit a *pessimistic explanatory style* are especially vulnerable to depression. These people tend to attribute their setbacks to their personal flaws instead of situational factors, and they tend to draw global, far-reaching conclusions about their personal inadequacies based on these setbacks.

Hopelessness theory builds on these insights by postulating a sense of hopelessness as the "final pathway" leading to depression and by incorporating additional factors that may interact with explanatory style to foster this sense of hopelessness (Abramson, Alloy, & Metalsky, 1995). According to hopelessness theory, a pessimistic explanatory style is just one of several or more factors—along with high stress, low self-esteem, and so forth—that may contribute to hopelessness, and thus depression. Although hopelessness theory casts a wider net than the learned helplessness model, it continues to emphasize the importance of people's *cognitive reactions* to the events in their lives.

In accord with this line of thinking, Susan Nolen-Hoeksema (1991, 2000) has found that depressed people who *ruminate* about their depression remain depressed longer than those who try to distract themselves. People who respond to depression with rumination repetitively focus their attention on their depressing feelings, thinking constantly about how sad, lethargic, and unmotivated they are. According to Nolen-Hoeksema (1995), excessive rumination tends to extend and amplify individuals' episodes of depression. As we noted earlier, she believes that women are more likely to ruminate than men and that this disparity may be one of the primary reasons why depression is more prevalent in women.

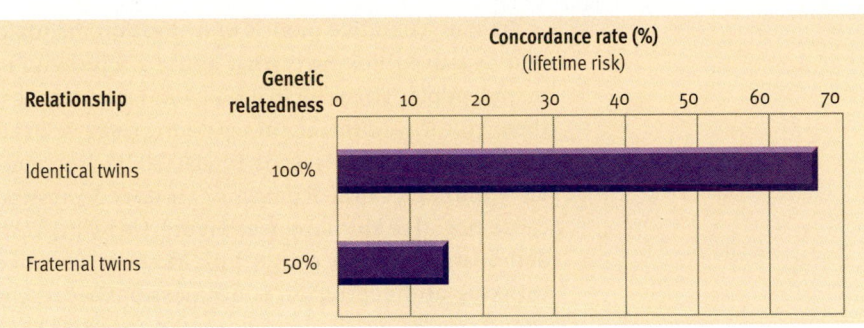

Figure 14.13

Twin studies of mood disorders. The concordance rate for mood disorders in identical twins is much higher than that for fraternal twins, who share less genetic overlap. These results suggest that there must be a genetic predisposition to mood disorders. (Data from Gershon, Berrettini, & Goldin, 1989)

"By adolescence, girls appear to be more likely than boys to respond to stress and distress with rumination—focusing inward on feelings of distress and personal concerns rather than taking action to relieve their distress."

SUSAN NOLEN-HOEKSEMA

In sum, cognitive models of depression maintain that negative thinking is what leads to depression in many people. The principal problem with cognitive theories is their difficulty in separating cause from effect (Rehm, Wagner, & Ivens-Tyndal, 2001). Does negative thinking cause depression? Or does depression cause negative thinking (see Figure 14.14)? A *clear* demonstration of a causal link between negative thinking and depression is not possible because it would require manipulating people's cognitive style (which is not easy to change) in sufficient degree to produce full-fledged depressive disorders (which would not be ethical). However, the research reported in our Featured Study provided impressive evidence consistent with a causal link between negative thinking and vulnerability to depression.

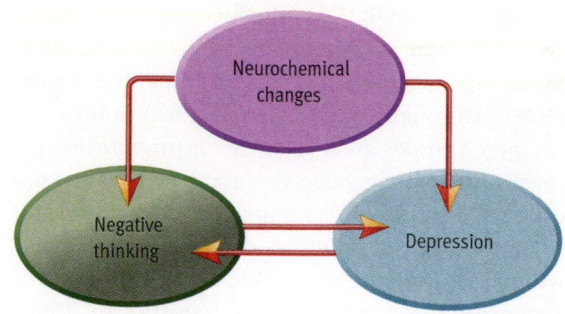

Figure 14.14

Interpreting the correlation between negative thinking and depression. Cognitive theories of depression assume that consistent patterns of negative thinking cause depression. Although these theories are highly plausible, depression could cause negative thoughts, or both could be caused by a third factor, such as neurochemical changes in the brain.

FEATURED STUDY | Does Negative Thinking *Cause* Depression?

Investigators: Lauren B. Alloy (Temple University), Lyn Y. Abramson (University of Wisconsin), Wayne G. Whitehouse (Temple University), Michael E. Hogan (University of Wisconsin), Nancy A. Tashman (University of Maryland), Dena L. Steinberg (New York State Psychiatric Institute), Donna T. Rose (Counseling Associates of Madison), and Patricia Donovan (University of Wisconsin).

Source: Depressogenic cognitive styles: Predictive validity, information processing and personality characteristics, and developmental origins. *Behavior Research and Therapy,* 1999, *37,* 503–531.

This article describes a series of studies conducted at Temple University and at the University of Wisconsin, collectively referred to as the Temple-Wisconsin Cognitive Vulnerability to Depression Project. Although the article provides a preliminary report on many facets of the project, we will focus on the study intended to test the hypothesis that a negative cognitive style is predictive of elevated vulnerability to depression.

Method

Participants. Over 5,000 first-year students at the two universities responded to two measures of negative thinking. Students who scored in the highest quartile on both measures were characterized as having a *high risk* for depression and those who scored in the lowest quartile on both measures were characterized as having a *low risk* for depression. Randomly selected subsets of these two groups were invited for additional screening to eliminate anyone who was currently depressed or suffering from any other major psychological disorder. The final sample consisted of 173 students in the high-risk group and 176 students in the low-risk group.

Follow-up assessments. Self-report measures and structured interviews were used to evaluate the mental health of the participants every 6 weeks for the first two years and then every 16 weeks for an additional three years. The assessments were conducted by interviewers who were blind regarding the subjects' risk group status. The present report summarized the followup data for the first two and one-half years of the study.

Results

The data for students who had no prior history of depression showed dramatic differences between the high-risk and low-risk groups in vulnerability to depression. During the relatively brief 2.5-year period, a major depressive disorder emerged in 17% of the high-risk students in comparison to only 1% of the low-risk students. The high-risk subjects also displayed a much greater incidence of minor depressive episodes, as you can see in the left panel of Figure 14.15. The right panel of Figure 14.15 shows the comparisons for participants who had a prior history of depression (but were not depressed or suffering from any other disorder at the beginning of the study). The data show that high-risk subjects were more vulnerable to a recurrence of both major and minor depression during the 2.5 year followup.

Discussion

The high-risk participants, who exhibited a negative cognitive style, were consistently found to have an elevated likelihood of developing depressive disorders. Hence, the authors conclude that their results provide strong support for the cognitive vulnerability hypothesis, which asserts that negative thinking makes people more vulnerable to depression.

Comment

Previous studies of the correlation between negative thinking and depression used *retrospective designs,* which look backward in time from known outcomes.

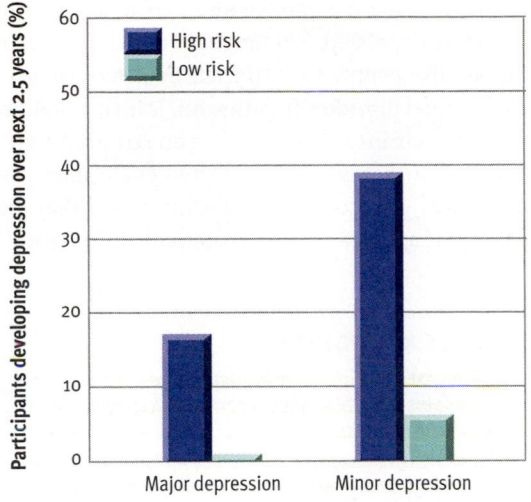

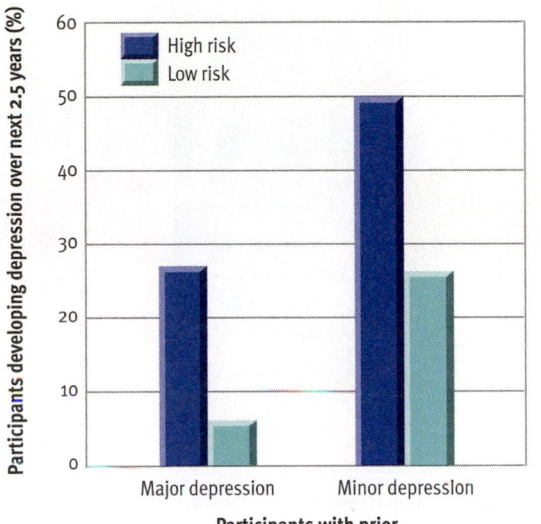

Participants with no prior
history of depression

Participants with prior
history of depression

For example, investigators might compare depressed subjects versus nondepressed subjects on some measure of negative thinking. What makes the design retrospective is that the researchers already know which people experienced the outcome of depression. Retrospective designs can yield useful information, but they don't provide much insight about causation. Why? Because if you find an association between depression and negative thinking you can't determine whether the negative thinking preceded the depression or the depression preceded the negative thinking. The present study used a *prospective design,* which moves forward in time, testing hypotheses about future outcomes. Prospective studies are much more difficult and time-consuming to conduct, but they can provide more insight about causation because they can show that one event (in this instance, the development of a negative cognitive style) preceded another (the occurrence of depression). The data are still correlational, so they cannot definitively establish a causal link, but they provide much stronger evidence in favor of causation than retrospective data. Thus, the research by Alloy and her colleagues provides the best evidence to date in support of the hypothesis that negative thinking contributes to the causation of depressive disorders. ∎

Interpersonal Roots

Behavioral approaches to understanding depression emphasize how inadequate social skills put people on the road to depressive disorders (see Figure 14.16 on the next page; Coyne, 1999). According to this notion, depression-prone people lack the social finesse needed to acquire many important kinds of reinforcers, such as good friends, top jobs, and desirable spouses. This paucity of reinforcers could understandably lead to negative emotions and depression. Consistent with this theory, researchers have found correlations between poor social skills and depression (Ingram, Scott, & Siegle, 1999).

Another interpersonal factor is that depressed people tend to be depressing (Joiner & Katz, 1999). Individuals suffering from depression often are irritable and pessimistic. They complain a lot and aren't particularly enjoyable companions. As a consequence, depressed people tend to court rejection from those around them (Joiner & Metalsky, 1995). Depressed people thus have fewer sources of social support than nondepressed people. Social rejection and lack of support may in turn aggravate and deepen a person's depression (Potthoff, Holahan, & Joiner, 1995). To compound these problems, evidence indicates that depressed people may gravitate to partners who view them unfavorably and hence reinforce their negative views of themselves (Joiner, 2002).

Precipitating Stress

Mood disorders sometimes appear mysteriously in people who are leading benign, nonstressful lives. For

Web Link 14.5

Dr. Ivan's Depression Central Some might suggest psychiatrist Ivan Goldberg's site would be better titled "Everything You Ever Wanted to Know About Depression." He offers a great depth of resources regarding mood disorders.

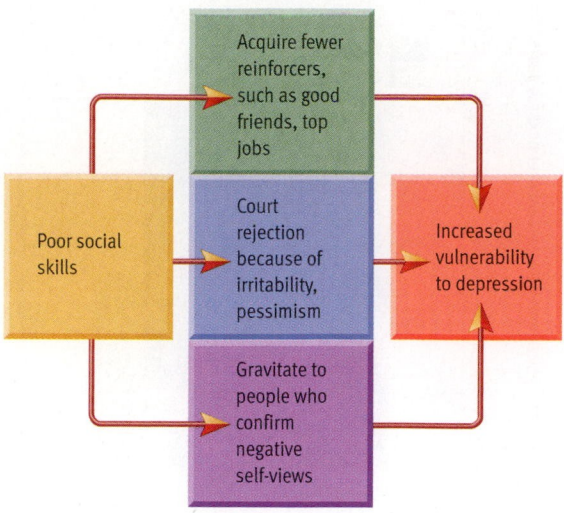

Figure 14.16

Interpersonal factors in depression. Behavioral theories about the etiology of depression emphasize how inadequate social skills may contribute to the development of the disorder through several mechanisms, as diagrammed here.

this reason, experts used to believe that mood disorders are not influenced much by stress. However, advances in the measurement of personal stress have altered this picture. The evidence available today suggests the existence of a moderately strong link between stress and the onset of mood disorders (Kendler, Karkowski, & Prescott, 1999; Kessler, 1997). Stress also appears to affect how people with mood disorders respond to treatment and whether they experience a relapse of their disorder (Monroe & Hadjiyannakis, 2002).

Of course, many people endure great stress without getting depressed. The impact of stress varies, in part, because people vary in their degree of *vulnerability* to mood disorders (Lewinsohn, Joiner, & Rohde, 2001). Similar interactions between stress and vulnerability probably influence the development of many kinds of disorders, including those that are next on our agenda—the schizophrenic disorders.

REVIEW OF KEY POINTS

- The principal mood disorders are depressive disorder, dysthymic disorder, bipolar disorder, and cyclothymic disorder. Mood disorders are episodic.

- Major depressive disorder is marked by profound sadness, slowed thought processes, low self-esteem, and loss of interest in previous sources of pleasure. Unipolar depression is more common than bipolar disorder, and it appears to be increasing in prevalence.

- Bipolar disorder is marked by the experience of both depressed and manic episodes. Manic episodes are characterized by inflated self-esteem, high energy, grandiose plans, and racing thoughts.

- Evidence indicates that people vary in their genetic vulnerability to mood disorders. These disorders are accompanied by changes in neurochemical activity in the brain. Abnormalities at norepinephrine and serotonin synapses appear particularly critical.

- Cognitive models posit that negative thinking contributes to depression. A pessimistic explanatory style has been implicated, as has a tendency to ruminate about one's problems. Our Featured Study reported impressive new evidence in support of the cognitive vulnerability hypothesis of depression.

- Interpersonal inadequacies may contribute to depressive disorders. Poor social skills may lead to a paucity of life's reinforcers and frequent rejection. The development of mood disorders is also affected by personal stress.

Schizophrenic Disorders ⬤SIM9

PREVIEW QUESTIONS
- What are the general symptoms of schizophrenia?
- What are the four subtypes of schizophrenic disorders, and what are their chief symptoms?
- What is known about the course and outcome of schizophrenia?
- Which biological factors have been implicated in schizophrenic disorders?
- What is the neurodevelopmental hypothesis of schizophrenia?
- How do family dynamics and stress contribute to schizophrenic disorders?

Literally, *schizophrenia* means "split mind." However, when Eugen Bleuler coined the term in 1911 he was referring to the fragmentation of thought processes seen in the disorder—not to a "split personality." Unfortunately, writers in the popular media often assume that the split-mind notion, and thus schizophrenia, refers to the rare syndrome in which a person manifests two or more personalities. As you have already learned, this syndrome is actually called *dissociative identity disorder* or *multiple-personality disorder*. Schizophrenia is a much more common, and altogether different, type of disorder.

Schizophrenic disorders **are a class of disorders marked by delusions, hallucinations, disorganized speech, and deterioration of adaptive behavior.** Peo-

ple with schizophrenic disorders often display some of the same symptoms seen in people with severe mood disorders; however, disturbed *thought* lies at the core of schizophrenic disorders, whereas disturbed *emotion* lies at the core of mood disorders.

How common is schizophrenia? Prevalence estimates suggest that about 1% of the population may suffer from schizophrenic disorders (Jablensky, 1999). That may not sound like much, but it means that in the United States alone there may be several million people troubled by schizophrenic disturbances. Moreover, schizophrenia is an extremely costly illness for society, because it is a severe, debilitating illness that tends to have an early onset and often requires lengthy hospital care (Buchanan & Carpenter, 2000).

General Symptoms

There are a number of distinct schizophrenic syndromes, but they share some general characteristics that we will examine before looking at the subtypes. Many of these characteristics are apparent in the following case history (adapted from Sheehan, 1982).

Sylvia was first given a diagnosis of schizophrenia at age 15. She has been in and out of many types of psychiatric facilities since then. She has never been able to hold a job for any length of time. During severe flare-ups of her disorder, her personal hygiene deteriorates. She rarely washes, she wears clothes that neither fit nor match, she smears makeup on heavily but randomly, and she slops food all over herself. Sylvia occasionally hears voices talking to her. She tends to be argumentative, aggressive, and emotionally volatile. Over the years, she has been involved in innumerable fights with fellow patients, psychiatric staff members, and strangers. Her thoughts can be highly irrational, as is apparent from the following quote, which was recorded while she was a patient in a psychiatric facility called Creedmoor:

"Mick Jagger wants to marry me. If I have Mick Jagger, I don't have to covet Geraldo Rivera. Mick Jagger is St. Nicholas and the Maharishi is Santa Claus. I want to form a gospel rock group called the Thorn Oil, but Geraldo wants me to be the music critic on Eyewitness News, so what can I do? Got to listen to my boyfriend. Teddy Kennedy cured me of my ugliness. I'm pregnant with the son of God. I'm going to marry David Berkowitz and get it over with. Creedmoor is the headquarters of the American Nazi Party. They're eating the patients here. Archie Bunker wants me to play his niece on his TV show. I work for Epic Records. I'm Joan of Arc. I'm Florence Nightingale. The door between the ward and the porch is the dividing line between New York and California. Divorce isn't a piece of paper, it's a feeling. Forget about Zip Codes. I need shock treatments. The body is run by electricity. My wiring is all faulty." (Sheehan, 1982, pp. 104–105)

Sylvia's case clearly shows that schizophrenic thinking can be bizarre and that schizophrenia can be a severe and debilitating disorder. Although no single symptom is inevitably present, the following symptoms are commonly seen in schizophrenia (Black & Andreasen, 1999; Cancro & Lehmann, 2000).

Delusions and Irrational Thought

Disturbed, irrational thought processes are the central feature of schizophrenic disorders. Various kinds of delusions are common. *Delusions* are false beliefs that are maintained even though they clearly are out of touch with reality. For example, one patient's delusion that he is a tiger (with a deformed body) persisted for more than 15 years (Kulick, Pope, & Keck, 1990). More typically, affected persons believe that their private thoughts are being broadcast to other people, that thoughts are being injected into their mind against their will, or that their thoughts are being controlled by some external force (Maher, 2001). In *delusions of grandeur,* people maintain that they are famous or important. Sylvia expressed an endless array of grandiose delusions, such as thinking that Mick Jagger wanted to marry her, that she had dictated the hobbit stories to J. R. R. Tolkien, and that she was going to win the Nobel prize for medicine.

Another characteristic of schizophrenia is that the person's train of thought deteriorates. Thinking becomes chaotic rather than logical and linear. There is a "loosening of associations," as people shift topics in disjointed ways. The quotation from Sylvia illustrates this symptom dramatically. The entire quote involves a wild flight of ideas, but at one point (beginning with the sentence "Creedmoor is the headquarters . . .") she rattles off ten consecutive sentences that have no apparent connection to each other.

Deterioration of Adaptive Behavior

Schizophrenia usually involves a noticeable deterioration in the quality of the person's routine functioning in work, social relations, and personal care. Friends will often make remarks such as "Hal just isn't himself anymore." This deterioration is readily apparent in Sylvia's inability to get along with others or to function in the work world. It's also apparent in her neglect of personal hygiene.

Hallucinations

A variety of perceptual distortions may occur with schizophrenia, the most common being auditory hallucinations. *Hallucinations* are sensory perceptions that occur in the absence of a real, external stimulus or are gross distortions of perceptual input. People with schizophrenia frequently report that they hear voices of nonexistent or absent people talking to them. Sylvia, for instance, said she heard messages from Paul McCartney. These voices often provide an insulting, running commentary on the person's behavior ("You're an idiot for shaking his hand"). They may be argumentative ("You don't need a bath"), and they may issue commands ("Prepare your home for visitors from outer space").

Courtesy of Nancy Andreasen

"Schizophrenia disfigures the emotional and cognitive faculties of its victims, and sometimes nearly destroys them."
NANCY ANDREASEN

Disturbed Emotion

Normal emotional tone can be disrupted in schizophrenia in a variety of ways. Although it may not be an accurate indicator of their underlying emotional experience (Kring, 1999), some victims show little emotional responsiveness, a symptom referred to as "blunted or flat affect." Others show inappropriate emotional responses that don't jibe with the situation or with what they are saying. For instance, a schizophrenic patient might cry over a silly cartoon and then laugh about a news story describing a child's tragic death. People with schizophrenia may also become emotionally volatile. This pattern was displayed by Sylvia, who often overreacted emotionally in erratic, unpredictable ways.

Subtypes, Course, and Outcome

Four subtypes of schizophrenic disorders are recognized, including a category for people who don't fit neatly into any of the first three categories. The major symptoms of each subtype are as follows (Black & Andreasen, 1999).

Paranoid Type

As its name implies, *paranoid schizophrenia* **is dominated by delusions of persecution, along with delusions of grandeur.** In this common form of schizophrenia, people come to believe that they have many enemies who want to harass and oppress them. They may become suspicious of friends and relatives or they may attribute the persecution to mysterious, unknown persons. They are convinced that they are being watched and manipulated in malicious ways. To make sense of this persecution, they often develop delusions of grandeur. They believe that they must be enormously important people, frequently seeing themselves as great inventors or as famous religious or political leaders. For example, in the case described at the beginning of the chapter, Ed's belief that he was president of the United States was a delusion of grandeur.

Catatonic Type

Catatonic schizophrenia **is marked by striking motor disturbances, ranging from muscular rigidity to random motor activity.** Some patients go into an extreme form of withdrawal known as a catatonic stupor. They may remain virtually motionless and seem oblivious to the environment around them for long periods of time. Others go into a state of catatonic excitement. They become hyperactive and incoher-

ent. Some alternate between these dramatic extremes. The catatonic subtype is not particularly common, and its prevalence seems to be declining.

Disorganized Type

In *disorganized schizophrenia,* **a particularly severe deterioration of adaptive behavior is seen.** Prominent symptoms include emotional indifference, frequent incoherence, and virtually complete social withdrawal. Aimless babbling and giggling are common. Delusions often center on bodily functions ("My brain is melting out my ears").

Undifferentiated Type

People who are clearly schizophrenic but who cannot be placed into any of the three previous categories are said to have *undifferentiated schizophrenia,* **which is marked by idiosyncratic mixtures of schizophrenic symptoms.** The undifferentiated subtype is fairly common.

Positive Versus Negative Symptoms

Many theorists have raised doubts about the value of dividing schizophrenic disorders into the four subtypes just described (Sanislow & Carson, 2001). Critics note that the catatonic subtype is disappearing and that undifferentiated cases aren't so much a subtype as a hodgepodge of "leftovers." Critics also point out that there aren't meaningful differences between the subtypes in etiology, prognosis, or response to treatment. The absence of such differences casts doubt on the value of the current classification scheme.

Because of such problems, Nancy Andreasen (1990) and others (Carpenter, 1992; McGlashan & Fenton, 1992) have proposed an alternative approach to subtyping. This new scheme divides schizophrenic disorders into just two categories based on the predominance of negative versus positive symptoms. *Negative symptoms* involve behavioral deficits, such as flattened emotions, social withdrawal, apathy, impaired attention, and poverty of speech. *Positive symptoms* involve behavioral excesses or peculiarities, such as hallucinations, delusions, bizarre behavior, and wild flights of ideas.

Theorists advocating this scheme hoped to find consistent differences between the two subtypes in etiology, prognosis, and response to treatment, and some progress along these lines *has* been made. For example, a predominance of positive symptoms is associated with better adjustment prior to the onset of schizophrenia and greater responsiveness to treatment (Cuesta, Peralta, & DeLeon, 1994; Fenton

& McGlashan, 1994). However, the assumption that patients can be placed into discrete categories based on this scheme now seems untenable. Most patients exhibit both types of symptoms and vary only in the *degree* to which positive or negative symptoms dominate (Black & Andreasen, 1999). Moreover, there is some debate about which symptoms should be classified as positive and which should be regarded as negative, and some theorists have proposed a third category of symptoms reflecting *disorganization* of behavior (Toomey et al., 1997). Although it seems fair to say that the distinction between positive and negative symptoms is enhancing our understanding of schizophrenia, it has not yielded a classification scheme that can replace the traditional subtypes of schizophrenia.

Course and Outcome

Schizophrenic disorders usually emerge during adolescence or early adulthood and only infrequently after age 45 (Howard et al., 1993). The emergence of schizophrenia may be sudden or gradual. Once it clearly emerges, the course of schizophrenia is variable (Norman & Malla, 1995), but patients tend to fall into three broad groups. Some patients, presumably those with milder disorders, are treated successfully and enjoy a full recovery. Other patients experience a partial recovery, but they have frequent relapses and are in and out of treatment facilities for much of the remainder of their lives. Finally, a third group of patients endure chronic illness that sometimes results in permanent hospitalization. Research suggests that perhaps as many as one-half of schizophrenic patients experience a reasonable recovery (Hegarty et al., 1994). For unknown reasons, gender is associated with the course and outcome of schizophrenia. The differences are modest, but in comparison to females, males tend to have an earlier onset of the disease, more hospitalizations, and higher relapse rates (Szymanski et al., 1995).

A number of factors are related to the likelihood of recovery from schizophrenic disorders (Cancro & Lehmann, 2000; Ho et al., 1998). A patient has a relatively *favorable prognosis* when (1) the onset of the disorder has been sudden rather than gradual, (2) the onset has occurred at a later age, (3) the patient's social and work adjustment were relatively good prior to the onset of the disorder, (4) the proportion of negative symptoms is relatively low, and (5) the patient has a relatively healthy, supportive family situation to return to. Most of these predictors are concerned with the etiology of schizophrenic illness, which is the matter we turn to next.

John Nash, the Nobel Prize-winning mathematician whose story was told in the film A Beautiful Mind, *has struggled with paranoid schizophrenia since 1959.*

Etiology of Schizophrenia

You can probably identify, at least to some extent, with people who suffer from mood disorders, somatoform disorders, and anxiety disorders. You can probably imagine events that could unfold that might leave you struggling with depression, grappling with anxiety, or worrying about your physical health. But what could possibly have led Ed to believe that he had been fighting space wars and vampires? What could account for Sylvia's thinking that she was Joan of Arc or that she had dictated the hobbit novels to Tolkien? As mystifying as these delusions may seem, you'll see that the etiology of schizophrenic disorders is not all that different from the etiology of other psychological disorders. We'll begin our discussion by examining the matter of genetic vulnerability.

Genetic Vulnerability

Evidence is plentiful that hereditary factors play a role in the development of schizophrenic disorders (Kendler, 2000). For instance, in twin studies, concordance rates average around 48% for identical twins, in comparison to about 17% for fraternal twins (Gottesman, 1991, 2001). Studies also indicate that a child born to two schizophrenic parents has about a 46% probability of developing a schizophrenic disorder

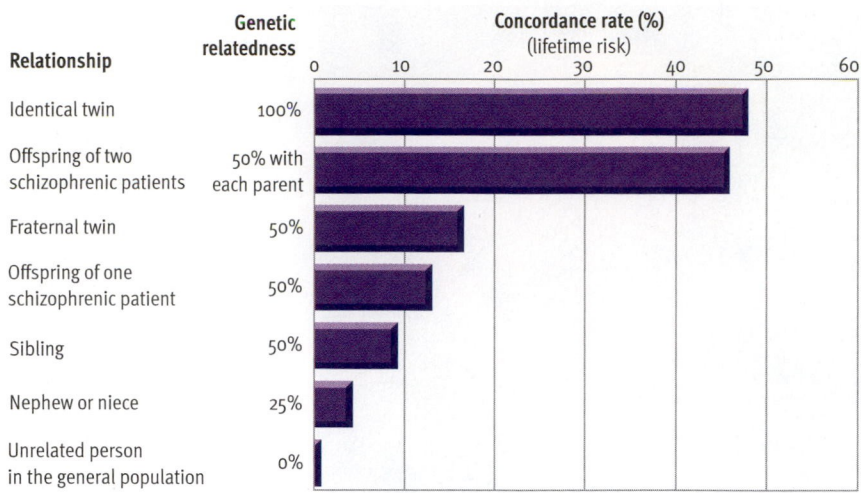

Relationship	Genetic relatedness	Concordance rate (%) (lifetime risk)
Identical twin	100%	
Offspring of two schizophrenic patients	50% with each parent	
Fraternal twin	50%	
Offspring of one schizophrenic patient	50%	
Sibling	50%	
Nephew or niece	25%	
Unrelated person in the general population	0%	

Figure 14.17

Genetic vulnerability to schizophrenic disorders. Relatives of schizophrenic patients have an elevated risk for schizophrenia. This risk is greater among closer relatives. Although environment also plays a role in the etiology of schizophrenia, the concordance rates shown here suggest that there must be a genetic vulnerability to the disorder. These concordance estimates are based on pooled data from 40 studies conducted between 1920 and 1987. (Data from Gottesman, 1991)

(as compared to the probability in the general population of about 1%). These and other findings that demonstrate the genetic roots of schizophrenia are summarized in Figure 14.17. Overall, the picture is similar to that seen for mood disorders. Several converging lines of evidence indicate that some people inherit a polygenically transmitted *vulnerability* to schizophrenia (Schneider & Deldin, 2001). Although some theorists suspect that genetic factors may account for as much as two-thirds of the variability in susceptibility to schizophrenia, genetic mapping studies have made little progress in identifying the specific genes at work (Levinson et al., 1998; Owen & O'Donovan, 2003).

Neurochemical Factors

 11c

Like mood disorders, schizophrenic disorders appear to be accompanied by changes in the activity of one or more neurotransmitters in the brain (Knable, Kleinman, & Weinberger, 1995). Excess *dopamine* activity has been implicated as a possible cause of schizophrenia, as discussed in Figure 14.18 (Abi-Dargham et al.,

Figure 14.18

The dopamine hypothesis as an explanation for schizophrenia. Decades of research have implicated overactivity at dopamine synapses as a key cause of schizophrenic disorders. However, the evidence on the exact mechanisms underlying this overactivity, which is summarized in this graphic, is complex and open to debate. Recent hypotheses about the neurochemical bases of schizophrenia go beyond the simple assumption that dopamine activity is increased. For example, one theory posits that schizophrenia may be accompanied by decreased dopamine activity in one area of the brain (the prefrontal cortex) and increased activity or dysregulation in other areas of the brain (Egan & Hyde, 2000). Moreover, abnormalities in other neurotransmitter systems may also contribute to schizophrenia.

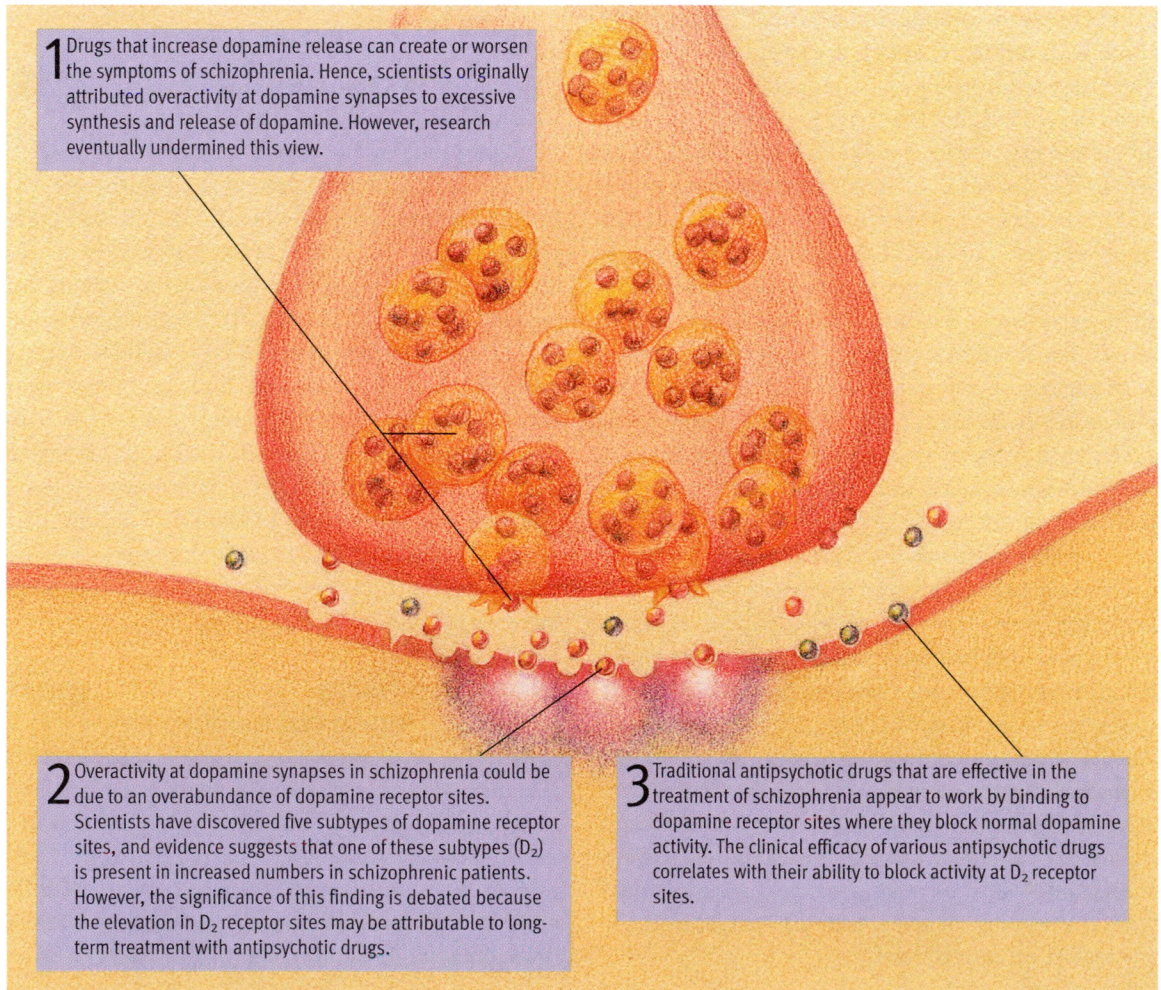

1 Drugs that increase dopamine release can create or worsen the symptoms of schizophrenia. Hence, scientists originally attributed overactivity at dopamine synapses to excessive synthesis and release of dopamine. However, research eventually undermined this view.

2 Overactivity at dopamine synapses in schizophrenia could be due to an overabundance of dopamine receptor sites. Scientists have discovered five subtypes of dopamine receptor sites, and evidence suggests that one of these subtypes (D_2) is present in increased numbers in schizophrenic patients. However, the significance of this finding is debated because the elevation in D_2 receptor sites may be attributable to long-term treatment with antipsychotic drugs.

3 Traditional antipsychotic drugs that are effective in the treatment of schizophrenia appear to work by binding to dopamine receptor sites where they block normal dopamine activity. The clinical efficacy of various antipsychotic drugs correlates with their ability to block activity at D_2 receptor sites.

1998). This hypothesis makes sense because most of the drugs that are useful in the treatment of schizophrenia are known to dampen dopamine activity in the brain (Tamminga, 1999). However, the evidence linking schizophrenia to high dopamine levels is riddled with inconsistencies, complexities, and interpretive problems (Egan & Hyde, 2000). Researchers are currently exploring how interactions between the dopamine and serotonin neurotransmitter systems may contribute to schizophrenia (Byne et al., 1999). Recent research has also suggested that abnormalities in neural circuits using *glutamate* as a neurotransmitter may play a role in schizophrenic disturbance (Goff & Coyle, 2001). Thus, investigators are gradually making progress in their search for the neurochemical bases of schizophrenia.

Structural Abnormalities in the Brain

11c

For decades, studies have suggested that individuals with schizophrenia exhibit a variety of deficits in attention, perception, and information processing (Bellack, Gearon, & Blanchard, 2000). These cognitive deficits suggest that schizophrenic disorders may be caused by neurological defects (Perry & Braff, 1994). Until recent decades this theory was based more on speculation than on actual research. Now, however, advances in brain-imaging technology have yielded mountains of intriguing data. The most reliable finding is that CT scans and MRI scans (see Chapter 3) suggest an association between enlarged brain ventricles (the hollow, fluid-filled cavities in the brain depicted in Figure 14.19) and schizophrenic disturbance (Egan & Hyde, 2000). Enlarged ventricles are assumed to reflect the degeneration of nearby brain tissue. The significance of enlarged ventricles is hotly debated, however. This structural deterioration (or failure to develop) could be a *consequence* of schizophrenia, or it could be a contributing *cause* of the illness.

Brain-imaging studies have also uncovered structural and metabolic abnormalities in the temporal and frontal lobes of individuals with schizophrenia. Although the research results are not entirely consistent, schizophrenia appears to be associated with reduced metabolic activity in an area of the prefrontal cortex and with increased metabolic activity in an area of the temporal lobe (Egan & Hyde, 2000). Theorists speculate that the frontal lobe dysfunction contributes to positive symptoms and that the temporal lobe dysfunction underlies negative symptoms (Conklin & Iacono, 2002). Scientists are also intrigued by the fact that a major dopamine pathway runs through the area in the prefrontal cortex where metabolic abnormalities have been found. There may be a connection between the abnormal dopamine activity implicated in schizophrenia and the dysfunctional metabolic activity seen in this area of the prefrontal cortex (Conklin & Iacono, 2002).

The Neurodevelopmental Hypothesis

In recent years, several new lines of evidence have led to the emergence of the *neurodevelopmental hypothesis* of schizophrenia, which posits that schizophrenia is caused in part by various disruptions in the normal maturational processes of the brain before or at birth (Brown, 1999). According to this hypothesis, insults to the brain during sensitive phases of prenatal development or during birth can cause subtle neurological damage that elevates individuals' vulnerability to schizophrenia years later in adolescence and early adulthood (see Figure 14.20). What are the sources of these early insults to the brain? Thus far, research has focused on viral infections or malnutrition during prenatal development and obstetrical complications during the birth process.

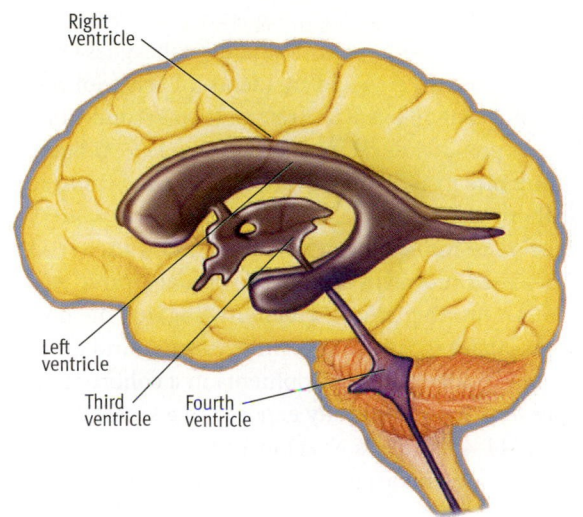

Figure 14.19

Schizophrenia and the ventricles of the brain. Cerebrospinal fluid (CSF) circulates around the brain and spinal cord. The hollow cavities in the brain filled with CSF are called ventricles. The four ventricles in the human brain are depicted here. Recent studies with CT scans and MRI scans suggest that there is an association between enlarged ventricles in the brain and the occurrence of schizophrenic disturbance.

SOURCE: Graphic adapted from Starr, C., & Taggart, R. (1998). *Biology: The unity and diversity of life.* Belmont, CA: Wadsworth. © 1998 Wadsworth Publishing. Reprinted by permission.

Figure 14.20

The neurodevelopmental hypothesis of schizophrenia. Recent findings have suggested that insults to the brain sustained during prenatal development or at birth may disrupt crucial maturational processes in the brain, resulting in subtle neurological damage that gradually becomes apparent as youngsters develop. This neurological damage is believed to increase both vulnerability to schizophrenia and the incidence of minor physical anomalies (slight anatomical defects of the head, face, hands, and feet).

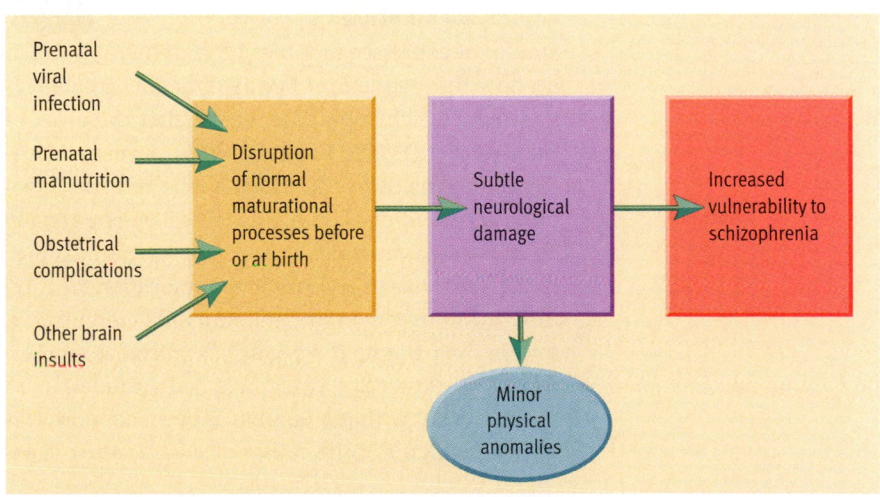

The evidence on viral infections has been building since Sarnoff Mednick and his colleagues (1988) discovered an elevated incidence of schizophrenia among individuals who were in their second trimester of prenatal development during a 1957 influenza epidemic in Finland. Several subsequent studies in other locations have also found a link between exposure to influenza during the second trimester and increased prevalence of schizophrenia (Torrey et al., 1994). Another study, which investigated the possible impact of prenatal malnutrition, found an elevated incidence of schizophrenia in a cohort of people who were prenatally exposed to a severe famine in 1944–45 due to a Nazi blockade of food deliveries in the Netherlands during World War II (Susser et al., 1996). A follow-up study of some schizophrenic patients exposed to this famine found increased brain abnormalities among the patients, as the neurodevelopmental hypothesis would predict (Hulshoff et al., 2000). Other research has shown that schizophrenic patients are more likely than control subjects to have a history of obstetrical complications (Geddes & Lawrie, 1995; Rosso et al., 2000). Finally, research suggests that minor physical anomalies (slight anatomical defects of the head, hands, feet, and face) that would be consistent with prenatal neurological damage are more common among people with schizophrenia than among others (McNeil, Canton-Graae, & Ismail, 2000; Schiffman et al., 2002).

Collectively, these diverse studies argue for a relationship between early neurological trauma and a predisposition to schizophrenia (Mednick et al., 1998). However, much remains to be learned. For example, a recent study suggests that early neurological damage may increase vulnerability to *mood disorders,* as well as schizophrenia (Brown et al., 2000). Nonetheless, this new line of inquiry promises to increase our understanding of the etiology of schizophrenia.

Expressed Emotion

Studies of expressed emotion have primarily focused on how this element of family dynamics influences the *course* of schizophrenic illness, after the onset of the disorder (Leff & Vaughn, 1985). *Expressed emotion (EE)* is the degree to which a relative of a schizophrenic patient displays highly critical or emotionally overinvolved attitudes toward the patient. Audiotaped interviews of relatives' communication are carefully evaluated for critical comments, resentment toward the patient, and excessive emotional involvement (overprotective, overconcerned attitudes).

Studies show that a family's expressed emotion is a good predictor of the course of a schizophrenic patient's illness (Hooley & Candela, 1999). After release from a hospital, people with schizophrenia who return to a family high in expressed emotion show relapse rates about three times that of patients who return to a family low in expressed emotion (see Figure 14.21; Hooley & Hiller, 1998). Part of the problem for patients returning to homes high in expressed emotion is that their families are probably sources of more stress than of social support (Cutting & Docherty, 2000). However, Rosenfarb et al. (1995) caution against placing all the blame on the families high in expressed emotion. They found that patients returning to high-EE homes exhibited more odd and disruptive behavior than patients returning to low-EE homes. Thus, the more critical, negative attitudes experienced by patients in high-EE homes may be caused in part by their own behavior.

Precipitating Stress

Most theories of schizophrenia assume that stress plays a key role in triggering schizophrenic disorders (Walker, Baum, & Diforio, 1998). According to this notion, various biological and psychological factors influence individuals' *vulnerability* to schizophrenia. High stress may then serve to precipitate a schizophrenic disorder in someone who is vulnerable (McGlashan & Hoffman, 2000). Research indicates that high stress can also trigger relapses in patients who have made progress toward recovery (Ventura et al., 1989).

Schizophrenia is the last of the major, Axis I diagnostic categories that we will consider. We'll complete our overview of various types of abnormal behavior with a brief look at the personality disorders. These disorders are recorded on Axis II in the DSM classification system.

Figure 14.21

Expressed emotion and relapse rates in schizophrenia.
Schizophrenic patients who return to a home that is high in expressed emotion have higher relapse rates than those who return to a home low in expressed emotion. Thus, unhealthy family dynamics can influence the course of schizophrenia. (Data adapted from Leff & Vaughn, 1981)

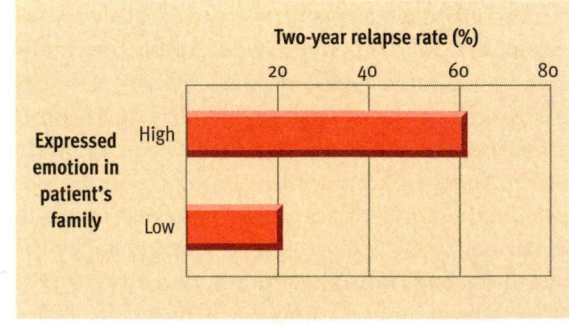

Distinguishing Schizophrenic and Mood Disorders

Check your understanding of the nature of schizophrenic and mood disorders by making preliminary diagnoses for the cases described below. Read each case summary and write your tentative diagnosis in the space provided. The answers are in Appendix A.

1. Max hasn't slept in four days. He's determined to write the "great American novel" before his class reunion, which is a few months away. He expounds eloquently on his novel to anyone who will listen, talking at such a rapid pace that no one can get a word in edgewise. He feels like he's wired with energy and is supremely confident about the novel, even though he's only written 10 to 20 pages. Last week, he charged $8000 worth of new computer software, which is supposed to help him write his book.

   Preliminary diagnosis: _____

2. Eduardo maintains that he invented the atomic bomb, even though he was born after its invention. He says he invented it to punish homosexuals, Nazis, and short people. It's short people that he's really afraid of. He's sure that all the short people on TV are talking about him. He thinks that short people are conspiring to make him look like a Republican. Eduardo frequently gets in arguments with people and is emotionally volatile. His grooming is poor, but he says it's okay because he's the secretary of state.

   Preliminary diagnosis: _____

3. Margaret has hardly gotten out of bed for weeks, although she's troubled by insomnia. She doesn't feel like eating and has absolutely no energy. She feels dejected, discouraged, spiritless, and apathetic. Friends stop by to try to cheer her up, but she tells them not to waste their time on "pond scum."

   Preliminary diagnosis: _____

REVIEW OF KEY POINTS

- Schizophrenic disorders are characterized by deterioration of adaptive behavior, irrational thought, delusions, hallucinations, and disturbed mood.
- Schizophrenic disorders are classified as paranoid, catatonic, disorganized, or undifferentiated. A new classification scheme based on the predominance of positive versus negative symptoms is under study. Schizophrenic disorders usually emerge during adolescence or young adulthood.
- Research has linked schizophrenia to a genetic vulnerability and changes in neurotransmitter activity at dopamine synapses. Structural abnormalities in the brain, such as enlarged ventricles, are associated with schizophrenia, but their significance is unclear.
- The neurodevelopmental hypothesis of schizophrenia asserts that schizophrenia is attributable to disruptions in the normal maturational processes of the brain before or at birth that are caused by prenatal viral infections, obstetrical complications, and other insults to the brain.
- Precipitating stress and unhealthy family dynamics (high expressed emotion), may also contribute to the development of schizophrenia.

Personality Disorders

We have seen repeatedly that it is often difficult to draw that imaginary line between healthy and disordered behavior. This is especially true in the case of personality disorders, which are relatively mild disturbances in comparison to most of the Axis I disorders. *Personality disorders* are a class of disorders marked by extreme, inflexible personality traits that cause subjective distress or impaired social and occupational functioning. Essentially, people with these disorders display certain personality traits to an excessive degree and in rigid ways that undermine their adjustment. Personality disorders usually emerge during late childhood or adolescence and often continue throughout adulthood. It is difficult to estimate the prevalence of these subtle disorders, but it is clear that they are common (Mattia & Zimmerman, 2001).

DSM-IV lists ten personality disorders. These disorders are described briefly in Table 14.2 on the next page. If you examine this table, you will find a diverse collection of maladaptive personality syndromes. You may also notice that some personality disorders essentially are mild versions of more severe Axis I disorders. Some of these disorders are more common in men and some in women, as the figures in the far right column of the table indicate.

PREVIEW QUESTIONS

- What are the three clusters of personality disorders?
- What is the major diagnostic challenge with personality disorders?
- What are the symptoms of antisocial personality disorder?
- What factors have been implicated in the etiology of antisocial personality disorders?

Table 14.2 Personality Disorders

Cluster	Disorder	Description	% Male/% Female
Anxious/fearful	Avoidant personality disorder	Excessively sensitive to potential rejection, humiliation, or shame; socially withdrawn in spite of desire for acceptance from others	50/50
	Dependent personality disorder	Excessively lacking in self-reliance and self-esteem; passively allowing others to make all decisions; constantly subordinating own needs to others' needs	31/69
	Obsessive-compulsive personality disorder	Preoccupied with organization, rules, schedules, lists, trivial details; extremely conventional, serious, and formal; unable to express warm emotions	50/50
Odd/eccentric	Schizoid personality disorder	Defective in capacity for forming social relationships; showing absence of warm, tender feelings for others	78/22
	Schizotypal personality disorder	Showing social deficits and oddities of thinking, perception, and communication that resemble schizophrenia	55/45
	Paranoid personality disorder	Showing pervasive and unwarranted suspiciousness and mistrust of people; overly sensitive; prone to jealousy	67/33
Dramatic/impulsive	Histrionic personality disorder	Overly dramatic; tending to exaggerated expressions of emotion; egocentric, seeking attention	15/85
	Narcissistic personality disorder	Grandiosely self-important; preoccupied with success fantasies; expecting special treatment; lacking interpersonal empathy	70/30
	Borderline personality disorder	Unstable in self-image, mood, and interpersonal relationships; impulsive and unpredictable	38/62
	Antisocial personality disorder	Chronically violating the rights of others; failing to accept social norms, to form attachments to others, or to sustain consistent work behavior; exploitive and reckless	82/18

Source: Estimated gender ratios from Millon (1981)

The ten personality disorders are grouped into three related clusters, as shown in Table 14.2. The three disorders in the *anxious/fearful cluster* are marked by maladaptive efforts to control anxiety and fear about social rejection. People with the three disorders in the *odd/eccentric cluster* are distrustful, socially aloof, and unable to connect with others emotionally. The four personality disorders in the *dramatic/impulsive cluster* have less in common with each other than those grouped in the first two clusters. The histrionic and narcissistic personalities share a flair for overdramatizing everything. Impulsiveness is the common ground shared by the borderline and antisocial personality disorders.

Diagnostic Problems

Many critics have argued that the personality disorders overlap too much with Axis I disorders and with each other (Dolan-Sewell, Krueger, & Shea, 2001).

The extent of this problem was documented in a study by Leslie Morey (1988). Morey reviewed the cases of 291 patients who had received a specific personality disorder diagnosis to see how many could have met the criteria for any of the other personality disorders. Morey found massive overlap among the diagnoses. For example, among patients with a diagnosis of histrionic personality disorder, 56% also qualified for a borderline disorder, 54% for a narcissistic disorder, 32% for an avoidant disorder, and 30% for a dependent disorder. Clearly, there are fundamental problems with Axis II as a classification system (Westen & Shedler, 1999). The overlap among the personality disorders makes it extremely difficult to achieve reliable diagnoses. Doubts have also been raised about the decision to place personality disorders on a separate axis, as there does not appear to be any fundamental distinction between personality disorders and Axis I disorders (Livesley, 2001).

In light of these problems, a variety of theorists have questioned the wisdom of the current *categorical approach* to describing personality disorders, which assumes (incorrectly, they argue) that people can reliably be placed in discontinuous (nonoverlapping) diagnostic categories (Trull & McCrae, 1994; Livesley, 2001). These theorists argue instead for a *dimensional approach,* which would describe personality disorders in terms of how people score on a limited number of continuous personality dimensions. The practical logistics of using a dimensional approach to describe personality disorders are formidable. In any event, debate about the classification of personality disorders is likely to continue and changes in the official diagnostic scheme will surely be seen in DSM-V (Widiger, 2001).

The difficulties involved in the diagnosis of personality disorders have clearly hindered research on their etiology and prognosis. The only personality disorder that has a long history of extensive research is the antisocial personality disorder, which we examine next.

Antisocial Personality Disorder

The antisocial personality disorder has a misleading name. The antisocial designation does *not* mean that people with this disorder shun social interaction. In fact, rather than shrinking from social interaction, many are sociable, friendly, and superficially charming. People with this disorder are *antisocial* in that they choose to *reject widely accepted social norms* regarding moral principles and behavior.

Description

People with antisocial personalities chronically violate the rights of others. They often use their social charm to cultivate others' liking or loyalty for purposes of exploitation. The ***antisocial personality disorder* is marked by impulsive, callous, manipulative, aggressive, and irresponsible behavior that reflects a failure to accept social norms.** Since they haven't accepted the social norms they violate, people with antisocial personalities rarely feel guilty about their transgressions. Essentially, they lack an adequate conscience. The antisocial personality disorder occurs much more frequently among males than females. Studies suggest that it is a moderately common disorder, seen in roughly 3%–4% of the population (Kessler et al., 1994).

Many people with antisocial personalities get involved in illegal activities. Moreover, antisocial personalities tend to begin their criminal careers at an early age, to commit offenses at a relatively high rate, and to be versatile offenders who get involved in many types of criminal activity (Hart & Hare, 1997). However, many people with antisocial personalities keep their exploitive, amoral behavior channeled within the boundaries of the law. Such people may even enjoy high status in our society. In other words, the concept of the antisocial personality disorder can apply to cut-throat business executives, scheming politicians, unprincipled lawyers, and money-hungry evangelists, as well as to con artists, drug dealers, thugs, burglars, and petty thieves.

People with antisocial personalities exhibit quite a variety of maladaptive traits (Hare, Cooke, & Hart, 1999; Sutker & Allain, 2001). Among other things, they rarely experience genuine affection for others. However, they may be skilled at faking affection so they can exploit people. Sexually, they are predatory and promiscuous. They also tend to be irresponsible and impulsive. They can tolerate little frustration, and they pursue immediate gratification. These characteristics make them unreliable employees, unfaithful spouses, inattentive parents, and undependable friends. Many people with antisocial personalities have a checkered history of divorce, child abuse, and job instability.

Etiology

Many theorists believe that biological factors contribute to the development of antisocial personality disorders. Twin and adoption studies suggest a genetic predisposition toward these disorders (Bock & Goode, 1996; Carey & Goldman, 1997). Hans Eysenck has noted that people with antisocial personalities lack the inhibitions that most of us have about violating moral standards. Their lack of inhibitions prompted Eysenck (1982) to theorize that such people might inherit relatively sluggish autonomic nervous systems, leading to slow acquisition of inhibitions through classical conditioning. The findings relating to this hypothesis are inconsistent, but the notion that antisocial personalities exhibit underarousal has received a fair amount of support (Raine, 1997). Research also suggests that subtle neurological damage that occurs during prenatal development or the early years of childhood is associated with an increased prevalence of antisocial behavior (Brennan & Mednick, 1997). As a whole, the evidence suggests that biological factors may create a genuine but weak predisposition toward antisocial behavior.

Efforts to relate psychological factors to antisocial behavior have emphasized inadequate socialization in dysfunctional family systems (Sutker, Bugg, & West,

Axis I category

Anxiety disorders

Edvard Munch's *The Scream* expresses overwhelming feelings of anxiety.

Mood disorders

Vincent van Gogh's *Portrait of Dr. Gachet* captures the profound dejection experienced in depressive disorders.

Schizophrenic disorders

The perceptual distortions seen in schizophrenia probably contributed to the bizarre imagery apparent in this portrait of a cat painted by Louis Wain.

Subtypes

Generalized anxiety disorder: Chronic, high level of anxiety not tied to any specific threat

Phobic disorder: Persistent, irrational fear of object or situation that presents no real danger

Panic disorder: Recurrent attacks of overwhelming anxiety that occur suddenly and unexpectedly

Obsessive-compulsive disorder: Persistent, uncontrollable intrusions of unwanted thoughts and urges to engage in senseless rituals

Major depressive disorder: Two or more major depressive episodes marked by feelings of sadness, worthlessness, despair

Bipolar disorder: One or more manic episodes marked by inflated self-esteem, grandiosity, and elevated mood and energy, usually accompanied by major depressive episodes

Paranoid schizophrenia: Delusions of persecution and delusions of grandeur; frequent auditory hallucinations

Catatonic schizophrenia: Motor disturbances ranging from immobility to excessive, purposeless activity

Disorganized schizophrenia: Flat or inappropriate emotions; disorganized speech and adaptive behavior

Undifferentiated schizophrenia: Idiosyncratic mixtures of schizophrenic symptoms that cannot be placed into above three categories

Prevalence/well-known victim

The famous industrialist Howard Hughes suffered from obsessive-compulsive disorder.

Actress Drew Barrymore has suffered from depression.

John Nash, the Nobel Prize-winning mathematician whose story was told in the film *A Beautiful Mind*, has struggled with schizophrenia.

Etiology: Biological factors

Genetic vulnerability: Twin studies and other evidence suggest a mild genetic predisposition to anxiety disorders.

Anxiety sensitivity: Oversensitivity to physical symptoms of anxiety may lead to overreactions to feelings of anxiety, so anxiety breeds more anxiety.

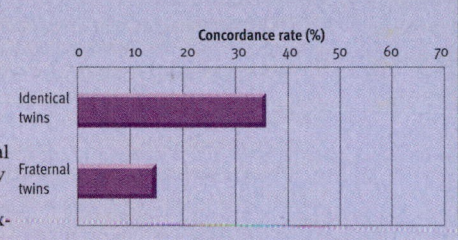

Concordance rate (%)

Neurochemical bases: Disturbances in neural circuits releasing GABA may contribute to some disorders; abnormalities at serotonin synapses have been implicated in panic and obsessive-compulsive disorders.

Genetic vulnerability: Twin studies and other evidence suggest a genetic predisposition to mood disorders.

Sleep disturbances: Disruption of biological rhythms and sleep patterns may lead to neurochemical changes that contribute to mood disorders.

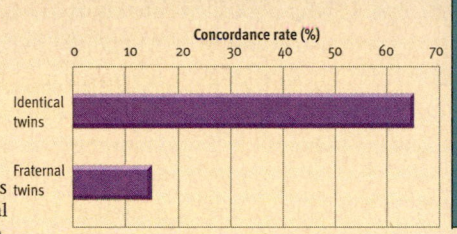

Concordance rate (%)

Neurochemical bases: Disturbances in neural circuits releasing norepinephrine may contribute to some mood disorders; abnormalties at serotonin synapses have also been implicated as a factor in depression.

Genetic vulnerability: Twin studies and other evidence suggest a genetic predisposition to schizophrenic disorders.

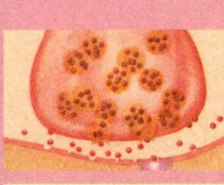
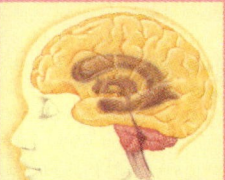

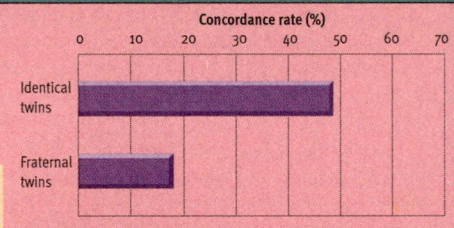

Concordance rate (%)

Neurochemical bases: Overactivity in neural circuits releasing dopamine is associated with schizophrenia; but abnormalities in other neurotransmitter systems may also contribute.

Structural abnormalities in brain: Enlarged brain ventricles are associated with schizophrenia, but they may be an effect rather than a cause of the disorder.

Etiology: Psychological factors

Learning: Many anxiety responses may be acquired through classical conditioning or observational learning; phobic responses may be maintained by operant reinforcement.

CS Snow

UCS Buried in avalanche

CR Fear UCR

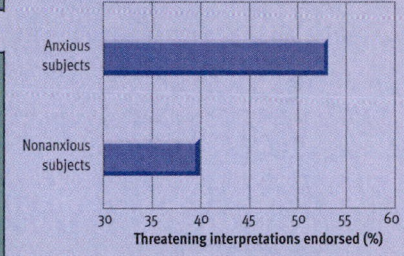

Threatening interpretations endorsed (%)

Stress: High stress may help to precipitate the onset of anxiety disorders.

Cognition: People who misinterpret harmless situations as threatening and who focus excessive attention on perceived threats are more vulnerable to anxiety disorders.

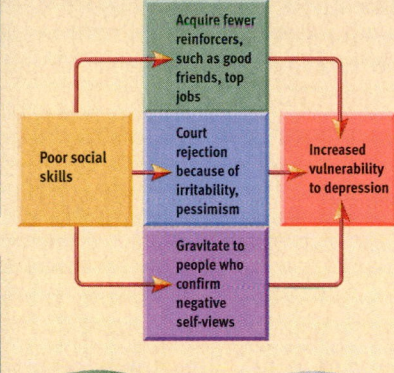

Poor social skills

Acquire fewer reinforcers, such as good friends, top jobs

Court rejection because of irritability, pessimism

Gravitate to people who confirm negative self-views

Increased vulnerability to depression

Negative thinking → Depression

Interpersonal roots: Behavioral theories emphasize how inadequate social skills can result in a paucity of reinforcers and other effects that make people vulnerable to depression.

Stress: High stress can act as precipitating factor that triggers depression or bipolar disorder.

Cognition: Negative thinking can contribute to the development of depression; rumination may extend and amplify depression.

Expressed emotion: A family's expressed emotion is a good predictor of the course of a schizophrenic patient's illness.

Stress: High stress can precipitate schizophrenic disorder in people who are vulnerable to schizophrenia.

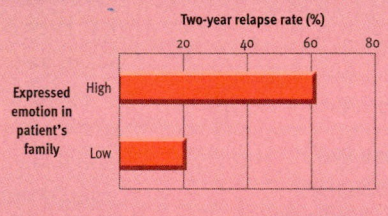

Two-year relapse rate (%)

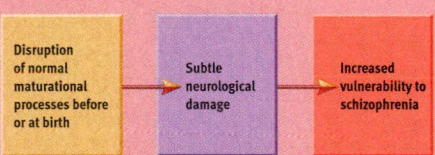

Disruption of normal maturational processes before or at birth

Subtle neurological damage

Increased vulnerability to schizophrenia

The neurodevelopmental hypothesis: Insults to the brain sustained during prenatal development or at birth may disrupt maturational processes in the brain resulting in elevated vulnerability to schizophrenia.

1993). It's easy to envision how antisocial traits could be fostered in homes where parents make haphazard or halfhearted efforts to socialize their children to be respectful, truthful, responsible, unselfish, and so forth. Consistent with this idea, studies find that individuals with antisocial personalities tend to come from homes where discipline is erratic or ineffective, and homes where they experience physical abuse and neglect (Luntz & Widom, 1994; Widom, 1997). Such people are also more likely to emerge from homes where one or both parents exhibit antisocial traits (Lahey et al., 1988). These parents presumably model exploitive, amoral behavior, which their children acquire through observational learning.

Psychological Disorders and the Law

Societies use laws to enforce their norms regarding appropriate behavior. Given this function, the law in our society has something to say about many issues related to abnormal behavior. In this section we examine the concepts of insanity and involuntary commitment.

Insanity

Insanity is *not* a diagnosis; it's a legal concept. *Insanity is a legal status indicating that a person cannot be held responsible for his or her actions because of mental illness.* Why is this an issue in the courtroom? Because criminal acts must be intentional. The law reasons that people who are "out of their mind" may not be able to appreciate the significance of what they're doing. The insanity defense is used in criminal trials by defendants who admit that they committed the crime but claim that they lacked intent.

No simple relationship exists between specific diagnoses of mental disorders and court findings of insanity. Most people with diagnosed psychological disorders would *not* qualify as insane. The people most likely to qualify are those troubled by severe disturbances that display delusional behavior. The courts apply various rules in making judgments about a defendant's sanity, depending on the jurisdiction. According to one widely used rule, called the *M'naghten rule, insanity exists when a mental disorder makes a person unable to distinguish right from wrong.* As you can imagine, evaluating insanity as defined in the M'naghten rule can be difficult for judges and jurors,

not to mention the psychologists and psychiatrists who are called into court as expert witnesses.

Although highly publicized and controversial, the insanity defense is actually used less frequently and less successfully than widely believed (see Figure 14.22). One study found that the general public estimates that the insanity defense is used in 37% of felony cases, when in fact it is used in less than 1% (Silver, Cirincione, & Steadman, 1994). Another study of over

Figure 14.22

The insanity defense: Public perceptions and actual realities. Silver, Cirincione, and Steadman (1994) collected data on the general public's beliefs about the insanity defense and the realities of how often it is used and how often it is successful (based on a large-scale survey of insanity pleas in eight states). Because of highly selective media coverage, there are dramatic disparities between public perceptions and actual realities, as the insanity defense is used less frequently and less successfully than widely assumed.

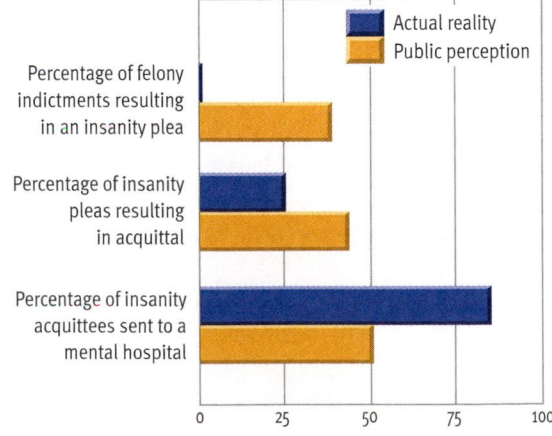

60,000 indictments in Baltimore found that only 190 defendants (0.31%) pleaded insanity, and of these, only 8 were successful (Janofsky et al., 1996).

Involuntary Commitment

The issue of insanity surfaces only in *criminal* proceedings. Far more people are affected by *civil* proceedings relating to involuntary commitment. **In *involuntary commitment* people are hospitalized in psychiatric facilities against their will.** What are the grounds for such a dramatic action? They vary some from state to state. Generally, people are subject to involuntary commitment when mental health professionals and legal authorities believe that a mental disorder makes them (1) dangerous to themselves (usually suicidal), (2) dangerous to others (potentially violent), or (3) in need of treatment (applied in cases of severe disorientation). In emergency situations psychologists and psychiatrists can authorize *temporary* commitment, usually for 24 to 72 hours. Orders for long-term involuntary commitment are usually set up for renewable six-month periods and can be issued by a court only after a formal hearing. Mental health professionals provide extensive input in these hearings, but the courts make the final decisions (Simon, 1999).

Most involuntary commitments occur because people appear to be *dangerous* to themselves or others. The difficulty, however, is in predicting dangerousness. Studies suggest that clinicians' short-term predictions about which patients are likely to become violent are only moderately accurate and that their long-term predictions of violent behavior are largely inaccurate (McNeil & Binder, 1995; Stone, 1999). This inaccuracy in predicting dangerousness is unfortunate, because involuntary commitment involves the *detention* of people for what they *might* do in the future. Such detention goes against the grain of the American legal principle that people are *innocent until proven guilty.* The inherent difficulty in predicting dangerousness makes involuntary commitment a complex and controversial issue.

Culture and Pathology

The legal rules governing insanity and involuntary commitment obviously are culture-specific. And we noted earlier that judgments of normality and abnormality are influenced by cultural norms and values. In light of these realities, would it be reasonable to infer that psychological disorders are culturally variable phenomena? Social scientists are sharply divided on the answer to this question. Some embrace a *relativistic view* of psychological disorders, whereas others subscribe to a *universalistic or pancultural view* (Tanaka-Matsumi, 2001). Theorists who embrace the *relativistic view* argue that the criteria of mental illness vary greatly across cultures and that there are no universal standards of normality and abnormality. According to the relativists, the DSM diagnostic system reflects an ethnocentric, Western, white, urban, middle- and upper-class cultural orientation that has limited relevance in other cultural contexts. In contrast, those who subscribe to the *pancultural view* argue that the criteria of mental illness are much the same around the world and that basic standards of normality and abnormality are universal across cultures. Theorists who accept the pancultural view of psychopathology typically maintain that Western diagnostic concepts have validity and utility in other cultural contexts.

The debate about culture and pathology basically boils down to two specific issues: (1) Are the psychological disorders seen in Western societies found throughout the world? (2) Are the symptom patterns of mental disorders invariant across cultures? Let's briefly examine the evidence on these questions and then reconsider the relativistic and pancultural views of psychological disorders.

Are Equivalent Disorders Found Around the World?

Most investigators agree that the principal categories of serious psychological disturbance—schizophrenia, depression, and bipolar illness—are identifiable in all cultures (Tsai et al., 2001). Most behaviors that are regarded as clearly abnormal in Western culture are also viewed as abnormal in other cultures. People who are delusional, hallucinatory, disoriented, or incoherent are thought to be disturbed in all societies, although there are cultural disparities in exactly what is considered delusional or hallucinatory.

Cultural variations are more apparent in the recognition of less severe forms of psychological disturbance (Tseng et al., 1986). Additional research is needed, but relatively mild types of pathology that do

PREVIEW QUESTIONS
- Are the same psychological disorders found in all cultures?
- Are the symptoms of psychological disorders influenced by culture?

not disrupt behavior in obvious ways appear to go unrecognized in many societies. Thus, syndromes such as generalized anxiety disorder, hypochondria, and narcissistic personality disorder, which are firmly established as diagnostic entities in the DSM, are viewed in some cultures as "run of the mill" difficulties and peculiarities rather than as full-fledged disorders.

Finally, researchers have discovered a small number of *culture-bound disorders* that further illustrate the diversity of abnormal behavior around the world (Griffith, Gonzalez, & Blue, 1999; Guarnaccia & Rogler, 1999). **Culture-bound disorders are abnormal syndromes found only in a few cultural groups.** For example, *koro,* an obsessive fear that one's penis will withdraw into one's abdomen, is seen only among Chinese males in Malaya and several other regions of southern Asia. *Windigo,* which involves an intense craving for human flesh and fear that one will turn into a cannibal, is seen only among Algonquin Indian cultures. And until fairly recently, the eating disorder *anorexia nervosa,* discussed in this chapter's Personal Application, was largely seen only in affluent Western cultures.

Are Symptom Patterns Culturally Invariant?

Do the major types of psychological disorders manifest themselves in the same way around the world? For the most part, yes. The constellations of symptoms associated with schizophrenia and bipolar illness are largely the same across widely disparate societies (Draguns, 1980, 1990). However, cultural variations in symptom patterns are also seen. For example, delusions are a common symptom of schizophrenia in all cultures, but the specific delusions that people report are tied to their cultural heritage (Brislin, 1993). In technologically advanced societies, schizophrenic patients report that thoughts are being inserted into their minds through transmissions from electric lines, satellites, or microwave ovens. Victims of schizophrenia in less technological societies experience the same phenomenon but blame sorcerers or demons. Of the major disorders, symptom patterns are probably most variable for depression. For example, profound feelings of guilt and self-deprecation lie at the core of depression in Western cultures but are far less central to depression in many other societies. In non-Western cultures, depression tends to be expressed in terms of somatic symptoms, such as complaints of fatigue, headaches, and backaches, more than psychological symptoms, such as dejection and low self-esteem (Tsai et al., 2001; Young, 1997). These differences presumably occur because people learn to express symptoms of psychological distress in ways that are acceptable in their culture.

So, what can we conclude about the validity of the relativistic versus pancultural views of psychological disorders? Both views appear to have some merit. As we have seen in other areas of research, psychopathology is characterized by both cultural variance and invariance. Investigators have identified some universal standards of normality and abnormality and found considerable similarity across cultures in the syndromes that are regarded as pathological and in their patterns of symptoms. However, researchers have also discovered many cultural variations in the recognition, definition, and symptoms of various psychological disorders. Given this extensive variability, the relativists' concerns about the ethnocentric nature of the DSM diagnostic system seem well founded.

Putting It in Perspective

PREVIEW QUESTIONS
- How did this chapter illustrate multifactorial causation?
- How did this chapter highlight the interaction of heredity and environment?
- How did this chapter show that psychology evolves in a sociohistorical context?
- How did this chapter illustrate the importance of cultural factors?

Our examination of abnormal behavior and its roots has highlighted four of our organizing themes: multifactorial causation, the interplay of heredity and environment, the sociohistorical context in which psychology evolves, and the influence of culture on psychological phenomena.

We can safely assert that every disorder described in this chapter has multiple causes. The development of mental disorders involves an interplay among a variety of psychological, biological, and social factors. We also saw that most psychological disorders depend on an interaction of genetics and experience. This interaction shows up most clearly in the *stress-vulnerability models* for mood disorders and schizophrenic disorders (see Figure 14.23). *Vulnerability* to these disorders seems to depend primarily on heredity, whereas stress is largely a function of environment. According to stress-vulnerability theories, disorders emerge when high vulnerability intersects with high stress. A high biological vulnerability may not be converted into a disorder if a person's stress is low. Similarly, high stress may not lead to a disorder if

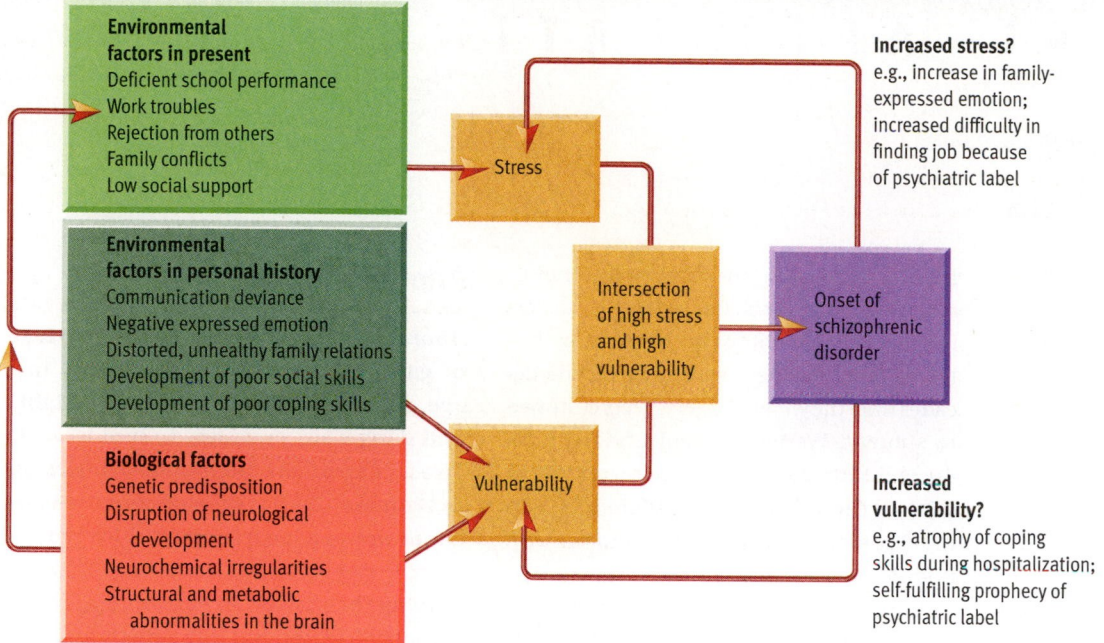

Figure 14.23

The stress-vulnerability model of schizophrenia. Multifactorial causation is readily apparent in current theories about the etiology of schizophrenic disorders. A variety of biological factors and personal history factors influence one's vulnerability to the disorder, which interacts with the amount of stress one experiences. Schizophrenic disorders appear to result from an intersection of high stress and high vulnerability.

vulnerability is low. Thus, the impact of heredity depends on the environment, and the effect of environment depends on heredity.

This chapter also demonstrated that psychology evolves in a sociohistorical context. We saw that modern conceptions of normality and abnormality are largely shaped by empirical research, but social trends, economic necessities, and political realities also play a role. Finally, our discussion of psychological disorders showed once again that psychological phenomena are shaped to some degree by cultural parameters. Although some standards of normality and abnormality transcend cultural boundaries, cultural norms influence many aspects of psychopathology. Indeed, the influence of culture will be apparent in our upcoming Personal Application on eating disorders. These disorders are largely a creation of modern, affluent, Western culture.

REVIEW OF KEY POINTS

- Insanity is a legal concept applied to people who cannot be held responsible for their actions because of mental illness. The insanity defense is used less frequently and less successfully than widely believed. When people appear to be dangerous to themselves or others, courts may rule that they are subject to involuntary commitment in a hospital.

- The principal categories of psychological disturbance are identifiable in all cultures. But milder disorders may go unrecognized in some societies, and culture-bound disorders further illustrate the diversity of abnormal behavior around the world. The symptoms associated with specific disorders are largely the same across different cultures, but cultural variations are seen in the details of how these symptoms are expressed.

- This chapter highlighted four of the text's unifying themes, showing that behavior is governed by multiple causes, that heredity and environment jointly influence mental disorders, that psychology evolves in a sociohistorical context, and that pathology is characterized by both cultural variance and invariance.

Understanding Eating Disorders

Answer the following "true" or "false."

____ 1 Although they have only attracted attention in recent years, eating disorders have a long history and have always been fairly common.

____ 2 People with anorexia nervosa are much more likely to recognize that their eating behavior is pathological than people suffering from bulimia nervosa are.

____ 3 The prevalence of eating disorders is twice as high in women as it is in men.

____ 4 The binge-and-purge syndrome seen in bulimia nervosa is not common in anorexia nervosa.

All of the above statements are false, as you will see in this Personal Application. The psychological disorders that we discussed in the main body of the chapter have largely been recognized for centuries and most of them are found in one form or another in all cultures and societies. Eating disorders present a sharp contrast to this picture; they have only been recognized in recent decades and they have largely been confined to affluent, Westernized cultures (G. F. M. Russell, 1995; Szmukler & Patton, 1995). In spite of these fascinating differences, eating disorders have much in common with traditional forms of pathology.

Eating disorders **are severe disturbances in eating behavior characterized by preoccupation with weight concerns and unhealthy efforts to control weight.** The vast majority of cases consist of two sometimes overlapping syndromes: *anorexia nervosa* and *bulimia nervosa.* Although most people don't seem to take eating disorders as seriously as other types of psychological disorders, you will see that they are very dangerous and debilitating (Striegel-Moore & Smolak, 2001).

Anorexia Nervosa

Anorexia nervosa **involves intense fear of gaining weight, disturbed body image, refusal to maintain normal weight, and dangerous measures to lose weight.** Two subtypes have been observed (Herzog & Delinsky, 2001). In *restricting type anorexia nervosa,* people drastically reduce their intake of food, sometimes literally starving themselves. In *binge-eating/purging type anorexia nervosa,* individuals attempt to lose weight by forcing themselves to vomit after meals, by misusing laxatives and diuretics, and by engaging in excessive exercise.

Both types suffer from disturbed body image. No matter how frail and emaciated they become, they insist that they are too fat. Their morbid fear of obesity means that they are never satisfied with their weight. If they gain a pound or two, they panic.

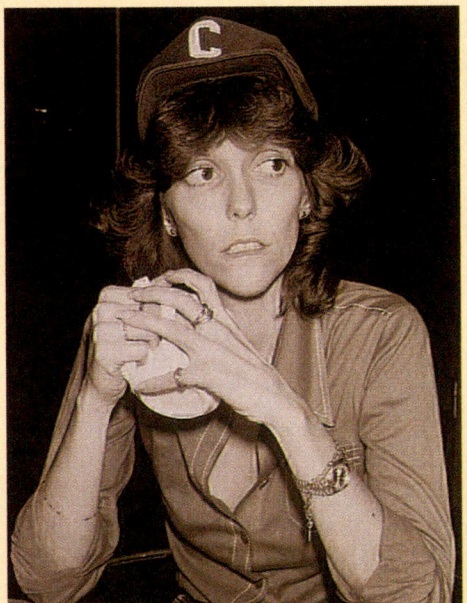

Eating disorders have become common and have been seen in many prominent women, such as Princess Diana (left), singer Karen Carpenter (middle), and gymnast Christy Henrich (right).

The only thing that makes them happy is to lose more weight. The frequent result is a relentless decline in body weight; people entering treatment for anorexia nervosa are typically 25%–30% below their normal weight (Hsu, 1990). Because of their disturbed body image, people suffering from anorexia generally do *not* appreciate the maladaptive quality of their behavior and rarely seek treatment on their own. They are typically coaxed or coerced into treatment by friends or family members who are alarmed by their appearance.

Anorexia nervosa eventually leads to a cascade of medical problems, including *amenorrhea* (a loss of menstrual cycles in women), gastrointestinal problems, low blood pressure, *osteoporosis* (a loss of bone density), and metabolic disturbances that can lead to cardiac arrest or circulatory collapse (Herzog & Becker, 1999; Pomeroy & Mitchell, 2002). Anorexia is a very serious illness that leads to death in 5%–10% of patients (Steinhausen, 2002).

Bulimia Nervosa

Bulimia nervosa **involves habitually engaging in out-of-control overeating followed by unhealthy compensatory efforts, such as self-induced vomiting, fasting, abuse of laxatives and diuretics, and excessive exercise.** The eating binges are usually carried out in secret and are followed by intense guilt and concern about gaining weight. These feelings motivate ill-advised strategies to undo the effects of the overeating. However, vomiting only prevents the absorption of about half of recently consumed food, and laxatives and diuretics have negligible impact on caloric intake, so people suffering from bulimia nervosa typically maintain a reasonably normal weight (Beumont, 2002; Kaye et al., 1993). Medical problems associated with bulimia nervosa include cardiac arrythmias, dental problems, metabolic deficiencies, and gastrointestinal problems (Halmi, 1999, 2002).

Obviously, bulimia nervosa shares many features with anorexia nervosa, such as a

morbid fear of becoming obese, preoccupation with food, and rigid, maladaptive approaches to controlling weight that are grounded in naive all-or-none thinking. However, the syndromes also differ in crucial ways. First and foremost, bulimia is a much less life-threatening condition. Second, although their appearance is usually more "normal" than that seen in anorexia, people with bulimia are much more likely to recognize that their eating behavior is pathological and are more prone to cooperate with treatment (Striegel-Moore, Silberstein, & Rodin, 1993).

History, Prevalence, and Course

Historians have been able to track down descriptions of anorexia nervosa that date back centuries, so the disorder is *not* entirely new, but anorexia nervosa did not become a common affliction until the middle part of the 20th century (G. F. M. Russell, 1995). Although binging and purging have a long history in some cultures, they were not part of pathological efforts to control weight, and bulimia nervosa appears to be a new syndrome that emerged gradually in the middle of the 20th century and was first recognized in the 1970s (Parry-Jones & Parry-Jones, 1995; G. F. M. Russell, 1997).

Both disorders are a product of modern, affluent, Western culture, where food is generally plentiful and the desirability of being thin is widely endorsed. Until recently, these disorders were not seen outside of Western cultures (Hoek, 2002). However, in recent years, advances in communication have exported Western culture to far-flung corners of the globe, and eating disorders have started showing up in many non-Western societies, especially affluent Asian countries (Lee & Katzman, 2002).

There is a huge gender gap in the likelihood of developing eating disorders. About 90%–95% of individuals with eating disorders are female (Hoek, 2002). This staggering discrepancy appears to be a result of cultural pressures rather than biological factors

(Smolak & Murnen, 2001). Western standards of attractiveness emphasize slenderness more for females than for males, and women generally experience greater pressure to be physically attractive than men do (Sobal, 1995). Eating disorders mostly afflict *young* women. The typical age of onset for anorexia is 14 to 18 and for bulimia it is 15 to 21 (see Figure 14.24 on the next page).

How common are eating disorders in Western societies? The prevalence of these disorders has increased substantially in recent decades, although this escalation may be leveling off (Steiger & Seguin, 1999). Studies of young women suggest that about 1%–1.5% develop anorexia nervosa (Walters & Kendler, 1995) and about 2%–3% develop bulimia nervosa (Romano & Quinn, 2001). These figures may seem small, but they mean that millions of young women wrestle with serious eating problems.

Virtually all of the approaches to treatment that we will discuss in the next chapter—such as insight therapy, group therapy, behavior therapy, and drug therapy—have been used in the treatment of eating disorders (Halmi, 2000). How successful are these therapeutic interventions? The picture is mixed. About 40%–50% of anorexia patients experience a full recovery, while treatment is largely a failure for about 20%–25% of patients (Steinhausen, 2002). The remaining patients fall somewhere in between, experiencing modest improvement along with continued struggles. The prognosis is better for bulimia nervosa, which has a recovery rate of about 70% (Sullivan, 2002).

Etiology of Eating Disorders

Like other types of psychological disorders, eating disorders are caused by multiple determinants that work interactively. Let's take a brief look at some of the factors that contribute to the development of anorexia nervosa and bulimia nervosa.

Genetic Vulnerability

The evidence is not nearly as strong or complete as it is for many other types of

Figure 14.24

Age of onset for anorexia nervosa. Eating disorders tend to emerge during adolescence, as these data for anorexia nervosa show. This graph shows how age of onset was distributed in a sample of 166 female patients from Minnesota. As you can see, over half the patients experienced the onset of their illness before the age of 20, with vulnerability clearly peaking between the ages of 15 and 19.

SOURCE: Adapted from Lucas, A. R., Beard, C. M., O'Fallon, W. M., & Kurland, L. T. (1991). 50-year trends in the incidence of anorexia nervosa in Rochester, Minn.: A population-based study. *American Journal of Psychiatry, 148*, 917–922. © 1991 American Psychiatric Association.

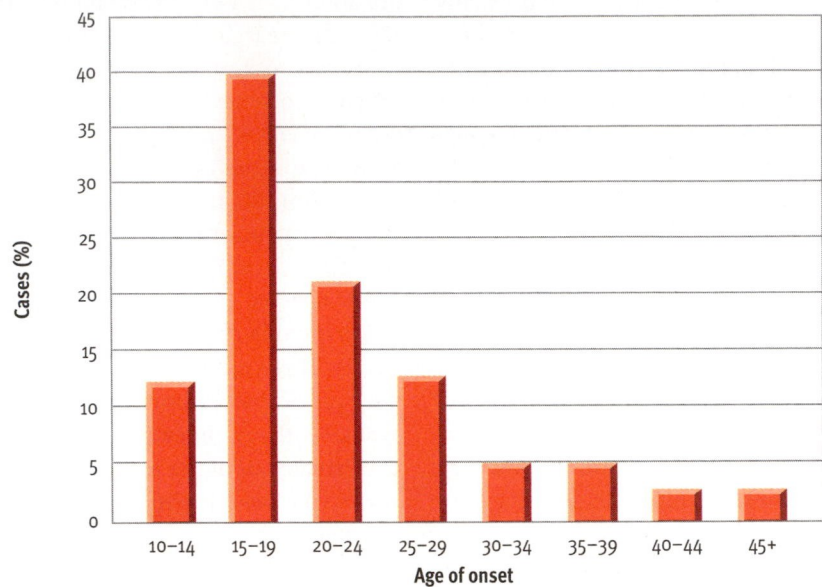

Eating disorders have become distressingly common. One contributing factor is that the models and actresses who dominate the media, such as Calista Flockhart, who is pictured here, tend to be remarkably slender. Thus, young girls are socialized to believe that they must be thin to be attractive.

psychopathology (such as anxiety, mood, and schizophrenic disorders), but some people may inherit a genetic vulnerability to eating disorders. Studies show that relatives of patients with eating disorders have elevated rates of anorexia nervosa and bulimia nervosa (Strober et al., 2000). And twin studies suggest that a genetic predisposition may be at work (Walters & Kendler, 1995).

Personality Factors

Certain personality traits may increase vulnerability to eating disorders. There are innumerable exceptions, but victims of anorexia nervosa tend to be obsessive, rigid, and emotionally restrained, whereas victims of bulimia nervosa tend to be impulsive, overly sensitive, and low in self-esteem (Wonderlich, 2002). Recent research also suggests that perfectionism is a risk factor for anorexia (Halmi et al., 2000).

Cultural Values

The contribution of cultural values to the increased prevalence of eating disorders can hardly be overestimated (Stice, 2001). In Western society, young women are socialized to believe that they must be attractive, and to be attractive they must be as thin as the actresses and fashion models that dominate the media (Lavine, Sweeney, & Wagner, 1999). As Figure 14.25 shows, the increased premium on being thin is reflected in statistics on Miss America contestants and *Playboy* centerfolds, whose average weight declined gradually between 1959 and 1988 (Garner et al., 1980; Wise-

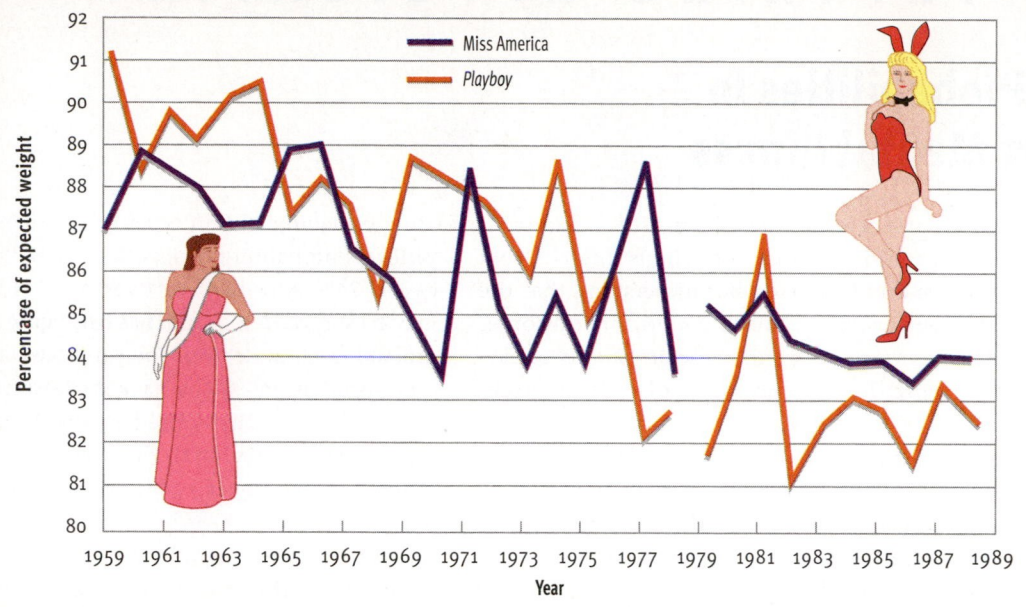

Figure 14.25

Weight trends among *Playboy* center- folds and Miss America contestants.
This graph charts how the average weight of *Playboy* centerfolds and Miss America contestants changed over the course of nearly 30 years (from 1959 to 1988). To control for age and height, each woman's weight was compared to the average weight for a woman of that age and height and expressed as a percentage of the expected weight. Given the small sam- ples, the figures are a little erratic, but overall, the data show a clear downward trend. (Data from Garner, et al., 1980; Wiseman, et al., 1992)

Source: Graphic adapted from Barlow. D. H., & Durand, V. M. (1999). *Abnormal psychology: An integrative approach.* Belmont, CA: Wadsworth. Copyright © 1999 Wadsworth Publishing. Reprinted by permission.

man et al., 1992). Thanks to this cultural milieu, many young women are dissatis- fied with their weight because the societal ideals promoted by the media are unattain- able for most of them (Thompson & Stice, 2001). Unfortunately, in a small portion of these women, the pressure to be thin, in combination with genetic vulnerability, family pathology, and other factors, leads to unhealthful efforts to control weight.

The Role of the Family

Quite a number of theorists emphasize how family dynamics can contribute to the development of anorexia nervosa and bu- limia nervosa in young women (Haworth- Hoeppner, 2000). Some theorists suggest that parents who are overly involved in their children's lives turn the normal ado- lescent push for independence into an unhealthy struggle (Minuchin, Rosman, & Baker, 1978). Needing to assert their auton- omy, some adolescent girls seek extreme

control over their body, leading to patho- logical patterns of eating (Bruch, 1978). Other theorists maintain that some moth- ers contribute to eating disorders simply by endorsing society's message that "you can never be too thin" and by modeling unhealthy dieting behaviors of their own (Pike & Rodin, 1991).

Cognitive Factors

Many theorists emphasize the role of dis- turbed thinking in the etiology of eating disorders (Williamson et al., 2001). For example, anorexic patients' typical belief that they are fat when they are really wast- ing away is a dramatic illustration of how thinking goes awry. Patients with eating disorders display rigid, all-or-none think- ing and many maladaptive beliefs, such as "I must be thin to be accepted," "If I am not in complete control, I will lose all con- trol," "If I gain one pound, I'll go on to gain enormous weight." Additional research

is needed to determine whether distorted thinking is a *cause* or merely a *symptom* of eating disorders.

REVIEW OF KEY POINTS

● The principal eating disorders are anorexia nervosa and bulimia nervosa. Both disorders reflect a morbid fear of gaining weight. Anorexia and bulimia both lead to a cascade of medical problems. Both disorders appear to be largely a product of modern, affluent, Westernized culture.

● Females account for 90%–95% of eating dis- orders. The typical age of onset is roughly 15 to 20. There appears to be a genetic vulnerability to eating disorders. Cultural pressures on young women to be thin clearly help to foster eating disorders. Unhealthy family dynamics, cer- tain personality traits, and disturbed thinking can also contribute to the development of eating disorders.

Working with Probabilities in Thinking About Mental Illness

As you read about the various types of psychological disorders, did you think to yourself that you or someone you know was being described? On the one hand, there is no reason to be alarmed. The tendency to see yourself and your friends in descriptions of pathology is a common one, sometimes called the *medical students' disease* because beginning medical students often erroneously believe that they or their friends have whatever diseases they are currently learning about. On the other hand, realistically speaking, it *is* quite likely that you know *many* people with psychological disorders because—as you learned in the main body of the chapter—the likelihood of anyone having at least one DSM disorder is estimated to be about 44% (consult Figure 14.5 on p. 567).

This estimate strikes most people as surprisingly high. Why is this so? One reason is that when people think about psychological disorders they tend to think of severe disorders, such as bipolar disorder or schizophrenia, which are relatively infrequent, rather than "run of the mill" disturbances, such as anxiety and depressive disorders, which are much more common. When it comes to mental illness, people tend to think of patients in straightjackets or of obviously psychotic homeless people who do not reflect the broad and diverse population of people who suffer from psychological disorders. In other words, their *prototypes* or "best examples" of mental illness consist of severe disorders that are infrequent, so they underestimate the prevalence of mental disorders. This distortion illustrates the influence of the ***representativeness heuristic*, which is basing the estimated probability of an event on how similar it is to the typical prototype of that event** (see Chapter 8).

Do you still find it hard to believe that the overall prevalence of psychological disorders is about 44%? Another reason this number seems surprisingly high is that many people do not understand that the probability of having *at least one* disorder is much higher than the probability of having the most prevalent disorder by itself. For example, the probability of having a substance-use disorder, the single most common type of disorder, is approximately 24%, but the probability of having a substance-use disorder *or* an anxiety disorder *or* a mood disorder *or* a schizophrenic disorder jumps to 44%. These "or" relationships represent *cumulative probabilities.* Yet another consideration that makes the prevalence figures seem high is that many people confuse different types of *prevalence rates.* The 44% estimate is for *lifetime prevalence,* which means it is the probability of having *any* disorder *at least once* at any time in one's lifetime. The lifetime prevalence rate is another example of "or" relationships. It is a value that takes into account the probability of having a psychological disorder in childhood *or* adolescence *or* adulthood *or* old age. *Point prevalence rates,* which estimate the percentage of people manifesting various disorders *at a particular point in time,* are much lower because many psychological disorders last only a few months to a few years.

What about "and" relationships—that is, relationships in which we want to know the probability of someone having condition A *and* condition B? For example, given the lifetime prevalence estimates (from Figure 14.5) for each category of disorder, which are shown in the parentheses, what is the probability of someone having a substance-use disorder (24% prevalence) *and* an anxiety disorder (19%) *and* a mood disorder (15%) *and* a schizophrenic disorder (1%) during his or her lifetime? Such "and" relationships represent *conjunctive probabilities.* Stop and think: what must be true about the proba-

bility of having all four types of disorders? Will this probability be less than 24%, between 24% and 44%, or over 44%? You may be surprised to learn that this figure is probably well under 1%. You can't have all four disorders unless you have the least frequent disorder (schizophrenia), which has a prevalence of 1%, so the answer *must* be 1% or less. Moreover, of all of the people with schizophrenia, only a tiny subset of them are likely to have all three of the other disorders, so the answer is probably well under 1% (see Figure 14.26). If this type of question strikes you as contrived, think again. Epidemiologists have devoted an enormous amount of research to the esti-

Figure 14.26

Conjunctive probabilities. The probability of someone having all four disorders depicted here cannot be greater than the probability of the least common condition by itself, which is 1% for schizophrenia. The intersection of all four disorders (shown in black) has to be a subset of schizophrenic disorders and is probably well under 1%. Efforts to think about probabilities can sometimes be facilitated by creating diagrams that show the relationships and overlap among various events.

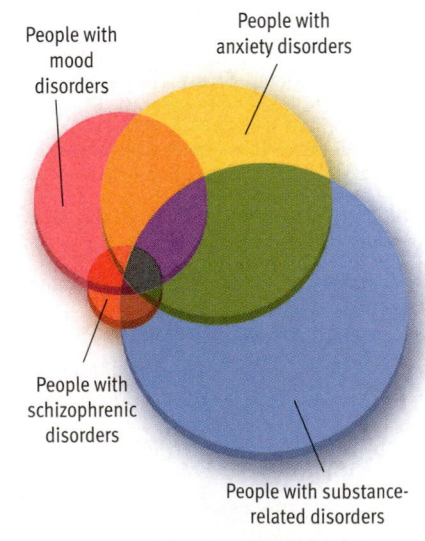

People with mood disorders

People with anxiety disorders

People with schizophrenic disorders

People with substance-related disorders

mation of *comorbidity*—the coexistence of two or more disorders—because it greatly complicates treatment issues.

These are two examples of using statistical probabilities as a critical thinking tool. Let's apply this type of thinking to another problem dealing with physical health. Here is a problem used in a study by Tversky and Kahneman (1983, p. 308) that many physicians got wrong:

A health survey was conducted in a sample of adult males in British Columbia, of all ages and occupations. Please give your best estimate of the following values:

What percentage of the men surveyed have had one or more heart attacks? _____

What percentage of the men surveyed both are over 55 years old and have had one or more heart attacks? _____

Fill in the blanks above with your best guesses. Of course, you probably have only a very general idea about the prevalence of heart attacks, but go ahead and fill in the blanks anyway.

The actual values are not as important in this example as the relative values are. Over 65% of the physicians who participated in the experiment by Tversky and Kahneman gave a higher percentage value for the second question than for the first. What is wrong with their answers? The second question is asking about the conjunctive probability of two events. Hopefully, you see why this figure *must* be less than the probability of either one of these events occurring alone. Of all of the men in the survey who had had a heart attack, only some of them are also over 55, so the second number must be smaller than the first. As we saw in Chapter 8, this common error in thinking is called the *conjunction fallacy*. **The conjunction fallacy occurs when people estimate that the odds of two uncertain events happening together are greater than the odds of either event happening alone.**

Why did so many physicians get this problem wrong? They were vulnerable to the conjunction fallacy because they were influenced by the *representativeness heuristic*, or the power of prototypes. When phy-

sicians think "heart attack," they tend to envision a man over the age of 55. Hence, the second scenario fit so well with their prototype of a heart attack victim, they carelessly overestimated its probability.

Let's consider some additional examples of erroneous reasoning about probabilities involving how people think about psychological disorders. Toward the beginning of the chapter, we discussed the fact that many people tend to stereotypically assume that mentally ill people are likely to be violent. Near the end of the chapter, we noted that people tend to wildly overestimate (37-fold in one study) how often the insanity defense is used in criminal trials. These examples reflect the influence of the *availability heuristic*, **which is basing the estimated probability of an event on the ease with which relevant instances come to mind.** Because of the availability heuristic, people tend to overestimate the probability of dramatic events that receive heavy media coverage, even when these events are rare, because examples of the events are easy to retrieve from memory. Violent acts by former psychiatric patients tend to get lots of attention in the press. And because of the *hindsight bias*, journalists tend to question why authorities couldn't foresee and prevent the violence (see the Critical Thinking Application for Chapter 12), so the mental illness angle tends to be emphasized. In a similar vein, press coverage

© Trippett/Sipa Press

Highly publicized insanity trials, such as that of John Hinckley, Jr., who tried to assassinate President Reagan, lead the public to greatly overestimate how often the insanity defense is used, illustrating the impact of the availability heuristic.

is usually intense when a defendant in a murder trial mounts an insanity defense.

In sum, the various types of statistics that come up in thinking about psychological disorders demonstrate that we are constantly working with probabilities, even though we may not realize it. Critical thinking requires a good understanding of the laws of probability because there are very few certainties in life.

Table 14.3 Critical Thinking Skills Discussed in This Application	
Skill	**Description**
Understanding the limitations of the representativeness heuristic	The critical thinker understands that focusing on prototypes can lead to inaccurate probability estimates.
Understanding cumulative probabilities	The critical thinker understands that the probability of at least one of several events occurring is additive, and increases with time and the number of events.
Understanding conjunctive probabilities	The critical thinker appreciates that the probability of two uncertain events happening together is less than the probability of either event happening alone.
Understanding the limitations of the availability heuristic	The critical thinker understands that the ease with which examples come to mind may not be an accurate guide to the probability of an event.

RECAP

Key Ideas

Abnormal Behavior: Myths, Realities, and Controversies

● The medical model assumes that it is useful to view abnormal behavior as a disease. This view has been criticized on the grounds that it turns ethical questions about deviance into medical questions.

● Three criteria are used in deciding whether people suffer from psychological disorders: deviance, personal distress, and maladaptive behavior. People with psychological disorders are not particularly bizarre or dangerous, and even the most severe disorders are potentially curable.

● DSM-IV is the official psychodiagnostic classification system in the United States. This system asks for information about patients on five axes, or dimensions. Psychological disorders are more common than widely believed.

Anxiety Disorders

● The anxiety disorders include generalized anxiety disorder, phobic disorder, panic disorder, and obsessive-compulsive disorder. Heredity, oversensitivity to the physiological symptoms of anxiety, and abnormalities in GABA or serotonin activity may contribute to these disorders.

● Many anxiety responses, especially phobias, may be caused by classical conditioning and maintained by operant conditioning. Cognitive theorists maintain that a tendency to overinterpret harmless situations as threatening may make some people vulnerable to anxiety disorders. Stress may also trigger anxiety disorders.

Somatoform Disorders

● Somatoform disorders include somatization disorder, conversion disorder, and hypochondriasis. These disorders often emerge in people with histrionic personalities and in people who focus excess attention on their internal physiological processes.

Dissociative Disorders

● Dissociative disorders include dissociative amnesia and fugue and dissociative identity disorder. These disorders are uncommon and their causes are not well understood.

Mood Disorders

● The principal mood disorders are major depressive disorder and bipolar disorder. Mood disorders are episodic. Depression is more common in females than males.

● Evidence indicates that people vary in their genetic vulnerability to mood disorders. These disorders are accompanied by changes in neurochemical activity in the brain. Cognitive mod-

els posit that negative thinking contributes to depression. Depression is often rooted in interpersonal inadequacies and stress.

Schizophrenic Disorders

● Schizophrenic disorders are characterized by deterioration of adaptive behavior, delusions, hallucinations, and disturbed mood. Research has linked schizophrenia to genetic vulnerability, changes in neurotransmitter activity, and structural abnormalities in the brain.

● The neurodevelopmental hypothesis asserts that schizophrenia is attributable to disruptions in the normal maturational processes of the brain before or at birth that are caused by prenatal viral infections, obstetrical complications, and other insults to the brain. Precipitating stress and unhealthful family dynamics, including high expressed emotion, may also modulate the course of schizophrenia.

Personality Disorders

● Ten personality disorders are allocated to Axis II in DSM. Personality disorders can be grouped into three clusters: anxious/fearful, odd/eccentric, and dramatic/impulsive.

● The antisocial personality disorder involves manipulative, impulsive, exploitive, aggressive behavior. Research on the etiology of this disorder has implicated genetic vulnerability, autonomic reactivity, inadequate socialization, and observational learning.

Psychological Disorders and the Law

● Insanity is a legal concept applied to people who cannot be held responsible for their actions because of mental illness. When people appear to be dangerous to themselves or others, courts may rule that they are subject to involuntary commitment in a hospital.

Culture and Pathology

● The principal categories of psychological disturbance are identifiable in all cultures. But milder disorders may go unrecognized in some societies. The symptoms associated with specific disorders are largely the same across different cultures, but some variability is seen.

Putting It in Perspective

● This chapter highlighted four of our unifying themes, showing that behavior is governed by multiple causes, that heredity and environment jointly influence mental disorders, that psychology evolves in a sociohistorical context, and that pathology is characterized by both cultural variance and invariance.

Personal Application ●
Understanding Eating Disorders

● The principal eating disorders are anorexia nervosa and bulimia nervosa. Both disorders

reflect a morbid fear of gaining weight and both appear to be largely a product of modern, affluent, Westernized culture. Females account for 90%–95% of eating disorders.

● There appears to be a genetic vulnerability to eating disorders. Cultural pressures on young women to be thin clearly help foster eating disorders. Unhealthful family dynamics and disturbed thinking can also contribute.

Critical Thinking Application ●
Working with Probabilities in Thinking About Mental Illness

● Probability estimates can be distorted by the representativeness heuristic and the availability heuristic. Cumulative probabilities are additive, whereas conjunctive probabilities are always less than the likelihood of any one of the events happening alone.

Key Terms

Agoraphobia
Anorexia nervosa
Antisocial personality disorder
Anxiety disorders
Availability heuristic
Bipolar disorder
Bulimia nervosa
Catatonic schizophrenia
Comorbidity
Concordance rate
Conjunction fallacy
Conversion disorder
Culture-bound disorders
Cyclothymic disorder
Delusions
Diagnosis
Disorganized schizophrenia
Dissociative amnesia
Dissociative disorders
Dissociative fugue
Dissociative identity disorder (DID)
Dysthymic disorder
Eating disorders
Epidemiology
Etiology
Generalized anxiety disorder
Hallucinations
Hypochondriasis
Insanity
Involuntary commitment
Major depressive disorder
Medical model
Mood disorders
Multiple-personality disorder
Negative symptoms
Obsessive-compulsive disorder (OCD)
Panic disorder
Paranoid schizophrenia
Personality disorders
Phobic disorder
Positive symptoms
Prevalence
Prognosis
Representativeness heuristic
Schizophrenic disorders
Somatization disorder
Somatoform disorders
Undifferentiated schizophrenia

Key People

Nancy Andreasen
Susan Nolen-Hoeksema
David Rosenhan
Martin Seligman
Thomas Szasz

PRACTICE TEST

1. According to Thomas Szasz, abnormal behavior usually involves:
   A. behavior that is statistically unusual.
   B. behavior that deviates from social norms.
   C. a disease of the mind.
   D. biological imbalance.

2. Although Sue is plagued by a high level of dread, worry, and anxiety, she still manages to meet her daily responsibilities. Sue's behavior:
   A. should not be considered abnormal, since her adaptive functioning is not impaired.
   B. should not be considered abnormal, since everyone sometimes experiences worry and anxiety.
   C. can still be considered abnormal, since she feels great personal distress.
   D. a and b.

3. The fact that people acquire phobias of ancient sources of threat (such as snakes) much more readily than modern sources of threat (such as electrical outlets) can best be explained by:
   A. classical conditioning.
   B. operant conditioning.
   C. observational learning.
   D. preparedness.

4. Which of the following statements about dissociative identity disorder is true?
   A. The original personality is always aware of the alternate personalities.
   B. The alternate personalities are usually unaware of the original personality.
   C. The personalities are typically all quite similar to one another.
   D. Starting in the 1970s, there was a dramatic increase in the diagnosis of dissociative identity disorder.

5. People with unipolar disorders experience _____; people with bipolar disorders are vulnerable to _____.
   A. alternating periods of depression and mania; mania only
   B. depression only; alternating periods of depression and mania
   C. mania only; alternating periods of depression and mania
   D. alternating periods of depression and mania; depression and mania simultaneously

6. A concordance rate indicates:
   A. the percentage of relatives who exhibit the same disorder.
   B. the percentage of people with a given disorder who are currently receiving treatment.
   C. the prevalence of a given disorder in the general population.
   D. the rate of cure for a given disorder.

7. People who consistently exhibit _____ thinking are more vulnerable to depression than others.
   A. overly optimistic
   B. negative, pessimistic
   C. delusional
   D. dysthymic

8. Mary believes that while she sleeps at night, space creatures are attacking her and invading her uterus, where they will multiply until they are ready to take over the world. Mary was chosen for this task, she believes, because she is the only one with the power to help the space creatures succeed. Mary would most likely be diagnosed as _____ schizophrenic.
   A. paranoid
   B. catatonic
   C. disorganized
   D. undifferentiated

9. As an alternative to the current classification scheme, it has been proposed that schizophrenic disorders be divided into just two categories based on:
   A. whether the prognosis is favorable or unfavorable.
   B. whether the disorder is mild or severe.

C. the predominance of thought disturbances.
D. the predominance of negative versus positive symptoms.

10. Most of the drugs that are useful in the treatment of schizophrenia are known to dampen _____ activity in the brain, suggesting that disruptions in the activity of this neurotransmitter may contribute to the development of the disorder.
    A. norepinephrine
    B. serotonin
    C. acetylcholine
    D. dopamine

11. The main problem with the current classification scheme for personality disorders is that:
    A. it falsely implies that nearly everyone has at least one personality disorder.
    B. the criteria for diagnosis are so detailed and specific that even extremely disturbed people fail to meet them.
    C. the categories often overlap, making diagnosis unreliable.
    D. it contains too few categories to be useful.

12. The diagnosis of antisocial personality disorder would apply to an individual who:
    A. withdraws from social interaction due to an intense fear of rejection or criticism.
    B. withdraws from social interaction due to a lack of interest in interpersonal intimacy.
    C. is emotionally cold, suspicious of everyone, and overly concerned about being slighted by others.
    D. is callous, impulsive, and manipulative.

13. Involuntary commitment to a psychiatric facility:
    A. can occur only after a mentally ill individual has been convicted of a violent crime.
    B. usually occurs because people appear to be a danger to themselves or others.
    C. no longer occurs under modern civil law.
    D. will be a lifelong commitment, even if the individual is no longer mentally ill.

14. Those who embrace a relativistic view of psychological disorders would agree that:
    A. the criteria of mental illness vary considerably across cultures.
    B. there are universal standards of normality and abnormality.
    C. Western diagnostic concepts have validity and utility in other cultural contexts.
    D. b and c.

15. About _____ of patients with eating disorders are female.
    A. 40%
    B. 50%–60%
    C. 75%
    D. 90%–95%

Answers

1 B p. 562	6 A p. 569	11 C p. 590
2 C pp. 562–563	7 B pp. 579–580	12 D p. 591
3 D p. 570	8 A p. 584	13 B p. 595
4 D pp. 574–575	9 D pp. 584–585	14 A p. 595
5 B p. 576	10 D pp. 586–587	15 D p. 599

ON THE WEB

For additional resources on the topics covered in this chapter, visit the *Psychology: Themes and Variations* Web site, where you will find practice quizzes, tutorials, Web links, simulations, critical thinking activities, flash cards, interactive exercises, and suggested readings available through INFOTRAC.

http://psychology.wadsworth.com/weiten_themes6e/

CHAPTER 15

© Kit Kittle/CORBIS

Treatment of Psychological Disorders

What do you picture when you hear the term *psychotherapy?* Unless you've had some personal exposure to therapy, your image of it has likely been shaped by depictions you've seen on television or in the movies. A good example is the 1999 film *Analyze This,* a comedy starring Billy Crystal as psychiatrist Ben Sobol and Robert De Niro as Paul Vitti, a mob boss who is suffering from "panic attacks." Complications ensue when Vitti—a man no one says "no" to—demands that Dr. Sobol cure him of his problem before his rivals in crime turn his "weakness" against him.

With his glasses and beard, Billy Crystal's Dr. Sobol resembles many people's picture of a therapist. Like many movie therapists, Dr. Sobol practices "talk therapy." He listens attentively as his patients talk about what is troubling them. Occasionally he offers comments that reflect their thoughts and feelings back to them or that offer some illuminating insight into their problems. We can get a feeling for his approach from a funny scene in which the uneducated Vitti turns Dr. Sobol's techniques on him:

Vitti: *Hey, let's see how you like it. Let's talk about your father.*
Sobol: *Let's not.*
Vitti: *What kind of work does your father do?*
Sobol: *It's not important.*
Vitti: *You paused.*
Sobol: *I did not.*
Vitti: *You just paused. That means you had a feeling, like a thought. . . .*
Sobol: *You know, we're running out of time. Let's not waste it talking about my problems.*
Vitti: *Your father's a problem?*
Sobol: *No!*
Vitti: *That's what you just said.*
Sobol: *I did not!*
Vitti: *Now you're upset.*
Sobol (getting upset): *I am not upset!*
Vitti: *Yes you are.*
Sobol: *Will you stop it!*
Vitti: *You know what, I'm getting good at this.*

As in this scene, the film derives much of its humor from popular conceptions—and misconceptions—about therapy. The technique that Vitti makes fun of does resemble one type of therapeutic process. Like Vitti, many people do associate needing therapy with a shameful weakness. Further, therapy is often of considerable benefit in assisting people to make significant changes in their lives—even if those changes are not as dramatic as Vitti's giving up his life of crime at the end of the movie. On the other hand, the film's comic exaggerations also highlight some misconceptions about therapy, including the following.

- Vitti is driven to see a "shrink" because he feels like he's "falling apart." In fact, therapists help people with all kinds of problems. People need not have severe symptoms of mental illness to benefit from therapy.
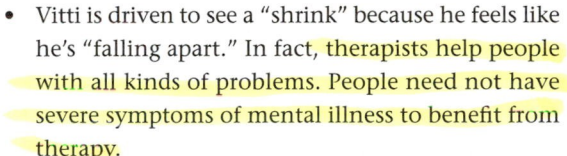
- Dr. Sobol is a psychiatrist, but most therapists are not. And although Dr. Sobol quotes Freud and the film's plot turns on interpreting a dream (in this case, it's the psychiatrist's dream!), many therapists make little or no use of Freudian techniques.
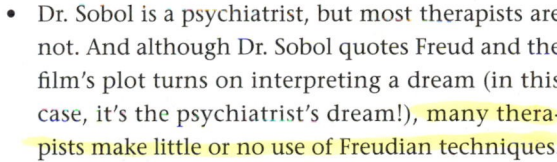

The popular film Analyze This *derived much of its humor from common misconceptions about the process of psychotherapy.*

- Dr. Sobol relies on "talk therapy" to produce insights that will help his patients overcome their troubles. In reality, this approach is only one of the many techniques used by therapists.
- Dr. Sobol "cures" Vitti by getting him to acknowledge a traumatic event in his childhood (the death of his father) that is at the root of his problems. But only rarely does therapy produce a single dramatic insight that results in wholesale change for the client.

In this chapter, we'll take a down-to-earth look at *psychotherapy,* using the term in its broadest sense, to refer to all the diverse approaches used in the treatment of mental disorders and psychological problems. We'll start by discussing some general questions about the provision of treatment. After considering these issues, we'll examine the goals, techniques, and effectiveness of some of the more widely used approaches to therapy and discuss recent trends and issues in treatment. In the Personal Application, we'll look at practical questions related to finding and choosing a therapist and getting the most out of therapy. And in the Critical Thinking Application we'll address problems involved in determining whether therapy actually helps.

The Elements of the Treatment Process

PREVIEW QUESTIONS
- What are the three major approaches to the treatment of psychological disorders?
- What are the correlates of treatment seeking?
- Why do only a portion of the people who need treatment receive it?
- What professions are involved in the treatment of psychological disorders?

Sigmund Freud is widely credited with launching modern psychotherapy. Ironically, the landmark case that inspired Freud was actually treated by one of his colleagues, Josef Breuer. Around 1880, Breuer began to treat a young woman referred to as Anna O (which was a pseudonym—her real name was Bertha Pappenheim). Anna exhibited a variety of physical maladies, including headaches, coughing, and a loss of feeling and movement in her right arm. Much to his surprise, Breuer discovered that Anna's physical symptoms cleared up when he encouraged her to talk about emotionally charged experiences from her past.

When Breuer and Freud discussed the case, they speculated that talking things through had enabled Anna to drain off bottled-up emotions that had caused her symptoms. Breuer found the intense emotional exchange in this treatment not to his liking, so he didn't follow through on his discovery. However, Freud applied Breuer's insight to other patients, and his successes led him to develop a systematic treatment procedure, which he called *psychoanalysis*. Anna O called her treatment "the talking cure." However, as you'll see, psychotherapy isn't always curative, and many modern treatments place little emphasis on talking.

Freud's breakthrough ushered in a century of progress for psychotherapy. Psychoanalysis spawned many offspring as Freud's followers developed their own systems of treatment. Since then, approaches to treatment have steadily grown more numerous, more diverse, and more effective. Today, people can choose from a bewildering array of therapies.

Treatments: How Many Types Are There?

In their efforts to help people, psychotherapists use many treatment methods. They included discussion, advice, emotional support, persuasion, conditioning procedures, relaxation training, role playing, drug therapy, biofeedback, and group therapy. No one knows exactly how many distinct types of psychotherapy there are. One expert (Kazdin, 1994) estimates that there may be over 400 approaches to treatment. Fortunately, we can impose some order on this chaos. As varied as therapists' procedures are, approaches to treatment can be classified into three major categories:

1. *Insight therapies*. Insight therapy is "talk therapy" in the tradition of Freud's psychoanalysis. In insight therapies, clients engage in complex verbal interactions with their therapists. The goal in these discussions is to pursue increased insight regarding the nature of the client's difficulties and to sort through possible solutions. Insight therapy can be conducted with an individual or with a group. Broadly speaking, family therapy and marital therapy fall in this category.

2. *Behavior therapies*. Behavior therapies are based on the principles of learning, which were introduced in Chapter 6. Instead of emphasizing personal insights, behavior therapists make direct efforts to alter problematic responses (phobias, for instance) and maladaptive habits (drug use, for instance). Behavior therapists work on changing clients' overt behaviors. They use different procedures for different kinds of problems. Most of their procedures involve classical conditioning, operant conditioning, or observational learning.

3. *Biomedical therapies*. Biomedical approaches to therapy involve interventions into a person's biological functioning. The most widely used procedures are drug therapy and electroconvulsive (shock) ther-

The case of Anna O., whose real name was Bertha Pappenheim, provided the inspiration for Sigmund Freud's invention of psychoanalysis.

Mary Evans/Sigmund Freud Copyrights

apy. As the name bio*medical* therapies suggests, these treatments have traditionally been provided only by physicians with a medical degree (usually psychiatrists). This situation may change, however, as psychologists have begun to campaign for prescription privileges (Gutierrez & Silk, 1998; Sammons et al., 2000). They have made some progress toward this goal, even though many psychologists have argued against pursuing the right to prescribe medication (Albee, 1998; Dobson & Dozois, 2001).

Clients: Who Seeks Therapy?

In the therapeutic triad (therapists, treatments, clients), the greatest diversity of all is seen among the clients. According to the 1999 Surgeon General's report on mental health (U.S. Department of Health and Human Services, 1999) about 15% of the U.S. population use mental health services in a given year. These people bring to therapy the full range of human problems: anxiety, depression, unsatisfactory interpersonal relations, troublesome habits, poor self-control, low self-esteem, marital conflicts, self-doubt, a sense of emptiness, and feelings of personal stagnation. The two most common presenting problems are excessive anxiety and depression (Narrow et al., 1993). Interestingly, people often delay for many years before finally seeking treatment for their psychological problems (Kessler, Olfson, & Berglund, 1998).

A client in treatment does *not* necessarily have an identifiable psychological disorder. Some people seek professional help for everyday problems (career

decisions, for instance) or vague feelings of discontent (Strupp, 1996). One surprising finding in the Surgeon General's report on mental health was that almost half of the people who use mental health services in a given year do not have a specific disorder.

People vary considerably in their willingness to seek psychotherapy. As you can see in Figure 15.1, women are more likely than men to receive therapy. Treatment is also more likely when people have medical insurance and when they have more education (Olfson & Pincus, 1996). *Unfortunately, it appears that many people who need therapy don't receive it* (Kessler et al., 1999). As Figure 15.2 on the next page shows, only a portion of the people who need treatment get it. People who could benefit from therapy do not seek it for a variety of reasons. Lack of health insurance and cost concerns appear to be major barriers to obtaining needed care for many people (Druss & Rosenheck, 1998). According to the Surgeon General's report, the biggest roadblock is the "stigma surrounding the receipt of mental health treatment." Unfortunately, many people equate seeking therapy with admitting personal weakness.

Therapists: Who Provides Professional Treatment?

People troubled by personal problems often solicit help from their friends, relatives, clergy, and primary care physicians. These sources of assistance may provide excellent advice, but their counsel does not qualify as therapy. Psychotherapy refers to *professional*

Web Link 15.1

How to Find Help with Life's Problems
This online brochure from the American Psychological Association provides guidance about how to seek out the best assistance for different kinds of human issues and difficulties.

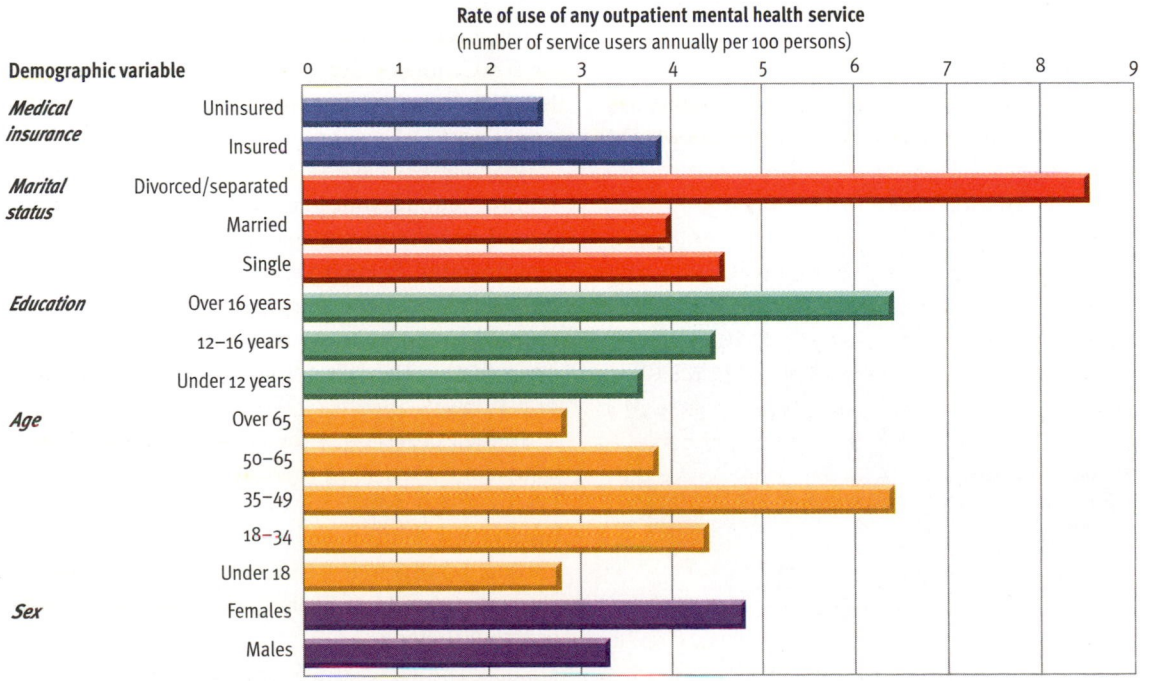

Rate of use of any outpatient mental health service
(number of service users annually per 100 persons)

Figure 15.1

Therapy utilization rates.
Olfson and Pincus (1996) gathered data on the use of non-hospital outpatient mental health services in the United States in relation to various demographic variables. As you can see, people are more likely to enter therapy if they have medical insurance than if they do not. In regard to marital status, utilization rates are particularly high among those who are divorced or separated. The use of therapy is greater among those who have more education and, in terms of age, utilization peaks in the 35–49 age bracket. Finally, females are more likely to pursue therapy than males are. (Data from Olfson & Pincus, 1996)

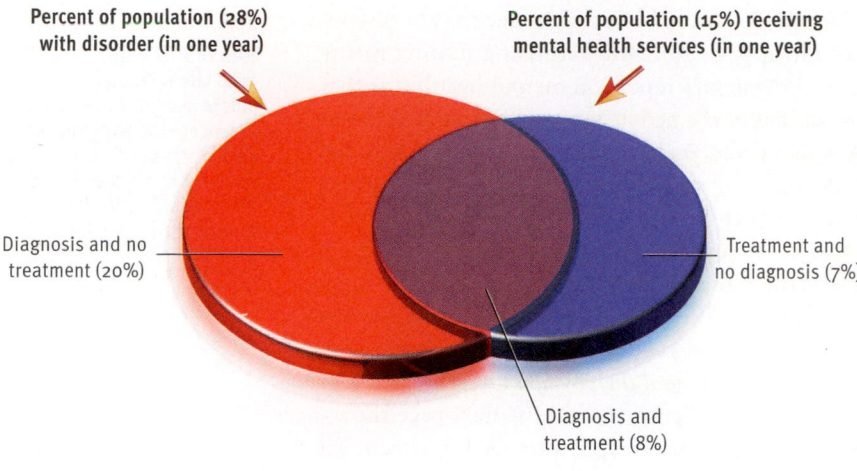

Percent of population (28%) with disorder (in one year)

Percent of population (15%) receiving mental health services (in one year)

Diagnosis and no treatment (20%)

Treatment and no diagnosis (7%)

Diagnosis and treatment (8%)

Figure 15.2

Psychological disorders and professional treatment. Not everyone who has a psychological disorder receives professional treatment and not everyone who seeks treatment has a clear disorder. This graph, from the Surgeon General's report on mental health, shows that 15% of the U.S. adult population receive mental health treatment each year. Almost half of these people (7%) do not receive a psychiatric diagnosis, although some of them probably have milder disorders that are not assessed in epidemiological research. This graph also shows that over two-thirds of the people who *do* have disorders do *not* receive professional treatment. (Data from *Mental Health: A Report of the Surgeon General*, U.S. Public Health Service, 1999)

Figure 15.3

Who people see for therapy.
Based on a national survey by Olfson and Pincus (1994), this pie chart shows how therapy visits were distributed among psychologists, psychiatrists, other mental health professionals (social workers, counselors, and such) and general medical professionals (typically physicians specializing in family practice and internal medicine). As you can see, psychologists and psychiatrists account for about 62% of outpatient treatment. (Data from Olfson & Pincus, 1994)

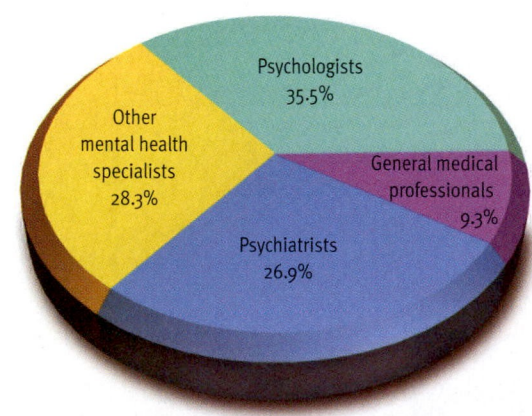

Psychologists
35.5%

Other mental health specialists
28.3%

General medical professionals
9.3%

Psychiatrists
26.9%

treatment by someone with special training. However, a common source of confusion about psychotherapy is the variety of "helping professions" available to offer assistance (Murstein & Fontaine, 1993). Psychology and psychiatry are the principal professions involved in the provision of psychotherapy (see Figure 15.3). However, therapy is increasingly provided by clinical social workers, psychiatric nurses, counselors, and marriage and family therapists. Let's look at the various mental health professions.

Psychologists

Two types of psychologists may provide therapy. *Clinical psychologists* and *counseling psychologists* specialize in the diagnosis and treatment of psychological disorders and everyday behavioral problems. Clinical psychologists' training emphasizes the treatment of full-fledged disorders. In contrast, counseling psychologists' training is slanted toward the treatment of everyday adjustment problems. In practice, however, there is quite a bit of overlap between clinical and counseling psychologists in training, skills, and the clientele that they serve.

Both types of psychologists must earn a doctoral degree (Ph.D., Psy.D., or Ed.D.). A doctorate in psychology requires about five to seven years of training beyond a bachelor's degree. The process of gaining admission to a Ph.D. program in clinical psychology is highly competitive (about as difficult as getting into medical school). Psychologists receive most of their training in universities or independent professional schools. They then serve a one-year internship in a clinical setting, such as a hospital, usually followed by one or two years of postdoctoral fellowship training.

In providing therapy, psychologists use either insight or behavioral approaches. In comparison to psychiatrists, they are more likely to use behavioral techniques and less likely to use psychoanalytic methods. Clinical and counseling psychologists do psychological testing as well as psychotherapy, and many also conduct research.

Psychiatrists

Psychiatrists are physicians who specialize in the diagnosis and treatment of psychological disorders. Many psychiatrists also treat everyday behavioral problems. However, in comparison to psychologists, psychiatrists devote more time to relatively severe disorders (schizophrenia, mood disorders) and less time to everyday marital, family, job, and school problems.

Psychiatrists have an M.D. degree. Their graduate training requires four years of coursework in medical school and a four-year apprenticeship in a residency at a hospital. Their psychotherapy training occurs during their residency, since the required coursework in medical school is essentially the same for everyone, whether they are going into surgery, pediatrics, or psychiatry.

In their provision of therapy, psychiatrists increasingly emphasize drug therapies (Olfson, Marcus, & Pincus, 1999), which the other, nonmedical helping professions cannot provide. In comparison to psychologists, psychiatrists are more likely to use psychoanalysis and less likely to use group therapies or behavior therapies.

Other Mental Health Professionals

Several other mental health professions also provide psychotherapy services, and some of these professions are growing rapidly. In hospitals and other institutions, *clinical social workers* and *psychiatric nurses* often work as part of a treatment team with a psychologist or psychiatrist. Psychiatric nurses, who may have a bachelor's or master's degree in their field, play a large role in hospital inpatient treatment. Clinical social workers generally have a master's degree and typically work with patients and their families to ease the patient's integration back into the community. Although social workers and psychiatric nurses have traditionally worked in institutional settings, they increasingly provide a wide range of therapeutic services as independent practitioners.

Many kinds of *counselors* also provide therapeutic services. Counselors are usually found working in schools, colleges, and assorted human service agencies (youth centers, geriatric centers, family planning centers, and so forth). Counselors typically have a master's degree. They often specialize in particular types of problems, such as vocational counseling, marital counseling, rehabilitation counseling, and drug counseling.

Although there are clear differences among the helping professions in education and training, their roles in the treatment process overlap considerably.

In this chapter, we will refer to psychologists or psychiatrists as needed, but otherwise we'll use the terms *clinician, therapist,* and *provider* to refer to mental health professionals of all kinds, regardless of their professional degree.

Now that we have discussed the basic elements in psychotherapy, we can examine specific approaches to treatment in terms of their goals, procedures, and effectiveness. We'll begin with a few representative insight therapies.

REVIEW OF KEY POINTS

● Approaches to treatment are diverse, but they can be grouped into three categories: insight therapies, behavior therapies, and biomedical therapies.

● Clients bring a wide variety of problems to therapy and do not necessarily have a disorder. People vary in their willingness to seek treatment, and many people who need therapy do not receive it.

● Therapists come from a variety of professional backgrounds. Clinical and counseling psychologists, psychiatrists, clinical social workers, psychiatric nurses, and counselors are the principal providers of therapeutic services.

● Each of these professions shows different preferences for approaches to treatment. Psychologists typically practice insight or behavior therapy. Psychiatrists rely more heavily on drug therapies.

Web Link 15.2

Online Dictionary of Mental Health
This thematically arranged "dictionary" at the University of Sheffield (UK) Medical School comprises diverse links related to many forms of psychotherapy, the treatment of psychological disorders, and general issues of mental health.

Insight Therapies

There are many schools of thought about how to do insight therapy. Therapists with various theoretical orientations use different methods to pursue different kinds of insights. However, what these varied approaches have in common is that *insight therapies involve verbal interactions intended to enhance clients' self-knowledge and thus promote healthful changes in personality and behavior.*

Although there may be hundreds of insight therapies, the leading eight or ten approaches appear to account for the lion's share of treatment. In this section, we'll delve into psychoanalysis, related psychodynamic approaches, client-centered therapy, and cognitive therapy. We'll also discuss how insight therapy can be done with groups as well as individuals.

Psychoanalysis

After the case of Anna O, Sigmund Freud worked as a psychotherapist for almost 50 years in Vienna.

Through a painstaking process of trial and error, he developed innovative techniques for the treatment of psychological disorders and distress. His system of *psychoanalysis* came to dominate psychiatry for many decades. Although the dominance of psychoanalysis has eroded in recent years, a diverse collection of psychoanalytic approaches to therapy continue to evolve and to remain influential today (Eagle & Wolitzky, 1992; Ursano & Silberman, 1999).

Psychoanalysis is an insight therapy that emphasizes the recovery of unconscious conflicts, motives, and defenses through techniques such as free association and transference. To appreciate the logic of psychoanalysis, we have to look at Freud's thinking about the roots of mental disorders. Freud mostly treated anxiety-dominated disturbances, such as phobic, panic, obsessive-compulsive, and conversion disorders, which were then called *neuroses.*

Freud believed that neurotic problems are caused by unconscious conflicts left over from early child-

PREVIEW QUESTIONS

● What are the goals and techniques of psychoanalysis?

● What are the goals and techniques of client-centered therapy?

● What are the goals and techniques of cognitive therapy?

● How is group therapy conducted?

● What is the evidence on the efficacy of insight therapy?

National Library of Medicine

"The news that reaches your consciousness is incomplete and often not to be relied on."
SIGMUND FREUD

hood. As explained in Chapter 12, he thought that these inner conflicts involve battles among the id, ego, and superego, usually over sexual and aggressive impulses. He theorized that people depend on defense mechanisms to avoid confronting these conflicts, which remain hidden in the depths of the unconscious (see Figure 15.4). However, he noted that defensive maneuvers often lead to self-defeating behavior. Furthermore, he asserted that defenses tend to be only partially successful in alleviating anxiety, guilt, and other distressing emotions. With this model in mind, let's take a look at the therapeutic procedures used in psychoanalysis.

Probing the Unconscious

Given Freud's assumptions, we can see that the logic of psychoanalysis is quite simple. The analyst attempts to probe the murky depths of the unconscious to discover the unresolved conflicts causing the client's neurotic behavior. In a sense, the analyst functions as a "psychological detective." In this effort to explore the unconscious, the therapist relies on two techniques: free association and dream analysis.

In *free association* clients spontaneously express their thoughts and feelings exactly as they occur, with as little censorship as possible. In free associating, clients expound on anything that comes to mind, regardless of how trivial, silly, or embarrassing it might be. Gradually, most clients begin to let everything pour out without conscious censorship. The analyst studies these free associations for clues about what is going on in the client's unconscious.

In *dream analysis* the therapist interprets the symbolic meaning of the client's dreams. Freud saw dreams as the "royal road to the unconscious," the most direct means of access to patients' innermost conflicts, wishes, and impulses. Clients are encouraged and trained to remember their dreams, which they describe in therapy. The therapist then analyzes the symbolism in these dreams to interpret their meaning.

To better illustrate these matters, let's look at an actual case treated through psychoanalysis (adapted from Greenson, 1967, pp. 40–41). Mr. N was troubled by an unsatisfactory marriage. He claimed to love his wife, but he preferred sexual relations with

prostitutes. Mr. N reported that his parents also endured lifelong marital difficulties. His childhood conflicts about their relationship appeared to be related to his problems. Both dream analysis and free association can be seen in the following description of a session in Mr. N's treatment:

Mr. N reported a fragment of a dream. All that he could remember is that he was waiting for a red traffic light to change when he felt that someone had bumped into him from behind. . . . The associations led to Mr. N's love of cars, especially sports cars. He loved the sensation, in particular, of whizzing by those fat, old expensive cars. . . . His father always hinted that he had been a great athlete, but he never substantiated it. . . . Mr. N doubted whether his father could really perform. His father would flirt with a waitress in a cafe or make sexual remarks about women passing by, but he seemed to be showing off. If he were really sexual, he wouldn't resort to that.

As is characteristic of free association, Mr. N's train of thought meandered about with little direction. Nonetheless, clues about his unconscious conflicts are apparent. What did Mr. N's therapist extract from this session? The therapist saw sexual overtones in the dream fragment, where Mr. N was bumped from behind. The therapist also inferred that Mr. N had a competitive orientation toward his father, based on the free association about whizzing by fat, old expensive cars. As you can see, analysts must *interpret* their clients' dreams and free associations. This is a critical process throughout psychoanalysis.

Interpretation

Interpretation refers to the therapist's attempts to explain the inner significance of the client's thoughts, feelings, memories, and behaviors. Contrary to popular belief, analysts do not interpret everything, and they generally don't try to dazzle clients with startling revelations. Instead, analysts move forward inch by inch, offering interpretations that should be just out of the client's own reach. Mr. N's therapist eventually offered the following interpretations to his client:

I said to Mr. N near the end of the hour that I felt he was struggling with his feelings about his father's sexual life. He seemed to be saying that his father was sexually not a very potent man. . . . He also recalls that he once found a packet of condoms under his father's pillow when he was an adolescent and he thought, "My father must be going to prostitutes." I then intervened and pointed out that the condoms under his father's pillow seemed to indicate more obviously that his father used the condoms

Figure 15.4

Freud's view of the roots of disorders. According to Freud, unconscious conflicts between the id, ego, and superego sometimes lead to anxiety. This discomfort may lead to pathological reliance on defensive behavior.

Intrapsychic conflict (between id, ego, and superego) → Anxiety → Reliance on defense mechanisms

with his mother, who slept in the same bed. However, Mr. N wanted to believe his wish-fulfilling fantasy: mother doesn't want sex with father and father is not very potent. The patient was silent and the hour ended.

As you may have already guessed, the therapist concluded that Mr. N's difficulties were rooted in an Oedipal complex (see Chapter 12). The man had unresolved sexual feelings toward his mother and hostile feelings about his father. These unconscious conflicts, rooted in Mr. N's childhood, were distorting his intimate relations as an adult.

Resistance

How would you expect Mr. N to respond to the therapist's suggestion that he was in competition with his father for the sexual attention of his mother? Obviously, most clients would have great difficulty accepting such an interpretation. Freud fully expected clients to display some resistance to therapeutic efforts. *Resistance* **refers to largely unconscious defensive maneuvers intended to hinder the progress of therapy.** Why would clients try to resist the helping process? Because they don't want to face up to the painful, disturbing conflicts that they have buried in their unconscious. Although they have sought help, they are reluctant to confront their real problems.

Resistance can take many forms. Clients may show up late for their sessions, may merely pretend to engage in free association, or may express hostility toward their therapist. For instance, Mr. N's therapist

In psychoanalysis, the therapist encourages the client to reveal thoughts, feelings, dreams, and memories, which can then be interpreted in relation to the client's current problems.

noted that after the session just described, "The next day he [Mr. N] began by telling me that he was furious with me . . ." Analysts use a variety of strategies to deal with their clients' resistance. Often, a key consideration is the handling of transference, which we consider next.

Transference

Transference **occurs when clients unconsciously start relating to their therapist in ways that mimic critical relationships in their lives.** Thus, a client might start relating to a therapist as if the therapist were an overprotective mother, a rejecting brother, or a passive spouse. In a sense, the client *transfers* conflicting feelings about important people onto the therapist. For instance, in his treatment, Mr. N transferred some of the competitive hostility he felt toward his father onto his analyst.

Psychoanalysts often encourage transference so that clients can reenact relations with crucial people in the context of therapy. These reenactments can help bring repressed feelings and conflicts to the surface, allowing the client to work through them. The therapist's handling of transference is complicated and difficult, because transference may arouse confusing, highly charged emotions in the client.

Undergoing psychoanalysis is not easy. It can be a slow, painful process of self-examination that routinely requires three to five years of hard work. Ultimately, if resistance and transference can be handled effectively, the therapist's interpretations should lead the client to profound insights. For instance, Mr. N eventually admitted, "The old boy is probably right, it does tickle me to imagine that my mother preferred me and I could beat out my father. Later, I wondered whether this had something to do with my own screwed-up sex life with my wife." According to Freud, once clients recognize the unconscious sources of conflicts, they can resolve these conflicts and discard their neurotic defenses.

Modern Psychodynamic Therapies

Though still available, classical psychoanalysis as done by Freud is not widely practiced anymore. Freud's psychoanalytic method was geared to a particular kind of clientele that he was seeing in Vienna many years ago. As his followers fanned out across Europe and America, many found it necessary to adapt psychoanalysis to different cultures, changing times, and new kinds of patients. Thus, many variations on Freud's original approach to psychoanalysis have developed over the years. These descendants of psychoanalysis are collectively known as *psychodynamic approaches* to therapy.

Some of these adaptations, such as those made by Carl Jung (1917) and Alfred Adler (1927), were sweeping revisions based on fundamental differences in theory. Other variations, such as those devised by Melanie Klein (1948) and Heinz Kohut (1971), made substantial changes in theory while retaining certain central ideas. Still other revisions (Alexander, 1954; Stekel, 1950) simply involved efforts to modernize and streamline psychoanalytic techniques. Hence, today we have a rich diversity of psychodynamic approaches to therapy.

Client-Centered Therapy

You may have heard of people going into therapy to "find themselves" or to "get in touch with their real feelings." These now-popular phrases emerged out of the human potential movement, which was stimulated in part by the work of Carl Rogers (1951, 1986). Using a humanistic perspective, Rogers devised client-centered therapy (also known as person-centered therapy) in the 1940s and 1950s.

Client-centered therapy is an insight therapy that emphasizes providing a supportive emotional climate for clients, who play a major role in determining the pace and direction of their therapy. You may wonder why the troubled, untrained client is put in charge of the pace and direction of the therapy. Rogers (1961) provides a compelling justification:

It is the client who knows what hurts, what directions to go, what problems are crucial, what experiences have been deeply buried. It began to occur to me that unless I had a need to demonstrate my own cleverness and learning, I would do better to rely upon the client for the direction of movement in the process. (pp. 11–12)

Rogers's theory about the principal causes of neurotic anxieties is quite different from the Freudian explanation. As discussed in Chapter 12, Rogers maintains that most personal distress is due to inconsistency, or "incongruence," between a person's self-concept and reality (see Figure 15.5). According to

his theory, incongruence makes people feel threatened by realistic feedback about themselves from others. For example, if you inaccurately viewed yourself as a hard-working, dependable person, you would feel threatened by contradictory feedback from friends or co-workers. According to Rogers, anxiety about such feedback often leads to reliance on defense mechanisms, to distortions of reality, and to stifled personal growth. Excessive incongruence is thought to be rooted in clients' overdependence on others for approval and acceptance.

Given Rogers's theory, client-centered therapists stalk insights that are quite different from the repressed conflicts that psychoanalysts go after. Client-centered therapists help clients to realize that they do not have to worry constantly about pleasing others and winning acceptance. They encourage clients to respect their own feelings and values. They help people restructure their self-concept to correspond better to reality. Ultimately, they try to foster self-acceptance and personal growth.

Therapeutic Climate

According to Rogers, the *process* of therapy is not as important as the emotional *climate* in which the therapy takes place. He believes that it is critical for the therapist to provide a warm, supportive, accepting climate. This creates a safe environment in which clients can confront their shortcomings without feeling threatened. The lack of threat should reduce clients' defensive tendencies and thus help them open up. To create this atmosphere of emotional support, client-centered therapists must provide three conditions:

1. *Genuineness*. The therapist must be genuine with the client, communicating honestly and spontaneously. The therapist should not be phony or defensive.

2. *Unconditional positive regard*. The therapist must also show complete, nonjudgmental acceptance of the client as a person. The therapist should provide warmth and caring for the client, with no strings attached. This does not mean that the therapist must approve of everything that the client says or does.

"*To my mind, empathy is in itself a healing agent.*"
CARL ROGERS

Figure 15.5

Rogers's view of the roots of disorders. Rogers's theory posits that anxiety and self-defeating behavior are rooted in an incongruent self-concept that makes one prone to recurrent anxiety, which triggers defensive behavior, which fuels more incongruence.

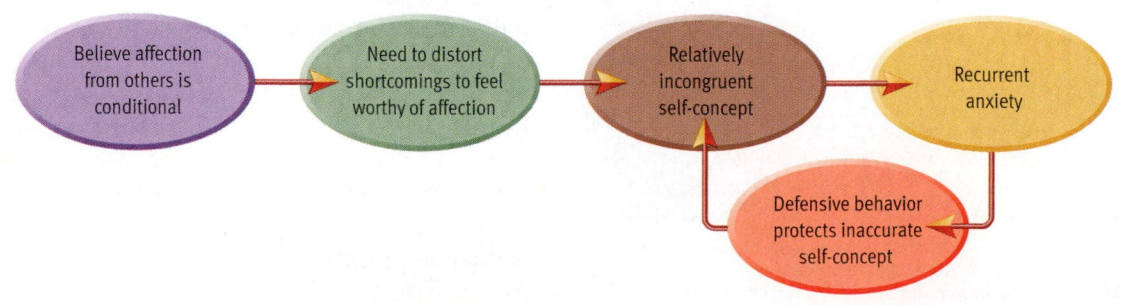

A therapist can disapprove of a particular behavior while continuing to value the client as a human being.

3. *Empathy*. Finally, the therapist must provide accurate empathy for the client. This means that the therapist must understand the client's world from the client's point of view. Furthermore, the therapist must be articulate enough to communicate this understanding to the client.

Rogers firmly believed that a supportive emotional climate is the critical force promoting healthy changes in therapy. More recently, however, some client-centered therapists have begun to place more emphasis on the therapeutic process (Rice & Greenberg, 1992).

Therapeutic Process

In client-centered therapy, the client and therapist work together as equals. The therapist provides relatively little guidance and keeps interpretation and advice to a minimum. So, just what does the client-centered therapist do, besides creating a supportive climate? Primarily, the therapist provides feedback to help clients sort out their feelings. The therapist's key task is *clarification*. Client-centered therapists try to function like a human mirror, reflecting statements back to their clients, but with enhanced clarity. They help clients become more aware of their true feelings by highlighting themes that may be obscure in the clients' rambling discourse.

By working with clients to clarify their feelings, client-centered therapists hope to gradually build toward more far-reaching insights. In particular, they try to help clients better understand their interpersonal relationships and become more comfortable with their genuine selves. Obviously, these are ambitious goals. Client-centered therapy resembles psychoanalysis in that both seek to achieve a major reconstruction of a client's personality. We'll see more limited and specific goals in cognitive therapy, which we consider next.

Cognitive Therapy

In Chapter 13, we saw that people's cognitive interpretations of events make all the difference in how well they handle stress. In Chapter 14, we learned that cognitive factors play a key role in the development of depression and other disorders. Citing the importance of findings such as these, two former psychoanalysts—Aaron Beck (1976, 1987) and Albert Ellis (1973, 1989)—independently devised cognitive-oriented therapies that became highly influential (Arnkoff & Glass, 1992). Since we covered the main ideas

Client-centered therapists emphasize the importance of a supportive emotional climate in therapy. They also work to clarify, rather than interpret, the feelings expressed by their patients.

underlying Ellis's *rational-emotive therapy* in our discussion of coping strategies (see the Personal Application for Chapter 13), we'll focus on Beck's system of *cognitive therapy* here. **Cognitive therapy is an insight therapy that emphasizes recognizing and changing negative thoughts and maladaptive beliefs.**

In recent years cognitive therapy has been applied fruitfully to a wide range of disorders (Beck, 1991; Rush & Beck, 2000), but it was originally devised as a treatment for depression. According to cognitive therapists, depression is caused by "errors" in thinking (see Figure 15.6). They assert that depression-prone people tend to (1) blame their setbacks on personal inadequacies without considering circumstantial explanations, (2) focus selectively on negative events

Web Link 15.3

The Albert Ellis Institute
Rational-emotive therapy, developed by Albert Ellis, is an influential cognitive-behavioral approach to treatment (see the Personal Application for Chapter 13). This site demonstrates how rational-emotive therapy has grown over the last 40 years.

Figure 15.6

Beck's view of the roots of disorders. Beck's theory initially focused on the causes of depression, although it was gradually broadened to explain other disorders. According to Beck, depression is caused by the types of negative thinking shown here.

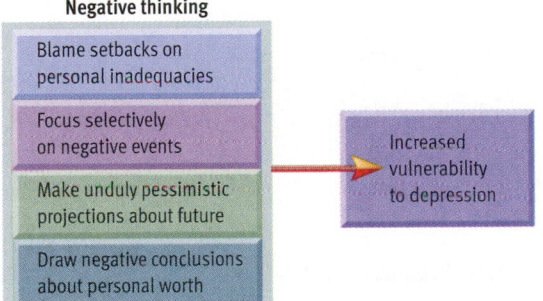

"Most people are barely aware of the automatic thoughts which precede unpleasant feelings or automatic inhibitions."
AARON BECK

while ignoring positive events, (3) make unduly pessimistic projections about the future, and (4) draw negative conclusions about their worth as a person based on insignificant events. For instance, imagine that you got a low grade on a minor quiz in a class. If you made the kinds of errors in thinking just described, you might blame the grade on your woeful stupidity, dismiss comments from a classmate that it was an unfair test, gloomily predict that you will surely flunk the course, and conclude that you are not genuine college material.

Goals and Techniques

The goal of cognitive therapy is to change the way clients think. To begin, clients are taught to detect their automatic negative thoughts—the self-defeating statements they tend to make when analyzing problems. Examples might include "I'm just not smart enough," "No one really likes me," or "It's all my fault." Clients are then trained to subject these automatic thoughts to reality testing. The therapist helps them see how unrealistically negative the thoughts are.

The therapist's goal is not to promote unwarranted optimism but rather to help the client use more reasonable standards of evaluation. For example, a cognitive therapist might point out that a client's failure to get a desired promotion at work can be attributable to many factors and that this setback doesn't mean that the client is incompetent. Gradually, the therapist digs deeper, looking for the unrealistic assumptions that underlie clients' constant negative thinking. These, too, must be changed.

Cognitive therapy tends to be a relatively short-term treatment, typically lasting 4 to 20 sessions (Beck, 1995). Unlike client-centered therapists, cognitive therapists are actively involved in determining the pace and direction of treatment. They usually talk extensively in the therapy sessions. They may even argue openly with clients as they try to persuade them to alter their patterns of thinking.

Kinship with Behavior Therapy

Cognitive therapy borrows extensively from behavioral approaches to treatment (Wright & Beck, 1999), which we will discuss shortly. Specifically, cognitive therapists often use "homework assignments" that focus on changing clients' overt behaviors. Clients may be instructed to engage in overt responses on their own, outside of the clinician's office. For example, one shy, insecure young man in cognitive therapy was told to go to a singles bar and engage three different women in conversations for up to five minutes each (Rush, 1984). He was instructed to record his thoughts before and after each of the conversations. This assignment elicited various maladaptive patterns of thought that gave the young man and his therapist plenty to talk about in subsequent sessions. As this example illustrates, cognitive therapy is a creative blend of "talk therapy" and behavior therapy, although it is primarily an insight therapy.

Cognitive therapy was originally designed as a treatment for individuals. However, it has recently been adapted for use with groups (Rose, 1999). Most insight therapies can be conducted on either an individual or a group basis (Kaplan & Sadock, 1993), so let's take a look at the dynamics of group therapy.

Group Therapy

Although it dates back to the early part of the 20th century, group therapy came of age during World War II and its aftermath in the 1950s (Rosenbaum, Lakin, & Roback, 1992). During this period, the expanding demand for therapeutic services forced clinicians to use group techniques (Scheidlinger, 1993). *Group therapy* is the simultaneous treatment of several clients in a group. Most major insight therapies have been adapted for use with groups. In fact, the ideas underlying Rogers's client-centered therapy spawned the much-publicized encounter group movement. Although group therapy can be conducted in a variety of ways, we can provide a general overview of the process as it usually unfolds with outpatient populations (see Vinogradov, Cox, & Yalom, 1994; Yalom, 1995).

Participants' Roles

A therapy group typically consists of 4 to 15 people, with 8 participants regarded as an ideal number. The

---

CONCEPT **CHECK 15.1**

Understanding Therapists' Conceptions of Disorders

Check your understanding of the three approaches to insight therapy covered in the text by matching each approach with the appropriate explanation of the typical origins of clients' psychological disorders. The answers are in Appendix A.

Theorized causes of disorders

_____ **1.** Problems rooted in pervasive negative thoughts about self and errors in thinking

_____ **2.** Problems rooted in unconscious conflicts left over from childhood

_____ **3.** Problems rooted in inaccurate self-concept and excessive concern about pleasing others

Therapy

a. Psychoanalysis

b. Client-centered therapy

c. Cognitive therapy

---

therapist usually screens the participants, excluding persons who seem likely to be disruptive. Some theorists maintain that judicious selection of participants is crucial to effective group treatment (Salvendy, 1993). There is some debate about whether it is best for the group to be homogeneous—made up of people who are similar in age, sex, and psychological problem. Practical necessities usually dictate that groups are at least somewhat diversified.

In group therapy, participants essentially function as therapists for one another. Group members describe their problems, trade viewpoints, share experiences, and discuss coping strategies. Most important, they provide acceptance and emotional support for each other. In this supportive atmosphere, group members work at peeling away the social masks that cover their insecurities. Once their problems are exposed, members work at correcting them. As members come to value one another's opinions, they work hard to display healthy changes to win the group's approval.

In group treatment, the therapist's responsibilities include selecting participants, setting goals for the group, initiating and maintaining the therapeutic process, and protecting clients from harm (Weiner, 1993). The therapist often plays a relatively subtle role in group therapy, staying in the background and focusing mainly on promoting group cohesiveness (although this strategy will vary depending on the nature of the group). The therapist models supportive behaviors for the participants and tries to promote a healthy climate. He or she always retains a special status, but the therapist and clients are usually on much more equal footing in group therapy than in individual therapy. The leader in group therapy expresses emotions, shares feelings, and copes with challenges from group members.

Advantages of the Group Experience

Group therapies obviously save time and money, which can be critical in understaffed mental hospitals and other institutional settings. Therapists in private practice usually charge less for group than individual therapy, making therapy affordable for more people. However, group therapy is *not* just a less costly substitute for individual therapy. For many types of patients and problems, group therapy can be just as effective as individual treatment (Piper, 1993). Moreover, group therapy has unique strengths of its own (Yalom, 1995). For example, in group therapy participants often come to realize that their misery is not unique. They are reassured to learn that many other

Group treatments have proven particularly helpful when members share similar problems, such as alcoholism, overeating, or having been sexually abused as a child. Many approaches to insight therapy that were originally designed for individuals—such as cognitive therapy—have been adapted for treatment of groups.

people have similar or even worse problems. Another advantage is that group therapy provides an opportunity for participants to work on their social skills in a safe environment. Yet another advantage is that certain types of problems and clients respond especially well to the social support that group therapy can provide.

Whether insight therapies are conducted on a group or an individual basis, clients usually invest considerable time, effort, and money. Are these therapies worth the investment? Let's examine the evidence on their effectiveness.

Evaluating Insight Therapies

In 1952 Hans Eysenck shocked mental health professionals by reporting that there was no sound evidence that insight therapy actually helped people. What was the basis for this startling claim? Eysenck reviewed numerous studies of therapeutic outcome for clients suffering from what were then called neurotic disorders (mostly anxiety, somatoform, and mild depressive disorders, in contemporary terminology). He found that about two-thirds of the clients recovered. A two-thirds recovery rate sounds reasonable, except that Eysenck found the same recovery rate among *untreated* neurotics. As we noted in Chapter 14, psychological disorders sometimes clear up on their own. A *spontaneous remission* is a recovery from a disorder that occurs without formal treatment. His estimate of the spontaneous remission rate for neurotic disorders led Eysenck to conclude that the therapeutic effects of insight therapy are small or nonexistent.

In the ensuing years, critics pounced on Eysenck's article looking for flaws (Jacobson & Christensen, 1996). They found a variety of shortcomings in his data. For instance, Eysenck used different time frames in comparing the recovery rates of treated and untreated individuals (Strupp & Howard, 1992). Moreover, the treated and untreated groups were not matched in terms of the severity of their disorders, their attitudes and expectations about therapy and recovery, or any other relevant variables that might influence therapeutic outcomes. After reexamining Eysenck's data, Bergin (1971) argued that the data really suggested that the spontaneous remission rate for neurotic problems was in the vicinity of 30% to 40%. Although Eysenck's conclusions were unduly pessimistic, he made an important contribution to the mental health field by sparking debate and research on the effectiveness of insight therapy.

Evaluating the effectiveness of any approach to treatment is a complex challenge (Howard, Krasner, & Saunders, 2000; Nathan, Stuart, & Dolan, 2000). This is especially true for insight therapies. If you were to undergo insight therapy, how would you judge its effectiveness? By how you felt? By looking at your behavior? By asking your therapist? By consulting your friends and family? What would you be looking for? Various schools of thought pursue entirely different goals. And clients' ratings of their progress are likely to be slanted toward a favorable evaluation because they want to justify their effort, their heartache, their expense, and their time. Another problem that crops up in studies of the relative efficacy of different treatments is the *allegiance effect*—researchers comparing different therapies tend to obtain results that favor the therapeutic approach they champion (Luborsky et al., 1999). Allegiance effects are probably due in part to the normal human tendency to see what one wants to see when making subjective evaluations. Allegiance effects may also occur because research teams often have more expertise in supervising and delivering their preferred therapy than the competing approaches under study (Hollon, 1999; Thase, 1999). In any event, allegiance effects further complicate the daunting task of assessing the effectiveness of various insight therapies. In sum, evaluations of therapeutic outcomes tend to be subjective, with little consensus about the best way to assess clients' progress (Lambert & Hill, 1994).

In spite of these difficulties, hundreds of therapy outcome studies have been conducted since Eysenck prodded researchers into action. These studies have examined a broad range of specific clinical problems and used diverse methods to assess therapeutic outcomes, including scores on psychological tests and ratings by family members, as well as therapists' and clients' ratings. These studies consistently indicate that insight therapy *is* superior to no treatment or to placebo treatment and that the effects of therapy are reasonably durable (Kopta et al., 1999; Lambert & Bergin, 1994; Lipsey & Wilson, 1993). In one widely discussed study that focused on patients' self-reports, the vast majority of the respondents subjectively felt that they had derived considerable benefit from their therapy (Seligman, 1995).

Although there is considerable evidence that insight therapy tends to produce positive effects for a sizable majority of clients, there is vigorous debate about the *mechanisms of action* underlying these positive effects. The advocates of various therapies tend to attribute the benefits of therapy to the particular methods and procedures used by each specific approach to therapy (Chambless & Hollon, 1998). In essence, they argue that different therapies achieve similar benefits through different processes. An alternative view espoused by many theorists is that the diverse approaches to therapy share certain *common factors* and that these common factors account for much of the improvement experienced by clients (Frank & Frank, 1991). Evidence supporting the common factors view has mounted in recent years (Ahn & Wampold, 2001; Lambert & Barley, 2001).

What are the common denominators that lie at the core of diverse approaches to therapy? The models proposed to answer to this question vary considerably, but there is some consensus. The most widely cited common factors include (1) the development of a therapeutic alliance with a professional helper, (2) the provision of emotional support and empathic understanding by the therapist, (3) the cultivation of hope and positive expectations in the client, (4) the provision of a rationale for the client's problems and a plausible method for ameliorating them, and (5) the opportunity to express feelings, confront problems, gain new insights, and learn new patterns of behavior (Grencavage & Norcross, 1990; Weinberger, 1995). How important are the common factors in therapy? Some theorists argue that common factors account for virtually *all* of the progress that clients make in therapy (Wampold, 2001). It seems more likely that the benefits of therapy represent the combined effects of common factors and specific procedures (Beutler & Harwood, 2002). Either way, it is clear that common factors play a significant role in insight therapy.

Web Link 15.4

The Effectiveness of Psychotherapy: The *Consumer Reports* Study
In 1995 *Consumer Reports* concluded that psychotherapy is effective in the treatment of psychological problems and disorders. Well-known psychologist Martin Seligman reviews the study's methods and compares it to other ways of judging psychotherapy's effects.

- Insight therapies involve verbal interactions intended to enhance self-knowledge. Freudian approaches to therapy assume that neuroses originate from unresolved conflicts lurking in the unconscious. Therefore, in psychoanalysis free association and dream analysis are used to explore the unconscious.

- When an analyst's probing hits sensitive areas, resistance can be expected. The transference relationship may be used to overcome this resistance so that the client can handle interpretations that lead to insight. Classical psychoanalysis is not widely practiced anymore, but Freud's legacy lives on in a rich diversity of modern psychodynamic therapies.

- Rogers's client-centered therapy assumes that neurotic anxieties are derived from incongruence between a person's self-concept and reality. Accordingly, the client-centered therapist tries to provide a supportive climate in which clients can restructure their self-concept. The process of client-centered therapy emphasizes clarification of the client's feelings and self-acceptance.

- Beck's cognitive therapy concentrates on changing the way clients think about events in their lives. Cognitive therapists reeducate clients to detect and challenge automatic negative thoughts that cause depression and anxiety.

- Most theoretical approaches to insight therapy have been adapted for use with groups. Participants in group therapy essentially act as therapists for one another, exchanging insights and emotional support. Group therapy has unique advantages in comparison to individual therapy.

- Eysenck's work in the 1950s raised doubts about the effectiveness of insight therapy and stimulated research on its efficacy. Evaluating the effectiveness of any approach to therapy is complex and difficult. Nonetheless, the weight of modern evidence suggests that insight therapies are superior to no treatment or to placebo treatment. Much of the improvement seen in clients in therapy may be attributable to the operation of common factors.

Behavior Therapies

Behavior therapy is different from insight therapy in that behavior therapists make no attempt to help clients achieve grand insights about themselves. Why not? Because behavior therapists believe that such insights aren't necessary to produce constructive change. For example, consider a client troubled by compulsive gambling. The behavior therapist doesn't care whether this behavior is rooted in unconscious conflicts or parental rejection. What the client needs is to get rid of the maladaptive behavior. Consequently, the therapist simply designs a program to eliminate the compulsive gambling. Actually, behavior therapists may work with clients to attain some limited insights about how situational factors evoke troublesome behaviors (Franks & Barbrack, 1983). This information can be helpful in designing a behavior therapy program.

The crux of the difference between insight therapy and behavior therapy is this: Insight therapists treat pathological symptoms as signs of an underlying problem, whereas behavior therapists think that the symptoms *are* the problem. Thus, *behavior therapies* involve the application of learning principles to direct efforts to change clients' maladaptive behaviors.

Behaviorism has been an influential school of thought in psychology since the 1920s. Nevertheless, behaviorists devoted little attention to clinical issues until the 1950s, when behavior therapy emerged out of three independent lines of research fostered by B. F. Skinner and his colleagues (Skinner, Solomon, & Lindsley, 1953) in the United States; by Hans Eysenck (1959) and his colleagues in Britain; and by Joseph Wolpe (1958) and his colleagues in South Africa (Glass & Arnkoff, 1992). Since then, there has been an explosion of interest in behavioral approaches to psychotherapy.

Behavior therapies are based on certain assumptions (Agras & Berkowitz, 1999). *First, it is assumed that behavior is a product of learning.* No matter how self-defeating or pathological a client's behavior might be, the behaviorist believes that it is the result of past learning and conditioning. *Second, it is assumed that what has been learned can be unlearned.* The same learning principles that explain how the maladaptive behavior was acquired can be used to get

PREVIEW QUESTIONS
- What assumptions are behavior therapies based on?
- How do behavior therapists treat phobias?
- How does aversion therapy work?
- What are the goals and techniques of social skills training?
- What is the evidence on the efficacy of behavior therapy?

CONCEPT CHECK 15.2

Understanding Therapists' Goals

Check your understanding of therapists' goals by matching various therapies with the appropriate description. The answers are in Appendix A.

Principal therapeutic goals

_____ 1. Elimination of maladaptive behaviors or symptoms

_____ 2. Acceptance of genuine self, personal growth

_____ 3. Recovery of unconscious conflicts, character reconstruction

_____ 4. Detection and reduction of negative thinking

Therapy

a. Psychoanalysis

b. Client-centered therapy

c. Cognitive therapy

d. Behavior therapy

rid of it. Thus, behavior therapists attempt to change clients' behavior by applying the principles of classical conditioning, operant conditioning, and observational learning.

Systematic Desensitization

Devised by Joseph Wolpe (1958), systematic desensitization revolutionized psychotherapy by giving therapists their first useful alternative to traditional "talk therapy" (Fishman & Franks, 1992). *Systematic desensitization is a behavior therapy used to reduce phobic clients' anxiety responses through counterconditioning*. The treatment assumes that most anxiety responses are acquired through classical conditioning (as we discussed in Chapter 14). According to this model, a harmless stimulus (for instance, a bridge) may be paired with a fear-arousing event (lightning striking it), so that it becomes a conditioned stimulus eliciting anxiety. The goal of systematic desensitization is to weaken the association between the conditioned stimulus (the bridge) and the conditioned response of anxiety (see Figure 15.7). Systematic desensitization involves three steps.

First, the therapist helps the client build an anxiety hierarchy. The hierarchy is a list of anxiety-arousing stimuli related to the specific source of anxiety, such as flying, academic tests, or snakes. The client ranks the stimuli from the least anxiety arousing to the most anxiety arousing. This ordered list of stimuli is the *anxiety hierarchy*. An example of an anxiety hierarchy for one woman's fear of heights is shown in Figure 15.8.

The second step involves training the client in deep muscle relaxation. This second phase may begin during early sessions while the therapist and client are still constructing the anxiety hierarchy. Various therapists use different relaxation training procedures. Whatever procedures are used, the client must learn to engage in deep, thorough relaxation on command from the therapist.

In the third step, the client tries to work through the hierarchy, learning to remain relaxed while imagining each stimulus. Starting with the least anxiety-arousing stimulus, the client imagines the situation as vividly as possible while relaxing. If the client experiences strong anxiety, he or she drops the imaginary scene and concentrates on relaxation. The client keeps repeating this process until he or she can imagine a scene with little or no anxiety. Once a particular scene is conquered, the client moves on to the next stimulus situation in the anxiety hierarchy. Gradually, over a number of therapy sessions, the client progresses through the hierarchy, unlearning troublesome anxiety responses.

Courtesy of Joseph Wolpe

"*Neurotic anxiety is nothing but a conditioned response.*"
JOSEPH WOLPE

© Steve McCarroll

Systematic desensitization is a behavioral treatment for phobias. Early studies of the procedure's efficacy often used people who had snake phobias as research subjects because people with snake phobias were relatively easy to find. This research showed that systematic desensitization is generally an effective treatment.

Figure 15.7

The logic underlying systematic desensitization. Behaviorists argue that many phobic responses are acquired through classical conditioning, as in the example diagrammed here. Systematic desensitization targets the conditioned associations between phobic stimuli and fear responses.

As clients conquer *imagined* phobic stimuli, they may be encouraged to confront the *real* stimuli. Although desensitization to imagined stimuli *can* be effective by itself, contemporary behavior therapists usually follow it up with direct exposures to the real anxiety-arousing stimuli (Emmelkamp & Scholing, 1990). Indeed, behavioral interventions emphasizing direct exposures to anxiety-arousing situations have become behavior therapists' treatment of choice for phobic and other anxiety disorders (Goldfried, Greenberg, & Marmar, 1990). Usually, these real-life confrontations prove harmless and individuals' anxiety responses decline.

According to Wolpe (1958, 1990), the principle at work in systematic desensitization is simple. Anxiety and relaxation are incompatible responses. The trick is to recondition people so that the conditioned stimulus elicits relaxation instead of anxiety. This is *counterconditioning*—an attempt to reverse the process of classical conditioning by associating the crucial stimulus with a new conditioned response. Although Wolpe's explanation of how systematic desensitization works has been questioned, the technique's effectiveness in eliminating specific anxieties has been well documented (Spiegler & Guevremont, 1998).

Aversion Therapy

Aversion therapy is far and away the most controversial of the behavior therapies. It's not something that you would sign up for unless you were pretty desperate. Psychologists usually suggest it only as a treatment of last resort, after other interventions have failed. What's so terrible about aversion therapy? The client has to endure decidedly unpleasant stimuli, such as shocks or drug-induced nausea.

Aversion therapy is a behavior therapy in which an aversive stimulus is paired with a stimulus that elicits an undesirable response. For example, alcoholics have had an *emetic drug* (one that causes nausea and vomiting) paired with their favorite drinks during therapy sessions (Landabaso et al., 1999). By pairing the drug with alcohol, the therapist hopes to create a conditioned aversion to alcohol (see Figure 15.9).

Aversion therapy takes advantage of the automatic nature of responses produced through classical conditioning. Admittedly, alcoholics treated with aversion therapy know that they won't be given an emetic outside of their therapy sessions. However, their reflex response to the stimulus of alcohol may be changed so they respond to it with nausea and distaste (remember the "sauce béarnaise syndrome" described in Chapter 6?). Obviously, this response should make it much easier to resist the urge to drink.

Aversion therapy is not a widely used technique, and when it is used it is usually only one element in a larger treatment program. Troublesome behaviors treated successfully with aversion therapy have included drug and alcohol abuse, sexual deviance, gambling, shoplifting, stuttering, cigarette smoking, and overeating (Emmelkamp, 1994; Sandler, 1975; Smith, Frawley, & Polissar, 1997; Wolpe, 1990).

Social Skills Training

Many psychological problems grow out of interpersonal difficulties. Behavior therapists point out that people are not born with social finesse—they acquire social skills through learning. Unfortunately, some people have not learned how to be friendly, how to make conversation, how to express anger appropriately, and so forth. Social ineptitude can contribute to anxiety, feelings of inferiority, and various kinds of disorders. In light of these findings, therapists are increasingly using social skills training in efforts to improve clients' social abilities. This approach to therapy has yielded promising results in the treatment of social anxiety (Shear & Beidel, 1998), autism (Gonzalez-Lopez & Kamps, 1997), and schizophrenia (Wallace, 1998).

Social skills training is a behavior therapy designed to improve interpersonal skills that emphasizes modeling, behavioral rehearsal, and shaping. This type of behavior therapy can be conducted with individual clients or in groups. Social skills training depends on the principles of operant conditioning and observational learning. With *modeling,* the client is encouraged to watch socially skilled friends and colleagues in order to acquire appropriate responses (eye contact, active listening, and so on) through observation. In *behavioral rehearsal,* the client tries to practice social techniques in structured role-playing exercises. The therapist provides corrective feedback

An Anxiety Hierarchy for Systematic Desensitization	
Degree of fear	
5	I'm standing on the balcony of the top floor of an apartment tower.
10	I'm standing on a stepladder in the kitchen to change a light bulb.
15	I'm walking on a ridge. The edge is hidden by shrubs and treetops.
20	I'm sitting on the slope of a mountain, looking out over the horizon.
25	I'm crossing a bridge 6 feet above a creek. The bridge consists of an 18-inch-wide board with a handrail on one side.
30	I'm riding a ski lift 8 feet above the ground.
35	I'm crossing a shallow, wide creek on an 18-inch-wide board, 3 feet above water level.
40	I'm climbing a ladder outside the house to reach a second-story window.
45	I'm pulling myself up a 30-degree wet, slippery slope on a steel cable.
50	I'm scrambling up a rock, 8 feet high.
55	I'm walking 10 feet on a resilient, 18-inch-wide board, which spans an 8-foot-deep gulch.
60	I'm walking on a wide plateau, 2 feet from the edge of a cliff.
65	I'm skiing an intermediate hill. The snow is packed.
70	I'm walking over a railway trestle.
75	I'm walking on the side of an embankment. The path slopes to the outside.
80	I'm riding a chair lift 15 feet above the ground.
85	I'm walking up a long, steep slope.
90	I'm walking up (or down) a 15-degree slope on a 3-foot-wide trail. On one side of the trail the terrain drops down sharply; on the other side is a steep upward slope.
95	I'm walking on a 3-foot-wide ridge. The slopes on both sides are long and more than 25 degrees steep.
100	I'm walking on a 3-foot-wide ridge. The trail slopes on one side. The drop on either side of the trail is more than 25 degrees.

Figure 15.8

Example of an anxiety hierarchy. Systematic desensitization requires the construction of an anxiety hierarchy like the one shown here, which was developed for a woman who had a fear of heights but wanted to go hiking in the mountains.

SOURCE: Rudestam, K. E. (1980). *Methods of self-change: An ABC primer.* Belmont, CA: Wadsworth. Copyright © 1980 by Wadsworth Publishing. Reprinted by permission of the author.

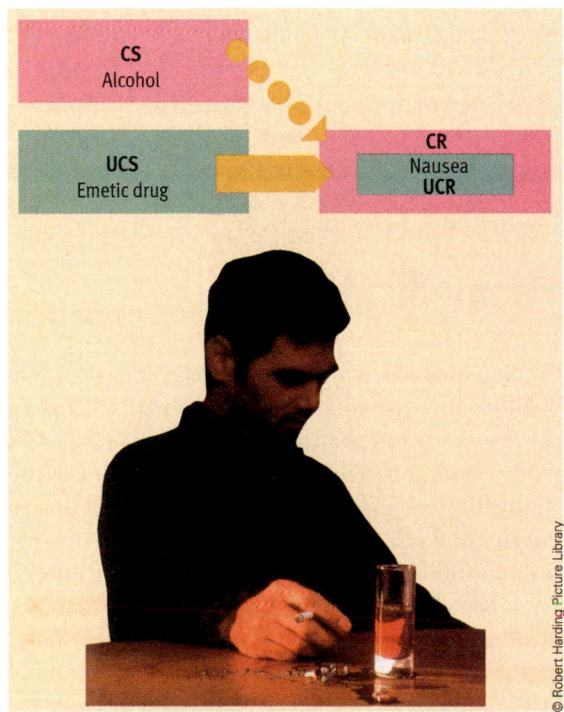

Figure 15.9

Aversion therapy. Aversion therapy uses classical conditioning to create an aversion to a stimulus that has elicited problematic behavior. For example, in the treatment of drinking problems, alcohol may be paired with a nausea-inducing drug to create an aversion to drinking.

and uses approval to reinforce progress. Eventually, of course, clients try their newly acquired skills in real-world interactions. Usually, they are given specific homework assignments. *Shaping* is used in that clients are gradually asked to handle more complicated and delicate social situations. For example, a nonassertive client may begin by working on making requests of friends. Only much later will he be asked to tackle standing up to his boss at work.

Evaluating Behavior Therapies

Behavior therapists have historically placed more emphasis on the importance of measuring therapeutic outcomes than insight therapists have. Hence, there is ample evidence attesting to the effectiveness of behavior therapy (Lambert & Bergin, 1992). Of course, behavior therapies are not well suited to the treatment of some types of problems (vague feelings of discontent, for instance). Furthermore, it's misleading to make global statements about the effectiveness of behavior therapies, because they include many types of procedures designed for very different purposes. For example, the value of systematic desensitization for phobias has no bearing on the value of aversion therapy for sexual deviance.

For our purposes, it is sufficient to note that there is favorable evidence on the efficacy of most of the widely used behavioral interventions (Jacob & Pelham, 2000). Behavior therapies can make important contributions to the treatment of phobias, obsessive-compulsive disorders, sexual dysfunction, schizophrenia, drug-related problems, eating disorders, psychosomatic disorders, hyperactivity, autism, and mental retardation (Agras & Berkowitz, 1999; Emmelkamp, 1994).

Many of these problems would not be amenable to treatment with the biomedical therapies, which we consider next. To some extent, the three major approaches to treatment have different strengths. Let's see where the strengths of the biomedical therapies lie.

CONCEPT CHECK 15.3

Understanding the Types of Behavior Therapy

Check your understanding of the varieties of behavior therapy discussed in the text by matching the therapies with the appropriate description. Choose from the following: (a) systematic desensitization, (b) social skills training, and (c) aversion therapy. The answers are in Appendix A.

_____ **1.** Anxiety is reduced by conditioning the client to respond positively to stimuli that previously aroused anxiety.

_____ **2.** Unwanted behaviors are eliminated by conditioning the client to have an unpleasant response to stimuli that previously triggered the behavior.

_____ **3.** Behavioral techniques are used to teach the client new behaviors aimed at enhancing the quality of their interactions with others.

REVIEW OF KEY POINTS

- Behavior therapies use the principles of learning in direct efforts to change specific aspects of behavior. Wolpe's systematic desensitization, a treatment for phobias, involves the construction of an anxiety hierarchy, relaxation training, and step-by-step movement through the hierarchy, pairing relaxation with each phobic stimulus.

- In aversion therapy, a stimulus associated with an unwanted response is paired with an unpleasant stimulus in an effort to eliminate the maladaptive response. Social skills training can improve clients' interpersonal skills through shaping, modeling, and behavioral rehearsal.

- Biofeedback involves providing information about bodily functions to a person so that he or she can attempt to exert some control over those physiological processes. There is ample evidence that behavior therapies are effective in the treatment of a wide variety of disorders.

Biomedical Therapies

PREVIEW QUESTIONS

- What are the principal types of psychiatric drugs, and what disorders are they used for?
- How effective are psychiatric drugs, and what are their disadvantages?
- What is ECT and what is it used for?
- How effective is ECT and what are the risks?

In the 1950s, a French surgeon looking for a drug that would reduce patients' autonomic response to surgical stress noticed that chlorpromazine produced a mild sedation. Based on this observation, Delay and Deniker (1952) decided to give chlorpromazine to hospitalized schizophrenic patients. They wanted to see whether the drug would have calming effects. Their experiment was a dramatic success. Chlorpromazine became the first effective antipsychotic drug, and a revolution in psychiatry was begun. Hundreds of thousands of severely disturbed patients who had appeared doomed to spend the remainder of their lives in mental hospitals were gradually sent home, thanks to the therapeutic effects of antipsychotic drugs. Today, biomedical therapies such as drug treatment lie at the core of psychiatric practice.

Biomedical therapies are physiological interventions intended to reduce symptoms associated with psychological disorders. These therapies assume that psychological disorders are caused, at least in part, by biological malfunctions. As we discussed in the previous chapter, this assumption clearly has merit for many disorders, especially the more severe ones. We will discuss two biomedical approaches to psychotherapy: drug therapy and electroconvulsive (shock) therapy.

Treatment with Drugs

Psychopharmacotherapy **is the treatment of mental disorders with medication.** We will refer to this kind of treatment more simply as *drug therapy*. The three main categories of therapeutic drugs for psychological problems are: (1) antianxiety drugs, (2) antipsychotic drugs, and (3) antidepressant drugs. Of these drugs, the antidepressant drugs have surpassed the antianxiety agents as the most widely prescribed psychiatric drugs (Pincus et al., 1998).

Antianxiety Drugs

Most of us know someone who pops pills to relieve anxiety. The drugs involved in this common coping strategy are *antianxiety drugs,* **which relieve tension, apprehension, and nervousness.** The most popular of these drugs are Valium and Xanax. These are the trade names (the proprietary names that pharmaceutical companies use in marketing drugs) for diazepam and alprazolam, respectively.

Valium, Xanax, and other drugs in the *benzodiazepine* family are often called *tranquilizers*. These drugs exert their effects almost immediately, and they can be fairly effective in alleviating feelings of anxiety (Ballenger, 2000). However, their effects are measured in hours, so their impact is relatively short-lived. Antianxiety drugs are routinely prescribed for people with anxiety disorders, but they are also given to millions of people who simply suffer from chronic nervous tension. In the mid-1970s, pharmacists in the United States were filling nearly *100 million* prescriptions each year for Valium and similar antianxiety drugs. Many critics characterized this level of use as excessive (Lickey & Gordon, 1991).

All the drugs used to treat psychological problems have potentially troublesome side effects that show up in some patients but not others. The antianxiety drugs are no exception. The most common side effects of Valium and Xanax are listed in Table 15.1. Some of these side effects—such as drowsiness, depression, nausea, and confusion—present serious problems for some patients. These drugs also have potential for abuse, drug dependence, and overdose, although these risks have probably been exaggerated in the press (Ballenger, 2000; Silberman, 1998).

Table 15.1 Side Effects of Xanax and Valium

Side Effects	Patients Experiencing Side Effects (%)	
	Xanax	Valium
Drowsiness	36.0	49.4
Lightheadedness	18.6	24.0
Dry mouth	14.9	13.0
Depression	11.9	17.0
Nausea, vomiting	9.3	10.0
Constipation	9.3	11.3
Insomnia	9.0	6.7
Confusion	9.3	14.1
Diarrhea	8.5	10.5
Tachycardia, palpitations	8.1	7.2
Nasal congestion	8.1	7.2
Blurred vision	7.0	9.1

SOURCE: Evans, R. L. (1981). New drug evaluations: Alprazolam. *Drug Intelligence and Clinical Pharmacy, 15*, 633–637. Copyright © 1981 by Harvey Whitney Books Company. Reprinted by permission.

Another drawback is that patients who have been on antianxiety drugs for a while often experience withdrawal symptoms when their drug treatment is stopped (Danton & Antonuccio, 1997).

A newer antianxiety drub called Buspar (buspirone), that does not belong to the benzodiazepine family, appears useful in the treatment of generalized anxiety disorder (Brawman-Mintzer, Lydiard, & Ballenger, 2000). Unlike Valium, Buspar is slow acting, exerting its effects in one to three weeks, but with fewer sedative side effects.

Antipsychotic Drugs

Antipsychotic drugs are used primarily in the treatment of schizophrenia. They are also given to people with severe mood disorders who become delusional. The trade names (and generic names) of some classic drugs in this category are Thorazine (chlorpromazine), Mellaril (thioridazine), and Haldol (haloperidol). *Antipsychotic drugs* **are used to gradually reduce psychotic symptoms, including hyperactivity, mental confusion, hallucinations, and delusions.** The traditional antipsychotics appear to decrease activity at dopamine synapses, although the exact relationship between their neurochemical effects and their clinical effects remains obscure (Egan & Hyde, 2000).

Studies suggest that antipsychotics reduce psychotic symptoms in about 70% of patients, albeit in varied degrees (Marder, 2000). When antipsychotic

Web Link 15.5

Psych Central
The work of John Grohol, Psych Central is a superb source for learning about all aspects of mental health, including psychological disorders and treatment, professional issues, and information for mental health care consumers. Almost 2000 annotated listings to information sources are offered here.

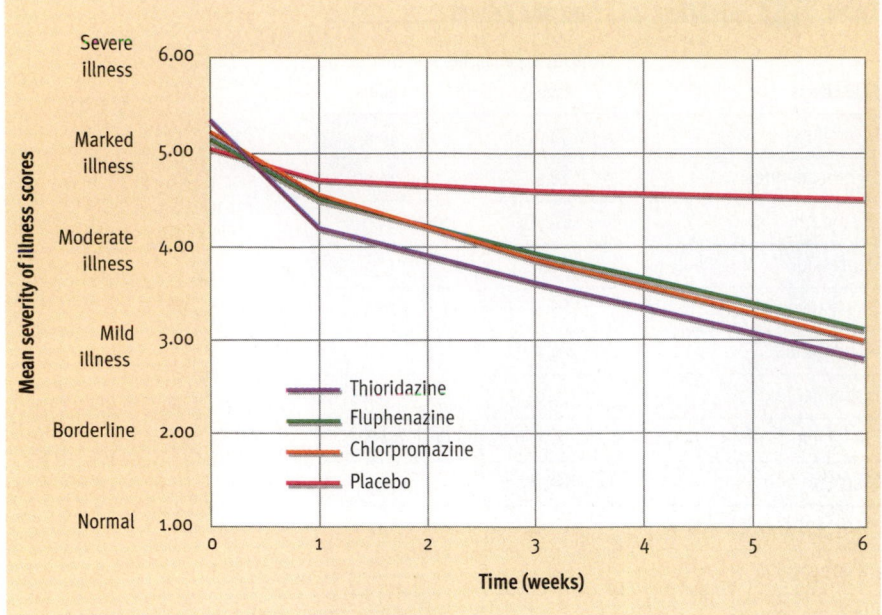

Figure 15.10

The time course of antipsychotic drug effects. Antipsychotic drugs reduce psychotic symptoms gradually, over a span of weeks, as graphed here. In contrast, patients given placebo medication show little improvement.

Source: Cole, J. O., Goldberg, S. C., & Davis, J. M. (1966). Drugs in the treatment of psychosis. In P. Solomon (Ed.), *Psychiatric drugs*. New York: Grune & Stratton. From data in the NIMH-PSC Collaborative Study I. Reprinted by permission of J. M. Davis.

about 20–30% of patients who receive long-term treatment with traditional antipsychotics (Marder, 2000). *Tardive dyskinesia* **is a neurological disorder marked by involuntary writhing and ticlike movements of the mouth, tongue, face, hands, or feet.** Once this debilitating syndrome emerges, there is no cure, although spontaneous remission sometimes occurs after the discontinuation of antipsychotic medication (Pi & Simpson, 2000).

Psychiatrists are currently enthusiastic about a new class of antipsychotic agents called *atypical antipsychotic drugs* (such as clozapine, olanzapine, and quetiapine). These drugs are roughly as effective as traditional antipsychotics (Fleischhacker, 2002) and they can help some patients who do not respond to conventional antipsychotic medications (Volavka et al., 2002). Moreover, the atypical antipsychotics produce fewer unpleasant side effects and carry less risk for tardive dyskinesia (Pi & Simpson, 2000; Stip, 2000). Of course, like all powerful drugs, they are not without their risks, as they appear to increase patients' vulnerability to diabetes and cardiovascular problems (Meltzer et al., 2002).

Antidepressant Drugs

As their name suggests, *antidepressant drugs* gradually elevate mood and help bring people out of a depression. Prior to 1987, there were two principal classes of antidepressants: *tricyclics* (such as Elavil) and *MAO inhibitors* (such as Nardil). These two sets of drugs affect neurochemical activity in different ways (see Figure 15.11) and tend to work with different patients. Overall, they are beneficial for about two-thirds of depressed patients (Gitlin, 2002), although only about one-third of treated patients experience a *complete resolution* of their symptoms (Shulman, 2001). The tricyclics have fewer problems with side effects and complications than the MAO inhibitors (Rush, 2000). Like antipsychotic drugs, antidepressants exert their effects gradually over a period of weeks.

Today, psychiatrists are more likely to prescribe a newer class of antidepressants, called *selective serotonin reuptake inhibitors (SSRIs)*, which slow the reuptake process at serotonin synapses. The drugs in this class, which include Prozac (fluoxetine), Paxil (paroxetine), and Zoloft (sertraline), seem to yield rapid therapeutic gains in the treatment of depression while producing fewer unpleasant or dangerous side effects (Marangell, Yudofsky, & Silver, 1999). SSRIs have also proven valuable in the treatment of obsessive-compulsive disorders, panic disorders, and

drugs are effective, they work their magic gradually, as shown in Figure 15.10. Patients usually begin to respond within two days to a week. Further improvement may occur for several months. Many schizophrenic patients are placed on antipsychotics indefinitely because these drugs can reduce the likelihood of a relapse into an active schizophrenic episode (Marder & van Kammen, 2000).

Antipsychotic drugs undeniably make a huge contribution to the treatment of severe mental disorders, but they are not without problems. They have many unpleasant side effects (Cohen, 1997). Drowsiness, constipation, and cotton mouth are common. The drugs may also produce effects that resemble the symptoms of Parkinson's disease, including muscle tremors, muscular rigidity, and impaired motor coordination. After being released from a hospital, many schizophrenic patients, supposedly placed on antipsychotics indefinitely, discontinue their drug regimen because of the disagreeable side effects. Unfortunately, a relapse eventually occurs in most patients after they stop taking antipsychotic medication (Gitlin et al., 2001). In addition to their nuisance side effects, antipsychotics may cause a more severe and lasting problem called *tardive dyskinesia*, which is seen in

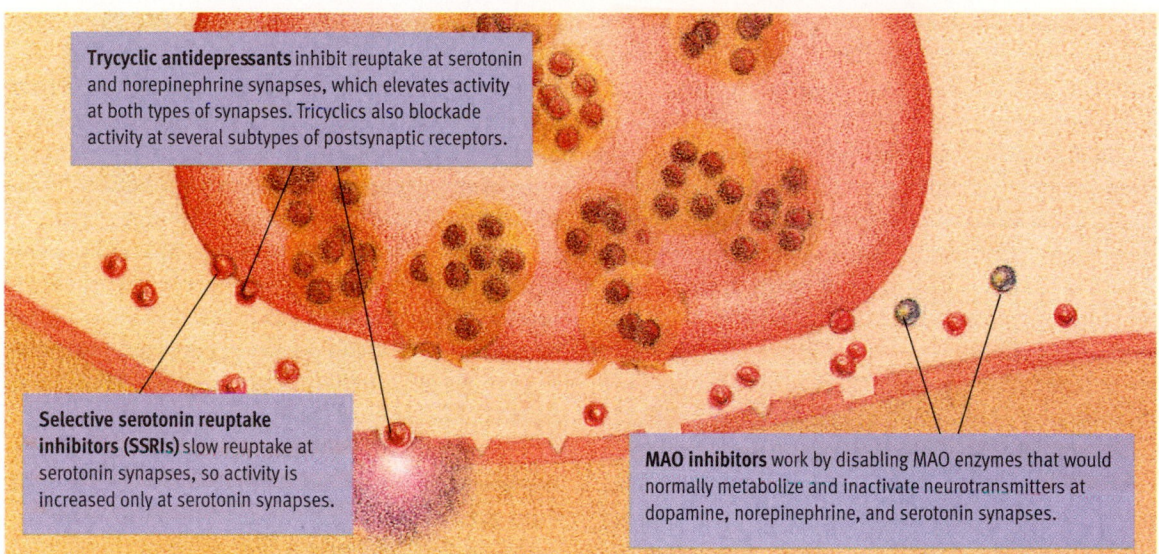

Trycyclic antidepressants inhibit reuptake at serotonin and norepinephrine synapses, which elevates activity at both types of synapses. Tricyclics also blockade activity at several subtypes of postsynaptic receptors.

Selective serotonin reuptake inhibitors (SSRIs) slow reuptake at serotonin synapses, so activity is increased only at serotonin synapses.

MAO inhibitors work by disabling MAO enzymes that would normally metabolize and inactivate neurotransmitters at dopamine, norepinephrine, and serotonin synapses.

Figure 15.11

Antidepressant drugs' mechanisms of action. The three types of antidepressant drugs all increase activity at serotonin synapses, which is probably the principal basis for their therapeutic effects. However, they increase serotonin activity in different ways, with different spillover effects (Marangell et al. 1999). Tricyclics and MAO inhibitors have effects at a much greater variety of synapses, which presumably explains why they have more side effects. The more recently developed SSRIs are much more specific in targeting serotonin synapses.

other anxiety disorders (Rivas-Vazquez, 2001). However, Prozac and the other SSRIs are not "miracle drugs," as suggested by some popular magazines. Like all drugs for psychological disorders, the SSRIs have side effects and risks that must be carefully weighed against their benefits (Baldessarini, 2001). Although early reports blaming SSRIs for incidents of suicide and homicide have not been substantiated (Slaby, 1997; Tardiff, Marzuk, & Leon, 2002), the drugs are associated with weight gain, sleep problems, and sexual dysfunctions (Ferguson, 2001).

Lithium and Other Mood Stabilizers

Lithium is a chemical used to control mood swings in patients with bipolar mood disorders. Lithium can help to prevent *future* episodes of both mania and depression in patients with bipolar illness (Maj et al., 1998; Tondo et al., 1998). Lithium can also be used in efforts to bring patients with bipolar illness out of *current* manic or depressive episodes. However, antipsychotics and antidepressants are more frequently used for these purposes. On the negative side of the ledger, lithium does have some dangerous side effects if its use isn't managed skillfully (Jefferson & Greist, 2000). Lithium levels in the patient's blood must be monitored carefully because high concentrations can be highly toxic and even fatal. Kidney and thyroid gland complications are the major problems associated with lithium therapy.

In recent years a number of alternatives to lithium have been developed. Collectively, these drugs are referred to as *mood stabilizers*. The most popular of these drugs is an anticonvulsant agent called *valproic acid,* which has become about as widely used as lithium in the treatment of bipolar disorders (Blanco et al., 2002). Valproic acid appears to be roughly as effective as lithium in efforts to treat current manic episodes and to prevent future affective disturbances (McElroy, Pope, & Keck, 2000). The advantage provided by valproic acid is that it produces fewer adverse effects than lithium and is better tolerated by patients.

Evaluating Drug Therapies

Drug therapies can produce clear therapeutic gains for many kinds of patients. What's especially impressive is that they can be effective with disorders that otherwise defy therapeutic endeavors. Nonetheless, drug therapies are controversial. Critics of drug therapy have raised a number of issues (Cohen & McCubbin, 1990; Lickey & Gordon, 1991). First, some critics argue that drug therapies are not as effective as advertised and that they often produce superficial, short-lived curative effects (Greenberg & Fisher, 1997). For example, Valium does not really solve problems with anxiety; it merely provides temporary relief from an unpleasant symptom. Moreover, relapse rates are substantial when drug regimens are discontinued. Second, critics charge that many drugs are overprescribed and many patients overmedicated. According to these critics, a number of physicians routinely hand out prescriptions without giving adequate consideration to more complicated and difficult interventions. Third, some critics charge that the damaging side effects of therapeutic drugs are underestimated by psychiatrists and that these side effects are often worse than the illnesses that the drugs are supposed to cure (Breggin, 1990, 1991; Whitaker, 2002). Consistent with this assertion, research suggests that over 2 million people experience serious adverse drug effects (from all types of medications, not just psychiatric drugs) in the United States each year and that adverse medication effects are responsible for over 100,000 deaths annually, making adverse drug reactions the fourth to sixth leading cause of death in the United States (Lazarou, Pomeranz, & Corey, 1998).

Critics maintain that the negative effects of psychiatric drugs are not fully appreciated because the pharmaceutical industry has managed to gain undue influence over the research enterprise as it relates to drug testing (Angell, 2000; Carpenter, 2002). Today, most researchers who investigate the benefits and risks of medications and write treatment guidelines have lucrative financial arrangements with the pharmaceutical industry (Bodenheimer, 2000; Choudhry, Stelfox, & Detsky, 2002). Their studies are funded by drug companies and they often receive substantial consulting fees. These financial arrangements have become so common, the prestigious *New England Journal of Medicine* had to relax its conflict-of-interest rules because it had difficulty finding expert reviewers who did not have financial ties to the drug industry (Drazen & Curfman, 2002). Unfortunately, these financial ties appear to undermine the objectivity required in scientific research, as studies funded by drug companies are far less likely to report unfavorable results than nonprofit-funded studies (Friedberg et al., 1999; Rennie & Luft, 2000). Industry-financed drug trials also tend to be much too brief to detect the long-term risks associated with new drugs (O'Brien, 1996). And research designs are often slanted in a multitude of ways so as to exaggerate the positive effects and minimize the negative effects of the drugs under scrutiny (Carpenter, 2002; Rennie, 1999). The conflicts of interest that appear to be pervasive in contemporary drug research raise grave concerns that require attention from researchers, universities, and federal agencies.

Obviously, drug therapies have stirred up some debate. However, this controversy pales in comparison to the furious debates inspired by electroconvulsive (shock) therapy (ECT). ECT is so controversial that the residents of Berkeley, California, voted in 1982 to outlaw ECT in their city. However, in subsequent lawsuits, the courts ruled that scientific questions cannot be settled through a vote, and they overturned the law. What makes ECT so controversial? You'll see in the next section.

Electroconvulsive Therapy (ECT)

In the 1930s, a Hungarian psychiatrist named Ladislas von Meduna speculated that epilepsy and schizophrenia could not coexist in the same body. On the basis of this observation, which turned out to be inaccurate, von Meduna theorized that it might be useful to induce epileptic-like seizures in schizophrenic patients. Initially, a drug was used to trigger these seizures. However, by 1938 a pair of Italian psychiatrists (Cerletti & Bini, 1938) demonstrated that it was safer to elicit the seizures with electric shock. Thus, modern electroconvulsive therapy was born.

Electroconvulsive therapy (ECT) is a biomedical treatment in which electric shock is used to produce a cortical seizure accompanied by convulsions. In ECT, electrodes are attached to the skull over the temporal lobes of the brain (see the photo below). A light anesthesia is induced, and the patient is given a variety of drugs to minimize the likelihood of complications. An electric current is then applied either to the right side or to both sides of the brain

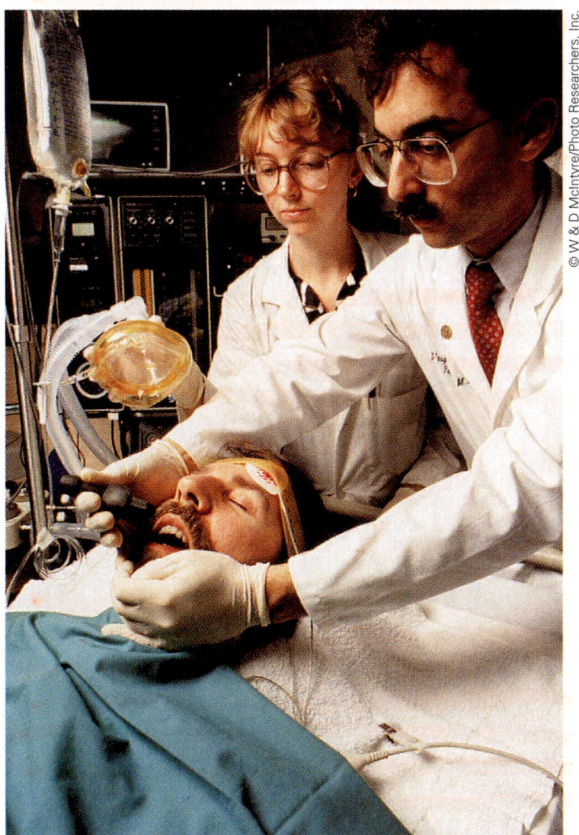

This patient is being prepared for electroconvulsive therapy (ECT). In ECT an electric shock is used to elicit a brief cortical seizure. The shock is delivered through electrodes attached to the patient's skull.

for about a second. Unilateral shock delivered to the right hemisphere is the preferred method of treatment today (Abrams, 2000). The current triggers a brief (about 30 seconds) convulsive seizure. The patient normally awakens in an hour or two and manifests some confusion, disorientation, and nausea, which usually clear up in a matter of hours. People typically receive between 6 and 20 treatments at a hospital (Fink, 1992).

The clinical use of ECT peaked in the 1940s and 1950s, before effective drug therapies were widely available. ECT has long been controversial, and its use did decline in the 1960s and 1970s. Nonetheless, there has been a resurgence in the use of ECT, and it is not a rare form of therapy. Although only about 8% of psychiatrists administer ECT (Hermann et al., 1998), it is estimated that about 100,000 people receive ECT treatments yearly in the United States (Hermann et al., 1995). Some critics argue that ECT is overused because it is a lucrative procedure that boosts psychiatrists' income while consuming relatively little of their time in comparison to insight therapy (Frank, 1990). Conversely, some ECT advocates argue that ECT is underutilized because the public harbors many misconceptions about its risks and side effects (Farah, 1997).

Controversy about ECT is also fueled by patients' reports that the treatment is painful, dehumanizing, and terrifying. Substantial improvements in the administration of ECT have made it less disagreeable than it once was (Bernstein et al., 1998). Nonetheless, some patients continue to report that they find the treatment extremely aversive (Johnstone, 1999).

Effectiveness of ECT

The evidence on the therapeutic efficacy of ECT is open to varied interpretations. Proponents of ECT maintain that it is a remarkably effective treatment for major depression (Prudic & Sackeim, 1999; Swartz, 1993). Moreover, they note that many patients who do not benefit from antidepressant medication improve in response to ECT (Isenberg & Zorumski, 2000). However, opponents of ECT argue that the available studies are flawed and inconclusive and that ECT is probably no more effective than a placebo (Breggin, 1991; Friedberg, 1983). Overall, there does seem to be enough favorable evidence to justify *conservative* use of ECT in treating severe mood disorders in patients who have not responded to medication (Metzger, 1999; Rudorfer & Goodwin, 1993). Unfortunately, relapse rates after ECT are distressingly high. Over 50% of patients relapse within 6 to 12 months, although relapse rates can be reduced by giving ECT patients antidepressant drugs (Sackeim et al., 2001).

Curiously, to the extent that ECT may be effective, no one is sure why. The discarded theories about how ECT works could fill several books. Many ECT advocates theorize that the treatment must affect neurotransmitter activity in the brain. However, the evidence supporting this view is fragmentary, inconsistent, and inconclusive (Abrams, 1992; Kapur & Mann, 1993). ECT opponents have a radically different, albeit equally unproven, explanation for why ECT might *appear* to be effective: They maintain that some patients find ECT so aversive that they muster all their willpower to climb out of their depression to avoid further ECT treatments.

Risks Associated with ECT

Even ECT proponents acknowledge that memory losses are common short-term side effects of electroconvulsive therapy (Lisanby et al., 2000; Weiner, 2000). However, ECT proponents assert that these deficits are mild and usually disappear within a month or two (Glass, 2001). A recent American Psychiatric Association (2001) task force concluded that there is no objective evidence that ECT causes structural damage in the brain or that it has any lasting negative effects on the ability to learn and remember information. In contrast, ECT critics maintain that ECT-induced cognitive deficits are often significant and sometimes permanent (Breggin, 1991; Frank, 1990), although their evidence seems to be largely anecdotal. Given the doubts that have been raised about the efficacy and risks of ECT, it appears that this treatment will remain controversial for some time to come.

CONCEPT CHECK 15.4

Understanding Biomedical Therapies

Check your understanding of biomedical therapies by matching each treatment with its chief use. The answers are in Appendix A.

Treatment

_____ **1.** Antianxiety drugs

_____ **2.** Antipsychotic drugs

_____ **3.** Antidepressant drugs

_____ **4.** Lithium

_____ **5.** Electroconvulsive therapy (ECT)

Chief purpose

a. To reduce psychotic symptoms

b. To bring a major depression to an end

c. To suppress tension, nervousness, and apprehension

d. To prevent future episodes of mania or depression in bipolar disorders

Overview of Five Major Approaches to Treatment

Therapy/founder

Roots of disorders

Psychoanalysis

National Library of Medicine

Developed by Sigmund Freud in Vienna, from the 1890s through the 1930s

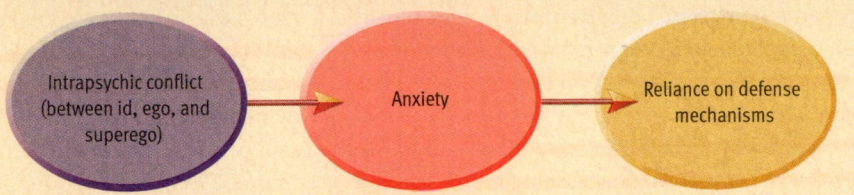

Intrapsychic conflict (between id, ego, and superego) → Anxiety → Reliance on defense mechanisms

Unconscious conflicts resulting from fixations in earlier development cause anxiety, which leads to defensive behavior. The repressed conflicts typically center on sex and aggression.

Client-centered therapy

Courtesy of Center for Studies of the Person

Created by Carl Rogers at the University of Chicago during the 1940s and 1950s

Need to distort shortcomings to feel worthy of affection → Relatively incongruent self-concept → Recurrent anxiety → Defensive behavior protects inaccurate self-concept

Overdependence on acceptance from others fosters incongruence, which leads to anxiety and defensive behavior and thwarts personal growth.

Cognitive therapy

Courtesy of Aaron T. Beck

Devised by Aaron Beck at the University of Pennsylvania in the 1960s and 1970s

- Blame setbacks on personal inadequacies
- Focus selectively on negative events
- Make unduly pessimistic projections about future
- Draw negative conclusions about personal worth

→ Increased vulnerability to depression

Pervasive negative thinking about events related to self fosters anxiety and depression.

Behavior therapy

Courtesy of Dr. Joseph Wolpe

Launched primarily by South African Joseph Wolpe's description of systematic desensitization in 1958

CS Bridge

UCS Lightning strikes

CR Fear UCR

Maladaptive patterns of behavior are acquired through learning. For example, many phobias are thought to be created through classical conditioning and maintained by operant conditioning.

Biomedical therapy

Many researchers contributed; key breakthroughs in drug treatment made around 1950 by John Cade in Australia, Henri Laborit in France, and Jean Delay and Pierre Deniker, also in France

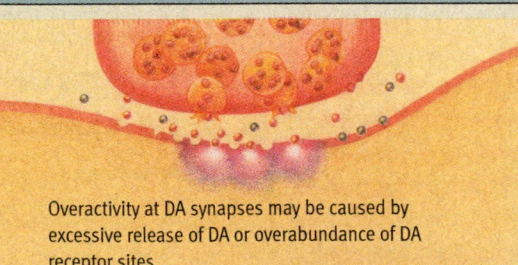

Overactivity at DA synapses may be caused by excessive release of DA or overabundance of DA receptor sites.

Most disorders are attributed to genetic predisposition and physiological malfunctions, such as abnormal neurotransmitter activity. For example, schizophrenia appears to be associated with overactivity at dopamine synapses.

Therapeutic Goals

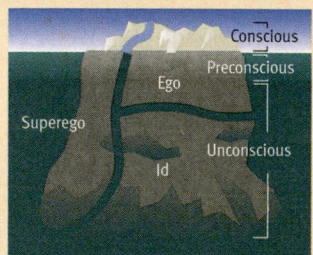

Insights regarding unconscious conflicts and motives; resolution of conflicts; personality reconstruction

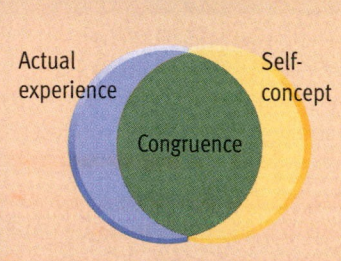

Increased congruence between self-concept and experience; acceptance of genuine self; self-determination and personal growth

Reduction of negative thinking; substitution of more realistic thinking

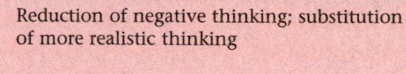
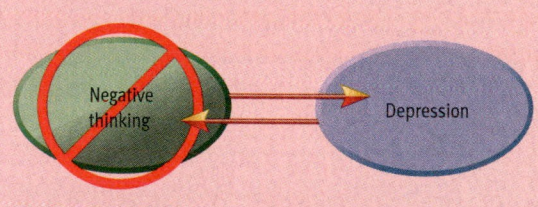

Elimination of maladaptive symptoms; acquisition of more adaptive responses

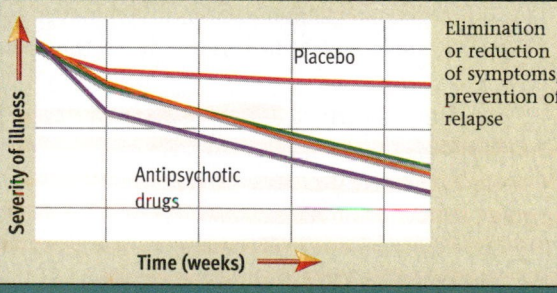

Elimination or reduction of symptoms; prevention of relapse

Therapeutic Techniques

Free association, dream analysis, interpretation, transference.

Genuineness, empathy, uncon- ditional positive regard, clarification, reflecting back to client

Thought stopping, recording of automatic thoughts, refuting of negative thinking, homework assignments

Classical and operant conditioning, systematic desensitization, aversive conditioning, social skills training, reinforcement, shaping, punishment, extinction, biofeedback

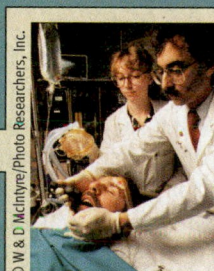
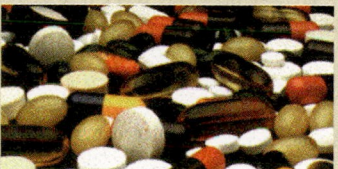

Antianxiety, antidepressant, and anti-psychotic drugs; lithium; electroconculsive therapy

PhotoDisc, Inc.

Treatment of Psychological Disorders   629

REVIEW OF KEY POINTS

- Biomedical therapies are physiological interventions for psychological problems. A great variety of disorders are treated with drugs. Antianxiety drugs are used to relieve excessive apprehension.

- Antipsychotic drugs are used primarily in the treatment of schizophrenia. Antidepressants are used to bring people out of episodes of depression. Lithium and other mood stabilizers are used to prevent the recurrence of episodes of disturbance in people with bipolar mood disorders.

- Drug therapies can be quite effective, but they have their drawbacks. All of the drugs produce side effects, and some

of these side effects can be very troublesome. Some critics maintain that drugs' curative effects are superficial and that some drugs are overprescribed. Disturbing questions have been raised about the scientific impartiality of contemporary research on therapeutic drugs.

- Electroconvulsive therapy (ECT) is used to trigger a cortical seizure that is believed to have therapeutic value for mood disorders, especially depression. Evidence about the effectiveness and risks of ECT is contradictory, but the overall evidence seems sufficient to justify conservative use of the procedure.

Current Trends and Issues in Treatment

PREVIEW QUESTIONS

- How has managed care affected mental health care?

- What are the pros and cons of empirically supported treatments?

- What have researchers found when they have combined insight therapy and drug therapy?

- What is eclecticism in therapy?

- Why is therapy underutilized by some ethnic groups?

The controversy about ECT is only one of many contentious issues and shifting trends in the world of mental health care. In this section, we will discuss the impact of managed care on psychotherapy, the vigorous debate about empirical validation of specific treatments, the continuing trend toward blending various approaches to therapy, and efforts to respond more effectively to increasing cultural diversity in Western societies.

Grappling with the Constraints of Managed Care

The 1990s brought a dramatic shift in how people in the United States pay for their health care. Alarmed by skyrocketing health care costs, huge numbers of employers and individuals moved from traditional fee-for-service arrangements to managed care health plans (Kiesler, 2000). In the *fee-for-service* system, hospitals, physicians, psychologists, and other providers charged fees for whatever health care services were needed, and most of these fees were reimbursed by private insurance or the government (through medicaid, medicare, and other programs). In *managed care systems* people enroll in prepaid plans with small co-payments for services, typically run by health maintenance organizations (HMOs), which agree to provide ongoing health care for a specific sum of money. Managed care usually involves a tradeoff: Consumers pay lower prices for their care, but they give up much of their freedom to choose their providers and to obtain whatever treatments they believe necessary. If an HMO's treatment expenses become excessive, it won't turn a profit, so HMOs have powerful financial incentives to hold treatment costs down. The HMOs originally promised individuals and employers that they would be able to hold costs

down, without having a negative impact on the quality of care, by negotiating lower fees from providers, reducing inefficiency, and cracking down on medically unnecessary services. During the 1990s, managed care *was* successful in reducing the acceleration of medical costs in the United States (Fuchs, 1997). However, critics charge that managed care systems have squeezed all the savings they can out of the "fat" that existed in the old system and that they have responded to continued inflation in their costs and the need to be profitable by rationing care and limiting access to medically *necessary* services (Duckworth & Borus, 1999; Giles & Marafiote, 1998; Karon, 1995).

The possibility that managed care is having a negative effect on the quality of care is a source of concern throughout the health care professions, but the issue is especially sensitive in the domain of mental health care (Campbell, 2000). Critics maintain that mental health care has suffered particularly severe cuts in services because the question of what is "medically necessary" can be more subjective than in other treatment specialties (such as internal medicine or ophthalmology) and because patients who are denied psychotherapy services are relatively unlikely to complain (Duckworth & Borus, 1999). For example, a business executive who is trying to hide his depression or cocaine addiction from his employer will be reluctant to complain to his employer if therapeutic services are denied.

According to critics, the restriction of mental health services sometimes involves outright denial of treatment, but it often takes more subtle forms, such as underdiagnosing conditions, failing to make needed referrals to mental health specialists, and arbitrarily limiting the length of treatment (Miller, 1996). Long-term therapy is becoming a thing of the past unless patients can pay for it out of pocket, and the goal of treatment has been reduced to reestablishing a reasonable level of functioning (Zatzick, 1999). Many managed care systems hold down costs by erecting *barriers to access*, such as requiring referrals from primary care physicians who don't have appointments available for weeks or months, or authorizing only a few sessions of therapy at a time. Another cost-cutting strategy is the rerouting of patients from highly trained providers, such as psychiatrists and doctoral-level psychologists, to less well-trained providers, such as masters-level counselors, who may not be adequately prepared to handle serious psychological disorders (Seligman & Levant, 1998). Cost containment is also achieved by requiring physicians to prescribe older antidepressant and antipsychotic drugs instead of the newer and much more expensive SSRIs and atypical antipsychotics, even though the newer drugs have fewer side effects and are more effective for some types of patients (Docherty, 1999).

The extensive utilization review procedures required by managed care have also raised concerns about providers' autonomy and clients' confidentiality (Plante, 1999). Clinicians who have to "sell" their treatment plans to managed care bureaucrats who may know little about mental health care often feel that they have lost control over their professional practice. They also worry that the need to divulge the details of clients' problems to justify treatment may breach the confidentiality of the therapist-client relationship.

Given these realities, it is not surprising that 79% of the psychologists in one national survey indicated that managed care had negatively affected the quality of their treatment efforts (Phelps, Eisman, & Kohout, 1998). Unfortunately, there are no simple solutions to these problems on the horizon. Restraining the burgeoning cost of health care without compromising the quality of care, consumers' freedom of choice, and providers' autonomy is an enormously complex and daunting challenge. At this juncture, it is difficult to predict what the future holds. However, it is clear that economic realities have ushered in an era of transition for the treatment of psychological disorders and problems.

Identifying Empirically Supported Treatments

One potentially positive outgrowth of grappling with the constraints of managed care systems—which often demand evidence that treatments are cost effective— has been for clinicians to increase their efforts to demonstrate the efficacy of their interventions. Psychologists have organized a process for identifying *empirically supported treatments* that have a solid research base attesting to their effectiveness. To qualify as empirically supported, procedures generally must have been found to be superior to placebo or no treatment, for a specific type of problem or disorder, in several or more carefully controlled experiments conducted by at least two or more independent research teams (Chambless & Hollon, 1998). To ensure that a specific *treatment* is tested, the therapists in these studies have to administer a "pure" version of the therapy (no mixing in strategies from other approaches), and they must adhere to detailed treatment manuals that spell out exactly how the therapy should unfold. Working with these standards, quite a variety of empirically supported treatments have been identified (Chambless & Ollendick, 2001; Nathan & Gorman, 1998). Although subjective judgments about research evidence remain an unavoidable problem (Beutler, 2000), the new emphasis on documenting the efficacy of treatments for specific problems seems to be a step in the right direction that promises to make therapeutic interventions more scientific and more reliable (Barlow, 1996; Wilson, 1996)

That said, the movement toward empirically supported treatments has also raised concerns in some quarters. Critics assert that in the real world patients come with unique mixtures of multiple problems that require creative therapeutic interventions. Hence, they argue that the manualized application of pure treatments to single problems does not reflect the complexity of the real world or the flexibility with which therapists must practice their craft (Garfield, 1996; Goldfried & Wolfe, 1998). In other words, they maintain that the emerging "gold standard" for judging therapy may be a highly artificial standard. They also worry that identifying a limited number of manualized therapies as "validated" will give the bureaucrats who run managed care systems even more control over how therapy is conducted (Henry, 1998). Finally, some clinicians argue that the movement toward empirically supported treatments runs counter to an important and healthy trend in treatment, the eclectic blending of therapeutic approaches (Fensterheim & Raw, 1996), which we will discuss next.

Blending Approaches to Treatment

In this chapter we have reviewed many approaches to treatment. However, there is no rule that a client must be treated with just one approach. Often, a clinician will use several techniques in working with a client. For example, a depressed person might receive cognitive therapy (an insight therapy), social skills training (a behavior therapy), and antidepressant medication (a biomedical therapy). Multiple approaches are particularly likely when a treatment team provides therapy. Studies suggest that combining approaches to treatment has merit, as you will see in our Featured Study for this chapter.

Investigators: Charles F. Reynolds III, Ellen Frank, James F. Perel, Stanley D. Imber, Cleon Cornes, Mark D. Miller, Sati Mazumdar, Patricia R. Houck, Mary Amanda Dew, Jacqueline A. Stack, Bruce G. Pollock, and David J. Kupfer (University of Pittsburgh Medical Center)

Source: Nortriptyline and interpersonal psychotherapy as maintenance therapies for recurrent major depression: A randomized controlled trial in patients older than 59 years. *Journal of the American Medical Association,* 1999, *281,* 39–45.

FEATURED STUDY

Combining Insight Therapy and Medication

Depression is common in older people and contributes to physical health problems, chronic disability, and increased mortality among the elderly. Geriatric depression is also a highly recurrent problem. After successful treatment of depression, elderly patients tend to relapse more quickly and more frequently than younger clients. The purpose of this study was to determine whether a combination of insight therapy and antidepressant medication could reduce the recurrence of depression in an elderly population.

Method

Participants. The participants were 107 elderly patients diagnosed with recurrent, unipolar, major depression. The minimum age of the patients was 60 and the mean age at the beginning of the study was 67.6. The subjects had all been successfully treated for a recent episode of depression and had remained stable for 4 months.

Treatments. The medication employed in the study was *nortriptyline,* a tricyclic antidepressant that appears to be relatively effective and well tolerated in elderly populations. The insight therapy was *interpersonal psychotherapy (IPT),* an approach to therapy that emphasizes the social roots of depression and focuses on how improved social relations can protect against depression (Klerman & Weissman, 1993). Clients learn how social isolation and unsatisfying interpersonal relationships can provoke depression and how confidants and supportive interactions can decrease vulnerability to depression.

Design. The subjects were randomly assigned to one of four maintenance treatment conditions: (1) monthly interpersonal therapy and medication, (2) medication alone, (3) monthly interpersonal therapy and placebo medication, and (4) placebo medication alone. A *double-blind* procedure was employed, so the clinicians who provided the treatments did not know which subjects were getting genuine medication as opposed to placebo pills. Patients remained in maintenance treatment for three years or until a recurrence of a major depressive episode.

Results

The relapse rates for the four treatment conditions are shown in Figure 15.12. The relapse rate for the combination of interpersonal therapy and medication was significantly less than that for either medication alone or interpersonal therapy alone (with placebo medication). The prophylactic value of the combined therapy proved most valuable to patients over 70 years of age and during the first year of the study, during which most relapses occurred.

Discussion

The authors conclude that "the continuation of combined medication and psychotherapy may represent the best long-term treatment strategy for preserving recovery in elderly patients with recurrent major depression" (p. 44). They speculate that the combined treatment may be "best-suited for dealing with both the biological and psychosocial substrates of old-age depression" (p. 45). However, they acknowledge the need for further research and recommend additional studies with

Figure 15.12

Relapse rates in the Reynolds et al. (1999) study. Following up over a period of three years, Reynolds et al. (1999) compared the preventive value of (1) monthly interpersonal therapy and medication, (2) medication alone, (3) monthly interpersonal therapy and placebo medication, and (4) placebo medication alone in a sample of elderly patients prone to recurrent depression. The combined treatment of insight therapy and medication yielded the lowest relapse rates and thus proved superior to either insight therapy or drug therapy alone. (Data from Reynolds et al., 1999)

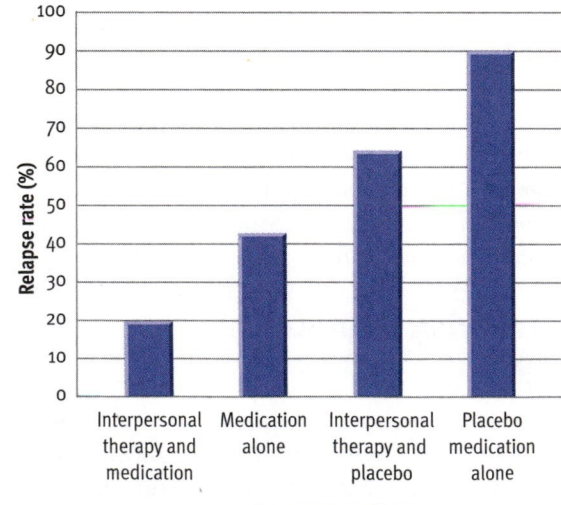

newer antidepressant drugs (the SSRIs) that are increasingly popular.

Comment

This study was featured because it illustrated how to conduct a well-controlled experimental evaluation of the efficacy of therapeutic interventions. It also high-lighted the value of combining approaches to treatment, which is a laudable trend in the treatment of psychological disorders. The fact that the study was published in the highly prestigious *Journal of the American Medical Association* also demonstrates how prominent and important research on therapeutic efficacy has become in the era of managed care. ∎

The value of multiple approaches to treatment may explain why a significant trend seems to have crept into the field of psychotherapy: a movement away from strong loyalty to individual schools of thought and a corresponding move toward integrating various approaches to therapy (Norcross & Gold-fried, 1992; D. A. Smith, 1999). Most clinicians used to depend exclusively on one system of therapy while rejecting the utility of all others. This era of fragmentation may be drawing to a close. In recent surveys of psychologists' theoretical orientations, researchers have been surprised to find that the greatest proportion of respondents describe themselves as *eclectic* in approach (Garfield & Bergin, 1994).

Eclecticism in the practice of therapy involves drawing ideas from two or more systems of therapy instead of committing to just one system. Therapists can be eclectic in a number of ways (Arkowitz, 1992). Two common approaches are theoretical integration and technical eclecticism. In *theoretical integration,* two or more systems of therapy are combined or blended to take advantage of the strengths of each. Paul Wachtel's (1977, 1991) efforts to blend psycho-dynamic and behavioral therapies is a prominent example. *Technical eclecticism* involves borrowing ideas, insights, and techniques from a variety of sources while tailoring one's intervention strategy to the unique needs of each client. Advocates of technical eclecticism, such as Arnold Lazarus (1989, 1992, 1995), maintain that therapists should ask themselves, "What is the best approach for this specific client, problem, and situation?" and then adjust their strategy accordingly.

Increasing Multicultural Sensitivity in Treatment

Modern psychotherapy emerged during the second half of the 19th century in Europe and America, spawned in part by a cultural milieu that viewed the self as an independent, reflective, rational being, capable of self-improvement (Cushman, 1992). Psy-chological disorders were assumed to have natural causes like physical diseases and to be amenable to medical treatments derived from scientific research. But the individualized, medicalized institution of modern psychotherapy reflects Western cultural values that are far from universal (Sue & Sue, 1999). In many nonindustrialized societies, psychological disorders are attributed to supernatural forces (possession, witchcraft, angry gods, and so forth), and victims seek help from priests, shamans, and folk healers, rather than doctors (Wittkower & Warnes, 1984). Thus, efforts to export Western psychotherapies to non-Western cultures have met with mixed success. Indeed, as the Surgeon General's report on mental health emphasizes, the highly culture-bound origins of modern therapies have raised questions about their applicability to ethnic minorities *within* Western culture.

Research on how cultural factors influence the process and outcome of psychotherapy has burgeoned in recent years, motivated in part by the need to improve mental health services for ethnic minority groups in American society (Lee & Ramirez, 2000). The data are ambiguous for a couple of ethnic groups, but studies suggest that American minority groups generally underutilize therapeutic services (Mays & Albee, 1992; Vega et al., 1999; Wells et al., 2001). Why? A variety of barriers appear to contribute to this problem, including the following (Sue, Zane, & Young, 1994; Takeuchi, Uehara, & Maramba, 1999; U.S. Department of Health and Human Services, 1999):

1. *Cultural barriers.* In times of psychological distress, some cultural groups are reluctant to turn to formal, professional sources of assistance. Given their socialization, they prefer to rely on informal assistance from family members, the clergy, respected elders, herbalists, acupuncturists, and so forth, who share their cultural heritage. Many members of minority groups have a history of frustrating interactions with American bureaucracies and are distrustful of large, intimidating, foreign institutions, such

as hospitals and community mental health centers (Pierce, 1992).

2. *Language barriers*. Effective communication is crucial to the provision of psychotherapy, yet most hospitals and mental health agencies are not adequately staffed with therapists who speak the languages used by minority groups in their service areas. The resulting communication problems make it awkward and difficult for many minority group members to explain their problems and to obtain the type of help that they need.

3. *Access barriers*. Many minority groups suffer from elevated rates of joblessness and poverty. In our society, people who are unemployed or employed in economically marginal jobs typically do not have health insurance. Thus, poverty and lack of health insurance severely restricts the options of many minorities in pursuing treatment for psychological problems (Miranda & Green, 1999).

4. *Institutional barriers*. When all is said and done, Stanley Sue and Nolan Zane (1987) argue that the "single most important explanation for the problems in service delivery involves the inability of therapists to provide culturally responsive forms of treatment" (p. 37). The vast majority of therapists have been trained almost exclusively in the treatment of white, middle-class Americans and are not familiar with the cultural backgrounds and unique characteristics of various ethnic groups. This culture gap often leads to misunderstandings and ill-advised treatment strategies (Hughes, 1993). Unfortunately, there is a grievous shortage of ethnic therapists to meet the needs of various ethnic groups (Mays & Albee, 1992).

What can be done to improve mental health services for American minority groups? Researchers in this area have offered a variety of suggestions (Homma-True et al., 1993; Hong, Garcia, & Soriano, 2000; Pedersen, 1994; Yamamoto et al., 1993). Discussions of possible solutions usually begin with the

need to recruit and train more ethnic minority therapists. Studies show that ethnic minorities are more likely to go to mental health facilities that are staffed by a higher proportion of people who share their ethnic background (Snowden & Hu, 1996; Sue et al., 1994). Furthermore, clients' satisfaction with therapy tends to be greater when they are treated by therapists from their own culture. Therapists can also be given special training to work more effectively with people from different cultural backgrounds. Finally, most authorities urge further investigation of how traditional approaches to therapy can be modified and tailored to be more compatible with specific cultural groups' attitudes, values, norms, and traditions.

REVIEW OF KEY POINTS

● Many clinicians and their clients believe that managed care has restricted access to mental health care and undermined its quality. Managed care has also raised concerns about providers' autonomy and clients' confidentiality. One response to the demands of managed care has been to increase research efforts to validate the efficacy of specific treatments for specific problems.

● Combinations of insight, behavioral, and biomedical therapies are often used fruitfully in the treatment of psychological disorders. For example, our Featured Study showed how the tandem of interpersonal therapy and antidepressant medication could be valuable in preventing additional depressive episodes in an elderly population. Many modern therapists are eclectic, using specific ideas, techniques, and strategies gleaned from a number of theoretical approaches.

● The highly culture-bound origins of Western therapies have raised doubts about their applicability to other cultures and even to ethnic groups in Western society. Because of cultural, language, and access barriers, therapeutic services are underutilized by ethnic minorities in America.

● More culturally responsive approaches to treatment will require more minority therapists, special training for therapists, and additional investigation of how traditional therapies can be tailored to be more compatible with specific ethnic groups' cultural heritage.

Institutional Treatment in Transition

PREVIEW QUESTIONS
● What led to the community mental health movement?
● What is deinstitutionalization, and what problems has it been blamed for?
● Is increased homelessness a mental health problem or an economic problem?

Traditionally, much of the treatment of mental illness has been carried out in institutional settings, primarily in mental hospitals. A *mental hospital is a medical institution specializing in providing inpatient care for psychological disorders*. In the United States, a national network of state-funded mental hospitals started to emerge in the 1840s through the efforts of Dorothea Dix and other reformers (see Figure 15.13). Prior to these reforms,

the mentally ill who were poor were housed in jails and poorhouses or were left to wander the countryside. Today, mental hospitals continue to play an important role in the delivery of mental health services. However, since World War II, institutional care for mental illness has undergone a series of major transitions—and the dust hasn't settled yet. Let's look at how institutional care has evolved in recent decades.

Disenchantment with Mental Hospitals

By the 1950s, it had become apparent that public mental hospitals were not fulfilling their goals very well (Mechanic, 1980). Experts began to realize that hospitalization often *contributed* to the development of pathology instead of curing it.

What were the causes of these unexpected negative effects? Part of the problem was that the facilities were usually underfunded (Bloom, 1984). The lack of adequate funding meant that the facilities were overcrowded and understaffed. Hospital personnel were undertrained and overworked, making them hard-pressed to deliver minimal custodial care. Despite gallant efforts at treatment, the demoralizing conditions made most public mental hospitals decidedly nontherapeutic (Scull, 1990). These problems were aggravated by the fact that state mental hospitals served large geographic regions but were rarely placed near major population centers. Hence, most patients were uprooted from their community and isolated from their social support networks.

Disenchantment with the public mental hospital system inspired the *community mental health movement* that emerged in the 1960s (Duckworth & Borus, 1999). The community mental health movement emphasizes (1) local, community-based care, (2) reduced dependence on hospitalization, and (3) the prevention of psychological disorders. The community mental health movement jumped into prominence in 1963 when John F. Kennedy became the first American president ever to address the nation on the subject of mental health. Kennedy outlined an ambitious plan to build a national network of community mental health centers. Thus, in the 1960s much of the responsibility for the treatment of psychological disorders was turned over to community mental health centers, which supplement mental hospitals with decentralized and more accessible services.

Deinstitutionalization

Mental hospitals continue to care for many people troubled by chronic mental illness, but their role in patient care has diminished. Since the 1960s, a policy of deinstitutionalization has been followed in the United States, as well as most other Western countries. *Deinstitutionalization* refers to transferring the treatment of mental illness from inpatient institutions to community-based facilities that emphasize outpatient care. This shift in responsibility was made possible by two developments: (1) the emergence of effective drug therapies for severe disor-

ders and (2) the deployment of community mental health centers to coordinate local care (Goff & Gudeman, 1999).

The exodus of patients from mental hospitals has been dramatic. In the United States, the average inpatient population in state and county mental hospitals dropped from a peak of nearly 550,000 in the mid-1950s to around 70,000 in the late 1990s, as shown in Figure 15.14. These trends do *not* mean that hospitalization for mental illness has become a thing of the past. A great many people are still hospitalized, but there's been a shift toward placing them in local general hospitals for brief periods instead of distant psychiatric hospitals for long periods (Kiesler, 1992). In keeping with the philosophy of deinstitutionalization, these local facilities try to get

Figure 15.13

Dorothea Dix and the advent of mental hospitals in America. During the 19th century, Dorothea Dix (inset) campaigned tirelessly to obtain funds for building mental hospitals. Many of these hospitals, such as the New York State Lunatic Asylum, were extremely large facilities. Although public mental hospitals improved the care of the mentally ill, they had a variety of shortcomings, which eventually prompted the deinstitutionalization movement.

SOURCE: Culver Pictures, Inc.; (inset) Detail of painting in Harrisburg State Hospital, photo by Ken Smith/LLR Collection.

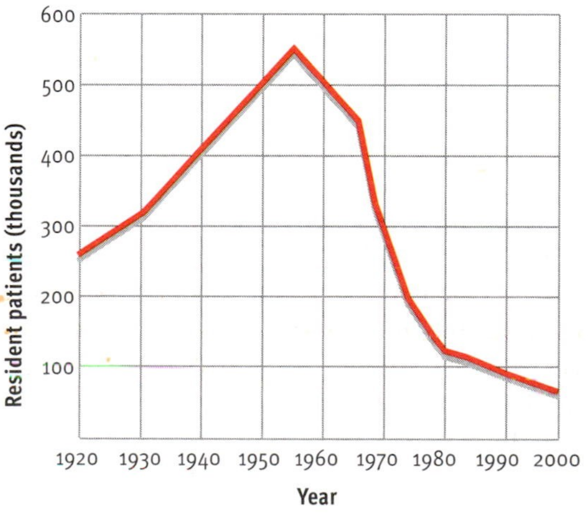

Figure 15.14

Declining inpatient population at state and county mental hospitals. The inpatient population in public mental hospitals has declined dramatically since the late 1950s, as a result of deinstitutionalization and the development of effective antipsychotic medication. (Data from the National Institute of Mental Health)

patients stabilized and back into the community as swiftly as possible.

How has deinstitutionalization worked out? It gets mixed reviews. On the positive side, many people have benefited by avoiding or shortening disruptive and unnecessary hospitalization. Ample evidence suggests that alternatives to hospitalization can be both as effective as and less costly than inpatient care (McGrew et al., 1999; Reinharz, Lesage, & Contandriopoulos, 2000). Moreover, follow-up studies of discharged patients reveal that a substantial majority prefer the greater freedom provided by community-based treatment (Leff, Trieman, & Gooch, 1996).

Nonetheless, some unanticipated problems have arisen (Elpers, 2000; Munk-Jorgensen, 1999). Many patients suffering from chronic psychological disorders had nowhere to go when they were released. They had no families, friends, or homes to return to. Many had no work skills and were poorly prepared to live on their own. These people were supposed to be absorbed by "halfway houses," sheltered workshops, and other types of intermediate care facilities. Unfortunately, many communities were never able to fund and build the planned facilities (H. Lamb, 1998). Coordination of support services for the chronically mentally ill has often been poor, and former patients have not been integrated effectively into their communities (Dewees, Pulice, & McCormick, 1996). Thus, deinstitutionalization left two major problems in its wake: a "revolving door" population of people who flow in and out of psychiatric facilities, and a sizable population of homeless mentally ill people.

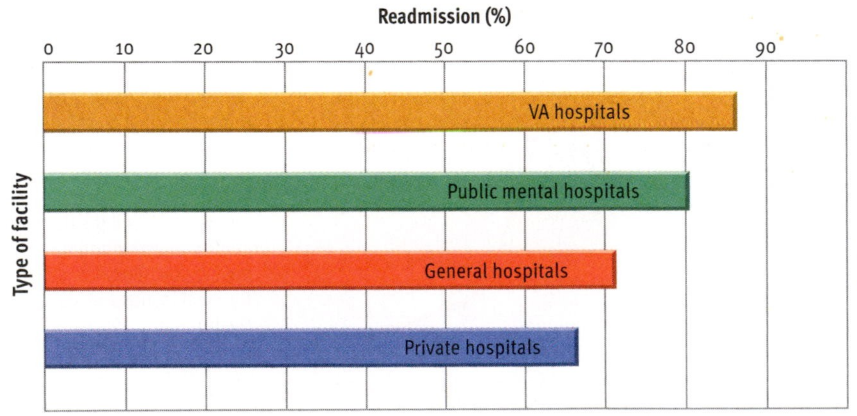

Mental Illness, the Revolving Door, and Homelessness

Although the proportion of hospital days attributable to mental illness has dwindled, admission rates for psychiatric hospitalization have actually climbed.

What has happened? Deinstitutionalization and drug therapy have created a revolving door through which many mentally ill people pass again and again (Geller, 1992; Langdon et al., 2001).

Most of the people caught in the mental health system's revolving door suffer from chronic, severe disorders that frequently require hospitalization (Haywood et al., 1995). They respond well to drug therapies in the hospital, but once they're stabilized through drug therapy, they no longer qualify for expensive hospital treatment according to the new standards created by deinstitutionalization. Thus, they're sent back out the door, into communities that often aren't prepared to provide adequate outpatient care. Because they lack appropriate care and support, their condition deteriorates and they soon require readmission to a hospital, where the cycle begins once again. Over two-thirds of all psychiatric inpatient admissions involve rehospitalizing a former patient, as Figure 15.15 shows.

Deinstitutionalization has also been blamed for the growing population of homeless people. Studies have consistently found elevated rates of mental illness among the homeless. Taken as a whole, the evidence suggests that roughly one-third of the homeless suffer from severe mental illness (schizophrenic and mood disorders), that another one-third or more are struggling with alcohol and drug problems, and that many qualify for multiple diagnoses (Bassuk et al., 1998; Haugland et al., 1997; Vazquez, Munoz, & Sanz, 1997).

The popular media routinely equate homelessness with mental illness, and it is widely assumed that deinstitutionalization is largely responsible for the rapid growth of homelessness in America. Although deinstitutionalization probably has *contributed* to the growth of homelessness, many experts in this area maintain that it is misleading to blame the problem of homelessness chiefly on deinstitutionalization (Main, 1998; Sullivan, Burnam, & Koegel, 2000).

Those who criticize the tendency to equate homelessness with mental illness worry that this equation diverts attention from the real causes of the homelessness crisis (Kiesler, 1991). They marshal evidence to show that the sharp increase in the homeless population is due to a variety of economic, social, and political trends, including increased unemployment and poverty, decreased support for welfare and subsidized housing programs, the loss of much low-income housing to urban renewal, and so forth (Cohen & Thompson, 1992; McCarty et al., 1991; Rossi, 1990). They maintain that homelessness is primarily an economic problem and that it requires economic solutions.

Figure 15.15

Percentage of psychiatric inpatient admissions that are readmissions. The extent of the revolving door problem is apparent from these figures on the percentage of inpatient admissions that are readmissions at various types of facilities. (Data from the National Institute of Mental Health)

Readmission (%)

Type of facility	
VA hospitals	~80
Public mental hospitals	~75
General hospitals	~65
Private hospitals	~50

In light of the revolving door problem and homelessness among the mentally ill, what can we conclude about deinstitutionalization? It appears to be a worthwhile idea that has been poorly executed (H. Lamb, 1998). Overall, the policy has probably been a benefit to countless people with milder disorders but a cruel trick on many others with severe, chronic disorders. Ultimately, it's clear that our society is not providing adequate care for a sizable segment of the mentally ill population (Elpers, 2000; Torrey, 1996). That's not a new development. Inadequate care for mental illness has always been the norm. Societies always struggle with the problem of what to do with the mentally ill and how to pay for their care (Duckworth & Borus, 1999).

What's the solution? Virtually no one advocates returning to the era of custodial warehouses. Many do advocate increasing the quality and availability of intermediate care facilities and programs (Lamb, 1999). Research shows that intermediate care initiatives (such as outreach and case management programs) can be effective, but they require significant funding (Rosenheck, 2000). Only time will tell whether American society will be willing to make the financial commitment to follow through on this recommendation.

Putting It in Perspective

In our discussion of psychotherapy, one of our unifying themes—the value of theoretical diversity—was particularly prominent, and one other theme—the importance of culture—surfaced briefly. Let's discuss the latter theme first. The approaches to treatment described in this chapter are products of modern, white, middle-class, Western culture. Some of these therapies have proven useful in some other cultures, but many have turned out to be irrelevant or counterproductive when used with different cultural groups, including ethnic minorities in Western society. Thus, we have seen once again that cultural factors influence psychological processes and that Western psychology cannot assume that its theories and practices have universal applicability.

As for theoretical diversity, its value can be illustrated with a rhetorical question: Can you imagine what the state of modern psychotherapy would be if everyone in psychology and psychiatry had simply accepted Freud's theories about the nature and treatment of psychological disorders? If not for theoretical diversity, psychotherapy might still be in the dark ages. Psychoanalysis can be a useful method of therapy, but it would be a tragic state of affairs if it were the *only* treatment available. Multitudes of people have benefited from alternative approaches to treatment that emerged out of tensions between psychoanalytic theory and other theoretical perspectives. People have diverse problems, rooted in varied origins, that call for the pursuit of different therapeutic goals. Thus, it's fortunate that people can choose from a diverse array of approaches to treatment. The graphic overview on pages 628–629 summarizes and compares the approaches that we've discussed in this chapter. This summary chart shows that the major approaches to treatment each have their own vision of the nature of human discontent and the ideal remedy.

Of course, diversity can be confusing. The range and variety of available treatments in modern psychotherapy leaves many people puzzled about their options. Thus, in our Personal Application we'll sort through the practical issues involved in selecting a therapist.

PREVIEW QUESTIONS
● How did this chapter illustrate the importance of cultural factors?
● How did this chapter illustrate the value of theoretical diversity?

REVIEW OF KEY POINTS

● Disenchantment with the negative effects of mental hospitals led to the advent of more localized community mental health centers and a policy of deinstitutionalization. Long-term hospitalization for mental disorders is largely a thing of the past.

● Unfortunately, deinstitutionalization has left some unanticipated problems in its wake, including the revolving door problem and increased homelessness, although some theorists argue that homelessness is primarily an economic problem.

● Our discussion of psychotherapy highlighted the value of theoretical diversity. Conflicting theoretical orientations have generated varied approaches to treatment. Our coverage of therapy also showed once again that cultural factors shape psychological processes.

Looking for a Therapist

Answer the following "true" or "false."

_____ **1** Psychotherapy is an art as well as a science.

_____ **2** Psychotherapy can be harmful or damaging to a client.

_____ **3** Psychotherapy does not have to be expensive.

_____ **4** The type of professional degree that a therapist holds is relatively unimportant.

All of these statements are true. Do any of them surprise you? If so, you're in good company. Many people know relatively little about the practicalities of selecting a therapist.

The task of finding an appropriate therapist is complex. Should you see a psychologist or psychiatrist? Should you opt for individual therapy or group therapy? Should you see a client-centered therapist or a behavior therapist? The unfortunate part of this situation is that people seeking psychotherapy often feel overwhelmed by personal problems. The last thing they need is to be confronted by yet another complex problem.

Nonetheless, the importance of finding a good therapist cannot be overestimated. Treatment can sometimes have harmful rather than helpful effects. We have already discussed how drug therapies and ECT can sometimes be damaging, but problems are not limited to these interventions. Talking about your problems with a therapist may sound pretty harmless, but studies indicate that insight therapies can also backfire (Lambert & Bergin, 1994; Singer & Lalich, 1996). Although a great many talented therapists are available, psychotherapy, like any other profession, has incompetent practitioners as well. Therefore, you should shop for a skilled therapist, just as you would for a good attorney or a good mechanic.

In this application, we'll go over some information that should be helpful if you ever have to look for a therapist for yourself or for a friend or family member (based on Beutler, Bongar, & Shurkin, 1998; Bruckner-Gordon, Gangi, & Wallman, 1988; Ehrenberg & Ehrenberg, 1994; Pittman, 1994).

Where Do You Find Therapeutic Services?

Psychotherapy can be found in a variety of settings. Contrary to general belief, most therapists are not in private practice. Many work in institutional settings such as community mental health centers, hospitals, and human service agencies. The principal sources of therapeutic services are described in Table 15.2. The exact configuration of therapeutic services available will vary from one community to another. To find out what your community has to offer, it is a good idea to consult your friends, your local phone book, or your local community mental health center.

Is the Therapist's Profession or Sex Important?

Psychotherapists may be trained in psychology, psychiatry, social work, counseling, psychiatric nursing, or marriage and family therapy. Researchers have *not* found any reliable associations between therapists' professional background and therapeutic efficacy (Beutler, Machado, & Neufeldt, 1994), probably because many talented therapists can be found in all of these professions. Thus, the kind of degree that a therapist holds doesn't need to be a crucial

Table 15.2 Principal Sources of Therapeutic Services

Source	Comments
Private practitioners	Self-employed therapists are listed in the Yellow Pages under their professional category, such as psychologists or psychiatrists. Private practitioners tend to be relatively expensive, but they also tend to be highly experienced therapists.
Community mental health centers	Community mental health centers have salaried psychologists, psychiatrists, and social workers on staff. The centers provide a variety of services and often have staff available on weekends and at night to deal with emergencies.
Hospitals	Several kinds of hospitals provide therapeutic services. There are both public and private mental hospitals that specialize in the care of people with psychological disorders. Many general hospitals have a psychiatric ward, and those that do not usually have psychiatrists and psychologists on staff and on call. Although hospitals tend to concentrate on inpatient treatment, many provide outpatient therapy as well.
Human service agencies	Various social service agencies employ therapists to provide short-term counseling. Depending on your community, you may find agencies that deal with family problems, juvenile problems, drug problems, and so forth.
Schools and workplaces	Most high schools and colleges have counseling centers where students can get help with personal problems. Similarly, some large businesses offer in-house counseling to their employees.

Finding the right therapist is no easy task. You need to take into account the therapist's training and orientation, fees charged, and personality. An initial visit should give you a good idea of what a particular therapist is like.

consideration in your selection process. At the present time, it is true that psychiatrists are the only type of therapists who can prescribe drugs. However, other types of therapists can refer you to a psychiatrist if they think that drug therapy would be helpful.

Whether a therapist's sex is important depends on your attitude. If *you* feel that the therapist's sex is important, then for you it is. The therapeutic relationship must be characterized by trust and rapport. Feeling uncomfortable with a therapist of one sex or the other could inhibit the therapeutic process. Hence, you should feel free to look for a male or female therapist if you prefer to do so. This point is probably most relevant to female clients whose troubles may be related to the extensive sexism in our society (A. Kaplan, 1985). It is entirely reasonable for women to seek a therapist with a feminist perspective if that would make them feel more comfortable.

Speaking of sex, you should be aware that sexual exploitation is an occasional problem in the context of therapy. Studies indicate that a small minority of therapists

take advantage of their clients sexually (Pope, Keith-Spiegel, & Tabachnick, 1986). These incidents almost always involve a

male therapist making advances to a female client. The available evidence indicates that these sexual liaisons are usually very harmful to clients (Gabbard, 1994; Williams, 1992). There are absolutely no situations in which therapist-client sexual relations are an ethical therapeutic practice. If a therapist makes sexual advances, a client should terminate treatment.

Is Treatment Always Expensive?

Psychotherapy does not have to be prohibitively expensive. Private practitioners tend to be the most expensive, charging between $75 and $140 per (50-minute) hour. These fees may seem high, but they are in line with those of similar professionals, such as dentists and attorneys. Community mental health centers and social service agencies are usually supported by tax dollars. Hence, they can charge lower fees than most therapists in private practice. Many of these organizations use a sliding scale, so that clients are charged according to how much they can afford to pay. Thus, most communities have inexpensive opportunities

Therapy is both a science and an art. It is scientific in that practitioners are guided in their work by a huge body of empirical research. It is an art in that therapists often have to be creative in adapting their treatment procedures to individual patients and their idiosyncrasies.

Figure 15.16

Estimates of the effectiveness of various approaches to psychotherapy. Smith and Glass (1977) reviewed nearly 400 studies in which clients who were treated with a specific type of therapy were compared with a control group made up of individuals with similar problems who went untreated. The bars indicate the percentile rank (on outcome measures) attained by the average client treated with each type of therapy when compared to control subjects. The higher the percentile, the more effective the therapy was. As you can see, the various approaches were fairly similar in their overall effectiveness.

Source: Adapted from Smith, M. L., & Glass, G. V. (1977). Meta-analysis of psychotherapy outcome series. *American Psychologist, 32,* 752–760. Copyright © 1977 by the American Psychological Association. Adapted by permission of the author.

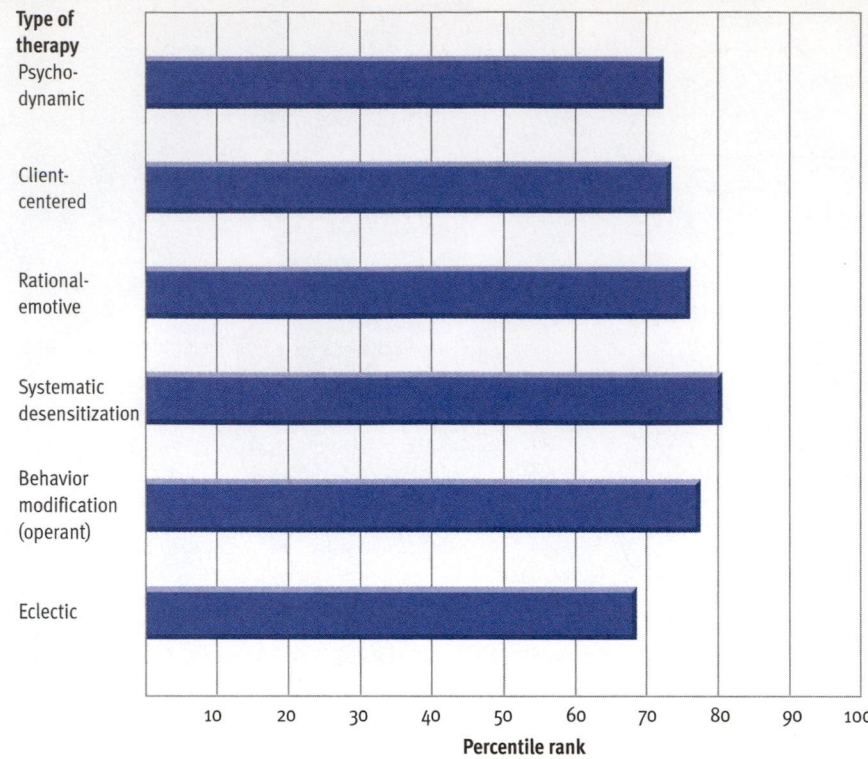

Is the Therapist's Theoretical Approach Important?

Logically, you might expect that the diverse approaches to therapy vary in effectiveness. For the most part, this is *not* what researchers find, however. After reviewing many studies of therapeutic efficacy, Jerome Frank (1961) and Lester Luborsky and his colleagues (1975) both quote the dodo bird who has just judged a race in *Alice in Wonderland:* "*Everybody* has won, and *all* must have prizes." Improvement rates for various theoretical orientations usually come out pretty close in most studies (Lambert & Bergin, 1994; Luborsky et al., 2002; Wampold, 2001; see Figure 15.16).

However, these findings are a little misleading, as the estimates of overall effectiveness have been averaged across many types of patients and many types of problems. Most experts seem to think that *for certain types of problems, some approaches to therapy are more effective than others* (Beutler, 2002; Crits-Christoph, 1997; Norcross, 1995). For example, Martin Seligman (1995) asserts that panic disorders respond best to cognitive therapy, that specific phobias are most amenable to treatment with systematic desensitization, and that obsessive-compulsive disorders are best treated with behavior therapy or medication. Thus, for a specific type of problem, a therapist's theoretical approach *may* make a difference.

It is also important to point out that the finding that different approaches to therapy are roughly equal in overall efficacy does not mean that all *therapists* are created equal. Some therapists unquestionably are more effective than others. However, these variations in effectiveness appear to depend on individual therapists' personal skills rather than on their theoretical orientation (Beutler et al., 1994). Good, bad, and mediocre therapists are found within each school of thought.

The key point is that effective therapy requires skill and creativity. Arnold Lazarus, who devised multimodal therapy, emphasizes that therapists "straddle the fence between science and art." Therapy is scientific in that interventions are based on extensive theory and empirical research (Forsyth & Strong, 1986). Ultimately, though, each client is a unique human being, and the therapist has to creatively fashion a treatment program that will help that individual.

What Should You Look For in a Prospective Therapist?

Some clients are timid about asking prospective therapists questions about their training, approach, fees, and so forth. However, these are reasonable questions, and the vast majority of therapists will be most accommodating in providing answers. Usually, you can ask your preliminary questions over the phone. If things seem promising, you may decide to make an appointment

for psychotherapy. Moreover, most health insurance plans and HMOs provide coverage for at least some forms of mental health care.

for an interview (for which you will probably have to pay). In this interview, the therapist will gather more information to determine the likelihood of helping you, given his or her training and approach to treatment. At the same time, you should be making a similar judgment about whether *you* believe the therapist can help you with your problems.

What should you look for? First, you should look for personal warmth and sincere concern. Try to judge whether you will be able to talk to this person in a candid, nondefensive way. Second, look for empathy and understanding. Is the person capable of appreciating your point of view? Third, look for self-confidence. Self-assured therapists will communicate a sense of competence without trying to intimidate you with jargon or boasting needlessly about what they can do for you. When all is said and done, you should *like* your therapist. Otherwise, it will be difficult to establish the needed rapport.

What If There Isn't Any Progress?

If you feel that your therapy isn't going anywhere, you should probably discuss these feelings with your therapist. Don't be surprised, however, if the therapist suggests that it may be your own fault. The concept of *resistance* originally described by Freud has some validity (Beutler et al., 2001). Some clients *do* have difficulty facing up to their problems. Thus, if your therapy isn't progressing, you may need to *consider* whether your resistance may be slowing progress. This self-examination isn't easy, as you are not an unbiased observer. Some common signs of resistance identified by Ehrenberg and Ehrenberg (1994) are listed in Figure 15.17.

Given the very real possibility that poor progress may be due to resistance, you should not be too quick to leave therapy when dissatisfied. However, it *is* possible that your therapist isn't sufficiently skilled or that the two of you are incompatible. Thus, after careful and deliberate consideration, you should feel free to terminate your therapy.

What Is Therapy Like?

It is important to have realistic expectations about therapy, or you may be unnecessarily disappointed. Some people expect miracles. They expect to turn their life around quickly with little effort. Others expect their therapist to run their lives for them. These are unrealistic expectations.

Therapy is usually a slow process. Your problems are not likely to melt away quickly. Moreover, therapy is hard work, and your therapist is only a facilitator. Ultimately, *you* have to confront the challenge of changing your behavior, your feelings, or your personality. This process may not be pleasant. You may have to face up to some painful truths about yourself. As Ehrenberg and Ehrenberg (1986) point out, "Psychotherapy takes time, effort, and courage."

REVIEW OF KEY POINTS

● Therapeutic services are available in many settings, and such services need not be expensive. Both excellent and mediocre therapists can be found in all of the mental health professions. Thus, therapists' personal skills are more important than their professional degree.

● The various theoretical approaches to therapy appear to be fairly similar in overall effectiveness. However, for certain types of problems, some approaches are probably more effective than others, and all therapists are not created equal.

● In selecting a therapist, warmth, empathy, confidence, and likability are desirable traits, and it is reasonable to insist on a therapist of one sex or the other. If progress is slow, your own resistance may be the problem.

Figure 15.17

Signs of resistance. Resistance in therapy may be subtle, but Ehrenberg and Ehrenberg (1994) have identified some telltale signs to look for.

Signs of resistance in therapy
If you're dissatisfied with your progress in therapy, resistance may be the problem when:
1   You have nothing specific or concrete to complain about.
2   Your attitude about therapy changes suddenly just as you reach the truly sensitive issues.
3   You've had the same problem with other therapists in the past.
4   Your conflicts with the therapist resemble those that you have with other people.
5   You start hiding things from your therapist.

From Crisis to Wellness— But Was It the Therapy?

It often happens this way. Problems seem to go from bad to worse—the trigger could be severe pressures at work, an acrimonious fight with your spouse, or a child's unruly behavior spiraling out of control. At some point, you recognize that it might be prudent to seek professional assistance from a therapist, but where do you turn? If you are like most people, you will probably hesitate before actively seeking professional help. People hesitate because therapy carries a stigma, because the task of finding a therapist is daunting, and because they hope that their psychological problems will clear up on their own—which *does* happen with some regularity. When people finally decide to pursue mental health care, it is often because they feel like they have reached rock bottom in terms of their functioning and they have no choice. Motivated by their crisis, they enter into treatment, looking for a ray of hope. Will therapy help them feel better?

It may surprise you to learn that the answer *generally* would be "yes," even if professional treatment itself were utterly worthless and totally ineffectual. There are two major reasons that people entering therapy are likely to get better, regardless of whether their treatment is effective. You can probably guess one of these reasons, which has been mentioned repeatedly in the chapter: the power of the *placebo*. **Placebo effects** occur when people's expectations lead them to experience some change even though they receive a fake treatment** (like getting a sugar pill instead of a real drug). Clients generally enter therapy with expectations that it will have positive effects, and as we have emphasized throughout this text, *people have a remarkable tendency to see what they expect to see*. Because of this factor, studies of the efficacy of medical drugs always include a placebo condition in which subjects are given fake medication (see Chapter 2). Research-

ers are often quite surprised by just how much the placebo subjects improve (Fisher & Greenberg, 1997; Walsh et al., 2002). Placebo effects can be very powerful and should be taken into consideration whenever efforts are made to evaluate the efficacy of some approach to treatment.

The other factor at work is the main focus in this Application. It is an interesting statistical phenomenon that we have not discussed previously: *regression toward the mean*. **Regression toward the mean occurs when people who score extremely high or low on some trait are measured a second time and their new scores fall closer to the mean (average).** Regression effects work in both directions: On the second measurement high scorers tend to fall back toward the mean and low scorers tend to creep upward toward the mean. For example, let's say we wanted to evaluate the effectiveness of a one-day coaching program intended to improve performance on the SAT test. We reason that coaching is most likely to help students who have performed poorly on the test, so we recruit a sample of high school students who have previously scored in the bottom 20% on

the SAT. Thanks to regression toward the mean, most of these students will score higher if they take the SAT a second time, so our coaching program may *look* effective even if it has no value. By the way, if we set out to see whether our coaching program could increase the performance of high scorers, regression effects would be working *against* us. If we recruited a sample of students who had scored in the upper 20% on the SAT, there would be a tendency for their scores to move downward when tested a second time, which could cancel out most or all of the beneficial effects of the coaching program. The processes underlying regression toward the mean are complex matters of probability, but they can be approximated by a simple principle: If you are near the bottom, there's almost nowhere to go but up, and if you are near the top, there's almost nowhere to go but down.

What does all of this have to do with the effects of professional treatment for psychological problems and disorders? Well, chance variations in the ups and downs of life occur for all of us. But recall that most people enter psychotherapy during a time of severe crisis, when they are at a really

Placebo effects and regression toward the mean are two prominent factors that make it difficult to evaluate the efficacy of various approaches to therapy.

© International Stock/Robert Harding Picture Library

Placebo effects and regression toward the mean are two prominent factors that make it difficult to evaluate the efficacy of various approaches to therapy.

low point in their lives. If you measure the mental health of a group of people entering therapy, they will mostly get relatively low scores. If you measure their mental health again a few months later, chances are that most of them will score higher—with or without therapy—because of regression toward the mean. This is not a matter of idle speculation. Studies of untreated subjects demonstrate that poor scores on measures of mental health regress toward the mean when participants are assessed a second time (Flett, Vredenburg, & Krames, 1995; Hsu, 1995).

Does the fact that most people will get better even if there is no therapy mean that there is no sound evidence that psychotherapy works? No, regression effects, along with placebo effects, do create major headaches for researchers evaluating the efficacy of various therapies, but these problems *can* be circumvented. Control groups, random assignment, placebo conditions, and statistical adjustments can be used to control for regression and placebo effects, as well as for other threats to validity. As discussed in the main body of the chapter, researchers have accumulated rigorous evidence that most approaches to therapy have demonstrated efficacy. However, our discussion of placebo and regression effects shows you some of the factors that make this type of research far more complicated and challenging than might be anticipated.

Recognizing how regression to the mean can occur in a variety of contexts is an important critical thinking skill, so let's look at some additional examples. Think about an outstanding young pro baseball player who has a fabulous first season and is named "Rookie of the Year." What sort of performance would you predict for this athlete for the next year? Before you make your prediction, think about regression to the mean. Statistically speaking, our Rookie of the Year is likely to perform well above average the next year, but not as well as he did in his first year. If you are a sports fan, you may recognize this pattern as the "sophomore slump." Many sports columnists have written about the sophomore slump, which they typically blame on the athlete's personality or motivation ("He got lazy,'" "He got cocky," "The money and fame went to his head," and so forth). A simple appeal to regression toward the mean could explain this sort of outcome, with no need to denigrate the personality or motivation of the athlete. Of course, sometimes the Rookie of the Year performs even better during his second year. Thus, our baseball example can be used to emphasize an important point. Regression to the mean is not an inevitability. It is a statistical tendency that predicts what will happen far more often than not, but it is merely a matter of probability—which means it is a much more reliable principle when applied to groups (say, the top ten rookies in a specific year) rather than to individuals.

Let's return to the world of therapy for one last thought about the significance of both regression and placebo effects. Over the years, a host of quacks, charlatans, con artists, herbalists, and faith healers have marketed and sold an endless array of worthless treatments for both psychological problems and physical maladies. In many instances, people who have been treated with these phony therapies have expressed satisfaction or even praise and gratitude. For instance, you may have heard someone sincerely rave about some herbal remedy or psychic advice that you were pretty sure was really worthless. If so, you were probably puzzled by their glowing testimonials. Well, you now have two highly plausible explanations for why people can honestly believe that they have derived great benefit from harebrained, bogus treatments: placebo effects and regression effects. The people who provide testimonials for worthless treatments may have experienced *genuine* improvements in their conditions, but those improvements were probably the results of placebo effects and regression toward the mean. Placebo and regression effects add to the many reasons that you should always be skeptical about anecdotal evidence. And they help explain why charlatans can be so successful and why unsound, ineffective treatments can have sincere proponents.

Table 15.3 Critical Thinking Skills Discussed in This Application

Skill	Description
Recognizing situations in which placebo effects might occur	The critical thinker understands that if people have expectations that a treatment will produce a certain effect, they may experience that effect even if the treatment was fake or ineffectual.
Recognizing situations in which regression toward the mean may occur	The critical thinker understands that when people are selected for their extremely high or low scores on some trait, their subsequent scores will probably fall closer to the mean.
Recognizing the limitations of anecdotal evidence	The critical thinker is wary of anecdotal evidence, which consists of personal stories used to support one's assertions. Anecdotal evidence tends to be unrepresentative, inaccurate, and unreliable.

RECAP

Key Ideas

The Elements of the Treatment Process

● Approaches to treatment are diverse, but they can be grouped into three categories: insight therapies, behavior therapies, and biomedical therapies.

● Therapists come from a variety of professional backgrounds. Clinical and counseling psychologists, psychiatrists, clinical social workers, psychiatric nurses, counselors, and marriage and family therapists are key providers of therapeutic services.

Insight Therapies

● Insight therapies involve verbal interactions intended to enhance self-knowledge. In psychoanalysis, free association and dream analysis are used to explore the unconscious. When an analyst's probing hits sensitive areas, resistance can be expected.

● The transference relationship may be used to overcome this resistance so that the client can handle interpretations that lead to insight. Classical psychoanalysis is not widely practiced anymore, but Freud's legacy lives on in a rich diversity of modern psychodynamic therapies.

● The client-centered therapist tries to provide a supportive climate in which clients can restructure their self-concept. The process of therapy emphasizes clarification of the client's feelings and self-acceptance.

● Beck's cognitive therapy concentrates on changing the way clients think about events in their lives. Cognitive therapists reeducate clients to detect and challenge automatic negative thoughts that cause depression and anxiety.

● Most theoretical approaches to insight therapy have been adapted for use with groups. Evaluating the effectiveness of any approach to treatment is complex and difficult. Nonetheless, the weight of the evidence suggests that insight therapies are superior to no treatment or placebo treatment. Studies suggest that common factors make a significant contribution to the benefits of various therapies.

Behavior Therapies

● Behavior therapies use the principles of learning in direct efforts to change specific aspects of behavior. Wolpe's systematic desensitization is a counterconditioning treatment for phobias. In aversion therapy, a stimulus associated with an unwanted response is paired with an unpleasant stimulus in an effort to eliminate the maladaptive response.

● Social skills training can improve clients' interpersonal skills through shaping, modeling, and behavioral rehearsal. There is ample evidence that behavior therapies are effective in the treatment of a wide variety of disorders.

Biomedical Therapies

● Biomedical therapies are physiological interventions for psychological problems. Antianxiety drugs are used to relieve excessive apprehension. Antipsychotic drugs are used primarily in the treatment of schizophrenia. Antidepressants are used to bring people out of episodes of depression. Bipolar mood disorders are treated with lithium and other mood stabilizers.

● Drug therapies can be quite effective, but they have their drawbacks. All of the drugs produce problematic side effects. The adverse effects of psychiatric drugs may be underestimated because pharmaceutical research is not as impartial as it should be.

● Electroconvulsive therapy (ECT) is used to trigger a cortical seizure that is believed to have therapeutic value for mood disorders, especially depression. There is contradictory evidence about the effectiveness and risks of ECT.

Current Trends and Issues in Treatment

● Many clinicians and their clients believe that managed care has restricted access to mental health care and undermined its quality. Managed care has also raised concerns about providers' autonomy and clients' confidentiality. One response to the demands of managed care has been to increase research efforts to validate the efficacy of specific treatments.

● Combinations of insight, behavioral, and biomedical therapies are often used fruitfully in the treatment of psychological disorders. Many modern therapists are eclectic, using specific ideas, techniques, and strategies gleaned from a number of theoretical approaches.

● Because of cultural, language, and access barriers, therapeutic services are underutilized by ethnic minorities in America. However, the crux of the problem is the failure of institutions to provide culturally sensitive and responsive forms of treatment for ethnic minorities.

Institutional Treatment in Transition

● Disenchantment with the negative effects of mental hospitals led to the advent of more localized community mental health centers and a policy of deinstitutionalization. Long-term hospitalization for mental disorders is largely a thing of the past.

● Unfortunately, deinstitutionalization has left some unanticipated problems in its wake, such as the revolving door problem and increased homelessness. However, many theorists believe that homelessness is primarily an economic problem.

Putting It in Perspective

● Our discussion of psychotherapy highlighted the value of theoretical diversity. Conflicting theoretical orientations have generated varied approaches to treatment. Our cover-

age of therapy also showed once again that cultural factors shape psychological processes.

Personal Application ●
Looking for a Therapist

● Therapeutic services are available in many settings, and such services need not be expensive. Excellent therapists and mediocre therapists can be found in all of the mental health professions, using the full range of therapeutic approaches.

● In selecting a therapist, warmth, empathy, confidence, and likability are desirable traits, and it is reasonable to insist on a therapist of one sex or the other. If progress is slow, your own resistance may be the problem.

Critical Thinking Application ●
From Crisis to Wellness—
But Was It the Therapy?

● People entering therapy are likely to get better even if their treatment is ineffective because of placebo effects and regression toward the mean.

● Regression toward the mean occurs when people selected for their extremely high or low scores on some trait are measured a second time and their new scores fall closer to the mean. Regression and placebo effects may also help explain why people can often be deceived by phony, ineffectual treatments.

Key Terms

Antianxiety drugs
Antidepressant drugs
Antipsychotic drugs
Aversion therapy
Behavior therapies
Biomedical therapies
Client-centered
  therapy
Clinical psychologists
Cognitive therapy
Counseling
  psychologists
Deinstitutionalization
Dream analysis
Eclecticism
Electroconvulsive
  therapy (ECT)
Free association
Group therapy
Insight therapies
Interpretation
Lithium
Mental hospital
Placebo effects
Psychiatrists
Psychoanalysis
Psychopharmaco-
  therapy
Regression toward the
  mean
Resistance
Social skills training
Spontaneous
  remission
Systematic
  desensitization
Tardive dyskinesia
Transference

Key People

Aaron Beck
Dorothea Dix
Hans Eysenck
Sigmund Freud
Carl Rogers
Joseph Wolpe

1. The goal of behavior therapy is to:
   A. identify the early childhood unconscious conflicts that are the source of the client's symptoms.
   B. change the client's thought patterns so that negative emotions can be controlled.
   C. alter the frequency of specific problematic responses by using conditioning techniques.
   D. alter the client's brain chemistry by prescribing specific drugs.

2. After undergoing psychoanalysis for several months, Karen has suddenly started "forgetting" to attend her therapy sessions. Karen's behavior is most likely a form of:
   A. resistance.   C. insight.
   B. transference.   D. catharsis.

3. Because Suzanne has an unconscious sexual attraction to her father, she behaves seductively toward her therapist. Suzanne's behavior is most likely a form of:
   A. resistance.
   B. transference.
   C. misinterpretation.
   D. an unconscious defense mechanism.

4. The key task of the client-centered therapist is:
   A. interpretation of the client's thoughts, feelings, memories, and behaviors.
   B. clarification of the client's feelings.
   C. confrontation of the client's irrational thoughts.
   D. modification of the client's problematic behaviors.

5. A therapist openly challenges a client's statement that she is a failure as a woman because her boyfriend left her, insisting that she justify it with evidence. Which type of therapy is probably being used?
   A. psychodynamic therapy   C. behavior therapy
   B. client-centered therapy   D. cognitive therapy

6. Based on a review of numerous studies of therapeutic outcome, Eysenck (1952) concluded that the recovery rate for neurotics treated with:
   A. insight therapy was about the same as the spontaneous remission rate for neurotic disorders.
   B. insight therapy was significantly higher than the spontaneous remission rate for neurotic disorders.
   C. group therapy was significantly higher than the recovery rate for neurotics treated with individual therapy.
   D. individual therapy was significantly higher than the recovery rate for neurotics treated with group therapy.

7. Systematic desensitization is particularly effective for the treatment of _____ disorders.
   A. generalized anxiety   C. obsessive-compulsive
   B. panic   D. phobic

8. Linda's therapist has her practice active listening skills in structured role-playing exercises. Later, Linda is gradually asked to practice these skills with family members, friends, and finally, her boss. Linda is undergoing:
   A. systematic desensitization.   C. a token economy procedure.
   B. biofeedback.   D. social skills training.

9. After being released from a hospital, many schizophrenic patients stop taking their antipsychotic medication because:
   A. their mental impairment causes them to forget.
   B. of the unpleasant side effects.
   C. most schizophrenics don't believe they are ill.
   D. all of the above.

10. Selective serotonin reuptake inhibitors (SSRIs) can be effective in the treatment of _____ disorders.
    A. depressive   C. obsessive-compulsive
    B. schizophrenic   D. both a and c

11. Modern psychotherapy:
    A. was spawned by a cultural milieu that viewed the self as an independent, rational being.
    B. embraces universal cultural values.
    C. has been successfully exported to many non-Western cultures.
    D. both b and c.

12. The community mental health movement emphasizes:
    A. segregation of the mentally ill from the general population.
    B. increased dependence on long-term inpatient care.
    C. local care and the prevention of psychological disorders.
    D. all of the above.

13. Many people repeatedly go in and out of mental hospitals. Typically, such people are released because _____; they are eventually readmitted because _____.
    A. they have been stabilized through drug therapy; their condition deteriorates once again because of inadequate outpatient care
    B. they run out of funds to pay for hospitalization; they once again can afford it
    C. they have been cured of their disorder; they develop another disorder
    D. they no longer want to be hospitalized; they voluntarily recommit themselves

14. The type of professional training a therapist has:
    A. is the most important indicator of his or her competence.
    B. should be the major consideration in choosing a therapist.
    C. is not all that important, since talented therapists can be found in all of the mental health professions.
    D. both a and b.

15. Which of the following could be explained by regression toward the mean?
    A. You get an average bowling score in one game and a superb score in the next game.
    B. You get an average bowling score in one game and a very low score in the next game.
    C. You get an average bowling score in one game and another average score in the next game.
    D. You get a terrible bowling score in one game and an average score in the next game.

Answers

1	C p. 608	**6**	A p. 617	**11**	A p. 633
2	A p. 613	**7**	D p. 620	**12**	C p. 635
3	B p. 613	**8**	D pp. 621–622	**13**	A p. 636
4	B p. 615	**9**	B p. 624	**14**	C pp. 638–639
5	D p. 616	**10**	D pp. 624–625	**15**	D pp. 642–643

WWW **ON THE WEB**

For additional resources on the topics covered in this chapter, visit the *Psychology: Themes and Variations* Web site, where you will find practice quizzes, tutorials, Web links, simulations, critical thinking activities, flash cards, interactive exercises, and suggested readings available through INFOTRAC.

http://psychology.wadsworth.com/weiten_themes6e/

CHAPTER 16

© Scott Barrow, Inc./SuperStock

Social Behavior

When Muffy, "the quintessential yuppie," met Jake, "the ultimate working-class stiff," her friends got very nervous.

Muffy is a 28-year-old stockbroker and a self-described "snob" with a group of about ten close women friends. Snobs all. They're graduates of fancy business schools. All consultants, investment bankers, and CPAs. All "cute, bright, fun to be with, and really intelligent," according to Muffy. They're all committed to their high-powered careers, but they all expect to marry someday, too.

Unfortunately, most of them don't date much. In fact, they spend a good deal of time "lamenting the dearth of 'good men'" Well, lucky Muffy actually met one of those "good men." Jake is a salesman. He comes from a working-class neighborhood. His clothes come from Sears.

He wasn't like the usual men Muffy dated. He treats Muffy the way she's always dreamed of being treated. He listens; he cares; he remembers. "He makes me feel safe and more cherished than any man I've ever known," she says.

So she decided to bring him to a little party of about 30 of her closest friends. . . .

Perhaps it was only Jake's nerves that caused him to commit some truly unforgivable faux pas that night. His sins were legion. Where do we start? First of all, he asked for a beer when everyone else was drinking white wine. He wore a worn turtleneck while everyone else had just removed the Polo tags from their clothing. He smoked. . . .

"The next day at least half of the people who had been at the party called to give me their impressions. They all said that they felt they just had to let me know that they thought Jake 'lacked polish' or 'seemed loud' or 'might not be a suitable match,'" Muffy says.

Now, you may think that Muffy's friends are simply very sensitive, demanding people. But you'd be wrong. Actually, they've been quite accepting of some of the other men that Muffy has brought to their little parties. Winston, for example, was a great favorite.

"He got drunk, ignored me, and asked for other women's phone numbers right in front of me. But he was six-foot-four, the classic preppie, with blond hair, horn-rimmed glasses, and Ralph Lauren clothes."

So now Muffy is confused. "Jake is the first guy I've been out with in a long time that I've really liked. I was excited about him and my friends knew that. I was surprised by their reaction. I'll admit there's some validity in all their comments, but it's hard to express how violent it was. It made me think about what these women really want in a man. Whatever they say, what they really want is someone they can take to a business dinner. They want someone who comes with a tux. Like a Ken doll."

Muffy may have come to a crossroads in her young life. It's clear that there's no way she can bring Jake among her friends for a while.

"I don't want their reaction to muddy my feelings until I get them sorted out," she says.

(Excerpt from *Tales from the Front* by Cheryl Lavin and Laura Kavesh, Copyright © 1988 by Cheryl Lavin and Laura Kavesh. Used by permission of Doubleday, a division of Random House, Inc.)

The preceding account is a real story, taken from a book about contemporary intimate relationships (Kavesh & Lavin, 1988, pp. 118–121). Muffy is on the horns of a difficult dilemma. Romantic relationships are important to most people, but so are friendships, and Muffy may have to choose between the two. Muffy's story illustrates the significance of social relations in people's lives. It also foreshadows each of the topics that we'll cover in this chapter, as we look at behavior in its social context.

Social psychology **is the branch of psychology concerned with the way individuals' thoughts, feelings, and behaviors are influenced by others.** Our coverage of social psychology will focus on six broad topics highlighted in Muffy's story:

- *Person perception.* The crux of Muffy's problem is that Jake didn't make a very good impression on her friends, primarily because her friends have preconceived views of "working-class stiffs." To what extent do people's expectations color their impressions of others?

- *Attribution processes.* Muffy is struggling to understand her friends' rejection of Jake. When she implies that Jake's rejection is due to their snotty elitism, she's engaging in attribution, making an inference about the causes of her friends' behavior. How do people use attributions to explain social behavior?

- *Interpersonal attraction.* Jake and Muffy are different in many important ways—is it true that opposites attract? Why does Jake's lack of similarity to Muffy's friends lead to such disdain?
- *Attitudes.* Muffy's girlfriends have negative attitudes about working-class men. How are attitudes formed? What leads to attitude change? How do attitudes affect people's behavior?
- *Conformity and obedience.* Muffy's friends discourage her from dating Jake, putting her under pressure to conform to their values. What factors influence conformity? Can people be coaxed into doing things that contradict their values?
- *Behavior in groups.* Muffy belongs to a tight-knit group of friends who think along similar lines. Do people behave differently when they are in groups as opposed to when they are alone? Why do people in groups often think alike?

Social psychologists study how people are affected by the actual, imagined, or implied presence of others. Their interest is not limited to individuals' interactions with others, as people can engage in social behavior even when they're alone. For instance, if you were driving by yourself on a deserted highway and tossed your trash out your car window, your littering would be a social action. It would defy social norms, reflect your socialization and attitudes, and have repercussions (albeit, small) for other people in your society. Social psychologists often study individual behavior in a social context. This interest in understanding individual behavior should be readily apparent in our first section, on person perception.

Person Perception: Forming Impressions of Others

PREVIEW QUESTIONS
- How do aspects of physical appearance sway impressions of others?
- What are social schemas and stereotypes?
- How do illusory correlations and other phenomena illustrate subjectivity in person perception?
- How do evolutionary psychologists explain biases in person perception?

Can you remember the first meeting of your introductory psychology class? What impression did your professor make on you that day? Did your instructor appear to be confident? Easygoing? Pompous? Open-minded? Cynical? Friendly? Were your first impressions supported or undermined by subsequent observations? When you interact with people, you're constantly engaged in *person perception, the process of forming impressions of others.* People show considerable ingenuity in piecing together clues about others' characteristics. However, impressions are often inaccurate because of the many biases and fallacies that occur in person perception. In this section we consider some of the factors that influence, and often distort, people's perceptions of others.

Effects of Physical Appearance

"You shouldn't judge a book by its cover." "Beauty is only skin deep." People know better than to let physical attractiveness determine their perceptions of others' personal qualities. Or do they? Studies have shown that judgments of others' personality are often swayed by their appearance, especially their physical attractiveness. People tend to ascribe desirable personality characteristics to those who are good looking, seeing them as more sociable, friendly, poised, warm, and well adjusted than those who are less attractive (Eagly et al., 1991; Wheeler & Kim, 1997). In reality, research findings suggest that there is little correlation between attractiveness and personality traits (Feingold, 1992). Why do we inaccurately assume that a connection exists between good looks and personality? One reason is that extremely attractive people are vastly overrepresented in the entertainment media, where they are mostly portrayed in a highly favorable light (Smith, McIntosh, & Bazzini, 1999).

You might guess that physical attractiveness would influence perceptions of competence less than perceptions of personality, but the data suggest otherwise. A recent review of the relevant research found that people have a surprisingly strong tendency to view good-looking individuals as more competent than less attractive individuals (Langlois et al., 2000). This bias literally pays off for good-looking people, as they tend to secure better jobs and earn higher salaries than less attractive individuals (Collins & Zebrowitz, 1995; Frieze, Olson, & Russell, 1991). Good looks seem to have relatively little impact on perceptions of honesty and integrity (Eagly et al., 1991). However, people tend to view those with *baby-faced features*—such as large eyes, smooth skin, and a rounded chin—as more honest and trustworthy (Zebrowitz, Voinescu, & Collins, 1996). Baby-faced individuals are also seen as relatively warm, submissive, helpless, and naive (Zebrowitz, 1996), although evidence suggests that there is no association between

In general, people have a bias toward viewing good-looking men and women as bright, competent, and talented. However, people sometimes downplay the talent of successful women who happen to be attractive, attributing their success to their good looks instead of to their competence.

baby-faced features and these traits (Zebrowitz, Collins, & Dutta, 1998).

Observers are also quick to draw inferences about people based on how they move, talk, and gesture—that is, their style of nonverbal expressiveness—and these inferences tend to be fairly accurate (Ambady & Rosenthal, 1993). For example, based on a mere 10 seconds of videotape, participants can guess strangers' sexual orientation (heterosexual-homosexual) with decent accuracy (Ambady, Hallahan, & Conner, 1999). It is also widely believed that it is reasonable to draw inferences about someone's personality based on their handshake. Surprisingly little research has been conducted on handshaking and person perception, but preliminary evidence suggests that a firm, vigorous handshake is associated with relatively favorable first impressions (Chaplin et al., 2000).

Cognitive Schemas

Even though every individual is unique, people tend to categorize one another. For instance, in our opening story, Muffy is characterized as "the quintessential yuppie," and Jake as a "working-class stiff." Such labels reflect the use of cognitive schemas in person perception. As we discussed in the chapter on memory (Chapter 7), *schemas* are cognitive structures that guide information processing. Individuals use schemas to organize the world around them—including their social world. *Social schemas* are organized clusters of ideas about categories of social events and people. People have social schemas for events such as dates, picnics, committee meetings, and family reunions, as well as for certain categories of people, such as "dumb jocks," "social climbers," "frat rats," and "wimps" (see Figure 16.1). Individuals depend on social schemas because the schemas help them to efficiently process and store the wealth of information that they take in about others in their interactions. Hence, people routinely place one another in categories, and these categories influence the process of person perception (Macrae & Bodenhausen, 2000).

Stereotypes

Some of the schemas that individuals apply to people are unique products of their personal experiences, while other schemas may be part of their shared cultural background. *Stereotypes* are special types of schemas that fall into the latter category. *Stereotypes are widely held beliefs that people have certain characteristics because of their membership in a particular group*.

The most common stereotypes in our society are those based on sex, age, and membership in ethnic or occupational groups. People who subscribe to traditional *gender stereotypes* tend to assume that women are emotional, submissive, illogical, and passive, while men are unemotional, dominant, logical, and aggressive. *Age stereotypes* suggest that elderly people are slow, feeble, rigid, forgetful, and asexual. Notions that Jews are mercenary, Germans are methodical, and Italians are passionate are examples of common *ethnic stereotypes*. *Occupational stereotypes* suggest that

Figure 16.1

Examples of social schemas. Everyone has social schemas for various "types" of people, such as sophisticated professionals or working-class stiffs. Social schemas are clusters of beliefs that guide information processing.

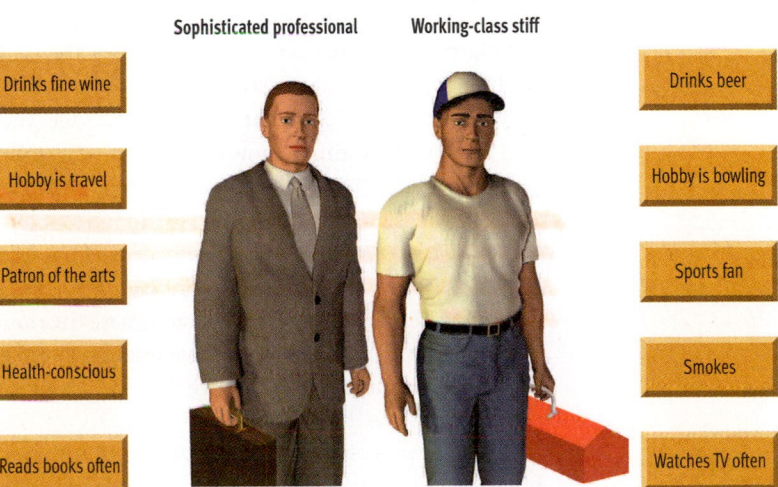

Sophisticated professional | Working-class stiff

Drinks fine wine

Hobby is travel

Patron of the arts

Health-conscious

Reads books often

Drinks beer

Hobby is bowling

Sports fan

Smokes

Watches TV often

Web Link 16.1

Social Psychology Network
Wesleyan University social psychologist Scott Plous offers a broad collection of resources related to all aspects of social (and general) psychology as well as information about careers and graduate study in this field.

lawyers are manipulative, accountants are conforming, artists are moody, and so forth.

Stereotyping is a normal cognitive process that is frequently automatic and that saves on the time and effort required to get a handle on people individually (Devine & Monteith, 1999; Operario & Fiske, 2001). Stereotypes save energy by simplifying our social world. However, this conservation of energy often comes at some cost in terms of accuracy. Stereotypes frequently are broad overgeneralizations that ignore the diversity within social groups and foster inaccurate perceptions of people (Hilton & von Hippel, 1996). Obviously, not all males, Jews, and lawyers behave alike. Most people who subscribe to stereotypes realize that not all members of a group are identical. For instance, they may admit that some men aren't competitive, some Jews aren't mercenary, and some lawyers aren't manipulative. However, they may still tend to assume that males, Jews, and lawyers are *more likely* than others to have these characteristics. Even if stereotypes mean only that people think in terms of slanted *probabilities*, their expectations may lead them to misperceive individuals with whom they interact. As we've noted in previous chapters, perception is subjective, and people often see what they expect to see.

Subjectivity in Person Perception

Stereotypes and other schemas create biases in person perception that frequently lead to confirmation of people's expectations about others. If someone's behavior is ambiguous, people are likely to interpret what they see in a way that's consistent with their expectations (Olson, Roese, & Zanna, 1996). Thus, after dealing with a pushy female customer, a salesman who holds traditional gender stereotypes might characterize the woman as "emotional." In contrast, he might characterize a male who exhibits the same pushy behavior as "aggressive."

People not only see what they expect to see, they also tend to overestimate how often they see it (Johnson & Mullen, 1994; Shavitt et al., 1999). *Illusory correlation* occurs when people estimate that they have encountered more confirmations of an association between social traits than they have actually seen. People also tend to underestimate the number of disconfirmations they have encountered, as illustrated by statements like "I've never met an honest lawyer."

Memory processes can contribute to confirmatory biases in person perception in a variety of ways. Of-

ten, individuals selectively recall facts that fit with their schemas and stereotypes (Fiske, 1998). Evidence for such a tendency was found in a study by Cohen (1981). In this experiment, participants watched a videotape of a woman, described as either a waitress or a librarian, who engaged in a variety of activities, including listening to classical music, drinking beer, and watching TV. When asked to recall what the woman did during the filmed sequence, participants tended to remember activities consistent with their stereotypes of waitresses and librarians. For instance, subjects who thought the woman was a waitress tended to recall her beer drinking, while subjects who thought she was a librarian tended to recall her listening to classical music.

Further evidence for the subjectivity of social perception comes from a phenomenon called the *spotlight effect*—people's tendency to assume that the social spotlight shines more brightly on them than it actually does (Gilovich & Savitsky, 1999). Recent studies show that people frequently overestimate the degree to which others pay attention to their appearance and behavior. For example, in one study some college students were induced to wear an embarrassing Barry Manilow T-shirt in interactions with other participants and were subsequently asked to estimate the percentage of the other subjects who had noticed the shirt. Their estimates were over twice as high as the actual percentage of subjects who noticed the embarrassing T-shirt (see Figure 16.2; Gilovich, Medvec, & Savitsky, 2000). The bad news about the spotlight effect is that it occurs in moments of triumph as well as moments of embarrassment, so our successes and accomplishments often garner less attention from others than we believe they do. The good news is that our blunders and failures are less salient to others than we think they are and that people's inferences about us based on these blunders are not as harsh as widely assumed (Savitsky, Epley, & Gilovich, 2001).

A similar type of subjective perception is apparent in research on the *illusion of asymmetric insight*—the finding that people tend to think that their knowledge of their peers is greater than their peers' knowledge of them (Pronin et al., 2001). For example, in a study of college roommates the participants tended to believe that they knew their roommates better than their roommates knew them. Additional research is needed to pinpoint the processes underlying this phenomenon. Pronin and her colleagues (2001) speculate that most of us have had many experiences where we feel that our behavior has been misinterpreted or our motives misunderstood, so we

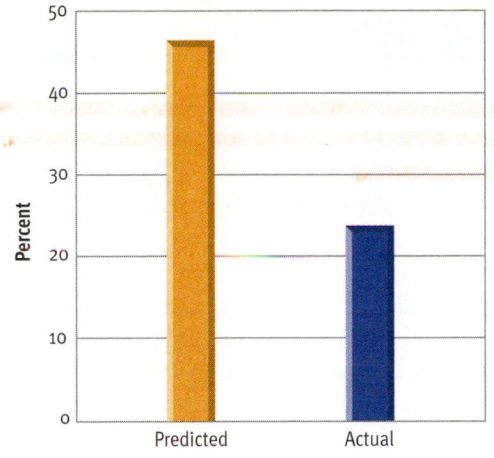

Figure 16.2

The spotlight effect. In a study of the spotlight effect, Gilovich, Medvec, and Savitsky (2000) induced college students to wear an embarrassing T-shirt while interacting with other participants. The shirt depicted Barry Manilow, a singer who was characterized by the authors as "not terribly popular among college students." The subjects who wore the Manilow shirt were asked to predict what percentage of the other participants would notice the shirt. As you can see, their predictions far exceeded the actual number of participants who noticed the embarrassing shirt.

SOURCE: Adapted from Gilovich, T., Medvec, V. H., & Savitsky, K. (2000). The spotlight effect in social judgment: An egocentric bias in estimates of the salience of one's own actions and appearance. *Journal of Personality and Social Psychology, 78,* 211–222. Copyright © 2000 by the American Psychological Association. Used by permission of the author.

develop doubts that anyone can really know us, but most of us fail to appreciate that this insight also applies to our perceptions of others. Consistent with this analysis, a subsequent study found that people tend to recognize biased social perception in others much more readily than in themselves (Pronin, Lin, & Ross, 2002).

An Evolutionary Perspective on Bias in Person Perception

Why is the process of person perception riddled with bias? Evolutionary psychologists argue that many of the biases seen in social perception were adaptive in humans' ancestral environment (Krebs & Denton, 1997). For example, they argue that person perception is swayed by physical attractiveness because attractiveness was associated with reproductive potential in women and with health, vigor, and the accumulation of material resources in men. What about baby-faced features? Evolutionary theorists assert that the tendency to view babies as helpless creatures requiring nurture would be highly adaptive and has probably been preprogrammed in humans by natural selection (Springer & Berry, 1997). The tendency to view

baby-faced adults as naive, submissive, and honest may simply be a spillover effect from humans' evolutionary heritage.

What about the human tendency to automatically categorize others? Evolutionary theorists attribute this behavior to our distant ancestors' need to quickly separate friend from foe. They assert that humans are programmed by evolution to immediately classify people as members of an *ingroup*—a group that one belongs to and identifies with, or as members of an *outgroup*—a group that one does not belong to or identify with. This crucial categorization is thought to structure subsequent perceptions. As Krebs and Denton (1997) put it, "It is as though the act of classifying others as ingroup or outgroup members activates two quite different brain circuits" (p. 27). Ingroup members tend to be viewed in a favorable light, whereas outgroup members tend to be viewed in terms of various negative stereotypes. According to Krebs and Denton, these negative stereotypes ("They are inferior; they are all alike; they will exploit us") move outgroups out of our domain of empathy, so we feel justified in not liking them or discriminating against them.

Thus, evolutionary psychologists ascribe much of the bias in person perception to cognitive mechanisms that have been shaped by natural selection. Their speculation is thought provoking, but empirical work is needed to test their hypotheses.

REVIEW OF KEY POINTS

- People's perceptions of others can be distorted by a variety of factors, including physical appearance. People tend to attribute desirable characteristics, such as intelligence, competence, warmth, and friendliness, to those who are good looking.

- Baby-faced people are viewed as honest. Perceptions of people are also influenced by their style of nonverbal expressiveness. People use social schemas to categorize others into types. Stereotypes are widely held social schemas that lead people to expect that others will have certain characteristics because of their membership in a specific group.

- Gender, age, ethnic, and occupational stereotypes are common. In interacting with others, stereotypes may lead people to see what they expect to see and to overestimate how often they see it. The spotlight effect and the illusion of asymmetric insight illustrate the subjective nature of social perception.

- Evolutionary psychologists argue that many biases in person perception were adaptive in humans' ancestral past. The human tendency to automatically categorize others may reflect the primitive need to quickly separate friend from foe.

Attribution Processes: Explaining Behavior

PREVIEW QUESTIONS

- What are attributions, and how do internal and external attributions differ?
- What types of factors influence the likelihood of internal versus external attributions?
- How do actors and observers differ in their patterns of attribution?
- What is defensive attribution and the self-serving bias?
- How do individualism and collectivism influence attribution bias?

It's Friday evening and you're sitting around at home feeling bored. You call a few friends to see whether they'd like to go out. They all say that they'd love to go, but they have other commitments and can't. Their commitments sound vague, and you feel that their reasons for not going out with you are rather flimsy. How do you explain these rejections? Do your friends really have commitments? Are they worn out by school and work? When they said that they'd love to go, were they being sincere? Or do they find you boring? Could they be right? Are you boring? These questions illustrate a process that people engage in routinely: the explanation of behavior. *Attributions* play a key role in these explanatory efforts, and they have significant effects on social relations.

What are attributions? *Attributions are inferences that people draw about the causes of events, others' behavior, and their own behavior.* If you conclude that a friend turned down your invitation because she's overworked, you have made an attribution about the cause of her behavior (and, implicitly, have rejected other possible explanations). If you conclude that you're stuck at home with nothing to do because you failed to plan ahead, you've made an attribution about the cause of an event (being stuck at home). If you conclude that you failed to plan ahead because you're a procrastinator, you've made an attribution about the cause of your own behavior. People make attributions mainly because they have a strong need to understand their experiences. They want to make sense out of their own behavior, others' actions, and the events in their lives. In this section, we'll take a look at some of the patterns seen when people make attributions.

Internal Versus External Attributions

Fritz Heider (1958) was the first to describe how people make attributions. He asserted that people tend to locate the cause of behavior either *within a person,* attributing it to personal factors, or *outside a person,* attributing it to environmental factors.

Elaborating on Heider's insight, various theorists have agreed that explanations of behavior and events can be categorized as internal or external attributions (Jones & Davis, 1965; Kelley, 1967; Weiner, 1974). *Internal attributions* ascribe the causes of behavior to personal dispositions, traits, abilities, and feel-

ings. *External attributions* ascribe the causes of behavior to situational demands and environmental constraints. For example, if a friend's business fails, you might attribute it to his or her lack of business acumen (an internal, personal factor) or to negative trends in the nation's economic climate (an external, situational explanation). Parents who find out that their teenage son has just banged up the car may blame it on his carelessness (a personal disposition) or on slippery road conditions (a situational factor).

Internal and external attributions can have a tremendous impact on everyday interpersonal interactions. Blaming a friend's business failure on poor business acumen as opposed to a poor economy will have a great impact on how you view your friend. Likewise, if parents attribute their son's automobile accident to slippery road conditions, they're likely to deal with the event very differently than if they attribute it to his carelessness.

Attributions for Success and Failure

Some psychologists have sought to discover additional dimensions of attributional thinking besides the internal-external dimension. After studying the attributions that people make in explaining success and failure, Bernard Weiner (1980, 1986, 1994) concluded that people often focus on the *stability* of the causes underlying behavior. According to Weiner, the stable-unstable dimension in attribution cuts across the internal-external dimension, creating four types of attributions for success and failure, as shown in Figure 16.3.

Let's apply Weiner's model to a concrete event. Imagine that you're contemplating why you failed to get a job that you wanted. You might attribute your setback to internal factors that are stable (lack of ability) or unstable (inadequate effort to put together an eye-catching résumé). Or you might attribute your setback to external factors that are stable (too much outstanding competition) or unstable (bad luck). If you got the job, your explanations for your success would fall into the same four categories: internal-stable (your excellent ability), internal-unstable (your hard work to assemble a superb résumé), external-stable (lack of top-flight competition), and external-unstable (good luck).

University of Kansas

"*Often the momentary situation which, at least in part, determines the behavior of a person is disregarded and the behavior is taken as a manifestation of personal characteristics.*"

FRITZ HEIDER

Bias in Attribution

Attributions are only inferences. Your attributions may not be the correct explanations for events. Paradoxical as it may seem, people often arrive at inaccurate explanations even when they contemplate the causes of *their own behavior*. Attributions ultimately represent *guesswork* about the causes of events, and these guesses tend to be slanted in certain directions. Let's look at the principal biases seen in attribution.

Actor-Observer Bias

Your view of your own behavior can be quite different from the view of someone else observing you. When an actor and an observer draw inferences about the causes of the actor's behavior, they often make different attributions. A common form of bias seen in observers is the *fundamental attribution error*, which refers to observers' bias in favor of internal attributions in explaining others' behavior. Of course, in many instances, an internal attribution may not be an "error." However, observers have a curious tendency to overestimate the likelihood that an actor's behavior reflects personal qualities rather than situational factors. Why? One reason is that situational pressures may not be readily apparent to an observer. As Gilbert and Malone (1995) put it, "When one tries to point to a situation, one often stabs empty air" (p. 25). Another reason is that attributing

others' behavior to their dispositions is a relatively simple, effortless process that borders on automatic (Trope & Liberman, 1993). In contrast, explaining people's behavior in terms of situational factors is a more complex process that requires more thought and effort (see Figure 16.4 on the next page; Krull & Erickson, 1995).

To illustrate the gap that often exists between actors' and observers' attributions, imagine that you're visiting your bank and you fly into a rage over a mistake made on your account. Observers who witness your rage are likely to make an internal attribution and infer that you are surly, temperamental, and quarrelsome. They may be right, but if asked, you'd probably attribute your rage to the frustrating situation. Perhaps you're normally a calm, easygoing person,

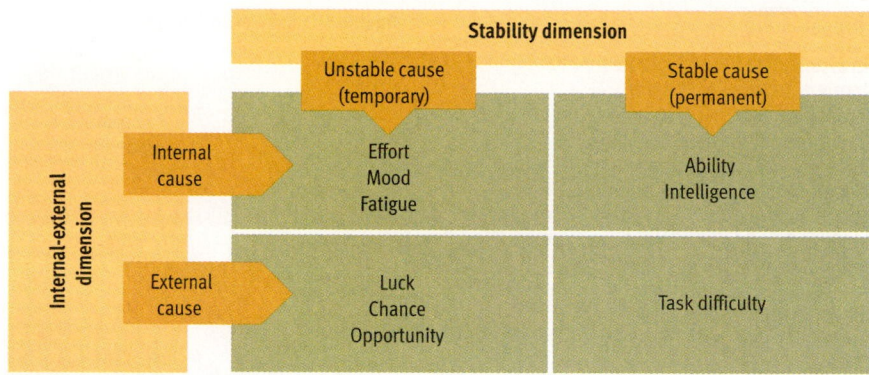

	Stability dimension	
	Unstable cause (temporary)	Stable cause (permanent)
Internal cause	Effort Mood Fatigue	Ability Intelligence
External cause	Luck Chance Opportunity	Task difficulty

Internal-external dimension

Figure 16.3

Weiner's model of attributions for success and failure.
Weiner's model assumes that people's explanations for success and failure emphasize internal versus external causes and stable versus unstable causes. Examples of causal factors that fit into each of the four cells in Weiner's model are shown in the diagram.

SOURCE: Weiner, B., Friese, I., Kukla, A., Reed, L., & Rosenbaum, R. M. (1972). Perceiving the causes of success and failure. In E. E. Jones, D. E. Kanouse, H. H. Kelley, R. E. Nisbett, S. Valins, & B. Weiner (Eds.), *Perceiving the causes of behavior.* Morristown, NJ: General Learning Press. Used by permission of Bernard Weiner.

CONCEPT CHECK 16.1

Analyzing Attributions

Check your understanding of attribution processes by analyzing possible explanations for an athletic team's success. Imagine that the women's track team at your school has just won a regional championship that qualifies it for the national tournament. Around the campus, you hear people attribute the team's success to a variety of factors. Examine the attributions shown below and place each of them in one of the cells of Weiner's model of attribution (just record the letter inside the cell). The answers are in Appendix A.

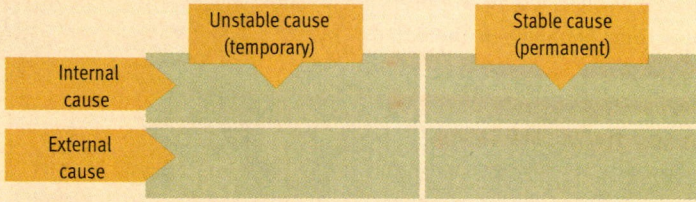

	Unstable cause (temporary)	Stable cause (permanent)
Internal cause		
External cause		

a. "They won only because the best two athletes on Central State's team were out with injuries—talk about good fortune!"
b. "They won because they have some of the best talent in the country."
c. "Anybody could win this region; the competition is far below average in comparison to the rest of the country."
d. "They won because they put in a great deal of last-minute effort and practice, and they were incredibly fired up for the regional tourney after last year's near miss."

Figure 16.4

An alternative view of the fundamental attribution error.
According to Gilbert (1989) and others, the nature of attribution processes favor the *fundamental attribution error*. Traditional models of attribution assume that internal and external attributions are an either-or proposition requiring equal amounts of effort. In contrast, Gilbert posits that people tend to automatically make internal attributions with little effort, and then they *may* expend additional effort to adjust for the influence of situational factors, which can lead to an external attribution. Thus, external attributions for others' behavior require more thought and effort, which makes them less frequent than personal attributions.

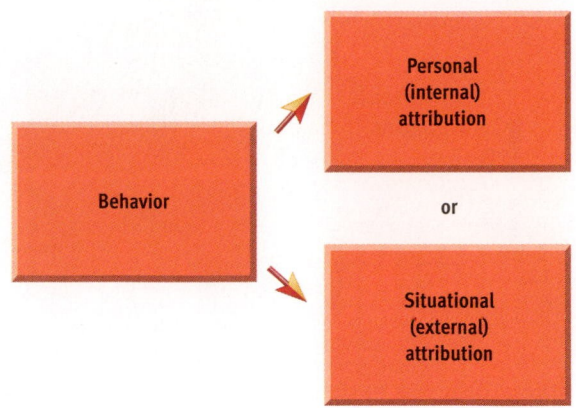

Traditional model of attribution

Behavior → Personal (internal) attribution

or

Situational (external) attribution

Alternative two-step model of attribution

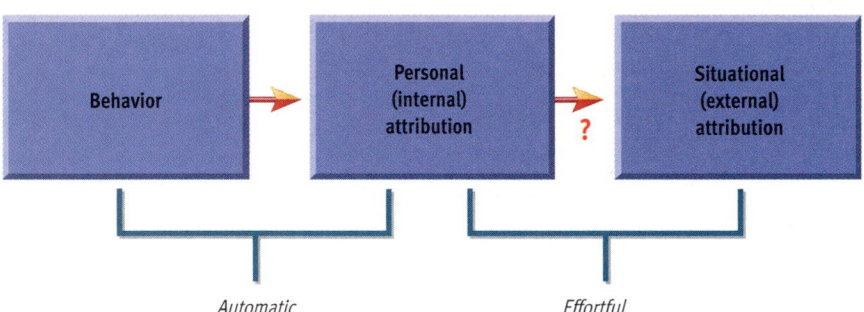

Behavior → Personal (internal) attribution → **?** → Situational (external) attribution

Automatic   *Effortful*

but today you've been in line for 20 minutes, you just straightened out a similar error by the same bank last week, and you're being treated rudely by the teller. Observers are often unaware of historical and situational considerations such as these, so they tend to make internal attributions for another's behavior (Gilbert, 1998).

In contrast, the circumstances that have influenced an actor's behavior tend to be more salient to the actor. Hence, actors are more likely than observers to locate the cause of their behavior in the situation. In general, then, *actors favor external attributions for their behavior, whereas observers are more likely to explain the same behavior with internal attributions* (Jones & Nisbett, 1971; Krueger, Ham, & Linford, 1996).

Defensive Attribution 12a

In attempting to explain the calamities and setbacks that befall other people, an observer's tendency to make internal attributions may become even stronger than normal. Let's say that a friend gets mugged and severely beaten. You may attribute the mugging to your friend's carelessness or stupidity ("He should have known better than to be in that neighborhood at

that time") rather than to bad luck. Why? Because if you attribute your friend's misfortune to bad luck, you have to face the ugly reality that it could just as easily happen to you. To avoid disturbing thoughts such as these, people often attribute mishaps to victims' negligence (Salminen, 1992; Thornton, 1984, 1992). *Defensive attribution* is a tendency to blame victims for their misfortune, so that one feels less likely to be victimized in a similar way. *Hindsight bias* probably contributes to this tendency, but blaming victims also helps people maintain their belief that they live in a just world, where they're unlikely to experience similar troubles (Lerner & Goldberg, 1999). The bias toward making defensive attributions can have unfortunate consequences. Blaming victims for their setbacks causes them to be seen in a negative light, and undesirable traits are unfairly attributed to them. Thus, it is assumed that burglary victims must be careless, that people who get fired must be incompetent, that poor people must be lazy, that rape victims must be seductive ("She probably asked for it"), and so on. As you can see, defensive attribution can lead to unwarranted derogation of victims of misfortune.

Self-Serving Bias 12a

The self-serving bias in attribution comes into play when people attempt to explain success and failure.

A common example of defensive attribution is the tendency to blame the homeless for their plight.

This bias may either strengthen or weaken one's normal attributional tendencies, depending on whether one is trying to explain positive or negative outcomes (Brown & Rogers, 1991; Campbell & Sedikides, 1999). The *self-serving bias* is the tendency to attribute one's successes to personal factors and one's failures to situational factors. Interestingly, this bias grows stronger as time passes after an event, so that people tend to take progressively more credit for their successes and less responsibility for their failures (Burger, 1986).

In explaining *failure,* the usual actor-observer biases are apparent. Actors tend to make external attributions, blaming their failures on unfavorable situational factors, while observers attribute the same failures to the actors' personal shortcomings. Thus, if you fail an exam, you may place the blame on the poorly constructed test items, lousy teaching, distractions in the hallway, or a bad week at work (all external attributions). However, an observer is more likely to attribute your failure to your lack of ability or lack of study (both internal attributions). In explaining success, the usual actor-observer differences are reversed to some degree. Thus, if you get a high exam score, you'll probably make an internal attribution and point to your ability or your hard work (Forsyth & McMillan, 1981).

Culture and Attributional Tendencies

Do the patterns of attribution observed in subjects from Western societies transcend culture? More research is needed, but the preliminary evidence suggests not. Some interesting cultural disparities have emerged in research on attribution processes.

According to Harry Triandis (1989, 1994, 2001), cultural differences in *individualism* versus *collectivism* influence attributional tendencies as well as other aspects of social behavior. *Individualism* involves putting personal goals ahead of group goals and defining one's identity in terms of personal attributes rather than group memberships. In contrast, *collectivism* involves putting group goals ahead of personal goals and defining one's identity in terms of the groups one belongs to (such as one's family, tribe, work group, social class, caste, and so on). In comparison to individualistic cultures, collectivist cultures place a higher priority on shared values and resources, cooperation, mutual interdependence, and concern for how one's actions will affect other group members. Child-rearing patterns in collectivist cultures emphasize the importance of

obedience, reliability, and proper behavior, whereas individualistic cultures emphasize the development of independence, self-esteem, and self-reliance.

A variety of factors influence whether societies cherish individualism as opposed to collectivism. Among other things, increases in a culture's affluence, education, urbanization, and social mobility tend to foster more individualism (Triandis, 1994). Many contemporary societies are in transition, but generally speaking, North American and Western European cultures tend to be individualistic, whereas Asian, African, and Latin American cultures tend to be higher in collectivism (Hofstede, 1980, 1983, 2001) (see Figure 16.5).

How does individualism versus collectivism relate to patterns of attribution? The evidence suggests that collectivist cultures may promote different attributional biases than individualistic cultures. For example, people from collectivist societies appear to be less prone to the *fundamental attribution error* than those from individualistic societies (Choi, Nisbett, & Norenzayan, 1999; Triandis, 2001). In Western cultures, people are viewed as autonomous individuals who are responsible for their actions. Endorsing be-

Figure 16.5

Individualism versus collectivism around the world. Hofstede (1980, 1983, 2001) used survey data from over 100,000 employees of a large, multinational corporation to estimate the emphasis on individualism versus collectivism in 50 nations and 3 regions. His large, diverse international sample remains unequaled to date. In the figure, cultures are ranked in terms of how strongly they embraced the values of individualism. As you can see, Hofstede's estimates suggest that North American and Western European nations tend to be relatively individualistic, whereas more collectivism is found in Asian, African, and Latin American countries.

SOURCE: Adapted from Hofstede, G. (2001). *Culture's consequences* (2nd Ed., p. 215). Thousand Oaks, CA: Sage. Copyright © 2001 Sage Publications. Adapted by permission of Dr. Geert Hofstede.

Hofstede's rankings of national cultures' individualism		
Individualistic cultures	**Intermediate cultures**	**Collectivist cultures**
1. United States	19. Israel	37. Hong Kong
2. Australia	20. Spain	38. Chile
3. Great Britain	21. India	40. Singapore
4. Canada	22. Argentina	40. Thailand
4. Netherlands	22. Japan	40. West Africa region
6. New Zealand	24. Iran	42. El Salvador
7. Italy	25. Jamaica	43. South Korea
8. Belgium	26. Arab region	44. Taiwan
9. Denmark	26. Brazil	45. Peru
10. France	28. Turkey	46. Costa Rica
11. Sweden	29. Uruguay	47. Indonesia
12. Ireland	30. Greece	47. Pakistan
13. Norway	31. Philippines	49. Columbia
14. Switzerland	32. Mexico	50. Venezuela
15. West Germany	34. East Africa region	51. Panama
16. South Africa	34. Portugal	52. Ecuador
17. Finland	34. Yugoslavia	53. Guatemala
18. Austria	36. Malaysia	

Recognizing Bias in Social Cognition

Check your understanding of bias in social cognition by identifying various types of errors that are common in person perception and attribution. Imagine that you're a nonvoting student member of a college committee at Southwest State University that is hiring a new political science professor. As you listen to the committee's discussion, you hear examples of (a) the illusory correlation effect, (b) stereotyping, (c) the fundamental attribution error, and (d) defensive attribution. Indicate which of these is at work in the excerpts from committee members' deliberations below. The answers are in Appendix A.

_____ **1.** "I absolutely won't consider the fellow who arrived 30 minutes late for his interview. Anybody who can't make a job interview on time is either irresponsible or hopelessly disorganized. I don't care what he says about the airline messing up his reservations."

_____ **2.** "You know, I was very, very impressed with the young female applicant, and I would love to hire her, but every time we add a young woman to the faculty in liberal arts, she gets pregnant within the first year." The committee chairperson, who has heard this line from this professor before replies, "You always say that, so I finally did a systematic check of what's happened in the past. Of the last 14 women hired in liberal arts, only one has become pregnant within a year."

_____ **3.** "The first one I want to rule out is the guy who's been practicing law for the last ten years. Although he has an excellent background in political science, I just don't trust lawyers. They're all ambitious, power-hungry, manipulative cutthroats. He'll be a divisive force in the department."

_____ **4.** "I say we forget about the two candidates who lost their faculty slots in the massive financial crisis at Western Polytechnic last year. I know it sounds cruel, but they brought it on themselves with their fiscal irresponsibility over at Western. Thank goodness we'll never let anything like that happen around here. As far as I'm concerned, if these guys couldn't see that crisis coming, they must be pretty dense."

Web Link 16.2

Social Cognition Paper Archive and Information Center
Eliot R. Smith at Purdue University maintains a popular site that includes information about papers (abstracts, mostly), people, and links to the wider social psychological research community.

liefs such as "You can do anything you put your mind to" or "You have no one to blame but yourself," Westerners typically explain behavior in terms of people's personality traits and unique abilities. In contrast, collectivists, who value interdependence and obedience, are more likely to assume that one's behavior reflects adherence to group norms.

Although the *self-serving bias* has been documented in a variety of cultures (Fletcher & Ward, 1988), it may be particularly prevalent in individualistic, Western societies, where an emphasis on competition and high self-esteem motivates people to try to impress others, as well as themselves. In contrast, Japanese subjects exhibit a *self-effacing bias* in explaining success (Akimoto & Sanbonmatsu, 1999; Markus & Kitayama, 1991), as they tend to attribute their successes to help they receive from others or to the ease of the task, while downplaying the importance of their ability. When they fail, Japanese subjects tend to be more self-critical than subjects from individualistic cultures (Heine & Renshaw, 2002). They are more likely to accept responsibility for their failures and to use their setbacks as an impetus for self-improvement (Heine et al, 2001). Studies have also failed to find the usual self-serving bias in Nepalese and Chinese samples (Lee & Seligman, 1997; Smith & Bond, 1994).

A great deal of additional research is needed before any broad conclusions can be drawn, but collectivism may put a different spin on attributional bias.

REVIEW OF KEY POINTS

- Attributions are inferences about the causes of events and behavior. Individuals make attributions to understand their social world. Attributions can be classified as internal or external. Internal attributions ascribe behavior to personal dispositions and traits, whereas external attributions locate the cause of behavior in the environment.

- Weiner's model proposes that attributions for success and failure should be analyzed in terms of the stability of causes, as well as along the internal-external dimension. Observers favor internal attributions to explain another's behavior (the fundamental attribution error), while actors favor external attributions to explain their own behavior.

- In defensive attribution, people unfairly blame victims for their misfortune (with internal attributions) to reduce their own feelings of vulnerability. The self-serving bias is the tendency to attribute one's good outcomes to personal factors and one's bad outcomes to situational factors.

- Cultures vary in their emphasis on individualism as opposed to collectivism, and these differences appear to influence attributional tendencies. The fundamental attribution error and the self-serving bias in attribution may be by-products of Western cultures' individualism.

Close Relationships: Liking and Loving

"I just don't know what she sees in him. She could do so much better for herself. I suppose he's a nice guy, but they're just not right for each other." Can't you imagine Muffy's friends making these comments in discussing her relationship with Jake? You've probably heard similar remarks on many occasions. These comments illustrate people's interest in analyzing the dynamics of attraction. *Interpersonal attraction refers to positive feelings toward another.* Social psychologists use this term broadly to encompass a variety of experiences, including liking, friendship, admiration, lust, and love. In this section, we'll analyze key factors that influence attraction and examine some theoretical perspectives on the mystery of love.

Key Factors in Attraction

Many factors influence who is attracted to whom. Here we'll discuss factors that promote the development of liking, friendship, and love. Although these are different types of attraction, the interpersonal dynamics at work in each are largely similar.

Physical Attractiveness

Although people often say that "beauty is only skin deep," the empirical evidence suggests that most people don't really believe that homily. The importance of physical attractiveness was demonstrated in a study of college students in which unacquainted men and women were sent off on a "get-acquainted" date (Sprecher & Duck, 1994). The investigators were mainly interested in how communication might affect the process of attraction, but to put this factor in context they also measured subjects' perceptions of their date's physical attractiveness and similarity to themselves. They found that the quality of communication during the date did have some effect on females' interest in friendship, but the key determinant of romantic attraction for both sexes was the physical attractiveness of the other person. Many other studies have demonstrated the singular prominence of physical attractiveness in the initial stage of dating and have shown that it continues to influence the course of commitment as dating relationships evolve (Hendrick & Hendrick, 1992). In the realm of romance, being physically attractive appears to be more important for females than males (Feingold, 1990). For example, in a study of college students (Speed & Gangestad, 1997), the correlation between romantic popularity (assessed by peer ratings) and physical attractiveness was higher for females (.76) than for males (.47).

Although people prefer physically attractive partners in romantic relationships, they may consider their own level of attractiveness in pursuing dates. What people want in a partner may be different from what they are willing to settle for (Regan, 1998). The *matching hypothesis* proposes that males and females of approximately equal physical attractiveness are likely to select each other as partners. The matching hypothesis is supported by evidence that married couples tend to be very similar in level of physical attractiveness (Feingold, 1988b). Interestingly, people expect that individuals who are similar in attractiveness will be more satisfied as couples and less likely to break up (Garcia & Khersonsky, 1996).

Similarity Effects

Is it true that "birds of a feather flock together," or do "opposites attract"? Research provides far more support for the former than the latter. Married and dating couples tend to be similar in age, race, religion, social class, personality, education, intelligence, physical attractiveness, and attitudes (Kalmijn, 1998; Knox, Zusman, & Nieves, 1997). In married couples, personality similarity appears to be associated with greater marital happiness (Caspi & Herbener, 1990). Similarity is also seen among friends. For instance, adult friends tend to be relatively similar in terms of

According to the matching hypothesis, males and females who are similar in physical attractiveness are likely to be drawn together. This type of matching may also influence the formation of friendships.

PREVIEW QUESTIONS

- To what extent are good looks, similarity, reciprocity, and ideals important in interpersonal attraction?
- How do theorists distinguish among different types of love?
- How are attachment patterns related to intimate relations?
- How does culture influence patterns of mating?
- How have mating strategies been shaped by evolution?

income, education, occupational status, ethnicity, and religion (Blieszner & Adams, 1992).

The most obvious explanation for these correlations is that similarity causes attraction. Laboratory experiments on *attitude similarity,* conducted by Donn Byrne and his colleagues, suggest that similarity *does* cause attraction (Byrne, 1997; Byrne, Clore, & Smeaton, 1986). However, research also suggests that attraction can foster similarity, as Davis and Rusbult (2001) found that dating partners gradually modify their attitudes in ways that make them more congruent, a phenomenon they called *attitude alignment.* Moreover, people in stable, satisfying intimate relationships tend to subjectively overestimate how similar they and their partners are (Murray et al., 2002). Wanting to believe that they have found a kindred spirit, they tend to assume that their partners are mirrors of themselves.

Reciprocity Effects

In his book *How to Win Friends and Influence People,* Dale Carnegie (1936) suggested that people can gain others' liking by showering them with praise and flattery. However, we've all heard that "flattery will get you nowhere." Which advice is right? The evidence suggests that flattery will get you somewhere, with some people, some of the time.

In interpersonal attraction, *reciprocity* involves liking those who show that they like you. In general, research indicates that we tend to like those who show that they like us and that we tend to see others as liking us more if we like them. Thus, it appears that liking breeds liking and loving promotes loving (Sprecher, 1998). Reciprocating attraction generally entails providing friends and intimate partners with positive feedback that results in a *self-enhancement* effect—in other words, you help them feel good about themselves (Sedikides & Strube, 1997). However, studies suggest that people are also interested in *self-verification*—that is, they seek feedback that matches and supports their self-concepts (Bosson & Swann, 2001).

Romantic Ideals

In the realm of romance, people want their partner to measure up to their ideals. These ideals spell out the personal qualities that one hopes to find in a partner, such as warmth, good looks, loyalty, high status, a sense of humor, and so forth. According to Simpson, Fletcher, and Campbell (2001), people routinely evaluate how close their intimate partners come to matching these ideal standards, and these evaluations influence how relationships progress. Consistent with this theory, research shows that the more

closely individuals' perceptions of their partners match their ideals, the more satisfied they tend to be with their relationship—both in the early stages of dating (Fletcher, Simpson, & Thomas, 2000) and in stable, long-term relationships (Fletcher et al., 1999). Moreover, the size of the discrepancy between ideals and perceptions predicts whether a dating relationship will continue or dissolve (Fletcher et al., 2000).

Of course, these evaluations of how our partners compare to our ideals are subjective, leaving room for distortion. When people are highly invested in a relationship they can reduce the discrepancy between their ideals and their perceptions either by lowering their standards or by making charitable evaluations of their partners. Research suggests that the latter strategy is more common. For example, in a study of 180 couples, Murray, Holmes, and Griffin (1996a) found that most participants viewed their partners more favorably than the partners viewed themselves. Individuals' perceptions of their romantic partners seemed to reflect their ideals for a partner more than reality. Moreover, the data showed that people were happier in their relationship when they idealized their partners and when their partners idealized them. A follow-up study found that relationships were more likely to persist—even in the face of conflicts and doubts—when partners idealized each other (Murray, Holmes, & Griffin, 1996b). Another study found that individuals who are satisfied with their romantic relationships tend to focus on their partners' virtues, and to minimize and rationalize their partners' faults (Murray & Holmes, 1999). This line of research suggests that small, positive illusions about one's partner may foster happier and more resilient romantic relationships (Murray, 2001).

Perspectives on the Mystery of Love

Love has proven to be an elusive subject of study. It's difficult to define, difficult to measure, and frequently difficult to understand. Nonetheless, psychologists have begun to make some progress in their study of love. Let's look at their theories and research.

Passionate and Companionate Love

Two early pioneers in research on love were Elaine Hatfield (formerly Walster) and Ellen Berscheid (Berscheid, 1988; Berscheid & Walster, 1978; Hatfield & Rapson, 1993). They have proposed that romantic relationships are characterized by two kinds of love: passionate love and companionate love. *Passionate love* is a complete absorption in another that includes tender sexual feelings and the agony and

"*The emotion of romantic love seems to be distressingly fragile. As a 16th-century sage poignantly observed, 'the history of a love affair is the drama of its fight against time.'*"
ELLEN BERSCHEID

ecstasy of intense emotion. *Companionate love* is warm, trusting, tolerant affection for another whose life is deeply intertwined with one's own. Passionate and companionate love *may* coexist, but they don't necessarily go hand in hand.

The distinction between passionate and companionate love has been further refined by Robert Sternberg (1988a), who suggests that love has three facets rather than just two. He subdivides companionate love into intimacy and commitment. *Intimacy* refers to warmth, closeness, and sharing in a relationship. *Commitment* is an intent to maintain a relationship in spite of the difficulties and costs that may arise. Sternberg has mapped out the probable relations between the passage of time and the three components of love, as shown in Figure 16.6. Like Hatfield and Berscheid, he suspects that passion reaches its zenith in the early phases of love and then erodes. He believes that intimacy and commitment increase with time, although at different rates.

Research suggests that commitment is a crucial facet of love that is predictive of relationship stability. For example, declining commitment is associated with an increased likelihood of infidelity in dating relationships (Drigotas, Safstrom, & Gentilia, 1999). In another study of dating couples who were followed for four years, Sprecher (1999) found that participants' feelings of commitment were more predictive of whether they broke up than were their ratings of their overall love. Interestingly, the participants who broke up indicated that their love had remained reasonably stable, but their commitment and satisfaction had declined.

Love as Attachment

In another groundbreaking analysis of love, Cindy Hazan and Phillip Shaver (1987) have looked not at the components of love but at similarities between love and *attachment relationships* in infancy. We noted in our chapter on human development (Chapter 11) that infant-caretaker bonding, or attachment, emerges in the first year of life. Early attachments vary in quality, and infants tend to fall into one of three groups, which depend in part on parents' caregiving styles (Ainsworth et al., 1978). Most infants develop a *secure attachment*. However, some are very anxious when separated from their caretaker, a syndrome called *anxious-ambivalent attachment*. A third group of infants, characterized by *avoidant attachment*, never bond very well with their caretaker (see Figure 16.7 on the next page).

According to Hazan and Shaver, romantic love is an attachment process, and people's intimate relationships in adulthood follow the same form as their

attachments in infancy. According to their theory, a person who had an anxious-ambivalent attachment in infancy will tend to have romantic relations marked by anxiety and ambivalence in adulthood. In other words, people relive their early bonding with their parents in their adult romantic relationships.

Hazan and Shaver's (1987) initial survey study provided striking support for their theory. They found that adults' love relationships could be sorted into groups that paralleled the three patterns of attachment seen in infants. *Secure adults* (56% of the subjects) found it relatively easy to get close to others, described their love relations as trusting, rarely worried about being abandoned, and reported the fewest divorces. *Anxious-ambivalent adults* (20% of the subjects) reported a preoccupation with love accompanied by expectations of rejection and described their love relations as volatile and marked by jealousy. *Avoidant adults* (24% of the subjects) found it difficult to get close to others and described their love relations as lacking intimacy and trust. Consistent with their theory, Hazan and Shaver (1987) found that the percentage of adults falling into each category was roughly the same as the percentage of infants in each comparable category—a finding that was subsequently replicated with a nationally representative sample of American adults (Mickelson, Kessler, & Shaver, 1997). Also, subjects' recollections of their childhood relations with their parents were consistent with the idea that people relive their infant attachment experiences in adulthood.

Understandably, Hazan and Shaver's theory has attracted considerable interest and has generated a number of studies within a relatively short period of time. For example, research has shown that securely attached individuals have more committed, satisfying,

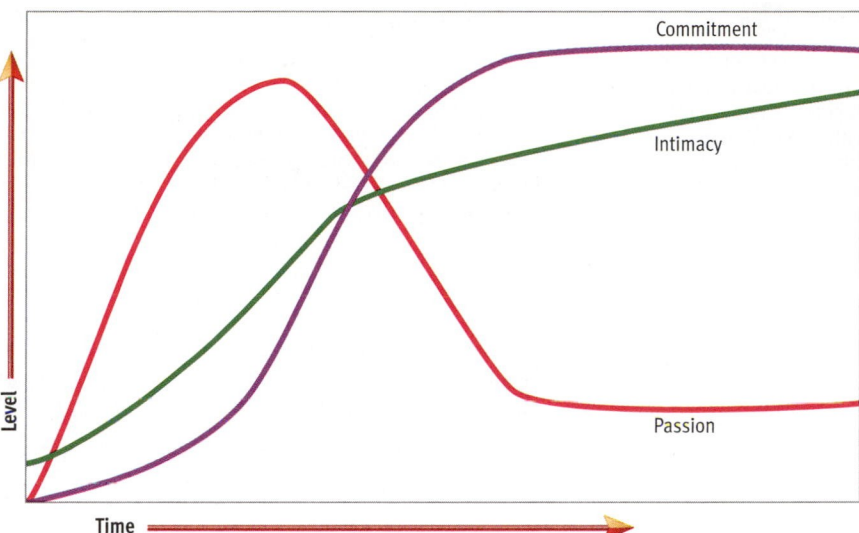

Figure 16.6

Sternberg's view of love over time. In his theory of love, Robert Sternberg (1988a) hypothesizes that the various elements of love progress in different ways over the course of time. According to Sternberg, passion peaks early in a relationship, whereas intimacy and commitment typically continue to build gradually. (Graphs adapted from Trotter, 1986)

Courtesy of Elaine Hatfield

"Passionate love is like any other form of excitement. By its very nature, excitement involves a continuous interplay between elation and despair, thrills and terror."
ELAINE HATFIELD

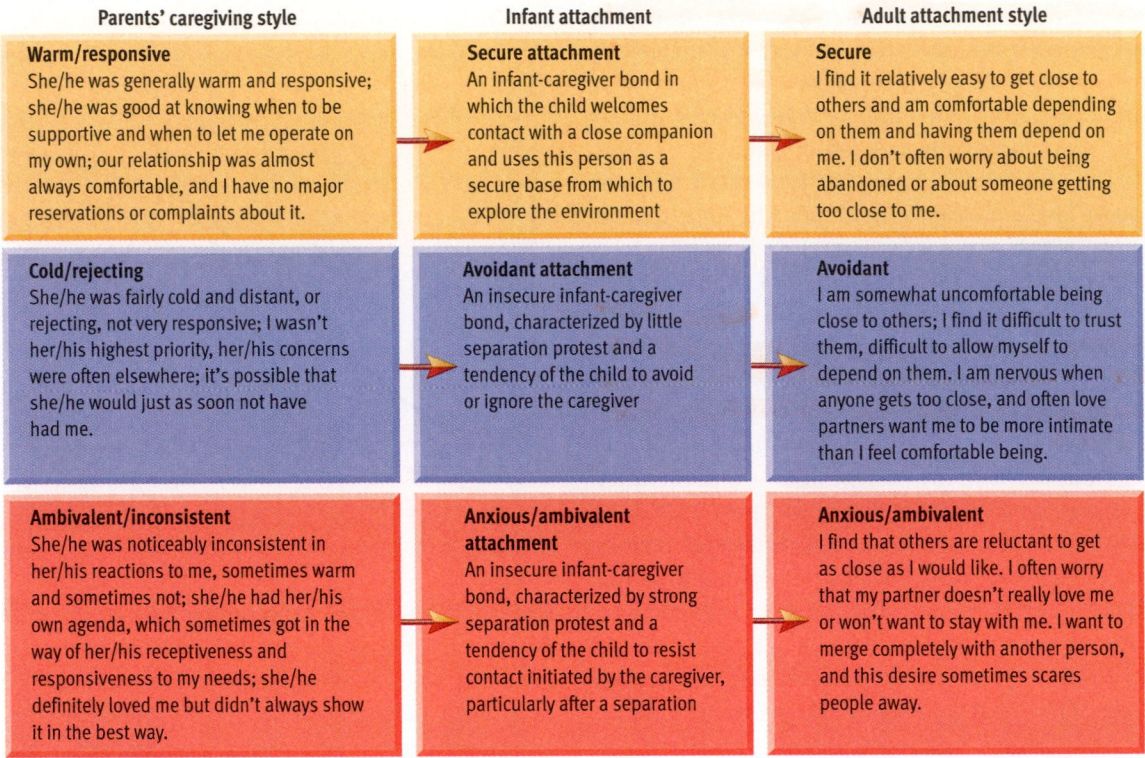

Figure 16.7

Infant attachment and romantic relationships.
According to Hazan and Shaver (1987), people's romantic relationships in adulthood are similar in form to their attachment patterns in infancy, which are determined in part by parental caregiving styles. The theorized relations between parental styles, attachment patterns, and intimate relations are outlined here. (Data for parental caregiving styles and adult attachment styles based on Hazan and Shaver, 1986, 1987; infant attachment patterns adapted from Shaffer, 1985)

Parents' caregiving style	Infant attachment	Adult attachment style
Warm/responsive She/he was generally warm and responsive; she/he was good at knowing when to be supportive and when to let me operate on my own; our relationship was almost always comfortable, and I have no major reservations or complaints about it.	**Secure attachment** An infant-caregiver bond in which the child welcomes contact with a close companion and uses this person as a secure base from which to explore the environment	**Secure** I find it relatively easy to get close to others and am comfortable depending on them and having them depend on me. I don't often worry about being abandoned or about someone getting too close to me.
Cold/rejecting She/he was fairly cold and distant, or rejecting, not very responsive; I wasn't her/his highest priority, her/his concerns were often elsewhere; it's possible that she/he would just as soon not have had me.	**Avoidant attachment** An insecure infant-caregiver bond, characterized by little separation protest and a tendency of the child to avoid or ignore the caregiver	**Avoidant** I am somewhat uncomfortable being close to others; I find it difficult to trust them, difficult to allow myself to depend on them. I am nervous when anyone gets too close, and often love partners want me to be more intimate than I feel comfortable being.
Ambivalent/inconsistent She/he was noticeably inconsistent in her/his reactions to me, sometimes warm and sometimes not; she/he had her/his own agenda, which sometimes got in the way of her/his receptiveness and responsiveness to my needs; she/he definitely loved me but didn't always show it in the best way.	**Anxious/ambivalent attachment** An insecure infant-caregiver bond, characterized by strong separation protest and a tendency of the child to resist contact initiated by the caregiver, particularly after a separation	**Anxious/ambivalent** I find that others are reluctant to get as close as I would like. I often worry that my partner doesn't really love me or won't want to stay with me. I want to merge completely with another person, and this desire sometimes scares people away.

interdependent, well-adjusted, and longer-lasting relationships compared to people with either anxious-ambivalent or avoidant attachment styles (Feeney, 1999). Moreover, studies have shown attachment patterns are reasonably stable over time (Fraley, 2002) and that people with different attachment styles are predisposed to think, feel, and behave differently in their relationships (Collins & Allard, 2001). For example, anxious-ambivalent people tend to report more intense emotional highs and lows in their romantic relationships. They also find conflicts with a partner more stressful than conflicts with others and feel more negative about their relationship after dealing with a conflict (Simpson, Rholes, & Phillips, 1996). Avoidant individuals tend to engage in more casual sex than others because this strategy allows them to get physically close without incurring the vulnerability of genuine intimacy (Brennan & Shaver, 1995). How do people with various attachment styles tend to pair up? More data are needed to answer this interesting question, but preliminary evidence suggests that avoidant and anxious-ambivalent people are not drawn to their mirror images. In an analysis of 240 couples, Kirkpatrick and Davis (1994) did not find *any* pairings between two avoidant people or two anxious-ambivalent people.

Studies have also suggested that attachment patterns may have far-reaching repercussions that extend into many aspects of people's lives besides their romantic relationships. For instance, people with secure attachments tend to have high self-esteem and to be relatively well adjusted. In contrast, people with avoidant or anxious-ambivalent attachments tend to be overrepresented in groups suffering from depression, eating disorders, and other types of psychopathology (Crowell, Fraley, & Shaver, 1999). Researchers have also found correlations between attachment styles and job satisfaction, gender roles, religious beliefs, and attitudes about work (Shaver & Hazan, 1993, 1994). Thus, Hazan and Shaver's innovative ideas about the long-term effects of infant attachment experiences have triggered an avalanche of thought-provoking research.

Culture and Close Relationships

Relatively little cross-cultural research has been conducted on the dynamics of close relationships. The limited evidence suggests both similarities and differences between cultures in romantic relationships (Hendrick & Hendrick, 2000). For the most part, similarities have been seen when research has focused on what people look for in prospective mates. As we discussed in Chapter 10, David Buss (1989, 1994a) has collected data on mate preferences in 37 divergent cultures and found that people all over the world value mutual attraction, kindness, intelligence, emotional stability, dependability, and good health in a

Marriages based on romantic love are the norm in Western cultures, whereas arranged marriages prevail in collectivist cultures.

mate. Buss also found that gender differences in mating priorities were nearly universal, with males placing more emphasis on physical attractiveness and females putting a higher priority on social status and financial resources.

Cultures vary, however, in their emphasis on love—especially passionate love—as a prerequisite for marriage. Love as the basis for marriage is an 18th-century invention of Western culture (Stone, 1977). As Hatfield and Rapson (1993) note, "Marriage-for-love represents an ultimate expression of individualism" (p. 2). In contrast, marriages arranged by families and other go-betweens remain common in cultures high in collectivism, including India (Gupta, 1992), Japan (Iwao, 1993), and China (Xiaghe & Whyte, 1990). This practice is declining in some societies as a result of Westernization, but in collectivist societies people contemplating marriage still tend to think in terms of "What will my parents and other people say?" rather than "What does my heart say?" (Triandis, 1994). Studies show that attitudes about love in collectivist societies reflect these cultural priorities. For example, in comparison to Western participants, subjects from Eastern countries report that romantic love is less important for marriage (Levine et al., 1995; Medora et al., 2002).

An Evolutionary Perspective on Attraction

Evolutionary psychologists have a great deal to say about heterosexual attraction. For example, they assert that physical appearance is an influential determinant of attraction because certain aspects of good looks can be indicators of sound health, good genes, and high fertility, all of which can contribute to re-

productive potential (Miller, 1998). Consistent with this analysis, recent research has found that some standards of attractiveness are more consistent across cultures than previously believed (Cunningham, Druen, & Barbee, 1997). For example, *facial symmetry* seems to be a key element of attractiveness in highly diverse cultures (Cunningham et al., 1995). Facial symmetry is thought to be valued because a host of environmental insults and developmental abnormalities are associated with physical asymmetries, which may serve as markers of relatively poor genes or health (Jones et al., 2001). Another facet of appearance that may transcend culture is *women's waist-to-hip ratio*. Around the world, men seem to prefer women with a waist-to-hip ratio around .70–.80, which appears to be a meaningful correlate of females' reproductive potential (Singh, 1993).

Evolutionary theorists also maintain that the unexpected correlations between infants' attachment patterns and adults' romantic relationships can be explained in terms of adaptive pressures. As discussed in Chapter 11, in ancestral societies infant attachment patterns may have reflected how safe and rich in resources local environments were and fostered mindsets about interpersonal relations and reproductive strategies that were adaptive, given the conditions in the local environments (Belsky, 1999b). Thus, the fascinating connections between attachment and intimate relations may reflect the influence of evolutionary processes (Zeifman & Hazan, 1997).

The most thoroughly documented findings on the evolutionary bases of heterosexual attraction are the findings on gender differences in humans' mating preferences. Consistent with the notion that humans are programmed by evolution to behave in ways that enhance their reproductive fitness, evidence indicates that men generally are more interested than women in seeking youthfulness and physical attractiveness in their mates because these traits should be associated with greater reproductive potential (see Chapter 10). On the other hand, research shows that women place a greater premium on prospective mates' ambition, social status, and financial potential because these traits should be associated with the ability to invest material resources in children (Buss & Kenrick, 1998; Li et al., 2002).

Does the gender gap in mating priorities influence the tactics people actually use in pursuing romantic relationships? Research suggests that the answer is yes. Buss (1988) asked 208 newlywed individuals to describe the things they did when they first met their spouse, and during the remainder of their courtship, to make themselves more appealing to their partner.

Web Link 16.3

Y? The National Forum on People's Differences
Did you ever want to ask a sensitive question of someone who was different from you—another race or religion or sexual orientation—but were too embarrassed or shy? In a cyberforum with clear rules for courteous and respectful dialogue, newspaper writer and editor Philip J. Milano allows visitors to share differences openly and frankly and to learn about topics that are frequently kept quiet.

He found that men were more likely than women to emphasize their material resources by doing such things as flashing lots of money, buying nice gifts, showing off expensive possessions, and bragging about their importance at work (see Figure 16.8). In contrast, women were more likely than men to work at enhancing their appearance by dieting, wearing stylish clothes, trying new hairstyles, and getting a tan.

Research suggests that people adjust their tactics of attraction depending on whether they are pursuing a short-term or long-term relationship, in ways that make sense from an evolutionary perspective (Schmitt & Buss, 1996; Schmitt, Couden, & Baker, 2001). For example, in the context of short-term relationships, men are thought to face the adaptive problem of finding sexually accessible women. In this context, the tactics of attraction rated most effective for women are those that signal sexual availability (such as flirting or dressing seductively) or that raise doubts about the availability of a rival (such as claiming that the rival is just a tease). In contrast, in the context of long-term relationships, men supposedly face the adaptive problem of maintaining exclusive sexual access to be certain of the paternity of any children. In this context, the tactics of attraction that are rated most effective for women are those that signal sexual exclusivity (such as rejecting sexual overtures from other men) or that raise doubts about a rival's fidelity (such as saying that the rival is promiscuous). Men are likely to make similar adjustments in their tactics of attraction (Schmitt & Buss, 1996). In the context of short-term relationships, tactics that involve giving resources immediately are rated as most effective, whereas for long-term relationships tactics that show potential for accumulating material resources or that raise doubts about a rival's resource potential are assumed to be optimal.

The tactics used by both sexes may include efforts at deception. A recent study found that many men and women indicated that they would be willing to lie about their personality, income, past relationships, career skills, and intelligence to impress a prospective date who was attractive (Rowatt, Cunningham, & Druen, 1999). Another study found that females anticipate more deception from prospective dates than males do (Keenan et al., 1997). Perhaps this is the reason women tend to underestimate the strength of men's relationship commitment (Haselton & Buss, 2000). Men do not appear to show a similar bias, but they do show a tendency to overestimate women's sexual interest. These cognitive biases seem to be designed to reduce the probability that ancestral women would consent to sex and then be abandoned and to

Tactics of attraction	Mean frequency (N = 102)	Mean frequency (N = 106)
Tactics used significantly more by males	Men	Women
Display resources	0.67	0.44
Brag about resources	0.73	0.60
Display sophistication	**1.18**	0.88
Display strength	0.96	0.44
Display athleticism	**1.18**	0.94
Show off	0.70	0.47
Tactics used significantly more by females	Men	Women
Wear makeup	0.02	**1.63**
Keep clean and groomed	**2.27**	**2.44**
Alter appearance—general	0.39	**1.27**
Wear stylish clothes	**1.22**	**2.00**
Act coy	0.54	0.73
Wear jewelry	0.25	**2.21**
Wear sexy clothes	0.68	0.91
Tactics for which no significant sex differences were found	Men	Women
Act provocative	0.77	0.90
Flirt	**2.13**	2.09
Keep hair groomed	**2.20**	**2.31**
Increase social exposure	0.89	0.90
Act nice	**1.77**	**1.86**
Display humor	**2.42**	**2.28**
Act promiscuous	0.30	0.21
Act submissive	**1.24**	1.11
Dissemble (feign agreement)	**1.26**	1.09
Touch	**2.26**	**2.16**

Figure 16.8

Similarities and differences between the sexes in tactics of attraction. Buss (1988) asked newlywed subjects to rate how often they had used 23 tactics of attraction to make themselves more appealing to their partner. The tactics used by one sex significantly more often than the other are listed in the first two sections of the figure. Although there were significant differences between the sexes, there were also many similarities. The 11 tactics used most frequently by each sex (those above the median) are boldfaced, showing considerable overlap between males and females in the tactics they use most. (Note: Higher means in the data reflect higher frequency of use, but the numbers do not indicate frequency per day or week.)

SOURCE: Adapted from Buss, D. M. (1988). The evolution of human intrasexual competition: Tactics of mate attraction. *Journal of Personality and Social Psychology, 54*, 616–628. Copyright © 1988 by the American Psychological Association. Adapted by permission of the author.

minimize the likelihood that ancestral men would overlook sexual opportunities (Buss, 2001). Thus, evolutionary psychologists analyze romantic relationships in terms of the adaptive problems they have presented over the course of human history.

REVIEW OF KEY POINTS

● People tend to like and love others who are physically attractive. The matching hypothesis asserts that people who are similar in physical attractiveness are more likely to be drawn together than those who are not.

● Byrne's research suggests that similarity causes attraction, although attitude alignment may also be at work. Reciprocity involves liking those who show that they like you. In intimate relationships, romantic ideals influence the progress of relationships. Romantic partners often idealize each other.

● Berscheid and Hatfield have distinguished between passionate and companionate love. Sternberg builds on their distinction by dividing companionate love into intimacy and commitment.

● Hazan and Shaver's theory suggests that love relationships in adulthood mimic attachment patterns in infancy. People tend to be secure, avoidant, or anxious-ambivalent in their

romantic relationships. Those who are secure tend to have more committed, satisfying relationships.

● The characteristics that people seek in prospective mates are much the same around the world. The gender differences in mating preferences seen in Western societies also appear to transcend culture. However, cultures vary considerably in their emphasis on passionate love as a prerequisite for marriage.

● According to evolutionary psychologists, certain aspects of good looks influence attraction because they are indicators of reproductive fitness. Consistent with evolutionary theory, men tend to seek youthfulness and attractiveness in their mates, whereas women emphasize prospective mates' financial potential and willingness to invest material resources in children. These preferences are reflected in people's courtship tactics, which vary depending on whether they are seeking short-term or long-term relationships.

Attitudes: Making Social Judgments

In our chapter-opening story, Muffy's friends exhibited decidedly negative attitudes about working-class men. Their example reveals a basic feature of attitudes: they're evaluative. Social psychology's interest in attitudes has a much longer history than its interest in attraction. Indeed, in its early days social psychology was defined as the study of attitudes. In this section we'll discuss the nature of attitudes, efforts to change attitudes through persuasion, and theories of attitude change.

What are attitudes? **Attitudes are positive or negative evaluations of objects of thought.** "Objects of thought" may include social issues (capital punishment or gun control, for example), groups (liberals, farmers), institutions (the Lutheran church, the Supreme Court), consumer products (yogurt, computers), and people (the president, your next-door neighbor).

Components and Dimensions of Attitudes

Social psychologists have traditionally viewed attitudes as being made up of three components: a cognitive component, an affective component, and a behavioral component. However, it gradually became apparent that many attitudes do not include all three components (Olson & Zanna, 1993), so it is more accurate to say that *attitudes may include up to three types of components*. The *cognitive component* of an attitude is made up of the beliefs that people hold about the object of an attitude. The *affective component* of an attitude consists of the *emotional feelings* stimulated by an object of thought. The *behavioral*

component of an attitude consists of *predispositions to act* in certain ways toward an attitude object. Figure 16.9 on the next page provides concrete examples of how someone's attitude about gun control might be divided into its components.

Attitudes vary along several crucial dimensions, including their *strength, accessibility,* and *ambivalence* (Olson & Zanna, 1993). Definitions of *attitude strength* differ, but they generally view strong attitudes as ones that are firmly held (resistant to change), durable over time, and that have a powerful impact on behavior (Krosnick & Petty, 1995). The *accessibility* of an attitude refers to how often one thinks about it and how quickly it comes to mind. Highly accessible attitudes are quickly and readily available (Fazio, 1995). Attitude accessibility is correlated with attitude strength, as highly accessible attitudes *tend* to be strong, but the concepts are distinct and there is no one-to-one correspondence. *Ambivalent attitudes* are conflicted evaluations that include both positive and negative feelings about an object of thought (Thompson, Zanna, & Griffin, 1995). Like attitude strength, attitude ambivalence has been measured in different ways (Priester & Petty, 2001). Generally speaking, ambivalence increases as the ratio of positive to negative evaluations gets closer to being equal. When ambivalence is low, an attitude tends to be more predictive of behavior and less pliable in the face of persuasion (Armitage & Conner, 2000).

Recent years have brought a great deal of research on the determinants and correlates of attitude strength. One determinant is *importance*—the subjective sense of caring and significance that a person attaches to an attitude. Attitudes that are important

PREVIEW QUESTIONS
● What are the key components and dimensions of attitudes?
● What factors influence the effectiveness of persuasive efforts?
● How do various theories explain attitude change?

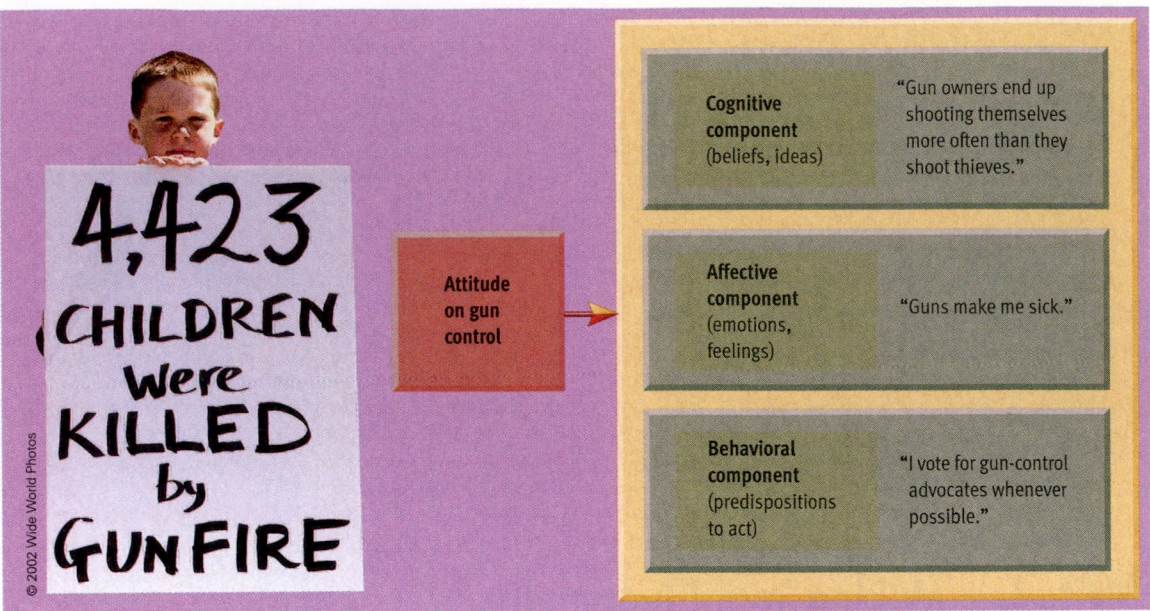

Figure 16.9

The possible components of attitudes. Attitudes may include cognitive, affective, and behavioral components, as illustrated here for a hypothetical person's attitude about gun control.

to people tend to be relatively strong (Boninger et al., 1995). Another factor is whether a person has a *vested interest* in an attitude. A vested interest exists when an attitude relates to an issue that can affect an individual's personal outcomes. For example, college students tend to have a vested interest in how localities regulate the legal age for drinking alcohol and physicians have a vested interest in whether managed care systems continue to become more influential in the practice of medicine. A vested interest in an attitude tends to make it stronger (Crano, 1995). Yet another consideration is one's knowledge of an attitude object. The more *knowledge and information* one has about an object of thought, the stronger one's attitude about it tends to be (Wood, Rhodes, & Biek, 1995). Perhaps this is true because thinking carefully about an attitude object can increase attitude strength (Petty, Haugtvedt, & Smith, 1995).

Attitudes and Behavior

In the early 1930s, when prejudice against Asians was common in the United States, Richard LaPiere journeyed across the country with a Chinese couple. He was more than a little surprised when they weren't turned away from any of the restaurants they visited in their travels—184 restaurants in all. About six months after his trip, LaPiere surveyed the same restaurants and asked whether they would serve Chinese customers. Roughly half of the restaurants replied to the survey, and over 90% of them indicated that they would not seat Chinese patrons. Thus, LaPiere (1934) found that people who voice prejudicial atti-

tudes may not behave in discriminatory ways. Since then, theorists have often asked: Why don't attitudes predict behavior better?

Admittedly, LaPiere's study had a fundamental flaw that you may already have detected. The person who seated LaPiere and his Chinese friends may not have been the same person who responded to the mail survey sent later. Nonetheless, numerous follow-up studies, using more sophisticated methods, have shown that attitudes are mediocre predictors of people's behavior (McGuire, 1985). That's not to say that they are irrelevant or meaningless. Kraus (1995) reviewed 88 attitude-behavior studies and found that the average correlation between attitudes and behavior was .38. That figure is high enough to justify Eagly's (1992) conclusion that researchers have identified "many conditions under which attitudes are substantial predictors of behavior" (p. 697). But on the whole, social psychologists have been surprised by how often a favorable attitude toward a candidate or product does not translate into a vote or a purchase.

Why aren't attitude-behavior relations more consistent? One consideration is that until recently researchers had failed to take variations in *attitude strength* into account. Accumulating evidence indicates that attitude strength influences the connection between attitudes and behavior. Stronger attitudes are more predictive of behavior (Eagly & Chaiken, 1998), but this factor has been left uncontrolled in decades of research on attitudes.

Another reason for the inconsistent relations between attitudes and behavior is that behavior depends on situational constraints—especially your subjective perceptions of how people expect you to behave. Thus, Icek Ajzen (1985, 1991) maintains that attitudes interact with situational norms to shape people's intentions, which then determine their behavior. Although you may be strongly opposed to marijuana use, you may not say anything when friends start passing a joint around at a party because you don't want to turn the party into an argument. However, in another situation governed by different norms, such as a class discussion, you may speak out forcefully against marijuana use. If so, you may be trying to change others' attitudes, the process we'll discuss next.

Trying to Change Attitudes: Factors in Persuasion

The fact that attitudes aren't always good predictors of a person's behavior doesn't stop others from trying to change those attitudes. Indeed, every day you're bombarded by efforts to alter your attitudes. To illustrate, let's trace the events of an imaginary morning. You may not even be out of bed before you start hearing radio advertisements intended to influence your attitudes about specific mouthwashes, computers, athletic shoes, and telephone companies. When you unfurl your newspaper, you find not only more ads but quotes from government officials and special interest groups, carefully crafted to shape your opinions. When you arrive at school, you encounter a group passing out leaflets that urge you to repent your sins and join them in worship. In class, your economics professor champions the wisdom of free markets in international trade. At lunch, the person you've been dating argues about the merits of an "open relationship." Your discussion is interrupted by someone who wants both of you to sign a petition. "Doesn't it ever let up?" you wonder. When it comes to persuasion, the answer is "no." As Anthony Pratkanis and Elliot Aronson (2000) put it, we live in

the "age of propaganda." In light of this reality, let's examine some of the factors that determine whether persuasion works.

The process of persuasion includes four basic elements: source, receiver, message, and channel (see Figure 16.10). **The *source* is the person who sends a communication, and the *receiver* is the person to whom the message is sent.** Thus, if you watch a presidential news conference on TV, the president is the source, and you and millions of other viewers are the receivers. **The *message* is the information transmitted by the source, and the *channel* is the medium through which the message is sent.** Although the research on communication channels is interesting, we'll confine our discussion to source, message, and receiver variables, which are most applicable to persuasion.

Source Factors

Occasional exceptions to the general rule are seen, but persuasion tends to be more successful when the source has high *credibility* (Petty, Wegener, & Fabrigar, 1997). What gives a person credibility? Either expertise or trustworthiness. *Expertise* tends to be more influential when arguments are ambiguous (Chaiken & Maheswaran, 1994). People try to convey their expertise by mentioning their degrees, their training, and their experience or by showing an impressive grasp of the issue at hand.

Expertise is a plus, but *trustworthiness* can be even more important. Many people tend to accept messages from trustworthy sources with little scrutiny (Priester & Petty, 1995). If you were told that your state needs to reduce corporate taxes to stimulate its economy, would you be more likely to believe it from the president of a huge corporation in your state or from an economics professor from out of state? Probably the latter. Trustworthiness is undermined when a source, such as the corporation president, appears to have something to gain. In contrast, trustworthi-

Figure 16.10

Overview of the persuasion process. The process of persuasion essentially boils down to *who* (the source) communicates *what* (the message) *by what means* (the channel) *to whom* (the receiver). Thus, there are four sets of variables that influence the process of persuasion: source, message, channel, and receiver factors. The diagram lists some of the more important factors in each category (including some that are not discussed in the text due to space limitations). (Adapted from Lippa, 1994)

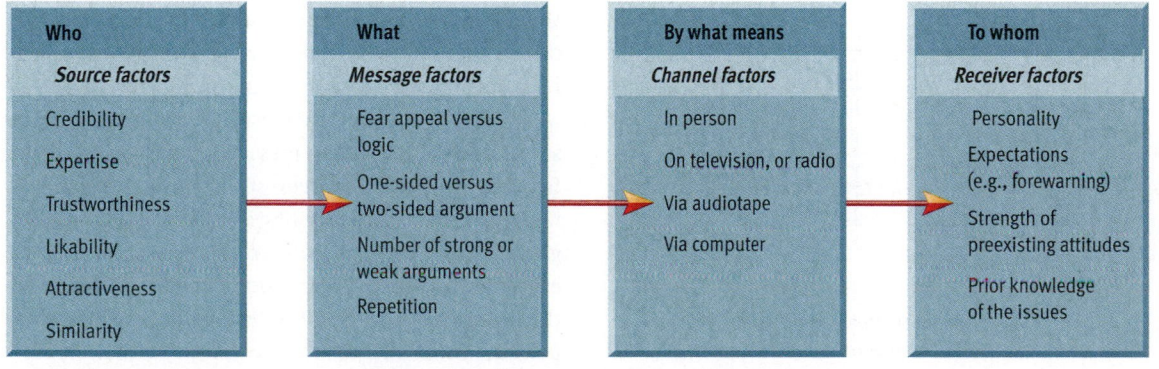

Who	What	By what means	To whom
Source factors	**Message factors**	**Channel factors**	**Receiver factors**
Credibility	Fear appeal versus logic	In person	Personality
Expertise	One-sided versus two-sided argument	On television, or radio	Expectations (e.g., forewarning)
Trustworthiness	Number of strong or weak arguments	Via audiotape	Strength of preexisting attitudes
Likability	Repetition	Via computer	Prior knowledge of the issues
Attractiveness			
Similarity			

ness is enhanced when people appear to argue against their own interests (Hunt, Smith, & Kernan, 1985). This effect explains why salespeople often make remarks like, "Frankly, my snowblower isn't the best. They have a better brand down the street. Of course, you'll have to spend quite a bit more . . ."

Likability also increases the effectiveness of a persuasive source (Roskos-Ewoldsen & Fazio, 1992), and some of the factors at work in attraction therefore have an impact on persuasion. Thus, the favorable effect of *physical attractiveness* on likability can make persuasion more effective (Shavitt et al., 1994). We also respond better to sources who share *similarity* with us in ways that are relevant to the issue at hand (Mackie, Worth, & Asuncion, 1990).

The importance of source variables can be seen in advertising. Many companies spend a fortune to obtain an ideal spokesperson, such as Bill Cosby, who combines trustworthiness, expertise (a doctorate in education), and likability. Companies quickly abandon spokespersons when their likability declines.

Message Factors

If you were going to give a speech to a local community group advocating a reduction in state taxes on corporations, you'd probably wrestle with a number of questions about how to structure your message. Should you look at both sides of the issue, or should you present just your side? Should you use all of the arguments at your disposal, or should you concentrate on the stronger arguments? Should you deliver a low-key, logical speech? Or should you try to strike fear into the hearts of your listeners? These questions are concerned with message factors in persuasion.

Let's assume that you're aware that there are two sides to the taxation issue. On the one hand, you're convinced that lower corporate taxes will bring new companies to your state and stimulate economic growth. On the other hand, you realize that reduced tax revenues may hurt the quality of education and roads in your state (but you think the benefits will outweigh the costs). Should you present a *one-sided argument* that ignores the possible problems for education and road quality? Or should you present a *two-sided argument* that acknowledges concern about education and road quality and then downplays the probable magnitude of these problems? The optimal strategy depends on a variety of considerations, but overall, two-sided arguments tend to be more effective (Petty & Wegener, 1998). Just mentioning that there are two sides to an issue can increase your credibility with an audience.

In presenting your side, should you use every argument you can think of, or should you focus on the stronger points? One study suggests that it is wise to concentrate on your strong arguments (Friedrich et al., 1996). The investigators exposed students to a variety of weak and strong arguments advocating a new senior comprehensive exam at their school. They found that adding strong arguments paid off, but adding weak arguments hurt rather than helped (see Figure 16.11). It appears that weak arguments may actually raise doubts rather than add to your case.

On the other hand, raw repetition of a message does seem to be an effective strategy. The *validity effect* refers to the finding that simply repeating a statement causes it to be perceived as more valid or true. It doesn't matter whether the statement is true, false, or clearly just an opinion; if you repeat something often enough, some people come to believe it (Boehm, 1994).

Persuasive messages frequently attempt to arouse fear. Opponents of nuclear power scare us with visions of meltdowns. Antismoking campaigns emphasize the threat of cancer, and deodorant ads highlight the risk of embarrassment. You could follow their lead and argue that if corporate taxes aren't reduced, your state will be headed toward economic ruin and massive unemployment. *Do appeals to fear work?* Yes—if they are successful in arousing fear. Research reveals that many messages intended to induce fear fail to do so. However, studies involving a wide range of issues (nuclear policy, auto safety, dental hygiene, and so on) have shown that messages that are effective in arousing fear tend to increase persuasion (Block & Keller, 1997; Witte & Allen, 2000). Fear appeals are most likely to work when your listeners view

Figure 16.11

The effect of adding weak arguments to one's case.
Friedrich et al. (1996) exposed students to various arguments in favor of requiring a new comprehensive exam for seniors at their school. This graph shows the effects of adding zero, three, or nine weak arguments to three or nine strong arguments. As you can see, in this instance, adding weak arguments generally had a negative effect on overall persuasion. (Data from Friedrich et al., 1996)

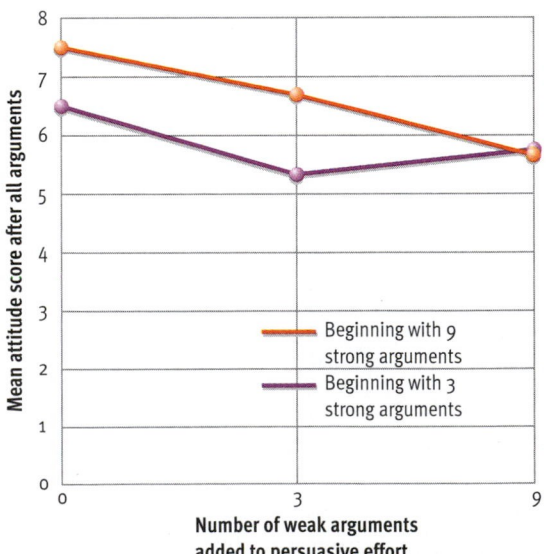

the dire consequences that you describe as exceedingly unpleasant, fairly probable if they don't take your advice, and avoidable if they do (Rogers, 1983; Witte et al., 1998).

Receiver Factors

What about the receiver of the persuasive message? Are some people easier to persuade than others? Undoubtedly, but researchers have not found any personality traits that are reliably associated with susceptibility to persuasion (Petty & Wegener, 1998). Other factors, such as the forewarning a receiver gets about a persuasive effort and the receiver's initial position on an issue, generally seem to be more influential than the receiver's personality.

An old saying suggests that "to be forewarned is to be forearmed." The value of *forewarning* applies to targets of persuasive efforts (Johnson, 1994). When you shop for a new TV, you *expect* salespeople to work at persuading you, and to some extent this forewarning reduces the impact of their arguments. Considerations that stimulate counterarguing in the receiver tend to increase resistance to persuasion (Jain, Buchanan, & Maheswaran, 2000).

A receiver's resistance to persuasion will depend in part on the nature of the attitude or belief that the source is trying to change. Obviously, resistance is greater when you have to advocate a position that is incompatible with the receiver's existing attitudes or beliefs. In general, people display a *disconfirmation bias* in evaluating arguments (Edwards & Smith, 1996). Arguments that are in conflict with one's prior attitudes are scrutinized longer and subjected to more skeptical analysis than arguments that are consistent with one's prior beliefs.

Furthermore, studies show that *stronger attitudes are more resistant to change* (Eagly & Chaiken, 1998). Strong attitudes may be tougher to alter because they tend to be embedded in networks of beliefs and values that might also require change (Erber, Hodges, & Wilson, 1995). Strong attitudes may also generate more biased and selective processing of persuasive arguments. *Prior knowledge about the issue* at hand also affects the difficulty experienced in trying to change someone's attitude. People who have more issue-relevant knowledge tend to scrutinize arguments more carefully and be more resistant to persuasion (Petty & Wegener, 1998).

Our review of source, message, and receiver variables has shown that attempting to change attitudes through persuasion involves a complex interplay of factors—and we haven't even looked beneath the

Web Link 16.4

Social Influence and Persuasion
How are people influenced or affected by other people? Shelley Wu has assembled a collection of web resources that seek to answer this question. Included are such topics as cults, propaganda, and healthy approaches to influencing other people.

CONCEPT CHECK 16.3

Understanding Attitudes and Persuasion

Check your understanding of the possible components of attitudes and the elements of persuasion by analyzing hypothetical political strategies. Imagine you're working on a political campaign and you're invited to join the candidate's inner circle in strategy sessions, as staff members prepare the candidate for upcoming campaign stops. During the meetings, you hear various strategies discussed. For each strategy below, indicate which component of voters' attitudes (cognitive, affective, or behavioral) is being targeted for change, and indicate which element in persuasion (source, message, or receiver factors) is being manipulated. The answers are in Appendix A.

1. "You need to convince this crowd that your program for regulating nursing homes is sound. Whatever you do, don't acknowledge the two weaknesses in the program that we've been playing down. I don't care if you're asked point blank. Just slide by the question and keep harping on the program's advantages."

_____

_____

2. "You haven't been smiling enough lately, especially when the TV cameras are rolling. Remember, you can have the best ideas in the world, but if you don't seem likable, you're not gonna get elected. By the way, I think I've lined up some photo opportunities that should help us create an image of sincerity and compassion."

_____

_____

3. "This crowd is already behind you. You don't have to alter their opinions on any issue. Get right to work convincing them to contribute to the campaign. I want them lining up to give money."

_____

_____

surface yet. How do people acquire attitudes in the first place? What dynamic processes within people produce attitude change? We turn to these theoretical issues next.

Theories of Attitude Formation and Change

Many theories have been proposed to explain the mechanisms at work in attitude change, whether or not it occurs in response to persuasion. We'll look at four theoretical perspectives: learning theory, dissonance theory, self-perception theory, and the elaboration likelihood model.

Learning Theory

We've seen repeatedly that *learning theory* can help explain a wide range of phenomena, from conditioned fears to the acquisition of sex roles to the development of personality traits. Now we can add attitude formation and change to our list.

The affective, or emotional, component in an attitude can be created through *classical conditioning,* just as other emotional responses can (Olson & Fazio, 2001, 2002). As we discussed in Chapter 6, advertisers routinely try to take advantage of classical conditioning by pairing their products with stimuli that elicit pleasant emotional responses, such as extremely attractive models, highly likable spokespersons, and cherished events, such as the Olympics (Grossman & Till, 1998). This conditioning process is diagrammed in Figure 16.12.

Operant conditioning may come into play when you openly express an attitude, such as "I believe that husbands should do more housework." Some people may endorse your view, while others may jump down your throat. Agreement from other people generally functions as a reinforcer, strengthening your tendency to express a specific attitude (Bohner & Schwarz, 2001). Disagreement often functions as a form of punishment, which may gradually weaken your commitment to your viewpoint.

Another person's attitudes may rub off on you through *observational learning* (Oskamp, 1991). If you hear your uncle say, "Republicans are nothing but puppets of big business" and your mother heartily agrees, your exposure to your uncle's attitude and your mother's reinforcement of your uncle may influence your attitude toward the Republican party. Studies show that parents and their children tend to have similar political attitudes (Sears, 1975). Observational learning presumably accounts for much of this similarity. The opinions of teachers, coaches, co-workers, talk-show hosts, rock stars, and so forth are

Figure 16.12

Classical conditioning of attitudes in advertising. Advertisers routinely pair their products with likable celebrities in the hope that their products will come to elicit pleasant emotional responses. See the Critical Thinking Application in Chapter 6 for a more in-depth discussion of this practice.

also likely to sway people's attitudes through observational learning.

Dissonance Theory

Leon Festinger's *dissonance theory* assumes that inconsistency among attitudes propels people in the direction of attitude change. Dissonance theory burst into prominence in 1959 when Festinger and J. Merrill Carlsmith published a famous study of counterattitudinal behavior. Let's look at their findings and at how dissonance theory explains them.

Festinger and Carlsmith (1959) had male college students come to a laboratory, where they worked on excruciatingly dull tasks such as turning pegs repeatedly. When a subject's hour was over, the experimenter confided that some participants' motivation was being manipulated by telling them that the task was interesting and enjoyable before they started it. Then, after a moment's hesitation, the experimenter asked if the subject could help him out of a jam. His usual helper was delayed and he needed someone to testify to the next "subject" (really an accomplice) that the experimental task was interesting. He offered to pay the subject if he would tell the person in the adjoining waiting room that the task was enjoyable and involving.

This entire scenario was enacted to coax participants into doing something that was inconsistent with their true feelings—that is, to engage in *counterattitudinal behavior*. Some participants received a token payment of $1 for their effort, while others received a more substantial payment of $20 (an amount equivalent to about $80–$90 today, in light of inflation). Later, a second experimenter inquired about the subjects' true feelings regarding the dull experimental task. Figure 16.13 summarizes the design of the Festinger and Carlsmith study.

Who do you think rated the task more favorably—the subjects who were paid $1 or those who were paid $20? Both common sense and learning theory would predict that the subjects who received the greater reward ($20) should come to like the task more. In reality, however, the subjects who were paid $1 exhibited more favorable attitude change—just as Festinger and Carlsmith had predicted. Why? Dissonance theory provides an explanation.

According to Festinger (1957), **cognitive dissonance exists when related cognitions are inconsistent— that is, when they contradict each other.** Cognitive dissonance is thought to create an unpleasant state of tension that motivates people to reduce their dissonance—usually by altering their cognitions. In the study by Festinger and Carlsmith, the subjects' contradictory cognitions were "The task is boring" and "I told someone the task was enjoyable." The subjects who were paid $20 for lying had an obvious reason for behaving inconsistently with their true attitudes, so these subjects experienced little dissonance. In contrast, the subjects paid $1 had no readily apparent justification for their lie and experienced high dissonance. To reduce it, they tended to persuade themselves that the task was more enjoyable than they had originally thought. Thus, dissonance theory sheds light on why people sometimes come to believe their own lies.

Cognitive dissonance is also at work when people turn attitudinal somersaults to justify efforts that haven't panned out, a syndrome called *effort justification*. Aronson and Mills (1959) studied effort justification by putting college women through a "severe initiation" before they could qualify to participate in what promised to be an interesting discussion of sexuality. In the initiation, the women had to read obscene passages out loud to a male experimenter. After all that, the highly touted discussion of sexuality turned out to be a boring, taped lecture on reproduction in lower animals. Subjects in the severe initiation condition experienced highly dissonant cog-

nitions ("I went through a lot to get here" and "This discussion is terrible"). How did they reduce their dissonance? Apparently by changing their attitude about the discussion, since they rated it more favorably than subjects in two control conditions. Effort justification may be at work in many facets of everyday life. For example, people who wait in line for an hour or more to get into an exclusive restaurant often praise the restaurant afterward even if they have been served a mediocre meal.

Dissonance theory has been tested in hundreds of studies with mixed, but largely favorable, results. The dynamics of dissonance appear to underlie many important types of attitude changes (Draycott & Dabbs, 1998; Hosseini, 1997; Keller & Block, 1999). Research has supported Festinger's claim that dissonance involves genuine psychological discomfort and even physiological arousal (Croyle & Cooper, 1983; Devine et al., 1999). However, dissonance effects are not among the most reliable phenomena in social psy-

❝*Cognitive dissonance is a motivating state of affairs. Just as hunger impels a person to eat, so does dissonance impel a person to change his opinions or his behavior.*❞
LEON FESTINGER

Figure 16.13

Design of the Festinger and Carlsmith (1959) study. The sequence of events in this landmark study of counterattitudinal behavior and attitude change is outlined here. The diagram omits a third condition (no dissonance), in which subjects were not induced to lie. The results in the nondissonance condition were similar to those found in the low-dissonance condition.

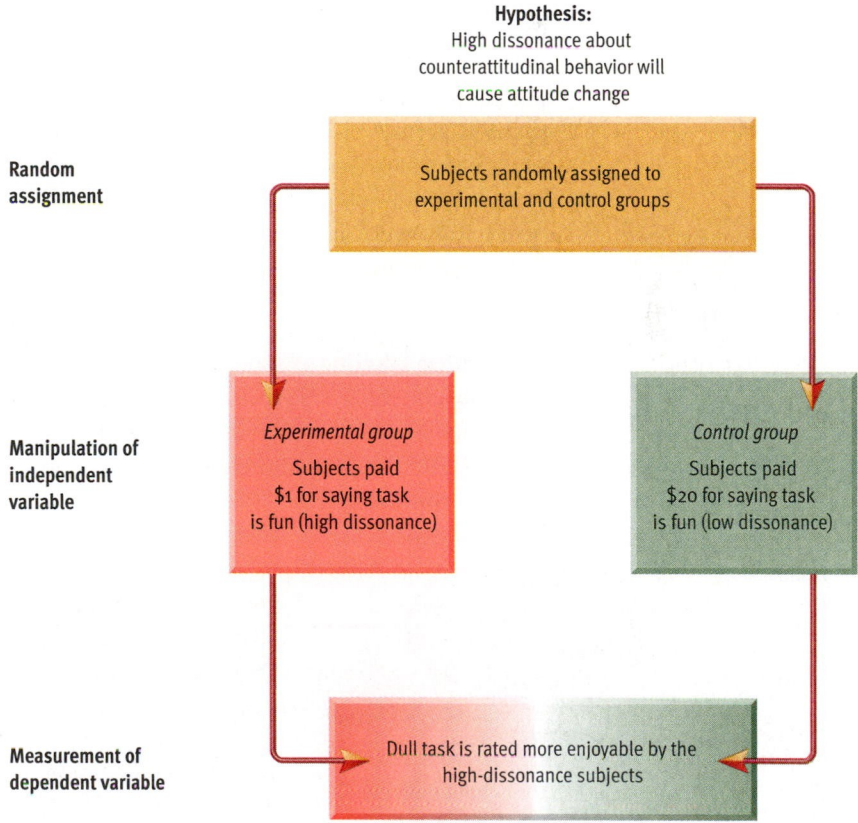

Hypothesis:
High dissonance about counterattitudinal behavior will cause attitude change

Random assignment
Subjects randomly assigned to experimental and control groups

Manipulation of independent variable

Experimental group
Subjects paid $1 for saying task is fun (high dissonance)

Control group
Subjects paid $20 for saying task is fun (low dissonance)

Measurement of dependent variable
Dull task is rated more enjoyable by the high-dissonance subjects

Conclusion:
Dissonance about counterattitudinal behavior does cause attitude change

chology, perhaps because people vary in the need for cognitive consistency (Cialdini, Trost, & Newsom, 1995). Moreover, even when people exhibit a clear preference for consistency, it's difficult to predict when dissonance will occur and what really motivates it.

Self-Perception Theory

After taking a close look at studies of counterattitudinal behavior, Daryl Bem (1967) concluded that self-perception, rather than dissonance, explains why people sometimes come to believe their own lies. According to Bem's *self-perception theory,* people often *infer* their attitudes from their behavior. Thus, Bem argued that in the study by Festinger and Carlsmith (1959), the subjects paid $1 probably thought to themselves, "A dollar isn't enough money to get me to lie, so I must have found the task enjoyable."

This thinking isn't much different from what dissonance theory would predict. Both theories suggest that people often think, "If I said it, it must be true." But the two theories propose that similar patterns of thought unfold for entirely different reasons. According to dissonance theory, subjects think along these lines because they're struggling to reduce tension caused by inconsistency among their cognitions. According to self-perception theory, subjects are engaged in normal attributional efforts to better understand their own behavior. Bem originally believed that most findings explained by dissonance were really due to self-perception. However, studies eventually showed that self-perception is at work primarily when subjects do not have well-defined attitudes regarding the issue at hand (Olson & Roese, 1995). Although self-perception theory did not replace dissonance theory, Bem's work demonstrated that attitudes are sometimes inferred from one's own behavior (see Figure 16.14).

Elaboration Likelihood Model

The *elaboration likelihood model* of attitude change, originally proposed by Richard Petty and John Cacioppo (1986), asserts that there are two basic "routes"

to persuasion (Petty & Wegener, 1999). The *central route* is taken when people carefully ponder the content and logic of persuasive messages. The *peripheral route* is taken when persuasion depends on nonmessage factors, such as the attractiveness and credibility of the source, or on conditioned emotional responses (see Figure 16.15). For example, a politician who campaigns by delivering carefully researched speeches that thoughtfully analyze complex issues is following the central route to persuasion. In contrast, a politician who depends on marching bands, flag waving, celebrity endorsements, and emotional slogans is following the peripheral route.

Both routes can lead to persuasion. However, according to the elaboration likelihood model, the durability of attitude change depends on the extent to which people elaborate on (think about) the contents of persuasive communications. Studies suggest that the central route to persuasion leads to more enduring attitude change than the peripheral route (Petty & Wegener, 1998). Research also suggests that attitudes changed through central processes predict behavior better than attitudes changed through peripheral processes (Petty, Wegener, & Fabrigar, 1997).

REVIEW OF KEY POINTS

● Attitudes may be made up of cognitive, affective, and behavioral components. Attitudes and behavior aren't as consistent as one might assume, in part because attitude strength varies and in part because attitudes only create predispositions to behave in certain ways.

● A source of persuasion who is credible, expert, trustworthy, likable, and physically attractive tends to be relatively effective in stimulating attitude change.

● Although there are some situational limitations, two-sided arguments and fear arousal are effective elements in persuasive messages. Repetition is helpful, but adding weak arguments to one's case may hurt more than help.

● Persuasion is undermined when a receiver is forewarned, when the sender advocates a position that is incompatible with the receiver's existing attitudes, or when strong attitudes are targeted.

● Attitudes may be shaped through classical conditioning, operant conditioning, and observational learning. Festinger's dissonance theory asserts that inconsistent attitudes cause tension and that people alter their attitudes to reduce cognitive dissonance.

● Dissonance theory has been used to explain attitude change following counterattitudinal behavior and efforts that haven't panned out. Some of these results can be explained by self-perception theory, which posits that people may infer their attitudes from their behavior.

● The elaboration likelihood model of persuasion holds that the central route to persuasion tends to yield longer-lasting attitude change than the peripheral route.

Figure 16.14

Bem's self-perception theory. The traditional view is that attitudes determine behavior. However, Bem stood conventional logic on its head when he proposed that behavior often determines (or causes people to draw inferences about) their attitudes. Subsequent research on attribution has shown that sometimes people *do* infer their attitudes from their behavior.

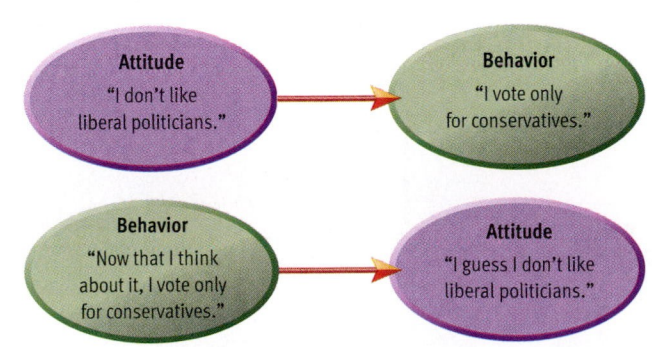

Traditional view
Attitudes determine behavior

Attitude
"I don't like liberal politicians."

Behavior
"I vote only for conservatives."

Bem's self-perception theory
Behavior determines attitudes

Behavior
"Now that I think about it, I vote only for conservatives."

Attitude
"I guess I don't like liberal politicians."

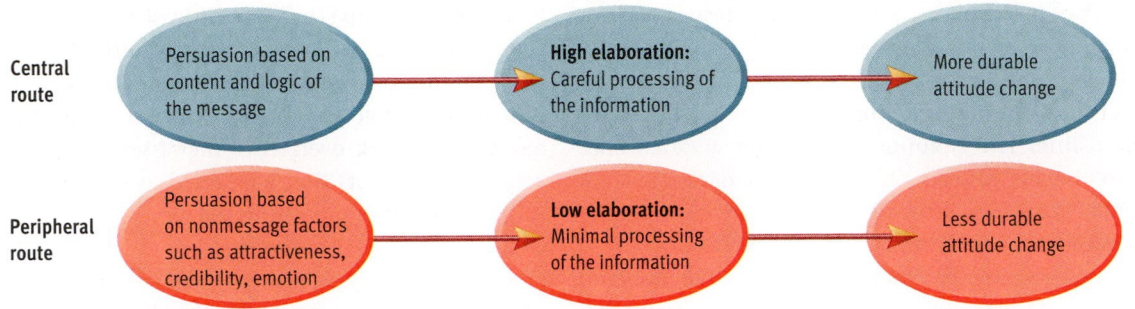

Figure 16.15

The elaboration likelihood model. According to the elaboration likelihood model (Petty & Cacioppo, 1986), the central route to persuasion leads to more elaboration of message content and more enduring attitude change than the peripheral route to persuasion.

Central route: Persuasion based on content and logic of the message → High elaboration: Careful processing of the information → More durable attitude change

Peripheral route: Persuasion based on nonmessage factors such as attractiveness, credibility, emotion → Low elaboration: Minimal processing of the information → Less durable attitude change

Conformity and Obedience: Yielding to Others

A number of years ago, the area that I lived in experienced a severe flood that required the mobilization of the National Guard and various emergency services. At the height of the crisis, a young man arrived at the scene of the flood, announced that he was from an obscure state agency that no one had ever heard of, and proceeded to take control of the emergency. City work crews, the fire department, local police, municipal officials, and the National Guard followed his orders with dispatch for several days, evacuating entire neighborhoods—until an official thought to check and found out that the man was just someone who had walked in off the street. The imposter, who had had small armies at his beck and call for several days, had no training in emergency services, just a history of unemployment and psychological problems.

After news of the hoax spread, people criticized red-faced local officials for their compliance with the imposter's orders. However, many of the critics probably would have cooperated in much the same way if they had been in the officials' shoes. For most people, willingness to obey someone in authority is the rule, not the exception. In this section, we'll analyze the dynamics of social influence at work in conformity and obedience.

Conformity

If you keep a well-manicured lawn, are you exhibiting conformity? According to social psychologists, it depends on whether your behavior is the result of group pressure. *Conformity* **occurs when people yield to real or imagined social pressure.** For example, if you maintain a well-groomed lawn only to avoid complaints from your neighbors, you're conforming to social pressure. However, if you maintain

a nice lawn because you genuinely prefer a nice lawn, that's *not* conformity.

In the 1950s, Solomon Asch (1951, 1955, 1956) devised a clever procedure that reduced ambiguity about whether subjects were conforming, allowing him to investigate the variables that govern conformity. Let's re-create one of Asch's (1955) classic experiments, which have become the most widely replicated studies in the history of social psychology (Markus, Kitayama, & Heiman, 1996). The subjects are male undergraduates recruited for a study of visual perception. A group of seven subjects are shown a large card with a vertical line on it and are then asked to indicate which of three lines on a second card matches the original "standard line" in length (see Figure 16.16). All seven subjects are given a turn at the task, and they announce their choice to the group. The subject in the sixth chair doesn't know it, but everyone else in the group is an accomplice of the experimenter, and they're about to make him wonder whether he has taken leave of his senses.

- How did Asch study conformity, and what did he learn?
- How did Milgram study obedience, and what did he learn?
- Why were Milgram's findings so controversial?
- How well do American findings on conformity and obedience generalize to other cultures?

Figure 16.16

Stimuli used in Asch's conformity studies. Subjects were asked to match a standard line (top) with one of three other lines displayed on another card (bottom). The task was easy—until experimental accomplices started responding with obviously incorrect answers, creating a situation in which Asch evaluated subjects' conformity.

1 2 3

Source: Adapted from Asch, S. (1955). Opinion and social pressure. *Scientific American, 193* (5), 31–35. Based on illustrations by Sara Love. Copyright © 1955 by Scientific American, Inc. All rights reserved.

Courtesy of Solomon Asch

"*That we have found the tendency to conformity in our society so strong that reasonably intelligent and well-meaning young people are willing to call white black is a matter of concern.*"
SOLOMON ASCH

Figure 16.17

Conformity and group size.
This graph shows the percentage of trials on which participants conformed as a function of group size in Asch's research. Asch found that conformity became more frequent as group size increased up to about four, and then conformity leveled off. (Data from Asch, 1955)

SOURCE: Adapted from Asch, S. (1955). Opinion and social pressure. *Scientific American, 193* (5), 31–35. Based on illustrations by Sara Love. Copyright © 1955 by Scientific American, Inc. All rights reserved.

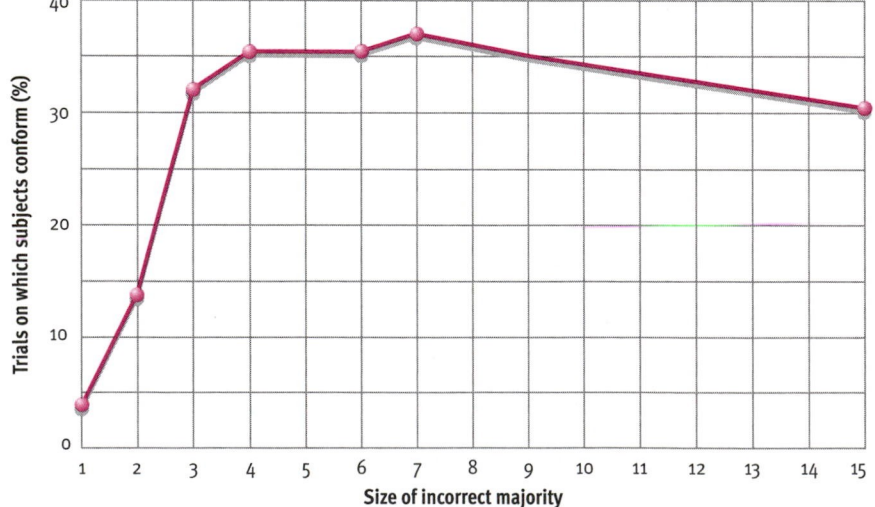

The accomplices give accurate responses on the first two trials. On the third trial, line number 2 clearly is the correct response, but the first five "subjects" all say that line number 3 matches the standard line. The genuine subject is bewildered and can't believe his ears. Over the course of the next 15 trials, the accomplices all give the same incorrect response on 11 of them. How does the real subject respond? The line judgments are easy and unambiguous. So, if the participant consistently agrees with the accomplices, he isn't making honest mistakes—he's conforming.

Averaging across all 50 participants, Asch (1955) found that the young men conformed on 37% of the trials. The subjects varied considerably in their tendency to conform, however. Of the 50 participants, 13 never caved in to the group, while 14 conformed on more than half the trials. One could argue that the results show that people confronting a unanimous majority generally tend to *resist* the pressure to conform, but given how clear and easy the line judgments were, most social scientists viewed the findings as a dramatic demonstration of humans' propensity to conform (Levine, 1999).

In subsequent studies, Asch (1956) found that *group size* and *group unanimity* are key determinants of conformity. To examine the impact of group size, Asch repeated his procedure with groups that included from 1 to 15 accomplices. Little conformity was seen when a subject was pitted against just one person, but conformity increased rapidly as group size went from 2 to 4, and then leveled off (see Figure 16.17). Thus, Asch reasoned that as groups grow larger, conformity increases—up to a point, a conclusion that has been echoed by other researchers (Cialdini & Trost, 1998).

However, group size made little difference if just one accomplice "broke" with the others, wrecking their unanimous agreement. The presence of another dissenter lowered conformity to about one-quarter of its peak, even when the dissenter made *inaccurate* judgments that happened to conflict with the majority view. Apparently, the subjects just needed to hear someone else question the accuracy of the group's perplexing responses. The importance of unanimity in fostering conformity has been replicated in subsequent research (Nemeth & Chiles, 1988).

What additional factors influence the likelihood of conformity? Among other things, people are more likely to conform when they are in ambiguous situations or when they have reasons to doubt their own judgments (Campbell, Tesser, & Fairey, 1986). Interestingly, if the situation is ambiguous, increasing the importance of the judgment—that is, the incentives for being accurate—only serves to heighten participants' tendency to conform (Baron, Vandello, & Brunsman, 1996). In other words, when the pressure is on, people tend to follow the leader.

Obedience

Obedience **is a form of compliance that occurs when people follow direct commands, usually from someone in a position of authority.** To a surprising extent, when an authority figure says, "Jump!" many people simply ask, "How high?" For most people, willingness to obey someone in authority is the rule, not the exception.

Milgram's Studies
Stanley Milgram wanted to study this tendency to obey authority figures. Like many other people after World War II, he was troubled by how readily the citizens of Germany had followed the orders of dictator Adolf Hitler, even when the orders required morally repugnant actions, such as the slaughter of millions of Jews. Milgram, who had worked with Solomon Asch, set out to design a standard laboratory procedure for the study of obedience, much like Asch's procedure for studying conformity. The clever experiment that Milgram devised became one of the most famous and controversial studies in the annals of psychology. It has been hailed as a "monumental contribution" to science and condemned as "dangerous, dehumanizing, and unethical research" (Ross, 1988). Decades after the research was conducted, it still generates spirited debate (Berkowitz, 1999; Lutsky, 1995). Because of its importance, it's our Featured Study for this chapter.

"I Was Just Following Orders"

Investigator: Stanley Milgram
(Yale University)

Source: Behavioral study of
obedience. *Journal of Abnormal and Social Psychology*,
1963, *67*, 371–378.

"I was just following orders." That was the essence of Adolf Eichmann's defense when he was tried for his war crimes, which included masterminding the Nazis' attempted extermination of European Jews. Milgram wanted to determine the extent to which people are willing to follow authorities' orders. In particular, he wanted to identify the factors that lead people to follow commands that violate their ethics, such as commands to harm an innocent stranger.

Method

The participants were a diverse collection of 40 men from the local community, recruited through advertisements to participate in a study at Yale University. When a subject arrived at the lab, he met the experimenter and another subject, a likable, 47-year-old accountant, who was actually an accomplice of the experimenter. The "subjects" were told that the study would concern the effects of punishment on learning. They drew slips of paper from a hat to get their assignments, but the drawing was fixed so that the real subject always became the "teacher" and the accomplice the "learner."

The participant then watched as the learner was strapped into an electrified chair through which a shock could be delivered to the learner whenever he made a mistake on the task (left photo in Figure 16.18). The subject was told that the shocks would be painful but

"would not cause tissue damage," and he was then taken to an adjoining room that housed the shock generator that he would control in his role as the teacher. This elaborate apparatus (right photo in Figure 16.18) had 30 switches designed to administer shocks varying from 15 to 450 volts, with labels ranging from "Slight shock" to "Danger: severe shock" and "XXX." Although the apparatus looked and sounded realistic, it was a fake, and the learner was never shocked.

As the "learning experiment" proceeded, the accomplice made many mistakes that necessitated shocks from the teacher, who was instructed to increase the shock level after each wrong answer. At "300 volts," the learner began to pound on the wall between the two rooms in protest and soon stopped responding to the teacher's questions. At this point, participants ordinarily turned to the experimenter for guidance. The experimenter, a 31-year-old male in a gray lab coat, firmly indicated that no response was the same as a wrong answer and that the teacher should continue to give stronger and stronger shocks to the now silent learner. If the participant expressed unwillingness to continue, the experimenter responded sternly with one of four prearranged prods, such as, "It is absolutely essential that you continue."

When a participant refused to obey the experimenter, the session came to an end. The dependent variable

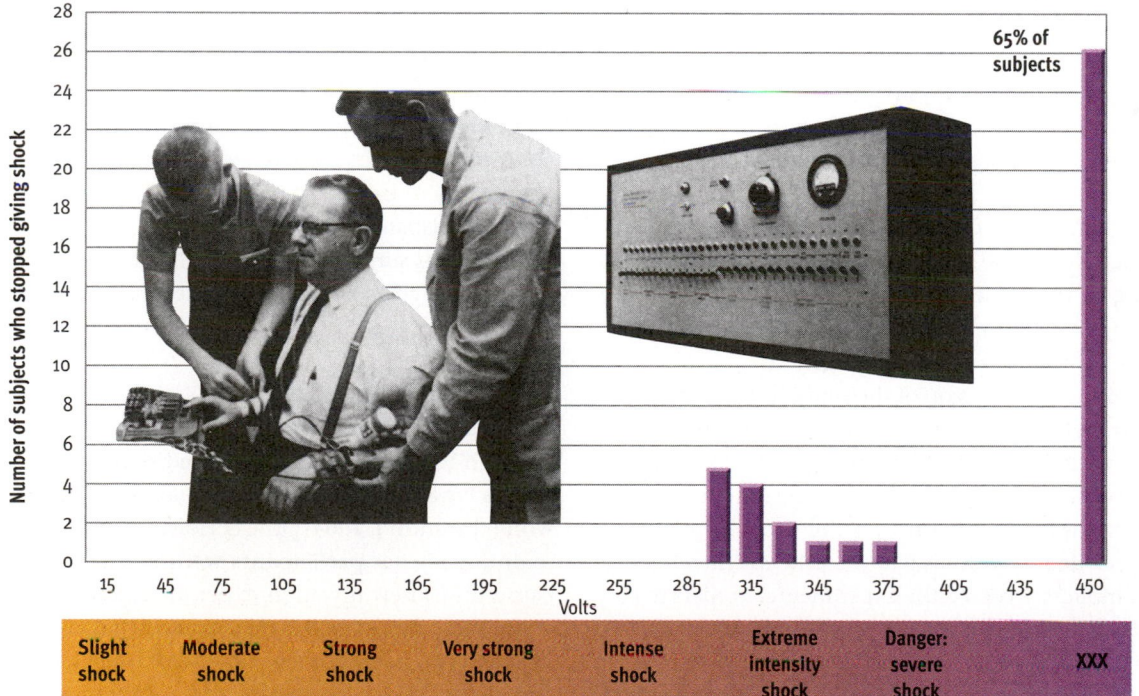

Figure 16.18

Milgram's experiment on obedience. The photo on the left shows the "learner" being connected to the shock generator during one of Milgram's experimental sessions. The photo on the right shows the fake shock generator used in the study. The surprising results of the Milgram (1963) study are summarized in the bar graph. Although subjects frequently protested, the vast majority (65%) delivered the entire series of shocks to the learner.

SOURCE: Photos copyright © 1965 by Stanley Milgram. From the film *Obedience*, distributed by The Pennsylvania State University. Reprinted by permission of Alexandra Milgram.

was the maximum shock the participant was willing to administer before refusing to cooperate. After each session, the true purpose of the study was explained to the subject, who was reassured that the shock was fake and the learner was unharmed.

Results

No participant stopped cooperating before the learner reached the point of pounding on the wall, but 5 quit at that point. As the graph in Figure 16.18 shows, only 14 out of 40 subjects defied the experimenter before the full series of shocks was completed. Thus, 26 of the 40 subjects (65%) administered all 30 levels of shock. Although they tended to obey the experimenter, many participants voiced and displayed considerable distress about harming the learner. The horrified subjects groaned, bit their lips, stuttered, trembled, and broke into a sweat, but they continued administering the shocks.

Discussion

Based on these results, Milgram concluded that obedience to authority is even more common than he or others had anticipated. Before the study was conducted, Milgram had described it to 40 psychiatrists and had asked them to predict how much shock subjects would be willing to administer to their innocent victims. Most of the psychiatrists had predicted that fewer than 1% of the subjects would continue to the end of the series of shocks!

In interpreting his results, Milgram argued that strong pressure from an authority figure can make decent people do indecent things to others. Applying this insight to Nazi war crimes and other travesties, Milgram asserted that some sinister actions may not be due to actors' evil character so much as to situational pressures that can lead normal people to engage in acts of treachery and violence. Thus, he arrived at the disturbing conclusion that given the right circumstances, anyone might obey orders to inflict harm on innocent strangers.

Comment

In itself, obedience is not necessarily bad or wrong. Social groups of any size depend on obedience to function smoothly. Life would be chaotic if orders from police, parents, physicians, bosses, generals, and presidents were routinely ignored. However, Milgram's study suggests that many people are overly willing to submit to the orders of someone in command.

If you're like most people, you're probably confident that you wouldn't follow an experimenter's demands to inflict harm on a helpless victim. But the empirical findings indicate that you're probably wrong. After many replications, the results are deplorable, but clear: Most people can be coerced into engaging in actions that violate their morals and values. This finding is disheartening, but it sharpens our understanding of moral atrocities, such as the Nazi persecutions of Jews. ■

"The essence of obedience is that a person comes to view himself as the instrument for carrying out another person's wishes, and he therefore no longer regards himself as responsible for his actions."

STANLEY MILGRAM

After his initial demonstration, Milgram (1974) tried about 20 variations on his experimental procedure, looking for factors that influence participants' obedience. In one variation, Milgram moved the study away from Yale's campus to see if the prestige of the university was contributing to the subjects' obedience. When the study was run in a seedy office building by the "Research Associates of Bridgeport," only a small decrease in obedience was observed (48% of the subjects gave all the shocks).

In another version of the study, Milgram borrowed a trick from Asch's conformity experiments and set up teams of three teachers that included two more accomplices. When they drew lots, the real subject was always selected to run the shock apparatus in consultation with his fellow teachers. When both accomplices accepted the experimenter's orders to continue shocking the learner, the pressure increased obedience a bit. However, if an accomplice defied the experimenter and supported the subject's objec-

tions, obedience declined dramatically (only 10% of the subjects gave all the shocks), just as conformity had dropped rapidly when dissent surfaced in Asch's conformity studies. Dissent from another "teacher" turned out to be one of the few variations that reduced participants' obedience appreciably. As a whole, Milgram was surprised at how high subjects' obedience remained as he changed various aspects of his experiment.

The Ensuing Controversy

Milgram's study evoked a controversy that continues through today. Some critics argued that Milgram's results couldn't be generalized to apply to the real world (Baumrind, 1964; Orne & Holland, 1968). They maintained that participants went along only because they knew it was an experiment and "everything must be okay." Or they argued that subjects who agree to participate in a scientific study *expect to obey* orders from an experimenter. Milgram (1964,

1968) replied by arguing that if subjects had thought "everything must be okay," they wouldn't have experienced the enormous distress that they clearly showed.

As for the idea that research participants expect to follow an experimenter's commands, Milgram pointed out that so do real-world soldiers and bureaucrats who are accused of villainous acts performed in obedience to authority. "I reject Baumrind's argument that the observed obedience doesn't count because it occurred where it is appropriate," said Milgram (1964). "That is precisely why it *does* count." Overall, the evidence supports the generalizability of Milgram's results, which were consistently replicated for many years, in diverse settings, with a variety of subjects and procedural variations (Blass, 1999; Miller, 1986).

Critics also questioned the ethics of Milgram's procedure (Baumrind, 1964; Kelman, 1967). They noted that without prior consent, subjects were exposed to extensive deception that could undermine their trust in people and to severe stress that could leave emotional scars. Moreover, most participants also had to confront the disturbing fact that they caved in to the experimenter's commands to inflict harm on an innocent victim.

Milgram's defenders argued that the brief distress experienced by his subjects was a small price to pay for the insights that emerged from his obedience studies. Looking back, however, many psychologists seem to share the critics' concerns about the ethical implications of Milgram's work. His procedure is questionable by contemporary standards of research ethics, and no replications of his obedience study have been conducted in the United States since the mid-1970s (Blass, 1991)—a bizarre epitaph for what may be psychology's best-known experiment.

Cultural Variations in Conformity and Obedience

Are conformity and obedience unique to American culture? By no means. The Asch and Milgram experiments have been repeated in many societies, where they have yielded results roughly similar to those seen in the United States. Thus, the phenomena of conformity and obedience seem to transcend culture.

The replications of Milgram's obedience study have largely been limited to industrialized nations similar to the United States. Comparisons of the results of these studies must be made with caution because the composition of the samples and the experimental procedures have varied somewhat. But many of the studies have reported even higher obedience rates than those seen in Milgram's American samples. For example, obedience rates of over 80% have been reported for samples from Italy, Germany, Austria, Spain, and Holland (Smith & Bond, 1994). Thus, the surprisingly high level of obedience observed by Milgram does not appear to be peculiar to the United States.

The Asch experiment has been repeated in a more diverse range of societies than the Milgram experiment. Like many other cultural differences in social behavior, variations in conformity appear to be related to the degree of *individualism versus collectivism* seen in a society. Various theorists have argued that collectivistic cultures, which emphasize respect for group norms, cooperation, and harmony, probably encourage more conformity than individualistic cultures (Schwartz, 1990) and have a more positive view of conformity (Kim & Markus, 1999). As Matsumoto (1994, p. 162) puts it, "To conform in American culture is to be weak or deficient somehow. But this is not true in other cultures. Many cultures foster more collective, group-oriented values, and concepts of conformity, obedience, and compliance enjoy much higher status." Consistent with this analysis, studies *have* found higher levels of conformity in collectivistic cultures than in individualistic cultures (Bond & Smith, 1996; Smith, 2001).

REVIEW OF KEY POINTS

- Conformity involves yielding to social pressure. Asch found that subjects often conform to the group, even when the group reports inaccurate judgments on a simple line-judging task. Conformity becomes more likely as group size increases, up to a group size of four, and then levels off. If a small group isn't unanimous, conformity declines rapidly.

- In Milgram's landmark study of obedience to authority, adult men drawn from the community showed a remarkable tendency, in spite of their misgivings, to follow orders to shock an innocent stranger. Milgram concluded that situational pressures can make decent people do indecent things.

- Critics asserted that Milgram's results were not generalizable to the real world and that his methods were unethical. The generalizability of Milgram's findings has stood the test of time, but his work also helped to stimulate stricter ethical standards for research.

- The Asch and Milgram experiments have been replicated in many cultures. These replications have uncovered modest cultural variations in the propensity to conform or to obey an authority figure.

Behavior in Groups: Joining with Others

PREVIEW QUESTIONS
- What is the bystander effect?
- What processes contribute to reduced individual productivity in larger groups?
- What is group polarization?
- What are the antecedent conditions and symptoms of groupthink?

Social psychologists study groups as well as individuals, but exactly what is a group? Are all the divorced fathers living in Baltimore a group? Are three strangers moving skyward in an elevator a group? What if the elevator gets stuck? How about four students from your psychology class who study together regularly? A jury deciding a trial? The Boston Celtics? The U.S. Congress? Some of these collections of people are groups and others aren't. Let's examine the concept of a group to find out which of these collections qualify.

In social psychologists' eyes, **a *group* consists of two or more individuals who interact and are interdependent.** The divorced fathers in Baltimore aren't likely to qualify on either count. Strangers sharing an elevator might interact briefly, but they're not interdependent. However, if the elevator got stuck and they had to deal with an emergency together, they could suddenly become a group. Your psychology classmates who study together are a group, as they interact and depend on each other to achieve shared goals. So do the members of a jury, a sports team such as the Celtics, and a large organization such as the U.S. Congress. Historically, most groups have interacted on a face-to-face basis, but advances in telecommunications are changing that reality. In the era of the Internet, people can interact, become interdependent, and develop a group identity, without ever meeting in person (McKenna & Bargh, 1998).

Groups vary in many ways. Obviously, a study group, the Celtics, and Congress are very different in terms of size, purpose, formality, longevity, similarity of members, and diversity of activities. Can anything meaningful be said about groups if they're so diverse? Yes. In spite of their immense variability, groups share certain features that affect their functioning. Among other things, most groups have *roles* that allocate special responsibilities to some members, *norms* about suitable behavior, a *communication structure* that reflects who talks to whom, and a *power structure* that determines which members wield the most influence (Forsyth, 1999).

Thus, when people join together in a group, they create a social organism with unique characteristics and dynamics that can take on a life of its own. One of social psychology's enduring insights is that in a given situation you may behave quite differently when you're in a group than when you're alone. To illustrate this point, let's look at some interesting research on helping behavior.

Behavior Alone and in Groups: The Case of the Bystander Effect

Imagine that you have a precarious medical condition and that you must go through life worrying about whether someone will leap forward to provide help if the need ever arises. Wouldn't you feel more secure when around larger groups? After all, there's "safety in numbers." Logically, as group size increases, the probability of having a "good Samaritan" on the scene increases. Or does it?

We've seen before that human behavior isn't necessarily logical. When it comes to helping behavior, many studies have uncovered an apparent paradox called the *bystander effect:* **People are less likely to provide needed help when they are in groups than when they are alone.** Evidence that your probability of getting help *declines* as group size increases was first described by John Darley and Bibb Latané (1968), who were conducting research on the determinants of helping behavior. In the Darley and Latané study, students in individual cubicles connected by an intercom participated in discussion groups of three sizes. (The separate cubicles allowed the researchers to examine each individual's behavior in a group context, a technique that minimizes confounded variables in individual-group comparisons.) Early in the discussion, a student who was an experimental accomplice hesitantly mentioned that he was prone to seizures. Later in the discussion, the same accomplice feigned a severe seizure and cried out for help. Although a majority of subjects sought assistance for the student, the tendency to seek help *declined* with increasing group size.

Similar trends have been seen in many other experiments, in which over 6000 subjects have had opportunities to respond to apparent emergencies, including fires, asthma attacks, faintings, crashes, and flat tires, as well as less pressing needs to answer a door or to pick up objects dropped by a stranger (Latané & Nida, 1981). Many of the experiments have been highly realistic studies conducted in subways, stores, and shopping malls, and many have compared individuals against groups in face-to-face interaction. Pooling the results of this research, Latané and Nida (1981) estimated that subjects who were alone provided help 75% of the time, whereas subjects in the presence of others provided help only 53% of the time. They concluded that the only significant limiting condition

Web Link 16.5

The Psychology of Cyberspace

As the Internet continues to develop into an ever more important part of our lives, a number of social scientists have begun to examine human behavior in the computer-mediated environment called "cyberspace." John Suler's site at Rider University presents a major overview of the research being carried out in this new field.

on the bystander effect is that it is less likely to occur when the need for help is not ambiguous.

What accounts for the bystander effect? A number of factors may be at work. Bystander effects are most likely in ambiguous situations because people look around to see whether others think there's an emergency. If everyone hesitates, their inaction suggests that there's no real need for help. The *diffusion of responsibility* that occurs in a group is also important. If you're by yourself when you encounter someone in need of help, the responsibility to provide help rests squarely on your shoulders. However, if other people are present, the responsibility is divided among you, and you may all say to yourselves, "Someone else will help." A reduced sense of responsibility may contribute to other aspects of behavior in groups, as we'll see in the next section.

Group Productivity and Social Loafing

Have you ever driven through a road construction project—at a snail's pace, of course—and become irritated because so many workers seem to be just standing around? Maybe the irony of the posted sign "Your tax dollars at work" made you imagine that they were all dawdling. And then again, perhaps not. Individuals' productivity often *does* decline in larger groups (Karau & Williams, 1993). This fact is unfortunate, as many important tasks can only be accomplished in groups. Group productivity is crucial to committees, sports teams, firefighting crews, sororities, study groups, symphonies, and work teams of all kinds, from the morning crew in a little diner to the board of directors of a Fortune 500 company.

Two factors appear to contribute to reduced individual productivity in larger groups. One factor is *reduced efficiency* resulting from the *loss of coordination* among workers' efforts. As you put more people on a yearbook staff, for instance, you'll probably create more and more duplication of effort and increase how often group members end up working at cross purposes.

The second factor contributing to low productivity in groups involves *effort* rather than efficiency. *Social loafing* is a reduction in effort by individuals when they work in groups as compared to when they work by themselves. To investigate social loafing, Latané and his colleagues (1979) measured the sound output produced by subjects who were asked to cheer or clap as loud as they could. So they couldn't see or hear other group members, subjects were told that the study concerned the importance of sensory

feedback and were asked to don blindfolds and put on headphones through which loud noise was played. This maneuver permitted a simple deception: Subjects were *led to believe* that they were working alone or in a group of two or six, when in fact *individual* output was actually measured.

When participants *thought* that they were working in larger groups, their individual output declined. Since lack of coordination could not affect individual output, the subjects' decreased sound production had to be due to reduced effort. Latané and his colleagues also had the same subjects clap and shout in genuine groups of two and six and found an additional decrease in production that was attributed to loss of coordination. Figure 16.19 shows how social loafing and loss of coordination combined to reduce productivity as group size increased.

The social-loafing effect has been replicated in numerous studies in which subjects have worked on a variety of tasks, including cheering, pumping air, swimming in a relay race, solving mazes, evaluating editorials, and brainstorming for new ideas (Karau & Williams, 1995; Levine & Moreland, 1998). Social loafing and the bystander effect appear to share a common cause: diffusion of responsibility in groups (Comer, 1995; Latané, 1981). As group size increases, the responsibility for getting a job done is divided among more people, and many group members ease up because their individual contribution is less recognizable. Thus, social loafing occurs in situations where individuals can "hide in the crowd" (Karau & Williams, 1993).

Social loafing is *not* inevitable. Social loafing is less likely when group members are convinced that individual performance is crucial to group performance

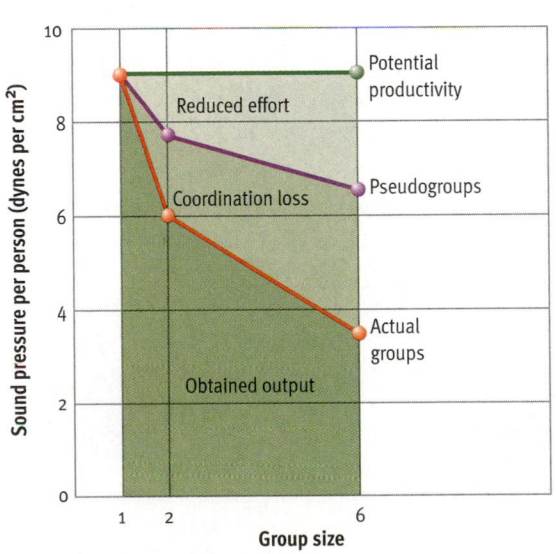

Figure 16.19

The effect of loss of coordination and social loafing on group productivity. The amount of sound produced per person declined noticeably when people worked in actual groups of two or six (orange line). This decrease in productivity reflects both loss of coordination and social loafing. Sound per person also declined when subjects merely thought they were working in groups of two or six (purple line). This smaller decrease in productivity is due to social loafing.

SOURCE: Adapted from Latané, B., Williams, K., & Harkins, S. (1979). Many hands make light the work: The causes and consequences of social loafing. *Journal of Personality and Social Psychology, 37,* 822–832. Copyright © 1979 by the American Psychological Association. Adapted by permission of the author.

Web Link 16.6

Group Dynamics
Donelson Forsyth of Virginia Commonwealth University maintains this excellent site devoted to the dynamics of group interaction. Topics of interest include group structure, group cohesiveness, influence in groups, conflict in groups, and the history of research on groups. The site also houses a rich set of links to organizations that study groups.

and that excellent group performance will lead to valued outcomes (Shepperd & Taylor, 1999). And social loafing is reduced when people work in cohesive, close-knit, committed groups (Karau & Hart, 1998). Cultural factors may also influence the likelihood of social loafing. Studies with subjects from Japan, China, and Taiwan suggest that social loafing may be less prevalent in collectivistic cultures, which place a high priority on meeting group goals and contributing to ones' ingroups (Karau & Williams, 1995; Smith, 2001).

Decision Making in Groups

Productivity is not the only issue that commonly concerns groups. When people join together in groups, they often have to make decisions about what the group will do and how it will use its resources. Whether it's your study group deciding what type of pizza to order, a jury deciding on a verdict, or Congress deciding on whether to pass a bill, groups make decisions.

Evaluating decision making is often more complicated than evaluating productivity. In many cases, the "right" decision may not be readily apparent. Who can say whether your study group ordered the right pizza or whether Congress passed the right bills? Nonetheless, social psychologists have discovered some interesting tendencies in group decision mak-

ing. We'll take a brief look at *group polarization* and *groupthink.*

Group Polarization

Who leans toward more cautious decisions: individuals or groups? Common sense suggests that groups will work out compromises that cancel out members' extreme views. Hence, the collective wisdom of the group should yield relatively conservative choices. Is common sense correct? To investigate this question, Stoner (1961) asked individual subjects to give their recommendations on tough decisions and then asked the same subjects to engage in group discussion to arrive at joint recommendations. When Stoner compared individuals' average recommendation against their group decision generated through discussion, he found that groups arrived at *riskier* decisions than individuals did. Stoner's finding was replicated in other studies (Pruitt, 1971), and the phenomenon acquired the name *risky shift.*

However, investigators eventually determined that groups can shift either way, toward risk or caution, depending on which way the group is leaning to begin with (Friedkin, 1999; Myers & Lamm, 1976). A shift toward a more extreme position, an effect called *polarization,* is often the result of group discussion. Thus, **group polarization occurs when group discussion strengthens a group's dominant point of view and produces a shift toward a more extreme decision in that direction** (see Figure 16.20). Group polarization does *not* involve widening the gap between factions in a group, as its name might suggest. In fact, group polarization can contribute to consensus in a group, as we'll see in our upcoming discussion of groupthink.

Why does group polarization occur? One reason is that group discussion often exposes group members to persuasive arguments that they had not thought about previously (Stasser, 1991). Another reason is that when people discover that their views are shared by others, they tend to express even stronger views because they want to be liked by their ingroups (Hogg, Turner, & Davidson, 1990).

Groupthink

In contrast to group polarization, which is a normal process in group dynamics, groupthink is more like a "disease" that can infect decision making in groups. **Groupthink occurs when members of a cohesive group emphasize concurrence at the expense of critical thinking in arriving at a decision.** As you might imagine, groupthink doesn't produce very effective decision making. Indeed, groupthink can lead to major blunders that may look incompre-

Figure 16.20

Group polarization. Two examples of group polarization are diagrammed here. In the first example (top) a group starts out mildly opposed to an idea, but after discussion sentiment against the idea is stronger. In the second example (bottom), a group starts out with a favorable disposition toward an idea, and this disposition is strengthened by group discussion.

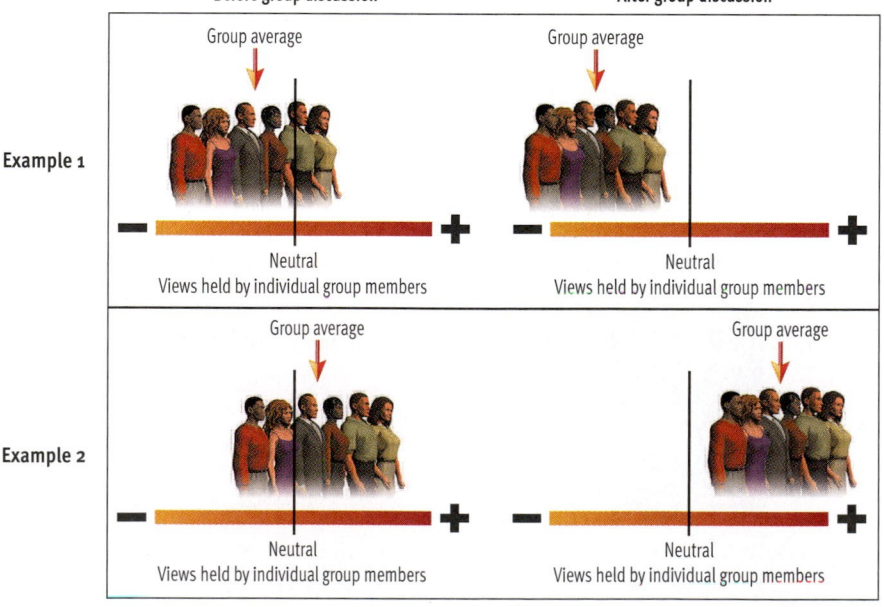

Before group discussion · After group discussion
Group average · Group average
Example 1 — Neutral — Views held by individual group members
Example 2 — Neutral — Views held by individual group members

hensible after the fact. Irving Janis (1972) first described groupthink in his effort to explain how President John F. Kennedy and his advisers could have miscalculated so badly in deciding to invade Cuba at the Bay of Pigs in 1961. The attempted invasion failed miserably and, in retrospect, seemed remarkably ill-conceived.

Applying his many years of research and theory on group dynamics to the Bay of Pigs fiasco, Janis developed a model of groupthink, which is summarized in Figure 16.21. When groups get caught up in groupthink, members suspend their critical judgment and the group starts censoring dissent as the pressure to conform increases. Soon, everyone begins to think alike. Moreover, "mind guards" try to shield the group from information that contradicts the group's view.

If the group's view is challenged from outside, victims of groupthink tend to think in simplistic "us versus them" terms. Members begin to overestimate the ingroup's unanimity, and they begin to view the outgroup as the enemy. Groupthink also promotes incomplete gathering of information. Like individuals, groups often display a confirmation bias, as they tend to seek and focus on information that supports their initial views (Schulz-Hardt et al., 2000).

Recent research has uncovered another factor that may contribute to groupthink—individual members often fail to share information that is unique to them (Postmes, Spears, & Cihangir, 2001). Sound decision making depends on group members combining their information effectively (Winquist & Larson, 1998). However, when groups discuss issues, they have an interesting tendency to focus mainly on the information that the members already share as opposed to encouraging offers of information unique to individual members (Stasser, Vaughn, & Stewart, 2000). Additional research is needed to determine why groups are mediocre at pooling members' information.

What causes groupthink? According to Janis, a key precondition is high group cohesiveness. **Group cohesiveness** refers to the strength of the liking relationships linking group members to each other and to the group itself. Members of cohesive groups are close-knit, are committed, have "team spirit," and are very loyal to the group. Cohesiveness itself isn't bad. It can facilitate group productivity (Mullen & Copper, 1994) and help groups achieve great things. But Janis maintains that the danger of groupthink is greater when groups are highly cohesive. Groupthink is also more likely when a group works in relative isolation, when the group's power structure is dominated by a strong, directive leader, and when the group is under stress to make a major decision (see Figure 16.21). Under these conditions, group discus-

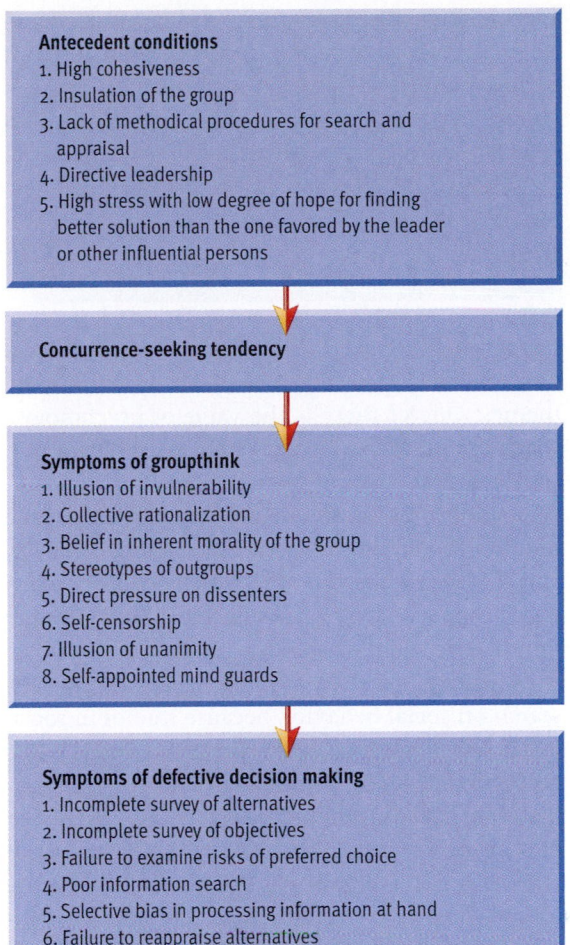

Figure 16.21

Overview of Janis's model of groupthink. The antecedent conditions, symptoms, and resultant effects of groupthink postulated by Janis (1972) are outlined here. His model of groupthink has been very influential, but practical difficulties have limited research on the theory.

Source: Adapted from Janis, I. L., & Mann, L. (1977). *Decision making: A psychological analysis of conflict, choice and commitment.* New York: Free Press. Adapted with permission of The Free Press, a Division of Simon & Schuster. Copyright © 1977 by The Free Press.

sions can easily lead to group polarization, strengthening the group's dominant view.

A relatively small number of experiments have been conducted to test Janis's theory, because the antecedent conditions thought to foster groupthink—

CONCEPT CHECK 16.4

Scrutinizing Common Sense

Check your understanding of the implications of research in social psychology by indicating whether the commonsense assertions listed below have been supported by empirical findings. Do the trends in research summarized in this chapter indicate that the following statements are true or false? The answers are in Appendix A.

_____ 1. Generally, in forming their impressions of others, people don't judge a book by its cover.

_____ 2. When it comes to attraction, birds of a feather flock together.

_____ 3. In the realm of love, opposites attract.

_____ 4. If you're the target of persuasion, to be forewarned is to be forearmed.

_____ 5. When you need help, there's safety in numbers.

such as high decision stress, strong group cohesiveness, and dominating leadership—are difficult to create effectively in laboratory settings (Aldag & Fuller, 1993). The evidence on groupthink consists mostly of retrospective case studies of major decision-making fiascos (Eaton, 2001). Thus, Janis's model of groupthink should probably be characterized as an innovative, sophisticated, intuitively appealing theory that needs to be subjected to much more empirical study (Esser, 1998).

Putting It in Perspective

PREVIEW QUESTIONS
- How did this chapter illustrate the value of empiricism?
- How did this chapter highlight the importance of cultural factors?
- How did this chapter demonstrate that human experience is highly subjective?

Our discussion of social psychology has provided a final embellishment on three of our seven unifying themes. One of these is the value of psychology's commitment to empiricism—that is, its reliance on systematic observation through research to arrive at conclusions. The second theme that stands out is the importance of cultural factors in shaping behavior, and the third is the extent to which people's experience of the world is highly subjective. Let's consider the virtues of empiricism first.

It's easy to question the need to do scientific research on social behavior, because studies in social psychology often seem to verify common sense. While most people wouldn't presume to devise their own theory of color vision, question the significance of REM sleep, or quibble about the principal causes of schizophrenia, everyone has beliefs about the nature of love, how to persuade others, and people's willingness to help in times of need. Thus, when studies demonstrate that credibility enhances persuasion, or that good looks facilitate attraction, it's tempting to conclude that social psychologists go to great lengths to document the obvious, and some critics say, "Why bother?"

You saw why in this chapter. Research in social psychology has repeatedly shown that the predictions of logic and common sense are often wrong. Consider just a few examples. Even psychiatric experts failed to predict the remarkable obedience to authority uncovered in Milgram's research. The bystander effect in helping behavior violates cold-blooded mathematical logic. Dissonance research has shown that after a severe initiation, the bigger the letdown, the more favorable people's feelings are. These principles defy common sense. Thus, research on social behavior provides dramatic illustrations of why psychologists put their faith in empiricism.

Our coverage of social psychology also demonstrated once again that, cross-culturally, behavior is characterized by both variance and invariance. Thus, we saw substantial cultural differences in patterns of attribution, the role of love in mating relationships, attitudes about conformity, the tendency to obey authority figures, and the likelihood of social loafing.

Although basic social phenomena such as stereotyping, attraction, obedience, and conformity probably occur all over the world, cross-cultural studies of social behavior show that research findings based on American samples may not generalize precisely to other cultures.

Research in social psychology is also uniquely well suited for making the point that people's view of the world is highly personal and subjective. In this chapter we saw how physical appearance can color perception of a person's ability or personality, how social schemas can lead people to see what they expect to see in their interactions with others, how pressure to conform can make people begin to doubt their senses, and how groupthink can lead group members down a perilous path of shared illusions.

The subjectivity of social perception will surface once again in our Applications for the chapter. The Personal Application focuses on prejudice, a practical problem that social psychologists have shown great interest in, whereas the Critical Thinking Application examines aspects of social influence.

REVIEW OF KEY POINTS
- People who help someone in need when they are alone are less likely to provide help when a group is present. This phenomenon, called the bystander effect, occurs primarily because a group creates diffusion of responsibility.
- Individuals' productivity often declines in larger groups because of loss of coordination and because of social loafing. Social loafing seems to be due mostly to diffusion of responsibility and may be less prevalent in collectivist cultures.
- Group polarization occurs when discussion leads a group to shift toward a more extreme decision in the direction the group was already leaning. In groupthink, a cohesive group suspends critical judgment in a misguided effort to promote agreement in decision making.
- Social psychology illustrates the value of empiricism because research in this area often proves that common sense is wrong. Cross-cultural research on social behavior illustrates that findings based on American samples may not generalize precisely to other cultures. Additionally, several lines of research on social perception demonstrate that people's experience of the world is highly subjective.

PERSONAL APPLICATION

Understanding Prejudice

Answer the following "true" or "false."

_____ **1** Prejudice and discrimination amount to the same thing.

_____ **2** Stereotypes are always negative or unflattering.

_____ **3** Ethnic and racial groups are the only widespread targets of prejudice in modern society.

_____ **4** People see members of their own ingroup as being more alike than the members of outgroups.

Prejudice is a major social problem. It harms victims' self-concepts, suppresses human potential, creates tension and strife between groups, and even instigates wars. The first step toward reducing prejudice is to understand its roots. Hence, in this Application, we'll try to achieve a better understanding of why prejudice is so common. Along the way, you'll learn the answers to the true-false questions above.

Prejudice and discrimination are closely related concepts, and the terms have become nearly interchangeable in popular use. Social scientists, however, prefer to define their terms precisely, so let's clarify which is which. *Prejudice* **is a negative attitude held toward members of a group.** Like many other attitudes, prejudice can include three components (see Figure 16.22): beliefs ("Indians are mostly alcoholics"), emotions ("I despise Jews"), and behavioral dispositions ("I wouldn't hire a Mexican"). Racial prejudice receives the lion's share of publicity, but prejudice is *not* limited to ethnic groups. Women, homosexuals, the aged, the handicapped, and the mentally ill are also targets of widespread prejudice. Thus, many people hold prejudicial attitudes toward one group or another, and many have been victims of prejudice.

Prejudice may lead to *discrimination,* **which involves behaving differently, usually unfairly, toward the members of a group.** Prejudice and discrimination tend to go hand in hand, but as LaPiere's (1934) pioneering study of discrimination in restaurant seating showed, attitudes and behavior do not necessarily correspond (see Figure 16.23). In our discussion, we'll concentrate primarily on the attitude of prejudice. Let's begin by looking at processes in person perception that promote prejudice.

Stereotyping and Subjectivity in Person Perception

Perhaps no factor plays a larger role in prejudice than *stereotypes.* That's not to say that stereotypes are inevitably negative. Although it's an overgeneralization, it's hardly insulting to assert that Americans are ambitious or that the Japanese are industrious. Unfortunately, many people do subscribe to derogatory stereotypes of various ethnic groups. Although studies suggest that negative racial stereotypes have diminished over the last 50 years, they're not a thing of the past (Gaertner et al., 1999; Madon et al., 2001). According to a variety of investigators, modern racism has merely become more subtle (Devine, Plant, & Blair, 2001; Dovidio & Gaertner, 1999). Many people carefully avoid overt expressions of prejudicial attitudes but covertly continue to harbor negative views of racial minorities. These people endorse racial equality as an abstract principle but often oppose concrete programs intended to promote equality, on the grounds that discrimination is no longer a problem. Recent studies suggest that modern sexism has become subtle in much the same way as racism (Swim & Campbell, 2001).

Figure 16.22

The three potential components of prejudice as an attitude. Attitudes can consist of up to three components. The tricomponent model of attitudes, applied to prejudice against women, would view sexism as negative beliefs about women (cognitive component) that lead to a feeling of dislike (affective component), which in turn leads to a readiness to discriminate against women (behavioral component).

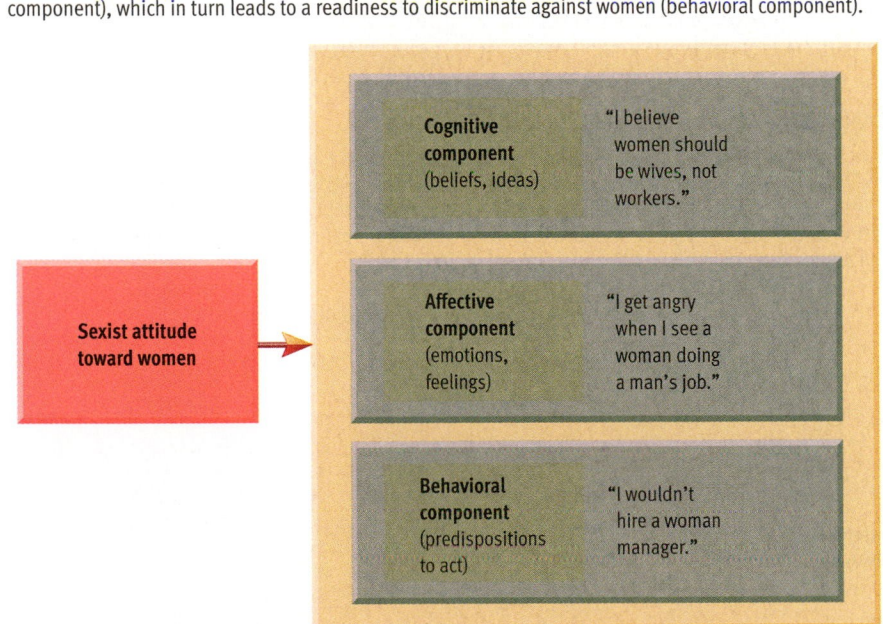

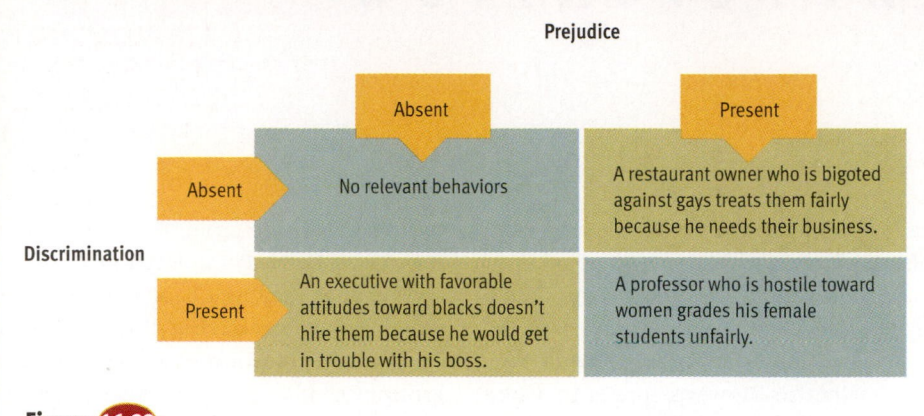

Prejudice

		Absent	Present
Discrimination	Absent	No relevant behaviors	A restaurant owner who is bigoted against gays treats them fairly because he needs their business.
	Present	An executive with favorable attitudes toward blacks doesn't hire them because he would get in trouble with his boss.	A professor who is hostile toward women grades his female students unfairly.

Figure 16.23

Relationship between prejudice and discrimination. As these examples show, prejudice can exist without discrimination and discrimination without prejudice. In the green cells, there is a disparity between attitude and behavior.

Research indicates that stereotypes are so pervasive and insidious they are often activated automatically (Bargh, 1999; Fiske, 2000). According to Devine and Monteith (1999), prejudicial stereotypes are highly accessible cognitive schemas that can be activated automatically, even in people who truly renounce prejudice. Thus, a man who rejects prejudice against homosexuals may still feel uncomfortable sitting next to a gay male on a bus, even though he regards his reaction as inappropriate.

Unfortunately, stereotypes are highly resistant to change. When people encounter members of a group that they view with prejudice who deviate from the stereotype of that group, they often discount this evidence by assuming that the atypical group members constitute a distinct subtype of that group, such as wealthy African Americans or conservative homosexuals (Kunda & Oleson, 1995, 1997). Consigning deviants to a subtype that is viewed as unrepresentative of the group allows people to preserve their stereotype of the group.

Stereotypes also persist because the *subjectivity* of person perception makes it likely that people will see what they expect to see when they actually come into contact with groups that they view with prejudice (Dunning & Sherman, 1997). For example, Duncan (1976) had white subjects watch and evaluate interaction on a TV monitor that was supposedly live (actually it was a videotape) and varied the race of a person who gets into an argument and gives another

person a slight shove. The shove was coded as "violent behavior" by 73% of the subjects when the actor was black but by only 13% of the subjects when the actor was white. As we've noted before, people's perceptions are highly subjective. Because of stereotypes, even "violence" may lie in the eye of the beholder.

Memory biases are also tilted in favor of confirming people's prejudices (Ybarra, Stephan, Schaberg, 2000). For example, if a man believes that "women are not cut out for leadership roles," he may dwell with delight on his female supervisor's mistakes and quickly forget about her achievements. Thus, the *illusory correlation effect* can contribute

to the maintenance of prejudicial stereotypes (McConnell, Leibold, & Sherman, 1997).

Biases in Attribution 12d

Attribution processes can also help perpetuate stereotypes and prejudice. Research taking its cue from Weiner's (1980) model of attribution has shown that people often make *biased attributions for success and failure*. For example, men and women don't get equal credit for their successes (Swim & Sanna, 1996). Observers often discount a woman's success by attributing it to good luck, sheer effort, or the ease of the task (except on traditional feminine tasks). In comparison, a man's success is more likely to be attributed to his outstanding ability (see Figure 16.24). These biased patterns of attribution help sustain the stereotype that men are more competent than women. Similar patterns of bias have been seen in attributional explanations of ethnic minorities' successes and failures (Jackson, Sullivan, & Hodge, 1993; Kluegel, 1990). Generally, when minorities experience stereotype-inconsistent success, it is discounted by attributing it to external factors or to unstable, internal causes.

Recall that the *fundamental attribution error* is a bias toward explaining events by pointing to the personal characteristics of the actors as causes (internal attributions). Research suggests that people are particu-

Figure 16.24

Bias in the attributions used to explain success and failure by men and women. Attributions about the two sexes often differ. For example, men's successes tend to be attributed to their ability and intelligence (blue cell), whereas women's successes tend to be attributed to hard work, good luck, or low task difficulty (green cells). These attributional biases help to perpetuate the belief that men are more competent than women.

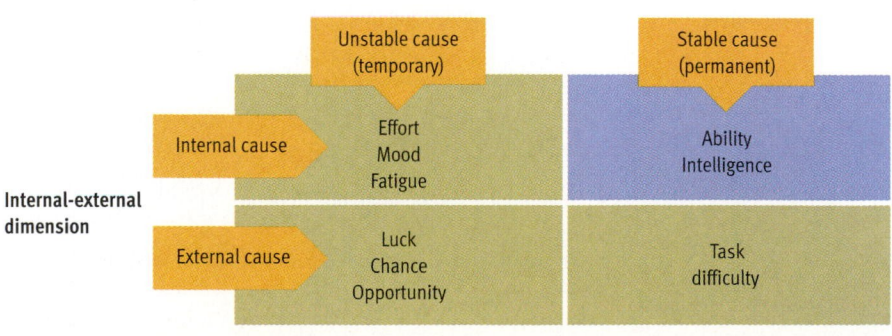

Stability dimension

		Unstable cause (temporary)	Stable cause (permanent)
Internal-external dimension	Internal cause	Effort Mood Fatigue	Ability Intelligence
	External cause	Luck Chance Opportunity	Task difficulty

larly likely to make this error when evaluating targets of prejudice (Hewstone, 1990). Thus, when people take note of ethnic neighborhoods dominated by crime and poverty, the personal qualities of the residents are blamed for these problems, while other explanations emphasizing situational factors (job discrimination, poor police service, and so on) are downplayed or ignored. The old saying "They should be able to pull themselves up by their bootstraps" is a blanket dismissal of how situational factors may make it especially difficult for minorities to achieve upward mobility.

Defensive attribution, which involves unjustly blaming victims of misfortune for their adversity, can also contribute to prejudice. A prominent example in recent years has been the assertion by some people that homosexuals brought the AIDS crisis on themselves and so deserve their fate (Anderson, 1992). By blaming AIDS on gays' alleged character flaws, heterosexuals may be unknowingly seeking to reassure themselves that they're immune to a similar fate.

Forming and Preserving Prejudicial Attitudes

If prejudice is an attitude, where does it come from? Many prejudices appear to be handed down as a legacy from parents (Ponterotto & Pedersen, 1993). Prejudicial attitudes can be found in children as young as ages 4 or 5 (Aboud & Amato, 2001). This transmission of prejudice across generations presumably depends to some extent on *observational learning.* For example, if a young boy hears his father ridicule homosexuals, his exposure to his father's attitude is likely to affect his attitude about gays. If the young boy then goes to school and makes disparaging remarks about gays that are reinforced by approval from peers, his prejudice will be strengthened through *operant conditioning.* Consistent with this analysis, one study found that college students' opinions on racial issues were swayed by overhearing others voice racist or antiracist sentiments (Blanchard, Lilly, & Vaughn, 1991). Of course, prejudicial attitudes are not acquired only through direct experience. Stereotypic portrayals of various groups in the media can also foster preju-

dicial attitudes (Herrett-Skjellum & Allen, 1996; Williams & Giles, 1998).

Another problem is that when people meet individuals who behave in ways that conform to prejudicial expectations, they are all too willing to generalize from the individual to the group. For example, one study showed that encountering a single African American person who performs a negative or stereotypical action can reaffirm whites' stereotypes of blacks (Henderson-King & Nisbett, 1996). The investigators attribute the inordinately large influence of a single person to a common pitfall in reasoning—*belief in the law of small numbers* (see the Personal Application for Chapter 8).

Dividing the World into Ingroups and Outgroups

As noted in the main body of the chapter, when people join together in groups, they sometimes divide the social world into "us versus them," or *ingroups versus outgroups.* These social dichotomies can promote **ethnocentrism—a tendency to view one's own group as superior to others and as the standard for judging the worth of foreign ways.**

As you might anticipate, people tend to evaluate outgroup members less favorably than ingroup members (Krueger, 1996). One reason is that when people derogate an outgroup, they tend to feel superior as a result, and this feeling helps to affirm their self-worth (Fein & Spencer, 1997). The more strongly one identifies with an ingroup, the more one tends to note outgroup membership, and the more one tends to be prejudiced toward competing outgroups (Blascovich et al., 1997; Perreault & Bourhis, 1999). People also tend to think simplistically about outgroups. They tend to see diversity among the members of their ingroup but to overestimate the homogeneity of the outgroup (Oakes, 2001; Ostrom & Sedikides, 1992). At a simple, concrete level, the essence of this process is captured by the statement "They all look alike." The illusion of homogeneity in the outgroup makes it easier to sustain stereotypic beliefs about its members (Ryan, Park, Judd, 1996). This point disposes of our last unanswered question from the list that opened the Ap-

plication. Just in case you missed one of the answers, the statements all were false.

In modern societies that endorse egalitarian attitudes, the prejudices that most people harbor tend to be subtle, unconscious, automatic, covert biases that mostly result in ingroup favoritism. Only a small minority of people (perhaps 10%) appear to be extremists who harbor blatant, conscious, overt, prejudices against outgroups that lead to hatred and aggression (Fiske, 2002). Still, 10% of the population adds up to an enormous number of people who can inflict great harm. Moreover, even subtle prejudices can foster a hostile, stressful environment for outgroup members (Fiske, 2002).

Our discussion has shown that a plethora of processes conspire to create and maintain personal prejudices against a diverse array of outgroups. Most of the factors at work reflect normal, routine processes in social behavior. Thus, it is understandable that most people—whether privileged or underprivileged, minority members or majority members—probably harbor some prejudicial attitudes. Our analysis of the causes of prejudice may have permitted you to identify prejudices of your own or their sources. Perhaps it's wishful thinking on my part, but an enhanced awareness of your personal prejudices may help you become a little more tolerant of the endless diversity seen in human behavior. If so, that alone would mean that my efforts in writing this book have been amply rewarded.

REVIEW OF KEY POINTS

- Prejudice is supported by selectivity and memory biases in person perception and stereotyping. Stereotypes are highly resistant to change.

- Attributional biases, such as the tendency to assume that others' behavior reflects their dispositions, can contribute to prejudice. The tendency to attribute others' failures to personal factors and the tendency to derogate victims can also foster prejudice.

- Negative attitudes about groups are often acquired through observational learning and strengthened through operant conditioning. The tendency to favor one's ingroups promotes ethnocentrism. The propensity to see outgroups as homogenous serves to strengthen prejudice.

Whom Can You Trust? Analyzing Credibility and Social Influence Tactics

You can run, but you cannot hide. This statement aptly sums up the situation that exists when it comes to persuasion and social influence. There is no way to successfully evade the constant, pervasive, omnipresent efforts of others to shape your attitudes and behavior. In this Application we will discuss two topics that can enhance your resistance to manipulation. First, we will outline some ideas that can be useful in evaluating the credibility of a persuasive source. Second, we will describe some widely used social influence strategies that it pays to know about.

Evaluating Credibility

The salesperson at your local health food store swears that a specific herb combination improves memory and helps people stay healthy. A popular singer touts a psychic hotline, where the operators can "really help" with the important questions in life. Speakers at a "historical society" meeting claim that the Holocaust never happened. These are just a few real-life examples of how people are always attempting to persuade the public to believe something. In these examples, the "something" people are expected to believe runs counter to the conventional or scientific view, but who is to say who is right? After all, people are entitled to their own opinions, aren't they?

Yes, people *are* entitled to their own opinions, but that does not mean that all opinions are equally valid. Some opinions are just plain wrong, and others are highly dubious. Every person is not equally believable. In deciding what to believe, it is important to carefully examine the evidence presented and the logic of the argument that supports the conclusion (see the Critical Thinking Application for Chapter 10). In deciding what to believe, you also need to decide *whom* to believe, a task that requires assessing the *credibility* of the source

of the information. Let's look at some questions that can provide guidance in this decision-making process.

Does the source have a vested interest in the issue at hand? If the source is likely to benefit in some way from convincing you of something, you need to take a skeptical attitude. In the examples provided here, it is easy to see how the sales clerk and popular singer will benefit if you buy the products they are selling, but what about the so-called historical society? How would members benefit by convincing large numbers of people that the Holocaust never happened? Like the sales clerk and singer, they are also selling something, in this case a particular view of history that they hope will influence future events in certain ways. Someone does *not* have to have a financial gain at stake to have a vested interest in an issue. Of course, the fact that these sources have a vested interest does not necessarily mean that the information they are providing is false or that their arguments are invalid. But a source's credibility needs to be evaluated with extra caution when the person or group has something to gain.

What are the source's credentials? Does the person have any special training, an advanced degree, or any other basis for claiming special knowledge about the topic? The usual training for a sales clerk or singer does not include how to assess research results in medical journals or claims of psychic powers. The Holocaust deniers are more difficult to evaluate. Some of them have studied history and written books on the topic, but the books are mostly self-published and few of these "experts" hold positions at reputable universities where scholars are subject to peer evaluation. That's *not* to say that legitimate credentials ensure a source's credibility. A number of popular diets that are widely regarded by nutritional experts as worthless, if not hazardous (Drewnewski, 1995; Dwyer, 1995), were created and

marketed by genuine physicians. Of course, these physicians have a *vested interest* in the diets, as they have made millions of dollars from them.

Is the information grossly inconsistent with the conventional view on the issue? Just being different from the mainstream view certainly does *not* make a conclusion wrong. But claims that vary radically from most other information on a subject should raise a red flag that leads to careful scrutiny. Bear in mind that charlatans and hucksters are often successful because they typically try to persuade people to believe things that they want to believe. Wouldn't it be great if we could effortlessly enhance our memory, foretell the future, eat all we *want* and still lose weight, and earn hundreds of dollars per hour working at home? And wouldn't it be nice if the Holocaust never happened? It pays to be wary of wishful thinking.

What was the method of analysis used in reaching the conclusion? The purveyors of miracle cures and psychic advice inevitably rely on anecdotal evidence. But you have already learned about the perils and unreliability of anecdotal evidence (see Chapter 2). One method frequently used by charlatans is to undermine the credibility of conventional information by focusing on trivial inconsistencies. This is one of the many strategies used by the people who argue that the Holocaust never occurred. They question the credibility of thousands of historical documents, photographs, and artifacts, and the testimony of countless people, by highlighting small inconsistencies among historical records relating to trivial matters, such as the number of people transported to a concentration camp in a specific week, or the number of bodies that could be disposed of in a single day (Shermer, 1997). Some inconsistencies are exactly what one should expect based on piecing together multiple accounts from sources working with different portions of incomplete information. But the strategy of focusing on trivial inconsistencies is a standard method for raising doubts about credible information. For example, this strategy was employed brilliantly by the defense attorneys in the O. J. Simpson murder trial.

Recognizing Social Influence Strategies

It pays to understand social influence strategies because advertisers, salespeople, and fundraisers—not to mention our friends and neighbors—frequently rely on them to manipulate our behavior. Let's look at four basic strategies: the foot-in-the-door technique, misuse of the reciprocity norm, the lowball technique, and feigned scarcity.

Door-to-door salespeople have long recognized the importance of gaining a *little* cooperation from sales targets (getting a "foot in the door") before hitting them with the real sales pitch. **The *foot-in-the-door* technique involves getting people to agree to a small request to increase the chances that they will agree to a larger request later.** This technique is widely used in all walks of life. For example, groups seeking donations often ask people to simply sign a petition first.

In an early study of the foot-in-the-door technique (Freedman & Fraser, 1966), the large request involved asking homemakers whether a team of six men doing consumer research could come into their home to classify *all* their household products. Only 22% of the control subjects agreed to this outlandish request. However, when the same request was made three days after a small request (to answer a few questions about soap preferences), 53% of the participants agreed to the large request. Why does the foot-in-the-door technique work? According to Burger (1999), quite a variety of processes contribute to its effectiveness,

including people's tendency to try to behave consistently (with their initial response) and their reluctance to renege on their sense of commitment to the person who made the initial request.

Most of us have been socialized to believe in the *reciprocity norm*—the rule that we should pay back in kind what we receive from others. Robert Cialdini (2001) has written extensively about how the reciprocity norm is used in social influence efforts. For example, groups seeking donations routinely send address labels, key rings, and other small gifts with their pleas. Salespeople using the reciprocity principle distribute free samples to prospective customers. When they return a few days later, most of the customers feel obligated to buy some of their products. The reciprocity rule is meant to promote fair exchanges in social interactions. However, when people manipulate the reciprocity norm, they usually give something of minimal value in hopes of getting far more in return (Howard, 1995).

The lowball technique is even more deceptive. The name for this technique derives from a common practice in automobile sales, in which a customer is offered a terrific bargain on a car. The bargain price gets the customer to commit to buying the car. Soon after this commitment is made, however, the dealer starts revealing some hidden costs. Typically, the customer learns that options assumed to be included in the

original price are actually going to cost extra. Once they have committed to buying a car, most customers are unlikely to cancel the deal. Thus, the *lowball technique* involves getting someone to commit to an attractive proposition before its hidden costs are revealed. Car dealers aren't the only ones who use this technique. For instance, a friend might ask whether you want to spend a week with him at his charming backwoods cabin. After you accept this seemingly generous proposition, he may add, "Of course there's some work for us to do. We need to repair the pier, paint the exterior, and . . ." Lowballing is a surprisingly effective strategy (Cialdini & Trost, 1998).

A number of years ago, Jack Brehm (1966) demonstrated that telling people they can't have something only makes them want it more. This phenomenon helps explain why companies often try to create the impression that their products are in scarce supply. Scarcity threatens your freedom to choose a product, thus creating an increased desire for the scarce commodity. Advertisers frequently feign scarcity to drive up the demand for products. Thus, we constantly see ads that scream "limited supply available," "for a limited time only," "while they last," and "time is running out." Like genuine scarcity, feigned scarcity *can* enhance the desirability of a commodity (Highhouse et al., 1998; Lynn, 1992).

Table 16.1 Critical Thinking Skills Discussed in This Application

Skill	Description
Judging the credibility of an information source	The critical thinker understands that credibility and bias are central to determining the quality of information and looks at factors such as vested interests, credentials, and appropriate expertise.
Recognizing social influence strategies	The critical thinker is aware of manipulative tactics such as the foot-in-the-door and lowball techniques, misuse of the reciprocity norm, and feigned scarcity.

RECAP

Key Ideas

Person Perception: Forming Impressions of Others

● People tend to attribute desirable characteristics to those who are good looking. Perceptions of people are also influenced by their style of nonverbal expressiveness.

● Stereotypes are widely held social schemas that lead people to expect that others will have certain characteristics because of their membership in a specific group. In interacting with others, stereotypes may lead people to see what they expect to see and to overestimate how often they see it.

Attribution Processes: Explaining Behavior

● Internal attributions ascribe behavior to personal traits, whereas external attributions locate the cause of behavior in the environment. Weiner's model proposes that attributions for success and failure should be analyzed in terms of the stability of causes, as well as along the internal-external dimension.

● Observers favor internal attributions to explain another's behavior (the fundamental attribution error), while actors favor external attributions to explain their own behavior. Cultures vary in their emphasis on individualism as opposed to collectivism, and these differences appear to influence attributional tendencies.

Close Relationships: Liking and Loving

● People tend to like and love others who are similar, who reciprocate expressions of affection, and who are physically attractive. In intimate relationships, romantic ideals influence the progress of relationships.

● Berscheid and Hatfield have distinguished between passionate and companionate love. Sternberg builds on their distinction by dividing companionate love into intimacy and commitment. Hazan and Shaver's theory suggests that love relationships in adulthood mimic attachment patterns in infancy.

● The characteristics that people seek in prospective mates are much the same around the world. However, cultures vary considerably in their emphasis on passionate love as a prerequisite for marriage.

● According to evolutionary psychologists, certain aspects of good looks influence attraction because they are indicators of reproductive fitness. Consistent with evolutionary theory, gender differences in mating preferences appear to transcend culture.

Attitudes: Making Social Judgments

● Attitudes may be made up of cognitive, affective, and behavioral components. Attitudes vary in strength, accessibility, and ambivalence.

Attitudes and behavior aren't as consistent as one might assume.

● A source of persuasion who is credible, expert, trustworthy, likable, and physically attractive tends to be relatively effective. Two-sided arguments and fear arousal are effective elements in persuasive messages.

● Attitudes may be shaped through classical conditioning, operant conditioning, and observational learning. Festinger's dissonance theory asserts that inconsistent attitudes cause tension and that people alter their attitudes to reduce cognitive dissonance.

● Self-perception theory posits that people may infer their attitudes from their behavior. The elaboration likelihood model of persuasion holds that the central route to persuasion tends to yield longer-lasting attitude change than the peripheral route.

Conformity and Obedience: Yielding to Others

● Asch found that conformity becomes more likely as group size increases, up to a group size of four, and then levels off. If a small group isn't unanimous, conformity declines rapidly.

● In Milgram's study of obedience, subjects showed a remarkable tendency to follow orders to shock an innocent stranger. The generalizability of Milgram's findings has stood the test of time, but his work also helped to stimulate stricter ethical standards for research.

● The Asch and Milgram experiments have been replicated in many cultures. These replications have uncovered modest cultural variations in the propensity to conform or to obey an authority figure.

Behavior in Groups: Joining with Others

● The bystander effect occurs primarily because a group creates diffusion of responsibility. Individuals' productivity often declines in larger groups because of loss of coordination and because of social loafing.

● Group polarization occurs when discussion leads a group to shift toward a more extreme decision in the direction the group was already leaning. In groupthink, a cohesive group suspends critical judgment in a misguided effort to promote agreement in decision making.

Putting It in Perspective

● Our study of social psychology illustrated the value of empiricism, the cultural limits of research based on American samples, and the subjectivity of perception.

Personal Application ●
Understanding Prejudice

● Prejudice is supported by selectivity and memory biases in person perception and stereotyping. Attributional biases, such as the tendency to assume that others' behavior reflects their dispositions, can contribute to prejudice.

● The tendency to attribute others' failures to personal factors and the tendency to derogate victims can also foster prejudice. The tendency to favor one's ingroups promotes ethnocentrism. The propensity to see outgroups as homogenous serves to strengthen prejudice.

Critical Thinking Application ●
Whom Can You Trust? Analyzing Credibility and Social Influence Tactics

● Useful criteria in judging credibility include whether a source has vested interests or appropriate credentials. One should also consider the method of analysis used in reaching conclusions and why information might not coincide with conventional wisdom.

● To resist manipulative efforts, it helps to be aware of social influence tactics, such as the foot-in-the-door technique, misuse of the reciprocity norm, the lowball technique, and feigned scarcity.

Key Terms

Attitudes
Attributions
Bystander effect
Channel
Cognitive dissonance
Collectivism
Commitment
Companionate love
Conformity
Defensive attribution
Discrimination
Ethnocentrism
External attributions
Foot-in-the-door
  technique
Fundamental
  attribution error
Group
Group cohesiveness
Group polarization
Groupthink
Illusory correlation
Individualism
Ingroup
Internal attributions
Interpersonal
  attraction
Intimacy
Lowball technique

Matching hypothesis
Message
Obedience
Outgroup
Passionate love
Person perception
Prejudice
Receiver
Reciprocity
Reciprocity norm
Self-serving bias
Social loafing
Social psychology
Social schemas
Source
Stereotypes

Key People

Solomon Asch
Ellen Berscheid
David Buss
Leon Festinger
Elaine Hatfield
Cindy Hazan and
  Philip Shaver
Fritz Heider
Irving Janis
Stanley Milgram
Bernard Weiner

1. Stereotypes are:
   A. special types of schemas that are part of people's shared cultural background.
   B. widely held beliefs that people have certain characteristics because of their membership in a particular group.
   C. equivalent to prejudice.
   D. both a and b.

2. You believe that short men have a tendency to be insecure. The concept of illusory correlation implies that you will:
   A. overestimate how often short men are insecure.
   B. underestimate how often short men are insecure.
   C. overestimate the frequency of short men in the population.
   D. falsely assume that shortness in men causes insecurity.

3. A father suggests that his son's low marks in school are due to the child's laziness. The father has made a (an) _____ attribution.
   A. external   C. situational
   B. internal   D. high consensus

4. Bob explains his failing grade on a term paper by saying that he really didn't work very hard at it. According to Weiner's model, Bob is making an _____ attribution about his failure.
   A. internal-stable   C. external-stable
   B. internal-unstable   D. external-unstable

5. The fundamental attribution error refers to the tendency of:
   A. observers to favor external attributions in explaining the behavior of others.
   B. observers to favor internal attributions in explaining the behavior of others.
   C. actors to favor external attributions in explaining the behavior of others.
   D. actors to favor situational attributions in explaining the behavior of others.

6. According to Hazan and Shaver (1987):
   A. romantic relationships in adulthood follow the same form as attachment relationships in infancy.
   B. those who had ambivalent attachments in infancy are doomed never to fall in love as adults.
   C. those who had avoidant attachments in infancy often over-compensate by becoming excessively intimate in their adult love relationships.
   D. all of the above.

7. Cross-cultural similarities are most likely to be found in which of the following areas?
   A. what people look for in prospective mates
   B. the overall value of romantic love
   C. passionate love as a prerequisite for marriage
   D. the tradition of prearranged marriages

8. Cognitive dissonance theory predicts that after people engage in counterattitudinal behavior, they will:
   A. convince themselves they really didn't perform the behavior.
   B. change their attitude to make it more consistent with their behavior.
   C. change their attitude to make it less consistent with their behavior.
   D. do nothing.

9. "I always choose romance novels rather than biographies. I guess I must like romance novels better." This thought process illustrates the premise of _____ theory.
   A. cognitive dissonance
   B. learning
   C. evolutionary
   D. self-perception

10. The elaboration likelihood model of attitude change suggests that:
    A. the peripheral route results in more enduring attitude change.
    B. the central route results in more enduring attitude change.
    C. only the central route to persuasion can be effective.
    D. only the peripheral route to persuasion can be effective.

11. The results of Milgram's (1963) study imply that:
    A. in the real world, most people will refuse to follow orders to inflict harm on a stranger.
    B. many people will obey an authority figure even if innocent people get hurt.
    C. most people are willing to give obviously wrong answers when ordered to do so.
    D. most people stick to their own judgment, even when group members unanimously disagree.

12. According to Latané (1981), social loafing is due to:
    A. social norms that stress the importance of positive interactions among group members.
    B. duplication of effort among group members.
    C. diffusion of responsibility in groups.
    D. a bias toward making internal attributions about the behavior of others.

13. Groupthink occurs when members of a cohesive group:
    A. are initially unanimous about an issue.
    B. stress the importance of caution in group decision making.
    C. emphasize concurrence at the expense of critical thinking in arriving at a decision.
    D. shift toward a less extreme position after group discussion.

14. Discrimination:
    A. refers to a negative attitude toward members of a group.
    B. refers to unfair behavior toward the members of a group.
    C. is the same thing as prejudice.
    D. is all of the above.

15. The foot-in-the-door technique involves asking people to agree to a _____ request first to increase the likelihood that they will comply with a _____ request later.
    A. large; small
    B. small: large
    C. large; large
    D. large; larger

Answers

1	D	p. 649	6	A	pp. 659–660	11	B	p. 674
2	A	p. 650	7	A	pp. 660–661	12	C	pp. 676–677
3	B	p. 652	8	B	pp. 668–669	13	C	pp. 678–679
4	B	pp. 652–653	9	D	p. 670	14	B	p. 681
5	B	p. 653	10	B	pp. 670–671	15	B	p. 685

ON THE WEB

For additional resources on the topics covered in this chapter, visit the *Psychology: Themes and Variations* Web site, where you will find practice quizzes, tutorials, Web links, simulations, critical thinking activities, flash cards, inter-active exercises, and suggested readings available through INFOTRAC.

http://psychology.wadsworth.com/weiten_themes6e/

Chapter 1

Concept Check 1.1

1. c. John B. Watson (1930, p. 103), dismissing the importance of genetic inheritance while arguing that traits are shaped entirely by experience.

2. a. Wilhelm Wundt (1874/1904, p. v), campaigning for a new, independent science of psychology.

3. b. William James (1890), commenting negatively on the structuralists' efforts to break consciousness into its elements and his view of consciousness as a continuously flowing stream.

Concept Check 1.2

1. b. B. F. Skinner (1971, p. 17), explaining why he believes that freedom is an illusion.

2. a. Sigmund Freud (1905, pp. 77–78), arguing that it is possible to probe into the unconscious depths of the mind.

3. c. Carl Rogers (1961, p. 27), commenting on others' assertion that he had an overly optimistic (Polly-annaish) view of human potential and discussing humans' basic drive toward personal growth.

Concept Check 1.3

a. 2. Psychology is theoretically diverse.

b. 6. Heredity and environment jointly influence behavior.

c. 4. Behavior is determined by multiple causes.

d. 7. Our experience of the world is highly subjective.

Chapter 2

Concept Check 2.1

1. IV: Film violence (present versus absent)

   DV: Heart rate and blood pressure (there are two DVs)

2. IV: Courtesy training (training versus no training)

   DV: Number of customer complaints

3. IV: Stimulus complexity (high versus low) and stimulus contrast (high versus low) (there are two IVs)

   DV: Length of time spent staring at the stimuli

4. IV: Group size (large versus small)

   DV: Conformity

Concept Check 2.2

1. d. Survey. You would distribute a survey to obtain information on subjects' social class, education, and attitudes about nuclear disarmament.

2. c. Case study. Using a case study approach, you could interview people with anxiety disorders, interview their parents, and examine their school records to look for similarities in childhood experiences. As a second choice, you might have people with anxiety disorders fill out a survey about their childhood experiences.

3. b. Naturalistic observation. To answer this question properly, you would want to observe baboons in their natural environment, without interference.

4. a. Experiment. To demonstrate a causal relationship, you would have to conduct an experiment. You would manipulate the presence or absence of food-related cues in controlled circumstances where subjects had an opportunity to eat some food, and monitor the amount eaten.

Concept Check 2.3

1. b and e. The other three conclusions all equate correlation with causation.

2. a. Negative. As age increases, more people tend to have visual problems and acuity tends to decrease.

   b. Positive. Studies show that highly educated people tend to earn higher incomes and that people with less education tend to earn lower incomes.

   c. Negative. As shyness increases, the size of one's friendship network should decrease. However, research suggests that this inverse association may be weaker than widely believed.

Concept Check 2.4

Methodological flaw	Study 1	Study 2
Sampling bias	✓	✓
Placebo effects	✓	
Confounding of variables	✓	
Distortions in self-report data		✓
Experimenter bias	✓	

Explanations for Study 1. Sensory deprivation is an unusual kind of experience that may intrigue certain potential subjects, who may be more adventurous or more willing to take risks than the population at large. Using the first 80 students who sign up for this study may not yield a sample that is representative of the population. Assigning the first 40 subjects who sign up to the experimental group may confound these extraneous variables with the treatment (students who sign up most quickly may be the most adventurous). In announcing that he will be examining the *detrimental* effects of sensory deprivation, the experimenter has created expectations in the subjects. These expectations could lead to placebo effects. The experimenter has also revealed that he has a bias about the outcome of the study. Since he supervises the treatments, he knows which subjects are in the experimental and control groups, thus aggravating potential problems with experimenter bias. For example, he might unintentionally give the control group subjects better instructions on how to do the pursuit-rotor task and thereby slant the study in favor of finding support for his hypothesis.

Explanations for Study 2. Sampling bias is a problem because the researcher has sampled only subjects from a low-income, inner-city neighborhood. A sample obtained in this way is not likely to be representative of the population at large. People are sensitive about the issue of racial prejudice, so distortions in self-report data are also likely. Many subjects may be swayed by social desirability bias and rate themselves as less prejudiced than they really are.

Chapter 3

Concept Check 3.1
1. d. Dendrite
2. f. Myelin
3. b. Neuron
4. e. Axon
5. a. Glia
6. g. Terminal button
7. h. Synapse

Concept Check 3.2
1. d. Serotonin
2. b. and d. Serotonin and norepinephrine
3. e. Endorphins
4. c. Dopamine
5. a. Acetylcholine

Concept Check 3.3
1. Left hemisphere damage, probably to Wernicke's area
2. Deficit in dopamine synthesis in an area of the midbrain
3. Degeneration of myelin sheaths surrounding axons
4. Disturbance in dopamine activity, possibly associated with enlarged ventricles in the brain

Please note that neuropsychological assessment is not as simple as this introductory exercise may suggest. There are many possible causes of most disorders, and we discussed only a handful of leading causes for each.

Concept Check 3.4
1. Closer relatives; more distant relatives
2. Identical twins; fraternal twins
3. Biological parents; adoptive parents
4. Genetic overlap or closeness; trait similarity

Chapter 4

Concept Check 4.1

1.

Dimension	Rods	Cones
Physical shape	Elongated	Stubby
Number in the retina	125 million	6.4 million
Area of the retina in which they are dominant receptor	Periphery	Center/fovea
Critical to color vision	No	Yes
Critical to peripheral vision	Yes	No
Sensitivity to dim light	Strong	Weak
Speed of dark adaptation	Slow	Rapid

2. Consider the responses of two ganglion cells in the retina whose firing is affected by light falling in center-surround receptive fields, like those drawn onto the grid in the lower right corner. An identical amount of light falls in the center of each receptive field. However, more light is falling in the surround of the receptive field on the left. Hence, the cell for this receptive field responds at a lower level than its neighbor because of greater inhibition by the surround (thanks to lateral antagonism). This reduced responding translates into the dark spots that you see. Why don't you see a dark spot at the intersection you are staring at? Because when you stare directly at a point, the image falls on the fovea, where receptive fields are much smaller, like the one drawn in the lower left corner. This receptive field does not produce a reduced response because an equal amount of light is falling in the center and the surround.

Concept Check 4.2
✓ 1. Interposition. The arches in front cut off part of the corridor behind them.
✓ 2. Height in plane. The back of the corridor is higher on the horizontal plane than the front of the corridor is.
✓ 3. Texture gradient. The more distant portions of the hallway are painted in less detail than the closer portions are.
✓ 4. Relative size. The arches in the distance are smaller than those in the foreground.
✓ 5. Light and shadow. Light shining in from the crossing corridor (it's coming from the left) contrasts with shadow elsewhere.
✓ 6. Linear perspective. The lines of the corridor converge in the distance.

Concept Check 4.3

Dimension	Vision	Hearing
1. Stimulus	Light waves	Sound waves
2. Elements of stimulus and related perceptions	Wavelength/hue Amplitude/brightness Purity/saturation	Frequency/pitch Amplitude/loudness Purity/timbre

3. Receptors	Rods and cones	Hair cells
4. Location of receptors	Retina	Basilar membrane
5. Main location of processing in brain	Occipital lobe, visual cortex	Temporal lobe, auditory cortex
6. Spatial aspect of perception	Depth perception	Auditory localization

Concept Check 4.4

Dimension	Taste	Smell	Touch
1. Stimulus	Soluble chemicals in saliva	Volatile chemicals in air	Mechanical, thermal, and chemical energy due to external contact
2. Receptors	Clusters of taste cells	Olfactory cilia (hairlike structures)	Many (at least 6) types
3. Location of receptors	Taste buds on tongue	Upper area of nasal passages	Skin
4. Basic elements of perception	Sweet, sour, salty, bitter	No satisfactory classification scheme	Pressure, hot, cold, pain

Chapter 5

Concept Check 5.1

Characteristic	REM sleep	NREM sleep
1. Type of EEG activity	"Wide awake" brain waves, mostly beta	Varied, lots of delta waves
2. Eye movements	Rapid, lateral	Slow or absent
3. Dreaming	Frequent, vivid	Less frequent
4. Depth (difficulty in awakening)	Varied, generally difficult to awaken	Varied, generally easier to awaken
5. Percentage of total sleep (in adults)	About 20%	About 80%
6. Increases or decreases (as percentage of sleep) during childhood	Percent decreases	Percent increases
7. Timing in sleep (dominates early or late)	Dominates late in cycle	Dominates early in cycle

Concept Check 5.2

1. Beta. Video games require alert information processing, which is associated with beta waves.

2. Alpha. Meditation involves relaxation, which is associated with alpha waves, and studies show increased alpha in meditators.

3. Theta. In stage 1 sleep, theta waves tend to be prevalent.

4. Delta. Sleepwalking usually occurs in deep NREM sleep, which is dominated by delta activity.

5. Beta. Nightmares are dreams, so you're probably in REM sleep, which paradoxically produces "wide awake" beta waves.

Chapter 6

Concept Check 6.1

1. CS: Fire in fireplace
   UCS: Pain from burn   CR/UCR: Fear

2. CS: Brake lights in rain
   UCS: Car accident   CR/UCR: Tensing up

3. CS: Sight of cat
   UCS: Cat dander   CR/UCR: Wheezing

Concept Check 6.2

1. FR. Each sale is a response and every third response earns reinforcement.

2. VI. A varied amount of time elapses before the response of doing yardwork can earn reinforcement.

3. VR. Reinforcement occurs after a varied number of unreinforced casts (time is irrelevant; the more casts Martha makes, the more reinforcers she will receive).

4. CR. The designated response (reading a book) is reinforced (with a gold star) every time.

5. FI. A fixed time interval (three years) has to elapse before Skip can earn a salary increase (the reinforcer).

Concept Check 6.3

1. Punishment.

2. Positive reinforcement.

3. Punishment.

4. Negative reinforcement (for Audrey); the dog is positively reinforced for its whining.

5. Negative reinforcement.

6. Extinction. When Sharma's co-workers start to ignore her complaints, they are trying to extinguish the behavior (which had been positively reinforced when it won sympathy).

Concept Check 6.4

1. Classical conditioning. Midori's blue windbreaker is a CS eliciting excitement in her dog.

2. Operant conditioning. Playing new songs leads to negative consequences (punishment), which weaken the tendency to play new songs. Playing old songs leads to positive reinforcement, which gradually strengthens the tendency to play old songs.

3. Classical conditioning. The song was paired with the passion of new love so that it became a CS eliciting emotional, romantic feelings.

4. Both. Ralph's workplace is paired with criticism so that his workplace becomes a CS eliciting anxiety. Calling in sick is operant behavior that is strengthened through negative reinforcement (because it reduces anxiety).

Chapter 7

Concept Check 7.1

Feature	Sensory memory	Short-term memory	Long-term memory
Encoding format	Copy of input	Largely phonemic	Largely semantic
Storage capacity	Limited	Small (7 ± 2 chunks)	No known limit
Storage duration	About ¼ second	Up to 20 seconds	Minutes to years

Concept Check 7.2

1. Ineffective encoding due to lack of attention

2. Retrieval failure due to motivated forgetting

3. Proactive interference (previous learning of Joe Cocker's name interferes with new learning)

4. Retroactive interference (new learning of sociology interferes with older learning of history)

Concept Check 7.3

1. a. Declarative memory

2. e. Long-term memory

3. j. Sensory memory

4. d. Implicit memory

5. b. Episodic memory

6. f. Procedural memory

7. i. Semantic memory

8. g. Prospective memory

9. k. Short-term memory

Chapter 8

Concept Check 8.1

1. 1. One-word utterance in which the word is overextended to refer to a similar object.

2. 4. Words are combined into a sentence, but the rule for past tense is overregularized.

3. 3. Telegraphic sentence.

4. 5. Words are combined into a sentence, and past tense is used correctly.

5. 2. One-word utterance without overextension.

6. 6. "Longer" sentence with metaphor.

Concept Check 8.2

1. Functional fixedness

2. Forming subgoals

3. Insight

4. Searching for analogies

5. Arrangement problem

Concept Check 8.3

1. Elimination by aspects

2. Availability heuristic

3. Shift to additive strategy

Chapter 9

Concept Check 9.1

1. Test-retest reliability

2. Criterion-related validity

3. Content validity

Concept Check 9.2

1. H. Given that the identical twins were reared apart, their greater similarity in comparison to fraternals reared together can only be due to heredity. This comparison is probably the most important piece of evidence supporting the genetic determination of IQ.

2. E. We tend to associate identical twins with evidence supporting heredity, but in this comparison genetic similarity is held constant since both sets of twins are identical. The only logical explanation for the greater similarity in identicals reared together is the effect of their being reared together (environment).

3. E. This comparison is similar to the previous one. Genetic similarity is held constant and a shared environment produces greater similarity than being reared apart.

4. B. This is nothing more than a quantification of Galton's original observation that intelligence runs in families. Since families share both genes and environment, either or both could be responsible for the observed correlation.

5. B. The similarity of adopted children to their biological parents can only be due to shared genes, and the similarity of adopted children to their foster parents can only be due to shared environment, so these correlations show the influence of both heredity and environment.

Concept Check 9.3

1. b. Gardner

2. a. Galton

3. c. Jensen

4. d. Scarr

5. e. Sternberg

Chapter 10

Concept Check 10.1

1. I. Early studies indicated that lesioning the ventromedial nucleus of the hypothalamus leads to overeating (although it is an oversimplification to characterize the VMH as the brain's "stop eating" center).

2. I. According to Mayer, hunger increases when the amount of glucose in the blood decreases.

3. I or ?. Food cues generally trigger hunger and eating, but reactions vary among individuals.

4. D. Food preferences are mostly learned, and we tend to like what we are accustomed to eating. Most people will not be eager to eat a strange-looking food.

5. D. When leptin levels are increased, hunger tends to decrease.

6. I. Reactions vary, but stress generally tends to increase eating.

7. I. Research on dietary restraint suggests that when people feel that they have cheated on their diet, they tend to become disinhibited and eat to excess.

Concept Check 10.2

1. d. Fear of failure

2. c. Incentive value of success

3. b. Perceived probability of success

4. a. Need for achievement

Concept Check 10.3

2. James-Lange theory

3. Schachter's two-factor theory

4. Evolutionary theories

Chapter 11

Concept Check 11.1

	Event	Stage	Organism	Time span
1.	Uterine implantation	Germinal	Zygote	0–2 weeks
2.	Muscle and bone begin to form	Fetal	Fetus	2 months to birth
3.	Vital organs and body systems begin to form	Embryonic	Embryo	2 weeks to 2 months

Concept Check 11.2

1. b. Animism is characteristic of the preoperational period.

2. c. Mastery of hierarchical classification occurs during the concrete operational period.

3. a. Lack of object permanence is characteristic of the sensorimotor period.

Concept Check 11.3

1. c. Commitment to personal ethics is characteristic of postconventional reasoning.

2. b. Concern about approval of others is characteristic of conventional reasoning.

3. a. Emphasis on positive or negative consequences is characteristic of preconventional reasoning.

Chapter 12

Concept Check 12.1

1. Regression

2. Projection

3. Reaction formation

4. Repression

5. Rationalization

Concept Check 12.2

1. Bandura's observational learning. Sarah imitates a role model from television.

2. Maslow's need for self-actualization. Yolanda is striving to realize her fullest potential.

3. Freud's Oedipal complex. Vladimir shows preference for his opposite-sex parent and emotional distance from his same-sex parent.

Concept Check 12.3

1. Maslow (1971, p. 36), commenting on the need for self-actualization.

2. Eysenck (1977, pp. 407–408), commenting on the biological roots of personality.

3. Freud (in Malcolm, 1980), commenting on the repression of sexuality.

Chapter 13

Concept Check 13.1

1. b. A choice between two unattractive options

2. c. Weighing the positive and negative aspects of a single goal

3. a. A choice between two attractive options

Concept Check 13.2

1. a. Frustration due to delay

2. d. Pressure to perform

3. c. Change associated with leaving school and taking a new job

4. a. Frustration due to loss of job

c. Change in life circumstances

d. Pressure to perform (in quickly obtaining new job)

Concept Check 13.3

1. Denial of reality

2. Undoing

3. Fantasy

4. Overcompensation

5. Intellectualization

Chapter 14

Concept Check 14.1

	Deviance	Maladaptive behavior	Personal distress
1. Alan	_____	✓	_____
2. Monica	_____	_____	✓
3. Boris	✓	_____	_____
4. Natasha	✓	✓	✓

Concept Check 14.2

1. Obsessive-compulsive disorder (key symptoms: frequent rituals, ruminations about school)

2. Somatization disorder (key symptoms: history of physical complaints involving many different organ systems)

3. Conversion disorder (key symptoms: loss of function in single organ system)

Concept Check 14.3

1. Bipolar disorder, manic episode (key symptoms: extravagant plans, hyperactivity, reckless spending)

2. Paranoid schizophrenia (key symptoms: delusions of persecution and grandeur, along with deterioration of adaptive behavior)

3. Major depression (key symptoms: feelings of despair, low self-esteem, lack of energy)

Chapter 15

Concept Check 15.1

1. c   **2.** a   **3.** b

Concept Check 15.2

1. d   **2.** b   **3.** a   **4.** c

Concept Check 15.3

1. a. Systematic desensitization

2. c. Aversion therapy

3. b. Social skills training

Concept Check 15.4

1. c   **2.** a   **3.** b   **4.** d   **5.** b

Chapter 16

Concept Check 16.1

	Unstable	Stable
Internal	d	b
External	a	c

Concept Check 16.2

1. c. Fundamental attribution error (assuming that arriving late reflects personal qualities)

2. a. Illusory correlation effect (overestimating how often one has seen confirmations of the assertion that young, female professors get pregnant soon after being hired)

3. b. Stereotyping (assuming that all lawyers have certain traits)

4. d. Defensive attribution (derogating the victims of misfortune to minimize the apparent likelihood of a similar mishap)

Concept Check 16.3

1. *Target:* Cognitive component of attitudes (beliefs about program for regulating nursing homes)

   Persuasion: Message factor (advice to use one-sided instead of two-sided arguments)

2. *Target:* Affective component of attitudes (feelings about candidate)

   Persuasion: Source factor (advice on appearing likable, sincere, and compassionate)

3. *Target:* Behavioral component of attitudes (making contributions)

   Persuasion: Receiver factor (considering audience's initial position regarding the candidate)

Concept Check 16.4

1. False   **2.** True   **3.** False   **4.** True   **5.** False

Appendix B Statistical Methods

Empiricism depends on observation; precise observation depends on measurement; and measurement requires numbers. Thus, scientists routinely analyze numerical data to arrive at their conclusions. Over 3000 empirical studies are cited in this text, and all but a few of the simplest ones required a statistical analysis. *Statistics* is the use of mathematics to organize, summarize, and interpret numerical data. We discussed statistics briefly in Chapter 2, but in this Appendix we take a closer look.

To illustrate statistics in action, let's assume that we want to test a hypothesis that has generated quite an argument in your psychology class. The hypothesis is that college students who watch a great deal of television aren't as bright as those who watch TV infrequently. For the fun of it, your class decides to conduct a correlational study of itself, collecting survey and psychological test data. Your classmates all agree to respond to a short survey on their TV viewing habits. Because everyone at your school has had to take the SAT, the class decides to use scores on the SAT verbal subtest as an index of how bright students are. All of them agree to allow the records office at the college to furnish their SAT scores to the professor, who replaces each student's name with a subject number (to protect students' right to privacy). Let's see how we could use statistics to analyze the data collected in our pilot study (a small, preliminary investigation).

Graphing Data

After collecting our data, our next step is to organize the data to get a quick overview of our numerical re-

sults. Let's assume that there are 20 students in your class, and when they estimate how many hours they spend per day watching TV, the results are as follows:

3	2	0	3	1
3	4	0	5	1
2	3	4	5	2
4	5	3	4	6

One of the simpler things that we can do to organize data is to create a *frequency distribution—an orderly arrangement of scores indicating the frequency of each score or group of scores.* Figure B.1(a) shows a frequency distribution for our data on TV viewing. The column on the left lists the possible scores (estimated hours of TV viewing) in order, and the column on the right lists the number of subjects with each score. Graphs can provide an even better overview of the data. One approach is to portray the data in a *histogram, which is a bar graph that presents data from a frequency distribution.* Such a histogram, summarizing our TV viewing data, is presented in Figure B.1(b).

Another widely used method of portraying data graphically is the *frequency polygon—a line figure used to present data from a frequency distribution.* Figures B.1(c) and B.1(d) show how our TV viewing data can be converted from a histogram to a frequency polygon. In both the bar graph and the line figure, the horizontal axis lists the possible scores and the vertical axis is used to indicate the frequency of each score. This use of the axes is nearly universal for frequency polygons, although sometimes it is reversed in histograms (the vertical axis lists possible scores, so the bars become horizontal).

Figure B.1

Graphing data. (a) Our raw data are tallied into a frequency distribution. (b) The same data are portrayed in a bar graph called a histogram. (c) A frequency polygon is plotted over the histogram. (d) The resultant frequency polygon is shown by itself.

Score	Tallies	Frequency
6	I	1
5	III	3
4	IIII	4
3	THL	5
2	III	3
1	II	2
0	II	2

(a) Frequency distribution

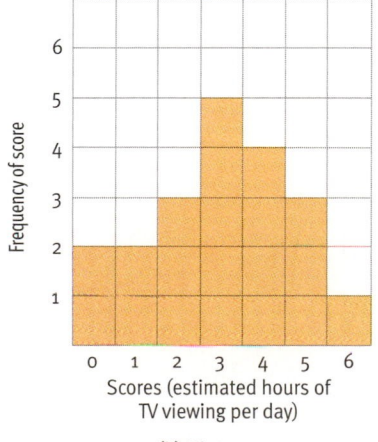

(b) Histogram

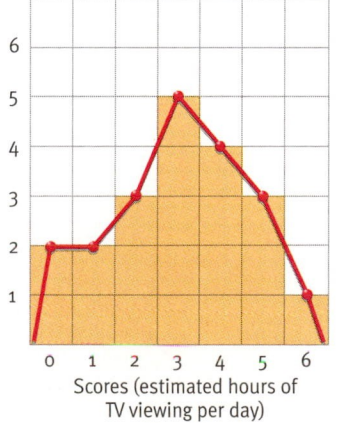

(c) Conversion of histogram into frequency polygon

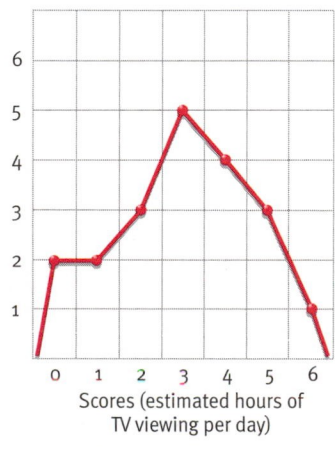

(d) Frequency polygon

Measures of central tendency. Although the mean, median, and mode sometimes yield different results, they usually converge, as in the case of our TV viewing data.

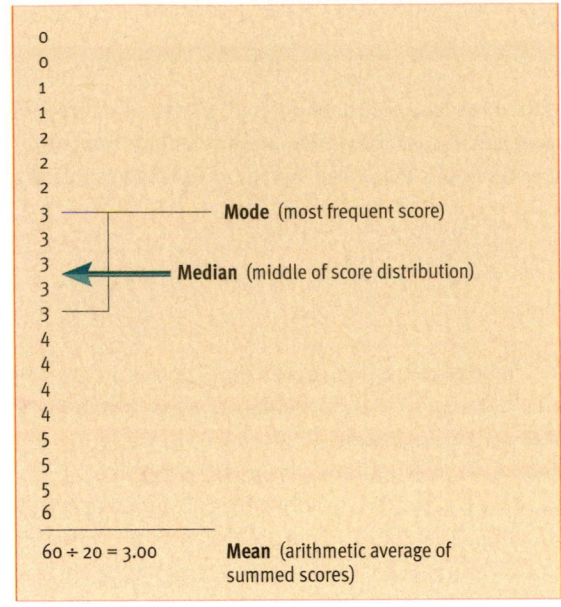

```
0
0
1
1
2
2
2
3 ──────── Mode (most frequent score)
3
3 ◄──────── Median (middle of score distribution)
3
3
4
4
4
4
5
5
5
6
─────────
60 ÷ 20 = 3.00   Mean (arithmetic average of
                  summed scores)
```

Our graphs improve on the jumbled collection of scores that we started with, but *descriptive statistics, which are used to organize and summarize data,* provide some additional advantages. Let's see what the three measures of central tendency tell us about our data.

Figure B.3

Measures of central tendency in skewed distributions. In a symmetrical distribution (**a**), the three measures of central tendency converge. However, in a negatively skewed distribution (**b**) or in a positively skewed distribution (**c**), the mean, median, and mode are pulled apart as shown here. Typically, in these situations the median provides the best index of central tendency.

Measuring Central Tendency

In examining a set of data, it's routine to ask "What is a typical score in the distribution?" For instance, in this case we might compare the average amount of TV watching in our sample to national estimates, to determine whether our subjects appear to be representative of the population. The three measures of central tendency—the median, the mean, and the mode—give us indications regarding the typical score in a data set. As explained in Chapter 2, **the *median***

is the score that falls in the center of a distribution, the *mean* is the arithmetic average of the scores, and the *mode* is the score that occurs most frequently.

All three measures of central tendency are calculated for our TV viewing data in Figure B.2. As you can see, in this set of data, the mean, median, and mode all turn out to be the same score, which is 3. Although our example in Chapter 2 emphasized that the mean, median, and mode can yield different estimates of central tendency, the correspondence among them seen in our TV viewing data is quite common. Lack of agreement usually occurs when a few extreme scores pull the mean away from the center of the distribution, as shown in Figure B.3. The curves plotted in Figure B.3 are simply "smoothed out" frequency polygons based on data from many subjects. They show that when a distribution is symmetric, the measures of central tendency fall together, but this is not true in skewed or unbalanced distributions.

Figure B.3(b) shows a *negatively skewed distribution,* in which most scores pile up at the high end of the scale (the negative skew refers to the direction in which the curve's "tail" points). A *positively skewed distribution,* in which scores pile up at the low end of the scale, is shown in Figure B.3(c). In both types of skewed distributions, a few extreme scores at one end pull the mean, and to a lesser degree the median, away from the mode. In these situations, the mean may be misleading and the median usually provides the best index of central tendency.

In any case, the measures of central tendency for our TV viewing data are reassuring, since they all agree and they fall reasonably close to national estimates regarding how much young adults watch TV (Nielsen Media Research, 1998). Given the small size of our group, this agreement with national norms

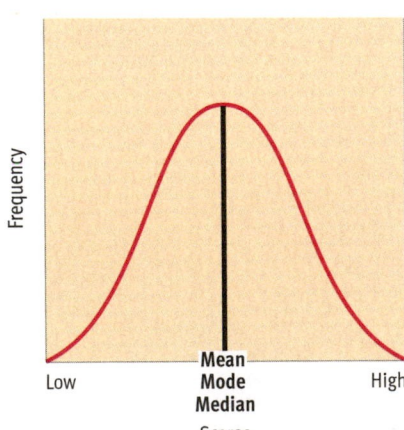

(a) Symmetrical distribution

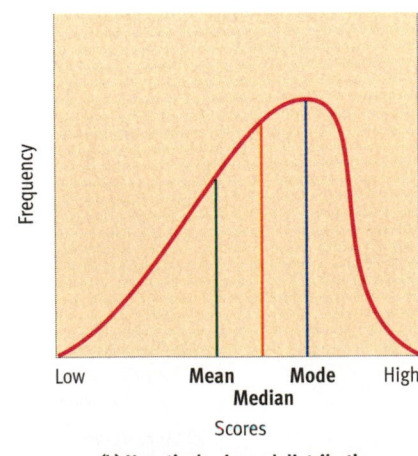

(b) Negatively skewed distribution

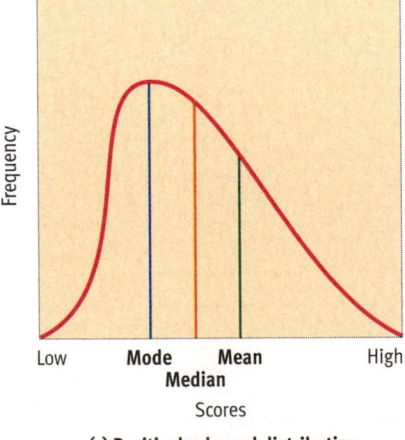

(c) Positively skewed distribution

doesn't *prove* that our sample is representative of the population, but at least there's no obvious reason to believe that it is unrepresentative.

Measuring Variability

Of course, the subjects in our sample did not report identical TV viewing habits. Virtually all data sets are characterized by some variability. **Variability refers to how much the scores tend to vary or depart from the mean score.** For example, the distribution of golf scores for a mediocre, erratic golfer would be characterized by high variability, while scores for an equally mediocre but consistent golfer would show less variability.

The *standard deviation* **is an index of the amount of variability in a set of data.** It reflects the dispersion of scores in a distribution. This principle is portrayed graphically in Figure B.4, where the two distributions of golf scores have the same mean but the

upper one has less variability because the scores are "bunched up" in the center (for the consistent golfer). The distribution in Figure B.4(b) is characterized by more variability, as the erratic golfer's scores are more spread out. This distribution will yield a higher standard deviation than the distribution in Figure B.4(a).

The formula for calculating the standard deviation is shown in Figure B.5, where *d* stands for each score's deviation from the mean and Σ stands for summation. A step-by-step application of this formula to our TV viewing data, shown in Figure B.5, reveals that the standard deviation for our TV viewing data is 1.64. The standard deviation has a variety of uses. One of these uses will surface in the next section, where we discuss the normal distribution.

The Normal Distribution

The hypothesis in our study is that brighter students watch less TV than relatively dull students. To test this hypothesis, we're going to correlate TV viewing with SAT scores. But to make effective use of the SAT data, we need to understand what SAT scores mean, which brings us to the normal distribution.

Figure B.4

The standard deviation and dispersion of data. Although both these distributions of golf scores have the same mean, their standard deviations will be different. In **(a)** the scores are bunched together and there is less variability than in **(b)**, yielding a lower standard deviation for the data in distribution **(a)**.

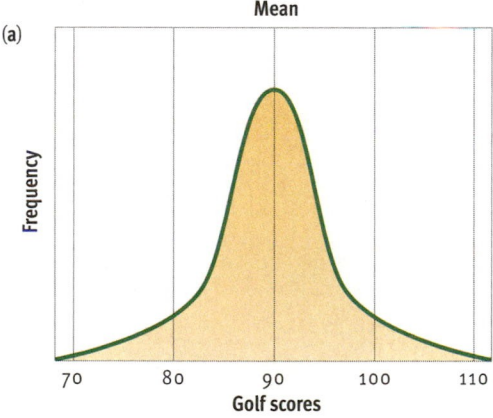

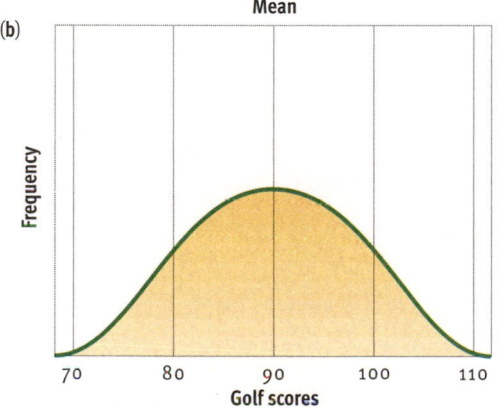

TV viewing score (X)	Deviation from mean (d)	Deviation squared (d²)
0	−3	9
0	−3	9
1	−2	4
1	−2	4
2	−1	1
2	−1	1
2	−1	1
3	0	0
3	0	0
3	0	0
3	0	0
3	0	0
4	+1	1
4	+1	1
4	+1	1
4	+1	1
5	+2	4
5	+2	4
5	+2	4
N = 20 6	+3	9
ΣX = 60		Σd² = 54

$$\text{Mean} = \frac{\Sigma X}{N} = \frac{60}{20} = 3.0$$

$$\text{Standard deviation} = \sqrt{\frac{\Sigma d^2}{N}} = \sqrt{\frac{54}{20}}$$

$$= \sqrt{2.70} = 1.64$$

Figure B.5

Steps in calculating the standard deviation. (1) Add the scores (ΣX) and divide by the number of scores (N) to calculate the mean (which comes out to 3.0 in this case). (2) Calculate each score's deviation from the mean by subtracting the mean from each score (the results are shown in the second column). (3) Square these deviations from the mean and total the results to obtain (Σd²) as shown in the third column. (4) Insert the numbers for N and Σd² into the formula for the standard deviation and compute the results.

The *normal distribution* is a symmetric, bell-shaped curve that represents the pattern in which many human characteristics are dispersed in the population. A great many physical qualities (for example, height, nose length, and running speed) and psychological traits (intelligence, spatial reasoning ability, introversion) are distributed in a manner that closely resembles this bell-shaped curve. When a trait is normally distributed, most scores fall near the center of the distribution (the mean), and the number of scores gradually declines as one moves away from the center in either direction. The normal distribution is *not* a law of nature. It's a mathematical function, or theoretical curve, that approximates the way nature seems to operate.

The normal distribution is the bedrock of the scoring system for most psychological tests, including the SAT. As we discuss in Chapter 9, psychological tests are *relative measures;* they assess how people score on a trait in comparison to other people. The normal distribution gives us a precise way to measure how people stack up in comparison to each other. The scores under the normal curve are dispersed in a fixed pattern, with the standard deviation serving as the unit of measurement, as shown in Figure B.6. About 68% of the scores in the distribution fall within

plus or minus 1 standard deviation of the mean, while 95% of the scores fall within plus or minus 2 standard deviations of the mean. Given this fixed pattern, if you know the mean and standard deviation of a normally distributed trait, you can tell where any score falls in the distribution for the trait.

Although you may not have realized it, you probably have taken many tests in which the scoring system is based on the normal distribution. On the SAT, for instance, raw scores (the number of items correct on each subtest) are converted into standard scores that indicate where you fall in the normal distribution for the trait measured. In this conversion, the mean is set arbitrarily at 500 and the standard deviation at 100, as shown in Figure B.7. Therefore, a score of 400 on the SAT verbal subtest means that you scored 1 standard deviation below the mean, while an SAT score of 600 indicates that you scored 1 standard deviation above the mean. Thus, SAT scores tell you how many standard deviations above or below the mean your score was. This system also provides the metric for IQ scales and many other types of psychological tests (see Chapter 9).

Test scores that place examinees in the normal distribution can always be converted to percentile scores, which are a little easier to interpret. A *percentile score*

Figure B.6

The normal distribution.

Many characteristics are distributed in a pattern represented by this bell-shaped curve (each dot represents a case). The horizontal axis shows how far above or below the mean a score is (measured in plus or minus standard deviations). The vertical axis shows the number of cases obtaining each score. In a normal distribution, most cases fall near the center of the distribution, so that 68.26% of the cases fall within plus or minus 1 standard deviation of the mean. The number of cases gradually declines as one moves away from the mean in either direction, so that only 13.59% of the cases fall between 1 and 2 standard deviations above or below the mean, and even fewer cases (2.14%) fall between 2 and 3 standard deviations above or below the mean.

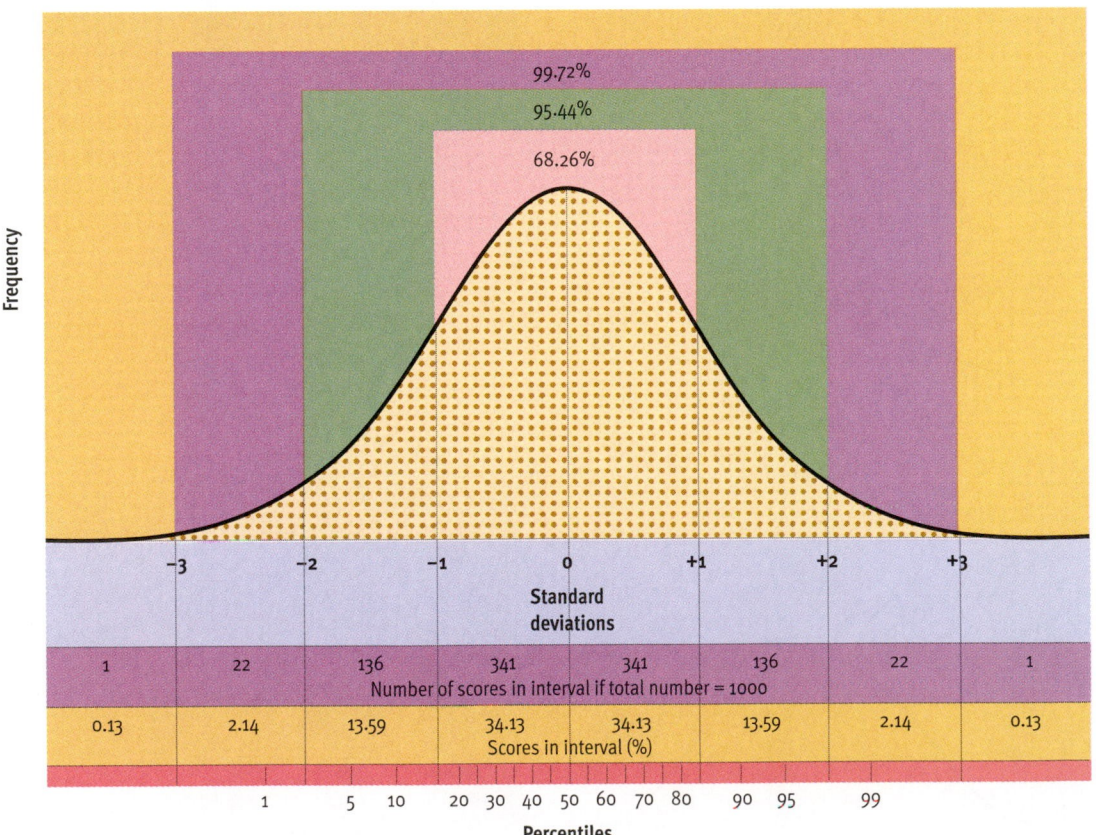

indicates the percentage of people who score at or below the score you obtained. For example, if you score at the 60th percentile, 60% of the people who take the test score the same or below you, while the remaining 40% score above you. There are tables available that permit us to convert any standard deviation placement in a normal distribution into a precise percentile score. Figure B.6 gives some percentile conversions for the normal curve.

Of course, not all distributions are normal. As we saw in Figure B.3, some distributions are skewed in one direction or the other. As an example, consider what would happen if a classroom exam were much too easy or much too hard. If the test were too easy, scores would be bunched up at the high end of the scale, as in Figure B.3(b). If the test were too hard, scores would be bunched up at the low end, as in Figure B.3(c).

Measuring Correlation  1d

To determine whether TV viewing is related to SAT scores, we have to compute a *correlation coefficient*—a numerical index of the degree of relationship between two variables. As discussed in Chapter 2, a *positive* correlation means that two variables—say X and Y—co-vary in the *same* direction. This means that high scores on variable X are associated with high scores on variable Y and that low scores on X are associated with low scores on Y. A *negative* correlation indicates that two variables co-vary in the *opposite* direction. This means that people who score high on variable X tend to score low on variable Y, whereas those who score low on X tend to score high on Y. In our study, we hypothesized that as TV view-

ing increases, SAT scores will decrease, so we should expect a negative correlation between TV viewing and SAT scores.

The *magnitude* of a correlation coefficient indicates the *strength* of the association between two variables. This coefficient can vary between 0 and ±1.00. The coefficient is usually represented by the letter r (for example, $r = .45$). A coefficient near 0 tells us that there is no relationship between two variables. A coefficient of +1.00 or −1.00 indicates that there is a perfect, one-to-one correspondence between two variables. A perfect correlation is found only rarely when working with real data. The closer the coefficient is to either −1.00 or +1.00, the stronger the relationship is.

The direction and strength of correlations can be illustrated graphically in scatter diagrams (see Figure B.8). A *scatter diagram* is a graph in which paired X and Y scores for each subject are plotted as sin-

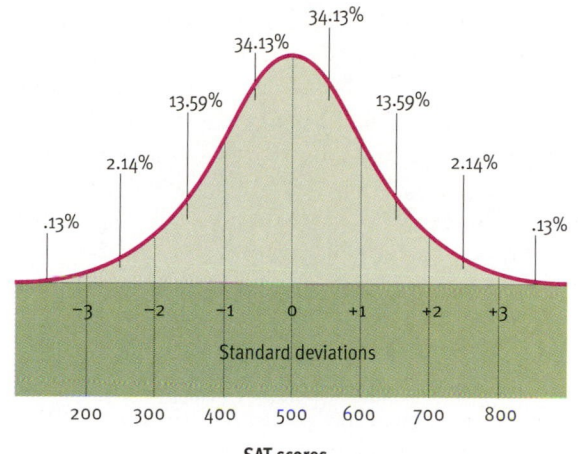

Figure B.7

The normal distribution and SAT scores. The normal distribution is the basis for the scoring system on many standardized tests. For example, on the SAT, the mean is set at 500 and the standard deviation at 100. Hence, an SAT score tells you how many standard deviations above or below the mean you scored. For example, a score of 700 means you scored 2 standard deviations above the mean.

Figure B.8

Scatter diagrams of positive and negative correlations. Scatter diagrams plot paired X and Y scores as single points. Score plots slanted in the opposite direction result from positive (top row) as opposed to negative (bottom row) correlations. Moving across both rows (to the right), you can see that progressively weaker correlations result in more and more scattered plots of data points.

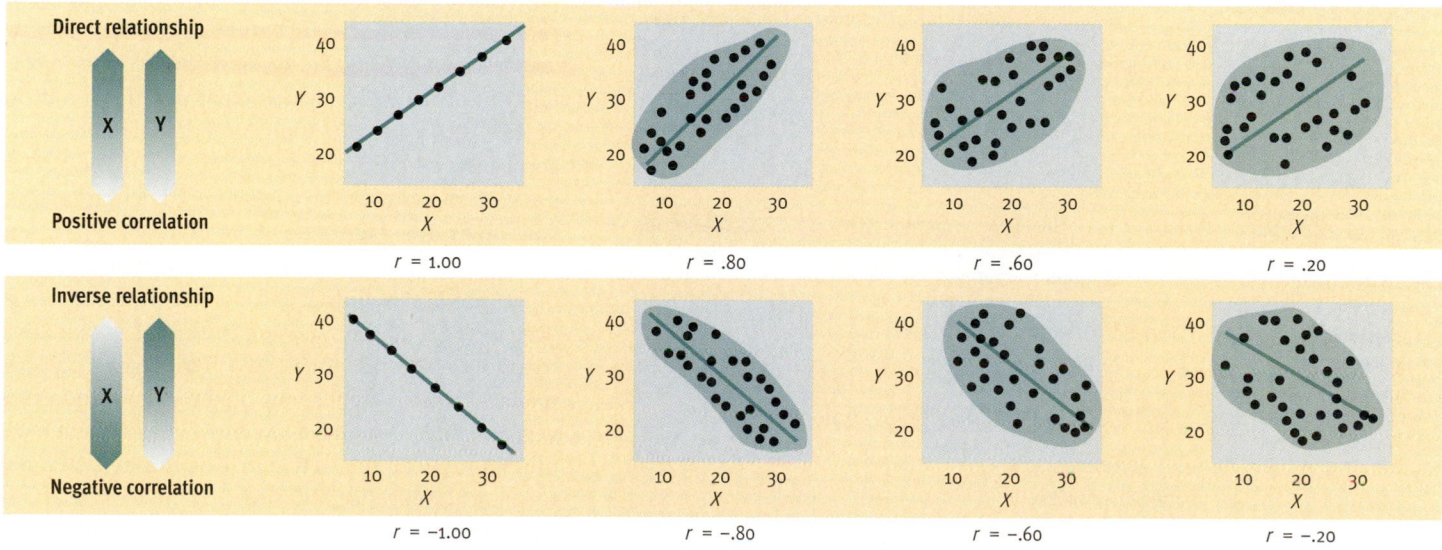

Figure B.9

Scatter diagram of the correlation between TV viewing and SAT scores. Our hypothetical data relating TV viewing to SAT scores are plotted in this scatter diagram. Compare it to the scatter diagrams seen in Figure B.8 and see whether you can estimate the correlation between TV viewing and SAT scores in our data (see the text for the answer).

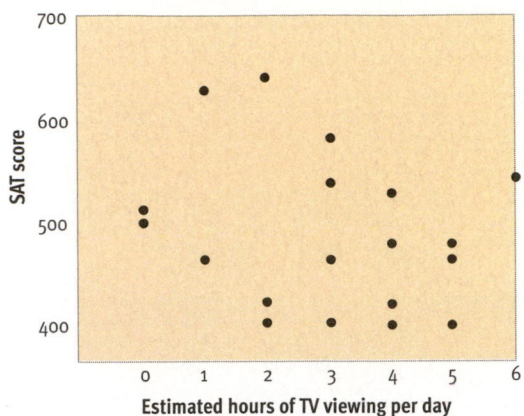

Figure B.10

Computing a correlation coefficient. The calculations required to compute the Pearson product-moment coefficient of correlation are shown here. The formula looks intimidating, but it's just a matter of filling in the figures taken from the sums of the columns shown above the formula.

gle points. Figure B.8 shows scatter diagrams for positive correlations in the upper half and for negative correlations in the bottom half. A perfect positive correlation and a perfect negative correlation are shown on the far left. When a correlation is perfect, the data points in the scatter diagram fall exactly in a straight line. However, positive and negative correlations yield lines slanted in the opposite direction

because the lines map out opposite types of associations. Moving to the right in Figure B.8, you can see what happens when the magnitude of a correlation decreases. The data points scatter farther and farther from the straight line that would represent a perfect relationship.

What about our data relating TV viewing to SAT scores? Figure B.9 shows a scatter diagram of these data. Having just learned about scatter diagrams, perhaps you can estimate the magnitude of the correlation between TV viewing and SAT scores. The scatter diagram of our data looks a lot like the one seen in the bottom right corner of Figure B.8, suggesting that the correlation will be in the vicinity of –.20.

The formula for computing the most widely used measure of correlation—the Pearson product-moment correlation—is shown in Figure B.10, along with the calculations for our data on TV viewing and SAT scores. The data yield a correlation of $r = -.24$. This coefficient of correlation reveals that we have found a weak inverse association between TV viewing and performance on the SAT. Among our participants, as TV viewing increases, SAT scores decrease, but the trend isn't very strong. We can get a better idea of how strong this correlation is by examining its predictive power.

Correlation and Prediction

As the magnitude of a correlation increases (gets closer to either –1.00 or +1.00), our ability to predict one variable based on knowledge of the other variable steadily increases. This relationship between the magnitude of a correlation and predictability can be quantified precisely. All we have to do is square the correlation coefficient (multiply it by itself) and this gives us the *coefficient of determination*, **the percentage of variation in one variable that can be predicted based on the other variable.** Thus, a correlation of .70 yields a coefficient of determination of .49 (.70 × .70 = .49), indicating that variable X can account for 49% of the variation in variable Y. Figure B.11 shows how the coefficient of determination goes up as the magnitude of a correlation increases.

Unfortunately, a correlation of .24 doesn't give us much predictive power. We can account only for a little over 6% of the variation in variable Y. So, if we tried to predict individuals' SAT scores based on how much TV they watched, our predictions wouldn't be very accurate. Although a low correlation doesn't have much practical, predictive utility, it may still have theoretical value. Just knowing that there is a relationship between two variables can be theoretically interesting. However, we haven't yet addressed the ques-

Subject number	TV viewing score (X)	X²	SAT score (Y)	Y²	XY
1	0	0	500	250,000	0
2	0	0	515	265,225	0
3	1	1	450	202,500	450
4	1	1	650	422,500	650
5	2	4	400	160,000	800
6	2	4	675	455,625	1350
7	2	4	425	180,625	850
8	3	9	400	160,000	1200
9	3	9	450	202,500	1350
10	3	9	500	250,000	1500
11	3	9	550	302,500	1650
12	3	9	600	360,000	1800
13	4	16	400	160,000	1600
14	4	16	425	180,625	1700
15	4	16	475	225,625	1900
16	4	16	525	275,625	2100
17	5	25	400	160,000	2000
18	5	25	450	202,500	2250
19	5	25	475	225,625	2375
20	6	36	550	302,500	3300
	$N = 20$	$\Sigma X = 60$	$\Sigma X^2 = 234$	$\Sigma Y = 9815$	$\Sigma Y^2 = 4,943,975$	$\Sigma XY = 28,825$

Formula for Pearson product-moment correlation coefficient

$$r = \frac{(N)\Sigma XY - (\Sigma X)(\Sigma Y)}{\sqrt{[(N)\Sigma X^2 - (\Sigma X)^2][(N)\Sigma Y^2 - (\Sigma Y)^2]}}$$

$$= \frac{(20)(28,825) - (60)(9815)}{\sqrt{[(20)(234) - (60)^2][(20)(4,943,975) - (9815)^2]}}$$

$$= \frac{-12,400}{\sqrt{[1080][2,545,275]}}$$

$$= -.237$$

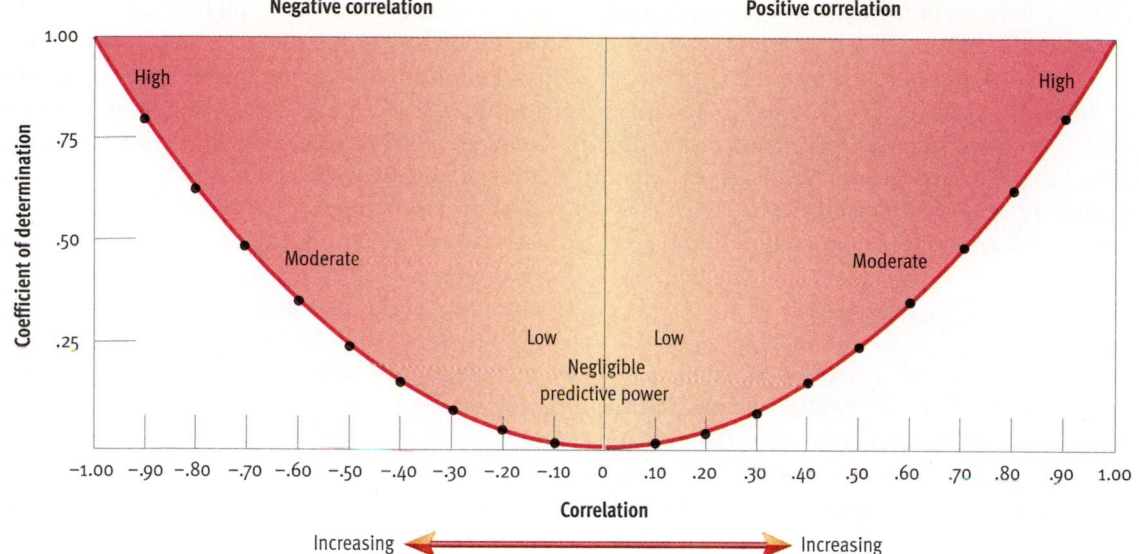

Figure **B.11**

Correlation and the coefficient of determination. The coefficient of determination is an index of a correlation's predictive power. As you can see, whether positive or negative, stronger correlations yield greater predictive power.

Negative correlation

Positive correlation

High

High

Moderate

Moderate

Low

Low

Negligible predictive power

Increasing

Increasing

Correlation

Coefficient of determination

tion of whether our observed correlation is strong enough to support our hypothesis that there is a relationship between TV viewing and SAT scores. To make this judgment, we have to turn to *inferential statistics* and the process of hypothesis testing.

Hypothesis Testing

Inferential statistics go beyond the mere description of data. **Inferential statistics are used to interpret data and draw conclusions.** They permit researchers to decide whether their data support their hypotheses.

In Chapter 2, we showed how inferential statistics can be used to evaluate the results of an experiment; the same process can be applied to correlational data. In our study of TV viewing we hypothesized that we would find an inverse relationship between amount of TV watched and SAT scores. Sure enough, that's what we found. However, we have to ask ourselves a critical question: Is this observed correlation large enough to support our hypothesis, or might a correlation of this size have occurred by chance?

We have to ask a similar question nearly every time we conduct a study. Why? Because we are working only with a sample. In research, we observe a limited *sample* (in this case, 20 participants) to draw conclusions about a much larger *population* (college students in general). There's always a possibility that if we drew a different sample from the population, the results might be different. Perhaps our results are unique to our sample and not generalizable to the larger population. If we were able to collect data on the entire population, we would not have to wrestle with this problem, but our dependence on a sample necessitates the use of inferential statistics to pre-

cisely evaluate the likelihood that our results are due to chance factors in sampling. Thus, inferential statistics are the key to making the inferential leap from the sample to the population (see Figure B.12).

Although it may seem backward, in hypothesis testing we formally test the *null hypothesis*. As applied to correlational data, the *null hypothesis* **is the assumption that there is no true relationship between the variables observed.** In our study, the null hypothesis is that there is no genuine association between TV viewing and SAT scores. We want to determine whether our results will permit us to *reject* the null hypothesis and thus conclude that our *research hypothesis* (that there *is* a relationship between the variables) has been supported. Why do we directly test the null hypothesis instead of the research hy-

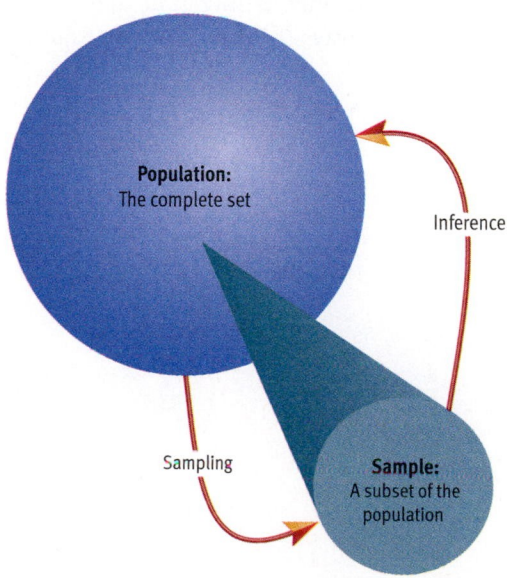

Figure **B.12**

The relationship between the population and the sample. In research, we are usually interested in a broad population, but we can observe only a small sample from the population. After making observations of our sample, we draw inferences about the population, based on the sample. This inferential process works well as long as the sample is reasonably representative of the population.

Population: The complete set

Inference

Sampling

Sample: A subset of the population

pothesis? Because our probability calculations depend on assumptions tied to the null hypothesis. Specifically, we compute the probability of obtaining the results that we have observed if the null hypothesis is indeed true. The calculation of this probability hinges on a number of factors. A key factor is the amount of variability in the data, which is why the standard deviation is an important statistic.

Statistical Significance

When we reject the null hypothesis, we conclude that we have found *statistically significant* results. **Statistical significance is said to exist when the probability that the observed findings are due to chance is very low, usually less than 5 chances in 100.** This means that if the null hypothesis is correct and we conduct our study 100 times, drawing a new sample from the population each time, we will get results such as those observed only 5 times out of 100. If our calculations allow us to reject the null hypothesis, we conclude that our results support our research hypothesis. Thus, statistically significant results typically are findings that *support* a research hypothesis.

The requirement that there be less than 5 chances in 100 that research results are due to chance is the *minimum* requirement for statistical significance. When this requirement is met, we say the results are significant at the .05 level. If researchers calculate that there is less than 1 chance in 100 that their results are due to chance factors in sampling, the results are significant at the .01 level. If there is less than a 1 in 1000 chance that findings are attributable to sampling error, the results are significant at the .001 level. Thus, there are several *levels* of significance that you may see cited in scientific articles.

Because we are only dealing in matters of probability, there is always the possibility that our decision to accept or reject the null hypothesis is wrong. The various significance levels indicate the probability of erroneously rejecting the null hypothesis (and inaccurately accepting the research hypothesis). At the .05 level of significance, there are 5 chances in 100 that we have made a mistake when we conclude that our results support our hypothesis, and at the .01 level of significance the chance of an erroneous conclusion is 1 in 100. Although researchers hold the probability of this type of error quite low, the probability is never zero. This is one of the reasons that competently executed studies of the same question can yield contradictory findings. The differences may be due to chance variations in sampling that can't be prevented.

What do we find when we evaluate our data linking TV viewing to students' SAT scores? The calculations indicate that, given our sample size and the variability in our data, the probability of obtaining a correlation of –.24 by chance is greater than 20%. That's not a high probability, but it's *not* low enough to reject the null hypothesis. Thus, our findings are not strong enough to allow us to conclude that we have supported our hypothesis.

Statistics and Empiricism

In summary, conclusions based on empirical research are a matter of probability, and there's always a possibility that the conclusions are wrong. However, two major strengths of the empirical approach are its precision and its intolerance of error. Scientists can give you precise estimates of the likelihood that their conclusions are wrong, and because they're intolerant of error, they hold this probability extremely low. It's their reliance on statistics that allows them to accomplish these goals.

Appendix C Industrial/Organizational Psychology

By Paul M. Muchinsky (University of North Carolina at Greensboro)

Throughout this book we have seen many examples of how psychology has been applied to practical problems in a wide variety of settings. But we have yet to discuss in earnest one setting that has received a great deal of attention from the earliest beginnings of psychology—the work setting. **Industrial and organizational (I/O) psychology is the branch of psychology concerned with the application of psychological principles in the workplace.** I/O psychology is studied throughout the world, although its name varies some from one locale to the next. For example, in the United Kingdom it is called *occupational psychology,* in many European countries *work and organizational psychology,* and in Australia *organisational psychology.* The Society for Industrial and Organizational Psychology (SIOP), which is the major professional organization for I/O psychologists, has approximately 6,000 members, who reside in 39 countries. The society has more than doubled in size in recent years, and it appears that this growth will continue. I/O psychologists are mostly found in four work settings: industry, universities, government, and consulting firms (see Figure C.1).

People devote an enormous part of their lives to occupational activities. Thus, I/O psychology is devoted to understanding one of the major domains of human behavior. In broad terms, I/O psychology is concerned with behavior in work situations. There are two sides of I/O psychology: science and practice. On the one hand, I/O psychology is a productive, fascinating area of scientific inquiry, concerned with advancing knowledge about behavior in the workplace. In this respect, I/O psychology is an academic discipline that seeks to test hypotheses, gather data, and make generalizations about work-related behavior. On the other hand, I/O psychology is a profession concerned with the application of knowledge to solve real problems in the world of work. I/O psychologists strive to help organizations to hire better employees, reduce absenteeism, improve communication at work, increase job satisfaction, and solve countless other problems. Accordingly, the education of I/O psychologists is founded on the *scientist-practitioner model,* which trains them in both scientific inquiry and practical applications.

I/O psychology was originally called *industrial psychology.* During its early years (roughly the first half of the 20th century), the field focused primarily on recruiting and selecting employees, training, evaluating job performance, and leadership in the workplace. In the 1950s and 1960s psychologists in this area became more concerned with the organizational context in which work occurs. This shift in emphasis was also fueled by changes in the United States economy, which gradually moved from a predominately manufacturing economy to more of a service economy. Because of these trends, the field's name was officially changed to industrial/organizational psychology in 1970. This name change is not merely cosmetic, as it captures the essence of the field. The topics of interest to contemporary I/O psychology generally fall into the traditional domain of *industrial psychology* or the more recently emerging domain of *organizational psychology.* Our coverage will reflect this reality, as we begin by discussing topics in industrial psychology and then turn to topics in organizational psychology.

Industrial Psychology

Industrial psychology focuses on topics associated with personnel matters. It is concerned with picking the right people for the right jobs and cultivating a productive workforce. We will discuss five topics of interest in the field of industrial psychology: recruitment, selection, employment discrimination, training, and performance appraisal.

Recruitment

Recruitment is the process of attracting people to apply for a job. Organizations can select from only those candidates who apply for their positions. If few people apply for a job, the odds of finding a strong candidate are lower than if many candidates apply.

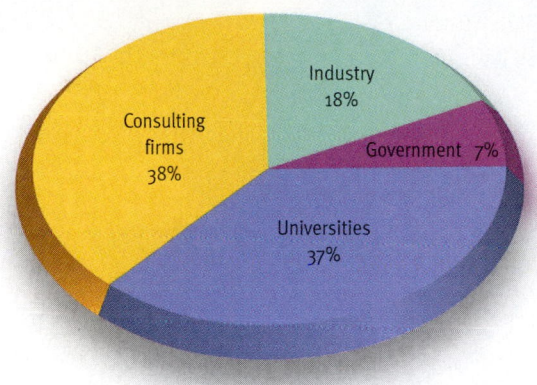

Figure C.1

Principal work settings of industrial/organizational psychologists. I/O psychologists are mainly found in the four work settings identified here. As the pie chart shows, about three-quarters of I/O psychologists work either in universities or at consulting firms. (Based on Society for Industrial and Organizational Psychology 2001 member database)

Source: Muchinsky, P. M. (2003). *Psychology applied to work.* Belmont, CA: Wadsworth. Reprinted by permission.

The interviewing of prospective employees needs to be handled with finesse as the recruitment process is mutual. Companies sometimes lose talented prospects because of inappropriate interviewing techniques.

With the growing acceptability of conducting business via the Internet, organizations are now developing websites to attract job applicants. Online recruiting is the fastest growing medium for attracting job applicants and is particularly popular among candidates in their 20s and 30s (Graham, 2000).

There is a relationship between the recruitment of job applicants and broad-based economic conditions. When the economy is stagnating or contracting, jobs are generally scarce and typically there will be many applicants for each opening. In contrast, when the economy is growing, competition among employers for qualified job applicants can be intense. Rynes (1993) noted that most of the emphasis on personnel decisions from an I/O psychology perspective centers on how employers can make better decisions in assessing applicants. However, as Rynes observed, the process can be viewed from the opposite perspective—that is, the extent to which applicants consider the company to be a desirable employer. Specifically, what impressions of the company are generated by the company's recruitment and assessment practices? Applicant reactions to assessment procedures are often vivid and highly emotional, as the following examples from Rynes (1993) illustrate:

A married graduate student with a 3.9 grade point average reported that the first three questions in a company's psychological assessment procedure involved inquiries about her personal relationship with her husband and children. Although the company asked her what she thought of the procedure before she left, she lied because she was afraid that telling the truth would eliminate her from future consideration. Because of dual-career constraints, she continued to pursue an offer, but noted that if she got one, her first on-the-job priority would be to try to get the assessor fired.

The first interview question asked of a female student was, "We're a pretty macho organization . . . Does that bother you?" Unfortunately it did, and she simply wrote the company out of her future interviewing plans. (p. 242)

These examples show that job applicants are not merely passive recipients of personnel selection procedures. Rather, applicants react to what they are asked to do or say to get a job. Sometimes a negative experience results in withdrawal from the application process. Companies and applicants should realize that the recruitment process is *mutual*—both parties are engaged in assessing the degree of fit with each other. L. Harris (2000) asserts that it might be wise for organizations to explain to rejected candidates why they were denied employment in a way that reduces negative feelings and damage to self-esteem rather than to provide explanations that are designed to protect the companies from potential litigation.

Selection

The process of personnel selection consists of deciding which of the job applicants will be extended an offer of employment. The selection process should be based on careful consideration of the knowledge, skills, and abilities possessed by each applicant. The goal is to get a good match or fit between the work demands of the job and the personal attributes of the applicant.

Schmitt and Chan (1998) identified five major changes in modern society that have affected the ways personnel selection decisions are made in many organizations. The first is the *speed of technological change*. With computer-based technology, work today is often conducted in ways that people couldn't even imagine 25 years ago. This rapid rate of change compels companies to hire workers who can adapt to ever-evolving work conditions. Emphasis is thus placed on a person's willingness and capacity to learn new job skills on a continuous basis. Second is the growing reliance on the *use of teams to accomplish work*. More and more work tasks require coordinated efforts by teams of employees as opposed to individual workers and their supervisors. The cultural values of the United States have traditionally rewarded individual achievement, and personnel selection methods have been geared toward that mentality. Today, organizations increasingly need to select employees who can fit well into the team concept. The third factor consists of *changes in communication technology*. Faxes, e-mail, and hand-held electronic devices permit workers to communicate with others instantaneously around the world. It is no longer necessary to meet face to face or even communicate by telephone. These new, impersonal methods of communication have implications for classic organizational issues, such as the bond between co-workers, worker morale, and employee commitment. The fourth change is that *most large corporations are now global*. For example, over half of the Ford Motor Company's employees work outside the United States. The products of many U.S. companies are sold and serviced throughout the world. Hence, companies need to select employees who are adaptable and open to cultures other than their own. Finally, the U.S. economy is continuing its long-running *transition from a manufacturing orientation to a service orientation*. Organizations that provide services must strive to hire employees who are likely to be sensitive to the customers' needs and adept at satisfying them. This objective has increased the emphasis on applicants' interpersonal skills.

These trends are likely to lead companies in the 21st century to select employees with somewhat different qualities than the companies sought in the past. If jobs are constantly changing, organizations will probably increase their emphasis on hiring candidates with high intelligence. Teaching them the specific knowledge or skills required on the job can be left to post-hiring training. If jobs are increasingly service oriented, companies will want to hire people who are conscientious and interpersonally flexible. However, as Behling (1998) has noted, these skills are most appropriate when new employees will have to do a lot of problem solving, will have a lot of autonomy, will learn skills on the job that are more important than those brought to the job, and will need to adapt rapidly. Of course, many jobs in modern society do not fit this description. In some jobs it is still critical to pursue a match between the specific skills applicants already have and specific job requirements. Thus, in a rapidly changing work environment the desired match is more between the *person* and the *organization*, whereas in a stable work environment the desired match is more between the *person* and the *job*.

I/O psychologists use a diverse array of personnel selection tools, including personality and intelligence tests, performance tests (for example, a typing test), interviews, tests of physical ability, letters of recommendation, and drug tests. These techniques are all designed to gauge candidates' suitability for employment. I/O psychologists strive to devise selection methods that are accurate predictors of future job performance, legally defensible, appropriate for the job, and cost-efficient. Obviously, selection decisions can have profound effects on job candidates' lives. These decisions can also be critical to the success of organizations.

Employment Discrimination

The tasks of employee recruitment and selection are intimately intertwined with the sometimes controversial issue of employment discrimination. Understanding this topic necessitates an awareness of the cultural and social evolution of the United States, which was founded through the confluence of people from other countries arriving in this country seeking a chance at a better life. The United States is a melting pot of people from various nations, cultures, races, and religions. However, over the course of history, some groups have been treated less equitably than others. The injustice of discrimination became a prominent concern in the late 1950s and early 1960s. Up until that time it was acceptable, for example, to pay a woman less money than a man even though they had equal job performance and seniority. In response to changing values and mounting political pressures, Congress passed the 1964 Civil Rights Act, which had far-reaching implications for life in the United States. The law was designed to reduce illegal discrimination in many areas of life, including the world of work. The Civil Rights Act outlawed discrimination based on race, color, religion, national origin, and sex. Subsequent laws prohibited discrimination based on age and disability.

This legislation had dramatic effects on the field of industrial psychology, making it accountable to many new legal standards. In addition to ensuring that their employee recruitment and selection methods represent sound science and sound business practice, contemporary I/O psychologists must strive to ensure that their practices are legally sound.

Training

Organizations select employees on the basis of their predicted likelihood of succeeding on the job. Although some employees are expected to perform their jobs well immediately, the vast majority of employees are given some time to grow into their jobs. This growth process is expedited by formal organizational training processes. Training is designed to help new employees acquire the skills, rules, concepts, or attitudes that result in improved job performance.

Training is important because the knowledge and skill demands of work are continually escalating. Martocchio and Baldwin (1997) expressed this perspective clearly: "In an age of technological innovation in which robots, telecommunications, artificial intelligence, software, and lasers perform routine tasks, worker skills soon become obsolete. Put bluntly, today's jobs require new and different skills at all levels of an organization" (p. 6). One major reason for the increased emphasis on training is the growing reliance on computers in the conduct of work. Computer-assisted manufacturing and computer-assisted design are two major technological innovations in production. Manufacturing employees are now often expected to have some fluency in computer-based operations. The acquisition of such skills often depends on post-hire training programs.

The U.S. government has sponsored activities for providing better vocational training to high school students. The Secretary's Commission on Achieving Necessary Skills (SCANS) is a national project started in 1990 by the Department of Labor. The SCANS Commission contends that more than half of the people leaving high school do not have the knowledge or foundation required to find or hold a good job. SCANS identified a set of competencies common across a broad range of occupations. The SCANS Commission (1991) concluded that high school students need to learn not only basic academic skills but also workplace know-how skills. Its report defined workplace competencies, foundation skills, and personal qualities necessary for worker success.

Pressures are growing in all areas of work to operate more efficiently and to enhance the overall quality of goods and services. Such changes require enhanced organizational performance in increasingly competitive markets. Training, therefore, is a process to improve the fit between job demands and employee attributes. Training needs to occur in virtually all organizations on a continuous basis. Thus, it might be advisable to think of your college years as "learning through education" and of your working years as "learning through training."

Obviously, training programs vary in their effectiveness. Successful training initiatives depend on four main considerations. First, the organization must value training, encourage employees to participate in training, and then design work so the training can be used back on the job. Second, there must be a clear understanding about what kind of training needs to occur, how it will benefit the organization, and which employees should receive the training. Third, there should be an approximate match between training methods and training needs. Some training methods are more geared to technical skill enhancement, while others are more suited for enhancing interpersonal skills. Fourth, there must be clear support systems in place to ensure that what is learned in training generalizes back to the job. The extent to which training actually improves job performance is the ultimate test of training effectiveness.

Performance Appraisal

With or without the input of I/O psychologists, employees continually have their job performance evaluated. Informal appraisals may be made from haphazard observations, memory, hearsay, or intuition. I/O psychologists endeavor to design performance appraisal methods that are formal, rational, systematic, accurate, fair, and useful to all concerned.

Performance appraisals serve many purposes for both employers and employees, as outlined in Figure C.2. Murphy and Cleveland (1995) maintain that effective performance appraisals can help organizations in several ways. First, they can enhance the quality of organizational decisions, ranging from pay raises to promotions to discharge. The purpose of the human resource function in an organization is to maximize the contributions of employees to the goals of the organization, and assessments of employee job performance can play a major role in accomplishing that function.

Second, performance appraisals can improve the quality of individual decisions, ranging from career choices to the development of future strengths. Accurate performance feedback is an important component of effective training and provides critical input for realistic self-assessments by employees. Performance feedback is also a key factor in promoting high levels of motivation in the workforce.

Third, performance appraisals can affect employees' views of, and attachment to, their organization. A fair and effective appraisal system can help build employee morale and satisfaction. In contrast, employees who believe that an organization's performance appraisals are irrational or unfair are unlikely to develop a strong commitment to that organization.

Finally, formal performance appraisals provide a legally defensible basis for personnel decisions, which cannot be capricious. Organizations must have reasonable explanations for why some employees are promoted, discharged, or receive differential pay raises compared to others.

Performance appraisal often requires evaluations of many aspects of job performance. At the lower level of complexity, jobs typically require employees to show up for work on time, cooperate with co-workers, and so forth. At higher levels of complexity, jobs may require the demonstration of technical expertise or leadership capability. I/O psychologists assist in deciding which aspects of job performance should be appraised and in designing the appraisal methods. They also try to find ways to deal with the fact that many employees don't like to be appraised and some supervisors don't like to evaluate their colleagues. The challenge for I/O psychologists is to help foster an atmosphere within the organization that recognizes the legitimate need for all parties to provide honest and accurate performance appraisals.

Organizational Psychology

Organizational psychology is the branch of I/O psychology concerned with how the collective social context of the work environment affects workers' behavior and attitudes. We will examine five topics that are important in contemporary organizational psychology: organizational culture, work teams, the psychological contract between employers and their employees, work motivation, and leadership.

Organizational Culture

The concept of *culture* has long been used to describe the customs, values, and norms of *societies,* but I/O psychologists have also found the concept useful in the description of *organizations.* An *organizational cul-*

Employer and employee reasons for conducting appraisals

Employer perspective

1. Despite imperfect measurement, individual differences in performance make a difference.
2. Documentation of performance appraisal and feedback may be needed for legal defense.
3. Appraisal provides a rational basis for constructing a bonus or merit system.
4. Appraisal dimensions and standards can operationalize strategic goals and clarify performance expectations.
5. Providing individual feedback is part of a performance management process.
6. Despite the traditional individual focus, appraisal criteria can include teamwork and teams can be the focus of appraisal.

Employee perspective

1. Performance feedback is needed and desired.
2. Improvement in performance requires assessment.
3. Fairness requires that differences in performance levels across workers be measured and have an impact on outcomes.
4. Assessment and recognition of performance levels can motivate improved performance.

ture consists of the language, values, attitudes, beliefs, and customs shared by the employees of a company. An organization's culture gives it its unique "flavor" or "personality." Several definitions of organizational culture have been proposed, but the most succinct was offered by Deal and Kennedy (1982): "The way we do things around here."

Furnham and Gunter (1993) proposed three features of organizational culture. First, an organization's culture can often be traced to its founders. These people often possess dynamic personalities, strong values, and a clear vision of what the organization should look like. They play a big role in the initial hiring of employees, and their ideas and values are readily transmitted to new employees. Second, culture often develops out of an organization's experience with the external environment. Every organization must establish its own identity in its industry and in the marketplace where it operates. As it struggles to do so, it may find that some values and practices are more effective than others. Third, an organizational culture develops from the need to maintain effective working relationships among employees. Depending on the nature of the organization's business and the characteristics of the people it hires, different expectations and values develop.

Deeply ingrained within organizational culture are communication processes, for it is through communication that culture is transmitted. Interactions with long-time organizational members ensure that new recruits are enculturated. New employees learn the language and appropriate behavior of the group, hear its stories and legends, and observe the organi-

Figure C.2

Employer and employee perspectives on performance appraisals. I/O psychologists often play an important role in designing performance appraisal systems. Although sometimes awkward for the people involved, performance appraisals serve many important purposes for both employers and employees. Some of the reasons that both organizations and workers desire fair and accurate appraisals are outlined here.

Source: Cardy, R. L. (1998). Performance appraisal in a quality context: A new look at an old problem. In J. W. Smither (Ed.), *Performance appraisal.* San Francisco: Jossey-Bass. Reprinted by permission.

The organizational culture of a company can have an enormous influence on employee productivity and satisfaction. This reality will weigh heavily on the minds of Hewlett-Packard executives as they manage their huge merger with Compaq Computer. Carly Fiorina, the CEO of Hewlett-Packard, is shown here with other employees celebrating the merger.

© 2002 APWide World Photos

zation's rites and rituals. The culture of an organization can best be understood by analyzing its tangible and visible rites, including rites of passage (hiring and basic training), degradation (dismissal), conflict reduction (grievance committees), and integration (office holiday party). New members must determine what is appropriate dress, how to arrange their office, and how much latitude they have in being on time for appointments and in making deadlines. Culture may also be communicated through other channels, such as in-house memos, official policies, statements of corporate philosophy, and any other means of expressing values. Schein (1996) asserted that understanding the culture of an organization is critical to making sense of the behavior observed in the organization. A description of behavior divorced from the cultural context in which it occurs is of limited value.

Schneider (1996) emphasizes that it is the people who populate the organization who most define its culture. That is, employees are not actors who fill predetermined roles in an established culture, but rather their personalities, values, and interests make the organization what it is. Schneider (1987) proposed what he calls the *attraction-selection-attrition (ASA) cycle.* In this cycle, people with similar person-

alities and values are recruited by (*attraction*) and hired into certain organizations (*selection*); those who don't fit into the pattern of shared values eventually leave the organization (*attrition*). The ASA cycle is assumed to unfold gradually over time. It is often difficult to bring about a change in organizational culture because that would necessitate altering underlying values and beliefs that may be deeply entrenched. In any event, a full understanding of an organization requires some appreciation of its culture.

Work Teams

Historically, I/O psychologists have focused their attention on *individuals*—finding the right person for a job, training the person, and subsequently monitoring the individual's performance. However, recent years have seen an upsurge of interest in *work groups*.

Teams are bounded social units that work within a larger social system—the organization. A team has identifiable members (that is, members and nonmembers know who is a member and who is not) and an identifiable task or set of tasks to perform. The team's work requires that members interact by exchanging information, sharing resources, and coordinating activities, so there is always some degree of interdependence among the members of a team. Organizations tend to give teams more decision authority than comparable employees working individually. The team members often must decide among themselves who will do what, where, when, and how.

What underlies the new emphasis on teams? Three factors are critical. The first is the burgeoning amount of information and knowledge available. Huge amounts of information from multiple sources often have to be absorbed to respond to complex business issues. Because no one person can have technical expertise in all areas of knowledge, a team approach, representing a pooling of mental resources, becomes more tenable. Second, the working population is becoming better educated and trained. When the traditional organizational structures of 100 years ago were created, the workforce was relatively uneducated. The members of the traditional working class were monitored by members of "management," who often possessed much more education or training than their subordinates. However, the workers of today are more highly qualified and better able to serve in the types of leadership roles called for in work teams. As an employee who now works in a production team in a manufacturing organization stated, "I'm no longer expected to check my brain at the front gate when I enter the factory." The third factor is the rate of change in work activities and responsibilities. For many years workers tended to have well-defined job responsibilities that rarely changed. In the current work world, there are pressures to make new products, modify services, alter processes to improve quality, and in general be in a continual state of transformation. Work teams are thought to be more adaptable to these ever-changing conditions of work.

The evolution of teams and teamwork has compelled I/O psychology to address a host of new issues (Ilgen, 1999). Some of what we have learned about individuals in the workplace generalizes to teams, but other issues are more specific to teams. However, teams are *not* universally superior to individuals for conducting work across all relevant performance indices. For example, teams do not necessarily produce better decisions than some individuals do. There is nothing magical about transforming individuals into work teams. Teams are merely one means of performing work.

I/O psychologists are concerned with the structure of teams, including their size, roles filled by various members, and the planned length of their existence. Issues relating to team processes include how older team members socialize new members, as well as matters of team communication, conflict, cohe-sion, and trust. Some teams have members that have never met face to face. They interact only electronically and belong to "virtual teams." Some of what I/O psychologists have learned regarding the selection, training, and appraisal of individuals also applies to teams, but some aspects of team functioning require new concepts, insights, and research.

The Psychological Contract Between Employers and Employees

Rousseau (1995) has noted that employers and their employees enter into a *psychological contract*. It is not a formal written contract between the two parties but an implied relationship based on perceptions of mutual contributions and reciprocal obligations. Employees have beliefs about the organization's obligations to them as well as their obligations to the organization. Thus, employees may believe that the organization has agreed to provide job security and promotion opportunities in exchange for hard work and loyalty from the employee. The psychological contract is oriented toward the future. Without the promise of future exchange, neither party has incentive to contribute anything to the other, and the relationship may not endure.

The psychological contract is composed of a belief that some form of a promise has been made and that the terms and conditions of the contract have been accepted by both parties. However, this belief does not necessarily mean that both parties share a common understanding of all contract terms. The psychological contract is revised throughout the employee's tenure in the organization. The longer the relationship endures and the two parties interact, the broader the array of contributions that might be included in the contract. Rousseau and Parks (1993) found that employment itself is perceived as a promise (the implied contract of continued future employment) and that an employee's performance is perceived as a contribution (a way of paying for the promise). Robinson, Kraatz, and Rousseau (1994) examined how psychological contracts change over time. They found that during the first two years of employment, employees came to perceive that they owed less to their employer while the employers in turn owed them more.

There is an element of power in all contracts. Unequal power is most common in employment relationships. Power inequities affect the perceived voluntariness of the exchange relationship, dividing the two parties into contract makers (relatively powerful) and contract takers (relatively powerless). As contract takers, employees cannot easily exit the employment relationship. This situation may result in a perceived loss of control in the relationship, which is likely to intensify feelings of mistreatment and injustice when violations are perceived. Because the employer is the more powerful party, the terms of the contract can be dictated to the less powerful employee, who must either accept them or exit the relationship.

The psychological contract is violated when one party in a relationship perceives the other as failing to fulfill promised obligations. The failure of one party to meet its obligations to another can be expected to undermine their mutual relationship. Violations by an employer may affect not only what an employee feels he or she is owed by the employer but also what an employee feels obligated to offer in return. Violation of a psychological contract undermines the very factors (such as trust) that led to emergence of a relationship. If the employer reneges on an implied promise, the employer's integrity is questioned. A violation signals that the employer's original motives to build and maintain a mutually beneficial relationship have changed or were false from the beginning. The psychological contract binds the employee and the employer—a form of guarantee that if each does his or her part, then the relationship will be mutually beneficial. Thus, violations weaken this bond.

In recent decades, the changing nature of the psychological contract between employers and employees has required employees to assume greater responsibility for their own career development. Organizations are now far less likely to offer the implicit promise to provide career-advancing opportunities. Consider the following message found posted on the bulletin board of a plant experiencing widespread layoffs (as reported by Hall & Mirvis, 1995, p. 326):

We can't promise you how long we'll be in business.
We can't promise you that we won't be bought by another company.
We can't promise that there'll be room for promotion.
We can't promise that your job will exist until you reach retirement age.
We can't promise that the money will be available for your pension.
We can't expect your undying loyalty and we aren't sure we want it.

Based on a multinational study, Rousseau and Schalk (2000) concluded that the psychological contract as a promise-based exchange is widely generalizable to a variety of societies. Given the rise of global business, it is likely that the nature of cultural differences in the psychological contract will continue to evolve. For example, people from Asian cultures generally prefer to first establish a relationship between parties and then carry out business transactions. In contrast, people from Western cultures generally prefer to create a relationship through repeated business transactions. In the future it is likely both styles will manifest themselves in new and varied forms.

Work Motivation

Have you ever observed a person who appears driven to perform well or succeed? Perhaps you would describe yourself in that way. Such people may or may not have more ability than others, but it appears they are willing to work harder or expend more effort than their peers. Psychologists refer to this attribute or trait as *ambition* or *motivation*. Motivation is not directly observable; it must be inferred from patterns of behavior.

According to Pinder (1998), *work motivation* refers to the set of forces that initiate work-related behavior and determine its direction, intensity, and duration. There are three noteworthy components to this definition. First, *direction* addresses the choice of activities people make in expending effort. That is, people may choose to work diligently at some tasks and not at others. Second, *intensity* implies people have the potential to exert various levels of effort, depending on how much is needed. Third, *duration* reflects persistence of motivation over time. Motivation can thus be conceptualized along three dimensions: direction, intensity, and persistence. Each dimension has its associated issues that are relevant to both the organization and the individual. Direction pertains to those activities you focus your energy on. Organizations want employees who will direct themselves to their work responsibilities, and many employees want jobs that will inspire their motivation and commitment. Intensity pertains to the amount of motivation that is expended in pursuit of an activity. Organizations want employees who will exhibit high levels of energy. Such people are often referred to as "self-starters," implying they do not require organizational inducements to work hard. Likewise, many employees hope to find jobs that are sufficiently appealing to invite large commitments of energy. The third dimension, persistence, pertains to sustained energy over time. Researchers know the least about this dimension, but it is the focus of more recent motivational theories. You can think of a career as an interrelated series of jobs through which individuals manifest their energies over a working lifetime. Organizations want employees who will persevere through good times and bad. Likewise, employees want jobs that will sustain their interests over the long haul. Each of the three dimensions of motivation has direct implications for both organizations and individuals.

Work motivation depends on a constellation of factors, which can often become blurred. Chief among these factors are the following:

- *Behavior.* The overt actions from which motivation can be inferred. The behavior in question may be typing, preparing a meal, organizing a stockroom, communicating with customers, or engaging in an endless array of other work-related activities.
- *Performance.* Evaluation of behavior. The basic unit of observation is behavior, but it is coupled with an assessment of the behavior as judged against some standard. Thus, if the behavior is typing, a judgment can be made as to whether a person's typing speed and accuracy are adequate to hold a job. The level of performance that is adequate for one job may be inadequate for another job. Most organizational theories tend to be concerned with performance, not just behavior.
- *Ability.* One of three determinants of behavior and performance. It is generally regarded as fairly stable within an individual and may be represented by a broad construct such as intelligence or a more specific construct such as physical coordination.
- *Situational constraints.* The second determinant of behavior. These are environmental factors and opportunities that facilitate or undermine performance. Examples include tools, equipment, procedures, and the like, which may enhance or hinder performance.
- *Motivation.* The third determinant of behavior. You can think of ability as reflecting what you *can* do, motivation as what you *will* do (given your ability), and the situational constraints as what you are *allowed* to do.

Each of the three components is critical to the manifestation of behavior and performance. Maximum performance is observed when a person has high ability, exhibits high motivation, and is in a supportive environment. The judgment of "poor performance" could be attributed to four factors. First, the organization in which the behavior occurs may have high standards, which in another organization might result in a more positive evaluation of performance. Second, the individual may lack the ability required for the desired behavior. Third, the individual may lack the motivation to exhibit the desired behavior. Fourth, the individual may lack needed equipment or other crucial elements of support.

Motivation is one of the most complex concepts that I/O psychologists study. People can be motivated by different factors, and the same person can be motivated by different factors during different stages of his or her career. Most organizations believe it is critical to their success to have a highly motivated workforce.

Leadership

When you think of *leadership,* many ideas may come to mind. Your thoughts might relate to power, authority, or influence. Maybe you think of actual people, such as Abraham Lincoln, John F. Kennedy, or Martin Luther King. In short, leadership is a multidimensional concept.

I/O psychologists have tried to grapple with the multifaceted concept of leadership as it relates to behavior in the world of work. Investigators have approached the concept from various perspectives. Some research has examined what strong leaders are like as people by looking at demographic variables, personality traits, special skills, and so on. Without followers, there can be no leaders; accordingly, some research has examined leader-follower relationships. Presumably strong leaders accomplish things that weak leaders do not. Thus, other research has examined the effects of leadership. An interesting question concerns how contextual factors affect leadership—for example, is leadership of a prison more demanding than leadership of a business organization? Thus, the situation in which leadership occurs has attracted much attention. Other areas of interest within the domain of leadership research have also been investigated. While such diversity of interest expands our understanding, it also creates ambiguity as to exactly what leadership is all about. Table C.1 on the next page identifies research topics of interest to I/O psychologists in studying leadership.

Despite the diversity of approaches used in exploring leadership, Yukl (1994) noted that there is some convergence in the empirical findings. Yukl identified three consistent themes in leadership research. First, influence is the essence of leadership. Much of the activity of leaders involves attempts to influence the attitudes and behaviors of people, including subordinates, peers, and outsiders. Motivating behavior includes a variety of social influence techniques for developing commitment to organizational objectives and compliance with requests. Much of the influence behavior of charismatic leaders falls into the motivating category, including inspiring commitment to new objectives and strategies, modeling exemplary behavior for followers to imitate, and appealing to values and aspirations. Some of the traits and skills that predict leader effectiveness relate to the use of power. Leaders with high need for

Table C.1 Research Topics and Associated Issues in Leadership Research

Research Topic	Unit of Analysis	Variables of Interest	Research Questions
Positional power	Organizational roles and positions	Influence tactics; use of power	Under what conditions will organizations resort to strong influence attempts?
The leader	Individual leaders	Personality characteristics; leader behaviors	What traits and behaviors differentiate effective and ineffective leaders?
The led	Work groups and subordinates	Group size; experience of subordinates	What types of subordinates desire close supervision?
Influence process	Superior-subordinate interface	Receptivity to influence; nature of influence attempts	Under what conditions are leaders most susceptible to subordinate influence attempts?
The situation	Environment or context in which leadership occurs	Situational effects on leader behavior; factors defining favorable situations	How do various situations modify behavior?
Leader emergence versus effectiveness	Individual and/or groups	Group dynamics and individual characteristics	How do individuals become recognized as leaders?

SOURCE: Muchinsky, P. M. (2003). *Psychology applied to work*. Belmont, CA: Wadsworth. Reprinted by permission.

power and high self-confidence make more influence attempts. Self-confidence, persuasive ability, relevant expertise, and political insight facilitate the effectiveness of influence attempts. Interpersonal skills are necessary to articulate an appealing vision and persuade people of the need for change.

Second, effective leaders establish cooperative relationships characterized by high levels of mutual trust and loyalty. Research has shown that subordinates are usually more satisfied with a leader who is friendly and helpful, shows trust and respect, and demonstrates concern for their needs and feelings. Several of the traits and skills predictive of leadership effectiveness appear important for developing favorable relationships with subordinates, peers, and superiors. Relevant interpersonal talents include tact and diplomacy, listening skills, and social sensitivity. A leader with a positive regard for others is more likely to develop friendly relationships with people. Leaders who are preoccupied with personal ambition tend to do things that jeopardize relationships with people, such as betraying a trust or reneging on a promise.

Third, much of the activity of leaders involves decision making, but leaders seldom make important decisions at a single point in time, except for problem solving in immediate crises. In dealing with day-to-day decisions, effective leaders are guided by their long-term objectives and strategies. People who effectively solve problems or develop successful strategies gain in status and power as a result. The reputa-

tion for expertise gained from successful decisions made in the past gives a person greater influence over subsequent decisions. Several of the traits and skills predictive of leadership effectiveness are relevant for decision making. Leaders with extensive technical knowledge and cognitive skills are more likely to make high-quality decisions. These skills are important for analyzing problems, identifying causal patterns and trends, and forecasting likely outcomes of different strategies for attaining objectives. Self-confidence and tolerance for ambiguity and stress help leaders cope with the responsibility for making major decisions on the basis of incomplete information.

Putting It All Together: A Case Study

Let's take a look at a recent, very real, and extremely important problem to see how the diverse aspects of I/O psychology are relevant to the world of work. The problem involves how to improve the screening of airport passengers and their baggage. You will see how many of the topics discussed in this appendix are germane to this daunting problem.

The Problem: Improving Airport Screening

The terrorist attacks of September 11, 2001 focused attention on airport security personnel and their performance. These employees are entrusted with the responsibility of screening all passengers and their luggage in order to detect any objects that might be a security risk to the flight personnel or passengers. Such objects include guns and knives but also everyday objects that potentially could be used as a weapon, such as scissors or corkscrews. There are typically four jobs that contribute to the screening process—two devoted to passengers and two devoted to luggage. One person is responsible for ensuring that each passenger goes through the metal detector. If a passenger activates the metal detector, the passenger must step aside and be rescreened with a portable, hand-held metal detector, called a "wand." A second employee is in charge of conducting this screening. The usual items that activate the metal detector are jewelry, metal belt buckles, and metal supports in shoes. The second employee's job is to identify the reason the metal detector was activated and to ensure that the cause is benign.

The third employee is responsible for examining the contents of passengers' luggage via an X-ray machine. As hand-carried items pass through the X-ray machine on a conveyor belt, the third employee peers at a monitor. If the employee sees an object that looks suspicious, that piece of luggage is subject to a manual search of its contents. A fourth employee is in charge of this manual search and verifying that the contents of the luggage are harmless.

Of these four jobs, one in particular is the source of errors: visually examining the monitor of the X-ray machine. Luggage moves along the conveyor belt quickly, about 6 pieces per minute, 360 pieces per hour—almost 3,000 pieces in an 8-hour workday. The examiner has but a few seconds to visually inspect the contents of each bag. The overwhelming majority of passengers do not pack dangerous items in their luggage. Occasionally there will be a suspicious-looking object, but it usually turns out (on manual inspection) to be harmless. If a potentially dangerous object is spotted, it is confiscated by airport security personnel. Because passengers know that potentially dangerous objects will not be allowed on the airplane, the vast majority pack only items that are not potentially harmful to others. The consequence of this pattern of behavior is that the X-ray machine screener is looking for a rare object. With hundreds of pieces of luggage passing through the machine every hour, it is difficult for screeners to remain vigilant and focused. Their attention begins to wander after viewing so many pieces of luggage that look alike. Hence, it is not surprising that dangerous objects sometimes make it through the screening process. In some cases airport authorities have intentionally "planted" knives in luggage just to see whether they would be detected. Most are, but some are not. Given the enormous importance of this screening

The task of improving airport screening of passengers and their baggage illustrates how problems in the workplace are often multifaceted. As the text explains, a host of strategies may be relevant to this extremely complicated and important challenge.

© 2002 AP/Wide World Photos

task, even a small error rate of, for example, .01% (that is, one potentially dangerous object per 10,000 cases), is considered unacceptable. In other words, if 99.99% of all luggage is screened properly, the error rate (.01%) is still too high to meet desired safety standards! Thus, our question is: What types of solutions might an I/O psychologist propose to help improve the performance of airport security inspectors?

Possible Solutions

The topics discussed in this appendix are all potentially relevant to this problem. Let's begin with the process of recruitment. Perhaps if the airports attracted a higher quality of applicant pool from which to draw their employees, fewer errors would be made by the inspectors. If the wage level for airport security personnel were raised, perhaps more skilled individuals would be attracted to the jobs. Alternatively, it is possible the quality of the applicant pool is satisfactory, but what is needed are better personnel selection methods to identify the best candidates. Perhaps special types of visual acuity tests could be used, or tests that measure the capacity for sustained mental alertness. Perhaps the solution lies not so much with how the employees are chosen as how they are trained. It is possible that current training methods are insufficient or fail to capture the need for sustained vigilance over an 8-hour workday. Finally, little is known about the degree to which airports reward security officers for effective performance. Perhaps if supervisors appraised the job performance of their security officers and acknowledged their successes, their failures would decline. There are also legal issues to consider. Passengers of certain nationalities or races cannot indiscriminately be singled out for closer scrutiny without just cause. Engaging in such a practice would be an example of "racial profiling," which is frowned upon.

There is a rich organizational component to this problem that must also be considered before a solution becomes evident. The organizational culture of airport security operations tells us something about the nature of flying, passengers, and safety precautions. Many airports are now staffed with uniformed military personnel carrying exposed weapons. Passengers see these military figures and their weapons and realize they are entering a potentially dangerous environment. Although passengers accept the need for airport security, no one likes to be hassled and intimidated. Airport security personnel are "just doing their job," but what they do can produce stress for passengers. If passengers become sufficiently dissatisfied with the emotional experiences associated with flying, some of them will either stop flying altogether or fly far less frequently. A reduction in the number of passengers can (and has) led some airlines to lose so much money they have had to declare bankruptcy. While it is possible that different methods of recruitment, personnel selection, training, and performance appraisal may help alleviate the problem encountered in this situation, it is also true that staring into a monitor over a prolonged time period is boring. Perhaps what needs to be done is lessen the time period of visual inspection from eight hours to two hours. Since four jobs are involved in passenger and baggage screening, perhaps the four employees could be viewed as a team, and the team members could rotate assignments every two hours to break the tedium. Such a solution would presume that all four team members are equally suited to perform each of the four jobs. This approach attempts to solve the problem of boredom and fatigue by limiting the length of time an employee is exposed to the conditions that produce them.

The psychological contract between the airport and its security personnel must also be considered. The flying passengers, our society, and the government demand a "zero-tolerance" policy for errors in screening passengers and luggage. The consequence of making errors in airport security can be extremely tragic. However, there are few jobs where a 99.99% success rate is judged to be not good enough. The airport security personnel are under stress from two sources. One source is the need to remain highly vigilant and attentive in what is a repetitive and boring job. The second is that they know they are responsible for the safety and welfare of the flying public. The airport as an organization must walk a fine line between demanding very high standards of performance yet being sensitive to the conditions under which their security personnel operate. If such sensitivity and support are not shown, the security personnel would probably exhibit little loyalty to an employer that demands so much of its employees. The needed support for the security personnel can come in the form of encouraging motivation and leadership. Supervisors who are present at the security area (or nearby) can provide attention, encouragement, and recognition to the security personnel. The supervisors can serve to break the tedium of the security jobs by establishing their presence, asking questions, acknowledging the contributions of the security officers, and in general providing recognition for employees performing highly stressful work. Finally, all of these actions must be taken within yet a broader context, that of increasing security without unduly inconveniencing the flying public.

There is no reason to believe there is *one* correct solution to the problem facing airport security personnel. In reality an I/O psychologist would probably invoke many of the possible solutions to this case, not just one. It is also possible that a solution lies in more sophisticated X-ray technology that reduces the role of human judgment in assessing potential risk. Such equipment is currently being developed, but it is extremely expensive and thus unlikely to be used in all airports. While such technology may reduce the human element, it will never eliminate it.

Conclusion

I/O psychologists must be prepared to use the full complement of their skills to solve problems in the workplace that are increasing in complexity. I/O psychology is a most rewarding and useful field that endeavors to improve the quality of worklife. Students interested in learning more about this field are encouraged to read P. M. Muchinsky's *Psychology Applied to Work* (2003) and to visit the SIOP web site (www.siop.org) to learn about career opportunities.

Appendix D Evaluating the Quality of Web-Based Resources

By Vincent W. Hevern (Le Moyne College)

Toward the end of every semester in my abnormal psychology course, my students conduct a public policy forum about an important but controversial topic in psychology. To prepare for the forum, I give students a research assignment. They must gather information from various types of sources: scholarly articles in journals, professional books, popular magazines, and sites on the Internet ("the Net"). However, to complete the Net part of the assignment, students must hand in two types of information: Some material must come from a "good" or "excellent" website, while other material must be from a "terrible" or "poor" website. Further, students must also tell me *why* these sites are either excellent or poor. Students regularly tell me later on that they had never paid attention before to whether a web page might be "good" or "bad." Many students actually say they appreciate learning how to recognize the difference between sites of high versus low quality.

What students tell me supports the comments that I hear from many college professors: They wish students would realize that research done with Internet-based resources can be both dangerous and misleading unless students recognize the issue of quality. Further, as psychology teachers across the California State University system recently noted, an important educational goal for student learning is developing the competence to "locate appropriate sources by searching electronic and traditional databases and providing evidence of the search" (Allen et al., 2000, p. 4). The important phrase is "appropriate sources." Which resources online are appropriate, and which should you avoid? Students and all other researchers need to think carefully about the quality of data or reference sources found online. Your teachers will expect it, and in the emerging Information Economy, so will many employers.

Criteria for Quality on the Net

So, what are the standards or criteria by which you can judge the quality of a web page or resource? What can you actually *do* to increase the chances that the material you take from the Net is worth your effort? In recent years, information specialists have researched how people browsing the Internet can tell the difference. For example, University of Georgia Professor Gene Wilkinson and two doctoral students, Kevin Oliver and Lisa Bennett, conducted an inten-

sive study of 125 criteria by polling the webmasters of highly regarded online resource sites, while reference librarians Janet E. Alexander and Marsha Ann Tate at Widener University's Wolfgram Memorial Library consulted intensively with their colleagues across the world (Alexander & Tate, 1999). Although these and other specialists have gathered standards in slightly different ways, they are in substantial agreement about what characteristics are associated with quality on the Web. I've summarized their findings and my own experience in Figure D.1 on the next page, and I elaborate on each criterion in this appendix. Some of these standards relate to an entire website from which material may be drawn, while others relate to a specific document in which the researcher may be interested. Users of the Net must weigh both kinds of criteria. In simplest terms, the key to finding quality resources online will always be a researcher's *active exercise of judgment and critical thinking*.

Identity and Qualifications of the Authors

The Internet is a kind of worldwide democracy. Pretty much anyone can construct a web page and put online what they want to say. With so few restrictions on Net publishing, the range and quality of online resources is bound to vary, from invaluable to completely worthless. So, researchers who turn to the Net need to ask two related questions: *Who has written this material?* and *What are their qualifications for so doing?* The answers to these questions are probably the two most important guides to quality among online resources.

Sometimes you will find no clue to the identity of the author of a particular site or resource—no name, no organizational affiliation, nothing that reveals the authorship of the material. In such cases, you should be skeptical about relying on the information. It's hard to defend the quality of a work when "Anonymous" is the author. One exception may be some "first person" accounts dealing with sensitive personal issues such as sexuality, child abuse, and the like. Some authors understandably prefer to use pseudonyms to protect themselves. In such cases, researchers must look for other clues to quality.

Suppose one or more authors are listed by name. The next task is to discover the *qualifications* of these authors. Do they have some type of expertise to justify writing the online material or constructing the

Questions to Ask in Evaluating Materials on the Internet

1. **Identity and qualifications of the author(s)**
   - Who is the author of the material? Is the author identified or anonymous?
   - What is the author's academic or professional background and experience?
   - Is the author writing within or outside his/her area of expertise and skill?
   - If the material is the product of a group (a committee, governmental agency, or the like), what is that group's qualifications or expertise regarding this subject?
2. **Publisher or sponsor of the website**
   - Is the material self-published by the author or is there some recognized organization (university, medical center, government agency, nonprofit foundation, and so forth) that sponsors the website for the material?
   - Does the site's sponsor or publisher have a positive reputation?
3. **Balance, objectivity, and independence**
   - Does the material or website strive for balance and objectivity rather than use extreme, inflammatory, or highly subjective language or opinions?
   - Is more than one point of view evident at the site?
   - If the material takes a strong stand on one side of a controversial issue, does the author or site acknowledge there may be another side to the matter?
   - Is the website sponsored by any commercial or political organization that advocates for a particular point of view?
   - Does the author have any financial or commercial interest that might conflict with a fair or objective presentation of the topic?
   - Is the material drawn from a site that sells a product or solicits customers for a service?
4. **Quality of online presentation**
   - Is the site well organized or designed so that browsers can easily visit and retrieve information?
   - Does the site or online material show care in its preparation, such as proper spelling and good grammar in all posted materials?
   - Does the site work effectively, so that the links to subpages and external sites are accurate and helpful?
   - How recently has the site been updated? Does the site show evidence that someone regularly attends to it with corrections, new materials, and so forth?
5. **Other cues to quality**
   - Does the material contain clear and useful references to other scholarship from journals, professional books, and recognized research studies?
   - Have supporting references in the material been published in recent years, or do they include mostly out-of-date, or possibly obsolete sources?
   - Have any editors or external reviewers judged the quality of the material at the site?

Figure D.1

Evaluating online resources. The questions listed here, which draw heavily on the work of Alexander and Tate (1999), can help you to evaluate the quality and reliability of resource materials found on the internet.

site? You should look for a statement of an author's academic credentials (such as a Ph.D. or an M.D. degree) or appropriate work experience (such as "director of personnel" at a company or "senior researcher" at a laboratory). If the data appear on a personal home page, you can discover other evidence of expertise elsewhere at the site, such as a bibliography of past writings or a résumé that demonstrates the author's competence to write about the topic under review. You should also try to determine whether the author has published on a similar topic in reputable, peer-reviewed journals or belongs to professional or scholarly organizations concerned with the subject.

There are other cautions for researchers to keep in mind. Some authors may be qualified to comment on one topic but go beyond their area of expertise into other domains of knowledge. For example, a physician may comment on economics or a biologist may pontificate on educational methods. Researchers need to be cautious about writers who move too far away from their fields of specialization. Another consideration is whether authors may also have a financial stake or commercial interest in the issue that might compromise their objectivity.

Finally, suppose the "author" of a web-based publication is a corporation or an organization, such as a professional association, a government agency, or a nonprofit organization. How should qualifications be weighed in such cases? Certainly the overall reputation of the corporate author should be recognized. For example, a consensus statement on a treatment approach produced by the National Institute of Mental Health or a report on the employment characteristics of psychologists issued by the American Psychological Association would probably be an excellent reference source. Most such reports include a list of individual contributors or committee members who worked to produce the material released under the name of an organization. It is important to inquire whether these persons may also have the credentials or professional status to render their work trustworthy. Alternatively, you might look for a broad corporate board of editors or advisers associated with an institutional voice on the Net. Beware of fancy-sounding "Institutes" or "Commissions" or "Associations" that may in fact be the product of a single person or a handful of individuals and serve only to artificially embellish the opinions of their creators.

Publisher or Sponsor of the Website

Book authors traditionally use print publishers to promote and distribute their writings. In turn, publishers place their reputations on the line by issuing new books. Discerning readers rely on a publisher's overall standing when they consider whether to acquire new works. Especially in academic publishing, readers know that an editorial and review process usually precedes publication, in an effort to ensure a high level of quality for the published material. Indeed, the essence of academic scholarship lies in a willingness to submit scholarly work to the early critiques of knowledgeable colleagues. Occasionally, though, an author circumvents the editorial and peer review process and pays to have his or her book published. This practice, called "vanity publishing," is usually looked down on by other scholars.

In a practice reminiscent of vanity publishing, many web authors post materials online directly through commercial or free Internet service providers. Because these writings have not been edited or evaluated prior to their publication, you must be cautious in judging their quality. This is not to disparage all self-published resources on the web. Clearly, there are valuable resources that experts have labored to bring to cyberspace. But, in the absence of a clear process of scholarly peer review, you must look for other indicators of quality. For this reason, the overall qualifications of an author as an expert may be crucial in determining whether to use a resource.

Sites sponsored by academic institutions, government agencies, and nonprofit or scholarly organizations have URLs that end with the designation *.edu, .gov,* or *.org* rather than *.com* or *.net.* Such sites would be expected to offer some assurance of higher quality for data posted there. A particular clue to quality at corporate sites may be a copyright notice by a sponsoring organization rather than a single individual. Often located at the bottom of a web page, this notice may signal that the organization is willing to put its reputation behind the resource. For example, online health information centers range in quality from the dismal to the superb. At one excellent site, *Alice! Columbia University's Health Education Program* (see Web Link 10.3), it is significant to find the notice on its title page "Copyright © 2000 by The Trustees of Columbia University."

Balance, Objectivity, and Independence

At the checkout line in a supermarket, shoppers often face a set of tabloid newspapers with outrageous headlines and the promise of lurid stories inside. Many people pick up a copy of their favorite tabloid as entertainment, something to be read purely for relaxation and enjoyment but not as an objective or reliable source of information or reporting about the world. Although tabloid papers are an extreme example, other sources of information should arouse similar suspicions because of their subjective, unbalanced, and biased style of presentation. Certainly, the presence of language, graphic images, or opinions that are extreme, inflammatory, or highly subjective on a website suggests that the material should be treated with some skepticism. The more extreme, vulgar, or intemperate the manner of presentation, the less likely that the resource is reliable and trustworthy.

A more difficult case arises from material found on sites clearly advocating a particular point of view, such as those for a lobbying group, political movement, or professional advocacy or commercial trade

association. Researchers should expect that resources available at these sites will support the point of view of the group. This fact does not necessarily disqualify the importance of materials found there. The sponsoring organization may provide valuable information for visitors to their sites. Greater reliance can probably be given to resources found on a site that acknowledges there is more than one side to a controversial issue. Some sites even offer links to the opposing side of a disputed topic. This openness should inspire confidence by users because it suggests fairness.

A challenge to researchers of psychological topics comes from commercial sites that stand to make money or gain new customers on the basis of what they post online. These sites may be businesses (with a *.com* Net address) or may be allied with the professional office or practice of individuals such as psychotherapists or physicians. Sometimes these sites offer a "Resource Center" or similar area filled with articles relating to the product or service of the site's sponsor. These articles may include scientific-sounding titles, and many come from magazines, journals, or books that seem to be similarly professional. Most evaluators warn researchers to be careful when using materials from any site that has a direct financial motivation in sharing information. A close examination of the actual reference sources cited in online articles may give a clue as to how much credence a researcher should put in them. For example, are the references only for the author's own works, or do they include reputable journal articles written by a range of other scholars? Finding quality in online materials is always a judgment call, and the more you know about a topic from other sources, the better you can make that call at commercial sites.

Quality of Online Presentation

Another important index of quality is the care with which sites and materials have been organized and maintained. You should consider how easily you can use a site. Do the hypertext links within the site work, or do they point to empty or missing pages? Can browsers easily find the information they are looking for? Is there evidence that the design of the site was carefully considered and executed? Similarly, the actual text of materials retrieved from the Net should be free from any gross errors. Poor grammar and improper spelling usually indicate that something is amiss. Frankly, reputable scholars are fanatical about eliminating sloppiness or careless mistakes in what they write. They believe any such errors would suggest a parallel sloppiness in their thinking. Thus, the presence of mechanical and stylistic mistakes at a website or in a document should raise doubts about how reputable the actual content of the resource may be. Finally, more credibility can be assigned to materials retrieved from sites that are frequently updated and carefully corrected. You should look for clear dates on pages containing important information. Ideally, one date will indicate when the page was first posted online and another when it was last changed or revised.

Other Cues to Quality

When I use the Net for research purposes, I use at least three further cues to evaluate the quality of the material or sites I find. First, in articles or papers online, I look at the references used by the author and consider whether they include scholarly materials from journals, professional books, or other recognized research sources. Second, I examine the dates of the supporting references. How recent are they? Do they include sources published in the last several years? Or do they include only older and possibly out-of-date materials? Finally, I look for evidence that the site itself has been recognized by an outside reviewer as possessing significant quality. For example, evaluation sites such as the Argus Clearinghouse (http://www.clearinghouse.net) provide an estimate of the overall quality of Internet subject guides. If a site is listed with high ratings, I am more likely to value the materials posted there. You should be alert to any designation by a website that it has received a favorable review by such an evaluation source.

A Final Note of Advice

I hope the suggestions summarized here make it clear that any researcher must actively exercise judgment and critical thinking skills in evaluating online resources. Such skills are enormously enhanced when the researcher chooses a balanced overall research strategy. It is one thing to seek a quick fact or a simple definition through a website; it is another to rely on the Internet as the sole data source for a major paper or research project. Yes, for many people, the Net is an easily "surfable" medium, one that can quickly lead to information of varying levels of quality. The very ease of conducting research online often seduces student researchers to skip more difficult, but crucially important steps offline.

The most important strategy a student can bring to any research project is to develop an overall per-spective, or a broad vantage point, regarding the topic of the project. And that means using sources of different types—scholarly books, journal and magazine articles, and printed research reports—*in addition to* materials retrieved from the Internet. It is both easy to understand, but embarrassing in the long run, when a student hands in a paper with only Internet-based sources and later discovers, in a professor's grading, that the Net provided a biased or slanted view of the topic. Without the counterbalance of non-Net sources, a student risks seriously misjudging how psychologists, medical researchers, and other scientists actually approach an issue. So, my final suggestion about research is a simple rule of thumb: The longer and more important the research project or paper, the broader the kinds of references you must use to answer the research question.

For Further Reference and Reading

To further explore the question of identifying quality in online materials and sites, consider the outstanding text by Janet Alexander and Marsha Tate: *Web Wisdom: How to Evaluate and Create Information Quality on the Web* (Mahwah, NJ: Erlbaum, 1999). An earlier but helpful version of this resource is posted online:

Evaluating web resources homepage *[Online document]. Chester, PA: Widener University, Wolfgram Memorial Library. Available on the World Wide Web at <http://www2.widener.edu/Wolfgram-Memorial-Library/webevaluation/webeval.htm>.*

Two other excellent web-based resources on this topic are:

Engle, M. (1999). Evaluating web wites: Criteria and tools *[online document]. Ithaca, NY: Cornell University, Olin-Kroch-Uris Libraries, Reference Division. Available on the World Wide Web at <http://www.library.cornell.edu/okuref/research/webeval.html>.*

Grassian, E. (1999). Thinking critically about world wide web resources *[online document]. Los Angeles, CA: UCLA College Library Instruction. Available on the World Wide Web at <http://www.library.ucla.edu/college/help/critical/index.htm>.*

The recommended Web Links sprinkled throughout the chapters in this text are intended to spark your interest in further exploration of psychological issues on the World Wide Web. We chose to not include the addresses (URLs) in the annotated Web Links because the Web is a fluid, dynamic medium in which change is the only constant. Many of the URLs for suggested sites will change before this book makes it off the printing press.

If you are interested in accessing some of the recommended websites, we suggest that you do so through the *Psychology: Themes & Variations* home page (http://psychology.wadsworth.com/weiten_theme6e/). Links to all of the recommended sites are maintained there, and the Wadsworth webmaster periodically updates the URLs.

Nonetheless, recognizing that you may want to go directly to a specific site or give a suggested URL to a friend, we have compiled a list of the current URLs for all the recommended sites. They are organized by chapter and are listed in the order of their appearance in the book.

Website	Web Address (URL)
Chapter 1: The Evolution of Psychology	
1.1 HistPsyc: History of Psychology Headlines Index	http://www.unb.ca/psychology/likely/headlines/
1.2 Mind and Body: René Descartes to William James	http://serendip.brynmawr.edu/Mind/Table.html
1.3 History and Philosophy of Psychology Web Resources	http://www.psych.yorku.ca/orgs/resource.htm
1.4 Museum of the History of Psychological Instrumentation	http://www.chss.montclair.edu/psychology/museum/museum.html
1.5 American Psychological Association	http://www.apa.org/
1.6 Marky Lloyd's Career Page	http://www.psywww.com/careers/index.htm
1.7 A Student's Guide to Careers in the Helping Professions	http://www.lemoyne.edu/OTRP/otrpresources/helping-online.html
1.8 Approaches to Psychology	http://www.ryerson.ca/~glassman/approach.html
1.9 Encyclopedia of Psychology	http://www.psychology.org/
Chapter 2: The Research Enterprise in Psychology	
2.1 PubMed	http://www.ncbi.nlm.nih.gov/PubMed/
2.2 PsycINFO Direct	http://www.apa.org/psycinfo/
2.3 Psychological Research on the Net	http://psych.hanover.edu/APS/exponnet.html
2.4 PSYCLine: Your Guide to Psychology and Social Science Journals on the Web	http://www.psycline.org/journals/psycline.html
2.5 HyperStat Online	http://davidmlane.com/hyperstat/index.html
2.6 The Troubling Legacy of the Tuskegee Syphilis Study	http://www.med.virginia.edu/hs-library/historical/apology/index.html
2.7 Animal Welfare Information Center	http://www.nal.usda.gov/awic/
2.8 Office of Research Integrity	http://ori.dhhs.gov/index.htm
Chapter 3: The Biological Bases of Behavior	
3.1 Neuropsychology Central	http://www.neuropsychologycentral.com/index.html
3.2 Molecular Neurobiology: A Gallery of Animations	http://www.neuroguide.com/cajal_gallery.html
3.3 Neurosciences on the Internet	http://www.neuroguide.com/
3.4 The Visible Human Project	http://www.nlm.nih.gov/research/visible/visible_human.html
3.5 The Whole Brain Atlas	http://www.med.harvard.edu/AANLIB/home.html
3.6 The Society for Neuroscience	http://web.sfn.org/Template.cfm?Section=PublicResources
3.7 Human Behavior and Evolution Society	http://www.hbes.com/

Website	Web Address (URL)
Chapter 4: Sensation and Perception	
4.1 Vision Science: An Internet Resource for Research	http://www.visionscience.com/in Human and Animal Vision
4.2 The Joy of Visual Perception: A Web Book	http://www.yorku.ca/eye/thejoy.htm
4.3 Sensation and Perception Tutorials	http://psych.hanover.edu/Krantz/sen_tut.html
4.4 IllusionWorks	http://psylux.psych.tudresden.de/i1/kaw/diverses%20Material/ www.illusionworks.com/index.html
4.5 The Moon Illusion Explained	http://facstaff.uww.edu/mccreadd/index.html
4.6 American Speech-Language-Hearing Association	http://www.asha.org/index.cfm
4.7 The Cochlea: Graphic Tour of the Inner Ear's Machinery	http://www.bp.sissa.it/cochlea/the Inner Ear's Machinery
4.8 Seeing, Hearing, and Smelling the World	http://www.hhmi.org/senses/
Chapter 5: Variations in Consciousness	
5.1 NSF Center for Biological Timing	http://www.cbt.virginia.edu/
5.2 The Sleep Well	http://www.stanford.edu/~dement/
5.3 National Sleep Foundation	http://www.sleepfoundation.org/
5.4 Sleep Medicine Homepage	http://www.users.cloud9.net/~thorpy/
5.5 States of Consciousness	http://www.psywww.com/asc/asc.html
5.6 Web of Addictions	http://www.well.com/user/woa/
5.7 National Institute on Alcohol Abuse and Alcoholism	http://www.niaaa.nih.gov/
Chapter 6: Learning Through Conditioning	
6.1 Behaviour Analysis and Learning	http://psych.athabascau.ca/html/aupr/ba.shtml
6.2 The B. F. Skinner Foundation	http://www.lafayette.edu/allanr/skinner.html
6.3 Cambridge Center for Behavioral Studies	http://www.behavior.org/
6.4 Animal Behavior and Welfare Sites	http://www.erols.com/mandtj/
6.5 *Journal of the Experimental Analysis of Behavior* and *Journal of Applied Behavioral Analysis*	http://www.envmed.rochester.edu/wwwrap/behavior/jeabjaba.htm
Chapter 7: Human Memory	
7.1 The Magic Number Seven Plus or Minus Two	http://www.well.com/user/smalin/miller.html
7.2 Memory Principles	http://www.mtsu.edu/~studskl/mem.html
7.3 Mind Tools—Tools for Improving Your Memory	http://www.mindtools.com/memory.html
7.4 False Memory Syndrome Foundation (FMSF) Online	http://www.fmsfonline.org/
7.5 False Memory Syndrome Facts	http://www.fmsf.org/
7.6 Alzheimer Page	http://www.biostat.wustl.edu/alzheimer/
Chapter 8: Language and Thought	
8.1 John Lawler's Homepage (Linguistics and Language)	http://www-personal.umich.edu/~jlawler/index.html
8.2 Critical Thinking Consortium	http://www.criticalthinking.org/
8.3 Online Decision Research Center Experiments	http://psych.fullerton.edu/mbirnbaum/exp.htm
8.4 Has Natural Selection Shaped How Humans Reason?	http://online.itp.ucsb.edu/online/colloq/cosmides1/
8.5 Simple Minds—Smart Choices	http://www.sciencenews.org/sn_arc99/5_29_99/bob2.htm

Website	Web Address (URL)
Chapter 9: Intelligence and Psychological Testing	
9.1 ERIC/AE Test Locator	http://ericae.net/testcol.htm
9.2 ERIC Clearinghouse on Assessment and Evaluation	http://ericae.net/
9.3 Finding Information About Psychological Tests	http://www.apa.org/science/faq-findtests.html
9.4 History of the Influences in the Development of Intelligence Theory & Testing	http://www.indiana.edu/~intell/index.html
9.5 Educational Psychology Interactive: Intelligence	http://chiron.valdosta.edu/whuitt/col/cogsys/intell.html
9.6 The ARC	http://www.thearc.org/
9.7 Upstream Issues: The Bell Curve	http://www.mugu.com/cgi-bin/Upstream/Issues/bell-curve/index.html

Website	Web Address (URL)
Chapter 10: Motivation and Emotion	
10.1 American Obesity Association	http://www.obesity.org/
10.2 The Evolutionary Psychology FAQ	http://www.anth.ucsb.edu/projects/human/evpsychfaq.html
10.3 Go Ask Alice!	http://www.alice.columbia.edu/
10.4 Queer Resources Directory (QRD)	http://www.qrd.org/QRD/
10.5 UCSC Perceptual Science Laboratory	http://mambo.ucsc.edu/

Website	Web Address (URL)
Chapter 11: Human Development Across the Life Span	
11.1 PBS: The Whole Child	http://www.pbs.org/wholechild/
11.2 Early Childhood Care and Development	http://www.ecdgroup.com/
11.3 Child Development Abstracts and Bibliography (CDAB) Online Edition	http://WWW.SRCD.ORG/cdab/default.shtml
11.4 Erik Erikson Tutorial Homepage	http://snycorva.cortland.edu/~ANDERSMD/ERIK/WELCOME.HTML
11.5 Adolescence Directory OnLine	http://education.indiana.edu/cas/adol/adol.html
11.6 Adolescent Health and Mental Health	http://www.fenichel.com/adolhealth.shtml
11.7 National Parent Information Network (NPIN)	http://npin.org/
11.8 Adult Development and Aging (APA Division 20)	http://www.iog.wayne.edu/apadiv20/apadiv20.htm
11.9 USDHHS: Administration on Aging	http://www.aoa.gov/

Website	Web Address (URL)
Chapter 12: Personality: Theory, Research, and Assessment	
12.1 The Victorian Web	http://www.stg.brown.edu/projects/hypertext/landow/victorian/victov.html
12.2 Sigmund Freud Museum, Vienna, Austria	http://freud.to.or.at/
12.3 C. G. Jung, Analytical Psychology, and Culture	http://www.cgjungpage.org/
12.4 Television and Violence—Media and Communications Studies Site	http://www.aber.ac.uk/~dgc/tv07.html
12.5 The Personality Project	http://pmc.psych.nwu.edu/personality.html
12.6 Great Ideas in Personality	http://www.personalityresearch.org/

Website	Web Address (URL)

Chapter 13: Stress, Coping, and Health

13.1 The Web's Stress Management and Emotional Wellness Page	http://imt.net/~randolfi/StressPage.html
13.2 Stress Management	http://tc.unl.edu/stress/
13.3 National Center for PTSD	http://www.dartmouth.edu/dms/ptsd/Index.html
13.4 Disaster Psychiatry	http://www.psych.org/pract_of_psych/disaster_psych.cfm
13.5 David Baldwin's Trauma Information Pages	http://www.trauma-pages.com/
13.6 healthfinder®	http://www.healthfinder.gov/
13.7 Exercise and Sport Psychology	http://www.psyc.unt.edu/apadiv47/

Chapter 14: Psychological Disorders

14.1 Mental Health Net	http://mentalhelp.net/
14.2 National Alliance for the Mentally Ill (NAMI)	http://www.nami.org/
14.3 Mental Health: A Report of the Surgeon General	http://www.surgeongeneral.gov/library/mentalhealth/index.html
14.4 National Institute of Mental Health: For the Public	http://www.nimh.nih.gov/publicat/index.cfm
14.5 Dr. Ivan's Depression Central	http://www.psycom.net/depression.central.html
14.6 Doctor's Guide to the Internet: Schizophrenia	http://www.pslgroup.com/SCHIZOPHR.HTM
14.7 David Willshire's Forensic Psychology and Psychiatry Links	http://members.optushome.com.au/dwillsh/index.html

Chapter 15: Treatment of Psychological Disorders

15.1 How to Find Help with Life's Problems	http://helping.apa.org/brochure/index.html
15.2 Online Dictionary of Mental Health	http://www.shef.ac.uk/~psysc/psychotherapy/index.html
15.3 The Albert Ellis Institute	http://www.rebt.org/
15.4 The Effectiveness of Psychotherapy: The *Consumer Reports* Study	http://www.apa.org/journals/seligman.html
15.5 Psych Central	http://psychcentral.com/grohol.htm
15.6 Dr. Bob's Psychopharmacology Tips	http://uhs.bsd.uchicago.edu/~bhsiung/tips/tips.html

Chapter 16: Social Behavior

16.1 Social Psychology Network	http://www.socialpsychology.org/
16.2 Social Cognition Paper Archive and Information Center	http://www.psych.purdue.edu/~esmith/scarch.html
16.3 Y? The National Forum on People's Differences	http://www.yforum.com/index.html
16.4 Social Influence and Persuasion	http://psychology.about.com/msub_soinflu.htm
16.5 The Psychology of Cyberspace	http://www.rider.edu/users/suler/psycyber/psycyber.html
16.6 Group Dynamics	http://www.has.vcu.edu/group/gdynamic.htm

Glossary

A

Absolute refractory period The minimum length of time after an action potential during which another action potential cannot begin.

Absolute threshold The minimum amount of stimulation that an organism can detect for a specific type of sensory input.

Accommodation Changing existing mental structures to explain new experiences.

Acculturation The degree to which a person is socially and psychologically integrated into a new culture.

Achievement motive The need to master difficult challenges, to outperform others, and to meet high standards of excellence.

Achievement tests Tests that gauge a person's mastery and knowledge of various subjects.

Acquired immune deficiency syndrome (AIDS) A disorder in which the immune system is gradually weakened and eventually disabled by the human immunodeficiency virus (HIV).

Acquisition The formation of a new conditioned response tendency.

Action potential A brief change in a neuron's electrical charge.

Adaptation An inherited characteristic that increased in a population (through natural selection) because it helped solve a problem of survival or reproduction during the time it emerged.

Additive color mixing Formation of colors by superimposing lights, putting more light in the mixture than exists in any one light by itself.

Adoption studies Research studies that assess hereditary influence by examining the resemblance between adopted children and both their biological and their adoptive parents.

Afferent nerve fibers Axons that carry information inward to the central nervous system from the periphery of the body.

Affiliation motive The need to associate with others and maintain social bonds.

Afterimage A visual image that persists after a stimulus is removed.

Age of viability The age at which a baby can survive in the event of a premature birth.

Aggression Any behavior that is intended to hurt someone, either physically or verbally.

Agonist A chemical that mimics the action of a neurotransmitter.

Agoraphobia A fear of going out to public places.

Alcohol A variety of beverages containing ethyl alcohol.

Algorithm A methodical, step-by-step procedure for trying all possible alternatives in searching for a solution to a problem.

Alternative outcomes effect Phenomenon that occurs when people's belief about whether an outcome will occur changes depending on how alternative outcomes are distributed, even though the assumed probability of the alternative outcomes is held constant.

Amnesia A significant memory loss that is too extensive to be due to normal forgetting. See also *Anterograde amnesia, Retrograde amnesia*.

Androgens The principal class of gonadal hormones in males.

Anecdotal evidence Personal stories about specific incidents and experiences.

Animism The belief that all things are living.

Anorexia nervosa Eating disorder characterized by intense fear of gaining weight, disturbed body image, refusal to maintain normal weight, and dangerous measures to lose weight.

Antagonist A chemical that opposes the action of a neurotransmitter.

Antecedents In behavior modification, events that typically precede the target response.

Anterograde amnesia Loss of memories for events that occur after a head injury.

Antianxiety drugs Medications that relieve tension, apprehension, and nervousness.

Antidepressant drugs Medications that gradually elevate mood and help bring people out of a depression.

Antipsychotic drugs Medications used to gradually reduce psychotic symptoms, including hyperactivity, mental confusion, hallucinations, and delusions.

Antisocial personality disorder A type of personality disorder marked by impulsive, callous, manipulative, aggressive, and irresponsible behavior that reflects a failure to accept social norms.

Anxiety disorders A class of disorders marked by feelings of excessive apprehension and anxiety.

Applied psychology The branch of psychology concerned with everyday, practical problems.

Approach-approach conflict A conflict situation in which a choice must be made between two attractive goals.

Approach-avoidance conflict A conflict situation in which a choice must be made about whether to pursue a single goal that has both attractive and unattractive aspects.

Aptitude tests Psychological tests used to assess talent for specific types of mental ability.

Archetypes According to Jung, emotionally charged images and thought forms that have universal meaning.

Argument One or more premises used to provide support for a conclusion.

Ascending reticular activating system (ARAS) The afferent fibers running through the reticular formation that influence physiological arousal.

Assimilation Interpreting new experiences in terms of existing menal structures without changing them.

Assumptions Premises for which no proof or evidence is offered.

Attachment A close, emotional bond of affection between infants and their caregivers.

Attention Focusing awareness on a narrowed range of stimuli or events.

Attitudes Orientations that locate objects of thought on dimensions of judgment.

Attributions Inferences that people draw about the causes of events, others' behavior, and their own behavior.

Auditory localization Locating the source of a sound in space.

Autonomic nervous system (ANS) The system of nerves that connect to the heart, blood vessels, smooth muscles, and glands.

Availability heuristic Basing the estimated probability of an event on the ease with which relevant instances come to mind.

Aversion therapy A behavior therapy in which an aversive stimulus is paired with a stimulus that elicits an undesirable response.

Avoidance-avoidance conflict A conflict situation in which a choice must be made between two unattractive goals.

Avoidance learning Learning that has occurred when an organism engages in a response that prevents aversive stimulation from occurring.

Axon A long, thin fiber that transmits signals away from the neuron cell body to other neurons, or to muscles or glands.

B

Basilar membrane A structure that runs the length of the cochlea in the inner ear and holds the auditory receptors, called hair cells.

Behavior Any overt (observable) response or activity by an organism.

Behavior modification A systematic approach to changing behavior through the application of the principles of conditioning.

Behavior therapies Application of the principles of learning to direct efforts to change clients' maladaptive behaviors.

Behavioral contract A written agreement outlining a promise to adhere to the contingencies of a behavior modification program.

Behavioral genetics An interdisciplinary field that studies the influence of genetic factors on behavioral traits.

Behaviorism A theoretical orientation based on the premise that scientific psychology should study only observable behavior.

Belief perseverance The tendency to hang onto beliefs in the face of contradictory evidence.

Bilingualism The acquisition of two languages that use different speech sounds, vocabularies, and grammatical rules.

Binocular depth cues Clues about distance based on the differing views of the two eyes.

Biological rhythms Periodic fluctuations in physiological functioning.

Biomedical therapies Physiological interventions intended to reduce symptoms associated with psychological disorders.

Biopsychosocial model A model of illness that holds that physical illness is caused by a complex interaction of biological, psychological, and sociocultural factors.

Bipolar disorder (formerly known as manic-depressive disorder) Mood disorder marked by the experience of both depressed and manic periods.

Bisexuals Persons who seek emotional-sexual relationships with members of either sex.

Body mass index (BMI) Weight (in kilograms) divided by height (in meters) squared (kg/m^2).

Bottom-up processing In form perception, progression from individual elements to the whole.

Bulimia nervosa Eating disorder characterized by habitually engaging in out-of-control overeating followed by unhealthy compensatory efforts, such as self-induced vomiting, fasting, abuse of laxatives and diuretics, and excessive exercise.

Burnout Physical, mental, and emotional exhaustion that is attributable to work-related stress.

Bystander effect A paradoxical social phenomenon in which people are less likely to provide needed help when they are in groups than when they are alone.

C

Cannabis The hemp plant from which marijuana, hashish, and THC are derived.

Case study An in-depth investigation of an individual subject.

Catastrophic thinking Unrealistically pessimistic appraisals of stress that exaggerate the magnitude of one's problems.

Catatonic schizophrenia A type of schizophrenia marked by striking motor disturbances, ranging from muscular rigidity to random motor activity.

Catharsis The release of emotional tension.

Central nervous system (CNS) The brain and the spinal cord.

Centration The tendency to focus on just one feature of a problem, neglecting other important aspects.

Cephalocaudal trend The head-to-foot direction of motor development.

Cerebral cortex The convoluted outer layer of the cerebrum.

Cerebral hemispheres The right and left halves of the cerebrum.

Cerebrospinal fluid (CSF) A solution that fills the hollow cavities (ventricles) of the brain and circulates around the brain and spinal cord.

Channel The medium through which a message is sent.

Chromosomes Threadlike strands of DNA (deoxyribonucleic acid) molecules that carry genetic information.

Chunk A group of familiar stimuli stored as a single unit.

Circadian rhythms The 24-hour biological cycles found in humans and many other species.

Classical conditioning A type of learning in which a neutral stimulus acquires the ability to evoke a response that was originally evoked by another stimulus.

Client-centered therapy An insight therapy that emphasizes providing a supportive emotional climate for clients, who play a major role in determining the pace and direction of their therapy.

Clinical psychologists Psychologists who specialize in the diagnosis and treatment of psychological disorders and everyday behavioral problems.

Clinical psychology The branch of psychology concerned with the diagnosis and treatment of psychological problems and disorders.

Clustering The tendency to remember similar or related items in groups.

Cochlea The fluid-filled, coiled tunnel in the inner ear that contains the receptors for hearing.

Coefficient of determination The percentage of variation in one variable that can be predicted based on the other variable.

Cognition The mental processes involved in acquiring knowledge.

Cognitive development Transitions in youngsters' patterns of thinking, including reasoning, remembering, and problem solving.

Cognitive dissonance A psychological state that exists when related cognitions are inconsistent.

Cognitive therapy An insight therapy that emphasizes recognizing and changing negative thoughts and maladaptive beliefs.

Collective unconscious According to Jung, a storehouse of latent memory traces inherited from people's ancestral past.

Collectivism Putting group goals ahead of personal goals and defining one's identity in terms of the groups one belongs to.

Color blindness Deficiency in the ability to distinguish among colors.

Commitment An intent to maintain a relationship in spite of the difficulties and costs that may arise.

Comorbidity The coexistence of two or more disorders.

Companionate love Warm, trusting, tolerant affection for another whose life is deeply intertwined with one's own.

Comparitors People, objects, events, and other standards that are used as a baseline for comparisons in making judgments.

Compensation According to Adler, efforts to overcome imagined or real inferiorities by developing one's abilities.

Complementary colors Pairs of colors that produce gray tones when added together.

Conceptual hierarchy A multilevel classification system based on common properties among items.

Concordance rate The percentage of twin pairs or other pairs of relatives that exhibit the same disorder.

Concurrent schedules of reinforcement Two or more reinforcement schedules that operate simultaneously and independently, each for a different response.

Conditioned reinforcers. See *Secondary reinforcers.*

Conditioned response (CR) A learned reaction to a conditioned stimulus that occurs because of previous conditioning.

Conditioned stimulus (CS) A previously neutral stimulus that has, through conditioning, acquired the capacity to evoke a conditioned response.

Cones Specialized visual receptors that play a key role in daylight vision and color vision.

Confirmation bias The tendency to seek information that supports one's decisions and beliefs while ignoring disconfirming information.

Conflict A state that occurs when two or more incompatible motivations or behavioral impulses compete for expression.

Conformity The tendency for people to yield to real or imagined social pressure.

Confounding of variables A condition that exists whenever two variables are linked together in a way that makes it difficult to sort out their independent effects.

Conjunction fallacy An error that occurs when people estimate that the odds of two uncertain events happening together are greater than the odds of either event happening alone.

Connectionist models. See *parallel distributed processing (PDP) models.*

Conscious Whatever one is aware of at a particular point in time.

Conservation Piaget's term for the awareness that physical quantities remain constant in spite of changes in their shape or appearance.

Consolidation A hypothetical process involving the gradual conversion of information into durable memory codes stored in long-term memory.

Construct validity The extent to which there is evidence that a test measures a particular hypothetical construct.

Constructive coping Relatively healthful efforts that people make to deal with stressful events.

Content validity The degree to which the content of a test is representative of the domain it's supposed to cover.

Continuous reinforcement Reinforcing every instance of a designated response.

Control group Subjects in a study who do not receive the special treatment given to the experimental group.

Convergence A cue to depth that involves sensing the eyes converging toward each other as they focus on closer objects.

Convergent thinking Narrowing down a list of alternatives to converge on a single correct answer.

Conversion disorder A somatoform disorder characterized by a significant loss of physical function (with no apparent organic basis), usually in a single organ system.

Coping Active efforts to master, reduce, or tolerate the demands created by stress.

Corpus callosum The structure that connects the two cerebral hemispheres.

Correlation The extent to which two variables are related to each other.

Correlation coefficient A numerical index of the degree of relationship between two variables.

Counseling psychologists Psychologists who specialize in the treatment of everyday adjustment problems.

Creativity The generation of ideas that are original, novel, and useful.

Criterion-related validity Test validity that is estimated by correlating subjects' scores on a test with their scores on an independent criterion (another measure) of the trait assessed by the test.

Critical period A limited time span in the development of an organism when it is optimal for certain capacities to emerge because the organism is especially responsive to certain experiences.

Critical thinking The use of cognitive skills and strategies that increase the probability of a desired outcome.

Cross-sectional design A research design in which investigators compare groups of subjects of differing age who are observed at a single point in time.

Crystallized intelligence One's ability to apply acquired skills and knowledge in problem solving.

Culture The widely shared customs, beliefs, values, norms, institutions, and other products of a community that are transmitted socially across generations.

Culture-bound disorders Abnormal syndromes found only in a few cultural groups.

Cumulative recorder A graphic record of reinforcement and responding in a Skinner box as a function of time.

Cyclothymic disorder Exhibiting chronic but relatively mild symptoms of bipolar disturbance.

D

Dark adaptation The process in which the eyes become more sensitive to light in low illumination.

Data collection techniques Procedures for making empirical observations and measurements.

Decay theory The idea that forgetting occurs because memory traces fade with time.

Decision making The process of evaluating alternatives and making choices among them.

Declarative memory system Memory for factual information.

Defense mechanisms Largely unconscious reactions that protect a person from unpleasant emotions such as anxiety and guilt.

Defensive attribution The tendency to blame victims for their misfortune, so that one feels less likely to be victimized in a similar way.

Deinstitutionalization Transferring the treatment of mental illness from inpatient institutions to community-based facilities that emphasize outpatient care.

Delusions False beliefs that are maintained even though they are clearly out of touch with reality.

Dementia An abnormal condition marked by multiple cognitive defects that include memory impairment.

Dendrites Branchlike parts of a neuron that are specialized to receive information.

Dependent variable In an experiment, the variable that is thought to be affected by the manipulation of the independent variable.

Depth perception Interpretation of visual cues that indicate how near or far away objects are.

Descriptive statistics Statistics that are used to organize and summarize data.

Development The sequence of age-related changes that occur as a person progresses from conception to death.

Developmental norms The average age at which individuals display various behaviors and abilities.

Deviation IQ scores Scores that locate subjects precisely within the normal distribution, using the standard deviation as the unit of measurement.

Diagnosis Distinguishing one illness from another.

Discrimination Behaving differently, usually unfairly, toward the members of a group.

Discriminative stimuli Cues that influence operant behavior by indicating the probable consequences (reinforcement or nonreinforcement) of a response.

Dishabituation An increase in the strength of a habituated response elicited by a new stimulus.

Disorganized schizophrenia A type of schizophrenia in which particularly severe deterioration of adaptive behavior is seen.

Displacement Diverting emotional feelings (usually anger) from their original source to a substitute target.

Display rules Cultural norms that regulate the appropriate expressions of emotions.

Dissociation A splitting off of mental processes into two separate, simultaneous streams of awareness.

Dissociative amnesia A sudden loss of memory for important personal information that is too extensive to be due to normal forgetting.

Dissociative disorders A class of disorders in which people lose contact with portions of their consciousness or memory, resulting in disruptions in their sense of identity.

Dissociative fugue A disorder in which people lose their memory for their entire lives along with their sense of personal identity.

Dissociative identity disorder (DID) A type of dissociative disorder characterized by the coexistence in one person of two or more largely complete, and usually very different, personalities. Also called multiple-personality disorder.

Distal stimuli Stimuli that lie in the distance (that is, in the world outside the body).

Divergent thinking Trying to expand the range of alternatives by generating many possible solutions.

Dominant gene A gene that is expressed when paired genes are heterozygous (different).

Door-in-the-face technique Making a large request that is likely to be turned down as a way to increase the chances that people will agree to a smaller request later.

Double-blind procedure A research strategy in which neither subjects nor experimenters know which subjects are in the experimental or control groups.

Dream analysis A psychoanalytic technique in which the therapist interprets the symbolic meaning of the client's dreams.

Drive An internal state of tension that motivates an organism to engage in activities that should reduce the tension.

Dual-coding theory Paivio's theory that memory is enhanced by forming semantic and visual codes, since either can lead to recall.

Dysthymic disorder A chronic depression that is insufficient in severity to merit diagnosis of a major depressive episode.

E

Eating disorders Severe disturbances in eating behavior characterized by preoccupation with weight concerns and unhealthy efforts to control weight.

Eclecticism In psychotherapy, drawing ideas from two or more systems of therapy instead of committing to just one system.

Efferent nerve fibers Axons that carry information outward from the central nervous system to the periphery of the body.

Ego According to Freud, the decision-making component of personality that operates according to the reality principle.

Egocentrism A limited ability to share another person's viewpoint.

Elaboration Linking a stimulus to other information at the time of encoding.

Electrical stimulation of the brain (ESB) Sending a weak electric current into a brain structure to stimulate (activate) it.

Electroconvulsive therapy (ECT) A biomedical treatment in which electric shock is used to produce a cortical seizure accompanied by convulsions.

Electroencephalograph (EEG) A device that monitors the electrical activity of the brain over time by means of recording electrodes attached to the surface of the scalp.

Electromyograph (EMG) A device that records muscular activity and tension.

Electrooculograph (EOG) A device that records eye movements.

Elicit To draw out or bring forth.

Embryonic stage The second stage of prenatal development, lasting from two weeks until the end of the second month.

Emit To send forth.

Emotion A subjective conscious experience (the cognitive component) accompanied by bodily arousal (the physiological component) and by characteristic overt expressions (the behavioral component).

Emotional intelligence The ability to perceive and express emotion, assimilate emotion in thought, understand and reason with emotion, and regulate emotion.

Empiricism The premise that knowledge should be acquired through observation.

Encoding Forming a memory code.

Encoding specificity principle The idea that the value of a retrieval cue depends on how well it corresponds to the memory code.

Endocrine system A group of glands that secrete chemicals into the bloodstream that help control bodily functioning.

Endorphins The entire family of internally produced chemicals that resemble opiates in structure and effects.

Epidemiology The study of the distribution of mental or physical disorders in a population.

Episodic memory system Chronological, or temporally dated, recollections of personal experiences.

Escape learning A type of learning in which an organism acquires a response that decreases or ends some aversive stimulation.

Estrogens The principal class of gonadal hormones in females.

Ethnocentrism The tendency to view one's own group as superior to others and as the standard for judging the worth of foreign ways.

Etiology The apparent causation and developmental history of an illness.

Evolutionary psychology Theoretical perspective that examines behavioral processes in terms of their adaptive value for a species over the course of many generations.

Excitatory PSP An electric potential that increases the likelihood that a postsynaptic neuron will fire action potentials.

Experiment A research method in which the investigator manipulates a variable under carefully controlled conditions and observes whether any changes occur in a second variable as a result.

Experimental group The subjects in a study who receive some special treatment in regard to the independent variable.

Experimenter bias A phenomenon that occurs when a researcher's expectations or preferences about the outcome of a study influence the results obtained.

Explicit memory Intentional recollection of previous experiences.

External attributions Ascribing the causes of behavior to situational demands and environmental constraints.

Extinction The gradual weakening and disappearance of a conditioned response tendency.

Extraneous variables Any variables other than the independent variable that seem likely to influence the dependent variable in a specific study.

Extraverts People who tend to be interested in the external world of people and things.

F

Factor analysis Statistical analysis of correlations among many variables to identify closely related clusters of variables.

Family life cycle A sequence of stages that families tend to progress through.

Family studies Scientific studies in which researchers assess hereditary influence by examining blood relatives to see how much they resemble each other on a specific trait.

Farsightedness A vision deficiency in which distant objects are seen clearly but close objects appear blurry.

Fast mapping The process by which children map a word onto an underlying concept after only one exposure to the word.

Feature analysis The process of detecting specific elements in visual input and assembling them into a more complex form.

Feature detectors Neurons that respond selectively to very specific features of more complex stimuli.

Fechner's law A psychophysical law stating that larger and larger increases in stimulus intensity are required to produce perceptible increments in the magnitude of sensation.

Fetal alcohol syndrome A collection of congenital (inborn) problems associated with excessive alcohol use during pregnancy.

Fetal stage The third stage of prenatal development, lasting from two months through birth.

Field dependence-independence Individuals' tendency to rely primarily on external versus internal frames of reference when orienting themselves in space.

Fight-or-flight response A physiological reaction to threat in which the autonomic nervous system mobilizes the organism for attacking (fight) or fleeing (flight) an enemy.

Fitness The reproductive success (number of descendants) of an individual organism relative to the average reproductive success of the population.

Fixation According to Freud, failure to move forward from one psychosexual stage to another as expected.

Fixed-interval (FI) schedule A reinforcement schedule in which the reinforcer is given for the first response that occurs after a fixed time interval has elapsed.

Fixed-ratio (FR) schedule A reinforcement schedule in which the reinforcer is given after a fixed number of nonreinforced responses.

Flashbulb memories Unusually vivid and detailed recollections of momentous events.

Fluid intelligence One's reasoning ability, memory capacity, and speed of information processing.

Foot-in-the-door technique Getting people to agree to a small request to increase the chances that they will agree to a larger request later.

Forebrain The largest and most complicated region of the brain, encompassing a variety of structures, including the thalamus, hypothalamus, limbic system, and cerebrum.

Forgetting curve A graph showing retention and forgetting over time.

Fovea A tiny spot in the center of the retina that contains only cones; visual acuity is greatest at this spot.

Framing How issues are posed or how choices are structured.

Fraternal twins Twins that result when two eggs are fertilized simultaneously by different sperm cells, forming two separate zygotes. Also called *Dizygotic twins*.

Free association A psychoanalytic technique in which clients spontaneously express their thoughts and feelings exactly as they occur, with as little censorship as possible.

Frequency distribution An orderly arrangement of scores indicating the frequency of each score or group of scores.

Frequency polygon A line figure used to present data from a frequency distribution.

Frequency theory The theory that perception of pitch corresponds to the rate, or frequency, at which the entire basilar membrane vibrates.

Frustration The feeling that people experience in any situation in which their pursuit of some goal is thwarted.

Functional fixedness The tendency to perceive an item only in terms of its most common use.

Functionalism A school of psychology based on the belief that psychology should investigate the function or purpose of consciousness, rather than its structure.

Fundamental attribution error Observers' bias in favor of internal attributions in explaining others' behavior.

G

Galvanic skin response (GSR) An increase in the electrical conductivity of the skin that occurs when sweat glands increase their activity.

Gambler's fallacy The belief that the odds of a chance event increase if the event hasn't occurred recently.

Gate-control theory The idea that incoming pain sensations must pass through a "gate" in the spinal cord that can be closed, thus blocking pain signals.

Gender Culturally constructed distinctions between masculinity and femininity.

Gender differences Actual disparities between the sexes in typical behavior or average ability.

Gender roles Expectations about what is appropriate behavior for each sex.

Gender stereotypes Widely held beliefs about males' and females' abilities, personality traits, and behavior.

General adaptation syndrome Selye's model of the body's stress response, consisting of three stages: alarm, resistance, and exhaustion.

Generalized anxiety disorder A psychological disorder marked by a chronic, high level of anxiety that is not tied to any specific threat.

Genes DNA segments that serve as the key functional units in hereditary transmission.

Genetic mapping The process of determining the location and chemical sequence of specific genes on specific chromosomes.

Genotype A person's genetic makeup.

Germinal stage The first phase of prenatal development, encompassing the first two weeks after conception.

Gestalt psychology A theoretical orientation based on the idea that the whole is greater than the sum of its parts.

Glucose A simple sugar that is an important source of energy.

Glucostats Neurons sensitive to glucose in the surrounding fluid.

Group Two or more individuals who interact and are interdependent.

Group cohesiveness The strength of the liking relationships linking group members to each other and to the group itself.

Group polarization A phenomenon that occurs when group discussion strengthens a group's dominant point of view and produces a shift toward a more extreme decision in that direction.

Group therapy The simultaneous treatment of several clients in a group.

Groupthink A process in which members of a cohesive group emphasize concurrence at the expense of critical thinking in arriving at a decision.

Gustatory system The sensory system for taste.

H

Habituation A gradual reduction in the strength of a response when a stimulus event is presented repeatedly.

Hallucinations Sensory perceptions that occur in the absence of a real, external stimulus, or gross distortions of perceptual input.

Hallucinogens A diverse group of drugs that have powerful effects on mental and emotional functioning, marked most prominently by distortions in sensory and perceptual experience.

Health psychology The subfield of psychology concerned with how psychosocial factors relate to the promotion and maintenance of health and with the causation, prevention, and treatment of illness.

Hedonic adaptation An effect that occurs when the mental scale that people use to judge the pleasantness-unpleasantness of their experiences shifts so that their neutral point, or baseline for comparison, changes.

Heritability ratio An estimate of the proportion of trait variability in a population that is determined by variations in genetic inheritance.

Heterosexuals Persons who seek emotional-sexual relationships with members of the other sex.

Heterozygous condition The situation that occurs when two genes in a specific pair are different.

Heuristic A strategy, guiding principle, or rule of thumb used in solving problems or making decisions.

Hierarchy of needs Maslow's systematic arrangement of needs according to priority, which assumes that basic needs must be met before less basic needs are aroused.

Higher-order conditioning A type of conditioning in which a conditioned stimulus functions as if it were an unconditioned stimulus.

Hindbrain The part of the brain that includes the cerebellum and two structures found in the lower part of the brainstem: the medulla and the pons.

Hindsight bias The tendency to mold one's interpretation of the past to fit how events actually turned out.

Histogram A bar graph that presents data from a frequency distribution.

Homeostatsis A state of physiological equilibrium or stability.

Homosexuals Persons who seek emotional-sexual relationships with members of the same sex.

Homozygous condition The situation that occurs when two genes in a specific pair are the same.

Hormones The chemical substances released by the endocrine glands.

Humanism A theoretical orientation that emphasizes the unique qualities of humans, especially their freedom and their potential for personal growth.

Hypnosis A systematic procedure that typically produces a heightened state of suggestibility.

Hypochondriasis A somatoform disorder characterized by excessive preoccupation with health concerns and incessant worry about developing physical illnesses.

Hypothalamus A structure found near the base of the forebrain that is involved in the regulation of basic biological needs.

Hypothesis A tentative statement about the relationship between two or more variables.

I

Id According to Freud, the primitive, instinctive component of personality that operates according to the pleasure principle.

Identical twins Twins that emerge from one zygote that splits for unknown reasons. Also called *Monozygotic twins.*

Identification Bolstering self-esteem by forming an imaginary or real alliance with some person or group.

Illusory correlation A misperception that occurs when people estimate that they have encountered more confirmations of an association between social traits than they have actually seen.

Immune response The body's defensive reaction to invasion by bacteria, viral agents, or other foreign substances.

Implicit memory Type of memory apparent when retention is exhibited on a task that does not require intentional remembering.

Impossible figures Objects that can be represented in two-dimensional pictures but cannot exist in three-dimensional space.

Incentive An external goal that has the capacity to motivate behavior.

Inclusive fitness The sum of an individual's own reproductive success plus the effects the organism has on the reproductive success of related others.

Incongruence The degree of disparity between one's self-concept and one's actual experience.

Independent variable In an experiment, a condition or event that an experimenter varies in order to see its impact on another variable.

Individualism Putting personal goals ahead of group goals and defining one's identity in terms of personal attributes rather than group memberships.

Industrial and organizational (I/O) psychology The branch of psychology concerned with the application of psychological principles to the workplace.

Inferential statistics Statistics that are used to interpret data and draw conclusions.

Ingroup The group that people belong to and identify with.

Inhibitory PSP An electric potential that decreases the likelihood that a postsynaptic neuron will fire action potentials.

Insanity A legal status indicating that a person cannot be held responsible for his or her actions because of mental illness.

Insight In problem solving, the sudden discovery of the correct solution following incorrect attempts based primarily on trial and error.

Insight therapies Psychotherapy methods characterized by verbal interactions intended to enhance clients' self-knowledge and thus promote healthful changes in personality and behavior.

Insomnia Chronic problems in getting adequate sleep.

Instinctive drift The tendency for an animal's innate responses to interfere with conditioning processes.

Instrumental learning. See *Operant conditioning.*

Intelligence quotient (IQ) A child's mental age divided by chronological age, multiplied by 100.

Intelligence tests Psychological tests that measure general mental ability.

Interference theory The idea that people forget information because of competition from other material.

Intermittent reinforcement A reinforcement schedule in which a designated response is reinforced only some of the time.

Internal attributions Ascribing the causes of behavior to personal dispositions, traits, abilities, and feelings.

Internet addiction Spending an inordinate amount of time on the Internet and being unable to control online use.

Interpersonal attraction Positive feelings toward another.

Interpretation In psychoanalysis, the therapist's attempts to explain the inner significance of the client's thoughts, feelings, memories, and behaviors.

Intimacy Warmth, closeness, and sharing in a relationship.

Introspection Careful, systematic observation of one's own conscious experience.

Introverts People who tend to be preoccupied with the internal world of their own thoughts, feelings, and experiences.

Involuntary commitment A civil proceeding in which people are hospitalized in psychiatric facilities against their will.

Irreversibility The inability to envision reversing an action.

J

Journal A periodical that publishes technical and scholarly material, usually in a narrowly defined area of inquiry.

Just noticeable difference (JND) The smallest difference in the amount of stimulation that a specific sense can detect.

K

Keyword method A mnemonic technique in which one associates a concrete word with an abstract word and generates an image to represent the concrete word.

Kinesthetic system The sensory system that monitors the positions of the various parts of one's body.

L

Language A set of symbols that convey meaning, and rules for combining those symbols, that can be used to generate an infinite variety of messages.

Language acquisition device (LAD) An innate mechanism or process that facilitates the learning of language.

Latent content According to Freud, the hidden or disguised meaning of the events in a dream.

Lateral antagonism A process in the retina that occurs when neural activity in a cell opposes activity in surrounding cells.

Law of effect The principle that if a response in the presence of a stimulus leads to satisfying effects, the association between the stimulus and the response is strengthened.

Learned helplessness Passive behavior produced by exposure to unavoidable aversive events.

Learning A relatively durable change in behavior or knowledge that is due to experience.

Lens The transparent eye structure that focuses the light rays falling on the retina.

Lesioning Destroying a piece of the brain.

Levels-of-processing theory The theory holding that deeper levels of mental processing result in longer-lasting memory codes.

Lie detector. See *Polygraph.*

Life changes Any noticeable alterations in one's living circumstances that require readjustment.

Light adaptation The process whereby the eyes become less sensitive to light in high illumination.

Limbic system A densely connected network of structures roughly located along the border between the cerebral cortex and deeper subcortical areas.

Linguistic relativity The theory that one's language determines the nature of one's thought.

Link method Forming a mental image of items to be remembered in a way that links them together.

Lithium A chemical used to control mood swings in patients with bipolar mood disorders.

Long-term memory (LTM) An unlimited capacity store that can hold information over lengthy periods of time.

Long-term potentiation (LTP) A long-lasting increase in neural excitability in synapses along a specific neural pathway.

Longitudinal design A research design in which investigators observe one group of subjects repeatedly over a period of time.

Lowball technique Getting someone to commit to an attractive proposition before revealing the hidden costs.

Lucid dreams Dreams in which people can think clearly about the circumstances of waking life and the fact that they are dreaming, yet they remain asleep in the midst of a vivid dream.

M

Major depressive disorder Mood disorder characterized by persistent feelings of sadness and despair and a loss of interest in previous sources of pleasure.

Manifest content According to Freud, the plot of a dream at a surface level.

Matching hypothesis The idea that males and females of approximately equal physical attractiveness are likely to select each other as partners.

Matching law The fact that, under concurrent schedules of reinforcement, organisms' relative rate of responding to each alternative tends to match each alternative's relative rate of reinforcement.

Maturation Development that reflects the gradual unfolding of one's genetic blueprint.

MDMA A compound drug related to both amphetamines and hallucinogens, especially mescaline; commonly called "ecstasy."

Mean The arithmetic average of the scores in a distribution.

Mean length of utterance (MLU) The average length of children's spoken statements (measured in phonemes).

Median The score that falls exactly in the center of a distribution of scores.

Medical model The view that it is useful to think of abnormal behavior as a disease.

Meditation A family of mental exercises in which a conscious attempt is made to focus attention in a nonanalytical way.

Menarche The first occurrence of menstruation.

Mental age In intelligence testing, a score that indicates that a child displays the mental ability typical of a child of that chronological (actual) age.

Mental hospital A medical institution specializing in providing inpatient care for psychological disorders.

Mental retardation Subnormal general mental ability accompanied by deficiencies in everyday living skills originating prior to age 18.

Mental set Persisting in using problem-solving strategies that have worked in the past.

Message The information transmitted by a source.

Meta-analysis Combining the statistical results of many studies of the same question, yielding an estimate of the size and consistency of a variable's effects.

Metalinguistic awareness The ability to reflect on the use of language.

Method of loci A mnemonic device that involves taking an imaginary walk along a familiar path where images of items to be remembered are associated with certain locations.

Midbrain The segment of the brain stem that lies between the hindbrain and the forebrain.

Midlife crisis A difficult, turbulent period of doubts and reappraisal of one's life.

Mnemonic devices Strategies for enhancing memory.

Mode The score that occurs most frequently in a distribution.

Model A person whose behavior is observed by another.

Monocular depth cues Clues about distance based on the image from either eye alone.

Monogamy A mating system in which one male and one female mate exclusively, or almost exclusively, with each other.

Mood disorders A class of disorders marked by emotional disturbances of varied kinds that may spill over to disrupt physical, perceptual, social, and thought processes.

Morphemes The smallest units of meaning in a language.

Motion parallax Cue to depth that involves images of objects at different distances moving across the retina at different rates.

Motivated forgetting Purposeful suppression of memories.

Motivation Goal-directed behavior.

Motor development The progression of muscular coordination required for physical activities.

Multiple-personality disorder See *Dissociative identity disorder.*

Mutation A spontaneous, heritable change in a piece of DNA that occurs in the individual organism.

Myelin sheath Insulating material, derived from glial cells, that encases some axons of neurons.

N

Narcolepsy A disease marked by sudden and irresistible onsets of sleep during normal waking periods.

Narcotics (opiates) Drugs derived from opium that are capable of relieving pain.

Natural selection Principle stating that heritable characteristics that provide a survival reproductive advantage are more likely than alternative characteristics to be passed on to subsequent generations and thus come to be "selected" over time.

Naturalistic observation A descriptive research method in which the researcher engages in careful, usually prolonged, observation of behavior without intervening directly with the subjects.

Nearsightedness A vision deficiency in which close objects are seen clearly but distant objects appear blurry.

Need for self-actualization The need to fulfill one's potential.

Negative reinforcement The strengthening of a response because it is followed by the removal of an aversive (unpleasant) stimulus.

Negative symptoms Schizophrenic symptoms that involve behavioral deficits, such as flattened emotions, social withdrawal, apathy, impaired attention, and poverty of speech.

Negatively skewed distribution A distribution in which most scores pile up at the high end of the scale.

Nerves Bundles of neuron fibers (axons) that are routed together in the peripheral nervous system.

Neurons Individual cells in the nervous system that receive, integrate, and transmit information.

Neurotransmitters Chemicals that transmit information from one neuron to another.

Night terrors Abrupt awakenings from NREM sleep accompanied by intense autonomic arousal and feelings of panic.

Nightmares Anxiety-arousing dreams that lead to awakening, usually from REM sleep.

Non-REM (NREM) sleep Sleep stages 1 through 4, which are marked by an absence of rapid eye movements, relatively little dreaming, and varied EEG activity.

Nondeclarative memory system Memory for actions, skills, and operations.

Normal distribution A symmetric, bell-shaped curve that represents the pattern in which many characteristics are dispersed in the population.

Null hypothesis In inferential statistics, the assumption that there is no true relationship between the variables being observed.

O

Obedience A form of compliance that occurs when people follow direct commands, usually from someone in a position of authority.

Obesity The condition of being overweight.

Object permanence Recognizing that objects continue to exist even when they are no longer visible.

Observational learning A type of learning that occurs when an organism's responding is influenced by the observation of others, who are called models.

Obsessive-compulsive disorder (OCD) A type of anxiety disorder marked by persistent, uncontrollable intrusions of unwanted thoughts (obsessions) and urges to engage in senseless rituals (compulsions).

Oedipal complex According to Freud, children's manifestation of erotically tinged desires for their opposite-sex parent, accompanied by feelings of hostility toward their same-sex parent.

Olfactory system The sensory system for smell.

Operant chamber. See *Skinner box.*

Operant conditioning A form of learning in which voluntary responses come to be controlled by their consequences.

Operational definition A definition that describes the actions or operations that will be made to measure or control a variable.

Opiates. See *Narcotics.*

Opponent process theory The theory that color perception depends on receptors that make antagonistic responses to three pairs of colors.

Optic chiasm The point at which the optic nerves from the inside half of each eye cross over and then project to the opposite half of the brain.

Optic disk A hole in the retina where the optic nerve fibers exit the eye.

Optical illusion An apparently inexplicable discrepancy between the appearance of a visual stimulus and its physical reality.

Optimal foraging theory The idea that the food-seeking behaviors of many animals maximize the nutrition gained in relation to the energy expended to locate, secure, and consume various foods.

Optimism A general tendency to expect good outcomes.

Orgasm The release of sexual tension that occurs when arousal reaches its peak intensity and is discharged in a series of muscular contractions that pulsate through the pelvic area.

Outgroup People who are not part of the ingroup.

Overextensions Using a word incorrectly to describe a wider set of objects or actions than it is meant to.

Overlearning Continued rehearsal of material after one first appears to have mastered it.

Overregularization In children, incorrect generalization of grammatical rules to irregular cases where they do not apply.

P

Panic disorder A type of anxiety disorder characterized by recurrent attacks of overwhelming anxiety that usually occur suddenly and unexpectedly.

Parallel distributed processing (PDP) models Models of memory that assume cognitive processes depend on patterns of activation in highly interconnected computational networks that resemble neural networks. Also called *connectionist models*.

Parallel processing Simultaneously extracting different kinds of information from the same input.

Paranoid schizophrenia A type of schizophrenia that is dominated by delusions of persecution along with delusions of grandeur.

Parasympathetic division The branch of the autonomic nervous system that generally conserves bodily resources.

Parental investment What each sex invests—in terms of time, energy, survival risk, and forgone opportunities—to produce and nurture offspring.

Partial reinforcement. See *Intermittent reinforcement*.

Participants See *Subjects*.

Passionate love A complete absorption in another that includes tender sexual feelings and the agony and ecstasy of intense emotion.

Pavlovian conditioning. See *Classical conditioning*.

Percentile score A figure that indicates the percentage of people who score below the score one has obtained.

Perception The selection, organization, and interpretation of sensory input.

Perceptual asymmetries Left-right imbalances between the cerebral hemispheres in the speed of visual or auditory processing.

Perceptual constancy A tendency to experience a stable perception in the face of continually changing sensory input.

Perceptual hypothesis An inference about which distal stimuli could be responsible for the proximal stimuli sensed.

Perceptual set A readiness to perceive a stimulus in a particular way.

Peripheral nervous system All those nerves that lie outside the brain and spinal cord.

Person perception The process of forming impressions of others.

Personal unconscious According to Jung, the level of awareness that houses material that is not within one's conscious awareness because it has been repressed or forgotten.

Personality An individual's unique constellation of consistent behavioral traits.

Personality disorders A class of psychological disorders marked by extreme, inflexible personality traits that cause subjective distress or impaired social and occupational functioning.

Personality tests Psychological tests that measure various aspects of personality, including motives, interests, values, and attitudes.

Personality trait A durable disposition to behave in a particular way in a variety of situations.

Phenomenological approach The assumption that one must appreciate individuals' personal, subjective experiences to truly understand their behavior.

Phenotype The ways in which a person's genotype is manifested in observable characteristics.

Phi phenomenon The illusion of movement created by presenting visual stimuli in rapid succession.

Phobias Irrational fears of specific objects or situations.

Phobic disorder A type of anxiety disorder marked by a persistent and irrational fear of an object or situation that presents no realistic danger.

Phonemes The smallest units of sound in a spoken language.

Physical dependence The condition that exists when a person must continue to take a drug to avoid withdrawal illness.

Pictorial depth cues Clues about distance that can be given in a flat picture.

Pituitary gland The "master gland" of the endocrine system; it releases a great variety of hormones that fan out through the body, stimulating actions in the other endocrine glands.

Place theory The idea that perception of pitch corresponds to the vibration of different portions, or places, along the basilar membrane.

Placebo effects The fact that subjects' expectations can lead them to experience some change even though they receive an empty, fake, or ineffectual treatment.

Placenta A structure that allows oxygen and nutrients to pass into the fetus from the mother's bloodstream and bodily wastes to pass out to the mother.

Pleasure principle According to Freud, the principle upon which the id operates, demanding immediate gratification of its urges.

Polyandry A mating system in which each female seeks to mate with multiple males, while each male mates with only one female.

Polygenic traits Characteristics that are influenced by more than one pair of genes.

Polygraph A device that records autonomic fluctuations while a subject is questioned, in an effort to determine whether the subject is telling the truth.

Polygyny A mating system in which each male seeks to mate with multiple females, while each female mates with only one male.

Population The larger collection of animals or people from which a sample is drawn and that researchers want to generalize about.

Positive reinforcement Reinforcement that occurs when a response is strengthened because it is followed by the presentation of a rewarding stimulus.

Positive symptoms Schizophrenic symptoms that involve behavioral excesses or peculiarities, such as hallucinations, delusions, bizarre behavior, and wild flights of ideas.

Positively skewed distribution A distribution in which scores pile up at the low end of the scale.

Postsynaptic potential (PSP) A voltage change at the receptor site on a postsynaptic cell membrane.

Posttraumatic stress disorder Disturbed behavior that is attributed to a major stressful event but that emerges after the stress is over.

Preconscious According to Freud, the level of awareness that contains material just beneath the surface of conscious awareness that can easily be retrieved.

Prejudice A negative attitude held toward members of a group.

Premises The reasons presented to persuade someone that a conclusion is true or probably true.

Prenatal period The period from conception to birth, usually encompassing nine months of pregnancy.

Preparedness A species-specific predisposition to be conditioned in certain ways and not others.

Pressure Expectations or demands that one behave in a certain way.

Prevalence The percentage of a population that exhibits a disorder during a specified time period.

Primary reinforcers Events that are inherently reinforcing because they satisfy biological needs.

Primary sex characteristics The sexual structures necessary for reproduction.

Proactive interference A memory problem that occurs when previously learned information interferes with the retention of new information.

Problem solving Active efforts to discover what must be done to achieve a goal that is not readily available.

Problem space The set of possible pathways to a solution considered by the problem solver.

Procedural memory system The repository of memories for actions, skills, and operations.

Prognosis A forecast about the probable course of an illness.

Projection Attributing one's own thoughts, feelings, or motives to another.

Projective tests Psychological tests that ask subjects to respond to vague, ambiguous stimuli in ways that may reveal the subjects' needs, feelings, and personality traits.

Prospective memory The ability to remember to perform actions in the future.

Proximal stimuli The stimulus energies that impinge directly on sensory receptors.

Proximodistal trend The center-outward direction of motor development.

Psychiatrists Physicians who specialize in the diagnosis and treatment of psychological disorders.

Psychiatry A branch of medicine concerned with the diagnosis and treatment of psychological problems and disorders.

Psychoactive drugs Chemical substances that modify mental, emotional, or behavioral functioning.

Psychoanalysis An insight therapy that emphasizes the recovery of unconscious conflicts, motives, and defenses through techniques such as free association and transference.

Psychoanalytic theory A theory developed by Freud that attempts to explain personality, motivation, and mental disorders by focusing on unconscious determinants of behavior.

Psychodynamic theories All the diverse theories descended from the work of Sigmund Freud that focus on unconscious mental forces.

Psychological dependence The condition that exists when a person must continue to take a drug in order to satisfy intense mental and emotional craving for the drug.

Psychological test A standardized measure of a sample of a person's behavior.

Psychology The science that studies behavior and the physiological and cognitive processes that underlie it, and the profession that applies the accumulated knowledge of this science to practical problems.

Psychopharmacotherapy The treatment of mental disorders with medication.

Psychophysics The study of how physical stimuli are translated into psychological experience.

Psychosexual stages According to Freud, developmental periods with a characteristic sexual focus that leave their mark on adult personality.

Psychosomatic diseases Physical ailments with a genuine organic basis that are caused in part by psychological factors, especially emotional distress.

Puberty The period of early adolescence marked by rapid physical growth and the development of sexual (reproductive) maturity.

Pubescence The two-year span preceding puberty during which the changes leading to physical and sexual maturity take place.

Punishment An event that follows a response that weakens or suppresses the tendency to make that response.

Pupil The opening in the center of the iris that helps regulate the amount of light passing into the rear chamber of the eye.

R

Random assignment The constitution of groups in a study such that all subjects have an equal chance of being assigned to any group or condition.

Rational-emotive therapy An approach to therapy that focuses on altering clients' patterns of irrational thinking to reduce maladaptive emotions and behavior.

Rationalization Creating false but plausible excuses to justify unacceptable behavior.

Reaction formation Behaving in a way that's exactly the opposite of one's true feelings.

Reaction range Genetically determined limits on IQ or other traits.

Reality monitoring The process of deciding whether memories are based on external sources (our perceptions of actual events) or internal sources (our thoughts and imaginations).

Reality principle According to Freud, the principle on which the ego operates, which seeks to delay gratification of the id's urges until appropriate outlets and situations can be found.

Recall A memory test that requires subjects to reproduce information on their own without any cues.

Receiver The person to whom a message is sent.

Receptive field of a visual cell The retinal area that, when stimulated, affects the firing of that cell.

Recessive gene A gene whose influence is masked when paired genes are different (heterozygous).

Reciprocal determinism The assumption that internal mental events, external environmental events, and overt behavior all influence each other.

Reciprocity Liking those who show that they like you.

Reciprocity norm The rule that people should pay back in kind what they receive from others.

Recognition A memory test that requires subjects to select previously learned information from an array of options.

Refractory period A time following orgasm during which males are largely unresponsive to further stimulation.

Regression A reversion to immature patterns of behavior.

Regression toward the mean Effect that occurs when people who score extremely high or low on some trait are measured a second time and their new score falls closer to the mean (average).

Rehearsal The process of repetitively verbalizing or thinking about information to be stored in memory.

Reification Giving an abstract concept a name and then treating it as though it were a concrete, tangible object.

Reinforcement An event following a response that strengthens the tendency to make that response.

Reinforcement contingencies The circumstances or rules that determine whether responses lead to the presentation of reinforcers.

Relearning A memory test that requires a subject to memorize information a second time to determine how much time or effort is saved by having learned it before.

Reliability The measurement consistency of a test (or of other kinds of measurement techniques).

REM sleep A deep stage of sleep marked by rapid eye movements, high-frequency brain waves, and dreaming.

Replication The repetition of a study to see whether the earlier results are duplicated.

Representativeness heuristic Basing the estimated probability of an event on how similar it is to the typical prototype of that event.

Repression Keeping distressing thoughts and feelings buried in the unconscious.

Research methods Differing approaches to the manipulation and control of variables in empirical studies.

Resistance Largely unconscious defensive maneuvers a client uses to hinder the progress of therapy.

Resistance to extinction In operant conditioning, the phenomenon that occurs when an organism continues to make a response after delivery of the reinforcer for it has been terminated.

Response set A tendency to respond to questions in a particular way that is unrelated to the content of the questions.

Respondent conditioning. See *Classical conditioning.*

Resting potential The stable, negative charge of a neuron when it is inactive.

Retention The proportion of material retained (remembered).

Retina The neural tissue lining the inside back surface of the eye; it absorbs light, processes images, and sends visual information to the brain.

Retinal disparity A cue to the depth based on the fact that objects within 25 feet project images to slightly different locations on the left and right retinas, so the right and left eyes see slightly different views of the object.

Retrieval Recovering information from memory stores.

Retroactive interference A memory problem that occurs when new information impairs the retention of previously learned information.

Retrograde amnesia Loss of memories for events that occurred prior to a head injury.

Retrospective memory The ability to remember events from the past or previously learned information.

Reuptake A process in which neurotransmitters are sponged up from the synaptic cleft by the presynaptic membrane.

Reversible figure A drawing that is compatible with two different interpretations that can shift back and forth.

Risky decision making Making choices under conditions of uncertainty.

Rods Specialized visual receptors that play a key role in night vision and peripheral vision.

S

Sample The collection of subjects selected for observation in an empirical study.

Sampling bias A problem that occurs when a sample is not representative of the population from which it is drawn.

Scatter diagram A graph in which paired X and Y scores for each subject are plotted as single points.

Schedule of reinforcement A specific presentation of reinforcers over time.

Schema An organized cluster of knowledge about a particular object or sequence of events.

Schizophrenic disorders A class of psychological disorders marked by disturbances in thought that spill over to affect perceptual, social, and emotional processes.

Script A type of schema that organizes what people know about common activities.

Secondary (conditioned) reinforcers Stimulus events that acquire reinforcing qualities by being associated with primary reinforcers.

Secondary sex characteristics Physical features that are associated with gender but that are not directly involved in reproduction.

Sedatives Sleep-inducing drugs that tend to decrease central nervous system activation and behavioral activity.

Self-actualizing persons People with exceptionally healthy personalities, marked by continued personal growth.

Self-concept A collection of beliefs about one's own nature, unique qualities, and typical behavior.

Self-efficacy One's belief about one's ability to perform behaviors that should lead to expected outcomes.

Self-esteem A person's overall assessment of her or his personal adequacy or worth.

Self-monitoring The degree to which people attend to and control the impression they make on others in social interactions.

Self-referent encoding Deciding how or whether information is personally relevant.

Self-report inventories Personality tests that ask individuals to answer a series of questions about their characteristic behavior.

Self-serving bias The tendency to attribute one's successes to personal factors and one's failures to situational factors.

Semantic memory system General knowledge that is not tied to the time when the information was learned.

Semantic network Concepts joined together by links that show how the concepts are related.

Semantics The area of language concerned with understanding the meaning of words and word combinations.

Sensation The stimulation of sense organs.

Sensation seeking A generalized preference for high or low levels of sensory stimulation.

Sensory adaptation A gradual decline in sensitivity to prolonged stimulation.

Sensory memory The preservation of information in its original sensory form for a brief time, usually only a fraction of a second.

Separation anxiety Emotional distress seen in many infants when they are separated from people with whom they have formed an attachment.

Serial-position effect In memory tests, the fact that subjects show better recall for items at the beginning and end of a list than for items in the middle.

Set-point theory The idea that the body monitors fat-cell levels to keep them (and weight) fairly stable).

Settling-point theory The idea that weight tends to drift around a level at which the constellation of factors that determine food consumption and energy expenditure achieve an equilibrium.

Sex The biologically based categories of male and female.

Sexual orientation A person's preference for emotional and sexual relationships with individuals of the same sex, the other sex, or either sex.

Shaping The reinforcement of closer and closer approximations of a desired response.

Short-term memory (STM) A limited-capacity store that can maintain unrehearsed information for about 20 to 30 seconds.

Signal-detection theory A psychophysiological theory proposing that the detection of stimuli involves decision processes as well as sensory processes, which are influenced by a variety of factors besides the physical intensity of a stimulus.

Skinner box A small enclosure in which an animal can make a specific response that is systematically recorded while the consequences of the response are controlled.

Sleep apnea A sleep disorder characterized by frequent reflexive gasping for air that awakens a person and disrupts sleep.

Slow-wave sleep (SWS) Sleep stages 3 and 4, during which low-frequency delta waves become prominent in EEG recordings.

Social comparison theory The idea that people compare themselves with others to understand and evaluate their own behavior.

Social desirability bias A tendency to give socially approved answers to questions about oneself.

Social loafing A reduction in effort by individuals when they work in groups as compared to when they work by themselves.

Social psychology The branch of psychology concerned with the way individuals' thoughts, feelings, and behaviors are influenced by others.

Social schemas Organized clusters of ideas about categories of social events and people.

Social skills training A behavior therapy designed to improve interpersonal skills that emphasizes shaping, modeling, and behavioral rehearsal.

Social support Various types of aid and succor provided by members of one's social networks.

Socialization The acquisition of the norms, roles, and behaviors expected of people in a particular society.

Soma The cell body of a neuron; it contains the nucleus and much of the chemical machinery common to most cells.

Somatic nervous system The system of nerves that connect to voluntary skeletal muscles and to sensory receptors.

Somatization disorder A type of somatoform disorder marked by a history of diverse physical complaints that appear to be psychological in origin.

Somatoform disorders A class of psychological disorders involving physical ailments with no authentic organic basis that are due to psychological factors.

Somnambulism (sleepwalking) Arising and wandering about while remaining asleep.

Source The person who sends a communication.

Source monitoring The process of making attributions about the origins of memories.

Source-monitoring error An error that occurs when a memory derived from one source is misattributed to another source.

Split-brain surgery A procedure in which the bundle of fibers that connects the cerebral hemispheres (the corpus callosum) is cut to reduce the severity of epileptic seizures.

Spontaneous recovery In classical conditioning, the reappearance of an extinguished response after a period of nonexposure to the conditioned stimulus.

Spontaneous remission Recovery from a disorder without formal treatment.

SQ3R A study system designed to promote effective reading by means of five steps: survey, question, read, recite, and review.

Stage A developmental period during which characteristic patterns of behavior are exhibited and certain capacities become established.

Standard deviation An index of the amount of variability in a set of data.

Standardization The uniform procedures used in the administration and scoring of a test.

Statistical significance The condition that exists when the probability that the observed findings are due to chance is very low.

Statistics The use of mathematics to organize, summarize, and interpret numerical data. See also *Descriptive statistics, Inferential statistics.*

Stereotypes Widely held beliefs that people have certain characteristics because of their membership in a particular group.

Stimulants Drugs that tend to increase central nervous system activation and behavioral activity.

Stimulus Any detectable input from the environment.

Stimulus discrimination The phenomenon that occurs when an organism that has learned a response to a specific stimulus does not respond in the same way to stimuli that are similar to the original stimulus.

Stimulus generalization The phenomenon that occurs when an organism that has learned a response to a specific stimulus responds in the same way to new stimuli that are similar to the original stimulus.

Storage Maintaining encoded information in memory over time.

Stress Any circumstances that threaten or are perceived to threaten one's well-being and that thereby tax one's coping abilities.

Striving for superiority According to Adler, the universal drive to adapt, improve oneself, and master life's challenges.

Structuralism A school of psychology based on the notion that the task of psychology is to analyze consciousness into its basic elements and to investigate how these elements are related.

Subjective contours The perception of contrours where none actually exist.

Subjective well-being Individuals' perceptions of their overall happiness and life satisfaction.

Subjects The persons or animals whose behavior is systematically observed in a study.

Subliminal perception The registration of sensory input without conscious awareness.

Subtractive color mixing Formation of colors by removing some wavelengths of light, leaving less light than was originally there.

Superego According to Freud, the moral component of personality that incorporates social standards about what represents right and wrong.

Survey A descriptive research method in which researchers use questionnaires or interviews to gather information about specific aspects of subjects' behavior.

Sympathetic division The branch of the autonomic nervous system that mobilizes the body's resources for emergencies.

Synapse A junction where information is transmitted from one neuron to the next.

Synaptic cleft A microscopic gap between the terminal button of a neuron and the cell membrane of another neuron.

Syntax A system of rules that specify how words can be combined into phrases and sentences.

Systematic desensitization A behavior therapy used to reduce clients' anxiety responses through counterconditioning.

T

Tactile system The sensory system for touch.

Tardive dyskinesia A neurological disorder marked by chronic tremors and involuntary spastic movements.

Telegraphic speech Speech that consists mainly of content words; articles, prepositions, and other less critical words are omitted.

Temperament An individual's characteristic mood, activity level, and emotional reactivity.

Terminal buttons Small knobs at the end of axons that secrete chemicals called neurotransmitters.

Test norms Standards that provide information about where a score on a psychological test ranks in relation to other scores on that test.

Testwiseness The ability to use the characteristics and format of a cognitive test to maximize one's score.

Thalamus A structure in the forebrain through which all sensory information (except smell) must pass to get to the cerebral cortex.

Theory A system of interrelated ideas that is used to explain a set of observations.

Theory of bounded rationality Simon's assertion that people tend to use simple strategies in decision making that focus on only a few facets of available options and often result in "irrational" decisions that are less than optimal.

Threshold A dividing point between energy levels that do and do not have a detectable effect.

Tip-of-the-tongue phenomenon A temporary inability to remember something accompanied by a feeling that it's just out of reach.

Token economy A system for doling out symbolic reinforcers that are exchanged later for a variety of genuine reinforcers.

Tolerance A progressive decrease in a person's responsiveness to a drug.

Top-down processing In form perception, a progression from the whole to the elements.

Transfer-appropriate processing The situation that occurs when the initial processing of information is similar to the type of processing required by the subsequent measures of attention.

Transference In therapy, the phenomenon that occurs when clients start relating to their therapists in ways that mimic critical relationships in their lives.

Trial In classical conditioning, any presentation of a stimulus or pair of stimuli.

Trial and error Trying possible solutions sequentially and discarding those that are in error until one works.

Trichromatic theory The theory of color vision holding that the human eye has three types of receptors with differing sensitivities to different wavelengths.

Twin studies A research design in which hereditary influence is assessed by comparing the resemblance of identical twins and fraternal twins with respect to a trait.

Type A personality Personality characterized by (1) a strong competitive orientation, (2) impatience and time urgency, and (3) anger and hostility.

Type B personality Personality characterized by relatively relaxed, patient, easygoing, amicable behavior.

U

Unconditioned response (UCR) An unlearned reaction to an unconditioned stimulus that occurs without previous conditioning.

Unconditioned stimulus (UCS) A stimulus that evokes an unconditioned response without previous conditioning.

Unconscious According to Freud, thoughts, memories, and desires that are well below the surface of conscious awareness but that nonetheless exert great influence on behavior.

Underextensions Errors that occur when a child incorrectly uses a word to describe a narrower set of objects or actions than it is meant to.

Undifferentiated schizophrenia A type of schizophrenia marked by idiosyncratic mixtures of schizophrenic symptoms.

V

Validity The ability of a test to measure what it was designed to measure.

Variability The extent to which the scores in a data set tend to vary from each other and from the mean.

Variable-interval (VI) schedule A reinforcement schedule in which the reinforcer is given for the first response after a variable time interval has elapsed.

Variable-ratio (VR) schedule A reinforcement schedule in which the reinforcer is given after a variable number of nonreinforced responses.

Variables Any measurable conditions, events, characteristics, or behaviors that are controlled or observed in a study.

Vasocongestion Engorgement of blood vessels.

Vestibular system The sensory system that responds to gravity and keeps people informed of their body's location in space.

Visual agnosia An inability to recognize objects.

Volley principle The theory holding that groups of auditory nerve fibers fire neural impulses in rapid succession, creating volleys of impulses.

W

Weber's law The theory stating that the size of a just noticeable difference is a constant proportion of the size of the initial stimulus.

Z

Zygote A one-celled organism formed by the union of a sperm and an egg.

Abel, E. L. (1998). *Fetal alcohol abuse syndrome.* New York: Plenum.

Abel, M. H. (1998). Interaction of humor and gender in moderating relationships between stress and outcomes. *Journal of Psychology, 132,* 267–276.

Abi-Dargham, A., Gil, R., Krystal, J., Baldwin, R. M., Seibyl, J. P., Bowers, M., van Dyck, C. H., Charney, D. S., Innis, R. B., & Laruelle, M. (1998). Increased striatal dopamine transmission in schizophrenia: Confirmation in a second cohort. *American Journal of Psychiatry, 155,* 761–767.

Aboud, F. E., & Amato, M. (2001). Developmental and socialization influences on intergroup bias. In R. Brown & S. L. Gaertner (Eds.), *Blackwell handbook of social psychology: Intergroup processes.* Malden, MA: Blackwell.

Abramowitz, A. J., & O'Leary, S. G. (1990). Effectiveness of delayed punishment in an applied setting. *Behavior Therapy, 21,* 231–239.

Abrams, R. (1992). *Electroconvulsive therapy.* New York: Oxford University Press.

Abrams, R. (2000). Electroconvulsive therapy requires higher dosage levels: Food and Drug Administration action is required. *General Psychiatry, 57,* 445–446.

Abramson, L. Y., Alloy, L. B., & Metalsky, J. I. (1995). Hopelessness depression. In J. N. Buchanan & M. E. P. Seligman (Eds.), *Explanatory style.* Hillsdale, NJ: Erlbaum.

Abramson, L. Y., Alloy, L. B., Hankin, B. L., Haeffel, G. J., MacCoon, D. G., & Gibb, B. E. (2002). Cognitive vulnerability-stress models of depression in a self-regulatory and pychobiological context. In I. H. Gotlib & C. L. Hammen (Eds.), *Handbook of depression.* New York: Guilford.

Abramson, L. Y., Seligman, M. E. P., & Teasdale, J. (1978). Learned helplessness in humans: Critique and reformulation. *Journal of Abnormal Psychology, 87,* 32–48.

Acker, M. M., & O'Leary, S. G. (1996). Inconsistency of mothers' feedback and toddlers' misbehavior and negative affect. *Journal of Abnormal Child Psychology, 24,* 703–714.

Adamopoulos, J., & Lonner, W. J. (2001). Culture and psychology at a crossroad: Historical perspective and theoretical analysis. In D. Matsumoto (Ed.), *The handbook of culture and psychology.* New York: Oxford University Press.

Adams, G., Gullotta, T., & Montemayor, R. (1992). *Adolescent identity formation.* Newbury Park, CA: Sage.

Adams, H. E., Luscher, K. A., & Bernat, J. A. (2001). The classification of abnormal behavior: An overview. In P. B. Sutker & H. E. Adams (Eds.), *Comprehensive handbook of psychopathology.* New York: Kluwer Academic/Plenum.

Adams, H. E., Wright, L. W., Jr., & Lohr, B. A. (1996). Is homophobia associated with homosexual arousal? *Journal of Abnormal Psychology, 105,* 440–445.

Adams, J. L. (1980). *Conceptual blockbusting.* San Francisco: W. H. Freeman.

Adcock, C. J. (1965). Thematic Apperception Test. In O. K. Buros (Ed.), *Sixth Mental Measurements Yearbook.* Highland Park, NY: Gryphon Press.

Ader, R. (2001). Psychoneuroimmunology. *Current Directions in Psychological Science, 10*(3), 94–98.

Ader, R., & Cohen, N. (1984). Behavior and the immune system. In W. D. Gentry (Ed.), *Handbook of behavioral medicine.* New York: Guilford.

Ader, R., & Cohen, N. (1993). Psychoneuroimmunology: Conditioning and stress. *Annual Review of Psychology, 44,* 53–85.

Adler, A. (1917). *Study of organ inferiority and its psychical compensation.* New York: Nervous and Mental Diseases Publishing Co.

Adler, A. (1927). *Practice and theory of individual psychology.* New York: Harcourt, Brace & World.

Adler, L. L. (Ed.). (1993). *International handbook on gender roles.* Westport, CT: Greenwood.

Affleck, G., Tennen, H., Urrows, S., & Higgins, P. (1994). Person and contextual features of daily stress reactivity: Individual differences in relations of undesirable daily events with mood disturbance and chronic pain intensity. *Journal of Personality and Social Psychology, 66,* 329–340.

Agnoli, F., & Krantz, D. H. (1989). Suppressing natural heuristics by formal instruction: The case of the conjunction fallacy. *Cognitive Psychology, 21,* 515–550.

Agras, W. S., & Berkowitz, R. I. (1999). Behavior therapies. In R. E. Hales, S. C. Yudofsky, & J. A. Talbott (Eds.), *American Psychiatric Press textbook of psychiatry.* Washington, DC: American Psychiatric Press.

Ahn, H., & Wampold, B. E. (2001). Where oh where are the specific ingredients? A meta-analysis of component studies in counseling and psychotherapy. *Journal of Counseling Psychology, 48,* 251–257.

Ainsworth, M. D. S. (1979). Attachment as related to mother-infant interaction. In J. S. Rosenblatt, R. A. Hinde, C. Beer, & M. Busnel (Eds.), *Advances in the study of behavior* (Vol. 9). New York: Academic Press.

Ainsworth, M. D. S., Blehar, M. C., Waters, E., & Wall, S. (1978). *Patterns of attachment: A psychological study of the strange situation.* Hillsdale, NJ: Erlbaum.

Ajzen, I. (1985). From intentions to actions: A theory of planned behavior. In J. Kuhl & J. Beckman (Eds.), *Action-control: From cognition to behavior.* Heidelberg: Springer.

Ajzen, I. (1991). The theory of planned behavior. *Organizational Behavior and Human Decision Processes, 50,* 179–211.

Akerstedt, T., Hume, K., Minors, D., & Waterhouse, J. (1997). Good sleep—its timing and physiological sleep characteristics. *Journal of Sleep Research, 6,* 221–229.

Akimoto, S. A., & Sanbonmatsu, D. M. (1999). Differences in self-effacing behavior between European and Japanese Americans: Effect on competence evaluations. *Journal of Cross-Cultural Psychology, 30,* 159–177.

Akiskal, H. S. (2000). Mood disorders: Clinical features. In B. J. Sadock & V. A. Sadock (Eds.), *Kaplan and Sadock's comprehensive textbook of psychiatry* (7th ed., Vol. 1, pp. 1338–1376). Philadelphia: Lippincott/Williams & Wilkins.

Albee, G. W. (1998). Fifty years of clinical psychology: Selling our soul to the devil. *Applied and Preventive Psychology, 7*(3), 189–194.

Albert, C. M., Ma, J., Rifai, N., Stampfer, M. J., & Ridker, P. M. (2002). Prospective study of C-reactive protein, homocysteine, and plasma lipid levels as predictors of sudden cardiac death. *Circulation, 105,* 2595–2599.

Albert, M. S., & Killiany, R. J. (2001). Age-related cognitive change and brain-behavior relationships. In J. E. Birren & K. W. Schaie (Eds.), *Handbook of the psychology of aging* (5th ed., pp. 160–184). San Diego, CA: Academic Press.

Albert, R. D. (1988). The place of culture in modern psychology. In P. Bronstein & K. Quina (Eds.), *Teaching a psychology of people: Resources for gender and sociocultural awareness.* Washington, DC: American Psychological Association.

Alcock, J. (1998). *Animal behavior: An evolutionary approach.* Sunderland, MA: Sinauer Associates.

Aldag, R. J., & Fuller, S. R. (1993). Beyond fiasco: A reappraisal of the groupthink phenomenon and a new model of group decision processes. *Psychological Bulletin, 113,* 533–552.

Aldrich, M. S. (2000). Cardinal manifestations of sleep disorders. In M. H. Kryger, T. Roth & W. C. Dement (Eds), *Principles and practice of sleep medicine.* Philadelphia: Saunders.

Alexander, C. N., Davies, J. L., Dixon, C. A., Dillbeck, M. C., Druker, S. M., Oetzel, R. M., Muehlman, J. M., & Orme-Johnson, D. W. (1990). Growth of higher states of consciousness: The Vedic psychology of human development. In C. N. Alexander & E. J. Langer (Eds.), *Higher stages of human development: Perspectives on adult growth.* New York: Oxford University Press.

Alexander, C. N., Robinson, P., Orme-Johnson, D. W., Schneider, R. H., et al. (1994). The effects of transcendental meditation compared with other methods of relaxation and meditation in reducing risk factors, morbidity, and mortality. *Homeostasis in Health & Disease, 35,* 243–263.

Alexander, F. (1954). Psychoanalysis and psychotherapy. *Journal of the American Psychoanalytic Association, 2,* 722–733.

Alexander, J., & Tate, M. (1999). *Web wisdom: How to evaluate and create information quality on the web.* Mahwah, NJ: Erlbaum.

Alexander, R. D., Hoogland, J. L., Howard, R. D., Noonan, K. M., & Sherman, P. W. (1979). Sexual dimorphism and breeding systems in pinnipeds, ungulates, primates, and humans. In N. A. Chagnon & W. Irons (Eds.), *Evolutionary biology and human social behavior.* North Scituate, MA: Duxbury Press.

Allan, R. W. (1998). Operant-respondent interactions. In W. O'Donohue (Ed.), *Learning and behavior therapy.* Boston: Allyn & Bacon.

Allen, C. T., & Shimp, T. A. (1990). On using classical conditioning methods for researching the impact of ad-evoked feelings. In S. J. Agres, J. A. Edell, & T. M. Dubitsky (Eds.), *Emotion in advertising: Theoretical and practical explorations.* New York: Quorum Books.

Allen, M. J., Noel, R., Degan, J., Halpern, D. F., & Crawford, C. (2000). *Goals and objectives for the undergraduate psychology major: Rec-*

ommendations from a meeting of the California State University psychology faculty. Distributed by the Office of Teaching Resources in Psychology, Society for the Teaching of Psychology: Available on the World Wide Web: <http://www.lemoyne.edu/OTRP/otrpresources/otrpoutcomes.html>.

Allen, M., Emmers, T., Gebhardt, L., & Giery, M. A. (1995). Exposure to pornography and acceptance of rape myths. *Journal of Communication, 45,* 5–26.

Allgood, W. P., Risko, V. J., Alvarez, M. C., & Fairbanks, M. M. (2000). Factors that influence study. In R. F. Flippo & D. C. Caverly (Eds.), *Handbook of college reading and study strategy research.* Mahwah, NJ: Erlbaum.

Allison, D. B., Fontaine, K. R., Manson, J. E., Stevens, J., & Van-Itallie, T. B. (1999). Annual deaths attributable to obesity in the United States. *Journal of the American Medical Association, 282,* 1530–1538.

Allison, D. B., Heshka, S., Neale, M. C., Lykken, D. T., & Heymsfield, S. B. (1994). A genetic analysis of relative weight among 4,020 twin pairs, with an emphasis on sex effects. *Health Psychology, 13,* 362–365.

Alloy, L. B., Abramson, L. Y., Whitehouse, W. G., Hogan, M. E., Tashman, N. A., Steinberg, D. L., Rose, D. T., & Donovan, P. (1999). Depressogenic cognitive styles: Predictive validity, information processing and personality characteristics, and developmental origins. *Behavioral Research and Therapy, 37,* 503–531.

Allport, G. W. (1937). *Personality: A psychological interpretation.* New York: Holt.

Altman, I. (1990). Centripetal and centrifugal trends in psychology. In L. Brickman & H. Ellis (Eds.), *Preparing psychologists for the 21st century: Proceedings of the National Conference on Graduate Education in Psychology.* Hillsdale, NJ: Erlbaum.

Alvarez, P., & Squire, L. (1994). Memory consolidation and the medial temporal lobe: A simple network model. *Proceedings of the National Academy of Sciences, USA, 91,* 7041–7045.

Amabile, T. M. (1983). *The social psychology of creativity.* New York: Springer-Verlag.

Amabile, T. M. (1990). Within you, without you: The social psychology of creativity, and beyond. In M. A. Runco & R. S. Albert (Eds.), *Theories of creativity.* Newbury Park, CA: Sage.

Amabile, T. M. (1996). *Creativity in context.* Boulder, CO: Westview.

Amato, P. R., & Keith, B. (1991). Parental divorce and adult well-being: A meta-analysis. *Journal of Marriage and the Family, 53,* 43–58.

Ambady, N., & Rosenthal, R. (1993). Half a minute: Predicting teacher evaluations from thin slices of nonverbal behavior and physical attractiveness. *Journal of Personality and Social Psychology, 64,* 431–441.

Ambady, N., Hallahan, M., & Conner, B. (1999). Accuracy of judgments of sexual orientation from thin slices of behavior. *Journal of Personality and Social Psychology, 77,* 538–547.

Ambrósio, A. M., Kennedy, J. L., Macciardi, F., Macedo, A., Azevedo, M. H., Oliveira, C. R., Pato, M. T., Schindler, K. M., & Pato, C. N. (2001). Candidate gene studies of bipolar disorder with further analysis of serotonergic system genes in a Portuguese population. *Primary Psychiatry, 8*(9), 61–64.

American Association on Mental Retardation. (1992). *Mental retardation: Definition, classification, and systems of supports.* Washington, DC: Author.

American Psychiatric Association. (1952). *Diagnostic and statistical manual of mental disorders.* Washington, DC: Author.

American Psychiatric Association. (1968). *Diagnostic and statistical manual of mental disorders* (2nd ed.). Washington, DC: Author.

American Psychiatric Association. (1980). *Diagnostic and statistical manual of mental disorders* (3rd ed.). Washington, DC: Author.

American Psychiatric Association. (1987). *Diagnostic and statistical manual of mental disorders* (3rd ed., rev.). Washington, DC: Author.

American Psychiatric Association. (1994). *Diagnostic and statistical manual of mental disorders* (4th ed.). Washington, DC: Author.

American Psychiatric Association. (2000). *Diagnostic and statistical manual of mental disorders* (4th ed. Text revision). Washington, DC: Author.

American Psychiatric Association Task Force on Electroconvulsive Therapy. (2001). *The practice of electroconvulsive therapy: Recommendations for treatment* (2nd ed.). Washington, DC: American Psychiatric Association.

American Psychological Association. (1984). *Behavioral research with animals.* Washington, DC: Author.

American Psychological Association. (1992). Ethical principles of psychologists and code of conduct. *American Psychologist, 47,* 1597–1611.

Anand, B. K., & Brobeck, J. R. (1951). Hypothalamic control of food intake in rats and cats. *Yale Journal of Biology and Medicine, 24,* 123–140.

Anch, A. M., Browman, C. P., Mitler, M. M., & Walsh, J. K. (1988). *Sleep: A scientific perspective.* Englewood Cliffs, NJ: Prentice-Hall.

Anderson, B. F. (1980). *The complete thinker.* Englewood Cliffs, NJ: Prentice-Hall.

Anderson, C., John, O. P., Keltner, D., & Kring, A. M. (2001). Who attains social status? Effects of personality and physical attractiveness in social groups. *Journal of Personality and Social Psychology, 81*(1), 116–132.

Anderson, K. J. (1990). Arousal and the inverted-U hypothesis: A critique of Neiss's "reconceptualizing arousal." *Psychological Bulletin, 107,* 96–100.

Anderson, M. C., & Neely, J. H. (1996). Interference and inhibition in memory retrieval. In E. L. Bjork & R. A. Bjork (Eds.), *Memory.* San Diego: Academic Press.

Anderson, V. L., Levinson, E. M., Barker, W., & Kiewra, K. R. (1999). The effects of meditation on teacher perceived occupational stress, state and trait anxiety and burnout. *School Psychology Quarterly, 14,* 3–25.

Anderson, V. N. (1992). For whom is this world just? Sexual orientation and AIDS. *Journal of Applied Social Psychology, 22*(3), 248–259.

Andersson, B. E. (1992). Effects of day-care on cognitive and socioemotional competence of thirteen-year-old Swedish schoolchildren. *Child Development, 63,* 20–36.

Andreasen, N. C. (1987). Creativity and mental illness: Prevalence rates in writers and their first-degree relatives. *American Journal of Psychiatry, 144,* 1288–1292.

Andreasen, N. C. (1990). Positive and negative symptoms: Historical and conceptual aspects. In N. C. Andreasen (Ed.), *Modern problems of pharmacopsychiatry: Positive and negative symptoms and syndromes.* Basel: Karger.

Andreasen, N. C. (1996). Creativity and mental illness: A conceptual and historical overview. In J. J. Schildkraut & A. Otero (Eds.), *Depression and the spiritual in modern art: Homage to Miro.* New York: Wiley.

Andreasen, N. C. (2001). *Brave new brain: Conquering mental illness in the era of the human genome.* New York: Oxford University Press.

Andres, R. L., & Day, M.-C. (2000). Perinatal complications associated with maternal tobacco use. *Seminars in Neonatology, 5,* 231–241.

Angell, M. (2000). Is academic medicine for sale? *New England Journal of Medicine, 342,* 1516–1518.

Anglin, J. M. (1993). Vocabulary development: A morphological analysis. *Monographs of the Society for Research in Child Development, 58.*

Angoff, W. H. (1988). The nature-nurture debate, aptitudes, and group differences. *American Psychologist, 43*(9), 713–720.

Angst, J., & Preizig, M. (1995). Course of a clinical cohort of unipolar, bipolar and schizoaffective patients: Results of a prospective study from 1959–1985. *Schweiz Archives of Neurology and Psychiatry, 146,* 1–16.

Ansbacher, H. (1970, February). Alfred Adler, individual psychology. *Psychology Today,* pp. 42–44, 66.

Anthenelli, R. M., & Schuckit, M. A. (1997). Genetics. In J. H. Lowinson, P. Ruiz, R. B. Millman, & J. G. Langrod (Eds.), *Substance abuse: A comprehensive textbook.* Baltimore: Williams & Wilkins.

Antrobus, J. (1993). Characteristics of dreams. In M. A. Carskadon (Ed.), *Encyclopedia of sleep and dreaming.* New York: Macmillan.

Antrobus, J. (2000). Theories of dreaming. In M. H. Kryger, T. Roth & W. C. Dement (Eds.), *Principles and practice of sleep medicine.* Philadelphia: Saunders.

Archer, J. (1996). Sex differences in social behavior: Are the social role and evolutionary explanations compatible? *American Psychologist, 51,* 909–917.

Arendt, J. (1996). Melatonin: Claims made in the popular media are mostly nonsense. *British Medical Journal, 312,* 1242–1243.

Arendt, J., Stone, B., & Skene, D. (2000). Jet lag and sleep disruption. In M. H. Kryger, T. Roth & W. C. Dement (Eds.), *Principles and practice of sleep medicine.* Philadelphia: Saunders.

Argyle, M. (1987). *The psychology of happiness.* London: Metheun.

Argyle, M. (1999). Causes and correlates of happiness. In D. Kahneman, E. Diener & N. Schwarz (Eds.), *Well-being: The foundations of hedonic psychology.* New York: Russell Sage Foundation.

Arkes, H. R., Wortmann, R. L., Saville, P. D., & Harkness, A. R. (1981). Hindsight bias among physicians weighing the likelihood of diagnoses. *Journal of Applied Psychology, 66,* 252–254.

Arkowitz, H. (1992). Integrative theories of therapy. In D. K. Freedheim (Ed.), *History of psychotherapy: A century of change.* Washington, DC: American Psychological Association.

Armbruster, B. B. (2000). Taking notes from lectures. In R. F. Flippo & D. C. Caverly (Eds.), *Handbook of college reading and study strategy research.* Mahwah, NJ: Erlbaum.

Armitage, C. J., & Conner, M. (2000). Attitudinal ambivalence: A test of three key hypotheses. *Personality and Social Psychology Bulletin, 26,* 1421–1432.

Armony, J. L., & LeDoux, J. E. (2000). How danger is encoded: Toward a systems, cellular, and computational understanding of cognitive-emotional interactions in fear. In M. S. Gazzaniga (Ed.), *The new cognitive neurosciences* (2nd ed., pp. 1067–1080). Cambridge, MA: MIT Press.

Arnett, J. J. (1992). Reckless behavior in adolescence: A developmental perspective. *Developmental Review, 12*, 339–373.

Arnett, J. J. (1995). The young and the reckless: Adolescent reckless behavior. *Current Directions in Psychological Science, 4*, 67–71.

Arnett, J. J. (1996). Sensation seeking, aggressiveness, and adolescent reckless behavior. *Personality & Individual Differences, 20*, 693–702.

Arnett, J. J. (1999). Adolescent storm and stress, reconsidered. *American Psychologist, 54*, 317–326.

Arnkoff, D. B., & Glass, C. R. (1992). Cognitive therapy and psychotherapy. In D. K. Freedheim (Ed.), *History of psychotherapy: A century of change.* Washington, DC: American Psychological Association.

Arnold, L. M. (2000). Psychocutaneous disorders. In B. J. Sadock & V. A. Sadock (Eds.), *Kaplan and Sadock's comprehensive textbook of psychiatry* (7th ed., pp. 1818–1827). Philadelphia: Lippincott/Williams & Wilkins.

Aronson, E., & Mills, J. (1959). The effect of severity of initiation on liking for a group. *Journal of Abnormal and Social Psychology, 59*, 177–181.

Aronson, J., Lustina, M. J., Good, C., Keough, K., Steele, C. M., & Brown, J. (1999). When white men can't do math: Necessary and sufficient factors in stereotype threat. *Journal of Experimental Social Psychology, 35*, 29–46.

Arrigo, J. M., & Pezdek, K. (1997). Lessons from the study of psychogenic amnesia. *Current Directions in Psychological Science, 6*, 148–152.

Asch, S. E. (1955). Opinions and social pressures. *Scientific American, 193*(5), 31–35.

Asch, S. E. (1956). Studies of independence and conformity: A minority of one against a unanimous majority. *Psychological Monographs, 70*(9, Whole No. 416).

Asendorpf, J. B., & Ostendorf, F. (1998). Is self-enhancement healthy? Conceptual, psychometric, and empirical analysis. *Journal of Personality and Social Psychology, 74*, 955–966.

Aserinsky, E., & Kleitman, N. (1953). Regularly occurring periods of eye mobility and concomitant phenomena during sleep. *Science, 118*, 273–274.

Ashford, J. W., Mattson, M., & Kumar, V. (1998). Neurobiological systems disrupted by Alzheimer's disease and molecular biological theories of vulnerability. In V. Kumar & C. Eisdorfer (Eds.), *Advances in the diagnosis and treatment of Alzheimer's disease.* New York: Springer Publishing Company.

Aslin, R. N. (1993). Perception of visual direction in human infants. In C. E. Granrud (Ed.), *Visual perception and cognition in infancy.* Hillsdale, NJ: Erlbaum.

Aslin, R. N., Saffran, J. R., & Newport, E. L. (1999). Statistical learning in linguistic and nonlinguistic domains. In B. MacWhinney (Ed.), *The emergence of language* (pp. 359–380). Mahwah, NJ: Erlbaum.

Aspinwall, L. G., Richter, L., & Hoffman R. R., III. (2001). Understanding how optimism works: An examination of optimists' adaptive moderation of belief and behavior. In E. C. Chang (Ed.), *Optimism and pessimism: Implications for theory, research, and practice* (pp. 217–238). Washington, DC: American Psychological Association.

Atkinson, J. W. (1974). The mainsprings of achievement-oriented activity. In J. W. Atkinson & J. O. Raynor (Eds.), *Motivation and achievement.* New York: Wiley.

Atkinson, J. W. (1981). Studying personality in the context of an advanced motivational psychology. *American Psychologist, 36*, 117–128.

Atkinson, J. W. (1992). Motivational determinants of thematic apperception. In C. P. Smith (Ed.), *Motivation and personality: Handbook of thematic content analysis.* New York: Cambridge University Press.

Atkinson, J. W., & Birch, D. (1978). *Introduction to motivation.* New York: Van Nostrand.

Atkinson, J. W., & Litwin, G. H. (1960). Achievement motive and test anxiety conceived as motive to approach success and to avoid failure. *Journal of Abnormal and Social Psychology, 60*, 52–63.

Atkinson, R. C., & Shiffrin, R. M. (1968). Human memory: A proposed system and its control processes. In K. W. Spence & J. T. Spence (Eds.), *The psychology of learning and motivation* (Vol. 2). New York: Academic Press.

Atkinson, R. C., & Shiffrin, R. M. (1971). The control of short-term memory. *Scientific American, 225*, 82–90.

Austin, J. T., & Hanisch, K. A. (1990). Occupational attainment as a function of abilities and interests: A longitudinal analysis using Project TALENT data. *Journal of Applied Psychology, 75*, 77–86.

Averill, J. A. (1980). A constructivist view of emotion. In R. Plutchik & H. Kellerman (Eds.), *Emotion: Theory, research, and experience: Vol. 1. Theories of emotion.* New York: Academic Press.

Avis, N. E. (1999). Women's health at midlife. In S. L. Willis & J. D. Reid (Eds.), *Life in the middle: Psychological and social development in middle age* (pp. 105–146). San Diego, CA: Academic Press.

Axel, R. (1995, April). The molecular logic of smell. *Scientific American, 273*, 154–159.

Ayanian, J. Z., & Cleary, P. D. (1999). Perceived risks of heart disease and cancer amoung cigarette smokers. *Journal of the American Medical Association, 281*, 1019–1021.

Ayers, M. S., & Reder, L. M. (1998). A theoretical review of the misinformation effect: Predictions from an activation-based memory model. *Psychonomic Bulletin & Review, 5*, 1–21.

Ayres, J. J. B. (1998). Fear conditioning and avoidance. In W. O'Donohue (Ed.), *Learning and behavior therapy.* Boston: Allyn & Bacon.

Baars, B. J. (1986). *The cognitive revolution in psychology.* New York: Guilford.

Bäckman, L., Small, B. J., & Wahlin, Å. (2001). Aging and memory: Cognitive and biological perspectives. In J. E. Birren & K. W. Schaie (Eds.), *Handbook of the psychology of aging* (5th ed., pp. 348–376). San Diego, CA: Academic Press.

Bäckman, L., Small, B. J., Wahlin, Å., & Larsson, M. (1999). Cognitive functioning in very old age. In F. I. M. Craik & T. A. Salthouse (Eds.), *Handbook of cognitive aging* (Vol. 2, pp. 499–558). Mahwah, NJ: Erlbaum.

Baddeley, A. D. (1986). *Working memory.* New York: Oxford University Press.

Baddeley, A. D. (1989). The uses of working memory. In P. R. Soloman, G. R. Goethals, C. M. Kelley, & B. R. Stephens (Eds.), *Memory: Interdisciplinary approaches.* New York: Springer-Verlag.

Baddeley, A. D. (1992). Working memory. *Science, 255*, 556–559.

Baddeley, A. D. (2001). Is working memory still working? *American Psychologist, 56*, 851–864.

Baddeley, A. D., & Hitch, G. (1974). Working memory. In G. H. Bower (Ed.), *The psychology of learning and motivation* (Vol. 8). New York: Academic Press.

Badia, P. (1990). Memories in sleep: Old and new. In R. R. Bootzin, J. F. Kihlstrom, & D. L. Schacter (Eds.), *Sleep and cognition.* Washington, DC: American Psychological Association.

Baenninger, M., & Newcombe, N. (1995). Environmental input to the development of sex-related differences in spatial and mathematical ability. *Learning & Individual Differences, 7*, 363–379.

Baenninger, R. (1997). On yawing and its functions. *Psychonomic Bulletin & Review, 4*, 198–207.

Baer, J. (1994). Divergent thinking is not a general trait: A multi-domain training experiment. *Creativity Research Journal, 7*, 35–36.

Bahrick, H. P. (2000). Long-term maintenance of knowledge. In E. Tulving & F. I. M. Craik (Eds.), *The Oxford handbook of memory* (pp. 347–362). New York: Oxford University Press.

Bailey, J. M., & Pillard, R. C. (1991). A genetic study of male homosexual orientation. *Archives of General Psychology, 48*, 1089–1097.

Bailey, J. M., & Zucker, K. J. (1995). Childhood sex-typed behavior and sexual orientation: A conceptual analysis and quantitative review. *Developmental Psychology, 31*, 43–55.

Bailey, J. M., Dunne, M. P., & Martin, N. G. (2000). Genetic and environmental influences on sexual orientation and its correlates in an Australian twin sample. *Journal of Personality and Social Psychology, 78*, 524–536.

Bailey, J. M., Pillard, R. C., Neale, M. C. I., & Agyei, Y. (1993). Heritable factors influence sexual orientation in women. *Archives of General Psychiatry, 50*, 217–223.

Baillargeon, R. (1987). Object permanence in 3.5- and 4.5-month-old infants. *Developmental Psychology, 23*, 655–664.

Baillargeon, R. (1994). How do infants learn about the physical world? *Current Directions in Psychological Science, 3*, 133–140.

Bakan, P. (1971, August). The eyes have it. *Psychology Today*, pp. 64–69.

Baker, F., Ainsworth, S. R., Dye, J. T., Crammer, C., Thun, M. J., Hoffmann, D., Repace, J. L., Henningfield, J. E., Slade, J., Pinney, J., Shanks, T., Burns, D. M., Connolly, G. N., & Shopland, D. R. (2000). Health risks associated with cigar smoking. *Journal of the American Medical Association, 284*, 735–740.

Baldessarini, R. J. (2001). Drugs and the treatment of psychiatric disorders: Depression and the anxiety disorders. In J. G. Hardman & L. E. Limbird (Eds.), *Goodman & Gilman's the pharmacological basis of therapeutics.* New York: McGraw-Hill.

Baldwin, E. (1993). The case for animal research in psychology. *Journal of Social Issues, 49*(1), 121–131.

Baldwin, W. (2000). Information no one else knows: The value of self-report. In A. A. Stone, J. S. Turkkan, C. A. Bachrach, J. B. Jobe, H. S. Kurtzman & V. Cain (Eds.), *The science of* self-report: Implications for research and practice. Mahwah, NJ: Erlbaum.

Ball, H. L., Hooker, E., & Kelly, P. J. (2000). Parent-infant co-sleeping: Father's roles and perspectives. *Infant and Child Development, 9*(2), 67–74.

Ballenger, J. C. (1995). Benzodiazepines. In A. F. Schatzberg & C. B. Nemeroff (Eds.), *The American Psychiatric Press textbook of psychopharmacology.* Washington, DC: American Psychiatric Press.

Ballenger, J. C. (2000). Benzodiazepine receptor agonists and antagonists. In B. J. Sadock & V. A. Sadock (Eds.), *Kaplan and Sadock's comprehensive textbook of psychiatry.* Philadelphia: Lippincott/Williams & Wilkins.

Balon, R. (1997). Seratonin reuptake inhibitors and sexual dysfunction. *Primary Psychiatry, 4,* 28–33.

Balsam, P. D. (1988). Selection, representation, and equivalence of controlling stimuli. In R. C. Atkinson, R. J. Herrnstein, G. Lindzey, & R. D. Luce (Eds.), *Stevens' handbook of experimental psychology.* New York: Wiley.

Baltes, P. B., Staudinger, U. M., & Lindenberger, U. (1999). Lifespan psychology: Theory and application to intellectual functioning. *Annual Review of Psychology, 50,* 471–507.

Bandura, A. (1973). *Aggression: A social learning analysis.* Englewood Cliffs, NJ: Prentice-Hall.

Bandura, A. (1977). *Social learning theory.* Englewood Cliffs, NJ: Prentice-Hall.

Bandura, A. (1982). The psychology of chance encounters and life paths. *American Psychologist, 37,* 747–755.

Bandura, A. (1986). *Social foundations of thought and action: A social-cognitive theory.* Englewood Cliffs, NJ: Prentice-Hall.

Bandura, A. (1990). Perceived self-efficacy in the exercise of personal agency. *Journal of Applied Sport Psychology, 2*(2), 128–163.

Bandura, A. (1993). Perceived self-efficacy in cognitive development and functioning. *Educational Psychologist, 28*(2), 117–148.

Bandura, A. (1995). Exercise of personal and collective efficacy in changing societies. In A. Bandura (Ed.), *Self-efficacy in changing societies.* New York: Cambridge University Press.

Bandura, A. (1999a). Social cognitive theory of personality. In L. A. Pervin, & O. P. John (Eds.), *Handbook of personality: Theory and research.* New York: Guilford.

Bandura, A. (1999b). A sociocognitive analysis of substance abuse: An agentic perspective. *Psychological Science, 10*(3), 214–217.

Bandura, A. (2001). Social cognitive theory: An agentic perspective. *Annual Review of Psychology, 52,* 1–26.

Banich, M. T., & Heller, W. (1998). Evolving perspectives on lateralization of function. *Current Directions in Psychological Science, 7,* 1.

Banks, W. P., & Krajicek, D. (1991). Perception. *Annual Review of Psychology, 42,* 305–331.

Banyard, V. L., & Williams, L. M. (1999). Memories for child sexual abuse and mental health functioning: Findings on a sample of women and implications for future research. In L. M. Williams & V. L. Banyard (Eds.), *Trauma & memory.* Thousand Oaks, CA: Sage Publications.

Bar, M., & Biederman, I. (1998). Subliminal visual priming. *Psychological Science, 9,* 464–469.

Barba, G. D., Parlato, V., Jobert, A., Samson, Y., & Pappata, S. (1998). Cortical networks implicated in semantic and episodic memory: Common or unique. *Cortex, 34,* 547–561.

Barber, B. K. (1994). Cultural, family, and personal contexts of parent-adolescent conflict. *Journal of Marriage and the Family, 56,* 375–386.

Barber, T. X. (1979). Suggested ("hypnotic") behavior: The trance paradigm versus an alternative paradigm. In E. Fromm & R. E. Shor (Eds.), *Hypnosis: Developments in research and new perspectives.* New York: Aldine.

Barber, T. X. (1986). Realities of stage hypnosis. In B. Zilbergeld, M. G. Edelstien, & D. L. Araoz (Eds.), *Hypnosis: Questions and answers.* New York: Norton.

Bard, P. (1934). On emotional experience after decortication with some remarks on theoretical views. *Psychological Review, 41,* 309–329.

Bargh, J. A. (1999). The cognitive monster: The case against the controllability of automatic stereotype effects. In S. Chaiken & Y. Trope (Eds.), *Dual-process theories in social psychology.* New York: Guilford.

Bar-Hillel, M. (1989). Discussion: How to solve probability teasers. *Philosophy of Science, 56,* 348–358.

Bar-Hillel, M., & Falk, R. (1982). Some teasers concerning conditional probabilities. *Cognition,* 109–122.

Barlett, D. L., & Steele, J. B. (1979). *Empire: The life, legend and madness of Howard Hughes.* New York: Norton.

Barlow, D. H. (1996). The effectiveness of psychotherapy: Science and policy. *Clinical Psychology: Science & Practice, 3,* 236–240.

Barlow, D. H., & Durand, V. M. (1999). *Abnormal psychology: An investigative approach.* Belmont, CA: Wadsworth.

Barnes, V. A., Treiber, F., & Davis, H. (2001). The impact of Transcendental Meditation on cardiovascular function at rest and during acute stress in adolescents with high normal blood pressure. *Journal of Psychosomatic Research, 51,* 597–605.

Barnett, W. S. (1995). Long-term effects of early childhood programs on cognitive and school outcomes. *Future of Children, 5,* 25–50.

Barnier, A. J., & McConkey, K. M. (1998). Posthypnotic responding away from the hypnotic setting. *Psychological Science, 9,* 256–262.

Baron, R. S., Vandello, J. A., & Brunsman, B. (1996). The forgotten variable in conformity research: Impact of task importance on social influence. *Journal of Personality and Social Psychology, 71,* 915–927.

Barrett, D. (1988–1989). Dreams of death. *Omega, 19*(2), 95–101.

Barrett, M. (1995). Early lexical development. In P. Fletcher & B. MacWhinney (Eds.), *The handbook of child language.* Cambridge, MA: Blackwell.

Barsky, A. J. (1988). The paradox of health. *New England Journal of Medicine, 318,* 414–418.

Barsky, A. J. (2001). Somatosensory amplification and hypochondriasis. In V. Starcevic & D. R. Lipsitt (Eds.), *Hypochondriasis: Modern perspectives on an ancient malady.* New York: Oxford University Press.

Barsky, A. J., Coeytaux, R. R., Sarnie, M. K., & Cleary, P. D. (1993). Hypochondriacal patients' beliefs about good health. *American Journal of Psychiatry, 150,* 1085–1090.

Bartlett, F. C. (1932). *Remembering: A study in experimental and social psychology.* New York: Macmillan.

Bartoshuk, L. M. (1993a). Genetic and pathological taste variation: What can we learn from animal models and human disease? In D. Chadwick, J. Marsh, & J. Goode (Eds.), *The molecular basis of smell and taste transduction.* New York: Wiley.

Bartoshuk, L. M. (1993b). The biological basis of food perception and acceptance. *Food Quality and Preference, 4,* 21–32.

Bartoshuk, L. M., & Beauchamp, G. K. (1994). Chemical senses. *Annual Review of Psychology, 45,* 419–449.

Bartoshuk, L. M., Duffy, V. B., & Miller, I. J. (1994). PTC/PROP taste: Anatomy, psychophysics, and sex effects. *Physiology & Behavior, 56,* 1165–1171.

Bartsch, K., & Wellman, H. M. (1995). *Children talk about the mind.* New York: Oxford University Press.

Basbaum, A. I., & Jessel, T. M. (2000). The perception of pain. In E. R. Kandel, J. H. Schwartz, & T. M. Jessell (Eds.), *Principles of neural science.* New York: McGraw-Hill.

Bashore, T. R., Ridderinkhof, K. R., & van der Molen, M. W. (1997). The decline of cognitive processing speed in old age. *Current Directions in Psychological Science, 6,* 163–169.

Basow, S. A. (1992). *Gender: Stereotypes and roles.* Pacific Grove, CA: Brooks/Cole.

Bassiri, A. B., & Guilleminault, C. (2000). Clinical features and evaluation of obstructive sleep apnea-hypopnea syndrome. In M. H. Kryger, T. Roth & W. C. Dement (Eds.), *Principles and practice of sleep medicine.* Philadelphia: Saunders.

Bassuk, E. L., Buckner, J. C., Perloff, J. N., & Bassuk, S. S. (1998). Prevalence of mental health and substance use disorders among homeless and low-income housed mothers. *American Journal of Psychiatry, 155,* 1561–1564.

Bassuk, E. L., Rubin, L., & Lauriat, A. (1984). Is homelessness a mental health problem? *American Journal of Psychiatry, 141,* 1546–1550.

Bastardi, A., & Shafir, E. (1998). On the pursuit and misuse of useless information. *Journal of Personality and Social Psychology, 75,* 19–32.

Bastardi, A., & Shafir, E. (2000). Nonconsequential reasoning and its consequences. *Current Directions in Psychological Science, 9,* 216–219.

Bates, E. (1999). Plasticity, localization, and language development. In S. H. Broman & J. M. Fletcher (Eds.), *The changing nervous system: Neurobehavioral consequences of early brain disorders* (pp. 214–247). New York: Oxford University Press.

Bates, E., & Carnevale, G. (1993). New directions in research on language development. *Developmental Review, 13,* 436–70.

Bates, E., Devescovi, A., & Wulfeck, B. (2001). Psycholinguistics: A cross-language perspective. *Annual Review of Psychology, 52,* 369–396.

Bates, M. S., Edwards, W. T., & Anderson, K. O. (1993). Ethnocultural influences on variation in chronic pain perception. *Pain, 52*(1), 101–112.

Bauer, M. I., & Johnson-Laird, P. N. (1993). How diagrams can improve reasoning. *Psychological Science, 4,* 372–378.

Baum, A. S., & Burnes, D. W. (1993). *A nation in denial: The truth about homelessness.* Boulder, CO: Westview Press.

Baum, A., Grunberg, N. E., & Singer, J. E. (1992). Biochemical measurements in the study of emotion. *Psychological Science, 3,* 56–60.

Baumeister, R. F. (1984). Choking under pressure: Self-consciousness and paradoxical effects of incentives on skillful performance. *Journal of Personality and Social Psychology, 46,* 610–620.

Baumeister, R. F. (1989). The optimal margin of illusion. *Journal of*

Social and Clinical Psychology, 8, 176–189.

Baumeister, R. F. (1995). Disputing the effects of championship pressures and home audiences. *Journal of Personality and Social Psychology, 68,* 644–648.

Baumeister, R. F., & Steinhilber, A. (1984). Paradoxical effects of supportive audiences on performance under pressure: The home field disadvantage in sports championships. *Journal of Personality and Social Psychology, 47,* 85–93.

Baumeister, R. F., & Twenge, J. M. (2002). Cultural suppression of female sexuality. *Review of General Psychology, 6,* 166–203.

Baumeister, R. F., Bratslavsky, E., Finkenauer, C., & Vohs, K. D. (2001). Bad is stronger than good. *Review of General Psychology, 5,* 323–370.

Baumeister, R. F., Catanese, K. R., & Vohs, K. D. (2001). Is there a gender difference in strength of sex drive? Theoretical views, conceptual distinctions and a review of relevant evidence. *Personality and Social Psychology Review, 5,* 242–273.

Baumeister, R. J., & Leary, M. R. (1995). The need to belong: Desire for interpersonal attachments as a fundamental human motivation. *Psychological Bulletin, 117,* 497–529.

Baumrind, D. (1964). Some thoughts on the ethics of reading Milgram's "Behavioral study of obedience." *American Psychologist, 19,* 421–423.

Baumrind, D. (1985). Research using intentional deception: Ethical issues revisited. *American Psychologist, 40,* 165–174.

Bauserman, R. (1996). Sexual aggression and pornography: A review of correlational research. *Basic and Applied Social Psychology, 18,* 405–427.

Baylis, G. C., & Driver, J. (1995). One-sided edge assignment in vision: 1. Figure-ground segmentation and attention to objects. *Current Directions in Psychological Science, 4,* 140–146.

Beahrs, J. O. (1983). Co-consciousness: A common denominator in hypnosis, multiple personality and normalcy. *American Journal of Clinical Hypnosis, 26*(2), 100–113.

Beck, A. T. (1976). *Cognitive therapy and the emotional disorders.* New York: International Universities Press.

Beck, A. T. (1987). Cognitive therapy. In J. K. Zeig (Ed.), *The evolution of psychotherapy.* New York: Brunner/Mazel.

Beck, A. T. (1991). Cognitive therapy: A 30-year retrospective. *American Psychologist, 46,* 368–375.

Beck, A. T. (1997). Cognitive therapy: Reflections. In J. K. Zeig (Ed.), *The evolution of psychotherapy: The third conference.* New York: Brunner/Mazel.

Beck, A. T., Rush, A. J., Shaw, B. F., & Emery, G. (1979). *Cognitive therapy of depression.* New York: Guilford.

Beck, J. (1995). *Cognitive therapy: Basics and beyond.* New York: Guilford.

Becker, A. E., & Kleinman, A. (2000). Anthropology and psychiatry. In B. J. Sadock & V. A. Sadock (Eds.), *Kaplan and Sadock's comprehensive textbook of psychiatry.* Philadelphia: Lippincott/Williams & Wilkins.

Beckham, J. C., Moore, S. D., Feldman, M. E., Hertzberg, M. A., Kirby, A. C., & Fairbank, J. A. (1998). Health status, somatization, and severity of posttraumatic stress disorder in Vietnam combat veterans with posttraumatic stress disorder. *American Journal of Psychiatry, 155,* 1565–1569.

Beeman, M. J., & Chiarello, C. (1998). Complementary right and left hemisphere language comprehension. *Current Directions in Psychological Science, 7,* 2–7.

Beer, J. M., Arnold, R. D., & Loehlin, J. C. (1998). Genetic and environmental influences on MMPI Factor Scales: Joint model fitting to twin and adoption data. *Journal of Personality and Social Psychology, 74,* 818–827.

Beers, M., Lassiter, G. D., & Flannery, B. C. (1997). Individual differences in person memory: Self-monitoring and the recall of consistent and inconsistent behavior. *Journal of Social Behavior and Personality, 12,* 811–820.

Behling, O. (1998). Employee selection: Will intelligence and conscientiousness do the job? *Academy of Management, 12,* 77–86.

Beilin, H. (1992). Piaget's enduring contribution to developmental psychology. *Developmental Psychology, 28,* 191–204.

Beisecker, A. E. (1990). Patient power in doctor-patient communication: What do we know? *Health Communication, 2,* 105–122.

Békésy, G. von. (1947). The variation of phase along the basilar membrane with sinusoidal vibrations. *Journal of the Acoustical Society of America, 19,* 452–460.

Bell, A. P., Weinberg, M. S., & Hammersmith, S. K. (1981). *Sexual preference: Its development in men and women.* Bloomington: Indiana University Press.

Bellack, A. S., Gearon, J. S., & Blanchard, J. J. (2000). Schizophrenia: Psychopathology. In M. Hersen & A. S. Bellack (Eds.), *Psychopathology in adulthood.* Boston: Allyn & Bacon.

Beller, M., & Gafni, N. (1996). The 1991 international assessment of educational progress in mathematics and sciences: The gender differences perspective. *Journal of Educational Psychology, 88,* 365–377.

Bellezza, F. S. (1996). Mnemonic methods to enhance storage and retrieval. In E. L. Bjork & R. A. Bjork (Eds.), *Memory.* San Diego: Academic Press.

Belli, R. F., Winkielman, P., Read, J. D., Schwarz, N., & Lynn, S. J. (1998). Recalling more childhood events leads to judgments of poorer memory: Implications for the recovered/false memory debate. *Psychonomic Bulletin & Review, 5,* 318–323.

Bellinger, D. C., & Adams, H. F. (2001). Environmental pollutant exposures and children's cognitive abilities. In R. J. Sternberg & E. L. Grigorenko (Eds.), *Environmental effects on cognitive abilities.* Mahwah, NJ: Erlbaum.

Belsky, J. (1988). The "effects" of infant day care reconsidered. *Early Childhood Research Quarterly, 3,* 235–272.

Belsky, J. (1990). Children and marriage. In F. D. Fincham & T. N. Bradbury (Eds.), *The psychology of marriage: Basic issues and applications.* New York: Guilford.

Belsky, J. (1992). Consequences of child care for children's development: A deconstructionist view. In A. Booth (Ed.), *Child care in the 1990s.* Hillsdale, NJ: Erlbaum.

Belsky, J. (1999a). Interactional and contextual determinants of attachment security. In J. Cassidy & P. R. Shaver (Eds.), *Handbook of attachment: Theory, research and clinical applications.* New York: Guilford.

Belsky, J. (1999b). Modern evolutionary theory and patterns of attachment. In J. Cassidy & P. R. Shaver (Eds.), *Handbook of attachment: Theory, research and clinical applications.* New York: Guilford.

Belsky, J., & Kelly, J. (1994). *The transition to parenthood.* New York: Dell.

Belsky, J., Steinberg, L., & Draper, P. (1991). Childhood experience, interpersonal development, and reproductive strategy: An evolutionary theory of socialization. *Child Development, 62,* 647–670.

Bem, D. J. (1967). Self-perception: An alternative interpretation of cognitive dissonance phenomena. *Psychological Review, 74,* 183–200.

Bem, S. L. (1985). Androgyny and gender schema theory: A conceptual and empirical integration. In T. B. Sonderegger (Ed.), *Nebraska symposium on motivation, 1984: Psychology and gender* (Vol. 32). Lincoln: University of Nebraska Press.

Bem, S. L. (1993). *The lenses of gender: Transforming the debate on sexual inequality.* New Haven: Yale University Press.

Benca, R. M. (2001). Consequences of insomnia and its therapies. *Journal of Clinical Psychiatry, 62*(suppl 10), 33–38.

Bender, R., Jockel, K. H., Trautner, C., Spraul, M., & Berger, M. (1999). Effect of age on excess mortality in obesity. *Journal of the American Medical Association, 281,* 1498–1504.

Bendersky, M., & Lewis, M. (1999). Prenatal cocaine exposure and neonatal condition. *Infant Behavior & Development, 22,* 353–366.

Benet, V., & Waller, N. G. (1995). The big seven factor model of personality description: Evidence for its cross-cultural generality in a Spanish sample. *Journal of Personality and Social Psychology, 69,* 701–718.

Benjamin, L. T., Jr., Cavell, T. A., & Shallenberger, W. R., III. (1984). Staying with initial answers on objective tests: Is it a myth? *Teaching of Psychology, 11,* 133–141.

Bennett, H. L. (1993). The mind during surgery: The uncertain effects of anesthesia. *Advances, 9*(1), 5–16.

Benson, H. (1975). *The relaxation response.* New York: Morrow.

Benson, H., & Klipper, M. Z. (1988). *The relaxation response.* New York: Avon.

Bentler, P. M., & Woodward, J. A. (1978). A Head Start reevaluation: Positive effects are not yet demonstrable. *Evaluation Quarterly, 2,* 493–510.

Bereczkei, T. (2000). Evolutionary psychology: A new perspective in the behavioral sciences. *European Psychologist, 5*(3), 175–190.

Berenbaum, S. A., & Snyder, E. (1995). Early hormonal influences on childhood sex-typed activity and playmate preferences: Implications for the development of sexual orientation. *Developmental Psychology, 31,* 31–42.

Bergin, A. E. (1971). The evaluation of therapeutic outcomes. In A. E. Bergin & S. L. Garfield (Eds.), *Handbook of psychotherapy and behavior change: An empirical analysis.* New York: Wiley.

Berkowitz, L. (1989). Frustration-aggression hypothesis: Examination and reformulation. *Psychological Bulletin, 106,* 59–73.

Berkowitz, L. (1999). Evil is more than banal: Situationism and concept of evil. *Personality and Social Psychology Review, 3,* 246–253.

Berliner, L., & Briere, J. (1999). Trauma, memory, and clinical practice. In L. M. Williams & V. L. Banyard (Eds.), *Trauma & memory.* Thousand Oaks, CA: Sage Publications.

Berman, R. F. (1991). Electrical brain stimulation used to study mechanisms and models of memory. In J. L. Martinez Jr. & R. P. Kesner (Eds.), *Learning and memory: A biological view.* San Diego: Academic Press.

Bernhardt, P. C. (1997). Influences of serotonin and testosterone in aggression and dominance: Convergence with social psychology. *Current Directions in Psychological Science, 6*, 44–48.

Bernstein, H. J., Beale, M. D., Burns, C., & Kellner, C. H. (1998). Patient attitudes about ECT after treatment. *Psychiatric Annuals*, 524–527.

Berquier, A., & Ashton, R. (1992). Characteristics of the frequent nightmare sufferer. *Journal of Abnormal Psychology, 101*, 246–250.

Berridge, K. C., & Robinson, T. E. (1998). What is the role of dopamine in reward: Hedonic impact, reward learning, or incentive salience? *Brain Research Reviews, 28*, 309–369.

Berry, D. T. R., Wetter, M. W., & Baer, R. A. (1995). Assessment of malingering. In J. N. Butcher (Ed.), *Clinical personality assessment: Practical approaches*. New York: Oxford University Press.

Berry, J. W. (1990). Cultural variations in cognitive style. In S. P. Wapner (Ed.), *Bio-psycho-social factors in cognitive style*. Hillsdale, NJ: Erlbaum.

Berry, J. W. (1994). Cross-cultural variations in intelligence. In R. J. Sternberg (Ed.), *Encyclopedia of human intelligence*. New York: Macmillan.

Berry, J. W., Poortinga, Y., Segall, M., & Dasen, P. (1992). *Cross-cultural psychology*. New York: Cambridge University Press.

Berscheid, E. (1988). Some comments on love's anatomy: Or, whatever happened to old-fashioned lust. In R. J. Sternberg & M. L. Barnes (Eds.), *The psychology of love*. New Haven: Yale University Press.

Berscheid, E., & Reis, H. T. (1998). Attraction and close relationships. In D. T. Gilbert, S. T. Fiske, & G. Lindzey (Eds.), *The handbook of social psychology*. New York: McGraw-Hill.

Berscheid, E., & Walster, E. (1978). *Interpersonal attraction*. Reading, MA: Addison-Wesley.

Bertenthal, B. I., & Clifton, R. K. (1998). Perception and action. In W. Damon (Ed.), *Handbook of child psychology (Vol. 2): Cognition, perception, and language*. New York: Wiley.

Berzonsky, M., & Adams, G. (1999). Commentary: Reevaluating the identity status paradigm: Still useful after 35 years. *Developmental Review, 19*, 557–590.

Beumont, P. J. V. (2002). Clinical presentation of anorexia nervosa and bulimia nervosa. In C. G. Fairburn & K. D. Brownell (Eds.), *Eating disorders and obesity: A comprehensive handbook*. New York: Guilford.

Beumont, P. J. V., Garner, D. M., & Touyz, S. W. (1994). Diagnosis of eating or dieting disorders: What

may we learn from past mistakes? *International Journal of Eating Disorders, 16*, 349–362.

Beutler, L. E. (2000). David and Goliath: When empirical and clinical standards of practice meet. *American Psychologist, 55*, 997–1007.

Beutler, L. E. (2002). The dodo bird is extinct. *Clinical Psychology: Science & Practice, 9*(1), 30–34.

Beutler, L. E., & Harwood, T. M. (2002). What is and can be attributed to the therapeutic relationship? *Journal of Contemporary Psychotherapy, 32*(1), 25–33.

Beutler, L. E., Bongar, B., & Shurkin, J. N. (1998). *Am I crazy, or is it my shrink?* New York: Oxford University Press.

Beutler, L. E., Machado, P. P. P., & Neufeldt, S. A. (1994). Therapist variables. In A. E. Bergin & S. L. Garfield (Eds.), *Handbook of psychotherapy and behavior change* (4th ed.). New York: Wiley.

Beutler, L. E., Rocco, F., Moleiro, C. M., & Talebi, H. (2001). Resistance. *Psychotherapy: Theory, Research, Practice, Training, 38*, 431–436.

Bhattachary, S., & Powell, J. H. (2001). Recreational use of 3,4-methylenedioxymethamphetamine (MDMA) or "ecstasy": Evidence for cognitive impairment. *Psychological Medicine, 31*, 647–658.

Bialystok, E. (1999). Cognitive complexity and attentional control in the bilingual mind. *Child Development, 70*, 636–644.

Biederman, I., Hilton, H. J., & Hummel, J. E. (1991). Pattern goodness and pattern recognition. In G. R. Lockhead & J. R. Pomerantz (Eds.), *The perception of structure*. Washington, DC: American Psychological Association.

Biehl, M., Matsumoto, D., Ekman, P., Hearn, V., Heider, K., Kudoh, T., & Ton, V. (1997). Matsumoto and Ekman's Japanese and Caucasian Facial Expressions of Emotion (JACFEE): Reliability data and cross-national differences. *Journal of Nonverbal Behavior, 21*, 3–21.

Bierut, L. J., Heath, A. C., Bucholz, K. K., Dinwiddie, S. H., Madden, P. A. F., Statham, D. J., Dunne, M. P., & Martin, N. G. (1999). Major depressive disorder in a community-based twin sample. *Archives of General Psychiatry, 56*, 557–563.

Bigler, E. D., Blatter, D. D., Anderson, C. V., Johnson, S. C., Gale, S. D., Hopkins, R. O., & Burnett, B. (1997). Hippocampal volume in normal aging and traumatic brain injury. *American Journal of Neuroradiology, 18*, 11–23.

Binet, A. (1911). Nouvelle recherches sur la mesure du niveau intellectuel chez les enfants d'école. *L'Année Psychologique, 17*, 145–201.

Binet, A., & Simon, T. (1905). Méthodes nouvelles pour le diagnostic du niveau intellectuel des anormaux. *L'Année Psychologique, 11*, 191–244.

Binet, A., & Simon, T. (1908). Le développement de l'intelligence chez les enfants. *L'Année Psychologique, 14*, 1–94.

Birch, L. L., & Fisher, J. A. (1996). The role of experience in the development of children's eating behavior. In E. D. Capaldi (Ed.), *Why we eat what we eat: The psychology of eating* (pp. 113–143). Washington, DC: American Psychological Association.

Birdsong, D. (1999). Introduction: Whys and why nots of the critical period hypothesis for second language acquisition. In D. Birdsong (Ed.), *Second language acquisition and the critical period hypothesis* (pp. 1–22). Mahwah, NJ: Erlbaum.

Bishop, K. M., & Wahlsten, D. (1997). Sex differences in the human corpus callosum: Myth or reality? *Neuroscience and Biobehavioral Reviews, 12*, 581–601.

Bishop, S. R. (2002). What do we really know about mindfulness-based stress reduction? *Psychosomatic Medicine, 64*(1), 71–83.

Bjork, R. A. (1992). Interference and forgetting. In L. R. Squire (Ed.), *Encyclopedia of learning and memory*. New York: Macmillan.

Bjorklund, D. F. (1997). In search of a metatheory for cognitive development (or, Piaget is dead and I don't feel so good myself). *Child Development, 68*, 144–148.

Bjorklund, D. F. (2000). *Children's thinking: Developmental function and individual differences*. Belmont, CA: Wadsworth.

Björntorp, P. (2002). Definition and classification of obesity. In C. G. Fairburn & K. D. Brownell (Eds.), *Eating disorders and obesity: A comprehensive handbook* (pp. 377–381). New York: Guilford.

Black, D. W., & Andreasen, N. C. (1994). Schizophrenia, schizophreniform disorder, and delusional (paranoid) disorder. In R. E. Hales, S. C. Yudofsky, & J. A. Talbott (Eds.), *The American Psychiatric Press textbook of psychiatry* (2nd ed.). Washington, DC: American Psychiatric Press.

Black, D. W., & Andreasen, N. C. (1999). Schizophrenia, schizophreniform disorder, and delusional (paranoid) disorders. In R. E. Hales, S. C. Yudofsky, & J. A. Talbott (Eds.), *American Psychiatric Press textbook of psychiatry* (3rd ed.). Washington, DC: American Psychiatric Press.

Blacker, D., & Tsuang, M. T. (1999). Classification and DSM-IV. In A. M. Nicholi (Ed.), *The Harvard guide to psychiatry*. Cambridge, MA: Harvard University Press.

Blacker, L. (1999). The launching phase of the life cycle. In B. Carter & M. McGoldrick (Eds.), *The expanded family life cycle: Individual, family, and social perspectives* (3rd ed., pp. 287–306). Boston: Allyn & Bacon.

Blagrove, M. (1992). Dreams as a reflection of our waking concerns and abilities: A critique of the problem-solving paradigm in dream research. *Dreaming, 2*, 205–220.

Blagrove, M. (1996). Problems with the cognitive psychological modeling of dreaming. *Journal of Mind and Behavior, 17*, 99–134.

Blair, S. L. (1993). Employment, family, and perceptions of marital quality among husbands and wives. *Journal of Family Issues, 14*, 189–212.

Blair, S. N., Kohl, H. W., Gordon, N. F., & Paffenbarger, R. S. (1992). How much physical activity is good for health? In G. S. Omenn, J. E. Fielding, & L. B. Lave (Eds.), *Annual review of public health* (Vol. 13). Palo Alto, CA: Annual Reviews.

Blair, S. N., Kohl, H. W., Paffenbarger, R. S., Clark, D. G., Cooper, K. H., & Gibbons, L. W. (1989). Physical fitness and all-cause mortality: A prospective study of healthy men and women. *Journal of the American Medical Association, 262*, 2395–2401.

Blakeslee, T. R. (1980). *The right brain*. Garden City, NY: Doubleday/Anchor.

Blanchard, F. A., Lilly, T., & Vaughn, L. A. (1991). Reducing the expression of racial prejudice. *Psychological Science, 2*, 101–105.

Blanchard, R., Zucker, K. J., Bradley, S. J., & Hume, C. S. (1995). Birth order and siblings sex ratio in homosexual male adolescents and probably prehomosexual feminine boys. *Developmental Psychology, 31*, 22–30.

Blanco, C., Laje, G., Olfson, M., Marcus, S. C., & Pincus, H. A. (2002). Trends in the treatment of bipolar disorder by outpatient psychiatrists. *American Journal of Psychiatry, 159*, 1005–1010.

Blankenhorn, D. (1995). *Fatherless America: Confronting our most urgent social problem*. New York: Basic Books.

Blascovich, J., Wyer, N. A., Swart, L. A., & Kibler, J. L. (1997). Racisim and racial categorization. *Journal of Personality and Social Psychology, 72*, 1364–1372.

Blashfield, R. K., & Livesley, W. J. (1999). Classification. In T. Millon, P. H. Blaney, & R. D. Davis (Eds.), *Oxford textbook of psychopathology*. New York: Oxford University Press.

Blass, T. (1991). Understanding behavior in the Milgram obedience experiment: The role of personality, situations, and their interactions.

Journal of Personality and Social Psychology, 60, 398–413.

Blass, T. (1999). The Milgram Paradigm after 35 years: Some things we now know about obedience to authority. *Journal of Applied Social Psychology, 29,* 955–978.

Blau, Z. S. (1981). *Black children/white children: Competence, socialization and social structure.* New York: Free Press.

Blazer, D. G. (2000). Mood disorders: Epidemiology. In B. J. Sadock & V. A. Sadock (Eds.), *Kaplan and Sadock's Comprehensive textbook of psychiatry* (7th ed., Vol. 1, pp. 1298–1307). Philadelphia: Lippincott/Williams & Wilkins.

Bleuler, E. (1911). *Dementia praecox or the group F schizophrenias.* New York: International Universities Press.

Blieszner, R., & Adams, R. G. (1992). *Adult friendship.* Newbury Park, CA: Sage.

Bliwise, D. L. (2000). Normal aging. In M. H. Kryger, T. Roth, & W. C. Dement (Eds.), *Principles and practice of sleep medicine.* Philadelphia: Saunders.

Block, J. (1981). Some enduring and consequential structures of personality. In A. I. Rabins, J. Aronoff, A. Barclay, & R. Zucker (Eds.), *Further explorations in personality.* New York: Wiley.

Block, J. (1995). A contrarian view of the five-factor approach to personality description. *Psychological Bulletin, 117,* 187–215.

Block, J. R., & Yuker, H. E. (1992). *Can you believe your eyes?: Over 250 illusions and other visual oddities.* New York: Brunner/Mazel.

Block, L. G., & Keller, P. A. (1997). Effects of self-efficacy and vividness on the persuasiveness of health communication. *Journal of Consumer Psychology, 6,* 31–54.

Bloodworth, R. C. (1987). Major problems associated with marijuana abuse. *Psychiatric Medicine, 3*(3), 173–184.

Bloom, B. L. (1984). *Community mental health: A general introduction.* Pacific Grove, CA: Brooks/Cole.

Bloom, B. S. (Ed.). (1985). *Developing talent in young people.* New York: Ballantine.

Bloom, F. E. (1995). Cellular mechanisms active in emotion. In M. S. Gazzaniga (Ed), *The cognitive neurosciences.* Cambridge, MA: MIT Press.

Bloomfield, H. H., & Kory, R. B. (1976). *Happiness: The TM program, psychiatry, and enlightenment.* New York: Simon & Schuster.

Blum, R., & Rinehart, P. (2000). *Reducing the risk: Connections that make a difference in the lives of youth.* Minneapolis: University of Minne-

sota, Division of General Pediatrics and Adolescent Health.

Blundell, J. E., & Halford, J. C. G. (1998). Serotonin and appetite regulation: Implications for the pharmacological treatment of obesity. *CNS Drugs, 9,* 473–495.

Bock, G. R., & Goode, J. A. (Eds.). (1996). *Genetics of criminal and antisocial behavior.* Chichester, England: Wiley.

Boden, J. M., & Baumeister, R. F. (1997). Repressive coping: Distraction using pleasant thoughts and memories. *Journal of Personality and Social Psychology, 73,* 45–62.

Bodenheimer, T. (2000). Uneasy alliance: Clinical investigators and the pharmaceutical industry. *New England Journal of Medicine, 342,* 1539–1544.

Boehm, L. E. (1994). The validity effect: A search for mediating variables. *Personality and Social Psychology Bulletin, 20,* 285–293.

Bogartz, R. S., & Shinskey, J. L. (1998). On perception of a partially occluded object in 6-month-olds. *Cognitive Development, 13,* 141–163.

Bogen, J. E. (1985). The dual brain: Some historical and methodological aspects. In D. F. Benson & E. Zaidel (Eds.), *The dual brain: Hemispheric specialization in humans.* New York: Guilford.

Bogen, J. E. (1990). Partial hemispheric independence with the neocommissures intact. In C. Trevarthen (Ed.), *Brain circuits and functions of the mind. Essays in honor of Roger W. Sperry.* Cambridge, MA: Cambridge University Press.

Boggild, H., & Knutsson, A. (1999). Shift work, risk factors and cardiovascular disease. *Scandinavian Journal of Work, Environment & Health, 25*(2), 85–99.

Bohannon, J. N., III, & Bonvillian, J. D. (2001). Theoretical approaches to language acquisition. In J. B. Gleason (Ed.), *The development of language* (5th ed., pp. 254–314). Boston: Allyn & Bacon.

Bohannon, J. N., III, & Warren-Leubecker, A. (1989). Theoretical approaches to language acquisition. In J. Berko Gleason (Ed.), *The development of language.* Columbus, OH: Merrill.

Bohannon, J. N., III, MacWhinney, B., & Snow, C. (1990). No negative evidence revisited: Beyond learnability or who has to prove what to whom. *Developmental Psychology, 26,* 221–226.

Bohner, G., & Schwarz, N. (2001). Attitudes, persuasion, and behavior. In A. Tesser & N. Schwarz (Eds.), *Blackwell handbook of social psychology: Intraindividual processes.* Malden, MA: Blackwell.

Bohning, D. E., Lorberbaum, J. P., Shastri, A., Nahas, Z., & George, M. S. (1998). Structural brain imaging (CT and MRI) in primary psychiatry. *Primary Psychiatry, 5,* 46–51.

Boland, R. J., & Keller, M. B. (2002). Course and outcome of depression. In I. H. Gotlib & C. L. Hammen (Eds.), *Handbook of depression.* New York: Guilford.

Bolger, N. (1990). Coping as a personality process: A prospective study. *Journal of Personality and Social Psychology, 59,* 525–537.

Bolles, R. C. (1975). *Theory of motivation.* New York: Harper & Row.

Bolles, R. C. (1990). A functionalistic approach to feeding. In E. D. Capaldi & T. L. Powley (Eds.), *Taste, experience, and feeding* (pp. 3–13). Washington, DC: American Psychological Association.

Bolles, R. C., & Fanselow, M. S. (1980). A perceptual-defensive-recuperative model of fear and pain. *Behavioral and Brain Sciences, 3,* 291–323.

Bond, C. F., Jr., Pitre, U., & Van Leeuwen, M. D. (1991). Encoding operations and the next-in-line effect. *Personality and Social Psychology Bulletin, 17,* 435–441.

Bond, R., & Smith, P. B. (1996). Culture and conformity: A meta-analysis of studies using Asch's line judgment task. *Psychological Bulletin, 119,* 111–137.

Boninger, D. S., Krosnick, J. A., Berent, M. K., & Fabrigar, L. R. (1995). The causes and consequences of attitude importance. In R. E. Petty & J. A. Krosnick (Eds.), *Attitude strength: Antecedents and consequences.* Mahwah, NJ: Erlbaum.

Bonn, D. (1996). Melatonin's multifarious marvels: Miracle or myth? *Lancet, 347,* 184.

Bonnet, M. H. (1991). Sleep deprivation. In M. Kryger, T. Roth, & W. C. Dement (Eds.), *Principles and practice of sleep medicine* (2nd ed.). Philadelphia: Saunders.

Bonnet, M. H. (2000). Sleep deprivation. In M. H. Kryger, T. Roth, & W. C. Dement (Eds.), *Principles and practice of sleep medicine.* Philadelphia: Saunders.

Booth, C. L., Clarke-Stewart, K. A., Vandell, D. L., McCartney, K., & Owen, M. T. (2002). Child-care usage and mother-infant "quality time." *Journal of Marriage and Family, 64,* 16–26.

Booth, D. (1994). Palatability and the intake of food and drinks. In M. S. Westerterp-Plantenga, E. W. H. M. Frederix, & A. B. Steffens (Eds.), *Food intake and energy expenditure.* Boca Raton, FL: CRC Press.

Bootzin, R. R., Manber, R., Loewy, D. H., Kuo, T. F., & Franzen, P. L.

(2001). Sleep disorders. In P. B. Sutker & H. E. Adams (Eds.), *Comprehensive handbook of psychopathology.* New York: Kluwer Academic/Plenum.

Borbely, A. A. (1986). *Secrets of sleep.* New York: Basic Books.

Borbely, A. A. (1994). Sleep homeostasis and models of sleep regulation. In M. H. Kryger, T. Roth, & W. C. Dement (Eds.), *Principles and practice of sleep medicine* (2nd ed.). Philadelphia: Saunders.

Borbely, A. A., & Achermann, P. (2000). Sleep homeostasis and models of sleep regulation. In M. H. Kryger, T. Roth & W. C. Dement (Eds.), *Principles and practice of sleep medicine.* Philadelphia: Saunders.

Borges, B., Goldstein, D. G., Ortmann, A., & Gigerenzer, G. (1999). Can ignorance beat the stock market? In G. Gigerenzer, P. M. Todd & ABC Research Group (Eds.), *Simple heuristics that make us smart* (pp. 59–74). New York: Oxford University Press.

Borgida, E., & Nisbett, R. E. (1977). The differential impact of abstract vs. concrete information on decisions. *Journal of Applied Social Psychology, 7,* 258–271.

Boring, E. G. (1966). A note on the origin of the word *psychology. Journal of the History of the Behavioral Sciences, 2,* 167.

Bornstein, B. H., & Zickafoose, D. J. (1999). "I know I know it, I know I saw it": The stability of the confidence-accuracy relationship across domains. *Journal of Experimental Psychology: Applied, 5,* 76–88.

Bosson, J. K., & Swann, W. B. (2001). The paradox of the sincere chameleon: Strategic self-verification in close relationships. In J. H. Harvey & A. Wenzel (Eds.), *Close romantic relationships: Maintenance and enhancement.* Mahwah, N.J.: Erlbaum.

Bouchard, C. (2002). Genetic influences on body weight. In C. G. Fairburn & K. D. Brownell (Eds.), *Eating disorders and obesity: A comprehensive handbook* (pp. 16–21). New York: Guilford.

Bouchard, T. J., Jr. (1997). IQ similarity in twins reared apart: Findings and responses to critics. In R. J. Sternberg, & E. L. Grigorenko (Eds.), *Intelligence, heredity, and environment.* New York: Cambridge University Press.

Bouchard, T. J., Jr. (1998). Genetic and environmental influences on adult intelligence and special mental abilities. *Human Biology, 70,* 257–279.

Bouchard, T. J., Jr., Lykken, D. T., McGue, M., Segal, N. L., & Tellegen, A. (1990). Sources of human psychological differences: The Minnesota study of twins reared apart. *Science, 250,* 223–228.

Boudreaux, E., Carmack, C. L., Scarinci, I. C., & Brantley, P. J. (1998). Predicting smoking stage of change among a sample of low socioeconomic status, primary care outpatients: Replication and extension using decisional balance and self-efficacy theories. *International Journal of Behavioral Medicine, 5,* 148–165.

Bouman, T. K., Eifert, G. H., & Lejeuz, C. W. (1999). Somatoform disorders. In T. Millon, P. H. Blaney, & R. D. Davis (Eds.), *Oxford textbook of psychopathology* (pp. 444–465). New York: Oxford University Press.

Bourguignon, E. (1972). Dreams and altered states of consciousness in anthropological research. In F. L. K. Hsu (Ed.), *Psychological anthropology* (2nd ed.). Cambridge, MA: Schenkman.

Bousfield, W. A. (1953). The occurrence of clustering in the recall of randomly arranged associates. *Journal of General Psychology, 49,* 229–240.

Bouton, M. E. (1994). Context, ambiguity, and classical conditioning. *Current Directions in Psychological Science, 3,* 49–53.

Bouton, M. E., & Nelson, J. B. (1998). The role of context in classical conditioning: Some implications for cognitive behavior therapy. In W. O'Donohue (Ed.), *Learning and behavior therapy.* Boston: Allyn & Bacon.

Bowd, A. D., & Shapiro, K. J. (1993). The case against laboratory animal research in psychology. *Journal of Social Issues, 49*(1), 133–142.

Bower, G. H. (1970). Organizational factors in memory. *Cognitive Psychology, 1,* 18–46.

Bower, G. H. (2000). A brief history of memory research. In E. Tulving & F. I. M. Craik (Eds.), *The Oxford handbook of memory* (pp. 3–32). New York: Oxford University Press.

Bower, G. H., & Clark, M. C. (1969). Narrative stories as mediators of serial learning. *Psychonomic Science, 14,* 181–182.

Bower, G. H., & Springston, F. (1970). Pauses as recoding points in letter series. *Journal of Experimental Psychology, 83,* 421–430.

Bower, G. H., Clark, M. C., Lesgold, A. M., & Winzenz, D. (1969). Hierarchical retrieval schemes in recall of categorized word lists. *Journal of Verbal Learning and Verbal Behavior, 8,* 323–343.

Bowlby, J. (1969). *Attachment and loss: Vol. 1. Attachment.* New York: Basic Books.

Bowlby, J. (1973). *Attachment and loss: Vol. 2. Separation, anxiety and anger.* New York: Basic Books.

Bowlby, J. (1980). *Attachment and loss: Vol. 3. Sadness and depression.* New York: Basic Books.

Boynton, R. M. (1990). Human color perception. In K. N. Leibovic (Ed.), *Science of vision.* New York: Springer-Verlag.

Bozarth, M. A., & Wise, R. A. (1985). Toxicity associated with long-term intravenous heroin and cocaine self-administration in the rat. *Journal of the American Medical Association, 254*(1), 81–83.

Bradbury, T. N. (1998). *The developmental course of marital dysfunction.* New York: Cambridge University Press.

Bradshaw, J. L. (1981). In two minds. *Behavioral and Brain Sciences, 4,* 101–102.

Bradshaw, J. L. (1989). *Hemispheric specialization and psychological function.* New York: Wiley.

Brady, K. T., Myrick, H., & Malcolm, R. (1999). Sedative-hypnotic and anxiolytic agents. In B. S. McCrady & E. E. Epstein (Eds.), *Addictions: A comprehensive guidebook.* New York: Oxford University Press.

Braffman, W., & Kirsch, I. (1999). Imaginative suggestibility and hypnotizability: An empirical analysis. *Journal of Personality and Social Psychology, 77,* 578–587.

Braginsky, D. D. (1985). Psychology: Handmaiden to society. In S. Koch & D. E. Leary (Eds.), *A century of psychology as science.* New York: McGraw-Hill.

Brainerd, C. J. (1996). Piaget: A centennial celebration. *Psychological Science, 7,* 191–195.

Bransford, J. D., & Stein, B. S. (1993). *The IDEAL problem solver.* New York: W. H. Freeman.

Brase, G. L., Cosmides, L., & Tooby, J. (1998). Individuation, counting, and statistical inference: The role of frequency and whole-object representations in judgment under certainty. *Journal of Experimental Psychology: General, 127,* 3–21.

Brawman-Mintzer, O., Lydiard, R. B., & Ballenger, J. C. (2000). Buspirone. In B. J. Sadock & V. A. Sadock (Eds.), *Kaplan and Sadock's comprehensive textbook of psychiatry* (7th ed., Vol. 1, pp. 2329–2333). Philadelphia: Lippincott/Williams & Wilkins.

Breedlove, S. M. (1992). Sexual differentiation of the brain and behavior. In J. B. Becker, S. M. Breedlove, & D. Crews (Eds.), *Behavioral endocrinology.* Cambridge, MA: MIT Press.

Breedlove, S. M. (1994). Sexual differentiation of the human nervous system. *Annual Review of Psychology, 45,* 389–418.

Breggin, P. R. (1990). Brain damage, dementia and persistent cognitive dysfunction associated with neuroleptic drugs: Evidence, etiology, implications. *The Journal of Mind and Behavior, 11*(3/4), 425–464.

Breggin, P. R. (1991). *Toxic psychiatry.* New York: St. Martin's Press.

Brehm, J. W. (1966). *A theory of psychological reactance.* New York: Academic Press.

Breland, K., & Breland, M. (1961). The misbehavior of organisms. *American Psychologist, 16,* 681–684.

Breland, K., & Breland, M. (1966). *Animal behavior.* New York: Macmillan.

Bremner, J. G. (2001). Cognitive development: Knowledge of the physical world. In G. Bremner & A. Fogel (Eds.), *Blackwell handbook of infant development* (pp. 99–138). Malden, MA: Blackwell.

Brende, J. O. (2000). Stress effects of floods. In G. Fink (Ed.), *Encyclopedia of stress* (Vol. 2, pp. 153–157). San Diego: Academic Press.

Brennan, K. A., & Shaver, P. R. (1995). Dimensions of adult attachment, affect regulation, and romantic relationship functioning. *Personality and Social Psychology Bulletin, 21,* 267–283.

Brennan, P. A., & Mednick, S. A. (1997). Medical histories of antisocial individuals. In D. M. Stoff, J. Breiling & J. D. Maser (Eds.), *Handbook of antisocial behavior.* New York: Wiley.

Breslau, N., Kilbey, M. M., & Andreski, P. (1991). Nicotine dependence, major depression, and anxiety in young adults. *Archives of General Psychiatry, 48,* 1069–1074.

Breslau, N., Kilbey, M. M., & Andreski, P. (1993). Nicotine dependence and major depression: New evidence from a prospective investigation. *Archives of General Psychiatry, 50,* 31–35.

Bretl, D. J., & Cantor, J. (1988). The portrayal of men and women in U.S. television commercials: A recent content analysis and trend over 15 years. *Sex Roles, 18,* 595–609.

Brewer, W. F., & Treyens, J. C. (1981). Role of schemata in memory for places. *Cognitive Psychology, 13,* 207–230.

Brewster, K. L., & Padavic, I. (2000). Change in gender-ideology, 1977–1996: The contributions of intracohort change and population turnover. *Journal of Marriage and the Family, 62,* 477–487.

Brickman, P., Coates, D., & Janoff-Bulman, R. (1978). Lottery winners and accident victims: Is happiness relative? *Journal of Personality and Social Psychology, 36,* 917–927.

Briere, J., & Conte, J. R. (1993). Self-reported amnesia for abuse in adults molested as children. *Journal of Traumatic Stress, 6*(1), 21–31.

Bringmann, W. G., & Balk, M. M. (1992). Another look at Wilhelm Wundt's publication record. *History of Psychology Newsletter, 24*(3/4), 50–66.

Brislin, R. (1993). *Understanding culture's influence on behavior.* Fort Worth: Harcourt Brace College Publishers.

Broadbent, D. E. (1958). *Perception and communication.* New York: Pergamon Press.

Brobeck, J. R., Tepperman, T., & Long, C. N. (1943). Experimental hypothalamic hyperphagia in the albino rat. *Yale Journal of Biology and Medicine, 15,* 831–853.

Bröder, A. (1998). Deception can be acceptable. *American Psychologist, 53,* 805–806.

Brody, N. (1992). *Intelligence.* San Diego: Academic Press.

Brody, N. (2000). History of theories and measurements of intelligence. In R. J. Sternberg (Ed.), *Handbook of intelligence* (pp. 16–33). New York: Cambridge University Press.

Brody, N., & Crowley, M. J. (1995). Environmental (and genetic) influences on personality and intelligence. In D. H. Saklofske & M. Zeidner (Eds.), *International handbook of personality and intelligence.* New York: Plenum.

Bromage, B. K., & Mayer, R. E. (1986). Quantitative and qualitative effects of repetition on learning from technical text. *Journal of Educational Psychology, 78,* 271–278.

Bronstein, P., & Quina, K. (1988). Perspectives on gender balance and cultural diversity in the teaching of psychology. In P. Bronstein & K. Quina (Eds.), *Teaching a psychology of people: Resources for gender and sociocultural awareness.* Washington, DC: American Psychological Association.

Brooks-Gunn, J. (1991). Maturational timing variations in adolescent girls, antecedents of. In R. M. Lerner, A. C. Petersen, & J. Brooks-Gunn (Eds.), *Encyclopedia of adolescence.* New York: Garland.

Brooks-Gunn, J., & Reiter, E. O. (1990). The role of pubertal process. In S. S. Feldman & G. R. Elliot (Eds.), *At the threshold: The developing adolescent.* Cambridge, MA: Harvard University Press.

Broughton, R. (1994). Important underemphasized aspects of sleep onset. In R. D. Ogilvie & J. R. Harsh (Eds.), *Sleep onset: Normal and abnormal processes.* Washington, DC: American Psychological Association.

Brown, A. S. (1991). A review of the tip-of-the-tongue experience. *Psychological Bulletin, 109,* 204–223.

Brown, A. S. (1999). New perspectives on the neurodevelopmental hypothesis of schizophrenia. *Psychiatric Annals, 29*(3), 128–130.

Brown, A. S., van Os, J., Driessens, C., Hoek, H. W., & Susser, E. S. (2000). Further evidence of relation between prenatal famine and major affective disorder. *American Journal of Psychiatry, 157,* 190–195.

Brown, D., Scheflin, A. W., & Hammond, D. C. (1998). *Memory, trauma treatment, and the law.* New York: Norton.

Brown, D., Scheflin, A. W., & Whitfield, C. L. (1999). Recovered memories: The current weight of the evidence in science and in the courts. *Journal of Psychiatry & Law, 27,* 5–156.

Brown, E. J., Juster, H. R., Heimberg, R. G., & Winning, C. D. (1998). Stressful life events and personality styles: Relation to impairment and treatment outcome in patients with social phobia. *Journal of Anxiety Disorders, 12,* 233–251.

Brown, H. D., & Kosslyn, S. M. (1993). Cerebral lateralization. *Current Opinion in Neurobiology, 3,* 183–186.

Brown, J. D., & Rogers, R. J. (1991). Self-serving attributions: The role of physiological arousal. *Personality and Social Psychology Bulletin, 17,* 501–506.

Brown, M. (1974). Some determinants of persistence and initiation of achievement-related activities. In J. W. Atkinson & J. O. Raynor (Eds.), *Motivation and achievement.* Washington, DC: Halsted.

Brown, R. (1973). *A first language: The early stages.* Cambridge, MA: Harvard University Press.

Brown, R., & Hanlon, C. (1970). Derivational complexity and order of acquisition. In J. R. Hayes (Ed.), *Cognition and the development of language.* New York: Wiley.

Brown, R., & Kulik, J. (1977). Flashbulb memories. *Cognition, 5,* 73–79.

Brown, R., & McNeill, D. (1966). The "tip-of-the-tongue" phenomenon. *Journal of Verbal Learning and Verbal Behavior, 5*(4), 325–337.

Brown, R. D., Goldstein, E., & Bjorklund, D. F. (2000). The history and zeitgeist of the repressed–false-memory debate: Scientific and sociological perspectives on suggestibility and childhood memory. In D. F. Bjorklund (Ed.), *False-memory creation in children and adults* (pp. 1–30). Mahwah, NJ: Erlbaum.

Brown, R. T. (1989). Creativity: What are we to measure? In J. A. Glover, R. R. Ronning, & C. R. Reynolds (Eds.), *Handbook of creativity.* New York: Plenum.

Brown, S. C., & Craik, F. I. M. (2000). Encoding and retrieval of information. In E. Tulving & F. I. M. Craik (Eds.), *The Oxford handbook of memory* (pp. 93–108). New York: Oxford University Press.

Browne, A., & Finkelhor, D. (1998). The impact of child sexual abuse: A review of the research. In R. A. Baker (Ed.), *Child sexual abuse and false memory syndrome.* Amherst, NY: Prometheus Books.

Brownell, H. H., & Gardner, H. (1981). Hemisphere specialization: Definitions not incantations. *Behavioral and Brain Sciences, 4,* 64–65.

Brownell, K. D. (2002). The environment and obesity. In C. G. Fairburn & K. D. Brownell (Eds.), *Eating disorders and obesity: A comprehensive handbook* (pp. 433–438). New York: Guilford.

Brownell, K. D., & Wadden, T. A. (2000). Obesity. In B. J. Sadock & V. A. Sadock (Eds.), *Kaplan and Sadock's comprehensive textbook of psychiatry* (7th ed., Vol. 2, pp. 1787–1796). Philadelphia: Lippincott Williams & Wilkins.

Bruce, D., Dolan, A., & Phillips-Grant, K. (2000). On the transition from childhood amnesia to the recall of personal memories. *Psychological Science, 11,* 360–364.

Bruch, H. (1978). *The golden cage: The enigma of anorexia nervosa.* Cambridge, MA: Harvard University Press.

Bruckner-Gordon, F., Gangi, B. K., & Wallman, G. U. (1988). *Making therapy work: Your guide to choosing, using, and ending therapy.* New York: Harper & Row.

Bruer, J. T. (1999). *The myth of the first three years: A new understanding of early brain development and lifelong learning.* New York: Free Press.

Bruggerman, E. L., & Hart, K. J. (1996). Cheating, lying, and moral reasoning by religious and secular high school students. *Journal of Educational Research, 89,* 340–344.

Bruner, J. S. (1974). Concluding comments and summary of conference. In J. L. M. Dawson & W. J. Lonner (Eds.), *Readings in cross-cultural psychology.* Hong Kong: University of Hong Kong Press.

Bryden, M. P. (1982). *Laterality: Functional asymmetry in the intact brain.* New York: Academic Press.

Buchanan, R. W., & Carpenter, W. T. (2000). Schizophrenia: Introduction and overview. In B. J. Sadock & V. A. Sadock (Eds.), *Kaplan and Sadock's comprehensive textbook of psychiatry* (7th ed., Vol. 1). Philadelphia: Lippincott/Williams & Wilkins.

Buck, L. B. (2000). Smell and taste: The chemical senses. In E. R. Kandel, J. H. Schwartz, & T. M. Jessell (Eds.), *Principles of neural science.* New York: McGraw-Hill.

Bühler, C., & Allen, M. (1972). *Introduction to humanistic psychology.* Pacific Grove, CA: Brooks/Cole.

Bull, D. L. (1999). A verified case of recovered memories of sexual abuse. *American Journal of Psychotherapy, 53,* 221–224.

Bunce, S. C., Bernat, E., Wong, P. S., & Shevrin, H. (1999). Further evidence for unconscious learning: Preliminary support for the conditioning of facial EMG to subliminal stimuli. *Journal of Psychiatric Research, 33,* 341–347.

Bunch, B. (1994). Mainstreaming. In R. J. Sternberg (Ed.), *Encyclopedia of human intelligence.* New York: Macmillan.

Burger, J. M. (1986). Temporal effects on attributions: Actor and observer differences. *Social Cognition, 4,* 377–387.

Burger, J. M. (1997). *Personality.* Pacific Grove: Brooks/Cole.

Burger, J. M. (1999). The foot-in-the-door compliance procedure: A multiple process analysis review. *Personality and Social Psychology Review, 3,* 303–325.

Burgess, C., O'Donohoe, A., & Gill, M. (2000). Agony and ecstasy: A review of MDMA effects and toxicity. *European Psychiatry, 15,* 287–294.

Burnstein, E., Crandall, C., & Kitayama, S. (1994). Some neo-Darwinian decision rules for altruism: Weighing cues for inclusive fitness as a function of the biological importance of the decision. *Journal of Personality and Social Psychology, 67,* 773–789.

Buss, D. M. (1985). Human mate selection. *American Scientist, 73,* 47–51.

Buss, D. M. (1988). The evolution of human intrasexual competition: Tactics of mate attraction. *Journal of Personality and Social Psychology, 54,* 616–628.

Buss, D. M. (1989). Sex differences in human mate preferences: Evolutionary hypotheses tested in 37 cultures. *Behavioral and Brain Sciences, 12,* 1–49.

Buss, D. M. (1991). Evolutionary personality psychology. *Annual Review of Psychology, 42,* 459–491.

Buss, D. M. (1994a). *The evolution of desire: Strategies of human mating.* New York: Basic Books.

Buss, D. M. (1994b). Mate preferences in 37 cultures. In W. J. Lonner & R. S. Malpass (Eds.), *Psychology and culture.* Boston: Allyn & Bacon.

Buss, D. M. (1995). Evolutionary psychology: A new paradigm for psychological science. *Psychological Inquiry, 6,* 1–30.

Buss, D. M. (1996). The evolutionary psychology of human social strategies. In E. T. Higgins & A. W. Kruglanski (Eds.), *Social psychology: Handbook of basic principles.* New York: Guilford.

Buss, D. M. (1997). Evolutionary foundation of personality. In R. Hogan, J. Johnson, & S. Briggs (Eds.), *Handbook of personality psychology.* San Diego: Academic Press.

Buss, D. M. (1998). The psychology of human mate selection: Exploring the complexity of the strategic repertoire. In C. Crawford, & D. L. Krebs (Eds.), *Handbook of evolutionary psychology: Ideas, issues, and applications.* Mahwah, NJ: Erlbaum.

Buss, D. M. (1999). *Evolutionary psychology: The new science of the mind.* Boston: Allyn & Bacon.

Buss, D. M. (2001). Cognitive biases and emotional wisdom in the evolution of conflict between the sexes. *Current Directions in Psychological Science, 10,* 219–223.

Buss, D. M., & Kenrick, D. T. (1998). Evolutionary social psychology. In D. T. Gilbert, S. T. Fiske, & G. Lindzey (Eds.), *The handbook of social psychology.* New York: McGraw-Hill.

Buss, D. M., & Schmitt, D. P. (1993). Sexual strategies theory: A contextual evolutionary analysis of human mating. *Psychological Review, 100,* 204–232.

Bussey, K., & Bandura, A. (1984). Influence of gender constancy and social power on sex-linked modeling. *Journal of Personality and Social Psychology, 47,* 1292–1302.

Bussey, K., & Bandura, A. (1999). Social cognitive theory of gender development and differentiation. *Psychological Review, 106,* 676–713.

Butcher, J. N. (1990). *The MMPI-2 in psychological treatment.* New York: Oxford University Press.

Butcher, J. N., & Keller, L. S. (1984). Objective personality assessment. In G. Goldstein & M. Hersen (Eds.), *Handbook of psychological assessment.* New York: Pergamon Press.

Butler, J. L., & Baumeister, R. F. (1998). The trouble with friendly faces: Skilled performance with a supportive audience. *Journal of Personality and Social Psychology, 75,* 1213–1230.

Buxton, M. N., Arkey, Y., Lagos, J., Deposito, F., Lowenthal, F., & Simring, S. (1981). Stress and platelet aggregation in hemophiliac children and their family members. *Research Communications in Psychology, Psychiatry and Behavior, 6*(1), 21–48.

Byne, W., & Parsons, B. (1993). Human sexual orientation: The biological theories reappraised. *Archives of General Psychiatry, 50,* 228–239.

Byne, W., Kemether, E., Jones, L., Haroutunian, V., & Davis, K. L. (1999). The neurochemistry of schizophrenia. In D. S. Charney, E. J. Nestler & B. S. Bunney (Eds.), *Neurobiology of mental illness* (pp. 236–245). New York: Oxford University Press.

Byrne, D. (1997). An overview (and underview) of research and theory within the attraction paradigm. *Journal of Social and Personal Relationships, 14,* 417–431.

Byrne, D., Clore, G. L., & Smeaton, G. (1986). The attraction hypothesis: Do similar attitudes affect anything? *Journal of Personality and Social Psychology, 51,* 1167–1170.

Byrnes, J. P., Miller, D. C., & Schafer, W. D. (1999). Gender differences in risk taking: A meta-analysis. *Psychological Bulletin, 125,* 367–383.

Cabrera, N. J., Tamis-LeMonda, C. S., Bradley, R. H., Hofferth, S., & Lamb, M. E. (2000). Fatherhood in the twenty-first century. *Child Development, 71,* 127–136.

Cacioppo, J. T., & Berntson, G. G. (1999). The affect system: Architecture and operating characteristics. *Current Directions in Psychological Science, 8,* 133–137.

Cacioppo, J. T., & Gardner, W. L. (1999). Emotion. *Annual Review of Psychology, 50,* 191–214.

Cacioppo, J. T., Klein, D. J., Berntson, G. G., & Hatfield, E. (1993). The psychophysiology of emotions. In M. Lewis & J. M. Haviland (Eds.), *Handbook of emotions.* New York: Guilford.

Cahill, L., & McGaugh, J. L. (1998). Mechanisms of emotional arousal and lasting declarative memory. *Trends in Neurosciences, 21,* 294–299.

Cain, W. S. (1979). To know with the nose: Keys to odor identification. *Science, 203,* 467–470.

Cain, W. S. (1988). Olfaction. In R. C. Atkinson, R. J. Herrnstein, G. Lindzey, & R. D. Luce (Eds.), *Stevens' handbook of experimental psychology: Perception and motivation* (Vol. 1). New York: Wiley.

Caine, E. D., & Lyness, J. M. (2000). Delirium, dementia, and amnestic and other cognitive disorders. In B. J. Sadock & V. A. Sadock (Eds.), *Kaplan and Sadock's comprehensive textbook of psychiatry.* Philadelphia: Lippincott/Williams & Wilkins.

Calev, A., Phil, D., Pass, H. L., Shapira, B., Fink, M., Tubi, N., & Lerer, B. (1993). ECT and memory. In C. E. Coffey (Ed.), *The clinical science of electroconvulsive therapy.* Washington, DC: American Psychiatric Press.

Calhoun, L. G., & Tedeschi, R. G. (2001). Posttraumatic growth: The positive lessons of loss. In R. A. Neimeyer (Ed.), *Meaning reconstruction and the experience of loss* (pp. 157–172). Washington, DC: American Psychological Association.

Calkins, S. D., Fox, N. A., & Marshall, T. R. (1996). Behavioral and physiological antecedents of inhibited and uninhibited behavior. *Child Development, 67,* 523–540.

Callahan, C. M. (2000). Intelligence and giftedness. In R. J. Sternberg (Ed.), *Handbook of intelligence* (pp. 159–175). New York: Cambridge University Press.

Calof, D. (1998). Facing the truth about false memory. In R. A. Baker (Ed.), *Child sexual abuse and false memory syndrome.* Amherst, NY: Prometheus Books.

Calvert, C. (1997). Hate speech and its harms: A communication theory perspective. *Journal of Communication, 47,* 4–19.

Cameron, L., Leventhal, E. A., & Leventhal, H. (1993). Symptom representations and affect as determinants of care seeking in a community-dwelling, adult sample population. *Health Psychology, 12,* 171–179.

Cameron, N. (1963). *Personality development and psychopathology.* Boston: Houghton Mifflin.

Campbell, J. (1971). *Hero with a thousand faces.* New York: Harcourt Brace Jovanovich.

Campbell, J. D., Tesser, A., & Fairey, P. J. (1986). Conformity and attention to stimulus: Some temporal and contextual dynamics. *Journal of Personality and Social Psychology, 51,* 315–324.

Campbell, R., & Sais, E. (1995). Accelerated metalinguistic (phonological) awareness in bilingual children. *British Journal of Developmental Psychology, 13,* 61–68.

Campbell, R. J. (2000). Managed care. In B. J. Sadock & V. A. Sadock (Eds.), *Kaplan and Sadock's comprehensive textbook of psychiatry* (7th ed., Vol. 2). Philadelphia: Lippincott/Williams & Wilkins.

Campbell, W. K., & Sedikides, C. (1999). Self-threat magnifies the self-serving bias: A meta-analytic integration. *Review of General Psychology, 3,* 23–43.

Campfield, L. A. (2002). Leptin and body weight regulation. In C. G. Fairburn & K. D. Brownell (Eds.), *Eating disorders and obesity: A comprehensive handbook* (pp. 32–36). New York: Guilford.

Cancro, R., & Lehmann, H. E. (2000). Schizophrenia: Clinical features. In B. J. Sadock & V. A. Sadock (Eds.), *Kaplan and Sadock's comprehensive textbook of psychiatry* (7th ed., Vol. 1, pp. 1169–1198). Philadelphia: Lippincott/Williams & Wilkins.

Cannon, W. B. (1927). The James-Lange theory of emotions: A critical examination and an alternate theory. *American Journal of Psychology, 39,* 106–124.

Cannon, W. B. (1929). *Bodily changes in pain, hunger, fear and rage.* New York: Appleton.

Cannon, W. B. (1932). *The wisdom of the body.* New York: Norton.

Cannon, W. B., & Washburn, A. L. (1912). An explanation of hunger. *American Journal of Physiology, 29,* 444–454.

Cao, Y., Vikingstad, E. M., Huttenlocher, P. R., Towle, V. L., & Levin, D. N. (1994). Functional magnetic resonance imaging studies of the reorganization of the human head sensorimotor area after unilateral brain injury. *Proceeding of the National Academy of Sciences of the United States of America, 91,* 9612–9616.

Capaldi, E. D. (1996). Conditioned food preferences. In E. D. Capaldi (Ed.), *Why we eat what we eat: The psychology of eating* (pp. 53–81). Washington, DC: American Psychological Association.

Capaldi, E. D., & VandenBos, G. R. (1991). Taste, food exposure, and eating behavior. *Hospital and Community Psychiatry, 42*(8), 787–789.

Capelli, C. A., Nakagawa, N., & Madden, C. M. (1990). How children understand sarcasm: The role of context and intonation. *Child Development, 61,* 1824–1841.

Caporael, L. R., & Brewer, M. B. (1995). Hierarchical evolutionary theory: There is an alternative, and it's not creationism. *Psychological Inquiry, 6,* 31–34.

Carey, G., & Goldman, D. (1997). The genetics of antisocial behavior. In D. M. Stoff, J. Breiling, & J. D. Maser (Eds.), *Handbook of antisocial behavior.* New York: Wiley.

Carli, L. L. (1999). Cognitive, reconstruction, hindsight, and reactions to victims and perpetrators. *Personality & Social Psychology Bulletin, 25,* 966–979.

Carnegie, D. (1936). *How to win friends and influence people.* New York: Simon & Schuster.

Caro, R. M. (1986). The functions of stotting in Thomson's gazelles: Some tests of the predictions. *Animal Behavior, 34,* 663–684.

Carpenter, W. T. (1992). The negative symptom challenge. *Archives of General Psychiatry, 49,* 236–237.

Carpenter, W. T. (2002). From clinical trial to prescription. *Archives of General Psychology, 59,* 282–285.

Carrington, P. (1987). Managing meditation in clinical practice. In M. A. West (Ed.), *The psychology of meditation.* Oxford: Clarendon Press.

Carroll, J. M., & Russell, J. A. (1997). Facial expressions in Hollywood's portrayal of emotion. *Journal of Personality and Social Psychology, 72,* 164–176.

Carroll, M. E., & Overmier, J. B. (2001). *Animal research and human health.* Washington, DC: American Psychological Association.

Carskadon, M. A., & Dement, W. C. (2000). Normal human sleep: An overview. In M. H. Kryger, T. Roth, & W. C. Dement (Eds.), *Principles and practice of sleep medicine.* Philadelphia: Saunders.

Carskadon, M. A., & Rechtschaffen, A. (2000). Monitoring and staging human sleep. In M. H. Kryger, T. Roth, & W. C. Dement (Eds.), *Principles and practice of sleep medicine.* Philadelphia: Saunders.

Carson, R. C., & Butcher, C. N., & Coleman, J. C. (1988). *Abnormal psychology and modern life.* Glenview, IL: Scott, Foresman.

Carson, R. C., & Sanislow, C. A., III. (1993). The schizophrenias. In P. B. Sutker & H. E. Adams (Eds.), *Comprehensive handbook of psychopathology* (2nd ed.). New York: Plenum.

Carter, B. (1999). Becoming parents: The family with young children. In B. Carter & M. McGoldrick (Eds.), *The expanded family life cycle: Individual, family, and social perspectives* (3rd ed., pp. 249–273). Boston: Allyn & Bacon.

Carter, B., & McGoldrick, M. (1999). Overview: The expanded family life cycle: Individual, family, and social perspectives. In B. Carter & M. McGoldrick (Eds.), *The expanded family life cycle: Individual, family, and social perspectives* (3rd ed., pp. 1–26). Boston: Allyn & Bacon.

Carter, E. A., & McGoldrick, M. (1988). Overview: The changing family life cycle—A framework for family therapy. In E. A. Carter & M. McGoldrick (Eds.), *The changing family cycle: A framework for family therapy* (2nd ed.). New York: Gardner Press.

Carter, R. (1998). *Mapping the mind.* Berkeley: University of California Press.

Cartwright, R. D. (1994). Dreams and their meaning. In M. H. Kryger, T. Roth, & W. C. Dement (Eds.), *Principles and practice of sleep medicine* (2nd ed.). Philadelphia: Saunders.

Cartwright, R. D., & Lamberg, L. (1992). *Crisis dreaming.* New York: HarperCollins.

Cartwright, R. D. (1977). *Night life: Explorations in dreaming.* Englewood Cliffs, NJ: Prentice-Hall.

Cartwright, R. D. (1991). Dreams that work: The relation of dream incorporation to adaptation to stressful events. *Dreaming, 1,* 3–9.

Carver, C. S., & Scheier, M. F. (1994). Situational coping and coping dispositions in a stressful transaction. *Journal of Personality and Social Psychology, 66,* 184–195.

Carver, C. S., & Scheier, M. F. (1999). Optimism. In C. R. Snyder (Ed.), *Coping: The psychology of what works.* New York: Oxford University Press.

Carver, C. S., Scheier, M. F., & Weintraub, J. K. (1989). Assessing coping strategies: A theoretically based approach. *Journal of Personality and Social Psychology, 56,* 267–283.

Carver, C. S., Pozo, C., Harris, S. D., Noriega, V., Scheier, M. F., Robinson, D. S., Ketcham, A. S., Moffat, F. L., Jr., & Clark, K. C. (1993). How coping mediates the effect of optimism on distress: A study of women with early stage breast cancer. *Jour-*

nal of Personality and Social Psychology, 65, 375–390.

Case, D. A., Fantino, E., & Goodie, A. S. (1999). Base-rate training without case cues reduces base-rate neglect. Psychonomic Bulletin & Review, 6, 310–327.

Casey, R., & Rozin, P. (1989). Changing children's food preferences: Parent opinions. Appetite, 12, 171–182.

Caspi, A., & Herbener, E. S. (1990). Continuity and change: Assortative marriage and the consistency of personality in adulthood. Journal of Personality and Social Psychology, 58(2), 250–258.

Cassel, R. N. (2000). Third force psychology and person-centered theory: From ego-status to ego-ideal. Psychology: A Journal of Human Behavior, 37(3), 44–48.

Cassidy, J. (1999). The nature of the child's ties. In J. Cassidy & P. R. Shaver (Eds.), Handbook of attachment: Theory, research, and clinical applications. New York: Guilford.

Catalano, E. M. (1990). Getting to sleep. Oakland, CA: New Harbinger.

Catania, A. C. (1992). Reinforcement. In L. R. Squire (Ed.), Encyclopedia of learning and memory. New York: Macmillan.

Catania, J. A., Binson, D., Dolcini, M. M., Moskowitz, J. T., & van der Straten, A. (2001). In A. Baum, T. A. Revenson, & J. E. Singer (Eds.), Handbook of health psychology. Mahwah, NJ: Erlbaum.

Cattell, R. B. (1950). Personality: A systematic, theoretical and factual study. New York: McGraw-Hill.

Cattell, R. B. (1957). Personality and motivation: Structure and measurement. New York: Harcourt, Brace & World.

Cattell, R. B. (1963). Theory of fluid and crystallized intelligence: A critical experiment. Journal of Educational Psychology, 54, 1–22.

Cattell, R. B. (1965). The scientific analysis of personality. Baltimore: Penguin.

Cattell, R. B. (1966). The scientific analysis of personality. Chicago: Aldine.

Cattell, R. B. (1990). Advances in Cattellian personality theory. In L. A. Pervin (Ed.), Handbook of personality: Theory and research. New York: Guilford.

Cattell, R. B., Eber, H. W., & Tatsuoka, M. M. (1970). Handbook of the Sixteen Personality Factor Questionnaire (16PF). Champaign, IL: Institute for Personality and Ability Testing.

Catz, S. L., & Kelly, J. A. (2001). Living with HIV disease. In A. Baum, T. A. Revenson, & J. E. Singer (Eds.), Handbook of health psychology (pp. 841–850). Mahwah, NJ: Erlbaum.

Cavanaugh, J. C. (1993). Adult development and aging (2nd ed.). Pacific Grove, CA: Brooks/Cole.

Caverly, D. C., Orlando, V. P., & Mullen, J. L. (2000). Textbook study reading. In R. F. Flippo & D. C. Caverly (Eds.), Handbook of college reading and study strategy research. Mahwah, NJ: Erlbaum.

Ceci, S. J. (1990). On intelligence . . . more or less: A bio-ecological treatise on intellectual development. Englewood Cliffs, NJ: Prentice-Hall.

Ceci, S. J. (1991). How much does schooling influence general intelligence and its cognitive components? A reassessment of the evidence. Developmental Psychology, 27, 703–722.

Ceci, S. J., & Bruck, M. (1993). Suggestibility of the child witness: A historical review and synthesis. Psychological Bulletin, 113, 403–439.

Ceci, S. J., & Williams, W. M. (1997). Schooling, intelligence, and income. American Psychologist, 52, 1051–1058.

Ceci, S. J., Rosenblum, T., de Bruyn, E., & Lee, D. Y. (1997). A bio-ecological model of intellectual development: Moving beyond h2. In R. J. Sternberg & E. L. Grigorenko (Eds.), Intelligence, heredity, and environment. New York: Cambridge University Press.

Cerletti, U., & Bini, L. (1938). Un nuovo metodo di shockterapie "L'elettro-shock". Boll. Acad. Med. Roma, 64, 136–138.

Chaiken, S., & Maheswaran, D. (1994). Heuristic processing can bias systematic processing: Effects of source credibility, argument ambiguity, and task importance on attitude judgment. Journal of Personality and Social Psychology, 66, 460–473.

Chambers, K. C., & Phoenix, C. H. (1987). Differences among ovariectomized female rhesus macaques in the display of sexual behavior without and with estradiol treatment. Behavioral Neuroscience, 101, 303–308.

Chambless, D. L., & Hollon, S. D. (1998). Defining empirically supported therapies. Journal of Consulting & Clinical Psychology, 66, 7–18.

Chambless, D. L., & Ollendick, T. H. (2001). Empirically supported psychological interventions: Controversies and evidence. Annual Review of Psychology, 52, 685–716.

Chan, J. W. C., & Vernon, P. E. (1988). Individual differences among the peoples of China. In S. H. Irvine & J. W. Berry (Eds.), Human abilities in cultural context. New York: Cambridge University Press.

Chance, P. (2001, September/October). The brain goes to school: Why neuroscience research is going to the head of the class. Psychology Today, p. 72.

Chandler, C. C. (1991). How memory for an event is influenced by related events: Interference in modified recognition tests. Journal of Experimental Psychology: Learning, Memory, & Cognition, 17, 115–125.

Chandler, C. C., & Fisher, R. P. (1996). Retrieval processes and witness memory. In E. L. Bjork & R. A. Bjork (Eds.), Memory. San Diego: Academic Press.

Chao, R. (2001). Integrating culture and attachment. American Psychologist, 56, 822–823.

Chaplin, W. F., Phillips, J. B., Brown, J. D., Clanton, N. R., & Stein, J. L. (2000). Handshaking, gender, personality, and first impressions. Journal of Personality and Social Psychology, 79(1), 110–117.

Chapman, P. D. (1988). Schools as sorters: Lewis M. Terman, applied psychology, and the intelligence testing movement. New York: New York University Press.

Charney, D. S., Nagy, L. M., Bremer, J. D., Goddard, A. W., Yehuda, R., & Southwich, S. M. (1996). Neurobiological mechanisms of human anxiety. In B. S. Fogel, R. B. Schiffer, & S. M. Rao (Eds.), Neuropsychiatry. Baltimore: Williams & Wilkins.

Chemers, M. M., Hu, L., & Garcia, B. F. (2001). Academic self-efficacy and first year college student performance and adjustment. Journal of Educational Psychology, 93(1), 55–64.

Chess, S., & Thomas, A. (1996). Temperament: Theory and practice. New York: Brunner/Mazel.

Chiappelli, F., & Hodgson, D. (2000). Immune suppression. In G. Fink (Ed.), Encyclopedia of stress (Vol. 2, pp. 531–535). San Diego: Academic Press.

Chiriboga, D. A. (1989). Mental health at the midpoint: Crisis, challenge, or relief? In S. Hunter & M. Sundel (Eds.), Mid life myths: Issues, findings, and practice implications. Newbury Park, CA: Sage.

Chisholm, J. S. (1996). The evolutionary ecology of attachment organization. Human Nature, 7, 1–38.

Cho, K., Ennaceur, A., Cole, J. C., & Kook Suh, C. (2000). Chronic jet lag produces cognitive deficits. Journal of Neuroscience, 20(6), RC66.

Choi, I., Nisbett, R. E., & Norenzayan, A. (1999). Causal attribution across cultures: Variation and universality. Psychological Bulletin, 125, 47–63.

Chomsky, N. (1957). Syntactic structures. The Hague: Mouton.

Chomsky, N. (1959). A review of B. F. Skinner's "Verbal Behavior." Language, 35, 26–58.

Chomsky, N. (1965). Aspects of theory of syntax. Cambridge, MA: MIT Press.

Chomsky, N. (1975). Reflections on language. New York: Pantheon.

Chomsky, N. (1986). Knowledge of language: Its nature, origins, and use. New York: Praeger.

Choudhry, N. K., Stelfox, H. T., & Detsky, A. S. (2002). Relationships between authors of clinical practice guidelines and the pharmaceutical industry. Journal of the American Medical Association, 287(5), 612–617.

Christensen, L. (1988). Deception in psychological research: When is its use justified? Personality and Social Psychology Bulletin, 14, 664–675.

Christoph, R. T., Schoenfeld, G. A., & Tansky, J. W. (1998). Overcoming barriers to training utilizing technology: The influence of self-efficacy factors on multimedia-based training receptiveness. Human Resource Development Quarterly, 9, 25–38.

Chu, J. A., Frey, L. M., Ganzel, B. L., & Matthews, J. A. (1999). Memories of childhood abuse: Dissociation, amnesia, and corroboration. American Journal of Psychiatry, 156, 749–755.

Chun, M. M., & Wolfe, J. M. (2001). Visual attention. In E. B. Goldstein (Ed.), Blackwell handbook of perception. Malden, MA: Blackwell.

Church, A. T. (1994). Relating to Tellegen and five-factor models of personality structure. Journal of Personality and Social Psychology, 67, 898–909.

Church, A. T., & Lonner, W. J. (1998). The cross-cultural perspective in the study of personality: Rationale and current research. Journal of Cross-Cultural Psychology, 29, 32–62.

Church, R. M. (1989). Theories of timing behavior. In S. P. Klein & R. R. Mowrer (Eds.), Contemporary learning theories: Instrumental conditioning theory and the impact of biological constraints on learning. Hillsdale, NJ: Erlbaum.

Cialdini, R. B. (1993). Influence: Science and practice. Glenview, IL: HarperCollins.

Cialdini, R. B. (2001). Influence: Science and practice. Boston: Allyn & Bacon.

Cialdini, R. B., & Trost, M. R. (1998). Social influence: Social norms, conformity, and compliance. In D. T. Gilbert, S. T. Fiske, & G. Lindzey (Eds.), The handbook of social psychology. New York: McGraw-Hill.

Cialdini, R. B., Trost, M. R., & Newsom, J. T. (1995). Preference for consistency: The development of a valid measure and the discovery of surprising behavioral implications. Journal of Personality and Social Psychology, 69, 318–328.

Ciarrochi, J., Dean, F. P., & Anderson, S. (2002). Emotional intelligence moderates the relationship between stress and mental health. Personality & Individual Differences, 32, 197–209.

Clancy, S. A., Schacter, D. L., McNally, R. J., & Pitman, R. K. (2000). False recognition in women reporting recovered memories of sexual abuse. *Psychological Science, 11*, 26–31.

Clark, A. (1997). From text to process: Connectionism's contribution to the future of cognitive science. In D. M. John & C. E. Erneling (Eds.), *The future of the cognitive revolution.* New York: Oxford University Press.

Clark, E. V. (1995). Later lexical development and word formation. In P. Fletcher & B. MacWhinney (Eds.), *The handbook of child language.* Cambridge, MA: Blackwell.

Clark, L. F. (1993). Stress and the cognitive-conversational benefits of social interaction. *Journal of Social and Clinical Psychology, 12*, 25–55.

Clayton, T., & Craig, P. (2001). *Diana: Story of a princess.* New York: Pocket Books.

Cloninger, C. R., Adolfsson, R., & Svrakic, D. (1996). Mapping genes for human personality. *Nature Genetics, 12*, 3–4.

Coates, T. J., & Collins, C. (1998). Preventing HIV infection. *Scientific American, 279*(1), 96–97.

Coenen, A. (1998). Neuronal phenomena associated with vigilance and consciousness: From cellular mechanisms to electroencephalographic patterns. *Consciousness & Cognition: An International Journal, 7*, 42–53.

Cohen, C. E. (1981). Person categories and social perception: Testing some boundaries of the processing effects of prior knowledge. *Journal of Personality and Social Psychology, 40*, 441–452.

Cohen, C. I., & Thompson, K. S. (1992). Homeless mentally ill or mentally ill homeless? *American Journal of Psychiatry, 149*, 816–823.

Cohen, D. (1997). A critique of the use of neuroleptic drugs in psychiatry. In S. Fisher & R. P. Greenberg (Eds.), *From placebo to panacea: Putting psychiatric drugs to the test.* New York: Wiley.

Cohen, D., & McCubbin, M. (1990). The political economy of tardive dyskinesia: Asymmetries in power and responsibility. *The Journal of Mind and Behavior, 11*(3/4), 465–488.

Cohen, D. B. (1999). *Stranger in the nest: Do parents really shape their child's personality, intelligence, or character?* New York: Wiley.

Cohen, H. W., & Alderman, M. H. (2001). The association between depression and cardiovascular disease in patients with hypertension. *Primary Psychiatry, 8*(7), 39–54.

Cohen, M. N. (2002). An anthropologist looks at "race" and IQ testing. In J. M. Fish (Ed.), *Race and intelligence: Separating science from myth* (pp. 201–224). Mahwah, NJ: Erlbaum.

Cohen, N. J., Ryan, J., Hunt, C., Romine, L., Wszalek, T., & Nash, C. (1999). Hippocampal system and declarative (relational) memory: Summarizing the data from functional neuroimaging studies. *Hippocampus, 9*, 83–98.

Cohen, S., & Lichtenstein, E. (1990). Perceived stress, quitting smoking, and smoking relapse. *Health Psychology, 9*, 466–478.

Cohen, S., & Williamson, G. M. (1991). Stress and infectious disease in humans. *Psychological Bulletin, 109*(1), 5–24.

Cohen, S., Kessler, R. C., & Gordon, L. U. (1995). Strategies for measuring stress in studies of psychiatric and physical disorders. In S. Cohen, R. C. Kessler, & L. U. Gordon (Eds.), *Measuring stress: A guide for health and social scientists* (pp. 3–28). New York: Oxford University Press.

Cohen, S., Tyrrell, D. A. J., & Smith, A. P. (1993). Negative life events, perceived stress, negative affect, and susceptibility to the common cold. *Journal of Personality and Social Psychology, 64*, 131–140.

Cohen, S., Lichtenstein, E., Prochaska, J. O., Rossi, J. S., Gritz, E. R., Carr, C. R., Orleans, C. T., Schoenbach, V. J., Biener, L., Abrams, D., DiClemente, C., Curry, S., Marlatt, G. A., Cummings, K. M., Emont, S. L., Giovino, A., & Ossip-Klien, D. (1989). Debunking myths about self-quitting: Evidence from 10 prospective studies of persons who attempt to quit smoking by themselves. *American Psychologist, 44*, 1355–1365.

Cohn, E., Cohn, S., & Bradley, J. (1995). Notetaking, working memory, and learning principles of economics. *Journal of Economics Education, 26*, 291–307.

Coie, J. D., & Dodge, K. A. Aggression and antisocial behavior. In W. Damon & N. Eisenberg (Eds.), *Handbook of child psychology* (Vol. 3). New York: Wiley.

Colby, A., & Kohlberg, L. (1987). *The measurement of moral judgment* (Vols. 1–2). New York: Cambridge University Press.

Colder, C. R. (2001). Life stress, physiological and subjective indexes of negative emotionality and coping reasons for drinking: Is there evidence for a self-medication model of alcohol use? *Psychology of Addictive Behaviors, 15*, 237–245.

Cole, J. O., Goldberg, S. C., & Davis, J. M. (1966). Drugs in the treatment of psychosis. In P. Solomon (Ed.), *Psychiatric drugs.* New York: Grune & Stratton.

Cole, M. (1999). Culture in development. In M. H. Bornstein & M. E. Lamb (Eds.), *Developmental psychology: An advanced textbook* (4th ed.). Hillsdale, NJ: Erlbaum.

Cole, M., Gay, J., Glick, J. A., Sharp, D. W. (1971). *The cultural context of learning and thinking: An exploration in experimental anthropology.* New York: Basic Books.

Cole, S. W., Kemeny, M. E., Taylor, S. E., & Visscher, B. R. (1996). Elevated physical health risk among gay men who conceal their homosexual identity. *Health Psychology, 15*, 243–251.

Coles, R. (1970). *Erik H. Erikson: The growth of his work.* Boston: Little, Brown.

Collaer, M. L., & Hines, M. (1995). Human behavioral sex differences: A role for gonadal hormones during early development? *Psychological Bulletin, 118*, 55–107.

Collins, A. M., & Loftus, E. F. (1975). A spreading activation theory of semantic processing. *Psychological Review, 82*, 407–428.

Collins, F. S., & McKusick, V. A. (2001). Implications of the human genome project for medical science. *Journal of the American Medical Association, 285*, 540–544.

Collins, M. A., & Zebrowitz, L. A. (1995). The contributions of appearance to occupational outcomes in civilian and military settings. *Journal of Applied Social Psychology, 25*, 129–163.

Collins, N. L., & Allard, L. M. (2001). Cognitive representations of attachment: The content and function of working models. In G. J. O. Fletcher & M. S. Clark (Eds.), *Blackwell handbook of social psychology: Interpersonal processes.* Malden, MA: Blackwell.

Collins, W. A., Maccoby, E. E., Steinberg, L., Hetherington, E. M., & Bornstein, M. H. (2000). Contemporary research in parenting: The case for nature and nurture. *American Psychologist, 55*, 218–232.

Coltrane, S. (2001). Research on household labor: Modeling and measuring the social embeddedness of routine family work. In R. M. Milardo (Ed.), *Understanding families into the new millennium: A decade in review* (pp. 427–452). Minneapolis, MN: National Council on Family Relations.

Colvin, C. R., Block, J., & Funder, D. C. (1995). Overly positive self-evaluations and personality: Negative implications for mental health. *Journal of Personality and Social Psychology, 68*, 1152–1162.

Colwill, R. M. (1993). An associative analysis of instrumental learning. *Current Directions in Psychological Science, 2*(4), 111–116.

Comer, D. R. (1995). A model of social loafing in real work groups. *Human Relations, 48*, 647–667.

Compton, D. M., Dietrich, K. L., & Smith, J. S. (1995). Animal rights activism and animal welfare concerns in the academic setting: Levels of activism and perceived importance of research with animals. *Psychological Reports, 76*, 23–31.

Conklin, H. M., & Iacono, W. G. (2002). Schizophrenia: A neurodevelopmental perspective. *Current Directions in Psychological Science, 11*, 33–37.

Cook, C. A. L., Selig, K. L., Wedge, B. J., & Gohn-Baube, E. A. (1999). Access barriers and the use of prenatal care by low-income, inner-city women. *Social Work, 44*, 129–139.

Coontz, S. (2000). *The way we never were: American families and the nostalgia trap.* New York: Basic Books.

Cooper, A., Scherer, C. R., Boies, S. C., & Gordon, B. L. (1999). Sexuality on the Internet: From sexual exploration to pathological expression. *Professional Psychology: Research and Practice, 30*(2), 154–164.

Cooper, E. (1991). A critique of six measures for assessing creativity. *Journal of Creative Behavior, 25*(3), 194–204.

Cooper, H., Okamura, L., & Gurka, V. (1992). Social activity and subjective well-being. *Personality and Individual Differences, 13*, 573–583.

Cooper, J. R., Bloom, F. E., & Roth, R. H. (1996). *The biochemical basis of neuropharmacology.* New York: Oxford University Press.

Cooper, Z. (1995). The development and maintenance of eating disorders. In K. D. Brownell & C. G. Fairburn (Eds.), *Eating disorders and obesity: A comprehensive handbook.* New York: Guilford.

Corballis, M. C. (1991). *The lopsided ape.* New York: Oxford University Press.

Coren, S. (1992). *The left-hander syndrome: The causes and consequences of left-handedness.* New York: Free Press.

Coren, S. (1996). *Sleep thieves: An eye-opening exploration into the science and mysteries of sleep.* New York: Free Press.

Coren, S., & Aks, D. J. (1990). Moon illusion in pictures: A multimechanism approach. *Journal of Experimental Psychology: Human Perception and Performance, 16*, 365–380.

Coren, S., & Girgus, J. S. (1978). *Seeing is deceiving: The psychology of visual illusions.* Hillsdale, NJ: Erlbaum.

Corkin, S. (1984). Lasting consequences of bilateral medial temporal lobectomy: Clinical course and experimental findings in H. M. *Seminars in Neurology, 4*, 249–259.

Cornell, D. G. (1997). Post hoc explanation is not prediction. *American Psychologist, 52*, 1380.

Cornoldi, C., & De Beni, R. (1996). Mnemonics and metacognition. In D. J. Herrmann, C. McEvoy, C. Hertzog, P. Hertel, & M. K. Johnson (Eds.), *Basic and applied memory* research: Practical applications. Mahwah, NJ: Erlbaum.

Cosmides, L. L., & Tooby, J. (1989). Evolutionary psychology and the generation of culture. Part II. Case study: A computational theory of social exchange. *Ethology and Sociobiology, 10,* 51–97.

Cosmides, L., & Tooby, J. (1994). Beyond intuition and instinct blindness: Toward an evolutionarily rigorous cognitive science. *Cognition, 50,* 41–77.

Cosmides, L., & Tooby, J. (1996). Are humans good intuitive statisticians after all? Rethinking some conclusions from the literature on judgment under uncertainty. *Cognition, 58,* 1–73.

Costa, G. (1996). The impact of shift and night work on health. *Applied Ergonomics, 27,* 9–16.

Costa, P. T., Jr., & McCrae, R. R. (1985). *NEO Personality Inventory.* Odessa, FL: Psychological Assessment Resources.

Costa, P. T., Jr., & McCrae, R. R. (1992). *Revised NEO Personality Inventory: NEO PI and NEO Five-Factor Inventory* (Professional Manual). Odessa, FL: Psychological Assessment Resources.

Costa, P. T., Jr., & McCrae, R. R. (1994). Set like plaster? Evidence for the stability of adult personality. In T. F. Heatherton & J. L. Weinberger (Eds.), *Can personality change?* Washington, DC: American Psychological Association.

Costa, P. T., Jr., & McCrae, R. R. (1997). Longitudinal stability of adult personality. In R. Hogan, J. Johnson, & S. Briggs (Eds.), *Handbook of personality psychology.* San Diego: Academic Press.

Costa, P. T., Jr., Terracciano, A., & McCrae, R. R. (2001). Gender differences in personality traits across cultures: Robust and surprising findings. *Journal of Personality and Social Psychology, 81,* 322–331.

Coutts, A. (2000). Nutrition and the life cycle. 1: Maternal nutrition and pregnancy. *British Journal of Nursing, 9,* 1133–1138.

Cowan, N. (1988). Evolving conceptions of memory storage, selective attention, and their mutual constraints within the human information-processing system. *Psychological Bulletin, 104,* 163–191.

Cowan, N. (1995). *Attention and memory: An integrated framework.* New York: Oxford University Press.

Cowan, N., Wood, N. L., Nugent, L. D., & Treisman, M. (1997). There are two word-length effects in verbal short-term memory: Opposed effects on duration and complexity. *Psychological Science, 8,* 290–295.

Cowart, B. J., & Rawson, N. E. (2001). Olfaction. In E. B. Goldstein

(Ed.), *Blackwell handbook of perception.* Malden, MA: Blackwell.

Cowey, A. (1994). Cortical visual areas and the neurobiology of higher visual processes. In M. J. Farah & G. Ratcliff (Eds.), *The neuropsychology of high-level vision: Collected tutorial essays.* Hillsdale, NJ: Erlbaum.

Cox, M. J., Paley, B., Burchinal, M., & Payne, C. (1999). Marital perceptions and interactions across the transition to parenthood. *Journal of Marriage and the Family, 61,* 611–625.

Coyne, J. C. (1999). Thinking interactionally about depression: A radical restatement. In T. E. Joiner & J. C. Coyne (Eds.), *Interpersonal processes in depression* (pp. 369–392). Washington, DC: American Psychological Association.

Craig, J. C., & Rollman, G. B. (1999). Somesthesis. *Annual Review of Psychology, 50,* 305–331.

Craik, F. I. M. (2001). Effects of dividing attention on encoding and retrieval processes. In H. L. Roediger III, J. S. Nairne, I. Neath, & A. M. Surprenant (Eds.), *The nature of remembering: Essays in honor of Robert G. Crowder* (pp. 55–68). Washington, DC: American Psychological Association.

Craik, F. I. M., & Kester, J. D. (2000). Divided attention and memory: Impairment of processing or consolidation? In E. Tulving (Ed.), *Memory, consciousness, and the brain: The Tallinn conference* (pp. 38–51). Philadelphia: Psychology Press.

Craik. F. I. M., & Lockhart, R. S. (1972). Levels of processing: A framework for memory research. *Journal of Verbal Learning and Verbal Behavior, 11,* 671–684.

Craik, F. I. M., & Tulving, E. (1975). Depth of processing and the retention of words in episodic memory. *Journal of Experimental Psychology: General, 104,* 268–294.

Craik, F. I. M., Govoni, R., Naveh-Benjamin, M., & Anderson, N. D. (1996). The effects of divided attention on encoding and retrieval processes in human memory. *Journal of Experimental Psychology: General, 125,* 159–180.

Craik, F. I. M., Moroz, T. M., Moscovitch, M., Stuss, D. T., Winocur, G., Tulving, E., & Kapur, S. (1999). In search of the self: A positron emission tomography study. *Psychological Science, 10,* 26–34.

Crain, S. (1991). Language acquisition in the absence of experience. *Behavioral and Brain Sciences, 14,* 597–650.

Cramer, P. (2000). Defense mechanisms in psychology today: Further processes for adaptation. *American Psychologist, 55*(6), 637–646.

Cramer, P. (2001). The unconscious status of defense mechanisms. *American Psychologist, 56,* 762–763.

Crano, W. D. (1995). Attitude strength and vested interest. In R. E. Petty & J. A. Krosnick (Eds.), *Attitude strength: Antecedents and consequences.* Mahwah, NJ: Erlbaum.

Cravens, H. (1992). A scientific project locked in time: The Terman Genetic Studies of Genius, 1920s–1950s. *American Psychologist, 47,* 183–189.

Creed, F. (1989). Appendectomy. In G. W. Brown & T. O. Harris (Eds.), *Life events and illness.* New York: Guilford.

Creed, T. L. (1987). Subliminal deception: Pseudoscience on the college lecture circuit. *The Skeptical Inquirer, 11,* 358–366.

Crick, N. R., & Rose, A. J. (2000). Toward a gender-balanced approach to the study of social-emotional development: A look at relational aggression. In R. G. Geen & E. Donnerstein (Eds.), *Human aggression: Theories, research, and implications for social policy* (pp. 153–168). San Diego, CA: Academic Press.

Crick, N. R., Casas, J. F., & Mosher, M. (1997). Relational and overt aggression in preschool. *Developmental Psychology, 33,* 579–588.

Critelli, J. W., & Ee, J. S. (1996). Stress and physical illness: Development of an integrative model. In T. W. Miller (Ed.), *Theory and assessment of stressful life events.* Madison, CT: International Universities Press.

Crits-Christoph, P. (1997). Limitations of the dodo bird verdict and the role of clinical trials in psychotherapy research: Comment on Wampold et al (1997). *Psychological Bulletin, 122,* 216–220.

Crockett, H. (1962). The achievement motive and differential occupational mobility in the United States. *American Sociological Review, 27,* 191–204.

Croizet, J., & Claire, T. (1998). Extending the concept of stereotype threat to social class: The intellectual underperformance of students from low socioeconomic backgrounds. *Personality and Social Psychology Bulletin, 24,* 588–594.

Cronbach, L. J. (1992). *Acceleration among the Terman males: Correlates in midlife and after.* Paper presented at the Symposium in Honor of Julian Stanley, San Francisco.

Cropley, A. J. (2000). Defining and measuring creativity: Are creativity tests worth using? *Roeper Review, 23,* 72–79.

Cross, S. E., & Markus, H. R. (1993). Gender in thought, belief, and action: A cognitive approach. In A. E. Beall & R. J. Sternberg (Eds.), *The psychology of gender.* New York: Guilford.

Cross, S. E., & Markus, H. R. (1999). The cultural constitution of personality. In L. A. Pervin & O. P. John

(Eds.), *Handbook of personality: Theory and research.* New York: Guilford.

Crowder, R. G. (1993). Short-term memory: Where do we stand? *Memory & Cognition, 21,* 142–45.

Crowder, R. G., & Greene, R. L. (2000). Serial learning: Cognition and behavior. In E. Tulving & F. I. M. Craik (Eds.), *The Oxford handbook of memory* (pp. 125–136). New York: Oxford University Press.

Crowell, J. A., Fraley, R. C., & Shaver, P. R. (1999). Measurement of individual differences in adolescent and adult attachment. In J. Cassidy & P. R. Shaver (Eds.), *Handbook of attachment: Theory, research, and clinical applications.* New York: Guilford.

Crowley, K., Callanan, M. A., Tenenbaum, H. R., & Allen, E. (2001). Parents explain more often to boys than to girls during shared scientific thinking. *Psychological Science, 12,* 258–261.

Croyle, R. T., & Cooper, J. (1983). Dissonance arousal: Physiological evidence. *Journal of Personality and Social Psychology, 45,* 782–791.

Cruz, C., della Rocco, P., & Hackworth, C. (2000). Effects of quick rotating schedules on the health and adjustment of air traffic controllers. *Aviation, Space, & Environmental Medicine, 71,* 400–407.

Csikszentmihalyi, M. (1994). Creativity. In R. J. Sternberg (Ed.), *Encyclopedia of human intelligence.* New York: Macmillan.

Csikszentmihalyi, M. (1999). Implications of a systems perspective for the study of creativity. In R. J. Sternberg (Ed.), *Handbook of creativity.* New York: Cambridge University Press.

Cuesta, M. J., Peralta, B., & DeLeon, J. (1994). Schizophrenic syndromes associated with treatment response. *Progress in Neurology, Psychopharmacology, and Biological Psychiatry, 18,* 87–99.

Culbertson, F. M. (1997). Depression and gender: An international review. *American Psychologist, 52,* 25–31.

Culnane, M., Fowler, M. G., Lee, S. S., McSherry, G., Brady, M., & O'Donnell, K. (1999). Lack of long-term effects of in utero exposure to zidovudine among uninfected children born to HIV-infected women. *Journal of the American Medical Association, 281,* 151–157.

Cunningham, M. R., Druen, P. B., & Barbee, A. P. (1997). Angels, mentors, and friends: Trade-offs among evolutionary, social, and individual variables in physical appearance. In J. A. Simpson & D. T. Kenrick (Eds.), *Evolutionary social psychology.* Mahwah, NJ: Erlbaum.

Cunningham, M. R., Roberts, A. R., Barbee, A. P., Druen, P. B., & Wu, C.

(1995). "Their ideas of beauty are, on the whole, the same as ours": Consistency and variability in the cross-cultural perception of female physical attractiveness. *Journal of Personality and Social Psychology, 68*, 261–279.

Cushman, P. (1992). Psychotherapy to 1992: A historically situated interpretation. In D. K. Freedheim (Ed.), *History of psychotherapy: A century of change*. Washington, DC: American Psychological Association.

Cutler, B. L., & Penrod, S. D. (1995). *Mistaken identification: The eyewitness, psychology, and the law*. New York: Cambridge University Press.

Cutting, L. P., & Docherty, N. M. (2000). Schizophrenia outpatients' perceptions of their parents: Is expressed emotion a factor? *Journal of Abnormal Psychology, 109*, 266–272.

Czeisler, C. A., & Khalsa, S. B. S. (2000). The human circadian timing system and sleep-wake regulation. In M. H. Kryger, T. Roth, & W. C. Dement (Eds.), *Principles and practice of sleep medicine*. Philadelphia: Saunders.

Czeisler, C. A., Cajochen, C., & Turek, F. W. (2000). Melatonin in the regulation of sleep and circadian rhythms. In M. H. Kryger, T. Roth, & W. C. Dement (Eds.), *Principles and practice of sleep medicine*. Philadelphia: Saunders.

Dallman, M. F., Bhatnagar, S., & Viau, V. (2000). Hypothalamo-pituitary-adrenal axis. In G. Fink (Ed.), *Encyclopedia of stress* (Vol. 2, pp. 468–476). San Diego: Academic Press.

Daly, M., & Wilson, M. (1985). Child abuse and other risks of not living with both parents. *Ethology and Sociobiology, 6*, 197–210.

Daly, M., & Wilson, M. (1988). *Homicide*. Hawthorne, NY: Aldine.

Dan, B. A., & Gleason, J. B. (2001). Semantic development: Learning the meanings of words. In J. B. Gleason (Ed.), *The development of language* (5th ed., pp. 125–161). Boston: Allyn & Bacon.

D'Andrade, R. G. (1961). Anthropological studies of dreams. In F. Hsu (Ed.), *Psychological anthropology: Approaches to culture and personality*. Homewood, IL: Dorsey Press.

Daniel, M. H. (1997). Intelligence testing: Status and trends. *American Psychologist, 52*, 1038–1045.

Danton, W. G., & Antonuccio, D. O. (1997). A focused empirical analysis of treatments for panic and anxiety. In S. Fisher & R. P. Greenberg (Eds.), *From placebo to panacea: Putting psychiatric drugs to the test*. New York: Wiley.

Danziger, K. (1990). *Constructing the subject: Historical origins of psychological research*. Cambridge, England: Cambridge University Press.

Darley, J. M., & Latané, B. (1968). Bystander intervention in emergencies: Diffusion of responsibility. *Journal of Personality and Social Psychology, 8*, 377–383.

Darwin, C. (1859). *On the origin of species*. London: Murray.

Darwin, C. (1871). *Descent of man*. London: Murray.

Darwin, C. (1872). *The expression of emotions in man and animals*. New York: Philosophical Library.

Das, J. P. (1992). Beyond a unidimensional scale of merit. *Intelligence, 16*(2), 137–149.

Das, J. P. (1994). Eastern views of intelligence. In R. J. Sternberg (Ed.), *Encyclopedia of human intelligence*. New York: Macmillan.

Dasen, P. R. (1994). Culture and cognitive development from a Piagetian perspective. In W. J. Lonner & R. Malpass (Eds.), *Psychology and culture*. Boston: Allyn & Bacon.

Davidson, R. J., Jackson, D. C., & Kalin, N. H. (2000). Emotion, plasticity, context, and regulation: Perspectives from affective neuroscience. *Psychological Bulletin, 126*, 890–909.

Davis, D. M. (1990). Portrayals of women in prime-time network television: Some demographic characteristics. *Sex Roles, 23*, 325–332.

Davis, J. L., & Rusbult, C. E. (2001). Attitude alignment in close relationships. *Journal of Personality and Social Psychology, 81*(1), 65–84.

Davis, M. H., Morris, M. M., & Kraus, L. A. (1998). Relationship-specific and global perceptions of social support: Associations with well-being and attachment. *Journal of Personality and Social Psychology, 74*, 468–481.

Davis, S. (2000). Testosterone and sexual desire in women. *Journal of Sex Education & Therapy, 25*, 25–32.

Dawod, N. (1995). Stressors encountered by junior high school students and their relation to grade point average, sex and grade. *Dirasat, 22A* (Supplement), 3671–3706.

Dawson, W. A. (1993). Aboriginal dreaming. In M. A. Carskadon (Ed.), *Encyclopedia of sleep and dreaming*. New York: Macmillan.

Day, R. H. (1965). Inappropriate constancy explanation of spatial distortions. *Nature, 207*, 891–893.

Deary, I. J. (2000). Simple information processing and intelligence. In R. J. Sternberg (Ed.), *Handbook of intelligence* (pp. 267–284). New York: Cambridge University Press.

Deary, I. J., & Stough, C. (1996). Intelligence and inspection time: Achievements, prospects, and problems. *American Psychologist, 51*, 599–608.

Deary, I. J., Caryl, P. G., & Gibson, G. J. (1993). Nonstationarity and the measurement of psychological response in a visual inspection time task. *Perception, 22*, 1245–1256.

Deaux, K. (1993). Commentary: Sorry, wrong number—A reply to Gentile's call. *Psychological Science, 4*, 125–126.

De Boysson-Bardies, B., & Vihman, M. (1991). Adaptation to language: Evidence from babbling and early words in four languages. *Language, 61*, 297–319.

DeCarvalho, R. J. (1991). *The founders of humanistic psychology*. New York: Praeger.

deCharms, R., & Moeller, G. H. (1962). Values expressed in American children's readers: 1800–1950. *Journal of Abnormal and Social Psychology, 64*, 136–142.

Deeks, S. G., Smith, M., Holodniy, M., & Kahn, J. O. (1997). HIV-1 protease inhibitors: A review for clinicians. *Journal of the American Medical Association, 277*, 145–154.

DeFrain, J., & Olson, D. H. (1999). Contemporary family patterns and relationships. In M. B. Sussman, S. K. Steinmetz, & G. W. Peterson (Eds.), *Handbook of marriage and the family* (pp. 309–326). New York: Plenum.

de Houwer, A. (1995). Bilingual language acquisition. In P. Fletcher & B. MacWhinney (Eds.), *The handbook of child language*. Oxford, OH: Basil Blackwell.

de Houwer, J., Hendrickx, H., & Baeyens, F. (1997). Evaluative learning with "subliminally" presented stimuli. *Consciousness & Cognition: An International Journal, 6*, 87–107.

de Jong, P. J., & Merckelbach, H. (2000). Phobia-relevant illusory correlations: The role of phobic responsivity. *Journal of Abnormal Psychology, 109*, 597–601.

De Koninck, J. (2000). Waking experiences and dreaming. In M. H. Kryger, T. Roth, & W. C. Dement (Eds.), *Principles and practice of sleep medicine*. Philadelphia: Saunders.

Delay, J., & Deniker, P. (1952). *Trente-huit cas de psychoses traitees par la cure prolongee et continue de 4560 RP*. Paris: Masson et Cie.

Delis, D. C., & Lucas, J. A. (1996). Memory. In B. S. Fogel, R. B. Schiffer, & S. M. Rao (Eds.), *Neuropsychiatry*. Baltimore: Williams & Wilkins.

DelMonte, M. M. (2000). Retrieved memories of childhood sexual abuse. *British Journal of Medical Psychology, 73*, 1–13.

DeLong, M. R. (2000). The basal ganglia. In E. R. Kandel, J. H. Schwartz, & T. M. Jessell (Eds.), *Principles of neural science* (pp. 853–872). New York: McGraw-Hill.

DeLongis, A., Folkman, S., & Lazarus, R. S. (1988). The impact of daily stress on health and mood: Psychological and social resources as mediators. *Journal of Personality and Social Psychology, 54*, 486–495.

Delprato, D. J., & Midgley, B. D. (1992). Some fundamentals of B. F. Skinner's behaviorism. *American Psychologist, 47*, 1507–1520.

DeMaio, T. J. (1984). Social desirability and survey measurement: A review. In C. F. Turner & E. Martin (Eds.), *Surveying subjective phenomena* (Vol. 2). New York: Russell Sage Foundation.

Dement, W. C. (1978). *Some must watch while some must sleep*. New York: Norton.

Dement, W. C. (1992). *The sleepwatchers*. Stanford, CA: Stanford Alumni Association.

Dement, W. C. (1997). The perils of drowsy driving. *New England Journal of Medicine, 337*, 783–784.

Dement, W. C. (2000). History of sleep physiology and medicine. In M. H. Kryger, T. Roth, & W. C. Dement (Eds.), *Principles and practice of sleep medicine*. Philadelphia: Saunders.

Dement, W. C., & Vaughan, C. (1999). *The promise of sleep*. New York: Delacorte Press.

Dement, W. C., & Wolpert, E. (1958). The relation of eye movements, bodily motility, and external stimuli to dream content. *Journal of Experimental Psychology, 53*, 543–553.

Demo, D. H. (1992). Parent-child relations: Assessing recent changes. *Journal of Marriage and the Family, 54*, 104–117.

Dempster, F. N. (1996). Distributing and managing the conditions of encoding and practice. In E. L. Bjork & R. A. Bjork (Eds.), *Memory*. San Diego: Academic Press.

Dennerstein, L. (1996). Well-being, symptoms and the menopausal transition. *Maturitas, 23*, 147–157.

Dennis, W. (1966). Age and creative productivity. *Journal of Gerontology, 21*(1), 1–8.

Derogatis, L. R., & Coons, H. L. (1993). Self-report measures of stress. In L. Goldberger & S. Breznitz (Eds.), *Handbook of stress: Theoretical and clinical aspects* (2nd ed.). New York: Free Press.

Desimone, R. (1991). Face selective cells in the temporal cortex of monkeys. *Journal of Cognitive Neuroscience, 3*, 1–8.

Des Jarlais, D. C., Hagan, H., & Friedman, S. R. (1997). Epidemiology and emerging public health perspectives. In J. H. Lowinson, P. Ruiz, R. B. Millman, & J. G. Langrod (Eds.), *Substance abuse: A comprehensive textbook*. Baltimore: Williams & Wilkins.

Detterman, L. T., Gabriel, L. T., & Ruthsatz, J. M. (2000). Intelligence and mental retardation. In R. J.

Sternberg (Ed.), *Handbook of intelligence* (pp. 141–158). New York: Cambridge University Press.

Deutch, J. A. (1990). Food intake: Gastric factors. In E. M. Stricker (Ed), *Handbook of behavioral neurobiology: Vol 10. Neurobiology of food and fluid intake*. New York: Plenum.

DeValois, R. L., & Jacobs, G. H. (1984). Neural mechanisms of color vision. In I. Darian-Smith (Ed.), *The nervous system* (Vol. 3). Baltimore: Williams & Wilkins.

De Villiers, P. (1977). Choice in concurrent schedules and a quantitative formulation of the law of effect. In W. K. Honig & J. E. R. Staddon (Eds.), *Handbook of operant behavior*. Englewood Cliffs, NJ: Prentice-Hall.

de Villiers, P. A. & de Villiers, J. G. (1992). Language development. In M. H. Bornstein & M. E. Lamb (Eds.), *Developmental psychology: An advanced textbook* (3rd ed.). Hillsdale, NJ: Erlbaum.

Devine, P. G., & Baker, S. M. (1991). Measurements of racial stereotypes subtyping. *Personality and Social Psychology Bulletin, 17*, 44–50.

Devine, P. G., & Monteith, M. J. (1999). Automaticity and control in stereotyping. In S. Chaiken & Y. Trope (Eds.), *Dual-process theories in social psychology*. New York: Guilford.

Devine, P. G., Plant, E. A., & Blair, I. V. (2001). Classic and contemporary analysis of racial prejudice. In R. Brown & S. L. Gaertner (Eds.), *Blackwell handbook of social psychology: Intergroup processes*. Malden, MA: Blackwell.

Devine, P. G., Tauer, J. M., Barron, K. E., Elliot, A. J., & Vance, K. M. (1999). Moving beyond attitude change in the study of dissonance-related processes. In E. Harmon-Jones & J. Mills (Eds.), *Cognitive dissonance: Progress on a pivotal theory in social psychology*. Washington, DC: American Psychological Association.

Devlin, B., Daniels, M., & Roeder, K. (1997). The heritability of IQ. *Nature, 388*, 468–471.

Devlin, B., Fienberg, S. E., Resnick, D. P., & Roeder, K. (2002). Intelligence and success: Is it all in the genes? In J. M. Fish (Ed.), *Race and intelligence: Separating science from myth* (pp. 355–368). Mahwah, NJ: Erlbaum.

Devlin, M. J., Yanovski, S. Z., & Wilson, G. T. (2000). Obesity: What mental health professionals need to know. *American Journal of Psychiatry, 157*, 854–866.

Dew, M. A., Bromet, E. J., & Switzer, G. E. (2000). Epidemiology. In M. Hersen & A. S. Bellack (Eds.), *Psychopathology in adulthood*. Boston: Allyn & Bacon.

Dewees, M., Pulice, R. T., & McCormick, L. L. (1996). Community integration of former state hospital patients: Outcomes of a policy shift in Vermont. *Psychiatric Services, 47*, 1088–1092.

de Wijk, R. A., Schab, F. R., & Cain, W. S. (1995). Odor identification. In F. R. Schab & R. G. Crowder (Eds.), *Memory for odors*. Mahwah, NJ: Erlbaum.

de Wolff, M. S., & van IJzendoorn, M. H. (1997). Sensitivity and attachment: A meta-analysis on parental antecedents of infant attachment. *Child Development, 68*, 571–591.

Deal, T., & Kennedy, A. (1982). *Corporate cultures*. Reading, MA: Addison-Wesley.

Dewsbury, D. A. (1981). Effects of novelty of copulatory behavior: The Coolidge effect and related phenomena. *Psychological Bulletin, 89*, 464–482.

Deyoub, P. L. (1984). Hypnotic stimulation of antisocial behavior: A case report. *International Journal of Clinical and Experimental Hypnosis, 32*(3), 301–306.

Di Chiara, G. (1999). Drug addiction as a dopamine-dependent associative learning disorder. *European Journal of Pharmacology, 375*, 13–30.

Dickens, W. T., & Flynn, J. R. (2001). Heritability estimates versus large environmental effects: The IQ paradox resolved. *Psychological Review, 108*, 346–369.

Diener, E. (1984). Subjective well-being. *Psychological Bulletin, 93*, 542–575.

Diener, E., & Diener, C. (1996). Most people are happy. *Psyhological Science, 7*, 181–185.

Diener, E., & Diener, M. (1995). Cross-cultural correlates of life satisfaction and self-esteem. *Journal of Personality and Social Psychology, 68*, 653–663.

Diener, E., & Lucas, R. E. (1999). Personality and subjective well-being. In D. Kahneman, E. Diener, & N. Schwarz (Eds.), *Well-being: The foundations of hedonic psychology*. New York: Russell Sage Foundation.

Diener, E., & Seligman, E. P. (2002). Very happy people. *Psychological Science, 13*, 81–84.

Diener, E., Diener, M., & Diener, C. (1995). Factors predicting the subjective well-being of nations. *Journal of Personality and Social Psychology, 69*, 851–864.

Diener, E., Gohm, C. L., Suh, E., & Oishi, S. (2000). Similarity of the relations between marital status and subjective well-being across cultures. *Journal of Cross-Cultural Psychology, 31*, 419–436.

Diener, E., Sandvik, E., Seidlitz, L., & Diener, M. (1993). The relationship between income and subjective well-being. Relative or absolute? *Social Indicators Research, 28*, 195–223.

Diener, E., Suh, E., Smith, H., & Shao, L. (1995). National differences in reported subjective well-being: Why do they occur? *Social Indicators Research, 34*, 7–32.

Diener, E., Wolsic, B., & Fujita, F. (1995). Physical attractiveness and subjective well-being. *Journal of Personality and Social Psychology, 69*, 120–129.

Dillbeck, M. C., & Orme-Johnson, D. W. (1987). Physiological differences between transcendental meditation and rest. *American Psychologist, 42*, 879–881.

Dilsaver, S. C., Chen, Y. R., Shoaib, A. M., & Swann, A. C. (1999). Phenomenology of mania: Evidence for distinct depressed, dysphoric, and euphoric presentations. *American Journal of Psychiatry, 156*, 426–430.

DiMatteo, M. R. (1991). *The psychology of health, illness, and medical care: An individual perspective*. Pacific Grove, CA: Brooks/Cole.

DiMatteo, M. R. (1994). Enhancing patient adherence to medical recommendations. *Journal of the American Medical Association, 271*, 79–83.

DiMatteo, M. R. (1997). Health behaviors and care decisions: An overview of professional-patient communication. In D. S. Gochman (Ed.), *Handbook of health behavior research II: Provider determinants*. New York: Plenum.

DiMatteo, M. R., & Friedman, H. S. (1982). *Social psychology and medicine*. Cambridge, MA: Oelgeschlager, Gunn & Hain.

Dinges, D. F. (1989). Napping patterns and effects in human adults. In D. F. Dinges & R. J. Broughton (Eds.), *Sleep and alertness: Chronobiological, behavioral, and medical aspects of napping*. New York: Raven.

Dinges, D. F. (1993). Napping. In M.A. Carskadon (Ed.), *Encyclopedia of sleep and dreaming*. New York: Macmillan.

Dinges, D. F. (1995). Overview of sleepiness and accidents. *Journal of Sleep Research, 4*, 4–14.

DiNicola, D. D., & DiMatteo, M. R. (1984). Practitioners, patients, and compliance with medical regimens: A social psychological perspective. In A. Baum, S. E. Taylor, & J. E. Singer (Eds.), *Handbook of psychology and health: Vol. 4. Social psychological aspects of health*. Hillsdale, NJ: Erlbaum.

Dinsmoor, J. A. (1992). Setting the record straight: The social views of B. F. Skinner. *American Psychologist, 47*, 1454–1463.

Dinsmoor, J. A. (1998). Punishment. In W. O'Donohue (Ed.), *Learning and behavior therapy*. Boston: Allyn & Bacon.

Dixon, M., & Laurence, J. R. (1992). Two hundred years of hypnosis research: Questions resolved? Questions unanswered! In E. Fromm & M. R. Nash (Eds.), *Contemporary hypnosis research*. New York: Guilford.

Dobson, K. S., & Dozois, D. J. A. (2001). Professional psychology and the prescription debate: Still not ready to go to the altar. *Canadian Psychology, 42*, 131–135.

Dobzhansky, T. (1937). *Genetics and the origin of species*. New York: Columbia University Press.

Docherty, J. P. (1999). Cost of treating mental illness from a managed care perspective. *Journal of Clinical Psychiatry, 60*, 49–53.

Doerr, P., Pirke, K. M., Kockott, G., & Dittmor, F. (1976). Further studies on sex hormones in male homosexuals. *Archives of General Psychiatry, 33*, 611–614.

Doghramji, P. P. (2001). Detection of insomnia in primary care. *Journal of Clinical Psychiatry, 62*(suppl 10), 18–26.

Dolan, M., Anderson, I. M., & Deakin, J. F. W. (2001). Relationship between 5-HT function and impulsivity and aggression in male offenders with personality disorders. *British Journal of Psychiatry, 178*, 352–359.

Dolan-Sewell, R. T., Krueger, R. F., & Shea, M. T. (2001). Co-occurrence with syndrome disorders. In W. J. Livesley (Ed.), *Handbook of personality disorders: Theory, research, and treatment*. New York: Guilford.

Dollard, J., & Miller, N. E. (1950). *Personality and psychotherapy: An analysis in terms of learning, thinking and culture*. New York: McGraw-Hill.

Dollard, J., Doob, L. W., Miller, N. E., Mowrer, O. H., & Sears, R. R. (1939). *Frustration and aggression*. New Haven: Yale University Press.

Domhoff, G. W. (2000). Methods and measures for the study of dream content. In M. H. Kryger, T. Roth, & W. C. Dement (Eds.), *Principles and practice of sleep medicine*. Philadelphia: Saunders.

Domhoff, G. W. (2001). A new neurocognitive theory of dreams. *Dreaming, 11*, 13–33.

Dominowski, R. L., & Bourne, L. E., Jr. (1994). History of research on thinking and problem solving. In R. J. Sternberg (Ed.), *Thinking and problem solving*. San Diego: Academic Press.

Domjan, M. (1992). Adult learning and mate choice: Possibilities and experimental evidence. *American Zoologist, 32*, 48–61.

Domjan, M. (1994). Formulation of a behavior system for sexual conditioning. *Psychonomic Bulletin & Review, 1*, 421–428.

Domjan, M. (1998). *The principles of learning and behavior.* Pacific Grove: Brooks/Cole.

Domjan, M., & Purdy, J. E. (1995). Animal research in psychology: More than meets the eye of the general psychology student. *American Psychologist, 50,* 496–503.

Domjan, M., Blesbois, E., & Williams, J. (1998). The adaptive significance of sexual conditioning: Pavlovian control of sperm release. *Psychological Science, 9,* 411–415.

Donn, L. (1988). *Freud and Jung: Years of friendship, years of loss.* New York: Scribner's.

Donnerstein, E., & Malamuth, N. (1997). Pornography: Its consequences on the observer. In L. B. Schlesinger & E. Revitch (Eds.), *Sexual dynamics of anti-social behavior.* Springfield, IL: Charles C. Thomas.

Donnerstein, E., Linz, D., & Penrod, S. (1987). *The question of pornography: Research findings and policy implications.* New York: Free Press.

Dorfman, D. D. (1995). Soft science with a neoconservative agenda. *Contemporary Psychology, 40,* 418–421.

Dorn, L. D., Nottelmann, E. D., Susman, E. J., Inoff-Germain, G., Cutler, G. B., & Chrousos, G. P. (1999). Variability in hormone concentrations and self-reported menstrual histories in young adolescents: Menarche as an integral part of a developmental process. *Journal of Youth and Adolescence, 28,* 283–304.

Dorner, G. (1988). Neuroendocrine response to estrogen and brain differentiation. *Archives of Sexual Behavior, 17*(1), 57–75.

Doty, R. L. (1991). Olfactory system. In T. V. Getchell, R. L. Doty, L. M. Bartoshuk, & J. B. Snow, Jr. (Eds.), *Smell and taste in health and disease.* New York: Raven.

Doty, R. L. (2001). Olfaction. *Annual Review of Psychology, 52,* 423–452.

Dougall, A. L., & Baum, A. (2001). Stress, health, and illness. In A. Baum, T. A. Revenson & J. E. Singer (Eds.), *Handbook of health psychology* (pp. 321–338). Mahwah, NJ: Erlbaum.

Dovidio, J. F., & Gaertner, S. L. (1999). Reducing prejudice: Combating intergroup biases. *Current Directions in Psychological Science, 8,* 101–105.

Draguns, J. G. (1979). Culture and personality. In A. J. Marsella, R. G. Tharp, & T. J. Ciborowski (Eds.), *Perspectives on cross-cultural psychology.* New York: Academic Press.

Draguns, J. G. (1980). Psychological disorders of clinical severity. In H. C. Triandis & J. Draguns (Eds.), *Handbook of cross-cultural psychology* (Vol. 6). Boston: Allyn & Bacon.

Draguns, J. G. (1990). Applications of cross-cultural psychology in the field of mental health. In R. Brislin (Ed.), *Applied cross-cultural psychology.* Newbury Park, CA: Sage.

Draijer, N., & Langeland, W. (1999). Childhood trauma and perceived parental dysfunction in the etiology of dissociative symptoms in psychiatric inpatients. *American Journal of Psychiatry, 156,* 379–385.

Draine, S. C., & Greenwald, A. G. (1998). Replicable unconscious semantic processing. *Journal of Experimental Psychology: General, 127,* 286–303.

Draycott, S., & Dabbs, A. (1998). Cognitive dissonance 1: An overview of the literature and its integration into theory and practice of clinical psychology. *British Journal of Clinical Psychology, 37,* 341–353.

Drazen, J. M., & Curfman, G. D. (2002). Financial associations of authors. *New England Journal of Medicine, 346,* 1901–1902.

Drewnowski, A. (1995). Standards for the treatment of obesity. In K. D. Brownell, & C. G. Fairburn (Eds.), *Eating disorders and obesity: A comprehensive handbook.* New York: Guilford.

Drigotas, S. M., Safstrom, C. A., & Gentilia, T. (1999). An investment model prediction of dating infidelity. *Journal of Personality and Social Psychology, 77,* 509–524.

Driskell, J. E., Willis, R. P., & Copper, C. (1992). Effect of overlearning on retention. *Journal of Applied Psychology, 77*(5), 615–622.

Druss, B. G., & Rosenheck, R. A. (1998). Mental disorders and access to medical care in the United States. *American Journal of Psychiatry, 155,* 1775–1777.

Dubovsky, S. L., & Buzan, R. (1999). Mood disorders. In R. E. Hales, S. C. Yudofsky, & J. A. Talbott (Eds.), *American Psychiatric Press Textbook of Psychiatry.* Washington, DC: American Psychiatric Press.

Duckworth, K., & Borus, J. F. (1999). Population-based psychiatry in the public sector and managed care. In A. M. Nicholi (Ed.), *The Harvard guide to psychiatry.* Cambridge, MA: Harvard University Press.

Duggal, S., & Sroufe, L. A. (1998). Recovered memory of childhood sexual trauma: A documented case from a longitudinal study. *Journal of Traumatic Stress, 11,* 301–321.

Dunbar, R. (1996). *Grooming, gossip, and the evolution of language.* Cambridge, MA: Harvard University Press.

Dunbar-Jacob, J., & Schlenk, E. (2001). Patient adherence to treatment regimen. In A. Baum, T. A. Revenson, & J. E. Singer (Eds.), *Handbook of health psychology* (pp. 571–580). Mahwah, NJ: Erlbaum.

Duncan, B. L. (1976). Differential social perception and attribution of intergroup violence: Testing the lower limits of stereotyping of blacks. *Journal of Personality and Social Psychology, 34,* 590–598.

Dunkel-Schetter, C., Gurung, R. A. R., Lobel, M., & Wadhwa, P. D. (2001). Stress processes in pregnancy and birth: Psychological, biological, and sociocultural influences. In A. Baum, T. A. Revenson, & J. E. Singer (Eds.), *Handbook of health psychology* (pp. 495–518). Mahwah, NJ: Erlbaum.

Dunning, D., & Sherman, D. A. (1997). Stereotypes and tacit inference. *Journal of Personality and Social Psychology, 73,* 459–471.

Durlach, N. I., & Colburn, H. S. (1978). Binaural phenomenon. In E. C. Carterette & M. P. Friedman (Eds.), *Handbook of perception* (Vol. 4). New York: Academic Press.

Dwyer, J. (1995). Popular diets. In K. D. Brownell & C. G. Fairburn (Eds.), *Eating disorders and obesity.* New York: Guilford.

Eacott, M. J., & Crawley, R. A. (1998). The offset of childhood amnesia: Memory for events that occurred before age three. *Journal of Experimental Psychology: General, 127,* 22–23.

Eagle, M. N., & Wolitzky, D. L. (1992). Psychoanalytic theories of psychotherapy. In D. K. Freedheim (Ed.), *History of psychotherapy: A century of change.* Washington, DC: American Psychological Association.

Eagly, A. H. (1992). Uneven progress: Social psychology and the study of attitudes. *Journal of Personality and Social Psychology, 63,* 693–710.

Eagly, A. H. (1995). The science and politics of comparing women and men. *American Psychologist, 50,* 145–158.

Eagly, A. H., & Chaiken, S. (1995). Attitude strength, attitude structure, and resistance to change. In R. E. Petty & J. A. Krosnick (Eds.), *Attitude strength: Antecedents and consequences.* Mahwah, NJ: Erlbaum.

Eagly, A. H., & Chaiken, S. (1998). Attitude structure and function. In D. T. Gilbert, S. T. Fiske, & G. Lindzey (Eds.), *The handbook of social psychology.* New York: McGraw-Hill.

Eagly, A. H., & Wood, W. (1999). The origins of sex differences in human behavior: Evolved dispositions versus social roles. *American Psychologist, 54,* 408–423.

Eagly, A. H., Ashmore, R. D., Makhijani, M. G., & Longo, L. C. (1991). What is beautiful is good, but . . .: A meta-analytic review of research on the physical attractiveness stereotype. *Psychological Bulletin, 110,* 109–128.

Eals, M., & Silverman, I. (1994). The hunter-gatherer theory of spatial sex differences: Proximate factors mediating the female advantage in recall of object arrays. *Ethology and Sociobiology, 15,* 95–115.

Easterlin, B. L., & Cardena, E. (1999). Cognitive and emotional differences between short- and long-term Vipassana meditators. *Imagination, Cognition and Personality, 18*(1), 68–81.

Eaton, J. (2001). Management communication: The threat of groupthink. *Corporate Communications, 6,* 183–192.

Eaton, W. W., Dryman, A., & Weissman, M. M. (1991). Panic and phobia. In L. N. Robins & D. A. Regier (Eds.), *Psychiatric disorders in America: The epidemiologic catchment area study.* New York: Free Press.

Ebbinghaus, H. (1885/1964). *Memory: A contribution to experimental psychology* (H. A. Ruger & E. R. Bussemius, Trans.). New York: Dover. (Original work published 1885)

Eckensberger, L., & Zimba, R. (1997). The development of moral judgment. In J. W. Berry, P. R. Dasen, & T. S. Saraswathi (Eds.), *Handbook of cross-cultural psychology.* Boston: Allyn & Bacon.

Edberg, P. (1990). Rorschach assessment. In A. Goldstein & M. Hersen (Eds.), *Handbook of psychological assessment.* New York: Pergamon Press.

Edlin, G., & Golanty, E. (1992). *Health and wellness: A holistic approach.* Boston: Jones and Bartlett.

Edwards, A. (1999). *Ever after: Diana and the life she led.* New York: St. Martin's Press.

Edwards, K., & Smith, E. E. (1996). A disconfirmation bias in the evaluation of arguments. *Journal of Personality an Social Psychology, 71,* 5–24.

Efron, R. (1990). *The decline and fall of hemispheric specialization.* Hillsdale, NJ: Erlbaum.

Egan, J. P. (1975). *Signal detection theory and ROC-analysis.* New York: Academic Press.

Egan, M. F., & Hyde, T. M. (2000). Schizophrenia: Neurobiology. In B. J. Sadock & V. A. Sadock (Eds.), *Kaplan and Sadock's comprehensive textbook of psychiatry* (7th ed., Vol. 1, pp. 1129–1146). Philadelphia: Lippincott/ Williams & Wilkins.

Egeland, B., & Hiester, M. (1995). The long-term consequences of infant day-care and mother-infant attachment. *Child Development, 66,* 474–485.

Ehrenberg, O., & Ehrenberg, M. (1986). *The psychotherapy maze.* Northvale, NJ: Aronson.

Ehrenberg, O., & Ehrenberg, M. (1994). *The psychotherapy maze: A consumer's guide to getting in and out of therapy.* Northvale, NJ: Jason Aronson.

Ehrenreich, H., Rinn, T., Kunert, H. J., Moeller, M. R., Poser, W.,

Schilling, L., Gigerenzer, G., & Hoehe, M. R. (1999). Specific attentional dysfunction in adults following early start of cannabis use. *Psychopharmacology, 142*, 295–301.

Eibl-Eibesfeldt, I. (1975). *Ethology: The biology of behavior.* New York: Holt, Rinehart & Winston.

Eich, E. (1990). Learning during sleep. In R. R. Bootzin, J. F. Kihlstrom, & D. L. Schacter (Eds.), *Sleep and cognition.* Washington, DC: American Psychological Association.

Eich, E., Macaulay, D., Loewenstein, R. J., & Dihle, P. H. (1997). Memory, amnesia, and dissociative identity disorder. *Psychological Science, 8*, 417–422.

Eichenbaum, H. (1997). Declarative memory: Insights from cognitive neurobiology. *Annual Review of Psychology, 48*, 547–572.

Eid, M., & Diener, E. (2001). Norms for experiencing emotions in different cultures: Inter- and intranational differences. *Journal of Personality and Social Psychology, 81*, 869–885.

Einstein, G. O., & McDaniel, M. A. (1996). Remembering to do things: Remembering a forgotten topic. In D. J. Herrmann, C. McEvoy, C. Hertzog, P. Hertel, & M. K. Johnson (Eds.), *Basic and applied memory research: Practical applications* (Vol. 2). Mahwah, NJ: Erlbaum.

Einstein, G. O., McDaniel, M. A., Smith, R. E., & Shaw, P. (1998). Habitual prospective memory and aging: Remembering intentions and forgetting actions. *Psychological Science, 9*, 284–288.

Eisler, R. M., & Ragsdale, K. (1992). Masculine gender role and midlife transition in men. In V. B. Van Hasselt & M. Hersen (Eds.), *Handbook of social development: A lifespan perspective.* New York: Plenum.

Ekman, P. (1992). Facial expressions of emotion: New findings, new questions. *Psychological Science, 3*, 34–38.

Ekman, P. (1993). Facial expression and emotion. *American Psychologist, 48*, 384–392.

Ekman, P., & Friesen, W. V. (1975). *Unmasking the face.* Englewood Cliffs, NJ: Prentice-Hall.

Ekman, P., & Friesen, W. V. (1984). *Unmasking the face.* Palo Alto: Consulting Psychologists Press.

Elbert, T., Pantev, C., Weinbruch, C., Rockstroh, B., & Taub, E. (1995). Increased cortical representation of the fingers of the left hand in string players. *Science, 270*, 305–307.

Eldred, L., & Chaisson, R. (1996). The clinical course of HIV infection in women. In R. R. Faden & N. E. Kass (Eds.), *HIV, AIDS, and childbearing.* New York: Oxford University Press.

Elicker, J., Englund, M., & Sroufe, L. A. (1992). Predicting peer compe-tence and peer relationships in child-hood from early parent-child relation-ships. In R. D. Parke & G. W. Ladd (Eds.), *Family-peer relationships: Modes of linkage.* Hillsdale, NJ: Erlbaum.

Ellis, A. (1973). *Humanistic psycho-therapy: The rational-emotive approach.* New York: Julian Press.

Ellis, A. (1977). *Reason and emotion in psychotherapy.* Seacaucus, NJ: Lyle Stuart.

Ellis, A. (1985). *How to live with and without anger.* New York: Citadel Press.

Ellis, A. (1987). The evolution of rational-emotive therapy (RET) and cognitive behavior therapy (CBT). In J. K. Zeig (Ed.), *The evolution of psycho-therapy.* New York: Brunner/Mazel.

Ellis, A. (1989). Rational-emotive therapy. In R. J. Corsini & D. Wedding (Eds.), *Current Psychotherapies.* Itasca, IL: F. E. Peacock.

Ellis, A. (1996). How I learned to help clients feel better and get better. *Psychotherapy, 33*, 149–151.

Ellis, B. J., McFadyen-Ketchum, S., Dodge, K. A., Pettit, G. S., & Bates, J. E. (1999). Quality of early family relationships and individual differ-ences in the timing of pubertal ma-turation in girls: A longitudinal test of an evolutionary model. *Journal of Personality and Social Psychology, 77*, 387–401.

Elman, J. L. (1999). The emergence of language: A conspiracy theory. In B. MacWhinney (Ed.), *The emergence of language* (pp. 1–28). Mahwah, NJ: Erlbaum .

Elpers, J. R. (2001). Public psychia-try. In B. J. Sadock & V. A. Sadock (Eds.), *Kaplan and Sadock's compre-hensive textbook of psychiatry* (7th ed., Vol. 2). Philadelphia: Lippincott/Williams & Wilkins.

Emavardhana, T., & Tori, C. D. (1997). Changes in self-concept, ego defense mechanisms, and religiosity following seven-day Vipassana medi-tation retreats. *Journal for the Scien-tific Study of Religion, 36*, 194–206.

Emmelkamp, P. M. G. (1994). Be-havior therapy with adults. In A. E. Bergin & S. L. Garfield (Eds.), *Hand-book of psychotherapy and behavior change* (4th ed.). New York: Wiley.

Emmelkamp, P. M. G., & Scholing, A. (1990). Behavioral treatment for simple and social phobias. In R. Noyes, Jr., M. Roth, & G. D. Burrows (Eds.), *Handbook of anxiety: The treat-ment of anxiety* (Vol. 4). Amsterdam: Elsevier.

Epley, N., & Huff, C. (1998). Suspi-cion, affective response, and educa-tional benefit as a result of deception in psychology research. *Personality and Social Psychology Bulletin, 24*, 759–768.

Epstein, L. H., Valoski, A. M., Vara, L. S., McCurley, J., Wisniewski, L., Kalarchian, M. A., Klein, K. R., & Shrager, L. R. (1995). Effects of decreasing sedentary behavior and increasing activity on weight change in obese children. *Health Psychology, 14*, 109–115.

Epstein, S., Donovan, S., & Denes-Raj, V. (1999). The missing link in the paradox of the Linda conjunc-tion problem: Beyond knowing and thinking of the conjunction rule, the intrinsic appeal of heuristic pro-cessing. *Personality and Social Psy-chology Bulletin, 25*, 204–214.

Epstein, S. P. (1980). The stability of confusion: A reply to Mischel and Peake. *Psychological Review, 90*, 179–184.

Epstein, S. P. (1986). Does aggrega-tion produce spuriously high esti-mates of behavior stability? *Journal of Personality and Social Psychology, 50*, 1199–1210.

Erber, M. W., Hodges, S. D., & Wil-son, T. D. (1995). Attitude strength, attitude stability, and the effects of analyzing reasons. In R. E. Petty & J. A. Krosnick (Eds.), *Attitude strength: Antecedents and consequences.* Mah-wah, NJ: Erlbaum.

Erdberg, P. (1990). Rorschach assess-ment. In G. Goldstein & M. Hersen (Eds.), *Handbook of psychological assessment* (2nd ed.). New York: Per-gamon Press.

Erdelyi, M. H. (2001). Defense pro-cesses can be conscious or uncon-scious. *American Psychologist, 56*, 761–762.

Erickson, R. P., DiLorenzo, P. M., & Woodbury, M. A. (1994). Classifica-tion of taste responses in brain stem: Membership in fuzzy sets. *Journal of Neurophysiology, 71*, 2139–2150.

Ericsson, K. A., & Lehman, A. C. (1996). Expert and exceptional per-formance: Evidence of maximal adap-tation to task constraints. *Annual Review of Psychology, 47*, 273–305.

Ericsson, K. A., & Polson, P. G. (1988). An experimental analysis of the mechanisms of a memory skill. *Journal of Experimental Psychology: Learning, Memory and Congnition, 14*, 305–316.

Erikson, E. (1963). *Childhood and society.* New York: Norton.

Erikson, E. (1968). *Identity: Youth and crisis.* New York: Norton.

Eriksson, P. S., Perfilieva, E., Bjork-Eriksson, T., Alborn, A. M., Nord-borg, C., Peterson, D. A., & Gage, F. H. (1998). Neurogenesis in the adult human hippocampus. *Nature Medicine, 4*, 1313–1317.

Ernst, C., & Angst, J. (1983). Birth order: Its influence on personality. *Behavioral and Brain Sciences, 10*(1), 55.

Esser, J. K. (1998). Alive and well after twenty-five years: A review of groupthink research. *Organizational Behavior & Human Decision Processes, 73*, 116–141.

Esterson, A. (1993). *Seductive mirage: An exploration of the work of Sigmund Freud.* Chicago: Open Court.

Estes, R. E., Coston, M. L., & Four-net, G. P. (1990). *Rankings of the most notable psychologists by department chairpersons.* Unpublished manuscript.

Estes, W. K. (1999). Models of hu-man memory: A 30-year retrospec-tive. In C. Izawa (Ed.), *On human memory: Evolution, progress, and re-flections on the 30th anniversary of the Atkinson-Shiffrin model.* Mahwah, NJ: Erlbaum.

Etaugh, C., & Liss, M. B. (1992). Home, school, and playroom: Train-ing grounds for adult gender roles. *Sex Roles, 26*, 129–147.

Evans, C. E., & Haynes, R. B. (1990). Patient compliance. In R. E. Rakel (Ed.), *Textbook of family practice.* Philadelphia: Saunders.

Evans, F. J. (1990). Behavioral re-sponses during sleep. In R. R. Bootzin, J. F. Kihlstrom, & D. L. Schacter (Eds.), *Sleep and cognition.* Washing-ton, DC: American Psychological Association.

Evans, R. L. (1981). New drug evaluations: Alprazolam. *Drug Intel-ligence and Clinical Pharmacy, 15*, 633–637.

Everly, G. S., Jr. (2000). Five princi-ples of crisis intervention: Reducing the risk of premature crisis interven-tion. *International Journal of Emer-gency Mental Health, 2*, 1–4.

Eysenck, H. J. (1952). The effects of psychotherapy: An evaluation. *Journal of Consulting Psychology, 16*, 319–324.

Eysenck, H. J. (1959). Learning the-ory and behaviour therapy. *Journal of Mental Science, 195*, 61–75.

Eysenck, H. J. (1967). *The biological basis of personality.* Springfield, IL: Charles C. Thomas.

Eysenck, H. J. (1977). *Crime and personality.* London: Routledge & Kegan Paul.

Eysenck, H. J. (1982). *Personality, genetics and behavior: Selected papers.* New York: Praeger.

Eysenck, H. J. (1988). The concept of "intelligence": Useful or useless? *Intelligence, 12*(1), 1–16.

Eysenck, H. J. (1989). Discrimina-tion reaction time and "*g*": A reply to Humphreys. *Intelligence, 13*(4), 325–326.

Eysenck, H. J. (1990a). Biological dimensions of personality. In L. A. Pervin (Ed.), *Handbook of personal-ity: Theory and research.* New York: Guilford.

Eysenck, H. J. (1990b). *Decline and fall of the Freudian empire.* Washing-ton, DC: Scott-Townsend.

Eysenck, H. J. (1991). Dimensions of personality: 16, 5, or 3?—Criteria for a taxonomic paradigm. *Personality and Individual Differences, 12,* 773–790.

Eysenck, H. J., & Kamin, L. (1981). *The intelligence controversy.* New York: Wiley.

Eysenck, M. W. (1984). *A handbook of cognitive psychology.* Hillsdale, NJ: Erlbaum.

Eysenck, M. W., Mogg, K., May, J., Richards, A., & Mathews, A. (1991). Bias in interpretation of ambiguous sentences related to threat in anxiety. *Journal of Abnormal Psychology, 100,* 144–150.

Fabes, R. A., Carlo, G., Kupanoff, K., & Laible, D. (1999). Early adolescence and prosocial/moral behavior I: The role of individual processes. *Journal of Early Adolescence, 19,* 5–16.

Fagot, B. I., Hagan, R., Leinbach, M. D., & Kronsberg, S. (1985). Differential reactions to assertive and communicative acts of toddler boys and girls. *Child Development, 56,* 1499–1505.

Fagot, B. I., Leinbach, M. D., & O'Boyle, C. (1992). Gender labeling, gender stereotyping, and parenting behaviors. *Developmental Psychology, 28,* 225–230.

Fahey, P. J., & Gallagher-Allred, C. (1990). Nutrition. In R. E. Rakel (Ed.), *Textbook of family practice* (4th ed.). Philadelphia: Saunders.

Falls, W. A. (1998). Extinction: A review of therapy and the evidence suggesting that memories are not erased with nonreinforcement. In W. O'Donohue (Ed.), *Learning and behavior therapy.* Boston: Allyn & Bacon.

Falsetti, S. A., & Ballenger, J. C. (1998). Stress and anxiety disorders. In J. R. Hubbard & E. A. Workman (Eds.), *Handbook of stress medicine: An organ system approach.* New York: CRC Press.

Fancher, R. E. (1979). *Pioneers of psychology.* New York: Norton.

Fancher, R. E. (2000). Snapshot of Freud in America, 1899–1999. *American Psychologist, 55,* 1025–1028.

Faraday, A. (1974). *The dream game.* New York: Harper & Row.

Farah, A. (1997). An overview of ECT. *Primary Psychiatry, 4,* 58–62.

Faravelli, C., & Pallanti, S. (1989). Recent life events and panic disorders. *American Journal of Psychiatry, 146,* 622–626.

Farrar, M. J. (1990). Discourse and the acquisition of grammatical morphemes. *Journal of Child Language, 17,* 607–624.

Fausto-Sterling, A. (1992). *Myths of gender.* New York: Basic Books.

Fazio, R. H. (1995). Attitudes as object-evaluation associations: De-terminants, consequences, and correlates of attitude accessibility. In R. E. Petty & J. A. Krosnick (Eds.), *Attitude strength: Antecedents and consequences.* Mahwah, NJ: Erlbaum.

Fechner, G. T. (1860). *Elemente der psychophysik* (Vol. 1). Leipzig: Breit-kopf & Harterl.

Federal Bureau of Investigation. (1999). *Uniform crime reports for the United States.* Washington, DC: U.S. Government Printing Office.

Feeney, D. M. (1987). Human rights and animal welfare. *American Psychologist, 42,* 593–599.

Feeney, J. A. (1999). Adult romantic attachment and couple relationships. In J. Cassidy & P. R. Shaver (Eds.), *Handbook of attachment: Theory, research, and clinical applications.* New York: Guilford.

Fein, S., & Spencer, S. J. (1997). Prejudice as self-image maintenance: Affirming the self through derogating others. *Journal of Personality and Social Psychology, 73,* 31–44.

Feingold, A. (1988a). Cognitive gender differences are disappearing. *American Psychologist, 43,* 95–103.

Feingold, A. (1988b). Matching for attractiveness in romantic partners and same-sex friends: A meta-analysis and theoretical critique. *Psychological Bulletin, 104,* 226–235.

Feingold, A. (1990). Gender differences in effects of physical attractiveness on romantic attraction: A comparison across five research paradigms. *Journal of Personality and Social Psychology, 59,* 981–993.

Feingold, A. (1992). Good-looking people are not what we think. *Psychological Bulletin, 111,* 304–341.

Feingold, A. (1994). Gender differences in personality: A meta-analysis. *Psychological Bulletin, 116,* 429–456.

Feist, G. J. (1998). A meta-analysis of personality in scientific and artistic creativity. *Personality and Social Psychology Review, 2,* 290–309.

Feldman, D. H. (1988). Creativity: Dreams, insights, and transformations. In R. J. Sternberg (Ed.), *The nature of creativity: Contemporary psychological perspectives.* Cambridge: Cambridge University Press.

Feldman, D. H. (1999). The development of creativity. In R. J. Sternberg (Ed.), *Handbook of creativity.* New York: Cambridge University Press.

Feldman, P. J., Cohen, S., Doyle, W. J., Skoner, D. P., & Gwaltney, J. M., Jr. (1999). The impact of personality on the reporting of unfounded symptoms and illness. *Journal of Personality and Social Psychology, 77,* 370–378.

Felker, B., & Hubbard, J. R. (1998). Influence of mental stress on the endocrine system. In J. R. Hubbard & E. A. Workman (Eds.), *Handbook of stress medicine: An organ system approach.* New York: CRC Press.

Fenson, L., Dale, P., Reznick, J., Bates, E., Thal, D., & Pethick, S. (1994). Variability in early communicative development. *Monographs of the Society for Research in Child Development, 59*(5, Serial No. 242), 1–173.

Fensterheim, H., & Raw, S. D. (1996). Empirically validated treatments, psychotherapy integration, and the politics of psychotherapy. *Journal of Psychotherapy Integration, 6,* 207–215.

Fenton, W. S., & McGlashan, T. H. (1994). Antecedents, symptom progression, and long-term outcome of the deficit syndrome in schizophrenia. *American Journal of Psychiatry, 151,* 351–356.

Fenwick, P. (1987). Meditation and the EEG. In M. A. West (Ed.), *The psychology of meditation.* Oxford: Clarendon Press.

Ferguson, J. M. (2001). SSRI antidepressant medications: Adverse effects and tolerability. *Primary Care Companion Journal of Clinical Psychiatry, 3,* 22–27.

Ferguson, T. (1993). Working with your doctor. In D. Goleman & J. Gurin (Eds.), *Mind-body medicine: How to use your mind for better health.* Yonkers, NY: Consumer Reports Books.

Ferster, C. S., & Skinner, B. F. (1957). *Schedules of reinforcement.* New York: Appleton-Century-Crofts.

Festinger, L. (1957). *A theory of cognitive dissonance.* Stanford, CA: Stanford University Press.

Festinger, L., & Carlsmith, J. M. (1959). Cognitive consequences of forced compliance. *Journal of Abnormal and Social Psychology, 58,* 203–210.

Fields, H. L., & Levine, J. D. (1984). Placebo analgesia: A role for endorphins. *Trends in Neuroscience, 7,* 271–273.

Fifer, W. P., Monk, C. E., & Grose-Fifer, J. (2001). Prenatal development and risk. In G. Bremner & A. Fogel (Eds.), *Blackwell handbook of infant development* (pp. 505–542). Malden, MA: Blackwell.

Fincham, F. D., & Bradbury, T. N. (1993). Marital satisfaction, depression, and attributions: A longitudinal analysis. *Journal of Personality and Social Psychology, 63,* 442–452.

Fincham, F. D., Bradbury, T. N., Arias, I., Byrne, C. A., & Karney, B. R. (1997). Marital violence, marital distress, and attributions. *Journal of Family Psychology, 11,* 367–372.

Fine, R. (1990). *The history of psychoanalysis.* New York: Continuum.

Finer, B. (1980). Hypnosis and anaesthesia. In G. D. Burrows & L. Dennerstein (Eds.), *Handbook of hypnosis and psychosomatic medicine.* Amsterdam: Elsevier/North Holland Biomedical Press.

Fink, M. (1992). Electroconvulsive therapy. In E. S. Paykel (Ed.), *Handbook of affective disorders* (2nd ed.). New York: Guilford.

Finnegan, L. P., & Kandall, S. R. (1997). Maternal and neonatal effects of alcohol and drugs. In J. H. Lowinson, P. Ruiz, R. B. Millman, & J. G. Langrod (Eds.), *Substance abuse: A comprehensive textbook.* Baltimore: Williams & Wilkins.

Fiorino, D. F., Coury, A., & Phillips, A. G. (1997). Dynamic changes in nucleus accumbens dopamine efflux during the Coolidge effect in male rats. *Journal of Neuroscience, 17,* 4849–4855.

Fischer, K. W., & Bidell, T. (1991). Constraining nativist inferences about cognitive capacities. In S. Carey & R. Gelman (Eds.), *The epigenesis of mind: Essays on biology and cognition.* Hillsdale, NJ: Erlbaum.

Fischer, K. W., & Hencke, R. W. (1996). Infants' construction of actions in context: Piaget's contribution to research on early development. *Psychological Science, 7,* 204–210.

Fischhoff, B. (1982). Debiasing. In D. Kahneman, P. Slovic, & A. Tversky (Eds.), *Judgment under uncertainty: Heuristics and biases.* Cambridge, MA: Cambridge University Press.

Fischhoff, B. (1988). Judgment and decision making. In R. J. Sternberg & E. E. Smith (Eds.), *The psychology of human thought.* Cambridge: Cambridge University Press.

Fisher, C., & Fyrberg, D. (1994). College students weigh the costs and benefits of deceptive research. *American Psychologist, 49,* 417–427.

Fisher, S., & Greenberg, R. P. (1985). *The scientific credibility of Freud's theories and therapy.* New York: Columbia University Press.

Fisher, S., & Greenberg, R. P. (1996). *Freud scientifically reappraised: Testing the theories and therapy.* New York: Wiley.

Fisher, S., & Greenberg, R. P. (1997). The curse of the placebo: Fanciful pursuit of a pure biological therapy. In S. Fisher & R. P. Greenberg (Eds.), *From placebo to panacea: Putting psychiatric drugs to the test.* New York: Wiley.

Fisher, W. A., Byrne, D., White, L. A., & Kelley, K. (1988). Erotophobia-erotophilia as a dimension of personality. *Journal of Sex Research, 25*(1), 123–151.

Fishman, D. B., & Franks, C. M. (1992). Evolution and differentiation within behavior therapy: A theoretical epistemological review. In D. K. Freedheim (Ed.), *History of psychotherapy: A century of change.*

Washington, DC: American Psychological Association.

Fiske, S. T. (1998). Stereotyping, prejudice, and discrimination. In D. T. Gilbert, S. T. Fiske, & G. Lindzey (Eds.), *The handbook of social psychology.* New York: McGraw-Hill.

Fiske, S. T. (2000). Stereotyping, prejudice, and discrimination at the seam between the centuries: Evolution, culture, mind and brain. *European Journal of Social Psychology, 30,* 299–322.

Fiske, S. T. (2002). What we know now about bias and intergroup conflict, the problem of the century. *Current Directions in Psychological Science, 11*(4), 123–128.

Flannery, R. B., Jr. (1999). Psychological trauma and posttraumatic stress disorder: A review. *International Journal of Mental Health, 1,* 135–140.

Flavell, J. H. (1992). Cognitive development: Past, present, and future. *Developmental Psychology, 28,* 998–1005.

Flavell, J. H. (1996). Piaget's legacy. *Psychological Science, 7,* 200–203.

Flavell, J. H. (1999). Cognitive development: Children's knowledge about the mind. *Annual Review of Psychology, 50,* 21–45.

Flavell, J. H., & Miller, P. H. (1998). Social cognition. In W. Damon (Ed.), *Handbook of child psychology (Vol. 2): Cognition, perception, and language.* New York: Wiley.

Fleischhacker, W. W. (2002). Second generation antipsychotics. *Psychopharmacology, 162*(1), 90–91.

Fletcher, G. J. O., & Ward, C. (1988). Attribution theory and processes: A cross-cultural perspective. In M. H. Bond (Ed.), *The cross-cultural challenge to social psychology.* Newbury Park, CA: Sage.

Fletcher, G. J. O., Simpson, J. A., & Thomas, G. (2000). Ideals, perceptions, and evaluations in early relationship development. *Journal of Personality and Social Psychology, 79,* 933–940.

Fletcher, G. J. O., Simpson, J. A., Thomas, G., & Giles, L. (1999). Ideals in intimate relationships. *Journal of Personality and Social Psychology, 76,* 72–89.

Flett, G. L., Vredenburg, K., & Krames, L. (1995). The stability of depressive symptoms in college students: An empirical demonstration of regression to the mean. *Journal of Psychopathology & Behavioral Assessment, 17,* 403–415.

Flippo, R. F., Becker, M. J., & Wark, D. M. (2000). Preparing for and taking tests. In R. F. Flippo & D. C. Caverly (Eds.), *Handbook of college reading and study strategy research.* Mahwah, NJ: Erlbaum.

Flum, H. (1994). Styles of identity formation in early and middle adolescence. *Genetic, Social, and General Psychology Monographs, 120,* 435–467.

Flynn, J. R. (1987). Massive IQ gains in 14 nations: What IQ tests really measure. *Psychological Bulletin, 101,* 171–191.

Flynn, J. R. (1994). IQ gains over time. In R. J. Sternberg (Ed.), *The encyclopedia of human intelligence.* New York: Macmillan.

Flynn, J. R. (1998). IQ gains over time: Toward finding the causes. In U. Neisser (Ed.), *The rising curve: Long-term gains in IQ and related measures.* Washington, DC: American Psychological Association.

Flynn, J. R. (1999). Searching for justice: The discovery of IQ gains over time. *American Psychologist, 54,* 5–20.

Foa, E. B., & Kozak, M. J. (1995). DSM-IV field trial: Obsessive-compulsive disorder. *American Journal of Psychiatry, 152,* 90–96.

Fodor, E. M., & Carver, R. A. (2000). Achievement and power motives, performance feedback, and creativity. *Journal of Research in Personality, 34,* 380–396.

Folkman, S. (1997). Positive psychological states and coping with severe stress. *Social Science and Medicine, 45,* 1207–1221.

Folkman, S., & Moskowitz, J. T. (2000). Positive affect and the other side of coping. *American Psychologist, 55,* 647–654.

Folkman, S., Moskowitz, J. T., Ozer, E. M., & Park, C. L. (1997). Positive meaningful events and coping in the context of HIV/AIDS. In B. H. Gottlieb (Ed.), *Coping with chronic stress* (pp. 293–314). New York: Plenum.

Ford, D. E., Mead, L. A., Chang, P. P., Cooper-Patrick, L., Wang, N. Y., & Klag, M. J. (1998). Depression is a risk factor for coronary artery disease in men: The precursors study. *Archives of Internal Medicine, 158,* 1422–1426.

Forsén, T., Eriksson, J., Tuomilehto, J., Reunanen, A., Osmond, C., & Barker, D. (2000). The fetal and childhood growth of persons who develop type 2 diabetes. *Annals of Internal Medicine, 133,* 176–182.

Forsyth, D. R. (1999). *An introduction to group dynamics.* Belmont, CA: Wadsworth.

Forsyth, D. R., & McMillan, J. H. (1981). Attributions, affect, and expectations: A test of Weiner's three-dimensional model. *Journal of Educational Psychology, 73,* 393–403.

Forsyth, D. R., & Strong, S. R. (1986). The scientific study of counseling and psychotherapy: A unificationist view. *American Psychologist, 41,* 113–119.

Foulkes, D. (1982). *Children's dreams.* New York: Wiley.

Foulkes, D. (1985). *Dreaming: A cognitive-psychological analysis.* Hillsdale, NJ: Erlbaum.

Foulkes, D. (1996). Dream research: 1953–1993. *Sleep, 19,* 609–624.

Foulkes, D. (1999). *Children's dreaming and the development of consciousness.* Cambridge: Harvard University Press.

Fowers, B. J., & Richardson, F. C. (1996). Why is multiculturalism good? *American Psychologist, 51,* 609–621.

Fowler, R. D. (1986, May). Howard Hughes: A psychological autopsy. *Psychology Today,* pp. 22–33.

Fowler, R. D. (1990). Report of the chief executive officer: A year of recovery. *American Psychologist, 45,* 803–806.

Fowles, D. C. (1992). Schizophrenia: Diathesis-stress revisited. *Annual Review of Psychology, 43,* 303–336.

Fozard, J. L. (1990). Vision and hearing in aging. In J. E. Birren & K. W. Schaie (Eds.), *Handbook of the psychology of aging* (3rd ed.). San Diego: Academic Press.

Fozard, J. L., & Gordon-Salant, S. (2001). Changes in vision and hearing with aging. In J. E. Birren & K. W. Schaie (Eds.), *Handbook of the psychology of aging* (5th ed., pp. 240–265). San Diego, CA: Academic Press.

Fraley, R. C. (2002). Attachment stability from infancy to adulthood: Meta-analysis and dynamic modeling of developmental mechanisms. *Personality and Social Psychology Review, 6,* 123–151.

Francis, M. E., & Pennebaker, J. W. (1992). Putting stress into words: The impact of writing on psychological, absentee and self-reported emotional well-being measures. *American Journal of Health Promotion, 6,* 280–287.

Franco, S. E., Hubbard, J. R., & Martin, P. R. (1998). Stress and addiction. In J. R. Hubbard & E. A. Workman (Eds.), *Handbook of stress medicine: An organ system approach.* New York: CRC Press.

Frank, J. D. (1961). *Persuasion and healing.* Baltimore: Johns Hopkins University Press.

Frank, J. D., & Frank, J. B. (1991). *Persuasion and healing: A comparison study of psychotherapy.* Baltimore: Johns Hopkins University Press.

Frank, L. K. (1939). Projective methods for the study of personality. *Journal of Psychology, 8,* 343–389.

Frank, L. R. (1990). Electroshock: Death, brain damage, memory loss, and brainwashing. *The Journal of Mind and Behavior, 11*(3/4), 489–512.

Franke, T. (2000). The role of attachment as a protective factor in adolescent violent behavior. *Adolescent and Family Health, 1,* 40–51.

Franken, R. E. (1993). Sensation seeking and keeping your options open. *Personality and Individual Differences, 14,* 247–249.

Franken, R. E., Gibson, K. J., & Rowland, G. L. (1992). Sensation seeking and the tendency to view the world as threatening. *Personality and Individual Differences, 13*(1), 31–38.

Franks, C. M., & Barbrack, C. R. (1983). Behavior therapy with adults: An integrative perspective. In M. Hersen, A. E. Kazdin, & A. S. Bellack (Eds.), *The clinical psychology handbook.* New York: Pergamon Press.

Frantom, C., & Sherman, M. F. (1999). At what price art? Affective instability within a visual art population. *Creativity Research Journal, 12,* 15–23.

Frazier, J. A. (1999). The person with mental retardation. In A. M. Nicholi (Ed.), *The Harvard guide to psychiatry* (3rd ed., pp. 660–671). Cambridge, MA: Harvard University Press.

Frederick, S., & Loewenstein, G. (1999). Hedonic adaptation. In D. Kahneman, E. Diener, & N. Schwarz (Eds.), *Well-being: The foundations of hedonic psychology.* New York: Russell Sage Foundation.

Frederickson, B. L. (1998). What good are positive emotions? *Review of General Psychology, 2,* 300–319.

Fredrickson, B. L. (2002). Positive emotions. In C. R. Snyder & S. J. Lopez (Eds.), *Handbook of positive psychology* (pp. 120–134). New York: Oxford University Press.

Fredrickson, B. L., & Branigan, C. (2001). Positive emotions. In T. J. Mayne & G. A. Bonanno (Eds.), *Emotions: Current issues and future directions* (pp. 123–151). New York: Guilford.

Fredrikson, M., Annas, P., & Wik, G. (1997). Parental history, aversive exposure and the development of snake and spider phobia in women. *Behavioral Research and Therapy, 35,* 23–28.

Freedman, J. L. (1978). *Happy people.* New York: Harcourt Brace Jovanovich.

Freedman, J. L., & Fraser, S. C. (1966). Compliance without pressure: The foot-in-the-door technique. *Journal of Personality and Social Psychology, 4,* 195–202.

Freese, J., Powell, B., & Steelman, L. C. (1999). Rebel without a cause or effect: Birth order and social attitudes. *American Sociological Review, 64,* 207–231.

Freud, S. (1900/1953). *The interpretation of dreams.* In J. Strachey (Ed.), *The standard edition of the complete psychological works of Sigmund Freud* (Vols. 4 and 5). London: Hogarth.

Freud, S. (1901/1960). *The psycho-pathology of everyday life*. In J. Strachey (Ed.), *The standard edition of the complete psychological works of Sigmund Freud* (Vol. 6). London: Hogarth.

Freud, S. (1905/1953). *Fragment of an analysis of a case of hysteria*. In J. Strachey (Ed.), *The standard edition of the complete psychological works of Sigmund Freud* (Vol. 7). London: Hogarth.

Freud, S. (1915/1959). Instincts and their vicissitudes. In E. Jones (Ed.), *The collected papers of Sigmund Freud* (Vol. 4). New York: Basic Books.

Freud, S. (1924). *A general introduction to psychoanalysis*. New York: Boni & Liveright.

Freud, S. (1933/1964). *New introductory lectures on psychoanalysis*. In J. Strachey (Ed.), *The standard edition of the complete psychological works of Sigmund Freud* (Vol. 22). London: Hogarth.

Freud, S. (1940). An outline of psychoanalysis. *International Journal of Psychoanalysis, 21*, 27–84.

Frey, K. S., & Ruble, D. N. (1992). Gender constancy and the cost of sex-typed behavior: A test of the conflict hypothesis. *Developmental Psychology, 28*, 714–721.

Freyd, J. J. (1996). *Betrayal trauma: The logic of forgetting childhood abuse*. Cambridge, MA: Harvard University Press.

Friedberg, J. M. (1983). Shock treatment II: Resistance in the 1970's. In R. F. Morgan (Ed.), *The iatrogenics handbook: A critical look at research and practice in the helping professions*. Fair Oaks, CA: Morgan Foundation Publishers.

Friedberg, M., Saffron, B., Stinson, T. J., Nelson, W., & Bennett, C. L. (1999). Evaluation of conflict of interest in economic analyses of new drugs used in oncology. *Journal of the American Medical Association, 282*, 1453–1457.

Friedkin, N. E. (1999). Choice shift and group polarization. *American Sociological Review, 64*, 856–875.

Friedman, H. S., Tucker, J. S., Schwartz, J. E., Martin, L. R., Tomlinson-Keasey, C., Wingard, D. L., & Criqui, M. H. (1995). Childhood conscientiousness and longevity: Health behaviors and cause of death. *Journal of Personality and Social Psychology, 68*, 696–703.

Friedman, H. S., Tucker, J. S., Tomlinson-Keasey, C., Schwartz, J. E., Wingard, D. L., & Criqui, M. H. (1993). Does childhood personality predict longevity? *Journal of Personality and Social Psychology, 65*, 176–185.

Friedman, M. (1996). *Type A behavior: Its diagnosis and treatment*. New York: Plenum.

Friedman, M., & Rosenman, R. F. (1974). *Type A behavior and your heart*. New York: Knopf.

Friedrich, J., Fetherstonhaugh, D., Casey, S., & Gallagher, D. (1996). Argument integration and attitude change: Suppression effects in the integration of one-sided arguments that vary in persuasiveness. *Personality and Social Psychology Bulletin, 22*, 179–191.

Frieze, I. H., Olson, J. E., & Russell, J. (1991). Attractiveness and income for men and women in management. *Journal of Applied Social Psychology, 21*, 1039–1057.

Frijda, N. H. (1999). Emotions and hedonic experience. In D. Kahneman, E. Diener, & N. Schwarz (Eds.), *Well-being: The foundations of hedonic psychology*. New York: Russell Sage Foundation.

Frishman, L. J. (2001). Basic visual processes. In E. B. Goldstein (Ed.), *Blackwell handbook of perception*. Malden, MA: Blackwell.

Fromholt, P., & Bruhn, P. (1999). Cognitive dysfunction and dementia. In I. H. Nordhus, G. R. VandenBos, S. Berg & P. Fromholt (Eds.), *Clinical geropsychology* (pp. 183–188). Washington, DC: American Psychological Association.

Fromm, E. (1979). The nature of hypnosis and other altered states of consciousness: An ego-psychological theory. In E. Fromm & R. E. Shor (Eds.), *Hypnosis: Developments in research and new perspectives*. New York: Aldine.

Fromm, E. (1992). An ego-psychological theory of hypnosis. In E. Fromm & M. R. Nash (Eds.), *Contemporary hypnosis research*. New York: Guilford.

Frumkes, T. E. (1990). Classical and modern psychophysical studies of dark and light adaptation and their relationship to underlying retinal function. In K. N. Leibovic (Ed.), *Science of vision*. New York: Springer-Verlag.

Fuchs, V. R. (1997). Managed care and merger mania. *Journal of the American Medical Association, 277*, 920–921.

Fullilove, M., & Dieudonne, I. (1996). Substance abuse in pregnancy. In *The Hatherleigh guide to treating substance abuse* (pp. 93–117). New York: Hatherleigh Press.

Funder, D. C. (2001). Personality. *Annual Review of Psychology, 52*, 197–221.

Furnham, A., & Gunter, B. (1993). Corporate culture: Definition, diagnosis, and change. In C. L. Cooper & I. T. Robertson (Eds.), *International review of industrial and organizational psychology* (Vol. 8, pp. 234–261). London: Wiley.

Furumoto, L. (1980). Mary Whiton Calkins (1863–1930). *Psychology of Women Quarterly, 5*, 55–68.

Furumoto, L., & Scarborough, E. (1986). Placing women in the history of psychology: The first American women psychologists. *American Psychologist, 41*, 35–42.

Fuster, J. M. (1996). Frontal lobe lesions. In B. S. Fogel, R. B. Schiffer, & S. M. Rao (Eds), *Neuropsychiatry*. Baltimore: Williams & Wilkins.

Fyer, A. J. (2000). Anxiety disorders: Genetics. In B. J. Sadock & V. A. Sadock (Eds.), *Kaplan and Sadock's comprehensive textbook of psychiatry* (7th ed., Vol. 1, pp. 1457–1463). Philadelphia: Lippincott/Williams & Wilkins.

Gabbard, G. O. (1994). Reconsidering the American Psychological Association's policy on sex with former patients: Is it justifiable? *Professional Psychology: Research and Practice, 25*, 329–335.

Gaertner, S. L., Dovidio, J. F., Nier, J. A., Ward, C. M., & Banker, B. S. (1999). Across cultural divides: The value of a superordinate identity. In D. A. Prentice & D. T. Miller (Eds.), *Cultural divides: Understanding and overcoming group conflict*. New York: Russell Sage Foundation.

Gaeth, G. J., & Shanteau, J. (2000). Reducing the influence of irrelevant information on experienced decision makers. In T. Connolly, H. R. Arkes, & K. R. Hammond (Eds.), *Judgment and decision making: An interdisciplinary reader* (2nd ed., pp. 305–323). New York: Cambridge University Press.

Galanter, E. (1962). Contemporary psychophysics. In R. Brown (Ed.), *New directions in psychology*. New York: Holt, Rinehart & Winston.

Galati, D., Scherer, K. R., & Ricci-Bitti, P. E. (1997). Voluntary facial expression of emotion: Comparing congenitally blind with normally sighted encoders. *Journal of Personality and Social Psychology, 73*, 1363–1379.

Gallagher, J. J., & Courtright, R. D. (1986). The educational definition of giftedness and its policy implications. In R. J. Sternberg & J. E. Davidson (Eds.), *Conceptions of giftedness*. Cambridge: Cambridge University Press.

Gallistel, C. R. (2000). The replacement of general-purpose learning models with adaptively specialized learning modules. In M. S. Gazzaniga (Ed.), *The new cognitive neurosciences* (2nd ed., pp. 1179–1192). Cambridge, MA: MIT Press.

Galton, F. (1869). *Hereditary genius: An inquiry into its laws and consequences*. New York: Appleton.

Gambone, J. C., Reiter, R. C., & DiMatteo, M. R. (1994). The PRE-PARED provider: A guide for improved patient communication. Beaverton, OR: Mosybl Great Performance.

Gangestad, S. W., & Simpson, J. A. (1993). Development of a scale measuring genetic variation related to expressive control. *Journal of Personality, 61*(2), 133–158.

Gangestad, S. W., & Snyder, M. (2000). Self-monitoring: Appraisal and reappraisal. *Psychological Bulletin, 126*, 530–555.

Gantt, W. H. (1975, April 25). Unpublished lecture, Ohio State University. Cited in D. Hothersall, (1984), *History of psychology*. New York: Random House.

Garb, H. N., Florio, C. M., & Grove, W. M. (1998). The validity of the Rorschach and the Minnesota Multiphasic Personality Inventory: Results form meta-analysis. *Psychological Science, 9*, 402–404.

Garcia, J. (1989). Food for Tolman: Cognition and cathexis in concert. In T. Archer & L. G. Nilsson (Eds.), *Aversion, avoidance, and anxiety: Perspectives on aversively motivated behavior*. Hillsdale, NJ: Erlbaum.

Garcia, J., & Koelling, R. A. (1966). Learning with prolonged delay of reinforcement. *Psychonomic Science, 5*, 121–122.

Garcia, J., & Rusiniak, K. W. (1980). What the nose learns from the mouth. In D. Muller-Schwarze & R. M. Silverstein (Eds.), *Chemical signals*. New York: Plenum.

Garcia, J., Clarke, J. C., & Hankins, W. G. (1973). Natural responses to scheduled rewards. In P. P. G. Bateson & P. Klopfer (Eds.), *Perspectives in ethology*. New York: Plenum.

Garcia, S. D., & Khersonsky, D. (1996). "They make a lovely couple": Perceptions of couple attractiveness. *Journal of Social Behavior and Personality, 11*, 667–682.

Gardner, E. L. (1997). Brain reward mechanisms. In J. H. Lowinson, P. Ruiz, R. B. Millman, & J. G. Langrod (Eds.), *Substance abuse: A comprehensive textbook*. Baltimore: Williams & Wilkins.

Gardner, E. P., & Kandel, E. R. (2000). Touch. In E. R. Kandel, J. H. Schwartz, & T. M. Jessell (Eds.), *Principles of neural science*. New York: McGraw-Hill.

Gardner, H. (1983). *Frames of mind: The theory of multiple intelligences*. New York: Basic Books.

Gardner, H. (1985). *The mind's new science: A history of the cognitive revolution*. New York: Basic Books.

Gardner, H. (1993). *Multiple intelligences: The theory in practice*. New York: Basic Books.

Gardner, H. (1998). A multiplicity of intelligences. *Scientific American Presents Exploring Intelligence, 9*, 18–23.

Gardner, R. A., & Gardner, B. T. (1969). Teaching sign language to a chimpanzee. *Science, 165*, 664–672.

Gardos, P. S., & Mosher, D. L. (1999). Gender differences in reactions to viewing pornographic vignettes: Essential or interpretive? *Journal of Psychology & Human Sexuality, 11*, 65–83.

Garfield, S. L. (1996). Some problems associated with "validated" forms of psychotherapy. *Clinical Psychology: Science & Practice, 3*, 218–229.

Garfield, S. L. (2001). Methodological issues in clinical diagnosis. In P. B. Sutker & H. E. Adams (Eds.), *Comprehensive handbook of psychopathology*. New York: Kluwer Academic/Plenum.

Garfield, S. L., & Bergin, A. E. (1994). Introduction and historical overview. In A. E. Bergin & S. L. Garfield (Eds.), *Handbook of psychotherapy and behavior change* (4th ed.). New York: Wiley.

Garland, A. F., & Zigler, E. (1993). Adolescent suicide prevention: Current research and social policy implications. *American Psychologist, 48*(2), 169–182.

Garland, A. F., & Zigler, E. (1999). Emotional and behavioral problems among highly intellectually gifted youth. *Roeper Review, 22*, 41–44.

Garlow, S. J., Musselman, D. L., & Nemeroff, C. B. (1999). The neurochemistry of mood disorders: Clinical studies. In D. S. Charney, E. J. Nestler & B. S. Bunney (Eds.), *Neurobiology of mental illness*. New York: Oxford University Press.

Garner, D. M., Garfindel, P. E., Schwartz, D., & Thompson, M. (1980). Cultural expectations of thinness in women. *Psychological Reports, 47*, 483–491.

Garnets, L., & Kimmel, D. (1991). Lesbian and gay male dimensions in the psychological study of human diversity. In J. D. Goodchilds (Ed.), *Psychological perspectives on human diversity in America*. Washington, DC: American Psychological Association.

Garvey, C. R. (1929). List of American psychology laboratories. *Psychological Bulletin, 26*, 652–660.

Gatewood, R., & Perloff, R. (1990). Testing and industrial application. In G. Goldstein & M. Hersen (Eds.), *Handbook of psychological assessment*. New York: Pergamon Press.

Gazzaniga, M. S. (1970). *The bisected brain*. New York: Appleton-Century-Crofts.

Gazzaniga, M. S., Bogen, J. E., & Sperry, R. W. (1965). Observations on visual perception after disconnection of the cerebral hemispheres in man. *Brain, 88*, 221–236.

Ge, X., Conger, R. D., & Elder, G. H. Jr. (1996). Coming of age too early: Pubertal influences on girls' vulnerability to psychological distress. *Child Development, 67*, 3386–3400.

Geddes, J. R., & Lawrie, S. M. (1995). Obstetrical complications and schizophrenia: A meta-analysis. *British Journal of Psychiatry, 167*, 786–793.

Geiger, M. A. (1997). An examination of the relationship between answer changing, testwiseness and examination performance. *Journal of Experimental Education, 66*, 49–60.

Geis, F. L. (1993). Self-fulfilling prophecies: A social psychological view of gender. In A. E. Beall & R. J. Sternberg (Eds.), *The psychology of gender*. New York: Guilford.

Geller, J. L. (1992). A historical perspective on the role of state hospitals viewed from the era of the "revolving door." *American Journal of Psychiatry, 149*, 1526–1533.

Geller, L. (1982). The failure of self-actualization theory: A critique of Carl Rogers and Abraham Maslow. *Journal of Humanistic Psychology, 22*, 56–73.

Gelman, R., & Williams, E. M. (1998). Enabling constraints for cognitive development and learning: Domain-specificity and epigenesis. In W. Damon (Ed.), *Handbook of child psychology (Vol. 2): Cognition, perception, and language*. New York: Wiley.

Gentner, D. (1988). Metaphor as structure mapping: The relational shift. *Child Development, 59*, 47–59.

Gentner, D., & Rattermann, M. J. (1991). Language and the career of similarity. In S. A. Gelman & J. P. Byrnes (Eds.), *Perspectives on language and thought: Interrelations in development*. Cambridge, MA: Cambridge University Press.

Gerard, M. (Ed.). (1968). *Dali*. Paris: Draeger.

Gergen, K. J., Gulerce, A., Lock, A., & Misra, G. (1996). Psychological science in cultural context. *American Psychologist, 51*, 496–503.

German, T. P., & Defeyter, M. A. (2000). Immunity to functional fixedness in young children. *Psychonomic Bulletin & Review, 7*, 707–712.

Gershberg, F. B., & Shimamura, A. P. (1998). The neuropsychology of human learning and memory. In J. L. Martinez, Jr. & R. P. Kesner (Eds.), *Neurobiology of learning and memory*. San Diego: Academic Press.

Gershon, E. S., Berrettini, W. H., & Goldin, L. R. (1989). Mood disorders: Genetic aspects. In H. I. Kaplan & B. J. Sadock (Eds.), *Comprehensive textbook of psychiatry/V*. Baltimore: Williams & Wilkins.

Geschwind, N., & Galaburda, A. M. (1987). *Cerebral lateralization: Biological mechanisms, associations, and pathology*. Cambridge, MA: MIT Press.

Gest, S. D. (1997). Behavioral inhibition: Stability and associations with adaptation from childhood to early adulthood. *Journal of Personality and Social Psychology, 72*, 467–475.

Ghez, C., & Thach, W. T. (2000). The cerebellum. In E. R. Kandel, J. H. Schwartz & T. M. Jessell (Eds.), *Principles of neural science* (pp. 832–852). New York: McGraw-Hill.

Ghiselin, B. (Ed.). (1952). *The creative process*. New York: Mentor.

Gibbon, J., & Fairhurst, S. (1994). Ratio versus difference comparators in choice. *Journal of the Experimental Analysis of Behavior, 62*, 409–434.

Gibbs, N. (1990, October 8). Shameful bequests to the next generation. *Time*, pp. 42–48.

Gibson, H. B., & Heap, M. (1991). *Hypnosis in therapy*. Hillsdale, NJ: Erlbaum.

Gigerenzer, G. (1997). Ecological intelligence: An adaption for frequencies. *Psychologische Beitraege, 39*, 107–125.

Gigerenzer, G. (2000). *Adaptive thinking: Rationality in the real world*. New York: Oxford University Press.

Gigerenzer, G., & Hoffrage, U. (1999). Overcoming difficulties in Bayesian reasoning: A reply to Lewis and Keren (1999) and Mellers and McGraw (1999). *Psychological Review, 106*, 425–430.

Gigerenzer, G., & Todd, P. M. (1999). Fast and frugal heuristics: The adaptive toolbox. In G. Gigerenzer, P. M. Todd, & ABC Research Group (Eds.), *Simple heuristics that make us smart* (pp. 3–36). New York: Oxford University Press.

Gilbert, D. T. (1989). Thinking lightly about others: Automatic components of the social inference process. In J. S. Uleman & J. A. Bargh (Eds.), *Unintended thought: Limits of awareness, intention, and control*. New York: Guilford.

Gilbert, C. D. (1993). Rapid dynamic changes in adult cerebral cortex. *Current Opinion in Neurobiology, 3*, 100–103.

Gilbert, D. T. (1998). Speeding with Ned: A personal view of the correspondence bias. In J. M. Darley & J. Cooper (Ed.), *Attribution and social interaction: The legacy of Edward E. Jones*. Washington, DC: American Psychological Association.

Gilbert, D. T., & Malone, P. S. (1995). The correspondence bias. *Psychological Bulletin, 117*, 21–38.

Giles, T. R., & Marafiote, R. A. (1998). Managed care and the practitioner: A call for unity. *Clinical Psychology: Science & Practice, 5*, 41–50.

Gilgen, A. R. (1982). *American psychology since World War II: A profile of the discipline*. Westport, CT: Greenwood Press.

Gilhooly, K. J. (1996). *Thinking: Directed, undirected and creative*. London: Academic Press.

Gillberg, M., & Akerstedt, T. (1998). Sleep loss and performance: No "safe" duration of a monotonous task. *Physiology & Behavior, 64*, 599–604.

Gillberg, M., Kecklund, G., Axelsson, J., & Akerstedt, T. (1996). The effects of a short daytime nap after restricted night sleep. *Sleep, 19*, 570–575.

Gillham, J. E., Shatté, A. J., Reivich, K. J., & Seligman, M. E. P. (2001). Optimism, pessimism, and explanatory style. In E. C. Chang (Ed.), *Optimism & pessimism: Implications for theory, research, and practice* (pp. 53–76). Washington, DC: American Psychological Association.

Gilovich, T., & Savitsky, K. (1999). The spotlight effect and the illusion of transparency: Egocentric assessments of how we're seen by others. *Current Directions in Psychological Science, 8*, 165–168.

Gilovich, T., Medvec, V. H., & Savitsky, K. (2000). The spotlight effect in social judgment: An egocentric bias in estimates of the salience of one's own actions and appearance. *Journal of Personality and Social Psychology, 78*, 211–222.

Gitlin, M. (2002). Pharmacological treatment of depression. In I. H. Gotlib & C. L. Hammen (Eds.), *Handbook of depression*. New York: Guilford.

Gitlin, M., Nuechterlein, K., Subotnik, K. L., Ventura, J., Mintz, J., Fogelson, D. L., Bartzokis, G., & Aravagiri, M. (2001). Clinical outcome following neuroleptic discontinuation in patients with remitted recent-onset schizophrenia. *American Journal of Psychiatry, 158*, 1835–1842.

Gladue, B. A. (1988). Hormones in relationship to homosexual/bisexual/heterosexual gender orientation. In J. M. A. Sitesen (Ed.), *Handbook of sexology: The pharmacology and endocrinology of sexual function* (Vol. 6). Amsterdam: Elsevier.

Gladue, B. A. (1994). The biopsychology of sexual orientation. *Current Directions in Psychological Science, 3*, 150–154.

Glaser, R. (1991). Intelligence as an expression of acquired knowledge. In H. A. H. Rowe (Ed.), *Intelligence: Reconceptualization and measurement*. Hillsdale, NJ: Erlbaum.

Glass, C. R., & Arnkoff, D. B. (1992). Behavior therapy. In D. K. Freedheim (Ed.), *History of psychotherapy: A century of change*. Washington, DC: American Psychological Association.

Glass, R. M. (2001). Electroconvulsive therapy. *Journal of the American Medical Association, 285,* 1346–1348.

Glassman, A. H., & Shapiro, P. A. (1998). Depression and the course of coronary artery disease. *American Journal of Psychiatry, 155,* 4–11.

Gleason, J. B., & Ratner, N. B. (1998). Language acquisition. In J. B. Gleason & N. B. Ratner (Eds.), *Psycholinguistics.* Fort Worth, TX: Harcourt College Publishers.

Gleaves, D. H. (1994). On "The reality of repressed memories." *American Psychologist, 49,* 440–441.

Gleaves, D. H., May, M. C., & Cardena, E. (2001). An examination of the diagnostic validity of dissociative identity disorders. *Clinical Psychology Review, 21,* 577–608.

Gleitman, L. R., & Newport, E. (1996). *The invention of language by children.* Cambridge, MA: MIT Press.

Glenberg, A. M. (1992). Distributed practice effects. In L. R. Squire (Ed.), *Encyclopedia of learning and memory.* New York: Macmillan.

Glenn, N. D. (1990). Quantitative research on marital quality in the 1980s: A critical review. *Journal of Marriage and the Family, 52,* 818–831.

Glenn, N. D. (1998). The course of marital success and failure in five American 10-year marriage cohorts. *Journal of Marriage and the Family, 60,* 569–576.

Gluck, M. A., & Myers, C. E. (1997). Psychobiological models of hippocampal function in learning and memory. *Annual Review of Psychology, 48,* 481–514.

Goddard, H. H. (1917). Mental tests and the immigrant. *Journal of Delinquency, 2,* 243–277.

Goff, D. C., & Coyle, J. T. (2001). The emerging role of glutamate in the pathophysiology and treatment of schizophrenia. *American Journal of Psychiatry, 158,* 1367–1377.

Goff, D. C., & Gudeman, J. E. (1999). The person with chronic mental illness. In A.M. Nicholi (Ed.), *The Harvard guide to psychiatry.* Cambridge, MA: Harvard University Press.

Gold, M. S. (1997). Cocaine (and crack): Clinical aspects. In J. H. Lowinson, P. Ruiz, R. B. Millman, & J. G. Langrod (Eds.), *Substance abuse: A comprehensive textbook.* Baltimore: Williams & Wilkins.

Gold, M. S., & Miller, N. S. (1997). Cocaine (and crack): Neurobiology. In J. H. Lowinson, P. Ruiz, R. B. Millman, & J. G. Langrod (Eds.), *Substance abuse: A comprehensive textbook.* Baltimore: Williams & Wilkins.

Goldberg, M. E., & Hudspeth, A. J. (2000). The vestibular system. In E. R. Kandel, J. H. Schwartz, & T. M. Jessell (Eds.), *Principles of neural science.* New York: McGraw-Hill.

Golden, C. J., Sawicki, R. F., & Franzen, M. D. (1990). Test construction. In G. Goldstein & M. Hersen (Eds.), *Handbook of psychological assessment.* New York: Pergamon Press.

Goldenberg, H. (1983). *Contemporary clinical psychology.* Pacific Grove, CA: Brooks/Cole.

Goldfield, B. A., & Reznick, J. S. (1990). Early lexical acquisition: Rate, content, and the vocabulary spurt. *Journal of Child Language, 17,* 171–183.

Goldfried, M. R., & Wolfe, B. E. (1998). Toward a more clinically valid approach to therapy research. *Journal of Consulting and Clinical Psychology, 66,* 143–150.

Goldfried, M. R., Greenberg, L. S., & Marmar, C. (1990). Individual psychotherapy: Process and outcome. *Annual Review of Psychology, 41,* 659–688.

Goldman-Rakic, P. S. (1993). Working memory and the mind. In *Mind and brain: Readings from* Scientific American *magazine.* New York: W. H. Freeman.

Goldman-Rakic, P. S. (1998). The prefrontal landscape: Implications of functional architecture for understanding human mentation and the central executive. In A. C. Roberts, T. W. Robbins, & L. Weiskrantz (Eds.), *The prefrontal cortex: Executive and cognitive functions.* New York: Oxford University Press.

Goldsmith, H. H., & Harman, C. (1994). Temperament and attachment; individuals and relationships. *Current Directions in Psychological Science, 3,* 53–57.

Goldstein, D. G., & Gigerenzer, G. (1999). The recognition heuristic: How ignorance makes us smart. In G. Gigerenzer, P. M. Todd, & ABC Research Group (Eds.), *Simple heuristics that make us smart* (pp. 37–58). New York: Oxford University Press.

Goldstein, D. G., & Gigerenzer, G. (2002). Models of ecological rationality: The recognition heuristic. *Psychological Review, 109,* 75–90.

Goldstein, E., & Farmer, K. (Eds.) (1993). *True stories of false memories.* Boca Raton, FL: Sir Publishing.

Goldstein, E. B. (1996). *Sensation and perception* (4th ed.). Pacific Grove, CA: Brooks/Cole.

Goldstein, E. B. (2001). Pictorial perception and art. In E. B. Goldstein (Ed.), *Blackwell handbook of perception.* Malden, MA: Blackwell.

Goldstein, W. M. (1990). Judgments of relative importance in decision making: Global vs. local interpretations of subjective weight. *Organizational Behavior and Human Decision Processes, 47,* 313–336.

Goldstein, W. M., & Hogarth, R. M. (1997). Judgement and decision research: Some historical context. In W. M. Goldstein, & R. M. Hogarth (Eds.), *Research on judgement and decision making.* New York: Cambridge University Press.

Goleman, D. (1995). *Emotional intelligence.* New York: Bantam Books.

Gonzalez-Lopez, A., & Kamps, D. M. (1997). Social skills training to increase social interactions between children with autism and their typical peers. *Focus on Autism & Other Developmental Disabilities, 12,* 2–14.

Goodenough, D. R. (1991). Dream recall: History and current status of the field. In S. J. Ellman & J. S. Antrobus (Eds.), *The mind in sleep: Psychology and psychophysiology* (2nd ed.). New York: Wiley.

Goodwin, C. J. (1991). Misportraying Pavlov's apparatus. *American Journal of Psychology, 104*(1), 135–141.

Goodwin, D. W., & Gabrielli, W. F. (1997). Alcohol: Clinical aspects. In J. H. Lowinson, P. Ruiz, R. B. Millman, & J. G. Langrod (Eds.), *Substance abuse: A comprehensive textbook.* Baltimore: Williams & Wilkins.

Goodwin, F. K., & Jamison, K. R. (1990). *Manic-depressive illness.* New York: Oxford University Press.

Gopnik, A., Meltzoff, A. N., & Kuhl, P. K. (1999). *The scientist in the crib: Minds, brains, and how children learn.* New York: Morrow.

Gordon, H. W. (1990). The neurobiological basis of hemisphericity. In C. Trevarthen (Ed.), *Brain circuits and functions of the mind. Essays in honor of Roger W. Sperry.* Cambridge, MA: Cambridge University Press.

Gordon, J., & Abramov, I. (2001). Color vision. In E. B. Goldstein (Ed.), *Blackwell handbook of perception.* Malden, MA: Blackwell.

Gorman, M. E. (1989). Error, falsification and scientific inference: An experimental investigation. *Quarterly Journal of Experimental Psychology, 41*(2–A), 385–412.

Gosden, C., Nicolaides, K., & Whitting, V. (1994). *Is my baby all right? A guide for expectant parents.* Oxford, England: Oxford University Press.

Gosling, S. D., Ko, S. J., Mannarelli, T., & Morris, M. E. (2002). A room with a cue: Personality judgments based on offices and bedrooms. *Journal of Personality and Social Psychology, 82,* 379–398.

Gottdiener, J. S., Krantz, D. S., Howell, R. H., Hecht, G. M., Klein, J., Falconer, J. J., & Rozanski, A. (1994). Induction of silent myocardial ischemia with mental stress testing: Relationship to the triggers of ischemia during daily life activities and to ischemic functional severity. *Journal of the American College of Cardiology, 24,* 1645–1651.

Gottesman, I. I. (1991). *Schizophrenia genesis: The origins of madness.* New York: W. H. Freeman.

Gottesman, I. I. (1993). Origins of schizophrenia: Past as prologue. In R. Plomin & G. E. McClearn (Eds.), *Nature, nurture and psychology.* Washington, DC: American Psychological Association.

Gottesman, I. I. (2001). Psychopathology through a life span-genetic prism. *American Psychologist, 56,* 867–878.

Gottesman, I. I., & Moldin, S. O. (1998). Genotypes, genes, genesis, and pathogenesis in schizophrenia. In M. F. Lenzenweger & R. H. Dworkin (Eds.), *Origins and development of schizophrenia: Advances in experimental psychopathology.* Washington, DC: American Psychological Association.

Gould, E., Reeves, A. J., Graziano, M. S. A., & Gross, C. G. (1999). Neurogenesis in the neocortex of adult primates. *Science, 286,* 548–552.

Gould, R. L. (1975, February). Adult life stages: Growth toward self-tolerance. *Psychology Today,* pp. 74–78.

Gould, R. L. (1978). *Transformations: Growth and change in adult life.* New York: Simon & Schuster.

Gould, S. J. (1993). The sexual politics of classification. *Natural History,* 20–29.

Gould, S. J., & Eldredge, N. (1977). Punctuated equilibria: The tempo and mode of evolution reconsidered. *Paleobiology, 3,* 115–151.

Gould, S. J., & Eldredge, N. (1993). Punctuated equilibrium comes of age. *Nature, 366,* 223–227.

Gouras, P. (1991). Color vision. In E. R. Kandel, J. H. Schwartz, & T. M. Jessell (Eds.), *Principles of neural science* (3rd ed.). New York: Elsevier.

Gouzoulis-Mayfrank, E., Daumann, J., Tuchtenhagen, F., Pelz, S., Becker, S., Kunert, H. J., Fimm, B., & Sass, H. (2000). Impaired cognition in drug free users of recreational ecstasy (MDMA). *Journal of Neurology, Neurosurgery, & Psychiatry, 68,* 719–725.

Gow, K. M. (1999). Recovered memories of abuse: Real, fabricated, or both? *Australian Journal of Clinical & Experimental Hypnosis, 27*(2), 81–97.

Graber, J. A., Brooks-Gunn, J., & Warren, M. P. (1995). The antecedents of menarcheal age: Heredity, family environment, and stressful life events. *Child Development, 66,* 346–359.

Graber, J. A., Brooks-Gunn, J., Paikoff, R. L., & Warren, M. P. (1994). Prediction of eating problems: An 8-year study of adolescent girls. *Developmental Psychology, 30,* 823–834.

Graber, J. A., Lewinsohn, P. M., Seeley, J. R., & Brooks-Gunn, J.

(1997). Is psychopathology associated with the timing of pubertal development? *Journal of the American Academy of Child & Adolescent Psychiatry, 36,* 1768–1776.

Graf, P., & Gallie, K. A. (1992). A transfer-appropriate processing account for memory and amnesia. In L. R. Squire & N. Butters (Eds.), *Neuropsychology of memory* (2nd ed.). New York: Guilford.

Graf, P., & Uttl, B. (2001). Prospective memory: A new focus for research. *Consciousness & Cognition: An International Journal, 10,* 437–450.

Graham, D. (2000). *Online recruiting.* Palo Alto, CA: Davies-Black.

Graham, J. R. (1990). *MMPI-2: Assessing personality and psychopathology.* New York: Oxford University Press.

Granberg, G., & Holmberg, S. (1991). Self-reported turnout and voter validation. *American Journal of Political Science, 35,* 448–459.

Grant, I., McDonald, W. I., Patterson, T., & Trimble, M. R. (1989). Multiple sclerosis. In G. W. Brown & T. O. Harris (Eds.), *Life events and illness.* New York: Guilford.

Grantham-McGregor, S., Ani, C., & Fernald, L. (2001). The role of nutrition in intellectual development. In R. J. Sternberg & E. L. Grigorenko (Eds.), *Environmental effects on cognitive abilities* (pp. 119–156). Mahwah, NJ: Erlbaum.

Gratton, A. (1996). In vivo analysis of the role of dopamine in stimulant and opiate self-administration. *Journal of Psychiatry & Neuroscience, 21,* 264–279.

Graziano, W. G. (1995). Evolutionary psychology: Old music, but now on CDs? *Psychological Inquiry, 6,* 41–44.

Graziano, W. G., & Eisenberg, N. H. (1997). Agreeableness: A dimension of personality. In R. Hogan, J. Johnson, & S. Briggs (Eds.), *Handbook of personality psychology.* San Diego: Academic Press.

Green, C. D., & Vervaeke, J. (1997). But what have you done for us lately? Some recent perspectives on linguistic nativism. In D. M. Johnson & C. E. Erneling (Eds.), *The future of the cognitive revolution.* New York: Oxford University Press.

Green, J. P. (1999). Hypnosis, context effects, and recall of early autobiographical memories. *International Journal of Clinical & Experimental Hypnosis, 47,* 284–300.

Green, L. W., Tryon W. W., Marks, B., & Huryn, J. (1986). Periodontal disease as a function of life events stress. *Journal of Human Stress, 12*(1), 32–36.

Greenberg, J. S. (1993). *Comprehensive stress management.* Dubuque, IA: William C. Brown.

Greenberg, M. A., Wortman, C. B., & Stone, A. A. (1996). Emotional expression and physical health: Revising traumatic memories or fostering self-regulation? *Journal of Personality and Social Psychology, 71,* 588–602.

Greenberg, R. P., & Fisher, S. (1997). Mood-mending medicines: Probing drug, psychotherapy and placebo solutions. In S. Fisher & R. P. Greenberg (Eds.), *From placebo to panacea: Putting psychiatric drugs to the test.* New York: Wiley.

Greene, R. L. (1992a). *Human memory: Paradigms and paradoxes.* Hillsdale, NJ: Erlbaum.

Greene, R. L. (1992b). Repetition and learning. In L. R. Squire (Ed.), *Encyclopedia of learning and memory.* New York: Macmillian.

Greene, W. A., & Swisher, S. N. (1969). Psychological and somatic variables associated with the development and course of monozygotic twins discordant for leukemia. *Annals of the New York Academy of Sciences, 164,* 394–408.

Greenfield, D. N. (1999). Psychological characteristics of compulsive Internet use: A preliminary analysis. *CyberPsychology and Behavior, 2,* 403–412.

Greenfield, P. M. (1997). You can't take it with you: Why ability assessments don't cross cultures. *American Psychologist, 52,* 1115–1124.

Greenfield, P. M. (1998). The cultural evolution of IQ. In U. Neisser (Ed.), *The rising curve: Long-term gains in IQ and related measures.* Washington, DC: American Psychological Association.

Greenfield, P. M., & Suzuki, L. K. (1998). Culture and human development: implications for parenting, education, pediatrics, and mental health. In W. Damon (Ed.), *Handbook of child psychology (Vol. 4): Child psychology in practice.* New York: Wiley.

Greeno, C. G., & Wing, R. R. (1994). Stress-induced eating. *Psychological Bulletin, 115,* 444–464.

Greeno, J. G. (1978). Nature of problem-solving abilities. In W. K. Estes (Ed.), *Handbook of learning and cognitive processes* (Vol. 5). Hillsdale, NJ: Erlbaum.

Greenough, W. T. (1975). Experiential modification of the developing brain. *American Scientist, 63,* 37–46.

Greenough, W. T. (1985). The possible role of experience-dependent synaptogenesis, or synapses on demand in the memory process. In N. M. Weinberger, J. L. McGaugh, & G. Lynch (Eds.), *Memory systems of the brain.* New York: Guilford.

Greenough, W. T. (1991). The animal rights assertions: A researcher's perspective. *Psychological Science Agenda, 4*(3), 10–12.

Greenough, W. T., & Volkmar, F. R. (1973). Pattern of dendritic branching in occipital cortex of rats reared in complex environments. *Experimental Neurology, 40,* 491–504.

Greenson, R. R. (1967). *The technique and practice of psychoanalysis* (Vol. 1). New York: International Universities Press.

Greenspan, S., & Driscoll, J. (1997). The role of intelligence in a broad model of personal competence. In D. P. Flanagan, J. L. Genshaft, & P. L. Harrison (Eds.), *Contemporary intellectual assessment: Theories, tests, and issues.* New York: Guilford.

Greenstein, T. N. (1996). Husbands' participation in domestic labor: Interactive effects of wives' and husbands' gender ideologies. *Journal of Marriage and the Family, 58,* 535–595.

Greenwald, A. G. (1992). New look 3: Unconscious cognition reclaimed. *American Psychologist, 47,* 766–779.

Greenwald, A. G., Spangenberg, E. R., Pratkanis, A. R., & Eskenazi, J. (1991). Double-blind tests of subliminal self-help audiotapes. *Psychological Science, 2,* 119–122.

Gregory, R. J. (1996). *Psychological testing: History, principles, and applications* (2nd ed.). Boston: Allyn & Bacon.

Gregory, R. L. (1973). *Eye and brain.* New York: McGraw-Hill.

Gregory, R. L. (1978). *Eye and brain* (2nd ed.). New York: McGraw-Hill.

Grencavage, L. M., & Norcross, J. C. (1990). Where are the commonalities among the therapeutic factors? *Professional Psychology: Research and Practice, 21,* 372–378.

Griffith, E. E. H., González, C. A., & Blue, H. C. (1999). The basics of cultural psychiatry. In R. E. Hales, S. C. Yudofsky, & J. A. Talbott (Eds.), *The American Psychiatric Press textbook of psychiatry.* Washington, DC: American Psychiatric Press.

Griffith, R. M., Miyago, M., & Tago, A. (1958). The universality of typical dreams: Japanese vs. Americans. *American Anthropologist, 60,* 1173–1179.

Griffiths, M. (1999). Internet addiction: Fact or fiction? *Psychologist, 12,* 246–250.

Grigorenko, E. L. (2000). Heritability and intelligence. In R. J. Sternberg (Ed.), *Handbook of intelligence* (pp. 53–91). New York: Cambridge University Press.

Grigorenko, E. L., & Sternberg, R. J. (2001). Analytical, creative, and practical intelligence as predictors of self-reported adaptive functioning: A case study in Russia. *Intelligence, 29,* 57–73.

Grinspoon, L., & Bakalar, J. B. (1997). Marihuana. In J. H. Lowinson, P. Ruiz, R. B. Millman, & J. G. Langrod (Eds.), *Substance abuse: A comprehensive textbook.* Baltimore: Williams & Wilkins.

Groat, H. T., Giordano, P. C., Cernkovich, S. A., Pugh, M. D., & Swinford, S. P. (1997). Attitudes toward childbearing among young parents. *Journal of Marriage and the Family, 59,* 568–581.

Grob, C. S., & Poland, R. E. (1997). MDMA. In J. H. Lowinson, P. Ruiz, R. B. Millman, & J. G. Langrod (Eds.), *Substance abuse: A comprehensive textbook.* Baltimore: Williams & Wilkins.

Grob, G. N. (1983). Disease and environment in American history. In D. Mechanic (Ed.), *Handbook of health, health care, and the health professions.* New York: Free Press.

Grob, G. N. (1991). Origins of DSM-I: A study in appearance and reality. *American Journal of Psychiatry, 148,* 421–431.

Grobbee, D. E., Rimm, E. B., Giovannucci, E., Colditz, G., Stampfer, M., & Willett, W. (1990). Coffee, caffeine, and cardiovascular disease in men. *New England Journal of Medicine, 323,* 1026–1032.

Gross, J. J. (1998). Antecedent and response focused emotion regulation: Divergent consequences for experience, expression, and physiology. *Journal of Personality and Social Psychology, 74,* 224–237.

Gross, J. J. (2001). Emotion regulation in adulthood: Timing is everything. *Current Directions in Psychological Science, 10,* 214–219.

Gross, J. J., & Levenson, R. W. (1997). Hiding feelings: The acute effects of inhibiting negative and positive emotion. *Journal of Abnormal Psychology, 106,* 95–103.

Grossarth-Maticek, R., & Eysenck, H. J. (1991). Coffee-drinking and personality as factors in the genesis of cancer and coronary heart disease. *Neuropsychobiology, 23,* 153–159.

Grossman, R. P., & Till, B. D. (1998). The persistence of classically conditioned brand attitudes. *Journal of Advertising, 27,* 23–31.

Grossman, S. P., Dacey, D., Halaris, A. E., Collier, T., & Routtenberg, A. (1978). Aphagia and adipsia after preferential desruction of nerve cell bodies in hypothalamus. *Science, 202,* 537–539.

Grossmann, K., Grossmann, K. E., Spangler, S., Suess, G., & Unzner, L. (1985). Maternal sensitivity and newborn orientation responses as related to quality of attachment in northern Germany. In I. Bretherton & E. Waters (Eds.), Growing points of attachment theory. *Monographs of* the Society for Research for Child Development, 50, (1–2, Serial No. 209).

Grossmann, K. E., & Grossmann, K. (1990). The wider concept of attachment in cross-cultural research. *Human Development, 33,* 31–47.

Grossmann, K. E., Grossmann, K., Huber, F., & Wartner, U. (1981). Children's behavior towards their mothers at 12 months and their fathers at 18 months in Ainsworth's Strange Situation. *International Journal of Behavioral Development, 4,* 157–181.

Grotevant, H. (1997). Adolescent development in family contexts. In N. Eisenberg (Ed.), *Handbook of child psychology. Vol. 3: Social, emotional, and personality development* (5th ed., pp. 1097–1149). New York: Wiley.

Groth-Marnat, G. (1997). *Handbook of psychological assessment.* New York: Wiley.

Gruen, R. J. (1993). Stress and depression: Toward the development of integrative models. In L. Goldberger & S. Breznitz (Eds.), *Handbook of stress: Theoretical and clinical aspects.* New York: Free Press.

Grunberg, N. E., & Straub, R. O. (1992). The role of gender and taste class in the effects of stress on eating. *Health Psychology, 11,* 97–100.

Grunberg, N. E., Faraday, M. M., & Rahman, M. A. (2001). The psychobiology of nicotine self-administration. In A. Baum, T. A. Revenson, & J. E. Singer (Eds.), *Handbook of health psychology* (pp. 249–262). Mahwah, NJ: Erlbaum.

Gruneberg, M. M., Sykes, R. N., & Gillett, E. (1994). The facilitating effects of mnemonic strategies on two learning disabled adults. *Neuropsychological Rehabilitation, 4,* 241–254.

Guarnaccia, P. J., & Rogler, L. H. (1999). Research on culture-bound syndromes: New directions. *American Journal of Psychiatry, 156,* 1322–1327.

Guenther, K. (1988). Mood and memory. In G. M. Davies & D. M. Thomson (Eds.), *Memory in context: Context in memory.* New York: Wiley.

Guggenheim, F. G. (2000). Somatoform disorders. In B. J. Sadock & V. A. Sadock (Eds.), *Kaplan and Sadock's comprehensive textbook of psychiatry* (7th ed., Vol. 1, pp. 1504–1532). Philadelphia: Lippincott/Williams & Wilkins.

Guilford, J. P. (1959). Three faces of intellect. *American Psychologist, 14,* 469–479.

Guilford, J. P. (1985). The structure-of-intellect model. In B. B. Wolman (Ed.), *Handbook of intelligence: Theories, measurements and applications.* New York: Wiley.

Guilleminault, C., & Anagnos, A. (2000). Narcolepsy. In M. H. Kryger, T. Roth, & W. C. Dement (Eds.),

Principles and practice of sleep medicine. Philadelphia: Saunders.

Gulletee, E. C. D., Blumenthal, J. A., Babyak, M., Jiang, W., Waugh, R. A., Frid, D. J., O'Connor, C. M., Morris, J. J., & Krantz, D. S. (1997). Effects of mental stress on myocardial ischema during daily life. *Journal of the American Medical Association, 277,* 1521–1526.

Gunn, D. V., Warm, J. S., Dember, W. N., & Temple, J. N. (2000). Subjective organization and the visibility of illusory contours. *American Journal of Psychology, 113,* 553–568.

Gupta, G. R. (1992). Love, arranged marriage, and the Indian social structure. In J. J. Macionis & N. V. Benokraitis (Eds.), *Seeing ourselves: Classic, contemporary and cross-cultural reading in sociology.* Englewood Cliffs, NJ: Prentice-Hall.

Gureje, O., Simon, G. E., Ustun, T. B., & Goldberg, D. P. (1997). Somatization in cross-cultural perspective: A world health organization study in primary care. *American Journal of Psychiatry, 154,* 989–995.

Gurm, H., & Litaker, D. G. (2000). Framing procedural risks to patients: Is 99% safe the same as a risk of 1 in 100? *Academic Medicine, 75,* 840–842.

Gutierrez, P. M., & Silk, K. R. (1998). Prescription privileges for psychologists: A review of the psychological literature. *Professional Psychology: Research and Practice, 29,* 213–222.

Guyton, A. C. (1991). *Textbook of medical physiology.* Philadelphia: Saunders.

Güzeldere, G., Flanagan, O., & Hardcastle, V. G. (2000). The nature and function of consciousness: Lessons from blindsight. In M. S. Gazzaniga (Ed.), *The new cognitive neurosciences.* Cambridge, MA: The MIT Press.

Haas, L. (1999). Families and work. In M. B. Sussman, S. K. Steinmetz, & G. W. Peterson (Eds.), *Handbook of marriage and the family* (pp. 571–612). New York: Plenum.

Hack, M., & Fanaroff, A. A. (1999). Outcomes of children of extremely low birthweight and gestational age in the 1990's. *Early Human Development, 53,* 193–218.

Hagerty, M. R. (2000). Social comparisons of income in one's community: Evidence from national surveys of income and happiness. *Journal of Personality and Social Psychology, 78,* 764–771.

Haith, M. M., & Benson, J. B. (1998). Infant cognition. In W. Damon (Ed.), *Handbook of child psychology (Vol. 2): Cognition, perception, and language.* New York: Wiley.

Hakuta, K. (1986). *Mirror of language.* New York: Basic Books.

Hakuta, K. (1999). The debate on bilingual education. *Journal of Developmental & Behavioral Pediatrics, 20,* 36–37.

Halaas, J. L., Gajiwala, K. S., Maffei, M., Cohen, S. L., Chait, B. T., Rabinowitz, D., Lallone, R. L., Burley, S. K., & Friedman, J. M. (1995). Weight-reducing effects of the plasma protein encoded by the obese gene. *Science, 269,* 543–546.

Hales, D. (1987). *How to sleep like a baby.* New York: Ballantine.

Halford, J. C. G., & Blundell, J. E. (2000). Separate systems for serotonin and leptin in appetite control. *Annals of Medicine, 32,* 222–232.

Hall, C. C. I. (1997). Cultural malpractice: The growing obsolescence of psychology with the changing U.S. population. *American Psychologist, 52,* 642–651.

Hall, C. S. (1966). *The meaning of dreams.* New York: McGraw-Hill.

Hall, C. S. (1979). The meaning of dreams. In D. Goleman & R. J. Davidson (Eds.), *Consciousness: Brain, states of awareness, and mysticism.* New York: Harper & Row.

Hall, C. S., & Nordby, V. J. (1972). *The individual and his dreams.* New York: Mentor.

Hall, D. T., & Mirvis, P. H. (1995). Careers as lifelong learning. In A. Howard (Ed.), *The changing nature of work* (pp. 323–381). San Francisco: Jossey-Bass.

Hall, E. (1987). *Growing and changing: What the experts say.* New York: Random House.

Hall, G. S. (1904). *Adolescence.* New York: Appleton.

Hall, J. A. (1990). *Nonverbal sex differences: Communication accuracy and expressive style* (2nd ed.). Baltimore: Johns Hopkins University Press.

Hall, J. A. (1998). How big are nonverbal sex differences? The case of smiling and sensitivity to nonverbal cues. In D. J. Canary & K. Dindia (Eds.), *Sex differences and similarities in communication: Critical essays and empirical investigations of sex and gender in interaction* (pp. 155–177). Mahwah, NJ: Erlbaum.

Hall, J. A., Roter, D. L., & Katz, N. R. (1988). Meta-analysis of correlates of provider behavior in medical encounters. *Medical Care, 26,* 1–19.

Hall, W., Solowij, N., & Lemon, J. (1994). *The health and psychological consequences of cannabis use.* Canberra, Australia: Australian Government Publishing Service.

Halligan, S. L., & Yehuda, R. (2001). Cognitive and biologic components involved in the development of posttraumatic stress disorder. *Primary Psychiatry, 8*(10), 50–60.

Halmi, K. A. (1999). Eating disorders: Anorexia nervosa, bulimia nervosa,

and obesity. In R. E. Hales, S. C. Yudofsky, & J. A. Talbott (Eds.), *American Psychiatric Press Textbook of Psychiatry.* Washington, DC: American Psychiatric Press.

Halmi, K. A. (2000). Eating disorders. In B. J. Sadock & V. A. Sadock (Eds.), *Kaplan and Sadock's comprehensive textbook of psychiatry* (7th ed., Vol. 1, pp. 1663–1676). Philadelphia: Lippincott/Williams & Wilkins.

Halmi, K. A. (2002). Physiology of anorexia nervosa and bulimia nervosa. In C. G. Fairburn & K. D. Brownell (Eds.), *Eating disorders and obesity: A comprehensive handbook.* New York: Guilford.

Halmi, K. A., Sunday, S. R., Strober, M., Kaplan, A., Woodside, D. B., Fichter, M., Treasure, J., Berrettini, W. H., & Kaye, W. H. (2000). Perfectionism in anorexia nervosa: Variation by clinical subtype, obsessionality, and pathological eating behavior. *American Journal of Psychiatry, 157,* 1799–1805.

Halpern, C. T., Udry, J. R., & Suchindran, C. (1997). Testosterone predicts initiation of coitus in adolescent females. *Psychosomatic Medicine, 59,* 161–171.

Halpern, D. F. (1984). *Thought and knowledge: An introduction to critical thinking.* Hillsdale, NJ: Erlbaum.

Halpern, D. F. (1992). *Sex differences in cognitive abilities.* Hillsdale, NJ: Erlbaum.

Halpern, D. F. (1994). A national assessment of critical thinking skills in adults: Taking steps toward the goal. In A. Greenwood (Ed.), *The national assessment of college student learning: Identification of the skills to be taught, learned, and assessed.* Washington, DC: U. S. Department of Education, National Center for Education Statistics.

Halpern, D. F. (1996). *Thought and knowledge: An introduction to critical thinking.* Mahwah, NJ: Erlbaum.

Halpern, D. F. (1997). Sex differences in intelligence: Implications for education. *American Psychologist, 52,* 1091–1102.

Halpern, D. F. (1998). Teaching critical thinking for transfer across domains: Dispositions, skills, structure training, and metacognitive monitoring. *American Psychologist, 53,* 449–455.

Halpern, D. F. (2000). *Sex differences in cognitive abilities.* Mahwah, NJ: Erlbaum.

Halverson, C. F. Jr., & Wampler, K. S. (1997). Family influences on personality development. In R. Hogan, J. Johnson, & S. Briggs (Eds.), *Handbook of personality psychology.* San Diego: Academic Press.

Hamill, R., Wilson T. D., & Nisbett, R. E. (1980). Insensitivity to sample bias: Generalizing from atypical cases. *Journal of Personality and Social Psychology, 39,* 578–589.

Hamilton, W. D. (1964). The evolution of social behavior. *Journal of Theoretical Biology, 7,* 1–52.

Hamilton, W. D., & Zuk, M. (1982). Heritable true fitness and bright birds: A role for parasites. *Science, 218,* 384–387.

Hankin, B. L., Abramson, L. Y., Moffitt, T. E., Silva, P. A., McGee, R., & Angell, K. E. (1998). Development of depression from preadolescence to young adulthood: Emerging gender differences in a 10-year longitudinal study. *Journal of Abnormal Psychology, 107,* 128–140.

Hannigan, J. H., & Armant, D. R. (2000). Alcohol in pregnancy and neonatal outcome. *Seminars in Neonatology, 5,* 243–254.

Hanson, F. A. (1993). *Testing testing: Social consequences of the examined life.* Berkeley: University of California Press.

Hare, R. D. (1983). Diagnosis of antisocial personality disorder in criminals. *American Journal of Psychiatry, 140,* 887–890.

Hare, R. D. (1993). *Without conscience: The disturbing world of the psychopaths among us.* New York: Pocket Books.

Hare, R. D., Cooke, D. J., & Hart, S. D. (1999). Psychopathy and sadistic personality disorder. In T. Millon, P. H. Blaney, & R. D. Davis (Eds.), *Oxford textbook of psychopathology.* New York: Oxford University Press.

Harmsen, P., Rosengren, A., Tsipogianni, A., & Wilhelmsen, L. (1990). Risk factors for stroke in middle-aged men in Goteborg, Sweden. *Stroke, 21,* 23–29.

Harrington, M. E., & Mistlberger, R. E. (2000). Anatomy and physiology of the mammalian circadian system. In M. H. Kryger, T. Roth, & W. C. Dement (Eds.), *Principles and practice of sleep medicine.* Philadelphia: Saunders.

Harris, J. E. (1984). Remembering to do things: A forgotten topic. In J. E. Harris & P. E. Morris (Eds.), *Everyday memory, actions, and absent-mindedness.* New York: Academic Press.

Harris, J. R. (1998). *The nurture assumption: Why children turn out the way they do.* New York: Free Press.

Harris, J. R. (2000). Context-specific learning, personality, and birth order. *Current Directions in Psychological Science, 9*(5), 174–177.

Harris, L. (2000). Procedural justice and perceptions of fairness in selection practice. *International Journal of Selection and Assessment, 8,* 148–157.

Harrower, M. R. (1936). Some factors determining figure-ground

articulation. *British Journal of Psychology, 26*(4), 407–424.

Hart, S. D., & Hare, R. D. (1997). Psychopathology: Assessment and association with criminal conduct. In D. M. Stoff, J. Breiling, & J. D. Maser (Eds.), *Handbook of antisocial behavior.* New York: Wiley.

Harvey, M. H. (1999). Memory research and clinical practice: A critique of three paradigms and a framework for psychotherapy with trauma survivors. In L. M. Williams & V. L. Banyard (Eds.), *Trauma & memory.* Thousand Oaks, CA: Sage Publications.

Haselton, M. G., & Buss, D. M. (2000). Error management theory: A new perspective on biases in cross-sex mind reading. *Journal of Personality and Social Psychology, 78,* 81–91.

Haslam, N. (1997). Evidence that male sexual orientation is a matter of degree. *Journal of Personality and Social Psychology, 73,* 862–870.

Hastorf, A., & Cantril, H. (1954). They saw a game: A case study. *Journal of Abnormal and Social Psychology, 49,* 129–134.

Hatfield, E., & Rapson, R. L. (1993). *Love, sex, and intimacy: Their psychology, biology, and history.* New York: HarperCollins.

Hathaway, S. R., & McKinley, J. C. (1943). *Manual for the Minnesota Multiphasic Personality Inventory.* New York: Psychological Corporation.

Haugland, G., Siegel, C., Hopper, K., & Alexander, M. J. (1997). Mental illness among homeless individuals in a suburban county. *Psychiatric Services, 48,* 504–509.

Hauri, P. J. (2000). Primary insomnia. In M. H. Kryger, T. Roth, & W. C. Dement (Eds.), *Principles and practice of sleep medicine.* Philadelphia: Saunders.

Hauri, P. J. (2002). Psychological and psychiatric issues in the etiopathogenesis of insomnia. *Journal of Clinical Psychiatry, 4*(suppl 1), 17–20.

Hauser, M., & Carey, S. (1998). Building a cognitive creature from a set of primitives: Evolutionary and developmental insights. In D. D. Cummins & C. Allen (Eds.), *The evolution of mind.* New York: Oxford University Press.

Hawkins, S. A., & Hastie, R. (1990). Hindsight: Biased judgments of past events after the outcomes are known. *Psychological Bulletin, 107,* 311–327.

Haworth-Hoeppner, S. (2000). The critical shapes of body image: The role of culture and family in the production of eating disorders. *Journal of Marriage and the Family, 62,* 212–227.

Hayashi, M., Watanabe, M., & Hori, T. (1999). The effects of a 20-minute nap in the mid-afternoon on mood, performance and EEG activity. *Clinical Neurophysiology, 110,* 272–279.

Hayes, J. R. (1989). Cognitive processes in creativity. In J. A. Glover, R. R. Ronning, & C. R. Reynolds (Eds.), *Handbook of creativity.* New York: Plenum.

Hayes, K. J., & Hayes, C. (1951). The intellectual development of a home-raised chimpanzee. *Proceedings of the American Philosophical Society, 95,* 105–109.

Hayes, S. C., & Heiby, E. (1996). Psychology's drug problem: Do we need a fix or should we just say no? *American Psychologist, 51,* 198–206.

Hays, K. F. (1999). *Working it out: Using exercise in psychotherapy.* Washington, DC: American Psychological Association.

Haywood, T. W., Kravitz, H. M., Grossman, L. S., Cavanaugh, J. L., Jr., Davis, J. M., & Lewis, D. A. (1995). Predicting the "revolving door" phenomenon among patients with schizophrenic, schizoaffective, and affective disorders. *American Journal of Psychiatry, 152,* 861–956.

Hazan, C., & Shaver, P. (1986). *Parental caregiving style questionnaire.* Unpublished questionnaire.

Hazan, C., & Shaver, P. (1987). Romantic love conceptualized as an attachment process. *Journal of Personality and Social Psychology, 52,* 511–524.

He, J., Ogden, L. G., Vupputuri, S., Bazzano, L. A., Loria, C., & Whelton, P. K. (1999). Dietary sodium intake and subsequent risk of cardiovascular disease in overweight adults. *Journal of the American Medical Association, 282,* 2027–2034.

Healy, A. F., & McNamara, D. S. (1996). Verbal learning and memory: Does the modal model still work? *Annual Review of Psychology, 47,* 143–72.

Hearst, E. (1988). Fundamentals of learning and conditioning. In R. C. Atkinson, R. J. Herrnstein, G. Lindzey, & R. D. Luce (Eds.), *Stevens' handbook of experimental psychology.* New York: Wiley.

Heatherton, T. F., Striepe, M., & Wittenberg, L. (1998). Emotional distress and disinhibited eating: The role of self. *Personality and Social Psychology Bulletin, 24,* 301–313.

Heaton, T. B., Jacobson, C. K., & Holland, K. (1999). Persistence and change in decisions to remain childless. *Journal of Marriage and the Family, 61,* 531–539.

Hegarty, J. D., Balderssarini, R. J., Tohen, M., Waternaux, C., & Oepen, G. (1994). One hundred years of schizophrenia: A meta-analysis of the outcome literature. *American Journal of Psychiatry, 151,* 1409–1416.

Heider, F. (1958). *The psychology of interpersonal relations.* New York: Wiley.

Heine, S. J., & Renshaw, K. (2002). Interjudge agreement, self-

enhancement, and liking: Cross-cultural divergences. *Personality and Social Psychology Bulletin, 28*(5), 578–587.

Heine, S. J., Kitayama, S., Lehman, D. R., Takata, T., Ide, E., Leung, C., & Matsumoto, H. (2001). Divergent consequences of success and failure in Japan and North America: An investigation of self-improving motivations and malleable selves. *Journal of Personality and Social Psychology, 81,* 599–615.

Heine, S. J., Lehman, D. R., Markus, H. R., & Kitayama, S. (2000). Is there a universal need for positive self-regard? *Psychological Review, 106,* 766–794.

Heller, W., Nitschke, J. B., Etienne, M. A., & Miller, G. A. (1997). Patterns of regional brain activity differentiate types of anxiety. *Journal of Abnormal Psychology, 106,* 376–385.

Hellige, J. B. (1990). Hemispheric asymmetry. *Annual Review of Psychology, 41,* 55–80.

Hellige, J. B. (1993a). Unity of thought and action: Varieties of interaction between left and right cerebral hemispheres. *Current Directions in Psychological Science, 2*(1), 21–25.

Hellige, J. B. (1993b). *Hemispheric asymmetry: What's right and what's left.* Cambridge, MA: Harvard University Press.

Helmholtz, H. von. (1852). On the theory of compound colors. *Philosophical Magazine, 4,* 519–534.

Helmholtz, H. von. (1863). *On the sensations of tone as a physiological basis for the theory of music* (A. J. Ellis, Trans.). New York: Dover.

Helms, J. E. (1992). Why is there no study of cultural equivalence in standard cognitive ability testing? *American Psychologist, 47,* 1083–1101.

Helson, R., & Moane, G. (1987). Personality change in women from college to midlife. *Journal of Personality and Social Psychology, 53,* 176–186.

Henderson-King, E. I., & Nisbett, R. E. (1996). Anti-black prejudice as a function of exposure to the negative behavior of a single black person. *Journal of Personality and Social Psychology, 71,* 654–664.

Hendrick, S. S., & Hendrick, C. (1992). *Liking, loving, and relating* (2nd ed.). Pacific Grove, CA: Brooks/Cole.

Hendrick, S. S., & Hendrick, C. (2000). Romantic love. In S. S. Hendrick & C. Hendrick (Eds.), *Close relationships.* Thousand Oaks, CA: Sage.

Hennessy, D. A., & Wiesenthal, D. L. (1999). Traffic congestion, driver stress, and driver aggression. *Aggressive Behavior, 25,* 409–423.

Henriksson, M. M., Aro, H. M., Marttunen, M. J., Heikkinen, M. E.,

Isometsa, E. T., Kuoppasalmi, K. I., & Lonnqvist, J. K. (1993). Mental disorders and commorbidity of suicide. *American Journal of Psychiatry, 150,* 935–940.

Henry, K. R. (1984). Cochlear damage resulting from exposure to four different octave bands of noise at three different ages. *Behavioral Neuroscience, 1,* 107–117.

Henry, W. P. (1998). Science, politics, and the politics of science: The use and misuse of empirically validated treatment research. *Psychotherapy Research, 8,* 126–140.

Herek, G. M. (1996). Heterosexism and homophobia. In R. P. Cabaj & T. S. Stein (Eds.), *Textbook of homosexuality and mental health.* Washington, DC: American Psychiatric Press.

Herek, G. M. (2000). The psychology of sexual prejudice. *Current Directions in Psychological Science, 9,* 19–22.

Herek, G. M., Gillis, J. R., Cogan, J. C., & Glunt, E. K. (1997). Hate crime victimization among lesbian, gay, and bisexual adults. *Journal of Interpersonal Violence, 12,* 195–215.

Hering, E. (1878). *Zür lehre vom lichtsinne.* Vienna: Gerold.

Herman, C. P., Ostovich, J. M., & Polivy, J. (1999). Effects of attentional focus on subjective hunger ratings. *Appetite, 33,* 181–193.

Herman, J. L. (1992). *Trauma and recovery.* New York: Basic Books.

Herman, J. L. (1994). Presuming to know the truth. *Nieman Reports, 48,* 43–45.

Herman, L. M., Kuczaj, S. A., & Holder, M. D. (1993). Responses to anomalous gestural sequences by a language-trained dolphin: Evidence for processing of semantic relations and syntactic information. *Journal of Experimental Psychology: General, 122,* 184–194.

Hermann, R. C., Dorwart, R. A., Hoover, C. W., & Brody, J. (1995). Variation in ECT use in the United States. *American Journal of Psychiatry, 152,* 869–875.

Hermann, R. C., Ettner, S. L., Dorwart, R. A., Hoover, C. W., & Yeung, E. (1998). Characteristics of psychiatrists who perform ECT. *American Journal of Psychiatry, 155,* 889–894.

Hermans, H. J. M., & Kempen, H. J. G. (1998). Moving cultures: The perilous problems of cultural dichotomies in a globalizing society. *American Psychologist, 53,* 1111–1120.

Hernandez, D. J. (1993). *America's children: Resources from family, government, and the economy.* New York: Russell Sage Foundation.

Herrett-Skjellum, J., & Allen, M. (1996). Television programming and sex stereotyping: A meta-analysis. In

B. R. Burleson (Ed.), *Communication yearbook 19* (pp. 157–185). Thousand Oaks, CA: Sage.

Herrnstein, R. J., & Murray, C. (1994). *The bell curve: Intelligence and class structure in American life.* New York: Free Press.

Hertwig, R., & Gigerenzer, G. (1999). The "conjunction fallacy" revisited: How intelligent inferences look like reasoning errors. *Journal of Behavioral Decision Making, 12,* 275–306.

Herzog, D. B., & Becker, A. E. (1999). Eating disorders. In A. M. Nicholi (Ed.), *The Harvard guide to psychiatry.* Cambridge, MA: Harvard University Press.

Herzog, D. B., & Delinski, S. S. (2001). Classification of eating disorders. In R. H. Striegel-Moore & L. Smolak (Eds.), *Eating disorders* (pp. 31–50). Washington, DC: American Psychological Association.

Herzog, T. A., Abrams, D. B., Emmons, K. M., Linnan, L. A., & Shadel, W. G. (1999). Do processes of change predict smoking stage movements? A prospective analysis of the transtheoretical model. *Health Psychology, 18,* 369–375.

Heshka, S., & Heymsfield, S. B. (2002). Pharmacological treatments on the horizon. In C. G. Fairburn & K. D. Brownell (Eds.), *Eating disorders and obesity: A comprehensive handbook* (pp. 557–561). New York: Guilford.

Heszen-Niejodek, I. (1997). Coping style and its role in coping with stressful encounters. *European Psychologist, 2,* 342–351.

Hetherington, E. M., Bridges, M., & Insabella, G. M. (1998). What matters? What does not? Five perspectives on the association between marital transitions and children's adjustments. *American Psychologist, 53,* 167–184.

Hetherington, E. M., Reiss, D., & Plomin, R. (1994). *Separate social worlds of siblings: The impact of nonshared environment on development.* Hillsdale, NJ: Erlbaum.

Hetherington, M. M., & Rolls, B. J. (1996). Sensory-specific satiety: Theoretical frameworks and central characteristics. In E. D. Capaldi (Ed.), *Why we eat what we eat: The psychology of eating* (267–290). Washington, DC: American Psychological Association.

Hettema, J. M., Neale, M. C., & Kendler, K. S. (2001). A review and meta-analysis of the genetic epidemiology of anxiety disorders. *American Journal of Psychiatry, 158,* 1568–1578.

Hettich, P. I. (1998). *Learning skills for college and career.* Pacific Grove, CA: Brooks/Cole.

Hewstone, M. (1990). The "ultimate attribution error"? A review of the literature on intergroup causal attribution. *European Journal of Social Psychology, 20,* 311–335.

Highhouse, S., Beadle, D., Gallo, A., & Miller, L. (1998). Get 'em while they last! Effects of scarcity information in job advertisements. *Journal of Applied Social Psychology, 28,* 779–795.

Hilgard, E. R. (1965). *Hypnotic susceptibility.* New York: Harcourt, Brace & World.

Hilgard, E. R. (1986). *Divided consciousness: Multiple controls in human thought and action.* New York: Wiley.

Hilgard, E. R. (1987). *Psychology in America: A historical survey.* San Diego: Harcourt Brace Jovanovich.

Hilgard, E. R. (1989). The early years of intelligence measurement. In R. L. Linn (Ed.), *Intelligence: Measurement, theory, and public policy.* Urbana: University of Illinois Press.

Hilgard, E. R. (1992). Dissociation and theories of hypnosis. In E. Fromm & M. R. Nash (Eds.), *Contemporary hypnosis research.* New York: Guilford.

Hill, A. J. (2002). Prevalence and demographics of dieting. In C. G. Fairburn & K. D. Brownell (Eds.), *Eating disorders and obesity: A comprehensive handbook* (pp. 80–83). New York: Guilford.

Hill, J. O., & Peters, J. C. (1998). Environmental contributions to the obesity epidemic. *Science, 280,* 1371–1374.

Hilliard, A. G., III. (1984). IQ testing as the emperor's new clothes: A critique of Jensen's *Bias in Mental Testing.* In C. R. Reynolds & R. T. Brown (Eds.), *Perspectives on bias in mental testing.* New York: Plenum.

Hilton, J. L., & von Hippel, W. (1996). Stereotypes. *Annual Review of Psychology, 47,* 237–271.

Hineline, P. N. (1981). The several roles of stimuli in negative reinforcement. In P. Harzem & M. D. Zeiler (Eds.), *Predictability, correlation and continuity.* Chichester, England: Wiley.

Hirsh, I. J., & Watson, C. S. (1996). Auditory psychophysics and perception. *Annual Review of Psychology, 47,* 461–484.

Hirt, E. R., McDonald, H. E., & Markman, K. D. (1998). Expectancy effects in reconstructive memory: When the past is just what we expected. In S. J. Lynn & K. M. McConkey (Eds.), *Truth in memory.* New York: Guilford.

Ho, B. C., Nopoulos, P., Flaum, M., Arndt, S., & Andreasen, N. C. (1998). Two-year outcome in first-episode schizophrenia: Predictive value of symptoms for quality of life. *American Journal of Psychiatry, 155,* 1196–1201.

Hobson, J. A. (1988). *The dreaming brain.* New York: Basic Books.

Hobson, J. A. (1989). *Sleep.* New York: Scientific American Library.

Hobson, J. A. (1995). *Sleep.* New York: Scientific American Library.

Hobson, J. A., & McCarley, R. W. (1977). The brain as a dream state generator: An activation-synthesis hypothesis of the dream process. *American Journal of Psychiatry, 134,* 1335–1348.

Hobson, J. A., Pace-Schott, E. F., & Stickgold, R. (2000). Dreaming and the brain: Toward a cognitive neuroscience of conscious states. *Behavioral and Brain Sciences, 23,* 793–842; 904–1018; 1083–1121.

Hocevar, D., & Bachelor, P. (1989). A taxonomy and critique of measurements used in the study of creativity. In J. A. Glover, R. R. Ronning, & C. R. Reynolds (Eds.), *Handbook of creativity.* New York: Plenum.

Hochberg, J. (1988). Visual perception. In R. C. Atkinson, R. J. Herrnstein, G. Lindzey, & R. D. Luce (Eds.), *Stevens' handbook of experimental psychology* (2nd ed., Vol. 1). New York: Wiley.

Hock, E., Schirtzinger, M. B., Lutz, W. J., & Widaman, K. (1995). Maternal depressive symptomatology over the transition to parenthood: Assessing the influence of marital satisfaction and marital sex role traditionalism. *Journal of Family Psychology, 9,* 79–88.

Hodapp, R. M. (1994). Cultural-familial mental retardation. In R. J. Sternberg (Ed.), *Encyclopedia of human intelligence.* New York: Macmillan.

Hodgkin, A. L., & Huxley, A. F. (1952). Currents carried by sodium and potassium ions through the membrane of the giant axon of Loligo. *Journal of Physiology, 116,* 449–472.

Hoek, H. W. (1995). The distribution of eating disorders. In K. D. Brownell, & C. G. Fairburn (Eds.), *Eating disorders and obesity: A comprehensive handbook.* New York: Guilford.

Hoek, H. W. (2002). Distribution of eating disorders. In C. G. Fairburn & K. D. Brownell (Eds.), *Eating disorders and obesity: A comprehensive handbook.* New York: Guilford.

Hoff, E. (2001). *Language development.* Belmont, CA: Wadsworth.

Hoffman, E. (1994). *The drive for self: Alfred Adler and the founding of individual psychology.* Reading, MA: Addison-Wesley.

Hofstede, G. (1980). *Culture's consequences: International differences in work-related values.* Beverly Hills, CA: Sage.

Hofstede, G. (1983). Dimensions of national cultures in fifty countries and three regions. In J. Deregowski, S. Dzuirawiec, & R. Annis (Eds.), *Explications in cross-cultural psychology.* Lisse: Swets and Zeitlinger.

Hofstede, G. (2001). *Culture's consequences: Comparing values, behaviors, institutions, and organizations across nations.* Thousand Oaks, CA: Sage.

Hogan, J., & Ones, D. S. (1997). Conscientiousness and integrity at work. In R. Hogan, J. Johnson, & S. Briggs (Eds.), *Handbook of personality psychology.* San Diego: Academic Press.

Hogan, R., Hogan, J., & Roberts, B. W. (1996). Personality measurement and employment decisions. *American Psychologist, 51,* 469–477.

Hogarth, R. M. (1987). *Judgement and choice.* New York: Wiley.

Hogg, M. A., Turner, J. C., & Davidson, B. (1990). Polarized norms and social frames of reference: A test of the self-categorization theory of group polarization. *Basic and Applied Social Psychology, 11,* 77–100.

Hokanson, J. E., & Burgess, M. (1962). The effects of three types of aggression on vascular processes. *Journal of Abnormal and Social Psychology, 65,* 446–449.

Holahan, C. J., & Moos, R. H. (1985). Life stress and health: Personality, coping, and family support in stress resistance. *Journal of Personality and Social Psychology, 49,* 739–747.

Holahan, C. J., & Moos, R. H. (1990). Life stressors, resistance factors, and improved psychological functioning: An extension of the stress resistance paradigm. *Journal of Personality and Social Psychology, 58,* 909–917.

Holahan, C. J., & Moos, R. H. (1994). Life stressors and mental health: Advances in conceptualizing stress resistance. In W. R. Avison & J. H. Gotlib (Eds.), *Stress and mental health: Contemporary issues and prospects for the future.* New York: Plenum.

Holahan, C., & Sears, R. (1995). *The gifted group in later maturity.* Stanford, CA: Stanford University Press.

Holden, C. (1986, October). The rational optimist. *Psychology Today,* pp. 55–60.

Holen, A. (2000). Posttraumatic stress disorder, delayed. In G. Fink (Ed.), *Encyclopedia of stress* (Vol. 3, pp. 179–180). San Diego: Academic Press.

Hollan, D. (1989). The personal use of dream beliefs in the Toraja Highlands. *Ethos, 17,* 166–186.

Holland, J. C., & Lewis, S. (1993). Emotions and cancer: What do we really know? In D. Goleman & J. Gurin (Eds.), *Mind/body medicine: How to use your mind for better health.*

Yonkers, NY: Consumer Reports Books.

Hollander, E., Simeon, D., & Gorman, J. M. (1999). Anxiety disorders. In R. E. Hales, S. C. Yudofsky, & J. A. Talbott (Eds.), *American Psychiatric Press Textbook of Psychiatry.* Washington, DC: American Psychiatric Press.

Hollands, C. (1989). Trivial and questionable research on animals. In G. Langley (Ed.), *Animal experimentation: The consensus changes.* New York: Chapman & Hall.

Hollingworth, L. S. (1914). *Functional periodicity: An experimental study of the mental and motor abilities of women during menstruation.* New York: Teachers College, Columbia University.

Hollingworth, L. S. (1916). Sex differences in mental tests. *Psychological Bulletin, 13,* 377–383.

Hollis, K. L. (1997). Contemporary research on Pavlovian conditioning: A "new" functional analysis. *American Psychologist, 52,* 956–965.

Hollister, L. E. (1988). Marijuana and immunity. *Journal of Psychoactive Drugs, 20,* 3–7.

Hollon, S. D. (1999). Allegiance effects in treatment research: A commentary. *Clinical Psychology: Science & Practice, 6,* 107–112.

Hollon, S. D., & Beck, A. T. (1994). Cognitive and cognitive-behavioral therapies. In A. E. Bergin & S. L. Garfield (Eds.), *Handbook of psychotherapy and behavior change* (4th ed.). New York: Wiley.

Holmes, D. S. (1987). The influence of meditation versus rest on physiological arousal: A second examination. In M. A. West (Ed.), *The psychology of meditation.* Oxford: Clarendon Press.

Holmes, D. S. (1990). The evidence for repression: An examination of sixty years of research. In J. Singer (Ed.), *Repression and dissociation: Implications for personality, theory, psychopathology, and health.* Chicago: University of Chicago Press.

Holmes, T. H., & Rahe, R. H. (1967). The Social Readjustment Rating Scale. *Journal of Psychosomatic Research, 11,* 213–218.

Holyoak, K. J. (1995). Problem solving. In E. E. Smith & D. N. Osherson (Eds.), *Thinking* (2nd ed., pp. 267–295). Cambridge, MA: MIT Press.

Holyoak, K. J., & Thagard, P. (1997). The analogical mind. *American Psychologist, 52,* 35–44.

Homma-True, R., Greene, B., Lopez, S. R., & Trimble, J. E. (1993). Ethnocultural diversity in clinical psychology. *The Clinical Psychologist, 46*(2), 50–63.

Hong, G. K., Garcia, M., & Soriano, M. (2000). Responding to the chal-

lenge: Preparing mental health professionals for the new millennium. In I. Cuellar & F. A. Paniagua (Eds.), *Handbook of multicultural mental health: Assessment and treatment of diverse populations.* San Diego: Academic Press.

Honig, W. K., & Alsop, B. (1992). Operant behavior. In L. R. Squire (Ed.), *Encyclopedia of learning and memory.* New York: Macmillan.

Hooley, J. M., & Candela, S. F. (1999). Interpersonal functioning in schizophrenia. In T. Millon, P. H. Blaney, & R. D. Davis (Eds.), *Oxford textbook of psychopathology* (pp. 311–338). New York: Oxford University Press.

Hooley, J. M., & Hiller, J. B. (1998). Expressed emotion and the pathogenesis of relapse in schizophrenia. In M. F. Lenzenweger & R. H. Dworkin (Eds.), *Origins and development of schizophrenia: Advances in experimental psychopathology.* Washington DC: American Psychological Association.

Hooper, J., & Teresi, D. (1986). *The 3-pound universe—The brain.* New York: Laurel.

Hopkins, B., & Westra, T. (1988). Maternal handling and motor development: An intracultural study. *Genetic, Social and General Psychology Monographs, 14,* 377–420.

Hopkins, B., & Westra, T. (1990). Motor development, maternal expectations, and the role of handling. *Infant Behavior and Development, 13,* 117–122.

Horn, J. L. (1979). Trends in the measurement of intelligence. In R. J. Sternberg & D. K. Detterman (Eds.), *Human intelligence: Perspectives on its theory and measurement.* Norwood, NJ: Ablex.

Horn, J. L. (1985). Remodeling old models of intelligence. In B. B. Wolman (Ed.), *Handbook of intelligence.* New York: Wiley.

Horn, J. L. (2002). Selections of evidence, misleading assumptions, and oversimplifications: The political message of *The Bell Curve.* In J. M. Fish (Ed.), *Race and intelligence: Separating science from myth* (pp. 297–326). Mahwah, NJ: Erlbaum.

Horn, J. L., & Hofer, S. M. (1992). Major abilities and development in the adult period. In R. J. Sternberg & C. A. Berg (Eds.), *Intellectual development.* Cambridge: Cambridge University Press.

Hornstein, G. A. (1992). The return of the repressed: Psychology's problematic relations with psychoanalysis, 1909–1960. *American Psychologist, 47,* 254–263.

Horowitz, F. D. (1992). John B. Watson's legacy: Learning and environment. *Developmental Psychology, 28,* 360–367.

Horwath, E., & Weissman, M. M. (2000). Anxiety disorders: Epidemiology. In B. J. Sadock & V. A. Sadock (Eds.), *Kaplan and Sadock's comprehensive textbook of psychiatry* (7th ed., Vol. 1, pp. 1441–1449). Philadelphia: Lippincott/Williams & Wilkins.

Hossain, J. L., & Shapiro, C. M. (1999). Considerations and possible consequences of shift work. *Journal of Psychosomatic Research, 47,* 293–296.

Hosseini, H. (1997). Cognitive dissonance as a means of explaining economics of irrationality and uncertainty. *Journal of Socio-Economics, 26,* 181–189.

Houts, A. C. (2002). Discovery, invention, and the expansion of the modern *Diagnostic and Statistical Manuals of Mental Disorders.* In L. E. Beutler & M. L. Malik (Eds.), *Rethinking the DSM.* Washington, DC: American Psychological Association.

Howard, A., Pion, G. M., Gottfredson, G. D., Flattau, P. E., Oskamp, S., Pfafflin, S. M., Bray, D. W., & Burstein, A. G. (1986). The changing face of American psychology: A report from the committee on employment and human resources. *American Psychologist, 41,* 1311–1327.

Howard, D. J. (1995). "Chaining" the use of influence strategies for producing compliance behavior. *Journal of Social Behavior and Personality, 10,* 169–185.

Howard, G., Wagenknecht, L. E., Burke, G. L., Diez-Roux, A., Evans, G. W., McGovern, P., Nieto, J., & Tell, G. S. (1998). Cigarette smoking and progression of atherosclerosis: The atherosclerosis risk in communities (ARIC) study. *Journal of the American Medical Association, 279,* 119–124.

Howard, K., Flora, J., & Griffin, M. (1999). Violence-prevention programs in schools: State of the science and implications for future research. *Applied and Preventive Psychology, 8,* 197–215.

Howard, K. I., Krasner, R. F., & Saunders, S. M. (2000). Evaluation of psychotherapy. In B. J. Sadock & V. A. Sadock (Eds.), *Kaplan and Sadock's comprehensive textbook of psychiatry* (7th ed., Vol. 1, pp. 2217–2224). Philadelphia: Lippincott/Williams & Wilkins.

Howard, K. I., Moras, K., Brill, P. L., Martinovich, Z., & Lutz, W. (1996). Evaluation of psychotherapy: Efficacy, effectiveness, and patient progress. *American Psychologist, 51,* 1059–1064.

Howard, R., Castle, D., Wessely, S., & Murray, R. (1993). A comparative study of 470 cases of early-onset and late-onset schizophrenia. *British Journal of Psychiatry, 163,* 352–357.

Howe, M. J. A. (1999). *The psychology of high abilities.* New York: New York University Press.

Hrdy, S. B. (1997). Raising Darwin's consciousness: Female sexuality and the prehominid origins of patriarchy. *Human Nature: An Interdiciplinary Biosocial Perspective, 8,* 1–49.

Hsu, L. K. G. (1990). *Eating disorders.* New York: Guilford.

Hsu, L. K. G. (1995). Outcome of bulimia nervosa. In K. D. Brownell, & C. G. Fairburn (Eds.), *Eating disorders and obesity: A comprehensive handbook.* New York: Guilford.

Hsu, L. M. (1995). Regression toward the mean associated with measurement error and identification of improvement and deterioration in psychotheray. *Journal of Consulting & Clinical Psychology, 63,* 141–144.

Hubbard, J. R., & Workman, E. A. (1998). *Handbook of stress medicine: An organ system approach.* New York: CRC Press.

Hubel, D. H., & Wiesel, T. N. (1962). Receptive fields, binocular interaction and functional architecture in the cat's visual cortex. *Journal of Physiology, 160,* 106–154.

Hubel, D. H., & Wiesel, T. N. (1963). Receptive fields of cells in striate cortex of very young visually inexperienced kittens. *Journal of Neurophysiology, 26,* 994–1002.

Hubel, D. H., & Wiesel, T. N. (1979). Brain mechanisms of vision. In Scientific American (Eds.), *The brain.* San Franciso: W. H. Freeman.

Hublin, C. G. M., & Partinen, M. M. (2002). The extent and impact of insomnia as a public health problem. *Journal of Clinical Psychiatry, 4*(suppl 1), 8–12.

Hudson, W. (1960). Pictorial depth perception in sub-cultural groups in Africa. *Journal of Social Psychology, 52,* 183–208.

Hudson, W. (1967). The study of the problem of pictorial perception among unacculturated groups. *International Journal of Psychology, 2,* 89–107.

Hudspeth, A. J. (2000). Sensory transduction in the ear. In E. R. Kandel, J. H. Schwartz, & T. M. Jessell (Eds.), *Principles of neural science.* New York: McGraw-Hill.

Hughes, C. C. (1993). Culture in clinical psychiatry. In A. C. Gaw (Ed.), *Culture, ethnicity, and mental illness.* Washington, DC: American Psychiatric Press.

Hughes, J., Smith, T. W., Kosterlitz, H. W., Fothergill, L. A., Morgan, B. A., & Morris, H. R. (1975). Identification of two related pentapeptides from the brain with the potent opiate agonist activity. *Nature, 258,* 577–579.

Hughes, J. R., Gulliver, S. B., Fenwick, J. W., Valliere, W. A., Cruser, K., Pepper, S., Shea, P., Solomon, L. J., & Flynn, B. S. (1992). Smoking cessation among self-quitters. *Health Psychology, 11,* 331–334.

Hughes, R. J., & Badia, P. (1997). Sleep-promoting and hypothermic effects of daytime melatonin administration in humans. *Sleep, 20,* 124–131.

Hull, C. L. (1943). *Principles of behavior.* New York: Appleton.

Hulshoff, H. E., Hoek, H. W., Susser, E., Brown, A. S., Dingemans, A., Schnack, H. G., van Haren, N. E. M., Ramos, L. M. P., Gispen-de Wied, C. C., & Kahn, R. S. (2000). Prenatal exposure to famine and brain morphology in schizophrenia. *American Journal of Psychiatry, 157,* 1170–1172.

Hunt, C., & Andrews, G. (1995). Comorbidity in the anxiety disorders: The use of a life-chart approach. *Journal of Psychiatric Research, 29,* 467–480.

Hunt, E. (1994). Problem solving. In R. J. Sternberg (Ed.), *Thinking and problem solving.* San Diego: Academic Press.

Hunt, E. (2001). Multiple views of multiple intelligence [Review of the book *Intelligence reframed: Multiple intelligence in the 21st century*]. *Contemporary Psychology, 46,* 5–7.

Hunt, E., & Agnoli, F. (1991). The Whorfian hypothesis: A cognitive psychology perspective. *Psychological Review, 98,* 377–389.

Hunt, E., Streissguth, A. P., Kerr, B., & Olsen, H. C. (1995). Mothers' alcohol consumption during pregnancy: Effects on spatial-visual reasoning in 14-year-old children. *Psychological Science, 6,* 339–342.

Hunt, H. (1989). *The multiplicity of dreams: Memory, imagination and consciousness.* New Haven: Yale University Press.

Hunt, J. M., Smith, M. F., & Kernan, J. B. (1985). The effects of expectancy disconfirmation and argument strength on message processing level: An application to personal selling. In E. C. Hirschman & M. B. Holbrook (Eds.), *Advances in consumer research* (Vol. 12). Provo, UT: Association for Consumer Research.

Hunt, W. A., & Matarazzo, J. D. (1982). Changing smoking behavior: A critique. In R. J. Gatchel, A. Baum, & J. E. Singer (Eds.), *Handbook of psychology and health: Vol. 1. Clinical psychology and behavioral medicine, overlapping disciplines.* Hillsdale, NJ: Erlbaum.

Hunter, J. E., & Schmidt, F. L. (1996). Intelligence and job performance: Economic and social implications. *Psychology, Public Policy, & Law, 2,* 447–472.

Hunter, J. E., & Schmidt, F. L. (2000). Racial and gender bias in ability and achievement tests: Resolving the apparent paradox. *Psychology, Public Policy, and Law, 6,* 151–158.

Hurvich, L. M. (1981). *Color vision.* Sunderland, MA: Sinnauer Associates.

Huston, A. C., & Wright, J. C. (1982). Effects of communications media on children. In C. B. Kopp & J. B. Krakow (Eds.), *The child: Development in a social context.* Reading, MA: Addison-Wesley.

Huttenlocher, P. R. (1979). Synaptic density in human frontal cortex: Developmental changes of ageing. *Brain Research, 163,* 195–205.

Huttenlocher, P. R. (1994). Synaptogenesis in human cerebral cortex. In G. Dawson & K. W. Fischer (Eds.), *Human behavior and the developing brain.* New York: Guilford.

Huyser, B., & Parker, J. C. (1998). Stress and rheumatoid arthritis: An integrative review. *Arthritis Care and Research, 11,* 135–145.

Hyde, J. S., Fennema, E., & Lamon, S. J. (1990). Gender differences in mathematics performance: A meta-analysis. *Psychological Bulletin, 107,* 139–155.

Hyman, I. E., Jr., & Kleinknecht, E. E. (1999). False childhood memories: Research, theory, and applications. In L. M. Williams, & V. L. Banyard (Eds.), *Trauma & memory.* Thousand Oaks, CA: Sage Publications.

Hyman, I. E., Jr., Husband, T. H., & Billings, J. F. (1995). False memories of childhood experiences. *Applied Cognitive Psychology, 9,* 181–197.

Iacono, W. G., & Lykken, D. T. (1997). The validity of the lie detector: Two surveys of scientific opinion. *Journal of Applied Psychology, 82,* 426–433.

Iacono, W. G., & Patrick, C. J. (1999). Polygraph ("lie detector") testing: The state of the art. In A. K. Hess & I. B. Weiner (Eds.), *The handbook of forensic psychology* (pp. 440–473). New York: Wiley.

Ickovics, J. R., Thayaparan, B., & Ethier, K. A. (2001). Women and AIDS: A contextual analysis. In A. Baum, T. A. Revenson, & J. E. Singer (Eds.), *Handbook of health psychology* (pp. 817–840). Mahwah, NJ: Erlbaum.

Iezzi, T., Duckworth, M. P., & Adams, H. E. (2001). Somatoform and factitious disorders. In P. B. Sutker & H. E. Adams (Eds.), *Comprehensive handbook of psychopathology* (3rd ed., pp. 211–258). New York: Kluwer Academic/Plenum Publishers.

Ilgen, D. R. (1999). Teams embedded in organizations: Some implications. *American Psychologist, 54,* 129–139.

Infante, J. R., Torres-Avisbal, M., Pinel, P., Vallejo. J. A., Peran, F., Gonzalez, F., Contreras, P., Pacheco, C., Roldan, A., & Latre, J. M. (2001). Catecholamine levels in practitioners of the transcendental meditation technique. *Physiology & Behavior, 72*(1-2), 141–146.

Inglehart, R. (1990). *Culture shift in advanced industrial society.* Princeton, NJ: Princeton University Press.

Ingram, R. E., Scott, W., & Siegle, G. (1999). Depression: Social and cognitive aspects. In T. Millon, P. H. Blaney, & R. D. Davis (Eds.), *Oxford textbook of psychopathology* (pp. 203–226). New York: Oxford University Press.

Innocenti, G. M. (1994). Some new trends in the study of the corpus callosum. *Behavioral and Brain Research, 64,* 1–8.

Inoff-Germain, G., Arnold, G. S., Nottelman, E. D., Susman, E. J., Cutler, G. B., Jr., & Chrousos, G. P. (1988). Relations between hormone levels and observational measures of aggressive behavior of young adolescents in family interactions. *Developmental Psychology, 24,* 129–139.

Iribarren, C., Sidney, S., Bild, D. E., Liu, K., Markovitz, J. H., Roseman, J. M., & Matthews, K. (2000). Association of hostility with coronary artery calcification in young adults: The CARDIA study. *Journal of the American Medical Association, 283,* 2546–2551.

Ironson, G., Klimas, N. G., Antoni, M., Friedman, A., Simoneau, J., LaPerriere, A., Baggett, L., August, S., Arevalo, F., Schneiderman, N., & Fletcher, M. A. (1994). Distress, denial, and low adherence to behavioral interventions predict faster disease progression in gay men infected with human immunodeficiency virus. *International Journal of Behavioral Medicine, 1,* 90–98.

Ironson, G., Wynings, C., Schneiderman, N., Baum, A., Rodriguez, M., Greenwood, D., Benight, C., Antoni, M., LaPerriere, A., Huang, H. S., Klimas, N., & Fletcher, M. A. (1997). Post-traumatic stress symptoms, intrusive thoughts, loss, and immune function after Hurricane Andrew. *Psychosomatic Medicine, 59,* 128–141.

Irvine, S. H., & Berry, J. W. (1988). *Human abilities in cultural context.* New York: Cambridge University Press.

Irwin, S., & Irwin, T. (2001). *The crocodile hunter: The incredible life and adventures of Steve and Terri Irwin.* New York: Penguin.

Irwin, W., Davidson, R. J., Lowe, M. J., Mock, B. J., Sorenson, J. A., & Turski, P. A. (1996). Human amygdala activation detected with echoplanar functional magnetic resonance imaging. *NeuroReport, 7,* 1765–1769.

Isaac, R. J., & Armat, V. C. (1990). *Madness in the streets: How psychiatry and the law abandoned the mentally ill.* New York: Free Press.

Isabella, R. A. (1995). The origins of infant-mother attachment: Maternal behavior and infant development. In R. Vasta (Ed.), *Annals of child development*. London: Jessica Kingsley.

Isada, N. B., & Grossman, J. H., III. (1991). Perinatal infections. In S. G. Gabbe, J. R. Niebyl, & J. L. Simpson (Eds.), *Obstetrics: Normal and problem pregnancies*. New York: Churchill Livingstone.

Isenberg, K. E., & Zorumski, C. F. (2000). Electroconvulsive therapy. In B. J. Sadock & V. A. Sadock (Eds.), *Kaplan and Sadock's Comprehensive textbook of psychiatry* (7th ed., Vol. 1, pp. 2503–2515). Philadelphia: Lippincott/Williams & Wilkins.

Ismail, M. A. (1993). Maternal-fetal infections. In C. Lin, M. S. Verp, & R. E. Sabbagha (Eds.), *The high-risk fetus: Pathophysiology, diagnosis, management*. New York: Springer-Verlag.

Isometsa, E. T., Heikkinen, M. E., Marttunen, M. J., Henriksson, M. M., Aro, H. M., & Lonnqvist, J. K. (1995). The last appointment before suicide: Is suicide intent communicated? *American Journal of Psychiatry, 152*, 919–922.

Iversen, S., Iversen, L., & Saper, C. B. (2000). The autonomic nervous system and the hypothalamus. In E. R. Kandel, J. H. Schwartz, & T. M. Jessell (Eds.), *Principles of neural science* (pp. 960–981). New York: McGraw-Hill.

Iwao, S. (1993). *The Japanese woman: Traditional image and changing reality*. New York: Free Press.

Iwawaki, S., & Vernon, P. E. (1988). Japanese abilities and achievements. In S. H. Irvine & J. W. Berry (Eds.), *Human abilities in cultural context*. New York: Cambridge University Press.

Izard, C. E. (1984). Emotion-cognition relationships and human development. In C. E. Izard, J. Kagan, & R. B. Zajonc (Eds.), *Emotions, cognition and behavior*. Cambridge, England: Cambridge University Press.

Izard, C. E. (1990). Facial expressions and the regulation of emotions. *Journal of Personality and Social Psychology, 58*, 487–498.

Izard, C. E. (1991). *The psychology of emotions*. New York: Plenum.

Izard, C. E. (1994). Innate and universal facial expressions: Evidence from developmental and cross-cultural research. *Psychological Bulletin, 115*, 288–299.

Izard, C. E. (2001). Emotional intelligence or adaptive emotions? *Emotion, 1*, 249–257.

Izard, C. E., & Saxton, P. M. (1988). Emotions. In R. C. Atkinson, R. J. Herrnstein, G. Lindzey, & R. D. Luce (Eds.), *Stevens' handbook of experimental psychology* (Vol. 1). New York: Wiley.

Jablensky, A. (1999). The 100-year epidemiology of schizophrenia. *Schizophrenia Research, 28*, 111–125.

Jackson, L. A., Sullivan, L. A., & Hodge, C. N. (1993). Stereotype effects on attributions, predictions, and evaluations: No two social judgments are quite alike. *Journal of Personality and Social Psychology, 65*, 69–84.

Jacob, R. G., & Pelham, W. H. (2000). Behavior therapy. In B. J. Sadock & V. A. Sadock (Eds.), *Kaplan and Sadock's comprehensive textbook of psychiatry* (7th ed., Vol. 1, pp. 2080–2127). Philadelphia: Lippincott/Williams & Wilkins.

Jacobs, H. S. (2001). Idea of male menopause is not useful. *Medical Crossfire, 3*, 52–55.

Jacobson, E. (1938). *Progressive relaxation*. Chicago: University of Chicago Press.

Jacobson, J. W., & Mulick, J. A. (1992). A new definition of mental retardation or a new definition of practice? *Psychology in Mental Retardation and Developmental Disabilities, 18*, 9–14.

Jacobson, N. S., & Christensen, A. (1996). Studying the effectiveness of psychotherapy: How well can clinical trials do the job? *American Psychologist, 51*, 1031–1039.

Jacoby, L. L. (1988). Memory observed and memory unobserved. In U. Neisser & E. Winograd (Eds.), *Remembering reconsidered: Ecological and traditional approaches to the study of memory*. Cambridge: Cambridge University Press.

Jacoby, L. L., Hessels, S., & Bopp, K. (2001). Proactive and retroactive effects in memory performance: Dissociating recollection and accessibility bias. In H. L. Roediger, J. S. Nairne, I. Neath, & A. M. Surprenant (Eds.), *The nature of remembering: Essays in honor of Robert G. Crowder* (pp. 35–54). Washington, DC: American Psychological Association.

Jain, S. P., Buchanan, B., & Maheswaran, D. (2000). Comparative versus noncomparative advertising. *Journal of Consumer Psychology, 9*, 201–211.

James, W. (1884). What is emotion? *Mind, 19*, 188–205.

James, W. (1890). *The principles of psychology*. New York: Holt.

James, W. (1902). *The varieties of religious experience*. New York: Modern Library.

Jamison, K. R. (1988). Manic-depressive illness and accomplishment: Creativity, leadership, and social class. In F. K. Goodwin & K. R. Jamison (Eds.), *Manic-depressive illness*. Oxford, England: Oxford University Press.

Janis, I. L. (1958). *Psychological stress*. New York: Wiley.

Janis, I. L. (1972). *Victims of groupthink*. Boston: Houghton Mifflin.

Janis, I. L. (1993). Decision making under stress. In L. Goldberger & S. Breznitz (Eds.), *Handbook of stress: Theoretical and clinical aspects* (2nd ed.). New York: Free Press.

Janis, I. L., & Mann, L. (1977). *Decision making: A psychological analysis of conflict, choice, and commitment*. New York: Free Press.

Janofsky, J. S., Dunn, M. H., Roskes, E. J., Briskin, J. K., & Rudolph, M. S. L. (1996). Insanity defense pleas in Baltimore city: An analysis of outcome. *American Journal of Psychiatry, 153*, 1464–1468.

Janowsky, J. S., Oviatt, S. K., & Orwoll, E. S. (1994). Testosterone influences spatial cognition in older men. *Behavioral Neuroscience, 108*, 325–332.

Janus, S. S., & Janus, C. L. (1993). *The Janus report on sexual behavior*. New York: Wiley.

Jaroff, L. (1993, November 29). Lies of the mind. *Time*, pp. 52–59.

Jarvik, M. E., & Schneider, N. G. (1992). Nicotine. In J. H. Lowinson, P. Ruiz, & R. B. Millman (Eds.), *Substance abuse: A comprehensive textbook* (2nd ed.). Baltimore: Williams & Wilkins.

Jefferson, J. W., & Greist, J. H. (2000). Lithium. In B. J. Sadock & V. A. Sadock (Eds.), *Kaplan and Sadock's comprehensive textbook of psychiatry* (7th ed., Vol. 1, pp. 2377–2389). Philadelphia: Lippincott/Williams & Wilkins.

Jeffrey, R. W. (2001). Public health strategies for obesity treatment and prevention. *American Journal of Health Behavior, 25*, 252–259.

Jemmott, J. B., III, & Magloire, K. (1988). Academic stress, social support, and secretory immunoglobin A. *Journal of Personality and Social Psychology, 55*, 803–810.

Jensen, A. R. (1969). How much can we boost IQ and scholastic achievement? *Harvard Educational Review, 39*, 1–23.

Jensen, A. R. (1980). *Bias in mental testing*. New York: Free Press.

Jensen, A. R. (1982). Reaction time and psychometric g. In H. J. Eysenck (Ed.), *A model for intelligence*. New York: Springer-Verlag.

Jensen, A. R. (1987). Process differences and individual difference in some cognitive tasks. *Intelligence, 11*, 107–136.

Jensen, A. R. (1992a). The Cyril Burt scandal, research taboos, and the media. *The General Psychologist, 28*(3), 16–21.

Jensen, A. R. (1992b). The importance of intraindividual variation in reaction time. *Personality and Individual Differences, 13*, 869–881.

Jensen, A. R. (1993a). Test validity: g versus "tacit knowledge." *Current Directions in Psychological Science, 2*(1), 9–10.

Jensen, A. R. (1993b). Why is reaction time correlated with psychometric g? *Current Directions in Psychological Science, 2*(2), 53–56.

Jensen, A. R. (1994a). Francis Galton. In R. J. Sternberg (Ed.), *Encyclopedia of human intelligence*. New York: Macmillan.

Jensen, A. R. (1994b). Race and IQ scores. In R. J. Sternberg (Ed.), *Encyclopedia of human intelligence*. New York: Macmillan.

Jensen, A. R. (1998). *The g factor: The science of mental ability*. Westport, CT: Praeger.

Jensen, E. (2000a). *Brain-based learning*. San Diego: Brain Store.

Jensen, A. R. (2000b). Testing: The dilemma of group differences. *Psychology, Public Policy, and Law, 6*, 121–127.

Jessell, T. M., & Kelly, D. D. (1991). Pain and analgesia. In E. R. Kandel, J. H. Schwartz, & T. M. Jessell (Eds.), *Principles of neural science* (3rd ed.). New York: Elsevier.

Jex, S. M., Bliese, P. D., Buzzell, S., & Primeau, J. (2001). The impact of self-efficacy on stressor-strain relations: Coping style as an explanatory mechanism. *Journal of Applied Psychology, 86*, 401–409.

Ji, L.-J., Peng, K., & Nisbett, R. E. (2000). Culture, control, and perception of relationships in the environment. *Journal of Personality and Social Psychology, 78*, 943–955.

John, O. P., & Srivastava, S. (1999). The big five trait taxonomy: History, measurement, and theoretical perspectives. In L. A. Pervin & O. P. John (Eds.), *Handbook of personality: Theory and research*. New York: Guilford.

Johnson, B. T. (1994). Effects of outcome-relevant involvement and prior information on persuasion. *Journal of Experimental Social Psychology, 30*, 556–579.

Johnson, C., & Mullen, B. (1994). Evidence for the accessibility of paired distinctiveness in distinctiveness-based illusory correlation in stereotyping. *Personality and Social Psychology Bulletin, 20*, 65–70.

Johnson, D. (1990). Animal rights and human lives: Time for scientists to right the balance. *Psychological Science, 1*, 213–214.

Johnson, J. G., & Sherman, M. F. (1997). Daily hassles mediate the relationship between major life events and psychiatric symptomatology: Longitudinal findings from an adolescent sample. *Journal of Social and Clinical Psychology, 16*, 389–404.

Johnson, J. S., & Newport, E. L. (1989). Critical period effects in second language learning: The influence of maturational state on the acquisition of English as a second language. *Cognitive Psychology, 21,* 60–99.

Johnson, M. E., & Dowling-Guyer, S. (1996). Effects of inclusive vs. exclusive language on evaluations of the counselor. *Sex Roles, 34,* 407–418.

Johnson, M. K. (1996). Fact, fantasy, and public policy. In D. J. Herrmann, C. McEvoy, C. Hertzog, P. Hertel, & M. K. Johnson (Eds.), *Basic and applied memory research: Theory in context* (Vol. 1). Mahwah, NJ: Erlbaum.

Johnson, M. K., & Raye, C. L. (1981). Reality monitoring. *Psychological Review, 88,* 67–85.

Johnson, M. K., Hashtroudi, S., & Lindsay, D. S. (1993). Source monitoring. *Psychological Bulletin, 114,* 3–28.

Johnson, M. K., Kahan, T. L., & Raye, C. L. (1984). Dreams and reality monitoring. *Journal of Experimental Psychology: General, 113,* 329–344.

Johnston, J. C., & McClelland, J. L. (1974). Perception of letters in words: Seek not and ye shall find. *Science, 184,* 1192–1194.

Johnston, L. D., O'Malley, P. M., & Bachman, J. G. (2001). *Monitoring the Future national survey results on drug use, 1975–2000.* Bethesda MD: National Institute of Drug Abuse.

Johnstone, L. (1999). Adverse psychological effects of ECT. *Journal of Mental Health (UK), 8,* 69–85.

Joiner, T. E. (2002). Depression in its interpersonal context. In I. H. Gotlib & C. L. Hammen (Eds.), *Handbook of depression.* New York: Guilford.

Joiner, T. E., & Katz, J. (1999). Contagion of depressive symptoms and mood: Meta-analytic review and explanations from cognitive, behavioral, and interpersonal viewpoints. *Clinical Psychology: Science and Practice, 6,* 149–164.

Joiner, T. E., Jr., & Metalsky, G. I. (1995). A prospective test of an integrative interpersonal theory of depression: A naturalistic study of college students. *Journal of Personality and Social Psychology, 69,* 778–788.

Jonah, B. A. (1997). Sensation seeking and risky driving: A review and synthesis of the literature. *Accident Analysis & Prevention, 29,* 651–665.

Jones, B. C., Little, A. C., Penton-Voak, I. S., Tiddeman, B. P., Burt, D. M., & Perrett, D. I. (2001). Facial symmetry and judgments of apparent health: Support for a "good genes" explanation of the attractiveness-symmetry relationship. *Evolution and Human Behavior, 22,* 417–429.

Jones, B. E. (2000). Basic mechanisms of sleep-wake states. In M. H. Kryger, T. Roth, & W. C. Dement (Eds.), *Principles and practice of sleep medicine.* Philadelphia: Saunders.

Jones, E. E., & Davis, K. E. (1965). From acts to dispositions: The attribution process in person perception. In L. Berkowitz (Ed.), *Advances in experimental social psychology* (Vol. 2). New York: Academic Press.

Jones, E. E., & Nisbett, R. E. (1971). The actor and the observer: Divergent perceptions of the causes of behavior. In E. E. Jones, D. E. Kanouse, H. H. Kelley, R. E. Nisbett, S. Valins, & B. Weiner (Eds.), *Attribution: Perceiving the causes of behavior.* Morristown, NJ: General Learning Press.

Jones, G. V. (1990). Misremembering a common object: When left is not right. *Memory & Cognition, 18*(2), 174–182.

Jordan, B. (1983). *Birth in four cultures.* Quebec, Canada: Eden Press.

Jorgensen, R. S., Johnson, B. T., Kolodziej, M. E., & Schreer, G. E. (1996). Elevated blood pressure and personality: A meta-analytic review. *Psychological Bulletin, 120,* 293–320.

Joseph, R. (1992). *The right brain and the unconscious.* New York: Plenum.

Joshipura, K. J., Ascherio, A., Manson, J. E., Stampfer, M. J., Rimm, E. B., Speizer, F. E., Hennekens, C. H., Speigelman, D., & Willett, W. C. (1999). Fruit and vegetable intake in relation to risk of ischemic stroke. *Journal of the American Medical Association, 282,* 1233–1239.

Judge, T. A., & Bono, J. E. (2000). Five-factor model of personality and transformational leadership. *Journal of Applied Psychology, 85,* 751–765.

Julien, R. M. (1998). *A primer of drug action.* New York: Freeman.

Julien, R. M. (2001). *A primer of drug action.* New York: Freeman.

Jung, C. G. (1917/1953). *On the psychology of the unconscious.* In H. Read, M. Fordham, & G. Adler (Eds.), *Collected works of C. G. Jung* (Vol. 7). Princeton, NJ: Princeton University Press.

Jung, C. G. (1921/1960). *Psychological types.* In H. Read, M. Fordham, & G. Adler (Eds.), *Collected works of C. G. Jung* (Vol. 6). Princeton, NJ: Princeton University Press.

Jung, C. G. (1933). *Modern man in search of a soul.* New York: Harcourt, Brace & World.

Jusczyk, P., & Hohne, E. (1997). Infants' memory for spoken words. *Science, 277,* 1984–1986.

Kaas, J. H. (2000). The reorganization of sensory and motor maps after injury in adult mammals. In M. S. Gazzaniga (Ed.), *The new cognitive neurosciences.* Cambridge, MA: The MIT Press.

Kaemingk, K., & Paquette, A. (1999). Effects of prenatal alcohol exposure on neuropsychological functioning. *Developmental Neuropsychology, 15,* 111–140.

Kagan, J. (1998, November/December). A parent's influence is peerless. *Harvard Education Letter.*

Kagan, J., & Snidman, N. (1999). Early childhood predictors of adult anxiety disorders. *Biological Psychiatry, 46,* 1536–1541.

Kagan, J., & Snidman, N. (1991). Temperamental factors in human development. *American Psychologist, 46,* 856–862.

Kagan, J., Reznik, J. S., & Snidman, N. (1999). Biological basis of childhood shyness. In A. Slater & D. Muir (Eds.), *The Blackwell reader in developmental psychology* (pp. 65–78). Malden, MA: Blackwell.

Kagan, J., Snidman, N., & Arcus, D. M. (1992). Initial reactions to unfamiliarity. *Current Directions in Psychological Science, 1*(6), 171–174.

Kahan, T. L., & Johnson, M. K. (1992). Self-effects in memory for person information. *Social Cognition, 10*(1), 30–50.

Kahan, T. L., & LaBerge, S. (1994). Lucid dreaming as metacognition: Implications for cognitive science. *Consciousness and Cognition, 3,* 246–264.

Kahan, T. L., & LaBerge, S. (1996). Cognition and metacognition in dreaming and waking: Comparisons of first- and third-person ratings. *Dreaming, 6,* 235–249.

Kahan, T., Mohsen, R., Tandez, J., & McDonald, J. (1999). Discriminating memories for actual and imagined taste experiences: A reality monitoring approach. *American Journal of Psychology, 112,* 97–112.

Kahane, H. (1992). *Logic and contemporary rhetoric: The use of reason in everyday life.* Belmont, CA: Wadsworth.

Kahneman, D. (1991). Judgment and decision making: A personal view. *Psychological Science, 2,* 142–145.

Kahneman, D. (1999). Objective happiness. In D. Kahneman, E. Diener, & N. Schwarz (Eds.), *Well-being: The foundations of hedonic psychology.* New York: Russell Sage Foundation.

Kahneman, D., & Tversky, A. (1973). On the psychology of prediction. *Psychological Review, 80,* 237–251.

Kahneman, D., & Tversky, A. (1982). Subjective probability: A judgment of representativeness. In D. Kahneman, P. Slovic, & A. Tversky (Eds.), *Judgment under uncertainty: Heuristics and biases.* Cambridge: Cambridge University Press.

Kahneman, D., & Tversky, A. (1984). Choices, values, and frames. *American Psychologist, 39,* 341–350.

Kahneman, D., & Tversky, A. (2000). *Choices, values, and frames.* New York: Cambridge University Press.

Kako, E. (1999). Elements of syntax in the systems of three language-trained animals. *Animal Learning and Behavior, 27,* 1–14.

Kalat, J. W. (2001). *Biological psychology.* Belmont, CA: Wadsworth.

Kales, J. D., Kales, A., Bixler, E. O., Soldatos, C. R., Cadieux, R. J., Kashurba, G. J., & Vela-Bueno, A. (1984). Biopsychobehavioral correlates of insomnia: V. Clinical characteristics and behavioral correlates. *American Journal of Psychiatry, 141,* 1371–1376.

Kalichman, S. C. (1995). *Understanding AIDS: A guide for mental health professionals.* Washington, DC: American Psychological Association.

Kalichman, S. C., Roffman, R. A., Picciano, J. F., & Bolan, M. (1998). Risk for HIV infection among bisexual men seeking HIV-prevention services and risks posed to their female partners. *Health Psychology, 17,* 320–327.

Kalidindi, S., & McGuffin, P. (2003). The genetics of affective disorders: Present and future. In R. Plomin, J. C. Defries, I. W. Craig, & P. McGuffin (Eds.), *Behavioral genetics in the postgenomic era.* Washington, DC: American Psychological Association.

Kalmijn, M. (1998). Intermarriage and homogamy: Causes, patterns, trends. *Annual Review of Sociology, 24,* 395–421.

Kalmuss, D., Davidson, A., & Cushman, L. (1992). Parenting expectations, experiences, and adjustment to parenthood: A test of the violated expectations framework. *Journal of Marriage and the Family, 52,* 516–526.

Kamin, L. J. (1974). *The science and politics of IQ.* Hillsdale, NJ: Erlbaum.

Kandel, E. R. (2000). Nerve cells and behavior. In E. R. Kandel, J. H. Schwartz, & T. M. Jessell (Eds.), *Principles of neural science* (pp. 19–35). New York: McGraw-Hill.

Kandel, E. R., & Jessell, T. M. (1991). Touch. In E. R. Kandel, J. H. Schwartz, & T. M. Jessell (Eds.), *Principles of neural science* (3rd ed.). New York: Elsevier.

Kandel, E. R., & Schwartz, J. H. (1982). Molecular biology of learning: Modification of transmitter release. *Science, 218,* 433–442.

Kandel, E. R., & Siegelbaum, S. A. (2000). Synaptic integration. In E. R. Kandel, J. H. Schwartz & T. M. Jessell (Eds.), *Principles of neural science* (pp. 207–228). New York: McGraw-Hill.

Kandel, E. R., & Wurtz, R. H. (2000). Constructing visual images. E. R. Kandel, J. H. Schwartz, & T. M. Jessell (Eds.), *Principles of neural science.* New York: McGraw-Hill.

Kandell, J. J. (1998). Internet addiction on campus: The vulnerability of college students. *CyberPsychology and Behavior, 1*(1), 11–17.

Kane, J. (1991). *Be sick well: A healthy approach to chronic illness.* Oakland, CA: New Harbinger Publications.

Kane, T. D., Marks, M. A., Zaccaro, S. J., & Blair, V. (1996). Self-efficacy, personal goals, and wrestlers' self-regulation. *Journal of Sport & Exercise Psychology, 18,* 36–48.

Kaplan, A. G. (1985). Female or male therapists for women patients: New formulations. *Psychiatry, 48,* 111–121.

Kaplan, H., & Dove, H. (1987). Infant development among the Ache of Eastern Paraguay. *Developmental Psychology, 23,* 190–198.

Kaplan, H. I. (1989). History of psychosomatic medicine. In H. I. Kaplan & B. J. Sadock (Eds.), *Comprehensive textbook of psychiatry* (5th ed.). Baltimore: Williams & Wilkins.

Kaplan, H. I., & Sadock, B. J. (Eds.). (1993). *Comprehensive group psychotherapy.* Baltimore: Williams & Wilkins.

Kaplan, R. M. (1985). The controversy related to the use of psychological tests. In B. B. Wolman (Ed.), *Handbook of intelligence: Theories, measurements, and applications.* New York: Wiley.

Kapp, B. S., Supple, W. F., & Whalen, P. J. (1994). Effects of electrical stimulation of the amygdaloid central nucleus on neocortical arousal in the rabbit. *Behavioral Neuroscience, 108,* 81–93.

Kaprio, J., Rimpela, A., Winter, T., Viken, R. J., Rimpela, M., & Rose, R. J. (1995). Common genetic influence on BMI and age at menarche. *Human Biology, 67,* 739–753.

Kapur, S., & Mann, J. J. (1993). Antidepressant action and the neurobiologic effects of ECT: Human studies. In C. E. Coffey (Ed.), *The clinical science of electroconvulsive therapy.* Washington, DC: American Psychiatric Press.

Karau, S. J., & Hart, J. W. (1998). Group cohesiveness and social loafing: Effects of a social interaction manipulation on individual motivation within groups. *Group Dynamics, 2,* 185–191.

Karau, S. J., & Williams, K. D. (1993). Social loafing: A meta-analytic review and theoretical integration. *Journal of Personality and Social Psychology, 65,* 681–706.

Karau, S. J., & Williams, K. D. (1995). Social loafing: Research findings, implications, and future directions. *Current Directions in Psychological Science, 4,* 134–140.

Kardiner, A., & Linton, R. (1945). *The individual and his society.* New York: Columbia University Press.

Karon, B. P. (1995). Provision of psychotherapy under managed health care: A growing crisis and national nightmare. *Professional Psychology: Research and Practice, 26,* 5–9.

Karon, B. P., & Widener, A. J. (1997). Repressed memories and World War II: Lest we forget! *Professional Psychology: Research & Practice, 28,* 338–340.

Kasser, T., & Sharma, Y. S. (1999). Reproductive freedom, educational equality, and females' preference for resource-aquisition characteristics in mates. *Psychological Science, 10,* 374–377.

Kassin, S. M., Tubb, V. A., Hosch, H. M., & Memon, A. (2001). On the "general acceptance" of eyewitness testimony research: A new survey of the experts. *American Psychologist, 56,* 405–416.

Katigbak, M. S., Church, A. T., Guanzon-Lapena, M. A., Carlota, A. J. & del Pilar, G. H. (2002). Are indigenous personality dimensions culture specific? Philippine inventories and the five-factor model. *Journal of Personality and Social Psychology, 82,* 89–101.

Kaufman, A. S. (2000). Tests of intelligence. In R. J. Sternberg (Ed.), *Handbook of intelligence* (pp. 445–476). New York: Cambridge University Press.

Kaufman, L., & Rock, I. (1962). The moon illusion I. *Science, 136,* 953–961.

Kavesh, L., & Lavin, C. (1988). *Tales from the front.* New York: Doubleday.

Kaye, W. H., Weltzin, T. E., Hsu, L. K. G., McConaha, C. W., & Bolton, B. (1993). Amount of calories retained after binge eating and vomiting. *American Journal of Psychiatry, 150,* 969–971.

Kazdin, A. E. (1982). History of behavior modification. In A. S. Bellack, M. Hersen, & A. E. Kazdin (Eds.), *International handbook of behavior modification and behavior therapy.* New York: Plenum.

Kazdin, A. E. (1994). Methodology, design, and evaluation in psychotherapy research. In A. E. Bergin & S. L. Garfield (Eds.), *Handbook of psychotherapy and behavior change* (4th ed.). New York: Wiley.

Keefauver, S. P., & Guilleminault, C. (1994). Sleep terrors and sleepwalking. In M. H. Kryger, T. Roth, & W. C. Dement (Eds.), *Principles and practice of sleep medicine* (2nd ed.). Philadelphia: Saunders.

Keenan, J. P., Gallup, G. G. Jr., Goulet, N., & Kulkarni, M. (1997). Attributions of deception in human mating strategies. *Journal of Social Behavior and Personality, 12,* 45–52.

Keesey, R. E. (1993). Physiological regulation of body energy: Implications for obesity. In A. J. Stunkard & T. A. Wadden (Eds.), *Obesity theory and therapy.* New York: Raven.

Keesey, R. E. (1995). A set point model of body weight regulation. In K. D. Brownell & C. G. Fairburn (Eds.), *Eating disorders and obesity: A comprehensive handbook.* New York: Guilford.

Keesey, R. E., & Powley, T. L. (1975). Hypothalamic regulation of body weight. *American Scientist, 63,* 558–565.

Kehoe, E. J., & Macrae, M. (1998). Classical conditioning. In W. O'Donohue (Ed.), *Learning and behavior therapy.* Boston, Allyn & Bacon.

Keinan, G. (1987). Decision making under stress: Scanning of alternatives under controllable and uncontrollable threats. *Journal of Personality and Social Psychology, 52,* 639–644.

Keinan, G., Friedland, N., Kahneman, D., & Roth, D. (1999). The effect of stress on the suppression of erroneous competing responses. *Anxiety, Stress & Coping: An International Journal, 12,* 455–476.

Keller, F. S. (1968). Goodbye teacher. . . . *Journal of Applied Behavior Analysis, 1,* 79–89.

Keller, L. S., Butcher, J. N., & Slutske, W. S. (1990). Objective personality assessment. In G. Goldstein & M. Hersen (Eds.), *Handbook of psychological assessment.* New York: Pergamon Press.

Keller, P. A., & Block, L. G. (1999). The effect of affect-based dissonance versus cognition-based dissonance on motivated reasoning and health-related persuasion. *Journal of Experimental Psychology: Applied, 5,* 302–313.

Kelley, H. H. (1950). The warm-cold variable in first impressions of persons. *Journal of Personality, 18,* 431–439.

Kelley, H. H. (1967). Attributional theory in social psychology. *Nebraska Symposium on Motivation, 15,* 192–241.

Kellogg, J. S., Hopko, D. R., & Ashcraft, M. H. (1999). The effects of time pressure on arithmetic performance. *Journal of Anxiety Disorders, 13,* 591–600.

Kelly, J. P. (1991). The sense of balance. In E. R. Kandel, J. H. Schwartz, & T. M. Jessell (Eds.), *Principles of neural science* (3rd ed.). New York: Elsevier.

Kelly, K. M., & Schramke, C. J. (2000). Epilepsy. In G. Fink (Ed.), *Encyclopedia of stress* (pp. 66–70). San Diego: Academic Press.

Kelly, S. J., Day, N., & Streissguth, A. P. (2000). Effects of prenatal alcohol exposure on social behavior in humans and other species. *Neurotoxicology & Teratology, 22,* 143–149.

Kelman, H. C. (1967). Human use of human subjects: The problem of deception in social psychological experiments. *Psychological Bulletin, 67,* 1–11.

Kelman, H. C. (1982). Ethical issues in different social science methods. In T. L. Beauchamp, R. R. Faden, R. J. Wallace, Jr., & L. Walters (Eds.), *Ethical issues in social science research.* Baltimore: Johns Hopkins University Press.

Kelsoe, J. R. (2000). Mood disorders: Genetics. In B. J. Sadock & V. A. Sadock (Eds.), *Kaplan and Sadock's comprehensive textbook of psychiatry* (7th ed., Vol. 1, pp. 1308–1317). Philadelphia: Lippincott/Williams & Wilkins.

Kendler, K. S. (2000). Schizophrenia: Genetics. In B. J. Sadock & V. A. Sadock (Eds.), *Kaplan and Sadock's comprehensive textbook of psychiatry* (7th ed., Vol. 1, pp. 1147–1158). Philadelphia: Lippincott/Williams & Wilkins.

Kendler, K. S., & Gardner, C. O., Jr. (1998). Boundaries of major depression: An evaluation of DSM-IV criteria. *American Journal of Psychiatry, 155,* 172–177.

Kendler, K. S., Karkowski, L. M., & Prescott, C. A. (1999). Causal relationship between stressful life events and the onset of major depression. *American Journal of Psychiatry, 156,* 837–841.

Kendler, K. S., Thornton, L. M., Gilman, S. E., & Kessler, R. C. (2000). Sexual orientation in a U.S. national sample of twin and nontwin sibling pairs. *American Journal of Psychiatry, 157,* 1843–1846.

Kennedy, T. E., Hawkins, R. D., & Kandel, E. R. (1992). Molecular interrelationships between short- and long-term memory. In L. R. Squire & N. Butters (Eds.), *Neuropsychology of Memory* (2nd ed.). New York: Wiley.

Kenrick, D. T. (1995). Evolutionary theory versus the confederacy of dunces. *Psychological Inquiry, 6,* 56–62.

Kenrick, D. T., & Funder, D. C. (1991). The person-situation debate: Do personality traits really exist? In N. J. Derlega, B. A. Winstead, & W. H. Jones (Eds.), *Personality: Contemporary theory and research.* Chicago: Nelson-Hall.

Kenrick, D. T., & Gutierres, S. E. (1980). Contrast effects and judgments of physical attractiveness: When beauty becomes a social problem. *Journal of Personality and Social Psychology, 38,* 131–140.

Kenrick, D. T., & Trost, M. R. (1993). The evolutionary perspective. In A. E. Beall & R. J. Sternberg (Eds.), *The psychology of gender.* New York: Guilford.

Kenrick, D. T., Sadalla, E. K., Groth, G., & Trost, M. R. (1990). Evolution, traits, and the stages of human courtship: Qualifying the parental investment model. *Journal of Personality, 58,* 97–116.

Keren, G. (1990). Cognitive aids and debiasing methods: Can cognitive pills cure cognitive ills? In J. P. Caverni, J. M. Fabre, & M. Gonzalez (Eds.), *Cognitive biases.* Amsterdam: North-Holland.

Kerfoot, P., Sakoulas, G., & Hyman, S. E. (1996). Cocaine. In L. S. Friedman, N. F. Fleming, D. H. Roberts, & S. E. Hyman (Eds.), *Source book of substance abuse and addiction.* Baltimore: Williams & Wilkins.

Kesner, R. P. (1998). Neural mediation of memory for time: Role of the hippocampus and medial prefrontal cortex. *Pscyhonomic Bulletin & Review, 5,* 585–596.

Kessen, W. (1996). American psychology just before Piaget. *Psychological Science, 7,* 196–199.

Kessler, R. C. (1997). The effects of stressful life events on depression. *Annual Review of Psychology, 48,* 191–214.

Kessler, R. C. (2002). Epidemiology of depression. In I. H. Gotlib & C. L. Hammen (Eds.), *Handbook of depression.* New York: Guilford.

Kessler, R. C., & Zhao, S. (1999). The prevalence of mental illness. In A. V. Horvitz & T. L. Scheid (Eds.), *A handbook for the study of mental health: Social contexts, theories, and systems.* New York: Cambridge University Press.

Kessler, R. C., McGonagle, K. A., Zhao, S., Nelson, C. B., Hughes, M., Eshleman, S., Wittchen, H. U., & Kendler, K. S. (1994). Lifetime and 12–month prevalence of DSM-III-R psychiatric disorders in the United States: Results from the National Comorbidity Survey. *Archives of General Psychiatry, 51,* 8–19.

Kessler, R. C., Olfson, M., & Berglund, P. A. (1998). Patterns and predictors of treatment contact after first onset of psychiatric disorders. *American Journal of Psychiatry, 155,* 62–69.

Kessler, R. C., Zhao, S., Katz, S. J., Kouzis, A. C., Frank, R. G., Edlund, M., & Leaf, P. (1999). Past-year use of outpatient services for psychiatric problems in the National Comorbidity Survey. *American Journal of Psychiatry, 156,* 115–123.

Ketterer, M. W., & Randall, M. (2000). Atherosclerosis. In G. Fink (Ed.), *Encyclopedia of stress* (pp. 258–261). San Diego: Academic Press.

Key, W. B. (1973). *Subliminal seduction.* Englewood Cliffs, NJ: Prentice-Hall.

Key, W. B. (1976). *Media sexploitation.* Englewood Cliffs, NJ: Prentice-Hall.

Key, W. B. (1980). *The clam-plate orgy and other subliminal techniques for manipulating your behavior.* Englewood Cliffs, NJ: Prentice-Hall.

Kiecolt-Glaser, J. K., & Glaser, R. (1995). Measurement of immune response. In S. Cohen, R. C. Kessler, & L. U. Gordon (Eds.), *Measuring stress: A guide for health and social scientists.* New York: Oxford University Press.

Kiecolt-Glaser, J. K., Garner, W., Speicher, C., Penn, G. M., Holliday, J., & Glaser, R. (1984). Psychosocial modifiers of immunocompetence in medical students. *Psychosomatic Medicine, 46*(1), 7–14.

Kiecolt-Glaser, J. K., Kennedy, S., Malkoff, S., Fisher, L., Speicher, C. E., & Glaser, R. (1988). Marital discord and immunity in males. *Psychosomatic Medicine, 50,* 213–229.

Kiecolt-Glaser, J. K., McGuire, L., Robles, T. F., & Glaser, R. (2002). Emotions, morbidity, and mortality: New perspectives from psychoneuroimmunology. *Annual Review of Psychology, 53,* 83–107.

Kiesler, C. A. (1991). Homelessness and public policy priorities. *American Psychologist, 46,* 1245–1252.

Kiesler, C. A. (1992). U.S. mental health policy: Doomed to fail. *American Psychologist, 47,* 1077–1082.

Kiesler, C. A. (2000). The next wave of change for psychology and mental health services in the health care revolution. *American Psychologist, 55,* 481–487.

Kiesler, D. J. (1999). *Beyond the disease model of mental disorders.* New York: Praeger Publishers.

Kihlstrom, J. F. (1985). Hypnosis. *Annual Review of Psychology, 36,* 385–418.

Kihlstrom, J. F. (1998a). Dissociations and dissociation theory in hypnosis: Comment on Kirsch and Lynn (1998). *Psychological Bulletin, 123,* 186–191.

Kihlstrom, J. F. (1998b). Exhumed memory. In S. J. Lynn, & K. M. McConkey (Eds.), *Truth in memory.* New York: Guilford.

Kihlstrom, J. F. (2001). Dissociative disorders. In P. B. Sutker & H. E. Adams (Eds.), *Comprehensive handbook of psychopathology* (3rd ed., pp. 259–276). New York: Kluwer Academic/Plenum Publishers.

Kihlstrom, J. F., Barnhardt, T. M., & Tataryn, D. J. (1992). Implicit perception. In R. F. Bornstein & T. S. Pittman (Eds.), *Perception without awareness: Cognitive, clinical, and social perspectives.* New York: Guilford.

Kihlstrom, J. F., Glisky, M. L., & Angiulo, M. J. (1994). Dissociative tendencies and dissociative disorders. *Journal of Abnormal Psychology, 103,* 117–124.

Kihlstrom, J. F., Tataryn, D. J., & Hoyt, I. P. (1993). Dissociative disorders. In P. B. Sutker & H. E. Adams (Eds.), *Comprehensive handbook of psychopathology* (2nd ed.). New York: Plenum.

Kihlstrom, J. F., Schacter, D. L., Cork, R. C., Hurt, C. A., & Behr, S. E. (1990). Implicit and explicit memory following surgical anesthesia. *Psychological Science, 1,* 303–306.

Killeen, P. R. (1981). Learning as causal inference. In M. L. Commons & J. A. Nevin (Eds.), *Quantitative analyses of behavior: Vol. 1. Discriminative properties of reinforcement schedules.* Cambridge, MA: Ballinger.

Kilpatrick, D. G., Edmunds, C. N., & Seymour, A. (1992). *Rape in America.* Arlington, VA: National Victim Center.

Kim, H., & Markus, H. R. (1999). Deviance or uniqueness, harmony or conformity? A cultural analysis. *Journal of Personality and Social Psychology, 77,* 785–800.

Kim, K., & Spelke, E. S. (1992). Infants' sensitivity to effects of gravity on visible object motion. *Journal of Experimental Psychology: Human Perception and Performance, 18,* 385–393.

Kimberg, D. Y., D'Esposito, M., & Farah, M. J. (1997). Cognitive functions in the prefrontal cortex— Working memory and executive control. *Current Directions in Psychological Science, 6,* 185–192.

Kimmel, A. J. (1996). *Ethical issues in behavioral research: A survey.* Cambridge, MA: Blackwell.

Kimmel, M. S., & Linders, A. (1996). Does censorship make a difference? An aggregate empirical analysis of pornography and rape. *Journal of Psychology and Human Sexuality, 8,* 1–20.

Kimura, D. (1973). The asymmetry of the human brain. *Scientific American, 228,* 70–78.

Kimura, D. (1999). *Sex and cognition.* Cambridge, MA: MIT Press.

Kimura, D., & Hampson, E. (1993). Neural and hormonal mechanisms mediating sex differences in cognition. In P. A. Vernon (Ed.), *Biological approaches to the study of human intelligence.* Norwood, NJ: Ablex.

King, A. C., Taylor, C. B., & Haskell, W. L. (1993). Effects of differing intensities and formats of 12 months of exercise training on psychological outcomes in older adults. *Health Psychology, 12,* 292–300.

King, A. C., Oman, R. F., Brassington, G. S., Bliwise, D. L., & Haskell, W. L. (1997). Moderate-intensity exercise and self-rated quality of sleep in older adults: A randomized controlled trial. *Journal of the American Medical Association, 277,* 32–37.

King, B. H., Hodapp, R. M., & Dykens, E. M. (2000). Mental retardation. In B. J. Sadock & V. A. Sadock (Eds.), *Kaplan and Sadock's comprehensive textbook of psychiatry* (7th ed., pp. 2587–2613). Philadelphia: Lippincott/Williams & Wilkins.

King, G. R., & Ellinwood, E. H. Jr. (1997). Amphetamines and other stimulants. In J. H. Lowinson, P. Ruiz, R. B. Millman, & J. G. Langrod (Eds.), *Substance abuse: A comprehensive textbook.* Baltimore: Williams & Willkins.

King, L. A., & Emmons, R. A. (1990). Conflict over emotional expression: Psychological and physical correlates. *Journal of Personality and Social Psychology, 58,* 864–877.

King, L. A., & Emmons, R. A. (1991). Psychological, physical, and interpersonal correlates of emotional expressiveness, conflict and control. *European Journal of Personality, 5,* 131–150.

King, L. A., King, D. W., Fairbank, J. A., Keane, T. M., & Adams, G. A. (1998). Resilience-recovery factors in post-traumatic stress disorder among female and male Vietnam veterans: Hardiness, postwar social support, and additional stressful life events. *Journal of Personality and Social Psychology, 74,* 420–434.

King, N. J., Eleonora, G., & Ollendick, T. H. (1998). Etiology of childhood phobias: Current status of Rachman's three pathways theory. *Behaviour Research and Therapy, 36,* 297–309.

Kinsbourne, M. (1980). If sex differences in brain lateralization exist, they have yet to be discovered. *Behavioral and Brain Sciences, 3,* 241–242.

Kinsbourne, M. (1997). What qualifies a representation for a role in consciousness? In J. D. Cohen & J. W. Schooler (Eds.), *Scientific approaches to consciousness.* Mahwah, NJ: Erlbaum.

Kinsey, A. C., Pomeroy, W. B., & Martin, C. E. (1948). *Sexual behavior in the human male.* Philadelphia: Saunders.

Kinsey, A. C., Pomeroy, W. B., Martin, C. E., & Gebhard, P. H. (1953). *Sexual behavior in the human female.* Philadelphia: Saunders.

Kirchner, J. T. (2001, September). Ten things primary care physicians should know about HIV/AIDS. *Medical Aspects of Human Sexuality, 7–9.*

Kirkpatrick, L. A. (1999). Attachment and religious representations and behavior. In J. Cassidy & P. R. Shaver (Eds.), *Handbook of attachment: Theory, research and clinical applications.* New York: Guilford.

Kirkpatrick, L. A., & Davis, K. E. (1994). Attachment style, gender, and relationship stability: A longitudinal study. *Journal of Personality and Social Psychology, 66,* 502–512.

Kirmayer, L. J., Robbins, J. M., & Paris, J. (1994). Somatoform disorders: Personality and the social matrix of somatic distress. *Journal of Abnormal Psychology, 103,* 125–136.

Kirsch, I. (1997). Response expectancy theory and application: A decennial review. *Applied and Preventive Psychology, 6,* 69–79.

Kirsch, I., & Braffman, W. (2001). Imaginative suggestibility and hypnotizability. *Current Directions in Psychological Science, 10*(2), 57–61.

Kirsch, I., & Council, J. R. (1992). Situational and personality correlates of hypnotic responsiveness. In E. Fromm & M. R. Nash (Eds.), *Contemporary hypnosis research.* New York: Guilford.

Kirsch, I., & Lynn, S. J. (1998). Dissociation theories of hypnosis. *Psychological Bulletin, 123,* 100–115.

Kitayama, S., Markus, H. R., Matsumoto, H., & Norasakkunkit, V. (1997). Individual and collective processes in the constuction of the self: Self-enhancement in the United States and self-criticism in Japan. *Journal of Personality and Social Psychology, 72,* 1245–1267.

Kitchens, A. (1991). Left brain/right brain theory: Implications for developmental math instruction. *Review of Research in Developmental Education, 8,* 20–23.

Kitigbak, M. S., Church, A. T., Guanzon-Lapeña, M. A., Carlota, A. J., & del Pilar, G. H. (2002). Are indigenous personality dimensions culture specific? Philippine inventories and the five factor model. *Journal of Personality and Social Psychology, 82,* 89–101.

Kittler, P. G., & Sucher, K. P. (1998). *Food and culture in America: A nutrition handbook.* St. Paul: West.

Klahr, D., & Simon, H. A. (1999). Studies of scientific discovery: Complementary approaches and convergent findings. *Psychological Bulletin, 125,* 524–543.

Kleiman, D. G. (1977). Monogamy in mammals. *Quarterly Review of Biology, 52,* 39–69.

Klein, K., & Boals, A. (2001). The relationship of life event stress and working memory capacity. *Applied Cognitive Psychology, 15,* 565–579.

Klein, M. (1948). *Contributions to psychoanalysis.* London: Hogarth.

Klein, P. D. (1997). Multiplying the problems of intelligence by eight: A critique of Gardner's theory. *Canadian Journal of Education, 22,* 377–394.

Kleinke, C. L., Peterson, T. R., & Rutledge, T. R. (1998). Effects of self-generated facial expressions on mood. *Journal of Personality and Social Psychology, 74,* 272–279.

Kleinmuntz, B. (1980). *Essentials of abnormal psychology.* San Francisco: Harper & Row.

Kleinmuntz, B. (1985). *Personality and psychological assessment.* Malabar, FL: Robert E. Krieger.

Klerman, E. B. (1993). Deprivation, selective: NREM sleep. In M. A. Carskadon (Ed.), *Encyclopedia of sleep and dreaming.* New York: Macmillan.

Klerman, G. L., & Weissman, M. M. E. (1993). *New applications of interpersonal therapy.* Washington, DC: American Psychiatric Press.

Kline, P. (1991). *Intelligence: The psychometric view.* New York: Routledge, Chapman, & Hall.

Kline, P. (1995). A critical review of the measurement of personality and intelligence. In D. H. Saklofske & M. Zeidner (Eds.), *International handbook of personality and intelligence.* New York: Plenum.

Kling, K. C., Hyde, J. S., Showers, C. J., & Buswell, B. N. (1999). Gender differences in self-esteem: A meta-analysis. *Psychological Bulletin, 125,* 470–500.

Kluckhohn, C., & Murray, H. A. (1948). *Personality in nature, society and culture.* New York: Knopf.

Kluegel, J. R. (1990). Trends in whites' explanations of the black-white gap in socioeconomic status. *American Sociological Review, 55,* 512–525.

Kluft, R. P. (1996). Dissociative identity disorder. In L. K. Michelson & W. J. Ray (Eds.), *Handbook of dissociation: Theoretical, empirical, and clinical perspectives.* New York: Plenum.

Kluft, R. P. (1999). True lies, false truths, and naturalistic raw data: Applying clinical research findings to the false memory debate. In L. M. Williams & V. L. Banyard (Eds.), *Trauma & memory.* Thousand Oaks, CA: Sage Publications.

Knable, M. B., Kleinman, J. E., & Weinberger, D. R. (1995). Neurobiology of schizophrenia. In A. F. Schatzberg & C. B. Nemeroff (Eds.), *The American Psychiatric Press textbook of psychopharmacology.* Washington, DC: American Psychiatric Press.

Knight, G. P., Fabes, R. A., & Higgins, D. A. (1996). Concerns about drawing causal inference from meta-analysis: An example in the study of gender differences in aggression. *Psychological Bulletin, 119,* 410–421.

Knowles, J. A., Kaufmann, C. A., & Rieder, R. O. (1999). Genetics. In R. E. Hales, S. C. Yudofsky, & J. A. Talbott (Eds.), *American Psychiatric Press textbook of Psychiatry.* Washington, DC: American Psychiatric Press.

Knox, D., Zusman, M., & Nieves, W. (1997). College students' homogamous preferences for a date and mate. *College Student Journal, 31,* 445–448.

Kobak, R. (1999). The emotional dynamics of disruptions in attachment relationships: Implications for theory, research, and clinical intervention. In J. Cassidy & P. R. Shaver (Eds.), *Handbook of attachment.* New York: Guilford.

Kochanska, G. (2001). Emotional development in children with different attachment histories: The first three years. *Child Development, 72,* 474–490.

Koehler, J. J. (1996). The base rate fallacy reconsidered: Descriptive, normative, and methodological challenges. *Behavioral Brain Sciences, 19,* 1–53.

Koester, J., & Siegelbaum, S. A. (2000). Propagated signaling: The action potential. In E. R. Kandel, J. H. Schwartz, & T. M. Jessell (Eds.), *Principles of neural science* (pp. 150–174). New York: McGraw-Hill.

Koestner, R., & McClelland, D. C. (1992). The affiliation motive. In C. P. Smith (Ed.), *Motivation and personality: Handbook of thematic content analysis.* New York: Cambridge University Press.

Kogan, N. (1990). Personality and aging. In J. E. Birren & K. W. Schaie (Eds.), *Handbook of the psychology of aging.* San Diego: Academic Press.

Kohlberg, L. (1963). The development of children's orientations toward a moral order: I. Sequence in the development of moral thought. *Vita Humana, 6,* 11–33.

Kohlberg, L. (1969). Stage and sequence: The cognitive-developmental approach to socialization. In D. A. Goslin (Ed.), *Handbook of socialization theory and research.* Chicago: Rand McNally.

Kohlberg, L. (1976). Moral stages and moralization: Cognitive-developmental approach. In T. Lickona (Ed.), *Moral development and behavior: Theory, research and social issues.* New York: Holt, Rinehart & Winston.

Kohlberg, L. (1984). *Essays on moral development: Vol. 2. The psychology of moral development.* San Francisco: Harper & Row.

Kohn, P. M., Lafreniere, K., & Gurevich, M. (1991). Hassles, health, and personality. *Journal of Personality and Social Psychology, 61,* 478–482.

Kohut, H. (1971). *Analysis of the self.* New York: International Universities Press.

Kolb, B., & Whishaw, I. Q. (1998). Brain plasticity and behavior. *Annual Review of Psychology, 49,* 43–64.

Kondo-Ikemura, K. (2001). Insufficient evidence. *American Psychologist, 56,* 825–826.

Koob, G. F. (1997). Neurochemical explanations for addiction. *Hospital Practice, April,* 12–14.

Koob, G. F., & Bloom, F. E. (1988). Cellular and molecular mechanisms of drug dependence. *Science, 242,* 715–723.

Kop, W. J., Gottdiener, J. S., & Krantz, D. S. (2001). Stress and silent ischemia. In A. Baum, T. A. Revenson, & J. E. Singer (Eds.), *Handbook of health psychology* (pp. 669–682). Mahwah, NJ: Erlbaum.

Kopta, S. M., Lueger, R. J., Saunders, S. M., & Howard, K. I. (1999). Individual psychotherapy outcome and process research: Challenges leading to greater turmoil or a positive transition? *Annual Review of Psychology, 50,* 441–69.

Koren, D., Arnon, I., & Klein, E. (1999). Acute stress response and posttraumatic stress disorder in traffic accident victims: A one-year prospective, follow-up study. *American Journal of Psychiatry, 156,* 367–373.

Koriat, A., & Melkman, R. (1987). Depth of processing and memory organization. *Psychological Research, 49,* 183–188.

Koriat, A., Goldsmith, M., & Pansky, A. (2000). Toward a psychology of memory accuracy. *Annual Review of Psychology, 51,* 481–537.

Koriat, A., Lichtenstein, S., & Fischhoff, B. (1980). Reasons for confidence. *Journal of Experimental Psychology, 6,* 107–118.

Korn, J. H. (1987). Judgements of acceptability of deception in psychological research. *Journal of General Psychology, 114,* 205–216.

Korn, J. H. (1997). *Illusions of reality: A history of deception in social psychology.* Albany: State University of New York Press.

Korn, J. H., Davis, R., & Davis, S. F. (1991). Historians' and chairpersons' judgements of eminence among psychologists. *American Psychologist, 46,* 789–792.

Korn, M. L. (2001). Trauma related disorders: Conversations with the experts—Posttraumatic stress disorder: An interview with Marilyn Bowman. Retrieved November 20, 2001 from Medscape Mental Health Website: http://www.medscape.com/ Medscape/psychiatry/journal/2001/ v06.n0 6.n05/myh5/mh1002.01. yehu /mh1002.01.yehu.html. *Medscape Mental Health, 6*(5).

Kortenhaus, C. M., & Demarest, J. (1993). Gender role stereotyping in children's literature: An update. *Sex Roles, 3,* 219–232.

Koss, M. P. (1993). Rape: Scope, impact, interventions, and public policy responses. *American Psychologist, 48,* 1062–1069.

Koss, M. P., Gidycz, C. A., & Wisniewski, N. (1988). The scope of rape: Incidence and prevalence of sexual aggression and victimization in a national sample of higher education students. *Journal of Consulting and Clinical Psychology, 55,* 162–170.

Kotovsky, K., Hayes, J. R., & Simon, H. A. (1985). Why are some problems hard? Evidence from Tower of Hanoi. *Cognitive Psychology, 17,* 248–294.

Kotulak, R. (1996). *Inside the brain: Revolutionary discoveries of how the mind works.* Kansas City, MO: Andrews McMeel.

Koukounas, E., & McCabe, M. (1997). Sexual and emotional variables influencing sexual response to erotica. *Behaviour Research and Therapy, 35,* 221–230.

Kracke, W. (1991). Myths in dreams, thought in images: An Amazonian contribution to the psychoanalytic theory of primary process. In B. Tedlock (Ed.), *Dreaming: Anthropological and psychological interpretations.* Santa Fe, NM: School of American Research Press.

Krakauer, J. (1998). *Into thin air: A personal account of the Mount Everest disaster.* New York: Villard.

Kramer, M. (1994). The scientific study of dreaming. In M. H. Kryger, T. Roth, & W. C. Dement (Eds.), *Principles and practice of sleep medicine* (2nd ed.). Philadelphia: Saunders.

Krantz, D. S., & McCeney, M. K. (2002). Effects of psychological and social factors on organic disease: A critical assessment of research on coronary heart disease. *Annual Review of Psychology, 53,* 341–369.

Krantz, D. S., Sheps, D. S., Carney, R. M., & Natelson, B. H. (2000). Effects of mental stress in patients with coronary artery disease. *Journal of the American Medical Association, 283,* 1800–1802.

Kraus, S. J. (1995). Attitudes and the prediction of behavior: A meta-analysis of the empirical literature. *Personality and Social Psychology Bulletin, 21,* 58–75.

Krebs, D. L., & Denton, K. (1997). Social illusions and self-deception: The evolution of biases in person perception. In J. A. Simpson & D. T. Kenrick (Eds.), *Evolutionary social psychology.* Mahwah, NJ: Erlbaum.

Krebs, J. R., & McCleery, R. H. (1984). Optimization in behavioral ecology. In J. R. Krebs & N. B. Davies (Eds.), *Behavioral ecology* (2nd ed.). Sunderland, MA: Sinauer.

Kribbs, N. B. (1993). Siesta. In M. A. Carskadon (Ed.), *Encyclopedia of sleep and dreaming.* New York: Macmillan.

Kring, A. M. (1999). Emotion in schizophrenia: Old mystery, new understanding. *Current Directions in Psychological Science, 8,* 160–163.

Kris, E. (1952). *Psychoanalytic explorations in art.* New York: International Universities Press.

Krishnan, K. R. R., & Hamilton, M. A. (1997). Obesity. *Primary Psychiatry, 5,* 49–53.

Kroger, J. (1995). The differentiation of "firm" and "developmental" foreclosure identity statuses: A longitudinal study. *Journal of Adolescent Research, 10,* 317–337.

Kroger, J. (1996). Identity, regression, and development. *Journal of Adolescence, 19,* 203–222.

Krosnick, J. A. (1999). Survey research. *Annual Review Psychology, 50,* 537–567.

Krosnick, J. A., & Fabrigar, L. R. (1998). *Designing good questionnaires: Insights from psychology.* New York: Oxford University Press.

Krosnick, J. A., & Petty, R. E. (1995). Attitude strength: An overview. In R. E. Petty & J. A. Krosnick (Eds.), *Attitude strength: Antecedents and consequences.* Mahwah, NJ: Erlbaum.

Krosnick, J. A., Betz, A. L., Jussim, L. J., & Lynn, A. R. (1992). Subliminal conditioning of attitudes. *Personality and Social Psychology Bulletin, 18,* 152–162.

Krueger, J. (1996). Personal beliefs and cultural stereotypes about racial characteristics. *Journal of Personality and Social Psychology, 71,* 536–548.

Krueger, J., Ham, J. J., & Linford, K. M. (1996). Perceptions of behavioral consistency: Are people aware of the actor-observer effect? *Psychological Science, 7,* 259–264.

Krueger, L. E. (1989). Reconciling Fechner and Stevens: Toward a unified psychophysical law. *Behavioral and Brain Sciences, 12,* 251–320.

Krueger, W. C. F. (1929). The effect of overlearning on retention. *Journal of Experimental Psychology, 12,* 71–78.

Krull, D. S., & Erickson, D. J. (1995). Inferential hopscotch: How people draw social inferences from behavior. *Current Directions in Psychological Science, 4,* 35–38.

Kryger, M. H. (1993). Snoring. In M. A. Carskadon (Ed.), *Encyclopedia of sleep and dreaming.* New York: Macmillan.

Kryger, M. H., Roth, T., & Dement, W. C. (2000). *Principles and practice of sleep medicine.* Philadelphia: Saunders.

Kuhl, P. K., & Meltzoff, A. N. (1997). Evolution, nativism and learning in the development of language and speech. In M. Gopnik (Ed.), *The inheritance and innateness of grammars* (pp. 7–44). New York: Oxford University Press.

Kulick, A. R., Pope, H. G., & Keck, P. E. (1990). Lycanthropy and self-identification. *Journal of Nervous & Mental Disease, 178*(2), 134–137.

Kunda, Z., & Oleson, K. C. (1995). Maintaining stereotypes in the face of disconfirmation: Constructing grounds for subtyping deviants. *Journal of Personality and Social Psychology, 68,* 565–579.

Kunda, Z., & Oleson, K. C. (1997). When exceptions prove the rule: How extremity of deviance determines the impact of deviant examples on stereotypes. *Journal of Personality and Social Psychology, 72,* 965–979.

Kupfermann, I., Kandel, E. R., & Iversen, S. (2000). Motivational and addictive states. In E. R. Kandel, J. H. Schwartz, & T. M. Jessell (Eds.), *Principles of neural science.* New York: McGraw-Hill.

Kutchins, H., & Kirk, S. A. (1997). *Making us crazy: DSM—The psychiatric Bible and the creation of mental disorders.* New York: Free Press.

Kutchinsky, B. (1991). Pornography and rape: Theory and practice? Evidence from crime data in four countries where pornography is easily available. *International Journal of Law and Psychiatry, 14,* 47–64.

Kwan, V. S. Y., Bond, M. H., & Singelis, T. M. (1997). Pancultural explanations for life satisfaction: Adding relationship harmony to self-esteem. *Journal of Personality and Social Psychology, 73,* 1038–1051.

LaBerge, S. (1988). Lucid dreaming in Western literature. In J. Gackenbach & S. LaBerge (Eds.), *Conscious mind, sleeping brain: Perspectives on lucid dreaming.* New York: Plenum.

LaBerge, S. (1990). Lucid dreaming: Psychophysiological studies of consciousness during REM sleep. In R. R. Bootzin, J. F. Kihlstrom, & D. L. Schacter (Eds.), *Sleep and cognition.* Washington, DC: American Psychological Association.

LaBerge, S., Nagel, L., Dement, W. C., & Zarcone, V., Jr. (1981). Lucid dreaming verified by volitional communication during REM sleep. *Perceptual and Motor Skills, 52,* 727–732.

LaBine, S. J., & LaBine, G. (1996). Determinations of negligence and the hindsight bias. *Law & Human Behavior, 20,* 501–516.

La Cerra, P., & Kurzban, R. (1995). The structure of scientific revolutions and the nature of the adapted mind. *Psychological Inquiry, 6,* 62–65.

Lachman, S. J. (1996). Processes in perception: Psychological transformations of highly structured stimulus material. *Perceptual and Motor Skills, 83,* 411–418.

Lack, D. (1968). *Ecological adaptations for breeding in birds.* London: Meuthen.

Lader, M. H. (2002). Managing dependence and withdrawal with newer hypnotic medications in the treatment of insomnia. *Journal of Clinical Psychiatry, 4*(suppl 1), 33–37.

Lahey, B. B., Piancentini, J. C., McBurnett, K., Stone, P., Hartdagen, S., & Hynd, G. (1988). Psychopathology in the parents of children with conduct disorder and hyperactivity. *Journal of the American Academy of Child and Adolescent Psychiatry, 27,* 163–170.

Laitinen, J., Ek, E., & Sovio, U. (2002). Stress-related eating and drinking behavior and body mass index and predictors of this behavior. *Preventive Medicine: An International Journal Devoted to Practice & Theory, 34,* 29–39.

Lakein, A. (1996). *How to get control of your time and your life.* New York: New American Library.

Lam, L. T., & Kirby, S. L. (2002). Is emotional intelligence an advantage? An exploration of the impact of emotional and general intelligence on individual performance. *Journal of Social Psychology, 142,* 133–143.

Lamb, H. R. (1998). Deinstitutionalization at the beginning of the new millenium. *Harvard Review of Psychiatry, 6,* 1–10.

Lamb, H. R. (1999). Public psychiatry and prevention. In R. E. Hales, S. C. Yudofsky, & J. A. Talbott (Eds.), *American Psychiatric Press textbook of psychiatry.* Washington, DC: American Psychiatric Press.

Lamb, M. E. (1998). Nonparental child care: context, quality, correlates, and consequences. In W. Damon (Ed.), *Handbook of child psychology (Vol. 4): Child psychology in practice.* New York: Wiley.

Lamb, M. E., Hwang, C. P., Ketterlinus, R. D., & Fracasso, M. P. (1999). Parent-child relationships: Development in the context of the family. In M. H. Bornstein & M. E. Lamb (Eds.), *Developmental psychology and advanced textbook.* Mahwah, NJ: Erlbaum.

Lamb, M. E., Ketterlinus, R. D., & Fracasso, M. P. (1992). Parent-child relationships. In M. H. Bornstein & M. E. Lamb (Eds.), *Developmental psychology: An advanced textbook* (3rd ed.). Hillsdale, NJ: Erlbaum.

Lamb, M. E., Sternberg, K. J., & Prodromidis, M. (1992). Nonmaternal care and the security of infant-mother attachment: A reanalysis of the data. *Infant Behavior and Development, 15,* 71–83.

Lambert, M. J., & Barley, D. E. (2001). Research summary on the therapeutic relationship and psychotherapy outcome. *Psychotherapy: Theory, Research, Practice, Training, 38,* 357–361.

Lambert, M. J., & Bergin, A. E. (1992). Achievements and limitations of psychotherapy research. In D. K. Freedheim (Ed.), *History of psychotherapy: A century of change.* Washington, DC: American Psychological Association.

Lambert, M. J., & Bergin, A. E. (1994). The effectiveness of psychotherapy. In A. E. Bergin & S. L. Garfield (Eds.), *Handbook of psychotherapy and behavior change* (4th ed.). New York: Wiley.

Lambert, M. J., & Hill, C. E. (1994). Assessing psychotherapy outcomes and processes. In A. E. Bergin & S. L.

Garfield (Eds.), *Handbook of psychotherapy and behavior change* (4th ed.). New York: Wiley.

Lambert, W. E. (1990). Persistent issues in bilingualism. In B. Harley, P. Allen, J. Cummins, & M. Swain (Eds.), *The development of second language proficiency*. Cambridge, England: Cambridge University Press.

Lampe, A., Soellner, W., Krismer, M., Rumpold, G., Kantner-Rumplmair, W., Ogon, M., & Rathner, G. (1998). The impact of stressful life events on exacerbation of chronic low-back pain. *Journal of Psychosomatic Research, 44*, 555–563.

Lampinen, J. M., Neuschatz, J. S., & Payne, D. G. (1999). Source attributions and false memories: A test of the demand characteristics account. *Psychonomic Bulletin & Review, 6*, 130–135.

Lampl, M., Veldhuis, J. D., & Johnson, M. L. (1992). Saltation and stasis: A model of human growth. *Science, 258*, 801–803.

Landabaso, M. A., Iraurgi, I., Sanz, J., Calle, R., Ruiz de Apodaka, J., Jimenez-Lerma, J. M., & Gutierrez-Fraile, M. (1999). Naltrexone in the treatment of alcoholism. Two-year follow up results. *European Journal of Psychiatry, 13*, 97–105.

Landau, J. D., & Marsh, R. L. (1997). Monitoring source in an unconscious plagiarism paradigm. *Psychonomic Bulletin & Review, 4*, 265–270.

Landesman, S., & Ramey, C. (1989). Developmental psychology and mental retardation: Integrating scientific principles with treatment practices. *American Psychologist, 44*, 409–415.

Landy, F. J., Shankster, L. J., & Kohler, S. S. (1994). Personnel selection and placement. *Annual Review of Psychology, 45*, 261–296.

Lang, P. J. (1995). The emotion probe: Studies of motivation and attention. *American Psychologist, 50*, 372–385.

Langdon, P. E., Yagueez, L., Brown, J., & Hope, A. (2001). Who walks through the "revolving door" of a British psychiatric hospital? *Journal of Mental Health (UK), 10*, 525–533.

Lange, C. (1885). One leuds beveegelser. In K. Dunlap (Ed.), *The emotions*. Baltimore: Williams & Wilkins.

Langlois, J. H., Kalakanis, L., Rubenstein, A. J., Larson, A., Hallam, M., & Smoot, M. (2000). Maxims or myths of beauty? A meta-analytic and theoretical review. *Psychological Bulletin, 126*, 390–423.

Lanyon, R. I., & Goodstein, L. D. (1997). *Personality assessment*. New York: Wiley.

LaPiere, R. T. (1934). Attitude and actions. *Social Forces, 13*, 230–237.

Larkin, J. A. (1988). Are good teachers perceived as high self-monitors? *Personality and Social Psychology Bulletin, 13*, 64–72.

Larson, R., & Richards, M. H. (1994). *Divergent realities: The emotional lives of mothers, fathers, and adolescents*. New York: Basic Books.

Larson, R., Richards, M., Moneta, G. , Holmbeck, G., & Duckett, E. (1996). Changes in adolescents' daily interactions with their families from ages 10 to 18: Disengagement and transformation. *Developmental Psychology, 32*, 744–754.

Larzelere, R. E., Schneider, W. N., Larson, D. B., & Pike, P. L. (1996). The effects of discipline responses in delaying toddler misbehavior recurrences. *Child and Family Behavior Therapy, 18*, 35–37.

Lash, T. L., & Aschengrau, A. (1999). Active and passive cigarette smoking and the occurrence of breast cancer. *American Journal of Epidemiology, 149*, 5–12.

Latané, B. (1981). The psychology of social impact. *American Psychologist, 36*, 343–356.

Latané, B., & Nida, S. A. (1981). Ten years of research on group size and helping. *Psychological Bulletin, 89*, 308–324.

Latané, B., Williams, K., & Harkins, S. (1979). Many hands make light the work: The causes and consequences of social loafing. *Journal of Personality and Social Psychology, 37*, 822–832.

Lattal, K. A. (1992). B. F. Skinner and psychology [Introduction to the Special Issue]. *American Psychologist, 27*, 1269–1272.

Latz, S., Wolf, A. W., & Lozoff, B. (1999). Cosleeping in context: Sleep practices and problems in young children in Japan and United States. *Archives of Pediatrics & Adolescent Medicine, 153*, 339–346.

Laughlin, H. (1967). *The neuroses*. Washington, DC: Butterworth.

Laughlin, H. (1979). *The ego and its defenses*. New York: Aronson.

Laumann, E. O., Gagnon, J. H., Michael, R. T., & Michaels, S. (1994). *The social organization of sexuality: Sexual practices in the United States*. Chicago: University of Chicago Press.

Laursen, B., Coy, K. C., & Collins, W. A. (1998). Reconsidering changes in parent-child conflict across adolescence: A meta-analysis. *Child Development, 69*, 817–832.

Lavie, P. (1997). Melatonin: Role in gating nocturnal rise in sleep propensity. *Journal of Biological Rhythms, 12*, 657–665.

Lavie, P. (2001). Sleep-wake as a biological rhythm. *Annual Review of Psychology, 52*, 277–303.

Lavine, H., Sweeney, D., & Wagner, S. H. (1999). Depicting women as sex objects in television advertising: Effects on body dissatisfaction. *Personality and Social Psychology Bulletin, 25*, 1049–1058.

Lawless, H. T. (2001). Taste. In E. B. Goldstein (Ed.), *Blackwell handbook of perception*. Malden, MA: Blackwell.

Lazarou, J., Pomeranz, B. H., & Corey, P. N. (1998). Incidence of adverse drug reactions in hospitalized patients: A meta-analysis of prospective studies. *Journal of the American Medical Association, 279*, 1200–1205.

Lazarus, A. A. (1989). Multimodal therapy. In R. J. Corsini & D. Wedding (Eds.), *Current Psychotherapies*. Itasca, IL: F. E. Peacock.

Lazarus, A. A. (1992). Multimodal therapy: Technical eclecticism with minimal integration. In J. C. Norcross & M. R. Goldfried (Eds.), *Handbook of psychotherapy integration*. New York: Basic Books.

Lazarus, A. A. (1995). Different types of eclecticism and integration: Let's be aware of the dangers. *Journal of Psychotherapy Integration, 5*, 27–39.

Lazarus, R. S. (1991). *Emotion and adaptation*. New York: Oxford University Press.

Lazarus, R. S. (1993). Why we should think of stress as a subset of emotion. In L. Goldberger & S. Breznitz (Eds.), *Handbook of stress: Theoretical and clinical aspects* (2nd ed.). New York: Free Press.

Lazarus, R. S. (1995). Vexing research problems inherent in cognitive-mediational theories of emotion— and some solutions. *Psychological Inquiry, 6*, 183–196.

Lazarus, R. S. (1999). *Stress and emotion: A new synthesis*. New York: Springer Publishing Company.

Leahey, T. H. (1987). *A history of psychology: Main currents in psychological thought* (2nd ed.). Englewood Cliffs, NJ: Prentice-Hall.

Leahey, T. H. (1991). *A history of modern psychology*. Englewood Cliffs, NJ: Prentice-Hall.

Leahey, T. H. (1992). The mythical revolutions of American psychology. *American Psychologist, 47*, 308–318.

Leavitt, F. (1995). *Drugs and behavior* (3rd ed.). Thousand Oaks, CA: Sage.

LeBoeuf, M. (1980, February). Managing time means managing yourself. *Business Horizons*, 41–46.

Leck, K., & Simpson, J. (1999). Feigning romantic interest: The role of self-monitoring. *Journal of Research in Personality, 33*, 69–91.

Leckman, J. F., Grice, D. E., Boardman, J., Zhang, H., Vitale, A., Bondi, C., Alsobrook, J., Peterson, B. S., Cohen, D. J., Rasmussen, S. A., Goodman, W. K., McDougle, C. J., & Pauls, D. (1997). Symptoms of obsessive-compulsive disorder. *American Journal of Psychiatry, 154*, 911–917.

LeDoux, J. E. (1986). The neurobiology of emotion. In J. E. LeDoux & W. Hirst (Eds.), *Mind and brain: Dialogues in cognitive neuroscience*. Cambridge, England: Cambridge University Press.

LeDoux, J. E. (1993). Emotional networks in the brain. In M. Lewis & J. M. Haviland (Eds.), *Handbook of emotions*. New York: Guilford.

LeDoux, J. E. (1994). Emotion, memory and the brain. *Scientific American, 270*, 50–57.

LeDoux, J. E. (1995). Emotion: Clues from the brain. *Annual Review of Psychology, 46*, 209–235.

LeDoux, J. E. (1996). *The emotional brain*. New York: Simon & Schuster.

Lee, I.-M., Hsieh, C., & Paffenbarger, R. S. Jr. (1995). Exercise intensity and longevity in men. *Journal of the American Medical Association, 273*, 1179–1184.

Lee, I.-M., Rexrode, K. M., Cook, N. R., Manson, J. E., & Buring, J. E. (2001). Physical activity and coronary heart disease in women: Is "no pain, no gain" passé? *Journal of the American Medical Association, 285*, 1447–1454.

Lee, I.-M., Karon, J. M., Selik, R., Neal, J. J., & Fleming, P. L. (2001). Survival after AIDS diagnosis in adolescents and adults during the treatment era, United States, 1984–1997. *Journal of the American Medical Association, 285*, 1308–1315.

Lee, R. M., & Ramirez, M. (2000). The history, current status, and future of multicultural psychotherapy. In I. Cuellar & F. A. Paniagua (Eds.), *Handbook of multicultural mental health: Assessment and treatment of diverse populations*. San Diego: Academic Press.

Lee, R. T., & Ashforth, B. E. (1996). A meta-analytic examination of the correlates of the three dimensions of job burnout. *Journal of Applied Psychology, 81*, 123–133.

Lee, S. (2000) *Wild thing*. [Web Page]. Retrieved July 2, 2002 from http://www.usaweekend.com/00_issues/000618/000618croc_hunter.html.

Lee, S., & Katzman, M. A. (2002). Cross-cultural perspectives on eating disorders. In C. G. Fairburn & K. D. Brownell (Eds.), *Eating disorders and obesity: A comprehensive handbook*. New York: Guilford.

Lee, Y. T., & Seligman, M. E. P. (1997). Are Americans more optimistic than the Chinese? *Personality and Social Psychology Bulletin, 23*, 32–40.

Leeper, R. W. (1935). A study of a neglected portion of the field of learning: The development of sensory organization. *Journal of Genetic Psychology, 46,* 41–75.

Lefcourt, H. M. (2001). The humor solution. In C. R. Snyder (Ed.), *Coping with stress: Effective people and processes* (pp. 68–92). New York: Oxford University Press.

Lefcourt, H. M., Davidson, K., Shepherd, R., Phillips, M., Prkachin, K., & Mills, D. (1995). Perspective-taking humor: Accounting for stress moderation. *Journal of Social and Clinical Psychology, 14,* 373–391.

Leff, J., & Vaughn, C. (1985). *Expressed emotion in families.* New York: Guilford.

Leff, J., Trieman, N., & Gooch, C. (1996). Team for the Assessment of Psychiatric Services (TAPS) Project 33: Prospective follow-up study of long-stay patients discharged from two psychiatric hospitals. *American Journal of Psychiatry, 153,* 1318–1324.

Lehrer, P. M., & Woolfolk, R. L. (1984). Are stress reduction techniques interchangeable, or do they have specific effects? A review of the comparative empirical literature. In R. L. Woolfolk & P. M. Lehrer (Eds.), *Principles and practice of stress management.* New York: Guilford.

Lehrer, P. M., & Woolfolk, R. L. (1993). Specific effects of stress management techniques. In P. M. Lehrer & R. L. Woolfolk (Eds.), *Principles and practice of stress management* (2nd ed.). New York: Guilford.

Leibovic, K. N. (1990). Vertebrate photoreceptors. In K. N. Leibovic (Ed.), *Science of vision.* New York: Springer-Verlag.

Leiter, M. P., & Maslach, C. (2001). Burnout and health. In A. Baum, T. A. Revenson, & J. E. Singer (Eds.), *Handbook of health psychology* (pp. 415–426). Mahwah, NJ: Erlbaum.

Lemack, G. E., Uzzo, R. G., & Poppas, D. P. (1998). Effects of stress on male reproductive function. In J. R. Hubbard & E. A. Workman (Eds.), *Handbook of stress medicine: An organ system approach.* New York: CRC Press.

LeMagnen, J. (1981). The metabolic basis of dual periodicity of feeding in rats. *Behavioral and Brain Sciences, 4,* 561–607.

Lemery, K. S., Goldsmith, H. H., Klinnert, M. D., & Mrazek, D. A. (1999). Developmental models of infant and childhood temperament. *Developmental Psychology, 35,* 189–204.

Lemme, B. H. (1999). *Development in adulthood.* Boston: Allyn & Bacon.

Lennie, P. (2000). Color vision. In E. R. Kandel, J. H. Schwartz, & T. M. Jessell (Eds.), *Principles of neural science.* New York: McGraw-Hill.

Leo, J. (1987, January). Exploring the traits of twins. *Time,* p. 63.

Lerman, H. (1986). *A mote in Freud's eye: From psychoanalysis to the psychology of women.* New York: Springer.

Lerner, M. J., & Goldberg, J. H. (1999). When do decent people blame victims? The differing effects of the explicit/rational and implicit/experiential cognitive systems. In S. Chaiken & Y. Trope (Eds.), *Dual-process theories in social psychology.* New York: Guilford.

Lesher, G. W. (1995). Illusory contours: Toward a neurally based perceptual theory. *Psychonomic Bulletin & Review, 2,* 279–321.

Leshner, A. I. (1997, April). Drug abuse and addiction are biomedical problems. *Hospital Practice,* 2–4.

Leslie, A. M. (1994). ToMM, ToBy, and agency: Core architecture and domain specificity in cognition and culture. In L. A. Hirschfeld & S. A. Gelman (Eds.), *Mapping the mind: Domain specificity in cognition and culture.* New York: Cambridge University Press.

LeVay, S. (1991). A difference in hypothalamic structure between heterosexual and homosexual men. *Science, 253,* 1034–1037.

LeVay, S. (1993). *The sexual brain.* Cambridge, MA: MIT Press.

LeVay, S. (1996). *Queer science: The use and abuse of research into homosexuality.* Cambridge, MA: MIT Press.

Levenson, J. L., McDaniel, J. S., Moran, M. G., & Stoudemire, A. (1999). Psychological factors affecting medical conditions. In R. E. Hales, S. C. Yudofsky & J. A. Talbott (Eds.), *Textbook of psychiatry* (3rd ed., pp. 635–662). Washington, DC: American Psychiatric Press, Inc.

Levenson, R. W. (1992). Autonomic nervous system differences among emotions. *Psychological Science, 3,* 23–27.

Leventhal, E. A., Hansell, S., Diefenbach, M., Leventhal, H., & Glass, D. C. (1996). Negative affect and self-report of physical symptoms: Two longitudinal studies of older adults. *Health Psychology, 15,* 193–199.

Leventhal, H., & Tomarken, A. J. (1986). Emotion: Today's problems. *Annual Review of Psychology, 37,* 565–610.

Levin, M. E., & Levin, J. R. (1990). Scientific mnemonomies: Methods for maximizing more than memory. *American Educational Research Journal, 27*(2), 301–321.

Levine, J. M. (1999). Solomon Asch's legacy for group research. *Personality and Social Psychology Review, 3,* 358–364.

Levine, J. M., & Moreland, R. L. (1998). Small groups. In D. T. Gilbert,

S. T. Fiske, & G. Lindzey (Eds.), *The handbook of social psychology.* New York: McGraw-Hill.

Levine, M. W. (2001). Principles of neural processing. In E. B. Goldstein (Ed.), *Blackwell handbook of perception.* Malden, MA: Blackwell.

Levine, R., & Norenzayan, A. (1999). The pace of life in 31 countries. *Journal of Cross-Cultural Psychology, 30,* 178–205.

Levine, R., Sata, S., Hashimoto, T., & Verma, J. (1995). Love and marriage in eleven cultures. *Journal of Cross-Cultural Psychology, 26,* 554–571.

Levinson, D. F., Mahtani, M. M., Nancarrow, D. J., Brown, D. M., Kruglyak, L., Kirby, A., Hayward, N. K., Crowe, R. R., Andreasen, N. C., Black, D. W., Silverman, J. M., Endicott, J., Sharpe, I., Mohs, R. C., Siever, L. J., Walters, M. K., Lennon, D. P., Jones, H. L., Nurs, B., Nertney, D. A., Daly, M. J., Gladis, M., & Mowry, B. J. (1998). Genome scan of schizophrenia. *American Journal of Psychiatry, 155,* 741–750.

Levinson, D. J., with Darrow, C. M., Klein, E. G., Levinson, M. H., & McKee, B. (1978). *The seasons of a man's life.* New York: Knopf.

Levinthal, C. F. (1999). *Drugs, behavior, and modern society.* Boston: Allyn & Bacon.

Levis, D. J. (1989). The case for a return to a two-factor theory of avoidance: The failure of non-fear interpretations. In S. B. Klein & R. R. Bowrer (Eds.), *Contemporary learning theories: Pavlovian conditioning and the status of traditional learning theory.* Hillsdale NJ: Erlbaum.

Levy, G. D., Taylor, M. G., & Gelman, S. A. (1995). Traditional and evaluative aspects of flexibility in gender roles, social conventions, moral rules, and physical laws. *Child Development, 66,* 515–531.

Levy, J. (1985, May). Right brain, left brain: Fact or fiction. *Psychology Today,* 38–44.

Levy, J., Trevarthen, C., & Sperry, R. W. (1972). Perception of bilateral chimeric figures following hemispheric disconnection. *Brain, 95,* 61–78.

Levy, S. M., Herberman, R. B., Simons, A., Whiteside, T., Lee, J., McDonald, R., & Beadle, M. (1989). Persistently low natural killer cell activity in normal adults: Immunological, hormonal and mood correlates. *Natural Immune Cell Growth Regulation, 8,* 173–186.

Lewicki, P., Hill, T., & Czyzewska, M. (1992). Nonconscious acquisition of information. *American Psychologist, 47,* 796–801.

Lewin, K. (1935). *A dynamic theory of personality.* New York: McGraw-Hill.

Lewinsohn, P. M., Joiner, T. E., Jr., & Rohde, P. (2001). Evaluation of cognitive diathesis-stress models in predicting major depressive disorder in adolescents. *Journal of Abnormal Psychology, 110,* 203–215.

Lewinsohn, P. M., Rohde, P., Seeley, J. R., & Fischer, S. A. (1993). Age-cohort changes in the lifetime occurrence of depression and other mental disorders. *Journal of Abnormal Psychology, 102,* 110–120.

Lewis, D. O., Yeager, C. A., Swica, Y., Pincus, J. H., & Lewis, M. (1997). Objective documentation of child abuse and dissociation in 12 murderers with dissociative identity disorder. *American Journal of Psychiatry, 154,* 1703–1710.

Lewis, M., & Feiring, C. (1989). Infant, mother, and mother-infant interaction behavior and subsequent attachment. *Child Development, 60,* 831–837.

Ley, P. (1997). Compliance among patients. In A. Baum, S. Newman, J. Weiman, R. West, & C. McManus (Eds.), *Cambridge handbook of psychology, health, and medicine.* Cambridge, England: Cambridge University Press.

Li, N. P., Bailey, J. M., Kenrick, D. T., & Linsenmeier, J. A. W. (2002). The necessities and luxuries of mate preferences: Testing the tradeoffs. *Journal of Personality and Social Psychology, 82,* 947–955.

Libby, P., Ridker, P. M., & Maseri, A. (2002). Inflammation and atherosclerosis. *Circulation, 105,* 1135–1143.

Lichtenstein, S., Fischhoff, B., & Phillips, L. (1982). Calibration of probabilities: The state of the art to 1980. In D. Kahneman, P. Slovic, & A. Tversky (Eds.), *Judgment under uncertainty: Heuristics and biases.* Cambridge, England: Cambridge University Press.

Lickey, M. E., & Gordon, B. (1991). *Medicine and mental illness: The use of drugs in psychiatry.* New York: W. H. Freeman.

Lieberman, M. A. (1993). Self-help groups. In H. I. Kaplan & B. J. Sadock (Eds.), *Comprehensive group psychotherapy.* Baltimore: Williams & Wilkins.

Liebert, R. M., & Liebert, L. L. (1998). *Liebert & Spiegler's personality strategies and issues.* Pacific Grove: Brooks/Cole.

Liebert, R. M., & Sprafkin, J. (1988). *The early window: Effects of television on children and youth.* Oxford, England: Pergamon Press.

Lilienfeld, S. O., Lynn, S. J., Kirsch, I., Chaves, J. F., Sarbin, T. R., Ganaway, G. K., & Powell, R. A. (1999). Dissociative identity disorder and the sociocognitive model: Recalling the lessons of the past. *Psychological Bulletin, 125,* 507–523.

Lilienfeld, S. O., & Marino, L. (1999). Essentialism revisited: Evolutionary theory and the concept of mental disorder. *Journal of Abnormal Psychology, 108,* 400–411.

Lilienfeld, S. O., Wood, J. M., & Garb, H. N. (2000). The scientific status of projective tests. *Psychological Science in the Public Interest, 1*(2), 27–66.

Lin, C. (1998). Comparison of the effects of perceived self-efficacy on coping with chronic cancer pain and coping with chronic low back pain. *Clinical Journal of Pain, 14,* 303–310.

Lindgren, H. C. (1969). *The psychology of college success: A dynamic approach.* New York: Wiley.

Lindsay, D. S. (1993). Eyewitness suggestibility. *Current Directions in Psychological Science, 2*(3), 86–89.

Lindsay, D. S. (1998). Depolarizing views on recovered memory experiences. In S. J. Lynn & K. M. McConkey (Eds.), *Truth in memory.* New York: Guilford.

Lindsay, D. S., & Johnson, M. K. (1989). The eyewitness suggestibility effects and memory for source. *Memory & Cognition, 17,* 349–358.

Lindsay, D. S., & Poole, D. A. (1995). Remembering childhood sexual abuse in therapy: Psychotherapists' self–reported beliefs, practices, and experiences. *Journal of Psychiatry & Law,* 461–476.

Lindsay, D. S., & Read, J. D. (1994). Psychotherapy and memories of childhood sexual abuse: A cognitive perspective. *Applied Cognitive Psychology, 8,* 281–338.

Lindsay, P. H., & Norman, D. A. (1977). *Human information processing.* New York: Academic Press.

Lippa, R. A. (1994). *Introduction to social psychology.* Pacific Grove, CA: Brooks/Cole.

Lipsey, M. W., & Wilson, D. B. (1993). The efficacy of psychological, educational, and behavioral treatment: Confirmation from meta-analysis. *American Psychologist, 48,* 1181–1209.

Lipsitt, L. P., & Behl, G. (1990). Taste-mediated differences in the sucking behavior of human newborns. In E. D. Capaldi & T. L. Powley (Eds.), *Taste, experience, and feeding.* Washington, DC: American Psychological Association.

Lisanby, S. H., Maddox, J. H., Prudic, J., Devanand, D. P., & Sackeim, H. A. (2000). The effects of electroconvulsive therapy on memory of autobiographical and public events. *General Psychiatry, 57,* 581–590.

Litt, I. F., & Vaughan, V. C., III. (1992). Adolescence. In R. E. Behrman (Ed.), *Nelson textbook of pediatrics.* Philadelphia: Saunders.

Liu, S., Siegel, P. Z., Brewer, R. D., Mokdad, A. H., Sleet, D. A., & Serdula, M. (1997). Prevalence of alcohol-impaired driving: Results from a national self-reported survey of health behaviors. *Journal of the American Medical Association, 277,* 122–125.

Livesley, W. J. (2001). Conceptual and taxonomic issues. In W. J. Livesley (Ed.), *Handbook of personality disorders: Theory, research, and treatment.* New York: Guilford.

Lloyd, G. D., Fletcher, A., & Minchin, M. C. W. (1992). GABA agonists as potential anxiolytics. In G. D. Burrows, S. M. Roth, & R. Noyes Jr. (Eds.), *Handbook of anxiety.* Oxford: Elsevier.

Lockhart, R. S. (1992). Measurement of memory. In L. R. Squire (Ed.), *Encyclopedia of learning and memory.* New York: Macmillan.

Lockhart, R. S. (2000). Methods of memory research. In E. Tulving & F. I. M. Craik (Eds.), *The Oxford handbook of memory* (pp. 45–58). New York: Oxford University Press.

Lockhart, R. S., & Craik, F. I. (1990). Levels of processing: A retrospective commentary on a framework for memory research. *Canadian Journal of Psychology, 44*(1), 87–112.

Locurto, C. (1990). The malleability of IQ as judged from adoption studies. *Intelligence, 14,* 275–292.

Locurto, C. (1991). *Sense and nonsense about IQ: The case for uniqueness.* New York: Praeger.

Loehlin, J. C. (1989). Partitioning environmental and genetic contributions to behavioral development. *American Psychologist, 44,* 1285–1292.

Loehlin, J. C. (1992). *Genes and environment in personality development.* Newbury Park, CA: Sage.

Loehlin, J. C. (1994). Behavior genetics. In R. J. Sternberg (Ed.), *Encyclopedia of human intelligence.* New York: Macmillan.

Loehlin, J. C. (2000). Group differences in intelligence. In R. J. Sternberg (Ed.), *Handbook of intelligence* (pp. 176–195). New York: Cambridge University Press.

Loehlin, J. C., Horn, J. M., & Willerman, L. (1997). Heredity, environment, and IQ in the Texas Adoption Project. In R. J. Sternberg & E. L. Grigorenko (Eds.), *Intelligence, heredity, and environment.* New York: Cambridge University Press.

Loewenstein, R. J. (1996). Dissociative amnesia and dissociative fugue. In L. K. Michelson & W. J. Ray (Eds.), *Handbook of dissociation: Theoretical, empirical, and clinical perspectives.* New York: Plenum.

Loftus, E. F. (1979). *Eyewitness testimony.* Cambridge, MA: Harvard University Press.

Loftus, E. F. (1992). When a lie becomes memory's truth: Memory distortion after exposure to misinformation. *Current Directions in Psychological Science, 1,* 121–123.

Loftus, E. F. (1993a). Psychologist in the eyewitness world. *American Psychologist, 48,* 550–552.

Loftus, E. F. (1993b). The reality of repressed memories. *American Psychologist, 48,* 518–537.

Loftus, E. F. (1994). The repressed memory controversy. *American Psychologist, 49,* 443–445.

Loftus, E. F. (1997, September). Creating false memories. *Scientific American,* 71–75.

Loftus, E. F. (1998). Remembering dangerously. In R. A. Baker (Ed.), *Child sexual abuse and false memory syndrome.* Amherst, NY: Prometheus Books.

Loftus, E. F. (2000). Remembering what never happened. In E. Tulving (Ed.), *Memory, consciousness, and the brain: The Tallinn conference* (pp. 106–118). Philadelphia: Psychology Press.

Loftus, E. F., & Ketcham, K. (1994). *The myth of repressed memory: False memories and allegations of sexual abuse.* New York: St. Martin's Press.

Loftus, E. F., & Klinger, M. R. (1992). Is the unconscious smart or dumb? *American Psychologist, 47,* 761–765.

Loftus, E. F., & Mazzoni, G. A. L. (1998). Using imagination and personalized suggestion to change people. *Behavior Therapy, 29,* 691–706.

Loftus, E. F., & Palmer, J. C. (1974). Reconstruction of automobile destruction: An example of the interaction between language and memory. *Journal of Verbal Learning and Verbal Behavior, 13,* 585–589.

Loftus, E. F., Garry, M., & Feldman, J. (1998). Forgetting sexual trauma: What does it mean when 38% forget? In R. A. Baker (Ed.), *Child sexual abuse and false memory syndrome.* Amherst, NY: Prometheus Books.

Logue, A. W. (1991). *The psychology of eating and drinking* (2nd ed.). New York: W. H. Freeman.

Lohman, D. F. (1989). Human intelligence: An introduction to advances in theory and research. *Review of Educational Research, 59*(4), 333–373.

LoLordo, V. M., & Droungas, A. (1989). Selective associations and adaptive specializations: Taste aversions and phobias. In S. B. Klein & R. R. Mower (Eds.), *Contemporary learning theories: Instrumental conditioning theory and the impact of biological constraints on learning.* Hillsdale, NJ: Erlbaum.

Longman, D. G., & Atkinson, R. H. (2002). *College learning and study skills.* Belmont, CA: Wadsworth.

Longo, L. P. (1998). Anxiety: Neurobiologic underpinnings. *Psychiatric Annals, 28,* 130–138.

Loranger, A. W. (1984). Sex difference in age at onset of schizophrenia. *Archives of General Psychiatry, 41,* 157–161.

Lorberbaum, J. P., Bohning, D. E., Shastri, A., Nahas, Z., & George, M. S. (1998). Functional magnetic resonance imaging (fMRI) for the psychiatrist. *Primary Psychiatry, 5,* 60–71.

Lott, B. (1987). *Women's lives.* Pacific Grove, CA: Brooks/Cole.

Lott, B. (2002). Cognitive and behavioral distancing from the poor. *American Psychologist, 57,* 100–110.

Lott, B., & Maluso, D. (1993). The social learning of gender. In A. E. Beall & R. J. Sternberg (Eds.), *The psychology of gender.* New York: Guilford.

Lovallo, W. R., a'Absi, M., Pincomb, G. A., Everson, S. A., Sung, B. E., Passey, R. B., & Wilson, M. F. (1996). Caffeine and behavioral stress effects on blood pressure in borderline hypertensive caucasian men. *Health Psychology, 15,* 11–17.

Lowe, M. R. (2002). Dietary restraint and overeating. In C. G. Fairburn & K. D. Brownell (Eds.), *Eating disorders and obesity: A comprehensive handbook* (pp. 88–92). New York: Guilford.

Lowinson, J. H., Ruiz, P., Millman, R. B., & Langrod, J. G. (Eds.). (1997). *Substance abuse: A comprehensive textbook.* Baltimore: Williams & Wilkins.

Luborsky, L., Singer, B., & Luborsky, L. (1975). Comparative studies of psychotherapies: Is it true that everyone has won and all must have prizes? *Archives of General Psychiatry, 32,* 995–1008.

Luborsky, L., Diguer, L., Seligman, D. A., Rosenthal, R., Krause, E. D., Johnson, S., Halperin, G., Bishop, M., Berman, J. S., & Schweizer, E. (1999). The researcher's own therapy allegiance: A "wild card" in comparisons of treatment efficacy. *Clinical Psychology: Science & Practice, 6*(1), 95–106.

Luborsky, L., Rosenthal, R., Diguer, L., Andrusyna, T. P., Berman, J. S., Levitt, J. T., Seligman, D. A., & Krause, E. D. (2002). The dodo bird verdict is alive and well—mostly. *Clinical Psychology: Science & Practice, 9,* 2–12.

Lucas, A. R., Beard, C. M., O'Fallon, W. M., & Kurland, L. T. (1991). 50-year trends in the incidence of anorexia nervosa in Rochester, Minn.: A population-based study. *American Journal of Psychiatry, 148,* 917–922.

Lucas, R. E., Diener, E., & Suh, E. (1996). Discriminant validity of well-being measures. *Journal of Personality and Social Psychology, 71,* 616–628.

Luchins, A. S. (1942). Mechanization in problem solving. *Psychological Monographs, 54* (6, Whole No. 248).

Ludwig, A. M. (1994). Mental illness and creative activity in female writers. *American Journal of Psychiatry, 151,* 1650–1656.

Ludwig, A. M. (1995). *The price of greatness: Resolving the creativity and madness controversy.* New York: Guilford.

Ludwig, A. M. (1998). Method and madness in the arts and sciences. *Creativity Research Journal, 11,* 93–101.

Ludwig, D. S., Pereira, M. A., Kroenke, C. H., Hilner, J. E., Van Horn, L., Slattery, M. L., & Jacobs, D. R., Jr. (1999). Dietary fiber, weight gain, and cardiovascular disease risk factors in young adults. *Journal of the American Medical Association, 282,* 1539–1546.

Luecke-Aleksa, D., Anderson, D. R., Collins, P. A., & Schmitt, K. L. (1995). Gender constancy and television viewing. *Developmental Psychology, 31,* 773–780.

Luengo, M. A., Otero, J. M., Carillo-de-la-Pena, M. T., & Miron, L. (1994). Dimensions of antisocial behaviour in juvenile delinquency: A study of personality variables. *Psychology, Crime & Law, 1*(1), 27–37.

Lugaresi, E., Cirignotta, F., Montagna, P., & Sforza, E. (1994). Snoring: Pathogenic, clinical, and therapeutic aspects. In M. H. Kryger, T. Roth, & W. C. Dement (Eds.), *Principles and practice of sleep medicine* (2nd ed.). Philadelphia: Saunders.

Luh, C. W. (1922). The conditions of retention. *Psychological Monographs, 31.*

Lundberg, U. (2000). Catecholamines. In G. Fink (Ed.), *Encyclopedia of stress* (Vol. 1, pp. 408–413). San Diego: Academic Press.

Luntz, B. K., & Widom, C. S. (1994). Antisocial personality disorder in abused and neglected children grown up. *Journal of Psychiatry, 151,* 670–674.

Lutsky, N. (1995). When is "obedience" obedience? Conceptual and historical commentary. *Journal of Social Issues, 51,* 55–65.

Lutz, C. (1987). Goals, events and understanding in Ifaluk emotion theory. In N. Quinn & D. Holland (Eds.), *Cultural models in language and thought.* Cambridge, England: Cambridge University Press.

Lutz, D. J., & Sternberg, R. J. (1999). Cognitive development. In M. H. Bornstein & M. E. Lamb (Eds.), *Developmental psychology an advanced textbook.* Mahwah, NJ: Erlbaum.

Lutz, W. (1989). *Doublespeak.* New York: Harper Perennial.

Lye, D. N., & Biblarz, T. J. (1993). The effects of attitudes toward family life and gender roles on marital satisfaction. *Journal of Family Issues, 14,* 157–188.

Lykken, D., & Tellegen, A. (1996). Happiness is a stochastic phenomenon. *Psychological Science, 7,* 186–189.

Lykken, D. T. (1998). *A tremor in the blood: Uses and abuses of the lie detector.* New York: Plenum Press.

Lykken, D. T., McGue, M., Tellegen, A., & Bouchard, T. J., Jr. (1992). Emergenesis: Genetic traits that may not run in families. *American Psychologist, 47,* 1565–1577.

Lynn, M. (1992). Scarcity's enhancement of desirability: The role of naive economic theories. *Basic & Applied Social Psychology, 13,* 67–78.

Lynn, R. (1996). Racial and ethnic differences in intelligence in the U.S. on the Differential Ability Scale. *Personality and Individual Differences, 20,* 271–273.

Lynn, R. (1998). In support of the Nutrition Theory. In U. Neisser (Ed.), *The rising curve: Long-term gains in IQ and related measures.* Washington, DC: American Psychological Association.

Lynn, S. J., & Nash, M. (1994). Truth in memory: Ramifications for psychotherapy and hypnotherapy. *Journal of Clinical Hypnosis, 36,* 194–208.

Lynn, S. J., Kirsch, I., Barabasz, A., Cardena, E., & Patterson, D. (2000). Hypnosis as an empirically supported clinical intervention: The state of the evidence and a look to the future. *International Journal of Clinical & Experimental Hypnosis, 48,* 239–259.

Lynn, S. J., Lock, T. G., Myers, B., & Payne D. G. (1997). Recalling the unrecallable: Should hypnosis be used to recover memories in psychotherapy? *Current Directions in Psychological Science, 6,* 79–83.

Lytton, H., & Romney, D. M. (1991). Parents' differential socialization of boys and girls: A meta-analysis. *Psychological Bulletin, 109,* 267–296.

Lyznicki, J. M., Doege, T. C., Davis, R. M., & Williams, M. A. (1998). Sleepiness, driving, and motor vehicle crashes. *Journal of the American Medical Association, 279,* 1908–1913.

Maas, J. B. (1998). *Power sleep.* New York: Harper Perennial.

Maccoby, E. E. (1990). Gender and relationships: A developmental account. *American Psychologist, 45,* 513–520.

Maccoby, E. E. (1998). *The two sexes: Growing up apart, coming together.* Cambridge, MA: Belknap Press.

Maccoby, E. E. (2000). Parenting and its effects on children: On reading and misreading behavior genetics. *Annual Review of Psychology, 51,* 1–27.

MacCoun, R. J. (1998). Biases in the interpretation and use of research results. *Annual Review Psychology, 49,* 259–287.

MacDonald, K. (1998). Evolution, culture, and the five-factor model. *Journal of Cross-Cultural Psychology, 29,* 119–149.

Machover, K. (1949). *Personality projection in the drawing of the human figure.* Springfield, IL: Charles C Thomas.

Macht, M., & Simons, G. (2000). Emotions and eating in everyday life. *Appetite, 35,* 65–71.

Mack, A., & Rock, I. (1998). *Inattentional blindness.* Cambridge, MA: MIT Press.

Mackie, D. M., Worth, L. T., & Asuncion, A. G. (1990). Processing of persuasive in-group messages. *Journal of Personality and Social Psychology, 58,* 812–822.

MacLean, P. D. (1954). Studies on limbic system ("viosceal brain") and their bearing on psychosomatic problems. In E. D. Wittkower & R. A. Cleghorn (Eds.), *Recent developments in psychosomatic medicine.* Philadelphia: Lippincott.

MacLean, P. D. (1993). Cerebral evolution of emotion. In M. Lewis & J. M. Haviland (Eds.), *Handbook of emotions.* New York: Guilford.

MacMillan, H. L., Fleming, J. E., Streiner, D. L., Lin, E., Boyle, M. H., Jamieson, E., Duku, E. K., Walsh, C. A., Wong, M. Y. Y., & Beardslee, W. R. (2001). Childhood abuse and lifetime psychopathology in a community sample. *American Journal of Psychiatry, 158,* 1878–1883.

MacMillan, H. L., Fleming, J. E., Trocme, N., Boyle, M. H., Wong, M., Racine, Y. A., Beardslee, W. R., & Offord, D. R. (1997). Prevalence of child physical and sexual abuse in the community: Results from the Ontario health supplement. *Journal of the American Medical Association, 278,* 131–135.

Macmillan, M. (1991). *Freud evaluated: The completed arc.* Amsterdam: North-Holland.

MacQueen, G., Marshall, J., Perdue, M., Siegel, S., & Bienenstock, J. (1989). Pavlovian conditioning of rat mucosal mast cells to secrete rat mast cell protease II. *Science, 243,* 83–86.

Macrae, C. N., & Bodenhausen, G. V. (2000). Social cognition: Thinking categorically about others. *Annual Review of Psychology, 51,* 93–120.

MacWhinney, B. (1998). Models of the emergence of language. *Annual Review of Psychology, 49,* 199–227.

MacWhinney, B. (1999). The emergence of language from embodiment. In B. MacWhinney (Ed.), *The emergence of language* (pp. 213–256). Mahwah, NJ: Erlbaum.

Maddi, S. R. (1989). *Personality theories: A comparative analysis.* Chicago, IL: Dorsey Press.

Madon, S., Guyll, M., Aboufadel, K., Montiel, E., Smith, A., Palumbo, P., & Jussim, L. (2001). Ethnic and national stereotypes: The Princeton trilogy revisited and revised. *Personality and Social Psychology Bulletin, 27,* 996–1010.

Madsen, K. B. (1968). *Theories of motivation.* Copenhagen: Munksgaard.

Madsen, K. B. (1973). Theories of motivation. In B. B. Wolman (Ed.), *Handbook of general psychology.* Englewood Cliffs, NJ: Prentice-Hall.

Magnusson, D., & Stattin, H. (1998). Person-context interaction theories. In W. Damon (Ed.), *Handbook of child psychology (Vol. 1): Theoretical models of human development.* New York: Wiley.

Maguire, W., Weisstein, N., & Klymenko, V. (1990). From visual structure to perceptual function. In K. N. Leibovic (Ed.), *Science of vision.* New York: Springer-Verlag.

Maher, B. A. (2001). Delusions. In P. B. Sutker & H. E. Adams (Eds.), *Comprehensive handbook of psychopathology* (3rd ed., pp. 309–370). New York: Kluwer Academic/Plenum Publishers.

Mahowald, M. W. (1993). Sleepwalking. In M. A. Carskadon (Ed.), *Encyclopedia of sleep and dreaming.* New York: Macmillan.

Maier, N. R. F. (1931). Reasoning and learning. *Psychological Review, 38,* 332–346.

Main, D. M., & Main, E. K. (1991). Preterm birth. In S. G. Gabbe, J. R. Niebyl, & J. L. Simpson (Eds.), *Obstetrics: Normal and problem pregnancies.* New York: Churchill Livingstone.

Main, T. (1998). How to think about homelessness: Balancing structural and individual causes. *Journal of Social Distress & the Homeless, 7,* 41–54.

Maj, M., Pirozzi, R., Magliano, L., & Bartoli, L. (1998). Long-term outcome of lithium prophylaxis in bipolar disorder: A 5-year prospective study on 402 patients at a lithium clinic. *American Journal of Psychiatry, 155,* 30–35.

Malamuth, N. M. (1996). Sexually explicit media, gender differences, and evolutionary theory. *Journal of Communication, 46,* 8–31.

Malamuth, N. M., Addison, T., & Koss, M. (2000). Pornography and sexual aggression: Are there reliable effects and can we understand them?

Annual Review of Sex Research, 11, 26–91.

Malcolm, J. (1980: Pt. 1, Nov. 24; Pt. 2, Dec. 1). The impossible profession. *The New Yorker,* pp. 55–133, 54–152.

Malhotra, A. K., & Goldman, D. (1999). Benefits and pitfalls encountered in psychiatric genetic association studies. *Biological Psychiatry, 45,* 541–550.

Malina, R. M. (1990). Physical growth and performance during the transitional years (9–16). In G. R. Adams & T. P. Gullota (Eds.), *From childhood to adolescence: A transitional period?* Newbury Park, CA: Sage.

Malle, B. F., & Knobe, J. (1997). Which behaviors do people explain? A basic actor-observer asymmetry. *Journal of Personality and Social Psychology, 72,* 288–304.

Malloy, M. H., Kao, T., & Lee, Y. J. (1992). Analyzing the effect of prenatal care on pregnancy outcome: A conditional approach. *American Journal of Public Health, 82,* 448–453.

Maltzman, I. (1994). Why alcoholism is a disease. *Journal of Psychoactive Drugs, 26,* 13–31.

Mandler, G. (1984). *Mind and body.* New York: Norton.

Mandler, G. (1989). Memory: Conscious and unconscious. In P. R. Soloman, G. R. Goethals, C. M. Kelley, & B. R. Stephens (Eds.), *Memory: Interdisciplinary approaches.* New York: Springer-Verlag.

Mandler, G. (1993). Thought, memory, and learning: Effects of emotional stress. In L. Goldberger & S. Breznitz (Eds.), *Handbook of stress: Theoretical and clinical aspects* (2nd ed.). New York: Free Press.

Mangelsdorf, S., Gunnar, M., Kestenbaum, R., Lang, S., & Andreas, D. (1990). Infant proneness-to-distress temperament, maternal personality, and mother-infant attachment: Associations and goodness of fit. *Child Development, 61,* 830–831.

Manson, J. E., Skerrett, P. J., & Willett, W. C. (2002). Epidemiology of health risks associated with obesity. In C. G. Fairburn & K. D. Brownell (Eds.), *Eating disorders and obesity: A comprehensive handbook* (pp. 422–428). New York: Guilford.

Marangell, L. B., Silver, J. M., & Yudofsky, S. C. (1999). Psychopharmocology and electroconvulsive therapy. In R. E. Hales, S. C. Yudofsky, & J. A. Talbott (Eds.), *American Psychiatric Press textbook of psychiatry.* Washington, DC: American Psychiatric Press.

Maratsos, M. (1983). Some current issues in the study of the acquisition of grammar. In J. H. Flavell & E. M.

Markman (Eds.), *Handbook of child psychology* (Vol. 3). New York: Wiley.

Marcel, A. (1983). Conscious and unconscious perception: Experiments on visual masking and word recognition. *Cognitive Psychology, 15,* 197–237.

Marcelino, A. S., Adam, A. S., Couronne, T., Koester, E. P., & Sieffermann, J. M. (2001). Internal and external determinants of eating initiation in humans. *Appetite, 36,* 9–14.

Marcenes, W. G., & Sheiham, A. (1992). The relationship between work stress and oral health status. *Social Science and Medicine, 35,* 1511.

Marcia, J. E. (1966). Development and validation of ego identity status. *Journal of Personality and Social Psychology, 3,* 551–558.

Marcia, J. E. (1980). Identity in adolescence. In J. Adelson (Ed.), *Handbook of adolescent psychology.* New York: Wiley.

Marcia, J. E. (1994). The empirical study of ego identity. In H. A. Bosma, T. L. G. Graafsma, H. D. Grotevant, & D. J. de Levita (Eds.), *Identity and development: An interdisciplinary approach.* Thousand Oaks, CA: Sage.

Marcia, J. E., Waterman, A. S., Matteson, D. R., Archer, S. L., & Orlofsky, J. L. (1993). *Ego identity: A handbook for psychosocial research.* New York: Springer-Verlag.

Marcus, B. H., Bock, B. C., & Pinto, B. M. (1997). Initiation and maintenance of exercise behavior. In D. S. Gochman (Ed.), *Handbook of health behavior research II: Provider determinants.* New York: Plenum.

Marcus, G. F. (1996). Why do children say "breaked"? *Current Directions in Psychological Science, 5,* 81–85.

Marcus-Newhall, A., Pedersen, W. C., Carlson, M., & Miller, N. (2000). Displaced aggression is alive and well: A meta-analytic review. *Journal of Personality and Social Psychology, 78,* 670–689.

Marder, S. R. (2000). Schizophrenia: Somatic treatment. In B. J. Sadock & V. A. Sadock (Eds.), *Kaplan and Sadock's comprehensive textbook of psychiatry* (7th ed., Vol. 1, pp. 1199–1209). Philadelphia: Lippincott/ Williams & Wilkins.

Marder, S. R., & van Kammen, D. P. (2000). Dopamine receptor antagonists (typical antipsychotics). In B. J. Sadock & V. A. Sadock (Eds.), *Kaplan and Sadock's comprehensive textbook of psychiatry* (7th ed., Vol. 1, pp. 2356–2376). Philadelphia: Lippincott/ Williams & Wilkins.

Maris, R. W., Berman, A. L., & Silverman, M. M. (2000). *Comprehensive textbook of suicidology.* New York: Guilford.

Mark, V. (1996). Conflicting communicative behavior in a split-brain patient: Support for dual consciousness. In S. R. Hameroff, A. W. Kaszniak, & A. C. Scott (Eds.), *Toward a science of consciousness. The first Tucson discussions and debates.* Cambridge, MA: MIT Press.

Markowitsch, H. J. (2000). Neuroanatomy of memory. In E. Tulving & F. I. M. Craik (Eds.), *The Oxford handbook of memory* (pp. 465–484). New York: Oxford University Press.

Markus, H. R., & Kitayama, S. (1991). Culture and the self: Implications for cognition, emotion, and motivation. *Psychological Review, 98,* 224–253.

Markus, H. R., & Kitayama, S. (1994). The cultural construction of self and emotion: Implications for social behavior. In S. Kitayama & H. R. Markus (Eds.), *Emotions and culture: Empirical studies of mutual influence.* Washington, DC: American Psychological Association.

Markus, H. R., & Kitayama, S. (1998). The cultural psychology of personality. *Journal of Cross-Cultural Psychology, 29,* 63–87.

Markus, H. R., Kitayama, S., & Heiman, R. J. (1996). Culture and "basic" psychological principles. In E. T. Higgins, & A. W. Kruglanski (Eds.), *Social Psychology: Handbook of basic principles.* New York: Guilford.

Marschark, M. (1992). Coding processes: Imagery. In L. R. Squire (Ed.), *Encyclopedia of learning and memory.* New York: Macmillan.

Martin, C. L., & Fabes, R. A. (2001). The stability and consequences of young children's same-sex peer interactions. *Developmental Psychology, 37,* 431–446.

Martin, J. H. (1991). The collective electrical behavior of cortical neurons: The electroencephalogram and the mechanisms of epilepsy. In E. R. Kandel, J. H. Schwartz, & T. M. Jessell (Eds.), *Principles of neural science* (3rd ed.). New York: Elsevier.

Martin, L. (1986). "Eskimo words for snow": A case study in the genesis and decay of an anthropological example. *American Psychologist, 88,* 418–423.

Martin, R. L., & Yutzy, S. H. (1999). Somatoform disorders. In R. E. Hales, S. C. Yudofsky, & J. A. Talbott (Eds.), *American Psychiatric Press Textbook of Psychiatry.* Washington, DC: American Psychiatric Press.

Martinez, J. L., Jr., Barea-Rodriguez, E. J., & Derrick, B. E. (1998). Long-term potentiation, long-term depression, and learning. In J. L. Martinez, Jr., & R. P. Kesner (Eds.), *Neurobiology of learning and memory.* San Diego: Academic Press.

Martocchio, J. J., & Baldwin, T. T. (1997). The evolution of strategic organizational training: New objectives and research agenda. In G. R. Ferris (Ed.), *Research in personnel and human resources management* (Vol. 11, pp. 259–329). Greenwich, CT: JAI Press.

Maslach, C., & Leiter, M. P. (1997). *The truth about burnout.* San Francisco: Jossey-Bass.

Maslach, C., & Leiter, M. P. (2000). Burnout. In G. Fink (Ed.), *Encyclopedia of stress* (Vol. 1, pp. 358–362). San Diego: Academic Press.

Maslow, A. H. (1954). *Motivation and personality.* New York: Harper & Row.

Maslow, A. H. (1968). *Toward a psychology of being.* New York: Van Nostrand.

Maslow, A. H. (1970). *Motivation and personality.* New York: Harper & Row.

Massaro, D. W., & Loftus, G. R. (1996). Sensory and perceptual storage: Data and theory. In E. L. Bjork & R. A. Bjork (Eds.), *Memory.* San Diego: Academic Press.

Masters, R. D. (1995). Mechanism and function in evolutionary psychology: Emotion, cognitive neuroscience, and personality. *Psychological Inquiry, 6,* 65–68.

Masters, W. H., & Johnson, V. E. (1966). *Human sexual response.* Boston: Little, Brown.

Masters, W. H., & Johnson, V. E. (1970). *Human sexual inadequacy.* Boston: Little, Brown.

Masuda, T., & Nisbett, R. E. (2001). Attending holistically versus analytically: Comparing the context sensitivity of Japanese and Americans. *Journal of Personality and Social Psychology, 81,* 922–934.

Matlin, M. W. (1989). *Cognition.* New York: Holt, Rinehart & Winston.

Matsumoto, D. (1994). *People: Psychology from a cultural perspective.* Pacific Grove, CA: Brooks/Cole.

Matsumoto, D. (2001). Culture and emotion. In D. Matsumoto (Ed.), *The handbook of culture and psychology* (pp. 171–194). New York: Oxford University Press.

Matthey, S. (1998). P<.05—But is it clinically *significant*?: Practical examples for clinicians. *Behaviour Change, 15,* 140–146.

Mattia, J. I., & Zimmerman, M. (2001). Epidemiology. In W. J. Livesley (Ed.), *Handbook of personality disorders: Theory, research, and treatment.* New York: Guilford.

Matute, H., & Miller, R. R. (1998). Detecting causal relations. In W. O'Donohue (Ed.), *Learning and behavior therapy.* Boston, Allyn & Bacon.

Mauro, R., Sato, K., & Tucker, J. (1992). The role of appraisal in human emotions: A cross-cultural study. *Journal of Personality and Social Psychology, 62,* 301–317.

Mayer, J. (1955). Regulation of energy intake and the body weight: The glucostatic theory and the lipostatic hypothesis. *Annals of the New York Academy of Science, 63,* 15–43.

Mayer, J. (1968). *Overweight: Causes and control.* Englewood Cliffs, NJ: Prentice-Hall.

Mayer, J. D., & Salovey, P. (1997). What is emotional intelligence? In P. Salovey & D. Sluyter (Eds.), *Emotional development and emotional intelligence: Educational implications.* New York: Basic Books.

Mayer, J. D., Caruso, D. R., & Salovey, P. (1999). Emotional intelligence meets traditional standards for an intelligence. *Intelligence, 27,* 267–298.

Mayer, J. D., Salovey, P., & Caruso, D. (2000). Models of emotional intelligence. In R. J. Sternberg (Ed.), *Handbook of intelligence* (pp. 396–420). New York: Cambridge University Press.

Mayer, J. D., Perkins, D. M., Caruso, D. R., & Salovey, P. (2001). Emotional intelligence and giftedness. *Roeper Review, 23,* 131–137.

Mayer, R. E. (1995). The search for insight: Grappling with Gestalt psychology's unanswered questions. In R. J. Sternberg, & J. E. Davidson (Eds.), *The nature of insight.* Cambridge, MA: The MIT Press.

Mays, V. M., & Albee, G. W. (1992). Psychotherapy and ethnic minorities. In D. K. Freedheim (Ed.), *History of psychotherapy: A century of change.* Washington, DC: American Psychological Association.

Mays, V. M., Rubin, J., Sabourin, M., & Walker, L. (1996). Moving toward a global psychology: Changing theories and practice to meet the needs of a changing world. *American Psychologist, 51,* 485–487.

Mazur, J. E. (1993). Predicting the strength of a conditioned reinforcer: Effects of delay and uncertainty. *Current Directions in Psychological Science, 2*(3), 70–74.

McAdams, D. P. (1992). The five-factor model in personality: A critical appraisal. *Journal of Personality, 60,* 329–361.

McAdams, D. P., & Constantian, C. A. (1983). Intimacy and affiliation motives in daily living: An experience sampling analysis. *Journal of Personality and Social Psychology, 45,* 851–861.

McAdams, D. P., de St. Aubin, E., & Logan, R. (1993). Generativity in young, midlife, and older adults. *Psychology and Aging, 8,* 221–230.

McAllister, L. E., & Boyle, J. S. (1998). Without money, means, or men: African American women receiving prenatal care in a housing project. *Family & Community Health, 21,* 67–79.

McAllister, W. R., & McAllister, D. E. (1995). Two-factor fear theory: Implications from understanding anxiety-based clinical phenomena. In W. O'Donohue & L. Krasner (Eds.), *Theories of behavior therapy: Exploring behavior change.* Washington, DC: American Psychological Association.

McBride-Chang, C., & Jacklin, C. N. (1993). Early play arousal, sex-typed play, and activity level as precursors to later rough-and-tumble play. *Early Education & Development, 4,* 99–108.

McBurney, D. H. (1996). How to think like a psychologist: Critical thinking in psychology. Upper Saddle River, NJ: Prentice-Hall.

McCann, T. S. (1981). Aggression and sexual activity of male southern elephant seals, *Mirounga leonina. Journal of Zoology, 195,* 295–310.

McCarley, R. W. (1994). Dreams and the biology of sleep. In M. H. Kryger, T. Roth, & W. C. Dement (Eds.), *Principles and practice of sleep medicine* (2nd ed.). Philadelphia: Saunders.

McCarley, R. W., Wible, C. G., Frumin, M., Hirayasu, Y., Levitt, J. J., Fischer, I. A., & Shenton, M. E. (1999). MRI anatomy of schizophrenia. *Biological Psychiatry, 45,* 1099–1119.

McCartt, A. T., Ribner, S. A., Pack, A. I., & Hammer, M. C. (1996). The scope and nature of the drowsy driving problem in New York State. *Accident Analysis and Prevention, 28,* 511–517.

McCarty, D., Argeriou, M., Huebner, R. B., & Lubran, B. (1991). Alcoholism, drug abuse, and the homeless. *American Psychologist, 46,* 1139–1148.

McCauley, M. E., Eskes, G., & Moscovitch, M. (1996). The effect of imagery on explicit and implicit tests of memory in young and old people: A double dissociation. *Canadian Journal of Experimental Psychology, 50,* 34–41.

McClelland, D. C. (1961). *The achieving society.* Princeton, NJ: Van Nostrand.

McClelland, D. C. (1975). *Power: The inner experience.* New York: Irvington.

McClelland, D. C. (1985). How motives, skills and values determine what people do. *American Psychologist, 40,* 812–825.

McClelland, D. C. (1987). Characteristics of successful entrepreneurs. *Journal of Creative Behavior, 3,* 219–233.

McClelland, D. C. (1993). Intelligence is not the best predictor of job performance. *Current Directions in Psychological Science, 2*(1), 5–6.

McClelland, D. C., & Boyatzis, R. E. (1982). The leadership motive pattern and long-term success in management. *Journal of Applied Psychology, 67,* 737–743.

McClelland, D. C., & Koestner, R. (1992). The achievement motive. In C. P. Smith (Ed.), *Motivation and personality: Handbook of thematic content analysis.* New York: Cambridge University Press.

McClelland, D. C., & Winter, D. G. (1969). *Motivating economic achievement.* New York: Free Press.

McClelland, D. C., Atkinson, J. W., Clark, R. A., & Lowell, E. L. (1953). *The achievement motive.* New York: Appleton-Century-Crofts.

McClelland, D. C., Koestner, R., & Weinberger, J. (1992). How do self-attributed and implicit motives differ? In C. P. Smith (Ed.), *Motivation and personality: Handbook of thematic content analysis.* New York: Cambridge University Press.

McClelland, J. L. (1992). Parallel-distributed processing models of memory. In L. R. Squire (Ed.), *Encyclopedia of learning and memory.* New York: Macmillan.

McClelland, J. L. (2000). Connectionist models of memory. In E. Tulving & F. I. M. Craik (Eds.), *The Oxford handbook of memory* (pp. 583–596). New York: Oxford University Press.

McClelland, J. L., & Rumelhart, D. E. (1985). Distributed memory and the representation of general and specific information. *Journal of Experimental Psychology: General, 114,* 159–188.

McCloskey, M. (1992). Special versus ordinary memory mechanisms in the genesis of flashbulb memories. In E. Winograd & U. Neisser (Eds.), *Affect and accuracy in recall: Studies of "flashbulb" memories.* New York: Cambridge University Press.

McClure, E. B. (2000). A meta-analytic review of sex differences in facial expression processing and their development in infants, children, and adolescents. *Psychological Bulletin, 126,* 424–453.

McConkey, K. M. (1992). The effects of hypnotic procedures on remembering: The experimental findings and their implications for forensic hypnosis. In E. Fromm & M. R. Nash (Eds.), *Contemporary hypnosis research.* New York: Guilford.

McConkey, K. M., Barnier, A. J., & Sheehan, P. W. (1998). Hypnosis and pseudomemory: Understanding the findings and their implications. In S. J. Lynn & K. M. McConkey (Eds.), *Truth in memory.* New York: Guilford.

McConnell, A. R., Leibold, J. M., & Sherman, S. J. (1997). Within-target illusory correlations and the formation of context-dependent attitudes. *Journal of Personality and Social Psychology, 73,* 675–686.

McConnell, J. V., Cutler, R. L., & McNeil, E. B. (1958). Subliminal stimulation: An overview. *American Psychologist, 13,* 229–242.

McConnell, J. V. (1962). Memory transfer through cannibalism in planarians. *Journal of Neuropsychiatry, 3*(Suppl. 1), 542–548.

McCoul, M. D., & Haslam, N. (2001). Predicting high-risk sexual behaviour in heterosexual and homosexual men: The roles of impulsivity and sensation seeking. *Personality & Individual Differences, 31,* 1303–1310.

McCrae, R. R. (1984). Situational determinants of coping responses: Loss, threat and challenge. *Journal of Personality and Social Psychology, 46,* 919–928.

McCrae, R. R. (1996). Social consequences of experimental openness. *Psychological Bulletin, 120,* 323–337.

McCrae, R. R. (2001). Trait psychology and culture: Exploring intercultural comparisons. *Journal of Personality, 69,* 819–846.

McCrae, R. R., & Costa, P. T., Jr. (1984). *Emerging lives, enduring dispositions: Personality in adulthood.* Boston: Little, Brown.

McCrae, R. R., & Costa., P. T., Jr. (1985). Updating Norman's "adequate taxonomy": Intelligence and personality dimensions in natural language and in questionnaires. *Journal of Personality and Social Psychology, 49,* 710–721.

McCrae, R. R., & Costa, P. T., Jr. (1987). Validation of the five-factor model of personality across instruments and observers. *Journal of Personality and Social Psychology, 52,* 81–90.

McCrae, R. R., & Costa, P. T., Jr. (1990). *Personality in adulthood.* New York: Guilford.

McCrae, R. R., & Costa, P. T., Jr. (1997). Personality trait structure as a human universal. *American Psychologist, 52,* 509–516.

McCrae, R. R., & Costa, P. T., Jr. (1999). A five-factor theory of personality. In L. A. Pervin & O. P. John (Eds.), *Handbook of personality: Theory and research.* New York: Guilford.

McCullough, M. E. (2001). Forgiving. In C. R. Snyder (Ed.), *Coping with stress: Effective people and processes* (pp. 93–113). New York: Oxford University Press.

McCullough, M. E., Bellah, C. G., Kilpatrick, S. D., & Johnson, J. L. (2001). Vengefulness: Relationships with forgiveness, rumination, well-being, and the Big Five. *Personality and Social Psychology Bulletin, 27,* 601–610.

McDaniel, M. A., & Einstein, G. O. (1986). Bizarre imagery as an effective memory aid: The importance of distinctiveness. *Journal of Experimental Psychology: Learning, Memory & Cognition, 12,* 54–65.

McDaniel, M. A., Waddill, P. J., & Shakesby, P. S. (1996). Study strategies, interest, and learning from text: The application of material appropriate processing. In D. J. Herrmann, C. McEvoy, C. Hertzog, P. Hertel, & M. K. Johnson (Eds.), *Basic and applied memory research: Theory in context* (Vol. 1). Mahwah, NJ: Erlbaum.

McElroy, S. L., Pope, H. G., & Keck, P. E. (2001). Valproate. In B. J. Sadock & V. A. Sadock (Eds.), *Kaplan and Sadock's comprehensive textbook of psychiatry* (7th ed., Vol. 2). Philadelphia: Lippincott/Williams & Wilkins.

McGaugh, J. L. (1992). Hormones and memory. In L. R. Squire (Ed.), *Encyclopedia of learning and memory.* New York: Macmillan.

McGaugh, J. L. (1995). Emotional activation, neuromodulatory systems, and memory. In D. L. Schacter, J. T. Coyle, G. D. Fischbach, M. Mesulam, & L. E. Sullivan (Eds.), *Memory distortion.* Cambridge, MA: Harvard University Press.

McGaugh, J. L. (2000). Memory: A century of consolidation. *Science, 287,* 248–251.

McGaugh, J. L., Cahill, L., & Roozendaal, B. (1996). Involvement of the amygdala in memory storage—Interaction with other brain systems. *Proceedings of the National Academy of Sciences of the United States of America, 93,* 13508–13514.

McGaugh, J. L., Roozendaal, B., & Cahill, L. (2000). Modulation of memory storage by stress hormones and the amygdaloid complex. In M. S. Gazzaniga (Ed.), *The new cognitive neurosciences* (2nd ed., pp. 1081–1098). Cambridge, MA: MIT Press.

McGeoch, J. A., & McDonald, W. T. (1931). Meaningful relation and retroactive inhibition. *American Journal of Psychology, 43,* 579–588.

McGinty, D. (1993). Thermoregulation. In M. A. Carskadon (Ed.), *Encyclopedia of sleep and dreaming.* New York: Macmillan.

McGlashan, T. H., & Fenton, W. S. (1992). The positive-negative distinction in schizophrenia: Review of natural history validators. *Archives of General Psychiatry, 49,* 63–72.

McGlashan, T. H., & Hoffman, R. E. (2000). Schizophrenia: Psychodynamic to neurodynamic theories. In B. J. Sadock & V. A. Sadock (Eds.), *Kaplan and Sadock's comprehensive textbook of psychiatry* (7th ed., Vol. 1, pp. 1159–1168). Philadelphia: Lippincott/Williams & Wilkins.

McGrew, J. H., Wright, E. R., Pescosolido, B. A., & McDonel, E. C. (1999). The closing of Central State Hospital: Long-term outcomes for persons with severe mental illness. *Journal of Behavioral Health Services & Research, 26,* 246–261.

McGue, M., Bouchard, T. J., Jr., Iacono, W. G., & Lykken, D. T. (1993). Behavioral genetics of cognitive ability: A life-span perspective. In R. Plomin & G. E. McClearn (Eds.), *Nature, nurture and psychology.* Washington, DC: American Psychological Association.

McGuire, W. J. (1985). Attitudes and attitude change. In G. Lindzey & E. Aronson (Eds.), *Handbook of social psychology* (Vol. 2). New York: Random House.

McHale, S. M., Bartko, W. T., Crouter, A. C., & Perry-Jenkins, M. (1990). Children's housework and psychosocial functioning: The mediating effects of parents' sex-role behaviors and attitudes. *Child Development, 61,* 1413–1426.

McHugh, P. R. (1995). Dissociative identity disorder as a socially constructed artifact. *Journal of Practical Psychiatry and Behavioral Health, 1,* 158–166.

McKean, K. (1985, June). Decisions, decisions. *Discover,* pp. 22–31.

McKenna, J. J. (1993). Co-sleeping. In M. A. Carskadon (Ed.), *Encyclopedia of sleep and dreaming.* New York: Macmillan.

McKenna, K. Y. A., & Bargh, J. A. (1998). Coming out in the age of the Internet: Identity "demarginalization" through virtual group participation. *Journal of Personality and Social Psychology, 75,* 681–694.

McLean, D. E., & Link, B. G. (1994). Unraveling complexity: Strategies to refine concepts, measures, and research designs in the study of life events and mental health. In W. R. Avison & I. H. Gotlib (Eds.), *Stress and mental health: Contemporary issues and prospects for the future.* New York: Plenum.

McLellan, A. T., Lewis, D. C., O'Brien, C. P., & Kleber, H. D. (2000). Drug dependence, a chronic mental illness: Implications for treatment, insurance, and outcome evaluation. *Journal of the American Medical Association, 284,* 1689–1695.

McLoyd, V. C. (1998). Socioeconomic disadvantage and child development. *American Psychologist, 53,* 185–204.

McNally, R. J. (1994). Cognitive bias in panic disorder. *Current Directions in Psychological Science, 3,* 129–132.

McNally, R. J. (1996). *Panic disorder: A critical analysis.* New York: Guilford.

McNally, R. J. (1999). Posttraumatic stress disorder. In T. Millon, P. H. Blaney, & R. D. Davis (Eds.), *Oxford textbook of psychopathology* (pp. 144–165). New York: Oxford University Press.

McNeil, D. E., & Binder, R. L. (1995). Correlates of accuracy in the assessment of psychiatric inpatients' risk of violence. *American Journal of Psychiatry, 152,* 901–906.

McNeil, T. F., Cantor-Graae, E., & Ismail, B. (2000). Obstetrics complications and congenital malformation in schizophrenia. *Brain Research Reviews, 31,* 166–178.

McNeill, D. (1970). *The acquisition of language: The study of developmental psycholinguistics.* New York: Harper & Row.

Mebert, C. J. (1991). Dimensions of subjectivity in parents' ratings of infant temperament. *Child Development, 62,* 352–361.

Mechanic, D. (1980). *Mental health and social policy.* Englewood Cliffs, NJ: Prentice-Hall.

Mechanic, D. (1999). Mental health and mental illness. In A. V. Horvitz & T. L. Scheid (Eds.), *A handbook for the study of mental health: Social contexts, theories, and systems.* New York: Cambridge University Press.

Mednick, S. A., & Mednick, M. T. (1967). *Examiner's manual, Remote Associates Test.* Boston: Houghton Mifflin.

Mednick, S. A., Machon, R. A., Huttunen, M. O., & Bonett, D. (1988). Adult schizophrenia following prenatal exposure to an influenza epidemic. *Archives of General Psychiatry, 45,* 189–192.

Mednick, S. A., Watson, J. B., Huttunen, M., Cannon, T. D., Katila, H., Machon, R., Mednick, B., Hollister, M., Parnas, J., Schulsinger, F., Sajaniemi, N., Voldsgaard, P., Pyhala, R., Gutkind, D., & Wang, X. (1998). A two-hit working model of the etiology of schizophrenia. In M. F. Lenzenweger & R. H. Dworkin (Eds.), *Origins and development of schizophrenia: Advances in experimental psychopathology.* Washington DC: American Psychological Association.

Medora, N. P., Larson, J. H., Hortacsu, N., & Dave, P. (2002). Perceived attitudes towards romanticism: A cross-cultural study of American, Asian-Indian, and Turkish young adults. *Journal of Comparative Family Studies, 33,* 155–178.

Meeus, W. (1996). Studies on identity development in adolescence: An overview of research and some new data. *Journal of Youth & Adolescence, 25,* 569–598.

Meeus, W., Iedema, J., Helsen, M., & Vollebergh, W. (1999). Patterns of adolescent identity development: Review of literature and longitudinal analysis. *Developmental Review, 19,* 419–461.

Mega, M. S., Cummings, J. L., Salloway, S., & Malloy, P. (1997). The limbic system: An anatomic, phylogenetic, and clinical perspective. *Journal of Neuropsychiatry & Clinical Neurosciences, 9,* 315–330.

Meilman, P. W. (1979). Cross-sectional age changes in ego identity status during adolescence. *Developmental Psychology, 15,* 230–231.

Meiser, T., & Klauer, K. C. (1999). Working memory and changing-state hypothesis. *Journal of Experimental Psychology: Learning, Memory, & Cognition, 25,* 1272–1299.

Mellers, B., Hertwig, R., & Kahneman, D. (2001). Do frequency representations eliminate conjunction effects? An exercise in adversarial collaboration. *Psychological Science, 12,* 269–275.

Mellers, B. A., Schwartz, A. & Cooke, A. D. J. (1998). Judgment and decision making. *Annual Review of Psychology, 49,* 447–477.

Mellers, B. A., Schwartz, A., Ho, K., & Ritov, I. (1997). Decision affect theory: Emotional reactions to the outcomes of risky options. *Psychological Science, 8,* 423–429.

Meltzer, H. Y., Davidson, M., Glassman, A. H., & Vieweg, V. R. (2002). Assessing cardiovascular risks versus clinical benefits of atypical antipsychotic drug treatment. *Journal of Clinical Psychiatry, 63*(9), 25–29.

Meltzoff, A. N., & Gopnik, A. (1989). On linking nonverbal imitation, representation, and language learning in the first two years of life. In G. E. Speidel & K. E. Nelson (Eds.), *The many faces of imitation in language learning.* New York: Springer-Verlag.

Melzack, R., & Wall, P. D. (1965). Pain mechanisms: A new theory. *Science, 150,* 971–979.

Melzack, R., & Wall, P. D. (1982). *The challenge of pain.* New York: Basic Books.

Mendelson, W. B. (2000). Hypnotics: Basic mechanisms and pharmacology. In M. H. Kryger, T. Roth & W. C. Dement (Eds.), *Principles and practice of sleep medicine.* Philadelphia: Saunders.

Mendelson, W. B. (2001). Neurotransmitters and sleep. *Journal of Clinical Psychiatry, 62*(suppl 10), 5–8.

Mennella, J. A., & Beauchamp, G. K. (1996). The early development of human flavor preferences. In E. D. Capaldi (Ed.), *Why we eat what we eat: The psychology of eating* (pp. 83–112). Washington, DC: American Psychological Association.

Mentzer, R. L. (1982). Response biases in multiple-choice test item files. *Educational and Psychological Measurement, 42,* 437–448.

Menyuk, P., Liebergott, J. W., & Schultz, M. C. (1995). *Early language development in full-term and premature infants.* Hillsdale, NJ: Erlbaum.

Merikle, P. M., & Daneman, M. (1998). Psychological investigations of unconscious perception. *Journal of Consciousness Studies, 5,* 5–18.

Mervis, C. B., & Bertrand, J. (1994). Acquisition of the novel name-nameless category principle. *Child Development, 65,* 1646–1662.

Mesquita, B. (2001). Culture and emotion: Different approaches to the question. In T. J. Mayne & G. A. Bonanno (Eds.), *Emotions: Current issues and future directions.* New York: Guilford.

Mesquita, B., & Frijda, N. H. (1992). Cultural variations in emotions: A review. *Psychological Bulletin, 112,* 179–204.

Messerli, F. H., Schmieder, R. E., & Weir, M. R. (1997). Salt: A perpetrator of hypertensive target organ disease? *Archive of Internal Medicine, 157,* 2449–2452.

Metzger, E. D. (1999). Electroconvulsive therapy. In A. M. Nicholi (Ed.), *The Harvard guide to psychiatry.* Cambridge, MA: Harvard University Press.

Meyer, D. E., & Schvaneveldt, R. W. (1976). Meaning, memory structure, and mental processes. *Science, 192,* 27–33.

Meyer, R. E. (1996). The disease called addiction: Emerging evidence in a 200-year debate. *The Lancet, 347,* 162–166.

Meyer, R. G. (1992). *Practical clinical hypnosis: Techniques and applications.* New York: Lexington Books.

Meyer-Bahlburg, H. F. L., Ehrhardt, A. A., Rosen, L. R., Gruen, R. S., Veridiano, N. P., Vann, F. H., & Neuwalder, H. F. (1995). Prenatal estrogens and the development of homosexual orientation. *Developmental Psychology, 31,* 12–21.

Michaels, S. (1996). The prevalence of homosexuality in the United States. In R. P. Cabaj & T. S. Stein (Eds.), *Textbook of homosexuality and mental health.* Washington, DC: American Psychiatric Press.

Mickelson, K. D., Kessler, R. C., & Shaver, P. R. (1997). Adult attachment in a nationally representative sample. *Journal of Personality and Social Psychology, 73,* 1092–1106.

Mignot, E. (2000). Pathophysiology of narcolepsy. In M. H. Kryger, T. Roth, & W. C. Dement (Eds.), *Principles and practice of sleep medicine.* Philadelphia: Saunders.

Milar, K. S. (2000). The first generation of women psychologists and the psychology of women. *American Psychologist, 55,* 616–619.

Milberger, S., Biederman, J., Faraone, S. V., & Jones, J. (1998). Further evidence of an association between maternal smoking during pregnancy and attention-deficit hyperactivity disorder: Findings from a high-risk sample of siblings. *Journal of Clinical Child Psychology, 27,* 352–358.

Milgram, S. (1963). Behavioral study of obedience. *Journal of Abnormal and Social Psychology, 67,* 371–378.

Milgram, S. (1964). Issues in the study of obedience. *American Psychologist, 19,* 848–852.

Milgram, S. (1968). Reply to the critics. *International Journal of Psychiatry, 6,* 294–295.

Milgram, S. (1974). *Obedience to authority.* New York: Harper & Row.

Millburn, M. A., Mather, R., & Conrad, S. D. (2000). The effects of viewing R-rated movie scenes that objectify women on perceptions of date rape. *Sex Roles, 43,* 645–664.

Miller, A. G. (1986). *The obedience experiments: A case study of controversy in social science.* New York: Praeger.

Miller, G. A. (1956). The magical number seven, plus or minus two: Some limits on our capacity for processing information. *Psychological Review, 63,* 81–97.

Miller, G. A. (1991). *The science of words.* New York: Scientific American Library.

Miller, G. F. (1998). How mate choice shaped human nature: A review of sexual selection and human evolution. In C. Crawford & D. L. Krebs (Eds.), *Handbook of evolutionary psychology: Ideas, issues, and applications.* Mahwah, NJ: Erlbaum.

Miller, I. J. (1996). Managed care is harmful to outpatient mental health services: A call for accountability. *Professional Psychology: Research and Practice, 27,* 349–363.

Miller, I. J., & Reedy, F. E. Jr. (1990). Variations in human taste-bud density and taste intensity perception. *Physiological Behavior, 47,* 1213–1219.

Miller, J. G. (1999). Cultural psychology: Implications for basic psychological theory. *Psychological Science, 10,* 85–91.

Miller, J. G. (2001). Culture and moral development. In D. Matsumoto (Ed.), *The handbook of culture and psychology* (pp. 151–170). New York: Oxford University Press.

Miller, N. E. (1941). The frustration-aggression hypothesis. *Psychological Review, 48,* 337–342.

Miller, N. E. (1944). Experimental studies of conflict. In J. M. Hunt (Ed.), *Personality and the behavior disorders* (Vol. 1). New York: Ronald.

Miller, N. E. (1951). Learnable drives and rewards. In S. S. Stevens (Ed.), *Handbook of experimental psychology.* New York: Wiley.

Miller, N. E. (1959). Liberalization of basic S-R concepts: Extension to conflict behavior, motivation, and social learning. In S. Koch (Ed.), *Psychology: A study of a science* (Vol. 2). New York: McGraw-Hill.

Miller, N. E. (1985). The value of behavioral research on animals. *American Psychologist, 40,* 423–440.

Millman, J., Bishop, C. H., & Ebel, R. (1965). An analysis of test-wiseness. *Educational and Psychological Measurement, 25,* 707–726.

Millon, T. (1981). *Disorders of personality: DSM-III, axis II.* New York: Wiley.

Millstone, E. (1989). Methods and practices of animal experimentation. In G. Langley (Ed.), *Animal experimentation: The consensus changes.* New York: Chapman & Hall.

Milner, B., Corkin, S., & Teuber, H. (1968). Further analysis of the hippocampal amnesic syndrome: 14-year follow-up study of H. M. *Neuropsychologia, 6,* 215–234.

Milstone, C. (1997). Sybil minds. *Saturday Night, 112,* 35–42.

Mineka, S., & Hamida, S. (1998). Observational and nonconscious learning. In W. O'Donohue (Ed.), *Learning and behavior therapy.* Boston: Allyn & Bacon.

Minuchin, S., Rosman, B. L., & Baker, L. (1978). *Psychosomatic families: Anorexia nervosa in context.* Cambridge, MA: Harvard University Press.

Miranda, J., & Green, B. L. (1999). The need for mental health services research focusing on poor young women. *Journal of Mental Health Policy and Economics, 2,* 73–89.

Mischel, W. (1961). Delay of gratification, need for achievement, and acquiescence in another culture. *Journal of Abnormal and Social Psychology, 62,* 543–552.

Mischel, W. (1968). *Personality and assessment.* New York: Wiley.

Mischel, W. (1973). Toward a cognitive social learning conceptualization of personality. *Psychological Review, 80,* 252–283.

Mischel, W. (1984). Convergences and challenges in the search for consistency. *American Psychologist, 39,* 351–364.

Mischel, W., & Shoda, Y. (1999). Integrating dispositions and processing dynamics within a unified theory of personality: The cognitive-affective personality system. In L. A. Pervin & O. P. John (Eds.), *Handbook of personality: Theory and research.* New York: Guilford.

Mishra, R. C. (2001). Cognition across cultures. In D. Matsumoto (Ed.), *The handbook of culture and psychology* (pp. 119–136). New York: Oxford University Press.

Mitchell, K. J., & Johnson, M. K. (2000). Source monitoring: Attributing mental experiences. In E. Tulving & F. I. M. Craik (Eds.), *The Oxford handbook of memory* (pp. 179–196). New York: Oxford University Press.

Mitka, M. (1999). Slowing decline in AIDS deaths prompts concern. *Journal of the American Medical Association, 282,* 1216–1217.

Mitler, M. M., Dinges, D. F., & Dement, W. C. (1994). Sleep medicine, public policy, and public health. In M. H. Kryger, T. Roth, & W. C. Dement (Eds.), *Principles and practice of sleep medicine* (2nd ed.). Philadelphia: Saunders.

Mitler, M. M., Dement, W. C., & Dinges, D. F. (2000). Sleep medicine, public policy, and public health. In M. H. Kryger, T. Roth, & W. C. Dement (Eds.), *Principles and practice of sleep medicine.* Philadelphia: Saunders.

Mitler, M. M. (1993). Public safety in the workplace. In M. A. Carskadon (Ed.), *Encyclopedia of sleep and dreaming.* New York: Macmillan.

Moak, D. H., & Anton, R. F. (1999). Alcohol. In B. S. McCrady & E. E. Epstein (Eds.), *Addictions: A comprehensive guidebook.* New York: Oxford University Press.

Modestin, J. (1992). Multiple personality disorder in Switzerland. *American Journal of Psychiatry, 149,* 88–92.

Moghaddam, F. M., Taylor, D. M., & Wright, S. C. (1993). *Social psychology in cross-cultural perspective.* New York: W. H. Freeman.

Mokdad, A. H., Serdula, M. K., Dietz, W. H., Bowman, B. A., Marks, J. S., & Koplan, J. P. (1999). The spread of the obesity epidemic in the United States, 1991–1998. *Journal of the American Medical Association, 282,* 1519–1522.

Moline, M. L. (1993). Jet lag. In M. A. Carskadon (Ed.), *Encyclopedia of sleep and dreaming.* New York: Macmillan.

Möller, J., Hallqvist, J., Diderichsen, F., Theorell, T., Reuterwall, C., & Ahlbom, A. (1999). Do episodes of anger trigger myocardial infarction? A case-crossover analysis in the Stockholm heart epidemiology program (SHEEP). *Psychosomatic Medicine, 61,* 842–849.

Mollon, J. D. (1989). "Tho' she kneel'd in that place where they grew . . ." *Journal of Experimental Biology, 146,* 21–38.

Monahan, J. (1997). Major mental disorders and violence to others. In D. M. Stoff, J. Breiling, & J. D. Maser (Eds.), *Handbook of antisocial behavior.* New York: Wiley.

Monahan, J. L., Murphy, S. T., & Zajonc, R. B. (2000). Subliminal mere exposure: Specific, general, and diffuse effects. *Psychological Science, 11,* 462–466.

Monk, T. H. (2000). Shift work. In M. H. Kryger, T. Roth, & W. C. Dement (Eds.), *Principles and practice of sleep medicine*. Philadelphia: Saunders.

Monroe, S. M., & Hadjiyannakis, K. (2002). The social environment and depression: Focusing on severe life stress. In I. H. Gotlib & C. L. Hammen (Eds.), *Handbook of depression*. New York: Guilford.

Monroe, S. M., & McQuaid, J. R. (1994). Measuring life stress and assessing its impact on mental health. In W. R. Avison & I. H. Gotlib (Eds.), *Stress and mental health: Contemporary issues and prospects for the future*. New York: Plenum.

Montgomery, G. H., DuHamel, K. N., & Redd, W. H. (2000). A meta-analysis of hypnotically induced analgesia: How effective is hypnosis? *International Journal of Clinical & Experimental Hypnosis, 48*, 138–153.

Moore, B. C. J. (2001). Basic auditory processes. In E. B. Goldstein (Ed.), *Blackwell handbook of perception*. Malden, MA: Blackwell.

Moore, K. L., & Persaud, T. V. N. (1998). *Before we are born*. Philadelphia: Saunders.

Moos, R. H., & Schaefer, J. A. (1993). Coping resources and processes: Current concepts and measures. In L. Goldberger & S. Breznitz (Eds.), *Handbook of stress: Theoretical and clinical aspects* (2nd ed.). New York: Free Press.

Morahan-Martin, J., & Schumacher, P. (2000). Incidence and correlates of pathological Internet use among college students. *Computers in Human Behavior, 16*(1), 13–29.

Morey, L. C. (1988). Personality disorders in DSM-III and DSM-III-R: Convergence, coverage, and internal consistency. *American Journal of Psychiatry, 145*, 573–577.

Morgan, C. D., & Murray, H. A. (1935). A method for investigating fantasies: The Thematic Apperception Test. *Archives of Neurology and Psychiatry, 34*, 289–306.

Morgan, H. (1996). An analysis of Gardner's theory of multiple intelligence. *Roeper Review, 18*, 263–269.

Morgan, M. J. (2000). Ecstacy (MDMA): A review of its possible persistent psychological effects. *Psychopharmacology, 152*, 230–248.

Mori, E., Ikeda, M., Hirono, N., Kitagaki, H., Imamura, T., & Shimomura, T. (1999). Amygdalar volume and emotional memory in Alzheimer's disease. *American Journal of Psychiatry, 156*, 216–222.

Moriarity, J. L., Boatman, D., Krauss, G. L., Storm, P. B., & Lenz, F. A. (2001). Human "memories" can be evoked by stimulation of the lateral temporal cortex after ipsilateral medical temporal lobe resection.

Journal of Neurology, Neurosurgery & Psychiatry, 71, 549–551.

Morin, C. M. (2002). Contributions of cognitive-behavioral approaches to the clinical management of insomnia. *Journal of Clinical Psychiatry, 4*(suppl 1), 21–26.

Morin, C. M., Colecchi, C., Stone, J., Sood, R., & Brink, D. (1999). Behavioral and pharmacological therapies for late-life insomnia: A randomized controlled trial. *Journal of the American Medical Association, 281*, 991–999.

Morley, J. E. (2001). Male menopause is underdiagnosed and undertreated. *Medical Crossfire, 3*(1), 46–47, 51.

Morokoff, P. J., Quina, K., Harlow, L. L., Whitmire, L., Grimley, D. M., Gibson, P. R., & Burkholder, G. J. (1997). Sexual assertivenes scale (SAS) for women: Development and validation. *Journal of Personality and Social Psychology, 73*, 790–804.

Morris, C. D., Bransford, J. D., & Franks, J. J. (1977). Levels of processing versus transfer appropriate processing. *Journal of Verbal Learning and Verbal Behavior, 16*, 519–533.

Morris, J. S., Frith, C. D., Perrett, D. I., Rowland, D., Young, A. W., Calder, A. J., & Dolan, R. J. (1996). A differential neural response in the human amygdala to fearful and happy facial expressions. *Nature, 383*, 812–815.

Morris, P. E., Jones, S., & Hampson, P. (1978). An imagery mnemonic for the learning of people's names. *British Journal of Psychology, 69*, 335–336.

Mortensen, M. E., Sever, L. E., & Oakley, G. P., Jr. (1991). Teratology and the epidemiology of birth defects. In S. G. Gabbe, J. R. Niebyl, & J. L. Simpson (Eds.), *Obstetrics: Normal and problem pregnancies*. New York: Churchill Livingstone.

Morton, A. (1998). *Diana: Her true story. The commemorative edition*. New York: Pocket Books.

Moruzzi, G. (1964). Reticular influences on the EEG. *Electroencephalography and Clinical Neurophysiology, 16*, 2–17.

Mosher, D., & Maclan, P. (1994). College men and women respond to X-rated videos intended for male or female audiences: Gender and sexual scripts. *Journal of Sex Research, 31*, 99–113.

Moss, P. (1994). Validity. In R. J. Sternberg (Ed.), *Encyclopedia of human intelligence*. New York: Macmillan.

Most, S. B., Simons, D. J., Scholl, B. J., Jimenez, R., Clifford, E., & Chabris, C. F. (2001). How not to be seen: The contribution of similarity and selective ignoring to sustained inattentional blindness. *Psychological Science, 12*(1), 9–17.

Mott, S. R., Fazekas, N. F., & James, S. R. (1985). *Nursing care of children and families: A holistic approach*. Reading, MA: Addison-Wesley.

Mowrer, O. H. (1947). On the dual nature of learning: A reinterpretation of "conditioning" and "problem-solving." *Harvard Educational Review, 17*, 102–150.

Moynihan, J. A., & Ader, R. (1996). Psychoneuroimmunology: Animal models of disease. *Psychosomatic Medicine, 58*, 546–558.

Muchinsky, P. M. (2003). *Psychology applied to work* (7th ed.). Belmont, CA: Wadsworth.

Mullen, B., & Copper, C. (1994). The relation between group cohesiveness and performance: An integration. *Psychological Bulletin, 115*, 210–227.

Mulligan, N. W. (1998). The role of attention during encoding in implicit and explicit memory. *Journal of Experimental Psychology: Learning, Memory, & Cognition, 24*, 27–47.

Mullin, C. R., & Linz, D. (1995). Desensitization and resensitization to violence against women: Effects of exposure to sexually violent films on judgments of domestic violence victims. *Journal of Personality and Social Psychology, 69*, 449–459.

Mulvey, E. P., & Cauffman, E. (2001). The inherent limits of predicting school violence. *American Psychologist, 56*, 797–802.

Munck, A. (2000). Corticosteroids and stress. In G. Fink (Ed.), *Encyclopedia of stress* (Vol. 1, pp. 570–577). San Diego: Academic Press.

Munk-Jorgensen, P. (1999). Has deinstitutionalization gone too far? *European Archives of Psychiatry & Clinical Neuroscience, 249*(3), 136–143.

Murdock, B. (2001). Analysis of the serial position curve. In H. L. Roediger III, J. S. Nairne, I. Neath, & A. M. Surprenant (Eds.), *The nature of remembering: Essays in honor of Robert G. Crowder* (pp. 151–170). Washington, DC: American Psychological Association.

Muris, P. (2002). Relationships between self-efficacy and symptoms of anxiety disorders and depression in a normal adolescent sample. *Personality and Individual Differences, 32*, 337–348.

Murison, R. (2001). Is there a role for psychology in ulcer disease? *Integrative Physiological and Behavioral Science, 36*(1), 75–83.

Murphy, J. M., Tohen, M., & Tsuang, M. T. (1999). Psychiatric epidemiology. In A. M. Nicholi (Ed.), *The Harvard guide to psychiatry*. Cambridge, MA: Harvard University Press.

Murphy, K. R., & Cleveland, J. N. (1995). *Understanding performance*

appraisal: Social, organizational, and goal-based perspectives. Thousand Oaks, CA: Sage.

Murray, H. A. (1938). *Explorations in personality*. New York: Oxford University Press.

Murray, H. A. (1943). *Thematic Apperception Test—Manual*. Cambridge, MA: Harvard University Press.

Murray, J. B. (1995). Evidence for acupuncture's analgesic effectiveness and proposals for the physiological mechanisms involved. *Journal of Psychology, 129*, 443–461.

Murray, S. L. (2001). Seeking a sense of conviction: Motivated cognition in close relationships. In G. J. O. Fletcher & M. S. Clark (Eds.), *Blackwell handbook of social psychology: Interpersonal processes*. Malden, MA: Blackwell.

Murray, S. L., & Holmes, J. G. (1999). The (mental) ties that bind: Cognitive structures that predict relationship resilience. *Journal of Personality and Social Psychology, 77*, 1228–1244.

Murray, S. L., Holmes, J. G., & Griffin, D. W. (1996a). The benefits of positive illusions: Idealization and the construction of satisfaction in close relationships. *Journal of Personality and Social Psychology, 70*, 79–98.

Murray, S. L., Holmes, J. G., & Griffin, D. W. (1996b). The self-fulfilling nature of positive illusions in romantic relationships: Love is not blind, but prescient. *Journal of Personality and Social Psychology, 71*, 1155–1180.

Murray, S. L., Holmes, J. G., Bellavia, G., Griffin, D. W., & Dolderman, D. (2002). Kindred spirits? The benefits of egocentrism in close relationships. *Journal of Personality and Social Psychology, 82*, 563–581.

Murstein, B. I., & Fontaine, P. A. (1993). The public's knowledge about psychologists and other mental health professionals. *American Psychologist, 48*, 839–845.

Myers, D. G. (1992). *The pursuit of happiness: Who is happy—and why*. New York: Morrow.

Myers, D. G. (1999). Close relationships and quality of life. In D. Kahneman, E. Diener, & N. Schwarz (Eds.), *Well-being: The foundations of hedonic psychology*. New York: Russell Sage Foundation.

Myers, D. G., & Diener, E. (1995). Who is happy? *Psychological Science, 6*, 10–19.

Myers, D. G., & Diener, E. (1997). The pursuit of happiness. *Scientific American Special Issue, 7*, 40–43.

Myers, D. G., & Lamm, H. (1976). The group polarization phenomenon. *Psychological Bulletin, 83*, 602–627.

Myerson, J., Rank, M. R., Raines, F. Q., & Schnitzler, M. A. (1998).

Race and general cognitive ability: The myth of diminishing returns to education. *Psychological Science, 9,* 139–142.

Mynatt, C. R., Doherty, M. E., & Tweney, R. D. (1978). Consequences of confirmation and disconfirmation in a simulated research environment. *Quarterly Journal of Experimental Psychology, 30,* 395–406.

Nadel, L., & Jacobs, W. J. (1998). Traumatic memory in special. *Current Directions in Psychological Science, 7 ,* 154–157.

Nahas, Z., George, M. S., Lorberbaum, J. P., Risch, S. C., & Spicer, K. M. (1998). SPECT and PET in neuropsychiatry. *Primary Psychiatry, 5,* 52–59.

Nairne, J. S. (1996). Short-term/working memory. In E. L. Bjork & R. A. Bjork (Eds.), *Memory.* San Diego: Academic Press.

Nairne, J. S. (2001). A functional analysis of primary memory. In H. L. I. Roediger III, J. S. Nairne, I. Neath, & A. M. Surprenant (Eds.), *The nature of remembering: Essays in honor of Robert G. Crowder* (pp. 283–296). Washington, DC: American Psychological Association.

Nairne, J. S. (2002). Remembering over the short-term: The case against the standard model. *Annual Review of Psychology, 53,* 53–81.

Nairne, J. S., Neath, I., & Serra, M. (1997). Proactive interference plays a role in the word-length effect. *Psychonomic Bulletin & Review, 4,* 541–545.

Nakajima, S., & Patterson, R. L. (1997). The involvement of dopamine D2 receptors, but not D3 or D4 receptors, in the rewarding effect of brain stimulation in the rat. *Brain Research, 760,* 74–79.

Narrow, W. E., Regier, D. A., Rae, D. S., Manderscheid, R. W., & Locke, B. Z. (1993). Use of services by persons with mental and addictive disorders: Findings from the National Institute of Mental Health Epidemiologic Catchment Area Program. *Archives of General Psychiatry, 50,* 95–107.

Nash, M. R. (2001, July). The truth and hype of hypnosis. *Scientific American, 285,* 36–43.

Nathan, P. E., & Gorman, J. M. (1998). *A guide to treatments that work.* New York: Oxford University Press.

Nathan, P. E., Stuart, S. P., & Dolan, S. L. (2000). Research on psychotherapy efficacy and effectiveness: Between Scylla and Charybdis? *Psychological Bulletin, 126,* 964–981.

Neiss, R. (1988). Reconceptualizing arousal: Psychobiological states in motor performance. *Psychological Bulletin, 103,* 345–366.

Neiss, R. (1990). Ending arousal's reign of error: A reply to Anderson. *Psychological Bulletin, 107,* 101–105.

Neisser, U. (1967). *Cognitive psychology.* New York: Appleton-Century-Crofts.

Neisser, U. (1998). Introduction: Rising test scores and what they mean. In U. Neisser (Ed.), *The rising curve: Long-term gains in IQ and related measures.* Washington, DC: American Psychological Association.

Neisser, U., & Harsch, N. (1992). Phantom flashbulbs: False recollections of hearing the news about *Challenger.* In E. Winograd & U. Neisser (Eds.), *Affect and accuracy in recall: Studies of "flashbulb" memories.* New York: Cambridge University Press.

Neisser, U., Boodoo, G., Bouchard, T. J., Jr., Boykin, A. W., Brody, N., Ceci, S. J., Halpern, D. F., Loehlin, J. C., Perloff, R., Sternberg, R. J., & Urbina, S. (1996). Intelligence: Knowns and unknowns. *American Psychologist, 51,* 77–101.

Nelson, R. J., & Chiavegatto, S. (2001). Molecular basis of aggression. *Trends in Neuroscience, 24,* 713–719.

Nemeroff, C. B. (1998). The neurobiology of depression. *Scientific American, June,* 42–49.

Nemes, I. (1992). The relationship between pornography and sex crimes. *Journal of Psychiatry and Law, 20,* 459–481.

Nemeth, C., & Chiles, C. (1988). Modelling courage: The role of dissent in fostering independence. *European Journal of Social Psychology, 18,* 275–280.

Nemiah, J. C. (1985). Somatoform disorders. In H. I. Kaplan & B. J. Sadock (Eds.), *Comprehensive textbook of psychiatry* (4th ed.). Baltimore: Williams & Wilkins.

Nesse, R. M., & Young, E. A. (2000). Evolutionary origins and functions of the stress response. In G. Fink (Ed.), *Encyclopedia of stress* (Vol. 2, pp. 79–83). San Diego: Academic Press.

Neubauer, D. N. (1999). Sleep problems in the elderly. *American Family Physician, 59,* 2551–2558.

Neugebauer, R., Dohrenwend, B. P., & Dohrenwend, B. S. (1980). Formulation of hypotheses about the true prevalence of functional psychiatric disorders among adults in the United States. In B. P. Dohrenwend, B. S. Dohrenwend, M. S. Gould, B. Link, R. Neugebauer, & R. Wunsch-Hitzig (Eds.), *Mental illness in the United States: Epidemiological estimates.* New York: Praeger.

Nevin, J. A. (1998). Choice and behavior momentum. In W. O'Donohue (Ed.), *Learning and behavior therapy.* Boston: Allyn & Bacon.

Newberg, A., Alavi, A., Baime, M., Pourdehnad, M., Santanna, J., & D'Aquili. E. (2001). The measurement of regional cerebral blood flow during the complex cognitive task of meditation: A preliminary SPECT study. *Psychiatry Research: Neuroimaging, 106*(2), 113–122.

Newcombe, N., & Huttenlocher, J. (1992). Children's early ability to solve perspective-taking problems. *Developmental Psychology, 28,* 635–643.

Newell, A., & Simon, H. A. (1972). *Human problem solving.* Englewood Cliffs, NJ: Prentice-Hall.

Newell, A., Shaw, J. C., & Simon, H. A. (1958). Elements of a theory of human problem solving. *Psychological Review, 65,* 151–166.

Newman, L. S., Duff, K. J., & Baumeister, R. F. (1997). A new look at defensive projection: Thought suppression, accessibility, and biased person perception. *Journal of Personality and Social Psychology, 72,* 980–1001.

Newsom, C., Favell, J. E., & Rincover, A. (1983). Side effects of punishment. In S. Axelrod & J. Apsche (Eds.), *The effects of punishment on human behavior.* New York: Academic Press.

Nicholson, A. N., Pascoe, P. A., Spencer, M. B., Stone, B. M., Roehis, T., & Roth, T. (1986). Sleep after transmeridian flights. *Lancet, 2,* 1205–1208.

Nickerson, R. S. (1998). Confirmation bias: A ubiquitous phenomenon in many guises. *Review of General Psychology, 2,* 175–220.

Nickerson, R. S. (1999). Enhancing creativity. In R. J. Sternberg (Ed.), *Handbook of creativity.* New York: Cambridge University Press.

Nickerson, R. S., & Adams, M. J. (1979). Long-term memory for a common object. *Cognitive Psychology, 11,* 287–307.

Nicoladis, E., & Genesee, F. (1997). Language development in preschool bilingual children. *Journal of Speech-Language Pathology & Audiology, 21,* 258–270.

Niebyl, J. R. (1991). Drugs in pregnancy and lactation. In S. G. Gabbe, J. R. Niebyl, & J. L. Simpson (Eds.), *Obstetrics: Normal and problem pregnancies.* New York: Churchill Livingstone.

Nielsen Media Research. (1998). *Report on television: 1998.* New York: Author.

Nielsen, T. A., & Zadra, A. (2000). Dreaming disorders. In M. H. Kryger, T. Roth, & W. C. Dement (Eds.), *Principles and practice of sleep medicine.* Philadelphia: Saunders.

Nikelly, A. G. (1994). Alcoholism: Social as well as psycho-medical problem—The missing "big picture." *Journal of Alcohol & Drug Education, 39,* 1–12.

Nikles, C. D., Brecht, D. L., Klinger, E., & Bursell, A. L. (1998). The effects of current concern- and nonconcern-related waking suggestions on nocturnal dream content. *Journal of Personality and Social Psychology, 75,* 242–255.

Nisbett, R. E. (Ed.). (1993). *Rules for reasoning.* Hillsdale, NJ: Erlbaum.

Nisbett, R. E., Peng, K., Choi, I., & Norenzayan, A. (2001). Culture and systems of thought: Holistic versus analytic cognition. *Psychological Review, 108,* 291–310.

Nishino, S., Mignot, E., & Dement, W. C. (1995). Sedative-hypnotics. In A. F. Schatzberg & C. B. Nemeroff (Eds.), *American Psychiatric Press textbook of psychopharmacology.* Washington, D.C.: American Psychiatric Press.

Nist, S. L., & Holschuh, J. L. (2000). Comprehension strategies at the college level. In R. F. Flippo & D. C. Caverly (Eds.), *Handbook of college reading and study strategy research.* Mahwah, NJ: Erlbaum.

Noddings, N. (1992). Gender and the curriculum. In P. W. Jackson (Ed.), *Handbook of research on curriculum.* New York: Macmillan.

Nolen-Hoeksema, S. (1991). Responses to depression and their effects on the duration of depressive episodes. *Journal of Abnormal Psychology, 100,* 569–582.

Nolen-Hoeksema, S. (1995). Gender differences in coping with depression across the lifespan. *Depression, 3,* 81–90.

Nolen-Hoeksema, S. (2000). The role of rumination in depressive disorders and mixed anxiety/depressive symptoms. *Journal of Abnormal Psychology, 109,* 504–511.

Nolen-Hoeksema, S. (2001). Gender differences in depression. *Current Directions in Psychological Science, 10,* 173–176.

Nolen-Hoeksema, S. (2002). Gender differences in depression. In I. H. Gotlib & C. L. Hammen (Eds.), *Handbook of depression.* New York: Guilford.

Norcross, J. C. (1995). Dispelling the dodo bird verdict and the exclusivity myth in psychotherapy. *Psychotherapy, 32,* 500–504.

Norcross, J. C., & Goldfried, M. R. (Eds.). (1992). *Handbook of psychotherapy integration.* New York: Basic Books.

Norman, R. M. G., & Malla, A. K. (1995). Prodromal symptoms of relapse in schizophrenia: A review. *Schizophrenia Bulletin, 21,* 527–539.

Norris, F. H., with Byrne, C. M., Diaz, E., & Kaniasty, K. (2001). *Risk factors for adverse outcomes in natural and human-caused disasters: A review of the empirical literature.* Retrieved November 21, 2001 from U.S. Department of Veterans Affairs National Center for PTSD Website: http://www.ncptsd.org/facts/disasters/fs_riskfactors.html.

North, C. S., Nixon, S. J., Shariat, S., Mallonee, S., McMillen, J. C., Spitznagel, E. L., & Smith, E. M. (1999). Psychiatric disorders among survivors of the Oklahoma City bombing. *Journal of the American Medical Association, 282,* 755–762.

Nourse, C. B., & Butler, K. M. (1998). Perinatal transmission of HIV and diagnosis of HIV infection in infants: A review. *Irish Journal of Medical Science, 167,* 28–32.

Nurnberger, J. I., & Zimmerman, J. (1970). Applied analysis of human behavior: An alternative to conventional motivational inferences and unconscious determination in therapeutic programming. *Behavior Therapy, 1,* 59–69.

Oakes, M. E., & Slotterback, C. S. (2000). Self-reported measures of appetite in relation to verbal cues about many foods. *Current Psychology: Developmental, Learning, Personality, Social, 19,* 137–142.

Oakes, P. (2001). The root of all evil in intergroup relations? Unearthing the categorization process. In R. Brown & S. L. Gaertner (Eds.), *Blackwell handbook of social psychology: Intergroup processes.* Malden, MA: Blackwell.

O'Brien, B. (1996). Economic evaluation of pharmaceuticals. *Medical Care, 34,* 99–108.

Ochse, R. (1990). *Before the gates of excellence: The determinants of creative genius.* Cambridge, England: Cambridge University Press.

O'Donnell, A., & Dansereau, D. F. (1993). Learning from lectures: Effects of cooperative review. *Journal of Experimental Education, 61,* 116–125.

O'Donohue, W. (1998). Conditioning and third generation behavior therapy. In W. O'Donohue (Ed.), *Learning and behavior therapy.* Boston: Allyn & Bacon.

Ogilvie, R. D., Wilkinson, R.T., & Allison, S. (1989). The detection of sleep onset: Behavioral, physiological, and subjective convergence. *Sleep, 12*(5), 458–474.

Okagaki, L. (1994). Socialization of intelligence. In R. J. Sternberg (Ed.), *Encyclopedia of human intelligence.* New York: Macmillan.

Okin, R. L., Borus, J. F., Baer, L., & Jones, A. L. (1995). Long-term outcome of state hospital patients discharged into structured community residential settings. *Psychiatric Services, 46,* 73–78.

Olden, K. W. (1998). Stress and the gastrointestinal tract. In J. R. Hubbard, & E. A. Workman (Eds.), *Handbook of stress medicine: An organ system approach.* New York: CRC Press.

Olds, J. (1956). Pleasure centers in the brain. *Scientific American, 193,* 105–116.

Olds, J., & Milner, P. (1954). Positive reinforcement produced by electrical stimulation of the septal area and other regions of the rat brain. *Journal of Comparative and Physiological Psychology, 47,* 419–427.

Olds, M. E., & Fobes, J. L. (1981). The central basis of motivation: Intracranial self-stimulation studies. *Annual Review of Psychology, 32,* 523–574.

O'Leary, K. D., Kent, R. N., & Kanowitz, J. (1975). Shaping data collection congruent with experimental hypotheses. *Journal of Applied Behavior Analysis, 8,* 43–51.

Olfson, M., & Pincus, H. A. (1994). Outpatient psychotherapy in the United States, I: Volume, costs, and user characteristics. *American Journal of Psychiatry, 151,* 1281–1288.

Olfson, M., & Pincus, H. A. (1996). Outpatient mental health care in nonhospital settings: Distribution of patients across provider groups. *American Journal of Psychiatry, 153,* 1353–1356.

Olfson, M., Marcus, S. C., & Pincus, H. A. (1999). Trends in office-based psychiatric practice. *American Journal of Psychiatry, 156,* 451–457.

Olio, K. (1994). Truth in memory. *American Psychologist, 49,* 442–443.

Oliver, M. B., & Hyde, J. S. (1993). Gender differences in sexuality: A meta-analysis. *Psychological Bulletin, 114,* 29–51.

Olson, J. M., & Roese, N. J. (1995). The perceived funniness of humorous stimuli. *Personality and Social Psychology Bulletin, 21,* 908–913.

Olson, J. M., & Zanna, M. P. (1993). Attitudes and attitude change. *Annual Review of Psychology, 44,* 117–154.

Olson, J. M., Roese, N. J., & Zanna, M. P. (1996). Expectancies. In E. T. Higgins & A. W. Kruglanski (Eds.), *Social psychology: Handbook of basic principles.* New York: Guilford.

Olson, M. A., & Fazio, R. H. (2001). Implicit attitude formation through classical conditioning. *Psychological Science, 12,* 413–417.

Olson, M. A., & Fazio, R. H. (2002). Implicit acquisition and manifestation of classically conditioned attitudes. *Social Cognition, 20*(2), 89–104.

Operario, D., & Fiske, S. T. (2001). Stereotypes: Content, structures, processes, and context. In R. Brown & S. L. Gaertner (Eds.), *Blackwell handbook of social psychology: Interpersonal processes.* Malden, MA: Blackwell.

Orbuch, T. L., House, J. S., Mero, R. P., & Webster, P. S. (1996). Marital quality over the life course. *Social Psychology Quarterly, 59,* 162–171.

Organista, P. B., & Miranda, J. (1991). Psychosomatic symptoms in medical outpatients: An investigation of self-handicapping theory. *Health Psychology, 10,* 427–431.

Oring, L. W. (1985). Avian polyandry. *Current Ornithology, 3,* 309–351.

Orne, M. T. (1951). The mechanisms of hypnotic age regression: An experimental study. *Journal of Abnormal and Social Psychology, 46,* 213–225.

Orne, M. T., & Dinges, D. F. (1989). Hypnosis. In H. I. Kaplan & B. J. Sadock (Eds.), *Comprehensive textbook of psychiatry* (5th ed., Vol. 2). Baltimore: Williams & Wilkins.

Orne, M. T., & Holland, C. C. (1968). On the ecological validity of laboratory deceptions. *International Journal of Psychiatry, 6,* 282–293.

Ornstein, R. E. (1977). *The psychology of consciousness.* New York: Harcourt Brace Jovanovich.

Ornstein, R. E. (1997). *The right mind: Making sense of the hemispheres.* San Diego: Harcourt.

Ornstein, R. E., & Dewan, T. (1991). *The evolution of consciousness: Of Darwin, Freud, and cranial fire—The origins of the way we think.* New York: Prentice-Hall.

Orth-Gomer, K., Wamala, S. P., Horsten, M., Schenck-Gustafsson, K., Schneiderman, N., & Mittleman, M. A. (2000). Marital stress worsens prognosis in women with coronary heart disease: The Stockholm female coronary risk study. *Journal of the American Medical Association, 284,* 3008–3014.

Ortmann, A., & Hertwig, R. (1997). Is deception acceptable? *American Psychologist, 52,* 746–747.

Oskamp, S. (1991). *Attitudes and opinions.* Englewood Cliffs, NJ: Prentice-Hall.

Oskamp, S., Kaufman, K., & Wolterbeek, L. A. (1996). Gender role portrayals in preschool picture books. *Journal of Social Behavior and Personality, 11,* 27–39.

Osrin, D., & de L Costello, A. M. (2000). Maternal nutrition and fetal growth: Practical issues in international health. *Seminars in Neonatology, 5,* 209–219.

Ostir, G. V., Peek, M. K., Markides, K. S., & Goodwin, J. S. (2001). The association between emotional well being and future risk of myocardial infarction in older adults. *Primary Psychiatry, 8*(7), 34–38.

Ostrom, T. M., & Sedikides, C. (1992). Outgroup homogeneity effects in natural and minimal groups. *Psychological Bulletin, 112,* 536–552.

Oswald, I., & Adam, K. (1980). The man who had not slept for ten years. *British Medical Journal, 281,* 1684–1685.

Ott, P. J., Tarter, R. E., & Ammerman, R. T. (1999). *Sourcebook on substance abuse: Etiology, epidemiology, assessment, and treatment.* Boston: Allyn & Bacon.

Otto, M. W., Pollack, M. H., Jenike, M. A., & Rosenbaum, J. F. (1999). Anxiety disorders and their treatment. In A. M. Nicholi (Ed.), *The Harvard guide to psychiatry* (3rd ed., pp. 220–239). Cambridge, MA: Harvard University Press.

Owen, M. J., & O'Donovan, M. C. (2003). Schizophrenia and genetics. In R. Plomin, J. C. Defries, I. W. Craig & P. McGuffin (Eds.), *Behavioral genetics in the postgenomic era.* Washington, DC: American Psychological Association.

Ozer, D. J., & Reise, S. P. (1994). Personality assessment. *Annual Review of Psychology, 45,* 357–388.

Padgett, D. A., & Sheridan, J. F. (2000). Herpesviruses. In G. Fink (Ed.), *Encyclopedia of stress* (pp. 357–363). San Diego: Academic Press.

Pagel, J. F., Blagrove, M., Levin, R., States, B., Stickgold, B., & White, S. (2001). Definitions of dream: A paradigm for comparing field descriptive specific studies of dream. *Dreaming: Journal of the Association for the Study of Dreams, 11,* 195–202.

Paivio, A. (1969). Mental imagery in associative learning and memory. *Psychological Review, 76,* 241–263.

Paivio, A. (1986). *Mental representations: A dual coding approach.* New York: Oxford University Press.

Paivio, A., Khan, M., & Begg, I. (2000). Concreteness of relational effects on recall of adjective-noun pairs. *Canadian Journal of Experimental Psychology, 54*(3), 149–160.

Paivio, A., Smythe, P. E., & Yuille, J. C. (1968). Imagery versus meaningfulness of nouns in paired-associate learning. *Canadian Journal of Psychology, 22,* 427–441.

Palladino, J. J., & Carducci, B. J. (1984). Students' knowledge of sleep and dreams. *Teaching of Psychology, 11,* 189–191.

Palmer, L. K., Frantz, C. E., Armsworth, M. W., Swank, P., Copley, J. V., & Bush, G. A. (1999). Neuropsychological sequelae of chronically psychologically traumatized children: Specific findings in memory and higher cognitive functions. In L. M. Williams & V. L. Banyard (Eds.), *Trauma & memory.* Thousand Oaks, CA: Sage Publications.

Palmere, M., Benton, S. L., Glover, J. A., & Ronning, R. (1983). Elaboration and recall of main ideas in prose. *Journal of Educational Psychology, 75,* 898–907.

Panksepp, J. (1991). Affective neuroscience: A conceptual framework for the neurobiological study of emotions. In K. T. Strongman (Ed.), *International review of studies on emotion.* Chichester, England: Wiley.

Paradiso, S. P., Robinson, R. G., Andreasen, N. C., Downhill, J. E., Davidson, R. J., Kirchner, P. T.,

Watkins, G. L., Boles Ponto, L. L., & Hichwa, R. D. (1997). Emotional activation of limbic circuitry in elderly normal subjects in a PET study. *American Journal of Psychiatry, 154*, 384–389.

Parent, E. C., & Newman, D. L. (1999). The role of sensation-seeking in alcohol use and risk-taking behavior among college women. *Journal of Alcohol & Drug Education, 44*(2), 12–28.

Paris, J. (1999). *Genetics and psychopathology: Predisposition-stress interactions*. Washington, DC: American Psychiatric Press.

Park, C. L. (1998). Stress-related growth and thriving through coping: The roles of personality and cognitive processes. *Journal of Social Issues, 54*, 267–277.

Park, C. W., Jun, S. Y., & Macinnis, D. J. (2000). Choosing what I want versus rejecting what I do not want: An application of decision framing to product option choice decisions. *Journal of Marketing Research, 37*, 187–202.

Parke, R. D., & Slaby, R. G. (1983). The development of aggression. In E. M. Hetherington (Ed.), *Handbook of child psychology: Socialization, personality, and social development* (Vol. 4). New York: Wiley.

Parker, D. E. (1980). The vestibular apparatus. *Scientific American, 243*(5), 118–135.

Parker, G. A., & Smith, J. M. (1990). Optimality theory in evolutionary biology. *Nature, 348*, 27–33.

Parkinson, B. (1997). Untangling the appraisal-emotion connection. *Personality and Social Psychology Review, 1*, 62–79.

Parks, T. E. (1984). Illusory figures: A (mostly) atheoretical review. *Psychological Bulletin, 95*, 282–300.

Parrot, A., & Bechhofer, L. (1991). *Acquaintance rape: The hidden crime*. New York: Wiley.

Parrot, A. C. (2000). Human research on MDMA (3,4-Methylenedioxymethamphetamine) neurotoxicity: Cognitive and behavioral indices of change. *Neuropsychobiology, 42*(1), 17–24.

Parry-Jones, B., & Parry-Jones, W. L. (1995). History of bulimia and bulimia nervosa. In K. D. Brownell & C. G. Fairburn (Eds.), *Eating disorders and obesity: A comprehensive handbook*. New York: Guilford.

Partinen, M., & Hublin, C. (2000). Epidemiology of sleep disorders. In M. H. Kryger, T. Roth, & W. C. Dement (Eds.), *Principles and practice of sleep medicine*. Philadelphia: Saunders.

Pashler, H., & Carrier, M. (1996). Stuctures, processes, and the flow of information. In E. L. Bjork & R. A.

Bjork (Eds.), *Memory*. San Diego: Academic Press.

Pashler, H., Johnston, J. C., & Ruthruff, E. (2001). Attention and performance. *Annual Review of Psychology, 52*, 629–651.

Pauk, W. (1990). *How to study in college*. Boston: Houghton Mifflin.

Paulhus, D. L. (1991). Measurement and control of response bias. In J. P. Robinson, P. Shaver, & L. S. Wrightsman (Eds.), *Measures of personality and social psychological attitudes*. San Diego: Academic Press.

Paulhus, D. L., Fridhandler, B., & Hayes, S. (1997). Psychological defense: Contemporary theory and research. In R. Hogan, J. Johnson, & S. Briggs (Eds.), *Handbook of personality psychology*. San Diego: Academic Press.

Paulhus, D. L., Trapnell, P. D., & Chen, D. (1999). Birth order effects on personality and achievement within families. *Psychological Science, 10*, 482–488.

Paulos, J. A. (1995). *A mathematician reads the newspaper*. New York: Doubleday.

Paunonen, S. V. (1998). Hierarchical organization of personality and prediction of behavior. *Journal of Personality and Social Psychology, 74*, 538–556.

Paunonen, S. V., & Ashton, M. C. (1998). The structured assessment of personality across cultures. *Journal of Cross-Cultural Psychology, 29*, 150–170.

Pavlov, I. P. (1906). The scientific investigation of psychical faculties or processes in the higher animals. *Science, 24*, 613–619.

Pavlov, I. P. (1927). *Conditioned reflexes* (G. V. Anrep, Trans.). London: Oxford University Press.

Payne, D. G., & Blackwell, J. M. (1998). Truth in memory: Caveat emptor. In S. J. Lynn & K. M. McConkey (Eds.), *Truth in memory*. New York: Guilford.

Payne, D. G., & Wenger, M. J. (1996). Practice effects in memory: Data, theory, and unanswered questions. In D. J. Herrmann, C. McEvoy, C. Hertzog, P. Hertel, & M. K. Johnson (Eds.), *Basic and applied memory research: Practical applications* (Vol. 2). Mahwah, NJ: Erlbaum.

Payne, J. W. (1976). Task complexity and contingent processing in decision making: An information search and protocol analysis. *Organizational Behavior and Human Performance, 16*, 366–387.

Payne, J. W., Bettman, J. R., & Johnson, E. J. (1992). Behavioral decision research: A constructive processing perspective. *Annual Review of Psychology, 43*, 87–131.

Pearce, L. (1974). Duck! It's the new journalism. *New Times, 2*(10), 40–41.

Pearson, B. Z., Fernandez, S. C., & Oller, D. K. (1993). Lexical development in bilingual infants and toddler: Comparison to monolingual norms. *Language Learning, 43*, 93–120.

Pearson, S. E., & Pollack, R. H. (1997). Female response to sexually explicit films. *Journal of Psychology and Human Sexuality, 9*, 73–88.

Pedersen, N. L., Plomin, R., Nesselroade, J. R., & McClearn, G. E. (1992). A quantitative genetic analysis of cognitive abilities during the second half of the life span. *Psychological Science, 3*, 346–353.

Pedersen, P. (1994). A culture-centered approach to counseling. In W. J. Lonner & R. Malpass (Eds.), *Psychology and culture*. Boston: Allyn & Bacon.

Peele, S. (1989). *Diseasing of America: Addiction treatment out of control*. Lexington, MA: Lexington Books.

Peirce, R. S., Frone, M. R., Russell, M., & Cooper, M. L. (1996). Financial stress, social support, and alcohol involvement: A longitudinal test of the buffering hypothesis in a general population survey. *Health Psychology, 15*, 38–47.

Penfield, W., & Perot, P. (1963). The brain's record of auditory and visual experience. *Brain, 86*, 595–696.

Pennebaker, J. W., Colder, M., & Sharp, L. K. (1990). Accelerating the coping process. *Journal of Personality and Social Psychology, 58*, 528–537.

Pennisi, E. (2001). The human genome. *Science, 291*, 1177–1180.

Pepperberg, I. M. (1993). Cognition and communication in an African Grey parrot (*Psittacus erithacus*): Studies on a nonhuman, nonprimate, nonmammalian subject. In H. L. Roitblat, L. H. Herman, & P. E. Nachtigall (Eds.), *Language and communication: Comparative perspectives*. Hillsdale, NJ: Erlbaum.

Pepperberg, I. M. (1990). Cognition in an African gray parrot (*Psittacus erithacus*): Further evidence for comprehension of categories and labels. *Journal of Comparative Psychology, 104*, 41–52.

Perlman, M. D., & Kaufman, A. S. (1990). Assessment of child intelligence. In G. Goldstein & M. Hersen (Eds.), *Handbook of psychological assessment*. New York: Pergamon Press.

Perone, M., Galizio, M., & Baron, A. (1988). The relevance of animal-based principles in the laboratory study of human operant conditioning. In G. Davey & C. Cullen (Eds.), *Human operant conditioning and behavior modification*. New York: Wiley.

Perreault, S., & Bourhis, R. Y. (1999). Ethnocentrism, social identification, and discrimination. *Personality and Social Psychology Bulletin, 25*, 92–103.

Perry, C., Nadon, R., & Button, J. (1992). The measurement of hypnotic ability. In E. Fromm & M. R. Nash (Eds.), *Contemporary hypnosis research*. New York: Guilford.

Perry, D. G., Kusel, S. J., & Perry, L. C. (1988). Victims of peer aggression. *Developmental Psychology, 24*, 807–814.

Perry, W., & Braff, D. L. (1994). Information-processing deficits and thought disorder in schizophrenia. *American Journal of Psychiatry, 151*, 363–367.

Person, E. S. (1990). The influence of values in psychoanalysis: The case of female psychology. In C. Zanardi (Ed.), *Essential papers in psychoanalysis*. New York: New York University Press.

Pert, C. B., & Snyder, S. H. (1973). Opiate receptor: Demonstration in the nervous tissue. *Science, 179*, 1011–1014.

Perugini, E. M., Kirsch, I., Allen, S. T., Coldwell, E., Meredith, J. M., Montgomery, G. H., & Sheehan, J. (1998). Surreptitious observation of response to hypnotically suggested hallucinations: A test of the compliance hypothesis. *International Journal of Clinical & Experimental Hypnosis, 46*, 191–203.

Pervin, L. A. (1994). Personality stability, personality change, and the question of process. In T. F. Heatherton & J. L. Weinberger (Eds.), *Can personality change?* Washington, DC: American Psychological Association.

Peterhans, E., & Von Der Heydt, R. (1991). Elements of form perception in monkey prestriate cortex. In A. Gorea, Y. Fregnac, Z. Kapoula, & J. Findlay (Eds.), *Representations of vision—Trends and tacit assumptions in vision research*. Cambridge, MA: Cambridge University Press.

Petersen, A. C., Compas, B. E., Brooks-Gunn, J., Stemmler, M., Ey, S., & Grant, K. E. (1993). Depression in adolescence. *American Psychologist, 48*, 155–168.

Peterson, C., & Bossio, L. M. (2001). Optimism and physical well-being. In E. C. Chang (Ed.), *Optimism and pessimism: Implications for theory, research, and practice* (pp. 127–146). Washington, DC: American Psychological Association.

Peterson, C., Seligman, M. E. P., & Vaillant, G. E. (1988). Pessimistic explanatory style is a risk factor for physical illness: A thirty-five-year longitudinal study. *Journal of Personality and Social Psychology, 55*, 23–27.

Peterson, C., Seligman, M. E. P., Yurko, K. H., Martin, L. R., & Friedman, H. S. (1998). Catastrophizing and untimely death. *Psychological Science, 9*, 127–130.

Peterson, L. R., & Peterson, M. J. (1959). Short-term retention of individual verbal items. *Journal of Experimental Psychology, 58,* 193–198.

Petrie, K. J., Booth, R. J., & Pennebaker, J. W. (1998). The immunological effects of thought suppression. *Journal of Personality and Social Psychology, 75,* 1264–1272.

Petty, R. E., & Cacioppo, J. T. (1986). *Communication and persuasion: Central and peripheral routes to attitude change.* New York: Springer-Verlag.

Petty, R. E., & Wegener, D. T. (1998). Attitude change: Multiple roles for persuasion variables. In D. T. Gilbert, S. T. Fiske, & G. Lindzey (Eds.), *The handbook of social psychology.* New York: McGraw-Hill.

Petty, R. E., & Wegener, D. T. (1999). The elaboration likelihood model: Current status and controversies. In S. Chaiken & Y. Trope (Eds.), *Dual-process theories in social psychology.* New York: Guilford.

Petty, R. E., Haugtvedt, C. P., & Smith, S. M. (1995). Elaboration as a determinant of attitude strength: Creating attitudes that are persistent, resistant, and predictive of behavior. In R. E. Petty & J. A. Krosnick (Eds.), *Attitude strength: Antecedents and consequences.* Mahwah, NJ: Erlbaum.

Petty, R. E., Wegener, D. T., & Fabrigar, L. R. (1997). Attitudes and attitude change. *Annual Review of Psychology, 48,* 609–647.

Pfau, M., Kenski, H. C., Nitz, M., & Sorenson, J. (1990). Efficacy of inoculation strategies in promoting resistance to political attack messages: Application to direct mail. *Communication Monographs, 57,* 25–43.

Pfaus, J. G., Kippin, T. E., & Centeno, S. (2001). Conditioning and sexual behavior: A review. *Hormones & Behavior, 40,* 291–321.

Pfefferbaum, B., Seale, T. W., McDonald, N. B., Brandt, E. N., Rainwater, S. M., Maynard, B. T., Meierhoefer, B., & Miller, P. D. (2000). Posttraumatic stress two years after the Oklahoma City bombing in youths geographically distant from the explosion. *Psychiatry, 63,* 358–370.

Phares, V. (1996). *Fathers and developmental psychopathology.* New York: Wiley.

Phelps, R., Eisman, E. J., & Kohout, J. (1998). Psychological practice and managed care: Results of the CAPP practitioner survey. *Professional Psychology: Research and Practice, 29,* 31–36.

Phillips, W. T., Kiernan, M., & King, A. C. (2001). The effects of physical activity on physical and psychological health. In A. Baum, T. A. Revenson, & J. E. Singer (Eds.), *Handbook of health psychology* (pp. 627–660). Mahwah, NJ: Erlbaum.

Pi, E. H., & Simpson, G. M. (2001). Medication-induced movement disorders. In B. J. Sadock & V. A. Sadock (Eds.), *Kaplan and Sadock's comprehensive textbook of psychiatry* (7th ed., Vol. 2). Philadelphia: Lippincott/Williams & Wilkins.

Piaget, J. (1929). *The child's conception of the world.* New York: Harcourt, Brace.

Piaget, J. (1932). *The moral judgment of the child.* Glencoe, IL: Free Press.

Piaget, J. (1952). *The origins of intelligence in children.* New York: International Universities Press.

Piaget, J. (1954). *The construction of reality in the child.* New York: Basic Books.

Piaget, J. (1983). Piaget's theory. In P. H. Mussen (Ed.), *Handbook of child psychology* (Vol. 1). New York: Wiley.

Pickering, T. G., Devereux, R. B., James, G. D., Gerin, W., Landsbergis, P., Schnall, P. L., & Schwartz, J. E. (1996). Environmental influences on blood pressure and the role of job strain. *Journal of Hypertension, 14,* S179–S185.

Pickles, J. O. (1988). *An introduction to the physiology of hearing* (2nd ed.). London: Academic Press.

Pierce, C. M. (1992). Contemporary psychiatry: Racial perspectives on the past and future. In A. Kales, C. M. Pierce, & M. Greenblatt (Eds.), *The mosaic of contemporary psychiatry in perspective.* New York: Springer-Verlag.

Pihl, R. O. (1999). Substance abuse: Etiological considerations. In T. Millon, P. H. Blaney, & R. D. Davis (Eds.), *Oxford textbook of psychopathology.* New York: Oxford University Press.

Pike, A., Manke, B., Reiss, D., & Plomin, R. (2000). A genetic analysis of differential experiences of adolescent siblings across three years. *Social Development, 9,* 96–114.

Pike, K. M., & Rodin, J. (1991). Mothers, daughters, and disordered eating. *Journal of Abnormal Psychology, 100,* 198–294.

Pilcher, J. J., & Huffcutt, A. I. (1996). Effects of sleep deprivation on performance: A meta-analysis. *Sleep, 19,* 318–326.

Pilcher, J. J., & Walters, A. S. (1997). How sleep deprivation affects psychological variables related to college students' cognitive performance. *Journal of American College Health, 46,* 121–126.

Pilcher, J. J., Ginter, D. R., & Sadowsky, B. (1997). Sleep quality versus sleep quantity: Relationships between sleep and measures of health, well-being and sleepiness in college students. *Journal of Psychosomatic Research, 42,* 583–596.

Pillow, D. R., Zautra, A. J., & Sandler, I. (1996). Major life events and minor stressors: Identifying mediational links in the stress process. *Journal of Personality and Social Psychology, 70,* 381–394.

Pilowsky, I. (1993). Aspects of abnormal illness behaviour. *Psychotherapy and Psychosomatics, 60,* 62–74.

Pincus, H. A., Tanielian, T. L., Marcus, S. C., Olfson, M., Zarin, D. A., Thompson, J., & Zito, J. M. (1998). Prescribing trends in psychotropic medications: Primary care, psychiatry, and other medical specialties. *Journal of the American Medical Association, 279,* 526–531.

Pinder, C. C. (1998). *Work motivation in organizational behavior.* Upper Saddle River, NJ: Prentice-Hall.

Pine, D. S. (2000). Anxiety disorders: Clinical features. In B. J. Sadock & V. A. Sadock (Eds.), *Kaplan and Sadock's comprehensive textbook of psychiatry* (7th ed., Vol. 1, pp. 1476–1489). Philadelphia: Lippincott/Williams & Wilkins.

Pinel, J. P. J., Assanand, S., & Lehman, D. R. (2000). Hunger, eating, and ill health. *American Psychologist, 55,* 1105–1116.

Pines, A. M. (1993). Burnout. In L. Goldberger, & S. Breznitz (Eds.), *Handbook of stress: Theoretical and clinical aspects.* New York: Free Press.

Pinker, S. (1990). Language acquisition. In D. N. Osherson & H. Lasnik (Eds.), *Language: An invitation to cognitive science* (Vol. 1). Cambridge, MA: MIT Press.

Pinker, S. (1994). *Language is to us as flying is to geese.* New York: Morrow.

Pinker, S., & Bloom, P. (1992). Natural language and natural selection. In J. H. Barkow, L. Cosmides, & J. Tooby (Eds.), *The adapted mind: Evolutionary psychology and the generation of culture.* New York: Oxford University Press.

Piper, W. E. (1993). Group psychotherapy research. In H. I. Kaplan & B. J. Sadock (Eds.), *Comprehensive group psychotherapy.* Baltimore: Williams & Wilkins.

Pi-Sunyer, F. X. (2002). Medical complications of obesity in adults. In C. G. Fairburn & K. D. Brownell (Eds.), *Eating disorders and obesity: A comprehensive handbook* (pp. 467–472). New York: Guilford.

Pittman, F., III. (1994, January/February). A buyer's guide to psychotherapy. *Psychology Today,* 50–53, 74–81.

Pivik, R. T. (2000). Psychophysiology of dreams. In M. H. Kryger, T. Roth, & W. C. Dement (Eds.), *Principles and practice of sleep medicine.* Philadelphia: Saunders.

Plante, T. G. (1999a). *Contemporary clinical psychology.* New York: Wiley & Sons, Inc.

Plante, T. G. (1999b). Could the perception of fitness account for many of the mental and physical health benefits of exercise? *Advances in Mind-Body Medicine, 15,* 291–295.

Plante, T. G., Caputo, D., & Chizmar, L. (2000). Perceived fitness and responses to laboratory-induced stress. *International Journal of Stress Management, 7*(1), 61–73.

Plomin, R. (1993). Nature and nurture: Perspective and prospective. In R. Plomin & G. E. McClearn (Eds.), *Nature, nurture and psychology.* Washington, DC: American Psychological Association.

Plomin, R. (1994). Nature, nurture, and development. In R. J. Sternberg (Ed.), *Encyclopedia of human intelligence.* New York: Macmillan.

Plomin, R., & Caspi, A. (1999). Behavioral genetics and personality. In L. A. Pervin & O. P. John (Eds.), *Handbook of personality: Theory and research.* New York: Guilford.

Plomin, R., & Crabbe, J. (2000). DNA. *Psychological Bulletin, 126,* 806–828.

Plomin, R., & Petrill, S. A. (1997). Genetics and intelligence: What's new? *Intelligence, 24,* 53–77.

Plomin, R., & Rende, R. (1991). Human behavioral genetics. *Annual Review of Psychology, 42,* 161–190.

Plomin, R., DeFries, J. C., McClearn, G. E., & McGuffin, P. (2001). *Behavioral genetics.* New York: Freeman.

Plotkin, H. (1998). *Evolution in mind: An introduction to evolutionary psychology.* Cambridge, MA: Harvard University Press.

Plous, S. (1991). An attitude survey of animal rights activists. *Psychological Science, 2,* 194–196.

Plucker, J. A., & Renzulli, J. S. (1999). Psychometric approaches to the study of human creativity. In R. J. Sternberg (Ed.), *Handbook of creativity.* New York: Cambridge University Press.

Plutchik, R. (1980, February). A language for the emotions. *Psychology Today,* pp. 68–78.

Plutchik, R. (1984). Emotions: A general psychoevolutionary theory. In K. R. Scherer & P. Ekman (Eds.), *Approaches to emotion.* Hillsdale, NJ: Erlbaum.

Plutchik, R. (1993). Emotions and their vicissitudes: Emotions and psychopathology. In M. Lewis & J. M. Haviland (Eds.), *Handbook of emotions.* New York: Guilford.

Policastro, E., & Gardner, H. (1999). From case studies to robust generalizations: An approach to the study of creativity. In R. J. Sternberg (Ed.), *Handbook of creativity.* New York: Cambridge University Press.

Polivy, J., & Herman, C. P. (1995). Dieting and its relation to eating disorders. In K. D. Brownell & C. G.Fairburn (Eds.), *Eating disorders and obesity: A comprehensive handbook.* New York: Guilford.

Poloma, M., & Pendleton, B. F. (1990). Religious domains and general well-being. *Social Indicators Research, 22,* 255–276.

Pomeroy, C., & Mitchell, J. E. (2002). Medical complications of anorexia nervosa and bulimia nervosa. In C. G. Fairburn & K. D. Brownell (Eds.), *Eating disorders and obesity: A comprehensive handbook.* New York: Guilford.

Ponterotto, J. G., & Pedersen, P. B. (1993). *Preventing prejudice: A guide for counselors and educators.* Newbury Park, CA: Sage.

Pope, H. G., Gruber, A. J., & Yurgelun-Todd, D. (2001). Residual neuropsychologic effects of cannabis. *Current Psychiatry Report, 3,* 507–512.

Pope, H. G., Gruber, A. J., Hudson, J. I., Huestis, M. A., & Yurgelun-Todd, D. (2001). Neuropsychological performance in long-term cannabis users. *Archives of General Psychiatry, 58,* 909–915.

Pope, H. G., Jr., & Hudson, J. I. (1998). Can memories of childhood sexual abuse be repressed? In R. A. Baker (Ed.), *Child sexual abuse and false memory syndrome.* Amherst, NY: Prometheus Books.

Pope, H. G., Jr., Oliva, P. S., Hudson, J. I., Bodkin, J. A., & Gruber, A. J. (1999). Attitudes toward DSM-IV dissociative disorders diagnoses among board-certified American psychiatrists. *American Journal of Psychiatry, 156,* 321–323.

Pope, K. S. (1996). Memory, abuse, and science: Questioning claims about the false memory syndrome epidemic. *American Psychologist, 51,* 957–974.

Pope, K. S., & Brown, L. (1996). *Recovered memories of abuse: Assessment, thereapy, forensics.* Washington, D.C.: American Psychological Association.

Pope, K. S., Keith-Spiegel, P., & Tabachnick, B. G. (1986). Sexual attraction to clients. *American Psychologist, 41,* 147–158.

Popenoe, D. (1996). *Life without father.* New York: Pressler Press.

Popper, C. W., & Steingard, R. J. (1994). Disorders usually first diagnosed in infancy, childhood, or adolescence. In R. E. Hales, S. C. Yudofsky, & J. A. Talbott (Eds.), *The American Psychiatric Press textbook of psychiatry.* Washington, DC: American Psychiatric Press.

Popper, C. W., & West, S. A. (1999). Disorders usually first diagnosed in infancy, childhood, or adolescence. In R. E. Hales, S. C. Yudofsky, & J. A. Talbott (Eds.), *The American Psychiatric Press textbook of psychiatry* (3rd ed., pp. 825–954). Washington, DC: American Psychiatric Press.

Posada, G., & Jacobs, A. (2001). Child-mother attachment relationships and culture. *American Psychologist, 56,* 821–822.

Posner, M. I., & DiGirolamo, G. J. (2000). Attention in cognitive neuroscience: An overview. In M. S. Gazzaniga (Ed.), *The new cognitive neurosciences* (2nd ed., pp. 623–632). Cambridge, MA: MIT Press.

Posner, M. I., & Raichle, M. E. (1994). *Images of mind.* New York: Scientific American Library.

Post, F. (1996). Verbal creativity, depression and alcoholism: An investigation of one hundred American and British writers. *British Journal of Psychiatry, 168,* 545–555.

Postman, L. (1985). Human learning and memory. In G. A. Kimble & K. Schlesinger (Eds.), *Topics in the history of psychology.* Hillsdale, NJ: Erlbaum.

Postmes, T., Spears, R., & Cihangir, S. (2001). Quality of decision making and group norms. *Journal of Personality and Social Psychology, 80,* 918–930.

Potthoff, J. G., Holahan, C. J., & Joiner, T. E., Jr. (1995). Reassurance-seeking, stress generation, and depressive symptoms: An integrative model. *Journal of Personality and Social Psychology, 68,* 664–670.

Poulton, E. C. (1994). *Behavioral decision theory: A new approach.* Cambridge, England: Cambridge University Press.

Powell, R. A., & Boer, D. P. (1995). Did Freud misinterpret reported memories of sexual abuse as fantasies? *Psychological Reports, 77,* 563–570.

Powell, R. A., & Gee, T. L. (1999). The effects of hypnosis on dissociative identity disorder: A reexamination of the evidence. *Canadian Journal of Psychiatry, 44,* 914–916.

Powell, R. A., Symbaluk, D. G., & MacDonald, S. E. (2002). *Introduction to learning and behavior.* Belmont, CA: Wadsworth.

Pratkanis, A. R., & Aronson, E. (2000). *Age of propaganda: The everyday use and abuse of persuasion.* New York: Freeman.

Pratt, L. A., Ford, D. E., Crum, R. M., Armenian, H. K., Gallo, J. J., & Eaton, W. W. (1996). Depression, psychotropic medication, and risk of myocardinal infarction: Prospective data from Baltimore ECA follow-up. *Archives of Internal Medicine, 94,* 3123–3129.

Premack, D. (1985). "Gavagai!" or the future history of the animal language controversy. *Cognition, 19,* 207–296.

Prentky, R. A. (1980). *Creativity and psychopathology: A neurocognitive perspective.* New York: Praeger.

Prentky, R. (1989). Creativity and psychopathology: Gamboling at the seat of madness. In J. A. Glover, R. R. Ronning, & C. R. Reynolds (Eds.), *Handbook of creativity.* New York: Plenum.

Prentky, R. A. (1997). Arousal reduction in sexual offenders: A review of antiandrogen interventions. *Sexual Abuse: Journal of Research and Treatment, 9,* 335–347.

Priester, J. R., & Petty, R. E. (1995). Source attributions and persuasion; Perceived honesty as a determinant of message scrutiny. *Personality and Social Psychology Bulletin, 21,* 637–654.

Priester, J. R., & Petty, R. E. (2001). Extending the bases of subjective attitudinal ambivalence: Interpersonal and intrapersonal antecedents of evaluative tension. *Journal of Personality and Social Psychology, 80,* 19–34.

Prifitera, A. (1994). Wechsler scales of intelligence. In R. J. Sternberg (Ed.), *Encyclopedia of human intelligence.* New York: Macmillan.

Prince, G. (1978). Putting the other half to work. *Training: The Magazine of Human Resources Development, 15,* 57–61.

Prochaska, J. O. (1994). Strong and weak principles for progressing from precontemplation to action on the basis of twelve problem behaviors. *Health Psychology, 13,* 47–51.

Proffitt, D. R., Bhalla, M., Gossweiler, R., & Midgett, J. (1995). Perceiving geographical slant. *Psychonomic Bulletin & Review, 2,* 409–428.

Pronin, E., Kruger, J., Savitsky, K., & Ross, L. (2001). You don't know me, but I know you: The illusion of asymmetric insight. *Journal of Personality and Social Psychology, 81,* 639–656.

Pronin, E., Lin, D. Y., & Ross, L. (2002). The bias blind spot: Perceptions of bias in self versus others. *Personality and Social Psychology Bulletin, 28,* 369–381.

Provine, R. R. (1989). Faces as releasers of contagious yawning: An approach to face detection using normal human subjects. *Bulletin of the Psychonomic Society, 27,* 211–214.

Provine, R. R. (1993). Yawning. In M. A. Carskadon (Ed.), *Encyclopedia of sleep and dreaming.* New York: Macmillan.

Prudic, J., & Sackeim, H. A. (1999). Electroconvulsive therapy and suicide risk. *Journal of Clinical Psychiatry, 60,* 104–110.

Pruitt, D. G. (1971). Choice shifts in group discussion: An introductory review. *Journal of Personality and Social Psychology, 20,* 339–360.

Pucetti, R. (1981). The case for mental duality: Evidence from split brain data and other considerations. *Behavioral and Brain Sciences, 4,* 93–123.

Puente, A. E. (1990). Psychological assessment of minority group members. In G. Goldstein & M. Hersen (Eds.), *Handbook of psychological assessment.* New York: Pergamon Press.

Pullum, G. K. (1991). *The Great Eskimo vocabulary hoax.* Chicago: University of Chicago Press.

Quinn, P. C., & Eimas, P. D. (1996). Perceptual cues that permit categorical differentiation of animal species by infants. *Journal of Experimental Child Psychology, 63,* 189–211.

Quinn, P. C., & Eimas, P. D. (1998). Evidence for a global categorical representation of humans by young infants. *Journal of Experimental Child Psychology, 69,* 151–174.

Quitkin, F. M. (1999). Placebos, drug effects, and study design: A clinician's guide. *American Journal of Psychiatry, 156,* 829–836.

Rabins, P. V., Lyketsos, C. G., & Steele, C. D. (1999). *Practical dementia care.* New York: Oxford University Press.

Rabkin, J. G., Wagner, G. J., & Rabkin, R. (2000). A double-blind, placebo-controlled trial of testosterone therapy for HIV-positive men with hypogonadal symptoms. *Archives of General Psychiatry, 57,* 141–147.

Rachman, S. J. (1990). *Fear and courage.* New York: W. H. Freeman.

Rachman, S. J. (1992). Behavior therapy. In L. R. Squire (Ed.), *Encyclopedia of learning and memory.* New York: Macmillan.

Racine, R. J., & deJonge, M. (1988). Short-term and long-term potentiation in projection pathways and local circuits. In P. W. Landfield & S. A. Deadwyler (Eds.), *Long-term potentiation: From biophysics to behavior.* New York: Liss.

Ragland, D. R., & Brand, R. J. (1988). Type A behavior and mortality from coronary heart disease. *The New England Journal of Medicine, 318*(2), 65–69.

Rahe, R. H., & Arthur, R. H. (1978). Life change and illness studies. *Journal of Human Stress, 4*(1), 3–15.

Raichle, M. E. (1994). Images of the mind: Studies with modern imaging techniques. *Annual Review of Psychology, 45,* 333–356.

Raine, A. (1997). Antisocial behavior and psychophysiology: A biosocial perspective and a prefrontal dysfunction hypothesis. In D. M. Stoff, J. Breiling, & J. D. Maser (Eds.), *Handbook of antisocial behavior.* New York: Wiley.

Rains, G. D. (2002). *Principles of human neuropsychology.* New York: McGraw-Hill.

Rainville, P., Duncan, G. H., Price, D. D., Carrier, B., & Bushnell, M. C. (1997). Pain affect encoded in human anterior cingulate but not somatosensory cortex. *Science, 277,* 968–971.

Rakic, P., Bourgeois, J. P., & Goldman-Rakic, P. S. (1994). Synaptic development of the cerebral cortex: Implications for learning, memory, and mental illness. *Progress in brain research.*

Ramadan, N. M. (2000). Migraine. In G. Fink (Ed.), *Encyclopedia of stress* (pp. 757–770). San Diego: Academic Press.

Ramaekers, J. G., Robbe, H. W. J., & O'Hanlon, J. F. (2000). Marijuana, alcohol and actual driving performance. *Human Psychopharmacology: Clinical & Experimental, 15,* 551–558.

Ramey, C. T., & Ramey, S. L. (2000). Intelligence and public policy. In R. J. Sternberg (Ed.), *Handbook of intelligence* (pp. 534–548). New York: Cambridge University Press.

Ramey, C. T., Ramey, S. L., & Lanzi, R. G. (2001). Intelligence and experience. In R. J. Sternberg & E. L. Grigorenko (Eds.), *Environmental effects on cognitive abilities* (pp. 83–116). Mahwah, NJ: Erlbaum.

Ramey, S. L. (1999). Head Start and preschool education: Toward continued improvement. *American Psychologist, 54,* 344–346.

Ramsay, D. S., Seeley, R. J., Bolles, R. C., & Woods, S. C. (1996). Ingestive homeostasis: The primacy of learning. In E. D. Capaldi (Ed.), *Why we eat what we eat: The psychology of eating* (pp. 11–29). Washington, DC: American Psychological Association.

Rapaport, D., Gill, M., & Schafer, R. (1968). *Diagnostic psychological testing.* New York: International Universities Press.

Rapee, R. M., & Barlow, D. H. (2001). Generalized anxiety disorders, panic disorders, and phobias. In P. B. Sutker & H. E. Adams (Eds.), *Comprehensive handbook of psychopathology* (3rd ed., pp. 131–154). New York: Kluwer Academic/Plenum Publishers.

Raphael, B., & Dobson, M. (2000). Effects of public disasters. In G. Fink (Ed.), *Encyclopedia of stress* (Vol. 1, pp. 699–705). San Diego: Academic Press.

Rasmussen, C., Knapp, T. J., & Garner, L. (2000). Driving-induced stress in urban college students. *Perceptual & Motor Skills, 90,* 437–443.

Rasmussen, T., & Milner, B. (1977). The role of early left brain injury in determining lateralization of cerebral speech functions. *Annals of the New York Academy of Sciences, 299,* 355–369.

Ratner, N. B., Gleason, J. B., & Narasimhan, B. (1998). An introduction to psycholinguistics: What do language users know? In J. B. Gleason & N. B. Ratner (Eds.), *Psycholinguistics* (2nd ed., pp. 1–40).

Fort Worth, TX: Harcourt College Publishers.

Rauscher, F. H., Shaw, G. L., & Ky, K. N. (1993). Music and spatial task performance. *Nature, 365,* 611.

Rauscher, F. H., Shaw, G. L., & Ky, K. N. (1995). Listening to Mozart enhances spatial-temporal reasoning: Towards a neurophysiological basis. *Neuroscience Letters, 185,* 44–47.

Raynor, J. O., & Entin, E. E. (1982). Future orientation and achievement motivation. In J. O. Raynor & E. E. Entin (Eds.), *Motivation, career striving, and aging.* New York: Hemisphere.

Raz, S. (1993). Structural cerebral pathology in schizophrenia: Regional or diffuse? *Journal of Abnormal Psychology, 102,* 445–452.

Read, C. R. (1991). Achievement and career choices: Comparisons of males and females. *Roeper Review, 13,* 188–193.

Real, L. (1991). Animal choice behavior and the evolution of cognitive architecture. *Science, 253,* 980–986.

Recanzone, G. H. (2000). Cerebral cortical plasticity: Perception and skill acquisition. In M. S. Gazzaniga (Ed.), *The new cognitive neurosciences.* Cambridge, MA: The MIT Press.

Recht, L. D., Lew, R. A., & Schwartz, W. J. (1995). Baseball teams beaten by jet lag. *Nature, 377,* 583.

Rechtschaffen, A. (1994). Sleep onset: Conceptual issues. In R. D. Ogilvie & J. R. Harsh (Eds.), *Sleep onset: Normal and abnormal processes.* Washington, DC: American Psychological Association.

Reddy, B. S. (1999). Role of dietary fiber in colon cancer: An overview. *American Journal of Medicine, 106*(1A), 16S–19S.

Ree, M. J., & Earles, J. A. (1992). Intelligence is the best predictor of job performance. *Current Directions in Psychological Science, 1,* 86–89.

Reed, J. G., & Baxter P. M. (1992). *Library use: A handbook for psychology.* Washington, DC: American Psychological Association.

Regan, P. C. (1998). What if you can't get what you want? Willingness to compromise ideal mate selection standards as a function of sex, mate value, and relationship context. *Personality and Social Psychology Bulletin, 24,* 1294–1303.

Regan, T. (1989). Ill-gotten gains. In G. Langley (Ed.), *Animal experimentation: The consensus changes.* New York: Chapman & Hall.

Regan, T. (1997). The rights of humans and other animals. *Ethics & Behavior, 7*(2), 103–111.

Regier, D. A., & Burke, J. D. (2000). Epidemiology. In B. J. Sadock & V. A. Sadock (Eds.), *Kaplan and Sadock's comprehensive textbook of psychiatry.*

Philadelphia: Lippincott/Williams & Wilkins.

Regier, D. A., & Kaelber, C. T. (1995). The Epidemiologic Catchment Area (ECA) program: Studying the prevalence and incidence of psychopathology. In M. T. Tsuang, M. Tohen, & G. E. P. Zahner (Eds.), *Textbook in psychiatric epidemiology.* New York: Wiley.

Rehm, L. P., Wagner, A., & Ivens-Tyndal, Co. (2001). Mood disorders: Unipolar and bipolar. In P. B. Sutker & H. E. Adams (Eds.), *Comprehensive handbook of psychopathology* (pp. 277–308). New York: Kluwer Academic/Plenum.

Reibel, D. K., Greeson, J. M., Brainard, G. C., & Rosenzweig, S. (2001). Mindfulness-based stress reduction and health-related quality of life in a heterogeneous patient population. *General Hospital Psychiatry, 23*(4), 183–192.

Reinharz, D., Lesage, A. D., & Contandriopoulos, A. P. (2000). Cost-effectiveness analysis of psychiatric deinstitutionalization. *Canadian Journal of Psychiatry, 45,* 533–538.

Reisner, A. D. (1998). Repressed memories: True and false. In R. A. Baker (Ed.), *Child sexual abuse and false memory syndrome.* Amherst, NY: Prometheus Books.

Reiss, S. (1991). Expectancy model of fear, anxiety and panic. *Clinical Psychology Review, 11,* 141–154.

Rennie, D. (1999). Fair conduct and fair reporting of clinical trials. *Journal of the American Medical Association, 282,* 1766–1768.

Rennie, D., & Luft, H. S. (2000). Making them transparent, making them credible. *Journal of the American Medical Association, 283,* 2516–2521.

Renzulli, J. S. (1986). The three-ring conception of giftedness: A developmental model for creative productivity. In R. J. Sternberg & J. E. Davidson (Eds.), *Conceptions of giftedness.* Cambridge: Cambridge University Press.

Renzulli, J. S. (1999). What is this thing called giftedness, and how do we develop it? A twenty-five year perspective. *Journal for the Education of the Gifted, 23,* 3–54.

Renzulli, J. S. (2002). Emerging conceptions of giftedness: Building a bridge to the new century. *Exceptionality, 10,* 67–75.

Rescorla, R. A. (1978). Some implications of a cognitive perspective on Pavlovian conditioning. In S. H. Hulse, H. Fowler, & W. K. Honig (Eds.), *Cognitive processes in animal behavior.* Hillsdale, NJ: Erlbaum.

Rescorla, R. A. (1980). *Pavlovian second-order conditioning.* Hillsdale, NJ: Erlbaum.

Rescorla, R. A., & Solomon, R. L. (1967). Two-process learning theory: Relationships between Pavlovian conditioning and instrumental learning. *Psychological Review, 74,* 151–182.

Rescorla, R. A., & Wagner, A. R. (1972). A theory of Pavlovian conditioning: Variations in the effectiveness of reinforcement and nonreinforcement. In A. H. Black & W. F. Prokasky (Eds.), *Classical conditioning: II. Current research and theory.* New York: Appleton-Century-Crofts.

Rest, J. R. (1986). *Moral development: Advances in research and theory.* New York: Praeger.

Reuter-Lorenz, P. A., & Miller, A. C. (1998). The cognitive neuroscience of human laterality: Lessons from the bisected brain. *Current Directions in Psychological Science, 7,* 15–20.

Reynolds, A. J., Temple, J. T., Robertson, D. L., & Mann, E. A. (2001). Long-term effects of an early childhood intervention on educational achievement and juvenile arrest: A 15-year follow-up of low-income children in public schools. *Journal of the American Medical Association, 285,* 2339–2346.

Reynolds, C. F., III, Frank, E., Perel, J. M., Imber, S. D., Cornes, C., Miller, M. D., Mazumdar, S., Houck, P. R., Dew, M. A., Stack, J. A., Pollock, B. G., & Kupfer, D. J. (1999). Nortriptyline and interpersonal psychotherapy as maintenance therapies for recurrent major depression: A randomized controlled trial in patients older than 50 years. *Journal of the American Medical Association, 28,* 39–45.

Reynolds, C. F., III, Kupfer, D. J., Buysse, D. J., Coble, P. A., & Yeager, A. (1991). Subtyping DSM-III-R primary insomnia: A literature review by the DSM-IV work group on sleep disorders. *American Journal of Psychiatry, 148,* 432–438.

Reynolds, C. R. (1994). Reliability. In R. J. Sternberg (Ed.), *Encyclopedia of human intelligence.* New York: Macmillan.

Reynolds, C. R. (2000). Why is psychometric research on bias in mental testing so often ignored? *Psychology, Public Policy, and Law, 6,* 144–150.

Riazi, A., & Bradley, C. (2000). Diabetes, Type I. In G. Fink (Ed.), *Encyclopedia of stress* (pp. 688–693). San Diego: Academic Press.

Rice, L. N., & Greenberg, L. S. (1992). Humanistic approaches to psychotherapy. In D. K. Freedheim (Ed.), *History of psychotherapy: A century of change.* Washington, DC: American Psychological Association.

Richardson, G. S. (1993). Circadian rhythms. In M. A. Carskadon (Ed.), *Encyclopedia of sleep and dreaming.* New York: Macmillan.

Rich-Edwards, J. W., Stampfer, M. J., Manson, J. E., Rosner, B., Hankinson, S. E., Colditz, G. A., Willett, W. C., & Hennekens, C. H. (1997). Birth weight and risk of cardiovascular disease in a cohort of women followed up since 1976. *British Medical Journal, 315,* 396–400.

Richert, E. S. (1997). Excellence with equity in identification and programming. In N. Colangelo, & G. A. Davis (Eds.), *Handbook of gifted education.* Boston: Allyn & Bacon.

Ridker, P. M. (2001). High-sensitivity C-reactive protein: Potential adjunct for global risk assessment in the primary prevention of cardiovascular disease. *Circulation, 103,* 1813–1818.

Rieber, R. W. (1998). The assimilation of psychoanalysis in America: From popularization to vulgarization. In R. W. Rieber & K. D. Salzinger (Eds.), *Psychology: Theoretical-historical perspectives.* Washington, DC: American Psychological Association.

Riemann, R., Angleitner, A., & Strelau, J. (1997). Genetic and environmental influences on personality: A study of twins reared together using the self-and peer report NEO-FFI scales. *Journal of Personality, 65,* 449–476.

Rieskamp, J., & Hoffrage, U. (1999). When do people use simple heuristics, and how can we tell? In G. Gigerenzer, P. M. Todd, & ABC Research Group (Eds.), *Simple heuristics that make us smart* (pp. 141–168). New York: Oxford University Press.

Rilling, M. (1996). The mystery of the vanished citations: James McConnell's forgotten 1960s quest for planarian learning, a biochemical engram, and celebrity. *American Psychologist, 51,* 589–598.

Rimal R. N. (2001). Longitudinal influences of knowledge and self-efficacy on exercise behavior: Tests of a mutual reinforcement model. *Journal of Health Psychology, 6,* 31–46.

Rivas-Vazquez, R. A. (2001). Antidepressants as first-line agents in the current pharmacotherapy of anxiety disorders. *Professional Psychology: Research & Practice, 32*(1), 101–104.

Roazen, P. (1976). *Erik H. Erikson: The power and limits of a vision.* New York: Free Press.

Roberts, B. W., & DelVecchio, W. F. (2000). The rank-order consistency of personality traits from childhood to old age: A quantitative review of longitudinal studies. *Psychological Bulletin, 126,* 3–25.

Roberts, B. W., Caspi, A., & Moffitt, T. E. (2001). The kids are alright: Growth and stability in personality development from adolescence to adulthood. *Journal of Personality and Social Psychology, 81,* 670–683.

Roberts, L. (2001). Controversial from the start. *Science, 291,* 1182–1188.

Roberts, R. D., Zeidner, M., & Matthews, G. (2001). Does emotional intelligence meet traditional standards for an intelligence? Some new data and conclusions. *Emotion, 1,* 196–231.

Robins, L. N., & Regier, D. A. (1991). *Psychiatric disorders in America: The epidemiologic catchment area study.* New York: Free Press.

Robins, L. N., Locke, B. Z., & Regier, D. A. (1991). An overview of psychiatric disorders in America. In L. N. Robins & D. A. Regier (Eds.), *Psychiatric disorders in America: The epidemiologic catchment area study.* New York: Free Press.

Robins, R. W., Gosling, S. D., & Craik, K. H. (1999). An empirical analysis of trends in psychology. *American Psychologist, 54,* 117–128.

Robinson, A., & Clinkenbeard, P. R. (1998). Giftedness: An exceptionality examined. *Annual Review of Psychology, 49,* 117–139.

Robinson, F. P. (1970). *Effective study* (4th ed.). New York: Harper & Row.

Robinson, J. P., & Godbey, G. (1997). *Time for life: The surprising ways Americans use their time.* University Park: Pennsylvania State University Press.

Robinson, S. L., Kraatz, M. S., & Rousseau, D. M. (1994). Changing obligations and the psychological contract: A longitudinal study. *Academy of Management Journal, 37,* 137–152.

Rock, I. (1986). The description and analysis of object and event perception. In K. R. Boff, L. Kaufman, & J. P. Thomas (Eds.), *Handbook of perception and human performance* (Vol. 2). New York: Wiley.

Rodgers, J. E. (1982). The malleable memory of eyewitnesses. *Science Digest, 3,* 32–35.

Rodin, J. (1985). Insulin levels, hunger, and food intake: An example of feedback loops in body weight regulation. *Health Psychology, 4,* 1–24.

Roediger, H. L., III. (1980). Memory metaphors in cognitive psychology. *Memory & Cognition, 8,* 231–246.

Roediger, H. L., III. (1990). Implicit memory: Retention without remembering. *American Psychologist, 45,* 1043–1056.

Roediger, H. L., III. (2000). Why retrieval is the key process in understanding human memory. In E. Tulving (Ed.), *Memory, consciousness, and the brain: The Tallinn conference* (pp. 52–75). Philadelphia: Psychology Press.

Roediger, H. L., III, & Guynn, M. J. (1996). Retrieval processes. In E. L. Bjork & R. A. Bjork (Eds.), *Memory.* San Diego: Academic Press.

Roediger, H. L., III, & McDermott, K. B. (1995). Creating false memories: Remembering words not presented in lists. *Journal of Experimental Psychology: Learning, Memory, and Cognition, 21,* 803–814.

Roediger, H. L., III, & McDermott, K. B. (2000). Tricks of memory. *Current Directions in Psychological Science, 9,* 123–127.

Roediger, H. L., III, Wheeler, M. A., & Rajaram, S. (1993). Remembering, knowing, and reconstructing the past. In D. L. Medin (Ed.), *The psychology of learning and motivation: Advances in research and theory.* San Diego: Academic Press.

Roehrs, T., & Roth, T. (2000). Hypnotics: Efficacy and adverse effects. In M. H. Kryger, T. Roth, & W. C. Dement (Eds.), *Principles and practice of sleep medicine.* Philadelphia: Saunders.

Roehrs, T., Carskadon, M. A., Dement, W. C., & Roth, T. (2000). Daytime sleepiness and alertness. In M. H. Kryger, T. Roth, & W. C. Dement (Eds.), *Principles and practice of sleep medicine.* Philadelphia: Saunders.

Roehrs, T., Zorick, F. J., & Roth, T. (2000). Transient and short term insomnias. In M. H. Kryger, T. Roth, & W. C. Dement (Eds.), *Principles and practice of sleep medicine.* Philadelphia: Saunders.

Roffwarg, H. P., Muzio, J. N., & Dement, W. C. (1966). Ontogenetic development of the human sleep-dream cycle. *Science, 152,* 604–619.

Rogers, C. R. (1951). *Client-centered therapy: Its current practice, implications, and theory.* Boston: Houghton Mifflin.

Rogers, C. R. (1961). *On becoming a person: A therapist's view of psychotherapy.* Boston: Houghton Mifflin.

Rogers, C. R. (1980). *A way of being.* Boston: Houghton Mifflin.

Rogers, C. R. (1986). Client-centered therapy. In I. L. Kutash & A. Wolf (Eds.), *Psychotherapist's casebook.* San Francisco: Jossey-Bass.

Rogers, M. P., Fricchione, G., & Reich, P. (1999). Psychosomatic medicine and consultation-liaison psychiatry. In A. M. Nicholi (Ed.), *The Harvard guide to psychiatry* (3rd ed., pp. 362–389). Cambridge, MA: Harvard University Press.

Rogers, P. (1998). The cognitive psychology of lottery gambling: A theoretical review. *Journal of Gambling Studies, 14,* 111–134.

Rogers, R. W. (1983). Cognitive and physiological processes in fear appeals and attitude change: A revised theory of protection motivation. In J. Cacioppo & R. Petty (Eds.), *Social psychophysiology.* New York: Guilford.

Rogers, T. B., Kuiper, N. A., & Kirker, W. S. (1977). Self-reference and the encoding of personal information. *Journal of Personality and Social Psychology, 35,* 677–688.

Rogers, W. T., & Yang, P. (1996). Test-wiseness: Its nature and application. *European Journal of Psychological Assessment, 12,* 247–259.

Rogoff, B. (1990). *Apprenticeship in thinking.* New York: Oxford University Press.

Rohner, R. P., & Veneziano, R. A. (2001). The importance of father love: History and contemporary evidence. *Review of General Psychology, 5,* 382–405.

Roivainen, M., Viik-Kajander, M., Palosuo, T., Toivanen, P., Leinonen, M., Saikku, P., Tenkanen, L., Manninen, V., Hovi, T., & Mänttäri, M. (2000). Infections, inflammation, and the risk of coronary heart disease. *Circulation, 101,* 252–257.

Rojahn, K., & Pettigrew, T. F. (1992). Memory for schema-relevant information: A meta-analytic resolution. *British Journal of Social Psychology, 31,* 81–109.

Rollins, B., & Feldman, H. (1970). Marital satisfaction over the family life cycle. *Journal of Marriage and the Family, 32,* 20–28.

Rollman, G. B. (1992). Cognitive effects in pain and pain judgements. In D. Algom (Ed.), *Psychophysical approaches to cognition.* Amsterdam: North Holland.

Rolls, E. T. (1990). A theory of emotion, and its application to understanding the neural basis of emotion. *Cognitive and Emotion, 4,* 161–190.

Rolls, E. T., & Tovee, M. T. (1995). Sparseness of the neuronal representation of stimuli in the primate temporal visual cortex. *Journal of Neurophysiology, 73,* 713–726.

Romano, S. J., & Quinn, L. (2001). Evaluation and treatment of bulimia nervosa. *Primary Psychiatry, 8*(2), 57–62.

Rorschach, H. (1942). *Psychodiagnostics: A diagnostic test based on perception.* Berne: Huber.

Rosch, E. H. (1973). Natural categories. *Cognitive Psychology, 4,* 328–350.

Rose, D. P. (1997). Dietary fatty acids and cancer. *American Journal of Clinical Nutrition, 66,* 998S–1003S.

Rose, H., & Rose, S. E. (2000). *Alas, poor Darwin: Arguments against evolutionary psychology.* New York: Harmony Books.

Rose, R. J. (1995). Genes and human behavior. *Annual Review of Psychology, 46,* 625–654.

Rose, S. D. (1999). Group therapy: A cognitive-behavioral approach. In J. R. Price & D. R. Hescheles (Ed.), *A guide to starting psychotherapy groups.* San Diego: Academic Press.

Rose, S. P. R. (1992). Protein synthesis in long-term memory in vertebrates. In L. R. Squire (Ed.), *Encyclopedia of learning and memory*. New York: Macmillan.

Rosenbaum, M., Lakin, M., & Roback, H. B. (1992). Psychotherapy in groups. In D. K. Freedheim (Ed.), *History of psychotherapy: A century of change*. Washington, DC: American Psychological Association.

Rosenberg, P. S., & Biggar, R. J. (1998). Trends in HIV incidence among young adults in the United States. *Journal of the American Medical Association, 279*, 1894–1899.

Rosenberg, S. D., Rosenberg, H. J., & Farrell, M. P. (1999). Midlife crisis revisited. In S. L. Willis & J. D. Reid (Eds.), *Life in the middle: Psychological and social development in middle age* (pp. 47–70). San Diego, CA: Academic Press.

Rosenfarb, I. S., Goldstein, M. J., Mintz, J., & Nuechterlein, K. H. (1995). Expressed emotion and subclinical psychopathology observable within the transactions between schizophrenic patients and their family members. *Journal of Abnormal Psychology, 104*, 259–267.

Rosenhan, D. L. (1973). On being sane in insane places. *Science, 179*, 250–258.

Rosenheck, R. (2000). Cost-effectiveness of services for mentally ill homeless people: The application of research to policy and practice. *American Journal of Psychiatry, 157*, 1563–1570.

Rosenman, R. H. (1993). Relationships of the Type A behavior pattern with coronary heart disease. In L. Goldberger & S. Breznitz (Eds.), *Handbook of stress: Theoretical and clinical aspects* (2nd ed.). New York: Free Press.

Rosenthal, R. (1976). *Experimenter effects in behavioral research*. New York: Halsted.

Rosenthal, R. (1994). Interpersonal expectancy effects: A 30-year perspective. *Current Directions in Psychological Science, 3*, 176–179.

Rosenthal, R., & Fode, K. L. (1963). Three experiments in experimenter bias. *Psychological Reports, 12*, 491–511.

Rosenzweig, M. R. (1996). Aspects of the search for neural mechanisms of memory. *Annual Review of Psychology, 47*, 1–32.

Rosenzweig, M. R., & Bennet, E. L. (1996). Psychobiology of plasticity: Effects of training and experience on brain and behavior. *Behavioural Brain Research, 78*(5), 57–65.

Rosenzweig, M. R., Krech, D., & Bennett, E. L. (1961). Heredity, environment, brain biochemistry, and learning. In *Current trends in*

psychological theory. Pittsburgh: University of Pittsburgh Press.

Rosenzweig, M., Krech, D., Bennett, E. L., & Diamond, M. (1962). Effects of environmental complexity and training on brain chemistry and anatomy: A replication and extension. *Journal of Comparative and Physiological Psychology, 55*, 429–437.

Rosenzweig, S. (1985). Freud and experimental psychology: The emergence of idiodynamics. In S. Koch & D. E. Leary (Eds.), *A century of psychology as a science*. New York: McGraw-Hill.

Roskos-Ewoldsen, D. R., & Fazio, R. H. (1992). The accessibility of source likability as a determinant of persuasion. *Personality and Social Psychology Bulletin, 18*, 19–25.

Ross, B. (1991). William James: Spoiled child of American psychology. In G. A. Kimble, M. Wertheimer, & C. White (Eds.), *Portraits of pioneers in psychology*. Hillsdale, NJ: Erlbaum.

Ross, C. A. (1999). Dissociative disorders. In T. Millon, P. H. Blaney, & R. D. Davis (Eds.), *Oxford textbook of psychopathology* (pp. 466–484). New York: Oxford University Press.

Ross, C. E., & Van Willigen, M. (1997). Education and the subjective quality of life. *Journal of Health and Social Behavior, 38*, 275–297.

Ross, L. D., & Anderson, C. A. (1982). Shortcomings in the attribution process: On the origins and maintenance of erroneous social assessments. In D. Kahneman, P. Slovic, & A. Tversky (Eds.), *Judgement under uncertainty: Heuristics and biases*. Cambridge: Cambridge University Press.

Ross, L. D. (1988). The obedience experiments: A case study of controversy. *Contemporary Psychology, 33*, 101–104.

Rosse, J. G., Stecher, M. D., Miller, J. L., & Levin, R. A. (1998). The impact of response distortion on preemployment personality testing and hiring decisions. *Journal of Applied Psychology, 83*, 634–644.

Rossi, P. H. (1990). The old homeless and the new homelessness in historical perspective. *American Psychologist, 45*(8), 954–959.

Rosso, I. M., Cannon, T. D., Huttunen, T., Huttunen, M. O., Lönnqvist, J., & Gasperoni, T. L. (2000). Obstetric risk factors for early-onset schizophrenia in a Finnish birth cohort. *American Journal of Psychiatry, 157*, 801–807.

Rothbart, M. K., & Bates, J. E. (1998). Temperament. In W. Damon (Ed.), *Handbook of child psychology (Vol. 3): Social, emotional, and personality development*. New York: Wiley.

Rothbart, M. K., Ahadi, S. A., & Evans, D. E. (2000). Temperament and personality: Origins and out-

comes. *Journal of Personality and Social Psychology, 78*, 122–135.

Rothbaum, F., Weisz, J., Pott, M., Miyake, K., & Morelli, G. (2000). Attachment and culture: Security in the United States and Japan. *American Psychologist, 55*, 1093–1104.

Rothenberg, A. (1990). *Creativity and madness*. Baltimore: John Hopkins University Press.

Rothschild, A. J. (1999). Mood disorders. In A. M. Nicholi, Jr. (Ed.), *The Harvard guide to psychiatry* (3rd ed., pp. 281–307). Cambridge, MA: Harvard University Press.

Rotter, J. B. (1982). *The development and application of social learning theory*. New York: Praeger.

Rotter, J. B., & Rafferty, J. E. (1950). *Manual: The Rotter incomplete sentence blank*. New York: Psychological Corporation.

Rouiller, E. M. (1997). Functional organization of the auditory pathways. In G. Ehret & R. Romand (Eds.), *The central auditory system*. Oxford, England: Oxford University Press.

Rousseau, D. M. (1995). *Psychological contracts in organizations*. Thousand Oaks, CA: Sage.

Rousseau, D. M., & Parks, J. M. (1993). The contracts of individuals and organizations. In B. M. Staw & L. L. Cummings (Eds.), *Research in organizational behavior* (Vol. 15, pp. 1–43). Greenwich, CT: JAI Press.

Rousseau, D. M., & Schalk, R. (2000). Learning from cross-national perspectives on psychological contracts. In D. M. Rousseau & R. Schalk (Eds.), *Psychological contracts in employment: Cross-national perspectives* (pp. 283–403). Thousand Oaks, CA: Sage.

Rowatt, W. C., Cunningham, M. R., & Druen, P. B. (1999). Lying to get a date: The effect of facial physical attractiveness on the willingness to deceive prospective dating partners. *Journal of Social & Personal Relationships, 16*, 209–223.

Rowe, D. (1994). *The limits of family influence: Genes, experience, and behavior*. New York: Guilford.

Rowe, D. C. (1997). Genetics, temperament, and personality. In R. Hogan, J. Johnson, & S. Briggs (Eds.), *Handbook of personality psychology*. San Diego: Academic Press.

Rozanski, A., Blumenthal, J. A., & Kaplan, J. (1999). Impact of psychological factors on the pathogenesis of cardiovascular disease and implications for therapy. *Circulation, 99*, 2192–2197.

Rozin, P. (1990). The importance of social factors in understanding the acquisition of food habits. In E. D. Capaldi & T. L. Powley (Eds.), *Taste, experience, and feeding*. Wash-

ington, DC: American Psychological Association.

Rozin, P. (1996). Towards a psychology of food and eating: From motivation to module to model to marker, morality, meaning, and metaphor. *Current Directions in Psychological Science, 5*, 18–24.

Rozin, P., Dow, S., Moscovitch, M., & Rajaram, S. (1998). What causes humans to begin and end a meal? A role for memory for what has been eaten, as evidenced by a study of multiple meal eating in amnesic patients. *Psychological Science, 9*, 392–396.

Ruble, D. N., & Martin, C. L. (1998). Gender development. In W. Damon (Ed.), *Handbook of child psychology (Vol. 3): Social, emotional, and personality development*. New York: Wiley.

Ruble, T. L. (1983). Sex stereotypes: Issues of change in the 70s. *Sex Roles, 9*, 397–402.

Rudorfer, M. V., & Goodwin, F. K. (1993). Introduction. In C. E. Coffey (Ed.), *The clinical science of electroconvulsive therapy*. Washington, DC: American Psychiatric Press.

Rush, A. J. (1984). Cognitive therapy. In T. B. Karasu (Ed.), *The psychiatric therapies*. Washington, DC: American Psychiatric Press.

Rush, A. J. (2000). Mood disorders: Treatment of depression. In B. J. Sadock & V. A. Sadock (Eds.), *Kaplan and Sadock's comprehensive textbook of psychiatry* (7th ed., Vol. 1, pp. 1377–1384). Philadelphia: Lippincott/Williams and Wilkins.

Rush, A. J., & Beck, A. T. (2000). Cognitive therapy. In B. J. Sadock & V. A. Sadock (Eds.), *Kaplan and Sadock's comprehensive textbook of psychiatry* (7th ed., Vol. 1, pp. 2167–2177). Philadelphia: Lippincott/Williams & Wilkins.

Russell, G. F. M. (1995). Anorexia nervosa through time. In G. Szmukler, C. Dare, & J. Treasure (Eds.), *Handbook of eating disorders: Theory, treatment, and research*. New York: Wiley.

Russell, G. F. M. (1997). The history of bulimia nervosa. In D. M. Garner, & P. E. Garfinkel (Eds.), *Handbook of treatment for eating disorders*. New York: Guilford.

Russell, J. A. (1991). Culture and the categorization of emotions. *Psychological Bulletin, 110*, 426–450.

Russell, J. A. (1994). Is there universal recognition of emotion from facial expression? A review of the cross-cultural studies. *Psychological Bulletin, 115*, 102–141.

Russell, J. A. (1995). Facial expressions of emotion: What lies beyond minimal universality? *Psychological Bulletin, 118*, 379–391.

Russo, N. F., & Denmark, F. L. (1987). Contributions of women to psychology. *Annual Review of Psychology, 38,* 279–298.

Rutherford, A. (2000). Radical behaviorism and psychology's public: B. F. Skinner in the popular press, 1934–1990. *History of Psychology, 3,* 371–395.

Rutherford, W. (1886). A new theory of hearing. *Journal of Anatomy and Physiology, 21,* 166–168.

Rutter, M., & O'Connor, T. G. (1999). Implications of attachment theory for child care policies. In J. Cassidy & P. R. Shaver (Eds.), *Handbook of attachment: Theory, research and clinical applications.* New York: Guilford.

Rutter, M. L. (1997). Nature-nurture intergration: The example of antisocial behavior. *American Psychologist, 52,* 390–398.

Ryan, C. S., Park, B., & Judd, C. M. (1996). Assessing stereotype accuracy: Implications for understanding the stereotyping process. In C. N. Macrae, C. Stangor, & M. Hewstone (Eds.), *Stereotypes and stereotyping.* New York: Guilford.

Ryan, R. M., & Deci, E. L. (2001). On happiness and human potentials: A review of research on hedonic and eudaimonic well-being. *Annual Review of Psychology, 52,* 141–166.

Rynes, S. S. (1993). Who's selecting whom? Effects of selection practices on applicant attitudes and behavior. In N. Schmitt & W. C. Borman (Eds.), *Personnel selection in organizations* (pp. 240–274). San Francisco: Jossey-Bass.

Sachs, J. (1985). Prelinguistic development. In J. B. Gleason (Ed.), *The development of language.* Columbus: Charles E. Merrill.

Sackeim, H. A., Haskett, R. F., Mulsant, B. H., Thase, M. E., Mann, J. J., Pettinati, H. M., Greenberg, R. M., Crowe, R. R., Cooper, T. B., & Prudic, J. (2001). Continuation pharmacotherapy in the prevention of relapse following electroconvulsive therapy: A randomized controlled trial. *Journal of the American Medical Association, 285,* 1299–1307.

Sacks, O. (1987). *The man who mistook his wife for a hat.* New York: Harper & Row.

Sadker, M., & Sadker, D. (1994). *Failing at fairness: How America's schools cheat girls.* New York: Scribners.

Salkovskis, P. M., & Warwick, H. M. C. (2001). Meaning, misinterpretations, and medicine: A cognitive-behavioral approach to understanding health anxiety and hypochondriasis. In V. Starcevic & D. R. Lipsitt (Eds.), *Hypochondriasis: Modern perspectives on an ancient malady.* New York: Oxford University Press.

Salminen, S. (1992). Defensive attribution hypothesis and serious occu-pational accidents. *Psychological Reports, 70,* 1195–1199.

Salovey, P., & Mayer, J. D. (1990). Emotional intelligence. *Imagination, Cognition, and Personality, 9,* 185–211.

Salthouse, T. A. (1991). Mediation of adult age differences in cognition by reductions in working memory and speed of processing. *Psychological Science, 2,* 179–183.

Salthouse, T. A. (1994). The nature of the influence of speed on adult age differences in cognition. *Developmental Psychology, 30,* 240–259.

Salthouse, T. A. (1996). The processing-speed theory of adult age differences in cognition. *Psychological Review, 103,* 403–428.

Salthouse, T. A. (2000). Aging and measures of processing speed. *Biological Psychology, 54,* 35–54.

Salvendy, J. T. (1993). Selection and preparation of patients and organization of the group. In H. I. Kaplan & B. J. Sadock (Eds.), *Comprehensive group psychotherapy.* Baltimore: Williams & Wilkins.

Samelson, F. (1981). Struggle for scientific authority: The reception of Watson's behaviorism, 1913–1920. *Journal of the History of the Behavioral Sciences, 17,* 399–425.

Samelson, F. (1994). John B. Watson in 1913: Rhetoric and practice. In J. T. Todd & E. K. Morris (Eds.), *Modern perspectives on John B. Watson and classical behaviorism.* Westport, CT: Greenwood Press.

Samet, J. M. (1992). The health benefits of smoking cessation. *Medical Clinics of North America, 76,* 399–414.

Sammons, M. T., Gorny, S. W., Zinner, E. S., & Allen, R. P. (2000). Prescriptive authority for psychologists: A consensus of support. *Professsional Psychology: Research and Practice, 31,* 604–609.

Sanderson, W. C., & Barlow, D. H. (1990). A description of patients diagnosed with DSM-III-R generalized anxiety disorder. *Journal of Nervous and Mental Disease, 178,* 588–591.

Sandler, J. (1975). Aversion methods. In F. H. Kanfer & A. P. Goldstein (Eds.), *Helping people change: A textbook of methods.* New York: Pergamon Press.

Sanislow, C. A., & Carson, R. C. (2001). Schizophrenia: A critical examination. In P. B. Sutker & H. E. Adams (Eds.), *Comprehensive handbook of psychopathology* (3rd ed., pp. 403–444). New York: Kluwer Academic/Plenum.

Sanz, J., Sanchez-Bernardos, M. L., & Avia, M. D. (1996). Self-monitoring and the prediction of one's own and others' personality test scores. *European Journal of Personality, 10,* 173–184.

Saper, C. B. (2000). Brain stem, reflexive behavior, and the cranial nerves. In E. R. Kandel, J. H. Schwartz, & T. M. Jessell (Eds.), *Principles of neural science* (pp. 873–888). New York: McGraw-Hill.

Sapolsky, R. M. (1992). Neuroendocrinology and the stress-response. In J. B. Becker, S. M. Breedlove, & D. Crews (Eds.), *Behavioral endocrinology.* Cambridge, MA: MIT Press.

Sarason, I. G., & Sarason, B. G. (1987). *Abnormal psychology: The problem of maladaptive behavior.* Englewood Cliffs, NJ: Prentice-Hall.

Savage-Rumbaugh, E. S. (1991). Language learning in the bonobo: How and why they learn. In N. A. Krasnegor, D. M. Rumbaugh, & R. L. Schiefelbusch/M. Studdert-Kennedy (Eds.), *Biological and behavioral determinants of language development.* Hillsdale, N.J.: Erlbaum.

Savage-Rumbaugh, S., McDonald, K., Sevcik, R. A., Hopkins, W. D., & Rupert, E. (1986). Spontaneous symbol acquisition and communication use by pygmy chimpanzees (*Pan paniscus*). *Journal of Experimental Psychology: General, 115,* 211–235.

Savage-Rumbaugh, S., Shanker, S. G., & Taylor, T. J. (1998). *Apes, language, and the human mind.* New York: Oxford University Press.

Savitsky, K., Epley, N., & Gilovich, T. (2001). Do others judge us as harshly as we think? Overestimating the impact of our failures, shortcomings, and mishaps. *Journal of Personality and Social Psychology, 81,* 44–56.

Saxe, G. N., van der Kolk, B. A., Berkowitz, R., Chinman, G., Hall, K., Lieberg, G., & Schwartz, J. (1993). Dissociative disorders in psychiatric inpatients. *American Journal of Psychiatry, 150,* 1037–1042.

Saxe, L. (1994). Detection of deception: Polygraph and integrity tests. *Current Directions in Psychological Science, 3,* 69–73.

Saxe, L., & Ben-Shakhar, G. (1999). Admissibility of polygraph tests: The application of scientific standards post-Daubert. *Psychology, Public Policy, and Law, 5,* 203–223.

Saxton, M., Kulcsar, B., Marshall, G., & Rupra, M. (1998). Longer-term effects of corrective input: An experimental approach. *Journal of Child Language, 25,* 701–721.

Scarr, S. (1991). *Theoretical issues in investigating intellectual plasticity.* S. E. Brauth, W. S. Hall, & R. Dooling (Eds.), *Plasticity of development.* Cambridge, MA: MIT Press.

Scarr, S. (1997). Behavior-genetic and socialization theories of intelligence: Truce and reconciliation. In R. J. Sternberg & E. L. Grigorenko (Eds.), *Intelligence, heredity, and environment.* New York: Cambridge University Press.

Scarr, S. (1998). American child care today. *American Psychologist, 53,* 95–108.

Scarr, S., & Weinberg, R. A. (1977). Intellectual similarities within families of both adopted and biological children. *Intelligence, 32,* 170–190.

Scarr, S., & Weinberg, R. A. (1983). The Minnesota adoption studies: Genetic differences and malleability. *Child Development, 54,* 260–267.

Schachter, S. (1959). *The psychology of affiliation.* Stanford, CA: Stanford University Press.

Schachter, S. (1964). The interaction of cognitive and physiological determinants of emotional state. In L. Berkowitz (Ed.), *Advances in experimental social psychology* (Vol. 1). New York: Academic Press.

Schachter, S. (1971). *Emotion, obesity and crime.* New York: Academic Press.

Schachter, S., & Rodin, J. (1974). *Obese humans and rats.* Hillsdale, NJ: Erlbaum.

Schachter, S., & Singer, J. E. (1962). Cognitive, social and physiological determinants of emotional state. *Psychological Review, 69,* 379–399.

Schachter, S., & Singer, J. E. (1979). Comments on the Maslach and Marshall-Zimbardo experiments. *Journal of Personality and Social Psychology, 37,* 989–995.

Schacter, D. L. (1987). Implicit memory: History and current status. *Journal of Experimental Psychology: Learning, Memory and Cognition, 14,* 501–518.

Schacter, D. L. (1989). On the relation between memory and consciousness: Dissociable interactions and conscious experience. In H. L. Roediger III & F. I. M. Craik (Eds.), *Varieties of memory and consciousness.* Hillsdale, NJ: Erlbaum.

Schacter, D. L. (1992). Understanding implicit memory: A cognitive neuroscience approach. *American Psychologist, 47,* 559–569.

Schacter, D. L. (1994). Priming and multiple memory systems: Perceptual mechanisms of implicit memory. In D. L. Schacter & E. Tulving (Eds.), *Memory systems.* Cambridge, MA: MIT Press.

Schacter, D. L. (1996). *Searching for memory: The brain, the mind, and the past.* New York: Basic Books.

Schacter, D. L. (1999). The seven sins of memory: Insights from psychology and cognitive neuroscience. *American Psychologist, 54,* 182–203.

Schacter, D. L., Chiu, C. Y. P., & Ochsner, K. N. (1993). Implicit memory: A selective review. *Annual Review of Neuroscience, 16,* 159–182.

Schaeffer, N. C. (2000). Asking questions about threatening topics:

A selective overview. In A. A. Stone, J. S. Turkkan, C. A. Bachrach, J. B. Jobe, H. S. Kurtzman, & V. Cain (Eds.), *The science of self-report: Implications for research and practice.* Mahwah, NJ: Erlbaum.

Schafe, G. E., & Bernstein, I. E. (1996). Taste aversion learning. In E. D. Capaldi (Ed.), *Why we eat what we eat: The psychology of eating* (pp. 31–52). Washington, DC: American Psychological Association.

Schaie, K. W. (1983). The Seattle longitudinal study: A twenty-one year exploration of psychometric intelligence in adulthood. In K. W. Schaie (Ed.), *Longitudinal studies of adult psychological development.* New York: Guilford.

Schaie, K. W. (1990). Intellectual development in adulthood. In J. E. Birren & K. W. Schaie (Eds.), *Handbook of the psychology of aging* (3rd ed.). San Diego: Academic Press.

Schaie, K. W. (1993). The Seattle longitudinal studies of adult intelligence. *Current Directions, 2,* 171–175.

Schaie, K. W. (1994). The course of adult intellectual development. *American Psychologist, 49,* 304–313.

Schaie, K. W. (1996). *Adult intellectual development: The Seattle longitudinal study.* New York: Cambridge University Press.

Scheidlinger, S. (1993). History of group psychotherapy. In H. I. Kaplan & B. J. Sadock (Eds.), *Comprehensive group psychotherapy.* Baltimore: Williams & Wilkins.

Scheier, M. F., & Carver, C. S. (1985). Optimism, coping and health: Assessment and implications of generalized expectancies. *Health Psychology, 4,* 219–247.

Schein, E. H. (1996). Culture: The missing concept in organizational studies. *Administrative Science Quarterly, 41,* 229–240.

Scherer, K. R. (1997). The role of culture in emotion-antecedent appraisal. *Journal of Personality and Social Psychology, 73,* 902–922.

Scherer, K. R., & Wallbott, H. G. (1994). Evidence for universality and cultural variation of differential emotion response patterning. *Journal of Personality and Social Psychology, 66,* 310–328.

Schiavi, R. C., White, D., Mandeli, J., & Levine, A. C. (1997). Effect of testosterone administration on sexual behavior and mood in men with erectile dysfunction. *Archives of Sexual Behavior, 26,* 231–241.

Schiff, M., & Lewontin, R. (1986). *Education and class: The irrelevance of IQ genetic studies.* Oxford: Clarendon Press.

Schiffman, J., Ekstrom, M., LaBrie, J., Schulsinger, F., Sorenson, H., & Mednick, S. (2002). Minor physical anomalies and schizophrenia spectrum disorders: A prospective investigation. *American Journal of Psychiatry, 159,* 238–243.

Schiffman, S. S., Graham, B. G., Sattely-Miller, E. A., & Warwick, Z. S. (1998). Orosensory perception of dietary fat. *Current Directions in Psychological Science, 7,* 137–143.

Schildkraut, J. J., Hirshfeld, A. J., & Murphy, J. M. (1994). Mind and mood in modern art, II: Depressive disorders, spirituality, and early deaths in the abstract expressionist artists of the New York School. *American Journal of Psychiatry, 151,* 482–488.

Schlaadt, R. G., & Shannon, P. T. (1994). *Drugs: Use, misuse, and abuse* (4th ed.). Englewood Cliffs, NJ: Prentice-Hall.

Schlaepfer, T. E., Pearlson, G. D., Wong. D. F., Marenco, S., & Dannals, R. F. (1997). PET study of competition between intravenous cocaine and [11C] raclopride at dopamine receptors in human subjects. *American Journal of Psychiatry, 154,* 1209–1213.

Schlegel, A., & Barry, H., III. (1991). *Adolescence: An anthropological inquiry.* New York: Free Press.

Schlenger, W. E., Kulka, R. A., Fairbank, J. A., Hough, R. L., Jordan, B. K., Marmar, C. R., & Weiss, D. S. (1992). The prevalence of post-traumatic stress disorder in the Vietnam generation: A multimethod, multisource assessment of psychiatric disorder. *Journal of Traumatic Stress, 5*(3), 333–363.

Schlosberg, H. (1954). Three dimensions of emotion. *Psychological Review, 61,* 81–88.

Schmidt, F. L., & Hunter, J. E. (1998). The validity and utility of selection methods in personnel psychology: Practical and theoretical implications of 85 years of research findings. *Psychological Bulletin, 124,* 262–274.

Schmidt, F. L., Ones, D. S., & Hunter, J. E. (1992). Personnel selection. *Annual Review of Psychology, 43,* 627–670.

Schmitt, D. P., & Buss, D. M. (1996). Strategic self-promotion and competitor derogation: Sex and context effects on the perceived effectiveness of mate attraction tactics. *Journal of Personality and Social Psychology, 70,* 1185–1204.

Schmitt, D. P., Couden, A., & Baker, M. (2001). The effects of sex and temporal context on feelings of romantic desire: An experimental evaluation of sexual strategies theory. *Personality and Social Psychology Bulletin, 27,* 833–847.

Schmitt, N., & Chan, D. (1998). *Personnel selection: A theoretical approach.* Thousand Oaks, CA: Sage.

Schmitz, J. M., Jarvik, M. E., & Schneider, N. G. (1997). Nicotine. In J. H. Lowinson, P. Ruiz, R. B. Millman, & J. G. Langrod (Eds.), *Substance abuse: A comprehensive textbook.* Baltimore: Williams & Wilkins.

Schmolck, H., Buffalo, E. A., & Squire, L. R. (2000). Memory distortions develop over time: Recollections of the O. J. Simpson trial verdict after 15 and 32 months. *Psychological Science, 11,* 39–45.

Schneewind, K. A. (1995). Impact of family processes on control beliefs. In A. Bandura (Ed.), *Self-efficacy in changing societies.* New York: Cambridge University Press.

Schneider, B. (1987). The people make the place. *Personnel Psychology, 40,* 437–454.

Schneider, B. (1996). When individual differences aren't. In K. R. Murphy (Ed.), *Individual differences and behaviors in organizations* (pp. 548–572). San Francisco: Jossey-Bass.

Schneider, B. H., Atkinson, L., & Tardif, C. (2001). Child-parent attachment and children's peer relations: A quantitative review. *Developmental Psychology, 37,* 86–100.

Schneider, F., & Deldin, P. J. (2001). Genetics and schizophrenia. In P. B. Sutker & H. E. Adams (Eds.), *Comprehensive handbook of psychopathology* (3rd ed., pp. 371–402). New York: Kluwer Academic/Plenum.

Schonemann, P. H. (1994). Heritability. In R. J. Sternberg (Ed.), *Encyclopedia of human intelligence.* New York: Macmillan.

Schooler, J. W. (1999). Seeking the core: The issues and evidence surrounding recovered accounts of sexual trauma. In L. M. Williams & V. L. Banyard (Eds.), *Trauma & memory.* Thousand Oaks, CA: Sage Publications.

Schooler, J. W., & Fiore, S. M. (1997). Consciousness and the limits of language: You can't always say what you think or think what you say. In J. D. Cohen & J. W. Schooler (Eds.), *Scientific Approaches to consciousness.* Mahwah, NJ: Erlbaum.

Schreiber, F. R. (1973). *Sybil.* New York: Warner.

Schultz, J. H., & Luthe, W. (1959). *Autogenic training.* New York: Grune & Stratton.

Schulz-Hardt, S., Frey, D., Luethgens, C., & Moscovici, S. (2000). Biased information search in group decision making. *Journal of Personality & Social Psychology, 78,* 655–669.

Schuman, H., & Kalton, G. (1985). Survey methods. In G. Lindzey & E. Aronson (Eds.), *Handbook of social psychology* (3rd ed.). New York: Random House.

Schumann, J. (1978). The acculturation model for second language acquisition. In R. C. Gingras (Ed.), *Second-language acquisition and foreign language teaching.* Washington, DC: Center for Applied Linguistics.

Schumann, J. (1993). Some problems with falsification: An illustration from SLA research. *Applied Linguistics, 14,* 295–306.

Schusterman, R. J., & Gisiner, R. (1988). Artificial language comprehension in dolphins and sea lions: The essential cognitive skills. *Psychological Record, 38,* 311–348.

Schwartz, B., & Robbins, S. J. (1995). *Psychology of learning and behavior* (4th ed.). New York: Norton.

Schwartz, B. L. (1999). Sparkling at the end of the tongue: The etiology of tip-of-the-tongue phenomenology. *Psychonomic Bulletin & Review, 6,* 379–393.

Schwartz, J. H. (2000). Neurotransmitters. In E. R. Kandel, J. H. Schwartz, & T. M. Jessell (Eds.), *Principles of neural science.* New York: McGraw-Hill.

Schwartz, J. H., & Westbrook, G. L. (2000). The cytology of neurons. In E. R. Kandel, J. H. Schwartz, & T. M. Jessell (Eds.), *Principles of neural science* (pp. 67–104). New York: McGraw-Hill.

Schwartz, L., Slater, M. A., & Birchler, G. R. (1994). Interpersonal stress and pain behaviors in patients with chronic pain. *Journal of Consulting and Clinical Psychology, 62,* 861–864.

Schwartz, M. W., & Seeley, R. J. (1997). The new biology of body weight regulation. *Journal of the American Dietetic Association, 97,* 54–58.

Schwartz, M. W., Peskind, E., Raskind, M., Nicolson, M., Moore, J., Morawiecki, A., Boyko, E. J., & Porte, D. J. (1996). Cerebrospinal fluid leptin levels: Relationship to plasma levels and to adiposity in humans. *Nature Medicine, 2,* 589–593.

Schwartz, N., & Strack, F. (1999). Reports of subjective well-being: Judgmental processes and their methodological implications. In D. Kahneman, E. Diener, & N. Schwarz (Eds.), *Well-being: The foundations of hedonic psychology.* New York: Russell Sage Foundation.

Schwartz, S. H. (1990). Individualism-collectivism: Critique and proposed refinements. *Journal of Cross-Cultural Psychology, 21,* 139–157.

Schwartz, W. J. (1996). Internal timekeeping. *Science & Medicine, 3,* 44–53.

Schwarz, N. (1999). Self-reports: How the questions shape the answers. *American Psychologist, 54,* 93–105.

Scott, T. R. (1990). The effect of physiological need on taste. In E. D. Capaldi & T. L. Powley (Eds.), *Taste,* *experience, and feeding.* Washington, DC: American Psychological Association.

Scoville, W. B., & Milner, B. (1957). Loss of recent memory after bilateral hippocampal lesions. *Journal of Neurology, Neurosurgery & Psychiatry, 20*, 11–21.

Scroppo, J. C., Drob, S. L., Weinberger, J. L., & Eagle, P. (1998). Identifying dissociative identity disorder: A self-report and projective study. *Journal of Abnormal Psychology, 107*, 272–284.

Scull, A. (1990). Deinstitutionalization: Cycles of despair. *The Journal of Mind and Behavior, 11*(3/4), 301–312.

Scully, J. A., Tosi, H., & Banning, K. (2000). Life event checklists: Revisiting the social readjustment rating scale after 30 years. *Educational & Psychological Measurement, 60*, 864–876.

Searle, A., & Bennett, P. (2001). Psychological factors and inflammatory bowel disease: A review of a decade of literature. *Psychology, Health and Medicine, 6*, 121–135.

Searleman, A. (1996). Personality variables and prospective memory performance. In D. J. Herrmann, C. McEvoy, C. Hertzog, P. Hertel, & M. K. Johnson (Eds.), *Basic and applied memory research: Practical applications* (Vol. 2). Mahwah, NJ: Erlbaum.

Searleman, A., & Herrmann, D. (1994). *Memory from a broader perspective.* New York: McGraw-Hill.

Sears, D. O. (1975). Political socialization. In F. I. Greenstein & N. W. Polsby (Eds.), *Handbook of political science* (Vol. 2). Reading, MA: Addison-Wesley.

Sears, D. O. (1986). College sophomores in the laboratory: Influences of a narrow database on social psychology's view of human nature. *Journal of Personality and Social Psychology, 51*, 515–530.

Secretary's Commission on Achieving Necessary Skills (1991). *What work requires of schools: SCANS report for America 2000.* Washington, DC: U.S. Government Printing Office.

Sedikides, C., & Strube, M. J. (1997). Self-evaluation: To thine own self be good, to thine own self be sure, to thine own self be true, and to thine own self be better. In M. P. Zanna (Ed.), *Advances in experimental social psychology.* New York: Academic Press.

Seeley, R. J., & Schwartz, M. W. (1997). Regulation of energy balance: Peripheral endocrine signals and hypothalamic neuropeptides. *Current Directions in Psychological Science, 6*, 39–44.

Seeley, R. J., Matson, C. A., Chavez, M., Woods, S. C., & Schwartz, M. W. (1996). Behavioral, endocrine and hypothalamic responses to involuntary overfeeding. *American Journal of Physiology, 271*, R819–R823.

Seeman, P., & Tallerico, T. (1999). Rapid release of antipsychotic drugs from dopamine D2 receptors: An explanation for low receptor occupancy and early clinical relapse upon withdrawal of clozapine or quetiapine. *American Journal of Psychiatry, 156*, 876–884.

Segall, M. H., Campbell, D. T., Herskovits, M. J. (1966). *The influence of culture on visual perception.* Indianapolis: Bobbs-Merrill.

Segall, M. H., Dasen, P. R., Berry, J. W., & Poortinga, Y. H. (1990). *Human behavior in global perspective: An introduction to cross-cultural psychology.* New York: Pergamon Press.

Segall, M. H., Lonner, W. J., & Berry, J. W. (1998). Cross-cultural psychology as a scholarly discipline: On the flowering of culture in behavioral research. *American Psychologist, 53*, 1101–1110.

Segerstrom, S. C., Taylor, S. E., Kemeny, M. E., & Fahey, J. L. (1998). Optimism is associated with mood, coping and immune change in response to stress. *Journal of Personality and Social Psychology, 74*, 1646–1655.

Seibyl, J. P., Scanley, E., Krystal, J. H., & Innis, R. B. (1999). Neuroimaging methodologies. In D. S. Charney, E. J. Nestler, & B. S. Bunney (Eds.), *Neurobiology of mental illness.* New York: Oxford University Press.

Seidenberg, M. S., & Petitto, L. A. (1986). Communication, symbolic communication, and language: Comment on Savage-Rumbaugh, McDonald, Sevcik, Hopkins, and Rupert (1986). *Journal of Experimental Psychology, 116*, 279–287.

Seidlitz, L., & Diener, E. (1993). Memory for positive versus negative life events: Theories for the differences between happy and unhappy persons. *Journal of Personality and Social Psychology, 64*, 654–664.

Seifer, R. (2001). Socioeconomic status, multiple risks, and development of intelligence. In R. J. Sternberg & E. L. Grigorenko (Eds.), *Environmental effects on cognitive abilities* (pp. 59–82). Mahwah, NJ: Erlbaum.

Seifer, R., Schiller, M., Sameroff, A. J., Resnick, S., & Riordan, K. (1996). Attachment, maternal sensitivity, and infant temperament during the first year of life. *Developmental Psychology, 32*, 12–25.

Self, D. W. (1997). Neurobiological adaptations to drug use. *Hospital Practice*, April, 5–9.

Self, D. W. (1998). Neural substrates of drug craving and relapse in drug addiction. *Annals of Medicine, 30*, 379–389.

Seligman, M. E. P. (1971). Phobias and preparedness. *Behavior Therapy, 2*, 307–321.

Seligman, M. E. P. (1974). Depression and learned helplessness. In R. J. Friedman & M. M. Katz (Eds.), *The psychology of depression: Contemporary theory and research.* New York: Wiley.

Seligman, M. E. P. (1990). *Learned optimism.* New York: Pocket Books.

Seligman, M. E. P. (1992). *Helplessness: On depression, development, and death.* New York: Freeman.

Seligman, M. E. P. (1995). The effectiveness of psychotherapy. *American Psychologist, 50*, 965–974.

Seligman, M. E. P. (2002). Positive psychology, positive prevention, and positive therapy. In C. R. Snyder & S. J. Lopez (Eds.), *Handbook of positive psychology* (pp. 3–11). New York: Oxford University Press.

Seligman, M. E. P., & Csikszentmihalyi, M. (2000). Positive psychology: An introduction. *American Psychologist, 55*, 5–14.

Seligman, M. E. P., & Hager, J. L. (1972, August). Biological boundaries of learning (The sauce béarnaise syndrome). *Psychology Today*, pp. 59–61, 84–87.

Seligman, M. E. P., & Isaacowitz, D. M. (2000). Learned helplessness. In G. Fink (Ed.), *Encyclopedia of stress* (Vol. 2, pp. 599–602). San Diego: Academic Press.

Seligman, M. E. P., & Levant, R. F. (1998). Managed care policies rely on inadequate science. *Professional Psychology: Research and Practice, 29*, 211–212.

Selye, H. (1936). A syndrome produced by diverse nocuous agents. *Nature, 138*, 32.

Selye, H. (1956). *The stress of life.* New York: McGraw-Hill.

Selye, H. (1973). The evolution of the stress concept. *American Scientist, 61*(6), 672–699.

Selye, H. (1974). *Stress without distress.* New York: Lippincott.

Selye, H. (1982). History and present status of the stress concept. In L. Goldberger & S. Breznitz (Eds.), *Handbook of stress: Theoretical and clinical aspects.* New York: Free Press.

Serbin, L. A., Powlishta, K. K., & Gulko, J. (1993). *The development of sex typing in middle childhood.* Chicago: University of Chicago Press.

Servan-Schreiber, D., Kolb, R., & Tabas, G. (1999). The somatizing patient. *Primary Care, 26*, 225–242.

Seta, J. J., Seta, C. E., & Wang, M. A. (1991). Feelings of negativity and stress: An averaging-summation analysis of impressions of negative life experiences. *Personality and Social Psychology Bulletin, 17*, 376–384.

Seto, M. C., Maric, A., & Barbaree, H. E. (2001). The role of pornography in the etiology of sexual aggression. *Aggression & Violent Behavior, 6*, 35–53.

Shafer, G., & Tversky, A. (1988). Languages and designs for probability judgement. In D. E. Bell, H. Raiffa, & A. Tversky (Eds.), *Decision making: Descriptive, normative, and prescriptive interactions.* New York: Cambridge University Press.

Shaffer, D. R. (1985). *Developmental psychology: Theory, research, and applications.* Pacific Grove, CA: Brooks/Cole.

Shafir, E., & LeBoeuf, R. A. (2002). Rationality. *Annual Review of Psychology, 53*, 491–517.

Shalev, A. Y. (2001). Posttraumatic stress disorder. *Primary Psychiatry, 8*(10), 41–46.

Shank, R. P., Smith-Swintosky, V. L., & Twyman, R. E. (2000). Amino acid neurotransmitters. In B. J. Sadock & V. A. Sadock (Eds), *Comprehensive textbook of psychiatry* (Vol. 1). New York: Lippincott/Williams & Wilkins.

Shapiro, A. F., Gottman, J. M., & Carrère. (2000). The baby and marriage: Identifying factors that buffer against decline in marital satisfaction after the first baby arrives. *Journal of Family Psychology, 14*, 59–70.

Shapiro, D. H., Jr. (1984). Overview: Clinical and physiological comparison of meditation with other self-control strategies. In D. H. Shapiro, Jr., & R. N. Walsh (Eds.), *Meditation: Classic and contemporary perspectives.* New York: Aldine.

Shapiro, D. H., Jr. (1987). Implications of psychotherapy research for the study of meditation. In M. A. West (Ed.), *The psychology of meditation.* Oxford: Clarendon Press.

Shapiro, S. L., Schwartz, G. E. R., & Santerre, C. (2002). Meditation and positive psychology. In C. R. Snyder & S. J. Lopez (Eds.), *Handbook of positive psychology.* New York: Oxford University Press.

Shapley, R. (1995). Parallel neural pathways and visual function. In M. S. Gazzaniga (Ed.), *The cognitive neurosciences.* Cambridge, MA: MIT Press.

Sharpe, D., Adair, J. G., & Roese, N. J. (1992). Twenty years of deception research: A decline in subjects' trust? *Personality and Social Psychology Bulletin, 18*, 585–590.

Sharps, M. J., & Wertheimer, M. (2000). Gestalt perspectives on cognitive science and on experimental psychology. *Review of General Psychology, 4*, 315–336.

Shatz, C. J. (1992, September). The developing brain. *Scientific American*, 60–67.

Shaver P. R., & Hazan, C. (1993). Adult attachment: Theory and research. In W. Jones & D. Perlman

(Eds.), *Advances in personal relationships* (Vol. 4). London: Jessica Kingsley.

Shaver, P. R., & Hazan, C. (1994). Attachment. In A. L. Weber & J. H. Harvey (Eds.), *Perspectives on close relationships*. Boston: Allyn & Bacon.

Shavitt, S., Sanbonmatsu, D. M., Smittipatana, S., & Posavac, S. S. (1999). Broadening the conditions for illusory correlation formation: Implications for judging minority groups. *Basic & Applied Social Psychology, 21,* 263–279.

Shavitt, S., Swan, S., Lowery, T. M., & Wanke, M. (1994). The interaction of endorser attractiveness and involvement in persuasion depends on the goal that guides message processing. *Journal of Consumer Psychology, 3,* 137–162.

Shear, J., & Jevning, R. (1999). Pure consciousness: Scientific exploration of meditation techniques. *Journal of Consciousness Studies, 6,* 189–209.

Shear, M. K., & Beidel, D. C. (1998). Psychotherapy in the overall management strategy for social anxiety disorder. *Journal of Clinical Psychiatry, 59,* 39–46.

Shedler, J., Mayman, M., & Manis, M. (1993). The illusion of mental health. *American Psychologist, 48,* 1117–1131.

Sheehan, S. (1982). *Is there no place on earth for me?* Boston: Houghton Mifflin.

Sheldon, K. M., & Kasser, T. (2001). Goals, congruence, and positive well-being: New empirical support for humanistic theories. *Journal of Humanistic Psychology, 41*(1), 30–50.

Shepard, R. N. (1990). *Mind sights.* New York: W. H. Freeman.

Shepperd, J. A., & McNulty, J. K. (2002). The affective consequences of expected and unexpected outcomes. *Psychological Science, 13,* 85–88.

Shepperd, J. A., & Taylor, K. M. (1999). Social loafing and expectancy-value theory. *Personality and Social Psychology Bulletin, 25,* 1147–1158.

Sherman, C. B. (1992). The health consequences of cigarette smoking: Pulmonary diseases. *Medical Clinics of North America, 76,* 355–375.

Sherman, M., & Key, C. B. (1932). The intelligence of isolated mountain children. *Child Development, 3,* 279–290.

Shermer, M. (1997). *Why people believe weird things: Pseudoscience, superstition, and other confusions of our time.* New York: W. H. Freeman.

Sherry, D. F. (1992). Evolution and learning. In L. R. Squire (Ed.), *Encyclopedia of learning and memory.* New York: Macmillan.

Shettleworth, S. J. (1998). *Cognition, evolution, and behavior.* New York: Oxford University Press.

Shiffrin, R. M. (1988). Attention. In R. C. Atkinson, R. J. Herrnstein, G. Lindzey, & R. D. Luce (Eds.), *Stevens' handbook of experimental psychology* (Vol. 2). New York: Wiley.

Shike, M. (1999). Diet and lifestyle in the prevention of colorectal cancer: An overview. *American Journal of Medicine, 106*(1A), 11S–15S, 50S–51S.

Shimamura, A. P. (1995). Memory and the prefrontal cortex. In J. Grafman, K. J. Holyoak, & F. Boller (Eds), *Structure and functions of the human prefrontal cortex.* New York: New York Academy of Sciences.

Shimamura, A. P. (1996). Unraveling the mystery of the frontal lobes: Explorations in cognitive neuroscience. *Psychological Science Agenda,* September-October, 8–9.

Shimamura, A. P., Berry, J. M., Mangels, J. A., Rusting, C. L., & Jurica, P. J. (1995). Memory and cognitive abilities in university professors: Evidence for successful aging. *Psychological Science, 6,* 271–277.

Shulman, R. B. (2001). Response versus remission in the treatment of depression: Understanding residual symptoms. *Primary Psychiatry, 8*(5), 28–30, 34.

Shweder, R. A., Mahapatra, M., & Miller, J. G. (1990). Culture and moral development. In J. W. Stigler, R. A. Shweder, & G. Herdt (Eds.), *Cultural psychology.* New York: Cambridge University Press.

Siebert, A. (1995). *Student success: How to succeed in college and still have time for your friends.* Fort Worth: Harcourt Brace Jovanovich.

Siegel, J. M. (2000). Brainstem mechanisms generating REM sleep. In M. H. Kryger, T. Roth, & W. C. Dement (Eds.), *Principles and practice of sleep medicine.* Philadelphia: Saunders.

Siegel, S. (2001). Pavlovian conditioning and drug overdose: When tolerance fails. *Addiction Research & Theory, 9,* 503–513.

Siegel, S., & Allan, L. G. (1998). Learning and homeostasis: Drug addiction and the McCollough effect. *Psychological Bulletin, 124,* 230–239.

Siegler, I. C., & Brummett, B. H. (2000). Associations among NEO personality assessments and well-being at mid-life: Facet-level analyses. *Psychology & Aging, 15,* 710–714.

Siegler, R. S. (1992). The other Alfred Binet. *Developmental Psychology, 28,* 179–190.

Siegler, R. S. (1994). Cognitive variability: A key to understanding cognitive development. *Current Directions in Psychological Science, 3*(1), 1–5.

Siegler, R. S. (1998). *Children's thinking.* Upper Saddle River, NJ: Prentice-Hall.

Siegler, R. S., & Ellis, S. (1996). Piaget on childhood. *Psychological Science, 7,* 211–215.

Siegler, R. S., & Kotovsky, K. (1986). Two levels of giftedness: Shall ever the twain meet? In R. J. Sternberg & J. E. Davidson (Eds.), *Conceptions of giftedness.* Cambridge: Cambridge University Press.

Sigman, M., & Whaley, S. E. (1998). The role of nutrition in the development of intelligence. In U. Neisser (Ed.), *The rising curve: Long-term gains in IQ and related measures.* Washington, DC: American Psychological Association.

Signorielli, N. (1993). Television, the portrayal of women, and children's attitudes. In G. Berry & J. K. Asamen (Eds.), *Children and television: Images in a changing sociocultural world.* Newbury Park, CA: Sage.

Signorielli, N., & Bacue, A. (1999). Recognition and respect: A content analysis of prime-time television characters across three decades. *Sex Roles, 40,* 527–544.

Signorielli, N., McLeod, D., & Healy, E. (1994). Gender stereotypes in MTV commercials: The beat goes on. *Journal of Broadcasting & Electronic Media, 38,* 91–101.

Siiter, R. J. (1999). *Introduction to animal behavior.* Pacific Grove: Brooks/Cole.

Silberman, E. K. (1998). Psychiatrists' and internists' beliefs. *Primary Psychiatry, 5,* 65–71.

Silver, E., Cirincon, C., & Steadman, H. J. (1994). Demythologizing inaccurate perceptions of the insanity defense. *Law & Human Behavior, 18,* 63–70.

Silverman, I., & Eals, M. (1992). Sex differences in spatial ability: Evolutionary theory and data. In J. Barkow, L. Cosmides, & J. Tooby (Eds.), *The adapted mind.* New York: Oxford University Press.

Silverman, I., & Phillips, K. (1998). The evolutionary psychology of spatial sex differences. In C. Crawford & D.L. Krebs (Eds.), *Handbook of evolutionary psychology: Ideas, issues, and applications.* Mahwah, NJ: Erlbaum.

Silverman, I., Choi, J., Mackewn, A., Fisher, M., Moro, J., & Olshansky, E. (2000). Evolved mechanisms underlying wayfinding: Further studies on the hunter-gatherer theory of spatial sex differences. *Evolution and Human Behavior, 21,* 201–213.

Silverstein, L. B., & Auerbach, C. F. (1999). Deconstructing the essential father. *American Psychologist, 54,* 397–407.

Simon, G. E., & VonKorff, M. (1997). Prevalence, burden, and treatment of insomnia in primary care. *American Journal Psychiatry, 154,* 1417–1423.

Simon, H. A. (1957). *Models of man.* New York: Wiley.

Simon, H. A. (1974). How big is a chunk? *Science, 183,* 482–488.

Simon, H. A. (1992). Alternative representations for cognition: Search and reasoning. In H. L. Pick, Jr., P. Van Den Broek, & D. C. Knill (Eds.), *Cognition: Conceptual and methodological issues.* Washington, DC: American Psychological Association.

Simon, H. A., & Reed, S. K. (1976). Modeling strategy shifts in a problem-solving task. *Cognitive Psychology, 8,* 86–97.

Simon, R. I. (1999). The law and psychiatry. In R. E. Hales, S. C. Yudofsky, & J. A. Talbott (Eds.), *American Psychiatric Press Textbook of Psychiatry.* Washington, DC: American Psychiatric Press.

Simonoff, E., Bolton, P., & Rutter, M. (1998). Genetic perspectives on mental retardation: A short introduction. In J. A. Burack, R. M. Hodapp, & E. Zigler (Eds.), *Handbook of mental retardation and development.* New York: Cambridge University Press.

Simons, D. K., & Chabris, C. F. (1999). Gorillas in our midst: Sustained inattentional blindness for dynamic events. *Perception, 28,* 1059–1074.

Simonton, D. K. (1990). Creativity and wisdom in aging. In J. E. Birren & K. W. Schaie (Eds.), *Handbook of the psychology of aging.* San Diego: Academic Press.

Simonton, D. K. (1997). Creative productivity: A predictive and explanatory model of career trajectories and landmarks. *Psychological Review, 104,* 66–89.

Simonton, D. K. (1999a). Creativity and genius. In L. A. Pervin & O. John (Eds.), *Handbook of personality theory and research.* New York: Guilford.

Simonton, D. K. (1999b). Talent and its development: An emergenic and epigenetic model. *Psychological Review, 106,* 435–457.

Simonton, D. K. (2001). Totally made, not at all born [Review of the book *The psychology of high abilities*]. *Contemporary Psychology, 46,* 176–179.

Simpson, J. A. (1990). Influence of attachment styles on romantic relationships. *Journal of Personality and Social Psychology, 59,* 971–980.

Simpson, J. A. (1999). Attachment theory in modern evolutionary perspective. In J. Cassidy & P. R. Shaver (Eds.), *Handbook of attachment: Theory, research, and clinical applications.* New York: Guilford.

Simpson, J. A., Fletcher, G. J. O., & Campbell, L. (2001). The structure and function of ideal standards in close relationships. In G. J. O. Fletcher & M. S. Clark (Eds.), *Blackwell hand-*

book of social psychology: Interpersonal processes. Malden, MA: Blackwell.

Simpson, J. A., Rholes, W. S., & Phillips, D. (1996). Conflict in close relationships: An attachment perspective. *Journal of Personality and Social Psychology, 71,* 899–914.

Simpson, J. L. (1991). Fetal wastage. In S. G. Gabbe, J. R. Niebyl, & J. L. Simpson (Eds.), *Obstetrics: Normal and problem pregnancies.* New York: Churchill Livingstone.

Simpson, S. (2001) Interview with Crocodile Hunter Steve Irwin [Web Page]. Retrieved July 2, 2002 from http://www.sciam.com/article.cfm?articleID=00067984-6FE2-1C70-84A9809EC588EF21&pageNumber=1&catID=2.

Sinclair, D. (1981). *Mechanisms of cutaneous stimulation.* Oxford, England: Oxford University Press.

Sinclair, R. C., Hoffman, C., Mark, M. M., Martin, L. L., & Pickering, T. L. (1994). Construct accessibility and the misattribution of arousal: Schachter and Singer revisited. *Psychological Science, 5,* 15–19.

Singer, L. T., Arendt, R., Minnes, S., Farkas, K., Salvator, A., Kirchner, H. L., & Kliegman, R. (2002). Cognitive and motor outcomes of cocaine-exposed infants. *Journal of the American Medical Association, 287,* 1952–1960.

Singer, M. T., & Lalich, J. (1996). *Crazy therapies: What are they? Do they work?* San Francisco: Jossey-Bass.

Singh, D. (1993). Adaptive significance of female physical attractiveness: Role of waist-to-hip ratio. *Journal of Personality and Social Psychology, 65,* 293–307.

Sinha, D. (1983). Human assessment in the Indian context. In S. H. Irvine & J. W. Berry (Eds.), *Human assessment and cultural factors.* New York: Plenum.

Skinner, B. F. (1938). *The behavior of organisms.* New York: Appleton-Century-Crofts.

Skinner, B. F. (1953). *Science and human behavior.* New York: Macmillan.

Skinner, B. F. (1957). *Verbal behavior.* New York: Appleton-Century-Crofts.

Skinner, B. F. (1967). Autobiography. In E. G. Boring & G. Lindzey (Eds.), *A history of psychology in autobiography* (Vol. 5). New York: Appleton-Century-Crofts.

Skinner, B. F. (1969). *Contingencies of reinforcement.* New York: Appleton-Century-Crofts.

Skinner, B. F. (1971). *Beyond freedom and dignity.* New York: Knopf.

Skinner, B. F. (1974). *About behaviorism.* New York: Knopf.

Skinner, B. F. (1984). Selection by consequences. *Behavioral and Brain Sciences, 7*(4), 477–510.

Skinner, B. F., Solomon, H. C., & Lindsley, O. R. (1953). *Studies in behavior therapy: Status report I.* Waltham, MA: Unpublished report, Metropolitan State Hospital.

Skodak, M., & Skeels, H. M. (1947). A follow-up study of one hundred adopted children in Iowa. *American Psychologist, 2,* 278.

Slaby, A. E. (1997). Beyond reasonable doubt: The case for SSRI's. *Primary Psychiatry, 4,* 26–27.

Slamecka, N. J. (1985). Ebbinghaus: Some associations. *Journal of Experimental Psychology: Learning, Memory and Cognition, 11,* 414–435.

Slamecka, N. J. (1992). Forgetting. In L. R. Squire (Ed.), *Encyclopedia of learning and memory.* New York: Macmillan.

Slater, E., & Shields, J. (1969). Genetical aspects of anxiety. In M. H. Lader (Ed.), *Studies of anxiety.* Ashford, England: Headley Brothers.

Slaughter, M. (1990). The vertebrate retina. In K. N. Leibovic (Ed.), *Science of vision.* New York: Springer-Verlag.

Slavney, P. R. (1990). *Perspectives on hysteria.* Baltimore: Johns Hopkins University Press.

Slobin, D. I. (1985). *A cross-linguistic study of language acquisition.* Hillsdale, NJ: Erlbaum.

Slobin, D. I. (1992). *The crosslinguistic study of language acquisition.* Hillsdale, NJ: Erlbaum.

Slovic, P. (1990). Choice. In D. N. Osherson & E. E. Smith (Eds.), *Thinking: An invitation to cognitive science* (Vol. 3). Cambridge, MA: MIT Press.

Slovic, P., & Fischhoff, B. (1977). On the psychology of experimental surprises. *Journal of Experimental Psychology: Human Perception and Performance, 3,* 544–551.

Slovic, P., Fischhoff, B., & Lichtenstein, S. (1982). Facts versus fears: Understanding perceived risk. In D. Kahneman, P. Slovic, & A. Tversky (Eds.), *Judgment under uncertainty: Heuristics and biases.* Cambridge, England: Cambridge University Press.

Slovic, P., Lichtenstein, S., & Fischhoff, B. (1988). Decision making. In R. C. Atkinson, R. J. Herrnstein, G. Lindzey, & R. D. Luce (Eds.), *Stevens' handbook of experimental psychology* (Vol. 2). New York: Wiley.

Smail, B. (1983). Spatial visualization skills and technical crafts education. *Educational Research, 25,* 230–231.

Smart, R. (1965). Social-group membership, leadership and birth order. *Journal of Social Psychology, 67,* 221–225.

Smedley, S. R., & Eisner, T. (1996). Sodium: A male moth's gift to its offspring. *Proceedings of the National Academy of Sciences, 93,* 809–813.

Smilkstein, G. (1990). Psychosocial influences on health. In R. E. Rakel (Ed.), *Textbook of family practice.* Philadelphia: Saunders.

Smith, A. L., & Weissman, M. M. (1992). Epidemiology. In E. S. Paykel (Ed.), *Handbook of affective disorders* (2nd ed.). New York: Guilford.

Smith, C. A., & Lazarus, R. S. (1993). Appraisal components, core relational themes, and the emotions. *Cognition and Emotion, 7,* 233–269.

Smith, C. P. (1992). Reliability issues. In C. P. Smith (Ed.), *Motivation and personality: Handbook of thematic content analysis.* New York: Cambridge University Press.

Smith, D. A. (1999). The end of theoretical orientations? *Applied & Preventative Psychology, 8,* 269–280.

Smith, E. E. (2000). Neural bases of human working memory. *Current Directions in Psychological Science, 9,* 45–49.

Smith, F. J., & Campfield, L. A. (1993). Meal initiation occurs after experimental induction of transient declines in blood glucose. *American Journal of Physiology, 265,* 1423–1429.

Smith, G. N., Flynn, S. W., Kopala, L. C., Bassett, A. S., Lapointe, J. S., Falkai, P., & Honer, W. G. (1997). A comprehensive method of assessing routine CT scans in schizophrenia. *Acta Psychiatrica Scandinavica, 96,* 395–401.

Smith, G. S., Dewey, S. L., Brodie, J. D., Logan, J., Vitkun, S. A., Simkowitz, P., Schloesser, R., Alexoff, D. A., Hurley, A., Cooper, T., & Volkow, N. D. (1997). Serotonergic modulation of dopamine measured with [11C] raclopride and PET in normal human subjects. *American Journal of Psychiatry, 154,* 490–496.

Smith, J. C. (1975). Meditation and psychotherapy: A review of the literature. *Psychological Bulletin, 32,* 553–564.

Smith, J. W., Frawley, P. J., & Polissar, N. L. (1997). Six- and twelve-month abstinence rates in inpatient alcoholics treated with either faradic aversion or chemical aversion compared with matched inpatients from a treatment registry. *Journal of Addictive Diseases, 16 ,* 5–24.

Smith, M., & Pazder, L. (1980). *Michelle remembers.* New York: Pocket Books.

Smith, M. L., & Glass, G. V. (1977). Meta-analysis of psychotherapy outcome studies. *American Psychologist, 32,* 752–760.

Smith, M. T., Perlis, M. L., Park, A., Smith, M. S., Pennington, J., Giles, D. E., & Buysse, D. J. (2002). Comparative meta-analysis of pharmacotherapy and behavior therapy for persistent insomnia. *American Journal of Psychiatry, 159,* 5–11.

Smith, P. B. (2001). Cross-cultural studies of social influence. In D. Matsumoto (Ed.), *The handbook of culture and psychology.* New York: Oxford University Press.

Smith, P. B., & Bond, M. H. (1994). *Social psychology across cultures: Analysis and perspectives.* Boston: Allyn & Bacon.

Smith, S. (1988). Environmental context-dependent memory. In G. M. Davies & D. M. Thomson (Eds.), *Memory in context: Context in memory.* New York: Wiley.

Smith, S. B. (2000). *Diana in search of herself: Portrait of a troubled princess.* New York: Signet.

Smith, S. M. (1995). Getting into and out of mental ruts: A theory of fixation, incubation, and insight. In R. J. Sternberg & J. E. Davidson (Eds.), *The nature of insight* (pp. 229–251). Cambridge, MA: MIT Press.

Smith, S. M., McIntosh, W. D., & Bazzini, D. G. (1999). Are the beautiful good in Hollywood? An investigation of the beauty-and-goodness stereotype on film. *Basic & Applied Social Psychology, 21,* 69–80.

Smith, T. W. (1999). *The emerging 21st century American family.* Chicago: University of Chicago, National Opinion Research Center.

Smith, T. W., & Gallo, L. C. (2001). Personality traits as risk factors for physical illness. In A. Baum, T. A. Revenson, & J. E. Singer (Eds.), *Handbook of health psychology* (pp. 139–174). Mahwah, NJ: Erlbaum.

Smith, T. W., Pope, M. K., Sanders, J. D., Allred, K. D., & O'Keefe, J. L. (1988). Cynical hostility at home and work: Psychosocial vulnerability across domains. *Journal of Research in Personality, 22,* 525–548.

Smith, W. P., Compton, W. C., & West, W. B. (1995). Meditation as an adjunct to a happiness enhancement program. *Journal of Clinical Psychology, 51,* 269–273.

Smolak, L., & Murnen, S. K. (2001). Gender and eating problems. In R. H. Striegel-Moore & L. Smolak (Eds.), *Eating disorders: Innovative directions in research and practice* (pp. 91–110). Washington, DC: American Psychological Association.

Smolensky, P. (1995). On the proper treatment of connectionism. In C. Madonald, & G. Macdonald (Eds.), *Connectionism: Debates on psychological explanation.* Cambridge, USA: Blackwell.

Smyth, J., Litcher, L., Hurewitz, A., & Stone, A. (2001). Relaxation training and cortisol secretion in adult asthmatics. *Journal of Health Psychology, 6,* 217–227.

Smyth, J. M., & Pennebaker, J. W. (1999). Sharing one's story: Translating emotional experiences into words as a coping tool. In C. R. Snyder

(Ed.), *Coping: The psychology of what works*. New York: Oxford University Press.

Smyth, J. M., & Pennebaker, J. W. (2001). What are the health effects of disclosure? In A. Baum, T. A. Revenson & J. E. Singer (Eds.), *Handbook of health psychology* (pp. 339–348). Mahwah, NJ: Erlbaum.

Snarey, J. R. (1995). In a communitarian voice: The sociological expansion of Kohlbergian theory, research and practice. In W. M. Kurtines & J. L. Gewirtz (Eds.), *Moral development: An introduction*. Boston: Allyn & Bacon.

Snow, C. E. (1998). Bilingualism and second language acquisition . In J. B. Gleason & N. B. Ratner (Eds.), *Psycholinguistics*. Fort Worth, TX: Harcourt College Publishers.

Snow, R. E. (1986). Individual differences in the design of educational programs. *American Psychologist, 41,* 1029–1039.

Snowden, L. R., & Hu, T. W. (1996). Outpatient service use in minority-serving mental health programs. *Administration and Policy in Mental Health, 24,* 149–159.

Snyder, A. (1989). *Relationship excellence: Right brain relationship skills for left brain personalities.* Seattle: Gresham Publishing.

Snyder, M. (1979). Self-monitoring processes. In L. Berkowitz (Ed.), *Advances in experimental social psychology* (Vol. 12). New York: Academic Press.

Snyder, M. (1987). *Public appearances/Private realities: The psychology of self-monitoring.* New York: W. H. Freeman.

Snyder, S. H. (1996). *Drugs and the brain.* New York: Scientific American Library.

Snyder, S. H., & Ferris, C. D. (2000). Novel neurotransmitters and their neuropsychiatric relevance. *American Journal of Psychiatry, 157,* 1738–1751.

Snyderman, M., & Rothman, S. (1987). Survey of expert opinion on intelligence and aptitude testing. *American Psychologist, 42,* 137–144.

So, K. T., & Orme-Johnson, D. W. (2001). Three randomized experiments on the longitudinal effects of the Transcendental Meditation technique on cognition. *Intelligence, 29,* 419–440.

Sobal, J. (1995). Social influences on body weight. In K. D. Brownell & C. G. Fairburn (Eds.), *Eating disorders and obesity: A comprehensive handbook.* New York: Guilford.

Solomon, D. A., Keller, M. B., Leon, A. C., Mueller, T. I., Shea, M. T., Warshaw, M., Maser, J. D., Coryell, W., & Endicott, J. (1997). Recovery from major depression: A 10-year prospective follow-up across multiple episodes. *Archives of General Psychiatry, 54,* 1001–1006.

Solomon, D. A., Keller, M. B., Leon, A. C., Mueller, T. I., Lavori, P. W., Shea, M. T., Coryell, W., Warshaw, M., Turvey, C., Maser, J. D., & Endicott, J. (2000). Multiple recurrences of major depressive disorder. *American Journal of Psychiatry, 157,* 229–233.

Solowij, N., Stephens, R. S., Roffman, R. A., Babor, T., Kadden, R., Miller, M., Christiansen. K., McRee, B., & Vendetti, J. (2002). Cognitive functioning of long-term heavy cannabis users seeking treatment. *Journal of the American Medical Association, 287,* 1123–1131.

Solso, R. L. (1994). *Cognition and the visual arts.* Cambridge, MA: MIT Press.

Sommer, B. (1987). *Not another diet book: A right-brain program for successful weight management.* Alameda, CA: Hunter House.

Sotiriou, P. E. (2002). *Integrating college study skills: Reasoning in reading, listening, and writing.* Belmont, CA: Wadsworth.

Sousa, D. A. (2000). *How the brain learns: A classroom teacher's guide.* Thousand Oaks, CA: Corwin Press.

Spangler, W. D. (1992). Validity of questionnaire and TAT measures of need for achievement: Two meta-analyses. *Psychological Bulletin, 112,* 140–154.

Spanos, N. P. (1986). Hypnotic behavior: A social-psychological interpretation of amnesia, analgesia, and "trance logic." *Behavioral & Brain Sciences, 9*(3), 449–467.

Spanos, N. P. (1994). Multiple identity enactments and multiple personality disorder: A sociocognitive perspective. *Psychological Bulletin, 116,* 143–165.

Spanos, N. P. (1996). *Multiple identities and false memories.* Washington, DC: American Psychological Association.

Spanos, N. P., & Coe, W. C. (1992). A social-psychological approach to hypnosis. In E. Fromm & M. R. Nash (Eds.), *Contemporary hypnosis research.* New York: Guilford.

Spear, P. (2000). The adolescent brain and age-related behavioral manifestations. *Neuroscience and Biobehavioral Reviews, 24,* 417–463.

Spearman, C. (1904). "General intelligence" objectively determined and measured. *American Journal of Psychology, 15,* 201–293.

Spearman, C. (1923). *The nature of "intelligence" and the principles of cognition.* London: Macmillan.

Speed, A., & Gangestad, S. W. (1997). Romantic popularity and mate preferences: A peer-nomination study. *Personality and Social Psychology Bulletin, 23,* 928–936.

Spelke, E. S. (1994). Initial knowledge: Six suggestions. *Cognition, 50,* 431–455.

Spelke, E. S., & Newport, E. L. (1998). Nativism, empiricism, and the development of knowledge. In W. Damon (Ed.), *Handbook of child psychology (Vol. 1): Theoretical models of human development.* New York: Wiley.

Spencer, S. J., Steele, C. M., & Quinn, D. M. (1999). Stereotype threat and women's math performance. *Journal of Experimental Social Psychology, 35,* 4–28.

Sperling, G. (1960). The information available in brief visual presentations. *Psychological Monographs, 74*(11, Whole No. 498).

Sperry, R. W. (1982). Some effects of disconnecting the cerebral hemispheres. *Science, 217,* 1223–1226, 1250.

Spiegel, D. (1994). Dissociative disorders. In R. E. Hales, S. C. Yudofsky, & J. A. Talbott (Eds.), *The American Psychiatric Press textbook of psychiatry* (2nd ed.). Washington, DC: American Psychiatric Press.

Spiegel, D., & Maldonado, J. R. (1999). Dissociative disorders. In R. E. Hales, S. C. Yudofsky, & J. A. Talbott (Eds.), *American Psychiatric Press Textbook of Psychiatry,* (3rd ed.). Washington, DC: American Psychiatric Press.

Spiegel, D., Cutcomb, S., Ren, C., & Pribram, K. (1985). Hypnotic hallucination alters evoked potentials. *Journal of Abnormal Psychology, 94,* 249–255.

Spiegel, H., Greenleaf, M., & Spiegel, D. (2000). Hypnosis. In B. J. Sadock & V. A. Sadock (Eds.), *Kaplan and Sadock's comprehensive textbook of psychiatry.* Philadelphia: Lippincott/Williams & Wilkins.

Spiegler, M. D., & Guevremont, D. C. (1998). *Contemporary behavior therapy.* Pacific Grove, CA: Brooks/Cole.

Spielberger, C. D., & Sydeman, S. J. (1994). Anxiety. In R. J. Sternberg (Ed.), *Encyclopedia of human intelligence.* New York: Macmillan.

Spitzer, R. L., Terman, M., Williams, J. B. W., Terman, J. S., Malt, U. F., Singer, F., & Lewy, A. J. (1999). Jet lag: Clinical features, validation of a new syndrome-specific scale, and lack of response to melatonin in a randomized, double-blind trial. *American Journal Psychiatry, 156,* 1392–1396.

Sprecher, S. (1998). Insiders' perspectives on reasons for attraction to a close other. *Social Psychology Quarterly, 61,* 287–300.

Sprecher, S. (1999). "I love you more today than yesterday": Romantic partners' perceptions of changes in love and related affect over time. *Journal of Personality and Social Psychology, 76,* 46–53.

Sprecher, S., & Duck, S. (1994). Sweet talk: The importance of perceived communication for romantic and friendship attraction experienced during a get-acquainted date. *Personality and Social Psychology Bulletin, 20,* 391–400.

Sprecher, S., Sullivan, Q., & Hatfield, E. (1994). Mate selection preferences: Gender differences examined in a national sample. *Journal of Personality and Social Psychology, 66,* 1074–1080.

Sprenger, M. (2001). *Becoming a "wiz" at brain-based teaching: From translation to application.* Thousand Oaks, CA: Corwin Press.

Springer, K., & Berry, D. S. (1997). Rethinking the role of evolution in the ecological model of social perception. In J. A. Simpson & D. T. Kenrick (Eds.), *Evolutionary psychology.* Mahwah, NJ: Erlbaum.

Springer, S. P., & Deutsch, G. (1998). *Left brain, right brain.* New York: W. H. Freeman.

Squire, L. R. (1987). *Memory and brain.* New York: Oxford University Press.

Squire, L. R. (1994). Declarative and nondeclarative memory: Multiple brain systems supporting learning and memory. In D. L. Schacter & E. Tulving (Eds.), *Memory systems.* Cambridge, MA: MIT Press.

Squire, L. R., & Knowlton, B. J. (2000). The medial temporal lobe, the hippocampus, and the memory systems of the brain. In M. S. Gazzaniga (Ed.), *The new cognitive neurosciences* (2nd ed., pp. 765–780). Cambridge, MA: MIT Press.

Squire, L. R., & Zola, S. M. (1996). Structure and function of declarative and nondeclarative memory systems. *Proceedings of the National Academy of Sciences, USA, 93,* 13515–13522.

Squire, L. R., Knowlton, B., & Musen, G. (1993). The structure and organization of memory. *Annual Review of Psychology, 44,* 453–495.

Sriram, T. G., & Silverman, J. J. (1998). The effects of stress on the respiratory system. In J. R. Hubbard & E. A. Workman (Eds.), *Handbook of stress medicine: An organ system approach.* New York: CRC Press.

Staal, W. G., Hulshoff Pol, H. E., Schnack, H. G., Hoogendoorn, M. L. C., Jellema, K., & Kahn, R. S. (2000). Structural brain abnormalities in patients with schizophrenia and their healthy siblings. *American Journal of Psychiatry, 157,* 416–421.

Staats, A. W., & Staats, C. K. (1963). *Complex human behavior.* New York: Holt, Rinehart & Winston.

Stahl, S. M. (1998). Getting stoned without inhaling: Anandamide is the brain's natural marijuana. *Journal of Clinical Psychiatry, 59,* 566–567.

Stainton, J. (1999). *The crocodile hunter: Steve's story* (Videotape). Santa Monica, CA: Artisan Home Entertainment.

Stajkovic, A. D., & Luthans, F. (1998). Self-efficacy and work-related performance: A meta-analysis. *Psychological Bulletin, 124,* 240–261.

Stalling, R. B. (1992). Mood and pain: The influence of positive and negative affect on reported body aches. *Journal of Social Behavior and Personality, 7*(2), 323–334.

Stamler, J., Daviglus, M. L., Garside, D. B., Dyer, A. R., Greenland, P., & Neaton, J. D. (2000). Relationship of baseline serum cholesterol levels in three large cohorts of younger men to long-term coronary, cardiovascular, and all-cause mortality and to longevity. *Journal of the American Medical Association, 284,* 311–318.

Stanovich, K. E. (1999). *Who is rational? Studies of individual differences in reasoning.* Mahwah, NJ: Erlbaum.

Starcevic, V. (2001). Clinical features and diagnosis of hypochondriasis. In V. Starcevic & D. R. Lipsitt (Eds.), *Hypochondriasis: Modern perspectives on an ancient malady.* New York: Oxford University Press.

Stasser, G. (1991). Pooling of unshared information during group discussion. In S. Worchel, W. Wood, & J. Simpson (Eds.), *Group process and productivity.* Beverly Hills, CA: Sage.

Stasser, G., Vaughan, S. I., & Stewart, D. D. (2000). Pooling unshared information: The benefits of knowing how access to information is distributed among group members. *Organizational Behavior and Human Decision Processes, 82,* 102–116.

Stattin, H., & Magnusson, D. (1990). *Pubertal maturation in female development.* Hillsdale, NJ: Erlbaum.

Steele, C. M. (1992, April). Race and the schooling of black Americans. *The Atlantic Monthly,* pp. 68–78.

Steele, C. M. (1997). A threat in the air: How stereotypes shape intellectual identity and performance. *American Psychologist, 52,* 613–629.

Steele, C. M., & Aronson, J. (1995). Stereotype threat and the intellectual test performance of African Americans. *Journal of Personality and Social Psychology, 69,* 797–811.

Steele, K. M., Bass, K. E., & Crook, M. D. (1999). The mystery of the Mozart Effect: Failure to replicate. *Psychological Science, 10,* 366–369.

Steiger, H., & Seguin, J. R. (1999). Eating disorders: Anorexia nervosa and bulimia nervosa. In T. Millon, P. H. Blaney, & R. D. Davis (Eds.),

Oxford textbook of psychopathology (pp. 365–389). New York: Oxford University Press.

Stein, B. E., & Meredith, M. A. (1993). *Vision, touch, and audition: Making sense of it all.* Cambridge, MA: MIT Press.

Stein, B. E., Wallace, M. T., & Stanford, T. R. (2000). Merging sensory signals in the brain: The development of multisensory integration in the superior colliculus. In M. S. Gazzaniga (Ed.), *The new cognitive neurosciences.* Cambridge, MA: The MIT Press.

Stein, B. E., Wallace, M. T., & Stanford, T. R. (2001). Brain mechanisms for synthesizing information from different sensory modalities. In E. B. Goldstein (Ed.), *Blackwell handbook of perception.* Malden, MA: Blackwell.

Stein, M. B., Forde, D. R., Anderson, G., & Walker, J. R. (1997a). Obsessive-compulsive disorder in the community: An epidemiologic survey with clinical reappraisal. *American Journal of Psychiatry, 154,* 1120–1126.

Stein, M. B., Walker, J. R., Hazen, A. L., & Forde, D. R. (1997b). Full and partial posttraumatic stress disorder: Findings from a community survey. *American Journal of Psychiatry, 154,* 1114–1119.

Steinberg, L. (2000, April). Youth violence: Do parents and families make a difference? *National Institute of Justice Journal,* 30–38.

Steinberg, L. (2001). We know some things: Adolescent-parent relationships in retrospect and prospect. *Journal of Research on Adolescence, 11,* 1–20.

Steinberg, L., & Levine, A. (1997). *You and your adolescent: A parents' guide for ages 10 to 20.* New York: Harper Perennial.

Steinberg, L., & Morris, A. S. (2001). Adolescent development. *Annual Review of Psychology, 52,* 83–110.

Steinberg, L., & Steinberg, W. (1994). *Crossing paths: How your child's adolescence triggers your own crisis.* New York: Simon & Schuster.

Steinhausen, H. (2002). The outcome of anorexia nervosa in the 20th century. *American Journal of Psychiatry, 159,* 1284–1293.

Steinmetz, H., Staiger, J. F., Schluag, G., Huang, Y., & Jancke, L. (1995). Corpus callosum and brain volume in women and men. *Neuroreport, 6,* 1002–1004.

Steinmetz, J. E. (1998). The localization of a simple type of learning and memory: The cerebellum and classical eyeblink conditioning. *Current Directions in Psychological Science, 7,* 72–77.

Stekel, W. (1950). *Techniques of analytical psychotherapy.* New York: Liveright.

Stellar, E. (1954). The physiology of motivation. *Psychological Review, 61,* 5–22.

Stemberger, R. T., Turner, S. M., Beidel, D. C., & Calhoun, K. S. (1995). Social phobia: An analysis of possible developmental factors. *Journal of Abnormal Psychology, 104,* 526–531.

Stepanski, E. J. (2000). Behavioral therapy for insomnia. In M. H. Kryger, T. Roth, & W. C. Dement (Eds.), *Principles and practice of sleep medicine.* Philadelphia: Saunders.

Stephens, R. S. (1999). Cannabis and hallucinogens. In B. S. McCrady & E. E. Epstein (Eds.), *Addictions: A comprehensive guidebook.* New York: Oxford University Press.

Stephens, T. W., Basinski, M., Bristow, P. K., Bue-Valleskey, J. M., Burgett, S. G., Craft, L., Hale, J., Hoffman, J., Hsiung, H. M., Kriauciunas, A., MacKellar, W., Rosteck, P. R., Jr., Schoner, B., Smith, D., Tinsley, F. C., Zhang, W. Y., & Heiman, M. (1995). The role of neuropeptide Y in the antiobesity action of the obese gene product. *Nature, 377,* 530–532.

Steraide, M. (2000). Brain electrical activity and sensory processing during waking and sleep states. In M. H. Kryger, T. Roth, & W. C. Dement (Eds.), *Principles and practice of sleep medicine.* Philadelphia: Saunders.

Stern, W. (1914). *The psychological method of testing intelligence.* Baltimore: Warwick & York.

Sternberg, R. J. (1985). *Beyond IQ: A triarchic theory of human intelligence.* New York: Cambridge University Press.

Sternberg, R. J. (1986). *Intelligence applied: Understanding and increasing your intellectual skills.* New York: Harcourt Brace Jovanovich.

Sternberg, R. J. (1988a). A three-facet model of creativity. In R. J. Sternberg (Ed.), *The nature of creativity: Contemporary psychological perspectives.* Cambridge, England: Cambridge University Press.

Sternberg, R. J. (1988b). *The triarchic mind: A new theory of human intelligence.* New York: Viking.

Sternberg, R. J. (1991). Theory-based testing of intellectual abilities: Rationale for the triarchic abilities test. In H. A. H. Rowe (Ed.), *Intelligence: Reconceptualization and measurement.* Hillsdale, NJ: Erlbaum.

Sternberg, R. J. (1995). For whom The Bell Curve tolls: A review of *The Bell Curve. Psychological Science, 6,* 257–261.

Sternberg, R. J. (1997). Educating intelligence: Infusing the triarchic theory into school instruction. In R. J. Sternberg & E. L. Grigorenko (Eds.), *Intelligence, heredity, and*

environment. New York: Cambridge University Press.

Sternberg, R. J. (1998). How intelligent is intelligence testing? *Scientific American Presents Exploring Intelligence, 9,* 12–17.

Sternberg, R. J. (1999). The theory of successful intelligence. *Review of General Psychology, 3,* 292–316.

Sternberg, R. J. (2000a). Creativity is a decision. In A. L. Costa (Ed.), *Teaching for intelligence II* (pp. 85–106). Arlington Heights, IL: Skylight Training.

Sternberg, R. J. (2000b). Successful intelligence: A unified view of giftedness. In C. F. M. van Lieshout & P. G. Heymans (Eds.), *Developing talent across the life span* (pp. 43–65). Philadelphia: Psychology Press.

Sternberg, R. J. (2001). What is the common thread of creativity? Its dialectical relation to intelligence and wisdom. *American Psychologist, 56,* 360–362.

Sternberg, R. J., & Kaufman, J. C. (1998). Human abilities. *Annual Review of Psychology, 49,* 479–502.

Sternberg, R. J., & Lubart, T. I. (1992). Buy low and sell high: An investment approach to creativity. *Current Directions in Psychological Science, 1*(1), 1–5.

Sternberg, R. J., & O'Hara, L. A. (1999). Creativity and intelligence. In R. J. Sternberg (Ed.), *Handbook of creativity.* New York: Cambridge University Press.

Sternberg, R. J., & Wagner, R. K. (1993). The *g*-ocentric view of intelligence and job performance is wrong. *Current Directions in Psychological Science, 2*(1), 1–5.

Sternberg, R. J., Castejon, J. L., Prieto, M. D., Hautamaeki, J., & Grigorenko, E. L. (2001). Confirmatory factor analysis of the Sternberg Triarchic Abilities Test in three international samples: An empirical test of the triarchic theory of intelligence. *European Journal of Psychological Assessment, 17,* 1–16.

Sternberg, R. J., Conway, B. E., Ketron, J. L., & Bernstein, M. (1981). People's conceptions of intelligence. *Journal of Personality and Social Psychology, 41,* 37–55.

Sternberg, R. J., Grigorenko, E. L., Ferrari, M., & Clinkenbeard, P. (1999). A triarchic analysis of an aptitude interaction. *European Journal of Psychological Assessment, 15,* 1–11.

Sternberg, R. J., Wagner, R. K., Williams, W. M., & Horvath, J. A. (1995). Testing common sense. *American Psychologist, 50,* 912–927.

Stevens, S. S. (1955). The measurement of loudness. *Journal of the Acoustical Society of America, 27,* 815–819.

Stevens, S. S. (1957). On the psychophysical law. *Psychological Review, 64,* 153–181.

Stevens, S. S. (1975). *Psychophysics: Introduction to its perceptual, neural, and social prospects.* New York: Wiley.

Stewart, A. J., & Ostrove, J. M. (1998). Women's personality in middle age: Gender, history, and midcourse corrections. *American Psychologist, 53,* 1185–1194.

Stice, E. (2001). Risk factors for eating pathology: Recent advances and future directions. In R. H. Striegel-Moore & L. Smolak (Eds.), *Eating disorders: Innovative directions in research and practice* (pp. 51–74). Washington, DC: American Psychological Association.

Stich, S. P. (1990). Rationality. In D. N. Osherson & E. E. Smith (Eds.), *Thinking: An invitation to cognitive science* (Vol. 3). Cambridge, MA: MIT Press.

Stickgold, R., James, L., & Hobson, J. A. (2000). Visual discrimination learning requires sleep after training. *Nature Neuroscience, 3,* 1237–1238.

Stickgold, R., Whidbee, D., Schirmer, B., Patel, V., & Hobson, J. A. (2000). Visual discrimination task improvement: A multi-step process occurring during sleep. *Journal of Cognitive Neuroscience, 12,* 246–254.

Stine, S. M., & Kosten, T. R. (1999). Opioids. In B. S. McCrady, & E. E. Epstein (Eds.), *Addictions: A comprehensive guidebook.* New York: Oxford University Press.

Stip, E. (2000). Novel antipsychotics: Issues and controversies. Typicality of atypical antipsychotics. *Journal of Psychiatry & Neuroscience, 25,* 137–153.

Stoddard, G. (1943). *The meaning of intelligence.* New York: Macmillan.

Stoddard, J. J., & Miller, T. (1995). Impact of parental smoking on the prevalence of wheezing respiratory illness in children. *American Journal of Epidemiology, 141,* 96–102.

Stoleru, S., Ennaji, A., Cournot, A., & Spira, A. (1993). LH pulsatile secretion and testosterone blood levels are influenced by sexual arousal in human males. *Psychoneuroendocrinology, 18,* 205–218.

Stone, A. A. (1999). Psychiatry and the law. In A. M. Nicholi (Ed.), *The Harvard guide to psychiatry.* Cambridge, MA: Harvard University Press.

Stone, A. A., Bovbjerg, D. H., Neale, J. M., Napoli, A., Valdimarsdottir, H., Cox, D., Hayden, F. G., & Gwaltney, J. M. (1992). Development of the common cold symptoms following experimental rhinovirus infection is related to prior stressful events. *Behavioral Medicine, 18,* 115–120.

Stone, L. (1977). *The family, sex and marriage in England 1500–1800.* New York: Harper & Row.

Stoner, J. A. F. (1961). *A comparison of individual and group decisions involving risk.* Unpublished master's thesis, Massachusetts Institute of Technology.

Stoohs, R. A., Blum, H. C., Haselhorst, M., Duchna, H. W., Guilleminault, C., & Dement, W. C. (1998). Normative data on snoring: A comparison between younger and older adults. *European Respiratory Journal, 11,* 451–457.

Stoolmiller, M. (1999). Implications of the restricted range of family environments for estimates of heritability and nonshared environment in behavior-genetic adoption studies. *Psychological Bulletin, 125,* 392–409.

Stormshak, E. A., Bierman, K. L., McMahon, R. J., & Lengua, L. J. (2000). Parenting practices and child disruptive behavior problems in early elementary school. *Journal of Clinical Child Psychology, 29*(1), 17–29.

Straus, M. A., & Kantor, G. K. (1994). Corporal punishment of adolescents by parents: A risk factor in the epidemiology of depression, suicide, alcohol abuse, child abuse, and wife beating. *Adolescence, 29,* 543–561.

Strayer, D. L., & Johnston, W. A. (2001). Driven to distraction: Dual-task studies of simulated driving and conversing on a cellular telephone. *Psychological Science, 12,* 462–466.

Streissguth, A. P., Barr, H. M., Bookstein, F. L., Sampson, P. D., & Olson, H. C. (1999). The long-term neurocognitive consequences of prenatal alcohol exposure: A 14-year study. *Psychological Science, 10,* 186–190.

Streissguth, A. P., Barr, H. M., Sampson, P. D., Darby, B. L., & Martin, D. C. (1989). IQ at age 4 in relation to maternal alcohol use and smoking during pregnancy. *Developmental Psychology, 25,* 3–11.

Striegel-Moore, R. H., & Rodin, J. (1986). The influence of psychological variables in obesity. In K. D. Brownell & J. P. Foreyt (Eds.), *Handbook of eating disorders: Physiology, psychology, and treatment of obesity, anorexia and bulimia.* New York: Basic Books.

Striegel-Moore, R. H., & Smolak, L. (2001). Introduction. In R. H. Striegel-Moore & L. Smolak (Eds.), *Eating disorders: Innovative directions in research and practice* (pp. 3–8). Washington, DC: American Psychological Association.

Striegel-Moore, R. H., Silberstein, L. R., & Rodin, J. (1993). The social self in bulimia nervosa: Public self-consciousness, social anxiety, and perceived fraudulence. *Journal of Abnormal Psychology, 102.*

Strober, M., Freeman, R., Lampert, C., Diamond, J., & Kaye, W. (2000). Controlled family study of anorexia nervosa and bulimia nervosa: Evidence of shared liability and transmission of partial syndromes. *American Journal of Psychiatry, 157,* 393–401.

Strupp, H. H. (1996). The tripartite model and the *Consumer Reports* study. *American Psychologist, 51,* 1017–1024.

Strupp, H. H., & Howard, K. I. (1992). A brief history of psychotherapy research. In D. K. Freedheim (Ed.), *History of psychotherapy: A century of change.* Washington, DC: American Psychological Association.

Stuart, E. W., Shimp, T. A., & Engle, R. W. (1987). Classical conditioning of consumer attitudes: Four experiments in an advertising context. *Journal of Consumer Research, 14,* 334–349.

Stumpf, H., & Stanley, J. C. (1996). Gender-related differences on the College Board's Advanced Placement and Achievement Tests, 1982–1992. *Journal of Educational Psychology, 88,* 353–364.

Stunkard, A. J., Harris, J. R., Pederson, N. L., & McClearn, G. E. (1990). The body-mass index of twins who have been reared apart. *New England Journal of Medicine, 322,* 1483–1487.

Stunkard, A. J., Sorensen, T., Hanis, C., Teasdale, T. W., Chakraborty, R., Schull, W. J., & Schulsinger, F. (1986). An adoption study of human obesity. *New England Journal of Medicine, 314,* 193–198.

Subrahmanyam, K., & Greenfield, P. M. (1996). Effect of video game practice on spatial skills in girls and boys. In P. M. Greenfield, & R. R. Cocking (Eds.), *Interacting with video.* Norwood, NJ: Ablex Publishing Corp.

Sue, D. W., & Sue, D. (1999). *Counseling the culturally different: Theory and practice.* New York: Wiley.

Sue, D. W., Bingham, R. P., Porche-Burke, L., & Vasquez, M. (1999). The diversification of psychology: A multicultural revolution. *American Psychologist, 54,* 1061–1069.

Sue, S. (1991). Ethnicity and culture in psychological research and practice. In J. D. Goodchilds (Ed.), *Psychological perspectives on human diversity in America.* Washington, DC: American Psychological Association.

Sue, S., & Zane, N. (1987). The role of culture and cultural techniques in psychotherapy: A critique and reformulation. *American Psychologist, 42,* 37–45.

Sue, S., Zane, N., & Young, K. (1994). Research on psychotherapy with culturally diverse populations. In A. E. Bergin & S. L. Garfield (Eds.), *Handbook of psychotherapy and behavior change* (4th ed.). New York: Wiley.

Suh, E., Diener, E., Oishi, S., & Triandis, H. C. (1998). The shifting basis of life satisfaction judgments across cultures: Emotions versus norms. *Journal of Personality and Social Psychology, 74,* 482–493.

Suinn, R. M. (1984). *Fundamentals of abnormal psychology.* Chicago: Nelson-Hall.

Sullivan, G., Burnam, A., & Koegel, P. (2000). Pathways to homelessness among the mentally ill. *Social Psychiatry & Psychiatric Epidemiology, 35,* 444–450.

Sullivan, G. M., & Coplan, J. D. (2000). Anxiety disorders: Biochemical aspects. In B. J. Sadock & V. A. Sadock (Eds.), *Kaplan and Sadock's comprehensive textbook of psychiatry,* (7th ed., Vol. 1). Philadelphia: Lippincott/Williams & Wilkins.

Sullivan, P. F. (2002). Course and outcome of anorexia nervosa and bulimia nervosa. In C. G. Fairburn & K. D. Brownell (Eds.), *Eating disorders and obesity: A comprehensive handbook.* New York: Guilford.

Sullivan, P. F., Neale, M. C., & Kendler, K. S. (2000). Genetic epidemiology of major depression: Review and meta-analysis. *American Journal of Psychiatry, 157,* 1552–1562.

Sulloway, F. J. (1995). Birth order and evolutionary psychology: A meta-analytic overview. *Psychological Inquiry, 6,* 75–80.

Sulloway, F. J. (1996). *Born to rebel: Birth order, family dynamics, and creative lives.* New York: Pantheon Books.

Super, C. M. (1976). Environmental effects on motor development: A case of African infant precocity. *Developmental Medicine and Child Neurology, 18,* 561–567.

Susser, E. B., Brown, A., & Matte, T. D. (1999). Prenatal factors and adult mental and physical health. *Canadian Journal of Psychiatry, 44,* 326–334.

Susser, E. B., Neugebauer, R., Hoek, H. W., Brown, A. S., Lin, S., Labovitz, D., & Gorman, J. M. (1996). Schizophrenia after prenatal famine: Further evidence. *Archives of General Psychiatry, 53,* 25–31.

Sutker, P. B., & Allain, A. N. (2001). Antisocial personality disorder. In P. B. Sutker & H. E. Adams (Eds.), *Comprehensive handbook of psychopathology.* New York: Kluwer Academic/Plenum.

Sutker, P. B., Bugg, F. & West, J. A. (1993). Antisocial personality disorder. In P. B. Sutker & H. E. Adams (Eds.),. *Comprehensive handbook of psychopathology* (2nd ed.). New York: Plenum.

Suzuki, L. A., & Valencia, R. R. (1997). Race-ethnicity and measured intelligence: Educational implications. *American Psychologist, 52,* 1103–1114.

Suzuki, L. A., & Vraniak, D. A. (1994). Ethnicity, race, and measured intelligence. In R. J. Sternberg

(Ed.), *Encyclopedia of human intelligence*. New York: Macmillan.

Swartz, C. M. (1993). Clinical and laboratory predictors of ECT response. In C. E. Coffey (Ed.), *The clinical science of electroconvulsive therapy*. Washington, DC: American Psychiatric Press.

Swets, J. A., Tanner, W. P., & Birdsall, T. G. (1961). Decision processes in perception. *Psychological Review, 68*, 301–340.

Swim, J. K. (1994). Perceived versus meta-analytic effect sizes: An assessment of the accuracy of gender stereotypes. *Journal of Personality and Social Psychology, 66*, 21–36.

Swim, J. K., & Campbell, B. (2001). Sexism: Attitudes, beliefs, and behaviors. In R. Brown & S. L. Gaertner (Eds.), *Blackwell handbook of social psychology: Intergroup processes*. Malden, MA: Blackwell.

Swim, J. K., & Sanna, L. J. (1996). He's skilled, she's lucky: A meta-analysis of observers' attributions for women's and men's successes and failures. *Personality and Social Psychology Bulletin, 22*, 507–519.

Swim, J. K., Aikin, K. J., Hall, W. S., & Hunter, B. A. (1995). Sexism and racism: Old-fashioned and modern prejudices. *Journal of Personality and Social Psychology, 68*, 199–214.

Symons, C. S., & Johnson, B. T. (1997). The self-reference effect in memory: A meta-analysis. *Psychological Bulletin, 121*, 371–394.

Szasz, T. (1974). *The myth of mental illness*. New York: Harper & Row.

Szasz, T. (1990). Law and psychiatry: The problems that will not go away. *The Journal of Mind and Behavior, 11*(3/4), 557–564.

Szechtman, H., Woody, E., Bowers, K. S., & Nahmias, C. (1998). Where the imaginal appears real: A positron emission tomography study of auditory hallucinations. *Proceedings of the National Academy of Sciences, 95*, 1956–1960.

Szmukler, G. I., & Patton, G. (1995). Sociocultural models of eating disorders. In G. Szmukler, C. Dare, & J. Treasure (Eds.), *Handbook of eating disorders: Theory, treatment, and research*. New York: Wiley.

Szymanski, S., Lieberman, J. A., Alvir, J. M., Mayerhoff, D., Loebel, A., Geisler, S., Chakos, M., Koreen, A., Jody, D., Kane, J., Woerner, M., & Cooper, T. (1995). Gender differences in onset of illness, treatment response, course, and biologic indexes in first-episode schizophrenic patients. *American Journal of Psychiatry, 152*, 698–703.

Takahashi, K. (1986). Examining the Strange Situation procedure with Japanese mothers and 12-month-old infants. *Developmental Psychology, 19*, 184–191.

Takahashi, K. (1990). Are the key assumptions of the "Strange Situation" procedure universal? *Human Development, 33*, 23–30.

Takeuchi, D. T., Uehara, E., & Maramba, G. (1999). Cultural diversity and mental health treatment. A. V. Horwitz & T. L. Scheid (Eds.), *A handbook for the study of mental health*. New York: Cambridge University Press.

Talwar, S. K., Xu, S., Hawley, E. S., Weiss, S. A., Moxon, K. A., & Chapin, J. K. (2002). Behavioural neuroscience: Rat navigation guided by remote control. *Nature, 417*, 37–38.

Tamminga, C. A. (1999). Principles of the pharmacotherapy of schizophrenia. In D. S. Charney, E. J. Nestler, & B. S. Bunney (Eds.), *Neurobiology of mental illness* (pp. 272–290). New York: Oxford University Press.

Tanaka-Matsumi, J. (2001). Abnormal psychology and culture. In D. Matsumoto (Ed.), *The handbook of culture & psychology*. New York: Oxford University Press.

Tang, I. T., & Glatt, A. E. (2001, September). The new approach to antiretroviral therapy. *Medical Aspects of Human Sexuality*, 27–33.

Tanner, J. M. (1978). *Fetus into man: Physical growth from conception to maturity*. Cambridge, MA: Harvard University Press.

Tardiff, K. (1999). Violence. In R. E. Hales, S. C. Yudofsky, & J. A. Talbott (Eds.), *American Psychiatric Press textbook of psychiatry*. Washington, DC: American Psychiatric Press.

Tardiff, K., Marzuk, P. M., & Leon, A. C. (2002). Role of anitdepressants in murder and suicide. *American Journal of Psychiatry, 159*, 1248–1249.

Tart, C. T. (1988). From spontaneous event to lucidity: A review of attempts to consciously control nocturnal dreaming. In J. Gackenbach & S. LaBerge (Eds.), *Conscious mind, sleeping brain: Perspectives on lucid dreaming*. New York: Plenum.

Tart, C. T. (1990). Toward the experimental control of dreaming: A review of the literature. In C. T. Tart (Ed.), *Altered states of consciousness* (3rd ed.). San Francisco: Harper.

Taub, S. (1996). The legal treatment of recovered memories of child sexual abuse. *Journal of Legal Medicine, 17*, 183–214.

Tavris, C. (1982). *Anger: the misunderstood emotion*. New York: Simon & Schuster.

Tavris, C. (1989). *Anger: The misunderstood emotion* (2nd ed.). New York: Simon & Schuster.

Tavris, C. (1992). *The mismeasure of woman*. New York: Simon & Schuster.

Tavris, C. (1998, September 13). Peer pressure (Review of *The Nurture Assumption*). *The New York Times Book Review, 103*, p. 14.

Taylor, E. (1999). An intellectual renaissance of humanistic psychology. *Journal of Humanistic Psychology, 39*, 7–25.

Taylor, E. (2001). Positive psychology and humanistic psychology: A reply to Seligman. *Journal of Humanistic Psychology, 41*(1), 13–29.

Taylor, I., & Taylor, M. M. (1990). *Psycholinguistics: Learning and using language*. Englewood Cliffs, NJ: Prentice-Hall.

Taylor, J. H., & Walker, L. J. (1997). Moral climate and the development of moral reasoning: The effects of dyadic discussions between young offenders. *Journal of Moral Education, 26*, 21–43.

Taylor, S. E., & Brown, J. D. (1988). Illusion and well-being: A social psychological perspective on mental health. *Psychological Bulletin, 103*, 193–210.

Taylor, S. E., & Brown, J. D. (1994). Positive illusions and well-being revisited: Separating fact from fiction. *Psychological Bulletin, 116*, 21–27.

Teachman, J. D., Polonko, K. A., & Scanzoni, J. (1999). Demography and families. In M. B. Sussman, S. K. Steinmetz, & G. W. Peterson (Eds.), *Handbook of marriage and the family* (pp. 39–76). New York: Plenum.

Teasdale, J. D., Howard, R. J., Cox, S. G., Ha, Y., Brammer, M. J., Williams, S. C. R., & Checkley, S. A. (1999). Functional MRI study of the cognitive generation of affect. *American Journal of Psychiatry, 156*, 209–215.

Tedeschi, R. G., Park, C. L., & Calhoun, L. G. (1998). Posttraumatic growth: Conceptual issues. In R. G. Tedeschi, C. L. Park, & L. G. Calhoun (Eds.), *Posttraumatic growth: Positive changes in the aftermath of crisis* (pp. 1–22). Mahwah, NJ: Erlbaum.

Tedlock, L. B. (1992). Zuni and Quiche dream sharing and interpreting. In B. Tedlock (Ed.), *Dreaming: Anthropoligical and psychological interpretations*. Santa Fe, NM: School of American Research Press.

Tellegen, A., Lykken, D. T., Bouchard, T. J., Jr., Wilcox, K. J., Segal, N. L., & Rich, S. (1988). Personality similarity in twins reared apart and together. *Journal of Personality and Social Psychology, 54*, 1031–1039.

Tennen, H., & Affleck, G. (1999). Finding benefits in adversity. In C. R. Snyder (Ed.), *Coping: The psychology of what works*. New York: Oxford University Press.

Tepper, B. J., & Nurse, R. J. (1997). Fat perception is related to PROP taster status. *Physiology & Behavior, 61*, 949–954.

Terman, L. M. (1916). *The measurement of intelligence*. Boston: Houghton Mifflin.

Terman, L. M. (1925). *Genetic studies of genius: Vol. 1. Mental and physical traits of a thousand gifted children*. Stanford, CA: Stanford University Press.

Terman, L. M., & Oden, M. H. (1959). *Genetic studies of genius: Vol. 5. The gifted group at mid-life*. Stanford, CA: Stanford University Press.

Terr, L. (1994). *Unchained memories*. New York: Basic Books.

Terrace, H. S. (1986). *Nim: A chimpanzee who learned sign language*. New York: Columbia University Press.

Tessier-Lavigne, M. (2000). Visual processing by the retina. In E. R. Kandel, J. H. Schwartz, & T. M. Jessell (Eds.), *Principles of neural science*. New York: McGraw-Hill.

Testa, K. (1996). Church to pay $1 million in false-memory case. *San Jose Mercury News*, 8A.

Teuber, M. (1974). Sources of ambiguity in the prints of Maurits C. Escher. *Scientific American, 231*, 90–104.

Thase, M. E. (1999). What is the investigator allegiance effect and what should we do about it? *Clinical Psychology: Science & Practice, 6*(1), 113–115.

Thase, M. E., Jindal, R., & Howland, R. H. (2002). Biological aspects of depression. In I. H. Gotlib & C. L. Hammen (Eds.), *Handbook of depression*. New York: Guilford.

Thayer, R. E. (1996). *The origin of everyday moods*. New York: Oxford University Press.

Thelen, E. (1995). Motor development: A new synthesis. *American Psychologist, 50*, 79–95.

Thomas, A., & Chess, S. (1977). *Temperament and development*. New York: Brunner/Mazel.

Thomas, A., & Chess, S. (1989). Temperament and personality. In G. A. Kohnstamm, J. E. Bates, & M. K. Rothbart (Eds.), *Temperament in childhood*. New York: Wiley.

Thomas, A., Chess, S., & Birch, H. G. (1970). The origin of personality. *Scientific American, 223*(2), 102–109.

Thomas, D. R. (1992). Discrimination and generalization. In L. R. Squire (Ed.), *Encyclopedia of learning and memory*. New York: Macmillan.

Thomas, R. M. (2000). *Comparing theories of child development*. Belmont, CA: Wadsworth.

Thomason, B. T., Brantkey, P. J., Jones, G. N., Dyer, H. R., & Morris, J. L. (1992). The relation between stress and disease activity in rheumatoid arthritis. *Journal of Behavioral Medicine, 15*, 215–220.

Thompson, J. K., & Stice, E. (2001). Thin-ideal internalization: Mounting evidence for a new risk factor for body-image disturbance and eating pathology. *Current Directions in Psychological Science, 10*(5), 181–183.

Thompson, M. M., Zanna, M. P., & Griffin, D. W. (1995). Let's not be indifferent about (attitudinal) ambivalence. In R. E. Petty & J. A. Krosnick (Eds.), *Attitude strength: Antecedents and consequences.* Mahwah, NJ: Erlbaum.

Thompson, R. A. (1999). The individual child: Temperament, emotion, self, and personality. In M. H. Bornstein & M. E. Lamb (Eds.), *Developmental psychology: An advanced textbook.* Mahwah, NJ: Erlbaum.

Thompson, R. A., & Nelson, C. A. (2001). Developmental science and the media: Early brain development. *American Psychologist, 56,* 5–15.

Thompson, R. F. (1992). Memory. *Current Opinion in Neurobiology, 2,* 203–208.

Thompson, R. F. (1989). A model system approach to memory. In P. R. Solomon, G. R. Goethals, C. M. Kelley, & B. R. Stephens (Eds.), *Memory: Interdisciplinary approaches.* New York: Springer-Verlag.

Thompson, W. F., Schellenberg, E. G., & Husain, G. (2001). Arousal, mood and the Mozart effect. *Psychological Science, 12,* 248–251.

Thoresen, C. E., Harris, A. H. S., & Luskin, F. (1999). Forgiveness and health: An unanswered question. In M. E. McCullough, K. I. Pargament & C. E. Thoresen (Eds.), *Forgiveness: Theory, research, and practice* (pp. 254–280). New York: Guilford.

Thorndike, E. L. (1913). *Educational psychology: The psychology of learning* (Vol. 2). New York: Teachers College.

Thorndike, R. L., Hagen, E. P., & Sattler, J. M. (1986). *The Stanford-Binet intelligence scale: Fourth edition technical manual.* Chicago: Riverside.

Thorndyke, P. W., & Hayes-Roth, B. (1979). The use of schemata in the acquisition and transfer of knowledge. *Cognitive Psychology, 11,* 83–106.

Thorne, B. M., & Henley, T. B. (1997). *Connections in the history and systems of psychology.* Boston: Houghton Mifflin.

Thornhill, R. (1976). Sexual selection and nuptial feeding behavior in *Bittacus apicalis* (Insecta: Mecoptera). *American Naturalist, 110,* 529–548.

Thornton, B., & Moore, S. (1993). Physical attractiveness contrast effect: Implications for self-esteem and evaluations of the social self. *Personality and Social Psychology Bulletin, 19,* 474–480.

Thornton, B. (1984). Defensive attribution of responsibility: Evidence for an arousal-based motivational bias. *Journal of Personality and Social Psychology, 46,* 721–734.

Thornton, B. (1992). Repression and its mediating influence on the defensive attribution of responsibility. *Journal of Research in Personality, 26,* 44–57.

Thorpe, S. J., & Salkozskis, P. M. (1995). Phobia beliefs: Do cognitive factors play a role in specific phobias? *Behavioral Research and Therapy, 33,* 805–816.

Thun, M. J., Apicella, L. F., & Henley, S. J. (2000). Smoking vs. other risk factors as the cause of smoking-attributable deaths: Confounding in the courtroom. *Journal of the American Medical Association, 284,* 706–712.

Thune, I., Brenn, T., Lund, E., & Gaard, M. (1997). Physical activity and the risk of breast cancer. *New England Journal of Medicine, 336,* 1269–1275.

Thurstone, L. L. (1938). *Primary mental abilities* (Psychometric Monographs No. 1). Chicago: University of Chicago Press.

Thurstone, L. L. (1955). *The differential growth of mental abilities* (Psychometric Laboratory Rep. No. 14). Chapel Hill: University of North Carolina.

Tice, D. M., Bratslavsky, E., & Baumeister, R. F. (2001). Emotional distress regulation takes precedence over impulse control: If you feel bad, do it! *Journal of Personality and Social Psychology, 80,* 53–67.

Tietzel, A. J., & Lack, L. C. (2001). The short-term benefits of brief and long naps following nocturnal sleep restriction. *Sleep: Journal of Sleep Research & Sleep Medicine, 24,* 293–300.

Todd, J. T., & Morris, E. K. (1992). Case histories in the great power of steady misrepresentation. *American Psychologist, 47,* 1441–1453.

Todd, P. M., & Gigerenzer, G. (2000). Precis of simple heuristics that make us smart. *Behavioral & Brain Sciences, 23,* 727–780.

Todes, D. P. (1997). From the machine to the ghost within: Pavlov's transition from digestive physiology to conditional reflexes. *American Psychologist, 52,* 947–955.

Tohen, M., & Goodwin, F. K. (1995). Epidemiology of bipolar disorder. In M. T. Tsuang, M. Tohen, & G. E. P. Zahner (Eds.), *Textbook in psychiatric epidemiology.* New York: Wiley.

Tolman, E. C. (1922). A new formula for behaviorism. *Psychological Review, 29,* 44–53.

Tolman, E. C. (1932). *Purposive behavior in animals and men.* New York: Appleton-Century-Crofts.

Tomkins, S. S. (1980). Affect as amplification: Some modifications in theory. In R. Plutchik & H. Kellerman (Eds.), *Emotion: Theory, research and experience* (Vol. 1). New York: Academic Press.

Tomkins, S. S. (1991). *Affect, imagery, consciousness: 3. Anger and fear.* New York: Springer-Verlag.

Tondo, L., Baldessarini, R. J., Hennen, J., & Floris, G. (1998). Lithium maintenance treatment of depression and mania in bipolar I and bipolar II disorders. *American Journal of Psychiatry, 155,* 638–645.

Tooby, J., & Cosmides, L. (1989). Evolutionary psychology and the generation of culture: Part 1. Theoretical considerations. *Ethology and Sociobiology, 10,* 29–49.

Tooby, J., & Cosmides, L. (1990). On the universality of human nature and the uniqueness of the individual: The role of genetics and adaptation. *Journal of Personality, 58,* 17–68.

Toomey, R., Kremen, W. S., Simpson, J. C., Samson, J. A., Seidman, L. J., Lyons, M. J., Faraone, S. V., & Tsuang, M. T. (1997). Revisiting the factor structure for positive and negative symptoms: Evidence from a large heterogeneous group of psychiatric patients. *American Journal of Psychiatry, 154,* 371–377.

Torgersen, S. (1979). The nature and origin of common phobic fears. *British Journal of Psychiatry, 119,* 343–351.

Torgersen, S. (1983). Genetic factors in anxiety disorders. *Archives of General Psychiatry, 40,* 1085–1089.

Torrey, E. F. (1992). *Freudian fraud: The malignant effect of Freud's theory on American thought and culture.* New York: Harper Perennial.

Torrey, E. F. (1996). *Out of the shadows.* New York: Wiley.

Torrey, E. F., Bowler, A. E., Taylor, E. H., & Gottesman, I. I. (1994). *Schizophrenia and manic-depressive disorder.* New York: Basic Books.

Toufexis, A. (1990, December 17). Drowsy America. *Time,* pp. 78–85.

Trasti, N., Vik, T., Jacobson, G., & Bakketeig, L. S. (1999). Smoking in pregnancy and children's mental and motor development at age 1 and 5 years. *Early Human Development, 55,* 137–147.

Travis, F. (2001). Autonomic and EEG patterns distinguish transcending from other experiences during Transcendental Meditation practice. *International Journal of Psychophysiology, 42,* 1–9.

Travis, F., & Pearson, C. (2000). Pure consciousness: Distinct phenomenological and physiological correlates of "consciousness itself." *International Journal of Neuroscience, 100*(1-4), 77–89.

Treisman, G. J. (1999). AIDS education for psychiatrists. *Primary Psychiatry, 6*(5), 71–73.

Triandis, H. C. (1989). Self and social behavior in differing cultural contexts. *Psychological Review, 96,* 269–289.

Triandis, H. C. (1994). *Culture and social behavior.* New York: McGraw-Hill.

Triandis, H. C. (2001). Individualism and collectivism: Past, present, and future. In D. Matsumoto (Ed.), *The handbook of culture and psychology.* New York: Oxford University Press.

Triandis, H. C., & Suh, E. M. (2002). Cultural influences on personality. *Annual Review of Psychology, 53,* 133–160.

Trivers, R. L. (1971). The evolution of reciprocal altruism. *Quarterly Review of Biology, 46,* 35–57.

Trivers, R. L. (1972). Parental investment and sexual selection. In B. Campbell (Ed.), *Sexual selection and the descent of man.* Chicago: Aldine.

Trope, Y., & Liberman, A. (1993). The use of trait conceptions to identify other people's behavior and to draw inferences about their personalities. *Personality and Social Psychology Bulletin, 19,* 553–562.

Trotter, R. J. (1986, September). The three faces of love. *Psychology Today,* pp. 46–54.

Trull, T. J., & McCrae, R. R. (1994). A five-factor perspective on personality disorder research. In P. T. Costa, Jr. & T. A. Widiger (Eds.), *Personality disorders and the five-factor model of personality.* Washington, DC: American Psychological Association.

Tsai, J. L., Butcher, J. N., Muñoz, R. F., & Vitousek, K. (2001). Culture, ethnicity, and psychopathology. In P. B. Sutker & H. E. Adams (Eds.), *Comprehensive handbook of psychopathology.* New York: Kluwer Academic/Plenum.

Tseng, W. S. (1997). Overview: Culture and psychopathology. In W. S. Tseng & J. Streltzer (Eds.), *Culture and psychopathology: A guide to clinical assessment.* New York: Brunner/Mazel.

Tulving, E. (1986). What kind of a hypothesis is the distinction between episodic and semantic memory? *Journal of Experimental Psychology: Learning, Memory and Cognition, 12,* 307–311.

Tulving, E. (1993). What is episodic memory? *Current Directions in Psychological Science, 2*(3), 67–70.

Tulving, E. (2001). Origin of autonoesis in episodic memory. In H. L. Roediger III, J. S. Nairne, I. Neath, & A. M. Surprenant (Eds.), *The nature of remembering: Essays in honor of Robert G. Crowder* (pp. 17–34). Washington, DC: American Psychological Association.

Tulving, E., & Schacter, D. L. (1990). Priming and human memory systems. *Science, 247,* 301–306.

Tulving, E., & Thomson, D. M. (1973). Encoding specificity and retrieval processes in episodic memory. *Psychological Review, 80,* 352–373.

Turk, D. C. (1994). Perspectives on chronic pain: The role of psychological factors. *Current Directions in Psychological Science, 3,* 45–48.

Turkheimer, E. (1991). Individual and group differences in adoption studies of IQ. *Psychological Bulletin, 110*, 392–405.

Turkheimer, E. (2000). Three laws of behavior genetics and what they mean. *Current Directions in Psychological Science, 9*(5), 160–164.

Turkheimer, E., & Waldron, M. (2000). Nonshared environment: A theoretical, methodological, and quantitative review. *Psychological Bulletin, 126*, 78–108.

Turkkan, J. S. (1989). Classical conditioning: The new hegemony. *Behavioral and Brain Sciences, 12*, 121–179.

Turner, J. R., & Wheaton, B. (1995). Checklist measurement of stressful life events. In S. Cohen, R. C. Kessler, & L. U. Gordon (Eds.), *Measuring stress: A guide for health and social scientists*. New York: Oxford University Press.

Turner, P. J., & Gervai, J. (1995). A multidimensional study of gender typing in preschool children and their parents: Personality, attitudes, preferences, behavior, and cultural differences. *Developmental Psychology, 31*, 759–772.

Turner, S. M., Beidel, D. C., Stanley, M. A., & Heiser, N. (2001). Obsessive-compulsive disorder. In P. B. Sutker & H. E. Adams (Eds.), *Comprehensive textbook of psychiatry* (3rd ed., pp. 155–182). New York: Kluwer Academic/Plenum.

Turner-Bowker, D. M. (1996). Gender stereotyped descriptions in children's picture books: Does "curious Jane" exist in the literature? *Sex Roles, 35*, 461–488.

Tversky, A. (1972). Elimination by aspects: A theory of choice. *Psychological Review, 79*, 281–299.

Tversky, A., & Kahneman, D. (1971). Belief in the law of small numbers. *Psychological Bulletin, 76*, 105–110.

Tversky, A., & Kahneman, D. (1973). Availability: A heuristic for judging frequency and probability. *Cognitive Psychology, 5*, 207–232.

Tversky, A., & Kahneman, D. (1974). Judgments under uncertainty: Heuristics and biases. *Science, 185*, 1124–1131.

Tversky, A., & Kahneman, D. (1982). Judgment under uncertainty: Heuristics and biases. In D. Kahneman, P. Slovic, & A. Tversky (Eds.), *Judgment under uncertainty: Heuristics and biases*. New York: Cambridge University Press.

Tversky, A., & Kahneman, D. (1983). Extensional versus intuitive reasoning: The conjunction fallacy in probability judgment. *Psychological Review, 90*, 283–315.

Tversky, A., & Kahneman, D. (1988). Rational choice and the framing of decisions. In D. E. Bell, H. Raiffa, & A. Tversky (Eds.), *Decision making: Descriptive, normative, and prescriptive interactions*. New York: Cambridge University Press.

Tversky, A., & Kahneman, D. (1991). Loss aversion in riskless choice: A reference-dependent model. *Quarterly Journal of Economics, 106*, 1039–1061.

Tversky, A., & Shafir, E. (1992). Choice under conflict: The dynamics of deferred decision. *Psychological Science, 3*, 358–361.

Uchino, B. N., Uno, D., & Holt-Lunstad, J. (1999). Social support, physiological processes, and health. *Current Directions in Psychological Science, 8*, 145–148.

Ulrich, R. E. (1991). Animal rights, animal wrongs and the question of balance. *Psychological Science, 2*, 197–201.

Umbel, V. M., Pearson, B. Z., Fernandez, S. C., & Oller, D. K. (1992). Measuring bilingual children's receptive vocabularies. *Child Development, 63*, 1012–1020.

Underwood, B. J. (1961). Ten years of massed practice on distributed practice. *Psychological Review, 68*, 229–247.

Underwood, B. J. (1970). A breakdown of the total-time law in free-recall learning. *Journal of Verbal Learning and Verbal Behavior, 9*, 573–580.

Unger, R. K., & Crawford, M. (1992). *Women and gender: A feminist psychology*. New York: McGraw-Hill.

Ungerleider, L. G., & Haxby, J. V. (1994). "What" and "where" in the human brain. *Current Opinion in Neurobiology, 4*, 157–165.

Ursano, R. J., & Silberman, E. K. (1999). Psychoanalysis, psychoanalytic psychotherapy, and supportive psychotherapy. In R. E. Hales, S. C. Yudofsky, & J. A. Talbott (Eds.), *American Psychiatric Press textbook of psychiatry*. Washington, DC: American Psychiatric Press.

Ursano, R. J., Fullerton, C. S., & Norwood, A. E. (2001). *Psychiatric dimensions of disaster: Patient care, community consultation, and preventive medicine*. Retrieved November 20, 2001 from American Psychiatric Association Web site: http:www.psych.org/pract_of_psych/disaster.cfm.

Ursano, R. J., Fullerton, C. S., Vance, K., & Kao, T. C. (1999). Posttraumatic stress disorder and identification in disaster workers. *American Journal of Psychiatry, 156*, 353–359.

U.S. Department of Health and Human Services. (1990). *The health benefits of smoking cessation: A report of the surgeon general*. Washington, DC: U.S. Government Printing Office.

U.S. Department of Health and Human Services. (1999). *Mental health: A report of the Surgeon General*. Washington, DC: U.S. Government Printing Office.

Vaillant, G. E. (1992). *Ego mechanisms of defense: A guide for clinicians and researchers*. Washington, DC: American Psychiatric Press.

Vaillant, G. E. (1994). Ego mechanisms of defense and personality psychopathology. *Journal of Abnormal Psychology, 103*, 44–50.

Vaillant, G. E. (2000). Adaptive mental mechanisms: Their role in a positive psychology. *American Psychologist, 55*, 89–98.

Valenstein, E. S. (1973). *Brain control*. New York: Wiley.

Valleroy, L. A., MacKellar, D. A., Karon, J. M., Rosen, D. H., McFarland, W., Shehan, D. A., Stoyanoff, S. R., LaLota, M., Celentano, D. D., Koblin, B. A., Thiede, H., Katz, M. H., Torian, L. V., & Janssen, R. S. (2000). HIV prevalence and associated risks in young men who have sex with men. *Journal of the American Medical Association, 284*, 198–204.

Vallone, R. P., Griffin, D. W., Lin, S., & Ross, L. (1990). Overconfident prediction of future actions and outcomes by self and others. *Journal of Personality and Social Psychology, 58*, 582–592.

Van Cauter, E., Leproult, R., & Plat, L. (2000). Age-related changes in slow wave sleep and REM sleep and relationship with growth hormone and cortisol levels in healthy men. *Journal of the American Medical Association, 284*, 861–868.

Van de Castle, R. L. (1993). Content of dreams. In M. A. Carskadon (Ed.), *Encyclopedia of sleep and dreaming*. New York: Macmillan.

Van de Castle, R. L. (1994). *Our dreaming mind*. New York: Ballantine Books.

van den Boom, D. C. (1994). The influence of temperament and mothering on attachment and exploration: An experimental manipulation of sensitive responsiveness among lower-class mothers and irritable infants. *Child Development, 65*, 1457–1477.

VanderPlate, C., Aral, S. O., & Magder, L. (1988). The relationship among genital herpes simplex virus, stress, and social support. *Health Psychology, 7*, 159–168.

van der Post, L. (1975). *Jung and the story of our time*. New York: Vintage Books.

VanderStoep, S. W., & Seifert, C. M. (1994). Problem solving, transfer, and thinking. In P. R. Pintrich, D. R. Brown, & C. E. Weinstein (Eds.), *Student motivation, cognition, and learning: Essays in honor of Wilbert J. McKeachie* (pp. 27–49). Hillsdale, NJ: Erlbaum.

Van Dongen, H. P. A., & Dinges, D. F. (2000). Circadian rhythms in fatigue, alertness and performance. In M. H. Kryger, T. Roth, & W. C. Dement (Eds.), *Principles and practice of sleep medicine*. Philadelphia: Saunders.

Vane, J. R., & Motta, R. W. (1990). Group intelligence tests. In G. Goldstein & M. Hersen (Eds.), *Handbook of psychological assessment*. New York: Pergamon Press.

van Eck, M., Nicolson, N. A., & Berkhof, J. (1998). Effects of stressful daily events on mood states: Relationship to global perceived stress. *Journal of Personality and Social Psychology, 75*, 1572–1585.

Van Hoesen, G. W., Morecraft, R. J., & Semendeferi, K. (1996). Functional neuroanatomy of the limbic system and prefrontal cortex. In B. S. Fogel, R. B. Schiffer, & S. M. Rao (Eds), *Neuropsychiatry*. Baltimore: Williams & Wilkins.

Van Houten, R. (1983). Punishment: From the animal laboratory to the applied setting. In S. Axelrod & J. Apsche (Eds.), *The effects of punishment on human behavior*. New York: Academic Press.

van IJzendoorn, M. H., & Sagi, A. (1999). Cross-cultural patterns of attachment: Universal and contextual dimensions. In J. Cassidy & P. R. Shaver (Eds.), *Handbook of attachment: Theory, research, and clinical applications*. New York: Guilford.

Vaughn, B. E., & Bost, K. K. (1999). Attachment and temperament: Redundant, independent, or interacting influences on interpersonal adaptation and personality development? In J. Cassidy & P. R. Shaver (Eds.), *Handbook of attachment: Theory, research, and clinical applications*. New York: Guilford.

Vazquez, C., Munoz, M., & Sanz, J. (1997). Lifetime and 12-month prevalence of DSM-III-R mental disorders among the homeless in Madrid: A European study using the CIDI. *Acta Psychiatrica Scandinavica, 95*, 523–530.

Veenhoven, R. (1993). *Happiness in nations*. Rotterdam, Netherlands: Risbo.

Vega, W. A., Kolody, B., Aguilar-Gaxiola, S., & Catalano, R. (1999). Gaps in service utilization by Mexican Americans with mental health problems. *American Journal of Psychiatry, 156*, 928–934.

Ventura, J., Nuechterlein, K. H., Lukoff, D., & Hardesty, J. P. (1989). A prospective study of stressful life events and schizophrenic relapse. *Journal of Abnormal Psychology, 98*, 407–411.

Verdone, P. (1993). Psychophysiology of dreaming. In M. A. Carskadon (Ed.), *Encyclopedia of dreaming*. New York: Macmillan.

Verhaeghen, P., & Salthouse, T. A. (1997). Meta-analyses of age-cognition relations in adulthood: Estimates of linear and nonlinear age effects and structural models. *Psychological Bulletin, 122,* 231–249.

Vernberg, E. M., La Greca, A. M., Silverman, W. K., & Prinstein, M. J. (1996). Prediction of posttraumatic stress symptoms in children after Hurricane Andrew. *Journal of Abnormal Psychology, 105,* 237–248.

Vernon, P. E. (1982). *The abilities and achievements of Orientals in North America.* New York: Academic Press.

Vgontzas, A. N., Bixler, E. O., & Kales, A. K. (2000). Sleep, sleep disorders, and stress. In G. Fink (Ed.), *Encyclopedia of stress* (Vol. 3, p. 449–457). San Diego: Academic Press.

Vierck, C. (1978). Somatosensory system. In R. B. Masterston (Ed.), *Handbook of sensory neurobiology.* New York: Plenum.

Vinogradov, S., Cox, P. D., & Yalom, I. D. (1999). Group therapy. In R. E. Hales, S. C. Yudofsky, & J. A. Talbott (Eds.), *American Psychiatric Press textbook of psychiatry.* Washington, DC: American Psychiatric Press.

Vinters, H. V. (2001). Aging and the human nervous system. In J. E. Birren & K. W. Schaie (Eds.), *Handbook of the psychology of aging* (5th ed., pp. 134–159). San Diego, CA: Academic Press.

Vodelholzer, U., Homyak, M., Thiel, B., Huwig-Poppe, C., Kiemen, A., Konig, A., Backhaus, J., Reimann, D., Berger, M., & Hohagen, R. (1998). Impact of experimentally induced serotonin deficiency by tryphophan depletion on sleep EEG in healthy subjects. *Neuropsychopharmacology, 18,* 112–124.

Vokey, J. R., & Read, J. D. (1985). Subliminal messages: Between the devil and the media. *American Psychologist, 40,* 1231–1239.

Volavka, J., Czobor, P., Sheitman, B., Lindenmayer, J. P., Citrome, L., McEvoy, J. P., Cooper, T. B. , Chakos, M., & Lieberman, J. A. (2002). Clozapine, olanzapine, risperidone, haloperidol in the treatment of patients with chronic schizophrenia and schizoaffective disorder. *American Journal of Psychiatry, 159,* 255–262.

Voyer, D. (1996). On the magnitude of laterality effects and sex differences in functional lateralities. *Laterality, 1,* 51–83.

Voyer, D., Voyer, S., & Bryden, M. P. (1995). Magnitude of sex differences in spatial abilities: A meta-analysis and consideration of critical variables. *Psychological Bulletin, 117,* 250–270.

Wachtel, P. L. (1977). *Psychoanalysis and behavior therapy: Toward an integration.* New York: Basic Books.

Wachtel, P. L. (1991). From eclectism to synthesis: Toward a more seamless psychotherapeutic integra-tion. *Journal of Psychotherapy Integration, 1,* 43–54.

Wagner, H. (1989). The physiological differentiation of emotions. In H. Wagner & A. Manstead (Eds), *Handbook of social psychophysiology.* New York: Wiley.

Wagner, M. E., Schubert, H. J. P., & Schubert, D. S. P. (1993). Sex-of-sibling effects: Part 1. Gender role, intelligence, achievement, and creativity. In H. W. Reese (Ed.), *Advances in child development and behavior* (Vol. 24). San Diego: Academic Press.

Wagner, R. K. (1997). Intelligence, training, and employment. *American Psychologist, 52,* 1059–1069.

Wahlsten, D. (1997). The malleability of intelligence is not constrained by heritability. In B. Devlin, S. E. Fienberg, D. P. Resnick, & K. Roeder (Eds.), *Intelligence, genes, and success: Scientists respond to The Bell Curve.* New York: Springer-Verlag.

Wahlsten, D. (1999). Single-gene influences on brain and behavior. *Annual Review of Psychology, 50,* 599–624.

Wakefield, J. C. (1992). The concept of mental disorder: On the boundary between biological facts and social values. *American Psychologist, 47,* 373–388.

Wakefield, J. C. (1999a). Evolutionary versus prototype analyses of the concept of disorder. *Journal of Abnormal Psychology, 108,* 374–399.

Wakefield, J. C. (1999b). The measurement of mental disorder. In A. V. Horvitz & T. L. Scheid (Eds.), *A handbook for the study of mental health: Social contexts, theories, and systems.* New York: Cambridge University Press.

Wald, G. (1964). The receptors of human color vision. *Science, 145,* 1007–1017.

Waldman, I. D. (1997). Unresolved questions and future directions in behavior-genetic studies of intelligence. In R. J. Sternberg, & E. L. Grigorenko (Eds.), *Intelligence, heredity, and environment.* New York: Cambridge University Press.

Waldrop, D., Lightsey, O. R., Ethington, C. A., Woemmel, C. A., & Coke, A. L. (2001). Self-efficacy, optimism, health competence, and recovery from orthopedic surgery. *Journal of Counseling Psychology, 48,* 233–238.

Walker, E. F., Baum, K. M., & Diforio, D. (1998). Developmental changes in behavioral expression and vulnerability for schizophrenia. In M. F. Lenzenweger & R. H. Dworkin (Eds.), *Origins and development of schizophrenia: Advances in experimental psychopathology.* Washington DC: American Psychological Association.

Walker, I., & Hulme, C. (1999). Concrete words are easier to recall than abstract words: Evidence for a semantic contribution to short-term serial recall. *Journal of Experimental Psychology: Learning, Memory, & Cognition, 25,* 1256–1271.

Walker, L. J. (1988). The development of moral reasoning. In R. Vasta (Ed.), *Annals of child development* (Vol. 5). Greenwich, CT: JAI Press.

Walker, L. J. (1989). A longitudinal study of moral reasoning. *Child Development, 60,* 157–166.

Walker, L. J. (1995). Sexism in Kohlberg's moral psychology? In W. M. Kurtines & J. L. Gewirtz (Eds.), *Moral development: An introduction.* Boston: Allyn & Bacon.

Walker, L. J., & Moran, T. J. (1991). Moral reasoning in a Communist Chinese society. *Journal of Moral Education, 20,* 139–155.

Walker, L. J., & Taylor, J. H. (1991). Strange transitions in moral reasoning: A longitudinal study of developmental processes. *Developmental Psychology, 27,* 330–337.

Wall, P. D. (1993). Pain and the placebo response. In G. R. Bock & J. Marsh (Eds.), *Experimental and theoretical studies of consciousness.* Chichester, England: Wiley.

Wallace, B., & Fisher, L. E. (1999). *Consciousness and behavior.* Boston: Allyn & Bacon.

Wallace, C. J. (1998). Social skills training in psychiatric rehabilitation: Recent findings. *International Review of Psychiatry, 10,* 9–10.

Wallace, R. K., & Benson, H. (1972). The physiology of meditation. *Scientific American, 226,* 84–90.

Wallbott, H. G., & Scherer, K. R. (1988). How universal and specific is emotional experience? Evidence from 27 countries. In K. R. Scherer (Ed.), *Facets of emotions.* Hillsdale, NJ: Erlbaum.

Wallen, K. (1989). Mate selection: Economics and affection. *Behavioral and Brain Sciences, 12,* 37–38.

Wallman, J. (1992). *Aping language.* Cambridge, England: Cambridge University Press.

Walraven, J., Enroth-Cugell, C., Hood, D. C., MacLeod, D. I. A., & Schnapf, J. L. (1990). The control of visual sensitivity: Receptoral and postreceptoral processes. In L. Spillmann & J. S. Werner (Eds.), *Visual perception: The neurophysiological foundations.* San Diego: Academic Press.

Walsh, B. T., Seidman, S. N., Sysko, R., & Gould, M. (2002). Placebo response studies of major depression: Variable, substantial and growing. *Journal of the American Medical Association, 287,* 1840–1847.

Walsh, F. (1999). Families in later life: Challenges and opportunities. In B. Carter & M. McGoldrick (Eds.), *The expanded family life cycle: Individ-ual, family, and social perspectives* (3rd ed., pp. 307–326). Boston: Allyn & Bacon.

Walsh, J. K., & Scweitzer, P. K. (1999). Ten-year trends in the pharmacological treatment of insomnia. *Sleep: Journal of Sleep Research & Sleep Medicine, 22,* 371–375.

Walter, T., & Siebert, A. (1990). *Student success: How to succeed in college and still have time for your friends.* Fort Worth: Holt, Rinehart & Winston.

Walters, E. E., & Kendler, K. S. (1995). Anorexia nervosa and anorexic-like syndromes in a population-based female twin sample. *American Journal of Psychiatry, 152,* 64–71.

Waltz, J. A., Knowlton, B. J., Holyoak, K. J., Boone, K. B., Mishkin, F. S., de Menezes Santos, M., Thomas, C. R., & Miller, B. L. (1999). A system for relational reasoning in human prefrontal cortex. *Psychological Science, 10,* 119–125.

Wampold, B. E. (2001). *The great psychotherapy debate.* Mahwah, NJ: Erlbaum.

Wangensteen, O. H., & Carlson, A. J. (1931). Hunger sensation after total gastrectomy. *Proceedings of the Society for Experimental Biology, 28,* 545–547.

Wardle, J., Steptoe, A., Oliver, G., & Lipsey, Z. (2000). Stress, dietary restraint and food intake. *Journal of Psychosomatic Research, 48,* 195–202.

Wark, G. R., & Krebs, D. L. (1996). Gender and dilemma differences in real-life moral judgment. *Developmental Psychology, 32,* 220–230.

Warr, P. (1999). Well-being and the workplace. In D. Kahneman, E. Diener, & N. Schwarz (Eds.), *Wellbeing: The foundations of hedonic psychology.* New York: Russell Sage Foundation.

Warrington, E. K., & Weiskrantz, L. (1970). Amnesic syndrome: Consolidation or retrieval? *Nature, 228,* 629–630.

Warshaw, M. G., Fierman, E., Pratt, L., Hunt, M., Yonkers, K. A., Massion, A. O., & Keller, M. B. (1993). Quality of life and dissociation in anxiety disorder patients with histories of trauma or PTSD. *American Journal of Psychiatry, 150,* 1512–1516.

Warwick, D. P. (1975, February). Social scientists ought to stop lying. *Psychology Today,* pp. 38, 40, 105–106.

Watanabe, M. (1998). The relationship between sensation seeking and health risk behavior: A survey on traffic-related risk behavior, cigarette smoking and alcohol drinking among university students. *Japanese Journal of Health Psychology, 11,* 28–38.

Waterman, A., & Archer, S. (1990). A life-span perspective on identity formation: Development in form, function, and process. In P. B. Baltes, D. L. Featherman, & R. M. Lerner (Eds.), *Life-span development and behavior* (Vol. 10). Hillsdale, NJ: Erlbaum.

Watkins, C. E., Campbell, V. L., Nieberding, R., & Hallmark, R. (1995). Contemporary practice of psychological assessment by clinical psychologists. *Professional Psychology: Research and Practice, 26,* 54–60.

Watson, D. L., & Tharp, R. G. (1997). *Self-directed behavior: Self-modification for personal adjustment* (6th ed.). Pacific Grove, CA: Brooks/Cole.

Watson, D. L., & Tharp, R. G. (2002). *Self-directed behavior: Self-modification for personal adjustment.* Belmont, CA: Wadsworth.

Watson, D., & Clark, L. A. (1997). Extraversion and its positive emotional core. In R. Hogan, J. Johnson, & S. Briggs (Eds.), *Handbook of personality psychology.* San Diego: Academic Press.

Watson, D., & Pennebaker, J. W. (1989). Health complaints, stress, and distress: Exploring the central role of negative affectivity. *Psychological Review, 96,* 234–254.

Watson, D., David, J. P., & Suls, J. (1999). Personality, affectivity, and coping. In C. R. Snyder (Ed.), *Coping: The psychology of what works.* New York: Oxford University Press.

Watson, D., Suls, J., & Haig, J. (2002). Global self-esteem in relation to structural models of personality and affectivity. *Journal of Personality and Social Psychology, 83,* 185–197.

Watson, J. B., & Rayner, R. (1920). Conditioned emotional reactions. *Journal of Experimental Psychology, 3,* 1–14.

Watson, J. B. (1913). Psychology as the behaviorist views it. *Psychological Review, 20,* 158–177.

Watson, J. B. (1919). *Psychology from the standpoint of a behaviorist.* Philadelphia: Lippincott.

Watson, J. B. (1924). *Behaviorism.* New York: Norton.

Watson, J. B. (1930). *Behaviorism.* New York: Norton.

Waugh, N. C., & Norman, D. A. (1965). Primary memory. *Psychological Review, 72,* 89–104.

Weatherall, A. (1992). Gender and languages: Research in progress. *Feminism & Psychology, 2,* 177–181.

Weaver, C. A., III. (1993). Do you need a "flash" to form a flashbulb memory? *Journal of Experimental Psychology: General, 122,* 39–46.

Weaver, M. F., & Schnoll, S. H. (1999). Stimulants: Amphetamines and cocaine. In B. S. McCrady & E. E. Epstein (Eds.), *Addictions: A comprehensive guidebook.* New York: Oxford University Press.

Webb, W. B., & Dinges, D. F. (1989). Cultural perspectives on napping and the siesta. In D. F. Dinges & R. J. Broughton (Eds.), *Sleep and alertness: Chronobiological, behavioral, and medical aspects of napping.* New York: Raven.

Webb, W. B. (1992a). Developmental aspects and a behavioral model of human sleep. In C. Stampi (Ed.), *Why we nap: Evolution, chronobiology, and functions of polyphasic and ultrashort sleep.* Boston: Birkhaeuser.

Webb, W. B. (1992b). *Sleep: The gentle tyrant.* Bolton, MA: Anker.

Wechsler, D. (1939). *The measurement of adult intelligence.* Baltimore: Williams & Wilkins.

Wechsler, D. (1949). *Wechsler intelligence scale for children.* New York: Psychological Corporation.

Wechsler, D. (1955). *Manual, Wechsler adult intelligence scale.* New York: Psychological Corporation.

Wechsler, D. (1967). *Manual for the Wechsler preschool and primary scale of intelligence.* New York: Psychological Corporation.

Wechsler, D. (1981). *Manual for the Wechsler adult intelligence scale—revised.* New York: Psychological Corporation.

Wechsler, D. (1991). *WISC-III manual.* San Antonio: Psychological Corporation.

Weems, C. F., Hayward, C., Killen, J., & Taylor, C. B. (2002). A longitudinal investigation of anxiety sensitivity in adolescence. *Journal of Abnormal Psychology, 111,* 471–477.

Wegner, D. M. (1997). Why the mind wanders. In J. D. Cohen & J. W. Schooler (Eds.), *Scientific approaches to consciousness.* Mahwah, NJ: Erlbaum.

Weinberg, R. A. (1989). Intelligence and IQ: Landmark issues and great debates. *American Psychologist, 44,* 98–104.

Weinberger, D. A. (1990). The construct validity of the repressive coping style. In J. L. Singer (Ed.), *Repression and dissociation.* Chicago: University of Chicago Press.

Weinberger, D. A., & Davidson, M. A. (1994). Styles of inhibiting emotional expression: Distinguishing repressive coping from impression management. *Journal of Personality, 62,* 589–611.

Weinberger, J. (1992). Validating and demystifying subliminal psychodynamic activation. In R. F. Bornstein & T. S. Pittman (Eds.), *Perception without awareness: Cognitive, clinical, and social perspectives.* New York: Guilford.

Weinberger, J. (1995). Common factors aren't so common: The common factors dilemma. *Clinical Psychology: Science and Practice, 2,* 45–69.

Weiner, B. (Ed). (1974). *Achievement motivation and attribution theory.* Morristown, NJ: General Learning Press.

Weiner, B. (1980). *Human motivation.* New York: Holt, Rinehart & Winston.

Weiner, B. (1986). *An attributional theory of motivation and emotion.* New York: Springer-Verlag.

Weiner, B. (1994). Integrating social and personal theories of achievement striving. *Review of Educational Research, 64,* 557–573.

Weiner, H. (1992). *Perturbing the organism: The biology of stressful experience.* Chicago: University of Chicago Press.

Weiner, M. F. (1993). Role of the leader in group psychotherapy. In H. I. Kaplan & B. J. Sadock (Eds.), *Comprehensive group psychotherapy.* Baltimore: Williams & Wilkins.

Weiner, R. D. (2000). Retrograde amnesia with eletroconvulsive therapy: Characteristics and implications. *General Psychiatry, 57,* 591–592.

Weinfield, N. S., Sroufe, L. A., Egeland, B., & Carlson, E. A. (1999). The nature of individual differences in infant-caregiver attachment. In J. Cassidy & P. R. Shaver (Eds.), *Handbook of attachment: Theory, research, and clinical applications.* New York: Guilford.

Weinger, M. B., & Ancoli-Israel, S. (2002). Sleep deprivation and clinical performance. *Journal of the American Medical Association, 287,* 955–957.

Weinstein, L. N., Schwartz, D. G., & Arkin, A. M. (1991). Qualitative aspects of sleep mentation. In S. J. Ellman & J. S. Antrobus (Eds.), *The mind in sleep: Psychology and psychophysiology* (2nd ed.). New York: Wiley.

Weinstein, N. D. (1984). Why it won't happen to me: Perceptions of risk factors and susceptibility. *Health Psychology, 3,* 431–458.

Weinstein, N. D., & Klein, W. M. (1995). Resistance of personal risk perceptions to debiasing interventions. *Health Psychology, 14,* 132–140.

Weinstein, N. D., & Klein, W. M. (1996). Unrealistic optimism: Present and future. *Journal of Social and Clinical Psychology, 15,* 1–8.

Weisberg, R. W. (1986). *Creativity: Genius and other myths.* New York: W. H. Freeman.

Weisberg, R. W. (1993). *Creativity: Beyond the myth of genius.* New York: W. H. Freeman.

Weisberg, R. W. (1999). Creativity and knowledge: A challenge to theories. In R. J. Sternberg (Ed.), *Handbook of creativity.* New York: Cambridge University Press.

Weisner, T. S., & Wilson-Mitchell, J. E. (1990). Nonconventional family life-styles and sex typing in six-year-olds. *Child Development, 61,* 1915–1933.

Weiten, W. (1984). Violation of selected item-construction principles in educational measurement. *Journal of Experimental Education, 51,* 46–50.

Weiten W. (1988a). Objective features of introductory psychology textbooks as related to professors' impressions. *Teaching of Psychology, 15,* 10–16.

Weiten, W. (1988b). Pressure as a form of stress and its relationship to psychological symptomatology. *Journal of Social and Clinical Psychology, 6*(1), 127–139.

Weiten, W. (1998). Pressure, major life events, and psychological symptoms. *Journal of Social Behavior and Personality, 13,* 51–68.

Weiten, W. Guadagno, R. E., & Beck, C. A. (1996). Students' perceptions of textbook pedagogical aids. *Teaching of Psychology, 23,* 105–107.

Weiten, W., & Diamond, S. S. (1979). A critical review of the jury-simulation paradigm: The case of defendant characteristics. *Law and Human Behavior, 3,* 71–93.

Weiten, W., & Wight, R. D. (1992). Portraits of a discipline: An examination of introductory psychology textbooks in America. In A. E. Puente, J. R. Matthews, & C. L. Brewer (Eds.), *Teaching psychology in America: A history.* Washington, DC: American Psychological Association.

Well, A. D., Pollatsek, A., & Boyce, S. J. (1990). Understanding the effects of sample size on the variability of the mean. *Organizational Behavior and Human Decision Processes, 47,* 289–312.

Wellman, H. M., & Gelman, S. A. (1998). Knowledge acquisition in foundational domians. In W. Damon (Ed.), *Handbook of child psychology (Vol. 2): Cognition, perception, and language.* New York: Wiley.

Wells, A. J. (1998). Lung cancer from passive smoking at work. *American Journal of Public Health, 88,* 1025–1029.

Wells, C. G. (1991). *Right-brain sex: How to reach the heights of sensual pleasure by releasing the erotic power of your mind.* New York: Avon.

Wells, G. L., & Bradfield, A. L. (1998). "Good, you identified the suspect": Feedback to eyewitnesses disorts their reports of the witnessing experience. *Journal of Applied Psychology, 83,* 360–376.

Wells, K., Klap, R., Koike, A., & Sherbourne, C. (2001). Ethnic disparities in unmet need for alcoholism, drug abuse, and mental health care. *American Journal of Psychiatry, 158,* 2027–2032.

Werbach, M. R. (1988). *Nutritional influences on illness: A sourcebook of* clinical research. Tarzana, CA: Third Line Press.

Werker, J. F., & Desjardins, R. N. (1995). Listening to speech in the 1st year of life: Experiential influences on phoneme perception. *Current Directions in Psychological Science, 4,* 76–81.

Wertheimer, M. (1912). Experimentelle studien über das sehen von bewegung. *Zeitschrift für Psychologie, 60,* 312–378.

Wertz, F. J. (1998). The role of the humanistic movement in the history of psychology. *Journal of Humanistic Psychology, 38,* 42–70.

Wesson, D. R., Smith, D. E., Ling, W., & Seymour, R. B. (1997). Sedative-hypnotics and tricyclics. In J. H. Lowinson, P. Ruiz, R. B. Millman, & J. G. Langrod (Eds.), *Substance abuse: A comprehensive textbook.* Baltimore: Williams & Wilkin.

West, R. F., & Stanovich, K. E. (1997). The domain specificity and generality of overconfidence: Individual differences in performance estimation bias. *Psychonomic Bulletin & Review, 4,* 387–392.

Westen, D. (1998). The scientific legacy of Sigmund Freud: Toward a psychodynamically informed psychological science. *Psychological Bulletin, 124,* 333–371.

Westen, D., & Gabbard, G. O. (1999). Psychoanalytic approaches to personality. In L. A. Pervin & O. P. John (Eds.), *Handbook of personality: Theory and research.* New York: Guilford.

Westen, D., & Shedler, J. (1999). Revising and assessing Axis II, Part II: Toward an empirically based and clinically useful classification of personality disorders. *American Journal of Psychiatry, 156,* 273–285.

Westneat, D. F., Sherman, P. W., & Morton, M. L. (1990). The ecology and evolution of extra-pair copulations in birds. *Current Ornithology, 7,* 330–369.

Wethington, E. (2000). Life events scale. In G. Fink (Ed.), *Encyclopedia of stress* (Vol. 1, pp. 618–622). San Diego: Academic Press.

Wever, E. G., & Bray, C. W. (1937). The perception of low tones and the resonance-volley theory. *Journal of Psychology, 3,* 101–114.

Wexler, B. E., Gottschalk, C. H., Fulbright, R. K., Prohovnik, I., Lacadie, C. M., Rounsaville, B. J., & Gore, J. C. (2001). Functional magnetic resonance imaging of cocaine craving. *American Journal of Psychiatry, 158,* 86–95.

Whalen, P. J. (1998). Fear, vigilance, and ambiguity: Initial neuroimaging studies of the human amygdala. *Current Directions in Psychological Science, 7,* 177–188.

Wheeler, L., & Kim, Y. (1997). What is beautiful is culturally good: The physical attractiveness stereotype has different content in collectivistic cultures. *Personality and Social Psychology Bulletin, 23,* 795–800.

Wheeler, M. A., Stuss, D. T., & Tulving, E. (1997). Toward a theory of episodic memory: The frontal lobes and autonoetic consciousness. *Psychological Bulletin, 121,* 331–354.

Whitaker, R. (2002). *Mad in America: Bad science, bad medicine, and the enduring mistreatment of the mentally ill.* New York: Perseus Publishing.

Whitbourne, S. K. (1999). Physical changes. In J. C. Cavanaugh & S. K. Whitbourne (Eds.), *Gerontology: Interdisciplinary perspectives* (pp. 91–122). New York: Oxford University Press.

Whitbourne, S. K., Zuschlag, M. K., Elliot, L. B., & Waterman, A. S. (1992). Psychosocial development in adulthood: A 22-year sequential study. *Journal of Personality and Social Psychology, 63,* 260–271.

White, S. H. (2000). Conceptual foundations of IQ testing. *Psychology, Public Policy, and Law, 6,* 33–43.

White, W. (1997) Croco%#@! Dundee [Web Page]. Retrieved July 2, 2002 from http://www.outsidemag.com/magazine/1197/9711out.html.

Whitehouse, W. G., & Dinges, D. F., Orne, E. C., & Orne, M. T. (1988). Hypnotic hyperamnesia: Enhanced memory accessibility or report bias? *Journal of Abnormal Psychology, 97,* 298–295.

Whitfield, C. L. (1995). *Memory and abuse: Remembering and healing the effects of trauma.* Deerfield Beach, FL: Health Communications.

Whiting, J. W. M., Burbank, V. K., & Ratner, M. S. (1986). The duration of maidenhood. In J. B. Lancaster & B. A. Hamburg (Eds.), *School age pregnancy and parenthood.* Hawthorne, NY: Aldine de Gruyter.

Whitley, B. E., Jr. (1988). *College students' reasons for sexual intercourse: A sex role perspective.* Paper presented at the 96th Annual Meeting of the American Psychological Association, Atlanta.

Whorf, B. L. (1956). Science and linguistics. In J. B. Carroll (Ed.), *Language, thought and reality: Selected writings of Benjamin Lee Whorf.* Cambridge, MA: MIT Press.

Wickens, T. D. (1999). Measuring the time course of retention. In C. Izawa (Ed.), *On human memory: Evolution, progress, and reflections on the 30th anniversary of the Atkinson-Shiffrin model.* Mahwah, NJ: Erlbaum.

Widiger, T. A. (2001). Official classification systems. In W. J. Livesley (Ed.), *Handbook of personality disorders: Theory, research, and treatment.* New York: Guilford.

Widiger, T. A., & Clark, L. A. (2000). Toward DSM-V and the classification of psychopathology. *Psychological Bulletin, 126,* 946–963.

Widiger, T. A., & Sankis, L. M. (2000). Adult psychopathology: Issues and controversies. *Annual Review of Psychology, 51,* 377–404.

Widom, C. S. (1997). Child abuse, neglect, and witnessing violence. In D. M. Stoff, J. Breiling, & J. D. Maser (Eds.), *Handbook of antisocial behavior.* New York: Wiley.

Wiederman, M. W. (1993). Evolved gender differences in mate preferences: Evidence from personal advertisements. *Ethology and Sociobiology, 14,* 331–352.

Wiesel, T. N., & Hubel, D. H. (1963). Single-cell responses in striate cortex of kittens deprived of vision in one eye. *Journal of Neurophysiology, 26,* 1003–1017.

Wiesel, T. N., & Hubel, D. H. (1965). Extent of recovery from the effects of visual deprivation in kittens. *Journal of Neurophysiology, 28,* 1060–1072.

Wiggins, J. S. (1992). Have model, will travel. *Journal of Personality, 60,* 527–532.

Wiggins, J. S., & Trapnell, P. D. (1997). Personality structure: The return of the big five. In R. Hogan, J. Johnson, & S. Briggs (Eds.), *Handbook of personality psychology.* San Diego, CA: Academic Press.

Wiggs, C. L., Weisberg, J., & Martin, A. (1999). Neural correlates of semantic and episodic memory retrieval. *Neuropsychologia, 37,* 103–118.

Wilcox, A. J., Weinberg, C. R., O'Connor, J. F., Baurd, D. D., Schlatterer, J. P., Canfield, R. E., Armstrong, E. G., & Nisula, B. C. (1988). Incidence of early loss of pregnancy. *New England Journal of Medicine, 319,* 189–194.

Wilding, J., & Valentine, E. (1996). Memory expertise. In D. J. Herrmann, C. McEvoy, C. Hertzog, P. Hertel, & M. K. Johnson (Eds.), *Basic and applied memory research: Theory in context* (Vol. 1). Mahwah, NJ: Erlbaum.

Wiley, J. L. (1999). Cannabis: Discrimination of "internal bliss"? *Pharmacology, Biochemistry & Behavior, 64,* 257–260.

Willett, W. C., & Manson, J. E. (1995). Epidemiologic studies of health risks due to excess weight. In K. D. Brownell & C. G. Fairburn (Eds.), *Eating disorders and obesity: A comprehensive handbook.* New York: Guilford.

Williams, A., & Giles, H. (1998). Communication of ageism. In M. C. Hecht (Ed.), *Communicating prejudice* (pp. 136–160). Thousand Oaks, CA: Sage.

Williams, B. A. (1988). Reinforcement, choice, and response strength. In R. C. Atkinson, R. J. Herrnstein, G. Lindzey, & R. D. Luce (Eds.), *Stevens' handbook of experimental psychology.* New York: Wiley.

Williams, B. A. (1994). Conditioned reinforcement: Neglected or outmoded explanatory construct? *Psychonomic Bulletin & Review, 1,* 457–475.

Williams, C. D. (1959). The elimination of tantrum behavior by extinction procedures. *Journal of Abnormal and Social Psychology, 59,* 269.

Williams, G. C. (1966). *Adaptation and natural selection.* Princeton, NJ: Princeton University Press.

Williams, J. B. W. (1994). Psychiatric classification. In R. E. Hales, S. C. Yudofsky, & J. A. Talbott (Eds.), *The American Psychiatric Press textbook of psychiatry* (2nd ed.). Washington, DC: American Psychiatric Press.

Williams, J. B. W. (1999). Psychiatric classification. In R.E. Hales, S. C. Yudofsky, & J. A. Talbott (Eds.), *American Psychiatric Press textbook of psychiatry* (3rd ed.). Washington, DC: American Psychiatric Press.

Williams, J. E., Paton, C. C., Siegler, I. C., Eigenbrodt, M. L., Neito, F. J., & Tyroler, H. A. (2000). Anger proneness predicts coronary heart disease risk. *Circulation, 101,* 2034–2039.

Williams, J. M. G., Watts, F. N., MacLeod, C., & Mathews, A. (1997). *Cognitive psychology and emotional disorders.* Chichester, England: Wiley.

Williams, K. E., & Bond, M. J. (2002). The roles of self-efficacy, outcome expectancies and social support in the self-care behaviors of diabetics. *Psychology, Health & Medicine, 7(2),* 127–141.

Williams, L. M. (1994). Recall of childhood trauma: A prospective study of women's memories of child sexual abuse. *Journal of Consulting and Clinical Psychology, 62,* 1167–1176.

Williams, L. V. (1986). *Teaching for the two-sided mind: A guide to right brain–left brain education.* New York: Simon & Schuster.

Williams, M. H. (1992). Exploitation and inference: Mapping the damage from therapist-patient sexual involvement. *American Psychologist, 47,* 412–421.

Williams, N. A., & Deffenbacher, J. L. (1983). Life stress and chronic yeast infections. *Journal of Human Stress, 9(1),* 26–31.

Williams, R., & Stockmyer, J. (1987). *Unleashing the right side of the brain: The LARC creativity program.* New York: Viking Penguin.

Williams, R. B. (2001). Hostility (and other psychosocial risk factors): Effects on health and the potential for successful behavioral approaches to prevention and treatment. In A. Baum, T. A. Revenson, & J. E. Singer (Eds.), *Handbook of health psychology* (pp. 661–668). Mahwah, NJ: Erlbaum.

Williams, R. B., & Williams, V. P. (2001). Managing hostile thoughts, feelings, and actions: The lifeskills approach. In C. R. Snyder (Ed.), *Coping with stress: Effective people and processes* (pp. 137–153). New York: Oxford University Press.

Williams, R. L., Dotson, W., Dow, P., & Williams, W. S. (1980). The war against testing: A current status report. *Journal of Negro Education, 49*, 263–273.

Williams, W. M. (1998). Are we raising smarter children today? School-and-home-related infuences on IQ. In U. Neisser (Ed.), *The rising curve: Long-term gains in IQ and related measures*. Washington, DC: American Psychological Association.

Williams, W. M., & Ceci, S. J. (1997). Are Americans becoming more or less alike?: Trends in race, class, and ability differences in intelligence. *American Psychologist, 52*, 1226–1235.

Williamson, D. A., Zucker, N. L., Martin, C. K., & Smeets, M. A. M. (2001). Etiology and management of eating disorders. In P. B. Sutker & H. E. Adams (Eds.), *Comprehensive handbook of psychopathology*. New York: Kluwer Academic/Plenum.

Willis, W. D. (1985). *The pain system. The neural basis of nociceptive transmission in the mammalian nervous system*. Basel: Karger.

Willoughby, T., Motz, M., & Wood, E. (1997). The impact of interest and strategy use on memory performance for child, adolescent, and adult learners. *Alberta Journal of Educational Research, 43*, 127–141.

Wills, T. A., & Fegan, M. (2001). Social networks and social support. In A. Baum, T. A. Revenson, & J. E. Singer (Eds.), *Handbook of health psychology* (pp. 209–234). Mahwah, NJ: Erlbaum.

Wilson, G. T. (1982). Alcohol and anxiety: Recent evidence on the tension reduction theory of alcohol use and abuse. In K. R. Blankstein & J. Polivy (Eds.), *Self-control and self-modification of emotional behavior*. New York: Plenum.

Wilson, G. T. (1996). Empirically validated treatments: Realities and resistance. *Clinical Psychology: Science & Practice, 3*, 241–244.

Wilson, M. (1993). DSM-III and the transformation of American psychiatry: A history. *American Journal of Psychiatry, 150*, 399–410.

Windham, G. C., Eaton, A., & Hopkins, B. (1999). Evidence for an association between environmental tobacco smoke exposure and birth-weight: A meta-analysis and new data.

Paediatrics and Perinatal Epidemiology, 13, 35–37.

Windholz, G. (1997). Ivan P. Pavlov: An overview of his life and psychological work. *American Psychologist, 52*, 941–946.

Windschitl, P. D., & Wells, G. L. (1998). The alternative-outcomes effect. *Journal of Personality and Social Psychology, 75*, 1411–1423.

Winick, C. (1992). Epidemiology of alcohol and drug abuse. In J. H. Lowinson, P. Ruiz, & R. B. Millman (Eds.), *Substance abuse: A comprehensive textbook*. Baltimore: Williams & Wilkins.

Winick, C., & Evans, J. T. (1996). The relationship between nonenforcement of state pornography laws and rates of sex crime arrests. *Archives of Sexual Behavior, 25*, 439–453.

Winn, P. (1995). The lateral hypothalmus and motivated behavior: An old syndrome reassessed and a new perspective gained. *Current Directions in Psychological Science, 4*, 182–187.

Winner, E. (1997). Exceptionally high intelligence and schooling. *American Psychologist, 52*, 1070–1081.

Winner, E. (1998). Uncommon talents: Gifted children, prodigies and savants. *Scientific American Presents Exploring Intelligence, 9*, 32–37.

Winner, E. (2000). The origins and ends of giftedness. *American Psychologist, 55*, 159–169.

Winograd, T. (1975). Frame representations and the declarative-procedural controversy. In D. Bobrow & A. Collins (Eds.), *Representation and understanding: Studies in cognitive science*. New York: Academic Press.

Winquist, J. R., & Larson, J. R. Jr. (1998). Information pooling: When it impacts group decision making. *Journal of Personality and Social Psychology, 74*, 371–377.

Winter, D. G. (1992). Content analysis of archival materials, personal documents, and everyday verbal productions. In C. P. Smith (Ed.), *Motivation and personality: Handbook of thematic content analysis*. New York: Cambridge University Press.

Winzelberg, A. J., & Luskin, F. M. (1999). The effect of a meditation training in stress levels in secondary school teachers. *Stress Medicine, 15*, 69–77.

Wise, M. G., Gray, K. F., & Seltzer, B. (1999). Delirium, dementia, and amnestic disorders. In R. E. Hales, S. C. Yudofsky, & J. A. Talbott (Eds.), *The American Psychiatric Press textbook of psychiatry* (3rd ed., pp. 317–362). Washington, DC: American Psychiatric Press.

Wise, R. (1995). D-sub-1– and D-sub-2–type contributions to psychomotor sensitization and reward: Implications for pharmacological treatment

strategies. *Clinical Neuropharmacology, 18*, S74–S83.

Wise, R. A. (1999). Animal models of addiction. In D. S. Charney, E. J. Nestler, & B. S. Bunney (Eds.), *Neurobiology of mental illness*. New York: Oxford University Press.

Wiseman, C. V., Gray, J. J., Mosimann, J. E., & Ahrens, A. H. (1992). Cultural expectations of thinness in women: An update. *International Journal of Eating Disorders, 11*, 85–89.

Witkin, H. A. (1950). Individual differences in ease of perception of embedded figures. *Journal of Personality, 19*, 1–15.

Witkin, H. A., & Goodenough, D. (1981). *Cognitive styles: Essence and origins*. New York: International Universities Press.

Witkin, H. A., Dyk, R. B., Paterson, H. F., Goodenough, D. R., & Karp, S. (1962). *Psychological differentiation*. New York: Wiley.

Witte, K., & Allen, M. (2000). A meta-analysis of fear appeals: Implications for effective public health campaigns. *Health Education & Behavior, 27*, 591–615.

Witte, K., Berkowitz, J. M., Cameron, K. A., & McKeon, J. K. (1998). Preventing the spread of genital warts: Using fear appeals to promote self-protective behaviors. *Health Education & Behavior, 25*, 571–585.

Wittkower, E. D., & Warnes, H. (1984). Cultural aspects of psychotherapy. In J. E. Mezzich & C. E. Berganza (Eds.), *Culture and psychopathology*. New York: Columbia University Press.

Wolk, A., Manson, J. E., Stampfer, M. J., Colditz, G. A., Hu, F. B., Speizer, F. E., Hennekens, C. H., & Willett, W. C. (1999). Long-term intake of dietary fiber and decreased risk of coronary heart disease among women. *Journal of the American Medical Association, 281*, 1998–2004.

Wolpe, J. (1958). *Psychotherapy by reciprocal inhibition*. Stanford, CA: Stanford University Press.

Wolpe, J. (1990). *The practice of behavior therapy*. Elmsford, NY: Pergamon Press.

Wonder, J. (1992). *Whole brain thinking: Working both sides of the brain to achieve peak job performance*. New York: Morrow.

Wonderlich, S. A. (2002). Personality and eating disorders. In C. G. Fairburn & K. D. Brownell (Eds.), *Eating disorders and obesity: A comprehensive handbook*. New York: Guilford.

Wood, F., Ebert, V., & Kinsbourne, M. (1982). The episodic-semantic memory distinction in memory and amnesia: Clinical and experimental observations. In L. Cermak (Ed.), *Human memory and amnesia*. Hillsdale, NJ: Erlbaum.

Wood, J. M., Nezworski, M. T., & Stejskal, W. J. (1996). The comprehensive system for the Rorschach: A critical examination. *Psychological Science, 7*, 3–10.

Wood, N. L., & Cowan, N. (1995). The cocktail party phenomenon revisited: Attention and memory in the classic selective listening procedure of Cherry (1953). *Journal of Experimental Psychology: Learning, Memory, & Cognition, 21*, 255–260.

Wood, W., Rhodes, N., & Biek, M. (1995). Working knowledge and attitude strength: An information-processing analysis. In R. E. Petty & J. A. Krosnick (Eds.), *Attitude strength: Antecedents and consequences*. Mahwah, NJ: Erlbaum.

Woodcock, R. W. (1994). Norms. In R. J. Sternberg (Ed.), *Encyclopedia of human intelligence*. New York: Macmillan.

Woods, S. C., Schwartz, M. W., Baskin, D. G., & Seeley, R. J. (2000). Food intake and the regulation of body weight. *Annual Review of Psychology, 51*, 255–277.

Woolfolk, R. L., & Richardson, F. C. (1978). *Stress, sanity and survival*. New York: Sovereign/Monarch.

Woolsey, C. N. (1981). *Cortical sensory organization*. Clifton, NJ: Humana Press.

Worthen, J. B., & Wade, C. E. (1999). Direction of travel and visiting team athletic performance: Support for a circadian dysrhythmia hypothesis. *Journal of Sport Behavior, 22*, 279–287.

Worthington-Roberts, B. S., & Klerman, L. V. (1990). Maternal nutrition. In I. R. Merkatz & J. E. Thompson (Eds.), *New perspectives on prenatal care*. New York: Elsevier.

Wright, J. H., & Beck, A. T. (1999). Cognitive therapies. In R. E. Hales, S. C. Yudofsky, & J. A. Talbott (Eds.), *American Psychiatric Press textbook of psychiatry*. Washington, DC: American Psychiatric Press.

Wu-Holt, P., & Boutte, J. (1994). The relationship between daily hassles, ways of coping, and menstrual cycle symptomatology. *International Journal of Stress Management, 1*, 173–183.

Wundt, W. (1874/1904). *Principles of physiological psychology*. Leipzig: Engelmann.

Wurtz, R. H., & Kandel, E. R. (2000). Central visual pathways. In E. R. Kandel, J. H. Schwartz, & T. M. Jessell (Eds.), *Principles of neural science*. New York: McGraw-Hill.

Wylie, M. S. (1998). The shadow of a doubt. In R. A. Baker (Ed.), *Child sexual abuse and false memory syndrome*. Amherst, NY: Prometheus Books.

Wynder, E. L., Cohen, L. A., Muscat, J. E., Winters, B., Dwyer, J. T., & Blackburn, G. (1997). Breast cancer: Weighing the evidence for a promoting role of dietary fat. *Journal of the National Cancer Institute, 89,* 766–775.

Wynn, K. (1992). Addition and subtraction by human infants. *Nature, 358,* 749–750.

Wynn, K. (1996). Infants' individuation and enumeration of sequential actions. *Psychological Science, 7,* 164–169.

Wynn, K. (1998). An evolved capacity for number. In D. D. Cummins & C. Allen (Eds.), *The evolution of mind.* New York: Oxford University Press.

Xiaghe, X., & Whyte, M. K. (1990). Love matches and arranged marriages: A Chinese replication. *Journal of Marriage and the Family, 52,* 709–722.

Yalom, I. D. (1995). *The theory and practice of group psychotherapy* (4th ed.). New York: Basic Books.

Yamamoto, J., Silva, J. A., Justice, L. R., Chang, C. Y., & Leong, G. B. (1993). Cross-cultural psychotherapy. In A. C. Gaw (Ed.), *Culture, ethnicity, and mental illness.* Washington, DC: American Psychiatric Press.

Yang, H., Liu, T., & Zang, D. (2000). A study of stressful life events before the onset of hypothyroidism. *Chinese Mental Health Journal, 14,* 201–202.

Yapko, M. D. (1994). *Suggestions of abuse: True and false memories of childhood sexual trauma.* New York: Simon & Schuster.

Yapko, M. D. (1998). The seductions of memory. In R. A. Baker (Ed.), *Child sexual abuse and false memory syndrome.* Amherst, NY: Prometheus Books.

Yates, F. A. (1966). *The art of memory.* London: Routledge & Kegan Paul.

Ybarra, O., Stephan, W. G., & Schaberg, L. (2000). Misanthropic memory for the behavior of group members. *Personality and Social Psychology Bulletin, 26,* 1515–1525.

Yerkes, R. M. (1921). *Memories of the National Academy of Sciences: Psychological examining in the United States Army* (Vol. 15). Washington, DC: U.S. Government Printing Office.

Yerkes, R. M., & Morgulis, S. (1909). The method of Pavlov in animal psychology. *Psychological Bulletin, 6,* 257–273.

Yost, W. A. (2000). *Fundamentals of hearing: An introduction.* San Diego, CA: Academic Press.

Yost, W. A. (2001). Auditory, localization, and scene perception. In E. B. Goldstein (Ed.), *Blackwell handbook of perception.* Malden, MA: Blackwell.

Young, D. M. (1997). Depression. In W. S. Tseng & J. Streltzer (Eds.), *Culture and psychopathology: A guide to clinical assessment.* New York: Brunner/Mazel.

Young, K. S. (1996, August). *Internet addiction: The emergence of a new clinical disorder.* Paper presented at the meeting of the American Psychological Association: Toronto, Ontario, Canada.

Young, K. S. (1998). *Caught in the net: How to recognize the signs of Internet addiction-and a winning strategy for recovery.* New York: Wiley.

Yudofsky, S. C. (1999). Parkinson's disease, depression, and electrical stimulation of the brain. *New England Journal of Medicine, 340,* 1500–1502.

Yukl, G. A. (1994). *Leadership in organizations* (3rd ed.). Englewood Cliffs, NJ: Prentice-Hall.

Zajonc, R. B. (1980). Feeling and thinking: Preferences need no inferences. *American Psychologist, 35,* 151–175.

Zakzanis, K. K., & Young, D. A. (2001). Memory impairment in abstinent MDMA ("Ecstasy") users: A longitudinal investigation. *Neurology, 56,* 966–969.

Zarcone, V. P., Jr. (2000). Sleep hygiene. In M. H. Kryger, T. Roth, & W. C. Dement (Eds.), *Principles and practice of sleep medicine.* Philadelphia: Saunders.

Zatzick, D. F. (1999). Managed care and psychiatry. In R. E. Hales, S. C. Yudofsky, & J. A. Talbott (Eds.), *American Psychiatric Press textbook of psychiatry.* Washington, DC: American Psychiatric Press.

Zatzick, D. F., & Dimsdale, J. E. (1990). Cultural variations in response to painful stimuli. *Psychosomatic Medicine, 52*(5), 544–557.

Zebrowitz, L. A. (1996). *Reading faces.* Boulder, CO: Westview Press.

Zebrowitz, L. A., Collins, M. A., & Dutta, R. (1998). The relationship between appearance and personality across the life span. *Personality and Social Psychology Bulletin, 24,* 736–749.

Zebrowitz, L. A., Voinescu, L., & Collins, M. A. (1996). "Wide-eyed" and "crooked-face": Determinants of perceived and real honesty across the life span. *Personality and Social Psychology Bulletin, 22,* 1258–1269.

Zechmeister, E. B., & Nyberg, S. E. (1982). *Human memory: An introduction to research and theory.* Pacific Grove, CA: Brooks/Cole.

Zeifman, D., & Hazan, C. (1997). Attachment: The bond in pair-bonds.

In J. A. Simpson & D. T. Kenrick (Eds.), *Evolutionary social psychology.* Mahwah, NJ: Erlbaum.

Zeiler, M. (1977). Schedules of reinforcement: The controlling variables. In W. K. Honig & J. E. R. Staddon (Eds.), *Handbook of operant behavior.* Englewood Cliffs, NJ: Prentice-Hall.

Zeki, S. (1993). The visual association cortex. *Current Opinion in Neurobiology, 3,* 155–159.

Zellner, D. A. (1991). How foods get to be liked: Some general mechanisms and some special cases. In R. C. Bolles (Ed.), *The hedonics of taste.* Hillsdale, NJ: Erlbaum.

Zenhausen, R. (1978). Imagery, cerebral dominance and style of thinking: A unified field model. *Bulletin of the Psychonomic Society, 12,* 381–384.

Zepelin, H. (1993). Internal alarm clock. In M. A. Carskadon (Ed.), *Encyclopedia of sleep and dreaming.* New York: Macmillan.

Zepelin, H. (2000). Mammalian sleep. In M. H. Kryger, T. Roth, & W. C. Dement (Eds.), *Principles and practice of sleep medicine.* Philadelphia: Saunders.

Zigler, E., & Seitz, V. (1982). Social policy and intelligence. In R. J. Sternberg (Ed.), *Handbook of human intelligence.* Cambridge, MA: Cambridge University Press.

Zigler, E., & Styfco, S. J. (1994). Head Start: Criticisms in a constructive context. *American Psychologist, 49,* 127–132.

Zillmann, D., & Bryant, J. (1984). Effects of massive exposure to pornography. In N. M. Malamuth & E. Donnerstein (Eds.), *Pornography and sexual aggression.* New York: Academic Press.

Zillmann, D., & Bryant, J. (1988). Pornography's impact on sexual satisfaction. *Journal of Applied Social Psychology, 18,* 438–453.

Zillmann, D., & Weaver, J. B. (1989). Pornography and men's sexual callousness toward women. In D. Zillmann & J. Bryant (Eds.), *Pornography: Research advances and policy considerations.* Hillsdale, NJ: Erlbaum.

Zillmann, D., Bryant, J., & Huston, A. C. (1994). *Media, family, and children.* Hillsdale, NJ: Erlbaum.

Zillmer, E. A., & Spiers, M. V. (2001). *Principles of neuropsychology.* Belmont, CA: Wadsworth.

Zimmerman, B. J. (1995). Self-efficacy and educational development. In A. Bandura (Ed.), *Self-*

efficacy in changing societies. New York: Cambridge University Press.

Zimmerman, I. L., & Woo-Sam, J. M. (1984). Intellectual assessment of children. In G. Goldstein & M. Hersen (Eds.), *Handbook of psychological assessment.* New York: Pergamon Press.

Zoellner, L. A., Foa, E. B., Brigidi, B. D., & Przeworski, A. (2000). Are trauma victims susceptible to "false memories"? *Journal of Abnormal Psychology, 109,* 517–524.

Zola, S. M., & Squire, L. R. (2000). The medial temporal lobe and the hippocampus. In E. Tulving & F. I. M. Craik (Eds.), *The Oxford handbook of memory* (pp. 485–500). New York: Oxford University Press.

Zorick, F. J., & Walsh, J. K. (2000). Evaluation and management of insomnia: An overview. In M. H. Kryger, T. Roth, & W. C. Dement (Eds.), *Principles and practice of sleep medicine.* Philadelphia: Saunders.

Zrenner, E., Abramov, I., Akita, M., Cowey, A., Livingstone, M., & Valberg, A. (1990). Color perception: Retina to cortex. In L. Spillman & J. S. Werner (Eds.), *Visual perception: The neurophysiological foundations.* San Diego: Academic Press.

Zuckerman, M. (1971). Dimensions of sensation seeking. *Journal of Consulting and Clinical Psychology, 36,* 45–52.

Zuckerman, M. (1979). *Sensation seeking: Beyond the optimal level of arousal.* Hillsdale, NJ: Erlbaum.

Zuckerman, M. (1984). Experience and desire: A new format for sensation seeking scales. *Journal of Behavioral Assessment, 6,* 101–114.

Zuckerman, M. (1990). The psychophysiology of sensation seeking. *Journal of Personality, 58*(1), 313–345.

Zuckerman, M. (1991). *Psychobiology of personality.* New York: Cambridge University Press.

Zuckerman, M. (1994). *Behavioral expressions and biosocial bases of sensation seeking.* New York: Cambridge University Press.

Zuckerman, M. (1996). The psychobiological model for impulsive unsocialized sensation seeking: A comparative approach. *Neuropsychobiology, 34,* 125–129.

Zuckerman, M., & Kuhlman, D. M. (2000). Personality and risk-taking: Common biosocial factors. *Journal of Personality, 68,* 999–1029.

Zwislocki, J. J. (1981). Sound analysis in the ear: A history of discoveries. *American Scientist, 69,* 184–192.

Name Index

Subject Index

cerebral laterality, 98–101, 115–117
cerebral specialization, 98, 100–101, 115–117, 469–470
cerebrospinal fluid (CSF), 85, 86
cerebrum, 92, 93, 94–97
change, as source of stress, 524–526
channels, for persuasive messages, 665
charismatic leaders, A-23
Charles, Prince of Wales, 425
chastity, 396
chemical senses, 159–162
chichlid fish, 112
child abuse
  psychological disorders and, 575
  repressed memories of, 283–286
child custody, 70
Child Development Abstracts & Bibliography, 437
child-rearing practices, 23, 502, 517
  culture and, 438, 655
childlessness, 458
children (childhood), 431, 462–463
  cognitive development in, 441–446, 462–463
  day care for, 437
  deprived environments and, 359–360, 363–364
  dreams in, 194
  eating behavior in, 387
  effect of father absence on, 472–473
  emotional development in, 435–439
  gender-role socialization of, 470–471
  gifted, 355–357
  home environment of, 502
  language development in, 306–308
  mental retardation and, 354–355
  motor development in, 432–433, 462, 463
  observational learning in, 493–494
  personality development in, 439–440, 484–486, 505
  sleep patterns in, 185, 186
  sleep problems in, 192
  understanding of mental states in, 446
chimpanzees, 310–311
China, 353, 508, 661, 678
chloride ions, 77, 78
chlorpromazine, 622, 623, 624
choices
  among alternatives, 323–324, 557
  among concurrent reinforcement schedules, 238–239
  rational, 323
  See also decision making
cholesterol, 538, 539, 545
chromosomes, 102–103, 426
chronic diseases, 521, 522
chunking, 269
cigar smoking, 544
cigarette smoking, 56, 429, 531, 544–545
circadian rhythms, 180–182, 211

circular reasoning, 215, 421
Civil Rights Act of 1964, A-17–A-18
clarification, in client-centered therapy, 615
Clark University, 8
class attendance, grades and, 29, 30
classical conditioning, 220–228, 250–251
  acquisition in, 225, 234
  in advertising, 256, 257
  of anxiety responses, 570
  of attitudes, 668
  in aversion therapy, 621
  of avoidance, 240–241
  basic processes in, 225–228
  biological constraints on, 243–246
  in business negotiations, 256–257
  cognitive processes in, 246
  compared with operant conditioning, 229, 234
  defined, 220
  discrimination in, 227–228, 234
  extinction in, 225, 234
  of emotional responses, 222–223
  of fear responses, 234, 408
  generalization in, 227, 234
  of physiological responses, 223–224
  in politics, 257
  of sexual arousal, 224–225
  spontaneous recovery in, 225
  in systematic desensitization, 620
  of taste aversion, 244–245
  of taste preferences, 387
  terminology for, 221
classical music, for infants, 119
claustrophobia, 568
client-centered therapy, 614–615, 628, 640
climate, pace of life and, 48–49, 53
clinical psychologists, 50, 610
clinical psychology, 11, 12, 20, 21
clinical social workers, 611
closure, as Gestalt principle, 143, 144
Clouser, Ronald, 298
clozapine, 624
clustering, 272–273
cocaine, 82, 89, 94, 203–204, 205, 206, 207, 429
cochlea, 156, 157
cocktail party phenomenon, 263
codeine, 203
cognition, 12, 303
cognitive abilities, 366–367, 369
  aging and, 460–461
  gender differences in, 467–468
  innate, 446
  marijuana use and, 208
  See also problem solving; reasoning; thinking
Cognitive Abilities Test, 349
cognitive appraisal
  of emotions, 406, 410

of stressful events, 522–523, 527
cognitive development, 441–446, 462–465
  evolutionary perspective on, 446
  in infants, 118–119
  moral development and, 447
  nativist theories of, 445–446
cognitive dissonance, 669
Cognitive Interference Questionnaire, 188
cognitive needs, 498
cognitive processes
  in conditioning, 245–246
  parallel-distributed processing model of, 274–275
  See also memory; problem solving; thinking
cognitive psychology, 10, 12–13, 19, 20, 304
cognitive revolution, 303–304
cognitive schemas, 649, 682
cognitive style
  culture and, 320–322
  hemispheric specialization and, 117
  negative, 580–581
cognitive theories
  of anxiety disorders, 570, 571
  of gender-role development, 470–471
  of intelligence, 369
  of intelligent behavior, 369
  of language development, 313
  of mood disorders 579–581
  of somatoform disorders, 573
cognitive therapy, 615–616, 628
cohesiveness, group, 679
coins, 261
collective unconscious, 486–487
collectivism, 418, 655–656, 661, 675, 678
college students
  date rape among, 392
  as research subjects, 58–59
  sleep deprivation and, 188–189
  study habits of, 27
color blindness, 139
color circle, 139
color mixing, 138, 167
color solid, 137
color vision, 132, 137–140
  opponent process theory of, 139, 140
  trichromatic theory, 138–139, 140
colors
  complementary, 139
  primary, 139
  purity of, 129, 137
  saturation of, 129, 137
  terms for, 314
Columbia University, 5
Columbine High School, 453
commitment
  involuntary, 595
  in relationships, 454, 659
common cold, stress and, 541–542
common sense
  fallibility of, 680

scientific approach vs., 41
communication
  in animals, 310–311
  in groups, 676, 679
  with health providers, 549–550
  in organizations, A-19–A-20
  persuasive, 665–668
  See also language
communication technology, A-17
community-based treatment, 636
community mental health centers, 638, 639
community mental health movement, 635
comorbidity, 603
companionate love, 658–659
comparitors, 172–173
compensation, 488
competence, 648
complementary colors, 139
compliance, 672–675
compulsions, 568, 569
computerized tomography (CT) scans, 88, 90
computers, in workplace, A-18
conception, 426
concepts, abstract, 443
conceptual hierarchies, 272–273
conclusions
  based on data, 40–41
  drawing, 420–421
  jumping to, 535
concordance rate
  for anxiety disorders, 569
  for gay sexual orientation, 399
  for mood disorders, 678–579
  for schizophrenia, 585–586
concrete operational period, 441, 443
concurrent schedules of reinforcement, 237–238
conditionability, 500
conditional love, 496
conditioned reflex, 221
conditioned response (CR), 221, 222, 223, 224, 227, 228, 244, 226, 227, 228, 244, 570, 620, 621, 668
conditioned stimulus (CS), 221, 222, 223, 224, 227, 228, 244, 226, 227, 228, 244, 570, 620, 621, 668
  higher-order conditioning and, 228
  predictive value of, 246
conditioning, 219
  of anxiety responses, 570
  of attitudes, 668, 683
  cognitive processes in, 246–247
  constraints on, 243–245
  of emotional responses, 222, 223
  higher-order, 228
  immune system and, 223–224
  overview of, 250–251
  of physiological responses, 223–224
  subliminal, 128
  See also classical conditioning; operant conditioning
cones, 131, 132, 133, 139–140

confidence levels, 334, 335
confidence ratings, 299
confirmation bias, 333, 650
conflict
  internal, 523, 482–483, 611–612
  types of, 523–524
  parent-child, 453, 459
conformity, 648
  Asch's studies of, 671–672
  cultural variations in, 675
  defined, 671
confounding variables, 44
congenital adrenal hyperplasia, 469
congruence, 496, 614
conjunction fallacy, 327, 603
conjunctive probabilities, 602
connectionist model, of memory, 274–275
conscientiousness, 479, 501, 502, 503, 544
conscious, Freud's view of, 481
consciousness
  altered, 199, 202–209
  behaviorists and, 6
  brain activity and, 179
  divided, 200
  evolutionary roots of, 178–179
  nature of, 178–179
  stream of, 5, 115, 178
  study of, 3, 5, 177–178
  subjective nature of, 209
  unity of, 117
conservation tasks, 442, 44
consistency
  as aspect of personality, 478
  cognitive, 670
  cross-situational, 494–495
consolidation, memory, 190, 288–289
constancies, perceptual, 150
constraint, 479
  unnecessary, 317
construct validity, 345–346
constructive coping, 534, 552–555
contagious diseases, 521, 522
content validity, 345
context
  leadership and, A-23
  perception and, 146, 171
  as retrieval cue, 276, 278
contingencies, reinforcement, 230–231, 247, 254, 494
continuity, as Gestalt principle, 144
continuous reinforcement, 235
contrast, visual processing and, 134
contrast effects, in persuasion, 172–173
control, as goal of scientific approach, 38
control group, 43, 44, 45
conventional thinking, 447
convergence, 146
convergent thinking, 373
conversion disorder, 572
Coolidge effect, 393
coping, 530–534
  adaptive, 530
  constructive, 534, 552–555
  defensive, 532–534
  defined, 530

posttraumatic stress disorder and, 536
  sleep and, 191
  stress and, 537
drugs, 531
  medical uses of, 203
  method of ingestion, 203
  overdose of, 205, 207
  physical dependence on, 205, 206–207
  psychoactive, 202–209
  psychological dependence on, 205, 207
  recreational, 202
  side effects of, 203
  synergistic effects of, 206
  tolerance for, 205
  See also specific drugs
DSM-IV, 565, 566
dual-coding theory, 265
Duchamp, Marcel, 168–169
dysthymic disorder, 577

E

ear, sensory processing in, 155–157
eardrum, 156
earlobes, attached vs. detached, 103
easy children, 435
eating behavior, 531
  biological factors in, 384–386
  environmental factors in, 386–388
  hypothalamus and, 93
  neurotransmitters and, 82
  obesity and, 388–390
  restrained, 390
eating binges, 598, 599
eating disorders, 598–601
  etiology of, 599–601
  history of, 599
  prevalence of, 599
  stress and, 537
  treatment of, 599
eclecticism, 633, 640
economy, U.S., A-17
ecstasy, 204, 208–209
educational and school psychology, 20, 21
educational enrichment programs, 376–377
Educational Testing Service (ETS), 342
efferent nerve fibers, 84
effort justification, 669
egg, 105, 106, 426
ego, 481, 483
egocentrism, 443, 444
ejaculation, 401
elaboration, 264–265
elaboration likelihood model, 670, 671
Elavil, 624
electrical stimulation of the brain (ESB), 12, 87–88, 93, 94, 270, 287
electroconvulsive therapy (ECT), 626–627
electrodes, 87, 94
electroencephalograph (EEG), 87, 177, 178, 183
electromyogrph (EMG), 183
electrooculopgrah (EOG), 183
elephant seals, 113
elicit, 221
elimination by aspects, 323–324

embryonic stage, 427
emergencies, helping in, 676
emergentist theories, 313
emetic drugs, 620–621
eminence, 357–358, 375
emit, 230
emotion(s), 405–411
  in adolescence, 452–453
  behavioral component of, 409
  biology of, 93–94
  classical conditioning of, 668
  cognitive component of, 406
  components of, 405
  culture and, 409–411
  defined, 405
  evolutionary perspective on, 413–414
  expressed, 588
  expressing, 553
  fundamental, 409, 413–414
  manipulation of, 256–257
  mixed, 406
  negative, 406, 411, 553–554
  physiological component of, 406–409
  theories of, 412–414
  positive, 406, 527–528
  in schizophrenia, 584
  suppression of, 553
emotional development, 435–439
Emotional Intelligence (Goleman), 371
emotional intelligence, 371–372
emotional responses
  conditioning of, 222, 223, 240–241, 245, 256–257, 408, 570
  heart disease and, 539–540
  semantics and, 336
  to stress, 552, 527–528
empathy, of therapist, 615
empirically validated treatments, 631
empiricism, 22, 37, 64, 114, 330, 680, A-14
employer-employee relationship, A-21–A-22
employment recruiting, A-15–A-16
employment testing, 353, A-17
empty nest, 459
encoding, 261, 262–266
  enriching, 264–266
  ineffective, 280–281
  levels of, 263–264
  self-referent, 265–266
encoding specificity principle, 282
encounter group movement, 616
endocrine disorders, 469
endocrine system, 93, 101–102, 529, 530
  See also hormones
endorphins, 81, 82–83, 163, 164, 206
English titmouse, 248, 249
entertainment, business, 256–257
environment
  brain development and, 118–119
  deprived, 359–360, 363–364
  enriched, 97, 118, 119, 360

heredity and, 25, 107–108, 114, 330, 466
  IQ scores and, 359–360, 363–366
  See also nature vs. nurture
environmental tobacco smoke, 545
Epidemiological Catchment Area studies, 567
epidemiology, 566, 602
epilepsy, 100
episodic memory, 291–292, 461
equilibrium, 91, 164
  physiological, 382
ERIC Clearinghouse on Assessment and Evaluation, 343
erotic materials, 391–392
escape learning, 239–240
Escher, M. C., 169, 170
Eskimos, 160, 313, 411
essay exams, 31
esteem needs, 498
estrogens, 391, 450
ethical dilemmas, 61–62
ethics, in psychological research, 61–64, 675
ethnic groups
  IQ differences in, 361–366
  psychotherapy and, 633–634
  stereotypes of, 649–650, 681–682
  in U.S. population, 14
ethnocentrism, 14, 683
etiology, 562, 567
euphoria
  drug-induced, 203, 204
  in manic-depressive disorder, 578
evidence
  anecdotal, 70–71
  contradictory, 33
  disconfirming, 299
  evaluating, 71
evolution
  face detection and, 136
  of color vision, 137
  sensory adaptation and, 128
  taste sensitivity and, 161
evolutionary perspective, 10
  on affiliation need, 402
  on attachment, 438–439
  on attraction, 661–662
  on consciousness, 178–179
  on decision making, 329, 332
  on emotions, 413–414
  on fight-or-flight response, 529
  on gender differences, 468–469
  on human sexual behavior, 393–397
  on innate cognitive abilities, 446
  on language, 311
  on learning, 245–246
  on motivation, 383
  on obesity, 388–389
  on orgasm, 401
  on person perception, 651
  on personality, 502–503, 517
  on sexual arousal, 225
  on sexual maturation, 451–452
  on sleep, 187
  on taste aversion, 245

evolutionary psychology, 14–15, 32–33, 108–114
evolutionary theory, 38
  Darwin's, 4–5, 108–109
  refinements to, 109–111
examples, as memory aid, 264–265
excitatory postsynaptic potential (EPSP), 79, 80
excitement phase, of human sexual response, 400–401
exercise
  lack of, 389, 546
  sleep and, 211
  for stress reduction, 554–555
exhaustion, 535
exorcism, 562
expectancy-value models, 383
expectations
  drug effects and, 204–205
  of experimenter, 60–61
  happiness and, 419
  for parenthood, 458
  perceptions and, 145–146
  person perception and, 25–26, 650
expected value, 325
experiment, 42, 52
  basic elements in, 42–43
  variations in design of, 44–45
experimental group, 43, 44
experimental psychology, 19, 20
experimental research, 42–47, 52
experimenter bias, 60–61
expertise, 666, 684
  of web authors, A-27–A-28
explanations, alternative, 33
explicit memory, 289–290
expressed emotion, 588
external ear, 156
extinction
  in classical conditioning, 226, 234
  in operant conditioning, 232–233, 234
  resistance to, 232–233, 236, 240
extrapolation, 118–119
extraversion, 106, 419, 479, 487, 500, 501, 502, 503
eye, structure of, 130–135
eye movements, during sleep, 177, 183
eyeblink responses, 288
eyewitness recall, 276, 298–299

F

face detectors, 136
facial expressions, 409, 411
facial feedback hypothesis, 409, 410
facial symmetry, 661
factor analysis, 366, 478
failure, 523
  attributions for, 652, 653, 655, 682
  fear of, 405
fallacies, 376, 421, 473
false beliefs, 446
false dichotomy, 421, 473
False Memory Syndrome Foundation, 285
family
  alternative forms of, 472
  dysfunctional, 591, 594

eating disorders and, 601
  expressed emotion in, 588
  gender-role socialization and, 471
  role of father in, 472–473
  See also children; marriage; parents
family environment, personality and, 502
family life cycle, 457–459
family studies, 105
  of anxiety disorders, 569
  of intelligence, 357–358
family values, 473
fantasy, 532, 533
farsightedness, 131
fast mapping, 307, 312
fat, dietary, 110, 546
fat cells, 386
fatalism, 531
fathers, absence of, 472–473
fatigue
  chronic, 535
  circadian rhythms and, 181
  perception and, 150
fear(s)
  appeals to, 666–667
  behavior therapy for, 620
  conditioned, 222, 240–241, 245, 408, 570
  of failure, 405
  irrational, 568
  learned, 93, 289
feature analysis, 141–143, 168
feature detectors, 136, 142, 162
Fechner's law, 126
fee-for-service system, 630
feedback, negative, 102
Fellini, Federico, 193
femininity, 467
fetal alcohol syndrome, 429
fetal stage, 428
fetishism, transvestic, 562
fetus, 427, 428
fiber, in diet, 546
field dependence-independence, 321–322
fight-or-flight response, 85, 110, 101, 407, 528–529
figure-ground, 143
finches, 393
Fiorina, Carly, A-20
firstborns, 488
fitness
  inclusive, 110–111
  physical, 546l, 554–555
  reproductive, 109, 110
five-factor model, of personality, 479
  See also Big Five personality traits
fixation, 485
fixed-interval schedules, 236, 237
fixed-ratio schedules, 236, 237
flashbulb memories, 270–271
flattery, 658
flatworms, 287
flavor, perception of, 161
Flockhart, Calista, 600
fluid intelligence, 367, 460
fluoxetine, 624
fluphenazine, 624
Flynn effect, 360
fMRI, 89
food preferences, 159, 160, 387

food-related cues, 386
foot-in-the-door technique, 685
foraging behavior, 238–239
Ford Motor Company, A-17
Fore (New Guinea), 410
forebrain, 92, 93–97, 385
forewarning, 257, 667
forgetting, 279–286
  aging and, 460
  causes of, 280–282
  measures of, 279–280
  motivated, 282, 483
forgetting curve, 279
forgiving, 553–554
form, perception of, 140–146
formal operational period, 441, 443
fovea, 130, 132
framing of questions, 334–335
Francesco, S., 166
fraternal twins, 104, 105–106
  intelligence and, 358
  See also twin studies
free association, 612
free will, 9, 490, 495
freebasing, 204
frequency
  of brain waves, 179
  of sound waves, 154, 155
frequency distribution, A-7
frequency polygon, A-7
frequency theory, of auditory perception, 1577, 158
Freudian slips, 7–8, 481
friendship, 657–658
frontal lobe, 95, 96, 98, 587
frustration, 485, 523, 526, 531
frustration-aggression hypothesis, 531
fugue, dissociative, 574
functional fixedness, 316
functional magnetic resonance imaging (fMRI), 89
functionalism, 4–5
fundamental attribution error, 653, 654, 655, 682–683
Futurism, 168

G
g, Spearman's, 366, 367
GABA, 81, 82, 187, 191, 206, 569
galvanic skin response (GSR), 407
gambler's fallacy, 332
gambling, 236, 237, 325
gamma-aminobutyric acid. See GABA
Gandhi, Mohandas, 193
ganglion cells, 131, 134, 140
gate-control theory, 163
Gates, Bill, 352
Gathani, Nirav, 356
gender, defined, 467
gender differences, 467–471
  in attributions for success, 682
  biological origins of, 468–470
  in brain organization, 469–470
  in cognitive abilities, 467–468
  in depression, 577
  in dream content, 194
  in eating disorders, 599

environmental origins of, 470–471
evolutionary perspective on, 468–469
  in mate preferences, 394–397, 661, 662
  in odor recognition, 162
  in orgasm consistency, 401
  in patterns of sexual activity, 394
  in personality, 468
  in rumination, 579
  in sexual thoughts, 394
  in social behavior, 468
  in tactics of attraction, 662
  in taste sensitivity, 161
  in visual-spatial ability, 15, 32–33
  study of, 5
gender roles, 470–471
  in marriage, 457–458
gender stereotypes, 467, 471, 649, 682
  test performance and, 364
gene flow, 109
gene pool, 109, 359
general adaptation syndrome, 529
generalization
  in classical conditioning, 227, 234
  in operant conditioning, 234
generalization gradients, 227, 228
generalized anxiety disorders, 567–568, 592, 623
generativity vs. self-absorption, 456, 457
genes, 15, 102–103, 426
genetic drift, 109
genetic mapping, 107, 586
genetic predisposition/vulnerability
  to anxiety disorders, 569
  to eating disorders, 599–601
  to homosexuality, 400
  to mood disorders, 578–579, 593
  to obesity, 389
  to sensation seeking, 506
  to schizophrenia, 90, 108
genetic relatedness, 104, 105
genetics, principles of, 102–104
genital herpes, 430, 540
genital stage, 485, 486
genius, 356
  hereditary, 347
genotype, 104
genuineness, of therapist, 614
geographical slant, perception of, 148–150
Germany, 437–438
germinal stage, 427
Gestalt principles, 143–144
  applied to art, 168–169
Gestalt psychology, 7, 143, 144
giftedness, 5, 355–357
glia, 76
globalization, of business, A-17
glove anesthesia, 572
glucose, 385
glucostats, 385
glutamate, 587
glycine, 82

goals
  motivation toward, 382
  of scientific approach, 38–39
gonadotropins, 102
gonads, 102, 391, 450
Goodwin, Doris Kearns, 278
Graduate Record Exam (GRE), 341
grandeur, delusions of, 583, 584
graphing, of data, A-7–A-8
grasshoppers, 111
gratification
  delaying, 481
  excessive, 485
group cohesiveness, 679
group intelligence tests, 348–349
group polarization, 678
group therapy, 616–617
groups
  behavior in, 676–680
  bystander effect and, 676–677
  conformity to, 671–672
  decision making in, 678–680
  defined, 676
  diffusion of responsibility in, 677
  identity and, 508
  productivity in, 677
groupthink, 678–679
growth hormone, fluctuations in, 180
growth needs, 497
growth spurt
  in adolescence, 102, 449
  in childhood, 432
guilt, 481, 484, 527, 532
gustatory system, 159–161

H
H. M., 288
habitual tasks, 292–293
habituation, 445
hair cells
  for balance, 164
  for hearing, 156, 157
Haldol, 623
halfway houses, 636
hallucinations, 583
  hypnosis-induced, 199
Hallucinogenic Toreador (Dali), 169
hallucinogens, 203, 204, 205
handedness, 116, 117
handshaking, 649
happiness, 416–419
  marriage and, 458
  measurement of, 416
  moderate predictors of, 417–418
  nonpredictors of, 416–417
  strong predictors of, 418–419
haptic measures, 149
Harvard Group Scale of Hypnotic Susceptibility, 197
Harvard University, 5
hashish, 203, 204
hassles, 522, 541
hawk, Galapagos, 113
Head Start, 376
health
  biopsychosocial factors in, 521, 551
  happiness and, 417
health care costs, 630
health-impairing behavior, 327, 544–548

health maintenance organizations (HMOs), 630
health providers, communicating with, 549–550
health psychology, 521
health statistics, 556–557
Healthfinder, 540
hearing, 154–158
  absolute threshold for, 125, 155
  aging and, 459
  brain centers for, 98
  theories of, 157
hearsay, 71
heart attack, 538, 539, 540
heart disease, 388, 521, 522, 527, 538–540, 545
hedonic adaptation, 419
hedonic treadmill, 419
height in plane, 147, 166
Heinz's dilemma, 446–447
helping behavior, 676
helplessness, 527, 531, 579
hemispheres, cerebral, 95, 96, 98–101
hemispheric specialization, 98, 100–101, 115–117, 469–470
Henrich, Christy, 598
Hereditary Genius (Galton), 347
heredity
  anxiety disorders and, 569
  environment and, 25, 107–108, 114, 330, 466
  homosexuality and, 399
  intelligence and, 357–359, 362–363
  mechanisms of, 102–108
  mental retardation and, 355
  mood disorders and, 578–579
  obesity and, 389
  personality and, 500–502, 503
  schizophrenia and, 585–586
  See also nature vs. nurture
heritability
  of body weight, 389
  of intelligence, 359, 362–363
  of personality, 501–502, 503
heritability ratios, 359, 377
Hermann grid, 134
heroin, 203, 207, 429
hertz (Hz), 154
heterosexuality, 397
heterozygotic twins, 106
heterozygous condition, 103
heuristics, 319
  fast and frugal, 329–330
  in judging probabilities, 325–326
Hewlett-Packard, A-20
"hidden observer," 200
hierarchical classification, 443
hierarchy of needs, 497–498
hierarchy of traits, 500
higher-order conditioning, 228
highly active antiretroviral therapy, 547
highway hypnosis, 200
hills, perceived steepness of, 148–150
Hinckley, John, Jr., 564, 603
hindbrain, 91, 92, 287
hindsight bias, 298–299, 516–517, 603, 654

hippocampus, 92, 93, 97, 460
  memory and, 287, 288–289, 291
hiring, A-15–A-17
Hispanic Americans, 14
  IQ scores of, 362, 364
  See also ethnic groups
histogram, A-7
HistPsyc, 3
histrionic personality, 573, 590
hobbits and orcs problem, 315
holistic cognitive style, 322
home environment, IQ and, 360
homelessness, 636–637
homeostasis, 382
homophobia, 484
homosexuality, 397–400
  AIDS and, 547
  biological theories of, 399–400
  concealment of, 39–40
  environmental theories of, 398–399
  prevalence of, 397–398
homozygotic twins, 105
homozygous condition, 103
honesty, 648
hopelessness, 577
hopelessness theory, 579
horizontal cells, 131
hormones, 101–102
  in adolescence, 449, 450
  aging and, 459
  emotional responses and, 407, 409
  homosexuality and, 399–400
  hunger regulation and, 386
  memory and, 287
  sex, 391–392, 450, 469
  stress and, 529–530
hostility
  coronary risk and, 538
  managing, 553
house finches, 112
housework, 457, 471
How to Sleep Like a Baby (Hales), 212
How to Win Friends and Influence People (Carnegie), 658
Howe, Elias, 193
hue, wavelength and, 129, 137–138
Hughes, Howard, 568, 569, 573
Human Behavior and Evolution Society, 111
Human Genome Project, 107
human immunodeficiency virus (HIV), 546–547
human nature, 499
  evolutionary theory and, 110
  humanists' view of, 10
human potential movement, 496
human resources function, A-18
humanism, 10–11
humanistic theories of personality, 495–499, 504–505
  evaluation of, 499–500
  Maslow's, 497–498
  Rogers's, 496–497, 505
humor, as stress reducer, 553

hunger, regulation of, 93, 384–388
hunting and gathering societies, 15, 33, 469
Huntington's disease, 460
hydrocephaly, 355
hydrophobia, 568
hypertension, 546
hypnic jerks, 183
hypnosis, 197–200
  as altered state, 200
  for anesthesia, 198–199
  highway, 200
  memory and, 200, 276, 285
  misconceptions about, 198
  phenomena found with, 198–199
  as role playing, 199–200
  theories of, 199–200
hypochondriasis, 572–573
hypogonadism, 391
hypothalamus, 92, 101, 102, 399
  circadian rhythms and, 181
  hunger regulation and, 385
  sex hormones and, 391
  stress and, 529–530
hypotheses, 38, 39
  null, A-13–A-14
  perceptual, 144–146, 153
  testing, 47, A-13–A-14
hypothetical constructs, 345, 377

I

"I have a friend who . . ." syndrome, 71
"I knew it all along" effect, 516
id, 481, 482
idealization, of romantic partners, 658
identical twins, 104, 105–106, 500, 501
  intelligence and, 358
  See also twin studies
identification, 483, 484
identity
  adolescent search for, 453–455
  loss of, 574
  mistaken, 298
identity statuses, 454–455
identity vs. confusion, 454
Ifaluk, 411
ignorance, appeal to, 376–377
illness
  biopsychosocial model of, 521, 551
  life change and, 525–526
  reactions to, 549–550
  stress and, 538–543
  See also disease; specific illnesses
illusion of asymmetric insight, 650–651
illusions
  about romantic partners, 658
  optical, 150–154, 169–170
  positive, 533–534
IllusionWorks, 152
illusory correlation, 650, 682
imagery, as memory aid, 265
imaginativeness, 198
imitation, of models, 493–494, 470
immigrants
  intelligence testing of, 366

language learning of, 309
immune functioning, 223
  AIDS and, 546–547
  emotional suppression and, 553
  marijuana and, 208
  optimism and, 543
  stress and, 541–542, 543
immunosuppression, 223–224
implantation, 427
implicit memory, 289–290, 291
impossible figures, 151–153, 169–170
impotence, marijuana use and, 208
impression formation, 648–651
impression management, 506–507
Impressionism, 166, 167
improbable, overestimating, 333
inattentional blindness, 141
incentives, 383, 404
inclines, estimating, 149
inclusive fitness, 110–111
income, happiness and, 416
incongruence, 496, 614
Incurably Ill for Animal Research, 64
independence, 438
independent variables, 42, 43, 44
independent view of the self, 508, 509
India, 24, 353, 661
individual differences
  in need for achievement, 403–404
  measuring, 342
  personality and, 478
individual psychology, 487–490
individualism, 418, 655–656, 661, 675
inducing structure, problems of, 314
induction, hypnotic, 197–198
industrial and organizational (I/O) psychology, 12, 20, 21, A-15–A-26
industrial psychology, A-15–A-19
industry vs. inferiority, 440
infant mortality, 430
infants
  attachment in, 435–439, 660–661
  cognitive development in, 442, 462
  educational programs for, 119
  language development in, 306
  math abilities of, 445
  motor development in, 432–433, 462
  neural development in, 118
  personality development in, 439, 440
  sleep patterns in, 185, 186
  temperament of, 434–435
infectious diseases, 521, 522
  during pregnancy, 430
inferences, from givens, 330
inferential statistics, 56–57, A-13

inferiority complex, 488
inflammation, heart disease and, 538, 539
inflammatory bowel disease, 541
influenza, prenatal, 588
information
  conflicting, 557
  irrelevant, 316
  organization of, 295
  useless, 324
information processing, 369
  connectionist model of, 274–275
  in nervous system, 75
  in retina, 132–134
  in visual cortex, 135–137
information-processing theories, 266, 267
infrared spectrum, 129, 130
ingroups, 651, 683
inhibitory postsynaptic potential (IPSP), 79, 82
inhibited temperament, 435
inhibitions, lack of, 199, 506, 591
initiative vs. guilt, 439, 440
inner ear, 156
insanity, 594–595
insanity defense, 594
insects, behavior of, 112
insight, 315, 373
insight therapies, 608, 611–618
  client-centered, 614–615, 628
  cognitive, 615–616, 628
  combining medication with, 632–633
  effectiveness of, 617–618, 640
  psychoanalytic, 608, 611–614, 628–629
insomnia, 182, 190–192, 211–212
  causes of, 191
  prevalence of, 190–191
  stress and, 537
  treatment of, 191–192
inspection time, 368–369
instinctive drift, 243–244
instrumental learning, 229
insulin, 101, 386
integrity vs. despair, 456–457
intellectualization, 532, 533
intelligence
  adoption studies of, 106–107, 358–359
  aging and, 460
  biological indexes of, 367–369
  cognitive perspective on, 369–370
  creativity and, 374–375
  emotional, 371–372
  environmental factors in, 359–360, 363–366
  ethnic/cultural differences in, 361–366, 376
  exceptional, 355–357
  expanding the concept of, 370–371
  facets of, 370
  fluid vs. crystallized, 367, 460
  happiness and, 417
  heredity and, 357–359, 362–363
  heritability of, 359, 362–363

interaction of heredity and environment, 360–361
  reification of, 377
  triarchic theory of, 369
  twin studies of, 106, 107, 358
  types of, 352, 367, 370–372
intelligence quotient. See IQ scores
intelligence tests, 341, 342
  cultural bias in, 365–366
  culture and, 353
  group, 348–349
  history of, 347–349
  new directions in, 366–372
  questions on, 349, 350
  reliability of, 351
  school performance and, 352
  validity of, 352
  vocational success and, 352–353
  what they measure, 351
interactionist theories, of language acquisition, 312
interdependent view of the self, 508, 509
interference, 268, 272, 294
  proactive, 282
  retroactive, 281–282
interference theory, 281–282
intermittent reinforcement, 235–236
International School of Advanced Studies (Trieste), 156
Internet
  addiction to, 531–532
  databases on, 67
  evaluating resources on, A-27–A-30
  sexual pursuits on, 51
interpersonal attraction, 648, 657–662
  cultural differences in, 660–661
  evolutionary perspective on, 661–662
interpersonal psychotherapy, 632
interposition, 147, 166
interpretation, in psychoanalysis, 612–613
interval schedules, 236, 237
interviews, 60
  for data collection, 40
intimacy, love and, 659
intimacy vs. isolation, 456
intravenous drug use, 207–208, 547
introspection, 4, 303, 446
introversion, 487
inventive activity, 403
inverted-U hypothesis, 527
involuntary commitment, 595
ions, 77, 78
Iowa Writers Workshop, 375
IQ scores, 347–348
  cultural differences in, 361–366
  generational changes in, 360
  giftedness and, 355–357
  happiness and, 417
  improvement in, 376–377
  mental retardation and, 354–355
  significance of, 349–351
  See also intelligence tests
iris, 130, 131

irrational thinking, 583
irreversibility, 443
Irwin, Steve, 477–478

J

jacana, northern, 113
Jamaica, 433
James-Lange theory, 412
Japan (Japanese), 186, 322, 353, 411, 437–438, 508, 656, 661, 678
Japanese quail, 224–225
jealousy, 402, 659
jet lag, 181
job applicants, A-15–A-16
job performance, A-18–A-19
  IQ and, 353
job recruitment, A-15–A-16
job skills, A-17, A-18
Johns Hopkins University, 3
Johnson, Lyndon, 193
joints, receptors in, 164
Jordan, Michael, 404
journal articles, researching, 66–69
journals, psychology, 3, 19, 41, 50, 66–69
judgments, contrast effects in, 172–173
juries, 47, 299
just noticeable difference (JND), 125
juvenile crime, 453

K

Kanzi, 310
Kennedy, John F., 635, 679
keyword method, 296, 297
kinesthetic system, 164
Kinetic Art, 171
Kipsigis, 432–433
knowledge, intelligence tests and, 351
Koppel, Ted, 352
koro, 596
Korsakoff's syndrome, 215
Krakauer, Jon, 361
Kreskin, 199
Kung San, 433

L

labeling, 215
labeling theory, Schachter's, 412, 413
language, 304–314
  adaptive value of, 311
  ambiguities in, 308
  animal use of, 310–311
  behaviorist theories of, 311–312
  bilingualism and, 308–309
  brain areas for, 98
  culture and, 313–314
  defined, 304
  evolutionary view of, 311
  interactionist theories of, 311–313
  nativist theories of, 312
  second, 309
  structure of, 304–306
language acquisition device, 312
language development, 306–308
  theories of, 311–313
latency stage, 485, 486
latent content, of dreams, 213
lateral antagonism, 133–134

mood swings, 578
moon illusion, 152, 153
moral reasoning, development of, 446–448
morality, 481
morphemes, 305, 308, 312
morphine, 82, 164, 203
mortality rates, 333, 521, 522
  infant, 430
  for smokers, 545
mother-infant attachment, 435–439
moths, 112
motion, perception of, 143
motion parallax, 147
motivated forgetting, 282, 483
motivation
  Adler's view of, 488
  creativity and, 374
  defined, 382
  drive theories of, 382–383
  evolutionary theories of, 383
  of hunger and eating, 384–390
  incentive theories of, 383
  IQ and, 356
  Maslow's theory of, 497–498
  observational learning and, 248
  personality and, 504
  sexual, 391–401
  of workers, A-22–A-23
motive(s)
  achievement, 403–405
  affiliation, 402–403
  biological, 383–384
  perception and, 26
  social, 383–384
motor cortex, 95, 96
motor development, 432–433, 462–463
movement, coordination of, 91, 95
Mozart effect, 119
MRI scans, 89, 90
Müller-Lyer illusion, 150, 151, 152–153
multiaxial evaluation, on DSM, 566
multicultural sensitivity, in psychotherapy, 633–634
Multifactor Emotional Intelligence Scale (MEIS), 371
multifactorial causation, 23–24, 550–551
  of drug effects, 204–205
  in memory processes, 293
  in psychological disorders, 596–597
multiple-choice tests, 31, 280
multiple personality disorder, 574–575
multiple sclerosis, 76
Munch, Edward, 592
Murrah Federal Building, 536
muscles
  control of, 84, 86
  during sleep, 184
  kinesthetic monitoring of, 164
mutations, 103, 109
myelin sheath, 76

N

name calling, 337
names
  memory for, 262
  used as explanations, 215

napping, 186
narcissistic personality disorder, 590
narcolepsy, 192
narcotics, 203, 205, 207, 429
Nardil, 624
narrative methods, for remembering, 295–296
Nash, John, 585
National Alliance for the Mentally Ill, 566
national character, 507
National Comorbidity Study, 567
National Forum on People's Differences, 661
National Institute of Child Health and Human Development, 437
National Institute of Mental Health, 570
National Library of Medicine, 41, 87
National Sleep Foundation, 190
Native Americans, IQ scores of, 362
nativist theories
  of cognitive development, 446
  of language, 312
natural selection, 4–5, 15, 108–109, 111
  of cognitive abilities, 446
  defined, 109
  face detection and, 136
  of gender differences, 468–469
  human language and, 311
  learning processes and, 245
  mating systems and, 113
  of mother-infant attachment, 438–439
  of motives, 383
  of personality traits, 502
  sensory adaptation and, 128
  taste aversions and, 245
  See also evolutionary perspective
naturalistic observation, 48–49, 52
nature vs. nurture, 6, 25, 347
  in homosexuality, 400
  in intelligence, 357–366
  in language acquisition, 311–313
  in shaping behavior, 249
  See also environment; heredity
Nazi Germany, 257, 673
nearsightedness, 130–131
Necker cube, 145–146, 170
need(s)
  for achievement, 403–405
  for affiliation, 42–43, 402–403
  child's, 485
  hierarchy of, 497–498
  for self-actualization, 497–498
negative emotionality, 479
negative feedback systems, 102
negative reinforcement, 239–240, 241, 253, 570
negative self-talk, 531
negative thinking, 552–553, 580–581, 615, 616
negatively skewed distribution, A-8

negotiations, classical conditioning in, 256–257
NEO Personality Inventory, 512–513
nerve endings, free, 162
nerve fibers, 84
nerves, 84, 86
nervous system
  cells in, 76–77
  communication in, 75–83
  organization of, 83–86
neural impulse, 77, 78
neural reorganization, 97
neurodevelopmental hypothesis, of schizophrenia, 587–588
neurons, 75–76
  aging and, 460
  memory formation and, 288
  new, 97
  number of, 83
  in pain pathways, 162–163
  structure of, 76
  in visual cortex, 136
  See also synapses
neuropeptide Y, 385, 386
Neuropsychology Central, 77
neuroscientists, 86
neuroses, 611
neuroticism, 479, 500, 501, 502, 503, 542, 549, 573
neurotransmitters, 76, 79–80
  anxiety disorders and, 569
  in depressive disorders, 624–625
  drug effects and, 205–206
  hormones and, 101
  hunger and, 385
  memory and, 287
  mood disorders and, 579, 593
  regulating sleep and waking, 187
  schizophrenia and, 586–587
  types of, 81–83
neutral stimulus, 220, 222
New England Journal of Medicine, 626
New York State Lunatic Asylum, 635
Newsweek, 115, 517
next-in-line effect, 262
nicotine, 82, 203, 211
night terrors, 192
night vision, 132
nightmares, 192
nine-dot problem, 317
noise, in signal detection, 126
nominal fallacy, 215
non-REM (NREM) sleep, 184, 192, 193
non sequiturs, 421
nonsense syllables, 279
nonverbal communication, 409
  of emotions, 409, 411
  gender differences in, 468
norepinephrine, 81, 82, 101, 205, 579, 625
normal distribution, 348, 349, 350, 351, A-9–A-11
normality, 562–563
norms
  cultural, 562
  developmental, 432
  group, 676
  social, 481
  test, 343–344

Northwestern University, 499
nortryptiline, 632
nose, smell receptors in, 161
notable events, memories for, 270–271
note taking, 29–30
nouns, 307
NREM sleep, 184, 192, 193
nucleus, cell, 76
nucleus accumbens, 206
Nude Descending a Staircase (Duchamp), 168–169
null hypotheses, A-13–A-14
Nurture Assumption, The (Harris), 517
nutritional habits, 545–546

O

obedience, 648, 672
  cultural variations in, 675
  Milgram's studies of, 672–675
obesity, 388–390
  fear of, 598
object permanence, 442, 444
objectivity, in research, 60
observation, as research technique, 40, 48–49, 52
observational learning, 247–249, 250–251
  antisocial personality and, 594
  of attitudes, 668, 683
  of conditioned fears, 570
  of eating habits, 387
  of gender roles, 470
  personality and, 493–494
  in social skills training, 621
observations, as basis of behaviorism, 6, 8–9
obsessions, 568
obsessive-compulsive disorder (OCD), 568–569, 592
  treatment for, 624, 640
obsessive-compulsive personality disorder, 590
occipital lobe, 95, 96, 134, 135
occupational attainment, IQ scores and, 352–353
occupational stereotypes, 649–650
octopus, 75
odors, 161–162
Oedipal complex, 486
offspring, parental investment in, 112–113
Oklahoma City, 536
olanzapine, 624
olfactory bulb, 161
olfactory cilia, 161
olfactory nerve, 161
olfactory system, 161–162
On the Origin of the Species (Darwin), 108
openness to experience, 479, 501, 502, 503
operant chamber, 230
operant conditioning, 229–243, 250–251
  acquisition in, 232, 234
  of anxiety responses, 570
  of attitudes, 668, 683
  basic processes in, 231–234
  biological constraints on, 243–245
  cognitive processes in, 245–246
  compared with classical conditioning, 234

defined, 229
discrimination in, 233, 234
distinguished from classical conditioning, 229
extinction in, 232, 234
of gender roles, 470
generalization in, 234
personality and, 490–491
schedules of reinforcement in, 235–237
shaping in, 232
in social skills training, 621
terminology of, 230–231
See also reinforcement
operational definition, 39, 48
operations, mental, 443
opiates, 203, 205
opinion surveys, 51
opponent process theory, of color vision, 139, 140
optic chiasm, 134, 135
optic disk, 130, 131, 132
optic nerve, 130, 133, 135
optical illusions, 150–154, 169–170
optimal foraging theory, 238–239
optimal level of arousal, 527
optimism, 419, 543–544
optimistic explanatory style, 544
oral stage, 485
organizational culture, A-19–A-20
organizational psychology, A-15, A-19–A-24
orgasm phase, of human sexual response, 401
oscilloscope, 78
ossicles, 156
osteoporosis, 546, 599
Otis-Lennon School Ability Test, 349
outcomes, alternative, 327–329
outgroups, 651, 683
outlining, 295
outpatient care, 635
oval window, 156
ovaries, 102
overcompensation, 532, 533
overconfidence effect, 299, 334
overeating, 599
overextension, 307
overextrapolation, 118–119
overlearning, 294
overregularization, 308, 312
ovulation, 391

P

pace of life, cultural differences in, 48–49, 53
Pagano, Bernard, 298
pain
  hypnosis for, 198–199
  perception of, 162–164
  stress and, 540
painting, principles of perception and, 166–171
palatability, hunger and, 386
pancreas, 102
pancultural viewpoint, 595
panic attacks, 568
panic disorder, 568, 571, 592
  treatment for, 624, 640
papillae, for taste, 160
Pappenheim, Bertha, 608
parahippocampal region, 288

parallel processing
in auditory cortex, 157
of information, 274–275
visual, 134
parallel-distributed processing model, 274–275, 289
paralysis, from spinal cord damage, 83
paranoid personality disorder, 590
paranoid schizophrenia, 584
parasympathetic division, 85, 529, 407
parathyroid glands, 102
paraventricular nucleus (PVN), 385, 386
parental investment theory, 112–113, 393
parent-child conflicts, 453, 459
parenthood
adjusting to, 458–459
happiness and, 417
parenting, pubertal timing and, 451–452
parents
affection of, 496–497
antisocial personality and, 594
attachment to, 435–439
caregiving styles of, 659–660
child's self-efficacy and, 494
disciplining by, 248–249
gender-role socialization and, 471
influence on children, 502, 517
parietal lobe, 95, 96, 162, 201
Parkinson's disease, 82, 460
paroxetine, 624
partial reinforcement, 235–236
participants, 40, 43
deception of, 62
parvocellular channel, 134
passionate love, 658–659, 661
passive behavior, 531
passive resistance, 550
pathology, 561
patient-provider communication, 549–550
patterns, perception of, 140–146
Pavlovian conditioning, 220
Paxil, 624
PBS: The Whole Child, 432
peacocks, 112
Pearson product-moment correlation, A-12
penis envy, 486, 489
pennies, 261
percentile scores, 343, 347, A-10–A-11
perception, 165
auditory, 157–158
of color, 137–140
context and, 146
contrast effects in, 172–173
cultural factors in, 163, 165
defined, 123
depth, 146–148
distinguished from sensation, 124
expectations and, 25–26
of forms and patterns, 140–146
of geographical slant, 148–150

Gestalt principles of, 143–144
of pain, 162–164
person, 25–26, 648–651
study of, 4
subjectivity of, 25–26, 141, 154, 165, 680
subliminal, 45–46, 127–128
tactile, 149
perceptual asymmetries, 100, 116
perceptual constancies, 150
perceptual hypotheses, 144–146, 153
perceptual-motor tasks, memory for, 290–291
perceptual set, 141, 145
perfectionism, 600
perform, pressure to, 526
performance
academic, 55–56, 352, 364–365, 537
group, 677–678
task, 403, 527, 534–535
performance appraisal, A-18–A-19
periaqueductal gray (PAG), 164
periodontal disease, 541
peripheral nerves, 86
peripheral nervous system, 84–85
persecution, delusions of, 584
person-centered theory, 496–497, 504–505
person perception, 25–26, 506–507, 647, 648–651
biases in, 650–651
cognitive schemas in, 649
evolutionary perspective on, 651
physical appearance and, 648–649, 651
of romantic partners, 658
stereotypes and, 649–650
subjectivity in, 650–651, 680, 681–682
person-situation controversy, 494–495
personal ads, 396
personal distress, as criterion for abnormal behavior, 563
personal unconscious, 486
personality
achievement motivation and, 403
Adler's individual approach to, 487–490
Bandura's view of, 491–494
behavioral genetics and, 501–502, 503
behavioral perspective on, 490–495, 504–505
biological perspective on, 500–503, 504–505
creativity and, 374
culture and, 507–509
defined, 478
eating disorders and, 600
evolutionary approach to, 502–503, 517
Eysenck's theory of, 500–501
five-factor model of, 479
Freud's psychoanalytic theory of, 480–486, 489, 504–505
gender differences in, 468
giftedness and, 356

happiness and, 418–419
heart disease and, 538–540
heredity and, 500–502, 503
hindsight and, 516–517
humanistic theories of, 495–499, 504–505
hypnotizability and, 198
Jung's analytic approach to, 486–487
longevity and, 544
Maslow's view of, 497–498
Mischel's view of, 494–495
multiple, 574–575
nature of, 478–480
observational learning and, 493–494
psychodynamic view of, 480–489
Rogers's theory of, 496–497, 504–505
of rooms, 492–493
social cognitive theory of, 491–494
somatoform disorders and, 573
stability in, 455–456
twin studies of, 106, 107
personality development, 462–465
Adler's view of, 488
in adolescence, 453–455, 464
in adulthood, 455–457, 464–465
family environment and, 502
Freud's view of, 484–486, 505
Rogers's view of, 497, 505
Skinner's view of, 490–491, 505
personality disorders, 589–591, 594
diagnostic problems with, 590
etiology of, 591, 594
prevalence of, 591
types of, 590
personality inventories, 60
Personality Project, 499
personality psychology, 19, 20
personality structure
Eysenck's view of, 500, 505
Freud's view of, 481, 505
Rogers's view of, 496–497, 505
Skinner's view of, 490, 505
personality tests, 342, 511–515
in employment screening, 353
projective, 514–515
self-report, 511–514
uses of, 511
personality traits, 439, 478–479, 500
of attractive people, 648
culture and, 502
evolutionary perspective on, 502–503, 517
of leaders, A-23–A-24
modern approaches to, 506–507
of self-actualizing persons, 498
stability of, 456
See also Big Five personality traits

personnel selection, 511, A-16–A-17
perspective, linear, 147, 151, 166
persuasion, 665–668
classical conditioning in, 256–257
elaboration likelihood model of, 670, 671
message factors in, 666–667
receiver factors in, 667–668
resistance to, 667
source factors in, 665–666
tactics of, 172–173, 685
pessimistic explanatory style, 544, 579
PET scans, 88–89
pharmaceutical industry, 626
phenomenological approach, 496
phenotype, 104
phenylketonuria, 355
phi phenomenon, 143
Philadelphia Zoo, 238
philosophy, psychology and, 2
phobias, 220, 222, 240–241, 568, 570
behavior therapy for, 620
conditioning of, 570
preparedness and, 245
treatment for, 640
phobic disorder, 568, 592
phonemes, 304–305
phonemic encoding, 263–264, 269, 272, 281, 282
phonological rehearsal loop, 269
physical appearance, person perception and, 648–649, 651
physical attractiveness
attraction and, 657
comparative effects and, 173
eating disorders and, 599, 600–601
happiness and, 417
mate selection and, 396
person perception and, 648–649, 651
of persuasive source, 666
physical development, 462–465
in adolescence, 449–455
in adulthood, 459–460
in childhood, 432–433
prenatal, 426–428
physiological arousal, emotions and, 406–408, 412–413
physiological needs, 497
physiological psychology, 19, 20
physiological recording, 40
physiology, psychology and, 2, 13
Picasso, Pablo, 167–168
pictorial depth cues, 147, 166, 167, 171
piecework, 236, 237
pineal gland, 102, 181
pinna, 156
pitch, of sounds, 154, 155, 157–158
pituitary gland, 92, 101, 102, 391, 450, 530
place theory, of auditory perception, 1577, 158

placebo effects, 59, 163, 205, 642
placenta, 427, 430
plagiarism, 278
plateau phase, of human sexual response, 401
Plato, 266
Playboy centerfolds, 600, 601
pleasure centers, in brain, 94
pleasure principle, 481
Poggendorff illusion, 151
pointillism, 166–167
polarization, group, 678
political attitudes, 479, 668
politics, classical conditioning in, 257
polyandry, 113
polygenic inheritance, 104, 107
polygraph, 407–408
polygyny, 113
pons, 91, 92, 186
Ponzo illusion, 150, 151
population, in research, 58, A-13
populations, evolution of, 109
pornography, 392, 394
Portrait of Dr. Gachet (van Gogh), 592
positive emotionality, 479
positive emotions, 527–528
positive illusions, 533–534
positive psychology movement, 406, 499, 537
positively skewed distribution, A-8
positron emission tomography (PET) scanning, 88–89
postconventional thinking, 447
posthypnotic suggestion, 199
postpartum stress, 458
postsynaptic neurons, 79, 81
postsynaptic potential (PSP), 79
posttraumatic stress disorder (PTSD), 535–536, 543
potassium ions, 77, 78
poverty, 473, 634
prenatal health care and, 430–431
power
in employment relationships, A-21–A-22
in groups, 676
practical intelligence, 352
practice, distributed vs. massed, 294, 295
Pragnanz, 143
preconscious, 481–482
preconventional thinking, 447
predators, avoiding, 111
prediction
correlation and, 55–56, A-12–A-13
as goal of scientific approach, 38
hypotheses as, 39
preferences, choices about, 323–324
prefrontal cortex, 95, 96, 97, 289, 289, 587
pregnancy, 426–431
drug use during, 429
health care during, 430–431
illness during, 430, 588
prejudice, 664, 681–683
attributions and, 682–683

defined, 681
discrimination and, 681, 682
racial, 681
stereotype vulnerability and, 364
stereotypes and, 681–682
premature birth, 430, 431
premises, 420
prenatal development, 426–431
antisocial personality and, 591
brain insults during, 587–588
course of, 427–428
environmental factors in, 428–431
homosexuality and, 399–400
hormones and, 102, 469
prenatal period, 426
preoperational period, 441, 442–443
preparedness, 245, 570
pressure (social), 671–672
choking under, 535
as source of stress, 526
pressure (tactile), 162
Pressure Inventory (PI), 526
presynaptic neurons, 79
prevalence, of psychological disorders, 566–567, 602–603
primary-process thinking, 481
Princess Diana, 425–426, 598
Principles of Psychology (James), 4
Priscilla, the Fastidious Pig, 232, 233
probabilities, 325–326
conjunctive, 602
cumulative, 602
erroneous reasoning about, 602–603
evaluating, 556
subjectivity of, 325, 327–328
probability
laws of, 56–57
statistical significance and, A-14
problem solving, 314–322, 369, 441, 443
aging and, 461
approaches to, 317–320
barriers to, 316–317
culture and, 320–322
defined, 314
dreams as, 196
positive emotions and, 527
problem space, 317
problems
changing representation of, 319–320
confronting, 534
types of, 314–315
problems in living, 562
procedural memory, 290–291, 461
procrastination, 549
productivity
aging and, 461
conscientiousness and, 479
creative, 374
in groups, 677
Profile of Mood States, 188
prognosis, 562
progressive relaxation, 212

projection, 483, 484
projective hypothesis, 514
projective tests, 402, 514–515
promiscuity, 662
prospective design, 581
prospective memory, 292–293
protein synthesis, 287
prototypes, 602, 603
proximal stimuli, 144–145, 154
proximity, as Gestalt principle, 143, 144
proximodistal development, 432
Prozac, 624, 625
pseudoforgetting, 280
pseudopatients, 564
psilocybin, 203, 204
Psych Central, 623
psyche, 2
psychiatric nurses, 611
psychiatrists, 20, 21, 610, 638, 639
psychiatry, 20
psychic reflexes, 220
psychoactive drugs, 202–209
psychoanalysis, 7, 608, 611–614, 628–629
psychoanalytic theory, 8, 10, 13, 480–486, 489
criticism of, 489, 517
cultural limits of, 507
of homosexuality, 398
psychodiagnosis, 564–566
psychodynamic activation, 128
psychodynamic theory
Adler's, 487–490
evaluation of, 489
Freud's, 480–486, 504–505
Jung's, 486–487
Psychological Abstracts, 67
psychological autopsies, 50
psychological contract, in employment, A-21–A-22
psychological disorders
Beck's view of, 615–616, 628
biomedical treatment for, 622–627, 628–629
classification of, 564–566
culture and, 595–596
empirically validated treatments for, 631
Freud's view of, 611–612, 628
institutional care for, 634–637
legal aspects of, 594–595
multifactorial causation of, 596–597
prevalence of, 566–567, 602–603
recovery from, 617–618
Rogers's view of, 614, 628
stereotypes about, 564
stress and, 536–537
testing for, 512
Psychological Screening Inventory (PSI), 346
psychological tests (testing), 23, 341, A-10
achievement, 342
aptitude, 342, 343
of creativity, 373–374
defined, 342
for employment, A-17
history of, 11
personality, 342
reliability of, 344

standardization of, 342–343
types of, 342
validity of, 344–346
See also intelligence tests
psychologists, 50, 610
work settings for, 19
psychology
applied, 11, 12, 20, 38, A-15–A-26
cognitive revolution in, 303-304
defined, 18
diversity of, 1
empirical nature of, 22
history of, 2–18
important figures in, 9
industrial, A-15–A-19
nature of, 1–2
organizational, A-15, A-19–A-24
origins of word, 2
practicality of, 1
as profession, 11–12, 20
professionalization of, 12
research areas in, 19–20
schools of thought in, 4–11
scientific approach to, 37–42
sociohistorical context for, 22–23
specialization areas in, 19, 20
as undergraduate major, 18, 19
women pioneers in, 5
psychometrics, 19, 20
Psychology Applied to Work (Muchinsky), A-26
psychopharmacotherapy, 623, 624
psychophysical scaling, 125–126
psychophysics, 124–128
psychosexual stages, 484–486
psychosocial crises, 439
psychosomatic disorders, 538, 571
psychotherapy, 608
benefits of, 618
blending approaches to, 631–633
bogus, 643
clients for, 609
cost of, 639
cultural factors in, 633–634
eclecticism in, 633
effectiveness of, 617–618, 622, 631, 640, 642–643
elements of, 608–611
empirically validated treatments in, 631
expectations for, 642
group, 616–617
interpersonal, 632
misconceptions about, 607–608
practitioners of, 609–611
psychoanalytic approach to, 611–614
psychodynamic approaches to, 613–614
realistic expectations for, 641
settings for, 638
sexual exploitation in, 639
types of, 608–609
utilization rates for, 609
willingness to seek, 609
See also therapists
psychoticism, 500

PsychWeb, 199
PsycINFO, 41, 66, 67–69
PSYCLine, 50
puberty, 102, 450, 451
pubescence, 449
punctuality, culture and, 24
punishment, 491
as disciplinary measure, 241–242, 248–249, 485
in operant conditioning, 241–243
in self-modification programs, 255
physical, 242, 248–249
pupil, 130, 131
purity
of light waves, 129, 137
of sound waves, 154, 155
push vs. pull theories, 383

Q

quackery, 643
quail, 224–225
Queer Resources Directory, 399
questionnaires, 40, 59
questions
framing of, 334–335
on intelligence tests, 349
quetiapine, 624

R

raccoons, 244
race, IQ scores and, 362–366
racial stereotypes, 681–682, 683
racism, 681
radar screens, signal detection of, 126
radical behaviorism, 490, 495
random assignment, 44
rape, 392
rapid eye movements, 177, 183, 184
ratio schedules, 236, 237
rational thinking, 552–553
rational-emotive therapy, 552, 615, 640
rationality, bounded, 323, 328
rationalization, 483
reaction formation, 483, 484
reaction range, 361
reaction time, 367–368
reading
form perception and, 142
improving, 29
Reagan, Ronald, 71, 564
reality monitoring, 278
reality principle, 481
reasoning, 441
in animals, 247
circular, 215
errors in, 329, 332–335
moral, 446–448
prefrontal lobe and, 97
reasons, irrelevant, 421
rebound insomnia, 191
recall, 279
eyewitness, 276, 277, 298–299
flashbulb memories and, 270–271
imagery and, 265
improving, 294
receiver factors, in persuasion, 667–668
receptive fields
of cells in visual cortex, 136
for cones, 140

for touch, 162
of visual cells, 133
receptor sites, 79, 80, 81, 206
receptors
for hearing, 156, 157
for kinesthesis, 164
for smell, 161
in skin, 162
for taste, 159
for vestibular sense, 164
for vision, 131, 132, 138–140
recessive gene, 103–104
reciprocal determinism, 491–492
reciprocity effects, 658
reciprocity norm, 257, 685
recognition, 279–280
recognition heuristic, 330
reconstructive memory processes, 276–277, 278, 298
recovery, spontaneous, 226
recovery rate, from psychological disorders, 617–618
recruitment, employment, A-15–A-16
references, in journal articles, 69
reflexes, 91
conditioned, 221, 287
"psychic," 220
refractory period,
in neurons, 77, 78
in sexual response, 401
regression, 483, 484
regression toward the mean, 642–643
rehearsal, 268, 294
rehearsal loop, 269
reification, 377
reinforcement, 232, 234–235
attitudes and, 668
conditioned, 235
continuous, 235
defined, 230
delayed, 235
of gender-appropriate behavior, 470
language learning and, 312
negative, 239–240, 241, 253, 570
observational learning, 248
positive, 239
response-outcome relations and, 247
schedules of, 235–237
in self-modification programs, 254–255
reinforcement contingencies, 230–231, 247, 254, 494
rejection, 581, 659
fear of, 402, 403
relationship harmony, 418
relationships, close, 657–662
relative size, 147, 166
relativistic viewpoint, 595
relativity
contrast effects and, 172–173
of well-being, 419
relaxation, 212
for insomnia, 192
meditation and, 202
for stress, 554
in systematic desensitization, 620
relearning, 280
relevance, memory and, 266

Credits

Contents **xxxiii:** © Kevin R. Morris/CORBIS; **xxiv:** © Digital Vision/Getty Images; **xxv:** © Francisco Cruz/SuperStock; **xxvi:** © Diana Ong/SuperStock; **xxvii:** © Keren Su/CORBIS; **xxviii:** © Katy Kootz/Mira.com. All rights reserved.; **xxix:** © A. Woolfitt/Robert Harding Picture Library, London; **xxx:** © Sally Brown/Index Stock Imagery; **xxxi:** © Adalberto Rios Szalay/Sexto Sol/PhotoDisc-Getty Images; **xxxii:** © Gary Buss/Taxi-Getty Images; **xxxiii:** © Adam Crowley/PhotoDisc-Getty Images; **xxxiv:** © Bruce Stoddard/Taxi-Getty Images; **xxxv:** © Kevin R. Morris/CORBIS; **xxxvi:** © Ed Freeman/Image Bank-Getty Images; **xxxvii:** © Kit Kittle/CORBIS; **xxxviii:** © Scott Barlow, Inc./SuperStock.

Chapter 1 **xlv:** © Kevin R. Morris/CORBIS; **1:** © Kevin R. Morris/CORBIS; **2:** (top left) © 2002 AP/Wide World Photos; **2:** (top right) © Tom Rosenthal/SuperStock; **4:** Archives of the History of American Psychology, University of Akron, Akron, Ohio; **5:** (all) Archives of the History of American Psychology, University of Akron, Akron, Ohio; **8:** Courtesy of the Clark University Archives; **9:** Copyright © 1971 Time Inc. Reprinted by permission; **10:** (both) Archives of the History of American Psychology University of Akron, Akron, Ohio; **16:** (telephone) Culver Pictures, Inc., (Wundt & others) Archives of the History of American Psychology, University of Akron, Akron, Ohio, Compliments of Clark University, Worcester, Massachusetts, (auto) Culver Pictures, Inc, (Washburn) Courtesy of the Archives of the History of American Psychology, University of Akron, Akron, Ohio, (airplane) Stock Montage, Inc., (James book) Courtesy of the Archives of the History of American Psychology, University of Akron, Akron, Ohio, (Hollingworth) Courtesy of the Archives of the History of American Psychology, University of Akron, Akron, Ohio, (Pavlov lab) Bettmann-CORBIS, (suffragettes) Culver Pictures, Inc., (lightbulb) Culver Pictures, Inc., (intelligence test) CORBIS-Bettmann; **17:** (atomic bomb) Culver Pictures, Inc., (Maccoby) Stan-

ford University News Service, (shuttle) NASA, (Kenneth Clark) © CORBIS-Bettmann, (therapy) © Karen Preuss from *Life Time: A New Image of Aging*, published by Unity Press, Santa Cruz, California, 1978, (TV viewing) Culver Pictures, Inc., (Erikson) AP/Wide World Photos, (Vietnam) AP/Wide World Photos, (brain) Wadsworth Collection; **19:** © Jim Cummins/CORBIS; **23:** © Bob Daemmrich/Stock, Boston; **25:** Preferred Stock and Gazelle Technologies; **28:** © Paul A. Souders/CORBIS.

Chapter 2 **36:** © Digital Vision/Getty Images; **37:** © Digital Vision/Getty Images; **49:** (left) © Rafael Macia/Photo Researchers, Inc.; **49:** (right) © Carl & Ann Purcell/CORBIS; **51:** © David Young-Wolff/PhotoEdit; **59:** © Spencer Grant/PhotoEdit; **61:** Courtesy of Robert Rosenthal; **63:** © James J. Broderick/International Stock; **63:** Yale University; **66:** Craig McClain; **71:** (left) © Wally McNamee/CORBIS; **71:** (right) © Douglas Kirkland/CORBIS.

Chapter 3 **74:** © Francisco Cruz/SuperStock; **75:** © Francisco Cruz/SuperStock; **82:** (bottom) © Dan McCoy/Rainbow; **82:** (top) © 1991 Analisa Kraft; **87:** © Science Photo Library/Photo Researchers, Inc.; **88:** (bottom left) © Alvis Upitis/Image Bank-Getty Images; **88:** (bottom right) © Dan McCoy/Rainbow; **89:** © Wellcome Dept of Cognitive Neurology/Science Photo Library/Photo Researchers, Inc.; **89:** (bottom left) © ISM-Sovereign/PhotoTake; **89:** (bottom right) Courtesy and by permission of Dr. Jack Belliveau, Chief, NMR, MGH; **92:** Wadsworth Collection; **95:** Wadsworth Collection; **99:** Courtesy of Roger Sperry; **103:** (both) © Laura Dwight; **106:** (top right) © Marina Jefferson/Taxi-Getty Images; **106:** (center right) © Mary Kate Denny/PhotoEdit; **108:** The Pennsylvania State University Center for Development and Health Genetics; **109:** CORBIS-Bettmann; **110:** John Dominis, Life Magazine © Time Inc.; **111:** (left) Courtesy of John Alcock; **111:** (right) © Mitch Reardon/National Audubon Society Collection/Photo Researchers, Inc.; **113:** © C. K. Lorenz/Photo Researchers, Inc.

Chapter 4 **122:** © Diana Ong/SuperStock; **123:** (center right) © Diane Padys/FPG International-Getty Images; **123:** (top right) © Diana Ong/SuperStock; **125:** Archives of the History of American Psychology, University of Akron, Akron, Ohio; **126:** © Fernado Serna/CORBIS; **127:** Wilson Bryan Key/Mediaprobe, Inc.; **131:** Craig McClain; **135:** © Ira Wyman/CORBIS-Sygma; **143:** Archives of the History of American Psychology, University of Akron,

Akron, Ohio; **147:** (bottom center) © John Elk III/Stock, Boston; **147:** (center) © Christopher Talbot Frank; **147:** (center left) © Peter Turner/Image Bank-Getty Images; **147:** (bottom right) U.S. Department of Energy; **147:** (center right) © Deborah Davis/PhotoEdit; **147:** (bottom left) © Deborah Davis/PhotoEdit; **148:** van Gogh, Vincent, *Corridor in the Asylum* (1889), gouache and watercolor, 24-3/8 x 18-1/2 inches (61.5 x 47 cm). Metropolitan Museum of Art. Bequest of Abby Aldrich Rockefeller, 1948.(48.190.2) Photograph © 1998 The Metropolitan Museum of Art.; **152:** © Wayne Weiten; **153:** (top right) © N. R. Rowan/The Image Works; **153:** (bottom right) © Peter Menzel/Stock, Boston; **155:** © Robert Harding Picture Library; **157:** Stock Montage, Inc.; **160:** (bottom left) © Malcolm S. Kirk; **160:** (bottom center) © Guy Mary-Rousseliere/Catholic Mission, Northwest, Canada; **160:** (bottom right) © Danielle Pellegrini/Science Source/Photo Researchers, Inc.; **161:** Courtesy of the Yale School of Medicine; **166:** *Maestro della cattura di Cristo, Cattura di Cristo*, parte centrale, Assisi, S. Francisco, Scala/Art Resource, New York; **167:** (top) *Brera Predica di S. Marco Pinacoteca*, by Gentile and Giovanni Belini in Egitto Scala/Art Resource, New York; **167:** (bottom) Monet, Claude, *Palazzo da Mula, Venice* 1908. Photo by Richard Carafelli. Chester Dale Collection, © 2000 Board of Trustees, National Gallery of Art; **168:** (top-both) Georges Seurat, French, 1859-1891, *Sunday Afternoon on the Island of La Grande Jatte*, (and detail) oil on canvas, 1884–1886, 207.6 x 308 cm, Helen Birch Bartlett Memorial Collection, 1926.224, © 1990 The Art Institute of Chicago, all rights reserved; **168:** (bottom) Pablo Picasso, *Violin and Grapes, Céret and Sorgues* (spring-early fall 1912), oil on canvas, 20 x 24 inches (50.6 x 61 cm), collection, The Museum of Modern Art, New York, Mrs. David M. Levy Bequest. © 2000 Estate of Pablo Picasso/Artists Rights Society (ARS), New York; **169:** (left) Duchamp, Marcel, 1912, "Nude Descending a Staircase, No. 2," oil on canvas, 58" x 35". Philadelphia Museum of Art: Louise and Walter Arensburg Collection, # '50-134-69. Reproduced by permission. © 2000 Artists Rights Society (ARS), New York/ADAGP, Paris/Estate of Marcel Duchamp.; **169:** (right) Dali, Salvador, *The Hallucinogenic Toreador* (1969-70), oil on canvas, 157x119 inches(398.7 x 302.3 cm) Collection of The Salvador Dali Museum, St. Petersburg, Florida, Copyright © 2000 The Salvador Dali Museum, Inc. © 2000 Foundation Gala-Salvador Dali/VEGAP/Artists Rights Society (ARS), New York; **170:** (both) Courtesy of Haags Gemeentemuseum,

© 1988 M. C. Escher, Cordon Art, Baarn; **171:** (top left) Vasarely, Victor: *Vega-Tek*. Wool Aubusson tapestry. 1969. Copyright Art Resource, NY Private Collection. © 2000 Artists Rights Society (ARS), New York/ADAGP, Paris; **171:** (top left) Magritte, Rene, *Les Promenades d'Euclide*, The Minneapolis Institute of Arts, The William Hood Dunwoody Fund. Copyright © 2000 Charly Herscovic, Brussels/Artists Rights Society (ARS) New York.

Chapter 5 **176:** © Keren Su/CORBIS; **177:** © Keren Su/CORBIS; **182:** © Andrew Holmgren/Peter Arnold, Inc.; **184:** Courtesy of William Dement; **190:** © Joseph Sohm/ChromoSohm-CORBIS; **195:** National Library of Medicine; **196:** Rush Presbyterian St. Luke's Medical Center; **199:** Biomedical Research Foundation; **199:** (bottom) AP/Wide World Photos; **200:** Courtesy of Ernest R. Hilgard; **204:** © Paul A. Souders/CORBIS; **208:** © Henry Diltz/CORBIS; **211:** © Topham/The Image Works.

Chapter 6 **218:** © Katy Kootz/Mira.com. All rights reserved; **219:** © Katy Kootz/Mira.com. All rights reserved; **220:** © Corbis-Bettmann; **221:** Sovfoto/Eastfoto; **223:** (bottom left) Craig McClain; **223:** (top) © Bill Aron/PhotoEdit; **227:** (both) Archives of the History of American Psychology, University of Akron, Akron, Ohio; **231:** © Richard Wood/Index Stock Imagery; **232:** Courtesy of B. F. Skinner; **233:** (left) Courtesy of Animal Behavior Enterprises, Inc.; **233:** (right) © Gerald Davis by permission of Karen Davis; **236:** (bottom left) © David Woods/CORBIS-The Stock Market; **236:** (bottom right) © Rick Doyle/Uniphoto-PICTOR; **236:** (top left) © Julian Cotton/International Stock; **236:** (top right) © David Falconer/Folio, Inc.; **238:** (bottom left) © Art Wolfe/Photo Researchers, Inc.; **238:** (bottom right) © Stephen J. Krasemann/DRK Photo; **242:** © Jonathan Nourok/PhotoEdit; **244:** Courtesy of John Garcia; **245:** (right) © John Gerlach/Animals, Animals/Earth Science; **245:** (left) Tom McCarthy/SKA; **247:** University of Pennsylvania; **248:** Courtesy of Albert Bandura; **249:** (top right) © J. Markham/Bruce Coleman, Inc.; **249:** (top left) © Laura Dwight/CORBIS; **251:** CORBIS-Bettmann; **251:** (top right) Archives of the History of American Psychology, University of Akron, Akron, Ohio; **251:** (center left) © Gerald Davis by permission of Karen Davis; **251:** (center right) © David Falconer/Folio, Inc.; **251:** (bottom left) © J. Markham/Bruce Coleman, Inc.; **251:** (bottom right) © Laura Dwight/CORBIS; **253:** © Donna Day/Stone-Getty Images; **256:** ©

Robert Harding Picture Library; **257:** © C. J. Gunther/Sipa Press.

Chapter 7   260: © A. Woolfitt/Robert Harding Picture Library, London; **261:** © A. Woolfitt/Robert Harding Picture Library, London; **266:** © Wayne Weiten; **269:** Courtesy of George Miller; **270:** © 2002 AP/Wide World Photos; **271:** © 2002 AP/Wide World Photos; **273:** Courtesy of W. F. Brewer. Brewer, W. F., and Treyens, J. C., "Role of schemata in memory of places," Cognitive Psychology, 1981, 13, 207–230; **277:** University of Washington News and Information Office; **278:** (top left) Denise Applewhite/Communications Department, Princeton University; **278:** (bottom) © Seth Resnick-CORBIS; **280:** Wellcome Institute for the History of Medicine, London; **284:** AP/Wide World Photos; **287:** Wadsworth Collection; **289:** Montreal Neurological Institute; **290:** Courtesy of Endel Tulving; **291:** © 2002 AP/Wide World Photos; **298:** (both) CORBIS/Bettmann-UPI; **298:** CORBIS/Bettmann-UPI; **299:** © Jeff Cadge/Image Bank-Getty Images.

Chapter 8   302: © Sally Brown/Index Stock Imagery; **303:** (bottom right) Carnegie-Mellon University; **303:** (top right) © Sally Brown/Index Stock Imagery; **307:** Courtesy of Wayne Weiten; **309:** © Michael Newman/PhotoEdit; **310:** © Michael Nichols/Magnum Photos; **311:** (top right) Courtesy of Sue Savage-Rumbaugh, GSU Language Research Center; **311:** (center right) MIT photo by Donna Coveney, courtesy of Steven Pinker; **312:** MIT photo by Donna Coveney/MIT News Office; **313:** © Wayne R Bilenduke/Stone-Getty Images; **321:** Craig McClain; **322:** Craig McClain; **324:** © Arthur Tilley/Taxi-Getty Images; **325:** Courtesy of Daniel Kahneman; **326:** (top) Stanford University News and Publication Service; **329:** (right-both) Courtesy of Leda Cosmides & John Tooby; **329:** Courtesy of Leda Cosmides & John Tooby **330:** Courtesy of Gerd Gigerenzer;; **333:** © 2002 AP/Wide World Photos; **336:** © Les Stone/CORBIS-Sygma; **337:** © Reza/CORBIS-Sygma.

Chapter 9   340: © Adalberto Rios Szalay/Sexto Sol/PhotoDisc-Getty Images; **341:** (bottom right) © Tony Freeman/PhotoEdit; **341:** (top right) © Adalberto Rios Szalay/Sexto Sol/PhotoDisc-Getty Images; **347:** Wellcome Institute for the History of Medicine, London; **347:** (bottom right) CORBIS-Bettmann; **348:** (bottom right) © Lew Merrim; **348:** (top left) Archives of the History of American Psychology, University of Akron, Akron, Ohio; **348:** (bottom left) Archives of the History of American Psychology, University of Akron, Akron, Ohio; **352:** (bottom left) © 2002 AP/Wide World Photos; **352:** (bottom center) © Spencer Platt/Getty Images; **352:** (bottom right) © Rufus F.

Folkks/CORBIS; **356:** (left) © Topham/The Image Works; **356:** Courtesy of Ellen Winner; **360:** Courtesy of Sandra Scarr; **362:** Courtesy of Arthur R. Jensen; **364:** Department of Psychology, Stanford University; **369:** Michael Marsland/Yale University; **370:** Courtesy of Howard Gardner, photo © Jay Gardner; **375:** (bottom right) Rembrandt, Harmensz, van Rijn, *Self-Portrait with Beard.* Museo de Arte, Sao Paulo, Brazil. Giraudon/Art Resource, NY; **375:** (bottom right) Pomerian, 16th cent. *Portrait of Nicolas Copernicus.* Museum, Torun, Poland. Erich Lessing/Art Resource, NY **375:** (bottom center) Delacroix, Eugene, *Portrait of Chopin,* Louvre, Paris: Giraudon/Art Resource, NY; **376:** AP/Wide World Photos; **377:** Cover of *Naked in Cyberspace* by Carole A. Lane: Reproduced by courtesy and permission of Information Today, Inc., Medford, NJ.

Chapter 10   380: © Gary Buss/Taxi-Getty Images; **381:** (center right) Copyright © by Klev Schoening; **381:** (top right) © Gary Buss/Taxi-Getty Images; **384:** © Yoav Levy/PhotoTake; **386:** (top left) Courtesy of Judith Rodin; **386:** (bottom right) © Jeff Greenberg/PhotoEdit; **387:** (both) © Michael Freeman/Aurora Photos; **387:** © Michael Freeman/Aurora Photos; **395:** © George DeSota/Newsmakers-Getty Images; **396:** Courtesy of David M. Buss; **399:** © Amy Etra/PhotoEdit; **401:** © John Chaisson/Gamma Liason-Getty Images; **403:** Courtesy of David C. McClelland **404:** © Getty Images; **406:** © Bob Dammerich/The Image Works; **407:** © Mark C. Burnett/Stock, Boston; **408:** Courtesy of Joseph LeDoux, New York University; **408:** (snake) © C. H. Wooley; **411:** From Unmasking the Face, © 1975 by Paul Ekman, photograph courtesy of Paul Ekman; **413:** © Bill Apple, courtesy of Stanley Schachter; **417:** © Carlos Alvarez/Getty Images.

Chapter 11   424: © Adam Crowley/PhotoDisc-Getty Images; **425:** (bottom) © Tim Graham/CORBIS; **425:** (top right) © Adam Crowley/PhotoDisc-Getty Images; **427:** (top left) © Petit Format/Science Source/Photo Researchers, Inc.; **427:** (bottom left) © Petit Format/Guigoz/Science Source/Photo Researchers, Inc.; **427:** (right) © Petit Format/Nestle/Science Source/Photo Researchers, Inc.; **430:** Courtesy of Wayne Weiten; **433:** © Konner/AnthroPhoto; **436:** Erik Hesse; **437:** © David Young-Woff/PhotoEdit; **440:** (top left) © AP/Wide World Photos; **440:** (right) © Bill Bachman/PhotoEdit; **442:** © Yves de Braine/Black Star; **447:** Courtesy of Harvard University News Office; **449:** © Tony Freeman/PhotoEdit; **453:** Paul Conklin/PhotoEdit; **459:** © Alan Becker/Image Bank-Getty Images; **461:** Courtesy of Wayne Weiten; **462:** © George Silver/The Stock Market-CORBIS; **463:** (bottom left) © David Young-Wolff/PhotoEdit; **463:** (bottom right) © Jon Feingersh/

The Stock Market-CORBIS; **464:** (bottom left) © David Young-Wolff/PhotoEdit; **464:** (bottom right) © Jeffry W. Myers/Stock, Boston; **465:** (bottom left) © Tony Freeman/PhotoEdit; **465:** (bottom right) © John Henley/The Stock Market-CORBIS; **473:** Digital Vision-Getty Images.

Chapter 12   476: © Bruce Stoddard/Taxi-Getty Images; **477:** (bottom) © 2002 AP/Wide World Photos; **477:** (top right) © Bruce Stoddard/Taxi-Getty Images; **480:** National Library of Medicine; **482:** © Peter Aprahamian/CORBIS; **485:** © Michael Newman/PhotoEdit; **486:** Culver Pictures, Inc.; **487:** (bottom center) Images from C. G. Jung Bild Und Wort, © Walter-Verlag AG, Olten, Switzerland, 1977; **487:** (right) Culver Pictures, Inc.; **488:** Bettmann/CORBIS; **491:** Courtesy of B.F. Skinner; **491:** (bottom left) © Jacobs Stock Photography/CORBIS; **491:** (bottom right) Courtesy of Professor Albert Bandura; **494:** University photographer Joe Pineiro, Columbia University; **496:** Courtesy of Center for Studies of the Person; **497:** Wadsworth Collection; **500:** Mark Gerson, FPIPP, London, courtesy of Hans Eysenck; **501:** © Daly & Newton/Stone-Getty Images; **503:** Courtesy of David M. Buss; **504:** (Freud's couch) © Peter Aprahamian/CORBIS; **504:** (Lab rat) © Richard Wood/Index Stock; **504:** (Therapy) © Tom Stewart/CORBIS; **504:** (Twins) © Daly & Newton/Stone-Getty Images; **505:** (Potty training) © Michael Newman/PhotoEdit; **505:** (Women) © Jacobs Stock Photography/CORBIS; **505:** (Father) © Stephanie Rausser/Taxi-Getty Images; **508:** (top left) Photo and Campus Services, University of Michigan; **508:** (center left) Courtesy of Shinobu Kitayama; **508:** (bottom left) © Keren Su/Stone-Getty Images; **510:** Salvador Dali, *Soft Construction with Boiled Beans . . . .* Photo by Graydon Wood, 1995, Philadelphia Museum of Art: The Louise and Walter Arensberg Collection. © 2000 Foundation Gala-Salvador Dali/VEGAP/Artists Rights Society (ARS), New York; **515:** (bottom) © Laura Dwight/PhotoEdit; **515:** (top) Reprinted by permission of the publishers from Henry A. Murray, Thematic Apperception Test, Cambridge, Mass.: Harvard University Press, Copyright © 1943 by The President and Fellows of Harvard College, © 1971 by Henry A. Murray; **516:** © 2002 AP/Wide World Photos.

Chapter 13   520: © Kevin R. Morris/CORBIS; **521:** © Kevin R. Morris/CORBIS; **522:** Courtesy of Richard S. Lazarus; **529:** © Yousuf Karsh/Hans Selve/Woodfin Camp & Associates; **531:** Courtesy of Albert Ellis; **532:** © Rob Meinychuk/PhotoDisc-Getty Images; **533:** Courtesy of Shelly Taylor; **537:** © Chin Allan/CORBIS Sygma; **539:** Digital Vision/Getty Images; **544:** Courtesy of Martin E. P. Seligman; **545:**

© Bonnie Kamin/PhotoEdit; **549:** © Ryan McVay/PhotoDisc-Getty Images; **550:** Steve Walag, University of California, Riverside; **554:** © Paul Francis Photo; **555:** (right) © Michael Newman/PhotoEdit; **555:** (left) © Paul Francis Photo; **555:** (center) © C. H. Wooley.

Chapter 14   560: © Ed Freeman/Image Bank-Getty Images; **561:** © Ed Freeman/Image Bank-Getty Images; **562:** (bottom left) Courtesy of Thomas Szasz; **562:** (top) Culver Pictures, Inc.; **562:** (center) *St. Catherine of Siena Exorcising a Possessed Woman,* c. 1500–1510. Girolamo Di Benvenuto. Denver Art Museum Collection, Gift of Samuel H. Kress Foundation Collection, 1961.171 © Denver Art Museum 2003; **563:** © 2002 AP/Wide World Photos; **564:** Stanford University News Service; **569:** (top) CORBIS-Bettmann; **569:** (center right) © 2002 AP/Wide World Photos; **577:** (top left) © Frazer Harrison/Getty Images; **577:** (top right) © 2002 AP/Wide World Photos; **579:** Courtesy of Susan Nolen-Hoeksema; **584:** Courtesy of Nancy Andreasen; **585:** © Reuters New Media Inc./CORBIS; **592:** (top left) Munch, Edvard: *The Scream.* National Gallery, Oslo, Norway/Art Resource/NY; **592:** (center left) van Gogh, Vincent: *Portrait of Dr. Gachet.* Musee d'Orsay, Paris. Erich Lessing/Art Resource, NY **592:** (bottom left) Derek Bayes, *Life Magazine,* © Time, Inc.; **592:** (top right) CORBIS-Bettmann; **592:** (center right) © Frazer Harrison/Getty Images; **592:** (bottom right) © Reuters News Media, Inc./CORBIS; **598:** (left) © T. Grahm/CORBIS-Sygma; **598:** (center) © Bonnie Schiffman; **598:** (right) © *Kansas City Star*/Gamma Liaison-Getty Images; **600:** © 2002 AP/Wide World Photos; **603:** © Trippett/Sipa Press.

Chapter 15   606: © Kit Kittle/CORBIS; **607:** Warner Bros./Shooting Star; **607:** © Kit Kittle/CORBIS; **608:** Mary Evans/Sigmund Freud Copyrights; **612:** National Library of Medicine; **613:** © Bruce Ayres/Stone-Getty Images; **614:** Courtesy of Center for Studies of the Person; **615:** (top) © Zigy Kaluzny/Stone-Getty Images; **615:** (bottom right) Courtesy of Aaron T. Beck; **617:** © Bob Daemmrich/The Image Works; **620:** Courtesy of Dr. Joseph Wolpe; **620:** © Steve McCarroll; **621:** © Robert Harding Picture Library; **626:** © W & D McIntyre/Photo Researchers, Inc.; **628:** National Library of Medicine; **628:** (top center) Courtesy of Center for Studies of the Person; **628:** (bottom center) Courtesy of Aaron T. Beck; **628:** (bottom) Courtesy of Dr. Joseph Wolpe; **629:** (group therapy) © Bob Daemmrich/The Image Works; **629:** (female client) © Zigy Kaluzny/Stone-Getty Images; **629:** (woman w/snake) © Steve McCarroll; **629:** (ECT) © W & D McIntyre/Photo Researchers, Inc.; **629:** (capsules) PhotoDisc, Inc.; **635:** (inset) Detail of painting in Harrisburg State Hospital, photo by Ken

Smith/LLR Collection; **635:** (right) Culver Pictures, Inc.; **639:** (top) © Tom McCarthy/SKA; **639:** (bottom) © Tom Stewart/CORBIS; **642:** © International Stock/Robert Harding Picture Library; **643:** © Tony Freeman/PhotoEdit.

Chapter 16 646: © Scott Barlow, Inc./SuperStock; **647:** © Scott Barlow, Inc./SuperStock; **649:** © Andrew Wakeford/PhotoDisc-Getty Images; **652:** University of Kansas; **654:** © Steve Raymer/CORBIS; **657:** © Alamy Images; **658:** Courtesy of Ellen Berscheid; **659:** Courtesy of Elaine Hatfield; **661:** © Earl & Nazima Kowalt/CORBIS; **664:** © 2002 Wide World Photos; **668:** © Photo Courtesy of ABC/Getty Images; **669:** Photo by Karen Zabulon, © 1982 courtesy of New School for Social Research, by permission of Trudy Festinger; **672:** Courtesy of Solomon Asch; **673:** Photos copyright © 1965 by Stanley Milgram. From the film *Obedience*, distributed by The Pennsylvania State University. Obedience, distributed by The Pennsylvania State University. Reprinted by permission of Alexandra Milgram; **674:** Photo by Eric Kroll, courtesy of the Alexandra Milgram.

Appendix A-16: © Michael Newman/PhotoEdit; **A-20:** © 2002 AP/Wide World Photos; **A-25:** © 2002 AP/Wide World Photos.

Figure Credits

Chapter 1 9: Figure 1.3: Adapted from Korn, J. H., Davis, R., & Davis, S. F. (1991) "Historians' and Chairpersons' Judgments of Eminence Among Psychologists," [with data from "Rankings of the Most Notable Psychologists by Department Chairpersons," by R. E. Estes, M. L. Coston & G. P Fournet, 1990, unpublished manuscript.], *American Psychologist, 46* (7), 789–792. Copyright © 1991 by the American Psychological Association. Reprinted by permission of the author. **13:** Figure 1.4: Adapted from Robins, E. W., Gosling, S. D., & Craik, K. H. (1999) "An Empirical Analysis of Trends in Psychology," *American Psychologist, 54* (2), 117–128. Copyright © 1999 by the American Psychological Association. Reprinted by permission of the author. **18:** Figure 1.6: Adapted from data from the American Psychological Association by permission **25:** Figure 1.11: Description from H. H. Kelley (1950) "The Warm-Cold Variable in First Impressions of Persons," *Journal of Personality, 8,* 431–439. Copyright © 1950 by the Ecological Society of America. Reprinted by permission. **28:** Figure 1.13: From questionnaire "Managing Time Means Managing Yourself," by LeBoeuf, 1980, p. 45. *Business Horizons Magazine,* 1980, 23 (1) February, Table 3. Reprinted with permission from Business Horizons. Copyright © 1980 by the Board of Trustees at of Indiana University, Kelley School of Business. **30:** Figure 1.14:

Adapted from *The Psychology of College Success: A Dynamic Approach* by H.C. Lindgren, 1969. John Wiley & Sons. Copyright © 1969 by Henry Clay Lindgren. Adapted by permission of H.C. Lindgren. **30:** Figure 1.15: Adapted from "Staying With Initial Answers on Objective Tests: Is It a Myth?," L.T. Benjamin, Jr., T.A. Cavell & W. R. Shallenberger III, 1984, *Teaching of Psychology, 11* (3), 133–141. Lawrence Erlbaum Associates, Inc. **30:** Figure 1.16: Adapted from "Staying With Initial Answers on Objective Tests: Is It a Myth?," by L.T. Benjamin, Jr., T.A. Cavell & W. R. Shallenberger III, 1984, *Teaching of Psychology, 11* (3), 133–141. Lawrence Erlbaum Associates, Inc. **33:** Figure 1.17: From Form AA, 1962, *Identical Blocks,* by R. E. Stafford and H. Gullikson.

Chapter 2 41: Figure 2.3: Data from Cole, S. W., Taylor, M. E., & Visscher, B.R., "Elevated Physical Health Risk Among Gay Men Who Conceal Their Homosexual Identity," 1996, *Health Psychology, 15,* 243–251. **46:** Figure 2.7: Adapted from Greenwald, A. G., Spangenberg, E. R., Pratkanis, A. R., & Eskenazi, J. (1991). "Double-blind Tests of Subliminal Self-help Audiotapes," *Psychological Science, 2,* 119–122. Copyright © 1991 by Cambridge University Press. Reprinted by permission. **46:** Figure 2.8: Adapted from Greenwald, A. G., Spangenberg, E. R., Pratkanis, A. R., & Eskenazi, J. (1991). Double-blind Tests of Subliminal Self-help Audiotapes. *Psychological Science, 2,* 119–122. Copyright © 1991 by Cambridge University Press. Reprinted by permission.; **49:** Table 2.2: Adapted from Levine, R. V., and Norenzayan, A., "The Pace of Life in 31 Countries", 1999, *Journal of Cross-Cultural Psychology, 30* (2), 178–205. Copyright © 1999 Sage Publications. Reprinted by permission.; **50:** Figure 2.9: From Greenfeld, D. (1985). *The Psychotic Patient: Medication and Psychotherapy,* New York: The Free Press. Copyright © 1985 by David Greenfeld. Reprinted by permission of the author.; **67:** Figure 2.19: Sample record reprinted with permission of the American Psychological Association, publisher of the PsycINFO (r) database. Copyright © 1887–present, American Psychological Association. All rights reserved. For more information contact psycinfo. apa.org.; **68:** Figure 2.20: Sample record reprinted with permission of the American Psychological Association, publisher of PsycINFO(R) Database (Copyright 1887–present by the American Psychological Association). All rights reserved. For more information contact psycinfo@apa.org.

Chapter 3 81: Figure 3.5: Data based on Huttenlocher, P. R. (1994). "Synaptogenesis in Human Cerebral Cortex." In G. Dawson & K. W. Fischer (Eds.), *Human Behavior and the Developing Brain.* New York: Guilford Press. Graphic adapted from Kolb, B. &

Whishaw, I. Q. (2001). *An Introduction to Brain and Behavior.* New York: Worth Publishers.; **84:** Figure 3.7: From Nairne, J. S. (2000), *Psychology: The Adaptive Mind.* Wadsworth © 2000 Wadsworth. Reprinted by permission.; **86:** Figure 3.9: From Starr C., and Taggart, R. (1998) *Biology The Unite and Diversity of Life with Infotrac and 2.1 CD, 8th edition,* © 1998 Wadsworth Publishing. Reprinted by permission.; **87:** Figure 3.10: EEG read-out from "Current Concepts: The Sleep Disorders," by P. Hauri, 1982, The Upjohn Company, Kalamazoo, Michigan. Reprinted by permission.; **96:** Figure 3.20: From Sternberg, R. J. (2001). *Psychology: In Search of the Human Mind,* p. 84. Harcourt. Reprinted by permission of Wadsworth Publishing.; **102:** Figure 3.24: From Starr, C. & Taggart, R. (1998). *Biology: The Unity and Diversity of Life.* © 1998 Wadsworth Publishing. Reprinted by permission.; **103:** Figure 3.26: Graphic adapted from *Introduction to Psychology, 3rd edition* by J. W. Kalat © 1993. Wadsworth. Reprinted by permission.; **105:** Figure 3.28: Based on *Schizophrenia Genesis: The Origins of Madness,* by I.I. Gottesman, 1991. Copyright © 1991 W. H. Freeman Company.; **106:** Figure 3.29: Adapted from Kalat, J. W., *Introduction to Psychology, 4th edition,* © 1996 Wadsworth. Reprinted by permission.; **107:** Figure 3.30: Based on data from "Behavioral Genetics of Cognitive Ability: A Life-Span Perspective," by M. McGue, T.J. Bouchard, W.G. Iacono & D.T. Lykken, 1993. In R. Plomin & G.E. McClearn (Eds.), *Nature, Nurture and Psychology.* American Psychological Association. Extraversion data based on *Genes and Environment in Personality Development,* by J. C. Loehlin, 1992, Sage Publications.; **112:** Table 3.2: Adapted from *Animal Behavior* by John Alcock, 1998, p. 463. Copyright © 1998 John Alcock. Reprinted by permission of Sinauer Associates and the author.; **113:** Figure 3.31: Data from McCann, T.S., "Aggression and Sexual Activity of Male Southern Elephant Seals, Mirounga leonina," 1981, *Journal of Zoology, 195,* 295–310. Copyright © 1981.; **115:** Figure 3.32: Cartoon courtesy of Roy Doty; **116:** Figure 3.33: Data from "The Asymmetry of the Human Brain," by D. Kimura, 1973, *Scientific American, 228,* 70–78.; **117:** Figure 3.34: Adapted from Rasmussen, T., and Milner, B., "The Role of Early Left Brain Injury in Determining Lateralization of Cerebral Speech Functions," 1977, *Annals of the New York Academy of Sciences, 299,* 355–369.

Chapter 4 125: Table 4.1: From "Contemporary Psychophysics," by E. Galanter, 1962, in *New Directions in Psychology,* R. Brown (Ed.). Holt, Rinehart & Winston. © 1962 Eugene Galanter. Reprinted by permission.; **128:** Figure 4.5: Based on Figure 4.6 in *Introduction to Psychology,* by James Kalat. Copyright © 1986 Wadsworth Pub-

lishing. **137:** Figure 4.16: Courtesy of BASF; **140:** Figure 4.20: Based on data from Wald, G., & Brown, P. K. (1965) "Human Color Vision and Color Blindness," *Symposium Cold Spring Harbor Laboratory of Quantitative Biology, 30,* 345–359 (p. 351). Copyright © 1965. Reprinted by permission of the author.; **148:** Figure 4.35: Adapted by permission from an illustration by Ilil Arbel on page 83 of "Pictorial Perception and Culture," by Jan B. Deregowski in *Scientific American, 227* (5) November 1972. Copyright © 1972 by Scientific American, Inc. All rights reserved.; **149:** Figure 4.36: Adapted from Proffitt, D. R., Bhalla, M., Gossweiler, R., & Midgett, R., (1995) "Perceiving Geographical Slant," *Psychonomic Bulletin & Review, 214,* 409–428. Copyright ©1995 by Psychonomic Society Publications. Reprinted by permission.; **149:** Figure 4.37: Adapted from Proffitt, D. R., Bhalla, M., Gossweiler, R., & Midgett, R., (1995) "Perceiving Geographical Slant," *Psychonomic Bulletin & Review, 214,* 409–428. Copyright © 1995 by Psychonomic Society Publications. Reprinted by permission.; **151:** Figure 4.41: From Shepard, R., *Mind Sights.* New York: W. H. Freeman. Copyright © 1990 by Roger N. Shepard. Used by permission of Henry Holt & Co., Inc.; **153:** Figure 4.44: From Shepard, R., *Mind Sights.* New York: W. H. Freeman. Copyright © 1990 by Roger N. Shepard. Used by permission of Henry Holt & Co., Inc.; **155:** Figure 4.46: Decibel level examples from Atkinson, R. L., Atkinson R. C., Smith, E. F., & Hilgard, E. R., *Introduction to Psychology, Ninth Edition,* San Diego: Harcourt, copyright © 1987. Reprinted by permission of Wadsworth Publishing.; **160:** Figure 4.50: Adapted from Bartoshuk, L. M. (1993) "Genetic and Pathological Taste Variation: What Can We Learn from Animal Models and Human Disease?." In D. Chadwick, J. Marsh & J. Goode (Eds.), *The Molecular Basis of Smell and Taste Transduction,* pp. 251–267. John Wiley & Sons, Inc.; **173:** Figure 4.67: From Alber, Joseph, *Interaction of Color.* Copyright © 1963 and Reprinted by permission of the publisher, Yale University Press.

Chapter 5 180: Figure 5.2: (Adapted) from *Wide Awake at 3:00 AM,* by Richard M. Coleman. Copyright © 1986 by Richard M. Coleman. Used with permission of Henry Holt & Co., Inc.; **181:** Figure 5.3: Adapted from Kalat, J. W. (2001). *Biological Psychology, 7/e* (based on data of Recht, Law & Schwartz, 1995). © 2001 Wadsworth. Adapted by permission.; **183:** Figure 5.4: Figure from Hauri, P., "Current Concepts: The Sleep Disorders," 1982, The Upjohn Company, Kalamazoo, Michigan. Reprinted by permission; **186:** Figure 5.6: Figure adapted from an updated revision of a figure in Roffwarg, H. P., Muzio, J N., and Dement, W. C., "Ontogenetic

American Life, by R. J. Hernstein and M. Murray, Jacket, Copyright © 1994 by Simon & Schuster, Inc. By permission of The Free Press, a division of Simon & Schuster, Inc.; **365:** Figure 9.17: Adapted from Steele, C. M., & Aronson, J. (1995) "Stereotype Threat and the Intellectual Test Performance of African American," *Journal of Personality and Social Psychology, 69,* 797–811. Copyright © 1995 American Psychological Association. Adapted by permission of the author; **368:** Figure 9.21: Reprinted with permission of THE RIVERSIDE PUBLISHING CO. from Stanford-Binet Intelligence Scale Guide for Administering and Scoring, The Fourth Edition by R. L. Thorndike, E. P. Hagen & J. M. Sattler. THE RIVERSIDE PUBLISHING CO., 8420 W. Bryn Mawr Avenue, Chicago, IL 60631. Copyright © 1986; **368:** Figure 9.22: Graph adapted from Deary, I. J., Caryl P. G., & Gibson, G. J. (1993) "Nonstationarity and the Measurement of Psychophysical Response in a Visual Inspection Time Task," *Perception, 22* p. 1250. Copyright © 1993 by Pion Ltd. Adapted by permission; **370:** Table 9.3: Adapted from Gardner, H. & Hatch, T., (1989) "Multiple Intelligences Go to School: Educational Implications of the Theory of Multiple Intelligences," *Educational Researcher, 18* (8), 4–10. American Educational Research Association. Additional data from Gardner, 1998; **374:** Figure 9.23: From Matlin, M. W. (1994). *Cognition (3rd Ed.).* Fort Worth, TX: Harcourt Brace. Reprinted by permission of the author; **375:** Figure 9.24: From Matlin, M. W. (1994). *Cognition (3rd Ed.).* Fort Worth, TX: Harcourt Brace. Reprinted by permission of the author.

Chapter 10 **389:** Figure 10.5: Data from Stunkard, A. J., Harris, J. R., Pederson, N. L., & McClearn, G. E. (1990) "The Body-Mass Index of Twins Who Have Been Reared Apart," *New England Journal of Medicine, 322,* 1483–1487; **394:** Figure 10.9: From Buss, D. M., & Schmitt, D. P. (1993) "Sexual Strategies Theory: An Evolutionary Perspective on Human Mating," *Psychological Review, 100,* 204–232. Copyright © 1993 by the American Psychological Association. Reprinted by permission of the author; **396:** Figure 10.10: Data from Buss, D. M. (1989) "Sex Differences in Human Mate Preferences: Evolutionary Hypotheses Tested in 37 Cultures," *Behavioral and Brain Sciences, 12,* 1–49; **396:** Figure 10.11: Data from "Sex Differences in Human Mate Preferences: Evolutionary Hypotheses Tested in 37 Cultures," by D. M. Buss, 1989, *Behavioral and Brain Sciences, 12,* 1–49; **400:** Figure 10.15: Based on *Human Sexual Response,* by W.H. Masters and V.E. Johnson, 1966. Copyright © (1966) Little, Brown and Company; **402:** Figure 10.17: Descriptions reprinted by permission of Dr. David McClelland; **410:** Figure 10.22: Adapted from Smith,

R. E. (1993) *Psychology,* figure 13.15, p. 416. Copyright © 1993 by West Publishing. Reprinted by permission of Wadsworth Publishing; **411:** Figure 10.23: From *Unmasking the Face,* © 1975 by Paul Ekman, photograph courtesy of Paul Ekman; **414:** Figure 10.26: Based on art in "A Language for Emotions," by R. Plutchik, 1980, *Psychology Today, 13* (9), 68–78. Reprinted with permission from Psychology Today Magazine. Copyright © 1980 (Sussex Publishers, Inc.); **418:** Figure 10.29: Reproduced from "Marital Status and Happiness," by David G. Myers. In *Well-Being, The Foundations of Hedonic Psychology,* edited by Daniel Kahneman, Ed Diener, and Norbert Schwarz. Copyright © 1999 Russell Sage Foundation, 112 East 64th Street, New York, NY 10021. Reprinted by permission; **420:** Figure 10.31: From Halpern, D. F., (1996) *Thought & Knowledge: An Introduction to Critical Thinking,* p. 181, figure 5.1. Copyright © 1996 Lawrence Erlbaum Associates. Reprinted by permission of Lawrence Erlbaum Associates.

Chapter 11 **429:** Figure 11.2: Figure adapted from Moore, K.L. & Persaud, T. V. N (1998) *Before We Are Born: Essentials of Embryology and Birth Defects, 5/E.* Copyright © 1998 Elsevier Science (USA). All rights reserved. Reprinted by permission of Elsevier Science; **430:** Figure 11.3: Adapted from Berk, L. E. (2002), *Infants, Children, and Adolescents.* Copyright © 2002 by Allyn & Bacon. Reprinted by permission; **431:** Figure 11.4: From a chart by Steve Hart in *Time* Magazine, October 8, 1990, p. 45. Copyright © 1990 by Time Inc. Reproduced by permission; **436:** Figure 11.7: Adapted from Shaver, P. R., & Hazan, C., "Attachment," (1994). In A. Weber and J.H. Harvey (Eds.), *Perspectives on Close Relationships.* Copyright © 1994 by Allyn and Bacon. Reprinted by permission; **438:** Table 11.1: From Cole, M. (1999) "Culture in Development." In M. H. Bornstein & M. E. Lamb (Eds.). *Developmental Psychology: An Advanced Textbook.* Mahwah, NJ, Erlbaum. Copyright © 1999 Lawrence Erlbaum Associates. Reprinted by permission; **445:** Figure 11.14: From Wynn, K. "Addition and Subtraction by Human Infants," (1992), *Nature, 358,* 749–750. Copyright © 1992 Macmillan Magazines, Ltd. Reprinted with permission from Nature; **448:** Figure 11.16: Adapted from Kohlberg, L. J., (1963) "The Development of Children's Orientations Toward a Moral Order: I: Sequence in the Development of Moral Thought," *Vita Humana, 6,* 11–33. Copyright © 1963 by S. Karger AG, Basel. Reprinted by permission; **453:** Figure 11.20: Data based on FBI Uniform Crime Reports for the United States, 1999. Adapted from Steinberg, L. (2002). *Adolescence.* New York: McGraw-Hill; **454:** Figure 11.21: Adapted from "Identity in Adolescence," by J.E. Marcia,

1980. In J. Adelson (Ed.), *Handbook of Adolescent Psychology,* pp. 159–210. Copyright © 1980 by John Wiley & Sons, Inc. Adapted by permission of John Wiley & Sons, Inc.; **455:** Figure 11.22: Adapted from Meilman, P. W. (1979). "Cross-sectional Age Changes in Ego Identity Status During Adolescence," *Developmental Psychology, 15,* 230–231. Copyright © American Psychological Association. Reprinted by permission of the author; **458:** Figure 11.24: Adapted from "Marital Satisfaction Over the Family Cycle," by Boyd C. Rollins and Harold Feldman, *Journal of Marriage and Family, 32* (February 1970), p. 25. Copyright © 1975 by the National Council on Family Relations, 3989 Central Ave., N.E., Suite 550, Minneapolis, MN 55421. Reprinted by permission; **461:** Figure 11.25: From Schaie, K. W. (1990) "Intellectual Development in Adulthood." In J.E. Birren and K. W. Schaie (Eds.), *Handbook of the Psychology of Aging, 3rd ed.* pp. 291–309. Copyright © 1990 Elsevier Science (USA), reproduced with permission from the publisher; **467:** Table 11.2: Adapted from Ruble, T. L. (1983) "Sex Stereotypes: Issues of Change in the 70s", *Sex Roles, 9,* 397–402. Copyright © 1983 Plenum Publishing Group. Adapted by permission.

Chapter 12 **493:** Figure 12.4: Adapted from Adams, H. E., Wright Jr., L. W., & Lohr, B. A. (1996) "Is Homophobia Associated with Homosexual Arousal?," *Journal of Abnormal Psychology, 105,* 440–445. Copyright © 1996 by American Psychological Association. Reprinted by permission of the author; **498:** Figure 12.12: Adapted from Potkay, C. R., & Allen, B. P. (1986), *Personality: Theory, Research and Application,* p. 246. Brooks/Cole Publishing Company. Copyright © 1986 by C.R. Potkay & Bem Allen. Adapted by permission of the author; **500:** Figure 12.13: From Eysenck, H. J. (1976) *The Biological Basis of Personality, 1st Ed.,* p. 36. Courtesy of Charles C. Thomas, Publisher, Springfield, Illinois. [Reprinted by permission]; **502:** Figure 12.15: Based on Plomin R., & Caspi, A. (1999), "Behavioral genetics and personality." In L. A. Pervin, & O. P. John (Eds.), *Handbook of Personality: Theory and Research.* New York: The Guilford Press; **507:** Figure 12.16: From Grasha, A. F., & Kirschenbaum, D. S. (1986) *Adjustment and Competence: Concepts and Applications,* © 1986 Wadsworth. Reprinted with permission of Anthony F. Grasha; **509:** Figure 12.17: Adapted from Markus, H. R., & Kitayama, S. (1991) "Culture and the Self: Implications for Cognition, Emotion, and Motivation," *Psychological Review, 98,* 224–253. Copyright © 1991 by the American Psychological Association. Adapted by permission of the author; **512:** Table 12.3: [Adaptation] Reprinted with permission from Keller, L. S., Butcher, J.N., & Slutske,

W.S. (1990), "Objective Personality Assessment." In G. Goldstein and M. Hersen (Eds.), *Handbook of Psychological Assessment,* pp 345–386. Copyright © 1990 Pergamon Press, Ltd.; **513:** Figure 12.20: From R. B. Cattell in "Personality Pinned Down," *Psychology Today (July)* 1973, 40–46. Reprinted by permission from Psychology Today Magazine. Copyright © 1973 (Sussex Publishers, Inc.).

Chapter 13 **525:** Table 13.1: Reprinted with permission from *Journal of Psychosomatic Research, 11,* 213–218, by T.H. Holmes and R. Rahe in "The Social Readjustment Rating Scale," 1967, Elsevier Science Publishing Co., Inc.; **532:** Figure 13.2: Adapted from Carson, R. C., Butcher, J. N., & Coleman, J. C., (1988). *Abnormal Psychology and Modern Life (8th Ed.)* pp 64–65, 1988. Copyright © 1988 by Scott, Foresman and Company. Adapted by permission of the publisher; **536:** Figure 13.8: Adapted from Stein, M. B., Walker, J. R., Hazen, A. L., & Forde, D. R., (1997) "Full and Partial Posttraumatic Stress Disorder: Findings from a Community Survey," *American Journal of Psychiatry, 154,* 1114–1119. © 1977 American Psychiatric Association; **539:** Figure 13.9: Adapted from Ridker, P. M. (2002). "High Sensitivity C-reactive Protein: Potential Adjunct for Global Risk Assessment in Primary Prevention of Cardiovascular Disease," *Circulation, 103,* 1813–1818. Copyright © 2002 American Heart Association. Adapted by permission of the publisher Lippincott Williams & Willams and the author; **542:** Figure 13.11: From Cohen, S., Tyrrell, D. A. J., & Smith, A. P. (1993) "Negative Life Events, Perceived Stress, Negative Affect, and Susceptibility to the Common Cold," *Journal of Personality and Social Psychology, 64,* 131–140. Copyright © 1993 by the American Psychological Association. Reprinted by permission of the author; **545:** Figure 13.14: Adapted from *The Health Benefits of Smoking Cessation: A Report of the Surgeon General 1990,* pp. V–VII. U. S. Department of Health and Printing Office, Washington, D.C.; **547:** Figure 13.15: From Mann, J., Tarantola, D. J. M., & Netter, T. W. (1992) *A Global Report: AIDS in the World,* Copyright © 1992 by Oxford University Press. Reprinted by permission; **548:** Figure 13.16: Adapted from Kalichman, S. C., (1995) *Understanding AIDS: A Guide for Mental Health Professionals.* Copyright © 1995 American Psychological Association. Reprinted by permission of the author; **554:** Figure 13.19: "Relaxation Procedure" from *The Relaxation Response,* by Herbert Benson, M.D. and Miriam Z. Klipper. Copyright © 1975 by William Morrow & Company, Inc. By permission of HarperCollins Publishers, Inc.; **555:** Figure 13.20: Based on data from Blair, S. N., Kohl, W. H., Paffenbarger, R.S., Clark,

D.G., Cooper, K.H., & Gibbons, L.W., (1989) "Physical Fitness and All-Cause Mortality," *Journal of the American Medical Association, 262,* 2395–2401. Copyright © 1989 American Medical Association. Reprinted by permission.

Chapter 14 **565:** Figure 14.3: Reprinted with permission from the *Diagnostic and Statistical Manual of Mental Disorders, DSM-TR.* Copyright © 2000 American Psychiatric Association; **571:** Adapted from Faravelli, C., & Pallanti, S. (1989) "Recent Life Events and Panic Figure 14.9: Disorders," *American Journal of Psychiatry, 146,* 622–626. Copyright © 1989 by the American Psychiatric Association. Adapted by permission; **577:** Table 14.1: From Sarason I. G., & Sarason, B. G. (1987) *Abnormal Psychology: The Problem of Maladaptive Behavior, 5/E,* (c) 1987, p. 283. Reprinted by permission of Prentice-Hall, Inc., Englewood Cliffs, NJ.; **578:** Figure 14.12: Figure 6-1, "Age of Onset for Bipolar Mood Disorder", from *Manic-Depressive Illness,* by Frederick K. Goodwin and Kay R. Jamison [p. 132]. Copyright © 1990 by Oxford University Press., Inc. Used by permission of Oxford University Press; **579:** Figure 14.13: Based on data from "Mood Disorders: Genetic Aspects," by E.S. Gershon, W.H Berrettini & L.R. Goldin, 1989. In H.I. Kaplan & B.J. Sadock (Eds.) *Comprehensive Textbook of Psychiatry.* Williams & Wilkins; **581:** Figure 14.15: Data from Alloy, L.B., Abramson, L. Y., Whitehouse, W. G., Hogan, M. E., Tashman, N. A., Steinberg, D. L., Rose, D. L., & Donovan, P. (1999) "Depressogenic Cognitive Styles: Predictive Validity, Information Processing and Personality Characteristics, and Developmental Origins," *Behavioral Research and Therapy, 37,* 503–531. Elsevier Science; **586:** Figure 14.17: Adapted from *Schizophrenia Genesis: The Origins of Madness,* by I.I. Gottesman, 1991. Copyright © 1991 by W.H. Freeman; **587:** Figure 14.19: Graphic adapted from Starr, C. & Taggart, R. (1998). *Biology: The Unity and Diversity of Life.* © 1998 Wadsworth Publishing. Reprinted by permission; **588:** Figure 14.21: Data adapted from Leff, J., & Vaughn, C. (1981) "The Role of Maintenance Therapy and Relatives' Expression Emotion in Relapse of Schizophrenia: A Two-Year Follow-Up," *British Journal of Psychiatry, 138,* 102–104; **600:** Figure 14.24: Data adapted from Lucas, A. R., Beard, C. M., O'Fallon,W. M., & Kurland, L. T. (1991) "50-Year Trends in the Incidence of Anorexia Nervosa in Rochester, Minn., A Population-based Study," *American Journal of Psychiatry, 148,* 917–922. American Psychiatric Association; **601:** Figure 14.25: Data from Garner, D. M., Garfinkel, P. E., Schwartz, D., & Thompson, M. (1980) "Cultural Expectations of Thinness in Women, *Psychological Reports, 47,* 483–491. Copyright © 1980 Psychological Reports; and from Wiseman, C. V., Gray, J.J., Mosimann, J. E., & Ahrens, A. H. (1992) "Cultural Expectations of Thinness in Women: An Update," *International Journal of Eating Disorders, 11,* 85–89, Copyright © 1992 John Wiley & Sons. Graphic adapted from Barlow, D. H., & Durand, V. M. (1999) *Abnormal Psychology: An Investigative Approach.* Copyright © 1999 Wadsworth Publishing Company. Reprinted by permission.

Chapter 15 **609:** Figure 15.1: Data from Olfson, M., & Pincus, H. A. (1996) "Outpatient Mental Health Care in Nonhospital Settings: Distribution of Patients Across Provider Groups," *American Journal of Psychiatry, 153,* pp. 1353–1356; **610:** Figure 15.3: Data from Olfson, M., & Pincus, H. A. (1994). "Outpatient Psychotherapy in the United States, I: Volume, Costs, and User Characteristics," *American Journal of Psychiatry, 151,* 1281–1288; **612:** Excerpt p. 612: Adapted from *The Technique and Practice of Psychoanalysis, Vol. 1,* by R. R. Greenson, pp. 40–41, 1967. Copyright © 1967 International Universities Press; **621:** Figure 15.8: From Rudestam K. E. (1980) *Methods of Self-Change: An ABC Primer,* pp. 42–43, Copyright © 1980 by Wadsworth, Inc. Reprinted by permission of the author; **623:** Table 15.1: From "New Drug Evaluations: Alprazolam," by R. L. Evans, 1981. Drug Intelligence and Clinical Pharmacy, 15, 633–637. Copyright © 1981 by Harvey Whitney Books Company. Reprinted by permission; **624:** Figure 15.10: From data in *NIMH-PSC Collaborative Study I* and reported in "Drugs in the Treatment of Psychosis," by J.O. Cole, S.C. Goldberg & J.M. Davis, 1966, 1985. In P. Solomon (Ed.) *Psychiatric Drugs,* Grune & Stratton. Reprinted by permission of J.M. Davis; **640:** Figure 15.16: Adapted from Smith, M.L. and Glass, G. V. (1977) "Meta Analysis of Psychotherapy Outcome Series," *American Psychologist, 32 (Sept),* 752–760. Copyright © 1977 by the American Psychological Association. Adapted by permission of the author; **641:** Figure 15.17: Based on *The Psychotherapy Maze,* by O. Ehrenberg and M. Ehrenberg, 1986. Copyright © 1986 by Jason Aronson, Inc.

Chapter 16 **647:** Excerpt from: *Tales from the Front* by Cheryl Lavin and Laura Kavesh, copyright © 1988 by Cheryl Lavin and Laura Kavesh. Used by permission of Doubleday, a division of Random House, Inc.; **651:** Figure 16.2: Adapted from Gilovich, T., Medvec, V. H., & Savitsky, K. (2000). "The Spotlight Effect in Social Judgment: An Egocentric Bias in Estimates of the Salience of One's Own Actions and Appearance," *Journal of Personality and Social Psychology, 78,* 211–222. Copyright © 2000 by the American Psychological Association. Adapted by permission of the author; **653:** Figure 16.3: Based on "Perceiving the Causes of Success and Failure," by B. Weiner, I. Friese, A. Kukla, L. Reed & R.M. Rosenbaum. In E.E. Jones, D.E. Kanuouse, H.H. Kelley, R.E. Nisbett, S. Valins & B. Weiner (Eds.) *Perceiving the Causes of Behavior,* 1972. General Learning Press. Used by permission of Dr. Bernard Weiner; **655:** Figure 16.5: Adapted from Hofstede, G. (2001). *Culture's Consequences, 2/e,* p. 215. Copyright © 2001 Sage Publications. Adapted by permission of Dr. Geert Hofstede; **662:** Figure 16.8: Adapted from Buss, D. M. (1988) "The Evolution of Human Intrasexual Competition: Tactics of Mate Attraction," *Journal of Personality and Social Psychology, 54,* (4), 616–628. Copyright © 1988 by the American Psychological Association. Adapted by permission of the author; **665:** Figure 16.10: Based on Lippa, R. A. (1994) *Introduction to Social Psychology,* Brooks/Cole Publishing Company. Copyright © 1994 by Wadsworth. Reprinted by permission; **666:** Figure 16.11: Data from Friedrich, J., Fetherstonhaugh, D., Casey, S., Gallagher, D. (1996) "Argument Integration and Attitude Change: Suppression Effects in the Integration of One-sided Arguments That Vary in Persuasiveness," *Personality and Social Psychology Bulletin, 22,* 179–191. American Psychological Association; **671:** Adapted from Asch, Solomon (1955) "Opinion and Social Pressure," *Scientific American, November* 1955, from illustrations by Sara Love on p.32. Copyright © 1955 by Scientific American, Inc. All rights reserved; **672:** Adapted from Asch, Solomon (1955) "Opinion and Social Pressure," *Scientific American, November* 1955, from illustration by Sara Love on p. 35. Copyright © 1955 by Scientific American, Inc. All rights reserved; **677:** Adapted from Latane, B., Williams, K., & Harkins, S. (1979) "Many Hands Make Light the Work: The Causes and Consequences of Social Loafing," *Journal of Personality and Social Psychology, 37,* 822–832. Copyright © 1979 by the American Psychological Association. Adapted by permission of the author; **679:** Adapted with permission of The Free Press, a Division of Simon & Schuster, from *Decision Making: A Psychological Analysis of Conflict, Choice and Commitment,* by Irving J. Janis and Leon Mann. Copyright © 1977 by The Free Press.

Appendix **A-15:** Figure C.1: Data from Society for Industrial and Organizational Psychology database, 2001. Figure adapted from Muchinsky, P. M. (2003). *Psychology Applied to Work.* Copyright © 2003 Wadsworth. Reprinted by permission; **A-19:** Figure C. 2: From Cardy, R. L., "Performance Appraisal in a Quality Context: A New Look at an Old Problem," (1998). In J. W. Smither, Ed., *Performance Appraisal,* p. 142. Jossey-Bass. Reprinted by permission of John Wiley & Sons, Inc.; **A-24:** Table C.1: From Muchinsky, P. M. (2003). *Psychology Applied to Work.* Copyright © 2003 Wadsworth. Reprinted by permission.